PETERSON'S PRIVATE SECONDARY SCHOOLS 2012–13

About Peterson's Publishing

Peterson's Publishing provides the accurate, dependable, high-quality education content and guidance you need to succeed. No matter where you are on your academic or professional path, you can rely on Peterson's print and digital publications for the most up-to-date education exploration data, expert test-prep tools, and top-notch career success resources—everything you need to achieve your goals.

Visit us online at **www.petersonspublishing.com** and let Peterson's help you achieve your goals.

For more information, contact Peterson's Publishing, 2000 Lenox Drive, Lawrenceville, NJ 08648; 800-338-3282 Ext. 54229; or find us on the World Wide Web at www.petersonspublishing.com.

Previous editions published as *Peterson's Guide to Independent Secondary Schools* © 1980, 1981, 1982, 1983, 1984, 1985, 1986, 1987, 1988, 1989, 1990, 1991, 1992 and as *Peterson's Private Secondary Schools* © 1993, 1994, 1995, 1996, 1997, 1998, 1999, 2000, 2001, 2002, 2003, 2004, 2005, 2006, 2007, 2008, 2009, 2010, 2011

Bernadette Webster, Director of Publishing; Jill C. Schwartz, Editor; Christine Lucas, Research Project Manager; James Ranish, Research Associate; Phyllis Johnson, Software Engineer; Ray Golaszewski, Publishing Operations Manager; Linda M. Williams, Composition Manager; Karen Mount, Fulfillment Coordinator

ISSN 1544-2330
ISBN-13: 978-0-7689-3437-3
ISBN-10: 0-7689-3437-0

Printed in the United States of America

10 9 8 7 6 5 4 3 2 1   14 13 12

Thirty-third Edition

By producing this book on recycled paper (40% post-consumer waste) 91 trees were saved.

Certified Chain of Custody

60% Certified Fiber Sourcing and
40% Post-Consumer Recycled

www.sfiprogram.org

*This label applies to the text stock.

Sustainability—Its Importance to Peterson's Publishing

What does sustainability mean to Peterson's? As a leading publisher, we are aware that our business has a direct impact on vital resources—most especially the trees that are used to make our books. Peterson's Publishing is proud that its products are certified by the Sustainable Forestry Initiative (SFI) and that all of its books are printed on paper that is 40% post-consumer waste.

Being a part of the Sustainable Forestry Initiative (SFI) means that all of our vendors—from paper suppliers to printers—have undergone rigorous audits to demonstrate that they are maintaining a sustainable environment.

Peterson's Publishing continuously strives to find new ways to incorporate sustainability throughout all aspects of its business.

Contents

INDEX

A Note from the Editors of Peterson's Publishing

Peterson's Private Secondary Schools 2012–13 is the authoritative source of information for parents and students who are exploring the alternative of privately provided education. In this edition, you will find information for more than 1,200 schools worldwide. The data published in this guide are obtained directly from the schools themselves to help you make a fully informed decision.

If you've decided to look into private schooling for your son or daughter but aren't sure how to begin, relax. You won't have to go it alone. **What You Should Know About Private Education** can help you plan your search and demystify the admission process. In the articles that follow, you'll find valuable advice from admission experts about applying to private secondary schools and choosing the school that's right for your child.

Schools will be pleased to know that Peterson's helped you in your private secondary school selection.

In "Why Choose an Independent School?" Patrick F. Bassett, President of the National Association of Independent Schools (NAIS), describes the reasons why an increasing number of families are considering private schooling.

If you want a private education for your child but are hesitant about sending him or her away to a boarding school, read "Another Option: Independent Day Schools" where Lila Lohr, former Head of School at Princeton Day School in Princeton, New Jersey, discusses the benefits of day schools.

From Howard and Matthew Greenes' "The Contemporary Boarding School: Change and Adaptability" to The Association of Boarding Schools' (TABS) "Study Confirms Benefits of Boarding School"—if you are having doubts about boarding schools, you'll want to check out these articles!

Mark Meyer-Braun, Head of School at the Outdoor Academy, offers "Semester Schools: Great Opportunities," which explores various options for students to spend an exciting semester in a new "school-away-from-school."

If you are considering a special needs or therapeutic school for your child, you will want to read "Why a Therapeutic or Special Needs School?" by Diederik van Renesse, an educational consultant who specializes in this area.

To help you compare private schools and make the best choice for your child, check out "Finding the Perfect Match" by Helene Reynolds, a former educational planning and placement counselor.

"Plan a Successful School Search" gives you an overview of the admission process.

If the admission application forms have you baffled and confused, read "Understanding the Admission Application Form," by Gregg W. M. Maloberti, Dean of Admission at The Lawrenceville School.

For the lowdown on standardized testing, Heather Hoerle, Executive Director of the Secondary School Admission Test Board (SSATB), describes the two tests most often required by private schools and the role that tests play in admission decisions in "About Standardized Tests."

In "Paying for a Private Education," Mark Mitchell, Vice President, School Information Services at NAIS, shares some thoughts on financing options.

Finally, "How to Use This Guide" gives you all the information you need on how to make *Peterson's Private Secondary Schools 2012–13* work for you!

Next up, the **Quick-Reference Chart,** "Private Secondary Schools At-a-Glance," lists schools by state, U.S. territory, or country and provides essential information about a school's students, range of grade levels, enrollment figures, faculty, and special offerings.

The **School Profiles** follow, and it's here you can learn more about particular schools. *Peterson's Private Secondary Schools 2012–13* contains three **School Profiles** sections—one for traditional college-preparatory and general academic schools, one for special needs schools that serve students with a variety of special learning and social needs, and one for junior boarding schools that serve students in middle school grades. Many schools have chosen to submit a display ad, which appears near their profile and offers specific information the school wants you to know.

Close-Ups follow each **School Profiles** section and feature expanded two-page school descriptions written exclusively for this guide. There is a reference at the end of a profile directing you to that school's **Close-Up.**

Summer programs are more important than ever for teens. Aside from looking good on a college application, they can be extremely transformative—helping students develop leadership skills, gain greater self-knowledge, and cultivate friendships with peers from across the country or around the world. Finding meaningful summer programs for teens can often be challenging. This year, *Peterson's Private Secondary Schools* has a NEW **Summer Programs** section, which includes two-page descriptions, complete with photos, of exciting opportunities taking place at private schools in the United States and abroad during the summer months. You'll find great information about program offerings, facilities, staff, costs, and much more.

The **Specialized Directories** are generated from responses to Peterson's annual school survey. These directories group schools by the categories considered most important when choosing a private school, including type, entrance requirements, curricula, financial aid data, and special programs.

Finally, in the **Index** you'll find the "Alphabetical Listing of Schools" for the page references of schools that have already piqued your interest.

At the end of the book, don't miss the special section of ads placed by Peterson's preferred clients. Their financial support helps make it possible for Peterson's Publishing to continue to provide you with the highest-quality educational exploration, test-prep, financial aid, and career-preparation resources you need to succeed on your educational journey.

Peterson's publishes a full line of resources to help guide you and your family through the private secondary school admission process. Peterson's publications can be found at your local bookstore and library and your school guidance office, and you can access us online at www.petersonspublishing.com. Peterson's books are now also available as eBooks.

Join Peterson's Private Schools conversation at www.facebook.com/petersonspublishing. The resources of Peterson's Publishing are available to help you with your private school search.

We welcome any comments or suggestions you may have about this publication. Write to us at:

Publishing Department
Peterson's, a Nelnet company
2000 Lenox Drive
Lawrenceville, NJ 08648

Your feedback will help us make your educational dreams possible.

Schools will be pleased to know that Peterson's Publishing helped you in your private secondary school selection. Admission staff members are more than happy to answer questions, address specific problems, and help in any way they can. The editors at Peterson's Publishing wish you great success in your search!

NOTICE: Certain portions of or information contained in this book have been submitted and paid for by the educational institution identified, and such institutions take full responsibility for the accuracy, timeliness, completeness and functionality of such content. Such portions or information include (i) each display ad in the "Profiles" sections, which include pages 52–577, 714–738, and 746–753 and comprise a half page of information covering a single educational institution, and (ii) each two-page description in the "Close-Up" sections, which include pages 578–711, 740–743, 756–765, and 768–779.

What You Should Know About Private Education

Why Choose an Independent School?

Patrick F. Bassett
President of the National Association of Independent Schools (NAIS)

Why do families choose independent private schools for their children? Many cite the intimate school size and setting, individualized attention, and high academic standards.

Recent research highlights the success of independent school graduates, who outperform graduates from all other types of schools in a whole host of categories, reflecting exceptional preparation for academic and civic life.

Although nearly all independent school graduates go on to attend college, *The Freshman Survey Trends Report*, a study conducted by the Higher Education Research Institute, found that 85 percent of students who attended independent schools that belong to the National Association of Independent Schools (NAIS) went on to attend "very high" or "highly selective" colleges and universities. This "persistence factor" is largely attributable to attending a school with high expectations for all students and a culture that reinforces achievement. The ethos of independent schools contributes to this equation, since everybody is expected to work hard and succeed academically.

NAIS school graduates were also more engaged with their communities than students from other types of schools. Forty-one percent of NAIS graduates said they expected to participate in volunteer or community activities in college, compared to just 24 percent of the whole group. NAIS graduates were also far more inclined to consider "keeping up-to-date with political affairs" essential (46 percent NAIS, 31 percent all).

Another study, the *National Educational Longitudinal Study* (conducted by the U.S. Department of Education) tracked students from public schools, parochial schools, NAIS independent schools, and other private schools from the time they were eighth graders in 1988 until the year 2000. Nearly all of the NAIS students in the NELS study had pursued postsecondary education by their mid-20s. More than three quarters had graduated from a college or university, including 8 percent who completed master's degrees, and 1.5 percent who achieved a Ph.D. or professional degree (e.g., M.D. or LL.B.) by their mid-20s.

Perhaps the most significant factor that distinguished NAIS graduates from graduates of other types of schools was the strength of their commitment to community service and active civic participation. While slightly more than 1 out of 5 survey participants reported volunteering for civic events, nearly one third of NAIS school graduates said that they regularly participated in voluntary activities in their communities. NAIS students were also nearly twice as likely to volunteer to work for political campaigns and political causes. And NAIS students were committed to exercising their civic duty as voters. Whereas slightly more than half of all NELS participants voted in the presidential election before the study, more than 75 percent of NAIS school graduates registered their voices.

With independent schools, you have the opportunity to choose a school with a philosophy, values, and approach to teaching that is the right fit for your child.

Another factor that contributes to the success of students in independent schools is the partnership with families. This coalescing of parental and school voices helps children prosper because the key adults in their lives reinforce a common set of values and speak with a common voice. Indeed, the great achievement of American education is that it offers families many choices of schooling so that they can find a school with a voice and vision to match their own.

Each independent school has a unique mission, culture, and personality. There are day schools, boarding schools, and combination day-boarding schools. Some independent schools have a few dozen students; others have several thousand. Some are coed;

others are single-sex. Some independent schools have a religious affiliation; some are nonsectarian. Most serve students of average to exceptional academic ability, but some serve exclusively those with learning differences, and others serve highly gifted students. The vast majority of independent schools are college-prep.

With independent schools, you have the opportunity to choose a school with a philosophy, values, and approach to teaching that is the right fit for your child.

Make the choice of a lifetime. Choose an independent school.

Another Option: Independent Day Schools

Lila Lohr

For those of us who are fortunate enough to be able to send our children to an independent day school, it seems to offer the best of both worlds. Our children are able to reap the enormous benefits of an independent school education and we, as parents, are able to continue to play a vital, daily role in the education of our children. Parents enjoy being seen as partners with day schools in educating their children.

As more and more independent day schools have sprung up in communities across the country, more and more parents are choosing to send their children to them, even when it might involve a lengthy daily commute. Contrary to some old stereotypes, parents of independent school students are not all cut from the same mold, living in the same neighborhood with identical dreams and aspirations for their children. Independent school parents represent a wide range of interests, attitudes, and parenting styles.

They also have several things in common. Most parents send their children to independent day schools because they think their children will get a better education in a safe, value-laden environment. Many parents are willing to pay substantial annual tuition because they believe their children will be held to certain standards, challenged academically, and thoroughly prepared for college.

This willingness to make what are, for many, substantial financial sacrifices reflects the recognition that much of one's character is formed in school. Concerned parents want their children to go to schools where values are discussed and reinforced. They seek schools that have clear expectations and limits. The nonpublic status allows independent schools to establish specific standards of behavior and performance and to suspend or expel students who don't conform to those expectations.

Understanding the power of adolescent peer pressure, parents are eager to have their children go to school with other teens who are academically ambitious and required to behave. They seek an environment where it is "cool" to be smart, to work hard, and to be involved in the school community. In independent day schools, students spend their evenings doing homework, expect to be called on in class, and participate in sports or clubs.

Successful independent schools, whether elementary or high school, large or small, single-sex or coed, recognize the importance of a school-parent partnership in educating each child. Experienced faculty members and administrators readily acknowledge that, while they are experts on education, parents are the experts on their own children. Gone are the days when parents simply dropped their children off in the morning, picked them up at the end of the day, and assumed the school would do the educating. Clearly, children benefit enormously when their parents and teachers work together, sharing their observations and concerns openly and frequently.

Most independent schools welcome and encourage parental involvement and support.

Independent schools encourage this two-way give-and-take and are committed to taking it well beyond the public school model. Annual back-to-school nights are attended by more than 90 percent of parents. Teacher-parent and student-teacherparent conferences, extensive written comments as part of the report cards, and adviser systems that encourage close faculty-student relationships are all structures that facilitate this parent-school partnership. Although more and more independent school parents work full-time, they make time for these critical opportunities to sit down and discuss their children's progress.

Most independent schools welcome and encourage parental involvement and support. Although the individual structures vary from school to school, most include opportunities beyond making cookies and chaperoning dances. Many parents enjoy being involved in community service projects, working on school fund raisers, participating in admission activities, sharing their expertise in appropriate academic classes, and even offering student internships. Most schools have made a concerted effort to structure specific opportunities for working parents to participate in the life of the school.

Independent day schools recognize the benefits of parent volunteers and of extending themselves so that parents feel that they are an important part of the school family. Buddy systems that pair new parents with families who have been at the school for several years help ease the transition for families who are new to the independent school sector.

Independent schools have also responded to increased parental interest in programs focusing on parenting skills. Recognizing the inherent difficulties of raising children, independent day schools have provided forums for discussing and learning about drugs, depression, stress management, peer pressure, and the like. Book groups, panel discussions, and workshops provide important opportunities for parents to share their concerns and to get to know the parents of their children's classmates. Schools recognize that this parent-to-parent communication and networking strengthens the entire school community.

Many current day school parents would contend that when you choose an independent day school for your child you are really choosing a school for the entire family. The students become so involved in their academic and extracurricular activities and the parents spend so much time at school supporting those activities that it does become the entire family's school.

Lila Lohr is a former Head of School at Princeton Day School in Princeton, New Jersey, and the Friends School of Baltimore in Baltimore, Maryland. She has been a teacher and an administrator in independent day schools for more than thirty years and is the mother of 3 independent day school graduates.

The Contemporary Boarding School: Change and Adaptability

Howard Greene
Matthew Greene

One of the most telling characteristics of the independent schools since their inception has been their ability to adapt to the significant social, political, and economic movements that have defined the evolutionary unfolding of an extraordinary nation. Those boarding schools that have survived and flourished over time have done so by adapting their curricula, the composition of their student bodies, and their facilities and resources to continue their role in training future leaders, regardless of their social, religious, and economic backgrounds.

How does this continuous state of adaptation and development translate to contemporary boarding school programs and populations? What do these schools stand for? How do they accomplish their primary goals? Here are the key features you should take note of as you consider this unique form of education.

Diversity

The American boarding school is viewed worldwide as an outstanding venue for students to obtain a first-rate education while they interact with a broad mix of other people. The resources and facilities are unmatched in any other country. Currently, more than 11,000 of the enrolled students in NAIS boarding schools are foreign nationals. Some of the larger, internationally recognized American schools enroll a large number of geographically diverse students.

The modern boarding school is, in fact, far more diverse than the local public schools that the majority of American students attend. Significant socioeconomic and continuing racial and ethnic segregation has resulted in homogeneous student bodies in many public school districts across the country. By contrast, boarding schools have a commitment to enroll outstanding students of all economic and social circumstances.

A Sense of Community

School leaders, when asked what defines their particular school, often refer to the power of community that envelops students, teachers, deans and administrators, coaches, and staff members. How valuable this is to all parties, especially to young men and women caught up in today's frenzied, competitive, and disjointed culture where it is easy to feel overwhelmed and uncertain. The desire to be in an environment where peers and adults are engaged with one another in a caring and supportive culture is a driving force for many who feel disconnected from, or simply not fully engaged with, the people and programs in their current school.

A Beacon of Educational Standards

Boarding schools have always set their own standards of educational attainment and pedagogy. Since they are not regulated by state educational bodies or influenced by the agendas of individual or party politics, the school professionals can design an academic and nonacademic curriculum that reflects the standards and goals they have set for their students.

Building Character

While all boarding schools have as their historic mission preparing students for university entrance and a successful academic experience, most have loftier goals in mind. Character is as important as acquired information and credits. Schools emphasize the development of critical thinking and analytical skills, an open mind to new and different ideas and opinions, excellent writing and oral skills, and an ability to think in mathematical and scientific terms. Most boarding schools look beyond these critical intellectual skills to the emotional, social, moral, and intellectual components of the education of the students in their charge. The residential community becomes a vital and active force in developing and honing these crucial skills. Every day, an individual might be called upon to make a decision in the classroom, on the playing field, or in the dormitory or dining hall that can have either a negative or positive impact on another student or the larger community.

The ultimate goal of the boarding school is not to create privileged adolescents who think and act alike but rather to consider the whole child at a critical stage in his or her moral and social development. There is a powerful force of stated ideals in the community at large that can be drawn on to help guide a young woman or man who has to decide how to behave in social situations, the classroom, the playing field, the dormitory, or even at home.

Boarding Schools as a Partnership

The Board of Trustees' Role

The members of the Board of Trustees are committed volunteers who have been elected to work as a cohesive group in overseeing the well-being of the school. The board is a legal entity charged with the responsibility of making certain the school is in sound fiscal and administrative condition and is fulfilling its stated mission. The board oversees the work of the head of school in the broadest sense and determines if he or she is responsibly managing the school. Typically, board members are recent and older graduates, parents of past and current students, or professional experts, all of whom work together to ensure that the school functions soundly on both an educational and financial basis. Boards generally choose their own members on the basis of a commitment to that institution's mission and purposes.

An independent school that is functioning well is, in large measure, the result of a healthy working relationship between the board and the senior management of the school. Together they review the annual operating budget, consider current and long-term strategic planning, and oversee fund-raising—in particular, capital campaigns to enlarge the school's endowment and physical facilities.

A number of schools include students in board meetings and specific committees. Typically, this includes the president of the student council who attends the general board meetings and student leaders who are active members of the student life committee. Their voices play a helpful role in determining school policies, rules, activities, and programs. In addition to the value added to the school community, these students gain a significant learning experience from such a deliberative process.

The School Head's Role

The head of school, reporting to the Board of Trustees, is the chief executive officer and is responsible for the operation of the school. It is his or her responsibility to execute the broad range of academic and noncurricular programs with the assistance of the faculty and other senior administrators, to hire and fire, to lead the faculty, to maintain a sound fiscal operation, to raise money from outside sources, and to serve as the educational visionary for the institution. A successfully run boarding school is a reflection of the mutual respect and effective working relationship between the head and the trustees.

In reviewing the merits of any boarding school for your child, be certain to learn about the relationship between the school head and the board, as well as the composition of the board. The days of a head staying at a school for twenty or thirty years are long gone, though some sitting heads have been in their position for close to that length of time. The norm these days is closer to the decade mark for a successful head running a well-managed school. A long-established or new head is not necessarily a sign either of school strength or weakness. Look beyond a head's tenure to seek out his or her experience level, accomplishments, energy, philosophy, and personal impact on a school.

The Faculty's Role

The opportunity to teach, counsel, and coach students in an intimate setting is what attracts most teachers to boarding schools. It is common practice for a faculty member in her role as dormitory parent, adviser, classroom teacher, coach, or administrator to seek out students whom she identifies as needing her help through the daily interaction that is part and parcel of the boarding life.

Boarding school teachers play an active and respected role in the affairs of their school. They serve on committees that set academic programs, grading standards, requirements for graduation, and standards of behavior. Faculty members work through academic departments to be certain that students are gaining a comprehensive and coherent education.

It is not happenstance that the great majority of boarding school teachers are graduates of strong liberal arts colleges and, most frequently, have graduate degrees in their particular discipline. A great many also played a sport at the intercollegiate level or were actively engaged in campus governance or the arts. The boarding school offers the teacher who loves her academic subject and has other talents the opportunity to share her enthusiasm with her students. The independent status of the school encourages the dedicated teacher to create and deliver a stimulating, effective curriculum that is usually free of topics, content, or lesson plans mandated by outside sources and without an end goal of preparation for standardized testing.

The Students' Role

Despite its traditions and culture, a school can, and often in large part does, reinvent itself every four years as new classes of students enter the school, gradually assume leadership responsibilities, and graduate, making room for new students to take their places. What an individual school "is" represents a shifting target because of the constant influx and egress of students. For prospective students, who those students are when they arrive constitutes one of the most significant influences on the boarding school experience and whether or not it is a good one.

Students in boarding schools today sit in on board meetings, judge fellow students on disciplinary committees, edit papers and yearbooks, serve as proctors or resident advisers in dormitories, and captain sports teams. They also conduct independent study projects, work with faculty as teaching assistants, guide tours on campus, talk with accreditation committees, and babysit faculty members' children. Students are active in community service projects on campus, in town, and around the world. They start new clubs, raise money for capital campaigns, and publish scientific research. They protest, vote, and serve as peer mediators and advisers. They sit around seminar tables discussing advanced literature and historical topics. They speak their minds, challenging faculty and administrators to improve courses, revise standards, and maintain their composure. Students at boarding schools are clearly not passive recipients; rather they are active participants in all aspects of school and community life.

The Parents' Role

One of the major changes in the boarding school partnership in recent years is the more active role that parents play. In past generations when the schools were more homogeneous in their student composition, parents were basically expected to leave the care and education of their children to the school's head and faculty. They were reassured that the moral, spiritual, and intellectual training of their offspring would be seen to. This is a far cry from the relationship contemporary parents, school administrators, and teachers understand as a partnership. Parents expect regular communications from their child's teachers and house advisers regarding student progress or any personal or academic difficulties. Heads of school and deans acknowledge that there is a regular flow of telephone calls and e-mails from the concerned parent. There is greater communication with parents regarding campus events and specific information about their child's engagement and performance.

Parenting a boarding school student involves a balancing act between being overly involved and too distant. Parents should neither assume that boarding schools will take over all parental and educational responsibilities for their children nor seek to insinuate themselves into every aspect of a student's school life. Parents should be watchful, involved, supportive, and attuned to the messages both the school and student are sending regarding the most appropriate and desirable level of engagement.

Schools also acknowledge that past and current parents are a major source of the financial support that enables them to carry on their stated purposes at the highest level of quality. Parents play a significant role in supporting fund-raising efforts and sponsoring events for current and prospective students and their parents. Most boarding schools have established parent committees that help to keep an open line of communication with the school's administrative leaders regarding parental concerns and recommendations for effective support of the students.

The Student Experience

Rather than interpreting discipline strictly as a punitive concept, schools use discipline as a teaching and learning tool. The community of faculty, deans, and students works together to establish agreeable rules of behavior. Each student must abide by this community ethos and, in the process of doing so, learns much about the interests and needs of others, the responsibility of an individual toward the common good, and the self-discipline and restraint that make this possible. The rewards are ample: a sense of responsibility and empowerment and the freedom to carry on one's daily life of activities and studies and time for friends. Those who break the rules find there is a response from the community and that appropriate action is taken.

Students play a major role in the smooth running of their school. Any school head will quickly confirm that his or her students are never shy or reluctant to make their voices heard on issues that affect their lives. Boarding students take it as fact that articulating their opinions to their teachers and administrators is a fundamental right.

Howard R. Greene, M.A., M.Ed., and Matthew W. Greene, Ph.D., have been providing personalized admissions counseling to guide students to the right secondary school, college, or graduate school for more than 35 years. They are the hosts of two PBS specials on college admission and have written numerous books, including the ***Greenes' Guides to Educational Planning Series.***

Originally published in a slightly different form in The Greenes' Guide to Boarding Schools (Princeton: Peterson's, 2006), 9-19. Reprinted by permission of the authors.

Study Confirms Benefits of Boarding School

Many people have long sung the praises of the boarding school experience. The high-level academics, the friendships, and the life lessons learned are without rival at private day or public schools, they say.

Now, a study released by The Association of Boarding Schools (TABS), a nonprofit organization of independent, college-preparatory schools, validates these claims. Not only do boarding school students spend more time studying (and less time watching TV), they are also better prepared for college and progress more quickly in their careers than their counterparts who attended private day or public schools.

The survey, which was conducted by the Baltimore-based research firm the Art & Science Group, involved interviews with 1,000 students and alumni from boarding schools, 1,100 from public schools, and 600 from private day schools (including independent day and parochial schools).

The results not only affirm the benefits enjoyed by boarding school graduates but those bestowed upon current boarding school students as well. "The study helps us better understand how the opportunities for interaction and learning beyond the classroom found at boarding schools impact a student's life at school and into adulthood," explained Steve Ruzicka, former TABS executive director. Ruzicka said the survey also provides boarding school alumni with empirical data to help when considering their children's educational options.

Rigorous Academics Prevail

Why do students apply to boarding schools? The TABS study found that the primary motivation for both applicants and their parents is the promise of a better education. And, happily, the vast majority of current and past students surveyed reported that their schools deliver on this promise. Current students indicated significantly higher levels of satisfaction with their academic experience at boarding schools than their peers at public and private day schools by more than ten percentage points (54 percent of boarding students versus 42 percent of private day students and 40 percent of public school students). Boarders reported in greater relative percentages that they find their schools academically challenging, that their peers are more motivated, and the quality of teaching is very high.

But the boarding environment is valued just as much for the opportunities for interaction and learning beyond the classroom. Interactions in the dining room, the dormitory, and on the playing field both complement and supplement academics, exposing students to a broad geographic and socioeconomic spectrum, challenging their boundaries, and broadening their vision of the world.

The Boarding School Boost

The 24/7 life at boarding schools also gives students a significant leg up when they attend college, the survey documents.

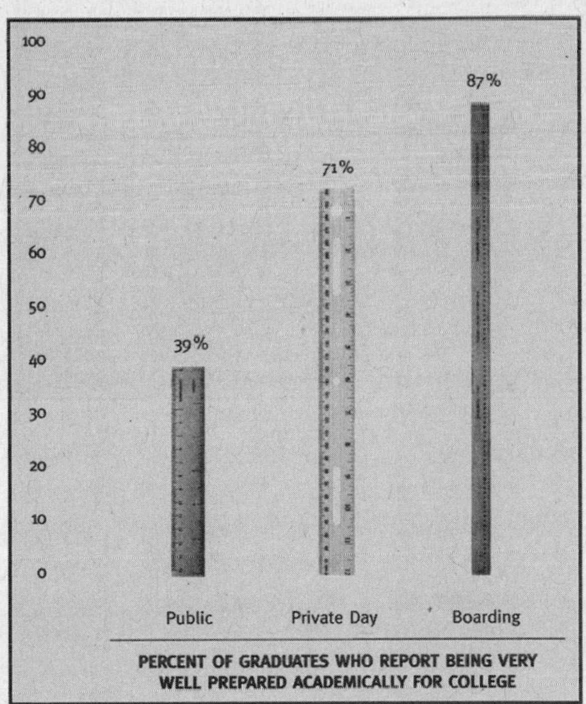

PERCENT OF GRADUATES WHO REPORT BEING VERY WELL PREPARED ACADEMICALLY FOR COLLEGE

Some 87 percent of boarding school graduates said they were very well prepared academically for college, with only 71 percent of private day and just 39 percent of public school alumni saying the same. And 78 percent of boarders reported that their schools also helped better prepare them to face the nonacademic aspects of college life, such as independence, social life, and time management. Only 36 percent of private day graduates and 23 percent of public school graduates said the same.

The TABS survey also documented that a larger percentage of boarding school graduates go on to earn advanced degrees once they finish college: 50 percent, versus 36 percent of private day and 21 percent of public school alumni.

Beyond college, boarding school graduates also reap greater benefits from their on-campus experiences, advancing faster and further in their careers comparatively. The study scrutinized former boarders versus private day and public school graduates in terms of achieving positions in top management and found that by midcareer, 44 percent of boarding school graduates had reached positions in top management versus 33 percent of private day school graduates and 27 percent of public school graduates.

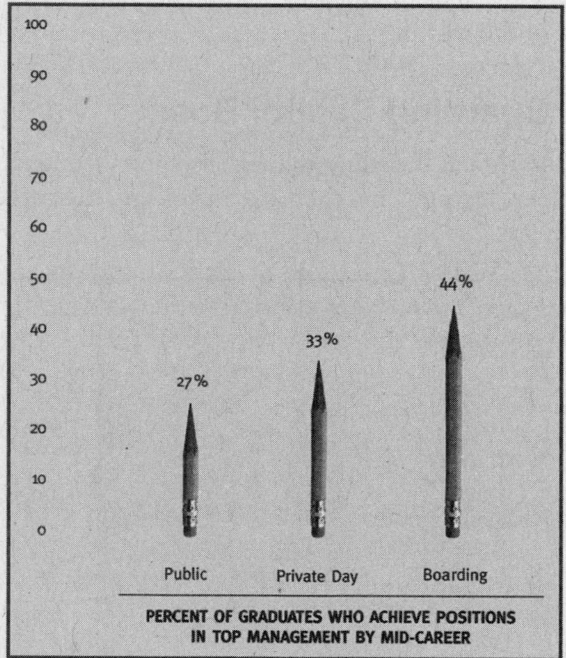

PERCENT OF GRADUATES WHO ACHIEVE POSITIONS IN TOP MANAGEMENT BY MID-CAREER

By late in their careers, more than half of the surveyed boarding school sample, 52 percent, held positions in top management as opposed to 39 percent of private day and 27 percent of public school graduates.

But perhaps the most compelling statistic that the study produced is the extremely high percentage—some 90 percent—of boarding school alumni who say they would, if given the opportunity, repeat their boarding school experience. This alone is a strong argument that validates the enduring value of the boarding school model. It is hoped that the study will help dispel many of the myths and stereotypes that have dogged the image of boarding schools over the last century and spread the good news that boarding schools today are diverse, exciting places for bright, well-adjusted students who are looking for success in their academic lives—and beyond.

For more information on TABS visit the Web site at www.schools.com.

Used by permission of The Association of Boarding Schools.

Semester Schools: Great Opportunities

Mark Meyer-Braun
Head of School The Outdoor Academy

Over the last twenty years, there has been tremendous growth in the range of educational opportunities available to young Americans. The advent of semester schools has played no small part in this trend. Similar in many ways to semester-abroad programs, semester schools provide secondary school students the opportunity to leave their home school for half an academic year to have a very different kind of experience—the experience of living and learning within a small community, among diverse students, and in a new and different place. The curricula of such schools tend to be thematic, interdisciplinary, rigorous, and experiential.

At semester schools, students have a full-immersion experience in a tightly knit learning community.

What Are the Benefits?

As a starting point for their programs, semester schools have embraced many of the qualities typical of independent schools. In fact, a number of semester schools were developed as extension programs by existing independent schools, providing unusual opportunities to their own students and those from other schools. Other semester schools have grown from independent educational organizations or foundations that bring their own educational interests and expertise to their semester programs. In both cases, semester schools provide the kind of challenging environment for which independent schools are known.

Across the board, semester school programs provide students with exceptional opportunities for contact with their teachers. Individual instruction and intimate classes are common, as is contact with teachers outside the classroom. At semester schools, students have a full-immersion experience in a tightly knit learning community. In such a setting, teachers are able to challenge each student in his or her own area of need, mentoring students to both academic and personal fulfillment.

Semester schools have developed around specialized curricular interests, often involving unique offerings or nontraditional subjects. In almost every case, these specialized curricula are related to the school's location. Indeed, place-based learning is a common thread in semester school education. Whether in New York City or the Appalachian Mountains, semester schools enable students to cultivate a sense of place and develop greater sensitivity to their surroundings. This is often accomplished through a combination of experiential education and traditional instruction. Students develop academic knowledge and practical skills in tandem through active participation in intellectual discourse, creative projects, hands-on exercises, and service learning opportunities. Throughout, emphasis is placed on the importance of combining intellectual exploration with thoughtful self-reflection, often facilitated by journaling exercises or group processing activities.

At semester schools, students inevitably learn their most important lessons through their membership in the school community. Living closely with peers and teachers and working together for the benefit of the group enables students to develop extraordinary communication skills and high levels of interpersonal accountability. Through this experience, students gain invaluable leadership and cooperation skills.

Ultimately, semester schools seek to impart translatable skills to their students. The common goal is for students to return to their schools and families with greater motivation, empathy, self-knowledge, and self-determination. These skills help to prepare students for the college experience and beyond. In addition, semester school participants report that their experiences helped to distinguish them in the college application process. Semester school programs are certainly not for everybody, but they serve an important role for students who are seeking something beyond the ordinary—students who wish to know themselves and the world in a profound way. All of the following semester school programs manifest these same values in their own distinctive way.

CITYterm

CITYterm, founded in 1996, is an interdisciplinary, experience-based program that takes 30 juniors and seniors from across the country and engages them in a semester-long study of New York City. CITYterm students typically spend three days a week in the classroom, reading, writing, and thinking about New York City, and three days a week in the city working on projects, studying diverse neighborhoods, or meeting with politicians, urban historians, authors, artists, actors, and various city experts. Much of the excitement of CITYterm comes from experiencing firsthand in the city what has been studied in the classroom. Many of the projects are done in collaborative teams where the groups engage not only in formal academic research at the city's libraries but also use the resources of New York City's residents and institutions to gather the information necessary for presentations. Students come to see themselves as the active creators of their own learning both in the classroom and in the world. Learn more about CITYterm by visiting www.cityterm.org.

Conserve School

Conserve School is a semester school for high school juniors that is focused on the theme of environmental stewardship. Attending Conserve School gives high school students a one-semester opportunity to step out of their regular school and into a unique educational setting, while still continuing their required academic studies. Conserve School's challenging, college-prep curriculum immerses high school juniors in environmental history, nature literature, and the science of conservation. Because Conserve School is located on a 1,200-acre wilderness campus, a significant portion of the curriculum is delivered via outdoors, hands-on, active learning. Conserve School is located just west of Land O' Lakes, Wisconsin, near the border of Michigan's Upper Peninsula. Learn more about the Conserve School at www.conserveschool.org/.

The Island School

The Island School, founded in 1999 by The Lawrenceville School, is an independent academic program in the Bahamas for high school sophomores or juniors. The fourteen-week academic course of study includes honors classes in science, field research (a laboratory science), history, math, art, English literature, and physical/outdoor education and a weekly community service component. All courses are place-based and explicitly linked, taking advantage of the school's surroundings to both deepen understandings of complex academic and social issues and to make those understandings lasting by connecting course content with experience. Students apply their investigative, interpretive, and problem-solving skills during four- and eight-day kayaking expeditions, SCUBA diving opportunities, teaching environmental issues to local students, and in daily life at the school. In addition to traditional

classroom assessments, students conduct research on mangrove communities, coastal management, artificial reefs, permaculture, and marine protected areas. These projects support national research and are conducted under the auspices of the Bahamian government. At the conclusion of the semester, students present their work to a panel of visiting scientists and educators, including local and national government officials from the Bahamas. The opportunity to interact with the local community through research, outreach, and the rigorous physical and academic schedule creates a transformative experience for students. The admissions process is competitive, and selected students demonstrate solid academic performance, leadership potential, and a high degree of self-motivation. Contact The Island School for more information at www.islandschool.org.

Chewonki Semester School

The Chewonki Semester School (formerly Maine Coast Semester) offers a small group of eleventh-grade students the chance to live and work on a 400-acre saltwater peninsula with the goal of exploring the natural world through courses in natural science, environmental issues, literature and writing, art, history, mathematics, and foreign language. Since 1988, this semester school has welcomed students from more than 230 public and private schools across the country and in Canada. The Chewonki community is small—39 students and 20 faculty members—and the application process is competitive. In addition to their studies, students work for several hours each afternoon on an organic farm, in a wood lot, or on maintenance and construction projects. Students who attend are highly motivated, capable, and willing to take the risk of leaving friends and family for a portion of their high school career. They enjoy hard work, both intellectual and physical, and they demonstrate a tangible desire to contribute to the world. Chewonki students return to their schools with self-confidence, an appreciation for the struggles and rewards of community living, and an increased sense of ownership of their education. For information on the Chewonki Semester School, go to www.chewonki.org.

The Mountain School

The Mountain School of Milton Academy, founded in 1984, hosts 45 high school juniors from private and public schools throughout the United States who have chosen to spend four months on a working organic farm in Vermont. Courses provide a demanding and integrated learning experience, taking full advantage of the school's small size and mountain campus. Students and adults develop a social contract of mutual trust that expects individual and communal responsibility, models the values of simplicity and sustainability, and challenges teenagers to engage in meaningful work. Students live with teachers in small houses and help make important decisions concerning how to live together and manage the farm. Courses offered include English, environmental science, U.S. history, and all levels of math, physics, chemistry, Spanish, French, Latin, studio art, and humanities. To learn more, please visit the Web site at www. mountainschool.org.

The Outdoor Academy of the Southern Appalachians

The Outdoor Academy offers tenth grade and select eleventh-grade students from across the country a semester away in the mountains of North Carolina. Arising from more than eighty years of experiential education at Eagle's Nest Foundation, this school-away-from-school provides a college-preparatory curriculum along with special offerings in environmental education, outdoor leadership, the arts, and community service. Each semester, up to 35 students embrace the Southern Appalachians as a unique ecological, historical, and cultural American region. In this setting, students and teachers live as a close-knit community, and lessons of cooperation and responsibility abound. Students develop a healthy work ethic as course work and projects are pursued both in and out of the classroom. Courses in English, mathematics, science, history, foreign language, visual and performing arts, and music emphasize hands-on and cooperative learning. Classes often meet outside on the 180-acre wooded campus or in nearby national wilderness areas, where the natural world enhances intellectual pursuits. On weekends and extended trips, the outdoor leadership program teaches hiking, backpacking, caving, canoeing, and rock-climbing skills. The Outdoor Academy is open to students from both public and private secondary schools and is accredited by the Southern Association of Colleges and Schools. Learn more about The Outdoor Academy at www.enf.org/outdoor_academy/academic_program.

The Oxbow School

The Oxbow School in Napa, California, is a one-semester visual arts program for high school juniors and seniors from public and private schools nationwide. Oxbow offers students a unique educational experience focused on in-depth study in sculpture, printmaking, drawing and painting, and photography and digital media, including animation. The interdisciplinary, project-based curriculum emphasizes experiential learning, critical thinking, and the development of research skills as a means of focused artistic inquiry. Each semester, 2 Visiting Artists are invited to work collaboratively with students and teachers. By engaging students in the creative process, Oxbow fosters a deep appreciation for creativity in all areas of life beyond the classroom. Since its founding in 1998, students who have spent a semester at The Oxbow School have matriculated to leading universities, colleges, and independent colleges of art and design around the country. Learn more at www.oxbowschool.org.

The Rocky Mountain Semester

The Rocky Mountain Semester (RMS) at the High Mountain Institute is an opportunity for high school juniors to examine the human relationship to the natural world through a combination of rigorous academics and extended wilderness expeditions. During the 110-day program, up to 38 students spend five weeks backpacking, skiing, and studying throughout the wilderness of Colorado and Utah. The remainder of the semester is spent on campus near Leadville, Colorado, where students pursue a rigorous course of study and learn how to live successfully in a small community environment. While at the RMS, most students take five or six classes—the only required elective is Practices and Principles: Ethics of the Natural World. It is in this class that students are taught the theoretical foundations for all that is done in the field, examine the human relationship to the natural world, and learn the skills necessary to travel safely and comfortably in remote settings. Students may also take literature of the natural world, natural science, U.S. history or AP U.S. history, Spanish or French, and mathematics.

Interested students can learn more about The Rocky Mountain Semester at www.hminet.org/RockyMountainSemester.

The Woolman Semester

The Woolman Semester is a community-based, sixteen-week, interdisciplinary program for high school juniors and seniors and first-year postgraduates. The mission of the school is to weave together peace, sustainability, and social action into an intensely rigorous academic experience. The school is located at the Sierra Friends

Center in Nevada City, California, on a 230-acre campus complete with forests, fields, gardens, and livestock to use as a living laboratory, as well as for the wood chopping and lettuce harvesting of daily life. Classes generally meet in the morning, while labs, study groups, and farm work take place in the afternoon. Students and faculty members also participate in a two-week service project and a one-week wilderness trip. Get all the information on The Woolman Semester program at www.woolman.org.

The author wishes to acknowledge and thank all the semester school programs for contributing their school profiles and collaborating in order to spread the word about semester school education.

Why a Therapeutic or Special Needs School?

Diederik van Renesse

Families contact me when a son or daughter is experiencing increased difficulties in school or has shown a real change in attitude at home. Upon further discussion, parents often share the fact that they have spoken with their child's teachers and have held meetings to establish support systems in the school and at home. Evaluations, medications, therapists, and motivational counseling are but a few of the multiple approaches that parents and educators take—yet in some cases, the downward spiral continues. Anxiety builds in the student and family members; school avoidance and increased family turmoil reach a point where the situation is intolerable, and alternatives must be explored—be it a special needs school, a therapeutic school, or a combination of both.

Some families seek the help of an independent education consultant to identify the most appropriate setting.

But should that school be a day or residential school, and how do parents decide which will best meet their child's needs? Resources such as *Peterson's Private Secondary Schools*, the Internet, guidance/school counselors, and therapists are valuable; however, the subtle nuances involved in determining the environment that will best serve the child are difficult to ascertain. Some families seek the help of an independent education consultant to identify the most appropriate setting. Many independent education consultants specialize in working with children who have special needs such as learning differences, anxiety disorders, emotional issues, ADHD, opposition, defiance, school phobia, drug or alcohol abuse, Asperger Syndrome, autism, and more. Consultants have frequent contact with the schools, and they work closely with parents during the enrollment process.

Given the broad spectrum of needs presented by individual students, many parents question whether there is indeed a day school that can meet the needs of their child. The answer often depends on location, space availability, willingness to relocate, and appropriateness of the options. While there are many day school options throughout the United States, there are even more residential or boarding options. Clearly the decision to have your child attend a residential school is not made easily. As a family you may feel as though you do not have a choice—but you should undertake a thorough assessment of all the day options and how they might meet the majority of your child's needs.

When the primary concerns are learning differences, many local options (though often small and issue-specific) are available to families. Local counselors are often valuable resources as are local chapters of national LD organizations. If you come up with a variety of options, carefully compare them by visiting the schools and meeting with the specialists at each school—those individuals who will work directly with your child.

With the day options, it is important to keep the following factors in mind: program and staff credentials, transportation time to and from the school, availability of additional resources (support services) in or outside the school setting, sports and extracurricular offerings, facilities and accessibility, and your child's potential peer group. You will also need to assess many of these factors when considering residential schools, although most residential schools are more self-contained than day schools. Also significant is whether the school has been approved by and accepts funding from its state and/or school district.

For families who cannot avail themselves of local day options or whose child is best served in a residential setting, an even greater spectrum of options is available. These range from traditional boarding schools with built-in academic support services to therapeutic boarding schools, wilderness or outdoor therapeutic programs, emotional growth or behavior modification schools, transitional or independent living programs, and even residential treatment centers, hospitals, or other health facilities.

Given the breadth of the residential schools or programs, most families are best served by a team that includes not only the parents (and at times the student), but also the professionals who have taught, counseled, and worked closely with the child. Together, the team can identify the specific needs, deficits, or behavioral issues that must be addressed, and they can work together to match those with the appropriate schools. As with day schools, you should arrange to visit the facilities so that you are well-informed about each option and will be comfortable with your final decision. These visits are not only opportunities for you to meet the staff and students, but also for you and your child to begin a relationship that will continue when your child is enrolled.

There is no question that seeking alternative options, whether they are special needs or therapeutic, is a daunting task. However, with the help of expert resources and reliable professionals, the right school can make a significant and lasting impact on your child's health and well-being.

Diederik van Renesse is a Senior Partner at Steinbrecher & Partners Educational Consulting Services in Westport, Connecticut. A former teacher, admission director, and private school counselor, he now specializes in helping families throughout the United States and abroad with youngsters who require special needs or alternative schools or who need interventions and therapeutic settings.

Finding the Perfect Match

Helene Reynolds

One of the real benefits of independent education is that it allows you to deliberately seek out and choose a school community for your child. If you are like most parents, you want your child's school years to reflect an appropriate balance of academic challenge, social development, and exploration into athletics and the arts. You hope that through exposure to new ideas and sound mentoring your child will develop an awareness of individual social responsibility, as well as the study skills and work ethic to make a contribution to his or her world. It is every parent's fondest wish to have the school experience spark those areas of competence that can be pursued toward excellence and distinction.

An increasing number of parents realize that this ideal education is found outside their public school system, that shrinking budgets, divisive school boards, and overcrowded classrooms have resulted in schools where other agendas vie with education for attention and money. In this environment there is less time and energy for teachers to focus on individual needs.

The decision to choose a private school can be made for as many different reasons as there are families making the choice. Perhaps your child would benefit from smaller classes or accelerated instruction. Perhaps your child has needs or abilities that can be more appropriately addressed in a specialized environment. Perhaps you are concerned about the academic quality of your local public school and the impact it may have on your child's academic future. Or perhaps you feel that a private school education is a gift you can give your child to guide him or her toward a more successful future.

Every child is an individual, and this makes school choice a process unique to each family. The fact that your father attended a top-flight Eastern boarding school to prepare for the Ivy League does not necessarily make this educational course suitable for all of his grandchildren. In addition to determining the school's overall quality, you must explore the appropriateness of philosophy, curriculum, level of academic difficulty, and style before making your selection. The right school is the school where your child will thrive, and a famous name and a hallowed reputation are not necessarily the factors that define the right environment. The challenge is in discovering what the factors are that make the match between your child and his or her school the right one.

No matter how good its quality and reputation, a single school is unlikely to be able to meet the needs of all children. The question remains: How do families begin their search with confidence so they will find what they are looking for? How do they make the right connection?

As a parent, there are a number of steps you can follow to establish a reasoned and objective course of information gathering that will lead to a subjective discussion of this information and the way it applies to the student in question. This can only occur if the first step is done thoroughly and in an orderly manner. Ultimately, targeting a small group of schools, any of which could be an excellent choice, is only possible after information gathering and discussion have taken place. With work and a little luck, the result of this process is a school with an academically sound and challenging program based on an educational philosophy that is an extension of the family's views and which will provide an emotionally and socially supportive milieu for the child.

Step 1: Identify Student Needs

Often the decision to change schools seems to come out of the blue, but, in retrospect, it can be seen as a decision the family has been leading up to for some time. I would urge parents to decide on their own goals for the search first and to make sure, if possible, that they can work in concert toward meeting these goals before introducing the idea to their child. These goals are as different as the parents who hold them. For one parent, finding a school with a state-of-the-art computer program is a high priority. For another, finding a school with a full dance and music program is important. Others will be most concerned about finding a school that has the best record of college acceptances and highest SAT or ACT scores.

Once you have decided your own goals for the search, bring the child into the discussion. I often say to parents that the decision to explore is *not* the decision to change schools but only the decision to gather information and consider options. It is important to be aware that everyone has an individual style of decision making and that the decision to make a change is loaded with concerns, many of which will not be discovered until the process has begun.

If you have already made the decision to change your child's school, it is important to let your child know that this aspect of the decision is open to discussion but not to negotiation. It is equally important that you let your child know that he or she will have responsibility in choosing the specific school. Without that knowledge, your son or daughter may feel that he or she has no control over the course of his or her own life.

Some students are responsible enough to take the lead in the exploration; some are too young to do so. But in all cases, children need reassurance about their future and clarity about the reasons for considering other school settings. Sometimes the situation is fraught with disparate opinions that can turn school choice into a family battleground, one in which the child is the ultimate casualty. It is always important to keep in mind that the welfare of the child is the primary goal.

If you have already made the decision to change your child's school, it is important to let your child know that this aspect of the decision is open to discussion but not to negotiation.

The knowledge that each individual has his or her own agenda and way of making decisions should be warning enough to pursue some preliminary discussion so that you, as parents, can avoid the pitfall of conflicting goals and maintain a united front and a reasonably directed course of action. The family discussion should be energetic, and differences of opinion should be encouraged as healthy and necessary and expressed in a climate of trust and respect.

There are many reasons why you may, at this point, decide to involve a professional educational consultant. Often this choice is made to provide a neutral ground where you and your child can both speak and be heard. Another reason is to make sure that you have established a sound course of exploration that takes both your own and your child's needs into consideration. Consultants who are up-to-date on school information, who have visited each campus, and who are familiar with the situations of their clients can add immeasurably to the process. They can provide a reality check, reinforcement of personal impressions, and experience-based information support for people who are doing a search of this type for the first time. All the research in the world cannot replace the experience and industry knowledge of a seasoned professional. In addition, if the specific circumstances of the placement are delicate, the educational consultant is in a position to advocate for your child during the placement process. There are also situations in which a family in crisis doesn't have the time or the ability to approach school choice in a deliberate and objective manner.

These are some of the many reasons to engage the services of a consultant, but it is the family guidance aspect that most families overlook at the start of the process and value most highly after they have completed it. A good consultant provides neutral ground and information backup that are invaluable.

Step 2: Evaluate Your Child's Academic Profile

If your child's academic profile raises questions about his or her ability, learning style, or emotional profile, get a professional evaluation to make sure that your expectations for your child are congruent with the child's actual abilities and needs.

Start gathering information about your child from the current school. Ask guidance counselors and teachers for their observations, and request a formal meeting to review the standardized testing that virtually every school administers. Question their views of your child's behavior, attentiveness, and areas of strength and weakness. Make sure you fully understand the reasons behind their recommendations. Do not feel shy about calling back to ask questions at a later date, after you have had time to think and consider this important information. Your child's future may depend on the decisions you are making; don't hesitate to keep asking until you have the information you need.

If a picture of concern emerges, ask the guidance counselor, other parents, or your pediatrician for suggestions regarding learning specialists or psychologists in the community who work with children and can provide an evaluation of their academic ability, academic achievement, and learning style. The evaluation should be reviewed in-depth with the specialist, who should be asked about specific recommendations for changes in the youngster's schooling.

Remember, as the parent, it is ultimately your responsibility to weigh the ideas of others and to decide if the difficulty lies with your child or the environment, either of which could indicate a need for a change of school.

Step 3: Review the Goals of Placement

Discuss your differences of opinion about making a change: Identify a list of schools that creates a ballpark of educational possibilities. (An educational consultant can also be helpful at this stage.)

It is important that both you and your child take the time to consider what characteristics, large and small, you would like in the new school and which you would like to avoid. As you each make lists of priorities and discuss them, the process of school choice enters the subjective arena. The impersonal descriptions of school environments transform into very personal visualizations of the ways you and your child view the child in a new setting.

A chance to play ice hockey, a series of courses in Mandarin Chinese, the opportunity to take private flute lessons, or a desire to meet others from all over the world may sound like a bizarre mix of criteria, but the desire to explore and find all of these options in a single environment expresses the expansiveness of the student's mind and the areas he or she wants to perfect, try out, or explore. Don't expect perfectly logical thinking from your child as he or she considers options; don't take everything he or she says literally or too seriously. Open and respectful discussion will allow a child to embrace a new possibility one day and reject it the next—this is part of the process of decision making and affirmation and part of the fun of exploration.

Step 4: Set an Itinerary

Set an itinerary for visits and interviews so that you and your child can compare campuses and test your preconceived ideas of the schools you have researched against the reality of the campus community; forward standardized testing scores and transcripts to the schools prior to visits so that the admission office has pertinent information in advance of your meeting.

In order to allow your child the freedom to form opinions about the schools you visit, you may want to keep these pointers in mind:

- Parents should allow their child to be front and center during the visits and interviews—allow your child to answer questions, even if they leave out details you think are important.
- Parents should stay in the background and have confidence that the admission officers know how to engage kids in conversation.
- This may be the first time your child has been treated by a school as an individual and responsible person—enjoy watching him or her adjust to this as an observer, not as a protector or participant.
- Don't let your own anxiety ruin your child's experience.
- Discuss dress in advance so it doesn't become the issue and focus of the trip.

Keep your ideas and impressions to yourself and allow your child first shot at verbalizing opinions. Remember that immediate reactions are not final decisions; often the first response is only an attempt to process the experience.

Step 5: Use the Application Process for Personal Guidance

Make sure your child uses the application process not only to satisfy the school's need for information but also to continue the personal guidance process of working through and truly understanding his or her goals and expectations.

Application questions demand your child's personal insight and exploration. Addressing questions about significant experiences, people who have influenced his or her life, or selecting four words that best describe him or her are ways of coming to grips with who your child is and what he or she wants to accomplish both at the new school and in life. Although parents want their children to complete seamless and perfect applications, it is important to remember that the application must be the work of the child and that the parent has an excellent opportunity to discuss the questions and answers to help guide the student in a positive and objective self-review.

It is more important that the application essays accurately reflect the personality and values of the student than that they be technically flawless. Since the school is basing part of its acceptance decision on the contents of the application, the school needs to meet the real student in the application. The child's own determination of what it is important for the school to know about them is crucial to this process. That being said, parents can play an important role in helping the child understand the difference between unnecessarily brutal honesty and putting his or her best foot forward.

Step 6: Trust Your Observations

Although the process of school exploration depends on objectivity, it is rare that a family will embrace a school solely because of its computer labs, endowment, library, SAT or ACT scores, or football team. These objective criteria frame the search, but it tends to be the intangibles that determine the decision. It is the subjective—instinctive responses to events on campus, people met, quality of interview, unfathomable vibes—that makes the match.

It is important to review what aspects of the school environment made you feel at home. These questions apply equally to parent and child. Did you like the people you met on campus? Was the tour informational but informal, with students stopping to greet you or the tour guide? Was the tone of the campus (austere or homey, modern or traditional) consistent with the kind of educational atmosphere you are looking for? Are the sports facilities beyond your wildest expectation? Does the college-sending record give you confidence that your child will find an intellectually comfortable peer group? How long do the teachers tend to stay with the school, and do they send their own children there? If it is a boarding school, do teachers live on campus? How homey is the dorm setup?

The most fundamental questions are: Do people in the school community like where they are, trust each other, have respect for each other, and feel comfortable there? Is it a family you would care to join? These subjective responses will help you recognize which schools will make your child feel he or she is part of the community, where he or she will fit in and be respected for who he or she is and wants to become.

Helene Reynolds is a former educational consultant from Princeton, New Jersey.

Plan a Successful School Search

Application deadlines, entrance exams, interviews, and acceptance or rejection letters—these are some of the challenges you can expect to encounter when applying to private schools. The school search may seem daunting, but it doesn't have to be. Here are some tips to help get you on your way.

The first step is to gather information, preferably in the spring before you plan on applying. *Peterson's Private Secondary Schools,* with vital statistics on more than 1,200 leading private schools in the United States and abroad, can help you evaluate schools, clarify your choices, and hone your search.

If you're considering boarding schools, you may also want to obtain a free copy of the *Boarding Schools Directory* from The Association of Boarding Schools (TABS) by calling 828-258-5354 or visiting TABS's Web site (www.boardingschools.com).

Visiting Schools

The next step is to start a list of schools that pique your or your child's interest. You'll want to call, fax, e-mail, or write to admission offices for catalogs and applications. At this stage, don't let cost rule out choices. You'll learn more about the school later—the financing resources it makes available to students and its policies of awarding aid.

With school brochures and catalogs in hand, start planning fall visits and interviews. Review your school calendar, noting Saturdays, holidays, and vacations. Try to plan interviews for these days off. Each interview could last about 3 hours, as campus tours and other activities are often included.

Once you have determined which schools you want to see, where they are, and in what order you want to see them, call each school to set the interview date and time.

Keep in mind that there is no "magic number" of schools to see. Some students interview at and apply to only one school, feeling that if they are not accepted, they will stay at their current school. Some students interview at many, thinking that considering a large number and a variety of schools will help them focus on real needs and desires.

After you've made an appointment to visit the school, reread the school's catalog and, if possible, its description in this guide, and check out its Web site so that facts about the school will be fresh in your mind when you visit.

The Application Process

Once the fact-finding is completed, your child will need to work on applications. Most schools have January or February deadlines, so it pays to begin filling out forms in November.

Applications may ask for all or some of the following: school records, references from teachers, a student statement, a writing sample or essay, an application fee, and medical history form.

If you are working with a hard-copy form, make photocopies of all application pages before your child begins to complete them. That way, he or she will have at least one copy for use as a rough draft. Also make copies of each completed application for your records.

References are usually written on specific school forms and are considered confidential. To ensure confidentiality, people providing references mail their comments directly to the school. A school may require four or five references—three academic references, usually from an English teacher, a math teacher, and one other teacher, and one or two references from other evaluators who know your child's strengths in areas other than academics. Ask these people in advance if they will write on your child's behalf. Give reference-writers appropriate forms with any special instructions and stamped envelopes addressed to the school; be sure to provide as much lead time before the deadline as possible.

Most schools have January or February deadlines, so it pays to begin filling out forms in November.

The student application is completed on a special form and consists of factual family information, as well as some long or short essay questions. As tempting as it may be to help, let your child do the writing. The schools need to see the student's style, mechanical skills, and the way he or she looks at life and education. Some schools require a corrected writing sample from an English assignment. In this case, have your child ask his or her English teacher to help choose his or her best work.

For additional information on applications, including the common application forms, check out "Understanding the Admission Application Form" on page 25.

Once the applications are mailed or submitted online, the hard part is done. Ask admission officers when you can expect to hear their decisions. Most schools will let you know in early March. While you wait, you may want to remind your son or daughter that being turned down by a school is not a statement about his or her worth. Schools have many different objectives in putting a class together. And that's a lesson that will come in handy when you face the college application process.

Understanding the Admission Application Form

Gregg W. M. Maloberti
Dean of Admission
The Lawrenceville School
Lawrenceville, New Jersey

Students applying to independent schools are presented with a myriad of options when it comes time to choose the method of completing the application process. Where once each school issued and required its own paper application, many schools now accept common applications such as the Secondary Schools Application from SSAT (Secondary School Admission Test), the Admission Application Form from TABS (The Association of Boarding Schools), or various other online application forms sponsored by individual schools and placement programs. With so many options, many applicants and parents are perplexed as to which method to employ, and others worry that the choice of one method over another may have a negative effect on their chances of admission. Understanding more about why these changes came about and how they save applicants and schools time and money may help applicants and their parents make an informed choice about which method to use.

The recent developments and innovations in independent school applications mirror the changes that have occurred at the college level. The College Board's Common Application is accepted at over 300 colleges and is available online. The Internet has accelerated the interest in online applications. At the same time, students are much more accustomed to writing on a computer than they once were with pen and paper. Concerns about the financial and environmental costs of a paper-based application that travels from the printer to the school, to the candidate, to the candidate's school, and back to the admission office by mail or courier contribute to the idea that the time of an online commonly accepted application has come.

The Standard Application Online (SAO) is available on the SSAT Web site at www.ssat.org/ssat/apply-appservice.html. The Boarding Schools Admission Application Form is available in the TABS Boarding Schools Directory and in electronic form from the TABS Web site: http://www.boardingschools.com/how-to-apply/application.aspx.

There are a few schools that accept only the recommendation forms from the Admission Application Form. It's best to check with each school to find out which forms are preferred. The list of schools accepting the Secondary Schools Application from SSAT is available at this SSAT Web site: www.ssat.org/ssat/apply-appservice.html.

Common Applications Make Sense

Anxious parents' lingering doubts about the use of one of the common application forms are hard to ignore: Will the substitution of the common application for the individual school's application cause the admission committee to be offended and compromise my child's chances for admission? Parents should rest assured that schools agreeing to accept the common application forms believe that a fair and effective admission decision can be made on the basis of the common form and that its use in no way erodes the quality of their selection process.

How Does the Common Application Differ?

All applications begin with a biographical sketch of the candidate: name, address, birth date, mailing address, parents' names, and schools attended. Information regarding sibling or legacy relationships, interest in financial aid, citizenship, language spoken, and even racial and ethnic diversity is collected as well. Except for the order in which these questions appear, there is little variation in these question types from one school's application to another. The common application forms certainly relieve candidates of the burden of providing the very same biographical information over and over again.

The second section of an application generally reveals a candidate's accomplishments and ambitions. Often, the applicants are asked to catalog their interests and activities in list or narrative form. Schools want to know what the candidate has done, for how long, with whom, and to what distinction, if any. In a few cases, some schools ask for a series of short answers to a combination of questions or look for the applicant to complete a sentence. There are generally no "right" answers to these questions—but honest answers can help the school begin to characterize the applicant's curiosity, maturity, ambition, and self-esteem. Here again, great similarity exists in the manner and style with which this information is gathered. While the common application forms ask these question types in a more direct manner, they are no less effective than the individual school's application, and their use affords a candidate a genuine measure of efficiency without compromising individuality.

Schools that advocate the use of their own applications over that of the common application forms often bitterly defend the third and final portion of their applications since it generally includes essay questions. With few exceptions, these questions, while occasionally posed in a unique or original manner, seek to probe much the same territory covered by the three choices listed in the essay section of the common application forms:

1. Describe a person you admire or who has influenced you a great deal.
2. What makes you the interesting person that you are?
3. Explain the impact of an event or activity that has created a change in your life or in your way of thinking.

Many schools that use the common applications require a supplement that affords an opportunity for candidates to provide information that is not requested by the common applications.

While the candidate's ability to write well is certainly under review in the essay question, the exercise investigates a candidate's values and explores the individual experiences that have shaped his or her character. These questions give candidates a chance to reveal such qualities as independence, self-reliance, creativity, originality, humility, generosity, curiosity, and genius. Viewed in this light, answering these questions becomes a tall order. The best advice may be to just answer them. In addition, candidates should recognize that although the content of their essays is always of interest, grammar, spelling, punctuation, organization, and the inclusion of evidence or examples are of equal importance.

Candidates who come from disadvantaged backgrounds often find this section of the application the most challenging and occasionally exclusionary. Some schools assume that all applicants have access to opportunities such as summer camps, music instruction, and periodicals and newspapers. Whatever the case, the common application forms attempt to be more inclusive of a broader set of experiences. In fact, many outreach agencies who seek to identify and place disadvantaged students in independent schools have either used one of the existing common application forms or have developed their own applications in lieu of individual school application forms.

If a student fears that using one of the common applications will somehow fail to convey a unique aspect of his or her individuality or that the essay question answers will not speak to the unique qualities of why a particular school might be a good match, he or she may want to think about including an extra essay. Just because a candidate uses a common application does not mean that he or she must use a common approach to completing it. Imagine how welcome a splash of creativity might be to an individual reader or committee of admission officers who may read hundreds or even thousands of applications each admission season. An application that parrots the list of school courses, sports, and activities offers little insight into the candidate. A well-written application will be as unique as the individual who wrote it.

Using a common application makes the process of applying to multiple schools a much more manageable endeavor.

Applicants and their parents are not the only winners when a common application form is used. The teachers who dutifully complete countless recommendation forms enjoy the convenience of having to complete only one form for each of their students applying to independent schools. Practically speaking, if there is ever a time that a student wants to be in good favor with his or her teacher, it is the moment at which a reference is being given. Using a common application makes the process of applying to multiple schools a much more manageable endeavor. When there is only one form to complete, most teachers will provide longer and more informative answers that are far more helpful to admission officers. Common applications are a great remedy for the fatigue and frustration endured by teachers who have been overwhelmed by a barrage of recommendation forms. Currently, there are even more schools accepting common recommendation forms than there are schools accepting the entire Secondary School Application or the Admission Application Form. Before discounting the benefits of a common application, be sure to consider at least the use of the recommendation forms.

Counselors and Consultants Speak Out

Lee Carey, Director of Admissions and Secondary School Counseling at Shore Country Day School in Beverly, Massachusetts, has been advising eighth-graders for many years and finds the workload associated with the application process unreasonable for most of her students. "It is inconceivable to expect a 14-year-old student to write upwards of eight individual essays, all of top quality. From taking time for school visits, making up missed schoolwork, organizing forms, completing paperwork, and polishing writing, the act of applying to secondary schools becomes a whole second job for eighth- and ninth-grade students." Considering that the average application includes up to ten documents, some of which must pass between the applicant, the sending school, and back to the applicant or the receiving school, an eighth grader and his or her parents are now looking at completing more than eighty documents! On top of the testing process and applying for financial aid, this amounts to an enormous administrative challenge.

Karl Koenigsbauer, Director of Secondary School Placement, Eaglebrook School in Deerfield, Massachusetts, agrees that the common application forms make the process more efficient, but he worries about how they might erode the process as well. "My goal is to help students find the school that will be the best match for their abilities and interests. The essay questions from some schools really help the candidate to understand more about what qualities of mind and spirit a school values. When a candidate comes to me and says a particular question is too difficult, too simplistic, or just plain confusing, it gives me an opportunity to help him or her see how that question represents the identity of that particular school and why it may or may not be a good match. I worry that the common application forms will homogenize the application process to the point where I lose this opportunity to fine-tune the placement process."

Faith Howland, an independent educational consultant in Boston, Massachusetts, and a member of the Independent Educational Consultants Association (IECA), works with families to find the right school and is also often contacted for help when a student's first round of applications has not been successful. "The application process can be near overwhelming for 13- and 14-year-olds. To write as many as eight different applications, each with different essays, just when you are expected to get great grades and continue your sports commitments and other extracurricular activities—not to mention working to prepare for entrance tests. This is high stress! Use of a common application form would be supportive to students and would be extremely helpful in streamlining the teacher recommendations. For those kids who need to submit a second round of applications, the common application forms could be invaluable. These youngsters are coping with disappointment while needing to research new possibilities. If schools were willing to share the common application forms, it's conceivable that many more students who might simply give up if not successful on their first applications could be placed."

Many Schools, One Application

Increased acceptance of the Secondary Schools Application and the Admission Application Form could lead to a marked increase in applications. Common applications are especially helpful to the candidate who fails to earn any acceptance letters at the end of the application process. Traditionally, if a candidate wants to apply to a new list of schools, he or she must start from scratch and complete a new set of forms. Common applications certainly speed up this process, and in the case of the Secondary School Application from SSAT, sending an application to an additional school is as easy as sending the test scores. Candidates simply sign in to their accounts and select another school.

More than half of the candidates who apply to independent schools come from public schools and may not enjoy the benefit of placement counselors at their schools nor do they seek the advice of independent counselors. Regardless, most candidates are well served in using one of the common application forms when applying to multiple schools. One strategy may be to complete a few individual applications and then submit one of the common application forms to a few other schools—identifying some additional options and increasing the likelihood of having meaningful choices after the decision letters are mailed. Many candidates find it much easier to figure out which school they want once they know which school wants them.

Few schools realize how difficult the application process can be for families who are applying to more than one school. Common application forms make the process of applying to multiple schools a much more manageable endeavor. The use of a common application form affords families much more time and energy to devote to other aspects of the application and interview process. By reducing the duplicated paperwork of recommendations and the need to complete so many essays, applicants and their parents are granted a greater opportunity to discuss the real issues surrounding school selection, such as the compatibility of curriculum, style of teaching, and program offerings. Rather than creating folders for each school and chasing down multiple letters of recommendation, applicants and their parents can focus on just a few essays and remove the stress associated with sorting and tracking multiple documents.

Candidates and their families can be assured of the professionalism of admission officers and feel free to use one of the common applications. The Secondary School Application and the Admission Application Form represent the efforts of the very best admission officers who have put the interests of the applicant at the fore—shifting the focus away from the school and back to the candidate. Candidates can be confident that the common application form will more than adequately allow them to make a strong case for their own admission at any school accepting the form.

About Standardized Tests

Heather Hoerle
Executive Director
Secondary School Admission Test Board (SSATB)

Mention the word "testing" to even the most capable student, and he or she is likely to freeze in fear. It's no wonder, then, that standardized testing in the independent school admission process causes nail-biting among students and parents alike.

You may be wondering why private schools test prospective students in the first place. In most cases, standardized testing is used to evaluate a student's ability to perform outside of the classroom. Often, testing helps schools to understand whether they have an appropriate program for applicants. In some cases, private schools find they are best equipped to serve students with test results that fit within a specific range or percentile. Note that standardized testing is also used to place accepted students into appropriate classes in their new school.

Often, testing helps schools to understand whether they have an appropriate program for applicants.

Years ago, I took the Secondary School Admission Test (SSAT) as part of the admission process to a boarding school. After my scores came back, my grim-faced mother called the boarding school's admission director to discuss the results. Much to her relief and surprise, I was accepted by the school in spite of mediocre quantitative testing. Indeed, the strength of my application assured school officials that I was ready for their academic challenge, despite the "average" test results. The SSAT, while an important part of my application, did not tell admission officials about my motivation, nor did it yield any information about my academic and creative achievements.

While it is true that some schools assign a great deal of importance to standardized testing, it is just as true that many schools regard testing as only one part of the application process. Many private schools place equal value on the applicant's campus interview, the student's record of achievement, teacher recommendations, and student/parent written statements. In short, test scores cannot tell an individual's full story, and admission officials recognize this limitation, even as they require standardized testing.

The tests that are most frequently used by private secondary schools are the Secondary School Admission Test Board's SSAT and the Educational Records Bureau's Independent School Entrance Exam (ISEE).

Taking the SSAT

The SSAT, which is used to evaluate applicants for admission to grades 5–11, is a multiple-choice test that measures students' abilities in math and verbal areas and enables counselors to compare students' scores with those of private school applicants and the national school population. The SSAT takes more than 2 hours to complete. Two levels are administered. The lower level exam is taken by students in grades 5–7. The upper level is administered to students in grades 8–11. Students' scores are compared only to students in the same grade. The exam contains multiple-choice questions and a writing sample.

The SSAT is given nationally at more than 600 test sites in all fifty states on selected Saturdays during the school year (in October, November, December, January, February, March, April, and June). It is also given internationally in November, December, January, March, and April.

Applicants can arrange to have SSAT scores sent to several different schools. Registration forms and details about specific test sites, dates, and fees are available at www.ssat.org or by calling 609-683-4440. You can download a free copy of the *SSAT Student Guide* from the Web site. The Secondary School Admission Test Board also sells *Preparing and Applying for Independent School Admission and the SSAT,* a sample test booklet that contains an actual test form for student practice, for a small fee.

Taking the ISEE

The ISEE is used to assess the math and verbal abilities and achievement of students entering grades 5 through 12. The test is administered at three levels: a lower level for students applying to grades 5 and 6; a middle level for those students applying to grades 7 and 8; and an upper level for students applying to grades 9 through 12. Students' scores are compared only to students in the same grade.

The test, which takes about 3 hours to complete, has two components—a multiple-choice segment and a 30-minute essay. The essay, although not scored, gives schools a chance to see a student's writing on an informal topic. The turnaround time for score reporting is seven to ten business days.

The ISEE is administered at sites across the United States and abroad on dates chosen by the schools. Families can obtain test dates and locations by requesting a free student guide from the Educational Records Bureau online at http://erblearn.org. The Educational Records Bureau also publishes *What to Expect on the ISEE*, a sample test booklet that contains half-length practice tests.

How Important Are the Tests?

Parents may want to assure their child that his or her fate does not rely solely on test performance. According to admission counselors, test results are only one part of the admission process. Test scores may not directly relate to the grades a student is capable of achieving in school, and tests cannot measure motivation. Because admission representatives know that a student can contribute to the life of the school community in many different ways, they are careful to keep all of an applicant's talents, abilities, and achievements in mind when evaluating his or her potential for success.

Attention Students: Worried About Taking the SSAT or ISEE?

Here are a few tips to help ban the testing blues.

- Get plenty of rest the day before the test. You will need all of your concentration on the test date, and fatigue can wreak havoc on your ability to focus.
- Eat a meal before you take the test. Your brain needs the energy that food provides!
- Carefully read the materials provided by the sponsoring test group several days before testing is scheduled. Often a "practice test" is included in your registration materials and can be helpful in preparing you for the upcoming test.
- Be well prepared. Advance registration materials offer plenty of guidance on what you will need to bring to the test, such as your registration ticket and No. 2 pencils.
- Allow plenty of time to get to your test site. Be sure that you have directions to the test center, and arrive ahead of the test administration time in order to register on-site, find a bathroom, and get acclimated to the setting.
- As you are taking the test, do not get hung up on hard questions. Skip them and move on. If you have time at the end of each test section, return to unanswered questions and try again.
- Don't forget personal "comfort" items. If you have a cold, be sure to bring tissues and cough drops along. Have extra money on hand, since you may want something to drink during the break. Wear layers, just in case you get too hot or too cold while taking the test.
- Finally, relax! While it is important to do your best work on standardized tests, your future does not depend solely on your test results.

Paying for a Private Education

Mark J. Mitchell

Vice President, School Information Services National Association of Independent Schools (NAIS)

Imagine asking a car dealer to sell you a $15,000 sedan for $5000 because that is all you can afford. When you buy a car, you know that you will be paying more than it cost to design, build, ship, and sell the car. The sales staff will not offer you a price based on your income. At best, you may receive discounts, rebates, or other incentives that allow you to pay the lowest price the dealer is willing to accept. As a buyer, you even accept the notion that the car's value will depreciate as soon as you drive it off the lot. No matter how you look at it, you pay more than the car cost to make and ultimately more than it's worth.

Tuition at many private schools can easily approach the cost of a new car; however, paying for a private school education is not the same as buying a car. One difference is the availability of financial aid at thousands of schools in the United States and abroad to help offset the tuition. Imagine asking a school to accept $5000 for a $15,000 tuition because that is all you can afford to pay. That is exactly what private schools that provide need-based financial aid programs accomplish. Learning about the financing options and procedures available at private schools can make this imagined scenario a reality for many families.

Need-Based Financial Aid

Many private schools offer assistance to families who demonstrate financial need. In fact, for a recent academic year, schools that belonged to the National Association of Independent Schools (NAIS) provided more than $1 trillion in need-based financial aid to nearly 18 percent of their students. For 2010–11, the average grant for boarding school students was $20,630 and the average grant for day school students was $10,054. These need-based grants do not need to be repaid and are used to offset the school's tuition. Schools make this substantial commitment as one way of ensuring a socioeconomically diverse student body and to help ensure that every student qualified for admission has the best chance to enroll, regardless of his or her financial circumstances.

How Financial Need Is Determined

Many schools use a process of determining financial need that requires the completion of applications and the submission of tax forms and other documentation to help them decide how much help each family needs. Currently, more than 2,400 schools nationwide ask families to complete The School and Student Service (SSS) Parents' Financial Statement (PFS) online at www.nais.org to determine eligibility for aid. The PFS gathers information about family size, income and expenses, parents' assets and indebtedness, and the child's assets. From this and other information, schools are provided with an estimate of the amount of discretionary income (after several allowances are made for basic necessities) available for education costs. Schools review each case individually and use this estimate, along with such supporting documentation as most recent income tax forms, to make a final decision on your need for a financial aid grant. For more information, please visit www.nais.org/go/parents.

The amount of a need-based financial aid award varies from person to person and school to school. Just as individuals have different financial resources and obligations that dictate their need for assistance, schools have different resources and policies that dictate their ability to meet your financial need. Tuition costs, endowment incomes, and the school's philosophy about financial aid are a few of the things that can affect how much aid a school can offer. If your decision to send your child to a private school depends heavily on getting financial help, you would benefit from applying for aid at more than one school.

Merit-Based Awards

While the majority of aid offered is based on a family's financial situation, not everyone who receives financial assistance must demonstrate financial need. Private schools offer millions of dollars in merit-based scholarships to thousands of students. In the 2009–10 academic year, 275 NAIS-member schools awarded an average annual merit award worth $4597 to students, totaling more than $35.7 million. Even with this level of commitment, such awards are rare (just 5.4 percent of all enrolled students receive this type of aid) and, therefore, highly competitive. They may serve to reward demonstrated talents or achievements in areas ranging from academics to athletics to the arts.

Some additional resources may be available from organizations and agencies in your community. Civic and religious groups, foundations, and even your employer may sponsor scholarships for students at private schools. Unfortunately, these options tend to be few and far between, limited in number and size of award. Be sure to ask a financial aid officer at the school(s) in which you are interested if he or she is aware of such organizations and opportunities.

The financial aid officer at the school is the best source of information about your options.

Whether it is offered by the school or a local organization, be sure to understand the requirements or conditions on which a merit-based scholarship is based. Ask if the award is renewable and, if so, under what conditions. Often, certain criteria must be met (such as minimum GPA, community service, or participation in activities) to ensure renewal of the award in subsequent years. (Some merit awards are available for just one year.)

Tuition Financing Options

Whether or not you qualify for grants or scholarships, another way to get financial help involves finding ways to make tuition payments easier on your family's monthly budget. One common option is the tuition payment plan. These plans allow you to spread tuition payments (less any forms of financial aid you receive) over a period of eight to ten months. In most cases, payments start before the school year begins, but this method can be more feasible than coming up with one or two lump sum payments before the beginning of the school year. Payment plans may be administered by the schools themselves or by a private company approved by the school. They do not normally require credit checks or charge interest; however, they typically charge an application or service fee, which may include tuition insurance. Additional information about tuition payment plans is available on the NAIS Web site at www.nais.org/about/index.cfm?ItemNumber=145882.

Since a high-quality education is one of the best investments they can make in their child's future, many parents finance the cost just as they would any other important expense. A number of schools, banks, and other agencies offer tuition loan programs specifically for elementary and secondary school expenses. While such loans are subject to credit checks and must be repaid with interest, they tend to offer rates and terms that are more favorable than those of other consumer loans. It pays to compare the details of more than one type of loan program to find the best one for your needs. Although they should always be regarded as an option of last resort, tuition loan programs can be helpful. Of course, every family must consider both the short- and long-term costs of borrowing and make its decision part of a larger plan for education financing.

A Final Word

Although the primary responsibility to pay for school costs rests with the family, there are options available if you need help. As you can see, financing a private school education can result in a partnership between the family, the school, and sometimes outside agencies or companies, with each making an effort to provide ways to meet the costs. The financial aid officer at the school is the best source of information about your options and is willing to help you in every way he or she can. Always go to the financial aid officer at a school in which you are interested whenever you have any questions or concerns about programs or the application process. Understanding your responsibilities, meeting deadlines, and learning about the full range of options is your best strategy for obtaining assistance. Although there are no guarantees, with proper planning and by asking the right questions, your family just might get the high-quality private education for less.

How to Use This Guide

Quick-Reference Chart

"Private Secondary Schools At-a-Glance" presents data listed in alphabetical order by state and U.S. territories; schools in Canada and other countries follow state listings. If your search is limited to a specific state, turn to the appropriate section and scan the chart for quick information about each school in that state: Are students boarding, day, or both? Is it coeducational? What grade levels are offered? How many students are enrolled? What is the student/faculty ratio? How many sports are offered? Does the school offer Advanced Placement test preparation?

School Profiles and Displays

The **School Profiles** and **Displays** contain basic information about the schools and are listed alphabetically in each section. An outline of a **School Profile** follows. The items of information found under each section heading are defined and displayed. Any item discussed below that is omitted from a **School Profile** either does not apply to that particular school or is one for which no information was supplied.

Heading Name and address of school, along with the name of the Head of School.

General Information Type (boys', girls', coeducational, boarding/day, distance learning) and academic emphasis, religious affiliation, grades, founding date, campus setting, nearest major city, housing, campus size, total number of buildings, accreditation and memberships, languages of instruction, endowment, enrollment, upper school average class size, upper school faculty-student ratio, number of required school days per year (Upper School), number of days per week Upper School students typically attend, and length of the average school day.

Upper School Student Profile Breakdown by grade, gender, boarding/day, geography, and religion.

Faculty Total number; breakdown by gender, number with advanced degrees, and number who reside on campus.

Subjects Offered Academic and general subjects.

Graduation Requirements Subjects and other requirements, including community service.

Special Academic Programs Honors and Advanced Placement courses, accelerated programs, study at local college for college credit, study abroad, independent study, ESL programs, programs for gifted/remedial students and students with learning disabilities.

College Admission Counseling Number of recent graduates, representative list of colleges attended. May include mean or median SAT/ACT scores and percentage of students scoring over 600 on each section of the SAT, over 1800 on the combined SAT, or over 26 on the composite ACT.

Student Life Dress code, student council, discipline, and religious service attendance requirements.

Summer Programs Programs offered and focus; location; open to boys, girls, or both and availability to students from other schools; usual enrollment; program dates and application deadlines.

Tuition and Aid Costs, available financial aid.

Admissions New-student figures, admissions requirements, application deadlines, fees.

Athletics Sports, levels, and gender; number of PE instructors, coaches, and athletic trainers.

Computers List of classes that use computers, campus technology, and availability of student e-mail accounts, online student grades, and a published electronic and media policy.

Contact Person to whom inquiries should be addressed.

Displays, provided by school administrators, present information designed to complement the data already appearing in the **School Profile.**

Close-Ups

Close-Ups, written expressly for Peterson's Publishing by school administrators, provide in-depth information about the schools that have chosen to submit them. These descriptions are all in the same format to provide maximum comparability. **Close-Ups** follow each **School Profile** section; there is a page reference at the end of a **School Profile** directing you to that school's **Close-Up** as well as its **Summer Program Close-Up,** if one was provided. Schools are listed alphabetically in each section.

Special Needs Schools

One of the great strengths of private schools is their variety. This section is dedicated to the belief that there is an appropriate school setting for every child, one in which he or she will thrive academically, socially, and emotionally. The task for parents, counselors, and educators is to know the child's needs and the schools' resources well enough to make the right match.

Schools in this section serve those students who may have special challenges, including learning differences, dyslexia, language delay, attention deficit disorders, social maladjustment to family and surroundings, or emotional disturbances; these students may need individual attention or are underachieving for some other reason. Parents of children who lag significantly behind their grade level in basic academic skills or who have little or no motivation for schoolwork will also want to consult this section. (For easy reference, schools that offer extra help for students are identified in two directories: "Schools Reporting Programs for Students with Special Needs" and "Schools Reporting That They Accommodate Underachievers.") The schools included here chose to be in this section because they consider special needs education to be their primary focus. It is the mission of these schools, whose curricula and methodologies vary widely, to uncover a student's strengths and, with appropriate academic, social, and psychological counseling, enable him or her to succeed.

Junior Boarding Schools

As parents know, the early adolescent years are ones of tremendous physical and emotional change. Junior boarding schools specialize in this crucial period by taking advantage of children's natural curiosity, zest for learning, and growing self-awareness. While junior boarding schools enroll students with a wide range of academic abilities and levels of emotional self-assurance, their goal is to meet each youngster's individual needs within a supportive community. They accomplish this through low student-teacher ratios and enrollment numbers deliberately kept low.

The boarding schools featured in this section serve students in the middle school grades (6–9); some offer primary programs as well. For more information about junior boarding schools, visit the Junior Boarding Schools Association Web site at www. jbsa.org.

Summer Programs

The Summer Programs section, which is brand new this year, offers Close-Ups of exciting summer programs that are taking place at private schools throughout the United States and abroad. These two-page in-depth descriptions provide details on the summer program's background and philosophy, program offerings, location, staff, facilities, daily schedule, extra opportunities and activities, medical care, transportation, costs, financial aid, application timetable, and contact information. The photos included in the Summer Program Close-Ups offer a glimpse of the facilities, surroundings, and faces of program participants. Those schools whose summer program descriptions are included in this section have paid a fee to Peterson's Publishing to provide this information to you.

Specialized Directories

These directories are compiled from the information gathered in *Peterson's Annual Survey of Private Secondary Schools.* The schools that did not return a survey or provided incomplete data are not fully represented in these directories. For ease of reference, the directories are grouped by category: type, curricula, financial data, special programs, and special needs.

Index

The "Alphabetical Listing of Schools" shows page numbers for School Profiles in regular type, page numbers for Displays in italics, and page numbers for Close-Ups in boldface type.

Data Collection Procedures

The data contained in *Peterson's Private Secondary Schools 2012–13* **School Profiles, Quick-Reference Chart, Specialized Directories,** and **Index** were collected through *Peterson's Annual Survey of Private Secondary Schools* during fall 2011. Also included were schools that submitted information for the 2010–11 data collection effort but did not submit updates in the fall of 2011. Questionnaires were posted online. With minor exceptions, data for those schools that responded to the questionnaire were submitted by officials at the schools themselves. All usable information received in time for publication has been included. The omission of a particular item from a **School Profile** means that it is either not applicable to that school or not available or usable. Because of Peterson's extensive system of checking data, we believe that the information presented in this guide is accurate. However, errors and omissions are possible in a data collection and processing endeavor of this scope. Therefore, students and parents should check with a specific school at the time of application to verify all pertinent information.

Criteria for Inclusion in This Book

Most schools in this book have curricula that are primarily college preparatory. If a school is accredited or is a candidate for accreditation by a regional accrediting group, including the European Council of International Schools, and/or is approved by a state Department of Education, and/or is a member of the National Association of Independent Schools or the European Council of International Schools, then such accreditation, approval, or membership is stated. Schools appearing in the **Special Needs Schools** section may not have such accreditation or approval.

Quick-Reference Chart

Private Secondary Schools At-a-Glance

	STUDENTS ACCEPTED: BOARDING		STUDENTS ACCEPTED: DAY		GRADES			STUDENT/FACULTY			SCHOOL OFFERINGS	
	Boys	Girls	Boys	Girls	Lower	Middle	Upper	Total	Upper	Student/Faculty Ratio	Advanced Placement Preparation	Sports
UNITED STATES												
Alabama												
Bayside Academy, Daphne			X	X	PK–6	7–8	9–12	753	250	7:1	X	29
Briarwood Christian High School, Birmingham			X	X	K–6	7–8	9–12	1,970	589	23:1	X	18
Edgewood Academy, Elmore					K–5	6–8	9–12	257	91	14:1	X	11
Indian Springs School, Indian Springs	X	X	X	X			8–12	261	261	7:1	X	18
John T. Morgan Academy, Selma			X	X						22:1		27
Lyman Ward Military Academy, Camp Hill	X				6–8		9–12	115	85	15:1	X	34
Madison Academy, Madison			X	X	PS–6		7–12	900	450	15:1		7
Marion Academy, Marion			X	X	K–3	4–6	7–12	84	44	8:1		8
Mars Hill Bible School, Florence			X	X	K–4	5–8	9–12	574	220	14:1	X	11
Pickens Academy, Carrollton			X	X	K4–6		7–12	247	128	20:1		12
Tuscaloosa Academy, Tuscaloosa			X	X	PK–4	5–8	9–12	418	110	15:1	X	14
Westminster Christian Academy, Huntsville			X	X	K–5	6–8	9–12	733	264	13:1	X	17
Arizona												
Blueprint Education, Glendale											X	
Brophy College Preparatory, Phoenix			X			6–6	9–12	1,322	1,290	15:1	X	44
Copper Canyon Academy, Rimrock		X					9–12	95	95	10:1		19
Immaculate Heart High School, Oro Valley			X	X			9–12	91	91	10:1	X	13
Phoenix Country Day School, Paradise Valley			X	X	PK–4	5–8	9–12	722	243	7:1	X	22
St. Gregory College Preparatory School, Tucson			X	X		6–8	9–12	305	177	9:1	X	23
Saint Mary's High School, Phoenix			X	X			9–12	501	501	17:1	X	19
Seton Catholic High School, Chandler			X	X			9–12	553	553	13:1	X	21
Southwestern Academy, Rimrock	X	X	X	X			9–PG	32	32	3:1	X	37
Valley Lutheran High School, Phoenix			X	X			9–12	184	184	10:1	X	16
Arkansas												
Episcopal Collegiate School, Little Rock			X	X	PK–5	6–8	9–12	730	216	10:1	X	16
California												
Academy of Our Lady of Peace, San Diego				X			9–12	750	750	14:1	X	11
Anacapa School, Santa Barbara			X	X	7–8		9–12	49	37	9:1	X	23
Archbishop Mitty High School, San Jose			X	X			9–12	1,640	1,640	17:1	X	27
Armona Union Academy, Armona			X	X	K–4	5–8	9–12	138	49	10:1		11
Army and Navy Academy, Carlsbad	X		X		7–9		10–12	310	223	15:1	X	30
The Athenian School, Danville	X	X	X	X		6–8	9–12	471	306	10:1	X	15
Berean Christian High School, Walnut Creek			X	X			9–12	430	430	14:1	X	11
Bishop Conaty-Our Lady of Loretto High School, Los Angeles				X			9–12	359	359	16:1	X	5
Bishop Montgomery High School, Torrance			X	X			9–12	1,063	1,063	22:1	X	17
Bishop Mora Salesian High School, Los Angeles			X				9–12	454	454	15:1		20
The Bishop's School, La Jolla			X	X		6–8	9–12	780	546	13:1	X	18
Brentwood School, Los Angeles			X	X	K–6	7–8	9–12	990	460	7:1	X	41
Bridgemont High School, Daly City			X	X			9–12	40	40	4:1		12
Bridges Academy, Studio City			X	X		5–8	9–12	129	77	8:1		3
Calvary Chapel High School, Downey			X	X	K–5	6–8	9–12	683	309	19:1	X	16
Calvin Christian High School, Escondido			X	X	PK–5	6–8	9–12	487	149	17:1	X	11
Campbell Hall (Episcopal), North Hollywood			X	X	K–6	7–8	9–12	1,085	533	8:1	X	20
Capistrano Valley Christian Schools, San Juan Capistrano			X	X	JK–6	7–8	9–12	440	175	13:1	X	15
Carondelet High School, Concord				X			9–12	800	800	15:1	X	22
Central Catholic High School, Modesto			X	X			9–12	406	406	14:1	X	15
Chadwick School, Palos Verdes Peninsula			X	X	K–6	7–8	9–12	845	366	6:1	X	19
Chaminade College Preparatory, West Hills			X	X		6–8	9–12	2,042	1,320	16:1	X	25
Children's Creative and Performing Arts Academy of San Diego, San Diego	X	X	X	X	K–5	6–8	9–12	265	115	15:1	X	33
Chinese Christian Schools, Alameda			X	X	K–5	6–8	9–12	696	216	8:1	X	17
Crossroads School for Arts & Sciences, Santa Monica			X	X	K–5	6–8	9–12	1,147	499	11:1		21
Damien High School, La Verne			X				9–12	962	962	22:1	X	27
De La Salle High School, Concord			X				9–12	1,028	1,028	28:1	X	19
Eldorado Emerson Private School, Orange	X	X	X	X	K–6		7–12	180	110	18:1	X	8
Faith Christian High School, Yuba City			X	X			9–12	100	100	12:1	X	7
Flintridge Preparatory School, La Canada Flintridge			X	X		7–8	9–12	500	400	10:1	X	17
Fresno Christian Schools, Fresno			X	X	K–6	7–8	9–12	612	185	12:1	X	17
The Frostig School, Pasadena			X	X	1–5	6–8	9–12	91	41	6:1		4

Private Secondary Schools At-a-Glance

	STUDENTS ACCEPTED				GRADES			STUDENT/FACULTY			SCHOOL OFFERINGS	
	BOARDING		DAY									
	Boys	Girls	Boys	Girls	Lower	Middle	Upper	Total	Upper	Student/Faculty Ratio	Advanced Placement Preparation	Sports
Garces Memorial High School, Bakersfield			X	X			9–12	622	622	28:1	X	17
Grace Brethren School, Simi Valley			X	X	K–6	7–8	9–12	810	290	11:1	X	17
The Grauer School, Encinitas			X	X		6–8	9–12	152	86	6:1	X	44
The Harker School, San Jose			X	X	K–5	6–8	9–12	1,791	715	16:1	X	21
Head-Royce School, Oakland			X	X	K–5	6–8	9–12	832	340	9:1	X	20
Hebrew Academy, Huntington Beach			X	X	N–5	6–8	9–12	257	14	4:1	X	14
Highland Hall Waldorf School, Northridge			X	X	N–6	7–8	9–12	296	90	6:1		6
Hillcrest Christian School, Thousand Oaks			X	X	K–6	7–8	9–12	288	71	8:1	X	7
Horizon Christian Academy Junior/Senior High School, San Diego												12
Idyllwild Arts Academy, Idyllwild	X	X	X	X			9–PG	295	295	12:1	X	38
Immaculate Heart High School and Middle School, Los Angeles				X		6–8	9–12	550	550	18:1		
International High School, San Francisco			X	X	PK–5	6–8	9–12	1,009	329	10:1		24
Junipero Serra High School, Gardena			X	X			9–12	686	68	25:1	X	14
Junipero Serra High School, San Mateo			X				9–12	900	900	27:1	X	29
Kings Christian School, Lemoore			X	X	PK–6	7–8	9–12	294	105	11:1	X	16
La Jolla Country Day School, La Jolla			X	X	N–4	5–8	9–12	1,158	486	15:1	X	29
La Salle High School, Pasadena			X	X			9–12	732	732	11:1	X	20
Laurel Springs School, Ojai					K–5	6–8	9–12	1,529	876	1:1	X	
Le Lycee Francais de Los Angeles, Los Angeles			X	X	PS–5	6–8	9–12	729	149	15:1	X	12
Liberty Christian School, Huntington Beach			X	X	K–5	6–8	9–12	204	84	6:1	X	7
Lodi Academy, Lodi			X	X			9–12	101	101	13:1	X	5
Los Angeles Baptist Middle School/High School, North Hills			X	X		6–8	9–12	753	485	22:1	X	11
Los Angeles Lutheran High School, Sylmar			X	X	K–6	7–8	9–12	440	167	10:1	X	20
Louisville High School, Woodland Hills				X			9–12	428	428	25:1	X	14
Lutheran High School of San Diego, Chula Vista			X	X			9–12	75	75	12:1	X	6
Maranatha High School, Pasadena			X	X			9–12	635	635	12:1	X	15
The Marin School, Sausalito			X	X			9–12	100	100	7:1		9
Marlborough School, Los Angeles				X		7–9	10–12	530	274	8:1	X	12
Marymount High School, Los Angeles				X			9–12	369	369	7:1	X	20
Mary Star of the Sea High School, San Pedro			X	X			9–12	317	317	17:1	X	11
Mercy High School College Preparatory, San Francisco				X			9–12	442	442	14:1	X	11
Mesa Grande Seventh-Day Academy, Calimesa			X	X	K–6	7–8	9–12	264	114	10:1		9
Midland School, Los Olivos	X	X					9–12	82	82	5:1		20
Moreau Catholic High School, Hayward			X	X			9–12	896	896	18:1	X	21
Notre Dame Academy, Los Angeles				X			9–12	400	400	13:1	X	8
Oak Grove School, Ojai	X	X	X	X	PK–6	7–8	9–12	197	45	7:1	X	15
Ojai Valley School, Ojai	X	X	X	X	PK–5	6–8	9–12	291	113	6:1	X	31
Orinda Academy, Orinda			X	X		7–8	9–12	81	73	9:1	X	4
Pacific Hills School, West Hollywood			X	X		6–8	9–12	207	150	10:1	X	11
Palma School, Salinas			X			7–8	9–12	534	402	15:1	X	13
Paradise Adventist Academy, Paradise			X	X	K–4	5–8	9–12	182	88	8:1		4
Providence High School, Burbank			X	X			9–12	401	401	12:1	X	17
Redwood Christian Schools, Castro Valley			X	X	K–5	6–8	9–12	648	260	10:1	X	8
Rincon Valley Christian School, Santa Rosa					PK–5	6–8	9–12	270	85			
Ripon Christian Schools, Ripon			X	X	K–5	6–8	9–12	659	224	18:1	X	12
Rolling Hills Preparatory School, San Pedro			X	X		6–8	9–12	235	135	9:1	X	21
Sacramento Adventist Academy, Carmichael			X	X	K–6	7–8	9–12	222	107	12:1	X	6
Sacramento Country Day School, Sacramento			X	X	PK–5	6–8	9–12	468	131	9:1	X	15
Saddleback Valley Christian School, San Juan Capistrano			X	X	JK–6	7–8	9–12	855	338	15:1	X	14
Sage Hill School, Newport Coast			X	X			9–12	443	443	10:1	X	14
Saint Anthony High School, Long Beach			X	X			9–12	440	440	15:1	X	23
St. Bernard's Catholic School, Eureka	X	X	X	X	K–8		9–12	300	150	12:1	X	11
St. Catherine's Academy, Anaheim	X		X		K–6	7–8		161	86	8:1		24
Saint Elizabeth High School, Oakland			X	X			9–12	165	165	15:1	X	7
Saint Francis High School, La Canada Flintridge			X				9–12	658	658	15:1	X	9
Saint Mary's College High School, Berkeley			X	X			9–12	625	625	16:1	X	14
St. Michael's Preparatory School of the Norbertine Fathers, Silverado	X						9–12	62	62	3:1	X	11
Saint Patrick - Saint Vincent High School, Vallejo			X	X			9–12	534	534	30:1	X	15
Salesian High School, Richmond			X	X			9–12	527	527	23:1	X	15
Santa Catalina School, Monterey		X		X			9–12	244	244	7:1	X	31
Sonoma Academy, Santa Rosa			X	X			9–12	236	226	12:1	X	26
Southwestern Academy, San Marino	X	X	X	X		6–8	9–PG	139	122	6:1	X	22
Squaw Valley Academy, Olympic Valley	X	X	X	X			9–12	100	100	8:1	X	68
Stevenson School, Pebble Beach	X	X	X	X	K–5	6–8	9–12	745	518	10:1	X	34
Summerfield Waldorf School, Santa Rosa			X	X	K–6	7–8	9–12	390	95	7:1		5
The Thacher School, Ojai	X	X	X	X			9–12	250	250	6:1	X	40

Private Secondary Schools At-a-Glance

	STUDENTS ACCEPTED				GRADES			STUDENT/FACULTY			SCHOOL OFFERINGS	
	BOARDING		DAY									
	Boys	Girls	Boys	Girls	Lower	Middle	Upper	Total	Upper	Student/Faculty Ratio	Advanced Placement Preparation	Sports
Tri-City Christian Schools, Vista			X	X	PK–6	7–8	9–12	614	245	12:1	X	22
Valley Christian High School, Dublin			X	X		6–8	9–12	471	298	13:1		14
Valley Christian High School, San Jose			X	X	K–5	6–8	9–12	2,280	1,320	17:1	X	20
Westmark School, Encino			X	X	3–5	6–8	9–12			12:1		12
Westridge School, Pasadena				X	4–6	7–8	9–12	487	279	6:1	X	19
Windward School, Los Angeles			X	X		7–8	9–12	541	369	7:1	X	5
York School, Monterey			X	X			8–12	230	230	8:1	X	19
Colorado												
Alexander Dawson School, Lafayette			X	X	K–4	5–8	9–12	453	183	7:1	X	43
The Colorado Springs School, Colorado Springs			X	X	PK–5	6–8	9–12	294	113	6:1	X	21
Denver Christian High School, Denver			X	X			9–12	179	179	14:1		11
Fountain Valley School of Colorado, Colorado Springs	X	X	X	X			9–12	244	244	6:1	X	41
Front Range Christian High School, Littleton			X	X	PK–6	7–8	9–12	391	169	12:1	X	11
Humanex Academy, Englewood			X	X		6–8	9–12	63	56	7:1		16
Telluride Mountain School, Telluride			X	X	PK–4	5–8	9–12	109	9			32
Vail Mountain School, Vail			X	X	K–5	6–8	9–12	349	106	8:1	X	46
Connecticut												
Brunswick School, Greenwich			X		PK–4	5–8	9–12	939	357	5:1	X	20
Cheshire Academy, Cheshire	X	X	X	X		7–8	9–PG	355	325	7:1	X	22
Convent of the Sacred Heart, Greenwich				X	PS–4	5–8	9–12	777	290	7:1	X	23
Eagle Hill-Southport, Southport			X	X				112	38	4:1		9
The Ethel Walker School, Simsbury		X		X		6–8	9–12	239	208	6:1	X	43
The Glenholme School, Devereux Connecticut, Washington	X	X	X	X	5–6	7–8	9–PG	88	74	10:1		44
Greenwich Academy, Greenwich				X	PK–4	5–8	9–12	805	348	6:1	X	34
Hamden Hall Country Day School, Hamden			X	X	PS–6	7–8	9–12	545	264	8:1	X	18
Holy Cross High School, Waterbury			X	X			9–12	698	698	15:1	X	23
Hopkins School, New Haven			X	X		7–8	9–12	687	530	6:1	X	43
The Hotchkiss School, Lakeville	X	X	X	X			9–PG	599	599	6:1	X	46
Hyde School, Woodstock	X	X	X	X			9–12	178	178	12:1	X	17
King Low Heywood Thomas, Stamford			X	X	PK–5	6–8	9–12	684	314	7:1	X	21
Kingswood-Oxford School, West Hartford			X	X		6–8	9–12	496	346	8:1	X	20
The Loomis Chaffee School, Windsor	X	X	X	X			9–PG	682	682	5:1	X	50
The Marvelwood School, Kent	X	X	X	X			9–12	165	165	4:1	X	34
The Master's School, West Simsbury			X	X	K–5	6–8	9–12	330	110	7:1	X	22
Mercy High School, Middletown				X			9–12	651	651	13:1	X	15
Miss Porter's School, Farmington		X		X			9–12	331	331	8:1	X	40
Northwest Catholic High School, West Hartford			X	X			9–12	643	643	12:1	X	32
The Norwich Free Academy, Norwich			X	X			9–12	2,315		22:1	X	32
The Oxford Academy, Westbrook	X						9–PG	38	38	1:1	X	13
The Rectory School, Pomfret	X	X	X	X	1–4	5–9		248	178	4:1		36
St. Bernard High School, Uncasville			X	X		6–8	9–12	373	281			24
Suffield Academy, Suffield	X	X	X	X			9–PG	412	412	5:1	X	31
The Taft School, Watertown	X	X	X	X			9–PG	585	585	5:1	X	46
Watkinson School, Hartford			X	X		6–8	9–PG	247	163	6:1		30
Wellspring Foundation, Bethlehem	X	X	X	X				52				
Westminster School, Simsbury	X	X	X	X			9–PG	390	390	6:1	X	34
Westover School, Middlebury		X		X			9–12	209	209	8:1	X	48
The Williams School, New London			X	X		7–8	9–12	259	217	6:1	X	18
The Woodhall School, Bethlehem	X		X				9–PG	38	38	4:1	X	35
Delaware												
St. Andrew's School, Middletown	X	X					9–12	297	297	5:1		34
St. Mark's High School, Wilmington			X	X			9–12	1,100	1,100	11:1	X	22
Salesianum School, Wilmington			X				9–12	981	981	12:1	X	22
Sanford School, Hockessin			X	X	PK–4	5–8	9–12	599	239	8:1	X	13
Tower Hill School, Wilmington			X	X	PS–4	5–8	9–12	753	236	6:1	X	21
Wilmington Christian School, Hockessin			X	X	PK–5	6–8	9–12	476	205	15:1	X	12
District of Columbia												
Edmund Burke School, Washington			X	X		6–8	9–12	275	207	6:1	X	17
Gonzaga College High School, Washington			X				9–12	957	957	15:1	X	33
Maret School, Washington			X	X	K–4	5–8	9–12	635	310	7:1	X	25
St. Albans School, Washington	X		X		4–8		9–12	578	312	7:1	X	34
Florida												
Academy at the Lakes, Land O'Lakes			X	X	PK–4	5–8	9–12	404	126	5:1	X	18
Allison Academy, North Miami Beach			X	X		6–8	9–12	91	70	10:1	X	16
American Academy, Plantation			X	X	1–6	7–8	9–12	306	152	12:1		21
American Heritage School, Delray Beach			X	X	PK–8		9–12				X	17

Private Secondary Schools At-a-Glance

	STUDENTS ACCEPTED				GRADES			STUDENT/FACULTY			SCHOOL OFFERINGS	
	BOARDING		DAY									
	Boys	Girls	Boys	Girls	Lower	Middle	Upper	Total	Upper	Student/Faculty Ratio	Advanced Placement Preparation	Sports
American Heritage School, Plantation			X	X	PK–6		7–12	2,278	1,565	15:1	X	19
Atlantis Academy, Miami			X	X	K–3	4–6	7–12	156	103	8:1		6
Belen Jesuit Preparatory School, Miami			X			6–8	9–12	1,472	900	13:1	X	19
Berkeley Preparatory School, Tampa			X	X	PK–5	6–8	9–12	1,250	550	8:1	X	28
Bishop John J. Snyder High School, Jacksonville			X	X			9–12	468	468	15:1	X	16
The Bolles School, Jacksonville	X	X	X	X	PK–5	6–8	9–12	1,648	781	10:1	X	18
Canterbury School, Fort Myers			X	X	PK–6	7–8	9–12	580	199	10:1	X	13
Cardinal Newman High School, West Palm Beach			X	X			9–12	572	572	25:1	X	18
Carrollton School of the Sacred Heart, Miami				X	PK–3	4–6	7–12	800	432	9:1	X	14
Chaminade-Madonna College Preparatory, Hollywood			X	X			9–12	594	594	19:1	X	19
Christian Home and Bible School, Mount Dora			X	X	K–5	6–8	9–12	533	207	15:1	X	15
Christopher Columbus High School, Miami			X				9–12	1,380	1,380	17:1	X	18
Clearwater Central Catholic High School, Clearwater			X	X						16:1	X	19
The Community School of Naples, Naples			X	X	PK–5	6–8	9–12	725	281	7:1	X	18
Father Lopez High School, Daytona Beach			X	X			9–12	348	348	15:1	X	16
The First Academy, Orlando			X	X	K4–5	6–8	9–12	973	379	13:1	X	22
Forest Lake Academy, Apopka	X	X	X	X			9–12	377	377	22:1		6
Fort Lauderdale Preparatory School, Fort Lauderdale			X	X	PK–6		7–12	195	100	8:1	X	
Foundation Academy, Winter Garden			X	X	K–5	6–8	9–12	537	120	16:1	X	12
The Geneva School, Winter Park			X	X	K4–6	7–8	9–12	454	104	9:1	X	9
Glades Day School, Belle Glade			X	X	PK–6	7–8	9–12	335	171	15:1	X	12
Immaculata-La Salle High School, Miami			X	X			9–12	758	758	15:1	X	23
Jesuit High School of Tampa, Tampa			X				9–12	733	733	13:1	X	18
John Paul II Catholic High School, Tallahassee			X	X			9–12	119	119	8:1	X	9
Out-Of-Door-Academy, Sarasota			X	X	PK–6	7–8	9–12	615	230	13:1	X	20
Pine Crest School, Fort Lauderdale			X	X	PK–5	6–8	9–12	1,755	806	10:1	X	21
The Pine School, Hobe Sound										9:1	X	
Rabbi Alexander S. Gross Hebrew Academy, Miami Beach			X	X	N–5	6–8	9–12	468	153	4:1	X	4
Ransom Everglades School, Miami			X	X		6–8	9–12	1,079	607	10:1	X	22
Saddlebrook Preparatory School, Wesley Chapel	X	X	X	X	3–5	6–8	9–12	97	80	9:1		1
St. Brendan High School, Miami			X	X			9–12	1,181	1,181	15:1	X	11
Saint Edward's School, Vero Beach			X	X	PK–5	6–8	9–12	500	221	7:1	X	20
St. Joseph Academy, St. Augustine			X	X			9–12	260	260	11:1	X	18
St. Thomas Aquinas High School, Fort Lauderdale			X	X			9–12	2,190	2,190	18:1	X	27
Trinity Preparatory School, Winter Park			X	X		6–8	9–12	836	501	10:1	X	21
University School of Nova Southeastern University, Fort Lauderdale			X	X	PK–5	6–8	9–12	1,897	714	11:1	X	20
Windermere Preparatory School, Windermere	X		X	X	PK–5	6–8	9–12	1,043	349	11:1	X	23
Georgia												
Atlanta International School, Atlanta			X	X	PK–5	6–8	9–12	934	277	8:1		11
Augusta Christian School (I), Martinez			X	X	K–5	6–8	9–12	537	246	10:1	X	13
Augusta Preparatory Day School, Martinez			X	X	PS–4	5–8	9–12	528	201	9:1		8
Ben Franklin Academy, Atlanta			X	X			9–12	130	130	2:1	X	6
Blessed Trinity High School, Roswell			X	X			9–12	965	965	14:1	X	17
Brookstone School, Columbus			X	X	PK–5	6–8	9–12	789	278	10:1	X	12
Bulloch Academy, Statesboro			X	X	PK–5	6–8	9–12	464	144	17:1	X	17
Chatham Academy, Savannah			X	X	1–4	5–8	9–12	78	28	10:1		20
Darlington School, Rome	X	X	X	X	PK–4	5–8	9–PG	880	481	13:1	X	42
Deerfield-Windsor School, Albany			X	X	PK–5	6–8	9–12	836	245	18:1	X	18
Excel Christian Academy, Cartersville			X	X	K–5	6–8	9–12	297	101	18:1	X	7
First Presbyterian Day School, Macon			X	X	PK–5	6–8	9–12	976	353	12:1	X	17
Flint River Academy, Woodbury			X	X		6–8	9–12	313	90	14:1	X	15
The Galloway School, Atlanta			X	X	P3–4	5–8	9–12	724	259	8:1	X	13
George Walton Academy, Monroe			X	X	K4–5	6–8	9–12	945	340	12:1	X	19
Holy Innocents' Episcopal School, Atlanta			X	X	PS–5	6–8	9–12	1,302	444	7:1	X	20
The Howard School, Atlanta			X	X	PK–5	6–8	9–12	232	76	8:1		6
King's Ridge Christian School, Alpharetta			X	X	PK–5	6–8	9–12	713	160	8:1	X	17
Landmark Christian School, Fairburn			X	X	K4–5	6–8	9–12	805	224	9:1	X	15
The Lovett School, Atlanta			X	X	K–5	6–8	9–12	1,589	605	7:1	X	45
Marist School, Atlanta			X	X			7–12	1,079	1,079	11:1	X	19
Mill Springs Academy, Alpharetta			X	X	1–5	6–8	9–12	305	116	4:1		23
North Cobb Christian School, Kennesaw			X	X	PK–5	6–8	9–12	841	245	10:1	X	22
The Paideia School, Atlanta			X	X	PK–6	7–8	9–12	975	415	9:1	X	22
Pinecrest Academy, Cumming			X	X	PK–5	6–8	9–12	830	235	10:1	X	11
Riverside Military Academy, Gainesville	X		X			7–8	9–12	349	300	14:1	X	56
St. Pius X Catholic High School, Atlanta			X	X			9–12	1,100	1,100	12:1	X	23
Southland Academy, Inc., Americus			X	X		6–8	9–12	565	179			13
Stratford Academy, Macon					1–5	6–8	9–12	934	305	13:1	X	17
The Walker School, Marietta			X	X	PK–5	6–8	9–12	1,049	380	15:1	X	22
Woodward Academy, College Park			X	X	PK–6	7–8	9–12	2,662	1,035		X	20

Private Secondary Schools At-a-Glance

	STUDENTS ACCEPTED				GRADES			STUDENT/FACULTY			SCHOOL OFFERINGS	
	BOARDING		DAY									
	Boys	Girls	Boys	Girls	Lower	Middle	Upper	Total	Upper	Student/Faculty Ratio	Advanced Placement Preparation	Sports
Hawaii												
ASSETS School, Honolulu			X	X	K–8		9–12	349	111	8:1		30
Hawaiian Mission Academy, Honolulu	X	X	X	X			9–12	118	118	15:1		3
Hawaii Baptist Academy, Honolulu			X	X	K–6	7–8	9–12	1,121	473	11:1	X	22
Kauai Christian Academy, Kilauea			X	X	PS–3	4–6	7–12	79	30	8:1		
Lutheran High School of Hawaii, Honolulu			X	X			9–12	86	86	7:1	X	23
Mid-Pacific Institute, Honolulu			X	X	K–5	6–8	9–12	1,550	840	20:1	X	31
Punahou School, Honolulu			X	X	K–5	6–8	9–12	3,743	1,714	11:1	X	21
St. Andrew's Priory School, Honolulu				X	K–5	6–8	9–12	401	123	8:1	X	36
St. Anthony's Junior-Senior High School, Wailuku			X	X		7–8	9–12	140	101	10:1	X	29
Saint Francis School, Honolulu			X	X	K–6	7–8	9–12	445	278	20:1	X	22
Saint Joseph Junior-Senior High School, Hilo			X	X		7–8	9–12	193	143	12:1	X	14
Seabury Hall, Makawao			X	X		6–8	9–12	444	310	11:1	X	15
Idaho												
Bishop Kelly High School, Boise			X	X			9–12	675	675	18:1	X	18
Illinois												
Benet Academy, Lisle			X	X			9–12	1,299	1,299	18:1	X	22
Boylan Central Catholic High School, Rockford			X	X			9–12	1,152	1,152	13:1	X	30
The Chicago Academy for the Arts, Chicago			X	X			9–12	140	140	12:1	X	
Elgin Academy, Elgin			X	X	PS–4	5–8	9–12	424	135	5:1	X	13
The Governor French Academy, Belleville	X	X	X	X	K–8		9–12	171	52	6:1	X	6
Holy Trinity High School, Chicago			X	X			9–12	270	270	12:1	X	15
Immaculate Conception School, Elmhurst			X	X			9–12	340	340	12:1	X	19
Josephinum Academy, Chicago				X			9–12	150	150	9:1	X	8
Keith Country Day School, Rockford			X	X	PK–5	6–8	9–12	290	87	6:1	X	9
The Latin School of Chicago, Chicago			X	X	JK–4	5–8	9–12	1,110	430	8:1	X	25
Marian Central Catholic High School, Woodstock			X	X			9–12	694	694	17:1	X	17
Mooseheart High School, Mooseheart	X	X	X	X	K–5	6–8	9–12	210	120	6:1		9
Mother McAuley High School, Chicago				X			9–12	1,362	1,362	17:1	X	20
Nazareth Academy, LaGrange Park			X	X			9–12	824	824	18:1	X	16
Notre Dame College Prep, Niles			X				9–12	802	802	17:1	X	27
Sacred Heart/Griffin High School, Springfield			X	X			9–12	774	773	17:1	X	15
Saint Anthony High School, Effingham			X	X			9–12	190	190	10:1	X	13
Saint Joseph High School, Westchester			X	X			9–12	605	605	20:1	X	18
Saint Patrick High School, Chicago			X				9–12	816	816	17:1	X	16
St. Scholastica Academy, Chicago				X			9–12	250	250	9:1	X	10
Saint Viator High School, Arlington Heights			X	X			9–12	990	990	18:1		18
Timothy Christian High School, Elmhurst			X	X	K–6	7–8	9–12	1,051	380	13:1	X	12
The University of Chicago Laboratory Schools, Chicago			X	X	N–4	5–8	9–12	1,819	510	10:1	X	16
Wheaton Academy, West Chicago			X	X			9–12	640	640	15:1	X	33
The Willows Academy, Des Plaines				X		6–8	9–12	225	150	10:1	X	7
Indiana												
Concordia Lutheran High School, Fort Wayne			X	X			9–12	684	684	22:1	X	19
The Culver Academies, Culver	X	X	X	X			9–PG	802	802	9:1	X	92
Lutheran High School, Indianapolis			X	X			9–12	235	235	15:1	X	17
Marian High School, Mishawaka			X	X			9–12	719	719	24:1	X	30
Reitz Memorial High School, Evansville			X	X			9–12	781	781	14:1	X	23
Shawe Memorial Junior/Senior High School, Madison			X	X	K–6	7–8	9–12	342	111	9:1	X	12
Iowa												
Alpha Omega Academy, Rock Rapids			X	X	K–5	6–8	9–12	2,243	1,509	35:1		
Maharishi School of the Age of Enlightenment, Fairfield	X	X	X	X	PS–6	7–9	10–12	204	61			33
Rivermont Collegiate, Bettendorf			X	X	PS–5	6–8	9–12	192	35	2:1	X	6
Kansas												
Hyman Brand Hebrew Academy of Greater Kansas City, Overland Park			X	X	K–5	6–8	9–12	240	48	5:1	X	4
Independent School, Wichita			X	X	PK–5	6–8	9–12	547	212	10:1	X	16
Saint Thomas Aquinas High School, Overland Park			X	X			9–12	982	982	15:1	X	20
Kentucky												
Beth Haven Christian School, Louisville			X	X	K4–5	6–8	9–12	210	75	8:1		7
Community Christian Academy, Independence			X	X	PS–6	7–8	9–12	254	53	15:1		6
Covington Catholic High School, Park Hills			X				9–12	502	502	14:1	X	16
Kentucky Country Day School, Louisville			X	X	JK–4	5–8	9–12	947	286	7:1	X	20
Landmark Christian Academy, Louisville			X	X	K4–6	7–8	9–12	130	28	11:1		4
Lexington Catholic High School, Lexington			X	X			9–12	807	807	13:1	X	23
Louisville Collegiate School, Louisville			X	X	JK–5	6–8	9–12	693		8:1	X	15
Oneida Baptist Institute, Oneida	X	X	X	X		6–8	9–12	300	225	11:1	X	10

Private Secondary Schools At-a-Glance

	STUDENTS ACCEPTED				GRADES			STUDENT/FACULTY			SCHOOL OFFERINGS	
	BOARDING		DAY									
	Boys	Girls	Boys	Girls	Lower	Middle	Upper	Total	Upper	Student/Faculty Ratio	Advanced Placement Preparation	Sports
Sayre School, Lexington			X	X	PK–5	6–8	9–12	549	214	9:1	X	13
Trinity High School, Louisville			X				9–12	1,333	1,333	12:1	X	48
Whitefield Academy, Louisville			X	X	PS–5	6–8	9–12	731	199	20:1	X	17
Louisiana												
Academy of the Sacred Heart, Grand Coteau		X	X	X	PK–4	5–8	9–12	481	136	10:1	X	17
Academy of the Sacred Heart, New Orleans				X	1–4	5–8	9–12	619	201	16:1	X	22
Archbishop Rummel High School, Metairie			X				8–12	815	815	14:1	X	22
Holy Savior Menard Catholic High School, Alexandria			X	X		7–8	9–12	480	298	12:1	X	14
Jesuit High School of New Orleans, New Orleans			X			8	9–12	1,354	1,089	22:1	X	27
St. Joseph's Academy, Baton Rouge				X			9–12	976	976	14:1	X	25
St. Martin's Episcopal School, Metairie			X	X	PK–5	6–8	9–12	515	235	8:1	X	15
Teurlings Catholic High School, Lafayette			X	X			9–12	658	658	21:1		22
Maine												
Cheverus High School, Portland			X	X			9–12	507	507	12:1	X	26
George Stevens Academy, Blue Hill	X	X	X	X			9–12	304	304	10:1	X	49
Gould Academy, Bethel	X	X	X	X			9–PG	232	232	6:1	X	12
Hyde School, Bath	X	X	X	X			9–12	143	143	6:1		40
Lincoln Academy, Newcastle			X	X			9–12	547	547	13:1	X	17
Maine Central Institute, Pittsfield	X	X	X	X			9–PG	464	464	14:1	X	26
Saint Dominic Academy, Auburn			X	X	PK–6	7–8	9–12	598	242	12:1	X	10
Waynflete School, Portland			X	X	PK–5	6–8	9–12	555	253	12:1		23
Maryland												
Academy of the Holy Cross, Kensington				X			9–12	550	550	14:1	X	19
Archbishop Curley High School, Baltimore			X				9–12	526	526	14:1	X	19
The Baltimore Actors' Theatre Conservatory, Baltimore			X	X	3–5	7–8	9–12	24	11	3:1	X	
Baltimore Lutheran School, Towson			X	X		6–8	9–12	295	220	12:1	X	18
Barrie School, Silver Spring			X	X	N–5	6–8	9–12	299	70	8:1	X	12
The Bryn Mawr School for Girls, Baltimore			X	X	K–5	6–8	9–12	711	295	6:1	X	41
Calvert Hall College High School, Baltimore			X				9–12	1,225	1,225	12:1	X	33
The Calverton School, Huntingtown			X	X	PS–5	6–8	9–12	416	165		X	7
The Catholic High School of Baltimore, Baltimore				X			9–12	313	313	12:1	X	17
Chelsea School, Silver Spring			X	X		5–8	9–12	71	59	8:1		5
DeMatha Catholic High School, Hyattsville			X				9–12	896	896	13:1	X	24
Elizabeth Seton High School, Bladensburg				X			9–12	606	606	13:1	X	38
Georgetown Preparatory School, North Bethesda	X		X				9–12	484	484	8:1	X	51
Gilman School, Baltimore			X		K–5	6–8	9–12	1,022	465	8:1	X	26
Glenelg Country School, Ellicott City			X	X	PK–5	6–8	9–12	778	289	6:1	X	27
Griggs International Academy, Silver Spring			X	X	PK–6	7–8	9–12	728	434			
The Gunston School, Centreville			X	X			9–12	136	136	6:1	X	16
Institute of Notre Dame, Baltimore				X			9–12	246	246	12:1	X	32
Landon School, Bethesda			X		3–5	6–8	9–12	691	338	8:1	X	25
Loyola-Blakefield, Baltimore			X			6–8	9–12	1,004	741	11:1	X	24
McDonogh School, Owings Mills	X	X	X	X	K–4	5–8	9–12	1,296	585	9:1	X	28
The Nora School, Silver Spring			X	X			9–12	60	60	6:1		24
The Park School of Baltimore, Brooklandville			X	X	PK–5	6–8	9–12	863	333	7:1	X	17
Roland Park Country School, Baltimore				X	K–5	6–8	9–12	650	287	7:1	X	25
Saint Mary's High School, Annapolis			X	X			9–12	480	480	15:1	X	20
Saints Peter and Paul High School, Easton			X	X			9–12	214	214	9:1	X	11
St. Timothy's School, Stevenson		X		X			9–12	150	150	5:1		22
Sandy Spring Friends School, Sandy Spring	X	X	X	X	PK–5	6–8	9–12	572	263	8:1	X	41
Severn School, Severna Park			X	X		6–8	9–12	582	397	8:1	X	23
Takoma Academy, Takoma Park			X	X			9–12	230	230	12:1	X	3
Washington Waldorf School, Bethesda			X	X	PS–4	5–8	9–12	236	47	7:1	X	10
Worcester Preparatory School, Berlin			X	X	PK–5	6–8	9–12	535	212	9:1	X	13
Massachusetts												
Berkshire School, Sheffield	X	X	X	X			9–PG		380	5:1	X	36
Bishop Stang High School, North Dartmouth			X	X			9–12	713	713	13:1	X	39
Boston University Academy, Boston			X	X			9–12	159	159	8:1		15
Brimmer and May School, Chestnut Hill			X	X	PK–5	6–8	9–12	393	128	6:1	X	18
Brooks School, North Andover	X	X	X	X			9–12	371	371	5:1	X	19
Buxton School, Williamstown	X	X	X	X			9–12	90	90	4:1		24
The Cambridge School of Weston, Weston	X	X	X	X			9–PG	339	339	6:1	X	44
Cape Cod Academy, Osterville			X	X	PK–5	6–8	9–12	327	167	4:1	X	17
Central Catholic High School, Lawrence			X	X			9–12	1,355	1,355	24:1	X	32
Chapel Hill–Chauncy Hall School, Waltham	X	X	X	X			9–12	165	165	6:1	X	24
Commonwealth School, Boston			X	X			9–12	149	149	5:1	X	16
Concord Academy, Concord	X	X	X	X			9–12	363	363	6:1		35
Cushing Academy, Ashburnham	X	X	X	X			9–PG	445	445	8:1	X	40

Private Secondary Schools At-a-Glance

	STUDENTS ACCEPTED				GRADES			STUDENT/FACULTY			SCHOOL OFFERINGS	
	BOARDING		DAY									
	Boys	Girls	Boys	Girls	Lower	Middle	Upper	Total	Upper	Student/Faculty Ratio	Advanced Placement Preparation	Sports
Dana Hall School, Wellesley		X		X		6–8	9–12	475	355	9:1	X	41
Deerfield Academy, Deerfield	X	X	X	X			9–PG	630	630	6:1	X	41
Eaglebrook School, Deerfield	X		X			6–9		265	246	4:1		64
Falmouth Academy, Falmouth			X	X		7–8	9–12	190	116	4:1	X	3
Fay School, Southborough	X	X	X	X	PK–6		7–9	461	210	8:1		39
The Fessenden School, West Newton	X		X		K–4	5–6	7–9	475	197	7:1		24
Gann Academy (The New Jewish High School of Greater Boston), Waltham			X	X			9–12	331	331	5:1	X	14
Groton School, Groton	X	X	X	X			8–12	370	370	7:1	X	38
Holyoke Catholic High School, Chicopee			X	X			9–12	301	301	11:1	X	19
The John Dewey Academy, Great Barrington	X	X					10–PG	20	20	3:1		
The Judge Rotenberg Educational Center, Canton	X	X							130			3
Landmark School, Prides Crossing	X	X	X	X	1–5	6–8	9–12	459	309	3:1		16
Lawrence Academy, Groton	X	X	X	X			9–12	399	399	5:1	X	29
Malden Catholic High School, Malden			X				9–12	700	700	13:1	X	35
Matignon High School, Cambridge			X	X			9–12	442	442	15:1	X	25
Middlesex School, Concord	X	X	X	X			9–12	372	372	6:1	X	22
Milton Academy, Milton	X	X	X	X	K–5	6–8	9–12	980	675	5:1	X	28
Miss Hall's School, Pittsfield		X		X			9–12	180	180	5:1	X	30
Noble and Greenough School, Dedham	X	X	X	X		7–8	9–12	589	467	7:1	X	8
Phillips Academy (Andover), Andover	X	X	X	X			9–PG	1,105	1,105	5:1	X	48
The Pingree School, South Hamilton			X	X			9–12	340	340	7:1	X	32
Pioneer Valley Christian School, Springfield			X	X	PS–5	6–8	9–12	270	89	5:1	X	11
The Rivers School, Weston			X	X		6–8	9–12	469	350	6:1	X	18
The Roxbury Latin School, West Roxbury			X				7–12	297	297	8:1	X	10
St. John's Preparatory School, Danvers			X				9–12	1,200	1,200	11:1	X	47
St. Sebastian's School, Needham			X			7–8	9–12	360	260	7:1	X	18
Stoneleigh–Burnham School, Greenfield		X		X		7–8	9–PG	127	92	6:1	X	21
The Sudbury Valley School, Framingham			X	X				160		16:1		
Tabor Academy, Marion	X	X	X	X			9–12	519	519	6:1	X	27
Valley View School, North Brookfield	X					5–8	9–12	56	26	6:1		43
Waldorf High School of Massachusetts Bay, Belmont			X	X			9–12	50	50	4:1		4
Walnut Hill School, Natick	X	X	X	X			9–12	298	298	6:1	X	11
Waring School, Beverly			X	X		6–8	9–12	152	95	8:1	X	9
The Williston Northampton School, Easthampton	X	X	X	X		7–8	9–PG	529	441	7:1	X	37
The Winsor School, Boston				X		5–8	9–12	434	241	5:1	X	13
The Woodward School, Quincy				X		6–8	9–12	140	98	8:1	X	3
Michigan												
Academy of the Sacred Heart, Bloomfield Hills			X	X	N–4	5–8	9–12	493	129	7:1	X	11
Brother Rice High School, Bloomfield Hills			X				9–12	674	674	13:1	X	26
Cardinal Mooney Catholic College Preparatory High School, Marine City			X	X			9–12	180	180	10:1	X	12
Gabriel Richard High School, Riverview			X	X			9–12	334	334	14:1	X	17
Interlochen Arts Academy, Interlochen	X	X	X	X			9–PG	474	474	6:1	X	
Ladywood High School, Livonia				X			9–12	316	316	12:1	X	20
Lutheran High School Northwest, Rochester Hills			X	X			9–12	298	298	15:1	X	20
Powers Catholic High School, Flint			X	X			9–12	542	542	19:1	X	29
The Roeper School, Bloomfield Hills			X	X	PK–5	6–8	9–12	551	191	6:1	X	11
St. Mary's Preparatory School, Orchard Lake	X		X				9–12	480	480	10:1	X	44
Southfield Christian High School, Southfield			X	X	PK–5	6–8	9–12	547	182	20:1	X	19
University of Detroit Jesuit High School and Academy, Detroit			X			7–8	9–12	882	740	14:1	X	18
The Valley School, Swartz Creek			X	X	PK–4	5–8	9–12	57	17	8:1		9
West Catholic High School, Grand Rapids			X	X			9–12	506	506	28:1	X	22
Minnesota												
Academy of Holy Angels, Richfield			X	X			9–12	845	845	13:1	X	14
Breck School, Minneapolis			X	X	PK–4	5–8	9–12	1,143	390	11:1	X	19
Cotter Schools, Winona	X	X	X	X		7–8	9–12	380	298	11:1		24
St. Croix Schools, West St. Paul	X	X	X	X		6–8	9–12	500	440	15:1	X	34
Saint John's Preparatory School, Collegeville	X	X	X	X	6–6	7–8	9–PG	313	231	10:1	X	50
St. Paul Academy and Summit School, St. Paul			X	X	K–5	6–8	9–12	869	363	7:1		25
Saint Thomas Academy, Mendota Heights			X			7–8	9–12	675	559	10:1	X	30
Shattuck-St. Mary's School, Faribault	X	X	X	X		6–8	9–PG	438	398	9:1	X	29
Mississippi												
Chamberlain-Hunt Academy, Port Gibson	X		X	X		7–9	10–12	90	54	5:1		43
Hillcrest Christian School, Jackson			X	X	K–6		7–12	590	256	11:1	X	13
Jackson Preparatory School, Jackson			X	X		6–9	10–12	815	398	13:1	X	15
Lee Academy, Clarksdale					1–5	6–8	9–12	357	177	20:1		7
Madison-Ridgeland Academy, Madison			X	X	K–5	6–8	9–12	906	254	13:1	X	14

Private Secondary Schools At-a-Glance

	STUDENTS ACCEPTED				GRADES			STUDENT/FACULTY			SCHOOL OFFERINGS	
	BOARDING		DAY									
	Boys	Girls	Boys	Girls	Lower	Middle	Upper	Total	Upper	Student/Faculty Ratio	Advanced Placement Preparation	Sports
Our Lady Academy, Bay St. Louis				X		7–8	9–12	220	150	13:1	X	12
St. Patrick Catholic High School, Biloxi			X	X			7–12	474	474	14:1	X	18
Vicksburg Catholic School, Vicksburg			X	X	PK–6		7–12	569	258	10:1	X	14
Missouri												
Chaminade College Preparatory School, St. Louis	X		X			6–8	9–12	791	498	10:1	X	21
John Burroughs School, St. Louis			X	X		7–8	9–12	600	402	7:1	X	27
Lutheran High School North, St. Louis			X	X			9–12	314	314	10:1	X	13
Missouri Military Academy, Mexico	X		X			6–8	9–PG	232	186	11:1	X	42
MU High School, Columbia			X	X							X	
Nerinx Hall, Webster Groves				X			9–12	627	627	12:1	X	13
New Covenant Academy, Springfield			X	X	JK–6	7–8	9–12	342	97	10:1		6
Saint Teresa's Academy, Kansas City				X			9–12	561	561	12:1	X	25
Thomas Jefferson School, St. Louis	X	X	X	X		7–8	9–PG	89	72	6:1	X	9
Valle Catholic High School, Ste. Genevieve			X	X			9–12	137	137	9:1	X	14
Villa Duchesne and Oak Hill School, St. Louis			X	X	JK–6	7–8	9–12	680	324	9:1	X	13
Visitation Academy of St. Louis County, St. Louis			X	X	PK–6		7–12	633	458	9:1	X	15
Montana												
Butte Central Catholic High School, Butte	X		X	X			9–12	121	121	10:1	X	11
Manhattan Christian High School, Manhattan			X	X	PK–5	6–8	9–12	290	87	10:1	X	8
Nebraska												
Mercy High School, Omaha				X			9–12	360	360	12:1	X	25
Mount Michael Benedictine School, Elkhorn	X		X				9–12	220	220	10:1	X	22
Nebraska Christian Schools, Central City	X	X	X	X	K–6	7–8	9–12	210	123	10:1		6
Scotus Central Catholic High School, Columbus			X	X		7–8	9–12	401	258	14:1	X	13
Nevada												
The Dr. Miriam and Sheldon G. Adelson Educational Campus, The Adelson Upper School, Las Vegas			X	X	PS–4	5–8	9–12	482	88	10:1		10
Faith Lutheran High School, Las Vegas			X	X		6–8	9–12	1,371	721	17:1	X	22
The Meadows School, Las Vegas			X	X	PK–5	6–8	9–12	900	270	11:1	X	16
Sage Ridge School, Reno			X	X		5–8	9–12	224	76	6:1	X	15
New Hampshire												
Bishop Brady High School, Concord			X	X			9–12	365	365	15:1	X	30
Bishop Guertin High School, Nashua			X	X			9–12	900	900		X	35
Brewster Academy, Wolfeboro	X	X	X	X			9–PG	364	364	6:1	X	32
The Derryfield School, Manchester			X	X		6–8	9–12	368	238	8:1	X	22
Dublin Christian Academy, Dublin	X	X	X	X	K–6	7–8	9–12	88	52	8:1	X	9
Hampshire Country School, Rindge	X				3–6	7–8	9–12	23	7	2:1		24
Kimball Union Academy, Meriden	X	X	X	X			9–PG	314	314	9:1	X	38
The Oliverian School, Haverhill	X	X	X	X			9–PG	50	50	2:1	X	54
Phillips Exeter Academy, Exeter	X	X	X	X			9–PG	1,062	1,062	5:1	X	20
St. Thomas Aquinas High School, Dover			X	X			9–12	643	643	14:1	X	18
Tilton School, Tilton	X	X	X	X			9–PG	250	250	6:1	X	28
Trinity High School, Manchester			X	X			9–12	417	417	12:1	X	22
New Jersey												
The American Boychoir School, Princeton	X		X		4–5	6–8		51	30	5:1		2
Bishop Eustace Preparatory School, Pennsauken			X	X			9–12	750	750	13:1	X	20
Blair Academy, Blairstown	X	X	X	X			9–PG	450	450	7:1	X	43
Christian Brothers Academy, Lincroft			X				9–12	958	958	16:1	X	15
Delbarton School, Morristown			X			7–8	9–12	555	489	10:1	X	28
DePaul Catholic High School, Wayne			X	X						19:1	X	38
Gill St. Bernard's School, Gladstone			X	X	PK–4	5–8	9–12	695	309	15:1	X	23
Hawthorne Christian Academy, Hawthorne			X	X	PS–5	6–8	9–12	464	146	7:1		10
Immaculate Conception High School, Lodi				X			9–12	162	162	10:1	X	15
Kent Place School, Summit			X	X	N–5	6–8	9–12	636	277	7:1	X	17
The Lawrenceville School, Lawrenceville	X	X	X	X			9–PG	810	810	8:1		51
Marylawn of the Oranges, South Orange				X		7–8	9–12	146	120	15:1	X	13
Monsignor Donovan High School, Toms River			X	X			9–12	787	787	15:1	X	23
Montclair Kimberley Academy, Montclair			X	X	PK–3	4–8	9–12	1,043	434	6:1	X	22
Moorestown Friends School, Moorestown			X	X	PS–4	5–8	9–12	713	289	9:1	X	17
Morristown-Beard School, Morristown			X	X		6–8	9–12	547	396	7:1	X	21
Newark Academy, Livingston			X	X		6–8	9–12	568	399	12:1	X	32
Our Lady of Mercy Academy, Newfield				X			9–12	147	147	11:1		19
Peddie School, Hightstown	X	X	X	X			9–PG	550	550	6:1	X	24
The Pingry School, Martinsville			X	X	K–5	6–8	9–12	1,079	548	8:1	X	25
Pope John XXIII Regional High School, Sparta			X	X			8–12	974	974	13:1		19
Ranney School, Tinton Falls			X	X	N–5	6–8	9–12	821	253	9:1	X	24
Saint Augustine Preparatory School, Richland			X				9–12	682	682	13:1	X	23

Private Secondary Schools At-a-Glance

	STUDENTS ACCEPTED				GRADES			STUDENT/FACULTY			SCHOOL OFFERINGS	
	BOARDING		DAY									
	Boys	Girls	Boys	Girls	Lower	Middle	Upper	Total	Upper	Student/Faculty Ratio	Advanced Placement Preparation	Sports
St. Benedict's Preparatory School, Newark			X		7–8		9–12	562	471	11:1		21
Saint Joseph High School, Hammonton			X	X			9–12	380	380	17:1		27
Saint Joseph's High School, Metuchen			X				9–12	761	761	16:1	X	24
St. Peter's Preparatory School, Jersey City			X				9–12	966	966	12:1	X	32
SciCore Academy, Hightstown			X	X	K–4	5–8	9–12	95	30	7:1	X	8
Villa Victoria Academy, Ewing				X	PK–6	7–8	9–12	202	67	6:1	X	10
Villa Walsh Academy, Morristown				X		7–8	9–12	257	230	8:1	X	11
New Mexico												
Menaul School, Albuquerque	X	X	X	X		6–8	9–12	185	122	9:1	X	9
The United World College - USA, Montezuma	X	X							212	9:1		50
New York												
Allendale Columbia School, Rochester			X	X	N–5	6–8	9–12	325	123	4:1	X	12
The Beekman School, New York			X	X			9–PG	80	80	8:1	X	
The Birch Wathen Lenox School, New York			X	X	K–5	6–8	9–12	550	170	15:1	X	24
The Brearley School, New York				X	K–4	5–8	9–12	701	218	6:1	X	26
The Browning School, New York			X		K–4	5–8	9–12	408	113	4:1	X	9
Cascadilla School, Ithaca	X	X	X	X			9–PG	50	50	6:1	X	51
Cathedral High School, New York				X			9–12	600	600	17:1	X	5
Christian Brothers Academy, Syracuse			X	X			7–12	750	750		X	18
Christian Central Academy, Williamsville			X	X	K–5	6–8	9–12	389	116	10:1	X	11
Collegiate School, New York			X		K–4	5–8	9–12	648	229	4:1	X	13
The Dalton School, New York			X	X	K–3	4–8	9–12	1,311	461	7:1	X	16
Doane Stuart School, Rensselaer			X	X	N–4	5–8	9–12	290	127	7:1	X	23
Dominican Academy, New York				X			9–12	224	224	9:1	X	9
Emma Willard School, Troy		X		X			9–PG	323	323	6:1	X	37
The Family Foundation School, Hancock	X	X					9–12	120	120			28
Fontbonne Hall Academy, Brooklyn				X			9–12	527	527	14:1	X	17
Fordham Preparatory School, Bronx			X				9–12	990	990	11:1	X	23
French-American School of New York, Mamaroneck			X	X	N–5	6–8	9–12	869	193	7:1	X	8
Friends Academy, Locust Valley			X	X	N–5	6–8	9–12	777	379	8:1	X	17
Hackley School, Tarrytown	X	X	X	X	K–4	5–8	9–12	842	390	6:1	X	35
The Harley School, Rochester			X	X	N–4	5–8	9–12	520	163	7:1	X	15
The Harvey School, Katonah	X	X	X	X		6–8	9–12	338	255	6.5:1	X	23
Hebrew Academy-the Five Towns, Cedarhurst			X	X			9–12	388	388		X	7
Holy Cross High School, Flushing			X				9–12	900	900			11
Holy Trinity Diocesan High School, Hicksville			X	X			9–12	1,496	1,496		X	24
Hoosac School, Hoosick	X	X	X	X			8–PG	125	125	5:1	X	35
Houghton Academy, Houghton	X	X	X	X		6–8	9–PG	142	117	8:1	X	15
Iona Preparatory School, New Rochelle			X				9–12	785	785	13:1	X	36
The Karafin School, Mount Kisco			X	X			9–12	78	78	6:1	X	36
The Kew-Forest School, Forest Hills			X	X					134	12:1	X	6
La Scuola D'Italia Guglielmo Marconi, New York	X	X	X	X	PK–5	6–8	9–12	247	43		X	3
Long Island Lutheran Middle and High School, Brookville			X	X		6–8	9–12	596	408	9:1	X	23
Martin Luther High School, Maspeth			X	X		6–8	9–12	217	186	12:1	X	19
The Masters School, Dobbs Ferry	X	X	X	X		5–8	9–12	603	438	8:1	X	32
Millbrook School, Millbrook	X	X	X	X			9–12	272	272	5:1	X	30
Nichols School, Buffalo			X	X		5–8	9–12	582	389	8:1	X	20
North Country School, Lake Placid	X	X	X	X		4–9		88	60	3:1		47
Northwood School, Lake Placid	X	X	X	X			9–12	182	182	6:1	X	49
Our Lady of Mercy High School, Rochester				X		7–8	9–12	691	554	11:1	X	17
Professional Children's School, New York			X	X		6–8	9–12	198	165	8:1		
Regis High School, New York			X				9–12	530	530	15:1	X	8
Riverdale Country School, Bronx			X	X	PK–5	6–8	9–12	1,138	496	8:1		22
Robert Louis Stevenson School, New York			X	X			7–PG	60	60	5:1		27
Ross School, East Hampton	X	X	X	X	N–4	5–8	9–12	483	249	7:1	X	19
Rye Country Day School, Rye			X	X	PK–4	5–8	9–12	886	393	7:1	X	32
Saint Agnes Boys High School, New York			X						255	16:1	X	8
St. Thomas Choir School, New York	X				3–6		7–8	35	21	5:1		21
Seton Catholic Central High School, Binghamton			X	X			7–12	380	380	23:1	X	20
Smith School, New York			X	X		7–8	9–12	53	39	4:1		7
Soundview Preparatory School, Yorktown Heights			X	X		6–8	9–12	75	64	5:1	X	8
The Spence School, New York				X	K–4	5–8	9–12	704	223	3:1	X	13
Storm King School, Cornwall-on-Hudson	X	X	X	X		8–8	9–12	132	125	6:1	X	59
Trinity-Pawling School, Pawling	X		X			7–8	9–PG	272	248	8:1	X	39
United Nations International School, New York			X	X	K–4	5–8	9–12	1,542	468	3:1		48
The Windsor School, Flushing			X	X		6–8	9–13	160	149	14:1	X	11
Winston Preparatory School, New York			X	X		6–8	9–12	197	159	3:1		15

Private Secondary Schools At-a-Glance

	STUDENTS ACCEPTED				GRADES			STUDENT/FACULTY			SCHOOL OFFERINGS	
	BOARDING		DAY									
	Boys	Girls	Boys	Girls	Lower	Middle	Upper	Total	Upper	Student/Faculty Ratio	Advanced Placement Preparation	Sports
Xaverian High School, Brooklyn			X				9–12	1,200			X	29
York Preparatory School, New York			X	X		6–8	9–12	351	250	6:1	X	26
North Carolina												
Arendell Parrott Academy, Kinston			X	X	PK–5	6–8	9–12	788	242		X	19
Auldern Academy, Siler City		X				8–8	9–12	60	54	10:1	X	32
Bishop McGuinness Catholic High School, Kernersville			X	X			9–12	549	549	15:1	X	15
Cannon School, Concord			X	X	PK–4	5–8	9–12	825	316	9:1	X	21
Cape Fear Academy, Wilmington			X	X	PK–5	6–8	9–12	628	238	8:1	X	11
Carolina Day School, Asheville			X	X	PK–5	6–8	9–12	655	181	6:1	X	14
Charlotte Christian School, Charlotte			X	X	JK–5	6–8	9–12	1,018	360	11:1	X	22
Charlotte Country Day School, Charlotte			X	X	PK–4	5–8	9–12	1,619	489	12:1		21
Charlotte Latin School, Charlotte			X	X	K–5	6–8	9–12	1,388	492	12:1	X	20
Durham Academy, Durham			X	X	PK–4	5–8	9–12	1,146	397	12:1	X	24
Fayetteville Academy, Fayetteville			X	X	PK–5	6–8	9–12	393	154	14:1	X	12
Forsyth Country Day School, Lewisville			X	X	PK–4	5–8	9–12	846	353	12:1	X	17
Gaston Day School, Gastonia			X	X	PS–4	5–8	9–12	503	143	6:1	X	19
Greenfield School, Wilson			X	X	PS–4	5–8	9–12	307	74	3:1	X	7
Greensboro Day School, Greensboro			X	X	K–5	6–8	9–12	904	357	13:1	X	18
Harrells Christian Academy, Harrells			X	X	K–5	6–8	9–12	395	144	9:1	X	9
The Hill Center, Durham Academy, Durham			X	X	K–5	6–8	9–12	135	49	4:1		
Kerr-Vance Academy, Henderson			X	X	PK–6	7–8	9–12	472	132	10:1	X	15
Noble Academy, Greensboro			X	X	K–5	6–8	9–12	150	53	9:1		8
Oak Ridge Military Academy, Oak Ridge	X	X	X	X		7–8	9–12	65	50	11:1		25
The O'Neal School, Southern Pines			X	X	PK–4	5–8	9–12	430	156	12:1	X	11
Providence Day School, Charlotte			X	X	PK–5	6–8	9–12	1,501	534	12:1	X	23
Ravenscroft School, Raleigh			X	X	PK–5	6–8	9–12	1,237	458	8:1	X	22
Saint Mary's School, Raleigh		X		X			9–12	247	247	8:1	X	15
Salem Academy, Winston-Salem		X		X			9–12	167	167	7:1	X	22
Westchester Country Day School, High Point			X	X	K–5	6–8	9–12	396	150	6:1	X	15
Ohio												
Archbishop Hoban High School, Akron			X	X			9–12	849	849	13:1	X	23
Benedictine High School, Cleveland			X				9–12	352	352	11:1	X	22
Bishop Fenwick High School, Franklin			X	X			9–12	541	541	14:1	X	23
Cincinnati Country Day School, Cincinnati			X	X	PK–5	6–8	9–12	820	260	9:1	X	14
The Columbus Academy, Gahanna			X	X	PK–4	5–8	9–12	1,077	361	8:1	X	15
Columbus School for Girls, Columbus				X	PK–5	6–8	9–12	611	210	9:1	X	44
Gilmour Academy, Gates Mills	X	X	X	X	PK–6	7–8	9–12	693	430	10:1	X	37
Hawken School, Gates Mills			X	X	PS–5	6–8	9–12	971	432	9:1	X	16
Lawrence School, Sagamore Hills			X	X	1–6	7–8	9–12	291	143	11:1		11
Lehman High School, Sidney			X	X			9–12	211	211	15:1	X	15
Magnificat High School, Rocky River				X			9–12	800	800	12:1	X	14
Padua Franciscan High School, Parma			X	X			9–12	837	837	19:1	X	43
St. Francis de Sales High School, Toledo			X				9–12	629	629	14:1	X	17
Saint Ursula Academy, Toledo				X		7–8	9–12	549	522	16:1	X	30
The Seven Hills School, Cincinnati			X	X	PK–5	6–8	9–12	1,000	280	9:1	X	13
Stephen T. Badin High School, Hamilton			X	X			9–12	455	455	18:1	X	18
Trinity High School, Garfield Heights			X	X			9–12	330	330	10:1	X	15
Western Reserve Academy, Hudson	X	X	X	X			9–PG	389	389	6:1	X	43
Oklahoma												
Bishop McGuinness Catholic High School, Oklahoma City			X	X	9–10		11–12	722	346	14:1	X	18
Oregon												
Blanchet School, Salem			X	X		6–8	9–12	368	253	15:1	X	15
Canyonville Christian Academy, Canyonville	X	X	X	X						15:1	X	11
The Catlin Gabel School, Portland			X	X	PS–5	6–8	9–12	728	287	8:1		49
Northwest Academy, Portland			X	X		6–8	9–12	137	63	7:1		8
Oak Hill School, Eugene			X	X	K–5	6–8	9–12	151	34	10:1	X	10
Oregon Episcopal School, Portland	X	X	X	X	PK–5	6–8	9–12	845	305	7:1	X	22
Pacific Crest Community School, Portland			X	X		6–8	9–12	80	60	9:1		12
St. Mary's School, Medford	X	X	X	X		6–8	9–12	433	299	11:1	X	25
Salem Academy, Salem			X	X	K–5	6–8	9–12	594	228	9:1	X	11
Western Mennonite School, Salem	X	X	X	X		6–8	9–12	230	154	14:1		6
Pennsylvania												
Academy of the New Church Boys' School, Bryn Athyn	X		X				9–12	124	124	8:1	X	6
Academy of the New Church Girls' School, Bryn Athyn		X		X				84	84	8:1	X	9
Blue Mountain Academy, Hamburg	X	X	X	X			9–12	158	158	9:1	X	6
Camphill Special School, Glenmoore	X	X	X	X	K–7		9–13	110	59	5:1		

Private Secondary Schools At-a-Glance

	STUDENTS ACCEPTED				GRADES			STUDENT/FACULTY			SCHOOL OFFERINGS	
	BOARDING		DAY									
	Boys	Girls	Boys	Girls	Lower	Middle	Upper	Total	Upper	Student/Faculty Ratio	Advanced Placement Preparation	Sports
Cardinal O'Hara High School, Springfield			X	X						21:1	X	21
CFS, The School at Church Farm, Exton	X		X			7–8	9–12	190	154	6:1	X	16
Christopher Dock Mennonite High School, Lansdale			X	X			9–12	364	364	11:1	X	12
The Concept School, Westtown			X	X		6–8	9–12	33	24	8:1		11
Country Day School of the Sacred Heart, Bryn Mawr				X	PK–4	5–8	9–12	321	184	8:1	X	11
Devon Preparatory School, Devon			X			6–8	9–12	260	190	10:1	X	10
DuBois Central Catholic High School/Middle School, DuBois			X	X		6–8	9–12	241	161	14:1		
The Ellis School, Pittsburgh				X	PK–4	5–8	9–12	448	177	6:1	X	10
The Episcopal Academy, Newtown Square			X	X	PK–5	6–8	9–12	1,223	509	7:1	X	30
Friends' Central School, Wynnewood			X	X	N–4	5–8	9–12	890	390	8:1		25
Germantown Friends School, Philadelphia			X	X	K–5	6–8	9–12	855	348	9:1		16
The Grier School, Tyrone		X		X		7–8	9–PG	262	223	7:1	X	38
The Haverford School, Haverford			X		PK–5	6–8	9–12	991	418	7:1		24
The Hill School, Pottstown	X	X	X	X			9–PG	494	494	7:1	X	25
The Hill Top Preparatory School, Rosemont			X	X		5–9	9–12	75	45	4:1		40
Holy Ghost Preparatory School, Bensalem			X				9–12	498	498	11:1	X	18
Jack M. Barrack Hebrew Academy, Bryn Mawr			X	X		6–8	9–12	274	205	15:1	X	14
Lancaster Mennonite High School, Lancaster	X	X	X	X	PK–5	6–8	9–12	1,446	648	15:1	X	11
Lansdale Catholic High School, Lansdale			X	X			9–12	785	785		X	24
Lehigh Valley Christian High School, Catasauqua			X	X			9–12	131	131	11:1	X	7
Mercyhurst Preparatory School, Erie			X	X			9–12	624	624	13:1		20
Merion Mercy Academy, Merion Station				X			9–12	482	482	9:1	X	15
MMI Preparatory School, Freeland			X	X		6–8	9–12	248	164	11:1	X	11
Moravian Academy, Bethlehem			X	X	PK–5	6–8	9–12	779	186	7:1	X	14
Mount Saint Joseph Academy, Flourtown				X			9–12	560	560	10:1	X	14
Nativity B.V.M. High School, Pottsville							9–12	189	189	10:1	X	12
North Catholic High School, Pittsburgh			X	X				250	250		X	12
Notre Dame Junior/Senior High School, East Stroudsburg			X	X			7–12	233	233	15:1	X	14
The Oakland School, Pittsburgh			X	X			8–12	55	55	6:1		32
The Pathway School, Norristown			X	X					73	6:1		5
Philadelphia-Montgomery Christian Academy, Erdenheim			X	X	PK–5	6–8	9–12	298	118	10:1	X	8
Saint Basil Academy, Jenkintown				X			9–12	324	324	10:1	X	12
St. Joseph's Preparatory School, Philadelphia			X				9–12	993	993	16:1	X	27
Sewickley Academy, Sewickley			X	X	PK–5	6–8	9–12	702	294	7:1	X	15
Shady Side Academy, Pittsburgh	X	X	X	X	PK–5	6–8	9–12	928	487	8:1	X	25
The Shipley School, Bryn Mawr			X	X	PK–5	6–8	9–12	838	344	7:1	X	25
Springside Chestnut Hill Academy, Philadelphia			X	X	PK–4	5–8	9–12	1,129	448	6:1	X	30
Villa Joseph Marie High School, Holland				X			9–12	366	366	14:1	X	13
Villa Maria Academy, Erie			X	X			9–12	301	301	10:1	X	13
Villa Maria Academy, Malvern				X			9–12	425	425	9:1		15
Winchester Thurston School, Pittsburgh			X	X	PK–5	6–8	9–12	643	244	8:1	X	25
York Catholic High School, York			X	X		7–8	9–12	636	440			20
York Country Day School, York			X	X	PS–5	6–8	9–12	217	61	6:1	X	13
Puerto Rico												
Colegio San Jose, San Juan			X			7–8	9–12	483	359		X	13
Fowlers Academy, Guaynabo			X	X		7–8	9–12	68	54	15:1		7
Guamani Private School, Guayama			X	X	1–6	7–8	9–12	606	164	13:1	X	6
Wesleyan Academy, Guaynabo			X	X	PK–6	7–8	9–12	922	332	23:1	X	9
Rhode Island												
Lincoln School, Providence			X	X	N–5	6–8	9–12	352	165	4:1	X	9
Mount Saint Charles Academy, Woonsocket			X	X			7–12	874	874	18:1	X	27
Providence Country Day School, East Providence			X	X		6–8	9–12	216	178	7:1	X	19
St. Andrew's School, Barrington	X	X	X	X	3–5	6–8	9–12	218	173	5:1	X	32
The Wheeler School, Providence			X	X	N–5	6–8	9–12	801	317	6:1	X	14
South Carolina												
The Byrnes Schools, Florence			X	X	PK–5	6–8	9–12	192	64	9:1	X	14
Christ Church Episcopal School, Greenville			X	X	K–4	5–8	9–12	1,025	342	9:1		17
Porter-Gaud School, Charleston			X	X	1–5	6–8	9–12	903	341	15:1	X	21
St. Joseph's Catholic School, Greenville			X	X		6–8	9–12	611	355	12:1	X	16
Spartanburg Day School, Spartanburg			X	X	PK–4	5–8	9–12	449	134	9:1	X	16
Wilson Hall, Sumter			X	X	PS–5	6–8	9–12	837	250	13:1	X	33
South Dakota												
Freeman Academy, Freeman	X	X	X	X	5–8		9–12	69	45	5:1		7
Sunshine Bible Academy, Miller	X	X	X	X	K–5	6–8	9–12	100	77	9:1		12

Private Secondary Schools At-a-Glance

	STUDENTS ACCEPTED				GRADES			STUDENT/FACULTY			SCHOOL OFFERINGS	
	BOARDING		DAY									
	Boys	Girls	Boys	Girls	Lower	Middle	Upper	Total	Upper	Student/Faculty Ratio	Advanced Placement Preparation	Sports
Tennessee												
Bachman Academy, McDonald	X	X	X	X		6–8	9–PG	31	25	3:1		27
Battle Ground Academy, Franklin			X	X	K–4	5–8	9–12	880	343	11:1	X	30
Baylor School, Chattanooga	X	X	X	X		6–8	9–12	1,070	756	8:1	X	50
Briarcrest Christian High School, Eads			X	X	PK–5	6–8	9–12	1,670	593	14:1	X	19
Chattanooga Christian School, Chattanooga			X	X	K–5	6–8	9–12	1,145	457	17:1	X	49
Clarksville Academy, Clarksville			X	X	PK–5	6–8	9–12	557	196	7:1	X	12
Collegedale Academy, Collegedale			X	X			9–12	361	361	18:1	X	11
Columbia Academy, Columbia			X	X	K–6		7–12	578	253	11:1	X	15
Currey Ingram Academy, Brentwood			X	X	K–4	5–8	9–12	320	80	4:1		10
Davidson Academy, Nashville			X	X	PK–6	7–8	9–12				X	15
Donelson Christian Academy, Nashville			X	X	K4–5	6–8	9–12	715	264	16:1	X	18
Ezell-Harding Christian School, Antioch			X	X	K–4	5–8	9–12	631	224	12:1	X	15
Father Ryan High School, Nashville			X	X			9–12	939	939	12:1	X	30
Girls Preparatory School, Chattanooga				X		6–8	9–12	603	358	8:1	X	45
Harding Academy, Memphis			X	X	PS–6		7–12	1,222	537	13:1	X	13
Harding Academy, Nashville			X	X	K–5	6–8		480	100			24
The King's Academy, Seymour	X	X	X	X	K4–5	6–8	9–12	451	158	14:1	X	25
Lausanne Collegiate School, Memphis			X	X	PK–4	5–8	9–12	809	319	9:1	X	26
Memphis University School, Memphis			X		7–8		9–12	660	456	8:1	X	13
Montgomery Bell Academy, Nashville			X			7–8	9–12	715	486	8:1	X	35
Notre Dame High School, Chattanooga			X	X			9–12	407	407	10:1	X	42
St. Andrew's–Sewanee School, Sewanee	X	X	X	X		6–8	9–12	255	187	4:1	X	61
St. Benedict at Auburndale, Cordova			X	X			9–12	982	982	16:1	X	23
St. George's Independent School, Collierville			X	X	PK–5	6–8	9–12	1,207	386	7:1	X	15
St. Mary's Episcopal School, Memphis				X	PK–4	5–8	9–12	845	234	13:1	X	12
Trinity Christian Academy, Jackson			X	X	K4–5	6–8	9–12	734	236	9:1		11
University School of Jackson, Jackson			X	X	PK–5	6–8	9–12	1,232	348	13:1	X	15
The Webb School, Bell Buckle	X	X	X	X		6–8	9–PG	304	227	7:1	X	42
Webb School of Knoxville, Knoxville			X	X	K–5	6–8	9–12	1,047	477	10:1	X	18
Texas												
The Canterbury Episcopal School, DeSoto			X	X	K–6	7–8	9–12	265	83	14:1	X	10
Carrollton Christian Academy, Carrollton			X	X	PK–5	6–8	9–12	375				14
Central Catholic High School, San Antonio			X				9–12	556	556	20:1	X	20
Cistercian Preparatory School, Irving			X			5–8	9–12	355	177	7:1	X	14
Episcopal High School, Bellaire			X	X			9–12	677	677	9:1	X	23
Fairhill School, Dallas			X	X	1–5	6–8	9–12	219	66	12:1		8
First Baptist Academy, Dallas			X	X	K–5	6–8	9–12	285	108	8:1	X	14
Fort Worth Country Day School, Fort Worth			X	X	K–4	5–8	9–12	1,110	407	10:1	X	26
Greenhill School, Addison			X	X	PK–4	5–8	9–12	1,270	464	7:1	X	29
Happy Hill Farm Academy, Granbury	X	X	X	X	K–5	6–8	9–12	165	65	7:1		17
Hill School of Fort Worth, Fort Worth			X	X	1–6	7–8	9–12	169	87	9:1		4
The Hockaday School, Dallas		X		X	PK–4	5–8	9–12	1,085	477	14:1	X	42
Huntington-Surrey School, Austin			X	X			9–12	36	32	4:1		
Jesuit College Preparatory School, Dallas			X				9–12	1,072	1,072	11:1	X	28
Key School, Fort Worth			X	X	K–3	4–8	9–12	87	27	4:1		
Lakehill Preparatory School, Dallas			X	X	K–4	5–8	9–12	400	110	10:1	X	14
Loretto Academy, El Paso			X	X	PK–5	6–8	9–12	648	365	20:1	X	14
Marine Military Academy, Harlingen	X						8–12	250	250	12:1	X	36
The Oakridge School, Arlington			X	X	PS–4	5–8	9–12	876	306	10:1	X	28
Presbyterian Pan American School, Kingsville	X	X	X	X			9–12	158	158	9:1		19
Prestonwood Christian Academy, Plano			X	X	PK–4	5–8	9–12	1,439	467	11:1	X	13
Providence Catholic School, The College Preparatory School for Girls Grades 6-12, San Antonio				X		6–8	9–12	346	206	11:1	X	21
St. Agnes Academy, Houston				X			9–12	871	871	15:1	X	19
St. Anthony Catholic High School, San Antonio	X	X	X	X			9–12	402	402	12:1	X	15
St. Mark's School of Texas, Dallas			X		1–4	5–8	9–12	852	374	8:1	X	41
Saint Mary's Hall, San Antonio			X	X	PK–5	6–8	9–PG	990	385	6:1	X	21
St. Stephen's Episcopal School, Austin	X	X	X	X		6–8	9–12	668	460	8:1	X	34
St. Thomas High School, Houston			X				9–12	738	738	14:1	X	18
San Marcos Baptist Academy, San Marcos	X	X	X	X		7–8	9–12	294	242	6:1	X	26
Shelton School and Evaluation Center, Dallas			X	X	PS–4	5–8	9–12	868	256	8:1		9
Strake Jesuit College Preparatory, Houston			X				9–12	904	904	11:1	X	13
The Tenney School, Houston			X	X		6–8	9–12	62	49	2:1	X	
Trinity School of Texas, Longview			X	X	PK–5	6–8	9–12	300	50	8:1	X	12
Trinity Valley School, Fort Worth			X	X	K–4	5–8	9–12	957	337	8:1	X	11
Tyler Street Christian Academy, Dallas			X	X	P3–6	7–8	9–12	198	47	17:1	X	12
Westbury Christian School, Houston			X	X	PK–6	7–8	9–12	545	242	10:1	X	14
The Winston School San Antonio, San Antonio			X	X	K–6	7–8	9–12	185	83	8:1		14

Private Secondary Schools At-a-Glance

	STUDENTS ACCEPTED				GRADES			STUDENT/FACULTY			SCHOOL OFFERINGS	
	BOARDING		DAY									
	Boys	Girls	Boys	Girls	Lower	Middle	Upper	Total	Upper	Student/Faculty Ratio	Advanced Placement Preparation	Sports
Utah												
Intermountain Christian School, Salt Lake City			X	X	PK–5	6–8	9–12	277	61	7:1	X	5
Realms of Inquiry, Salt Lake City			X	X		7–8	9–12	22	12	10:1		67
Rowland Hall, Salt Lake City			X	X	PK–5	6–8	9–12	1,001	296	8:1	X	30
Wasatch Academy, Mt. Pleasant	X	X	X	X			8–12	285	285	10:1	X	69
The Waterford School, Sandy			X	X	PK–5	6–8	9–12	900	243	5:1	X	25
Vermont												
Burr and Burton Academy, Manchester	X	X	X	X			9–12	680	680	12:1	X	21
The Greenwood School, Putney						6–8	9–12	45	26	2:1		68
Rock Point School, Burlington	X	X	X	X			9–12	29	29	5:1		35
Stratton Mountain School, Stratton Mountain	X	X	X	X		6–8	9–PG	140	106	6:1		15
Thetford Academy, Thetford			X	X		7–8	9–12	300	238	7:1		11
Virgin Islands												
Kingshill School, St. Croix			X	X		7–8	9–PG	30	29	5:1		25
St. Croix Country Day School, Kingshill			X	X	N–6	7–8	9–12	413	144	12:1	X	12
Virginia												
Benedictine High School, Richmond			X				9–12	277	277	9:1	X	27
Bishop Ireton High School, Alexandria			X	X			9–12	827	827	14:1	X	26
Blessed Sacrament Hugenot, Powhatan			X	X	PS–5	6–8	9–12	337	111	6:1	X	11
The Blue Ridge School, St. George	X						9–12	195	195	6:1		49
Cape Henry Collegiate School, Virginia Beach			X	X	PK–5	6–8	9–12	852	371	10:1	X	45
Carlisle School, Axton	X	X	X	X	PK–5	6–8	9–12	549	174	7:1	X	18
Chatham Hall, Chatham		X		X			9–12	140	140	7:1	X	19
Christchurch School, Christchurch	X		X	X	1–4	5–8	9–PG	220	220	6:1	X	37
The Collegiate School, Richmond			X	X	K–4	5–8	9–12	1,597	516	15:1	X	24
Episcopal High School, Alexandria	X	X					9–12	435	435	6:1	X	44
Flint Hill School, Oakton			X	X	JK–4	5–8	9–12	1,116	501	8:1	X	35
Foxcroft School, Middleburg		X		X			9–12	154	154	7:1	X	27
Fuqua School, Farmville			X	X	PK–5	6–8	9–12	431	145	16:1	X	13
Hampton Roads Academy, Newport News			X	X	PK–4	5–8	9–12	589	274	10:1	X	24
Hargrave Military Academy, Chatham	X		X			7–9	10–PG	310	260	12:1	X	50
Little Keswick School, Keswick	X							34		4:1		17
Miller School, Charlottesville	X	X	X	X		8–8	9–12	145	137	6:1	X	40
Norfolk Academy, Norfolk			X	X	1–6	7–9	10–12	1,229	370	10:1	X	22
Oak Hill Academy, Mouth of Wilson	X	X	X	X			8–12	122	122	10:1		34
Oakland School, Keswick	X	X	X	X						5:1		44
The Potomac School, McLean			X	X	K–3	4–8	9–12	1,007	410	6:1	X	26
Randolph-Macon Academy, Front Royal	X	X	X	X		6–8	9–PG	367	294	9:1	X	27
St. Anne's–Belfield School, Charlottesville	X	X	X	X	PK–4	5–8	9–12	892	350	8:1	X	21
St. Christopher's School, Richmond			X		JK–5	6–8	9–12	956	293	6:1	X	26
St. Stephen's & St. Agnes School, Alexandria			X	X	JK–5	6–8	9–12	1,140	445	9:1	X	28
Tandem Friends School, Charlottesville			X	X		5–8	9–12	196	110	6:1	X	10
Tidewater Academy, Wakefield			X	X	PK–5	6–7	8–12	179	68	15:1	X	7
Wakefield School, The Plains			X	X	PS–5	6–8	9–12	432	143	16:1	X	16
Washington												
Annie Wright School, Tacoma		X	X	X	PS–5	6–8	9–12	441	156	7:1		5
Bishop Blanchet High School, Seattle			X	X			9–12	989	989	13:1	X	23
Chrysalis School, Woodinville			X	X	K–6	7–8	9–12	169	116	5:1		
Eastside Catholic School, Sammamish			X	X		6–8	9–12			13:1	X	19
Gonzaga Preparatory School, Spokane			X	X			9–12	902	902	14:1	X	24
Holy Names Academy, Seattle				X			9–12	675	675			
King's High School, Seattle			X	X	PK–6	7–8	9–12	1,130	471	15:1	X	13
Lakeside School, Seattle			X	X		5–8	9–12	797	538	9:1		19
Northwest Yeshiva High School, Mercer Island			X	X			9–12	87	87	4:1		5
The Overlake School, Redmond			X	X		5–8	9–12	535	302	9:1	X	34
Seattle Academy of Arts and Sciences, Seattle			X	X		6–8	9–12	648	409	9:1		23
Seattle Christian Schools, Seattle			X	X	K–6	7–8	9–12	538	213	10:1	X	19
Shoreline Christian, Shoreline			X	X	PS–6	7–8	9–12	222	71	7:1		6
University Prep, Seattle			X	X		6–8	9–12	510	298	9:1	X	33
West Sound Academy, Poulsbo	X	X	X	X		6–8	9–12	76	44	7:1		5
West Virginia												
The Linsly School, Wheeling	X	X	X	X	5–8		9–12	450	296	9:1	X	47
Wisconsin												
Fox Valley Lutheran High School, Appleton			X	X			9–12	569	569	14:1		14
The Prairie School, Racine			X	X	PK–4	5–8	9–12	687	265	17:1	X	10
University School of Milwaukee, Milwaukee			X	X	PK–4	5–8	9–12	1,058	341	9:1	X	16

Private Secondary Schools At-a-Glance

	STUDENTS ACCEPTED				GRADES			STUDENT/FACULTY			SCHOOL OFFERINGS	
	BOARDING		DAY									
	Boys	Girls	Boys	Girls	Lower	Middle	Upper	Total	Upper	Student/Faculty Ratio	Advanced Placement Preparation	Sports
CANADA												
The Academy for Gifted Children (PACE), Richmond Hill, ON			X	X	1–3	4–7	8–12	295	108	15:1	X	43
Académie Ste Cécile International School, Windsor, ON	X	X	X	X	JK–8		9–12	236	113	15:1	X	25
Armbrae Academy, Halifax, NS			X	X	K–6		7–12	258	124	9:1	X	11
Arrowsmith School, Toronto, ON			X	X	1–5	6–9	10–12	75	20	10:1		
Balmoral Hall School, Winnipeg, MB		X		X	N–5	6–8	9–12	451	165	7:1	X	67
Bearspaw Christian School, Calgary, AB			X	X	K–6	7–9	10–12	577	115	20:1		13
Bishop's College School, Sherbrooke, QC	X	X	X	X		7–9	10–12	212	155	5:1	X	47
The Bishop Strachan School, Toronto, ON		X		X	JK–6	7–8	9–12	891	461	9:1	X	52
Branksome Hall, Toronto, ON		X		X	JK–6	7–8	9–12	880	462	9:1		42
Calgary Academy Collegiate, Calgary, AB			X	X	6–6	7–9	10–12	176	80	8:1	X	14
Central Alberta Christian High School, Lacombe, AB			X	X			10–12	113	113	14:1		22
Columbia International College of Canada, Hamilton, ON	X	X	X	X		7–9	10–12	1,622	1,418	20:1	X	42
The Country Day School, King City, ON			X	X	JK–6	7–8	9–12	720	300	10:1	X	25
Covenant Canadian Reformed School, Neerlandia, AB			X	X	K–6	7–9	10–12	188	28	10:1		17
Crawford Adventist Academy, Willowdale, ON			X	X	JK–6	7–8	9–12	266	185	16:1	X	13
Eastside Christian Academy, Calgary, AB			X	X	K–6	7–9	10–12	82	14	25:1		8
Edison School, Okotoks, AB			X	X	K–4	5–8	9–12	198	48	12:1	X	5
Foothills Academy, Calgary, AB			X	X	1–6	7–8	9–12	200	114	12:1		46
Glen Eden School, Vancouver, BC			X	X						5:1		
Glenlyon Norfolk School, Victoria, BC			X	X	JK–5	6–8	9–12	691	273	10:1		27
Great Lakes Christian High School, Beamsville, ON	X	X	X	X			9–12	95	95	10:1		19
Heritage Christian Academy, Calgary, AB			X	X	K–5	6–9	10–12	568	97	9:1		17
Heritage Christian School, Jordan, ON			X	X	K–8		9–12	571	171	15:1		5
Highroad Academy, Chilliwack, BC					K–6	7–8	9–12	392	123	10:1		
King's-Edgehill School, Windsor, NS	X	X	X	X		6–9	10–12	290	200	10:1		33
Lakefield College School, Lakefield, ON	X	X	X	X		7–8	9–12	368	347	7:1	X	31
Lighthouse Christian School, Sylvan Lake, AB			X	X	PK–5	6–9	10–12	84	22	15:1		
Linden Christian School, Winnipeg, MB			X	X	K–4	5–8	9–12	887	274	13:1		20
Luther College High School, Regina, SK	X	X	X	X			9–12	370	370	16:1		21
MacLachlan College, Oakville, ON			X	X	PK–8		9–12	344	133	10:1	X	39
Miss Edgar's and Miss Cramp's School, Montreal, QC				X	K–5	6–8	9–11	335	115	9:1	X	26
MPS Etobicoke, Toronto, ON			X	X	JK–6	7–8	9–12	318	145	14:1		27
New Tribes Mission Academy, Durham, ON			X	X	K–6	7–8	9–11	21	4	3:1		14
Niagara Christian Community of Schools, Fort Erie, ON	X	X	X	X	JK–6	7–8	9–12	254	179	17:1		21
North Toronto Christian School, Toronto, ON			X	X	JK–6	7–8	9–12	504	220	15:1		27
Peoples Christian Academy, Markham, ON			X	X	JK–6		7–12	339	178	10:1		9
Pickering College, Newmarket, ON	X	X	X	X	JK–8		9–12	373	217	9:1		44
Pic River Private High School, Heron Bay, ON			X	X						10:1		
Pinehurst School, St. Catharines, ON	X	X			7–8	9–10	11–12	23	14	10:1		68
Providence Christian School, Monarch, AB			X	X	K–6	7–9	10–12	120	21	11:1		
Queen Margaret's School, Duncan, BC		X	X	X	PS–7		8–12	302	152	8:1		71
Quinte Christian High School, Belleville, ON			X	X			9–12	161	161	15:1		8
Ridley College, St. Catharines, ON	X	X	X	X	JK–8		9–PG	591	416	7:1	X	77
Robert Land Academy, Wellandport, ON	X				6–8	9–10	11–12	125	73	14:1		69
Rosseau Lake College, Rosseau, ON	X	X	X	X		7–8	9–12	81	64	6:1		82
Rothesay Netherwood School, Rothesay, ND	X	X	X	X		6–8	9–12	270	208	8:1		48
Royal Canadian College, Vancouver, BC			X	X		9–10	11–12	70	52	15:1		5
Rundle College, Calgary, AB			X	X	PK–6	7–9	10–12	783	245			23
Sacred Heart School of Halifax, Halifax, NS			X	X	K–6		7–12	485	295	15:1	X	17
St. Andrew's College, Aurora, ON	X		X			6–8	9–12	591	458	9:1	X	62
St. Andrew's Regional High School, Victoria, BC			X	X		8–9	10–12			14:1		8
Saint Clement Academy, Ottawa, ON			X	X		7–8	9–12	20	13	3:1		11
St. Clement's School, Toronto, ON				X	1–6	7–9	10–12	473	194	7:1	X	37
St. George's School of Montreal, Montreal, QC			X	X	K–6		7–11	442	256	17:1	X	45
St. John's-Ravenscourt School, Winnipeg, MB	X	X	X	X	K–5	6–8	9–12	830	370	9:1	X	15
St. Jude's School, Kitchener, ON			X	X	1–6	7–9	10–12	30	10	6:1		13
St. Michael's College School, Toronto, ON			X			7–8	9–12	1,054	862	16:1	X	27
St. Patrick's Regional Secondary, Vancouver, BC			X	X				500	500		X	6
St. Paul's High School, Winnipeg, MB			X				9–12	599	599	14:1	X	21
Scholar's Hall Preparatory School, Kitchener, ON			X	X	JK–3	4–8	9–12	105	35	10:1		23
Shawnigan Lake School, Shawnigan Lake, BC	X	X	X	X			8–12	453	453	8:1	X	46
Solomon College, Edmonton, AB			X	X				25	25	10:1		
Toronto District Christian High School, Woodbridge, ON			X	X			9–12	430	421	14:1		10
Trafalgar Castle School, Whitby, ON		X		X		5–8	9–12	181	123	9:1	X	29

Private Secondary Schools At-a-Glance

	STUDENTS ACCEPTED				GRADES			STUDENT/FACULTY			SCHOOL OFFERINGS	
	BOARDING		DAY									
	Boys	Girls	Boys	Girls	Lower	Middle	Upper	Total	Upper	Student/Faculty Ratio	Advanced Placement Preparation	Sports
Trinity College School, Port Hope, ON	X	X	X	X		5–8	9–12	545	450	8:1	X	41
United Mennonite Educational Institute, Leamington, ON			X	X			9–12	50	50	15:1		13
Westgate Mennonite Collegiate, Winnipeg, MB			X	X		7–9	10–12	340	172	15:1	X	32
West Island College, Calgary, AB			X	X		7–9	10–12	463	239	17:1	X	35
Willow Wood School, Don Mills, ON			X	X	1–6	7–8	9–12	190	122	7:1		34
INTERNATIONAL												
Bermuda												
Saltus Grammar School, Hamilton			X	X	K–5	6–8	9–12	961	198	13:1	X	29
Brazil												
Escola Americana de Campinas, Campinas-SP			X	X	PK–5	6–8	9–12	648	151	7:1	X	27
Colombia												
Colegio Nueva Granada, Bogota			X	X	PK–5	6–8	9–12	1,801	527	22:1	X	8
Denmark												
Copenhagen International School, 2900 Hellerup			X	X	PK–5		6–12	602	308	7:1		5
Ecuador												
Alliance Academy, Quito	X	X	X	X	PK–6	7–8	9–12	604	208	7:1	X	27
Germany												
International School Hamburg, Hamburg			X	X	PK–5	6–8	9–12	694	152	8:1		19
Munich International School, Starnberg			X	X	PK–4	5–8	9–12	1,212	420	6:1		23
Italy												
Marymount International School, Rome			X	X	PK–5	6–8	9–12	655	230	15:1		7
St. Stephen's School, Rome, Rome	X	X	X	X			9–PG	258	258	7:1	X	8
Japan												
Saint Maur International School, Yokohama			X	X	PK–5	6–8	9–12	380	104	4:1	X	8
Seisen International School, Tokyo			X	X	K–6	7–8	9–12	628	158	3:1		12
Mexico												
The American School Foundation, Mexico City, D.F.			X	X	1–5	6–8	9–12	2,565	719	13:1	X	8
Netherlands												
International School of Amsterdam, Amstelveen			X	X	PS–5	6–8	9–12	992	244	5:1		17
Philippines												
International School Manila, 1634 Taguig City			X	X	PK–4	5–8	9–12	1,966	722	9:1	X	19
Switzerland												
Neuchatel Junior College, Neuchtel	X	X					12	56	56	10:1	X	18
TASIS, The American School in Switzerland, Montagnola-Lugano	X	X	X	X	1–5	6–8	9–PG	642	339	5:1	X	35
Taiwan												
Taipei American School, Taipei			X	X	PK–5	6–8	9–12	2,192	886	10:1	X	12
Thailand												
International School Bangkok, Pakkret			X	X	PK–5	6–8	9–12	1,840	703	10:1	X	15
United Kingdom												
The American School in London, London			X	X	PK–4	5–8	9–12	1,350	468	10:1	X	17
The International School of London, London			X	X	K–5	6–10	11–12	340	60	8:1		7
Merchiston Castle School, Edinburgh	X		X						174	9:1		43
TASIS The American School in England, Thorpe, Surrey	X	X	X	X	N–4	5–8	9–13	750	390	8:1	X	44

Traditional Day and Boarding Schools

THE ACADEMY AT CHARLEMONT

1359 Route 2

The Mohawk Trail

Charlemont, Massachusetts 01339

Head of School: Mr. Todd A. Sumner

General Information Coeducational day college-preparatory and arts school. Grades 7–PG. Founded: 1981. Setting: rural. Nearest major city is Springfield. 52-acre campus. 3 buildings on campus. Approved or accredited by New England Association of Schools and Colleges and Massachusetts Department of Education. Member of National Association of Independent Schools. Endowment: $307,000. Total enrollment: 114. Upper school average class size: 17. Upper school faculty-student ratio: 1:7. There are 166 required school days per year for Upper School students. Upper School students typically attend 5 days per week. The average school day consists of 7 hours.

Upper School Student Profile Grade 9: 20 students (12 boys, 8 girls); Grade 10: 20 students (12 boys, 8 girls); Grade 11: 19 students (10 boys, 9 girls); Grade 12: 16 students (7 boys, 9 girls).

Faculty School total: 18. In upper school: 9 men, 9 women; 6 have advanced degrees.

Subjects Offered Algebra, American legal systems, American literature, art, art history, biology, calculus, chemistry, computer science, creative writing, drama, earth science, ecology, English, English literature, environmental science, ethics, European history, expository writing, fine arts, French, geography, geometry, government/civics, grammar, health, history, Latin, mathematics, music, philosophy, photography, physical education, physics, religion, Russian, science, social studies, Spanish, speech, theater, trigonometry, world history, world literature, zoology.

Graduation Requirements Algebra, American government, American literature, American studies, arts and fine arts (art, music, dance, drama), biology, calculus, chemistry, civics, computer literacy, English, foreign language, four units of summer reading, geography, geometry, Latin, mathematics, physics, pre-calculus, science, senior project, social studies (includes history), Year-long senior project equal to one full course, requiring outside evaluation and a presentation.

Special Academic Programs Independent study; study abroad.

College Admission Counseling 15 students graduated in 2010; all went to college, including Berklee College of Music; Guilford College; Middlebury College; Skidmore College; University of Vermont; Williams College. Mean SAT critical reading: 657, mean SAT math: 591, mean SAT writing: 634, mean combined SAT: 1881, mean composite ACT: 27.

Student Life Upper grades have specified standards of dress, student council, honor system. Discipline rests primarily with faculty.

Tuition and Aid Day student tuition: $22,600. Tuition installment plan (monthly payment plans, individually arranged payment plans). Need-based scholarship grants available. In 2010–11, 70% of upper-school students received aid. Total amount of financial aid awarded in 2010–11: $1,000,000.

Admissions Traditional secondary-level entrance grade is 9. For fall 2010, 40 students applied for upper-level admission, 38 were accepted, 28 enrolled. School's own test and writing sample required. Deadline for receipt of application materials: February 15. Application fee required: $30. On-campus interview required.

Athletics Interscholastic: alpine skiing (boys, girls), basketball (b,g), cross-country running (b,g), lacrosse (b,g), skiing (downhill) (b,g), soccer (b,g), ultimate Frisbee (b,g); intramural: indoor soccer (b,g); coed interscholastic: basketball; coed intramural: aerobics/dance, alpine skiing, basketball, bicycling, bocce, canoeing/kayaking, cooperative games, croquet, hiking/backpacking, kayaking, outdoor activities, outdoor recreation, rafting, skiing (cross-country), skiing (downhill), soccer, tennis, ultimate Frisbee, yoga. 7 coaches.

Computers Computers are regularly used in all classes. Computer network features include on-campus library services, Internet access, wireless campus network, Internet filtering or blocking technology, school Website for schedules and other administrative information. Student e-mail accounts and computer access in designated common areas are available to students. Students grades are available online. The school has a published electronic and media policy.

Contact Sandy Warren, Director of Admissions. 413-339-4912. Fax: 413-339-4324. E-mail: swarren@charlemont.org. Web site: www.charlemont.org.

ACADEMY AT THE LAKES

2331 Collier Parkway

Land O'Lakes, Florida 34639

Head of School: Mr. Mark Heller

General Information Coeducational day college-preparatory and arts school. Grades PK–12. Founded: 1992. Setting: suburban. Nearest major city is Tampa. 9-acre campus. 9 buildings on campus. Approved or accredited by Southern Association of Colleges and Schools and Florida Department of Education. Member of National Association of Independent Schools and Secondary School Admission Test Board. Total enrollment: 404. Upper school average class size: 14. Upper school faculty-student ratio: 1:5. There are 176 required school days per year for Upper School students. Upper School students typically attend 5 days per week. The average school day consists of 7 hours and 15 minutes.

Upper School Student Profile Grade 9: 30 students (14 boys, 16 girls); Grade 10: 33 students (13 boys, 20 girls); Grade 11: 40 students (23 boys, 17 girls); Grade 12: 23 students (12 boys, 11 girls).

Faculty School total: 57. In upper school: 12 men, 16 women; 19 have advanced degrees.

Graduation Requirements Standard curriculum.

Special Academic Programs 9 Advanced Placement exams for which test preparation is offered; honors section; ESL (10 students enrolled).

College Admission Counseling 30 students graduated in 2011; all went to college, including Gettysburg College; Rollins College; The University of Tampa; University of South Florida; Wake Forest University.

Student Life Upper grades have specified standards of dress, student council, honor system. Discipline rests primarily with faculty.

Tuition and Aid Day student tuition: $16,990. Tuition installment plan (monthly payment plans). Merit scholarship grants, need-based scholarship grants available. In 2011–12, 24% of upper-school students received aid.

Admissions Traditional secondary-level entrance grade is 9. For fall 2011, 44 students applied for upper-level admission, 36 were accepted, 26 enrolled. SSAT required. Deadline for receipt of application materials: none. Application fee required: $50. Interview required.

Athletics Interscholastic: baseball (boys), basketball (b,g), cheering (g), cross-country running (b,g), football (b), golf (b,g), physical fitness (b,g), physical training (b,g), soccer (b,g), softball (g), strength & conditioning (b,g), swimming and diving (b,g), tennis (b,g), touch football (b), track and field (b,g), volleyball (g), weight training (b,g), winter soccer (b,g); coed interscholastic: physical fitness, physical training, soccer, strength & conditioning, weight training. 3 PE instructors, 11 coaches, 1 athletic trainer.

Computers Computer network features include on-campus library services, Internet access, wireless campus network, Internet filtering or blocking technology. Students grades are available online. The school has a published electronic and media policy.

Contact Mrs. Melissa Starkey, Associate Director of Admissions. 813-909-7919. Fax: 813-949-0563. E-mail: mstarkey@academyatthelakes.org. Web site: www.academyatthelakes.org/.

THE ACADEMY FOR GIFTED CHILDREN (PACE)

12 Bond Crescent

Richmond Hill, Ontario L4E 3K2, Canada

Head of School: Barbara Rosenberg

General Information Coeducational day college-preparatory and intellectually gifted school. Grades 1–12. Founded: 1993. Setting: suburban. Nearest major city is Toronto, Canada. 3-acre campus. 1 building on campus. Approved or accredited by Ontario Ministry of Education and Ontario Department of Education. Language of instruction: English. Total enrollment: 295. Upper school average class size: 17. Upper school faculty-student ratio: 1:15. There are 187 required school days per year for Upper School students. Upper School students typically attend 5 days per week. The average school day consists of 6 hours.

Upper School Student Profile Grade 8: 24 students (16 boys, 8 girls); Grade 9: 23 students (11 boys, 12 girls); Grade 10: 27 students (17 boys, 10 girls); Grade 11: 13 students (7 boys, 6 girls); Grade 12: 21 students (12 boys, 9 girls).

Faculty School total: 27. In upper school: 6 men, 7 women; 3 have advanced degrees.

Subjects Offered 20th century world history, Advanced Placement courses, algebra, analytic geometry, biology, calculus, calculus-AP, Canadian geography, Canadian history, Canadian law, career education, chemistry, chemistry-AP, civics, computer programming, computer science, computer science-AP, computer studies, dramatic arts, English, finite math, French, French as a second language, geometry, health education, language, law, literature, mathematics, modern Western civilization, music, philosophy, physical education, physics, science, sociology, visual arts, world civilizations, writing.

Graduation Requirements Advanced chemistry, advanced math, algebra, analytic geometry, biology, calculus, Canadian geography, Canadian history, Canadian literature, career education, chemistry, civics, English literature, French as a second language, healthful living, law, music, philosophy, pre-algebra, pre-calculus, science, scuba diving, senior humanities, social sciences, sociology, theater arts, visual arts, minimum of 40 hours of community service, OSSLT.

Special Academic Programs 5 Advanced Placement exams for which test preparation is offered; honors section; academic accommodation for the gifted.

College Admission Counseling 22 students graduated in 2011; all went to college, including Harvard University; McMaster University; Queen's University at Kingston; The University of Western Ontario; University of Toronto; University of Waterloo. Median SAT critical reading: 780, median SAT math: 800, median SAT writing: 780, median combined SAT: 2360. 100% scored over 600 on SAT critical reading, 100% scored over 600 on SAT math, 100% scored over 600 on SAT writing, 100% scored over 1800 on combined SAT.

Student Life Upper grades have specified standards of dress, student council, honor system. Discipline rests primarily with faculty.

Tuition and Aid Day student tuition: CAN$11,250. Tuition installment plan (monthly payment plans).

Admissions Traditional secondary-level entrance grade is 8. For fall 2011, 14 students applied for upper-level admission, 6 were accepted, 6 enrolled. Psychoeducational evaluation, Wechsler Individual Achievement Test, WISC III or other aptitude measures; standardized achievement test and WISC-R required. Deadline for receipt of application materials: none. No application fee required. On-campus interview required.
Athletics Interscholastic: badminton (boys, girls), ball hockey (b), baseball (b,g), basketball (b,g), flag football (b), floor hockey (b), golf (b,g), independent competitive sports (b,g), indoor soccer (b,g), soccer (b,g), softball (b,g), track and field (b,g), volleyball (b,g), winter soccer (b,g); intramural: badminton (b,g), basketball (b,g), soccer (b,g), softball (b,g); coed interscholastic: badminton, baseball, bowling, cross-country running, flag football, Frisbee, indoor soccer, ultimate Frisbee; coed intramural: alpine skiing, badminton, ball hockey, basketball, blading, climbing, cooperative games, cross-country running, curling, dance, diving, floor hockey, handball, ice skating, indoor soccer, jogging, jump rope, life saving, martial arts, outdoor activities, outdoor education, outdoor skills, physical fitness, rock climbing, ropes courses, scuba diving, skiing (downhill), snowboarding, snowshoeing, ultimate Frisbee, volleyball, wall climbing, yoga. 2 PE instructors, 10 coaches.
Computers Computers are regularly used in career exploration, desktop publishing, digital applications, English, information technology, keyboarding, news writing, newspaper, photography, programming, science, technology, theater, writing, yearbook classes. Computer network features include Internet access, wireless campus network. Computer access in designated common areas is available to students. The school has a published electronic and media policy.
Contact Barbara Rosenberg, Director. 905-773-3997. Fax: 905-773-4722. Web site: www.pace.on.ca.

ACADEMY OF HOLY ANGELS

6600 Nicollet Avenue South

Richfield, Minnesota 55423-2498

Head of School: Mr. Thomas C. Shipley

General Information Coeducational day college-preparatory, arts, business, religious studies, and technology school, affiliated with Roman Catholic Church. Grades 9–12. Founded: 1877. Setting: suburban. Nearest major city is Minneapolis. 26-acre campus. 2 buildings on campus. Approved or accredited by North Central Association of Colleges and Schools. Endowment: $1 million. Total enrollment: 845. Upper school average class size: 20. Upper school faculty-student ratio: 1:13.
Upper School Student Profile 80% of students are Roman Catholic.
Faculty School total: 63. In upper school: 30 men, 30 women; 29 have advanced degrees.
Subjects Offered Algebra, American history, American literature, anatomy, art, art history, astronomy, Bible studies, biology, broadcasting, business, business skills, calculus, ceramics, chemistry, computer math, computer programming, computer science, dance, drafting, drama, economics, electronics, English, English literature, environmental science, ethics, European history, expository writing, fine arts, French, geography, geometry, German, government/civics, grammar, health, history, home economics, industrial arts, journalism, mathematics, mechanical drawing, music, photography, physical education, physics, physiology, psychology, religion, Russian, science, social sciences, social studies, sociology, Spanish, speech, theater, theology, trigonometry, typing, world history, world literature, writing.
Graduation Requirements Arts and fine arts (art, music, dance, drama), business skills (includes word processing), English, mathematics, physical education (includes health), religion (includes Bible studies and theology), science, social sciences, social studies (includes history).
Special Academic Programs Advanced Placement exam preparation; honors section; independent study; study at local college for college credit; study abroad; academic accommodation for the gifted, the musically talented, and the artistically talented.
College Admission Counseling 183 students graduated in 2011; 174 went to college, including College of Saint Benedict; Iowa State University of Science and Technology; Saint John's University; University of Minnesota, Duluth; University of Minnesota, Twin Cities Campus; University of Wisconsin–Madison. Other: 2 went to work, 2 entered military service, 5 had other specific plans. Mean SAT critical reading: 577, mean SAT math: 606, mean composite ACT: 25.
Student Life Upper grades have uniform requirement, student council, honor system. Discipline rests equally with students and faculty. Attendance at religious services is required.
Summer Programs Sports, art/fine arts programs offered; session focuses on activities geared toward 9th grade recruiting; held both on and off campus; held at nearby tennis courts; accepts boys and girls; open to students from other schools. 450 students usually enrolled. 2012 schedule: June 12 to July 20. Application deadline: May 26.
Tuition and Aid Day student tuition: $11,875. Tuition installment plan (monthly payment plans, individually arranged payment plans, quarterly payment plan). Need-based scholarship grants, minority student scholarships, single-parent family scholarships available. In 2011–12, 37% of upper-school students received aid. Total amount of financial aid awarded in 2011–12: $1,000,000.
Admissions Traditional secondary-level entrance grade is 9. For fall 2011, 325 students applied for upper-level admission, 320 were accepted, 206 enrolled. ACT-Explore required. Deadline for receipt of application materials: January 21. No application fee required. Interview recommended.
Athletics Interscholastic: baseball (boys), basketball (b,g), cross-country running (b,g), danceline (g), football (b), golf (b,g), ice hockey (b,g), soccer (b,g), softball (g), tennis (b,g), track and field (b,g), volleyball (g); intramural: lacrosse (g); coed interscholastic: bowling; coed intramural: football. 3 PE instructors, 27 coaches, 1 athletic trainer.
Computers Computers are regularly used in English, foreign language, mathematics, science, yearbook classes. Computer network features include on-campus library services, online commercial services, Internet access. The school has a published electronic and media policy.
Contact Ms. Meg Angevine, Assistant Director of Admissions. 612-798-0764. Fax: 612-798-2610. E-mail: mangevine@academyofholyangels.org. Web site: www.academyofholyangels.org.

ACADEMY OF NOTRE DAME DE NAMUR

560 Sproul Road

Villanova, Pennsylvania 19085-1220

Head of School: Mrs. Veronica Collins Harrington

General Information Girls' day college-preparatory school, affiliated with Roman Catholic Church. Grades 6–12. Founded: 1856. Setting: suburban. Nearest major city is Philadelphia. 38-acre campus. 9 buildings on campus. Approved or accredited by Middle States Association of Colleges and Schools, National Catholic Education Association, and Pennsylvania Department of Education. Member of National Association of Independent Schools. Endowment: $4 million. Total enrollment: 513. Upper school average class size: 15. Upper school faculty-student ratio: 1:8. There are 170 required school days per year for Upper School students. Upper School students typically attend 5 days per week. The average school day consists of 6 hours and 45 minutes.
Upper School Student Profile Grade 9: 88 students (88 girls); Grade 10: 107 students (107 girls); Grade 11: 100 students (100 girls); Grade 12: 94 students (94 girls). 88% of students are Roman Catholic.
Faculty School total: 59. In upper school: 8 men, 45 women; 39 have advanced degrees.
Subjects Offered Advanced biology, American history-AP, Bible, biology, biology-AP, calculus, calculus-AP, ceramics, chemistry, chemistry-AP, choral music, Christian and Hebrew scripture, Christian ethics, comparative government and politics-AP, computer skills, computer-aided design, contemporary history, dance, economics, English, English literature, English literature and composition-AP, environmental science, French, French language-AP, geometry, government and politics-AP, health, health education, Hebrew scripture, instrumental music, journalism, Latin, Latin-AP, literature, literature and composition-AP, mathematics, multimedia design, music, music performance, music theory, music theory-AP, music-AP, physical education, physics-AP, pre-algebra, pre-calculus, SAT/ACT preparation, Spanish, Spanish language-AP, Spanish-AP, studio art-AP, U.S. government and politics-AP, U.S. history-AP, United States government-AP, video film production, visual and performing arts, vocal music, world cultures.
Graduation Requirements Art, dance, English, foreign language, guidance, mathematics, music, physical education (includes health), religion (includes Bible studies and theology), science, social studies (includes history), trigonometry, 40 hours of social service.
Special Academic Programs Honors section; independent study; study at local college for college credit; study abroad.
College Admission Counseling 96 students graduated in 2010; all went to college, including Penn State University Park; Saint Joseph's University; University of Delaware; University of Pittsburgh; Villanova University. Median SAT critical reading: 580, median SAT math: 600, median SAT writing: 620, median combined SAT: 1780, median composite ACT: 25. 50% scored over 600 on SAT critical reading, 44% scored over 600 on SAT math, 57% scored over 600 on SAT writing, 50% scored over 1800 on combined SAT, 40% scored over 26 on composite ACT.
Student Life Upper grades have uniform requirement, student council, honor system. Discipline rests primarily with faculty. Attendance at religious services is required.
Tuition and Aid Day student tuition: $17,500–$18,700. Tuition installment plan (monthly payment plans, quarterly and semi-annual payment plans). Merit scholarship grants, need-based scholarship grants available. In 2010–11, 32% of upper-school students received aid; total upper-school merit-scholarship money awarded: $370,500. Total amount of financial aid awarded in 2010–11: $449,500.
Admissions Traditional secondary-level entrance grade is 9. For fall 2010, 210 students applied for upper-level admission, 168 were accepted, 48 enrolled. High School Placement Test required. Deadline for receipt of application materials: December 17. Application fee required: $40. Interview recommended.
Athletics Interscholastic: basketball, crew, cross-country running, diving, field hockey, golf, lacrosse, soccer, softball, swimming and diving, tennis, track and field, volleyball, winter (indoor) track; intramural: dance, kickball, modern dance. 3 PE instructors, 31 coaches, 1 athletic trainer.
Computers Computers are regularly used in all classes. Computer network features include on-campus library services, online commercial services, Internet access, Internet filtering or blocking technology, Smart Boards in classrooms. Student e-mail

accounts are available to students. Students grades are available online. The school has a published electronic and media policy.
Contact Mrs. Diane Sander, Director of Admissions. 610-971-0498. Fax: 610-687-1912. E-mail: dsander@ndapa.org. Web site: www.ndapa.org.

ACADEMY OF OUR LADY OF MERCY–LAURELTON HALL

200 High Street

Milford, Connecticut 06460

Head of School: Dr. Antoinette Iadarola

General Information Girls' day college-preparatory, arts, religious studies, and technology school, affiliated with Roman Catholic Church. Grades 9–12. Founded: 1905. Setting: suburban. Nearest major city is New Haven. 30-acre campus. 5 buildings on campus. Approved or accredited by Connecticut Association of Independent Schools, Mercy Secondary Education Association, New England Association of Schools and Colleges, and Connecticut Department of Education. Total enrollment: 437. Upper school average class size: 18. Upper school faculty-student ratio: 1:12. There are 165 required school days per year for Upper School students. Upper School students typically attend 5 days per week. The average school day consists of 6 hours and 15 minutes.
Upper School Student Profile Grade 9: 124 students (124 girls); Grade 10: 113 students (113 girls); Grade 11: 111 students (111 girls); Grade 12: 89 students (89 girls). 77% of students are Roman Catholic.
Faculty School total: 38. In upper school: 2 men, 35 women; 29 have advanced degrees.
Subjects Offered Algebra, American history, American literature, anatomy, art, biology, business, calculus, chemistry, computer math, computer programming, English, English literature, environmental science, European history, fine arts, French, geometry, government/civics, health, history, journalism, Latin, mathematics, music, physical education, physics, physiology, religion, science, social studies, Spanish, trigonometry, world history, writing.
Graduation Requirements Arts and fine arts (art, music, dance, drama), English, foreign language, mathematics, physical education (includes health), religion (includes Bible studies and theology), science, social studies (includes history). Community service is required.
Special Academic Programs Honors section; study at local college for college credit.
College Admission Counseling 104 students graduated in 2010; all went to college, including Boston College; College of the Holy Cross; Fairfield University; Loyola University Maryland; Quinnipiac University; University of Connecticut. Mean SAT critical reading: 536, mean SAT math: 537, mean SAT writing: 555.
Student Life Upper grades have uniform requirement, student council, honor system. Discipline rests primarily with faculty. Attendance at religious services is required.
Tuition and Aid Day student tuition: $14,250. Tuition installment plan (FACTS Tuition Payment Plan, 1- and 2-payment plans). Tuition reduction for siblings, merit scholarship grants, need-based scholarship grants available. In 2010–11, 28% of upper-school students received aid; total upper-school merit-scholarship money awarded: $125,000. Total amount of financial aid awarded in 2010–11: $300,000.
Admissions Traditional secondary-level entrance grade is 9. For fall 2010, 323 students applied for upper-level admission, 247 were accepted, 124 enrolled. High School Placement Test required. Deadline for receipt of application materials: none. Application fee required: $60.
Athletics Interscholastic: basketball, cheering, cross-country running, diving, field hockey, golf, gymnastics, ice hockey, indoor track, lacrosse, running, skiing (downhill), soccer, softball, swimming and diving, tennis, track and field, volleyball; intramural: basketball. 1 PE instructor, 27 coaches, 1 athletic trainer.
Computers Computers are regularly used in mathematics classes. Computer network features include on-campus library services, online commercial services, Internet access, wireless campus network, Internet filtering or blocking technology. Campus intranet, student e-mail accounts, and computer access in designated common areas are available to students. The school has a published electronic and media policy.
Contact Mrs. Kathleen O. Shine, Director of Admissions and Financial Aid. 203-877-2786 Ext. 125. Fax: 203-876-9760. E-mail: kshine@lauraltonhall.org. Web site: www.lauraltonhall.org.

ACADEMY OF OUR LADY OF PEACE

4860 Oregon Street

San Diego, California 92116-1393

Head of School: Sr. Dolores Anchondo

General Information Girls' day college-preparatory, arts, and religious studies school, affiliated with Roman Catholic Church. Grades 9–12. Founded: 1882. Setting: urban. 20-acre campus. 7 buildings on campus. Approved or accredited by Western Association of Schools and Colleges, Western Catholic Education Association, and California Department of Education. Endowment: $250,000. Total enrollment: 750. Upper school average class size: 28. Upper school faculty-student ratio: 1:14. There are 180 required school days per year for Upper School students. Upper School students typically attend 5 days per week. The average school day consists of 6 hours and 45 minutes.
Upper School Student Profile Grade 9: 193 students (193 girls); Grade 10: 181 students (181 girls); Grade 11: 190 students (190 girls); Grade 12: 186 students (186 girls). 91% of students are Roman Catholic.
Faculty School total: 53. In upper school: 11 men, 42 women; 35 have advanced degrees.
Subjects Offered Algebra, American literature, art, Bible studies, biology, biology-AP, British literature, calculus, calculus-AP, campus ministry, ceramics, chemistry, chemistry-AP, dance, drama, economics, English, English language and composition-AP, English literature and composition-AP, ethics, fitness, French, French language-AP, French-AP, genetics, geometry, government, graphic arts, health, marine science, music appreciation, music theory-AP, painting, physical education, physics, pre-calculus, psychology, Spanish, Spanish language-AP, Spanish literature-AP, speech, studio art-AP, study skills, U.S. government and politics-AP, U.S. history, U.S. history-AP, Western civilization, yearbook, yoga.
Graduation Requirements Arts and fine arts (art, music, dance, drama), English, foreign language, mathematics, physical education (includes health), religion (includes Bible studies and theology), science, social sciences, social studies (includes history), speech, 75 hours of community service, 9-11 reflection paper required for seniors.
Special Academic Programs 13 Advanced Placement exams for which test preparation is offered; honors section.
College Admission Counseling 161 students graduated in 2011; 160 went to college, including Loyola Marymount University; San Diego State University; Sonoma State University; The University of Arizona; University of San Diego; University of San Francisco. Other: 1 had other specific plans. Median SAT critical reading: 540, median SAT math: 520, median SAT writing: 550, median combined SAT: 1610. 34% scored over 600 on SAT critical reading, 22% scored over 600 on SAT math, 37% scored over 600 on SAT writing, 50% scored over 1800 on combined SAT, 10% scored over 26 on composite ACT.
Student Life Upper grades have uniform requirement, student council, honor system. Discipline rests equally with students and faculty. Attendance at religious services is required.
Summer Programs Enrichment, advancement programs offered; session focuses on advancement and remediation/make-up; held on campus; accepts girls; open to students from other schools. 200 students usually enrolled. 2012 schedule: June 11 to July 20. Application deadline: May 1.
Tuition and Aid Day student tuition: $12,960. Tuition installment plan (FACTS Tuition Payment Plan). Need-based scholarship grants available. In 2011–12, 47% of upper-school students received aid. Total amount of financial aid awarded in 2011–12: $2,100,000.
Admissions Traditional secondary-level entrance grade is 9. For fall 2011, 248 students applied for upper-level admission, 223 were accepted, 210 enrolled. High School Placement Test required. Deadline for receipt of application materials: none. Application fee required: $50. On-campus interview required.
Athletics Interscholastic: basketball, cheering, cross-country running, golf, gymnastics, soccer, softball, swimming and diving, tennis, track and field, volleyball. 4 PE instructors, 16 coaches.
Computers Computers are regularly used in computer applications, media production, music, music technology, photography, Web site design, word processing classes. Computer network features include on-campus library services, online commercial services, Internet access, wireless campus network, Internet filtering or blocking technology. Campus intranet, student e-mail accounts, and computer access in designated common areas are available to students. Students grades are available online. The school has a published electronic and media policy.
Contact Mrs. Sue De Winter, Administrative Assistant/Registrar. 619-725-9118. Fax: 619-297-2473. E-mail: admissions@aolp.org. Web site: www.aolp.org.

ACADEMY OF SAINT ELIZABETH

Box 297

Convent Station, New Jersey 07961-0297

Head of School: Sr. Patricia Costello, OP

General Information Girls' day college-preparatory, arts, religious studies, and technology school, affiliated with Roman Catholic Church. Grades 9–12. Founded: 1860. Setting: suburban. Nearest major city is Morristown. 200-acre campus. 2 buildings on campus. Approved or accredited by Middle States Association of Colleges and Schools, National Catholic Education Association, and New Jersey Association of Independent Schools. Total enrollment: 245. Upper school average class size: 15. Upper school faculty-student ratio: 1:9.
Upper School Student Profile Grade 9: 75 students (75 girls); Grade 10: 67 students (67 girls); Grade 11: 49 students (49 girls); Grade 12: 54 students (54 girls). 90% of students are Roman Catholic.
Faculty School total: 30. In upper school: 6 men, 22 women; 12 have advanced degrees.

Subjects Offered 20th century American writers, algebra, American history, American literature, art, Bible studies, biology, calculus, ceramics, chemistry, dance, drama, driver education, ecology, English, English literature, environmental science, European history, expository writing, fine arts, French, geometry, grammar, health, history, journalism, Latin, mathematics, music, photography, physical education, physics, psychology, religion, science, social sciences, social studies, sociology, Spanish, theater, theology, trigonometry, word processing, world history, world literature.

Graduation Requirements Arts and fine arts (art, music, dance, drama), computer education, English, foreign language, mathematics, physical education (includes health), religion (includes Bible studies and theology), science, social sciences, social studies (includes history), senior independent study.

Special Academic Programs Advanced Placement exam preparation; honors section; independent study; study at local college for college credit.

College Admission Counseling 57 students graduated in 2010; all went to college, including American University; Boston College; College of the Holy Cross; Seton Hall University; University of Notre Dame; Villanova University.

Student Life Upper grades have uniform requirement, student council, honor system. Discipline rests primarily with faculty. Attendance at religious services is required.

Tuition and Aid Day student tuition: $11,000. Tuition installment plan (monthly payment plans, individually arranged payment plans). Merit scholarship grants, need-based scholarship grants available. In 2010–11, 35% of upper-school students received aid.

Admissions Traditional secondary-level entrance grade is 9. For fall 2010, 150 students applied for upper-level admission, 115 were accepted, 75 enrolled. School's own exam required. Deadline for receipt of application materials: January 15. Application fee required: $100. On-campus interview recommended.

Athletics Interscholastic: aquatics, basketball, cross-country running, field hockey, lacrosse; intramural: aerobics, aerobics/dance, alpine skiing, dance, equestrian sports, horseback riding, independent competitive sports. 1 PE instructor, 9 coaches.

Computers Computers are regularly used in English, foreign language, history, mathematics, science, study skills classes. Computer network features include on-campus library services, online commercial services, Internet access. The school has a published electronic and media policy.

Contact Sr. Patricia Costello, OP, Principal. 973-290-5200. Fax: 973-290-5232. Web site: academyofsaintelizabeth.org.

ACADEMY OF THE HOLY CROSS

4920 Strathmore Avenue

Kensington, Maryland 20895-1299

Head of School: Dr. Claire M. Helm

General Information Girls' day college-preparatory, arts, and religious studies school, affiliated with Roman Catholic Church. Grades 9–12. Founded: 1868. Setting: suburban. Nearest major city is Rockville. 28-acre campus. 2 buildings on campus. Approved or accredited by Association of Independent Schools of Greater Washington, International Baccalaureate Organization, Middle States Association of Colleges and Schools, National Catholic Education Association, and Maryland Department of Education. Upper school average class size: 20. Upper school faculty-student ratio: 1:14. There are 176 required school days per year for Upper School students. Upper School students typically attend 5 days per week. The average school day consists of 7 hours.

Upper School Student Profile Grade 9: 141 students (141 girls); Grade 10: 156 students (156 girls); Grade 11: 115 students (115 girls); Grade 12: 138 students (138 girls). 87% of students are Roman Catholic.

Faculty School total: 50. In upper school: 11 men, 39 women.

Subjects Offered Acting, Advanced Placement courses, African studies, algebra, American history, American literature, Arabic, art, art history-AP, Asian studies, biology, biology-AP, calculus, calculus-AP, ceramics, chemistry, chemistry-AP, Christian scripture, computer science, concert choir, creative writing, design, drama, drawing, earth science, economics, English, English language and composition-AP, English literature, English literature and composition-AP, environmental science, ethnic studies, expository writing, fine arts, forensics, French, genetics, geography, geometry, government/civics, grammar, health, Hebrew scripture, history, history of the Catholic Church, honors English, honors geometry, humanities, instrumental music, jazz dance, Latin, Latin American studies, madrigals, mathematics, moral theology, music, music appreciation, musical theater, musical theater dance, painting, peace studies, personal finance, photography, physical education, physical science, physics, physiology, precalculus, psychology, public speaking, religion, religious studies, science, sculpture, Shakespeare, social sciences, social studies, Spanish, sports medicine, statistics, studio art, studio art-AP, tap dance, technology, theater, theater design and production, theology, trigonometry, U.S. government, U.S. government and politics-AP, U.S. history, U.S. history-AP, Web site design, world history, world studies.

Graduation Requirements Art, electives, English, foreign language, mathematics, performing arts, physical education (includes health), science, senior project, social sciences, social studies (includes history), theology, Christian service commitment, Senior Project Internship.

Special Academic Programs International Baccalaureate program; Advanced Placement exam preparation; honors section; independent study; academic accommodation for the gifted and the artistically talented.

College Admission Counseling 137 students graduated in 2011; all went to college, including Saint Joseph's University; Salisbury University; University of Maryland, Baltimore County; University of Maryland, College Park; University of South Carolina. Mean SAT critical reading: 562, mean SAT math: 546, mean SAT writing: 574, mean combined SAT: 1682, mean composite ACT: 24.

Student Life Upper grades have uniform requirement, student council, honor system. Discipline rests equally with students and faculty. Attendance at religious services is required.

Summer Programs Enrichment, advancement, sports, art/fine arts, computer instruction programs offered; session focuses on enrichment and athletic skill-building; held on campus; accepts girls; open to students from other schools. 200 students usually enrolled. 2012 schedule: June 18 to July 13. Application deadline: May 31.

Tuition and Aid Day student tuition: $17,650. Tuition installment plan (individually arranged payment plans). Tuition reduction for siblings, merit scholarship grants, need-based scholarship grants, alumnae stipends available. In 2011–12, 54% of upper-school students received aid.

Admissions Traditional secondary-level entrance grade is 9. High School Placement Test required. Deadline for receipt of application materials: December 15. Application fee required: $50. On-campus interview required.

Athletics Interscholastic: archery, basketball, crew, cross-country running, diving, equestrian sports, field hockey, golf, lacrosse, soccer, softball, swimming and diving, tennis, track and field, volleyball; intramural: basketball, cheering, dance, dance team, kayaking, lacrosse, soccer. 2 PE instructors, 35 coaches, 1 athletic trainer.

Computers Computers are regularly used in art, foreign language, mathematics, science, social sciences classes. Computer network features include on-campus library services, online commercial services, Internet access, wireless campus network, Internet filtering or blocking technology. Students grades are available online. The school has a published electronic and media policy.

Contact Mrs. Gracie Smith, Director of Admissions. 301-929-6442. Fax: 301-929-6440. E-mail: admissions@ahctartans.org. Web site: www.ahctartans.org.

ACADEMY OF THE HOLY NAMES

3319 Bayshore Boulevard

Tampa, Florida 33629-8899

Head of School: Dr. Harry Purpur

General Information Coeducational day college-preparatory, arts, religious studies, and technology school, affiliated with Roman Catholic Church. Boys grades PK–8, girls grades PK–12. Founded: 1881. Setting: urban. 19-acre campus. 6 buildings on campus. Approved or accredited by Florida Council of Independent Schools, National Catholic Education Association, Southern Association of Colleges and Schools, and Florida Department of Education. Endowment: $4 million. Total enrollment: 801. Upper school average class size: 18. Upper school faculty-student ratio: 1:15. Upper School students typically attend 5 days per week. The average school day consists of 7 hours and 25 minutes.

Upper School Student Profile Grade 6: 41 students (13 boys, 28 girls); Grade 7: 54 students (22 boys, 32 girls); Grade 8: 70 students (24 boys, 46 girls); Grade 9: 108 students (108 girls); Grade 10: 76 students (76 girls); Grade 11: 78 students (78 girls); Grade 12: 77 students (77 girls). 70% of students are Roman Catholic.

Faculty School total: 95. In upper school: 3 men, 36 women; 24 have advanced degrees.

Subjects Offered 20th century history, accounting, algebra, American history, American history-AP, anatomy and physiology, art history-AP, biology, biology-AP, calculus, calculus-AP, ceramics, chemistry, chemistry-AP, Christian and Hebrew scripture, communications, computer applications, computer science, contemporary history, economics, English, English literature and composition-AP, environmental science-AP, ethics, French, French-AP, geometry, government, government-AP, honors algebra, honors English, honors geometry, honors U.S. history, honors world history, journalism, Latin, Latin-AP, law studies, marine biology, marketing, media, music, physical education, physics, physics-AP, psychology, religious education, social justice, Spanish, Spanish-AP, speech, statistics, studio art-AP, U.S. government and politics-AP, world history, world religions.

Graduation Requirements 100 community service hours.

Special Academic Programs 16 Advanced Placement exams for which test preparation is offered; honors section.

College Admission Counseling 76 students graduated in 2010; all went to college, including Boston College; College of Charleston; Florida State University; University of Florida; University of South Florida; Vanderbilt University. Mean SAT critical reading: 567, mean SAT math: 558, mean SAT writing: 579, mean composite ACT: 25.

Student Life Upper grades have uniform requirement, student council, honor system. Discipline rests primarily with faculty. Attendance at religious services is required.

Tuition and Aid Day student tuition: $14,980. Tuition installment plan (monthly payment plans). Merit scholarship grants, need-based scholarship grants, paying campus jobs available. In 2010–11, 29% of upper-school students received aid; total upper-school merit-scholarship money awarded: $40,320. Total amount of financial aid awarded in 2010–11: $515,525.

Admissions Traditional secondary-level entrance grade is 9. For fall 2010, 140 students applied for upper-level admission, 110 were accepted, 74 enrolled. High School Placement Test (closed version) from Scholastic Testing Service or Stanford Achievement Test required. Deadline for receipt of application materials: December 10. Application fee required: $50. On-campus interview required.

Athletics Interscholastic: aerobics/dance (girls), aquatics (g), basketball (g), cheering (g), crew (g), cross-country running (g), dance (g), dance squad (g), dance team (g), diving (g), golf (g), physical fitness (g), softball (g), swimming and diving (g), tennis (g), track and field (g), volleyball (g), winter soccer (g); coed interscholastic: soccer. 3 PE instructors, 10 coaches, 1 athletic trainer.

Computers Computers are regularly used in all academic classes. Computer network features include on-campus library services, Internet access, Internet filtering or blocking technology. Students grades are available online. The school has a published electronic and media policy.

Contact Mrs. Pam Doherty, Enrollment Assistant. 813-839-5371 Ext. 307. Fax: 813-839-1486. E-mail: pdoherty@holynamestpa.org. Web site: www.holynamestpa.org.

ACADEMY OF THE NEW CHURCH BOYS' SCHOOL

2815 Benade Circle

Box 707

Bryn Athyn, Pennsylvania 19009

Head of School: Mr. Jeremy T. Irwin

General Information Boys' boarding and day college-preparatory, arts, and religious studies school, affiliated with Church of the New Jerusalem. Grades 9–12. Founded: 1887. Setting: suburban. Nearest major city is Philadelphia. Students are housed in single-sex dormitories. 200-acre campus. 8 buildings on campus. Approved or accredited by Middle States Association of Colleges and Schools and Pennsylvania Department of Education. Endowment: $200 million. Total enrollment: 124. Upper school average class size: 15. Upper school faculty-student ratio: 1:8. There are 175 required school days per year for Upper School students. Upper School students typically attend 5 days per week. The average school day consists of 7 hours and 15 minutes.

Upper School Student Profile Grade 9: 28 students (28 boys); Grade 10: 26 students (26 boys); Grade 11: 36 students (36 boys); Grade 12: 34 students (34 boys). 35% of students are boarding students. 75% are state residents. 18 states are represented in upper school student body. 3% are international students. International students from China and Republic of Korea; 2 other countries represented in student body. 85% of students are Church of the New Jerusalem.

Faculty School total: 40. In upper school: 20 men, 20 women; 35 have advanced degrees; 10 reside on campus.

Subjects Offered Advanced chemistry, Advanced Placement courses, African-American literature, algebra, American history, American history-AP, American literature, American literature-AP, anatomy, anatomy and physiology, ancient world history, art, art history, Bible studies, biology, British literature, calculus, calculus-AP, ceramics, chemistry, civics, computer programming, computer science, creative writing, dance, drama, ecology, English, English literature, English literature-AP, environmental science, European history, expository writing, fine arts, French, geometry, German, government/civics, grammar, health, history, honors U.S. history, industrial arts, journalism, Latin, mathematics, music, music theater, musical theater, philosophy, photography, physical education, physical science, physics, physiology, portfolio art, pre-calculus, printmaking, probability and statistics, religion, religious education, religious studies, science, sculpture, senior project, social sciences, social studies, sociology, Spanish, speech, statistics, studio art, theater, theater arts, theater design and production, theater production, theology, trigonometry, U.S. history-AP, vocal ensemble, vocal music, women in literature, world history, world literature.

Graduation Requirements Arts and fine arts (art, music, dance, drama), English, foreign language, mathematics, physical education (includes health), religion (includes Bible studies and theology), science, social sciences, social studies (includes history).

Special Academic Programs Advanced Placement exam preparation; honors section; independent study; study at local college for college credit; academic accommodation for the gifted, the musically talented, and the artistically talented; remedial reading and/or remedial writing; remedial math; programs in English, mathematics, general development for dyslexic students; ESL (6 students enrolled).

College Admission Counseling 31 students graduated in 2011; 30 went to college, including Bryn Athyn College of the New Church; Gettysburg College; Penn State University Park; University of Pennsylvania; Virginia Polytechnic Institute and State University; West Chester University of Pennsylvania. Other: 1 entered military service. Median SAT critical reading: 540, median SAT math: 560, median SAT writing: 530, median combined SAT: 1630. 28% scored over 600 on SAT critical reading, 33% scored over 600 on SAT math, 31% scored over 600 on SAT writing, 31% scored over 1800 on combined SAT.

Student Life Upper grades have specified standards of dress, student council. Discipline rests primarily with faculty. Attendance at religious services is required.

Summer Programs Enrichment, advancement, sports, art/fine arts, computer instruction programs offered; session focuses on enrichment; held on campus; accepts boys and girls; open to students from other schools. 110 students usually enrolled. 2012 schedule: July 11 to August 1. Application deadline: June 1.

Tuition and Aid Day student tuition: $11,901; 7-day tuition and room/board: $17,055. Tuition installment plan (monthly payment plans, individually arranged payment plans, term payment plan). Need-based scholarship grants, middle-income loans available. In 2011–12, 60% of upper-school students received aid. Total amount of financial aid awarded in 2011–12: $510,000.

Admissions Traditional secondary-level entrance grade is 9. For fall 2011, 110 students applied for upper-level admission, 40 were accepted, 12 enrolled. Iowa Subtests, PSAT, SAT or SSAT required. Deadline for receipt of application materials: none. Application fee required: $50. Interview required.

Athletics Interscholastic: baseball, basketball, football, ice hockey, lacrosse, wrestling. 1 PE instructor, 6 coaches, 1 athletic trainer.

Computers Computers are regularly used in English, foreign language, history, mathematics, science classes. Computer network features include on-campus library services, online commercial services, Internet access, wireless campus network, Internet filtering or blocking technology. Campus intranet and student e-mail accounts are available to students.

Contact Denise DiFiglia, Director of Admissions. 267-502-4855. Web site: www.ancss.org.

ACADEMY OF THE NEW CHURCH GIRLS' SCHOOL

2815 Benade Circle

Box 707

Bryn Athyn, Pennsylvania 19009

Head of School: Susan O. Odhner

General Information Girls' boarding and day college-preparatory, general academic, arts, and religious studies school, affiliated with Church of the New Jerusalem, Christian faith. Grades 9–12. Founded: 1884. Setting: suburban. Nearest major city is Philadelphia. Students are housed in single-sex dormitories. 200-acre campus. 8 buildings on campus. Approved or accredited by Middle States Association of Colleges and Schools and Pennsylvania Department of Education. Member of National Association of Independent Schools. Endowment: $200 million. Total enrollment: 84. Upper school average class size: 15. Upper school faculty-student ratio: 1:8. There are 175 required school days per year for Upper School students. Upper School students typically attend 5 days per week. The average school day consists of 7 hours and 15 minutes.

Upper School Student Profile Grade 9: 18 students (18 girls); Grade 10: 17 students (17 girls); Grade 11: 23 students (23 girls); Grade 12: 26 students (26 girls). 33% of students are boarding students. 75% are state residents. 13 states are represented in upper school student body. 13% are international students. International students from Canada, China, and Republic of Korea. 85% of students are Church of the New Jerusalem, Christian.

Faculty School total: 40. In upper school: 20 men, 20 women; 36 have advanced degrees; 10 reside on campus.

Subjects Offered Advanced chemistry, Advanced Placement courses, African-American literature, algebra, American history, American history-AP, American literature, anatomy, ancient history, ancient world history, art, art history, Bible studies, biology, British literature, calculus, calculus-AP, chemistry, civics, computer science, creative writing, drafting, drama, dramatic arts, drawing, ecology, ecology, environmental systems, economics, English, English literature, English literature-AP, English-AP, European history, expository writing, film studies, fine arts, French, geometry, government/civics, grammar, health, history, honors algebra, honors English, honors geometry, honors U.S. history, human anatomy, Latin, mathematics, medieval history, music, painting, philosophy, photography, physical education, physical science, physics, physiology, pre-calculus, printmaking, religion, science, sculpture, senior project, social sciences, social studies, Spanish, speech, stained glass, statistics-AP, theater, theology, trigonometry, women in literature, world history, world literature.

Graduation Requirements Arts and fine arts (art, music, dance, drama), English, foreign language, mathematics, physical education (includes health), religion (includes Bible studies and theology), science, social sciences, social studies (includes history).

Special Academic Programs Advanced Placement exam preparation; honors section; independent study; study at local college for college credit; academic accommodation for the gifted, the musically talented, and the artistically talented; remedial reading and/or remedial writing; remedial math; special instructional classes for students with Attention Deficit Disorder and learning-disabled children; ESL (8 students enrolled).

College Admission Counseling 78 students graduated in 2011; they went to Bryn Athyn College of the New Church; Gettysburg College; Penn State University Park; University of Pennsylvania; Virginia Polytechnic Institute and State University; West Chester University of Pennsylvania. Other: 1 went to work. Median SAT critical reading: 540, median SAT math: 560, median SAT writing: 530, median combined SAT: 1630. 28% scored over 600 on SAT critical reading, 33% scored over 600 on SAT math, 31% scored over 600 on SAT writing, 31% scored over 1800 on combined SAT.

Student Life Upper grades have uniform requirement, student council. Discipline rests primarily with faculty. Attendance at religious services is required.

Summer Programs Enrichment, advancement, art/fine arts, computer instruction programs offered; session focuses on enrichment; held on campus; accepts boys and girls; open to students from other schools. 130 students usually enrolled. 2012 schedule: July 11 to August 1. Application deadline: June 1.

Tuition and Aid Day student tuition: $11,901; 7-day tuition and room/board: $17,055. Tuition installment plan (monthly payment plans, individually arranged payment plans, term payment plan). Need-based scholarship grants, need-based loans, middle-income loans available. In 2011–12, 53% of upper-school students received aid. Total amount of financial aid awarded in 2011–12: $400,000.

Admissions Traditional secondary-level entrance grade is 9. For fall 2011, 92 students applied for upper-level admission, 75 were accepted, 70 enrolled. Iowa Subtests, PSAT, SAT or SSAT required. Deadline for receipt of application materials: none. Application fee required: $50. Interview required.

Athletics Interscholastic: basketball, dance team, field hockey, ice hockey, lacrosse, soccer, softball, tennis, volleyball. 1 PE instructor, 6 coaches, 1 athletic trainer.

Computers Computers are regularly used in English, foreign language, history, mathematics, science classes. Computer network features include on-campus library services, online commercial services, Internet access, wireless campus network, Internet filtering or blocking technology. Campus intranet and student e-mail accounts are available to students.

Contact Denise DiFiglia, Director of Admissions. 267-502-4855. Fax: 267-502-2617. Web site: www.ancss.org.

ACADEMY OF THE SACRED HEART

1821 Academy Road

Grand Coteau, Louisiana 70541

Head of School: Sr. Lynne Lieux, RSCJ

General Information Girls' boarding and coeducational day college-preparatory, arts, religious studies, bilingual studies, technology, and liberal arts and sciences school, affiliated with Roman Catholic Church. Boarding girls grades 7–12, day boys grades PK–9, day girls grades PK–12. Founded: 1821. Setting: small town. Nearest major city is Lafayette. Students are housed in single-sex dormitories. 250-acre campus. 9 buildings on campus. Approved or accredited by Independent Schools Association of the Southwest, Ohio Catholic Schools Accreditation Association (OCSAA), and Louisiana Department of Education. Endowment: $8 million. Total enrollment: 481. Upper school average class size: 18. Upper school faculty-student ratio: 1:10. There are 180 required school days per year for Upper School students. Upper School students typically attend 5 days per week. The average school day consists of 6 hours.

Upper School Student Profile Grade 9: 49 students (9 boys, 40 girls); Grade 10: 29 students (29 girls); Grade 11: 28 students (28 girls); Grade 12: 30 students (30 girls). 19% of students are boarding students. 80% are state residents. 6 states are represented in upper school student body. 5% are international students. International students from Brazil, China, Mexico, Republic of Korea, and Taiwan. 90% of students are Roman Catholic.

Faculty School total: 50. In upper school: 6 men, 20 women; 14 have advanced degrees; 3 reside on campus.

Subjects Offered Advanced math, Advanced Placement courses, algebra, American literature, art appreciation, biology, biology-AP, British literature, British literature (honors), calculus, calculus-AP, chemistry, chorus, creative dance, creative writing, dance, drama, English, English literature-AP, environmental science, equestrian sports, equine science, ESL, ethical decision making, fine arts, French, French language-AP, French-AP, geometry, government-AP, government/civics, health, independent study, mathematics, moral reasoning, music theater, photography, physical education, physics, play production, pottery, pre-algebra, religion and culture, scripture, social justice, social sciences, Spanish, Spanish language-AP, Spanish-AP, studio art, theater, U.S. government, U.S. government and politics-AP, U.S. history, U.S. history-AP, women's studies, world history, world history-AP, yearbook.

Graduation Requirements Arts and fine arts (art, music, dance, drama), English, foreign language, mathematics, physical education (includes health), religion (includes Bible studies and theology), science, social sciences, social studies (includes history), May project. Community service is required.

Special Academic Programs International Baccalaureate program; Advanced Placement exam preparation; honors section; independent study; term-away projects; study at local college for college credit; domestic exchange program; study abroad; academic accommodation for the gifted, the musically talented, and the artistically talented; ESL (13 students enrolled).

College Admission Counseling 29 students graduated in 2011; all went to college, including Baylor University; Louisiana State University and Agricultural and Mechanical College; Loyola University New Orleans; Tulane University; University of Louisiana at Lafayette. Mean composite ACT: 25.

Student Life Upper grades have uniform requirement, student council, honor system. Discipline rests primarily with faculty. Attendance at religious services is required.

Summer Programs Rigorous outdoor training programs offered; session focuses on summer fun; held on campus; accepts boys and girls; open to students from other schools. 2012 schedule: June 4 to June 29. Application deadline: none.

Tuition and Aid Day student tuition: $11,350–$12,600; 5-day tuition and room/board: $15,700; 7-day tuition and room/board: $17,000–$18,000. Tuition installment plan (monthly payment plans, individually arranged payment plans, 1 ayment, 2 payments, monthly payment plan for day students). Tuition reduction for siblings, merit scholarship grants, need-based scholarship grants available. In 2011–12, 16% of upper-school students received aid; total upper-school merit-scholarship money awarded: $7500.

Admissions Traditional secondary-level entrance grade is 9. For fall 2011, 34 students applied for upper-level admission, 30 were accepted, 28 enrolled. Metropolitan Achievement Short Form and Stanford Achievement Test required. Deadline for receipt of application materials: none. Application fee required: $100. Interview recommended.

Athletics Interscholastic: aquatics (girls), baseball (b), basketball (b,g), cheering (g), cross-country running (g), dance (g), dance team (g), dressage (b,g), equestrian sports (b,g), golf (b,g), horseback riding (b,g), soccer (b,g), softball (g), swimming and diving (b,g), tennis (b,g), track and field (b,g), volleyball (g). 3 PE instructors, 5 coaches.

Computers Computers are regularly used in all academic classes. Computer network features include on-campus library services, online commercial services, Internet access, wireless campus network, Internet filtering or blocking technology. Student e-mail accounts and computer access in designated common areas are available to students. Students grades are available online. The school has a published electronic and media policy.

Contact D'Lane Wimberley Thomas, Director of Admissions. 337-662-5275 Ext. 5009. Fax: 337-662-3011. E-mail: admissions@sshcoteau.org. Web site: www.sshcoteau.org.

ACADEMY OF THE SACRED HEART

4521 St. Charles Avenue

New Orleans, Louisiana 70115-4831

Head of School: Dr. Timothy Matthew Burns

General Information Girls' day college-preparatory, arts, religious studies, bilingual studies, and technology school, affiliated with Roman Catholic Church. Grades PK–12. Founded: 1887. Setting: urban. 7-acre campus. 3 buildings on campus. Approved or accredited by Independent Schools Association of the Southwest, National Catholic Education Association, Network of Sacred Heart Schools, Southern Association of Colleges and Schools, and Louisiana Department of Education. Member of National Association of Independent Schools. Endowment: $10.1 million. Total enrollment: 619. Upper school average class size: 16. Upper school faculty-student ratio: 1:16. There are 180 required school days per year for Upper School students. Upper School students typically attend 5 days per week. The average school day consists of 6 hours and 15 minutes.

Upper School Student Profile Grade 9: 57 students (57 girls); Grade 10: 56 students (56 girls); Grade 11: 45 students (45 girls); Grade 12: 43 students (43 girls). 88% of students are Roman Catholic.

Faculty School total: 101. In upper school: 7 men, 22 women; 19 have advanced degrees.

Subjects Offered Advanced chemistry, algebra, American government, American history, American history-AP, American literature, American literature-AP, anatomy and physiology, art, astronomy, athletics, basketball, biology, biology-AP, calculus, calculus-AP, campus ministry, Catholic belief and practice, ceramics, cheerleading, chemistry, chemistry-AP, clayworking, college admission preparation, college awareness, college counseling, college planning, computer applications, computer education, computer processing, computer resources, computer science, computer skills, computer studies, creative writing, drawing, electives, English, English literature, English literature-AP, English-AP, foreign language, French, French-AP, geometry, government, government-AP, guidance, history of the Catholic Church, honors algebra, honors English, honors geometry, honors U.S. history, honors world history, painting, peer counseling, pre-calculus, religion, robotics, social justice, Spanish, Spanish-AP, U.S. government, U.S. government and politics-AP, U.S. history, U.S. history-AP, video communication, Web site design, world history, world history-AP, world religions, zoology.

Graduation Requirements Advanced Placement courses, algebra, American government, American literature, arts and fine arts (art, music, dance, drama), athletics, Basic programming, British literature, calculus, career/college preparation, computer applications, computer literacy, electives, English, foreign language, geometry, guidance, moral theology, peer counseling, physical education (includes health), physics, religion (includes Bible studies and theology), robotics, science, scripture, social justice, social studies (includes history), U.S. government, yearbook, senior speech, 50 hours of required community service.

Special Academic Programs Advanced Placement exam preparation; honors section; study at local college for college credit; domestic exchange program (with Network of Sacred Heart Schools).

College Admission Counseling 66 students graduated in 2011; all went to college, including Louisiana State University and Agricultural and Mechanical College; The University of Alabama at Birmingham; University of Georgia; University of Louisiana at Lafayette; University of Mississippi; University of Virginia.

Student Life Upper grades have uniform requirement, student council, honor system. Discipline rests equally with students and faculty. Attendance at religious services is required.

Summer Programs Enrichment, sports, art/fine arts programs offered; session focuses on arts, creative writing, robotics, strength and conditioning; held both on and off campus; held at Upper School Campus, gym, area tracks; accepts girls; not open to students from other schools. 18 students usually enrolled. 2012 schedule: June to August.

Tuition and Aid Day student tuition: $13,900. Tuition installment plan (The Tuition Plan, individually arranged payment plans, bank loan). Merit scholarship grants, need-based scholarship grants available. In 2011–12, 24% of upper-school students received aid; total upper-school merit-scholarship money awarded: $16,995. Total amount of financial aid awarded in 2011–12: $241,400.

Admissions Traditional secondary-level entrance grade is 9. For fall 2011, 20 students applied for upper-level admission, 18 were accepted, 10 enrolled. Achievement tests, admissions testing, ERB, OLSAT/Stanford or PSAT or SAT for applicants to grade 11 and 12 required. Deadline for receipt of application materials: none. Application fee required: $50. Interview required.

Athletics Interscholastic: aerobics, ballet, baseball, basketball, cheering, cross-country running, fitness, golf, indoor track & field, physical fitness, sailing, soccer, softball, strength & conditioning, swimming and diving, tennis, track and field, volleyball; intramural: aerobics, cooperative games, fitness, jogging, outdoor activities, outdoor recreation, physical fitness. 5 PE instructors, 14 coaches, 1 athletic trainer.

Computers Computers are regularly used in all classes. Computer network features include on-campus library services, online commercial services, Internet access, wireless campus network, Internet filtering or blocking technology. Campus intranet, student e-mail accounts, and computer access in designated common areas are available to students. Students grades are available online. The school has a published electronic and media policy.

Contact Ms. Christy Sevante, Admission Director. 504-269-1214. Fax: 504-896-7880. E-mail: csevante@ashrosary.org. Web site: www.ashrosary.org.

ACADEMY OF THE SACRED HEART

1250 Kensington Road

Bloomfield Hills, Michigan 48304-3029

Head of School: Bridget Bearss, RSCJ

General Information Coeducational day college-preparatory, arts, religious studies, technology, experiential learning, and community service school, affiliated with Roman Catholic Church. Boys grades N–8, girls grades N–12. Founded: 1851. Setting: suburban. Nearest major city is Detroit. 44-acre campus. 1 building on campus. Approved or accredited by Independent Schools Association of the Central States, Network of Sacred Heart Schools, and the Michigan Department of Education. Endowment: $3.7 million. Total enrollment: 493. Upper school average class size: 12. Upper school faculty-student ratio: 1:7. There are 180 required school days per year for Upper School students. Upper School students typically attend 5 days per week. The average school day consists of 7 hours.

Upper School Student Profile Grade 9: 39 students (39 girls); Grade 10: 29 students (29 girls); Grade 11: 27 students (27 girls); Grade 12: 32 students (32 girls). 63% of students are Roman Catholic.

Faculty School total: 79. In upper school: 11 men, 13 women; 14 have advanced degrees.

Subjects Offered 20th century history, Advanced Placement courses, algebra, American literature, art, art history, biology, calculus, calculus-AP, chemistry, child development, clayworking, community service, computer applications, computer graphics, concert band, concert choir, crafts, creative writing, earth science, economics, English literature, English literature-AP, English-AP, environmental science, European history, European history-AP, forensics, French, genetics, geometry, global studies, government/civics, health, health and wellness, honors algebra, honors geometry, interior design, jewelry making, Latin, literature, mathematics, photography, physical education, physical science, physics, pre-calculus, psychology, publications, social studies, sociology, Spanish, theater, theology, U.S. history, U.S. history-AP, video, Web site design, world history, world literature.

Graduation Requirements Arts and fine arts (art, music, dance, drama), computer applications, foreign language, government, health and wellness, literature, mathematics, physical education (includes health), science, social studies (includes history), theology, U.S. government, U.S. history, world history, world literature, Project Term, First Year Experience (arts lab). Community service is required.

Special Academic Programs 3 Advanced Placement exams for which test preparation is offered; honors section; independent study; term-away projects; domestic exchange program (with Network of Sacred Heart Schools); academic accommodation for the gifted, the musically talented, and the artistically talented.

College Admission Counseling 34 students graduated in 2011; all went to college, including Dartmouth College; Fordham University; Michigan State University; University of Michigan; Washington University in St. Louis. Mean SAT critical reading: 545, mean SAT math: 527, mean SAT writing: 563, mean composite ACT: 25.

Student Life Upper grades have uniform requirement, student council, honor system. Discipline rests primarily with faculty. Attendance at religious services is required.

Summer Programs Enrichment, sports, art/fine arts, computer instruction programs offered; session focuses on enrichment/day camp; held on campus; accepts boys and girls; open to students from other schools. 75 students usually enrolled. 2012 schedule: June 25 to August 5. Application deadline: none.

Tuition and Aid Day student tuition: $20,200. Tuition installment plan (Sallie Mae Tuition Pay). Tuition reduction for siblings, merit scholarship grants, need-based scholarship grants available. In 2011–12, 40% of upper-school students received aid; total upper-school merit-scholarship money awarded: $7000. Total amount of financial aid awarded in 2011–12: $626,915.

Admissions Traditional secondary-level entrance grade is 9. For fall 2011, 35 students applied for upper-level admission, 29 were accepted, 17 enrolled. Scholastic Testing Service High School Placement Test or Stanford Achievement Test required. Deadline for receipt of application materials: none. Application fee required: $50. On-campus interview required.

Athletics Interscholastic: basketball, dance team, equestrian sports, field hockey, figure skating, golf, lacrosse, skiing (downhill), softball, tennis, volleyball. 1 PE instructor, 13 coaches.

Computers Computers are regularly used in all academic classes. Computer network features include on-campus library services, online commercial services, Internet access, wireless campus network, Internet filtering or blocking technology, tablet PC program with wireless network and print services, classroom multimedia services, computer in each classroom. Campus intranet, student e-mail accounts, and computer access in designated common areas are available to students. Students grades are available online. The school has a published electronic and media policy.

Contact Barbara Lopiccolo, Director of Admissions. 248-646-8900 Ext. 129. Fax: 248-646-4143. E-mail: blopiccolo@ashmi.org. Web site: www.ashmi.org.

ACADÉMIE STE CÉCILE INTERNATIONAL SCHOOL

925 Cousineau Road

Windsor, Ontario N9G 1V8, Canada

Head of School: Mlle. Thérèse H. Gadoury

General Information Coeducational boarding and day college-preparatory, arts, and bilingual studies school, affiliated with Roman Catholic Church. Boarding grades 6–12, day grades JK–12. Founded: 1993. Setting: suburban. Nearest major city is Toronto, Canada. Students are housed in single-sex by floor dormitories. 30-acre campus. 2 buildings on campus. Approved or accredited by International Baccalaureate Organization, Ontario Ministry of Education, The Association of Boarding Schools, and Ontario Department of Education. Languages of instruction: English and French. Total enrollment: 236. Upper school average class size: 15. Upper school faculty-student ratio: 1:15. There are 180 required school days per year for Upper School students. Upper School students typically attend 5 days per week. The average school day consists of 6 hours and 15 minutes.

Upper School Student Profile Grade 9: 24 students (8 boys, 16 girls); Grade 10: 22 students (7 boys, 15 girls); Grade 11: 32 students (26 boys, 6 girls); Grade 12: 34 students (17 boys, 17 girls). 60% of students are boarding students. 2% are province residents. 2 provinces are represented in upper school student body. 50% are international students. International students from Barbados, China, Hong Kong, Mexico, and Taiwan; 3 other countries represented in student body. 70% of students are Roman Catholic.

Faculty School total: 50. In upper school: 13 men, 11 women; 10 have advanced degrees; 4 reside on campus.

Subjects Offered Accounting, advanced chemistry, advanced computer applications, advanced math, algebra, art, art education, art history, audio visual/media, ballet, basketball, biology, business technology, calculus, campus ministry, career education, careers, Catholic belief and practice, chemistry, choir, choral music, civics, classical music, computer information systems, computer programming, computer science, concert band, concert bell choir, concert choir, creative dance, creative drama, creative thinking, creative writing, critical thinking, critical writing, dance, dance performance, decision making skills, desktop publishing, desktop publishing, ESL, discrete mathematics, drama performance, drama workshop, dramatic arts, drawing, drawing and design, driver education, earth science, economics, English, English literature, environmental studies, ethics, expository writing, family living, French, French studies, geography, geometry, German, golf, handbells, health and wellness, health education, history, history of dance, history of music, history of religion, history of the Catholic Church, honors algebra, honors English, honors geometry, honors world history, instrumental music, International Baccalaureate courses, Internet, Internet research, intro to computers, Italian, jazz band, jazz dance, journalism, keyboarding, Latin, leadership, library skills, Life of Christ, literature, literature and composition-AP, mathematics, media studies, music, music appreciation, music composition, music history, music performance, music theory, organ, painting, philosophy, photography, physical education, physics, piano, poetry, prayer/spirituality, pre-algebra, pre-calculus, probability and statistics, public speaking, reading, reading/study skills, religion, research skills, SAT preparation, science, sculpture, Shakespeare, social studies, softball, Spanish, stage and body movement, stained glass, strings, student government, swimming, tennis, TOEFL preparation, track and field, values and decisions, visual arts, vocal ensemble, voice, volleyball, wind ensemble, wind instruments, world religions, writing, yearbook.

Graduation Requirements Ontario Ministry of Education requirements.

Special Academic Programs International Baccalaureate program; Advanced Placement exam preparation; honors section; accelerated programs; academic accommodation for the gifted, the musically talented, and the artistically talented; remedial reading and/or remedial writing; remedial math; ESL (60 students enrolled).
College Admission Counseling 42 students graduated in 2011; they went to McMaster University; The University of British Columbia; The University of Western Ontario; University of Toronto; University of Waterloo; University of Windsor. Other: 1 went to work, 40 entered a postgraduate year, 1 had other specific plans. Mean SAT critical reading: 593, mean SAT math: 724, mean SAT writing: 615. 67% scored over 600 on SAT critical reading, 83% scored over 600 on SAT math, 67% scored over 600 on SAT writing.
Student Life Upper grades have uniform requirement, student council, honor system. Discipline rests primarily with faculty.
Summer Programs Remediation, enrichment, advancement, ESL, art/fine arts programs offered; session focuses on ESL; held on campus; accepts boys and girls; open to students from other schools. 25 students usually enrolled. 2012 schedule: July 2 to August 31. Application deadline: May 31.
Tuition and Aid Day student tuition: CAN$13,850; 7-day tuition and room/board: CAN$45,500. Tuition installment plan (Insured Tuition Payment Plan). Tuition reduction for siblings, merit scholarship grants available. In 2011–12, 5% of upper-school students received aid; total upper-school merit-scholarship money awarded: CAN$4500. Total amount of financial aid awarded in 2011–12: CAN$15,000.
Admissions Traditional secondary-level entrance grade is 9. For fall 2011, 25 students applied for upper-level admission, 21 were accepted, 18 enrolled. Deadline for receipt of application materials: none. Application fee required: CAN$300. Interview recommended.
Athletics Interscholastic: aquatics (boys, girls), badminton (b,g), basketball (b,g), equestrian sports (b,g), golf (b,g), horseback riding (b,g), ice hockey (g), independent competitive sports (b,g), modern dance (b,g), physical fitness (b,g), soccer (b,g), softball (b,g), swimming and diving (b,g), tennis (b,g), volleyball (b,g); intramural: aquatics (b,g), badminton (b,g), ballet (g), basketball (b,g), bowling (b,g), cross-country running (b,g), dance (b,g), dressage (b,g), equestrian sports (b,g), golf (b,g), horseback riding (b,g), paddle tennis (b,g), soccer (b,g), softball (b,g), swimming and diving (b,g), table tennis (b,g), tennis (b,g), volleyball (b,g); coed interscholastic: aquatics, badminton, basketball, dressage, equestrian sports, fitness, golf, horseback riding, indoor track & field, modern dance, physical fitness, soccer, softball, swimming and diving, tennis, volleyball; coed intramural: aquatics, badminton, basketball, bowling, cross-country running, dance, dressage, equestrian sports, floor hockey, golf, horseback riding, modern dance, soccer, softball, swimming and diving, tennis, volleyball. 2 PE instructors, 8 coaches.
Computers Computers are regularly used in accounting, business, desktop publishing, ESL, information technology, mathematics classes. Computer network features include Internet access, wireless campus network.
Contact Ms. Gwen A. Gatt, Admissions Clerk. 519-969-1291. Fax: 519-969-7953. E-mail: info@stececile.ca. Web site: www.stececile.ca.

ADELPHI ACADEMY

8515 Ridge Boulevard

Brooklyn, New York 11209

General Information Coeducational day college-preparatory, arts, technology, and writing school; primarily serves students with learning disabilities, individuals with Attention Deficit Disorder, individuals with emotional and behavioral problems, and dyslexic students. Grades PK–12. Founded: 1863. Setting: urban. Nearest major city is New York. 1-acre campus. 3 buildings on campus. Approved or accredited by New York Department of Education. Candidate for accreditation by Middle States Association of Colleges and Schools. Endowment: $2.6 million. Total enrollment: 110. Upper school average class size: 14. Upper school faculty-student ratio: 1:6. There are 153 required school days per year for Upper School students. Upper School students typically attend 5 days per week. The average school day consists of 7 hours.

ADMIRAL FARRAGUT ACADEMY

501 Park Street North

St. Petersburg, Florida 33710

Head of School: Capt. Robert J. Fine Jr.

General Information Coeducational boarding and day college-preparatory, Naval Junior ROTC, aviation, and military school. Boarding grades 6–12, day grades P3–12. Founded: 1933. Setting: suburban. Students are housed in single-sex by floor dormitories. 35-acre campus. 20 buildings on campus. Approved or accredited by Florida Council of Independent Schools, Southern Association of Colleges and Schools, The Association of Boarding Schools, and Florida Department of Education. Member of National Association of Independent Schools and Secondary School Admission Test Board. Endowment: $2 million. Total enrollment: 358. Upper school average class size: 16. Upper school faculty-student ratio: 1:8. There are 189 required school days per year for Upper School students. Upper School students typically attend 5 days per week. The average school day consists of 7 hours.
Upper School Student Profile Grade 9: 40 students (27 boys, 13 girls); Grade 10: 51 students (39 boys, 12 girls); Grade 11: 63 students (51 boys, 12 girls); Grade 12: 67 students (51 boys, 16 girls). 50% of students are boarding students. 73% are state residents. 14 states are represented in upper school student body. 30% are international students. International students from China, Colombia, Japan, Republic of Korea, Russian Federation, and Spain; 14 other countries represented in student body.
Faculty School total: 63. In upper school: 20 men, 14 women; 20 have advanced degrees; 20 reside on campus.
Subjects Offered ACT preparation, advanced math, algebra, American history, American literature, analytic geometry, anatomy and physiology, art, art history, aviation, band, biology, boating, British literature, business communications, calculus, calculus-AP, chemistry, Chinese, chorus, community service, computer programming, computer science, computer science-AP, creative writing, drama, driver education, earth science, economics, English, English composition, English language-AP, English literature, environmental science, ESL, ethics and responsibility, fine arts, French, geography, geometry, government/civics, grammar, health, history, journalism, keyboarding, Latin, library assistant, marching band, marine biology, mathematics, meteorology, military science, music, music history, navigation, NJROTC, oceanography, physical education, physics, pre-algebra, science, sign language, social studies, sociology, Spanish, Spanish language-AP, speech, statistics, swimming test, trigonometry, world history, world literature, yearbook.
Graduation Requirements Arts and fine arts (art, music, dance, drama), economics, English, ethics, foreign language, government, health education, mathematics, NJROTC, physical education (includes health), science, social studies (includes history), U.S. history, world history, Qualified Boat Handler (QBH) test, 80 hours of community service.
Special Academic Programs Advanced Placement exam preparation; honors section; study at local college for college credit; academic accommodation for the gifted; remedial reading and/or remedial writing; remedial math; ESL (10 students enrolled).
College Admission Counseling 53 students graduated in 2010; 52 went to college, including Florida State University; Georgia Institute of Technology; Syracuse University; United States Naval Academy; University of Florida; University of South Florida. Other: 1 entered military service. Mean SAT critical reading: 488, mean SAT math: 520, mean SAT writing: 478, mean composite ACT: 20. 10% scored over 600 on SAT critical reading, 20% scored over 600 on SAT math, 3% scored over 600 on SAT writing, 15% scored over 26 on composite ACT.
Student Life Upper grades have uniform requirement, student council. Discipline rests equally with students and faculty.
Tuition and Aid Day student tuition: $17,070; 5-day tuition and room/board: $29,610; 7-day tuition and room/board: $35,400. Tuition installment plan (monthly payment plans, individually arranged payment plans, AFA Payment Plan). Tuition reduction for siblings, need-based scholarship grants, tuition reduction for children of faculty available. In 2010–11, 22% of upper-school students received aid. Total amount of financial aid awarded in 2010–11: $500,000.
Admissions Traditional secondary-level entrance grade is 10. For fall 2010, 200 students applied for upper-level admission, 122 were accepted, 106 enrolled. Any standardized test required. Deadline for receipt of application materials: none. Application fee required: $100. Interview required.
Athletics Interscholastic: aquatics (boys, girls), baseball (b), basketball (b,g), cross-country running (b,g), diving (b,g), drill team (b,g), football (b,g), golf (b,g), riflery (b,g), soccer (b,g), softball (g), swimming and diving (b,g), tennis (b,g), track and field (b,g), volleyball (g), wrestling (b); intramural: badminton (b,g), fishing (b,g), fitness walking (b,g), jogging (b,g), kayaking (b,g), riflery (b,g), running (b,g), wall climbing (b,g), weight training (b,g); coed interscholastic: aquatics, bowling, cheering, drill team, football, golf, JROTC drill, marksmanship, riflery; coed intramural: badminton, basketball, bicycling, billiards, canoeing/kayaking, fitness, flag football, Frisbee, martial arts, paint ball, physical training, sailing, scuba diving, strength & conditioning, table tennis, volleyball. 4 PE instructors, 3 coaches, 1 athletic trainer.
Computers Computers are regularly used in aviation, computer applications, English, foreign language, history, keyboarding, NJROTC, programming, science, writing, yearbook classes. Computer network features include on-campus library services, online commercial services, Internet access, wireless campus network, Internet filtering or blocking technology, faculty Web pages, Cisco Networking Academy. Students grades are available online. The school has a published electronic and media policy.
Contact Cmdr. Gretchen Herbst, Director of Admissions. 727-384-5500 Ext. 220. Fax: 727-347-5160. E-mail: gherbst@farragut.org. Web site: www.farragut.org.

ALEXANDER DAWSON SCHOOL

10455 Dawson Drive

Lafayette, Colorado 80026

Head of School: Mr. Brian Johnson

General Information Coeducational day college-preparatory, arts, technology, and engineering school. Grades K–12. Founded: 1970. Setting: rural. Nearest major city is Boulder. 113-acre campus. 11 buildings on campus. Approved or accredited by Association of Colorado Independent Schools and Colorado Department of Education. Member of National Association of Independent Schools and Secondary School Admission Test Board. Total enrollment: 453. Upper school average class size: 15. Upper school faculty-student ratio: 1:7. There are 172 required school days per year for Upper School students. Upper School students typically attend 5 days per week. The average school day consists of 9 hours and 30 minutes.

Upper School Student Profile Grade 9: 62 students (27 boys, 35 girls); Grade 10: 43 students (23 boys, 20 girls); Grade 11: 44 students (25 boys, 19 girls); Grade 12: 44 students (17 boys, 27 girls).

Faculty School total: 53. In upper school: 17 men, 10 women; 23 have advanced degrees.

Subjects Offered Algebra, American history, American literature, art, art history, biology, calculus, ceramics, chemistry, Chinese, computer math, computer multimedia, computer programming, computer science, creative writing, dance, drafting, drama, earth science, economics, English, English literature, European history, expository writing, fine arts, French, geography, geometry, government-AP, government/civics, grammar, health, history, industrial arts, journalism, Latin, mathematics, mechanical drawing, music, photography, physical education, physics, science, social sciences, social studies, Spanish, speech, theater, trigonometry, world history, world literature, writing.

Graduation Requirements Arts and fine arts (art, music, dance, drama), computer science, English, foreign language, history, mathematics, science, sports.

Special Academic Programs 15 Advanced Placement exams for which test preparation is offered; honors section; independent study; term-away projects; study at local college for college credit; study abroad; academic accommodation for the gifted, the musically talented, and the artistically talented; remedial reading and/or remedial writing; remedial math; special instructional classes for deaf students.

College Admission Counseling 27 students graduated in 2011; all went to college, including Middlebury College; Pomona College; University of Denver; Wellesley College. Mean SAT critical reading: 616, mean SAT math: 620, mean composite ACT: 27.

Student Life Upper grades have specified standards of dress, student council, honor system. Discipline rests equally with students and faculty.

Tuition and Aid Day student tuition: $19,200. Tuition installment plan (Insured Tuition Payment Plan, monthly payment plans, individually arranged payment plans). Need-based scholarship grants, need-based loans available. In 2011–12, 13% of upper-school students received aid. Total amount of financial aid awarded in 2011–12: $905,000.

Admissions Traditional secondary-level entrance grade is 9. For fall 2011, 45 students applied for upper-level admission, 31 were accepted, 24 enrolled. Deadline for receipt of application materials: none. Application fee required: $100. Interview required.

Athletics Interscholastic: baseball (boys), basketball (b,g), lacrosse (b), soccer (b,g), swimming and diving (b,g), synchronized swimming (g), tennis (b,g), track and field (b,g), volleyball (g); intramural: lacrosse (b); coed interscholastic: bicycling, canoeing/kayaking, cross-country running, equestrian sports, golf, kayaking, martial arts, paddling, skiing (downhill), Special Olympics; coed intramural: aerobics, aerobics/dance, backpacking, Circus, climbing, dance, equestrian sports, fitness, flag football, football, Frisbee, golf, hiking/backpacking, indoor soccer, martial arts, modern dance, outdoor activities, outdoor education, outdoor recreation, outdoor skills, physical fitness, rafting, rock climbing, ropes courses, running, strength & conditioning, weight lifting. 3 PE instructors, 22 coaches, 1 athletic trainer.

Computers Computers are regularly used in art, engineering, mathematics, science classes. Computer network features include on-campus library services, online commercial services, Internet access, wireless campus network, Internet filtering or blocking technology. Student e-mail accounts and computer access in designated common areas are available to students. Students grades are available online. The school has a published electronic and media policy.

Contact Ms. Denise LaRusch, Assistant to the Director of Admissions. 303-665-6679. Fax: 303-381-0415. E-mail: dlarusch@dawsonschool.org. Web site: www.dawsonschool.org.

ALLENDALE COLUMBIA SCHOOL

519 Allens Creek Road

Rochester, New York 14618-3405

Head of School: David Blanchard

General Information Coeducational day college-preparatory school. Grades N–12. Founded: 1890. Setting: suburban. 33-acre campus. 5 buildings on campus. Approved or accredited by New York State Association of Independent Schools. Member of National Association of Independent Schools. Endowment: $15 million. Total enrollment: 325. Upper school average class size: 7. Upper school faculty-student ratio: 1:4. There are 165 required school days per year for Upper School students. Upper School students typically attend 5 days per week. The average school day consists of 6 hours and 30 minutes.

Upper School Student Profile Grade 9: 33 students (15 boys, 18 girls); Grade 10: 28 students (17 boys, 11 girls); Grade 11: 28 students (14 boys, 14 girls); Grade 12: 34 students (17 boys, 17 girls).

Faculty School total: 59. In upper school: 11 men, 17 women; 23 have advanced degrees.

Subjects Offered Advanced Placement courses, advanced studio art-AP, algebra, American history, American history-AP, American literature, American literature-AP, art, art-AP, astronomy, bioethics, biology, biology-AP, calculus, calculus-AP, chemistry, chemistry-AP, composition-AP, computer science, discrete mathematics, earth science, economics, English, English language and composition-AP, English literature, environmental science, environmental science-AP, European history, European history-AP, expository writing, French, French-AP, genetics, geology, geometry, government/civics, grammar, health, history, history of China and Japan, jazz ensemble, Latin, Latin-AP, mathematics, mathematics-AP, music, photography, physical education, physics, physics-AP, pre-calculus, probability and statistics, science, social studies, Spanish, Spanish-AP, statistics-AP, U.S. history, U.S. history-AP, world history, writing.

Graduation Requirements Art, arts, computer science, English, foreign language, history, mathematics, physical education (includes health), science, participation in at least one team sport in both 9th and 10th grade.

Special Academic Programs 19 Advanced Placement exams for which test preparation is offered; independent study.

College Admission Counseling 36 students graduated in 2011; 32 went to college, including Harvard University; Ithaca College; Rochester Institute of Technology; University of California, Berkeley; University of Rochester; Yale University. Other: 4 had other specific plans. Mean SAT critical reading: 612, mean SAT math: 646, mean SAT writing: 618. 50% scored over 600 on SAT critical reading, 62% scored over 600 on SAT math, 59% scored over 600 on SAT writing.

Student Life Upper grades have specified standards of dress, student council. Discipline rests primarily with faculty.

Summer Programs Enrichment, sports, art/fine arts programs offered; session focuses on athletics and arts; held on campus; accepts boys and girls; open to students from other schools. 600 students usually enrolled. 2012 schedule: June 11 to August 3. Application deadline: none.

Tuition and Aid Day student tuition: $6700–$19,475. Tuition installment plan (FACTS Tuition Payment Plan). Need-based scholarship grants available. In 2011–12, 46% of upper-school students received aid. Total amount of financial aid awarded in 2011–12: $645,341.

Admissions Traditional secondary-level entrance grade is 9. For fall 2011, 40 students applied for upper-level admission, 26 were accepted, 21 enrolled. ERB - verbal abilities, reading comprehension, quantitative abilities (level F, form 1), ERB Reading and Math, essay, math and English placement tests, school's own exam or writing sample required. Deadline for receipt of application materials: none. Application fee required: $50. Interview required.

Athletics Interscholastic: baseball (boys), basketball (b,g), cross-country running (b,g), soccer (b,g), softball (g), tennis (b,g), track and field (b,g), volleyball (g); coed interscholastic: bowling, golf, running, swimming and diving. 4 PE instructors.

Computers Computers are regularly used in all academic classes. Computer network features include on-campus library services, Internet access, wireless campus network, Internet filtering or blocking technology, county-wide library services. Student e-mail accounts and computer access in designated common areas are available to students. The school has a published electronic and media policy.

Contact Sara Scharr, Director of Admissions. 585-381-4560. Fax: 585-383-1191. E-mail: sscharr@allendalecolumbia.org. Web site: www.allendalecolumbia.org.

ALL HALLOWS HIGH SCHOOL

111 East 164th Street

Bronx, New York 10452-9402

Head of School: Mr. Paul P. Krebbs

General Information Boys' day college-preparatory, general academic, business, and religious studies school, affiliated with Roman Catholic Church. Grades 9–12. Founded: 1909. Setting: urban. 1 building on campus. Approved or accredited by Christian Brothers Association, Middle States Association of Colleges and Schools, and New York Department of Education. Total enrollment: 640. Upper school average class size: 27. Upper school faculty-student ratio: 1:15. There are 180 required school days per year for Upper School students. The average school day consists of 6 hours and 8 minutes.

Upper School Student Profile 85% of students are Roman Catholic.

Faculty School total: 42. In upper school: 37 men, 5 women; 33 have advanced degrees.

Subjects Offered Algebra, American history, art, Bible studies, biology, calculus, chemistry, computer science, economics, English, English literature, environmental science, geometry, government/civics, grammar, history, humanities, Latin, mathematics, media studies, physical education, physics, political science, religion, science, social studies, Spanish, speech, trigonometry.

Graduation Requirements Arts and fine arts (art, music, dance, drama), business skills (includes word processing), computer science, English, foreign language, mathematics, physical education (includes health), religion (includes Bible studies and theology), science, social sciences, social studies (includes history). Community service is required.

Special Academic Programs Remedial reading and/or remedial writing; remedial math.
College Admission Counseling 154 students graduated in 2010; all went to college.
Student Life Upper grades have specified standards of dress, student council, honor system. Discipline rests primarily with faculty. Attendance at religious services is required.
Admissions Cooperative Entrance Exam (McGraw-Hill) and school's own exam required. Deadline for receipt of application materials: none. No application fee required. On-campus interview required.
Athletics Interscholastic: baseball, basketball, bowling, cross-country running, dance, fencing, golf, handball, indoor track, indoor track & field, martial arts, soccer, swimming and diving, track and field; intramural: field hockey, indoor soccer, lacrosse, tennis. 1 PE instructor, 3 athletic trainers.
Computers Computers are regularly used in English, history, mathematics, media studies, science classes. Computer resources include on-campus library services, Internet access.
Contact Sean Sullivan, Principal. 718-293-4545. Fax: 718-293-8634. E-mail: alhallow@aol.com. Web site: www.allhallows.org.

ALLIANCE ACADEMY

Casilla 17-11-06186

Quito, Ecuador

Head of School: Dr. David Wells

General Information Coeducational boarding and day and distance learning college-preparatory, arts, and religious studies school, affiliated with Christian faith. Boarding grades 7–12, day grades PK–12. Distance learning grades 10–12. Founded: 1929. Setting: urban. Students are housed in single-sex by floor dormitories and mission agency dormitories. 8-acre campus. 6 buildings on campus. Approved or accredited by Association of American Schools in South America, Association of Christian Schools International, and Southern Association of Colleges and Schools. Language of instruction: English. Total enrollment: 604. Upper school average class size: 15. Upper school faculty-student ratio: 1:7. There are 180 required school days per year for Upper School students. Upper School students typically attend 5 days per week. The average school day consists of 6 hours and 30 minutes.
Upper School Student Profile Grade 9: 51 students (27 boys, 24 girls); Grade 10: 60 students (26 boys, 34 girls); Grade 11: 44 students (14 boys, 30 girls); Grade 12: 53 students (27 boys, 26 girls). 1% of students are boarding students. 34% are international students. International students from Canada, China, Japan, Republic of Korea, Taiwan, and United States; 9 other countries represented in student body. 40% of students are Christian faith.
Faculty School total: 91. In upper school: 21 men, 24 women; 14 have advanced degrees.
Subjects Offered Algebra, American history, American history-AP, American literature, art, auto mechanics, band, Bible, Bible as literature, Bible studies, biology, biology-AP, business, calculus, calculus-AP, chemistry, choir, Christian doctrine, Christian ethics, Christian studies, church history, computer applications, computer art, computer math, computer programming, computer science, computer science-AP, concert band, creative writing, debate, desktop publishing, drama, earth science, economics, English, English as a foreign language, English language-AP, English literature, English literature-AP, ESL, family and consumer science, fine arts, French, French as a second language, geography, geometry, government/civics, grammar, health, health education, history, home economics, industrial arts, jazz band, journalism, keyboarding, Life of Christ, marching band, mathematics, music, novels, photography, physical education, physics, piano, pre-algebra, pre-calculus, public speaking, religion, religion and culture, science, senior seminar, small engine repair, social sciences, social studies, Spanish, Spanish literature, Spanish literature-AP, speech, speech and debate, theater, trigonometry, U.S. history-AP, video communication, vocal ensemble, woodworking, world geography, world history, world religions, writing, yearbook.
Graduation Requirements 1 1/2 elective credits, algebra, arts and fine arts (art, music, dance, drama), comparative government and politics, computer applications, English, foreign language, health education, mathematics, physical education (includes health), religion (includes Bible studies and theology), science, social sciences, social studies (includes history), U.S. government and politics, U.S. history.
Special Academic Programs 12 Advanced Placement exams for which test preparation is offered; independent study; academic accommodation for the gifted and the artistically talented; remedial reading and/or remedial writing; remedial math; programs in English, mathematics, general development for dyslexic students; special instructional classes for students with developmental and/or learning disabilities; ESL (52 students enrolled).
College Admission Counseling 45 students graduated in 2011; 35 went to college, including Azusa Pacific University; Calvin College; John Brown University; Simpson University; Worcester Polytechnic Institute. Other: 3 went to work, 2 entered military service, 5 had other specific plans. Median SAT critical reading: 495, median SAT math: 517, median SAT writing: 496, median combined SAT: 1508, median composite ACT: 22. 36% scored over 600 on SAT critical reading, 29% scored over 600 on SAT math, 30% scored over 600 on SAT writing, 32% scored over 1800 on combined SAT, 26% scored over 26 on composite ACT.
Student Life Upper grades have specified standards of dress, student council, honor system. Discipline rests primarily with faculty. Attendance at religious services is required.
Summer Programs Remediation, ESL, sports programs offered; session focuses on ESL; held on campus; accepts boys and girls; not open to students from other schools. 27 students usually enrolled. 2012 schedule: June 25 to August 3. Application deadline: June 12.
Tuition and Aid Day student tuition: $8900. Tuition installment plan (monthly payment plans, individually arranged payment plans). Tuition reduction for siblings, need-based scholarship grants, paying campus jobs, tuition reduction for children of missionaries, two full scholarships for children of Ecuadorian military personnel available. In 2011–12, 30% of upper-school students received aid. Total amount of financial aid awarded in 2011–12: $800,000.
Admissions Traditional secondary-level entrance grade is 9. For fall 2011, 81 students applied for upper-level admission, 61 were accepted, 58 enrolled. English entrance exam, English proficiency, WRAT or writing sample required. Deadline for receipt of application materials: none. Application fee required: $100. On-campus interview required.
Athletics Interscholastic: basketball (boys, girls), soccer (b,g), volleyball (b,g); intramural: badminton (b,g), ball hockey (b), horseshoes (b), in-line hockey (b), modern dance (g), table tennis (b,g); coed intramural: backpacking, basketball, bocce, climbing, croquet, field hockey, flag football, floor hockey, football, hiking/backpacking, indoor soccer, kickball, martial arts, outdoor adventure, paddle tennis, running, soccer, softball, strength & conditioning, table tennis, volleyball, wall climbing. 2 PE instructors, 1 coach.
Computers Computers are regularly used in basic skills, business education, career exploration, college planning, computer applications, design, desktop publishing, desktop publishing, ESL, digital applications, graphic design, independent study, information technology, introduction to technology, keyboarding, lab/keyboard, language development, media arts, media production, media services, photography, photojournalism, programming, publications, technology, video film production, word processing, writing, yearbook classes. Computer network features include on-campus library services, online commercial services, Internet access, wireless campus network, Internet filtering or blocking technology. Campus intranet, student e-mail accounts, and computer access in designated common areas are available to students. Students grades are available online. The school has a published electronic and media policy.
Contact Mrs. Alexandra Chavez, Director of Admissions. 593 2 226-6985. Fax: 593-2 226 4350. E-mail: achavez@alliance.k12.ec. Web site: www.alliance.k12.ec.

ALLISON ACADEMY

1881 Northeast 164th Street

North Miami Beach, Florida 33162

Head of School: Dr. Sarah F. Allison

General Information Coeducational day college-preparatory, general academic, arts, business, and English for Speakers of Other Languages school. Grades 6–12. Founded: 1983. Setting: urban. Nearest major city is Miami. 1-acre campus. 2 buildings on campus. Approved or accredited by Association of Independent Schools of Florida, National Council for Private School Accreditation, Southern Association of Colleges and Schools, and Florida Department of Education. Total enrollment: 91. Upper school average class size: 15. Upper school faculty-student ratio: 1:10. There are 180 required school days per year for Upper School students. Upper School students typically attend 5 days per week. The average school day consists of 5 hours and 50 minutes.
Upper School Student Profile Grade 9: 17 students (13 boys, 4 girls); Grade 10: 17 students (12 boys, 5 girls); Grade 11: 15 students (12 boys, 3 girls); Grade 12: 21 students (13 boys, 8 girls).
Faculty School total: 11. In upper school: 5 men, 6 women; 5 have advanced degrees.
Subjects Offered Advanced Placement courses, algebra, American government, American history, art history, arts, biology, chemistry, chorus, computer science, consumer mathematics, creative drama, drama, drawing, ecology, environmental systems, economics, economics and history, English, English language and composition-AP, English literature, environmental science, ESL, fine arts, French, French language-AP, general math, geography, geometry, health education, history, humanities, life management skills, life skills, mathematics, painting, peer counseling, physical education, physical science, physics, pre-calculus, psychology, reading, reading/study skills, SAT/ACT preparation, science, social sciences, social studies, Spanish, sports, trigonometry, world cultures, writing, yearbook.
Graduation Requirements Algebra, American government, arts and fine arts (art, music, dance, drama), business skills (includes word processing), chemistry, computer applications, computer science, creative writing, current events, drama, earth and space science, economics, English, English literature, environmental education, foreign language, health education, life management skills, mathematics, physical education (includes health), psychology, SAT/ACT preparation, science, social sciences, social studies (includes history), Spanish, U.S. history, world history, 75 hours of community service.

Special Academic Programs 1 Advanced Placement exam for which test preparation is offered; honors section; accelerated programs; study at local college for college credit; academic accommodation for the gifted, the musically talented, and the artistically talented; remedial reading and/or remedial writing; remedial math; programs in English, mathematics, general development for dyslexic students; special instructional classes for students with learning disabilities, dyslexia, and Attention Deficit Disorder; ESL (3 students enrolled).
College Admission Counseling 22 students graduated in 2011; 17 went to college, including Barry University; Broward College; Florida International University; Miami Dade College. Other: 2 went to work, 1 entered military service, 2 had other specific plans. Median SAT critical reading: 500, median SAT math: 510, median composite ACT: 19. 16% scored over 600 on SAT critical reading, 15% scored over 600 on SAT math, 8% scored over 26 on composite ACT.
Student Life Upper grades have uniform requirement, student council. Discipline rests primarily with faculty.
Summer Programs Remediation, enrichment, advancement, ESL programs offered; session focuses on academics for credit courses, remedial reading, and ESL; held on campus; accepts boys and girls; open to students from other schools. 2012 schedule: June 18 to July 26. Application deadline: June 18.
Tuition and Aid Day student tuition: $14,000. Tuition installment plan (Insured Tuition Payment Plan, monthly payment plans, individually arranged payment plans). Tuition reduction for siblings, merit scholarship grants, need-based scholarship grants available. In 2011–12, 26% of upper-school students received aid; total upper-school merit-scholarship money awarded: $32,000. Total amount of financial aid awarded in 2011–12: $105,000.
Admissions Traditional secondary-level entrance grade is 9. Admissions testing, CAT, CTBS (or similar from their school), Woodcock-Johnson or Woodcock-Johnson Revised Achievement Test required. Deadline for receipt of application materials: none. Application fee required: $450. Interview required.
Athletics Interscholastic: basketball (boys), swimming and diving (b), tennis (b,g), walking (g), weight training (b); intramural: basketball (b,g), golf (b), martial arts (b,g), soccer (b,g), softball (b,g), swimming and diving (b,g), table tennis (b,g), tennis (b,g), walking (g); coed interscholastic: bowling, flag football, kickball, physical fitness, tennis; coed intramural: badminton, martial arts, physical fitness, soccer, softball, swimming and diving, table tennis, tennis, volleyball. 2 PE instructors, 2 coaches.
Computers Computers are regularly used in art, business applications, computer applications, current events, drawing and design, English, foreign language, geography, health, history, keyboarding, life skills, mathematics, psychology, reading, SAT preparation, science, Spanish, word processing classes. Computer resources include on-campus library services, online commercial services, Internet access, wireless campus network. Computer access in designated common areas is available to students. Students grades are available online. The school has a published electronic and media policy.
Contact Margaret Sheriff, Administrator. 305-940-3922. Fax: 305-940-1820. E-mail: thenewsheriff@gmail.com. Web site: www.allisonacademy.com.

ALMA HEIGHTS CHRISTIAN HIGH SCHOOL

1030 Linda Mar Boulevard

Pacifica, California 94044

Head of School: David Gross

General Information Coeducational day college-preparatory, general academic, arts, religious studies, and technology school, affiliated with Christian faith. Grades K–12. Founded: 1955. Setting: suburban. Nearest major city is San Francisco. 40-acre campus. 5 buildings on campus. Approved or accredited by Association of Christian Schools International, Western Association of Schools and Colleges, and California Department of Education. Upper school average class size: 22. Upper school faculty-student ratio: 1:10. There are 176 required school days per year for Upper School students. Upper School students typically attend 5 days per week. The average school day consists of 7 hours and 45 minutes.
Upper School Student Profile Grade 9: 30 students (17 boys, 13 girls); Grade 10: 38 students (18 boys, 20 girls); Grade 11: 31 students (13 boys, 18 girls); Grade 12: 29 students (17 boys, 12 girls). 80% of students are Christian.
Faculty School total: 17. In upper school: 10 men, 7 women; 4 have advanced degrees.
Special Academic Programs International Baccalaureate program; 6 Advanced Placement exams for which test preparation is offered; honors section; accelerated programs; special instructional classes for students with ADD and dyslexia.
College Admission Counseling 34 students graduated in 2010; 32 went to college, including Biola University; Skyline College; University of California, Berkeley; University of California, Davis; University of California, Irvine; Whitworth University. Other: 2 went to work. Mean SAT critical reading: 574, mean SAT math: 559, mean SAT writing: 585.
Student Life Upper grades have uniform requirement, student council, honor system. Discipline rests primarily with faculty. Attendance at religious services is required.
Tuition and Aid Day student tuition: $9400. Tuition installment plan (monthly payment plans, individually arranged payment plans). Tuition reduction for siblings, merit scholarship grants, need-based scholarship grants, paying campus jobs available. In 2010–11, 5% of upper-school students received aid.
Admissions Placement test required. Deadline for receipt of application materials: none. Application fee required: $75. Interview required.
Athletics Interscholastic: baseball (boys), basketball (b,g), football (b), soccer (b), softball (g), volleyball (b,g); intramural: flag football (b), indoor soccer (b); coed interscholastic: cross-country running, soccer. 3 PE instructors, 6 coaches.
Computers Computer resources include on-campus library services, online commercial services, Internet access, wireless campus network, Internet filtering or blocking technology. Campus intranet, student e-mail accounts, and computer access in designated common areas are available to students. Students grades are available online. The school has a published electronic and media policy.
Contact 650-355-1935. Fax: 650-355-3488. Web site: www.almaheights.org.

ALPHA OMEGA ACADEMY

804 North Second Avenue East

Rock Rapids, Iowa 51246

Head of School: Mr. Gary O'Neill

General Information Coeducational day and distance learning college-preparatory, general academic, and distance learning school, affiliated with Christian faith. Grades K–12. Distance learning grades K–12. Founded: 1992. Setting: small town. Approved or accredited by CITA (Commission on International and Trans-Regional Accreditation) and North Central Association of Colleges and Schools. Total enrollment: 2,243. Upper school faculty-student ratio: 1:35. Upper School students typically attend 5 days per week.
Faculty School total: 66. In upper school: 25 men, 38 women; 12 have advanced degrees.
Subjects Offered Accounting, algebra, American government, American history, American literature, art, Bible, biology, British literature, calculus, career planning, chemistry, civics, consumer mathematics, earth science, English, English composition, English literature, French, general math, general science, geography, geometry, health, history, home economics, language arts, mathematics, music appreciation, music theory, physical fitness, science, Spanish, state history, world geography, world history.
Graduation Requirements 1 1/2 elective credits, algebra, biology, chemistry, language arts, mathematics, physical education (includes health), science, social studies (includes history), one credit of Bible.
Special Academic Programs Accelerated programs; independent study; remedial math.
College Admission Counseling 250 students graduated in 2011.
Student Life Discipline rests equally with students and faculty.
Tuition and Aid Day student tuition: $600–$3000. Tuition installment plan (Six Month Payment Plan, Two Payment Plan). Tuition reduction for siblings available.
Admissions Traditional secondary-level entrance grade is 9. Placement test required. Deadline for receipt of application materials: none. Application fee required: $185. Interview required.
Athletics 2 PE instructors.
Computers Computers are regularly used in accounting, Bible studies, business skills, college planning, English, foreign language, French, geography, health, history, mathematics, music, science, social sciences, social studies, Spanish classes. Students grades are available online. The school has a published electronic and media policy.
Contact Mrs. Kelli Hoogers, Academy Services Department Head. 800-682-7396 Ext. 1736. Fax: 712-472-6830. E-mail: khoogers@aoacademy.com. Web site: www.aoacademy.com.

AMERICAN ACADEMY

Plantation, Florida

See Special Needs Schools section.

THE AMERICAN BOYCHOIR SCHOOL

Princeton, New Jersey

See Junior Boarding Schools section.

AMERICAN COMMUNITY SCHOOLS OF ATHENS

129 Aghias Paraskevis Street

Halandri

Athens 152 34, Greece

Head of School: Dr. Stefanos Gialamas

General Information Coeducational day college-preparatory, arts, and technology school. Grades JK–12. Founded: 1945. Setting: suburban. 3-hectare campus. 4 buildings on campus. Approved or accredited by CITA (Commission on International and Trans-Regional Accreditation) and Middle States Association of Colleges and

Schools. Language of instruction: English. Total enrollment: 859. Upper school average class size: 17. Upper school faculty-student ratio: 1:17. There are 180 required school days per year for Upper School students. Upper School students typically attend 5 days per week. The average school day consists of 6 hours and 30 minutes.

Upper School Student Profile Grade 9: 77 students (35 boys, 42 girls); Grade 10: 87 students (43 boys, 44 girls); Grade 11: 96 students (41 boys, 55 girls); Grade 12: 82 students (43 boys, 39 girls).

Faculty School total: 95. In upper school: 15 men, 37 women; 40 have advanced degrees.

Subjects Offered Algebra, American history, American literature, analysis, Arabic, art, art history, band, biology, business skills, calculus, chemistry, Chinese, computer programming, computer science, dance, drama, earth science, economics, English, English literature, environmental science, ESL, European history, expository writing, fine arts, French, geometry, German, government/civics, grammar, Greek, history, humanities, information technology, journalism, mathematics, music, peer counseling, photography, physical education, physical science, physics, psychology, science, social sciences, social studies, sociology, Spanish, speech, statistics, theater, theory of knowledge, trigonometry, writing.

Graduation Requirements Arts and fine arts (art, music, dance, drama), computer science, English, foreign language, mathematics, physical education (includes health), science, social sciences, social studies (includes history).

Special Academic Programs International Baccalaureate program; 4 Advanced Placement exams for which test preparation is offered; honors section; accelerated programs; independent study; study at local college for college credit; academic accommodation for the gifted; remedial reading and/or remedial writing; remedial math; programs in English, mathematics, general development for dyslexic students; special instructional classes for deaf students, blind students, mild learning disabilities; ESL (17 students enrolled).

College Admission Counseling 97 students graduated in 2010; 96 went to college, including Boston College; Boston University; Columbia University; Georgetown University; New York University; Tufts University. Other: 1 had other specific plans. Mean SAT critical reading: 543, mean SAT math: 550, mean SAT writing: 579. 27% scored over 600 on SAT critical reading, 25% scored over 600 on SAT math, 26% scored over 600 on SAT writing.

Student Life Upper grades have specified standards of dress, student council. Discipline rests primarily with faculty.

Tuition and Aid Day student tuition: €11,758. Tuition installment plan (individually arranged payment plans, semester and quarterly payment plans). Tuition reduction for siblings, need-based scholarship grants available. In 2010–11, 1% of upper-school students received aid. Total amount of financial aid awarded in 2010–11: €60,000.

Admissions Traditional secondary-level entrance grade is 9. For fall 2010, 340 students applied for upper-level admission, 307 were accepted, 219 enrolled. English for Non-native Speakers or math and English placement tests required. Deadline for receipt of application materials: none. No application fee required. Interview required.

Athletics Interscholastic: basketball (boys, girls), cross-country running (b,g), soccer (b,g), softball (b,g), swimming and diving (b,g), tennis (b,g), track and field (b,g), volleyball (b,g), wrestling (b); coed interscholastic: gymnastics; coed intramural: martial arts. 2 PE instructors, 3 coaches.

Computers Computers are regularly used in all academic classes. Computer network features include on-campus library services, Internet access. Campus intranet, student e-mail accounts, and computer access in designated common areas are available to students. Students grades are available online.

Contact John G. Papadakis, Director of Enrollment, Communications and Technology. 30-210-639-3200. Fax: 30-210-639-0051. E-mail: papadakisj@acs.gr. Web site: www.acs.gr.

AMERICAN HERITAGE SCHOOL

6200 Linton Boulevard

Delray Beach, Florida 33484

Head of School: Robert Stone

General Information Coeducational day college-preparatory, arts, and pre-medical, pre-law, pre-engineering school. Grades PK–12. Founded: 1994. Setting: suburban. Nearest major city is Fort Lauderdale. 40-acre campus. Approved or accredited by Association of Independent Schools of Florida, CITA (Commission on International and Trans-Regional Accreditation), Southern Association of Colleges and Schools, and Florida Department of Education. Upper school average class size: 17.

Subjects Offered Acting, algebra, American government, American history, American history-AP, American legal systems, American literature, American literature-AP, anatomy and physiology, architectural drawing, art, art history-AP, band, biology, biology-AP, calculus-AP, ceramics, chemistry, chemistry-AP, Chinese, chorus, community service, computer graphics, computer science, computer science-AP, constitutional law, costumes and make-up, creative writing, dance, drama, drawing, economics, economics-AP, engineering, English, English language and composition-AP, English literature, English literature and composition-AP, environmental science, environmental science-AP, ESL, European history-AP, film and literature, fine arts, forensics, French, French-AP, geometry, graphic design, guitar, honors algebra, honors English, honors geometry, honors U.S. history, honors world history, journalism, law studies, mathematics, music theory, music theory-AP, oceanography, orchestra, painting, photography, physical education, physics, physics-AP, portfolio art, pre-algebra, pre-calculus, probability and statistics, psychology, psychology-AP, public policy, research skills, SAT/ACT preparation, science, sculpture, set design, sociology, Spanish, Spanish-AP, speech and debate, sports medicine, stagecraft, statistics-AP, studio art, theater, U.S. government and politics-AP, vocal music, Web site design, weight training, word processing, world history, world history-AP, world literature, world religions, writing, writing, yearbook.

Graduation Requirements Arts and fine arts (art, music, dance, drama), English, foreign language, mathematics, physical education (includes health), science, social studies (includes history), acceptance to a 4-year college. Community service is required.

Special Academic Programs Advanced Placement exam preparation; honors section; academic accommodation for the gifted, the musically talented, and the artistically talented; ESL.

College Admission Counseling Median SAT critical reading: 570, median SAT math: 590, median SAT writing: 560. 36% scored over 600 on SAT critical reading, 36% scored over 600 on SAT math, 33% scored over 600 on SAT writing.

Student Life Upper grades have uniform requirement, student council. Discipline rests primarily with faculty.

Tuition and Aid Tuition installment plan (monthly payment plans, semester payment plan, yearly). Tuition reduction for siblings, merit scholarship grants, need-based scholarship grants available.

Admissions Traditional secondary-level entrance grade is 9. Slossen Intelligence and Stanford Achievement Test required. Deadline for receipt of application materials: none. Application fee required: $100. On-campus interview required.

Athletics Interscholastic: baseball (boys), basketball (b,g), cross-country running (b,g), diving (b,g), football (b), golf (b,g), soccer (b,g), softball (g), swimming and diving (b,g), tennis (b,g), track and field (b,g), volleyball (g), weight training (b,g), winter soccer (b,g), wrestling (b); coed interscholastic: cheering, physical fitness.

Computers Computers are regularly used in computer applications, desktop publishing, digital applications, drafting, drawing and design, economics, engineering, English, ESL, French, geography, graphic design, history, keyboarding, library, literary magazine, mathematics, media arts, media production, multimedia, music, music technology, newspaper, photography, programming, psychology, reading, SAT preparation, social sciences, Spanish, speech, Web site design, writing, yearbook classes. Computer network features include on-campus library services, online commercial services, Internet access, wireless campus network, Internet filtering or blocking technology, Questia. Computer access in designated common areas is available to students. Students grades are available online. The school has a published electronic and media policy.

Contact 561-495-7272. Web site: http://www.ahschool.com/BocaDelraynew/ahhome/ahhomepage.html.

See Display on next page and Close-Up on page 578.

AMERICAN HERITAGE SCHOOL

12200 West Broward Boulevard

Plantation, Florida 33325

Head of School: William R. Laurie

General Information Coeducational day college-preparatory, arts, and pre-medical, pre-law, pre-engineering, bio-medical, arts school. Grades PK–12. Founded: 1969. Setting: suburban. Nearest major city is Fort Lauderdale. 40-acre campus. 5 buildings on campus. Approved or accredited by Association of Independent Schools of Florida, CITA (Commission on International and Trans-Regional Accreditation), Southern Association of Colleges and Schools, and Florida Department of Education. Total enrollment: 2,278. Upper school average class size: 18. Upper school faculty-student ratio: 1:15. There are 175 required school days per year for Upper School students. Upper School students typically attend 5 days per week. The average school day consists of 7 hours and 15 minutes.

Upper School Student Profile Grade 7: 158 students (91 boys, 67 girls); Grade 8: 198 students (104 boys, 94 girls); Grade 9: 320 students (186 boys, 134 girls); Grade 10: 323 students (161 boys, 162 girls); Grade 11: 299 students (141 boys, 158 girls); Grade 12: 267 students (131 boys, 136 girls).

Faculty School total: 170. In upper school: 42 men, 71 women; 62 have advanced degrees.

Subjects Offered Acting, algebra, American government, American history, American history-AP, American legal systems, American literature, American literature-AP, anatomy and physiology, architectural drawing, architecture, art, art history-AP, band, biology, biology-AP, business law, calculus-AP, ceramics, chemistry, chemistry-AP, Chinese, chorus, community service, computer graphics, computer science, computer science-AP, constitutional law, costumes and make-up, creative writing, dance, drama, drawing, economics, economics-AP, engineering, English, English language and composition-AP, English literature, English literature and composition-AP, environmental science, environmental science-AP, ESL, European history-AP, film and literature, fine arts, forensics, French, French language-AP, French-AP, geometry, government-AP, graphic design, guitar, honors algebra, honors English, honors geometry, honors U.S. history, honors world history, human geography - AP, journalism, law studies, literary magazine, mathematics, music theory, music theory-AP, oceanography, orchestra, organic chemistry, painting, photography, physical education, physics, physics-AP, portfolio art, pre-algebra, pre-calculus, probability and statistics, psychology, psychology-AP, public policy, public speaking, research, research skills, SAT preparation, SAT/ACT preparation, science, sculpture, set design, sociology, Spanish, Spanish-AP, speech and debate, stage design, stagecraft, statistics-AP, studio art, technical theater, theater, U.S. government and politics-AP, video film production, visual arts, vocal music, Web site design, weight training, word processing, world history, world history-AP, world literature, writing, writing, yearbook.

Graduation Requirements Arts and fine arts (art, music, dance, drama), English, foreign language, mathematics, physical education (includes health), science, social studies (includes history), acceptance to a 4-year college. Community service is required.

Special Academic Programs Advanced Placement exam preparation; honors section; academic accommodation for the gifted, the musically talented, and the artistically talented; ESL (87 students enrolled).

College Admission Counseling 242 students graduated in 2011; all went to college, including Florida Gulf Coast University; Florida State University; Nova Southeastern University; University of Central Florida; University of Florida; University of Miami. Median SAT critical reading: 576, median SAT math: 595, median SAT writing: 600. 43% scored over 600 on SAT critical reading, 49% scored over 600 on SAT math, 49% scored over 600 on SAT writing.

Student Life Upper grades have uniform requirement, student council. Discipline rests primarily with faculty.

Summer Programs Remediation, enrichment, advancement, ESL, art/fine arts, computer instruction programs offered; session focuses on academics; held on campus; accepts boys and girls; open to students from other schools. 500 students usually enrolled. 2012 schedule: June 11 to August 10. Application deadline: none.

Tuition and Aid Day student tuition: $20,402–$22,019. Tuition installment plan (monthly payment plans, Semester payment plan, yearly). Tuition reduction for siblings, merit scholarship grants, need-based scholarship grants available. In 2011–12, 22% of upper-school students received aid; total upper-school merit-scholarship money awarded: $3,800,000. Total amount of financial aid awarded in 2011–12: $3,800,000.

Admissions Traditional secondary-level entrance grade is 9. Slossen Intelligence and Stanford Achievement Test required. Deadline for receipt of application materials: none. Application fee required: $100. On-campus interview required.

Athletics Interscholastic: baseball (boys), basketball (b,g), cross-country running (b,g), diving (b,g), football (b), golf (b,g), lacrosse (b,g), soccer (b,g), softball (g), swimming and diving (b,g), tennis (b,g), track and field (b,g), volleyball (b,g), weight training (b,g), winter soccer (b,g), wrestling (b); coed interscholastic: cheering, physical fitness, physical training. 4 PE instructors, 6 coaches.

Computers Computers are regularly used in all academic, computer applications, creative writing, desktop publishing, digital applications, drafting, drawing and design, economics, engineering, English, ESL, foreign language, French, geography, graphic arts, graphic design, history, human geography - AP, journalism, keyboarding, library, literary magazine, mathematics, media arts, media production, multimedia, music, music technology, newspaper, photography, programming, psychology, reading, SAT preparation, science, social sciences, social studies, Spanish, speech, theater arts, Web site design, writing, writing, yearbook classes. Computer network features include on-campus library services, online commercial services, Internet access, wireless campus network, Internet filtering or blocking technology, Questia, iPads used by students and teachers on school Intranet. Campus intranet, student e-mail accounts, and computer access in designated common areas are available to students. Students grades are available online. The school has a published electronic and media policy.

Contact William R. Laurie, President. 954-472-0022 Ext. 3062. Fax: 954-472-3088. E-mail: admissions@ahschool.com. Web site: www.ahschool.com.

See Display below and Close-Up on page 578.

AMERICAN INTERNATIONAL SCHOOL, DHAKA

PO Box 6106

Gulshan

Dhaka, Bangladesh

Head of School: Mr. Richard E. Boerner

General Information Coeducational day college-preparatory school. Grades PK–12. Founded: 1972. Setting: suburban. 4-acre campus. 1 building on campus. Approved or accredited by New England Association of Schools and Colleges. Language of instruction: English. Total enrollment: 753. Upper school average class size: 18. Upper school faculty-student ratio: 1:15. There are 180 required school days per year for Upper School students. Upper School students typically attend 5 days per week. The average school day consists of 6 hours and 42 minutes.

Upper School Student Profile Grade 9: 53 students (34 boys, 19 girls); Grade 10: 56 students (27 boys, 29 girls); Grade 11: 41 students (18 boys, 23 girls); Grade 12: 58 students (30 boys, 28 girls).

Faculty School total: 102. In upper school: 29 men, 17 women; 38 have advanced degrees.

Subjects Offered Algebra, American literature, art, biology, chemistry, choir, choral music, computer science, concert band, creative writing, critical writing, digital photography, drawing, economics, electives, English, English literature, environmental science, ESL, fine arts, fitness, French, geography, geometry, language arts, mathe-

matics, media arts, model United Nations, modern languages, modern world history, music, music theory, painting, physical education, physics, printmaking, psychology, science, sculpture, senior project, social studies, Spanish, speech, sports, study skills, symphonic band, theater arts, theory of knowledge, trigonometry, visual arts, women in literature, yearbook.
Special Academic Programs International Baccalaureate program; ESL.
College Admission Counseling 53 students graduated in 2010; all went to college, including Franklin & Marshall College; McGill University; The George Washington University; University of Toronto; Wellesley College. Mean SAT critical reading: 519, mean SAT math: 573, mean SAT writing: 516, mean combined SAT: 1608, mean composite ACT: 22. 27% scored over 600 on SAT critical reading, 42% scored over 600 on SAT math, 19% scored over 600 on SAT writing, 19% scored over 1800 on combined SAT, 18% scored over 26 on composite ACT.
Student Life Upper grades have student council, honor system. Discipline rests primarily with faculty.
Tuition and Aid Day student tuition: $18,820.
Admissions For fall 2010, 69 students applied for upper-level admission, 57 were accepted, 57 enrolled. School's own test required. Deadline for receipt of application materials: none. Application fee required: $50. On-campus interview required.
Athletics Interscholastic: basketball (boys, girls), cricket (b), soccer (b,g), swimming and diving (b,g), tennis (b,g), track and field (b,g), volleyball (b,g); intramural: basketball (b,g), soccer (b,g), swimming and diving (b,g), volleyball (b,g).
Computers Computers are regularly used in all academic classes. Computer network features include on-campus library services, online commercial services, Internet access, wireless campus network. Student e-mail accounts are available to students. Students grades are available online. The school has a published electronic and media policy.
Contact Mrs. Kanwal Bhagat, Registrar. 880-2 882 2452 Ext. 139. Fax: 880-2 882 3175. E-mail: aisdadmissions@ais-dhaka.net. Web site: www.ais-dhaka.net.

AMERICAN INTERNATIONAL SCHOOL OF COSTA RICA

Apartado Postal 4941-1000

Cariari

San Jose, Costa Rica

Head of School: Mr. Charles Ernest Prince

General Information Coeducational day college-preparatory, general academic, arts, technology, Spanish as a Second language, and English as a Second language school. Grades PK–12. Founded: 1970. Setting: suburban. 6-acre campus. 5 buildings on campus. Approved or accredited by Southern Association of Colleges and Schools, The College Board, and US Department of State. Languages of instruction: English and Spanish. Total enrollment: 199. Upper school average class size: 25. Upper school faculty-student ratio: 1:10. There are 184 required school days per year for Upper School students. Upper School students typically attend 5 days per week. The average school day consists of 6 hours.
Upper School Student Profile Grade 7: 15 students (7 boys, 8 girls); Grade 8: 13 students (5 boys, 8 girls); Grade 9: 13 students (8 boys, 5 girls); Grade 10: 14 students (7 boys, 7 girls); Grade 11: 9 students (5 boys, 4 girls); Grade 12: 11 students (8 boys, 3 girls).
Faculty School total: 32. In upper school: 10 men, 4 women; 6 have advanced degrees.
Subjects Offered Algebra, American literature, art, biology, biology-AP, chemistry, civics, college counseling, computer applications, computer skills, earth science, economics, English, English composition, environmental science, ESL, geometry, government/civics, health, history, language arts, mathematics, physical education, precalculus, science, social studies, Spanish, Spanish language-AP, Spanish-AP, technology, U.S. government, U.S. history, world history, yearbook.
Graduation Requirements American government, British literature, foreign language, music, physical education (includes health).
Special Academic Programs 5 Advanced Placement exams for which test preparation is offered; accelerated programs; independent study; remedial reading and/or remedial writing; remedial math; programs in English, mathematics, general development for dyslexic students; ESL (12 students enrolled).
College Admission Counseling 15 students graduated in 2010; 13 went to college, including University of Victoria. Other: 2 had other specific plans. Mean SAT critical reading: 460, mean SAT math: 600, mean SAT writing: 520, mean combined SAT: 1580. 5% scored over 600 on SAT critical reading, 10% scored over 600 on SAT math.
Student Life Upper grades have uniform requirement, student council, honor system. Discipline rests primarily with faculty.
Tuition and Aid Day student tuition: $6910. Tuition installment plan (monthly payment plans, annual payments with 10% discount, Semester payment with 5% discount). Tuition reduction for siblings available.
Admissions For fall 2010, 17 students applied for upper-level admission, 13 were accepted, 13 enrolled. School placement exam required. Deadline for receipt of application materials: none. No application fee required. On-campus interview required.
Athletics Interscholastic: basketball (boys, girls), football (b,g), gymnastics (g), outdoor activities (b,g), physical training (b,g), soccer (b,g), volleyball (b,g); intramural: basketball (b,g), football (b,g), soccer (b,g), volleyball (b,g). 1 PE instructor, 1 coach.
Computers Computers are regularly used in English, ESL, history, mathematics, science, Spanish, word processing, writing, yearbook classes. Computer network features include on-campus library services, Internet access, wireless campus network, Internet filtering or blocking technology, equipment support and software. Campus intranet and computer access in designated common areas are available to students. Students grades are available online. The school has a published electronic and media policy.
Contact Mrs. Ivania Quesada, Counselor. 011-506-2293-2567. Fax: 011-506-2239-0625. E-mail: counselor@aiscr.com. Web site: www.aiscr.com.

THE AMERICAN SCHOOL FOUNDATION

Bondojito 215

Colonia Las Americas

Mexico City, D.F. 01120, Mexico

Head of School: Mr. Paul Williams

General Information Coeducational day college-preparatory, arts, bilingual studies, and technology school. Grades PK–12. Founded: 1888. Setting: urban. Nearest major city is Mexico City, Mexico. 17-acre campus. 4 buildings on campus. Approved or accredited by International Baccalaureate Organization and Southern Association of Colleges and Schools. Affiliate member of National Association of Independent Schools. Languages of instruction: English and Spanish. Endowment: 102.5 million Mexican pesos. Total enrollment: 2,565. Upper school average class size: 18. Upper school faculty-student ratio: 1:13. There are 181 required school days per year for Upper School students. Upper School students typically attend 5 days per week. The average school day consists of 6 hours and 45 minutes.
Upper School Student Profile Grade 9: 180 students (78 boys, 102 girls); Grade 10: 174 students (82 boys, 92 girls); Grade 11: 183 students (98 boys, 85 girls); Grade 12: 182 students (98 boys, 84 girls).
Faculty School total: 252. In upper school: 29 men, 28 women, 39 have advanced degrees.
Subjects Offered Advanced Placement courses, algebra, American history, American literature, anatomy, art, art history, biology, calculus, ceramics, chemistry, community service, computer programming, computer science, drafting, drama, earth science, ecology, economics, English, English literature, European history, expository writing, film, fine arts, French, geography, geometry, government/civics, grammar, health, history, humanities, journalism, mathematics, Mexican history, music, philosophy, photography, physical education, physics, physiology, psychology, religion, science, social sciences, social studies, Spanish, speech, statistics, trigonometry, typing, world history, world literature, writing.
Graduation Requirements English, foreign language, foreign policy, mathematics, physical education (includes health), science, social sciences, social studies (includes history), IB Personal Project (10th grade).
Special Academic Programs International Baccalaureate program; 12 Advanced Placement exams for which test preparation is offered; independent study; remedial reading and/or remedial writing; remedial math; programs in English, mathematics, general development for dyslexic students; special instructional classes for learning disabilities (LD), Attention Deficit Hyperactivity Disorder (ADHD), and speech and language disorders.
College Admission Counseling 182 students graduated in 2011; 151 went to college, including Northeastern University; Savannah College of Art and Design; Universidad Iberoamericana; The University of British Columbia; The University of Texas at San Antonio. Other: 31 had other specific plans. Median SAT critical reading: 570, median SAT math: 580, median SAT writing: 580, median combined SAT: 1720, median composite ACT: 26. 38.7% scored over 600 on SAT critical reading, 45.9% scored over 600 on SAT math, 40.2% scored over 600 on SAT writing, 41.2% scored over 1800 on combined SAT, 53% scored over 26 on composite ACT.
Student Life Upper grades have specified standards of dress, student council. Discipline rests primarily with faculty.
Summer Programs Remediation programs offered; session focuses on remediation only at Upper School level; held on campus; accepts boys and girls; open to students from other schools. 11 students usually enrolled. 2012 schedule: June 18 to July 27. Application deadline: none.
Tuition and Aid Day student tuition: 154,800 Mexican pesos. Tuition installment plan (monthly payment plans, Tuition Insurance). Merit scholarship grants, need-based scholarship grants available. In 2011–12, 39% of upper-school students received aid. Total amount of financial aid awarded in 2011–12: 9,000,000 Mexican pesos.
Admissions Traditional secondary-level entrance grade is 10. For fall 2011, 205 students applied for upper-level admission, 101 were accepted, 97 enrolled. Deadline for receipt of application materials: none. Application fee required: 1000 Mexican pesos. On-campus interview required.
Athletics Interscholastic: basketball (boys, girls), dance team (g), football (b), soccer (b,g), swimming and diving (b,g), volleyball (g); coed interscholastic: running, tennis. 2 PE instructors, 23 coaches, 1 athletic trainer.

Computers Computers are regularly used in all academic classes. Computer network features include on-campus library services, online commercial services, Internet access, wireless campus network, Internet filtering or blocking technology. Campus intranet, student e-mail accounts, and computer access in designated common areas are available to students. Students grades are available online. The school has a published electronic and media policy.

Contact Patricia Hubp, Director of Admission. 52-555-227-4900. Fax: 52-55273-4357. E-mail: martindehubp@asf.edu.mx. Web site: www.asf.edu.mx.

THE AMERICAN SCHOOL IN LONDON

One Waverley Place

London NW8 0NP, United Kingdom

Head of School: Coreen R. Hester

General Information Coeducational day college-preparatory school. Grades PK–12. Founded: 1951. Setting: urban. 3-acre campus. 1 building on campus. Approved or accredited by Middle States Association of Colleges and Schools. Affiliate member of National Association of Independent Schools; member of Secondary School Admission Test Board. Language of instruction: English. Endowment: £12 million. Total enrollment: 1,350. Upper school average class size: 15. Upper school faculty-student ratio: 1:10. There are 172 required school days per year for Upper School students. Upper School students typically attend 5 days per week. The average school day consists of 5 hours and 50 minutes.

Upper School Student Profile Grade 9: 127 students (68 boys, 59 girls); Grade 10: 123 students (66 boys, 57 girls); Grade 11: 115 students (67 boys, 48 girls); Grade 12: 103 students (56 boys, 47 girls).

Faculty School total: 112. In upper school: 17 men, 30 women; 36 have advanced degrees.

Subjects Offered Acting, African studies, algebra, American literature, anatomy and physiology, Arabic, architectural drawing, art, art history-AP, astronomy, biology, biology-AP, British literature, calculus, calculus-AP, chemistry, chemistry-AP, Chinese, Chinese studies, computer applications, computer science-AP, concert band, concert choir, dance, digital imaging, digital music, digital photography, drawing, ecology, economics, environmental science, European history, European history-AP, film, French, French language-AP, French literature-AP, genetics, geometry, German, health, human geography - AP, independent study, Japanese, jazz band, journalism, Latin, macro/microeconomics-AP, Middle East, modern European history-AP, music theory-AP, mythology, orchestra, painting, photography, physical education, physics-AP, play production, poetry, pre-calculus, psychology, psychology-AP, Russian, Russian literature, Russian studies, Shakespeare, Spanish, Spanish language-AP, Spanish literature-AP, statistics-AP, studio art-AP, trigonometry, U.S. history, U.S. history-AP, video and animation, video film production, world civilizations, world geography, writing, yearbook.

Graduation Requirements Arts and fine arts (art, music, dance, drama), English, foreign language, mathematics, physical education (includes health), science, social studies (includes history), technology.

Special Academic Programs Advanced Placement exam preparation; independent study; programs in general development for dyslexic students; ESL (41 students enrolled).

College Admission Counseling 111 students graduated in 2011; 109 went to college, including Brown University; Emory University, Oxford College; Georgetown University; New York University; Princeton University; University of Southern California. Other: 2 had other specific plans. Mean SAT critical reading: 659, mean SAT math: 669, mean SAT writing: 669.

Student Life Upper grades have student council, honor system. Discipline rests primarily with faculty.

Tuition and Aid Day student tuition: £22,550. Tuition installment plan (monthly payment plans, individually arranged payment plans). Need-based scholarship grants available. In 2011–12, 5% of upper-school students received aid. Total amount of financial aid awarded in 2011–12: £411,850.

Admissions ERB, ISEE, PSAT or SAT required. Deadline for receipt of application materials: none. Application fee required: £150.

Athletics Interscholastic: baseball (boys), basketball (b,g), cheering (g), crew (b,g), cross-country running (b,g), dance (g), field hockey (g), rugby (b), soccer (b,g), softball (g), swimming and diving (b,g), tennis (b,g), track and field (b,g), volleyball (b,g); coed interscholastic: golf; coed intramural: badminton, kickball, soccer, swimming and diving, tennis. 3 PE instructors, 52 coaches.

Computers Computers are regularly used in animation, English, foreign language, journalism, mathematics, media arts, media production, science, social studies, video film production, Web site design, yearbook classes. Computer network features include on-campus library services, Internet access, wireless campus network. Student e-mail accounts are available to students. Students grades are available online.

Contact Jodi Coats, Dean of Admissions. 44-20-7449-1221. Fax: 44-20-7449-1350. E-mail: admissions@asl.org. Web site: www.asl.org.

See Display below and Close-Up on page 580.

AMERICAN SCHOOL OF BOMBAY

SF2, G Block
Bandra Kurla Complex Road
Mumbai 400 098, India

Head of School: Mr. Craig Johnson

General Information Coeducational day college-preparatory school. Grades PK–12. Founded: 1981. Setting: urban. 2-acre campus. 1 building on campus. Approved or accredited by Middle States Association of Colleges and Schools and National Independent Private Schools Association. Member of European Council of International Schools. Language of instruction: English. Total enrollment: 700. Upper school average class size: 18. Upper school faculty-student ratio: 1:5. There are 183 required school days per year for Upper School students. Upper School students typically attend 5 days per week. The average school day consists of 5 hours and 40 minutes.

Upper School Student Profile Grade 6: 41 students (23 boys, 18 girls); Grade 7: 51 students (30 boys, 21 girls); Grade 8: 60 students (31 boys, 29 girls); Grade 9: 51 students (26 boys, 25 girls); Grade 10: 42 students (12 boys, 30 girls); Grade 11: 44 students (18 boys, 26 girls); Grade 12: 43 students (19 boys, 24 girls).

Faculty School total: 100. In upper school: 18 men, 23 women; 35 have advanced degrees.

Special Academic Programs International Baccalaureate program; ESL (16 students enrolled).

College Admission Counseling 30 students graduated in 2010; 29 went to college. Other: 1 had other specific plans. Median SAT critical reading: 600, median SAT math: 600, median SAT writing: 635, median combined SAT: 1845.

Student Life Upper grades have specified standards of dress, student council, honor system. Discipline rests primarily with faculty.

Admissions For fall 2010, 43 students applied for upper-level admission, 29 were accepted, 25 enrolled. Deadline for receipt of application materials: none. Application fee required: $250.

Athletics Interscholastic: aquatics (boys, girls), badminton (b,g), basketball (b,g), soccer (b,g), tennis (b,g), track and field (b,g), volleyball (b,g); coed intramural: cricket, floor hockey, Frisbee, indoor track, juggling, life saving. 4 PE instructors, 20 coaches.

Computers Computer resources include on-campus library services, online commercial services, Internet access, wireless campus network, Internet filtering or blocking technology, 1-1 laptop program. Campus intranet and student e-mail accounts are available to students. Students grades are available online. The school has a published electronic and media policy.

Contact Ms. Vanita Barrett, Admissions Assistant. 91-22-6772-7272 Ext. 322. Fax: 91-22-2652-6666. E-mail: admissionassistant@asbindia.org. Web site: www.asbindia.org.

THE AMERICAN SCHOOL OF MADRID

Apartado 80
Madrid 28080, Spain

Head of School: Mr. William D. O'Hale

General Information Coeducational day college-preparatory, arts, and technology school. Grades PK–12. Founded: 1961. Setting: suburban. 4-hectare campus. 2 buildings on campus. Approved or accredited by International Baccalaureate Organization and Middle States Association of Colleges and Schools. Affiliate member of National Association of Independent Schools; member of European Council of International Schools. Language of instruction: English. Total enrollment: 868. Upper school average class size: 20. Upper school faculty-student ratio: 1:8. There are 175 required school days per year for Upper School students. Upper School students typically attend 5 days per week. The average school day consists of 6 hours and 45 minutes.

Upper School Student Profile Grade 9: 67 students (37 boys, 30 girls); Grade 10: 72 students (38 boys, 34 girls); Grade 11: 73 students (38 boys, 35 girls); Grade 12: 72 students (31 boys, 41 girls).

Faculty School total: 103. In upper school: 20 men, 15 women; 30 have advanced degrees.

Subjects Offered 3-dimensional art, algebra, American history, American literature, art, biology, business studies, calculus, chemistry, choir, computer math, computer science, computer skills, computer-aided design, creative writing, debate, earth science, English, English literature, environmental science, European history, expository writing, French, geography, geometry, government/civics, health, history, instrumental music, jazz band, journalism, mathematics, music, orchestra, philosophy, physical education, physics, psychology, science, social studies, Spanish, speech, U.S. history, world history, world literature, world wide web design, yearbook.

Graduation Requirements Electives, English, foreign language, information technology, mathematics, physical education (includes health), science, social studies (includes history).

Special Academic Programs International Baccalaureate program; independent study; ESL (50 students enrolled).

College Admission Counseling 65 students graduated in 2010; 63 went to college, including Georgetown University; New York University; Saint Louis University; Suffolk University; The University of Tampa. Other: 2 entered military service. Mean SAT critical reading: 551, mean SAT math: 566, mean SAT writing: 558.

Student Life Upper grades have specified standards of dress, student council, honor system. Discipline rests equally with students and faculty.

Tuition and Aid Day student tuition: €17,415. Tuition installment plan (monthly payment plans, individually arranged payment plans, semester payment plan). Tuition reduction for siblings, need-based scholarship grants, scholarships for children of employees available. In 2010–11, 5% of upper-school students received aid.

Admissions Traditional secondary-level entrance grade is 11. For fall 2010, 83 students applied for upper-level admission, 50 were accepted, 50 enrolled. Achievement/Aptitude/Writing, Comprehensive Test of Basic Skills, ERB, independent norms, Iowa Tests of Basic Skills, PSAT or TAP required. Deadline for receipt of application materials: none. Application fee required: €140. On-campus interview required.

Athletics Interscholastic: basketball (boys, girls), soccer (b,g), volleyball (b,g); coed interscholastic: golf, gymnastics, martial arts, tennis; coed intramural: weight lifting. 2 PE instructors, 7 coaches.

Computers Computers are regularly used in all classes. Computer network features include on-campus library services, Internet access, wireless campus network, Internet filtering or blocking technology. Campus intranet is available to students. The school has a published electronic and media policy.

Contact Ms. Sholeh Farpour, Admissions Head. 34-91 740 1904. Fax: 34-91 357 2678. E-mail: admissions@asmadrid.org. Web site: www.asmadrid.org.

AMERICAN SCHOOL OF MILAN

Via K. Marx 14
Noverasco di Opera, Milan 20090, Italy

Head of School: Dr. Alan Austen

General Information Coeducational day college-preparatory, bilingual studies, and International Baccalaureate school. Grades N–12. Founded: 1962. Setting: suburban. Nearest major city is Milan, Italy. 9-acre campus. 1 building on campus. Approved or accredited by Department of Defense Dependents Schools, International Baccalaureate Organization, Middle States Association of Colleges and Schools, and US Department of State. Affiliate member of National Association of Independent Schools; member of European Council of International Schools. Language of instruction: English. Total enrollment: 658. Upper school average class size: 20. Upper school faculty-student ratio: 1:9. Upper School students typically attend 5 days per week.

Faculty School total: 74. In upper school: 7 men, 18 women; 19 have advanced degrees.

Subjects Offered Algebra, art, biology, business studies, calculus, chemistry, community service, computer programming, computer science, creative writing, ecology, economics, English, English literature, ESL, European history, expository writing, fine arts, French, geology, geometry, grammar, history, Italian, mathematics, music, physical education, physics, psychology, science, social sciences, social studies, theory of knowledge, trigonometry, world history, world literature, writing.

Graduation Requirements Arts and fine arts (art, music, dance, drama), computer science, English, foreign language, mathematics, physical education (includes health), science, social sciences, social studies (includes history), 100 hours of CAS (Creativity, Action, Service) each year.

Special Academic Programs International Baccalaureate program; independent study; remedial reading and/or remedial writing; remedial math; ESL (14 students enrolled).

College Admission Counseling 49 students graduated in 2010; 47 went to college. Other: 2 had other specific plans.

Student Life Upper grades have specified standards of dress, student council, honor system. Discipline rests primarily with faculty.

Tuition and Aid Day student tuition: €8290–€17,150. Tuition installment plan (individually arranged payment plans).

Admissions Traditional secondary-level entrance grade is 9. For fall 2010, 229 students applied for upper-level admission, 183 were accepted, 178 enrolled. Admissions testing, English for Non-native Speakers, English proficiency and mathematics proficiency exam required. Deadline for receipt of application materials: none. Application fee required: €250. On-campus interview recommended.

Athletics Interscholastic: basketball (boys, girls), cross-country running (b,g), dance team (g), soccer (b,g), tennis (b,g), track and field (b,g), volleyball (b,g); intramural: golf (b,g); coed interscholastic: aerobics/dance; coed intramural: aerobics/dance, ballet, basketball, martial arts, soccer, softball, swimming and diving, table tennis, tennis, volleyball. 3 PE instructors, 4 coaches.

Computers Computers are regularly used in college planning, desktop publishing, ESL, English, ESL, history, humanities, journalism, library, library skills, literary magazine, mathematics, media arts, research skills, science, technology, writing, yearbook classes. Computer network features include on-campus library services, online commercial services, Internet access, wireless campus network, Internet filtering or blocking technology. Student e-mail accounts and computer access in designated common areas are available to students. Students grades are available online. The school has a published electronic and media policy.

Contact Ms. Neda Buncic, Admissions Assistant. 39-02-53000015. Fax: 39-02-93660932. E-mail: admissions@asmilan.org. Web site: www.asmilan.org.

AMERICAN SCHOOL OF THE HAGUE

Rijksstraatweg 200

Wassenaar 2241 BX, Netherlands

Head of School: Richard Spradling

General Information Coeducational day college-preparatory, arts, technology, and applied and performing arts school. Grades PS–12. Founded: 1953. Setting: suburban. Nearest major city is The Hague, Netherlands. 11-acre campus. 1 building on campus. Approved or accredited by International Baccalaureate Organization, Middle States Association of Colleges and Schools, The College Board, and US Department of State. Language of instruction: English. Total enrollment: 1,035. Upper school average class size: 18. Upper school faculty-student ratio: 1:7. There are 183 required school days per year for Upper School students. Upper School students typically attend 5 days per week. The average school day consists of 6 hours.

Upper School Student Profile Grade 9: 77 students (35 boys, 42 girls); Grade 10: 86 students (48 boys, 38 girls); Grade 11: 104 students (51 boys, 53 girls); Grade 12: 96 students (58 boys, 38 girls).

Faculty School total: 144. In upper school: 24 men, 29 women; 42 have advanced degrees.

Subjects Offered Advanced chemistry, advertising design, algebra, American literature, art history, art-AP, band, biology, biology-AP, calculus, calculus-AP, chemistry, chemistry-AP, choir, comparative government and politics, computer applications, computer multimedia, computer music, computer science, computer-aided design, creative writing, current events, dance, debate, dramatic arts, Dutch, economics, economics-AP, English, English literature, English-AP, environmental systems, ESL, European history, French, French-AP, geometry, German, German-AP, global studies, guidance, health and wellness, honors algebra, honors geometry, human geography - AP, information technology, instrumental music, international affairs, International Baccalaureate courses, jazz band, math analysis, math methods, mathematics-AP, multimedia, music composition, music technology, music theory-AP, music-AP, orchestra, peer counseling, photography, physical education, physics, physics-AP, pre-calculus, programming, psychology, public speaking, senior composition, sociology, Spanish, Spanish-AP, speech and debate, stagecraft, student publications, studio art, theater arts, theater design and production, theory of knowledge, trigonometry, U.S. history, U.S. history-AP, video film production, Web site design, Western civilization, world history, writing, yearbook.

Graduation Requirements Arts, computer information systems, electives, English, health and wellness, human issues, lab science, mathematics, modern languages, physical education (includes health), science, service learning/internship, social studies (includes history), technology.

Special Academic Programs International Baccalaureate program; Advanced Placement exam preparation; honors section; independent study; academic accommodation for the gifted, the musically talented, and the artistically talented; remedial reading and/or remedial writing.

College Admission Counseling 89 students graduated in 2010; 87 went to college, including Massachusetts Institute of Technology; Parsons The New School for Design; Queen's University at Kingston; United States Air Force Academy; Vassar College; Virginia Polytechnic Institute and State University. Other: 1 entered military service, 1 had other specific plans. Mean SAT critical reading: 570, mean SAT math: 597, mean SAT writing: 560, mean combined SAT: 1727.

Student Life Upper grades have specified standards of dress, student council, honor system. Discipline rests primarily with faculty.

Tuition and Aid Day student tuition: €17,320. Tuition installment plan (individually arranged payment plans).

Admissions For fall 2010, 84 students applied for upper-level admission, 78 were accepted, 65 enrolled. Deadline for receipt of application materials: none. No application fee required. Interview recommended.

Athletics Interscholastic: baseball (boys), basketball (b,g), cross-country running (b,g), soccer (b,g), softball (g), swimming and diving (b,g), tennis (b,g), track and field (b,g), volleyball (b,g); intramural: baseball (b), basketball (b,g), cheering (g), cross-country running (b,g), dance team (g), soccer (b,g), softball (g), volleyball (b,g); coed intramural: cheering. 2 PE instructors, 9 coaches.

Computers Computers are regularly used in all classes. Computer network features include on-campus library services, online commercial services, Internet access, wireless campus network, Internet filtering or blocking technology. Campus intranet, student e-mail accounts, and computer access in designated common areas are available to students. Students grades are available online. The school has a published electronic and media policy.

Contact Admissions Office. 31-70-512-1080. Fax: 31-70-512-1076. E-mail: admissions@ash.nl. Web site: www.ash.nl.

ANACAPA SCHOOL

814 Santa Barbara Street

Santa Barbara, California 93101

Head of School: Mr. Gordon Sichi

General Information Coeducational day college-preparatory and arts school. Grades 7–12. Founded: 1981. Setting: urban. 2 buildings on campus. Approved or accredited by Western Association of Schools and Colleges and California Department of Education. Total enrollment: 49. Upper school average class size: 12. Upper school faculty-student ratio: 1:9. Upper School students typically attend 5 days per week. The average school day consists of 7 hours and 10 minutes.

Upper School Student Profile Grade 9: 13 students (6 boys, 7 girls); Grade 10: 4 students (2 boys, 2 girls); Grade 11: 8 students (6 boys, 2 girls); Grade 12: 12 students (4 boys, 8 girls).

Faculty School total: 12. In upper school: 5 men, 5 women; 4 have advanced degrees.

Special Academic Programs Advanced Placement exam preparation.

College Admission Counseling 11 students graduated in 2011; all went to college, including Santa Barbara City College; University of California, Los Angeles; Westmont College.

Student Life Upper grades have specified standards of dress, student council, honor system. Discipline rests primarily with faculty.

Tuition and Aid Day student tuition: $23. Tuition installment plan (individually arranged payment plans). Merit scholarship grants, need-based scholarship grants, paying campus jobs available. In 2011–12, 69% of upper-school students received aid.

Admissions Traditional secondary-level entrance grade is 9. For fall 2011, 6 students applied for upper-level admission, 6 were accepted, 5 enrolled. Deadline for receipt of application materials: none. Application fee required: $100. On-campus interview required.

Athletics Coed Intramural: aquatics, backpacking, basketball, canoeing/kayaking, dance, fitness, flag football, hiking/backpacking, jogging, kayaking, outdoor activities, outdoor adventure, running, sailing, scuba diving, skiing (downhill), soccer, softball, squash, surfing, swimming and diving, table tennis, yoga.

Computers Computer resources include Internet access, wireless campus network, Internet filtering or blocking technology. Computer access in designated common areas is available to students.

Contact Ms. Sheryn Sears, Executive Administrator. 805-965-0228. Fax: 805-899-2758. E-mail: anacapa@anacapaschool.org. Web site: www.anacapaschool.org.

ANNIE WRIGHT SCHOOL

827 North Tacoma Avenue

Tacoma, Washington 98403

Head of School: Mr. Christian Sullivan

General Information Girls' boarding and coeducational day college-preparatory, arts, technology, and mathematics, science and music school, affiliated with Episcopal Church. Boarding girls grades 9–12, day boys grades PS–8, day girls grades PS–12. Founded: 1884. Setting: suburban. Nearest major city is Seattle. Students are housed in single-sex dormitories. 10-acre campus. 2 buildings on campus. Approved or accredited by National Association of Episcopal Schools, National Independent Private Schools Association, Northwest Association of Schools and Colleges, Pacific Northwest Association of Independent Schools, The Association of Boarding Schools, and Washington Department of Education. Member of National Association of Independent Schools and Secondary School Admission Test Board. Endowment: $13 million. Total enrollment: 441. Upper school average class size: 11. Upper school faculty-student ratio: 1:7.

Upper School Student Profile Grade 9: 40 students (40 girls); Grade 10: 42 students (42 girls); Grade 11: 41 students (41 girls); Grade 12: 33 students (33 girls). 51% of students are boarding students. 64% are state residents. 7 states are represented in upper school student body. 33% are international students. International students from Bermuda, China, Republic of Korea, Romania, Taiwan, and Venezuela; 7 other countries represented in student body. 10% of students are members of Episcopal Church.

Faculty School total: 74. In upper school: 12 men, 17 women; 15 have advanced degrees; 6 reside on campus.

Subjects Offered Algebra, American history, American literature, anatomy, art, art history, biology, calculus, ceramics, chemistry, computer programming, computer science, creative writing, dance, drama, earth science, economics, English, English literature, ESL, fine arts, French, geometry, government/civics, health, history, Japanese, mathematics, music, music history, physical education, physics, religion, science, social studies, Spanish, theater, world history, world literature.

Graduation Requirements Arts and fine arts (art, music, dance, drama), computer science, English, foreign language, mathematics, physical education (includes health), religion (includes Bible studies and theology), science, social studies (includes history), swim safety test.

Special Academic Programs International Baccalaureate program; independent study; term-away projects; study abroad; ESL (55 students enrolled).

College Admission Counseling 16 students graduated in 2011; 15 went to college, including Brown University; Cornell University; Macalester College; Rhode Island School of Design; Rice University; University of Michigan–Dearborn. Other: 1 had other specific plans. Mean SAT critical reading: 585, mean SAT math: 661, mean SAT writing: 622, mean combined SAT: 1860.

Student Life Upper grades have uniform requirement, student council, honor system. Discipline rests equally with students and faculty.

Tuition and Aid Day student tuition: $22,750; 5-day tuition and room/board: $32,950; 7-day tuition and room/board: $46,950. Tuition installment plan (monthly payment plans, individually arranged payment plans). Merit scholarship grants, need-based scholarship grants available. In 2011–12, 33% of upper-school students received aid; total upper-school merit-scholarship money awarded: $300,000. Total amount of financial aid awarded in 2011–12: $300,000.

Admissions Traditional secondary-level entrance grade is 9. ISEE and TOEFL required. Deadline for receipt of application materials: January 20. Application fee required: $100. Interview required.

Athletics Interscholastic: basketball, crew, cross-country running, golf, soccer. 5 PE instructors, 10 coaches, 1 athletic trainer.

Computers Computers are regularly used in all academic classes. Computer network features include on-campus library services, Internet access. Student e-mail accounts are available to students.

Contact Ms. Stacey Guadnola, Director of Admissions. 253-284-8601. Fax: 253-572-3616. E-mail: stacey_guadnola@aw.org. Web site: www.aw.org.

ARCHBISHOP ALTER HIGH SCHOOL

940 East David Road

Kettering, Ohio 45429-5512

Head of School: Mrs. Nicole Brainard

General Information Coeducational day college preparatory, general academic, and arts school, affiliated with Roman Catholic Church. Grades 9–12. Founded: 1962. Setting: suburban. Nearest major city is Dayton. 3 buildings on campus. Approved or accredited by North Central Association of Colleges and Schools, Ohio Catholic Schools Accreditation Association (OCSAA), and Ohio Department of Education. Total enrollment: 650. Upper school average class size: 25. Upper school faculty-student ratio: 1:15. There are 185 required school days per year for Upper School students.

Upper School Student Profile Grade 9: 164 students (92 boys, 72 girls); Grade 10: 170 students (84 boys, 86 girls); Grade 11: 170 students (90 boys, 80 girls); Grade 12: 146 students (69 boys, 77 girls). 90% of students are Roman Catholic.

Faculty School total: 62. In upper school: 19 men, 30 women; 38 have advanced degrees.

Subjects Offered Accounting, advanced chemistry, advanced math, Advanced Placement courses, algebra, American Civil War, American government, American history, American history-AP, American literature, American literature-AP, analysis and differential calculus, analytic geometry, anatomy and physiology, band, Basic programming, biology-AP, British literature, business, business law, calculus, calculus-AP, Catholic belief and practice, chemistry, chemistry-AP, choir, choral music, Christian and Hebrew scripture, church history, Civil War, civil war history, costumes and make-up, ecology, environmental systems, economics, English, English literature, French, health, history, history of the Catholic Church, honors algebra, honors English, honors geometry, honors U.S. history, integrated mathematics, introduction to theater, keyboarding, Latin, marching band, mechanical drawing, music appreciation, personal finance, physical fitness, physics, physics-AP, pre-calculus, public speaking, reading/study skills, Spanish, speech, theater arts, U.S. government and politics-AP, U.S. history, U.S. history-AP.

Graduation Requirements Arts and fine arts (art, music, dance, drama), English, health, keyboarding, mathematics, physical education (includes health), science, social studies (includes history), speech, theology, word processing, Additional requirements for students enrolled in the Alter Scholars Program or Conservatory for the Arts.

Special Academic Programs Advanced Placement exam preparation; honors section; study at local college for college credit.

College Admission Counseling 156 students graduated in 2010; 153 went to college, including Miami University; Ohio University; The Ohio State University; University of Cincinnati; University of Dayton; Wright State University. Other: 2 went to work, 1 had other specific plans. Mean SAT critical reading: 580, mean SAT math: 600, mean SAT writing: 560, mean combined SAT: 1180, mean composite ACT: 25.

Student Life Upper grades have uniform requirement, student council, honor system. Discipline rests equally with students and faculty. Attendance at religious services is required.

Tuition and Aid Day student tuition: $5750–$8095. Tuition installment plan (FACTS Tuition Payment Plan). Tuition reduction for siblings, merit scholarship grants, need-based scholarship grants available. In 2010–11, 15% of upper-school students received aid; total upper-school merit-scholarship money awarded: $32,000. Total amount of financial aid awarded in 2010–11: $150,000.

Admissions Traditional secondary-level entrance grade is 9. For fall 2010, 190 students applied for upper-level admission, 185 were accepted, 170 enrolled. Scholastic Testing Service High School Placement Test (open version) or STS required. Deadline for receipt of application materials: none. Application fee required: $100.

Athletics Interscholastic: baseball (boys), basketball (b,g), bowling (b,g), cheering (g), cross-country running (b,g), dance team (g), diving (b,g), football (b), golf (b,g), gymnastics (g), ice hockey (b,g), lacrosse (b), soccer (b,g), softball (g), strength & conditioning (b,g), swimming and diving (b,g), tennis (b,g), track and field (b,g), volleyball (b,g), wrestling (b). 2 PE instructors, 3 coaches, 1 athletic trainer.

Computers Computer network features include Internet access, wireless campus network, Internet filtering or blocking technology. Campus intranet and student e-mail accounts are available to students. Students grades are available online. The school has a published electronic and media policy.

Contact Mrs. Mary Ruth Shearer, Director of Enrollment Management and Marketing. 937-428-5394. Fax: 937-434-0507. E-mail: mshearer@alterhighschool.org. Web site: www.alterhighschool.org.

ARCHBISHOP CURLEY HIGH SCHOOL

3701 Sinclair Lane

Baltimore, Maryland 21213

Head of School: Fr. Joseph Benicewicz

General Information Boys' day college-preparatory school, affiliated with Roman Catholic Church. Grades 9–12. Founded: 1961. Setting: urban. 33-acre campus. 3 buildings on campus. Approved or accredited by Middle States Association of Colleges and Schools and Maryland Department of Education. Endowment: $3.2 million. Total enrollment: 526. Upper school average class size: 22. Upper school faculty-student ratio: 1:14. Upper School students typically attend 5 days per week. The average school day consists of 6 hours and 30 minutes.

Upper School Student Profile Grade 9: 135 students (135 boys); Grade 10: 135 students (135 boys); Grade 11: 132 students (132 boys); Grade 12: 124 students (124 boys). 70% of students are Roman Catholic.

Faculty School total: 52. In upper school: 41 men, 11 women; 24 have advanced degrees.

Subjects Offered 20th century world history, 3-dimensional design, accounting, advanced chemistry, advanced computer applications, advanced math, algebra, American government, American history, American history-AP, American literature, analytic geometry, art, art appreciation, astronomy, band, Basic programming, biology, biology-AP, British literature, British literature (honors), business law, business mathematics, calculus, calculus-AP, campus ministry, Catholic belief and practice, chemistry, chemistry-AP, choral music, Christian and Hebrew scripture, Christian doctrine, Christian ethics, computer applications, computer studies, concert band, consumer law, consumer mathematics, earth science, English, English literature and composition-AP, environmental science, ethical decision making, European history, fine arts, French, freshman seminar, geography, geometry, government, government-AP, health, history of the Catholic Church, HTML design, instrumental music, jazz band, journalism, keyboarding, Latin, Life of Christ, music theory, photography, physical science, physics, physics-AP, pre-algebra, pre-calculus, probability and statistics, psychology, psychology-AP, reading/study skills, SAT/ACT preparation, Spanish, Spanish language-AP, U.S. government and politics-AP.

Graduation Requirements Algebra, American government, American history, art appreciation, biology, British literature, chemistry, church history, computer applications, English, foreign language, geometry, keyboarding, Life of Christ, physical fitness, physics, world history, world religions, 30 hours of community service with a written paper.

Special Academic Programs Advanced Placement exam preparation; honors section; independent study; study at local college for college credit; remedial reading and/or remedial writing; remedial math; programs in English, mathematics for dyslexic students.

College Admission Counseling 139 students graduated in 2011; they went to Frostburg State University; Loyola University Maryland; Mount St. Mary's University; Stevenson University; Towson University; York College of Pennsylvania.

Student Life Upper grades have specified standards of dress, student council, honor system. Discipline rests primarily with faculty. Attendance at religious services is required.

Summer Programs Remediation, enrichment, advancement, sports, art/fine arts, computer instruction programs offered; held on campus; accepts boys and girls; open to students from other schools. 2012 schedule: June 15 to August 20. Application deadline: June 15.

Tuition and Aid Day student tuition: $11,200. Tuition installment plan (Academic Management Services Plan, monthly payment plans, individually arranged payment plans). Tuition reduction for siblings, merit scholarship grants, need-based scholarship grants, paying campus jobs available.

Admissions Traditional secondary-level entrance grade is 9. For fall 2011, 300 students applied for upper-level admission, 135 enrolled. High School Placement Test (closed version) from Scholastic Testing Service required. Deadline for receipt of application materials: December 31. Application fee required: $10. Interview required.

Athletics Interscholastic: baseball, basketball, cross-country running, football, golf, indoor track & field, lacrosse, soccer, tennis, track and field, volleyball, wrestling; intramural: basketball, flag football, Frisbee, handball, martial arts, touch football, weight lifting, weight training. 2 PE instructors, 32 coaches, 1 athletic trainer.

Computers Computers are regularly used in creative writing, English, graphic arts, journalism, library, photography, SAT preparation, science, technology classes. Computer network features include on-campus library services, Internet access, wireless campus network, Internet filtering or blocking technology. Student e-mail accounts are available to students. Students grades are available online. The school has a published electronic and media policy.

Contact Mr. John Tucker, Admissions Director. 410-485-5000 Ext. 289. Fax: 410-485-1090. E-mail: jtucker@archbishopcurley.org. Web site: www.archbishopcurley.org.

ARCHBISHOP HOBAN HIGH SCHOOL

1 Holy Cross Boulevard

Akron, Ohio 44306

Head of School: Br. Kenneth Haders, CSC

General Information Coeducational day college-preparatory, arts, business, religious studies, technology, and family and consumer sciences school, affiliated with Roman Catholic Church. Grades 9–12. Founded: 1953. Setting: urban. 75-acre campus. 3 buildings on campus. Approved or accredited by National Catholic Education Association, North Central Association of Colleges and Schools, Ohio Catholic Schools Accreditation Association (OCSAA), and Ohio Department of Education. Endowment: $6 million. Total enrollment: 849. Upper school average class size: 23. Upper school faculty-student ratio: 1:13. There are 178 required school days per year for Upper School students. Upper School students typically attend 5 days per week. The average school day consists of 6 hours and 55 minutes.

Upper School Student Profile Grade 9: 220 students (109 boys, 111 girls); Grade 10: 215 students (110 boys, 105 girls); Grade 11: 197 students (95 boys, 102 girls); Grade 12: 216 students (96 boys, 120 girls). 82% of students are Roman Catholic.

Faculty School total: 56. In upper school: 26 men, 30 women; 48 have advanced degrees.

Subjects Offered Advanced Placement courses, advanced studio art-AP, algebra, American literature, anatomy and physiology, art, astronomy, biology, biology-AP, British literature, calculus-AP, Catholic belief and practice, ceramics, chemistry, chemistry-AP, child development, Chinese, choir, Christian and Hebrew scripture, church history, computer applications, computer graphics, conceptual physics, concert choir, desktop publishing, digital imaging, digital music, drawing, earth science, economics, electronic music, engineering, English, English literature and composition-AP, ensembles, environmental science, European history-AP, fine arts, food and nutrition, French, geometry, guitar, health education, history of the Catholic Church, honors algebra, honors English, honors geometry, honors world history, human anatomy, Italian, Latin, learning strategies, moral and social development, newspaper, orchestra, painting, philosophy, physical education, physics, physics-AP, pre-algebra, pre-calculus, printmaking, social justice, Spanish, statistics-AP, studio art, television, trigonometry, U.S. government, U.S. history, U.S. history-AP, values and decisions, Web site design, world cultures, world literature, yearbook.

Graduation Requirements Algebra, arts and fine arts (art, music, dance, drama), biology, economics, electives, English, health education, mathematics, physical education (includes health), religious studies, science, social studies (includes history), U.S. government, Christian service totaling 75 hours over four years.

Special Academic Programs 9 Advanced Placement exams for which test preparation is offered; honors section; academic accommodation for the gifted; remedial reading and/or remedial writing; remedial math.

College Admission Counseling 214 students graduated in 2011; 212 went to college, including Kent State University; Ohio University; The Ohio State University; The University of Akron; The University of Toledo; University of Dayton. Other: 1 went to work, 1 entered military service. Median SAT critical reading: 570, median SAT math: 570, median SAT writing: 560, median combined SAT: 1720, median composite ACT: 24. 44% scored over 600 on SAT critical reading, 46% scored over 600 on SAT math, 39% scored over 600 on SAT writing, 39% scored over 1800 on combined SAT, 40% scored over 26 on composite ACT.

Student Life Upper grades have specified standards of dress, student council, honor system. Discipline rests primarily with faculty. Attendance at religious services is required.

Tuition and Aid Day student tuition: $8880. Tuition installment plan (FACTS Tuition Payment Plan, individually arranged payment plans, Semester Payment Plan, Quarterly Payment Plan). Tuition reduction for siblings, merit scholarship grants, need-based scholarship grants, paying campus jobs available. In 2011–12, 40% of upper-school students received aid; total upper-school merit-scholarship money awarded: $250,000. Total amount of financial aid awarded in 2011–12: $2,200,000.

Admissions Traditional secondary-level entrance grade is 9. For fall 2011, 305 students applied for upper-level admission, 250 were accepted, 240 enrolled. High School Placement Test required. Deadline for receipt of application materials: none. No application fee required. Interview recommended.

Athletics Interscholastic: baseball (boys), basketball (b,g), bowling (b,g), cross-country running (b,g), dance team (g), football (b), golf (b,g), gymnastics (g), ice hockey (b), indoor track & field (b), lacrosse (b), soccer (b,g), softball (g), swimming and diving (b,g), tennis (b,g), track and field (b,g), volleyball (b,g), wrestling (b); intramural: flag football (g); coed interscholastic: cheering; coed intramural: basketball, strength & conditioning, ultimate Frisbee, weight training. 1 PE instructor, 1 athletic trainer.

Computers Computers are regularly used in desktop publishing, graphic design, newspaper, science, video film production, Web site design, yearbook classes. Computer network features include on-campus library services, Internet access, wireless campus network, Internet filtering or blocking technology. Campus intranet, student e-mail accounts, and computer access in designated common areas are available to students. Students grades are available online. The school has a published electronic and media policy.

Contact Mr. Christopher Fahey, Admissions Counselor. 330-773-6658 Ext. 215. Fax: 330-773-9100. E-mail: Faheyc@hoban.org. Web site: www.hoban.org.

ARCHBISHOP MCNICHOLAS HIGH SCHOOL

6536 Beechmont Avenue

Cincinnati, Ohio 45230-2098

Head of School: Mr. Gregory R. Saelens

General Information Coeducational day college-preparatory, general academic, arts, business, technology, and services for the Learning Disabled school, affiliated with Roman Catholic Church. Grades 9–12. Founded: 1951. Setting: suburban. 48-acre campus. 3 buildings on campus. Approved or accredited by North Central Association of Colleges and Schools, Ohio Catholic Schools Accreditation Association (OCSAA), and Ohio Department of Education. Total enrollment: 677. Upper school average class size: 19. Upper school faculty-student ratio: 1:14. There are 180 required school days per year for Upper School students. Upper School students typically attend 5 days per week. The average school day consists of 7 hours.

Upper School Student Profile Grade 9: 171 students (79 boys, 92 girls); Grade 10: 177 students (90 boys, 87 girls); Grade 11: 156 students (80 boys, 76 girls); Grade 12: 173 students (84 boys, 89 girls). 92% of students are Roman Catholic.

Faculty School total: 51. In upper school: 19 men, 32 women; 24 have advanced degrees.

Subjects Offered Accounting, advanced computer applications, advanced math, Advanced Placement courses, advanced studio art-AP, algebra, American history, American history-AP, American legal systems, American literature, anatomy and physiology, architectural drawing, band, Basic programming, biology, biology-AP, British literature, business applications, calculus-AP, Catholic belief and practice, ceramics, chemistry, choir, church history, civics, communication skills, computer art, computer processing, computer programming, computer programming-AP, computer technologies, computer-aided design, concert band, concert choir, creative writing, design, developmental math, digital photography, directing, drama, drawing and design, English, English literature and composition-AP, European history-AP, French, government and politics-AP, guitar, health, honors algebra, honors English, honors geometry, integrated science, intro to computers, journalism, Latin, Latin-AP, Life of Christ, marching band, moral theology, music appreciation, music theory-AP, Native American studies, photography, physical education, physical science, physics, physics-AP, portfolio art, pottery, pre-algebra, pre-calculus, reading, reading/study skills, skills for success, Spanish, Spanish language-AP, Spanish literature-AP, speech and debate, street law, studio art, studio art-AP, theater, U.S. government and politics-AP, video film production, Web site design, world history, world religions, writing.

Graduation Requirements Algebra, American government, American history, American literature, arts and fine arts (art, music, dance, drama), biology, British literature, Catholic belief and practice, civics, communication skills, computer applications, English, foreign language, geometry, mathematics, religion (includes Bible studies and theology), science, social justice, world history, senior-year retreat, a minimum of 40 hours of community service.

Special Academic Programs Advanced Placement exam preparation; honors section; academic accommodation for the gifted, the musically talented, and the artistically talented; remedial reading and/or remedial writing; remedial math; programs in English, mathematics, general development for dyslexic students.

College Admission Counseling 183 students graduated in 2010; 181 went to college, including Miami University; Northern Kentucky University; Ohio University; University of Cincinnati; University of Dayton; Xavier University. Other: 2 went to work. Median SAT critical reading: 549, median SAT math: 549, median combined SAT: 1090. 24% scored over 26 on composite ACT.

Student Life Upper grades have uniform requirement, student council. Discipline rests primarily with faculty. Attendance at religious services is required.

Tuition and Aid Day student tuition: $8375. Tuition installment plan (FACTS Tuition Payment Plan). Tuition reduction for siblings, merit scholarship grants, need-based scholarship grants available. In 2010–11, 14% of upper-school students received aid; total upper-school merit-scholarship money awarded: $330,000. Total amount of financial aid awarded in 2010–11: $480,000.

Admissions Traditional secondary-level entrance grade is 9. High School Placement Test (closed version) from Scholastic Testing Service required. Deadline for receipt of application materials: December 10. No application fee required.

Athletics Interscholastic: baseball (boys), basketball (b,g), bowling (b,g), cheering (g), dance team (g), football (b), golf (b,g), soccer (b,g), softball (g), track and field (b,g), volleyball (b,g), wrestling (b); coed interscholastic: cross-country running, swimming and diving, track and field; coed intramural: bicycling, flag football, skiing (downhill), snowboarding. 44 coaches, 3 athletic trainers.

Computers Computers are regularly used in computer applications, data processing, English, foreign language, French, graphic design, history, journalism, mathematics, multimedia, photography, programming, publications, reading, religion, science, Spanish, video film production, Web site design, writing classes. Computer network features include on-campus library services, Internet access, Internet filtering or blocking technology, student files, Edline. Campus intranet and student e-mail accounts are available to students. Students grades are available online. The school has a published electronic and media policy.

Contact Mrs. Catherine H. Sherrick, Director of Admissions. 513-231-3500 Ext. 5817. Fax: 513-231-1351. E-mail: csherrick@mcnhs.org. Web site: www.mcnhs.org.

ARCHBISHOP MITTY HIGH SCHOOL

5000 Mitty Avenue

San Jose, California 95129

Head of School: Mr. Tim Brosnan

General Information Coeducational day college-preparatory, arts, religious studies, and technology school, affiliated with Roman Catholic Church. Grades 9–12. Founded: 1964. Setting: suburban. 24-acre campus. 11 buildings on campus. Approved or accredited by National Catholic Education Association, Western Association of Schools and Colleges, and California Department of Education. Endowment: $8 million. Total enrollment: 1,640. Upper school average class size: 27. Upper school faculty-student ratio: 1:17. There are 180 required school days per year for Upper School students. Upper School students typically attend 5 days per week. The average school day consists of 6 hours and 45 minutes.

Upper School Student Profile Grade 9: 471 students (221 boys, 250 girls); Grade 10: 421 students (199 boys, 222 girls); Grade 11: 396 students (182 boys, 214 girls); Grade 12: 391 students (173 boys, 218 girls). 75% of students are Roman Catholic.

Faculty School total: 110. In upper school: 55 men, 55 women; 70 have advanced degrees.

Subjects Offered 3-dimensional art, acting, American history-AP, American literature-AP, ancient world history, art, biology, biology-AP, British literature, calculus, calculus-AP, Catholic belief and practice, chemistry, chemistry-AP, choral music, chorus, church history, college placement, college writing, community service, computer graphics, computer multimedia, concert band, concert choir, drawing, economics and history, English, English language and composition-AP, English literature, English literature-AP, French, French language-AP, French literature-AP, French studies, French-AP, geometry, history-AP, honors algebra, honors English, honors geometry, honors U.S. history, honors world history, music, music appreciation, music theory-AP, philosophy, physics, physics-AP, political science, religion, social sciences, Spanish, Spanish language-AP, Spanish literature, Spanish literature-AP, student government, theater arts, U.S. government and politics, U.S. government and politics-AP, U.S. history, U.S. history-AP, U.S. literature, visual and performing arts, visual arts, world history.

Graduation Requirements Art, English, foreign language, mathematics, philosophy, physical education (includes health), religious studies, science, social sciences, 100 hours of Christian service.

Special Academic Programs 18 Advanced Placement exams for which test preparation is offered, honors section, study at local college for college credit, academic accommodation for the gifted, the musically talented, and the artistically talented.

College Admission Counseling 400 students graduated in 2011; all went to college, including California Polytechnic State University, San Luis Obispo; Santa Clara University; Stanford University; University of California, Berkeley; University of California, Davis; University of California, Los Angeles. Mean SAT critical reading: 580, mean SAT math: 590, mean SAT writing: 601.

Student Life Upper grades have specified standards of dress, student council, honor system. Discipline rests primarily with faculty. Attendance at religious services is required.

Summer Programs Remediation, enrichment, advancement, sports, art/fine arts, computer instruction programs offered; session focuses on academics and athletics; held on campus; accepts boys and girls; open to students from other schools. 500 students usually enrolled. 2012 schedule: June 11 to July 21. Application deadline: May 31.

Tuition and Aid Day student tuition: $14,900. Tuition installment plan (SMART Tuition Payment Plan). Need-based scholarship grants, paying campus jobs available. In 2011–12, 20% of upper-school students received aid. Total amount of financial aid awarded in 2011–12: $2,800,000.

Admissions Traditional secondary-level entrance grade is 9. For fall 2011, 1,400 students applied for upper-level admission, 470 were accepted, 470 enrolled. High School Placement Test required. Deadline for receipt of application materials: December 16. Application fee required: $75.

Athletics Interscholastic: aquatics (boys, girls), badminton (b,g), baseball (b), basketball (b,g), cross-country running (b,g), dance team (g), diving (b,g), field hockey (g), football (b), golf (b,g), lacrosse (b), soccer (b,g), softball (g), swimming and diving (b,g), tennis (b,g), track and field (b,g), volleyball (b,g), water polo (b,g), weight training (b,g), winter soccer (b,g); intramural: roller hockey (b,g); coed interscholastic: physical fitness, strength & conditioning, wrestling; coed intramural: basketball, ice hockey, in-line hockey, table tennis. 4 PE instructors, 110 coaches, 2 athletic trainers.

Computers Computers are regularly used in all classes. Computer network features include on-campus library services, online commercial services, Internet access, wireless campus network, Internet filtering or blocking technology. Campus intranet, student e-mail accounts, and computer access in designated common areas are available to students. Students grades are available online. The school has a published electronic and media policy.

Contact Mrs. Lori Robowski, Assistant for Admissions. 408-342-4300. Fax: 408-342-4308. E-mail: admissions@mitty.com. Web site: www.mitty.com/.

ARCHBISHOP RUMMEL HIGH SCHOOL

1901 Severn Avenue

Metairie, Louisiana 70001-2893

Head of School: Mr. Michael Scalco

General Information Boys' day college-preparatory, arts, religious studies, and technology school, affiliated with Roman Catholic Church. Grades 8–12. Founded: 1962. Setting: suburban. Nearest major city is New Orleans. 20-acre campus. 10 buildings on campus. Approved or accredited by Association for Experiential Education, National Catholic Education Association, Southern Association of Colleges and Schools, and Louisiana Department of Education. Total enrollment: 815. Upper school average class size: 27. Upper school faculty-student ratio: 1:14. There are 181 required school days per year for Upper School students. Upper School students typically attend 5 days per week. The average school day consists of 7 hours.

Upper School Student Profile Grade 8: 121 students (121 boys); Grade 9: 174 students (174 boys); Grade 10: 172 students (172 boys); Grade 11: 162 students (162 boys); Grade 12: 186 students (186 boys). 90% of students are Roman Catholic.

Faculty School total: 57. In upper school: 30 men, 27 women; 7 have advanced degrees.

Subjects Offered ACT preparation, advanced biology, advanced chemistry, advanced computer applications, advanced math, advanced studio art-AP, algebra, American government, American history, American history-AP, American literature, American literature-AP, anatomy, anatomy and physiology, ancient world history, art, art appreciation, art-AP, band, biology, British literature, British literature (honors), British literature-AP, calculus, calculus-AP, campus ministry, Catholic belief and practice, ceramics, chemistry, chemistry-AP, civics, computer applications, computer literacy, computer science, creative writing, economics, English, English language and composition-AP, English literature, English literature and composition-AP, environmental science, European history, European literature, fine arts, French, geography, geometry, government-AP, health education, history of the Catholic Church, honors algebra, honors English, honors geometry, honors U.S. history, honors world history, human anatomy, instrumental music, language arts, Latin, moral theology, physics, psychology, reading, sociology, Spanish, Spanish literature, speech, statistics-AP, street law, studio art, studio art-AP, U.S. government and politics-AP, U.S. history, U.S. history-AP, U.S. literature, United States government-AP, Web site design, Western civilization, world geography.

Graduation Requirements ACT preparation, advanced math, American history, art appreciation, biology, Catholic belief and practice, chemistry, civics, computer applications, computer literacy, computer science, English, environmental science, foreign language, geography, health education, history of the Catholic Church, physical education (includes health), physical science, physics, reading, U.S. history, Western civilization, world geography.

Special Academic Programs Advanced Placement exam preparation; honors section; programs in general development for dyslexic students.

College Admission Counseling 210 students graduated in 2011; 200 went to college, including Louisiana State University and Agricultural and Mechanical College; Loyola University New Orleans; Nicholls State University; University of Louisiana at Lafayette; University of New Orleans. Other: 2 entered military service.

Student Life Upper grades have uniform requirement, student council, honor system. Discipline rests primarily with faculty. Attendance at religious services is required.

Summer Programs Remediation, enrichment, advancement, sports, art/fine arts, rigorous outdoor training, computer instruction programs offered; session focuses on student involvement and fun; held on campus; accepts boys and girls; open to students from other schools. 200 students usually enrolled. 2012 schedule: June 2 to July 18.

Tuition and Aid Day student tuition: $7150. Tuition installment plan (monthly payment plans). Merit scholarship grants, need-based scholarship grants, paying campus jobs available. In 2011–12, 20% of upper-school students received aid.

Admissions High School Placement Test required. Deadline for receipt of application materials: January 8. Application fee required: $20. Interview required.

Athletics Interscholastic: baseball, basketball, bowling, cheering, cross-country running, field hockey, football, Frisbee, golf, hockey, in-line hockey, jogging, power lifting, rugby, soccer, strength & conditioning, swimming and diving, tennis, track and field, whiffle ball, wrestling; intramural: flag football. 10 PE instructors, 25 coaches, 2 athletic trainers.

Computers Computers are regularly used in computer applications, creative writing, English, multimedia, programming, reading, science classes. Computer resources include on-campus library services, Internet access, Internet filtering or blocking technology. Students grades are available online. The school has a published electronic and media policy.

Contact Joseph A. Serio, Director of Communications. 504-834-5592 Ext. 263. Fax: 504-833-2232. E-mail: jserio@rummelraiders.com. Web site: www.rummelraiders.com.

THE ARCHER SCHOOL FOR GIRLS

11725 Sunset Boulevard

Los Angeles, California 90049

Head of School: Elizabeth English

General Information Girls' day college-preparatory school. Grades 6–12. Founded: 1995. Setting: suburban. 6-acre campus. 1 building on campus. Approved or accredited by California Association of Independent Schools, The College Board, Western Association of Schools and Colleges, and California Department of Education. Endowment: $2.6 million. Total enrollment: 440. Upper school average class size: 16. Upper school faculty-student ratio: 1:8. The average school day consists of 5 hours and 45 minutes.

Faculty School total: 60. In upper school: 15 men, 45 women; 40 have advanced degrees.

Subjects Offered 20th century history, acting, advanced chemistry, advanced math, algebra, American literature, ancient history, archaeology, architectural drawing, art, art appreciation, art history, art history-AP, biology, biology-AP, calculus, calculus-AP, career/college preparation, ceramics, chemistry, chemistry-AP, Chinese, choir, classical studies, college admission preparation, college counseling, community service, computer applications, computer graphics, computer literacy, critical studies in film, dance, debate, digital imaging, drama, drawing and design, earth and space science, English, English composition, English language-AP, English literature, English literature-AP, environmental science-AP, experiential education, film appreciation, fitness, French, French language-AP, geometry, history, honors U.S. history, human development, human geography - AP, independent study, intro to computers, journalism, Latin, law studies, literary magazine, marine biology, marine ecology, media literacy, modern world history, music, orchestra, painting, performing arts, photography, physics, portfolio art, pre-algebra, pre-calculus, psychology, robotics, Roman civilization, self-defense, senior seminar, Spanish, Spanish language-AP, speech and debate, statistics-AP, student government, student publications, studio art, theater, theater arts, U.S. history, U.S. history-AP, wilderness experience, yearbook.

Graduation Requirements Arts and fine arts (art, music, dance, drama), English, fitness, foreign language, history, human development, mathematics, performing arts, science, annual participation in Arrow Week (experiential education program). Community service is required.

Special Academic Programs 14 Advanced Placement exams for which test preparation is offered; honors section.

College Admission Counseling 65 students graduated in 2010; all went to college, including Barnard College; University of California, Berkeley; University of Southern California; Wesleyan University; Yale University. Median SAT critical reading: 600, median SAT math: 575, median SAT writing: 645, median combined SAT: 1820.

Student Life Upper grades have uniform requirement, student council, honor system. Discipline rests primarily with faculty.

Tuition and Aid Day student tuition: $28,750. Tuition installment plan (FACTS Tuition Payment Plan). Need-based scholarship grants available. In 2010–11, 24% of upper-school students received aid. Total amount of financial aid awarded in 2010–11: $2,500,000.

Admissions Traditional secondary-level entrance grade is 9. ISEE required. Deadline for receipt of application materials: December 10. Application fee required: $115. On-campus interview required.

Athletics Interscholastic: basketball, cross-country running, equestrian sports, soccer, softball, swimming and diving, tennis, track and field, volleyball. 5 PE instructors, 16 coaches.

Computers Computers are regularly used in all academic classes. Computer network features include on-campus library services, online commercial services, Internet access, wireless campus network, 1 to 1 laptop program for grades 6 and 9. Student e-mail accounts are available to students. The school has a published electronic and media policy.

Contact Beth Kemp, Director of Admissions. 310-873-7037. Fax: 310-873-7052. E-mail: bkemp@archer.org. Web site: www.archer.org/.

ARENDELL PARROTT ACADEMY

PO Box 1297

Kinston, North Carolina 28503-1297

Head of School: Mr. Peter Cowen

General Information Coeducational day college-preparatory school. Grades PK–12. Founded: 1964. Setting: small town. 80-acre campus. 6 buildings on campus. Approved or accredited by Southern Association of Colleges and Schools and North Carolina Department of Education. Total enrollment: 788. Upper school average class size: 18. There are 178 required school days per year for Upper School students. Upper School students typically attend 5 days per week. The average school day consists of 6 hours and 20 minutes.

Faculty School total: 60. In upper school: 10 men, 21 women; 20 have advanced degrees.

Special Academic Programs Advanced Placement exam preparation; honors section; study at local college for college credit.

College Admission Counseling 54 students graduated in 2011; all went to college. Mean SAT critical reading: 611, mean SAT math: 600, mean SAT writing: 602, mean combined SAT: 1813.

Student Life Upper grades have specified standards of dress, student council, honor system. Discipline rests primarily with faculty.

Tuition and Aid Day student tuition: $9500. Tuition installment plan (monthly payment plans, individually arranged payment plans). Need-based scholarship grants available. In 2011–12, 17% of upper-school students received aid. Total amount of financial aid awarded in 2011–12: $260,000.

Admissions Traditional secondary-level entrance grade is 9. Deadline for receipt of application materials: none. Application fee required: $550. Interview required.

Athletics Interscholastic: baseball (boys), basketball (b,g), canoeing/kayaking (g), cross-country running (b,g), dance squad (g), field hockey (g), football (b), lacrosse (b), soccer (b,g), softball (g), swimming and diving (b,g), tennis (b,g), volleyball (g); coed interscholastic: dance, fitness, golf, physical fitness, physical training, strength & conditioning.

Computers Computer network features include on-campus library services, Internet access, wireless campus network, Internet filtering or blocking technology. Computer access in designated common areas is available to students. Students grades are available online. The school has a published electronic and media policy.

Contact Julie Rogers, Director of Admissions. 252-522-0410 Ext. 202. Fax: 919-522-0672. E-mail: jrogers@parrottacademy.org. Web site: www.parrottacademy.org.

ARMBRAE ACADEMY

1400 Oxford Street

Halifax, Nova Scotia B3H 3Y8, Canada

Head of School: Gary D. O'Meara

General Information Coeducational day college-preparatory school. Grades K–12. Founded: 1887. Setting: urban. 2-acre campus. 3 buildings on campus. Approved or accredited by Canadian Association of Independent Schools, Canadian Educational Standards Institute, and Nova Scotia Department of Education. Language of instruction: English. Endowment: CAN$1 million. Total enrollment: 258. Upper school average class size: 22. Upper school faculty-student ratio: 1:9. There are 185 required school days per year for Upper School students. Upper School students typically attend 5 days per week. The average school day consists of 5 hours and 30 minutes.

Faculty School total: 35. In upper school: 5 men, 8 women; 5 have advanced degrees.

Subjects Offered Algebra, American history, art, biology, calculus, chemistry, computer science, earth science, economics, English, English literature, European history, French, geography, geology, geometry, government/civics, grammar, health, history, keyboarding, Mandarin, mathematics, music, physical education, physics, science, social studies, study skills, trigonometry, world literature, writing.

Graduation Requirements Computer science, English, foreign language, mathematics, physical education (includes health), science, social studies (includes history), 6 courses each in grades 11 and 12.

Special Academic Programs Advanced Placement exam preparation; accelerated programs; study at local college for college credit; academic accommodation for the artistically talented.

College Admission Counseling 20 students graduated in 2011; they went to Acadia University; Carleton University; Dalhousie University; McGill University; Queen's University at Kingston; St. Francis Xavier University.

Student Life Upper grades have uniform requirement, student council. Discipline rests equally with students and faculty.

Tuition and Aid Day student tuition: CAN$11,870. Tuition installment plan (monthly payment plans, term payment plan). Tuition reduction for siblings, bursaries, merit scholarship grants available. In 2011–12, 4% of upper-school students received aid; total upper-school merit-scholarship money awarded: CAN$2000. Total amount of financial aid awarded in 2011–12: CAN$60,000.

Admissions Traditional secondary-level entrance grade is 10. For fall 2011, 25 students applied for upper-level admission, 22 were accepted, 15 enrolled. CTBS (or similar from their school) required. Deadline for receipt of application materials: none. Application fee required: CAN$150. On-campus interview required.

Athletics Interscholastic: badminton (boys, girls), basketball (b,g), cross-country running (b,g), field hockey (g), ice hockey (b), soccer (b,g), swimming and diving (b,g), tennis (b,g), track and field (b,g), volleyball (b,g); intramural: badminton (b,g), cross-country running (b,g); coed interscholastic: curling, ice hockey; coed intramural: ice hockey. 2 PE instructors, 4 coaches.

Computers Computers are regularly used in all classes. Computer network features include on-campus library services, online commercial services, Internet access, wireless campus network. Campus intranet and student e-mail accounts are available to students. Students grades are available online. The school has a published electronic and media policy.

Contact Gary D. O'Meara, Headmaster. 902-423-7920. Fax: 902-423-9731. E-mail: head@armbrae.ns.ca. Web site: www.armbrae.ns.ca.

ARMONA UNION ACADEMY

14435 Locust Street

PO Box 397

Armona, California 93202

Head of School: Mr. Erik Borges

General Information Coeducational day college-preparatory, general academic, and religious studies school, affiliated with Seventh-day Adventists. Grades K–12. Founded: 1904. Setting: small town. Nearest major city is Fresno. 20-acre campus. 5 buildings on campus. Approved or accredited by Western Association of Schools and Colleges and California Department of Education. Member of Secondary School Admission Test Board. Endowment: $98,000. Total enrollment: 138. Upper school average class size: 15. Upper school faculty-student ratio: 1:10. There are 180 required school days per year for Upper School students. Upper School students typically attend 5 days per week. The average school day consists of 7 hours and 45 minutes.

Upper School Student Profile 85% of students are Seventh-day Adventists.

Faculty School total: 13. In upper school: 5 men, 1 woman; 3 have advanced degrees.

Subjects Offered Algebra, American history, American literature, art, Bible studies, biology, chemistry, choir, community service, computer science, economics, English, English literature, geometry, government, mathematics, physical education, physical science, physics, religion, science, Spanish, world history, world literature, yearbook.

Graduation Requirements Arts and fine arts (art, music, dance, drama), business skills (includes word processing), computer science, English, foreign language, mathematics, physical education (includes health), religion (includes Bible studies and theology), science, social sciences, social studies (includes history). Community service is required.

Special Academic Programs Study at local college for college credit.

College Admission Counseling 11 students graduated in 2011; 9 went to college, including La Sierra University; Southern Adventist University; West Hills Community College. Other: 1 went to work, 1 entered military service.

Student Life Upper grades have specified standards of dress, student council. Discipline rests primarily with faculty. Attendance at religious services is required.

Tuition and Aid Day student tuition: $5140. Guaranteed tuition plan. Tuition installment plan (monthly payment plans, individually arranged payment plans). Tuition reduction for siblings, need-based scholarship grants available. In 2011–12, 60% of upper-school students received aid. Total amount of financial aid awarded in 2011–12: $50,000.

Admissions Traditional secondary-level entrance grade is 9. For fall 2011, 11 students applied for upper-level admission, 7 were accepted, 7 enrolled. Deadline for receipt of application materials: August 15. Application fee required: $75. Interview required.

Athletics Interscholastic: basketball (boys, girls), flag football (b,g), football (b,g), volleyball (b,g); intramural: basketball (b,g), flag football (b,g); coed interscholastic: baseball, outdoor education, soccer, softball, track and field; coed intramural: baseball, outdoor education, paddle tennis, soccer, softball, table tennis, track and field, volleyball.

Computers Computers are regularly used in English, history, mathematics, science, yearbook classes. Computer network features include on-campus library services, online commercial services, Internet access, wireless campus network, Internet filtering or blocking technology. Students grades are available online. The school has a published electronic and media policy.

Contact Mrs. Aniesha Kleinhammer, Registrar. 559-582-4468 Ext. 10. Fax: 559-582-6609. E-mail: auaregistrar@gmail.com. Web site: www.auaweb.com.

ARMY AND NAVY ACADEMY

2605 Carlsbad Boulevard

PO Box 3000

Carlsbad, California 92018-3000

Head of School: Brig. Gen. Stephen M. Bliss, Retd.

General Information Boys' boarding and day college-preparatory, Junior ROTC, and military school. Grades 7–12. Founded: 1910. Setting: small town. Nearest major city is San Diego. Students are housed in single-sex dormitories. 16-acre campus. 34 buildings on campus. Approved or accredited by California Association of Independent Schools and Western Association of Schools and Colleges. Member of National Association of Independent Schools and Secondary School Admission Test Board. Endowment: $462,608. Total enrollment: 310. Upper school average class size: 12. Upper school faculty-student ratio: 1:15. There are 180 required school days per year for Upper School students. Upper School students typically attend 5 days per week. The average school day consists of 6 hours and 45 minutes.

Upper School Student Profile Grade 10: 66 students (66 boys); Grade 11: 91 students (91 boys); Grade 12: 66 students (66 boys). 91% of students are boarding students. 63% are state residents. 9 states are represented in upper school student body. 26% are international students. International students from China, Kuwait, Mexico, Russian Federation, Taiwan, and Viet Nam; 5 other countries represented in student body.

Faculty School total: 30. In upper school: 16 men, 14 women; 17 have advanced degrees; 1 resides on campus.

Subjects Offered Advanced studio art-AP, algebra, art, biology, biology-AP, calculus-AP, chemistry, chemistry-AP, composition-AP, drama, economics, English, English literature-AP, English-AP, ESL, European history-AP, French, French-AP, geography, geometry, guitar, independent study, JROTC, marching band, media studies, music appreciation, music technology, photography, physical education, physics, physics-AP, pre-calculus, psychology-AP, Spanish, Spanish-AP, statistics-AP, studio art-AP, study skills, U.S. government, U.S. history, U.S. history-AP, video film production, weight training, world history, yearbook.

Graduation Requirements Arts and fine arts (art, music, dance, drama), electives, English, foreign language, lab science, leadership education training, mathematics, physical education (includes health), social studies (includes history).

Special Academic Programs 8 Advanced Placement exams for which test preparation is offered; honors section; independent study; special instructional classes for students with Attention Deficit Disorder and learning disabilities; ESL (30 students enrolled).

College Admission Counseling 58 students graduated in 2011; all went to college, including California State University, Fullerton; California State University, San Marcos; Marymount College, Palos Verdes, California; University of California, Irvine; University of California, Los Angeles; University of Nevada, Reno. Median SAT critical reading: 480, median SAT math: 520, median SAT writing: 470.

Student Life Upper grades have uniform requirement, student council, honor system. Discipline rests primarily with faculty.

Summer Programs Remediation, enrichment, ESL, sports, art/fine arts, rigorous outdoor training, computer instruction programs offered; session focuses on academic, JROTC leadership, and recreation; held on campus; accepts boys and girls; open to students from other schools. 300 students usually enrolled. 2012 schedule: June 30 to August 2. Application deadline: none.

Tuition and Aid Day student tuition: $19,500; 7-day tuition and room/board: $32,850. Tuition installment plan (individually arranged payment plans). Tuition reduction for siblings, need-based scholarship grants, Military Discount available. In 2011–12, 17% of upper-school students received aid. Total amount of financial aid awarded in 2011–12: $377,300.

Admissions Traditional secondary-level entrance grade is 10. For fall 2011, 136 students applied for upper-level admission, 97 were accepted, 68 enrolled. ISEE, Otis-Lennon School Ability Test, SSAT, Star-9 or TOEFL or SLEP required. Deadline for receipt of application materials: none. Application fee required: $100. Interview required.

Athletics Interscholastic: aquatics, baseball, basketball, cross-country running, drill team, football, golf, in-line hockey, marksmanship, riflery, roller hockey, ropes courses, soccer, surfing, swimming and diving, tennis, track and field, water polo, weight lifting, wrestling; intramural: aquatics, combined training, fitness, hockey, independent competitive sports, JROTC drill, outdoor activities, outdoor recreation, physical fitness, physical training, roller hockey, strength & conditioning, surfing. 15 coaches, 1 athletic trainer.

Computers Computers are regularly used in media, music technology, video film production, yearbook classes. Computer network features include on-campus library services, Internet access, wireless campus network, Internet filtering or blocking technology. Computer access in designated common areas is available to students. Students grades are available online. The school has a published electronic and media policy.

Contact Candice Heidenrich, Director of Admissions. 888-762-2338. Fax: 760-434-5948. E-mail: admissions@armyandnavyacademy.org. Web site: www.armyandnavyacademy.org.

ARROWSMITH SCHOOL

Toronto, Ontario, Canada

See Special Needs Schools section.

ARTHUR MORGAN SCHOOL

Burnsville, North Carolina

See Junior Boarding Schools section.

ASPEN RANCH

Loa, Utah

See Special Needs Schools section.

ASSETS SCHOOL

Honolulu, Hawaii

See Special Needs Schools section.

THE ATHENIAN SCHOOL

2100 Mount Diablo Scenic Boulevard

Danville, California 94506

Head of School: Eric Feron Niles

General Information Coeducational boarding and day college-preparatory school. Boarding grades 9–12, day grades 6–12. Founded: 1965. Setting: suburban. Nearest major city is San Francisco. Students are housed in single-sex dormitories. 75-acre campus. 25 buildings on campus. Approved or accredited by California Association of Independent Schools, The Association of Boarding Schools, The College Board, Western Association of Schools and Colleges, and California Department of Education. Member of National Association of Independent Schools and Secondary School Admission Test Board. Endowment: $7 million. Total enrollment: 471. Upper school average class size: 15. Upper school faculty-student ratio: 1:10. Upper School students typically attend 5 days per week. The average school day consists of 5 hours and 35 minutes.

Upper School Student Profile Grade 9: 74 students (37 boys, 37 girls); Grade 10: 78 students (39 boys, 39 girls); Grade 11: 79 students (36 boys, 43 girls); Grade 12: 75 students (37 boys, 38 girls). 14% of students are boarding students. 90% are state residents. 1 state is represented in upper school student body. 13% are international students. International students from China, Indonesia, Japan, Republic of Korea, Taiwan, and Viet Nam; 5 other countries represented in student body.

Faculty School total: 55. In upper school: 27 men, 24 women; 37 have advanced degrees; 20 reside on campus.

Subjects Offered African-American studies, algebra, American history, American literature, American literature-AP, anatomy, art, art history, Asian history, Asian literature, biology, calculus-AP, ceramics, chemistry, classical studies, college writing, community service, comparative cultures, comparative religion, computer programming, computer science, computer skills, contemporary history, creative writing, dance, dance performance, debate, drama, drama performance, drama workshop, drawing, earth science, ecology, economics, economics and history, English, English as a foreign language, English literature, English-AP, environmental studies, ESL, ethics, European history, European history-AP, expository writing, fencing, fine arts, French, French-AP, geography, geology, geometry, government/civics, graphic design, health, history, humanities, introduction to technology, jazz band, jewelry making, literary magazine, literature seminar, literature-AP, mathematics, modern European history-AP, music, music history, music performance, musical theater, painting, philosophy, photography, physical education, physics, science, science project, sculpture, sociology, Spanish, Spanish literature-AP, Spanish-AP, stained glass, statistics, statistics-AP, theater, theater design and production, trigonometry, U.S. history-AP, wilderness experience, world cultures, world history, world literature, writing, yearbook, yoga.

Graduation Requirements American history, arts and fine arts (art, music, dance, drama), English, foreign language, history, literature, mathematics, physical education (includes health), science, wilderness experience, world history. Community service is required.

Special Academic Programs Advanced Placement exam preparation; honors section; independent study; term-away projects; study at local college for college credit; domestic exchange program; study abroad; ESL (8 students enrolled).

College Admission Counseling 77 students graduated in 2011; 74 went to college, including Lewis & Clark College; The George Washington University; University of California, Berkeley; University of California, Santa Cruz; University of Colorado Boulder; Willamette University. Other: 2 went to work, 1 had other specific plans. Median SAT critical reading: 610, median SAT math: 640, median SAT writing: 630, median combined SAT: 1890. 55% scored over 600 on SAT critical reading, 74% scored over 600 on SAT math, 66% scored over 600 on SAT writing, 62% scored over 1800 on combined SAT.

Student Life Upper grades have specified standards of dress, student council. Discipline rests equally with students and faculty.

Summer Programs Enrichment, advancement, ESL, sports, art/fine arts, computer instruction programs offered; session focuses on academic enrichment, sports, and ESL; held on campus; accepts boys and girls; open to students from other schools. 200 students usually enrolled. 2012 schedule: June 13 to August 3. Application deadline: none.

Tuition and Aid Day student tuition: $30,750; 5-day tuition and room/board: $48,500; 7-day tuition and room/board: $48,500. Tuition installment plan (Insured Tuition Payment Plan, monthly payment plans). Need-based scholarship grants available. In 2011–12, 22% of upper-school students received aid. Total amount of financial aid awarded in 2011–12: $2,002,000.

Admissions Traditional secondary-level entrance grade is 9. For fall 2011, 514 students applied for upper-level admission, 122 were accepted, 51 enrolled. International English Language Test, ISEE, SSAT or TOEFL required. Deadline for receipt of application materials: January 12. Application fee required: $75. Interview required.

Athletics Interscholastic: baseball (boys), basketball (b,g), cross-country running (b,g), golf (b), soccer (b,g), softball (g), swimming and diving (b,g), tennis (b,g); coed interscholastic: volleyball, wrestling; coed intramural: basketball, climbing, cross-country running, dance, fencing, weight training, yoga. 12 coaches.

Computers Computers are regularly used in English, foreign language, graphic design, history, humanities, information technology, library science, literary magazine, mathematics, publications, science, yearbook classes. Computer network features include on-campus library services, online commercial services, Internet access, wireless campus network, Internet filtering or blocking technology. Student e-mail accounts and computer access in designated common areas are available to students. Students grades are available online. The school has a published electronic and media policy.

Contact Beverly Gomer, Associate Director of Admission. 925-362-7223. Fax: 925-362-7228. E-mail: bgomer@athenian.org. Web site: www.athenian.org.

See Display on next page and Close-Up on page 582.

ATLANTA INTERNATIONAL SCHOOL

2890 North Fulton Drive

Atlanta, Georgia 30305

Head of School: Mr. Kevin Glass

General Information Coeducational day college-preparatory, bilingual studies, and International Baccalaureate school. Grades PK–12. Founded: 1984. Setting: urban. 10-acre campus. 4 buildings on campus. Approved or accredited by French Ministry of Education, Georgia Independent School Association, International Baccalaureate Organization, National Independent Private Schools Association, Southern Association of Colleges and Schools, Southern Association of Independent Schools, and Georgia Department of Education. Member of National Association of Independent Schools and European Council of International Schools. Endowment: $7.3 million. Total enrollment: 934. Upper school average class size: 16. Upper school faculty-student ratio: 1:8. Upper School students typically attend 5 days per week. The average school day consists of 6 hours and 30 minutes.

Upper School Student Profile Grade 9: 66 students (42 boys, 24 girls); Grade 10: 70 students (33 boys, 37 girls); Grade 11: 76 students (39 boys, 37 girls); Grade 12: 65 students (24 boys, 41 girls).

Faculty School total: 134.

Subjects Offered American history, art, biology, chemistry, Chinese, choir, chorus, computer science, contemporary issues, economics, English, English literature, ESL, fine arts, French, French as a second language, geography, German, health, integrated mathematics, International Baccalaureate courses, jazz band, lab/keyboard, Latin, math methods, mathematics, model United Nations, physical education, physics, SAT preparation, science, science and technology, social studies, Spanish, theater, theater arts, theory of knowledge, world history, yearbook.

Graduation Requirements Arts and fine arts (art, music, dance, drama), English, foreign language, mathematics, physical education (includes health), science, social studies (includes history), theory of knowledge, extended essay/research project. Community service is required.

Special Academic Programs International Baccalaureate program; independent study; term-away projects; study abroad; ESL (45 students enrolled).

College Admission Counseling 73 students graduated in 2011; 72 went to college, including Emory University; Georgetown University; Georgia Institute of Technology; McGill University; New York University; University of Georgia. Other: 1 had other specific plans. Mean SAT critical reading: 650, mean SAT math: 627.

Student Life Upper grades have specified standards of dress, student council. Discipline rests primarily with faculty.

Summer Programs Remediation, enrichment, advancement, ESL, sports, art/fine arts, computer instruction programs offered; session focuses on language acquisition (French, Spanish, German, Chinese, ESL), day camps, sport camps, theater, robotics, chess; held on campus; accepts boys and girls; open to students from other schools. 150 students usually enrolled. 2012 schedule: June 15 to July 31. Application deadline: May 1.

Tuition and Aid Day student tuition: $18,092–$20,640. Tuition installment plan (Insured Tuition Payment Plan). Need-based scholarship grants available. In 2011–12, 14% of upper-school students received aid.

Admissions Traditional secondary-level entrance grade is 9. For fall 2011, 57 students applied for upper-level admission, 47 were accepted, 31 enrolled. Deadline for receipt of application materials: none. Application fee required: $100. Interview recommended.

Athletics Interscholastic: baseball (boys), basketball (b,g), cross-country running (b,g), soccer (b,g), swimming and diving (b,g), tennis (b,g), track and field (b,g), volleyball (g); intramural: strength & conditioning (b,g), track and field (b,g); coed intramural: basketball, fitness, jogging, volleyball. 9 PE instructors, 7 coaches, 3 athletic trainers.

Computers Computers are regularly used in all academic classes. Computer network features include Internet access, Internet filtering or blocking technology, server space for file storage, online classroom, multi-user learning software. Student e-mail accounts and computer access in designated common areas are available to students. Students grades are available online. The school has a published electronic and media policy.

Contact Ms. Charlotte Smith, Associate Director of Admission and Financial Aid. 404-841-3891. Fax: 404-841-3873. E-mail: csmith@aischool.org. Web site: www.aischool.org.

ATLANTIS ACADEMY

Miami, Florida

See Special Needs Schools section.

AUGUSTA CHRISTIAN SCHOOL (I)

313 Baston Road

Martinez, Georgia 30907

Head of School: Dr. David M. Piccolo

General Information Coeducational day college-preparatory, arts, religious studies, and technology school. Grades K–12. Founded: 1958. Setting: suburban. Nearest major city is Augusta. 26-acre campus. 10 buildings on campus. Approved or accredited by Association of Christian Schools International, Southern Association of Colleges and Schools, and Georgia Department of Education. Total enrollment: 537. Upper school average class size: 18. Upper school faculty-student ratio: 1:10. There are 100 required school days per year for Upper School students. Upper School students typically attend 5 days per week. The average school day consists of 7 hours and 5 minutes.

Upper School Student Profile Grade 9: 62 students (34 boys, 28 girls); Grade 10: 52 students (28 boys, 24 girls); Grade 11: 58 students (35 boys, 23 girls); Grade 12: 74 students (46 boys, 28 girls).

Faculty School total: 55. In upper school: 13 men, 13 women; 3 have advanced degrees.

Subjects Offered Advanced chemistry, advanced computer applications, advanced math, Advanced Placement courses, algebra, American government, American history, American history-AP, American literature, anatomy and physiology, art, athletic training, athletics, band, baseball, basketball, Bible, Bible studies, biology, biology-AP, British literature, British literature-AP, calculus-AP, ceramics, cheerleading, chemistry, choir, choral music, chorus, Christian education, Christian studies, college counseling, comparative religion, computer education, computer skills, drama, drama performance, earth science, ecology, economics and history, electives, English, English composition, English literature, English literature-AP, English-AP, European history, French, general science, geography, geometry, government, grammar, health, history, instrumental music, keyboarding, life skills, mathematics, mathematics-AP, music appreciation, musical productions, New Testament, physics, piano, pre-algebra, pre-calculus, public speaking, reading, remedial/makeup course work, SAT preparation, science, social studies, Spanish, speech, sports, state history, student government, swimming, U.S. government, U.S. history, U.S. history-AP, U.S. literature, volleyball, weight training, weightlifting, world history, wrestling, yearbook.

Graduation Requirements Bible, computers, electives, English, foreign language, mathematics, physical education (includes health), science, social studies (includes history), speech.

Special Academic Programs Advanced Placement exam preparation; honors section; study at local college for college credit; programs in English, mathematics for dyslexic students.

College Admission Counseling 52 students graduated in 2011; all went to college, including Augusta State University; Georgia Institute of Technology; Georgia Southern University; University of Georgia.

Student Life Upper grades have specified standards of dress, student council. Discipline rests primarily with faculty. Attendance at religious services is required.

Summer Programs Remediation programs offered; session focuses on academics; held on campus; accepts boys and girls; open to students from other schools.

Tuition and Aid Day student tuition: $1500–$9216. Tuition installment plan (Insured Tuition Payment Plan, monthly payment plans, individually arranged payment plans). Tuition reduction for siblings, need based scholarship grants available.

Admissions Traditional secondary-level entrance grade is 9. Stanford Achievement Test required. Deadline for receipt of application materials: none. Application fee required: $100. Interview required.

Athletics Interscholastic: baseball (boys), basketball (b,g), cheering (g), cross-country running (b,g), football (b), golf (b), soccer (b,g), softball (g), swimming and diving (b,g), tennis (b,g), track and field (b,g), volleyball (g), wrestling (b). 3 PE instructors.

Computers Computers are regularly used in computer applications, keyboarding, yearbook classes. Computer network features include on-campus library services, Internet access, Internet filtering or blocking technology. Campus intranet is available to students. Students grades are available online. The school has a published electronic and media policy.

Contact Mrs. Lauren Banks, Director of Admissions. 706-863-2905 Ext. 111. Fax: 706-860-6618. E-mail: laurenbanks@augustachristian.org. Web site: www.augustachristian.org.

AUGUSTA PREPARATORY DAY SCHOOL

285 Flowing Wells Road

Martinez, Georgia 30907

Head of School: Becky Gilmore

General Information Coeducational day college-preparatory school. Grades PS–12. Founded: 1960. Setting: suburban. Nearest major city is Augusta. 52-acre campus. 6 buildings on campus. Approved or accredited by Georgia Independent School Association, Southern Association of Colleges and Schools, and Southern Association of Independent Schools. Member of National Association of Independent Schools and Secondary School Admission Test Board. Endowment: $4 million. Total enrollment: 528. Upper school average class size: 11. Upper school faculty-student ratio: 1:9. There are 180 required school days per year for Upper School students. Upper School students typically attend 5 days per week. The average school day consists of 7 hours and 15 minutes.

Upper School Student Profile Grade 9: 62 students (31 boys, 31 girls); Grade 10: 42 students (22 boys, 20 girls); Grade 11: 44 students (22 boys, 22 girls); Grade 12: 53 students (27 boys, 26 girls).

Faculty School total: 65. In upper school: 15 men, 10 women; 18 have advanced degrees.

Subjects Offered 20th century world history, Advanced Placement courses, advanced studio art-AP, algebra, American history, American literature, art, biology, biology-AP, calculus, calculus-AP, chemistry, chemistry-AP, computer programming, debate, drama, ecology, economics, English, English literature, English literature-AP, European history-AP, French, French-AP, geometry, government, government/civics, grammar, Latin, Latin-AP, marine science, physics, pre-calculus, senior project, Spanish, Spanish-AP, statistics-AP, studio art-AP, theater design and production, U.S. history-AP, world history, zoology.

Graduation Requirements American government, American history, arts and fine arts (art, music, dance, drama), English, foreign language, mathematics, science, social studies (includes history).

Special Academic Programs Honors section; independent study; term-away projects; academic accommodation for the gifted.

College Admission Counseling 54 students graduated in 2011; all went to college, including Augusta State University; College of Charleston; Furman University; Georgia Institute of Technology; Mercer University; University of Georgia. Median SAT critical reading: 602, median SAT math: 602, median SAT writing: 603, median combined SAT: 1807, median composite ACT: 27. 50% scored over 600 on SAT critical reading, 50% scored over 600 on SAT math, 50% scored over 600 on SAT writing, 50% scored over 1800 on combined SAT, 50% scored over 26 on composite ACT.

Student Life Upper grades have specified standards of dress, student council, honor system. Discipline rests equally with students and faculty.

Summer Programs Enrichment, sports, art/fine arts programs offered; session focuses on enrichment/sports; held on campus; accepts boys and girls; open to students from other schools. 2012 schedule: June 6 to August 1.

Admissions Traditional secondary-level entrance grade is 9. For fall 2011, 30 students applied for upper-level admission, 28 were accepted, 18 enrolled. ERB CTP III required. Deadline for receipt of application materials: none.

Athletics Interscholastic: baseball (boys), basketball (b,g), cheering (g), cross-country running (b,g), fitness (b,g), football (b), golf (b), physical training (b,g). 3 PE instructors, 1 athletic trainer.

Computers Computers are regularly used in all classes. Computer network features include on-campus library services, online commercial services, Internet access, wireless campus network, Internet filtering or blocking technology. Campus intranet and computer access in designated common areas are available to students. Students grades are available online. The school has a published electronic and media policy.

Contact Rosie Herrmann, Director of Admission. 706-863-1906 Ext. 201. Fax: 706-863-6198. E-mail: admissions@augustaprep.org. Web site: www.augustaprep.org.

AULDERN ACADEMY

990 Glovers Grove Church Road

Siler City, North Carolina 27344

Head of School: Ms. Jane Samuel

General Information Girls' boarding college-preparatory and arts school; primarily serves underachievers, students with learning disabilities, individuals with Attention Deficit Disorder, and individuals with emotional and behavioral problems. Grades 8–12. Founded: 2001. Setting: rural. Nearest major city is Chapel Hill. Students are housed in single-sex dormitories. 86-acre campus. 4 buildings on campus. Approved or accredited by National Independent Private Schools Association, Southern Association of Colleges and Schools, and North Carolina Department of Education. Total enrollment: 60. Upper school average class size: 10. Upper school faculty-student ratio: 1:10. There are 225 required school days per year for Upper School students. Upper School students typically attend 5 days per week. The average school day consists of 6 hours.

Upper School Student Profile Grade 9: 6 students (6 girls); Grade 10: 12 students (12 girls); Grade 11: 16 students (16 girls); Grade 12: 20 students (20 girls). 100% of students are boarding students. 10% are state residents. 18 states are represented in upper school student body.

Faculty School total: 7. In upper school: 4 men, 3 women; 1 has an advanced degree.

Subjects Offered Advanced math, Advanced Placement courses, algebra, American literature, art, arts and crafts, biology, biology-AP, British literature, ceramics, chemistry, choir, clayworking, college planning, dance, discrete mathematics, drawing, earth science, economics, English, English composition, English language and composition-AP, environmental science, environmental science-AP, equestrian sports, geometry, health, health education, honors algebra, honors English, honors geometry, honors U.S. history, honors world history, jewelry making, library assistant, life skills, nutrition, oil painting, painting, photography, physical education, physical fitness, pottery, pre-algebra, pre-calculus, printmaking, SAT preparation, science, sex education, sociology, Spanish, study skills, U.S. government, U.S. history, U.S. history-AP, world history.

Graduation Requirements Art, electives, English, foreign language, mathematics, physical education (includes health), science, social studies (includes history), 30 hours of community service.

Special Academic Programs Advanced Placement exam preparation; honors section; accelerated programs; independent study; academic accommodation for the gifted; remedial reading and/or remedial writing; remedial math; programs in English, mathematics for dyslexic students; special instructional classes for students with mild learning disabilities, mild Attention Deficit Disorder, mild behavioral and/or emotional problems (anxiety, depression).

College Admission Counseling 16 students graduated in 2011; 13 went to college, including Guilford College; High Point University; Meredith College; William Peace University. Other: 3 went to work. Mean SAT critical reading: 580, mean SAT math: 550.

Student Life Upper grades have specified standards of dress, student council, honor system. Discipline rests primarily with faculty.

Summer Programs Remediation, enrichment, advancement, art/fine arts, computer instruction programs offered; session focuses on academics; held on campus; accepts girls; not open to students from other schools. 35 students usually enrolled. 2012 schedule: June 18 to August 9.

Tuition and Aid 7-day tuition and room/board: $69,000. Guaranteed tuition plan. Tuition installment plan (monthly payment plans, individually arranged payment plans, Clark Educational Loans, Serenity Loans). Need-based scholarship grants available.

Admissions Traditional secondary-level entrance grade is 11. Battery of testing done through outside agency, comprehensive educational evaluation, psychoeducational evaluation, Stanford Achievement Test and WISC-III and Woodcock-Johnson required. Deadline for receipt of application materials: none. Application fee required: $1500. Interview recommended.

Athletics Intramural: basketball, bicycling, billiards, cheering, combined training, cooperative games, croquet, dance, fishing, fitness, fitness walking, flag football, horseback riding, indoor soccer, jogging, kickball, outdoor activities, outdoor adventure, outdoor education, outdoor recreation, physical fitness, roller skating, running, soccer, softball, strength & conditioning, table tennis, tennis, volleyball, walking, weight training, yoga.

Computers Computer resources include on-campus library services, Internet access, Internet filtering or blocking technology. Campus intranet, student e-mail accounts, and computer access in designated common areas are available to students.

Contact Ms. Amanda Woolard, Admission Coordinator. 919-837-2336 Ext. 200. Fax: 919-837-5284. E-mail: anamda.woolard@sequeltsi.com. Web site: www.auldern.com.

THE AWTY INTERNATIONAL SCHOOL

7455 Awty School Lane

Houston, Texas 77055

Head of School: Mr. Peter Cooper

General Information Coeducational day college-preparatory and bilingual studies school. Grades PK–12. Founded: 1956. Setting: urban. 25-acre campus. 15 buildings on campus. Approved or accredited by French Ministry of Education, Independent Schools

Association of the Southwest, International Baccalaureate Organization, and Texas Department of Education. Member of National Association of Independent Schools, Secondary School Admission Test Board, and European Council of International Schools. Languages of instruction: English, Spanish, and French. Endowment: $2.8 million. Total enrollment: 1,230. Upper school average class size: 18. Upper school faculty-student ratio: 1:18.

Upper School Student Profile Grade 9: 92 students (46 boys, 46 girls); Grade 10: 86 students (34 boys, 52 girls); Grade 11: 93 students (41 boys, 52 girls); Grade 12: 86 students (32 boys, 54 girls).

Faculty School total: 145. In upper school: 31 men, 52 women; 39 have advanced degrees.

Subjects Offered Algebra, American history, Arabic, art, biology, calculus, chemistry, community service, computer programming, computer science, computer studies, drama, Dutch, English, ESL, fine arts, French, geography, geometry, German, grammar, history, Italian, Mandarin, mathematics, music, Norwegian, philosophy, physical education, physics, science, social sciences, social studies, Spanish, theater, theory of knowledge, trigonometry, world history, world literature, writing.

Graduation Requirements Arts and fine arts (art, music, dance, drama), computer science, English, foreign language, mathematics, physical education (includes health), science, social sciences, social studies (includes history), 4000-word extended essay. Community service is required.

Special Academic Programs International Baccalaureate program; ESL (20 students enrolled).

College Admission Counseling 84 students graduated in 2010; 82 went to college, including Boston University; Carnegie Mellon University; Duke University; McGill University; Rice University; University of Houston.

Student Life Upper grades have uniform requirement, student council, honor system. Discipline rests primarily with faculty.

Tuition and Aid Day student tuition: $18,927. Tuition installment plan (monthly payment plans, semiannual payment plan, Dewar Tuition Refund Plan). Need-based financial aid available. In 2010–11, 7% of upper-school students received aid. Total amount of financial aid awarded in 2010–11: $287,033.

Admissions Traditional secondary-level entrance grade is 9. For fall 2010, 170 students applied for upper-level admission, 76 were accepted, 46 enrolled. ISEE, OLSAT, ERB and writing sample required. Deadline for receipt of application materials: none. Application fee required: $100. On-campus interview required.

Athletics Interscholastic: basketball (boys, girls), cheering (g), cross-country running (b,g), soccer (b,g), tennis (b,g), track and field (b,g), volleyball (g), winter soccer (g); intramural: dance (g), dance squad (g), dance team (g), flag football (b); coed interscholastic: golf, swimming and diving; coed intramural: badminton. 3 PE instructors, 20 coaches.

Computers Computers are regularly used in foreign language, science classes. Computer network features include on-campus library services, Internet access. The school has a published electronic and media policy.

Contact Mrs. Erika Benavente, Director of Admissions. 713-686-4850. Fax: 713-579-0003. E-mail: ebenavente@awty.org. Web site: www.awty.org.

BACHMAN ACADEMY

McDonald, Tennessee

See Special Needs Schools section.

THE BALDWIN SCHOOL

701 West Montgomery Avenue

Bryn Mawr, Pennsylvania 19010

Head of School: Mrs. Sally M. Powell

General Information Girls' day college-preparatory, arts, technology, and athletics school. Grades PK–12. Founded: 1888. Setting: suburban. Nearest major city is Philadelphia. 25-acre campus. 5 buildings on campus. Approved or accredited by Middle States Association of Colleges and Schools and Pennsylvania Association of Independent Schools. Member of National Association of Independent Schools and Secondary School Admission Test Board. Endowment: $7 million. Total enrollment: 560. Upper school average class size: 14. Upper school faculty-student ratio: 1:7. There are 171 required school days per year for Upper School students. Upper School students typically attend 5 days per week. The average school day consists of 7 hours.

Upper School Student Profile Grade 9: 54 students (54 girls); Grade 10: 44 students (44 girls); Grade 11: 37 students (37 girls); Grade 12: 58 students (58 girls).

Faculty School total: 90. In upper school: 9 men, 31 women; 34 have advanced degrees.

Subjects Offered Advanced Placement courses, algebra, American history, American history-AP, American literature, anthropology, architecture, art, art history, art history-AP, athletics, basketball, bell choir, biology, biology-AP, calculus, calculus-AP, ceramics, chemistry, chemistry-AP, chorus, classical Greek literature, college admission preparation, college counseling, community service, computer resources, computer science, computer studies, contemporary issues, creative writing, current history, dance, digital photography, drama, drama performance, dramatic arts, earth and space science, earth science, English, English literature, environmental studies, ethics, European history, fine arts, French, French literature-AP, geometry, golf, handbells, health, health education, history, history-AP, honors algebra, human development, Latin, library skills, life science, Mandarin, mathematics, mentorship program, model United Nations, music, peer counseling, performing arts, photography, photojournalism, physical education, physics, physics-AP, play production, playwriting, public speaking, SAT preparation, science, senior internship, social studies, softball, Spanish, speech, squash, swimming, swimming competency, tennis, theater, trigonometry, U.S. history, U.S. history-AP, vocal ensemble, volleyball, world history, world literature.

Graduation Requirements Arts, English, foreign language, history, life skills, mathematics, physical education (includes health), science, U.S. history.

Special Academic Programs Advanced Placement exam preparation; honors section; independent study; academic accommodation for the gifted, the musically talented, and the artistically talented.

College Admission Counseling 49 students graduated in 2010; all went to college, including Cornell University; Franklin & Marshall College; New York University; Princeton University; The Johns Hopkins University; University of Pennsylvania. Mean SAT critical reading: 660, mean SAT math: 660, mean SAT writing: 682. 100% scored over 600 on SAT critical reading, 100% scored over 600 on SAT math, 100% scored over 600 on SAT writing.

Student Life Upper grades have uniform requirement, student council, honor system. Discipline rests equally with students and faculty.

Tuition and Aid Day student tuition: $28,000. Tuition installment plan (monthly payment plans, individually arranged payment plans). Need-based scholarship grants available. In 2010–11, 35% of upper-school students received aid. Total amount of financial aid awarded in 2010–11: $1,700,000.

Admissions Traditional secondary-level entrance grade is 9. For fall 2010, 60 students applied for upper-level admission, 34 were accepted, 12 enrolled. ISEE, SSAT, Wechsler Intelligence Scale for Children or writing sample required. Deadline for receipt of application materials: February 1. Application fee required: $50. On-campus interview required.

Athletics Interscholastic: aquatics, basketball, crew, cross-country running, dance, field hockey, golf, independent competitive sports, indoor track, lacrosse, rowing, running, soccer, softball, squash, swimming and diving, tennis, volleyball, winter (indoor) track. 7 PE instructors, 40 coaches, 1 athletic trainer.

Computers Computers are regularly used in all academic classes. Computer network features include on-campus library services, Internet access, wireless campus network. Campus intranet, student e-mail accounts, and computer access in designated common areas are available to students. The school has a published electronic and media policy.

Contact Sarah J. Goebel, Director of Admissions and Financial Aid. 610-525-2700 Ext. 251. Fax: 610-581-7231. E-mail: sgoebel@baldwinschool.org. Web site: www.baldwinschool.org.

BALMORAL HALL SCHOOL

630 Westminster Avenue

Winnipeg, Manitoba R3C 3S1, Canada

Head of School: Mrs. Joanne Kamins

General Information Girls' boarding and day college-preparatory, arts, technology, and athletics/prep hockey school. Boarding grades 6–12, day grades N–12. Founded: 1901. Setting: urban. Students are housed in apartment-style residence. 12-acre campus. 2 buildings on campus. Approved or accredited by Canadian Association of Independent Schools, Canadian Educational Standards Institute, International Baccalaureate Organization, The Association of Boarding Schools, and Manitoba Department of Education. Affiliate member of National Association of Independent Schools; member of Secondary School Admission Test Board. Language of instruction: English. Endowment: CAN$860,000. Total enrollment: 451. Upper school average class size: 18. Upper school faculty-student ratio: 1:7. There are 185 required school days per year for Upper School students. Upper School students typically attend 5 days per week. The average school day consists of 5 hours.

Upper School Student Profile Grade 9: 34 students (34 girls); Grade 10: 45 students (45 girls); Grade 11: 53 students (53 girls); Grade 12: 34 students (34 girls). 13% of students are boarding students. 85% are province residents. 2 provinces are represented in upper school student body. 10% are international students. International students from China, Hong Kong, Mexico, Republic of Korea, Taiwan, and Tunisia; 2 other countries represented in student body.

Faculty School total: 47. In upper school: 5 men, 19 women; 7 have advanced degrees; 5 reside on campus.

Subjects Offered Acting, advanced math, Advanced Placement courses, advanced studio art-AP, advanced TOEFL/grammar, aerobics, art, art-AP, biology, biology-AP, business, calculus, calculus-AP, career and personal planning, career/college preparation, chemistry, chemistry-AP, choir, college planning, communications, community service, computer science, computer science-AP, consumer mathematics, dance performance, debate, desktop publishing, digital art, digital photography, drama, driver education, English, English language and composition-AP, English literature, English literature and composition-AP, English literature-AP, English/composition-AP, ESL, ethics, European history, French, French language-AP, French literature-AP, general science, geography, health, history, history-AP, jazz ensemble, journalism, mathematics, mathematics-AP, media arts, modern Western civilization, multimedia, music, musical theater, performing arts, personal development, physical education, physics, physics-AP, pre-calculus, psychology-AP, SAT/ACT preparation, science, social studies, Spanish, Spanish-AP, studio art-AP, technology, vocal ensemble, world affairs, world history.

Graduation Requirements Minimum of 10 hours per year of Service Learning participation in grades 9 through 12.

Special Academic Programs Advanced Placement exam preparation; honors section; accelerated programs; study at local college for college credit; academic accommodation for the gifted; ESL (15 students enrolled).

College Admission Counseling 46 students graduated in 2011; all went to college, including McGill University; Queen's University at Kingston; The University of Western Ontario; The University of Winnipeg; University of Manitoba; University of Toronto.

Student Life Upper grades have uniform requirement, student council, honor system. Discipline rests primarily with faculty.

Tuition and Aid Tuition installment plan (The Tuition Plan, international students must pay in full prior to official letter of acceptance). Tuition reduction for siblings, merit scholarship grants available. In 2011–12, 45% of upper-school students received aid. Total amount of financial aid awarded in 2011–12: CAN$135,000.

Admissions Traditional secondary-level entrance grade is 9. School's own exam required. Deadline for receipt of application materials: none. Application fee required: CAN$150. Interview recommended.

Athletics Interscholastic: badminton, basketball, cross-country running, curling, Frisbee, golf, ice hockey, indoor track & field, outdoor skills, running, soccer, speedskating, track and field, ultimate Frisbee, volleyball; intramural: aerobics, aerobics/dance, aerobics/Nautilus, alpine skiing, backpacking, badminton, ballet, baseball, basketball, bicycling, bowling, broomball, cooperative games, Cosom hockey, cross-country running, curling, dance, dance team, fencing, field hockey, figure skating, fitness, fitness walking, flag football, floor hockey, Frisbee, golf, gymnastics, handball, hiking/backpacking, hockey, ice hockey, ice skating, in-line skating, indoor hockey, indoor track & field, jogging, jump rope, modern dance, netball, outdoor activities, outdoor education, outdoor skills, physical fitness, physical training, roller blading, rowing, rugby, running, skiing (cross-country), skiing (downhill), snowboarding, snowshoeing, soccer, softball, speedskating, strength & conditioning, swimming and diving, table tennis, tennis, track and field, ultimate Frisbee, volleyball, walking, wall climbing, weight training, yoga. 2 PE instructors, 4 coaches.

Computers Computers are regularly used in all classes. Computer network features include on-campus library services, Internet access, wireless campus network, Internet filtering or blocking technology. Campus intranet, student e-mail accounts, and computer access in designated common areas are available to students. Students grades are available online. The school has a published electronic and media policy.

Contact Ms. Bin Dong Jiang, Day Admissions Administrator. 204-784-1608. Fax: 204-774-5534. E-mail: bdjiang@balmoralhall.com. Web site: www.balmoralhall.com.

THE BALTIMORE ACTORS' THEATRE CONSERVATORY

The Dumbarton House

300 Dumbarton Road

Baltimore, Maryland 21212-1532

Head of School: Walter E. Anderson

General Information Coeducational day and distance learning college-preparatory and arts school. Grades K–12. Distance learning grades 9–12. Founded: 1979. Setting: suburban. 35-acre campus. 3 buildings on campus. Approved or accredited by Association of Independent Maryland Schools, Middle States Association of Colleges and Schools, and Maryland Department of Education. Endowment: $200,000. Total enrollment: 24. Upper school average class size: 6. Upper school faculty-student ratio: 1:3. There are 175 required school days per year for Upper School students. Upper School students typically attend 5 days per week. The average school day consists of 7 hours and 30 minutes.

Upper School Student Profile Grade 9: 4 students (2 boys, 2 girls); Grade 10: 4 students (2 boys, 2 girls); Grade 11: 2 students (2 girls); Grade 12: 1 student (1 girl).

Faculty School total: 12. In upper school: 2 men, 8 women; 9 have advanced degrees.

Subjects Offered Acting, algebra, American history-AP, ballet, biology-AP, British literature, chemistry, English language-AP, environmental science-AP, French, geometry, health science, music history, music theory-AP, novels, physics, pre-calculus, psychology, sociology, theater history, trigonometry, world history, world history-AP.

Graduation Requirements Algebra, American history, ballet, chemistry, English, French, geometry, modern dance, music history, music theory, physical science, psychology, sociology, theater history, world history, students are required to complete graduation requirements in the three performing arts areas of music, drama, and dance.

Special Academic Programs Advanced Placement exam preparation; honors section; accelerated programs; independent study; study at local college for college credit; academic accommodation for the gifted, the musically talented, and the artistically talented.

College Admission Counseling 2 students graduated in 2011; all went to college. Median SAT critical reading: 600, median SAT math: 570, median composite ACT: 26.

Student Life Upper grades have uniform requirement, student council, honor system. Discipline rests primarily with faculty.

Summer Programs Remediation, art/fine arts programs offered; session focuses on music, drama, dance, and art; held off campus; held at theatre in Oregon Ridge Park, Hunt Valley, Maryland; accepts boys and girls; open to students from other schools. 30 students usually enrolled. 2012 schedule: July 24 to August 8. Application deadline: none.

Tuition and Aid Day student tuition: $10,000. Tuition installment plan (SMART Tuition Payment Plan, FACTS Tuition Payment Plan, individually arranged payment plans). Need-based scholarship grants available. In 2011–12, 10% of upper-school students received aid. Total amount of financial aid awarded in 2011–12: $12,000.

Admissions Traditional secondary-level entrance grade is 9. For fall 2011, 50 students applied for upper-level admission, 15 were accepted, 7 enrolled. Any standardized test, English, French, and math proficiency and writing sample required. Deadline for receipt of application materials: April 3. Application fee required: $50. On-campus interview required.

Computers Computers are regularly used in college planning, creative writing, dance, desktop publishing, English, historical foundations for arts, history, independent study, introduction to technology, keyboarding, music, music technology, psychology, senior seminar, theater, theater arts, word processing, writing classes. Computer network features include Internet access, wireless campus network, Internet filtering or blocking technology. Student e-mail accounts are available to students. The school has a published electronic and media policy.

Contact Mr. Walter E. Anderson, Headmaster. 410-337-8519. Fax: 410-337-8582. E-mail: batpro@baltimoreactorstheatre.org. Web site: www.baltimoreactorstheatre.org.

BALTIMORE LUTHERAN SCHOOL

1145 Concordia Drive

Towson, Maryland 21286-1796

Head of School: Mr. Alan Freeman

General Information Coeducational day and distance learning college-preparatory, arts, religious studies, and technology school, affiliated with Lutheran Church–Missouri Synod. Grades 6–12. Distance learning grades 9–12. Founded: 1965. Setting: suburban. Nearest major city is Baltimore. 25-acre campus. 5 buildings on campus. Approved or accredited by Association of Independent Maryland Schools, Middle States Association of Colleges and Schools, and Maryland Department of Education. Endowment: $1.3 million. Total enrollment: 295. Upper school average class size: 16. Upper school faculty-student ratio: 1:12. There are 174 required school days per year for Upper School students. Upper School students typically attend 5 days per week. The average school day consists of 6 hours and 45 minutes.

Upper School Student Profile 30% of students are Lutheran Church–Missouri Synod.

Faculty School total: 36. In upper school: 14 men, 15 women; 16 have advanced degrees.

Subjects Offered 20th century history, 3-dimensional art, acting, advanced biology, Advanced Placement courses, algebra, American government, American history, American literature, analytic geometry, anatomy, art, Bible studies, biology, biology-AP, brass choir, British literature, British literature (honors), calculus, chemistry, Chesapeake Bay studies, Christian doctrine, Christian scripture, church history, college counseling, college planning, computer education, computer graphics, computer programming, computers, concert band, concert choir, creative writing, digital photography, drama, drama performance, dramatic arts, drawing, drawing and design, earth science, ecology, economics, economics and history, English, English literature, English literature-AP, expository writing, French, geometry, German, government/civics, grammar, graphic arts, graphic design, health, honors English, independent study, intro to computers, jazz band, journalism, keyboarding, Latin, law, mathematics, music, painting, photography, physical education, physics, pre-algebra, psychology, religion, SAT/ACT preparation, science, social studies, Spanish, Spanish-AP, speech, studio art, theater, theology, trigonometry, Web site design, word processing, world history, world history-AP, world literature, writing, yearbook.

Graduation Requirements Arts and fine arts (art, music, dance, drama), English, foreign language, mathematics, physical education (includes health), religion (includes Bible studies and theology), science, social studies (includes history), technology.

Special Academic Programs 5 Advanced Placement exams for which test preparation is offered; honors section; independent study; study at local college for college credit; academic accommodation for the gifted; programs in English, mathematics for dyslexic students.

College Admission Counseling 79 students graduated in 2011; 78 went to college, including Brown University; Loyola University Maryland; The Johns Hopkins University; Towson University; University of Maryland, Baltimore County; University of Maryland, College Park. Other: 1 went to work. Mean SAT critical reading: 539, mean SAT math: 522, mean SAT writing: 545.

Student Life Upper grades have uniform requirement, student council, honor system. Discipline rests primarily with faculty. Attendance at religious services is required.

Summer Programs Remediation, sports programs offered; session focuses on general activities; held on campus; accepts boys and girls; open to students from other schools. 2012 schedule: June 12 to August 11.
Tuition and Aid Day student tuition: $10,950. Tuition installment plan (FACTS Tuition Payment Plan). Tuition reduction for siblings, merit scholarship grants, need-based scholarship grants, Academic merit scholarships for students from Christian schools available. In 2011–12, 25% of upper-school students received aid; total upper-school merit-scholarship money awarded: $18,000. Total amount of financial aid awarded in 2011–12: $70,000.
Admissions Traditional secondary-level entrance grade is 9. For fall 2011, 95 students applied for upper-level admission, 80 were accepted, 60 enrolled. ISEE, school placement exam, TOEFL or SLEP and writing sample required. Deadline for receipt of application materials: none. Application fee required: $50. On-campus interview required.
Athletics Interscholastic: baseball (boys), basketball (b,g), cheering (g), cross-country running (b,g), field hockey (g), football (b), golf (b), indoor soccer (g), lacrosse (b,g), soccer (b,g), softball (g), tennis (b,g), track and field (b,g), volleyball (g), winter soccer (g), wrestling (b); coed intramural: skiing (downhill), snowboarding. 2 PE instructors, 5 coaches, 1 athletic trainer.
Computers Computers are regularly used in English, graphic design, history, independent study, journalism, library, mathematics, newspaper, photography, SAT preparation, social sciences, technology, writing, yearbook classes. Computer network features include on-campus library services, online commercial services, Internet access, wireless campus network, Internet filtering or blocking technology. Student e-mail accounts are available to students. Students grades are available online. The school has a published electronic and media policy.
Contact Mrs. Ruth A. Heilman, Director of Admissions. 410-825-2323 Ext. 272. Fax: 410-825-2506. E-mail: rheilman@baltimorelutheran.org. Web site: www.baltimorelutheran.org.

BARRIE SCHOOL

13500 Layhill Road

Silver Spring, Maryland 20906

Head of School: Mr. Charles Abelmann

General Information Coeducational day college-preparatory school. Grades N–12. Founded: 1932. Setting: suburban. Nearest major city is Washington, DC. 45-acre campus. 8 buildings on campus. Approved or accredited by Middle States Association of Colleges and Schools and Maryland Department of Education. Member of National Association of Independent Schools and Secondary School Admission Test Board. Endowment: $1 million. Total enrollment: 299. Upper school average class size: 15. Upper school faculty-student ratio: 1:8. There are 174 required school days per year for Upper School students. Upper School students typically attend 5 days per week. The average school day consists of 7 hours and 20 minutes.
Upper School Student Profile Grade 9: 22 students (8 boys, 14 girls); Grade 10: 15 students (8 boys, 7 girls); Grade 11: 12 students (8 boys, 4 girls); Grade 12: 22 students (8 boys, 14 girls).
Faculty School total: 19. In upper school: 10 men, 9 women; 13 have advanced degrees.
Subjects Offered Algebra, art, biology, Buddhism, calculus, calculus-AP, ceramics, chemistry, community service, computer programming, drama, drawing, environmental science-AP, fitness, French, French-AP, geometry, health, health and wellness, history, humanities, illustration, instrumental music, journalism, music, painting, performing arts, physics, pre-algebra, pre-calculus, reading, robotics, science, sculpture, service learning/internship, Spanish, statistics-AP, studio art, world geography, world history, writing, yearbook.
Graduation Requirements Algebra, art, biology, chemistry, English, foreign language, health, history, humanities, mathematics, physics, pre-algebra, science, sports, U.S. history, 96 hours of community service.
Special Academic Programs 11 Advanced Placement exams for which test preparation is offered; independent study.
College Admission Counseling 22 students graduated in 2011; 21 went to college, including Babson College; Earlham College; St. Mary's College of Maryland; The College of Wooster; University of Maryland, Baltimore County; University of Maryland, College Park. Other: 1 had other specific plans. Mean SAT critical reading: 536, mean SAT math: 525, mean SAT writing: 541, mean combined SAT: 1602, mean composite ACT: 25. 21% scored over 600 on SAT critical reading, 26% scored over 600 on SAT math, 21% scored over 600 on SAT writing, 21% scored over 1800 on combined SAT, 17% scored over 26 on composite ACT.
Student Life Upper grades have student council. Discipline rests primarily with faculty.
Summer Programs Sports programs offered; session focuses on day camp; held on campus; accepts boys and girls; open to students from other schools. 700 students usually enrolled. 2012 schedule: June 20 to August 12. Application deadline: none.
Tuition and Aid Day student tuition: $25,793. Tuition installment plan (FACTS Tuition Payment Plan, monthly payment plans, The Tuition Refund Plan). Need-based scholarship grants, need-based financial aid grants available. In 2011–12, 34% of upper-school students received aid. Total amount of financial aid awarded in 2011–12: $814,427.
Admissions Traditional secondary-level entrance grade is 9. For fall 2011, 28 students applied for upper-level admission, 9 were accepted, 7 enrolled. ISEE, SSAT, Wechsler Intelligence Scale for Children III or WISC-R required. Deadline for receipt of application materials: January 14. Application fee required: $100. Interview required.
Athletics Interscholastic: basketball (boys, girls), lacrosse (g), soccer (b,g); coed interscholastic: cross-country running, equestrian sports, horseback riding, outdoor activities, physical fitness, running, tennis, track and field, ultimate Frisbee. 6 coaches.
Computers Computer network features include Internet access, wireless campus network, Internet filtering or blocking technology. Campus intranet, student e-mail accounts, and computer access in designated common areas are available to students. The school has a published electronic and media policy.
Contact Ms. Alyssa Jahn, Director of Admission. 301-576-2839. Fax: 301-576-2803. E-mail: ajahn@barrie.org. Web site: www.barrie.org.

BATTLE GROUND ACADEMY

PO Box 1889

Franklin, Tennessee 37065-1889

Head of School: Dr. John W. Griffith

General Information Coeducational day college-preparatory, arts, and technology school. Grades K–12. Founded: 1889. Setting: suburban. Nearest major city is Nashville. 55-acre campus. 11 buildings on campus. Approved or accredited by Southern Association of Colleges and Schools, Southern Association of Independent Schools, Tennessee Association of Independent Schools, and Tennessee Department of Education. Member of National Association of Independent Schools. Endowment: $8 million. Total enrollment: 880. Upper school average class size: 16. Upper school faculty-student ratio: 1:11.
Faculty School total: 110. In upper school: 26 men, 20 women; 27 have advanced degrees.
Subjects Offered Accounting, algebra, American history, American literature, art, art history, biology, calculus, chemistry, chorus, computer applications, computer programming, computer science, drama, early childhood, economics, English, English literature, English literature and composition-AP, European history, fine arts, French, French-AP, geography, geometry, government/civics, grammar, health, history, Latin, mathematics, modern European history-AP, music, music history, physical education, physics, science, social studies, Spanish, speech, technical theater, theater, trigonometry, U.S. history, U.S. history-AP, world history, world history-AP, world literature, writing.
Graduation Requirements Arts and fine arts (art, music, dance, drama), computer science, English, foreign language, mathematics, physical education (includes health), science, social studies (includes history). Community service is required.
Special Academic Programs Advanced Placement exam preparation; honors section.
College Admission Counseling 87 students graduated in 2011; all went to college. Median combined SAT: 1200, median composite ACT: 25.
Student Life Upper grades have uniform requirement, student council, honor system. Discipline rests primarily with faculty.
Summer Programs Remediation, enrichment, sports, art/fine arts, computer instruction programs offered; session focuses on remediation, enrichment, and sports; held both on and off campus; held at local farm; accepts boys and girls; open to students from other schools. 350 students usually enrolled. 2012 schedule: June 5 to August 4. Application deadline: none.
Tuition and Aid Day student tuition: $17,080. Tuition installment plan (The Tuition Plan, FACTS Tuition Payment Plan, individually arranged payment plans). Merit scholarship grants, need-based scholarship grants, paying campus jobs available. In 2011–12, 15% of upper-school students received aid; total upper-school merit-scholarship money awarded: $750,000. Total amount of financial aid awarded in 2011–12: $750,000.
Admissions Traditional secondary-level entrance grade is 9. ISEE required. Deadline for receipt of application materials: none. Application fee required: $50. Interview required.
Athletics Interscholastic: baseball (boys), basketball (b,g), cheering (g), cross-country running (b,g), dance team (g), fitness (b,g), football (b), golf (b,g), physical fitness (b,g), physical training (b,g), soccer (b,g), softball (g), strength & conditioning (b,g), swimming and diving (b,g), tennis (b,g), track and field (b,g), volleyball (g), weight training (b,g), wrestling (b); intramural: baseball (b,g), basketball (b,g), fitness (b,g), football (b), softball (g); coed interscholastic: bowling, fitness, marksmanship, riflery, trap and skeet; coed intramural: fitness, flag football, hiking/backpacking, mountain biking, outdoor activities, outdoor adventure, physical training, rock climbing, ropes courses, soccer. 4 PE instructors, 2 coaches, 1 athletic trainer.
Computers Computers are regularly used in art, college planning, desktop publishing, English, foreign language, geography, history, library, literary magazine, mathematics, newspaper, photography, SAT preparation, science, social studies, Spanish, study skills, technology, theater, writing classes. Computer network features include on-campus library services, online commercial services, Internet access, wireless campus network, Internet filtering or blocking technology. Campus intranet, student e-mail accounts, and

computer access in designated common areas are available to students. Students grades are available online. The school has a published electronic and media policy.
Contact Ms. Cathy Irwin, Director of Admissions. 615-567-9014. E-mail: cathy.irwin@mybga.org. Web site: www.battlegroundacademy.org.

BAVARIAN INTERNATIONAL SCHOOL

Schloss Haimhausen
Hauptstrasse 1
Haimhausen D-85778, Germany

Head of School: Bryan Nixon

General Information Coeducational day college-preparatory, general academic, arts, business, bilingual studies, technology, and physical education school. Grades PK–12. Founded: 1991. Setting: small town. Nearest major city is Munich, Germany. 10-acre campus. 5 buildings on campus. Approved or accredited by International Baccalaureate Organization and New England Association of Schools and Colleges. Language of instruction: English. Total enrollment: 854. Upper school average class size: 19. Upper school faculty-student ratio: 1:7. There are 190 required school days per year for Upper School students. Upper School students typically attend 5 days per week. The average school day consists of 7 hours.
Upper School Student Profile Grade 9: 57 students (28 boys, 29 girls); Grade 10: 68 students (35 boys, 33 girls); Grade 11: 63 students (34 boys, 29 girls); Grade 12: 54 students (28 boys, 26 girls).
Faculty School total: 110. In upper school: 9 men, 26 women; 24 have advanced degrees.
Subjects Offered Art, chemistry, community service, computer science, English, fine arts, French, French language-AP, geography, German, history, Japanese, mathematics, music, physical education, physics, science, social studies, theater.
Graduation Requirements Youth culture.
Special Academic Programs International Baccalaureate program; independent study; remedial reading and/or remedial writing; remedial math; programs in English, mathematics, general development for dyslexic students; special instructional classes for students with learning disabilities and dyslexia; ESL (40 students enrolled).
Student Life Upper grades have specified standards of dress, student council, honor system. Discipline rests primarily with faculty.
Tuition and Aid Day student tuition: €13,900–€14,100. Tuition installment plan (yearly payment plan, 2-payment plan). Tuition reduction for siblings available.
Admissions English proficiency or mathematics proficiency exam required. Deadline for receipt of application materials: none. No application fee required. On-campus interview required.
Athletics Interscholastic: cheering (girls); coed interscholastic: aerobics, aerobics/dance, alpine skiing, badminton, ball hockey, ballet, baseball, basketball, climbing, combined training, cooperative games, cricket, cross-country running, dance, field hockey, football, golf, gymnastics, handball, indoor hockey, indoor soccer, indoor track & field, jogging, judo, netball, outdoor activities, outdoors, physical training, rock climbing, rugby, running, skiing (downhill), snowboarding, soccer, softball, swimming and diving, tennis, track and field, volleyball, winter soccer. 3 PE instructors, 6 coaches.
Computers Computers are regularly used in art, business, English, ESL, information technology, photography, science, typing, video film production, writing, yearbook classes. Computer network features include on-campus library services, online commercial services, Internet access, wireless campus network, Internet filtering or blocking technology. Campus intranet, student e-mail accounts, and computer access in designated common areas are available to students. The school has a published electronic and media policy.
Contact Katharina Lippacher, Registrar. 49-8133-917 Ext. 121. Fax: 49-8133-917 Ext. 182. E-mail: k.lippacher@bis-school.com. Web site: www.bis-school.com.

BAYLOR SCHOOL

171 Baylor School Road
Chattanooga, Tennessee 37405

Head of School: Mr. Scott Wilson

General Information Coeducational boarding and day college-preparatory and arts school. Boarding grades 9–12, day grades 6–12. Founded: 1893. Setting: suburban. Nearest major city is Atlanta, GA. Students are housed in single-sex dormitories. 670-acre campus. 30 buildings on campus. Approved or accredited by Southern Association of Colleges and Schools, Southern Association of Independent Schools, The Association of Boarding Schools, and Tennessee Department of Education. Member of National Association of Independent Schools and Secondary School Admission Test Board. Endowment: $90 million. Total enrollment: 1,070. Upper school average class size: 14. Upper school faculty-student ratio: 1:8. There are 180 required school days per year for Upper School students. Upper School students typically attend 5 days per week. The average school day consists of 7 hours and 30 minutes.
Upper School Student Profile Grade 9: 165 students (84 boys, 81 girls); Grade 10: 200 students (103 boys, 97 girls); Grade 11: 199 students (101 boys, 98 girls); Grade 12: 192 students (102 boys, 90 girls). 38% of students are boarding students. 74% are state residents. 21 states are represented in upper school student body. 10% are international students. International students from Bermuda, China, Germany, Mexico, Republic of Korea, and Taiwan; 24 other countries represented in student body.
Faculty School total: 144. In upper school: 77 men, 67 women; 91 have advanced degrees; 45 reside on campus.
Subjects Offered Algebra, American history, American literature, anthropology, art, art history, art history-AP, art-AP, astronomy, biology, biology-AP, calculus-AP, ceramics, chemistry, chemistry-AP, computer math, computer science, computer science-AP, creative writing, dance, drama, driver education, economics, English, English language-AP, English literature, English literature-AP, environmental science, environmental science-AP, ethics, European history, European history-AP, film, fine arts, finite math, forensics, French, French-AP, genetics, geography, geometry, German, German-AP, government/civics, history, human geography - AP, Latin, Latin-AP, mathematics, music, photography, physical education, physics, physics-AP, religion, science, social studies, Spanish, Spanish-AP, speech, statistics, statistics-AP, theater, trigonometry, U.S. history-AP, video, world history, world literature.
Graduation Requirements Arts and fine arts (art, music, dance, drama), English, foreign language, mathematics, physical education (includes health), science, social studies (includes history), Leadership Baylor, summer reading, iPad School.
Special Academic Programs 22 Advanced Placement exams for which test preparation is offered; honors section; study abroad; academic accommodation for the gifted, the musically talented, and the artistically talented; special instructional classes for deaf students.
College Admission Counseling 162 students graduated in 2011; all went to college, including Georgia Institute of Technology; Sewanee: The University of the South; The University of Alabama; The University of Tennessee; University of Georgia; University of Illinois at Urbana–Champaign.
Student Life Upper grades have specified standards of dress, student council, honor system. Discipline rests primarily with faculty.
Summer Programs Enrichment, sports, art/fine arts, rigorous outdoor training, computer instruction programs offered; session focuses on sports, arts, wilderness activities; held both on and off campus; held at locations near Chattanooga and various locations throughout the U.S.; accepts boys and girls; open to students from other schools. 500 students usually enrolled. 2012 schedule: June 6 to July 29. Application deadline: none.
Tuition and Aid Day student tuition: $19,985; 7-day tuition and room/board: $40,705. Tuition installment plan (The Tuition Plan, Insured Tuition Payment Plan, Key Tuition Payment Plan, FACTS Tuition Payment Plan, monthly payment plans, individually arranged payment plans). Merit scholarship grants, need-based scholarship grants available. In 2011–12, 35% of upper-school students received aid; total upper-school merit-scholarship money awarded: $350,000. Total amount of financial aid awarded in 2011–12: $2,500,000.
Admissions Traditional secondary-level entrance grade is 9. For fall 2011, 89 students applied for upper-level admission, 47 were accepted, 38 enrolled. ISEE, SSAT or TOEFL required. Deadline for receipt of application materials: none. Application fee required: $75. Interview required.
Athletics Interscholastic: aquatics (boys, girls), baseball (b), basketball (b,g), bowling (b,g), cheering (g), crew (b,g), cross-country running (b,g), dance (g), dance team (g), diving (b,g), fencing (b,g), football (b), golf (b,g), lacrosse (b,g), modern dance (g), soccer (b,g), softball (g), swimming and diving (b,g), tennis (b,g), track and field (b,g), volleyball (g), wrestling (b); intramural: ballet (g), dance (g), weight lifting (b,g); coed interscholastic: aerobics/dance, rowing, running, strength & conditioning; coed intramural: backpacking, bicycling, canoeing/kayaking, climbing, fitness, fly fishing, Frisbee, hiking/backpacking, kayaking, mountain biking, mountaineering, ocean paddling, outdoor activities, outdoor adventure, outdoor education, physical fitness, rafting, rock climbing, scuba diving, ultimate Frisbee, wall climbing, wilderness survival. 4 PE instructors, 10 coaches, 2 athletic trainers.
Computers Computers are regularly used in art, English, history, mathematics, photography, publications, science, Spanish, technology, theater arts, writing, yearbook classes. Computer network features include on-campus library services, online commercial services, Internet access, wireless campus network, Internet filtering or blocking technology. Student e-mail accounts and computer access in designated common areas are available to students. Students grades are available online. The school has a published electronic and media policy.
Contact Ms. Cindy Clark, Boarding Admission Associate. 423-267-8505 Ext. 220. Fax: 423-757-2525. E-mail: cclark@baylorschool.org. Web site: www.baylorschool.org.

BAYSIDE ACADEMY

303 Dryer Avenue
Daphne, Alabama 36526

Head of School: Mr. Thomas F. Johnson

General Information Coeducational day college-preparatory, arts, and technology school. Grades PK–12. Founded: 1970. Setting: small town. Nearest major city is Mobile. 44-acre campus. 9 buildings on campus. Approved or accredited by Southern Association of Colleges and Schools, Southern Association of Independent Schools, and Alabama Department of Education. Endowment: $1.4 million. Total enrollment: 753. Upper school average class size: 19. Upper school faculty-student ratio: 1:7. There

are 178 required school days per year for Upper School students. The average school day consists of 7 hours.
Faculty School total: 108. In upper school: 17 men, 21 women; 32 have advanced degrees.
Subjects Offered Advanced Placement courses, algebra, American history, American literature, art, art history, biology, biology-AP, calculus, chemistry, chemistry-AP, computer programming, computer science, creative writing, drama, economics, English, English literature, environmental science, European history, film, fine arts, French, genetics, geography, geometry, government/civics, grammar, histology, history, Latin, marine biology, mathematics, multimedia, music, photography, physical education, physics, science, social studies, Spanish, speech, theater, trigonometry, world history, world literature, writing.
Graduation Requirements Arts and fine arts (art, music, dance, drama), computer science, English, foreign language, mathematics, physical education (includes health), science, social studies (includes history).
Special Academic Programs 15 Advanced Placement exams for which test preparation is offered; honors section; independent study; study abroad; programs in English, mathematics, general development for dyslexic students.
College Admission Counseling 62 students graduated in 2011; all went to college, including Auburn University; College of Charleston; Rhodes College; The University of Alabama; Tulane University; Vanderbilt University. 80% scored over 26 on composite ACT.
Student Life Upper grades have uniform requirement, student council, honor system. Discipline rests primarily with faculty.
Tuition and Aid Day student tuition: $9900. Tuition installment plan (monthly payment plans, individually arranged payment plans). Need-based scholarship grants available. In 2011–12, 15% of upper-school students received aid.
Admissions Traditional secondary-level entrance grade is 9. For fall 2011, 31 students applied for upper-level admission, 22 were accepted, 19 enrolled. Otis-Lennon School Ability Test, Stanford Achievement Test and Stanford Achievement Test, Otis-Lennon School Ability Test required. Deadline for receipt of application materials: none. Application fee required: $100. Interview required.
Athletics Interscholastic: aerobics/dance (girls), aquatics (b,g), baseball (b), basketball (b,g), cheering (g), cross-country running (b,g), dance (g), dance squad (g), dance team (g), football (b), golf (b,g), indoor track (b,g), indoor track & field (b,g), soccer (b,g), softball (g), swimming and diving (b,g), tennis (b,g), track and field (b,g), volleyball (g); intramural: ballet (g), dance (g), dance team (g), football (b), soccer (b,g); coed intramural: ballet, basketball, bicycling, canoeing/kayaking, dance, equestrian sports, physical training, sailing, scuba diving, soccer, strength & conditioning, track and field, weight training, yoga. 6 PE instructors, 26 coaches, 1 athletic trainer.
Computers Computer network features include on-campus library services, online commercial services, Internet access, wireless campus network, Internet filtering or blocking technology. Campus intranet is available to students. Students grades are available online.
Contact Alan M. Foster, Director of Admissions. 251-338-6415. Fax: 251-338-6310. E-mail: afoster@baysideacademy.org. Web site: www.baysideacademy.org.

BEARSPAW CHRISTIAN SCHOOL

15001 69 Street NW

Calgary, Alberta T3R 1C5, Canada

Head of School: Mr. Kelly Blake

General Information Coeducational day and distance learning college-preparatory, general academic, and religious studies school, affiliated with Christian faith. Grades K–12. Distance learning grades 10–12. Founded: 1991. Setting: rural. 40-acre campus. 3 buildings on campus. Approved or accredited by Association of Christian Schools International, Association of Independent Schools and Colleges of Alberta, and Alberta Department of Education. Language of instruction: English. Total enrollment: 577. Upper school average class size: 21. Upper school faculty-student ratio: 1:20. There are 176 required school days per year for Upper School students. Upper School students typically attend 5 days per week. The average school day consists of 6 hours and 45 minutes.
Upper School Student Profile Grade 10: 40 students (14 boys, 26 girls); Grade 11: 38 students (14 boys, 24 girls); Grade 12: 37 students (19 boys, 18 girls). 90% of students are Christian faith.
Faculty School total: 36. In upper school: 6 men, 15 women; 2 have advanced degrees.
Subjects Offered 20th century history, 20th century world history, acting, advanced chemistry, advanced math, algebra, applied music, art, athletic training, athletics, Bible studies, biology, business education, calculus, Canadian history, Canadian law, career education, chemistry, Christian education, computer applications, English composition, food and nutrition, foreign language, French as a second language, general math, health and wellness, keyboarding, media arts, physical education, physics, science, social studies, Spanish, world history.
Graduation Requirements Bible, English, mathematics, science, social studies (includes history).
Special Academic Programs Honors section; special instructional classes for students with learning disabilities, Attention Deficit Disorder, emotional problems, and dyslexia.
College Admission Counseling 34 students graduated in 2011; they went to Trinity Western University; University of Alberta; University of Calgary; University of Victoria.
Student Life Upper grades have uniform requirement, student council. Discipline rests primarily with faculty. Attendance at religious services is required.
Tuition and Aid Day student tuition: CAN$5040. Tuition installment plan (monthly payment plans, individually arranged payment plans). Tuition reduction for siblings, need-based scholarship grants available. In 2011–12, 21% of upper-school students received aid. Total amount of financial aid awarded in 2011–12: CAN$137,342.
Admissions Traditional secondary-level entrance grade is 10. For fall 2011, 13 students applied for upper-level admission, 9 were accepted, 9 enrolled. Achievement tests, admissions testing, CTB/McGraw-Hill/Macmillan Co-op Test, WAIS, WICS, Woodcock-Johnson and writing sample required. Deadline for receipt of application materials: September 30. Application fee required: CAN$400. Interview required.
Athletics Interscholastic: badminton (boys, girls), basketball (b,g), cross-country running (b,g), floor hockey (b,g), golf (b,g), indoor soccer (b,g), track and field (b,g), volleyball (b,g), wrestling (b); intramural: aerobics/dance (b,g), badminton (b,g), basketball (b,g), cross-country running (b,g), flag football (b,g), floor hockey (b,g), track and field (b,g), volleyball (b,g), wrestling (b); coed interscholastic: badminton, indoor soccer, soccer; coed intramural: aerobics/dance, badminton, basketball, flag football, strength & conditioning, volleyball. 2 PE instructors, 1 athletic trainer.
Computers Computers are regularly used in all academic classes. Computer network features include Internet access, wireless campus network, Internet filtering or blocking technology. Student e-mail accounts and computer access in designated common areas are available to students. Students grades are available online. The school has a published electronic and media policy.
Contact Mrs. Amie Lee, Registrar. 403-295-2566 Ext. 1102. Fax: 403-275-8170. E-mail: alee@bearspawschool.com. Web site: www.bearspawschool.com.

BEAUMONT SCHOOL

3301 North Park Boulevard

Cleveland Heights, Ohio 44118

Head of School: Mrs. Mary Whelan

General Information Girls' day college-preparatory, arts, and religious studies school, affiliated with Roman Catholic Church. Grades 9–12. Founded: 1850. Setting: suburban. Nearest major city is Cleveland. 21-acre campus. 2 buildings on campus. Approved or accredited by North Central Association of Colleges and Schools, Ohio Catholic Schools Accreditation Association (OCSAA), and Ohio Department of Education. Endowment: $7.5 million. Total enrollment: 442. Upper school average class size: 20. Upper school faculty-student ratio: 1:12. There are 180 required school days per year for Upper School students. Upper School students typically attend 5 days per week. The average school day consists of 6 hours and 30 minutes.
Upper School Student Profile Grade 9: 107 students (107 girls); Grade 10: 107 students (107 girls); Grade 11: 115 students (115 girls); Grade 12: 113 students (113 girls). 80% of students are Roman Catholic.
Faculty School total: 52. In upper school: 4 men, 42 women; 40 have advanced degrees.
Subjects Offered Algebra, American history, American history-AP, American literature, analysis, anatomy, applied arts, art, art appreciation, art history, astronomy, biology, biology-AP, British literature, British literature (honors), business skills, calculus, calculus-AP, campus ministry, Catholic belief and practice, ceramics, chemistry, chemistry-AP, choir, Christian and Hebrew scripture, Christian testament, church history, college counseling, college planning, community service, comparative government and politics, comparative politics, comparative religion, competitive science projects, computer applications, computer art, computer education, computer graphics, computer multimedia, computer programming, computer science, creative writing, critical thinking, critical writing, culinary arts, desktop publishing, drama, dramatic arts, drawing and design, economics, economics and history, electives, English, English literature, English literature-AP, English-AP, ethics, fashion, film history, fine arts, foreign language, French, French language-AP, French-AP, genetics, geology, geometry, government, government and politics-AP, government-AP, guidance, health, health education, Hebrew scripture, history, history-AP, honors algebra, honors English, honors geometry, honors U.S. history, honors world history, human relations, instrumental music, integrated science, journalism, keyboarding, lab science, language arts, Latin, Latin-AP, leadership and service, Life of Christ, mathematics, mathematics-AP, media production, media studies, music, music appreciation, music history, music theater, music theory, mythology, New Testament, peace and justice, peer ministry, performing arts, personal development, photo shop, photography, physical education, physical fitness, physical science, physics, piano, play production, pottery, prayer/spirituality, pre-calculus, probability and statistics, psychology, public speaking, reading/study skills, religion, religious studies, SAT preparation, SAT/ACT preparation, science, senior project, service learning/internship, social sciences, social studies, sociology, Spanish, Spanish language-AP, Spanish literature-AP, speech, speech and debate, speech and oral interpretations, stagecraft, student government, studio art, study skills, theater history, theater production, theology, trigonometry, U.S. history-AP, voice, voice ensemble, Web site design, world affairs, world geography, world history, world literature, world studies, writing, writing, yearbook.

Graduation Requirements Arts and fine arts (art, music, dance, drama), computer science, English, foreign language, health, mathematics, physical education (includes health), religion (includes Bible studies and theology), science, social sciences, social studies (includes history), Senior Project R.E.A.L, junior career shadowing day. Community service is required.

Special Academic Programs Advanced Placement exam preparation; honors section; independent study; study at local college for college credit; academic accommodation for the gifted, the musically talented, and the artistically talented.

College Admission Counseling 120 students graduated in 2010; all went to college, including Cleveland State University; John Carroll University; Miami University; Ohio University; The Ohio State University; University of Dayton. Mean SAT critical reading: 559, mean SAT math: 548, mean composite ACT: 23. 25% scored over 600 on SAT critical reading, 25% scored over 600 on SAT math, 36% scored over 26 on composite ACT.

Student Life Upper grades have uniform requirement, student council, honor system. Discipline rests primarily with faculty. Attendance at religious services is required.

Tuition and Aid Day student tuition: $10,700. Tuition installment plan (monthly payment plans, individually arranged payment plans, Quarterly). Tuition reduction for siblings, merit scholarship grants, need-based scholarship grants, paying campus jobs available. In 2010–11, 41% of upper-school students received aid. Total amount of financial aid awarded in 2010–11: $1,200,000.

Admissions Traditional secondary-level entrance grade is 9. For fall 2010, 188 students applied for upper-level admission, 175 were accepted, 137 enrolled. High School Placement Test required. Deadline for receipt of application materials: none. No application fee required. On-campus interview required.

Athletics Interscholastic: basketball, cross-country running, diving, lacrosse, softball, swimming and diving, tennis, track and field, volleyball, winter (indoor) track. 1 PE instructor, 11 coaches, 1 athletic trainer.

Computers Computers are regularly used in English, foreign language, keyboarding, media, publications, science, social studies, yearbook classes. Computer network features include on-campus library services, Internet access, wireless campus network, Internet filtering or blocking technology. Student e-mail accounts are available to students. Students grades are available online. The school has a published electronic and media policy.

Contact Ms. Kaitlin Daly, Recruitment and Admission Associate. 216-325-7336. Fax: 216-325-1688. E-mail: kdaly@beaumontschool.org. Web site: www.beaumontschool.org.

THE BEEKMAN SCHOOL

220 East 50th Street

New York, New York 10022

Head of School: George Higgins

General Information Coeducational day college-preparatory, general academic, arts, and technology school. Grades 9–PG. Founded: 1925. Setting: urban. 1 building on campus. Approved or accredited by New York State Board of Regents and New York Department of Education. Total enrollment: 80. Upper school average class size: 8. Upper school faculty-student ratio: 1:8. There are 165 required school days per year for Upper School students. Upper School students typically attend 5 days per week. The average school day consists of 6 hours and 15 minutes.

Upper School Student Profile Grade 9: 15 students (8 boys, 7 girls); Grade 10: 19 students (11 boys, 8 girls); Grade 11: 21 students (12 boys, 9 girls); Grade 12: 25 students (13 boys, 12 girls); Postgraduate: 2 students (1 boy, 1 girl).

Faculty School total: 13. In upper school: 4 men, 9 women; 10 have advanced degrees.

Subjects Offered Advanced Placement courses, algebra, American history, ancient world history, art, astronomy, bioethics, biology, business mathematics, calculus, calculus-AP, chemistry, computer animation, computer art, computer science, conceptual physics, creative writing, drama, drawing, Eastern religion and philosophy, ecology, economics, electronics, English, environmental science, ESL, European history, film, French, geometry, government, health, modern politics, modern world history, photography, physical education, physical science, physics, poetry, pre-calculus, psychology, SAT preparation, sculpture, Spanish, TOEFL preparation, trigonometry, U.S. history, video film production, Web site design, Western philosophy.

Graduation Requirements Art, computer technologies, electives, English, foreign language, health education, mathematics, physical education (includes health), science, social studies (includes history).

Special Academic Programs Advanced Placement exam preparation; honors section; accelerated programs; independent study; academic accommodation for the gifted, the musically talented, and the artistically talented; remedial reading and/or remedial writing; remedial math; programs in English, mathematics, general development for dyslexic students; ESL (4 students enrolled).

College Admission Counseling 28 students graduated in 2011; 27 went to college, including Arizona State University; Boston University; Fordham University; New York University; Sarah Lawrence College; University of Vermont. Other: 1 had other specific plans. Mean SAT critical reading: 556, mean SAT math: 519, mean SAT writing: 543. 33% scored over 600 on SAT critical reading, 27% scored over 600 on SAT math, 30% scored over 600 on SAT writing.

Student Life Upper grades have student council, honor system. Discipline rests primarily with faculty.

Summer Programs Remediation, enrichment, advancement, ESL programs offered; session focuses on academics; held on campus; accepts boys and girls; open to students from other schools. 35 students usually enrolled. 2012 schedule: July 2 to August 14. Application deadline: June 29.

Tuition and Aid Day student tuition: $33,000. Tuition installment plan (monthly payment plans, individually arranged payment plans).

Admissions Traditional secondary-level entrance grade is 9. For fall 2011, 39 students applied for upper-level admission, 38 were accepted, 33 enrolled. Deadline for receipt of application materials: none. No application fee required. On-campus interview required.

Athletics 1 PE instructor.

Computers Computer resources include online commercial services, Internet access.

Contact George Higgins, Headmaster. 212-755-6666. Fax: 212-888-6085. E-mail: georgeh@beekmanschool.org. Web site: www.BeekmanSchool.org.

See Display on previous page and Close-Up on page 584.

BELEN JESUIT PREPARATORY SCHOOL

500 Southwest 127th Avenue

Miami, Florida 33184

Head of School: Fr. Pedro A. Suarez, SJ

General Information Boys' day college-preparatory and religious studies school, affiliated with Roman Catholic Church. Grades 6–12. Founded: 1854. Setting: urban. 32-acre campus. 3 buildings on campus. Approved or accredited by CITA (Commission on International and Trans-Regional Accreditation), Jesuit Secondary Education Association, National Catholic Education Association, Southern Association of Colleges and Schools, and Florida Department of Education. Endowment: $8 million. Total enrollment: 1,472. Upper school average class size: 25. Upper school faculty-student ratio: 1:13. There are 175 required school days per year for Upper School students. Upper School students typically attend 5 days per week. The average school day consists of 8 hours.

Upper School Student Profile Grade 9: 246 students (246 boys); Grade 10: 228 students (228 boys); Grade 11: 204 students (204 boys); Grade 12: 222 students (222 boys). 98% of students are Roman Catholic.

Faculty School total: 120. In upper school: 43 men, 34 women; 67 have advanced degrees.

Subjects Offered Art, art history, biology, chemistry, composition, computers, English, English literature, French, history, mathematics, music, philosophy, physical education, physics, religion, science, social studies, Spanish.

Graduation Requirements Arts and fine arts (art, music, dance, drama), electives, English, foreign language, mathematics, philosophy, physical education (includes health), religion (includes Bible studies and theology), science, social sciences, social studies (includes history). Community service is required.

Special Academic Programs Advanced Placement exam preparation; honors section; study at local college for college credit.

College Admission Counseling 224 students graduated in 2011; all went to college, including Florida International University; Florida State University; Miami Dade College; University of Central Florida; University of Florida; University of Miami. Median SAT critical reading: 560, median SAT math: 570. Mean composite ACT: 24. 27% scored over 600 on SAT critical reading, 26% scored over 600 on SAT math.

Student Life Upper grades have uniform requirement, student council. Discipline rests primarily with faculty.

Summer Programs Remediation, enrichment programs offered; session focuses on make-up courses; held on campus; accepts boys; not open to students from other schools. 200 students usually enrolled. 2012 schedule: June 20 to July 20.

Tuition and Aid Day student tuition: $12,800. Tuition installment plan (monthly payment plans). Need-based scholarship grants available. In 2011–12, 35% of upper-school students received aid. Total amount of financial aid awarded in 2011–12: $400,000.

Admissions Traditional secondary-level entrance grade is 9. For fall 2011, 108 students applied for upper-level admission, 71 were accepted, 54 enrolled. School's own exam required. Deadline for receipt of application materials: none. Application fee required: $60.

Athletics Interscholastic: baseball, basketball, crew, cross-country running, football, golf, lacrosse, soccer, swimming and diving, tennis, track and field, volleyball, water polo, wrestling; intramural: bowling, fencing, fishing, in-line hockey, weight training. 6 PE instructors, 22 coaches, 1 athletic trainer.

Computers Computers are regularly used in art, English, foreign language, history, mathematics, music, science classes. Computer network features include on-campus library services, online commercial services, Internet access, wireless campus network, Internet filtering or blocking technology. Campus intranet is available to students. Students grades are available online. The school has a published electronic and media policy.

Contact Mrs. Chris Besil, Admissions Secretary. 786-621-4032. Fax: 305-227-2565. E-mail: admissions@belenjesuit.org. Web site: belenjesuit.org.

BELLARMINE COLLEGE PREPARATORY

960 West Hedding Street

San Jose, California 95126

Head of School: Mr. Chris Meyercord

General Information Boys' day college-preparatory, arts, religious studies, and technology school, affiliated with Roman Catholic Church. Grades 9–12. Founded: 1851. Setting: suburban. 21-acre campus. 14 buildings on campus. Approved or accredited by National Catholic Education Association and Western Association of Schools and Colleges. Endowment: $50 million. Total enrollment: 1,600. Upper school average class size: 25. Upper school faculty-student ratio: 1:18. There are 170 required school days per year for Upper School students. Upper School students typically attend 5 days per week. The average school day consists of 6 hours and 25 minutes.

Upper School Student Profile Grade 9: 415 students (415 boys); Grade 10: 410 students (410 boys); Grade 11: 390 students (390 boys); Grade 12: 385 students (385 boys). 75% of students are Roman Catholic.

Faculty School total: 90. In upper school: 60 men, 30 women; 65 have advanced degrees.

Subjects Offered Algebra, American history, American literature, anatomy, art, arts, biology, calculus, ceramics, chemistry, community service, computer science, drama, English, English literature, ethics, European history, expository writing, fine arts, French, geography, geometry, government/civics, history, international relations, Latin, Mandarin, mathematics, music, physical education, physics, psychology, religion, science, social sciences, social studies, Spanish, speech, theater, theology, trigonometry, world history, world literature, writing.

Graduation Requirements Arts and fine arts (art, music, dance, drama), English, foreign language, mathematics, physical education (includes health), religion (includes Bible studies and theology), science, social sciences, social studies (includes history), 75 hours of Christian service.

Special Academic Programs Advanced Placement exam preparation; honors section; independent study; study at local college for college credit; special instructional classes for students with learning disabilities and Attention Deficit Disorder.

College Admission Counseling 392 students graduated in 2010; 390 went to college, including California Polytechnic State University, San Luis Obispo; San Jose State University; Santa Clara University; University of California, Berkeley; University of California, Davis; University of Southern California. Other: 1 entered a postgraduate year, 1 had other specific plans. Mean combined SAT: 1884, mean composite ACT: 27.

Student Life Upper grades have specified standards of dress, student council, honor system. Discipline rests primarily with faculty. Attendance at religious services is required.

Tuition and Aid Day student tuition: $15,250. Tuition installment plan (FACTS Tuition Payment Plan, semester payment plan, 10-installment plan). Need-based scholarship grants available. In 2010–11, 23% of upper-school students received aid. Total amount of financial aid awarded in 2010–11: $3,200,000.

Admissions Traditional secondary-level entrance grade is 9. For fall 2010, 950 students applied for upper-level admission, 500 were accepted, 415 enrolled. High School Placement Test required. Deadline for receipt of application materials: December 15. Application fee required: $70.

Athletics Interscholastic: aquatics, baseball, basketball, cross-country running, diving, football, golf, ice hockey, in-line hockey, indoor hockey, lacrosse, soccer, swimming and diving, tennis, track and field, volleyball, water polo, wrestling; intramural: basketball, flag football, in-line hockey, soccer, softball, tai chi, yoga. 4 PE instructors, 15 coaches, 2 athletic trainers.

Computers Computers are regularly used in art, English, foreign language, mathematics, music, science classes. Computer network features include on-campus library services, online commercial services, Internet access, wireless campus network. Student e-mail accounts are available to students. Students grades are available online. The school has a published electronic and media policy.

Contact Terry Council, Admissions Assistant. 408-294-9224. Fax: 408-294-1894. E-mail: admissions@bcp.org. Web site: www.bcp.org.

BELLARMINE-JEFFERSON HIGH SCHOOL

465 East Olive Avenue

Burbank, California 91501-2176

Head of School: Sr. Cheryl Milner

General Information Coeducational day college-preparatory, arts, business, religious studies, and technology school, affiliated with Roman Catholic Church. Grades 9–12. Founded: 1940. Setting: urban. 4 buildings on campus. Approved or accredited by Western Association of Schools and Colleges and California Department of Education. Upper school average class size: 20.

Faculty In upper school: 30 have advanced degrees.

Special Academic Programs International Baccalaureate program; Advanced Placement exam preparation; honors section.
College Admission Counseling 91 students graduated in 2010; they went to California State University, Fullerton; California State University, Long Beach; California State University, Los Angeles; California State University, Monterey Bay; California State University, Northridge; California State University, Sacramento.
Student Life Upper grades have uniform requirement, student council, honor system. Discipline rests primarily with faculty. Attendance at religious services is required.
Tuition and Aid Tuition installment plan (The Tuition Plan). Tuition reduction for siblings, merit scholarship grants, need-based scholarship grants available.
Admissions High School Placement Test required. Deadline for receipt of application materials: January 16. Application fee required: $50. Interview required.
Athletics Interscholastic: aerobics (girls), baseball (b); coed interscholastic: basketball.
Computers The school has a published electronic and media policy.
Contact 818-972-1400. Web site: www.bell-jeff.net.

THE BEMENT SCHOOL

Deerfield, Massachusetts

See Junior Boarding Schools section.

BENEDICTINE HIGH SCHOOL

2900 Martin Luther King, Jr. Drive

Cleveland, Ohio 44104

Head of School: Mr. Joseph Gressock

General Information Boys' day college-preparatory and religious studies school, affiliated with Roman Catholic Church. Grades 9–12. Founded: 1927. Setting: urban. 13-acre campus. 3 buildings on campus. Approved or accredited by National Catholic Education Association, North Central Association of Colleges and Schools, Ohio Catholic Schools Accreditation Association (OCSAA), and Ohio Department of Education. Total enrollment: 352. Upper school average class size: 15. Upper school faculty-student ratio: 1:11. There are 180 required school days per year for Upper School students. Upper School students typically attend 5 days per week. The average school day consists of 6 hours and 30 minutes.
Upper School Student Profile Grade 9: 90 students (90 boys); Grade 10: 68 students (68 boys); Grade 11: 90 students (90 boys); Grade 12: 82 students (82 boys). 80% of students are Roman Catholic.
Faculty School total: 37. In upper school: 32 men, 5 women; 31 have advanced degrees.
Subjects Offered Advanced chemistry, advanced math, Advanced Placement courses, aesthetics, algebra, American literature, American literature-AP, analysis and differential calculus, analytic geometry, Ancient Greek, ancient history, ancient world history, art, athletic training, band, Basic programming, Bible studies, biology, biology-AP, British literature-AP, business education, business law, calculus, calculus-AP, Catholic belief and practice, Central and Eastern European history, ceramics, chemistry, choir, chorus, church history, Civil War, civil war history, classical Greek literature, classical language, computer education, computer graphics, computer information systems, computer literacy, computer programming, computer skills, computer-aided design, concert band, concert choir, current events, drawing, drawing and design, economics, electives, English, English literature and composition-AP, European history-AP, film studies, foreign language, French, geometry, German, government, government-AP, government/civics, government/civics-AP, graphic design, health, honors algebra, honors English, honors geometry, honors U.S. history, honors world history, human geography - AP, jazz band, journalism, keyboarding, lab science, Latin, Latin-AP, Life of Christ, marching band, marketing, moral theology, music, music appreciation, New Testament, painting, physical education, pre-calculus, probability and statistics, psychology, Russian, Shakespeare.
Graduation Requirements 1 1/2 elective credits, 20th century American writers, 20th century history, 20th century world history, algebra, American government, American history, American literature, ancient history, ancient world history, art, biology, British literature, chemistry, church history, computer applications, English, foreign language, geometry, physical education (includes health), physics, senior project, theology, U.S. history, world history, community service hours.
Special Academic Programs 8 Advanced Placement exams for which test preparation is offered; honors section; independent study; study at local college for college credit; study abroad; remedial reading and/or remedial writing; remedial math.
College Admission Counseling 79 students graduated in 2011; 75 went to college, including Bowling Green State University; Case Western Reserve University; Cleveland State University; Kent State University; The University of Akron; University of Dayton. Other: 2 went to work, 2 entered military service. Mean SAT critical reading: 554, mean SAT math: 526, mean SAT writing: 542, mean combined SAT: 1622, mean composite ACT: 22.
Student Life Upper grades have specified standards of dress, student council, honor system. Discipline rests primarily with faculty. Attendance at religious services is required.
Summer Programs Enrichment, sports, computer instruction programs offered; held on campus; accepts boys and girls; open to students from other schools. 150 students usually enrolled. 2012 schedule: June 8 to July 24. Application deadline: June 1.
Tuition and Aid Day student tuition: $9000. Tuition installment plan (monthly payment plans, individually arranged payment plans). Tuition reduction for siblings, merit scholarship grants, need-based scholarship grants, paying campus jobs available. In 2011–12, 73% of upper-school students received aid.
Admissions Traditional secondary-level entrance grade is 9. For fall 2011, 250 students applied for upper-level admission, 175 were accepted, 90 enrolled. High School Placement Test required. Deadline for receipt of application materials: none. Application fee required: $150. Interview recommended.
Athletics Interscholastic: baseball, basketball, bowling, cross-country running, football, golf, hockey, ice hockey, lacrosse, soccer, swimming and diving, track and field, wrestling; intramural: baseball, basketball, flag football, football, physical fitness, physical training, skiing (downhill), snowboarding, strength & conditioning, volleyball, weight lifting, weight training. 10 coaches, 2 athletic trainers.
Computers Computers are regularly used in computer applications, creative writing, current events, data processing, design, English, graphic design, history, independent study, information technology, library, mathematics, newspaper, technical drawing, yearbook classes. Computer network features include on-campus library services, online commercial services, Internet access, wireless campus network, Internet filtering or blocking technology. Student e-mail accounts are available to students. Students grades are available online. The school has a published electronic and media policy.
Contact Mr. Kieran Patton, Admissions and Advancement Director. 216-421-2080 Ext. 356. Fax: 216-421-1100. E-mail: patton@cbhs.net. Web site: www.cbhs.net.

BENEDICTINE HIGH SCHOOL

304 North Sheppard Street

Richmond, Virginia 23221

Head of School: Mr. Jesse Grapes

General Information Boys' day college-preparatory, arts, religious studies, Junior ROTC, and military school, affiliated with Roman Catholic Church. Grades 9–12. Founded: 1911. Setting: urban. 1-acre campus. 3 buildings on campus. Approved or accredited by National Catholic Education Association and Virginia Department of Education. Member of National Association of Independent Schools. Endowment: $1.5 million. Total enrollment: 277. Upper school average class size: 15. Upper school faculty-student ratio: 1:9. There are 180 required school days per year for Upper School students. Upper School students typically attend 5 days per week. The average school day consists of 7 hours and 30 minutes.
Upper School Student Profile Grade 9: 72 students (72 boys); Grade 10: 66 students (66 boys); Grade 11: 61 students (61 boys); Grade 12: 78 students (78 boys). 65% of students are Roman Catholic.
Faculty School total: 34. In upper school: 24 men, 10 women; 14 have advanced degrees.
Subjects Offered 3-dimensional art, advanced biology, advanced studio art-AP, algebra, American literature, anatomy and physiology, art, art-AP, band, biology, biology-AP, calculus, calculus-AP, Catholic belief and practice, chemistry, Christian doctrine, Christian scripture, communication arts, creative writing, discrete mathematics, economics, engineering, English, English literature, English literature and composition-AP, geography, geometry, graphic arts, human anatomy, journalism, JROTC, Latin, Latin-AP, moral theology, photography, photojournalism, physical education, physical science, physics, pre-calculus, psychology, religion, robotics, Spanish, statistics, U.S. and Virginia government, U.S. government, U.S. government and politics, U.S. government and politics-AP, U.S. history, U.S. history-AP, United States government-AP, world history, world literature, yearbook.
Graduation Requirements Arts and fine arts (art, music, dance, drama), electives, English, JROTC, lab science, language, mathematics, physical education (includes health), religion (includes Bible studies and theology), social studies (includes history), community service requirement.
Special Academic Programs Advanced Placement exam preparation; honors section; academic accommodation for the gifted and the artistically talented; remedial math.
College Admission Counseling 69 students graduated in 2011; 68 went to college, including The College of William and Mary; University of Notre Dame; University of Virginia; Virginia Polytechnic Institute and State University. Other: 1 went to work. Mean combined SAT: 1580, mean composite ACT: 22.
Student Life Upper grades have uniform requirement, student council, honor system. Discipline rests equally with students and faculty. Attendance at religious services is required.
Summer Programs Enrichment, sports, art/fine arts programs offered; session focuses on providing a fun learning experience while learning about Benedictine; held both on and off campus; held at The Benedictine Abbey; accepts boys and girls; open to students from other schools. 300 students usually enrolled. 2012 schedule: June 20 to August 5.
Tuition and Aid Day student tuition: $14,700. Tuition installment plan (FACTS Tuition Payment Plan). Merit scholarship grants, need-based scholarship grants, full time employee tuition discount (1/2 price) for sons available. In 2011–12, 35% of

upper-school students received aid; total upper-school merit-scholarship money awarded: $50,000. Total amount of financial aid awarded in 2011–12: $500,000.

Admissions Traditional secondary-level entrance grade is 9. For fall 2011, 138 students applied for upper-level admission, 115 were accepted, 89 enrolled. SSAT required. Deadline for receipt of application materials: none. Application fee required: $50. Interview required.

Athletics Interscholastic: baseball, basketball, boxing, cross-country running, football, golf, indoor track & field, JROTC drill, lacrosse, marksmanship, outdoor skills, riflery, soccer, swimming and diving, tennis, track and field, winter (indoor) track, wrestling; intramural: Frisbee, outdoor adventure, outdoor education, strength & conditioning, volleyball, weight lifting, weight training, wilderness survival, wildernessways. 27 coaches, 1 athletic trainer.

Computers Computers are regularly used in graphic arts, journalism, photojournalism, programming, yearbook classes. Computer resources include on-campus library services, Internet access, wireless campus network, Internet filtering or blocking technology. Student e-mail accounts are available to students. Students grades are available online. The school has a published electronic and media policy.

Contact Mrs. Sandy M. Carli, Associate Director of Admission. 804-342-1314. Fax: 804-342-1349. E-mail: scarli@benedictinecollegeprep.org. Web site: www.benedictinecollegeprep.org.

BENET ACADEMY

2200 Maple Avenue

Lisle, Illinois 60532

Head of School: Mr. Stephen A. Marth

General Information Coeducational day college-preparatory, arts, and religious studies school, affiliated with Roman Catholic Church. Grades 9–12. Founded: 1887. Setting: suburban. Nearest major city is Chicago. 54-acre campus. 8 buildings on campus. Approved or accredited by North Central Association of Colleges and Schools and Illinois Department of Education. Total enrollment: 1,299. Upper school average class size: 27. Upper school faculty-student ratio: 1:18. There are 176 required school days per year for Upper School students. Upper School students typically attend 5 days per week. The average school day consists of 6 hours and 20 minutes.

Upper School Student Profile Grade 9: 352 students (188 boys, 164 girls); Grade 10: 333 students (171 boys, 162 girls); Grade 11: 331 students (163 boys, 168 girls); Grade 12: 338 students (149 boys, 189 girls). 97% of students are Roman Catholic.

Faculty School total: 76. In upper school: 45 men, 31 women; 73 have advanced degrees.

Subjects Offered Algebra, American history, American literature, art history, biology, business, calculus, chemistry, computer programming, computer science, creative writing, drama, driver education, economics, English, European history, French, geography, geometry, German, government/civics, health, history, Latin, mathematics, music, physical education, physics, religion, science, Spanish, speech, statistics, trigonometry, U.S. history-AP, world history, world literature, writing.

Graduation Requirements Computer science, English, foreign language, mathematics, physical education (includes health), religion (includes Bible studies and theology), science, social studies (includes history).

Special Academic Programs Advanced Placement exam preparation; honors section; study at local college for college credit; academic accommodation for the gifted.

College Admission Counseling 326 students graduated in 2011; all went to college, including Northwestern University; The University of Iowa; University of Illinois; University of Notre Dame. Mean SAT critical reading: 632, mean SAT math: 647, mean SAT writing: 622, mean composite ACT: 28.

Student Life Upper grades have uniform requirement, student council. Discipline rests primarily with faculty. Attendance at religious services is required.

Summer Programs Computer instruction programs offered; session focuses on computer literacy skills for incoming freshmen; held on campus; accepts boys and girls; not open to students from other schools. 300 students usually enrolled.

Tuition and Aid Day student tuition: $9300. Tuition installment plan (monthly payment plans). Tuition reduction for siblings, need-based scholarship grants available. In 2011–12, 5% of upper-school students received aid.

Admissions Traditional secondary-level entrance grade is 9. For fall 2011, 625 students applied for upper-level admission, 430 were accepted, 352 enrolled. High School Placement Test required. Deadline for receipt of application materials: January 14. Application fee required: $35. On-campus interview required.

Athletics Interscholastic: baseball (boys), basketball (b,g), cheering (g), cross-country running (b,g), dance team (g), fishing (b), football (b), golf (b,g), lacrosse (b,g), pom squad (g), soccer (b,g), softball (g), strength & conditioning (b), swimming and diving (b,g), tennis (b,g), track and field (b,g), volleyball (b,g); coed interscholastic: ice hockey; coed intramural: basketball, bowling, flag football, Frisbee, table tennis. 3 PE instructors, 30 coaches, 1 athletic trainer.

Computers Computers are regularly used in English, history, mathematics, science, Spanish classes. Computer network features include on-campus library services, online commercial services, Internet access, Internet filtering or blocking technology. The school has a published electronic and media policy.

Contact Mr. James E. Brown, Assistant Principal. 630-969-6550. Fax: 630-719-2849. E-mail: jbrown@benet.org.

BEN FRANKLIN ACADEMY

1585 Clifton Road

Atlanta, Georgia 30329

Head of School: Dr. Wood Smethurst

General Information Coeducational day college-preparatory school. Grades 9–12. Founded: 1987. Setting: urban. 3-acre campus. 2 buildings on campus. Approved or accredited by Georgia Independent School Association, Southern Association of Colleges and Schools, Southern Association of Independent Schools, and Georgia Department of Education. Total enrollment: 130. Upper school average class size: 1. Upper school faculty-student ratio: 1:2. There are 180 required school days per year for Upper School students. Upper School students typically attend 5 days per week. The average school day consists of 3 hours and 30 minutes.

Faculty School total: 29. In upper school: 12 men, 17 women; 15 have advanced degrees.

Subjects Offered 1 1/2 elective credits.

Graduation Requirements We have a work-study component in addition to the academic requirements.

Special Academic Programs Advanced Placement exam preparation; honors section; accelerated programs; academic accommodation for the gifted.

College Admission Counseling 40 students graduated in 2011; all went to college.

Student Life Upper grades have specified standards of dress. Discipline rests primarily with faculty.

Tuition and Aid Day student tuition: $23,250–$29,750. Tuition installment plan (individually arranged payment plans). Tuition reduction for siblings, need-based scholarship grants available. In 2011–12, 20% of upper-school students received aid.

Admissions Traditional secondary-level entrance grade is 10. Deadline for receipt of application materials: none. No application fee required. On-campus interview required.

Athletics Interscholastic: cross-country running (boys, girls), golf (b,g); coed interscholastic: basketball, cross-country running, Frisbee, golf, tennis, ultimate Frisbee.

Computers Computer resources include on-campus library services, Internet access, Internet filtering or blocking technology. Campus intranet and student e-mail accounts are available to students. The school has a published electronic and media policy.

Contact Dr. Martha B. Burdette, Dean of Studies. 404-633-7404. Fax: 404-321-0610. E-mail: bfa@benfranklinacademy.org. Web site: www.benfranklinacademy.org.

BEREAN CHRISTIAN HIGH SCHOOL

245 El Divisadero Avenue

Walnut Creek, California 94598

Head of School: Mr. Nelson M. Noriega

General Information Coeducational day college-preparatory and religious studies school, affiliated with Baptist Church. Grades 9–12. Founded: 1969. Setting: suburban. Nearest major city is Oakland. 5-acre campus. 5 buildings on campus. Approved or accredited by Western Association of Schools and Colleges and California Department of Education. Total enrollment: 430. Upper school average class size: 430. Upper school faculty-student ratio: 1:14. There are 180 required school days per year for Upper School students. Upper School students typically attend 5 days per week. The average school day consists of 6 hours and 30 minutes.

Upper School Student Profile 50% of students are Baptist.

Faculty School total: 31. In upper school: 14 men, 17 women; 11 have advanced degrees.

Subjects Offered Algebra, anatomy, art, arts, Bible studies, biology, chemistry, choir, computer literacy, computer science, drama, economics, English, ethics, fine arts, geometry, government, health, mathematics, physical education, physics, physiology, pre-calculus, religion, science, social studies, Spanish, trigonometry, U.S. history, world history, world religions.

Special Academic Programs Advanced Placement exam preparation; independent study; study abroad.

College Admission Counseling 105 students graduated in 2011; 103 went to college. Other: 2 went to work.

Student Life Upper grades have specified standards of dress, student council, honor system. Discipline rests primarily with faculty.

Summer Programs Enrichment programs offered; session focuses on biology, study abroad; held on campus; accepts boys and girls; not open to students from other schools. 25 students usually enrolled. 2012 schedule: June to July.

Tuition and Aid Day student tuition: $7500. Tuition reduction for siblings, need-based scholarship grants available. In 2011–12, 5% of upper-school students received aid.

Admissions Traditional secondary-level entrance grade is 9. For fall 2011, 205 students applied for upper-level admission, 125 were accepted, 125 enrolled. Deadline for receipt of application materials: March. Application fee required: $345. On-campus interview required.

Athletics Interscholastic: baseball (boys), basketball (b,g), cheering (g), cross-country running (b,g), football (b), soccer (b,g), softball (g), swimming and diving (b,g), tennis (g), volleyball (b,g); coed interscholastic: golf. 2 PE instructors, 42 coaches.

Computers Computer network features include on-campus library services, Internet access, wireless campus network, Internet filtering or blocking technology. Student e-mail accounts are available to students. Students grades are available online.

Contact Nelson M. Noriega, Principal. 925-945-6464. E-mail: nnoriega@berean-eagles.org. Web site: www.berean-eagles.org.

BERKELEY PREPARATORY SCHOOL

4811 Kelly Road

Tampa, Florida 33615

Head of School: Joseph W. Seivold

General Information Coeducational day college-preparatory, arts, religious studies, bilingual studies, and technology school, affiliated with Episcopal Church. Grades PK–12. Founded: 1960. Setting: suburban. 80-acre campus. 8 buildings on campus. Approved or accredited by Florida Council of Independent Schools, National Association of Episcopal Schools, Southern Association of Colleges and Schools, Southern Association of Independent Schools, The College Board, and Florida Department of Education. Member of National Association of Independent Schools and Secondary School Admission Test Board. Total enrollment: 1,250. Upper school average class size: 15. Upper school faculty-student ratio: 1:8. Upper School students typically attend 5 days per week. The average school day consists of 7 hours.

Upper School Student Profile Grade 9: 143 students (75 boys, 68 girls); Grade 10: 140 students (71 boys, 69 girls); Grade 11: 119 students (61 boys, 58 girls); Grade 12: 146 students (81 boys, 65 girls).

Faculty School total: 176. In upper school: 30 men, 38 women; 45 have advanced degrees.

Subjects Offered African history, algebra, American government, American history, American literature, art, art history, biology, biology-AP, calculus, calculus-AP, ceramics, chemistry, chemistry-AP, China/Japan history, community service, computer math, computer programming, computer science, creative writing, dance, drama, drama performance, drama workshop, early childhood, economics, English, English literature, English-AP, environmental science-AP, etymology, European history, expository writing, fine arts, French, French-AP, freshman seminar, geography, geometry, government/civics, grammar, guitar, health, history, history of China and Japan, honors algebra, honors English, honors geometry, instruments, Latin, Latin American history, Latin-AP, logic, Mandarin, math analysis, mathematics, media arts, microbiology, modern European history, modern European history-AP, music, performing arts, philosophy, physical education, physics, physics-AP, pre-calculus, psychology, religious studies, SAT preparation, science, social studies, Spanish, Spanish-AP, speech, stage design, statistics, statistics-AP, technical theater, television, theater, theater production, U.S. history, U.S. history-AP, video, video film production, Western civilization, world history, world literature, writing.

Graduation Requirements Arts and fine arts (art, music, dance, drama), computer science, English, foreign language, mathematics, physical education (includes health), religious studies, science, social studies (includes history). Community service is required.

Special Academic Programs Advanced Placement exam preparation; honors section; independent study; study abroad.

College Admission Counseling 144 students graduated in 2011; all went to college, including Boston College; Duke University; Florida State University; University of Florida; University of Michigan; Wake Forest University. Mean SAT critical reading: 629, mean SAT math: 642, mean SAT writing: 642, mean combined SAT: 1913, mean composite ACT: 28.

Student Life Upper grades have specified standards of dress, student council, honor system. Discipline rests equally with students and faculty.

Summer Programs Remediation, enrichment, advancement, sports, art/fine arts, computer instruction programs offered; session focuses on setting a fun pace for excellence; held on campus; accepts boys and girls; open to students from other schools. 2,000 students usually enrolled. 2012 schedule: June 4 to July 27. Application deadline: none.

Tuition and Aid Day student tuition: $19,420. Tuition installment plan (8-installment plan). Need-based scholarship grants available.

Admissions Traditional secondary-level entrance grade is 9. Otis-Lennon Mental Ability Test and SSAT required. Deadline for receipt of application materials: January 30. Application fee required: $50. On-campus interview required.

Athletics Interscholastic: baseball (boys), basketball (b,g), cheering (g), crew (b,g), cross-country running (b,g), dance squad (g), dance team (g), diving (b,g), football (b), golf (b,g), lacrosse (b), rowing (b,g), soccer (b,g), softball (g), swimming and diving (b,g), tennis (b,g), track and field (b,g), volleyball (b,g); coed interscholastic: ice hockey, weight lifting, wrestling; coed intramural: physical fitness, physical training, power lifting, project adventure, strength & conditioning, wall climbing, weight training. 14 PE instructors, 74 coaches, 2 athletic trainers.

Computers Computers are regularly used in art, English, foreign language, history, mathematics, music, science classes. Computer network features include on-campus library services, online commercial services, Internet access, wireless campus network, Internet filtering or blocking technology. Student e-mail accounts are available to students. Students grades are available online. The school has a published electronic and media policy.

Contact Janie McIlvaine, Director of Admissions. 813-885-1673. Fax: 813-886-6933. E-mail: mcilvjan@berkeleyprep.org. Web site: www.berkeleyprep.org.

BERKSHIRE SCHOOL

245 North Undermountain Road

Sheffield, Massachusetts 01257

Head of School: Michael J. Maher

General Information Coeducational boarding and day college-preparatory, arts, and technology school. Grades 9–PG. Founded: 1907. Setting: rural. Nearest major city is Hartford, CT. Students are housed in single-sex dormitories. 500-acre campus. 36 buildings on campus. Approved or accredited by Association of Independent Schools in New England, New England Association of Schools and Colleges, and The Association of Boarding Schools. Member of National Association of Independent Schools and Secondary School Admission Test Board. Endowment: $94 million. Upper school average class size: 12. Upper school faculty-student ratio: 1:5. Upper School students typically attend 6 days per week. The average school day consists of 6 hours and 45 minutes.

Upper School Student Profile Grade 9: 60 students (40 boys, 20 girls); Grade 10: 96 students (51 boys, 45 girls); Grade 11: 108 students (60 boys, 48 girls); Grade 12: 100 students (55 boys, 45 girls); Postgraduate: 16 students (12 boys, 4 girls). 88% of students are boarding students. 14% are state residents. 30 states are represented in upper school student body. 19% are international students. International students from Canada, China, Germany, Republic of Korea, Spain, and Viet Nam; 18 other countries represented in student body.

Faculty School total: 61. In upper school: 40 men, 21 women; 37 have advanced degrees; 49 reside on campus.

Subjects Offered 3-dimensional design, acting, Advanced Placement courses, algebra, American government, American history, American literature, anatomy, ancient history, animal behavior, art, art history, aviation, biology, calculus, ceramics, chemistry, Chinese, choral music, chorus, comparative government and politics, comparative religion, computer programming, computer science, constitutional law, creative writing, dance, digital art, drama, drawing and design, economics, English, English literature, environmental science, ESL, ethics, European history, expository writing, French, geology, geometry, health, history, instrumental music, Latin, mathematics, music, music technology, painting, philosophy, photography, physics, pre-calculus, psychology, science, Spanish, studio art, theater, trigonometry, world religions, writing.

Graduation Requirements Arts and fine arts (art, music, dance, drama), English, foreign language, history, introduction to technology, mathematics, science. Community service is required.

Special Academic Programs 16 Advanced Placement exams for which test preparation is offered; honors section; independent study; study abroad; ESL (8 students enrolled).

College Admission Counseling 113 students graduated in 2011; 107 went to college, including Boston College; Emory University; Georgetown University; St. Lawrence University; Tufts University; Union College. Other: 2 entered a postgraduate year, 4 had other specific plans.

Student Life Upper grades have specified standards of dress, student council, honor system. Discipline rests equally with students and faculty.

Tuition and Aid Day student tuition: $38,100; 7-day tuition and room/board: $48,100. Tuition installment plan (Key Tuition Payment Plan, monthly payment plans). Need-based scholarship grants available. In 2011–12, 32% of upper-school students received aid. Total amount of financial aid awarded in 2011–12: $4,175,000.

Admissions Traditional secondary-level entrance grade is 9. For fall 2011, 975 students applied for upper-level admission, 346 were accepted, 146 enrolled. ACT, PSAT, SAT, SSAT or TOEFL required. Deadline for receipt of application materials: January 15. Application fee required: $75. Interview required.

Athletics Interscholastic: baseball (boys), basketball (b,g), crew (b,g), cross-country running (b,g), field hockey (g), football (b), ice hockey (b,g), lacrosse (b,g), soccer (b,g), softball (g), squash (b,g), tennis (b,g), track and field (b,g), volleyball (g); coed interscholastic: alpine skiing, golf, mountain biking; coed intramural: alpine skiing, canoeing/kayaking, climbing, dance, fly fishing, hiking/backpacking, kayaking, modern dance, mountaineering, outdoor adventure, outdoor education, outdoor skills, rappelling, rock climbing, ropes courses, skiing (cross-country), skiing (downhill), snowboarding, wilderness, wilderness survival. 2 athletic trainers.

Computers Computers are regularly used in art, English, foreign language, mathematics, music, science, technology classes. Computer network features include on-campus library services, online commercial services, Internet access, wireless campus network, Internet filtering or blocking technology, network printing, interactive Polyvision white boards (smart boards). Campus intranet and student e-mail accounts are available to students. Students grades are available online. The school has a published electronic and media policy.

Contact Mr. Andrew L. Bogardus, Director of Admission. 413-229-1003. Fax: 413-229-1016. E-mail: admission@berkshireschool.org. Web site: www.berkshireschool.org.

See Display below and Close-Up on page 586.

BERLIN INTERNATIONAL SCHOOL

Lentzeallee 8 - 14

Berlin 14195, Germany

Head of School: Mr. Hubert Keulers

General Information Coeducational day college-preparatory, general academic, arts, business, and bilingual studies school. Founded: 1998. Setting: suburban. 3 buildings on campus. Approved or accredited by International Baccalaureate Organization and New England Association of Schools and Colleges. Languages of instruction: English and German. Total enrollment: 820. Upper school average class size: 22. Upper school faculty-student ratio: 1:11. There are 180 required school days per year for Upper School students. Upper School students typically attend 5 days per week. The average school day consists of 8 hours and 45 minutes.

Faculty School total: 75. In upper school: 15 men, 28 women; 35 have advanced degrees.

Subjects Offered Advanced biology, advanced chemistry, advanced math, advanced studio art-AP, art, art history, art-AP, biology, biology-AP, British literature-AP, business studies, chemistry, chemistry-AP, computer studies, drama, economics, economics-AP, English, English as a foreign language, English language-AP, English literature-AP, ESL, foreign language, French, French language-AP, geography, German, German-AP, history, history-AP, International Baccalaureate courses, mathematics-AP, music, music-AP, physical education, physics, physics-AP, SAT preparation, SAT/ACT preparation, senior thesis, service learning/internship, Spanish, Spanish-AP, student government, student publications, theory of knowledge, visual arts.

Special Academic Programs International Baccalaureate program; academic accommodation for the gifted; remedial reading and/or remedial writing; remedial math; ESL (80 students enrolled).

College Admission Counseling 30 students graduated in 2010; 27 went to college. Other: 3 had other specific plans.

Student Life Upper grades have student council, honor system. Discipline rests primarily with faculty.

Tuition and Aid Day student tuition: €10,000. Tuition installment plan (monthly payment plans, individually arranged payment plans, Scholarship programme for academically, artistically highly able and/or gifted students.). Tuition reduction for siblings, merit scholarship grants, need-based scholarship grants available. In 2010–11, 10% of upper-school students received aid.

Admissions Traditional secondary-level entrance grade is 11. For fall 2010, 65 students applied for upper-level admission, 33 were accepted, 33 enrolled. Admissions testing required. Deadline for receipt of application materials: none. Application fee required: €800. Interview recommended.

Athletics Interscholastic: badminton (boys, girls), basketball (b,g), cross-country running (b,g), field hockey (b,g), football (b,g), soccer (b,g), swimming and diving (b,g), tennis (b,g), track and field (b,g); intramural: handball (b,g), hockey (b,g), indoor hockey (b,g), indoor soccer (b,g), soccer (b,g), team handball (b,g), track and field (b,g), volleyball (b,g); coed interscholastic: basketball, cross-country running, field hockey, football, soccer, swimming and diving, tennis, track and field; coed intramural: handball, hockey, indoor hockey, indoor soccer, soccer, team handball, track and field, volleyball. 2 PE instructors.

Computers Computers are regularly used in all academic classes. Computer network features include on-campus library services, Internet access, wireless campus network, Internet filtering or blocking technology. Student e-mail accounts and computer access in designated common areas are available to students.

Contact Ms. Ute Harris. +49-30820077780. Fax: +49-30820077789. E-mail: admissions@berlin-international-school.de. Web site: www.berlin-international-school.de.

BERWICK ACADEMY

31 Academy Street

South Berwick, Maine 03908

Head of School: Gregory J. Schneider

General Information Coeducational day college-preparatory and arts school. Grades K–PG. Founded: 1791. Setting: small town. Nearest major city is Portsmouth, NH. 72-acre campus. 11 buildings on campus. Approved or accredited by New England Association of Schools and Colleges and Maine Department of Education. Member of National Association of Independent Schools and Secondary School Admission Test Board. Endowment: $21 million. Total enrollment: 567. Upper school average class size: 14. Upper school faculty-student ratio: 1:12. There are 169 required school days per year for Upper School students.

Upper School Student Profile Grade 9: 77 students (37 boys, 40 girls); Grade 10: 70 students (32 boys, 38 girls); Grade 11: 62 students (38 boys, 24 girls); Grade 12: 63 students (29 boys, 34 girls); Postgraduate: 3 students (2 boys, 1 girl).

Faculty School total: 89. In upper school: 13 men, 18 women; 16 have advanced degrees.

Subjects Offered Algebra, American history, American literature, art, art history, biology, calculus, chemistry, computer math, computer programming, computer science, dance, English, ethics, European history, fine arts, French, geometry, government/civics, health, history, journalism, Latin, mathematics, metalworking, music, physical education, physics, science, social studies, Spanish, statistics, theater arts, trigonometry, world history.

Graduation Requirements Algebra, analysis, arts and fine arts (art, music, dance, drama), biology, chemistry, computer science, English, English literature, European civilization, foreign language, languages, mathematics, physical education (includes health), physics, science, social studies (includes history).

Special Academic Programs Advanced Placement exam preparation; honors section; independent study; term-away projects; study abroad; academic accommodation for the gifted, the musically talented, and the artistically talented.

College Admission Counseling 63 students graduated in 2010; 59 went to college, including Connecticut College; Middlebury College; Rensselaer Polytechnic Institute; University of New Hampshire; University of Vermont; Worcester Polytechnic Institute. Other: 2 entered a postgraduate year, 2 had other specific plans. Mean SAT critical reading: 611, mean SAT math: 613, mean SAT writing: 627.

Student Life Upper grades have specified standards of dress, student council, honor system. Discipline rests equally with students and faculty.

Tuition and Aid Day student tuition: $23,250. Tuition installment plan (FACTS Tuition Payment Plan). Need-based scholarship grants, need-based loans available. In 2010–11, 33% of upper-school students received aid. Total amount of financial aid awarded in 2010–11: $2,200,000.

Admissions Traditional secondary-level entrance grade is 9. For fall 2010, 159 students applied for upper-level admission, 103 were accepted, 51 enrolled. ERB or SSAT or WISC III required. Deadline for receipt of application materials: January 31. Application fee required: $50. Interview required.

Athletics Interscholastic: alpine skiing (boys, girls), baseball (b), basketball (b,g), cross-country running (b,g), dance (b,g), field hockey (g), golf (b,g), hockey (b,g), ice hockey (b,g), lacrosse (b,g), modern dance (b,g), skiing (downhill) (b,g), soccer (b,g), softball (g), wilderness (b,g); intramural: wilderness (g); coed intramural: bicycling, wilderness. 3 PE instructors, 4 coaches, 2 athletic trainers.

Computers Computers are regularly used in art, dance, English, foreign language, graphic design, history, humanities, independent study, library, mathematics, SAT preparation, science, social studies, theater arts, writing, yearbook classes. Computer network features include on-campus library services, Internet access, wireless campus network, Internet filtering or blocking technology. Student e-mail accounts are available to students. The school has a published electronic and media policy.

Contact Diane M. Field, Director of Admission and Financial Aid. 207-384-2164 Ext. 2301. Fax: 207-384-3332. E-mail: dfield@berwickacademy.org. Web site: www.berwickacademy.org.

BESANT HILL SCHOOL

8585 Ojai Santa Paula Road

PO Box 850

Ojai, California 93023

General Information Coeducational boarding and day college-preparatory and arts school; primarily serves students with learning disabilities, individuals with Attention Deficit Disorder, and dyslexic students. Grades 9–12. Founded: 1946. Setting: small town. Nearest major city is Los Angeles. Students are housed in single-sex dormitories. 500-acre campus. 14 buildings on campus. Approved or accredited by California Association of Independent Schools, The Association of Boarding Schools, Western Association of Schools and Colleges, and California Department of Education. Member of National Association of Independent Schools and Secondary School Admission Test Board. Languages of instruction: English, Spanish, and French. Endowment: $1 million. Total enrollment: 100. Upper school average class size: 10. Upper school faculty-student ratio: 1:4. The average school day consists of 8 hours and 15 minutes.

See Display below, Close-Up on page 588, and Summer Program Close-Up on page 768.

BETH HAVEN CHRISTIAN SCHOOL

5515 Johnsontown Road

Louisville, Kentucky 40272

Head of School: Ms. Melissa Pace

General Information Coeducational day college-preparatory and religious studies school, affiliated with Baptist Church. Grades K4–12. Founded: 1971. Setting: suburban. 2-acre campus. 1 building on campus. Approved or accredited by Association of Christian Schools International and Kentucky Department of Education. Total enrollment: 210. Upper school average class size: 18. Upper school faculty-student ratio: 1:8. There are 177 required school days per year for Upper School students. Upper School students typically attend 5 days per week. The average school day consists of 7 hours and 5 minutes.

Upper School Student Profile Grade 9: 14 students (8 boys, 6 girls); Grade 10: 16 students (5 boys, 11 girls); Grade 11: 19 students (10 boys, 9 girls); Grade 12: 26 students (14 boys, 12 girls). 65% of students are Baptist.

Faculty School total: 18. In upper school: 5 men, 7 women; 4 have advanced degrees.

Subjects Offered ACT preparation, Advanced Placement courses, algebra, American history, American literature, analytic geometry, art appreciation, Bible studies, biology, British literature (honors), business mathematics, calculus-AP, chemistry, computer applications, drama, dramatic arts, earth science, economics, English, English composition, English language and composition-AP, health, honors algebra, honors English, honors geometry, honors U.S. history, honors world history, independent study, journalism, keyboarding, lab science, psychology, psychology-AP, senior seminar, Spanish, speech, trigonometry, U.S. government and politics-AP, world geography, world history, yearbook.

Graduation Requirements ACT preparation, algebra, American government, American history, American literature, analytic geometry, arts appreciation, Bible, biology, British literature, chemistry, earth science, economics, English, language, physical education (includes health), world geography, world history.

Special Academic Programs Honors section; independent study; study at local college for college credit.

College Admission Counseling 26 students graduated in 2011; 24 went to college, including Bellarmine University; Indiana University Bloomington; Jefferson Community and Technical College; Liberty University; University of Louisville. Other: 2 had other specific plans. Median composite ACT: 22. 5% scored over 26 on composite ACT.

Student Life Upper grades have uniform requirement, student council, honor system. Discipline rests primarily with faculty.

Summer Programs Remediation, sports programs offered; held on campus; accepts boys and girls; not open to students from other schools. 50 students usually enrolled. 2012 schedule: June 1 to August 21. Application deadline: June 1.

Tuition and Aid Day student tuition: $4450. Tuition installment plan (FACTS Tuition Payment Plan). Tuition reduction for siblings, need-based scholarship grants, two full-tuition memorial scholarships are awarded each year based on a combination of merit and need available. In 2011–12, 2% of upper-school students received aid. Total amount of financial aid awarded in 2011–12: $4450.

Admissions Traditional secondary-level entrance grade is 9. For fall 2011, 5 students applied for upper-level admission, 5 were accepted, 5 enrolled. Stanford Test of Academic Skills required. Deadline for receipt of application materials: none. Application fee required: $250. Interview required.

Athletics Interscholastic: baseball (boys), basketball (b,g), cheering (g), football (b), softball (g), volleyball (g); coed interscholastic: cross-country running. 1 PE instructor.

Computers Computers are regularly used in business applications, computer applications, English, journalism, yearbook classes. Computer network features include Internet access, Internet filtering or blocking technology. Computer access in designated common areas is available to students. Students grades are available online. The school has a published electronic and media policy.

Contact Ms. Lisa Vincent, Registrar. 502-937-3516. Fax: 502-937-3364. E-mail: lvincent@bethhaven.com.

THE BIRCH WATHEN LENOX SCHOOL

210 East 77th Street

New York, New York 10075

Head of School: Mr. Frank J. Carnabuci III

General Information Coeducational day college-preparatory school. Grades K–12. Founded: 1916. Setting: urban. 1 building on campus. Approved or accredited by New York Department of Education. Member of National Association of Independent Schools. Endowment: $7.4 million. Total enrollment: 550. Upper school average class size: 15. Upper school faculty-student ratio: 1:15. Upper School students typically attend 5 days per week. The average school day consists of 7 hours.

Upper School Student Profile Grade 9: 46 students (24 boys, 22 girls); Grade 10: 45 students (25 boys, 20 girls); Grade 11: 46 students (23 boys, 23 girls); Grade 12: 48 students (22 boys, 26 girls).

Faculty School total: 120. In upper school: 30 men, 85 women; 115 have advanced degrees.

Subjects Offered Algebra, American history, American history-AP, American literature, American literature-AP, art, art history, biology, calculus, ceramics, chemistry, community service, computer math, computer science, creative writing, dance, drama, driver education, economics, English, English literature, environmental science, European history, expository writing, fine arts, French, geography, geology, geometry, government/civics, grammar, industrial arts, Japanese, journalism, mathematics, music, philosophy, photography, physical education, physics, science, Shakespeare, social studies, Spanish, speech, swimming, theater, trigonometry, typing, world history, writing.

Graduation Requirements 20th century world history, arts and fine arts (art, music, dance, drama), computer science, English, foreign language, mathematics, physical education (includes health), science, social studies (includes history). Community service is required.

Special Academic Programs Advanced Placement exam preparation; honors section; independent study; study abroad; academic accommodation for the gifted, the musically talented, and the artistically talented.

College Admission Counseling 44 students graduated in 2011; all went to college, including Columbia University; Princeton University; Stanford University; University of Pennsylvania; Vanderbilt University; Williams College. Mean SAT critical reading: 650, mean SAT math: 650, mean SAT writing: 700.

Student Life Upper grades have uniform requirement, student council, honor system. Discipline rests equally with students and faculty.

Tuition and Aid Day student tuition: $36,915. Tuition installment plan (Key Tuition Payment Plan, monthly payment plans, individually arranged payment plans). Merit scholarship grants, need-based scholarship grants available. In 2011–12, 17% of upper-school students received aid; total upper-school merit-scholarship money awarded: $100,000. Total amount of financial aid awarded in 2011–12: $1,200,000.

Admissions Traditional secondary-level entrance grade is 9. For fall 2011, 100 students applied for upper-level admission, 30 were accepted, 20 enrolled. ERB, ISEE, Math Placement Exam or writing sample required. Deadline for receipt of application materials: none. Application fee required: $50. On-campus interview required.

Athletics Interscholastic: baseball (boys), basketball (b,g), cross-country running (b,g), field hockey (g), hockey (b), ice hockey (b), soccer (b,g), softball (g), swimming and diving (b,g), tennis (b,g), track and field (b,g), volleyball (b,g); intramural: aerobics (b,g), badminton (g), baseball (b), basketball (b,g), dance (b), ice hockey (b), indoor soccer (b), running (b,g), skiing (downhill) (b,g), soccer (b,g), softball (g), swimming and diving (b,g), tennis (b,g), track and field (b,g), volleyball (b,g); coed interscholastic: cross-country running, golf, indoor track & field, lacrosse; coed intramural: bicycling, dance, golf, gymnastics, indoor track & field, skiing (cross-country), skiing (downhill). 5 PE instructors, 8 coaches.

Computers Computers are regularly used in all academic classes. Computer network features include on-campus library services, Internet access, wireless campus network, MOBY, Smartboard. Student e-mail accounts are available to students.

Contact Billie Williams, Admissions Coordinator. 212-861-0404. Fax: 212-879-3388. E-mail: bwilliams@bwl.org. Web site: www.bwl.org.

BISHOP BLANCHET HIGH SCHOOL

8200 Wallingford Avenue North

Seattle, Washington 98103-4599

Head of School: Kristine Ann Bryuildsen-Smith, EdD

General Information Coeducational day college-preparatory, arts, religious studies, and technology school, affiliated with Roman Catholic Church. Grades 9–12. Founded: 1954. Setting: urban. 9-acre campus. 1 building on campus. Approved or accredited by National Catholic Education Association, Northwest Accreditation Commission, Northwest Association of Schools and Colleges, and Washington Department of Education. Endowment: $5 million. Total enrollment: 989. Upper school average class size: 20. Upper school faculty-student ratio: 1:13. There are 180 required school days per year for Upper School students. Upper School students typically attend 5 days per week. The average school day consists of 7 hours and 30 minutes.

Upper School Student Profile Grade 9: 264 students (138 boys, 126 girls); Grade 10: 262 students (152 boys, 110 girls); Grade 11: 223 students (118 boys, 105 girls); Grade 12: 241 students (132 boys, 109 girls). 82% of students are Roman Catholic.

Faculty School total: 81. In upper school: 36 men, 45 women; 52 have advanced degrees.

Subjects Offered 20th century American writers, 20th century world history, 3-dimensional design, American foreign policy, American history-AP, American literature, anatomy and physiology, applied arts, art, arts and crafts, ASB Leadership, band, biology, business applications, calculus, calculus-AP, Catholic belief and practice, ceramics, chamber groups, chemistry, chemistry-AP, choral music, comparative religion, contemporary history, desktop publishing, discrete mathematics, drama, drama performance, economics, English composition, English literature, ethics, ethnic literature, ethnic studies, European history, family living, French, German, government, guitar, health, history of rock and roll, history of the Catholic Church, instrumental music, Japanese, jazz band, language arts, Life of Christ, literature, marching band, math analysis, musical productions, performing arts, personal finance, philosophy, photography, physical education, physics, psychology, religion, scripture, set design, Spanish, U.S. history, vocal ensemble.

Graduation Requirements Art, business education, English, foreign language, lab science, mathematics, physical education (includes health), religion (includes Bible studies and theology), social studies (includes history).

Special Academic Programs Advanced Placement exam preparation; honors section; study at local college for college credit; programs in general development for dyslexic students.

College Admission Counseling 224 students graduated in 2011; 215 went to college, including Gonzaga University; The University of Montana Western; University of Washington; Washington State University; Western Washington University. Other: 4 went to work, 5 had other specific plans.

Student Life Upper grades have specified standards of dress, student council. Discipline rests primarily with faculty. Attendance at religious services is required.

Summer Programs Remediation programs offered; session focuses on students with learning needs; failed classes, cr. recovery; held on campus; accepts boys and girls; not open to students from other schools. 100 students usually enrolled. 2012 schedule: June 25 to July 27. Application deadline: June 25.

Tuition and Aid Day student tuition: $12,312. Tuition installment plan (monthly payment plans, individually arranged payment plans). Tuition reduction for siblings, merit scholarship grants, need-based scholarship grants, paying campus jobs available. In 2011–12, 40% of upper-school students received aid; total upper-school merit-scholarship money awarded: $120,000. Total amount of financial aid awarded in 2011–12: $1,600,000.

Admissions Traditional secondary-level entrance grade is 9. For fall 2011, 600 students applied for upper-level admission, 265 enrolled. ISEE required. Deadline for receipt of application materials: January 12. Application fee required: $25.

Athletics Interscholastic: baseball (boys), basketball (b,g), cheering (g), cross-country running (b,g), football (b), golf (b,g), lacrosse (b), soccer (b,g), softball (g), volleyball (g), wrestling (b); coed interscholastic: swimming and diving, tennis, track and field; coed intramural: alpine skiing, basketball, bowling, dance team, golf, hiking/backpacking, skiing (downhill), snowboarding, soccer, softball, strength & conditioning, table tennis, tennis, volleyball, weight lifting. 6 PE instructors, 1 athletic trainer.

Computers Computers are regularly used in accounting, business applications, business education, career exploration, college planning, computer applications, desktop publishing, foreign language, journalism, keyboarding, library skills, mathematics, newspaper, photography, science, video film production, word processing, yearbook classes. Computer network features include on-campus library services, online commercial services, Internet access, wireless campus network, Internet filtering or blocking technology, Internet Services with 2 ISP's totaling 60mbps bandwidth, Desktop monitoring software for library and labs, Web-based virtual classroom environment for all classes (Moodle. Student e-mail accounts and computer access in designated common areas are available to students. Students grades are available online. The school has a published electronic and media policy.

Contact Ann Alokolaro, Director of Admissions. 206-527-7741. Fax: 206-527-7712. E-mail: aalokola@bishopblanchet.org. Web site: www.bishopblanchet.org.

BISHOP BRADY HIGH SCHOOL

25 Columbus Avenue

Concord, New Hampshire 03301

Head of School: Mr. Trevor Bonat

General Information Coeducational day college-preparatory school, affiliated with Roman Catholic Church. Grades 9–12. Founded: 1963. Setting: suburban. 8-acre campus. 1 building on campus. Approved or accredited by National Catholic Education Association, New England Association of Schools and Colleges, and New Hampshire Department of Education. Total enrollment: 365. Upper school average class size: 17. Upper school faculty-student ratio: 1:15. There are 180 required school days per year for Upper School students. Upper School students typically attend 5 days per week. The average school day consists of 6 hours and 30 minutes.

Upper School Student Profile Grade 9: 93 students (45 boys, 48 girls); Grade 10: 84 students (43 boys, 41 girls); Grade 11: 93 students (43 boys, 50 girls); Grade 12: 95 students (47 boys, 48 girls). 70% of students are Roman Catholic.

Faculty School total: 34. In upper school: 14 men, 20 women; 25 have advanced degrees.

Subjects Offered Advanced chemistry, advanced math, algebra, anatomy and physiology, art appreciation, arts, biology, biology-AP, calculus-AP, career/college preparation, chemistry, chemistry-AP, Christian scripture, civics, college awareness, college counseling, computer education, conceptual physics, drama, English, English literature-AP, English-AP, film studies, French-AP, freshman seminar, geometry, guidance, health education, history, history-AP, honors English, Latin, moral theology, music appreciation, musical theater, physical education, physics-AP, pre-calculus, probability and statistics, psychology, religious studies, research and reference, SAT preparation, social justice, Spanish-AP, theology, trigonometry, U.S. history-AP, world religions, writing.

Graduation Requirements Algebra, American literature, arts and fine arts (art, music, dance, drama), biology, chemistry, computer education, English, geometry, languages, physical education (includes health), science, social studies (includes history), theology, 90 hours of community service.

Special Academic Programs 8 Advanced Placement exams for which test preparation is offered; honors section; independent study; study at local college for college credit; academic accommodation for the gifted; ESL (21 students enrolled).

College Admission Counseling 94 students graduated in 2011; 89 went to college, including Boston College; Georgetown University; Saint Anselm College; University of New Hampshire; University of Notre Dame. Other: 2 went to work, 3 entered military service. Mean SAT critical reading: 556, mean SAT math: 544, mean SAT writing: 552, mean composite ACT: 25. 30% scored over 600 on SAT critical reading, 30% scored over 600 on SAT math.

Student Life Upper grades have specified standards of dress, student council, honor system. Discipline rests primarily with faculty. Attendance at religious services is required.

Summer Programs Remediation, enrichment, advancement, sports programs offered; session focuses on football and conditioning, mathematics, study skills; held on campus; accepts boys and girls; open to students from other schools. 60 students usually enrolled. 2012 schedule: June 20 to August 15.

Tuition and Aid Day student tuition: $9300. Tuition installment plan (Insured Tuition Payment Plan, monthly payment plans, individually arranged payment plans). Tuition reduction for siblings, merit scholarship grants, need-based scholarship grants available. In 2011–12, 35% of upper-school students received aid.

Admissions Traditional secondary-level entrance grade is 9. For fall 2011, 135 students applied for upper-level admission, 130 were accepted, 81 enrolled. ACT-Explore or SSAT required. Deadline for receipt of application materials: June 15. Application fee required: $25. Interview required.

Athletics Interscholastic: alpine skiing (boys, girls), baseball (b), basketball (b,g), cheering (g), cross-country running (b,g), field hockey (g), football (b), golf (b,g), hockey (b), ice hockey (b), indoor track (b,g), lacrosse (b,g), skiing (downhill) (b,g), soccer (b,g), softball (g), swimming and diving (b,g), tennis (b,g), track and field (b,g); intramural: basketball (b,g); coed interscholastic: equestrian sports, juggling, outdoor activities, outdoor adventure; coed intramural: basketball, indoor track, outdoor activities, outdoor adventure, rock climbing, skiing (cross-country), skiing (downhill), snowboarding, strength & conditioning, table tennis, volleyball, weight lifting, weight training. 1 PE instructor.

Computers Computers are regularly used in business applications, college planning, journalism, literary magazine, newspaper classes. Computer network features include on-campus library services, online commercial services, Internet access, wireless campus network, Internet filtering or blocking technology. Student e-mail accounts and computer access in designated common areas are available to students. Students grades are available online. The school has a published electronic and media policy.

Contact Mrs. Lonna J. Abbott, Director of Admissions and Enrollment. 603-224-7419. Fax: 603-228-6664. E-mail: labbott@bishopbrady.edu. Web site: www.bishopbrady.edu.

BISHOP CONATY-OUR LADY OF LORETTO HIGH SCHOOL

2900 West Pico Boulevard

Los Angeles, California 90006

Head of School: Mr. Richard A. Spicer

General Information Girls' day college-preparatory, general academic, arts, religious studies, and technology school, affiliated with Roman Catholic Church. Grades 9–12. Founded: 1923. Setting: urban. 3-acre campus. 2 buildings on campus. Approved or accredited by National Catholic Education Association, The College Board, Western Catholic Education Association, and California Department of Education. Candidate for accreditation by Western Association of Schools and Colleges. Endowment: $598,721. Total enrollment: 359. Upper school average class size: 23. Upper school faculty-student ratio: 1:16. There are 182 required school days per year for Upper School students. Upper School students typically attend 5 days per week. The average school day consists of 4 hours and 30 minutes.

Upper School Student Profile Grade 9: 118 students (118 girls); Grade 10: 89 students (89 girls); Grade 11: 83 students (83 girls); Grade 12: 69 students (69 girls). 93% of students are Roman Catholic.

Faculty School total: 22. In upper school: 9 men, 13 women; 18 have advanced degrees.

Subjects Offered Aerobics, algebra, American literature, anatomy and physiology, ASB Leadership, athletics, biology, British literature, Catholic belief and practice, ceramics, chemistry, Christian and Hebrew scripture, computer literacy, dance, dance performance, drama, drawing, drawing and design, economics, English, English language and composition-AP, European history-AP, French, geometry, government, government and politics-AP, health, Holocaust studies, honors algebra, honors English, honors geometry, honors U.S. history, integrated science, linear algebra, moral reasoning, painting, physical education, physics, pre-calculus, religion, senior project, social justice, Spanish, Spanish language-AP, statistics, trigonometry, U.S. government, U.S. history, visual arts, Web site design, world history, world religions, yearbook.

Graduation Requirements Arts and fine arts (art, music, dance, drama), computer science, English, foreign language, mathematics, physical education (includes health), religion (includes Bible studies and theology), science, social studies (includes history), 100 hours of community service, senior project.

Special Academic Programs 4 Advanced Placement exams for which test preparation is offered; honors section; remedial reading and/or remedial writing; remedial math.

College Admission Counseling 60 students graduated in 2011; 52 went to college, including Loyola Marymount University; Marymount College, Palos Verdes, California; Mount St. Mary's College; Pasadena City College; Santa Monica College; University of California, Riverside. Other: 2 entered military service, 6 had other specific plans. Median SAT critical reading: 470, median SAT math: 450, median SAT writing: 440, median combined SAT: 1350, median composite ACT: 19. 3% scored over 600 on SAT critical reading, 11% scored over 600 on SAT math, 6% scored over 600 on SAT writing, 6% scored over 1800 on combined SAT.

Student Life Upper grades have uniform requirement, student council, honor system. Discipline rests primarily with faculty. Attendance at religious services is required.

Summer Programs Remediation, enrichment, advancement, art/fine arts, computer instruction programs offered; session focuses on make-up courses and strengthening incoming freshmen skills; held on campus; accepts boys and girls; open to students from other schools. 205 students usually enrolled. 2012 schedule: June 18 to July 20. Application deadline: June 11.

Tuition and Aid Day student tuition: $5995–$7800. Tuition installment plan (monthly payment plans, individually arranged payment plans). Tuition reduction for siblings, need-based scholarship grants, paying campus jobs available. In 2011–12, 92% of upper-school students received aid. Total amount of financial aid awarded in 2011–12: $627,618.

Admissions Traditional secondary-level entrance grade is 9. For fall 2011, 160 students applied for upper-level admission, 159 were accepted, 119 enrolled. High School Placement Test required. Deadline for receipt of application materials: August 15. Application fee required: $55. On-campus interview required.

Athletics Interscholastic: basketball, cross-country running, soccer, softball, volleyball. 3 coaches.

Computers Computers are regularly used in computer applications, Web site design, yearbook classes. Computer network features include on-campus library services, Internet access, wireless campus network, Internet filtering or blocking technology. Computer access in designated common areas is available to students. Students grades are available online. The school has a published electronic and media policy.

Contact Sr. Harriet Stellern, Director of Admissions. 323-737-0012 Ext. 103. Fax: 323-737-1749. E-mail: hstellern@bishopconatyloretto.org. Web site: www.bishopconatyloretto.org.

BISHOP CONNOLLY HIGH SCHOOL

373 Elsbree Street

Fall River, Massachusetts 02720

Head of School: Mr. Christopher Myron

General Information Coeducational day college-preparatory and religious studies school, affiliated with Roman Catholic Church. Grades 9–12. Founded: 1966. Setting: suburban. Nearest major city is Providence, RI. 72-acre campus. 1 building on campus. Approved or accredited by New England Association of Schools and Colleges and Massachusetts Department of Education. Total enrollment: 300. Upper school average class size: 18. Upper school faculty-student ratio: 1:16. There are 185 required school days per year for Upper School students. Upper School students typically attend 5 days per week. The average school day consists of 6 hours and 30 minutes.

Upper School Student Profile 90% of students are Roman Catholic.

Faculty School total: 30. In upper school: 18 men, 12 women; 22 have advanced degrees.

Subjects Offered Advanced Placement courses, algebra, American literature, American studies, anatomy and physiology, art, art history, Bible studies, biology, biology-AP, British literature, British literature (honors), calculus, calculus-AP, campus ministry, chemistry, chemistry-AP, choir, chorus, community service, computer programming, creative writing, desktop publishing, drama, English, English literature, English-AP, environmental science, European history-AP, French, French-AP, geometry, health, history, honors algebra, honors English, honors geometry, honors U.S. history, honors world history, human biology, instrumental music, keyboarding, math analysis, mathematics, music, music history, music theory, physical education, physics, Portuguese, psychology, religion, science, social studies, Spanish, theology, trigonometry, U.S. history-AP, world history, world literature.

Graduation Requirements English, foreign language, mathematics, religion (includes Bible studies and theology), science, social studies (includes history). Community service is required.

Special Academic Programs Advanced Placement exam preparation; honors section; independent study; study at local college for college credit.

College Admission Counseling 108 students graduated in 2010; they went to Bridgewater State University; Northeastern University; Providence College; Quinnipiac University; University of Massachusetts Dartmouth; University of Rhode Island. Mean SAT critical reading: 525, mean SAT math: 471. 13% scored over 600 on SAT critical reading, 11% scored over 600 on SAT math.

Student Life Upper grades have uniform requirement, student council. Discipline rests primarily with faculty. Attendance at religious services is required.

Tuition and Aid Day student tuition: $7600. Tuition installment plan (FACTS Tuition Payment Plan, monthly payment plans). Merit scholarship grants, need-based scholarship grants available. In 2010–11, 33% of upper-school students received aid.

Admissions Traditional secondary-level entrance grade is 9. High School Placement Test required. Deadline for receipt of application materials: none. No application fee required. Interview recommended.

Athletics Interscholastic: baseball (boys), basketball (b,g), cheering (b,g), cross-country running (b,g), football (b), ice hockey (b), lacrosse (b), soccer (b,g), softball (g), tennis (b,g), track and field (b,g), volleyball (g), winter (indoor) track (b,g); intramural: field hockey (g); coed interscholastic: golf, indoor soccer, indoor track & field. 2 PE instructors, 32 coaches, 1 athletic trainer.

Computers Computers are regularly used in all classes. Computer network features include online commercial services, Internet access, wireless campus network, Internet filtering or blocking technology. Computer access in designated common areas is available to students. The school has a published electronic and media policy.

Contact Mr. Anthony C. Ciampanelli, Director of Admissions/Alumni. 508-676-1071 Ext. 333. Fax: 508-676-8594. E-mail: aciampanelli@bishopconnolly.com. Web site: www.bishopconnolly.com.

BISHOP DENIS J. O'CONNELL HIGH SCHOOL

6600 Little Falls Road

Arlington, Virginia 22213

Head of School: Mrs. Katy Prebble

General Information Coeducational day college-preparatory, arts, business, religious studies, bilingual studies, and technology school, affiliated with Roman Catholic Church. Grades 9–12. Founded: 1957. Setting: suburban. Nearest major city is Washington, DC. 28-acre campus. 1 building on campus. Approved or accredited by National Catholic Education Association, Southern Association of Colleges and Schools, Southern Association of Independent Schools, Virginia Association of Independent Schools, and Virginia Department of Education. Member of Secondary School Admission Test Board. Total enrollment: 1,219. Upper school average class size: 21. Upper school faculty-student ratio: 1:12. Upper School students typically attend 5 days per week. The average school day consists of 6 hours and 50 minutes.

Upper School Student Profile Grade 9: 293 students (150 boys, 143 girls); Grade 10: 308 students (160 boys, 148 girls); Grade 11: 283 students (140 boys, 143 girls); Grade 12: 335 students (148 boys, 187 girls). 90% of students are Roman Catholic.

Faculty School total: 105.

Subjects Offered Accounting, algebra, American history, American literature, analysis, art, art history, athletic training, Basic programming, Bible studies, biology, biology-AP, business, calculus, calculus-AP, chemistry, chemistry-AP, choir, choral music, chorus, comparative government and politics-AP, computer graphics, computer multimedia, computer programming, computer science, computer science-AP, computer skills, creative writing, digital art, dramatic arts, driver education, earth science, East Asian history, economics, English, English language-AP, English literature, English literature-AP, environmental science-AP, European history, European history-AP, fine arts, forensics, French, French language-AP, geography, geometry, German, German-AP, government-AP, government/civics, guitar, health, history, honors English, honors geometry, honors U.S. history, honors world history, introduction to theater, Italian, jazz band, journalism, Latin, macroeconomics-AP, marketing, mathematics, media arts, microeconomics-AP, modern European history-AP, music, music theory-AP, New Testament, physical education, physics, physics-AP, piano, psychology-AP, public speaking, religion, remedial study skills, science, social sciences, social studies, sociology, Spanish, Spanish language-AP, Spanish literature-AP, speech, sports conditioning, statistics-AP, studio art-AP, theology, trigonometry, U.S. and Virginia history, U.S. government, U.S. history, U.S. history-AP, United States government-AP, voice ensemble, Web site design, world history, world literature.

Graduation Requirements Arts and fine arts (art, music, dance, drama), computer science, English, foreign language, mathematics, physical education (includes health), religion (includes Bible studies and theology), science, social sciences, social studies (includes history), community service program incorporated into graduation requirements.

Special Academic Programs Advanced Placement exam preparation; honors section; study at local college for college credit; academic accommodation for the gifted; remedial math; programs in general development for dyslexic students.

College Admission Counseling 330 students graduated in 2010; 327 went to college, including George Mason University; James Madison University; The College of William and Mary; University of Mary Washington; University of Virginia; Virginia Polytechnic Institute and State University. Other: 1 went to work, 1 entered military service, 1 entered a postgraduate year. Median SAT critical reading: 565, median SAT math: 551, median SAT writing: 559.

Student Life Upper grades have uniform requirement, student council, honor system. Discipline rests equally with students and faculty. Attendance at religious services is required.

Tuition and Aid Day student tuition: $9995–$14,665. Tuition installment plan (FACTS Tuition Payment Plan). Tuition reduction for siblings, merit scholarship grants, need-based scholarship grants, scholarship competition only for eighth graders currently enrolled in a Diocese of Arlington Catholic school available. In 2010–11, 20% of upper-school students received aid; total upper-school merit-scholarship money awarded: $30,000. Total amount of financial aid awarded in 2010–11: $1,400,000.

Admissions High School Placement Test required. Deadline for receipt of application materials: January 24. Application fee required: $50.

Athletics Interscholastic: baseball (boys), basketball (b,g), crew (b,g), cross-country running (b,g), dance team (g), diving (b,g), football (b), ice hockey (b), lacrosse (b,g), soccer (b,g), softball (g), swimming and diving (b,g), tennis (b,g), track and field (b,g), volleyball (g), wrestling (b); intramural: basketball (b,g), weight lifting (b,g); coed interscholastic: golf, sailing; coed intramural: crew, flag football, softball, ultimate Frisbee, volleyball. 7 PE instructors, 7 coaches, 1 athletic trainer.

Computers Computers are regularly used in art, business, computer applications, English, foreign language, health, history, mathematics, science, social sciences classes. Computer network features include on-campus library services, online commercial ser-

vices, Internet access, Internet filtering or blocking technology. Computer access in designated common areas is available to students. Students grades are available online. The school has a published electronic and media policy.
Contact Mrs. Mary McAlevy, Director of Admissions. 703-237-1433. Fax: 703-241-9066. E-mail: mmcalevy@bishopoconnell.org. Web site: www.bishopoconnell.org.

BISHOP EUSTACE PREPARATORY SCHOOL

5552 Route 70

Pennsauken, New Jersey 08109-4798

Head of School: Br. James Beamesderfer, SAC

General Information Coeducational day college-preparatory, arts, religious studies, and technology school, affiliated with Roman Catholic Church. Grades 9–12. Founded: 1954. Setting: suburban. Nearest major city is Philadelphia, PA. 32-acre campus. 7 buildings on campus. Approved or accredited by Middle States Association of Colleges and Schools and New Jersey Department of Education. Endowment: $3.3 million. Total enrollment: 750. Upper school average class size: 20. Upper school faculty-student ratio: 1:13. There are 166 required school days per year for Upper School students. Upper School students typically attend 5 days per week. The average school day consists of 6 hours and 20 minutes.
Upper School Student Profile 88% of students are Roman Catholic.
Faculty School total: 58. In upper school: 28 men, 30 women; 44 have advanced degrees.
Subjects Offered Advanced chemistry, advanced computer applications, Advanced Placement courses, algebra, American history, American history-AP, American literature, anatomy, anatomy and physiology, applied music, art and culture, art history, band, Bible studies, biology, biology-AP, British literature, British literature (honors), calculus, calculus-AP, campus ministry, career education, career exploration, career/college preparation, chemistry, chemistry-AP, choir, Christian doctrine, Christian education, Christian ethics, Christian scripture, clinical chemistry, college counseling, college placement, college planning, comparative religion, computer education, computer science, creative writing, driver education, economics and history, electives, English, English literature, English literature and composition-AP, environmental science, environmental science-AP, ethics, European history-AP, film, film and literature, fine arts, French, French as a second language, gender issues, genetics, geometry, German, government and politics-AP, government/civics, grammar, health, history, honors algebra, honors English, honors geometry, honors U.S. history, honors world history, instrumental music, journalism, Latin, law, law studies, macroeconomics-AP, mathematics, mathematics-AP, music, music composition, music history, music theory, music theory-AP, physical education, physical science, physics, physics-AP, physiology, pre-calculus, psychology, psychology-AP, science, sex education, social studies, sociology, Spanish, Spanish-AP, statistics-AP, theology, trigonometry, U.S. government and politics-AP, U.S. history, U.S. history-AP, vocal music, women's studies, world affairs, world history, world religions.
Graduation Requirements Arts and fine arts (art, music, dance, drama), career exploration, computer science, English, foreign language, mathematics, physical education (includes health), religion (includes Bible studies and theology), science, social studies (includes history). Community service is required.
Special Academic Programs 16 Advanced Placement exams for which test preparation is offered; honors section; independent study; study at local college for college credit; academic accommodation for the gifted and the musically talented.
College Admission Counseling 181 students graduated in 2011; 180 went to college, including Drexel University; Rutgers, The State University of New Jersey, New Brunswick; Saint Joseph's University; The Catholic University of America; University of Delaware; Villanova University. Other: 1 had other specific plans. 40% scored over 600 on SAT critical reading, 41% scored over 600 on SAT math, 34% scored over 600 on SAT writing.
Student Life Upper grades have uniform requirement, student council, honor system. Discipline rests primarily with faculty. Attendance at religious services is required.
Summer Programs Enrichment, advancement, sports programs offered; session focuses on student recruitment and enrichment for middle school students; advancement in math for current students; held on campus; accepts boys and girls; open to students from other schools. 150 students usually enrolled. 2012 schedule: June 25 to August 2. Application deadline: June 22.
Tuition and Aid Day student tuition: $14,900. Tuition installment plan (FACTS Tuition Payment Plan). Merit scholarship grants, need-based scholarship grants available. In 2011–12, 35% of upper-school students received aid; total upper-school merit-scholarship money awarded: $268,200. Total amount of financial aid awarded in 2011–12: $550,000.
Admissions Traditional secondary-level entrance grade is 9. Common entrance examinations, High School Placement Test, math and English placement tests or placement test required. Deadline for receipt of application materials: none. Application fee required: $60.
Athletics Interscholastic: baseball (boys), basketball (b,g), bowling (b,g), cheering (g), crew (b,g), cross-country running (b,g), field hockey (g), football (b), ice hockey (b), indoor track & field (b,g), lacrosse (b,g), running (b,g), soccer (b,g), softball (g), swimming and diving (b,g), tennis (b,g), track and field (b,g); coed interscholastic: aquatics, diving, golf. 3 PE instructors, 61 coaches, 1 athletic trainer.
Computers Computers are regularly used in all academic classes. Computer network features include on-campus library services, online commercial services, Internet access, wireless campus network, Internet filtering or blocking technology. Campus intranet and computer access in designated common areas are available to students. Students grades are available online. The school has a published electronic and media policy.
Contact Mr. Nicholas Italiano, Director of Institutional Advancement. 856-662-2160 Ext. 252. Fax: 856-665-2184. E-mail: nitaliano@eustace.org. Web site: www.eustace.org.

BISHOP FENWICK HIGH SCHOOL

4855 State Route 122

Franklin, Ohio 45005

Head of School: Mr. Michael Miller

General Information Coeducational day college-preparatory, arts, and religious studies school, affiliated with Roman Catholic Church. Grades 9–12. Founded: 1952. Setting: small town. Nearest major city is Cincinnati. 66-acre campus. 1 building on campus. Approved or accredited by National Catholic Education Association, North Central Association of Colleges and Schools, Ohio Catholic Schools Accreditation Association (OCSAA), and Ohio Department of Education. Upper school average class size: 24. Upper school faculty-student ratio: 1:14. There are 184 required school days per year for Upper School students. Upper School students typically attend 5 days per week. The average school day consists of 6 hours and 35 minutes.
Upper School Student Profile Grade 9: 135 students (77 boys, 58 girls); Grade 10: 157 students (96 boys, 61 girls); Grade 11: 122 students (61 boys, 61 girls); Grade 12: 124 students (56 boys, 68 girls). 85% of students are Roman Catholic.
Faculty School total: 39. In upper school: 22 men, 17 women; 24 have advanced degrees.
Subjects Offered Accounting, ACT preparation, algebra, American democracy, art, art-AP, athletic training, biology, botany, calculus-AP, career planning, cell biology, chemistry, choir, chorus, church history, college admission preparation, computer graphics, computer programming, concert band, creative writing, economics, engineering, English, English-AP, ensembles, film and literature, fine arts, French, functions, general business, geometry, government, government/civics-AP, health, honors algebra, honors English, honors geometry, integrated mathematics, jazz band, Latin, Latin-AP, leadership, marching band, mathematics, multimedia, music appreciation, mythology, physical education, physical science, physics, physiology, portfolio art, pre-algebra, psychology, publications, religion, science, social studies, Spanish, statistics, study skills, technology, theater, theater arts, trigonometry, U.S. history, U.S. history-AP, Web site design, world geography, world history, writing, yearbook, zoology.
Graduation Requirements Arts and fine arts (art, music, dance, drama), English, foreign language, mathematics, physical education (includes health), religion (includes Bible studies and theology), science, social studies (includes history), technology, community service, retreats, pass the Ohio Graduation Test.
Special Academic Programs Advanced Placement exam preparation; honors section; study at local college for college credit; special instructional classes for deaf students.
College Admission Counseling 139 students graduated in 2011; 138 went to college, including Miami University; Ohio University; The Ohio State University; University of Cincinnati; University of Dayton; Xavier University. Other: 1 entered military service. Median SAT critical reading: 550, median SAT math: 560, median SAT writing: 530, median combined SAT: 1640. Mean composite ACT: 24. 37% scored over 600 on SAT critical reading, 39% scored over 600 on SAT math, 26% scored over 600 on SAT writing, 33% scored over 1800 on combined SAT, 38% scored over 26 on composite ACT.
Student Life Upper grades have uniform requirement, student council, honor system. Discipline rests primarily with faculty. Attendance at religious services is required.
Tuition and Aid Day student tuition: $8050. Tuition installment plan (FACTS Tuition Payment Plan). Tuition reduction for siblings, merit scholarship grants, need-based scholarship grants, paying campus jobs available. In 2011–12, 13% of upper-school students received aid.
Admissions Traditional secondary-level entrance grade is 9. High School Placement Test required. Deadline for receipt of application materials: December 1. No application fee required.
Athletics Interscholastic: baseball (boys), basketball (b,g), cheering (g), cross-country running (b,g), dance team (g), football (b), golf (b,g), lacrosse (b,g), soccer (b,g), softball (g), tennis (b,g), volleyball (b,g), weight training (b,g), wrestling (b); intramural: basketball (b), weight training (b,g); coed interscholastic: bowling, in-line hockey, roller hockey, swimming and diving, track and field; coed intramural: freestyle skiing, paint ball, skiing (downhill), snowboarding. 1 PE instructor, 62 coaches, 1 athletic trainer.
Computers Computers are regularly used in career exploration, college planning, engineering, graphic arts, graphic design, introduction to technology, multimedia, photography, publications, technology, video film production, Web site design, yearbook classes. Computer network features include on-campus library services, Internet access, wireless campus network, Internet filtering or blocking technology, laptop carts, iPad cart. Campus intranet and computer access in designated common areas are available to

students. Students grades are available online. The school has a published electronic and media policy.
Contact Mrs. Betty Turvy, Director of Admissions. 513-428-0525. Fax: 513-727-1501. E-mail: bturvy@fenwickfalcons.org. Web site: www.fenwickfalcons.org.

BISHOP GUERTIN HIGH SCHOOL

194 Lund Road

Nashua, New Hampshire 03060-4398

Head of School: Br. Mark Hilton, SC

General Information Coeducational day college-preparatory and religious studies school, affiliated with Roman Catholic Church. Grades 9–12. Founded: 1963. Setting: suburban. Nearest major city is Boston, MA. 1 building on campus. Approved or accredited by New England Association of Schools and Colleges and New Hampshire Department of Education. Total enrollment: 900. Upper school average class size: 20.
Upper School Student Profile 80% of students are Roman Catholic.
Subjects Offered 20th century history, acting, advanced chemistry, advanced computer applications, advanced math, algebra, American literature-AP, analysis and differential calculus, anatomy and physiology, art appreciation, art history, band, Bible studies, biology, biology-AP, British history, British literature, British literature (honors), business law, calculus, calculus-AP, campus ministry, career/college preparation, chemistry, chemistry-AP, chorus, Christian and Hebrew scripture, Christian doctrine, Christian education, Christian ethics, Christianity, church history, civics, college admission preparation, college counseling, college writing, community service, comparative government and politics, comparative government and politics-AP, comparative religion, computer applications, computer art, computer education, computer literacy, computer multimedia, computer processing, computer programming, computer programming-AP, computer science, computer technologies, computer-aided design, constitutional history of U.S., consumer economics, contemporary history, CPR, creative writing, death and loss, debate, desktop publishing, digital photography, discrete mathematics, dramatic arts, drawing, driver education, economics, emergency medicine, English, English composition, English literature, English literature and composition-AP, English-AP, environmental science, ethics, European history, fine arts, foreign language, French, geography, geometry, government/civics, grammar, health, health and wellness, health education, history, honors geometry, honors U.S. history, honors world history, human anatomy, human biology, human sexuality, instrumental music, journalism, Latin, Latin-AP, law, literary magazine, marching band, mechanics of writing, moral reasoning, moral theology, music, philosophy, physical education, physics, pre-calculus, psychology, religion, religious studies, science, senior seminar, Shakespeare, social studies, Spanish, statistics, studio art, studio art-AP, The 20th Century, theater, trigonometry, U.S. government and politics, U.S. government and politics-AP, U.S. history, U.S. history-AP, U.S. literature, world history, world literature.
Graduation Requirements Arts and fine arts (art, music, dance, drama), computer science, physical education (includes health), religion (includes Bible studies and theology). Community service is required.
Special Academic Programs 13 Advanced Placement exams for which test preparation is offered; honors section; study at local college for college credit; academic accommodation for the gifted.
College Admission Counseling 211 students graduated in 2011; 208 went to college. Other: 2 entered military service, 1 entered a postgraduate year.
Student Life Attendance at religious services is required.
Summer Programs Held on campus; accepts boys and girls; not open to students from other schools. 40 students usually enrolled. 2012 schedule: July 1 to July 31. Application deadline: May 1.
Tuition and Aid Tuition installment plan (FACTS Tuition Payment Plan, individually arranged payment plans). Merit scholarship grants, need-based scholarship grants available. In 2011–12, 10% of upper-school students received aid.
Admissions Traditional secondary-level entrance grade is 9. High School Placement Test required. Deadline for receipt of application materials: January 6. Application fee required: $35.
Athletics Interscholastic: baseball (boys), basketball (b,g), cheering (b,g), cross-country running (b,g), field hockey (g), football (b), gymnastics (g), hockey (b,g), ice hockey (b,g), lacrosse (b), skiing (downhill) (b,g), soccer (b,g), softball (g), swimming and diving (b,g), tennis (b,g), track and field (b,g), volleyball (g), wrestling (b); intramural: crew (b,g); coed interscholastic: aquatics, cheering, golf, ice hockey, indoor track, nordic skiing, paint ball, skiing (downhill); coed intramural: aerobics/dance, basketball, bowling, crew, dance, fishing, freestyle skiing, golf, mountain biking, outdoor education, strength & conditioning, swimming and diving, table tennis, tennis, volleyball, weight lifting, weight training. 4 PE instructors, 55 coaches, 2 athletic trainers.
Computers Computers are regularly used in career education, career exploration, career technology, college planning, data processing, desktop publishing, independent study, information technology, introduction to technology, library, library science, library skills, literary magazine, multimedia, music, news writing, newspaper, programming, publications, publishing, research skills, stock market, technology, Web site design, word processing, yearbook classes. Computer network features include on-campus library services, online commercial services, Internet access, wireless campus network, Internet filtering or blocking technology. The school has a published electronic and media policy.
Contact Ms. Jamie Gregoire, Director of Admissions. 603-889-4107 Ext. 4304. Fax: 603-889-0701. E-mail: admit@bghs.org. Web site: www.bghs.org.

BISHOP IRETON HIGH SCHOOL

201 Cambridge Road

Alexandria, Virginia 22314-4899

Head of School: Mr. Timothy Hamer

General Information Coeducational day college-preparatory, arts, religious studies, and technology school, affiliated with Roman Catholic Church. Grades 9–12. Founded: 1964. Setting: suburban. 12-acre campus. 1 building on campus. Approved or accredited by National Catholic Education Association and Southern Association of Colleges and Schools. Total enrollment: 827. Upper school average class size: 24. Upper school faculty-student ratio: 1:14. There are 180 required school days per year for Upper School students. Upper School students typically attend 5 days per week. The average school day consists of 7 hours.
Upper School Student Profile Grade 9: 212 students (88 boys, 124 girls); Grade 10: 196 students (108 boys, 88 girls); Grade 11: 216 students (96 boys, 120 girls); Grade 12: 203 students (100 boys, 103 girls). 89% of students are Roman Catholic.
Faculty School total: 65. In upper school: 29 men, 36 women; 50 have advanced degrees.
Subjects Offered Advanced Placement courses, Catholic belief and practice, computer science, driver education, English, film, fine arts, foreign language, health, mathematics, physical education, religion, science, social studies.
Graduation Requirements Arts and fine arts (art, music, dance, drama), computer science, English, foreign language, mathematics, physical education (includes health), religion (includes Bible studies and theology), science, social studies (includes history), 60 hours of community service.
Special Academic Programs Advanced Placement exam preparation; honors section; academic accommodation for the musically talented; special instructional classes for students with Attention Deficit Disorder.
College Admission Counseling 206 students graduated in 2011; 204 went to college, including George Mason University; Radford University; The College of William and Mary; University of South Carolina; Virginia Commonwealth University; Virginia Polytechnic Institute and State University. Other: 2 had other specific plans. Mean SAT critical reading: 574, mean SAT math: 562, mean SAT writing: 580, mean combined SAT: 1716, mean composite ACT: 25.
Student Life Upper grades have uniform requirement, honor system. Discipline rests primarily with faculty. Attendance at religious services is required.
Summer Programs Remediation, enrichment, art/fine arts, computer instruction programs offered; session focuses on remediation; held on campus; accepts boys and girls; open to students from other schools. 50 students usually enrolled. 2012 schedule: June to July.
Tuition and Aid Day student tuition: $11,928–$16,065. Tuition installment plan (FACTS Tuition Payment Plan, monthly payment plans). Tuition reduction for siblings, merit scholarship grants, need-based scholarship grants available. In 2011–12, 15% of upper-school students received aid; total upper-school merit-scholarship money awarded: $128,000. Total amount of financial aid awarded in 2011–12: $622,000.
Admissions Traditional secondary-level entrance grade is 9. For fall 2011, 440 students applied for upper-level admission, 353 were accepted, 212 enrolled. High School Placement Test (closed version) from Scholastic Testing Service required. Deadline for receipt of application materials: January 23. Application fee required: $50.
Athletics Interscholastic: baseball (boys), basketball (b,g), field hockey (g), football (b), lacrosse (b,g), soccer (b,g), softball (g), swimming and diving (b,g), tennis (b,g), track and field (b,g), volleyball (g), water polo (b), winter (indoor) track (b,g), wrestling (b); intramural: weight training (b,g); coed interscholastic: cheering, crew, cross-country running, diving, golf, ice hockey, indoor track, water polo, weight training; coed intramural: dance team, freestyle skiing, skiing (downhill), table tennis. 4 PE instructors, 1 athletic trainer.
Computers Computers are regularly used in all academic classes. Computer network features include on-campus library services, online commercial services, Internet access, Internet filtering or blocking technology. Student e-mail accounts and computer access in designated common areas are available to students. Students grades are available online. The school has a published electronic and media policy.
Contact Mr. Peter J. Hamer, Director of Admissions. 703-212-5190. Fax: 703-212-8173. E-mail: hamerp@bishopireton.org. Web site: www.bishopireton.org.

BISHOP JOHN J. SNYDER HIGH SCHOOL

5001 Samaritan Way

Jacksonville, Florida 32210

Head of School: Deacon David Yazdiya

General Information Coeducational day college-preparatory school, affiliated with Worldwide Church of God. Grades 9–12. Founded: 2002. Setting: suburban. 50-acre campus. 14 buildings on campus. Approved or accredited by Southern Association of Colleges and Schools and Florida Department of Education. Upper school average class size: 21. Upper school faculty-student ratio: 1:15. There are 180 required school days per year for Upper School students. Upper School students typically attend 5 days per week. The average school day consists of 6 hours and 47 minutes.

Upper School Student Profile Grade 9: 128 students (76 boys, 52 girls); Grade 10: 124 students (55 boys, 69 girls); Grade 11: 111 students (46 boys, 65 girls); Grade 12: 105 students (65 boys, 40 girls). 80% of students are Worldwide Church of God.

Faculty School total: 33. In upper school: 18 men, 15 women; 15 have advanced degrees.

Subjects Offered Advanced biology, advanced chemistry, Advanced Placement courses, algebra, American government, American history, American history-AP, American literature, American literature-AP, anatomy and physiology, applied skills, art, athletics, Basic programming, Bible, biology, biology-AP, British literature, British literature (honors), calculus-AP, campus ministry, chemistry-AP, Chinese, choir, choral music, Christian doctrine, church history, college admission preparation, college awareness, college counseling, college planning, composition-AP, computer skills, creative writing, debate, economics, economics-AP, English, English composition, English language and composition-AP, English literature and composition-AP, French, geography, geometry, government, government-AP, guidance, history of the Catholic Church, honors algebra, honors English, honors geometry, honors U.S. history, honors world history, Latin, marine science, physics, religious education, Spanish, speech and debate, statistics, studio art, the Web, U.S. history, U.S. history-AP, world history, world history-AP.

Graduation Requirements 20th century world history.

Special Academic Programs 8 Advanced Placement exams for which test preparation is offered; remedial math.

College Admission Counseling 103 students graduated in 2011; 101 went to college, including Florida State University; University of Central Florida; University of Florida; University of North Florida; University of South Florida. Other: 1 went to work, 1 entered military service.

Student Life Upper grades have uniform requirement, student council, honor system. Discipline rests primarily with faculty. Attendance at religious services is required.

Tuition and Aid Day student tuition: $6700. Tuition installment plan (FACTS Tuition Payment Plan). Tuition reduction for siblings, need-based scholarship grants available. In 2011–12, 32% of upper-school students received aid. Total amount of financial aid awarded in 2011–12: $250,000.

Admissions Traditional secondary-level entrance grade is 11. For fall 2011, 500 students applied for upper-level admission, 485 were accepted, 468 enrolled. Explore required. Deadline for receipt of application materials: none. Application fee required: $375. Interview recommended.

Athletics Interscholastic: baseball (boys), basketball (b,g), cheering (b,g), cross-country running (b,g), diving (b,g), football (b), golf (b,g), lacrosse (b), soccer (b,g), softball (g), swimming and diving (b,g), tennis (b,g), track and field (b,g), volleyball (g), weight lifting (b), wrestling (b). 2 PE instructors, 23 coaches, 1 athletic trainer.

Computers Computers are regularly used in all academic classes. Computer resources include on-campus library services, Internet access, Internet filtering or blocking technology. Students grades are available online.

Contact Mrs. Mary Anne Briggs, Assistant to the Principal. 904-771-1029. Fax: 904-908-8988. E-mail: maryannebriggs@bishopsnyder.org. Web site: www.bishopsnyder.org.

BISHOP KELLY HIGH SCHOOL

7009 Franklin Road

Boise, Idaho 83709-0922

Head of School: Mr. Robert R. Wehde

General Information Coeducational day college-preparatory and religious studies school, affiliated with Roman Catholic Church. Grades 9–12. Founded: 1964. Setting: urban. 68-acre campus. 2 buildings on campus. Approved or accredited by National Catholic Education Association, Northwest Accreditation Commission, Western Catholic Education Association, and Idaho Department of Education. Endowment: $6.8 million. Total enrollment: 675. Upper school average class size: 21. Upper school faculty-student ratio: 1:18. There are 175 required school days per year for Upper School students. Upper School students typically attend 5 days per week. The average school day consists of 7 hours.

Upper School Student Profile Grade 9: 197 students (96 boys, 101 girls); Grade 10: 174 students (91 boys, 83 girls); Grade 11: 146 students (73 boys, 73 girls); Grade 12: 152 students (81 boys, 71 girls); Grade 13: 6 students (1 boy, 5 girls). 80% of students are Roman Catholic.

Faculty School total: 46. In upper school: 24 men, 22 women; 25 have advanced degrees.

Subjects Offered Advanced Placement courses, algebra, American government, American history-AP, art, art appreciation, art-AP, band, biology, biology-AP, calculus-AP, campus ministry, Catholic belief and practice, chemistry, chemistry-AP, choir, Christianity, comparative religion, computer applications, computer science-AP, conceptual physics, creative writing, drawing, earth science, ecology, economics, engineering, English, English-AP, fitness, French, geology, geometry, health, history of the Catholic Church, horticulture, instrumental music, journalism, literature, moral reasoning, painting, physical education, physics, physics-AP, pottery, pre-algebra, pre-calculus, psychology, reading/study skills, religious education, religious studies, senior seminar, service learning/internship, social justice, Spanish, Spanish-AP, speech, speech and debate, sports medicine, statistics-AP, theater, theater arts, theology, U.S. history, video film production, weight training, world history, yearbook.

Graduation Requirements Computer science, English, foreign language, mathematics, physical education (includes health), religion (includes Bible studies and theology), science, social studies (includes history), 30 hours of community service.

Special Academic Programs Advanced Placement exam preparation; honors section; independent study; study at local college for college credit.

College Admission Counseling 153 students graduated in 2011; 150 went to college, including Boise State University; Carroll College; The University of Arizona; University of Idaho; University of Utah; Westminster College. Mean SAT critical reading: 551, mean SAT math: 570, mean SAT writing: 540, mean combined SAT: 1661.

Student Life Upper grades have specified standards of dress, student council, honor system. Discipline rests primarily with faculty. Attendance at religious services is required.

Tuition and Aid Day student tuition: $6890. Tuition installment plan (The Tuition Plan, monthly payment plans, individually arranged payment plans). Need-based scholarship grants available. In 2011–12, 76% of upper-school students received aid. Total amount of financial aid awarded in 2011–12: $956,077.

Admissions Traditional secondary-level entrance grade is 9. For fall 2011, 675 students applied for upper-level admission, 675 were accepted, 675 enrolled. Deadline for receipt of application materials: none. Application fee required: $205.

Athletics Interscholastic: baseball (boys), basketball (b,g), cheering (g), cross-country running (b,g), football (b), golf (b,g), ice hockey (b), lacrosse (b,g), skiing (downhill) (b,g), snowboarding (b,g), soccer (b,g), softball (g), swimming and diving (b,g), tennis (b,g), track and field (b,g), volleyball (g), weight lifting (b,g), wrestling (b). 2 PE instructors, 11 coaches, 1 athletic trainer.

Computers Computers are regularly used in economics, English, foreign language, history, journalism, mathematics, science classes. Computer network features include on-campus library services, Internet access, Internet filtering or blocking technology, Blackboard. Student e-mail accounts and computer access in designated common areas are available to students. Students grades are available online. The school has a published electronic and media policy.

Contact Mrs. Kelly Shockey, Director of Admissions. 208-375-6010. Fax: 208-375-3626. E-mail: kshockey@bk.org. Web site: www.bk.org.

BISHOP KENNY HIGH SCHOOL

1055 Kingman Avenue

Jacksonville, Florida 32207

Head of School: Rev. Michael R. Houle

General Information Coeducational day college-preparatory school, affiliated with Roman Catholic Church. Grades 9–12. Founded: 1952. Setting: urban. 55-acre campus. 10 buildings on campus. Approved or accredited by Southern Association of Colleges and Schools. Total enrollment: 1,274. Upper school average class size: 22. Upper school faculty-student ratio: 1:15. There are 76 required school days per year for Upper School students. Upper School students typically attend 5 days per week. The average school day consists of 6 hours and 30 minutes.

Upper School Student Profile Grade 9: 285 students (128 boys, 157 girls); Grade 10: 339 students (169 boys, 170 girls); Grade 11: 337 students (170 boys, 167 girls); Grade 12: 313 students (155 boys, 158 girls). 85% of students are Roman Catholic.

Faculty In upper school: 28 men, 48 women; 36 have advanced degrees.

Subjects Offered Accounting, desktop publishing, technology, word processing.

Graduation Requirements Electives, English, foreign language, health, mathematics, performing arts, personal fitness, practical arts, religion (includes Bible studies and theology), science, social studies (includes history), service hour requirements.

Special Academic Programs Advanced Placement exam preparation; honors section.

College Admission Counseling 334 students graduated in 2010; 332 went to college, including Florida State University; University of Central Florida; University of Florida. Other: 2 went to work. Mean SAT critical reading: 526, mean SAT math: 517, mean SAT writing: 510, mean combined SAT: 1553, mean composite ACT: 23. 22% scored over 600 on SAT critical reading, 20% scored over 600 on SAT math, 18% scored over 600 on SAT writing.

Student Life Upper grades have uniform requirement, student council, honor system. Discipline rests primarily with faculty. Attendance at religious services is required.

Tuition and Aid Day student tuition: $6200. Tuition installment plan (FACTS Tuition Payment Plan, individually arranged payment plans). Tuition reduction for siblings, need-based scholarship grants available. In 2010–11, 20% of upper-school students received aid.

Admissions Traditional secondary-level entrance grade is 9. ACT-Explore or Explore required. Deadline for receipt of application materials: none. Application fee required. On-campus interview required.

Athletics Interscholastic: baseball (boys), basketball (b,g), cheering (g), cross-country running (b,g), diving (b,g), drill team (g), football (b), golf (b,g), JROTC drill (b,g), riflery (b,g), soccer (b,g), softball (g), swimming and diving (b,g), tennis (b,g), track and field (b,g), volleyball (g), weight lifting (b), wrestling (b).

Computers Computers are regularly used in computer applications, journalism, keyboarding, newspaper, yearbook classes. Computer resources include on-campus library services, Internet access, Internet filtering or blocking technology, design software for Journalism and MultiMedia, CS4 Suite, 5 computer labs. The school has a published electronic and media policy.

Contact Mrs. Sheila W. Marovich, Director of Admissions. 904-398-7545. Fax: 904-398-5728. E-mail: development@bishopkenny.org. Web site: www.bishopkenny.org.

BISHOP LUERS HIGH SCHOOL

333 East Paulding Road

Fort Wayne, Indiana 46816

Head of School: Mrs. Mary T. Keefer

General Information Coeducational day college-preparatory and religious studies school, affiliated with Roman Catholic Church. Grades 9–12. Founded: 1958. Setting: urban. 5-acre campus. 1 building on campus. Approved or accredited by National Catholic Education Association, North Central Association of Colleges and Schools, and Indiana Department of Education. Total enrollment: 545. Upper school average class size: 25. Upper school faculty-student ratio: 1:17. There are 180 required school days per year for Upper School students. Upper School students typically attend 5 days per week. The average school day consists of 6 hours and 35 minutes.

Upper School Student Profile Grade 9: 135 students (70 boys, 65 girls); Grade 10: 150 students (80 boys, 70 girls); Grade 11: 127 students (52 boys, 75 girls); Grade 12: 133 students (63 boys, 70 girls). 89% of students are Roman Catholic.

Faculty School total: 31. In upper school: 10 men, 21 women; 18 have advanced degrees.

Subjects Offered 3-dimensional art, accounting, algebra, Bible, biology, biology-AP, business, business law, calculus-AP, chamber groups, chemistry, chemistry-AP, chorus, church history, computer applications, computer programming, concert band, creative writing, drawing, economics, English, French, geometry, government, health education, honors algebra, honors English, honors geometry, honors U.S. history, honors world history, Latin, music appreciation, music theory, painting, physical education, physics, physiology, pre-calculus, probability and statistics, psychology, sculpture, sociology, Spanish, speech communications, student government, student publications, study skills, theater arts, theater production, theology, trigonometry, U.S. history, world civilizations, world geography, world history.

Graduation Requirements Computers, English, mathematics, physical education (includes health), religion (includes Bible studies and theology), science, social studies (includes history).

Special Academic Programs Advanced Placement exam preparation; honors section; study at local college for college credit; academic accommodation for the gifted and the musically talented; remedial reading and/or remedial writing; remedial math.

College Admission Counseling Colleges students went to include Indiana University–Purdue University Fort Wayne; Purdue University. Mean SAT critical reading: 513, mean SAT math: 507, mean SAT writing: 495.

Student Life Upper grades have specified standards of dress, student council. Discipline rests equally with students and faculty. Attendance at religious services is required.

Tuition and Aid Day student tuition: $3875. Tuition installment plan (FACTS Tuition Payment Plan). Tuition reduction for siblings, merit scholarship grants, need-based scholarship grants, paying campus jobs available. In 2010–11, 61% of upper-school students received aid.

Admissions Deadline for receipt of application materials: none. Application fee required: $120.

Athletics Interscholastic: baseball (boys), basketball (b,g), bowling (b,g), cheering (g), cross-country running (b,g), dance (g), dance team (g), diving (b,g), football (b), golf (b,g), lacrosse (b), riflery (b,g), running (b,g), soccer (b,g), softball (g), swimming and diving (b,g), tennis (b,g), track and field (b,g), volleyball (g), wrestling (g); intramural: lacrosse (b,g); coed intramural: lacrosse, riflery, weight training. 2 PE instructors, 25 coaches, 2 athletic trainers.

Computers Computers are regularly used in all academic, business, yearbook classes. Computer network features include on-campus library services, Internet access, Internet filtering or blocking technology. Students grades are available online. The school has a published electronic and media policy.

Contact Mrs. Jennifer Andorfer, Co-Director of Admissions and Public Relations. 260-456-1261 Ext. 3141. Fax: 260-456-1262. E-mail: jandorfer@bishopluers.org. Web site: www.bishopluers.org/.

BISHOP MCGUINNESS CATHOLIC HIGH SCHOOL

1725 NC Highway 66 South

Kernersville, North Carolina 27284

Head of School: Mr. George L. Repass

General Information Coeducational day college-preparatory, arts, and religious studies school, affiliated with Roman Catholic Church. Grades 9–12. Founded: 1959. Setting: small town. Nearest major city is Winston-Salem. 42-acre campus. 2 buildings on campus. Approved or accredited by National Catholic Education Association, Southern Association of Colleges and Schools, The College Board, and North Carolina Department of Education. Member of National Association of Independent Schools. Endowment: $100,000. Total enrollment: 549. Upper school average class size: 18. Upper school faculty-student ratio: 1:15. There are 180 required school days per year for Upper School students. Upper School students typically attend 5 days per week. The average school day consists of 6 hours and 50 minutes.

Upper School Student Profile Grade 9: 142 students (87 boys, 55 girls); Grade 10: 152 students (81 boys, 71 girls); Grade 11: 111 students (69 boys, 42 girls); Grade 12: 144 students (76 boys, 68 girls). 75% of students are Roman Catholic.

Faculty School total: 36. In upper school: 20 men, 16 women; 31 have advanced degrees.

Subjects Offered Algebra, American history, anatomy, art history, arts, biology, biology-AP, calculus, calculus-AP, chemistry, chemistry-AP, community service, computer science, computer science-AP, creative writing, earth science, English, English language-AP, English literature and composition-AP, environmental science, European history-AP, fine arts, French, French language-AP, French-AP, geometry, health, Latin, Latin-AP, mathematics, music, music theory-AP, photography, physical education, physical science, physics, political science, religion, science, social studies, Spanish, Spanish-AP, statistics-AP, trigonometry, U.S. history-AP, world history.

Graduation Requirements Arts and fine arts (art, music, dance, drama), English, foreign language, mathematics, physical education (includes health), religion (includes Bible studies and theology), science, social studies (includes history), all students must attend the retreat for their grade level; all seniors must complete the senior career project. Community service is required.

Special Academic Programs 15 Advanced Placement exams for which test preparation is offered; honors section; independent study; term-away projects; study at local college for college credit.

College Admission Counseling 134 students graduated in 2011; 131 went to college, including Appalachian State University; East Carolina University; North Carolina State University; The University of North Carolina at Chapel Hill; The University of North Carolina at Charlotte; The University of North Carolina Wilmington. Other: 3 had other specific plans. Mean SAT critical reading: 553, mean SAT math: 539, mean SAT writing: 534, mean combined SAT: 1626, mean composite ACT: 24. 30% scored over 600 on SAT critical reading, 29% scored over 600 on SAT math, 20% scored over 600 on SAT writing, 27% scored over 1800 on combined SAT, 29% scored over 26 on composite ACT.

Student Life Upper grades have specified standards of dress, student council, honor system. Discipline rests primarily with faculty. Attendance at religious services is required.

Tuition and Aid Day student tuition: $7069–$9877. Tuition installment plan (monthly payment plans, yearly, semester, and quarterly payment plans). Tuition reduction for siblings, need-based scholarship grants available. In 2011–12, 19% of upper-school students received aid. Total amount of financial aid awarded in 2011–12: $288,550.

Admissions Traditional secondary-level entrance grade is 9. For fall 2011, 182 students applied for upper-level admission, 172 were accepted, 154 enrolled. Achievement/Aptitude/Writing or High School Placement Test required. Deadline for receipt of application materials: none. Application fee required: $75. On-campus interview required.

Athletics Interscholastic: baseball (boys), basketball (b,g), cheering (g), football (b), lacrosse (b), soccer (b,g), softball (g), tennis (b,g), volleyball (g), wrestling (b); coed interscholastic: cross-country running, golf, swimming and diving, track and field, weight training. 3 PE instructors, 40 coaches, 1 athletic trainer.

Computers Computer resources include on-campus library services, Internet access, Internet filtering or blocking technology. Student e-mail accounts and computer access in designated common areas are available to students. Students grades are available online. The school has a published electronic and media policy.

Contact Mr. Robert Belcher, Admissions Director. 336-564-1011. Fax: 336-564-1060. E-mail: rb@bmhs.us. Web site: www.bmhs.us.

BISHOP MCGUINNESS CATHOLIC HIGH SCHOOL

801 Northwest 50th Street

Oklahoma City, Oklahoma 73118-6001

Head of School: Mr. David L. Morton

General Information Coeducational day college-preparatory, arts, business, religious studies, bilingual studies, and technology school, affiliated with Roman Catholic Church. Grades 9–12. Founded: 1950. Setting: urban. 20-acre campus. 4 buildings on campus. Approved or accredited by North Central Association of Colleges and Schools and Oklahoma Department of Education. Endowment: $1.2 million. Total enrollment: 722. Upper school average class size: 14. Upper school faculty-student ratio: 1:14. There are 177 required school days per year for Upper School students. Upper School students typically attend 5 days per week. The average school day consists of 6 hours and 10 minutes.

Upper School Student Profile Grade 11: 168 students (79 boys, 89 girls); Grade 12: 179 students (95 boys, 84 girls). 76% of students are Roman Catholic.

Faculty School total: 55. In upper school: 11 men, 15 women; 10 have advanced degrees.

Subjects Offered Algebra, American literature, American literature-AP, art, band, Bible studies, biology, biology-AP, business, business law, calculus-AP, Catholic belief and practice, ceramics, chemistry, chorus, church history, computer technologies, creative writing, culinary arts, current events, dance, debate, design, drama, drawing, economics, electives, English, English literature, English literature-AP, ethics, French, geography, geometry, German, government, government-AP, health and wellness, history of the Catholic Church, honors algebra, honors English, honors geometry, introduction to theater, Latin, leadership, learning lab, macroeconomics-AP, newspaper, orchestra, painting, personal finance, photography, physical education, physical science, physics, physics-AP, physiology, play production, practical arts, prayer/spirituality, pre-calculus, psychology, scripture, sociology, Spanish, speech, stagecraft, theater, U.S. history, U.S. history-AP, weight training, world history, world history-AP, world religions, writing workshop, yearbook.

Graduation Requirements Arts and fine arts (art, music, dance, drama), electives, English, foreign language, mathematics, physical education (includes health), practical arts, science, social studies (includes history), theology, 90 hours of Christian service.

Special Academic Programs 10 Advanced Placement exams for which test preparation is offered; honors section; academic accommodation for the gifted and the artistically talented; programs in English, mathematics for dyslexic students; special instructional classes for students with learning differences.

College Admission Counseling 174 students graduated in 2011; 165 went to college, including Oklahoma City University; Oklahoma State University; Texas Christian University; University of Arkansas; University of Oklahoma. Other: 1 went to work, 1 had other specific plans. Median SAT critical reading: 590, median SAT math: 570, median SAT writing: 580. Mean composite ACT: 25. 42% scored over 600 on SAT critical reading, 45% scored over 600 on SAT math, 48% scored over 600 on SAT writing, 46% scored over 1800 on combined SAT, 38% scored over 26 on composite ACT.

Student Life Upper grades have uniform requirement, student council, honor system. Discipline rests primarily with faculty. Attendance at religious services is required.

Tuition and Aid Day student tuition: $7800. Tuition installment plan (FACTS Tuition Payment Plan). Need-based scholarship grants, paying campus jobs available. In 2011–12, 23% of upper-school students received aid. Total amount of financial aid awarded in 2011–12: $264,300.

Admissions Traditional secondary-level entrance grade is 11. For fall 2011, 11 students applied for upper-level admission, 11 were accepted, 11 enrolled. School placement exam, STS or writing sample required. Deadline for receipt of application materials: May 1. Application fee required: $375. On-campus interview required.

Athletics Interscholastic: baseball (boys), basketball (b,g), bowling (b,g), cheering (g), cross-country running (b,g), dance team (b,g), football (b), golf (b,g), soccer (b,g), softball (g), swimming and diving (b,g), tennis (b,g), track and field (b,g), volleyball (g), weight training (b,g), winter (indoor) track (b,g), wrestling (b); coed interscholastic: bowling, physical fitness.

Computers Computers are regularly used in all academic classes. Computer network features include on-campus library services, online commercial services, Internet access, wireless campus network, Internet filtering or blocking technology, laptop classroom computers, wireless printing, eBooks, and My Road. Student e-mail accounts and computer access in designated common areas are available to students. Students grades are available online. The school has a published electronic and media policy.

Contact Ms. Amy Hanson, 9th Grade Counselor. 405-842-6638 Ext. 225. Fax: 405-858-9550. E-mail: ahanson@bmchs.org. Web site: www.bmchs.org.

BISHOP MONTGOMERY HIGH SCHOOL

5430 Torrance Boulevard

Torrance, California 90503

Head of School: Ms. Rosemary Distaso-Libbon

General Information Coeducational day college-preparatory, arts, religious studies, and technology school, affiliated with Roman Catholic Church. Grades 9–12. Founded: 1957. Setting: suburban. Nearest major city is Los Angeles. 27-acre campus. 8 buildings on campus. Approved or accredited by National Catholic Education Association, Western Association of Schools and Colleges, Western Catholic Education Association, and California Department of Education. Total enrollment: 1,063. Upper school average class size: 22. Upper school faculty-student ratio: 1:22. There are 180 required school days per year for Upper School students. Upper School students typically attend 5 days per week. The average school day consists of 6 hours and 10 minutes.

Upper School Student Profile Grade 9: 274 students (136 boys, 138 girls); Grade 10: 248 students (114 boys, 134 girls); Grade 11: 261 students (117 boys, 144 girls); Grade 12: 280 students (123 boys, 157 girls). 75% of students are Roman Catholic.

Faculty School total: 60. In upper school: 25 men, 33 women; 22 have advanced degrees.

Subjects Offered Advanced Placement courses, algebra, American history, American history-AP, American literature, anatomy, art, Bible studies, biology, calculus, chemistry, chorus, composition, computer science, drama, economics, English, English literature, English literature-AP, fine arts, French, geometry, government/civics, health, history, languages, literature, mathematics, physical education, physics, physics-AP, physiology, religion, science, social studies, Spanish, statistics, theater, weight training, world history, yearbook.

Graduation Requirements Arts and fine arts (art, music, dance, drama), business skills (includes word processing), computer science, English, mathematics, physical education (includes health), religion (includes Bible studies and theology), science, social studies (includes history).

Special Academic Programs Advanced Placement exam preparation; honors section.

College Admission Counseling 266 students graduated in 2011; all went to college, including California State University, Dominguez Hills; California State University, Long Beach; Loyola Marymount University; University of California, Irvine; University of California, Los Angeles; University of California, Riverside. Mean SAT critical reading: 527, mean SAT math: 527, mean SAT writing: 526.

Student Life Upper grades have uniform requirement, student council, honor system. Discipline rests primarily with faculty. Attendance at religious services is required.

Summer Programs Remediation, enrichment, advancement, sports, art/fine arts, computer instruction programs offered; session focuses on academic enrichment/remediation and athletic conditioning; held on campus; accepts boys and girls; not open to students from other schools. 900 students usually enrolled. 2012 schedule: June 20 to July 24. Application deadline: June 19.

Tuition and Aid Day student tuition: $7500. Tuition installment plan (monthly payment plans). Tuition reduction for siblings, financial need available. In 2011–12, 4% of upper-school students received aid. Total amount of financial aid awarded in 2011–12: $30,000.

Admissions Traditional secondary-level entrance grade is 9. High School Placement Test, Iowa Tests of Basic Skills and Stanford 9 required. Deadline for receipt of application materials: January 12. Application fee required: $75.

Athletics Interscholastic: baseball (boys), basketball (b,g), cheering (g), cross-country running (b,g), dance (g), dance team (g), football (b), golf (b,g), soccer (b,g), softball (g), strength & conditioning (b,g), tennis (b,g), volleyball (b,g); coed interscholastic: aerobics, surfing, swimming and diving, track and field. 3 PE instructors, 32 coaches, 2 athletic trainers.

Computers Computers are regularly used in library, newspaper, programming, publications, technology, Web site design classes. Computer network features include on-campus library services, Internet access, wireless campus network. Students grades are available online. The school has a published electronic and media policy.

Contact Mrs. Casey Dunn, Director of Admissions. 310-540-2021 Ext. 227. Fax: 310-543-5102. E-mail: cdunn@bmhs-la.org. Web site: www.bmhs-la.org.

BISHOP MORA SALESIAN HIGH SCHOOL

960 South Soto Street

Los Angeles, California 90023

Head of School: Mr. Samuel Robles

General Information Boys' day college-preparatory, general academic, and religious studies school, affiliated with Roman Catholic Church. Grades 9–12. Founded: 1958. Setting: urban. 2 buildings on campus. Approved or accredited by Accrediting Commission for Schools, Western Association of Schools and Colleges, Western Catholic Education Association, and California Department of Education. Upper school average class size: 28. Upper school faculty-student ratio: 1:15. There are 188 required school days per year for Upper School students. The average school day consists of 6 hours and 50 minutes.

Upper School Student Profile Grade 9: 131 students (131 boys); Grade 10: 116 students (116 boys); Grade 11: 105 students (105 boys); Grade 12: 102 students (102 boys). 98% of students are Roman Catholic.

Faculty School total: 32. In upper school: 24 men, 8 women; 28 have advanced degrees.

Subjects Offered Advanced biology, advanced chemistry, advanced math, Advanced Placement courses, algebra, American history, American history-AP, American literature, anatomy and physiology, applied music, art, arts appreciation, athletic training, athletics, baseball, basketball, Bible studies, biology, biology-AP, British history, British literature, British literature (honors), business, calculus, calculus-AP, Catholic belief and practice, chemistry, chemistry-AP, Christianity, church history, cinematography, college admission preparation, college awareness, college counseling, college placement, college planning, computer applications, computer science, creative writing, drama, drawing, economics, economics-AP, English, English literature, English-AP, environmental science, ethics, European history, expository writing, fine arts, geometry, government/civics, grammar, health, health education, Hispanic literature, history, mathematics, music, physical education, physical science, physics, physics-AP, pre-algebra, pre-calculus, psychology, psychology-AP, religion, science, social studies, Spanish, Spanish-AP, speech and debate, theater, trigonometry, U.S. government and politics-AP, volleyball, weight training, world history, world literature, writing.

Graduation Requirements Arts and fine arts (art, music, dance, drama), computer science, English, foreign language, mathematics, physical education (includes health), religion (includes Bible studies and theology), religious studies, science, social studies (includes history), Christian service program.

Special Academic Programs Study at local college for college credit; academic accommodation for the musically talented and the artistically talented; remedial reading and/or remedial writing.

College Admission Counseling 87 students graduated in 2011; 86 went to college, including California State University, Los Angeles; Loyola Marymount University; University of California, Los Angeles; University of California, Riverside; Whittier College. Other: 1 entered military service.

Student Life Upper grades have uniform requirement, student council, honor system. Discipline rests equally with students and faculty. Attendance at religious services is required.

Summer Programs Remediation, enrichment, advancement, sports, art/fine arts, rigorous outdoor training, computer instruction programs offered; session focuses on refresher course; held on campus; accepts boys and girls; open to students from other schools. 200 students usually enrolled. 2012 schedule: June 19 to July 31. Application deadline: May.

Tuition and Aid Day student tuition: $8900. Tuition installment plan (FACTS Tuition Payment Plan, monthly payment plans, individually arranged payment plans). Tuition reduction for siblings, merit scholarship grants, need-based scholarship grants available. In 2011–12, 75% of upper-school students received aid; total upper-school merit-scholarship money awarded: $2500. Total amount of financial aid awarded in 2011–12: $1,548,500.

Admissions Traditional secondary-level entrance grade is 9. ETS high school placement exam required. Deadline for receipt of application materials: April 1. Application fee required: $50. On-campus interview required.

Athletics Interscholastic: baseball, basketball, bicycling, cross-country running, football, golf, physical fitness, physical training, power lifting, running, soccer, track and field, volleyball, weight training, wrestling; intramural: aerobics/Nautilus, basketball, cheering, dance squad, dance team, soccer, yoga. 12 coaches, 1 athletic trainer.

Computers Computers are regularly used in design, desktop publishing, English, mathematics, word processing, writing, writing, yearbook classes. Computer network features include Internet access. Campus intranet and student e-mail accounts are available to students.

Contact Mr. Mark Johnson, Vice Principal/Director of Curriculum. 323-261-7124 Ext. 224. Fax: 213-261-7600. E-mail: johnson@mustangsla.org. Web site: www.mustangsla.org.

BISHOP O'DOWD HIGH SCHOOL

9500 Stearns Avenue

Oakland, California 94605-4799

Head of School: Dr. Stephen Phelps, EdD

General Information Coeducational day college-preparatory, arts, religious studies, and technology school, affiliated with Roman Catholic Church. Grades 9–12. Founded: 1951. Setting: urban. 8-acre campus. 12 buildings on campus. Approved or accredited by Western Association of Schools and Colleges, Western Catholic Education Association, and California Department of Education. Endowment: $1 million. Total enrollment: 1,125. Upper school average class size: 26. Upper school faculty-student ratio: 1:15. Upper School students typically attend 5 days per week. The average school day consists of 6 hours and 30 minutes.

Upper School Student Profile Grade 9: 257 students (118 boys, 139 girls); Grade 10: 282 students (151 boys, 131 girls); Grade 11: 314 students (153 boys, 161 girls); Grade 12: 276 students (127 boys, 149 girls). 55% of students are Roman Catholic.

Faculty School total: 78. In upper school: 41 men, 37 women; 55 have advanced degrees.

Subjects Offered Art, computer science, English, fine arts, foreign language, mathematics, physical education, religion, science, social studies.

Graduation Requirements Arts and fine arts (art, music, dance, drama), English, foreign language, mathematics, physical education (includes health), religion (includes Bible studies and theology), religious studies, science, social studies (includes history), 100 hour service learning project to be completed over all four years.

Special Academic Programs Advanced Placement exam preparation; honors section; academic accommodation for the gifted, the musically talented, and the artistically talented; remedial reading and/or remedial writing; remedial math; special instructional classes for students with ADD and dyslexia.

College Admission Counseling 296 students graduated in 2010; 294 went to college, including California Polytechnic State University, San Luis Obispo; San Francisco State University; University of California, Berkeley; University of California, Davis; University of California, Santa Cruz; University of Oregon. Other: 2 had other specific plans. Mean SAT critical reading: 561, mean SAT math: 566, mean SAT writing: 576.

Student Life Upper grades have specified standards of dress, student council. Discipline rests equally with students and faculty.

Tuition and Aid Day student tuition: $13,840. Tuition installment plan (monthly payment plans, individually arranged payment plans). Tuition reduction for siblings, merit scholarship grants, need-based scholarship grants available. In 2010–11, 30% of upper-school students received aid; total upper-school merit-scholarship money awarded: $15,000. Total amount of financial aid awarded in 2010–11: $2,100,000.

Admissions Traditional secondary-level entrance grade is 9. For fall 2010, 550 students applied for upper-level admission, 430 were accepted, 265 enrolled. High School Placement Test and High School Placement Test (closed version) from Scholastic Testing Service required. Deadline for receipt of application materials: none. Application fee required: $90.

Athletics Interscholastic: aquatics (boys, girls), baseball (b), basketball (b,g), cheering (g), cross-country running (b,g), diving (b,g), football (b), golf (b,g), lacrosse (b,g), rugby (b,g), soccer (b,g), softball (g), swimming and diving (b,g), tennis (b,g), track and field (b,g), volleyball (g), water polo (b,g); intramural: basketball (b,g), dance squad (g), physical training (b,g), soccer (b,g), weight training (b,g); coed interscholastic: cross-country running; coed intramural: aerobics, aerobics/dance, alpine skiing, backpacking, bicycling, combined training, flag football, Frisbee, hiking/backpacking, mountain biking, skiing (downhill), snowboarding, weight training. 5 PE instructors, 36 coaches, 1 athletic trainer.

Computers Computers are regularly used in all academic, career exploration, library, library skills, mathematics, media arts, media production, newspaper, programming, research skills, science, video film production, yearbook classes. Computer network features include on-campus library services, online commercial services, Internet access, wireless campus network, Internet filtering or blocking technology, one to one laptop program: every student has a laptop on campus. Student e-mail accounts are available to students. Students grades are available online. The school has a published electronic and media policy.

Contact Tyler Kreitz, Director of Admissions. 510-577-9100. Fax: 510-638-3259. E-mail: tkreitz@bishopodowd.org. Web site: www.bishopodowd.org.

BISHOP'S COLLEGE SCHOOL

80 Moulton Hill Road

PO Box 5001, Succ. Lennoxville

Sherbrooke, Quebec J1M 1Z8, Canada

Head of School: Mr. Ian Watt

General Information Coeducational boarding and day college-preparatory, arts, and bilingual studies school. Grades 7–12. Founded: 1836. Setting: small town. Nearest major city is Montreal, Canada. Students are housed in single-sex dormitories. 270-acre campus. 30 buildings on campus. Approved or accredited by Canadian Association of Independent Schools, Canadian Educational Standards Institute, Quebec Association of Independent Schools, The Association of Boarding Schools, and Quebec Department of Education. Affiliate member of National Association of Independent Schools. Languages of instruction: English and French. Endowment: CAN$15 million. Total enrollment: 212. Upper school average class size: 15. Upper school faculty-student ratio: 1:5. There are 180 required school days per year for Upper School students. Upper School students typically attend 6 days per week. The average school day consists of 8 hours.

Upper School Student Profile Grade 10: 48 students (30 boys, 18 girls); Grade 11: 61 students (40 boys, 21 girls); Grade 12: 45 students (31 boys, 14 girls). 75% of students are boarding students. 44% are province residents. 11 provinces are represented in upper school student body. 49% are international students. International students from Bahamas, China, France, Mexico, Saudi Arabia, and United States; 17 other countries represented in student body.

Faculty School total: 40. In upper school: 17 men, 13 women; 20 reside on campus.

Subjects Offered Algebra, art, biology, calculus, chemistry, computer science, creative writing, dance, drama, economics, English, environmental science, ESL, ethics, finite math, French, French as a second language, geography, geometry, history, mathematics, music, philosophy, physical education, physical science, physics, political science, religion, science, sociology, study skills, technology, theater, trigonometry, world history.

Graduation Requirements Follow Ministry of Quebec guidelines, Follow Ministry of Ontario guidelines.

Special Academic Programs Advanced Placement exam preparation; term-away projects; study at local college for college credit; study abroad; academic accommodation for the gifted, the musically talented, and the artistically talented; remedial reading and/or remedial writing; remedial math; ESL (31 students enrolled).

College Admission Counseling 44 students graduated in 2011; 42 went to college, including Carleton University; Ryerson University; University of Guelph; University of Toronto. Other: 2 had other specific plans.

Student Life Upper grades have uniform requirement, student council, honor system. Discipline rests equally with students and faculty.

Summer Programs Remediation, advancement, ESL programs offered; session focuses on English or French as a Second Language and Math; held on campus; accepts boys and girls; open to students from other schools. 150 students usually enrolled. 2012 schedule: July 1 to July 28. Application deadline: none.

Tuition and Aid Day student tuition: CAN$17,200; 7-day tuition and room/board: CAN$44,500. Tuition installment plan (monthly payment plans, individually arranged payment plans, single payment plan). Tuition reduction for siblings, bursaries, merit scholarship grants, need-based scholarship grants, need-based loans available.

Admissions Admissions testing or English for Non-native Speakers required. Deadline for receipt of application materials: none. Application fee required: CAN$100. Interview required.

Athletics Interscholastic: baseball (boys), football (b,g), gymnastics (g), hockey (b), ice hockey (b), softball (g); coed interscholastic: alpine skiing, aquatics, basketball, bicycling, climbing, cross-country running, equestrian sports, golf, horseback riding, independent competitive sports, nordic skiing, outdoor adventure, rugby, skiing (cross-country), skiing (downhill), soccer, swimming and diving, track and field; coed intramural: aerobics, alpine skiing, backpacking, badminton, basketball, climbing, Cosom hockey, curling, dance, figure skating, fitness, fitness walking, floor hockey, hiking/backpacking, hockey, horseback riding, ice hockey, ice skating, indoor hockey, jogging, mountain biking, outdoor activities, outdoor education, physical fitness, rock climbing, snowshoeing, squash, strength & conditioning, yoga. 1 PE instructor, 10 coaches, 1 athletic trainer.

Computers Computer network features include on-campus library services, Internet access, wireless campus network, Internet filtering or blocking technology, school-wide laptop initiative (included in tuition), fiber optic network. Student e-mail accounts are available to students. The school has a published electronic and media policy.

Contact Mrs. Ashli MacInnis, Director of Recruitment and Admissions. 819-566-0227 Ext. 296. Fax: 819-566-8123. E-mail: amacinnis@bishopscollegeschool.com. Web site: www.bishopscollegeschool.com.

THE BISHOP'S SCHOOL

7607 La Jolla Boulevard

La Jolla, California 92037

Head of School: Aimeclaire Roche

General Information Coeducational day college-preparatory, arts, religious studies, and technology school, affiliated with Episcopal Church. Grades 6–12. Founded: 1909. Setting: suburban. Nearest major city is San Diego. 11-acre campus. 7 buildings on campus. Approved or accredited by Western Association of Schools and Colleges and California Department of Education. Member of National Association of Independent Schools. Endowment: $27 million. Total enrollment: 780. Upper school average class size: 13. Upper school faculty-student ratio: 1:13. Upper School students typically attend 5 days per week. The average school day consists of 7 hours.

Upper School Student Profile Grade 9: 139 students (62 boys, 77 girls); Grade 10: 137 students (67 boys, 70 girls); Grade 11: 139 students (71 boys, 68 girls); Grade 12: 131 students (62 boys, 69 girls).

Faculty School total: 93. In upper school: 38 men, 45 women; 71 have advanced degrees.

Subjects Offered Acting, Advanced Placement courses, advanced studio art-AP, algebra, American history, American literature, art history, art history-AP, arts, ASB Leadership, biology, biology-AP, calculus, calculus-AP, ceramics, chemistry, chemistry-AP, Chinese, Chinese studies, chorus, community service, comparative government and politics-AP, comparative religion, computer programming, computer science, creative writing, dance, discrete mathematics, drama, drawing, earth science, ecology, economics, economics and history, economics-AP, English, English literature, environmental science, ethics, European history, European history-AP, forensics, French, French language-AP, French literature-AP, genetics, geography, geometry, government/civics, health, history, human anatomy, humanities, integrated mathematics, Internet, jazz band, journalism, Latin, Latin American studies, Latin-AP, literature and composition-AP, literature-AP, macro/microeconomics-AP, marine biology, mathematics, music, painting, philosophy, photography, physical education, physical science, physics, physics-AP, physiology, pre-algebra, pre-calculus, probability, programming, religious studies, Shakespeare, social studies, Spanish, Spanish language-AP, Spanish literature-AP, speech, speech and debate, stained glass, statistics, statistics-AP, studio art-AP, tap dance, theater, theater design and production, typing, U.S. government and politics-AP, U.S. history, U.S. history-AP, visual reality, world history, yearbook.

Graduation Requirements Arts and fine arts (art, music, dance, drama), computer science, English, foreign language, mathematics, physical education (includes health), religion (includes Bible studies and theology), science, social sciences, social studies (includes history), swimming test, computer proficiency. Community service is required.

Special Academic Programs Advanced Placement exam preparation; honors section; independent study; study abroad.

College Admission Counseling 148 students graduated in 2011; all went to college, including Princeton University; Stanford University; University of California, Berkeley; University of California, Los Angeles; University of California, Santa Barbara; University of Southern California. Mean SAT critical reading: 662, mean SAT math: 669, mean SAT writing: 686.

Student Life Upper grades have uniform requirement, student council, honor system. Discipline rests equally with students and faculty. Attendance at religious services is required.

Summer Programs Remediation, enrichment, advancement, sports, art/fine arts, computer instruction programs offered; held on campus; accepts boys and girls; open to students from other schools. 270 students usually enrolled. 2012 schedule: June 21 to July 21. Application deadline: June 21.

Tuition and Aid Day student tuition: $28,000. Tuition installment plan (FACTS Tuition Payment Plan, semester payment plans, Key Resources Achiever Loan). Need-based scholarship grants available. In 2011–12, 20% of upper-school students received aid. Total amount of financial aid awarded in 2011–12: $2,900,000.

Admissions Traditional secondary-level entrance grade is 9. For fall 2011, 155 students applied for upper-level admission, 125 were accepted, 101 enrolled. Admissions testing, ISEE and Otis-Lennon School Ability Test required. Deadline for receipt of application materials: February 1. Application fee required: $100. On-campus interview required.

Athletics Interscholastic: baseball (boys), basketball (b,g), cross-country running (b,g), equestrian sports (b,g), field hockey (g), football (b), golf (b,g), gymnastics (g), lacrosse (b,g), soccer (b,g), softball (g), swimming and diving (b,g), tennis (b,g), track and field (b,g), volleyball (b,g), water polo (b,g); intramural: weight training (b,g); coed interscholastic: sailing. 5 PE instructors, 38 coaches, 1 athletic trainer.

Computers Computers are regularly used in English, foreign language, history, journalism, library, music, science, yearbook classes. Computer network features include on-campus library services, online commercial services, Internet access.

Contact Kim Peckham, Director of Admission and Financial Aid. 858-459-4021 Ext. 409. Fax: 858-459-2990. E-mail: peckhamk@bishops.com. Web site: www.bishops.com.

BISHOP STANG HIGH SCHOOL

500 Slocum Road

North Dartmouth, Massachusetts 02747-2999

Head of School: Mrs. Theresa E. Dougall

General Information Coeducational day college-preparatory, arts, business, religious studies, technology, science, and arts school, affiliated with Roman Catholic Church. Grades 9–12. Founded: 1959. Setting: suburban. Nearest major city is New Bedford. 8-acre campus. 1 building on campus. Approved or accredited by New England Association of Schools and Colleges and Massachusetts Department of Education. Endowment: $2 million. Total enrollment: 713. Upper school average class size: 19. Upper school faculty-student ratio: 1:13. There are 180 required school days per year for Upper School students. Upper School students typically attend 5 days per week. The average school day consists of 6 hours and 30 minutes.

Upper School Student Profile Grade 9: 175 students (86 boys, 89 girls); Grade 10: 168 students (73 boys, 95 girls); Grade 11: 168 students (76 boys, 92 girls); Grade 12: 201 students (92 boys, 109 girls). 85% of students are Roman Catholic.

Faculty School total: 61. In upper school: 23 men, 38 women; 29 have advanced degrees.

Subjects Offered 3-dimensional design, advanced biology, algebra, American history, American literature, anatomy and physiology, art, biochemistry, bioethics, biology, biology-AP, calculus, calculus-AP, campus ministry, Catholic belief and practice, chemistry, chemistry-AP, chorus, church history, communications, community service, computer science, concert band, criminal justice, criminology, death and loss, driver education, ecology, English, English literature, English-AP, environmental science, fine arts, French, geometry, government/civics, health, history, history of the Catholic Church, instrumental music, introduction to theater, Latin, Life of Christ, marine biology, marketing, mathematics, mechanical drawing, media production, modern European history-AP, moral theology, music, oceanography, photography, physical education, physics, physics-AP, physiology, Portuguese, prayer/spirituality, psychology, psychology-AP, religion, religious studies, science, social sciences, social studies, sociology, Spanish, study skills, technical drawing, theater arts, trigonometry, Web authoring, world history, world literature, writing, yearbook.

Graduation Requirements Arts and fine arts (art, music, dance, drama), business skills (includes word processing), computer science, English, foreign language, mathematics, physical education (includes health), religion (includes Bible studies and theology), science, social sciences, social studies (includes history), service project. Community service is required.

Special Academic Programs 7 Advanced Placement exams for which test preparation is offered; honors section; remedial reading and/or remedial writing; remedial math; programs in English, mathematics, general development for dyslexic students.

College Admission Counseling 188 students graduated in 2011; 161 went to college, including Bryant University; Providence College; University of Massachusetts Amherst; University of Massachusetts Dartmouth; University of Rhode Island; Worcester Polytechnic Institute. Other: 5 went to work, 1 entered military service, 4 entered a postgraduate year. Mean SAT critical reading: 535, mean SAT math: 531, mean SAT writing: 525, mean combined SAT: 1591.

Student Life Upper grades have uniform requirement, student council, honor system. Discipline rests primarily with faculty. Attendance at religious services is required.

Summer Programs Enrichment, sports, art/fine arts, computer instruction programs offered; session focuses on sport and activity camps; held on campus; accepts boys and girls; open to students from other schools. 200 students usually enrolled. 2012 schedule: July 1 to August 19. Application deadline: June.

Tuition and Aid Day student tuition: $7900. Tuition installment plan (FACTS Tuition Payment Plan, monthly payment plans). Merit scholarship grants, need-based scholarship grants available. In 2011–12, 27% of upper-school students received aid; total upper-school merit-scholarship money awarded: $12,500. Total amount of financial aid awarded in 2011–12: $500,000.

Admissions Traditional secondary-level entrance grade is 9. For fall 2011, 275 students applied for upper-level admission, 261 were accepted, 175 enrolled. Scholastic Testing Service High School Placement Test required. Deadline for receipt of application materials: none. No application fee required. On-campus interview recommended.

Athletics Interscholastic: aquatics (boys, girls), baseball (b), basketball (b,g), cheering (g), cross-country running (b,g), diving (b,g), field hockey (g), football (b), golf (b,g), ice hockey (b), lacrosse (b,g), soccer (b,g), softball (g), swimming and diving (b,g), tennis (b,g), track and field (b,g), volleyball (g), winter (indoor) track (b,g); intramural: fitness (b,g); coed interscholastic: indoor track & field, sailing; coed intramural: backpacking, bicycling, canoeing/kayaking, climbing, crew, hiking/backpacking, kayaking, outdoor activities, outdoor adventure, physical training, rock climbing, sailing, skiing (downhill), snowboarding, strength & conditioning, ultimate Frisbee, wall climbing, weight lifting, weight training. 10 coaches, 1 athletic trainer.

Computers Computers are regularly used in all classes. Computer network features include on-campus library services, online commercial services, Internet access, wireless campus network, Internet filtering or blocking technology. Campus intranet and computer access in designated common areas are available to students. The school has a published electronic and media policy.

Contact Mrs. Christine Payette, Admissions Director. 508-996-5602 Ext. 424. Fax: 508-994-6756. E-mail: admits@bishopstang.com. Web site: www.bishopstang.com.

THE BISHOP STRACHAN SCHOOL

298 Lonsdale Road

Toronto, Ontario M4V 1X2, Canada

Head of School: Ms. Deryn Lavell

General Information Girls' boarding and day and distance learning college-preparatory, arts, business, religious studies, and technology school, affiliated with Anglican Church of Canada. Boarding grades 7–12, day grades JK–12. Distance learning grades 9–12. Founded: 1867. Setting: urban. Students are housed in single-sex dormitories. 7-acre campus. 1 building on campus. Approved or accredited by Canadian Association of Independent Schools, Canadian Educational Standards Institute, The Association of Boarding Schools, and Ontario Department of Education. Affiliate member of National Association of Independent Schools; member of Secondary School Admission Test Board. Language of instruction: English. Endowment: CAN$12 million. Total enrollment: 891. Upper school average class size: 20. Upper school faculty-student ratio: 1:9. There are 184 required school days per year for Upper School students. Upper School students typically attend 5 days per week. The average school day consists of 6 hours and 10 minutes.

Upper School Student Profile Grade 6: 44 students (44 girls); Grade 7: 82 students (82 girls); Grade 8: 100 students (100 girls); Grade 9: 118 students (118 girls); Grade 10: 123 students (123 girls); Grade 11: 115 students (115 girls); Grade 12: 105 students (105 girls). 16% of students are boarding students. 90% are province residents. 6 provinces are represented in upper school student body. 10% are international students. International students from Bahamas, China, Ghana, Nepal, Republic of Korea, and United States; 14 other countries represented in student body. 30% of students are members of Anglican Church of Canada.

Faculty School total: 111. In upper school: 20 men, 61 women; 30 have advanced degrees; 5 reside on campus.

Subjects Offered Accounting, algebra, American history, aquatics, art, art history, biology, biology-AP, business, business skills, calculus, calculus-AP, Canadian geography, Canadian history, career and personal planning, career education, chemistry, chemistry-AP, computer programming, computer science, computer science-AP, creative writing, drama, earth science, ecology, economics, English, English language-AP, English literature, English literature-AP, environmental science, ESL, ethics, European history, expository writing, fine arts, French, French language-AP, geography, geometry, government/civics, graphic arts, health, history, Italian, Latin, macroeconomics-AP, Mandarin, mathematics, microeconomics-AP, music, philosophy, physical education, physics, religion, science, social sciences, social studies, Spanish, Spanish language-AP, statistics-AP, theater, trigonometry, U.S. history-AP, world history.

Graduation Requirements Arts, Canadian geography, Canadian history, career education, civics, English, French, mathematics, physical education (includes health), science, 40 hours of community service, completion of 30 credits from grade 9-12.

Special Academic Programs Advanced Placement exam preparation; honors section; accelerated programs; independent study; term-away projects; study abroad; academic accommodation for the gifted, the musically talented, and the artistically talented; ESL (12 students enrolled).

College Admission Counseling 122 students graduated in 2011; 121 went to college, including Cornell University; McGill University; Queen's University at Kingston; University of Southern California; University of Toronto; Yale University. Other: 1 had other specific plans. Mean SAT critical reading: 609, mean SAT math: 610, mean SAT writing: 599.

Student Life Upper grades have uniform requirement, student council, honor system. Discipline rests primarily with faculty.

Summer Programs Enrichment, advancement, ESL, art/fine arts, rigorous outdoor training, computer instruction programs offered; session focuses on ESL, languages, science, math, economics, arts, geography, online courses (available through e-academy); held both on and off campus; held at France and worldwide; accepts boys and girls; open to students from other schools. 200 students usually enrolled. 2012 schedule: July 2 to July 29. Application deadline: June 15.

Tuition and Aid Day student tuition: CAN$26,410; 7-day tuition and room/board: CAN$47,860. Tuition installment plan (monthly payment plans, 3-installment plan). Bursaries, merit scholarship grants, need-based scholarship grants available. In 2011–12, 5% of upper-school students received aid; total upper-school merit-scholarship money awarded: CAN$95,000. Total amount of financial aid awarded in 2011–12: CAN$500,000.

Admissions Traditional secondary-level entrance grade is 9. For fall 2011, 450 students applied for upper-level admission, 244 were accepted, 165 enrolled. Admissions testing, SSAT or TOEFL required. Deadline for receipt of application materials: none. Application fee required: CAN$180. Interview required.

Athletics Interscholastic: alpine skiing, aquatics, archery, artistic gym, badminton, basketball, cross-country running, curling, field hockey, golf, gymnastics, hockey, ice hockey, nordic skiing, rhythmic gymnastics, skiing (downhill), soccer, softball, swimming and diving, tennis, track and field, volleyball; intramural: aerobics, aerobics/dance, backpacking, ballet, canoeing/kayaking, climbing, cooperative games, crew, dance, fencing, fitness, hiking/backpacking, kayaking, life saving, modern dance, outdoor adventure, outdoor education, outdoor recreation, physical training, rappelling, rock climbing, ropes courses, rowing, running, self defense, synchronized swimming, wall climbing, weight training, wilderness survival, yoga. 11 PE instructors.

Computers Computers are regularly used in art, business studies, career education, career exploration, economics, English, foreign language, geography, history, mathematics, music, science classes. Computer network features include on-campus library services, Internet access, wireless campus network, Internet filtering or blocking technology, laptop program (grades 9-12). Campus intranet and student e-mail accounts are available to students. Students grades are available online. The school has a published electronic and media policy.

Contact Ms. Jenna Parrett, Administrative Assistant. 416-483-4325 Ext. 1220. Fax: 416-481-5632. E-mail: studentrecruiting@bss.on.ca. Web site: www.bss.on.ca.

BISHOP WALSH MIDDLE HIGH SCHOOL

700 Bishop Walsh Road

Cumberland, Maryland 21502

Head of School: Sr. Phyllis McNally

General Information Coeducational day college-preparatory school, affiliated with Roman Catholic Church. Grades PK–12. Founded: 1966. Setting: small town. 10-acre campus. 1 building on campus. Approved or accredited by National Catholic Education Association and Maryland Department of Education. Total enrollment: 428. Upper school average class size: 20. Upper school faculty-student ratio: 1:15.

Upper School Student Profile Grade 9: 46 students (13 boys, 33 girls); Grade 10: 58 students (28 boys, 30 girls); Grade 11: 47 students (25 boys, 22 girls); Grade 12: 47 students (25 boys, 22 girls). 70% of students are Roman Catholic.

Faculty School total: 45. In upper school: 8 men, 12 women; 15 have advanced degrees.

Subjects Offered Western civilization.

Special Academic Programs Advanced Placement exam preparation; honors section; remedial reading and/or remedial writing; programs in English, general development for dyslexic students; ESL (6 students enrolled).

College Admission Counseling 54 students graduated in 2010; 52 went to college, including Frostburg State University; West Virginia University. Other: 2 entered military service. Median SAT critical reading: 505, median SAT math: 504, median SAT writing: 500, median combined SAT: 1509, median composite ACT: 25.

Student Life Upper grades have uniform requirement, student council. Discipline rests primarily with faculty. Attendance at religious services is required.

Tuition and Aid Day student tuition: $4900. Tuition installment plan (FACTS Tuition Payment Plan, monthly payment plans). Need-based scholarship grants available. In 2010–11, 50% of upper-school students received aid. Total amount of financial aid awarded in 2010–11: $30,000.

Admissions Traditional secondary-level entrance grade is 9. For fall 2010, 20 students applied for upper-level admission, 19 were accepted, 19 enrolled. Deadline for receipt of application materials: August 31. Application fee required: $30. Interview required.

Athletics Interscholastic: baseball (boys), basketball (b,g), bowling (b,g), cheering (g), football (b), golf (b), soccer (b,g), softball (g), tennis (b,g), volleyball (g), weight training (b,g); coed interscholastic: cross-country running, track and field. 2 PE instructors, 8 coaches, 1 athletic trainer.

Computers Computers are regularly used in all classes. Computer network features include Internet access. Students grades are available online. The school has a published electronic and media policy.

Contact Mrs. Erin Dale, Administrative Assistant. 301-724-5360 Ext. 104. Fax: 301-722-0555. E-mail: edale@bishopwalsh.org. Web site: www.bishopwalsh.org.

BLAIR ACADEMY

2 Park Street

Blairstown, New Jersey 07825

Head of School: T. Chandler Hardwick III

General Information Coeducational boarding and day college-preparatory and arts school, affiliated with Presbyterian Church. Boarding grades 9–PG, day grades 9–12. Founded: 1848. Setting: rural. Nearest major city is New York, NY. Students are housed in single-sex dormitories. 423-acre campus. 42 buildings on campus. Approved or accredited by Middle States Association of Colleges and Schools, The Association of Boarding Schools, and New Jersey Department of Education. Member of National Association of Independent Schools and Secondary School Admission Test Board. Endowment: $66.5 million. Total enrollment: 450. Upper school average class size: 11. Upper school faculty-student ratio: 1:7. Upper School students typically attend 6 days per week. The average school day consists of 6 hours and 45 minutes.

Upper School Student Profile Grade 9: 87 students (44 boys, 43 girls); Grade 10: 96 students (55 boys, 41 girls); Grade 11: 131 students (75 boys, 56 girls); Grade 12: 136 students (76 boys, 60 girls); Postgraduate: 13 students (8 boys, 5 girls). 22 states are represented in upper school student body. 17% are international students.

Faculty School total: 80. In upper school: 40 men, 27 women; 54 have advanced degrees; 74 reside on campus.

Subjects Offered 3-dimensional art, 3-dimensional design, advanced math, Advanced Placement courses, advanced studio art-AP, African history, algebra, American government, American history, American history-AP, American literature, anatomy, architectural drawing, architecture, art, art history-AP, art-AP, Asian studies, biochemistry, biology, biology-AP, biotechnology, calculus, calculus-AP, ceramics, chemistry, chemistry-AP, Chinese, comparative government and politics-AP, computer programming, computer science, computer science-AP, creative writing, dance, drafting, drama, drawing, drawing and design, driver education, economics, economics and history, economics-AP, English, English language-AP, English literature, English literature-AP, environmental science, environmental science-AP, ethics, European history, European history-AP, filmmaking, fine arts, French, French language-AP, geometry, government/civics, health, history, Japanese history, jazz band, Latin, marine biology, marine science, mathematics, mechanical drawing, music, music theory-AP, painting, philosophy, photography, physics, pre-calculus, psychology, religion, science, social studies, Spanish, Spanish language-AP, statistics-AP, theater, theology, world history, world history-AP, world literature, writing.

Graduation Requirements Arts and fine arts (art, music, dance, drama), biology, English, foreign language, mathematics, performing arts, religion (includes Bible studies and theology), science, social studies (includes history), U.S. history, athletic requirement.

Special Academic Programs 23 Advanced Placement exams for which test preparation is offered; honors section; independent study; study abroad.

College Admission Counseling 134 students graduated in 2011; 133 went to college, including Boston College; Lehigh University; New York University; Swarthmore College; Syracuse University; University of Pennsylvania. Other: 1 entered a postgraduate year. Mean SAT critical reading: 610, mean SAT math: 620, mean SAT writing: 630.

Student Life Upper grades have specified standards of dress, student council, honor system. Discipline rests equally with students and faculty.

Tuition and Aid Day student tuition: $33,800; 7-day tuition and room/board: $47,600. Tuition installment plan (Key Tuition Payment Plan, monthly payment plans). Need-based scholarship grants, need-based loans available. In 2011–12, 32% of upper-school students received aid. Total amount of financial aid awarded in 2011–12: $4,100,000.

Admissions Traditional secondary-level entrance grade is 9. For fall 2011, 777 students applied for upper-level admission, 249 were accepted, 145 enrolled. SSAT or TOEFL required. Deadline for receipt of application materials: February 1. Application fee required: $50. On-campus interview required.

Athletics Interscholastic: alpine skiing (boys, girls), baseball (b), basketball (b,g), crew (b,g), cross-country running (b,g), field hockey (g), football (b), golf (b,g), ice hockey (b), indoor track (b,g), lacrosse (b,g), rowing (b,g), running (b,g), skiing (downhill) (b,g), soccer (b,g), softball (g), squash (b,g), swimming and diving (b,g), tennis (b,g), track and field (b,g), volleyball (g), winter (indoor) track (b,g), wrestling (b); intramural: basketball (b,g), crew (b,g), ice hockey (g), rowing (b,g), volleyball (g); coed intramural: alpine skiing, bicycling, canoeing/kayaking, dance, equestrian sports, fitness, flag football, golf, horseback riding, kayaking, life saving, modern dance, mountaineering, outdoor activities, outdoor adventure, outdoor education, outdoor skills, physical fitness, skiing (downhill), snowboarding, squash, swimming and diving, tennis, weight lifting, weight training, wrestling, yoga. 3 athletic trainers.

Computers Computers are regularly used in architecture, drawing and design, English, foreign language, graphic arts, graphic design, history, information technology, mathematics, media production, science, video film production, writing classes. Computer network features include on-campus library services, online commercial services,

Internet access, Internet filtering or blocking technology. Campus intranet, student e-mail accounts, and computer access in designated common areas are available to students. The school has a published electronic and media policy.

Contact Nancy Klein, Administrative. 800-462-5247. Fax: 908-362-7975. E-mail: admissions@blair.edu. Web site: www.blair.edu.

See Display on previous page and Close-Up on page 590.

BLANCHET SCHOOL

4373 Market Street NE

Salem, Oregon 97305

Head of School: Mr. Anthony Guevara

General Information Coeducational day college-preparatory, arts, and religious studies school, affiliated with Roman Catholic Church. Grades 6–12. Founded: 1995. Setting: suburban. 22-acre campus. 2 buildings on campus. Approved or accredited by National Catholic Education Association, Northwest Association of Schools and Colleges, and Oregon Department of Education. Endowment: $265,400. Total enrollment: 368. Upper school average class size: 18. Upper school faculty-student ratio: 1:15. There are 175 required school days per year for Upper School students. Upper School students typically attend 5 days per week. The average school day consists of 7 hours.

Upper School Student Profile Grade 9: 55 students (29 boys, 26 girls); Grade 10: 57 students (30 boys, 27 girls); Grade 11: 75 students (36 boys, 39 girls); Grade 12: 66 students (27 boys, 39 girls). 70% of students are Roman Catholic.

Faculty School total: 25. In upper school: 8 men, 17 women; 21 have advanced degrees.

Subjects Offered Advanced Placement courses, algebra, American government, American history-AP, American literature, anatomy, anatomy and physiology, art, art education, band, Bible studies, biology, calculus, campus ministry, career and personal planning, Catholic belief and practice, chemistry, choir, civics, college counseling, college placement, comparative religion, composition, critical thinking, critical writing, debate, digital photography, drama, economics, economics and history, English literature, English literature and composition-AP, first aid, fitness, French, geometry, global studies, government, great books, health, health and safety, health and wellness, health education, history of the Catholic Church, history-AP, lab science, literature and composition-AP, mathematics, music, personal finance, photography, physical education, physical fitness, physical science, physics, pre-algebra, pre-calculus, psychology, publications, religion, religion and culture, SAT/ACT preparation, sociology, Spanish, speech and debate, U.S. government, U.S. history, U.S. history-AP, weight training, world history, world religions, World War II.

Graduation Requirements Applied arts, arts and fine arts (art, music, dance, drama), electives, English, foreign language, mathematics, physical education (includes health), religion (includes Bible studies and theology), science, social studies (includes history), 20 hours of community service for each year in attendance.

Special Academic Programs 2 Advanced Placement exams for which test preparation is offered; honors section; study at local college for college credit; special instructional classes for deaf students; ESL (6 students enrolled).

College Admission Counseling 65 students graduated in 2011; 63 went to college, including Chemeketa Community College; Gonzaga University; Oregon State University; University of Oregon; University of Portland; Willamette University. Other: 2 entered military service. Median SAT critical reading: 535, median SAT math: 525, median SAT writing: 521, median composite ACT: 24.

Student Life Upper grades have specified standards of dress, student council. Discipline rests primarily with faculty. Attendance at religious services is required.

Summer Programs Remediation, enrichment, sports programs offered; session focuses on preparation for the next academic year, athletic training; held on campus; accepts boys and girls; open to students from other schools. 75 students usually enrolled. 2012 schedule: June 13 to August 17.

Tuition and Aid Day student tuition: $7165. Tuition installment plan (FACTS Tuition Payment Plan). Tuition reduction for siblings, merit scholarship grants, need-based scholarship grants available. In 2011–12, 35% of upper-school students received aid; total upper-school merit-scholarship money awarded: $8500. Total amount of financial aid awarded in 2011–12: $240,000.

Admissions Traditional secondary-level entrance grade is 9. For fall 2011, 92 students applied for upper-level admission, 84 were accepted, 83 enrolled. Math Placement Exam required. Deadline for receipt of application materials: none. Application fee required: $100. Interview recommended.

Athletics Interscholastic: baseball (boys), basketball (b,g), cheering (g), cross-country running (b,g), fencing (b,g), football (b), golf (b,g), physical fitness (b,g), soccer (b,g), softball (g), swimming and diving (b,g), tennis (b,g), track and field (b,g), volleyball (g), weight training (b,g); intramural: weight training (b,g). 4 PE instructors, 60 coaches.

Computers Computers are regularly used in business, photography, science, social studies classes. Computer network features include online commercial services, Internet access, wireless campus network, Internet filtering or blocking technology. Computer access in designated common areas is available to students. Students grades are available online. The school has a published electronic and media policy.

Contact Mrs. Cathy McClaughry, Admissions Office. 503-485-4491. Fax: 503-399-1259. E-mail: cathy@blanchetcatholicschool.com. Web site: www.blanchetcatholicschool.com.

BLESSED SACRAMENT HUGENOT

2501 Academy Road

Powhatan, Virginia 23139

Head of School: Dr. Tracy Bonday-deLeon

General Information Coeducational day college-preparatory school, affiliated with Roman Catholic Church. Grades PS–12. Founded: 1954. Setting: rural. Nearest major city is Richmond. 46-acre campus. 5 buildings on campus. Approved or accredited by National Catholic Education Association, Southern Association of Colleges and Schools, and Virginia Department of Education. Total enrollment: 337. Upper school average class size: 120. Upper school faculty-student ratio: 1:6. There are 180 required school days per year for Upper School students. Upper School students typically attend 5 days per week. The average school day consists of 6 hours and 30 minutes.

Upper School Student Profile 35% of students are Roman Catholic.

Faculty School total: 36. In upper school: 6 men, 14 women; 12 have advanced degrees.

Subjects Offered Advanced math, Advanced Placement courses, algebra, American government, American history, American history-AP, American literature-AP, art, athletics, baseball, basketball, biology, calculus, calculus-AP, Central and Eastern European history, cheerleading, chemistry, Christian education, college admission preparation, college awareness, college counseling, college planning, college writing, community service, conceptual physics, drama, drama performance, English, English-AP, European history, foreign language, geography, geometry, government-AP, history of the Catholic Church, history-AP, honors algebra, honors English, honors geometry, honors U.S. history, honors world history, Latin, modern European history, physical education, religious education, SAT preparation, Spanish, student government, swimming, tennis, theology, trigonometry, U.S. and Virginia government, U.S. and Virginia government-AP, U.S. history-AP, world history.

Graduation Requirements Admission to a 4-year Institution, Community Service Hours.

Special Academic Programs Advanced Placement exam preparation; honors section.

College Admission Counseling 33 students graduated in 2011; all went to college, including Hampden-Sydney College; Longwood University, Radford University; University of Virginia; Virginia Polytechnic Institute and State University.

Student Life Upper grades have uniform requirement, student council, honor system. Discipline rests equally with students and faculty. Attendance at religious services is required.

Summer Programs Enrichment, sports, art/fine arts, computer instruction programs offered; session focuses on extracurricular activities, art enrichment, and sports enrichment; held on campus; accepts boys and girls; open to students from other schools. 200 students usually enrolled. 2012 schedule: June 11 to August 24. Application deadline: none.

Tuition and Aid Day student tuition: $10,725. Tuition installment plan (FACTS Tuition Payment Plan). Tuition reduction for siblings, need-based scholarship grants available. In 2011–12, 15% of upper-school students received aid. Total amount of financial aid awarded in 2011–12: $175,000.

Admissions Traditional secondary-level entrance grade is 9. For fall 2011, 25 students applied for upper-level admission, 20 were accepted, 16 enrolled. Deadline for receipt of application materials: none. Application fee required: $50. Interview required.

Athletics Interscholastic: baseball (boys), basketball (b,g), football (b), softball (g), volleyball (g); intramural: basketball (b,g), football (b), softball (g), volleyball (g); coed interscholastic: cheering, cross-country running, golf, soccer, swimming and diving, tennis; coed intramural: cross-country running, soccer, swimming and diving, tennis. 2 PE instructors, 20 coaches, 1 athletic trainer.

Computers Computer network features include Internet access, Internet filtering or blocking technology. Campus intranet is available to students. Students grades are available online. The school has a published electronic and media policy.

Contact Mrs. Christy M. Polster, Director of Admissions. 804-598-4211. Fax: 804-598-1053. E-mail: cpolster@bshknights.org. Web site: www.bshknights.org.

BLESSED TRINITY HIGH SCHOOL

11320 Woodstock Road

Roswell, Georgia 30075

Head of School: Mr. Frank Moore

General Information Coeducational day college-preparatory and religious studies school, affiliated with Roman Catholic Church. Grades 9–12. Founded: 2000. Setting: suburban. Nearest major city is Atlanta. 68-acre campus. 2 buildings on campus. Approved or accredited by Georgia Independent School Association, Southern Association of Colleges and Schools, and Georgia Department of Education. Upper school average class size: 20. Upper school faculty-student ratio: 1:14.

Upper School Student Profile 88% of students are Roman Catholic.
Faculty School total: 71. In upper school: 32 men, 39 women; 36 have advanced degrees.
Graduation Requirements American government, American history, American literature, ancient world history.
Special Academic Programs 22 Advanced Placement exams for which test preparation is offered.
College Admission Counseling 199 students graduated in 2011; all went to college, including Auburn University; Georgia College & State University; Georgia Institute of Technology; Georgia Southern University; The University of Alabama; University of Georgia.
Student Life Upper grades have uniform requirement, student council. Discipline rests primarily with faculty. Attendance at religious services is required.
Tuition and Aid Tuition installment plan (FACTS Tuition Payment Plan). Need-based scholarship grants available. In 2011–12, 18% of upper-school students received aid.
Admissions Traditional secondary-level entrance grade is 9. SSAT required. Deadline for receipt of application materials: February 1. Application fee required: $100.
Athletics Interscholastic: baseball (boys), basketball (b,g), cheering (g), cross-country running (b,g), dance (b,g), dance team (g), football (b), golf (b,g), lacrosse (b,g), soccer (b,g), softball (g), strength & conditioning (b,g), swimming and diving (b,g), tennis (b,g), track and field (b,g), volleyball (g), wrestling (b). 4 PE instructors, 1 athletic trainer.
Contact Mr. Brian Marks, Director of Admissions. 678-277-0983 Ext. 502. Fax: 678-277-9756. E-mail: bmarks@btcatholic.org. Web site: www.btcatholic.org.

BLUE MOUNTAIN ACADEMY

2363 Mountain Road

Hamburg, Pennsylvania 19526

Head of School: Mr. W. Craig Ziesmer

General Information Coeducational boarding and day college-preparatory, religious studies, leadership, and aviation school, affiliated with Seventh-day Adventists. Grades 9–12. Founded: 1955. Setting: rural. Students are housed in single-sex dormitories. 735-acre campus. 6 buildings on campus. Approved or accredited by Board of Regents, General Conference of Seventh-day Adventists and Middle States Association of Colleges and Schools. Total enrollment: 158. Upper school average class size: 22. Upper school faculty-student ratio: 1:9. There are 180 required school days per year for Upper School students. Upper School students typically attend 5 days per week. The average school day consists of 6 hours and 30 minutes.
Upper School Student Profile Grade 9: 27 students (12 boys, 15 girls); Grade 10: 41 students (17 boys, 24 girls); Grade 11: 39 students (23 boys, 16 girls); Grade 12: 51 students (30 boys, 21 girls). 81% of students are boarding students. 58% are state residents. 9 states are represented in upper school student body. 5% are international students. International students from Bermuda, Canada, China, Malaysia, Mexico, and Republic of Korea; 4 other countries represented in student body. 95% of students are Seventh-day Adventists.
Faculty School total: 17. In upper school: 12 men, 5 women; 12 have advanced degrees; all reside on campus.
Subjects Offered Accounting, Advanced Placement courses, algebra, anatomy and physiology, art, auto mechanics, band, bell choir, Bible, biology, business mathematics, chemistry, chemistry-AP, choir, computer applications, desktop publishing, digital photography, English, English literature and composition-AP, flight instruction, French, geometry, golf, gymnastics, health, home economics, honors English, honors world history, leadership, life science, music appreciation, music theory, organ, physical education, physics, piano, pre-algebra, pre-calculus, psychology, Spanish, U.S. government, U.S. history, U.S. history-AP, Western civilization, world history.
Graduation Requirements Algebra, arts, Bible, biology, computer applications, electives, English, foreign language, mathematics, physical education (includes health), science, social sciences, U.S. government, U.S. history, work-study, work study credit per semester enrolled.
Special Academic Programs 3 Advanced Placement exams for which test preparation is offered; honors section; accelerated programs; study at local college for college credit; academic accommodation for the musically talented; remedial reading and/or remedial writing; remedial math; programs in English, mathematics, general development for dyslexic students.
College Admission Counseling 66 students graduated in 2011; 60 went to college, including Andrews University; Southern Adventist University; Walla Walla University; Washington Adventist University. Mean SAT critical reading: 500, mean SAT math: 463, mean SAT writing: 500, mean composite ACT: 21.
Student Life Upper grades have specified standards of dress, student council, honor system. Discipline rests primarily with faculty. Attendance at religious services is required.
Tuition and Aid Day student tuition: $10,870; 7-day tuition and room/board: $17,510. Tuition installment plan (monthly payment plans). Tuition reduction for siblings, need-based scholarship grants, paying campus jobs available. In 2011–12, 45% of upper-school students received aid. Total amount of financial aid awarded in 2011–12: $287,000.
Admissions Traditional secondary-level entrance grade is 9. Math Placement Exam required. Deadline for receipt of application materials: none. Application fee required: $20. Interview recommended.
Athletics Intramural: basketball (boys, girls), flag football (b,g), soccer (b,g), softball (b,g), volleyball (b,g); coed intramural: basketball, flag football, gymnastics, soccer, softball, volleyball. 1 PE instructor.
Computers Computers are regularly used in desktop publishing, history, keyboarding, mathematics, photography, psychology, religion, science, yearbook classes. Computer network features include on-campus library services, Internet access, Internet filtering or blocking technology. Student e-mail accounts and computer access in designated common areas are available to students. Students grades are available online. The school has a published electronic and media policy.
Contact Mrs. Diana Engen, Registrar. 484-662-7000. Fax: 610-562-8050. E-mail: dengen@bma.us. Web site: www.bma.us.

BLUEPRINT EDUCATION

5651 West Talavi Boulevard

Suite 170

Glendale, Arizona 85306

Head of School: Doug Covey

General Information Distance learning only college-preparatory, general academic, technology, and distance learning school. Distance learning grades 7–12. Founded: 1969. Approved or accredited by CITA (Commission on International and Trans-Regional Accreditation), North Central Association of Colleges and Schools, and Arizona Department of Education.
Faculty School total: 4. In upper school: 1 man, 3 women; all have advanced degrees.
Subjects Offered Algebra, American government, American history, art, art history, auto mechanics, biology, British literature, calculus, career experience, career exploration, career planning, careers, chemistry, child development, computer applications, computer education, earth science, economics, English, English composition, entrepreneurship, foreign language, geometry, government, health and wellness, health education, independent study, interpersonal skills, mathematics, parenting, personal development, physical education, physical fitness, physics, pre-algebra, psychology, psychology-AP, reading, remedial/makeup course work, sociology, Spanish, speech, speech communications, statistics, travel, trigonometry, U.S. government, wellness, wilderness education, work experience, world geography, world history.
Graduation Requirements Arts and fine arts (art, music, dance, drama), computers, economics, English, foreign language, geography, health, mathematics, science, social studies (includes history), speech.
Special Academic Programs 1 Advanced Placement exam for which test preparation is offered; accelerated programs; independent study; academic accommodation for the musically talented and the artistically talented; remedial reading and/or remedial writing; remedial math.
College Admission Counseling Colleges students went to include Arizona State University; Northern Arizona University; Pima Community College; The University of Arizona; The University of North Carolina at Chapel Hill.
Student Life Upper grades have honor system.
Summer Programs Remediation, advancement programs offered; session focuses on remediation and advancement; held off campus; held at various locations for independent study; accepts boys and girls; open to students from other schools.
Tuition and Aid Need-based scholarship grants available.
Admissions Deadline for receipt of application materials: none. Application fee required: $39.
Computers Computers are regularly used in all academic classes. Computer resources include Internet access. Students grades are available online. The school has a published electronic and media policy.
Contact Brenda Baer, Distance Learning Director. 800-426-4952 Ext. 4834. Fax: 602-943-9700. E-mail: brendab@blueprinteducation.org. Web site: www.blueprinteducation.org.

THE BLUE RIDGE SCHOOL

273 Mayo Drive

St. George, Virginia 22935

Head of School: Dr. John R. O'Reilly

General Information Boys' boarding college-preparatory, general academic, arts, business, and technology school, affiliated with Episcopal Church; primarily serves underachievers. Grades 9–12. Founded: 1909. Setting: rural. Nearest major city is Charlottesville. Students are housed in single-sex dormitories. 750-acre campus. 11 buildings on campus. Approved or accredited by National Association of Episcopal Schools, Southern Association of Colleges and Schools, The Association of Boarding Schools, Virginia Association of Independent Schools, and Virginia Department of Education. Member of National Association of Independent Schools and Secondary School Admission Test Board. Endowment: $12 million. Total enrollment: 195. Upper school average class size: 8. Upper school faculty-student ratio: 1:6. There are 180 required

school days per year for Upper School students. Upper School students typically attend 6 days per week. The average school day consists of 6 hours.

Upper School Student Profile Grade 9: 26 students (26 boys); Grade 10: 57 students (57 boys); Grade 11: 47 students (47 boys); Grade 12: 65 students (65 boys). 100% of students are boarding students. 25% are state residents. 27 states are represented in upper school student body. 35% are international students. International students from Canada, China, Ghana, Nigeria, Republic of Korea, and Taiwan; 12 other countries represented in student body.

Faculty School total: 35. In upper school: 25 men, 7 women; 18 have advanced degrees; 27 reside on campus.

Subjects Offered Algebra, American history, American literature, anatomy, anatomy and physiology, art, astronomy, biology, calculus, chemistry, choir, decision making skills, discrete mathematics, drama, economics, English, environmental science, ESL, European history, French, geometry, guitar, health, honors English, honors geometry, honors U.S. history, integrated science, keyboarding, leadership, marketing, mathematics, music, music history, outdoor education, physics, pre-algebra, pre-calculus, Spanish, trigonometry, U.S. history, world history, world literature, writing, yearbook.

Graduation Requirements Algebra, American history, American literature, biology, decision making skills, English, foreign language, geometry, leadership, mathematics, physical education (includes health), science, social studies (includes history), three years of a single foreign language.

Special Academic Programs Honors section; independent study; study at local college for college credit; remedial reading and/or remedial writing; remedial math; programs in English, general development for dyslexic students; ESL (20 students enrolled).

College Admission Counseling 60 students graduated in 2011; all went to college, including Emory University; Franklin & Marshall College; Hampden-Sydney College; Kenyon College; The Johns Hopkins University; University of California, Berkeley.

Student Life Upper grades have specified standards of dress, student council, honor system. Discipline rests primarily with faculty. Attendance at religious services is required.

Tuition and Aid 7-day tuition and room/board: $38,500. Guaranteed tuition plan. Tuition installment plan (monthly payment plans). Merit scholarship grants, need-based scholarship grants, paying campus jobs available. In 2011–12, 45% of upper-school students received aid; total upper school merit-scholarship money awarded: $85,000. Total amount of financial aid awarded in 2011–12: $1,700,000.

Admissions For fall 2011, 313 students applied for upper-level admission, 138 were accepted, 88 enrolled. Deadline for receipt of application materials: none. Application fee required: $50. Interview required.

Athletics Interscholastic: baseball, basketball, cross-country running, football, golf, indoor soccer, lacrosse, mountain biking, soccer, table tennis, tennis, track and field, volleyball, wrestling; intramural: alpine skiing, aquatics, backpacking, bicycling, canoeing/kayaking, climbing, cooperative games, fishing, fitness, Frisbee, hiking/backpacking, kayaking, mountain biking, mountaineering, outdoor activities, outdoor adventure, outdoor education, outdoor recreation, outdoor skills, outdoors, paint ball, physical fitness, physical training, rafting, rappelling, rock climbing, ropes courses, skiing (downhill), snowboarding, soccer, strength & conditioning, tennis, ultimate Frisbee, wall climbing, weight lifting, weight training, wilderness, wilderness survival. 2 coaches, 2 athletic trainers.

Computers Computers are regularly used in business studies, English, ESL, foreign language, mathematics, science, study skills, word processing, writing, yearbook classes. Computer network features include on-campus library services, online commercial services, Internet access, wireless campus network, Internet filtering or blocking technology. Campus intranet, student e-mail accounts, and computer access in designated common areas are available to students. The school has a published electronic and media policy.

Contact Mr. Donald Smith, Assistant Headmaster for Enrollment and Marketing. 434-985-2811. Fax: 434-992-0536. E-mail: donsmith@blueridgeschool.com. Web site: www.blueridgeschool.com.

THE BOLLES SCHOOL

7400 San Jose Boulevard

Jacksonville, Florida 32217-3499

Head of School: John E. Trainer, Jr., PhD

General Information Coeducational boarding and day college-preparatory and arts school. Boarding grades 7–PG, day grades PK–PG. Founded: 1933. Setting: suburban. Students are housed in single-sex dormitories. 52-acre campus. 8 buildings on campus. Approved or accredited by Florida Council of Independent Schools, Southern Association of Colleges and Schools, Southern Association of Independent Schools, The Association of Boarding Schools, and Florida Department of Education. Member of National Association of Independent Schools and Secondary School Admission Test Board. Endowment: $10.7 million. Total enrollment: 1,648. Upper school average class size: 17. Upper school faculty-student ratio: 1:10. There are 175 required school days per year for Upper School students. Upper School students typically attend 5 days per week. The average school day consists of 6 hours.

Upper School Student Profile Grade 9: 183 students (100 boys, 83 girls); Grade 10: 196 students (113 boys, 83 girls); Grade 11: 195 students (101 boys, 94 girls); Grade 12: 193 students (112 boys, 81 girls). 10% of students are boarding students. 92% are state residents. 8 states are represented in upper school student body. 8% are international students. International students from Brazil, China, Colombia, Democratic People's Republic of Korea, Germany, and Mexico; 20 other countries represented in student body.

Faculty School total: 165. In upper school: 40 men, 51 women; 51 have advanced degrees; 9 reside on campus.

Subjects Offered Acting, algebra, American Civil War, American government, American history, American literature, anatomy, art, art history, art history-AP, art-AP, band, biology, biology-AP, British literature, calculus, calculus-AP, ceramics, chemistry, chemistry-AP, Chinese, chorus, comparative government and politics-AP, composition, computer applications, computer science, computer science-AP, contemporary history, creative writing, dance, data analysis, design, directing, drama, drawing, driver education, earth science, ecology, economics, English, English literature-AP, environmental science, ESL, European history, fine arts, fitness, French, French-AP, geography, geometry, German, government/civics, health, history, history-AP, humanities, Japanese, journalism, Latin, Latin-AP, life management skills, life skills, literature, marine science, mathematics, Middle Eastern history, modern European history-AP, multimedia, music, mythology, neurobiology, painting, performing arts, photography, physical education, physics, physics-AP, portfolio art, pre-algebra, pre-calculus, programming, psychology, public speaking, publications, science, sculpture, social sciences, social studies, Spanish, Spanish-AP, statistics, statistics-AP, studio art, theater, U.S. government and politics-AP, visual arts, Web site design, weight training, world cultures, world history.

Graduation Requirements Arts and fine arts (art, music, dance, drama), English, foreign language, mathematics, physical education (includes health), science, social studies (includes history).

Special Academic Programs Advanced Placement exam preparation; honors section; independent study; term-away projects; study at local college for college credit; ESL (45 students enrolled).

College Admission Counseling 200 students graduated in 2011; 192 went to college, including Florida State University; Tallahassee Community College; The University of Alabama; University of Central Florida; University of Florida; University of North Florida. Other: 2 entered a postgraduate year, 6 had other specific plans. 50% scored over 600 on SAT critical reading, 50% scored over 600 on SAT math, 49% scored over 600 on SAT writing, 47% scored over 1800 on combined SAT, 50% scored over 26 on composite ACT.

Student Life Upper grades have specified standards of dress, student council, honor system. Discipline rests primarily with faculty.

Summer Programs Enrichment, ESL, art/fine arts, computer instruction programs offered; held on campus; accepts boys and girls; open to students from other schools. 150 students usually enrolled. 2012 schedule: June 6 to July 22.

Tuition and Aid Day student tuition: $18,750; 7-day tuition and room/board: $38,950. Tuition installment plan (major increment payment plan, 10-month plan, June payment plan). Need-based scholarship grants, faculty tuition remission available. In 2011–12, 22% of upper-school students received aid. Total amount of financial aid awarded in 2011–12: $2,368,513.

Admissions Traditional secondary-level entrance grade is 9. For fall 2011, 378 students applied for upper-level admission, 164 were accepted, 94 enrolled. ISEE required. Deadline for receipt of application materials: none. Application fee required: $45. Interview required.

Athletics Interscholastic: baseball (boys), basketball (b,g), cheering (g), crew (b,g), cross-country running (b,g), dance (b,g), diving (b,g), football (b), golf (b,g), lacrosse (b), soccer (b,g), softball (g), swimming and diving (b,g), tennis (b,g), track and field (b,g), volleyball (g), weight lifting (b), wrestling (b). 2 PE instructors, 5 coaches, 1 athletic trainer.

Computers Computers are regularly used in all academic classes. Computer network features include on-campus library services, online commercial services, Internet access, wireless campus network, Internet filtering or blocking technology. Computer access in designated common areas is available to students. Students grades are available online. The school has a published electronic and media policy.

Contact Mark I. Frampton, Director of Upper School and Boarding Admission. 904-256-5032. Fax: 904-739-9929. E-mail: framptonm@bolles.org. Web site: www.bolles.org.

See Display on next page and Close-Up on page 592.

BOSTON COLLEGE HIGH SCHOOL

150 Morrissey Boulevard

Boston, Massachusetts 02125

Head of School: Mr. William Kemeza

General Information Boys' day college-preparatory, arts, and religious studies school, affiliated with Roman Catholic Church. Grades 7–12. Founded: 1863. Setting: urban. 40-acre campus. 5 buildings on campus. Approved or accredited by Association of Independent Schools in New England, Jesuit Secondary Education Association, National Catholic Education Association, New England Association of Schools and Colleges, and Massachusetts Department of Education. Member of Secondary School

Admission Test Board. Endowment: $40 million. Total enrollment: 1,591. Upper school average class size: 23. Upper school faculty-student ratio: 1:13. Upper School students typically attend 5 days per week. The average school day consists of 6 hours.

Upper School Student Profile Grade 9: 331 students (331 boys); Grade 10: 365 students (365 boys); Grade 11: 397 students (397 boys); Grade 12: 268 students (268 boys). 85% of students are Roman Catholic.

Faculty School total: 143. In upper school: 69 men, 50 women; 87 have advanced degrees.

Subjects Offered Acting, Advanced Placement courses, algebra, American history, American history-AP, American literature, anatomy and physiology, Ancient Greek, art, art history, astronomy, band, Bible studies, biology, biology-AP, British literature, British literature (honors), calculus, calculus-AP, calligraphy, chemistry, chemistry-AP, Chinese, choir, Christian doctrine, composition-AP, computer math, computer programming, computer science, computer science-AP, creative writing, digital photography, drafting, drama, dramatic arts, driver education, ecology, economics, economics-AP, electronics, English, English language and composition-AP, English literature, English literature and composition-AP, environmental science, environmental science-AP, environmental studies, ethics, European history, European history-AP, film, fine arts, forensics, French, French language-AP, French literature-AP, geometry, German, government and politics-AP, government/civics, grammar, graphic design, Greek, guitar, health, health and wellness, history, Homeric Greek, integrated science, Japanese, Latin, Latin-AP, marine biology, mathematics, modern world history, music, music theory-AP, physics, physics-AP, pre-calculus, printmaking, probability and statistics, psychology, religion, science, social justice, social studies, Spanish, Spanish language-AP, Spanish literature-AP, statistics-AP, trigonometry, U.S. government and politics-AP, U.S. history-AP, world history, world literature.

Graduation Requirements Arts and fine arts (art, music, dance, drama), English, foreign language, mathematics, religion (includes Bible studies and theology), science, social studies (includes history), 150+ hours of community service over 4 years.

Special Academic Programs 24 Advanced Placement exams for which test preparation is offered; honors section; independent study; term-away projects; study abroad; academic accommodation for the gifted; special instructional classes for blind students; ESL (10 students enrolled).

College Admission Counseling 283 students graduated in 2010; 278 went to college, including Boston College; Boston University; Fordham University; Loyola University Maryland; Northeastern University; University of Massachusetts Amherst. Other: 3 went to work, 1 entered military service, 1 entered a postgraduate year. Mean SAT critical reading: 598, mean SAT math: 611, mean SAT writing: 598, mean combined SAT: 1808.

Student Life Upper grades have specified standards of dress, student council. Discipline rests primarily with faculty.

Tuition and Aid Day student tuition: $15,900. Tuition installment plan (monthly payment plans). Merit scholarship grants, need-based scholarship grants, need-based loans, paying campus jobs available. In 2010–11, 35% of upper-school students received aid; total upper-school merit-scholarship money awarded: $140,000. Total amount of financial aid awarded in 2010–11: $4,300,000.

Admissions Traditional secondary-level entrance grade is 9. For fall 2010, 700 students applied for upper-level admission, 350 were accepted, 200 enrolled. Catholic High School Entrance Examination, High School Placement Test or SSAT required. Deadline for receipt of application materials: December 31. No application fee required.

Athletics Interscholastic: baseball, basketball, cross-country running, football, golf, ice hockey, lacrosse, rugby, sailing, skiing (downhill), soccer, swimming and diving, tennis, track and field, volleyball, winter (indoor) track; intramural: basketball, bicycling, crew, flag football, Frisbee, hiking/backpacking, tennis. 42 coaches, 1 athletic trainer.

Computers Computers are regularly used in English, foreign language, mathematics, religious studies, science, social sciences classes. Computer network features include on-campus library services, online commercial services, Internet access, wireless campus network, Internet filtering or blocking technology. Student e-mail accounts and computer access in designated common areas are available to students. Students grades are available online.

Contact Mr. Michael Brennan, Director of Admissions. 617-474-5010. Fax: 617-474-5015. E-mail: brennan@bchigh.edu. Web site: www.bchigh.edu/.

BOSTON UNIVERSITY ACADEMY

One University Road

Boston, Massachusetts 02215

Head of School: Mr. James Berkman

General Information Coeducational day college-preparatory and arts school. Grades 9–12. Founded: 1993. Setting: urban. 132-acre campus. 1 building on campus. Approved or accredited by Association of Independent Schools in New England, New England Association of Schools and Colleges, and Massachusetts Department of Education. Member of National Association of Independent Schools and Secondary School Admission Test Board. Total enrollment: 159. Upper school average class size: 12. Upper school faculty-student ratio: 1:8. There are 164 required school days per year for Upper School students. Upper School students typically attend 5 days per week. The average school day consists of 7 hours.

Upper School Student Profile Grade 9: 41 students (22 boys, 19 girls); Grade 10: 40 students (22 boys, 18 girls); Grade 11: 39 students (20 boys, 19 girls); Grade 12: 39 students (23 boys, 16 girls).
Faculty School total: 21. In upper school: 13 men, 8 women; 18 have advanced degrees.
Subjects Offered Advanced math, African American studies, algebra, American history, American literature, ancient history, anthropology, Arabic, archaeology, art, art history, astronomy, biochemistry, biology, calculus, chemistry, Chinese, classical studies, college counseling, community service, computer programming, drama, English, English literature, European history, French, geometry, German, Greek, Hebrew, history, Italian, Japanese, Latin, music, physical education, physics, robotics, Russian, sculpture, senior project, Spanish, statistics, theater, trigonometry, women's studies, writing.
Graduation Requirements Arts and fine arts (art, music, dance, drama), chemistry, English, Greek, history, Latin, mathematics, physical education (includes health), physics, two-semester senior thesis project, coursework at Boston University. Community service is required.
Special Academic Programs Honors section; accelerated programs; independent study; study at local college for college credit; academic accommodation for the gifted.
College Admission Counseling 34 students graduated in 2011; 33 went to college, including Boston University; Brandeis University; Harvey Mudd College; Massachusetts Institute of Technology; University of Chicago; University of Pennsylvania. Other: 1 had other specific plans. Mean SAT critical reading: 718, mean SAT math: 724, mean SAT writing: 722, mean combined SAT: 2164. 97% scored over 600 on SAT critical reading, 100% scored over 600 on SAT math, 94% scored over 600 on SAT writing.
Student Life Upper grades have student council, honor system. Discipline rests equally with students and faculty.
Tuition and Aid Day student tuition: $32,590. Tuition installment plan (Insured Tuition Payment Plan, Academic Management Services Plan, monthly payment plans). Need-based scholarship grants available. In 2011–12, 35% of upper-school students received aid. Total amount of financial aid awarded in 2011–12: $1,089,800.
Admissions Traditional secondary-level entrance grade is 9. For fall 2011, 189 students applied for upper-level admission, 96 were accepted, 46 enrolled. SSAT required. Deadline for receipt of application materials: January 31. Application fee required: $45. On-campus interview required.
Athletics Interscholastic: baseball (boys), basketball (b,g), crew (b,g); coed interscholastic: cross-country running, fencing, sailing, soccer, tennis, ultimate Frisbee; coed intramural: climbing, dance, fitness, hiking/backpacking, softball, volleyball. 10 PE instructors, 7 coaches.
Computers Computers are regularly used in art, English, foreign language, history, mathematics, science classes. Computer network features include on-campus library services, online commercial services, Internet access, Internet filtering or blocking technology, internal electronic bulletin board system. Campus intranet and student e-mail accounts are available to students. Students grades are available online. The school has a published electronic and media policy.
Contact Ms. Nicole White, Admission Coordinator. 617-358-2493. Fax: 617-353-8999. E-mail: nicole_white@buacademy.org. Web site: www.buacademy.org.

BOURGADE CATHOLIC HIGH SCHOOL

4602 North 31st Avenue

Phoenix, Arizona 85017

Head of School: Sr. Mary McGreevy, SSND

General Information Coeducational day college-preparatory, general academic, arts, and religious studies school, affiliated with Roman Catholic Church. Grades 9–12. Founded: 1962. Setting: urban. 27-acre campus. 6 buildings on campus. Approved or accredited by North Central Association of Colleges and Schools, Western Catholic Education Association, and Arizona Department of Education. Total enrollment: 406. Upper school average class size: 25. Upper school faculty-student ratio: 1:13. There are 184 required school days per year for Upper School students. Upper School students typically attend 5 days per week. The average school day consists of 6 hours.
Upper School Student Profile Grade 9: 130 students (65 boys, 65 girls); Grade 10: 90 students (38 boys, 52 girls); Grade 11: 96 students (50 boys, 46 girls); Grade 12: 90 students (41 boys, 49 girls). 94% of students are Roman Catholic.
Faculty School total: 33. In upper school: 18 men, 15 women; 22 have advanced degrees.
Subjects Offered Acting, advanced biology, advanced chemistry, algebra, American government, American history, American history-AP, American sign language, ancient world history, art, band, bell choir, biology, broadcasting, calculus, calculus-AP, Catholic belief and practice, chemistry, chemistry-AP, choir, Christian and Hebrew scripture, Christian doctrine, Christian ethics, church history, college admission preparation, comparative religion, computer graphics, constitutional history of U.S., creative dance, dance, desktop publishing, digital photography, drama performance, earth science, economics, English, English composition, foreign language, general science, geography, government, graphic design, health education, Hebrew scripture, honors algebra, honors English, honors geometry, honors U.S. history, honors world history, keyboarding, leadership and service, modern dance, New Testament, newspaper, photography, pre-algebra, psychology, reading, sexuality, social justice, Spanish, Spanish-AP, speech, study skills, theater arts, U.S. government, U.S. history, U.S. history-AP, video communication, world religions, yearbook, yoga.
Graduation Requirements Advanced Placement courses, arts and fine arts (art, music, dance, drama), English, foreign language, mathematics, physical education (includes health), religion (includes Bible studies and theology), science.
Special Academic Programs Advanced Placement exam preparation; honors section.
College Admission Counseling 86 students graduated in 2010; 82 went to college, including Arizona State University; Embry-Riddle Aeronautical University–Daytona; Grand Canyon University; Northern Arizona University; The University of Arizona. Other: 2 went to work, 2 entered military service.
Student Life Upper grades have uniform requirement, student council, honor system. Discipline rests primarily with faculty. Attendance at religious services is required.
Tuition and Aid Day student tuition: $8320–$10,450. Tuition installment plan (monthly payment plans). Tuition reduction for siblings, need-based scholarship grants, Catholic Tuition Organization Diocese of Phoenix (CTODP) available. In 2010–11, 80% of upper-school students received aid. Total amount of financial aid awarded in 2010–11: $800,000.
Admissions Traditional secondary-level entrance grade is 9. For fall 2010, 484 students applied for upper-level admission, 430 were accepted, 406 enrolled. ETS high school placement exam or Stanford 9 required. Deadline for receipt of application materials: February 10. Application fee required: $10,450. Interview required.
Athletics Interscholastic: baseball (boys), basketball (b,g), cheering (g), dance (g), dance squad (g), dance team (g), danceline (g), football (b), golf (b), soccer (b), softball (g), tennis (b,g), track and field (b,g), volleyball (g), wrestling (b); intramural: weight training (b,g). 2 PE instructors, 2 coaches, 1 athletic trainer.
Computers Computers are regularly used in all academic classes. Computer resources include Internet access.
Contact Mrs. Vicki Kilgarriff, Assistant Principal/Academic Director. 602-973-4000 Ext. 112. Fax: 602-973-5854. E-mail: vkilgarriff@bourgade.org. Web site: www.bourgadecatholic.org.

BOYLAN CENTRAL CATHOLIC HIGH SCHOOL

4000 Saint Francis Drive

Rockford, Illinois 61103-1699

Head of School: Rev. Paul Lipinski

General Information Coeducational day and distance learning college-preparatory, general academic, arts, business, vocational, religious studies, bilingual studies, and technology school, affiliated with Roman Catholic Church. Grades 9–12. Distance learning grades 9–12. Founded: 1960. Setting: urban. Nearest major city is Chicago. 60-acre campus. 3 buildings on campus. Approved or accredited by North Central Association of Colleges and Schools and Illinois Department of Education. Endowment: $3 million. Total enrollment: 1,152. Upper school average class size: 24. Upper school faculty-student ratio: 1:13. There are 176 required school days per year for Upper School students. Upper School students typically attend 5 days per week. The average school day consists of 7 hours.
Upper School Student Profile Grade 9: 287 students (142 boys, 145 girls); Grade 10: 280 students (146 boys, 134 girls); Grade 11: 272 students (140 boys, 132 girls); Grade 12: 313 students (159 boys, 154 girls). 87% of students are Roman Catholic.
Faculty School total: 86. In upper school: 33 men, 53 women; 62 have advanced degrees.
Subjects Offered 20th century history, 3-dimensional art, accounting, ACT preparation, acting, advanced computer applications, Advanced Placement courses, advanced studio art-AP, algebra, American history, American history-AP, American literature-AP, analysis and differential calculus, analytic geometry, anatomy and physiology, architectural drawing, architecture, art, art history, art history-AP, art-AP, athletics, auto mechanics, band, biology, bookkeeping, botany, British literature, British literature (honors), broadcast journalism, broadcasting, business, business education, business law, calculus, calculus-AP, career education, career exploration, career planning, Catholic belief and practice, cheerleading, chemistry, chemistry-AP, Chinese, choir, chorus, Christian and Hebrew scripture, Christian doctrine, Christian ethics, church history, college counseling, communications, comparative religion, composition-AP, computer multimedia, computer-aided design, concert band, concert choir, consumer economics, consumer education, consumer law, consumer mathematics, contemporary history, contemporary issues, contemporary studies, creative writing, critical thinking, culinary arts, debate, desktop publishing, drafting, drama, dramatic arts, earth science, economics-AP, English, English language-AP, English literature-AP, English/composition-AP, environmental science, European history, European history-AP, family and consumer science, family living, fashion, fiction, finite math, foods, French, French as a second language, French literature-AP, French-AP, freshman foundations, general math, geography, geometry, German, government, government-AP, graphics, guitar, health, health education, history of music, illustration, industrial technology, information processing, integrated science, jazz band, keyboarding, library assistant, marketing, music appreciation, music composition, music history, music technology, music theory, photo shop, physical science, physics, physics-AP, pre-algebra, pre-calculus, psychology, psychology-AP, religion, senior composition, Spanish, statistics, strings, studio art, swimming, technological applications, technology/design, trigonometry, U.S. history,

vocal music, Web authoring, Web site design, wood lab, woodworking, world geography, world history, world literature, writing, yearbook, zoology.

Graduation Requirements Consumer education, English, mathematics, physical education (includes health), religious studies, science, social studies (includes history), fine and applied arts, community service.

Special Academic Programs 12 Advanced Placement exams for which test preparation is offered; honors section; independent study; academic accommodation for the gifted, the musically talented, and the artistically talented; remedial reading and/or remedial writing; remedial math; programs in general development for dyslexic students; special instructional classes for deaf students, blind students.

College Admission Counseling 295 students graduated in 2011; 284 went to college, including Illinois State University; Loyola University Chicago; Marquette University; Northern Illinois University; The University of Iowa; University of Illinois at Urbana–Champaign. Other: 9 went to work, 2 entered military service. 40% scored over 26 on composite ACT.

Student Life Upper grades have uniform requirement, student council. Discipline rests primarily with faculty. Attendance at religious services is required.

Summer Programs Enrichment, sports, art/fine arts, rigorous outdoor training programs offered; session focuses on enrichment; held on campus; accepts boys and girls; open to students from other schools. 150 students usually enrolled. 2012 schedule: June 5 to July 30.

Tuition and Aid Day student tuition: $5100. Tuition installment plan (monthly payment plans, individually arranged payment plans, full-year or semester payment plan). Tuition reduction for siblings, need-based scholarship grants, paying campus jobs available. In 2011–12, 100% of upper-school students received aid. Total amount of financial aid awarded in 2011–12: $425,000.

Admissions Traditional secondary-level entrance grade is 9. For fall 2011, 300 students applied for upper-level admission, 300 were accepted, 287 enrolled. ETS HSPT (closed) required. Deadline for receipt of application materials: none. Application fee required: $100. Interview required.

Athletics Interscholastic: aerobics/dance (girls), baseball (b), basketball (b,g), bowling (b,g), cheering (g), cross-country running (b,g), dance team (g), diving (b,g), fishing (b,g), football (b), golf (b,g), ice hockey (b), soccer (b,g), softball (g), swimming and diving (b,g), tennis (b,g), track and field (b,g), volleyball (g), wrestling (b); intramural: aerobics (g), archery (b,g), fitness (b,g), golf (b,g), outdoor education (b,g), physical fitness (b,g), physical training (b,g), rowing (b,g), running (b,g), strength & conditioning (b,g), track and field (b,g), volleyball (b,g), weight training (b,g); coed intramural: dance. 6 PE instructors, 4 coaches, 2 athletic trainers.

Computers Computers are regularly used in all academic, architecture, business applications, computer applications, desktop publishing, drawing and design, keyboarding, music technology, photography, publications, technical drawing, technology, video film production, Web site design, word processing, yearbook classes. Computer network features include on-campus library services, online commercial services, Internet access, wireless campus network, Internet filtering or blocking technology. Campus intranet, student e-mail accounts, and computer access in designated common areas are available to students. Students grades are available online. The school has a published electronic and media policy.

Contact Mr. Dennis Hiemenz, Assistant Principal. 815-877-0531 Ext. 227. Fax: 815-877-2544. E-mail: dhiemenz@boylan.org. Web site: www.boylan.org.

BRANKSOME HALL

10 Elm Avenue

Toronto, Ontario M4W 1N4, Canada

Head of School: Karen Murton

General Information Girls' boarding and day college-preparatory and arts school. Boarding grades 8–12, day grades JK–12. Founded: 1903. Setting: urban. Students are housed in single-sex dormitories. 13-acre campus. 6 buildings on campus. Approved or accredited by Canadian Association of Independent Schools, Canadian Educational Standards Institute, International Baccalaureate Organization, Ontario Ministry of Education, The Association of Boarding Schools, and Ontario Department of Education. Affiliate member of National Association of Independent Schools; member of Secondary School Admission Test Board. Language of instruction: English. Endowment: CAN$13 million. Total enrollment: 880. Upper school average class size: 18. Upper school faculty-student ratio: 1:9. There are 180 required school days per year for Upper School students. Upper School students typically attend 5 days per week. The average school day consists of 8 hours.

Upper School Student Profile Grade 9: 107 students (107 girls); Grade 10: 121 students (121 girls); Grade 11: 115 students (115 girls); Grade 12: 119 students (119 girls). 16% of students are boarding students. 1% are province residents. 3 provinces are represented in upper school student body. 90% are international students. International students from China, Democratic People's Republic of Korea, Germany, Kenya, Saint Kitts and Nevis, and Taiwan; 12 other countries represented in student body.

Faculty School total: 115. In upper school: 15 men, 70 women; 40 have advanced degrees; 3 reside on campus.

Subjects Offered Accounting, acting, advanced math, algebra, all academic, American history, American literature, ancient history, ancient world history, Arabic, art, art and culture, art history, arts, athletics, band, biology, British history, British literature, business, calculus, Canadian geography, Canadian history, Canadian law, Canadian literature, Cantonese, career and personal planning, career exploration, career/college preparation, chemistry, Chinese, Chinese studies, classical civilization, classical Greek literature, computer multimedia, computer programming, computer science, critical thinking, critical writing, drama, drawing, economics, economics and history, English, English literature, environmental science, environmental systems, ethics, European history, European literature, expository writing, film studies, fine arts, food science, French, French studies, geography, geometry, German, government/civics, health, history, home economics, independent study, interdisciplinary studies, Latin, Mandarin, mathematics, music, physical education, physics, science, social sciences, social studies, Spanish, theater, theory of knowledge, trigonometry, typing, vocal ensemble, vocal music, world affairs, world arts, world civilizations, world cultures, world geography, world governments, world history, world issues, world literature, world religions, world studies, writing, writing workshop, yearbook.

Graduation Requirements Arts and fine arts (art, music, dance, drama), business skills (includes word processing), English, International Baccalaureate courses, language, mathematics, physical education (includes health), science, social sciences, social studies (includes history), IB diploma or certificate requirements.

Special Academic Programs International Baccalaureate program; honors section; academic accommodation for the gifted, the musically talented, and the artistically talented; ESL (20 students enrolled).

College Admission Counseling 112 students graduated in 2011; 111 went to college, including Dalhousie University; McGill University; Queen's University at Kingston; The University of British Columbia; The University of Western Ontario; University of Toronto. Other: 1 had other specific plans.

Student Life Upper grades have uniform requirement, student council, honor system. Discipline rests primarily with faculty.

Summer Programs Remediation, enrichment programs offered; session focuses on two-week summer academy in courses including math and English; held on campus; accepts boys and girls; open to students from other schools. 2012 schedule: August to September.

Tuition and Aid Day student tuition: CAN$26,265; 7-day tuition and room/board: CAN$49,000. Tuition installment plan (monthly payment plans, tri-annual payment, early payment option ($500 savings)). Bursaries, merit scholarship grants available. In 2011–12, 10% of upper-school students received aid; total upper-school merit-scholarship money awarded: CAN$12,500. Total amount of financial aid awarded in 2011–12: CAN$650,000.

Admissions Traditional secondary-level entrance grade is 9. For fall 2011, 350 students applied for upper-level admission, 220 were accepted, 170 enrolled. SSAT required. Deadline for receipt of application materials: December 16. Application fee required: CAN$200. Interview required.

Athletics Interscholastic: alpine skiing, aquatics, badminton, baseball, basketball, crew, cross-country running, field hockey, golf, hockey, ice hockey, indoor track, indoor track & field, rowing, rugby, skiing (downhill), soccer, softball, swimming and diving, synchronized swimming, tennis, track and field, volleyball; intramural: aerobics, aerobics/dance, aquatics, badminton, ball hockey, ballet, baseball, basketball, cheering, climbing, cooperative games, cross-country running, dance, dance squad, field hockey, fitness, gymnastics, outdoor activities, paddle tennis, physical fitness, physical training, rugby, soccer, softball, squash, strength & conditioning, swimming and diving, table tennis, tennis, track and field, volleyball, yoga. 6 PE instructors, 2 coaches, 1 athletic trainer.

Computers Computers are regularly used in art, geography, mathematics, music, science classes. Computer network features include on-campus library services, Internet access, wireless campus network, Internet filtering or blocking technology. Campus intranet, student e-mail accounts, and computer access in designated common areas are available to students. The school has a published electronic and media policy.

Contact Kimberly Carter, Associate Director of Admissions. 416-920-9741. Fax: 416-920-5390. E-mail: admissions@branksome.on.ca. Web site: www.branksome.on.ca.

THE BREARLEY SCHOOL

610 East 83rd Street

New York, New York 10028

Head of School: Dr. Priscilla Winn. Barlow

General Information Girls' day college-preparatory school. Grades K–12. Founded: 1884. Setting: urban. 2 buildings on campus. Approved or accredited by New York State Association of Independent Schools. Member of National Association of Independent Schools. Endowment: $101 million. Total enrollment: 701. Upper school average class size: 12. Upper school faculty-student ratio: 1:6. The average school day consists of 7 hours.

Upper School Student Profile Grade 9: 60 students (60 girls); Grade 10: 55 students (55 girls); Grade 11: 49 students (49 girls); Grade 12: 59 students (59 girls).

Faculty School total: 134. In upper school: 21 men, 53 women; 56 have advanced degrees.

Subjects Offered 20th century world history, advanced biology, advanced chemistry, African history, algebra, American history, American literature, applied music, art, art history, astronomy, biology, calculus, calculus-AP, chamber groups, chemistry, computer science, contemporary women writers, critical writing, drama, drama perfor-

mance, drawing, English, English literature, environmental science, equality and freedom, expository writing, fiction, finite math, French, French language-AP, French literature-AP, geometry, history, history of China and Japan, Homeric Greek, independent study, Latin, Mandarin, mathematics, modern European history, multimedia design, music, music history, oil painting, painting, physical education, physics, political thought, pre-calculus, senior project, Shakespeare, Spanish, Spanish literature, statistics, trigonometry, vocal music, water color painting, Web site design, world history.
Graduation Requirements Arts and fine arts (art, music, dance, drama), English, foreign language, history, mathematics, physical education (includes health), science.
Special Academic Programs 12 Advanced Placement exams for which test preparation is offered; independent study; term-away projects; study abroad.
College Admission Counseling 46 students graduated in 2011; all went to college, including Columbia University; Dartmouth College; Harvard University; Princeton University; University of Pennsylvania. Median SAT critical reading: 730, median SAT math: 690. 99% scored over 600 on SAT critical reading, 92% scored over 600 on SAT math.
Student Life Upper grades have specified standards of dress, student council. Discipline rests equally with students and faculty.
Tuition and Aid Day student tuition: $36,800. Tuition installment plan (Key Tuition Payment Plan, individually arranged payment plans). Need-based scholarship grants, need-based loans available. In 2011–12, 22% of upper-school students received aid. Total amount of financial aid awarded in 2011–12: $3,441,395.
Admissions Traditional secondary-level entrance grade is 9. For fall 2011, 121 students applied for upper-level admission, 21 were accepted, 13 enrolled. ISEE and school's own exam required. Deadline for receipt of application materials: December 1. Application fee required: $60. On-campus interview required.
Athletics Interscholastic: aquatics, badminton, basketball, cross-country running, field hockey, gymnastics, lacrosse, soccer, softball, squash, swimming and diving, tennis, track and field, volleyball; intramural: aquatics, badminton, basketball, cooperative games, cricket, dance, dance team, field hockey, fitness, gymnastics, jogging, lacrosse, modern dance, physical fitness, soccer, softball, strength & conditioning, swimming and diving, tai chi, team handball, track and field, volleyball, yoga. 12 PE instructors, 3 coaches, 2 athletic trainers.
Computers Computers are regularly used in classics, computer applications, foreign language, history, mathematics, multimedia, music, photography, science, theater arts, Web site design classes. Computer network features include on-campus library services, Internet access, wireless campus network, Britannica Online, EBSCO, SIRS Researcher, ProQuest, JSTOR, ArtStor, AtomicLearning.com (software tutorials), a file server. Student e-mail accounts and computer access in designated common areas are available to students. The school has a published electronic and media policy.
Contact Ms. Joan Kaplan, Director of Middle and Upper School Admission. 212-744-8582. Fax: 212-472-8020. E-mail: admission@brearley.org. Web site: www.brearley.org.

BRECK SCHOOL

123 Ottawa Avenue North

Minneapolis, Minnesota 55422

Head of School: Edward Kim

General Information Coeducational day college-preparatory, arts, and religious studies school, affiliated with Episcopal Church. Grades PK–12. Founded: 1886. Setting: suburban. 53-acre campus. 1 building on campus. Approved or accredited by Independent Schools Association of the Central States. Member of National Association of Independent Schools and Secondary School Admission Test Board. Endowment: $49 million. Total enrollment: 1,143. Upper school average class size: 17. Upper school faculty-student ratio: 1:11.
Upper School Student Profile 10% of students are members of Episcopal Church.
Faculty School total: 145. In upper school: 12 men, 17 women; 22 have advanced degrees.
Subjects Offered Algebra, American history, American literature, art, astronomy, biology, calculus, ceramics, chemistry, Chinese, chorus, community service, computer math, computer programming, creative writing, dance, drama, ecology, economics, English, English literature, environmental science, ethics, European history, expository writing, fine arts, French, geometry, health, history, mathematics, music, orchestra, physical education, physics, religion, science, social studies, Spanish, statistics, theater, theology, trigonometry, world history, world literature, writing.
Graduation Requirements Arts and fine arts (art, music, dance, drama), English, foreign language, mathematics, physical education (includes health), religion (includes Bible studies and theology), science, social studies (includes history), senior speech, May Program. Community service is required.
Special Academic Programs Advanced Placement exam preparation; honors section; independent study; term-away projects; academic accommodation for the gifted, the musically talented, and the artistically talented.
College Admission Counseling 94 students graduated in 2011; all went to college, including Amherst College; Boston University; Bowdoin College; Pitzer College; St. Olaf College; The Colorado College. Mean SAT critical reading: 638, mean SAT math: 618, mean SAT writing: 620.
Student Life Upper grades have specified standards of dress, student council, honor system. Discipline rests equally with students and faculty. Attendance at religious services is required.
Tuition and Aid Day student tuition: $24,290. Tuition installment plan (Key Tuition Payment Plan). Need-based scholarship grants available. In 2011–12, 22% of upper-school students received aid.
Admissions Traditional secondary-level entrance grade is 9. CTP III required. Deadline for receipt of application materials: February 1. Application fee required: $75. On-campus interview required.
Athletics Interscholastic: alpine skiing (boys, girls), baseball (b), basketball (b,g), cross-country running (b,g), diving (b,g), football (b), golf (b,g), gymnastics (g), ice hockey (b,g), lacrosse (b,g), nordic skiing (b,g), skiing (cross-country) (b,g), skiing (downhill) (b,g), soccer (b,g), softball (g), swimming and diving (b,g), tennis (b,g), track and field (b,g), volleyball (g). 6 PE instructors, 82 coaches, 1 athletic trainer.
Computers Computers are regularly used in all classes. Computer network features include on-campus library services, online commercial services, Internet access, wireless campus network, Internet filtering or blocking technology, multimedia imaging, video presentation, student laptop program. Campus intranet and student e-mail accounts are available to students. The school has a published electronic and media policy.
Contact Scott D. Wade, Director of Admissions. 763-381-8200. Fax: 763-381-8288. E-mail: scott.wade@breckschool.org. Web site: www.breckschool.org.

BRENTWOOD COLLEGE SCHOOL

2735 Mount Baker Road

Mill Bay, British Columbia V0R 2P1, Canada

Head of School: Mrs. Andrea M. Pennells

General Information Coeducational boarding and day college-preparatory, arts, and athletics, leadership, and citizenship school school. Grades 9–12. Founded: 1923. Setting: rural. Nearest major city is Victoria, Canada. Students are housed in single-sex dormitories. 47-acre campus. 15 buildings on campus. Approved or accredited by British Columbia Independent Schools Association, Canadian Association of Independent Schools, The Association of Boarding Schools, Western Boarding Schools Association, and British Columbia Department of Education. Affiliate member of National Association of Independent Schools. Language of instruction: English. Total enrollment: 435. Upper school average class size: 16. Upper school faculty-student ratio: 1:9.
Upper School Student Profile Grade 9: 83 students (53 boys, 30 girls); Grade 10: 115 students (61 boys, 54 girls); Grade 11: 124 students (62 boys, 62 girls); Grade 12: 113 students (62 boys, 51 girls). 81% of students are boarding students. 58% are province residents. 20 provinces are represented in upper school student body. 27% are international students. International students from Germany, Hong Kong, Mexico, Republic of Korea, Saudi Arabia, and United States; 12 other countries represented in student body.
Faculty School total: 50. In upper school: 24 men, 17 women; 13 have advanced degrees; 30 reside on campus.
Subjects Offered Advanced Placement courses, algebra, art history-AP, athletics, audio visual/media, band, basketball, biology, biology-AP, business, calculus, calculus-AP, Canadian geography, Canadian history, Canadian law, career and personal planning, ceramics, chemistry, chemistry-AP, choir, choreography, computer graphics, computer science, dance, dance performance, debate, design, drafting, drama, dramatic arts, drawing, economics, economics-AP, English, English literature, English literature-AP, French, French language-AP, geography, geometry, golf, government and politics-AP, health and wellness, history, human geography - AP, information technology, instrumental music, international studies, jazz band, jazz ensemble, marketing, mathematics, musical productions, musical theater, orchestra, outdoor education, painting, photography, physics, physics-AP, pottery, psychology, psychology-AP, public speaking, science, sculpture, sex education, social studies, Spanish, Spanish-AP, stagecraft, technical theater, tennis, theater design and production, video film production, visual and performing arts, vocal jazz, volleyball, yearbook.
Graduation Requirements Arts and fine arts (art, music, dance, drama), career and personal planning, English, foreign language, mathematics, physical education (includes health), science, social studies (includes history).
Special Academic Programs Advanced Placement exam preparation.
College Admission Counseling 112 students graduated in 2010; all went to college, including Duke University; McGill University; Queen's University at Kingston; The University of British Columbia; University of California, Berkeley; University of California, Los Angeles.
Student Life Upper grades have uniform requirement, student council, honor system. Discipline rests primarily with faculty.
Tuition and Aid Day student tuition: CAN$18,300; 7-day tuition and room/board: CAN$36,000–CAN$46,500. Tuition reduction for siblings available.
Admissions Traditional secondary-level entrance grade is 9. Henmon-Nelson or SSAT required. Deadline for receipt of application materials: none. Application fee required: CAN$2500. Interview required.
Athletics Interscholastic: basketball (boys, girls), crew (b,g), cross-country running (b,g), field hockey (g), hockey (g), rowing (b,g), rugby (b,g), running (b,g), soccer (b,g),

squash (b,g), tennis (b,g), volleyball (g); intramural: crew (b,g), cross-country running (b,g), field hockey (g), indoor hockey (g), soccer (b,g), squash (b,g), tennis (b,g), track and field (b,g), volleyball (g), weight training (g); coed interscholastic: badminton, ballet, canoeing/kayaking, fitness, golf, ice hockey, judo, kayaking, modern dance, ocean paddling, outdoor activities, rock climbing, sailing; coed intramural: aerobics, aerobics/dance, badminton, canoeing/kayaking, cooperative games, dance, fitness, floor hockey, hiking/backpacking, indoor soccer, kayaking, outdoor activities, physical fitness, physical training, rowing, rugby, running, skiing (downhill), snowboarding, strength & conditioning, table tennis, touch football, weight lifting, weight training. 6 PE instructors, 36 coaches.

Computers Computers are regularly used in photojournalism, video film production classes. Computer network features include on-campus library services, Internet access, wireless campus network, Internet filtering or blocking technology. Campus intranet and student e-mail accounts are available to students. The school has a published electronic and media policy.

Contact Mr. Clayton Johnston, Director of Admissions. 250-743-5521. Fax: 250-743-2911. E-mail: admissions@brentwood.bc.ca. Web site: www.brentwood.bc.ca.

BRENTWOOD SCHOOL

100 South Barrington Place

Los Angeles, California 90049

Head of School: Dr. Michael Riera

General Information Coeducational day college-preparatory school. Grades K–12. Founded: 1972. Setting: suburban. 30-acre campus. 12 buildings on campus. Approved or accredited by California Association of Independent Schools and Western Association of Schools and Colleges. Member of National Association of Independent Schools and Secondary School Admission Test Board. Endowment: $7 million. Total enrollment: 990. Upper school average class size: 17. Upper school faculty-student ratio: 1:7. Upper School students typically attend 5 days per week. The average school day consists of 8 hours.

Upper School Student Profile Grade 9: 121 students (60 boys, 61 girls); Grade 10: 123 students (62 boys, 61 girls); Grade 11: 111 students (61 boys, 50 girls); Grade 12: 108 students (56 boys, 52 girls).

Faculty School total: 125. In upper school: 45 men, 49 women; 70 have advanced degrees.

Subjects Offered Acting, Advanced Placement courses, advanced studio art-AP, algebra, American history, American literature, Ancient Greek, anthropology, art, art history, art history-AP, art-AP, astronomy, biology, biology-AP, calculus, calculus-AP, ceramics, chemistry, chemistry-AP, Chinese, choir, choral music, chorus, community service, comparative government and politics-AP, computer programming, computer programming-AP, computer science, computer science-AP, concert choir, creative writing, dance, digital photography, directing, drama, drawing, ecology, economics, economics-AP, English, English literature, environmental science-AP, European history, filmmaking, fine arts, French, French-AP, geometry, global studies, government and politics-AP, government-AP, history, honors algebra, honors English, honors geometry, human development, human geography - AP, Japanese, jazz band, jazz dance, journalism, language-AP, Latin, Latin-AP, literature-AP, math analysis, mathematics, music, music theater, music theory-AP, orchestra, organic chemistry, philosophy, photography, physical education, physics, physics-AP, probability and statistics, robotics, science, senior seminar, senior thesis, social sciences, social studies, Spanish, Spanish-AP, speech, speech and debate, stagecraft, stained glass, statistics-AP, studio art-AP, theater, U.S. government and politics-AP, U.S. history-AP, video, word processing, world history, world literature.

Graduation Requirements Arts and fine arts (art, music, dance, drama), English, foreign language, mathematics, physical education (includes health), science, senior seminar, social sciences, social studies (includes history). Community service is required.

Special Academic Programs 26 Advanced Placement exams for which test preparation is offered; honors section; independent study; study at local college for college credit; academic accommodation for the gifted and the artistically talented.

College Admission Counseling 115 students graduated in 2011; 114 went to college, including Brown University; Stanford University; The Johns Hopkins University; University of Pennsylvania; University of Southern California. Mean SAT critical reading: 660, mean SAT math: 670, mean SAT writing: 680, mean combined SAT: 2010.

Student Life Upper grades have specified standards of dress, student council, honor system. Discipline rests primarily with faculty.

Summer Programs Remediation, enrichment, advancement, sports, art/fine arts, computer instruction programs offered; session focuses on academic enrichment and sports; held on campus; accepts boys and girls; open to students from other schools. 350 students usually enrolled. 2012 schedule: June 25 to July 27. Application deadline: none.

Tuition and Aid Day student tuition: $31,250. Tuition installment plan (Insured Tuition Payment Plan, monthly payment plans, individually arranged payment plans). Need-based scholarship grants available. In 2011–12, 16% of upper-school students received aid. Total amount of financial aid awarded in 2011–12: $3,500,000.

Admissions Traditional secondary-level entrance grade is 9. For fall 2011, 171 students applied for upper-level admission, 25 were accepted, 20 enrolled. ISEE required. Deadline for receipt of application materials: January 13. Application fee required: $100. On-campus interview required.

Athletics Interscholastic: baseball (boys), basketball (b,g), cheering (g), cross-country running (b,g), dance squad (g), dance team (g), football (b), independent competitive sports (b,g), lacrosse (b,g), soccer (b,g), softball (g), swimming and diving (b,g), tennis (b,g), track and field (b,g), volleyball (b,g), water polo (b), wrestling (b); intramural: modern dance (g), ultimate Frisbee (b); coed interscholastic: dance, diving, drill team, equestrian sports, fencing, football, golf, swimming and diving, water polo; coed intramural: bicycling, fitness, Frisbee, jogging, mountain biking, outdoor activities, physical fitness, physical training, running, sailing, surfing, table tennis, ultimate Frisbee, weight lifting, weight training, wilderness, yoga. 6 PE instructors, 40 coaches, 2 athletic trainers.

Computers Computers are regularly used in college planning, computer applications, desktop publishing, digital applications, foreign language, graphic design, introduction to technology, journalism, literary magazine, mathematics, media arts, media production, photojournalism, programming, publications, research skills, science, technical drawing, technology, video film production, Web site design classes. Computer network features include on-campus library services, online commercial services, Internet access, wireless campus network, Internet filtering or blocking technology, Schoology (learning management system). Campus intranet, student e-mail accounts, and computer access in designated common areas are available to students. Students grades are available online. The school has a published electronic and media policy.

Contact Ms. Colleen Ward, Admissions Assistant. 310-889-2657. Fax: 310-476-4087. E-mail: cward@bwscampus.com. Web site: www.bwscampus.com.

BREWSTER ACADEMY

80 Academy Drive

Wolfeboro, New Hampshire 03894

Head of School: Dr. Michael E. Cooper

General Information Coeducational boarding and day college-preparatory, arts, and technology school. Grades 9–PG. Founded: 1820. Setting: small town. Nearest major city is Boston, MA. Students are housed in single-sex dormitories. 91-acre campus. 39 buildings on campus. Approved or accredited by Independent Schools of Northern New England, New England Association of Schools and Colleges, and The Association of Boarding Schools. Member of National Association of Independent Schools and Secondary School Admission Test Board. Endowment: $8.4 million. Total enrollment: 364. Upper school average class size: 12. Upper school faculty-student ratio: 1:6. There are 165 required school days per year for Upper School students. Upper School students typically attend 6 days per week. The average school day consists of 6 hours.

Upper School Student Profile Grade 9: 54 students (20 boys, 34 girls); Grade 10: 95 students (56 boys, 39 girls); Grade 11: 97 students (58 boys, 39 girls); Grade 12: 102 students (54 boys, 48 girls); Postgraduate: 16 students (14 boys, 2 girls). 80% of students are boarding students. 26% are state residents. 32 states are represented in upper school student body. 23% are international students. International students from Bermuda, Canada, China, Japan, Republic of Korea, and Taiwan; 11 other countries represented in student body.

Faculty School total: 62. In upper school: 33 men, 29 women; 34 have advanced degrees; 54 reside on campus.

Subjects Offered 3-dimensional design, acting, algebra, art, art history, astronomy, biology, biology-AP, calculus, calculus-AP, chemistry, chorus, community service, computer graphics, creative writing, dance, dance performance, digital photography, drama, driver education, ecology, environmental systems, economics, English, English language and composition-AP, English literature, English literature-AP, environmental science, ESL, filmmaking, French, geometry, jazz band, journalism, macroeconomics-AP, mathematics, media arts, music, music history, music technology, music theory, orchestra, physics, physics-AP, pottery, science, Spanish, statistics-AP, studio art, theater, U.S. history, U.S. history-AP, Web authoring, Web site design, wind ensemble, world history, writing.

Graduation Requirements English, foreign language, mathematics, science, social studies (includes history).

Special Academic Programs 9 Advanced Placement exams for which test preparation is offered; honors section; programs in English, mathematics, general development for dyslexic students; ESL (20 students enrolled).

College Admission Counseling 117 students graduated in 2011; 114 went to college, including Boston University; Hobart and William Smith Colleges; New York University; Northeastern University; Saint Michael's College; Susquehanna University. Other: 3 entered a postgraduate year. Median SAT critical reading: 500, median SAT math: 530, median SAT writing: 500, median combined SAT: 1560, median composite ACT: 22. 19% scored over 600 on SAT critical reading, 29% scored over 600 on SAT math, 15% scored over 600 on SAT writing, 17% scored over 1800 on combined SAT, 21% scored over 26 on composite ACT.

Student Life Upper grades have specified standards of dress, student council, honor system. Discipline rests primarily with faculty.

Summer Programs Enrichment, advancement, ESL, sports, art/fine arts, computer instruction programs offered; session focuses on humanities and math, study skills, technology in academics and the arts, outdoor adventure education; held on campus; accepts boys and girls; open to students from other schools. 60 students usually enrolled. 2012 schedule: June 23 to August 2. Application deadline: May 15.

Tuition and Aid Day student tuition: $27,985; 7-day tuition and room/board: $45,540. Tuition installment plan (FACTS Tuition Payment Plan, monthly payment plans). Need-based scholarship grants available. In 2011–12, 27% of upper-school students received aid. Total amount of financial aid awarded in 2011–12: $2,700,000.

Admissions Traditional secondary-level entrance grade is 9. For fall 2011, 531 students applied for upper-level admission, 297 were accepted, 146 enrolled. SSAT required. Deadline for receipt of application materials: February 1. Application fee required: $50. On-campus interview required.

Athletics Interscholastic: alpine skiing (boys, girls), baseball (b), basketball (b,g), crew (b,g), cross-country running (b,g), field hockey (g), ice hockey (b,g), lacrosse (b,g), running (b,g), skiing (downhill) (b,g), soccer (b,g), softball (g), tennis (b,g); coed interscholastic: golf, sailing, snowboarding; coed intramural: aerobics, alpine skiing, climbing, croquet, dance, equestrian sports, fitness, indoor soccer, outdoor skills, rock climbing, sailing, skiing (downhill), snowboarding, strength & conditioning, table tennis, tennis, touch football, ultimate Frisbee, wall climbing, weight training, yoga. 2 athletic trainers.

Computers Computers are regularly used in all classes. Computer network features include on-campus library services, online commercial services, Internet access, Internet filtering or blocking technology. Campus intranet, student e-mail accounts, and computer access in designated common areas are available to students. Students grades are available online. The school has a published electronic and media policy.

Contact Mary Roetger, Admission Coordinator. 603-569-7200. Fax: 603-569-7272. E-mail: mary_roetger@brewsteracademy.org. Web site: www.brewsteracademy.org.

BRIARCREST CHRISTIAN HIGH SCHOOL

76 S. Houston Levee Road

Eads, Tennessee 38028

Head of School: Mr. Eric Sullivan

General Information Coeducational day college-preparatory, arts, religious studies, and technology school, affiliated with Christian faith. Grades 9–12. Founded: 1973. Setting: suburban. Nearest major city is Memphis. 100-acre campus. 1 building on campus. Approved or accredited by Association of Christian Schools International, Southern Association of Colleges and Schools, Southern Association of Independent Schools, and Tennessee Department of Education. Total enrollment: 1,670. Upper school average class size: 18. Upper school faculty-student ratio: 1:14. There are 176 required school days per year for Upper School students. Upper School students typically attend 5 days per week. The average school day consists of 7 hours.

Upper School Student Profile Grade 9: 143 students (66 boys, 77 girls); Grade 10: 137 students (71 boys, 66 girls); Grade 11: 149 students (67 boys, 82 girls); Grade 12: 164 students (79 boys, 85 girls). 94% of students are Christian.

Faculty School total: 42. In upper school: 18 men, 24 women; 26 have advanced degrees.

Subjects Offered Algebra, American history, American literature, anatomy, art, Bible studies, biology, business, calculus, chemistry, computer math, computer programming, computer science, creative writing, drama, driver education, English, English literature, environmental science, European history, expository writing, French, geography, geometry, government/civics, grammar, health, history, Latin, mathematics, music, physical education, physics, physiology, psychology, religion, science, social sciences, social studies, sociology, Spanish, speech, theater, trigonometry, typing, world history, writing.

Graduation Requirements Arts and fine arts (art, music, dance, drama), business skills (includes word processing), English, foreign language, mathematics, physical education (includes health), religion (includes Bible studies and theology), science, social sciences, social studies (includes history).

Special Academic Programs Advanced Placement exam preparation; honors section; term-away projects; study at local college for college credit; academic accommodation for the gifted, the musically talented, and the artistically talented; programs in English, mathematics, general development for dyslexic students.

College Admission Counseling 129 students graduated in 2011; 122 went to college, including Mississippi State University; The University of Tennessee; The University of Tennessee at Chattanooga; University of Arkansas; University of Memphis; University of Mississippi. Other: 1 went to work, 5 entered military service, 1 had other specific plans. Median composite ACT: 25. 46% scored over 26 on composite ACT.

Student Life Upper grades have uniform requirement, student council, honor system. Discipline rests primarily with faculty. Attendance at religious services is required.

Tuition and Aid Day student tuition: $12,395. Tuition installment plan (Insured Tuition Payment Plan, monthly payment plans, individually arranged payment plans, 2-payment plan). Tuition reduction for siblings, need-based tuition assistance available. In 2011–12, 12% of upper-school students received aid.

Admissions Traditional secondary-level entrance grade is 9. For fall 2011, 110 students applied for upper-level admission, 100 were accepted, 56 enrolled. ISEE required. Deadline for receipt of application materials: none. Application fee required: $50. On-campus interview required.

Athletics Interscholastic: baseball (boys), basketball (b,g), cheering (g), cross-country running (b,g), drill team (g), football (b), golf (b,g), lacrosse (b,g), pom squad (g), soccer (b,g), softball (g), swimming and diving (b,g), tennis (b,g), track and field (b,g), trap and skeet (b,g), volleyball (g), weight lifting (b), wrestling (b); coed interscholastic: bowling, cross-country running, swimming and diving. 2 PE instructors.

Computers Computers are regularly used in accounting, art, English, history, journalism, keyboarding, lab/keyboard, language development, mathematics, newspaper, science, social sciences, social studies, Spanish, speech, yearbook classes. Computer network features include on-campus library services, Internet access, wireless campus network, Internet filtering or blocking technology. Campus intranet, student e-mail accounts, and computer access in designated common areas are available to students. Students grades are available online. The school has a published electronic and media policy.

Contact Mrs. Claire Foster, Admissions Coordinator. 901-765-4605. Fax: 901-765-4614. E-mail: cofoster@briarcrest.com. Web site: www.briarcrest.com.

BRIARWOOD CHRISTIAN HIGH SCHOOL

6255 Cahaba Valley Road

Birmingham, Alabama 35242

Head of School: Dr. Barrett Mosbacker

General Information Coeducational day college-preparatory, arts, and religious studies school, affiliated with Presbyterian Church in America. Grades K4–12. Founded: 1964. Setting: suburban. 85-acre campus. 5 buildings on campus. Approved or accredited by Association of Christian Schools International, Southern Association of Colleges and Schools, and Alabama Department of Education. Endowment: $500,000. Total enrollment: 1,970. Upper school average class size: 23. Upper school faculty-student ratio: 1:23. There are 177 required school days per year for Upper School students. Upper School students typically attend 5 days per week. The average school day consists of 6 hours and 10 minutes.

Upper School Student Profile Grade 9: 149 students (74 boys, 75 girls); Grade 10: 144 students (73 boys, 71 girls); Grade 11: 147 students (82 boys, 65 girls); Grade 12: 148 students (89 boys, 59 girls). 30% of students are Presbyterian Church in America.

Faculty School total: 125. In upper school: 30 men, 25 women; 35 have advanced degrees.

Subjects Offered Accounting, algebra, American history, American literature, art, band, Bible studies, biology, calculus, chemistry, community service, computer science, creative writing, debate, drama, driver education, economics, English, English literature, ethics, European history, French, geometry, government, grammar, health, history, mathematics, music, philosophy, photo shop, physical education, physics, psychology, religion, science, social sciences, social studies, Spanish, speech, trigonometry, world history, world literature.

Graduation Requirements 20th century history, business skills (includes word processing), computer science, English, foreign language, mathematics, physical education (includes health), religion (includes Bible studies and theology), science, social sciences, social studies (includes history). Community service is required.

Special Academic Programs Advanced Placement exam preparation; honors section; academic accommodation for the gifted; special instructional classes for students with learning disabilities, Attention Deficit Disorder.

College Admission Counseling 136 students graduated in 2011; all went to college, including Auburn University; Birmingham-Southern College; Samford University; The University of Alabama; Troy University; University of Mississippi. Mean combined SAT: 1183, mean composite ACT: 26.

Student Life Upper grades have specified standards of dress, student council. Discipline rests primarily with faculty. Attendance at religious services is required.

Summer Programs Remediation, advancement programs offered; session focuses on social studies and mathematics; held on campus; accepts boys and girls; not open to students from other schools. 50 students usually enrolled. 2012 schedule: June 11 to July 28. Application deadline: March 1.

Tuition and Aid Day student tuition: $6600. Tuition installment plan (monthly payment plans). Tuition reduction for siblings available. In 2011–12, 3% of upper-school students received aid. Total amount of financial aid awarded in 2011–12: $5000.

Admissions Traditional secondary-level entrance grade is 9. For fall 2011, 86 students applied for upper-level admission, 49 were accepted, 43 enrolled. SSAT required. Deadline for receipt of application materials: none. Application fee required: $75. On-campus interview required.

Athletics Interscholastic: baseball (boys), basketball (b,g), cheering (g), cross-country running (b,g), dance team (g), football (b), golf (b,g), indoor track (b,g), indoor track & field (b,g), outdoor activities (b,g), physical fitness (b,g), soccer (b,g), softball (g), strength & conditioning (b), swimming and diving (b,g), tennis (b,g), track and field (b,g), volleyball (g). 5 PE instructors, 15 coaches, 1 athletic trainer.

Computers Computers are regularly used in computer applications classes. Computer network features include on-campus library services, online commercial services, Internet access. Students grades are available online.

Contact Mrs. Kelly McCarthy Mooney, Director of Admissions. 205-776-5812. Fax: 205-776-5816. E-mail: kmooney@bcsk12.org. Web site: www.bcsk12.org.

BRIDGEMONT HIGH SCHOOL

444 East Market Street

Daly City, California 94014

Head of School: Mr. Peter Tropper

General Information Coeducational day college-preparatory, arts, religious studies, and technology school, affiliated with Christian faith. Grades 9–12. Founded: 1973. Setting: urban. Nearest major city is San Francisco. 1-acre campus. 3 buildings on campus. Approved or accredited by Association of Christian Schools International and Western Association of Schools and Colleges. Total enrollment: 40. Upper school average class size: 10. Upper school faculty-student ratio: 1:4. There are 176 required school days per year for Upper School students. Upper School students typically attend 5 days per week. The average school day consists of 6 hours and 25 minutes.

Upper School Student Profile Grade 9: 9 students (3 boys, 6 girls); Grade 10: 7 students (2 boys, 5 girls); Grade 11: 12 students (5 boys, 7 girls); Grade 12: 12 students (6 boys, 6 girls). 50% of students are Christian faith.

Faculty School total: 10. In upper school: 6 men, 3 women; 2 have advanced degrees.

Subjects Offered Advanced math, algebra, American history, American literature, art, arts, Bible studies, biology, calculus, chemistry, creative writing, drama, earth science, economics, English, English literature, European history, expository writing, fine arts, French, French as a second language, geography, geometry, government/civics, grammar, health, history, mathematics, music, physical education, physics, religion, science, social sciences, social studies, Spanish, study skills, theater, trigonometry, U.S. history, world history, world literature, writing, yearbook.

Graduation Requirements Arts and fine arts (art, music, dance, drama), English, foreign language, mathematics, physical education (includes health), religion (includes Bible studies and theology), science, social sciences, social studies (includes history), field studies.

Special Academic Programs Independent study.

College Admission Counseling 15 students graduated in 2011; all went to college, including California State University, Los Angeles; City College of San Francisco; San Francisco State University; San Jose State University; University of California, Davis; University of California, Irvine.

Student Life Upper grades have specified standards of dress, student council, honor system. Discipline rests primarily with faculty. Attendance at religious services is required.

Summer Programs Sports programs offered; session focuses on baseball and basketball; held both on and off campus; held at nearby gym and playing fields; accepts boys and girls; open to students from other schools. 25 students usually enrolled. 2012 schedule: June 20 to August 20. Application deadline: none.

Tuition and Aid Day student tuition: $10,800. Tuition installment plan (FACTS Tuition Payment Plan, monthly payment plans, Tuition Management Systems Plan). Tuition reduction for siblings, need-based scholarship grants available. In 2011–12, 90% of upper-school students received aid. Total amount of financial aid awarded in 2011–12: $108,660.

Admissions Traditional secondary-level entrance grade is 9. For fall 2011, 12 students applied for upper-level admission, 10 were accepted, 9 enrolled. Essay, math and English placement tests and writing sample required. Deadline for receipt of application materials: none. Application fee required: $60. On-campus interview required.

Athletics Interscholastic: baseball (boys, girls), basketball (b,g), flag football (b), soccer (b), softball (g), volleyball (g); intramural: basketball (b,g), flag football (b,g), weight lifting (b); coed intramural: flag football, floor hockey, football, judo, jump rope, physical training, volleyball. 1 PE instructor, 4 coaches.

Computers Computers are regularly used in yearbook classes. Computer resources include Internet access, wireless campus network, Internet filtering or blocking technology, independent study courses through Acellus and NovelStar. Computer access in designated common areas is available to students. Students grades are available online.

Contact Ms. Janelle Tropper, Director of Student Development. 650-746-2522. Fax: 650-746-2529. E-mail: admissions@bridgemont.org. Web site: www.bridgemont.org.

BRIDGES ACADEMY

Studio City, California

See Special Needs Schools section.

BRIMMER AND MAY SCHOOL

69 Middlesex Road

Chestnut Hill, Massachusetts 02467

Head of School: Anne Reenstierna

General Information Coeducational day college-preparatory, arts, technology, Creative Arts Diploma Program, and Global Studies Diploma Program school. Grades PK–12. Founded: 1880. Setting: suburban. Nearest major city is Boston. 7-acre campus. 7 buildings on campus. Approved or accredited by Association of Independent Schools in New England and New England Association of Schools and Colleges. Member of National Association of Independent Schools and Secondary School Admission Test Board. Total enrollment: 393. Upper school average class size: 12. Upper school faculty-student ratio: 1:6. There are 175 required school days per year for Upper School students. Upper School students typically attend 5 days per week. The average school day consists of 7 hours and 10 minutes.

Upper School Student Profile Grade 9: 27 students (15 boys, 12 girls); Grade 10: 36 students (15 boys, 21 girls); Grade 11: 35 students (17 boys, 18 girls); Grade 12: 30 students (9 boys, 21 girls).

Faculty School total: 68. In upper school: 15 men, 19 women; 24 have advanced degrees.

Subjects Offered Acting, adolescent issues, Advanced Placement courses, advanced studio art-AP, algebra, American history, American literature, art, biology, biology-AP, calculus, ceramics, chamber groups, chemistry, chorus, college counseling, community service, computer education, creative arts, creative writing, desktop publishing, drama, economics, economics-AP, English, English literature, English literature-AP, ESL, European history, expository writing, fine arts, French, geometry, grammar, health, health education, history, humanities, Internet research, mathematics, music, music theory, newspaper, participation in sports, performing arts, photography, physical education, physical science, physics, psychology, social studies, Spanish, theater, trigonometry, typing, U.S. history, video film production, world history, world literature, writing, yearbook.

Graduation Requirements Creative arts, English, foreign language, history, mathematics, physical education (includes health), science, technology, Senior Independent project, Senior Thesis Defense, Creative Art Diploma Program (optional). Community service is required.

Special Academic Programs 13 Advanced Placement exams for which test preparation is offered; honors section; independent study; study at local college for college credit; ESL (13 students enrolled).

College Admission Counseling 32 students graduated in 2011; all went to college, including Brown University; Connecticut College; Fordham University; Syracuse University; Wellesley College.

Student Life Upper grades have specified standards of dress, student council, honor system. Discipline rests equally with students and faculty.

Tuition and Aid Day student tuition: $36,850. Tuition installment plan (FACTS Tuition Payment Plan, monthly payment plans). Need-based scholarship grants available. In 2011–12, 43% of upper-school students received aid. Total amount of financial aid awarded in 2011–12: $1,467,825.

Admissions Traditional secondary-level entrance grade is 9. For fall 2011, 104 students applied for upper-level admission, 62 were accepted, 25 enrolled. ISEE, SSAT or TOEFL or SLEP required. Deadline for receipt of application materials: January 15. Application fee required: $50. On-campus interview required.

Athletics Interscholastic: baseball (boys), basketball (b,g), field hockey (g), lacrosse (b,g), soccer (b,g), softball (g), tennis (b,g); coed interscholastic: cross-country running, curling, golf; coed intramural: alpine skiing, fitness, outdoor education, physical fitness, skiing (downhill), snowboarding, strength & conditioning, tennis, weight training. 3 PE instructors, 20 coaches, 2 athletic trainers.

Computers Computers are regularly used in desktop publishing, foreign language, graphic design, humanities, journalism, media production, technology, typing, video film production, Web site design, yearbook classes. Computer network features include on-campus library services, online commercial services, Internet access, wireless campus network, Internet filtering or blocking technology. Campus intranet, student e-mail accounts, and computer access in designated common areas are available to students. Students grades are available online. The school has a published electronic and media policy.

Contact Myra Korin, Admissions Coordinator. 617-738-8695. Fax: 617-734-5147. E-mail: admissions@brimmer.org. Web site: www.brimmerandmay.org.

BROOKS SCHOOL

1160 Great Pond Road

North Andover, Massachusetts 01845-1298

Head of School: Mr. John R. Packard

General Information Coeducational boarding and day college-preparatory school, affiliated with Episcopal Church. Grades 9–12. Founded: 1926. Setting: suburban. Nearest major city is Boston. Students are housed in single-sex dormitories. 251-acre campus. 39 buildings on campus. Approved or accredited by Association of Independent Schools in New England, National Association of Episcopal Schools, New England Association of Schools and Colleges, The Association of Boarding Schools, and Massachusetts Department of Education. Member of National Association of Independent Schools and Secondary School Admission Test Board. Endowment: $58.7 million. Total enrollment: 371. Upper school average class size: 12. Upper school faculty-student ratio: 1:5. There are 180 required school days per year for Upper School students. Upper School students typically attend 5 days per week. The average school day consists of 7 hours.

Upper School Student Profile Grade 9: 73 students (36 boys, 37 girls); Grade 10: 107 students (53 boys, 54 girls); Grade 11: 103 students (60 boys, 43 girls); Grade 12: 89 students (49 boys, 40 girls). 70% of students are boarding students. 60% are state residents. 23 states are represented in upper school student body. 15% are international

students. International students from Canada, China, Hong Kong, Nigeria, Republic of Korea, and Thailand; 13 other countries represented in student body.
Faculty School total: 77. In upper school: 42 men, 35 women; 61 have advanced degrees; 47 reside on campus.
Subjects Offered Algebra, American history, American history-AP, American literature, art history, art history-AP, astronomy, Bible studies, biology, biology-AP, calculus, calculus-AP, ceramics, chemistry, chemistry-AP, Chinese, chorus, computer math, creative writing, drama, driver education, earth science, English, English literature, English-AP, environmental science-AP, ethics, European history, expository writing, film, fine arts, French, French language-AP, French literature-AP, French-AP, geometry, government and politics-AP, grammar, Greek, health, history, history-AP, honors algebra, honors geometry, honors world history, integrated arts, journalism, Latin, Latin-AP, life skills, Mandarin, mathematics, Middle East, music, music theory, painting, photography, physics, physics-AP, playwriting, poetry, psychology, public speaking, religion, rhetoric, robotics, senior project, senior seminar, Southern literature, Spanish, Spanish language-AP, Spanish literature, Spanish literature-AP, Spanish-AP, statistics, studio art, theater, theater design and production, theology, trigonometry, U.S. government and politics-AP, visual arts, world history, world history-AP, world literature, writing.
Graduation Requirements Arts and fine arts (art, music, dance, drama), English, foreign language, health, history, mathematics, religion (includes Bible studies and theology), science. Community service is required.
Special Academic Programs 14 Advanced Placement exams for which test preparation is offered; honors section; independent study; term-away projects; study abroad.
College Admission Counseling 91 students graduated in 2011; all went to college, including Boston University; Bowdoin College; Connecticut College; Massachusetts Institute of Technology; Tufts University; Tulane University. Mean SAT critical reading: 615, mean SAT math: 640, mean SAT writing: 615, mean composite ACT: 27.
Student Life Upper grades have specified standards of dress, student council. Discipline rests primarily with faculty. Attendance at religious services is required.
Summer Programs Enrichment, advancement, sports, computer instruction programs offered; session focuses on English, mathematics, and SAT preparation; held on campus; accepts boys and girls; open to students from other schools. 70 students usually enrolled. 2012 schedule: June 28 to August 20. Application deadline: none.
Tuition and Aid Day student tuition: $35,575; 7-day tuition and room/board: $47,555. Tuition installment plan (Academic Management Services Plan, individually arranged payment plans). Need-based scholarship grants available. In 2011–12, 22% of upper-school students received aid. Total amount of financial aid awarded in 2011–12: $2,600,000.
Admissions Traditional secondary-level entrance grade is 9. For fall 2011, 1,015 students applied for upper-level admission, 269 were accepted, 113 enrolled. ISEE, SSAT, ERB, PSAT, SAT, PLAN or ACT or TOEFL required. Deadline for receipt of application materials: February 1. Application fee required: $50. Interview required.
Athletics Interscholastic: baseball (boys), basketball (b,g), crew (b,g), cross-country running (b,g), field hockey (g), football (b), golf (b,g), hockey (b,g), ice hockey (b,g), lacrosse (b,g), soccer (b,g), softball (g), squash (b,g), tennis (b,g), wrestling (b); coed intramural: dance, fitness, sailing, skiing (downhill). 1 athletic trainer.
Computers Computers are regularly used in all academic classes. Computer network features include on-campus library services, online commercial services, Internet access, wireless campus network, Internet filtering or blocking technology. Campus intranet, student e-mail accounts, and computer access in designated common areas are available to students. Students grades are available online. The school has a published electronic and media policy.
Contact Mr. Andrew C. Hirt, Director of Admission. 978-725-6272. Fax: 978-725-6298. E-mail: admission@brooksschool.org. Web site: www.brooksschool.org.

BROOKSTONE SCHOOL

440 Bradley Park Drive

Columbus, Georgia 31904

Head of School: Brian D. Kennerly

General Information Coeducational day college-preparatory school. Grades PK–12. Founded: 1951. Setting: suburban. Nearest major city is Atlanta. 112-acre campus. 11 buildings on campus. Approved or accredited by Georgia Independent School Association, Southern Association of Colleges and Schools, Southern Association of Independent Schools, and Georgia Department of Education. Member of National Association of Independent Schools. Endowment: $20.1 million. Total enrollment: 789. Upper school average class size: 14. Upper school faculty-student ratio: 1:10. There are 176 required school days per year for Upper School students. Upper School students typically attend 5 days per week. The average school day consists of 5 hours and 20 minutes.
Upper School Student Profile Grade 9: 87 students (43 boys, 44 girls); Grade 10: 75 students (41 boys, 34 girls); Grade 11: 67 students (34 boys, 33 girls); Grade 12: 49 students (23 boys, 26 girls).
Faculty School total: 80. In upper school: 13 men, 15 women; 19 have advanced degrees.
Subjects Offered Advanced computer applications, Advanced Placement courses, algebra, American Civil War, American government, American history, American history-AP, American literature, anatomy and physiology, art, art-AP, band, biology, biology-AP, calculus, calculus-AP, chemistry, chemistry-AP, choral music, chorus, Civil War, communications, comparative government and politics-AP, comparative religion, computer applications, computer multimedia, computer programming, computer science, computers, concert band, concert choir, constitutional law, creative writing, drama, ecology, economics, economics-AP, English, English composition, English literature, English literature and composition-AP, European history, European history-AP, fine arts, French, French language-AP, French-AP, geometry, government and politics-AP, graphic design, health, history-AP, honors algebra, honors English, honors geometry, human geography - AP, humanities, Latin, Latin-AP, law, literature and composition-AP, literature-AP, macro/microeconomics-AP, marine biology, mathematics, mythology, neuroanatomy, ornithology, physical education, physics, pre-calculus, psychology, science, social sciences, social studies, Spanish, Spanish language-AP, Spanish-AP, statistics, statistics-AP, studio art-AP, theater, trigonometry, U.S. government, U.S. government and politics-AP, U.S. history, U.S. history-AP, weight training, world history, yearbook, zoology.
Graduation Requirements Algebra, American government, American history, arts and fine arts (art, music, dance, drama), biology, chemistry, computer science, economics, electives, English, foreign language, geometry, mathematics, physical education (includes health), science, social sciences, social studies (includes history), speech, world history, senior year speech.
Special Academic Programs 15 Advanced Placement exams for which test preparation is offered; honors section.
College Admission Counseling 72 students graduated in 2011; all went to college, including Auburn University; Columbus State University; Furman University; Samford University; The University of Alabama; University of Georgia. Median SAT critical reading: 620, median SAT math: 610, median SAT writing: 600, median combined SAT: 1820. 49% scored over 600 on SAT critical reading, 51% scored over 600 on SAT math, 47% scored over 600 on SAT writing, 51% scored over 1800 on combined SAT.
Student Life Upper grades have specified standards of dress, student council, honor system. Discipline rests equally with students and faculty.
Tuition and Aid Day student tuition: $13,985. Tuition installment plan (monthly payment plans, individually arranged payment plans, 3 payments in months July, October and January (no interest)). Tuition reduction for siblings, merit scholarship grants, need-based scholarship grants, need-based loans, middle income loans available. In 2011–12, 16% of upper-school students received aid; total upper-school merit-scholarship money awarded: $313,530. Total amount of financial aid awarded in 2011–12: $341,100.
Admissions Traditional secondary-level entrance grade is 9. For fall 2011, 87 students applied for upper-level admission, 68 were accepted, 40 enrolled. Otis-Lennon IQ Test or SSAT, ERB, PSAT, SAT, PLAN or ACT required. Deadline for receipt of application materials: none. Application fee required: $50. Interview required.
Athletics Interscholastic: baseball (boys), basketball (b,g), cheering (g), cross-country running (b,g), football (b), golf (b,g), soccer (b,g), softball (g), tennis (b,g), track and field (b,g), volleyball (g), wrestling (b); intramural: basketball (b,g). 6 PE instructors.
Computers Computers are regularly used in college planning, computer applications, creative writing, English, foreign language, French, geography, graphic arts, graphic design, history, human geography - AP, information technology, mathematics, media production, programming, publications, science, social studies, Spanish, video film production, Web site design, yearbook classes. Computer network features include on-campus library services, online commercial services, Internet access, wireless campus network, Internet filtering or blocking technology. Campus intranet and student e-mail accounts are available to students. Students grades are available online. The school has a published electronic and media policy.
Contact Mary S. Snyder, Enrollment Director. 706-324-1392. Fax: 706-571-0178. E-mail: msnyder@brookstoneschool.org. Web site: www.brookstoneschool.org.

BROPHY COLLEGE PREPARATORY

4701 North Central Avenue

Phoenix, Arizona 85012-1797

Head of School: Mr. Robert E. Ryan III

General Information Boys' day college-preparatory, arts, religious studies, and technology school, affiliated with Roman Catholic Church (Jesuit order). Grades 9–12. Founded: 1928. Setting: urban. 38-acre campus. 8 buildings on campus. Approved or accredited by Jesuit Secondary Education Association, National Catholic Education Association, and Western Catholic Education Association. Endowment: $19 million. Total enrollment: 1,322. Upper school average class size: 24. Upper school faculty-student ratio: 1:15. There are 178 required school days per year for Upper School students. Upper School students typically attend 5 days per week. The average school day consists of 6 hours and 40 minutes.
Upper School Student Profile Grade 9: 343 students (343 boys); Grade 10: 325 students (325 boys); Grade 11: 321 students (321 boys); Grade 12: 301 students (301 boys). 64% of students are Roman Catholic Church (Jesuit order).
Faculty School total: 94. In upper school: 66 men, 22 women; 76 have advanced degrees.
Subjects Offered Advanced Placement courses, advanced studio art-AP, algebra, American history, American literature, anatomy, art, Bible studies, biology, business,

calculus, chemistry, community service, computer math, computer programming, computer science, creative writing, drama, earth science, economics, engineering, English, English literature, ethics, European history, expository writing, fine arts, French, geography, geometry, government/civics, health, history, Latin, mathematics, mechanical drawing, music, physical education, physics, probability and statistics, psychology, religion, science, social sciences, social studies, sociology, Spanish, speech, theater, theology, trigonometry, video film production, world history, world literature.

Graduation Requirements Arts and fine arts (art, music, dance, drama), English, foreign language, mathematics, physical education (includes health), religion (includes Bible studies and theology), science, social studies (includes history). Community service is required.

Special Academic Programs Advanced Placement exam preparation; honors section; study at local college for college credit; study abroad.

College Admission Counseling 278 students graduated in 2011; all went to college, including Arizona State University; Gonzaga University; Loyola Marymount University; Saint Louis University; Seattle University; The University of Arizona. Median SAT critical reading: 585, median SAT math: 606, median SAT writing: 576, median combined SAT: 1767, median composite ACT: 26.

Student Life Upper grades have specified standards of dress, student council, honor system. Discipline rests primarily with faculty. Attendance at religious services is required.

Summer Programs Enrichment, advancement, sports, art/fine arts, computer instruction programs offered; session focuses on academic skills and sports; held both on and off campus; held at Manresa Retreat (Sedona, AZ), Brophy East Campus, and Brophy Sports Campus; accepts boys and girls; open to students from other schools. 1,300 students usually enrolled. 2012 schedule: June 1 to July 2. Application deadline: May 28.

Tuition and Aid Day student tuition: $12,800. Tuition installment plan (The Tuition Plan, monthly payment plans, individually arranged payment plans). Need-based scholarship grants, paying campus jobs available. In 2011–12, 29% of upper-school students received aid. Total amount of financial aid awarded in 2011–12: $2,241,937.

Admissions Traditional secondary-level entrance grade is 9. For fall 2011, 630 students applied for upper-level admission, 382 were accepted, 343 enrolled. STS required. Deadline for receipt of application materials: January 29. Application fee required: $50. On-campus interview required.

Athletics Interscholastic: aquatics, baseball, basketball, cross-country running, diving, flagball, football, golf, ice hockey, lacrosse, soccer, swimming and diving, tennis, track and field, volleyball, wrestling; intramural: aquatics, badminton, baseball, basketball, bicycling, bowling, cheering, climbing, crew, cricket, fishing, fitness, flag football, Frisbee, golf, handball, hockey, ice hockey, lacrosse, mountain biking, outdoor activities, physical fitness, physical training, rock climbing, skiing (downhill), softball, strength & conditioning, table tennis, touch football, ultimate Frisbee, volleyball, wall climbing, water polo, weight lifting, weight training. 2 PE instructors, 15 coaches, 2 athletic trainers.

Computers Computers are regularly used in all academic classes. Computer network features include on-campus library services, online commercial services, Internet access, wireless campus network, Blackboard, computer tablets. Student e-mail accounts are available to students. Students grades are available online. The school has a published electronic and media policy.

Contact Ms. Alana Dorsey, Assistant to Director of Admissions. 602-264-5291 Ext. 6233. Fax: 602-234-1669. E-mail: adorsey@brophyprep.org. Web site: www.brophyprep.org/.

BROTHER RICE HIGH SCHOOL

10001 South Pulaski Road

Chicago, Illinois 60655

Head of School: Mr. James P. Antos

General Information Boys' day college-preparatory school, affiliated with Roman Catholic Church. Grades 9–12. Founded: 1956. Setting: urban. 23-acre campus. 1 building on campus. Approved or accredited by North Central Association of Colleges and Schools and Illinois Department of Education. Total enrollment: 900. Upper school average class size: 30. Upper school faculty-student ratio: 1:15. There are 183 required school days per year for Upper School students. Upper School students typically attend 5 days per week. The average school day consists of 6 hours and 45 minutes.

Upper School Student Profile Grade 9: 245 students (245 boys); Grade 10: 231 students (231 boys); Grade 11: 225 students (225 boys); Grade 12: 200 students (200 boys). 75% of students are Roman Catholic.

Faculty School total: 75. In upper school: 35 men, 40 women; 40 have advanced degrees.

Subjects Offered 20th century history, 20th century physics, 20th century world history, accounting, ACT preparation, acting, advanced biology, advanced chemistry, advanced computer applications, advanced math, Advanced Placement courses, algebra, American Civil War, American democracy, American government, American history, American history-AP, American literature, American literature-AP, American studies, analytic geometry, anatomy and physiology, ancient history, ancient world history, art, astronomy, athletics, band, baseball, Basic programming, basic skills, basketball, Bible studies, biology, biology-AP, bowling, business law, calculus, calculus-AP, campus ministry, career and personal planning, career exploration, career planning, career/college preparation, careers, Catholic belief and practice, cell biology, chemistry, chemistry-AP, Christian education, civil war history, classical civilization, college admission preparation, college awareness, college counseling, college placement, college planning, college writing, community service, comparative government and politics, comparative government and politics-AP, comparative political systems-AP, composition, composition-AP, computer education, computer information systems, computer skills, concert band, constitutional history of U.S., developmental math, drama, drawing and design, driver education, economics, electives, English, English composition, English language and composition-AP, English language-AP, English literature, English literature and composition-AP, English literature-AP, English-AP, English/composition-AP, equality and freedom, fine arts, foreign language, French, general math, general science, geography, geometry, German, government, guidance, health education, history-AP, honors algebra, honors English, honors geometry, honors U.S. history, honors world history, journalism, language, language and composition, language arts, language-AP, languages, library, library assistant, library research, literature and composition-AP, logic, macro/microeconomics-AP, macroeconomics-AP, marching band, math analysis, math applications, math methods, math review, mathematics, mathematics-AP, Microsoft, participation in sports, performing arts, photography, physical education, physics, physics-AP, pre-algebra, pre-calculus, pre-college orientation, psychology, public service, publications, reading/study skills, religion, religious education, religious studies, remedial/makeup course work, science, social studies, Spanish, Spanish language-AP, Spanish-AP, student government, student publications, student teaching, swimming, swimming competency, swimming test, tennis, theater arts, track and field, trigonometry, U.S. government, U.S. government and politics, U.S. government and politics-AP, U.S. history, U.S. history-AP, Vietnam, Vietnam history, Vietnam War, volleyball, water polo, Western civilization, world civilizations, world cultures, world geography, world governments, world history, world history-AP, World War II, wrestling, yearbook.

Graduation Requirements 1 1/2 elective credits, 20th century history, algebra, American government, American history, ancient world history, biology, chemistry, Christian studies, civil war history, classical civilization, composition, computer literacy, constitutional history of U.S., electives, English, English composition, English literature, foreign language, general science, geometry, government, health education, history, intro to computers, language arts, mathematics, physical education (includes health), physical science, religious education, U.S. constitutional history, U.S. history, Western civilization, service hours required for all students.

Special Academic Programs 10 Advanced Placement exams for which test preparation is offered; honors section; study at local college for college credit; academic accommodation for the gifted; remedial reading and/or remedial writing; remedial math; programs in English, mathematics, general development for dyslexic students.

College Admission Counseling 278 students graduated in 2010; 256 went to college, including Eastern Illinois University; Illinois State University; Saint Xavier University; University of Illinois at Chicago; University of Illinois at Urbana–Champaign; Western Illinois University. Other: 10 went to work, 2 entered military service, 10 had other specific plans.

Student Life Upper grades have specified standards of dress, student council, honor system. Discipline rests primarily with faculty. Attendance at religious services is required.

Tuition and Aid Day student tuition: $9000. Tuition installment plan (monthly payment plans). Merit scholarship grants, need-based scholarship grants, need-based loans available. In 2010–11, 11% of upper-school students received aid; total upper-school merit-scholarship money awarded: $18,000. Total amount of financial aid awarded in 2010–11: $782,000.

Admissions Traditional secondary-level entrance grade is 9. For fall 2010, 1,000 students applied for upper-level admission, 900 were accepted, 900 enrolled. High School Placement Test (closed version) from Scholastic Testing Service required. Deadline for receipt of application materials: none. Application fee required: $200.

Athletics Interscholastic: baseball, basketball, bowling, cross-country running, fishing, football, golf, hockey, ice hockey, indoor track & field, lacrosse, rugby, soccer, swimming and diving, tennis, track and field, volleyball, water polo, wrestling. 3 PE instructors, 50 coaches, 1 athletic trainer.

Computers Computers are regularly used in all academic classes. Computer network features include on-campus library services, online commercial services, Internet access, Internet filtering or blocking technology. Campus intranet and student e-mail accounts are available to students. Students grades are available online. The school has a published electronic and media policy.

Contact Mr. Tim O'Connell, Recruitment Director. 773-429-4312. Fax: 773-779-5239. E-mail: tlyons@brrice.org. Web site: www.brrice.org.

BROTHER RICE HIGH SCHOOL

7101 Lahser Road

Bloomfield Hills, Michigan 48301

Head of School: Mr. John Birney

General Information Boys' day college-preparatory, arts, business, religious studies, and technology school, affiliated with Roman Catholic Church. Grades 9–12. Founded: 1960. Setting: suburban. Nearest major city is Detroit. 20-acre campus. 1 building on campus. Approved or accredited by North Central Association of Colleges and Schools and Michigan Department of Education. Total enrollment: 674. Upper school average class size: 22. Upper school faculty-student ratio: 1:13. Upper School students typically attend 5 days per week. The average school day consists of 6 hours and 51 minutes.

Upper School Student Profile Grade 9: 184 students (184 boys); Grade 10: 170 students (170 boys); Grade 11: 172 students (172 boys); Grade 12: 147 students (147 boys). 75% of students are Roman Catholic.

Faculty School total: 60. In upper school: 32 men, 10 women; 36 have advanced degrees.

Subjects Offered 20th century world history, accounting, algebra, American government, anatomy, anthropology, architectural drawing, art, band, biology, biology-AP, business law, calculus, calculus-AP, chemistry, Chinese, choir, church history, computer science, computer science-AP, computers, concert band, creative writing, death and loss, debate, drama, earth science, economics, electronics, engineering, English, English composition, English language-AP, ensembles, European history, family living, forensics, French, French-AP, geometry, German, global science, health, jazz band, Latin, library science, literature, mathematics, mechanical drawing, music, music history, music theory, organic chemistry, photography, photojournalism, physical education, physics, physiology, pre-calculus, probability and statistics, psychology, social justice, Spanish, Spanish-AP, speech, studio art-AP, theology, trigonometry, U.S. government and politics-AP, U.S. history, U.S. history-AP, Western civilization, world geography, world religions.

Graduation Requirements Computer science, electives, English, foreign language, mathematics, physical education (includes health), science, social studies (includes history), speech, theology.

Special Academic Programs Advanced Placement exam preparation; honors section; remedial reading and/or remedial writing; remedial math.

College Admission Counseling 174 students graduated in 2011; 173 went to college, including Central Michigan University; Michigan State University; University of Michigan. Median combined SAT: 1800, median composite ACT: 25.

Student Life Upper grades have specified standards of dress, student council, honor system. Discipline rests primarily with faculty. Attendance at religious services is required.

Summer Programs Remediation, enrichment, art/fine arts programs offered; session focuses on camps and enrichment; held on campus; accepts boys and girls; open to students from other schools. 400 students usually enrolled. 2012 schedule: June to August.

Tuition and Aid Day student tuition: $10,350. Tuition installment plan (The Tuition Plan, monthly payment plans, individually arranged payment plans). Tuition reduction for siblings, merit scholarship grants, need-based scholarship grants available. In 2011–12, 20% of upper-school students received aid; total upper-school merit-scholarship money awarded: $600,000. Total amount of financial aid awarded in 2011–12: $900,000.

Admissions Traditional secondary-level entrance grade is 9. For fall 2011, 465 students applied for upper-level admission, 265 were accepted, 184 enrolled. SAS, STS-HSPT required. Deadline for receipt of application materials: none. No application fee required. Interview required.

Athletics Interscholastic: alpine skiing, baseball, basketball, bowling, cross-country running, diving, football, golf, hockey, ice hockey, lacrosse, skiing (downhill), soccer, swimming and diving, tennis, track and field, wrestling; intramural: basketball, bowling, drill team, fitness, football, golf, ice hockey, paint ball, rugby, skiing (downhill), snowboarding, strength & conditioning, touch football, ultimate Frisbee, winter (indoor) track. 50 coaches, 1 athletic trainer.

Computers Computer resources include online commercial services, Internet access. The school has a published electronic and media policy.

Contact Mr. David D. Sofran, Director of Admissions. 248-647-2526 Ext. 123. Fax: 248-647-2532. E-mail: sofran@brrice.edu.

THE BROWNING SCHOOL

52 East 62nd Street

New York, New York 10065

Head of School: Stephen M. Clement III

General Information Boys' day college-preparatory school. Grades K–12. Founded: 1888. Setting: urban. 2 buildings on campus. Approved or accredited by New York State Association of Independent Schools. Member of National Association of Independent Schools and Secondary School Admission Test Board. Endowment: $30 million. Total enrollment: 408. Upper school average class size: 15. Upper school faculty-student ratio: 1:4. Upper School students typically attend 5 days per week. The average school day consists of 6 hours and 54 minutes.

Upper School Student Profile Grade 9: 28 students (28 boys); Grade 10: 30 students (30 boys); Grade 11: 27 students (27 boys); Grade 12: 28 students (28 boys).

Faculty School total: 59. In upper school: 21 men, 13 women; 33 have advanced degrees.

Subjects Offered Adolescent issues, advanced biology, advanced chemistry, advanced math, Advanced Placement courses, advanced studio art-AP, African drumming, algebra, American history, American history-AP, American literature, American literature-AP, anatomy and physiology, Ancient Greek, ancient world history, applied arts, applied music, art, art history, athletics, baseball, basketball, bell choir, biology, biology-AP, calculus, calculus-AP, ceramics, chemistry, chemistry-AP, chorus, college admission preparation, computer math, computer music, computer programming, computer science, drama, dramatic arts, English, English literature, English-AP, environmental science, environmental studies, ethics, European history, European history-AP, expository writing, fencing, filmmaking, fine arts, French, French language-AP, general science, geography, geometry, golf, government/civics, grammar, Greek, handbells, health, history, instruments, jazz ensemble, language arts, Latin, Latin-AP, mathematics, medieval/Renaissance history, mentorship program, model United Nations, music, peer counseling, philosophy, physical education, physics, physics-AP, political science, public speaking, science, senior project, social sciences, social studies, Spanish, Spanish language-AP, squash, statistics, technology, tennis, theater, track and field, trigonometry, U.S. history-AP, video film production, visual arts, wrestling, yearbook.

Graduation Requirements Arts and fine arts (art, music, dance, drama), computer science, English, foreign language, mathematics, physical education (includes health), public speaking, science, social sciences, social studies (includes history), senior community service project.

Special Academic Programs Advanced Placement exam preparation; honors section; independent study; academic accommodation for the gifted and the musically talented.

College Admission Counseling 25 students graduated in 2011; all went to college, including Cornell University; Dartmouth College; Georgetown University; University of Virginia; Williams College; Yale University. Median SAT critical reading: 636, median SAT math: 654, median SAT writing: 664, median combined SAT: 1954, median composite ACT: 27. 71% scored over 600 on SAT critical reading, 71% scored over 600 on SAT math, 83% scored over 600 on SAT writing, 75% scored over 1800 on combined SAT, 57% scored over 26 on composite ACT.

Student Life Upper grades have specified standards of dress, student council, honor system. Discipline rests primarily with faculty.

Tuition and Aid Day student tuition: $38,280. Tuition installment plan (Key Tuition Payment Plan). Need-based scholarship grants available. In 2011–12, 32% of upper-school students received aid. Total amount of financial aid awarded in 2011–12: $953,900.

Admissions Traditional secondary-level entrance grade is 9. For fall 2011, 72 students applied for upper-level admission, 26 were accepted, 9 enrolled. ERB, ISEE and SSAT required. Deadline for receipt of application materials: January 15. Application fee required: $50. On-campus interview required.

Athletics Interscholastic: baseball, basketball, soccer, tennis; intramural: basketball, cross-country running, ice hockey, soccer, softball, tai chi; coed intramural: fencing. 4 PE instructors, 6 coaches.

Computers Computers are regularly used in English, foreign language, history, mathematics, music technology, science, video film production classes. Computer network features include on-campus library services, online commercial services, Internet access, wireless campus network. Student e-mail accounts are available to students. The school has a published electronic and media policy.

Contact Liane Pei, Director of Admissions. 212-838-6280. Fax: 212-355-5602. E-mail: lpei@browning.edu. Web site: www.browning.edu.

BRUNSWICK SCHOOL

100 Maher Avenue

Greenwich, Connecticut 06830

Head of School: Thomas W. Philip

General Information Boys' day college-preparatory school. Grades PK–12. Founded: 1902. Setting: suburban. Nearest major city is New York, NY. 118-acre campus. 4 buildings on campus. Approved or accredited by New England Association of Schools and Colleges and Connecticut Department of Education. Member of National Association of Independent Schools. Endowment: $85 million. Total enrollment: 939. Upper school average class size: 15. Upper school faculty-student ratio: 1:5. The average school day consists of 9 hours and 30 minutes.

Upper School Student Profile Grade 9: 87 students (87 boys); Grade 10: 92 students (92 boys); Grade 11: 89 students (89 boys); Grade 12: 89 students (89 boys).

Faculty School total: 171. In upper school: 42 men, 14 women; 46 have advanced degrees.

Subjects Offered 20th century history, 3-dimensional design, acting, advanced chemistry, African-American literature, algebra, American history, American history-AP, American literature, anthropology, Arabic, architecture, art, art history, art history-AP, astronomy, biology, biology-AP, calculus, calculus-AP, ceramics, chemistry, chemistry-AP, Chinese, choir, community service, computer graphics, computer programming, computer programming-AP, creative writing, digital art, digital music, drama, earth science, economics, economics-AP, English, environmental science-AP, ethics, European history, European history-AP, film and literature, fine arts, French, French language-AP, French literature-AP, geometry, government-AP, Greek, Greek culture, health, history, honors algebra, honors geometry, human geography - AP, Italian, Japanese history, jazz, jazz band, jazz ensemble, Latin, Latin American literature, Latin-AP, mathematics, media studies, microeconomics, military history, music, oceanography, philosophy, photography, physical education, physics, physics-AP, poetry, pre-calculus, psychology, psychology-AP, science, senior seminar, Shakespeare, short story, social studies, Spanish, Spanish language-AP, Spanish literature-AP, speech and debate, statistics-AP, studio art, studio art-AP, theater, trigonometry, U.S. government and politics-AP, U.S. history-AP, world cultures, world history-AP, writing.

Graduation Requirements Arts and fine arts (art, music, dance, drama), English, foreign language, mathematics, physical education (includes health), science, social studies (includes history). Community service is required.

Special Academic Programs Advanced Placement exam preparation; honors section; independent study; term-away projects; academic accommodation for the gifted, the musically talented, and the artistically talented.

College Admission Counseling 81 students graduated in 2011; all went to college, including Cornell University; Dartmouth College; Duke University; Georgetown University; University of Virginia; Yale University. Mean SAT critical reading: 660, mean SAT math: 665, mean SAT writing: 670, mean combined SAT: 1985. 75% scored over 600 on SAT critical reading, 87% scored over 600 on SAT math, 88% scored over 600 on SAT writing, 85% scored over 1800 on combined SAT.

Student Life Upper grades have specified standards of dress, student council, honor system. Discipline rests equally with students and faculty.

Summer Programs Enrichment programs offered; session focuses on academic enrichment; held on campus; accepts boys and girls; open to students from other schools. 2012 schedule: June 13 to July 8. Application deadline: April 1.

Tuition and Aid Day student tuition: $34,500. Tuition installment plan (Key Tuition Payment Plan, monthly payment plans). Need-based scholarship grants available. In 2011–12, 11% of upper-school students received aid. Total amount of financial aid awarded in 2011–12: $1,250,000.

Admissions Traditional secondary-level entrance grade is 9. For fall 2011, 162 students applied for upper-level admission, 38 were accepted, 33 enrolled. ISEE, PSAT or SSAT required. Deadline for receipt of application materials: December 15. Application fee required: $75. On-campus interview required.

Athletics Interscholastic: baseball, basketball, crew, cross-country running, fencing, fitness, football, golf, ice hockey, lacrosse, sailing, soccer, squash, tennis, track and field, water polo, wrestling; intramural: basketball, softball, squash, touch football, ultimate Frisbee. 4 PE instructors, 2 athletic trainers.

Computers Computers are regularly used in career technology classes. Computer network features include online commercial services, Internet access, wireless campus network, Internet filtering or blocking technology. Campus intranet and student e-mail accounts are available to students. The school has a published electronic and media policy.

Contact Stephen Garnett, Director, Upper School Admission. 203-625-5842. Fax: 203-625-5863. E-mail: sgarnett@brunswickschool.org. Web site: www.brunswickschool.org.

THE BRYN MAWR SCHOOL FOR GIRLS

109 West Melrose Avenue

Baltimore, Maryland 21210

Head of School: Maureen E. Walsh

General Information Coeducational day (boys' only in lower grades) college-preparatory and arts school. Boys grade PK, girls grades PK–12. Founded: 1885. Setting: suburban. 26-acre campus. 9 buildings on campus. Approved or accredited by Association of Independent Maryland Schools and Maryland Department of Education. Member of National Association of Independent Schools. Endowment: $27 million. Total enrollment: 711. Upper school average class size: 14. Upper school faculty-student ratio: 1:6. There are 172 required school days per year for Upper School students. Upper School students typically attend 5 days per week. The average school day consists of 7 hours.

Upper School Student Profile Grade 9: 74 students (74 girls); Grade 10: 72 students (72 girls); Grade 11: 74 students (74 girls); Grade 12: 75 students (75 girls).

Faculty School total: 147. In upper school: 15 men, 38 women; 24 have advanced degrees.

Subjects Offered Accounting, acting, African studies, African-American history, African-American literature, algebra, American history, American literature, anatomy, anatomy and physiology, Arabic, architectural drawing, art, art history, art history-AP, astronomy, biology, biology-AP, British literature, calculus, ceramics, chemistry, chemistry-AP, Chinese, comparative religion, computer programming, computer science, computer science-AP, creative writing, dance, design, digital art, digital photography, drama, drawing, ecology, economics, emerging technology, English, English literature, English-AP, environmental science-AP, ethics, European history, fine arts, forensics, French, French literature-AP, genetics, geography, geology, geometry, German, grammar, Greek, health, Holocaust studies, Irish literature, Latin, Latin American history, mathematics, mechanical drawing, moral theology, music, music theory, mythology, Native American studies, orchestra, painting, personal finance, photography, physical education, physics, physics-AP, poetry, pre-calculus, public speaking, rite of passage, Russian, science, Shakespearean histories, short story, social studies, Spanish, statistics, strings, technology, theater, trigonometry, U.S. government and politics-AP, U.S. history, U.S. history-AP, urban studies, Vietnam War, world history, world history-AP, world literature, World War I, World War II, writing.

Graduation Requirements Arts and fine arts (art, music, dance, drama), emerging technology, English, foreign language, history, mathematics, physical education (includes health), public speaking, science, 50 hours of community service, convocation speech.

Special Academic Programs Advanced Placement exam preparation; honors section; independent study; term-away projects; study abroad; academic accommodation for the gifted, the musically talented, and the artistically talented.

College Admission Counseling 77 students graduated in 2011; 76 went to college, including Brown University; Dartmouth College; University of Maryland, College Park; University of Pennsylvania; Wake Forest University; Washington University in St. Louis. Other: 1 had other specific plans. Median SAT critical reading: 660, median SAT math: 635, median SAT writing: 670, median combined SAT: 1970, median composite ACT: 27. 78.7% scored over 600 on SAT critical reading, 69.3% scored over 600 on SAT math, 85.3% scored over 600 on SAT writing, 77.3% scored over 1800 on combined SAT, 55.6% scored over 26 on composite ACT.

Student Life Upper grades have uniform requirement, student council, honor system. Discipline rests equally with students and faculty.

Summer Programs Enrichment, sports, art/fine arts programs offered; session focuses on arts, crafts, language, culture, and sports; held on campus; accepts boys and girls; open to students from other schools. 740 students usually enrolled. 2012 schedule: June 18 to August 17. Application deadline: none.

Tuition and Aid Day student tuition: $24,630. Tuition installment plan (FACTS Tuition Payment Plan, individually arranged payment plans, Tuition Management Services, Semi-monthly Payroll Deduction (for employees only)). Need-based scholarship grants, need-based loans, middle-income loans available. In 2011–12, 29% of upper-school students received aid. Total amount of financial aid awarded in 2011–12: $1,241,190.

Admissions Traditional secondary-level entrance grade is 9. For fall 2011, 69 students applied for upper-level admission, 41 were accepted, 22 enrolled. ISEE required. Deadline for receipt of application materials: December 15. Application fee required: $60. On-campus interview required.

Athletics Interscholastic: badminton, ballet, basketball, crew, cross-country running, dance, field hockey, hockey, indoor soccer, indoor track & field, lacrosse, rowing, running, soccer, softball, squash, tennis, track and field, volleyball, winter (indoor) track, winter soccer; intramural: aerobics, aerobics/dance, aerobics/Nautilus, archery, badminton, ball hockey, basketball, bowling, cooperative games, croquet, cross-country running, dance, fitness, flag football, floor hockey, ice hockey, jogging, outdoor activities, physical training, pillo polo, ropes courses, running, strength & conditioning, tennis, touch football, weight training. 5 PE instructors, 28 coaches, 1 athletic trainer.

Computers Computers are regularly used in all academic, animation, art, computer applications, Web site design classes. Computer network features include on-campus library services, online commercial services, Internet access, off-campus email. Campus intranet and student e-mail accounts are available to students. Students grades are available online. The school has a published electronic and media policy.

Contact Talia Titus, Director of Admission and Financial Aid. 410-323-8800 Ext. 1237. Fax: 410-435-4678. E-mail: titust@brynmawrschool.org. Web site: www.brynmawrschool.org.

THE BUCKLEY SCHOOL

3900 Stansbury Avenue

Sherman Oaks, California 91423

Head of School: Larry W. Dougherty, EdD

General Information Coeducational day college-preparatory, arts, and technology school. Grades K–12. Founded: 1933. Setting: suburban. Nearest major city is Los Angeles. 20-acre campus. 8 buildings on campus. Approved or accredited by California Association of Independent Schools, Western Association of Schools and Colleges, and California Department of Education. Member of National Association of Independent Schools. Endowment: $2.7 million. Total enrollment: 770. Upper school average class size: 14. Upper school faculty-student ratio: 1:8. There are 180 required school days per year for Upper School students. Upper School students typically attend 5 days per week. The average school day consists of 6 hours and 15 minutes.

Upper School Student Profile Grade 9: 73 students (47 boys, 26 girls); Grade 10: 76 students (43 boys, 33 girls); Grade 11: 70 students (40 boys, 30 girls); Grade 12: 70 students (35 boys, 35 girls).

Faculty School total: 100. In upper school: 28 men, 27 women; 31 have advanced degrees.

Subjects Offered Algebra, American history, American literature, art history, biology, calculus, ceramics, chemistry, chorus, computer graphics, computer science, creative writing, dance, drama, ecology, English, English literature, fine arts, French, geology, geometry, government/civics, humanities, journalism, Latin, mathematics, music, music theory, orchestra, photography, physical education, physics, science, social sciences, Spanish, theater, trigonometry, world history, world literature, yoga.

Graduation Requirements Arts and fine arts (art, music, dance, drama), computer science, English, foreign language, humanities, mathematics, performing arts, physical education (includes health), science, social sciences. Community service is required.

Special Academic Programs Advanced Placement exam preparation; honors section; study abroad.

College Admission Counseling 74 students graduated in 2010; all went to college, including New York University; Stanford University; University of California, Berkeley; University of California, Los Angeles; University of Southern California.

Student Life Upper grades have uniform requirement, student council, honor system. Discipline rests primarily with faculty.

Tuition and Aid Day student tuition: $30,025. Tuition installment plan (Key Tuition Payment Plan, individually arranged payment plans, For families that qualify for Financial Aid). Need-based scholarship grants available. In 2010–11, 14% of upper-school students received aid. Total amount of financial aid awarded in 2010–11: $421,225.

Admissions Traditional secondary-level entrance grade is 9. ISEE required. Deadline for receipt of application materials: January 10. Application fee required: $100. On-campus interview required.

Athletics Interscholastic: baseball (boys), softball (g), volleyball (g); coed interscholastic: basketball, cross-country running, equestrian sports, soccer, swimming and diving, tennis. 12 PE instructors, 11 coaches, 2 athletic trainers.

Computers Computers are regularly used in art, English, graphic design, music, science, video film production classes. Computer network features include on-campus library services, online commercial services, Internet access, wireless campus network, Internet filtering or blocking technology, Web page design, online syllabi. Student e-mail accounts are available to students. The school has a published electronic and media policy.

Contact Carinne M. Barker, Director of Admission and Financial Aid. 818-783-1610 Ext. 709. Fax: 818-461-6714. E-mail: admissions@buckley.org. Web site: www.buckley.org.

BULLOCH ACADEMY

873 Westside Road

Statesboro, Georgia 30458

Head of School: Mrs. Leisa Houghton

General Information Coeducational day college-preparatory, arts, and technology school, affiliated with Christian faith, Baptist Church. Grades PK–12. Founded: 1971. Setting: small town. Nearest major city is Savannah. 35-acre campus. 4 buildings on campus. Approved or accredited by Georgia Accrediting Commission, Georgia Independent School Association, Southern Association of Colleges and Schools, and Southern Association of Independent Schools. Member of National Association of Independent Schools. Total enrollment: 464. Upper school average class size: 17. Upper school faculty-student ratio: 1:17. There are 180 required school days per year for Upper School students. Upper School students typically attend 5 days per week. The average school day consists of 8 hours.

Upper School Student Profile Grade 9: 36 students (16 boys, 20 girls); Grade 10: 21 students (13 boys, 8 girls); Grade 11: 29 students (20 boys, 9 girls); Grade 12: 27 students (8 boys, 19 girls). 98% of students are Christian, Baptist.

Faculty School total: 14. In upper school: 5 men, 9 women; 3 have advanced degrees.

Subjects Offered Advanced Placement courses, American government, American history, anatomy and physiology, art, art education, biology, calculus, chemistry, computer applications, computer science, earth science, economics, economics and history, English, ethics, geometry, government, government-AP, government/civics, health education, journalism, language and composition, language arts, literature-AP, mathematics-AP, music, performing arts, physical education, physics, pre-algebra, pre-calculus, research skills, science, social sciences, Spanish, speech and debate, technology, U.S. government and politics-AP, U.S. history, Web site design, world geography, world history.

Graduation Requirements Computer science, English, foreign language, mathematics, physical education (includes health), science, social sciences, social studies (includes history).

Special Academic Programs 6 Advanced Placement exams for which test preparation is offered; honors section; independent study; study at local college for college credit; academic accommodation for the gifted, the musically talented, and the artistically talented.

College Admission Counseling 33 students graduated in 2011; all went to college, including Furman University; Georgia College & State University; Georgia Institute of Technology; Georgia Southern University; United States Military Academy; University of Georgia. Median SAT critical reading: 584, median SAT math: 583, median SAT writing: 571, median combined SAT: 1738.

Student Life Upper grades have specified standards of dress, student council, honor system. Discipline rests primarily with faculty.

Tuition and Aid Day student tuition: $6515. Tuition installment plan (monthly payment plans, individually arranged payment plans). Tuition reduction for siblings, need-based scholarship grants, tuition assistance available. In 2011–12, 10% of upper-school students received aid. Total amount of financial aid awarded in 2011–12: $50,000.

Admissions Traditional secondary-level entrance grade is 9. For fall 2011, 14 students applied for upper-level admission, 12 were accepted, 12 enrolled. Any standardized test required. Deadline for receipt of application materials: none. Application fee required: $375. Interview recommended.

Athletics Interscholastic: baseball (boys), basketball (b,g), cheering (g), cross-country running (b,g), dance team (g), football (b), golf (b,g), physical fitness (b,g), running (b,g), soccer (b,g), softball (g), strength & conditioning (b,g), tennis (b,g), track and field (b,g), weight lifting (b,g), weight training (b,g), wrestling (b); intramural: cheering (g), cross-country running (b,g), football (b), physical fitness (b,g); coed interscholastic: physical fitness; coed intramural: basketball, football, physical fitness. 3 PE instructors, 7 coaches, 3 athletic trainers.

Computers Computers are regularly used in art, career education, career exploration, computer applications, creative writing, desktop publishing, economics, geography, history, independent study, keyboarding, technology classes. Computer network features include on-campus library services, Internet access, Internet filtering or blocking technology. Student e-mail accounts are available to students. Students grades are available online. The school has a published electronic and media policy.

Contact Mr. Leisa Houghton, Head of School. 912-764-6297. Fax: 912-764-3165. E-mail: lhoughton@bullochacademy.com. Web site: www.bullochacademy.com.

BURR AND BURTON ACADEMY

57 Seminary Avenue

Manchester, Vermont 05254

Head of School: Mr. Mark Tashjian

General Information Coeducational boarding and day college-preparatory, general academic, arts, and technology school. Grades 9–12. Founded: 1829. Setting: small town. Nearest major city is Albany, NY. Students are housed in single-sex dormitories and homes of host families. 29-acre campus. 7 buildings on campus. Approved or accredited by New England Association of Schools and Colleges and Vermont Department of Education. Member of National Association of Independent Schools. Total enrollment: 680. Upper school average class size: 19. Upper school faculty-student ratio: 1:12. There are 175 required school days per year for Upper School students. Upper School students typically attend 5 days per week. The average school day consists of 6 hours and 40 minutes.

Upper School Student Profile Grade 9: 178 students (95 boys, 83 girls); Grade 10: 163 students (83 boys, 80 girls); Grade 11: 157 students (82 boys, 75 girls); Grade 12: 182 students (101 boys, 81 girls). 8% are international students.

Faculty School total: 60. In upper school: 35 men, 25 women; 30 have advanced degrees.

Subjects Offered Algebra, American history, American literature, anatomy, art, art history, biology, business, calculus, chemistry, computer math, computer programming, computer science, drafting, drama, driver education, earth science, ecology, English, English literature, environmental science, expository writing, French, geometry, German, government/civics, health, history, industrial arts, mathematics, music, photography, physical education, physics, psychology, science, social studies, Spanish, theater, trigonometry, typing, world history, world literature.

Graduation Requirements Arts, computer literacy, English, mathematics, physical education (includes health), science, social studies (includes history), U.S. history. Community service is required.

Special Academic Programs 12 Advanced Placement exams for which test preparation is offered; honors section; independent study; term-away projects; study abroad; remedial reading and/or remedial writing; remedial math; programs in English, mathematics, general development for dyslexic students; special instructional classes for deaf students, blind students; ESL (20 students enrolled).

College Admission Counseling 154 students graduated in 2011; 111 went to college, including Elon University; St. Lawrence University; University of Vermont. Other: 20 went to work, 3 entered military service, 2 entered a postgraduate year, 18 had other specific plans. Mean SAT critical reading: 534, mean SAT math: 538, mean SAT writing: 533, mean combined SAT: 1605, mean composite ACT: 24.

Student Life Upper grades have specified standards of dress, student council. Discipline rests primarily with faculty.

Tuition and Aid Day student tuition: $15,100; 7-day tuition and room/board: $36,600. Tuition installment plan (individually arranged payment plans). Financial aid available to upper-school students. In 2011–12, 2% of upper-school students received aid.

Admissions Traditional secondary-level entrance grade is 9. School's own test and SLEP for foreign students required. Deadline for receipt of application materials: none. No application fee required. Interview recommended.

Athletics Interscholastic: alpine skiing (boys, girls), baseball (b), basketball (b,g), cross-country running (b,g), dance team (g), football (b), golf (b,g), ice hockey (b,g), lacrosse (b,g), nordic skiing (b,g), skiing (cross-country) (b,g), skiing (downhill) (b,g), soccer (b,g), softball (g), tennis (b,g), track and field (b,g); coed intramural: field hockey, floor hockey, outdoor adventure, outdoor education, volleyball. 3 PE instructors.

Computers Computers are regularly used in drafting, drawing and design, English, foreign language, graphic design, history, information technology, mathematics, science, video film production, Web site design, yearbook classes. Computer network features include on-campus library services, online commercial services, Internet access, Internet filtering or blocking technology.

Contact Mr. Philip G. Anton, Director of Admission and School Counseling. 802-362-1775 Ext. 125. Fax: 802-362-0574. E-mail: panton@burrburton.org. Web site: www.burrburton.org.

BUTTE CENTRAL CATHOLIC HIGH SCHOOL

9 South Idaho Street

Butte, Montana 59701

Head of School: Mr. Timothy Norbeck

General Information Boys' boarding and coeducational day college-preparatory, arts, business, vocational, religious studies, and technology school, affiliated with Roman Catholic Church. Boarding boys grades 9–12, day boys grades 9–12, day girls grades 9–12. Founded: 1892. Setting: small town. Nearest major city is Bozeman. 6-acre campus. 1 building on campus. Approved or accredited by National Catholic Education Association, Northwest Accreditation Commission, Northwest Association of Schools and Colleges, and Montana Department of Education. Endowment: $300,000. Total enrollment: 121. Upper school average class size: 15. Upper school faculty-student ratio: 1:10. There are 180 required school days per year for Upper School students. Upper School students typically attend 5 days per week. The average school day consists of 7 hours.

Upper School Student Profile Grade 9: 25 students (20 boys, 5 girls); Grade 10: 28 students (16 boys, 12 girls); Grade 11: 39 students (18 boys, 21 girls); Grade 12: 29 students (16 boys, 13 girls). 10% of students are boarding students. 90% are state residents. 1 state is represented in upper school student body. 10% are international students. International students from Brazil, China, Portugal, and Taiwan. 85% of students are Roman Catholic.

Faculty School total: 12. In upper school: 7 men, 5 women; 2 have advanced degrees.

Subjects Offered Accounting, advanced math, Advanced Placement courses, algebra, American literature-AP, animal behavior, art, athletic training, biology, calculus, calculus-AP, career education, chemistry, choir, college counseling, college placement, college planning, college writing, community service, computer science, computers, debate, desktop publishing, drama, English, English literature and composition-AP, foreign language, French, French as a second language, geometry, government/civics, health, history, honors algebra, honors English, honors geometry, human biology, integrated mathematics, keyboarding, mathematics, model United Nations, physical education, physics, pre-calculus, public speaking, reading, religion, science, social studies, Spanish, student government, trigonometry, Web site design, weightlifting, world history, writing, yearbook.

Graduation Requirements American government, American history, arts and fine arts (art, music, dance, drama), electives, English, foreign language, global studies, health education, keyboarding, mathematics, physical education (includes health), religion (includes Bible studies and theology), science, social studies (includes history), writing. Community service is required.

Special Academic Programs 2 Advanced Placement exams for which test preparation is offered; honors section; independent study; study at local college for college credit; remedial reading and/or remedial writing; remedial math.

College Admission Counseling 40 students graduated in 2011; 35 went to college, including Carroll University; Division of Technology of Montana Tech of The University of Montana; Gonzaga University; Montana State University; The University of Montana Western. Other: 5 went to work. Median composite ACT: 20. 7% scored over 26 on composite ACT.

Student Life Upper grades have specified standards of dress, student council, honor system. Discipline rests primarily with faculty. Attendance at religious services is required.

Tuition and Aid Day student tuition: $4000–$7000; 7-day tuition and room/board: $10,000–$15,000. Guaranteed tuition plan. Tuition installment plan (FACTS Tuition Payment Plan, monthly payment plans, individually arranged payment plans). Tuition reduction for siblings, need-based scholarship grants available. In 2011–12, 25% of upper-school students received aid. Total amount of financial aid awarded in 2011–12: $68,000.

Admissions Traditional secondary-level entrance grade is 9. Admissions testing required. Deadline for receipt of application materials: none. Application fee required: $125. Interview required.

Athletics Interscholastic: basketball (boys, girls), cheering (g), cross-country running (b,g), football (b), golf (b,g), softball (g), strength & conditioning (b,g), tennis (b,g), track and field (b,g), volleyball (g), wrestling (b). 1 PE instructor, 30 coaches, 1 athletic trainer.

Computers Computers are regularly used in all academic classes. Computer network features include on-campus library services, Internet access, Internet filtering or blocking technology. The school has a published electronic and media policy.

Contact Mr. Timothy Norbeck, Principal. 406-782-6761. Fax: 406-723-3873. E-mail: tim.norbeck@buttecentralschools.org. Web site: www.buttecentralschools.org.

BUXTON SCHOOL

291 South Street

Williamstown, Massachusetts 01267

Head of School: C. William Bennett and Peter Smith '74

General Information Coeducational boarding and day college-preparatory and arts school. Grades 9–12. Founded: 1928. Setting: small town. Nearest major city is Boston. Students are housed in single-sex dormitories. 150-acre campus. 20 buildings on campus. Approved or accredited by Association of Independent Schools in New England, New England Association of Schools and Colleges, The Association of Boarding Schools, and Massachusetts Department of Education. Member of National Association of Independent Schools and Secondary School Admission Test Board. Endowment: $1.9 million. Total enrollment: 90. Upper school average class size: 9. Upper school faculty-student ratio: 1:4. There are 221 required school days per year for Upper School students. Upper School students typically attend 7 days per week. The average school day consists of 5 hours and 15 minutes.

Upper School Student Profile Grade 9: 16 students (6 boys, 10 girls); Grade 10: 24 students (11 boys, 13 girls); Grade 11: 27 students (16 boys, 11 girls); Grade 12: 23 students (11 boys, 12 girls). 90% of students are boarding students. 14% are state residents. 11 states are represented in upper school student body. 25% are international students. International students from Bermuda, China, Japan, Mexico, Rwanda, and Venezuela; 2 other countries represented in student body.

Faculty School total: 22. In upper school: 12 men, 10 women; 5 have advanced degrees; 14 reside on campus.

Subjects Offered Advanced math, African dance, African drumming, African studies, algebra, American history, American literature, anatomy and physiology, anthropology, architecture, astronomy, biology, British literature, calculus, cell biology, ceramics, chemistry, costumes and make-up, creative writing, critical writing, dance performance, drama, drama performance, drawing, economics, English, English literature, ensembles, ESL, European history, expository writing, fiction, film history, French, geometry, grammar, history, improvisation, independent study, instruments, lab science, linear algebra, literary genres, literature, Mandarin, marine biology, music, music composition, music performance, music theory, oceanography, painting, performing arts, philosophy, photography, physics, poetry, pre-calculus, printmaking, psychology, set design, social sciences, Spanish, studio art, technical theater, TOEFL preparation, trigonometry, video film production, voice, writing workshop.

Graduation Requirements American history, English, foreign language, lab science, mathematics, social sciences.

Special Academic Programs Honors section; academic accommodation for the gifted, the musically talented, and the artistically talented; ESL (17 students enrolled).

College Admission Counseling 30 students graduated in 2011; 26 went to college, including Bard College; Barnard College; Bennington College; Guilford College; Oberlin College; Williams College. Other: 4 had other specific plans.

Student Life Discipline rests primarily with faculty.

Tuition and Aid Day student tuition: $28,000; 7-day tuition and room/board: $45,500. Tuition installment plan (individually arranged payment plans, Tuition Management Systems). Need-based scholarship grants, need-based loans with limited in-house financing available. In 2011–12, 49% of upper-school students received aid. Total amount of financial aid awarded in 2011–12: $1,300,000.

Admissions Traditional secondary-level entrance grade is 9. SSAT or TOEFL or SLEP required. Deadline for receipt of application materials: February 1. Application fee required: $50. Interview required.

Athletics Interscholastic: soccer (boys, girls); intramural: soccer (b,g); coed interscholastic: basketball, ultimate Frisbee; coed intramural: ballet, bicycling, dance, hiking/backpacking, horseback riding, ice skating, indoor soccer, jogging, martial arts, mountain biking, outdoor activities, physical training, running, skateboarding, skiing (downhill), snowboarding, soccer, squash, table tennis, tennis, ultimate Frisbee, weight lifting, yoga.

Computers Computers are regularly used in architecture, economics, ESL, French, history, language development, mathematics, media production, multimedia, music, photography, psychology, science, Spanish, video film production, writing, yearbook classes. Computer network features include Internet access, wireless campus network, Internet filtering or blocking technology. Campus intranet and computer access in designated common areas are available to students. The school has a published electronic and media policy.

Contact Admissions Office. 413-458-3919. Fax: 413-458-9428. E-mail: Admissions@BuxtonSchool.org. Web site: www.BuxtonSchool.org.

See Display on next page and Close-Up on page 594.

THE BYRNES SCHOOLS

1201 East Ashby Road

Florence, South Carolina 29506

Head of School: Mr. John W. Colby Jr.

General Information Coeducational day college-preparatory school. Grades PK–12. Founded: 1966. Setting: small town. 16-acre campus. 3 buildings on campus. Approved or accredited by South Carolina Independent School Association and Southern Association of Independent Schools. Candidate for accreditation by Southern Association of

Colleges and Schools. Endowment: $25,000. Total enrollment: 192. Upper school average class size: 13. Upper school faculty-student ratio: 1:9. There are 175 required school days per year for Upper School students. Upper School students typically attend 5 days per week. The average school day consists of 6 hours and 50 minutes.

Upper School Student Profile Grade 9: 12 students (5 boys, 7 girls); Grade 10: 15 students (10 boys, 5 girls); Grade 11: 16 students (10 boys, 6 girls); Grade 12: 21 students (10 boys, 11 girls).

Faculty School total: 28. In upper school: 5 men, 6 women; 5 have advanced degrees.

Subjects Offered Advanced Placement courses, algebra, American history, biology, biology-AP, calculus-AP, chemistry, computer science, earth science, economics, English, English-AP, environmental science, geography, geometry, government/civics, history-AP, mathematics, physical education, physics, science, social studies, Spanish, world history.

Graduation Requirements English, foreign language, mathematics, physical education (includes health), science, social studies (includes history).

Special Academic Programs Advanced Placement exam preparation; honors section; academic accommodation for the gifted.

College Admission Counseling 13 students graduated in 2011; all went to college, including Clemson University; Francis Marion University; Sewanee: The University of the South; University of South Carolina.

Student Life Upper grades have specified standards of dress, student council, honor system. Discipline rests primarily with faculty.

Tuition and Aid Day student tuition: $7100. Tuition installment plan (Insured Tuition Payment Plan, monthly payment plans). Need-based scholarship grants available. In 2011–12, 15% of upper-school students received aid. Total amount of financial aid awarded in 2011–12: $25,000.

Admissions Traditional secondary-level entrance grade is 9. For fall 2011, 2 students applied for upper-level admission, 2 were accepted, 2 enrolled. Metropolitan Achievement Test or Stanford Achievement Test required. Deadline for receipt of application materials: none. Application fee required: $50. On-campus interview required.

Athletics Interscholastic: baseball (boys), basketball (b,g), cheering (g), football (b), golf (b,g), soccer (b,g), softball (g), volleyball (g); intramural: aerobics/dance (g), strength & conditioning (b,g), weight lifting (b,g), weight training (b,g); coed interscholastic: cross-country running; coed intramural: tennis. 1 PE instructor, 1 athletic trainer.

Computers Computers are regularly used in mathematics, yearbook classes. Computer network features include Internet access. Students grades are available online. The school has a published electronic and media policy.

Contact Mr. John W. Colby Jr., Headmaster. 843-622-0131 Ext. 116. Fax: 843-669-2466. E-mail: JColby@byrnesschools.org. Web site: www.byrnesschools.org.

CALGARY ACADEMY COLLEGIATE

1677 93rd St Sw

Calgary, Alberta T3H 0R3, Canada

Head of School: Ms. Kim McLean

General Information Coeducational day college-preparatory, arts, and technology school; primarily serves students with learning disabilities, individuals with Attention Deficit Disorder, and dyslexic students. Grades 6–12. Founded: 1981. Setting: suburban. 17-acre campus. 3 buildings on campus. Approved or accredited by Association of Independent Schools and Colleges of Alberta and Alberta Department of Education. Language of instruction: English. Endowment: CAN$3 million. Total enrollment: 176. Upper school average class size: 17. Upper school faculty-student ratio: 1:8. There are 188 required school days per year for Upper School students. Upper School students typically attend 5 days per week. The average school day consists of 6 hours and 10 minutes.

Upper School Student Profile Grade 10: 30 students (20 boys, 10 girls); Grade 11: 30 students (19 boys, 11 girls); Grade 12: 35 students (21 boys, 14 girls).

Faculty School total: 25. In upper school: 10 men, 15 women; 10 have advanced degrees.

Subjects Offered Art history, athletics, band, biology, calculus, career and personal planning, character education, chemistry, computer animation, computer multimedia, drama, English composition, English literature, grammar, language arts, mathematics, outdoor education, physical education, physics, psychology, social studies, sociology, Spanish, study skills.

Graduation Requirements Biology, chemistry, English, mathematics, physics, social studies (includes history).

Special Academic Programs International Baccalaureate program; 1 Advanced Placement exam for which test preparation is offered.

College Admission Counseling 39 students graduated in 2011; 36 went to college, including Mount Royal University; University of Alberta; University of Calgary; University of Lethbridge. Other: 3 went to work.

Student Life Upper grades have specified standards of dress, student council, honor system. Discipline rests primarily with faculty.

Tuition and Aid Day student tuition: CAN$9500. Tuition installment plan (monthly payment plans, individually arranged payment plans). Bursaries available. In 2011–12, 5% of upper-school students received aid. Total amount of financial aid awarded in 2011–12: CAN$300,000.

Admissions Traditional secondary-level entrance grade is 10. For fall 2011, 50 students applied for upper-level admission, 30 were accepted, 20 enrolled. Achievement tests, Wechsler Individual Achievement Test or Wechsler Intelligence Scale for Children III required. Deadline for receipt of application materials: none. Application fee required: CAN$1500. On-campus interview required.

Athletics Interscholastic: badminton (boys, girls), ball hockey (b), basketball (b,g), cross-country running (b,g), golf (b,g), handball (b,g), track and field (b,g), volleyball (b,g), wrestling (b,g); intramural: ice hockey (b,g); coed interscholastic: badminton, curling, soccer; coed intramural: outdoor recreation, triathlon. 6 PE instructors, 30 coaches.

Computers Computers are regularly used in all academic classes. Computer network features include on-campus library services, Internet access, wireless campus network, Internet filtering or blocking technology. Computer access in designated common areas is available to students. Students grades are available online. The school has a published electronic and media policy.

Contact Ms. Joanne Endacott, Director of Admissions. 403-686-6444 Ext. 236. Fax: 403-686-3427. E-mail: jendacott@calgaryacademy.com.

THE CALHOUN SCHOOL

433 West End Avenue

New York, New York 10024

Head of School: Steven J. Nelson

General Information Coeducational day college-preparatory and arts school. Grades N–12. Founded: 1896. Setting: urban. 2 buildings on campus. Approved or accredited by New York State Association of Independent Schools and New York Department of Education. Member of National Association of Independent Schools. Endowment: $2.5 million. Total enrollment: 724. Upper school average class size: 15. Upper school faculty-student ratio: 1:6.

Upper School Student Profile Grade 9: 50 students (21 boys, 29 girls); Grade 10: 41 students (23 boys, 18 girls); Grade 11: 51 students (25 boys, 26 girls); Grade 12: 41 students (16 boys, 25 girls).

Faculty School total: 122. In upper school: 18 men, 18 women; 28 have advanced degrees.

Subjects Offered Acting, advanced biology, advanced chemistry, advanced computer applications, African-American literature, algebra, American history, American literature, anthropology, arts, biology, calculus, chemistry, child development, chorus, community service, computer math, computer programming, computer science, constitutional law, creative writing, English literature, English-AP, ethnic literature, French, geometry, healthful living, human sexuality, independent study, instrumental music, music history, peer counseling, photography, physical education, physics, pre-calculus, psychology, Shakespeare, Spanish, speech, studio art, theater, theater design and production, Web site design, world history, world literature.

Graduation Requirements Arts and fine arts (art, music, dance, drama), English, foreign language, mathematics, physical education (includes health), science, social studies (includes history), 9th grade Life Skills with peer leaders. Community service is required.

Special Academic Programs Independent study; domestic exchange program (with The Network Program Schools); academic accommodation for the gifted.

College Admission Counseling 48 students graduated in 2010; all went to college, including American University; Bard College; Bates College; Goucher College; New York University; Syracuse University. Mean SAT critical reading: 610, mean SAT math: 578, mean SAT writing: 608, mean combined SAT: 1796.

Student Life Upper grades have student council. Discipline rests primarily with faculty.

Tuition and Aid Day student tuition: $35,900. Tuition installment plan (Key Tuition Payment Plan, individually arranged payment plans, 60%/40% payment plan). Need-based scholarship grants, tuition reduction for faculty and staff available. In 2010–11, 35% of upper-school students received aid. Total amount of financial aid awarded in 2010–11: $1,800,000.

Admissions Traditional secondary-level entrance grade is 9. For fall 2010, 240 students applied for upper-level admission, 80 were accepted, 23 enrolled. Deadline for receipt of application materials: January 15. Application fee required: $65. On-campus interview required.

Athletics Interscholastic: baseball (boys, girls), basketball (b,g), cross-country running (b,g), track and field (b,g), volleyball (b,g); coed interscholastic: golf, soccer; coed intramural: aerobics, aerobics/Nautilus, basketball, fitness, golf, project adventure, sailing, soccer, strength & conditioning, tennis, weight training, yoga. 5 PE instructors, 2 coaches.

Computers Computers are regularly used in basic skills, mathematics, programming, video film production, Web site design classes. Computer network features include Internet access, MS Office, PowerPoint, Basic, Dreameaver, and Flash Software. Student e-mail accounts are available to students. The school has a published electronic and media policy.

Contact Jenny Eugenio, Director of Admissions, Upper School. 212-497-6510. Fax: 212-497-6531. E-mail: jenny.eugenio@calhoun.org. Web site: www.calhoun.org.

CALVARY CHAPEL HIGH SCHOOL

12808 Woodruff Avenue

Downey, California 90242

Head of School: Pastor Yuri Escandon

General Information Coeducational day college-preparatory, arts, business, religious studies, and technology school, affiliated with Christian faith. Grades K–12. Founded: 1978. Setting: suburban. Nearest major city is Los Angeles. 16-acre campus. 1 building on campus. Approved or accredited by Western Association of Schools and Colleges and California Department of Education. Total enrollment: 683. Upper school average class size: 19. Upper school faculty-student ratio: 1:19. There are 174 required school days per year for Upper School students. Upper School students typically attend 5 days per week. The average school day consists of 6 hours and 6 minutes.

Upper School Student Profile 100% of students are Christian faith.

Faculty School total: 35. In upper school: 18 men, 17 women; 5 have advanced degrees.

Subjects Offered Algebra, anatomy, art, arts, band, Bible studies, biology, calculus-AP, chemistry, choir, community service, computer science, creative writing, current events, drama, earth science, economics, English, ethics, fine arts, geometry, government, health, humanities, mathematics, media, music appreciation, physical education, physical science, physics, physiology, pre-calculus, religion, science, social studies, sociology, Spanish, speech, U.S. history, world history.

Graduation Requirements American sign language, anatomy and physiology, art-AP, computers.

Special Academic Programs Advanced Placement exam preparation; honors section; independent study; study at local college for college credit.

College Admission Counseling 92 students graduated in 2011; 90 went to college, including Azusa Pacific University; Biola University; California State University, Fullerton; California State University, Long Beach; Chapman University; Vanguard University of Southern California. Other: 1 entered military service, 1 had other specific plans. Mean SAT critical reading: 491, mean SAT math: 444, mean SAT writing: 484.

Student Life Upper grades have specified standards of dress, student council, honor system. Discipline rests primarily with faculty. Attendance at religious services is required.

Summer Programs Remediation, advancement, sports programs offered; held on campus; accepts boys and girls; not open to students from other schools. 45 students usually enrolled. 2012 schedule: June 16 to August 15. Application deadline: April 10.

Tuition and Aid Day student tuition: $8250. Guaranteed tuition plan. Tuition installment plan (monthly payment plans). Tuition reduction for siblings, need-based scholarship grants available. In 2011–12, 15% of upper-school students received aid.

Admissions Traditional secondary-level entrance grade is 9. Admissions testing required. Deadline for receipt of application materials: none. Application fee required: $125. Interview required.

Athletics Interscholastic: aquatics (boys, girls), baseball (b), basketball (b,g), cheering (g), cross-country running (b,g), football (b), outdoor activities (b,g), physical fitness (b,g), soccer (b,g), softball (g), strength & conditioning (b,g), swimming and diving (b,g), track and field (b,g), volleyball (b,g), weight training (b,g), wrestling (b); coed interscholastic: aquatics, swimming and diving. 4 PE instructors, 25 coaches, 1 athletic trainer.

Computers Computers are regularly used in all academic classes. Computer resources include on-campus library services, Internet access, Internet filtering or blocking technology. Computer access in designated common areas is available to students. Students grades are available online. The school has a published electronic and media policy.

Contact Diane Kirkhuff, Office/Admissions. 562-803-4076 Ext. 302. Fax: 562-803-1292. E-mail: dkirkhuff@calvarydowney.org. Web site: cccsdowney.org.

CALVARY CHRISTIAN SCHOOL

5955 Taylor Mill Road

Covington, Kentucky 41015

Head of School: Mr. Ed Ryan

General Information Coeducational day college-preparatory, arts, religious studies, and technology school, affiliated with Baptist Church. Grades K4–12. Founded: 1974. Setting: suburban. Nearest major city is Cincinnati, OH. 72-acre campus. 1 building on campus. Approved or accredited by Association of Christian Schools International, CITA (Commission on International and Trans-Regional Accreditation), Southern Association of Colleges and Schools, and Kentucky Department of Education. Total enrollment: 388. Upper school average class size: 17. Upper school faculty-student ratio: 1:10. There are 178 required school days per year for Upper School students. Upper School students typically attend 5 days per week. The average school day consists of 7 hours.

Upper School Student Profile Grade 9: 26 students (10 boys, 16 girls); Grade 10: 24 students (10 boys, 14 girls); Grade 11: 28 students (15 boys, 13 girls); Grade 12: 23 students (10 boys, 13 girls). 30% of students are Baptist.

Faculty School total: 30. In upper school: 10 men, 8 women; 15 have advanced degrees.

Subjects Offered Advanced math, algebra, American literature-AP, ancient history, art, art appreciation, Bible, biology, calculus, chemistry, chemistry-AP, choir, chorus,

Christian doctrine, Christian ethics, communication arts, computer applications, computer multimedia, computer science, concert band, concert choir, consumer mathematics, creative writing, cultural geography, drama, drama performance, earth science, economics, English, English composition, English language and composition-AP, English language-AP, English literature, English literature and composition-AP, English literature-AP, English-AP, ethics, European history-AP, fitness, food and nutrition, general math, general science, geography, geometry, government-AP, grammar, health education, home economics, honors algebra, independent study, journalism, Kentucky history, keyboarding, lab science, language arts, library assistant, literature-AP, logic, music theory, newspaper, physical education, physical science, physics-AP, pre-algebra, pre-calculus, rhetoric, Spanish, Spanish-AP, speech and debate, state history, student government, student publications, student teaching, U.S. government, U.S. government and politics-AP, U.S. history, U.S. history-AP, world governments, world history, yearbook.

Graduation Requirements Algebra, art appreciation, Bible, biology, chemistry, Christian doctrine, church history, civics, economics, English, English composition, English literature, European history, foreign language, geometry, health, physical science, U.S. government, U.S. history, world history, 4 years of HS Bible required for graduation.

Special Academic Programs Advanced Placement exam preparation; honors section; independent study; study at local college for college credit.

College Admission Counseling 38 students graduated in 2010; 35 went to college, including Eastern Kentucky University; Northern Kentucky University; University of Cincinnati; University of Kentucky; University of Louisville. Other: 1 went to work, 2 entered military service. Median composite ACT: 26. 25% scored over 26 on composite ACT.

Student Life Upper grades have uniform requirement, student council. Discipline rests primarily with faculty. Attendance at religious services is required.

Tuition and Aid Day student tuition: $5800. Tuition installment plan (FACTS Tuition Payment Plan, monthly payment plans, individually arranged payment plans). Tuition reduction for siblings, need-based scholarship grants, paying campus jobs available. In 2010–11, 9% of upper-school students received aid. Total amount of financial aid awarded in 2010–11: $25,000.

Admissions Traditional secondary-level entrance grade is 9. For fall 2010, 14 students applied for upper-level admission, 14 were accepted, 14 enrolled. Stanford Achievement Test required. Deadline for receipt of application materials: none. Application fee required: $285. Interview required.

Athletics Interscholastic: baseball (boys), basketball (b,g), bowling (b,g), cheering (g), cross-country running (b,g), diving (b,g), golf (b), horseback riding (b,g), physical fitness (b,g), soccer (b,g), softball (g), swimming and diving (b,g), volleyball (g), weight lifting (b), weight training (b); intramural: indoor soccer (b,g), strength & conditioning (b,g), weight training (b); coed intramural: bowling, gymnastics, physical fitness, running. 2 PE instructors, 15 coaches.

Computers Computers are regularly used in architecture, art, computer applications, design, desktop publishing, drafting, graphics, information technology, journalism, keyboarding, lab/keyboard, library, photography, photojournalism, science, Spanish, technical drawing, Web site design, yearbook classes. Computer network features include on-campus library services, Internet access, wireless campus network, Internet filtering or blocking technology. Campus intranet is available to students. Students grades are available online. The school has a published electronic and media policy.

Contact Mrs. Laurie Switzer, Registrar. 859-356-9201. Fax: 859-359-8962. E-mail: laurie.switzer@calvarychristianky.org. Web site: www.calvarychristianky.org.

CALVERT HALL COLLEGE HIGH SCHOOL

8102 LaSalle Road

Baltimore, Maryland 21286

Head of School: Br. Thomas Zoppo, FSC

General Information Boys' day college-preparatory, arts, business, religious studies, and technology school, affiliated with Roman Catholic Church. Grades 9–12. Founded: 1845. Setting: suburban. 32-acre campus. 6 buildings on campus. Approved or accredited by Christian Brothers Association, Middle States Association of Colleges and Schools, National Catholic Education Association, and Maryland Department of Education. Endowment: $4.3 million. Total enrollment: 1,225. Upper school average class size: 21. Upper school faculty-student ratio: 1:12. There are 174 required school days per year for Upper School students. Upper School students typically attend 5 days per week. The average school day consists of 6 hours and 20 minutes.

Upper School Student Profile Grade 9: 331 students (331 boys); Grade 10: 295 students (295 boys); Grade 11: 300 students (300 boys); Grade 12: 299 students (299 boys). 71% of students are Roman Catholic.

Faculty School total: 100. In upper school: 71 men, 26 women; 72 have advanced degrees.

Subjects Offered Algebra, American history, American literature, art, art history, band, Bible studies, biology, business, business skills, calculus, chemistry, chorus, computer programming, computer science, creative writing, drama, earth science, economics, engineering, English, English literature, ethics, European history, fine arts, French, geography, geometry, German, government/civics, graphic arts, history, journalism, Latin, leadership, mathematics, music, painting, philosophy, physical education, physics, psychology, religion, science, sculpture, social sciences, social studies, Spanish, speech, statistics, theater, theology, typing, world history, world literature, writing.

Graduation Requirements Arts and fine arts (art, music, dance, drama), English, foreign language, mathematics, physical education (includes health), religion (includes Bible studies and theology), science, social sciences, social studies (includes history).

Special Academic Programs 22 Advanced Placement exams for which test preparation is offered; honors section; academic accommodation for the gifted, the musically talented, and the artistically talented; programs in English, mathematics, general development for dyslexic students.

College Admission Counseling 301 students graduated in 2011; 297 went to college, including Loyola University Maryland; Salisbury University; Stevenson University; Towson University; University of Maryland, College Park. Other: 2 went to work, 2 entered military service. Median SAT critical reading: 555, median SAT math: 558, median SAT writing: 538.

Student Life Upper grades have specified standards of dress, student council, honor system. Discipline rests primarily with faculty. Attendance at religious services is required.

Summer Programs Remediation, enrichment, sports, art/fine arts, computer instruction programs offered; session focuses on remediation and make-up courses; held on campus; accepts boys and girls; open to students from other schools. 250 students usually enrolled. 2012 schedule: June 25 to July 27. Application deadline: June 15.

Tuition and Aid Day student tuition: $11,900. Tuition installment plan (monthly payment plans, individually arranged payment plans). Merit scholarship grants, need-based scholarship grants available. In 2011–12, 45% of upper-school students received aid; total upper-school merit-scholarship money awarded: $428,000. Total amount of financial aid awarded in 2011–12: $1,142,000.

Admissions Traditional secondary-level entrance grade is 9. For fall 2011, 685 students applied for upper-level admission, 577 were accepted, 331 enrolled. High School Placement Test (closed version) from Scholastic Testing Service required. Deadline for receipt of application materials: none. Application fee required: $20.

Athletics Interscholastic: aquatics, baseball, basketball, cross-country running, diving, football, golf, ice hockey, indoor track & field, lacrosse, rugby, soccer, squash, swimming and diving, tennis, track and field, volleyball, water polo, winter (indoor) track, wrestling; intramural: basketball, billiards, bocce, bowling, fitness, flag football, freestyle skiing, outdoor adventure, rock climbing, rugby, sailing, skiing (downhill), table tennis, ultimate Frisbee, weight lifting. 2 PE instructors, 12 coaches, 1 athletic trainer.

Computers Computers are regularly used in accounting, business, college planning, computer applications, digital applications, economics, English, foreign language, graphic design, history, independent study, journalism, keyboarding, library, literary magazine, mathematics, music, programming, religion, SAT preparation, science, social sciences, stock market, video film production, writing, yearbook classes. Computer network features include on-campus library services, Internet access, wireless campus network, Internet filtering or blocking technology. Campus intranet, student e-mail accounts, and computer access in designated common areas are available to students. Students grades are available online. The school has a published electronic and media policy.

Contact Chris Bengel, Director of Admissions. 410-825-4266 Ext. 126. Fax: 410-825-6826. E-mail: bengelc@calverthall.com. Web site: www.calverthall.com.

THE CALVERTON SCHOOL

300 Calverton School Road

Huntingtown, Maryland 20639

Head of School: Mr. Daniel Hildebrand

General Information Coeducational day college-preparatory, arts, and technology school. Grades PS–12. Founded: 1967. Setting: rural. Nearest major city is Annapolis. 159-acre campus. 3 buildings on campus. Approved or accredited by Association of Independent Maryland Schools, The College Board, and Maryland Department of Education. Member of National Association of Independent Schools. Total enrollment: 416. Upper school average class size: 18. The average school day consists of 7 hours and 20 minutes.

Faculty School total: 49.

Subjects Offered Advanced Placement courses, algebra, American history, American literature, art, art history, biology, calculus, chemistry, Chesapeake Bay studies, chorus, creative writing, drama, economics, English, English literature, environmental science, European civilization, fine arts, French, French-AP, geometry, government/civics, health, humanities, journalism, literature, mathematics, physical education, physics, pre-calculus, public speaking, publications, SAT/ACT preparation, science, social studies, Spanish, Spanish-AP, studio art-AP, theater, trigonometry, U.S. history, U.S. history-AP, visual and performing arts, world civilizations, world history, world literature, yearbook.

Graduation Requirements Algebra, arts and fine arts (art, music, dance, drama), biology, chemistry, English, English composition, English literature, foreign language, geometry, mathematics, physical education (includes health), physics, science, social studies (includes history), trigonometry, U.S. history, world history.

Special Academic Programs Advanced Placement exam preparation; honors section; independent study; ESL (10 students enrolled).
College Admission Counseling 44 students graduated in 2011; all went to college. Median SAT critical reading: 562, median SAT math: 570, median SAT writing: 475, median combined SAT: 1600, median composite ACT: 25. 29% scored over 600 on SAT critical reading, 29% scored over 600 on SAT math, 22% scored over 600 on SAT writing, 14% scored over 1800 on combined SAT, 40% scored over 26 on composite ACT.
Student Life Upper grades have uniform requirement, student council, honor system. Discipline rests equally with students and faculty.
Summer Programs Enrichment, advancement, sports, art/fine arts, computer instruction programs offered; session focuses on enrichment; held both on and off campus; held at various sites; accepts boys and girls; open to students from other schools. 125 students usually enrolled. 2012 schedule: June to August. Application deadline: none.
Tuition and Aid Day student tuition: $18,308. Tuition installment plan (Insured Tuition Payment Plan, FACTS Tuition Payment Plan, monthly payment plans, individually arranged payment plans). Need-based scholarship grants available.
Admissions Traditional secondary-level entrance grade is 9. Admissions testing required. Deadline for receipt of application materials: none. Application fee required: $100. On-campus interview required.
Athletics Interscholastic: basketball (boys, girls), cross-country running (b,g), lacrosse (b,g), soccer (b,g); coed interscholastic: field hockey, golf, tennis; coed intramural: basketball. 3 PE instructors, 10 coaches.
Computers Computers are regularly used in all academic classes. Computer network features include on-campus library services, online commercial services, Internet access, Internet filtering or blocking technology, research services and encyclopedia research programs. Student e-mail accounts are available to students.
Contact Mrs. Julie M. Simpson, Director of Admission. 888-678-0216 Ext. 1108. Fax: 410-535-6169. E-mail: jsimpson@CalvertonSchool.org. Web site: www.CalvertonSchool.org.

CALVIN CHRISTIAN HIGH SCHOOL

2000 North Broadway
Escondido, California 92026

Head of School: Mr. Terry D. Kok

General Information Coeducational day college-preparatory, arts, and religious studies school, affiliated with Reformed Church, Presbyterian Church. Grades PK–12. Founded: 1980. Setting: suburban. Nearest major city is San Diego. 24-acre campus. 2 buildings on campus. Approved or accredited by Christian Schools International, Western Association of Schools and Colleges, and California Department of Education. Endowment: $830,000. Total enrollment: 487. Upper school average class size: 18. Upper school faculty-student ratio: 1:17. There are 174 required school days per year for Upper School students. Upper School students typically attend 5 days per week. The average school day consists of 6 hours and 25 minutes.
Upper School Student Profile Grade 9: 47 students (30 boys, 17 girls); Grade 10: 42 students (24 boys, 18 girls); Grade 11: 27 students (13 boys, 14 girls); Grade 12: 32 students (18 boys, 14 girls). 35% of students are Reformed, Presbyterian.
Faculty School total: 15. In upper school: 8 men, 7 women; 8 have advanced degrees.
Subjects Offered Advanced Placement courses, algebra, American government, art, band, Bible, biology, biology-AP, business mathematics, calculus-AP, chemistry, choir, Christian doctrine, Christian ethics, Christian studies, church history, computer applications, computer programming, computers, dramatic arts, economics, electives, English, English literature-AP, geometry, health, instrumental music, intro to computers, media, modern history, photography, physical education, physical science, physics, pre-calculus, psychology, robotics, Spanish, Spanish-AP, speech, U.S. history, U.S. history-AP, world history, World War II, yearbook.
Graduation Requirements Advanced Placement courses, arts and fine arts (art, music, dance, drama), English, foreign language, mathematics, media, physical education (includes health), religion (includes Bible studies and theology), science, social studies (includes history), technology.
Special Academic Programs 5 Advanced Placement exams for which test preparation is offered; remedial reading and/or remedial writing.
College Admission Counseling 31 students graduated in 2011; all went to college, including California State University, San Marcos; Calvin College; Dordt College; Point Loma Nazarene University; Trinity Christian College; University of California, San Diego. Mean SAT critical reading: 568, mean SAT math: 570, mean SAT writing: 549, mean composite ACT: 24.
Student Life Upper grades have specified standards of dress, student council, honor system. Discipline rests primarily with faculty. Attendance at religious services is required.
Summer Programs Remediation, advancement, sports programs offered; session focuses on Bible courses and/or athletics; held on campus; accepts boys and girls; open to students from other schools. 60 students usually enrolled. 2012 schedule: June 11 to July 20. Application deadline: May 31.
Tuition and Aid Day student tuition: $8515. Tuition installment plan (monthly payment plans, individually arranged payment plans). Need-based scholarship grants, need-based loans available. In 2011–12, 20% of upper-school students received aid. Total amount of financial aid awarded in 2011–12: $225,000.
Admissions Traditional secondary-level entrance grade is 9. For fall 2011, 26 students applied for upper-level admission, 26 were accepted, 24 enrolled. Deadline for receipt of application materials: none. Application fee required: $200. Interview required.
Athletics Interscholastic: baseball (boys), basketball (b,g), cross-country running (b,g), football (b), soccer (b,g), softball (g), track and field (b,g), volleyball (g); coed interscholastic: golf, in-line hockey; coed intramural: weight training. 1 PE instructor, 16 coaches.
Computers Computers are regularly used in computer applications, keyboarding, photography, programming, science, yearbook classes. Computer network features include on-campus library services, Internet access, Internet filtering or blocking technology. Students grades are available online. The school has a published electronic and media policy.
Contact Mr. Frank Steidl, Principal. 760-489-6430. Fax: 760-489-7055. E-mail: franksteidl@calvinchristianescondido.org. Web site: www.calvinchristianescondido.org.

THE CAMBRIDGE SCHOOL OF WESTON

45 Georgian Road
Weston, Massachusetts 02493

Head of School: Jane Moulding

General Information Coeducational boarding and day college-preparatory and arts school. Grades 9–PG. Founded: 1886. Setting: suburban. Nearest major city is Boston. Students are housed in single-sex dormitories. 65-acre campus. 25 buildings on campus. Approved or accredited by Association of Independent Schools in New England, New England Association of Schools and Colleges, The Association of Boarding Schools, and The College Board. Member of National Association of Independent Schools and Secondary School Admission Test Board. Endowment: $7.8 million. Total enrollment: 339. Upper school average class size: 14. Upper school faculty-student ratio: 1:6. There are 160 required school days per year for Upper School students. Upper School students typically attend 5 days per week.
Upper School Student Profile Grade 9: 80 students (34 boys, 46 girls); Grade 10: 81 students (34 boys, 47 girls); Grade 11: 88 students (42 boys, 46 girls); Grade 12: 90 students (37 boys, 53 girls). 25% of students are boarding students. 81% are state residents. 12 states are represented in upper school student body. 12% are international students. International students from China, Hong Kong, Republic of Korea, Taiwan, Thailand, and United Kingdom; 5 other countries represented in student body.
Subjects Offered 20th century physics, 3-dimensional art, acting, Advanced Placement courses, aerospace science, African dance, African history, African literature, African studies, African-American history, African-American literature, African-American studies, algebra, American Civil War, American democracy, American history, American literature, American sign language, analytic geometry, anatomy, anatomy and physiology, animal behavior, animal science, art, art and culture, art history, Asian literature, athletics, backpacking, ballet, ballet technique, baseball, basketball, Bible as literature, biology, botany, calculus, calculus-AP, cell biology, ceramics, chemistry, child development, Chinese history, choir, choreography, chorus, Civil War, collage and assemblage, community service, computer animation, computer math, computer programming, computer science, computer skills, constitutional history of U.S., creative writing, dance, death and loss, digital art, digital photography, discrete mathematics, drama, drama performance, drawing, driver education, earth science, ecology, economics, electronic music, English, English composition, English literature, environmental science, environmental systems, ethics, ethnic literature, European history, European literature, expository writing, fashion, field ecology, film history, film studies, filmmaking, fine arts, foods, French, geography, geometry, government/civics, grammar, great books, Harlem Renaissance, health, health and wellness, history, history of ideas, history of music, history of science, independent study, interdisciplinary studies, Islamic history, Japanese history, jazz, jazz dance, jazz ensemble, jewelry making, journalism, keyboarding, Latin, Latin American history, Latin American literature, leadership education training, literature by women, logic, Mandarin, marine biology, martial arts, mathematical modeling, mathematics, Middle East, model United Nations, music, music theory, musical theater, musicianship, mythology, ornithology, painting, philosophy, photography, physical education, physics, physiology, playwriting, poetry, pre-calculus, printmaking, psychology, religion, Roman civilization, science, sculpture, senior project, set design, Shakespeare, short story, social studies, sociology, Spanish, sports nutrition, stagecraft, statistics, the Presidency, theater, trigonometry, U.S. constitutional history, U.S. history, Vietnam War, weight training, wilderness education, wilderness experience, woodworking, world history, world literature, World War II, writing, yearbook, zoology.
Graduation Requirements Arts and fine arts (art, music, dance, drama), English, foreign language, health education, history, mathematics, performing arts, physical education (includes health), science, senior project. Community service is required.
Special Academic Programs Advanced Placement exam preparation; independent study; term-away projects; study abroad.
College Admission Counseling 92 students graduated in 2011; 91 went to college, including Clark University; Oberlin College; Rhode Island School of Design; Skidmore College; Smith College; The George Washington University. Other: 1 had other specific

plans. 69% scored over 600 on SAT critical reading, 72% scored over 600 on SAT math, 77% scored over 600 on SAT writing.
Student Life Upper grades have student council. Discipline rests equally with students and faculty.
Summer Programs Art/fine arts programs offered; session focuses on visual and performing arts for ages 6 through 15; held on campus; accepts boys and girls; open to students from other schools. 100 students usually enrolled. 2012 schedule: June 25 to July 27. Application deadline: none.
Tuition and Aid Day student tuition: $36,400; 7-day tuition and room/board: $47,900. Tuition installment plan (Insured Tuition Payment Plan, Academic Management Services Plan, monthly payment plans, individually arranged payment plans). Tuition reduction for siblings, need-based scholarship grants, paying campus jobs available. In 2011–12, 27% of upper-school students received aid. Total amount of financial aid awarded in 2011–12: $2,598,100.
Admissions Traditional secondary-level entrance grade is 9. For fall 2011, 350 students applied for upper-level admission, 198 were accepted, 89 enrolled. ISEE, PSAT, SAT, SSAT or TOEFL required. Deadline for receipt of application materials: February 1. Application fee required: $50. Interview required.
Athletics Interscholastic: basketball (boys, girls), field hockey (g), lacrosse (g), soccer (b,g); coed interscholastic: baseball, cross-country running, Frisbee, running, tennis, ultimate Frisbee; coed intramural: alpine skiing, backpacking, ballet, bicycling, canoeing/kayaking, climbing, dance, dance team, fencing, fitness, Frisbee, golf, hiking/backpacking, indoor soccer, kayaking, martial arts, modern dance, nordic skiing, outdoor activities, physical fitness, physical training, rafting, rock climbing, running, skateboarding, skiing (downhill), snowboarding, snowshoeing, soccer, strength & conditioning, table tennis, tai chi, tennis, triathlon, ultimate Frisbee, volleyball, weight training, wilderness, yoga.
Computers Computers are regularly used in art, college planning, English, ESL, ethics, French, graphic design, history, humanities, independent study, journalism, keyboarding, Latin, library, literary magazine, mathematics, music, newspaper, photography, programming, psychology, publications, science, Spanish, word processing, writing, yearbook classes. Computer network features include on-campus library services, online commercial services, Internet access, wireless campus network, Internet filtering or blocking technology, laptops available for use in-class. Student e-mail accounts and computer access in designated common areas are available to students. Students grades are available online.
Contact Trish Saunders, Director of Admissions. 781-642-8650. Fax: 781-398-8344. E-mail: admissions@csw.org. Web site: www.csw.org.

CAMPBELL HALL (EPISCOPAL)

4533 Laurel Canyon Boulevard

North Hollywood, California 91607

Head of School: Rev. Julian Bull

General Information Coeducational day college-preparatory, arts, and technology school, affiliated with Episcopal Church. Grades K–12. Founded: 1944. Setting: suburban. Nearest major city is Los Angeles. 15-acre campus. 12 buildings on campus. Approved or accredited by California Association of Independent Schools, The College Board, Western Association of Schools and Colleges, and California Department of Education. Member of National Association of Independent Schools. Endowment: $5 million. Total enrollment: 1,085. Upper school average class size: 15. Upper school faculty-student ratio: 1:8. There are 140 required school days per year for Upper School students. Upper School students typically attend 5 days per week. The average school day consists of 7 hours and 15 minutes.
Upper School Student Profile Grade 9: 128 students (64 boys, 64 girls); Grade 10: 134 students (64 boys, 70 girls); Grade 11: 132 students (58 boys, 74 girls); Grade 12: 137 students (66 boys, 71 girls). 7% of students are members of Episcopal Church.
Faculty School total: 110. In upper school: 23 men, 32 women; 30 have advanced degrees.
Subjects Offered Algebra, American history, American literature, American studies, ancient history, art, art history, astronomy, band, biology, calculus, ceramics, chemistry, Chinese, community service, computer programming, computer science, creative writing, dance, drama, drawing, earth science, ecology, economics, English, English literature, environmental science, ethics, European history, filmmaking, fine arts, French, geography, geometry, government/civics, history, human development, humanities, instrumental music, Japanese, law, mathematics, music, orchestra, painting, philosophy, photography, physical education, physics, physiology, pre-calculus, printmaking, psychology, science, sculpture, senior seminar, social studies, sociology, Spanish, speech, statistics, theater, theater arts, trigonometry, voice, yearbook.
Graduation Requirements Arts and fine arts (art, music, dance, drama), computer science, English, foreign language, mathematics, physical education (includes health), science, social studies (includes history). Community service is required.
Special Academic Programs Advanced Placement exam preparation; honors section; independent study; study at local college for college credit.
College Admission Counseling 128 students graduated in 2011; all went to college, including Boston University; New York University; Syracuse University; University of California, Berkeley; University of California, Los Angeles; University of Southern California.
Student Life Upper grades have uniform requirement, student council, honor system. Discipline rests equally with students and faculty. Attendance at religious services is required.
Summer Programs Enrichment, advancement, sports, art/fine arts, computer instruction programs offered; session focuses on creative arts and sports; held on campus; accepts boys and girls; open to students from other schools. 200 students usually enrolled. 2012 schedule: June 18 to August 3. Application deadline: June 1.
Tuition and Aid Day student tuition: $28,310. Tuition installment plan (Insured Tuition Payment Plan, monthly payment plans, individually arranged payment plans). Need-based scholarship grants, Episcopal Credit Union tuition loans available. In 2011–12, 25% of upper-school students received aid. Total amount of financial aid awarded in 2011–12: $4,000,000.
Admissions Traditional secondary-level entrance grade is 9. ISEE required. Deadline for receipt of application materials: January 27. Application fee required: $125. Interview required.
Athletics Interscholastic: aerobics/dance (boys, girls), ballet (b,g), baseball (b), basketball (b,g), cheering (b,g), cross-country running (b,g), dance (b,g), dance squad (b,g), equestrian sports (b,g), flag football (b,g), football (b), golf (b,g), horseback riding (b,g), modern dance (b,g), soccer (b,g), softball (g), tennis (b,g), track and field (b,g), volleyball (b,g); intramural: weight lifting (b,g); coed interscholastic: aerobics/dance, ballet, cheering, cross-country running, dance, dance squad, golf, horseback riding, modern dance, track and field. 5 PE instructors, 13 coaches, 2 athletic trainers.
Computers Computers are regularly used in art, English, foreign language, history, humanities, mathematics, science, theater arts classes. Computer network features include on-campus library services, online commercial services, Internet access, wireless campus network, Internet filtering or blocking technology. Campus intranet, student e-mail accounts, and computer access in designated common areas are available to students. The school has a published electronic and media policy.
Contact Ms. Alice Fleming, Director of Admissions. 818-980-7280. Fax: 818-762-3269. Web site: www.campbellhall.org.

See Display on next page and Close-Up on page 596.

CAMPHILL SPECIAL SCHOOL

Glenmoore, Pennsylvania

See Special Needs Schools section.

CANADIAN ACADEMY

4-1 Koyo-cho Naka

Higashinada-ku

Kobe 658-0032, Japan

Head of School: Mr. Frederic Wesson

General Information Coeducational boarding and day college-preparatory school. Boarding grades 9–13, day grades PK–13. Founded: 1913. Setting: urban. Nearest major city is Osaka, Japan. Students are housed in single-sex dormitories. 3-hectare campus. 2 buildings on campus. Approved or accredited by International Baccalaureate Organization, Ministry of Education, Japan, The College Board, and Western Association of Schools and Colleges. Language of instruction: English. Total enrollment: 690. Upper school average class size: 15. Upper school faculty-student ratio: 1:10. There are 180 required school days per year for Upper School students. The average school day consists of 6 hours and 55 minutes.
Upper School Student Profile Grade 9: 58 students (31 boys, 27 girls); Grade 10: 58 students (29 boys, 29 girls); Grade 11: 48 students (28 boys, 20 girls); Grade 12: 58 students (23 boys, 35 girls); Grade 13: 1 student (1 girl).
Faculty School total: 87. In upper school: 20 men, 14 women; 20 have advanced degrees; 19 reside on campus.
Subjects Offered Algebra, art, biology, calculus, chemistry, choir, college writing, concert band, drama, economics, English, ESL, French, geometry, health, integrated mathematics, introduction to literature, Japanese, Japanese history, jazz band, music, orchestra, peer counseling, physical education, physics, publications, social studies, Spanish, theater arts, theory of knowledge, U.S. history, world literature.
Graduation Requirements Electives, English, health, mathematics, modern languages, performing arts, physical education (includes health), science, social studies (includes history), senior project.
Special Academic Programs International Baccalaureate program; Advanced Placement exam preparation; independent study; ESL (11 students enrolled).
College Admission Counseling 53 students graduated in 2010; 43 went to college, including Boston University; Cornell University; Northeastern University; Rhode Island School of Design; The University of British Columbia. Other: 1 had other specific plans. Mean SAT critical reading: 543, mean SAT math: 610, mean SAT writing: 572. 27% scored over 600 on SAT critical reading, 62% scored over 600 on SAT math, 49% scored over 600 on SAT writing.
Student Life Upper grades have specified standards of dress, student council, honor system. Discipline rests primarily with faculty.

Tuition and Aid Day student tuition: ¥1,962,000; 7-day tuition and room/board: ¥3,000,000. Tuition installment plan (semester payment plan). Need-based scholarship grants available. In 2010–11, 20% of upper-school students received aid. Total amount of financial aid awarded in 2010–11: ¥575,000.
Admissions Traditional secondary-level entrance grade is 9. For fall 2010, 27 students applied for upper-level admission, 20 were accepted, 19 enrolled. English for Non-native Speakers, essay, math and English placement tests or SLEP for foreign students required. Deadline for receipt of application materials: none. Application fee required: ¥61,000. On-campus interview required.
Athletics Interscholastic: baseball (boys), basketball (b,g), soccer (b,g), softball (g), tennis (b,g), volleyball (b,g); intramural: baseball (b), basketball (b,g), soccer (b,g), softball (g), table tennis (b,g), volleyball (b,g), weight training (b,g); coed interscholastic: dance, tennis. 4 PE instructors.
Computers Computers are regularly used in all classes. Computer network features include on-campus library services, online commercial services, Internet access, wireless campus network, Internet filtering or blocking technology. Campus intranet and student e-mail accounts are available to students. Students grades are available online. The school has a published electronic and media policy.
Contact Ms. Sandra Ota, Director of Admissions. 81-78-857-0100. Fax: 81-78-857-4095. E-mail: sandyo@canacad.ac.jp. Web site: www.canacad.ac.jp.

CANNON SCHOOL

5801 Poplar Tent Road
Concord, North Carolina 28027

Head of School: Mr. Matthew Gossage

General Information Coeducational day college-preparatory school. Grades PK–12. Founded: 1969. Setting: suburban. Nearest major city is Charlotte. 65-acre campus. 3 buildings on campus. Approved or accredited by Southern Association of Colleges and Schools and North Carolina Department of Education. Endowment: $2.8 million. Total enrollment: 825. Upper school average class size: 17. Upper school faculty-student ratio: 1:9.
Faculty School total: 97. In upper school: 18 men, 28 women; 27 have advanced degrees.
Subjects Offered Acting, advanced math, algebra, American history, American history-AP, American literature, anatomy and physiology, biology, biology-AP, British literature, calculus-AP, character education, chemistry, chemistry-AP, Chinese, chorus, college counseling, computer programming-AP, creative writing, dance, directing, discrete mathematics, drawing, English, English language-AP, English literature-AP, environmental science-AP, ethics, film and literature, film history, finance, French, French-AP, functions, geometry, jazz band, law and the legal system, marine science, mathematical modeling, painting, physics, physics-AP, playwriting, poetry, pre-calculus, psychology-AP, publications, sculpture, senior project, Spanish, Spanish language-AP, statistics-AP, strings, studio art-AP, theater design and production, trigonometry, U.S. government and politics-AP, visual arts, weight training, wind ensemble, world history, world literature, world religions, yearbook.
Graduation Requirements Arts and fine arts (art, music, dance, drama), biology, chemistry, computer literacy, English, foreign language, history, mathematics, physical education (includes health), science, senior project, trigonometry, U.S. history. Community service is required.
Special Academic Programs Advanced Placement exam preparation; honors section; independent study.
College Admission Counseling 72 students graduated in 2011; all went to college, including Appalachian State University; Clemson University; Emory University; Furman University; North Carolina State University; The University of North Carolina at Chapel Hill. Mean SAT critical reading: 610, mean SAT math: 624, mean SAT writing: 623, mean combined SAT: 1857, mean composite ACT: 27.
Student Life Upper grades have specified standards of dress, student council, honor system. Discipline rests primarily with faculty.
Summer Programs Enrichment, sports, art/fine arts, computer instruction programs offered; held on campus; accepts boys and girls; open to students from other schools. 2012 schedule: June 11 to July 27.
Tuition and Aid Day student tuition: $17,535. Tuition installment plan (Insured Tuition Payment Plan, monthly payment plans). Need-based scholarship grants available. In 2011–12, 10% of upper-school students received aid. Total amount of financial aid awarded in 2011–12: $310,000.
Admissions Traditional secondary-level entrance grade is 9. For fall 2011, 79 students applied for upper-level admission, 33 were accepted, 24 enrolled. Admissions testing and ISEE required. Deadline for receipt of application materials: none. Application fee required: $90. On-campus interview required.
Athletics Interscholastic: baseball (boys), basketball (b,g), cheering (g), cross-country running (b,g), dance (g), dance team (g), football (b), golf (b,g), lacrosse (b), physical fitness (b,g), running (b,g), soccer (b,g), softball (g), strength & conditioning (b,g), swimming and diving (b,g), tennis (b,g), track and field (b,g), volleyball (g), weight

training (b,g); coed interscholastic: fitness, golf, running, strength & conditioning, track and field, weight training; coed intramural: yoga. 6 PE instructors, 28 coaches, 1 athletic trainer.

Computers Computers are regularly used in all academic, art, music classes. Computer network features include on-campus library services, online commercial services, Internet access, wireless campus network, Internet filtering or blocking technology, productivity software. Campus intranet, student e-mail accounts, and computer access in designated common areas are available to students. Students grades are available online. The school has a published electronic and media policy.

Contact Mr. William D. Diskin, Director of Admission. 704-721-7164. Fax: 704-788-7779. E-mail: wdiskin@cannonschool.org. Web site: www.cannonschool.org.

THE CANTERBURY EPISCOPAL SCHOOL

1708 North Westmoreland Road

DeSoto, Texas 75115

Head of School: Mr. Raymond Doerge

General Information Coeducational day college-preparatory school, affiliated with Episcopal Church. Grades K–12. Founded: 1992. Setting: suburban. Nearest major city is Dallas. 36-acre campus. 2 buildings on campus. Approved or accredited by Southwest Association of Episcopal Schools and Texas Department of Education. Member of National Association of Independent Schools. Total enrollment: 265. Upper school average class size: 11. Upper school faculty-student ratio: 1:14. There are 173 required school days per year for Upper School students. Upper School students typically attend 5 days per week. The average school day consists of 6 hours and 50 minutes.

Upper School Student Profile Grade 9: 23 students (10 boys, 13 girls); Grade 10: 26 students (16 boys, 10 girls); Grade 11: 10 students (1 boy, 9 girls); Grade 12: 24 students (11 boys, 13 girls). 5% of students are members of Episcopal Church.

Faculty School total: 36. In upper school: 8 men, 11 women; 9 have advanced degrees.

Subjects Offered 1 1/2 elective credits, advanced chemistry, Advanced Placement courses, algebra, American government, American literature, anatomy and physiology, athletics, basketball, biology, biology-AP, calculus, calculus-AP, cheerleading, chemistry, chemistry-AP, college counseling, comparative religion, computer applications, debate, economics, English composition, English language and composition-AP, English literature, English literature and composition-AP, environmental science-AP, European history-AP, fine arts, foreign language, geometry, government, health, math applications, music, organic chemistry, personal money management, photography, physics-AP, Spanish, speech, theology, U.S. history-AP, visual and performing arts, world geography, yearbook.

Graduation Requirements 1 1/2 elective credits, algebra, anatomy and physiology, arts and fine arts (art, music, dance, drama), biology, calculus, chemistry, computer applications, economics, English, English composition, English language and composition-AP, English literature, European history, foreign language, geometry, government, math applications, physical education (includes health), physics, pre-calculus, religion (includes Bible studies and theology), trigonometry, U.S. history, world geography.

Special Academic Programs 9 Advanced Placement exams for which test preparation is offered; honors section; independent study; study at local college for college credit.

College Admission Counseling 17 students graduated in 2011; all went to college, including Oklahoma State University; University of Arkansas. Median SAT critical reading: 574, median SAT math: 553, median SAT writing: 574, median combined SAT: 1686, median composite ACT: 25. 35% scored over 600 on SAT critical reading, 18% scored over 600 on SAT math, 41% scored over 600 on SAT writing, 29% scored over 1800 on combined SAT, 33% scored over 26 on composite ACT.

Student Life Upper grades have uniform requirement, student council, honor system. Discipline rests primarily with faculty. Attendance at religious services is required.

Summer Programs Remediation, enrichment, sports programs offered; session focuses on providing programs based on the needs of our student population; held on campus; accepts boys and girls; open to students from other schools. 80 students usually enrolled. 2012 schedule: June 4 to August 15. Application deadline: May 14.

Tuition and Aid Day student tuition: $13,425. Tuition installment plan (FACTS Tuition Payment Plan, individually arranged payment plans). Tuition reduction for siblings, need-based scholarship grants available. In 2011–12, 45% of upper-school students received aid.

Admissions Traditional secondary-level entrance grade is 9. For fall 2011, 17 students applied for upper-level admission, 16 were accepted, 15 enrolled. OLSAT, Stanford Achievement Test required. Deadline for receipt of application materials: none. Application fee required: $150. Interview required.

Athletics Interscholastic: baseball (boys), basketball (b,g), cheering (g), softball (g), volleyball (g); intramural: flag football (b); coed interscholastic: soccer, swimming and diving, tennis, track and field. 1 PE instructor, 2 coaches, 1 athletic trainer.

Computers Computers are regularly used in computer applications, design, economics, photography, yearbook classes. Computer resources include Internet access, Internet filtering or blocking technology. Computer access in designated common areas is available to students. Students grades are available online.

Contact Ms. Libby Tadlock, Director of Admissions and Development. 972-572-7200 Ext. 106. Fax: 972-572-2470. E-mail: TadlockL@TheCanterburySchool.org. Web site: www.thecanterburyschool.org/.

CANTERBURY SCHOOL

8141 College Parkway

Fort Myers, Florida 33919

Head of School: Mr. John Anthony (Tony) Paulus II

General Information Coeducational day college-preparatory and liberal arts school. Grades PK–12. Founded: 1964. Setting: suburban. Nearest major city is Fort Myers-Sarasota. 33-acre campus. 7 buildings on campus. Approved or accredited by Council of Accreditation and School Improvement, Florida Council of Independent Schools, Southern Association of Colleges and Schools, Southern Association of Independent Schools, The College Board, and Florida Department of Education. Member of National Association of Independent Schools and Secondary School Admission Test Board. Endowment: $6.9 million. Total enrollment: 580. Upper school average class size: 18. Upper school faculty-student ratio: 1:10. There are 181 required school days per year for Upper School students. Upper School students typically attend 5 days per week. The average school day consists of 7 hours and 10 minutes.

Upper School Student Profile Grade 9: 62 students (36 boys, 26 girls); Grade 10: 54 students (23 boys, 31 girls); Grade 11: 46 students (21 boys, 25 girls); Grade 12: 37 students (18 boys, 19 girls).

Faculty School total: 95. In upper school: 21 men, 19 women; 22 have advanced degrees.

Subjects Offered Advanced Placement courses, algebra, American history, American history-AP, American literature, anatomy, art, art history, biology, biology-AP, British literature, calculus, calculus-AP, ceramics, chemistry, chemistry-AP, comparative government and politics-AP, computer programming, constitutional law, creative writing, critical writing, drama, earth science, ecology, economics, English, English literature, English literature-AP, environmental science-AP, European history, fine arts, French, French language-AP, geography, geometry, government-AP, government/civics, grammar, health, history, Latin, leadership, macroeconomics-AP, marine biology, mathematics, music, nationalism and ethnic conflict, photography, physical education, physics, physics-AP, physiology, SAT preparation, science, social studies, sociology, Spanish, Spanish language-AP, speech, statistics, theater, U.S. government and politics-AP, U.S. history, United Nations and international issues, world history, world literature, writing, yearbook.

Graduation Requirements Arts and fine arts (art, music, dance, drama), English, foreign language, mathematics, physical education (includes health), science, social studies (includes history), speech. Community service is required.

Special Academic Programs 15 Advanced Placement exams for which test preparation is offered; independent study; study at local college for college credit.

College Admission Counseling 47 students graduated in 2011; all went to college, including Boston College; Duke University; Stetson University; University of Florida; University of Miami; Yale University. Median SAT critical reading: 632, median SAT math: 627, median SAT writing: 615, median combined SAT: 1874, median composite ACT: 28.

Student Life Upper grades have specified standards of dress, student council, honor system. Discipline rests primarily with faculty.

Summer Programs Remediation, enrichment, advancement, sports, art/fine arts programs offered; session focuses on academic enrichment; held on campus; accepts boys and girls; open to students from other schools. 125 students usually enrolled. 2012 schedule: June 14 to July 30. Application deadline: none.

Tuition and Aid Day student tuition: $18,055. Tuition installment plan (Insured Tuition Payment Plan, monthly payment plans, individually arranged payment plans, quarterly payment plan). Merit scholarship grants, need-based scholarship grants available. In 2011–12, 50% of upper-school students received aid; total upper-school merit-scholarship money awarded: $240,475. Total amount of financial aid awarded in 2011–12: $709,284.

Admissions Traditional secondary-level entrance grade is 9. For fall 2011, 35 students applied for upper-level admission, 24 were accepted, 17 enrolled. ERB CTP IV or SSAT required. Deadline for receipt of application materials: none. Application fee required: $75. Interview required.

Athletics Interscholastic: baseball (boys), basketball (b,g), cheering (g), football (b), lacrosse (b,g), soccer (b,g), volleyball (g), winter soccer (b,g); intramural: volleyball (b); coed interscholastic: cross-country running, golf, swimming and diving, tennis, track and field. 5 PE instructors, 9 coaches, 1 athletic trainer.

Computers Computers are regularly used in art, college planning, English, foreign language, French, history, independent study, journalism, Latin, library, mathematics, science, social sciences, Spanish, speech, theater arts, yearbook classes. Computer network features include on-campus library services, Internet access, wireless campus network, Internet filtering or blocking technology. Campus intranet, student e-mail accounts, and computer access in designated common areas are available to students. Students grades are available online. The school has a published electronic and media policy.

Contact Ms. Julie A. Peters, Director of Admission. 239-415-8945. Fax: 239-481-8339. E-mail: jpeters@canterburyfortmyers.org. Web site: www.canterburyfortmyers.org.

See Display below and Close-Up on page 598.

THE CANTERBURY SCHOOL OF FLORIDA

990 62nd Avenue NE

St. Petersburg, Florida 33702

Head of School: Mr. Mac H. Hall

General Information Coeducational day college-preparatory, arts, and marine studies, international program school, affiliated with Episcopal Church. Grades PK–12. Founded: 1968. Setting: suburban. Nearest major city is Tampa. 20-acre campus. 5 buildings on campus. Approved or accredited by Florida Council of Independent Schools, National Association of Episcopal Schools, National Independent Private Schools Association, The College Board, and Florida Department of Education. Endowment: $115,000. Total enrollment: 402. Upper school average class size: 13. Upper school faculty-student ratio: 1:4.

Upper School Student Profile Grade 9: 49 students (24 boys, 25 girls); Grade 10: 38 students (12 boys, 26 girls); Grade 11: 33 students (13 boys, 20 girls); Grade 12: 33 students (14 boys, 19 girls). 5% of students are members of Episcopal Church.

Faculty School total: 60. In upper school: 12 men, 15 women; 18 have advanced degrees.

Subjects Offered 20th century world history, advanced computer applications, Advanced Placement courses, advanced studio art-AP, algebra, American government, American literature, anatomy, Ancient Greek, ancient world history, art, art history, art history-AP, astronomy, athletics, band, Basic programming, biology, biology-AP, British literature, British literature (honors), calculus, calculus-AP, career exploration, ceramics, character education, chemistry, chemistry-AP, choral music, chorus, classical language, classical studies, college counseling, college placement, community service, competitive science projects, computer multimedia, computer science, computer science-AP, computer skills, contemporary issues, creative writing, dance, dance performance, digital imaging, earth science, economics, English, English composition, English literature, English literature-AP, environmental science, environmental science-AP, environmental studies, ethics, European history, expository writing, film studies, fine arts, finite math, foreign language, French, French-AP, freshman seminar, geography, geometry, government/civics, grammar, Greek culture, guitar, health, history, history of music, history-AP, honors algebra, honors geometry, human geography - AP, independent living, interdisciplinary studies, journalism, keyboarding, Latin, Latin-AP, leadership, leadership and service, library skills, life science, life skills, macroeconomics-AP, marine biology, marine ecology, marine science, marine studies, mathematics, mathematics-AP, mechanical drawing, mentorship program, modern world history, multimedia, music, musical productions, musical theater, oceanography, outdoor education, personal and social education, personal fitness, photojournalism, physical education, physical science, physics, physics-AP, play production, portfolio art, pottery, prayer/spirituality, pre-algebra, pre-calculus, pre-college orientation, psychology, psychology-AP, reading/study skills, robotics, SAT preparation, SAT/ACT preparation, science, senior composition, senior seminar, senior thesis, Shakespeare, social sciences, social studies, Spanish, Spanish language-AP, Spanish literature-AP, Spanish-AP, speech, speech and debate, sports conditioning, stagecraft, statistics-AP, student government, student publications, student teaching, studio art-AP, technical theater, theater arts, theater design and production, theater history, U.S. history, U.S. history-AP, values and decisions, visual and performing arts, weight fitness, weight training, Western philosophy, world history, world literature, world religions, yearbook.

Graduation Requirements Arts and fine arts (art, music, dance, drama), career/college preparation, electives, English, ethics, foreign language, history, mathematics, physical education (includes health), research, science, senior seminar, writing, research and writing, miniterms, ethics and world religions. Community service is required.

Special Academic Programs Advanced Placement exam preparation; honors section; independent study; term-away projects; study at local college for college credit; study abroad.

College Admission Counseling 27 students graduated in 2010; all went to college.

Student Life Upper grades have specified standards of dress, student council, honor system. Discipline rests equally with students and faculty. Attendance at religious services is required.

Tuition and Aid Day student tuition: $15,100–$16,100. Tuition installment plan (Insured Tuition Payment Plan, monthly payment plans, individually arranged payment plans). Tuition reduction for siblings, need-based scholarship grants available. In 2010–11, 20% of upper-school students received aid. Total amount of financial aid awarded in 2010–11: $575,000.

Admissions Traditional secondary-level entrance grade is 9. For fall 2010, 35 students applied for upper-level admission, 30 were accepted, 28 enrolled. 3-R Achievement Test, any standardized test, ERB, SSAT or TOEFL required. Deadline for receipt of application materials: none. Application fee required: $75. On-campus interview required.

Athletics Interscholastic: baseball (boys), basketball (b,g), cross-country running (b,g), diving (g), football (b), golf (b), soccer (b,g), softball (g), swimming and diving (b,g), tennis (b,g), track and field (b,g), volleyball (g); intramural: strength & conditioning (b); coed interscholastic: cheering, cross-country running, golf, soccer; coed intramural: canoeing/kayaking, dance, fitness, flag football, floor hockey, hiking/backpacking, indoor hockey, kayaking, modern dance, outdoor activities, outdoor education, paddle tennis, physical fitness, ropes courses, ultimate Frisbee, weight training. 4 PE instructors, 21 coaches, 1 athletic trainer.

Computers Computers are regularly used in all academic classes. Computer network features include on-campus library services, online commercial services, Internet access, wireless campus network, Internet filtering or blocking technology, remote access to second campus. Computer access in designated common areas is available to students. Students grades are available online. The school has a published electronic and media policy.

Contact Dr. Ashley L. Gairing, Director of Advancement/Admission/Alumni. 727-521-5903. Fax: 727-521-5991. E-mail: agairing@canterbury-fl.org. Web site: www.canterbury-fl.org.

CANTON ACADEMY

Post Office Box 116

One Nancy Drive

Canton, Mississippi 39046

Head of School: Mr. Curt McCain

General Information Coeducational day college-preparatory school. Grades 6–12. Founded: 1965. Setting: small town. Nearest major city is Jackson. Students are housed in day school. 1 building on campus. Approved or accredited by Mississippi Private School Association, Southern Association of Independent Schools, and Mississippi Department of Education. Total enrollment: 323. Upper school average class size: 17. Upper school faculty-student ratio: 1:17. There are 175 required school days per year for Upper School students. Upper School students typically attend 5 days per week. The average school day consists of 7 hours and 20 minutes.

Upper School Student Profile Grade 6: 20 students (9 boys, 11 girls); Grade 7: 21 students (8 boys, 13 girls); Grade 8: 23 students (13 boys, 10 girls); Grade 9: 39 students (24 boys, 15 girls); Grade 10: 32 students (17 boys, 15 girls); Grade 11: 27 students (15 boys, 12 girls); Grade 12: 44 students (27 boys, 17 girls).

Faculty School total: 50. In upper school: 6 men, 7 women.

Graduation Requirements Accounting, Community Service Hours.

College Admission Counseling 32 students graduated in 2010; all went to college, including Delta State University; Millsaps College; Mississippi College; Mississippi State University; University of Mississippi; University of Southern Mississippi.

Student Life Upper grades have specified standards of dress, student council, honor system. Discipline rests primarily with faculty.

Tuition and Aid Tuition installment plan (monthly payment plans, individually arranged payment plans). Tuition reduction for siblings, need-based scholarship grants, paying campus jobs available. In 2010–11, 11% of upper-school students received aid. Total amount of financial aid awarded in 2010–11: $50,000.

Admissions Traditional secondary-level entrance grade is 10. Comprehensive Test of Basic Skills required. Deadline for receipt of application materials: January 26. Application fee required: $35. Interview recommended.

Athletics Interscholastic: aerobics/dance (girls), baseball (b,g), basketball (b,g), cheering (g), cross-country running (b,g), dance team (g), equestrian sports (b,g), football (b), golf (b), horseback riding (b,g), jogging (b,g), power lifting (b), running (b,g), soccer (b,g), softball (g), swimming and diving (b,g), tennis (b,g), weight training (b,g), yoga (g).

Contact 601-859-5231. Fax: 601-859-5232. Web site: www.cantonacademy.org.

CANYONVILLE CHRISTIAN ACADEMY

PO Box 1100

Canyonville, Oregon 97417-1100

Head of School: Mrs. Cathy Lovato

General Information Coeducational boarding and day college-preparatory, religious studies, and English for Speakers of Other Languages school, affiliated with Christian faith. Grades 9–12. Founded: 1924. Setting: rural. Nearest major city is Medford. Students are housed in single-sex dormitories. 10-acre campus. 11 buildings on campus. Approved or accredited by Association of Christian Schools International, Northwest Association of Schools and Colleges, The Association of Boarding Schools, and Oregon Department of Education. Upper school average class size: 20. Upper school faculty-student ratio: 1:15. There are 180 required school days per year for Upper School students. Upper School students typically attend 5 days per week. The average school day consists of 7 hours.

Upper School Student Profile 90% of students are boarding students. 5% are state residents. 3 states are represented in upper school student body. 85% are international students. International students from China, Hong Kong, Republic of Korea, Rwanda, and Taiwan; 6 other countries represented in student body. 70% of students are Christian faith.

Faculty School total: 11. In upper school: 5 men, 6 women; 3 have advanced degrees; 10 reside on campus.

Subjects Offered Advanced Placement courses, aerobics, algebra, American culture, American history, art, Bible, biology, calculus, calculus-AP, career/college preparation, chemistry, choir, Christian doctrine, composition, computer education, computer technologies, computers, consumer economics, desktop publishing, economics, English, English literature, ESL, foreign language, French as a second language, general science, government, grammar, health, integrative seminar, keyboarding, language and composition, library assistant, Life of Christ, mathematics, New Testament, physical education, physical science, physics, pre-calculus, religious education, Spanish, speech and debate, theology, U.S. government, U.S. history, United States government-AP, world history.

Graduation Requirements 1 1/2 elective credits, algebra, arts and fine arts (art, music, dance, drama), Bible, biology, economics, English, foreign language, government, health and wellness, mathematics, physical education (includes health), physical science, speech and debate, U.S. history, world history.

Special Academic Programs Advanced Placement exam preparation; honors section; accelerated programs; independent study; study at local college for college credit; ESL (50 students enrolled).

College Admission Counseling 30 students graduated in 2011; 25 went to college, including Oregon State University; Sarah Lawrence College; University of Illinois at Urbana–Champaign; University of Oregon; Washington State University. Other: 1 entered military service, 2 had other specific plans. Mean SAT critical reading: 380, mean SAT math: 576, mean SAT writing: 406, mean combined SAT: 1362.

Student Life Upper grades have specified standards of dress, student council, honor system. Discipline rests primarily with faculty. Attendance at religious services is required.

Tuition and Aid Day student tuition: $4600; 7-day tuition and room/board: $23,500. Tuition installment plan (monthly payment plans, individually arranged payment plans). Tuition reduction for siblings, merit scholarship grants, need-based scholarship grants, paying campus jobs available. In 2011–12, 15% of upper-school students received aid. Total amount of financial aid awarded in 2011–12: $390,000.

Admissions Traditional secondary-level entrance grade is 9. TOEFL or SLEP required. Deadline for receipt of application materials: none. Application fee required: $100. Interview recommended.

Athletics Interscholastic: basketball (boys, girls), cheering (g), cross-country running (b,g), soccer (b), tennis (b,g), track and field (b,g), volleyball (g); intramural: aerobics (g), soccer (b); coed interscholastic: soccer, tennis; coed intramural: badminton, basketball, billiards, table tennis, tennis, volleyball. 3 PE instructors, 9 coaches.

Computers Computers are regularly used in business applications, technology, yearbook classes. Computer network features include Internet access, wireless campus network, Internet filtering or blocking technology. Student e-mail accounts and computer access in designated common areas are available to students. Students grades are available online.

Contact Mr. Ed Lovato, Director of Admissions. 541-839-4401. Fax: 541-839-6228. E-mail: admissions@canyonville.net. Web site: www.canyonville.net.

CAPE COD ACADEMY

50 Osterville-West Barnstable Road

Osterville, Massachusetts 02655

Head of School: Mr. Philip Petru

General Information Coeducational day college-preparatory, arts, and technology school. Grades PK–12. Founded: 1976. Setting: small town. Nearest major city is Boston. 47-acre campus. 5 buildings on campus. Approved or accredited by Association of Independent Schools in New England and New England Association of Schools and Colleges. Member of National Association of Independent Schools and Secondary School Admission Test Board. Endowment: $2.2 million. Total enrollment: 327. Upper school average class size: 13. Upper school faculty-student ratio: 1:4. There are 172 required school days per year for Upper School students. Upper School students typically attend 5 days per week. The average school day consists of 6 hours and 30 minutes.

Upper School Student Profile Grade 9: 34 students (18 boys, 16 girls); Grade 10: 50 students (27 boys, 23 girls); Grade 11: 46 students (23 boys, 23 girls); Grade 12: 27 students (15 boys, 12 girls).

Faculty School total: 52. In upper school: 19 men, 20 women; 28 have advanced degrees.

Subjects Offered Advanced biology, advanced chemistry, advanced math, Advanced Placement courses, advanced studio art-AP, algebra, American history, American literature, art, art history, art history-AP, art-AP, biology, calculus, calculus-AP, ceramics, chemistry, chemistry-AP, community service, computer math, computer programming, computer science, digital photography, drama, earth science, English, English literature, English-AP, environmental science, ethics, European history, expository writing, fine arts, French, French-AP, geography, geometry, health, history, history-AP, honors algebra, honors geometry, Latin, mathematics, music, music composition, music history, music theory, philosophy, photography, physical education, physics, SAT preparation, science, senior internship, social sciences, social studies, Spanish, Spanish-AP, statistics-AP, studio art-AP, theater, trigonometry, world history, world literature.

Graduation Requirements Arts and fine arts (art, music, dance, drama), computer science, English, foreign language, history, independent study, mathematics, physical education (includes health), science. Community service is required.

Special Academic Programs 10 Advanced Placement exams for which test preparation is offered; honors section; independent study; term-away projects; study abroad.
College Admission Counseling 39 students graduated in 2011; all went to college, including Boston College; Boston University; Providence College; Tufts University; University of Massachusetts Amherst; University of Pennsylvania. Mean SAT critical reading: 595, mean SAT math: 624.
Student Life Upper grades have specified standards of dress, student council, honor system. Discipline rests primarily with faculty.
Tuition and Aid Day student tuition: $18,470–$22,270. Tuition installment plan (Academic Management Services Plan, monthly payment plans, individually arranged payment plans). Need-based scholarship grants available. In 2011–12, 35% of upper-school students received aid.
Admissions Traditional secondary-level entrance grade is 9. ISEE or SSAT required. Deadline for receipt of application materials: February 1. Application fee required: $95. On-campus interview required.
Athletics Interscholastic: baseball (boys), basketball (b,g), lacrosse (b,g), soccer (b,g), tennis (b,g); coed interscholastic: cross-country running, golf; coed intramural: aerobics, aerobics/Nautilus, archery, basketball, combined training, fitness, floor hockey, physical training, sailing, soccer, strength & conditioning, weight training. 1 PE instructor, 11 coaches, 1 athletic trainer.
Computers Computers are regularly used in all classes. Computer network features include on-campus library services, online commercial services, Internet access, wireless campus network, Internet filtering or blocking technology. Campus intranet, student e-mail accounts, and computer access in designated common areas are available to students. Students grades are available online. The school has a published electronic and media policy.
Contact Laurie Wyndham, Director of Admissions. 508-428-5400 Ext. 226. Fax: 508-428-0701. E-mail: lwyndham@capecodacademy.org. Web site: www.capecodacademy.org.

CAPE FEAR ACADEMY

3900 South College Road

Wilmington, North Carolina 28412

Head of School: Mr. John B. Meehl

General Information Coeducational day college-preparatory and arts school. Grades PK–12. Founded: 1967. Setting: suburban. 27-acre campus. 3 buildings on campus. Approved or accredited by Southern Association of Colleges and Schools, Southern Association of Independent Schools, and North Carolina Department of Education. Member of National Association of Independent Schools. Endowment: $659,800. Total enrollment: 628. Upper school average class size: 17. Upper school faculty-student ratio: 1:8. There are 177 required school days per year for Upper School students. Upper School students typically attend 5 days per week. The average school day consists of 7 hours and 20 minutes.
Upper School Student Profile Grade 9: 56 students (23 boys, 33 girls); Grade 10: 74 students (35 boys, 39 girls); Grade 11: 52 students (22 boys, 30 girls); Grade 12: 56 students (30 boys, 26 girls).
Faculty School total: 80. In upper school: 14 men, 15 women; 12 have advanced degrees.
Subjects Offered 3-dimensional art, Advanced Placement courses, algebra, American history, American history-AP, American literature, analysis, art, art history, band, biology, biology-AP, British literature, calculus-AP, chemistry, choral music, comparative government and politics-AP, computer science, conceptual physics, critical studies in film, discrete mathematics, drama, earth and space science, English, English language-AP, English literature, English literature-AP, environmental science, environmental science-AP, European history, European history-AP, film studies, finance, fine arts, fitness, geometry, global studies, government and politics-AP, government-AP, history, honors geometry, human anatomy, independent study, journalism, language, literature, marine science, mathematics, music, music theory-AP, musical theater, newspaper, organizational studies, photography, physical education, physics, pre-calculus, psychology, publications, religion, SAT preparation, science, sculpture, social studies, Spanish, student publications, theater, video film production, vocal ensemble, weight training, world history.
Graduation Requirements Arts and fine arts (art, music, dance, drama), biology, English, foreign language, mathematics, physical education (includes health), science, social studies (includes history), U.S. government, U.S. history, 72 hours of community service over 4 years. Community service is required.
Special Academic Programs 11 Advanced Placement exams for which test preparation is offered; honors section; independent study; study at local college for college credit; study abroad.
College Admission Counseling 56 students graduated in 2011; all went to college, including East Carolina University; North Carolina State University; The University of North Carolina at Chapel Hill; Wake Forest University. Mean combined SAT: 1803, mean composite ACT: 26.
Student Life Upper grades have specified standards of dress, student council, honor system. Discipline rests primarily with faculty.
Summer Programs Enrichment, sports, art/fine arts programs offered; session focuses on enrichment and sports; held on campus; accepts boys and girls; open to students from other schools. 250 students usually enrolled. 2012 schedule: June 11 to August 10. Application deadline: none.
Tuition and Aid Day student tuition: $12,525. Tuition installment plan (Insured Tuition Payment Plan, FACTS Tuition Payment Plan, monthly payment plans). Merit scholarship grants, need-based scholarship grants available. In 2011–12, 20% of upper-school students received aid; total upper-school merit-scholarship money awarded: $12,500. Total amount of financial aid awarded in 2011–12: $249,612.
Admissions Traditional secondary-level entrance grade is 9. For fall 2011, 42 students applied for upper-level admission, 32 were accepted, 24 enrolled. ERB, ISEE, PSAT or SAT or SSAT required. Deadline for receipt of application materials: none. Application fee required: $75. On-campus interview recommended.
Athletics Interscholastic: basketball (boys, girls), field hockey (g), lacrosse (b,g), soccer (b,g), tennis (b,g), volleyball (g); coed interscholastic: cheering, cross-country running, golf, surfing, swimming and diving. 2 PE instructors, 11 coaches, 1 athletic trainer.
Computers Computers are regularly used in all academic classes. Computer network features include on-campus library services, online commercial services, Internet access, wireless campus network, Internet filtering or blocking technology. Campus intranet, student e-mail accounts, and computer access in designated common areas are available to students. Students grades are available online. The school has a published electronic and media policy.
Contact Mrs. Susan Mixon Harrell, Director of Admission. 910-791-0287 Ext. 1015. Fax: 910-791-0290. E-mail: sharrell@capefearacademy.org. Web site: www.capefearacademy.org.

CAPE HENRY COLLEGIATE SCHOOL

1320 Mill Dam Road

Virginia Beach, Virginia 23454-2306

Head of School: Dr. John P. Lewis

General Information Coeducational day college-preparatory, arts, technology, and global education school. Grades PK–12. Founded: 1924. Setting: suburban. 30-acre campus. 9 buildings on campus. Approved or accredited by Virginia Association of Independent Schools. Member of National Association of Independent Schools. Endowment: $6 million. Total enrollment: 852. Upper school average class size: 14. Upper school faculty-student ratio: 1:10. Upper School students typically attend 5 days per week. The average school day consists of 7 hours and 20 minutes.
Upper School Student Profile Grade 9: 86 students (38 boys, 48 girls); Grade 10: 104 students (60 boys, 44 girls); Grade 11: 87 students (44 boys, 43 girls); Grade 12: 94 students (55 boys, 39 girls).
Faculty School total: 118. In upper school: 27 men, 35 women; 34 have advanced degrees.
Subjects Offered Algebra, American history, American literature, art, art history, biology, botany, business skills, calculus, ceramics, chemistry, community service, computer programming, computer science, creative writing, drama, driver education, earth science, ecology, economics, English, English literature, environmental science, European history, expository writing, fine arts, French, geography, geology, geometry, government/civics, health, history, journalism, Latin, law, marine biology, mathematics, music, oceanography, photography, physical education, physics, science, social sciences, social studies, sociology, Spanish, speech, statistics, theater, trigonometry, world history, world literature, writing.
Graduation Requirements Arts and fine arts (art, music, dance, drama), computer science, English, foreign language, mathematics, physical education (includes health), science, social sciences, social studies (includes history). Community service is required.
Special Academic Programs Advanced Placement exam preparation; honors section; independent study; academic accommodation for the gifted, the musically talented, and the artistically talented; ESL (15 students enrolled).
College Admission Counseling 84 students graduated in 2011; all went to college, including Hampden-Sydney College; James Madison University; The College of William and Mary; University of Virginia; Virginia Polytechnic Institute and State University; Washington and Lee University.
Student Life Upper grades have specified standards of dress, student council, honor system. Discipline rests equally with students and faculty.
Summer Programs Enrichment, advancement, ESL, sports, art/fine arts, computer instruction programs offered; session focuses on academics and enrichment; held on campus; accepts boys and girls; open to students from other schools. 1,200 students usually enrolled. 2012 schedule: June 8 to August 14. Application deadline: none.
Tuition and Aid Day student tuition: $17,165. Tuition installment plan (The Tuition Plan, Insured Tuition Payment Plan, monthly payment plans, individually arranged payment plans, 3-payment plan). Merit scholarship grants, need-based scholarship grants available. In 2011–12, 20% of upper-school students received aid; total upper-school merit-scholarship money awarded: $17,165.
Admissions Traditional secondary-level entrance grade is 9. For fall 2011, 169 students applied for upper-level admission, 151 were accepted, 107 enrolled. Brigance Test of Basic Skills, ERB CTP, ISEE or writing sample required. Deadline for receipt of application materials: February 15. Application fee required: $50. On-campus interview required.

Athletics Interscholastic: baseball (boys), basketball (b,g), crew (b,g), cross-country running (b,g), field hockey (g), golf (b,g), lacrosse (b,g), soccer (b,g), softball (g), tennis (b,g), volleyball (b,g), wrestling (b); intramural: baseball (b), basketball (b,g), crew (b,g), cross-country running (b,g), field hockey (g), floor hockey (b,g), wrestling (b); coed interscholastic: cheering, swimming and diving, track and field; coed intramural: aerobics, aerobics/dance, aerobics/Nautilus, archery, backpacking, badminton, ballet, cheering, dance, fishing, fitness, fitness walking, golf, hiking/backpacking, jogging, kayaking, lacrosse, modern dance, ocean paddling, outdoor activities, outdoor adventure, physical fitness, physical training, skiing (downhill), snowboarding, soccer, strength & conditioning, surfing, swimming and diving, table tennis, tennis, volleyball, weight lifting, weight training, wilderness, yoga. 3 PE instructors, 25 coaches, 1 athletic trainer.
Computers Computers are regularly used in computer applications, desktop publishing, graphic arts, information technology, literary magazine, newspaper, publications, technology, video film production, Web site design, word processing, yearbook classes. Computer network features include on-campus library services, online commercial services, Internet access, wireless campus network, Internet filtering or blocking technology. Student e-mail accounts and computer access in designated common areas are available to students. Students grades are available online. The school has a published electronic and media policy.
Contact Mrs. Angie Finley, Admissions Associate. 757-963-8234. Fax: 757-481-9194. E-mail: angiefinley@capehenry.org. Web site: www.capehenrycollegiate.org.

CAPISTRANO VALLEY CHRISTIAN SCHOOLS

32032 Del Obispo Street

San Juan Capistrano, California 92675

Head of School: Dr. Ron Sipus

General Information Coeducational day college-preparatory, arts, religious studies, bilingual studies, and technology school, affiliated with Christian faith. Grades JK–12. Founded: 1972. Setting: suburban. 8-acre campus. 2 buildings on campus. Approved or accredited by Association of Christian Schools International, Western Association of Schools and Colleges, and California Department of Education. Total enrollment: 440. Upper school average class size: 18. Upper school faculty-student ratio: 1:13. There are 180 required school days per year for Upper School students. Upper School students typically attend 5 days per week. The average school day consists of 6 hours.
Upper School Student Profile Grade 9: 38 students (20 boys, 18 girls); Grade 10: 40 students (19 boys, 21 girls); Grade 11: 46 students (22 boys, 24 girls); Grade 12: 51 students (25 boys, 26 girls). 80% of students are Christian faith.
Faculty School total: 45. In upper school: 9 men, 13 women; 9 have advanced degrees.
Subjects Offered ACT preparation, advanced biology, advanced chemistry, advanced computer applications, advanced math, Advanced Placement courses, advanced TOEFL/grammar, algebra, American government, American history, American history-AP, American literature, American literature-AP, anatomy, art, ASB Leadership, athletic training, athletics, Bible studies, biology, biology-AP, calculus-AP, career planning, chemistry, choir, college counseling, college placement, composition, composition-AP, computer animation, computer applications, computer education, computer information systems, computer literacy, computer multimedia, computer skills, computer technologies, desktop publishing, drama performance, ecology, economics, English, English literature-AP, English-AP, ESL, European history, freshman foundations, geometry, government, graphic design, health, history, honors algebra, honors English, independent study, Internet, intro to computers, journalism, keyboarding, lab science, leadership, physical education, physical science, physics, public speaking, research skills, Spanish, Spanish-AP, student government, U.S. government and politics-AP, U.S. history-AP, Web site design, world cultures, yearbook.
Graduation Requirements Algebra, American government, American history, American literature, arts and fine arts (art, music, dance, drama), Bible, biology, composition, computer skills, economics, electives, English, European history, foreign language, freshman foundations, geometry, physical education (includes health), research skills, speech, graduation requirements meet UC and CSU entrance requirements.
Special Academic Programs Advanced Placement exam preparation; honors section; independent study; special instructional classes for Oportunity School Program; ESL (24 students enrolled).
College Admission Counseling 56 students graduated in 2011; 54 went to college, including Azusa Pacific University; Biola University; Point Loma Nazarene University; University of California, Berkeley; University of California, Irvine; Westmont College. Other: 1 went to work, 1 had other specific plans. Median SAT critical reading: 537, median SAT math: 619, median SAT writing: 559, median combined SAT: 1715.
Student Life Upper grades have uniform requirement, student council, honor system. Discipline rests primarily with faculty. Attendance at religious services is required.
Summer Programs Remediation, advancement, sports programs offered; held on campus; accepts boys and girls; open to students from other schools. 35 students usually enrolled. 2012 schedule: July 11 to August 5. Application deadline: May 1.
Tuition and Aid Day student tuition: $11,330. Tuition installment plan (FACTS Tuition Payment Plan). Tuition reduction for siblings, merit scholarship grants, need-based scholarship grants available. In 2011–12, 40% of upper-school students received aid; total upper-school merit-scholarship money awarded: $12,000. Total amount of financial aid awarded in 2011–12: $225,000.
Admissions Traditional secondary-level entrance grade is 9. For fall 2011, 64 students applied for upper-level admission, 60 were accepted, 58 enrolled. ESOL English Proficiency Test, High School Placement Test, Stanford Test of Academic Skills or TOEFL required. Deadline for receipt of application materials: April 30. Application fee required: $100. On-campus interview required.
Athletics Interscholastic: baseball (boys), basketball (b,g), cheering (g), cross-country running (b,g), football (b), softball (g), tennis (b,g), volleyball (b,g), weight lifting (b); coed interscholastic: equestrian sports, golf, physical training, soccer, strength & conditioning, weight training. 3 PE instructors, 51 coaches, 4 athletic trainers.
Computers Computers are regularly used in all academic, Bible studies, data processing, design, journalism, yearbook classes. Computer network features include on-campus library services, Internet access, wireless campus network, Internet filtering or blocking technology, 1 to 1 tablet PC program. Campus intranet, student e-mail accounts, and computer access in designated common areas are available to students. Students grades are available online. The school has a published electronic and media policy.
Contact Jo Beveridge, Director of Admissions/Development. 949-493-5683 Ext. 109. Fax: 949-493-6057. E-mail: jbeveridge@cvcs.org. Web site: www.cvcs.org.

CARDIGAN MOUNTAIN SCHOOL

Canaan, New Hampshire

See Junior Boarding Schools section.

CARDINAL MOONEY CATHOLIC COLLEGE PREPARATORY HIGH SCHOOL

660 South Water Street

Marine City, Michigan 48039

Head of School: Ms. Celeste Conflitti

General Information Coeducational day college-preparatory school, affiliated with Roman Catholic Church. Grades 9–12. Founded: 1977. Setting: small town. Nearest major city is Mount Clemens. 1-acre campus. 1 building on campus. Approved or accredited by North Central Association of Colleges and Schools and Michigan Department of Education. Total enrollment: 180. Upper school average class size: 22. Upper school faculty-student ratio: 1:10. There are 186 required school days per year for Upper School students. Upper School students typically attend 5 days per week. The average school day consists of 6 hours and 25 minutes.
Upper School Student Profile Grade 9: 44 students (16 boys, 28 girls); Grade 10: 45 students (20 boys, 25 girls); Grade 11: 45 students (22 boys, 23 girls); Grade 12: 44 students (18 boys, 26 girls). 90% of students are Roman Catholic.
Faculty School total: 20. In upper school: 5 men, 13 women; 10 have advanced degrees.
Subjects Offered Advanced Placement courses, algebra, American literature, anatomy, art, biology, calculus, Catholic belief and practice, chemistry, choir, computer applications, computer skills, drama, economics, English, fiction, French, French language-AP, geography, geometry, government, government-AP, health, humanities, Italian, library science, moral and social development, mythology, physical education, physical science, physics, poetry, pre-calculus, Spanish, Spanish language-AP, statistics, study skills, U.S. history, U.S. history-AP, world history, world literature, yearbook.
Special Academic Programs 6 Advanced Placement exams for which test preparation is offered; honors section.
College Admission Counseling 49 students graduated in 2011; 47 went to college, including Central Michigan University; Grand Valley State University; Michigan State University; Oakland University; University of Detroit Mercy; University of Michigan. Other: 2 entered military service.
Student Life Upper grades have uniform requirement, student council, honor system. Discipline rests primarily with faculty. Attendance at religious services is required.
Tuition and Aid Tuition installment plan (monthly payment plans). Tuition reduction for siblings available.
Admissions Traditional secondary-level entrance grade is 9. For fall 2011, 48 students applied for upper-level admission, 48 were accepted, 48 enrolled. High School Placement Test required. Deadline for receipt of application materials: none. Application fee required: $250. Interview required.
Athletics Interscholastic: baseball (boys), basketball (b,g), bowling (b,g), cheering (g), cross-country running (b,g), equestrian sports (b,g), football (b), golf (b), soccer (b,g), softball (g), volleyball (g); coed interscholastic: cross-country running, track and field. 2 PE instructors, 6 coaches.
Computers Computers are regularly used in all academic, computer applications, data processing, desktop publishing, graphic design, library science, word processing, yearbook classes. Computer network features include on-campus library services, Internet access, Internet filtering or blocking technology. Computer access in designated common areas is available to students. Students grades are available online. The school has a published electronic and media policy.

Contact Ms. Celeste Conflitti, Principal. 810-765-8825 Ext. 14. Fax: 810-765-7164. E-mail: principal@cardinalmooneycatholic.com.

CARDINAL MOONEY CATHOLIC HIGH SCHOOL

4171 Fruitville Road

Sarasota, Florida 34232

Head of School: Mr. Stephen J. Christie

General Information Coeducational day college-preparatory, arts, and religious studies school, affiliated with Roman Catholic Church. Grades 9–12. Founded: 1959. Setting: suburban. Nearest major city is Tampa. 36-acre campus. 7 buildings on campus. Approved or accredited by Southern Association of Colleges and Schools. Endowment: $1.8 million. Total enrollment: 467. Upper school average class size: 18. Upper school faculty-student ratio: 1:13. There are 180 required school days per year for Upper School students. Upper School students typically attend 5 days per week. The average school day consists of 6 hours and 35 minutes.

Upper School Student Profile Grade 9: 91 students (46 boys, 45 girls); Grade 10: 132 students (57 boys, 75 girls); Grade 11: 119 students (72 boys, 47 girls); Grade 12: 125 students (74 boys, 51 girls). 80% of students are Roman Catholic.

Faculty School total: 45. In upper school: 20 men, 25 women; 25 have advanced degrees.

Subjects Offered Algebra, American government, American history, anatomy, art, biology, business, calculus, ceramics, chemistry, chorus, Christian and Hebrew scripture, community service, computer applications, computer graphics, contemporary history, creative writing, drama, earth science, economics, economics and history, English, English literature, environmental science, fine arts, French, geometry, guitar, health, history, instrumental music, integrated mathematics, journalism, keyboarding, learning strategies, marine biology, mathematics, music, physical education, physics, psychology, science, social justice, social studies, sociology, Spanish, speech, theology, trigonometry, U.S. government and politics-AP, world history, world literature, world religions.

Graduation Requirements Arts and fine arts (art, music, dance, drama), electives, English, foreign language, mathematics, musical theater, physical education (includes health), religion (includes Bible studies and theology), science, social sciences, social studies (includes history), 100 hours of community service.

Special Academic Programs 8 Advanced Placement exams for which test preparation is offered; honors section; academic accommodation for the musically talented and the artistically talented.

College Admission Counseling 147 students graduated in 2010; all went to college, including Florida Gulf Coast University; Florida State University; University of Central Florida; University of Florida; University of North Florida; University of South Florida. Median SAT critical reading: 510, median SAT math: 520, median SAT writing: 518, median composite ACT: 22. 31% scored over 600 on SAT critical reading, 41% scored over 600 on SAT math, 35% scored over 600 on SAT writing, 38% scored over 26 on composite ACT.

Student Life Upper grades have specified standards of dress, student council. Discipline rests primarily with faculty. Attendance at religious services is required.

Tuition and Aid Day student tuition: $7875–$10,300. Tuition installment plan (monthly payment plans, semester payment plan). Tuition reduction for siblings, merit scholarship grants, need-based scholarship grants, paying campus jobs available. In 2010–11, 15% of upper-school students received aid; total upper-school merit-scholarship money awarded: $12,250. Total amount of financial aid awarded in 2010–11: $200,000.

Admissions Traditional secondary-level entrance grade is 9. For fall 2010, 180 students applied for upper-level admission, 180 were accepted, 133 enrolled. Placement test or STS required. Deadline for receipt of application materials: none. No application fee required. On-campus interview required.

Athletics Interscholastic: baseball (boys), basketball (b,g), cheering (g), cross-country running (b,g), dance team (g), diving (b,g), football (b), golf (b,g), lacrosse (b,g), modern dance (g), soccer (b,g), softball (g), strength & conditioning (b,g), swimming and diving (b,g), track and field (b,g), volleyball (g), weight lifting (b,g), weight training (b,g); intramural: basketball (b,g), volleyball (b,g); coed intramural: volleyball. 4 PE instructors, 66 coaches, 1 athletic trainer.

Computers Computers are regularly used in art, computer applications, English, mathematics, science classes. Computer network features include on-campus library services, online commercial services, Internet access, wireless campus network. Students grades are available online. The school has a published electronic and media policy.

Contact Mrs. Joanne Mades, Registrar. 941-371-4917. Fax: 941-371-6924. E-mail: jmades@cmhs-sarasota.org. Web site: www.cmhs-sarasota.org.

CARDINAL NEWMAN HIGH SCHOOL

512 Spencer Drive

West Palm Beach, Florida 33409-3699

Head of School: Fr. David W. Carr

General Information Coeducational day college-preparatory and International Baccalaureate school, affiliated with Roman Catholic Church. Grades 9–12. Founded: 1961. Setting: suburban. Nearest major city is Miami. 50-acre campus. 5 buildings on campus. Approved or accredited by National Catholic Education Association, Southern Association of Colleges and Schools, and Florida Department of Education. Total enrollment: 572. Upper school average class size: 25. Upper school faculty-student ratio: 1:25. There are 180 required school days per year for Upper School students. Upper School students typically attend 5 days per week. The average school day consists of 6 hours and 40 minutes.

Upper School Student Profile Grade 9: 134 students (70 boys, 64 girls); Grade 10: 160 students (75 boys, 85 girls); Grade 11: 128 students (54 boys, 74 girls); Grade 12: 150 students (72 boys, 78 girls). 80% of students are Roman Catholic.

Faculty School total: 48. In upper school: 16 men, 32 women; 36 have advanced degrees.

Subjects Offered Algebra, American government, American history, American literature, anatomy and physiology, art, band, Bible studies, biology, biology-AP, calculus, calculus-AP, chemistry, chorus, church history, college writing, computer applications, computer science, creative writing, desktop publishing, drama, economics, English, English literature, English-AP, ethics, European history, fine arts, French, French-AP, geometry, government/civics, health, history, honors algebra, honors English, honors geometry, integrated science, International Baccalaureate courses, journalism, leadership, marine biology, mathematics, music appreciation, newspaper, physical education, physics, political science, pre-calculus, probability and statistics, religion, social justice, social studies, Spanish, speech, world history, world literature, writing, yearbook.

Graduation Requirements Arts and fine arts (art, music, dance, drama), English, foreign language, mathematics, physical education (includes health), religion (includes Bible studies and theology), science, social studies (includes history), 100-hour community service requirement.

Special Academic Programs International Baccalaureate program; Advanced Placement exam preparation; honors section; study at local college for college credit; academic accommodation for the gifted; remedial reading and/or remedial writing; remedial math.

College Admission Counseling 184 students graduated in 2011; 182 went to college, including Florida Atlantic University; Florida State University; Palm Beach State College; University of Central Florida; University of Florida; University of North Florida. Other: 1 entered a postgraduate year, 1 had other specific plans.

Student Life Upper grades have uniform requirement, student council, honor system. Discipline rests primarily with faculty. Attendance at religious services is required.

Summer Programs Remediation, enrichment, sports programs offered; session focuses on freshman preparation; held on campus; accepts boys and girls; not open to students from other schools. 75 students usually enrolled. 2012 schedule: June 15 to June 30.

Tuition and Aid Day student tuition: $9650–$10,650. Tuition installment plan (FACTS Tuition Payment Plan). Need-based scholarship grants available. In 2011–12, 18% of upper-school students received aid.

Admissions Traditional secondary-level entrance grade is 9. STS required. Deadline for receipt of application materials: none. Application fee required: $50. On-campus interview recommended.

Athletics Interscholastic: baseball (boys), basketball (b,g), bowling (b,g), cheering (g), cross-country running (b,g), dance team (g), diving (b,g), football (b), golf (b,g), lacrosse (b,g), physical fitness (b,g), soccer (b,g), softball (g), swimming and diving (b,g), tennis (b,g), track and field (b,g), volleyball (g), wrestling (b). 2 PE instructors, 1 athletic trainer.

Computers Computers are regularly used in all academic, Bible studies, yearbook classes. Computer resources include on-campus library services, online commercial services, Internet access, Internet filtering or blocking technology. Students grades are available online. The school has a published electronic and media policy.

Contact Mrs. Jan Joy, Admissions Coordinator. 561-242-2268. Fax: 561-683-7307. E-mail: jjoy@cardinalnewman.com. Web site: www.cardinalnewman.com.

CARDINAL O'HARA HIGH SCHOOL

1701 South Sproul Road

Springfield, Pennsylvania 19064-1199

Head of School: Mrs. Marie Rogai

General Information Coeducational day college-preparatory school, affiliated with Roman Catholic Church. Grades 9–12. Founded: 1963. Setting: suburban. Nearest major city is Philadelphia. 1 building on campus. Approved or accredited by Pennsylvania Department of Education. Upper school average class size: 30. Upper school faculty-student ratio: 1:21. There are 180 required school days per year for Upper School students. Upper School students typically attend 5 days per week. The average school day consists of 6 hours and 35 minutes.

Upper School Student Profile 83% of students are Roman Catholic.
Faculty School total: 76. In upper school: 42 men, 34 women; 31 have advanced degrees.
Special Academic Programs Advanced Placement exam preparation; academic accommodation for the musically talented.
Student Life Upper grades have uniform requirement, student council, honor system. Discipline rests primarily with faculty. Attendance at religious services is required.
Summer Programs Enrichment programs offered; held on campus; accepts boys and girls; not open to students from other schools. 75 students usually enrolled.
Tuition and Aid Day student tuition: $5600. Tuition installment plan (monthly payment plans). Need-based scholarship grants available.
Admissions Traditional secondary-level entrance grade is 9. Application fee required: $200.
Athletics Interscholastic: baseball (boys), basketball (b,g), bowling (b,g), cheering (g), cross-country running (b,g), field hockey (g), football (b), Frisbee (b,g), golf (b), ice hockey (b), indoor track (b,g), indoor track & field (b,g), lacrosse (b,g), rugby (b), soccer (b,g), softball (g), tennis (b,g), track and field (b,g), ultimate Frisbee (b,g), volleyball (g), wrestling (b).
Computers Computer resources include on-campus library services, Internet access, wireless campus network, Internet filtering or blocking technology. Students grades are available online. The school has a published electronic and media policy.
Contact Mrs. Patti Arnold, Admissions Director. 610-544-3800 Ext. 70. Fax: 610-544-1189. E-mail: pattiarnold@cohs.com. Web site: www.cohs.com.

CARLISLE SCHOOL

300 Carlisle Road

Axton, Virginia 24054

Head of School: Mr. Simon A. Owen-Williams

General Information Coeducational boarding and day college-preparatory, International Baccalaureate (IB), and IB Middle Years program and Primary Years program school. Boarding grades 9–12, day grades PK–12. Founded: 1968. Setting: rural. Nearest major city is Danville. Students are housed in single-sex dormitories. 50-acre campus. 5 buildings on campus. Approved or accredited by International Baccalaureate Organization, Southern Association of Colleges and Schools, and Virginia Department of Education. Member of National Association of Independent Schools. Endowment: $1.5 million. Total enrollment: 549. Upper school average class size: 18. Upper school faculty-student ratio: 1:7. There are 176 required school days per year for Upper School students. Upper School students typically attend 5 days per week. The average school day consists of 6 hours and 45 minutes.
Upper School Student Profile Grade 9: 31 students (20 boys, 11 girls); Grade 10: 44 students (28 boys, 16 girls); Grade 11: 49 students (20 boys, 29 girls); Grade 12: 50 students (35 boys, 15 girls). 24% of students are boarding students. 74% are state residents. 2 states are represented in upper school student body. 24% are international students. International students from China, Finland, Germany, Japan, Mexico, and Republic of Korea.
Faculty School total: 30. In upper school: 7 men, 18 women; 11 have advanced degrees; 3 reside on campus.
Subjects Offered Advanced computer applications, advanced math, Advanced Placement courses, algebra, American government, American history, American history-AP, American literature, art, arts, band, biology, biology-AP, calculus, calculus-AP, chemistry, chemistry-AP, choir, composition-AP, computer information systems, computer programming, computer science, computer science-AP, concert band, creative dance, creative drama, creative writing, dance, drama, earth science, economics, economics-AP, English, English language and composition-AP, English literature, English literature and composition-AP, English literature-AP, ESL, film studies, fine arts, geometry, government, government/civics, health, health and wellness, history, history of the Americas, honors algebra, honors English, honors geometry, HTML design, independent study, International Baccalaureate courses, intro to computers, jazz band, jazz ensemble, journalism, lab science, madrigals, mathematics, mathematics-AP, music, physical education, physics, play production, pre-algebra, pre-calculus, psychology, psychology-AP, publications, robotics, science, senior project, social studies, Spanish, statistics, statistics-AP, studio art, theater, theory of knowledge, U.S. government and politics-AP, U.S. history-AP, wind ensemble, world civilizations, world history, world history-AP, world wide web design, yearbook.
Graduation Requirements Advanced math, algebra, arts and fine arts (art, music, dance, drama), computer science, electives, English, foreign language, mathematics, physical education (includes health), science, social studies (includes history), U.S. and Virginia history, U.S. government, community and service, senior project.
Special Academic Programs International Baccalaureate program; Advanced Placement exam preparation; honors section; independent study; term-away projects; study at local college for college credit; ESL (17 students enrolled).
College Admission Counseling 31 students graduated in 2011; all went to college, including Lynchburg College; The College of William and Mary; The University of North Carolina at Chapel Hill; The University of North Carolina at Greensboro; University of Virginia; Virginia Commonwealth University. Median SAT critical reading: 546, median SAT math: 540, median SAT writing: 526. 33% scored over 600 on SAT critical reading, 37% scored over 600 on SAT math, 33% scored over 600 on SAT writing.
Student Life Upper grades have specified standards of dress, student council, honor system. Discipline rests equally with students and faculty.
Summer Programs Remediation, enrichment, advancement, ESL, sports, art/fine arts, computer instruction programs offered; session focuses on enrichment, academics, sports, fun; held on campus; accepts boys and girls; open to students from other schools. 60 students usually enrolled. 2012 schedule: June 15 to August 15. Application deadline: June 1.
Tuition and Aid Day student tuition: $9150; 7-day tuition and room/board: $29,900. Tuition installment plan (Insured Tuition Payment Plan, FACTS Tuition Payment Plan). Need-based scholarship grants available. In 2011–12, 50% of upper-school students received aid. Total amount of financial aid awarded in 2011–12: $250,000.
Admissions Traditional secondary-level entrance grade is 9. Nelson-Denny Reading Test, Woodcock-Johnson or writing sample required. Deadline for receipt of application materials: none. Application fee required: $50. On-campus interview required.
Athletics Interscholastic: basketball (boys, girls), cheering (g), field hockey (g), football (b), soccer (b,g), softball (g), tennis (b,g), volleyball (g); intramural: basketball (b,g), cheering (g), softball (g); coed interscholastic: baseball, cross-country running, dance, fencing, golf; coed intramural: aerobics/Nautilus, archery, basketball, Frisbee, table tennis, weight lifting. 2 PE instructors, 12 coaches.
Computers Computers are regularly used in all academic classes. Computer network features include on-campus library services, online commercial services, Internet access, wireless campus network, Internet filtering or blocking technology. Campus intranet and computer access in designated common areas are available to students. Students grades are available online. The school has a published electronic and media policy.
Contact Mrs. Jenna Martin, Admissions Assistant. 276-632-7288 Ext. 221. Fax: 276-632-9545. E-mail: jmartin@carlisleschool.org. Web site: www.carlisleschool.org.

CARLUCCI AMERICAN INTERNATIONAL SCHOOL OF LISBON

Rua António dos Reis, 95

Linhó 2710-301, Portugal

Head of School: Ms. Blannie M. Curtis

General Information Coeducational day college-preparatory and Portuguese Equivalia Program school. Grades PK–12. Founded: 1956. Setting: small town. Nearest major city is Lisbon, Portugal. 4-hectare campus. 4 buildings on campus. Approved or accredited by International Baccalaureate Organization, New England Association of Schools and Colleges, US Department of State, and state department of education. Language of instruction: English. Total enrollment: 523. Upper school average class size: 15. Upper school faculty-student ratio: 1:8. There are 180 required school days per year for Upper School students. Upper School students typically attend 5 days per week. The average school day consists of 5 hours and 30 minutes.
Upper School Student Profile Grade 9: 47 students (22 boys, 25 girls); Grade 10: 39 students (20 boys, 19 girls); Grade 11: 31 students (17 boys, 14 girls); Grade 12: 45 students (30 boys, 15 girls).
Faculty School total: 64. In upper school: 19 men, 16 women; 11 have advanced degrees.
Subjects Offered Algebra, art, biology, business studies, chemistry, choir, computer applications, computer art, economics, English, European history, French, geography, geometry, International Baccalaureate courses, journalism, model United Nations, modern civilization, music, physical education, physics, Portuguese, Portuguese literature, SAT preparation, Spanish, theory of knowledge, U.S. history, U.S. literature, writing workshop, yearbook.
Graduation Requirements Arts and fine arts (art, music, dance, drama), computer science, electives, English, foreign language, mathematics, physical education (includes health), science, social studies (includes history), International Baccalaureate diploma candidates have to complete 150 Community Action Service hours, plus Theory of Knowledge and Extended Essay.
Special Academic Programs International Baccalaureate program; honors section; independent study; academic accommodation for the gifted; remedial reading and/or remedial writing; remedial math; programs in general development for dyslexic students; ESL (57 students enrolled).
College Admission Counseling 27 students graduated in 2010; 26 went to college, including Amherst College; Boston University; California State University, Fullerton; Rensselaer Polytechnic Institute; Rollins College; Suffolk University. Other: 1 had other specific plans. Median SAT critical reading: 580, median SAT math: 565, median SAT writing: 600, median combined SAT: 1785.
Student Life Upper grades have specified standards of dress, student council. Discipline rests equally with students and faculty.
Tuition and Aid Day student tuition: €7064–€16,480. Tuition installment plan (monthly payment plans, individually arranged payment plans, early payment discount, quarterly payment plan). Tuition reduction for siblings, merit scholarship grants, need-based scholarship grants, merit-based scholarships are available to student residents in

Sintra, Portugal only available. In 2010–11, 7% of upper-school students received aid; total upper-school merit-scholarship money awarded: €115,072.

Admissions English for Non-native Speakers or Math Placement Exam required. Deadline for receipt of application materials: none. No application fee required. Interview recommended.

Athletics Interscholastic: basketball (boys, girls), cross-country running (b,g), soccer (b,g), track and field (b,g), volleyball (b,g); intramural: basketball (b,g), soccer (b,g); coed intramural: golf, volleyball. 4 PE instructors, 12 coaches.

Computers Computers are regularly used in computer applications, digital applications, graphic design classes. Computer resources include on-campus library services, Internet access, wireless campus network, Internet filtering or blocking technology. Campus intranet and computer access in designated common areas are available to students. Students grades are available online. The school has a published electronic and media policy.

Contact Ms. Cynthia Ferrell, Enrollment Coordinator. 351-21-923-9800. Fax: 351-21-923-9809. E-mail: admissions@caislisbon.org. Web site: www.caislisbon.org.

CARMEL HIGH SCHOOL

One Carmel Parkway

Mundelein, Illinois 60060-2499

Head of School: Judith Mucheck, PhD

General Information Coeducational day college-preparatory, arts, business, religious studies, and technology school, affiliated with Roman Catholic Church. Grades 9–12. Founded: 1962. Setting: suburban. Nearest major city is Libertyville. 45-acre campus. 1 building on campus. Approved or accredited by National Catholic Education Association, North Central Association of Colleges and Schools, and Illinois Department of Education. Total enrollment: 1,370. Upper school average class size: 25. Upper school faculty-student ratio: 1:16.

Upper School Student Profile 90% of students are Roman Catholic.

Faculty School total: 90. In upper school: 33 men, 57 women; 63 have advanced degrees.

Subjects Offered 20th century world history, accounting, advanced chemistry, advanced math, Advanced Placement courses, advanced studio art-AP, algebra, American government, American history, American literature, American literature-AP, anatomy and physiology, art, athletic training, band, biology, biology-AP, biotechnology, botany, British literature, British literature (honors), business, calculus, calculus-AP, chemistry, chemistry-AP, choir, choral music, chorus, community service, computer applications, computer programming, computer programming-AP, concert band, drama, drama performance, drawing, economics, English, English composition, English language and composition-AP, English literature, English literature-AP, European history-AP, French, French language-AP, French-AP, geography, geometry, government, government-AP, history of religion, honors algebra, honors English, honors geometry, honors U.S. history, honors world history, instrumental music, Internet research, intro to computers, jazz band, journalism, Latin, Latin-AP, marching band, music, music composition, music theory-AP, orchestra, performing arts, physical education, physical science, physics, physics-AP, pre-algebra, pre-calculus, probability and statistics, psychology, reading/study skills, religion, religious education, scripture, sociology, Spanish, strings, student government, student publications, student teaching, studio art, studio art-AP, theater arts, trigonometry, U.S. government and politics-AP, U.S. history, U.S. history-AP, Web site design, wind ensemble, women spirituality and faith, world history, world history-AP, world literature, yearbook, zoology.

Graduation Requirements Ministry requirement, 20 hours of ministry service per semester.

Special Academic Programs Honors section; special instructional classes for deaf students, blind students.

College Admission Counseling 320 students graduated in 2010; 316 went to college, including Marquette University; Purdue University; The University of Iowa; University of Illinois at Urbana–Champaign. Other: 1 went to work, 3 entered military service. Mean composite ACT: 25.

Student Life Upper grades have specified standards of dress, student council. Discipline rests primarily with faculty. Attendance at religious services is required.

Tuition and Aid Day student tuition: $8460. Tuition installment plan (FACTS Tuition Payment Plan). Merit scholarship grants, need-based scholarship grants available. In 2010–11, 10% of upper-school students received aid; total upper-school merit-scholarship money awarded: $16,000. Total amount of financial aid awarded in 2010–11: $82,000.

Admissions Traditional secondary-level entrance grade is 9. Explore required. Deadline for receipt of application materials: January 29. Application fee required: $350.

Athletics Interscholastic: baseball (boys), basketball (b,g), cheering (g), cross-country running (b,g), football (b), golf (b,g), gymnastics (g), ice hockey (b), pom squad (g), soccer (b,g), softball (g), tennis (b,g), track and field (b,g), volleyball (b,g), wrestling (b); intramural: basketball (b,g); coed intramural: Frisbee, volleyball, winter soccer, yoga.

Computers Computers are regularly used in all classes. Computer resources include on-campus library services, Internet access. Students grades are available online. The school has a published electronic and media policy.

Contact Mr. Brian Stith, Director of Admissions. 847-388-3320. Fax: 847-566-8465. E-mail: bstith@carmelhs.org. Web site: www.carmelhs.org.

CAROLINA DAY SCHOOL

1345 Hendersonville Road

Asheville, North Carolina 28803

Head of School: Thomas F. H. Trigg

General Information Coeducational day college-preparatory school. Grades PK–12. Founded: 1987. Setting: suburban. 60-acre campus. 9 buildings on campus. Approved or accredited by Southern Association of Colleges and Schools, Southern Association of Independent Schools, and North Carolina Department of Education. Member of National Association of Independent Schools. Endowment: $3.5 million. Total enrollment: 655. Upper school average class size: 12. Upper school faculty-student ratio: 1:6. There are 180 required school days per year for Upper School students. Upper School students typically attend 5 days per week. The average school day consists of 6 hours and 25 minutes.

Upper School Student Profile Grade 9: 44 students (27 boys, 17 girls); Grade 10: 37 students (19 boys, 18 girls); Grade 11: 44 students (20 boys, 24 girls); Grade 12: 55 students (25 boys, 30 girls).

Faculty School total: 116. In upper school: 14 men, 14 women; 19 have advanced degrees.

Subjects Offered Acting, advanced biology, advanced chemistry, advanced studio art-AP, algebra, American literature, art history, art history-AP, biology, biology-AP, calculus, calculus-AP, ceramics, chemistry, chemistry-AP, chorus, CPR, creative writing, debate, ecology, English language and composition-AP, English literature, environmental science-AP, European history-AP, fiction, French, French-AP, geometry, global studies, history, industrial arts, language and composition, linear algebra, linguistics, literature, literature and composition-AP, Mandarin, martial arts, music theory, music theory-AP, philosophy, photography, physical education, physics, physics-AP, pre-calculus, psychology-AP, reading/study skills, research, science, Spanish, Spanish-AP, speech, statistics-AP, studio art, theater, U.S. government and politics-AP, U.S. history, U.S. history-AP, world literature.

Graduation Requirements Algebra, arts and fine arts (art, music, dance, drama), biology, chemistry, electives, English, geometry, global studies, modern languages, physical education (includes health), public speaking, social studies (includes history), U.S. history, CPR/First Aid (non-credit class).

Special Academic Programs 17 Advanced Placement exams for which test preparation is offered; honors section; independent study.

College Admission Counseling 34 students graduated in 2011; all went to college, including High Point University; Mount Holyoke College; Northwestern University; The University of North Carolina at Chapel Hill; The University of North Carolina at Charlotte; Wofford College. Median SAT critical reading: 625, median SAT math: 615, median SAT writing: 615, median combined SAT: 1855.

Student Life Upper grades have specified standards of dress, student council, honor system. Discipline rests equally with students and faculty.

Summer Programs Enrichment, sports, art/fine arts, computer instruction programs offered; session focuses on recreation and enrichment; held on campus; accepts boys and girls; open to students from other schools. 220 students usually enrolled. 2012 schedule: June 18 to August 3. Application deadline: none.

Tuition and Aid Day student tuition: $17,910–$19,610. Tuition installment plan (Insured Tuition Payment Plan, FACTS Tuition Payment Plan, monthly payment plans, individually arranged payment plans, 1-payment plan or 2-installments plan (August and January)). Merit scholarship grants, need-based scholarship grants available. In 2011–12, 49% of upper-school students received aid; total upper-school merit-scholarship money awarded: $158,340. Total amount of financial aid awarded in 2011–12: $674,035.

Admissions Traditional secondary-level entrance grade is 9. For fall 2011, 35 students applied for upper-level admission, 23 were accepted, 18 enrolled. ERB, ISEE, PSAT or SAT or SSAT required. Deadline for receipt of application materials: none. Application fee required: $100. On-campus interview required.

Athletics Interscholastic: baseball (boys), basketball (b,g), cross-country running (b,g), field hockey (g), martial arts (b,g), soccer (b,g), swimming and diving (b,g), tennis (b,g), track and field (b,g), volleyball (g); coed interscholastic: golf; coed intramural: basketball, lacrosse, soccer, table tennis, touch football, volleyball. 2 PE instructors, 15 coaches, 1 athletic trainer.

Computers Computers are regularly used in all academic classes. Computer network features include on-campus library services, online commercial services, Internet access, wireless campus network, Internet filtering or blocking technology. Campus intranet, student e-mail accounts, and computer access in designated common areas are available to students. The school has a published electronic and media policy.

Contact Michelle Nailen, Assistant Director of Admissions. 828-274-0757. Fax: 828-274-0756. E-mail: admissions@cdschool.org. Web site: www.cdschool.org.

CARONDELET HIGH SCHOOL

1133 Winton Drive

Concord, California 94518

Head of School: Nancy Libby

General Information Girls' day college-preparatory, arts, religious studies, and technology school, affiliated with Roman Catholic Church. Grades 9–12. Founded: 1965. Setting: suburban. Nearest major city is Oakland. 9-acre campus. 5 buildings on campus. Approved or accredited by Western Association of Schools and Colleges. Total enrollment: 800. Upper school average class size: 30. Upper school faculty-student ratio: 1:15. The average school day consists of 7 hours.

Upper School Student Profile Grade 9: 200 students (200 girls); Grade 10: 200 students (200 girls); Grade 11: 200 students (200 girls); Grade 12: 200 students (200 girls). 90% of students are Roman Catholic.

Faculty School total: 61. In upper school: 13 men, 48 women; 30 have advanced degrees.

Subjects Offered Algebra, American studies, animation, architectural drawing, art, band, biology, calculus, calculus-AP, cartooning/animation, chemistry, chorus, church history, civics, community service, computer applications, concert band, concert choir, creative writing, criminal justice, dance, design, drafting, drawing, economics, English, English-AP, ethics, finite math, fitness, French, geometry, government-AP, health, honors algebra, honors English, honors geometry, Italian, jazz band, journalism, Latin, marching band, marine biology, music history, music theory, musical theater, orchestra, painting, physical education, physics, physics-AP, physiology, pre-algebra, pre-calculus, psychology, psychology-AP, relationships, sculpture, Spanish, Spanish-AP, sports medicine, statistics, studio art-AP, technical drawing, transition mathematics, U.S. history, U.S. history-AP, water color painting, Web site design, women's health, world arts, world civilizations, world religions, writing, yearbook.

Graduation Requirements Computer literacy, English, mathematics, modern languages, physical education (includes health), religious studies, science, social studies (includes history), visual and performing arts.

Special Academic Programs 12 Advanced Placement exams for which test preparation is offered; honors section; independent study; academic accommodation for the gifted.

College Admission Counseling 199 students graduated in 2011; all went to college, including California Polytechnic State University, San Luis Obispo; California State University, Chico; University of California, Berkeley. Mean SAT critical reading: 548, mean SAT math: 538, mean SAT writing: 556, mean composite ACT: 24.

Student Life Upper grades have uniform requirement, honor system. Discipline rests primarily with faculty. Attendance at religious services is required.

Tuition and Aid Day student tuition: $14,300. Tuition installment plan (SMART Tuition Payment Plan, monthly payment plans, prepayment plan, semester or quarterly payment plans). Need-based scholarship grants available. In 2011–12, 25% of upper-school students received aid. Total amount of financial aid awarded in 2011–12: $1,300,000.

Admissions Traditional secondary-level entrance grade is 9. For fall 2011, 380 students applied for upper-level admission, 240 were accepted, 220 enrolled. High School Placement Test required. Deadline for receipt of application materials: December 5. Application fee required: $100. On-campus interview recommended.

Athletics Interscholastic: aquatics, basketball, cheering, combined training, cross-country running, dance squad, dance team, diving, golf, lacrosse, soccer, softball, swimming and diving, tennis, volleyball, water polo; intramural: badminton, basketball, broomball, flag football, physical fitness, physical training, touch football, volleyball. 3 PE instructors, 40 coaches, 1 athletic trainer.

Computers Computers are regularly used in computer applications classes. Computer network features include on-campus library services, Internet access, wireless campus network, Internet filtering or blocking technology. Student e-mail accounts are available to students. Students grades are available online. The school has a published electronic and media policy.

Contact Ms. Kathy Harris, Director of Admissions. 925-686-5353 Ext. 161. Fax: 925-671-9429. E-mail: kharris@carondeleths.org. Web site: www.carondelet.net.

CARROLLTON CHRISTIAN ACADEMY

2205 East Hebron Parkway

Carrollton, Texas 75010

Head of School: Dr. Alex Ward

General Information Coeducational day college-preparatory, arts, religious studies, and technology school, affiliated with United Methodist Church. Grades PK–12. Founded: 1980. Setting: suburban. Nearest major city is Dallas/Fort Worth. 25-acre campus. 1 building on campus. Approved or accredited by Southern Association of Colleges and Schools, University Senate of United Methodist Church, and Texas Department of Education. Language of instruction: Spanish. Total enrollment: 375. Upper school average class size: 20.

Student Life Upper grades have uniform requirement, student council, honor system. Discipline rests primarily with faculty.

Tuition and Aid Tuition installment plan (FACTS Tuition Payment Plan). Tuition reduction for siblings, need-based scholarship grants available.

Admissions Stanford Achievement Test required. Application fee required. Interview required.

Athletics Interscholastic: baseball (boys), basketball (b,g), cheering (g), cross-country running (b,g), dance team (g), football (b), golf (b,g), soccer (b,g), softball (g), strength & conditioning (b,g), tennis (b,g), track and field (b,g), volleyball (g), winter soccer (b,g).

Contact Ms. Jane Funk, Admissions Coordinator. . 972-242-6688. Fax: 469-568-1396. E-mail: jane.funk@ccasaints.org. Web site: www.ccasaints.org.

CARROLLTON SCHOOL OF THE SACRED HEART

3747 Main Highway

Miami, Florida 33133

Head of School: Sr. Suzanne Cooke

General Information Girls' day college-preparatory, arts, religious studies, bilingual studies, and technology school, affiliated with Roman Catholic Church. Grades PK–12. Founded: 1961. Setting: urban. 17-acre campus. 5 buildings on campus. Approved or accredited by Florida Council of Independent Schools, Network of Sacred Heart Schools, and Southern Association of Colleges and Schools. Member of National Association of Independent Schools and Secondary School Admission Test Board. Endowment: $2 million. Total enrollment: 800. Upper school average class size: 16. Upper school faculty-student ratio: 1:9.

Upper School Student Profile 87% of students are Roman Catholic.

Faculty School total: 74. In upper school: 9 men, 24 women; 20 have advanced degrees.

Subjects Offered Algebra, American history, American literature, anatomy and physiology, art, art history, Bible studies, biology, British literature, calculus, chemistry, computer science, debate, drama, earth systems analysis, economics, English, English literature, environmental science, ethics, expository writing, fine arts, French, general science, geometry, government/civics, grammar, health, history, humanities, journalism, mathematics, music, photography, physical education, physical science, physics, pre-calculus, psychology, religion, science, scripture, social sciences, social studies, Spanish, speech, theater, trigonometry, vocal ensemble, world history, world literature.

Graduation Requirements Arts and fine arts (art, music, dance, drama), computer science, English, foreign language, mathematics, physical education (includes health), religion (includes Bible studies and theology), science, social studies (includes history). Community service is required.

Special Academic Programs International Baccalaureate program; Advanced Placement exam preparation; honors section; independent study; study at local college for college credit; domestic exchange program; study abroad.

College Admission Counseling 66 students graduated in 2011; all went to college, including Boston College; Massachusetts Institute of Technology; Northwestern University; University of Miami; Vanderbilt University. Median SAT math: 590, median composite ACT: 24. Mean SAT critical reading: 590. 51% scored over 600 on SAT critical reading, 47% scored over 600 on SAT math, 30% scored over 26 on composite ACT.

Student Life Upper grades have uniform requirement, student council, honor system. Discipline rests primarily with faculty. Attendance at religious services is required.

Tuition and Aid Day student tuition: $23,150. Tuition installment plan (Insured Tuition Payment Plan, monthly payment plans). Merit scholarship grants, need-based scholarship grants available. In 2011–12, 25% of upper-school students received aid; total upper-school merit-scholarship money awarded: $45,000. Total amount of financial aid awarded in 2011–12: $920,000.

Admissions Traditional secondary-level entrance grade is 9. For fall 2011, 132 students applied for upper-level admission, 37 were accepted, 30 enrolled. Admissions testing or ISEE required. Deadline for receipt of application materials: February 1. Application fee required: $50. On-campus interview required.

Athletics Interscholastic: aquatics, basketball, crew, cross-country running, golf, sailing, soccer, softball, swimming and diving, tennis, track and field, volleyball, water polo, winter soccer. 4 PE instructors, 8 coaches.

Computers Computers are regularly used in all academic classes. Computer network features include on-campus library services, online commercial services, Internet access, wireless campus network, Internet filtering or blocking technology, laptop program. Student e-mail accounts are available to students. The school has a published electronic and media policy.

Contact Ms. Ana J. Roye, Director of Admission and Financial Aid. 305-446-5673 Ext. 1224. Fax: 305-446-4160. E-mail: aroye@carrollton.org. Web site: www.carrollton.org.

CARY ACADEMY

1500 North Harrison Avenue

Cary, North Carolina 27513

Head of School: Mr. Donald S. Berger

General Information Coeducational day college-preparatory, arts, and technology school. Grades 6–12. Founded: 1996. Setting: suburban. Nearest major city is Raleigh. 55-acre campus. 6 buildings on campus. Approved or accredited by North Carolina Association of Independent Schools, Southern Association of Colleges and Schools, Southern Association of Independent Schools, and North Carolina Department of Education. Total enrollment: 710. Upper school average class size: 14. Upper school faculty-student ratio: 1:14. Upper School students typically attend 5 days per week. The average school day consists of 7 hours and 10 minutes.

Upper School Student Profile Grade 9: 104 students (54 boys, 50 girls); Grade 10: 106 students (61 boys, 45 girls); Grade 11: 100 students (52 boys, 48 girls); Grade 12: 98 students (45 boys, 53 girls).

Faculty School total: 77. In upper school: 29 men, 19 women; 38 have advanced degrees.

Subjects Offered Advanced Placement courses, algebra, American history, American history-AP, American literature, American literature-AP, anatomy and physiology, biology, biology-AP, calculus, calculus-AP, ceramics, chamber groups, chemistry, chemistry-AP, Chinese, computer programming, computer programming-AP, concert choir, debate, digital photography, drawing, economics, economics-AP, environmental science, environmental science-AP, film studies, forensics, French language-AP, French literature-AP, French-AP, genetics, geometry, German, German literature, German-AP, health education, instruments, jazz band, journalism, modern European history-AP, multimedia design, music composition, music theory, music theory-AP, orchestra, painting, photography, physical education, physics, physics-AP, pre-calculus, probability and statistics, programming, Spanish language-AP, Spanish literature, Spanish literature-AP, Spanish-AP, statistics-AP, studio art, studio art-AP, technical theater, theater production, trigonometry, U.S. government and politics-AP, video, voice, Web site design, wind ensemble, world arts, world history, world literature, yearbook.

Graduation Requirements Algebra, American history, American literature, biology, chemistry, foreign language, physical education (includes health), physics, world history, world literature.

Special Academic Programs Advanced Placement exam preparation; honors section; independent study; academic accommodation for the gifted, the musically talented, and the artistically talented.

College Admission Counseling 99 students graduated in 2010; all went to college, including Duke University; North Carolina State University; Princeton University; The University of North Carolina at Chapel Hill; The University of North Carolina Wilmington; University of Maryland, College Park. Mean SAT critical reading: 646, mean SAT math: 647, mean SAT writing: 639, mean combined SAT: 1932.

Student Life Upper grades have specified standards of dress, student council, honor system. Discipline rests equally with students and faculty.

Admissions Traditional secondary-level entrance grade is 9. For fall 2010, 82 students applied for upper-level admission, 50 were accepted, 37 enrolled. Achievement/Aptitude/Writing, ERB CTP IV or ISEE required. Deadline for receipt of application materials: none. Application fee required: $110. Interview required.

Athletics Interscholastic: aquatics (boys, girls), baseball (b), basketball (b,g), cheering (b,g), cross-country running (b,g), field hockey (g), golf (b), lacrosse (b), soccer (b,g), softball (g), swimming and diving (b,g), tennis (b,g), track and field (b,g), volleyball (g), wrestling (g); intramural: baseball (b), basketball (b,g), cooperative games (b,g), dance (b,g), dance squad (g), fitness (b,g), fitness walking (b,g), Fives (b,g), floor hockey (b,g), indoor soccer (b,g), modern dance (g), soccer (b,g), softball (g), strength & conditioning (b,g), tennis (b,g), touch football (b,g), track and field (b,g), ultimate Frisbee (b,g), volleyball (b,g), walking (b,g), weight lifting (b,g); coed intramural: aerobics, aerobics/dance, aerobics/Nautilus, badminton, basketball, billiards, bowling, cooperative games, dance, fitness, fitness walking, Fives, floor hockey, Frisbee, golf, gymnastics, handball, indoor soccer, jogging, jump rope, kickball, martial arts, modern dance, Newcombe ball, physical fitness, running, soccer, strength & conditioning, table tennis, tai chi, tennis, touch football, track and field, ultimate Frisbee, volleyball, walking, weight lifting, weight training, winter walking. 4 PE instructors, 40 coaches, 1 athletic trainer.

Computers Computers are regularly used in all academic, animation, desktop publishing, drawing and design, independent study, media arts, media production, music, theater arts, video film production, yearbook classes. Computer network features include on-campus library services, online commercial services, Internet access, wireless campus network, Internet filtering or blocking technology, each student is issued a free laptop computer. Campus intranet, student e-mail accounts, and computer access in designated common areas are available to students. Students grades are available online. The school has a published electronic and media policy.

Contact Ms. Denise Goodman, Director of Admissions. 919-228-4550. Fax: 919-677-4002. E-mail: denise_goodman@caryacademy.org. Web site: www.caryacademy.org.

CASCADE CHRISTIAN ACADEMY

600 North Western Avenue

Wenatchee, Washington 98801

Head of School: Mr. Brian Harris

General Information Coeducational day college-preparatory, arts, business, vocational, religious studies, bilingual studies, and technology school, affiliated with Seventh-day Adventist Church. Grades K–12. Founded: 1905. Setting: small town. Nearest major city is Seattle. 15-acre campus. 1 building on campus. Approved or accredited by Northwest Association of Schools and Colleges and Washington Department of Education. Endowment: $25,000. Total enrollment: 146. Upper school average class size: 10. Upper school faculty-student ratio: 1:5. There are 180 required school days per year for Upper School students. Upper School students typically attend 5 days per week. The average school day consists of 7 hours and 10 minutes.

Upper School Student Profile Grade 6: 13 students (7 boys, 6 girls); Grade 7: 11 students (6 boys, 5 girls); Grade 8: 9 students (3 boys, 6 girls); Grade 9: 11 students (3 boys, 8 girls); Grade 10: 9 students (4 boys, 5 girls); Grade 11: 9 students (6 boys, 3 girls); Grade 12: 9 students (4 boys, 5 girls). 45% of students are Seventh-day Adventists.

Faculty School total: 9. In upper school: 4 men, 3 women; 5 have advanced degrees.

Subjects Offered Accounting, algebra, American history, anatomy and physiology, arts, band, Bible, biology, calculus, chemistry, choir, computer science, drama, earth science, English, fine arts, foreign language, geometry, history, marine biology, mathematics, physical education, physics, science, social studies, world history.

Graduation Requirements Arts and fine arts (art, music, dance, drama), Bible, computer science, English, foreign language, mathematics, physical education (includes health), science, social studies (includes history).

Special Academic Programs Accelerated programs; independent study; remedial reading and/or remedial writing; remedial math; programs in English, mathematics, general development for dyslexic students.

College Admission Counseling 15 students graduated in 2010; 13 went to college, including Walla Walla University. Other: 2 went to work. Median SAT critical reading: 515, median SAT math: 495, median composite ACT: 19. 11% scored over 600 on SAT critical reading, 11% scored over 600 on SAT math.

Student Life Upper grades have uniform requirement, student council, honor system. Discipline rests primarily with faculty. Attendance at religious services is required.

Tuition and Aid Day student tuition: $6942. Tuition installment plan (monthly payment plans, individually arranged payment plans). Tuition reduction for siblings, need-based scholarship grants, paying campus jobs, church subsidy available. Total amount of financial aid awarded in 2010–11: $119,000.

Admissions Traditional secondary-level entrance grade is 10. For fall 2010, 10 students applied for upper-level admission, 10 were accepted, 10 enrolled. Deadline for receipt of application materials: none. Application fee required: $50. Interview required.

Athletics Interscholastic: basketball (boys, girls), volleyball (g); coed interscholastic: flag football, soccer; coed intramural: fitness, flag football, floor hockey, ice hockey, ice skating, skiing (downhill), snowboarding, soccer, softball, volleyball, weight training. 1 PE instructor, 4 coaches.

Computers Computers are regularly used in accounting, career education, desktop publishing, English, mathematics, publications classes. Computer network features include online commercial services, Internet access.

Contact Mrs. Ayrin Harris, Administrative Assistant/Registrar. 509-662-2723 Ext. 10. Fax: 509-662-5892. E-mail: ayrin.harris@ccawenatchee.org. Web site: ccawenatchee.org.

CASCADES ACADEMY OF CENTRAL OREGON

2150 NE Studio Road

Suite 2

Bend, Oregon 97701

Head of School: Blair Jenkins

General Information Distance learning only college-preparatory and experiential education school. Distance learning grades K–12. Founded: 2003. Setting: suburban. 1 building on campus. Approved or accredited by Northwest Accreditation Commission and Oregon Department of Education. Total enrollment: 109. Upper school average class size: 6. Upper school faculty-student ratio: 1:6. There are 168 required school days per year for Upper School students. Upper School students typically attend 5 days per week. The average school day consists of 7 hours and 15 minutes.

Upper School Student Profile Grade 6: 9 students (6 boys, 3 girls); Grade 7: 15 students (5 boys, 10 girls); Grade 8: 7 students (4 boys, 3 girls); Grade 9: 5 students (5 boys); Grade 10: 1 student (1 girl); Grade 12: 6 students (1 boy, 5 girls).

Faculty School total: 21. In upper school: 3 men, 3 women; 3 have advanced degrees.

Graduation Requirements 3-dimensional art, Internship.

College Admission Counseling 3 students graduated in 2010; all went to college.

Student Life Upper grades have honor system. Discipline rests primarily with faculty.

Tuition and Aid Day student tuition: $10,875. Tuition installment plan (monthly payment plans). Need-based scholarship grants available.

Admissions Traditional secondary-level entrance grade is 9. For fall 2010, 54 students applied for upper-level admission, 48 were accepted, 37 enrolled. Deadline for receipt of application materials: none. Application fee required: $50. On-campus interview required.
Computers The school has a published electronic and media policy.
Contact 541-382-0699. Fax: 541-382-0225. Web site: http://www.cascadesacademy.org/.

CASCADILLA SCHOOL

116 Summit Street

Ithaca, New York 14850

Head of School: Patricia T. Kendall

General Information Coeducational boarding and day college-preparatory, arts, bilingual studies, English/language arts (The Cascadilla Seminar/Cornell Univ.), and mathematics school. Grades 9–PG. Founded: 1870. Setting: urban. Nearest major city is Syracuse. Students are housed in single-sex dormitories. 2-acre campus. 3 buildings on campus. Approved or accredited by New York State Board of Regents, New York State University, The College Board, US Department of State, and New York Department of Education. Endowment: $1.2 million. Total enrollment: 50. Upper school average class size: 7. Upper school faculty-student ratio: 1:6. There are 185 required school days per year for Upper School students. Upper School students typically attend 5 days per week. The average school day consists of 7 hours and 40 minutes.
Upper School Student Profile Grade 9: 6 students (3 boys, 3 girls); Grade 10: 11 students (8 boys, 3 girls); Grade 11: 13 students (7 boys, 6 girls); Grade 12: 14 students (7 boys, 7 girls); Postgraduate: 6 students (2 boys, 4 girls). 30% of students are boarding students. 70% are state residents. 4 states are represented in upper school student body. 30% are international students. International students from Angola, China, Republic of Korea, Saudi Arabia, Taiwan, and Turkey; 4 other countries represented in student body.
Faculty School total: 14. In upper school: 7 men, 7 women; 13 have advanced degrees; 4 reside on campus.
Subjects Offered Advanced chemistry, Advanced Placement courses, advanced TOEFL/grammar, African literature, algebra, alternative physical education, American history, American literature, anatomy and physiology, art, biochemistry, biology, biology-AP, calculus, calculus-AP, career/college preparation, chemistry, chemistry-AP, college admission preparation, college awareness, college counseling, college placement, college planning, college writing, computer programming, computer science, creative writing, decision making skills, drama performance, earth science, economics, English, English as a foreign language, English composition, English literature, English literature and composition-AP, English literature-AP, environmental education, environmental science, ESL, ethics, European history, expository writing, fabric arts, French, French as a second language, geometry, government/civics, health, health and wellness, health education, history, honors algebra, honors English, honors geometry, honors U.S. history, honors world history, lab science, leadership, mathematics, philosophy, photography, physical education, physics, psychology, public speaking, reading, reading/study skills, SAT preparation, SAT/ACT preparation, science, Shakespeare, social studies, Spanish, trigonometry, typing, video film production, world history, world history-AP, world literature, writing.
Graduation Requirements Alternative physical education, arts, arts and fine arts (art, music, dance, drama), computer science, current events, debate, economics, economics and history, English, European history, foreign language, government, health education, international affairs, mathematics, physical education (includes health), political science, public speaking, research, research and reference, research seminar, science, senior seminar, social studies (includes history), study skills, U.S. government and politics, English V-The Cascadilla Seminar (for college research preparation). Community service is required.
Special Academic Programs 5 Advanced Placement exams for which test preparation is offered; honors section; accelerated programs; independent study; term-away projects; study at local college for college credit; academic accommodation for the gifted, the musically talented, and the artistically talented; remedial reading and/or remedial writing; remedial math; programs in English, mathematics for dyslexic students; special instructional classes for students with learning disabilities and Attention Deficit Disorder; ESL (26 students enrolled).
College Admission Counseling 7 students graduated in 2011; all went to college, including California State University, Monterey Bay; Cornell University; Parsons The New School for Design; State University of New York at Binghamton; University of Connecticut; University of Rochester. Median SAT critical reading: 600, median SAT math: 650, median SAT writing: 550. 50% scored over 600 on SAT critical reading, 50% scored over 600 on SAT math, 15% scored over 600 on SAT writing.
Student Life Upper grades have specified standards of dress, student council, honor system. Discipline rests equally with students and faculty.
Summer Programs Remediation, enrichment, advancement, ESL, art/fine arts programs offered; session focuses on academics; held on campus; accepts boys and girls; open to students from other schools. 40 students usually enrolled. 2012 schedule: July 1 to August 17. Application deadline: June 30.
Tuition and Aid Day student tuition: $14,000; 7-day tuition and room/board: $35,000. Tuition installment plan (monthly payment plans, individually arranged payment plans). Tuition reduction for siblings, merit scholarship grants, need-based scholarship grants available. In 2011–12, 40% of upper-school students received aid; total upper-school merit-scholarship money awarded: $50,000. Total amount of financial aid awarded in 2011–12: $60,000.
Admissions Traditional secondary-level entrance grade is 10. For fall 2011, 55 students applied for upper-level admission, 15 were accepted, 15 enrolled. English Composition Test for ESL students, English entrance exam, English for Non-native Speakers, English language, English proficiency, High School Placement Test, math and English placement tests, mathematics proficiency exam, non-standardized placement tests, Reading for Understanding, school's own exam, skills for ESL students or writing sample required. Deadline for receipt of application materials: none. Application fee required: $75. Interview recommended.
Athletics Interscholastic: crew (boys, girls), modern dance (g); intramural: crew (b,g), fencing (b), independent competitive sports (b,g), rowing (b,g), sailing (b,g), skiing (cross-country) (b,g), skiing (downhill) (b,g), soccer (b,g), tennis (b,g); coed interscholastic: aerobics, aerobics/Nautilus, alpine skiing, aquatics, backpacking, badminton, ballet, basketball, billiards, blading, bowling, climbing, combined training, fencing, fitness, fitness walking, Frisbee, hiking/backpacking, jogging, kayaking, nordic skiing, outdoor activities, outdoor adventure, outdoor education, physical fitness, physical training, swimming and diving, table tennis, weight lifting, yoga; coed intramural: aerobics, aerobics/dance, badminton, basketball, blading, bowling, horseback riding, independent competitive sports, jogging, Nautilus, nordic skiing, outdoor activities, outdoor adventure, physical fitness, physical training, pillo polo, racquetball, rowing, sailboarding, skiing (cross-country), skiing (downhill), snowboarding, strength & conditioning, tennis, volleyball, walking, wall climbing, windsurfing. 3 PE instructors.
Computers Computers are regularly used in career exploration, college planning, creative writing, desktop publishing, desktop publishing, ESL, ESL, French as a second language, literary magazine, mathematics, media arts, newspaper, photography, publishing, research skills, SAT preparation, senior seminar, Spanish, stock market, theater, theater arts, video film production, Web site design, word processing, writing, writing, yearbook classes. Computer network features include on-campus library services, online commercial services, Internet access, wireless campus network, Internet filtering or blocking technology. Student e-mail accounts and computer access in designated common areas are available to students. Students grades are available online.
Contact Donna W. Collins, Administrative Assistant. 607-272-3110. Fax: 607-272-0747. E-mail: admissions@cascadillaschool.org. Web site: www.cascadillaschool.org.

CASCIA HALL PREPARATORY SCHOOL

2520 South Yorktown Avenue

Tulsa, Oklahoma 74114-2803

Head of School: Mr. Roger C. Carter

General Information Coeducational day college-preparatory and liberal arts school, affiliated with Roman Catholic Church. Grades 6–12. Founded: 1926. Setting: urban. 40-acre campus. 10 buildings on campus. Approved or accredited by North Central Association of Colleges and Schools and Oklahoma Department of Education. Endowment: $7 million. Total enrollment: 574. Upper school average class size: 18. Upper school faculty-student ratio: 1:12. There are 180 required school days per year for Upper School students. Upper School students typically attend 5 days per week. The average school day consists of 6 hours and 30 minutes.
Upper School Student Profile Grade 9: 98 students (50 boys, 48 girls); Grade 10: 108 students (57 boys, 51 girls); Grade 11: 94 students (52 boys, 42 girls); Grade 12: 97 students (54 boys, 43 girls). 45% of students are Roman Catholic.
Faculty School total: 48. In upper school: 19 men, 20 women; 32 have advanced degrees.
Subjects Offered 20th century physics, ACT preparation, Advanced Placement courses, algebra, American history-AP, American literature, anatomy and physiology, ancient world history, art, art-AP, Asian studies, astronomy, Basic programming, Bible studies, biology, business, calculus, calculus-AP, career experience, career exploration, Catholic belief and practice, Central and Eastern European history, chemistry, chemistry-AP, Chinese, Chinese studies, chorus, Christian ethics, church history, college admission preparation, composition, computer science, CPR, creative writing, digital photography, drama, drawing, driver education, English language and composition-AP, English literature and composition-AP, environmental studies, ethics, European history, European history-AP, French, geography, geometry, German, government-AP, grammar, health, history of the Catholic Church, Holocaust studies, independent study, Latin, literature, philosophy, photography, physical science, physics, physics-AP, precalculus, probability and statistics, psychology, Russian studies, SAT/ACT preparation, senior seminar, senior thesis, Shakespeare, Spanish, Spanish language-AP, speech, speech and debate, theater, theology, trigonometry, U.S. government and politics-AP, U.S. history, world history, yearbook.
Graduation Requirements Arts and fine arts (art, music, dance, drama), career exploration, college admission preparation, computer science, English, foreign language, mathematics, religion (includes Bible studies and theology), science, senior seminar, social sciences, social studies (includes history), community service.
Special Academic Programs 11 Advanced Placement exams for which test preparation is offered; honors section; independent study; study at local college for college credit; study abroad; academic accommodation for the gifted.

College Admission Counseling 88 students graduated in 2010; all went to college, including Kansas State University; Oklahoma State University; Texas Christian University; University of Arkansas; University of Oklahoma; University of Tulsa. Median SAT critical reading: 611, median SAT math: 602, median SAT writing: 600, median composite ACT: 26. 56% scored over 600 on SAT critical reading, 56% scored over 600 on SAT math, 53% scored over 600 on SAT writing, 45% scored over 26 on composite ACT.

Student Life Upper grades have uniform requirement, student council. Discipline rests primarily with faculty. Attendance at religious services is required.

Tuition and Aid Day student tuition: $11,425. Tuition installment plan (monthly payment plans). Tuition reduction for siblings, need-based scholarship grants available. In 2010–11, 20% of upper-school students received aid. Total amount of financial aid awarded in 2010–11: $450,000.

Admissions Traditional secondary-level entrance grade is 9. For fall 2010, 75 students applied for upper-level admission, 59 were accepted, 44 enrolled. STS - Educational Development Series required. Deadline for receipt of application materials: none. Application fee required: $25. On-campus interview required.

Athletics Interscholastic: baseball (boys), basketball (b,g), bowling (b,g), cheering (g), cross-country running (b,g), dance team (g), football (b), golf (b,g), power lifting (b,g), soccer (b,g), softball (g), strength & conditioning (b,g), tennis (b,g), track and field (b,g), volleyball (g), weight training (b,g), wrestling (b); coed intramural: ultimate Frisbee. 1 PE instructor, 17 coaches, 1 athletic trainer.

Computers Computer network features include on-campus library services, online commercial services, Internet access, wireless campus network, Internet filtering or blocking technology, InfoTrac Search Bank, Internet access to local and state university library catalogues. Campus intranet, student e-mail accounts, and computer access in designated common areas are available to students. Students grades are available online. The school has a published electronic and media policy.

Contact Carol A. Bradley, Coordinator of Admissions and Communications. 918-746-2604. Fax: 918-746-2640. E-mail: cbradley@casciahall.org. Web site: www.casciahall.org.

CASTILLEJA SCHOOL

1310 Bryant Street

Palo Alto, California 94301

Head of School: Nanci Z. Kauffman

General Information Girls' day college-preparatory, arts, and technology school. Grades 6–12. Founded: 1907. Setting: suburban. Nearest major city is San Francisco/San Jose. 5-acre campus. 7 buildings on campus. Approved or accredited by California Association of Independent Schools, National Council for Private School Accreditation, and Western Association of Schools and Colleges. Member of National Association of Independent Schools and Secondary School Admission Test Board. Endowment: $35 million. Total enrollment: 415. Upper school average class size: 14. Upper school faculty-student ratio: 1:6. Upper School students typically attend 5 days per week. The average school day consists of 7 hours.

Upper School Student Profile Grade 9: 61 students (61 girls); Grade 10: 58 students (58 girls); Grade 11: 55 students (55 girls); Grade 12: 61 students (61 girls).

Faculty School total: 75. In upper school: 12 men, 34 women; 40 have advanced degrees.

Subjects Offered Advanced Placement courses, African studies, algebra, American history, American literature, art, art history, biology, calculus, ceramics, chemistry, computer math, computer science, creative writing, drama, economics, English, English literature, environmental science, European history, expository writing, fine arts, French, geometry, global issues, government/civics, grammar, health, history, journalism, Latin, marine biology, mathematics, music, philosophy, physical education, physics, psychology, Russian history, science, social studies, Spanish, speech, statistics, theater, trigonometry, world history, writing.

Graduation Requirements Arts and fine arts (art, music, dance, drama), English, foreign language, health and wellness, mathematics, science, social studies (includes history).

Special Academic Programs 16 Advanced Placement exams for which test preparation is offered; honors section; independent study; academic accommodation for the gifted.

College Admission Counseling 60 students graduated in 2010; all went to college, including Harvard University; Santa Clara University; Scripps College; Stanford University; Tufts University; University of California, Berkeley. Mean SAT critical reading: 706, mean SAT math: 693, mean SAT writing: 731.

Student Life Upper grades have uniform requirement, student council, honor system. Discipline rests equally with students and faculty.

Tuition and Aid Day student tuition: $32,250. Tuition installment plan (monthly payment plans, individually arranged payment plans). Need-based scholarship grants available. In 2010–11, 19% of upper-school students received aid. Total amount of financial aid awarded in 2010–11: $1,800,000.

Admissions Traditional secondary-level entrance grade is 9. For fall 2010, 122 students applied for upper-level admission, 26 were accepted, 18 enrolled. ISEE, SSAT or TOEFL required. Deadline for receipt of application materials: January 14. Application fee required: $75. On-campus interview required.

Athletics Interscholastic: basketball, cross-country running, golf, lacrosse, soccer, softball, swimming and diving, tennis, track and field, volleyball, water polo; intramural: climbing, fitness, rock climbing. 6 PE instructors, 15 coaches, 1 athletic trainer.

Computers Computers are regularly used in art, English, foreign language, history, mathematics, science classes. Computer network features include on-campus library services, online commercial services, Internet access, wireless campus network, Internet filtering or blocking technology, one to one laptop program. Campus intranet and student e-mail accounts are available to students. Students grades are available online. The school has a published electronic and media policy.

Contact Jill V.W. Lee, Director of Admission. 650-470-7731. Fax: 650-326-8036. E-mail: jlee@castilleja.org. Web site: www.castilleja.org.

CATHEDRAL HIGH SCHOOL

350 East 56th Street

New York, New York 10022-4199

Head of School: Ms. Maria Spagnuolo

General Information Girls' day college-preparatory, arts, business, religious studies, and technology school, affiliated with Roman Catholic Church. Grades 9–12. Founded: 1905. Setting: urban. 1 building on campus. Approved or accredited by Middle States Association of Colleges and Schools, National Catholic Education Association, New York Department of Education, New York State Board of Regents, The College Board, and New York Department of Education. Total enrollment: 600. Upper school average class size: 35. Upper school faculty-student ratio: 1:17. The average school day consists of 7 hours.

Upper School Student Profile 75% of students are Roman Catholic.

Subjects Offered Advanced Placement courses, algebra, art, band, biology, biology-AP, business law, business skills, business studies, calculus, calculus-AP, campus ministry, career education internship, career exploration, Catholic belief and practice, chemistry, chemistry-AP, choir, chorus, Christian doctrine, college admission preparation, college counseling, computer education, computer graphics, computers, constitutional history of U.S., crafts, drama, earth science, economics, electives, English composition, English literature, English-AP, English/composition-AP, fashion, fitness, foreign language, French, general math, geometry, government, guidance, health, health education, honors algebra, honors English, honors geometry, honors U.S. history, honors world history, HTML design, integrated mathematics, internship, lab science, law and the legal system, literature, mathematics-AP, physics, physics-AP, physiology, portfolio art, pre-algebra, pre-calculus, psychology, psychology-AP, religion, science, social education, sociology, Spanish literature, Spanish-AP, studio art, U.S. government, U.S. history, U.S. history-AP, world history, world wide web design.

Graduation Requirements Art, electives, English, foreign language, mathematics, music, physical education (includes health), religion (includes Bible studies and theology), science, social studies (includes history), New York State Regents.

Special Academic Programs 7 Advanced Placement exams for which test preparation is offered; honors section; remedial reading and/or remedial writing; remedial math.

Student Life Upper grades have uniform requirement, student council, honor system. Discipline rests primarily with faculty. Attendance at religious services is required.

Summer Programs Remediation programs offered; held on campus; accepts boys and girls; open to students from other schools. 2012 schedule: July to August. Application deadline: July.

Tuition and Aid Day student tuition: $6590. Tuition installment plan (monthly payment plans). Tuition reduction for siblings, merit scholarship grants, need-based scholarship grants available.

Admissions Traditional secondary-level entrance grade is 9. Catholic High School Entrance Examination required. Deadline for receipt of application materials: none. No application fee required.

Athletics Interscholastic: basketball, soccer, softball, volleyball; intramural: basketball, swimming and diving. 1 PE instructor, 3 coaches.

Computers Computers are regularly used in all academic classes. Computer network features include on-campus library services, Internet access, Internet filtering or blocking technology. Campus intranet, student e-mail accounts, and computer access in designated common areas are available to students. Students grades are available online.

Contact Mrs. Johanna Velez, Director of Recruitment. 212-688-1545 Ext. 224. Fax: 212-754-2024. E-mail: jcastex@cathedralhs.org. Web site: www.cathedralhs.org.

CATHOLIC CENTRAL HIGH SCHOOL

148 McHenry Street

Burlington, Wisconsin 53105

Head of School: Mr. Gregory J. Groth

General Information Coeducational day college-preparatory, arts, business, religious studies, bilingual studies, and technology school, affiliated with Roman Catholic Church. Grades 9–12. Founded: 1920. Setting: small town. Nearest major city is Milwaukee. 25-acre campus. 2 buildings on campus. Approved or accredited by North

Central Association of Colleges and Schools and Wisconsin Department of Education. Endowment: $1 million. Total enrollment: 141. Upper school average class size: 14. Upper school faculty-student ratio: 1:8. There are 180 required school days per year for Upper School students. Upper School students typically attend 5 days per week. The average school day consists of 7 hours.

Upper School Student Profile Grade 9: 40 students (26 boys, 14 girls); Grade 10: 39 students (24 boys, 15 girls); Grade 11: 30 students (17 boys, 13 girls); Grade 12: 32 students (20 boys, 12 girls); Postgraduate: 131 students (77 boys, 54 girls). 86% of students are Roman Catholic.

Faculty School total: 17. In upper school: 9 men, 8 women; 7 have advanced degrees.

Subjects Offered 20th century American writers, 3-dimensional art, 3-dimensional design, accounting, advanced biology, advanced chemistry, advanced computer applications, advanced math, Advanced Placement courses, algebra, American government, American history, American literature, American literature-AP, analytic geometry, anatomy, anatomy and physiology, Arabic, art, band, Bible, biology, botany, business, business education, calculus, calculus-AP, cartooning/animation, Catholic belief and practice, chemistry, Chinese, choir, college planning, composition, computer animation, computer graphics, computer skills, consumer education, digital photography, diversity studies, drawing, earth science, economics, English, environmental science, finance, forensics, French, geography, geometry, health, history of religion, history of the Catholic Church, human anatomy, human biology, integrated science, intro to computers, journalism, marketing, music theory, New Testament, painting, personal fitness, photography, physical fitness, physics, physiology, pre-calculus, probability and statistics, psychology, religion, religious studies, skills for success, social justice, Spanish, speech, theology, U.S. history, world religions, zoology.

Graduation Requirements Religious education.

Special Academic Programs International Baccalaureate program; Advanced Placement exam preparation; honors section; independent study; study at local college for college credit; study abroad; academic accommodation for the gifted.

College Admission Counseling 41 students graduated in 2010; all went to college, including Marquette University; University of Wisconsin–Eau Claire; University of Wisconsin–Madison; University of Wisconsin–Milwaukee; University of Wisconsin–Stevens Point; University of Wisconsin–Whitewater. Median composite ACT: 23. 21% scored over 26 on composite ACT.

Student Life Upper grades have specified standards of dress, student council, honor system. Discipline rests primarily with faculty. Attendance at religious services is required.

Tuition and Aid Day student tuition: $6950–$7600. Tuition installment plan (individually arranged payment plans). Tuition reduction for siblings, need-based scholarship grants, paying campus jobs available. In 2010–11, 75% of upper-school students received aid. Total amount of financial aid awarded in 2010–11: $113,000.

Admissions Traditional secondary-level entrance grade is 9. For fall 2010, 150 students applied for upper-level admission, 142 were accepted, 141 enrolled. ACT, ACT-Explore or PSAT required. Deadline for receipt of application materials: none. Application fee required: $80. On-campus interview required.

Athletics Interscholastic: baseball (boys), basketball (b,g), dance team (g), football (b), golf (b), softball (g), tennis (g), volleyball (g), wrestling (b); coed interscholastic: bowling, cheering, cross-country running, fitness, gymnastics, physical fitness, strength & conditioning, track and field; coed intramural: bicycling, dance, dance squad, table tennis, ultimate Frisbee, weight training. 1 PE instructor, 32 coaches, 1 athletic trainer.

Computers Computers are regularly used in accounting, business, economics, journalism, newspaper, typing, Web site design, writing classes. Computer network features include Internet access, Internet filtering or blocking technology. Student e-mail accounts and computer access in designated common areas are available to students. Students grades are available online. The school has a published electronic and media policy.

Contact Mrs. Joanne C. Kresken, Admissions Director. 262-763-1510 Ext. 225. Fax: 262-763-1509. E-mail: jkresken@cchsnet.org. Web site: www.cchsnet.org.

THE CATHOLIC HIGH SCHOOL OF BALTIMORE

2800 Edison Highway

Baltimore, Maryland 21213

Head of School: Dr. Barbara D. Nazelrod

General Information Girls' day and distance learning college-preparatory, general academic, arts, religious studies, and technology school, affiliated with Roman Catholic Church. Grades 9–12. Distance learning grades 9–12. Founded: 1939. Setting: urban. 6-acre campus. 1 building on campus. Approved or accredited by Association of Independent Maryland Schools, Middle States Association of Colleges and Schools, National Catholic Education Association, and Maryland Department of Education. Endowment: $3 million. Total enrollment: 313. Upper school average class size: 17. Upper school faculty-student ratio: 1:12. There are 175 required school days per year for Upper School students. Upper School students typically attend 5 days per week. The average school day consists of 6 hours and 45 minutes.

Upper School Student Profile Grade 9: 90 students (90 girls); Grade 10: 64 students (64 girls); Grade 11: 60 students (60 girls); Grade 12: 99 students (99 girls). 75% of students are Roman Catholic.

Faculty School total: 32. In upper school: 12 men, 15 women; 20 have advanced degrees.

Subjects Offered Algebra, American history, American literature, anatomy, art, band, biology, calculus, chemistry, community service, computer programming, computer science, creative writing, dance, drama, driver education, earth science, economics, English, English literature, expository writing, fine arts, French, geometry, government/civics, grammar, health, history, instrumental music, journalism, keyboarding, literature, mathematics, music, personal development, photography, physical education, physics, physiology, psychology, reading, religion, science, social studies, Spanish, speech, study skills, technology, theater, theology, world history, world literature.

Graduation Requirements Arts and fine arts (art, music, dance, drama), computer science, English, foreign language, mathematics, physical education (includes health), religion (includes Bible studies and theology), science, social studies (includes history). Community service is required.

Special Academic Programs Advanced Placement exam preparation; honors section; independent study; study at local college for college credit; remedial reading and/or remedial writing; remedial math; programs in English, mathematics, general development for dyslexic students.

College Admission Counseling 76 students graduated in 2011; 69 went to college, including George Mason University; Johnson & Wales University; Salisbury University; Stevenson University; Towson University. Other: 7 went to work. Median SAT critical reading: 510, median SAT math: 460, median SAT writing: 510. 21.8% scored over 600 on SAT critical reading, 9.1% scored over 600 on SAT math, 18.2% scored over 600 on SAT writing.

Student Life Upper grades have uniform requirement, student council, honor system. Discipline rests primarily with faculty. Attendance at religious services is required.

Summer Programs Enrichment, sports, art/fine arts, computer instruction programs offered; session focuses on enrichment; held both on and off campus; held at Sports Field; accepts girls; open to students from other schools. 100 students usually enrolled. 2012 schedule: June 18 to July 23. Application deadline: none.

Tuition and Aid Day student tuition: $10,700. Tuition installment plan (Insured Tuition Payment Plan, FACTS Tuition Payment Plan, biannual payment plan, annual payment plan). Tuition reduction for siblings, merit scholarship grants, need-based scholarship grants available. In 2011–12, 63% of upper-school students received aid; total upper-school merit-scholarship money awarded: $273,450. Total amount of financial aid awarded in 2011–12: $408,150.

Admissions Traditional secondary-level entrance grade is 9. For fall 2011, 206 students applied for upper-level admission, 190 were accepted, 90 enrolled. High School Placement Test required. Deadline for receipt of application materials: December 23. Application fee required: $40. On-campus interview required.

Athletics Interscholastic: basketball, cheering, cross-country running, dance team, field hockey, golf, indoor track & field, lacrosse, soccer, softball, swimming and diving, tennis, track and field, volleyball; intramural: aerobics, aerobics/dance, cooperative games. 1 PE instructor, 20 coaches.

Computers Computers are regularly used in art, English, foreign language, history, mathematics, music, science, theology classes. Computer network features include on-campus library services, online commercial services, Internet access, wireless campus network, Internet filtering or blocking technology. Campus intranet and student e-mail accounts are available to students. Students grades are available online. The school has a published electronic and media policy.

Contact Mrs. Barbara Czawlytko, Administrative Assistant. 410-732-6200 Ext. 213. Fax: 410-732-7639. E-mail: bczawlytko@thecatholichighschool.org. Web site: www.thecatholichighschool.org.

THE CATLIN GABEL SCHOOL

8825 SW Barnes Road

Portland, Oregon 97225

Head of School: Dr. Lark P. Palma

General Information Coeducational day college-preparatory, arts, technology, and sciences school. Grades PK–12. Founded: 1957. Setting: suburban. 54-acre campus. 13 buildings on campus. Approved or accredited by Northwest Association of Schools and Colleges and Pacific Northwest Association of Independent Schools. Member of National Association of Independent Schools and Secondary School Admission Test Board. Endowment: $19.5 million. Total enrollment: 728. Upper school average class size: 15. Upper school faculty-student ratio: 1:8. There are 169 required school days per year for Upper School students. Upper School students typically attend 5 days per week. The average school day consists of 7 hours and 10 minutes.

Upper School Student Profile Grade 9: 75 students (39 boys, 36 girls); Grade 10: 70 students (33 boys, 37 girls); Grade 11: 71 students (39 boys, 32 girls); Grade 12: 71 students (35 boys, 36 girls).

Faculty School total: 87. In upper school: 28 men, 22 women; 34 have advanced degrees.

Subjects Offered Acting, advanced chemistry, advanced computer applications, advanced math, algebra, American democracy, American history, American literature, ancient world history, applied music, art, art history, arts, astronomy, athletics, baseball, Basic programming, basketball, biology, bookmaking, bowling, calculus, ceramics, chemistry, Chinese, choir, college admission preparation, college counseling, comedy, computer art, computer graphics, computer programming, computer resources, computer science, computer skills, computer studies, concert choir, creative writing, critical studies in film, critical thinking, debate, digital imaging, digital photography, drama, drama performance, dramatic arts, drawing and design, driver education, ecology, economics, English, English literature, ensembles, ethics and responsibility, European history, expository writing, fiber arts, film studies, fine arts, foreign language, foreign policy, French, geometry, golf, government/civics, graphic arts, graphic design, health, history, human sexuality, Japanese, jazz band, mathematics, model United Nations, music, music theory, musical productions, ornithology, outdoor education, peer counseling, performing arts, photo shop, photography, physical education, physical fitness, physics, playwriting and directing, pre-calculus, probability and statistics, robotics, science, set design, Shakespeare, social studies, Spanish, Spanish literature, speech and debate, stage design, stagecraft, statistics, strings, studio art, study skills, technical theater, tennis, theater, theater arts, theater design and production, track and field, trigonometry, U.S. history, visual and performing arts, vocal ensemble, voice, voice ensemble, volleyball, weight fitness, weight training, woodworking, world affairs, world history, world literature, world wide web design, writing, writing workshop, yearbook.

Graduation Requirements Arts and fine arts (art, music, dance, drama), English, foreign language, mathematics, physical education (includes health), science, social studies (includes history). Community service is required.

Special Academic Programs Honors section; independent study; term-away projects; study at local college for college credit; study abroad; academic accommodation for the gifted, the musically talented, and the artistically talented.

College Admission Counseling 77 students graduated in 2011; 71 went to college, including Bard College; Boston College; Claremont McKenna College; Occidental College; Reed College; University of Oregon. Other: 6 had other specific plans. Mean SAT critical reading: 632, mean SAT math: 637, mean SAT writing: 627, mean combined SAT: 1896, mean composite ACT: 27. 89% scored over 600 on SAT critical reading, 87% scored over 600 on SAT math, 80% scored over 600 on SAT writing, 86% scored over 1800 on combined SAT, 96% scored over 26 on composite ACT.

Student Life Upper grades have student council, honor system. Discipline rests equally with students and faculty.

Summer Programs Enrichment, art/fine arts, computer instruction programs offered; session focuses on arts and enrichment; held both on and off campus; held at various outdoor areas - hiking, climbing, etc.; accepts boys and girls; open to students from other schools. 85 students usually enrolled. 2012 schedule: June 27 to August 5.

Tuition and Aid Day student tuition: $23,800. Tuition installment plan (Insured Tuition Payment Plan, monthly payment plans, individually arranged payment plans). Merit scholarship grants, need-based scholarship grants available. In 2011–12, 24% of upper-school students received aid. Total amount of financial aid awarded in 2011–12: $2,900,000.

Admissions Traditional secondary-level entrance grade is 9. For fall 2011, 64 students applied for upper-level admission, 50 were accepted, 29 enrolled. SSAT required. Deadline for receipt of application materials: February 6. Application fee required: $75. On-campus interview required.

Athletics Interscholastic: baseball (boys, girls), basketball (b,g), cross-country running (b,g), golf (b,g), racquetball (b,g), soccer (b,g), tennis (b,g), track and field (b,g), volleyball (g); coed interscholastic: racquetball; coed intramural: alpine skiing, backpacking, bicycling, bowling, canoeing/kayaking, climbing, fishing, fitness, Frisbee, hiking/backpacking, jogging, kayaking, mountain biking, mountaineering, nordic skiing, ocean paddling, outdoor activities, outdoor education, outdoor recreation, outdoors, paddling, physical fitness, physical training, rafting, rock climbing, ropes courses, running, skiing (cross-country), skiing (downhill), snowshoeing, strength & conditioning, telemark skiing, ultimate Frisbee, walking, wall climbing, weight lifting, weight training, wilderness, wilderness survival, yoga. 6 PE instructors, 20 coaches.

Computers Computers are regularly used in animation, art, English, foreign language, graphic design, mathematics, science, theater, writing classes. Computer network features include on-campus library services, online commercial services, Internet access, wireless campus network, laptop requirement for all upper school students, videoconferencing, SmartBoards. Campus intranet and student e-mail accounts are available to students. The school has a published electronic and media policy.

Contact Ms. Sara Nordhoff, Director of Admission and Financial Aid. 503-297-1894 Ext. 345. Fax: 503-297-0139. E-mail: nordhoffs@catlin.edu. Web site: www.catlin.edu.

CEDAR RIDGE ACADEMY

Roosevelt, Utah

See Special Needs Schools section.

CENTRAL ALBERTA CHRISTIAN HIGH SCHOOL

22 Eagle Road

Lacombe, Alberta T4L 1G7, Canada

Head of School: Mr. Mel Brandsma

General Information Coeducational day college-preparatory, general academic, religious studies, and bilingual studies school, affiliated with Christian Reformed Church. Grades 10–12. Founded: 1989. Setting: rural. Nearest major city is Red Deer, Canada. 1 building on campus. Approved or accredited by Christian Schools International and Alberta Department of Education. Language of instruction: English. Total enrollment: 113. Upper school average class size: 113. Upper school faculty-student ratio: 1:14. Upper School students typically attend 5 days per week. The average school day consists of 6 hours and 25 minutes.

Upper School Student Profile Grade 10: 41 students (20 boys, 21 girls); Grade 11: 38 students (19 boys, 19 girls); Grade 12: 34 students (17 boys, 17 girls). 75% of students are members of Christian Reformed Church.

Faculty School total: 9. In upper school: 4 men, 5 women; 1 has an advanced degree.

Subjects Offered Accounting, agriculture, all academic, art, career education, Christian ethics, computer education, drafting, foods, French as a second language, law studies, photography, physical education, work experience.

Graduation Requirements All academic, French.

College Admission Counseling 53 students graduated in 2011; they went to Redeemer University College.

Student Life Upper grades have student council, honor system. Discipline rests primarily with faculty.

Tuition and Aid Day student tuition: CAN$4950. Tuition installment plan (monthly payment plans, individually arranged payment plans). Tuition reduction for siblings available.

Admissions Traditional secondary-level entrance grade is 10. Deadline for receipt of application materials: none. No application fee required. Interview recommended.

Athletics Coed Interscholastic: badminton, basketball, bowling, climbing, cross-country running, fitness, ice skating, jogging, outdoor activities, physical fitness, physical training, running, soccer, softball, swimming and diving, track and field, volleyball, wall climbing, weight training, whiffle ball; coed intramural: basketball, broomball, cooperative games. 1 PE instructor, 1 coach.

Computers Computers are regularly used in all classes. Computer network features include Internet access, wireless campus network, Internet filtering or blocking technology. Campus intranet is available to students.

Contact Office. 403-782-4535. Fax: 403-782-5425. E-mail: office@cachs.ca.

CENTRAL CATHOLIC HIGH SCHOOL

200 South Carpenter Road

Modesto, California 95351

Head of School: Jim Pecchenino

General Information Coeducational day college-preparatory, arts, religious studies, bilingual studies, and technology school, affiliated with Roman Catholic Church. Grades 9–12. Founded: 1966. Setting: urban. Nearest major city is Sacramento. 21-acre campus. 13 buildings on campus. Approved or accredited by Western Association of Schools and Colleges and Western Catholic Education Association. Endowment: $1.7 million. Total enrollment: 406. Upper school average class size: 23. Upper school faculty-student ratio: 1:14. There are 191 required school days per year for Upper School students. Upper School students typically attend 5 days per week. The average school day consists of 6 hours.

Upper School Student Profile Grade 9: 99 students (57 boys, 42 girls); Grade 10: 104 students (50 boys, 54 girls); Grade 11: 101 students (51 boys, 50 girls); Grade 12: 102 students (52 boys, 50 girls). 81% of students are Roman Catholic.

Faculty School total: 30. In upper school: 9 men, 21 women; 11 have advanced degrees.

Subjects Offered Algebra, American history, American literature, art, Bible studies, biology, broadcast journalism, calculus, chemistry, choir, computer programming, computer science, creative writing, dance, drama, earth science, economics, English, English literature, environmental science, ethics, European history, expository writing, film appreciation, fine arts, geometry, government/civics, grammar, graphics, health, history, mathematics, music, music appreciation, philosophy, physical education, physical science, physics, pre-algebra, pre-calculus, psychology, psychology-AP, religion, science, social sciences, social studies, Spanish, speech, theater, theology, trigonometry, vocal ensemble, world history, world literature, writing, yearbook.

Graduation Requirements Arts and fine arts (art, music, dance, drama), computer science, English, mathematics, physical education (includes health), religion (includes Bible studies and theology), science, social sciences, social studies (includes history), speech, 100 Christian service hours. Community service is required.

Special Academic Programs Advanced Placement exam preparation; honors section; study at local college for college credit; academic accommodation for the gifted; remedial reading and/or remedial writing; remedial math; programs in English, mathematics, general development for dyslexic students.

College Admission Counseling 112 students graduated in 2011; 111 went to college, including California Polytechnic State University, San Luis Obispo; Saint Mary's College of California; San Francisco State University; United States Military Academy; University of California, Berkeley; University of the Pacific. Other: 1 entered military service. Mean SAT critical reading: 511, mean SAT math: 517, mean SAT writing: 509, mean combined SAT: 1537, mean composite ACT: 23.

Student Life Upper grades have specified standards of dress, student council, honor system. Discipline rests primarily with faculty. Attendance at religious services is required.

Summer Programs Remediation programs offered; session focuses on remediation and SAT Prep; held on campus; accepts boys and girls; open to students from other schools. 109 students usually enrolled. 2012 schedule: June 4 to July 6. Application deadline: May 11.

Tuition and Aid Day student tuition: $8995–$9378. Guaranteed tuition plan. Tuition installment plan (monthly payment plans, individually arranged payment plans, Tuition Management Systems Plan, quarterly and semiannual payment plans). Tuition reduction for siblings, merit scholarship grants, need-based scholarship grants, paying campus jobs available. In 2011–12, 19% of upper-school students received aid; total upper-school merit-scholarship money awarded: $10,350. Total amount of financial aid awarded in 2011–12: $196,598.

Admissions Traditional secondary-level entrance grade is 9. For fall 2011, 119 students applied for upper-level admission, 116 were accepted, 116 enrolled. Cognitive Abilities Test, Iowa Test of Educational Development or USC/UC Math Diagnostic Test required. Deadline for receipt of application materials: none. Application fee required: $45. On-campus interview required.

Athletics Interscholastic: baseball (boys), basketball (b,g), cheering (g), cross-country running (b,g), football (b), golf (b,g), soccer (b,g), softball (g), tennis (b,g), track and field (b,g), volleyball (g), wrestling (b); coed interscholastic: dance, swimming and diving, water polo. 2 PE instructors, 91 coaches.

Computers Computers are regularly used in English, foreign language, graphic arts, literacy, mathematics, science, social studies, technology, Web site design, yearbook classes. Computer network features include on-campus library services, Internet access, Internet filtering or blocking technology. Student e-mail accounts and computer access in designated common areas are available to students. Students grades are available online. The school has a published electronic and media policy.

Contact Jodi Tybor, Admissions Coordinator/Registrar. 209-524-9611 Ext. 104. Fax: 209-524-4913. E-mail: tybor@cchsca.org. Web site: www.cchsca.org.

CENTRAL CATHOLIC HIGH SCHOOL

300 Hampshire Street

Lawrence, Massachusetts 01841

Head of School: Mrs. Doreen A. Keller

General Information Coeducational day college-preparatory, arts, business, religious studies, and technology school, affiliated with Roman Catholic Church. Grades 9–12. Founded: 1935. Setting: urban. Nearest major city is Boston. 1 building on campus. Approved or accredited by Commission on Independent Schools, New England Association of Schools and Colleges, and Massachusetts Department of Education. Total enrollment: 1,355. Upper school average class size: 25. Upper school faculty-student ratio: 1:24. There are 165 required school days per year for Upper School students. Upper School students typically attend 5 days per week. The average school day consists of 6 hours and 15 minutes.

Upper School Student Profile Grade 9: 356 students (204 boys, 152 girls); Grade 10: 331 students (168 boys, 163 girls); Grade 11: 325 students (163 boys, 162 girls); Grade 12: 343 students (160 boys, 183 girls). 80% of students are Roman Catholic.

Faculty School total: 101. In upper school: 53 men, 48 women; 59 have advanced degrees.

Subjects Offered Art, arts, computer science, English, fine arts, French, health, mathematics, physical education, religion, science, social studies, Spanish.

Graduation Requirements Arts and fine arts (art, music, dance, drama), computer science, English, foreign language, mathematics, religion (includes Bible studies and theology), science, social studies (includes history).

Special Academic Programs Advanced Placement exam preparation; honors section; study at local college for college credit.

College Admission Counseling 324 students graduated in 2011; 315 went to college. Other: 2 went to work, 3 entered military service.

Student Life Upper grades have uniform requirement, student council, honor system. Discipline rests primarily with faculty. Attendance at religious services is required.

Tuition and Aid Day student tuition: $10,800. Tuition installment plan (FACTS Tuition Payment Plan, monthly payment plans). Merit scholarship grants, need-based scholarship grants available.

Admissions Traditional secondary-level entrance grade is 9. Archdiocese of Boston High School entrance exam provided by STS and High School Placement Test required. Deadline for receipt of application materials: none. No application fee required. Interview required.

Athletics Interscholastic: baseball (boys), basketball (b,g), bowling (b,g), cheering (g), cross-country running (b,g), dance squad (b,g), diving (b,g), equestrian sports (b,g), field hockey (g), figure skating (g), fishing (b,g), football (b), golf (b), gymnastics (g), hockey (b), ice hockey (b), ice skating (g), indoor hockey (g), indoor track (b,g), lacrosse (b,g), martial arts (b,g), modern dance (b,g), soccer (b,g), softball (g), swimming and diving (b,g), tennis (b,g), track and field (b,g), volleyball (b,g), wall climbing (b,g), winter (indoor) track (b,g), wrestling (b); coed interscholastic: dance team. 3 PE instructors, 1 athletic trainer.

Computers Computer network features include on-campus library services, Internet access, wireless campus network, Internet filtering or blocking technology. Campus intranet, student e-mail accounts, and computer access in designated common areas are available to students. The school has a published electronic and media policy.

Contact Mr. Thomas Sipsey, Assistant Director of Admissions. 978-682-0260 Ext. 623. Fax: 978-685-2707. E-mail: tsipsey@centralcatholic.net. Web site: www.centralcatholic.net.

CENTRAL CATHOLIC HIGH SCHOOL

4824 Tuscarawas Street West

Canton, Ohio 44708-5198

Head of School: Rev. Robert W. Kaylor

General Information Coeducational day college-preparatory school, affiliated with Roman Catholic Church. Grades 9–12. Founded: 1905. Setting: suburban. 65-acre campus. 1 building on campus. Approved or accredited by Ohio Catholic Schools Accreditation Association (OCSAA) and Ohio Department of Education. Total enrollment: 444. Upper school average class size: 25. Upper school faculty-student ratio: 1:16.

Upper School Student Profile Grade 9: 126 students (69 boys, 57 girls); Grade 10: 90 students (60 boys, 30 girls); Grade 11: 101 students (55 boys, 46 girls); Grade 12: 127 students (62 boys, 65 girls). 90% of students are Roman Catholic.

Faculty School total: 45. In upper school: 23 men, 22 women; 25 have advanced degrees.

Special Academic Programs Advanced Placement exam preparation.

College Admission Counseling 115 students graduated in 2010; 110 went to college, including Kent State University; Ohio University; The Ohio State University; The University of Akron. Other: 4 went to work, 1 entered military service. Mean SAT critical reading: 543, mean SAT math: 527, mean SAT writing: 527, mean composite ACT: 23.

Student Life Upper grades have specified standards of dress, student council, honor system. Discipline rests equally with students and faculty. Attendance at religious services is required.

Tuition and Aid Day student tuition: $5800–$6200. Tuition installment plan (FACTS Tuition Payment Plan, monthly payment plans, individually arranged payment plans). Tuition reduction for siblings, merit scholarship grants, need-based scholarship grants available. In 2010–11, 35% of upper-school students received aid; total upper-school merit-scholarship money awarded: $20,000. Total amount of financial aid awarded in 2010–11: $125,000.

Admissions Deadline for receipt of application materials: May 15. Application fee required: $15.

Athletics Interscholastic: baseball (boys), basketball (b,g), bowling (b,g), cheering (g), cross-country running (b,g), football (b), golf (b,g), soccer (b,g), softball (g), swimming and diving (b,g), tennis (b,g), volleyball (g), wrestling (b). 1 PE instructor.

Computers Computer resources include on-campus library services, Internet access. Campus intranet and student e-mail accounts are available to students. Students grades are available online. The school has a published electronic and media policy.

Contact 330-478-2131. Fax: 330-478-6086. Web site: www.cchsweb.com.

CENTRAL CATHOLIC HIGH SCHOOL

2550 Cherry Street

Toledo, Ohio 43608

Head of School: Rev. Dennis P. Hartigan

General Information Coeducational day college-preparatory, technology, and International Baccalaureate programme school, affiliated with Roman Catholic Church. Grades 9–12. Founded: 1920. Setting: urban. 25-acre campus. 3 buildings on campus. Approved or accredited by North Central Association of Colleges and Schools and Ohio Department of Education. Upper school average class size: 17. Upper school faculty-student ratio: 1:17. There are 181 required school days per year for Upper School students. Upper School students typically attend 5 days per week. The average school day consists of 7 hours.

Upper School Student Profile Grade 9: 250 students (130 boys, 120 girls); Grade 10: 264 students (135 boys, 129 girls); Grade 11: 260 students (116 boys, 144 girls); Grade 12: 296 students (157 boys, 139 girls). 75% of students are Roman Catholic.

Faculty School total: 74. In upper school: 31 men, 41 women; 24 have advanced degrees.

Special Academic Programs International Baccalaureate program; Advanced Placement exam preparation; honors section.

College Admission Counseling 222 students graduated in 2010; 210 went to college, including Bowling Green State University; Kent State University; Ohio University; The Ohio State University; The University of Toledo. Other: 1 went to work, 2 entered military service, 8 had other specific plans.

Student Life Upper grades have uniform requirement, student council, honor system. Discipline rests primarily with faculty. Attendance at religious services is required.

Tuition and Aid Day student tuition: $7400. Tuition installment plan (FACTS Tuition Payment Plan, monthly payment plans). Tuition reduction for siblings, merit scholarship grants, need-based scholarship grants, paying campus jobs available. In 2010–11, 80% of upper-school students received aid.

Admissions Traditional secondary-level entrance grade is 9. Catholic High School Entrance Examination required. Deadline for receipt of application materials: none. Application fee required. Interview required.

Computers Computer network features include on-campus library services, Internet access, wireless campus network, Internet filtering or blocking technology. Campus intranet and student e-mail accounts are available to students. Students grades are available online. The school has a published electronic and media policy.

Contact Mrs. Sandy Faunce, Registrar. 419-255-2280 Ext. 1107. Fax: 419-259-2848. E-mail: sfaunce@centralcatholic.org. Web site: www.centralcatholic.org.

CENTRAL CATHOLIC HIGH SCHOOL

4720 Fifth Avenue

Pittsburgh, Pennsylvania 15213

Head of School: Br. Richard F. Grzeskiewicz, FSC

General Information Boys' day college-preparatory, arts, business, and religious studies school, affiliated with Roman Catholic Church. Grades 9–12. Founded: 1927. Setting: urban. 2 buildings on campus. Approved or accredited by Middle States Association of Colleges and Schools and Pennsylvania Department of Education. Endowment: $6 million. Total enrollment: 835. Upper school average class size: 21. Upper school faculty-student ratio: 1:16.

Upper School Student Profile Grade 9: 192 students (192 boys); Grade 10: 226 students (226 boys); Grade 11: 225 students (225 boys); Grade 12: 223 students (223 boys). 83% of students are Roman Catholic.

Faculty School total: 54. In upper school: 44 men, 10 women; 23 have advanced degrees.

Subjects Offered 1968, accounting, algebra, American foreign policy, American literature, art, biology, biology-AP, British literature, British literature (honors), business, business mathematics, calculus, calculus-AP, chemistry, chemistry-AP, computer science, computers, consumer education, debate, economics-AP, electives, English, English-AP, environmental science, European history-AP, foreign language, French, geometry, German, health, history, honors algebra, honors English, honors geometry, instrumental music, Italian, Latin, law, marketing, math analysis, mathematics, music, music theory, physical education, physics, physics-AP, pre-calculus, probability and statistics, programming, psychology, religion, science, social studies, sociology, Spanish, Spanish-AP, studio art, theater arts, trigonometry, U.S. history, U.S. history-AP, vocal music, world history, world literature, writing.

Special Academic Programs Advanced Placement exam preparation; honors section; study at local college for college credit; academic accommodation for the gifted.

College Admission Counseling 191 students graduated in 2010; 187 went to college, including Carnegie Mellon University; Duquesne University; Miami University; Penn State University Park; University of Pittsburgh. Other: 3 went to work, 1 entered military service. Mean SAT critical reading: 549, mean SAT math: 563, mean SAT writing: 534, mean combined SAT: 1646. 35% scored over 600 on SAT critical reading, 35% scored over 600 on SAT math, 35% scored over 600 on SAT writing.

Student Life Upper grades have specified standards of dress, student council. Discipline rests primarily with faculty. Attendance at religious services is required.

Tuition and Aid Day student tuition: $7750. Tuition installment plan (SMART Tuition Payment Plan). Merit scholarship grants, need-based scholarship grants available. In 2010–11, 35% of upper-school students received aid; total upper-school merit-scholarship money awarded: $20,000. Total amount of financial aid awarded in 2010–11: $1,250,000.

Admissions Traditional secondary-level entrance grade is 9. For fall 2010, 300 students applied for upper-level admission, 240 were accepted, 192 enrolled. Scholastic Testing Service High School Placement Test or STS Examination required. Deadline for receipt of application materials: February 1. No application fee required. Interview recommended.

Athletics Interscholastic: baseball, basketball, bowling, crew, cross-country running, fencing, football, golf, hockey, ice hockey, in-line hockey, lacrosse, soccer, squash, swimming and diving, tennis, track and field, volleyball, wrestling; intramural: basketball, flag football, football, Frisbee, touch football. 2 PE instructors, 27 coaches, 2 athletic trainers.

Computers Computers are regularly used in business applications, college planning, data processing, library skills, mathematics, newspaper, yearbook classes. Computer network features include on-campus library services, online commercial services, Internet access, wireless campus network, Internet filtering or blocking technology. Campus intranet, student e-mail accounts, and computer access in designated common areas are available to students. Students grades are available online. The school has a published electronic and media policy.

Contact Mr. Brian Miller, Director of Admissions. 412-621-7505. Fax: 412-208-0555. E-mail: bmiller@centralcatholichs.com. Web site: www.centralcatholichs.com.

CENTRAL CATHOLIC HIGH SCHOOL

1403 North St. Mary's Street

San Antonio, Texas 78215-1785

Head of School: Br. Peter A. Pontolillo, S.M., PhD

General Information Boys' day college-preparatory school, affiliated with Roman Catholic Church. Grades 9–12. Founded: 1852. Setting: urban. 10-acre campus. 2 buildings on campus. Approved or accredited by National Catholic Education Association, Southern Association of Colleges and Schools, Texas Catholic Conference, and Texas Department of Education. Endowment: $1 million. Total enrollment: 556. Upper school average class size: 23. Upper school faculty-student ratio: 1:20. There are 180 required school days per year for Upper School students. Upper School students typically attend 5 days per week. The average school day consists of 6 hours and 30 minutes.

Upper School Student Profile Grade 9: 145 students (145 boys); Grade 10: 149 students (149 boys); Grade 11: 138 students (138 boys); Grade 12: 124 students (124 boys). 90% of students are Roman Catholic.

Faculty School total: 46. In upper school: 33 men, 13 women; 23 have advanced degrees.

Subjects Offered Algebra, American government, American history-AP, anatomy, art, biology, calculus-AP, ceramics, chemistry, chemistry-AP, chorus, Christian and Hebrew scripture, church history, community service, computer science, concert band, economics, English, English language and composition-AP, English language-AP, English literature and composition-AP, English literature-AP, environmental science, fine arts, geometry, health, honors algebra, honors English, honors geometry, honors world history, humanities, information technology, jazz band, journalism, JROTC, languages, Latin, marching band, physics, pre-calculus, probability and statistics, psychology, religion, science, social studies, Spanish, Spanish literature-AP, speech, trigonometry, world geography, world history.

Graduation Requirements Algebra, American government, American history, arts and fine arts (art, music, dance, drama), biology, chemistry, Christian and Hebrew scripture, Christian doctrine, computer information systems, computer science, economics, English, foreign language, geometry, health, JROTC, moral reasoning, religion (includes Bible studies and theology), religious education, social justice, speech, trigonometry, world civilizations, world geography, world history, world religions, requirements for Marianist Honors Diploma differ. Community service is required.

Special Academic Programs 6 Advanced Placement exams for which test preparation is offered; honors section; independent study; study at local college for college credit; study abroad.

College Admission Counseling 106 students graduated in 2011; 105 went to college, including Saint Mary's University; Texas A&M University; Texas Tech University; The University of Texas at Austin; The University of Texas at San Antonio; University of the Incarnate Word. Other: 1 entered military service. Mean SAT critical reading: 541, mean SAT math: 537, mean SAT writing: 528, mean combined SAT: 1606, mean composite ACT: 25.

Student Life Upper grades have specified standards of dress, student council, honor system. Discipline rests primarily with faculty. Attendance at religious services is required.

Summer Programs Remediation, enrichment, advancement, sports, computer instruction programs offered; session focuses on enrichment and make-up courses, sports; held on campus; accepts boys and girls; open to students from other schools. 300 students usually enrolled. 2012 schedule: June 11 to July 20. Application deadline: none.

Tuition and Aid Day student tuition: $8995. Tuition installment plan (monthly payment plans, semester payment plan, Tuition Management Systems). Tuition reduction for siblings, merit scholarship grants, need-based scholarship grants, paying campus jobs available. In 2011–12, 45% of upper-school students received aid; total upper-school merit-scholarship money awarded: $54,000. Total amount of financial aid awarded in 2011–12: $542,050.

Admissions Traditional secondary-level entrance grade is 9. Essay, Scholastic Testing Service High School Placement Test and writing sample required. Deadline for receipt of application materials: none. No application fee required. On-campus interview recommended.

Athletics Interscholastic: baseball, basketball, cheering (g), cross-country running, drill team, football, golf, JROTC drill, lacrosse, physical training, riflery, soccer, strength & conditioning, swimming and diving, tennis, track and field, weight training; intramural: basketball, bowling, football, softball, strength & conditioning, swimming and diving, volleyball. 1 PE instructor, 21 coaches, 1 athletic trainer.

Computers Computers are regularly used in college planning, drawing and design, information technology, journalism, newspaper, science, yearbook classes. Computer network features include on-campus library services, Internet access, Internet filtering or blocking technology, access to other libraries through Texas Library Connection. Students grades are available online. The school has a published electronic and media policy.

Contact Mrs. Veronica Beck, Director of Admissions and Tuition Assistance. 210-225-6794 Ext. 209. Fax: 210-227-9353. E-mail: admissions@cchs-satx.org. Web site: www.cchs-satx.org.

CENTRAL CATHOLIC MID-HIGH SCHOOL

1200 Ruby Avenue

Grand Island, Nebraska 68803-3799

Head of School: Mr. John Golka

General Information Coeducational day college-preparatory and religious studies school, affiliated with Roman Catholic Church. Grades 6–12. Founded: 1956. Setting: suburban. 1 building on campus. Approved or accredited by National Catholic Education Association, North Central Association of Colleges and Schools, The College Board, and Nebraska Department of Education. Total enrollment: 340. Upper school average class size: 17. Upper school faculty-student ratio: 1:15. There are 175 required school days per year for Upper School students. Upper School students typically attend 5 days per week. The average school day consists of 7 hours.

Upper School Student Profile Grade 9: 54 students (22 boys, 32 girls); Grade 10: 38 students (18 boys, 20 girls); Grade 11: 44 students (24 boys, 20 girls); Grade 12: 52 students (26 boys, 26 girls). 98% of students are Roman Catholic.

Faculty School total: 36. In upper school: 8 men, 28 women; 13 have advanced degrees.

Subjects Offered ACT preparation, advanced chemistry, Advanced Placement courses, algebra, American government, American history, art, audio visual/media, basketball, biology, calculus-AP, career education, careers, Catholic belief and practice, cheerleading, chemistry, college writing, commercial art, computer applications, concert band, concert choir, contemporary problems, CPR, desktop publishing, drama, driver education, economics, English, English composition, English/composition-AP, environmental science, general science, golf, government, guidance, health, history, human biology, instrumental music, jazz band, journalism, marching band, mechanical drawing, music, music theory, newspaper, novels, physical education, physics, pre-algebra, pre-calculus, psychology, public speaking, religious studies, senior seminar, sociology, Spanish, speech, tennis, U.S. government, video film production, vocal music, volleyball, Web site design, weight training, world history, world history-AP, wrestling, yearbook.

Graduation Requirements American government, American history, American literature, biology, composition, computer applications, English, English composition, English literature, English literature and composition-AP, English/composition-AP, geography, government, history, mathematics, physical education (includes health), religion (includes Bible studies and theology), science, senior seminar, world history, world history AP, community service.

Special Academic Programs Advanced Placement exam preparation; study at local college for college credit.

College Admission Counseling 38 students graduated in 2010; 36 went to college, including Creighton University; University of Nebraska–Lincoln; University of Nebraska at Kearney; University of Nebraska at Omaha. Other: 1 went to work, 1 entered military service. Median composite ACT: 24. 29% scored over 26 on composite ACT.

Student Life Upper grades have uniform requirement, student council. Discipline rests primarily with faculty. Attendance at religious services is required.

Tuition and Aid Tuition installment plan (monthly payment plans). Tuition reduction for siblings, need-based scholarship grants, paying campus jobs available.

Admissions Traditional secondary-level entrance grade is 9. Deadline for receipt of application materials: none. Application fee required: $100. Interview recommended.

Athletics Interscholastic: baseball (boys), basketball (b,g), cheering (g), cross-country running (b,g), dance team (g), football (b), golf (b,g), physical fitness (b,g), soccer (b,g), tennis (b,g), track and field (b,g), volleyball (g), weight lifting (b,g), weight training (b,g), wrestling (b); coed interscholastic: power lifting; coed intramural: volleyball. 2 PE instructors.

Computers Computers are regularly used in computer applications, desktop publishing, drafting, English, journalism, keyboarding, Web site design, writing, yearbook classes. Computer network features include on-campus library services, Internet access, Internet filtering or blocking technology. Computer access in designated common areas is available to students. Students grades are available online. The school has a published electronic and media policy.

Contact Admissions. 308-384-2440. Fax: 308-389-3274. Web site: www.gicentralcatholic.org/.

CFS, THE SCHOOL AT CHURCH FARM

1001 East Lincoln Highway

Exton, Pennsylvania 19341

Head of School: Rev. Edmund K. Sherrill II

General Information Boys' boarding and day college-preparatory, arts, and technology school, affiliated with Episcopal Church. Grades 7–12. Founded: 1918. Setting: suburban. Nearest major city is Philadelphia. Students are housed in single-sex dormitories. 150-acre campus. 19 buildings on campus. Approved or accredited by Middle States Association of Colleges and Schools, National Association of Episcopal Schools, The Association of Boarding Schools, and Pennsylvania Department of Education. Member of National Association of Independent Schools and Secondary School Admission Test Board. Endowment: $135 million. Total enrollment: 190. Upper school average class size: 12. Upper school faculty-student ratio: 1:6. There are 180 required school days per year for Upper School students. Upper School students typically attend 5 days per week. The average school day consists of 7 hours and 5 minutes.

Upper School Student Profile Grade 9: 43 students (43 boys); Grade 10: 38 students (38 boys); Grade 11: 35 students (35 boys); Grade 12: 38 students (38 boys). 92% of students are boarding students. 39% are state residents. 14 states are represented in upper school student body. 19% are international students. International students from China, Czech Republic, Italy, Nigeria, Republic of Korea, and Thailand; 3 other countries represented in student body. 15% of students are members of Episcopal Church.

Faculty School total: 30. In upper school: 22 men, 8 women; 17 have advanced degrees; 26 reside on campus.

Subjects Offered 20th century history, 3-dimensional design, African-American history, algebra, American government, American history, American history-AP, American literature, American studies, anatomy and physiology, art, art history, biology, biology-AP, British literature, calculus-AP, ceramics, chemistry, chemistry-AP, choir, choral music, clayworking, college writing, composition, computer science, construction, creative writing, design, drama, driver education, earth science, ecology, economics, English, English-AP, environmental science, ethics, European history, expository writing, film and literature, fine arts, French, geometry, government/civics, grammar, health, history, history of jazz, industrial arts, instrumental music, journalism, leadership, mathematics, medieval history, music, music history, music technology, musicianship, mythology, photography, physical education, physics, physics-AP, poetry, pre-calculus, psychology, public speaking, Russian history, science, Shakespeare, Shakespearean histories, social studies, sociology, Spanish, speech, statistics, technology, theater, trigonometry, Vietnam history, Vietnam War, weaving, Web site design, woodworking, world history, world literature, world religions, World War II, writing.

Graduation Requirements Arts and fine arts (art, music, dance, drama), English, foreign language, mathematics, physical education (includes health), religion (includes Bible studies and theology), science, social studies (includes history), technology, Challenge of Required Experience (combination of community service and outdoor educational experience).

Special Academic Programs 4 Advanced Placement exams for which test preparation is offered; honors section; accelerated programs; independent study; study at local college for college credit; study abroad; academic accommodation for the gifted, the musically talented, and the artistically talented.

College Admission Counseling 34 students graduated in 2011; all went to college, including Cornell University; Emory University; Massachusetts Institute of Technology; Northeastern University; Penn State University Park; Temple University. Median SAT critical reading: 550, median SAT math: 580, median SAT writing: 540, median combined SAT: 1700. 36% scored over 600 on SAT critical reading, 45% scored over 600 on SAT math, 33% scored over 600 on SAT writing, 39% scored over 1800 on combined SAT.

Student Life Upper grades have specified standards of dress, student council. Discipline rests primarily with faculty. Attendance at religious services is required.

Tuition and Aid Day student tuition: $16,550; 5-day tuition and room/board: $26,750; 7-day tuition and room/board: $26,750. Tuition installment plan (monthly payment plans, individually arranged payment plans). Need-based scholarship grants available. In 2011–12, 89% of upper-school students received aid. Total amount of financial aid awarded in 2011–12: $3,535,445.

Admissions Traditional secondary-level entrance grade is 9. For fall 2011, 247 students applied for upper-level admission, 90 were accepted, 62 enrolled. ISEE, SSAT or TOEFL required. Deadline for receipt of application materials: none. Application fee required: $25. Interview required.

Athletics Interscholastic: baseball, basketball, cross-country running, golf, indoor track, soccer, tennis, track and field, wrestling; intramural: fitness, floor hockey, indoor soccer, physical fitness, strength & conditioning, touch football, weight lifting. 6 coaches, 1 athletic trainer.

Computers Computers are regularly used in art, English, foreign language, history, mathematics, music, science, technology classes. Computer network features include on-campus library services, online commercial services, Internet access, wireless campus network, Internet filtering or blocking technology, 1:1 MacBook Program. Campus intranet and student e-mail accounts are available to students. Students grades are available online. The school has a published electronic and media policy.

Contact Mr. Bart Bronk, Director of Admissions. 610-363-5346. Fax: 610-280-6746. E-mail: bbronk@gocfs.net. Web site: www.gocfs.net.

CHADWICK SCHOOL

26800 South Academy Drive

Palos Verdes Peninsula, California 90274

Head of School: Frederick T. Hill

General Information Coeducational day college-preparatory, arts, and technology school. Grades K–12. Founded: 1935. Setting: suburban. Nearest major city is Los Angeles. 45-acre campus. 5 buildings on campus. Approved or accredited by Association for Experiential Education, California Association of Independent Schools, The College Board, Western Association of Schools and Colleges, and California Department of Education. Member of National Association of Independent Schools.

Endowment: $18 million. Total enrollment: 845. Upper school average class size: 17. Upper school faculty-student ratio: 1:6. There are 167 required school days per year for Upper School students. Upper School students typically attend 5 days per week. The average school day consists of 7 hours and 45 minutes.

Upper School Student Profile Grade 9: 95 students (45 boys, 50 girls); Grade 10: 84 students (43 boys, 41 girls); Grade 11: 92 students (44 boys, 48 girls); Grade 12: 95 students (44 boys, 51 girls).

Faculty School total: 71. In upper school: 26 men, 45 women; 50 have advanced degrees.

Subjects Offered 3-dimensional art, Advanced Placement courses, African history, algebra, American history, American literature, American studies, art, art history-AP, art-AP, Asian history, biology, calculus, calculus-AP, ceramics, chemistry, chemistry-AP, choral music, computer math, computer programming, computer science-AP, constitutional law, creative writing, dance, drama, economics, English, English literature, English literature-AP, environmental science, European history, expository writing, fine arts, forensics, French, French-AP, geometry, grammar, health, history, honors algebra, honors geometry, instrumental music, integrated science, Latin, Latin American history, Latin American studies, life science, Mandarin, marine biology, mathematics, Middle East, Middle Eastern history, music, music theory-AP, outdoor education, photography, physical education, physics, pre-calculus, probability, robotics, science, social studies, South African history, Spanish, Spanish-AP, speech, statistics, statistics-AP, theater, trigonometry, U.S. history-AP, wilderness education, world history, world literature, writing, yearbook.

Graduation Requirements Arts and fine arts (art, music, dance, drama), English, foreign language, history, mathematics, outdoor education, performing arts, physical education (includes health), science.

Special Academic Programs Advanced Placement exam preparation; honors section; independent study; term-away projects; study abroad; academic accommodation for the gifted, the musically talented, and the artistically talented.

College Admission Counseling 96 students graduated in 2011; all went to college, including Trinity College; Tufts University; University of California, Davis; University of Southern California; Washington University in St. Louis; Yale University. Mean SAT critical reading: 664, mean SAT math: 684, mean SAT writing: 692, mean combined SAT: 2040.

Student Life Upper grades have specified standards of dress, student council, honor system. Discipline rests equally with students and faculty.

Summer Programs Sports, art/fine arts, computer instruction programs offered; session focuses on visual and performing arts, academics, athletics, enrichment; held on campus; accepts boys and girls; open to students from other schools. 500 students usually enrolled. 2012 schedule: June 25 to July 27. Application deadline: April.

Tuition and Aid Day student tuition: $27,400. Tuition installment plan (Key Tuition Payment Plan, individually arranged payment plans). Need-based scholarship grants, paying campus jobs, Malone Scholarship (need/merit-based), MacFarlane Scholarship (need/merit-based) available. In 2011–12, 19% of upper-school students received aid. Total amount of financial aid awarded in 2011–12: $1,985,375.

Admissions Traditional secondary-level entrance grade is 9. ISEE required. Deadline for receipt of application materials: January 17. Application fee required: $125. On-campus interview required.

Athletics Interscholastic: baseball (boys), basketball (b,g), cheering (g), cross-country running (b,g), diving (b,g), football (b), golf (b,g), lacrosse (b,g), soccer (b,g), softball (g), swimming and diving (b,g), tennis (b,g), track and field (b,g), volleyball (b,g), water polo (b,g); intramural: aerobics/dance (g), dance (g), horseback riding (g); coed interscholastic: cheering, equestrian sports. 11 coaches, 3 athletic trainers.

Computers Computers are regularly used in art, computer applications, creative writing, drawing and design, economics, English, foreign language, geography, graphic arts, health, history, humanities, mathematics, music, newspaper, photography, photojournalism, publications, science, social studies, theater arts, Web site design, wilderness education, writing, yearbook classes. Computer network features include on-campus library services, Internet access, wireless campus network, Internet filtering or blocking technology. Campus intranet, student e-mail accounts, and computer access in designated common areas are available to students. Students grades are available online. The school has a published electronic and media policy.

Contact Rita Mills, Admission Manager. 310-377-1543 Ext. 4025. Fax: 310-377-0380. E-mail: admissions@chadwickschool.org. Web site: www.chadwickschool.org.

CHAMBERLAIN-HUNT ACADEMY

124 McComb Avenue

Port Gibson, Mississippi 39150

Head of School: Col. Jack Gardner West

General Information Boys' boarding and coeducational day college-preparatory, arts, religious studies, and military school, affiliated with Presbyterian Church, Reformed Church. Boarding boys grades 7–12, day boys grades 7–12, day girls grades 7–12. Founded: 1879. Setting: small town. Nearest major city is Vicksburg. Students are housed in single-sex dormitories. 230-acre campus. 11 buildings on campus. Approved or accredited by Assocaition of Classical Christian Schools, Mississippi Private School Association, Southern Association of Colleges and Schools, and Mississippi Department of Education. Endowment: $29 million. Total enrollment: 90. Upper school average class size: 5. Upper school faculty-student ratio: 1:5. There are 180 required school days per year for Upper School students. Upper School students typically attend 5 days per week. The average school day consists of 7 hours and 45 minutes.

Upper School Student Profile Grade 10: 21 students (19 boys, 2 girls); Grade 11: 27 students (25 boys, 2 girls); Grade 12: 17 students (17 boys). 95% of students are boarding students. 27% are state residents. 20 states are represented in upper school student body. 2% are international students. International students from China. 16% of students are Presbyterian, Reformed.

Faculty School total: 19. In upper school: 12 men, 2 women; 11 have advanced degrees; 11 reside on campus.

Subjects Offered ACT preparation, advanced math, Advanced Placement courses, algebra, American Civil War, American government, American history, American literature-AP, ancient history, art, Bible, biology, British literature, business, calculus, chemistry, choir, Christian doctrine, Christian ethics, church history, classical Greek literature, computer programming, computer skills, CPR, earth science, economics, English, English literature, English literature-AP, ethics, French, geometry, government, keyboarding, Latin, logic, men's studies, military history, physics, pre-algebra, rhetoric, Spanish, theology, U.S. government, U.S. history, vocal ensemble, wilderness experience, world history, world wide web design.

Graduation Requirements Algebra, American literature, anatomy and physiology, Bible, biology, British literature, chemistry, classical Greek literature, economics, electives, geometry, intro to computers, languages, medieval literature, rhetoric, state history, Talmud, U.S. government, U.S. history, world geography, world history, oral comprehensive exams, senior speech, worldview class.

Special Academic Programs International Baccalaureate program; honors section; accelerated programs; independent study; academic accommodation for the gifted, the musically talented, and the artistically talented; remedial reading and/or remedial writing; remedial math; ESL.

College Admission Counseling 10 students graduated in 2011; 7 went to college, including Auburn University; Hinds Community College; Louisiana State University and Agricultural and Mechanical College; Mississippi College; Palm Beach Atlantic University; University of the Ozarks. Other: 2 went to work, 1 entered military service. Median composite ACT: 22. 20% scored over 26 on composite ACT.

Student Life Upper grades have uniform requirement, student council, honor system. Discipline rests primarily with faculty. Attendance at religious services is required.

Summer Programs Remediation, enrichment, advancement, ESL, sports, rigorous outdoor training programs offered; session focuses on remediation and advancement courses along with weekend activities such as rafting, paintball, and ropes course; held both on and off campus; held at Kayaking and professional sporting events; accepts boys; open to students from other schools. 55 students usually enrolled. 2012 schedule: June 4 to June 30. Application deadline: May 31.

Tuition and Aid Day student tuition: $14,500; 7-day tuition and room/board: $24,000. Guaranteed tuition plan. Tuition installment plan (The Tuition Plan, monthly payment plans, individually arranged payment plans). Tuition reduction for siblings, merit scholarship grants, need-based scholarship grants available. In 2011–12, 33% of upper-school students received aid; total upper-school merit-scholarship money awarded: $10,000. Total amount of financial aid awarded in 2011–12: $250,000.

Admissions Traditional secondary-level entrance grade is 10. For fall 2011, 39 students applied for upper-level admission, 35 were accepted, 30 enrolled. Math and English placement tests required. Deadline for receipt of application materials: none. Application fee required: $50. Interview required.

Athletics Interscholastic: basketball (boys), golf (b), independent competitive sports (b), soccer (b), winter soccer (b); intramural: archery (b), baseball (b), basketball (b), canoeing/kayaking (b), climbing (b), cross-country running (b), field hockey (b), fishing (b), fitness (b), flag football (b), jogging (b), life saving (b), marksmanship (b), outdoor activities (b), outdoor adventure (b), outdoor education (b), outdoor recreation (b), outdoor skills (b), paint ball (b), physical fitness (b), physical training (b), pistol (b), rappelling (b), riflery (b), rock climbing (b), ropes courses (b), running (b), soccer (b), softball (b), strength & conditioning (b), table tennis (b), tennis (b), volleyball (b), wall climbing (b), weight lifting (b), weight training (b), wilderness (b), wilderness survival (b), wildernessways (b); coed interscholastic: cross-country running, track and field; coed intramural: track and field. 6 PE instructors, 4 coaches, 1 athletic trainer.

Computers Computers are regularly used in library skills, programming, typing, Web site design classes. Computer network features include on-campus library services, online commercial services, Internet access, wireless campus network, Internet filtering or blocking technology. Students grades are available online. The school has a published electronic and media policy.

Contact Mrs. Beth Cade, Director of Admissions. 601-437-8855 Ext. 239. Fax: 601-437-3212. E-mail: beth.cade@chamberlain-hunt.com. Web site: www.chamberlain-hunt.com/.

See Display on next page, Close-Up on page 600, and Summer Program Close-Up on page 770

CHAMINADE COLLEGE PREPARATORY

7500 Chaminade Avenue

West Hills, California 91304

Head of School: Br. Thomas Fahy

General Information Coeducational day college preparatory, arts, business, religious studies, and technology school, affiliated with Roman Catholic Church. Grades 9–12. Founded: 1952. Setting: suburban. Nearest major city is Los Angeles. 21-acre campus. 14 buildings on campus. Approved or accredited by Western Association of Schools and Colleges, Western Catholic Education Association, and California Department of Education. Endowment: $5.1 million. Total enrollment: 2,042. Upper school average class size: 27. Upper school faculty-student ratio: 1:16. There are 180 required school days per year for Upper School students. Upper School students typically attend 5 days per week. The average school day consists of 6 hours and 25 minutes.

Upper School Student Profile Grade 9: 344 students (176 boys, 168 girls); Grade 10: 317 students (161 boys, 156 girls); Grade 11: 344 students (189 boys, 155 girls); Grade 12: 315 students (162 boys, 153 girls). 50% of students are Roman Catholic.

Faculty School total: 81. In upper school: 33 men, 48 women; 47 have advanced degrees.

Subjects Offered Algebra, American history, American literature, anatomy, art, art history, athletic training, band, baseball, basketball, biology, biology AP, British literature, British literature (honors), calculus, calculus-AP, chemistry, chemistry-AP, Chinese, Christian and Hebrew scripture, community service, comparative government and politics-AP, composition, computer programming, computer programming-AP, computer science, creative writing, dance, dance performance, debate, drama, drawing, driver education, economics, economics and history, English, English language-AP, English literature and composition-AP, environmental science-AP, ethics, European history, expository writing, film studies, finance, fine arts, finite math, French, French language-AP, French literature-AP, geography, geometry, government-AP, government/civics, guitar, jazz ensemble, journalism, Latin, Latin-AP, literature and composition-AP, macroeconomics-AP, marching band, mathematics, microeconomics-AP, modern European history-AP, music, music appreciation, music performance, physical education, physical science, physics, physics-AP, physiology, play/screen writing, probability and statistics, psychology, psychology-AP, religion, science, science fiction, scripture, Shakespeare, social studies, Spanish, Spanish language-AP, Spanish literature-AP, speech, speech and debate, sports medicine, statistics-AP, studio art, theater, trigonometry, U.S. government, U.S. history, U.S. history-AP, United States government-AP, visual and performing arts, visual arts, Western philosophy, Western religions, women's studies, world history, world history-AP, world literature, writing.

Graduation Requirements Arts and fine arts (art, music, dance, drama), college writing, computer science, English, foreign language, mathematics, physical education (includes health), religious studies, science, social studies (includes history), speech. Community service is required.

Special Academic Programs Advanced Placement exam preparation; honors section.

College Admission Counseling 272 students graduated in 2011; 268 went to college, including Arizona State University; California State University, Northridge; Loyola Marymount University; The University of Arizona; University of California, Berkeley; University of Southern California. Other: 2 went to work, 2 had other specific plans. Mean SAT critical reading: 565, mean SAT math: 574, mean SAT writing: 582, mean combined SAT: 1721, mean composite ACT: 26. 37% scored over 600 on SAT critical reading, 39% scored over 600 on SAT math, 41% scored over 600 on SAT writing, 39% scored over 1800 on combined SAT, 45% scored over 26 on composite ACT.

Student Life Upper grades have uniform requirement, student council, honor system. Discipline rests primarily with faculty. Attendance at religious services is required.

Summer Programs Remediation, enrichment, advancement, sports, computer instruction programs offered; session focuses on remediation; held on campus; accepts boys and girls; open to students from other schools. 600 students usually enrolled. 2012 schedule: June 18 to July 27. Application deadline: none.

Tuition and Aid Day student tuition: $12,331. Tuition installment plan (monthly payment plans, 2-payment plan, discounted one-payment plan). Merit scholarship grants, need-based scholarship grants available. In 2011–12, 25% of upper-school students received aid; total upper-school merit-scholarship money awarded: $18,000. Total amount of financial aid awarded in 2011–12: $2,171,466.

Admissions Traditional secondary-level entrance grade is 9. For fall 2011, 274 students applied for upper-level admission, 234 were accepted, 155 enrolled. Non-standardized placement tests required. Deadline for receipt of application materials: January 13. Application fee required: $100. On-campus interview required.

Athletics Interscholastic: aquatics (boys, girls), baseball (b), basketball (b,g), cross-country running (b,g), equestrian sports (b,g), fencing (b,g), field hockey (g), football (b), golf (b,g), lacrosse (b,g), soccer (b,g), softball (g), strength & conditioning (b,g), swimming and diving (b,g), tennis (b,g), track and field (b,g), volleyball (b,g), weight training (b,g), wrestling (b); coed interscholastic: cheering, dance, equestrian sports, physical fitness, strength & conditioning, weight training; coed intramural: dance team, hiking/backpacking, table tennis. 5 PE instructors, 85 coaches, 2 athletic trainers.

Computers Computers are regularly used in creative writing, data processing, information technology, introduction to technology, literary magazine, news writing, newspaper, photojournalism, writing, writing, yearbook classes. Computer network features include on-campus library services, online commercial services, Internet access, wireless campus network, Internet filtering or blocking technology, laptops are issued to students in grades 9-12, Blackboard online learning system, Dyno. Student e-mail accounts are available to students. Students grades are available online. The school has a published electronic and media policy.

Contact Ms. Carrin Torres, Assistant to Admissions and Registrar. 818-347-8300 Ext. 355. Fax: 818-348-8374. E-mail: catorres@chaminade.org. Web site: www.chaminade.org.

CHAMINADE COLLEGE PREPARATORY SCHOOL

425 South Lindbergh Boulevard

St. Louis, Missouri 63131-2799

Head of School: Rev. Ralph A. Siefert, SM

General Information Boys' boarding and day college-preparatory, arts, business, religious studies, bilingual studies, and technology school, affiliated with Roman Catholic Church. Grades 6–12. Founded: 1910. Setting: suburban. Students are housed in single-sex dormitories. 55-acre campus. 12 buildings on campus. Approved or accredited by Independent Schools Association of the Central States, Midwest Association of Boarding Schools, National Catholic Education Association, North Central Association of Colleges and Schools, The Association of Boarding Schools, The College Board, and Missouri Department of Education. Member of National Association of Independent Schools and Secondary School Admission Test Board. Endowment: $8 million. Total enrollment: 791. Upper school average class size: 19. Upper school faculty-student ratio: 1:10. There are 174 required school days per year for Upper School students. Upper School students typically attend 5 days per week. The average school day consists of 7 hours.

Upper School Student Profile Grade 9: 137 students (137 boys); Grade 10: 117 students (117 boys); Grade 11: 125 students (125 boys); Grade 12: 119 students (119 boys). 8% of students are boarding students. 93% are state residents. 2 states are represented in upper school student body. 8% are international students. International students from China, Mexico, Republic of Korea, Rwanda, Taiwan, and Viet Nam; 2 other countries represented in student body. 83% of students are Roman Catholic.

Faculty School total: 88. In upper school: 67 men, 15 women; 62 have advanced degrees; 6 reside on campus.

Subjects Offered Accounting, algebra, American government, American history, American history-AP, American literature, architecture, art, art history, band, Bible studies, biology, biology-AP, botany, business, business law, business skills, calculus, calculus-AP, campus ministry, Catholic belief and practice, chemistry, chemistry-AP, Chinese, church history, civics, communication skills, communications, community service, comparative government and politics-AP, comparative political systems-AP, computer literacy, computer processing, computer programming, computer programming-AP, computer science, computer science-AP, concert band, creative writing, drama, dramatic arts, earth science, ecology, economics, economics-AP, engineering, English, English composition, English literature, English literature-AP, English/composition-AP, ESL, European history, European history-AP, expository writing, fine arts, French, French-AP, geography, geology, geometry, government/civics, grammar, health, history, industrial arts, keyboarding, Latin, Latin-AP, mathematics, music theory-AP, physical education, physics, physics-AP, psychology, psychology-AP, religion, science, social studies, sociology, Spanish, Spanish-AP, speech, statistics, statistics-AP, studio art-AP, theater, theology, trigonometry, weight training, world affairs, world history, world literature, writing.

Graduation Requirements Arts and fine arts (art, music, dance, drama), computer science, English, foreign language, mathematics, physical education (includes health), practical arts, religion (includes Bible studies and theology), science, social studies (includes history). Community service is required.

Special Academic Programs 23 Advanced Placement exams for which test preparation is offered; honors section; study at local college for college credit; academic accommodation for the gifted; ESL (27 students enrolled).

College Admission Counseling 125 students graduated in 2011; all went to college, including Purdue University; Saint Louis University; University of Dayton; University of Illinois at Urbana–Champaign; University of Missouri; Vanderbilt University.

Student Life Upper grades have specified standards of dress, honor system. Discipline rests primarily with faculty. Attendance at religious services is required.

Summer Programs Enrichment, sports, art/fine arts programs offered; held on campus; accepts boys; open to students from other schools. 500 students usually enrolled. 2012 schedule: June to July.

Tuition and Aid Day student tuition: $15,195; 5-day tuition and room/board: $30,780; 7-day tuition and room/board: $31,880. Tuition installment plan (FACTS Tuition Payment Plan). Merit scholarship grants, need-based scholarship grants, paying campus jobs available. In 2011–12, 30% of upper-school students received aid; total upper-school merit-scholarship money awarded: $80,000. Total amount of financial aid awarded in 2011–12: $1,600,000.

Admissions Traditional secondary-level entrance grade is 9. For fall 2011, 73 students applied for upper-level admission, 61 were accepted, 49 enrolled. SSAT required. Deadline for receipt of application materials: none. Application fee required: $50. Interview required.

Athletics Interscholastic: baseball, basketball, bowling, cross-country running, football, golf, ice hockey, lacrosse, racquetball, soccer, swimming and diving, tennis, track and field, ultimate Frisbee, volleyball, water polo, wrestling; intramural: in-line hockey, rugby, table tennis, weight training. 5 PE instructors, 30 coaches, 1 athletic trainer.

Computers Computers are regularly used in all academic classes. Computer network features include on-campus library services, online commercial services, Internet access, wireless campus network, Internet filtering or blocking technology. Campus intranet and student e-mail accounts are available to students. Students grades are available online. The school has a published electronic and media policy.

Contact Ms. Dianne Dunning-Gill, Associate Director of Admissions. 314-692-6640. Fax: 314-993-5732. E-mail: ddunning-gill@chaminade-stl.com. Web site: www.chaminade-stl.org.

CHAMINADE-MADONNA COLLEGE PREPARATORY

500 Chaminade Drive

Hollywood, Florida 33021-5800

Head of School: Fr. Larry Doersching, SM

General Information Coeducational day college-preparatory, arts, business, and religious studies school, affiliated with Roman Catholic Church. Grades 9–12. Founded: 1960. Setting: suburban. Nearest major city is Fort Lauderdale. 13-acre campus. 10 buildings on campus. Approved or accredited by Southern Association of Colleges and Schools and Florida Department of Education. Total enrollment: 594. Upper school average class size: 26. Upper school faculty-student ratio: 1:19. There are 180 required school days per year for Upper School students. Upper School students typically attend 5 days per week. The average school day consists of 6 hours and 45 minutes.

Upper School Student Profile Grade 9: 147 students (92 boys, 55 girls); Grade 10: 154 students (83 boys, 71 girls); Grade 11: 143 students (94 boys, 49 girls); Grade 12: 150 students (85 boys, 65 girls). 70% of students are Roman Catholic.

Faculty School total: 48. In upper school: 23 men, 24 women.

Subjects Offered Advanced chemistry, advanced computer applications, advanced math, advanced studio art-AP, algebra, American history, American literature, anatomy, art, art history, band, biology, business skills, calculus, ceramics, chemistry, choir, community service, computer applications, creative writing, design, directing, drama, economics, English, fine arts, French, geography, geometry, government/civics, health, history, international relations, journalism, keyboarding, marine biology, mathematics, music, philosophy, physical education, physics, physiology, play production, practical arts, pre-calculus, psychology, reading, religion, science, Shakespeare, social studies, sociology, Spanish, speech, stagecraft, theater, trigonometry, word processing, world history, writing, yearbook.

Graduation Requirements Arts and fine arts (art, music, dance, drama), business skills (includes word processing), English, foreign language, mathematics, physical education (includes health), practical arts, religion (includes Bible studies and theology), science, social studies (includes history), 80 community service hours.

Special Academic Programs 10 Advanced Placement exams for which test preparation is offered; honors section; study at local college for college credit; academic accommodation for the gifted, the musically talented, and the artistically talented; remedial reading and/or remedial writing; remedial math; programs in general development for dyslexic students; special instructional classes for students with learning disabilities, Attention Deficit Disorder, and dyslexia.

College Admission Counseling 156 students graduated in 2011; all went to college, including Florida Atlantic University; Florida International University; Florida State University; University of Central Florida; University of Florida; University of Miami. Mean SAT critical reading: 512, mean SAT math: 504, mean composite ACT: 20.

Student Life Upper grades have uniform requirement, student council, honor system. Discipline rests primarily with faculty. Attendance at religious services is required.

Summer Programs Remediation, enrichment programs offered; session focuses on remediation/make-up; held on campus; accepts boys and girls; not open to students from other schools.

Tuition and Aid Day student tuition: $9700. Tuition installment plan (FACTS Tuition Payment Plan). Tuition reduction for siblings, need-based scholarship grants available. In 2011–12, 33% of upper-school students received aid. Total amount of financial aid awarded in 2011–12: $400,000.

Admissions Traditional secondary-level entrance grade is 9. For fall 2011, 250 students applied for upper-level admission, 200 were accepted, 147 enrolled. High School Placement Test (closed version) from Scholastic Testing Service required. Deadline for receipt of application materials: January 20. Application fee required: $50. Interview required.

Athletics Interscholastic: baseball (boys), basketball (b,g), cheering (g), cross-country running (b,g), dance (g), dance team (g), flag football (g), football (b), golf (b,g), hockey (b,g), ice hockey (b,g), lacrosse (g), soccer (b,g), swimming and diving (b,g), track and field (b,g), volleyball (b,g), wrestling (b); intramural: aerobics/dance (g), danceline (g), football (b,g). 2 PE instructors, 1 athletic trainer.

Computers Computers are regularly used in English, mathematics, reading classes. Computer resources include on-campus library services, online commercial services, Internet access. The school has a published electronic and media policy.

Contact Mrs. Carol Manzella, Admissions Coordinator. 954-989-5150 Ext. 136. Fax: 954-983-4663. E-mail: cmanzella@cmlions.org. Web site: www.cmlions.org.

CHAPEL HILL–CHAUNCY HALL SCHOOL

785 Beaver Street

Waltham, Massachusetts 02452

Head of School: Mr. Lance Conrad

General Information Coeducational boarding and day college-preparatory and arts school. Grades 9–PG. Founded: 1828. Setting: suburban. Nearest major city is Boston. Students are housed in single-sex dormitories. 40-acre campus. 11 buildings on campus. Approved or accredited by New England Association of Schools and Colleges and Massachusetts Department of Education. Member of National Association of Independent Schools and Secondary School Admission Test Board. Endowment: $1.8 million. Total enrollment: 165. Upper school average class size: 11. Upper school faculty-student ratio: 1:6. Upper School students typically attend 5 days per week. The average school day consists of 7 hours.

Upper School Student Profile Grade 9: 25 students (12 boys, 13 girls); Grade 10: 41 students (21 boys, 20 girls); Grade 11: 36 students (24 boys, 12 girls); Grade 12: 47 students (24 boys, 23 girls). 45% of students are boarding students. 65% are state residents. 7 states are represented in upper school student body. 25% are international students. International students from China, Japan, Kazakhstan, Republic of Korea, Taiwan, and Viet Nam; 6 other countries represented in student body.

Faculty School total: 35. In upper school: 14 men, 16 women; 20 have advanced degrees; 20 reside on campus.

Subjects Offered 20th century history, 3-dimensional design, acting, adolescent issues, advanced biology, advanced chemistry, advanced studio art-AP, algebra, American history, American literature, anatomy and physiology, art, biology, calculus, ceramics, chamber groups, chemistry, chorus, comparative religion, creative writing, drama, economics, English, English literature, English-AP, ESL, European history, fine arts, geography, geometry, government/civics, grammar, health, history, journalism, Mandarin, mathematics, music, music theory, photography, physical education, physics, psychology, science, social studies, Spanish, theater, world history, world literature, writing.

Graduation Requirements Arts and fine arts (art, music, dance, drama), English, foreign language, mathematics, physical education (includes health), science, social studies (includes history), senior presentations, earn Charger Points for service. Community service is required.

Special Academic Programs Advanced Placement exam preparation; honors section; independent study; programs in general development for dyslexic students; special instructional classes for students with mild to moderate learning disabilities; ESL (12 students enrolled).

College Admission Counseling 48 students graduated in 2011; all went to college, including Clark University; Curry College; Drew University; Roger Williams University; University of Illinois at Urbana–Champaign; Wheaton College. Mean SAT critical reading: 520, mean SAT math: 540, mean SAT writing: 530.

Student Life Upper grades have student council. Discipline rests equally with students and faculty.

Tuition and Aid Day student tuition: $33,900; 7-day tuition and room/board: $46,000. Tuition installment plan (Key Tuition Payment Plan, monthly payment plans, individually arranged payment plans). Need-based scholarship grants available. In 2011–12, 22% of upper-school students received aid. Total amount of financial aid awarded in 2011–12: $850,000.

Admissions Traditional secondary-level entrance grade is 9. For fall 2011, 221 students applied for upper-level admission, 121 were accepted, 56 enrolled. SSAT or WISC III, TOEFL or SLEP or WISC or WAIS required. Deadline for receipt of application materials: February 1. Application fee required: $50. Interview required.

Athletics Interscholastic: baseball (boys), basketball (b,g), lacrosse (b,g), soccer (b,g), softball (g), volleyball (g), wrestling (b); coed interscholastic: climbing, combined training, cross-country running, fitness, Frisbee, golf, rock climbing, ropes courses, ultimate Frisbee; coed intramural: aerobics/dance, cooperative games, dance team, fitness, outdoor education, physical fitness, racquetball, rock climbing, ropes courses, swimming and diving, yoga. 1 PE instructor, 1 athletic trainer.

Computers Computers are regularly used in art, English, history, mathematics, multimedia, newspaper, yearbook classes. Computer network features include on-campus library services, online commercial services, Internet access, wireless campus network, Internet filtering or blocking technology. Campus intranet, student e-mail accounts, and computer access in designated common areas are available to students. Students grades are available online. The school has a published electronic and media policy.

Contact Ms. Lauren Lewis, Admissions Administrative Assistant. 781-314-0800. Fax: 781-894-5205. E-mail: llewis@chch.org. Web site: www.chch.org.

CHARLES WRIGHT ACADEMY

7723 Chambers Creek Road

Tacoma, Washington 98467-2099

Head of School: Mr. Robert Camner

General Information Coeducational day college-preparatory and arts school. Grades PK–12. Founded: 1957. Setting: suburban. Nearest major city is Seattle. 100-acre campus. 8 buildings on campus. Approved or accredited by Pacific Northwest Association of Independent Schools and Washington Department of Education. Member of National Association of Independent Schools. Endowment: $15 million. Total enrollment: 668. Upper school average class size: 14. Upper school faculty-student ratio: 1:8. There are 180 required school days per year for Upper School students. Upper School students typically attend 5 days per week. The average school day consists of 5 hours and 45 minutes.

Upper School Student Profile Grade 9: 62 students (43 boys, 19 girls); Grade 10: 65 students (43 boys, 22 girls); Grade 11: 77 students (43 boys, 34 girls); Grade 12: 70 students (35 boys, 35 girls).

Faculty School total: 77. In upper school: 25 men, 16 women; 26 have advanced degrees.

Subjects Offered Algebra, American history, American literature, art history, biology, calculus, ceramics, chemistry, choir, community service, computer programming, computer science, creative writing, criminology, drama, earth science, English, English literature, environmental science, European history, expository writing, French, geometry, government/civics, history, Japanese, journalism, mathematics, music, outdoor education, performing arts, photography, physical education, physics, science, social studies, Spanish, statistics, theater, trigonometry, visual arts, world history, world religions, yearbook.

Graduation Requirements 20th century history, arts and fine arts (art, music, dance, drama), English, foreign language, mathematics, outdoor education, performing arts, physical education (includes health), science, social studies (includes history), participation in Winterim courses, participation in outdoor education/experiences, participation in community service. Community service is required.

Special Academic Programs Advanced Placement exam preparation; honors section.

College Admission Counseling 76 students graduated in 2010; all went to college, including University of Oregon; University of Puget Sound; University of Washington; Western Washington University; Whitman College.

Student Life Upper grades have specified standards of dress, student council, honor system. Discipline rests equally with students and faculty.

Tuition and Aid Day student tuition: $20,900. Tuition installment plan (monthly payment plans). Need-based scholarship grants available. In 2010–11, 23% of upper-school students received aid. Total amount of financial aid awarded in 2010–11: $1,025,446.

Admissions Traditional secondary-level entrance grade is 9. For fall 2010, 67 students applied for upper-level admission, 38 were accepted, 28 enrolled. ISEE, SSAT, TOEFL or Woodcock-Johnson required. Deadline for receipt of application materials: none. Application fee required: $40. Interview required.

Athletics Interscholastic: baseball (boys), basketball (b,g), cross-country running (b,g), football (b), golf (b,g), soccer (b,g), tennis (b,g), track and field (b,g), volleyball (g); intramural: crew (b,g), strength & conditioning (b,g); coed intramural: backpacking, canoeing/kayaking, climbing, hiking/backpacking, kayaking, outdoor adventure, outdoor education, outdoors, physical fitness, strength & conditioning, ultimate Frisbee, weight training, yoga. 4 PE instructors, 7 coaches, 1 athletic trainer.

Computers Computer network features include on-campus library services, online commercial services, Internet access, wireless campus network, Internet filtering or blocking technology. Student e-mail accounts and computer access in designated common areas are available to students. Students grades are available online.

Contact Mrs. Sue Johnson, Admissions Secretary. 253-620-8373. Fax: 253-620-8357. E-mail: admissions@charleswright.org. Web site: www.charleswright.org.

CHARLOTTE CHRISTIAN SCHOOL

7301 Sardis Road

Charlotte, North Carolina 28270

Head of School: Mr. Barry Giller

General Information Coeducational day college-preparatory and arts school, affiliated with Christian faith. Grades JK–12. Founded: 1950. Setting: suburban. 55-acre campus. 4 buildings on campus. Approved or accredited by Association of Christian Schools International, Southern Association of Colleges and Schools, Southern Association of Independent Schools, and North Carolina Department of Education. Total enrollment: 1,018. Upper school average class size: 20. Upper school faculty-student ratio: 1:11. There are 172 required school days per year for Upper School students. Upper School students typically attend 5 days per week. The average school day consists of 7 hours.

Upper School Student Profile Grade 9: 94 students (61 boys, 33 girls); Grade 10: 89 students (54 boys, 35 girls); Grade 11: 84 students (48 boys, 36 girls); Grade 12: 93 students (42 boys, 51 girls). 100% of students are Christian faith.

Faculty School total: 121. In upper school: 18 men, 18 women; 14 have advanced degrees.

Subjects Offered Accounting, acting, advanced studio art-AP, algebra, American culture, American government, American literature, anatomy and physiology, art, art history-AP, athletic training, band, biology, biology-AP, British literature, business, business law, calculus-AP, chamber groups, chemistry, choir, choreography, Christian doctrine, Christian education, Christian ethics, church history, civil war history, computer applications, computer science-AP, computer-aided design, economics, English literature, environmental science-AP, European history-AP, French, French-AP, geometry, German, graphic arts, graphic design, health and wellness, language-AP, Latin, leadership, learning strategies, Life of Christ, literature and composition-AP, marketing, math applications, music composition, music theory-AP, newspaper, painting, photography, physical education, physical science, physics, physics-AP, pre-calculus, psychology, public speaking, research skills, SAT preparation, sign language, Spanish, Spanish-AP, speech and debate, sports medicine, stage design, statistics-AP, studio art-AP, theater, theater design and production, trigonometry, U.S. government and politics-AP, U.S. history, U.S. history-AP, video film production, voice, voice and diction, Web site design, weight training, wind ensemble, world civilizations, world literature, World War II, yearbook.

Graduation Requirements Arts and fine arts (art, music, dance, drama), Bible studies, English, foreign language, mathematics, physical education (includes health), SAT preparation, science, social studies (includes history), speech, service hours.

Special Academic Programs Advanced Placement exam preparation; honors section; study at local college for college credit.

College Admission Counseling 93 students graduated in 2011; 92 went to college, including Appalachian State University; Furman University; North Carolina State University; The University of North Carolina at Chapel Hill; University of South Carolina; Wake Forest University. Other: 1 had other specific plans.

Student Life Upper grades have specified standards of dress, student council, honor system. Discipline rests primarily with faculty. Attendance at religious services is required.

Summer Programs Enrichment, advancement, sports, art/fine arts, computer instruction programs offered; session focuses on enrichment; held both on and off campus; held at area museums, farms, science centers; accepts boys and girls; open to students from other schools. 300 students usually enrolled. 2012 schedule: June to August. Application deadline: none.

Tuition and Aid Day student tuition: $11,240–$16,125. Tuition installment plan (The Tuition Plan, Insured Tuition Payment Plan, monthly payment plans, individually arranged payment plans). Tuition reduction for siblings, need-based scholarship grants available. In 2011–12, 20% of upper-school students received aid. Total amount of financial aid awarded in 2011–12: $389,150.

Admissions Traditional secondary-level entrance grade is 9. Admissions testing, ISEE, Wechsler Intelligence Scale for Children III or Woodcock-Johnson required. Deadline for receipt of application materials: none. Application fee required: $90. On-campus interview required.

Athletics Interscholastic: baseball (boys), basketball (b,g), cheering (g), cross-country running (b,g), dance (g), football (b), golf (b), indoor track (b,g), lacrosse (b), soccer (b,g), softball (g), swimming and diving (b,g), tennis (b,g), track and field (b,g), volleyball (g), wrestling (b); intramural: basketball (b,g), cheering (g), jogging (g), lacrosse (b), volleyball (g); coed interscholastic: physical fitness, physical training, strength & conditioning, weight training; coed intramural: basketball, fencing, soccer, tennis, weight training. 2 PE instructors, 25 coaches, 1 athletic trainer.

Computers Computers are regularly used in computer applications, journalism, keyboarding, photography, publications, yearbook classes. Computer network features include on-campus library services, Internet access, wireless campus network, Internet filtering or blocking technology, NewsBank InfoWeb. Students grades are available online. The school has a published electronic and media policy.

Contact Mrs. Cathie Broocks, Director of Admissions. 704-366-5657. Fax: 704-366-5678. E-mail: cathie.broocks@charchrist.com. Web site: www.charlottechristian.com.

CHARLOTTE COUNTRY DAY SCHOOL

1440 Carmel Road

Charlotte, North Carolina 28226

Head of School: Mr. Mark Reed

General Information Coeducational day college-preparatory school. Grades JK–12. Founded: 1941. Setting: suburban. 60-acre campus. 10 buildings on campus. Approved or accredited by Southern Association of Colleges and Schools, Southern Association of Independent Schools, and North Carolina Department of Education. Member of National Association of Independent Schools and Secondary School Admission Test Board. Endowment: $18.6 million. Total enrollment: 1,619. Upper school average class size: 15. Upper school faculty-student ratio: 1:12. There are 170 required school days per year for Upper School students. Upper School students typically attend 5 days per week. The average school day consists of 7 hours and 15 minutes.

Upper School Student Profile Grade 9: 122 students (64 boys, 58 girls); Grade 10: 129 students (70 boys, 59 girls); Grade 11: 120 students (65 boys, 55 girls); Grade 12: 118 students (69 boys, 49 girls).

Faculty School total: 218. In upper school: 36 men, 35 women; 51 have advanced degrees.

Subjects Offered Algebra, American history, American history-AP, anatomy, art, art history-AP, astronomy, biology, biology-AP, biotechnology, calculus-AP, ceramics, chemistry, chemistry-AP, Chinese, computer graphics, computer science, computer science-AP, creative writing, dance, debate, discrete mathematics, drama, ecology, economics, English, English literature, English-AP, environmental science-AP, ESL, European history, European history-AP, French, French-AP, geography, geometry, German, German-AP, Japanese, journalism, Latin, Latin-AP, library studies, music, non-Western societies, novels, photography, physical education, physics, physics-AP, physiology, poetry, political science, pre-calculus, probability and statistics, psychology-AP, sculpture, Shakespeare, short story, Spanish, Spanish-AP, studio art-AP, theater, theory of knowledge, trigonometry, typing, visual arts, yearbook.

Graduation Requirements Arts and fine arts (art, music, dance, drama), computer science, English, foreign language, mathematics, physical education (includes health), science, social sciences, social studies (includes history). Community service is required.

Special Academic Programs International Baccalaureate program; honors section; independent study; term-away projects; study abroad; academic accommodation for the gifted; ESL (14 students enrolled).

College Admission Counseling 123 students graduated in 2011; all went to college, including Clemson University; College of Charleston; The University of North Carolina at Chapel Hill; University of Georgia; University of South Carolina; Vanderbilt University. Median SAT critical reading: 630, median SAT math: 650, median SAT writing: 630, median combined SAT: 1890, median composite ACT: 27. 58% scored over 600 on SAT critical reading, 74% scored over 600 on SAT math, 61% scored over 600 on SAT writing, 66% scored over 1800 on combined SAT, 54% scored over 26 on composite ACT.

Student Life Upper grades have specified standards of dress, student council, honor system. Discipline rests primarily with faculty.

Summer Programs Remediation, enrichment, advancement, ESL, sports, art/fine arts, computer instruction programs offered; session focuses on enrichment classes, academic courses, and sports camps; held on campus; accepts boys and girls; open to students from other schools. 200 students usually enrolled. 2012 schedule: June 11 to July 27. Application deadline: none.

Tuition and Aid Day student tuition: $20,815. Tuition installment plan (The Tuition Plan, Insured Tuition Payment Plan, monthly payment plans). Need-based scholarship grants available. In 2011–12, 20% of upper-school students received aid. Total amount of financial aid awarded in 2011–12: $1,530,035.

Admissions Traditional secondary-level entrance grade is 9. For fall 2011, 109 students applied for upper-level admission, 70 were accepted, 47 enrolled. CTP III, ERB or ISEE required. Deadline for receipt of application materials: January 15. Application fee required: $90. On-campus interview required.

Athletics Interscholastic: baseball (boys), basketball (b,g), cheering (g), crew (g), cross-country running (b,g), dance (g), dance team (g), field hockey (g), fitness (b,g), football (b), golf (b,g), lacrosse (b,g), soccer (b,g), softball (g), strength & conditioning (b,g), swimming and diving (b,g), tennis (b,g), track and field (b,g), volleyball (g), weight training (b,g), wrestling (b). 1 PE instructor, 38 coaches, 3 athletic trainers.

Computers Computers are regularly used in art, computer applications, English, foreign language, mathematics, photography, science, yearbook classes. Computer network features include on-campus library services, Internet access, wireless campus network, Internet filtering or blocking technology. Campus intranet and student e-mail accounts are available to students. Students grades are available online. The school has a published electronic and media policy.

Contact Nancy R. Ehringhaus, Director of Admissions. 704-943-4530 Ext. 4531. Fax: 704-943-4536. E-mail: nancy.ehringhaus@charlottecountryday.org. Web site: www.charlottecountryday.org.

CHARLOTTE LATIN SCHOOL

9502 Providence Road

Charlotte, North Carolina 28277-8695

Head of School: Mr. Arch N. McIntosh Jr.

General Information Coeducational day college-preparatory school. Grades K–12. Founded: 1970. Setting: suburban. 122-acre campus. 15 buildings on campus. Approved or accredited by Southern Association of Colleges and Schools, Southern Association of Independent Schools, and North Carolina Department of Education. Member of National Association of Independent Schools and Secondary School Admission Test Board. Endowment: $22.9 million. Total enrollment: 1,388. Upper school average class size: 16. Upper school faculty-student ratio: 1:12. There are 173 required school days per year for Upper School students. Upper School students typically attend 5 days per week. The average school day consists of 7 hours and 5 minutes.

Upper School Student Profile Grade 9: 132 students (64 boys, 68 girls); Grade 10: 124 students (63 boys, 61 girls); Grade 11: 122 students (57 boys, 65 girls); Grade 12: 114 students (60 boys, 54 girls).

Faculty School total: 180. In upper school: 29 men, 27 women; 39 have advanced degrees.

Subjects Offered 20th century American writers, 20th century history, 20th century physics, 20th century world history, 3-dimensional art, acting, advanced chemistry, Advanced Placement courses, algebra, American culture, American government, American history, American history-AP, American literature, anatomy, anatomy and physiology, art, biology, biology-AP, British literature, calculus, calculus-AP, ceramics, chemistry, chemistry-AP, college counseling, computer applications, computer math, computer programming, computer science, computer science-AP, conceptual physics, concert band, concert choir, creative writing, debate, discrete mathematics, drama, dramatic arts, earth science, ecology, economics, economics and history, engineering, English, English literature, English-AP, environmental science, European history, European history-AP, expository writing, finite math, French, French-AP, geography, geology, geometry, German, government/civics, grammar, Greek, health, history, Holocaust and other genocides, honors algebra, honors English, honors geometry, human rights, international relations, international studies, journalism, Latin, Latin-AP, leadership and service, mathematics, media literacy, music, music theory, music theory-AP, physical education, physics, physics-AP, pre-calculus, programming, psychology, science, social studies, Southern literature, Spanish, Spanish language-AP, Spanish-AP, speech, sports medicine, statistics-AP, studio art, technical theater, theater, trigonometry, U.S. government and politics-AP, Web site design, world history, world literature, world religions, writing, yearbook.

Graduation Requirements Electives, English, foreign language, history, mathematics, physical education (includes health), science.

Special Academic Programs 14 Advanced Placement exams for which test preparation is offered; honors section; study abroad; academic accommodation for the gifted.

College Admission Counseling 118 students graduated in 2011; all went to college, including Elon University; North Carolina State University; The University of Alabama; The University of North Carolina at Chapel Hill; University of Georgia; Wake Forest University. 56% scored over 600 on SAT critical reading, 67% scored over 600 on SAT math, 63% scored over 600 on SAT writing, 63% scored over 1800 on combined SAT, 67% scored over 26 on composite ACT.

Student Life Upper grades have specified standards of dress, student council, honor system. Discipline rests primarily with faculty.

Summer Programs Enrichment, sports, art/fine arts, computer instruction programs offered; session focuses on enrichment, sports camps; held both on and off campus; held at N.C. coast (offered for Charlotte Latin students only); accepts boys and girls; open to students from other schools. 850 students usually enrolled. 2012 schedule: June 11 to July 27. Application deadline: none.

Tuition and Aid Day student tuition: $19,250. Tuition installment plan (monthly payment plans, individually arranged payment plans). Merit scholarship grants, need-based scholarship grants available. In 2011–12, 15% of upper-school students received aid; total upper-school merit-scholarship money awarded: $197,690. Total amount of financial aid awarded in 2011–12: $817,525.

Admissions Traditional secondary-level entrance grade is 9. For fall 2011, 152 students applied for upper-level admission, 44 were accepted, 33 enrolled. ERB, ISEE, Wechsler Intelligence Scale for Children III or Woodcock-Johnson required. Deadline for receipt of application materials: none. Application fee required: $90. On-campus interview required.

Athletics Interscholastic: aquatics (boys, girls), baseball (b), basketball (b,g), cross-country running (b,g), dance team (g), field hockey (g), football (b), golf (b,g), independent competitive sports (b,g), indoor track (b,g), lacrosse (b,g), soccer (b,g), softball (g), swimming and diving (b,g), tennis (b,g), track and field (b,g), volleyball (g), wrestling (b); intramural: basketball (b,g), outdoor activities (b,g); coed interscholastic: ultimate Frisbee; coed intramural: outdoor activities. 3 PE instructors, 60 coaches, 3 athletic trainers.

Computers Computers are regularly used in all academic classes. Computer network features include on-campus library services, online commercial services, Internet access, wireless campus network, Internet filtering or blocking technology. Computer access in designated common areas is available to students. The school has a published electronic and media policy.

Contact Ms. Kathryn B. Booe, Director of Admissions. 704-846-7207. Fax: 704-847-8776. E-mail: kbooe@charlottelatin.org. Web site: www.charlottelatin.org.

See Display below and Close-Up on page 602.

CHATHAM ACADEMY

Savannah, Georgia

See Special Needs Schools section.

CHATHAM HALL

800 Chatham Hall Circle

Chatham, Virginia 24531

Head of School: Dr. Gary J. Fountain

General Information Girls' boarding and day college-preparatory and arts school, affiliated with Episcopal Church. Grades 9–12. Founded: 1894. Setting: small town. Nearest major city is Greensboro, NC. Students are housed in single-sex dormitories.

362-acre campus. 9 buildings on campus. Approved or accredited by National Association of Episcopal Schools, Southern Association of Colleges and Schools, The Association of Boarding Schools, and Virginia Association of Independent Schools. Member of Secondary School Admission Test Board. Endowment: $20 million. Total enrollment: 140. Upper school average class size: 8. Upper school faculty-student ratio: 1:7.

Upper School Student Profile 82% of students are boarding students. 34% are state residents. 20 states are represented in upper school student body. 14% are international students. International students from Bermuda, China, Costa Rica, Germany, Republic of Korea, and Taiwan; 12 other countries represented in student body. 20% of students are members of Episcopal Church.

Faculty School total: 34. In upper school: 11 men, 23 women; 19 have advanced degrees; 29 reside on campus.

Subjects Offered Algebra, American history-AP, American literature, art, art history, biology, biology-AP, calculus, calculus-AP, ceramics, chemistry, chemistry-AP, choir, college counseling, computer art, creative writing, dance, DNA science lab, drama, drama performance, earth science, economics, English, English language-AP, English literature, English-AP, ESL, ethics, European history, European history-AP, fine arts, French, French-AP, general science, geography, geometry, history, instrumental music, journalism, Latin, mathematics, medieval/Renaissance history, model United Nations, modern European history, modern European history-AP, music, music composition, music theory, music theory-AP, photography, physical education, physics, pre-calculus, psychology, religion, robotics, SAT/ACT preparation, science, service learning/internship, social studies, Spanish, Spanish-AP, studio art-AP, swimming, theater design and production, trigonometry, U.S. government and politics, U.S. history, veterinary science, Western civilization, world history, writing workshop, yearbook.

Graduation Requirements Arts and fine arts (art, music, dance, drama), English, ethics, foreign language, mathematics, physical education (includes health), religion (includes Bible studies and theology), science, social studies (includes history).

Special Academic Programs 13 Advanced Placement exams for which test preparation is offered; honors section; independent study; study abroad; academic accommodation for the gifted, the musically talented, and the artistically talented; ESL (3 students enrolled).

College Admission Counseling 38 students graduated in 2011; all went to college, including Cornell University; Dartmouth College; Duke University; Georgetown University; University of Virginia; Vanderbilt University. Median SAT critical reading: 605, median SAT math: 600. 61% scored over 600 on SAT critical reading, 55% scored over 600 on SAT math.

Student Life Upper grades have specified standards of dress, student council, honor system. Discipline rests equally with students and faculty. Attendance at religious services is required.

Summer Programs Sports programs offered; session focuses on horseback riding; held on campus; accepts girls; open to students from other schools. 30 students usually enrolled. 2012 schedule: July.

Tuition and Aid Day student tuition: $16,500; 7-day tuition and room/board: $38,000. Tuition installment plan (Key Tuition Payment Plan, increments of 45%, 30%, and 20% due July 1, September 1, and December 1 respectively). Merit scholarship grants, need-based scholarship grants available.

Admissions Traditional secondary-level entrance grade is 9. For fall 2011, 114 students applied for upper-level admission, 89 were accepted, 49 enrolled. ISEE, PSAT or SAT, SSAT or TOEFL required. Deadline for receipt of application materials: February 1. Application fee required: $50. Interview required.

Athletics Interscholastic: aquatics, basketball, cross-country running, diving, equestrian sports, field hockey, fitness, golf, horseback riding, soccer, swimming and diving, tennis, volleyball; intramural: aerobics, aquatics, ballet, basketball, dance, diving, equestrian sports, field hockey, fitness, horseback riding, lacrosse, modern dance, soccer, softball, swimming and diving, tennis, volleyball. 2 PE instructors, 3 coaches, 1 athletic trainer.

Computers Computers are regularly used in art, English, foreign language, graphic design, history, independent study, journalism, literary magazine, mathematics, music, newspaper, photography, science, yearbook classes. Computer network features include on-campus library services, online commercial services, Internet access, Internet filtering or blocking technology. Campus intranet, student e-mail accounts, and computer access in designated common areas are available to students. The school has a published electronic and media policy.

Contact Vicki Wright, Director of Admission and Financial Aid. 434-432-5613. Fax: 434-432-1002. E-mail: vwright@chathamhall.org. Web site: www.chathamhall.org.

See Display below and Close-Up on page 604.

CHATTANOOGA CHRISTIAN SCHOOL

3354 Charger Drive

Chattanooga, Tennessee 37409

Head of School: Mr. Chad Dirkse

General Information Coeducational day college-preparatory, arts, religious studies, technology, college-level (AP) courses, and dual enrollment courses school, affiliated with Christian faith. Grades K–12. Founded: 1970. Setting: urban. Nearest major city is Atlanta, GA. 60-acre campus. 6 buildings on campus. Approved or accredited by Christian Schools International, Southern Association of Colleges and Schools, and Tennessee Department of Education. Endowment: $10 million. Total enrollment: 1,145.

Upper school average class size: 17. Upper school faculty-student ratio: 1:17. There are 175 required school days per year for Upper School students. Upper School students typically attend 5 days per week. The average school day consists of 7 hours.

Upper School Student Profile Grade 9: 115 students (61 boys, 54 girls); Grade 10: 110 students (44 boys, 66 girls); Grade 11: 116 students (55 boys, 61 girls); Grade 12: 120 students (70 boys, 50 girls). 100% of students are Christian faith.

Faculty School total: 104. In upper school: 28 men, 21 women; 19 have advanced degrees.

Subjects Offered Advanced biology, advanced chemistry, advanced studio art-AP, algebra, American government, American history, American literature, anatomy, ancient history, art, art appreciation, art history, art-AP, astronomy, band, Bible, Bible studies, biology, biology-AP, calculus, calculus-AP, chemistry, choir, civil rights, community service, computer applications, computer programming, concert band, concert choir, creative writing, current events, dance, drama, drama performance, Eastern world civilizations, economics, English, English literature, English-AP, entrepreneurship, environmental science, environmental studies, ethics, European history, European history-AP, fine arts, foreign language, French, geometry, German, government, health, honors geometry, industrial arts, introduction to theater, Latin, leadership education training, mathematics, mathematics-AP, mechanical drawing, Microsoft, modern dance, modern European history-AP, music, music theory, New Testament, personal finance, physical education, physical science, physics, physics-AP, physiology, psychology, religion, science, shop, Spanish, statistics-AP, studio art-AP, theater, trigonometry, U.S. history-AP, Web site design, weight training, wellness, world literature, writing.

Graduation Requirements Arts and fine arts (art, music, dance, drama), computer science, English, foreign language, mathematics, physical education (includes health), religion (includes Bible studies and theology), science, social sciences, social studies (includes history). Community service is required.

Special Academic Programs Advanced Placement exam preparation; honors section; independent study; study at local college for college credit; academic accommodation for the gifted, the musically talented, and the artistically talented; remedial reading and/or remedial writing; remedial math.

College Admission Counseling 104 students graduated in 2011; 98 went to college, including Chattanooga State Community College; Covenant College; Middle Tennessee State University; The University of Tennessee; The University of Tennessee at Chattanooga. Other: 1 went to work, 2 entered military service, 3 had other specific plans. Mean SAT critical reading: 578, mean SAT math: 519, mean SAT writing: 540, mean composite ACT: 23. 32% scored over 600 on SAT critical reading, 24% scored over 600 on SAT math, 29% scored over 600 on SAT writing, 27% scored over 26 on composite ACT.

Student Life Upper grades have specified standards of dress, student council, honor system. Discipline rests primarily with faculty. Attendance at religious services is required.

Summer Programs Remediation, enrichment, sports, art/fine arts, computer instruction programs offered; session focuses on sports camps and arts camps; held on campus; accepts boys and girls; open to students from other schools. 100 students usually enrolled. 2012 schedule: June 4 to June 29. Application deadline: May 31.

Tuition and Aid Day student tuition: $9. Tuition installment plan (monthly payment plans, individually arranged payment plans). Tuition reduction for siblings, need-based scholarship grants, paying campus jobs available. In 2011–12, 21% of upper-school students received aid. Total amount of financial aid awarded in 2011–12: $122,300.

Admissions Traditional secondary-level entrance grade is 9. For fall 2011, 52 students applied for upper-level admission, 40 were accepted, 36 enrolled. Any standardized test required. Deadline for receipt of application materials: February 1. Application fee required: $100. Interview required.

Athletics Interscholastic: baseball (boys), basketball (b,g), bowling (b,g), cheering (g), cross-country running (b,g), football (b), golf (b,g), soccer (b,g), softball (g), strength & conditioning (b,g), tennis (b,g), track and field (b,g), volleyball (g), weight lifting (b,g), weight training (b,g), wrestling (b); intramural: badminton (b,g), basketball (b,g), fencing (b,g), field hockey (g), flag football (b,g), indoor soccer (b,g), lacrosse (b,g), paddle tennis (b,g), soccer (b,g), softball (g), speedball (b,g), table tennis (b,g), tennis (b,g), touch football (b), track and field (b,g), volleyball (g), weight lifting (b,g), wrestling (b); coed intramural: aerobics/dance, bowling, cooperative games, dance, fitness, Frisbee, handball, hockey, independent competitive sports, jump rope, kickball, modern dance, outdoor activities, outdoor adventure, outdoor education, outdoor recreation, paddle tennis, physical fitness, physical training, running, street hockey, strength & conditioning, swimming and diving, table tennis, ultimate Frisbee, wall climbing, weight training, whiffle ball. 3 PE instructors, 15 coaches, 1 athletic trainer.

Computers Computers are regularly used in all academic, drawing and design, English, foreign language, history, lab/keyboard, library, mathematics, psychology, science, technology classes. Computer network features include on-campus library services, Internet access, wireless campus network, Internet filtering or blocking technology. Students grades are available online. The school has a published electronic and media policy.

Contact Mrs. Debbie Grisham, Admission Director. 423-265-6411 Ext. 209. Fax: 423-756-4044. E-mail: dgrisham@ccsk12.com. Web site: www.ccsk12.com.

CHELSEA SCHOOL

Silver Spring, Maryland

See Special Needs Schools section.

CHESHIRE ACADEMY

10 Main Street

Cheshire, Connecticut 06410

Head of School: Douglas G. Rogers

General Information Coeducational boarding and day college-preparatory and bilingual studies school. Boarding grades 9–PG, day grades 8–PG. Founded: 1794. Setting: small town. Nearest major city is New Haven. Students are housed in single-sex dormitories. 104-acre campus. 24 buildings on campus. Approved or accredited by Connecticut Association of Independent Schools, International Baccalaureate Organization, New England Association of Schools and Colleges, and The Association of Boarding Schools. Member of National Association of Independent Schools and Secondary School Admission Test Board. Endowment: $8 million. Total enrollment: 355. Upper school average class size: 12. Upper school faculty-student ratio: 1:7. There are 171 required school days per year for Upper School students. Upper School students typically attend 5 days per week.

Upper School Student Profile Grade 9: 41 students (20 boys, 21 girls); Grade 10: 84 students (53 boys, 31 girls); Grade 11: 94 students (52 boys, 42 girls); Grade 12: 93 students (53 boys, 40 girls); Postgraduate: 13 students (13 boys). 62% of students are boarding students. 46% are state residents. 14 states are represented in upper school student body. 40% are international students. International students from China, Democratic People's Republic of Korea, Jamaica, and Taiwan; 8 other countries represented in student body.

Faculty School total: 70. In upper school: 26 men, 41 women; 47 have advanced degrees; 47 reside on campus.

Subjects Offered Acting, Advanced Placement courses, algebra, American Civil War, American government, American history, American literature, anatomy, art, art history, Asian studies, biology, calculus, ceramics, chemistry, Chinese, community service, computer programming, computer science, creative writing, digital imaging, drama, earth science, ecology, economics, English, English literature, environmental science, ESL, European history, expository writing, fine arts, French, geography, geometry, government/civics, grammar, health, history, International Baccalaureate courses, Latin American studies, mathematics, music, photography, physical education, physics, physiology, psychology, reading, science, social sciences, social studies, Spanish, speech, statistics, theater, Vietnam, world history, world literature, writing.

Graduation Requirements Arts and fine arts (art, music, dance, drama), computer science, electives, English, foreign language, mathematics, science, social sciences, social studies (includes history), senior speech, 10 hours of community service, Discover Week program.

Special Academic Programs International Baccalaureate program; Advanced Placement exam preparation; honors section; independent study; study abroad; academic accommodation for the musically talented and the artistically talented; remedial reading and/or remedial writing; remedial math; programs in English, mathematics, general development for dyslexic students; ESL (45 students enrolled).

College Admission Counseling 90 students graduated in 2011; all went to college, including Carnegie Mellon University; Furman University; Gettysburg College; School of the Art Institute of Chicago; University of Washington.

Student Life Upper grades have specified standards of dress, student council, honor system. Discipline rests primarily with faculty.

Summer Programs Enrichment, advancement, ESL, rigorous outdoor training programs offered; session focuses on accelerated study in the arts and sciences; held on campus; accepts boys and girls; open to students from other schools. 2012 schedule: July 7 to August 4. Application deadline: March 1.

Tuition and Aid Day student tuition: $32,360; 7-day tuition and room/board: $45,385. Tuition installment plan (Key Tuition Payment Plan, monthly payment plans). Merit scholarship grants, need-based scholarship grants, need-based loans available. In 2011–12, 30% of upper-school students received aid; total upper-school merit-scholarship money awarded: $120,000. Total amount of financial aid awarded in 2011–12: $2,000,000.

Admissions Traditional secondary-level entrance grade is 9. ACT, ISEE, PSAT, SAT, SSAT or TOEFL required. Deadline for receipt of application materials: February 1. Application fee required: $50. Interview required.

Athletics Interscholastic: baseball (boys), basketball (b,g), cross-country running (b,g), field hockey (g), football (b), lacrosse (b,g), soccer (b,g), softball (g), swimming and diving (b,g), tennis (b,g), track and field (b,g), volleyball (g), wrestling (b); coed interscholastic: archery, fencing, golf, ultimate Frisbee; coed intramural: fitness, indoor soccer, ropes courses, skiing (downhill), weight training. 1 PE instructor, 9 coaches, 2 athletic trainers.

Computers Computers are regularly used in art, classics, college planning, computer applications, creative writing, design, English, foreign language, mathematics, science classes. Computer network features include on-campus library services, online commercial services, Internet access, wireless campus network, Internet filtering or blocking technology. Campus intranet, student e-mail accounts, and computer access in

designated common areas are available to students. The school has a published electronic and media policy.
Contact Gayle Holt, Associate Director of Admission. 203-272-5396 Ext. 455. Fax: 203-250-7209. E-mail: gayle.holt@cheshireacademy.org. Web site: www.cheshireacademy.org.

CHEVERUS HIGH SCHOOL

267 Ocean Avenue

Portland, Maine 04103

Head of School: Mr. John H.R. Mullen

General Information Coeducational day college-preparatory, religious studies, technology, honors, and AP courses school, affiliated with Roman Catholic Church (Jesuit order). Grades 9–12. Founded: 1917. Setting: suburban. 32-acre campus. 2 buildings on campus. Approved or accredited by Association of Independent Schools in New England, Independent Schools of Northern New England, Jesuit Secondary Education Association, New England Association of Schools and Colleges, The College Board, and Maine Department of Education. Endowment: $3 million. Total enrollment: 507. Upper school average class size: 22. Upper school faculty-student ratio: 1:12. There are 173 required school days per year for Upper School students. Upper School students typically attend 5 days per week. The average school day consists of 6 hours and 30 minutes.
Upper School Student Profile Grade 9: 128 students (80 boys, 48 girls); Grade 10: 132 students (69 boys, 63 girls); Grade 11: 128 students (80 boys, 48 girls); Grade 12: 119 students (60 boys, 59 girls). 65% of students are Roman Catholic Church (Jesuit order).
Faculty School total: 50. In upper school: 26 men, 20 women; 28 have advanced degrees.
Subjects Offered Advanced Placement courses, algebra, American history, art, biology, calculus, chemistry, college counseling, creative writing, economics, English, European history, fine arts, French, geography, geometry, government/civics, history, journalism, Latin, library skills, mathematics, music, physics, religion, science, social studies, Spanish, statistics, trigonometry, world history, yearbook.
Graduation Requirements Arts and fine arts (art, music, dance, drama), computer science, English, foreign language, health, mathematics, science, social studies (includes history), theology, all seniors are required to fill a community service requirement. Community service is required.
Special Academic Programs Advanced Placement exam preparation; honors section; study at local college for college credit; programs in general development for dyslexic students.
College Admission Counseling 120 students graduated in 2011; 112 went to college, including Emmanuel College; Saint Anselm College; Saint Joseph's College of Maine; Southern Maine Community College; Tufts University; University of Maine. Other: 5 went to work, 1 entered military service, 1 entered a postgraduate year, 1 had other specific plans. Median SAT critical reading: 536, median SAT math: 535, median SAT writing: 537.
Student Life Upper grades have specified standards of dress, student council, honor system. Discipline rests primarily with faculty. Attendance at religious services is required.
Summer Programs Enrichment, sports programs offered; session focuses on enrichment; held on campus; accepts boys and girls; open to students from other schools. 50 students usually enrolled. 2012 schedule: June 21 to July 2. Application deadline: May 8.
Tuition and Aid Day student tuition: $14,605. Tuition installment plan (FACTS Tuition Payment Plan, monthly payment plans, individually arranged payment plans). Tuition reduction for siblings, merit scholarship grants, need-based scholarship grants, paying campus jobs available. In 2011–12, 66% of upper-school students received aid; total upper-school merit-scholarship money awarded: $12,500. Total amount of financial aid awarded in 2011–12: $1,888,610.
Admissions Traditional secondary-level entrance grade is 9. For fall 2011, 233 students applied for upper-level admission, 217 were accepted, 128 enrolled. English language and Math Placement Exam required. Deadline for receipt of application materials: none. Application fee required: $50. On-campus interview required.
Athletics Interscholastic: baseball (boys), basketball (b,g), cross-country running (b,g), diving (b,g), field hockey (g), football (b), golf (b,g), ice hockey (b,g), indoor track & field (b,g), lacrosse (b,g), sailing (b,g), skiing (downhill) (b,g), soccer (b,g), softball (g), swimming and diving (b,g), tennis (b,g), track and field (b,g), volleyball (g), winter (indoor) track (b,g), wrestling (b); intramural: basketball (b,g), flag football (b,g); coed interscholastic: alpine skiing, outdoor adventure; coed intramural: basketball, bicycling, flag football, hiking/backpacking, table tennis, volleyball. 82 coaches, 2 athletic trainers.
Computers Computers are regularly used in creative writing, economics, history, information technology, journalism, mathematics, SAT preparation, science, word processing, yearbook classes. Computer network features include on-campus library services, online commercial services, Internet access, wireless campus network. Student e-mail accounts and computer access in designated common areas are available to students. Students grades are available online. The school has a published electronic and media policy.
Contact Ms. Kate Luke-Jenkins, Admissions Assistant. 207-774-6238 Ext. 35. Fax: 207-321-0004. E-mail: luke-jenkins@cheverus.org. Web site: www.cheverus.org.

THE CHICAGO ACADEMY FOR THE ARTS

1010 West Chicago Avenue

Chicago, Illinois 60642

Head of School: Ms. Pamela Jordan

General Information Coeducational day college-preparatory and arts school. Grades 9–12. Founded: 1981. Setting: urban. 1-acre campus. 1 building on campus. Approved or accredited by Independent Schools Association of the Central States, North Central Association of Colleges and Schools, and Illinois Department of Education. Member of National Association of Independent Schools. Total enrollment: 140. Upper school average class size: 15. Upper school faculty-student ratio: 1:12. There are 163 required school days per year for Upper School students. Upper School students typically attend 5 days per week. The average school day consists of 8 hours.
Faculty School total: 43. In upper school: 21 men, 21 women; 21 have advanced degrees.
Subjects Offered Algebra, American history, anatomy, art history, arts, biology, calculus, chemistry, consumer law, creative writing, dance, drama, English, film, fine arts, French, geometry, historical foundations for arts, humanities, mathematics, music, physics, science, social sciences, Spanish, speech, theater.
Graduation Requirements Arts and fine arts (art, music, dance, drama), English, foreign language, mathematics, science, social sciences, U.S. history, requirements vary according to arts discipline.
Special Academic Programs Advanced Placement exam preparation; honors section; academic accommodation for the musically talented and the artistically talented; programs in general development for dyslexic students.
College Admission Counseling 44 students graduated in 2011; all went to college, including New England Conservatory of Music; New York University; Rhode Island School of Design; School of the Art Institute of Chicago; The Juilliard School; University of Michigan. Median composite ACT: 24.
Student Life Upper grades have student council, honor system. Discipline rests equally with students and faculty.
Tuition and Aid Day student tuition: $21,052. Tuition installment plan (FACTS Tuition Payment Plan, monthly payment plans). Merit scholarship grants, need-based scholarship grants available. In 2011–12, 48% of upper-school students received aid.
Admissions Traditional secondary-level entrance grade is 9. For fall 2011, 128 students applied for upper-level admission, 80 were accepted, 60 enrolled. ISEE required. Deadline for receipt of application materials: December 2. Application fee required: $65. On-campus interview required.
Computers Computers are regularly used in English, historical foundations for arts classes. Computer resources include online commercial services, Internet access, graphic design and production.
Contact Ms. Kaitlyn Myzwinski, Associate Director of Admissions. 312-421-0202 Ext. 21. Fax: 312-421-3816. E-mail: kmyzwinski@chicagoartsacademy.org. Web site: www.chicagoartsacademy.org.

CHICAGO WALDORF SCHOOL

1300 West Loyola Avenue

Chicago, Illinois 60626

Head of School: Mr. Leukos Goodwin

General Information Coeducational day college-preparatory, arts, vocational, service learning, and arts integrated into all core academic subjects school. Grades 1–12. Founded: 1974. Setting: urban. Students are housed in Day school. 2 buildings on campus. Approved or accredited by Independent Schools Association of the Central States and Illinois Department of Education. Total enrollment: 277. Upper school average class size: 25.
Upper School Student Profile Grade 6: 33 students (12 boys, 21 girls); Grade 7: 19 students (10 boys, 9 girls); Grade 8: 18 students (11 boys, 7 girls); Grade 9: 14 students (7 boys, 7 girls); Grade 10: 14 students (5 boys, 9 girls); Grade 11: 24 students (9 boys, 15 girls); Grade 12: 15 students (6 boys, 9 girls).
Subjects Offered All academic.
Special Academic Programs Independent study; study abroad.
College Admission Counseling 18 students graduated in 2010; all went to college, including DePaul University; Grinnell College; Knox College; Skidmore College; University of Illinois at Urbana–Champaign; Vassar College.
Student Life Upper grades have specified standards of dress, student council. Discipline rests primarily with faculty.
Tuition and Aid Day student tuition: $16,478. Tuition installment plan (monthly payment plans, individually arranged payment plans). Tuition reduction for siblings, need-based scholarship grants available. In 2010–11, 55% of upper-school students received aid. Total amount of financial aid awarded in 2010–11: $272,880.

Admissions Traditional secondary-level entrance grade is 9. For fall 2010, 18 students applied for upper-level admission, 13 were accepted, 9 enrolled. Deadline for receipt of application materials: none. Application fee required: $75. Interview required.
Athletics Interscholastic: basketball (boys, girls), soccer (g), volleyball (g); coed interscholastic: Circus, cross-country running, ultimate Frisbee. 1 PE instructor.
Computers Computers are regularly used in all academic classes. Computer network features include Internet access, wireless campus network. The school has a published electronic and media policy.
Contact Ms. Lisa Payton, Admissions Director. 773-465-2371. Fax: 773-465-6648. E-mail: lpayton@chicagowaldorf.org. Web site: http://www.chicagowaldorf.org/dir/highschool.aspx.

CHILDREN'S CREATIVE AND PERFORMING ARTS ACADEMY OF SAN DIEGO

3051 El Cajon Boulevard

San Diego, California 92104

Head of School: Mrs. Janet M. Cherif

General Information Coeducational boarding and day college-preparatory and arts school. Boarding grades 6–12, day grades K–12. Founded: 1981. Setting: urban. Students are housed in homestay families. 1-acre campus. 1 building on campus. Approved or accredited by Western Association of Schools and Colleges and California Department of Education. Total enrollment: 265. Upper school average class size: 16. Upper school faculty-student ratio: 1:15. There are 186 required school days per year for Upper School students. Upper School students typically attend 5 days per week. The average school day consists of 7 hours and 30 minutes.
Upper School Student Profile Grade 9: 31 students (11 boys, 20 girls); Grade 10: 28 students (12 boys, 16 girls); Grade 11: 28 students (13 boys, 15 girls); Grade 12: 28 students (15 boys, 13 girls). 20% of students are boarding students. 80% are state residents. 1 state is represented in upper school student body. 20% are international students. International students from China, Mexico, Republic of Korea, Taiwan, Thailand, and Viet Nam; 3 other countries represented in student body.
Faculty School total: 30. In upper school: 3 men, 14 women; 10 have advanced degrees.
Subjects Offered 3-dimensional art, 3-dimensional design, accounting, algebra, American government, anatomy and physiology, art, art history, art history-AP, art-AP, audition methods, ballet, band, biology, business skills, calculus, calculus-AP, ceramics, chamber groups, cheerleading, chemistry, Chinese, choir, choreography, chorus, communications, comparative government and politics-AP, computer applications, computer literacy, computer programming-AP, concert band, concert choir, creative writing, dance performance, digital photography, drama, drama performance, earth science, ecology, English, English literature-AP, English-AP, English/composition-AP, ensembles, environmental science-AP, ESL, European history-AP, film, fitness, French, French language-AP, French literature-AP, geometry, government and politics-AP, government/civics, government/civics-AP, graphic design, gymnastics, health, history of music, history-AP, honors algebra, honors English, honors geometry, honors U.S. history, honors world history, HTML design, human anatomy, humanities, instrumental music, Japanese, jazz band, jazz dance, jazz ensemble, journalism, Latin, library studies, mathematics, mathematics-AP, modern dance, music history, music performance, music theory-AP, orchestra, performing arts, physical education, physics, physics-AP, playwriting and directing, political science, portfolio art, pottery, pre-algebra, pre-calculus, psychology, reading/study skills, SAT preparation, SAT/ACT preparation, science, senior seminar, social sciences, social studies, Spanish, Spanish language-AP, Spanish literature-AP, speech, sports, stage design, statistics, studio art-AP, tap dance, tennis, theater design and production, TOEFL preparation, track and field, trigonometry, U.S. government and politics-AP, U.S. history, U.S. history-AP, vocal ensemble, vocal jazz, voice ensemble, volleyball, Web site design, Western civilization, world history, world history-AP, writing, writing workshop, yearbook.
Graduation Requirements Algebra, arts, biology, business skills (includes word processing), chemistry, choir, chorus, computer applications, computer skills, English, English composition, English literature, foreign language, government/civics, history, mathematics, modern world history, music, physical education (includes health), physics, science, social sciences, Spanish, sports, trigonometry, U.S. government, U.S. history, visual and performing arts, senior recital or project, 30 hours of community service per year of attendance. Community service is required.
Special Academic Programs 14 Advanced Placement exams for which test preparation is offered; honors section; accelerated programs; independent study; study at local college for college credit; academic accommodation for the gifted, the musically talented, and the artistically talented; remedial reading and/or remedial writing; remedial math; ESL (10 students enrolled).
College Admission Counseling 15 students graduated in 2011; all went to college, including San Diego State University; The George Washington University; The University of Texas at Austin; University of California, Berkeley; University of California, Davis; University of California, San Diego. Median SAT critical reading: 627, median SAT math: 677, median SAT writing: 590, median combined SAT: 1894. 50% scored over 600 on SAT critical reading, 50% scored over 600 on SAT math, 45% scored over 600 on SAT writing, 45% scored over 1800 on combined SAT.
Student Life Upper grades have uniform requirement, student council, honor system. Discipline rests primarily with faculty.
Summer Programs Remediation, enrichment, advancement, ESL, art/fine arts, computer instruction programs offered; session focuses on advancement and ESL; held on campus; accepts boys and girls; open to students from other schools. 40 students usually enrolled. 2012 schedule: June 21 to August 13. Application deadline: none.
Tuition and Aid Day student tuition: $9650; 7-day tuition and room/board: $16,900. Tuition installment plan (individually arranged payment plans, Pay by semester). Tuition reduction for siblings, merit scholarship grants, need-based scholarship grants, paying campus jobs, music scholarships. available. In 2011–12, 20% of upper-school students received aid; total upper-school merit-scholarship money awarded: $10,000. Total amount of financial aid awarded in 2011–12: $25,000.
Admissions Traditional secondary-level entrance grade is 9. For fall 2011, 20 students applied for upper-level admission, 8 were accepted, 8 enrolled. Admissions testing, any standardized test, audition, math and English placement tests, Math Placement Exam or writing sample required. Deadline for receipt of application materials: none. Application fee required: $200. Interview recommended.
Athletics Interscholastic: artistic gym (girls), baseball (b,g), basketball (b,g), cross-country running (b,g), flag football (b), gymnastics (g), indoor soccer (b,g), soccer (b,g), softball (g), track and field (b,g), volleyball (b,g); intramural: aerobics/dance (b,g), artistic gym (g), backpacking (b,g), badminton (b,g), ballet (b,g), baseball (b,g), basketball (b,g), bowling (b,g), cheering (g), dance (b,g), dance squad (b,g), dance team (b,g), fitness (b,g), flag football (b,g), floor hockey (b,g), gymnastics (b,g), hiking/backpacking (b,g), horseback riding (b,g), indoor soccer (b,g), jump rope (b,g), modern dance (b,g), outdoor activities (b,g), outdoor education (b,g), physical fitness (b,g), soccer (b,g), softball (b,g), surfing (b,g), swimming and diving (b,g), table tennis (b,g), tennis (b,g), track and field (b,g), volleyball (b,g); coed interscholastic: indoor soccer; coed intramural: aerobics/dance, backpacking, badminton, ballet, baseball, bowling, dance, dance squad, dance team, fitness, flag football, floor hockey, hiking/backpacking, indoor soccer, jump rope, modern dance, outdoor activities, outdoor education, physical fitness, softball, surfing, swimming and diving, table tennis, track and field. 2 PE instructors, 2 coaches.
Computers Computers are regularly used in architecture, business skills, commercial art, creative writing, data processing, desktop publishing, drawing and design, journalism, keyboarding, media arts, music, programming, SAT preparation, typing, video film production, Web site design, word processing, yearbook classes. Computer network features include Internet access, college credit classes online.
Contact Karen Peterson, Admissions Department. 619-584-2454. Fax: 619-584-2422. E-mail: jmcherif@yahoo.com. Web site: www.ccpaasd.com.

CHINESE CHRISTIAN SCHOOLS

1801 North Loop Road

Alameda, California 94502

Head of School: Mr. Robin S. Hom

General Information Coeducational day college-preparatory and religious studies school, affiliated with Bible Fellowship Church, Evangelical/Fundamental faith. Grades K–12. Founded: 1979. Setting: suburban. Nearest major city is Oakland. 10-acre campus. 3 buildings on campus. Approved or accredited by Association of Christian Schools International, The College Board, US Department of State, Western Association of Schools and Colleges, and California Department of Education. Languages of instruction: English and Mandarin. Endowment: $14,000. Total enrollment: 696. Upper school average class size: 20. Upper school faculty-student ratio: 1:8. There are 173 required school days per year for Upper School students. Upper School students typically attend 5 days per week. The average school day consists of 6 hours and 50 minutes.
Upper School Student Profile Grade 9: 44 students (27 boys, 17 girls); Grade 10: 51 students (20 boys, 31 girls); Grade 11: 70 students (43 boys, 27 girls); Grade 12: 51 students (19 boys, 32 girls). 20% of students are Bible Fellowship Church, Evangelical/Fundamental faith.
Faculty School total: 40. In upper school: 15 men, 20 women; 12 have advanced degrees.
Subjects Offered Advanced computer applications, Advanced Placement courses, aerobics, algebra, American government, American history, American history-AP, American literature, American literature-AP, applied music, art, art-AP, audio visual/media, Basic programming, basketball, Bible, Bible studies, biology, biology-AP, British literature, calculus, calculus-AP, career/college preparation, chemistry, Chinese, Chinese studies, choir, choral music, Christian doctrine, Christian ethics, Christian studies, civics, civics/free enterprise, college counseling, college placement, college planning, communications, community service, comparative religion, computer applications, computer graphics, computer science, computer science-AP, CPR, debate, drama, driver education, economics, economics-AP, electives, English, English language-AP, English literature, English literature-AP, ESL, European history-AP, first aid, foreign language, general science, geometry, government, government and politics-AP, government-AP, graphic arts, honors English, intro to computers, language arts, leadership and service, learning strategies, library assistant, literature and composition-AP, literature-AP, macro/microeconomics-AP, Mandarin, marching band, marine science, martial arts, mathematics-AP, microeconomics, microeconomics-AP, music, newspaper,

participation in sports, physical education, physics, physics-AP, pre-algebra, pre-calculus, probability and statistics, public speaking, religious education, religious studies, ROTC (for boys), SAT preparation, SAT/ACT preparation, science, science research, Spanish, speech, speech and debate, speech communications, sports, state history, statistics, student government, theater, theater arts, trigonometry, U.S. government, U.S. government and politics-AP, U.S. history, U.S. history-AP, visual and performing arts, volleyball, Web authoring, world history, world wide web design, yearbook.

Graduation Requirements Algebra, American government, American history, Bible, Chinese, CPR, driver education, economics, English, first aid, foreign language, geometry, history, lab science, Life of Christ, mathematics, physical education (includes health), physics, pre-algebra, science, visual and performing arts, world history, Mandarin I or Chinese Culture class.

Special Academic Programs 13 Advanced Placement exams for which test preparation is offered; honors section; term-away projects; study at local college for college credit; study abroad; academic accommodation for the gifted; remedial reading and/or remedial writing; ESL (15 students enrolled).

College Admission Counseling 61 students graduated in 2011; 60 went to college, including University of California, Berkeley; University of California, Davis; University of California, Irvine; University of California, Riverside; University of California, San Diego; University of the Pacific. Other: 1 entered military service. Mean SAT critical reading: 563, mean SAT math: 622, mean SAT writing: 558, mean combined SAT: 1743. 43% scored over 600 on SAT critical reading, 59% scored over 600 on SAT math, 39% scored over 600 on SAT writing, 38% scored over 1800 on combined SAT.

Student Life Upper grades have uniform requirement, student council. Discipline rests primarily with faculty. Attendance at religious services is required.

Summer Programs Remediation, enrichment, advancement, ESL, sports programs offered; session focuses on academic enrichment or remediation; held on campus; accepts boys and girls; open to students from other schools. 270 students usually enrolled. 2012 schedule: June 22 to July 22. Application deadline: May 15.

Tuition and Aid Day student tuition: $7250–$9400. Tuition installment plan (monthly payment plans, individually arranged payment plans, eTuition automatic electronic deposit). Tuition reduction for siblings, merit scholarship grants, need-based scholarship grants, paying campus jobs, tuition reduction for staff children, tuition reduction for children of full-time Christian ministers of like faith available. In 2011–12, 10% of upper-school students received aid; total upper-school merit-scholarship money awarded: $10,000. Total amount of financial aid awarded in 2011–12: $120,000.

Admissions Traditional secondary-level entrance grade is 9. For fall 2011, 28 students applied for upper-level admission, 25 were accepted, 22 enrolled. Achievement/Aptitude/Writing, admissions testing, California Achievement Test, CTBS (or similar from their school), Math Placement Exam, Stanford Achievement Test or writing sample required. Deadline for receipt of application materials: none. No application fee required. Interview required.

Athletics Interscholastic: badminton (boys, girls), baseball (b), basketball (b,g), cross-country running (b,g), drill team (b,g), JROTC drill (b,g), soccer (b,g), tennis (b,g), track and field (b,g), volleyball (b,g); intramural: basketball (b,g), drill team (b,g), martial arts (b,g), outdoor education (b,g), outdoor recreation (b,g), soccer (b,g), softball (b,g), street hockey (b,g), table tennis (b,g), volleyball (b,g); coed interscholastic: badminton, swimming and diving; coed intramural: outdoor education, outdoor recreation, softball, table tennis, volleyball. 2 PE instructors, 1 coach.

Computers Computers are regularly used in lab/keyboard, programming, science, senior seminar, Web site design classes. Computer network features include on-campus library services, Internet access, wireless campus network, Internet filtering or blocking technology. Student e-mail accounts are available to students. Students grades are available online. The school has a published electronic and media policy.

Contact Mrs. Cindy Loh, Admissions Director. 510-351-4957 Ext. 210. Fax: 510-351-1789. E-mail: CindyLoh@ccs-rams.org. Web site: www.ccs-rams.org.

CHOATE ROSEMARY HALL

333 Christian Street

Wallingford, Connecticut 06492-3800

Head of School: Edward J. Shanahan, PhD

General Information Coeducational boarding and day college-preparatory school. Grades 9–PG. Founded: 1890. Setting: small town. Nearest major city is New Haven. Students are housed in single-sex dormitories. 458-acre campus. 121 buildings on campus. Approved or accredited by Connecticut Association of Independent Schools, New England Association of Schools and Colleges, The Association of Boarding Schools, and Connecticut Department of Education. Member of National Association of Independent Schools and Secondary School Admission Test Board. Endowment: $240 million. Total enrollment: 850. Upper school average class size: 12. Upper school faculty-student ratio: 1:6. There are 166 required school days per year for Upper School students. Upper School students typically attend 5 days per week. The average school day consists of 5 hours.

Upper School Student Profile Grade 9: 148 students (72 boys, 76 girls); Grade 10: 217 students (115 boys, 102 girls); Grade 11: 228 students (111 boys, 117 girls); Grade 12: 235 students (112 boys, 123 girls); Postgraduate: 22 students (18 boys, 4 girls). 75% of students are boarding students. 47% are state residents. 40 states are represented in upper school student body. 12% are international students. International students from Canada, China, Hong Kong, Republic of Korea, Saudi Arabia, and Thailand; 39 other countries represented in student body.

Faculty School total: 130. In upper school: 67 men, 54 women; 89 have advanced degrees; 99 reside on campus.

Subjects Offered Algebra, American history, American literature, anatomy, Arabic, architecture, art, astronomy, biology, British history, calculus, calculus-AP, ceramics, chemistry, chemistry-AP, child development, Chinese, computer programming, computer science, computer science-AP, creative writing, dance, drama, ecology, economics, English, English literature, environmental science, environmental science-AP, European history-AP, fine arts, French, French language-AP, French studies, geometry, government and politics-AP, history, history-AP, Holocaust, interdisciplinary studies, international studies, Italian, language, Latin, Latin-AP, linear algebra, macroeconomics-AP, marine biology, mathematics, microbiology, microeconomics-AP, music, music composition, music history, music performance, music technology, music theater, music theory-AP, music-AP, musical productions, musical theater, musical theater dance, musicianship, philosophy, photography, physics, physics-AP, psychology, psychology-AP, public speaking, religion, Spanish, Spanish language-AP, Spanish literature, Spanish literature-AP, Spanish-AP, statistics, statistics-AP, studio art, theater, trigonometry, U.S. history, U.S. history-AP, visual arts, world history, world literature, world religions, world studies, wrestling, writing, writing, writing workshop.

Graduation Requirements Art, English, foreign language, global studies, history, mathematics, philosophy, physical education (includes health), science, 30 hours of community service.

Special Academic Programs 25 Advanced Placement exams for which test preparation is offered; honors section; independent study; term-away projects; study abroad; academic accommodation for the gifted, the musically talented, and the artistically talented.

College Admission Counseling 249 students graduated in 2010; 245 went to college, including Boston University; Cornell University; Georgetown University; New York University; Wesleyan University; Yale University. Other: 4 had other specific plans. Mean SAT critical reading: 668, mean SAT math: 678, mean SAT writing: 679, mean combined SAT: 2025, mean composite ACT: 29.

Student Life Upper grades have specified standards of dress, student council, honor system. Discipline rests primarily with faculty.

Tuition and Aid Day student tuition: $34,320; 7-day tuition and room/board: $45,070. Tuition installment plan (Insured Tuition Payment Plan, Key Tuition Payment Plan, monthly payment plans, individually arranged payment plans). Need-based scholarship grants, need-based loans available. In 2010–11, 33% of upper-school students received aid. Total amount of financial aid awarded in 2010–11: $8,500,000.

Admissions Traditional secondary-level entrance grade is 9. For fall 2010, 1,761 students applied for upper-level admission, 418 were accepted, 262 enrolled. ACT, ISEE, PSAT or SAT for applicants to grade 11 and 12, SSAT or TOEFL required. Deadline for receipt of application materials: January 10. Application fee required: $60. Interview required.

Athletics Interscholastic: baseball (boys), basketball (b,g), crew (b,g), cross-country running (b,g), diving (b,g), field hockey (g), football (b), golf (b,g), ice hockey (b,g), lacrosse (b,g), soccer (b,g), softball (g), squash (b,g), swimming and diving (b,g), tennis (b,g), track and field (b,g), volleyball (b,g), water polo (b,g), wrestling (b); intramural: crew (b,g), squash (b,g); coed interscholastic: archery; coed intramural: aerobics, aerobics/dance, aerobics/Nautilus, ballet, basketball, dance, dance squad, fitness, martial arts, modern dance, Nautilus, outdoor activities, physical fitness, physical training, rock climbing, running, soccer, softball, strength & conditioning, swimming and diving, tennis, ultimate Frisbee, volleyball, wall climbing, weight training, winter (indoor) track, yoga. 10 coaches, 3 athletic trainers.

Computers Computers are regularly used in all academic, art, college planning, computer applications, desktop publishing, drawing and design, graphic design, information technology, library skills, literary magazine, media production, music, newspaper, photography, programming, stock market, study skills, theater arts, video film production, word processing, yearbook classes. Computer network features include on-campus library services, online commercial services, Internet access, wireless campus network, Internet filtering or blocking technology. Campus intranet, student e-mail accounts, and computer access in designated common areas are available to students. Students grades are available online. The school has a published electronic and media policy.

Contact Raymond M. Diffley III, Director of Admission. 203-697-2239. Fax: 203-697-2629. E-mail: admission@choate.edu. Web site: www.choate.edu.

CHRIST CHURCH EPISCOPAL SCHOOL

245 Cavalier Drive

Greenville, South Carolina 29607

Head of School: Dr. Leonard Kupersmith

General Information Coeducational day college-preparatory, arts, religious studies, and technology school, affiliated with Episcopal Church. Grades K–12. Founded: 1959. Setting: suburban. Nearest major city is Charlotte, NC. 72-acre campus. 8 buildings on campus. Approved or accredited by International Baccalaureate Organization, National Association of Episcopal Schools, South Carolina Independent School Association, Southern Association of Colleges and Schools, Southern Association of Independent

Schools, and The College Board. Member of National Association of Independent Schools. Endowment: $12 million. Total enrollment: 1,025. Upper school average class size: 12. Upper school faculty-student ratio: 1:9. There are 175 required school days per year for Upper School students. Upper School students typically attend 5 days per week. The average school day consists of 7 hours.

Upper School Student Profile Grade 9: 88 students (53 boys, 35 girls); Grade 10: 90 students (48 boys, 42 girls); Grade 11: 93 students (44 boys, 49 girls); Grade 12: 71 students (40 boys, 31 girls). 28% of students are members of Episcopal Church.

Faculty School total: 121. In upper school: 15 men, 41 women; 33 have advanced degrees.

Subjects Offered Algebra, American history-AP, Ancient Greek, ancient history, art, art-AP, Bible studies, biology, biology-AP, calculus, calculus-AP, ceramics, chemistry, chemistry-AP, China/Japan history, comparative government and politics-AP, computer applications, computer graphics, computer programming, computer science, computer science-AP, contemporary issues, creative writing, digital applications, digital photography, economics, English, environmental science, environmental science-AP, ESL, ethics, European history, European history-AP, film appreciation, French, French-AP, geometry, German, government and politics-AP, government/civics, graphic arts, history of China and Japan, honors English, honors world history, instrumental music, International Baccalaureate courses, journalism, Latin, Latin-AP, literature-AP, Mandarin, mathematics, medieval history, military history, modern European history, music, music history, music theory, music theory-AP, physical education, physical fitness, physics, physics-AP, pre-calculus, probability and statistics, psychology, religion, SAT/ACT preparation, sculpture, senior thesis, service learning/internship, Southern literature, Spanish, Spanish-AP, sports conditioning, sports medicine, statistics, statistics-AP, theater, theater design and production, theology, theory of knowledge, U.S. history, U.S. history-AP, video communication, visual arts, voice, voice ensemble, Web authoring, Web site design, world religions, World War II, yearbook.

Graduation Requirements American history, arts and fine arts (art, music, dance, drama), electives, English, foreign language, mathematics, physical education (includes health), religion (includes Bible studies and theology), science, senior thesis, service learning/internship, extended essay (for IB diploma candidates), sophomore project (all students), senior thesis (for non-IB diploma candidates).

Special Academic Programs International Baccalaureate program; honors section; independent study; ESL (29 students enrolled).

College Admission Counseling 74 students graduated in 2011; all went to college, including Clemson University; College of Charleston; Furman University; University of South Carolina; Washington and Lee University; Wofford College. Mean SAT critical reading: 602, mean SAT math: 603, mean SAT writing: 592, mean combined SAT: 1796, mean composite ACT: 27.

Student Life Upper grades have specified standards of dress, student council, honor system. Discipline rests equally with students and faculty. Attendance at religious services is required.

Summer Programs Enrichment, advancement, sports programs offered; session focuses on enrichment, athletics, academics; held both on and off campus; held at Field trips to other locations; accepts boys and girls; open to students from other schools. 680 students usually enrolled. 2012 schedule: May 29 to August 10.

Tuition and Aid Day student tuition: $16,350. Tuition installment plan (Insured Tuition Payment Plan, FACTS Tuition Payment Plan, monthly payment plans). Merit scholarship grants, need-based scholarship grants available. In 2011–12, 20% of upper-school students received aid; total upper-school merit-scholarship money awarded: $139,941. Total amount of financial aid awarded in 2011–12: $488,705.

Admissions Traditional secondary-level entrance grade is 9. For fall 2011, 32 students applied for upper-level admission, 24 were accepted, 20 enrolled. PSAT required. Deadline for receipt of application materials: December 1. Application fee required: $150. On-campus interview required.

Athletics Interscholastic: baseball (boys), basketball (b,g), cheering (g), cross-country running (b,g), dance team (g), field hockey (g), football (b), golf (b,g), lacrosse (b,g), soccer (b,g), softball (g), swimming and diving (b,g), tennis (b,g), track and field (b,g), volleyball (g), wrestling (b); intramural: dance team (g), fencing (b). 8 PE instructors, 35 coaches, 1 athletic trainer.

Computers Computers are regularly used in all academic classes. Computer network features include on-campus library services, online commercial services, Internet access, wireless campus network, Internet filtering or blocking technology, classroom computers. Computer access in designated common areas is available to students. Students grades are available online. The school has a published electronic and media policy.

Contact Mrs. Kathy Jones, Director of Student Recruitment. 864-299-1522 Ext. 1208. Fax: 864-299-8861. E-mail: jonesk@cces.org. Web site: www.cces.org.

CHRISTCHURCH SCHOOL

49 Seahorse Lane

Christchurch, Virginia 23031

Head of School: Mr. John E. Byers

General Information Boys' boarding and coeducational day college-preparatory, marine and environmental sciences, and ESL school, affiliated with Episcopal Church. Boarding boys grades 9–PG, day boys grades 9–PG, day girls grades 9–PG. Founded: 1921. Setting: rural. Nearest major city is Richmond. Students are housed in single-sex dormitories. 125-acre campus. 14 buildings on campus. Approved or accredited by National Association of Episcopal Schools, The Association of Boarding Schools, The College Board, and Virginia Department of Education. Member of National Association of Independent Schools and Secondary School Admission Test Board. Endowment: $2 million. Total enrollment: 220. Upper school average class size: 12. Upper school faculty-student ratio: 1:6. There are 165 required school days per year for Upper School students. Upper School students typically attend 5 days per week. The average school day consists of 9 hours.

Upper School Student Profile Grade 9: 45 students (29 boys, 16 girls); Grade 10: 51 students (47 boys, 4 girls); Grade 11: 66 students (53 boys, 13 girls); Grade 12: 40 students (33 boys, 7 girls); Postgraduate: 2 students (2 boys). 54% of students are boarding students. 65% are state residents. 14 states are represented in upper school student body. 19% are international students. International students from Bermuda, China, Hong Kong, Republic of Korea, Taiwan, and Viet Nam; 2 other countries represented in student body. 17% of students are members of Episcopal Church.

Faculty School total: 39. In upper school: 25 men, 14 women; 26 have advanced degrees; 25 reside on campus.

Subjects Offered Advanced biology, advanced chemistry, algebra, ancient world history, art, biology, calculus, chemistry, Chesapeake Bay studies, Chinese, computer art, computer-aided design, conceptual physics, digital art, drawing and design, economics, English, English language and composition-AP, English literature and composition-AP, environmental science, environmental science-AP, ESL, fine arts, finite math, geography, geometry, health and wellness, honors U.S. history, honors world history, marine biology, modern world history, Native American history, physical education, physics, pre-calculus, probability and statistics, SAT/ACT preparation, Spanish, Spanish-AP, technology/design, theology, U.S. government, U.S. government and politics-AP, U.S. history, U.S. history-AP, world geography, world history.

Graduation Requirements Arts and fine arts (art, music, dance, drama), English, foreign language, health and wellness, mathematics, physical education (includes health), religion (includes Bible studies and theology), science, social studies (includes history), theology, Great Journeys Integrated Work.

Special Academic Programs 11 Advanced Placement exams for which test preparation is offered; honors section; independent study; academic accommodation for the gifted; ESL (18 students enrolled).

College Admission Counseling 62 students graduated in 2011; all went to college, including James Madison University; University of Mary Washington; Virginia Commonwealth University. Mean SAT critical reading: 521, mean SAT math: 554, mean SAT writing: 516, mean combined SAT: 1591. 25% scored over 600 on SAT critical reading, 25% scored over 600 on SAT math.

Student Life Upper grades have specified standards of dress, student council, honor system. Discipline rests equally with students and faculty. Attendance at religious services is required.

Summer Programs Enrichment, sports programs offered; session focuses on marine and environmental science, sailing, camping, fishing; held on campus; accepts boys and girls; open to students from other schools. 75 students usually enrolled. 2012 schedule: June 23 to July 21. Application deadline: none.

Tuition and Aid Day student tuition: $18,000; 7-day tuition and room/board: $42,500. Tuition installment plan (monthly payment plans, individually arranged payment plans, 10 month plan, 1st payment due 6/15, 4-payment plan, first payment due 6/15, 2-payment plan, first payment due 6/15). Need-based scholarship grants available. In 2011–12, 40% of upper-school students received aid. Total amount of financial aid awarded in 2011–12: $1,490,200.

Admissions Traditional secondary-level entrance grade is 9. For fall 2011, 194 students applied for upper-level admission, 136 were accepted, 93 enrolled. PSAT or SAT, SSAT, TOEFL or WISC/Woodcock-Johnson required. Deadline for receipt of application materials: none. Application fee required: $50. Interview required.

Athletics Interscholastic: baseball (boys), basketball (b,g), crew (b,g), field hockey (g), football (b), golf (b), lacrosse (b), sailing (b,g), soccer (b,g), tennis (b,g), volleyball (g); intramural: basketball (b), fencing (b), weight training (b,g); coed interscholastic: golf, sailing; coed intramural: backpacking, canoeing/kayaking, fishing, fitness, fly fishing, Frisbee, hiking/backpacking, indoor soccer, kayaking, mountain biking, outdoor activities, outdoor adventure, outdoor education, outdoor recreation, outdoor skills, outdoors, paint ball, physical training, rock climbing, sailing, skateboarding, skeet shooting, snowboarding, soccer, strength & conditioning, tennis, winter soccer. 1 athletic trainer.

Computers Computers are regularly used in all academic classes. Computer network features include on-campus library services, online commercial services, Internet access, wireless campus network, Internet filtering or blocking technology. Campus intranet, student e-mail accounts, and computer access in designated common areas are available to students. Students grades are available online. The school has a published electronic and media policy.

Contact Mr. Lawrence J. Jensen, Director of Admission. 804-758-2306. Fax: 804-758-0721. E-mail: admission@christchurchschool.org. Web site: www.christchurchschool.org.

CHRISTIAN BROTHERS ACADEMY

850 Newman Springs Road

Lincroft, New Jersey 07738

Head of School: Br. James Butler, FSC

General Information Boys' day college-preparatory school, affiliated with Roman Catholic Church. Grades 9–12. Founded: 1959. Setting: suburban. Nearest major city is New York, NY. 157-acre campus. 3 buildings on campus. Approved or accredited by Middle States Association of Colleges and Schools. Total enrollment: 958. Upper school average class size: 18. Upper school faculty-student ratio: 1:16. There are 180 required school days per year for Upper School students. Upper School students typically attend 5 days per week. The average school day consists of 6 hours and 15 minutes.

Upper School Student Profile Grade 9: 257 students (257 boys); Grade 10: 236 students (236 boys); Grade 11: 231 students (231 boys); Grade 12: 234 students (234 boys). 80% of students are Roman Catholic.

Faculty School total: 77. In upper school: 53 men, 24 women; 52 have advanced degrees.

Subjects Offered Algebra, American government, American history, anatomy and physiology, Bible studies, biology, business, business skills, calculus, chemistry, computer science, creative writing, driver education, economics, English, environmental science, European history, French, geometry, health, history, journalism, Latin, mathematics, physical education, physics, psychology, religion, science, social sciences, social studies, Spanish, theology, trigonometry, world history, world literature, writing.

Graduation Requirements Business skills (includes word processing), computer science, English, foreign language, mathematics, physical education (includes health), religion (includes Bible studies and theology), science, social sciences, social studies (includes history).

Special Academic Programs Advanced Placement exam preparation; honors section.

College Admission Counseling 220 students graduated in 2011; 218 went to college, including Fordham University; Manhattan College; Providence College; Rutgers, The State University of New Jersey, New Brunswick; Stevens Institute of Technology; University of Delaware. Other: 2 had other specific plans. Median SAT critical reading: 580, median SAT math: 606, median SAT writing: 580, median combined SAT: 1766.

Student Life Upper grades have specified standards of dress, student council. Discipline rests primarily with faculty. Attendance at religious services is required.

Tuition and Aid Day student tuition: $13,100. Tuition installment plan (Academic Management Services Plan, individually arranged payment plans). Merit scholarship grants, need-based scholarship grants available. In 2011–12, 20% of upper-school students received aid; total upper-school merit-scholarship money awarded: $300,000.

Admissions For fall 2011, 479 students applied for upper-level admission, 335 were accepted, 257 enrolled. School's own test required. Deadline for receipt of application materials: none. Application fee required: $75.

Athletics Interscholastic: baseball, basketball, bowling, cross-country running, golf, ice hockey, lacrosse, soccer, swimming and diving, tennis, track and field, winter (indoor) track, wrestling; intramural: baseball, basketball, bowling, Frisbee, soccer, tennis, volleyball. 3 PE instructors, 21 coaches, 1 athletic trainer.

Computers Computers are regularly used in mathematics, science classes. Computer network features include on-campus library services, Internet access.

Contact Br. James Butler, FSC, Principal. 732-747-1959 Ext. 100. Fax: 732-747-1643. Web site: www.cbalincroftnj.org.

CHRISTIAN BROTHERS ACADEMY

12 Airline Drive

Albany, New York 12205

Head of School: Mr. James P. Schlegel

General Information Boys' day college-preparatory, business, religious studies, Junior ROTC, and military school, affiliated with Roman Catholic Church. Grades 6–12. Founded: 1859. Setting: suburban. 120-acre campus. 1 building on campus. Approved or accredited by Middle States Association of Colleges and Schools and New York Department of Education. Endowment: $2 million. Total enrollment: 360. Upper school average class size: 17. Upper school faculty-student ratio: 1:17. There are 180 required school days per year for Upper School students. Upper School students typically attend 5 days per week. The average school day consists of 6 hours and 36 minutes.

Upper School Student Profile Grade 9: 63 students (63 boys); Grade 10: 69 students (69 boys); Grade 11: 76 students (76 boys); Grade 12: 71 students (71 boys). 71% of students are Roman Catholic.

Faculty School total: 31. In upper school: 22 men, 5 women; 10 have advanced degrees.

Subjects Offered Accounting, advanced computer applications, algebra, American government, art, band, biology, biology-AP, business law, calculus-AP, chemistry, driver education, earth science, economics, English, English-AP, forensics, geometry, global studies, health, life science, math analysis, mathematics, mechanical drawing, military science, music, physical education, physical science, physics, physics-AP, psychology, religion, science, sociology, Spanish, Spanish-AP, trigonometry, U.S. history, U.S. history-AP, world history-AP.

Graduation Requirements Arts and fine arts (art, music, dance, drama), English, foreign language, health education, lab science, mathematics, military science, physical education (includes health), religion (includes Bible studies and theology), social studies (includes history), a service requirement.

Special Academic Programs 8 Advanced Placement exams for which test preparation is offered; honors section; study at local college for college credit.

College Admission Counseling 64 students graduated in 2010; 62 went to college, including Clarkson University; Le Moyne College; Manhattan College; Rensselaer Polytechnic Institute; Rochester Institute of Technology; Siena College. Other: 1 entered military service, 1 entered a postgraduate year. Mean SAT critical reading: 505, mean SAT math: 523, mean SAT writing: 501.

Student Life Upper grades have uniform requirement, student council, honor system. Discipline rests primarily with faculty. Attendance at religious services is required.

Tuition and Aid Day student tuition: $10,900. Tuition installment plan (monthly payment plans). Tuition reduction for siblings, merit scholarship grants, need-based scholarship grants available. In 2010–11, 65% of upper-school students received aid; total upper-school merit-scholarship money awarded: $223,650. Total amount of financial aid awarded in 2010–11: $739,500.

Admissions Traditional secondary-level entrance grade is 9. For fall 2010, 72 students applied for upper-level admission, 66 were accepted, 47 enrolled. Iowa Test of Educational Development required. Deadline for receipt of application materials: none. No application fee required.

Athletics Interscholastic: baseball, basketball, bowling, cross-country running, football, golf, ice hockey, indoor track, indoor track & field, JROTC drill, lacrosse, marksmanship, riflery, skiing (downhill), soccer, swimming and diving, tennis, track and field, weight lifting, wrestling; intramural: hiking/backpacking, outdoor activities, outdoor adventure, outdoor education, skiing (downhill), speleology, weight lifting. 3 PE instructors, 18 coaches, 1 athletic trainer.

Computers Computers are regularly used in all academic, career exploration, college planning, computer applications, JROTC, yearbook classes. Computer network features include on-campus library services, Internet access, wireless campus network, Internet filtering or blocking technology.

Contact Mr. Martin McGraw, AIA, Director of Admissions. 518-452-9809 Ext. 110. Fax: 518-452-9806. E-mail: mcgrawmp@aol.com. Web site: www.cbaalbany.org.

CHRISTIAN BROTHERS ACADEMY

6245 Randall Road

Syracuse, New York 13214

Head of School: Br. Joseph Jozwiak, FSC

General Information Coeducational day college-preparatory and religious studies school, affiliated with Roman Catholic Church. Grades 7–12. Founded: 1900. Setting: suburban. 40-acre campus. 1 building on campus. Approved or accredited by Christian Brothers Association, Middle States Association of Colleges and Schools, and New York State Board of Regents. Endowment: $800,000. Total enrollment: 750. Upper school average class size: 25.

Upper School Student Profile 85% of students are Roman Catholic.

Faculty School total: 62. In upper school: 32 men, 30 women; 58 have advanced degrees.

Subjects Offered Advanced Placement courses, American history, American literature, art, biology, business, calculus, chemistry, chemistry-AP, earth science, economics, English, English literature, European history, expository writing, fine arts, French, government/civics, grammar, health, history, mathematics, music, physical education, physics, pre-calculus, psychology, religion, science, social sciences, social studies, Spanish, theology, world history, world literature.

Graduation Requirements Arts and fine arts (art, music, dance, drama), English, foreign language, mathematics, physical education (includes health), religion (includes Bible studies and theology), science, social sciences, social studies (includes history), community service for seniors.

Special Academic Programs Advanced Placement exam preparation; honors section.

College Admission Counseling 113 students graduated in 2011; all went to college, including Le Moyne College; Loyola University Maryland; New York University; Saint Joseph's University; Syracuse University. Mean SAT critical reading: 579, mean SAT math: 581, mean composite ACT: 26.

Student Life Upper grades have specified standards of dress, student council. Discipline rests primarily with faculty. Attendance at religious services is required.

Tuition and Aid Day student tuition: $8650. Tuition installment plan (SMART Tuition Payment Plan, individually arranged payment plans). Merit scholarship grants, need-based scholarship grants available. In 2011–12, 95% of upper-school students received aid; total upper-school merit-scholarship money awarded: $650,000.

Admissions Traditional secondary-level entrance grade is 9. For fall 2011, 50 students applied for upper-level admission, 38 were accepted, 38 enrolled. Admissions testing required. Deadline for receipt of application materials: February 1. Application fee required: $40. Interview recommended.

Athletics Interscholastic: baseball (boys), basketball (b,g), cheering (g), cross-country running (b,g), diving (b,g), football (b), golf (b,g), gymnastics (b), ice hockey (b), lacrosse (b,g), soccer (b,g), softball (g), swimming and diving (b,g), tennis (b,g), track and field (b,g), volleyball (g), wrestling (b); coed interscholastic: bowling. 3 PE instructors, 1 athletic trainer.

Computers Computer network features include on-campus library services, Internet access, Internet filtering or blocking technology. Students grades are available online. The school has a published electronic and media policy.

Contact Mr. Mark Person, Assistant Principal for Student Affairs. 315-446-5960 Ext. 1227. Fax: 315-446-3393. E-mail: mperson@cbasyracuse.org. Web site: www.cbasyracuse.org.

CHRISTIAN CENTRAL ACADEMY

39 Academy Street

Williamsville, New York 14221

Head of School: Mrs. Nurline Lawrence

General Information Coeducational day college-preparatory, arts, and religious studies school, affiliated with Christian faith. Grades K–12. Founded: 1949. Setting: suburban. Nearest major city is Buffalo. 5-acre campus. 4 buildings on campus. Approved or accredited by Association of Christian Schools International, Middle States Association of Colleges and Schools, New York State Board of Regents, and New York Department of Education. Member of Secondary School Admission Test Board. Endowment: $55,000. Total enrollment: 389. Upper school average class size: 20. Upper school faculty-student ratio: 1:10. There are 180 required school days per year for Upper School students. Upper School students typically attend 5 days per week. The average school day consists of 6 hours and 30 minutes.

Upper School Student Profile Grade 9: 29 students (12 boys, 17 girls); Grade 10: 25 students (10 boys, 15 girls); Grade 11: 27 students (9 boys, 18 girls); Grade 12: 35 students (24 boys, 11 girls). 100% of students are Christian faith.

Faculty School total: 39. In upper school: 5 men, 13 women; 9 have advanced degrees.

Subjects Offered Advanced computer applications, advertising design, algebra, art, band, Bible, biology, biology-AP, calculus-AP, career/college preparation, chemistry, chorus, communications, computer skills, drawing, driver education, earth science, economics, English, English language-AP, English literature-AP, European history-AP, geometry, global studies, government, health, honors English, independent study, journalism, mathematics, music, music theory, orchestra, painting, physical education, physics, physics-AP, pre-calculus, Spanish, studio art, trigonometry, U.S. history, U.S. history-AP, yearbook.

Graduation Requirements Algebra, American government, American history, American literature, arts and fine arts (art, music, dance, drama), Bible, biology, chemistry, earth science, economics, English, geometry, global studies, keyboarding, physical education (includes health), physics, pre-calculus, Spanish, trigonometry, writing, community service hours for all four years, completion of standardized NYS Regents exams, honors and high honors diplomas have more rigorous requirements.

Special Academic Programs 7 Advanced Placement exams for which test preparation is offered; honors section; independent study.

College Admission Counseling 26 students graduated in 2011; 25 went to college, including Buffalo State College, State University of New York; Canisius College; Houghton College; University at Buffalo, the State University of New York. Median SAT critical reading: 515, median SAT math: 520, median SAT writing: 505, median combined SAT: 1505. 19% scored over 600 on SAT critical reading, 23% scored over 600 on SAT math, 15% scored over 600 on SAT writing, 19% scored over 1800 on combined SAT.

Student Life Upper grades have specified standards of dress, student council, honor system. Discipline rests primarily with faculty. Attendance at religious services is required.

Summer Programs Sports programs offered; session focuses on basketball camp, soccer camp; held on campus; accepts boys and girls; open to students from other schools. 45 students usually enrolled. 2012 schedule: July 1 to July 1. Application deadline: June 1.

Tuition and Aid Day student tuition: $7636. Tuition installment plan (FACTS Tuition Payment Plan, monthly payment plans, prepayment discount plans, multiple-student discounts, pastors/full-time Christian service discounts). Tuition reduction for siblings, merit scholarship grants, need-based scholarship grants available. In 2011–12, 28% of upper-school students received aid; total upper-school merit-scholarship money awarded: $13,500. Total amount of financial aid awarded in 2011–12: $54,868.

Admissions Traditional secondary-level entrance grade is 9. For fall 2011, 21 students applied for upper-level admission, 19 were accepted, 15 enrolled. Admissions testing, Brigance Test of Basic Skills, essay, Iowa Subtests, school's own test or writing sample required. Deadline for receipt of application materials: none. Application fee required: $50. Interview recommended.

Athletics Interscholastic: baseball (boys), basketball (b,g), bowling (b), cheering (g), cross-country running (b,g), flag football (b), soccer (b,g), softball (g); intramural: basketball (b,g), physical fitness (b,g), soccer (b,g); coed interscholastic: cross-country running, soccer; coed intramural: basketball, track and field, volleyball. 2 PE instructors, 17 coaches.

Computers Computers are regularly used in college planning, computer applications, desktop publishing, drawing and design, English, journalism, library skills, photojournalism, yearbook classes. Computer resources include on-campus library services, Internet access, Internet filtering or blocking technology, teacher-guided use of programs in various subject areas. Computer access in designated common areas is available to students. The school has a published electronic and media policy.

Contact Deborah L. White, Director of Admissions and Public Relations. 716-634-4821 Ext. 107. Fax: 716-634-5851. E-mail: dwhitecca@gmail.com. Web site: www.christianca.com.

CHRISTIAN HOME AND BIBLE SCHOOL

301 West 13th Avenue

Mount Dora, Florida 32757

Head of School: Patrick Todd

General Information Coeducational day college-preparatory, general academic, arts, religious studies, and technology school, affiliated with Church of Christ. Grades PK–12. Founded: 1945. Setting: small town. Nearest major city is Orlando. 70-acre campus. 9 buildings on campus. Approved or accredited by National Christian School Association, Southern Association of Colleges and Schools, and Florida Department of Education. Total enrollment: 533. Upper school average class size: 21. Upper school faculty-student ratio: 1:15. There are 180 required school days per year for Upper School students. Upper School students typically attend 5 days per week. The average school day consists of 6 hours and 30 minutes.

Upper School Student Profile Grade 6: 40 students (22 boys, 18 girls); Grade 7: 40 students (22 boys, 18 girls); Grade 8: 54 students (20 boys, 34 girls); Grade 9: 37 students (22 boys, 15 girls); Grade 10: 58 students (32 boys, 26 girls); Grade 11: 42 students (30 boys, 12 girls); Grade 12: 47 students (27 boys, 20 girls). 20% of students are members of Church of Christ.

Faculty School total: 45. In upper school: 11 men, 14 women; 12 have advanced degrees.

Subjects Offered Algebra, American government, American history, anatomy and physiology, art, band, Bible, biology, calculus-AP, ceramics, chemistry, computer applications, computer skills, consumer mathematics, drama, drawing, economics, English, English literature-AP, European history, geography, geometry, government, health, honors algebra, honors English, honors geometry, honors world history, intro to computers, jazz band, journalism, life management skills, life skills, math applications, Microsoft, painting, personal fitness, photography, physical education, physical science, physics, pre-algebra, pre-calculus, probability and statistics, psychology, sculpture, sign language, Spanish, speech, state history, student publications, technology/design, television, theater, theater production, trigonometry, video communication, video film production, visual and performing arts, Web site design, weight training, word processing, world history.

Graduation Requirements Advanced math, algebra, American government, American history, arts and fine arts (art, music, dance, drama), Bible, biology, chemistry, economics, electives, English, foreign language, keyboarding, lab science, life skills, physical education (includes health), physical science, world history, 80 hours of community service.

Special Academic Programs 4 Advanced Placement exams for which test preparation is offered; honors section; independent study; study at local college for college credit.

College Admission Counseling 47 students graduated in 2011; 45 went to college, including Florida State University; Harding University; Lipscomb University; University of Central Florida; University of Florida; University of South Florida. Other: 2 went to work. Median SAT critical reading: 600, median SAT math: 580, median SAT writing: 540, median combined SAT: 1640, median composite ACT: 22. 47.6% scored over 600 on SAT critical reading, 42.8% scored over 600 on SAT math, 28.5% scored over 600 on SAT writing, 38% scored over 1800 on combined SAT, 20.3% scored over 26 on composite ACT.

Student Life Upper grades have specified standards of dress, student council. Discipline rests primarily with faculty. Attendance at religious services is required.

Summer Programs Remediation programs offered; session focuses on math; held on campus; accepts boys and girls; not open to students from other schools. 10 students usually enrolled. 2012 schedule: June 5 to June 20.

Tuition and Aid Day student tuition: $8044. Tuition installment plan (monthly payment plans). Tuition reduction for siblings, need-based scholarship grants, discount for members of the Churches of Christ available. In 2011–12, 17% of upper-school students received aid.

Admissions Traditional secondary-level entrance grade is 9. For fall 2011, 160 students applied for upper-level admission, 138 were accepted, 138 enrolled. Any standardized test required. Deadline for receipt of application materials: none. Application fee required: $100. On-campus interview required.

Athletics Interscholastic: baseball (boys), basketball (b,g), bowling (b,g), cheering (g), cross-country running (b,g), fitness (b,g), football (b), golf (b,g), physical fitness (b,g), physical training (b,g), softball (g), tennis (b,g), track and field (b,g), volleyball (g), weight training (b,g). 3 coaches.

Computers Computers are regularly used in independent study, journalism, library, mathematics, publications, reading, video film production, Web site design, yearbook classes. Computer network features include on-campus library services, Internet access, wireless campus network, Internet filtering or blocking technology, Net Classroom communication for students and parents, Desk Top Monitoring and manage software, Accelerated Reader Access. Computer access in designated common areas is available to students. Students grades are available online. The school has a published electronic and media policy.

Contact Natalie Yawn, Admissions Director. 352-383-2155 Ext. 261. Fax: 352-383-0098. E-mail: natalie.yawn@chbs.org. Web site: www.chbs.org.

CHRISTOPHER COLUMBUS HIGH SCHOOL

3000 Southwest 87th Avenue

Miami, Florida 33165-3293

Head of School: Br. Michael Brady, FMS

General Information Boys' day college-preparatory school, affiliated with Roman Catholic Church. Grades 9–12. Founded: 1958. Setting: suburban. 19-acre campus. 10 buildings on campus. Approved or accredited by National Catholic Education Association, Southern Association of Colleges and Schools, and Florida Department of Education. Total enrollment: 1,380. Upper school average class size: 25. Upper school faculty-student ratio: 1:17. There are 180 required school days per year for Upper School students. Upper School students typically attend 5 days per week. The average school day consists of 6 hours and 25 minutes.

Upper School Student Profile Grade 9: 358 students (358 boys); Grade 10: 373 students (373 boys); Grade 11: 304 students (304 boys); Grade 12: 345 students (345 boys). 95% of students are Roman Catholic.

Faculty School total: 82. In upper school: 56 men, 26 women; 35 have advanced degrees.

Subjects Offered 3-dimensional art, accounting, acting, advanced biology, advanced chemistry, advanced computer applications, advanced math, Advanced Placement courses, algebra, American government, American history, American history-AP, American literature, analysis, anatomy, ancient world history, architectural drawing, art, athletic training, athletics, band, Basic programming, Bible, biology, biology-AP, British literature (honors), business law, business skills, calculus, calculus-AP, campus ministry, Catholic belief and practice, chemistry, chemistry-AP, Christian and Hebrew scripture, Christian doctrine, Christian ethics, church history, college counseling, composition-AP, computer applications, computer information systems, computer programming, computer science, computer science-AP, computer-aided design, contemporary history, debate, drama, economics, economics-AP, English, English language and composition-AP, English literature, English literature-AP, English-AP, ethics, European history, European history-AP, French, French language-AP, French-AP, geometry, global studies, government, government and politics-AP, health, history of the Catholic Church, Holocaust studies, keyboarding, library assistant, marine biology, physical education, physical fitness, physics, physics-AP, pre-algebra, pre-calculus, psychology, Spanish, Spanish language-AP, Spanish literature, Spanish literature-AP, speech, U.S. government, U.S. government and politics, U.S. government and politics-AP, U.S. history, U.S. history-AP, Vietnam War, word processing, world governments, yearbook.

Graduation Requirements Algebra, arts and fine arts (art, music, dance, drama), computer applications, English, lab science, language, mathematics, personal fitness, physical education (includes health), practical arts, religion (includes Bible studies and theology), science, social studies (includes history), students must earn a Florida scale GPA of 2.0, students must complete 75 hours of community service during their four years of high school.

Special Academic Programs Advanced Placement exam preparation; honors section; study at local college for college credit; academic accommodation for the gifted; remedial reading and/or remedial writing.

College Admission Counseling Colleges students went to include Florida International University; The University of Alabama; University of Florida; University of Miami; University of Notre Dame; University of Pennsylvania.

Student Life Upper grades have uniform requirement, student council, honor system. Discipline rests primarily with faculty. Attendance at religious services is required.

Summer Programs Remediation, enrichment programs offered; session focuses on enrichment, remediation and study skills; held on campus; accepts boys; not open to students from other schools. 154 students usually enrolled. 2012 schedule: June 11 to June 29.

Tuition and Aid Tuition installment plan (monthly payment plans, individually arranged payment plans). Bursaries available. In 2011–12, 22% of upper-school students received aid. Total amount of financial aid awarded in 2011–12: $800,000.

Admissions Traditional secondary-level entrance grade is 9. For fall 2011, 484 students applied for upper-level admission, 354 were accepted, 354 enrolled. High School Placement Test required. Deadline for receipt of application materials: none. Application fee required: $50. Interview required.

Athletics Interscholastic: baseball, basketball, bowling, cross-country running, football, golf, lacrosse, soccer, swimming and diving, tennis, track and field, volleyball, water polo, wrestling; intramural: basketball, flag football, power lifting, roller hockey, weight training. 2 PE instructors, 25 coaches, 2 athletic trainers.

Computers Computers are regularly used in architecture, computer applications, history, journalism, keyboarding, media production, science, yearbook classes. Computer network features include on-campus library services, online commercial services, Internet access, wireless campus network, Internet filtering or blocking technology. Campus intranet and computer access in designated common areas are available to students. Students grades are available online. The school has a published electronic and media policy.

Contact Mrs. Rebecca Rafuls, Registrar. 305-223-5650 Ext. 2239. Fax: 305-559-4306. E-mail: rrafuls@columbushs.com. Web site: www.columbushs.com.

CHRISTOPHER DOCK MENNONITE HIGH SCHOOL

1000 Forty Foot Road

Lansdale, Pennsylvania 19446

Head of School: Dr. Conrad Swartzentruber

General Information Coeducational day college-preparatory, general academic, arts, vocational, religious studies, and technology school, affiliated with Mennonite Church. Grades 9–12. Founded: 1954. Setting: suburban. Nearest major city is Philadelphia. 75-acre campus. 6 buildings on campus. Approved or accredited by Mennonite Education Agency, Mennonite Schools Council, Middle States Association of Colleges and Schools, and Pennsylvania Department of Education. Endowment: $1.2 million. Total enrollment: 364. Upper school average class size: 21. Upper school faculty-student ratio: 1:11. There are 182 required school days per year for Upper School students. Upper School students typically attend 5 days per week. The average school day consists of 6 hours and 55 minutes.

Upper School Student Profile Grade 9: 77 students (28 boys, 49 girls); Grade 10: 97 students (45 boys, 52 girls); Grade 11: 80 students (39 boys, 41 girls); Grade 12: 111 students (59 boys, 52 girls). 49% of students are Mennonite.

Faculty School total: 33. In upper school: 19 men, 14 women; 24 have advanced degrees.

Subjects Offered Accounting, advanced biology, advanced chemistry, advanced math, Advanced Placement courses, algebra, American government, American history, American literature, anatomy, anatomy and physiology, art, art history, arts, arts appreciation, athletic training, athletics, Basic programming, Bible, Bible studies, biology, British literature, business, business mathematics, business skills, calculus, calculus-AP, career education internship, career technology, ceramics, chemistry, child development, choir, choral music, chorus, Christian and Hebrew scripture, Christian doctrine, Christian education, Christian ethics, Christian scripture, Christian studies, Christian testament, Christianity, church history, communication skills, communications, composition-AP, computer graphics, computer information systems, computer literacy, computer programming, computer science, computer skills, computer technologies, computers, concert choir, consumer economics, creative writing, design, digital art, digital imaging, digital music, digital photography, drama, driver education, early childhood, earth science, ecology, environmental systems, economics, economics and history, English, English language and composition-AP, English literature, environmental science, European history, family and consumer science, family living, family studies, fine arts, food science, foreign language, forensics, genetics, geography, geology, geometry, global studies, government/civics, grammar, graphic design, guitar, health, health and wellness, health education, history, honors English, honors geometry, instrumental music, instruments, international foods, jazz band, journalism, keyboarding, language and composition, Life of Christ, life saving, life science, mathematics, mathematics-AP, music, New Testament, oral communications, parent/child development, peace and justice, peace education, peace studies, personal finance, photography, physical education, physics, religion, religion and culture, religious education, religious studies, research and reference, rhetoric, science, science research, scripture, sculpture, senior internship, service learning/internship, social sciences, social studies, Spanish, Spanish language-AP, Spanish literature-AP, Spanish-AP, speech, speech communications, sports team management, stage and body movement, statistics, student government, student publications, theater, trigonometry, U.S. government, U.S. history, U.S. literature, Vietnam, vocal ensemble, vocal music, vocational skills, vocational-technical courses, Web site design, word processing, work-study, world cultures, world history, world literature.

Graduation Requirements Arts and fine arts (art, music, dance, drama), business skills (includes word processing), computer science, English, family and consumer science, mathematics, physical education (includes health), religion (includes Bible studies and theology), science, social sciences, social studies (includes history), three-day urban experience, senior independent study/service experience (one week), senior presentation.

Special Academic Programs Advanced Placement exam preparation; honors section; term-away projects; study at local college for college credit; remedial reading and/or remedial writing; programs in English for dyslexic students.

College Admission Counseling 94 students graduated in 2011; 83 went to college, including Eastern Mennonite University; Eastern University; Messiah College; Montgomery County Community College; Penn State University Park. Other: 4 went to work, 7 had other specific plans. Mean SAT critical reading: 552, mean SAT math: 566, mean SAT writing: 554, mean combined SAT: 1672. 32% scored over 600 on SAT critical reading, 33% scored over 600 on SAT math, 26% scored over 600 on SAT writing, 26% scored over 1800 on combined SAT, 44% scored over 26 on composite ACT.

Student Life Upper grades have specified standards of dress, student council, honor system. Discipline rests primarily with faculty. Attendance at religious services is required.

Tuition and Aid Day student tuition: $14,370. Tuition installment plan (monthly payment plans). Tuition reduction for siblings, need-based scholarship grants available. In 2011–12, 27% of upper-school students received aid. Total amount of financial aid awarded in 2011–12: $533,185.

Admissions Traditional secondary-level entrance grade is 9. For fall 2011, 120 students applied for upper-level admission, 115 were accepted, 97 enrolled. Deadline for receipt of application materials: none. Application fee required: $50. Interview required.

Athletics Interscholastic: baseball (boys), basketball (b,g), bowling (b,g), cheering (g), cross-country running (b,g), field hockey (g), golf (b), soccer (b,g), softball (g), tennis (b,g), track and field (b,g), volleyball (b,g); coed interscholastic: bowling, track and field. 3 PE instructors, 32 coaches, 1 athletic trainer.

Computers Computers are regularly used in accounting, art, design, digital applications, keyboarding, lab/keyboard, mathematics, music, programming, SAT preparation, science, Web site design, word processing, yearbook classes. Computer network features include on-campus library services, online commercial services, Internet access, wireless campus network, Internet filtering or blocking technology, PowerSchool, WinSNAP. Computer access in designated common areas is available to students. Students grades are available online. The school has a published electronic and media policy.

Contact Lois Boaman, Admissions Director. 215-362-2675 Ext. 106. Fax: 215-362-2943. E-mail: laboaman@dockhs.org. Web site: www.dockhs.org.

CHRIST SCHOOL

500 Christ School Road

Asheville, North Carolina 28704

General Information Boys' boarding and day college-preparatory, arts, religious studies, and technology school, affiliated with Episcopal Church. Grades 8–12. Founded: 1900. Setting: rural. Students are housed in single-sex dormitories. 500-acre campus. 15 buildings on campus. Approved or accredited by National Association of Episcopal Schools, North Carolina Association of Independent Schools, Southern Association of Colleges and Schools, Southern Association of Independent Schools, The Association of Boarding Schools, and North Carolina Department of Education. Member of National Association of Independent Schools and Secondary School Admission Test Board. Endowment: $10 million. Total enrollment: 227. Upper school average class size: 11. Upper school faculty-student ratio: 1:6.

See Display below and Close-Up on page 606.

CHRYSALIS SCHOOL

14241 North East Woodinville-Duvall Road

PMB 243

Woodinville, Washington 98072

Head of School: Karen Fogle

General Information Coeducational day college-preparatory, general academic, arts, and technology school. Grades 1–12. Founded: 1983. Setting: suburban. Nearest major city is Seattle. 1 building on campus. Approved or accredited by Northwest Accreditation Commission, Northwest Association of Schools and Colleges, and Washington Department of Education. Total enrollment: 169. Upper school average class size: 8. Upper school faculty-student ratio: 1:5.

Upper School Student Profile Grade 9: 29 students (17 boys, 12 girls); Grade 10: 25 students (18 boys, 7 girls); Grade 11: 29 students (20 boys, 9 girls); Grade 12: 33 students (19 boys, 14 girls).

Faculty School total: 41. In upper school: 13 men, 20 women; 30 have advanced degrees.

Subjects Offered Advanced biology, advanced chemistry, advanced computer applications, advanced math, art, audio visual/media, career planning, college counseling, computer technologies, drama, English, filmmaking, French, geography, German, graphics, history, Japanese, mathematics, physical education, SAT preparation, science, social sciences, Spanish.

Graduation Requirements Career and personal planning, computer literacy, English, foreign language, history, mathematics, physical education (includes health), science, portfolio.

Special Academic Programs Honors section; accelerated programs; study at local college for college credit; academic accommodation for the gifted; remedial reading and/or remedial writing; remedial math; programs in English, mathematics, general development for dyslexic students; special instructional classes for students with learning disabilities.

College Admission Counseling 73 students graduated in 2011; 65 went to college, including Bellevue College; Central Washington University; University of Washington; Washington State University; Western Washington University. Other: 2 went to work, 2 entered military service, 4 had other specific plans.

Student Life Upper grades have specified standards of dress, honor system. Discipline rests primarily with faculty.
Summer Programs Remediation, enrichment, advancement, computer instruction programs offered; session focuses on enrichment; held on campus; accepts boys and girls; open to students from other schools. 35 students usually enrolled. 2012 schedule: July 10 to August 23. Application deadline: June 1.
Tuition and Aid Tuition installment plan (monthly payment plans).
Admissions Traditional secondary-level entrance grade is 10. For fall 2011, 100 students applied for upper-level admission, 90 were accepted, 80 enrolled. Deadline for receipt of application materials: none. Application fee required: $450. On-campus interview required.
Computers Computers are regularly used in computer applications, English, foreign language, graphic arts, history, information technology, introduction to technology, keyboarding, mathematics, media, science, video film production, Web site design, word processing, yearbook classes. Computer resources include on-campus library services, online commercial services, Internet access, Internet filtering or blocking technology. Computer access in designated common areas is available to students.
Contact Wanda Metcalfe, Director of Student Services. 425-481-2228. Fax: 425-486-8107. E-mail: wanda@chrysalis-school.com. Web site: www.chrysalis-school.com.

CINCINNATI COUNTRY DAY SCHOOL

6905 Given Road

Cincinnati, Ohio 45243-2898

Head of School: Dr. Robert P. Macrae

General Information Coeducational day college-preparatory, arts, and technology school. Grades PK–12. Founded: 1926. Setting: suburban. 62-acre campus. 8 buildings on campus. Approved or accredited by Independent Schools Association of the Central States and Ohio Department of Education. Member of National Association of Independent Schools and Secondary School Admission Test Board. Endowment: $13.5 million. Total enrollment: 820. Upper school average class size: 15. Upper school faculty-student ratio: 1:9. There are 170 required school days per year for Upper School students. Upper School students typically attend 5 days per week. The average school day consists of 7 hours.
Upper School Student Profile Grade 9: 76 students (39 boys, 37 girls); Grade 10: 67 students (31 boys, 36 girls); Grade 11: 57 students (25 boys, 32 girls); Grade 12: 70 students (33 boys, 37 girls).
Faculty School total: 110. In upper school: 24 men, 16 women; 32 have advanced degrees.
Subjects Offered Acting, algebra, American history, American history-AP, American literature, analysis, art, art history, biology, biology-AP, calculus, calculus-AP, ceramics, chemistry, chemistry-AP, choir, computer graphics, computer programming, computer science, CPR, creative writing, dance, drama, earth science, English, English literature, European history, fine arts, French, French language-AP, French literature-AP, genetics, geometry, health, humanities, music, photography, physical education, physics, psychology, public speaking, Spanish, Spanish language-AP, Spanish literature-AP, speech, statistics, theater, trigonometry, world history.
Graduation Requirements Arts and fine arts (art, music, dance, drama), computer science, English, foreign language, history, mathematics, physical education (includes health), science, senior project. Community service is required.
Special Academic Programs Advanced Placement exam preparation; honors section; independent study; study abroad.
College Admission Counseling 53 students graduated in 2011; all went to college, including Dartmouth College; Miami University; Northwestern University; Vanderbilt University; Wake Forest University. Mean SAT critical reading: 630, mean SAT math: 630, mean SAT writing: 640, mean combined SAT: 1900, mean composite ACT: 27.
Student Life Upper grades have specified standards of dress, student council, honor system. Discipline rests equally with students and faculty.
Summer Programs Remediation, enrichment, advancement, sports, art/fine arts, computer instruction programs offered; session focuses on camps and academic programs; held on campus; accepts boys and girls; open to students from other schools. 500 students usually enrolled. 2012 schedule: June 18 to August 10. Application deadline: May 31.
Tuition and Aid Day student tuition: $21,090. Tuition installment plan (Insured Tuition Payment Plan, FACTS Tuition Payment Plan, monthly payment plans, individually arranged payment plans). Merit scholarship grants, need-based scholarship grants, parent loans, Sallie Mae loans available. In 2011–12, 20% of upper-school students received aid; total upper-school merit-scholarship money awarded: $210,000. Total amount of financial aid awarded in 2011–12: $1,200,000.
Admissions Traditional secondary-level entrance grade is 9. For fall 2011, 70 students applied for upper-level admission, 49 were accepted, 29 enrolled. ISEE, Otis-Lennon Ability or Stanford Achievement Test or SSAT, ERB, PSAT, SAT, PLAN or ACT required. Deadline for receipt of application materials: March 15. Application fee required: $25. Interview recommended.
Athletics Interscholastic: baseball (boys), basketball (b,g), crew (b,g), cross-country running (b,g), football (b), golf (b,g), gymnastics (g), lacrosse (b,g), softball (g), swimming and diving (b,g), tennis (b,g), track and field (b,g); intramural: dance team (g); coed interscholastic: crew, dance squad. 5 PE instructors, 1 athletic trainer.
Computers Computers are regularly used in all academic classes. Computer network features include on-campus library services, online commercial services, Internet access, wireless campus network, Internet filtering or blocking technology. Campus intranet, student e-mail accounts, and computer access in designated common areas are available to students. Students grades are available online. The school has a published electronic and media policy.
Contact Mr. Aaron B. Kellenberger, Director of Admission. 513-979-0220. Fax: 513-527-7614. E-mail: kellenbea@countryday.net. Web site: www.countryday.net.

CISTERCIAN PREPARATORY SCHOOL

3660 Cistercian Road

Irving, Texas 75039

Head of School: Fr. Peter Verhalen

General Information Boys' day college-preparatory, arts, and religious studies school, affiliated with Roman Catholic Church. Grades 5–12. Founded: 1962. Setting: suburban. Nearest major city is Dallas. 80-acre campus. 7 buildings on campus. Approved or accredited by Independent Schools Association of the Southwest, Texas Catholic Conference, and Texas Department of Education. Member of National Association of Independent Schools. Endowment: $5.9 million. Total enrollment: 355. Upper school average class size: 22. Upper school faculty-student ratio: 1:7. There are 180 required school days per year for Upper School students. Upper School students typically attend 5 days per week. The average school day consists of 8 hours.
Upper School Student Profile Grade 9: 44 students (44 boys); Grade 10: 43 students (43 boys); Grade 11: 42 students (42 boys); Grade 12: 48 students (48 boys). 82% of students are Roman Catholic.
Faculty School total: 54. In upper school: 23 men, 7 women; 23 have advanced degrees.
Subjects Offered Advanced biology, advanced chemistry, algebra, American history, American literature, art, athletics, baseball, basketball, biology, calculus, chemistry, computer science, creative writing, digital applications, drama, earth science, ecology, economics, English, English composition, English literature, epic literature, ethics, European history, expository writing, fine arts, French, geometry, government/civics, grammar, health, history, history of the Catholic Church, Latin, modern world history, music, performing arts, photography, physical education, physics, pre-algebra, pre-calculus, religion, science, senior project, social studies, Spanish, speech, studio art, swimming, tennis, Texas history, theology, trigonometry, world history, world literature.
Graduation Requirements Arts and fine arts (art, music, dance, drama), electives, English, foreign language, mathematics, physical education (includes health), science, senior project, social studies (includes history), theology, completion of an independent senior project during fourth quarter of senior year.
Special Academic Programs 18 Advanced Placement exams for which test preparation is offered; independent study; study at local college for college credit.
College Admission Counseling 42 students graduated in 2011; all went to college, including Baylor University; Creighton University; Rice University; Texas A&M University; University of Notre Dame; Vanderbilt University. Median SAT critical reading: 690, median SAT math: 720, median SAT writing: 710, median combined SAT: 2130, median composite ACT: 31. 98% scored over 600 on SAT critical reading, 95% scored over 600 on SAT math, 93% scored over 600 on SAT writing, 100% scored over 1800 on combined SAT, 91% scored over 26 on composite ACT.
Student Life Upper grades have uniform requirement, student council. Discipline rests primarily with faculty. Attendance at religious services is required.
Summer Programs Remediation, enrichment, sports, art/fine arts programs offered; session focuses on remediation and enrichment in mathematics and English, arts and fine arts, computers, and sports camp; held on campus; accepts boys; open to students from other schools. 125 students usually enrolled. 2012 schedule: June 11 to July 6. Application deadline: January 26.
Tuition and Aid Day student tuition: $13,900–$15,800. Tuition installment plan (FACTS Tuition Payment Plan). Need-based scholarship grants available. In 2011–12, 22% of upper-school students received aid. Total amount of financial aid awarded in 2011–12: $320,500.
Admissions Traditional secondary-level entrance grade is 9. For fall 2011, 33 students applied for upper-level admission, 4 were accepted, 4 enrolled. English language, High School Placement Test, Iowa Tests of Basic Skills, ITBS achievement test, Kuhlmann-Anderson, mathematics proficiency exam or writing sample required. Deadline for receipt of application materials: January 28. Application fee required: $75.
Athletics Interscholastic: baseball, basketball, cross-country running, football, physical training, soccer, swimming and diving, tennis, track and field; intramural: basketball, physical training, soccer, strength & conditioning, ultimate Frisbee, volleyball, weight lifting, weight training. 5 coaches, 1 athletic trainer.
Computers Computers are regularly used in college planning, computer applications, digital applications, library, literary magazine, newspaper, photography, programming, publications, yearbook classes. Computer network features include on-campus library services, Internet access, online college applications, numerous online databases, reference sources, Moodle. Student e-mail accounts and computer access in designated common areas are available to students. The school has a published electronic and media policy.

Contact Mrs. Lisa Richard, Assistant to Headmaster. 469-499-5402. Fax: 469-499-5440. E-mail: lrichard@cistercian.org. Web site: www.cistercian.org.

CLARKSVILLE ACADEMY

710 North Second Street

Clarksville, Tennessee 37040-2998

Head of School: Mrs. Kay D. Drew

General Information Coeducational day college-preparatory school. Grades PK–12. Founded: 1970. Setting: urban. 31-acre campus. 7 buildings on campus. Approved or accredited by Southern Association of Colleges and Schools and Tennessee Department of Education. Member of National Association of Independent Schools. Endowment: $1 million. Total enrollment: 557. Upper school average class size: 15. Upper school faculty-student ratio: 1:7. There are 175 required school days per year for Upper School students. Upper School students typically attend 5 days per week. The average school day consists of 7 hours.

Upper School Student Profile Grade 9: 43 students (22 boys, 21 girls); Grade 10: 45 students (25 boys, 20 girls); Grade 11: 56 students (34 boys, 22 girls); Grade 12: 52 students (33 boys, 19 girls).

Faculty School total: 56. In upper school: 12 men, 17 women; 15 have advanced degrees.

Subjects Offered American history, anatomy and physiology, art, art appreciation, Bible as literature, biology, calculus, calculus-AP, ceramics, chemistry, chemistry-AP, choir, chorus, college writing, computer education, computer science, debate, drama, driver education, ecology, economics, economics and history, English language and composition-AP, English literature and composition-AP, fitness, geography, geometry, German, government, graphic design, health, health education, honors algebra, honors English, honors geometry, honors U.S. history, honors world history, keyboarding, Latin, marketing, media arts, music, music theory-AP, mythology, personal finance, physical education, physical fitness, physics, physics-AP, physiology, piano, political science, pre-calculus, psychology, sculpture, Spanish, speech, statistics, statistics-AP, studio art, study skills, trigonometry, U.S. history, U.S. history AP, weight training, wellness, women's health, world history, writing, yearbook.

Graduation Requirements 24 credit, 4 years of high school math required.

Special Academic Programs 6 Advanced Placement exams for which test preparation is offered; honors section; independent study; study at local college for college credit.

College Admission Counseling 32 students graduated in 2011; all went to college, including Austin Peay State University; Lipscomb University; Rhodes College; The University of Tennessee; The University of Tennessee at Chattanooga; Vanderbilt University.

Student Life Upper grades have specified standards of dress, student council, honor system. Discipline rests primarily with faculty.

Summer Programs Remediation, enrichment, sports, art/fine arts, computer instruction programs offered; session focuses on enrichment and remediation; held both on and off campus; held at Sports Complex; accepts boys and girls; open to students from other schools. 2012 schedule: June 1 to August 13. Application deadline: May 20.

Tuition and Aid Tuition installment plan (monthly payment plans). Tuition reduction for siblings, paying campus jobs available.

Admissions Otis-Lennon School Ability Test required. Deadline for receipt of application materials: none. Application fee required: $75. On-campus interview required.

Athletics Interscholastic: baseball (boys), basketball (b,g), cheering (g), dance team (g), football (b), soccer (b,g), softball (g), volleyball (g), wrestling (b); coed interscholastic: bowling, golf, tennis. 4 PE instructors, 26 coaches, 1 athletic trainer.

Computers Computers are regularly used in all academic, art classes. Computer network features include on-campus library services, Internet access, wireless campus network, Internet filtering or blocking technology, 1:1 Apple Macbook Program. Campus intranet, student e-mail accounts, and computer access in designated common areas are available to students. Students grades are available online. The school has a published electronic and media policy.

Contact Mrs. Angie Henson, Business Office & Admissions. 931-647-6311. Fax: 931-906-0610. E-mail: ahenson@clarksvilleacademy.com. Web site: www.clarksvilleacademy.com.

CLEARWATER CENTRAL CATHOLIC HIGH SCHOOL

2750 Haines Bayshore Road

Clearwater, Florida 33760

Head of School: Dr. John A. Venturella

General Information Coeducational day college-preparatory, arts, religious studies, technology, and International Baccalaureate diploma programme school, affiliated with Roman Catholic Church. Grades 9–12. Founded: 1962. Setting: suburban. Nearest major city is Tampa. 40-acre campus. 7 buildings on campus. Approved or accredited by International Baccalaureate Organization, National Catholic Education Association, Southern Association of Colleges and Schools, The College Board, and Florida Department of Education. Upper school average class size: 25. Upper school faculty-student ratio: 1:16. There are 190 required school days per year for Upper School students. Upper School students typically attend 5 days per week. The average school day consists of 6 hours and 13 minutes.

Upper School Student Profile 80% of students are Roman Catholic.

Faculty School total: 41. In upper school: 14 men, 27 women; 32 have advanced degrees.

Subjects Offered Acting, advanced chemistry, Advanced Placement courses, aerobics, algebra, American government, American history, American history-AP, American literature, American literature-AP, American sign language, anatomy, architecture, Bible studies, biology, biology-AP, British literature, British literature (honors), calculus, calculus-AP, campus ministry, chemistry, chemistry-AP, choral music, chorus, church history, composition, computer processing, creative writing, desktop publishing, discrete mathematics, drama, drawing, drawing and design, ecology, economics, English, English literature and composition-AP, foreign language, French, general science, geometry, health, honors algebra, honors English, honors geometry, honors U.S. history, honors world history, information technology, journalism, keyboarding, language arts, law, law studies, leadership, learning strategies, life management skills, marine biology, music appreciation, oral communications, painting, personal fitness, philosophy, physical education, physics, pre-algebra, probability and statistics, psychology, sociology, Spanish, Spanish language AP, speech, speech and debate, theater, theology, trigonometry, U.S. government, U.S. government and politics-AP, U.S. history, U.S. history-AP, video, volleyball, Web site design, wellness, world history.

Graduation Requirements Algebra, biology, ceramics, chemistry, comparative government and politics-AP, economics, English, general science, geometry, global studies, physical education (includes health), physical fitness, physical science, physics, Spanish, theology, U.S. government, U.S. history, United States government-AP, visual and performing arts, world geography, world history, world religions, yearbook.

Special Academic Programs International Baccalaureate program; Advanced Placement exam preparation; honors section; study at local college for college credit; programs in English, mathematics, general development for dyslexic students.

College Admission Counseling 130 students graduated in 2011; all went to college, including Florida State University, University of Central Florida, University of Florida; University of South Florida.

Student Life Upper grades have uniform requirement, student council, honor system. Discipline rests primarily with faculty. Attendance at religious services is required.

Summer Programs Remediation, enrichment, advancement, sports, computer instruction programs offered; session focuses on work-ahead classes for credit; held on campus; accepts boys and girls; open to students from other schools. 225 students usually enrolled. 2012 schedule: June 9 to June 27. Application deadline: May 15.

Tuition and Aid Day student tuition: $9800–$11,775. Tuition installment plan (SMART Tuition Payment Plan). Tuition reduction for siblings, merit scholarship grants, need-based scholarship grants available. In 2011–12, 20% of upper-school students received aid.

Admissions Traditional secondary-level entrance grade is 9. For fall 2011, 230 students applied for upper-level admission, 200 were accepted, 170 enrolled. Explore required. Deadline for receipt of application materials: none. Application fee required: $100. Interview recommended.

Athletics Interscholastic: baseball (boys), basketball (b,g), cheering (g), cross-country running (b,g), diving (b,g), football (b), golf (b,g), physical fitness (b,g), running (b,g), soccer (b,g), softball (g), swimming and diving (b,g), tennis (b,g), track and field (b,g), volleyball (g), weight lifting (b,g), weight training (b,g), winter soccer (b,g), wrestling (b). 1 PE instructor, 43 coaches, 1 athletic trainer.

Computers Computer network features include on-campus library services, online commercial services, Internet access. The school has a published electronic and media policy.

Contact Mrs. Helen Lambert, Director of Admissions. 727-531-1449 Ext. 304. Fax: 727-451-0003. E-mail: hlambert@ccchs.org. Web site: www.ccchs.org.

COLEGIO FRANKLIN D. ROOSEVELT

Av. Las Palmeras 325, Urbanizacion Camacho La Molina

Lima 12, Peru

Head of School: Mr. Russel D. Junes

General Information Coeducational day college-preparatory, general academic, arts, and technology school. Grades N–12. Founded: 1946. Setting: suburban. Nearest major city is Lima, Peru. 23-acre campus. 5 buildings on campus. Approved or accredited by International Baccalaureate Organization and Southern Association of Colleges and Schools. Languages of instruction: English and Spanish. Total enrollment: 1,452. Upper school average class size: 20. Upper school faculty-student ratio: 1:11. There are 179 required school days per year for Upper School students. Upper School students typically attend 5 days per week. The average school day consists of 7 hours and 30 minutes.

Upper School Student Profile Grade 9: 109 students (57 boys, 52 girls); Grade 10: 89 students (51 boys, 38 girls); Grade 11: 97 students (56 boys, 41 girls); Grade 12: 93 students (47 boys, 46 girls).

Faculty School total: 182. In upper school: 20 men, 25 women; 26 have advanced degrees.
Subjects Offered Algebra, American history, American literature, art, biology, calculus, chemistry, computer programming, computer science, debate, digital photography, drama, drama performance, early childhood, earth science, economics, English, English literature, ESL, fine arts, French, geography, geometry, global issues, health, history, International Baccalaureate courses, mathematics, model United Nations, music, orchestra, photography, physical education, physical science, physics, psychology, science, social studies, Spanish, theater, theory of knowledge, trigonometry, U.S. history, world history, yearbook.
Graduation Requirements Arts and fine arts (art, music, dance, drama), English, foreign language, information technology, mathematics, physical education (includes health), science, social studies (includes history).
Special Academic Programs International Baccalaureate program; honors section; special instructional classes for students with mild learning disabilities; ESL (15 students enrolled).
College Admission Counseling 93 students graduated in 2010; 92 went to college, including Boston College; Michigan State University; Northwestern University; Purdue University; Texas A&M University; University of California, Berkeley. Other: 1 had other specific plans. Mean SAT critical reading: 548, mean SAT math: 576, mean SAT writing: 548, mean composite ACT: 23.
Student Life Upper grades have uniform requirement, student council, honor system. Discipline rests primarily with faculty.
Tuition and Aid Day student tuition: $9660–$10,980. Tuition installment plan (monthly payment plans). Need-based scholarship grants available. In 2010–11, 0% of upper-school students received aid. Total amount of financial aid awarded in 2010–11: $5490.
Admissions Traditional secondary-level entrance grade is 9. For fall 2010, 34 students applied for upper-level admission, 32 were accepted, 32 enrolled. ESL or math and English placement tests required. Deadline for receipt of application materials: none. Application fee required: $250. On-campus interview required.
Athletics Interscholastic: aquatics (boys, girls), basketball (b,g), field hockey (b), soccer (b,g), softball (b,g), swimming and diving (b,g), track and field (b,g), volleyball (b,g); intramural: aquatics (b,g), basketball (b,g), soccer (b,g), softball (b,g), swimming and diving (b,g), volleyball (b,g); coed interscholastic: aerobics, aquatics, dance, field hockey, fitness, floor hockey, martial arts, soccer, swimming and diving, track and field, volleyball, water polo; coed intramural: aerobics, aquatics, floor hockey, martial arts, outdoor adventure, soccer, swimming and diving, volleyball, wall climbing, water polo. 3 PE instructors, 18 coaches.
Computers Computers are regularly used in art, digital applications, English, history, mathematics, music, photography, science, technology classes. Computer network features include on-campus library services, online commercial services, Internet access, wireless campus network, Internet filtering or blocking technology. Campus intranet and student e-mail accounts are available to students. Students grades are available online. The school has a published electronic and media policy.
Contact Ms. Nora Marquez, Admissions Officer. 51-1-435-0890 Ext. 1004. Fax: 51-1-6199301. E-mail: nmarquez@amersol.edu.pe. Web site: www.amersol.edu.pe.

COLEGIO NUEVA GRANADA

Carrera 2E #70-20

Bogota, Colombia

Head of School: Dr. Eric H. Habegger

General Information Coeducational day college-preparatory, Colombian Bachillerato, and Advanced Placement school, affiliated with Roman Catholic Church, Jewish faith. Grades PK–12. Founded: 1938. Setting: urban. 10-hectare campus. 2 buildings on campus. Approved or accredited by Southern Association of Colleges and Schools. Languages of instruction: English and Spanish. Total enrollment: 1,801. Upper school average class size: 23. Upper school faculty-student ratio: 1:22. There are 183 required school days per year for Upper School students. Upper School students typically attend 5 days per week. The average school day consists of 7 hours.
Upper School Student Profile Grade 9: 160 students (77 boys, 83 girls); Grade 10: 127 students (58 boys, 69 girls); Grade 11: 119 students (61 boys, 58 girls); Grade 12: 121 students (64 boys, 57 girls).
Faculty School total: 233. In upper school: 28 men, 35 women; 27 have advanced degrees.
Subjects Offered Art, art history-AP, basketball, biology, biology-AP, calculus, chemistry, crafts, dance performance, drama, drawing, economics-AP, English, English-AP, ESL, ethics, European history-AP, French, graphic design, human geography - AP, macroeconomics-AP, Mandarin, mathematics, model United Nations, music, philosophy, photography, physical education, physics, pre-calculus, religion, science, sex education, social studies, Spanish, Spanish language-AP, studio art-AP, theater, U.S. history, U.S. history-AP, volleyball, weight training, world history, world history-AP.
Graduation Requirements Arts and fine arts (art, music, dance, drama), computer education, electives, English, foreign language, mathematics, physical education (includes health), science, social studies (includes history), senior independent project.
Special Academic Programs Advanced Placement exam preparation; honors section; independent study; academic accommodation for the gifted; programs in English, mathematics, general development for dyslexic students; special instructional classes for students with learning disabilities, students with emotional and behavioral problems, Attention Deficit Disorder; ESL (8 students enrolled).
College Admission Counseling 114 students graduated in 2011; 90 went to college, including Florida International University; Massachusetts Institute of Technology; Northeastern University; Penn State University Park; University of Miami; University of Pennsylvania. Other: 1 went to work, 23 had other specific plans. Median SAT critical reading: 470, median SAT math: 500, median SAT writing: 490, median combined SAT: 1470.
Student Life Upper grades have uniform requirement, student council, honor system. Discipline rests equally with students and faculty.
Tuition and Aid Day student tuition: 15,100,000 Colombian pesos–24,100,000 Colombian pesos. Tuition installment plan (5-installment plan, yearly). Need-based scholarship grants available.
Admissions For fall 2011, 50 students applied for upper-level admission, 38 were accepted, 38 enrolled. Academic Profile Tests, admissions testing, Reading for Understanding and writing sample required. Deadline for receipt of application materials: none. Application fee required: $85. On-campus interview required.
Athletics Interscholastic: aerobics/dance (girls), baseball (b), basketball (b,g), gymnastics (b,g), soccer (b,g), table tennis (b,g), volleyball (b,g); intramural: basketball (b,g), soccer (b,g), table tennis (b,g), volleyball (b,g), weight training (b,g); coed interscholastic: gymnastics; coed intramural: basketball, soccer, table tennis, volleyball, weight training. 5 PE instructors, 25 coaches.
Computers Computers are regularly used in desktop publishing, ESL, introduction to technology, mathematics, science, technology, video film production, Web site design classes. Computer network features include on-campus library services, Internet access, wireless campus network, Internet filtering or blocking technology, Sharepoint, SDS. Campus intranet, student e-mail accounts, and computer access in designated common areas are available to students. Students grades are available online.
Contact Laura De Brigard, Director of Admissions. 57-1-359-9344. Fax: 57-1-211-3720. E-mail: lbrigard@cng.edu. Web site: www.cng.edu.

COLEGIO SAN JOSE

PO Box 21300

San Juan, Puerto Rico 00928-1300

Head of School: Br. Francisco T. Gonzalez, DMD

General Information Boys' day college-preparatory, arts, business, religious studies, bilingual studies, technology, science, anatomy, and marine biology, and psychology, humanities, health, economy, political science school, affiliated with Roman Catholic Church. Grades 7–12. Founded: 1938. Setting: urban. 6-acre campus. 1 building on campus. Approved or accredited by Middle States Association of Colleges and Schools, National Catholic Education Association, The College Board, and Puerto Rico Department of Education. Languages of instruction: English and Spanish. Endowment: $217,000. Total enrollment: 483. Upper school average class size: 22. Upper School students typically attend 5 days per week. The average school day consists of 6 hours and 50 minutes.
Upper School Student Profile Grade 9: 92 students (92 boys); Grade 10: 115 students (115 boys); Grade 11: 74 students (74 boys); Grade 12: 78 students (78 boys). 90% of students are Roman Catholic.
Faculty School total: 43. In upper school: 24 men, 19 women; 24 have advanced degrees.
Subjects Offered Accounting, algebra, American history, American literature, anatomy, art, art history, biology, biology-AP, broadcasting, business skills, calculus, chemistry, choir, Christian ethics, computer education, computer science, ecology, English, English literature, ethics, European history, French, French as a second language, geography, geometry, government/civics, grammar, health, history, instrumental music, keyboarding, marine biology, mathematics, music, physical education, physics, pre-calculus, psychology, religion, science, social studies, Spanish, world history.
Graduation Requirements Business skills (includes word processing), computer science, English, foreign language, history, mathematics, physical education (includes health), religion (includes Bible studies and theology), science, social studies (includes history), Spanish, 40 hours of Christian community service.
Special Academic Programs International Baccalaureate program; Advanced Placement exam preparation; honors section.
College Admission Counseling 81 students graduated in 2011; all went to college, including University of Dayton; University of Puerto Rico, Mayagüez Campus; University of Puerto Rico, Río Piedras.
Student Life Upper grades have uniform requirement, student council, honor system. Discipline rests equally with students and faculty. Attendance at religious services is required.
Summer Programs Remediation programs offered; session focuses on remediation/make-up; held on campus; accepts boys and girls; open to students from other schools. 150 students usually enrolled. 2012 schedule: June 1 to June 30. Application deadline: May 31.
Tuition and Aid Day student tuition: $6850. Tuition installment plan (The Tuition Plan, individually arranged payment plans). Need-based scholarship grants available. In

2011–12, 11% of upper-school students received aid. Total amount of financial aid awarded in 2011–12: $216,000.
Admissions Traditional secondary-level entrance grade is 9. Catholic High School Entrance Examination required. Deadline for receipt of application materials: February 28. Application fee required: $10. On-campus interview required.
Athletics Interscholastic: baseball, basketball, bowling, cross-country running, fitness, golf, indoor soccer, physical fitness, soccer, swimming and diving, tennis, track and field, volleyball; intramural: cross-country running, indoor soccer, soccer, swimming and diving, tennis, track and field, volleyball. 3 PE instructors, 6 coaches, 1 athletic trainer.
Computers Computers are regularly used in accounting, art, data processing, English, foreign language, keyboarding, mathematics, music, psychology, science, Spanish, yearbook classes. Computer network features include on-campus library services, Internet access, wireless campus network, Internet filtering or blocking technology, Edline. Students grades are available online. The school has a published electronic and media policy.
Contact Mrs. Mar?E. Guzm? Guidance Advisor. 787-751-8177 Ext. 229. Fax: 866-955-7646. E-mail: mguzman@csj-rpi.org. Web site: www.csj-rpi.org.

COLLEGEDALE ACADEMY

PO Box 628

4855 College Drive East

Collegedale, Tennessee 37315

Head of School: Mr. Murray J. Cooper

General Information Coeducational day college-preparatory and arts school, affiliated with Seventh-day Adventists. Grades 9–12. Founded: 1892. Setting: small town. Nearest major city is Chattanooga. 20-acre campus. 3 buildings on campus. Approved or accredited by Southern Association of Colleges and Schools and Tennessee Department of Education. Endowment: $496,487. Total enrollment: 361. Upper school average class size: 25. Upper school faculty-student ratio: 1:18. There are 180 required school days per year for Upper School students. Upper School students typically attend 5 days per week. The average school day consists of 7 hours.
Upper School Student Profile Grade 9: 98 students (47 boys, 51 girls); Grade 10: 86 students (39 boys, 47 girls); Grade 11: 90 students (51 boys, 39 girls); Grade 12: 89 students (48 boys, 41 girls). 98% of students are Seventh-day Adventists.
Faculty School total: 39. In upper school: 19 men, 17 women; 22 have advanced degrees.
Subjects Offered Algebra, American history, American literature, anatomy, art, art appreciation, Bible studies, biology, calculus-AP, chemistry, choir, composition, computer skills, concert band, digital imaging, drawing, earth science, economics, English, English literature, environmental science, fine arts, French, geometry, government/civics, gymnastics, health and wellness, history, home economics, journalism, mathematics, music, music appreciation, personal fitness, physical education, physical science, physics, physiology, pre-calculus, religion, social studies, Spanish, woodworking, world history, yearbook.
Graduation Requirements Arts and fine arts (art, music, dance, drama), computer science, English, foreign language, mathematics, physical education (includes health), religion (includes Bible studies and theology), science, social studies (includes history).
Special Academic Programs 1 Advanced Placement exam for which test preparation is offered; accelerated programs; study at local college for college credit.
College Admission Counseling 89 students graduated in 2011; 85 went to college, including Chattanooga State Community College; Cleveland State University; Southern Adventist University; The University of Tennessee at Chattanooga. Other: 3 went to work, 1 entered military service. 24.5% scored over 26 on composite ACT.
Student Life Upper grades have uniform requirement, student council, honor system. Discipline rests primarily with faculty. Attendance at religious services is required.
Summer Programs Advancement programs offered; session focuses on U.S. history; held on campus; accepts boys and girls; open to students from other schools. 20 students usually enrolled. 2012 schedule: May 21 to July 6. Application deadline: none.
Tuition and Aid Day student tuition: $8760. Tuition installment plan (monthly payment plans). Need-based scholarship grants available. In 2011–12, 20% of upper-school students received aid. Total amount of financial aid awarded in 2011–12: $55,000.
Admissions Traditional secondary-level entrance grade is 9. Mathematics proficiency exam required. Deadline for receipt of application materials: August 1. Application fee required: $125. On-campus interview required.
Athletics Interscholastic: cross-country running (boys, girls), golf (b), tennis (b,g); intramural: basketball (b,g), soccer (b,g), track and field (b,g), volleyball (b,g); coed intramural: flag football, gymnastics, hiking/backpacking, paddle tennis, volleyball. 1 PE instructor, 2 coaches.
Computers Computers are regularly used in business applications, computer applications, digital applications, English, library, publications, yearbook classes. Computer network features include on-campus library services, Internet access, wireless campus network, Internet filtering or blocking technology. Student e-mail accounts and computer access in designated common areas are available to students. Students grades are available online. The school has a published electronic and media policy.
Contact Miss Kerre Conerly, Registrar. 423-396-2124 Ext. 415. Fax: 423-396-3363. E-mail: kconerly@collegedaleacademy.com. Web site: www.collegedaleacademy.com.

COLLEGIATE SCHOOL

260 West 78th Street

New York, New York 10024

Head of School: Dr. Lee M. Levison

General Information Boys' day college-preparatory and arts school. Grades K–12. Founded: 1628. Setting: urban. 4 buildings on campus. Approved or accredited by New York State Association of Independent Schools. Member of National Association of Independent Schools. Endowment: $70 million. Total enrollment: 648. Upper school average class size: 14. Upper school faculty-student ratio: 1:4. There are 164 required school days per year for Upper School students. Upper School students typically attend 5 days per week. The average school day consists of 6 hours and 45 minutes.
Upper School Student Profile Grade 9: 59 students (59 boys); Grade 10: 59 students (59 boys); Grade 11: 56 students (56 boys); Grade 12: 55 students (55 boys).
Faculty School total: 111. In upper school: 39 men, 22 women; 56 have advanced degrees.
Subjects Offered African drumming, African history, algebra, American history, Ancient Greek, applied music, architecture, art, art appreciation, art history, Asian history, athletics, biology, calculus, ceramics, chemistry, Chinese, chorus, contemporary issues in science, digital photography, drama, dramatic arts, drawing, drawing and design, East Asian history, economics, English, environmental science, European history, film, film appreciation, film studies, foreign policy, French, geometry, health and wellness, history, Latin, Latin American history, linear algebra, literature, logic, Mandarin, mathematics, Middle Eastern history, music, music composition, music theory, orchestra, painting, philosophy, photography, physical education, physics, play production, poetry, pre-calculus, religion, sculpture, senior project, Shakespeare, social studies, Spanish, technical theater, theater, U.S. history, Web site design, world history, world literature, world religions.
Graduation Requirements Drama, English, foreign language, history, mathematics, music, physical education (includes health), religion (includes Bible studies and theology), science, visual arts. Community service is required.
Special Academic Programs 15 Advanced Placement exams for which test preparation is offered; honors section; independent study; term-away projects; study abroad.
College Admission Counseling 55 students graduated in 2011; all went to college, including Brown University; Dartmouth College; University of Pennsylvania; Williams College; Yale University.
Student Life Upper grades have specified standards of dress, student council, honor system. Discipline rests equally with students and faculty.
Tuition and Aid Day student tuition: $37,500. Tuition installment plan (SMART Tuition Payment Plan). Need-based scholarship grants available. In 2011–12, 22% of upper-school students received aid. Total amount of financial aid awarded in 2011–12: $1,630,000.
Admissions Traditional secondary-level entrance grade is 9. ERB or ISEE required. Deadline for receipt of application materials: December 1. Application fee required: $50. On-campus interview required.
Athletics Interscholastic: baseball, basketball, cross-country running, indoor track & field, lacrosse, soccer, tennis, track and field, winter (indoor) track, wrestling; intramural: physical fitness, weight training, yoga. 3 PE instructors, 8 coaches, 2 athletic trainers.
Computers Computers are regularly used in all academic classes. Computer network features include on-campus library services, online commercial services, Internet access, wireless campus network, Internet filtering or blocking technology. Campus intranet, student e-mail accounts, and computer access in designated common areas are available to students. The school has a published electronic and media policy.
Contact Joanne P. Heyman, Director of Admissions and Financial Aid. 212-812-8552. Fax: 212-812-8547. E-mail: jheyman@collegiateschool.org. Web site: www.collegiateschool.org.

THE COLLEGIATE SCHOOL

North Mooreland Road

Richmond, Virginia 23229

Head of School: Keith A. Evans

General Information Coeducational day college-preparatory, arts, and technology school. Grades K–12. Founded: 1915. Setting: suburban. 211-acre campus. 13 buildings on campus. Approved or accredited by Southern Association of Colleges and Schools and Virginia Department of Education. Member of National Association of Independent Schools and Secondary School Admission Test Board. Endowment: $39.5 million. Total enrollment: 1,597. Upper school average class size: 15. Upper school faculty-student ratio: 1:15. There are 175 required school days per year for Upper School students. Upper School students typically attend 5 days per week. The average school day consists of 7 hours.

Upper School Student Profile Grade 9: 139 students (71 boys, 68 girls); Grade 10: 123 students (60 boys, 63 girls); Grade 11: 126 students (62 boys, 64 girls); Grade 12: 126 students (56 boys, 70 girls).

Faculty School total: 186. In upper school: 32 men, 34 women; 48 have advanced degrees.

Subjects Offered 20th century history, acting, advanced chemistry, algebra, American Civil War, American history, American history-AP, American literature, art, Asian literature, Bible as literature, biology, biology-AP, calculus-AP, ceramics, chemistry, chemistry-AP, community service, computer applications, creative writing, drama, driver education, earth science, economics, economics-AP, English, English literature, ethics, European history, film and literature, fine arts, French, French-AP, geometry, government and politics-AP, government/civics, health, journalism, Latin, music, photography, physics, physics-AP, religion, robotics, Russian literature, senior seminar, Spanish, Spanish language-AP, statistics, theater, trigonometry, world history, World War II.

Graduation Requirements Arts and fine arts (art, music, dance, drama), English, ethics, foreign language, government, history, mathematics, physical education (includes health), religion (includes Bible studies and theology), science, sports, senior speech. Community service is required.

Special Academic Programs 12 Advanced Placement exams for which test preparation is offered; honors section; independent study; study at local college for college credit; programs in general development for dyslexic students.

College Admission Counseling 117 students graduated in 2011; all went to college, including Elon University; High Point University; James Madison University; The College of William and Mary; University of Virginia; Virginia Polytechnic Institute and State University.

Student Life Upper grades have specified standards of dress, student council, honor system. Discipline rests equally with students and faculty.

Summer Programs Remediation, enrichment, advancement, sports, art/fine arts, computer instruction programs offered; session focuses on advancement, remediation, sports; held both on and off campus; held at various locations in metro Richmond; accepts boys and girls; open to students from other schools. 1,225 students usually enrolled. 2012 schedule: June 11 to August 3. Application deadline: none.

Tuition and Aid Day student tuition: $20,690. Tuition installment plan (Insured Tuition Payment Plan, monthly payment plans). Need-based scholarship grants available. In 2011–12, 14% of upper-school students received aid. Total amount of financial aid awarded in 2011–12: $850,330.

Admissions Traditional secondary-level entrance grade is 9. For fall 2011, 108 students applied for upper-level admission, 44 were accepted, 25 enrolled. PSAT and SAT for applicants to grade 11 and 12 or SSAT required. Deadline for receipt of application materials: none. Application fee required: $50. Interview required.

Athletics Interscholastic: baseball (boys), basketball (b,g), cross-country running (b,g), diving (b,g), field hockey (g), football (b), indoor track & field (b,g), lacrosse (b,g), soccer (b,g), softball (g), swimming and diving (b,g), tennis (b,g), track and field (b,g), volleyball (g), winter (indoor) track (b,g), wrestling (b); coed interscholastic: golf, indoor soccer; coed intramural: combined training, dance, dance squad, dance team, fitness, modern dance. 3 PE instructors, 48 coaches, 2 athletic trainers.

Computers Computers are regularly used in all academic classes. Computer network features include on-campus library services, Internet access, wireless campus network, Internet filtering or blocking technology. Student e-mail accounts are available to students. The school has a published electronic and media policy.

Contact Amanda L. Surgner, Director of Admission. 804-741-9722. Fax: 804-741-5472. E-mail: asurgner@collegiate-va.org. Web site: www.collegiate-va.org/.

THE COLORADO ROCKY MOUNTAIN SCHOOL

1493 County Road 106

Carbondale, Colorado 81623

Head of School: Jeff Leahy

General Information Coeducational boarding and day college-preparatory and arts school. Grades 9–12. Founded: 1953. Setting: small town. Nearest major city is Denver. Students are housed in single-sex dormitories. 350-acre campus. 23 buildings on campus. Approved or accredited by Association for Experiential Education, Association of Colorado Independent Schools, The Association of Boarding Schools, and Colorado Department of Education. Member of National Association of Independent Schools and Secondary School Admission Test Board. Endowment: $13.8 million. Total enrollment: 145. Upper school average class size: 12. Upper school faculty-student ratio: 1:5. Upper School students typically attend 5 days per week. The average school day consists of 8 hours.

Upper School Student Profile Grade 9: 32 students (21 boys, 11 girls); Grade 10: 38 students (20 boys, 18 girls); Grade 11: 53 students (33 boys, 20 girls); Grade 12: 33 students (16 boys, 17 girls). 64% of students are boarding students. 56% are state residents. 19 states are represented in upper school student body. 22% are international students. International students from China, Democratic People's Republic of Korea, Germany, Japan, Rwanda, and Venezuela; 7 other countries represented in student body.

Faculty School total: 42. In upper school: 21 men, 21 women; 21 have advanced degrees; 40 reside on campus.

Subjects Offered Advanced Placement courses, algebra, American literature, anthropology, art, art history, biology, botany, calculus, ceramics, chemistry, computer programming, computer science, creative writing, drama, earth science, ecology, English, English literature, environmental science, ESL, ethics, European history, expository writing, fine arts, French, gardening, geography, geology, geometry, geopolitics, government/civics, grammar, guitar, history, history of ideas, journalism, mathematics, music, philosophy, photography, physical education, physics, physiology, religion, science, Shakespeare, social studies, Spanish, theater, trigonometry, Western civilization, world history, world literature, writing.

Graduation Requirements Arts and fine arts (art, music, dance, drama), chemistry, English, foreign language, mathematics, science, senior project, social studies (includes history), participation in outdoor program. Community service is required.

Special Academic Programs Advanced Placement exam preparation; academic accommodation for the gifted, the musically talented, and the artistically talented; ESL (10 students enrolled).

College Admission Counseling 37 students graduated in 2010; all went to college, including Bates College; Lewis & Clark College; Middlebury College; The Colorado College; University of Pennsylvania; University of Vermont. Mean SAT critical reading: 576, mean SAT math: 582, mean SAT writing: 543, mean combined SAT: 1701, mean composite ACT: 24. 28% scored over 600 on SAT critical reading, 23% scored over 600 on SAT math, 25% scored over 600 on SAT writing, 25% scored over 1800 on combined SAT, 28% scored over 26 on composite ACT.

Student Life Upper grades have student council, honor system. Discipline rests equally with students and faculty.

Tuition and Aid Day student tuition: $23,375; 7-day tuition and room/board: $37,650. Tuition installment plan (monthly payment plans, individually arranged payment plans, 3rd party loan options). Merit scholarship grants, need-based scholarship grants, middle-income loans available. In 2010–11, 41% of upper-school students received aid; total upper-school merit-scholarship money awarded: $40,000. Total amount of financial aid awarded in 2010–11: $1,000,000.

Admissions Traditional secondary-level entrance grade is 9. For fall 2010, 143 students applied for upper-level admission, 108 were accepted, 66 enrolled. PSAT or SAT, SLEP, SSAT or TOEFL required. Deadline for receipt of application materials: February 15. Application fee required: $50. Interview required.

Athletics Intramural: aerobics/dance (girls), basketball (b,g), dance (b,g), fly fishing (b,g), freestyle skiing (b,g), kayaking (b,g); coed interscholastic: alpine skiing, bicycling, canoeing/kayaking, climbing, cross-country running, independent competitive sports, kayaking, nordic skiing; coed intramural: alpine skiing, backpacking, basketball, bicycling, canoeing/kayaking, climbing, cross-country running, dance, equestrian sports, fishing, fitness, floor hockey, fly fishing, freestyle skiing, Frisbee, hiking/backpacking, horseshoes, jogging, kayaking, martial arts, mountain biking, mountaineering, nordic skiing, outdoor adventure, outdoor education, outdoor recreation, outdoor skills, outdoors. 4 coaches.

Computers Computers are regularly used in art, college planning, ESL, mathematics, science classes. Computer network features include on-campus library services, online commercial services, Internet access, wireless campus network, Internet filtering or blocking technology. Students grades are available online. The school has a published electronic and media policy.

Contact Molly Dorais, Director of Admission and Financial Aid. 970-963-2562. Fax: 970-963-9865. E-mail: mdorais@crms.org. Web site: www.crms.org.

THE COLORADO SPRINGS SCHOOL

21 Broadmoor Avenue

Colorado Springs, Colorado 80906

Head of School: Mr. Kevin Reel

General Information Coeducational day college-preparatory, arts, and experiential learning school. Grades PK–12. Founded: 1962. Setting: suburban. 30-acre campus. 6 buildings on campus. Approved or accredited by Association of Colorado Independent Schools. Member of National Association of Independent Schools, Secondary School Admission Test Board, and National Association for College Admission Counseling. Endowment: $3.1 million. Total enrollment: 294. Upper school average class size: 16. Upper school faculty-student ratio: 1:6. There are 160 required school days per year for Upper School students. Upper School students typically attend 5 days per week. The average school day consists of 6 hours and 30 minutes.

Upper School Student Profile Grade 9: 23 students (9 boys, 14 girls); Grade 10: 28 students (19 boys, 9 girls); Grade 11: 34 students (11 boys, 23 girls); Grade 12: 28 students (15 boys, 13 girls).

Faculty School total: 46. In upper school: 11 men, 13 women; 18 have advanced degrees.

Subjects Offered 20th century history, acting, African history, African studies, algebra, American literature, anatomy and physiology, art history, band, biology, biology-AP, botany, calculus-AP, chemistry, choir, community service, composition, computer applications, directing, drama, drawing, economics, economics-AP, English, English literature-AP, environmental science, environmental science-AP, ethics, European history-AP, European literature, filmmaking, French, French language-AP, French literature-AP, functions, geography, geology, geometry, glassblowing, global studies, government and politics-AP, grammar, history, Latin American history, literature, macro/microeconomics-AP, microeconomics, music, music appreciation, painting, philosophy, photography, physical education, physics, playwriting, pottery, pre-calculus, printmaking, SAT/ACT preparation, sculpture, Spanish, Spanish literature, Spanish literature-AP, speech, statistics, statistics-AP, studio art-AP, textiles, theater, trigonometry, U.S. history, U.S. history-AP, Western civilization, world geography, world history, world literature, writing, writing workshop, yearbook.

Graduation Requirements Arts and fine arts (art, music, dance, drama), athletics, college admission preparation, English, experiential education, foreign language, mathematics, science, social studies (includes history), speech and oral interpretations, experience-centered seminar each year, college overview course, 24 hours of community service per each year of high school.

Special Academic Programs Advanced Placement exam preparation; honors section; independent study; term-away projects; academic accommodation for the gifted; programs in general development for dyslexic students; special instructional classes for deaf students.

College Admission Counseling 30 students graduated in 2011; all went to college, including Colorado State University; The Colorado College; University of Denver. Mean combined SAT: 1720, mean composite ACT: 26.

Student Life Upper grades have specified standards of dress, student council, honor system. Discipline rests equally with students and faculty.

Summer Programs Enrichment, advancement, sports, art/fine arts, computer instruction programs offered; session focuses on summer; held both on and off campus; held at various field trip locations; accepts boys and girls; open to students from other schools. 90 students usually enrolled. 2012 schedule: May 25 to August 19. Application deadline: none.

Tuition and Aid Day student tuition: $17,900. Tuition installment plan (Insured Tuition Payment Plan, monthly payment plans, individually arranged payment plans). Merit scholarship grants, need-based scholarship grants available. In 2011–12, 43% of upper-school students received aid; total upper-school merit-scholarship money awarded: $61,200. Total amount of financial aid awarded in 2011–12: $492,602.

Admissions Traditional secondary-level entrance grade is 9. For fall 2011, 28 students applied for upper-level admission, 23 were accepted, 11 enrolled. Otis-Lennon School Ability Test or SLEP for foreign students required. Deadline for receipt of application materials: none. Application fee required: $50. Interview required.

Athletics Interscholastic: basketball (boys, girls), cross-country running (b,g), golf (b), ice hockey (b), lacrosse (b), soccer (b,g), tennis (b,g), volleyball (g); intramural: archery (b,g), climbing (b,g), physical fitness (b,g), physical training (b,g); coed intramural: fly fishing, golf, mountaineering, outdoor activities, outdoor education, rock climbing, skiing (cross-country), skiing (downhill), wilderness, yoga. 2 PE instructors, 8 coaches.

Computers Computers are regularly used in all academic classes. Computer network features include on-campus library services, online commercial services, Internet access, wireless campus network, Internet filtering or blocking technology. Campus intranet, student e-mail accounts, and computer access in designated common areas are available to students. Students grades are available online. The school has a published electronic and media policy.

Contact Mrs. Nori Madrigal, Director of Admission and Financial Assistance. 719-475-9747 Ext. 524. Fax: 719-475-9864. E-mail: nmadrigal@css.org. Web site: www.css.org.

COLUMBIA ACADEMY

1101 West 7th Street

Columbia, Tennessee 38401

Head of School: Dr. James Thomas

General Information Coeducational day college-preparatory, arts, business, religious studies, and technology school, affiliated with Church of Christ. Grades K–12. Founded: 1978. Setting: small town. Nearest major city is Nashville. 67-acre campus. 6 buildings on campus. Approved or accredited by National Christian School Association, Southern Association of Colleges and Schools, and Tennessee Department of Education. Endowment: $1.5 million. Total enrollment: 578. Upper school average class size: 18. Upper school faculty-student ratio: 1:11. There are 175 required school days per year for Upper School students. Upper School students typically attend 5 days per week. The average school day consists of 7 hours.

Upper School Student Profile Grade 7: 36 students (16 boys, 20 girls); Grade 8: 44 students (24 boys, 20 girls); Grade 9: 52 students (24 boys, 28 girls); Grade 10: 43 students (23 boys, 20 girls); Grade 11: 27 students (13 boys, 14 girls); Grade 12: 51 students (37 boys, 14 girls). 60% of students are members of Church of Christ.

Faculty School total: 48. In upper school: 13 men, 12 women; 13 have advanced degrees.

Subjects Offered Accounting, advanced math, algebra, American history, American literature, anatomy and physiology, art, band, Bible, biology, British literature, calculus, chemistry, chorus, computer science, concert band, economics, English, English literature and composition-AP, environmental science, fine arts, geometry, government/civics, grammar, health, keyboarding, math review, music, personal finance, physical education, physics, pre-calculus, psychology, religion, Spanish, speech, U.S. history-AP, world geography, world history.

Graduation Requirements Arts and fine arts (art, music, dance, drama), computer science, economics, electives, English, foreign language, mathematics, physical education (includes health), religion (includes Bible studies and theology), science, social sciences, social studies (includes history), speech, successfully pass the state Gateway Exams in Algebra I, English II and Biology (required for students who were freshmen before 2009), four hours of approved service required for each quarter enrolled.

Special Academic Programs Advanced Placement exam preparation; honors section; independent study; study at local college for college credit.

College Admission Counseling 50 students graduated in 2011; 49 went to college, including Austin Peay State University; Columbia State Community College; Freed-Hardeman University; Harding University; Lipscomb University; The University of Tennessee. Other: 1 went to work. Median composite ACT: 23. 20% scored over 26 on composite ACT.

Student Life Upper grades have specified standards of dress, student council, honor system. Discipline rests primarily with faculty.

Summer Programs Remediation programs offered; session focuses on make-up or credit recovery for failing grades during the semsters.; held on campus; accepts boys and girls; not open to students from other schools. 5 students usually enrolled. 2012 schedule: May 29. Application deadline: May 11.

Tuition and Aid Day student tuition: $6100. Tuition installment plan (monthly payment plans, individually arranged payment plans). Tuition reduction for siblings, need-based scholarship grants, paying campus jobs available. In 2011–12, 6% of upper-school students received aid. Total amount of financial aid awarded in 2011–12: $26,250.

Admissions Traditional secondary-level entrance grade is 9. For fall 2011, 24 students applied for upper-level admission, 23 were accepted, 22 enrolled. Otis-Lennon School Ability Test required. Deadline for receipt of application materials: none. Application fee required: $50. On-campus interview recommended.

Athletics Interscholastic: baseball (boys), basketball (b,g), cheering (g), football (b), golf (b,g), soccer (b,g), softball (g), strength & conditioning (b), trap and skeet (b,g), volleyball (g); intramural: flag football (g); coed interscholastic: bowling, cross-country running, marksmanship, tennis. 1 PE instructor.

Computers Computers are regularly used in accounting, computer applications, keyboarding, library, yearbook classes. Computer network features include on-campus library services, Internet access, students in grades 7-12 are issued ipads. Campus intranet and student e-mail accounts are available to students. Students grades are available online. The school has a published electronic and media policy.

Contact Mrs. Emily Lansdell, Director of Admissions. 931-490-4302. Fax: 931-380-8506. E-mail: emily.lansdell@cabulldogs.org. Web site: www.columbia-academy.net.

COLUMBIA INTERNATIONAL COLLEGE OF CANADA

1003 Main Street West

Hamilton, Ontario L8S 4P3, Canada

Head of School: Mr. Ron Rambarran

General Information Coeducational boarding and day college-preparatory, general academic, arts, business, technology, Science, and Mathematics school. Grades 7–12. Founded: 1979. Setting: urban. Nearest major city is Toronto, Canada. Students are housed in single-sex dormitories. 12-acre campus. 3 buildings on campus. Approved or accredited by Ontario Ministry of Education and Ontario Department of Education. Language of instruction: English. Endowment: CAN$1 million. Total enrollment: 1,622. Upper school average class size: 20. Upper school faculty-student ratio: 1:20. There are 208 required school days per year for Upper School students. Upper School students typically attend 5 days per week. The average school day consists of 7 hours and 15 minutes.

Upper School Student Profile Grade 7: 44 students (22 boys, 22 girls); Grade 8: 60 students (30 boys, 30 girls); Grade 9: 96 students (48 boys, 48 girls); Grade 10: 214 students (130 boys, 84 girls); Grade 11: 321 students (206 boys, 115 girls); Grade 12: 887 students (499 boys, 388 girls). 80% of students are boarding students. 5% are province residents. 5 provinces are represented in upper school student body. 95% are international students. International students from China, Indonesia, Mexico, Nigeria, Russian Federation, and Viet Nam; 70 other countries represented in student body.

Faculty School total: 93. In upper school: 38 men, 55 women; 32 have advanced degrees.

Subjects Offered 20th century world history, accounting, advanced TOEFL/grammar, algebra, analytic geometry, anthropology, applied arts, art, band, biology, business, calculus, calculus-AP, Canadian geography, Canadian history, career education, chemistry, Chinese, choir, civics, computer programming, computer science, computer technologies, dance, discrete mathematics, dramatic arts, economics, English, English composition, English literature, ESL, family studies, food and nutrition, French, French as a second language, general business, general math, general science, geography, geometry, history, intro to computers, kinesiology, Korean, lab science, language arts, law, leadership, life skills, Mandarin, marketing, math applications, mathematics, mathematics-AP, music, physical education, physics, psychology, society challenge and change, sociology, Spanish, visual arts.

Graduation Requirements Arts, business, English, mathematics, science, social studies (includes history), Community Volunteer Hours, Ontario Secondary School Literacy Test.

Special Academic Programs 4 Advanced Placement exams for which test preparation is offered; accelerated programs; study at local college for college credit; academic accommodation for the gifted; ESL (316 students enrolled).

College Admission Counseling 770 students graduated in 2011; all went to college, including McMaster University; The University of Western Ontario; University of Alberta; University of Toronto; University of Waterloo; York University.

Student Life Upper grades have uniform requirement, student council. Discipline rests primarily with faculty.

Summer Programs Remediation, advancement, ESL, sports, art/fine arts, computer instruction programs offered; session focuses on academics, ESL, and leadership education; held both on and off campus; held at Bark Lake Outdoor Education and Leadership Centre; accepts boys and girls; open to students from other schools. 700 students usually enrolled. 2012 schedule: July 2 to August 12. Application deadline: May 31.

Tuition and Aid Day student tuition: CAN$12,516–CAN$20,446; 7-day tuition and room/board: CAN$18,621–CAN$33,046. Tuition reduction for siblings, merit scholarship grants, tuition reduction for Canadian citizens and permanent residents available. Total upper-school merit-scholarship money awarded for 2011–12: CAN$45,000.

Admissions Traditional secondary-level entrance grade is 11. For fall 2011, 1,800 students applied for upper-level admission, 1,100 were accepted, 1,046 enrolled. Math Placement Exam and SLEP required. Deadline for receipt of application materials: none. Application fee required: CAN$200. Interview recommended.

Athletics Interscholastic: badminton (boys, girls), basketball (b), indoor soccer (b), soccer (b); intramural: aerobics (g), aquatics (b,g), badminton (b,g), ball hockey (b,g), basketball (b,g), cheering (g), fitness (b,g), floor hockey (b), football (b), indoor soccer (b,g), martial arts (b), outdoor activities (b,g), soccer (b,g), squash (b), strength & conditioning (b), swimming and diving (b,g), table tennis (b,g), volleyball (b,g), weight training (b,g); coed interscholastic: badminton, indoor track & field; coed intramural: aquatics, badminton, ball hockey, canoeing/kayaking, cooperative games, cross-country running, floor hockey, golf, hiking/backpacking, ice skating, in-line skating, indoor track & field, jogging, kayaking, martial arts, outdoor activities, physical fitness, physical training, roller blading, ropes courses, running, self defense, skiing (cross-country), snowshoeing, squash, strength & conditioning, swimming and diving, table tennis, volleyball, wallyball, weight training, wilderness, wilderness survival, winter walking, yoga. 3 PE instructors, 4 coaches.

Computers Computers are regularly used in accounting, business, business applications, career education, economics, English, ESL, geography, information technology, music, SAT preparation, science classes. Computer network features include Internet access, wireless campus network. Computer access in designated common areas is available to students. Students grades are available online.

Contact Ms. Marina Rosas, Admissions Officer. 905-572-7883 Ext. 2835. Fax: 905-572-9332. E-mail: admissions02@cic-totalcare.com. Web site: www.cic-TotalCare.com.

THE COLUMBUS ACADEMY

4300 Cherry Bottom Road

Gahanna, Ohio 43230

Head of School: John M. Mackenzie

General Information Coeducational day college-preparatory school. Grades PK–12. Founded: 1911. Setting: suburban. Nearest major city is Columbus. 233-acre campus. 16 buildings on campus. Approved or accredited by Independent Schools Association of the Central States and Ohio Department of Education. Member of National Association of Independent Schools and Secondary School Admission Test Board. Endowment: $23.5 million. Total enrollment: 1,077. Upper school average class size: 14. Upper school faculty-student ratio: 1:8. The average school day consists of 7 hours and 5 minutes.

Upper School Student Profile Grade 9: 95 students (44 boys, 51 girls); Grade 10: 96 students (54 boys, 42 girls); Grade 11: 82 students (41 boys, 41 girls); Grade 12: 87 students (44 boys, 43 girls).

Faculty School total: 135. In upper school: 27 men, 22 women; 37 have advanced degrees.

Subjects Offered Advanced chemistry, advanced computer applications, advanced math, Advanced Placement courses, advanced studio art-AP, algebra, American history, American history-AP, American literature, analysis and differential calculus, art history, biology, biology-AP, British literature, calculus, calculus-AP, career/college preparation, ceramics, chemistry, chemistry-AP, China/Japan history, Chinese, choir, choral music, chorus, college counseling, comparative government and politics-AP, comparative political systems-AP, computer applications, computer education, computer programming-AP, computer science, computer science-AP, concert band, concert choir, creative writing, drawing and design, economics, economics-AP, English, European history, European history-AP, fine arts, French, French-AP, geology, geometry, government and politics-AP, government-AP, health education, history of China and Japan, instrumental music, Latin, Latin-AP, military history, photography, physical education, physics, physics-AP, pre-calculus, senior career experience, South African history, Spanish, Spanish language-AP, Spanish literature-AP, speech, statistics-AP, strings, theater, trigonometry, U.S. government and politics-AP, U.S. history-AP, United States government-AP, weight training, world history, world religions.

Graduation Requirements Arts and fine arts (art, music, dance, drama), English, foreign language, mathematics, science, social studies (includes history), formal speech delivered to the students and faculty of the upper school during junior year, community service requirement.

Special Academic Programs 23 Advanced Placement exams for which test preparation is offered; honors section; independent study; academic accommodation for the gifted.

College Admission Counseling 93 students graduated in 2011; all went to college, including Kenyon College; Miami University; Northwestern University; The Ohio State University; University of Chicago; University of Richmond. Median SAT critical reading: 640, median SAT math: 670, median SAT writing: 650, median combined SAT: 1970, median composite ACT: 27. 74% scored over 600 on SAT critical reading, 78% scored over 600 on SAT math, 78% scored over 600 on SAT writing, 78% scored over 1800 on combined SAT, 74% scored over 26 on composite ACT.

Student Life Upper grades have specified standards of dress, student council. Discipline rests equally with students and faculty.

Summer Programs Remediation, enrichment, advancement, art/fine arts, computer instruction programs offered; session focuses on academic enrichment, fine arts, fun and games; held on campus; accepts boys and girls; open to students from other schools. 400 students usually enrolled. 2012 schedule: June 15 to August 22.

Tuition and Aid Day student tuition: $20,200. Tuition installment plan (The Tuition Plan, Academic Management Services Plan, Tuition Management Systems Plan). Merit scholarship grants, need-based scholarship grants available. In 2011–12, 18% of upper-school students received aid. Total amount of financial aid awarded in 2011–12: $979,150.

Admissions Traditional secondary-level entrance grade is 9. For fall 2011, 57 students applied for upper-level admission, 34 were accepted, 29 enrolled. ISEE or SSAT required. Deadline for receipt of application materials: February 10. Application fee required: $50. On-campus interview required.

Athletics Interscholastic: baseball (boys), basketball (b,g), bowling (b,g), cross-country running (b,g), diving (b,g), field hockey (g), football (b), lacrosse (b,g), soccer (b,g), swimming and diving (b,g), tennis (b,g), track and field (b,g), volleyball (g), wrestling (b); coed intramural: bicycling. 3 PE instructors, 2 athletic trainers.

Computers Computers are regularly used in college planning, current events, economics, English, foreign language, humanities, journalism, Latin, learning cognition, library skills, mathematics, media production, multimedia, music, photography, publications, reading, research skills, SAT preparation, science, technology, theater, writing, yearbook classes. Computer network features include on-campus library services, online commercial services, Internet access, wireless campus network. Campus intranet, student e-mail accounts, and computer access in designated common areas are available to students. The school has a published electronic and media policy.

Contact John Wuorinen, Director of Admissions and Financial Aid. 614-509-2220. Fax: 614-475-0396. E-mail: admissions@columbusacademy.org. Web site: www.ColumbusAcademy.org.

COLUMBUS SCHOOL FOR GIRLS

56 South Columbia Avenue

Columbus, Ohio 43209

Head of School: Mrs. Elizabeth M. Lee

General Information Girls' day college-preparatory, arts, and technology school. Grades PK–12. Founded: 1898. Setting: urban. 80-acre campus. 1 building on campus. Approved or accredited by Independent Schools Association of the Central States and Ohio Association of Independent Schools. Member of National Association of Independent Schools. Endowment: $22.5 million. Total enrollment: 611. Upper school average class size: 13. Upper school faculty-student ratio: 1:9. There are 180 required school days per year for Upper School students. Upper School students typically attend 5 days per week. The average school day consists of 6 hours and 45 minutes.

Upper School Student Profile Grade 9: 49 students (49 girls); Grade 10: 51 students (51 girls); Grade 11: 60 students (60 girls); Grade 12: 51 students (51 girls).

Faculty School total: 77. In upper school: 7 men, 19 women; 21 have advanced degrees.

Subjects Offered Acting, Advanced Placement courses, algebra, American literature, astronomy, band, biology, biology-AP, British literature, calculus, calculus-AP, ceramics, chemistry, chemistry-AP, civics, college admission preparation, comparative government and politics-AP, computer science, concert choir, digital photography, discrete mathematics, drawing, economics, English, English language and composition-AP, English literature and composition-AP, European history-AP, fine arts, geometry, German, health, lab science, Latin, Latin-AP, Mandarin, modern European history-AP, music theory-AP, newspaper, philosophy, photography, physical education, physics, physics-AP, pre-calculus, public speaking, robotics, senior seminar, Spanish, Spanish language-AP, statistics, strings, studio art-AP, theater, trigonometry, U.S. government and politics-AP, U.S. history, visual arts, vocal ensemble, world history, world literature, world religions, yearbook.

Graduation Requirements Algebra, arts and fine arts (art, music, dance, drama), biology, civics, college planning, computer science, electives, English, foreign language, geometry, history, lab science, mathematics, physical education (includes

health), public speaking, science, technology, U.S. history, world history, Senior May program, service hours, self defense/water safety.
Special Academic Programs Advanced Placement exam preparation; honors section; independent study; study at local college for college credit.
College Admission Counseling 63 students graduated in 2011; all went to college, including Miami University; New York University; The College of Wooster; The Ohio State University; University of Kentucky; University of Richmond. Mean SAT critical reading: 606, mean SAT math: 597, mean SAT writing: 602, mean combined SAT: 1804, mean composite ACT: 27.
Student Life Upper grades have uniform requirement, student council, honor system. Discipline rests primarily with faculty.
Summer Programs Remediation, enrichment, advancement, sports, art/fine arts, rigorous outdoor training, computer instruction programs offered; session focuses on academic areas; held both on and off campus; held at various sites in community and CSG's Kirk Athletic Campus; accepts boys and girls; open to students from other schools. 600 students usually enrolled. 2012 schedule: June 18 to August 10. Application deadline: none.
Tuition and Aid Day student tuition: $19,200–$20,200. Tuition installment plan (Tuition Management Systems Plan). Tuition reduction for siblings, need-based scholarship grants, tuition reduction for three or more siblings available. In 2011–12, 33% of upper-school students received aid. Total amount of financial aid awarded in 2011–12: $720,655.
Admissions Traditional secondary-level entrance grade is 9. For fall 2011, 25 students applied for upper-level admission, 24 were accepted, 19 enrolled. CTP, ISEE or school's own test required. Deadline for receipt of application materials: February 11. Application fee required: $50. On-campus interview required.
Athletics Interscholastic: aquatics, basketball, cross-country running, diving, field hockey, golf, indoor track & field, lacrosse, running, soccer, swimming and diving, tennis, track and field, volleyball, winter (indoor) track; intramural: aquatics, badminton, basketball, bocce, climbing, cooperative games, cricket, field hockey, fitness, fitness walking, flag football, floor hockey, Frisbee, golf, indoor hockey, indoor soccer, indoor track, jogging, kickball, lacrosse, martial arts, physical fitness, physical training, rugby, running, self defense, soccer, softball, strength & conditioning, swimming and diving, synchronized swimming, table tennis, tennis, track and field, ultimate Frisbee, volleyball, walking, weight training, winter soccer, yoga. 4 PE instructors, 25 coaches, 1 athletic trainer.
Computers Computers are regularly used in art, English, foreign language, freshman foundations, health, history, mathematics, music, publications, science, technology, theater, yearbook classes. Computer network features include on-campus library services, online commercial services, Internet access, wireless campus network, Internet filtering or blocking technology. Campus intranet, student e-mail accounts, and computer access in designated common areas are available to students. Students grades are available online. The school has a published electronic and media policy.
Contact Jodie Moriarty, Interim Director of Admission and Financial Aid. 614-252-0781 Ext. 104. Fax: 614-252-0571. E-mail: jmoriarty@columbusschoolforgirls.org. Web site: www.columbusschoolforgirls.org.

COMMONWEALTH PARKVILLE SCHOOL

PO Box 70177

San Juan, Puerto Rico 00936-8177

Head of School: Mr. F. Richard Marracino

General Information Coeducational day college-preparatory, arts, and technology school. Grades PS–12. Founded: 1952. Setting: urban. 1-acre campus. 1 building on campus. Approved or accredited by Middle States Association of Colleges and Schools and Puerto Rico Department of Education. Endowment: $502,005. Total enrollment: 669. Upper school average class size: 13. Upper school faculty-student ratio: 1:7. There are 180 required school days per year for Upper School students. Upper School students typically attend 5 days per week. The average school day consists of 5 hours and 8 minutes.
Upper School Student Profile Grade 9: 39 students (19 boys, 20 girls); Grade 10: 54 students (36 boys, 18 girls); Grade 11: 46 students (26 boys, 20 girls); Grade 12: 39 students (26 boys, 13 girls).
Faculty School total: 30. In upper school: 12 men, 18 women; 13 have advanced degrees.
Subjects Offered Advanced Placement courses, algebra, American history, American literature, art, art history-AP, band, biology, business mathematics, calculus, ceramics, chemistry, chemistry-AP, civics, computer science, computer technologies, creative writing, drama, drawing, ecology, English, English language and composition-AP, English literature, ethics, European history, forensics, French, geometry, health, journalism, mathematics, modern world history, music, music appreciation, music history, painting, physical education, physics, play production, pre-calculus, sculpture, Spanish, Spanish-AP, stained glass, theater, trigonometry, world history.
Graduation Requirements Art, computer science, English, ethics, health, mathematics, music, physical education (includes health), Puerto Rican history, science, social studies (includes history), Spanish, community service hours.
Special Academic Programs 8 Advanced Placement exams for which test preparation is offered; honors section; independent study; domestic exchange program (with The Network Program Schools); study abroad; programs in English, mathematics, general development for dyslexic students; special instructional classes for students with mild learning disabilities and Attention Deficit Disorder.
College Admission Counseling 33 students graduated in 2010; all went to college, including Bentley University; New York University; Swarthmore College; Syracuse University; University of Puerto Rico, Río Piedras; Williams College. Mean SAT critical reading: 560, mean SAT math: 570, mean SAT writing: 575.
Student Life Upper grades have uniform requirement, student council, honor system. Discipline rests primarily with faculty.
Tuition and Aid Day student tuition: $10,204–$12,080. Tuition installment plan (monthly payment plans, individually arranged payment plans, annual and semester payment plans). Tuition reduction for siblings, merit scholarship grants, need-based scholarship grants available. In 2010–11, 16% of upper-school students received aid; total upper-school merit-scholarship money awarded: $36,720. Total amount of financial aid awarded in 2010–11: $81,560.
Admissions Traditional secondary-level entrance grade is 9. For fall 2010, 34 students applied for upper-level admission, 32 were accepted, 26 enrolled. Math and English placement tests, Stanford Achievement Test and writing sample required. Deadline for receipt of application materials: none. Application fee required: $85. Interview required.
Athletics Interscholastic: baseball (boys), basketball (b,g), cross-country running (b,g), football (b), indoor soccer (b,g), soccer (b,g), softball (g), track and field (b,g), volleyball (b,g); intramural: soccer (b,g), softball (b,g), volleyball (b,g); coed interscholastic: swimming and diving; coed intramural: badminton, basketball, cooperative games, field hockey, fitness, flag football, Frisbee, indoor soccer, jogging, outdoor activities, outdoor education, outdoor recreation, physical fitness, physical training, soccer, softball, strength & conditioning, table tennis, tennis, track and field, volleyball, walking. 3 PE instructors, 9 coaches.
Computers Computers are regularly used in all academic, music, yearbook classes. Computer network features include on-campus library services, Internet access, wireless campus network, Internet filtering or blocking technology. Campus intranet, student e-mail accounts, and computer access in designated common areas are available to students. Students grades are available online. The school has a published electronic and media policy.
Contact Mrs. Jo-Ann Aranguren, Director of Admissions. 787-765-4411 Ext. 232. Fax: 787-764-3809. E-mail: jaranguren@cpspr.org. Web site: www.cpspr.org.

COMMONWEALTH SCHOOL

151 Commonwealth Avenue

Boston, Massachusetts 02116

Head of School: Mr. William D. Wharton

General Information Coeducational day college-preparatory school. Grades 9–12. Founded: 1957. Setting: urban. 1 building on campus. Approved or accredited by Association of Independent Schools in New England, New England Association of Schools and Colleges, and Massachusetts Department of Education. Member of National Association of Independent Schools and Secondary School Admission Test Board. Endowment: $14 million. Total enrollment: 149. Upper school average class size: 12. Upper school faculty-student ratio: 1:5. Upper School students typically attend 5 days per week. The average school day consists of 6 hours and 30 minutes.
Upper School Student Profile Grade 9: 39 students (18 boys, 21 girls); Grade 10: 36 students (15 boys, 21 girls); Grade 11: 37 students (23 boys, 14 girls); Grade 12: 37 students (19 boys, 18 girls).
Faculty School total: 36. In upper school: 14 men, 19 women; 26 have advanced degrees.
Subjects Offered 20th century American writers, 20th century history, acting, advanced biology, advanced chemistry, advanced computer applications, advanced math, Advanced Placement courses, African-American literature, algebra, American history, American history-AP, American literature, analysis and differential calculus, analysis of data, analytic geometry, ancient history, ancient world history, art, art history, biology, biology-AP, calculus, calculus-AP, ceramics, chamber groups, chemistry, chemistry-AP, choral music, chorus, classics, college counseling, community service, computer programming, computer science, constitutional law, creative writing, current events, dance, drama, drawing, economics, economics-AP, English, English literature, English-AP, environmental science, environmental studies, ethics, European history, European history-AP, expository writing, film series, film studies, fine arts, foreign language, French, French language-AP, French literature-AP, French studies, French-AP, geometry, Greek, health and safety, Hispanic literature, history of the Americas, history-AP, honors algebra, honors English, honors geometry, honors U.S. history, Japanese history, jazz, jazz band, jazz ensemble, jazz theory, Latin, Latin American history, Latin-AP, mathematics, mathematics-AP, medieval history, medieval/Renaissance history, modern European history-AP, music, music theory, music theory-AP, orchestra, organic chemistry, painting, performing arts, philosophy, photography, physical education, physics, physics-AP, poetry, pottery, pre-calculus, printmaking, probability and statistics, psychology, Russian literature, science, short story, society, politics and law, Spanish, Spanish language-AP, Spanish literature, Spanish literature-AP, Spanish-AP, studio art, tap dance, theater, U.S. history-AP, visual and performing arts, visual arts, vocal music, voice, voice ensemble, writing.

Graduation Requirements Algebra, ancient history, art, biology, calculus, chemistry, English, ethics, foreign language, geometry, medieval history, physical education (includes health), physics, U.S. history, City of Boston course, completion of a one- to three-week project each year (with report), Health and Community. Community service is required.
Special Academic Programs Advanced Placement exam preparation; honors section; independent study; term-away projects; study abroad; academic accommodation for the gifted, the musically talented, and the artistically talented.
College Admission Counseling 37 students graduated in 2011; 36 went to college, including Brown University; Haverford College; Reed College; Smith College; University of Chicago. Other: 1 had other specific plans. Median SAT critical reading: 740, median SAT math: 740, median SAT writing: 720.
Student Life Discipline rests primarily with faculty.
Tuition and Aid Day student tuition: $33,080. Tuition installment plan (Key Tuition Payment Plan). Need-based scholarship grants, need-based loans available. In 2011–12, 34% of upper-school students received aid. Total amount of financial aid awarded in 2011–12: $1,108,002.
Admissions Traditional secondary-level entrance grade is 9. For fall 2011, 184 students applied for upper-level admission, 77 were accepted, 42 enrolled. ISEE or SSAT required. Deadline for receipt of application materials: February 1. Application fee required: $50. On-campus interview required.
Athletics Interscholastic: basketball (boys, girls), independent competitive sports (b,g), soccer (b,g); coed interscholastic: baseball, cross-country running, fencing, squash, ultimate Frisbee; coed intramural: aerobics/Nautilus, ballet, cross-country running, dance, fencing, fitness, martial arts, sailing, squash, tai chi, yoga. 12 coaches.
Computers Computers are regularly used in computer applications, photography, programming classes. Computer network features include on-campus library services, online commercial services, Internet access, wireless campus network, Internet filtering or blocking technology. Campus intranet, student e-mail accounts, and computer access in designated common areas are available to students. The school has a published electronic and media policy.
Contact Ms. Robyn Gibson, Assistant Director of Admissions. 617-266-7525. Fax: 617-266-5769. E-mail: admissions@commschool.org. Web site: www.commschool.org.

COMMUNITY CHRISTIAN ACADEMY

11875 Taylor Mill Road

Independence, Kentucky 41051

Head of School: Tara Montez Bates

General Information Coeducational day college-preparatory and religious studies school, affiliated with Pentecostal Church. Grades PS–12. Founded: 1983. Setting: rural. Nearest major city is Cincinnati, OH. 112-acre campus. 2 buildings on campus. Approved or accredited by International Christian Accrediting Association and Kentucky Department of Education. Total enrollment: 254. Upper school average class size: 15. Upper school faculty-student ratio: 1:15. There are 175 required school days per year for Upper School students. Upper School students typically attend 5 days per week. The average school day consists of 6 hours.
Upper School Student Profile Grade 9: 8 students (8 girls); Grade 10: 12 students (8 boys, 4 girls); Grade 11: 18 students (9 boys, 9 girls); Grade 12: 15 students (10 boys, 5 girls). 50% of students are Pentecostal.
Faculty School total: 14. In upper school: 1 man, 5 women; 2 have advanced degrees.
Subjects Offered Advanced biology, advanced math, algebra, American history, art appreciation, Bible, biology, business skills, calculus, chemistry, choral music, computer applications, cultural geography, English, geography, health, integrated science, life skills, literature, pre-algebra, pre-calculus, Spanish.
Graduation Requirements Bible, electives, English, foreign language, mathematics, physical education (includes health), science, social studies (includes history), statistics, visual and performing arts.
College Admission Counseling 11 students graduated in 2011; 9 went to college, including Cincinnati State Technical and Community College; Northern Kentucky University; University of Cincinnati. Other: 1 went to work, 1 entered military service. Mean composite ACT: 21. 20% scored over 26 on composite ACT.
Student Life Upper grades have uniform requirement, student council, honor system. Discipline rests primarily with faculty. Attendance at religious services is required.
Tuition and Aid Day student tuition: $3249. Guaranteed tuition plan. Tuition installment plan (The Tuition Plan, monthly payment plans). Financial aid available to upper-school students. In 2011–12, 5% of upper-school students received aid. Total amount of financial aid awarded in 2011–12: $9000.
Admissions Traditional secondary-level entrance grade is 9. For fall 2011, 12 students applied for upper-level admission, 9 were accepted, 9 enrolled. Admissions testing required. Deadline for receipt of application materials: none. Application fee required: $50. Interview required.
Athletics Interscholastic: basketball (boys, girls), cheering (g), golf (b), volleyball (g); coed interscholastic: archery, flag football. 2 PE instructors, 10 coaches.
Computers Computers are regularly used in foreign language classes. Computer network features include Internet access.
Contact Edie Carkeek, Secretary. 859-356-7990 Ext. 112. Fax: 859-356-7991. E-mail: edie.carkeek@ccaky.org. Web site: www.ccaky.org.

COMMUNITY HEBREW ACADEMY

200 Wilmington Avenue

Toronto, Ontario M3H 5J8, Canada

Head of School: Mr. Paul Shaviv

General Information Coeducational day college-preparatory, general academic, arts, religious studies, and technology school, affiliated with Jewish faith. Grades 9–12. Founded: 1964. Setting: urban. 6-acre campus. 2 buildings on campus. Approved or accredited by Ontario Department of Education. Language of instruction: English. Endowment: CAN$250,000. Total enrollment: 1,400. Upper school average class size: 22. Upper school faculty-student ratio: 1:8. There are 185 required school days per year for Upper School students. Upper School students typically attend 5 days per week. The average school day consists of 8 hours.
Upper School Student Profile 100% of students are Jewish.
Faculty School total: 195. In upper school: 85 men, 110 women; 40 have advanced degrees.
Subjects Offered Accounting, American history, art, athletics, biology, business, calculus, Canadian history, Canadian law, careers, chemistry, communications, computer information systems, computer technologies, creative writing, discrete mathematics, drama, economics, English, entrepreneurship, exercise science, first aid, French, general math, geography, health education, Hebrew, Hebrew scripture, Holocaust, information technology, interdisciplinary studies, Jewish history, mathematics, media studies, modern Western civilization, peer counseling, personal fitness, physical education, physics, Rabbinic literature, remedial study skills, social studies, Spanish, Talmud.
Graduation Requirements English, 72 hours of community service over 4 years.
Special Academic Programs ESL (2 students enrolled).
College Admission Counseling 300 students graduated in 2010; 270 went to college, including McGill University; Queen's University at Kingston; The University of Western Ontario; University of Guelph; University of Toronto; York University. Other: 30 had other specific plans.
Student Life Upper grades have specified standards of dress, student council. Discipline rests primarily with faculty.
Tuition and Aid Day student tuition: CAN$20,100. Tuition installment plan (monthly payment plans, individually arranged payment plans, individual payment plans). Need-based scholarship grants, need-based loans available. In 2010–11, 25% of upper-school students received aid. Total amount of financial aid awarded in 2010–11: CAN$2,000,000.
Admissions Traditional secondary-level entrance grade is 9. For fall 2010, 400 students applied for upper-level admission, 357 enrolled. Math and English placement tests and writing sample required. Deadline for receipt of application materials: January 14. Application fee required: CAN$150. On-campus interview required.
Athletics Interscholastic: baseball (boys), basketball (b,g), field hockey (g), flag football (b), ice hockey (b,g), rugby (b), soccer (b,g), softball (b), tennis (b,g), volleyball (b,g); coed interscholastic: alpine skiing, cross-country running, curling, golf, skiing (cross-country), skiing (downhill), snowboarding. 10 PE instructors.
Computers Computers are regularly used in business applications, information technology, media classes. Computer resources include on-campus library services, Internet access. Computer access in designated common areas is available to students. Students grades are available online.
Contact Ms. Jill Garazi, Admissions Coordinator. 905-787-8772 Ext. 2509. Fax: 905-787-8773. E-mail: jgarazi@tanenbaumchat.org. Web site: www.tanenbaumchat.org.

COMMUNITY HIGH SCHOOL

Teaneck, New Jersey

See Special Needs Schools section.

THE COMMUNITY SCHOOL OF NAPLES

13275 Livingston Road

Naples, Florida 34109

Head of School: Mr. John E. Zeller Jr.

General Information Coeducational day college-preparatory and arts school. Grades PK–12. Founded: 1982. Setting: suburban. Nearest major city is Miami. 110-acre campus. 3 buildings on campus. Approved or accredited by Florida Department of Education. Member of National Association of Independent Schools and Secondary School Admission Test Board. Endowment: $9.4 million. Total enrollment: 725. Upper school average class size: 12. Upper school faculty-student ratio: 1:7. There are 172 required school days per year for Upper School students. Upper School students typically attend 5 days per week. The average school day consists of 6 hours.

Upper School Student Profile Grade 9: 81 students (50 boys, 31 girls); Grade 10: 68 students (27 boys, 41 girls); Grade 11: 60 students (35 boys, 25 girls); Grade 12: 72 students (35 boys, 37 girls).
Faculty School total: 103. In upper school: 22 men, 25 women; 29 have advanced degrees.
Subjects Offered Algebra, American government, American history, American history-AP, American literature, American literature-AP, anatomy and physiology, art, band, biology, biology-AP, calculus, calculus-AP, chemistry, chemistry-AP, chorus, clayworking, comparative government and politics-AP, computer programming, computer science, computer science-AP, creative writing, digital photography, dramatic arts, drawing, economics, economics-AP, electives, English, English language and composition-AP, English language-AP, English literature and composition-AP, English literature-AP, English-AP, English/composition-AP, environmental science-AP, European history-AP, fine arts, French, French language-AP, French literature-AP, French-AP, geometry, government and politics-AP, government-AP, government/civics-AP, graphic design, health, history, history-AP, honors algebra, honors English, honors geometry, honors U.S. history, honors world history, Italian, jazz band, Latin, marine science, mathematics, mathematics-AP, music, music theory-AP, painting, performing arts, personal fitness, photography, physical education, physics, physics-AP, pre-calculus, psychology, science, Spanish, Spanish language-AP, Spanish literature-AP, Spanish-AP, statistics-AP, strings, studio art-AP, theater, U.S. government and politics-AP, U.S. history-AP, vocal music, Web site design, world history, world literature.
Graduation Requirements Arts and fine arts (art, music, dance, drama), computer science, electives, English, foreign language, history, mathematics, physical education (includes health), science, community service–20 per year.
Special Academic Programs 23 Advanced Placement exams for which test preparation is offered; honors section; independent study; study at local college for college credit; study abroad.
College Admission Counseling 75 students graduated in 2011; all went to college, including Eckerd College; Florida State University; Princeton University; University of Florida; University of Miami; Washington University in St. Louis. Mean SAT critical reading: 604, mean SAT math: 645, mean SAT writing: 612, mean combined SAT: 1861, mean composite ACT: 27. 37% scored over 600 on SAT critical reading, 45% scored over 600 on SAT math, 40% scored over 600 on SAT writing, 41% scored over 1800 on combined SAT, 38% scored over 26 on composite ACT.
Student Life Upper grades have specified standards of dress, student council, honor system. Discipline rests equally with students and faculty.
Summer Programs Remediation, enrichment, ESL, sports, art/fine arts programs offered; session focuses on mathematics, English, and SAT preparation, sports; held on campus; accepts boys and girls; open to students from other schools. 75 students usually enrolled. 2012 schedule: June 13 to August 9. Application deadline: April 15.
Tuition and Aid Day student tuition: $22,350. Tuition installment plan (Insured Tuition Payment Plan, monthly payment plans, individually arranged payment plans). Merit scholarship grants, need-based scholarship grants available. In 2011–12, 31% of upper-school students received aid; total upper-school merit-scholarship money awarded: $70,000. Total amount of financial aid awarded in 2011–12: $1,091,586.
Admissions Traditional secondary-level entrance grade is 9. For fall 2011, 56 students applied for upper-level admission, 50 were accepted, 39 enrolled. School's own exam or SSAT required. Deadline for receipt of application materials: February 1. Application fee required: $100. On-campus interview required.
Athletics Interscholastic: baseball (boys), basketball (b,g), cheering (g), cross-country running (b,g), diving (b,g), football (b), golf (b,g), lacrosse (b), soccer (b,g), softball (g), swimming and diving (b,g), tennis (b,g), track and field (b,g), volleyball (g), winter soccer (b,g); intramural: cheering (g), cross-country running (g), football (b), lacrosse (g); coed intramural: rock climbing, sailing, weight training. 4 PE instructors, 45 coaches, 1 athletic trainer.
Computers Computers are regularly used in art, computer applications, creative writing, design, desktop publishing, digital applications, English, foreign language, history, mathematics, music, science, Web site design, writing, writing, yearbook classes. Computer network features include on-campus library services, Internet access, wireless campus network, Internet filtering or blocking technology. Campus intranet, student e-mail accounts, and computer access in designated common areas are available to students. The school has a published electronic and media policy.
Contact Mr. Scott Vasey, Director of Admissions. 239-597-7575 Ext. 205. Fax: 239-598-2973. E-mail: Svasey@communityschoolnaples.org. Web site: www.communityschoolnaples.org.

THE CONCEPT SCHOOL

1120 E. Street Rd

PO Box 54

Westtown, Pennsylvania 19395

Head of School: Mrs. Lauren Vangieri

General Information Coeducational day college-preparatory, general academic, arts, vocational, and technology school. Grades 6–12. Founded: 1972. Setting: suburban. Nearest major city is Philadelphia. 10-acre campus. 1 building on campus. Approved or accredited by Pennsylvania Department of Education. Endowment: $75,000. Total enrollment: 33. Upper school average class size: 8. Upper school faculty-student ratio: 1:8. There are 180 required school days per year for Upper School students. Upper School students typically attend 5 days per week. The average school day consists of 6 hours and 30 minutes.
Upper School Student Profile Grade 9: 3 students (3 boys); Grade 10: 7 students (6 boys, 1 girl); Grade 11: 5 students (5 boys); Grade 12: 9 students (8 boys, 1 girl).
Faculty School total: 12. In upper school: 3 men, 4 women; 4 have advanced degrees.
Subjects Offered 20th century world history, acting, advanced computer applications, algebra, American history, art, art history, biology, career and personal planning, chemistry, computer graphics, consumer mathematics, criminal justice, cultural arts, earth science, economics, English, environmental science, film, film appreciation, fine arts, foreign language, general science, geometry, government, government/civics, health, history, human development, independent study, keyboarding, lab science, language arts, Latin, mathematics, physical education, physics, physiology, pre-algebra, pre-calculus, psychology, science, Shakespeare, social sciences, social studies, trigonometry, U.S. government, visual arts.
Graduation Requirements Arts and fine arts (art, music, dance, drama), computer science, English, mathematics, physical education (includes health), science, social sciences, social studies (includes history).
Special Academic Programs Accelerated programs; independent study; study at local college for college credit; academic accommodation for the gifted and the artistically talented; remedial reading and/or remedial writing; remedial math; programs in English, mathematics, general development for dyslexic students; special instructional classes for deaf students, blind students, students with learning differences, Attention Deficit Disorder, Asperger's Syndrome, school phobia, dyslexia, Attention Deficit Hyperactivity Disorder, and Non-verbal Learning Disorder.
College Admission Counseling 5 students graduated in 2011; 4 went to college, including Neumann University; Pennsylvania State University System. Other: 1 went to work. Mean SAT critical reading: 490, mean SAT math: 480, mean SAT writing: 470.
Student Life Upper grades have specified standards of dress, honor system. Discipline rests primarily with faculty.
Tuition and Aid Day student tuition: $18,500. Tuition installment plan (monthly payment plans). Tuition reduction for siblings available.
Admissions Traditional secondary-level entrance grade is 9. For fall 2011, 20 students applied for upper-level admission, 7 were accepted, 7 enrolled. Math and English placement tests, WAIS, WICS and WISC/Woodcock-Johnson required. Deadline for receipt of application materials: none. Application fee required: $50. On-campus interview required.
Athletics Coed Intramural: aerobics, basketball, bowling, ice skating, in-line skating, physical fitness, physical training, roller skating, skiing (downhill), snowboarding, yoga. 1 PE instructor.
Computers Computers are regularly used in all academic classes. Computer network features include on-campus library services, Internet access, wireless campus network, Internet filtering or blocking technology. Campus intranet is available to students. The school has a published electronic and media policy.
Contact Mrs. Carol McAdam, School Secretary. 610-399-1135. Fax: 610-399-0767. E-mail: cmcadam@theconceptschool.org. Web site: www.theconceptschool.org.

CONCORD ACADEMY

166 Main Street

Concord, Massachusetts 01742

Head of School: Rick Hardy

General Information Coeducational boarding and day college-preparatory and arts school. Grades 9–12. Founded: 1922. Setting: suburban. Nearest major city is Boston. Students are housed in single-sex dormitories. 39-acre campus. 29 buildings on campus. Approved or accredited by New England Association of Schools and Colleges, The Association of Boarding Schools, and Massachusetts Department of Education. Member of National Association of Independent Schools and Secondary School Admission Test Board. Endowment: $55 million. Total enrollment: 363. Upper school average class size: 12. Upper school faculty-student ratio: 1:6. Upper School students typically attend 5 days per week. The average school day consists of 6 hours and 30 minutes.
Upper School Student Profile Grade 9: 74 students (33 boys, 41 girls); Grade 10: 99 students (46 boys, 53 girls); Grade 11: 94 students (45 boys, 49 girls); Grade 12: 95 students (46 boys, 49 girls). 42% of students are boarding students. 73% are state residents. 12 states are represented in upper school student body. 10% are international students. International students from Canada, China, Indonesia, Republic of Korea, Taiwan, and Thailand; 2 other countries represented in student body.
Faculty School total: 63. In upper school: 29 men, 34 women; 46 have advanced degrees; 26 reside on campus.
Subjects Offered 20th century American writers, 3-dimensional art, advanced chemistry, advanced math, African history, African-American literature, algebra, American history, American literature, ancient history, ancient world history, anthropology, applied music, architecture, art, art history, Asian history, astronomy, astrophysics, batik, Bible as literature, biochemistry, biology, bookmaking, British literature, calculus, ceramics, chamber groups, chemistry, Chinese history, choreography, chorus, classical civilization, classical Greek literature, classical language, computer multi-

media, computer programming, computer science, computer studies, creative writing, critical studies in film, dance, dance performance, digital imaging, directing, drama, drama performance, drawing, earth science, economics, English, English literature, environmental science, environmental studies, European history, experimental science, expository writing, fiber arts, fiction, film, film history, filmmaking, forensics, French, freshman seminar, geology, geometry, German, German literature, guitar, health and wellness, history, history of China and Japan, history of music, Holocaust, HTML design, improvisation, instruments, introduction to digital multitrack recording techniques, Irish literature, Islamic history, jazz ensemble, journalism, Latin, Latin American history, Latin American literature, life management skills, literature seminar, math analysis, mathematics, medieval/Renaissance history, Middle East, Middle Eastern history, model United Nations, modern dance, modern European history, modern languages, music, music composition, music history, music technology, music theory, musical productions, neuroscience, newspaper, novels, oceanography, orchestra, painting, performing arts, philosophy, photography, physical education, physics, piano, play/screen writing, poetry, post-calculus, pre-calculus, printmaking, probability and statistics, Roman civilization, science, science fiction, sculpture, senior project, sex education, Shakespeare, Spanish, Spanish literature, statistics, student publications, studio art, technical theater, theater, theater design and production, theater history, trigonometry, U.S. history, urban studies, visual arts, voice, Web site design, wind ensemble, writing.

Graduation Requirements Computer science, English, foreign language, history, mathematics, performing arts, physical education (includes health), science, visual arts.

Special Academic Programs Honors section; independent study; term-away projects; study abroad; academic accommodation for the gifted, the musically talented, and the artistically talented.

College Admission Counseling 97 students graduated in 2011; all went to college, including Barnard College; Brown University; Columbia College; Skidmore College; Tufts University; Yale University. Mean SAT critical reading: 690, mean SAT math: 691, mean SAT writing: 691, mean combined SAT: 2071.

Student Life Upper grades have student council, honor system. Discipline rests equally with students and faculty.

Tuition and Aid Day student tuition: $38,850; 7-day tuition and room/board: $48,050. Guaranteed tuition plan. Tuition installment plan (Key Tuition Payment Plan, monthly payment plans). Need-based scholarship grants, need-based loans available. In 2011–12, 24% of upper-school students received aid. Total amount of financial aid awarded in 2011–12: $3,340,000.

Admissions Traditional secondary-level entrance grade is 9. For fall 2011, 776 students applied for upper-level admission, 256 were accepted, 100 enrolled. ISEE, SSAT or TOEFL required. Deadline for receipt of application materials: January 15. Application fee required: $50. Interview recommended.

Athletics Interscholastic: baseball (boys), basketball (b,g), cross-country running (b,g), field hockey (g), lacrosse (g), skiing (downhill) (b,g), soccer (b,g), squash (g), tennis (b,g), volleyball (g), wrestling (b); intramural: softball (g), squash (b); coed interscholastic: alpine skiing, golf, lacrosse, ultimate Frisbee; coed intramural: aerobics, aerobics/dance, ballet, canoeing/kayaking, combined training, cross-country running, dance, fencing, fitness, jogging, martial arts, modern dance, outdoor activities, physical fitness, physical training, sailing, self defense, skiing (downhill), strength & conditioning, track and field, ultimate Frisbee, weight training, yoga. 8 PE instructors, 35 coaches, 2 athletic trainers.

Computers Computers are regularly used in English, foreign language, history, library skills, mathematics, music, newspaper, science, social studies, technology, video film production, Web site design, yearbook classes. Computer network features include on-campus library services, online commercial services, Internet access, wireless campus network, Internet filtering or blocking technology. Campus intranet, student e-mail accounts, and computer access in designated common areas are available to students. Students grades are available online. The school has a published electronic and media policy.

Contact Marie D. Myers, Director of Admissions. 978-402-2250. Fax: 978-402-2345. E-mail: admissions@concordacademy.org. Web site: www.concordacademy.org.

CONCORDIA HIGH SCHOOL

7128 Ada Boulevard

Edmonton, Alberta T5B 4E4, Canada

Head of School: Mr. David Eifert

General Information Coeducational boarding and day college-preparatory, arts, and religious studies school, affiliated with Lutheran Church. Grades 9–12. Founded: 1921. Setting: urban. Students are housed in single-sex dormitories. 12-acre campus. 1 building on campus. Approved or accredited by Association of Independent Schools and Colleges of Alberta, Canadian Association of Independent Schools, and Alberta Department of Education. Languages of instruction: English and French. Total enrollment: 137. Upper school average class size: 16. Upper school faculty-student ratio: 1:10.

Upper School Student Profile 24% of students are boarding students. International students from Brazil, Hong Kong, Mexico, Republic of Korea, Thailand, and United States; 6 other countries represented in student body. 12% of students are Lutheran.

Faculty School total: 15. In upper school: 5 men, 10 women; 7 have advanced degrees.

Subjects Offered Art, athletics, biology, career and personal planning, chemistry, choir, Christian education, drama, drama performance, English, French, information processing, mathematics, media arts, physical education, physics, religious studies, service learning/internship, social studies.

Graduation Requirements Advanced chemistry, advanced math, arts and fine arts (art, music, dance, drama), Christian education, French, language, religious studies.

Special Academic Programs Study at local college for college credit.

College Admission Counseling 42 students graduated in 2010; 39 went to college. Other: 3 went to work.

Student Life Upper grades have uniform requirement, student council. Discipline rests primarily with faculty. Attendance at religious services is required.

Admissions TOEFL or SLEP required. Deadline for receipt of application materials: none. Application fee required: CAN$150. Interview required.

Athletics Interscholastic: basketball (boys, girls); intramural: basketball (b,g), soccer (b,g), volleyball (b,g); coed interscholastic: badminton, fitness, lacrosse; coed intramural: alpine skiing, canoeing/kayaking, cheering, cross-country running, curling, golf, outdoor activities, physical fitness.

Computers Computers are regularly used in media arts classes.

Contact Mr. Keith Kruse, Dean of Operations. 780-479-9392. Fax: 780-479-5050. E-mail: keith.kruse@concordia.ab.ca. Web site: www.concordiahighschool.com.

CONCORDIA LUTHERAN HIGH SCHOOL

1601 Saint Joe River Drive

Fort Wayne, Indiana 46805

Head of School: Mr. Terry Breininger

General Information Coeducational day college-preparatory and religious studies school, affiliated with Lutheran Church–Missouri Synod. Grades 9–12. Founded: 1935. Setting: urban. Nearest major city is Indianapolis. 3 buildings on campus. Approved or accredited by National Lutheran School Accreditation, North Central Association of Colleges and Schools, and Indiana Department of Education. Total enrollment: 684. Upper school average class size: 22. Upper school faculty-student ratio: 1:22. There are 180 required school days per year for Upper School students. Upper School students typically attend 5 days per week. The average school day consists of 7 hours and 5 minutes.

Upper School Student Profile Grade 9: 187 students (97 boys, 90 girls); Grade 10: 166 students (85 boys, 81 girls); Grade 11: 177 students (82 boys, 95 girls); Grade 12: 154 students (70 boys, 84 girls). 80% of students are Lutheran Church–Missouri Synod.

Faculty School total: 41. In upper school: 20 men, 21 women; 21 have advanced degrees.

Subjects Offered 3-dimensional art, Advanced Placement courses, algebra, American history, American literature, art, band, Bible studies, biology, biology-AP, broadcasting, business, calculus, calculus-AP, ceramics, chemistry, chemistry-AP, choir, computer science, creative writing, discrete mathematics, driver education, earth science, economics, English, English literature, English literature and composition-AP, entrepreneurship, environmental science, ethics, expository writing, family and consumer science, food and nutrition, French, geography, geometry, German, government/civics, grammar, health, health and safety, history, home economics, honors algebra, honors English, honors geometry, internship, journalism, JROTC, JROTC or LEAD (Leadership Education and Development), keyboarding, Latin, marching band, mathematics, media arts, media communications, microeconomics-AP, music, newspaper, painting, physical education, physics, physics-AP, psychology, religion, science, social sciences, social studies, sociology, Spanish, speech, statistics-AP, theater, theater arts, theology, typing, U.S. government, U.S. history, U.S. history-AP, video film production, weight training, world history, world literature, writing, yearbook.

Graduation Requirements English, foreign language, mathematics, physical education (includes health), religion (includes Bible studies and theology), science, social sciences, social studies (includes history). Community service is required.

Special Academic Programs Advanced Placement exam preparation; honors section; independent study; study at local college for college credit; programs in English, mathematics, general development for dyslexic students.

College Admission Counseling 146 students graduated in 2011; 135 went to college, including Ball State University; Indiana University–Purdue University Fort Wayne; Indiana University Bloomington; Purdue University; Valparaiso University. Other: 4 went to work, 3 entered military service, 4 had other specific plans. Mean SAT critical reading: 523, mean SAT math: 567, mean SAT writing: 511.

Student Life Upper grades have uniform requirement, student council. Discipline rests primarily with faculty. Attendance at religious services is required.

Summer Programs Remediation, advancement, sports, art/fine arts programs offered; session focuses on summer classes, drivers ed, summer conditioning and sports camps; held both on and off campus; held at various locations based on sport; accepts boys and girls; open to students from other schools.

Tuition and Aid Day student tuition: $6825–$8275. Tuition installment plan (FACTS Tuition Payment Plan, monthly payment plans, individually arranged payment plans, NBD bank loan). Tuition reduction for siblings, merit scholarship grants, need-based scholarship grants available.

Admissions Deadline for receipt of application materials: none. Application fee required: $35. On-campus interview recommended.

Athletics Interscholastic: baseball (boys), basketball (b,g), cheering (g), cross-country running (b,g), dance team (g), diving (b,g), football (b), golf (b,g), gymnastics (g), soccer (b,g), softball (g), swimming and diving (b,g), tennis (b,g), track and field (b,g), volleyball (g); coed interscholastic: bowling, crew, JROTC drill, riflery; coed intramural: volleyball. 3 PE instructors, 50 coaches, 1 athletic trainer.

Computers Computers are regularly used in all academic, English, mathematics, newspaper, religion, yearbook classes. Computer resources include on-campus library services, Internet access, wireless campus network. Student e-mail accounts and computer access in designated common areas are available to students. Students grades are available online.

Contact Mrs. Krista Friend, Enrollment Management Coordinator. 260-483-1102. Fax: 260-471-0180. E-mail: kfriend@clhscadets.com. Web site: www.clhscadets.com.

CONCORDIA PREPARATORY SCHOOL

4020 South 900 East

Salt Lake City, Utah 84124-1169

Head of School: Mr. Charles Gebhardt

General Information Coeducational day and distance learning college-preparatory, general academic, and religious studies school, affiliated with Lutheran Church. Grades 9–12. Distance learning grades 11–12. Founded: 1984. Setting: urban. 3-acre campus. 1 building on campus. Approved or accredited by National Lutheran School Accreditation, Northwest Accreditation Commission, Northwest Association of Schools and Colleges, and Utah Department of Education. Total enrollment: 58. Upper school average class size: 13. Upper school faculty-student ratio: 1:7. There are 180 required school days per year for Upper School students. Upper School students typically attend 5 days per week. The average school day consists of 6 hours and 45 minutes.

Upper School Student Profile Grade 9: 10 students (5 boys, 5 girls); Grade 10: 12 students (10 boys, 2 girls); Grade 11: 13 students (6 boys, 7 girls); Grade 12: 23 students (12 boys, 11 girls). 40% of students are Lutheran.

Faculty School total: 10. In upper school: 4 men, 6 women; 7 have advanced degrees.

Subjects Offered Advanced biology, advanced chemistry, advanced computer applications, advanced math, Advanced Placement courses, algebra, American history, American literature, art, band, bell choir, Bible studies, biology, calculus, chemistry, chorus, computer science, drama, English, general science, geography, geometry, government/civics, health, journalism, keyboarding, literature, mathematics, novels, physical education, physics, psychology, religion, science, social sciences, sociology, Spanish, speech, vocal music, word processing, world history, world literature.

Graduation Requirements Arts and fine arts (art, music, dance, drama), business skills (includes word processing), computer science, English, mathematics, physical education (includes health), religion (includes Bible studies and theology), science, social sciences.

Special Academic Programs Honors section; accelerated programs; independent study; academic accommodation for the gifted; remedial reading and/or remedial writing.

College Admission Counseling 22 students graduated in 2010; all went to college, including Boise State University; Concordia College; Southern Utah University; University of Utah; Utah State University; Westminster College. Median composite ACT: 24. 23% scored over 26 on composite ACT.

Student Life Upper grades have specified standards of dress, student council, honor system. Discipline rests equally with students and faculty. Attendance at religious services is required.

Tuition and Aid Day student tuition: $8300. Tuition installment plan (monthly payment plans). Tuition reduction for siblings, merit scholarship grants, need-based scholarship grants available. In 2010–11, 60% of upper-school students received aid; total upper-school merit-scholarship money awarded: $4000. Total amount of financial aid awarded in 2010–11: $99,000.

Admissions Traditional secondary-level entrance grade is 9. For fall 2010, 65 students applied for upper-level admission, 58 were accepted, 58 enrolled. School placement exam, SLEP for foreign students, TOEFL or SLEP or writing sample required. Deadline for receipt of application materials: none. Application fee required: $50. Interview required.

Athletics Interscholastic: baseball (boys), basketball (b,g), cross-country running (b,g), golf (b,g), soccer (b,g), swimming and diving (b,g), track and field (b,g), volleyball (g); coed interscholastic: cross-country running, golf, swimming and diving, track and field; coed intramural: badminton, basketball, cross-country running, fencing, golf, outdoors, physical fitness, physical training, soccer, track and field, volleyball, weight training. 3 coaches.

Computers Computers are regularly used in history, writing, yearbook classes. Computer network features include on-campus library services, Internet access.

Contact Mr. Charles Gebhardt, Principal/Executive Director. 801-266-6676. Fax: 801-266-1953. E-mail: charles.gebhardt@lhs-slc.org. Web site: www.lhs-slc.org.

CONVENT OF THE SACRED HEART

1177 King Street

Greenwich, Connecticut 06831

Head of School: Mrs. Pamela Juan Hayes

General Information Girls' day college-preparatory, arts, religious studies, and technology school, affiliated with Roman Catholic Church. Grades PS–12. Founded: 1848. Setting: suburban. Nearest major city is New York, NY. 110-acre campus. 10 buildings on campus. Approved or accredited by Network of Sacred Heart Schools, New England Association of Schools and Colleges, and Connecticut Department of Education. Member of National Association of Independent Schools and Secondary School Admission Test Board. Endowment: $22.8 million. Total enrollment: 777. Upper school average class size: 13. Upper school faculty-student ratio: 1:7. There are 163 required school days per year for Upper School students. Upper School students typically attend 5 days per week. The average school day consists of 7 hours and 15 minutes.

Upper School Student Profile Grade 9: 79 students (79 girls); Grade 10: 63 students (63 girls); Grade 11: 82 students (82 girls); Grade 12: 61 students (61 girls). 70% of students are Roman Catholic.

Faculty School total: 112. In upper school: 15 men, 36 women; 45 have advanced degrees.

Subjects Offered 20th century world history, advanced biology, advanced chemistry, advanced math, Advanced Placement courses, advanced studio art-AP, algebra, American literature, American literature-AP, Arabic, biology, biology-AP, broadcast journalism, calculus, calculus-AP, Catholic belief and practice, chemistry, chemistry-AP, Chinese, choir, choral music, Christian and Hebrew scripture, Christian education, Christian ethics, Christianity, college counseling, community service, comparative government and politics-AP, concert bell choir, design, drama, drawing, English language and composition-AP, English literature, English literature and composition-AP, environmental science-AP, ethics, European history, European history-AP, fine arts, French, French language-AP, geometry, health, honors algebra, honors geometry, honors U.S. history, HTML design, instrumental music, journalism, Latin, literary magazine, photography, physical education, physics, physics-AP, pre-calculus, SAT/ACT preparation, Spanish, Spanish language-AP, Spanish literature-AP, statistics, theology, trigonometry, U.S. history, U.S. history-AP, world cultures, world literature.

Graduation Requirements Arts and fine arts (art, music, dance, drama), electives, English, foreign language, mathematics, physical education (includes health), religion (includes Bible studies and theology), science, social studies (includes history). Community service is required.

Special Academic Programs 17 Advanced Placement exams for which test preparation is offered; honors section; independent study; term-away projects; study at local college for college credit; domestic exchange program (with Network of Sacred Heart Schools); study abroad; academic accommodation for the gifted and the artistically talented.

College Admission Counseling 60 students graduated in 2011; all went to college, including Georgetown University; New York University; Villanova University.

Student Life Upper grades have uniform requirement, student council, honor system. Discipline rests primarily with faculty. Attendance at religious services is required.

Tuition and Aid Day student tuition: $33,300. Tuition installment plan (Sallie May Payment Plan). Need-based scholarship grants available. In 2011–12, 22% of upper-school students received aid. Total amount of financial aid awarded in 2011–12: $1,404,800.

Admissions Traditional secondary-level entrance grade is 9. ISEE or SSAT required. Deadline for receipt of application materials: February 1. Application fee required: $50. On-campus interview required.

Athletics Interscholastic: basketball, cooperative games, crew, cross-country running, dance, diving, field hockey, fitness, golf, jogging, lacrosse, physical fitness, running, soccer, softball, squash, swimming and diving, tennis, volleyball; intramural: equestrian sports, fitness, independent competitive sports, physical training, strength & conditioning. 4 PE instructors, 34 coaches, 1 athletic trainer.

Computers Computers are regularly used in all academic classes. Computer network features include on-campus library services, online commercial services, Internet access, wireless campus network, Internet filtering or blocking technology, course selection online, laptops mandatory for students in grades 7 to 12. Campus intranet, student e-mail accounts, and computer access in designated common areas are available to students. The school has a published electronic and media policy.

Contact Mrs. Catherine Cullinane, Director of Admission. 203-532-3534. Fax: 203-532-3301. E-mail: admission@cshgreenwich.org. Web site: www.cshgreenwich.org.

See Display on next page and Close-Up on page 608.

CONVENT OF THE SACRED HEART

1 East 91st Street

New York, New York 10128-0689

Head of School: Dr. Joseph J. Ciancaglini

General Information Girls' day college-preparatory, arts, religious studies, bilingual studies, and technology school, affiliated with Roman Catholic Church. Grades PK–12. Founded: 1881. Setting: urban. 2 buildings on campus. Approved or accredited by Network of Sacred Heart Schools, New York State Association of Independent Schools, and New York Department of Education. Member of National Association of Independent Schools and Secondary School Admission Test Board. Endowment: $33.8 million. Total enrollment: 691. Upper school average class size: 16. Upper school faculty-student ratio: 1:16.

Upper School Student Profile Grade 8: 53 students (53 girls); Grade 9: 52 students (52 girls); Grade 10: 51 students (51 girls); Grade 11: 50 students (50 girls); Grade 12: 47 students (47 girls). 65% of students are Roman Catholic.

Faculty School total: 110. In upper school: 10 men, 30 women; 38 have advanced degrees.

Subjects Offered Advanced studio art-AP, algebra, American history, American literature, art, audio visual/media, biology, biology-AP, calculus, calculus-AP, campus ministry, ceramics, chemistry, chemistry-AP, chorus, computer applications, computer multimedia, creative writing, dance, desktop publishing, digital photography, drama, earth science, East European studies, English, English literature, English literature-AP, environmental science, ethics, European history, expository writing, film history, fine arts, finite math, forensics, French, French-AP, functions, geography, geometry, government/civics, handbells, health, history, journalism, Latin, madrigals, mathematics, model United Nations, multicultural literature, multimedia design, music, musical theater, performing arts, photography, physical education, physical science, physics, physics-AP, portfolio art, pottery, pre-calculus, religion, science, science research, social studies, Spanish, Spanish-AP, speech, statistics, statistics-AP, theater, theology, trigonometry, U.S. history-AP, visual arts, women's literature, world history, world issues, world literature, world religions, writing.

Graduation Requirements Arts and fine arts (art, music, dance, drama), computer science, English, foreign language, mathematics, physical education (includes health), religion (includes Bible studies and theology), science, social studies (includes history).

Special Academic Programs 15 Advanced Placement exams for which test preparation is offered; honors section; independent study; term-away projects; domestic exchange program (with Network of Sacred Heart Schools); study abroad.

College Admission Counseling 48 students graduated in 2010; all went to college, including Boston College; Georgetown University; Lehigh University; New York University; The George Washington University; University of Pennsylvania.

Student Life Upper grades have uniform requirement, student council. Discipline rests primarily with faculty. Attendance at religious services is required.

Tuition and Aid Day student tuition: $30,970. Tuition installment plan (Key Tuition Payment Plan). Need-based scholarship grants, need-based loans available. In 2010–11, 37% of upper-school students received aid. Total amount of financial aid awarded in 2010–11: $1,800,000.

Admissions Traditional secondary-level entrance grade is 9. For fall 2010, 200 students applied for upper-level admission, 35 were accepted, 16 enrolled. ERB or ISEE required. Deadline for receipt of application materials: November 15. Application fee required: $65. On-campus interview required.

Athletics Interscholastic: basketball, cross-country running, indoor track & field, lacrosse, soccer, softball, swimming and diving, tennis, track and field, volleyball, winter (indoor) track; intramural: aerobics/dance, aquatics, ballet, basketball, dance, fitness, gymnastics, jogging, physical training, roller blading, running, soccer, softball, swimming and diving, tennis, volleyball, weight lifting, weight training. 8 PE instructors, 8 coaches, 1 athletic trainer.

Computers Computers are regularly used in all academic classes. Computer network features include on-campus library services, online commercial services, Internet access, wireless campus network, Internet filtering or blocking technology. Campus intranet, student e-mail accounts, and computer access in designated common areas are available to students. The school has a published electronic and media policy.

Contact Evin Watson, Admissions Office Coordinator. 212-722-4745 Ext. 105. Fax: 212-996-1784. E-mail: ewatson@cshnyc.org. Web site: www.cshnyc.org.

COPENHAGEN INTERNATIONAL SCHOOL

Hellerupvej 22

2900 Hellerup, Denmark

Head of School: Walter Plotkin

General Information Coeducational day college-preparatory school. Grades 6–12. Founded: 1963. Setting: suburban. Nearest major city is Copenhagen, Denmark. 1-hectare campus. 2 buildings on campus. Approved or accredited by New England Association of Schools and Colleges. Member of European Council of International Schools. Language of instruction: English. Total enrollment: 602. Upper school average class size: 12. Upper school faculty-student ratio: 1:7. There are 185 required school days per year for Upper School students. Upper School students typically attend 5 days per week. The average school day consists of 7 hours and 10 minutes.

Upper School Student Profile Grade 6: 41 students (22 boys, 19 girls); Grade 7: 46 students (19 boys, 27 girls); Grade 8: 39 students (20 boys, 19 girls); Grade 9: 44 students (21 boys, 23 girls); Grade 10: 44 students (21 boys, 23 girls); Grade 11: 54 students (31 boys, 23 girls); Grade 12: 40 students (21 boys, 19 girls).
Faculty School total: 90. In upper school: 27 men, 23 women; 35 have advanced degrees.
Subjects Offered Anthropology, art, biology, chemistry, computer programming, Danish, English, English literature, ESL, European history, French, German, history, International Baccalaureate courses, mathematics, music, physics, science, social sciences, social studies, theory of knowledge.
Special Academic Programs International Baccalaureate program; special instructional classes for students with mild learning disabilities and dyslexia; ESL (4 students enrolled).
College Admission Counseling 47 students graduated in 2011; 40 went to college, including Harvard University; The University of North Carolina at Chapel Hill; Vanderbilt University. Other: 7 had other specific plans.
Student Life Upper grades have student council, honor system. Discipline rests equally with students and faculty.
Tuition and Aid Day student tuition: 114,000 Danish kroner. Tuition installment plan (monthly payment plans, individually arranged payment plans). Need-based scholarship grants available. In 2011–12, 15% of upper-school students received aid. Total amount of financial aid awarded in 2011–12: 4,000,000 Danish kroner.
Admissions Traditional secondary-level entrance grade is 11. For fall 2011, 59 students applied for upper-level admission, 57 were accepted, 56 enrolled. English for Non-native Speakers, math and English placement tests and writing sample required. Deadline for receipt of application materials: none. Application fee required: 25,000 Danish kroner. On-campus interview required.
Athletics Interscholastic: basketball (boys, girls), scooter football (b,g), soccer (b,g), softball (b,g), swimming and diving (b,g). 3 PE instructors, 3 coaches.
Computers Computers are regularly used in English, geography, history, humanities, information technology, lab/keyboard, library, mathematics, media arts, programming classes. Computer network features include on-campus library services, online commercial services, Internet access, wireless campus network, Internet filtering or blocking technology. Student e-mail accounts are available to students.
Contact Thomas Martin Nielsen, Admissions Officer. 45-39-46-33-00 Ext. 315. Fax: 45-39-61-22-30. E-mail: admission@cis.dk. Web site: www.cis-edu.dk.

COPPER CANYON ACADEMY

Rimrock, Arizona

See Special Needs Schools section.

COTTER SCHOOLS

1115 West Broadway

Winona, Minnesota 55987-1399

Head of School: Mrs. Jennifer Elfering

General Information Coeducational boarding and day college-preparatory, general academic, arts, religious studies, technology, and ESL school, affiliated with Roman Catholic Church. Boarding grades 9–12, day grades 7–12. Founded: 1911. Setting: small town. Nearest major city is Minneapolis. Students are housed in single-sex by floor dormitories. 75-acre campus. 7 buildings on campus. Approved or accredited by Midwest Association of Boarding Schools, National Catholic Education Association, North Central Association of Colleges and Schools, The Association of Boarding Schools, and Minnesota Department of Education. Endowment: $15 million. Total enrollment: 380. Upper school average class size: 18. Upper school faculty-student ratio: 1:11. There are 176 required school days per year for Upper School students. Upper School students typically attend 5 days per week. The average school day consists of 5 hours and 40 minutes.
Upper School Student Profile Grade 9: 58 students (31 boys, 27 girls); Grade 10: 88 students (46 boys, 42 girls); Grade 11: 78 students (40 boys, 38 girls); Grade 12: 74 students (41 boys, 33 girls). 31% of students are boarding students. 65% are state residents. 4 states are represented in upper school student body. 30% are international students. International students from China, Japan, Mexico, Republic of Korea, Taiwan, and Viet Nam; 7 other countries represented in student body. 66% of students are Roman Catholic.
Faculty School total: 38. In upper school: 18 men, 20 women; 32 have advanced degrees; 3 reside on campus.
Subjects Offered Algebra, American history, anatomy, art, band, Bible, biology, calculus, calculus-AP, campus ministry, chemistry, chorus, Christian and Hebrew scripture, Christian ethics, community service, computer science, death and loss, economics, English, environmental science, ESL, German, health, Hebrew scripture, honors English, learning lab, linear algebra, literature and composition-AP, math analysis, mathematics, media, painting, physical education, physical science, physics, psychology, science, Spanish, statistics, U.S. history, U.S. history-AP, visual arts, world geography, world religions.
Graduation Requirements English, foreign language, mathematics, performing arts, physical education (includes health), religion (includes Bible studies and theology), science, social studies (includes history), visual arts, 80 hours of community service.
Special Academic Programs Honors section; accelerated programs; independent study; term-away projects; study at local college for college credit; study abroad; academic accommodation for the gifted, the musically talented, and the artistically talented; remedial reading and/or remedial writing; remedial math; programs in English, mathematics for dyslexic students; ESL (25 students enrolled).
College Admission Counseling 80 students graduated in 2011; 78 went to college, including Saint John's University; Saint Mary's University of Minnesota; University of Illinois at Urbana–Champaign; University of Minnesota, Twin Cities Campus; University of St. Thomas; University of Wisconsin–Madison. Other: 1 went to work, 1 entered military service. Median composite ACT: 24. 50% scored over 26 on composite ACT.
Student Life Upper grades have specified standards of dress, student council. Discipline rests primarily with faculty. Attendance at religious services is required.
Summer Programs Remediation, enrichment, sports, art/fine arts programs offered; held on campus; accepts boys and girls; open to students from other schools. 150 students usually enrolled. 2012 schedule: June to July.
Tuition and Aid Day student tuition: $5975; 5-day tuition and room/board: $23,850; 7-day tuition and room/board: $29,700. Tuition installment plan (monthly payment plans, individually arranged payment plans). Tuition reduction for siblings, need-based scholarship grants available. In 2011–12, 60% of upper-school students received aid.
Admissions Traditional secondary-level entrance grade is 9. For fall 2011, 78 students applied for upper-level admission, 56 were accepted, 42 enrolled. SLEP for foreign students or TOEFL required. Deadline for receipt of application materials: none. Application fee required: $50. Interview required.
Athletics Interscholastic: aerobics/dance (girls), baseball (b), basketball (b,g), cheering (g), cross-country running (b,g), dance (g), dance team (g), danceline (g), football (b), golf (b,g), gymnastics (g), hockey (b,g), ice hockey (b,g), skiing (cross-country) (b,g), soccer (b,g), softball (g), swimming and diving (b,g), tennis (b,g), track and field (b,g), volleyball (g), wrestling (b); intramural: basketball (b,g), indoor soccer (b); coed intramural: badminton, basketball, canoeing/kayaking, indoor soccer. 2 PE instructors, 66 coaches, 1 athletic trainer.
Computers Computers are regularly used in art, technology classes. Computer network features include on-campus library services, Internet access, Internet filtering or blocking technology. Campus intranet, student e-mail accounts, and computer access in designated common areas are available to students. The school has a published electronic and media policy.
Contact Mr. Will Gibson, Director of Admissions and Resident Life. 507-453-5403. Fax: 507-453-5013. E-mail: wgibson@cotterschools.org. Web site: www.cotterschools.org.

THE COUNTRY DAY SCHOOL

13415 Dufferin Street

King City, Ontario L7B 1K5, Canada

Head of School: Mr. John Liggett

General Information Coeducational day college-preparatory, arts, business, and technology school. Grades JK–12. Founded: 1972. Setting: rural. Nearest major city is Toronto, Canada. 100-acre campus. 2 buildings on campus. Approved or accredited by Canadian Association of Independent Schools, Canadian Educational Standards Institute, Conference of Independent Schools of Ontario, and Ontario Department of Education. Language of instruction: English. Total enrollment: 720. Upper school average class size: 17. Upper school faculty-student ratio: 1:10.
Upper School Student Profile Grade 9: 80 students (40 boys, 40 girls); Grade 10: 80 students (40 boys, 40 girls); Grade 11: 80 students (40 boys, 40 girls); Grade 12: 80 students (40 boys, 40 girls).
Faculty School total: 79. In upper school: 28 men, 20 women.
Subjects Offered Advanced chemistry, advanced computer applications, advanced math, algebra, American history, anatomy and physiology, ancient history, ancient/medieval philosophy, art and culture, art history, athletics, band, biology, business studies, Canadian geography, Canadian history, Canadian literature, career education, career/college preparation, choir, comparative politics, computer programming, creative writing, English, environmental geography, European history, French, government/civics, history, languages, mathematics, modern Western civilization, performing arts, philosophy, physical education, physics, politics, science, society, world history.
Graduation Requirements Ministry Grade 10 Literacy Test (Government of Ontario).
Special Academic Programs Advanced Placement exam preparation; study abroad.
College Admission Counseling 79 students graduated in 2011; all went to college, including McGill University; McMaster University; Queen's University at Kingston; The University of Western Ontario; University of Toronto; Wilfrid Laurier University.
Student Life Upper grades have uniform requirement, student council, honor system. Discipline rests primarily with faculty.
Summer Programs Advancement, sports, art/fine arts programs offered; session focuses on advancement; held both on and off campus; held at Costa Rica, England, and

Galapagos Islands; accepts boys and girls; open to students from other schools. 20 students usually enrolled. 2012 schedule: July 2 to July 31. Application deadline: March 1.
Tuition and Aid Day student tuition: CAN$22,765.
Admissions Traditional secondary-level entrance grade is 9. For fall 2011, 97 students applied for upper-level admission, 58 were accepted, 37 enrolled. CAT 5 or SSAT required. Deadline for receipt of application materials: none. Application fee required: CAN$125. On-campus interview required.
Athletics Interscholastic: baseball (girls), basketball (b,g), cross-country running (b,g), golf (b,g), hockey (b,g), ice hockey (b,g), rugby (b,g), running (b,g), soccer (b,g), softball (b,g), track and field (b,g), volleyball (b,g); intramural: badminton (b,g), basketball (b,g), bowling (b,g), ice hockey (b), ice skating (b,g), physical fitness (b,g), skiing (downhill) (b,g), snowboarding (b,g), soccer (b,g), softball (b,g), volleyball (b,g); coed intramural: curling, Frisbee, physical fitness, physical training, rock climbing, strength & conditioning, swimming and diving, table tennis. 5 PE instructors.
Computers Computers are regularly used in accounting, business, career education, English, geography, history, mathematics, media, music, writing, yearbook classes. Computer network features include on-campus library services, Internet access, wireless campus network, Internet filtering or blocking technology, access to online library resources from home, access to homework online via Blackboard Software. Campus intranet is available to students.
Contact Mr. David Huckvale, Director of Admission. 905-833-1220. Fax: 905-833-1350. E-mail: admissions@cds.on.ca. Web site: www.cds.on.ca/.

COUNTRY DAY SCHOOL OF THE SACRED HEART

480 Bryn Mawr Avenue

Bryn Mawr, Pennsylvania 19010

Head of School: Sr. Matthew Anita MacDonald, SSJ

General Information Girls' day college-preparatory, arts, religious studies, and technology school, affiliated with Roman Catholic Church. Grades PK–12. Founded: 1865. Setting: suburban. Nearest major city is Philadelphia. 16-acre campus. 3 buildings on campus. Approved or accredited by Middle States Association of Colleges and Schools, Network of Sacred Heart Schools, and Pennsylvania Department of Education. Member of National Association of Independent Schools. Total enrollment: 321. Upper school average class size: 15. Upper school faculty-student ratio: 1:8. There are 180 required school days per year for Upper School students. The average school day consists of 7 hours.
Upper School Student Profile Grade 9: 53 students (53 girls); Grade 10: 41 students (41 girls); Grade 11: 40 students (40 girls); Grade 12: 50 students (50 girls). 75% of students are Roman Catholic.
Faculty School total: 44. In upper school: 5 men, 29 women; 21 have advanced degrees.
Subjects Offered Algebra, American history, American history-AP, American literature, art, arts, Bible studies, biology, calculus, chemistry, composition, computer science, economics, English, English literature, environmental science, ethics, European history, film, fine arts, French, geometry, government/civics, health, Latin, mathematics, media studies, physical education, physics, pre-calculus, religion, science, social sciences, social studies, Spanish, trigonometry, word processing, world history, world literature.
Graduation Requirements Arts and fine arts (art, music, dance, drama), English, foreign language, mathematics, physical education (includes health), religion (includes Bible studies and theology), science, social studies (includes history), two weeks of senior independent study with a working professional, 25 hours of community service per year.
Special Academic Programs 7 Advanced Placement exams for which test preparation is offered; honors section; independent study; term-away projects; study at local college for college credit; domestic exchange program (with Network of Sacred Heart Schools); study abroad; academic accommodation for the musically talented.
College Admission Counseling 44 students graduated in 2011; all went to college, including Drexel University; Fordham University; Georgetown University; Saint Joseph's University; The Catholic University of America; University of Pittsburgh. Mean SAT critical reading: 620, mean SAT math: 580, mean SAT writing: 650. 45% scored over 600 on SAT critical reading, 40% scored over 600 on SAT math, 50% scored over 600 on SAT writing.
Student Life Upper grades have uniform requirement, student council. Discipline rests equally with students and faculty. Attendance at religious services is required.
Tuition and Aid Day student tuition: $15,950. Tuition installment plan (SMART Tuition Payment Plan). Tuition reduction for siblings, merit scholarship grants, need-based scholarship grants available. In 2011–12, 72% of upper-school students received aid; total upper-school merit-scholarship money awarded: $415,900. Total amount of financial aid awarded in 2011–12: $424,500.
Admissions Traditional secondary-level entrance grade is 9. For fall 2011, 90 students applied for upper-level admission, 65 were accepted, 32 enrolled. High School Placement Test required. Deadline for receipt of application materials: none. Application fee required: $35. Interview required.
Athletics Interscholastic: basketball, crew, cross-country running, field hockey, golf, lacrosse, softball, tennis, track and field, volleyball; intramural: fitness walking. 2 PE instructors, 12 coaches, 1 athletic trainer.
Computers Computers are regularly used in English, foreign language, history, mathematics, science, technology classes. Computer network features include on-campus library services, online commercial services, Internet access, wireless campus network. Student e-mail accounts are available to students. Students grades are available online. The school has a published electronic and media policy.
Contact Mrs. Laurie Nowlan, Director of Admissions. 610-527-3915 Ext. 214. Fax: 610-527-0942. E-mail: lnowlan@cdssh.org. Web site: www.cdssh.org.

COVENANT CANADIAN REFORMED SCHOOL

3030 TWP Road 615A

PO Box 67

Neerlandia, Alberta T0G 1R0, Canada

Head of School: Mr. James Meinen

General Information Coeducational day college-preparatory, general academic, business, religious studies, and technology school, affiliated with Reformed Church. Grades K–12. Founded: 1977. Setting: rural. Nearest major city is Edmonton, Canada. 5-acre campus. 2 buildings on campus. Approved or accredited by Association of Independent Schools and Colleges of Alberta and Alberta Department of Education. Language of instruction: English. Total enrollment: 188. Upper school average class size: 10. Upper school faculty-student ratio: 1:10. There are 167 required school days per year for Upper School students. Upper School students typically attend 4 days per week. The average school day consists of 6 hours and 10 minutes.
Upper School Student Profile Grade 10: 9 students (6 boys, 3 girls); Grade 11: 11 students (2 boys, 9 girls); Grade 12: 8 students (3 boys, 5 girls). 100% of students are Reformed.
Faculty School total: 16. In upper school: 6 men, 3 women.
Subjects Offered Accounting, architectural drawing, Bible studies, biology, Canadian geography, career and personal planning, career technology, chemistry, child development, Christian education, computer information systems, computer skills, computer studies, consumer law, desktop publishing, digital photography, drama, drawing and design, early childhood, electronic publishing, English, ESL, French as a second language, geology, health education, history, HTML design, information processing, intro to computers, introduction to technology, keyboarding, mathematics, physical education, physics, prayer/spirituality, religious studies, science, sewing, social studies, theology and the arts, Web site design, Western religions, work experience, world geography, world religions, yearbook.
Graduation Requirements Must pass religious studies courses offered in grades 10, 11, and 12 for the years the student attended.
Special Academic Programs Independent study; remedial reading and/or remedial writing; remedial math.
College Admission Counseling 7 students graduated in 2011; 4 went to college, including University of Alberta; University of Calgary; University of Lethbridge. Other: 3 went to work.
Student Life Upper grades have specified standards of dress, student council. Discipline rests primarily with faculty.
Tuition and Aid Day student tuition: CAN$6000. Tuition installment plan (monthly payment plans, individually arranged payment plans). Tuition rates per family available.
Admissions Traditional secondary-level entrance grade is 10. Achievement tests or CTBS or ERB required. Deadline for receipt of application materials: none. No application fee required. Interview required.
Athletics Interscholastic: track and field (boys, girls), volleyball (b,g); coed intramural: badminton, ball hockey, baseball, basketball, flag football, floor hockey, football, Frisbee, hockey, ice hockey, indoor hockey, indoor soccer, lacrosse, soccer, softball, volleyball. 4 PE instructors, 6 coaches.
Computers Computers are regularly used in all classes. Computer network features include on-campus library services, Internet access, Internet filtering or blocking technology. Computer access in designated common areas is available to students. The school has a published electronic and media policy.
Contact Mr. James Meinen, Principal. 780-674-4774. Fax: 780-401-3295. E-mail: principal@covenantschool.ca.

COVINGTON CATHOLIC HIGH SCHOOL

1600 Dixie Highway

Park Hills, Kentucky 41011

Head of School: Mr. Robert Rowe

General Information Boys' day college-preparatory, arts, business, religious studies, bilingual studies, and technology school, affiliated with Roman Catholic Church. Grades 9–12. Founded: 1925. Setting: suburban. Nearest major city is Cincinnati, OH. 4 buildings on campus. Approved or accredited by Southern Association of Colleges and Schools and Kentucky Department of Education. Total enrollment: 502. Upper school faculty-student ratio: 1:14. Upper School students typically attend 5 days per week. The average school day consists of 6 hours and 40 minutes.

Upper School Student Profile Grade 9: 133 students (133 boys); Grade 10: 126 students (126 boys); Grade 11: 120 students (120 boys); Grade 12: 115 students (115 boys).

Faculty School total: 37. In upper school: 31 men, 5 women; 21 have advanced degrees.

Subjects Offered Algebra, American government, American history, American history-AP, anatomy and physiology, art, biology, business law, calculus-AP, career exploration, chemistry, chemistry-AP, chorus, church history, computer applications, computer programming, computer science, computer science-AP, computer-aided design, creative writing, current events, drama, economics, English, film, geometry, German, graphic design, health, journalism, Latin, modern European history, music appreciation, orchestra, personal finance, physical education, physical science, physics, pre-algebra, pre-calculus, probability and statistics, psychology, psychology-AP, reading, scripture, social justice, sociology, Spanish, Spanish-AP, speech, theology, Web site design, wood processing, world civilizations, world geography, world history-AP, writing workshop.

Graduation Requirements Arts and fine arts (art, music, dance, drama), electives, English, mathematics, physical education (includes health), science, social studies (includes history), community service requirement.

Special Academic Programs 10 Advanced Placement exams for which test preparation is offered; honors section; study at local college for college credit.

College Admission Counseling 127 students graduated in 2011, 124 went to college, including Bellarmine University; Miami University; University of Dayton; University of Kentucky; University of Louisville; Xavier University. Other: 2 went to work, 1 entered military service. Mean composite ACT: 25.

Student Life Upper grades have specified standards of dress, student council. Discipline rests primarily with faculty. Attendance at religious services is required.

Tuition and Aid Day student tuition: $5985–$6590. Tuition installment plan (monthly payment plans). Tuition reduction for siblings, merit scholarship grants, paying campus jobs available.

Admissions Traditional secondary-level entrance grade is 9. High School Placement Test required. Deadline for receipt of application materials: none. No application fee required.

Athletics Interscholastic: baseball, basketball, bowling, football, golf, soccer, swimming and diving, tennis, track and field; intramural: basketball, bicycling, fishing, Frisbee, lacrosse, skiing (downhill), ultimate Frisbee, whiffle ball. 1 PE instructor.

Computers Computers are regularly used in all academic classes. Computer network features include Internet access, wireless campus network, Internet filtering or blocking technology. Student e-mail accounts are available to students. Students grades are available online.

Contact Mr. Tony Barczak, Freshman/Sophomore Counselor. 859-491-2247 Ext. 2257. Fax: 859-448-2242. E-mail: tbarczak@covcath.org. Web site: www.covcath.org/.

CRANBROOK SCHOOLS

39221 Woodward Avenue

PO Box 801

Bloomfield Hills, Michigan 48303-0801

General Information Coeducational boarding and day college-preparatory and arts school. Boarding grades 9–12, day grades PK–12. Founded: 1922. Setting: suburban. Nearest major city is Detroit. Students are housed in single-sex dormitories. 315-acre campus. 10 buildings on campus. Approved or accredited by Independent Schools Association of the Central States, Midwest Association of Boarding Schools, The Association of Boarding Schools, The College Board, and Michigan Department of Education. Member of National Association of Independent Schools and Secondary School Admission Test Board. Endowment: $218 million. Total enrollment: 1,636. Upper school average class size: 16. Upper school faculty-student ratio: 1:8. There are 164 required school days per year for Upper School students. Upper School students typically attend 5 days per week. The average school day consists of 5 hours and 15 minutes.

See Display below and Close-Up on page 610.

CRAWFORD ADVENTIST ACADEMY

531 Finch Avenue West

Willowdale, Ontario M2R 3X2, Canada

Head of School: Mr. Norman Brown

General Information Coeducational day college-preparatory, arts, business, religious studies, bilingual studies, and technology school, affiliated with Seventh-day Adventist Church. Grades JK–12. Founded: 1954. Setting: urban. Nearest major city is Toronto, Canada. 5-acre campus. 1 building on campus. Approved or accredited by National Council for Private School Accreditation, Ontario Ministry of Education, and Ontario Department of Education. Language of instruction: English. Upper school average class size: 25. Upper school faculty-student ratio: 1:16. There are 196 required school days per year for Upper School students. Upper School students typically attend 5 days per week. The average school day consists of 7 hours.

Upper School Student Profile Grade 9: 52 students (26 boys, 26 girls); Grade 10: 49 students (27 boys, 22 girls); Grade 11: 47 students (22 boys, 25 girls); Grade 12: 37 students (18 boys, 19 girls). 90% of students are Seventh-day Adventists.
Faculty School total: 18. In upper school: 11 men, 6 women; 11 have advanced degrees.
Subjects Offered Advanced computer applications, band, Bible, biology, business, business technology, calculus, Canadian geography, Canadian history, chemistry, choir, civics, community service, computer applications, computer information systems, drama, dramatic arts, earth and space science, English, English composition, French, French as a second language, geography, guidance, independent study, information technology, marketing, mathematics, physical education, physics, religion, science, writing, yearbook.
Special Academic Programs 3 Advanced Placement exams for which test preparation is offered; remedial reading and/or remedial writing; programs in English for dyslexic students; ESL.
College Admission Counseling 32 students graduated in 2011; 4 went to college, including Andrews University; Oakwood University; Ryerson University; University of Toronto; University of Waterloo; York University. Other: 28 entered a postgraduate year. Median composite ACT: 20. 22% scored over 26 on composite ACT.
Student Life Upper grades have uniform requirement, student council, honor system. Discipline rests primarily with faculty. Attendance at religious services is required.
Tuition and Aid Day student tuition: CAN$8500. Guaranteed tuition plan. Tuition installment plan (monthly payment plans, individually arranged payment plans). Tuition reduction for siblings, need-based scholarship grants, paying campus jobs available. In 2011–12, 20% of upper-school students received aid. Total amount of financial aid awarded in 2011–12: CAN$35,000.
Admissions Traditional secondary-level entrance grade is 9. For fall 2011, 10 students applied for upper-level admission, 10 were accepted, 10 enrolled. CAT, CAT 2, CCAT or CTBS (or similar from their school) required. Deadline for receipt of application materials: none. Application fee required: CAN$50. On-campus interview required.
Athletics Interscholastic: basketball (boys, girls), weight lifting (b,g); intramural: basketball (b,g); coed interscholastic: cooperative games, outdoor recreation; coed intramural: basketball, flag football, floor hockey, indoor soccer, outdoor education, outdoor recreation, physical fitness, physical training, snowboarding, soccer, volleyball. 1 PE instructor, 1 coach.
Computers Computers are regularly used in accounting, business, computer applications, yearbook classes. Computer network features include Internet access, wireless campus network, Internet filtering or blocking technology. Student e-mail accounts and computer access in designated common areas are available to students. Students grades are available online. The school has a published electronic and media policy.
Contact Mr. Andrew Mark Thomas, Principal, 9-12. 416-633-0090 Ext. 223. Fax: 416-633-0467. E-mail: athomas@caasda.com.

CRESPI CARMELITE HIGH SCHOOL

5031 Alonzo Avenue

Encino, California 91316-3699

Head of School: Fr. Paul Henson, OCARM

General Information Boys' day college-preparatory, arts, and religious studies school, affiliated with Roman Catholic Church. Grades 9–12. Founded: 1959. Setting: suburban. Nearest major city is Los Angeles. 3-acre campus. 3 buildings on campus. Approved or accredited by Western Association of Schools and Colleges, Western Catholic Education Association, and California Department of Education. Total enrollment: 585. Upper school average class size: 23. Upper school faculty-student ratio: 1:23. There are 182 required school days per year for Upper School students. Upper School students typically attend 5 days per week. The average school day consists of 6 hours.
Upper School Student Profile Grade 9: 173 students (173 boys); Grade 10: 143 students (143 boys); Grade 11: 140 students (140 boys); Grade 12: 129 students (129 boys). 59% of students are Roman Catholic.
Faculty School total: 37. In upper school: 33 men, 4 women; 29 have advanced degrees.
Subjects Offered Advanced Placement courses, advanced studio art-AP, algebra, American history-AP, American literature-AP, anatomy and physiology, Ancient Greek, ancient world history, applied music, ASB Leadership, astronomy, athletic training, audio visual/media, baseball, Basic programming, basketball, biology, biology-AP, British literature, British literature-AP, business mathematics, calculus, calculus-AP, chemistry, Christian scripture, church history, classical Greek literature, computer graphics, constitutional law, drama performance, driver education, earth science, economics and history, economics-AP, English composition, English literature and composition-AP, environmental science, ethics, European history-AP, film studies, French language-AP, French-AP, geometry, golf, government, government and politics-AP, Greek, Greek culture, health, history of the Catholic Church, Holocaust, Holocaust studies, honors English, honors geometry, international studies, journalism, language and composition, Latin-AP, law, media arts, men's studies, model United Nations, moral and social development, music appreciation, music composition, photography, physical science, physics-AP, prayer/spirituality, pre-calculus, probability and statistics, psychology, Shakespeare, social justice, Spanish, Spanish language-AP, Spanish literature-AP, Spanish-AP, speech, sports, sports conditioning, statistics-AP, student government, student publications, U.S. history, U.S. history-AP, video film production, Vietnam War, visual arts, Web site design, weight training, Western civilization, Western religions, world cultures, world geography, world religions, yearbook, zoology.
Graduation Requirements Arts and fine arts (art, music, dance, drama), English, foreign language, mathematics, physical education (includes health), religion (includes Bible studies and theology), science, social sciences, social studies (includes history). Community service is required.
Special Academic Programs 13 Advanced Placement exams for which test preparation is offered; honors section.
College Admission Counseling 147 students graduated in 2010; 143 went to college, including California Polytechnic State University, San Luis Obispo; California State University, Northridge; University of California, Los Angeles; University of California, Santa Barbara; University of San Diego. Other: 3 entered military service, 1 had other specific plans. Median SAT critical reading: 520, median SAT math: 500, median SAT writing: 540, median composite ACT: 23.
Student Life Upper grades have specified standards of dress, student council, honor system. Discipline rests primarily with faculty. Attendance at religious services is required.
Tuition and Aid Day student tuition: $12,000. Tuition installment plan (FACTS Tuition Payment Plan, Tuition Management Systems Plan). Merit scholarship grants, need-based scholarship grants available. In 2010–11, 32% of upper-school students received aid; total upper-school merit-scholarship money awarded: $48,600. Total amount of financial aid awarded in 2010–11: $1,018,965.
Admissions Traditional secondary-level entrance grade is 9. For fall 2010, 295 students applied for upper-level admission, 286 were accepted, 173 enrolled. High School Placement Test required. Deadline for receipt of application materials: February 4. Application fee required: $100. On-campus interview required.
Athletics Interscholastic: aquatics, baseball, basketball, cross-country running, football, golf, lacrosse, soccer, swimming and diving, tennis, track and field, volleyball, water polo, wrestling; intramural: basketball, floor hockey, Frisbee, table tennis. 4 PE instructors, 2 athletic trainers.
Computers Computers are regularly used in business applications, business studies, economics, English, foreign language, history, mathematics, media production, science, video film production, yearbook classes. Computer network features include on-campus library services, online commercial services, Internet access, wireless campus network. Students grades are available online. The school has a published electronic and media policy.
Contact Mrs. Anita Rezzo, Assistant Admissions Director. 818-345-1672 Ext. 329. Fax: 818-705-0209. E-mail: arezzo@crespi.org. Web site: www.crespi.org.

CROSS CREEK PROGRAMS

LaVerkin, Utah

See Special Needs Schools section.

CROSSPOINT ACADEMY

4012 Chico Way NW

Bremerton, Washington 98312-1397

Head of School: Mr. James White

General Information Coeducational day college-preparatory, arts, religious studies, and technology school, affiliated with Christian faith. Grades K–12. Founded: 1991. Setting: small town. Nearest major city is Tacoma. 7-acre campus. 7 buildings on campus. Approved or accredited by Association of Christian Schools International, Northwest Accreditation Commission, and Washington Department of Education. Total enrollment: 242. Upper school average class size: 17. Upper school faculty-student ratio: 1:8. There are 171 required school days per year for Upper School students. Upper School students typically attend 5 days per week. The average school day consists of 6 hours and 45 minutes.
Upper School Student Profile Grade 7: 14 students (6 boys, 8 girls); Grade 8: 26 students (11 boys, 15 girls); Grade 9: 25 students (13 boys, 12 girls); Grade 10: 28 students (12 boys, 16 girls); Grade 11: 17 students (9 boys, 8 girls); Grade 12: 31 students (18 boys, 13 girls). 70% of students are Christian faith.
Faculty School total: 25. In upper school: 6 men, 10 women; 8 have advanced degrees.
Subjects Offered Algebra, American literature, art, band, Bible, biology, calculus-AP, chemistry, choir, computer animation, computers, creative writing, desktop publishing, digital photography, drama, drama performance, earth science, English, geography, geometry, health, introduction to theater, keyboarding, leadership, life science, life skills, physical fitness, physical science, physics, practical living, pre-algebra, pre-calculus, programming, religion, science, senior project, Spanish, speech, student government, technology, U.S. government and politics-AP, U.S. history, U.S. history-AP, video, vocal ensemble, Washington State and Northwest History, weight training, world history, world literature, world religions, world wide web design, yearbook.
Graduation Requirements Arts and fine arts (art, music, dance, drama), Bible, computer science, English, foreign language, mathematics, physical education (includes health), practical living, science, social studies (includes history), speech.

Special Academic Programs Study at local college for college credit.
College Admission Counseling 33 students graduated in 2010; 32 went to college, including Baylor University; Central Washington University; Georgia Institute of Technology; Olympic College; Seattle Pacific University; University of Washington. Other: 1 went to work. Mean SAT critical reading: 578, mean SAT math: 569, mean SAT writing: 557, mean combined SAT: 1704, mean composite ACT: 24. 36% scored over 600 on SAT critical reading, 24% scored over 600 on SAT math, 36% scored over 600 on SAT writing, 36% scored over 1800 on combined SAT, 14% scored over 26 on composite ACT.
Student Life Upper grades have specified standards of dress, student council, honor system. Discipline rests primarily with faculty. Attendance at religious services is required.
Tuition and Aid Day student tuition: $9430. Tuition installment plan (monthly payment plans, prepayment discount plan, active military discount, Pastor, church employee & Christian school employee discounts). Tuition reduction for siblings, need-based scholarship grants available. In 2010–11, 28% of upper-school students received aid. Total amount of financial aid awarded in 2010–11: $171,000.
Admissions Traditional secondary-level entrance grade is 7. For fall 2010, 21 students applied for upper-level admission, 20 were accepted, 19 enrolled. Comprehensive educational evaluation required. Deadline for receipt of application materials: none. Application fee required: $50. Interview required.
Athletics Interscholastic: basketball (boys, girls), cross country running (b,g), golf (b), soccer (b,g), softball (g), track and field (b,g), volleyball (g), weight training (b,g).
Computers Computers are regularly used in animation, computer applications, desktop publishing, digital applications, graphics, keyboarding, photography, publications, technology, video film production, Web site design, yearbook classes. Computer network features include Internet access, wireless campus network, Internet filtering or blocking technology. Student e-mail accounts are available to students. Students grades are available online. The school has a published electronic and media policy.
Contact Ms. Sherri M. Miller, Admissions and Marketing Coordinator. 360-377-7700 Ext. 5004. Fax: 360-377-7795. E-mail: smiller@crista.net. Web site: www.crosspointacademy.org.

CROSSROADS COLLEGE PREPARATORY SCHOOL

500 DeBaliviere Avenue
St. Louis, Missouri 63112

Head of School: William B. Handmaker

General Information Coeducational day college-preparatory and arts school. Grades 7–12. Founded: 1974. Setting: urban. 20-acre campus. 1 building on campus. Approved or accredited by Independent Schools Association of the Central States and Missouri Department of Education. Member of National Association of Independent Schools and Secondary School Admission Test Board. Total enrollment: 215. Upper school average class size: 14. Upper school faculty-student ratio: 1:9. Upper School students typically attend 5 days per week. The average school day consists of 7 hours and 30 minutes.
Upper School Student Profile Grade 9: 40 students (25 boys, 15 girls); Grade 10: 46 students (23 boys, 23 girls); Grade 11: 40 students (17 boys, 23 girls); Grade 12: 26 students (11 boys, 15 girls).
Faculty School total: 29. In upper school: 10 men, 11 women; 14 have advanced degrees.
Subjects Offered 3-dimensional art, advanced chemistry, African American history, African-American history, algebra, American literature, anatomy, art, art history, art history-AP, Asian history, biology, biology-AP, botany, calculus, calculus-AP, ceramics, chemistry, chemistry-AP, community service, comparative religion, computer applications, creative writing, drama, ecology, English, English literature, environmental science, environmental science-AP, environmental studies, European history, fine arts, French, geography, geology, geometry, history, journalism, keyboarding, Latin, literature and composition-AP, mathematics, music, music theater, photography, physical education, physics, psychology, SAT/ACT preparation, social sciences, sociology, Spanish, speech, studio art-AP, theater, trigonometry, U.S. history-AP, women's studies, word processing, world history, world literature.
Graduation Requirements American literature, arts and fine arts (art, music, dance, drama), biology, chemistry, classics, computer science, creative writing, earth science, electives, English composition, English literature, environmental science, foreign language, interdisciplinary studies, mathematics, non-Western literature, physical education (includes health), political science, practical arts, social sciences, social studies (includes history), U.S. government and politics, world cultures, one course taken at a local university or college during senior year.
Special Academic Programs Advanced Placement exam preparation; honors section; independent study; study at local college for college credit.
College Admission Counseling 36 students graduated in 2010; all went to college, including Grinnell College; Knox College; Saint Louis University; University of Chicago; Washington University in St. Louis; Wesleyan University. Mean SAT critical reading: 650, mean SAT math: 660, mean SAT writing: 630, mean composite ACT: 27.
Student Life Upper grades have specified standards of dress, student council, honor system. Discipline rests equally with students and faculty.
Tuition and Aid Day student tuition: $16,750. Tuition installment plan (FACTS Tuition Payment Plan, monthly payment plans, individually arranged payment plans). Merit scholarship grants, need-based scholarship grants available. In 2010–11, 43% of upper-school students received aid.
Admissions Traditional secondary-level entrance grade is 9. For fall 2010, 36 students applied for upper-level admission, 24 were accepted, 15 enrolled. SSAT required. Deadline for receipt of application materials: January 21. Application fee required: $40. On-campus interview required.
Athletics Interscholastic: baseball (boys), basketball (b,g), indoor soccer (b,g), soccer (b,g), tennis (b,g), track and field (b,g), volleyball (g); intramural: soccer (b,g); coed interscholastic: bicycling, dance, fitness, physical fitness, physical training, weight lifting, weight training; coed intramural: aquatics, basketball, bicycling, dance team, drill team, fencing, indoor soccer, table tennis, touch football, volleyball, wall climbing, weight training, yoga. 3 PE instructors, 10 coaches.
Computers Computers are regularly used in computer applications, English, foreign language, history, journalism, mathematics, newspaper, programming, science, Web site design, word processing, writing, yearbook classes. Computer network features include on-campus library services, Internet access, wireless campus network, Internet filtering or blocking technology, SmartBoard usage in every academic classroom. Computer access in designated common areas is available to students. Students grades are available online.
Contact Maggie Baisch, Director of Admission. 314-367-8101. Fax: 314-367-9711. E-mail: maggie@crossroadscollegeprep.org. Web site: www.crossroadscollegeprep.org.

CROSSROADS SCHOOL FOR ARTS & SCIENCES

1714 21st Street
Santa Monica, California 90404-3917

Head of School: Mr. Bob Riddle

General Information Coeducational day college-preparatory, arts, and technology school. Grades K–12. Founded: 1971. Setting: urban. Nearest major city is Los Angeles. 3-acre campus. 16 buildings on campus. Approved or accredited by Western Association of Schools and Colleges and California Department of Education. Member of National Association of Independent Schools. Endowment: $13 million. Total enrollment: 1,147. Upper school average class size: 15. Upper school faculty-student ratio: 1:11. There are 161 required school days per year for Upper School students. Upper School students typically attend 5 days per week. The average school day consists of 7 hours.
Upper School Student Profile Grade 9: 127 students (66 boys, 61 girls); Grade 10: 125 students (56 boys, 69 girls); Grade 11: 129 students (59 boys, 70 girls); Grade 12: 118 students (56 boys, 62 girls).
Faculty School total: 154. In upper school: 31 men, 35 women; 40 have advanced degrees.
Subjects Offered Algebra, American history, American studies, art history, biology, calculus, ceramics, chemistry, community service, computer programming, computer science, creative writing, critical studies in film, cultural arts, dance, earth and space science, English, environmental education, film studies, French, gender issues, geometry, graphic design, great books, Greek, human development, Japanese, jazz ensemble, jazz theory, journalism, Latin, marine biology, marine ecology, music appreciation, music theory, orchestra, photography, physical education, physics, physiology, pre-calculus, sculpture, Spanish, statistics, studio art, theater, trigonometry, video film production, world civilizations, yoga.
Graduation Requirements Arts and fine arts (art, music, dance, drama), English, foreign language, human development, mathematics, physical education (includes health), science, social studies (includes history). Community service is required.
Special Academic Programs Honors section; term-away projects; academic accommodation for the gifted, the musically talented, and the artistically talented.
College Admission Counseling 129 students graduated in 2011; all went to college, including Boston University; New York University; University of Colorado Boulder; University of Michigan; University of Southern California; University of Wisconsin–Madison. Mean SAT critical reading: 620, mean SAT math: 609, mean SAT writing: 655, mean combined SAT: 1884, mean composite ACT: 27.
Student Life Upper grades have student council. Discipline rests primarily with faculty.
Summer Programs Remediation, enrichment, advancement, sports, art/fine arts, computer instruction programs offered; session focuses on enrichment; held on campus; accepts boys and girls; open to students from other schools. 1,100 students usually enrolled. 2012 schedule: June 28 to August 6. Application deadline: none.
Tuition and Aid Day student tuition: $30,900. Tuition installment plan (individually arranged payment plans, In-House only - 2 payment plan for full pay students and 10, payment plan exclusively for financial aid students only). Merit scholarship grants, need-based scholarship grants, Tuition Reduction Fund-Need Based Financial Aid, Merit-based scholarships for Elizabeth Mandell Music Institute only available. In 2011–12, 27% of upper-school students received aid. Total amount of financial aid awarded in 2011–12: $3,128,946.
Admissions Traditional secondary-level entrance grade is 9. For fall 2011, 178 students applied for upper-level admission, 73 were accepted, 48 enrolled. ISEE or PSAT

required. Deadline for receipt of application materials: December 7. Application fee required: $130. On-campus interview required.

Athletics Interscholastic: baseball (boys), basketball (b,g), cross-country running (b,g), soccer (b,g), softball (g), tennis (b,g), track and field (b,g), volleyball (b,g); coed interscholastic: flag football, golf, swimming and diving; coed intramural: canoeing/kayaking, climbing, hiking/backpacking, kayaking, outdoor activities, outdoor education, rock climbing, ropes courses, snowshoeing, table tennis. 10 PE instructors, 29 coaches, 1 athletic trainer.

Computers Computers are regularly used in college planning, creative writing, foreign language, graphic design, journalism, Latin, mathematics, music, newspaper, programming, science classes. Computer network features include on-campus library services, online commercial services, Internet access, wireless campus network. Student e-mail accounts and computer access in designated common areas are available to students. Students grades are available online. The school has a published electronic and media policy.

Contact Celia Lee, Director of Admissions. 310-829-7391 Ext. 704. Fax: 310-392-9011. E-mail: clee@xrds.org. Web site: www.xrds.org.

CRYSTAL SPRINGS UPLANDS SCHOOL

400 Uplands Drive

Hillsborough, California 94010

Head of School: Ms. Amy Richards

General Information Coeducational day college-preparatory school. Grades 6–12. Founded: 1952. Setting: suburban. Nearest major city is San Francisco. 10-acre campus. 4 buildings on campus. Approved or accredited by California Association of Independent Schools, Western Association of Schools and Colleges, and California Department of Education. Member of National Association of Independent Schools and Secondary School Admission Test Board. Endowment: $15 million. Total enrollment: 358. Upper school average class size: 14. Upper school faculty-student ratio: 1:9.

Faculty School total: 44. In upper school: 18 men, 26 women; 24 have advanced degrees.

Subjects Offered Acting, advanced computer applications, algebra, American history, American history-AP, American literature, art, art history-AP, art-AP, astronomy, biology, biology-AP, calculus, calculus-AP, ceramics, chamber groups, chemistry, chorus, comparative cultures, computer math, computer programming, computer science, concert bell choir, creative writing, dance, dance performance, drama, English, English literature, ensembles, environmental science-AP, European history, European history-AP, fine arts, French, French language-AP, French literature-AP, geometry, government and politics-AP, graphic design, health, history, mathematics, multicultural literature, music, music theory-AP, photography, physical education, physics, physics-AP, poetry, post-calculus, pre-calculus, science, Shakespeare, Spanish, Spanish language-AP, Spanish literature-AP, statistics, theater, U.S. government and politics-AP, video film production, wellness, world history, world literature, writing.

Graduation Requirements Arts and fine arts (art, music, dance, drama), English, foreign language, history, mathematics, physical education (includes health), science, senior project.

Special Academic Programs 16 Advanced Placement exams for which test preparation is offered; honors section; term-away projects; domestic exchange program; study abroad.

College Admission Counseling 61 students graduated in 2010; all went to college, including Stanford University; University of California, Los Angeles; University of California, San Diego; University of Pennsylvania; University of Southern California. Mean SAT critical reading: 674, mean SAT math: 703, mean SAT writing: 688, mean combined SAT: 2067, mean composite ACT: 29.

Student Life Upper grades have specified standards of dress, student council, honor system. Discipline rests equally with students and faculty.

Tuition and Aid Day student tuition: $32,700. Tuition installment plan (Insured Tuition Payment Plan, monthly payment plans, Tuition Management Systems Plan). Need-based scholarship grants available. In 2010–11, 22% of upper-school students received aid. Total amount of financial aid awarded in 2010–11: $2,000,000.

Admissions Traditional secondary-level entrance grade is 9. ISEE or SSAT required. Deadline for receipt of application materials: January 13. Application fee required: $85. On-campus interview required.

Athletics Interscholastic: baseball (boys), basketball (b,g), cross-country running (b,g), football (b), soccer (b,g), swimming and diving (b,g), tennis (b,g), track and field (b,g), volleyball (b,g); coed interscholastic: badminton, dance, golf; coed intramural: dance, fitness, outdoors, rock climbing. 3 PE instructors, 14 coaches, 1 athletic trainer.

Computers Computers are regularly used in all academic classes. Computer network features include on-campus library services, online commercial services, Internet access, wireless campus network, Internet filtering or blocking technology. Campus intranet, student e-mail accounts, and computer access in designated common areas are available to students. The school has a published electronic and media policy.

Contact Aaron Whitmore, Director of Admission. 650-342-4175 Ext. 1517. Fax: 650-342-7611. E-mail: admission@csus.org. Web site: www.csus.org.

THE CULVER ACADEMIES

1300 Academy Road

Culver, Indiana 46511

Head of School: Mr. John N. Buxton

General Information Coeducational boarding and day college-preparatory and arts school. Grades 9–PG. Founded: 1894. Setting: small town. Nearest major city is South Bend. Students are housed in single-sex dormitories. 1,700-acre campus. 38 buildings on campus. Approved or accredited by Independent Schools Association of the Central States, North Central Association of Colleges and Schools, and Indiana Department of Education. Member of National Association of Independent Schools and Secondary School Admission Test Board. Endowment: $285 million. Total enrollment: 802. Upper school average class size: 13. Upper school faculty-student ratio: 1:9. There are 185 required school days per year for Upper School students. Upper School students typically attend 5 days per week. The average school day consists of 6 hours.

Upper School Student Profile Grade 9: 150 students (86 boys, 64 girls); Grade 10: 215 students (123 boys, 92 girls); Grade 11: 225 students (118 boys, 107 girls); Grade 12: 212 students (121 boys, 91 girls). 92% of students are boarding students. 30% are state residents. 41 states are represented in upper school student body. 32% are international students. International students from Canada, China, Mexico, Republic of Korea, Saudi Arabia, and Taiwan; 26 other countries represented in student body.

Faculty School total: 97. In upper school: 53 men, 44 women; 83 have advanced degrees; 16 reside on campus.

Subjects Offered Acting, advanced math, African-American history, algebra, American government, American history, American history-AP, American literature, anatomy, anatomy and physiology, art, art history, arts, ballet, Basic programming, biology, biology-AP, calculus, calculus-AP, career/college preparation, ceramics, character education, chemistry, chemistry-AP, Chinese, choir, church history, college admission preparation, college placement, college planning, comparative government and politics-AP, comparative religion, computer math, computer programming, computer science, computer science-AP, dance, drama, dramatic arts, driver education, economics, economics-AP, English, English language-AP, English literature, entrepreneurship, equestrian sports, equine science, equitation, ESL, ethics and responsibility, European history, film studies, fine arts, fitness, French, French-AP, geology, geometry, German, German literature, German-AP, global studies, government, government-AP, government/civics, health and wellness, honors English, honors geometry, humanities, instrumental music, integrated mathematics, integrated science, jazz band, Latin, Latin-AP, leadership, library research, macro/microeconomics-AP, mathematics, mentorship program, music, music theory, music theory-AP, photography, physical education, physics, physics-AP, physiology, piano, play production, pottery, pre-algebra, pre-calculus, science, science research, Shakespeare, social studies, Spanish, Spanish language-AP, Spanish-AP, speech, statistics-AP, strings, theater, trigonometry, U.S. government and politics-AP, U.S. history-AP, world history, world religions.

Graduation Requirements Arts and fine arts (art, music, dance, drama), English, foreign language, health education, history, leadership, mathematics, science, senior community service project.

Special Academic Programs 21 Advanced Placement exams for which test preparation is offered; honors section; academic accommodation for the gifted, the musically talented, and the artistically talented; ESL (24 students enrolled).

College Admission Counseling 204 students graduated in 2011; 197 went to college, including Indiana University Bloomington; Purdue University; Southern Methodist University; The University of North Carolina at Chapel Hill; Vanderbilt University. Other: 1 entered military service, 4 entered a postgraduate year, 2 had other specific plans.

Student Life Upper grades have uniform requirement, student council, honor system. Discipline rests equally with students and faculty. Attendance at religious services is required.

Summer Programs Enrichment, advancement, ESL, sports, art/fine arts, rigorous outdoor training, computer instruction programs offered; session focuses on leadership training, citizenship, lifetime interests and skills development; held on campus; accepts boys and girls; open to students from other schools. 1,385 students usually enrolled. 2012 schedule: June 25 to August 7. Application deadline: May 1.

Tuition and Aid Day student tuition: $28,000; 7-day tuition and room/board: $38,000. Guaranteed tuition plan. Tuition installment plan (Key Tuition Payment Plan). Merit scholarship grants, need-based scholarship grants available. In 2011–12, 46% of upper-school students received aid; total upper-school merit-scholarship money awarded: $7,850,000. Total amount of financial aid awarded in 2011–12: $8,900,000.

Admissions Traditional secondary-level entrance grade is 9. For fall 2011, 2,500 students applied for upper-level admission, 528 were accepted, 261 enrolled. SSAT or TOEFL required. Deadline for receipt of application materials: June 1. Application fee required: $30. Interview required.

Athletics Interscholastic: baseball (boys), basketball (b,g), cheering (g), crew (b,g), cross-country running (b,g), diving (b,g), equestrian sports (b,g), fencing (b,g), football (b), golf (b,g), hockey (b,g), horseback riding (b,g), ice hockey (b,g), indoor hockey (b,g), indoor track & field (b,g), lacrosse (b,g), polo (b,g), rugby (b,g), soccer (b,g), softball (g), swimming and diving (b,g), tennis (b,g), track and field (b,g), volleyball (g), winter (indoor) track (b,g), wrestling (b,g); intramural: aerobics (b,g), basketball (b,g), dance (b,g), dance squad (g), dance team (g), danceline (g), drill team (b,g), flag football (b,g), ice hockey (b,g), indoor soccer (b,g), marksmanship (b,g), modern dance (b,g), paint ball (b,g), racquetball (b,g), soccer (b,g); coed interscholastic: dressage, sailing, trap and skeet; coed intramural: aerobics, aerobics/dance, aerobics/Nautilus, alpine skiing, aquatics, archery, backpacking, badminton, ballet, broomball, climbing, combined training, cooperative games, cross-country running, figure skating, fitness, fitness walking, Frisbee, handball, hiking/backpacking, horseback riding, ice skating, independent competitive sports, indoor track, indoor track & field, jogging, life saving, Nautilus, outdoor activities, outdoor adventure, outdoor education, outdoor recreation, outdoor skills, outdoors, physical fitness, physical training, power lifting, project adventure, ropes courses, rowing, running, scuba diving, skeet shooting, skiing (downhill), snowboarding, strength & conditioning, swimming and diving, table tennis, tai chi, ultimate Frisbee, volleyball, walking, wall climbing, weight lifting, weight training, wilderness, yoga. 8 PE instructors, 4 athletic trainers.

Computers Computers are regularly used in all classes. Computer network features include on-campus library services, online commercial services, Internet access, wireless campus network, Internet filtering or blocking technology, each student is issued a laptop. Campus intranet, student e-mail accounts, and computer access in designated common areas are available to students. Students grades are available online. The school has a published electronic and media policy.

Contact Mr. Michael Turnbull, Director of Admissions. 574-842-7100. Fax: 574-842-8066. E-mail: turnbul@culver.org. Web site: culver.org.

CURREY INGRAM ACADEMY

6544 Murray Lane

Brentwood, Tennessee 37027

Head of School: Ms. Kathleen G. Rayburn

General Information Coeducational day college-preparatory, arts, technology, ethics and character education, and service learning school; primarily serves students with learning disabilities, individuals with Attention Deficit Disorder, dyslexic students, non-verbal learning disabilities, and speech and language disabilities. Grades K–12. Founded: 1968. Setting: suburban. Nearest major city is Nashville. 83-acre campus. 2 buildings on campus. Approved or accredited by Council of Accreditation and School Improvement, Southern Association of Colleges and Schools, Southern Association of Independent Schools, and Tennessee Department of Education. Member of National Association of Independent Schools. Total enrollment: 320. Upper school average class size: 7. Upper school faculty-student ratio: 1:4. There are 175 required school days per year for Upper School students. Upper School students typically attend 5 days per week. The average school day consists of 6 hours.

Upper School Student Profile Grade 9: 23 students (17 boys, 6 girls); Grade 10: 21 students (14 boys, 7 girls); Grade 11: 15 students (9 boys, 6 girls); Grade 12: 21 students (13 boys, 8 girls).

Faculty School total: 130.

Subjects Offered Algebra, American government, art, basic language skills, biology, British literature, character education, chemistry, cinematography, college admission preparation, college awareness, college counseling, college planning, community service, digital music, digital photography, drama performance, earth science, economics, electives, English composition, English literature, environmental science, ethics and responsibility, government, health, history, integrated technology fundamentals, learning strategies, life skills, literature, modern world history, music, newspaper, physical education, physics, pragmatics, pre-calculus, reading/study skills, social studies, sports, studio art, technology, video film production, vocal music, writing, writing workshop, yearbook.

Graduation Requirements Arts and fine arts (art, music, dance, drama), electives, English, ethics, foreign language, mathematics, physical education (includes health), science, social studies (includes history), students who need remediation in reading/writing take reading/writing workshop instead of foreign language, seniors must complete Service Learning credit plus 30 hours of community service.

Special Academic Programs Honors section; independent study; academic accommodation for the gifted, the musically talented, and the artistically talented; remedial reading and/or remedial writing; programs in English, mathematics, general development for dyslexic students.

College Admission Counseling 9 students graduated in 2011; all went to college.

Student Life Upper grades have uniform requirement, student council, honor system. Discipline rests primarily with faculty.

Summer Programs Enrichment, sports, art/fine arts programs offered; session focuses on camps for arts and athletics; held on campus; accepts boys and girls; open to students from other schools. 2012 schedule: June.

Tuition and Aid Day student tuition: $34,995. Tuition installment plan (monthly payment plans). Need-based scholarship grants available. In 2011–12, 35% of upper-school students received aid. Total amount of financial aid awarded in 2011–12: $1,200,000.

Admissions Traditional secondary-level entrance grade is 9. Psychoeducational evaluation required. Deadline for receipt of application materials: none. Application fee required: $250. Interview required.

Athletics Interscholastic: basketball (boys, girls), cheering (g), cross-country running (b,g), football (b), golf (b,g), softball (g), volleyball (g); intramural: dance (g), fitness (b,g); coed interscholastic: soccer.

Computers Computers are regularly used in all academic classes. Computer network features include on-campus library services, Internet access, wireless campus network, Internet filtering or blocking technology, iPods for instructional use in classrooms, 1:1 laptop program, assistive technology. Students grades are available online. The school has a published electronic and media policy.

Contact Ms. Amber Mogg, Director of Admission. 615-507-3173 Ext. 244. Fax: 615-507-3170. E-mail: amber.mogg@curreyingram.org. Web site: www.curreyingram.org.

CUSHING ACADEMY

39 School Street

PO Box 8000

Ashburnham, Massachusetts 01430-8000

Head of School: Dr. James Tracy

General Information Coeducational boarding and day college-preparatory, arts, and technology school. Grades 9–PG. Founded: 1865. Setting: small town. Nearest major city is Boston. Students are housed in single-sex dormitories. 162-acre campus. 31 buildings on campus. Approved or accredited by Association of Independent Schools in New England, New England Association of Schools and Colleges, and Massachusetts Department of Education. Member of National Association of Independent Schools and Secondary School Admission Test Board. Endowment: $29.2 million. Total enrollment: 445. Upper school average class size: 12. Upper school faculty-student ratio: 1:8. There are 152 required school days per year for Upper School students. Upper School students typically attend 5 days per week. The average school day consists of 7 hours.

Upper School Student Profile Grade 9: 65 students (41 boys, 24 girls); Grade 10: 107 students (67 boys, 40 girls); Grade 11: 140 students (71 boys, 69 girls); Grade 12: 110 students (70 boys, 40 girls); Postgraduate: 23 students (20 boys, 3 girls). 85% of students are boarding students. 31% are state residents. 28 states are represented in upper school student body. 30% are international students. International students from China, Germany, Mexico, Republic of Korea, Saudi Arabia, and Taiwan; 30 other countries represented in student body.

Faculty School total: 64. In upper school: 27 men, 37 women; 37 have advanced degrees; 47 reside on campus.

Subjects Offered Advanced biology, advanced math, Advanced Placement courses, aerobics, algebra, American government, American history, American literature, American literature-AP, anatomy, anatomy and physiology, architectural drawing, art, art history, athletic training, bioethics, biology, biology-AP, calculus, calculus-AP, career education internship, chemistry, chemistry-AP, Chinese, chorus, Civil War, community service, computer programming, computer science, creative arts, creative drama, creative writing, dance, developmental language skills, digital photography, discrete mathematics, drafting, drama, drawing, driver education, earth and space science, ecology, ecology, environmental systems, economics, economics and history, economics-AP, English, English literature, environmental science, ESL, ethics, European history, expository writing, fine arts, French, geometry, government/civics, grammar, graphic arts, health, health and wellness, history, honors algebra, honors English, honors geometry, honors U.S. history, honors world history, Latin, Latin-AP, Mandarin, marine biology, mathematics, mechanical drawing, music, music history, music theory, musical theater, photography, physics, physiology, pre-calculus, probability and statistics, psychology, SAT preparation, science, social studies, sociology, Spanish, Spanish-AP, speech, stagecraft, statistics-AP, student government, technology, The 20th Century, theater, theater history, trigonometry, U.S. government and politics-AP, U.S. history, United Nations and international issues, Vietnam War, visual arts, vocal music, wind instruments, world history, world literature, World-Wide-Web publishing, writing.

Graduation Requirements English, foreign language, health and wellness, mathematics, science, social studies (includes history).

Special Academic Programs 14 Advanced Placement exams for which test preparation is offered; honors section; independent study; term-away projects; academic accommodation for the gifted, the musically talented, and the artistically talented; remedial reading and/or remedial writing; remedial math; programs in English, mathematics, general development for dyslexic students; ESL (75 students enrolled).

College Admission Counseling 150 students graduated in 2011; 147 went to college, including Boston University; Northeastern University; Purdue University; Suffolk University; Syracuse University; University of New Hampshire. Other: 1 entered military service, 2 had other specific plans.

Student Life Upper grades have specified standards of dress, student council, honor system. Discipline rests primarily with faculty.

Summer Programs Remediation, enrichment, advancement, ESL, sports, art/fine arts, computer instruction programs offered; session focuses on enrichment; held on campus; accepts boys and girls; open to students from other schools. 320 students usually enrolled. 2012 schedule: July 1 to August 3.

Tuition and Aid Day student tuition: $34,900; 7-day tuition and room/board: $49,600. Tuition installment plan (Academic Management Services Plan, monthly payment plans). Merit scholarship grants, need-based scholarship grants available. In 2011–12, 26% of upper-school students received aid; total upper-school merit-scholarship money awarded: $100,000. Total amount of financial aid awarded in 2011–12: $3,200,000.

Admissions Traditional secondary-level entrance grade is 9. For fall 2011, 804 students applied for upper-level admission, 505 were accepted, 185 enrolled. ACT, PSAT,

SAT, SLEP, SSAT or TOEFL required. Deadline for receipt of application materials: February 1. Application fee required: $50. Interview required.
Athletics Interscholastic: baseball (boys), basketball (b,g), field hockey (g), football (b), hockey (b,g), ice hockey (b,g), lacrosse (b,g), running (b,g), skiing (downhill) (b,g), soccer (b,g), softball (g), tennis (b,g), track and field (b,g), volleyball (g); intramural: flag football (b); coed interscholastic: alpine skiing, cross-country running, golf, running; coed intramural: aerobics, aerobics/dance, alpine skiing, dance, equestrian sports, figure skating, fitness, horseback riding, ice hockey, ice skating, independent competitive sports, martial arts, modern dance, outdoor adventure, outdoor education, outdoor recreation, outdoor skills, physical fitness, physical training, ropes courses, skiing (downhill), snowboarding, strength & conditioning, wall climbing, weight training. 2 coaches, 2 athletic trainers.
Computers Computers are regularly used in all academic classes. Computer network features include on-campus library services, online commercial services, Internet access, wireless campus network, Internet filtering or blocking technology, CushNet (on-campus network), Cushing-designed iClass interactive tables, Digital Library. Campus intranet, student e-mail accounts, and computer access in designated common areas are available to students. Students grades are available online. The school has a published electronic and media policy.
Contact Mrs. Deborah A. Gustafson, Co-Director of Admissions. 978-827-7300. Fax: 978-827-6253. E-mail: admissions@cushing.org. Web site: www.cushing.org.

See Display on this page, Close-Up on page 612, and Summer Programs Close-Up on page 772.

DAKOTA CHRISTIAN SCHOOL

37614 Highway 44
Corsica, South Dakota 57328

Head of School: Ivan Groothuis

General Information Coeducational day college-preparatory, general academic, business, religious studies, and technology school, affiliated with Christian faith. Grades 9–12. Founded: 1955. Setting: rural. Nearest major city is Mitchell. 17-acre campus. 1 building on campus. Approved or accredited by Christian Schools International and South Dakota Department of Education. Endowment: $475,000. Total enrollment: 126. Upper school average class size: 15. Upper school faculty-student ratio: 1:8. There are 180 required school days per year for Upper School students.
Upper School Student Profile Grade 7: 10 students (5 boys, 5 girls); Grade 8: 7 students (3 boys, 4 girls); Grade 9: 12 students (7 boys, 5 girls); Grade 10: 9 students (3 boys, 6 girls); Grade 11: 11 students (2 boys, 9 girls); Grade 12: 18 students (10 boys, 8 girls). 80% of students are Christian faith.
Faculty School total: 9. In upper school: 5 men, 4 women; 4 have advanced degrees.
Subjects Offered Accounting, algebra, American history, American literature, ancient world history, Bible studies, biology, business law, chemistry, Christian ethics, church history, computer studies, concert band, concert choir, creative writing, earth science, English, English literature, fine arts, geometry, government/civics, grammar, history, home economics, keyboarding, mathematics, music, New Testament, personal finance, philosophy, physical education, physics, physiology, pre-calculus, psychology, religion, science, social studies, Spanish, speech, statistics, trigonometry, world history, world literature, yearbook.
Graduation Requirements Algebra, arts and fine arts (art, music, dance, drama), biology, computer studies, English, first aid, geography, geometry, keyboarding, music appreciation, philosophy, physical education (includes health), physical science, religion (includes Bible studies and theology), social sciences, sociology, speech, U.S. history, world history, writing, 10 hours of community service.
Special Academic Programs Independent study; study at local college for college credit.
College Admission Counseling 12 students graduated in 2010; 10 went to college, including Dordt College; South Dakota State University; The University of South Dakota; Trinity Christian College; University of Sioux Falls. Other: 2 went to work. Median composite ACT: 23.
Student Life Upper grades have specified standards of dress, student council, honor system. Discipline rests primarily with faculty. Attendance at religious services is required.
Tuition and Aid Day student tuition: $4700. Tuition installment plan (monthly payment plans, individually arranged payment plans). Tuition reduction for siblings, need-based scholarship grants available. In 2010–11, 100% of upper-school students received aid. Total amount of financial aid awarded in 2010–11: $300,000.
Admissions Traditional secondary-level entrance grade is 9. For fall 2010, 50 students applied for upper-level admission, 50 were accepted, 50 enrolled. Deadline for receipt of application materials: none. Application fee required: $100. Interview recommended.
Athletics Interscholastic: basketball (boys, girls), cheering (g), football (b), volleyball (g); intramural: baseball (b), kickball (b,g), softball (g); coed interscholastic: cross-country running, golf, track and field; coed intramural: archery, floor hockey, paddle tennis, soccer, touch football, volleyball. 5 coaches.
Computers Computers are regularly used in accounting, business applications, business skills, social studies, Spanish, typing, word processing, writing, yearbook classes. Computer network features include on-campus library services, Internet access, wireless campus network, Internet filtering or blocking technology. Students grades are available online. The school has a published electronic and media policy.

Contact ivan Groothuis, Principal. 605-243-2211. Fax: 605-243-2379. Web site: www.dchs.net.

DALLAS CHRISTIAN SCHOOL

1515 Republic Parkway

Mesquite, Texas 75150

Head of School: Dr. Colleen Netterville

General Information Coeducational day college-preparatory and religious studies school, affiliated with Church of Christ. Grades PK–12. Founded: 1957. Setting: suburban. Nearest major city is Dallas. 60-acre campus. 7 buildings on campus. Approved or accredited by National Christian School Association, Southern Association of Colleges and Schools, and Texas Department of Education. Total enrollment: 595. Upper school average class size: 25. Upper school faculty-student ratio: 1:12. There are 178 required school days per year for Upper School students. Upper School students typically attend 5 days per week. The average school day consists of 7 hours and 15 minutes.

Upper School Student Profile 36% of students are members of Church of Christ.

Faculty School total: 56. In upper school: 13 men, 17 women; 14 have advanced degrees.

Subjects Offered Algebra, American history, American literature, art, band, Bible studies, biology, calculus, cheerleading, chemistry, chorus, computer math, computer science, creative writing, drama, economics, English, English literature, fine arts, French, geography, geometry, government/civics, health, history, humanities, journalism, mathematics, newspaper, physical education, physics, religion, science, sign language, social studies, Spanish, speech, speech origins of English, theater, world history, world literature, yearbook.

Graduation Requirements Arts and fine arts (art, music, dance, drama), computer science, English, foreign language, mathematics, physical education (includes health), religion (includes Bible studies and theology), science, social studies (includes history), speech origins of English, seniors must take SAT or ACT.

Special Academic Programs Study at local college for college credit.

College Admission Counseling 71 students graduated in 2010; 70 went to college, including Abilene Christian University; Austin College; Baylor University; Dallas Baptist University; Pepperdine University; Texas A&M University. Mean SAT critical reading: 603, mean SAT math: 568, mean SAT writing: 595, mean composite ACT: 27.

Student Life Upper grades have uniform requirement, student council, honor system. Discipline rests primarily with faculty. Attendance at religious services is required.

Tuition and Aid Day student tuition: $12,450. Tuition installment plan (FACTS Tuition Payment Plan). Tuition reduction for siblings, need-based scholarship grants available. In 2010–11, 18% of upper-school students received aid. Total amount of financial aid awarded in 2010–11: $180,000.

Admissions Traditional secondary-level entrance grade is 9. For fall 2010, 32 students applied for upper-level admission, 20 were accepted, 18 enrolled. ERB IF, ERB Mathematics, ERB Reading and Math and Woodcock-Johnson Revised Achievement Test required. Deadline for receipt of application materials: none. Application fee required. On-campus interview required.

Athletics Interscholastic: baseball (boys), basketball (b,g), cheering (g), cross-country running (b,g), drill team (g), football (b), golf (b,g), soccer (b,g), softball (g), tennis (b,g), track and field (b,g), volleyball (g). 2 PE instructors.

Computers Computers are regularly used in computer applications, newspaper, Web site design, yearbook classes. Computer network features include on-campus library services, Internet access, Internet filtering or blocking technology. Student e-mail accounts are available to students. Students grades are available online.

Contact Mrs. Katie Neuroth, Admissions Assistant. 972-270-5495 Ext. 266. Fax: 972-686-9436. E-mail: kneuroth@dallaschristian.com. Web site: www.dallaschristian.com.

THE DALTON SCHOOL

108 East 89th Street

New York, New York 10128-1599

Head of School: Ellen C. Stein

General Information Coeducational day college-preparatory and arts school. Grades K–12. Founded: 1919. Setting: urban. 2 buildings on campus. Approved or accredited by New York State Association of Independent Schools. Member of National Association of Independent Schools and Secondary School Admission Test Board. Endowment: $65 million. Total enrollment: 1,311. Upper school average class size: 15. Upper school faculty-student ratio: 1:7.

Upper School Student Profile Grade 9: 116 students (59 boys, 57 girls); Grade 10: 119 students (61 boys, 58 girls); Grade 11: 117 students (59 boys, 58 girls); Grade 12: 109 students (52 boys, 57 girls).

Faculty School total: 203. In upper school: 60 men, 61 women; 58 have advanced degrees.

Subjects Offered Algebra, American history, American legal systems, American literature, architecture, art, art history, Asian literature, astronomy, biology, calculus, ceramics, chemistry, community service, computer programming, computer science, dance, earth science, ecology, economics, English, English literature, environmental science, ethics, European history, fine arts, French, geometry, government/civics, health, history, Latin, law, mathematics, music, philosophy, photography, physical education, physics, Russian literature, science, social studies, Spanish, theater, trigonometry, world history, world literature.

Graduation Requirements Arts and fine arts (art, music, dance, drama), computer science, English, foreign language, history, mathematics, physical education (includes health), science. Community service is required.

Special Academic Programs Advanced Placement exam preparation; honors section; independent study; study at local college for college credit.

College Admission Counseling 100 students graduated in 2011; all went to college, including Brown University; Cornell University; Harvard University; The George Washington University; University of Pennsylvania; Yale University. Median SAT critical reading: 690, median SAT math: 680, median SAT writing: 720.

Student Life Upper grades have student council. Discipline rests equally with students and faculty.

Tuition and Aid Day student tuition: $36,970. Tuition installment plan (FACTS Tuition Payment Plan, 2-payment plan). Need-based scholarship grants available. In 2011–12, 24% of upper-school students received aid. Total amount of financial aid awarded in 2011–12: $2,938,600.

Admissions Traditional secondary-level entrance grade is 9. For fall 2011, 394 students applied for upper-level admission, 50 were accepted, 30 enrolled. ISEE or SSAT required. Deadline for receipt of application materials: November 11. Application fee required: $60. On-campus interview required.

Athletics Interscholastic: baseball (boys), basketball (b,g), lacrosse (b,g), soccer (b,g), softball (g), tennis (b,g), track and field (b,g), wrestling (b); intramural: baseball (b), basketball (b,g); coed interscholastic: cross-country running, football, swimming and diving, volleyball; coed intramural: cheering, dance, football, modern dance, ultimate Frisbee. 10 PE instructors, 14 coaches, 1 athletic trainer.

Computers Computers are regularly used in English, foreign language, mathematics, science classes. Computer network features include on-campus library services, online commercial services, Internet access, wireless campus network, Internet filtering or blocking technology. Campus intranet, student e-mail accounts, and computer access in designated common areas are available to students.

Contact Jacqueline Katz, Associate Director, Middle and High School Admissions. 212-423-5262. Fax. 212-423-5259. E-mail: admissionsmshs@dalton.org. Web site: www.dalton.org.

DAMIEN HIGH SCHOOL

2280 Damien Avenue

La Verne, California 91750

Head of School: Rev. Peadar Cronin

General Information Boys' day college-preparatory school, affiliated with Roman Catholic Church. Grades 9–12. Founded: 1959. Setting: suburban. Nearest major city is Los Angeles. 23-acre campus. 9 buildings on campus. Approved or accredited by Western Association of Schools and Colleges, Western Catholic Education Association, and California Department of Education. Endowment: $2 million. Total enrollment: 962. Upper school average class size: 22. Upper school faculty-student ratio: 1:22. There are 180 required school days per year for Upper School students. Upper School students typically attend 5 days per week. The average school day consists of 7 hours.

Upper School Student Profile Grade 9: 267 students (267 boys); Grade 10: 230 students (230 boys); Grade 11: 231 students (231 boys); Grade 12: 234 students (234 boys). 63% of students are Roman Catholic.

Faculty School total: 70. In upper school: 60 men, 10 women; 60 have advanced degrees.

Subjects Offered 20th century history, 20th century physics, 20th century world history, 3-dimensional art, acting, advanced biology, advanced chemistry, advanced computer applications, advanced math, Advanced Placement courses, advanced studio art-AP, algebra, American Civil War, American democracy, American foreign policy, American government, American history, American history-AP, American literature, American literature-AP, analysis, analysis and differential calculus, analysis of data, analytic geometry, anatomy and physiology, ancient history, ancient world history, ancient/medieval philosophy, animation, applied arts, applied music, architectural drawing, architecture, art, art and culture, art appreciation, art education, art history, art history-AP, art-AP, arts, arts and crafts, arts appreciation, ASB Leadership, athletic training, athletics, audio visual/media, band, baseball, basic language skills, Basic programming, basketball, Bible, Bible as literature, Bible studies, biology, biology-AP, body human, bowling, British literature, British literature-AP, calculus, calculus-AP, campus ministry, Catholic belief and practice, chemistry, chemistry-AP, choir, choral music, chorus, Christian and Hebrew scripture, Christian doctrine, Christian education, Christian ethics, Christian scripture, Christian studies, Christian testament, Christianity, church history, civics, civil rights, Civil War, civil war history, comparative government and politics, comparative government and politics-AP, comparative political systems-AP, comparative politics, comparative religion, composition, composition-AP, computer animation, computer applications, computer art, computer education, computer graphics, computer information systems, computer literacy, computer multimedia, computer processing, computer programming, computer programming-AP, computer resources, computer science, computer science-AP, computer skills, computer studies, computer technologies, computer-aided design, computers, conceptual physics, concert band, constitutional history of U.S., constitutional law, contemporary art, creative writing, data analysis, data processing, debate, democracy in America, drama, drama performance, drama workshop, dramatic arts, drawing, drawing and design, economics, economics-AP, English, English composition, English language and composition-AP, English language-AP, English literature, English literature and composition-AP, English literature-AP, English-AP, English/composition-AP, environmental science-AP, equality and freedom, European history-AP, expository writing, film, film appreciation, film history, film studies, fine arts, foreign language, foreign policy, forensics, French, French language-AP, French literature-AP, French studies, French-AP, freshman seminar, functions, geometry, German, German literature, German-AP, global issues, government, government and politics-AP, government-AP, government/civics, government/civics-AP, grammar, guidance, health, health education, history, history of music, history of the Americas, history of the Catholic Church, history-AP, honors algebra, honors English, honors geometry, honors U.S. history, honors world history, HTML design, human anatomy, human biology, human geography - AP, human sexuality, Internet, intro to computers, jazz, jazz band, jazz ensemble, jazz theory, journalism, lab science, language, language and composition, language arts, language-AP, leadership and service, library, Life of Christ, life science, literature and composition-AP, literature-AP, logarithms, macro/microeconomics-AP, macroeconomics-AP, math applications, mathematical modeling, mathematics, mathematics-AP, medieval history, microeconomics, microeconomics-AP, modern European history, modern European history-AP, modern history, modern languages, modern political theory, modern politics, modern Western civilization, modern world history, moral and social development, moral reasoning, moral theology, music, music appreciation, music composition, music history, music performance, music theory, music theory-AP, music-AP, musical productions, Native American history, New Testament, newspaper, North American literature, philosophy, physical education, physics, physics-AP, physiology, political science, politics, prayer/spirituality, pre-calculus, probability and statistics, programming, psychology, psychology-AP, reading, reading/study skills, religion, religion and culture, religious education, religious studies, science, scripture, social doctrine, social justice, social sciences, Spanish, Spanish language-AP, Spanish literature, Spanish literature-AP, Spanish-AP, speech, speech and debate, statistics, statistics-AP, stock market, student government, student publications, studio art, studio art-AP, swimming, technology, tennis, the Web, theater, theater arts, theater design and production, theater history, theater production, theology, track and field, trigonometry, U.S. government, U.S. government and politics, U.S. government and politics-AP, U.S. history, U.S. history-AP, U.S. literature, U.S. Presidents, United States government-AP, video, Vietnam War, visual arts, vocal jazz, vocal music, water polo, weight fitness, weight training, weightlifting, Western civilization, Western literature, Western religions, wind ensemble, wind instruments, world geography, world governments, world history, world history-AP, world literature, world religions, world religions, World War I, World War II, world wide web design, wrestling, writing, writing, yearbook.

Special Academic Programs 18 Advanced Placement exams for which test preparation is offered; honors section; accelerated programs; independent study; study at local college for college credit; study abroad; remedial reading and/or remedial writing; remedial math.

College Admission Counseling 268 students graduated in 2011; 260 went to college, including Ball State University; California State University, Fullerton. Other: 2 entered military service, 6 had other specific plans. Median SAT critical reading: 480, median SAT math: 540. 40% scored over 600 on SAT critical reading, 50% scored over 600 on SAT math.

Student Life Upper grades have specified standards of dress, student council. Discipline rests primarily with faculty.

Summer Programs Remediation, enrichment, advancement, sports, art/fine arts, computer instruction programs offered; session focuses on academics; held on campus; accepts boys and girls; open to students from other schools. 600 students usually enrolled. 2012 schedule: June 18 to July 20. Application deadline: June 1.

Tuition and Aid Day student tuition: $6900. Guaranteed tuition plan. Tuition installment plan (The Tuition Plan, monthly payment plans, individually arranged payment plans). Tuition reduction for siblings, merit scholarship grants, need-based scholarship grants available. In 2011–12, 25% of upper-school students received aid; total upper-school merit-scholarship money awarded: $50,000. Total amount of financial aid awarded in 2011–12: $50,000.

Admissions Traditional secondary-level entrance grade is 9. For fall 2011, 340 students applied for upper-level admission, 340 were accepted, 267 enrolled. Scholastic Testing Service required. Deadline for receipt of application materials: none. Application fee required: $75. Interview required.

Athletics Interscholastic: baseball, basketball, billiards, bowling, cross-country running, diving, field hockey, fishing, football, golf, hockey, ice hockey, in-line hockey, indoor hockey, lacrosse, physical fitness, racquetball, roller hockey, running, soccer, surfing, swimming and diving, tennis, track and field, water polo, weight lifting, wrestling. 1 PE instructor, 30 coaches, 2 athletic trainers.

Computers Computer network features include on-campus library services, online commercial services, Internet access. Students grades are available online. The school has a published electronic and media policy.

Contact Mrs. Kay Manning, Registrar. 909-596-1946. Fax: 909-596-6112. E-mail: kay@damien-hs.edu. Web site: www.damien-hs.edu.

DAMIEN MEMORIAL SCHOOL

1401 Houghtailing Street

Honolulu, Hawaii 96817-2797

Head of School: Mr. Bernard Ho

General Information Boys' day college-preparatory, arts, business, religious studies, and technology school, affiliated with Roman Catholic Church. Grades 6–12. Founded: 1962. Setting: urban. 8-acre campus. 9 buildings on campus. Approved or accredited by National Catholic Education Association and Western Association of Schools and Colleges. Total enrollment: 407. Upper school average class size: 25. Upper school faculty-student ratio: 1:10. There are 180 required school days per year for Upper School students. Upper School students typically attend 5 days per week. The average school day consists of 6 hours and 30 minutes.

Upper School Student Profile Grade 7: 20 students (20 boys); Grade 8: 24 students (24 boys); Grade 9: 103 students (103 boys); Grade 10: 72 students (72 boys); Grade 11: 90 students (90 boys); Grade 12: 100 students (100 boys). 75% of students are Roman Catholic.

Faculty School total: 35. In upper school: 27 men, 8 women; 24 have advanced degrees.

Subjects Offered Advanced Placement courses, algebra, American history, American literature, art, band, biology, business, business skills, calculus, chemistry, computer programming, economics, engineering, English, English literature, geometry, government, grammar, Hawaiian history, health, history, Japanese, journalism, JROTC, mathematics, photography, physical education, physics, pre-calculus, psychology, religion, SAT/ACT preparation, science, social sciences, social studies, Spanish, speech, trigonometry, world history.

Graduation Requirements Business skills (includes word processing), English, foreign language, mathematics, physical education (includes health), religion (includes Bible studies and theology), science, social sciences, social studies (includes history).

Special Academic Programs Honors section; independent study; study at local college for college credit.

College Admission Counseling 120 students graduated in 2010; 116 went to college, including Pacific University. Other: 4 went to work.

Student Life Upper grades have specified standards of dress, student council. Discipline rests primarily with faculty. Attendance at religious services is required.

Tuition and Aid Day student tuition: $9875. Tuition installment plan (FACTS Tuition Payment Plan, monthly payment plans, individually arranged payment plans, 2-payment plan, 10-payment plan). Tuition reduction for siblings, merit scholarship grants, need-based scholarship grants available. In 2010–11, 50% of upper-school students received aid; total upper-school merit-scholarship money awarded: $100,000. Total amount of financial aid awarded in 2010–11: $600,000.

Admissions Traditional secondary-level entrance grade is 9. Educational Development Series or High School Placement Test required. Deadline for receipt of application materials: none. Application fee required: $50. On-campus interview recommended.

Athletics Interscholastic: baseball, basketball, bowling, canoeing/kayaking, cheering (g), cross-country running, football, golf, judo, soccer, strength & conditioning, tennis, track and field, volleyball, weight training, wrestling; intramural: basketball. 2 PE instructors, 15 coaches, 2 athletic trainers.

Computers Computers are regularly used in English, science, yearbook classes. Computer network features include on-campus library services, Internet access, wireless campus network, Internet filtering or blocking technology. Student e-mail accounts and computer access in designated common areas are available to students. Students grades are available online. The school has a published electronic and media policy.

Contact Mr. Brent Limos, Director of Admissions. 808-841-0195. Fax: 808-847-1401. E-mail: limos@damien.edu. Web site: www.damien.edu/.

DANA HALL SCHOOL

45 Dana Road

Wellesley, Massachusetts 02482

Head of School: Ms. Caroline Erisman, JD

General Information Girls' boarding and day college-preparatory and Forum- Life Skills school. Boarding grades 9–12, day grades 6–12. Founded: 1881. Setting: suburban. Nearest major city is Boston. Students are housed in single-sex dormitories. 55-acre campus. 34 buildings on campus. Approved or accredited by Association of Independent Schools in New England, Massachusetts Department of Education, New England Association of Schools and Colleges, The Association of Boarding Schools, and Massachusetts Department of Education. Member of National Association of Independent Schools and Secondary School Admission Test Board. Endowment: $18.4 million. Total enrollment: 475. Upper school average class size: 12. Upper school faculty-student ratio: 1:9. There are 160 required school days per year for Upper School students. Upper School students typically attend 5 days per week. The average school day consists of 7 hours and 30 minutes.

Upper School Student Profile Grade 9: 81 students (81 girls); Grade 10: 94 students (94 girls); Grade 11: 90 students (90 girls); Grade 12: 90 students (90 girls). 38% of students are boarding students. 69% are state residents. 16 states are represented in upper school student body. 17% are international students. International students from

China, Hong Kong, Mexico, Republic of Korea, Taiwan, and Thailand; 15 other countries represented in student body.

Faculty School total: 61. In upper school: 17 men, 28 women; 33 have advanced degrees; 34 reside on campus.

Subjects Offered Acting, African history, African studies, algebra, American history, American literature, architecture, art, art history, art-AP, astronomy, biology, calculus, ceramics, chemistry, chorus, community service, computer programming, computer science, creative writing, dance, dance performance, drama, drama workshop, drawing, East Asian history, economics, electives, English, English composition, English language and composition-AP, English/composition-AP, European history, European history-AP, fitness, French, French language-AP, French literature-AP, freshman foundations, geometry, government, government/civics, health, journalism, Latin, Latin American history, Latin-AP, leadership education training, library, Mandarin, marine biology, mathematics-AP, Middle Eastern history, music, music composition, music performance, music theory, photography, physics, physics-AP, public speaking, Russian studies, Spanish, Spanish-AP, statistics-AP, trigonometry, U.S. history-AP, U.S. literature, weight training, Western civilization, women in the classical world.

Graduation Requirements American history, area studies, computer science, English, fitness, foreign language, mathematics, performing arts, science, social studies (includes history), visual arts, 20 hours of community service.

Special Academic Programs 17 Advanced Placement exams for which test preparation is offered; honors section; independent study; term-away projects; study abroad.

College Admission Counseling 103 students graduated in 2011; all went to college, including Brandeis University; Connecticut College; New York University; The Johns Hopkins University; Trinity College; University of Pennsylvania. Mean SAT critical reading: 600, mean SAT math: 632, mean SAT writing: 632, mean combined SAT: 1864, mean composite ACT: 28. 47% scored over 600 on SAT critical reading, 64% scored over 600 on SAT math, 65% scored over 600 on SAT writing, 59% scored over 1800 on combined SAT, 66% scored over 26 on composite ACT.

Student Life Upper grades have specified standards of dress, student council, honor system. Discipline rests equally with students and faculty.

Summer Programs Enrichment, sports programs offered; session focuses on leadership training and confidence building for girls entering high school; held on campus; accepts girls; open to students from other schools. 32 students usually enrolled. 2012 schedule: June 23 to June 30. Application deadline: none.

Tuition and Aid Day student tuition: $38,496; 7-day tuition and room/board: $51,109. Tuition installment plan (monthly payment plans, K-12 Family Education Loan, AchieverLoan). Need-based scholarship grants, need-based loans available. In 2011–12, 19% of upper-school students received aid. Total amount of financial aid awarded in 2011–12: $3,163,219.

Admissions Traditional secondary-level entrance grade is 9. For fall 2011, 537 students applied for upper-level admission, 273 were accepted, 132 enrolled. ISEE, SSAT or TOEFL required. Deadline for receipt of application materials: February 1. Application fee required: $50. Interview required.

Athletics Interscholastic: basketball, cross-country running, equestrian sports, fencing, field hockey, golf, horseback riding, ice hockey, lacrosse, modern dance, soccer, softball, squash, swimming and diving, tennis, volleyball; intramural: aerobics, aerobics/dance, aquatics, ballet, crew, dance, equestrian sports, fitness, Frisbee, golf, hiking/backpacking, horseback riding, indoor track, life saving, martial arts, modern dance, Nautilus, outdoor activities, physical fitness, physical training, rock climbing, scuba diving, self defense, skiing (downhill), squash, strength & conditioning, swimming and diving, tennis, ultimate Frisbee, weight lifting, weight training, yoga. 5 PE instructors, 20 coaches, 1 athletic trainer.

Computers Computers are regularly used in art, English, French, history, Latin, mathematics, science, Spanish, Web site design, yearbook classes. Computer network features include on-campus library services, online commercial services, Internet access, wireless campus network, Internet filtering or blocking technology. Campus intranet, student e-mail accounts, and computer access in designated common areas are available to students.

Contact Mrs. Brenda Dowdell, Admission Office Manager. 781-235-3010 Ext. 2531. Fax: 781-239-1383. E-mail: admission@danahall.org. Web site: www.danahall.org.

DARLINGTON SCHOOL

1014 Cave Spring Road

Rome, Georgia 30161

Head of School: Thomas C. Whitworth III

General Information Coeducational boarding and day college-preparatory, arts, and technology school. Boarding grades 9–PG, day grades PK–PG. Founded: 1905. Setting: small town. Nearest major city is Atlanta. Students are housed in single-sex dormitories. 500-acre campus. 15 buildings on campus. Approved or accredited by Georgia Independent School Association, Southern Association of Colleges and Schools, Southern Association of Independent Schools, The Association of Boarding Schools, The College Board, and Georgia Department of Education. Member of National Association of Independent Schools and Secondary School Admission Test Board. Endowment: $32.7 million. Total enrollment: 880. Upper school average class size: 13. Upper school faculty-student ratio: 1:13. There are 176 required school days per year for Upper School students. Upper School students typically attend 5 days per week. The average school day consists of 7 hours and 30 minutes.

Upper School Student Profile Grade 9: 79 students (38 boys, 41 girls); Grade 10: 130 students (71 boys, 59 girls); Grade 11: 131 students (70 boys, 61 girls); Grade 12: 142 students (68 boys, 74 girls). 39% of students are boarding students. 79% are state residents. 17 states are represented in upper school student body. 19% are international students. International students from Bahamas, Bermuda, China, Germany, Mexico, and Republic of Korea; 38 other countries represented in student body.

Faculty School total: 94. In upper school: 30 men, 15 women; 32 have advanced degrees; 54 reside on campus.

Subjects Offered Advanced biology, advanced chemistry, Advanced Placement courses, advanced studio art-AP, algebra, ancient world history, art, art history, art history-AP, band, biology, biology-AP, calculus, calculus-AP, chemistry, chemistry-AP, choir, chorus, college counseling, computer programming, computer science, concert choir, creative writing, drama, drawing, economics, economics-AP, English, English language and composition-AP, English language-AP, English literature, English literature-AP, English-AP, ensembles, environmental science, environmental science-AP, ESL, fine arts, French, geometry, government-AP, graphic arts, graphic design, health, honors algebra, honors English, honors geometry, honors world history, humanities, jazz ensemble, journalism, lab science, macro/microeconomics-AP, macroeconomics-AP, modern European history-AP, music, music theory-AP, musical theater, newspaper, personal fitness, physical education, physics, physics-AP, pre-calculus, probability and statistics, psychology-AP, robotics, Spanish, Spanish language-AP, Spanish literature-AP, Spanish-AP, statistics-AP, studio art-AP, trigonometry, U.S. history, U.S. history-AP, video, video film production, vocal ensemble, wind ensemble, world cultures, world history, world history-AP, yearbook.

Graduation Requirements Arts and fine arts (art, music, dance, drama), English, foreign language, information technology, mathematics, physical education (includes health), science, social studies (includes history), community service/servant leadership program, after school activity.

Special Academic Programs 21 Advanced Placement exams for which test preparation is offered; honors section; academic accommodation for the musically talented; ESL (18 students enrolled).

College Admission Counseling 119 students graduated in 2011; all went to college, including Auburn University; Georgia Institute of Technology; Georgia Southern University; The University of Alabama; University of Georgia; University of Mississippi. Median SAT critical reading: 481, median SAT math: 549, median SAT writing: 501, median combined SAT: 1530.

Student Life Upper grades have uniform requirement, student council, honor system. Discipline rests equally with students and faculty.

Summer Programs Enrichment, ESL, sports, art/fine arts, computer instruction programs offered; session focuses on academic enrichment and specialized sports camps for all ages; held on campus; accepts boys and girls; open to students from other schools. 3,500 students usually enrolled. 2012 schedule: June 2 to August 5. Application deadline: none.

Tuition and Aid Day student tuition: $17,650; 7-day tuition and room/board: $40,600. Tuition installment plan (FACTS Tuition Payment Plan, monthly payment plans, individually arranged payment plans). Merit scholarship grants, need-based scholarship grants available. In 2011–12, 42% of upper-school students received aid; total upper-school merit-scholarship money awarded: $721,175. Total amount of financial aid awarded in 2011–12: $2,801,475.

Admissions Traditional secondary-level entrance grade is 9. For fall 2011, 255 students applied for upper-level admission, 203 were accepted, 100 enrolled. PSAT and SAT for applicants to grade 11 and 12, SSAT or WISC III or TOEFL required. Deadline for receipt of application materials: February 1. Application fee required: $50. Interview required.

Athletics Interscholastic: baseball (boys), basketball (b,g), cheering (g), crew (b,g), cross-country running (b,g), diving (b,g), football (b), golf (b,g), lacrosse (b,g), rowing (b,g), soccer (b,g), softball (g), swimming and diving (b,g), tennis (b,g), track and field (b,g), volleyball (g), wrestling (b); intramural: aerobics/dance (g), aquatics (b,g), basketball (b,g), cheering (g), dance squad (g), fitness (b,g), flag football (b,g), flagball (b,g), running (b,g), tennis (b,g), volleyball (b,g); coed intramural: aerobics, fishing, fly fishing, Frisbee, independent competitive sports, outdoor activities, outdoor education, outdoor recreation, physical fitness, physical training, skeet shooting, soccer, speleology, strength & conditioning, table tennis, ultimate Frisbee, water volleyball, weight lifting, weight training. 2 PE instructors, 11 coaches, 2 athletic trainers.

Computers Computers are regularly used in computer applications, English, foreign language, history, mathematics, science, Web site design classes. Computer network features include on-campus library services, Internet access, wireless campus network, Internet filtering or blocking technology. Campus intranet, student e-mail accounts, and computer access in designated common areas are available to students. Students grades are available online. The school has a published electronic and media policy.

Contact Mrs. Kila McCann, Director of Boarding Admission. 706-236-0447. Fax: 706-232-3600. E-mail: kmccann@darlingtonschool.org. Web site: www.darlingtonschool.org.

DAVID LIPSCOMB HIGH SCHOOL

3901 Granny White Pike

Nashville, Tennessee 37204-3951

Head of School: Dr. Michael P. Hammond

General Information Coeducational day college-preparatory and religious studies school, affiliated with Church of Christ. Grades PK–12. Founded: 1891. Setting: suburban. 10-acre campus. 4 buildings on campus. Approved or accredited by National Christian School Association, Southern Association of Colleges and Schools, Southern Association of Independent Schools, Tennessee Association of Independent Schools, and Tennessee Department of Education. Endowment: $95,000. Total enrollment: 1,386. Upper school average class size: 20. Upper school faculty-student ratio: 1:15. Upper School students typically attend 5 days per week.

Upper School Student Profile Grade 9: 137 students (65 boys, 72 girls); Grade 10: 119 students (69 boys, 50 girls); Grade 11: 135 students (73 boys, 62 girls); Grade 12: 147 students (72 boys, 75 girls). 64% of students are members of Church of Christ.

Faculty School total: 35. In upper school: 16 men, 19 women; 25 have advanced degrees.

Subjects Offered Accounting, advanced computer applications, algebra, American government, American history, anatomy and physiology, art, band, biology, biology-AP, calculus-AP, chemistry, chemistry-AP, chorus, computer science, current history, drama, economics, English, French, geography, geometry, health, home economics, honors algebra, honors English, honors geometry, interior design, journalism, keyboarding, Latin, mathematics, modern history, painting, photography, physical education, physics, pre-algebra, psychology, religion, science, science research, social studies, Spanish, Spanish-AP, speech, statistics, trigonometry, visual arts, world history.

Graduation Requirements Economics, English, foreign language, mathematics, physical education (includes health), religion (includes Bible studies and theology), science, social studies (includes history), research paper, 60 hours of community service.

Special Academic Programs 4 Advanced Placement exams for which test preparation is offered; honors section; accelerated programs; study at local college for college credit; programs in general development for dyslexic students.

College Admission Counseling 132 students graduated in 2010; 131 went to college, including Belmont University; Harding University; Lipscomb University; Middle Tennessee State University; The University of Alabama; The University of Tennessee. Other: 1 entered military service. Mean composite ACT: 24.

Student Life Upper grades have uniform requirement, student council. Discipline rests primarily with faculty. Attendance at religious services is required.

Tuition and Aid Day student tuition: $9500. Tuition installment plan (monthly payment plans, individually arranged payment plans). Tuition reduction for siblings, need-based scholarship grants available. In 2010–11, 1% of upper-school students received aid. Total amount of financial aid awarded in 2010–11: $46,840.

Admissions Traditional secondary-level entrance grade is 9. For fall 2010, 41 students applied for upper-level admission, 35 were accepted, 30 enrolled. TOEFL required. Deadline for receipt of application materials: none. Application fee required: $100. Interview required.

Athletics Interscholastic: baseball (boys), basketball (b,g), bowling (b,g), cheering (g), cross-country running (b,g), football (b), golf (b,g), soccer (b,g), softball (g), tennis (b,g), track and field (b,g), volleyball (g), wrestling (b); intramural: basketball (b,g); coed intramural: basketball. 2 PE instructors, 16 coaches, 1 athletic trainer.

Computers Computer network features include on-campus library services, online commercial services, Internet access, wireless campus network, Internet filtering or blocking technology. Student e-mail accounts and computer access in designated common areas are available to students. Students grades are available online. The school has a published electronic and media policy.

Contact Mrs. Kim Schow, Administrative Assistant. 615-966-6409. Fax: 615-966-7639. E-mail: kim.schow@lipscomb.edu. Web site: www.dlcs.lipscomb.edu.

DAVIDSON ACADEMY

1414 Old Hickory Boulevard

Nashville, Tennessee 37207-1098

Head of School: Dr. Bill Chaney

General Information Coeducational day college-preparatory, arts, religious studies, technology, and science, mathematics school, affiliated with Christian faith. Grades PK–12. Founded: 1980. 1 building on campus. Approved or accredited by Association of Christian Schools International, Southern Association of Colleges and Schools, and Tennessee Department of Education. Endowment: $25,000. Upper school average class size: 18.

Upper School Student Profile 99% of students are Christian faith.

Subjects Offered 3-dimensional art, ACT preparation, advanced math, Advanced Placement courses, algebra, American government, American history, American history-AP, art, art appreciation, audio visual/media, band, Bible, Bible studies, biology, calculus, calculus-AP, cheerleading, chemistry, choral music, chorus, church history, college admission preparation, college counseling, college placement, composition-AP, computer applications, computer skills, conceptual physics, concert band, concert choir, consumer economics, creative writing, drama, drama performance, dramatic arts, earth science, economics, English, English literature-AP, English-AP, English/composition-AP, film and new technologies, geography, geometry, government-AP, health and wellness, history, honors algebra, honors English, honors geometry, human anatomy, independent study, Latin, leadership and service, Life of Christ, literature, marching band, mathematics, mathematics-AP, music, musical productions, New Testament, newspaper, physical education, physical fitness, physical science, physics, physics-AP, poetry, pre-algebra, pre-calculus, pre-college orientation, probability and statistics, psychology, reading, religious studies, science, senior project, Spanish, speech, speech communications, trigonometry, U.S. history, U.S. history-AP, video film production, wellness, world geography, world history, writing, yearbook.

Graduation Requirements Algebra, art, biology, calculus, chemistry, computer technologies, drama, economics, electives, English, English composition, English literature, foreign language, geometry, government, literature, physical science, physics, senior project, trigonometry, U.S. history, wellness, world history, senior math topics, Old Testament, New Testament.

Special Academic Programs Advanced Placement exam preparation; honors section; independent study; study at local college for college credit; programs in general development for dyslexic students.

College Admission Counseling 66 students graduated in 2011; all went to college, including Austin Peay State University; Middle Tennessee State University; Tennessee Technological University; The University of Tennessee; Western Kentucky University.

Summer Programs Enrichment, advancement, sports, art/fine arts programs offered; session focuses on physical and mental growth through a caring, Christian, and learning-enriched environment; held on campus; accepts boys and girls; open to students from other schools. 250 students usually enrolled. 2012 schedule: May 30 to July 30. Application deadline: April 15.

Tuition and Aid Day student tuition: $7745. Tuition installment plan (monthly payment plans, individually arranged payment plans). Tuition reduction for siblings, need-based scholarship grants, need-based financial aid, tuition reduction for children of faculty and staff available. In 2011–12, 10% of upper-school students received aid.

Admissions Traditional secondary-level entrance grade is 9. For fall 2011, 63 students applied for upper-level admission, 52 were accepted, 44 enrolled. Admissions testing, any standardized test and WRAT required. Deadline for receipt of application materials: none. Application fee required: $100.

Athletics Interscholastic: baseball (boys), basketball (b,g), cheering (g), cross-country running (b,g), dance team (g), football (b), golf (b,g), soccer (b,g), softball (g), tennis (b,g), track and field (b,g), volleyball (g); intramural: ballet (g), dance (g), weight training (b). 1 athletic trainer.

Computers Computers are regularly used in computer applications, English, graphic arts, history, mathematics, media production, newspaper, yearbook classes. Computer network features include on-campus library services, Internet access, wireless campus network, Internet filtering or blocking technology, RenWeb, Accelerated Reader, CollegeView. Computer access in designated common areas is available to students. Students grades are available online.

Contact Mrs. Darlyne Kent, Director of Admissions. 615-860-5307. Fax: 615-868-7918. E-mail: dkent@davidsonacademy.com. Web site: www.davidsonacademy.com.

DEERFIELD ACADEMY

7 Boyden Lane

Deerfield, Massachusetts 01342

Head of School: Dr. Margarita O'Byrne Curtis

General Information Coeducational boarding and day college-preparatory school. Grades 9–PG. Founded: 1797. Setting: small town. Nearest major city is Hartford, CT. Students are housed in single-sex dormitories. 280-acre campus. 81 buildings on campus. Approved or accredited by Association of Independent Schools in New England, National Independent Private Schools Association, New England Association of Schools and Colleges, and Massachusetts Department of Education. Member of National Association of Independent Schools and Secondary School Admission Test Board. Endowment: $367 million. Total enrollment: 630. Upper school average class size: 12. Upper school faculty-student ratio: 1:6. There are 150 required school days per year for Upper School students. Upper School students typically attend 5 days per week. The average school day consists of 5 hours and 25 minutes.

Upper School Student Profile Grade 9: 101 students (52 boys, 49 girls); Grade 10: 150 students (73 boys, 77 girls); Grade 11: 180 students (86 boys, 94 girls); Grade 12: 179 students (90 boys, 89 girls); Postgraduate: 20 students (18 boys, 2 girls). 88% of students are boarding students. 23% are state residents. 39 states are represented in upper school student body. 14% are international students. International students from Canada, China, Jamaica, Republic of Korea, Singapore, and Thailand; 25 other countries represented in student body.

Faculty School total: 119. In upper school: 62 men, 57 women; 89 have advanced degrees; 115 reside on campus.

Subjects Offered Advanced chemistry, advanced computer applications, advanced math, advanced studio art-AP, algebra, American government, American history-AP, American studies, analytic geometry, anatomy, applied arts, applied music, Arabic, architectural drawing, architecture, art, art history, art history-AP, Asian history, Asian literature, Asian studies, astronomy, Basic programming, biochemistry, biology, biology-AP, Black history, calculus, calculus-AP, chemistry, chemistry-AP, Chinese, computer applications, computer math, computer programming, computer science, computer science-AP, concert band, creative writing, dance, dance performance, discrete mathematics, drama, drama performance, drama workshop, drawing and design, earth science, Eastern religion and philosophy, ecology, economics, economics-AP, English, English literature, English literature-AP, English-AP, environmental science, ethics, European history, expository writing, fine arts, French, geology, geometry, Greek, health, health education, history, instrumental music, journalism, Latin, literature, mathematics, modern European history, music, philosophy, photography, physics, physics-AP, physiology, probability and statistics, religion, science, social studies, Spanish, Spanish literature, studio art, studio art-AP, theater, theater arts, trigonometry, U.S. history, U.S. literature, video, vocal music, Western civilization, world civilizations, world governments, world history, world literature, world religions, writing.

Graduation Requirements Arts and fine arts (art, music, dance, drama), English, foreign language, history, mathematics, philosophy, science.

Special Academic Programs Advanced Placement exam preparation; honors section; independent study; term-away projects; study abroad; academic accommodation for the gifted, the musically talented, and the artistically talented.

College Admission Counseling 189 students graduated in 2011; 175 went to college, including Brown University; Dartmouth College; Georgetown University; Harvard University; Middlebury College; Yale University. Other: 1 entered military service, 1 entered a postgraduate year, 12 had other specific plans. Mean SAT critical reading: 653, mean SAT math: 662, mean SAT writing: 661.

Student Life Upper grades have specified standards of dress, student council, honor system. Discipline rests equally with students and faculty.

Tuition and Aid Day student tuition: $32,575; 7-day tuition and room/board: $45,450. Tuition installment plan (Educational Data Systems, Inc.). Need-based scholarship grants available. In 2011–12, 35% of upper-school students received aid. Total amount of financial aid awarded in 2011–12: $7,003,000.

Admissions Traditional secondary-level entrance grade is 9. For fall 2011, 2,361 students applied for upper-level admission, 312 were accepted, 203 enrolled. ACT, ISEE, PSAT, SAT, SSAT or TOEFL required. Deadline for receipt of application materials: January 13. Application fee required: $60. Interview required.

Athletics Interscholastic: alpine skiing (boys, girls), baseball (b), basketball (b,g), crew (b,g), cross-country running (b,g), diving (b,g), field hockey (g), football (b), golf (b), ice hockey (b,g), lacrosse (b,g), skiing (downhill) (b,g), soccer (b,g), softball (g), squash (b,g), swimming and diving (b,g), tennis (b,g), track and field (b,g), volleyball (g), water polo (b,g), wrestling (b); intramural: dance (b,g), fitness (b,g), modern dance (b,g); coed interscholastic: bicycling, diving, golf, indoor track & field, swimming and diving; coed intramural: aerobics, aerobics/dance, aerobics/Nautilus, alpine skiing, aquatics, ballet, canoeing/kayaking, dance, fitness, hiking/backpacking, life saving, modern dance, outdoor skills, paddle tennis, sailing, skiing (cross-country), skiing (downhill), snowboarding, soccer, squash, strength & conditioning, swimming and diving, tennis, volleyball, weight lifting. 1 coach, 2 athletic trainers.

Computers Computers are regularly used in architecture, mathematics, programming, science classes. Computer network features include on-campus library services, online commercial services, Internet access, wireless campus network. Campus intranet, student e-mail accounts, and computer access in designated common areas are available to students. Students grades are available online. The school has a published electronic and media policy.

Contact Patricia L. Gimbel, Dean of Admission and Financial Aid. 413-774-1400. Fax: 413-772-1100. E-mail: admission@deerfield.edu. Web site: www.deerfield.edu.

See Display on this page and Close-Up on page 614.

DEERFIELD-WINDSOR SCHOOL

2500 Nottingham Way
Albany, Georgia 31707

Head of School: Mr. David L. Davies

General Information Coeducational day college-preparatory, arts, and technology school; primarily serves students with learning disabilities and individuals with Attention Deficit Disorder. Grades PK–12. Founded: 1964. Setting: suburban. Nearest major city is Atlanta. 24-acre campus. 1 building on campus. Approved or accredited by Southern Association of Colleges and Schools, Southern Association of Independent Schools, and Georgia Department of Education. Member of National Association of Independent Schools. Endowment: $1 million. Total enrollment: 836. Upper school average class size: 18. Upper school faculty-student ratio: 1:18. There are 180 required school days per year for Upper School students. Upper School students typically attend 5 days per week. The average school day consists of 6 hours and 25 minutes.

Upper School Student Profile Grade 9: 61 students (35 boys, 26 girls); Grade 10: 68 students (33 boys, 35 girls); Grade 11: 61 students (28 boys, 33 girls); Grade 12: 71 students (39 boys, 32 girls).

Faculty School total: 56. In upper school: 9 men, 28 women; 22 have advanced degrees.

Subjects Offered Advanced studio art-AP, algebra, American history, American literature, art, art history, biology, calculus, chemistry, creative writing, drama, earth science, economics, English, English literature, environmental science, expository writing, French, geometry, government/civics, grammar, health, history, Latin, mathematics, music, physical education, physics, physiology, psychology, science, social sciences, social studies, Spanish, speech, theater, trigonometry, world history, world literature, writing, yearbook.

Graduation Requirements All academic, 55 volunteer hours of community service.

Special Academic Programs 10 Advanced Placement exams for which test preparation is offered; honors section; independent study; study at local college for college credit; academic accommodation for the gifted, the musically talented, and the artistically talented; remedial reading and/or remedial writing; remedial math; programs in general development for dyslexic students.

College Admission Counseling 68 students graduated in 2011; all went to college, including Auburn University; Georgia Institute of Technology; Georgia Southern University; University of Georgia; Valdosta State University. Mean SAT critical reading: 576, mean SAT math: 527, mean SAT writing: 587, mean combined SAT: 1690.

Student Life Upper grades have specified standards of dress, student council, honor system. Discipline rests primarily with faculty.

Tuition and Aid Day student tuition: $9800. Tuition installment plan (Insured Tuition Payment Plan, monthly payment plans, individually arranged payment plans, quarterly and semi-annual payment plans). Tuition reduction for siblings, merit scholarship grants, need-based scholarship grants, need-based tuition reduction available. In 2011–12, 7% of upper-school students received aid; total upper-school merit-scholarship money awarded: $25,200. Total amount of financial aid awarded in 2011–12: $350,000.

Admissions Traditional secondary-level entrance grade is 9. For fall 2011, 36 students applied for upper-level admission, 21 were accepted, 18 enrolled. ERB verbal, ERB math and Otis-Lennon Mental Ability Test required. Deadline for receipt of application materials: none. Application fee required: $50. On-campus interview recommended.

Athletics Interscholastic: aquatics (boys, girls), baseball (b), basketball (b,g), cross-country running (b,g), football (b), golf (b), running (b,g), soccer (b,g), softball (g), strength & conditioning (b,g), swimming and diving (b,g), tennis (b,g), track and field (b,g), wrestling (b); intramural: basketball (b,g), cheering (b,g), danceline (b,g), football (b), soccer (b,g), weight lifting (b,g); coed intramural: badminton. 5 PE instructors, 9 coaches, 1 athletic trainer.

Computers Computers are regularly used in mathematics, yearbook classes. Computer network features include on-campus library services, Internet access, wireless campus network. Student e-mail accounts and computer access in designated common areas are available to students. Students grades are available online.

Contact Mrs. DeeDee R. Willcox, College Counselor. 912-435-1301 Ext. 256. Fax: 912-888-6085. E-mail: deedee.willcox@deerfieldwindsor.com. Web site: www.deerfieldwindsor.com.

DE LA SALLE HIGH SCHOOL

1130 Winton Drive

Concord, California 94518-3528

Head of School: Br. Robert J. Wickman, FSC

General Information Boys' day college-preparatory, arts, and religious studies school, affiliated with Roman Catholic Church. Grades 9–12. Founded: 1965. Setting: suburban. Nearest major city is Oakland. 25-acre campus. 11 buildings on campus. Approved or accredited by Western Association of Schools and Colleges and Western Catholic Education Association. Endowment: $3.7 million. Total enrollment: 1,028. Upper school average class size: 30. Upper school faculty-student ratio: 1:28. There are 172 required school days per year for Upper School students. Upper School students typically attend 5 days per week. The average school day consists of 6 hours and 5 minutes.

Upper School Student Profile Grade 9: 260 students (260 boys); Grade 10: 262 students (262 boys); Grade 11: 253 students (253 boys); Grade 12: 253 students (253 boys). 80% of students are Roman Catholic.

Faculty School total: 73. In upper school: 50 men, 23 women; 41 have advanced degrees.

Subjects Offered Advanced studio art-AP, algebra, American history, anatomy, art, band, Bible studies, biology, calculus, chemistry, chorus, design, drafting, drawing, economics, English, English-AP, ethics, fine arts, first aid, French, geometry, government/civics, health, history, Italian, jazz, Latin, literature, marine biology, mathematics, music theory, painting, physical education, physics, physiology, pre-calculus, psychology, religion, science, sculpture, social studies, Spanish, Spanish-AP, sports medicine, statistics, statistics-AP, trigonometry, world history, world religions, writing.

Graduation Requirements Arts and fine arts (art, music, dance, drama), English, foreign language, mathematics, physical education (includes health), religion (includes Bible studies and theology), science, social studies (includes history).

Special Academic Programs Advanced Placement exam preparation; honors section; independent study; remedial math.

College Admission Counseling 257 students graduated in 2011; 254 went to college, including California Polytechnic State University, San Luis Obispo; California State University, Chico; Loyola Marymount University; Saint Mary's College of California; Santa Clara University; The University of Arizona. Other: 1 entered military service, 2 had other specific plans. Mean SAT critical reading: 565, mean SAT math: 573, mean SAT writing: 548, mean combined SAT: 1687, mean composite ACT: 25. 34% scored over 600 on SAT critical reading, 39% scored over 600 on SAT math, 28% scored over 600 on SAT writing, 35% scored over 1800 on combined SAT, 37% scored over 26 on composite ACT.

Student Life Upper grades have specified standards of dress, student council, honor system. Discipline rests primarily with faculty. Attendance at religious services is required.

Summer Programs Remediation programs offered; session focuses on remediation for incoming and/or conditionally accepted freshmen only; held on campus; accepts boys; not open to students from other schools. 40 students usually enrolled. 2012 schedule: June 11 to July 6. Application deadline: May 31.

Tuition and Aid Day student tuition: $14,750. Tuition installment plan (10-month). Need-based grants available. In 2011–12, 30% of upper-school students received aid.

Admissions Traditional secondary-level entrance grade is 9. For fall 2011, 448 students applied for upper-level admission, 302 were accepted, 260 enrolled. High School Placement Test required. Deadline for receipt of application materials: December 2. Application fee required: $75. On-campus interview required.

Athletics Interscholastic: baseball, basketball, cross-country running, diving, football, golf, lacrosse, rugby, soccer, swimming and diving, tennis, track and field, volleyball, water polo, wrestling; intramural: bowling, flag football, floor hockey, football, ultimate Frisbee. 2 PE instructors, 85 coaches, 2 athletic trainers.

Computers Computers are regularly used in animation, Web site design, yearbook classes. Computer network features include on-campus library services, Internet access, wireless campus network, Internet filtering or blocking technology. Student e-mail accounts and computer access in designated common areas are available to students. Students grades are available online. The school has a published electronic and media policy.

Contact Mr. Joseph Grantham, Director of Admissions. 925-288-8102. Fax: 925-686-3474. E-mail: granthamj@dlshs.org. Web site: www.dlshs.org.

DELAWARE VALLEY FRIENDS SCHOOL

Paoli, Pennsylvania

See Special Needs Schools section.

DELBARTON SCHOOL

230 Mendham Road

Morristown, New Jersey 07960

Head of School: Br. Paul Diveny, OSB

General Information Boys' day college-preparatory, arts, religious studies, and technology school, affiliated with Roman Catholic Church. Grades 7–12. Founded: 1939. Setting: suburban. Nearest major city is New York, NY. 200-acre campus. 7 buildings on campus. Approved or accredited by Middle States Association of Colleges and Schools, National Catholic Education Association, New Jersey Association of Independent Schools, and New Jersey Department of Education. Member of National Association of Independent Schools and Secondary School Admission Test Board. Endowment: $23.9 million. Total enrollment: 555. Upper school average class size: 15. Upper school faculty-student ratio: 1:10. There are 160 required school days per year for Upper School students. Upper School students typically attend 5 days per week. The average school day consists of 6 hours and 15 minutes.

Upper School Student Profile Grade 9: 118 students (118 boys); Grade 10: 133 students (133 boys); Grade 11: 119 students (119 boys); Grade 12: 120 students (120 boys). 80% of students are Roman Catholic.

Faculty School total: 92. In upper school: 77 men, 15 women; 55 have advanced degrees.

Subjects Offered Accounting, advanced chemistry, algebra, American history, American literature, art, art history, astronomy, biology, calculus, chemistry, computer math, computer programming, computer science, creative writing, driver education, economics, English, English literature, environmental science, ethics, European history, fine arts, French, geography, geometry, German, grammar, health, history, international relations, Latin, mathematics, music, philosophy, physical education, physics, religion, Russian, social studies, Spanish, speech, trigonometry, world history.

Graduation Requirements Arts and fine arts (art, music, dance, drama), computer science, English, foreign language, mathematics, physical education (includes health), religion (includes Bible studies and theology), science, social studies (includes history), speech.

Special Academic Programs Advanced Placement exam preparation; independent study.

College Admission Counseling 119 students graduated in 2011; all went to college, including Boston College; Columbia University; Cornell University; Duke University; Georgetown University; Villanova University.

Student Life Upper grades have specified standards of dress, student council, honor system. Discipline rests primarily with faculty. Attendance at religious services is required.

Summer Programs Enrichment, advancement, sports, computer instruction programs offered; session focuses on summer school (coed) and summer sports (boys); held on campus; accepts boys and girls; open to students from other schools. 1,000 students usually enrolled. 2012 schedule: June 20 to July 27. Application deadline: June 1.

Tuition and Aid Day student tuition: $27,800. Tuition installment plan (monthly payment plans, individually arranged payment plans). Need-based scholarship grants available. In 2011–12, 15% of upper-school students received aid. Total amount of financial aid awarded in 2011–12: $1,574,000.
Admissions Traditional secondary-level entrance grade is 9. For fall 2011, 302 students applied for upper-level admission, 108 were accepted, 84 enrolled. Stanford Achievement Test, Otis-Lennon School Ability Test, school's own exam required. Deadline for receipt of application materials: November 28. Application fee required: $65. On-campus interview required.
Athletics Interscholastic: baseball, basketball, bowling, cross-country running, football, golf, ice hockey, indoor track, lacrosse, soccer, squash, swimming and diving, tennis, track and field, winter (indoor) track, wrestling; intramural: bicycling, combined training, fitness, flag football, Frisbee, independent competitive sports, mountain biking, skiing (downhill), strength & conditioning, ultimate Frisbee, weight lifting, weight training. 3 PE instructors, 2 athletic trainers.
Computers Computers are regularly used in computer applications, music, science, word processing classes. Computer network features include on-campus library services, online commercial services, Internet access, wireless campus network. Student e-mail accounts are available to students. Students grades are available online.
Contact Mrs. Connie Curnow, Administrative Assistant, Office of Admissions. 973-538-3231 Ext. 3019. Fax: 973-538-8836. E-mail: ccurnow@delbarton.org. Web site: www.delbarton.org.

DEMATHA CATHOLIC HIGH SCHOOL

4313 Madison Street

Hyattsville, Maryland 20781

Head of School: Daniel J. McMahon, PhD

General Information Boys' day college-preparatory, arts, business, religious studies, technology, and music (instrumental and choral) school, affiliated with Roman Catholic Church. Grades 9–12. Founded: 1946. Setting: suburban. Nearest major city is Washington, DC. 6-acre campus. 5 buildings on campus. Approved or accredited by Association of Independent Schools of Greater Washington, Middle States Association of Colleges and Schools, National Catholic Education Association, and Maryland Department of Education. Total enrollment: 896. Upper school average class size: 22. Upper school faculty-student ratio: 1:13. There are 174 required school days per year for Upper School students. Upper School students typically attend 5 days per week. The average school day consists of 6 hours.
Upper School Student Profile Grade 9: 248 students (248 boys); Grade 10: 250 students (250 boys); Grade 11: 197 students (197 boys); Grade 12: 201 students (201 boys). 61% of students are Roman Catholic.
Faculty School total: 79. In upper school: 60 men, 19 women; 43 have advanced degrees.
Subjects Offered Accounting, Advanced Placement courses, algebra, American government, American history, American history-AP, anatomy and physiology, art, art history, art-AP, astronomy, band, biology, biology-AP, British literature, British literature-AP, business, business law, calculus, calculus-AP, campus ministry, chemistry, chemistry-AP, Chinese, choral music, chorus, Christian ethics, church history, college admission preparation, community service, computer applications, computer programming, computer science, computer science-AP, computer skills, computer studies, contemporary art, digital photography, English, English composition, English literature, environmental science, film studies, French, French language-AP, geology, geometry, German, German-AP, government, government-AP, Greek, health, health education, history, history of religion, history of rock and roll, honors algebra, honors English, honors geometry, honors U.S. history, honors world history, instrumental music, jazz, journalism, Latin, Latin American studies, Latin-AP, literature-AP, mathematics, modern languages, music, music performance, mythology, newspaper, photography, photojournalism, physical education, physical science, physics, physics-AP, pre-calculus, psychology, SAT preparation, science, science research, social studies, Spanish, Spanish-AP, speech, sports medicine, statistics, studio art, studio art-AP, study skills, symphonic band, theology, trigonometry, U.S. government, U.S. government and politics-AP, U.S. history, U.S. literature, vocal music, world history, writing, yearbook.
Graduation Requirements Arts, computer science, English, foreign language, mathematics, physical education (includes health), science, social studies (includes history), theology, 55 hours of Christian service, service reflection paper.
Special Academic Programs Advanced Placement exam preparation; honors section; independent study; academic accommodation for the gifted, the musically talented, and the artistically talented; remedial reading and/or remedial writing.
College Admission Counseling 223 students graduated in 2011; 217 went to college, including Howard University; Salisbury University; The Catholic University of America; Towson University; University of Maryland, Baltimore County; University of Maryland, College Park. Other: 4 went to work, 2 entered military service. Mean SAT critical reading: 521, mean SAT math: 527, mean SAT writing: 502.
Student Life Upper grades have uniform requirement, student council, honor system. Discipline rests primarily with faculty. Attendance at religious services is required.
Summer Programs Remediation, enrichment, sports, art/fine arts, computer instruction programs offered; session focuses on remediation/enrichment; held on campus; accepts boys and girls; open to students from other schools. 400 students usually enrolled. 2012 schedule: June 18 to July 20. Application deadline: June 10.
Tuition and Aid Day student tuition: $13,200. Tuition installment plan (FACTS Tuition Payment Plan). Tuition reduction for siblings, merit scholarship grants, need-based scholarship grants, paying campus jobs available. In 2011–12, 54% of upper-school students received aid; total upper-school merit-scholarship money awarded: $390,250. Total amount of financial aid awarded in 2011–12: $1,315,308.
Admissions Traditional secondary-level entrance grade is 9. For fall 2011, 555 students applied for upper-level admission, 441 were accepted, 250 enrolled. Archdiocese of Washington Entrance Exam, High School Placement Test or High School Placement Test (closed version) from Scholastic Testing Service required. Deadline for receipt of application materials: December 15. Application fee required: $50.
Athletics Interscholastic: baseball, basketball, crew, cross-country running, diving, football, golf, hockey, ice hockey, indoor track, indoor track & field, lacrosse, rugby, soccer, swimming and diving, tennis, track and field, ultimate Frisbee, water polo, winter (indoor) track, wrestling; intramural: basketball, paddle tennis, strength & conditioning, table tennis. 2 PE instructors, 1 coach, 2 athletic trainers.
Computers Computers are regularly used in computer applications, digital applications, English, independent study, lab/keyboard, library, newspaper, publishing, science, technology, Web site design, word processing, yearbook classes. Computer network features include on-campus library services, Internet access, wireless campus network, Internet filtering or blocking technology, ProQuest, SIRS, World Book. Computer access in designated common areas is available to students. Students grades are available online. The school has a published electronic and media policy.
Contact Mrs. Christine Thomas, Assistant Director of Admissions. 240-764-2210. Fax: 240-764-2277. E-mail: cthomas@dematha.org. Web site: www.dematha.org.

DENVER CHRISTIAN HIGH SCHOOL

2135 South Pearl Street

Denver, Colorado 80210

Head of School: Mr. Mark H. Swalley

General Information Coeducational day college-preparatory, general academic, arts, business, religious studies, bilingual studies, and technology school, affiliated with Christian Reformed Church. Grades 9–12. Founded: 1950. Setting: urban. 4-acre campus. 1 building on campus. Approved or accredited by Association of Christian Schools International, North Central Association of Colleges and Schools, and Colorado Department of Education. Endowment: $1.5 million. Total enrollment: 179. Upper school average class size: 15. Upper school faculty-student ratio: 1:14. There are 181 required school days per year for Upper School students. Upper School students typically attend 5 days per week. The average school day consists of 6 hours and 45 minutes.
Upper School Student Profile Grade 9: 46 students (25 boys, 21 girls); Grade 10: 34 students (17 boys, 17 girls); Grade 11: 51 students (24 boys, 27 girls); Grade 12: 48 students (23 boys, 25 girls). 20% of students are members of Christian Reformed Church.
Faculty School total: 22. In upper school: 10 men, 12 women; 16 have advanced degrees.
Subjects Offered Acting, advanced chemistry, advanced computer applications, advanced math, algebra, American government, American history, American literature, art, band, Bible, biology, British literature, calculus, chamber groups, chemistry, choir, Christian doctrine, Christian scripture, church history, composition, computer applications, concert band, concert choir, consumer economics, drama, driver education, earth science, European history, general math, government, grammar, health, introduction to literature, jazz band, keyboarding, personal fitness, physical education, physical fitness, physics, poetry, pre-algebra, pre-calculus, psychology, research, senior seminar, Shakespeare, Spanish, speech, studio art, symphonic band, the Web, trigonometry, U.S. government, U.S. history, Web site design, weight fitness, Western civilization, world geography, world history, yearbook.
Graduation Requirements Bible studies, veterinary science.
Special Academic Programs Honors section; independent study; special instructional classes for deaf students.
College Admission Counseling 48 students graduated in 2011; 44 went to college, including Azusa Pacific University; Calvin College; Colorado State University; Dordt College; University of Colorado Boulder. Other: 4 had other specific plans. Mean SAT critical reading: 560, mean SAT math: 545, mean composite ACT: 24.
Student Life Upper grades have specified standards of dress, student council. Discipline rests primarily with faculty. Attendance at religious services is required.
Tuition and Aid Day student tuition: $9110. Tuition installment plan (FACTS Tuition Payment Plan, monthly payment plans). Tuition reduction for siblings, merit scholarship grants, need-based scholarship grants available. In 2011–12, 45% of upper-school students received aid. Total amount of financial aid awarded in 2011–12: $72,000.
Admissions Traditional secondary-level entrance grade is 9. For fall 2011, 36 students applied for upper-level admission, 34 were accepted, 34 enrolled. WISC-III and Woodcock-Johnson, WISC/Woodcock-Johnson or Woodcock-Johnson Educational Evaluation, WISC III required. Deadline for receipt of application materials: none. Application fee required: $260. Interview required.

Athletics Interscholastic: baseball (boys), basketball (b,g), cheering (g), cross-country running (b,g), football (b), golf (b,g), soccer (b,g), track and field (b,g), volleyball (g); coed interscholastic: physical training, strength & conditioning. 1 PE instructor, 25 coaches.

Computers Computer network features include on-campus library services, Internet access, wireless campus network, Internet filtering or blocking technology. Student e-mail accounts are available to students. Students grades are available online. The school has a published electronic and media policy.

Contact Sheryl Vriesman, Admissions Secretary. 303-733-2421 Ext. 110. Fax: 303-733-7734. E-mail: sherylv@denver-christian.org.

DENVER LUTHERAN HIGH SCHOOL

3201 West Arizona Avenue

Denver, Colorado 80219

Head of School: Mr. Daniel Gehrke

General Information Coeducational day college-preparatory, general academic, arts, religious studies, and technology school, affiliated with Lutheran Church–Missouri Synod. Grades 9–12. Founded: 1955. Setting: urban. 12-acre campus. 1 building on campus. Approved or accredited by National Lutheran School Accreditation, North Central Association of Colleges and Schools, and Colorado Department of Education. Total enrollment: 182. Upper school average class size: 18. Upper school faculty-student ratio: 1:17. There are 175 required school days per year for Upper School students. Upper School students typically attend 5 days per week. The average school day consists of 6 hours.

Upper School Student Profile Grade 9: 51 students (24 boys, 27 girls); Grade 10: 42 students (24 boys, 18 girls); Grade 11: 36 students (18 boys, 18 girls); Grade 12: 53 students (30 boys, 23 girls). 65% of students are Lutheran Church–Missouri Synod.

Faculty School total: 18. In upper school: 15 men, 3 women; 6 have advanced degrees.

Subjects Offered 20th century history, algebra, art, band, biology, calculus, chemistry, chorus, computer programming, computer science, consumer mathematics, creative writing, English, fine arts, geography, geometry, literature, mathematics, physical education, physics, psychology, reading, religion, science, social sciences, social studies, Spanish, speech, trigonometry.

Graduation Requirements Algebra, American government, arts and fine arts (art, music, dance, drama), biology, chemistry, computer applications, electives, English, English composition, English literature, geography, mathematics, physical education (includes health), science, social sciences, social studies (includes history), religion class for each year enrolled.

Special Academic Programs Advanced Placement exam preparation; honors section; independent study; remedial reading and/or remedial writing; remedial math.

College Admission Counseling 47 students graduated in 2010; 44 went to college, including Colorado State University; Concordia University; Metropolitan State College of Denver; University of Colorado Boulder; University of Northern Colorado. Other: 2 went to work, 1 entered military service. Mean composite ACT: 23.

Student Life Upper grades have specified standards of dress, student council, honor system. Discipline rests primarily with faculty. Attendance at religious services is required.

Tuition and Aid Day student tuition: $7000. Need-based scholarship grants available. In 2010–11, 30% of upper-school students received aid.

Admissions Traditional secondary-level entrance grade is 9. High School Placement Test required. Deadline for receipt of application materials: none. Application fee required: $100. On-campus interview required.

Athletics Interscholastic: baseball (boys), basketball (b,g), floor hockey (b), football (b), golf (b,g), roller hockey (b), softball (g), tennis (g), track and field (b,g), volleyball (g), weight training (b,g), wrestling (b); intramural: field hockey (b). 3 PE instructors, 6 coaches, 1 athletic trainer.

Computers Computers are regularly used in art, geography, graphic arts, theater arts, Web site design, yearbook classes. Computer network features include online commercial services, Internet access. The school has a published electronic and media policy.

Contact Mr. Ryan Bredow, Admissions Director. 303-934-2345 Ext. 3306. Fax: 303-934-0455. Web site: www.denverlhs.org.

DEPAUL CATHOLIC HIGH SCHOOL

1512 Alps Road

Wayne, New Jersey 07470

Head of School: Fr. Mike Donovan

General Information Coeducational day college-preparatory, arts, religious studies, and technology school, affiliated with Roman Catholic Church. Grades 9–12. Founded: 1956. Setting: suburban. Nearest major city is New York, NY. 5-acre campus. 2 buildings on campus. Approved or accredited by National Catholic Education Association and New Jersey Department of Education. Upper school average class size: 22. Upper school faculty-student ratio: 1:19. There are 185 required school days per year for Upper School students. Upper School students typically attend 5 days per week. The average school day consists of 7 hours.

Upper School Student Profile 90% of students are Roman Catholic.

Faculty School total: 65. In upper school: 25 men, 40 women; 40 have advanced degrees.

Special Academic Programs International Baccalaureate program; Advanced Placement exam preparation; honors section; accelerated programs; remedial reading and/or remedial writing; remedial math; programs in general development for dyslexic students; special instructional classes for deaf students, blind students.

College Admission Counseling 195 students graduated in 2011; all went to college.

Student Life Upper grades have uniform requirement, student council, honor system. Discipline rests equally with students and faculty. Attendance at religious services is required.

Summer Programs Enrichment, advancement, sports, computer instruction programs offered; session focuses on academics and physical fitness; held on campus; accepts boys and girls; open to students from other schools. 300 students usually enrolled. 2012 schedule: June 20 to August 29.

Tuition and Aid Day student tuition: $10,300. Tuition installment plan (SMART Tuition Payment Plan, monthly payment plans, individually arranged payment plans). Tuition reduction for siblings, merit scholarship grants, need-based scholarship grants available.

Admissions Deadline for receipt of application materials: none. No application fee required. Interview recommended.

Athletics Interscholastic: baseball (boys), basketball (b,g), cheering (g), cross-country running (b,g), dance (g), dance squad (g), dance team (g), danceline (g), figure skating (g), football (b), gymnastics (g), ice skating (g), independent competitive sports (b,g), indoor track (b,g), indoor track & field (b,g), lacrosse (b,g), modern dance (g), soccer (b,g), softball (b), swimming and diving (b,g), tennis (b,g), track and field (b,g), volleyball (b,g), weight lifting (b,g), weight training (b,g), winter (indoor) track (b,g), wrestling (b); intramural: aerobics/dance (g), equestrian sports (g), strength & conditioning (b,g); coed interscholastic: alpine skiing, bowling, drill team, golf, ice hockey, skiing (downhill); coed intramural: backpacking, hiking/backpacking. 5 PE instructors, 40 coaches, 1 athletic trainer.

Computers Computer network features include on-campus library services, Internet access, wireless campus network, Internet filtering or blocking technology. Campus intranet, student e-mail accounts, and computer access in designated common areas are available to students. Students grades are available online. The school has a published electronic and media policy.

Contact Mr. John W. Merritt, Director of Admissions. 973-694-3702 Ext. 410. Fax: 973-694-3525. E-mail: merrittj@dpchs.org. Web site: www.depaulcatholic.org.

THE DERRYFIELD SCHOOL

2108 River Road

Manchester, New Hampshire 03104-1302

Head of School: Mr. Craig Sellers

General Information Coeducational day college-preparatory school. Grades 6–12. Founded: 1964. Setting: suburban. Nearest major city is Boston, MA. 84-acre campus. 3 buildings on campus. Approved or accredited by Association of Independent Schools in New England, Independent Schools of Northern New England, New England Association of Schools and Colleges, and New Hampshire Department of Education. Member of National Association of Independent Schools and Secondary School Admission Test Board. Endowment: $5 million. Total enrollment: 368. Upper school average class size: 14. Upper school faculty-student ratio: 1:8. There are 159 required school days per year for Upper School students. Upper School students typically attend 5 days per week. The average school day consists of 6 hours and 45 minutes.

Upper School Student Profile Grade 9: 67 students (33 boys, 34 girls); Grade 10: 63 students (32 boys, 31 girls); Grade 11: 56 students (24 boys, 32 girls); Grade 12: 57 students (26 boys, 31 girls).

Faculty School total: 44. In upper school: 15 men, 16 women; 16 have advanced degrees.

Subjects Offered 3-dimensional art, algebra, American literature, anatomy and physiology, ancient world history, art, biology, British literature, calculus, calculus-AP, chemistry, chemistry-AP, China/Japan history, Chinese, chorus, computer science, contemporary issues, creative writing, drafting, drama, driver education, earth science, economics, economics and history, engineering, English, English composition, English literature, English-AP, European history, expository writing, film, fine arts, freshman foundations, geography, geometry, global issues, government/civics, graphics, Greek, health, history, Holocaust, independent study, Latin, Latin-AP, mathematics, media, music, music theory, mythology, organic chemistry, philosophy, physical education, physics, physics-AP, pre-calculus, public speaking, robotics, science, sculpture, senior project, social studies, Spanish, Spanish language-AP, speech, statistics, statistics-AP, studio art, theater, trigonometry, U.S. history-AP, Western civilization, world history, world literature, writing.

Graduation Requirements Arts and fine arts (art, music, dance, drama), athletics, English, foreign language, health and wellness, history, mathematics, science.

Special Academic Programs Advanced Placement exam preparation; honors section; independent study; term-away projects.

College Admission Counseling 64 students graduated in 2011; all went to college, including Boston College; Northeastern University; Syracuse University; The College of William and Mary; University of New Hampshire; University of Vermont. Mean SAT critical reading: 633, mean SAT math: 611, mean SAT writing: 625, mean combined SAT: 1244, mean composite ACT: 26.

Student Life Upper grades have specified standards of dress, student council. Discipline rests equally with students and faculty.

Summer Programs Art/fine arts programs offered; session focuses on theater camp; held on campus; accepts boys and girls; open to students from other schools. 50 students usually enrolled. 2012 schedule: July to August. Application deadline: June.

Tuition and Aid Day student tuition: $26,435. Tuition installment plan (The Tuition Plan, FACTS Tuition Payment Plan). Merit scholarship grants, need-based scholarship grants available. In 2011–12, 26% of upper-school students received aid; total upper-school merit-scholarship money awarded: $71,000. Total amount of financial aid awarded in 2011–12: $1,041,927.

Admissions Traditional secondary-level entrance grade is 9. For fall 2011, 147 students applied for upper-level admission, 123 were accepted, 74 enrolled. SSAT required. Deadline for receipt of application materials: February 1. Application fee required: $50. On-campus interview required.

Athletics Interscholastic: alpine skiing (boys, girls), baseball (b), basketball (b,g), crew (b,g), cross-country running (b,g), field hockey (g), independent competitive sports (b,g), lacrosse (b,g), skiing (cross-country) (b,g), skiing (downhill) (b,g), soccer (b,g), softball (g), tennis (b,g); coed interscholastic: golf, swimming and diving; coed intramural: aerobics, aerobics/dance, cooperative games, physical training, ropes courses, weight training, yoga. 10 coaches, 1 athletic trainer.

Computers Computers are regularly used in all academic, college planning classes. Computer network features include on-campus library services, online commercial services, Internet access, wireless campus network, online computer linked to New Hampshire State Library. Student e-mail accounts and computer access in designated common areas are available to students. The school has a published electronic and media policy.

Contact Ms. Allison Price, Director of Admission and Financial Aid. 603-669-4524 Ext. 6201. Fax: 603-641-9521. E-mail: aprice@derryfield.org. Web site: www.derryfield.org.

See Display below and Close-Up on page 616.

DES MOINES CHRISTIAN SCHOOL

13007 Douglas Parkway

Urbandale, Iowa 50323

Head of School: Mr. John Steddom

General Information Coeducational day college-preparatory, arts, business, and religious studies school, affiliated with Christian faith. Grades PK–12. Founded: 1948. Setting: suburban. Nearest major city is Des Moines. 26-acre campus. 2 buildings on campus. Approved or accredited by Association of Christian Schools International, North Central Association of Colleges and Schools, and Iowa Department of Education. Endowment: $60,000. Total enrollment: 744. Upper school average class size: 20. Upper school faculty-student ratio: 1:18. There are 180 required school days per year for Upper School students. Upper School students typically attend 5 days per week. The average school day consists of 7 hours and 10 minutes.

Upper School Student Profile 90% of students are Christian faith.

Faculty School total: 27. In upper school: 11 men, 16 women; 13 have advanced degrees.

Subjects Offered 20th century world history, acting, advanced math, Advanced Placement courses, algebra, American government, American history, American history-AP, American literature, American literature-AP, applied music, art, Bible, biology, calculus-AP, chemistry, choir, choral music, chorus, Christian doctrine, Christian ethics, Christian scripture, Christian studies, Christian testament, Christianity, church history, civics, composition, composition-AP, computer applications, computer art, computer education, computer graphics, computer programming, concert band, concert choir, CPR, creative writing, decision making skills, drama, drawing, driver education, economics, economics and history, English, English literature, English literature and composition-AP, first aid, foreign language, general math, geometry, government, guidance, health, health and safety, health education, history-AP, human anatomy, integrated mathematics, jazz band, keyboarding, physical science, pre-algebra, pre-calculus, psychology, Spanish, speech, speech communications, student government, student publications.

Graduation Requirements Arts and fine arts (art, music, dance, drama), Bible, language arts, mathematics, physical education (includes health), science, social studies (includes history), speech, technology.

Special Academic Programs Advanced Placement exam preparation; accelerated programs; independent study; study at local college for college credit.

College Admission Counseling 36 students graduated in 2010; 31 went to college, including Iowa State University of Science and Technology; The University of Iowa; University of Northern Iowa. Other: 1 went to work, 2 entered military service. Median composite ACT: 25. 45% scored over 26 on composite ACT.

Student Life Upper grades have specified standards of dress, student council, honor system. Discipline rests primarily with faculty. Attendance at religious services is required.

Tuition and Aid Day student tuition: $6715. Tuition installment plan (monthly payment plans, individually arranged payment plans). Tuition reduction for siblings, need-based scholarship grants available. In 2010–11, 30% of upper-school students received aid. Total amount of financial aid awarded in 2010–11: $250,000.

Admissions Traditional secondary-level entrance grade is 9. For fall 2010, 22 students applied for upper-level admission, 21 were accepted, 21 enrolled. Iowa Test of Educational Development or Iowa Tests of Basic Skills required. Deadline for receipt of application materials: none. Application fee required: $250. Interview required.

Athletics Interscholastic: baseball (boys), basketball (b,g), cheering (g), football (b), golf (b,g), soccer (b), softball (g), track and field (b,g), volleyball (g); coed interscholastic: bowling, JROTC drill. 1 PE instructor, 17 coaches, 1 athletic trainer.

Computers Computers are regularly used in computer applications, media classes. Computer network features include on-campus library services, Internet access, wireless campus network, Internet filtering or blocking technology. Students grades are available online. The school has a published electronic and media policy.

Contact Mrs. Melanie Carlson, Administrative Assistant. 515-252-2490. Fax: 515-252-6972. E-mail: mcarlson@dmcs.org.

DEVON PREPARATORY SCHOOL

363 North Valley Forge Road

Devon, Pennsylvania 19333-1299

Head of School: Rev. James J. Shea, Sch.P

General Information Boys' day college-preparatory and religious studies school, affiliated with Roman Catholic Church. Grades 6–12. Founded: 1956. Setting: suburban. Nearest major city is Philadelphia. 20-acre campus. 7 buildings on campus. Approved or accredited by Middle States Association of Colleges and Schools and Pennsylvania Department of Education. Member of National Association of Independent Schools. Endowment: $600,000. Total enrollment: 260. Upper school average class size: 15. Upper school faculty-student ratio: 1:10. There are 180 required school days per year for Upper School students. Upper School students typically attend 5 days per week. The average school day consists of 6 hours.

Upper School Student Profile Grade 9: 59 students (59 boys); Grade 10: 43 students (43 boys); Grade 11: 39 students (39 boys); Grade 12: 49 students (49 boys). 84% of students are Roman Catholic.

Faculty School total: 33. In upper school: 23 men, 9 women; 21 have advanced degrees.

Subjects Offered Accounting, ACT preparation, Advanced Placement courses, algebra, American history, American literature, anatomy and physiology, art, biology, biology-AP, British literature, calculus, calculus-AP, chemistry, chemistry-AP, community service, computer science, computer science-AP, economics, English, environmental science, environmental science-AP, European history, forensics, French, French language-AP, geography, geometry, German, German-AP, health, human geography - AP, language-AP, Latin, literature and composition-AP, mathematics, modern European history, music, physical education, physics, physics-AP, political science, pre-calculus, religion, science, social studies, Spanish, Spanish-AP, trigonometry, U.S. history-AP, world cultures, world literature.

Graduation Requirements Computer science, English, foreign language, geography, Latin, mathematics, physical education (includes health), political science, religion (includes Bible studies and theology), science, social studies (includes history). Community service is required.

Special Academic Programs 18 Advanced Placement exams for which test preparation is offered.

College Admission Counseling 60 students graduated in 2011; all went to college, including Case Western Reserve University; Loyola University Maryland; New York University; Penn State University Park; The Catholic University of America; University of Pittsburgh. Median SAT critical reading: 643, median SAT math: 635, median SAT writing: 633.

Student Life Upper grades have specified standards of dress, student council. Discipline rests primarily with faculty. Attendance at religious services is required.

Tuition and Aid Day student tuition: $18,500. Tuition installment plan (monthly payment plans). Tuition reduction for siblings, merit scholarship grants, need-based scholarship grants available. In 2011–12, 20% of upper-school students received aid; total upper-school merit-scholarship money awarded: $475,000. Total amount of financial aid awarded in 2011–12: $700,000.

Admissions Traditional secondary-level entrance grade is 9. For fall 2011, 200 students applied for upper-level admission, 75 were accepted, 32 enrolled. Math and English placement tests required. Deadline for receipt of application materials: none. Application fee required: $50. On-campus interview recommended.

Athletics Interscholastic: baseball, basketball, cross-country running, golf, indoor track & field, lacrosse, soccer, swimming and diving, tennis, track and field. 2 PE instructors, 9 coaches, 1 athletic trainer.

Computers Computers are regularly used in all academic, newspaper, technology, writing, yearbook classes. Computer network features include on-campus library services, Internet access, wireless campus network, Internet filtering or blocking technology. Student e-mail accounts and computer access in designated common areas are available to students. Students grades are available online. The school has a published electronic and media policy.

Contact Mr. Patrick Parsons, Director of Admissions. 610-688-7337 Ext. 129. Fax: 610-688-2409. E-mail: pparsons@devonprep.com. Web site: www.devonprep.com.

DEXTER SCHOOL

20 Newton Street

Brookline, Massachusetts 02445

Head of School: Mr. Todd A. Vincent

General Information Boys' day college-preparatory and arts school. Grades 1–12. Founded: 1926. Setting: suburban. Nearest major city is Boston. 36-acre campus. 4 buildings on campus. Approved or accredited by Massachusetts Department of Education. Endowment: $24 million. Total enrollment: 444. Upper school average class size: 16. Upper school faculty-student ratio: 1:7. There are 172 required school days per year for Upper School students. Upper School students typically attend 5 days per week. The average school day consists of 6 hours and 45 minutes.

Upper School Student Profile Grade 6: 36 students (36 boys); Grade 7: 28 students (28 boys); Grade 8: 36 students (36 boys); Grade 9: 42 students (42 boys); Grade 10: 42 students (42 boys); Grade 11: 31 students (31 boys); Grade 12: 39 students (39 boys).

Faculty School total: 110. In upper school: 26 men, 23 women; 31 have advanced degrees.

Subjects Offered Acting, advanced studio art-AP, algebra, American government, American history-AP, American literature, American literature-AP, analysis and differential calculus, Ancient Greek, ancient history, art, art history, art history-AP, art-AP, astronomy, biology, biology-AP, British literature, British literature-AP, calculus, calculus-AP, Central and Eastern European history, ceramics, character education, chemistry, chemistry-AP, Chinese history, choral music, community service, computer graphics, computer music, conceptual physics, constitutional law, digital photography, drama workshop, earth and space science, economics, electronic music, English, English language-AP, English literature-AP, environmental science, ethics, European history, European history-AP, European literature, Far Eastern history, French, French language-AP, French literature-AP, French-AP, geometry, grammar, graphic arts, history of China and Japan, history of England, history of music, honors algebra, honors English, honors geometry, honors U.S. history, independent study, instrumental music, jazz ensemble, Latin, Latin-AP, marine biology, medieval history, Middle Eastern history, modern European history, music, music composition, music history, music technology, music theory, music theory-AP, music-AP, photography, physics, physics-AP, probability and statistics, public speaking, robotics, Russian history, SAT preparation, Spanish, Spanish language-AP, Spanish literature-AP, Spanish-AP, statistics, studio art, studio art-AP, U.S. history, U.S. history-AP, vocal music, woodworking, writing workshop.

Graduation Requirements Latin I.

Special Academic Programs 11 Advanced Placement exams for which test preparation is offered; honors section.

College Admission Counseling 19 students graduated in 2010; 17 went to college, including Boston College; Harvard University; Northeastern University; St. Lawrence University; Trinity College; Tufts University. Other: 1 went to work, 1 entered a postgraduate year.

Student Life Upper grades have specified standards of dress, student council, honor system. Discipline rests primarily with faculty. Attendance at religious services is required.

Tuition and Aid Day student tuition: $36,795. Tuition installment plan (monthly payment plans). Need-based scholarship grants available. In 2010–11, 29% of upper-school students received aid.

Admissions Traditional secondary-level entrance grade is 9. For fall 2010, 53 students applied for upper-level admission, 33 were accepted, 22 enrolled. ISEE, PSAT and SAT for applicants to grade 11 and 12 or SSAT required. Deadline for receipt of application materials: February 1. No application fee required. Interview required.

Athletics Interscholastic: baseball, basketball, crew, cross-country running, curling, fitness, football, golf, ice hockey, lacrosse, soccer, squash, swimming and diving, tennis. 6 coaches, 2 athletic trainers.

Computers Computers are regularly used in all classes. Computer network features include on-campus library services, online commercial services, Internet access, wireless campus network, Internet filtering or blocking technology, one-to-one laptop program. Campus intranet and student e-mail accounts are available to students. The school has a published electronic and media policy.

Contact Mrs. Jennifer DaPonte, Admissions Office Manager. 617-454-2721. Fax: 617-928-7696. E-mail: admissions@dexter.org. Web site: http://www.dexter.org.

DOANE STUART SCHOOL

199 Washington Avenue

Rensselaer, New York 12144

Head of School: Dr. Richard D. Enemark

General Information Coeducational day college-preparatory, arts, religious studies, Irish and peace studies, and bioethics school, affiliated with Episcopal Church. Grades N–12. Founded: 1852. Setting: urban. Nearest major city is Albany. 27-acre campus. 3 buildings on campus. Approved or accredited by National Association of Episcopal Schools and New York Department of Education. Member of National Association of Independent Schools and Secondary School Admission Test Board. Endowment: $1 million. Total enrollment: 290. Upper school average class size: 14. Upper school faculty-student ratio: 1:7. Upper School students typically attend 5 days per week. The average school day consists of 7 hours and 30 minutes.

Upper School Student Profile Grade 9: 43 students (19 boys, 24 girls); Grade 10: 27 students (13 boys, 14 girls); Grade 11: 26 students (10 boys, 16 girls); Grade 12: 31 students (23 boys, 8 girls). 10% of students are members of Episcopal Church.

Faculty School total: 50. In upper school: 11 men, 10 women; 13 have advanced degrees.

Subjects Offered 3-dimensional art, 3-dimensional design, accounting, advanced biology, advanced chemistry, advanced math, advanced studio art-AP, African-American literature, algebra, American history, American literature, art, bioethics, biology, Buddhism, calculus, campus ministry, ceramics, chemistry, choral music, college admission preparation, college counseling, college placement, college planning, college writing, community service, computer science, creative writing, earth science, economics, English, English literature, environmental science, ethics, fencing, fine arts, French, geometry, government/civics, health, history, independent study, instrumental music, instruments, international studies, internship, Irish literature, Irish studies, jazz band, jazz ensemble, journalism, literature, mathematics, mechanical drawing, media arts, medieval/Renaissance history, mentorship program, microeconomics, Middle Eastern history, music, music composition, music performance, music theory, newspaper, oil painting, opera, oral communications, oral expression, organ, painting, peace and justice, peace education, peace studies, performing arts, photography, physical education, physical fitness, physical science, physics, play production, play/screen writing, playwriting, playwriting and directing, poetry, policy and value, political economy, political science, politics, portfolio art, portfolio writing, pre-algebra, pre-calculus, psychology, psychology-AP, public service, public speaking, religion, SAT preparation, science, senior humanities, senior seminar, Shakespeare, social studies, Spanish, theater, trigonometry, world history, writing.

Special Academic Programs 30 Advanced Placement exams for which test preparation is offered; independent study; term-away projects; study at local college for college credit; domestic exchange program; study abroad; academic accommodation for the gifted, the musically talented, and the artistically talented.

College Admission Counseling 29 students graduated in 2011; all went to college, including Hampshire College; Northeastern University; Rensselaer Polytechnic Institute; Tufts University; Vassar College; Williams College.

Student Life Upper grades have uniform requirement, student council. Discipline rests primarily with faculty. Attendance at religious services is required.

Tuition and Aid Day student tuition: $20,105–$22,255. Tuition installment plan (Academic Management Services Plan). Need-based scholarship grants available. In 2011–12, 40% of upper-school students received aid. Total amount of financial aid awarded in 2011–12: $867,583.

Admissions Traditional secondary-level entrance grade is 9. For fall 2011, 86 students applied for upper-level admission, 47 were accepted, 28 enrolled. School's own test required. Deadline for receipt of application materials: none. Application fee required: $75. On-campus interview required.

Athletics Interscholastic: baseball (boys), basketball (b,g), crew (b,g), soccer (b,g), softball (g), volleyball (g); intramural: backpacking (b,g), independent competitive sports (b,g); coed interscholastic: crew, cross-country running, independent competitive sports, tennis; coed intramural: backpacking, crew, cross-country running, fencing, Frisbee, hiking/backpacking, independent competitive sports, jogging, outdoor adventure, outdoors, physical fitness, sailing, soccer, strength & conditioning, tai chi, ultimate Frisbee, walking, yoga. 2 PE instructors, 8 coaches.

Computers Computers are regularly used in accounting, architecture, art, basic skills, business, career exploration, college planning, creative writing, current events, data processing, desktop publishing, drawing and design, economics, English, ethics, foreign language, freshman foundations, geography, graphic arts, graphic design, graphics, health, historical foundations for arts, history, humanities, independent study, introduction to technology, journalism, keyboarding, language development, learning cognition, library science, library skills, literary magazine, mathematics, media arts, media production, mentorship program, multimedia, music, music technology, news writing, newspaper, philosophy, photography, programming, psychology, publications, publishing, reading, religion, religious studies, remedial study skills, research skills, SAT preparation, science, senior seminar, social sciences, social studies, study skills, technology, theater, theater arts, video film production, Web site design, writing, writing, yearbook classes. Computer resources include on-campus library services, online commercial services, Internet access, wireless campus network. Computer access in designated common areas is available to students. The school has a published electronic and media policy.

Contact Mr. Michael Green, Director of Admission. 518-465-5222 Ext. 241. Fax: 518-465-5230. E-mail: mgreen@doanestuart.org. Web site: www.doanestuart.org.

THE DR. MIRIAM AND SHELDON G. ADELSON EDUCATIONAL CAMPUS, THE ADELSON UPPER SCHOOL

9700 West Hillpoint Road

Las Vegas, Nevada 89134

Head of School: Mr. Paul Schiffman

General Information Coeducational day college-preparatory, arts, religious studies, and bilingual studies school, affiliated with Jewish faith. Grades PS–12. Founded: 1979. Setting: suburban. 30-acre campus. 1 building on campus. Approved or accredited by Pacific Northwest Association of Independent Schools and Nevada Department of Education. Member of National Association of Independent Schools. Languages of instruction: English and Hebrew. Total enrollment: 482. Upper school average class size: 16. Upper school faculty-student ratio: 1:10. There are 185 required school days per year for Upper School students. Upper School students typically attend 5 days per week. The average school day consists of 8 hours and 15 minutes.

Upper School Student Profile Grade 6: 33 students (19 boys, 14 girls); Grade 7: 35 students (19 boys, 16 girls); Grade 8: 21 students (11 boys, 10 girls); Grade 9: 26 students (12 boys, 14 girls); Grade 10: 24 students (12 boys, 12 girls); Grade 11: 21 students (4 boys, 17 girls); Grade 12: 17 students (7 boys, 10 girls). 80% of students are Jewish.

Faculty School total: 20. In upper school: 8 men, 12 women; all have advanced degrees.

Graduation Requirements Jewish studies.

College Admission Counseling 24 students graduated in 2011; all went to college.

Student Life Upper grades have uniform requirement, student council, honor system. Discipline rests primarily with faculty. Attendance at religious services is required.

Tuition and Aid Tuition reduction for siblings, need-based scholarship grants available. In 2011–12, 30% of upper-school students received aid.

Admissions ERB (CTP-Verbal, Quantitative) required. Deadline for receipt of application materials: none. Application fee required: $100. Interview required.

Athletics Interscholastic: aerobics/dance (girls), baseball (b), basketball (b,g), cross-country running (b,g), dance (b,g), dance team (b,g), soccer (b,g), swimming and diving (b,g), tennis (b,g), volleyball (b,g). 10 coaches.

Contact 702-255-4500. Fax: 702 255-7232. Web site: www.adelsoncampus.org.

DOMINICAN ACADEMY

44 East 68th Street

New York, New York 10065

Head of School: Sr. Barbara Kane, OP

General Information Girls' day college-preparatory, arts, religious studies, and technology school, affiliated with Roman Catholic Church. Grades 9–12. Founded: 1897. Setting: urban. 1 building on campus. Approved or accredited by Middle States Association of Colleges and Schools, National Catholic Education Association, New York State Board of Regents, and New York Department of Education. Member of National Association of Independent Schools and Secondary School Admission Test Board. Total enrollment: 224. Upper school average class size: 20. Upper school faculty-student ratio: 1:9. There are 180 required school days per year for Upper School students. Upper School students typically attend 5 days per week. The average school day consists of 6 hours and 30 minutes.

Upper School Student Profile Grade 9: 41 students (41 girls); Grade 10: 63 students (63 girls); Grade 11: 53 students (53 girls); Grade 12: 67 students (67 girls). 85% of students are Roman Catholic.

Faculty School total: 26. In upper school: 5 men, 21 women; 20 have advanced degrees.

Subjects Offered Algebra, American history, American history-AP, American literature, art history-AP, biology, biology-AP, calculus, calculus-AP, chemistry, chemistry-AP, chorus, communications, computer science, creative writing, dance, debate, drama, economics, economics-AP, English, English literature, English-AP, European history-AP, forensics, French, French-AP, geometry, global studies, government and politics-AP, government/civics, health, history, Latin, Latin-AP, library studies, logic, mathematics, music, music theory, physical education, physics, physics-AP, pre-calculus, psychology, religion, science, social studies, Spanish, Spanish-AP, world history.

Graduation Requirements Alternative physical education, arts and fine arts (art, music, dance, drama), English, foreign language, Latin, mathematics, religion (includes Bible studies and theology), science, social studies (includes history).

Special Academic Programs 11 Advanced Placement exams for which test preparation is offered.

College Admission Counseling 52 students graduated in 2011; all went to college, including Fairfield University; Fordham University; Providence College; St. John's University; The Catholic University of America; University of Notre Dame.

Student Life Upper grades have uniform requirement, student council. Discipline rests primarily with faculty. Attendance at religious services is required.

Summer Programs Remediation, enrichment, advancement programs offered; session focuses on Integrated Algebra Regents prep; held on campus; accepts girls; open to students from other schools. 15 students usually enrolled.

Tuition and Aid Day student tuition: $11,000. Tuition installment plan (FACTS Tuition Payment Plan, individually arranged payment plans, quarterly payment plan, semester payment plan). Tuition reduction for siblings, merit scholarship grants, need-based scholarship grants, paying campus jobs available. In 2011–12, 33% of upper-school students received aid; total upper-school merit-scholarship money awarded: $45,000.

Admissions Traditional secondary-level entrance grade is 9. For fall 2011, 350 students applied for upper-level admission, 185 were accepted, 42 enrolled. Catholic High School Entrance Examination required. Deadline for receipt of application materials: December 20. No application fee required.

Athletics Interscholastic: basketball, cross-country running, soccer, softball, tennis, track and field, volleyball; intramural: billiards, dance, soccer, volleyball. 1 PE instructor.

Computers Computers are regularly used in economics, health, history, Latin, library science, library studies, mathematics, religious studies, science, technology classes. Computer network features include on-campus library services, online commercial services, Internet access, wireless campus network, Internet filtering or blocking technology, T1 fiber optic network. Campus intranet, student e-mail accounts, and computer access in designated common areas are available to students. The school has a published electronic and media policy.

Contact Mrs. Jo Ann Fannon, Associate Director of Admissions. 212-744-0195 Ext. 31. Fax: 212-744-0375. E-mail: jfannon@dominicanacademy.org. Web site: www.dominicanacademy.org.

DONELSON CHRISTIAN ACADEMY

300 Danyacrest Drive

Nashville, Tennessee 37214

Head of School: Dr. Daniel W. Kellum Sr.

General Information Coeducational day college-preparatory, arts, religious studies, and technology school, affiliated with Christian faith. Grades K4–12. Founded: 1971. Setting: suburban. 50-acre campus. 3 buildings on campus. Approved or accredited by Association of Christian Schools International, Southern Association of Colleges and Schools, Tennessee Association of Independent Schools, and Tennessee Department of Education. Endowment: $78,000. Total enrollment: 715. Upper school average class size: 16. Upper school faculty-student ratio: 1:16. There are 180 required school days per year for Upper School students. Upper School students typically attend 5 days per week. The average school day consists of 6 hours and 50 minutes.

Upper School Student Profile Grade 9: 62 students (27 boys, 35 girls); Grade 10: 64 students (31 boys, 33 girls); Grade 11: 65 students (29 boys, 36 girls); Grade 12: 73 students (29 boys, 44 girls). 95% of students are Christian faith.

Faculty School total: 73. In upper school: 10 men, 15 women; 16 have advanced degrees.

Subjects Offered Advanced Placement courses, algebra, American history, American literature, anatomy, art, Bible studies, biology, business, business skills, calculus, chemistry, community service, computer science, drama, earth science, ecology, economics, English, English literature, environmental science, fine arts, French, geography, geometry, government/civics, grammar, health, history, journalism, keyboarding, Latin, mathematics, music, physical education, physics, physiology, psychology, religion, science, social sciences, social studies, sociology, Spanish, speech, theater, world history, world literature.

Graduation Requirements Arts and fine arts (art, music, dance, drama), Bible, chemistry, electives, English, foreign language, mathematics, physical education (includes health), science, social sciences, social studies (includes history), wellness, senior service (community service for 12th grade students).

Special Academic Programs 6 Advanced Placement exams for which test preparation is offered; honors section; independent study; study at local college for college credit; academic accommodation for the gifted; ESL (2 students enrolled).

College Admission Counseling 67 students graduated in 2011; all went to college, including Lipscomb University; Middle Tennessee State University; Tennessee Technological University; The University of Tennessee System; Trevecca Nazarene University; Western Kentucky University. Median SAT critical reading: 560, median SAT math: 505, median SAT writing: 525, median combined SAT: 1590, median composite ACT: 23. 50% scored over 600 on SAT critical reading, 25% scored over 600 on SAT math, 25% scored over 600 on SAT writing, 25% scored over 1800 on combined SAT, 22% scored over 26 on composite ACT.

Student Life Upper grades have uniform requirement, student council, honor system. Discipline rests primarily with faculty. Attendance at religious services is required.

Summer Programs Sports programs offered; session focuses on skill development; held on campus; accepts boys and girls; not open to students from other schools. 230 students usually enrolled. 2012 schedule: June 1 to August 1. Application deadline: none.

Tuition and Aid Day student tuition: $9340. Tuition installment plan (FACTS Tuition Payment Plan, monthly payment plans). Tuition reduction for siblings, need-based scholarship grants, paying campus jobs available. In 2011–12, 35% of upper-school students received aid. Total amount of financial aid awarded in 2011–12: $125,757.

Admissions Traditional secondary-level entrance grade is 9. For fall 2011, 30 students applied for upper-level admission, 27 were accepted, 22 enrolled. Achievement tests, Stanford Achievement Test or TOEFL or SLEP required. Deadline for receipt of application materials: none. Application fee required: $40. On-campus interview required.

Athletics Interscholastic: baseball (boys), basketball (b,g), bowling (b,g), cheering (g), cross-country running (b,g), football (b), golf (b,g), soccer (b,g), softball (g), tennis (b,g), track and field (b,g), volleyball (g), wrestling (b); intramural: basketball (b,g); coed interscholastic: physical fitness, swimming and diving, weight training; coed intramural: fitness, rappelling. 1 PE instructor, 2 coaches.

Computers Computers are regularly used in all academic, career exploration, college planning, creative writing, English, French, history, journalism, library, mathematics, newspaper, science, technology, yearbook classes. Computer network features include on-campus library services, Internet access, wireless campus network, Internet filtering or blocking technology. Campus intranet is available to students. Students grades are available online. The school has a published electronic and media policy.

Contact Mrs. Stephanie Craven, Admissions Assistant. 615-577-1215. Fax: 615-883-2998. E-mail: scraven@dcawildcats.org. Web site: www.dcawildcats.org.

DOWLING CATHOLIC HIGH SCHOOL

1400 Buffalo Road

West Des Moines, Iowa 50265

Head of School: Dr. Jerry M. Deegan

General Information Coeducational day college-preparatory, general academic, arts, business, religious studies, bilingual studies, technology, performing arts, and Advanced Placement school, affiliated with Roman Catholic Church. Grades 9–12. Founded: 1918. Setting: suburban. 60-acre campus. 1 building on campus. Approved or accredited by North Central Association of Colleges and Schools and Iowa Department of Education. Endowment: $9 million. Total enrollment: 1,372. Upper school average class size: 25. Upper school faculty-student ratio: 1:17.

Upper School Student Profile 94.5% of students are Roman Catholic.

Faculty School total: 79. In upper school: 39 men, 40 women; 40 have advanced degrees.

Subjects Offered 20th century world history, accounting, ACT preparation, acting, advanced chemistry, advanced computer applications, advanced math, Advanced Placement courses, advertising design, algebra, American government, American history, American history-AP, American literature, American literature-AP, applied arts, aquatics, art, art history, athletics, band, baseball, Basic programming, biology, biology-AP, brass choir, British literature, business, business communications, business law, calculus, calculus-AP, career and personal planning, career planning, career/college preparation, ceramics, chamber groups, cheerleading, chemistry, chemistry-AP, choir, choral music, chorus, church history, college counseling, college planning, composition, composition-AP, computer applications, computer information systems, computer processing, computer programming, computers, concert band, concert choir, creative writing, digital photography, drama, economics, economics-AP, engineering, English, English composition, English language and composition-AP, English literature, environmental science, European history, European history-AP, finance, fine arts, foreign language, French, general business, general science, geography, geometry, German, government, government-AP, health, health education, history, history-AP, honors algebra, honors English, honors geometry, honors U.S. history, honors world history, humanities, information processing, integrated mathematics, jazz band, journalism, keyboarding, Latin, life saving, literature, literature-AP, marching band, metalworking, modern European history, newspaper, painting, personal finance, physical education, physics, physics-AP, play production, poetry, pottery, pre-algebra, pre-calculus, probability and statistics, programming, religion, SAT/ACT preparation, scuba diving, social justice, sociology, Spanish, Spanish language-AP, speech and debate, swimming, tennis, theater production, theology, U.S. government, U.S. government and politics-AP, U.S. history, U.S. history-AP, visual arts, vocal jazz, weight training, world religions, yearbook.

Graduation Requirements Arts, business, electives, English, mathematics, reading, science, social studies (includes history), theology, Reading Across the Curriculum (RAC), 10 service hours per semester/20 per year, 10.5 credits of electives. Community service is required.

Special Academic Programs Advanced Placement exam preparation; honors section; accelerated programs; independent study; study at local college for college credit; academic accommodation for the gifted, the musically talented, and the artistically talented; remedial reading and/or remedial writing; remedial math; special instructional classes for blind students.

College Admission Counseling 295 students graduated in 2010; 294 went to college, including Creighton University; Iowa State University of Science and Technology; Loras College; The University of Iowa; University of Northern Iowa. Other: 1 went to work. Median SAT critical reading: 613, median SAT math: 618, median SAT writing: 583, median combined SAT: 605, median composite ACT: 24.

Student Life Upper grades have uniform requirement, student council, honor system. Discipline rests primarily with faculty. Attendance at religious services is required.

Tuition and Aid Day student tuition: $5908. Tuition installment plan (monthly payment plans, individually arranged payment plans). Need-based scholarship grants, paying campus jobs available. In 2010–11, 45% of upper-school students received aid. Total amount of financial aid awarded in 2010–11: $1,000,000.

Admissions Traditional secondary-level entrance grade is 9. Placement test required. Deadline for receipt of application materials: none. Application fee required: $90.

Athletics Interscholastic: aerobics/dance (girls), aquatics (b,g), baseball (b), basketball (b,g), bowling (b,g), cheering (g), cross-country running (b,g), dance team (b,g), diving (g), drill team (g), football (b), golf (b,g), hockey (b), soccer (b,g), softball (g), swimming and diving (b,g), tennis (b,g), track and field (b,g), volleyball (g), wrestling (b); coed interscholastic: cheering; coed intramural: ultimate Frisbee.

Computers Computers are regularly used in keyboarding classes. Computer network features include on-campus library services, Internet access, wireless campus network, Internet filtering or blocking technology. Computer access in designated common areas is available to students. Students grades are available online.

Contact Mrs. Tatia Eischeid, Admissions Assistant. 515-222-1047. Fax: 515-222-1056. E-mail: teischei@dowlingcatholic.org. Web site: www.dowlingcatholic.org.

DUBLIN CHRISTIAN ACADEMY

106 Page Road

Dublin, New Hampshire 03444

Head of School: Mr. Kevin E. Moody

General Information Coeducational boarding and day college-preparatory, arts, business, and religious studies school, affiliated with Christian faith, Bible Fellowship Church. Boarding grades 7–12, day grades K–12. Founded: 1964. Setting: rural. Nearest major city is Boston, MA. Students are housed in single-sex dormitories. 200-acre campus. 5 buildings on campus. Approved or accredited by American Association of Christian Schools and New Hampshire Department of Education. Total enrollment: 88. Upper school average class size: 15. Upper school faculty-student ratio: 1:8. There are 170 required school days per year for Upper School students. Upper School students typically attend 5 days per week. The average school day consists of 5 hours and 45 minutes.

Upper School Student Profile Grade 9: 10 students (5 boys, 5 girls); Grade 10: 15 students (9 boys, 6 girls); Grade 11: 7 students (2 boys, 5 girls), Grade 12: 18 students (8 boys, 10 girls). 33% of students are boarding students. 57% are state residents. 5 states are represented in upper school student body. 25% are international students. International students from China and Republic of Korea. 80% of students are Christian faith, Bible Fellowship Church.

Faculty School total: 22. In upper school: 7 men, 7 women; 7 have advanced degrees; 17 reside on campus.

Subjects Offered Accounting, algebra, art, Bible studies, biology, business, calculus, ceramics, chemistry, chorus, computer literacy, consumer mathematics, economics, English, geometry, history, home economics, instrumental music, law, mathematics, music, physics, piano, religion, science, social studies, Spanish, speech, studio art, study skills, U.S. history, voice, word processing, world history.

Graduation Requirements English, foreign language, mathematics, religion (includes Bible studies and theology), science, social studies (includes history), speech.

Special Academic Programs Advanced Placement exam preparation; academic accommodation for the musically talented and the artistically talented; remedial reading and/or remedial writing; remedial math.

College Admission Counseling 16 students graduated in 2011; 13 went to college, including Bob Jones University; Clearwater Christian College; Liberty University; The Master's College and Seminary. Other: 1 went to work. Mean SAT critical reading: 620, mean SAT math: 560, mean composite ACT: 23.

Student Life Upper grades have uniform requirement, student council, honor system. Discipline rests primarily with faculty. Attendance at religious services is required.

Tuition and Aid Day student tuition: $6500; 7-day tuition and room/board: $12,500. Tuition installment plan (FACTS Tuition Payment Plan). Need-based scholarship grants available. In 2011–12, 20% of upper-school students received aid. Total amount of financial aid awarded in 2011–12: $35,000.

Admissions Deadline for receipt of application materials: June 1. Application fee required: $35. Interview recommended.

Athletics Interscholastic: basketball (boys, girls), soccer (b), volleyball (g); intramural: cheering (g), flag football (b); coed intramural: alpine skiing, ice skating, snowboarding, softball.

Computers Computers are regularly used in accounting, business, English, foreign language, history, mathematics, music, science classes. Computer network features include on-campus library services, Internet access, Internet filtering or blocking technology.

Contact Mrs. Jenn Lawton, Admissions Secretary. 603-563-8505. Fax: 603-563-8008. E-mail: jlawton@dublinchristian.org. Web site: www.dublinchristian.org.

DUBLIN SCHOOL

Box 522

18 Lehmann Way

Dublin, New Hampshire 03444-0522

Head of School: Bradford D. Bates

General Information Coeducational boarding and day college-preparatory school. Grades 9–12. Founded: 1935. Setting: rural. Nearest major city is Boston, MA. Students are housed in single-sex dormitories. 300-acre campus. 22 buildings on campus. Approved or accredited by Independent Schools of Northern New England, New England Association of Schools and Colleges, and The Association of Boarding Schools. Member of National Association of Independent Schools and Secondary School Admission Test Board. Total enrollment: 127. Upper school average class size: 8. Upper school faculty-student ratio: 1:4. Upper School students typically attend 5 days per week. The average school day consists of 6 hours and 35 minutes.

Upper School Student Profile Grade 9: 29 students (17 boys, 12 girls); Grade 10: 37 students (21 boys, 16 girls); Grade 11: 36 students (25 boys, 11 girls); Grade 12: 25 students (14 boys, 11 girls). 72% of students are boarding students. 35% are state residents. 16 states are represented in upper school student body. 23% are international students. International students from China, Egypt, Japan, Mexico, Republic of Korea, and Spain; 6 other countries represented in student body.

Faculty School total: 29. In upper school: 15 men, 14 women; 18 have advanced degrees; 23 reside on campus.

Subjects Offered Acting, advanced math, African-American history, algebra, American foreign policy, American literature, anatomy and physiology, ancient world history, art, arts, biology, biology-AP, British literature, calculus, calculus-AP, carpentry, ceramics, chemistry, choir, chorus, college counseling, college placement, community service, computer education, computer literacy, computer programming, costumes and make-up, creative arts, creative dance, creative drama, cultural arts, dance performance, digital music, drama, drama performance, dramatic arts, drawing and design, electronic music, English, English composition, English literature, ESL, European civilization, European history, film history, fine arts, foreign policy, French, geology, geometry, guitar, honors U.S. history, instrumental music, Latin, library research, library skills, literature, marine biology, mathematics, modern dance, modern European history, music, music composition, music performance, music technology, music theory, musical productions, musical theater, musical theater dance, painting, personal and social education, personal development, philosophy, photography, physics, poetry, pre-algebra, pre-calculus, psychology, research, science, senior project, Shakespeare, social studies, Spanish, Spanish literature, stagecraft, statistics, student government, studio art, study skills, theater, theater arts, U.S. government and politics, U.S. history, U.S. history-AP, video film production, vocal ensemble, voice, weight training, world literature, writing, yearbook.

Graduation Requirements Art, arts, computer skills, English, general science, history, languages, mathematics, independent study in selected disciplines (for seniors), graduation requirements for honors diploma differ.

Special Academic Programs Advanced Placement exam preparation; honors section; independent study; term-away projects; domestic exchange program (with The Network Program Schools); programs in general development for dyslexic students; ESL (10 students enrolled).

College Admission Counseling 35 students graduated in 2010; 33 went to college, including Goucher College; Mount Holyoke College; Sacred Heart University; Smith College; The Johns Hopkins University; University of New Hampshire. Mean SAT critical reading: 563, mean SAT math: 549, mean SAT writing: 510, mean combined SAT: 1622, mean composite ACT: 21.

Student Life Upper grades have specified standards of dress, student council, honor system. Discipline rests primarily with faculty.

Tuition and Aid Day student tuition: $25,000; 7-day tuition and room/board: $43,000. Tuition installment plan (monthly payment plans). Need-based scholarship grants, need-based financial aid available. In 2010–11, 32% of upper-school students received aid. Total amount of financial aid awarded in 2010–11: $1,600,000.

Admissions Traditional secondary-level entrance grade is 9. For fall 2010, 143 students applied for upper-level admission, 97 were accepted, 48 enrolled. English, French, and math proficiency, SSAT, SSAT, ERB, PSAT, SAT, PLAN or ACT or TOEFL or SLEP required. Deadline for receipt of application materials: January 31. Application fee required: $50. Interview required.

Athletics Interscholastic: basketball (boys, girls), crew (b,g), freestyle skiing (b,g), lacrosse (b,g), skiing (downhill) (b,g), snowboarding (b,g), soccer (b,g), tennis (b,g); coed interscholastic: aerobics/dance, alpine skiing, crew, cross-country running, dance, dance team, equestrian sports, modern dance, nordic skiing, rowing, running, sailing, skiing (cross-country), skiing (downhill), snowboarding; coed intramural: aerobics/dance, alpine skiing, backpacking, basketball, bicycling, bowling, canoeing/kayaking, climbing, cooperative games, fencing, fishing, fitness, flagball, freestyle skiing, Frisbee, golf, hiking/backpacking, horseback riding, ice hockey, indoor soccer, martial arts, mountain biking, outdoor activities, outdoor adventure, outdoor education, outdoor recreation, physical fitness, physical training, rock climbing, ropes courses, sailing, skateboarding, skiing (cross-country), skiing (downhill), snowshoeing, softball, strength & conditioning, table tennis, telemark skiing, tennis, ultimate Frisbee, volleyball, wall climbing, weight lifting, weight training, whiffle ball, wrestling, yoga.

Computers Computers are regularly used in all academic classes. Computer network features include on-campus library services, Internet access, wireless campus network, Internet filtering or blocking technology. Student e-mail accounts are available to students. The school has a published electronic and media policy.

Contact Sheila Bogan, Director of Admission and Financial Aid. 603-563-1233. Fax: 603-563-8671. E-mail: admission@dublinschool.org. Web site: www.dublinschool.org/

DUBOIS CENTRAL CATHOLIC HIGH SCHOOL/ MIDDLE SCHOOL

PO Box 567

200 Central Christian Road

DuBois, Pennsylvania 15801

Head of School: Mrs. Dawn Bressler

General Information Coeducational day college-preparatory and general academic school, affiliated with Roman Catholic Church. Grades 6–12. Founded: 1961. Setting: small town. Nearest major city is Pittsburgh. 51-acre campus. 1 building on campus. Approved or accredited by Middle States Association of Colleges and Schools, National Catholic Education Association, Western Catholic Education Association, and Pennsylvania Department of Education. Endowment: $500,000. Total enrollment: 241. Upper school average class size: 20. Upper school faculty-student ratio: 1:14. There are 180 required school days per year for Upper School students. Upper School students typically attend 5 days per week. The average school day consists of 6 hours and 20 minutes.

Upper School Student Profile Grade 9: 35 students (18 boys, 17 girls); Grade 10: 39 students (12 boys, 27 girls); Grade 11: 42 students (22 boys, 20 girls); Grade 12: 45 students (17 boys, 28 girls). 86% of students are Roman Catholic.

Faculty School total: 30. In upper school: 9 men, 21 women; 13 have advanced degrees.

Subjects Offered 20th century American writers, 20th century history, 20th century physics, 20th century world history, 3-dimensional art, accounting, advanced biology, advanced chemistry, advanced computer applications, advanced math, Advanced Placement courses, algebra, American government, American history, American legal systems, American literature, analysis and differential calculus, anatomy and physiology, ancient world history, biology, biology-AP, British literature, calculus, calculus-AP, calligraphy, career and personal planning, career planning, career/college preparation, Catholic belief and practice, chemistry, chemistry-AP, Christian doctrine, Christian ethics, Christian scripture, Christian testament, civil war history, college admission preparation, college counseling, college placement, college planning, college writing, communications, computer applications, computer graphics, constitutional law, contemporary art, creative drama, creative writing, critical writing, debate, digital applications, digital imaging, drama, drama performance, driver education, earth science, ecology, ecology, environmental systems, economics, electives, English, English composition, English literature, English/composition-AP, environmental education, ethics and responsibility, expository writing, fitness, foreign language, forensics, French, general math, general science, geography, geometry, German, government, grammar, graphic arts, graphic design, guidance, health and wellness, health education, history of the Catholic Church, honors algebra, honors English, honors geometry, humanities, information technology, Internet, Internet research, journalism, keyboarding, lab science, language and composition, language arts, law, leadership and service, library, library assistant, library science, library skills, life management skills, Life of Christ, literature, marketing, mathematics, media communications, medieval/Renaissance history, methods of research, Microsoft, minority studies, moral and social development, moral theology, multicultural literature, music, music appreciation, music composition, music performance, music theater, musical productions, musical theater dance, mythology, Native American history, nature study, New Testament, news writing, newspaper, nutrition, oral communications, participation in sports, peer ministry, performing arts, personal fitness, philosophy, physical education, physical fitness, physical science, physics, piano, poetry, political systems, prayer/spirituality, pre-algebra, pre-calculus, probability and statistics, psychology, public speaking, publications, reading, reading/ study skills, religion and culture, research, research seminar, research skills, Roman culture, SAT preparation, science, science and technology, science project, science research, scripture, senior career experience, senior humanities, senior project, senior seminar, Shakespeare, Shakespearean histories, short story, skills for success, social issues, social justice, sociology, sophomore skills, Spanish, speech, speech and debate, speech communications, sports, standard curriculum, student government, student publications, student teaching, study skills, substance abuse, technology, telecommunications and the Internet, theater, trigonometry, U.S. government, U.S. history, U.S. literature, values and decisions, visual and performing arts, vocal ensemble, Web site design, wellness, Western religions, word processing, world cultures, world history, world literature, world religions, writing, writing workshop, yearbook.

Graduation Requirements Seniors must take an exit exam, service hours are mandated for each grade level from 6th through 12th.

Special Academic Programs International Baccalaureate program; honors section; independent study; study at local college for college credit.

College Admission Counseling 44 students graduated in 2011; 41 went to college, including Gannon University; Penn State University Park. Other: 1 entered military service, 2 had other specific plans.

Student Life Upper grades have uniform requirement, student council. Discipline rests primarily with faculty.

Tuition and Aid Tuition installment plan (FACTS Tuition Payment Plan, monthly payment plans, individually arranged payment plans). Tuition reduction for siblings, merit scholarship grants, need-based scholarship grants, Rotary Rebate Program uses 'scrips' both national & local;, Tuition Aid based on criteria selected by the donor, such as, from a certain parish, town, etc. available. In 2011–12, 46% of upper-school students received aid; total upper-school merit-scholarship money awarded: $448,000. Total amount of financial aid awarded in 2011–12: $448,000.

Admissions Traditional secondary-level entrance grade is 9. For fall 2011, 26 students applied for upper-level admission, 26 were accepted, 26 enrolled. ACT-Explore, Math Placement Exam, school's own exam or writing sample required. Application fee required: $25. On-campus interview required.

Athletics 2 PE instructors, 17 coaches.

Computers Computer network features include on-campus library services, Internet access, wireless campus network, Internet filtering or blocking technology, personal lap tops or notebooks mandated in 2011-12 for all 8th, 9th & 10th graders, soon all students in grades 6th through 12th will be required for curricular instruction. Campus intranet, student e-mail accounts, and computer access in designated common areas are available to students. Students grades are available online. The school has a published electronic and media policy.

Contact Mrs. Joyce Taylor, Director of Development. 814-371-3060 Ext. 606. Fax: 814-371-3215. E-mail: jtaylor@duboiscatholic.com. Web site: www.duboiscatholic.com.

DUCHESNE ACADEMY OF THE SACRED HEART

3601 Burt Street

Omaha, Nebraska 68131

Head of School: Mrs. Sheila Haggas

General Information Girls' day college-preparatory school, affiliated with Roman Catholic Church. Grades 9–12. Founded: 1881. Setting: urban. 13-acre campus. 3 buildings on campus. Approved or accredited by Network of Sacred Heart Schools, North Central Association of Colleges and Schools, and Nebraska Department of Education. Endowment: $4 million. Total enrollment: 303. Upper school average class size: 15. Upper school faculty-student ratio: 1:9. There are 173 required school days per year for Upper School students. Upper School students typically attend 5 days per week. The average school day consists of 7 hours.

Upper School Student Profile Grade 9: 86 students (86 girls); Grade 10: 82 students (82 girls); Grade 11: 59 students (59 girls); Grade 12: 76 students (76 girls). 90% of students are Roman Catholic.

Faculty School total: 38. In upper school: 10 men, 28 women; 26 have advanced degrees.

Subjects Offered 20th century history, 3-dimensional art, ACT preparation, acting, advanced chemistry, advanced math, algebra, American history, American literature, American literature-AP, anatomy and physiology, art, art history, bell choir, Bible as literature, biology, British literature, business, calculus, chemistry, chemistry-AP, child development, choir, choral music, Christian and Hebrew scripture, Christian ethics, Christian scripture, Christian testament, Christianity, church history, college counseling, community service, comparative government and politics, computer skills, constitutional history of U.S., constitutional law, creative writing, dance, digital photography, driver education, economics, English, environmental science, ethics, forensics, French, geometry, health, healthful living, Hebrew scripture, independent study, instrumental music, introduction to theater, journalism, Latin, modern European history, music theory, personal finance, photography, physical education, physics, physics-AP, pre-calculus, publications, SAT preparation, senior seminar, sociology, Spanish, speech, technical theater, theater, theater production, U.S. government and politics, world cultures, world literature, world religions, yearbook.

Graduation Requirements Arts and fine arts (art, music, dance, drama), computer literacy, English, foreign language, mathematics, physical education (includes health), religion (includes Bible studies and theology), science, social studies (includes history). Community service is required.

Special Academic Programs Advanced Placement exam preparation; honors section; independent study; term-away projects; study at local college for college credit; domestic exchange program (with Network of Sacred Heart Schools); study abroad; academic accommodation for the gifted; special instructional classes for deaf students, blind students.

College Admission Counseling 59 students graduated in 2010; all went to college, including Creighton University; Iowa State University of Science and Technology; Saint Louis University; The University of Iowa; University of Nebraska–Lincoln; University of Nebraska at Omaha. Median combined SAT: 1810, median composite ACT: 27.

Student Life Upper grades have uniform requirement, student council, honor system. Discipline rests primarily with faculty. Attendance at religious services is required.

Tuition and Aid Day student tuition: $8800. Tuition installment plan (monthly payment plans, quarterly payment plan, semester payment plan). Tuition reduction for siblings, merit scholarship grants, need-based scholarship grants, minority scholarships, reduced tuition for children of Creighton University employees available. In 2010–11, 48% of upper-school students received aid; total upper-school merit-scholarship money awarded: $50,000. Total amount of financial aid awarded in 2010–11: $117,000.
Admissions Traditional secondary-level entrance grade is 9. For fall 2010, 332 students applied for upper-level admission, 313 were accepted, 303 enrolled. Scholastic Testing Service required. Deadline for receipt of application materials: January 26. Application fee required: $35. On-campus interview required.
Athletics Interscholastic: basketball, cheering, cross-country running, dance squad, dance team, diving, golf, soccer, softball, swimming and diving, tennis, track and field, volleyball; intramural: aerobics, aerobics/dance, cheering, yoga. 2 PE instructors, 12 coaches, 1 athletic trainer.
Computers Computers are regularly used in all academic classes. Computer network features include on-campus library services, Internet access, wireless campus network, Internet filtering or blocking technology, computer network with other Sacred Heart schools, mandatory laptop purchase by 10th, 11th, and 12th grade students. Campus intranet and student e-mail accounts are available to students. Students grades are available online. The school has a published electronic and media policy.
Contact Mrs. Meg Jones, Recruitment Director/Exchange Coordinator. 402-558-3800 Ext. 1070. Fax: 402-558-0051. E-mail: mjones@duchesneacademy.org. Web site: www.duchesneacademy.org.

DUCHESNE ACADEMY OF THE SACRED HEART

10202 Memorial Drive
Houston, Texas 77024

Head of School: Sr. Jan Dunn, RSCJ

General Information Girls' day college-preparatory, arts, religious studies, and technology school, affiliated with Roman Catholic Church. Grades PK–12. Founded: 1960. Setting: suburban. 14-acre campus. 2 buildings on campus. Approved or accredited by Independent Schools Association of the Southwest, National Catholic Education Association, Network of Sacred Heart Schools, Texas Catholic Conference, Texas Education Agency, and Texas Department of Education. Endowment: $7 million. Total enrollment: 675. Upper school average class size: 14. Upper school faculty-student ratio: 1:7. There are 180 required school days per year for Upper School students. Upper School students typically attend 5 days per week. The average school day consists of 7 hours and 25 minutes.
Upper School Student Profile Grade 6: 60 students (60 girls); Grade 7: 61 students (61 girls); Grade 8: 39 students (39 girls); Grade 9: 56 students (56 girls); Grade 10: 62 students (62 girls); Grade 11: 62 students (62 girls); Grade 12: 60 students (60 girls). 64% of students are Roman Catholic.
Faculty School total: 92. In upper school: 3 men, 33 women; 28 have advanced degrees.
Subjects Offered Algebra, American literature, art history, arts, band, Bible studies, bioethics, biology, British literature, calculus, calculus-AP, ceramics, chemistry, chemistry-AP, community service, composition, computer graphics, computer programming, creative writing, desktop publishing, drawing, economics, English, English literature, European history, fine arts, French, French-AP, geometry, government/civics, health, human sexuality, Internet, Latin, mathematics, music, photography, physical education, physical fitness, physics, prayer/spirituality, pre-calculus, psychology, religious studies, science, scripture, sexuality, Shakespeare, social justice, social studies, Spanish, Spanish-AP, speech, statistics, statistics-AP, studio art, theater, theater production, theology, U.S. government and politics-AP, U.S. history, U.S. history-AP, Western literature, women's studies, world history, world literature, world religions, writing.
Graduation Requirements Arts and fine arts (art, music, dance, drama), computer science, English, foreign language, history, mathematics, physical education (includes health), religion (includes Bible studies and theology), science, completion of social awareness program. Community service is required.
Special Academic Programs 15 Advanced Placement exams for which test preparation is offered; honors section; independent study; domestic exchange program (with Network of Sacred Heart Schools); academic accommodation for the musically talented and the artistically talented.
College Admission Counseling 67 students graduated in 2010; all went to college, including Duke University; Southern Methodist University; Texas Christian University; The University of Texas at Austin; Trinity University; University of Houston. Median SAT critical reading: 600, median SAT math: 585, median SAT writing: 640, median combined SAT: 1845, median composite ACT: 27. 61% scored over 600 on SAT critical reading, 48% scored over 600 on SAT math, 78% scored over 600 on SAT writing, 59% scored over 1800 on combined SAT, 54% scored over 26 on composite ACT.
Student Life Upper grades have uniform requirement, student council, honor system. Discipline rests primarily with faculty. Attendance at religious services is required.
Tuition and Aid Day student tuition: $18,340. Tuition installment plan (monthly payment plans). Merit scholarship grants, need-based scholarship grants available. In 2010–11, 21% of upper-school students received aid; total upper-school merit-scholarship money awarded: $46,300. Total amount of financial aid awarded in 2010–11: $641,530.
Admissions Traditional secondary-level entrance grade is 9. For fall 2010, 101 students applied for upper-level admission, 68 were accepted, 29 enrolled. ISEE required. Deadline for receipt of application materials: February 1. Application fee required: $80. On-campus interview required.
Athletics Interscholastic: basketball, combined training, cross-country running, dance team, diving, field hockey, golf, soccer, softball, swimming and diving, tennis, track and field, volleyball, winter soccer. 5 PE instructors, 25 coaches, 2 athletic trainers.
Computers Computers are regularly used in all academic classes. Computer network features include on-campus library services, online commercial services, Internet access, wireless campus network, Internet filtering or blocking technology. Student e-mail accounts are available to students. Students grades are available online. The school has a published electronic and media policy.
Contact Mrs. Beth Speck, Director of Admission. 713-468-8211 Ext. 133. Fax: 713-465-9809. E-mail: beth.speck@duchesne.org. Web site: www.duchesne.org.

DURHAM ACADEMY

3601 Ridge Road
Durham, North Carolina 27705

Head of School: Mr. Edward Costello

General Information Coeducational day college-preparatory, arts, and technology school. Grades PK–12. Founded: 1933. Setting: suburban. 75-acre campus. 11 buildings on campus. Approved or accredited by North Carolina Association of Independent Schools, Southern Association of Colleges and Schools, Southern Association of Independent Schools, and North Carolina Department of Education. Member of National Association of Independent Schools and Secondary School Admission Test Board. Endowment: $9.6 million. Total enrollment: 1,146. Upper school average class size: 15. Upper school faculty-student ratio: 1:12. There are 179 required school days per year for Upper School students. Upper School students typically attend 5 days per week. The average school day consists of 6 hours.
Upper School Student Profile Grade 9: 97 students (42 boys, 55 girls); Grade 10: 102 students (49 boys, 53 girls); Grade 11: 106 students (50 boys, 56 girls); Grade 12: 92 students (41 boys, 51 girls).
Faculty School total: 198. In upper school: 24 men, 29 women; 36 have advanced degrees.
Subjects Offered 3-dimensional art, accounting, acting, advanced biology, advanced chemistry, advanced computer applications, advanced math, Advanced Placement courses, advanced studio art-AP, algebra, American history, American literature, art, art history, art history-AP, astronomy, biology, calculus, ceramics, chemistry, chemistry-AP, Chinese, chorus, community service, computer graphics, computer programming, computer science, computer science-AP, concert band, creative writing, dance, drama, ecology, economics, English, English literature, environmental science, fine arts, finite math, French, French language-AP, French-AP, geometry, German, history, Latin, mathematics, music, outdoor education, physical education, physics, psychology, science, social studies, Spanish, statistics, theater, U.S. history-AP.
Graduation Requirements Arts and fine arts (art, music, dance, drama), computer science, English, foreign language, mathematics, outdoor education, physical education (includes health), science, senior project, social studies (includes history), community service hours required for graduation.
Special Academic Programs Advanced Placement exam preparation; honors section; independent study; special instructional classes for students with learning disabilities and Attention Deficit Disorder.
College Admission Counseling 89 students graduated in 2011; all went to college, including Duke University; Harvard University; Stanford University; The University of North Carolina at Chapel Hill; The University of North Carolina Wilmington; Wake Forest University. Mean SAT critical reading: 672, mean SAT math: 667, mean SAT writing: 676.
Student Life Upper grades have specified standards of dress, student council, honor system. Discipline rests equally with students and faculty.
Summer Programs Remediation, enrichment, sports, art/fine arts, computer instruction programs offered; session focuses on academic enrichment, non-academic activities; held on campus; accepts boys and girls; open to students from other schools. 600 students usually enrolled. 2012 schedule: June 11 to July 27. Application deadline: none.
Tuition and Aid Day student tuition: $19,980. Tuition installment plan (Insured Tuition Payment Plan, monthly payment plans). Need-based scholarship grants available. In 2011–12, 41% of upper-school students received aid. Total amount of financial aid awarded in 2011–12: $805,415.
Admissions Traditional secondary-level entrance grade is 9. For fall 2011, 80 students applied for upper-level admission, 53 were accepted, 36 enrolled. ISEE required. Deadline for receipt of application materials: January 13. Application fee required: $55. Interview required.
Athletics Interscholastic: aquatics (boys, girls), baseball (b), basketball (b,g), cross-country running (b,g), dance team (g), field hockey (g), golf (b,g), lacrosse (b,g), soccer (b,g), softball (g), swimming and diving (b,g), tennis (b,g), track and field (b,g), volleyball (g), weight training (b,g); coed interscholastic: outdoor adventure, outdoor education, weight training; coed intramural: indoor soccer, judo, martial arts, modern

dance, physical fitness, physical training, winter soccer. 1 PE instructor, 6 coaches, 1 athletic trainer.
Computers Computers are regularly used in all academic, animation, computer applications, graphic arts, graphic design, introduction to technology, video film production, Web site design classes. Computer network features include on-campus library services, online commercial services, Internet access, wireless campus network, Internet filtering or blocking technology. Student e-mail accounts and computer access in designated common areas are available to students. The school has a published electronic and media policy.
Contact Ms. S. Victoria Muradi, Director of Admission and Financial Aid. 919-493-5787. Fax: 919-489-4893. E-mail: admissions@da.org. Web site: www.da.org.

EAGLEBROOK SCHOOL

Deerfield, Massachusetts

See Junior Boarding Schools section.

EAGLE HILL-SOUTHPORT

Southport, Connecticut

See Special Needs Schools section.

EASTERN CHRISTIAN HIGH SCHOOL

50 Oakwood Avenue

North Haledon, New Jersey 07508

Head of School: Mr. Thomas Dykhouse

General Information Coeducational day college-preparatory, general academic, arts, and technology school, affiliated with Christian Reformed Church. Grades PK–12. Founded: 1892. Setting: suburban. Nearest major city is New York, NY. 27-acre campus. 1 building on campus. Approved or accredited by Association of Christian Schools International, Christian Schools International, Middle States Association of Colleges and Schools, New Jersey Department of Education, and New Jersey Department of Education. Endowment: $6 million. Total enrollment: 757. Upper school average class size: 20. Upper school faculty-student ratio: 1:10. There are 185 required school days per year for Upper School students. Upper School students typically attend 5 days per week. The average school day consists of 6 hours and 40 minutes.
Upper School Student Profile Grade 6: 43 students (23 boys, 20 girls); Grade 7: 54 students (31 boys, 23 girls); Grade 8: 61 students (24 boys, 37 girls); Grade 9: 90 students (39 boys, 51 girls); Grade 10: 94 students (44 boys, 50 girls); Grade 11: 81 students (37 boys, 44 girls); Grade 12: 88 students (38 boys, 50 girls). 40% of students are members of Christian Reformed Church.
Faculty School total: 85. In upper school: 11 men, 22 women; 21 have advanced degrees.
Subjects Offered Accounting, advanced biology, algebra, American history, American legal systems, American literature, art, band, Bible studies, biology, business, business skills, calculus, chemistry, chorus, community service, composition, computer programming, computer science, computer-aided design, contemporary math, creative writing, driver education, English, English composition, English literature, entrepreneurship, ESL, European history, fine arts, French, geometry, government/civics, health, history, humanities, journalism, Latin, mathematics, music, orchestra, personal finance, physical education, physical science, physics, pre-calculus, psychology, science, social studies, sociology, Spanish, study skills, technical education, trigonometry, Web site design, world history, writing, writing workshop, yearbook.
Graduation Requirements Arts and fine arts (art, music, dance, drama), Bible, English, foreign language, lab science, leadership, mathematics, physical education (includes health), social studies (includes history), 50 hours of community service.
Special Academic Programs 1 Advanced Placement exam for which test preparation is offered; honors section; independent study; academic accommodation for the gifted, the musically talented, and the artistically talented; remedial reading and/or remedial writing; remedial math; programs in English, mathematics for dyslexic students; ESL (20 students enrolled).
College Admission Counseling 81 students graduated in 2010; 76 went to college, including Calvin College; Liberty University; Messiah College; Montclair State University; Palm Beach Atlantic University; William Paterson University of New Jersey. Other: 5 went to work. Median SAT critical reading: 540, median SAT math: 510, median SAT writing: 510. Mean composite ACT: 20. 28% scored over 600 on SAT critical reading, 24% scored over 600 on SAT math, 25% scored over 600 on SAT writing.
Student Life Upper grades have specified standards of dress, student council. Discipline rests primarily with faculty. Attendance at religious services is required.
Tuition and Aid Day student tuition: $11,230. Tuition installment plan (SMART Tuition Payment Plan, monthly payment plans). Tuition reduction for siblings, need-based scholarship grants available.
Admissions Traditional secondary-level entrance grade is 9. For fall 2010, 63 students applied for upper-level admission, 50 were accepted, 50 enrolled. Deadline for receipt of application materials: none. Application fee required: $100. On-campus interview required.
Athletics Interscholastic: baseball (boys), basketball (b,g), bowling (b,g), cheering (g), cross-country running (b,g), golf (b,g), soccer (b,g), softball (g), tennis (b,g), track and field (b,g), volleyball (g); intramural: aerobics (b,g), badminton (b,g), basketball (b,g), fitness walking (b,g), flag football (b,g), flagball (b,g), football (b,g), Frisbee (b,g), golf (b,g), gymnastics (b,g), indoor soccer (b,g), lacrosse (b,g), paddle tennis (b,g), physical fitness (b,g), roller hockey (b,g), running (b,g), skateboarding (b,g), skiing (downhill) (b,g), soccer (b,g), softball (b,g), street hockey (b,g), table tennis (b,g), volleyball (b,g), weight lifting (b,g); coed intramural: aerobics, badminton, baseball, basketball, fitness walking, flag football, flagball, football, golf, gymnastics, indoor soccer, lacrosse, paddle tennis, physical fitness, roller hockey, running, skateboarding, skiing (downhill), soccer, softball, street hockey, table tennis, volleyball, weight lifting. 2 PE instructors, 18 coaches.
Computers Computers are regularly used in all academic classes. Computer network features include on-campus library services, Internet access, wireless campus network, Internet filtering or blocking technology, Microsoft Office, Microsoft Visual Studio, AutoCAD LT 2000, Adobe Photoshop, Adobe GoLive, Adobe Illustrator, Adobe LiveMotion, Macromedia Dreamweaver, Adobe Premiere, Lego Mindstorms NXT. Computer access in designated common areas is available to students. Students grades are available online. The school has a published electronic and media policy.
Contact Mr. G. Anthony Cantalupo, Admission Director. 973-427-6244 Ext. 207. Fax: 973-427-9775. E-mail: admissions@easternchristian.org. Web site: www.easternchristian.org.

EASTSIDE CATHOLIC SCHOOL

232 228th Avenue SE

Sammamish, Washington 98074

Head of School: Sr. Mary E. Tracy

General Information Coeducational day college-preparatory, arts, business, religious studies, and technology school, affiliated with Roman Catholic Church. Grades 6–12. Founded: 1980. Setting: suburban. 50-acre campus. 2 buildings on campus. Approved or accredited by National Catholic Education Association, Northwest Association of Schools and Colleges, Pacific Northwest Association of Independent Schools, and Washington Department of Education. Upper school average class size: 20. Upper school faculty-student ratio: 1:13. There are 180 required school days per year for Upper School students. The average school day consists of 7 hours.
Upper School Student Profile 60% of students are Roman Catholic.
Faculty School total: 65. In upper school: 22 men, 30 women; 38 have advanced degrees.
Subjects Offered Advanced Placement courses, algebra, American government, American history, American literature, anatomy and physiology, art, ASB Leadership, athletic training, band, biology, biology-AP, British literature, calculus, calculus-AP, campus ministry, Catholic belief and practice, ceramics, chemistry, chemistry-AP, choir, church history, community service, computers, contemporary issues, creative writing, debate, digital photography, drama, drawing, economics, English, English literature, environmental science-AP, French, French-AP, geometry, government and politics-AP, graphic design, health, history, honors algebra, honors English, honors geometry, honors U.S. history, honors world history, journalism, law, literature and composition-AP, math analysis, music, music theory-AP, painting, performing arts, physical education, physics, physics-AP, religious education, social justice, Spanish, Spanish-AP, speech and debate, statistics-AP, studio art, studio art-AP, theology, trigonometry, U.S. history-AP, Web site design, world history, world history-AP, yearbook.
Graduation Requirements Arts and fine arts (art, music, dance, drama), business education, English, foreign language, health, history, information technology, lab science, mathematics, physical education (includes health), science, social sciences, theology, 100 hours of community service (over 4 years).
Special Academic Programs Advanced Placement exam preparation; honors section; study at local college for college credit; academic accommodation for the gifted; programs in English, mathematics, general development for dyslexic students.
College Admission Counseling 144 students graduated in 2011; 142 went to college, including Gonzaga University; Santa Clara University; University of Colorado Boulder; University of Portland; University of Washington; Washington State University. Other: 1 entered a postgraduate year, 1 had other specific plans.
Student Life Upper grades have specified standards of dress, student council, honor system. Discipline rests primarily with faculty. Attendance at religious services is required.
Tuition and Aid Day student tuition: $17,260. Tuition installment plan (monthly payment plans). Tuition reduction for siblings, merit scholarship grants, need-based scholarship grants available.
Admissions Traditional secondary-level entrance grade is 9. ISEE required. Deadline for receipt of application materials: January 12. Application fee required: $25. Interview recommended.
Athletics Interscholastic: baseball (boys), basketball (b,g), cheering (g), cross-country running (b,g), drill team (g), football (b), golf (b,g), lacrosse (b,g), soccer (b,g), softball

(g), swimming and diving (b,g), tennis (b,g), track and field (b,g), volleyball (g), wrestling (b); coed interscholastic: Special Olympics; coed intramural: strength & conditioning, weight lifting, weight training. 2 PE instructors, 43 coaches, 1 athletic trainer.

Computers Computers are regularly used in business education, digital applications, graphic design, technology, Web site design, yearbook classes. Computer network features include on-campus library services, online commercial services, Internet access, wireless campus network, Internet filtering or blocking technology. Students grades are available online.

Contact Sarah Dahleen, Director of Admissions. 425-295-3017. Fax: 425-392-5160. E-mail: sdahleen@eastsidecatholic.org. Web site: www.eastsidecatholic.org.

EASTSIDE CHRISTIAN ACADEMY

1320 Abbeydale Drive SE

Calgary, Alberta T2A 7L8, Canada

Head of School: Dr. Frank Moody

General Information Coeducational day and distance learning college-preparatory, general academic, religious studies, and music school, affiliated with Christian faith. Grades K–12. Distance learning grades 10–12. Founded: 1999. Setting: urban. 4-acre campus. 1 building on campus. Approved or accredited by Association of Independent Schools and Colleges of Alberta and Alberta Department of Education. Language of instruction: English. Total enrollment: 82. Upper school average class size: 20. Upper school faculty-student ratio: 1:25. There are 180 required school days per year for Upper School students. Upper School students typically attend 5 days per week. The average school day consists of 5 hours and 35 minutes.

Upper School Student Profile Grade 10: 7 students (2 boys, 5 girls); Grade 11: 1 student (1 boy); Grade 12: 6 students (3 boys, 3 girls). 100% of students are Christian faith.

Faculty School total: 4. In upper school: 2 men, 2 women; 1 has an advanced degree.

Subjects Offered Algebra, art, Bible studies, biology, business, business mathematics, Canadian geography, Canadian history, career/college preparation, chemistry, church history, civics, computer literacy, economics, English, etymology, French, geometry, Life of Christ, literature, music, natural history, physical education, physical science, physics, Spanish, speech, typing, world geography, world history.

Graduation Requirements Algebra, Bible studies, biology, business education, Canadian geography, Canadian history, chemistry, Christian scripture, Christian testament, church history, concert band, data processing, economics, electives, English, etymology, French, geometry, German, mathematics, music, physical education (includes health), physical science, physics, religious education, social studies (includes history), Spanish, speech and debate, vocal music, volleyball, world geography, world history.

Special Academic Programs Honors section; accelerated programs; independent study; study at local college for college credit; academic accommodation for the gifted and the musically talented; remedial reading and/or remedial writing; remedial math; ESL (2 students enrolled).

College Admission Counseling 4 students graduated in 2011; 3 went to college, including Mount Royal University; University of Alberta; University of Calgary.

Student Life Upper grades have uniform requirement, student council, honor system. Discipline rests primarily with faculty. Attendance at religious services is required.

Tuition and Aid Day student tuition: CAN$3600. Tuition installment plan (monthly payment plans, individually arranged payment plans). Tuition reduction for siblings, bursaries available. In 2011–12, 20% of upper-school students received aid. Total amount of financial aid awarded in 2011–12: CAN$8400.

Admissions Traditional secondary-level entrance grade is 10. Cognitive Abilities Test, Diagnostic Achievement Battery-2 (for applicants from non-U.S. curriculum) and school placement exam required. Deadline for receipt of application materials: June 29. Application fee required: CAN$60. On-campus interview required.

Athletics Interscholastic: badminton (boys, girls), ball hockey (b,g), basketball (b), curling (b,g), soccer (b,g), swimming and diving (b,g), track and field (b,g), volleyball (b,g); coed interscholastic: badminton, ball hockey, curling, soccer, swimming and diving, track and field, volleyball. 1 PE instructor, 1 coach.

Computers Computers are regularly used in career exploration, data processing, economics, English, French, geography, history, information technology, keyboarding, literacy, mathematics, media, reading, religion, religious studies, social studies, Spanish, speech, typing, word processing classes. Computer network features include Internet access, wireless campus network, Internet filtering or blocking technology. Computer access in designated common areas is available to students. Students grades are available online. The school has a published electronic and media policy.

Contact Mrs. LaDawn Hamilton, Administration Assistant. 403-569-1039 Ext. 200. Fax: 403-569-7557. E-mail: admin@ecaab.ca.

ECOLE D'HUMANITÉ

CH 6085 Hasliberg Goldern, Switzerland

Head of School: Mr. John Ashley Curtis

General Information Coeducational boarding and day college-preparatory, general academic, arts, vocational, and bilingual studies school. Ungraded, ages 12–19. Founded: 1934. Setting: rural. Nearest major city is Lucerne, Switzerland. Students are housed in coed dormitories. 5-acre campus. 13 buildings on campus. Approved or accredited by CITA (Commission on International and Trans-Regional Accreditation), Department of Education of Bern, North Central Association of Colleges and Schools, and Swiss Federation of Private Schools. Member of European Council of International Schools. Languages of instruction: English and German. Endowment: 1 million Swiss francs. Upper school average class size: 5. Upper school faculty-student ratio: 1:5. Upper School students typically attend 6 days per week. The average school day consists of 6 hours.

Upper School Student Profile 95% of students are boarding students. 49% are international students. International students from China, Germany, Italy, Russian Federation, Taiwan, and United States; 12 other countries represented in student body.

Faculty School total: 44. In upper school: 15 men, 19 women; 10 have advanced degrees; 37 reside on campus.

Subjects Offered Advanced Placement courses, algebra, American literature, art, art history, backpacking, band, batik, biology, biology-AP, calculus, calculus-AP, career and personal planning, carpentry, ceramics, chemistry, choir, choreography, chorus, college counseling, community service, computer programming, computer skills, costumes and make-up, crafts, creative dance, creative writing, culinary arts, cultural geography, current events, dance, dance performance, drama, drama workshop, drawing, ecology, environmental systems, English, English as a foreign language, English composition, English literature, English literature-AP, environmental science, ESL, European history, expository writing, fine arts, first aid, folk dance, French, French as a second language, gardening, geography, geometry, German, German-AP, grammar, guitar, gymnastics, health, history, home economics, independent study, jazz ensemble, jewelry making, Latin, mathematics, modern dance, music, music appreciation, music performance, musical productions, musical theater, musical theater dance, outdoor education, peer counseling, philosophy, photo shop, photography, physical education, physics, piano, poetry, pottery, pre-calculus, psychology, religion, research skills, SAT preparation, science, sewing, Shakespeare, single survival, social sciences, social studies, studio art, swimming, theater, TOEFL preparation, trigonometry, U.S. history, visual and performing arts, vocal ensemble, voice, volleyball, weaving, wind ensemble, women's studies, woodworking, world history, world history-AP, world literature, writing, yoga.

Graduation Requirements English, foreign language, independent study, mathematics, physical education (includes health), research skills, SAT preparation, science, social sciences, social studies (includes history), 2x term paper methodology course, balance of courses in arts, sports, handcrafts. Community service is required.

Special Academic Programs 5 Advanced Placement exams for which test preparation is offered; honors section; accelerated programs; independent study; term-away projects; academic accommodation for the gifted, the musically talented, and the artistically talented; remedial reading and/or remedial writing; remedial math; ESL (40 students enrolled).

College Admission Counseling 10 students graduated in 2010; 6 went to college, including Brandeis University; Brown University; New York University; The Colorado College. Other: 2 went to work, 2 had other specific plans. Median SAT critical reading: 600, median SAT math: 650, median SAT writing: 580.

Student Life Upper grades have student council, honor system. Discipline rests equally with students and faculty.

Tuition and Aid Day student tuition: 22,000 Swiss francs; 7-day tuition and room/board: 44,000 Swiss francs–48,000 Swiss francs. Guaranteed tuition plan. Tuition installment plan (monthly payment plans, individually arranged payment plans). Need-based scholarship grants, need-based loans, middle-income loans available. In 2010–11, 20% of upper-school students received aid. Total amount of financial aid awarded in 2010–11: 180,000 Swiss francs.

Admissions Traditional secondary-level entrance age is 16. For fall 2010, 50 students applied for upper-level admission, 46 were accepted, 46 enrolled. Deadline for receipt of application materials: none. No application fee required. Interview recommended.

Athletics Interscholastic: basketball (boys); intramural: basketball (b,g); coed intramural: aerobics, aerobics/dance, alpine skiing, archery, backpacking, badminton, ballet, baseball, basketball, bicycling, canoeing/kayaking, climbing, dance, fitness, freestyle skiing, Frisbee, gymnastics, hiking/backpacking, horseback riding, indoor soccer, jogging, juggling, kayaking, martial arts, modern dance, mountaineering, physical fitness, rock climbing, skiing (downhill), snowboarding, snowshoeing, soccer, softball, strength & conditioning, swimming and diving, table tennis, tennis, ultimate Frisbee, volleyball, yoga.

Computers Computers are regularly used in career exploration, college planning, creative writing, data processing, English, graphic design, independent study, library, newspaper, photography, typing, yearbook classes. Computer resources include Internet access. Computer access in designated common areas is available to students.

Contact John Ashley Curtis, Director. 41-33-972-9272. Fax: 41-33-972-9272. E-mail: admissions@ecole.ch. Web site: www.ecole.ch.

EDGEWOOD ACADEMY

5475 Elmore Road

PO Box 160

Elmore, Alabama 36025

Head of School: Mr. Frankie Mitchum

General Information Coeducational day college-preparatory, arts, business, religious studies, bilingual studies, and technology school. Founded: 1967. Setting: small town. Nearest major city is Montgomery. 30-acre campus. 4 buildings on campus. Approved or accredited by National Independent Private Schools Association, Southern Association of Colleges and Schools, and Alabama Department of Education. Total enrollment: 257. Upper school average class size: 18. Upper school faculty-student ratio: 1:14. There are 177 required school days per year for Upper School students. Upper School students typically attend 5 days per week. The average school day consists of 5 hours and 45 minutes.

Upper School Student Profile Grade 9: 19 students (11 boys, 8 girls); Grade 10: 11 students (6 boys, 5 girls); Grade 11: 33 students (20 boys, 13 girls); Grade 12: 28 students (15 boys, 13 girls).

Faculty School total: 20. In upper school: 4 men, 5 women; 7 have advanced degrees.

Graduation Requirements Advanced diploma requires 100 hours of community service, standard diplomas requires 50 hours of community service.

Special Academic Programs Advanced Placement exam preparation; study at local college for college credit.

College Admission Counseling 18 students graduated in 2011; they went to Auburn University Montgomery. Median composite ACT: 25.

Student Life Upper grades have specified standards of dress, student council.

Summer Programs Session focuses on driver education; held both on and off campus; held at Driving practice - random; accepts boys and girls; open to students from other schools. 15 students usually enrolled. 2012 schedule: June to July. Application deadline: May.

Tuition and Aid Day student tuition: $5500. Tuition installment plan (SMART Tuition Payment Plan). Tuition reduction for siblings available.

Admissions Admissions testing required. Deadline for receipt of application materials: none. No application fee required. Interview required.

Athletics Interscholastic: baseball (boys), basketball (b,g), cheering (g), football (b), physical fitness (b,g), physical training (b,g), softball (g), volleyball (g), weight lifting (b), weight training (b,g); coed interscholastic: track and field. 2 PE instructors, 3 coaches.

Computers Computers are regularly used in yearbook classes. Computer network features include on-campus library services, Internet access, wireless campus network, Internet filtering or blocking technology. Students grades are available online. The school has a published electronic and media policy.

Contact 334-567-5102. Fax: 334-567-8316. Web site: edgewoodacademy.org.

EDISON SCHOOL

Box 2, Site 11, RR2

Okotoks, Alberta T1S 1A2, Canada

Head of School: Mrs. Beth Chernoff

General Information Coeducational day college-preparatory and general academic school. Grades K–12. Founded: 1993. Setting: small town. Nearest major city is Calgary, Canada. 5-acre campus. 3 buildings on campus. Approved or accredited by Association of Independent Schools and Colleges of Alberta and Alberta Department of Education. Languages of instruction: English, Spanish, and French. Total enrollment: 198. Upper school average class size: 12. Upper school faculty-student ratio: 1:12. There are 185 required school days per year for Upper School students. Upper School students typically attend 5 days per week. The average school day consists of 6 hours and 15 minutes.

Upper School Student Profile Grade 9: 12 students (6 boys, 6 girls); Grade 10: 12 students (6 boys, 6 girls); Grade 11: 12 students (6 boys, 6 girls); Grade 12: 12 students (6 boys, 6 girls).

Faculty School total: 18. In upper school: 5 men, 1 woman; 4 have advanced degrees.

Subjects Offered Advanced Placement courses, art, biology, chemistry, English, French, mathematics, physical education, physics, science, social studies, Spanish, standard curriculum.

Graduation Requirements Alberta Learning requirements.

Special Academic Programs Advanced Placement exam preparation; accelerated programs; independent study; study at local college for college credit; academic accommodation for the gifted.

College Admission Counseling 8 students graduated in 2011; 7 went to college, including The University of British Columbia; University of Alberta; University of Calgary; University of Waterloo. Other: 1 went to work. Median composite ACT: 26. 58% scored over 26 on composite ACT.

Student Life Upper grades have uniform requirement, student council, honor system. Discipline rests primarily with faculty.

Tuition and Aid Day student tuition: CAN$7000. Tuition installment plan (monthly payment plans). Tuition reduction for siblings available.

Admissions Traditional secondary-level entrance grade is 9. For fall 2011, 20 students applied for upper-level admission, 4 were accepted, 4 enrolled. Achievement tests or admissions testing required. Deadline for receipt of application materials: none. No application fee required. On-campus interview required.

Athletics Interscholastic: badminton (boys, girls), basketball (b,g), cross-country running (b,g); intramural: badminton (b,g), basketball (b,g), cross-country running (b,g); coed interscholastic: badminton, flag football; coed intramural: badminton, flag football, outdoor education. 1 PE instructor, 1 coach.

Computers Computers are regularly used in all classes. Computer resources include Internet access. Computer access in designated common areas is available to students.

Contact Mrs. Beth Chernoff, Headmistress. 403-938-7670. Fax: 403-938-7224. E-mail: office@edisonschool.ca. Web site: www.edisonschool.ca.

EDMUND BURKE SCHOOL

4101 Connecticut Avenue NW

Washington, District of Columbia 20008

Head of School: Andrew Slater

General Information Coeducational day college-preparatory and arts school. Grades 6–12. Founded: 1968. Setting: urban. 2 buildings on campus. Approved or accredited by Association of Independent Schools of Greater Washington, Middle States Association of Colleges and Schools, and District of Columbia Department of Education. Member of National Association of Independent Schools and Secondary School Admission Test Board. Endowment: $829,556. Total enrollment: 275. Upper school average class size: 15. Upper school faculty-student ratio: 1:6. There are 185 required school days per year for Upper School students. Upper School students typically attend 5 days per week. The average school day consists of 5 hours.

Upper School Student Profile Grade 9: 42 students (19 boys, 23 girls); Grade 10: 52 students (29 boys, 23 girls); Grade 11: 53 students (30 boys, 23 girls); Grade 12: 60 students (29 boys, 31 girls).

Faculty School total: 45. In upper school: 19 men, 19 women; 25 have advanced degrees.

Subjects Offered African-American literature, algebra, American history, American literature, anatomy, anthropology, biology, calculus, ceramics, chemistry, computer science, creative writing, economics, English, English literature, European history, French, geography, geometry, health, history, journalism, Latin, linguistics, music, performing arts, philosophy, photography, physical education, physics, senior seminar, Spanish, theater, trigonometry, values and decisions, visual arts, women's studies, world history, writing.

Graduation Requirements English, foreign language, history, mathematics, physical education (includes health), science, social sciences, values and decisions, visual and performing arts, senior research seminar. Community service is required.

Special Academic Programs Advanced Placement exam preparation; independent study; term-away projects.

College Admission Counseling 65 students graduated in 2011; all went to college, including New York University; University of New Hampshire; University of Pittsburgh; University of Rhode Island; Wesleyan University. Median SAT critical reading: 651, median SAT math: 641, median SAT writing: 648.

Student Life Upper grades have student council, honor system. Discipline rests primarily with faculty.

Summer Programs Remediation, enrichment, advancement, ESL, art/fine arts, computer instruction programs offered; session focuses on academic programs and visual arts; held on campus; accepts boys and girls; open to students from other schools. 50 students usually enrolled. 2012 schedule: June 20 to August 21. Application deadline: none.

Tuition and Aid Day student tuition: $31,650. Tuition installment plan (The Tuition Plan, Insured Tuition Payment Plan, Academic Management Services Plan, individually arranged payment plans). Need-based scholarship grants available. In 2011–12, 29% of upper-school students received aid. Total amount of financial aid awarded in 2011–12: $978,185.

Admissions Traditional secondary-level entrance grade is 9. For fall 2011, 130 students applied for upper-level admission, 86 were accepted, 39 enrolled. ISEE or SSAT required. Deadline for receipt of application materials: January 13. Application fee required: $60. On-campus interview required.

Athletics Interscholastic: aquatics (boys, girls), basketball (b,g), cross-country running (b,g), golf (b,g), soccer (b,g), softball (g), swimming and diving (g), track and field (b,g), volleyball (b,g), wrestling (b,g); intramural: dance team (b,g), Frisbee (b,g), martial arts (b,g), physical fitness (b,g), weight lifting (b,g); coed interscholastic: swimming and diving; coed intramural: indoor soccer, jogging. 2 PE instructors, 2 coaches.

Computers Computers are regularly used in creative writing, English, foreign language, French, graphic arts, history, journalism, mathematics, science classes. Computer network features include on-campus library services, online commercial services, Internet access. Students grades are available online. The school has a published electronic and media policy.

Contact Admissions Office. 202-362-8882. Fax: 202-362-1914. E-mail: admissions@eburke.org. Web site: www.eburke.org.

ELDORADO EMERSON PRIVATE SCHOOL

4100 East Walnut Street

Orange, California 92869

Head of School: Dr. Glory Ludwick

General Information Coeducational boarding and day college-preparatory, general academic, and arts school. Boarding grades 7–12, day grades K–12. Founded: 1958. Setting: suburban. Nearest major city is Los Angeles. Students are housed in homes of host families. 5-acre campus. 8 buildings on campus. Approved or accredited by Western Association of Schools and Colleges and California Department of Education. Total enrollment: 180. Upper school average class size: 18. Upper school faculty-student ratio: 1:18. There are 180 required school days per year for Upper School students. Upper School students typically attend 5 days per week. The average school day consists of 6 hours.

Upper School Student Profile Grade 7: 5 students (2 boys, 3 girls); Grade 8: 14 students (10 boys, 4 girls); Grade 9: 21 students (11 boys, 10 girls); Grade 10: 13 students (7 boys, 6 girls); Grade 11: 29 students (16 boys, 13 girls); Grade 12: 24 students (11 boys, 13 girls). 20% of students are boarding students. 80% are state residents. 3 states are represented in upper school student body. 20% are international students. International students from China, Japan, Republic of Korea, and Viet Nam.

Faculty School total: 25. In upper school: 7 men, 6 women; 11 have advanced degrees.

Subjects Offered Acting, advanced chemistry, advanced math, advanced TOEFL/grammar, algebra, American government, American history-AP, analysis and differential calculus, anatomy, ancient world history, applied arts, applied music, Arabic, art, art and culture, art appreciation, art education, art history, Basic programming, biology, biology-AP, calculus, calculus-AP, cell biology, ceramics, chemistry, chemistry-AP, Chinese, civil war history, classical civilization, classical Greek literature, classical music, classics, clayworking, computer processing, computer programming, computer skills, concert band, contemporary art, contemporary history, creative drama, creative writing, cultural geography, current events, current history, drama workshop, drawing, earth science, economics and history, Egyptian history, English, English literature, ESL, fine arts, gardening, general math, geography, geometry, grammar, jazz band, keyboarding, library skills, Mandarin, math analysis, physics, physics-AP, pre-algebra, pre-calculus, reading, SAT preparation, science, Shakespeare, Spanish, TOEFL preparation, U.S. government and politics-AP, U.S. history, world history.

Graduation Requirements Art, English, foreign language, mathematics, music, physical education (includes health), science, social studies (includes history). Community service is required.

Special Academic Programs Advanced Placement exam preparation; honors section; accelerated programs; independent study; study at local college for college credit; academic accommodation for the gifted, the musically talented, and the artistically talented; ESL (50 students enrolled).

College Admission Counseling Colleges students went to include California State University, Fullerton; Chapman University; Occidental College; Purdue University; The Johns Hopkins University; University of California, Santa Cruz.

Student Life Upper grades have specified standards of dress, honor system. Discipline rests equally with students and faculty.

Tuition and Aid Day student tuition: $12,150; 7-day tuition and room/board: $20,000–$30,000. Tuition installment plan (monthly payment plans, individually arranged payment plans). Tuition reduction for siblings, need-based scholarship grants available. In 2011–12, 10% of upper-school students received aid. Total amount of financial aid awarded in 2011–12: $50,000.

Admissions Traditional secondary-level entrance grade is 10. For fall 2011, 100 students applied for upper-level admission, 80 were accepted, 75 enrolled. Achievement tests or any standardized test required. Deadline for receipt of application materials: none. Application fee required: $250. Interview required.

Athletics Coed Interscholastic: baseball, basketball, cross-country running, fitness, flag football, handball, kickball, physical fitness. 1 PE instructor, 4 coaches.

Computers Computers are regularly used in desktop publishing, graphic design, keyboarding, Web site design, word processing, yearbook classes. Computer resources include Internet access, Internet filtering or blocking technology.

Contact Mrs. Melinda Bently, Administration. 714-633-4774. Fax: 714-744-3304. E-mail: mbently@eldoradoemerson.org. Web site: www.eldorado-emerson.org.

ELGIN ACADEMY

350 Park Street

Elgin, Illinois 60120

Head of School: Dr. John W. Cooper

General Information Coeducational day college-preparatory, arts, and technology school. Grades PS–12. Founded: 1839. Setting: suburban. Nearest major city is Chicago. 20-acre campus. 8 buildings on campus. Approved or accredited by Independent Schools Association of the Central States. Member of National Association of Independent Schools and Secondary School Admission Test Board. Endowment: $10 million. Total enrollment: 424. Upper school average class size: 12. Upper school faculty-student ratio: 1:5. There are 183 required school days per year for Upper School students. Upper School students typically attend 5 days per week. The average school day consists of 6 hours and 30 minutes.

Upper School Student Profile Grade 9: 43 students (21 boys, 22 girls); Grade 10: 32 students (17 boys, 15 girls); Grade 11: 37 students (17 boys, 20 girls); Grade 12: 25 students (15 boys, 10 girls).

Subjects Offered Algebra, American history, American literature, anatomy and physiology, art, art history, biology, calculus, ceramics, chemistry, computer programming, computer science, creative writing, drama, English, English literature, environmental science, European history, expository writing, fine arts, finite math, French, geometry, government/civics, grammar, history, Latin, Latin-AP, mathematics, music, painting, photography, physical education, psychology, psychology-AP, science, social studies, Spanish, statistics, theater, trigonometry, world history, world literature, writing.

Graduation Requirements 20th century history, arts and fine arts (art, music, dance, drama), English, foreign language, mathematics, science, social studies (includes history).

Special Academic Programs 16 Advanced Placement exams for which test preparation is offered; honors section; independent study.

College Admission Counseling 29 students graduated in 2010; all went to college, including Lawrence University; New York University; Northwestern University; University of Notre Dame; Washington University in St. Louis; Wellesley College. Median SAT critical reading: 650, median SAT math: 600, median SAT writing: 650, median combined SAT: 1910, median composite ACT: 27.

Student Life Upper grades have specified standards of dress, student council, honor system. Discipline rests primarily with faculty.

Tuition and Aid Day student tuition: $17,725. Tuition installment plan (FACTS Tuition Payment Plan, 10-month payment plan). Tuition reduction for siblings, merit scholarship grants, need-based scholarship grants available. In 2010–11, 40% of upper-school students received aid; total upper-school merit-scholarship money awarded: $15,000.

Admissions Traditional secondary-level entrance grade is 9. ERB - verbal abilities, reading comprehension, quantitative abilities (level F, form 1) required. Deadline for receipt of application materials: none. Application fee required: $50. Interview required.

Athletics Interscholastic: field hockey (girls), golf (b); coed interscholastic: basketball, cross-country running, outdoors, soccer, tennis, track and field, volleyball, wilderness, wilderness survival; coed intramural: backpacking, canoeing/kayaking. 2 PE instructors.

Computers Computers are regularly used in art, English, foreign language, mathematics, science, social studies classes. Computer network features include on-campus library services, online commercial services, Internet access, wireless campus network. Campus intranet is available to students. Students grades are available online. The school has a published electronic and media policy.

Contact Mr. Shannon D. Howell, Director of Admission and Marketing. 847-695-0303. Fax: 847-695-5017. E-mail: showell@elginacademy.org. Web site: www.elginacademy.org.

See Display on next page and Close-Up on page 618.

ELIZABETH SETON HIGH SCHOOL

5715 Emerson Street

Bladensburg, Maryland 20710-1844

Head of School: Sr. Ellen Marie Hagar

General Information Girls' day college-preparatory, arts, religious studies, bilingual studies, technology, visual arts, and music school, affiliated with Roman Catholic Church. Grades 9–12. Founded: 1959. Setting: suburban. Nearest major city is Washington, DC. 24-acre campus. 2 buildings on campus. Approved or accredited by Middle States Association of Colleges and Schools, National Catholic Education Association, and Maryland Department of Education. Total enrollment: 606. Upper school average class size: 18. Upper school faculty-student ratio: 1:13. There are 180 required school days per year for Upper School students. Upper School students typically attend 5 days per week. The average school day consists of 6 hours and 30 minutes.

Upper School Student Profile Grade 9: 119 students (119 girls); Grade 10: 146 students (146 girls); Grade 11: 143 students (143 girls); Grade 12: 179 students (179 girls). 65% of students are Roman Catholic.

Faculty School total: 59. In upper school: 4 men, 55 women; 35 have advanced degrees.

Subjects Offered Accounting, advanced chemistry, advanced math, algebra, American history, American history-AP, American literature, analytic geometry, anatomy, art, art-AP, bioethics, biology, business, calculus, calculus-AP, ceramics, chemistry, choir, chorus, Christian and Hebrew scripture, Christianity, church history, community service, computer multimedia, computer programming, computer science, desktop publishing, earth science, economics, English, English literature, English literature and composition-AP, English literature-AP, environmental science, ethics, European history, film and literature, fine arts, French, geography, geometry, government-AP, government/civics, grammar, health, history, home economics, honors algebra, honors English, honors geometry, journalism, keyboarding, Latin, mathematics, music, newspaper, philosophy, photography, physical education, physics, physiology, pre-calculus, probability and statistics, psychology, psychology-AP, religion, science, social studies, sociology, Spanish, speech, symphonic band, theology, trigonometry, U.S. government and politics-AP, Web site design, world history, world literature, writing.

Graduation Requirements 1 1/2 elective credits, arts and fine arts (art, music, dance, drama), English, foreign language, health education, mathematics, physical education (includes health), religion (includes Bible studies and theology), science, social studies (includes history), technology. Community service is required.

Special Academic Programs Advanced Placement exam preparation; honors section; independent study; academic accommodation for the gifted, the musically talented, and the artistically talented; programs in general development for dyslexic students; special instructional classes for students with mild learning disabilities, organizational deficiencies, Attention Deficit Disorder, and dyslexia.

College Admission Counseling 159 students graduated in 2011; all went to college, including Frostburg State University; Salisbury University; Temple University; Towson University; University of Maryland, Baltimore County; University of Maryland, College Park. Mean SAT critical reading: 520, mean SAT math: 500, mean SAT writing: 550.

Student Life Upper grades have uniform requirement, student council, honor system. Discipline rests equally with students and faculty. Attendance at religious services is required.

Summer Programs Remediation, enrichment, sports, art/fine arts programs offered; held on campus; accepts girls; open to students from other schools. 2012 schedule: June to August.

Tuition and Aid Day student tuition: $10,950. Tuition installment plan (FACTS Tuition Payment Plan, monthly payment plans, individually arranged payment plans, quarterly payment plan). Tuition reduction for siblings, merit scholarship grants, need-based scholarship grants, paying campus jobs available. In 2011–12, 40% of upper-school students received aid; total upper-school merit-scholarship money awarded: $104,000. Total amount of financial aid awarded in 2011–12: $500,000.

Admissions Traditional secondary-level entrance grade is 9. For fall 2011, 247 students applied for upper-level admission, 156 were accepted, 120 enrolled. High School Placement Test required. Deadline for receipt of application materials: December 8. Application fee required: $50. On-campus interview required.

Athletics Interscholastic: basketball, cheering, crew, cross-country running, dance squad, dance team, equestrian sports, field hockey, golf, horseback riding, indoor track, lacrosse, modern dance, pom squad, rowing, running, soccer, softball, swimming and diving, tennis, volleyball, winter (indoor) track; intramural: aerobics, aerobics/dance, aerobics/Nautilus, combined training, cooperative games, cross-country running, dance, fitness, fitness walking, flag football, martial arts, ocean paddling, outdoor recreation, physical fitness, strength & conditioning, walking, weight training. 5 PE instructors, 32 coaches, 1 athletic trainer.

Computers Computers are regularly used in computer applications, desktop publishing, English, graphic design, independent study, keyboarding, lab/keyboard, literary magazine, multimedia, photojournalism, programming, research skills, science, typing, Web site design, word processing, yearbook classes. Computer network features include on-campus library services, online commercial services, Internet access, wireless campus network, Internet filtering or blocking technology. Campus intranet and student e-mail accounts are available to students. Students grades are available online. The school has a published electronic and media policy.

Contact Ms. Melissa Davey, Director of Admissions. 301-864-4532 Ext. 7115. Fax: 301-864-8946. E-mail: mdavey@setonhs.org. Web site: www.setonhs.org.

THE ELLIS SCHOOL

6425 Fifth Avenue

Pittsburgh, Pennsylvania 15206

Head of School: Mrs. A. Randol Benedict

General Information Girls' day college-preparatory and arts school. Grades PK–12. Founded: 1916. Setting: urban. 8-acre campus. 9 buildings on campus. Approved or accredited by Pennsylvania Association of Independent Schools and Pennsylvania Department of Education. Member of National Association of Independent Schools. Total enrollment: 448. Upper school average class size: 10. Upper school faculty-student ratio: 1:6. There are 167 required school days per year for Upper School students. Upper School students typically attend 5 days per week. The average school day consists of 6 hours.

Upper School Student Profile Grade 9: 31 students (31 girls); Grade 10: 60 students (60 girls); Grade 11: 43 students (43 girls); Grade 12: 43 students (43 girls).

Faculty School total: 78. In upper school: 10 men, 25 women; 23 have advanced degrees.

Subjects Offered Algebra, American history, American literature, anthropology, art, art history, biology, calculus, ceramics, chemistry, computer science, creative writing, dance, drama, English, English literature, European history, expository writing, fine arts, French, geometry, government/civics, health, history, journalism, Latin, linear algebra, mathematics, music, photography, physical education, physics, social studies, Spanish, speech, statistics, theater, trigonometry, world history, world literature, writing.

Graduation Requirements Arts and fine arts (art, music, dance, drama), computer literacy, English, first aid, foreign language, health education, mathematics, physical education (includes health), science, social studies (includes history), completion of three-week mini-course program (grades 9-11), senior projects.

Special Academic Programs Advanced Placement exam preparation; honors section; independent study; term-away projects; academic accommodation for the gifted.

College Admission Counseling 34 students graduated in 2011; all went to college, including Brown University; Davidson College; Harvard University; Indiana University of Pennsylvania; Northwestern University; University of Rochester. Mean SAT critical reading: 637, mean SAT math: 632, mean SAT writing: 635, mean combined SAT: 1902. 67% scored over 600 on SAT critical reading, 71% scored over 600 on SAT math, 71% scored over 600 on SAT writing, 76% scored over 1800 on combined SAT, 74% scored over 26 on composite ACT.

Student Life Upper grades have uniform requirement, student council, honor system. Discipline rests primarily with faculty.

Summer Programs Session focuses on geometry; held on campus; accepts boys and girls; open to students from other schools.

Tuition and Aid Day student tuition: $20,500. Tuition installment plan (FACTS Tuition Payment Plan, 10-month payment plan; two-payment plan). Need-based financial aid available. In 2011–12, 31% of upper-school students received aid. Total amount of financial aid awarded in 2011–12: $968,120.

Admissions Traditional secondary-level entrance grade is 9. For fall 2011, 44 students applied for upper-level admission, 31 were accepted, 15 enrolled. ISEE required. Deadline for receipt of application materials: none. Application fee required: $50. Interview required.

Athletics Interscholastic: basketball, crew, cross-country running, field hockey, gymnastics, lacrosse, soccer, softball, swimming and diving, tennis; intramural: crew, field hockey, lacrosse. 3 PE instructors, 4 coaches, 1 athletic trainer.

Computers Computers are regularly used in all classes. Computer network features include on-campus library services, online commercial services, Internet access, wireless campus network, Internet filtering or blocking technology. Student e-mail accounts are available to students. The school has a published electronic and media policy.

Contact Sara I. Leone, Director of Admissions. 412-661-4880. Fax: 412-661-7634. E-mail: admissions@theellisschool.org. Web site: www.theellisschool.org.

EMMA WILLARD SCHOOL

285 Pawling Avenue

Troy, New York 12180

Head of School: Ms. Trudy E. Hall

General Information Girls' boarding and day college-preparatory and arts school. Grades 9–PG. Founded: 1814. Setting: suburban. Nearest major city is Albany. Students are housed in single-sex dormitories. 137-acre campus. 23 buildings on campus. Approved or accredited by The Association of Boarding Schools and New York Department of Education. Member of National Association of Independent Schools and Secondary School Admission Test Board. Endowment: $86.1 million. Total enrollment: 323. Upper school average class size: 12. Upper school faculty-student ratio: 1:6. There are 154 required school days per year for Upper School students. Upper School students typically attend 5 days per week. The average school day consists of 7 hours and 20 minutes.

Upper School Student Profile Grade 9: 59 students (59 girls); Grade 10: 81 students (81 girls); Grade 11: 88 students (88 girls); Grade 12: 81 students (81 girls); Postgraduate: 2 students (2 girls). 63% of students are boarding students. 53% are state residents. 22 states are represented in upper school student body. 27% are international students. International students from China, Hong Kong, Japan, Mexico, Republic of Korea, and Taiwan; 26 other countries represented in student body.

Faculty School total: 69. In upper school: 16 men, 50 women; 51 have advanced degrees; 41 reside on campus.

Subjects Offered Advanced Placement courses, advanced studio art-AP, algebra, American history, American literature, ancient world history, art, art history, art history-AP, art-AP, ballet, bioethics, biology, biology-AP, calculus, calculus-AP, ceramics, chemistry, chemistry-AP, chorus, comparative government and politics-AP, computer programming, computer science, computer science-AP, conceptual physics, creative writing, dance, digital imaging, drama, drawing and design, economics, English, English literature, English literature and composition-AP, ESL, European history, expository writing, fiber arts, fine arts, forensics, French, French language-AP, geometry, government and politics-AP, government-AP, government/civics, health and wellness, history, internship, Latin-AP, mathematics, medieval/Renaissance history, music, neuroscience, orchestra, photography, physical education, physics, physics-AP, poetry, practicum, pre-calculus, SAT preparation, science, social sciences, Spanish, Spanish language-AP, Spanish-AP, statistics, statistics-AP, studio art-AP, theater, trigonometry, U.S. history-AP, weaving, world history, world literature.

Graduation Requirements Arts and fine arts (art, music, dance, drama), computer science, English, foreign language, mathematics, physical education (includes health), science, social studies (includes history). Community service is required.

Special Academic Programs 14 Advanced Placement exams for which test preparation is offered; independent study; term-away projects; domestic exchange program (with The Masters School); study abroad; academic accommodation for the gifted, the musically talented, and the artistically talented; ESL (17 students enrolled).

College Admission Counseling 84 students graduated in 2011; 77 went to college, including Cornell University; Rensselaer Polytechnic Institute; St. Lawrence University; Swarthmore College; Union College; University of Pennsylvania. Other: 7 entered a postgraduate year. Median SAT critical reading: 630, median SAT math: 620, median SAT writing: 640, median combined SAT: 1900, median composite ACT: 26.

Student Life Upper grades have specified standards of dress, student council, honor system. Discipline rests equally with students and faculty.

Tuition and Aid Day student tuition: $27,700; 7-day tuition and room/board: $43,650. Tuition installment plan (Key Tuition Payment Plan, monthly payment plans). Merit scholarship grants, need-based scholarship grants, Davis Scholars Program, Day Student /Capital District Scholarships available. In 2011–12, 53% of upper-school students received aid; total upper-school merit-scholarship money awarded: $219,650. Total amount of financial aid awarded in 2011–12: $3,881,300.

Admissions Traditional secondary-level entrance grade is 9. For fall 2011, 451 students applied for upper-level admission, 163 were accepted, 101 enrolled. ACT, PSAT or SAT, SAT, SSAT or TOEFL required. Deadline for receipt of application materials: February 1. Application fee required: $50. Interview required.

Athletics Interscholastic: aquatics, basketball, crew, cross-country running, diving, field hockey, lacrosse, rowing, soccer, softball, swimming and diving, tennis, track and field, volleyball; intramural: aerobics, aerobics/dance, ballet, basketball, dance, fencing, fitness, fitness walking, floor hockey, hiking/backpacking, jogging, martial arts, modern dance, outdoor activities, physical fitness, physical training, riflery, running, skiing (downhill), snowboarding, soccer, softball, strength & conditioning, swimming and diving, tennis, ultimate Frisbee, volleyball, water polo, weight training. 3 PE instructors, 3 coaches, 1 athletic trainer.

Computers Computers are regularly used in all classes. Computer network features include on-campus library services, online commercial services, Internet access, wireless campus network, Internet filtering or blocking technology. Campus intranet, student e-mail accounts, and computer access in designated common areas are available to students. Students grades are available online. The school has a published electronic and media policy.

Contact Ms. Sharon Busone, Officer Manager. 518-883-1327. Fax: 518-883-1805. E-mail: sbusone@emmawillard.org. Web site: www.emmawillard.org.

See Display on next page and Close-Up on page 620.

THE EPISCOPAL ACADEMY

1785 Bishop White Drive

Newtown Square, Pennsylvania 19073

Head of School: Mr. L. Hamilton Clark Jr.

General Information Coeducational day college-preparatory, arts, religious studies, and technology school, affiliated with Episcopal Church. Grades PK–12. Founded: 1785. Setting: suburban. Nearest major city is Philadelphia. 123-acre campus. 12 buildings on campus. Approved or accredited by Middle States Association of Colleges and Schools, Pennsylvania Association of Independent Schools, and Pennsylvania Department of Education. Member of National Association of Independent Schools and Secondary School Admission Test Board. Endowment: $16.5 million. Total enrollment: 1,223. Upper school average class size: 13. Upper school faculty-student ratio: 1:7. There are 172 required school days per year for Upper School students. Upper School students typically attend 5 days per week. The average school day consists of 9 hours and 30 minutes.

Upper School Student Profile Grade 9: 130 students (75 boys, 55 girls); Grade 10: 127 students (70 boys, 57 girls); Grade 11: 127 students (66 boys, 61 girls); Grade 12: 125 students (65 boys, 60 girls).

Faculty School total: 179. In upper school: 41 men, 38 women; 75 have advanced degrees.

Subjects Offered Algebra, American history, American history-AP, American literature, art, art history, biology, calculus, ceramics, chemistry, classical language, college counseling, computer art, computer graphics, computer information systems, computer programming, computer programming-AP, creative writing, drama, drawing, earth science, ecology, economics, English, English-AP, environmental science, ethics, European history, fine arts, French, French language-AP, French literature-AP, French studies, French-AP, geometry, government and politics-AP, Greek, health and safety, history, Latin, Latin-AP, mathematics, mechanical drawing, modern world history, music, painting, photography, physical education, physics, physics-AP, pre-calculus, psychology, religion, science, senior project, social studies, Spanish, Spanish language-AP, Spanish literature, Spanish literature-AP, Spanish-AP, statistics-AP, studio art, studio art-AP, theater history, theater production, theology, U.S. government and politics-AP, U.S. history, U.S. history-AP, Vietnam history, visual and performing arts, vocal ensemble, vocal music, water polo, weight training, woodworking, world cultures, world history, writing.

Graduation Requirements Arts and fine arts (art, music, dance, drama), English, foreign language, mathematics, physical education (includes health), religion (includes Bible studies and theology), science, senior project, social studies (includes history), participation in Outward Bound for 6 days.

Special Academic Programs Advanced Placement exam preparation; honors section; independent study; study abroad.

College Admission Counseling 122 students graduated in 2010; all went to college, including Bucknell University; Cornell University; Duke University; Georgetown University; Harvard University; University of Pennsylvania. Mean SAT critical reading: 664, mean SAT math: 660.
Student Life Upper grades have specified standards of dress, student council, honor system. Discipline rests primarily with faculty. Attendance at religious services is required.
Tuition and Aid Day student tuition: $27,300. Tuition installment plan (Key Tuition Payment Plan, monthly payment plans, 60% due July 1 - remainder by February 1). Need-based scholarship grants available. In 2010–11, 20% of upper-school students received aid. Total amount of financial aid awarded in 2010–11: $3,100,100.
Admissions Traditional secondary-level entrance grade is 9. For fall 2010, 235 students applied for upper-level admission, 107 were accepted, 46 enrolled. ISEE or SSAT required. Deadline for receipt of application materials: January 1. Application fee required: $50. On-campus interview required.
Athletics Interscholastic: baseball (boys), basketball (b,g), crew (b,g), cross-country running (b,g), dance (g), diving (b,g), field hockey (g), football (b), golf (b,g), indoor track (b,g), lacrosse (b,g), soccer (b,g), softball (g), squash (b,g), swimming and diving (b,g), tennis (b,g), track and field (b,g), winter (indoor) track (b,g); intramural: aerobics (g), aerobics/dance (g), dance (g), floor hockey (b); coed interscholastic: ice hockey, water polo; coed intramural: basketball, fencing, fitness, fitness walking, football, Frisbee, squash, trap and skeet, weight lifting, weight training. 1 PE instructor, 27 coaches, 2 athletic trainers.
Computers Computers are regularly used in art, English, foreign language, history, science, technology classes. Computer network features include on-campus library services, Internet access, wireless campus network, Internet filtering or blocking technology. Student e-mail accounts and computer access in designated common areas are available to students. The school has a published electronic and media policy.
Contact Ellen M. Hay, Director of Admission. 484-424-1400 Ext. 1444. Fax: 484-424-1604. E-mail: hay@episcopalacademy.org. Web site: www.episcopalacademy.org.

See Display on next page and Close-Up on page 622.

EPISCOPAL COLLEGIATE SCHOOL

Jackson T. Stephens Campus
1701 Cantrell Road
Little Rock, Arkansas 72201

Head of School: Mr. Steve Hickman

General Information Coeducational day college-preparatory, arts, and technology school, affiliated with Episcopal Church. Grades PK–12. Founded: 2000. Setting: suburban. Nearest major city is Memphis, TN. 34-acre campus. 3 buildings on campus. Approved or accredited by National Association of Episcopal Schools and Southwest Association of Episcopal Schools. Member of National Association of Independent Schools. Endowment: $31 million. Total enrollment: 730. Upper school average class size: 15. Upper school faculty-student ratio: 1:10. There are 179 required school days per year for Upper School students. Upper School students typically attend 5 days per week. The average school day consists of 7 hours and 30 minutes.
Upper School Student Profile Grade 6: 60 students (27 boys, 33 girls); Grade 7: 56 students (26 boys, 30 girls); Grade 8: 73 students (34 boys, 39 girls); Grade 9: 49 students (27 boys, 22 girls); Grade 10: 68 students (34 boys, 34 girls); Grade 11: 55 students (21 boys, 34 girls); Grade 12: 44 students (19 boys, 25 girls). 20% of students are members of Episcopal Church.
Faculty School total: 39. In upper school: 15 men, 24 women; 30 have advanced degrees.
Graduation Requirements Senior chapel talk.
Special Academic Programs 16 Advanced Placement exams for which test preparation is offered; honors section; independent study.
College Admission Counseling 43 students graduated in 2011; all went to college, including Hendrix College; Rhodes College; Sewanee: The University of the South; The University of Texas at Austin; Tulane University; University of Arkansas. Mean SAT critical reading: 637, mean SAT math: 610, mean SAT writing: 633, mean combined SAT: 1879, mean composite ACT: 27. 66% scored over 600 on SAT critical reading, 47% scored over 600 on SAT math, 63% scored over 600 on SAT writing, 63% scored over 1800 on combined SAT, 43% scored over 26 on composite ACT.
Student Life Upper grades have uniform requirement, student council, honor system. Discipline rests primarily with faculty. Attendance at religious services is required.
Summer Programs Enrichment, sports, art/fine arts, computer instruction programs offered; session focuses on enrichment; held on campus; accepts boys and girls; open to students from other schools. 150 students usually enrolled. 2012 schedule: June 1 to July 31. Application deadline: May 30.
Tuition and Aid Day student tuition: $10,235. Tuition installment plan (FACTS Tuition Payment Plan). Need-based scholarship grants available. In 2011–12, 22% of

upper-school students received aid. Total amount of financial aid awarded in 2011–12: $649,000.

Admissions Traditional secondary-level entrance grade is 9. Stanford 9 required. Deadline for receipt of application materials: none. Application fee required: $50. Interview required.

Athletics Interscholastic: baseball (boys), basketball (b,g), cross-country running (b,g), fishing (b,g), fitness (b,g), football (b), golf (b,g), physical fitness (b,g), physical training (b,g), soccer (b,g), tennis (b,g), track and field (b,g), volleyball (g), weight training (b,g), wrestling (b,g); coed interscholastic: cheering. 2 PE instructors, 8 coaches, 2 athletic trainers.

Computers Computers are regularly used in all academic classes. Computer network features include on-campus library services, online commercial services, Internet access, wireless campus network, Internet filtering or blocking technology. Campus intranet and student e-mail accounts are available to students. Students grades are available online. The school has a published electronic and media policy.

Contact Ms. Ashley Honeywell, Director of Admission. 501-372-1194 Ext. 2406. Fax: 501-372-2160. E-mail: ahoneywell@episcopalcollegiate.org. Web site: www.episcopalcollegiate.org.

EPISCOPAL HIGH SCHOOL

4650 Dissonnet

Bellaire, Texas 77401

Head of School: Mr. C. Edward Smith

General Information Coeducational day college-preparatory, arts, religious studies, and technology school, affiliated with Episcopal Church. Grades 9–12. Founded: 1984. Setting: urban. Nearest major city is Houston. 35-acre campus. 7 buildings on campus. Approved or accredited by Independent Schools Association of the Southwest, National Association of Episcopal Schools, and Texas Department of Education. Member of National Association of Independent Schools and Secondary School Admission Test Board. Total enrollment: 677. Upper school average class size: 15. Upper school faculty-student ratio: 1:9. Upper School students typically attend 5 days per week. The average school day consists of 8 hours.

Upper School Student Profile Grade 9: 166 students (80 boys, 86 girls); Grade 10: 169 students (73 boys, 96 girls); Grade 11: 171 students (80 boys, 91 girls); Grade 12: 171 students (75 boys, 96 girls). 23.4% of students are members of Episcopal Church.

Faculty School total: 90. In upper school: 43 men, 47 women; 57 have advanced degrees.

Subjects Offered Acting, algebra, anatomy, ancient history, art appreciation, art history, band, Bible studies, biology, biology-AP, calculus-AP, ceramics, chemistry, choir, civil rights, dance, debate, design, drawing, English, English-AP, ethics, European history, French, French-AP, geography, geology, geometry, government, government-AP, graphic design, health, history of science, instrumental music, journalism, Latin, Latin American studies, music theory, newspaper, oceanography, orchestra, painting, photography, physical education, physics, physics-AP, physiology, pre-calculus, sculpture, Spanish, Spanish-AP, speech, stagecraft, statistics, theater, theology, U.S. history, U.S. history-AP, video film production, Vietnam War, world religions, World War II, writing, yearbook.

Graduation Requirements Arts and fine arts (art, music, dance, drama), English, foreign language, mathematics, physical education (includes health), religion (includes Bible studies and theology), religious studies, science, social studies (includes history).

Special Academic Programs 14 Advanced Placement exams for which test preparation is offered; honors section; independent study; study at local college for college credit.

College Admission Counseling 156 students graduated in 2011; all went to college, including Baylor University; Southern Methodist University; Texas Christian University; The University of Texas at Austin.

Student Life Upper grades have uniform requirement, student council, honor system. Discipline rests equally with students and faculty. Attendance at religious services is required.

Summer Programs Remediation, enrichment, advancement, art/fine arts programs offered; session focuses on remediation, advancement, enrichment; held on campus; accepts boys and girls; open to students from other schools. 250 students usually enrolled. 2012 schedule: June 4 to July 13. Application deadline: May 10.

Tuition and Aid Day student tuition: $22,160. Tuition installment plan (Insured Tuition Payment Plan, SMART Tuition Payment Plan, monthly payment plans). Need-based scholarship grants, middle-income loans available. In 2011–12, 19% of upper-school students received aid. Total amount of financial aid awarded in 2011–12: $1,700,000.

Admissions Traditional secondary-level entrance grade is 9. For fall 2011, 469 students applied for upper-level admission, 323 were accepted, 181 enrolled. ISEE and Otis-Lennon Ability or Stanford Achievement Test required. Deadline for receipt of application materials: January 4. Application fee required: $60. On-campus interview required.

Athletics Interscholastic: ballet (boys, girls), baseball (b), basketball (b,g), cheering (b,g), cross-country running (b,g), dance (b,g), drill team (g), field hockey (b,g), fitness (b,g), football (b), golf (b,g), lacrosse (b,g), physical fitness (b,g), running (b,g), soccer (b,g), softball (g), strength & conditioning (b,g), swimming and diving (b,g), tennis (b,g), track and field (b,g), volleyball (b,g), weight training (b,g), wrestling (b). 7 PE instructors, 8 coaches, 1 athletic trainer.

Computers Computers are regularly used in art, English, foreign language, history, mathematics, music, religion, science classes. Computer network features include on-campus library services, online commercial services, Internet access, wireless campus network, CollegeView. Student e-mail accounts are available to students. Students grades are available online. The school has a published electronic and media policy.

Contact Audrey Koehler, Director of Admission. 713-512-3400. Fax: 713-512-3603. E-mail: kpiper@ehshouston.org. Web site: www.ehshouston.org/.

EPISCOPAL HIGH SCHOOL

1200 North Quaker Lane

Alexandria, Virginia 22302

Head of School: Mr. F. Robertson Hershey

General Information Coeducational boarding college-preparatory, arts, religious studies, and technology school, affiliated with Episcopal Church. Grades 9–12. Founded: 1839. Setting: urban. Nearest major city is Washington, DC. Students are housed in single-sex dormitories. 130-acre campus. 26 buildings on campus. Approved or accredited by Association of Independent Schools of Greater Washington, National Association of Episcopal Schools, Southern Association of Colleges and Schools, and Virginia Department of Education. Member of National Association of Independent Schools and Secondary School Admission Test Board. Endowment: $153 million. Total enrollment: 435. Upper school average class size: 12. Upper school faculty-student ratio: 1:6.

Upper School Student Profile Grade 9: 95 students (52 boys, 43 girls); Grade 10: 112 students (62 boys, 50 girls); Grade 11: 112 students (62 boys, 50 girls); Grade 12: 116 students (64 boys, 52 girls). 100% of students are boarding students. 35% are state residents. 30 states are represented in upper school student body. 7% are international students. International students from China, Republic of Korea, Saudi Arabia, Thailand, United Kingdom, and Zimbabwe; 11 other countries represented in student body. 40% of students are members of Episcopal Church.

Faculty School total: 68. In upper school: 42 men, 26 women; 61 have advanced degrees; 54 reside on campus.

Subjects Offered 3-dimensional art, 3-dimensional design, advanced chemistry, advanced math, Advanced Placement courses, advanced studio art-AP, algebra, American history, American literature, art, art history, art-AP, astronomy, biology, biology-AP, calculus, calculus-AP, ceramics, chemistry, chemistry-AP, Chinese, choir, composition-AP, computer programming, computer programming-AP, computer science, computer science-AP, creative writing, dance, drama, economics, economics-AP, English, English literature, English literature and composition-AP, English literature-AP, English-AP, English/composition-AP, environmental science, environmental science-AP, ethics, European history, European history-AP, fine arts, forensics, French, French language-AP, French literature-AP, geometry, German, German-AP, government-AP, government/civics, Greek, history, honors algebra, honors English, honors geometry, honors U.S. history, honors world history, international relations, Latin, Latin-AP, mathematics, microeconomics-AP, Middle Eastern history, modern European history-AP, music, music theory-AP, photography, physical education, physics, physics-AP, pre-calculus, psychology-AP, religion, science, senior internship, Shakespeare, social sciences, social studies, Spanish, Spanish literature-AP, statistics-AP, theater, theology, trigonometry, U.S. history-AP, world history, world history-AP, writing.

Graduation Requirements Arts and fine arts (art, music, dance, drama), computer studies, English, foreign language, mathematics, physical education (includes health), science, social studies (includes history), theology.

Special Academic Programs Advanced Placement exam preparation; honors section; independent study; term-away projects; study abroad; academic accommodation for the gifted, the musically talented, and the artistically talented.

College Admission Counseling 109 students graduated in 2011; all went to college, including The University of North Carolina at Chapel Hill; University of Virginia; Washington and Lee University. 64% scored over 600 on SAT critical reading, 68% scored over 600 on SAT math, 71% scored over 600 on SAT writing.

Student Life Upper grades have specified standards of dress, student council, honor system. Discipline rests primarily with faculty. Attendance at religious services is required.

Summer Programs Enrichment, advancement, sports, art/fine arts programs offered; session focuses on academic enrichment and athletic skills; held on campus; accepts boys and girls; open to students from other schools.

Tuition and Aid 7-day tuition and room/board: $45,300. Tuition installment plan (Insured Tuition Payment Plan, monthly payment plans). Merit scholarship grants, need-based scholarship grants, paying campus jobs available. In 2011–12, 32% of upper-school students received aid; total upper-school merit-scholarship money awarded: $145,000. Total amount of financial aid awarded in 2011–12: $4,300,000.

Admissions Traditional secondary-level entrance grade is 9. For fall 2011, 614 students applied for upper-level admission, 249 were accepted, 139 enrolled. ISEE, PSAT or SAT or SSAT required. Deadline for receipt of application materials: January 15. Application fee required: $60. Interview required.

Athletics Interscholastic: baseball (boys), basketball (b,g), crew (g), cross-country running (b,g), field hockey (g), football (b), golf (b), indoor track (b,g), indoor track & field (b,g), lacrosse (b,g), modern dance (g), rowing (g), soccer (b,g), softball (g), squash (b,g), tennis (b,g), track and field (b,g), volleyball (g), winter (indoor) track (b,g), wrestling (b); intramural: soccer (b), strength & conditioning (b,g); coed interscholastic: aerobics, aerobics/dance, aerobics/Nautilus, backpacking, ballet, canoeing/kayaking, climbing, dance, fitness, hiking/backpacking, kayaking, outdoor activities, outdoor adventure, outdoor education, outdoor recreation, outdoors, physical fitness, physical training, rock climbing, strength & conditioning, weight lifting, weight training; coed intramural: ballet, fitness, modern dance, outdoor activities, physical fitness, physical training, power lifting, wall climbing, weight lifting, weight training. 4 coaches, 2 athletic trainers.

Computers Computers are regularly used in all academic classes. Computer network features include on-campus library services, online commercial services, Internet access, wireless campus network, Internet filtering or blocking technology. Campus intranet and student e-mail accounts are available to students. Students grades are available online. The school has a published electronic and media policy.

Contact Ms. Emily M. Atkinson, Director of Admission. 703-933-4062. Fax: 703-933-3016. E-mail: admissions@episcopalhighschool.org. Web site: www.episcopalhighschool.org.

EPISCOPAL HIGH SCHOOL OF JACKSONVILLE

4455 Atlantic Boulevard

Jacksonville, Florida 32207

Head of School: Dale D. Regan

General Information Coeducational day college-preparatory, arts, religious studies, and technology school, affiliated with Episcopal Church. Grades 6–12. Founded: 1966. Setting: urban. 88-acre campus. 25 buildings on campus. Approved or accredited by Florida Council of Independent Schools, National Association of Episcopal Schools, Southern Association of Colleges and Schools, and Southern Association of Independent Schools. Member of National Association of Independent Schools. Endowment: $15.4 million. Total enrollment: 857. Upper school average class size: 17. Upper school faculty-student ratio: 1:10. There are 175 required school days per year for Upper School students. Upper School students typically attend 5 days per week. The average school day consists of 6 hours and 50 minutes.

Upper School Student Profile Grade 9: 140 students (76 boys, 64 girls); Grade 10: 142 students (73 boys, 69 girls); Grade 11: 140 students (73 boys, 67 girls); Grade 12: 144 students (77 boys, 67 girls). 25% of students are members of Episcopal Church.

Faculty School total: 93. In upper school: 35 men, 58 women; 53 have advanced degrees.

Subjects Offered Advanced studio art-AP, algebra, American history, American history-AP, American literature, ancient history, art, art history, art history-AP, band, Basic programming, biology, biology-AP, calculus, calculus-AP, ceramics, chemistry, chemistry-AP, Chinese, computer programming, computer science, computer science-AP, dance, drama, earth science, economics, electronic publishing, English, English language and composition-AP, English literature and composition-AP, English/composition-AP, environmental science-AP, European history-AP, fine arts, French, French language-AP, geography, geometry, German, German-AP, government and politics-AP, government/civics, health, history, journalism, Latin, Latin-AP, marine biology, mathematics, music, music history, music theory, music theory-AP, photography, physical education, physics, physics-AP, public speaking, religion, religious studies, science, social studies, Spanish, Spanish language-AP, statistics, statistics-AP, studio art-AP, technical theater, theater, theology, trigonometry, U.S. government and politics-AP, U.S. history-AP, world history, writing, yearbook.

Graduation Requirements Arts and fine arts (art, music, dance, drama), computer science, English, foreign language, leadership, library skills, mathematics, physical education (includes health), religion (includes Bible studies and theology), science, social studies (includes history), 75 community-service hours. Community service is required.

Special Academic Programs Advanced Placement exam preparation; honors section; independent study; study abroad; academic accommodation for the gifted.

College Admission Counseling 156 students graduated in 2010; all went to college, including Florida State University; University of Florida; University of North Florida. Median SAT critical reading: 579, median SAT math: 584, median SAT writing: 567, median combined SAT: 1729, median composite ACT: 26.

Student Life Upper grades have uniform requirement, student council, honor system. Discipline rests equally with students and faculty. Attendance at religious services is required.

Tuition and Aid Day student tuition: $17,400. Tuition installment plan (Insured Tuition Payment Plan, monthly payment plans). Need-based scholarship grants available. In 2010–11, 23% of upper-school students received aid. Total amount of financial aid awarded in 2010–11: $2,000,000.

Admissions Traditional secondary-level entrance grade is 9. For fall 2010, 89 students applied for upper-level admission, 58 were accepted, 38 enrolled. ISEE required. Deadline for receipt of application materials: January 11. Application fee required: $50. On-campus interview required.

Athletics Interscholastic: baseball (boys), basketball (b,g), crew (b,g), cross-country running (b,g), football (b), golf (b,g), lacrosse (b,g), modern dance (b,g), soccer (b,g), softball (g), swimming and diving (b,g), tennis (b,g), track and field (b,g), volleyball (g), weight lifting (b), weight training (b), wrestling (b); intramural: dance (g); coed interscholastic: cheering, dance, dance squad, dance team, wrestling; coed intramural: fencing. 7 PE instructors, 100 coaches, 4 athletic trainers.

Computers Computers are regularly used in all classes. Computer network features include on-campus library services, online commercial services, Internet access, wireless campus network, Internet filtering or blocking technology, Senior Systems: My BackPack online grading and student accounts, online parent portals, RSS feeds. Campus intranet, student e-mail accounts, and computer access in designated common areas are available to students. Students grades are available online. The school has a published electronic and media policy.

Contact Peggy P. Fox, Director of Admissions. 904-396-7104. Fax: 904-396-0981. E-mail: foxp@episcopalhigh.org. Web site: www.episcopalhigh.org.

ESCOLA AMERICANA DE CAMPINAS

Rua Cajamar, 35

Chácara da Barra

Campinas-SP 13090-860, Brazil

Head of School: Stephen A. Herrera

General Information Coeducational day college-preparatory, arts, bilingual studies, and technology school. Grades PK–12. Founded: 1956. Setting: urban. Nearest major city is São Paulo, Brazil. 4-acre campus. 4 buildings on campus. Approved or accredited by Association of American Schools in South America and Southern Association of Colleges and Schools. Affiliate member of National Association of Independent Schools; member of European Council of International Schools. Languages of instruction: English and Portuguese. Endowment: $350,000. Total enrollment: 648. Upper school average class size: 20. Upper school faculty-student ratio: 1:7.

Upper School Student Profile Grade 9: 43 students (18 boys, 25 girls); Grade 10: 47 students (23 boys, 24 girls); Grade 11: 34 students (18 boys, 16 girls); Grade 12: 27 students (6 boys, 21 girls).

Faculty School total: 68. In upper school: 12 men, 18 women; 20 have advanced degrees.

Subjects Offered Algebra, American history, American literature, art, biology, calculus, chemistry, computer science, creative writing, drama, economics, English, English literature, fine arts, geography, geometry, government/civics, grammar, history, journalism, mathematics, music, physical education, physics, Portuguese, psychology, science, social studies, speech, trigonometry, world history, world literature, writing.

Graduation Requirements Arts and fine arts (art, music, dance, drama), computer science, English, foreign language, mathematics, physical education (includes health), science, social studies (includes history). Community service is required.

Special Academic Programs Advanced Placement exam preparation; honors section; term-away projects; study at local college for college credit; study abroad; special instructional classes for students with mild learning differences; ESL (5 students enrolled).

College Admission Counseling 17 students graduated in 2011; 16 went to college, including Emerson College; Northwestern University; Southwestern University; The University of Tampa. Other: 1 entered a postgraduate year. Median SAT critical reading: 610, median SAT math: 640, median SAT writing: 540, median combined SAT: 1790.

Student Life Upper grades have student council, honor system. Discipline rests equally with students and faculty.

Tuition and Aid Day student tuition: 54,078 Brazilian reals. Tuition installment plan (monthly payment plans). Need-based scholarship grants available. In 2011–12, 10% of upper-school students received aid. Total amount of financial aid awarded in 2011–12: $51,000.

Admissions Traditional secondary-level entrance grade is 9. For fall 2011, 35 students applied for upper-level admission, 24 were accepted, 22 enrolled. Admissions testing, English Composition Test for ESL students, ERB CTP IV, Iowa Test, CTBS, or TAP, SAT and writing sample required. Deadline for receipt of application materials: September 3. No application fee required. On-campus interview required.

Athletics Interscholastic: basketball (boys, girls), canoeing/kayaking (g), cheering (g), indoor soccer (b,g), soccer (b,g), volleyball (g); intramural: ballet (g), basketball (b,g), canoeing/kayaking (g), cheering (g), climbing (b,g), indoor soccer (b,g), soccer (b,g); coed intramural: aerobics, baseball, basketball, climbing, cooperative games, fitness, flag football, Frisbee, gymnastics, handball, indoor soccer, jogging, judo, kickball, martial arts, physical fitness, self defense, soccer, softball, strength & conditioning, table tennis, track and field, ultimate Frisbee, volleyball. 6 PE instructors, 11 coaches.

Computers Computers are regularly used in art, English, history, independent study, mathematics, science, yearbook classes. Computer network features include on-campus library services, online commercial services, Internet access. Campus intranet is available to students.

Contact Davi Sanchez, High School Principal. 55-19-2102-1006. Fax: 55-19-2102-1016. E-mail: davi_sanchez@eac.com.br. Web site: www.eac.com.br.

THE ETHEL WALKER SCHOOL

230 Bushy Hill Road

Simsbury, Connecticut 06070

Head of School: Mrs. Elizabeth Cromwell Speers

General Information Girls' boarding and day college-preparatory and arts school. Boarding grades 9–12, day grades 6–12. Founded: 1911. Setting: suburban. Nearest major city is Hartford. Students are housed in single-sex dormitories. 300-acre campus. 9 buildings on campus. Approved or accredited by New England Association of Schools and Colleges, The Association of Boarding Schools, and Connecticut Department of Education. Member of National Association of Independent Schools and Secondary School Admission Test Board. Endowment: $17.3 million. Total enrollment: 239. Upper school average class size: 12. Upper school faculty-student ratio: 1:6. Upper School students typically attend 5 days per week. The average school day consists of 7 hours.

Upper School Student Profile Grade 9: 44 students (44 girls); Grade 10: 63 students (63 girls); Grade 11: 59 students (59 girls); Grade 12: 41 students (41 girls). 66% of students are boarding students. 34% are state residents. 18 states are represented in upper school student body. 22% are international students. International students from China, Germany, Japan, Mexico, Republic of Korea, and Spain; 12 other countries represented in student body.

Faculty School total: 45. In upper school: 10 men, 32 women; 28 have advanced degrees; 29 reside on campus.

Subjects Offered 3-dimensional art, acting, advanced studio art-AP, African history, African literature, African studies, algebra, American government, American history, American history-AP, American literature, anatomy and physiology, Ancient Greek, ancient world history, art, art history, art-AP, Asian history, astronomy, bell choir, biology, biology-AP, calculus, calculus-AP, Caribbean history, ceramics, chemistry, chemistry-AP, Chinese, choir, choral music, choreography, civil rights, computer literacy, computer science, computer science-AP, conceptual physics, concert bell choir, concert choir, creative writing, digital photography, directing, diversity studies, drama, drama performance, dramatic arts, drawing, drawing and design, East Asian history, economics, economics-AP, English, English composition, English literature, English literature and composition AP, English literature-AP, environmental science, environmental science-AP, environmental studies, equine science, ethics, European history, European history-AP, fiber arts, fiction, fine arts, forensics, French language-AP, geography, geometry, graphic design, health and wellness, history, history-AP, honors algebra, honors English, honors geometry, honors U.S. history, honors world history, independent study, instrumental music, Islamic studies, justice seminar, Latin, Latin American history, Latin-AP, leadership, macro/microeconomics-AP, Mandarin, Middle Eastern history, modern civilization, modern European history, modern European history-AP, music, music theory, musical theater, mythology, newspaper, painting, peace and justice, philosophy of government, photography, physics, physics-AP, playwriting, poetry, pre-calculus, psychology, psychology-AP, public speaking, religion and culture, Russian studies, sculpture, senior project, set design, Shakespeare, social justice, Spanish, Spanish language-AP, Spanish literature-AP, statistics-AP, student publications, studio art-AP, the Web, theater, trigonometry, U.S. history, U.S. history-AP, visual and performing arts, voice, Western civilization, women in literature, women's health, world history, world literature, world religions, writing, yearbook.

Graduation Requirements Arts and fine arts (art, music, dance, drama), English, ethics, foreign language, history, leadership, mathematics, performing arts, science, women's health, Junior/Senior project, community service hours. Community service is required.

Special Academic Programs 19 Advanced Placement exams for which test preparation is offered; honors section; independent study; term-away projects; study at local college for college credit; study abroad; academic accommodation for the gifted, the musically talented, and the artistically talented.

College Admission Counseling 62 students graduated in 2011; all went to college, including Amherst College; Dartmouth College; Hamilton College; New York University; Trinity College; University of Connecticut. Mean SAT critical reading: 570, mean SAT math: 570, mean SAT writing: 610, mean composite ACT: 25.

Student Life Upper grades have specified standards of dress, student council, honor system. Discipline rests equally with students and faculty.

Summer Programs Sports, art/fine arts programs offered; held on campus; accepts boys and girls; open to students from other schools. 2012 schedule: June to August. Application deadline: May.

Tuition and Aid Day student tuition: $34,900; 7-day tuition and room/board: $47,900. Tuition installment plan (monthly payment plans, individually arranged payment plans, 1-, 2-, and 10-payment plans). Need-based scholarship grants available. In 2011–12, 46% of upper-school students received aid. Total amount of financial aid awarded in 2011–12: $3,354,000.

Admissions Traditional secondary-level entrance grade is 9. For fall 2011, 256 students applied for upper-level admission, 169 were accepted, 80 enrolled. SSAT and TOEFL required. Deadline for receipt of application materials: February 1. Application fee required: $60. Interview required.

Athletics Interscholastic: alpine skiing, basketball, dance, dressage, equestrian sports, field hockey, golf, horseback riding, independent competitive sports, lacrosse, modern dance, nordic skiing, skiing (downhill), soccer, softball, squash, swimming and diving, tennis, volleyball; intramural: ballet, climbing, combined training, cross-country running, dance, dance team, equestrian sports, fitness, hiking/backpacking, jogging, kayaking, mountain biking, mountaineering, Nautilus, outdoor activities, outdoor adventure, physical fitness, physical training, rock climbing, ropes courses, running, strength & conditioning, wall climbing, weight lifting, weight training, yoga. 5 coaches, 1 athletic trainer.

Computers Computers are regularly used in all classes. Computer network features include on-campus library services, online commercial services, Internet access, wireless campus network, Internet filtering or blocking technology. Student e-mail accounts and computer access in designated common areas are available to students. Students grades are available online. The school has a published electronic and media policy.

Contact Ms. Margy Foulk, Director of Admission. 860-408-4200. Fax: 860-408-4201. E-mail: margy_foulk@ethelwalker.org. Web site: www.ethelwalker.org.

EXCEL CHRISTIAN ACADEMY

325 Old Mill Road

Cartersville, Georgia 30120

Head of School: Dr. Davis Nelson

General Information Coeducational day college-preparatory school, affiliated with Christian faith. Grades K–12. Founded: 1993. Setting: suburban. 15-acre campus. 3 buildings on campus. Approved or accredited by Association of Christian Schools International, Southern Association of Colleges and Schools, and Georgia Department of Education. Total enrollment: 297. Upper school average class size: 20. Upper school faculty-student ratio: 1:18. There are 177 required school days per year for Upper School students. Upper School students typically attend 5 days per week. The average school day consists of 7 hours and 25 minutes.

Upper School Student Profile Grade 9: 21 students (9 boys, 12 girls); Grade 10: 30 students (13 boys, 17 girls); Grade 11: 26 students (16 boys, 10 girls); Grade 12: 24 students (9 boys, 15 girls). 99% of students are Christian.

Faculty School total: 29. In upper school: 10 men, 10 women; 10 have advanced degrees.

Subjects Offered Algebra, American government, anatomy, art, band, Bible, British literature, broadcast journalism, business education, calculus-AP, chemistry, choir, chorus, computer applications, concert band, dance, drama, earth science, electives, English, English literature, foreign language, government, health, history, life science, literature, mathematics, music, personal fitness, physical education, physical science, physics, pre-algebra, psychology, reading, science, social studies, Spanish, trigonometry, U.S. government, U.S. history, U.S. history-AP, world geography, world history.

Graduation Requirements Advanced Placement courses, Bible, computer technologies, electives, English, foreign language, history, mathematics, physical education (includes health), science.

Special Academic Programs 2 Advanced Placement exams for which test preparation is offered; honors section; study at local college for college credit.

College Admission Counseling 18 students graduated in 2011; 17 went to college, including Georgia Institute of Technology; Kennesaw State University; Truett-McConnell College; Valdosta State University. Other: 1 had other specific plans. Median SAT critical reading: 480, median SAT math: 490, median SAT writing: 470. Mean combined SAT: 1481. 11% scored over 600 on SAT critical reading, 17% scored over 600 on SAT math, 17% scored over 600 on SAT writing, 17% scored over 1800 on combined SAT.

Student Life Upper grades have uniform requirement, student council, honor system. Discipline rests primarily with faculty.

Tuition and Aid Day student tuition: $8640. Tuition installment plan (monthly payment plans). Need-based scholarship grants available.

Admissions Traditional secondary-level entrance grade is 9. For fall 2011, 21 students applied for upper-level admission, 21 were accepted, 17 enrolled. Any standardized test required. Deadline for receipt of application materials: none. Application fee required: $100. Interview required.

Athletics Interscholastic: baseball (boys), basketball (b,g), cheering (g), cross-country running (b,g), softball (g); intramural: football (b); coed interscholastic: soccer. 2 PE instructors, 4 coaches.

Computers Computers are regularly used in business applications, computer applications, newspaper, yearbook classes. Computer network features include Internet access, wireless campus network, Internet filtering or blocking technology. Computer access in designated common areas is available to students. Students grades are available online. The school has a published electronic and media policy.

Contact Mrs. Krista K. Keefe, Counselor. 770-382-9488. Fax: 770-606-9884. E-mail: kkeefe@excelacademy.cc. Web site: www.excelacademy.cc.

EXPLORATIONS ACADEMY

PO Box 3014

Bellingham, Washington 98227

Head of School: Daniel Kirkpatrick

General Information Coeducational day college-preparatory, experiential education, and international field study expeditions school. Ungraded, ages 11–18. Founded: 1995. Setting: urban. Nearest major city is Vancouver, BC, Canada. 1-acre campus. 1 building on campus. Approved or accredited by Northwest Accreditation Commission, Northwest Association of Schools and Colleges, Pacific Northwest Association of Independent Schools, and Washington Department of Education. Total enrollment: 26. Upper school average class size: 9. Upper school faculty-student ratio: 1:7. There are 177 required school days per year for Upper School students. Upper School students typically attend 5 days per week. The average school day consists of 6 hours.

Faculty School total: 7. In upper school: 4 men, 3 women; 5 have advanced degrees.

Subjects Offered Agriculture, American literature, anatomy and physiology, anthropology, archaeology, art, boat building, botany, calculus, carpentry, chemistry, computer graphics, computer programming, conflict resolution, construction, creative writing, desktop publishing, drawing, earth science, ecology, environmental science, first aid, French, gardening, gender issues, geology, government, health, horticulture, human relations, journalism, Latin American studies, leadership, marine biology, media, meteorology, microbiology, music, music history, painting, philosophy, photography, physical education, physics, poetry, political science, psychology, sculpture, sexuality, short story, Spanish, technology, theater design and production, video film production, world cultures, world geography, world history, world literature, writing.

Graduation Requirements Arts and fine arts (art, music, dance, drama), computer science, English, foreign language, human relations, lab science, mathematics, occupational education, physical education (includes health), science, social sciences, social studies (includes history), U.S. government and politics, Washington State and Northwest History, world history, one term of self-designed interdisciplinary studies. Community service is required.

Special Academic Programs Advanced Placement exam preparation; honors section; accelerated programs; independent study; term-away projects; academic accommodation for the gifted.

College Admission Counseling 5 students graduated in 2010; 4 went to college, including The Evergreen State College; University of Washington; Western Washington University. Other: 1 went to work.

Student Life Upper grades have honor system. Discipline rests primarily with faculty.

Tuition and Aid Day student tuition: $10,500. Tuition installment plan (monthly payment plans, individually arranged payment plans, school's own payment plan). Tuition reduction for siblings, merit scholarship grants, need-based scholarship grants, need-based loans, low-interest loans with deferred payment available. In 2010–11, 40% of upper-school students received aid; total upper-school merit-scholarship money awarded: $35,000. Total amount of financial aid awarded in 2010–11: $81,000.

Admissions Traditional secondary-level entrance age is 14. For fall 2010, 30 students applied for upper-level admission, 25 were accepted, 24 enrolled. Non-standardized placement tests required. Deadline for receipt of application materials: none. Application fee required: $50. Interview required.

Computers Computers are regularly used in animation, art, English, French, graphics, mathematics, media production, publications, SAT preparation, science, writing, yearbook classes. Computer network features include online commercial services, Internet access, wireless campus network. Computer access in designated common areas is available to students. The school has a published electronic and media policy.

Contact Allison Roberts, Registrar. 360-671-8085. Fax: 360-671-2521. E-mail: info@explorationsacademy.org. Web site: www.ExplorationsAcademy.org.

EZELL-HARDING CHRISTIAN SCHOOL

574 Bell Road

Antioch, Tennessee 37013

Head of School: Mrs. Belvia Pruitt

General Information Coeducational day college-preparatory and religious studies school, affiliated with Church of Christ. Grades K–12. Founded: 1973. Setting: suburban. Nearest major city is Nashville. 30-acre campus. 1 building on campus. Approved or accredited by National Christian School Association, Southern Association of Colleges and Schools, and Tennessee Association of Independent Schools. Endowment: $100,000. Total enrollment: 631. Upper school average class size: 19. Upper school faculty-student ratio: 1:12. There are 176 required school days per year for Upper School students. Upper School students typically attend 5 days per week. The average school day consists of 7 hours.

Upper School Student Profile Grade 9: 50 students (22 boys, 28 girls); Grade 10: 57 students (16 boys, 41 girls); Grade 11: 66 students (33 boys, 33 girls); Grade 12: 51 students (28 boys, 23 girls). 40% of students are members of Church of Christ.

Faculty School total: 70. In upper school: 9 men, 10 women; 10 have advanced degrees.

Subjects Offered ACT preparation, advanced math, Advanced Placement courses, algebra, American history, anatomy and physiology, art, band, Bible, biology, broadcasting, calculus, calculus-AP, chemistry, chorus, economics, English literature and

composition-AP, European history, European history-AP, fitness, geography, geometry, government, humanities, keyboarding, microcomputer technology applications, physical science, psychology, sociology, Spanish, theater arts, trigonometry, wellness, world history.
Graduation Requirements American history, Bible, computers, economics, English, government, mathematics, physical education (includes health), science, wellness, world history.
Special Academic Programs 4 Advanced Placement exams for which test preparation is offered; honors section.
College Admission Counseling 70 students graduated in 2011; 68 went to college, including Freed-Hardeman University; Harding University; Lipscomb University; Middle Tennessee State University; The University of Tennessee; Trevecca Nazarene University. Other: 1 went to work, 1 entered military service. Median composite ACT: 25. 20% scored over 26 on composite ACT.
Student Life Upper grades have uniform requirement, student council. Discipline rests primarily with faculty.
Tuition and Aid Day student tuition: $6750. Tuition installment plan (The Tuition Plan, monthly payment plans). Need-based scholarship grants, paying campus jobs available.
Admissions Traditional secondary-level entrance grade is 9. For fall 2011, 40 students applied for upper-level admission, 28 were accepted, 20 enrolled. Deadline for receipt of application materials: none. Application fee required: $50. Interview recommended.
Athletics Interscholastic: baseball (boys), basketball (b,g), bowling (b,g), cheering (g), cross-country running (b,g), drill team (g), football (b), golf (b,g), hockey (b), soccer (b,g), softball (g), tennis (b,g), track and field (b,g), volleyball (g), weight training (b,g). 2 PE instructors, 6 coaches, 1 athletic trainer.
Computers Computer network features include on-campus library services, Internet access, wireless campus network, Internet filtering or blocking technology. Student e-mail accounts are available to students. Students grades are available online. The school has a published electronic and media policy.
Contact Mrs. Debbie S. Shaffer, Admissions Officer. 615-367-0532 Ext. 109. Fax: 615-399-8747. E-mail: debbie.shaffer@ezellharding.com. Web site: www.ezellharding.com.

FAIRHILL SCHOOL

Dallas, Texas

See Special Needs Schools section.

FAITH CHRISTIAN HIGH SCHOOL

3105 Colusa Highway

Yuba City, California 95993

Head of School: Mr. Stephen Finlay

General Information Coeducational day college-preparatory, arts, religious studies, and technology school, affiliated with Christian faith. Grades 9–12. Founded: 1975. Setting: small town. Nearest major city is Sacramento. 10-acre campus. 4 buildings on campus. Approved or accredited by Association of Christian Schools International, Western Association of Schools and Colleges, and California Department of Education. Total enrollment: 100. Upper school average class size: 25. Upper school faculty-student ratio: 1:12. There are 175 required school days per year for Upper School students. Upper School students typically attend 5 days per week. The average school day consists of 5 hours and 30 minutes.
Upper School Student Profile Grade 9: 20 students (10 boys, 10 girls); Grade 10: 26 students (13 boys, 13 girls); Grade 11: 29 students (13 boys, 16 girls); Grade 12: 25 students (13 boys, 12 girls). 99% of students are Christian.
Faculty School total: 15. In upper school: 11 men, 4 women; 4 have advanced degrees.
Subjects Offered Algebra, arts, Bible, biology, biology-AP, British literature, calculus-AP, chemistry, civics, computer science, computer studies, concert band, drama, economics, English, English composition, English literature, English-AP, geography, geometry, government, health, honors English, physical education, physical science, pre-calculus, senior project, Spanish, U.S. history, world geography, world history, yearbook.
Graduation Requirements Algebra, Bible, biology, civics, economics, English, geometry, health, physical science, senior project, U.S. history, world geography, world history.
Special Academic Programs Advanced Placement exam preparation; study at local college for college credit.
College Admission Counseling 26 students graduated in 2011; 23 went to college, including Azusa Pacific University; Point Loma Nazarene University; Simpson University; University of California, Davis; University of Nevada, Reno; University of the Pacific. Other: 1 entered military service, 2 had other specific plans. Median SAT critical reading: 580, median SAT math: 540, median SAT writing: 550, median combined SAT: 1640, median composite ACT: 20. 30% scored over 600 on SAT critical reading, 20% scored over 600 on SAT math, 30% scored over 600 on SAT writing, 30% scored over 1800 on combined SAT, 25% scored over 26 on composite ACT.
Student Life Upper grades have specified standards of dress, student council, honor system. Discipline rests primarily with faculty. Attendance at religious services is required.
Tuition and Aid Day student tuition: $7460. Tuition installment plan (monthly payment plans). Tuition reduction for siblings, need-based scholarship grants available. In 2011–12, 20% of upper-school students received aid. Total amount of financial aid awarded in 2011–12: $50,000.
Admissions Traditional secondary-level entrance grade is 9. For fall 2011, 18 students applied for upper-level admission, 17 were accepted, 17 enrolled. Achievement tests required. Deadline for receipt of application materials: none. Application fee required: $50. Interview required.
Athletics Interscholastic: baseball (boys), basketball (b,g), cheering (g), cross-country running (b,g), soccer (b,g), volleyball (g); coed interscholastic: golf. 1 PE instructor, 8 coaches.
Computers Computers are regularly used in all academic classes. Computer network features include on-campus library services, Internet access, Internet filtering or blocking technology. Students grades are available online. The school has a published electronic and media policy.
Contact Mrs. Sue Shorey, Secretary. 530-674-5474. Fax: 530-674-0194. E-mail: sshorey@fcs-k12.org. Web site: www.fcs-k12.org.

FAITH LUTHERAN HIGH SCHOOL

2015 South Hualapai Way

Las Vegas, Nevada 89117-6949

Head of School: Dr. Steve J. Buuck

General Information Coeducational day college-preparatory and religious studies school, affiliated with Lutheran Church–Missouri Synod, Evangelical Lutheran Church in America. Grades 6–12. Founded: 1979. Setting: suburban. 39-acre campus. 4 buildings on campus. Approved or accredited by Lutheran School Accreditation Commission, National Lutheran School Accreditation, Northwest Accreditation Commission, Northwest Association of Schools and Colleges, and Nevada Department of Education. Endowment: $1 million. Total enrollment: 1,371. Upper school average class size: 25. Upper school faculty-student ratio: 1:17. There are 180 required school days per year for Upper School students. Upper School students typically attend 5 days per week. The average school day consists of 7 hours.
Upper School Student Profile Grade 9: 178 students (69 boys, 109 girls); Grade 10: 186 students (88 boys, 98 girls); Grade 11: 184 students (90 boys, 94 girls); Grade 12: 156 students (71 boys, 85 girls). 24% of students are Lutheran Church–Missouri Synod, Evangelical Lutheran Church in America.
Faculty School total: 92. In upper school: 32 men, 54 women; 48 have advanced degrees.
Subjects Offered Algebra, American history, art, biology, chemistry, computer science, earth science, English, fine arts, fitness, geometry, German, health, mathematics, music, physical education, physical science, religion, SAT/ACT preparation, science, social studies, Spanish.
Graduation Requirements American history, arts and fine arts (art, music, dance, drama), computer science, English, foreign language, mathematics, physical education (includes health), religion (includes Bible studies and theology), science, social studies (includes history).
Special Academic Programs 7 Advanced Placement exams for which test preparation is offered; honors section; independent study; study at local college for college credit; academic accommodation for the musically talented.
College Admission Counseling 159 students graduated in 2011; 157 went to college, including Concordia University; University of Nevada, Las Vegas; University of Nevada, Reno. Other: 2 went to work. Median SAT critical reading: 540, median SAT math: 520, median SAT writing: 510, median combined SAT: 1570, median composite ACT: 23. 25% scored over 600 on SAT critical reading, 25% scored over 600 on SAT math, 20% scored over 600 on SAT writing, 23% scored over 1800 on combined SAT, 30% scored over 26 on composite ACT.
Student Life Upper grades have uniform requirement, student council. Discipline rests primarily with faculty. Attendance at religious services is required.
Tuition and Aid Day student tuition: $9300. Tuition installment plan (monthly payment plans, individually arranged payment plans). Tuition reduction for siblings, need-based scholarship grants available. In 2011–12, 12% of upper-school students received aid. Total amount of financial aid awarded in 2011–12: $300,000.
Admissions Traditional secondary-level entrance grade is 9. For fall 2011, 110 students applied for upper-level admission, 100 were accepted, 80 enrolled. High School Placement Test and Stanford 9 required. Deadline for receipt of application materials: none. Application fee required: $350. On-campus interview required.
Athletics Interscholastic: aerobics/dance (girls), aquatics (b,g), baseball (b), basketball (b,g), cheering (g), cross-country running (b,g), dance team (g), football (b), golf (b,g), lacrosse (b,g), soccer (b,g), softball (g), swimming and diving (b,g), tennis (b,g), track and field (b,g), volleyball (g), wrestling (b); intramural: strength & conditioning (b,g), weight training (b,g); coed interscholastic: strength & conditioning; coed intramural: skiing (downhill), snowboarding, ultimate Frisbee. 7 PE instructors, 26 coaches.
Computers Computers are regularly used in keyboarding, yearbook classes. Computer network features include on-campus library services, online commercial services,

Internet access, wireless campus network, Internet filtering or blocking technology. Student e-mail accounts and computer access in designated common areas are available to students. Students grades are available online. The school has a published electronic and media policy.
Contact Mrs. Julie Buuck, Admissions Coordinator. 702-562-7737. Fax: 702-804-4488. E-mail: buuckj@flhsemail.org. Web site: www.faithlutheranlv.org.

FALMOUTH ACADEMY

7 Highfield Drive

Falmouth, Massachusetts 02540

Head of School: Mr. David C. Faus

General Information Coeducational day college-preparatory and arts school. Grades 7–12. Founded: 1976. Setting: small town. Nearest major city is Boston. 34-acre campus. 3 buildings on campus. Approved or accredited by Association of Independent Schools in New England and New England Association of Schools and Colleges. Member of National Association of Independent Schools and Secondary School Admission Test Board. Endowment: $4 million. Total enrollment: 190. Upper school average class size: 12. Upper school faculty-student ratio: 1:4. There are 165 required school days per year for Upper School students. Upper School students typically attend 5 days per week. The average school day consists of 6 hours and 20 minutes.
Upper School Student Profile Grade 9: 35 students (14 boys, 21 girls); Grade 10: 22 students (10 boys, 12 girls); Grade 11: 28 students (9 boys, 19 girls); Grade 12: 31 students (14 boys, 17 girls).
Faculty School total: 35. In upper school: 14 men, 20 women; 26 have advanced degrees.
Subjects Offered Algebra, American history, American literature, art, biology, calculus, ceramics, chemistry, creative writing, drama, earth science, ecology, English, English literature, environmental science, European history, expository writing, fine arts, French, geography, geology, geometry, German, grammar, health, history, journalism, mathematics, music, photography, physical education, physics, science, sculpture, social studies, statistics, theater, trigonometry, woodworking, world history, world literature, writing.
Graduation Requirements Arts and fine arts (art, music, dance, drama), English, foreign language, history, mathematics, science.
Special Academic Programs 5 Advanced Placement exams for which test preparation is offered; independent study; term-away projects; study abroad.
College Admission Counseling 35 students graduated in 2011; 33 went to college, including Connecticut College; Sarah Lawrence College; Wake Forest University; Worcester Polytechnic Institute. Other: 2 had other specific plans. Mean SAT critical reading: 642, mean SAT math: 615, mean SAT writing: 660.
Student Life Upper grades have specified standards of dress, student council, honor system. Discipline rests primarily with faculty.
Tuition and Aid Day student tuition: $23,695. Merit scholarship grants, need-based scholarship grants, need-based loans available. In 2011–12, 40% of upper-school students received aid; total upper-school merit-scholarship money awarded: $6000. Total amount of financial aid awarded in 2011–12: $650,000.
Admissions Traditional secondary-level entrance grade is 9. For fall 2011, 18 students applied for upper-level admission, 11 were accepted, 6 enrolled. SSAT required. Deadline for receipt of application materials: March 1. Application fee required: $50. On-campus interview required.
Athletics Interscholastic: basketball (boys, girls), lacrosse (b,g), soccer (b,g). 1 PE instructor.
Computers Computers are regularly used in design, English, mathematics, science classes. Computer resources include on-campus library services, Internet access, Internet filtering or blocking technology. The school has a published electronic and media policy.
Contact Mr. Michael J. Earley, Assistant Headmaster/Director of Admissions. 508-457-9696 Ext. 224. Fax: 508-457-4112. E-mail: mearley@falmouthacademy.org. Web site: www.falmouthacademy.org.

THE FAMILY FOUNDATION SCHOOL

Hancock, New York

See Special Needs Schools section.

FATHER LOPEZ HIGH SCHOOL

3918 LPGA Boulevard

Daytona Beach, Florida 32124

Head of School: Mr. Lee Sayago

General Information Coeducational day college-preparatory and religious studies school, affiliated with Roman Catholic Church. Grades 9–12. Founded: 1959. Setting: suburban. 90-acre campus. 9 buildings on campus. Approved or accredited by National Catholic Education Association, Southern Association of Colleges and Schools, and Florida Department of Education. Total enrollment: 348. Upper school average class size: 15. Upper school faculty-student ratio: 1:15. There are 180 required school days per year for Upper School students. Upper School students typically attend 5 days per week. The average school day consists of 6 hours and 20 minutes.
Upper School Student Profile Grade 9: 114 students (61 boys, 53 girls); Grade 10: 71 students (39 boys, 32 girls); Grade 11: 95 students (48 boys, 47 girls); Grade 12: 68 students (31 boys, 37 girls). 66% of students are Roman Catholic.
Faculty School total: 23. In upper school: 10 men, 13 women; 10 have advanced degrees.
Subjects Offered Accounting, advanced biology, advanced chemistry, advanced math, Advanced Placement courses, aerobics, algebra, American government, American history, American history-AP, American literature, anatomy and physiology, applied skills, art, audio visual/media, biology, biology-AP, British literature, calculus, calculus-AP, Catholic belief and practice, chemistry, Chinese, Christian and Hebrew scripture, church history, classical Greek literature, computer applications, computer art, computer graphics, consumer mathematics, culinary arts, dance, dance performance, death and loss, design, digital photography, drama, drama performance, economics, English, English literature, English literature and composition-AP, film, film and literature, filmmaking, French, geometry, government, graphic design, health education, honors algebra, honors English, honors geometry, honors U.S. history, honors world history, human geography - AP, Latin, marine science, moral and social development, philosophy, photography, physical education, physical science, physics, precalculus, psychology, psychology-AP, social justice, sociology, Spanish, speech, statistics, studio art-AP, television, tennis, theology, trigonometry, U.S. government and politics-AP, U.S. history, U.S. history-AP, video film production, Web authoring, Web site design, weight training, weightlifting, world geography, world history, world history-AP, world religions, writing, yearbook.
Graduation Requirements Algebra, American history, American literature, arts and fine arts (art, music, dance, drama), biology, British literature, chemistry, economics, electives, English, English literature, foreign language, geometry, health and wellness, physical education (includes health), physics, U.S. government, world history, 100 hours of community service.
Special Academic Programs 10 Advanced Placement exams for which test preparation is offered; honors section; study at local college for college credit; ESL (14 students enrolled).
College Admission Counseling 72 students graduated in 2011; 71 went to college, including Florida State University; Stetson University; University of Central Florida; University of Florida; University of North Florida; University of South Florida. Other: 1 had other specific plans. Mean SAT critical reading: 541, mean SAT math: 515, mean SAT writing: 500, mean combined SAT: 1556, mean composite ACT: 23. 20% scored over 600 on SAT critical reading, 18% scored over 600 on SAT math, 14% scored over 600 on SAT writing, 18% scored over 1800 on combined SAT, 33% scored over 26 on composite ACT.
Student Life Upper grades have uniform requirement, student council, honor system. Discipline rests primarily with faculty. Attendance at religious services is required.
Tuition and Aid Day student tuition: $9800. Tuition installment plan (SMART Tuition Payment Plan). Merit scholarship grants, need-based scholarship grants, tiered tuition rate based on income available. In 2011–12, 57% of upper-school students received aid; total upper-school merit-scholarship money awarded: $17,900. Total amount of financial aid awarded in 2011–12: $780,000.
Admissions Traditional secondary-level entrance grade is 9. High School Placement Test required. Deadline for receipt of application materials: none. Application fee required: $50. Interview required.
Athletics Interscholastic: baseball (boys), basketball (b,g), cheering (g), cross-country running (b,g), dance team (g), football (b), golf (b,g), lacrosse (b), soccer (b,g), softball (g), swimming and diving (b,g), tennis (b,g), track and field (b,g), volleyball (g); coed intramural: table tennis, tennis, weight lifting. 2 PE instructors, 27 coaches, 1 athletic trainer.
Computers Computers are regularly used in all academic, computer applications, drawing and design, graphic arts, graphic design, media production, photography, video film production, yearbook classes. Computer network features include on-campus library services, Internet access, wireless campus network, Internet filtering or blocking technology. Student e-mail accounts and computer access in designated common areas are available to students. Students grades are available online. The school has a published electronic and media policy.
Contact Mrs. Carmen Rivera, Admissions Coordinator. 386-253-5213 Ext. 325. Fax: 386-252-6101. E-mail: crivera@fatherlopez.org. Web site: www.fatherlopez.org.

FATHER RYAN HIGH SCHOOL

700 Norwood Drive

Nashville, Tennessee 37204

Head of School: Mr. Jim McIntyre

General Information Coeducational day college-preparatory, arts, and religious studies school, affiliated with Roman Catholic Church. Grades 9–12. Founded: 1925. Setting: suburban. 40-acre campus. 9 buildings on campus. Approved or accredited by National Catholic Education Association, Southern Association of Colleges and Schools, Southern Association of Independent Schools, Tennessee Association of Independent Schools, and The College Board. Endowment: $5 million. Total enrollment: 939. Upper school average class size: 20. Upper school faculty-student ratio: 1:12. There are 180 required school days per year for Upper School students. Upper School students typically attend 5 days per week. The average school day consists of 7 hours and 10 minutes.

Upper School Student Profile Grade 9: 251 students (153 boys, 98 girls); Grade 10: 239 students (141 boys, 98 girls); Grade 11: 222 students (128 boys, 94 girls); Grade 12: 227 students (124 boys, 103 girls). 90% of students are Roman Catholic.

Faculty School total: 84. In upper school: 42 men, 40 women; 46 have advanced degrees.

Subjects Offered 3-dimensional design, Advanced Placement courses, aerobics, algebra, American government, American history, American history-AP, American literature, anatomy, art, art history, art-AP, Bible studies, biology, British literature, calculus, calculus-AP, Catholic belief and practice, chemistry, chemistry-AP, Chinese, Chinese studies, chorus, church history, college counseling, college planning, college writing, computer programming, computer science, computer studies, dance, dance performance, drama, drama performance, driver education, economics, English, English literature, English-AP, European history, European history-AP, film studies, French, French-AP, geography, geometry, government-AP, government/civics, grammar, health, history, honors geometry, honors U.S. history, journalism, Latin, mathematics, music, physical education, physics, physics-AP, physiology, psychology, psychology-AP, religion, SAT preparation, science, Shakespeare, social studies, Spanish, Spanish-AP, speech, statistics-AP, theater, theater production, theology, trigonometry, U.S. government and politics-AP, Web site design, wind ensemble, world history, world literature, world religions, writing.

Graduation Requirements Arts and fine arts (art, music, dance, drama), computer science, English, foreign language, health education, mathematics, physical education (includes health), religion (includes Bible studies and theology), science, social studies (includes history), service hours required each year.

Special Academic Programs 27 Advanced Placement exams for which test preparation is offered; honors section; academic accommodation for the gifted, the musically talented, and the artistically talented; programs in English, mathematics for dyslexic students.

College Admission Counseling 202 students graduated in 2011; 200 went to college, including Belmont University; Middle Tennessee State University; Tennessee Technological University; The University of Tennessee; Western Kentucky University. Other: 2 went to work. Median SAT critical reading: 553, median SAT math: 524, median composite ACT: 24. 20% scored over 26 on composite ACT.

Student Life Upper grades have uniform requirement, student council. Discipline rests primarily with faculty. Attendance at religious services is required.

Summer Programs Remediation, enrichment, advancement, sports, art/fine arts, computer instruction programs offered; held on campus; accepts boys and girls; open to students from other schools. 240 students usually enrolled. 2012 schedule: June 1 to June 30. Application deadline: none.

Tuition and Aid Day student tuition: $10,185. Tuition installment plan (FACTS Tuition Payment Plan, individually arranged payment plans). Tuition reduction for siblings, need-based scholarship grants available. In 2011–12, 13% of upper-school students received aid. Total amount of financial aid awarded in 2011–12: $536,000.

Admissions Traditional secondary-level entrance grade is 9. For fall 2011, 347 students applied for upper-level admission, 278 were accepted, 251 enrolled. High School Placement Test required. Deadline for receipt of application materials: none. Application fee required: $80. On-campus interview required.

Athletics Interscholastic: aquatics (boys, girls), baseball (b), basketball (b,g), bowling (b,g), cheering (g), cross-country running (b,g), dance (b,g), dance squad (b), dance team (g), diving (b,g), football (b), golf (b,g), ice hockey (b), lacrosse (b,g), modern dance (g), power lifting (b), soccer (b,g), softball (g), Special Olympics (b,g), strength & conditioning (b,g), swimming and diving (b,g), tennis (b,g), track and field (b,g), volleyball (g), weight lifting (b,g), weight training (b,g), wrestling (b); intramural: fishing (b,g), indoor soccer (b,g), physical fitness (b,g). 1 athletic trainer.

Computers Computers are regularly used in all academic classes. Computer network features include on-campus library services, online commercial services, Internet access, wireless campus network, Internet filtering or blocking technology. Computer access in designated common areas is available to students. Students grades are available online. The school has a published electronic and media policy.

Contact Ms. Kate Goetzinger, Director of Admissions. 615-383-4200. Fax: 615-783-0264. E-mail: goetzinferk@fatherryan.org. Web site: www.fatherryan.org.

FAYETTEVILLE ACADEMY

3200 Cliffdale Road

Fayetteville, North Carolina 28303

Head of School: Mr. Richard D. Cameron

General Information Coeducational day college-preparatory, arts, and technology school. Grades PK–12. Founded: 1970. Setting: suburban. 30-acre campus. 10 buildings on campus. Approved or accredited by Southern Association of Colleges and Schools, Southern Association of Independent Schools, The College Board, and North Carolina Department of Education. Member of National Association of Independent Schools. Endowment: $339,522. Total enrollment: 393. Upper school average class size: 14. Upper school faculty-student ratio: 1:14. There are 175 required school days per year for Upper School students. Upper School students typically attend 5 days per week. The average school day consists of 6 hours and 55 minutes.

Upper School Student Profile Grade 9: 39 students (17 boys, 22 girls); Grade 10: 34 students (11 boys, 23 girls); Grade 11: 41 students (21 boys, 20 girls); Grade 12: 40 students (20 boys, 20 girls).

Faculty School total: 62. In upper school: 7 men, 10 women; 11 have advanced degrees.

Subjects Offered Algebra, American history, American literature, anatomy, art, band, biology, biology-AP, calculus, calculus-AP, chemistry, chemistry-AP, chorus, communications, ecology, English, English language and composition-AP, English literature, English literature-AP, European history, European history-AP, geography, geometry, government/civics, history, honors geometry, mathematics, music, physical education, physics, physiology, pre-calculus, psychology, science, social studies, Spanish, Spanish-AP, statistics-AP, trigonometry, typing, U.S. history-AP, weight training, world history, world history-AP, yearbook.

Graduation Requirements Arts and fine arts (art, music, dance, drama), English, foreign language, history, lab science, mathematics, physical education (includes health), senior projects.

Special Academic Programs Advanced Placement exam preparation; honors section; independent study.

College Admission Counseling 32 students graduated in 2011; all went to college, including East Carolina University; Elon University; North Carolina State University; The University of North Carolina at Chapel Hill; The University of North Carolina at Greensboro; The University of North Carolina Wilmington. Mean SAT critical reading: 569, mean SAT math: 586, mean SAT writing: 562, mean combined SAT: 1717, mean composite ACT: 24.

Student Life Upper grades have specified standards of dress, student council, honor system. Discipline rests primarily with faculty.

Summer Programs Enrichment, sports, art/fine arts, computer instruction programs offered; session focuses on enrichment; held on campus; accepts boys and girls; open to students from other schools. 200 students usually enrolled. 2012 schedule: June 13 to August 1.

Tuition and Aid Day student tuition: $12,999. Tuition installment plan (monthly payment plans, payment in full, 3-payment plan). Need-based scholarship grants available. In 2011–12, 26% of upper-school students received aid. Total amount of financial aid awarded in 2011–12: $477,000.

Admissions Traditional secondary-level entrance grade is 9. For fall 2011, 36 students applied for upper-level admission, 33 were accepted, 28 enrolled. ERB and SSAT required. Deadline for receipt of application materials: none. Application fee required: $30. On-campus interview recommended.

Athletics Interscholastic: baseball (boys), basketball (b,g), cheering (g), cross-country running (b,g), golf (b), soccer (b,g), softball (g), tennis (b,g), track and field (b,g), volleyball (g); intramural: weight training (g); coed interscholastic: swimming and diving. 4 PE instructors, 10 coaches, 1 athletic trainer.

Computers Computers are regularly used in all classes. Computer network features include on-campus library services, online commercial services, Internet access. Students grades are available online. The school has a published electronic and media policy.

Contact Ms. Barbara E. Lambert, Director of Admissions. 910-868-5131 Ext. 3311. Fax: 910-868-7351. E-mail: blambert@fayettevilleacademy.com. Web site: www.fayettevilleacademy.com.

FAY SCHOOL

Southborough, Massachusetts

See Junior Boarding Schools section.

FENWICK HIGH SCHOOL

505 West Washington Boulevard

Oak Park, Illinois 60302

Head of School: Mr. Richard A. Borsch

General Information Coeducational day college-preparatory school, affiliated with Roman Catholic Church. Grades 9–12. Founded: 1929. Setting: suburban. Nearest major city is Chicago. 1-acre campus. 4 buildings on campus. Approved or accredited by North Central Association of Colleges and Schools and Illinois Department of Education. Endowment: $4.5 million. Total enrollment: 1,196. Upper school average class size: 25. Upper school faculty-student ratio: 1:16. There are 180 required school days per year for Upper School students. Upper School students typically attend 5 days per week. The average school day consists of 2 hours and 20 minutes.

Upper School Student Profile Grade 9: 311 students (163 boys, 148 girls); Grade 10: 304 students (171 boys, 133 girls); Grade 11: 294 students (170 boys, 124 girls); Grade 12: 287 students (161 boys, 126 girls). 86% of students are Roman Catholic.

Faculty School total: 85. In upper school: 57 men, 28 women; 63 have advanced degrees.

Subjects Offered Algebra, American history, American history-AP, American literature, anatomy, art, art history, arts, astronomy, band, Bible studies, biology, British literature, British literature (honors), calculus, calculus-AP, chemistry, chemistry-AP, chorus, computer math, computer programming, computer science, creative writing, critical studies in film, critical writing, economics, economics-AP, English, English language and composition-AP, English literature, English literature and composition-AP, environmental science, European history, European history-AP, fine arts, French, French-AP, geometry, German, government/civics, health, history, humanities, Italian, Latin, Latin-AP, literature and composition-AP, literature-AP, marine biology, mathematics, music, music appreciation, physical education, physics, physics-AP, religion, science, social studies, Spanish, Spanish-AP, speech, statistics, theology, trigonometry, U.S. history-AP, United States government-AP, world history, world history-AP, writing.

Graduation Requirements Arts and fine arts (art, music, dance, drama), computer science, English, foreign language, humanities, mathematics, physical education (includes health), religion (includes Bible studies and theology), science, social studies (includes history), speech, theology.

Special Academic Programs Advanced Placement exam preparation; honors section; study at local college for college credit; academic accommodation for the gifted.

College Admission Counseling 291 students graduated in 2010; all went to college, including DePaul University; Indiana University Bloomington; Loyola University Chicago; Marquette University; University of Illinois at Urbana–Champaign; University of Notre Dame. Median SAT critical reading: 580, median SAT math: 589, median SAT writing: 582, median combined SAT: 1750, median composite ACT: 27. 47% scored over 600 on SAT critical reading, 49% scored over 600 on SAT math, 46% scored over 600 on SAT writing, 48% scored over 1800 on combined SAT, 53% scored over 26 on composite ACT.

Student Life Upper grades have uniform requirement, student council. Discipline rests primarily with faculty. Attendance at religious services is required.

Tuition and Aid Day student tuition: $10,950. Tuition installment plan (monthly payment plans, quarterly and semi-annual payment plans). Tuition reduction for siblings, merit scholarship grants, need-based scholarship grants available. In 2010–11, 33% of upper-school students received aid; total upper-school merit-scholarship money awarded: $91,500. Total amount of financial aid awarded in 2010–11: $1,336,049.

Admissions Traditional secondary-level entrance grade is 9. For fall 2010, 585 students applied for upper-level admission, 317 were accepted, 311 enrolled. Archdiocese of Boston or STS or High School Placement Test required. Deadline for receipt of application materials: January 8. Application fee required: $25.

Athletics Interscholastic: aquatics (boys, girls), baseball (b), basketball (b,g), bowling (b,g), cheering (g), cross-country running (b,g), diving (b,g), football (b), golf (b,g), ice hockey (b,g), lacrosse (b,g), soccer (b,g), softball (g), swimming and diving (b,g), tennis (b,g), track and field (b,g), volleyball (g), water polo (b,g), wrestling (b); intramural: basketball (b,g), bowling (b), indoor soccer (b,g), martial arts (b,g), pom squad (g), table tennis (b,g), touch football (b), volleyball (g); coed intramural: canoeing/kayaking, climbing, Nautilus, outdoor adventure, physical training, rock climbing, roller blading, strength & conditioning, wall climbing, weight lifting, weight training. 4 PE instructors, 1 athletic trainer.

Computers Computers are regularly used in English, journalism, literary magazine, mathematics, newspaper, science, yearbook classes. Computer network features include on-campus library services, online commercial services, Internet access, wireless campus network, Internet filtering or blocking technology. Student e-mail accounts are available to students. Students grades are available online. The school has a published electronic and media policy.

Contact Francesca Rabchuk, Director of Admissions. 708-386-0127 Ext. 115. Fax: 708-386-4323. E-mail: frabchuk@fenwickfriars.com. Web site: fenwickfriars.com.

THE FESSENDEN SCHOOL

West Newton, Massachusetts

See Junior Boarding Schools section.

THE FIRST ACADEMY

2667 Bruton Boulevard

Orlando, Florida 32805

Head of School: Dr. Steve D. Whitaker

General Information Coeducational day college-preparatory, arts, religious studies, and technology school, affiliated with Christian faith. Grades K4–12. Founded: 1986. Setting: suburban. 140-acre campus. 1 building on campus. Approved or accredited by Association of Christian Schools International, Southern Association of Colleges and Schools, Southern Association of Independent Schools, and Florida Department of Education. Endowment: $2.5 million. Total enrollment: 973. Upper school average class size: 17. Upper school faculty-student ratio: 1:13. There are 180 required school days per year for Upper School students. Upper School students typically attend 5 days per week. The average school day consists of 6 hours.

Upper School Student Profile Grade 9: 117 students (64 boys, 53 girls); Grade 10: 102 students (50 boys, 52 girls); Grade 11: 85 students (42 boys, 43 girls); Grade 12: 85 students (45 boys, 40 girls). 100% of students are Christian.

Faculty School total: 85. In upper school: 14 men, 15 women; 14 have advanced degrees.

Subjects Offered Advanced chemistry, advanced computer applications, advanced math, Advanced Placement courses, advanced studio art-AP, algebra, American government, American history, American history-AP, American literature, American literature-AP, analytic geometry, anatomy, ancient world history, art, art-AP, athletics, audio visual/media, band, Bible, Bible studies, biology, biology-AP, broadcasting, calculus, calculus-AP, chemistry, chemistry-AP, choir, Christian doctrine, Christian ethics, Christian testament, comparative government and politics, composition, computer programming, computer science, creative writing, drama, economics, economics and history, electives, English, English composition, English literature, English literature-AP, English-AP, ethics, European history, European history-AP, expository writing, fine arts, genetics, geometry, government, grammar, health, history, history-AP, honors algebra, honors English, honors geometry, honors U.S. history, honors world history, integrated mathematics, journalism, keyboarding, Latin, life skills, literature, literature-AP, marine biology, mathematics, media communications, music, newspaper, physical education, physical science, physics, politics, pottery, pre-algebra, pre-calculus, religion, SAT/ACT preparation, science, social sciences, social studies, Spanish, Spanish-AP, speech, speech and debate, theater, trigonometry, U.S. government, U.S. government and politics-AP, world history, world history-AP, world literature, writing, yearbook.

Graduation Requirements Arts and fine arts (art, music, dance, drama), computer science, English, foreign language, mathematics, physical education (includes health), religion (includes Bible studies and theology), science, social sciences, social studies (includes history).

Special Academic Programs Advanced Placement exam preparation; honors section; independent study; study at local college for college credit; academic accommodation for the gifted.

College Admission Counseling 68 students graduated in 2011; all went to college, including Clemson University; Florida State University; Liberty University; Samford University; University of Central Florida; University of Florida.

Student Life Upper grades have uniform requirement, student council, honor system. Discipline rests primarily with faculty. Attendance at religious services is required.

Summer Programs Enrichment, advancement, sports, art/fine arts programs offered; session focuses on academics and athletic camps; held on campus; accepts boys and girls; open to students from other schools. 200 students usually enrolled. 2012 schedule: June 1 to July 31. Application deadline: March 1.

Tuition and Aid Day student tuition: $13,195–$13,495. Tuition installment plan (SMART Tuition Payment Plan, monthly payment plans). Need-based scholarship grants available.

Admissions Traditional secondary-level entrance grade is 9. Otis-Lennon School Ability Test and Stanford Achievement Test required. Deadline for receipt of application materials: none. Application fee required: $100. On-campus interview required.

Athletics Interscholastic: baseball (boys), basketball (b,g), cheering (g), cross-country running (b,g), diving (b,g), flag football (b), football (b), golf (b,g), lacrosse (b), physical fitness (b,g), physical training (b,g), power lifting (b), running (b,g), soccer (b,g), softball (g), strength & conditioning (b,g), swimming and diving (b,g), tennis (b,g), track and field (b,g), volleyball (g), weight lifting (b), wrestling (b); coed intramural: basketball. 6 PE instructors, 18 coaches, 1 athletic trainer.

Computers Computers are regularly used in art, computer applications, English, foreign language, history, journalism, keyboarding, library, library skills, mathematics, media production, science, yearbook classes. Computer network features include on-campus library services, Internet access, wireless campus network, Internet filtering or blocking technology. Campus intranet is available to students. Students grades are available online. The school has a published electronic and media policy.

Contact Janie Weber, Admissions Specialist. 407-206-8602. Fax: 407-206-8700. E-mail: janieweber@thefirstacademy.org. Web site: www.TheFirstAcademy.org.

FIRST BAPTIST ACADEMY

PO Box 868

Dallas, Texas 75221

Head of School: Mr. Brian Littlefield

General Information Coeducational day college-preparatory, arts, religious studies, and technology school, affiliated with Baptist Church, Southern Baptist Convention. Grades K4–12. Founded: 1972. Setting: urban. 1 building on campus. Approved or accredited by Accreditation Commission of the Texas Association of Baptist Schools, Association of Christian Schools International, Southern Association of Colleges and Schools, Texas Private School Accreditation Commission, and Texas Department of Education. Endowment: $2 million. Total enrollment: 285. Upper school average class size: 15. Upper school faculty-student ratio: 1:8. There are 176 required school days per year for Upper School students. Upper School students typically attend 5 days per week. The average school day consists of 7 hours.

Upper School Student Profile 50% of students are Baptist, Southern Baptist Convention.

Faculty School total: 49. In upper school: 12 men, 16 women; 11 have advanced degrees.
Subjects Offered Algebra, American history, Bible, biology, calculus, calculus-AP, chemistry, choir, computer skills, concert band, desktop publishing, drawing, economics, English, English literature-AP, English-AP, fine arts, geometry, government-AP, history, Latin, math analysis, photography, physics, pre-calculus, Spanish, theater arts, world history.
Graduation Requirements Algebra, American history, arts and fine arts (art, music, dance, drama), Basic programming, Bible studies, biology, chemistry, economics, electives, English, government, history, keyboarding, Latin, mathematics, physical education (includes health), physics, science, Spanish, U.S. history, world geography, service hours are required for graduation. Community service is required.
Special Academic Programs 4 Advanced Placement exams for which test preparation is offered; honors section.
College Admission Counseling 50 students graduated in 2011; all went to college, including Baylor University; Texas A&M University; Texas Tech University; The University of Texas at Austin; University of Mississippi.
Student Life Upper grades have uniform requirement, student council, honor system. Discipline rests primarily with faculty. Attendance at religious services is required.
Tuition and Aid Day student tuition: $12,065. Tuition installment plan (FACTS Tuition Payment Plan). Need-based scholarship grants available. In 2011–12, 22% of upper-school students received aid.
Admissions Traditional secondary-level entrance grade is 9. ERB (grade level), ISEE or Stanford Achievement Test required. Deadline for receipt of application materials: none. Application fee required: $75. Interview required.
Athletics Interscholastic: aquatics (boys, girls), baseball (b), basketball (b,g), cheering (g), diving (b,g), football (b), golf (b,g), softball (g), strength & conditioning (b,g), swimming and diving (b,g), tennis (b,g), track and field (b,g), volleyball (g), wrestling (b). 2 PE instructors, 25 coaches.
Computers Computers are regularly used in desktop publishing, yearbook classes. Computer resources include on-campus library services, Internet access. Students grades are available online. The school has a published electronic and media policy.
Contact Elizabeth Gore, Director of Admissions and Marketing. 214-969-7861. Fax: 214-969-7797. E-mail: egore@firstdallas.org.

FIRST PRESBYTERIAN DAY SCHOOL

5671 Calvin Drive

Macon, Georgia 31210

Head of School: Mr. Gregg E. Thompson

General Information Coeducational day college-preparatory, arts, and religious studies school, affiliated with Christian faith, Presbyterian Church in America. Grades PK–12. Founded: 1970. Setting: suburban. Nearest major city is Atlanta. 64-acre campus. 7 buildings on campus. Approved or accredited by Christian Schools International, Georgia Independent School Association, Southern Association of Colleges and Schools, Southern Association of Independent Schools, and Georgia Department of Education. Endowment: $3.1 million. Total enrollment: 976. Upper school average class size: 18. Upper school faculty-student ratio: 1:12. There are 180 required school days per year for Upper School students. Upper School students typically attend 5 days per week. The average school day consists of 7 hours.
Upper School Student Profile Grade 9: 90 students (44 boys, 46 girls); Grade 10: 85 students (43 boys, 42 girls); Grade 11: 96 students (47 boys, 49 girls); Grade 12: 82 students (42 boys, 40 girls). 96% of students are Christian, Presbyterian Church in America.
Faculty School total: 73. In upper school: 27 men, 39 women; 47 have advanced degrees.
Subjects Offered 3-dimensional design, accounting, advanced biology, advanced chemistry, Advanced Placement courses, advanced studio art-AP, algebra, American literature, anatomy and physiology, art, art appreciation, art-AP, band, Bible, biology, biology-AP, British literature, calculus-AP, chemistry, chorus, comparative religion, computer applications, debate, economics, English, English language and composition-AP, English literature and composition-AP, family living, French, geometry, government, government-AP, honors algebra, honors English, honors geometry, journalism, Latin, Latin-AP, logic, model United Nations, modern European history, music appreciation, physical science, physics, pre-calculus, psychology, Spanish, statistics, studio art-AP, theater, U.S. government and politics-AP, U.S. history, U.S. history-AP, world history.
Graduation Requirements Arts and fine arts (art, music, dance, drama), Bible, computer skills, electives, English, foreign language, mathematics, physical education (includes health), science, social studies (includes history), service to distressed populations.
Special Academic Programs 12 Advanced Placement exams for which test preparation is offered; honors section; ESL (4 students enrolled).
College Admission Counseling 92 students graduated in 2011; all went to college, including Auburn University; Georgia College & State University; Georgia Institute of Technology; Mercer University; Samford University; University of Georgia. 34% scored over 600 on SAT critical reading, 43% scored over 600 on SAT math, 38% scored over 600 on SAT writing, 36% scored over 1800 on combined SAT.
Student Life Upper grades have uniform requirement, student council, honor system. Discipline rests primarily with faculty. Attendance at religious services is required.
Summer Programs Remediation, enrichment, sports, art/fine arts programs offered; session focuses on reading and study skills, mathematics enrichment, science, sports; held on campus; accepts boys and girls; open to students from other schools. 200 students usually enrolled. 2012 schedule: June 10 to July 30. Application deadline: May 15.
Tuition and Aid Day student tuition: $11,300. Tuition installment plan (monthly payment plans). Tuition reduction for siblings, merit scholarship grants, need-based scholarship grants available. In 2011–12, 31% of upper-school students received aid; total upper-school merit-scholarship money awarded: $4000. Total amount of financial aid awarded in 2011–12: $874,000.
Admissions Traditional secondary-level entrance grade is 9. CTP, Math Placement Exam or writing sample required. Deadline for receipt of application materials: February 1. Application fee required: $50. Interview recommended.
Athletics Interscholastic: baseball (boys), basketball (b,g), cheering (g), cross-country running (b,g), dance team (g), football (b), golf (b,g), soccer (b,g), softball (g), swimming and diving (b,g), tennis (b,g), track and field (b,g), volleyball (g), wrestling (b,g); intramural: football (b), indoor soccer (b,g), soccer (b,g), strength & conditioning (b,g), weight training (b,g). 3 PE instructors, 5 coaches, 1 athletic trainer.
Computers Computers are regularly used in all classes. Computer network features include on-campus library services, online commercial services, Internet access, Internet filtering or blocking technology. Campus intranet and computer access in designated common areas are available to students. Students grades are available online. The school has a published electronic and media policy.
Contact Mrs. Cheri Frame, Director of Admissions. 478-477-6505 Ext. 107. Fax: 478-477-2804. E-mail: admissions@fpdmacon.org. Web site: www.fpdmacon.org.

FISHBURNE MILITARY SCHOOL

225 South Wayne Avenue

Waynesboro, Virginia 22980

Head of School: Col. Roy F. Zinser

General Information Boys' boarding and day college-preparatory, Army Junior ROTC, and military school. Grades 7–PG. Founded: 1879. Setting: small town. Nearest major city is Washington, DC. Students are housed in single-sex dormitories. 10-acre campus. 4 buildings on campus. Approved or accredited by Southern Association of Colleges and Schools, Virginia Association of Independent Schools, and Virginia Department of Education. Endowment: $1.3 million. Total enrollment: 170. Upper school average class size: 9. Upper school faculty-student ratio: 1:9.
Upper School Student Profile Grade 9: 35 students (35 boys); Grade 10: 45 students (45 boys); Grade 11: 50 students (50 boys); Grade 12: 45 students (45 boys); Postgraduate: 15 students (15 boys). 90% of students are boarding students. 17 states are represented in upper school student body. 5% are international students. International students from Aruba, Mexico, Republic of Korea, Russian Federation, Saudi Arabia, and Taiwan; 5 other countries represented in student body.
Faculty School total: 24. In upper school: 20 men, 4 women; 5 have advanced degrees; 6 reside on campus.
Subjects Offered Algebra, American history, American literature, biology, calculus, chemistry, computer programming, computer science, computer technologies, creative writing, driver education, earth science, English, English literature, environmental science, French, geography, geology, geometry, government/civics, grammar, health, history, JROTC, mathematics, military science, music, physical education, physics, science, social studies, Spanish, speech, trigonometry, world history.
Graduation Requirements Computer science, English, foreign language, JROTC, mathematics, physical education (includes health), science, social studies (includes history).
Special Academic Programs Advanced Placement exam preparation; honors section; study at local college for college credit; remedial reading and/or remedial writing; remedial math.
College Admission Counseling 47 students graduated in 2010; all went to college, including Miami University; Penn State University Park; United States Military Academy; University of Virginia; Virginia Military Institute; Virginia Polytechnic Institute and State University. Median SAT critical reading: 470, median SAT math: 530, median SAT writing: 540, median combined SAT: 1535. 4.5% scored over 600 on SAT critical reading, 11.4% scored over 600 on SAT math, 4.5% scored over 600 on SAT writing, 2.3% scored over 1800 on combined SAT.
Student Life Upper grades have uniform requirement, student council, honor system. Discipline rests equally with students and faculty.
Admissions Traditional secondary-level entrance grade is 10. For fall 2010, 200 students applied for upper-level admission, 180 were accepted, 65 enrolled. Deadline for receipt of application materials: none. Application fee required: $50. Interview required.
Athletics Interscholastic: aquatics, baseball, basketball, canoeing/kayaking, cooperative games, cross-country running, drill team; intramural: baseball, basketball, billiards, bowling, fitness. 1 PE instructor, 15 coaches, 1 athletic trainer.
Computers Computers are regularly used in English, foreign language, history, mathematics, science classes. Computer network features include on-campus library ser-

vices, Internet access, Internet filtering or blocking technology. Campus intranet and student e-mail accounts are available to students. The school has a published electronic and media policy.

Contact Mr. Brock Selkow, Director of Admissions. 800-946-7773. Fax: 540-946-7738. E-mail: bselkow@fishburne.org. Web site: www.fishburne.org.

FLINT HILL SCHOOL

3320 Jermantown Road

Oakton, Virginia 22124

Head of School: Mr. John Thomas

General Information Coeducational day college-preparatory, arts, technology, and athletics, community service school. Grades JK–12. Founded: 1956. Setting: suburban. Nearest major city is Washington, DC. 45-acre campus. 1 building on campus. Approved or accredited by Virginia Association of Independent Schools and Virginia Department of Education. Member of National Association of Independent Schools and Secondary School Admission Test Board. Endowment: $1.4 million. Total enrollment: 1,116. Upper school average class size: 12. Upper school faculty-student ratio: 1:8. There are 168 required school days per year for Upper School students. Upper School students typically attend 5 days per week. The average school day consists of 6 hours and 30 minutes.

Upper School Student Profile Grade 9: 132 students (70 boys, 62 girls); Grade 10: 121 students (65 boys, 56 girls); Grade 11: 128 students (78 boys, 50 girls); Grade 12: 120 students (70 boys, 50 girls).

Faculty School total: 164. In upper school: 28 men, 45 women; 54 have advanced degrees.

Subjects Offered 20th century history, advanced chemistry, algebra, anatomy, art, ballet, biology, biology-AP, British literature, calculus, calculus-AP, ceramics, chemistry, chemistry-AP, Chinese, choir, choral music, chorus, civil rights, community service, computer animation, computer graphics, computer programming, computer science-AP, concert band, concert choir, creative writing, digital imaging, discrete mathematics, drama, drawing, drawing and design, earth science, economics-AP, English, English literature, English literature and composition-AP, English-AP, environmental science, environmental science-AP, environmental studies, European civilization, European history, fine arts, French, French language-AP, French literature-AP, geometry, government-AP, history, history of music, honors English, improvisation, jazz band, jazz dance, Latin, Latin American studies, Latin-AP, macro/microeconomics-AP, marine science, modern European history-AP, music, music history, music theory, music theory-AP, orchestra, ornithology, photography, physical education, physics, physics-AP, physiology, playwriting, pre-calculus, psychology, psychology-AP, science, sculpture, senior project, Shakespeare, short story, Spanish, Spanish-AP, statistics-AP, studio art, study skills, symphonic band, theater, trigonometry, U.S. history, U.S. history-AP, world religions.

Graduation Requirements Arts and fine arts (art, music, dance, drama), athletics, English, foreign language, history, mathematics, physical education (includes health), science, senior project. Community service is required.

Special Academic Programs 23 Advanced Placement exams for which test preparation is offered; honors section; academic accommodation for the musically talented and the artistically talented.

College Admission Counseling 124 students graduated in 2011; 121 went to college, including Christopher Newport University; High Point University; James Madison University; Syracuse University; University of Virginia; Virginia Polytechnic Institute and State University. Other: 1 went to work, 2 had other specific plans. Median SAT critical reading: 590, median SAT math: 610, median SAT writing: 600, median combined SAT: 1830, median composite ACT: 27. 48% scored over 600 on SAT critical reading, 60% scored over 600 on SAT math, 52% scored over 600 on SAT writing, 54% scored over 1800 on combined SAT, 55% scored over 26 on composite ACT.

Student Life Upper grades have specified standards of dress, student council, honor system. Discipline rests primarily with faculty.

Summer Programs Remediation, enrichment, advancement, ESL, sports, art/fine arts, rigorous outdoor training, computer instruction programs offered; session focuses on academics, arts, enrichment, travel, athletics and service; held both on and off campus; held at various domestic and international locations; accepts boys and girls; open to students from other schools. 815 students usually enrolled. 2012 schedule: June 20 to July 29. Application deadline: none.

Tuition and Aid Day student tuition: $29,185. Tuition installment plan (Insured Tuition Payment Plan, FACTS Tuition Payment Plan, monthly payment plans, one payment, two payments, or ten payments). Need-based scholarship grants available. In 2011–12, 19% of upper-school students received aid. Total amount of financial aid awarded in 2011–12: $1,931,144.

Admissions Traditional secondary-level entrance grade is 9. For fall 2011, 242 students applied for upper-level admission, 152 were accepted, 88 enrolled. ISEE, PSAT, SAT or SSAT required. Deadline for receipt of application materials: January 18. Application fee required: $75. On-campus interview required.

Athletics Interscholastic: aerobics/dance (girls), baseball (b), basketball (b,g), cross-country running (b,g), dance (g), dance team (g), diving (b,g), football (b), lacrosse (b,g), self defense (g), soccer (b,g), softball (g), swimming and diving (b,g), tennis (b,g), track and field (b,g), volleyball (g); coed interscholastic: golf, hockey, ice hockey, independent competitive sports, physical fitness, running, strength & conditioning, yoga; coed intramural: aerobics/dance, canoeing/kayaking, climbing, dance, fitness, modern dance, mountaineering, outdoor activities, outdoor education, physical fitness, physical training, strength & conditioning, wall climbing, weight training, winter soccer. 16 coaches, 2 athletic trainers.

Computers Computers are regularly used in all academic classes. Computer network features include on-campus library services, online commercial services, Internet access, wireless campus network, Internet filtering or blocking technology. Campus intranet, student e-mail accounts, and computer access in designated common areas are available to students. Students grades are available online. The school has a published electronic and media policy.

Contact Mr. Chris Pryor, Director of Admission. 703-584-2300. Fax: 703-242-0718. E-mail: cpryor@flinthill.org. Web site: www.flinthill.org.

FLINTRIDGE PREPARATORY SCHOOL

4543 Crown Avenue

La Canada Flintridge, California 91011

Head of School: Peter H. Bachmann

General Information Coeducational day college-preparatory school. Grades 7–12. Founded: 1933. Setting: suburban. Nearest major city is Pasadena. 7-acre campus. 8 buildings on campus. Approved or accredited by California Association of Independent Schools, The College Board, and Western Association of Schools and Colleges. Member of National Association of Independent Schools. Total enrollment: 500. Upper school average class size: 13. Upper school faculty-student ratio: 1:10.

Upper School Student Profile Grade 9: 100 students (47 boys, 53 girls); Grade 10: 101 students (51 boys, 50 girls); Grade 11: 102 students (49 boys, 53 girls); Grade 12: 96 students (46 boys, 50 girls).

Faculty School total: 68. In upper school: 40 men, 24 women; 48 have advanced degrees.

Subjects Offered African history, algebra, American history, American history-AP, American literature, American literature-AP, American politics in film, analysis and differential calculus, art, art history, art-AP, Basic programming, biology, biology-AP, business applications, calculus, calculus-AP, career/college preparation, ceramics, chemistry, chemistry-AP, Chinese studies, choral music, computer literacy, computer math, computer programming, computer science, creative writing, dance, drama, driver education, earth science, economics, English, English literature, environmental studies, European history, expository writing, fine arts, French, geography, geometry, government-AP, government/civics, grammar, great books, history, jazz band, Latin, mathematics, music, photography, physical education, physics, physiology, psychology, science, social studies, Spanish, Spanish literature-AP, Spanish-AP, statistics, theater, trigonometry, world history, world literature, writing.

Graduation Requirements Arts and fine arts (art, music, dance, drama), English, foreign language, mathematics, science, social studies (includes history), community service.

Special Academic Programs Advanced Placement exam preparation; honors section; independent study; study abroad; academic accommodation for the gifted, the musically talented, and the artistically talented.

College Admission Counseling 104 students graduated in 2011; all went to college, including Cornell University; Tufts University; University of California, Berkeley; University of California, Los Angeles; University of California, San Diego; University of Southern California. Median SAT critical reading: 640, median SAT math: 700, median SAT writing: 720.

Student Life Upper grades have specified standards of dress, student council, honor system. Discipline rests equally with students and faculty.

Summer Programs Enrichment, advancement, sports, art/fine arts, rigorous outdoor training, computer instruction programs offered; session focuses on academic enrichment/advancement, fine arts, and athletics; held on campus; accepts boys and girls; open to students from other schools. 300 students usually enrolled. 2012 schedule: June 23 to August 1. Application deadline: June 23.

Tuition and Aid Day student tuition: $28,000. Need-based scholarship grants available.

Admissions Traditional secondary-level entrance grade is 9. ISEE required. Deadline for receipt of application materials: January 20. Application fee required: $85. On-campus interview required.

Athletics Interscholastic: aquatics (boys, girls), baseball (b), basketball (b,g), cheering (g), cross-country running (b,g), diving (b,g), football (b), soccer (b,g), softball (g), swimming and diving (b,g), tennis (b,g), track and field (b,g), volleyball (b,g), water polo (b,g), winter soccer (b,g); coed interscholastic: equestrian sports, golf. 4 PE instructors, 41 coaches, 1 athletic trainer.

Computers Computers are regularly used in foreign language, mathematics, photography, science classes. Computer network features include on-campus library services, online commercial services, Internet access, wireless campus network. Campus intranet, student e-mail accounts, and computer access in designated common areas are available to students. The school has a published electronic and media policy.

Contact Arthur Stetson, Director of Admissions. 818-949-5515. Fax: 818-952-6247. Web site: www.flintridgeprep.org.

FLINT RIVER ACADEMY

11556 East Highway 85

Woodbury, Georgia 30293

Head of School: Mrs. Michele Purvis

General Information Coeducational day college-preparatory, arts, and technology school. Grades PK–12. Founded: 1967. Setting: rural. Nearest major city is Atlanta. 8-acre campus, 1 building on campus. Approved or accredited by Georgia Accrediting Commission and Southern Association of Colleges and Schools. Total enrollment: 313. Upper school average class size: 18. Upper school faculty-student ratio: 1:14. There are 180 required school days per year for Upper School students. Upper School students typically attend 5 days per week. The average school day consists of 6 hours and 23 minutes.

Upper School Student Profile Grade 9: 23 students (11 boys, 12 girls); Grade 10: 27 students (16 boys, 11 girls); Grade 11: 18 students (9 boys, 9 girls); Grade 12: 22 students (10 boys, 12 girls).

Faculty School total: 45. In upper school: 2 men, 12 women; 10 have advanced degrees.

Subjects Offered Algebra, American history, American literature, art, biology, calculus, chemistry, creative writing, drama, earth science, economics, English, fine arts, geography, geometry, government/civics, grammar, health, history, mathematics, music, physical education, physics, physiology, science, social studies, Spanish, theater, trigonometry, typing, world history, world literature.

Graduation Requirements Arts and fine arts (art, music, dance, drama), business skills (includes word processing), computer science, English, foreign language, mathematics, physical education (includes health), science, social sciences, social studies (includes history).

Special Academic Programs Advanced Placement exam preparation; honors section; study at local college for college credit; academic accommodation for the musically talented and the artistically talented; remedial math.

College Admission Counseling 28 students graduated in 2011; all went to college, including Columbus State University; Georgia Institute of Technology; Georgia Southern University; Kennesaw State University; University of Georgia; Valdosta State University. Median SAT critical reading: 210, median SAT math: 527, median SAT writing: 513, median combined SAT: 1544, median composite ACT: 20.

Student Life Upper grades have specified standards of dress, student council, honor system. Discipline rests primarily with faculty.

Tuition and Aid Day student tuition: $6555. Tuition installment plan (monthly payment plans). Tuition reduction for third sibling available.

Admissions Traditional secondary-level entrance grade is 9. For fall 2011, 4 students applied for upper-level admission, 4 were accepted, 4 enrolled. ACT-Explore required. Deadline for receipt of application materials: none. Application fee required: $50. On-campus interview required.

Athletics Interscholastic: baseball (boys), basketball (b,g), cheering (g), cross-country running (b,g), football (b), golf (b,g), softball (g), tennis (b,g), track and field (b,g); intramural: baseball (b), basketball (b,g), cheering (g), dance team (g), golf (g), soccer (b), softball (g), tennis (b,g), volleyball (b,g), weight lifting (b,g), weight training (b); coed intramural: ropes courses. 2 coaches.

Computers Computer network features include on-campus library services, Internet access.

Contact Ms. Ida Ann Dunn, Guidance Counselor. 706-553-2541. Fax: 706-553-9777. E-mail: counselor@flintriveracademy.com. Web site: www.flintriveracademy.com.

FLORIDA AIR ACADEMY

1950 South Academy Drive

Melbourne, Florida 32901

Head of School: James Dwight

General Information Coeducational boarding and day college-preparatory, arts, technology, computer science, aerospace science, and military school. Grades 7–12. Founded: 1961. Setting: suburban. Nearest major city is Orlando. Students are housed in single-sex dormitories. 15-acre campus. 13 buildings on campus. Approved or accredited by Florida Council of Independent Schools, Southern Association of Colleges and Schools, and Florida Department of Education. Member of Secondary School Admission Test Board. Total enrollment: 237. Upper school average class size: 16. Upper school faculty-student ratio: 1:11.

Upper School Student Profile Grade 9: 19 students (13 boys, 6 girls); Grade 10: 52 students (40 boys, 12 girls); Grade 11: 61 students (49 boys, 12 girls); Grade 12: 66 students (49 boys, 17 girls). 65% of students are boarding students. 70% are state residents. 11 states are represented in upper school student body. 15% are international students. International students from Bahamas, Bermuda, Cayman Islands, China, Republic of Korea, and Taiwan; 34 other countries represented in student body.

Faculty School total: 28. In upper school: 18 men, 10 women; 5 have advanced degrees; 4 reside on campus.

Subjects Offered ACT preparation, advanced computer applications, aerospace education, aerospace science, algebra, American history, American literature, animation, applied music, art, band, biology, calculus, calculus-AP, chemistry, chorus, computer applications, computer art, computer graphics, computer programming, computer science, computer technology certification, driver education, economics, English, English literature and composition-AP, English literature-AP, English-AP, ESL, flight instruction, geometry, government/civics, graphic arts, graphic design, health education, history, history-AP, honors algebra, honors English, honors geometry, honors U.S. history, honors world history, JROTC, mathematics, music, music appreciation, oceanography, physical education, physics, physics-AP, pre-calculus, psychology, SAT preparation, science, scuba diving, social studies, sociology, Spanish, Spanish language-AP, TOEFL preparation, trigonometry, U.S. government, world history, yearbook.

Graduation Requirements Aerospace education, arts and fine arts (art, music, dance, drama), computer education, English, mathematics, physical fitness, ROTC, science, social sciences, Spanish, 100 community service hours.

Special Academic Programs Advanced Placement exam preparation; honors section; study at local college for college credit; academic accommodation for the gifted; remedial reading and/or remedial writing; remedial math; ESL (20 students enrolled).

College Admission Counseling 84 students graduated in 2010; 82 went to college, including Florida Atlantic University; Florida Institute of Technology; Florida International University; Florida State University; University of Central Florida; University of Florida. Other: 2 entered military service.

Student Life Upper grades have uniform requirement, student council, honor system. Discipline rests primarily with faculty.

Tuition and Aid Day student tuition: $10,500; 7-day tuition and room/board: $31,500. Tuition installment plan (individually arranged payment plans, student loan providers). Tuition reduction for siblings, need-based scholarship grants available. In 2010–11, 40% of upper-school students received aid. Total amount of financial aid awarded in 2010–11: $650,000.

Admissions Traditional secondary-level entrance grade is 9. For fall 2010, 310 students applied for upper-level admission, 261 were accepted, 237 enrolled. Achievement tests, admissions testing, any standardized test, PSAT and SAT for applicants to grade 11 and 12 or TOEFL required. Deadline for receipt of application materials: none. Application fee required: $100. Interview required.

Athletics Interscholastic: baseball (boys), basketball (b,g), cheering (g), cross-country running (b,g), football (b), golf (b), power lifting (b), soccer (b,g), softball (b,g), tennis (b,g), volleyball (b,g), weight lifting (b), winter soccer (b,g); intramural: aerobics/Nautilus (b), baseball (b), basketball (b,g), cooperative games (b), equestrian sports (b,g), flag football (b), floor hockey (b,g), football (b), Frisbee (b), golf (b), ice skating (b), power lifting (b), soccer (b,g), softball (b,g), touch football (b), volleyball (b,g), weight lifting (b), winter soccer (b,g); coed interscholastic: aerobics/dance, aquatics, climbing, drill team, JROTC drill, martial arts, Nautilus, physical fitness, physical training, rock climbing, running, scuba diving, strength & conditioning, swimming and diving, track and field, weight training, wrestling; coed intramural: billiards, bowling, canoeing/kayaking, independent competitive sports, jogging, JROTC drill, life saving, martial arts, Nautilus, outdoor activities, outdoor education, outdoor recreation, physical fitness, physical training, rock climbing, roller skating, ropes courses, running, scuba diving, self defense, skateboarding, street hockey, surfing, swimming and diving, table tennis, tai chi, tennis, ultimate Frisbee, weight training, windsurfing. 4 PE instructors, 6 coaches, 1 athletic trainer.

Computers Computers are regularly used in aerospace science, aviation, college planning, data processing, desktop publishing, English, foreign language, graphic arts, graphic design, information technology, mathematics, publishing, research skills, SAT preparation, science, social sciences, writing classes. Computer network features include on-campus library services, Internet access, wireless campus network, Internet filtering or blocking technology. Student e-mail accounts and computer access in designated common areas are available to students. Students grades are available online. The school has a published electronic and media policy.

Contact Tiffany D. Malcolm, Director of Admissions. 321-723-3211 Ext. 30012. Fax: 321-676-0422. E-mail: tmalcolm@flair.com. Web site: www.flair.com.

FONTBONNE HALL ACADEMY

9901 Shore Road

Brooklyn, New York 11209

Head of School: Sr. Dolores F. Crepeau, CSJ

General Information Girls' day college-preparatory, arts, religious studies, and technology school, affiliated with Roman Catholic Church. Grades 9–12. Founded: 1937. Setting: urban. Nearest major city is New York. 5 buildings on campus. Approved or accredited by Middle States Association of Colleges and Schools and New York State Board of Regents. Total enrollment: 527. Upper school average class size: 20. Upper school faculty-student ratio: 1:14. There are 180 required school days per year for Upper School students. Upper School students typically attend 5 days per week. The average school day consists of 6 hours and 30 minutes.

Upper School Student Profile Grade 9: 135 students (135 girls); Grade 10: 132 students (132 girls); Grade 11: 128 students (128 girls); Grade 12: 132 students (132 girls). 90% of students are Roman Catholic.

Faculty School total: 41. In upper school: 3 men, 38 women.

Subjects Offered Advanced chemistry, algebra, American literature-AP, anatomy and physiology, anthropology, art, biology-AP, calculus, calculus-AP, chemistry, chorus, computer multimedia, computers, earth science, economics, English, forensics, genetics, government, health, history-AP, Italian, Latin, marine science, mathematics, music, photography, physical education, physics, religion, Spanish, Spanish language-AP, U.S. history, world geography, world history.
Graduation Requirements Algebra, American government, American history, American literature, art, biology, British literature, chemistry, college counseling, college writing, computer applications, economics, electives, English, European civilization, foreign language, geometry, government, guidance, Internet research, lab science, music, physical education (includes health), religion (includes Bible studies and theology), science, world civilizations, Board of Regents requirements, 60 hours of service.
Special Academic Programs Advanced Placement exam preparation; honors section; study at local college for college credit.
College Admission Counseling 123 students graduated in 2011; all went to college, including Columbia University; Fordham University; Manhattan College; New York University; The Catholic University of America; United States Military Academy. Median SAT critical reading: 550, median SAT math: 550, median SAT writing: 600, median combined SAT: 1700.
Student Life Upper grades have uniform requirement, student council. Discipline rests primarily with faculty. Attendance at religious services is required.
Summer Programs Sports programs offered; session focuses on sports clinics; held on campus; accepts girls; open to students from other schools. 50 students usually enrolled. 2012 schedule: August 1 to August 12. Application deadline: June 27.
Tuition and Aid Day student tuition: $8100. Tuition installment plan (monthly payment plans, 3 payments per year). Tuition reduction for siblings, merit scholarship grants, Service Scholarships available. In 2011–12, 20% of upper-school students received aid; total upper-school merit-scholarship money awarded: $100,000. Total amount of financial aid awarded in 2011–12: $107,500.
Admissions Traditional secondary-level entrance grade is 9. For fall 2011, 437 students applied for upper-level admission, 276 were accepted, 135 enrolled. Diocesan Entrance Exam required. Deadline for receipt of application materials: February 4. Application fee required: $250.
Athletics Interscholastic: aquatics, baseball, basketball, cheering, cross-country running, dance, dance squad, drill team, fishing, golf, running, soccer, softball, swimming and diving, tennis, track and field, volleyball. 2 PE instructors, 10 coaches, 2 athletic trainers.
Computers Computers are regularly used in all academic classes. Computer network features include on-campus library services, Internet access, wireless campus network, Internet filtering or blocking technology. Campus intranet and computer access in designated common areas are available to students. The school has a published electronic and media policy.
Contact Sr. Dolores F. Crepeau, CSJ, Principal. 718-748-2244. Fax: 718-745-3841. E-mail: crepeau@fontbonne.org. Web site: www.fontbonne.org.

FOOTHILLS ACADEMY

Calgary, Alberta, Canada

See Special Needs Schools section.

FORDHAM PREPARATORY SCHOOL

East Fordham Road

Bronx, New York 10458-5175

Head of School: Rev. Kenneth J. Boller, SJ

General Information Boys' day college-preparatory school, affiliated with Roman Catholic Church. Grades 9–12. Founded: 1841. Setting: urban. Nearest major city is New York. 5-acre campus. 2 buildings on campus. Approved or accredited by Jesuit Secondary Education Association, Middle States Association of Colleges and Schools, National Catholic Education Association, and New York Department of Education. Endowment: $1.8 million. Total enrollment: 990. Upper school average class size: 24. Upper school faculty-student ratio: 1:11.
Upper School Student Profile Grade 9: 253 students (253 boys); Grade 10: 239 students (239 boys); Grade 11: 244 students (244 boys); Grade 12: 254 students (254 boys). 75% of students are Roman Catholic.
Faculty School total: 87. In upper school: 63 men, 24 women; 79 have advanced degrees.
Subjects Offered Advanced chemistry, algebra, American Civil War, American history, American history-AP, American literature, Ancient Greek, architectural drawing, art history-AP, biochemistry, biology, biology-AP, British literature, calculus, calculus-AP, chemistry, chemistry-AP, Chinese, computer graphics, computer programming, computer programming-AP, constitutional history of U.S., creative writing, economics, emerging technology, English, English language and composition-AP, English literature-AP, European history-AP, finite math, forensics, French, geometry, German, global studies, government and politics-AP, health, Italian, Latin, Latin-AP, macroeconomics-AP, media communications, modern history, modern world history, music, physical education, physics, physics-AP, poetry, pre-calculus, religious studies, science research, short story, Spanish, Spanish language-AP, Spanish literature-AP, statistics-AP, studio art, studio art-AP, trigonometry, world history-AP.
Graduation Requirements Arts and fine arts (art, music, dance, drama), English, foreign language, mathematics, physical education (includes health), religious studies, science, social studies (includes history), senior service project.
Special Academic Programs Advanced Placement exam preparation; honors section; study at local college for college credit.
College Admission Counseling 221 students graduated in 2011; 216 went to college, including Boston College; College of the Holy Cross; Fordham University; Manhattan College; New York University; The University of Scranton. Other: 1 entered military service, 1 entered a postgraduate year, 3 had other specific plans. Mean SAT critical reading: 585, mean SAT math: 590, mean SAT writing: 584.
Student Life Upper grades have specified standards of dress. Discipline rests primarily with faculty. Attendance at religious services is required.
Tuition and Aid Day student tuition: $15,820. Tuition installment plan (monthly payment plans). Merit scholarship grants, need-based scholarship grants available. In 2011–12, 35% of upper-school students received aid; total upper-school merit-scholarship money awarded: $400,000. Total amount of financial aid awarded in 2011–12: $2,200,000.
Admissions Traditional secondary-level entrance grade is 9. For fall 2011, 1,141 students applied for upper-level admission, 561 were accepted, 253 enrolled. Cooperative Entrance Exam (McGraw-Hill), Diocesan Entrance Exam, ISEE, SSAT or STS required. Deadline for receipt of application materials: December 15. No application fee required.
Athletics Interscholastic: baseball, basketball, bowling, crew, cross-country running, diving, football, golf, ice hockey, indoor track, lacrosse, rugby, soccer, swimming and diving, tennis, track and field, volleyball, winter (indoor) track, wrestling; intramural: basketball, fitness, Frisbee, rock climbing, weight training. 2 PE instructors, 16 coaches.
Computers Computers are regularly used in English, foreign language, history, mathematics, science classes. Computer network features include on-campus library services, online commercial services, Internet access, wireless campus network, Internet filtering or blocking technology, Rosetta Stone. Student e-mail accounts are available to students. The school has a published electronic and media policy.
Contact Christopher D. Lauber, Director of Admissions. 718-584-8367. Fax: 718-367-7598. E-mail: lauberc@fordhamprep.org. Web site: www.fordhamprep.org.

FOREST LAKE ACADEMY

500 Education Loop

Apopka, Florida 32703

Head of School: Gloria M. Becker

General Information Coeducational boarding and day and distance learning college-preparatory, arts, religious studies, and bilingual studies school, affiliated with Seventh-day Adventists. Grades 9–12. Distance learning grades 9–12. Founded: 1926. Setting: suburban. Nearest major city is Orlando. Students are housed in single-sex dormitories. 200-acre campus. 9 buildings on campus. Approved or accredited by CITA (Commission on International and Trans-Regional Accreditation), Middle States Association of Colleges and Schools, National Council for Private School Accreditation, and Florida Department of Education. Total enrollment: 377. Upper school average class size: 22. Upper school faculty-student ratio: 1:22. There are 176 required school days per year for Upper School students. Upper School students typically attend 5 days per week. The average school day consists of 6 hours and 35 minutes.
Upper School Student Profile Grade 9: 78 students (36 boys, 42 girls); Grade 10: 101 students (53 boys, 48 girls); Grade 11: 101 students (48 boys, 53 girls); Grade 12: 97 students (51 boys, 46 girls). 8% of students are boarding students. 84% are state residents. 13 states are represented in upper school student body. 1% are international students. International students from Argentina and Bermuda. 95% of students are Seventh-day Adventists.
Faculty School total: 29. In upper school: 18 men, 11 women; 12 have advanced degrees; 5 reside on campus.
Subjects Offered Algebra, American government, American literature, art, band, bell choir, Bible studies, biology, calculus, chemistry, choir, church history, computer applications, desktop publishing, digital photography, economics, English, environmental science, geometry, health, honors algebra, honors English, honors geometry, honors world history, integrated mathematics, life management skills, physical science, physics, play production, pre-calculus, psychology, SAT preparation, senior project, Spanish, statistics, strings, swimming, tennis, U.S. history, video film production, world geography, world history, world literature, writing, yearbook.
Graduation Requirements Algebra, American government, American literature, arts and fine arts (art, music, dance, drama), Bible studies, biology, chemistry, computer applications, computer science, economics, English, environmental science, fitness, foreign language, geometry, health education, life management skills, physical education (includes health), physical science, pre-calculus, religion (includes Bible studies and theology), science, social studies (includes history), Spanish, statistics, U.S. history, world history, world literature, writing, 20 hours of community service activity for each year enrolled.

Special Academic Programs Honors section; study at local college for college credit.

College Admission Counseling 107 students graduated in 2011; 100 went to college, including Andrews University; Florida Hospital College of Health Sciences; Oakwood University; Seminole State College of Florida; Southern Adventist University; University of Central Florida. Other: 7 went to work. Mean SAT critical reading: 487, mean SAT math: 485, mean SAT writing: 474, mean composite ACT: 21.

Student Life Upper grades have uniform requirement, student council, honor system. Discipline rests primarily with faculty.

Tuition and Aid Day student tuition: $10,760; 7-day tuition and room/board: $21,888. Tuition installment plan (FACTS Tuition Payment Plan, monthly payment plans, individually arranged payment plans). Merit scholarship grants, need-based scholarship grants, paying campus jobs available. In 2011–12, 57% of upper-school students received aid; total upper-school merit-scholarship money awarded: $7940. Total amount of financial aid awarded in 2011–12: $378,500.

Admissions Traditional secondary-level entrance grade is 9. For fall 2011, 488 students applied for upper-level admission, 430 were accepted, 377 enrolled. Deadline for receipt of application materials: none. Application fee required: $60. Interview recommended.

Athletics Interscholastic: basketball (boys, girls), golf (b), volleyball (g); intramural: golf (b); coed intramural: basketball, flag football, floor hockey, soccer, volleyball. 2 PE instructors, 1 coach.

Computers Computers are regularly used in computer applications, desktop publishing, photography, Web site design, writing, yearbook classes. Computer resources include Internet access, wireless campus network, Internet filtering or blocking technology, financial aid and grant search programs for college. Campus intranet, student e-mail accounts, and computer access in designated common areas are available to students. Students grades are available online. The school has a published electronic and media policy.

Contact Mrs. Claudia Dure C. Osorio, Director of Student Records. 407-862-8411 Ext. 743. Fax: 407-862-7050. E-mail: osorioc@forestlake.org. Web site: www.forestlakeacademy.org.

FORSYTH COUNTRY DAY SCHOOL

5501 Shallowford Road

PO Box 549

Lewisville, North Carolina 27023-0549

Head of School: Dr. Nan Wodarz

General Information Coeducational day college-preparatory school. Grades PK–12. Founded: 1970. Setting: suburban. Nearest major city is Winston-Salem. 80-acre campus. 7 buildings on campus. Approved or accredited by Southern Association of Colleges and Schools, Southern Association of Independent Schools, The College Board, and North Carolina Department of Education. Member of National Association of Independent Schools. Endowment: $16 million. Total enrollment: 846. Upper school average class size: 15. Upper school faculty-student ratio: 1:12. There are 175 required school days per year for Upper School students. Upper School students typically attend 5 days per week. The average school day consists of 5 hours and 45 minutes.

Upper School Student Profile Grade 9: 77 students (42 boys, 35 girls); Grade 10: 94 students (58 boys, 36 girls); Grade 11: 77 students (43 boys, 34 girls); Grade 12: 105 students (62 boys, 43 girls).

Faculty School total: 175. In upper school: 18 men, 29 women; 24 have advanced degrees.

Subjects Offered Advanced Placement courses, advanced studio art-AP, algebra, American history, American history-AP, American literature, art, astronomy, biology, calculus, calculus-AP, ceramics, chemistry, Chinese studies, community service, computer math, computer programming, computer science, creative writing, digital art, drama, English, English literature, European history, fine arts, foreign policy, French, freshman seminar, geometry, grammar, health, history, history of science, humanities, international relations, Japanese studies, journalism, Latin, Mandarin, mathematics, Middle Eastern history, music, photography, physical education, physics, psychology, SAT/ACT preparation, science, social studies, Spanish, statistics-AP, theater, yearbook.

Graduation Requirements Arts and fine arts (art, music, dance, drama), English, foreign language, history, mathematics, physical education (includes health), physical fitness, science. Community service is required.

Special Academic Programs 18 Advanced Placement exams for which test preparation is offered; honors section; academic accommodation for the gifted; programs in English, general development for dyslexic students; ESL (2 students enrolled).

College Admission Counseling 110 students graduated in 2011; all went to college, including Duke University; Elon University; North Carolina State University; The University of North Carolina at Chapel Hill; The University of North Carolina Wilmington; Wake Forest University. Median SAT critical reading: 600, median SAT math: 615. 70% scored over 600 on SAT critical reading, 68% scored over 600 on SAT math.

Student Life Upper grades have specified standards of dress, student council, honor system. Discipline rests equally with students and faculty.

Summer Programs Enrichment programs offered; session focuses on leadership training; held both on and off campus; held at various businesses and offices throughout the community; accepts boys and girls; open to students from other schools. 50 students usually enrolled. 2012 schedule: June 15 to July 31.

Tuition and Aid Day student tuition: $18,985. Tuition installment plan (Insured Tuition Payment Plan, monthly payment plans, individually arranged payment plans). Need-based scholarship grants available. In 2011–12, 23% of upper-school students received aid. Total amount of financial aid awarded in 2011–12: $914,455.

Admissions Traditional secondary-level entrance grade is 9. For fall 2011, 70 students applied for upper-level admission, 60 were accepted, 50 enrolled. ERB CTP IV, WRAT and writing sample required. Deadline for receipt of application materials: none. Application fee required: $100. On-campus interview recommended.

Athletics Interscholastic: baseball (boys), basketball (b,g), cheering (g), cross-country running (b,g), field hockey (g), football (b), golf (b,g), lacrosse (b,g), physical fitness (b,g), soccer (b,g), softball (g), tennis (b,g), track and field (b,g), volleyball (g), wrestling (b); coed interscholastic: swimming and diving; coed intramural: sailing. 4 PE instructors, 4 coaches, 1 athletic trainer.

Computers Computers are regularly used in art, English, foreign language, history, mathematics, music, science classes. Computer network features include on-campus library services, online commercial services, Internet access, wireless campus network, Internet filtering or blocking technology. Campus intranet, student e-mail accounts, and computer access in designated common areas are available to students. Students grades are available online. The school has a published electronic and media policy.

Contact Cindy C. Kluttz, Director of Admission. 336-945-3151 Ext. 340. Fax: 336-945-2907. E-mail: cindykluttz@fcds.org. Web site: www.fcds.org.

FORT LAUDERDALE PREPARATORY SCHOOL

3275 West Oakland Park Boulevard

Fort Lauderdale, Florida 33311

Head of School: Dr. Lawrence Berkowitz

General Information Coeducational day college-preparatory, general academic, arts, and technology school. Grades PK–12. Founded: 1986. Setting: urban. 5-acre campus. 1 building on campus. Approved or accredited by CITA (Commission on International and Trans-Regional Accreditation), National Council for Private School Accreditation, National Independent Private Schools Association, Southern Association of Colleges and Schools, and Florida Department of Education. Member of National Association of Independent Schools and European Council of International Schools. Languages of instruction: English and Spanish. Total enrollment: 195. Upper school average class size: 16. Upper school faculty-student ratio: 1:8. There are 177 required school days per year for Upper School students. Upper School students typically attend 5 days per week. The average school day consists of 7 hours.

Upper School Student Profile Grade 7: 18 students (8 boys, 10 girls); Grade 8: 17 students (9 boys, 8 girls); Grade 9: 17 students (8 boys, 9 girls); Grade 10: 17 students (7 boys, 10 girls); Grade 11: 15 students (7 boys, 8 girls); Grade 12: 16 students (8 boys, 8 girls).

Faculty School total: 28. In upper school: 11 men, 10 women; 9 have advanced degrees.

Subjects Offered Accounting, ACT preparation, advanced chemistry, advanced computer applications, advanced math, Advanced Placement courses, advanced studio art-AP, advanced TOEFL/grammar, algebra, American government, American history, American history-AP, American literature, American literature-AP, art, art appreciation, art history, art history-AP, art-AP, automated accounting, Basic programming, biology, biology-AP, bookkeeping, British literature, British literature (honors), business applications, business education, business mathematics, calculus, calculus-AP, career education, career/college preparation, character education, chemistry, chemistry-AP, U.S. government and politics-AP.

Special Academic Programs International Baccalaureate program; Advanced Placement exam preparation; honors section; accelerated programs; independent study; study at local college for college credit; academic accommodation for the gifted; remedial reading and/or remedial writing; remedial math; programs in English, mathematics, general development for dyslexic students; ESL (17 students enrolled).

College Admission Counseling 18 students graduated in 2011; 16 went to college, including Florida Atlantic University; Florida State University; Hunter College of the City University of New York; University of Florida; University of Miami; University of South Florida. Other: 1 went to work, 1 entered military service.

Student Life Upper grades have uniform requirement, student council, honor system. Discipline rests primarily with faculty.

Summer Programs Remediation, enrichment, advancement, ESL, computer instruction programs offered; session focuses on academics; held on campus; accepts boys and girls; open to students from other schools. 100 students usually enrolled. 2012 schedule: June 18 to July 26.

Tuition and Aid Day student tuition: $12,500. Tuition installment plan (monthly payment plans, individually arranged payment plans). Tuition reduction for siblings, merit scholarship grants, need-based scholarship grants available. In 2011–12, 50% of upper-school students received aid; total upper-school merit-scholarship money awarded: $200,000. Total amount of financial aid awarded in 2011–12: $1,000,000.

Admissions Traditional secondary-level entrance grade is 7. For fall 2011, 92 students applied for upper-level admission, 51 were accepted, 39 enrolled. Admissions testing, High School Placement Test, math and English placement tests, Math Placement Exam, school's own exam, standardized test scores, Stanford Achievement Test, TOEFL or writing sample required. Deadline for receipt of application materials: none. Application fee required: $50. Interview recommended.

Athletics 2 PE instructors.

Computers Computers are regularly used in all academic classes. Computer network features include on-campus library services, Internet access, wireless campus network, Internet filtering or blocking technology. Campus intranet is available to students. The school has a published electronic and media policy.

Contact Jonathan A. Lonstein, Director of Admissions. 954-485-7500. Fax: 954-485-1732. E-mail: admissions@flps.com. Web site: www.flps.com/.

FORT WORTH COUNTRY DAY SCHOOL

4200 Country Day Lane

Fort Worth, Texas 76109-4299

Head of School: Evan D. Peterson

General Information Coeducational day college-preparatory and arts school. Grades K–12. Founded: 1962. Setting: suburban. 100-acre campus. 13 buildings on campus. Approved or accredited by Accreditation Commission of the Texas Association of Baptist Schools and Independent Schools Association of the Southwest. Member of National Association of Independent Schools. Endowment: $42 million. Total enrollment: 1,110. Upper school average class size: 14. Upper school faculty-student ratio: 1:10. There are 174 required school days per year for Upper School students. Upper School students typically attend 5 days per week. The average school day consists of 8 hours.

Upper School Student Profile Grade 9: 102 students (51 boys, 51 girls); Grade 10: 108 students (61 boys, 47 girls); Grade 11: 101 students (51 boys, 50 girls); Grade 12: 96 students (44 boys, 52 girls).

Faculty School total: 128. In upper school: 16 men, 21 women; 29 have advanced degrees.

Subjects Offered 3-dimensional art, algebra, American history, American literature, art, art history, biology, calculus, ceramics, chemistry, comparative religion, computer math, computer programming, computer science, computer technologies, creative writing, dance, drama, driver education, earth science, ecology, economics, English, English literature, European history, expository writing, fine arts, French, geography, geology, geometry, government/civics, grammar, health, history, journalism, Latin, mathematics, modern problems, music, music history, photography, physical education, physics, psychology, science, social studies, Spanish, speech, study skills, technology, theater, trigonometry, typing, word processing, world history, writing.

Graduation Requirements Algebra, American government, arts and fine arts (art, music, dance, drama), biology, English, foreign language, lab science, mathematics, physical education (includes health), science, social studies (includes history), participation in athletics, Completion of a two year College Counseling Course. Community service is required.

Special Academic Programs 22 Advanced Placement exams for which test preparation is offered; honors section; independent study; study at local college for college credit; academic accommodation for the gifted, the musically talented, and the artistically talented.

College Admission Counseling 96 students graduated in 2011; all went to college, including Southern Methodist University; Texas A&M University; Texas Christian University; The University of Texas at Austin; University of Georgia; University of Oklahoma.

Student Life Upper grades have uniform requirement, student council, honor system. Discipline rests equally with students and faculty.

Summer Programs Remediation, enrichment, sports, art/fine arts programs offered; session focuses on athletics and enrichment; held both on and off campus; held at local golf course (for enrichment golf and golf team practice); accepts boys and girls; open to students from other schools. 300 students usually enrolled. 2012 schedule: June 1 to July 31. Application deadline: May 30.

Tuition and Aid Day student tuition: $18,810. Tuition installment plan (monthly payment plans, individually arranged payment plans). Merit scholarship grants, need-based scholarship grants, Malone Scholars Program available. In 2011–12, 21% of upper-school students received aid; total upper-school merit-scholarship money awarded: $185,778. Total amount of financial aid awarded in 2011–12: $867,400.

Admissions Traditional secondary-level entrance grade is 9. For fall 2011, 79 students applied for upper-level admission, 39 were accepted, 31 enrolled. ERB or ISEE required. Deadline for receipt of application materials: March 5. Application fee required: $75. Interview required.

Athletics Interscholastic: ballet (boys, girls), baseball (b), basketball (b,g), cheering (g), field hockey (g), football (b), lacrosse (b), track and field (b,g), volleyball (b,g), winter soccer (b,g), wrestling (b); intramural: lacrosse (b); coed interscholastic: ballet, cross-country running, dance, dance team, fitness, golf, independent competitive sports, outdoor education, outdoor recreation, physical fitness, physical training, ropes courses, strength & conditioning, swimming and diving, tennis, weight training. 12 PE instructors, 45 coaches, 2 athletic trainers.

Computers Computers are regularly used in architecture, college planning, computer applications, creative writing, desktop publishing, English, foreign language, history, humanities, introduction to technology, library skills, life skills, mathematics, music, newspaper, publications, reading, science, Web site design, writing, yearbook classes. Computer network features include on-campus library services, online commercial services, Internet access, wireless campus network, Internet filtering or blocking technology. Campus intranet, student e-mail accounts, and computer access in designated common areas are available to students. Students grades are available online. The school has a published electronic and media policy.

Contact Yolanda Espinoza, Admission Associate. 817-302-3209. Fax: 817-377-3425. E-mail: yolanda.espinoza@fwcd.org. Web site: www.fwcd.org.

FOUNDATION ACADEMY

15304 Tilden Road

Winter Garden, Florida 34787

Head of School: Mr. Shawn Minks

General Information Coeducational day college-preparatory, general academic, and arts school, affiliated with Baptist Church. Grades 6–12. Founded: 1958. Setting: suburban. Nearest major city is Orlando. 75-acre campus. 3 buildings on campus. Approved or accredited by Association of Christian Schools International and Southern Association of Colleges and Schools. Total enrollment: 537. Upper school average class size: 16. Upper school faculty-student ratio: 1:16. There are 180 required school days per year for Upper School students. Upper School students typically attend 5 days per week. The average school day consists of 6 hours and 20 minutes.

Upper School Student Profile Grade 9: 36 students (17 boys, 19 girls); Grade 10: 26 students (14 boys, 12 girls); Grade 11: 30 students (24 boys, 6 girls); Grade 12: 29 students (19 boys, 10 girls). 20% of students are Baptist.

Faculty School total: 30. In upper school: 8 men, 22 women; 9 have advanced degrees.

Subjects Offered Advanced Placement courses, anatomy and physiology, art, band, Bible, biology, biology-AP, business law, business mathematics, calculus, calculus-AP, chemistry, college admission preparation, computer processing, drama, economics and history, English, English composition, English literature, English literature-AP, French, geometry, government, health education, history-AP, journalism, physical education, physical fitness, SAT preparation, science, science project, social psychology, Spanish, speech, sports conditioning, studio art-AP, U.S. history, weight training.

Graduation Requirements Algebra, American government, American history, American literature, anatomy and physiology, arts and fine arts (art, music, dance, drama), Bible, biology, chemistry, college admission preparation, English, English composition, geography, geometry, government, history, human anatomy, languages, SAT preparation, science, U.S. history, 4 credits of Bible.

Special Academic Programs Advanced Placement exam preparation; honors section; independent study; study at local college for college credit; remedial reading and/or remedial writing; remedial math; programs in English, mathematics for dyslexic students.

College Admission Counseling 28 students graduated in 2011; all went to college, including Florida Gulf Coast University; Florida State University; Savannah College of Art and Design; The University of Arizona; University of Central Florida; Valencia College.

Student Life Upper grades have uniform requirement, student council. Discipline rests primarily with faculty. Attendance at religious services is required.

Summer Programs Remediation, enrichment, sports, art/fine arts programs offered; session focuses on sports camps, art; held on campus; accepts boys and girls; open to students from other schools. 100 students usually enrolled. 2012 schedule: June 1 to July 31.

Tuition and Aid Day student tuition: $9000. Guaranteed tuition plan. Tuition installment plan (SMART Tuition Payment Plan). Tuition reduction for siblings, need-based scholarship grants available. In 2011–12, 10% of upper-school students received aid.

Admissions For fall 2011, 60 students applied for upper-level admission, 55 were accepted, 50 enrolled. Admissions testing, Gates MacGinite Reading Tests, Math Placement Exam and Wide Range Achievement Test required. Deadline for receipt of application materials: none. Application fee required: $150. Interview required.

Athletics Interscholastic: baseball (boys), basketball (b,g), bowling (b,g), cheering (g), cross-country running (b,g), football (b), golf (b), soccer (b), softball (g), tennis (b,g), track and field (b,g), volleyball (g); intramural: bowling (b,g). 2 PE instructors, 50 coaches, 2 athletic trainers.

Computers Computers are regularly used in career exploration, college planning, computer applications, independent study, library skills, word processing, yearbook classes. Computer resources include on-campus library services, Internet access, Internet filtering or blocking technology. Campus intranet is available to students. Students grades are available online.

Contact Mrs. Stephanie Baysinger, Student Advisor. 407-877-2744. Fax: 407-877-1985. E-mail: sbaysinger@foundationacademy.net. Web site: www.foundationacademy.net.

FOUNTAIN VALLEY SCHOOL OF COLORADO

6155 Fountain Valley School Road

Colorado Springs, Colorado 80911

Head of School: Craig W. Larimer Jr.

General Information Coeducational boarding and day college-preparatory, arts, and technology school. Grades 9–12. Founded: 1930. Setting: suburban. Students are housed in single-sex dormitories. 1,100-acre campus. 42 buildings on campus. Approved or accredited by Association of Colorado Independent Schools, The Association of Boarding Schools, and Colorado Department of Education. Member of National Association of Independent Schools and Secondary School Admission Test Board. Endowment: $34 million. Total enrollment: 244. Upper school average class size: 11. Upper school faculty-student ratio: 1:6. Upper School students typically attend 5 days per week. The average school day consists of 9 hours and 15 minutes.

Upper School Student Profile Grade 9: 50 students (26 boys, 24 girls); Grade 10: 72 students (31 boys, 41 girls); Grade 11: 58 students (25 boys, 33 girls); Grade 12: 63 students (30 boys, 33 girls). 66% of students are boarding students. 52% are state residents. 27 states are represented in upper school student body. 22% are international students. International students from China, Germany, Japan, Mexico, Republic of Korea, and Taiwan; 15 other countries represented in student body.

Faculty School total: 44. In upper school: 20 men, 14 women; 25 have advanced degrees; 22 reside on campus.

Subjects Offered 3-dimensional art, 3-dimensional design, ACT preparation, advanced chemistry, Advanced Placement courses, advanced studio art-AP, algebra, American history, American history-AP, American literature, biology, biology-AP, British literature, calculus, calculus-AP, ceramics, chamber groups, chemistry, chemistry-AP, college counseling, Colorado ecology, composition, computer applications, computer multimedia, computer programming, creative writing, drama, English, English literature and composition-AP, environmental science-AP, ESL, fiction, film and literature, French, French language-AP, geology, geometry, honors algebra, honors English, honors geometry, instrumental music, jewelry making, literature, Mandarin, musical productions, outdoor education, photography, physics, physics-AP, pre-calculus, probability and statistics, robotics, senior project, senior seminar, Shakespeare, Shakespearean histories, short story, Spanish, Spanish language-AP, statistics-AP, strings, student government, student publications, studio art, studio art-AP, U.S. government and politics-AP, visual and performing arts, vocal ensemble, wilderness education, wind ensemble, world history, world history-AP, world literature, writing.

Graduation Requirements Arts and fine arts (art, music, dance, drama), computer science, English, foreign language, mathematics, physical education (includes health), science, social studies (includes history), community service hours, senior seminar.

Special Academic Programs 18 Advanced Placement exams for which test preparation is offered; honors section; independent study; academic accommodation for the gifted, the musically talented, and the artistically talented; ESL (17 students enrolled).

College Admission Counseling 74 students graduated in 2011; all went to college, including Bowdoin College; Colorado School of Mines; Colorado State University; The Colorado College; University of Colorado Boulder; Wesleyan University. Median SAT critical reading: 570, median SAT math: 610, median SAT writing: 540, median composite ACT: 25.

Student Life Upper grades have specified standards of dress, student council, honor system. Discipline rests equally with students and faculty.

Summer Programs Enrichment, ESL, sports, computer instruction programs offered; session focuses on outdoor education, natural sciences, leadership, sports camps, international student enrichment; held both on and off campus; held at FVS' 40-acre Mountain Campus and surrounding Mount Princeton region; accepts boys and girls; open to students from other schools. 100 students usually enrolled. 2012 schedule: June 5 to August 15. Application deadline: none.

Tuition and Aid Day student tuition: $23,900; 7-day tuition and room/board: $44,100. Tuition installment plan (Key Tuition Payment Plan, monthly payment plans, individually arranged payment plans). Merit scholarship grants, need-based scholarship grants available. In 2011–12, 41% of upper-school students received aid. Total amount of financial aid awarded in 2011–12: $1,870,000.

Admissions Traditional secondary-level entrance grade is 9. For fall 2011, 231 students applied for upper-level admission, 159 were accepted, 86 enrolled. SSAT or TOEFL required. Deadline for receipt of application materials: February 1. Application fee required: $50. Interview required.

Athletics Interscholastic: basketball (boys, girls), cross-country running (b,g), diving (g), hockey (b), ice hockey (b), lacrosse (b,g), soccer (b,g), swimming and diving (g), tennis (b,g), track and field (b,g), volleyball (b,g); coed interscholastic: climbing, equestrian sports, golf, horseback riding, independent competitive sports, rock climbing, rodeo, skiing (downhill), snowboarding, telemark skiing; coed intramural: aerobics/dance, alpine skiing, backpacking, climbing, dance, equestrian sports, fitness, Frisbee, hiking/backpacking, horseback riding, modern dance, mountain biking, mountaineering, outdoor activities, outdoor adventure, outdoor education, outdoor recreation, outdoor skills, physical fitness, rock climbing, skiing (downhill), snowboarding, strength & conditioning, table tennis, telemark skiing, tennis, ultimate Frisbee, weight training. 2 coaches, 1 athletic trainer.

Computers Computers are regularly used in all academic, college planning, multimedia, news writing, newspaper, photography, publications, Web site design, yearbook classes. Computer network features include on-campus library services, online commercial services, Internet access, wireless campus network, Internet filtering or blocking technology. Campus intranet, student e-mail accounts, and computer access in designated common areas are available to students. Students grades are available online. The school has a published electronic and media policy.

Contact Mr. Randy Roach, Director of Admission. 719-390-7035 Ext. 251. Fax: 719-390-7762. E-mail: admission@fvs.edu. Web site: www.fvs.edu.

See Display on next page and Close-Up on page 624.

FOWLERS ACADEMY

PO Box 921

Guaynabo, Puerto Rico 00970-0921

Head of School: Mrs. Nancy Santana

General Information Coeducational day general academic, arts, religious studies, music, and graphic art design school, affiliated with Christian faith; primarily serves underachievers. Grades 7–12. Founded: 1986. Setting: suburban. 2-acre campus. 2 buildings on campus. Approved or accredited by Comisión Acreditadora de Instituciones Educativas, The College Board, and Puerto Rico Department of Education. Languages of instruction: English and Spanish. Total enrollment: 68. Upper school average class size: 15. Upper school faculty-student ratio: 1:15. Upper School students typically attend 5 days per week. The average school day consists of 6 hours and 50 minutes.

Upper School Student Profile Grade 9: 9 students (5 boys, 4 girls); Grade 10: 14 students (10 boys, 4 girls); Grade 11: 13 students (9 boys, 4 girls); Grade 12: 16 students (14 boys, 2 girls).

Faculty School total: 7. In upper school: 5 men, 2 women; 3 have advanced degrees.

Subjects Offered Algebra, American history, ancient world history, art, athletics, basketball, Bible, character education, chemistry, Christian education, Christian ethics, Christian scripture, computer applications, computer art, computer education, computer graphics, computer literacy, computer skills, drama, drawing, earth science, electives, English, film appreciation, geometry, history, instrumental music, keyboarding, leadership, leadership and service, martial arts, mathematics, music, physical education, physics, pre-algebra, pre-college orientation, Puerto Rican history, science, sex education, Spanish, Spanish literature, theater, U.S. history, world history.

Graduation Requirements Algebra, ancient world history, biology, chemistry, Christian education, electives, English, geometry, physical education (includes health), physical science, physics, pre-college orientation, Puerto Rican history, Spanish, U.S. history, world history.

Special Academic Programs Accelerated programs; special instructional classes for students with ADD and LD.

College Admission Counseling 14 students graduated in 2011; 12 went to college, including University of Puerto Rico, Rio Piedras; University of Puerto Rico at Carolina. Other: 2 had other specific plans.

Student Life Upper grades have uniform requirement, student council, honor system. Discipline rests primarily with faculty.

Summer Programs Remediation, enrichment, advancement programs offered; session focuses on academic courses and remediation; held on campus; accepts boys and girls; open to students from other schools. 35 students usually enrolled. 2012 schedule: June 1 to June 28. Application deadline: May 31.

Tuition and Aid Day student tuition: $5900. Tuition installment plan (monthly payment plans, individually arranged payment plans). Tuition reduction for siblings, need-based scholarship grants available. In 2011–12, 5% of upper-school students received aid. Total amount of financial aid awarded in 2011–12: $5000.

Admissions Traditional secondary-level entrance grade is 9. For fall 2011, 21 students applied for upper-level admission, 19 were accepted, 19 enrolled. Psychoeducational evaluation required. Deadline for receipt of application materials: none. No application fee required. On-campus interview required.

Athletics Interscholastic: basketball (boys); intramural: basketball (b); coed interscholastic: archery, physical fitness; coed intramural: archery, fitness, physical fitness, soccer, table tennis, volleyball. 1 PE instructor.

Computers Computers are regularly used in English, graphic arts, graphic design, keyboarding, mathematics, religious studies, science, Spanish classes. Computer resources include Internet access, Internet filtering or blocking technology. Computer access in designated common areas is available to students.

Contact Mr. Lynette Montes, Registrar. 787-787-1350. Fax: 787-789-0055. E-mail: fowlersacademy@gmail.com.

FOXCROFT SCHOOL

22407 Foxhound Lane

P.O. Box 5555

Middleburg, Virginia 20118

Head of School: Mary Louise Leipheimer

General Information Girls' boarding and day college-preparatory school. Grades 9–12. Founded: 1914. Setting: rural. Nearest major city is Washington, DC. Students are housed in single-sex dormitories. 500-acre campus. 32 buildings on campus. Approved or accredited by The Association of Boarding Schools and Virginia Department of Education. Member of National Association of Independent Schools and Secondary School Admission Test Board. Endowment: $22.8 million. Total enrollment: 154. Upper school average class size: 12. Upper school faculty-student ratio: 1:7. There are 160 required school days per year for Upper School students. Upper School students typically attend 5 days per week. The average school day consists of 7 hours and 15 minutes.

Upper School Student Profile Grade 9: 32 students (32 girls); Grade 10: 44 students (44 girls); Grade 11: 40 students (40 girls); Grade 12: 38 students (38 girls). 67% of students are boarding students. 49% are state residents. 21 states are represented in upper school student body. 18% are international students. International students from China, India, Mexico, Nigeria, Republic of Korea, and Spain; 2 other countries represented in student body.

Faculty School total: 22. In upper school: 5 men, 17 women; 17 have advanced degrees; 16 reside on campus.

Subjects Offered 3-dimensional art, acting, advanced chemistry, algebra, American literature, anatomy and physiology, ancient world history, architecture, art, art history, astronomy, biology, British literature, calculus, calculus-AP, cell biology, ceramics, chemistry, chemistry-AP, choir, chorus, college counseling, community service, comparative religion, computer graphics, computer science, conceptual physics, constitutional law, creative dance, creative drama, creative writing, current events, dance, debate, digital photography, discrete mathematics, drama, drawing and design, economics, economics-AP, electives, English, English composition, English literature, English literature-AP, environmental science, European civilization, European history, European literature, expository writing, fine arts, fitness, French, French language-AP, general science, geology, geometry, grammar, health education, history, human anatomy, independent study, leadership, library, macroeconomics-AP, mathematics, microbiology, music, music theory, music theory-AP, painting, performing arts, photography, physical education, physics, piano, poetry, pottery, pre-calculus, probability and statistics, production, public speaking, SAT preparation, sculpture, senior project, social studies, Spanish, Spanish language-AP, Spanish literature, Spanish literature-AP, studio art, studio art-AP, technology, The 20th Century, trigonometry, U.S. history, U.S. history-AP, vocal ensemble, world cultures, world literature, writing, yearbook, yoga.

Graduation Requirements Arts and fine arts (art, music, dance, drama), English, foreign language, history, mathematics, physical education (includes health), science, senior thesis if student is not enrolled in AP English.

Special Academic Programs 11 Advanced Placement exams for which test preparation is offered; independent study; term-away projects; study abroad; academic accommodation for the gifted, the musically talented, and the artistically talented.

College Admission Counseling 44 students graduated in 2011; 43 went to college, including Sewanee: The University of the South; The College of William and Mary; The George Washington University; University of Mary Washington; University of Pennsylvania; Virginia Polytechnic Institute and State University. Other: 1 had other specific plans.

Student Life Upper grades have specified standards of dress, student council, honor system. Discipline rests equally with students and faculty.

Tuition and Aid Day student tuition: $35,640; 7-day tuition and room/board: $44,900. Tuition installment plan (Insured Tuition Payment Plan, Tuition Management Systems Plan (Monthly Payment Plan)). Merit scholarship grants, need-based scholarship grants, merit-based scholarship grants are offered to prosepctive 9th grade students available. In 2011–12, 25% of upper-school students received aid; total upper-school merit-scholarship money awarded: $31,000. Total amount of financial aid awarded in 2011–12: $1,200,000.

Admissions Traditional secondary-level entrance grade is 9. For fall 2011, 160 students applied for upper-level admission, 138 were accepted, 54 enrolled. SSAT or TOEFL required. Deadline for receipt of application materials: February 15. Application fee required: $50. Interview required.

Athletics Interscholastic: basketball, cross-country running, dressage, equestrian sports, field hockey, horseback riding, lacrosse, running, soccer, softball, swimming and diving, tennis, volleyball; intramural: aerobics, aerobics/dance, basketball, climbing, combined training, dance, dance team, dressage, equestrian sports, field hockey, fitness, horseback riding, modern dance, physical fitness, physical training, rock climbing, strength & conditioning, weight lifting, weight training. 3 coaches, 1 athletic trainer.

Computers Computers are regularly used in all classes. Computer resources include on-campus library services, online commercial services, Internet access, wireless campus network, Internet filtering or blocking technology. Campus intranet, student e-mail accounts, and computer access in designated common areas are available to students. The school has a published electronic and media policy.

Contact Gina B. Finn, Director of Admission and Financial Aid. 540-687-4340. Fax: 540-687-3627. E-mail: gina.finn@foxcroft.org. Web site: www.foxcroft.org.

FOX VALLEY LUTHERAN HIGH SCHOOL

5300 North Meade Street

Appleton, Wisconsin 54913-8383

Head of School: Mr. Paul Hartwig

General Information Coeducational day college-preparatory, general academic, arts, business, vocational, religious studies, and technology school, affiliated with Wisconsin Evangelical Lutheran Synod. Grades 9–12. Founded: 1953. Setting: suburban. 63-acre campus. 1 building on campus. Approved or accredited by Wisconsin Department of Education. Endowment: $2.9 million. Total enrollment: 569. Upper school average class size: 23. Upper school faculty-student ratio: 1:14. There are 180 required school days per year for Upper School students. Upper School students typically attend 5 days per week. The average school day consists of 6 hours and 30 minutes.

Upper School Student Profile Grade 9: 156 students (87 boys, 69 girls); Grade 10: 149 students (77 boys, 72 girls); Grade 11: 128 students (56 boys, 72 girls); Grade 12: 133 students (67 boys, 66 girls). 85% of students are Wisconsin Evangelical Lutheran Synod.

Faculty School total: 41. In upper school: 28 men, 13 women; 18 have advanced degrees.

Subjects Offered Accounting, advanced chemistry, advanced computer applications, advanced math, algebra, American government, American history, American literature, art, athletics, band, basic language skills, Basic programming, Bible, Bible studies, biology, British literature, British literature (honors), British literature-AP, business, business law, calculus, calculus-AP, choir, Christian doctrine, church history, communication skills, comparative religion, composition, computer applications, computer programming, computer skills, computer-aided design, concert band, concert choir, construction, critical writing, digital applications, digital photography, earth science, economics, economics-AP, English, English composition, foods, general science, geometry, German, government, graphic arts, health and wellness, honors English, keyboarding, language and composition, Latin, Life of Christ, modern Western civilization, modern world history, personal fitness, physical fitness, physics, piano, psychology, reading/study skills, religion, remedial/makeup course work, sewing, Spanish, statistics, symphonic band, woodworking, world geography, world history.

Graduation Requirements 1 1/2 elective credits, arts and fine arts (art, music, dance, drama), English, mathematics, physical education (includes health), religion (includes Bible studies and theology), science.

Special Academic Programs Honors section; accelerated programs; study at local college for college credit; academic accommodation for the gifted; remedial reading and/or remedial writing; remedial math.

College Admission Counseling 169 students graduated in 2011; 160 went to college, including Marquette University; Martin Luther College; University of Wisconsin–Fox Valley; University of Wisconsin–Oshkosh. Other: 5 went to work, 2 entered military service, 1 had other specific plans. Median composite ACT: 24.

Student Life Upper grades have specified standards of dress, student council, honor system. Discipline rests primarily with faculty. Attendance at religious services is required.

Summer Programs Remediation, advancement programs offered; session focuses on alleviate school year schedule conflicts; held on campus; accepts boys and girls. 30 students usually enrolled. 2012 schedule: June 1 to August 7. Application deadline: April 30.

Tuition and Aid Day student tuition: $4750–$7000. Tuition installment plan (FACTS Tuition Payment Plan). Tuition reduction for siblings, need-based scholarship grants available. In 2011–12, 25% of upper-school students received aid. Total amount of financial aid awarded in 2011–12: $325,000.

Admissions Traditional secondary-level entrance grade is 9. ACT-Explore or Explore required. Deadline for receipt of application materials: none. Application fee required: $25. Interview required.

Athletics Interscholastic: baseball (boys), basketball (b,g), cheering (g), cross-country running (b,g), dance team (g), football (b), golf (b,g), hockey (b,g), ice hockey (b,g), soccer (b,g), softball (g), track and field (b,g), volleyball (g), wrestling (b). 2 PE instructors, 1 athletic trainer.

Computers Computers are regularly used in business, current events, economics, English, graphic arts, keyboarding, science classes. Computer network features include on-campus library services, Internet access, Internet filtering or blocking technology. Campus intranet and student e-mail accounts are available to students. Students grades are available online. The school has a published electronic and media policy.

Contact Mrs. Gloria Knoll, Guidance Assistant. 920-739-4441. Fax: 920-739-4418. E-mail: gknoll@fvlhs.org. Web site: www.fvlhs.org.

FRANKLIN ACADEMY

East Haddam, Connecticut

See Special Needs Schools section.

FRANKLIN ROAD ACADEMY

4700 Franklin Road

Nashville, Tennessee 37220

Head of School: Dr. Margaret Wade

General Information Coeducational day college-preparatory, arts, religious studies, and technology school. Grades PK–12. Founded: 1971. Setting: suburban. 57-acre campus. 5 buildings on campus. Approved or accredited by Southern Association of Colleges and Schools, Southern Association of Independent Schools, Tennessee Association of Independent Schools, and Tennessee Department of Education. Member of National Association of Independent Schools. Endowment: $10.4 million. Total enrollment: 816. Upper school average class size: 8. Upper school faculty-student ratio: 1:8. There are 185 required school days per year for Upper School students. Upper School students typically attend 5 days per week. The average school day consists of 6 hours and 30 minutes.

Upper School Student Profile Grade 9: 60 students (30 boys, 30 girls); Grade 10: 60 students (30 boys, 30 girls); Grade 11: 60 students (30 boys, 30 girls); Grade 12: 60 students (30 boys, 30 girls).

Faculty School total: 100. In upper school: 21 men, 14 women; 20 have advanced degrees.

Subjects Offered Advanced chemistry, Advanced Placement courses, algebra, American history, American literature, anatomy and physiology, art, art-AP, band, baseball, basketball, Bible, Bible studies, biology, biology-AP, calculus, calculus-AP, chemistry, chemistry-AP, choral music, Civil War, college counseling, computer education, computer music, computer programming, computer science, current events, dance, drama, dramatic arts, economics, economics and history, electronic music, English, English language-AP, English literature, English literature-AP, environmental science, European history, European history-AP, fine arts, French, French language-AP, French literature-AP, geometry, government/civics, grammar, history, history-AP, honors algebra, honors English, honors geometry, honors U.S. history, human anatomy, jazz band, keyboarding, Latin, Latin-AP, Life of Christ, mathematics, mathematics-AP, model United Nations, music, music theory, personal development, physical education, physics, physics-AP, pottery, pre-calculus, SAT preparation, SAT/ACT preparation, science, social sciences, social studies, Spanish, Spanish language-AP, Spanish literature-AP, speech, statistics, statistics-AP, student government, student publications, technical theater, theater, theater production, track and field, trigonometry, U.S. government, U.S. history, U.S. history-AP, vocal music, volleyball, weight training, world history, world literature, wrestling, writing.

Graduation Requirements Arts and fine arts (art, music, dance, drama), computer science, English, foreign language, mathematics, physical education (includes health), religion (includes Bible studies and theology), science, social studies (includes history). Community service is required.

Special Academic Programs Advanced Placement exam preparation; honors section; independent study; term-away projects; academic accommodation for the gifted, the musically talented, and the artistically talented.

College Admission Counseling 56 students graduated in 2010; all went to college, including Auburn University; Belmont University; Middle Tennessee State University; The University of Tennessee; University of Georgia. 40% scored over 600 on SAT critical reading, 50% scored over 600 on SAT math, 50% scored over 26 on composite ACT.

Student Life Upper grades have uniform requirement, student council, honor system. Discipline rests primarily with faculty.

Tuition and Aid Day student tuition: $16,560. Tuition installment plan (Insured Tuition Payment Plan, FACTS Tuition Payment Plan, individually arranged payment plans). Need-based scholarship grants available. In 2010–11, 10% of upper-school students received aid. Total amount of financial aid awarded in 2010–11: $600,000.

Admissions Traditional secondary-level entrance grade is 9. For fall 2010, 104 students applied for upper-level admission, 65 were accepted, 23 enrolled. ISEE required. Deadline for receipt of application materials: none. Application fee required: $40. On-campus interview required.

Athletics Interscholastic: baseball (boys), basketball (b,g), bowling (b,g), cheering (g), cross-country running (b,g), dance (g), diving (b,g), football (b), golf (b,g), hockey (b), ice hockey (b), soccer (b,g), softball (g), swimming and diving (b,g), tennis (b,g), track and field (b,g), volleyball (g), wrestling (b); intramural: aerobics/dance (g), physical fitness (b,g), physical training (b,g), power lifting (b), strength & conditioning (b,g); coed intramural: aerobics/dance, riflery. 2 PE instructors, 2 coaches, 1 athletic trainer.

Computers Computers are regularly used in art, Bible studies, college planning, creative writing, economics, English, foreign language, French, history, journalism, keyboarding, Latin, library skills, literary magazine, mathematics, music, religious studies, science, social sciences, Spanish, technology, theater, theater arts, Web site design, writing, yearbook classes. Computer network features include on-campus library services, online commercial services, Internet access, wireless campus network, Internet filtering or blocking technology, networked instructional software. Campus intranet and student e-mail accounts are available to students. Students grades are available online. The school has a published electronic and media policy.

Contact Dr. Kenyetta Wynn, Director of Admissions. 615-832-8845. Fax: 615-834-4137. E-mail: wynnk@franklinroadacademy.com. Web site: www.franklinroadacademy.com.

FRASER ACADEMY

Vancouver, British Columbia, Canada

See Special Needs Schools section.

FREDERICA ACADEMY

200 Murray Way

St. Simons Island, Georgia 31522

Head of School: Ms. Ellen E. Fleming

General Information Coeducational day college-preparatory, arts, and technology school. Grades PK–12. Founded: 1970. Setting: small town. Nearest major city is Jacksonville, FL. 35-acre campus. 7 buildings on campus. Approved or accredited by Georgia Independent School Association, Southern Association of Colleges and Schools, and Georgia Department of Education. Member of National Association of Independent Schools. Endowment: $2 million. Total enrollment: 357. Upper school average class size: 18. Upper school faculty-student ratio: 1:9. There are 180 required school days per year for Upper School students. Upper School students typically attend 5 days per week. The average school day consists of 8 hours and 5 minutes.

Faculty School total: 50. In upper school: 6 men, 9 women; 10 have advanced degrees.

Subjects Offered Algebra, American history, American literature, anatomy, ancient history, art, biology, biology-AP, calculus-AP, chemistry, choral music, computer applications, drama, economics, English, English literature, environmental science, geometry, government/civics, grammar, keyboarding, literature-AP, photography, physical education, physical science, physics, pre-calculus, psychology, public speaking, science, Spanish, U.S. history-AP, world history, world literature, writing, yearbook.

Graduation Requirements Algebra, American government, American history, arts and fine arts (art, music, dance, drama), biology, chemistry, computer applications, economics, English literature, foreign language, geometry, physical education (includes health), world history.

Special Academic Programs Advanced Placement exam preparation; honors section.

College Admission Counseling 41 students graduated in 2010; all went to college, including Georgia Institute of Technology; University of Georgia. Mean SAT critical reading: 591, mean SAT math: 583, mean SAT writing: 584, mean combined SAT: 1758.

Student Life Upper grades have specified standards of dress, student council, honor system. Discipline rests primarily with faculty.

Tuition and Aid Day student tuition: $14,440. Merit scholarship grants, need-based scholarship grants, local bank financing available. In 2010–11, 30% of upper-school students received aid. Total amount of financial aid awarded in 2010–11: $300,000.

Admissions Traditional secondary-level entrance grade is 9. Any standardized test, Cognitive Abilities Test, OLSAT/Stanford and writing sample required. Deadline for receipt of application materials: none. Application fee required: $75. On-campus interview required.

Athletics Interscholastic: baseball (boys), basketball (b,g), cheering (g), cross-country running (b,g), golf (b,g), lacrosse (b), outdoor education (b,g), physical fitness (b,g), soccer (b,g), tennis (b,g), volleyball (g), weight training (b,g); coed interscholastic: cross-country running, golf, swimming and diving. 2 PE instructors, 5 coaches, 1 athletic trainer.

Computers Computers are regularly used in library skills, photography, yearbook classes. Computer network features include on-campus library services, online commercial services, Internet access, wireless campus network. Students grades are available online. The school has a published electronic and media policy.

Contact Mrs. Jennifer D. Wall, Director of Admission. 912-638-9981 Ext. 106. Fax: 912-638-1442. E-mail: jwall@fredericaacademy.org. Web site: www.fredericaacademy.org.

FREEMAN ACADEMY

748 South Main Street

PO Box 1000

Freeman, South Dakota 57029

Head of School: Ms. Pam Tieszen

General Information Coeducational boarding and day college-preparatory, arts, and religious studies school, affiliated with Mennonite Church. Boarding grades 9–12, day grades 5–12. Founded: 1900. Setting: rural. Nearest major city is Sioux Falls. Students are housed in coed dormitories and host family homes. 80-acre campus. 6 buildings on campus. Approved or accredited by Mennonite Schools Council, North Central Association of Colleges and Schools, and South Dakota Department of Education. Endowment: $378,000. Total enrollment: 69. Upper school average class size: 11. Upper school faculty-student ratio: 1:5. There are 180 required school days per year for Upper School students. Upper School students typically attend 5 days per week. The average school day consists of 8 hours.

Upper School Student Profile Grade 9: 12 students (5 boys, 7 girls); Grade 10: 9 students (6 boys, 3 girls); Grade 11: 15 students (8 boys, 7 girls); Grade 12: 9 students (3 boys, 6 girls). 13% of students are boarding students. 85% are state residents. 1 state is represented in upper school student body. 15% are international students. International students from China, Democratic People's Republic of Korea, Japan, Paraguay, and Thailand. 55% of students are Mennonite.

Faculty School total: 10. In upper school: 4 men, 6 women; 3 have advanced degrees.

Subjects Offered Computer science, English, fine arts, humanities, mathematics, music, religion, science, social sciences.

Graduation Requirements Arts and fine arts (art, music, dance, drama), computer science, English, foreign language, mathematics, religion (includes Bible studies and theology), science, social studies (includes history), humanities.

Special Academic Programs Independent study; academic accommodation for the musically talented and the artistically talented.

College Admission Counseling 16 students graduated in 2011; 15 went to college, including Bethel College; Dordt College; Goshen College; Hesston College; University of Sioux Falls. Other: 1 went to work. Median composite ACT: 25. 60% scored over 26 on composite ACT.

Student Life Upper grades have specified standards of dress, honor system. Discipline rests primarily with faculty. Attendance at religious services is required.

Tuition and Aid Day student tuition: $6135; 7-day tuition and room/board: $18,550. Tuition installment plan (FACTS Tuition Payment Plan, monthly payment plans, individually arranged payment plans, semester payment plan). Tuition reduction for siblings, merit scholarship grants, need-based scholarship grants available. In 2011–12, 13% of upper-school students received aid; total upper-school merit-scholarship money awarded: $500. Total amount of financial aid awarded in 2011–12: $24,000.

Admissions Traditional secondary-level entrance grade is 9. For fall 2011, 8 students applied for upper-level admission, 7 were accepted, 7 enrolled. Secondary Level English Proficiency required. Deadline for receipt of application materials: none. No application fee required. Interview recommended.

Athletics Interscholastic: basketball (boys, girls), cheering (g), cross-country running (b,g), golf (b,g), soccer (b,g), track and field (b,g), volleyball (g); coed interscholastic: soccer. 4 coaches.

Computers Computers are regularly used in English, keyboarding, mathematics, religion, science, social studies, speech, yearbook classes. Computer network features include on-campus library services, Internet access, wireless campus network, Internet filtering or blocking technology. Student e-mail accounts and computer access in designated common areas are available to students. Students grades are available online. The school has a published electronic and media policy.

Contact Ms. Bonnie Young, Enrollment Director. 605-925-4237 Ext. 225. Fax: 605-925-4271. E-mail: byoung@freemanacademy.org. Web site: www.freemanacademy.org.

FRENCH-AMERICAN SCHOOL OF NEW YORK

525 Fenimore Road

Mamaroneck, New York 10543

Head of School: Mr. Robert Leonhardt

General Information Coeducational day college-preparatory and bilingual studies school. Grades N–12. Founded: 1980. Setting: suburban. Nearest major city is White Plains. 1 building on campus. Approved or accredited by Middle States Association of Colleges and Schools and New York Department of Education. Languages of instruction: English and French. Total enrollment: 869. Upper school average class size: 18. Upper school faculty-student ratio: 1:7. There are 167 required school days per year for Upper School students. Upper School students typically attend 5 days per week. The average school day consists of 6 hours and 11 minutes.

Upper School Student Profile Grade 9: 59 students (24 boys, 35 girls); Grade 10: 55 students (22 boys, 33 girls); Grade 11: 44 students (17 boys, 27 girls); Grade 12: 35 students (22 boys, 13 girls).

Faculty School total: 121. In upper school: 17 men, 40 women; 33 have advanced degrees.

Subjects Offered Algebra, American history, American literature, art, biology, choir, civics, computer applications, computer multimedia, current events, earth science, ecology, economics, English, ESL, European history, expository writing, French, French language-AP, French literature-AP, French studies, geometry, German, government, health, Latin, mathematics, multimedia, music, newspaper, philosophy, physical education, physics, physics-AP, public speaking, science, social studies, Spanish, Spanish language-AP, world history, world literature, writing, yearbook.

Graduation Requirements 20th century history, algebra, American history, biology, calculus, chemistry, civics, computer studies, current events, English, European history, foreign language, French, geography, geology, geometry, mathematics, music, philosophy, physical education (includes health), physics, pre-algebra, pre-calculus, research seminar, social studies (includes history). Community service is required.

Special Academic Programs Advanced Placement exam preparation; honors section; ESL (21 students enrolled).

College Admission Counseling 25 students graduated in 2011; all went to college, including McGill University. Mean SAT critical reading: 625, mean SAT math: 641, mean SAT writing: 645.

Student Life Upper grades have specified standards of dress, student council. Discipline rests primarily with faculty.
Tuition and Aid Day student tuition: $24,200–$24,720. Tuition installment plan (Academic Management Services Plan). Need-based scholarship grants available. In 2011–12, 5% of upper-school students received aid. Total amount of financial aid awarded in 2011–12: $188,856.
Admissions Traditional secondary-level entrance grade is 9. For fall 2011, 43 students applied for upper-level admission, 17 were accepted, 15 enrolled. English, French, and math proficiency required. Deadline for receipt of application materials: none. Application fee required: $150. Interview recommended.
Athletics Interscholastic: baseball (boys), basketball (b,g), cross-country running (b,g), rugby (b,g), soccer (b,g), softball (g), tennis (b,g); coed intramural: fencing. 3 PE instructors, 3 coaches.
Computers Computers are regularly used in art, English, foreign language, French, history, mathematics, music, publications, science classes. Computer network features include on-campus library services, Internet access, Internet filtering or blocking technology, laptop use (in certain classes). Student e-mail accounts are available to students. The school has a published electronic and media policy.
Contact Mr. Antoine Agopian, Director of Admissions. 914-250-0400. Fax: 914-940-2214. E-mail: aagopian@fasny.org. Web site: www.fasny.org.

FRESNO ADVENTIST ACADEMY

5397 East Olive Avenue
Fresno, California 93727

Head of School: Pastor Daniel Kittle

General Information Coeducational day college-preparatory, general academic, arts, business, vocational, and religious studies school, affiliated with Seventh-day Adventist Church. Grades K–12. Founded: 1897. Setting: suburban. 40-acre campus. 7 buildings on campus. Approved or accredited by Board of Regents, General Conference of Seventh-day Adventists, Western Association of Schools and Colleges, and California Department of Education. Language of instruction: Spanish. Endowment: $875,000. Total enrollment: 193. Upper school average class size: 20. Upper school faculty-student ratio: 1:19. There are 147 required school days per year for Upper School students. Upper School students typically attend 4 days per week. The average school day consists of 7 hours and 35 minutes.
Upper School Student Profile Grade 9: 19 students (10 boys, 9 girls); Grade 10: 17 students (8 boys, 9 girls); Grade 11: 14 students (6 boys, 8 girls); Grade 12: 16 students (7 boys, 9 girls). 80% of students are Seventh-day Adventists.
Faculty School total: 23. In upper school: 6 men, 6 women; 7 have advanced degrees.
Subjects Offered Algebra, American government, American history, American literature, anatomy, art history, Bible, Bible studies, biology, business skills, ceramics, chemistry, choir, choral music, computer science, digital photography, economics, English, English literature, fine arts, geometry, government/civics, grammar, health, health education, history, home economics, industrial arts, keyboarding, life skills, mathematics, music, physical education, physical science, physics, physiology, pre-algebra, publications, religion, science, small engine repair, social sciences, social studies, Spanish, speech communications, typing, vocal ensemble, welding, work experience, world history.
Graduation Requirements Arts and fine arts (art, music, dance, drama), business skills (includes word processing), computer science, English, foreign language, mathematics, physical education (includes health), religion (includes Bible studies and theology), science, social sciences, social studies (includes history), work experience, service learning, work experience.
Special Academic Programs Advanced Placement exam preparation; honors section; accelerated programs; independent study; study at local college for college credit; programs in general development for dyslexic students; ESL (2 students enrolled).
College Admission Counseling 17 students graduated in 2010; 15 went to college, including Azusa Pacific University; California State University, Fresno; Fresno City College; La Sierra University; Oakwood University. Other: 2 went to work. 10% scored over 600 on SAT critical reading, 10% scored over 600 on SAT math, 10% scored over 26 on composite ACT.
Student Life Upper grades have specified standards of dress, student council, honor system. Discipline rests primarily with faculty. Attendance at religious services is required.
Tuition and Aid Day student tuition: $8000. Tuition installment plan (monthly payment plans, individually arranged payment plans). Tuition reduction for siblings, merit scholarship grants, need-based scholarship grants, paying campus jobs available. In 2010–11, 80% of upper-school students received aid. Total amount of financial aid awarded in 2010–11: $102,000.
Admissions Traditional secondary-level entrance grade is 9. For fall 2010, 14 students applied for upper-level admission, 14 were accepted, 13 enrolled. 3-R Achievement Test, ITBS achievement test, school's own exam or Test of Achievement and Proficiency required. Deadline for receipt of application materials: none. Application fee required: $25. Interview required.
Athletics Interscholastic: basketball (boys, girls), flag football (b,g), volleyball (b,g); intramural: basketball (b,g), flag football (b,g), soccer (b,g), track and field (b,g), volleyball (b,g); coed interscholastic: volleyball; coed intramural: flag football, soccer, track and field, volleyball. 1 PE instructor, 4 coaches.
Computers Computers are regularly used in art, business skills, computer applications, economics, English, foreign language, keyboarding, life skills, photography, science, yearbook classes. Computer network features include on-campus library services, Internet access, wireless campus network, Internet filtering or blocking technology. Student e-mail accounts are available to students. Students grades are available online.
Contact Mrs. Sue Schramm, Executive Assistant. 559-251-5548. Fax: 559-252-6495. E-mail: sschramm@faa.org. Web site: www.faa.org.

FRESNO CHRISTIAN SCHOOLS

7280 North Cedar Avenue
Fresno, California 93720

Head of School: Mrs. Debbie Siebert

General Information Coeducational day college-preparatory, arts, religious studies, and technology school, affiliated with Protestant-Evangelical faith. Grades K–12. Founded: 1977. Setting: suburban. 27-acre campus. 4 buildings on campus. Approved or accredited by Association of Christian Schools International, Western Association of Schools and Colleges, and California Department of Education. Endowment: $152,573. Total enrollment: 612. Upper school average class size: 28. Upper school faculty-student ratio: 1:12. There are 176 required school days per year for Upper School students. Upper School students typically attend 5 days per week. The average school day consists of 5 hours and 50 minutes.
Upper School Student Profile Grade 9: 52 students (25 boys, 27 girls); Grade 10: 45 students (25 boys, 20 girls); Grade 11: 37 students (16 boys, 21 girls); Grade 12: 52 students (29 boys, 23 girls). 86% of students are Protestant-Evangelical faith.
Faculty School total: 32. In upper school: 8 men, 8 women; 7 have advanced degrees.
Subjects Offered Advanced Placement courses, algebra, alternative physical education, American government, American history-AP, art, ASB Leadership, athletics, band, baseball, basketball, Bible, Bible studies, biology, biology-AP, British literature, calculus-AP, cheerleading, chemistry, choir, choral music, Christian education, civics, composition-AP, computer applications, computer graphics, computer literacy, concert band, drama, economics, English, English language and composition-AP, English literature and composition-AP, English-AP, ensembles, geometry, golf, home economics, honors algebra, honors English, honors geometry, humanities, jazz band, journalism, leadership, marching band, mathematics, mathematics-AP, physical education, physics, pre-calculus, softball, Spanish, sports, statistics-AP, student government, tennis, track and field, trigonometry, U.S. history, video film production, vocal music, volleyball, woodworking, work experience, world history, yearbook.
Graduation Requirements Arts and fine arts (art, music, dance, drama), electives, English, mathematics, physical education (includes health), religion (includes Bible studies and theology), science, social studies (includes history).
Special Academic Programs 5 Advanced Placement exams for which test preparation is offered; honors section; independent study; study at local college for college credit; remedial reading and/or remedial writing; remedial math; special instructional classes for students with learning disabilities.
College Admission Counseling 62 students graduated in 2011; 58 went to college, including Biola University; California State University, Fresno; Fresno City College; Harvard University; University of California, Irvine; University of Chicago. Other: 4 had other specific plans. Mean SAT critical reading: 544, mean SAT math: 546, mean SAT writing: 508, mean combined SAT: 1598.
Student Life Upper grades have specified standards of dress, student council, honor system. Discipline rests primarily with faculty. Attendance at religious services is required.
Tuition and Aid Day student tuition: $8274. Tuition installment plan (monthly payment plans, individually arranged payment plans). Tuition reduction for siblings, merit scholarship grants, need-based scholarship grants available. In 2011–12, 24% of upper-school students received aid; total upper-school merit-scholarship money awarded: $1000. Total amount of financial aid awarded in 2011–12: $218,577.
Admissions Traditional secondary-level entrance grade is 9. Stanford Achievement Test required. Deadline for receipt of application materials: none. Application fee required: $100. Interview required.
Athletics Interscholastic: baseball (boys), basketball (b,g), cheering (g), cross-country running (b,g), drill team (g), football (b), soccer (b,g), softball (g), strength & conditioning (b,g), tennis (b,g), track and field (b,g), volleyball (g), weight training (b,g); coed interscholastic: golf, physical training; coed intramural: badminton, basketball, outdoor recreation, volleyball. 2 PE instructors, 16 coaches, 1 athletic trainer.
Computers Computers are regularly used in media production, publications, yearbook classes. Computer network features include on-campus library services, online commercial services, Internet access, wireless campus network, Internet filtering or blocking technology. Computer access in designated common areas is available to students. Students grades are available online. The school has a published electronic and media policy.
Contact Mrs. Kerry Roberts, Registrar. 559-299-1695 Ext. 102. Fax: 559-299-1051. E-mail: kroberts@fresnochristian.com. Web site: www.fresnochristian.com.

FRIENDS ACADEMY

270 Duck Pond Road

Locust Valley, New York 11560

Head of School: Mr. William G. Morris Jr.

General Information Coeducational day college-preparatory school, affiliated with Society of Friends. Grades N–12. Founded: 1876. Setting: suburban. Nearest major city is New York. 65-acre campus. 8 buildings on campus. Approved or accredited by New York Department of Education. Member of National Association of Independent Schools and Secondary School Admission Test Board. Endowment: $30 million. Total enrollment: 777. Upper school average class size: 15. Upper school faculty-student ratio: 1:8. There are 165 required school days per year for Upper School students. Upper School students typically attend 5 days per week. The average school day consists of 7 hours.

Upper School Student Profile Grade 9: 93 students (56 boys, 37 girls); Grade 10: 86 students (43 boys, 43 girls); Grade 11: 99 students (57 boys, 42 girls); Grade 12: 101 students (44 boys, 57 girls). 1% of students are members of Society of Friends.

Faculty School total: 92. In upper school: 20 men, 25 women; 35 have advanced degrees.

Subjects Offered Advanced Placement courses, African studies, algebra, American history, American literature, art, art history, Bible studies, biology, calculus, ceramics, chemistry, community service, computer literacy, computer programming, computer science, creative writing, drama, driver education, English, English literature, environmental science, ethics, European history, expository writing, fine arts, French, geography, geometry, grammar, Greek, health, history, Italian, Latin, logic, mathematics, mechanical drawing, music, outdoor education, photography, physical education, physics, psychology, religion, science, social sciences, social studies, Spanish, speech, theater, trigonometry, Western civilization, world literature, writing.

Graduation Requirements Arts and fine arts (art, music, dance, drama), computer literacy, English, foreign language, mathematics, outdoor education, physical education (includes health), religion (includes Bible studies and theology), science, social sciences, social studies (includes history), speech, participation in on-campus work crew program, independent service program. Community service is required.

Special Academic Programs 18 Advanced Placement exams for which test preparation is offered; honors section; independent study; remedial reading and/or remedial writing; remedial math.

College Admission Counseling 87 students graduated in 2011; all went to college, including Barnard College; Bucknell University; Colgate University; Cornell University; Dartmouth College; Duke University.

Student Life Upper grades have specified standards of dress, student council. Discipline rests primarily with faculty. Attendance at religious services is required.

Summer Programs Art/fine arts programs offered; session focuses on arts/sports; held both on and off campus; held at off campus for golf, sailing and riding.; accepts boys and girls; open to students from other schools. 250 students usually enrolled. 2012 schedule: June 18 to July 21.

Tuition and Aid Day student tuition: $27,600. Tuition installment plan (Insured Tuition Payment Plan, monthly payment plans). Need-based scholarship grants, Quaker grants, Tuition remission for children of faculty and staff available. In 2011–12, 20% of upper-school students received aid. Total amount of financial aid awarded in 2011–12: $1,169,500.

Admissions Traditional secondary-level entrance grade is 9. For fall 2011, 123 students applied for upper-level admission, 44 were accepted, 36 enrolled. SSAT required. Deadline for receipt of application materials: January 15. Application fee required: $55. On-campus interview required.

Athletics Interscholastic: baseball (boys), basketball (b,g), crew (b,g), cross-country running (b,g), field hockey (g), football (b), golf (b,g), indoor track & field (b,g), lacrosse (b,g), soccer (b,g), softball (g), tennis (b,g), track and field (b,g), winter (indoor) track (b,g), wrestling (b); coed intramural: dance, volleyball. 8 PE instructors, 1 athletic trainer.

Computers Computers are regularly used in English, mathematics, science, technology classes. Computer network features include on-campus library services, online commercial services, Internet access, wireless campus network, Internet filtering or blocking technology, 6th Graders use an iPad in school. Campus intranet, student e-mail accounts, and computer access in designated common areas are available to students. The school has a published electronic and media policy.

Contact Joanna Kim, Admissions Assistant. 516-393-4244. Fax: 516-465-1718. E-mail: joanna_kim@fa.org. Web site: www.fa.org.

FRIENDS' CENTRAL SCHOOL

1101 City Avenue

Wynnewood, Pennsylvania 19096

Head of School: Joanne P. Hoffman

General Information Coeducational day college-preparatory school, affiliated with Society of Friends. Grades N–12. Founded: 1845. Setting: suburban. Nearest major city is Philadelphia. 23-acre campus. 7 buildings on campus. Approved or accredited by Pennsylvania Department of Education. Member of National Association of Independent Schools and Secondary School Admission Test Board. Endowment: $22 million. Total enrollment: 890. Upper school average class size: 18. Upper school faculty-student ratio: 1:8. There are 170 required school days per year for Upper School students. Upper School students typically attend 5 days per week. The average school day consists of 6 hours and 40 minutes.

Upper School Student Profile Grade 9: 91 students (45 boys, 46 girls); Grade 10: 96 students (53 boys, 43 girls); Grade 11: 106 students (51 boys, 55 girls); Grade 12: 97 students (55 boys, 42 girls). 3% of students are members of Society of Friends.

Faculty School total: 130. In upper school: 26 men, 26 women; 38 have advanced degrees.

Subjects Offered Advanced biology, advanced chemistry, advanced math, algebra, American history, American literature, Bible, biology, calculus, ceramics, chemistry, chorus, computer applications, computer programming, conflict resolution, drama, English, French, geometry, instrumental music, Latin, life skills, media studies, modern European history, music history, music theory, philosophy, photography, physical education, physical science, physics, pre-calculus, psychology, sexuality, Spanish, studio art, study skills, Western literature, women in world history, woodworking, world history, writing workshop.

Graduation Requirements Arts and fine arts (art, music, dance, drama), English, foreign language, mathematics, science, service learning/internship, U.S. history, world cultures.

Special Academic Programs Honors section; independent study; term-away projects.

College Admission Counseling 88 students graduated in 2011; 87 went to college, including Franklin & Marshall College; Indiana University Bloomington; Oberlin College; Temple University; The George Washington University; University of Pennsylvania. Other: 1 entered military service. Mean SAT critical reading: 640, mean SAT math: 629, mean SAT writing: 641.

Student Life Upper grades have specified standards of dress, student council. Discipline rests primarily with faculty. Attendance at religious services is required.

Summer Programs Remediation, advancement programs offered; held on campus; accepts boys and girls; open to students from other schools. 37 students usually enrolled. 2012 schedule: June 27 to August 5.

Tuition and Aid Day student tuition: $13,200–$27,400. Tuition installment plan (monthly payment plans, Higher Education Service, Inc). Need-based scholarship grants available. In 2011–12, 32% of upper-school students received aid. Total amount of financial aid awarded in 2011–12: $2,694,469.

Admissions Traditional secondary-level entrance grade is 9. For fall 2011, 141 students applied for upper-level admission, 68 were accepted, 26 enrolled. ISEE, SSAT or Wechsler Intelligence Scale for Children required. Deadline for receipt of application materials: January 15. Application fee required: $50. On-campus interview required.

Athletics Interscholastic: aquatics (boys, girls), baseball (b), basketball (b,g), cross-country running (b,g), field hockey (g), indoor track (b,g), lacrosse (b,g), soccer (b,g), softball (g), tennis (b,g), track and field (b,g), winter (indoor) track (b,g), wrestling (b,g); coed interscholastic: golf, squash, water polo; coed intramural: aerobics, aerobics/dance, aerobics/Nautilus, cheering, dance, fitness, flag football, life saving, table tennis. 8 PE instructors, 10 coaches, 1 athletic trainer.

Computers Computers are regularly used in college planning, foreign language, French, health, information technology, introduction to technology, Latin, mathematics, publishing, science, Spanish, technology, Web site design, yearbook classes. Computer network features include on-campus library services, online commercial services, Internet access, wireless campus network, Internet filtering or blocking technology, Intranet collaboration. Campus intranet and student e-mail accounts are available to students. The school has a published electronic and media policy.

Contact Barbara Behar, Director of Admission and Financial Aid. 610-645-5032. Fax: 610-658-5644. E-mail: admission@friendscentral.org. Web site: www.friendscentral.org.

FRIENDSHIP CHRISTIAN SCHOOL

5400 Coles Ferry Pike

Lebanon, Tennessee 37087

Head of School: Mr. Jon Shoulders

General Information Coeducational day college-preparatory, arts, business, religious studies, technology, and dual enrollment with Cumberland University school, affiliated with Christian faith. Grades PK–12. Founded: 1973. Setting: rural. Nearest major city is Nashville. 50-acre campus. 6 buildings on campus. Approved or accredited by National Christian School Association, Southern Association of Colleges and Schools, and Tennessee Department of Education. Endowment: $250. Total enrollment: 627. Upper school average class size: 20. Upper school faculty-student ratio: 1:15. There are 175 required school days per year for Upper School students. Upper School students typically attend 5 days per week. The average school day consists of 6 hours and 35 minutes.

Upper School Student Profile Grade 9: 56 students (27 boys, 29 girls); Grade 10: 50 students (23 boys, 27 girls); Grade 11: 50 students (29 boys, 21 girls); Grade 12: 47 students (20 boys, 27 girls). 80% of students are Christian faith.

Faculty School total: 50. In upper school: 9 men, 12 women; 18 have advanced degrees.

Subjects Offered Accounting, ACT preparation, advanced biology, advanced chemistry, advanced math, Advanced Placement courses, agriculture, algebra, American government, anatomy and physiology, Ancient Greek, art, athletic training, backpacking, band, Bible, Bible studies, biology, bowling, British literature (honors), business applications, calculus, calculus-AP, chemistry, choral music, chorus, college placement, college planning, computers, creative writing, drama, driver education, earth science, economics, English, English-AP, environmental science, geometry, honors algebra, honors English, honors geometry, Internet, journalism, keyboarding, mathematics, modern history, physical education, physical science, physics, physiology, pre-algebra, psychology, science project, science research, Spanish, speech, swimming, trigonometry, U.S. constitutional history, U.S. government, U.S. history, U.S. history-AP, U.S. Presidents, weight training, wellness, world geography, world history, yearbook.

Graduation Requirements ACT preparation, advanced chemistry, advanced math, Advanced Placement courses, algebra, American government, American history, American history-AP, applied arts, arts and fine arts (art, music, dance, drama), Bible, biology, chemistry, chemistry-AP, ecology, English language and composition-AP, English literature-AP, English-AP, foreign language, French, honors U.S. history, keyboarding, physical education (includes health), physics, pre-calculus, U.S. government and politics-AP, U.S. history-AP, weight training.

Special Academic Programs Advanced Placement exam preparation; honors section; study at local college for college credit.

College Admission Counseling 58 students graduated in 2010; all went to college, including Cumberland University; Lipscomb University; Tennessee Technological University; The University of Tennessee; United States Naval Academy; Vanderbilt University. Mean composite ACT: 23. 50% scored over 26 on composite ACT.

Student Life Upper grades have uniform requirement, student council, honor system. Discipline rests primarily with faculty.

Tuition and Aid Day student tuition: $7300. Tuition installment plan (FACTS Tuition Payment Plan). Tuition reduction for siblings, need-based scholarship grants, paying campus jobs available. In 2010–11, 2% of upper-school students received aid. Total amount of financial aid awarded in 2010–11: $5000.

Admissions Traditional secondary-level entrance grade is 9. For fall 2010, 163 students applied for upper-level admission, 160 were accepted, 117 enrolled. Otis-Lennon School Ability Test required. Deadline for receipt of application materials: none. Application fee required: $50. Interview recommended.

Athletics Interscholastic: baseball (boys), basketball (b,g), cheering (g), football (b), golf (b,g), physical fitness (b,g); coed interscholastic: bowling, cross-country running, golf, physical fitness. 2 PE instructors, 13 coaches, 1 athletic trainer.

Computers Computers are regularly used in accounting, all academic, business, college planning, creative writing, journalism, library, media, multimedia, newspaper, reading, remedial study skills, science, typing classes. Computer network features include on-campus library services, online commercial services, Internet access, wireless campus network, Internet filtering or blocking technology. Student e-mail accounts and computer access in designated common areas are available to students. Students grades are available online. The school has a published electronic and media policy.

Contact Terresia Williams, Director of Admissions. 615-449-1573 Ext. 207. Fax: 615-449-2769. E-mail: twilliams@friendshipchristian.org. Web site: www.friendshipchristian.org.

FRIENDS SELECT SCHOOL

17th & Benjamin Franklin Parkway

Philadelphia, Pennsylvania 19103-1284

Head of School: Rose Hagan

General Information Coeducational day college-preparatory, arts, and religious studies school, affiliated with Society of Friends. Grades PK–12. Founded: 1689. Setting: urban. 1-acre campus. 2 buildings on campus. Approved or accredited by Friends Council on Education. Member of National Association of Independent Schools and Secondary School Admission Test Board. Endowment: $8 million. Total enrollment: 536. Upper school average class size: 15. Upper school faculty-student ratio: 1:15. There are 167 required school days per year for Upper School students. Upper School students typically attend 5 days per week. The average school day consists of 6 hours and 20 minutes.

Upper School Student Profile Grade 9: 35 students (11 boys, 24 girls); Grade 10: 44 students (19 boys, 25 girls); Grade 11: 37 students (16 boys, 21 girls); Grade 12: 49 students (20 boys, 29 girls). 5% of students are members of Society of Friends.

Faculty School total: 74. In upper school: 14 men, 18 women; 27 have advanced degrees.

Subjects Offered 20th century American writers, 3-dimensional art, algebra, American history, American literature, art, art history, biology, calculus, chemistry, computer math, computer programming, computer science, creative writing, drama, drawing, earth science, ecology, economics, electronics, English, English literature, ethics, European history, expository writing, fine arts, French, geography, geology, geometry, government/civics, grammar, health, history, Italian, Latin, marine biology, mathematics, music, photography, physical education, physics, religion, science, sculpture, social studies, Spanish, statistics, theater, trigonometry, world history, world literature, writing.

Graduation Requirements Arts and fine arts (art, music, dance, drama), English, foreign language, mathematics, physical education (includes health), religion (includes Bible studies and theology), science, senior project, social studies (includes history), junior internship.

Special Academic Programs Advanced Placement exam preparation; independent study; academic accommodation for the musically talented and the artistically talented; ESL (10 students enrolled).

College Admission Counseling 38 students graduated in 2010; 37 went to college, including Arcadia University; Boston University; Drexel University; Northeastern University; The George Washington University; University of Pennsylvania. Other: 1 had other specific plans.

Student Life Upper grades have student council. Discipline rests primarily with faculty. Attendance at religious services is required.

Tuition and Aid Day student tuition: $25,825. Tuition installment plan (10-month payment plan, 2-payment plan). Tuition reduction for siblings, need-based scholarship grants, need-based loans, K-12 Family Education Loan Program (SLM Financial Group), AchieverLoans (Key Education Resources), tuition reduction for 3-plus siblings from same family; 5% reduction for children of alumni/alumnae available. In 2010–11, 43% of upper-school students received aid. Total amount of financial aid awarded in 2010–11: $888,006.

Admissions Traditional secondary-level entrance grade is 9. For fall 2010, 73 students applied for upper-level admission, 55 were accepted, 21 enrolled. ERB CTP IV, ISEE, PSAT and SAT for applicants to grade 11 and 12, SSAT or WISC or WAIS required. Deadline for receipt of application materials: none. Application fee required: $40. On-campus interview required.

Athletics Interscholastic: baseball (boys), basketball (b,g), crew (b,g), cross-country running (b,g), field hockey (g), soccer (b,g), softball (g), wrestling (b); coed interscholastic: crew, cross-country running, swimming and diving, tennis. 5 PE instructors, 28 coaches, 1 athletic trainer.

Computers Computers are regularly used in all academic, English, foreign language, mathematics, science classes. Computer network features include on-campus library services, online commercial services, Internet access, online learning center. Campus intranet, student e-mail accounts, and computer access in designated common areas are available to students. The school has a published electronic and media policy.

Contact Roger Dillow, Director of Enrollment Management and Director of Admission PK-8. 215-561-5900 Ext. 102. Fax: 215-864-2979. E-mail: rogerd@friends-select.org. Web site: friends-select.org.

FRONT RANGE CHRISTIAN HIGH SCHOOL

6637 West Ottawa Avenue

Littleton, Colorado 80128

Head of School: Dave Sherman

General Information Coeducational day college-preparatory, general academic, arts, business, vocational, religious studies, bilingual studies, technology, and science, math, language arts, media school, affiliated with Christian faith. Grades PK–12. Founded: 1994. Setting: suburban. Nearest major city is Denver. 20-acre campus. 3 buildings on campus. Approved or accredited by Association of Christian Schools International, North Central Association of Colleges and Schools, and Colorado Department of Education. Total enrollment: 391. Upper school average class size: 25. Upper school faculty-student ratio: 1:12.

Upper School Student Profile Grade 9: 47 students (22 boys, 25 girls); Grade 10: 42 students (16 boys, 26 girls); Grade 11: 34 students (17 boys, 17 girls); Grade 12: 46 students (25 boys, 21 girls). 100% of students are Christian faith.

Faculty School total: 41. In upper school: 9 men, 11 women; 10 have advanced degrees.

Subjects Offered ACT preparation, acting, advanced biology, advanced chemistry, advanced math, Advanced Placement courses, algebra, American history, American literature, anatomy and physiology, ancient world history, art, athletics, band, baseball, basketball, Bible, biology, British literature, calculus, career/college preparation, cheerleading, chemistry, choir, Christian doctrine, Christian scripture, composition, composition-AP, dance, drama, drama performance, earth science, electives, foreign language, forensics, geometry, golf, grammar, guitar, health education, home economics, junior and senior seminars, lab science, language arts, leadership and service, Life of Christ, music, musical productions, participation in sports, performing arts, photography, photojournalism, physical education, physical fitness, physics, pre-calculus, psychology, Spanish, speech, sports, statistics, trigonometry, video film production, vocal ensemble, volleyball, yearbook.

Special Academic Programs Advanced Placement exam preparation; honors section; academic accommodation for the gifted; remedial reading and/or remedial writing; remedial math; programs in English, mathematics, general development for dyslexic students; special instructional classes for deaf students, blind students.

College Admission Counseling 36 students graduated in 2011; 31 went to college, including Arapahoe Community College; Colorado State University; University of Northern Colorado. Other: 2 went to work, 1 entered military service, 2 had other specific plans.

Student Life Upper grades have specified standards of dress, student council, honor system. Discipline rests primarily with faculty. Attendance at religious services is required.

Tuition and Aid Day student tuition: $7950. Tuition installment plan (FACTS Tuition Payment Plan, monthly payment plans). Need-based scholarship grants, paying campus jobs available. In 2011–12, 100% of upper-school students received aid. Total amount of financial aid awarded in 2011–12: $180,000.

Admissions Traditional secondary-level entrance grade is 9. For fall 2011, 12 students applied for upper-level admission, 8 were accepted, 6 enrolled. English proficiency, essay or Math Placement Exam required. Deadline for receipt of application materials: none. Application fee required: $50. Interview required.

Athletics Interscholastic: baseball (boys), basketball (b,g), cheering (g), dance (b,g), football (b), golf (b), physical fitness (b,g), soccer (g), volleyball (g); intramural: basketball (b,g), soccer (b), volleyball (g); coed interscholastic: cross-country running; coed intramural: mountain biking. 1 PE instructor, 28 coaches.

Computers Computers are regularly used in basic skills, computer applications, data processing, introduction to technology, media arts, multimedia, yearbook classes. Computer network features include on-campus library services, Internet access, wireless campus network, Internet filtering or blocking technology, Renweb Parents access, 2nd semester of 2011/2012 year: 1-to-1 iPads. Computer access in designated common areas is available to students. Students grades are available online. The school has a published electronic and media policy.

Contact Sara Ogdon, Admissions Coordinator. 303-531-4541. Fax: 720-922-3296. E-mail: admissions@frcs.org. Web site: www.frcs.org.

THE FROSTIG SCHOOL

Pasadena, California

See Special Needs Schools section.

FUQUA SCHOOL

605 Fuqua Drive

PO Drawer 328

Farmville, Virginia 23901

Head of School: Ms. Ruth S. Murphy

General Information Coeducational day college-preparatory, arts, and business school. Grades PK–12. Founded: 1959. Setting: small town. Nearest major city is Richmond. 60-acre campus. 19 buildings on campus. Approved or accredited by Southern Association of Colleges and Schools and Virginia Department of Education. Member of Secondary School Admission Test Board. Endowment: $5.1 million. Total enrollment: 431. Upper school average class size: 16. Upper school faculty-student ratio: 1:16. There are 180 required school days per year for Upper School students. Upper School students typically attend 5 days per week. The average school day consists of 6 hours.

Upper School Student Profile Grade 9: 37 students (16 boys, 21 girls); Grade 10: 36 students (20 boys, 16 girls); Grade 11: 32 students (19 boys, 13 girls); Grade 12: 40 students (18 boys, 22 girls).

Faculty School total: 42. In upper school: 7 men, 12 women; 6 have advanced degrees.

Subjects Offered Agriculture, algebra, art, band, biology-AP, calculus-AP, chemistry, chemistry-AP, communications, composition, computer information systems, driver education, economics, English composition, English literature-AP, English-AP, environmental science, environmental studies, ethics, fitness, general business, geometry, government-AP, grammar, health, history-AP, industrial technology, personal finance, physics, pre-calculus, psychology, Spanish, theater, U.S. government, U.S. history-AP, United States government-AP, weight training, yearbook, zoology.

Graduation Requirements Arts and fine arts (art, music, dance, drama), communications, composition, computer information systems, driver education, English, fitness, foreign language, grammar, health education, mathematics, physical education (includes health), science, social studies (includes history). Community service is required.

Special Academic Programs Advanced Placement exam preparation; honors section; accelerated programs; independent study; study at local college for college credit.

College Admission Counseling 41 students graduated in 2011; all went to college, including James Madison University; Longwood University; Lynchburg College; University of Virginia; Virginia Polytechnic Institute and State University; Washington and Lee University. Median SAT critical reading: 570, median SAT math: 540, median SAT writing: 550, median composite ACT: 26. 42% scored over 600 on SAT critical reading, 41% scored over 600 on SAT math, 40% scored over 600 on SAT writing, 57% scored over 26 on composite ACT.

Student Life Upper grades have specified standards of dress, student council, honor system. Discipline rests primarily with faculty.

Summer Programs Enrichment, sports, art/fine arts programs offered; session focuses on sports and sport skills, arts, enrichment; held on campus; accepts boys and girls; open to students from other schools. 75 students usually enrolled. 2012 schedule: June 15 to July 31. Application deadline: May 15.

Tuition and Aid Day student tuition: $7325. Tuition installment plan (The Tuition Plan, Insured Tuition Payment Plan, monthly payment plans, individually arranged payment plans). Tuition reduction for siblings, merit scholarship grants, need-based scholarship grants available. In 2011–12, 44% of upper-school students received aid; total upper-school merit-scholarship money awarded: $7000. Total amount of financial aid awarded in 2011–12: $44,000.

Admissions Traditional secondary-level entrance grade is 9. For fall 2011, 9 students applied for upper-level admission, 9 were accepted, 9 enrolled. Placement test required. Deadline for receipt of application materials: none. Application fee required: $100. On-campus interview required.

Athletics Interscholastic: baseball (boys), basketball (b,g), cheering (g), football (b), softball (g), tennis (g), volleyball (g); intramural: lacrosse (b); coed interscholastic: cross-country running, golf, soccer, swimming and diving, track and field; coed intramural: basketball. 2 PE instructors, 38 coaches, 1 athletic trainer.

Computers Computer network features include on-campus library services, online commercial services, Internet access, wireless campus network, Internet filtering or blocking technology, video editing software, CD-ROM +RW and DVD +RW. Student e-mail accounts and computer access in designated common areas are available to students. The school has a published electronic and media policy.

Contact Mrs. Christy M. Murphy, Director of Admissions and Development. 434-392-4131 Ext. 273. Fax: 434-392-5062. E-mail: murphycm@fuquaschool.com. Web site: www.fuquaschool.com.

GABRIEL RICHARD HIGH SCHOOL

15325 Pennsylvania Road

Riverview, Michigan 48193

Head of School: Mr. Joseph J. Whalen

General Information Coeducational day college-preparatory school, affiliated with Roman Catholic Church. Grades 9–12. Founded: 1965. Setting: suburban. Nearest major city is Detroit. 23-acre campus. 1 building on campus. Approved or accredited by North Central Association of Colleges and Schools and Michigan Department of Education. Total enrollment: 334. Upper school average class size: 20. Upper school faculty-student ratio: 1:14. There are 180 required school days per year for Upper School students. Upper School students typically attend 5 days per week. The average school day consists of 6 hours and 35 minutes.

Upper School Student Profile Grade 9: 69 students (34 boys, 35 girls); Grade 10: 87 students (42 boys, 45 girls); Grade 11: 90 students (32 boys, 58 girls); Grade 12: 88 students (49 boys, 39 girls); Postgraduate: 334 students (157 boys, 177 girls). 90% of students are Roman Catholic.

Faculty School total: 24. In upper school: 6 men, 18 women; 13 have advanced degrees.

Subjects Offered 1 1/2 elective credits, 20th century American writers, 20th century history, 20th century world history, accounting, acting, advanced chemistry, advanced math, Advanced Placement courses, advanced studio art-AP, algebra, American Civil War, American democracy, American government, American history, American history-AP, American literature, American literature-AP, anatomy, anatomy and physiology, ancient history, ancient world history, animal science, art, band, basic language skills, biology, biology-AP, British literature (honors), business law, calculus, calculus-AP, campus ministry, Catholic belief and practice, ceramics, chemistry, chemistry-AP, Christian doctrine, Christian education, Christian scripture, Christian testament, Christianity, church history, Civil War, civil war history, clayworking, college planning, communications, comparative politics, comparative religion, constitutional history of U.S., constitutional law, digital art, digital photography, drama, drawing, earth science, economics, English literature, English-AP, environmental science, European history-AP, family living, foods, forensics, French, general business, general math, general science, geography, geometry, government, government-AP, health, history, history of the Catholic Church, history-AP, home economics, honors algebra, honors English, human anatomy, humanities, instrumental music, lab science, library assistant, logic, New Testament, participation in sports, peace and justice, peer ministry, photography, physical fitness, physics, physics-AP, portfolio art, pre-algebra, psychology-AP, publications, research, senior composition, sociology, Spanish, speech, sports, studio art-AP, theater arts, U.S. government and politics-AP, U.S. history, U.S. history-AP, United States government-AP, weight fitness, weight training, yearbook, zoology.

Graduation Requirements Arts and fine arts (art, music, dance, drama), English, mathematics, physical education (includes health), science, social studies (includes history), speech, theology.

Special Academic Programs Advanced Placement exam preparation; honors section; independent study.

College Admission Counseling 103 students graduated in 2011; all went to college, including Central Michigan University; Grand Valley State University; Michigan State University; University of Michigan; University of Michigan–Dearborn; Wayne State University. Median composite ACT: 24. 32% scored over 26 on composite ACT.

Student Life Upper grades have uniform requirement, student council, honor system. Discipline rests primarily with faculty. Attendance at religious services is required.

Tuition and Aid Tuition installment plan (The Tuition Plan, Academic Management Services Plan). Tuition reduction for siblings, merit scholarship grants, need-based scholarship grants available.
Admissions Traditional secondary-level entrance grade is 9. For fall 2011, 85 students applied for upper-level admission, 85 were accepted, 85 enrolled. High School Placement Test required. Deadline for receipt of application materials: none. Application fee required: $100. Interview required.
Athletics Interscholastic: baseball (boys), basketball (b,g), cheering (g), cross-country running (b,g), football (b), ice hockey (b), pom squad (g), soccer (b,g), softball (g), tennis (b,g), track and field (b,g), volleyball (g), wrestling (b); coed interscholastic: bowling, equestrian sports, figure skating, golf. 1 PE instructor.
Computers Computers are regularly used in digital applications, research skills, speech classes. Computer network features include on-campus library services, Internet access, Internet filtering or blocking technology. Computer access in designated common areas is available to students. Students grades are available online.
Contact Mr. Joseph J. Whalen, Principal. 734-284-1875. Fax: 734-284-9304. E-mail: whalenj@gabrielrichard.org. Web site: www.gabrielrichard.org.

THE GALLOWAY SCHOOL

215 West Wieuca Road NW

Atlanta, Georgia 30342

Head of School: Dr. Beth Farokhi

General Information Coeducational day college-preparatory, arts, and technology school. Grades PK–12. Founded: 1969. Setting: suburban. 8-acre campus. 4 buildings on campus. Approved or accredited by Academy of Orton-Gillingham Practitioners and Educators, Georgia Independent School Association, Southern Association of Colleges and Schools, Southern Association of Independent Schools, and Georgia Department of Education. Member of National Association of Independent Schools and Secondary School Admission Test Board. Endowment: $5 million. Total enrollment: 724. Upper school average class size: 12. Upper school faculty-student ratio: 1:8.
Subjects Offered 3-dimensional design, advanced computer applications, Advanced Placement courses, algebra, American culture, American history, American literature, analytic geometry, animation, biology, biology-AP, British literature, calculus, calculus-AP, chemistry, computer animation, computer applications, computer graphics, desktop publishing, digital art, digital music, digital photography, drama, economics, electives, English, English-AP, filmmaking, fine arts, French, geometry, guidance, history, integrated physics, language arts, Latin, library, mathematics, music, physical education, physical science, political science, pre-calculus, public speaking, science, senior composition, social studies, Spanish, technology, U.S. government and politics-AP, visual arts, world geography, world history, world literature.
Graduation Requirements Arts and fine arts (art, music, dance, drama), computers, electives, English, foreign language, mathematics, science, social studies (includes history).
Special Academic Programs Advanced Placement exam preparation; accelerated programs; independent study; study at local college for college credit; academic accommodation for the gifted, the musically talented, and the artistically talented.
College Admission Counseling 58 students graduated in 2011; all went to college, including Emory University; Emory University, Oxford College; Georgia Institute of Technology; University of Georgia.
Student Life Upper grades have student council, honor system. Discipline rests primarily with faculty.
Summer Programs Remediation, enrichment, advancement, sports programs offered; held both on and off campus; held at sports camps; accepts boys and girls; open to students from other schools. 55 students usually enrolled. 2012 schedule: June 16 to July 25. Application deadline: June 6.
Tuition and Aid Day student tuition: $18,430. Tuition installment plan (50/50). Need-based scholarship grants available. In 2011–12, 14% of upper-school students received aid. Total amount of financial aid awarded in 2011–12: $312,130.
Admissions Traditional secondary-level entrance grade is 9. SSAT required. Deadline for receipt of application materials: January 29. Application fee required: $75. Interview required.
Athletics Interscholastic: basketball (boys, girls), golf (b,g), soccer (b,g), softball (g), swimming and diving (b,g), tennis (b,g), volleyball (g); intramural: dance team (g); coed interscholastic: cross-country running, outdoor adventure, running, track and field, ultimate Frisbee. 1 PE instructor, 4 coaches, 1 athletic trainer.
Computers Computers are regularly used in art, desktop publishing, drawing and design, English, graphic arts, information technology, introduction to technology, journalism, keyboarding, literary magazine, mathematics, multimedia, music, newspaper, photography, publishing, research skills, science, technology, theater, Web site design, yearbook classes. Computer network features include on-campus library services, online commercial services, Internet access, wireless campus network, Internet filtering or blocking technology, print sharing. Campus intranet, student e-mail accounts, and computer access in designated common areas are available to students. Students grades are available online. The school has a published electronic and media policy.
Contact Polly Williams, Director of Admissions. 404-252-8389. Fax: 404-252-7770. E-mail: pwilliams@gallowayschool.org. Web site: www.gallowayschool.org.

GANN ACADEMY (THE NEW JEWISH HIGH SCHOOL OF GREATER BOSTON)

333 Forest Street

Waltham, Massachusetts 02452

Head of School: Rabbi Marc A. Baker

General Information Coeducational day college-preparatory, arts, and religious studies school, affiliated with Jewish faith. Grades 9–12. Founded: 1997. Setting: suburban. Nearest major city is Boston. 20-acre campus. 2 buildings on campus. Approved or accredited by New England Association of Schools and Colleges and Massachusetts Department of Education. Total enrollment: 331. Upper school average class size: 14. Upper school faculty-student ratio: 1:5. There are 165 required school days per year for Upper School students. Upper School students typically attend 5 days per week. The average school day consists of 8 hours.
Upper School Student Profile Grade 9: 89 students (37 boys, 52 girls); Grade 10: 93 students (45 boys, 48 girls); Grade 11: 65 students (29 boys, 36 girls); Grade 12: 84 students (39 boys, 45 girls). 100% of students are Jewish.
Faculty School total: 73. In upper school: 28 men, 45 women; 52 have advanced degrees.
Subjects Offered Advanced Placement courses, algebra, American history-AP, American literature-AP, art history, arts, Bible as literature, biology, calculus, calculus-AP, chemistry, creative arts, creative writing, drama, English, French, geometry, health and wellness, Hebrew, history, Jewish history, Judaic studies, Mandarin, music, photography, physics, pre-calculus, Rabbinic literature, Spanish.
Graduation Requirements Arts, athletics, Bible as literature, English, health, Hebrew, history, mathematics, Rabbinic literature, science, Jewish Thought, electives.
Special Academic Programs Advanced Placement exam preparation; study abroad.
College Admission Counseling 82 students graduated in 2011; 80 went to college, including Brandeis University; Emory University; The George Washington University; University of Maryland, Baltimore County; University of Massachusetts Amherst; University of Rochester. Other: 1 went to work, 1 had other specific plans. Median SAT critical reading: 640, median SAT math: 640, median SAT writing: 650, median combined SAT: 1965, median composite ACT: 27.
Student Life Upper grades have specified standards of dress, student council, honor system. Discipline rests primarily with faculty. Attendance at religious services is required.
Tuition and Aid Day student tuition: $30,750. Tuition installment plan (FACTS Tuition Payment Plan). Need-based scholarship grants available. In 2011–12, 39% of upper-school students received aid.
Admissions Traditional secondary-level entrance grade is 9. For fall 2011, 159 students applied for upper-level admission, 137 were accepted, 98 enrolled. SSAT required. Deadline for receipt of application materials: January 31. Application fee required: $100. On-campus interview required.
Athletics Interscholastic: baseball (boys), basketball (b,g), cross-country running (b,g), lacrosse (b,g), soccer (b,g), softball (g), tennis (b,g); intramural: basketball (b,g), tennis (b,g); coed interscholastic: juggling, ultimate Frisbee; coed intramural: fitness, golf, modern dance, table tennis, yoga. 26 coaches, 1 athletic trainer.
Computers Computer network features include on-campus library services, Internet access, wireless campus network, Internet filtering or blocking technology, computer lab. Student e-mail accounts and computer access in designated common areas are available to students. Students grades are available online. The school has a published electronic and media policy.
Contact Efraim Yudewitz, Director of Admissions. 781-642-6800 Ext. 101. Fax: 781-642-6805. E-mail: eyudewitz@gannacademy.org. Web site: www.gannacademy.org/.

GARCES MEMORIAL HIGH SCHOOL

2800 Loma Linda Drive

Bakersfield, California 93305

Head of School: Mrs. Kathleen B. Bears

General Information Coeducational day college-preparatory school, affiliated with Roman Catholic Church. Grades 9–12. Founded: 1947. Setting: suburban. Nearest major city is Los Angeles. 32-acre campus. 16 buildings on campus. Approved or accredited by Western Association of Schools and Colleges and Western Catholic Education Association. Endowment: $460,000. Total enrollment: 622. Upper school average class size: 25. Upper school faculty-student ratio: 1:28. There are 180 required school days per year for Upper School students. Upper School students typically attend 5 days per week. The average school day consists of 6 hours.
Upper School Student Profile Grade 9: 169 students (86 boys, 83 girls); Grade 10: 139 students (68 boys, 71 girls); Grade 11: 150 students (75 boys, 75 girls); Grade 12: 164 students (80 boys, 84 girls). 75% of students are Roman Catholic.
Faculty School total: 41. In upper school: 20 men, 21 women; 24 have advanced degrees.
Subjects Offered Algebra, American history, American literature, anatomy, art, biology, calculus, chemistry, community service, computer science, creative writing, drama, driver education, economics, English, English literature, ethics, fine arts, French, geography, geometry, government/civics, graphic arts, health, history, jour-

nalism, mathematics, music, physical education, physics, physiology, psychology, religion, science, social studies, Spanish, theater, world history, world literature.

Graduation Requirements Arts and fine arts (art, music, dance, drama), computer literacy, English, foreign language, health education, mathematics, physical education (includes health), religion (includes Bible studies and theology), science, social studies (includes history), 60 hours of community service.

Special Academic Programs Advanced Placement exam preparation; honors section; study at local college for college credit.

College Admission Counseling 149 students graduated in 2011; all went to college, including Bakersfield College; California Polytechnic State University, San Luis Obispo; California State University, Bakersfield; Texas Christian University; University of California, Santa Barbara; University of California, Santa Cruz. Mean SAT critical reading: 538, mean SAT math: 525, mean SAT writing: 529, mean composite ACT: 24. 15.3% scored over 600 on SAT critical reading, 16.9% scored over 600 on SAT math.

Student Life Upper grades have uniform requirement, student council. Discipline rests primarily with faculty. Attendance at religious services is required.

Summer Programs Remediation, enrichment, advancement, sports, art/fine arts, computer instruction programs offered; session focuses on mathematics and English; held on campus; accepts boys and girls; open to students from other schools. 800 students usually enrolled. 2012 schedule: June 4 to July 6. Application deadline: May 6.

Tuition and Aid Day student tuition: $7500–$8500. Tuition installment plan (monthly payment plans, individually arranged payment plans). Merit scholarship grants, need-based scholarship grants available. In 2011–12, 32% of upper-school students received aid; total upper-school merit-scholarship money awarded: $9035. Total amount of financial aid awarded in 2011–12: $312,000.

Admissions Traditional secondary-level entrance grade is 9. For fall 2011, 185 students applied for upper-level admission, 175 were accepted, 162 enrolled. CTBS/4 required. Deadline for receipt of application materials: January 31. Application fee required: $75. Interview required.

Athletics Interscholastic: baseball (boys), basketball (b,g), cheering (g), cross-country running (b,g), dance squad (g), dance team (g), diving (b,g), football (b), golf (b,g), soccer (b,g), softball (g), swimming and diving (b,g), tennis (b,g), track and field (b,g), volleyball (g), water polo (b,g), weight training (b); intramural: baseball (b), basketball (b,g), volleyball (b,g); coed intramural: basketball, volleyball. 3 PE instructors, 28 coaches, 1 athletic trainer.

Computers Computers are regularly used in graphic arts, journalism, keyboarding classes. Computer resources include Internet access.

Contact Mrs. Joan M. Richardson, Registrar. 661-327-2578 Ext. 109. Fax: 661-327-5427. E-mail: jrichardson@garces.org. Web site: www.garces.org.

GARRISON FOREST SCHOOL

300 Garrison Forest Road

Owings Mills, Maryland 21117

Head of School: Mr. G. Peter O'Neill Jr.

General Information Girls' boarding and day (coeducational in lower grades) college-preparatory, arts, and Women in Science & Engineering (WISE) school. Boarding girls grades 8–12, day boys grades N–K, day girls grades N–12. Founded: 1910. Setting: suburban. Nearest major city is Baltimore. Students are housed in single-sex dormitories. 110-acre campus. 18 buildings on campus. Approved or accredited by Association of Independent Maryland Schools, Middle States Association of Colleges and Schools, The Association of Boarding Schools, and Maryland Department of Education. Member of National Association of Independent Schools and Secondary School Admission Test Board. Endowment: $30 million. Total enrollment: 671. Upper school average class size: 14. Upper school faculty-student ratio: 1:7. The average school day consists of 6 hours and 45 minutes.

Upper School Student Profile Grade 6: 44 students (44 girls); Grade 7: 45 students (45 girls); Grade 8: 59 students (59 girls); Grade 9: 79 students (79 girls); Grade 10: 75 students (75 girls); Grade 11: 69 students (69 girls); Grade 12: 66 students (66 girls). 22% of students are boarding students. 7 states are represented in upper school student body. 12% are international students. International students from Bahamas, China, Mauritius, Mexico, Republic of Korea, and Taiwan.

Faculty School total: 104. In upper school: 6 men, 36 women; 39 have advanced degrees; 20 reside on campus.

Subjects Offered Algebra, American history, American literature, anatomy, animal behavior, art, art history, art history-AP, arts and crafts, biology, calculus, calculus-AP, ceramics, chemistry, chemistry-AP, child development, Chinese, Chinese studies, computer science, computer skills, creative writing, dance, decision making skills, design, drama, drawing, ecology, English, English literature, English-AP, ESL, ethics, fine arts, French, French-AP, geometry, history-AP, Latin, Latin-AP, life skills, mathematics, music, philosophy, photography, physical education, physics, physics-AP, portfolio art, science, Spanish, Spanish-AP, statistics, theater, trigonometry, U.S. history-AP, world history.

Graduation Requirements Arts and fine arts (art, music, dance, drama), decision making skills, English, foreign language, mathematics, physical education (includes health), science, social studies (includes history).

Special Academic Programs 11 Advanced Placement exams for which test preparation is offered; honors section; independent study; term-away projects; academic accommodation for the gifted, the musically talented, and the artistically talented; ESL (8 students enrolled).

College Admission Counseling 67 students graduated in 2010; all went to college, including Clemson University; Rensselaer Polytechnic Institute; University of Maryland, College Park; University of Vermont; University of Virginia; Washington and Lee University. 50% scored over 600 on SAT critical reading, 50% scored over 600 on SAT math, 50% scored over 600 on SAT writing.

Student Life Upper grades have uniform requirement, student council, honor system. Discipline rests equally with students and faculty.

Tuition and Aid Day student tuition: $23,350; 7-day tuition and room/board: $42,160. Tuition installment plan (FACTS Tuition Payment Plan). Need-based scholarship grants, need-based loans available. In 2010–11, 32% of upper-school students received aid. Total amount of financial aid awarded in 2010–11: $1,377,360.

Admissions Traditional secondary-level entrance grade is 9. For fall 2010, 119 students applied for upper-level admission, 74 were accepted, 40 enrolled. ISEE or SSAT required. Deadline for receipt of application materials: January 7. Application fee required: $50. Interview required.

Athletics Interscholastic: badminton, basketball, cross-country running, equestrian sports, field hockey, golf, horseback riding, indoor soccer, lacrosse, polo, soccer, softball, tennis, track and field, winter soccer; intramural: aerobics, aerobics/dance, bowling, dance, fitness, horseback riding, modern dance, physical fitness, squash, strength & conditioning, swimming and diving, yoga. 5 PE instructors, 12 coaches, 1 athletic trainer.

Computers Computers are regularly used in art, English, foreign language, history, mathematics, science classes. Computer network features include on-campus library services, Internet access, wireless campus network, Internet filtering or blocking technology, Moodle. Student e-mail accounts are available to students. The school has a published electronic and media policy.

Contact Mrs. Leslie D. Tinati, Director of Admission and Financial Aid. 410-559-3111. Fax: 410-363-8441. E-mail: gfsinfo@gfs.org. Web site: www.gfs.org.

GASTON DAY SCHOOL

2001 Gaston Day School Road

Gastonia, North Carolina 28056

Head of School: Dr. Richard E. Rankin

General Information Coeducational day college-preparatory and arts school. Grades PS–12. Founded: 1967. Setting: suburban. Nearest major city is Charlotte. 60-acre campus. 4 buildings on campus. Approved or accredited by Southern Association of Colleges and Schools, Southern Association of Independent Schools, and North Carolina Department of Education. Member of National Association of Independent Schools. Endowment: $2.1 million. Total enrollment: 503. Upper school average class size: 12. Upper school faculty-student ratio: 1:6. There are 180 required school days per year for Upper School students. Upper School students typically attend 5 days per week. The average school day consists of 7 hours and 15 minutes.

Upper School Student Profile Grade 9: 38 students (17 boys, 21 girls); Grade 10: 41 students (22 boys, 19 girls); Grade 11: 32 students (11 boys, 21 girls); Grade 12: 32 students (15 boys, 17 girls).

Faculty School total: 50. In upper school: 6 men, 17 women; 10 have advanced degrees.

Subjects Offered Advanced chemistry, Advanced Placement courses, advanced studio art-AP, algebra, American history-AP, American literature, anatomy and physiology, art, biology, biology-AP, British literature, British literature (honors), calculus-AP, chemistry, chemistry-AP, chorus, creative writing, drama, English language and composition-AP, English language-AP, English literature and composition-AP, environmental science, environmental science-AP, film and literature, fine arts, French, general science, geometry, government/civics, honors algebra, honors English, honors geometry, honors U.S. history, honors world history, jazz band, journalism, learning lab, physics, pre-calculus, senior internship, Spanish, Spanish-AP, statistics-AP, student government, studio art-AP, study skills, U.S. government, U.S. history, U.S. history-AP, United States government-AP, visual arts, weight training, world literature, yearbook.

Graduation Requirements Arts and fine arts (art, music, dance, drama), electives, English, foreign language, mathematics, physical education (includes health), science, social studies (includes history), 25 hours of community service per year, seniors must complete a senior project.

Special Academic Programs Advanced Placement exam preparation; honors section; independent study; academic accommodation for the gifted.

College Admission Counseling 40 students graduated in 2011; all went to college, including Appalachian State University; Auburn University; North Carolina State University; Princeton University; The University of North Carolina at Chapel Hill; Virginia Polytechnic Institute and State University. Mean SAT critical reading: 603, mean SAT math: 606, mean SAT writing: 613.

Student Life Upper grades have specified standards of dress, student council, honor system. Discipline rests primarily with faculty.

Summer Programs Remediation, enrichment, advancement, sports, art/fine arts programs offered; session focuses on academic enrichment, advancement in sports and arts; held on campus; accepts boys and girls; open to students from other schools. 200 students usually enrolled. 2012 schedule: June to August.

Tuition and Aid Day student tuition: $13,140. Tuition installment plan (monthly payment plans, individually arranged payment plans). Merit scholarship grants, need-based scholarship grants available. In 2011–12, 60% of upper-school students received aid; total upper-school merit-scholarship money awarded: $119,300. Total amount of financial aid awarded in 2011–12: $469,262.

Admissions Traditional secondary-level entrance grade is 9. For fall 2011, 26 students applied for upper-level admission, 20 were accepted, 14 enrolled. ISEE required. Deadline for receipt of application materials: none. Application fee required: $50. On-campus interview required.

Athletics Interscholastic: baseball (boys), basketball (b,g), cheering (g), cross-country running (b,g), soccer (b,g), softball (g), swimming and diving (b,g), tennis (b,g), track and field (b,g), volleyball (g); intramural: cooperative games (g), fitness (b,g), physical fitness (b,g), physical training (b,g), strength & conditioning (b,g), ultimate Frisbee (b,g), weight lifting (b,g), weight training (b,g); coed interscholastic: golf. 1 PE instructor, 25 coaches, 1 athletic trainer.

Computers Computers are regularly used in art, English, foreign language, history, journalism, mathematics, newspaper, science, yearbook classes. Computer network features include on-campus library services, online commercial services, Internet access, Internet filtering or blocking technology. Computer access in designated common areas is available to students. Students grades are available online.

Contact Mrs. Martha Jayne Rhyne, Director of Admission. 704-864-7744 Ext. 174. Fax: 704-865-3813. E-mail: mrhyne@gastonday.org. Web site: www.gastonday.org.

GATEWAY SCHOOL

Arlington, Texas

See Special Needs Schools section.

GEM STATE ACADEMY

16115 Montana Avenue

Caldwell, Idaho 83607

Head of School: Peter McPherson

General Information Coeducational boarding and day and distance learning college-preparatory, arts, religious studies, and technology school, affiliated with Seventh-day Adventist Church. Grades 9–12. Distance learning grade 9. Founded: 1918. Setting: rural. Nearest major city is Boise. Students are housed in single-sex dormitories. 4 buildings on campus. Approved or accredited by Northwest Association of Schools and Colleges and Idaho Department of Education. Total enrollment: 104. Upper school average class size: 24. Upper school faculty-student ratio: 1:9. There are 175 required school days per year for Upper School students. Upper School students typically attend 5 days per week. The average school day consists of 6 hours.

Upper School Student Profile Grade 9: 21 students (5 boys, 16 girls); Grade 10: 25 students (11 boys, 14 girls); Grade 11: 29 students (15 boys, 14 girls); Grade 12: 29 students (15 boys, 14 girls). 45% of students are boarding students. 84% are state residents. 7 states are represented in upper school student body. 1% are international students. International students from China. 95% of students are Seventh-day Adventists.

Faculty School total: 12. In upper school: 9 men, 3 women; 6 have advanced degrees; 2 reside on campus.

Subjects Offered Advanced computer applications, algebra, art, bell choir, Bible studies, biology, calculus-AP, chemistry, chorus, computer applications, consumer mathematics, economics, English, general science, geometry, graphic arts, gymnastics, health, Internet, keyboarding, music history, music theory, physical education, physics, piano, pre-algebra, pre-calculus, Spanish, speech, U.S. government, U.S. history, voice, work experience, world history, yearbook.

Graduation Requirements Arts and fine arts (art, music, dance, drama), computer education, economics, English, foreign language, humanities, mathematics, physical education (includes health), religion (includes Bible studies and theology), science, social studies (includes history), speech, U.S. government, U.S. history, senior project.

Special Academic Programs Advanced Placement exam preparation; study at local college for college credit.

College Admission Counseling 42 students graduated in 2010; 38 went to college, including Boise State University; Pacific Union College; Southern Adventist University; Walla Walla University.

Student Life Upper grades have specified standards of dress, student council, honor system. Discipline rests primarily with faculty. Attendance at religious services is required.

Tuition and Aid Day student tuition: $9244; 5-day tuition and room/board: $13,078; 7-day tuition and room/board: $14,612. Tuition installment plan (FACTS Tuition Payment Plan, monthly payment plans, individually arranged payment plans). Tuition reduction for siblings, merit scholarship grants, need-based scholarship grants, paying campus jobs available.

Admissions Traditional secondary-level entrance grade is 9. TOEFL or SLEP required. Deadline for receipt of application materials: none. No application fee required. Interview required.

Athletics Interscholastic: basketball (boys, girls), flag football (b), volleyball (g); intramural: basketball (b,g), flag football (b,g), floor hockey (b,g), soccer (b,g), softball (b,g); coed intramural: gymnastics, softball. 1 PE instructor, 1 coach.

Computers Computers are regularly used in all academic, art, business education, English, graphic arts, health, history, science, typing, writing classes. Computer network features include on-campus library services, online commercial services, Internet access, Internet filtering or blocking technology. Student e-mail accounts are available to students. Students grades are available online. The school has a published electronic and media policy.

Contact Karen Davies, Registrar. 208-459-1627. Fax: 208-454-9079. E-mail: kdavies@gemstate.org. Web site: www.gemstate.org.

THE GENEVA SCHOOL

2025 State Road 436

Winter Park, Florida 32792

Head of School: Rev. Robert Forrest Ingram

General Information Coeducational day college-preparatory, arts, and religious studies school, affiliated with Christian faith. Grades K4–12. Founded: 1993. Setting: suburban. Nearest major city is Orlando. 3-acre campus. 1 building on campus. Approved or accredited by Florida Council of Independent Schools. Total enrollment: 454. Upper school average class size: 18. Upper school faculty-student ratio: 1:9. There are 174 required school days per year for Upper School students. Upper School students typically attend 5 days per week. The average school day consists of 6 hours and 45 minutes.

Upper School Student Profile 95% of students are Christian faith.

Faculty School total: 53. In upper school: 17 men, 12 women; 19 have advanced degrees.

Subjects Offered Advanced Placement courses, advanced studio art-AP, aesthetics, algebra, American government, anatomy and physiology, Ancient Greek, ancient world history, art, Bible, biology, British literature (honors), calculus, calculus-AP, chemistry, chemistry-AP, choir, choral music, Christian ethics, classical Greek literature, classics, comparative religion, critical thinking, critical writing, debate, drama, earth science, economics, English language and composition-AP, English literature and composition-AP, ethics, European history, foreign language, French, French-AP, history, honors algebra, honors English, honors geometry, honors U.S. history, honors world history, independent study, instrumental music, Irish literature, journalism, Latin, life management skills, mathematics, medieval literature, music appreciation, oral communications, philosophy, photography, photojournalism, physical education, physical fitness, physical science, physics, physics-AP, pre-algebra, pre-calculus, reading/study skills, rhetoric, science, senior thesis, Shakespeare, Spanish, speech and debate, studio art-AP, theater, theater arts, trigonometry, U.S. history, U.S. history-AP, world history, yearbook.

Graduation Requirements Arts and fine arts (art, music, dance, drama), athletics, Bible, electives, English, foreign language, history, mathematics, rhetoric, science, classics.

Special Academic Programs 12 Advanced Placement exams for which test preparation is offered; honors section; independent study; study at local college for college credit; academic accommodation for the gifted, the musically talented, and the artistically talented.

College Admission Counseling 10 students graduated in 2011; 9 went to college, including Auburn University; Furman University; Rollins College; The University of Alabama; University of Central Florida; University of Florida. Other: 1 had other specific plans. Median SAT critical reading: 625, median SAT math: 581, median SAT writing: 593, median combined SAT: 1830, median composite ACT: 26.

Student Life Upper grades have uniform requirement, student council, honor system. Discipline rests primarily with faculty. Attendance at religious services is required.

Summer Programs Enrichment, sports, art/fine arts programs offered; session focuses on sports, arts, discovery; held on campus; accepts boys and girls; open to students from other schools. 200 students usually enrolled. 2012 schedule: June 1 to August 1. Application deadline: May 20.

Tuition and Aid Day student tuition: $11,590. Tuition installment plan (The Tuition Plan, monthly payment plans). Need-based scholarship grants available. In 2011–12, 30% of upper-school students received aid.

Admissions Traditional secondary-level entrance grade is 9. For fall 2011, 64 students applied for upper-level admission, 25 were accepted, 24 enrolled. ISEE required. Deadline for receipt of application materials: none. Application fee required: $100. Interview required.

Athletics Interscholastic: baseball (boys), basketball (b,g), cross-country running (b,g), flag football (b), soccer (b,g), softball (g), tennis (b,g), volleyball (g); coed interscholastic: golf. 3 PE instructors, 10 coaches, 1 athletic trainer.

Computers Computers are regularly used in all academic, college planning, journalism, photography, yearbook classes. Computer network features include on-campus library services, Internet access, wireless campus network, Internet filtering or blocking

technology. Students grades are available online. The school has a published electronic and media policy.
Contact Mrs. Patti Rader, Director of Admission. 407-332-6363 Ext. 204. Fax: 407-332-1664. E-mail: pnrader@genevaschool.org. Web site: www.genevaschool.org.

GEORGE SCHOOL

1690 Newtown Langhorne Road

PO Box 4460

Newtown, Pennsylvania 18940

Head of School: Nancy O. Starmer

General Information Coeducational boarding and day college-preparatory, arts, religious studies, bilingual studies, and technology school, affiliated with Society of Friends. Grades 9–12. Founded: 1893. Setting: suburban. Nearest major city is Philadelphia. Students are housed in single-sex dormitories. 265-acre campus. 19 buildings on campus. Approved or accredited by Friends Council on Education, International Baccalaureate Organization, Middle States Association of Colleges and Schools, Pennsylvania Association of Independent Schools, The Association of Boarding Schools, The College Board, and Pennsylvania Department of Education. Member of National Association of Independent Schools and Secondary School Admission Test Board. Endowment: $7 million. Total enrollment: 539. Upper school average class size: 14. Upper school faculty-student ratio: 1:7. Upper School students typically attend 5 days per week. The average school day consists of 6 hours.

Upper School Student Profile Grade 9: 112 students (51 boys, 61 girls); Grade 10: 144 students (72 boys, 72 girls); Grade 11: 143 students (71 boys, 72 girls); Grade 12: 140 students (66 boys, 74 girls). 53% of students are boarding students. 21 states are represented in upper school student body. International students from China, Hong Kong, Japan, Republic of Korea, Taiwan, and United Kingdom; 31 other countries represented in student body. 13% of students are members of Society of Friends.

Faculty School total: 82. In upper school: 54 have advanced degrees; 49 reside on campus.

Subjects Offered African-American history, algebra, American history-AP, American literature, American literature-AP, art, Asian history, astronomy, athletics, Bible studies, biology, biology-AP, calculus, calculus-AP, ceramics, chemistry, chemistry-AP, Chinese, community service, composition, computer science, dance, drama, drawing, driver education, English, English literature, English literature and composition-AP, English literature-AP, English-AP, environmental science, ESL, fine arts, French, French language-AP, geometry, global studies, health, history-AP, horticulture, Latin, Latin American history, life science, literature, mathematics, Middle Eastern history, modern dance, modern European history, music theory, orchestra, painting, philosophy, photography, physical education, physics, pre-calculus, probability and statistics, religion, Russian history, science, science and technology, Spanish, Spanish language-AP, stagecraft, statistics-AP, theater, theory of knowledge, video film production, visual arts, vocal ensemble, woodworking, work camp program, world history, world literature.

Graduation Requirements Arts and fine arts (art, music, dance, drama), English, foreign language, geometry, mathematics, performing arts, religion (includes Bible studies and theology), science, social studies (includes history), 65 hours of community service.

Special Academic Programs International Baccalaureate program; Advanced Placement exam preparation; honors section; independent study; ESL.

College Admission Counseling 124 students graduated in 2010; 120 went to college, including American University; Boston University; Connecticut College; McGill University; New York University; The George Washington University. Other: 1 entered military service, 3 had other specific plans.

Student Life Upper grades have specified standards of dress, student council, honor system. Discipline rests equally with students and faculty. Attendance at religious services is required.

Tuition and Aid Day student tuition: $30,850; 7-day tuition and room/board: $42,920. Tuition installment plan (monthly payment plans, individually arranged payment plans). Merit scholarship grants, need-based scholarship grants available. In 2010–11, 47% of upper-school students received aid; total upper-school merit-scholarship money awarded: $230,000. Total amount of financial aid awarded in 2010–11: $6,100,000.

Admissions Traditional secondary-level entrance grade is 9. For fall 2010, 538 students applied for upper-level admission, 261 were accepted, 148 enrolled. SSAT or TOEFL or SLEP required. Deadline for receipt of application materials: February 15. Application fee required: $50. Interview required.

Athletics Interscholastic: baseball (boys), basketball (b,g), cross-country running (b,g), field hockey (g), football (b), lacrosse (b,g), soccer (b,g), softball (g), swimming and diving (b,g), tennis (b,g), track and field (b,g), volleyball (g), wrestling (b,g); coed interscholastic: cheering, equestrian sports, golf, horseback riding, winter (indoor) track; coed intramural: aerobics/dance, aquatics, dance, horseback riding. 5 PE instructors, 5 coaches, 1 athletic trainer.

Computers Computers are regularly used in English, ESL, foreign language, history, mathematics, newspaper, photography, science, yearbook classes. Computer network features include on-campus library services, online commercial services, Internet access, wireless campus network, Internet filtering or blocking technology. Campus intranet and student e-mail accounts are available to students. The school has a published electronic and media policy.

Contact Christian Donovan, Director of Admission. 215-579-6547. Fax: 215-579-6549. E-mail: admission@georgeschool.org. Web site: www.georgeschool.org.

GEORGE STEVENS ACADEMY

23 Union Street

Blue Hill, Maine 04614

Head of School: Mr. Paul Perkinson

General Information Coeducational boarding and day college-preparatory, general academic, arts, vocational, and technology school. Grades 9–12. Founded: 1803. Setting: small town. Nearest major city is Bangor. Students are housed in single-sex dormitories and host family homes. 20-acre campus. 6 buildings on campus. Approved or accredited by Independent Schools of Northern New England, New England Association of Schools and Colleges, The College Board, and Maine Department of Education. Member of Secondary School Admission Test Board. Endowment: $7 million. Total enrollment: 304. Upper school average class size: 15. Upper school faculty-student ratio: 1:10. There are 180 required school days per year for Upper School students. Upper School students typically attend 5 days per week. The average school day consists of 6 hours and 30 minutes.

Upper School Student Profile Grade 9: 87 students (45 boys, 42 girls); Grade 10: 67 students (41 boys, 26 girls); Grade 11: 83 students (42 boys, 41 girls); Grade 12: 67 students (22 boys, 45 girls). 12% of students are boarding students. 87% are state residents. 2 states are represented in upper school student body. 13% are international students. International students from China, Ecuador, Germany, Japan, Panama, and Republic of Korea; 1 other country represented in student body.

Faculty School total: 34. In upper school: 17 men, 17 women; 18 have advanced degrees; 2 reside on campus.

Subjects Offered 20th century history, 3-dimensional design, advanced chemistry, advanced math, Advanced Placement courses, algebra, American literature, American literature-AP, art, art history, art-AP, arts and crafts, band, biology, British literature (honors), business mathematics, calculus-AP, carpentry, chamber groups, chemistry, computer applications, computer literacy, creative writing, critical thinking, desktop publishing, developmental language skills, drafting, drawing, driver education, earth science, electives, English, English-AP, environmental science, environmental science-AP, ESL, European history, fine arts, foreign language, forensics, French, general math, general science, geometry, German, health education, history, history-AP, honors algebra, honors English, honors geometry, honors U.S. history, human geography - AP, humanities, independent study, industrial arts, industrial technology, instrumental music, internship, jazz band, jazz ensemble, lab science, languages, Latin, literature, literature-AP, marine science, mathematics, mathematics-AP, mechanics, model United Nations, modern history, modern languages, modern problems, music, music theory, musical productions, mythology, personal fitness, photo shop, photography, physical education, physics, pre-algebra, pre-calculus, printmaking, psychology, reading/study skills, remedial study skills, science, senior project, shop, small engine repair, social issues, social sciences, Spanish, speech and debate, sports, statistics-AP, street law, student government, technology/design, TOEFL preparation, transportation technology, U.S. history, U.S. history-AP, Western civilization, wilderness education, woodworking, work-study, World-Wide-Web publishing, writing.

Graduation Requirements Arts and fine arts (art, music, dance, drama), electives, English, foreign language, history, mathematics, physical education (includes health), science, social sciences, U.S. history, senior debate.

Special Academic Programs Advanced Placement exam preparation; honors section; accelerated programs; independent study; term-away projects; academic accommodation for the gifted, the musically talented, and the artistically talented; remedial reading and/or remedial writing; remedial math; ESL (24 students enrolled).

College Admission Counseling 82 students graduated in 2011; 74 went to college, including College of the Atlantic; Husson University; Maine Maritime Academy; University of Maine; University of Southern Maine; Wellesley College. Other: 6 went to work, 2 entered military service. Median SAT critical reading: 540, median SAT math: 505, median SAT writing: 525, median combined SAT: 1570.

Student Life Upper grades have student council. Discipline rests primarily with faculty.

Summer Programs Remediation, enrichment, ESL, sports, art/fine arts programs offered; session focuses on ESL; held on campus; accepts boys and girls; open to students from other schools. 15 students usually enrolled. 2012 schedule: August 1 to August 26. Application deadline: May 15.

Tuition and Aid 7-day tuition and room/board: $35,000. Tuition installment plan (monthly payment plans, individually arranged payment plans). Need-based scholarship grants available. In 2011–12, 1% of upper-school students received aid.

Admissions Traditional secondary-level entrance grade is 9. International English Language Test, SSAT or TOEFL or SLEP required. Deadline for receipt of application materials: March 1. Application fee required: $75. Interview required.

Athletics Interscholastic: baseball (boys), basketball (b,g), cheering (b,g), cross-country running (b,g), golf (b,g), independent competitive sports (b,g), indoor track & field (b,g), running (b,g), sailing (b,g), soccer (b,g), softball (g), swimming and diving (b,g), tennis (b,g), track and field (b,g), winter (indoor) track (b,g), wrestling (b,g); coed intramural: backpacking, canoeing/kayaking, croquet, dance, dance team, fitness walking, flag football, floor hockey, Frisbee, hiking/backpacking, jogging, kayaking, modern dance, ocean paddling, outdoor activities, outdoor adventure, outdoor education, outdoor recreation, outdoor skills, physical fitness, physical training, skateboarding, skiing (cross-country), skiing (downhill), snowboarding, snowshoeing, table tennis, ultimate Frisbee, volleyball, walking, weight training, wilderness, yoga. 2 PE instructors, 26 coaches.

Computers Computers are regularly used in all academic, business skills, computer applications, creative writing, design, desktop publishing, drafting, English, foreign language, graphic design, photography, Web site design classes. Computer network features include on-campus library services, online commercial services, Internet access, wireless campus network, Internet filtering or blocking technology. Student e-mail accounts and computer access in designated common areas are available to students. Students grades are available online. The school has a published electronic and media policy.

Contact Ms. Libby Irwin, Director of Admissions. 207-374-2808 Ext. 134. Fax: 207-374-2982. E-mail: l.irwin@georgestevens.org. Web site: www.georgestevensacademy.org.

GEORGETOWN PREPARATORY SCHOOL

10900 Rockville Pike

North Bethesda, Maryland 20852-3299

Head of School: Mr. Jeff Jones

General Information Boys' boarding and day college-preparatory, arts, religious studies, and technology school, affiliated with Roman Catholic Church. Grades 9–12. Founded: 1789. Setting: suburban. Nearest major city is Washington, DC. Students are housed in single-sex dormitories. 92-acre campus. 8 buildings on campus. Approved or accredited by Jesuit Secondary Education Association, Middle States Association of Colleges and Schools, National Catholic Education Association, The Association of Boarding Schools, and Maryland Department of Education. Member of National Association of Independent Schools and Secondary School Admission Test Board. Endowment: $20 million. Total enrollment: 484. Upper school average class size: 16. Upper school faculty-student ratio: 1:8. Upper School students typically attend 5 days per week. The average school day consists of 6 hours and 30 minutes.

Upper School Student Profile Grade 9: 125 students (125 boys); Grade 10: 125 students (125 boys); Grade 11: 117 students (117 boys); Grade 12: 117 students (117 boys). 20% of students are boarding students. 60% are state residents. 17 states are represented in upper school student body. 30% are international students. International students from China, Indonesia, Mexico, Republic of Korea, Saudi Arabia, and Taiwan; 27 other countries represented in student body. 70% of students are Roman Catholic.

Faculty School total: 58. In upper school: 36 men, 22 women; 50 have advanced degrees; 18 reside on campus.

Subjects Offered Algebra, American history, American literature, art, art history, Bible studies, biology, calculus, chemistry, computer programming, computer science, drama, driver education, economics, English, English literature, ESL, ethics, European history, fine arts, French, geometry, German, government/civics, history, journalism, Latin, mathematics, music, philosophy, physical education, physics, psychology, religion, science, social studies, Spanish, speech, stained glass, theater, theology, trigonometry, world history, world literature.

Graduation Requirements Arts and fine arts (art, music, dance, drama), classics, English, foreign language, mathematics, music theory, religion (includes Bible studies and theology), science, social studies (includes history), two years of Latin. Community service is required.

Special Academic Programs 24 Advanced Placement exams for which test preparation is offered; honors section; independent study; term-away projects; study abroad; academic accommodation for the gifted; ESL (14 students enrolled).

College Admission Counseling 116 students graduated in 2011; all went to college, including Boston College; Georgetown University; Stanford University; University of Notre Dame; University of Pennsylvania; University of Virginia. Mean SAT critical reading: 620, mean SAT math: 643, mean SAT writing: 637, mean combined SAT: 1900, mean composite ACT: 27.

Student Life Upper grades have specified standards of dress, student council. Discipline rests primarily with faculty. Attendance at religious services is required.

Summer Programs Remediation, enrichment, advancement, ESL, sports programs offered; session focuses on ESL; held on campus; accepts boys and girls; open to students from other schools. 75 students usually enrolled. 2012 schedule: June 28 to August 6. Application deadline: March 1.

Tuition and Aid Day student tuition: $26,935; 7-day tuition and room/board: $46,020. Tuition installment plan (FACTS Tuition Payment Plan). Need-based scholarship grants, middle-income loans available. In 2011–12, 25% of upper-school students received aid. Total amount of financial aid awarded in 2011–12: $2,000,000.

Admissions Traditional secondary-level entrance grade is 9. For fall 2011, 392 students applied for upper-level admission, 170 were accepted, 135 enrolled. SSAT required. Deadline for receipt of application materials: January 16. Application fee required: $100. Interview required.

Athletics Interscholastic: baseball, basketball, cross-country running, diving, fencing, football, golf, ice hockey, indoor soccer, indoor track & field, lacrosse, rugby, running, soccer, swimming and diving, tennis, track and field, winter (indoor) track, wrestling; intramural: basketball, canoeing/kayaking, fitness, flag football, floor hockey, Frisbee, hiking/backpacking, ice skating, indoor hockey, kayaking, life saving, martial arts, mountain biking, Nautilus, ocean paddling, paddle tennis, paint ball, physical fitness, physical training, power lifting, racquetball, rappelling, rock climbing, ropes courses, scuba diving, skiing (downhill), snowboarding, soccer, softball, strength & conditioning, table tennis, tennis, ultimate Frisbee, volleyball, weight training. 16 coaches, 3 athletic trainers.

Computers Computers are regularly used in art, classics, data processing, English, French, history, Latin, mathematics, music, religious studies, science, Spanish, writing classes. Computer network features include on-campus library services, online commercial services, Internet access, wireless campus network, Internet filtering or blocking technology. Campus intranet, student e-mail accounts, and computer access in designated common areas are available to students. Students grades are available online. The school has a published electronic and media policy.

Contact Mr. Brian J. Gilbert, Dean of Admissions. 301-214-1215. Fax: 301-493-6128. E-mail: admissions@gprep.org. Web site: www.gprep.org.

GEORGETOWN VISITATION PREPARATORY SCHOOL

1524 35th Street NW

Washington, District of Columbia 20007

Head of School: Daniel M. Kerns Jr.

General Information Girls' day college-preparatory school, affiliated with Roman Catholic Church. Grades 9–12. Founded: 1799. Setting: urban. 23-acre campus. 7 buildings on campus. Approved or accredited by Association of Independent Schools of Greater Washington, Middle States Association of Colleges and Schools, National Independent Private Schools Association, and District of Columbia Department of Education. Member of National Association of Independent Schools. Endowment: $16.7 million. Total enrollment: 484. Upper school average class size: 15. Upper school faculty-student ratio: 1:10. There are 181 required school days per year for Upper School students. Upper School students typically attend 5 days per week. The average school day consists of 5 hours and 30 minutes.

Upper School Student Profile Grade 9: 124 students (124 girls); Grade 10: 117 students (117 girls); Grade 11: 121 students (121 girls); Grade 12: 122 students (122 girls). 93% of students are Roman Catholic.

Faculty School total: 54. In upper school: 12 men, 42 women; 39 have advanced degrees.

Subjects Offered Advanced Placement courses, advanced studio art-AP, algebra, American history, American literature, anthropology, art, art history, art history-AP, Bible studies, biology, biology-AP, calculus, calculus-AP, chemistry, comparative political systems-AP, computer programming, computer science, creative writing, dance, English, English language and composition-AP, English literature, English literature and composition-AP, environmental science, environmental science-AP, ethics, European history, European history-AP, expository writing, fine arts, French, French-AP, geography, geometry, government-AP, government/civics, health, history, Latin, mathematics, music, philosophy, physical education, physics, psychology, psychology-AP, religion, science, social sciences, social studies, Spanish, speech, theology, trigonometry, U.S. government and politics-AP, U.S. history-AP, world history.

Graduation Requirements Arts and fine arts (art, music, dance, drama), English, foreign language, mathematics, physical education (includes health), religion (includes Bible studies and theology), science, social sciences, social studies (includes history), 80 hours of community service.

Special Academic Programs Advanced Placement exam preparation; honors section; independent study; study at local college for college credit.

College Admission Counseling 122 students graduated in 2010; all went to college, including Boston College; Georgetown University; Princeton University; University of Notre Dame; University of Virginia. Mean SAT critical reading: 651, mean SAT math: 626.

Student Life Upper grades have uniform requirement, student council, honor system. Discipline rests primarily with faculty. Attendance at religious services is required.

Tuition and Aid Day student tuition: $22,500. Tuition installment plan (FACTS Tuition Payment Plan, individually arranged payment plans). Merit scholarship grants, need-based scholarship grants available. In 2010–11, 25% of upper-school students received aid; total upper-school merit-scholarship money awarded: $55,000. Total amount of financial aid awarded in 2010–11: $1,250,000.

Admissions Traditional secondary-level entrance grade is 9. For fall 2010, 430 students applied for upper-level admission, 160 were accepted, 126 enrolled. High School Placement Test or High School Placement Test (closed version) from Scholastic Testing Service required. Deadline for receipt of application materials: December 4. Application fee required: $50. On-campus interview required.

Athletics Interscholastic: basketball, crew, cross-country running, dance, diving, field hockey, fitness, indoor track, lacrosse, soccer, softball, swimming and diving, tennis, track and field, volleyball; intramural: cheering, flag football, strength & conditioning. 4 PE instructors, 23 coaches, 1 athletic trainer.

Computers Computers are regularly used in art, English, French, history, mathematics, religion, science, Spanish classes. Computer network features include on-campus library services, online commercial services, Internet access, wireless campus network, Internet filtering or blocking technology. Student e-mail accounts are available to students.

Contact Janet Keller, Director of Admissions. 202-337-3350 Ext. 2241. Fax: 202-333-3522. E-mail: jkeller@visi.org. Web site: www.visi.org.

GEORGE WALTON ACADEMY

One Bulldog Drive

Monroe, Georgia 30655

Head of School: William M. Nicholson

General Information Coeducational day college-preparatory, arts, and technology school. Grades K4–12. Founded: 1969. Setting: small town. Nearest major city is Atlanta. 54-acre campus. 8 buildings on campus. Approved or accredited by Georgia Independent School Association, Southern Association of Colleges and Schools, and Georgia Department of Education. Total enrollment: 945. Upper school average class size: 17. Upper school faculty-student ratio: 1:12. There are 180 required school days per year for Upper School students. Upper School students typically attend 5 days per week. The average school day consists of 6 hours and 45 minutes.

Upper School Student Profile Grade 9: 81 students (38 boys, 43 girls); Grade 10: 82 students (41 boys, 41 girls); Grade 11: 80 students (38 boys, 42 girls); Grade 12: 97 students (55 boys, 42 girls).

Faculty School total: 83. In upper school: 15 men, 38 women; 20 have advanced degrees.

Subjects Offered Algebra, American history, American literature, anatomy, art, art history, Bible studies, biology, calculus, chemistry, creative writing, drama, economics, English, English literature, environmental science, European history, fine arts, geography, geometry, government/civics, grammar, health, history, journalism, Latin, mathematics, music, photography, physical education, physics, psychology, science, social sciences, social studies, sociology, Spanish, trigonometry, world history, world literature, writing.

Graduation Requirements Arts and fine arts (art, music, dance, drama), composition, English, foreign language, mathematics, physical education (includes health), science, social sciences, social studies (includes history), all students must be accepted to a college or university to graduate.

Special Academic Programs 11 Advanced Placement exams for which test preparation is offered; honors section; academic accommodation for the musically talented and the artistically talented.

College Admission Counseling 80 students graduated in 2011; all went to college, including Georgia College & State University; Georgia Institute of Technology; Georgia Southern University; Georgia State University; North Georgia College & State University; University of Georgia.

Student Life Upper grades have uniform requirement, student council, honor system. Discipline rests primarily with faculty.

Summer Programs Enrichment, sports, art/fine arts programs offered; session focuses on academic and athletic enrichment; held on campus; accepts boys and girls; open to students from other schools. 500 students usually enrolled. 2012 schedule: May 29 to August 3.

Tuition and Aid Day student tuition: $8300. Tuition installment plan (monthly payment plans). Tuition reduction for siblings, need-based scholarship grants available. In 2011–12, 1% of upper-school students received aid.

Admissions Traditional secondary-level entrance grade is 9. ACT, CAT 5, CTBS, Stanford Achievement Test, any other standardized test, Otis-Lennon, Stanford Achievement Test, PSAT or SAT required. Deadline for receipt of application materials: none. Application fee required: $150. On-campus interview recommended.

Athletics Interscholastic: aquatics (boys, girls), baseball (b), basketball (b,g), cheering (g), cross-country running (b,g), dance squad (g), drill team (g), football (b), golf (b), physical fitness (b,g), soccer (b,g), softball (g), swimming and diving (b,g), tennis (b,g), track and field (b,g), volleyball (g), weight lifting (b), weight training (b,g), wrestling (b). 3 PE instructors, 8 coaches.

Computers Computers are regularly used in all academic classes. Computer network features include on-campus library services, Internet access, wireless campus network, Internet filtering or blocking technology. Computer access in designated common areas is available to students. Students grades are available online. The school has a published electronic and media policy.

Contact Ms. Chris Stancil, Director of Admissions. 770-207-5172 Ext. 234. Fax: 770-267-4023. E-mail: cstancil@gwa.com. Web site: www.gwa.com.

GERMANTOWN FRIENDS SCHOOL

31 West Coulter Street

Philadelphia, Pennsylvania 19144

Head of School: Richard L. Wade

General Information Coeducational day college-preparatory, arts, and technology school, affiliated with Society of Friends. Grades K–12. Founded: 1845. Setting: urban. 21-acre campus. 21 buildings on campus. Approved or accredited by Friends Council on Education, Middle States Association of Colleges and Schools, National Independent Private Schools Association, and Pennsylvania Association of Independent Schools. Member of National Association of Independent Schools and Secondary School Admission Test Board. Endowment: $24 million. Total enrollment: 855. Upper school average class size: 18. Upper school faculty-student ratio: 1:9. There are 172 required school days per year for Upper School students. Upper School students typically attend 5 days per week. The average school day consists of 6 hours and 25 minutes.

Upper School Student Profile Grade 9: 96 students (44 boys, 52 girls); Grade 10: 93 students (42 boys, 51 girls); Grade 11: 83 students (49 boys, 34 girls); Grade 12: 76 students (37 boys, 39 girls). 6.8% of students are members of Society of Friends.

Faculty School total: 135. In upper school: 28 men, 30 women; 39 have advanced degrees.

Subjects Offered 3-dimensional art, advanced chemistry, advanced math, algebra, American history, ancient history, art, art history, biology, calculus, chemistry, choir, chorus, comparative cultures, computer applications, computer programming, creative writing, drama, dramatic arts, drawing, English, environmental education, environmental science, European history, French, geometry, graphic arts, Greek, health, human sexuality, independent study, instrumental music, jazz ensemble, Latin, Latin History, madrigals, mathematics, music, music theory, orchestra, painting, philosophy, photography, physical education, physics, pre-calculus, science, social studies, Spanish, sports, stagecraft, statistics, studio art, theater, trigonometry, vocal music.

Graduation Requirements English, foreign language, history, lab science, mathematics, music, physical education (includes health), month-long off-campus independent project.

Special Academic Programs Honors section; independent study; term-away projects; domestic exchange program (with The Network Program Schools, The Catlin Gabel School); study abroad; academic accommodation for the gifted, the musically talented, and the artistically talented; ESL (3 students enrolled).

College Admission Counseling 90 students graduated in 2011; all went to college, including Brown University; Stanford University; University of Pennsylvania; University of Pittsburgh; Vanderbilt University; Wesleyan University. Mean SAT critical reading: 676, mean SAT math: 649, mean SAT writing: 674. 83% scored over 600 on SAT critical reading, 81% scored over 600 on SAT math, 84% scored over 600 on SAT writing.

Student Life Upper grades have student council. Discipline rests primarily with faculty. Attendance at religious services is required.

Summer Programs Enrichment programs offered; session focuses on partnership of public and private school, studying water as both environmental and social justice issues; held both on and off campus; held at various locations around Philadelphia; accepts boys and girls; open to students from other schools. 36 students usually enrolled. 2012 schedule: June 25 to August 3. Application deadline: March 1.

Tuition and Aid Day student tuition: $26,000–$27,500. Tuition installment plan (Academic Management Services Plan, Key Tuition Payment Plan, individually arranged payment plans). Need-based scholarship grants, need-based loans available. In 2011–12, 27% of upper-school students received aid. Total amount of financial aid awarded in 2011–12: $855,950.

Admissions Traditional secondary-level entrance grade is 9. For fall 2011, 103 students applied for upper-level admission, 46 were accepted, 24 enrolled. ISEE or SSAT required. Deadline for receipt of application materials: December 9. Application fee required: $40. On-campus interview required.

Athletics Interscholastic: baseball (boys), basketball (b,g), cross-country running (b,g), field hockey (g), indoor soccer (b,g), indoor track & field (b,g), lacrosse (g), soccer (b,g), softball (g), squash (b,g), tennis (b,g), track and field (b,g), wrestling (b); coed intramural: physical training, strength & conditioning, weight training. 5 PE instructors, 37 coaches, 1 athletic trainer.

Computers Computers are regularly used in art, English, foreign language, history, mathematics, music, photography, publications, science classes. Computer network features include on-campus library services, online commercial services, Internet access, wireless campus network, Internet filtering or blocking technology. Campus intranet, student e-mail accounts, and computer access in designated common areas are available to students.

Contact Laura Sharpless Myran, Director, Admissions and Financial Aid. 215-951-2346. Fax: 215-951-2370. E-mail: lauram@gfsnet.org. Web site: www.germantownfriends.org.

GILL ST. BERNARD'S SCHOOL

PO Box 604

St. Bernard's Road

Gladstone, New Jersey 07934

Head of School: Mr. S.A. Rowell

General Information Coeducational day college-preparatory school. Grades PK–12. Founded: 1900. Setting: small town. Nearest major city is New York, NY. 72-acre campus. 15 buildings on campus. Approved or accredited by Middle States Association of Colleges and Schools and New Jersey Association of Independent Schools. Member of National Association of Independent Schools and Secondary School Admission Test Board. Endowment: $7 million. Total enrollment: 695. Upper school average class size: 16. Upper school faculty-student ratio: 1:15. There are 175 required school days per year for Upper School students. Upper School students typically attend 5 days per week. The average school day consists of 7 hours.

Faculty School total: 99. In upper school: 22 men, 24 women; 27 have advanced degrees.

Subjects Offered 20th century world history, 3-dimensional art, advanced chemistry, advanced computer applications, advanced math, Advanced Placement courses, algebra, American democracy, American history, American history-AP, American literature, analysis and differential calculus, analytic geometry, art, astronomy, biology, biology-AP, British literature, British literature (honors), calculus, calculus-AP, chemistry, chemistry-AP, chorus, college counseling, comparative cultures, computer science, computer science-AP, contemporary issues, creative writing, earth science, economics, English, English literature, English literature-AP, environmental science, environmental science-AP, European history, European history-AP, fine arts, forensics, French, gender issues, geography, geometry, government/civics, health, history, honors English, human geography - AP, independent study, international relations, Latin, Latin American literature, literature, mathematics, music, oceanography, philosophy, photography, physical education, physics, portfolio art, psychology, science, social studies, Spanish, Spanish-AP, technology, theater, U.S. government and politics-AP, United States government-AP, woodworking, world history, world literature.

Graduation Requirements Arts and fine arts (art, music, dance, drama), English, foreign language, history, mathematics, science, The Unit: an intensive 2-week course each year of Upper School.

Special Academic Programs 15 Advanced Placement exams for which test preparation is offered; honors section; independent study; study abroad.

College Admission Counseling 75 students graduated in 2011; all went to college, including Boston College; Furman University; New York University; The George Washington University; Vanderbilt University; Villanova University. 65% scored over 600 on SAT critical reading, 65% scored over 600 on SAT math, 70% scored over 600 on SAT writing.

Student Life Upper grades have specified standards of dress, student council, honor system. Discipline rests primarily with faculty.

Summer Programs Enrichment, advancement, sports, art/fine arts programs offered; session focuses on academics, arts, sports, day and outdoor camping; held on campus; accepts boys and girls; open to students from other schools. 325 students usually enrolled. 2012 schedule: June 10 to August 20. Application deadline: none.

Tuition and Aid Day student tuition: $29,400. Tuition installment plan (The Tuition Plan, Insured Tuition Payment Plan). Merit scholarship grants, need-based scholarship grants available. In 2011–12, 12% of upper-school students received aid; total upper-school merit-scholarship money awarded: $40,000. Total amount of financial aid awarded in 2011–12: $1,200,000.

Admissions Traditional secondary-level entrance grade is 9. For fall 2011, 263 students applied for upper-level admission, 164 were accepted, 112 enrolled. ISEE or SSAT required. Deadline for receipt of application materials: January 25. Application fee required: $75. On-campus interview required.

Athletics Interscholastic: baseball (boys), basketball (b,g), cheering (g), cross-country running (b,g), fencing (b,g), ice hockey (b), indoor track & field (b,g), lacrosse (b,g), soccer (b,g), softball (g), tennis (b,g), track and field (b,g), winter (indoor) track (b,g); intramural: skiing (downhill) (b,g), strength & conditioning (b,g); coed interscholastic: golf, swimming and diving; coed intramural: backpacking, hiking/backpacking, outdoor adventure, outdoor recreation, physical fitness, physical training. 6 PE instructors, 37 coaches, 1 athletic trainer.

Computers Computers are regularly used in art, computer applications, design, desktop publishing, graphic arts, graphic design, independent study, information technology, introduction to technology, journalism, library, library skills, literary magazine, multimedia, news writing, newspaper, photography, programming, research skills, science, technology, Web site design, yearbook classes. Computer network features include on-campus library services, online commercial services, Internet access, wireless campus network, Internet filtering or blocking technology. Campus intranet and computer access in designated common areas are available to students. The school has a published electronic and media policy.

Contact Mrs. Ann Marie Blackman, Admission Office Manager. 908-234-1611 Ext. 245. Fax: 908-234-1712. E-mail: ablackman@gsbschool.org. Web site: www.gsbschool.org.

GILMAN SCHOOL

5407 Roland Avenue

Baltimore, Maryland 21210

Head of School: Mr. John E. Schmick

General Information Boys' day college-preparatory school. Grades K–12. Founded: 1897. Setting: suburban. 68-acre campus. 6 buildings on campus. Approved or accredited by Association of Independent Maryland Schools, Middle States Association of Colleges and Schools, and Maryland Department of Education. Member of National Association of Independent Schools and Secondary School Admission Test Board. Endowment: $83.5 million. Total enrollment: 1,022. Upper school average class size: 16. Upper school faculty-student ratio: 1:8. There are 172 required school days per year for Upper School students. Upper School students typically attend 5 days per week. The average school day consists of 9 hours.

Upper School Student Profile Grade 9: 116 students (116 boys); Grade 10: 116 students (116 boys); Grade 11: 118 students (118 boys); Grade 12: 115 students (115 boys).

Faculty School total: 145. In upper school: 58 men, 8 women; 50 have advanced degrees.

Subjects Offered Algebra, American history, American literature, anatomy, Arabic, art, art history, biology, calculus, chemistry, Chinese, community service, computer math, computer programming, computer science, creative writing, drafting, drama, ecology, economics, English, English literature, environmental science, European history, expository writing, fine arts, French, geometry, German, government/civics, Greek, history, industrial arts, Latin, mathematics, mechanical drawing, music, photography, physical education, physics, physiology, religion, Russian, science, social studies, Spanish, speech, statistics, theater, trigonometry, writing.

Graduation Requirements Art history, athletics, English, foreign language, history, mathematics, music appreciation, religion (includes Bible studies and theology), science, senior project.

Special Academic Programs 30 Advanced Placement exams for which test preparation is offered; honors section; independent study; term-away projects; academic accommodation for the gifted, the musically talented, and the artistically talented.

College Admission Counseling 106 students graduated in 2011; all went to college, including Dickinson College; Princeton University; University of Maryland, Baltimore County; University of Maryland, College Park; University of Virginia; Yale University. Mean SAT critical reading: 638, mean SAT math: 660, mean SAT writing: 637.

Student Life Upper grades have specified standards of dress, student council, honor system. Discipline rests primarily with faculty.

Summer Programs Remediation, enrichment, advancement, sports, art/fine arts, rigorous outdoor training programs offered; session focuses on remediation and enrichment; held on campus; accepts boys and girls; open to students from other schools. 250 students usually enrolled. 2012 schedule: June 18 to July 18. Application deadline: June 18.

Tuition and Aid Day student tuition: $24,340. Tuition installment plan (Insured Tuition Payment Plan, FACTS Tuition Payment Plan, monthly payment plans). Need-based scholarship grants, need-based loans available. In 2011–12, 25% of upper-school students received aid. Total amount of financial aid awarded in 2011–12: $1,839,100.

Admissions Traditional secondary-level entrance grade is 9. For fall 2011, 140 students applied for upper-level admission, 52 were accepted, 40 enrolled. ISEE required. Deadline for receipt of application materials: December 31. Application fee required: $50. On-campus interview required.

Athletics Interscholastic: baseball, basketball, cross-country running, football, golf, ice hockey, indoor track, lacrosse, soccer, squash, swimming and diving, tennis, track and field, volleyball, water polo, winter (indoor) track, wrestling; intramural: basketball, bicycling, cross-country running, fitness, flag football, Frisbee, golf, physical fitness, rugby, table tennis, tennis, touch football, weight lifting. 3 PE instructors, 2 athletic trainers.

Computers Computers are regularly used in all academic, computer applications, design, digital applications classes. Computer network features include on-campus library services, Internet access, wireless campus network, Internet filtering or blocking technology. Campus intranet, student e-mail accounts, and computer access in designated common areas are available to students. Students grades are available online. The school has a published electronic and media policy.

Contact Allison Conner, Admissions Assistant. 410-323-7169. Fax: 410-864-2825. E-mail: aconner@gilman.edu. Web site: www.gilman.edu.

GILMOUR ACADEMY

34001 Cedar Road

Gates Mills, Ohio 44040-9356

Head of School: Br. Robert E. Lavelle, CSC

General Information Coeducational boarding and day college-preparatory, arts, religious studies, and technology school, affiliated with Roman Catholic Church. Boarding grades 7–12, day grades PK–12. Founded: 1946. Setting: suburban. Nearest major city is Cleveland. Students are housed in coed dormitories and boys' wing and girls' wing dormitory. 144-acre campus. 15 buildings on campus. Approved or accredited by Independent Schools Association of the Central States, Midwest Association of Boarding Schools, National Catholic Education Association, North Central Association of Colleges and Schools, The Association of Boarding Schools, and Ohio Department of Education. Member of National Association of Independent Schools and Secondary School Admission Test Board. Endowment: $30 million. Total enrollment: 693. Upper school average class size: 14. Upper school faculty-student ratio: 1:10. Upper School students typically attend 5 days per week. The average school day consists of 7 hours and 20 minutes.

Upper School Student Profile 12% of students are boarding students. 88% are state residents. 15 states are represented in upper school student body. 35% are international students. International students from Canada, China, Mexico, and Republic of Korea; 1 other country represented in student body. 75% of students are Roman Catholic.

Faculty School total: 77. In upper school: 43 men, 34 women; 57 have advanced degrees; 4 reside on campus.

Subjects Offered Advanced Placement courses, advanced studio art-AP, algebra, American government, American history, American literature, art, band, Bible, biology, biology-AP, British literature, broadcast journalism, calculus, calculus-AP, ceramics, chemistry, chemistry-AP, chorus, community service, computer programming, computer science, computer science-AP, creative writing, drama, drawing, economics, English, English literature, English-AP, ensembles, ethics, European history, European history-AP, fine arts, French, French language-AP, French-AP, geometry, geometry with art applications, government, government-AP, government/civics, health, history, history of rock and roll, independent study, jazz ensemble, journalism, Latin, Latin-AP, law, leadership, mathematics, mathematics-AP, model United Nations, modern European history-AP, music, musical productions, oil painting, painting, photography, physical education, physical fitness, physics, physics-AP, pre-algebra, pre-calculus, religion, religious studies, SAT/ACT preparation, science, social studies, Spanish, Spanish language-AP, speech, speech and debate, statistics-AP, student government, student publications, studio art, studio art-AP, swimming, theater, trigonometry, U.S. history, U.S. history-AP, weight training, work-study, world history, writing, writing workshop, yearbook.

Graduation Requirements Arts and fine arts (art, music, dance, drama), English, foreign language, mathematics, physical education (includes health), religion (includes Bible studies and theology), science, social studies (includes history), speech, senior project. Community service is required.

Special Academic Programs Advanced Placement exam preparation; accelerated programs; independent study; study at local college for college credit; academic accommodation for the gifted, the musically talented, and the artistically talented.

College Admission Counseling 113 students graduated in 2011; 108 went to college, including Boston College; Case Western Reserve University; John Carroll University; Loyola University Chicago; Miami University; University of Dayton. Other: 1 entered a postgraduate year, 4 had other specific plans. Mean SAT critical reading: 531, mean SAT math: 536, mean SAT writing: 545, mean combined SAT: 1612, mean composite ACT: 24.

Student Life Upper grades have specified standards of dress, student council, honor system. Discipline rests equally with students and faculty. Attendance at religious services is required.

Summer Programs Enrichment, advancement, sports programs offered; session focuses on athletics and other opportunities available; held both on and off campus; held at Some universities; accepts boys and girls; open to students from other schools. 100 students usually enrolled. 2012 schedule: June to July. Application deadline: none.

Tuition and Aid Day student tuition: $10,495–$25,625; 7-day tuition and room/board: $37,875. Tuition installment plan (monthly payment plans, Tuition Management Systems). Tuition reduction for siblings, merit scholarship grants, need-based scholarship grants, need-based loans, paying campus jobs, endowed scholarships with criteria specified by donors available. In 2011–12, 55% of upper-school students received aid; total upper-school merit-scholarship money awarded: $85,000. Total amount of financial aid awarded in 2011–12: $3,200,000.

Admissions Traditional secondary-level entrance grade is 9. For fall 2011, 178 students applied for upper-level admission, 147 were accepted, 88 enrolled. ACT, ACT-Explore, ISEE, PSAT, SAT, SSAT or TOEFL required. Deadline for receipt of application materials: none. Application fee required: $35. Interview required.

Athletics Interscholastic: baseball (boys), basketball (b,g), cross-country running (b,g), football (b), gymnastics (g), hockey (b,g), ice hockey (b,g), lacrosse (b,g), running (b,g), soccer (b,g), softball (g), swimming and diving (b,g), tennis (b,g), track and field (b,g), volleyball (g), winter soccer (b,g); intramural: cheering (g), indoor soccer (b,g); coed interscholastic: figure skating, golf, indoor track, indoor track & field, winter (indoor) track; coed intramural: aerobics, alpine skiing, aquatics, basketball, bowling, broomball, figure skating, fitness, golf, ice skating, indoor track, paddle tennis, physical fitness, physical training, skiing (downhill), snowboarding, soccer, strength & conditioning, swimming and diving, tennis, volleyball, weight training, winter (indoor) track, winter soccer. 9 coaches, 3 athletic trainers.

Computers Computers are regularly used in all academic classes. Computer network features include on-campus library services, online commercial services, Internet access, wireless campus network, Internet filtering or blocking technology. Campus intranet, student e-mail accounts, and computer access in designated common areas are available to students. Students grades are available online. The school has a published electronic and media policy.

Contact Mr. Steve M. Scheidt, Director of Middle and Upper School Admissions. 440-473-8050. Fax: 440-473-8010. E-mail: admissions@gilmour.org. Web site: www.gilmour.org.

GIRARD COLLEGE

2101 South College Avenue

Box #121

Philadelphia, Pennsylvania 19121-4857

Head of School: Mrs. Autumn A. Graves

General Information Coeducational boarding college-preparatory and general academic school. Grades 1–12. Founded: 1848. Setting: urban. Students are housed in single-sex dormitories. 43-acre campus. 10 buildings on campus. Approved or accredited by Middle States Association of Colleges and Schools, The Association of Boarding Schools, and Pennsylvania Department of Education. Member of National Association of Independent Schools. Endowment: $355 million. Total enrollment: 530. Upper school average class size: 22. Upper school faculty-student ratio: 1:16.

Upper School Student Profile Grade 7: 55 students (24 boys, 31 girls); Grade 8: 56 students (29 boys, 27 girls); Grade 9: 60 students (24 boys, 36 girls); Grade 10: 64 students (29 boys, 35 girls); Grade 11: 59 students (29 boys, 30 girls); Grade 12: 56 students (23 boys, 33 girls). 100% of students are boarding students. 90% are state residents. 6 states are represented in upper school student body.

Faculty School total: 71. In upper school: 12 men, 9 women; 9 have advanced degrees; 1 resides on campus.

Subjects Offered Algebra, American history, American literature, anatomy, art, biology, calculus, chemistry, choir, college counseling, community service, computer literacy, earth science, English, English literature, European history, French, geometry, government/civics, health, honors algebra, honors English, honors geometry, honors U.S. history, instrumental music, jazz band, life management skills, mathematics, multicultural studies, music appreciation, physical education, physics, poetry, pre-calculus, SAT preparation, senior project, social studies, sociology, Spanish, video film production, world cultures.

Graduation Requirements College counseling, computer literacy, English, foreign language, mathematics, physical education (includes health), science, senior career experience, senior project, social sciences, social studies (includes history). Community service is required.

Special Academic Programs Advanced Placement exam preparation; honors section; study at local college for college credit; remedial reading and/or remedial writing; remedial math.

College Admission Counseling 41 students graduated in 2010; 40 went to college, including Columbia College; Howard University; Penn State University Park; Rutgers, The State University of New Jersey, New Brunswick; Temple University; Villanova University. Other: 1 had other specific plans. Mean SAT critical reading: 490, mean SAT math: 477.

Student Life Upper grades have uniform requirement, student council. Discipline rests primarily with faculty.

Tuition and Aid Full scholarships (if admission requirements met) available. In 2010–11, 100% of upper-school students received aid.

Admissions Traditional secondary-level entrance grade is 9. Admissions testing and math, reading, and mental ability tests required. Deadline for receipt of application materials: none. No application fee required. On-campus interview required.

Athletics Interscholastic: baseball (boys), basketball (b,g), cross-country running (b,g), soccer (b,g), softball (g), tennis (g), track and field (b,g), winter (indoor) track (b,g), wrestling (b); intramural: bicycling (b), strength & conditioning (b,g), yoga (g); coed interscholastic: cheering; coed intramural: aerobics, aerobics/dance, aquatics, dance, fitness, flag football, indoor track & field, jogging, jump rope, life saving, martial arts, outdoor activities, outdoor adventure, physical fitness, running, swimming and diving, walking, weight training, winter walking. 1 PE instructor, 11 coaches.

Computers Computers are regularly used in college planning, English, foreign language, history, library, mathematics, newspaper, reading, research skills, SAT preparation, science, social studies, study skills, word processing, writing, yearbook classes. Computer network features include on-campus library services, online commercial services, Internet access, Internet filtering or blocking technology. Student e-mail accounts are available to students. The school has a published electronic and media policy.

Contact Joan McGovern, Admissions Representative. 215-787-2621. Fax: 215-787-4402. E-mail: admissions@girardcollege.com. Web site: www.girardcollege.com.

GIRLS PREPARATORY SCHOOL

205 Island Avenue

Chattanooga, Tennessee 37405

Head of School: Mr. Stanley R. Tucker Jr.

General Information Girls' day college-preparatory, arts, and technology school. Grades 6–12. Founded: 1906. Setting: suburban. Nearest major city is Atlanta, GA. 55-acre campus. 8 buildings on campus. Approved or accredited by Southern Association of Colleges and Schools and Southern Association of Independent Schools. Member of

National Association of Independent Schools. Endowment: $27.7 million. Total enrollment: 603. Upper school average class size: 16. Upper school faculty-student ratio: 1:8. There are 180 required school days per year for Upper School students. Upper School students typically attend 5 days per week. The average school day consists of 7 hours and 45 minutes.

Upper School Student Profile Grade 9: 71 students (71 girls); Grade 10: 97 students (97 girls); Grade 11: 92 students (92 girls); Grade 12: 98 students (98 girls).

Faculty School total: 75. In upper school: 13 men, 28 women; 29 have advanced degrees.

Subjects Offered Advanced Placement courses, algebra, American history, American literature, art, art history, Basic programming, Bible studies, biology, calculus, chemistry, computer science, dance, drama, English, English literature, European history, fine arts, forensics, French, geometry, government/civics, graphic design, history, Latin, mathematics, music, orchestra, physical education, physics, pottery, pre-calculus, religion, science, Spanish, statistics, trigonometry, world history.

Graduation Requirements Arts and fine arts (art, music, dance, drama), electives, English, foreign language, history, mathematics, physical education (includes health), religion (includes Bible studies and theology), science.

Special Academic Programs 18 Advanced Placement exams for which test preparation is offered; honors section; independent study.

College Admission Counseling 108 students graduated in 2011; all went to college, including Auburn University; Birmingham-Southern College; Sewanee: The University of the South; The University of Tennessee; The University of Tennessee at Chattanooga; Washington University in St. Louis. Median SAT critical reading: 590, median SAT math: 590, median SAT writing: 610, median combined SAT: 1800, median composite ACT: 27. 47% scored over 600 on SAT critical reading, 45% scored over 600 on SAT math, 54% scored over 600 on SAT writing, 48% scored over 1800 on combined SAT, 64% scored over 26 on composite ACT.

Student Life Upper grades have uniform requirement, student council, honor system. Discipline rests primarily with faculty.

Summer Programs Remediation, enrichment, advancement, sports, art/fine arts, computer instruction programs offered; session focuses on summer fun and enrichment; held both on and off campus; held at Lupton Athletic fields and yacht club in Hixson, various locations throughout town, and Nantahala River Gorge; accepts boys and girls; open to students from other schools. 400 students usually enrolled. 2012 schedule: June 4 to July 20. Application deadline: June 1.

Tuition and Aid Day student tuition: $20,020. Tuition installment plan (Insured Tuition Payment Plan, FACTS Tuition Payment Plan, monthly payment plans, individually arranged payment plans, 60%/40% and 100% payment plans). Need-based scholarship grants available. In 2011–12, 38% of upper-school students received aid. Total amount of financial aid awarded in 2011–12: $1,310,040.

Admissions Traditional secondary-level entrance grade is 9. For fall 2011, 42 students applied for upper-level admission, 35 were accepted, 26 enrolled. Admissions testing, mathematics proficiency exam, Otis-Lennon School Ability Test and Reading for Understanding required. Deadline for receipt of application materials: none. Application fee required: $75. Interview recommended.

Athletics Interscholastic: basketball, bowling, cheering, crew, cross-country running, diving, golf, lacrosse, rowing, soccer, softball, swimming and diving, tennis, track and field, volleyball; intramural: backpacking, bicycling, canoeing/kayaking, climbing, dance, dance squad, fitness, fitness walking, Frisbee, hiking/backpacking, jogging, kayaking, life saving, modern dance, mountain biking, outdoor activities, outdoor education, outdoor skills, paddle tennis, physical fitness, rafting, rock climbing, running, self defense, strength & conditioning, ultimate Frisbee, walking, weight training, wilderness, yoga; coed interscholastic: cheering. 6 PE instructors, 24 coaches, 1 athletic trainer.

Computers Computers are regularly used in Bible studies, computer applications, dance, English, foreign language, history, mathematics, science classes. Computer network features include on-campus library services, online commercial services, Internet access, wireless campus network, Internet filtering or blocking technology, network printing. Campus intranet, student e-mail accounts, and computer access in designated common areas are available to students. Students grades are available online. The school has a published electronic and media policy.

Contact Debbie Bohner Young, Director of Admissions. 423-634-7647. Fax: 423-634-7643. E-mail: dyoung@gps.edu. Web site: www.gps.edu.

GLADES DAY SCHOOL

400 Gator Boulevard

Belle Glade, Florida 33430

Head of School: Dr. Robert Egley

General Information Coeducational day college-preparatory and general academic school. Grades PK–12. Founded: 1965. Setting: small town. Nearest major city is West Palm Beach. 21-acre campus. 4 buildings on campus. Approved or accredited by Florida Council of Independent Schools. Total enrollment: 335. Upper school average class size: 20. Upper school faculty-student ratio: 1:15. There are 180 required school days per year for Upper School students. Upper School students typically attend 5 days per week. The average school day consists of 6 hours and 35 minutes.

Upper School Student Profile Grade 9: 38 students (20 boys, 18 girls); Grade 10: 39 students (18 boys, 21 girls); Grade 11: 48 students (24 boys, 24 girls); Grade 12: 46 students (22 boys, 24 girls).

Faculty School total: 34. In upper school: 9 men, 14 women; 5 have advanced degrees.

Subjects Offered Agriculture, algebra, American government, American history, American literature, anatomy, ancient history, art, Bible studies, biology, calculus, calculus-AP, chemistry, computer applications, computer skills, computer technologies, earth science, economics, English, English language and composition-AP, English literature, English literature and composition-AP, European history, general math, geometry, government and politics-AP, grammar, health, health education, human geography - AP, journalism, keyboarding, literature and composition-AP, macro/microeconomics-AP, macroeconomics-AP, modern world history, music performance, physical education, pre-calculus, SAT/ACT preparation, Spanish, Spanish-AP, trigonometry, U.S. government and politics-AP, U.S. history, U.S. history-AP, weightlifting, world geography, world history, world history-AP, yearbook.

Graduation Requirements Algebra, American government, American literature, anatomy, ancient world history, arts and fine arts (art, music, dance, drama), biology, calculus, chemistry, computer applications, economics, English, English composition, English literature, geometry, health education, keyboarding, macroeconomics-AP, marine biology, modern world history, physical education (includes health), physical fitness, physical science, physics, pre-calculus, Spanish, U.S. history, world history.

Special Academic Programs 9 Advanced Placement exams for which test preparation is offered; honors section; independent study; study at local college for college credit; programs in general development for dyslexic students.

College Admission Counseling 52 students graduated in 2011; 50 went to college, including Florida Gulf Coast University; Florida State University; Palm Beach State College; Santa Fe College; University of Central Florida; University of Florida. Other: 2 went to work.

Student Life Upper grades have uniform requirement, student council, honor system. Discipline rests primarily with faculty.

Summer Programs Remediation programs offered; session focuses on remediation; held on campus; accepts boys and girls; not open to students from other schools. 15 students usually enrolled. 2012 schedule: June 7 to July 15. Application deadline: June 4.

Tuition and Aid Day student tuition: $6900–$7650. Tuition installment plan (FACTS Tuition Payment Plan, monthly payment plans, individually arranged payment plans). Tuition reduction for siblings, need-based scholarship grants available. In 2011–12, 10% of upper-school students received aid.

Admissions Traditional secondary-level entrance grade is 9. For fall 2011, 34 students applied for upper-level admission, 25 were accepted, 25 enrolled. Deadline for receipt of application materials: none. Application fee required: $400. On-campus interview required.

Athletics Interscholastic: baseball (boys), basketball (b,g), cheering (g), cross-country running (b,g), football (b), golf (b), soccer (b,g), softball (g), track and field (b,g), volleyball (g); intramural: strength & conditioning (b,g), weight training (b,g). 3 PE instructors, 2 coaches, 1 athletic trainer.

Computers Computers are regularly used in English, journalism, science, Spanish, Web site design, word processing, yearbook classes. Computer network features include on-campus library services, Internet access, wireless campus network. Campus intranet and student e-mail accounts are available to students. Students grades are available online. The school has a published electronic and media policy.

Contact Mrs. Irene Tellechea, High School Secretary. 561-996-6769 Ext. 10. Fax: 561-992-9274. E-mail: admissions@gladesdayschool.com. Web site: www.gladesdayschool.com.

GLEN EDEN SCHOOL

Vancouver, British Columbia, Canada

See Special Needs Schools section.

GLENELG COUNTRY SCHOOL

12793 Folly Quarter Road

Ellicott City, Maryland 21042

Head of School: Mr. Gregory J. Ventre

General Information Coeducational day college-preparatory, arts, and technology school. Grades PK–12. Founded: 1954. Setting: suburban. Nearest major city is Baltimore. 87-acre campus. 1 building on campus. Approved or accredited by Association of Independent Maryland Schools, Middle States Association of Colleges and Schools, and Maryland Department of Education. Member of National Association of Independent Schools. Endowment: $900,000. Total enrollment: 778. Upper school average class size: 15. Upper school faculty-student ratio: 1:6. There are 175 required school days per year for Upper School students. Upper School students typically attend 5 days per week. The average school day consists of 7 hours.

Upper School Student Profile Grade 9: 71 students (36 boys, 35 girls); Grade 10: 66 students (41 boys, 25 girls); Grade 11: 84 students (43 boys, 41 girls); Grade 12: 66 students (40 boys, 26 girls).

Faculty School total: 131. In upper school: 26 men, 21 women; 37 have advanced degrees.

Subjects Offered Algebra, American history, American literature, art, art history, biology, biology-AP, calculus, calculus-AP, chemistry, chemistry-AP, Chinese, chorus, computer science, creative writing, drama, English, English literature, English-AP, European history, expository writing, French, French-AP, geometry, history, humanities, integrative seminar, Latin, Latin-AP, mathematics, photography, physical education, physical science, physics, physics-AP, pre-calculus, psychology, publications, science, social studies, Spanish, Spanish-AP, statistics, studio art, theater, trigonometry, world affairs.

Graduation Requirements Civics, English, foreign language, integrative seminar, mathematics, physical education (includes health), science, social studies (includes history), participation in Civic Leadership Program, 25 hours of community service per year.

Special Academic Programs 17 Advanced Placement exams for which test preparation is offered; honors section; independent study; academic accommodation for the gifted.

College Admission Counseling 70 students graduated in 2011; all went to college, including Gettysburg College; University of Maryland, College Park; University of South Carolina; Wake Forest University. Mean SAT critical reading: 600, mean SAT math: 612, mean SAT writing: 611, mean combined SAT: 1823. 51% scored over 600 on SAT critical reading, 53% scored over 600 on SAT math, 56% scored over 600 on SAT writing, 57% scored over 1800 on combined SAT.

Student Life Upper grades have uniform requirement, student council, honor system. Discipline rests equally with students and faculty.

Summer Programs Sports programs offered; session focuses on athletics and CIT (Couselor-In-Training) programs; held on campus; accepts boys and girls; open to students from other schools. 300 students usually enrolled. 2012 schedule: June 18 to July 27. Application deadline: May 31.

Tuition and Aid Day student tuition: $23,460. Tuition installment plan (monthly payment plans, individually arranged payment plans, 2-payment plan). Merit scholarship grants, need-based scholarship grants available. In 2011–12, 40% of upper-school students received aid; total upper-school merit-scholarship money awarded: $140,000. Total amount of financial aid awarded in 2011–12: $1,800,000.

Admissions Traditional secondary-level entrance grade is 9. For fall 2011, 68 students applied for upper-level admission, 48 were accepted, 27 enrolled. ISEE or SSAT required. Deadline for receipt of application materials: January 15. Application fee required: $75. On-campus interview required.

Athletics Interscholastic: baseball (boys), basketball (b,g), cross-country running (b,g), field hockey (g), golf (b,g), ice hockey (b), indoor soccer (g), indoor track (b,g), lacrosse (b,g), soccer (b,g), tennis (b,g), volleyball (g), winter soccer (g), wrestling (b); coed interscholastic: golf, ice hockey, strength & conditioning; coed intramural: aerobics, aerobics/dance, dance, fitness, flag football, Frisbee, physical fitness, physical training, skiing (downhill), strength & conditioning, ultimate Frisbee, weight training, yoga. 5 PE instructors, 12 coaches, 1 athletic trainer.

Computers Computers are regularly used in all academic classes. Computer network features include on-campus library services, Internet access, wireless campus network. Campus intranet, student e-mail accounts, and computer access in designated common areas are available to students. Students grades are available online. The school has a published electronic and media policy.

Contact Mrs. Karen K. Wootton, Director of Admission and Financial Aid. 410-531-7346 Ext. 2203. Fax: 410-531-7363. E-mail: wootton@glenelg.org. Web site: www.glenelg.org.

THE GLENHOLME SCHOOL, DEVEREUX CONNECTICUT

Washington, Connecticut

See Special Needs Schools section.

GLENLYON NORFOLK SCHOOL

801 Bank Street

Victoria, British Columbia V8S 4A8, Canada

Head of School: Mr. Simon Bruce-Lockhart

General Information Coeducational day college-preparatory, arts, technology, and International Baccalaureate school. Grades JK–12. Founded: 1913. Setting: urban. 6-acre campus. 5 buildings on campus. Approved or accredited by International Baccalaureate Organization and British Columbia Department of Education. Affiliate member of National Association of Independent Schools. Language of instruction: English. Endowment: CAN$800,000. Total enrollment: 691. Upper school average class size: 18. Upper school faculty-student ratio: 1:10. There are 180 required school days per year for Upper School students. Upper School students typically attend 5 days per week. The average school day consists of 6 hours.

Upper School Student Profile Grade 9: 85 students (44 boys, 41 girls); Grade 10: 63 students (31 boys, 32 girls); Grade 11: 58 students (19 boys, 39 girls); Grade 12: 67 students (24 boys, 43 girls).

Faculty School total: 90. In upper school: 20 men, 21 women; 13 have advanced degrees.

Subjects Offered 20th century world history, art, band, biology, calculus, chemistry, choir, community service, comparative civilizations, concert band, creative writing, debate, directing, drama, English, English literature, European history, European literature, fine arts, French, geography, history, information technology, International Baccalaureate courses, jazz band, journalism, life skills, mathematics, music, newspaper, peer counseling, physical education, physics, public speaking, science, social studies, Spanish, stagecraft, theater arts, theory of knowledge, vocal jazz, world history, world literature, writing, yearbook.

Graduation Requirements Arts and fine arts (art, music, dance, drama), career planning, English, foreign language, information technology, mathematics, physical education (includes health), science, social studies (includes history). Community service is required.

Special Academic Programs International Baccalaureate program; honors section; term-away projects; ESL (10 students enrolled).

College Admission Counseling 58 students graduated in 2011; 52 went to college, including McGill University; The University of British Columbia; University of Calgary; University of Toronto; University of Victoria. Other: 6 went to work.

Student Life Upper grades have uniform requirement, student council, honor system. Discipline rests primarily with faculty.

Tuition and Aid Day student tuition: CAN$13,575–CAN$16,785. Guaranteed tuition plan. Tuition installment plan (monthly payment plans, individually arranged payment plans). Tuition reduction for siblings, bursaries, merit scholarship grants, tuition allowances for children of staff available. In 2011–12, 20% of upper-school students received aid; total upper-school merit-scholarship money awarded: CAN$23,050. Total amount of financial aid awarded in 2011–12: CAN$129,895.

Admissions Traditional secondary-level entrance grade is 9. SAT, SLEP, SSAT or writing sample required. Deadline for receipt of application materials: none. Application fee required: CAN$185. Interview recommended.

Athletics Interscholastic: backpacking (boys, girls), badminton (b,g), basketball (b,g), canoeing/kayaking (b,g), climbing (b,g), crew (b,g), cross-country running (b,g), field hockey (g), fitness (b,g), kayaking (b,g), rock climbing (b,g), rowing (b,g), rugby (b), soccer (b,g), squash (b,g), swimming and diving (b,g), tennis (b,g), track and field (b,g), volleyball (g); intramural: badminton (b,g), ball hockey (b), basketball (b,g), floor hockey (b), outdoor education (b,g), outdoor recreation (b,g), outdoor skills (b,g), swimming and diving (b,g), track and field (b,g), ultimate Frisbee (b,g); coed interscholastic: backpacking, badminton, canoeing/kayaking, crew, cross-country running, fitness, golf, kayaking, sailing, tennis; coed intramural: badminton, basketball, outdoor education, outdoor recreation, outdoor skills, swimming and diving, track and field, ultimate Frisbee. 4 PE instructors, 12 coaches.

Computers Computers are regularly used in all classes. Computer network features include on-campus library services, Internet access, wireless campus network, Internet filtering or blocking technology. Campus intranet and student e-mail accounts are available to students. The school has a published electronic and media policy.

Contact Ms. Andrea Hughes, Admissions Associate. 250-370-6801. Fax: 250-370-6811. E-mail: admissions@mygns.ca. Web site: www.glenlyonnorfolk.bc.ca.

GONZAGA COLLEGE HIGH SCHOOL

19 Eye Street NW

Washington, District of Columbia 20001

Head of School: Rev. Vincent Conti, SJ

General Information Boys' day college-preparatory, arts, religious studies, and technology school, affiliated with Roman Catholic Church. Grades 9–12. Founded: 1821. Setting: urban. 1-acre campus. 9 buildings on campus. Approved or accredited by Association of Independent Schools of Greater Washington, Jesuit Secondary Education Association, Middle States Association of Colleges and Schools, and District of Columbia Department of Education. Member of National Association of Independent Schools. Endowment: $9.1 million. Total enrollment: 957. Upper school average class size: 29. Upper school faculty-student ratio: 1:15. There are 166 required school days per year for Upper School students. Upper School students typically attend 5 days per week. The average school day consists of 6 hours and 35 minutes.

Upper School Student Profile Grade 9: 239 students (239 boys); Grade 10: 243 students (243 boys); Grade 11: 240 students (240 boys); Grade 12: 235 students (235 boys). 85% of students are Roman Catholic.

Faculty School total: 66. In upper school: 50 men, 16 women; 60 have advanced degrees.

Subjects Offered Advanced Placement courses, African-American literature, algebra, American history, American literature, applied music, art, band, biology, broadcasting, calculus, calculus-AP, Catholic belief and practice, chemistry, chemistry-AP, Chinese, choir, choral music, Christian and Hebrew scripture, Christian ethics, Christian scripture, communications, community service, computer applications, computer math, computer programming, computer science, concert band, concert choir, creative writing, driver education, earth science, economics, economics-AP, English, English literature, English literature and composition-AP, English literature-AP, English-AP, environmental science-AP, ethics, ethics and responsibility, European history, European history-AP, expository writing, film appreciation, film studies, fine arts, French, French-AP, functions, geometry, government, government/civics, grammar, Greek, health, health education, history, honors algebra, honors English, honors geometry, human geography - AP, independent study, Irish literature, jazz ensemble, Latin, Latin-AP, mathematics, media communications, music, musicianship, philosophy, photography, physical education, physics, physics-AP, piano, poetry, political science, political systems, psychology, psychology-AP, religion, Russian history, Russian studies, science, social justice, social sciences, social studies, Spanish, Spanish-AP, statistics, statistics-AP, studio art-AP, symphonic band, theology, trigonometry, U.S. government and politics-AP, Web site design, world history, world literature.

Graduation Requirements Arts and fine arts (art, music, dance, drama), English, ethics, foreign language, mathematics, physical education (includes health), religion (includes Bible studies and theology), science, social justice, social sciences, social studies (includes history). Community service is required.

Special Academic Programs Advanced Placement exam preparation; honors section.

College Admission Counseling 232 students graduated in 2011; 229 went to college, including Boston College; Fordham University; Georgetown University; James Madison University; University of Maryland, College Park; University of Virginia. Other: 1 entered a postgraduate year, 2 had other specific plans.

Student Life Upper grades have specified standards of dress, student council, honor system. Discipline rests primarily with faculty. Attendance at religious services is required.

Summer Programs Remediation, enrichment programs offered; session focuses on new student remediation, enrichment, and SAT preparation; held on campus; accepts boys and girls; open to students from other schools. 200 students usually enrolled. 2012 schedule: June 25 to July 20. Application deadline: June 1.

Tuition and Aid Day student tuition: $17,850. Tuition installment plan (Insured Tuition Payment Plan, monthly payment plans). Merit scholarship grants, need-based scholarship grants available. In 2011–12, 33% of upper-school students received aid; total upper-school merit-scholarship money awarded: $100,000. Total amount of financial aid awarded in 2011–12: $2,190,000.

Admissions Traditional secondary-level entrance grade is 9. For fall 2011, 650 students applied for upper-level admission, 300 were accepted, 239 enrolled. High School Placement Test (closed version) from Scholastic Testing Service required. Deadline for receipt of application materials: December 9. Application fee required: $35.

Athletics Interscholastic: baseball, basketball, crew, cross-country running, diving, football, golf, ice hockey, indoor track & field, lacrosse, rugby, soccer, squash, swimming and diving, tennis, track and field, water polo, winter (indoor) track, wrestling; intramural: basketball, bowling, fencing, fishing, football, Frisbee, hiking/backpacking, martial arts, physical training, skiing (downhill), softball, strength & conditioning, table tennis, volleyball, weight lifting, whiffle ball. 2 PE instructors, 30 coaches, 3 athletic trainers.

Computers Computer network features include on-campus library services, Internet access. Student e-mail accounts are available to students.

Contact Mr. Andrew C. Battaile, Director of Admission. 202-336-7101. Fax: 202-454-1188. E-mail: abattaile@gonzaga.org. Web site: www.gonzaga.org.

GONZAGA PREPARATORY SCHOOL

1224 East Euclid Avenue

Spokane, Washington 99207-2899

Head of School: Rev. Fr. Kevin Gerard Connell, SJ

General Information Coeducational day college-preparatory, general academic, and religious studies school, affiliated with Roman Catholic Church (Jesuit order). Grades 9–12. Founded: 1887. Setting: urban. 20-acre campus. 4 buildings on campus. Approved or accredited by Northwest Association of Schools and Colleges and Washington Department of Education. Endowment: $10 million. Total enrollment: 902. Upper school average class size: 19. Upper school faculty-student ratio: 1:14. There are 180 required school days per year for Upper School students. Upper School students typically attend 5 days per week. The average school day consists of 6 hours and 30 minutes.

Upper School Student Profile Grade 9: 222 students (116 boys, 106 girls); Grade 10: 216 students (104 boys, 112 girls); Grade 11: 223 students (121 boys, 102 girls); Grade 12: 241 students (119 boys, 122 girls). 70% of students are Roman Catholic Church (Jesuit order).

Faculty School total: 66. In upper school: 43 men, 23 women; 55 have advanced degrees.

Subjects Offered Algebra, American history, American literature, art, Bible studies, biology, calculus, ceramics, chemistry, computer programming, computer science, drama, earth science, English, English literature, environmental science, European history, fine arts, French, geography, geometry, government/civics, grammar, Greek, health, history, home economics, journalism, keyboarding, Latin, mathematics, music, philosophy, photography, physical education, physics, psychology, religion, science, single survival, social studies, Spanish, theater, theology, trigonometry, world history, world literature, writing, zoology.

Graduation Requirements Arts and fine arts (art, music, dance, drama), English, foreign language, mathematics, occupational education, physical education (includes health), religion (includes Bible studies and theology), science, social studies (includes history). Community service is required.

Special Academic Programs 13 Advanced Placement exams for which test preparation is offered; honors section; independent study; study at local college for college credit; academic accommodation for the gifted; remedial reading and/or remedial writing; remedial math; programs in English for dyslexic students; special instructional classes for deaf students, blind students; ESL (11 students enrolled).

College Admission Counseling 217 students graduated in 2011; 215 went to college, including Gonzaga University; Seattle University; University of Portland; University of Washington; Washington State University; Western Washington University. Other: 1 went to work, 1 entered military service. Median SAT critical reading: 552, median SAT math: 544, median SAT writing: 526, median composite ACT: 24. 32% scored over 600 on SAT critical reading, 29% scored over 600 on SAT math, 24% scored over 600 on SAT writing.

Student Life Upper grades have specified standards of dress, student council. Discipline rests primarily with faculty. Attendance at religious services is required.

Summer Programs Remediation, enrichment, art/fine arts, computer instruction programs offered; session focuses on development of basic skills; held on campus; accepts boys and girls; open to students from other schools. 140 students usually enrolled. 2012 schedule: June 20 to July 22. Application deadline: June 20.

Tuition and Aid Day student tuition: $9800. Tuition installment plan (monthly payment plans, individually arranged payment plans). Tuition reduction for siblings, merit scholarship grants, need-based scholarship grants, Fair Share Tuition Program available. In 2011–12, 60% of upper-school students received aid; total upper-school merit-scholarship money awarded: $5000. Total amount of financial aid awarded in 2011–12: $2,000,000.

Admissions Traditional secondary-level entrance grade is 9. Explore required. Deadline for receipt of application materials: December 3. Application fee required: $25.

Athletics Interscholastic: baseball (boys), basketball (b,g), cheering (g), cross-country running (b,g), dance team (g), football (b), golf (b,g), ice hockey (b), lacrosse (b,g), soccer (b,g), softball (g), tennis (b,g), track and field (b,g), volleyball (g), wrestling (b); intramural: lacrosse (b,g); coed interscholastic: aerobics/dance, dance, strength & conditioning; coed intramural: aerobics/dance, bowling, dance, dance squad, dance team, rock climbing, tennis, wall climbing, weight lifting, yoga. 2 PE instructors, 44 coaches, 1 athletic trainer.

Computers Computers are regularly used in Christian doctrine, computer applications, English, ethics, foreign language, French, health, history, Latin, mathematics, occupational education, photography, psychology, religious studies, remedial study skills, research skills, SAT preparation, science, social sciences, Spanish, speech, study skills, theater, theology, writing, yearbook classes. Computer network features include on-campus library services, online commercial services, Internet access, wireless campus network, Internet filtering or blocking technology. Computer access in designated common areas is available to students. Students grades are available online. The school has a published electronic and media policy.

Contact Mr. Derek Duchesne, Academic Vice Principal. 509-483-8511 Ext. 414. Fax: 509-483-3124. E-mail: dduchesne@gprep.com. Web site: www.gprep.com.

GOULD ACADEMY

PO Box 860

39 Church Street

Bethel, Maine 04217

Head of School: Daniel A. Kunkle

General Information Coeducational boarding and day college-preparatory, arts, and technology school. Grades 9–PG. Founded: 1836. Setting: small town. Nearest major city is Portland. Students are housed in single-sex dormitories. 456-acre campus. 30 buildings on campus. Approved or accredited by Association of Independent Schools in New England, Independent Schools of Northern New England, New England Association of Schools and Colleges, The Association of Boarding Schools, and Maine Department of Education. Member of National Association of Independent Schools and Secondary School Admission Test Board. Endowment: $9.5 million. Total enrollment: 232. Upper school average class size: 12. Upper school faculty-student ratio: 1:6. There are 175 required school days per year for Upper School students. Upper School students typically attend 5 days per week.

Upper School Student Profile Grade 9: 44 students (22 boys, 22 girls); Grade 10: 50 students (31 boys, 19 girls); Grade 11: 57 students (37 boys, 20 girls); Grade 12: 78 students (51 boys, 27 girls); Grade 13: 3 students (2 boys, 1 girl); Postgraduate: 4 students (4 boys). 71% of students are boarding students. 42% are state residents. 22 states are represented in upper school student body. 20% are international students. International students from China, Germany, Japan, Republic of Korea, Spain, and Taiwan; 2 other countries represented in student body.

Faculty School total: 44. In upper school: 23 men, 21 women; 25 have advanced degrees; 32 reside on campus.

Subjects Offered Acting, Advanced Placement courses, African-American literature, algebra, American foreign policy, American history, American literature, American literature-AP, analytic geometry, art, art history, athletic training, band, bioethics, DNA and culture, biology, biology-AP, British literature, British literature (honors), British literature-AP, calculus, calculus-AP, celestial navigation, ceramics, chemistry, chemistry-AP, chorus, Civil War, clayworking, college placement, computer information systems, computer music, computer programming, computer science, computers, conceptual physics, creative writing, debate, design, digital music, drama, drawing, earth science, Eastern religion and philosophy, ecology, economics, electives, electronic music, electronics, English, environmental science, environmental science-AP, ESL, European history, expository writing, foreign policy, French, geography, geometry, government and politics-AP, history, history-AP, honors algebra, honors English, honors world history, introduction to digital multitrack recording techniques, jazz band, jewelry making, Latin, learning strategies, literature by women, mathematics, music, music appreciation, music theory, musicianship, navigation, painting, philosophy, photography, physics, pottery, pre-calculus, printmaking, robotics, science, sculpture, Shakespeare, social studies, software design, Spanish, theater, U.S. government and politics-AP, video film production, women's literature, world history, writing.

Graduation Requirements English, foreign language, mathematics, physical education (includes health), science, social studies (includes history).

Special Academic Programs Advanced Placement exam preparation; honors section; independent study; academic accommodation for the gifted, the musically talented, and the artistically talented; ESL (25 students enrolled).

College Admission Counseling 61 students graduated in 2011; all went to college, including Bentley University; Lewis & Clark College; Rochester Institute of Technology; Saint Michael's College; University of Illinois at Urbana–Champaign; University of Vermont.

Student Life Upper grades have specified standards of dress, student council, honor system. Discipline rests equally with students and faculty.

Tuition and Aid Day student tuition: $28,170; 7-day tuition and room/board: $47,730. Tuition installment plan (individually arranged payment plans, full payment by August 15, 2/3 payment by August 12, 1/3 by December 1). Need-based scholarship grants, need-based loans available. In 2011–12, 38% of upper-school students received aid. Total amount of financial aid awarded in 2011–12: $1,355,000.

Admissions Traditional secondary-level entrance grade is 9. For fall 2011, 216 students applied for upper-level admission, 184 were accepted, 90 enrolled. SSAT required. Deadline for receipt of application materials: February 1. Application fee required: $30. Interview required.

Athletics Interscholastic: alpine skiing (boys, girls), baseball (b), basketball (b,g), bicycling (b,g), cross-country running (b,g), field hockey (g), freestyle skiing (b,g); coed interscholastic: climbing, dance, dressage, equestrian sports, golf; coed intramural: golf. 11 coaches, 1 athletic trainer.

Computers Computers are regularly used in English, foreign language, history, mathematics, music, science, technology classes. Computer network features include on-campus library services, Internet access, wireless campus network. Student e-mail accounts are available to students. Students grades are available online. The school has a published electronic and media policy.

Contact Todd Ormiston, Director of Admission. 207-824-7777. Fax: 207-824-2926. E-mail: todd.ormiston@gouldacademy.org. Web site: www.gouldacademy.org.

THE GOVERNOR FRENCH ACADEMY

219 West Main Street

Belleville, Illinois 62220-1537

Head of School: Mr. Phillip E. Paeltz

General Information Coeducational boarding and day college-preparatory and bilingual studies school. Boarding grades 9–12, day grades K–12. Founded: 1983. Setting: urban. Nearest major city is St. Louis, MO. Students are housed in homes of local families. 3 buildings on campus. Approved or accredited by CITA (Commission on International and Trans-Regional Accreditation), North Central Association of Colleges and Schools, and Illinois Department of Education. Endowment: $100,000. Total enrollment: 171. Upper school average class size: 15. Upper school faculty-student ratio: 1:6. There are 176 required school days per year for Upper School students. Upper School students typically attend 5 days per week. The average school day consists of 7 hours and 15 minutes.

Upper School Student Profile Grade 9: 13 students (9 boys, 4 girls); Grade 10: 16 students (9 boys, 7 girls); Grade 11: 15 students (6 boys, 9 girls); Grade 12: 8 students (5 boys, 3 girls). 1% of students are boarding students. 88% are state residents. 1 state is represented in upper school student body. 1% are international students. International students from China, Republic of Korea, and Taiwan.

Faculty School total: 14. In upper school: 2 men, 5 women; 7 have advanced degrees.

Subjects Offered Algebra, American history, American literature, biology, calculus, chemistry, creative writing, earth science, ecology, economics, English, English literature, environmental science, European history, expository writing, geography, geometry, government/civics, grammar, history, mathematics, physical education, physics, science, social sciences, social studies, theater arts, trigonometry, world history, world literature.

Graduation Requirements English, foreign language, mathematics, physical education (includes health), science, social sciences, vote of faculty.

Special Academic Programs 6 Advanced Placement exams for which test preparation is offered; accelerated programs; independent study; academic accommodation for the gifted and the artistically talented; programs in English for dyslexic students; ESL (2 students enrolled).

College Admission Counseling 20 students graduated in 2011; all went to college, including Saint Louis University; Southern Illinois University Edwardsville; University of Illinois at Urbana–Champaign. Median composite ACT: 25.

Student Life Upper grades have uniform requirement, honor system. Discipline rests primarily with faculty.

Summer Programs Remediation, enrichment, advancement programs offered; session focuses on academics; held on campus; accepts boys and girls; open to students from other schools. 30 students usually enrolled. 2012 schedule: June 18 to July 27. Application deadline: none.

Tuition and Aid Day student tuition: $5500; 7-day tuition and room/board: $22,200. Tuition installment plan (monthly payment plans). Tuition reduction for siblings available.

Admissions Traditional secondary-level entrance grade is 9. For fall 2011, 20 students applied for upper-level admission, 17 were accepted, 14 enrolled. School placement exam required. Deadline for receipt of application materials: none. No application fee required. Interview required.

Athletics Interscholastic: martial arts (boys, girls), volleyball (g); intramural: basketball (b), martial arts (b,g); coed interscholastic: basketball, soccer; coed intramural: independent competitive sports, softball.

Computers Computers are regularly used in computer applications, science, yearbook classes. Computer network features include Internet access, wireless campus network, Internet filtering or blocking technology. Computer access in designated common areas is available to students. The school has a published electronic and media policy.

Contact Ms. Carol S. Wilson, Director of Admissions. 618-233-7542. Fax: 618-233-0541. E-mail: admiss@governorfrench.com. Web site: www.governorfrench.com.

THE GOVERNOR'S ACADEMY (FORMERLY GOVERNOR DUMMER ACADEMY)

1 Elm Street

Byfield, Massachusetts 01922

Head of School: John Martin Doggett Jr.

General Information Coeducational boarding and day college-preparatory and arts school. Grades 9–12. Founded: 1763. Setting: rural. Nearest major city is Boston. Students are housed in single-sex dormitories. 450-acre campus. 48 buildings on campus. Approved or accredited by Association of Independent Schools in New England, New England Association of Schools and Colleges, and The Association of Boarding Schools. Member of National Association of Independent Schools and Secondary School Admission Test Board. Endowment: $63 million. Total enrollment: 395. Upper school average class size: 12. Upper school faculty-student ratio: 1:5. There are 158 required school days per year for Upper School students. Upper School students typically attend 5 days per week.

Upper School Student Profile Grade 9: 89 students (44 boys, 45 girls); Grade 10: 108 students (59 boys, 49 girls); Grade 11: 102 students (58 boys, 44 girls); Grade 12: 91 students (47 boys, 44 girls). 65% of students are boarding students. 50% are state residents. 21 states are represented in upper school student body. 12% are international students. International students from Bermuda, China, Republic of Korea, Singapore, Taiwan, and Thailand; 6 other countries represented in student body.

Faculty In upper school: 46 men, 36 women; 40 have advanced degrees; 60 reside on campus.

Subjects Offered Advanced chemistry, algebra, American history, American history-AP, American literature, anatomy, art, band, biology, biology-AP, calculus-AP, ceramics, chemistry, chemistry-AP, Chinese, chorus, civics, computer graphics, computer math, computer programming, computer science, computer science-AP, constitutional law, creative writing, dance, drama, driver education, ecology, economics, economics-AP, English language-AP, English literature, English literature and composition-AP, environmental science, ESL, European history, European history-AP, expository writing, filmmaking, fine arts, French, French-AP, geometry, German, health, history, Holocaust and other genocides, honors algebra, jazz band, Latin, Latin-AP, marine biology, marine science, mathematics, Middle Eastern history, modern European history, modern European history-AP, music, music history, music theory, photography, physics, physics-AP, psychology, religion, science, social studies, Spanish, Spanish language-AP, Spanish literature-AP, statistics-AP, studio art-AP, theater, trigonometry, visual and performing arts, women's studies, writing.

Graduation Requirements Arts and fine arts (art, music, dance, drama), English, foreign language, history, mathematics, science, 50 hours of community service.

Special Academic Programs Advanced Placement exam preparation; honors section; independent study; study abroad; ESL (5 students enrolled).

College Admission Counseling 96 students graduated in 2010; all went to college, including Boston University; Colby College; Harvard University; New York University; Tufts University. Mean SAT critical reading: 602, mean SAT math: 633, mean SAT writing: 603, mean combined SAT: 1829. 38% scored over 600 on SAT critical reading, 50% scored over 600 on SAT math, 42% scored over 600 on SAT writing, 42% scored over 1800 on combined SAT.

Student Life Upper grades have specified standards of dress, student council, honor system. Discipline rests primarily with faculty.

Tuition and Aid Day student tuition: $35,250; 7-day tuition and room/board: $44,550. Tuition installment plan (The Tuition Plan, Academic Management Services Plan, monthly payment plans). Need-based scholarship grants available. In 2010–11, 28% of upper-school students received aid. Total amount of financial aid awarded in 2010–11: $32,000,000.

Admissions Traditional secondary-level entrance grade is 9. For fall 2010, 775 students applied for upper-level admission, 234 were accepted, 110 enrolled. ISEE, SSAT or TOEFL required. Deadline for receipt of application materials: January 31. Application fee required: $50. Interview required.

Athletics Interscholastic: baseball (boys), basketball (b,g), cross-country running (b,g), field hockey (g), football (b), ice hockey (b,g), indoor track & field (b,g), lacrosse (b,g), soccer (b,g), softball (g), tennis (b,g), track and field (b,g), volleyball (g), wrestling (b); intramural: dance (g); coed interscholastic: golf; coed intramural: aerobics/dance, alpine skiing, dance, outdoor activities, outdoor recreation, skiing (downhill), tennis, yoga. 2 athletic trainers.

Computers Computers are regularly used in art, English, foreign language, history, mathematics, music, science classes. Computer network features include on-campus library services, online commercial services, Internet access, wireless campus network, Internet filtering or blocking technology, laptop sign-out in student center and library, Moodle Website for teachers and students to share course data, events, and discussions. Campus intranet, student e-mail accounts, and computer access in designated common areas are available to students. The school has a published electronic and media policy.

Contact Michael Kinnealey, Director of Admission. 978-499-3120. Fax: 978-462-1278. E-mail: admissions@thegovernorsacademy.org. Web site: www.thegovernorsacademy.org.

GRACE BAPTIST ACADEMY

7815 Shallowford Road

Chattanooga, Tennessee 37421

Head of School: Mr. David Patrick

General Information Coeducational day college-preparatory and religious studies school, affiliated with Baptist Church. Grades K4–12. Founded: 1985. Setting: suburban. 2 buildings on campus. Approved or accredited by Association of Christian Schools International, Southern Association of Colleges and Schools, and Tennessee Department of Education. Total enrollment: 704. Upper school average class size: 22. Upper school faculty-student ratio: 1:20. Upper School students typically attend 5 days per week. The average school day consists of 7 hours and 15 minutes.

Upper School Student Profile Grade 9: 53 students (23 boys, 30 girls); Grade 10: 45 students (18 boys, 27 girls); Grade 11: 49 students (20 boys, 29 girls); Grade 12: 42 students (20 boys, 22 girls). 75% of students are Baptist.

Faculty School total: 47. In upper school: 10 men, 9 women; 5 have advanced degrees.

Subjects Offered Advanced computer applications, algebra, American government, American history, American literature, ancient world history, art, band, Bible, Bible studies, biology, biology-AP, calculus, chemistry, choir, Christian doctrine, Christian ethics, Christian testament, computer applications, drama performance, dramatic arts, economics, English, English composition, English literature, environmental studies, fitness, general math, general science, geometry, global studies, health, health and safety, honors English, honors world history, keyboarding, language arts, Life of Christ, mathematics, music, New Testament, physical education, physics, pre-algebra, pre-calculus, SAT/ACT preparation, Spanish, speech, state history, study skills, U.S. government and politics, U.S. history, weight training, weightlifting, world geography, yearbook.

Graduation Requirements Algebra, American history, Bible, biology, chemistry, economics, English, English literature, geometry, global studies, government, physical education (includes health), Spanish, speech, U.S. history, visual and performing arts, 1/2 unit of speech.

Special Academic Programs Honors section; study at local college for college credit.

College Admission Counseling 58 students graduated in 2010; 56 went to college, including Chattanooga State Community College; The University of Tennessee at Chattanooga. Other: 2 went to work. Mean composite ACT: 22.

Student Life Upper grades have uniform requirement, student council, honor system. Discipline rests primarily with faculty. Attendance at religious services is required.

Tuition and Aid Tuition installment plan (FACTS Tuition Payment Plan, bank draft). Tuition reduction for siblings, need-based scholarship grants available. In 2010–11, 5% of upper-school students received aid.

Admissions Traditional secondary-level entrance grade is 9. For fall 2010, 26 students applied for upper-level admission, 25 were accepted, 25 enrolled. Latest standardized score from previous school required. Deadline for receipt of application materials: none. Application fee required: $300. On-campus interview required.

Athletics Interscholastic: baseball (boys), basketball (b,g), cheering (g), cross-country running (b,g), football (b), soccer (b,g), softball (g), tennis (b,g), track and field (b,g), volleyball (g), weight training (b,g); intramural: physical training (b,g), strength & conditioning (b,g), weight lifting (b), weight training (b); coed interscholastic: archery, golf. 2 PE instructors, 5 coaches, 1 athletic trainer.

Computers Computers are regularly used in computer applications, keyboarding, Web site design classes. Computer resources include on-campus library services, Internet access, Internet filtering or blocking technology. Students grades are available online.

Contact Mrs. Janine McCurdy, Admissions Director. 423-892-8222 Ext. 115. Fax: 423-892-1194. E-mail: jmccurdy@gracechatt.org. Web site: www.gracechatt.org.

GRACE BRETHREN SCHOOL

1350 Cherry Avenue

Simi Valley, California 93065

Head of School: Mr. John Hynes

General Information Coeducational day college-preparatory, arts, vocational, religious studies, and bilingual studies school, affiliated with Brethren Church, Christian faith. Grades PS–12. Founded: 1979. Setting: suburban. Nearest major city is Los Angeles. 12-acre campus. 9 buildings on campus. Approved or accredited by Association of Christian Schools International, Western Association of Schools and Colleges, and California Department of Education. Total enrollment: 810. Upper school average class size: 20. Upper school faculty-student ratio: 1:11.

Upper School Student Profile 90% of students are Brethren, Christian.

Faculty School total: 36. In upper school: 18 men, 18 women; 15 have advanced degrees.

Subjects Offered Accounting, Advanced Placement courses, algebra, American literature, American literature-AP, anatomy and physiology, ancient world history, art, ASB Leadership, athletic training, band, baseball, basketball, Bible, Bible studies, biology, British literature, British literature-AP, career/college preparation, cheerleading, chemistry, choir, college counseling, computer graphics, computer music, computer tools, concert choir, critical thinking, critical writing, digital photography, drama, drama performance, environmental science, film studies, forensics, geometry, government and politics-AP, health, home economics, jazz ensemble, New Testament, photography, physical education, physics, physics-AP, pre-algebra, pre-calculus, set design, softball, Spanish, Spanish language-AP, speech, stage design, statistics, statistics-AP, technical theater, U.S. government and politics, U.S. government and politics-AP, U.S. history, U.S. history-AP, visual and performing arts, volleyball, world cultures, world geography, world history, yearbook.

Graduation Requirements Bible studies, electives, English, foreign language, mathematics, physical education (includes health), science, social studies (includes history), visual and performing arts.

Special Academic Programs Advanced Placement exam preparation; honors section; independent study; study at local college for college credit; remedial math.

College Admission Counseling 55 students graduated in 2011; 53 went to college, including California State University, Northridge; Moorpark College; The Master's College and Seminary; University of California, Los Angeles; Westmont College. Other: 2 entered a postgraduate year. Median combined SAT: 1480. 15% scored over 1800 on combined SAT.

Student Life Upper grades have uniform requirement, student council, honor system. Discipline rests primarily with faculty. Attendance at religious services is required.

Summer Programs Remediation, advancement programs offered; session focuses on remediation; held on campus; accepts boys and girls; open to students from other schools. 45 students usually enrolled.

Tuition and Aid Day student tuition: $8376. Guaranteed tuition plan. Tuition installment plan (monthly payment plans). Tuition reduction for siblings, need-based scholarship grants available. In 2011–12, 5% of upper-school students received aid.

Admissions Traditional secondary-level entrance grade is 9. For fall 2011, 71 students applied for upper-level admission, 68 were accepted, 64 enrolled. Math Placement Exam, Stanford Achievement Test and writing sample required. Deadline for receipt of application materials: none. Application fee required: $385. On-campus interview required.

Athletics Interscholastic: aquatics (boys, girls), baseball (b), basketball (b,g), cheering (g), cross-country running (b,g), equestrian sports (b,g), flag football (b), football (b), golf (b,g), physical training (b,g), soccer (b,g), softball (g), strength & conditioning (b,g), swimming and diving (b,g), track and field (b,g), volleyball (g), weight training (b). 4 PE instructors, 16 coaches, 1 athletic trainer.

Computers Computers are regularly used in art, graphic arts, library, newspaper, photography, photojournalism, science, study skills, video film production, writing, yearbook classes. Computer network features include on-campus library services, Internet access, wireless campus network, Internet filtering or blocking technology. Computer access in designated common areas is available to students. Students grades are available online. The school has a published electronic and media policy.

Contact Mrs. Sheri Herr, Registrar. 805-522-4667 Ext. 2033. Fax: 805-522-5617. E-mail: sherr@gracebrethren.com. Web site: www.gracebrethrenschools.com.

GRACE CHRISTIAN SCHOOL

50 Kirkdale Road

Charlottetown, Prince Edward Island C1E 1N6, Canada

Head of School: Mr. Jason Biech

General Information Coeducational day college-preparatory, arts, and religious studies school, affiliated with Baptist Church, Evangelical faith. Grades JK–12. Founded: 1980. Setting: small town. 6-acre campus. 1 building on campus. Approved or accredited by Christian Schools International and Prince Edward Island Department of Education. Language of instruction: English. Endowment: CAN$100,000. Total enrollment: 124. Upper school average class size: 10. Upper school faculty-student ratio: 1:10. There are 185 required school days per year for Upper School students. Upper School students typically attend 5 days per week. The average school day consists of 6 hours.

Upper School Student Profile Grade 6: 14 students (4 boys, 10 girls); Grade 7: 13 students (7 boys, 6 girls); Grade 8: 10 students (5 boys, 5 girls); Grade 9: 12 students (8 boys, 4 girls); Grade 10: 8 students (5 boys, 3 girls); Grade 11: 7 students (1 boy, 6 girls); Grade 12: 10 students (5 boys, 5 girls). 70% of students are Baptist, members of Evangelical faith.

Faculty School total: 12. In upper school: 4 men, 3 women.

Graduation Requirements Bible, language, mathematics, Christian service requirements.

College Admission Counseling 10 students graduated in 2010; 9 went to college, including Acadia University. Other: 1 went to work.

Student Life Upper grades have specified standards of dress, student council. Discipline rests primarily with faculty. Attendance at religious services is required.

Tuition and Aid Day student tuition: CAN$3600. Tuition installment plan (monthly payment plans). Tuition reduction for siblings, bursaries available. In 2010–11, 5% of upper-school students received aid. Total amount of financial aid awarded in 2010–11: CAN$4000.

Admissions Traditional secondary-level entrance grade is 10. For fall 2010, 6 students applied for upper-level admission, 6 were accepted, 6 enrolled. Deadline for receipt of application materials: June 25. Application fee required: CAN$200. On-campus interview required.

Athletics Interscholastic: basketball (boys, girls), cross-country running (b,g), soccer (b,g); coed interscholastic: cross-country running, golf, track and field; coed intramural: cross-country running, track and field.

Computers Computer resources include Internet access.

Contact Mr. Jason Biech, Administrator. 902-628-1668 Ext. 223. Fax: 902-628-1668. E-mail: principal@gracechristianschool.ca.

THE GRAUER SCHOOL

1500 South El Camino Real

Encinitas, California 92024

Head of School: Dr. Stuart Robert Grauer, EdD

General Information Coeducational day college-preparatory, arts, technology, and All of our students graduate with Distinction in a subject. school. Grades 6–12. Founded: 1991. Setting: suburban. Nearest major city is San Diego. 5-acre campus. 6 buildings on campus. Approved or accredited by California Association of Independent Schools, Western Association of Schools and Colleges, and California Department of Education. Endowment: $150,000. Total enrollment: 152. Upper school average class size: 12. Upper school faculty-student ratio: 1:6. There are 178 required school days per year for Upper School students. Upper School students typically attend 5 days per week. The average school day consists of 6 hours and 30 minutes.

Upper School Student Profile Grade 6: 12 students (6 boys, 6 girls); Grade 7: 30 students (13 boys, 17 girls); Grade 8: 24 students (9 boys, 15 girls); Grade 9: 24 students (15 boys, 9 girls); Grade 10: 17 students (10 boys, 7 girls); Grade 11: 25 students (11 boys, 14 girls); Grade 12: 20 students (11 boys, 9 girls).

Faculty School total: 30. In upper school: 11 men, 15 women; 22 have advanced degrees.

Subjects Offered ACT preparation, advanced biology, advanced chemistry, advanced math, advanced TOEFL/grammar, algebra, alternative physical education, American government, American history, anatomy and physiology, ancient history, applied music, art, art appreciation, art history, art history-AP, ASB Leadership, athletic training, audio visual/media, backpacking, baseball, basketball, bell choir, biology, business mathematics, calculus, character education, chemistry, Chinese, choir, civics, classical music, college admission preparation, college planning, community service, computer applications, computer education, computer multimedia, computers, creative writing, culinary arts, drama, dramatic arts, earth and space science, economics, English literature, environmental education, ESL, ESL, experiential education, fencing, film studies, filmmaking, fitness, French, gardening, geography, geometry, global studies, health, high adventure outdoor program, honors algebra, honors English, honors geometry, honors U.S. history, honors world history, Japanese, keyboarding, Latin, leadership and service, marine science, multimedia, music, music appreciation, music performance, outdoor education, peace studies, personal fitness, photo shop, photography, physical education, physics, pre-algebra, pre-calculus, religion, religion and culture, robotics, SAT preparation, Spanish, speech and debate, studio art, study skills, surfing, tennis, theater arts, trigonometry, U.S. government, U.S. history, U.S. literature, world geography, world history, world religions.

Graduation Requirements Algebra, American history, art, biology, chemistry, college admission preparation, computer applications, computer skills, economics, English, experiential education, foreign language, French, geometry, life science, marine science, mathematics, non-Western literature, outdoor education, physical education (includes health), physical science, physics, science, senior project, social studies (includes history), studio art, U.S. government, U.S. history, U.S. literature, Western civilization, Western literature, wilderness education, world geography, world history, world literature, world religions, expeditionary learning in the field and 50 hours community service, all students graduate with distinction in a subject of their choice.

Special Academic Programs Advanced Placement exam preparation; honors section; independent study; study abroad; academic accommodation for the gifted, the musically talented, and the artistically talented; remedial math; special instructional classes for deaf students; ESL (7 students enrolled).

College Admission Counseling 14 students graduated in 2011; all went to college, including Bates College; Sarah Lawrence College; The College of Wooster; University of California, Irvine; University of California, San Diego; University of Colorado Boulder. Median SAT critical reading: 650, median SAT math: 600, median SAT writing: 600. 60% scored over 600 on SAT critical reading, 60% scored over 600 on SAT math, 60% scored over 600 on SAT writing.

Student Life Upper grades have specified standards of dress, student council, honor system. Discipline rests equally with students and faculty.

Summer Programs Remediation, enrichment, advancement, ESL, sports, art/fine arts, rigorous outdoor training, computer instruction programs offered; session focuses on academics and enrichment; held on campus; accepts boys and girls; open to students from other schools. 60 students usually enrolled. 2012 schedule: June 18 to July 27. Application deadline: June 1.

Tuition and Aid Day student tuition: $18,000. Tuition installment plan (individually arranged payment plans, 3 payment plans). Tuition reduction for siblings, need-based scholarship grants available. In 2011–12, 13% of upper-school students received aid. Total amount of financial aid awarded in 2011–12: $90,000.

Admissions Traditional secondary-level entrance grade is 9. For fall 2011, 36 students applied for upper-level admission, 19 were accepted, 16 enrolled. Admissions testing, any standardized test and writing sample required. Deadline for receipt of application materials: February 7. Application fee required: $100. Interview required.

Athletics Interscholastic: equestrian sports (girls), football (g), tennis (b,g), volleyball (g); intramural: baseball (b), basketball (b,g), equestrian sports (g), ice hockey (g), martial arts (g), soccer (b,g), tennis (b,g), triathlon (b,g), volleyball (b,g); coed interscholastic: cross-country running, sailing, soccer, tennis, track and field; coed intramural: aerobics/dance, alpine skiing, backpacking, bicycling, bowling, canoeing/kayaking, climbing, cross-country running, dance, dressage, fitness, fitness walking, flag football, football, golf, hiking/backpacking, independent competitive sports, jogging, kayaking, marksmanship, mountain biking, outdoor education, physical fitness, physical training, rock climbing, running, sailing, self defense, skiing (downhill), snowboarding, soccer, strength & conditioning, surfing, tennis, track and field, triathlon, volleyball, weight training, yoga. 5 PE instructors, 5 coaches.

Computers Computers are regularly used in English, ESL, foreign language, graphic arts, journalism, keyboarding, multimedia, photography, programming, SAT preparation, video film production, yearbook classes. Computer network features include Internet access, wireless campus network, Internet filtering or blocking technology. Campus intranet, student e-mail accounts, and computer access in designated common areas are available to students. Students grades are available online. The school has a published electronic and media policy.

Contact Mrs. Elizabeth Braymen, JD, Admissions Director. 760-274-2116. Fax: 760-944-6784. E-mail: admissions@grauerschool.com. Web site: www.grauerschool.com.

GREATER ATLANTA CHRISTIAN SCHOOLS

1575 Indian Trail Road

Norcross, Georgia 30093

Head of School: Dr. David Fincher

General Information Coeducational day college-preparatory, arts, religious studies, and technology school, affiliated with Christian faith, Christian faith. Grades P4–12. Founded: 1961. Setting: suburban. Nearest major city is Atlanta. 74-acre campus. 18 buildings on campus. Approved or accredited by Canadian Educational Standards Institute, Georgia Independent School Association, National Christian School Association, Southern Association of Colleges and Schools, Southern Association of Independent Schools, The College Board, and Georgia Department of Education. Endowment: $28.5 million. Total enrollment: 1,850. Upper school average class size: 13. Upper school faculty-student ratio: 1:13. There are 180 required school days per year for Upper School students. Upper School students typically attend 5 days per week. The average school day consists of 7 hours and 10 minutes.

Upper School Student Profile Grade 9: 186 students (96 boys, 90 girls); Grade 10: 201 students (99 boys, 102 girls); Grade 11: 177 students (97 boys, 80 girls); Grade 12: 155 students (78 boys, 77 girls).

Faculty School total: 150. In upper school: 35 men, 30 women; 39 have advanced degrees.

Subjects Offered 3-dimensional art, accounting, Advanced Placement courses, algebra, American history-AP, American literature, analysis, anatomy, art appreciation, art history, art-AP, audio visual/media, band, Bible, biology-AP, British literature, business, calculus-AP, chemistry-AP, chorus, composition, computer applications, computer math, computer programming, computer science-AP, dramatic arts, economics-AP, English language and composition-AP, environmental science, ethics, European history, European history-AP, expository writing, French, geometry, government-AP, graphic design, home economics, honors English, journalism, language arts, Latin, Latin-AP, music theory-AP, music-AP, newspaper, orchestra, painting, personal finance, philosophy, photography, physics-AP, physiology, pre-calculus, psychology-AP, religion, sculpture, sociology, Spanish, speech, speech communications, statistics, statistics-AP, studio art-AP, symphonic band, theology, trigonometry, U.S. history-AP, video film production, visual arts, Web site design, world history-AP, world literature, yearbook.

Graduation Requirements English, foreign language, mathematics, physical education (includes health), religious studies, science, social sciences, social studies (includes history), one year of Bible for each year of attendance.

Special Academic Programs 19 Advanced Placement exams for which test preparation is offered; honors section; study abroad; academic accommodation for the gifted, the musically talented, and the artistically talented.

College Admission Counseling 151 students graduated in 2010; all went to college, including Auburn University; Georgia Institute of Technology; Georgia Southern University; Lipscomb University; The University of Alabama; University of Georgia. Median SAT critical reading: 566, median SAT math: 581, median SAT writing: 568, median combined SAT: 1715, median composite ACT: 26.

Student Life Upper grades have uniform requirement, student council, honor system. Discipline rests primarily with faculty. Attendance at religious services is required.

Tuition and Aid Day student tuition: $14,400. Tuition installment plan (monthly payment plans, quarterly payment plan). Need-based scholarship grants available.

Admissions Traditional secondary-level entrance grade is 9. For fall 2010, 123 students applied for upper-level admission, 85 were accepted, 69 enrolled. California Achievement Test or Stanford 9 required. Deadline for receipt of application materials: none. Application fee required: $160. On-campus interview required.

Athletics Interscholastic: baseball (boys), dance team (g), flag football (b), football (b), golf (b,g), lacrosse (b,g), soccer (b,g), softball (g), tennis (b,g), volleyball (g), wrestling (b); intramural: aerobics (g), ballet (g), cheering (g), physical fitness (b,g), strength & conditioning (b,g), weight lifting (b), weight training (b,g); coed interscholastic: aquatics, basketball, cross-country running, diving, swimming and diving, track and field, water polo. 5 PE instructors, 1 athletic trainer.

Computers Computers are regularly used in college planning classes. Computer network features include on-campus library services, online commercial services, Internet access, wireless campus network, Internet filtering or blocking technology. Campus intranet is available to students. Students grades are available online. The school has a published electronic and media policy.

Contact Mrs. Linda Clovis, Director of Admissions. 770-243-2274. Fax: 770-243-2213. E-mail: lclovis@greateratlantachristian.org. Web site: www.greateratlantachristian.org.

GREAT LAKES CHRISTIAN HIGH SCHOOL

4875 King Street

Beamsville, Ontario L0R 1B6, Canada

Head of School: Mr. Don Rose

General Information Coeducational boarding and day college-preparatory, general academic, arts, and religious studies school, affiliated with Church of Christ. Grades 9–12. Founded: 1952. Setting: small town. Nearest major city is Hamilton, Canada. Students are housed in single-sex dormitories. 15-acre campus. 6 buildings on campus. Approved or accredited by Ontario Ministry of Education and Ontario Department of Education. Language of instruction: English. Endowment: CAN$500,000. Total enrollment: 95. Upper school average class size: 22. Upper school faculty-student ratio: 1:10. There are 180 required school days per year for Upper School students. Upper School students typically attend 5 days per week. The average school day consists of 6 hours and 10 minutes.

Upper School Student Profile Grade 9: 11 students (4 boys, 7 girls); Grade 10: 26 students (11 boys, 15 girls); Grade 11: 32 students (20 boys, 12 girls); Grade 12: 26 students (11 boys, 15 girls). 55% of students are boarding students. 60% are province residents. 5 provinces are represented in upper school student body. 30% are international students. International students from China, Hong Kong, Japan, Republic of Korea, Taiwan, and United States; 3 other countries represented in student body. 40% of students are members of Church of Christ.

Faculty School total: 11. In upper school: 7 men, 4 women; 4 have advanced degrees; 3 reside on campus.

Subjects Offered 20th century world history, accounting, algebra, arts appreciation, Bible, biology, calculus, career and personal planning, chemistry, computer science, computer technologies, dramatic arts, economics, English, English composition, English language and composition-AP, English literature, English-AP, ESL, family studies, finite math, French, geography, history, mathematics, mathematics-AP, media, music, music composition, physical education, physics, society, technology, world issues.

Graduation Requirements 20th century history, advanced math, art, Bible, business, Canadian geography, Canadian history, Canadian literature, career planning, civics, computer information systems, conceptual physics, critical thinking, current events, economics, English, English composition, English literature, French as a second language, geography, mathematics, physical education (includes health), science, society challenge and change, world geography, world history.

Special Academic Programs Independent study; ESL (13 students enrolled).

College Admission Counseling 23 students graduated in 2011; 17 went to college, including Carleton University; McMaster University; University of Ottawa; University of Toronto; Wilfrid Laurier University; York University. Other: 6 went to work.

Student Life Upper grades have uniform requirement, student council. Discipline rests primarily with faculty. Attendance at religious services is required.

Summer Programs ESL, sports, computer instruction programs offered; session focuses on skill levels improvement; held on campus; accepts boys and girls; open to students from other schools. 2012 schedule: June 25 to August 24. Application deadline: May 11.

Tuition and Aid Day student tuition: CAN$8000; 5-day tuition and room/board: CAN$13,400; 7-day tuition and room/board: CAN$15,200. Tuition installment plan (monthly payment plans, individually arranged payment plans). Tuition reduction for siblings, bursaries, merit scholarship grants, need-based scholarship grants, need-based loans, middle-income loans, paying campus jobs available. In 2011–12, 45% of upper-school students received aid; total upper-school merit-scholarship money awarded: CAN$8000. Total amount of financial aid awarded in 2011–12: CAN$150,000.

Admissions Traditional secondary-level entrance grade is 9. For fall 2011, 130 students applied for upper-level admission, 115 were accepted, 95 enrolled. CAT or SLEP required. Deadline for receipt of application materials: none. Application fee required: CAN$100. Interview recommended.

Athletics Interscholastic: badminton (boys, girls), basketball (b,g), cross-country running (b,g), golf (b), hockey (b,g), ice hockey (b,g), soccer (b,g), tennis (b,g), track and field (b,g), volleyball (b,g); intramural: aerobics (g), badminton (b,g), basketball (b,g), cooperative games (b,g), fitness (b,g), ice hockey (b,g), volleyball (b,g); coed interscholastic: badminton, indoor hockey, indoor soccer, netball; coed intramural: badminton, ball hockey, baseball, basketball, cooperative games, floor hockey, hockey, volleyball. 2 PE instructors, 2 coaches.

Computers Computers are regularly used in accounting, business, music, technology, typing classes. Computer network features include Internet access, Internet filtering or blocking technology, grades are available online to parents. Computer access in designated common areas is available to students. Students grades are available online.

Contact Mrs. Sandy McBay, Admissions Liaison. 905-563-5374 Ext. 230. Fax: 905-563-0818. E-mail: study@glchs.on.ca. Web site: www.glchs.on.ca.

GREENFIELD SCHOOL

PO Box 3525

Wilson, North Carolina 27895-3525

Head of School: Dr. Vincent M. Janney

General Information Coeducational day and distance learning college-preparatory school. Grades PS–12. Distance learning grades 11–12. Founded: 1969. Setting: small town. Nearest major city is Raleigh. 61-acre campus. 9 buildings on campus. Approved or accredited by Southern Association of Colleges and Schools and North Carolina Department of Education. Member of National Association of Independent Schools. Total enrollment: 307. Upper school average class size: 19. Upper school faculty-student ratio: 1:3. There are 180 required school days per year for Upper School students. Upper School students typically attend 5 days per week. The average school day consists of 6 hours and 45 minutes.

Upper School Student Profile Grade 9: 18 students (7 boys, 11 girls); Grade 10: 19 students (7 boys, 12 girls); Grade 11: 20 students (10 boys, 10 girls); Grade 12: 15 students (12 boys, 3 girls).

Faculty School total: 56. In upper school: 9 men, 15 women; 13 have advanced degrees.

Subjects Offered Advanced computer applications, advanced math, Advanced Placement courses, algebra, American history, American literature, ancient world history, art, athletics, biology, British literature, calculus, calculus-AP, chemistry, chorus, college awareness, community service, computer applications, computer education, computer graphics, computer information systems, computer math, computer multimedia, computer processing, computer programming, computer programming-AP, computer science, computer skills, computer technologies, desktop publishing, drama, earth science, economics, electives, English, English literature, fine arts, foreign language, geography, geometry, government/civics, grammar, health, history, honors algebra, honors English, honors geometry, honors world history, keyboarding, language arts, mathematics, music, physical education, physical science, physics, pre-algebra, pre-calculus, SAT preparation, science, social studies, Spanish, sports conditioning, trigonometry, Web site design, world geography, world history, writing, yearbook.

Graduation Requirements Arts and fine arts (art, music, dance, drama), computer science, English, foreign language, mathematics, physical education (includes health), science, social studies (includes history). Community service is required.

Special Academic Programs 5 Advanced Placement exams for which test preparation is offered; honors section; independent study; academic accommodation for the gifted; remedial reading and/or remedial writing; remedial math; programs in English, general development for dyslexic students.

College Admission Counseling 19 students graduated in 2011; all went to college, including Agnes Scott College; East Carolina University; Meredith College; North Carolina State University; The University of North Carolina at Chapel Hill; University of Kentucky. Median SAT critical reading: 520, median SAT math: 510, median SAT writing: 500, median combined SAT: 1540, median composite ACT: 23. 18% scored over 600 on SAT critical reading, 24% scored over 600 on SAT math, 29% scored over 600 on SAT writing, 24% scored over 1800 on combined SAT, 38% scored over 26 on composite ACT.

Student Life Upper grades have specified standards of dress, student council, honor system. Discipline rests primarily with faculty.

Summer Programs Enrichment, sports, art/fine arts, computer instruction programs offered; session focuses on academic enrichment, athletic development, and relaxation; held on campus; accepts boys and girls; open to students from other schools. 200 students usually enrolled. 2012 schedule: June 4 to August 3. Application deadline: none.

Tuition and Aid Day student tuition: $8730. Tuition installment plan (monthly payment plans). Tuition reduction for siblings, merit scholarship grants, need-based scholarship grants available.

Admissions Traditional secondary-level entrance grade is 9. For fall 2011, 15 students applied for upper-level admission, 12 were accepted, 7 enrolled. Brigance Test of Basic Skills, Comprehensive Test of Basic Skills or CTP III required. Deadline for receipt of application materials: none. Application fee required: $100. On-campus interview required.

Athletics Interscholastic: baseball (boys), basketball (b,g), cheering (g), soccer (b,g), tennis (b,g), volleyball (g); coed interscholastic: golf. 3 PE instructors, 11 coaches.

Computers Computers are regularly used in all academic classes. Computer resources include on-campus library services, Internet access, wireless campus network, Internet filtering or blocking technology. Computer access in designated common areas is available to students. The school has a published electronic and media policy.

Contact Diane Oliphant Hamilton, Director of Admissions and Community Relations. 252-237-8046. Fax: 252-237-1825. E-mail: hamiltond@greenfieldschool.org. Web site: www.greenfieldschool.org.

GREENHILL SCHOOL

4141 Spring Valley Road

Addison, Texas 75001

Head of School: Scott A. Griggs

General Information Coeducational day college-preparatory school. Grades PK–12. Founded: 1950. Setting: suburban. Nearest major city is Dallas. 78-acre campus. 8 buildings on campus. Approved or accredited by Independent Schools Association of the Southwest and Texas Department of Education. Member of National Association of Independent Schools and Secondary School Admission Test Board. Endowment: $28.2 million. Total enrollment: 1,270. Upper school average class size: 16. Upper school faculty-student ratio: 1:7. Upper School students typically attend 5 days per week. The average school day consists of 7 hours and 45 minutes.

Upper School Student Profile Grade 9: 112 students (55 boys, 57 girls); Grade 10: 117 students (56 boys, 61 girls); Grade 11: 117 students (59 boys, 58 girls); Grade 12: 118 students (59 boys, 59 girls).

Faculty School total: 167. In upper school: 40 men, 26 women; 54 have advanced degrees.

Subjects Offered Algebra, American history, American literature, art, art history, biology, calculus, ceramics, chemistry, Chinese, computer programming, computer science, creative writing, dance, drama, ecology, economics, English, English literature, European history, fine arts, French, geometry, government/civics, health, history, journalism, Latin, mathematics, music, philosophy, photography, physical education, physics, science, social studies, Spanish, speech, theater, trigonometry.

Graduation Requirements Arts and fine arts (art, music, dance, drama), classical language, computer studies, English, history, mathematics, modern languages, physical education (includes health), public speaking, science. Community service is required.

Special Academic Programs Advanced Placement exam preparation; honors section; independent study; term-away projects.

College Admission Counseling 104 students graduated in 2011; all went to college, including Duke University; Indiana University Bloomington; New York University; Southern Methodist University; The University of Texas at Austin; University of Southern California. Median SAT critical reading: 640, median SAT math: 630, median SAT writing: 630, median combined SAT: 1890, median composite ACT: 30. 69% scored over 600 on SAT critical reading, 60% scored over 600 on SAT math, 55% scored over 600 on SAT writing, 64% scored over 1800 on combined SAT, 85% scored over 26 on composite ACT.

Student Life Upper grades have specified standards of dress, student council, honor system. Discipline rests primarily with faculty.

Summer Programs Enrichment, sports, art/fine arts, computer instruction programs offered; session focuses on enrichment and sports; held on campus; accepts boys and girls; open to students from other schools. 1,300 students usually enrolled. 2012 schedule: May 29 to August 10. Application deadline: none.

Tuition and Aid Day student tuition: $23,100. Need-based scholarship grants available. In 2011–12, 20% of upper-school students received aid. Total amount of financial aid awarded in 2011–12: $1,424,960.

Admissions Traditional secondary-level entrance grade is 9. For fall 2011, 179 students applied for upper-level admission, 75 were accepted, 47 enrolled. ISEE required. Deadline for receipt of application materials: January 13. Application fee required: $175. Interview required.

Athletics Interscholastic: aquatics (boys, girls), baseball (b), basketball (b,g), cross-country running (b,g), field hockey (g), football (b), golf (b,g), lacrosse (b,g), running (b,g), soccer (b,g), softball (g), swimming and diving (b,g), tennis (b,g), track and field (b,g), volleyball (b,g), winter soccer (b,g); intramural: baseball (b), basketball (b,g), field hockey (g), fitness (b,g), football (b), lacrosse (b,g), physical fitness (b,g), running (b,g), soccer (b,g), softball (g), strength & conditioning (b,g), swimming and diving (b,g), tennis (b,g), track and field (b,g), volleyball (b,g), weight lifting (b,g), winter soccer (b,g); coed interscholastic: cheering; coed intramural: aquatics, ballet, cross-country running, dance, fitness, Frisbee, golf, physical fitness, running, soccer, strength & conditioning, swimming and diving, table tennis, tai chi, tennis, track and field, ultimate Frisbee, volleyball, weight lifting, weight training, winter soccer, yoga. 15 PE instructors, 4 athletic trainers.

Computers Computers are regularly used in computer applications, digital applications, independent study, programming, video film production, Web site design classes. Computer network features include on-campus library services, online commercial services, Internet access, wireless campus network, Internet filtering or blocking technology. Campus intranet, student e-mail accounts, and computer access in designated common areas are available to students. Students grades are available online. The school has a published electronic and media policy.

Contact Angela H. Woodson, Director of Admission. 972-628-5910. Fax: 972-404-8217. E-mail: admission@greenhill.org. Web site: www.greenhill.org.

GREENHILLS SCHOOL

850 Greenhills Drive

Ann Arbor, Michigan 48105

Head of School: Peter B. Fayroian

General Information Coeducational day college-preparatory and arts school. Grades 6–12. Founded: 1968. Setting: suburban. Nearest major city is Detroit. 30-acre campus. 1 building on campus. Approved or accredited by Independent Schools Association of the Central States and Michigan Department of Education. Member of National Association of Independent Schools and Secondary School Admission Test Board. Endowment: $6 million. Total enrollment: 538. Upper school average class size: 15. Upper school faculty-student ratio: 1:7. There are 165 required school days per year for Upper School students. Upper School students typically attend 5 days per week. The average school day consists of 7 hours.

Upper School Student Profile Grade 9: 70 students (28 boys, 42 girls); Grade 10: 79 students (44 boys, 35 girls); Grade 11: 89 students (30 boys, 59 girls); Grade 12: 79 students (29 boys, 50 girls).

Faculty School total: 70. In upper school: 24 men, 24 women; 42 have advanced degrees.

Subjects Offered 3-dimensional art, advanced chemistry, Advanced Placement courses, African-American literature, algebra, American history, American literature, ancient history, art, astronomy, biology, calculus, calculus-AP, ceramics, chemistry, Chinese, Chinese studies, chorus, community service, creative writing, discrete mathematics, drama, drawing, economics, economics and history, English, English literature, ethics, European history, expository writing, fine arts, French, geometry, government, health, history, jazz, journalism, Latin, mathematics, music, orchestra, painting, photography, physical education, physical science, physics, science, social studies, Spanish, theater, trigonometry, world history, world literature, writing.

Graduation Requirements Arts and fine arts (art, music, dance, drama), English, foreign language, mathematics, physical education (includes health), science, social studies (includes history), senior project. Community service is required.

Special Academic Programs Advanced Placement exam preparation; honors section; independent study; study at local college for college credit; academic accommodation for the gifted; programs in English, mathematics for dyslexic students; special instructional classes for blind students.

College Admission Counseling 80 students graduated in 2010; all went to college, including Pomona College; Princeton University; University of Michigan; Wesleyan University; Yale University. Median SAT critical reading: 659, median SAT math: 672, median SAT writing: 651, median combined SAT: 1982, median composite ACT: 29.

Student Life Upper grades have specified standards of dress, student council, honor system. Discipline rests equally with students and faculty.

Tuition and Aid Day student tuition: $18,225. Tuition installment plan (FACTS Tuition Payment Plan, monthly payment plans). Need-based scholarship grants available. In 2010–11, 21% of upper-school students received aid. Total amount of financial aid awarded in 2010–11: $1,000,000.

Admissions Traditional secondary-level entrance grade is 9. For fall 2010, 86 students applied for upper-level admission, 55 were accepted, 31 enrolled. SSAT or TOEFL required. Deadline for receipt of application materials: none. Application fee required: $50. Interview required.

Athletics Interscholastic: baseball (boys), basketball (b,g), cross-country running (b,g), field hockey (g), golf (b,g), soccer (b,g), softball (g), tennis (b,g), track and field (b,g), volleyball (g); intramural: basketball (b,g), cross-country running (b,g), field hockey (g), soccer (b,g); coed interscholastic: equestrian sports, swimming and diving; coed intramural: hiking/backpacking, outdoor activities, outdoor education. 3 PE instructors, 1 athletic trainer.

Computers Computers are regularly used in all academic classes. Computer network features include on-campus library services, online commercial services, Internet access, wireless campus network, Internet filtering or blocking technology. Campus intranet, student e-mail accounts, and computer access in designated common areas are available to students. Students grades are available online. The school has a published electronic and media policy.

Contact Betsy Ellsworth, Director of Admission and Financial Aid. 734-205-4061. Fax: 734-205-4056. E-mail: admission@greenhillsschool.org. Web site: www.greenhillsschool.org.

GREENSBORO DAY SCHOOL

5401 Lawndale Drive

Greensboro, North Carolina 27455

Head of School: Mr. Mark C. Hale

General Information Coeducational day college-preparatory, arts, and technology school. Grades K–12. Founded: 1970. Setting: suburban. 65-acre campus. 10 buildings on campus. Approved or accredited by North Carolina Association of Independent Schools and Southern Association of Colleges and Schools. Member of National Association of Independent Schools. Total enrollment: 904. Upper school average class size: 16. Upper school faculty-student ratio: 1:13. There are 182 required school days per year for Upper School students. Upper School students typically attend 5 days per week. The average school day consists of 6 hours and 15 minutes.

Upper School Student Profile Grade 9: 86 students (39 boys, 47 girls); Grade 10: 90 students (42 boys, 48 girls); Grade 11: 95 students (51 boys, 44 girls); Grade 12: 86 students (45 boys, 41 girls).

Faculty School total: 120. In upper school: 24 men, 26 women.

Subjects Offered Algebra, American government, American history, American literature, art, art appreciation, biology, biology-AP, calculus, calculus-AP, chemistry, chorus, college admission preparation, college counseling, college placement, computer programming, computer science-AP, creative writing, drama, economics, English, English language-AP, English literature, ESL, European history, European history-AP, fine arts, French, French language-AP, French literature-AP, geometry, government/civics, health, history, journalism, Latin, Latin-AP, mathematics, music, photography, physical education, physics, physics-AP, psychology, SAT preparation, science, social studies, Spanish, Spanish language-AP, Spanish literature-AP, sports medicine, statistics-AP, theater, trigonometry, U.S. history-AP, world history, writing, yearbook.

Graduation Requirements Arts and fine arts (art, music, dance, drama), English, foreign language, mathematics, physical education (includes health), science, social studies (includes history), senior project (four-week internship).

Special Academic Programs 11 Advanced Placement exams for which test preparation is offered; honors section; independent study; term-away projects; study abroad; academic accommodation for the gifted and the artistically talented; special instructional classes for students with learning disabilities and Attention Deficit Disorder; ESL (8 students enrolled).

College Admission Counseling 80 students graduated in 2011; all went to college, including Duke University; Elon University; The University of North Carolina at Chapel Hill; The University of North Carolina Wilmington; Wake Forest University. Median SAT critical reading: 610, median SAT math: 650, median SAT writing: 650.

Student Life Upper grades have specified standards of dress, student council, honor system. Discipline rests equally with students and faculty.

Summer Programs Remediation, enrichment, advancement, sports, art/fine arts, computer instruction programs offered; session focuses on enrichment and camps; held on campus; accepts boys and girls; open to students from other schools. 600 students usually enrolled.

Tuition and Aid Day student tuition: $8200–$18,980. Tuition installment plan (FACTS Tuition Payment Plan, monthly payment plans, individually arranged payment plans). Need-based scholarship grants available.

Admissions Traditional secondary-level entrance grade is 9. ERB (CTP-Verbal, Quantitative) required. Deadline for receipt of application materials: none. Application fee required: $50. On-campus interview required.

Athletics Interscholastic: baseball (boys), basketball (b,g), cheering (g), cross-country running (b,g), field hockey (g), lacrosse (b,g), soccer (b,g), swimming and diving (b,g), tennis (b,g), track and field (b,g), volleyball (g), wrestling (b); intramural: weight lifting (b,g); coed interscholastic: aquatics, golf; coed intramural: backpacking, badminton, basketball, ropes courses. 11 PE instructors, 20 coaches, 2 athletic trainers.

Computers Computers are regularly used in yearbook classes. Computer network features include on-campus library services, online commercial services, Internet access, wireless campus network, Internet filtering or blocking technology. Student e-mail accounts are available to students. Students grades are available online. The school has a published electronic and media policy.

Contact Robin Schenck, Director of Admission and Financial Aid. 336-288-8590 Ext. 106. Fax: 336-282-2905. E-mail: robinschenck@greensboroday.org. Web site: www.greensboroday.org.

GREENWICH ACADEMY

200 North Maple Avenue

Greenwich, Connecticut 06830-4799

Head of School: Molly H. King

General Information Girls' day college-preparatory and arts school. Grades PK–12. Founded: 1827. Setting: suburban. Nearest major city is New York, NY. 39-acre campus. 6 buildings on campus. Approved or accredited by New England Association of Schools and Colleges and Connecticut Department of Education. Member of National Association of Independent Schools and Secondary School Admission Test Board. Endowment: $61.9 million. Total enrollment: 805. Upper school average class size: 13. Upper school faculty-student ratio: 1:6. There are 164 required school days per year for Upper School students. Upper School students typically attend 5 days per week. The average school day consists of 5 hours.

Upper School Student Profile Grade 9: 83 students (83 girls); Grade 10: 85 students (85 girls); Grade 11: 91 students (91 girls); Grade 12: 89 students (89 girls).

Faculty School total: 139. In upper school: 29 men, 109 women; 41 have advanced degrees.

Subjects Offered Advanced Placement courses, advanced studio art-AP, African-American literature, algebra, American history, American history-AP, American literature, ancient history, Arabic, architecture, art, art history, art history-AP, art-AP, astronomy, biochemistry, biology, biology-AP, calculus, calculus-AP, ceramics, chemistry, chemistry-AP, Chinese, classics, computer science, creative writing, dance, dance performance, drama, drama performance, earth science, ecology, economics, economics-AP, English, English literature, environmental science, European history, European history-AP, expository writing, film, film and literature, fine arts, foreign language, French, French language-AP, French literature-AP, French-AP, geology, geometry, government and politics-AP, government/civics, health, history, history-AP, honors algebra, honors geometry, independent study, Italian, Latin, Latin-AP, mathematics, mathematics-AP, medieval history, microeconomics, microeconomics-AP, music, music performance, music theory-AP, oceanography, physical education, physics, pre-calculus, psychology, science, senior project, Spanish, Spanish-AP, speech, statistics, studio art-AP, theater, trigonometry, world history, world literature.

Graduation Requirements Arts and fine arts (art, music, dance, drama), English, foreign language, mathematics, physical education (includes health), science, social studies (includes history). Community service is required.

Special Academic Programs 26 Advanced Placement exams for which test preparation is offered; honors section; independent study; term-away projects; study abroad.

College Admission Counseling 77 students graduated in 2011; all went to college, including Boston College; Bowdoin College; New York University; Princeton University; Stanford University; Yale University. Mean SAT critical reading: 675, mean SAT math: 664, mean SAT writing: 700, mean combined SAT: 1900, mean composite ACT: 29. 84% scored over 600 on SAT critical reading, 82% scored over 600 on SAT math, 94% scored over 600 on SAT writing, 91% scored over 1800 on combined SAT, 91% scored over 26 on composite ACT.

Student Life Upper grades have uniform requirement, student council, honor system. Discipline rests equally with students and faculty.

Summer Programs Enrichment, sports, art/fine arts programs offered; session focuses on enrichment, arts/fine arts, and sports; held on campus; accepts boys and girls; open to students from other schools. 200 students usually enrolled. 2012 schedule: June 14 to August 15.

Tuition and Aid Day student tuition: $35,400. Tuition installment plan (Academic Management Services Plan, monthly payment plans). Need-based scholarship grants, middle-income loans, PLITT Loans, tuition reduction for children of faculty and staff available. In 2011–12, 20% of upper-school students received aid. Total amount of financial aid awarded in 2011–12: $1,351,850.

Admissions Traditional secondary-level entrance grade is 9. For fall 2011, 105 students applied for upper-level admission, 50 were accepted, 36 enrolled. ERB, ISEE or SSAT required. Deadline for receipt of application materials: December 15. Application fee required: $75. On-campus interview required.

Athletics Interscholastic: basketball, crew, cross-country running, dance, dance team, fencing, field hockey, golf, hockey, ice hockey, independent competitive sports, lacrosse, sailing, soccer, softball, squash, swimming and diving, tennis, volleyball; intramural: aerobics, aerobics/Nautilus, basketball, cooperative games, crew, dance, fitness, floor hockey, Frisbee, independent competitive sports, lacrosse, modern dance, Nautilus, physical fitness, physical training, running, self defense, soccer, strength & conditioning, tennis, volleyball, weight lifting, yoga. 7 PE instructors, 54 coaches, 1 athletic trainer.

Computers Computers are regularly used in art, English, foreign language, history, humanities, mathematics, music, science classes. Computer network features include on-campus library services, online commercial services, Internet access, wireless campus network, Internet filtering or blocking technology. Campus intranet and student

e-mail accounts are available to students. The school has a published electronic and media policy.
Contact Irene Mann, Admission Associate, Registrar. 203-625-8990. Fax: 203-625-8912. E-mail: imann@greenwichacademy.org. Web site: www.greenwichacademy.org.

THE GREENWOOD SCHOOL

Putney, Vermont

See Junior Boarding Schools section.

THE GRIER SCHOOL

PO Box 308

Tyrone, Pennsylvania 16686-0308

Head of School: Mrs. Gina Borst

General Information Girls' boarding and day college-preparatory, arts, and business school. Boarding grades 7–PG, day grades 8–12. Founded: 1853. Setting: rural. Nearest major city is Pittsburgh. Students are housed in single-sex dormitories. 320-acre campus. 12 buildings on campus. Approved or accredited by Middle States Association of Colleges and Schools, Pennsylvania Association of Independent Schools, and The Association of Boarding Schools. Member of National Association of Independent Schools and Secondary School Admission Test Board. Endowment: $11 million. Total enrollment: 262. Upper school average class size: 10. Upper school faculty-student ratio: 1:7. There are 160 required school days per year for Upper School students. Upper School students typically attend 5 days per week. The average school day consists of 7 hours.
Upper School Student Profile Grade 9: 52 students (52 girls); Grade 10: 67 students (67 girls); Grade 11: 54 students (54 girls); Grade 12: 50 students (50 girls). 90% of students are boarding students. 10% are state residents. 20 states are represented in upper school student body. 50% are international students. International students from China, Germany, Mexico, Republic of Korea, Russian Federation, and Viet Nam; 7 other countries represented in student body.
Faculty School total: 56. In upper school: 13 men, 43 women; 32 have advanced degrees; 18 reside on campus.
Subjects Offered 3-dimensional art, acting, advanced studio art-AP, advanced TOEFL/grammar, algebra, American history, American literature, anatomy, art, art history, art history-AP, art-AP, ballet, ballet technique, batik, biology, biology-AP, Broadway dance, calculus, calculus-AP, ceramics, chemistry, chemistry-AP, Chinese, choral music, choreography, civics, community service, computer graphics, computer math, computer programming, computer-aided design, costumes and make-up, creative writing, dance, desktop publishing, drama, dramatic arts, earth science, ecology, economics, economics-AP, English, English as a foreign language, English literature, English literature and composition-AP, environmental science, equine science, ESL, European history, European history-AP, fabric arts, fiber arts, fine arts, French, French language-AP, French-AP, geography, geometry, government/civics, graphic arts, guitar, health, history, honors algebra, honors English, honors geometry, honors U.S. history, honors world history, human anatomy, human biology, instrumental music, journalism, linguistics, macro/microeconomics-AP, mathematics, modern dance, music, music technology, music theory, musical theater, musical theater dance, newspaper, painting, photography, physical education, physics, physics-AP, physiology, piano, pre-algebra, precalculus, printmaking, probability and statistics, psychology, science, scuba diving, social studies, Spanish, Spanish language-AP, stagecraft, statistics-AP, studio art-AP, symphonic band, tap dance, theater, TOEFL preparation, trigonometry, typing, video film production, vocal ensemble, voice, weaving, women's studies, world history, world literature, writing, writing, writing workshop, yearbook.
Graduation Requirements Arts and fine arts (art, music, dance, drama), computer science, English, foreign language, mathematics, physical education (includes health), science, social sciences, social studies (includes history).
Special Academic Programs 16 Advanced Placement exams for which test preparation is offered; honors section; independent study; study abroad; academic accommodation for the gifted, the musically talented, and the artistically talented; remedial reading and/or remedial writing; remedial math; programs in English, general development for dyslexic students; special instructional classes for students with learning disabilities, Attention Deficit Disorder, and dyslexia; ESL (39 students enrolled).
College Admission Counseling 54 students graduated in 2011; all went to college, including Boston College; Lehigh University; Penn State University Park; Savannah College of Art and Design; University of California, San Diego; University of Washington. Median SAT critical reading: 600, median SAT math: 640. 25% scored over 600 on SAT critical reading, 20% scored over 600 on SAT math.
Student Life Upper grades have specified standards of dress, student council, honor system. Discipline rests primarily with faculty.
Summer Programs Enrichment, ESL, sports, art/fine arts programs offered; session focuses on recreation and ESL; held on campus; accepts girls; open to students from other schools. 25 students usually enrolled. 2012 schedule: June 16 to September 7. Application deadline: none.
Tuition and Aid Day student tuition: $23,000; 7-day tuition and room/board: $46,800. Tuition installment plan (individually arranged payment plans). Tuition reduction for siblings, merit scholarship grants, need-based scholarship grants, need-

based loans, paying campus jobs available. In 2011–12, 45% of upper-school students received aid; total upper-school merit-scholarship money awarded: $540,000. Total amount of financial aid awarded in 2011–12: $1,940,000.

Admissions Traditional secondary-level entrance grade is 9. For fall 2011, 223 students applied for upper-level admission, 147 were accepted, 102 enrolled. SSAT or WISC III required. Deadline for receipt of application materials: none. Application fee required: $50. Interview recommended.

Athletics Interscholastic: basketball, dance team, drill team, equestrian sports, martial arts, skiing (downhill), soccer, tennis, volleyball; intramural: aerobics, aerobics/dance, alpine skiing, aquatics, archery, badminton, ballet, basketball, bicycling, bowling, cheering, dance, dance team, equestrian sports, fencing, figure skating, fitness walking, fly fishing, gymnastics, hiking/backpacking, horseback riding, jogging, martial arts, modern dance, mountain biking, nordic skiing, ropes courses, scuba diving, skiing (cross-country), skiing (downhill), soccer, swimming and diving, tennis, volleyball, walking, weight training, yoga. 3 PE instructors, 3 coaches, 3 athletic trainers.

Computers Computers are regularly used in creative writing, English, foreign language, graphic arts, mathematics, music technology, newspaper, science, yearbook classes. Computer network features include on-campus library services, online commercial services, Internet access, wireless campus network, Internet filtering or blocking technology. Campus intranet and student e-mail accounts are available to students. The school has a published electronic and media policy.

Contact Mr. Andrew M. Wilson, Headmaster/Director of Admissions. 814-684-3000 Ext. 106. Fax: 814-684-2177. E-mail: admissions@grier.org. Web site: www.grier.org.

See Display on previous page and Close-Up on page 626.

GRIGGS INTERNATIONAL ACADEMY

12501 Old Columbia Pike

Silver Spring, Maryland 20904-6600

Head of School: Dr. Donald R. Sahly

General Information Coeducational day and distance learning college-preparatory, general academic, and religious studies school, affiliated with Seventh-day Adventist Church. Grades PK–PG. Distance learning grades K–12. Founded: 1909. Setting: suburban. Nearest major city is Washington, DC. 1 building on campus. Approved or accredited by Board of Regents, General Conference of Seventh-day Adventists, CITA (Commission on International and Trans-Regional Accreditation), Distance Education and Training Council, Middle States Association of Colleges and Schools, and Maryland Department of Education. Total enrollment: 728.

Upper School Student Profile 60% of students are Seventh-day Adventists.

Faculty School total: 34. In upper school: 14 men, 20 women; 19 have advanced degrees.

Subjects Offered Accounting, algebra, American government, American history, American literature, art appreciation, art history, arts, Bible studies, biology, business skills, chemistry, digital photography, earth science, English, English literature, fine arts, food science, French, geography, geometry, government/civics, health, home economics, keyboarding, mathematics, music appreciation, physics, pre-algebra, science, social studies, Spanish, word processing, world history, writing.

Graduation Requirements American government, arts and fine arts (art, music, dance, drama), English, health, history, keyboarding, language, mathematics, religion (includes Bible studies and theology), science, social studies (includes history), requirements for basic diploma differ. Community service is required.

Special Academic Programs Accelerated programs; independent study; study at local college for college credit.

College Admission Counseling 27 students graduated in 2010; they went to Andrews University; Loma Linda University; Southern Adventist University; Towson University; University of Maryland, Baltimore County; Washington Adventist University.

Student Life Upper grades have honor system. Discipline rests primarily with faculty.

Tuition and Aid Day student tuition: $1680–$2100. Tuition installment plan (monthly payment plans, individually arranged payment plans).

Admissions Deadline for receipt of application materials: none. Application fee required: $80.

Computers Computers are regularly used in word processing classes. Students grades are available online.

Contact Mrs. Angie Crews, Enrollment Services Director. 301-680-5170. Fax: 301-680-6577. E-mail: adeaver@griggs.edu. Web site: www.griggs.edu.

See Display belowand Close-Up on page 628.

GROTON SCHOOL

Box 991

Farmers Row

Groton, Massachusetts 01450

Head of School: Richard B. Commons

General Information Coeducational boarding and day college-preparatory, arts, and religious studies school, affiliated with Episcopal Church. Grades 8–12. Founded: 1884. Setting: rural. Nearest major city is Boston. Students are housed in single-sex dormitories. 410-acre campus. 17 buildings on campus. Approved or accredited by Association of Independent Schools in New England, New England Association of Schools and Colleges, and The Association of Boarding Schools. Member of National Association of Independent Schools and Secondary School Admission Test Board. Endowment: $265.6 million. Total enrollment: 370. Upper school average class size: 13. Upper school faculty-student ratio: 1:7. There are 182 required school days per year for Upper School students. Upper School students typically attend 6 days per week. The average school day consists of 6 hours and 30 minutes.

Upper School Student Profile Grade 8: 26 students (13 boys, 13 girls); Grade 9: 78 students (41 boys, 37 girls); Grade 10: 85 students (44 boys, 41 girls); Grade 11: 86 students (43 boys, 43 girls); Grade 12: 95 students (49 boys, 46 girls). 86% of students are boarding students. 27% are state residents. 31 states are represented in upper school student body. 13% are international students. International students from Bermuda, Canada, China, France, Republic of Korea, and United Arab Emirates; 4 other countries represented in student body.

Faculty School total: 52. In upper school: 30 men, 22 women; 45 have advanced degrees; all reside on campus.

Subjects Offered Advanced chemistry, advanced math, algebra, American literature, American literature-AP, analytic geometry, Ancient Greek, ancient world history, archaeology, art, art history, art history-AP, Bible studies, biology, biology-AP, botany, Buddhism, calculus, calculus-AP, cell biology, Central and Eastern European history, ceramics, chemistry, chemistry-AP, Chinese, choir, choral music, civil rights, Civil War, civil war history, classical Greek literature, classical language, classics, composition, composition-AP, creative writing, dance, discrete mathematics, drawing, earth science, ecology, environmental systems, economics, English, English composition, English-AP, environmental science, environmental science-AP, environmental studies, ethics, ethics and responsibility, European history, European history-AP, expository writing, fine arts, fractal geometry, French, French language-AP, French literature-AP, geography, geometry, government, grammar, Greek, health, history, Holocaust, honors algebra, honors English, honors geometry, honors U.S. history, honors world history, independent study, lab science, language-AP, Latin, Latin-AP, linear algebra, literature, literature and composition-AP, mathematics, mathematics-AP, modern European history, modern European history-AP, modern history, modern languages, modern world history, music, music history, music theory, organic biochemistry, painting, philosophy, photo shop, photography, physical science, physics, physics-AP, pre-algebra, pre-calculus, psychology, religion, religious education, religious studies, science, Shakespeare, social sciences, Spanish, Spanish language-AP, Spanish literature, Spanish literature-AP, sports medicine, statistics, studio art, studio art-AP, theology, trigonometry, U.S. constitutional history, U.S. government, U.S. government and politics, U.S. government and politics-AP, U.S. history, U.S. history-AP, vocal music, Western civilization, wood lab, woodworking, world history, world history-AP, writing.

Graduation Requirements Arts and fine arts (art, music, dance, drama), classical language, English, foreign language, mathematics, religious studies, science, social studies (includes history).

Special Academic Programs 13 Advanced Placement exams for which test preparation is offered; honors section; independent study; study abroad; academic accommodation for the gifted, the musically talented, and the artistically talented.

College Admission Counseling Colleges students went to include Georgetown University; Harvard University; Northwestern University; Stanford University; Tufts University; University of Virginia. Median SAT critical reading: 700, median SAT math: 700, median SAT writing: 710, median combined SAT: 2100, median composite ACT: 28. 92% scored over 600 on SAT critical reading, 95% scored over 600 on SAT math, 96% scored over 600 on SAT writing, 99% scored over 1800 on combined SAT, 78% scored over 26 on composite ACT.

Student Life Upper grades have specified standards of dress, student council, honor system. Discipline rests equally with students and faculty. Attendance at religious services is required.

Tuition and Aid Day student tuition: $38,420; 7-day tuition and room/board: $49,810. Tuition installment plan (Insured Tuition Payment Plan, Key Tuition Payment Plan, monthly payment plans, individually arranged payment plans). Need-based scholarship grants, Key Education Resources available. In 2011–12, 37% of upper-school students received aid. Total amount of financial aid awarded in 2011–12: $4,900,000.

Admissions Traditional secondary-level entrance grade is 9. For fall 2011, 1,120 students applied for upper-level admission, 138 were accepted, 92 enrolled. ISEE, SSAT or TOEFL required. Deadline for receipt of application materials: January 15. Application fee required: $50. Interview required.

Athletics Interscholastic: baseball (boys), basketball (b,g), crew (b,g), cross-country running (b,g), field hockey (g), Fives (b,g), football (b), hockey (b,g), ice hockey (b,g), lacrosse (b,g), rowing (b,g), soccer (b,g), squash (b,g), tennis (b,g); intramural: physical training (b,g), self defense (g), weight training (b,g); coed intramural: aerobics/dance, alpine skiing, dance, fitness, Fives, Frisbee, golf, ice skating, modern dance, nordic skiing, outdoor activities, running, skeet shooting, skiing (cross-country), skiing (downhill), snowboarding, strength & conditioning, swimming and diving, track and field, trap and skeet, ultimate Frisbee, yoga. 2 coaches, 1 athletic trainer.

Computers Computers are regularly used in all academic classes. Computer network features include on-campus library services, Internet access, wireless campus network, Internet filtering or blocking technology, campus-wide wireless environment. Campus intranet and student e-mail accounts are available to students. The school has a published electronic and media policy.

Contact Mr. Ian Gracey, Director of Admission. 978-448-7510. Fax: 978-448-9623. E-mail: igracey@groton.org. Web site: www.groton.org.

GUAMANI PRIVATE SCHOOL

PO Box 3000

Guayama, Puerto Rico 00785

Head of School: Mr. Eduardo Delgado

General Information Coeducational day college-preparatory and bilingual studies school. Grades 1–12. Founded: 1914. Setting: urban. Nearest major city is Caguas. 1-acre campus. 1 building on campus. Approved or accredited by Middle States Association of Colleges and Schools, National Catholic Education Association, and Puerto Rico Department of Education. Languages of instruction: English and Spanish. Total enrollment: 606. Upper school average class size: 20. Upper school faculty-student ratio: 1:13.

Faculty School total: 32. In upper school: 10 men, 10 women; 3 have advanced degrees.

Subjects Offered Advanced math, Advanced Placement courses, algebra, American government, American history, analysis and differential calculus, chemistry, civics, pre-algebra, pre-calculus, science project, science research, social sciences, social studies, sociology, Spanish, Spanish language-AP, U.S. literature, visual arts, world geography, world history.

Graduation Requirements Mathematics, science, social sciences, Spanish, acceptance into a college or university. Community service is required.

Special Academic Programs Advanced Placement exam preparation; honors section; independent study.

College Admission Counseling 23 students graduated in 2011; they went to Embry-Riddle Aeronautical University–Daytona; Syracuse University; University of Puerto Rico, Cayey University College; University of Puerto Rico, Mayagüez Campus; University of Puerto Rico, Río Piedras. Other: 23 entered a postgraduate year.

Student Life Upper grades have uniform requirement, student council, honor system. Discipline rests primarily with faculty.

Summer Programs Remediation, ESL programs offered; held on campus; accepts boys and girls; open to students from other schools. 30 students usually enrolled. 2012 schedule: June 1 to June 30. Application deadline: May 27.

Admissions Traditional secondary-level entrance grade is 9. For fall 2011, 30 students applied for upper-level admission, 21 were accepted, 20 enrolled. School's own test or Test of Achievement and Proficiency required. Deadline for receipt of application materials: none. Application fee required: $30. Interview required.

Athletics Interscholastic: aerobics/dance (girls), basketball (b,g), cheering (g), dance squad (g), volleyball (b,g); coed interscholastic: dance team. 3 PE instructors, 2 coaches.

Computers Computers are regularly used in English, mathematics, science, social sciences, Spanish, word processing classes. Computer resources include on-campus library services, Internet access, wireless campus network, Internet filtering or blocking technology. The school has a published electronic and media policy.

Contact Mrs. Digna Torres, Secretary. 787-864-6880. Fax: 787-866-4947. Web site: www.guamani.com.

GULLIVER PREPARATORY SCHOOL

6575 North Kendall Drive

Pinecrest, Florida 33156

Head of School: John W. Krutulis

General Information Coeducational day college-preparatory, arts, technology, International Baccalaureate, architectural design, and pre-engineering, law and litigation, biomedical sciences school. Grades PK–12. Founded: 1926. Setting: suburban. Nearest major city is Miami. 14-acre campus. 3 buildings on campus. Approved or accredited by CITA (Commission on International and Trans-Regional Accreditation), Florida Council of Independent Schools, Southern Association of Colleges and Schools, and Florida Department of Education. Member of Secondary School Admission Test Board. Total enrollment: 1,834. Upper school average class size: 14. Upper school faculty-student ratio: 1:8.

Faculty School total: 126. In upper school: 58 men, 68 women; 69 have advanced degrees.

Subjects Offered Algebra, American history, American literature, anatomy, architectural drawing, architecture, art, art history, biology, calculus, ceramics, chemistry, college admission preparation, college writing, computer animation, computer applications, computer processing, computer programming, computer programming-AP, computer science, computer science-AP, computer skills, computer studies, concert band, concert choir, creative writing, dance, desktop publishing, drafting, drama, economics, engineering, English, English literature, European history, fine arts, French, geometry, government/civics, history, Italian, keyboarding, Latin, marine biology, mathematics, mechanical drawing, music, newspaper, physical education, physics, psychology, science, social studies, Spanish, speech, statistics, theater, trigonometry, video, world history, world literature, yearbook, zoology.

Graduation Requirements Arts and fine arts (art, music, dance, drama), computer science, English, foreign language, mathematics, physical education (includes health), science, social studies (includes history). Community service is required.

Special Academic Programs International Baccalaureate program; Advanced Placement exam preparation; honors section; study at local college for college credit; academic accommodation for the gifted, the musically talented, and the artistically talented.

College Admission Counseling 180 students graduated in 2010; all went to college, including Boston University; Duke University; Florida International University; Florida State University; University of Florida; University of Miami. Mean SAT critical reading: 575, mean SAT math: 590, mean SAT writing: 578.

Student Life Upper grades have specified standards of dress, student council, honor system. Discipline rests primarily with faculty.

Tuition and Aid Day student tuition: $8500–$24,520. Tuition installment plan (monthly payment plans, school's own tuition recovery plan). Tuition reduction for siblings, need-based scholarship grants, application and matriculation fee waived for children of alumni available.

Admissions Traditional secondary-level entrance grade is 9. For fall 2010, 340 students applied for upper-level admission, 242 were accepted, 134 enrolled. School's own exam and SSAT required. Deadline for receipt of application materials: February 19. Application fee required: $100. Interview recommended.

Athletics Interscholastic: aerobics/Nautilus (girls), baseball (b), basketball (b,g), cross-country running (b,g), dance (g), dance squad (g), dance team (g), diving (b,g), football (b), golf (b,g), gymnastics (b,g), lacrosse (b), physical training (b,g), running (b,g), soccer (b,g), softball (g), swimming and diving (b,g), tennis (b,g), track and field (b,g), volleyball (g), water polo (b,g); intramural: boxing (b,g), weight training (b,g); coed interscholastic: aerobics, bowling, cheering, modern dance, yoga; coed intramural: aerobics/dance, aerobics/Nautilus, badminton, dance, dance squad, dance team, fitness, flag football, Frisbee, kickball, modern dance, netball, physical fitness, running, strength & conditioning, touch football, yoga. 6 PE instructors, 55 coaches, 2 athletic trainers.

Computers Computers are regularly used in architecture, art, college planning, drafting, English, graphic arts, graphic design, keyboarding, newspaper, programming, science, technology, word processing, yearbook classes. Computer network features include on-campus library services, online commercial services, Internet access, wireless campus network, Internet filtering or blocking technology, modified laptop program, SMART Boards and Audio enhancement systems. Students grades are available online. The school has a published electronic and media policy.

Contact Carol A. Bowen, Director of Admission. 305-666-7937 Ext. 1408. Fax: 305-665-3791. E-mail: bowc@gulliverschools.org. Web site: www.gulliverschools.org.

THE GUNSTON SCHOOL

911 Gunston Road

PO Box 200

Centreville, Maryland 21617

Head of School: Mr. John A. Lewis, IV

General Information Coeducational day college-preparatory, arts, and technology school. Grades 9–12. Founded: 1911. Setting: rural. Nearest major city is Annapolis. 32-acre campus. 4 buildings on campus. Approved or accredited by Association of Independent Maryland Schools, Middle States Association of Colleges and Schools, and Maryland Department of Education. Member of National Association of Independent Schools and Secondary School Admission Test Board. Endowment: $1 million. Total enrollment: 136. Upper school average class size: 10. Upper school faculty-student ratio: 1:6. There are 170 required school days per year for Upper School students. Upper School students typically attend 5 days per week. The average school day consists of 8 hours.

Upper School Student Profile Grade 9: 31 students (19 boys, 12 girls); Grade 10: 37 students (14 boys, 23 girls); Grade 11: 32 students (18 boys, 14 girls); Grade 12: 36 students (16 boys, 20 girls).

Faculty School total: 23. In upper school: 12 men, 11 women; 14 have advanced degrees.

Subjects Offered Advanced biology, advanced chemistry, advanced math, Advanced Placement courses, advanced studio art-AP, algebra, American government, American history, American literature, anatomy and physiology, ancient history, applied arts, art, art history, art history-AP, biology, biology-AP, British literature, British literature (honors), calculus, calculus-AP, calligraphy, ceramics, chemistry, chemistry-AP, Chesapeake Bay studies, chorus, college counseling, college placement, college planning, community service, computer applications, computer science, digital photography, drama performance, economics, English, English as a foreign language, English literature, environmental science, environmental science-AP, ethical decision making, ethics, European history-AP, fine arts, fitness, freshman seminar, geometry, golf, government, government-AP, government/civics, health, health and wellness, history, history-AP, honors algebra, honors English, honors geometry, ideas, lab science, Latin, Latin-AP, mathematics, mathematics-AP, medieval history, Microsoft, music, music appreciation, music composition, music theory, painting, performing arts, photography, physics, physics-AP, play production, poetry, pottery, pre-calculus, pre-college orientation, printmaking, psychology, SAT preparation, SAT/ACT preparation, science, sculpture, senior internship, senior project, senior thesis, short story, silk screening, Spanish, Spanish-AP, sports, studio art, studio art-AP, swimming, tennis, trigonometry, U.S. government, U.S. government and politics-AP, U.S. history, U.S. history-AP, weight training, wellness, woodworking, world history, writing workshop.

Graduation Requirements Arts and fine arts (art, music, dance, drama), athletics, computer science, English, foreign language, history, mathematics, science, social sciences. Community service is required.

Special Academic Programs Advanced Placement exam preparation; honors section; independent study; term-away projects; study at local college for college credit; study abroad; academic accommodation for the gifted, the musically talented, and the artistically talented; ESL (23 students enrolled).

College Admission Counseling 42 students graduated in 2011; all went to college, including Davidson College; Dickinson College; Lehigh University; University of Maryland, College Park; Virginia Polytechnic Institute and State University; Washington College.

Student Life Upper grades have specified standards of dress, student council, honor system. Discipline rests primarily with faculty.

Summer Programs Enrichment, advancement, sports, computer instruction programs offered; session focuses on student activities for ages 6-18; held on campus; accepts boys and girls; open to students from other schools. 75 students usually enrolled. 2012 schedule: June 17 to August 22. Application deadline: none.

Tuition and Aid Day student tuition: $21,730. Tuition installment plan (monthly payment plans, individually arranged payment plans, Sallie Mae, Tuition Management Solutions). Merit scholarship grants, need-based scholarship grants available. In 2011–12, 50% of upper-school students received aid; total upper-school merit-scholarship money awarded: $15,000. Total amount of financial aid awarded in 2011–12: $700,000.

Admissions Traditional secondary-level entrance grade is 9. For fall 2011, 83 students applied for upper-level admission, 76 were accepted, 54 enrolled. ISEE or SSAT required. Deadline for receipt of application materials: February 1. Application fee required: $50. On-campus interview required.

Athletics Interscholastic: basketball (boys, girls), field hockey (g), lacrosse (b,g), soccer (b,g), swimming and diving (b,g), tennis (b,g); intramural: independent competitive sports (b,g), tennis (b,g); coed interscholastic: crew, equestrian sports, golf, horseback riding, sailing, swimming and diving, tennis; coed intramural: badminton, equestrian sports, fitness, independent competitive sports, strength & conditioning, tennis, weight training. 4 coaches.

Computers Computers are regularly used in English, foreign language, history, mathematics, science classes. Computer network features include on-campus library services, online commercial services, Internet access, wireless campus network, Internet filtering or blocking technology. Campus intranet, student e-mail accounts, and computer access in designated common areas are available to students.

Contact David Henry, Director of Admission and Financial Aid. 410-758-0620. Fax: 410-758-0628. E-mail: dhenry@gunston.org. Web site: www.gunstondayschool.org/.

GWYNEDD MERCY ACADEMY

1345 Sumneytown Pike

PO Box 902

Gwynedd Valley, Pennsylvania 19437-0902

Head of School: Sr. Kathleen Boyce, RSM

General Information Girls' day college-preparatory, arts, religious studies, and technology school, affiliated with Roman Catholic Church. Grades 9–12. Founded: 1861. Setting: suburban. Nearest major city is Philadelphia. 48-acre campus. 1 building on campus. Approved or accredited by Mercy Secondary Education Association, Middle States Association of Colleges and Schools, National Catholic Education Association, and Pennsylvania Department of Education. Total enrollment: 387. Upper school average class size: 18. Upper school faculty-student ratio: 1:11. There are 178 required school days per year for Upper School students. Upper School students typically attend 5 days per week. The average school day consists of 6 hours and 5 minutes.

Upper School Student Profile Grade 9: 101 students (101 girls); Grade 10: 90 students (90 girls); Grade 11: 105 students (105 girls); Grade 12: 91 students (91 girls). 99% of students are Roman Catholic.

Faculty School total: 36. In upper school: 6 men, 30 women; 26 have advanced degrees.

Subjects Offered Accounting, Advanced Placement courses, algebra, American history, American history-AP, American literature, art, art appreciation, athletics, biology, business law, business skills, calculus, calculus-AP, chemistry, college counseling, computer science, computer skills, English, fine arts, French, geometry, health,

health education, history, honors English, human development, Latin, library studies, mathematics, music, music theory, physical education, physical science, physics, piloting, post-calculus, pre-calculus, religion, social studies, Spanish, statistics-AP, study skills, theology, trigonometry, U.S. government and politics-AP, word processing, world cultures, zoology.

Graduation Requirements English, foreign language, mathematics, physical education (includes health), religion (includes Bible studies and theology), science, social studies (includes history).

Special Academic Programs Advanced Placement exam preparation; honors section; study at local college for college credit; academic accommodation for the musically talented and the artistically talented.

College Admission Counseling 95 students graduated in 2010; all went to college, including Fordham University; Penn State University Park; Saint Joseph's University; Temple University; The University of Scranton. Mean SAT critical reading: 578, mean SAT math: 563, mean SAT writing: 579, mean combined SAT: 1710. 36% scored over 600 on SAT critical reading, 26% scored over 600 on SAT math, 43% scored over 600 on SAT writing, 35% scored over 1800 on combined SAT.

Student Life Upper grades have uniform requirement, student council, honor system. Discipline rests primarily with faculty. Attendance at religious services is required.

Tuition and Aid Day student tuition: $13,500. Tuition installment plan (monthly payment plans, individually arranged payment plans, quarterly and semi-annual payment plans). Tuition reduction for siblings, merit scholarship grants, need-based scholarship grants available. In 2010–11, 5% of upper-school students received aid; total upper-school merit-scholarship money awarded: $141,680. Total amount of financial aid awarded in 2010–11: $217,680.

Admissions Traditional secondary-level entrance grade is 9. For fall 2010, 272 students applied for upper-level admission, 230 were accepted, 103 enrolled. Scholastic Testing Service High School Placement Test (open version) required. Deadline for receipt of application materials: November 6. Application fee required: $50.

Athletics Interscholastic: basketball, cross-country running, diving, field hockey, golf, indoor track, lacrosse, soccer, softball, swimming and diving, tennis, track and field, volleyball; intramural: dance. 2 PE instructors, 24 coaches, 1 athletic trainer.

Computers Computers are regularly used in art, business, English, foreign language, French, history, Latin, library skills, mathematics, music, newspaper, publications, religion, science, technology, word processing, writing, yearbook classes. Computer network features include on-campus library services, online commercial services, Internet access, wireless campus network, Internet filtering or blocking technology. Student e-mail accounts and computer access in designated common areas are available to students. The school has a published electronic and media policy.

Contact Mrs. Kimberly Dunphy Scott, Director of Admissions. 215-646-8815 Ext. 329. Fax: 215-646-4361. E-mail: kscott@gmahs.org. Web site: www.gmahs.org.

HACKLEY SCHOOL

293 Benedict Avenue

Tarrytown, New York 10591

Head of School: Mr. Walter C. Johnson

General Information Coeducational boarding and day college-preparatory, arts, technology, and liberal arts, math and science school. Boarding grades 9–12, day grades K–12. Founded: 1899. Setting: suburban. Nearest major city is New York. Students are housed in single-sex dormitories. 285-acre campus. 15 buildings on campus. Approved or accredited by Middle States Association of Colleges and Schools, New York State Association of Independent Schools, New York State Board of Regents, and The Association of Boarding Schools. Member of National Association of Independent Schools and Secondary School Admission Test Board. Endowment: $28 million. Total enrollment: 842. Upper school average class size: 15. Upper school faculty-student ratio: 1:6. There are 169 required school days per year for Upper School students. Upper School students typically attend 5 days per week. The average school day consists of 7 hours.

Upper School Student Profile Grade 9: 102 students (59 boys, 43 girls); Grade 10: 101 students (49 boys, 52 girls); Grade 11: 98 students (48 boys, 50 girls); Grade 12: 90 students (45 boys, 45 girls). 3% of students are boarding students. 96% are state residents. 3 states are represented in upper school student body.

Faculty School total: 128. In upper school: 30 men, 34 women; 53 have advanced degrees; 43 reside on campus.

Subjects Offered 20th century world history, 3-dimensional art, acting, algebra, American history, American literature, ancient history, anthropology, architectural drawing, art, art history-AP, biology, biology-AP, British literature, calculus-AP, ceramics, chemistry, chemistry-AP, Chinese, chorus, computer graphics, computer programming, computer science, computer science-AP, concert band, contemporary issues, creative writing, driver education, ecology, economics, electronic publishing, English, environmental science-AP, European history, fine arts, finite math, French, French language-AP, French literature-AP, geometry, Greek, history, Italian, Latin, Latin-AP, marine biology, mathematics, modern European history, music, music theory, music theory-AP, orchestra, organic chemistry, performing arts, photography, physical education, physics, physics-AP, pre-calculus, science, Spanish, Spanish language-AP, Spanish literature-AP, statistics-AP, studio art-AP, trigonometry, U.S. government and politics-AP, world history.

Graduation Requirements Arts and fine arts (art, music, dance, drama), English, foreign language, history, mathematics, physical education (includes health), science.

Special Academic Programs 21 Advanced Placement exams for which test preparation is offered; honors section; independent study.

College Admission Counseling 96 students graduated in 2011; 95 went to college, including Colgate University; Columbia University; Cornell University; University of Michigan; University of Pennsylvania; Vanderbilt University. Median SAT critical reading: 670, median SAT math: 690, median SAT writing: 700, median combined SAT: 2080. 90% scored over 600 on SAT critical reading, 88% scored over 600 on SAT math, 90% scored over 600 on SAT writing, 90% scored over 1800 on combined SAT.

Student Life Upper grades have specified standards of dress, student council. Discipline rests primarily with faculty.

Summer Programs Sports programs offered; session focuses on sports (football and basketball); held on campus; accepts boys and girls; open to students from other schools. 50 students usually enrolled. 2012 schedule: June to June.

Tuition and Aid Day student tuition: $35,700; 5-day tuition and room/board: $46,800. Tuition installment plan (Insured Tuition Payment Plan, Academic Management Services Plan, Key Tuition Payment Plan, monthly payment plans). Need-based scholarship grants, need-based loans available. In 2011–12, 15% of upper-school students received aid. Total amount of financial aid awarded in 2011–12: $3,500,000.

Admissions Traditional secondary-level entrance grade is 9. For fall 2011, 217 students applied for upper-level admission, 96 were accepted, 51 enrolled. ERB, ISEE or SSAT required. Deadline for receipt of application materials: January 14. Application fee required: $65. On-campus interview required.

Athletics Interscholastic: baseball (boys), basketball (b,g), field hockey (g), football (b), golf (b,g), lacrosse (b,g), soccer (b,g), softball (g), squash (b,g), tennis (b,g), wrestling (b); intramural: squash (b,g); coed interscholastic: cross-country running, fencing, indoor track, strength & conditioning, swimming and diving, track and field; coed intramural: aerobics, aerobics/Nautilus, canoeing/kayaking, climbing, cooperative games, fencing, fitness, Frisbee, golf, kayaking, life saving, martial arts, outdoor education, outdoor recreation, physical fitness, physical training, ropes courses, scuba diving, weight training, yoga. 6 PE instructors, 9 coaches, 1 athletic trainer.

Computers Computers are regularly used in computer applications, desktop publishing, drawing and design, graphic arts, independent study, keyboarding, literary magazine, music, newspaper, photography, programming, Web site design, yearbook classes. Computer network features include on-campus library services, online commercial services, Internet access, wireless campus network, laptop loaner program. Campus intranet and computer access in designated common areas are available to students.

Contact Mrs. Lynn Hooley, Admissions Associate. 914-366-2642. Fax: 914-366-2636. E-mail: lhooley@hackleyschool.org. Web site: www.hackleyschool.org.

HAMDEN HALL COUNTRY DAY SCHOOL

1108 Whitney Avenue

Hamden, Connecticut 06517

Head of School: Mr. Robert J. Izzo

General Information Coeducational day college-preparatory school. Grades PS–12. Founded: 1912. Setting: suburban. Nearest major city is New Haven. 42-acre campus. 8 buildings on campus. Approved or accredited by Connecticut Association of Independent Schools, New England Association of Schools and Colleges, and Connecticut Department of Education. Member of National Association of Independent Schools and Secondary School Admission Test Board. Endowment: $8.2 million. Total enrollment: 545. Upper school average class size: 13. Upper school faculty-student ratio: 1:8. There are 165 required school days per year for Upper School students. Upper School students typically attend 5 days per week. The average school day consists of 4 hours and 45 minutes.

Upper School Student Profile Grade 9: 64 students (37 boys, 27 girls); Grade 10: 54 students (33 boys, 21 girls); Grade 11: 62 students (34 boys, 28 girls); Grade 12: 82 students (46 boys, 36 girls).

Faculty School total: 80. In upper school: 22 men, 21 women; 31 have advanced degrees.

Subjects Offered African-American history, algebra, American literature, anatomy, art history, astronomy, biology, British literature, calculus, ceramics, chamber groups, chemistry, chorus, computer graphics, computer multimedia, computer programming, computer science, constitutional law, creative writing, digital photography, drama, drawing, electronics, English language and composition-AP, European history-AP, expository writing, French, genetics, geology, geometry, improvisation, independent study, jazz, Latin, life science, Mandarin, marine biology, meteorology, multimedia design, music appreciation, music history, music theory, oceanography, painting, peer counseling, performing arts, physiology, playwriting, poetry, printmaking, sculpture, Spanish, speech, statistics, theater, trigonometry, U.S. history, video film production, Western civilization, women in literature, world history, world literature, zoology.

Graduation Requirements Arts and fine arts (art, music, dance, drama), computer science, English, foreign language, mathematics, physical education (includes health), science, social studies (includes history), participation in 2 athletic seasons each year.

Special Academic Programs Advanced Placement exam preparation; honors section; independent study; term-away projects; academic accommodation for the gifted.
College Admission Counseling 70 students graduated in 2011; all went to college, including Boston College; Brown University; Emory University; Lehigh University; Princeton University; University of Michigan. Median SAT critical reading: 600, median SAT math: 600, median SAT writing: 600, median combined SAT: 1800, median composite ACT: 26.
Student Life Upper grades have specified standards of dress, student council, honor system. Discipline rests equally with students and faculty.
Summer Programs Remediation, enrichment, advancement, sports, art/fine arts, computer instruction programs offered; held on campus; accepts boys and girls; open to students from other schools. 450 students usually enrolled. 2012 schedule: June 11 to August 17. Application deadline: none.
Tuition and Aid Day student tuition: $29,990. Tuition installment plan (monthly payment plans, Tuition Management Services). Need-based scholarship grants, need-based loans, paying campus jobs, Key Education Resources available. In 2011–12, 30% of upper-school students received aid. Total amount of financial aid awarded in 2011–12: $1,600,000.
Admissions Traditional secondary-level entrance grade is 9. For fall 2011, 128 students applied for upper-level admission, 80 were accepted, 33 enrolled. ISEE or SSAT required. Deadline for receipt of application materials: January 15. Application fee required: $50. Interview required.
Athletics Interscholastic: baseball (boys), basketball (b,g), field hockey (g), football (b), ice hockey (b), lacrosse (b,g), soccer (b,g), softball (g), tennis (b,g), volleyball (g), wrestling (b); coed interscholastic: cross-country running, golf, outdoors, physical fitness, swimming and diving; coed intramural: outdoors, physical fitness, running, weight training. 3 PE instructors, 15 coaches, 1 athletic trainer.
Computers Computers are regularly used in all academic, art, digital applications, graphic arts, graphic design, information technology, video film production, yearbook classes. Computer network features include on-campus library services, Internet access, wireless campus network, Internet filtering or blocking technology. Student e-mail accounts are available to students. The school has a published electronic and media policy.
Contact Janet B. Izzo, Director of Admissions. 203-752-2610. Fax: 203-752-2611. E-mail: jizzo@hamdenhall.org. Web site: www.hamdenhall.org.

HAMILTON DISTRICT CHRISTIAN HIGH

92 Glancaster Road

Ancaster, Ontario L9G 3K9, Canada

Head of School: Mr. George Van Kampen

General Information Coeducational day college-preparatory, general academic, arts, business, vocational, religious studies, and technology school, affiliated with Christian faith. Grades 9–12. Founded: 1956. Setting: suburban. Nearest major city is Hamilton, Canada. 22-acre campus. 1 building on campus. Approved or accredited by Christian Schools International, Ontario Ministry of Education, and Ontario Department of Education. Language of instruction: English. Total enrollment: 480. Upper school average class size: 19. Upper school faculty-student ratio: 1:19. There are 180 required school days per year for Upper School students. Upper School students typically attend 5 days per week. The average school day consists of 6 hours.
Upper School Student Profile Grade 9: 120 students (60 boys, 60 girls); Grade 10: 100 students (50 boys, 50 girls); Grade 11: 130 students (65 boys, 65 girls); Grade 12: 130 students (65 boys, 65 girls). 100% of students are Christian faith.
Faculty School total: 37. In upper school: 24 men, 13 women; 9 have advanced degrees.
Subjects Offered 20th century history, 3-dimensional art, 3-dimensional design, accounting, acting, adolescent issues, advanced chemistry, advanced computer applications, advanced math, ancient history, ancient world history, applied arts, architectural drawing, art, art history, Bible, biology, business technology, calculus, Canadian geography, Canadian history, Canadian law, career experience, carpentry, chemistry, choir, civics, computer applications, computer multimedia, computer programming, computer technologies, computer-aided design, concert band, creative writing, drafting, drama, economics, English literature, environmental science, ESL, family and consumer science, finite math, food and nutrition, French, geometry, guidance, history, instrumental music, keyboarding, leadership, mathematics, media, modern Western civilization, music, peer counseling, personal finance, physical education, physics, religious studies, science, sociology, trigonometry, woodworking.
Graduation Requirements Art, Bible, Canadian geography, Canadian history, career education, civics, English, French, history, keyboarding, mathematics, science, 40 hours of community service.
Special Academic Programs 6 Advanced Placement exams for which test preparation is offered; independent study; term-away projects; academic accommodation for the musically talented and the artistically talented; remedial reading and/or remedial writing; remedial math; ESL (20 students enrolled).
College Admission Counseling 108 students graduated in 2010; 95 went to college, including McMaster University; Queen's University at Kingston; Redeemer University College; The University of Western Ontario; University of Waterloo; Wilfrid Laurier University. Other: 8 went to work, 5 had other specific plans. Median composite ACT: 23. 25% scored over 26 on composite ACT.
Student Life Upper grades have uniform requirement, student council. Discipline rests primarily with faculty.
Tuition and Aid Day student tuition: CAN$11,360. Tuition installment plan (monthly payment plans, individually arranged payment plans). Merit scholarship grants, need-based scholarship grants, tuition assistance fund, family rate tuition: additional children at no extra charge, reduced rate for two-school tuition families and home school families available. In 2010–11, 6% of upper-school students received aid; total upper-school merit-scholarship money awarded: CAN$4000. Total amount of financial aid awarded in 2010–11: CAN$95,000.
Admissions Traditional secondary-level entrance grade is 9. For fall 2010, 140 students applied for upper-level admission, 139 were accepted, 130 enrolled. Deadline for receipt of application materials: none. No application fee required. Interview required.
Athletics Interscholastic: badminton (boys, girls), baseball (g), basketball (b,g), cross-country running (b,g), golf (b,g), hockey (b), ice hockey (b), lacrosse (b,g), running (b,g), soccer (b,g), softball (g), touch football (b), track and field (b,g), volleyball (b,g); intramural: ball hockey (b,g), basketball (b,g), flag football (b,g), floor hockey (b,g), volleyball (b,g), wallyball (b,g), whiffle ball (b,g); coed interscholastic: badminton, ultimate Frisbee; coed intramural: floor hockey, horseback riding, indoor soccer, mountain biking, weight lifting, weight training. 5 PE instructors, 6 coaches.
Computers Computers are regularly used in art, business studies, career education, career exploration, college planning, current events, desktop publishing, drafting, economics, English, ESL, ethics, geography, graphic arts, graphic design, history, independent study, keyboarding, library, literary magazine, mathematics, media production, music, news writing, newspaper, photography, religious studies, research skills, science, video film production, Web site design, writing, yearbook classes. Computer network features include on-campus library services, online commercial services, Internet access, wireless campus network, Internet filtering or blocking technology, course Web pages, course chat rooms. Campus intranet, student e-mail accounts, and computer access in designated common areas are available to students. Students grades are available online. The school has a published electronic and media policy.
Contact Ms. Janet Hagen, Office Manager. 905-648-6655 Ext. 103. Fax: 905-648-3139. E-mail: jhagen@hdch.org. Web site: www.hdch.org.

HAMPSHIRE COUNTRY SCHOOL

Rindge, New Hampshire

See Junior Boarding Schools section.

HAMPTON ROADS ACADEMY

739 Academy Lane

Newport News, Virginia 23602

Head of School: Mr. Peter Mertz

General Information Coeducational day college-preparatory school. Grades PK–12. Founded: 1959. Setting: suburban. 53-acre campus. 4 buildings on campus. Approved or accredited by Virginia Association of Independent Schools and Virginia Department of Education. Member of National Association of Independent Schools. Total enrollment: 589. Upper school average class size: 16. Upper school faculty-student ratio: 1:10. Upper School students typically attend 5 days per week. The average school day consists of 6 hours and 30 minutes.
Faculty School total: 70. In upper school: 13 men, 17 women; 19 have advanced degrees.
Subjects Offered African studies, algebra, American history, American literature, anatomy, art, biology, calculus, ceramics, chemistry, creative writing, drama, driver education, earth science, economics, English, English literature, European history, expository writing, fine arts, French, geography, geometry, government/civics, grammar, health, history, Latin, mathematics, music, photography, physical education, physics, physiology, science, social studies, Spanish, speech, statistics, theater, trigonometry, typing, world history, world literature, writing.
Graduation Requirements Arts and fine arts (art, music, dance, drama), English, foreign language, mathematics, physical education (includes health), science, social studies (includes history), community service. Community service is required.
Special Academic Programs 19 Advanced Placement exams for which test preparation is offered; honors section; independent study.
College Admission Counseling 71 students graduated in 2011; all went to college, including Hampden-Sydney College; James Madison University; The College of William and Mary; University of Virginia; Virginia Polytechnic Institute and State University. Median SAT critical reading: 600, median SAT math: 600, median SAT writing: 600, median combined SAT: 1800, median composite ACT: 22. 60% scored over 600 on SAT critical reading, 54% scored over 600 on SAT math, 56% scored over 600 on SAT writing, 57% scored over 1800 on combined SAT, 36% scored over 26 on composite ACT.
Student Life Upper grades have specified standards of dress, student council, honor system. Discipline rests primarily with faculty.

Summer Programs Enrichment, sports, art/fine arts, computer instruction programs offered; session focuses on K-8 students; held on campus; accepts boys and girls; open to students from other schools. 75 students usually enrolled. 2012 schedule: June 10 to July 30. Application deadline: none.

Tuition and Aid Day student tuition: $14,800. Tuition installment plan (SMART Tuition Payment Plan). Need-based scholarship grants available. In 2011–12, 18% of upper-school students received aid. Total amount of financial aid awarded in 2011–12: $800,000.

Admissions Traditional secondary-level entrance grade is 9. For fall 2011, 43 students applied for upper-level admission, 37 were accepted, 29 enrolled. ERB, school's own test and writing sample required. Deadline for receipt of application materials: none. Application fee required: $125. On-campus interview required.

Athletics Interscholastic: baseball (boys), basketball (b,g), cheering (g), cross-country running (b,g), field hockey (g), football (b), golf (b,g), lacrosse (b), physical training (b,g), sailing (b,g), soccer (b,g), softball (g), swimming and diving (b,g), tennis (b,g), track and field (b,g), volleyball (g), weight training (b,g); coed interscholastic: aquatics; coed intramural: equestrian sports, fitness, physical fitness, physical training, ropes courses, strength & conditioning, ultimate Frisbee, weight training. 3 PE instructors, 44 coaches, 1 athletic trainer.

Computers Computers are regularly used in English, mathematics, music, science, writing, yearbook classes. Computer network features include on-campus library services, online commercial services, Internet access, wireless campus network, Internet filtering or blocking technology. Student e-mail accounts are available to students. Students grades are available online. The school has a published electronic and media policy.

Contact Rebecca Bresee, Director of Admission. 757-884-9148. Fax: 757-884-9137. E-mail: RBrese@hra.org. Web site: www.hra.org.

HANALANI SCHOOLS

94-294 Anania Drive

Mililani, Hawaii 96789

Head of School: Mr. Mark Y. Sugimoto

General Information Coeducational day college-preparatory, arts, religious studies, bilingual studies, and technology school, affiliated with Christian faith. Grades PK–12. Founded: 1952. Setting: suburban. 6-acre campus. 6 buildings on campus. Approved or accredited by The Hawaii Council of Private Schools, Western Association of Schools and Colleges, and Hawaii Department of Education. Total enrollment: 769. Upper school average class size: 16. Upper school faculty-student ratio: 1:16. There are 175 required school days per year for Upper School students. Upper School students typically attend 5 days per week. The average school day consists of 7 hours and 5 minutes.

Upper School Student Profile Grade 6: 59 students (30 boys, 29 girls); Grade 7: 58 students (32 boys, 26 girls); Grade 8: 63 students (35 boys, 28 girls); Grade 9: 61 students (36 boys, 25 girls); Grade 10: 63 students (31 boys, 32 girls); Grade 11: 51 students (26 boys, 25 girls); Grade 12: 46 students (23 boys, 23 girls). 98% of students are Christian faith.

Faculty School total: 62. In upper school: 18 men, 14 women; 10 have advanced degrees.

Subjects Offered Advanced math, Advanced Placement courses, algebra, American government, American literature, art, band, basketball, Bible, Bible studies, biology, British literature, calculus, calculus-AP, cheerleading, chemistry, chemistry-AP, choir, chorus, Christian doctrine, Christian ethics, computer skills, concert band, consumer mathematics, drafting, drama, earth science, English composition, English literature, English-AP, ethics, geography, geometry, golf, grammar, handbells, intro to computers, Japanese, Japanese as Second Language, Japanese studies, journalism, keyboarding, language development, leadership, Life of Christ, life science, music, paleontology, physical education, physical science, physics, piano, pre-algebra, pre-calculus, robotics, SAT preparation, sign language, Spanish, speech, student government, student publications, study skills, theology, transition mathematics, trigonometry, U.S. history, U.S. history-AP, video, voice, volleyball, world history, writing, yearbook.

Graduation Requirements Arts and fine arts (art, music, dance, drama), Bible, Bible studies, electives, English, foreign language, guidance, mathematics, physical education (includes health), science, social studies (includes history), technology. Community service is required.

Special Academic Programs Advanced Placement exam preparation; honors section; independent study; remedial reading and/or remedial writing; remedial math.

College Admission Counseling 48 students graduated in 2010; 47 went to college, including Chaminade University of Honolulu; Hawai`i Pacific University; Pacific University; University of California, Davis; University of California, Irvine; University of Hawaii at Manoa. Other: 1 went to work.

Student Life Upper grades have uniform requirement, student council, honor system. Discipline rests primarily with faculty. Attendance at religious services is required.

Tuition and Aid Day student tuition: $8600. Tuition installment plan (SMART Tuition Payment Plan, monthly payment plans, lump sum payment, biannual payment). Tuition reduction for siblings, need-based scholarship grants, student referral credit available. In 2010–11, 14% of upper-school students received aid. Total amount of financial aid awarded in 2010–11: $164,045.

Admissions Traditional secondary-level entrance grade is 9. For fall 2010, 98 students applied for upper-level admission, 88 were accepted, 69 enrolled. SAT or SSAT required. Deadline for receipt of application materials: none. Application fee required: $75. Interview required.

Athletics Interscholastic: archery (boys), baseball (b), basketball (b,g), bowling (b,g), cheering (g), cross-country running (b,g), football (b), golf (b,g), outdoor education (b,g), soccer (b,g), track and field (b,g), volleyball (b,g), water polo (b); intramural: basketball (b,g), fitness (b,g), flag football (b,g), football (b,g), physical fitness (b,g), soccer (b,g), strength & conditioning (b,g), table tennis (b,g), track and field (b,g), volleyball (b,g), weight lifting (b,g), weight training (b,g); coed intramural: indoor soccer, jump rope, kickball, ropes courses, touch football. 3 PE instructors, 2 coaches.

Computers Computers are regularly used in all academic, journalism, newspaper, science, social sciences, yearbook classes. Computer network features include on-campus library services, online commercial services, Internet access, wireless campus network, Internet filtering or blocking technology, desktop publishing applications, Ebsco, Moodle. Campus intranet and student e-mail accounts are available to students. Students grades are available online. The school has a published electronic and media policy.

Contact Ms. Nancy J. Cowley, Admissions Director. 808-625-0737 Ext. 456. Fax: 808-625-0691. E-mail: admissions@hanalani.org. Web site: www.hanalani.org.

HANK HANEY INTERNATIONAL JUNIOR GOLF ACADEMY

55 Hospital Center Common

Hilton Head Island, South Carolina 29926

Head of School: Tina Sprouse

General Information Coeducational boarding and day college-preparatory, arts, business, and bilingual studies school. Grades 5–PG. Founded: 1995. Setting: suburban. Nearest major city is Savannah, GA. Students are housed in single-sex cottages. 5-acre campus. 2 buildings on campus. Approved or accredited by South Carolina Department of Education. Candidate for accreditation by Southern Association of Colleges and Schools. Total enrollment: 140. Upper school average class size: 9. Upper school faculty-student ratio: 1:10. Upper School students typically attend 5 days per week. The average school day consists of 4 hours and 30 minutes.

Upper School Student Profile 95% of students are boarding students. 28 states are represented in upper school student body. 50% are international students. International students from Canada, Denmark, Japan, Mexico, Republic of Korea, and United Kingdom; 28 other countries represented in student body.

Faculty School total: 14. In upper school: 2 men, 12 women; 5 have advanced degrees.

Special Academic Programs Advanced Placement exam preparation; honors section; ESL.

Student Life Upper grades have specified standards of dress, student council, honor system. Discipline rests equally with students and faculty.

Tuition and Aid Day student tuition: $38,900; 7-day tuition and room/board: $51,900. Guaranteed tuition plan. Tuition installment plan (individually arranged payment plans). Tuition reduction for siblings, Sallie Mae loans available.

Admissions Deadline for receipt of application materials: none. Application fee required: $50. Interview recommended.

Athletics Interscholastic: golf (boys, girls). 13 coaches.

Computers Computer resources include Internet access, wireless campus network. Computer access in designated common areas is available to students. Students grades are available online.

Contact Matt Bashaw, Director of Admissions. 843-686-1500. Fax: 843-785-5116. E-mail: admissions@ijga.com. Web site: www.ijga.com.

HANSON MEMORIAL HIGH SCHOOL

903 Anderson Street

Franklin, Louisiana 70538-0000

Head of School: Dr. Vincent Miholic

General Information Coeducational day and distance learning college-preparatory, general academic, arts, business, vocational, religious studies, and technology school, affiliated with Roman Catholic Church. Grades 6–12. Distance learning grades 9–12. Founded: 1925. Setting: rural. Nearest major city is Lafayette. 14-acre campus. 4 buildings on campus. Approved or accredited by National Catholic Education Association, Southern Association of Colleges and Schools, and Louisiana Department of Education. Total enrollment: 275. Upper school average class size: 27. Upper school faculty-student ratio: 1:13. There are 178 required school days per year for Upper School students.

Upper School Student Profile 80% of students are Roman Catholic.

Faculty School total: 20. In upper school: 4 men, 16 women; 5 have advanced degrees.

Subjects Offered 3-dimensional art, 3-dimensional design, addiction, ADL skills, Advanced Placement courses, advanced studio art-AP, advanced TOEFL/grammar, advertising design, aerobics, aerospace education, aerospace science, aesthetics, African American history, African American studies, African dance, African drumming, African history, African literature, African studies, African-American history, African-American literature, African-American studies, agriculture, agro-ecology, Alabama history and geography, algebra, alternative physical education, American biography, American Civil War, American culture, American democracy, American foreign policy, American government, American history-AP, American legal systems, American literature-AP, American minority experience, American politics in film, American sign language, American studies, anatomy, anatomy and physiology, Ancient Greek, ancient history, ancient/medieval philosophy, animal behavior, animal husbandry, animal science, animation, anthropology, applied arts, applied music, applied skills, aquatics, Arabic, Arabic studies, archaeology, architectural drawing, architecture, area studies, art and culture, art appreciation, art education, art history, art history-AP, art in New York, art-AP, arts, arts and crafts, arts appreciation, ASB Leadership, Asian history, Asian literature, Asian studies, astronomy, astrophysics, athletic training, athletics, atomic theory, audio visual/media, audition methods, auto mechanics, automated accounting, aviation, backpacking, bacteriology, ballet, ballet technique, band, banking, basic imaging, basic language skills, Basic programming, basic skills, batik, biochemistry, bioethics, bioethics, DNA and culture, biology-AP, biotechnology, bivouac, Black history, boat building, boating, body human, Bolivian history, Bolivian social studies, bookbinding, bookkeeping, bookmaking, botany, bowling, brass choir, Brazilian history, Brazilian social studies, Brazilian studies, British history, British literature (honors), British literature-AP, British National Curriculum, broadcast journalism, broadcasting, Broadway dance, Buddhism, business applications, business communications, business education, business law, business skills, business studies, cabinet making, calculus-AP, California writers, calligraphy, Canadian geography, Canadian history, Canadian law, Canadian literature, Cantonese, career and technology systems, career education, career education internship, career experience, career exploration, Career Passport, career planning, career technology, careers, Caribbean history, carpentry, cartography, cartooning/animation, celestial navigation, cell biology, Central and Eastern European history, ceramics, ceremonies of life, chamber groups, chaplaincy, chemistry-AP, Cherokee, Chesapeake Bay studies, Cheyenne history, Cheyenne language, child development, China/Japan history, Chinese, Chinese history, Chinese literature, Chinese studies, choral music, choreography, chorus, cinematography, circus acts, civics/free enterprise, civil rights, Civil War, classical Greek literature, classical language, classical music, classical studies, classics, claywoking, clinical chemistry, collage and assemblage, college counseling, college writing, Colorado ecology, comedy, Coming of Age in the 20th Century, commercial art, communication skills, communications, community garden, community service, comparative civilizations, comparative cultures, comparative government and politics, comparative government and politics-AP, comparative political systems-AP, comparative politics, comparative religion, competitive science projects, composition-AP, computer animation, computer applications, computer art, computer education, computer graphics, computer literacy, computer math, computer multimedia, computer music, computer processing, computer programming, computer programming-AP, computer resources, computer science, computer science-AP, computer studies, computer technologies, computer technology certification, computer tools, computer-aided design, computers, conceptual physics, concert band, concert bell choir, concert choir, conflict resolution, conservation, constitutional history of U.S., constitutional law, construction, consumer economics, consumer education, consumer law, consumer mathematics, contemporary art, contemporary issues, contemporary issues in science, contemporary math, contemporary problems, contemporary studies, contemporary technique, contemporary women writers, costumes and make-up, CPR, crafts, creation science, creative arts, creative dance, creative drama, criminal justice, criminology, critical studies in film, critical thinking, critical writing, culinary arts, cultural arts, cultural criticism, cultural geography, current events, dance, dance performance, Danish, data analysis, data processing, death and loss, debate, design, desktop publishing, desktop publishing, ESL, developmental language skills, developmental math, digital applications, digital art, digital imaging, digital music, digital photography, directing, discrete mathematics, diversity studies, DNA, DNA research, DNA science lab, drafting, drama workshop, dramatic arts, drawing, drawing and design, driver education, Dutch, early childhood, earth and space science, earth systems analysis, East Asian history, East European studies, Eastern religion and philosophy, Eastern world civilizations, Easterner in the West, ecology, environmental systems, economics, economics and history, economics-AP, education, Egyptian history, electronic imagery, electronic music, electronic publishing, electronic research, electronics, emergency medicine, emerging technology, engineering, English as a foreign language, English language and composition-AP, English language-AP, English literature and composition-AP, English literature-AP, English-AP, English/composition-AP, ensembles, entomology, entrepreneurship, environmental education, environmental geography, environmental science-AP, environmental studies, environmental systems, epic literature, equestrian sports, equine management, equine science, equitation, ESL, ESL, essential learning systems, ethical decision making, ethics, ethics and responsibility, ethnic literature, ethnic studies, ethology, etymology, European civilization, European history, European history-AP, European literature, eurythmics (guard), eurythmy, evolution, exercise science, existentialism, experiential education, experimental science, expository writing, expressive arts, fabric arts, family and consumer science, family living, family studies, Far Eastern history, Farsi, fashion, female experience in America, fencing, fiber arts, fiction, field ecology, Filipino, film, film and literature, film and new technologies, film appreciation, film history, film series, film studies, filmmaking, finance, fine arts, Finnish, first aid, fitness, flight instruction, folk art, folk dance, folk music, food and nutrition.

Special Academic Programs Study at local college for college credit.
College Admission Counseling 38 students graduated in 2010; 36 went to college, including Louisiana State University and Agricultural and Mechanical College; Nicholls State University. Other: 2 went to work.
Student Life Upper grades have uniform requirement, student council, honor system. Discipline rests primarily with faculty. Attendance at religious services is required.
Tuition and Aid Guaranteed tuition plan. Tuition installment plan (monthly payment plans). Tuition reduction for siblings, need-based scholarship grants available. In 2010–11, 10% of upper-school students received aid.
Admissions Traditional secondary-level entrance grade is 9. ACT required. Deadline for receipt of application materials: February. Application fee required. On-campus interview required.
Athletics Interscholastic: baseball (boys), basketball (b,g), cheering (b,g), cross-country running (b,g), drill team (g), football (b), golf (b,g), softball (g), strength & conditioning (b,g), track and field (b,g), weight lifting (b,g); intramural: tennis (b,g); coed interscholastic: cheering, cross-country running, golf; coed intramural: tennis. 7 coaches.
Computers Computers are regularly used in all academic classes. Computer network features include on-campus library services, online commercial services, Internet access, wireless campus network, Internet filtering or blocking technology. Students grades are available online. The school has a published electronic and media policy.
Contact Mrs. Kim Adams, Dean of Students. 337-828-3487. Fax: 337-828-0787. E-mail: kadams@hansonmemorial.com. Web site: www.hansonmemorial.com.

HAPPY HILL FARM ACADEMY

3846 North Highway 144

Granbury, Texas 76048

Head of School: Dr. Marc Evans

General Information Coeducational boarding and day and distance learning college-preparatory, arts, and agriculture/FFA school, affiliated with Christian faith. Grades K–12. Distance learning grade X. Founded: 1975. Setting: rural. Nearest major city is Dallas. Students are housed in single-sex residences. 500-acre campus. 1 building on campus. Approved or accredited by Association of Christian Schools International, Christian Schools International, Southern Association of Colleges and Schools, and The Association of Boarding Schools. Total enrollment: 165. Upper school average class size: 8. Upper school faculty-student ratio: 1:7. There are 182 required school days per year for Upper School students. Upper School students typically attend 5 days per week. The average school day consists of 6 hours and 30 minutes.
Upper School Student Profile 70% of students are boarding students. 70% are state residents. 8 states are represented in upper school student body. 10% are international students. International students from China, Hong Kong, Nigeria, Russian Federation, and Taiwan; 3 other countries represented in student body. 65% of students are Christian.
Faculty School total: 28. In upper school: 4 men, 24 women; 8 have advanced degrees; 10 reside on campus.
Subjects Offered 1 1/2 elective credits, advanced math, Advanced Placement courses, agriculture, algebra, all academic, American history, American literature, animal husbandry, animal science, applied music, art, athletics, basketball, Bible, biology, calculus, cheerleading, chemistry, choir, classical music, computer education, computer literacy, computer skills, concert choir, desktop publishing, drawing, driver education, economics, economics-AP, electives, English, English literature, English-AP, fine arts, gardening, general math, general science, geometry, golf, government, government-AP, guitar, health, history, horticulture, instruments, journalism, language arts, library, life science, mathematics, mathematics-AP, music, music appreciation, music performance, music theory, newspaper, physical education, physics, pottery, pre-algebra, pre-calculus, science, scripture, social studies, Spanish, speech, sports, tennis, track and field, trigonometry, U.S. government, U.S. history, vocal ensemble, volleyball, weight training, woodworking, world history, yearbook.
Special Academic Programs Honors section; independent study; study at local college for college credit; academic accommodation for the gifted, the musically talented, and the artistically talented; ESL (14 students enrolled).
College Admission Counseling 11 students graduated in 2011; 10 went to college, including Southwestern University; Texas A&M University; Texas Christian University; Texas State University–San Marcos; Texas Wesleyan University; United States Air Force Academy. Other: 1 entered military service.
Student Life Upper grades have uniform requirement, student council, honor system. Discipline rests primarily with faculty. Attendance at religious services is required.
Summer Programs Remediation, enrichment, ESL, sports, art/fine arts programs offered; session focuses on enrichment; held on campus; accepts boys and girls; not open to students from other schools. 160 students usually enrolled. 2012 schedule: June 4 to July 13.
Tuition and Aid Day student tuition: $3000–$8400; 7-day tuition and room/board: $1200–$36,000. Tuition installment plan (monthly payment plans, individually arranged payment plans). Tuition reduction for siblings, need-based scholarship grants available. In 2011–12, 90% of upper-school students received aid.
Admissions Traditional secondary-level entrance grade is 10. Achievement tests, English for Non-native Speakers, Stanford Achievement Test or writing sample

required. Deadline for receipt of application materials: none. Application fee required: $60. Interview required.

Athletics Interscholastic: baseball (boys), basketball (b,g), cheering (g), cross-country running (b,g), football (b), golf (b,g), horseback riding (b,g), outdoor education (b,g), physical fitness (b,g), running (b,g), soccer (g), softball (g), strength & conditioning (b,g), tennis (b,g), track and field (b,g), volleyball (g), weight training (b,g). 2 PE instructors, 4 coaches.

Computers Computers are regularly used in computer applications, creative writing, desktop publishing, English, journalism, library, newspaper, yearbook classes. Computer resources include on-campus library services, Internet access, wireless campus network, Internet filtering or blocking technology. Computer access in designated common areas is available to students. Students grades are available online.

Contact Mr. Todd L. Shipman, President/Chief Financial Officer. 254-897-4822. Fax: 254-897-7650. E-mail: todd@happyhillfarm.org. Web site: www.happyhillfarm.org.

HARDING ACADEMY

1100 Cherry Road

Memphis, Tennessee 38117

Head of School: Mr. Allen Gillespie

General Information Coeducational day college-preparatory, arts, and religious studies school, affiliated with Christian faith. Grades PS–12. Founded: 1952. Setting: urban. 28-acre campus. 3 buildings on campus. Approved or accredited by National Christian School Association, Southern Association of Colleges and Schools, and Tennessee Department of Education. Endowment: $2 million. Total enrollment: 1,222. Upper school average class size: 19. Upper school faculty-student ratio: 1:13. There are 175 required school days per year for Upper School students. Upper School students typically attend 5 days per week. The average school day consists of 6 hours and 45 minutes.

Upper School Student Profile Grade 7: 82 students (38 boys, 44 girls); Grade 8: 93 students (48 boys, 45 girls); Grade 9: 84 students (37 boys, 47 girls); Grade 10: 75 students (37 boys, 38 girls); Grade 11: 100 students (54 boys, 46 girls); Grade 12: 100 students (52 boys, 48 girls). 47% of students are Christian.

Faculty School total: 45. In upper school: 18 men, 27 women; 23 have advanced degrees.

Subjects Offered Accounting, algebra, American government, American history, American history-AP, American literature, art, art-AP, band, Bible, biology, biology-AP, British literature, calculus-AP, chemistry, chorus, computer applications, concert band, drama, earth science, English, English language and composition-AP, English literature and composition-AP, etymology, French, geography, geometry, grammar, humanities, journalism, keyboarding, physical fitness, Spanish, Spanish language-AP, speech, statistics, world history.

Graduation Requirements Algebra, American government, American history, American literature, arts and fine arts (art, music, dance, drama), Bible, biology, British literature, English, fitness, foreign language, geometry, speech, world history.

Special Academic Programs 8 Advanced Placement exams for which test preparation is offered; honors section.

College Admission Counseling 64 students graduated in 2011; 63 went to college, including Harding University; Lipscomb University; The University of Tennessee; The University of Tennessee at Chattanooga; University of Memphis. Other: 1 entered military service. Mean SAT critical reading: 534, mean SAT math: 499, mean SAT writing: 540, mean composite ACT: 24.

Student Life Upper grades have uniform requirement, student council, honor system. Discipline rests primarily with faculty. Attendance at religious services is required.

Summer Programs Remediation, enrichment, sports, art/fine arts, computer instruction programs offered; held on campus; accepts boys and girls; open to students from other schools.

Tuition and Aid Day student tuition: $9795–$10,795. Tuition installment plan (monthly payment plans, individually arranged payment plans). Tuition reduction for siblings, need-based scholarship grants available. In 2011–12, 18% of upper-school students received aid. Total amount of financial aid awarded in 2011–12: $191,824.

Admissions Traditional secondary-level entrance grade is 7. For fall 2011, 74 students applied for upper-level admission, 62 were accepted, 56 enrolled. Metropolitan Achievement Short Form and Otis-Lennon School Ability Test required. Deadline for receipt of application materials: none. Application fee required: $50. Interview required.

Athletics Interscholastic: baseball (boys), basketball (b,g), bowling (b,g), cheering (g), cross-country running (b,g), fitness (b,g), football (b), golf (b,g), soccer (b,g), softball (g), tennis (b,g), track and field (b,g), volleyball (g). 2 PE instructors, 45 coaches, 1 athletic trainer.

Computers Computers are regularly used in accounting, keyboarding classes. Computer network features include on-campus library services, online commercial services, Internet access. Students grades are available online. The school has a published electronic and media policy.

Contact Mrs. Karen Sills, Administrative Assistant in Admissions. 901-767-4494 Ext. 113. Fax: 901-763-4949. E-mail: sills.karen@hardinglions.org. Web site: www.hardinglions.org.

HARDING ACADEMY

170 Windsor Drive

Nashville, Tennessee 37205

Head of School: Ian Craig

General Information Coeducational day college-preparatory, general academic, arts, and technology school. Grades K–8. Founded: 1971. Setting: suburban. 15-acre campus. Approved or accredited by Southern Association of Colleges and Schools, Southern Association of Independent Schools, and Tennessee Department of Education. Endowment: $2.2 million. Total enrollment: 480.

Upper School Student Profile Grade 6: 50 students (25 boys, 25 girls); Grade 7: 50 students (25 boys, 25 girls); Grade 8: 50 students (25 boys, 25 girls).

Faculty School total: 61.

Subjects Offered Algebra, art, chorus, civics, computers, dance, drama, English, French, history, jazz band, lab science, library, mathematics, music, physical education, pre-algebra, science.

Student Life Upper grades have specified standards of dress, honor system. Discipline rests primarily with faculty.

Summer Programs Enrichment, sports programs offered; held on campus; accepts boys and girls; open to students from other schools. 2012 schedule: June to August. Application deadline: May.

Tuition and Aid Day student tuition: $15,310. Tuition installment plan (Key Tuition Payment Plan, monthly payment plans). Need-based scholarship grants available.

Admissions Achievement/Aptitude/Writing, CTP III, ERB, Gates MacGinite (vocab) and Stanford Achievement Test (math), ISEE, Otis-Lennon School Ability Test or writing sample required. Deadline for receipt of application materials: none. Application fee required: $100. On-campus interview required.

Athletics Interscholastic: baseball (boys), basketball (b,g), cheering (g), football (b), lacrosse (b,g), soccer (b,g), tennis (b,g), track and field (b,g), volleyball (g), wrestling (b); coed interscholastic: cross-country running, diving, golf, swimming and diving; coed intramural: ballet, climbing, dance, floor hockey, Frisbee, indoor soccer, modern dance, running, table tennis, ultimate Frisbee. 4 PE instructors, 15 coaches.

Computers Computer resources include on-campus library services, online commercial services, Internet access, wireless campus network, Internet filtering or blocking technology. Campus intranet and student e-mail accounts are available to students. Students grades are available online.

Contact Rebecca P. Arnold, Director of Admission and Financial Aid. 615-356-2974. Fax: 615-356-0441. E-mail: arnoldb@hardingacademy.org. Web site: www.hardingacademy.org.

HARGRAVE MILITARY ACADEMY

200 Military Drive

Chatham, Virginia 24531

Head of School: Brig. Gen. Don Broome, USA (Ret.)

General Information Boys' boarding and day college-preparatory, general academic, arts, religious studies, technology, academic post-graduate, leadership and ethics, and military school, affiliated with Baptist General Association of Virginia. Grades 7–PG. Founded: 1909. Setting: small town. Nearest major city is Danville. Students are housed in single-sex dormitories. 276-acre campus. 13 buildings on campus. Approved or accredited by Southern Association of Colleges and Schools, The Association of Boarding Schools, and Virginia Association of Independent Schools. Member of National Association of Independent Schools. Endowment: $3.5 million. Total enrollment: 310. Upper school average class size: 11. Upper school faculty-student ratio: 1:12. Upper School students typically attend 5 days per week.

Upper School Student Profile 94% of students are boarding students. 24% are state residents. 29 states are represented in upper school student body. 12% are international students. International students from China, Nigeria, Republic of Korea, Saudi Arabia, Taiwan, and United Kingdom; 24 other countries represented in student body. 20% of students are Baptist General Association of Virginia.

Faculty School total: 30. In upper school: 18 men, 12 women; all have advanced degrees; 12 reside on campus.

Subjects Offered Advanced biology, advanced chemistry, advanced math, Advanced Placement courses, algebra, American government, American history, American literature, art, astronomy, Bible studies, biology, calculus, chemistry, creative writing, debate, English, English literature, environmental science, ESL, French, geometry, government/civics, health, history, journalism, leadership, leadership and service, leadership education training, mathematics, media production, physical education, physics, psychology, reading, religion, SAT/ACT preparation, science, social studies, sociology, Spanish, speech, study skills, TOEFL preparation, trigonometry.

Graduation Requirements English, foreign language, mathematics, physical education (includes health), religion (includes Bible studies and theology), science, social studies (includes history).

Special Academic Programs Advanced Placement exam preparation; honors section; independent study; study at local college for college credit; remedial reading and/or remedial writing; remedial math; programs in general development for dyslexic students; special instructional classes for students with Attention Deficit Disorder; ESL (8 students enrolled).

College Admission Counseling 63 students graduated in 2011; all went to college, including Hampden-Sydney College; The University of North Carolina at Charlotte; United States Military Academy; Virginia Military Institute; Virginia Polytechnic Institute and State University.

Student Life Upper grades have uniform requirement, student council, honor system. Discipline rests equally with students and faculty. Attendance at religious services is required.

Summer Programs Remediation, enrichment, advancement, ESL, sports, rigorous outdoor training, computer instruction programs offered; session focuses on academics/sports camps; held on campus; accepts boys; open to students from other schools. 140 students usually enrolled. 2012 schedule: July 1 to July 29. Application deadline: June 30.

Tuition and Aid Day student tuition: $12,750; 5-day tuition and room/board: $28,600; 7-day tuition and room/board: $28,600. Tuition installment plan (monthly payment plans, individually arranged payment plans). Tuition reduction for siblings, merit scholarship grants, need-based scholarship grants, need-based loans, Sallie Mae available. In 2011–12, 32% of upper-school students received aid; total upper-school merit-scholarship money awarded: $52,000. Total amount of financial aid awarded in 2011–12: $525,000.

Admissions Traditional secondary-level entrance grade is 10. Math and English placement tests required. Deadline for receipt of application materials: none. Application fee required: $75. Interview recommended.

Athletics Interscholastic: aquatics, baseball, basketball, cross-country running, diving, football, golf, independent competitive sports, lacrosse, marksmanship, riflery, soccer, swimming and diving, tennis, wrestling; intramural: aquatics, backpacking, billiards, canoeing/kayaking, climbing, cross-country running, drill team, fishing, fitness, fitness walking, hiking/backpacking, independent competitive sports, jogging, jump rope, kayaking, lacrosse, life saving, marksmanship, mountaineering, Nautilus, outdoor activities, outdoor adventure, outdoor recreation, paint ball, physical fitness, physical training, rappelling, riflery, rock climbing, ropes courses, running, scuba diving, skeet shooting, skiing (downhill), strength & conditioning, swimming and diving, table tennis, tennis, trap and skeet, walking, water polo, weight lifting, weight training. 1 PE instructor, 10 coaches, 1 athletic trainer.

Computers Computers are regularly used in all academic classes. Computer network features include on-campus library services, online commercial services, Internet access, wireless campus network, Internet filtering or blocking technology. Campus intranet, student e-mail accounts, and computer access in designated common areas are available to students. Students grades are available online. The school has a published electronic and media policy.

Contact Mrs. Amy Walker, Director of Admissions. 434-432-2481 Ext. 2130. Fax: 434-432-3129. E-mail: admissions@hargrave.edu. Web site: www.hargrave.edu.

THE HARKER SCHOOL

500 Saratoga Avenue

San Jose, California 95129

Head of School: Christopher Nikoloff

General Information Coeducational day college preparatory, arts, technology, and gifted students school. Grades K–12. Founded: 1893. Setting: urban. 16-acre campus. 7 buildings on campus. Approved or accredited by Western Association of Schools and Colleges and California Department of Education. Member of National Association of Independent Schools. Total enrollment: 1,791. Upper school average class size: 16. Upper school faculty-student ratio: 1:16. Upper School students typically attend 5 days per week.

Upper School Student Profile Grade 9: 187 students (97 boys, 90 girls); Grade 10: 181 students (101 boys, 80 girls); Grade 11: 175 students (85 boys, 90 girls); Grade 12: 172 students (95 boys, 77 girls).

Faculty School total: 187. In upper school: 40 men, 51 women; 80 have advanced degrees.

Subjects Offered Acting, advanced math, aerobics, algebra, American literature, anatomy and physiology, architecture, art history-AP, Asian history, Asian literature, astronomy, baseball, basketball, biology, biology-AP, British literature, British literature (honors), calculus-AP, ceramics, chemistry, chemistry-AP, choir, college counseling, community service, computer programming, computer science-AP, contemporary women writers, dance, dance performance, debate, discrete mathematics, drawing, ecology, economics, electronics, engineering, English literature and composition-AP, environmental science-AP, ethics, European history-AP, evolution, expository writing, fencing, film and literature, fitness, French, French language-AP, French literature-AP, golf, graphic arts, honors algebra, honors geometry, instrumental music, international affairs, Japanese, Latin, Latin-AP, linear algebra, literary magazine, macro/microeconomics-AP, macroeconomics-AP, Mandarin, medieval literature, mentorship program, music, music theory-AP, newspaper, orchestra, organic chemistry, painting, physics, physics-AP, play production, political thought, pre-calculus, psychology-AP, public policy, public speaking, radio broadcasting, robotics, scene study, sculpture, self-defense, Shakespeare, softball, Spanish, Spanish language-AP, Spanish literature-AP, statistics, stone carving, student government, studio art-AP, study skills, swimming, technical theater, tennis, theater arts, track and field, trigonometry, U.S. government and politics-AP, U.S. history, U.S. history-AP, video and animation, visual arts, vocal ensemble, volleyball, weight training, Western philosophy, women in world history, world history, wrestling, yearbook, yoga.

Graduation Requirements Algebra, arts and fine arts (art, music, dance, drama), biology, chemistry, computer science, English, foreign language, geometry, physical education (includes health), physics, public speaking, trigonometry, U.S. history, world history, 30 total hours of community service.

Special Academic Programs Advanced Placement exam preparation; honors section; independent study; academic accommodation for the gifted.

College Admission Counseling 164 students graduated in 2011; all went to college, including Harvard University; Stanford University; University of California, Berkeley; University of California, Los Angeles; University of California, San Diego; University of Southern California. Mean SAT critical reading: 708, mean SAT math: 735, mean SAT writing: 731.

Student Life Upper grades have specified standards of dress, student council, honor system. Discipline rests primarily with faculty.

Summer Programs Enrichment, advancement programs offered; session focuses on academics; held both on and off campus; held at venues abroad for upper school students; accepts boys and girls; open to students from other schools. 700 students usually enrolled. 2012 schedule: June 25 to August 10.

Tuition and Aid Day student tuition: $36,435. Need-based scholarship grants, need-based loans available. In 2011–12, 10% of upper-school students received aid.

Admissions Traditional secondary-level entrance grade is 9. ERB CTP IV, essay, ISEE or SSAT required. Deadline for receipt of application materials: January 13. Application fee required: $75. Interview required.

Athletics Interscholastic: baseball (boys), basketball (b,g), cross-country running (b,g), football (b), golf (b,g), lacrosse (g), soccer (b,g), softball (g), swimming and diving (b,g), tennis (b,g), track and field (b,g), volleyball (b,g), water polo (b,g), wrestling (b,g); coed interscholastic: cheering, football; coed intramural: aerobics/dance, dance, fencing, fitness, physical fitness, tennis, yoga. 4 PE instructors, 62 coaches, 1 athletic trainer.

Computers Computers are regularly used in all academic, graphic arts, newspaper, programming, yearbook classes. Computer network features include on-campus library services, online commercial services, Internet access, wireless campus network, Internet filtering or blocking technology, ProQuest, Gale Group, InfoTrac, Facts On File. Student e-mail accounts are available to students. The school has a published electronic and media policy.

Contact Ruth Tebo, Assistant to the Director of Admission. 408-249-2510. Fax: 408-984-2325. E-mail: rutht@harker.org. Web site: www.harker.org.

See Display on next page and Close-Up on page 630.

THE HARLEY SCHOOL

1981 Clover Street

Rochester, New York 14618

Head of School: Dr. Timothy Cottrell

General Information Coeducational day college-preparatory and arts school. Grades N–12. Founded: 1917. Setting: suburban. 25-acre campus. 3 buildings on campus. Approved or accredited by National Independent Private Schools Association and New York State Association of Independent Schools. Member of National Association of Independent Schools. Endowment: $9.2 million. Total enrollment: 520. Upper school average class size: 7. Upper school faculty-student ratio: 1:7. There are 180 required school days per year for Upper School students. Upper School students typically attend 5 days per week. The average school day consists of 6 hours and 50 minutes.

Upper School Student Profile Grade 9: 42 students (18 boys, 24 girls); Grade 10: 40 students (20 boys, 20 girls); Grade 11: 35 students (11 boys, 24 girls); Grade 12: 46 students (22 boys, 24 girls).

Faculty School total: 90. In upper school: 14 men, 14 women; 28 have advanced degrees.

Subjects Offered 3-dimensional art, Advanced Placement courses, algebra, American history, anthropology, art, art history, art-AP, band, biology, calculus, calculus-AP, ceramics, chamber groups, chemistry, Chinese, choir, chorus, community service, comparative government and politics-AP, computer graphics, computer math, computer programming, computer science, creative writing, debate, desktop publishing, drama, drawing, driver education, economics-AP, English, English language and composition-AP, English literature, environmental science, ethics, European history, expository writing, film, fine arts, foreign language, French, gardening, geometry, graphic arts, Greek, health, jazz band, language-AP, Latin, mathematics, multimedia, music, music theory, orchestra, organic gardening, outdoor education, photography, physical education, physics, psychology, SAT preparation, science, Shakespeare, social studies, Spanish, speech, student government, study skills, theater, theater arts, theater production, U.S. history-AP, voice, world history, writing, yoga.

Graduation Requirements Arts and fine arts (art, music, dance, drama), computer science, English, foreign language, internship, mathematics, physical education (includes health), science, social studies (includes history), participation in team sports. Community service is required.

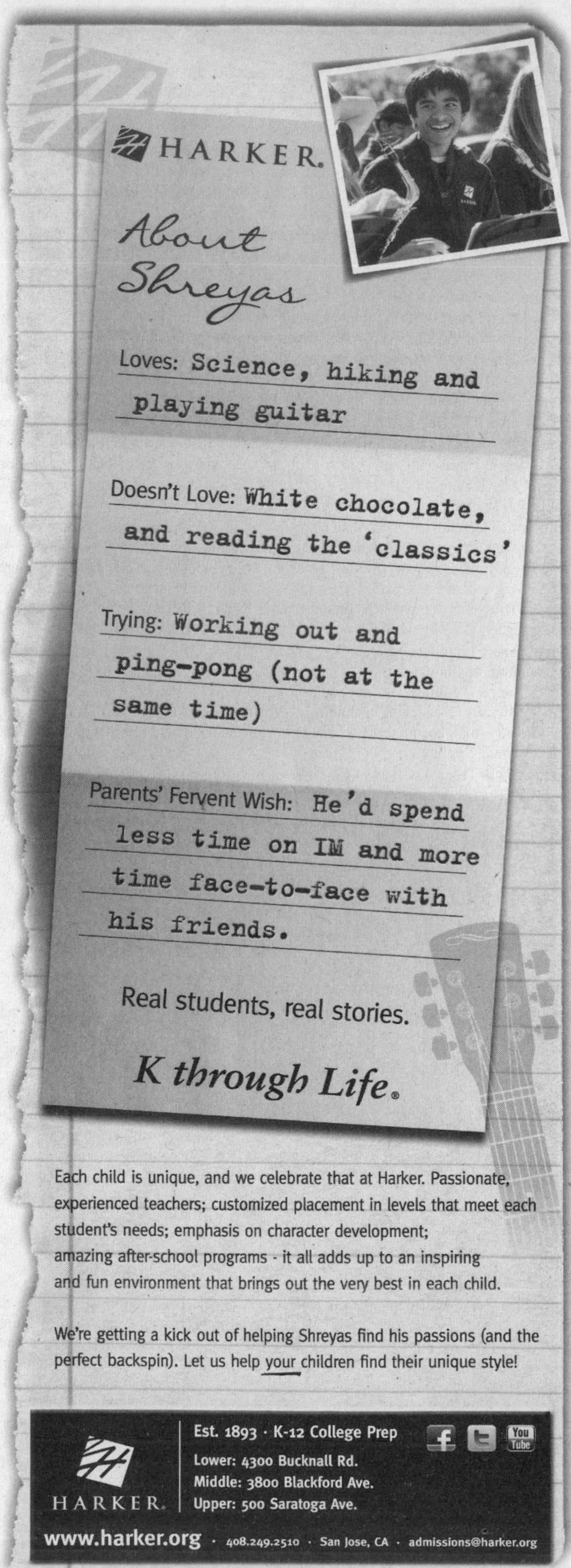

Special Academic Programs 17 Advanced Placement exams for which test preparation is offered.

College Admission Counseling 41 students graduated in 2011; 40 went to college, including Bucknell University; Carleton College; Cornell University; Drexel University; Duke University; Tufts University. Other: 1 entered a postgraduate year. Mean SAT critical reading: 601, mean SAT math: 608, mean SAT writing: 597.

Student Life Upper grades have student council, honor system. Discipline rests primarily with faculty.

Summer Programs Remediation, enrichment, sports, art/fine arts, computer instruction programs offered; session focuses on day camp, outdoor skills, swimming, tennis, writing, college prep; held both on and off campus; held at field house, classrooms, grounds, field trips; accepts boys and girls; open to students from other schools. 150 students usually enrolled. 2012 schedule: June 11 to August 3. Application deadline: May.

Tuition and Aid Day student tuition: $19,500–$20,200. Tuition installment plan (Insured Tuition Payment Plan, Key Tuition Payment Plan, monthly payment plans, 2-payment plan, prepaid discount plan). Tuition reduction for siblings, need-based scholarship grants available. In 2011–12, 33% of upper-school students received aid.

Admissions Traditional secondary-level entrance grade is 9. For fall 2011, 28 students applied for upper-level admission, 23 were accepted, 21 enrolled. Essay and Math Placement Exam required. Deadline for receipt of application materials: none. Application fee required: $50. On-campus interview required.

Athletics Interscholastic: baseball (boys), basketball (b,g), bowling (b,g), golf (b), skiing (downhill) (b,g), soccer (b,g), softball (b,g), swimming and diving (b,g), tennis (b,g), track and field (b,g), volleyball (b,g); coed interscholastic: cross-country running, outdoor education, running, yoga. 3 PE instructors, 11 coaches.

Computers Computers are regularly used in all academic, art classes. Computer network features include Internet access, wireless campus network. The school has a published electronic and media policy.

Contact Ms. Valerie Myntti, Director of Admissions. 585-442-1770. Fax: 585-442-5758. E-mail: vmyntti@harleyschool.org. Web site: www.harleyschool.org.

HARMONY HEIGHTS RESIDENTIAL AND DAY SCHOOL

Oyster Bay, New York

See Special Needs Schools section.

HARRELLS CHRISTIAN ACADEMY

360 Tomahawk Highway

PO Box 88

Harrells, North Carolina 28444

Head of School: Dr. Ronald L. Montgomery

General Information Coeducational day college-preparatory, arts, religious studies, and technology school, affiliated with Christian faith. Grades K–12. Founded: 1969. Setting: rural. Nearest major city is Wilmington. 32-acre campus. 7 buildings on campus. Approved or accredited by Southern Association of Colleges and Schools, Southern Association of Independent Schools, and North Carolina Department of Education. Total enrollment: 395. Upper school average class size: 13. Upper school faculty-student ratio: 1:9. There are 180 required school days per year for Upper School students. Upper School students typically attend 5 days per week. The average school day consists of 6 hours and 16 minutes.

Upper School Student Profile Grade 9: 42 students (25 boys, 17 girls); Grade 10: 33 students (17 boys, 16 girls); Grade 11: 33 students (21 boys, 12 girls); Grade 12: 36 students (21 boys, 15 girls). 96% of students are Christian.

Faculty School total: 19. In upper school: 5 men, 14 women; 5 have advanced degrees.

Subjects Offered Algebra, animal science, art, art education, biology, botany, calculus, ceramics, chemistry, computer art, earth science, English, English language and composition-AP, English literature, English literature and composition-AP, French, government/civics, history, journalism, Latin, mathematics, painting, photography, physical education, physical science, religion, social studies, Spanish, U.S. history-AP, weightlifting, yearbook.

Graduation Requirements Biology, computer applications, electives, English, environmental science, foreign language, mathematics, physical education (includes health), physical science, religious studies, social studies (includes history). Community service is required.

Special Academic Programs 3 Advanced Placement exams for which test preparation is offered; honors section; study at local college for college credit; programs in English, mathematics, general development for dyslexic students.

College Admission Counseling 31 students graduated in 2011; all went to college, including East Carolina University; North Carolina State University; The University of North Carolina at Chapel Hill; The University of North Carolina Wilmington. Median SAT critical reading: 530, median SAT math: 490, median SAT writing: 490, median combined SAT: 1510, median composite ACT: 22. 21% scored over 600 on SAT critical reading, 14% scored over 600 on SAT math, 11% scored over 600 on SAT writing, 7% scored over 1800 on combined SAT, 23% scored over 26 on composite ACT.

Student Life Upper grades have specified standards of dress, honor system. Discipline rests primarily with faculty. Attendance at religious services is required.

Tuition and Aid Day student tuition: $7950. Tuition installment plan (FACTS Tuition Payment Plan, individually arranged payment plans). Tuition reduction for siblings available. In 2011–12, 10% of upper-school students received aid. Total amount of financial aid awarded in 2011–12: $32,500.

Admissions Traditional secondary-level entrance grade is 9. For fall 2011, 7 students applied for upper-level admission, 7 were accepted, 7 enrolled. Admissions testing or Stanford 9 required. Deadline for receipt of application materials: none. Application fee required: $35. On-campus interview required.

Athletics Interscholastic: baseball (boys), basketball (b,g), cheering (g), football (b), soccer (b,g), softball (g), tennis (g), volleyball (g); coed interscholastic: golf. 1 PE instructor, 1 coach.

Computers Computers are regularly used in art, computer applications, English, journalism, yearbook classes. Computer network features include Internet access, wireless campus network, Internet filtering or blocking technology. Students grades are available online. The school has a published electronic and media policy.

Contact Mrs. Susan Frederick, Administrative Assistant. 910-532-4575 Ext. 221. Fax: 910-532-2958. E-mail: sfrederick@harrellsca.org. Web site: www.harrellschristianacademy.com.

HARROW SCHOOL

5 High Street

Harrow on the Hill

Middlesex HAI 3HT, United Kingdom

Head of School: Barnaby J. Lenon

General Information Boys' boarding college-preparatory school, affiliated with Church of England (Anglican). Grades 9–13. Founded: 1572. Setting: suburban. Nearest major city is London, United Kingdom. Students are housed in individual or double rooms. 250-acre campus. 50 buildings on campus. Approved or accredited by Boarding Schools Association (UK). Language of instruction: English. Total enrollment: 820. Upper school average class size: 10. Upper school faculty-student ratio: 1:8.

Upper School Student Profile Grade 9: 160 students (160 boys); Grade 10: 160 students (160 boys); Grade 11: 160 students (160 boys), Grade 12: 175 students (175 boys); Grade 13: 175 students (175 boys). 100% of students are boarding students. 20% are international students. International students from Australia, China, Germany, Malaysia, Republic of Korea, and United States; 32 other countries represented in student body. 70% of students are members of Church of England (Anglican).

Faculty School total: 100. In upper school: 85 men, 15 women; all reside on campus.

Subjects Offered Advanced chemistry, advanced math, algebra, ancient history, Arabic, art, art history, Bible studies, biology, British literature, business studies, calculus, calculus-AP, career education internship, ceramics, character education, chemistry, chemistry-AP, computer science, creative writing, drama, ecology, economics, English, English literature, European history, French, geography, geometry, German, grammar, Greek, history, Italian, Japanese, Latin, mathematics, music, photography, physics, religion, Spanish, statistics, theater, trigonometry, zoology.

Graduation Requirements Completion of at least three advanced level (AP) courses.

Special Academic Programs Advanced Placement exam preparation; academic accommodation for the gifted, the musically talented, and the artistically talented; programs in general development for dyslexic students; ESL (15 students enrolled).

College Admission Counseling 160 students graduated in 2010.

Student Life Upper grades have uniform requirement, honor system. Discipline rests primarily with faculty.

Tuition and Aid 7-day tuition and room/board: £30,000. Tuition installment plan (individually arranged payment plans). Tuition reduction for siblings, bursaries, merit scholarship grants available. In 2010–11, 20% of upper-school students received aid.

Admissions Traditional secondary-level entrance grade is 12. For fall 2010, 200 students applied for upper-level admission, 26 were accepted, 26 enrolled. Cognitive Abilities Test and common entrance examinations required. Deadline for receipt of application materials: January. Application fee required: £250. On-campus interview required.

Athletics Interscholastic: alpine skiing, archery, badminton, ball hockey, basketball, biathlon, climbing, cricket, croquet, cross-country running, equestrian sports, fencing, field hockey, fishing, fitness, Fives, fly fishing, golf, hockey, indoor soccer, jogging, judo, life saving, marksmanship, martial arts, physical fitness, physical training, pistol, polo, riflery, rock climbing, rugby, running, sailing, scuba diving, skiing (downhill), soccer, squash, strength & conditioning, swimming and diving, table tennis, tennis, track and field, triathlon, volleyball, wall climbing, water polo, weight training, winter soccer; intramural: alpine skiing, archery, backpacking, badminton, biathlon, canoeing/kayaking, climbing, cricket, croquet, cross-country running, drill team, fencing, field hockey, fishing, fly fishing, golf, hiking/backpacking, hockey, independent competitive sports, jogging, kayaking, life saving, marksmanship, martial arts, mountaineering, outdoor adventure, physical fitness, rock climbing, rugby, running, soccer, squash, strength & conditioning, swimming and diving, tennis, track and field, wall climbing, water polo, weight training. 1 PE instructor, 8 coaches, 2 athletic trainers.

Computers Computers are regularly used in all academic classes. Computer network features include on-campus library services, online commercial services, Internet access, wireless campus network, Internet filtering or blocking technology. Student e-mail accounts are available to students. Students grades are available online. The school has a published electronic and media policy.

Contact Mr. Rob Taylor, Registrar. 44-208-8728007. Fax: 44-208-8728012. E-mail: admissions@harrowschool.org.uk. Web site: www.harrowschool.org.uk.

HARVARD-WESTLAKE SCHOOL

3700 Coldwater Canyon

North Hollywood, California 91604

Head of School: Thomas C. Hudnut

General Information Coeducational day college-preparatory school, affiliated with Episcopal Church. Grades 7–12. Founded: 1989. Setting: urban. Nearest major city is Los Angeles. 26-acre campus. 12 buildings on campus. Approved or accredited by Western Association of Schools and Colleges. Member of National Association of Independent Schools. Endowment: $39.5 million. Total enrollment: 1,609. Upper school average class size: 16. Upper school faculty-student ratio: 1:8. Upper School students typically attend 5 days per week. The average school day consists of 6 hours and 35 minutes.

Upper School Student Profile Grade 10: 297 students (152 boys, 145 girls); Grade 11: 296 students (158 boys, 138 girls); Grade 12: 282 students (154 boys, 128 girls).

Faculty School total: 122. In upper school: 72 men, 50 women; 85 have advanced degrees.

Subjects Offered 3-dimensional art, advanced studio art-AP, algebra, American history, American literature, American literature-AP, anatomy, architecture, art, art history, art history-AP, Asian studies, astronomy, biology, biology-AP, calculus, calculus-AP, ceramics, chemistry, chemistry-AP, Chinese, choreography, chorus, classics, community service, comparative government and politics-AP, computer animation, computer programming, computer science, computer science-AP, creative writing, dance, drama, drawing, economics, economics-AP, electronics, English, English language and composition-AP, English literature, English literature-AP, environmental science, environmental science-AP, European history, expository writing, film, film studies, fine arts, French, French language-AP, French literature-AP, geography, geology, geometry, government and politics-AP, government/civics, grammar, health, human development, human geography - AP, Japanese, jazz, journalism, Latin, Latin-AP, logic, macro/microeconomics-AP, Mandarin, mathematics, music, music history, music theory-AP, oceanography, orchestra, painting, photography, physical education, physics, physics-AP, physiology, political science, pre-calculus, psychology, Russian, science, senior project, Shakespeare, social studies, Spanish, Spanish language-AP, Spanish literature-AP, statistics, statistics-AP, studio art-AP, technical theater, theater, trigonometry, U.S. government and politics-AP, U.S. history-AP, video, women's studies, world history, world history-AP, world literature, yearbook, zoology.

Graduation Requirements English, foreign language, history, human development, mathematics, performing arts, physical education (includes health), science, visual arts. Community service is required.

Special Academic Programs 30 Advanced Placement exams for which test preparation is offered; honors section; independent study; term-away projects; study at local college for college credit; study abroad; academic accommodation for the gifted, the musically talented, and the artistically talented.

College Admission Counseling 280 students graduated in 2010; 278 went to college, including Columbia University; Cornell University; New York University; University of Michigan; University of Pennsylvania; University of Southern California. Other: 2 had other specific plans. Mean SAT critical reading: 663, mean SAT math: 681, mean SAT writing: 676. 90% scored over 600 on SAT critical reading, 91% scored over 600 on SAT math.

Student Life Upper grades have specified standards of dress, student council, honor system. Discipline rests primarily with faculty.

Tuition and Aid Day student tuition: $29,200. Tuition installment plan (monthly payment plans, semiannual payment plan, triennial payment plan). Need-based scholarship grants, short-term loans (payable by end of year in which loan is made) available. In 2010–11, 16% of upper-school students received aid. Total amount of financial aid awarded in 2010–11: $6,846,600.

Admissions Traditional secondary-level entrance grade is 10. For fall 2010, 56 students applied for upper-level admission, 17 were accepted, 15 enrolled. ISEE required. Deadline for receipt of application materials: January 24. Application fee required: $200. On-campus interview required.

Athletics Interscholastic: baseball (boys), basketball (b,g), cross-country running (b,g), field hockey (g), football (b), golf (b,g), gymnastics (g), lacrosse (b), soccer (b,g), softball (g), swimming and diving (b,g), tennis (b,g), track and field (b,g), volleyball (b,g), water polo (b,g), wrestling (b); coed interscholastic: diving, equestrian sports, fencing, martial arts; coed intramural: badminton. 6 PE instructors, 32 coaches, 3 athletic trainers.

Computers Computers are regularly used in art, foreign language, history, mathematics, music, science classes. Computer resources include on-campus library services, Internet access, wireless campus network, music composition and editing, foreign language lab, science lab. Campus intranet, student e-mail accounts, and computer access in designated common areas are available to students. Students grades are available online.

Contact Elizabeth Gregory, Director of Admission. 310-274-7281. Fax: 310-288-3212. E-mail: egregory@hw.com. Web site: www.harvardwestlake.com.

THE HARVEY SCHOOL

260 Jay Street

Katonah, New York 10536

Head of School: Mr. Barry W. Fenstermacher

General Information Coeducational boarding and day and distance learning college-preparatory school. Boarding grades 9–12, day grades 6–12. Distance learning grades 6–12. Founded: 1916. Setting: suburban. Students are housed in single-sex dormitories. 125-acre campus. 14 buildings on campus. Approved or accredited by New York State Association of Independent Schools. Member of National Association of Independent Schools. Endowment: $1.9 million. Total enrollment: 338. Upper school average class size: 12. Upper school faculty-student ratio: 1:7. There are 165 required school days per year for Upper School students. Upper School students typically attend 5 days per week. The average school day consists of 8 hours and 50 minutes.

Upper School Student Profile Grade 9: 56 students (30 boys, 26 girls); Grade 10: 74 students (43 boys, 31 girls); Grade 11: 61 students (36 boys, 25 girls); Grade 12: 64 students (38 boys, 26 girls). 12% of students are boarding students. 75% are state residents. 3 states are represented in upper school student body.

Faculty School total: 62. In upper school: 22 men, 18 women; 20 have advanced degrees; 30 reside on campus.

Subjects Offered Algebra, American history, American literature, art, art history, biology, calculus, ceramics, chemistry, composition-AP, computer programming-AP, creative writing, drama, English, English literature, European history, expository writing, fine arts, French, general science, geology, geometry, government/civics, grammar, Greek, history, Japanese, Latin, mathematics, music, photography, physics, religion, science, social studies, Spanish, theater, trigonometry, world history, writing.

Graduation Requirements Arts and fine arts (art, music, dance, drama), computer literacy, English, foreign language, mathematics, science, social sciences, social studies (includes history).

Special Academic Programs 11 Advanced Placement exams for which test preparation is offered; honors section; independent study.

College Admission Counseling 63 students graduated in 2011; all went to college, including Barnard College; Bentley University; Cornell University; University of Connecticut; Villanova University.

Student Life Upper grades have specified standards of dress, student council. Discipline rests primarily with faculty.

Summer Programs Remediation, advancement programs offered; session focuses on on-line academic course; held both on and off campus; held at via distance learning; accepts boys and girls; open to students from other schools. 2012 schedule: June 20 to August 10. Application deadline: May 1.

Tuition and Aid Day student tuition: $31,000–$31,950; 5-day tuition and room/board: $38,500–$38,950. Tuition installment plan (FACTS Tuition Payment Plan, individually arranged payment plans). Need-based scholarship grants available. In 2011–12, 28% of upper-school students received aid. Total amount of financial aid awarded in 2011–12: $2,010,500.

Admissions Traditional secondary-level entrance grade is 9. For fall 2011, 134 students applied for upper-level admission, 94 were accepted, 59 enrolled. Deadline for receipt of application materials: none. Application fee required: $50. Interview required.

Athletics Interscholastic: baseball (boys), basketball (b,g), football (b), ice hockey (b), lacrosse (b,g), rugby (b), soccer (b,g), softball (g), volleyball (g); coed interscholastic: cross-country running, tennis, weight lifting; coed intramural: aerobics, dance, figure skating, fitness, fitness walking, Frisbee, golf, modern dance, strength & conditioning, tai chi, yoga. 1 athletic trainer.

Computers Computers are regularly used in English, foreign language, history, mathematics, science classes. Computer resources include on-campus library services, online commercial services, Internet access. The school has a published electronic and media policy.

Contact Mr. William Porter, Director of Admissions. 914-232-3161 Ext. 113. Fax: 914-232-6034. E-mail: wporter@harveyschool.org. Web site: www.harveyschool.org.

THE HAVERFORD SCHOOL

450 Lancaster Avenue

Haverford, Pennsylvania 19041

Head of School: Dr. Joseph T. Cox

General Information Boys' day college-preparatory and arts school. Grades PK–12. Founded: 1884. Setting: suburban. Nearest major city is Philadelphia. 32-acre campus. 7 buildings on campus. Approved or accredited by Middle States Association of Colleges and Schools, Pennsylvania Association of Independent Schools, and Pennsylvania Department of Education. Member of National Association of Independent Schools and Secondary School Admission Test Board. Endowment: $40 million. Total enrollment: 991. Upper school average class size: 16. Upper school faculty-student ratio: 1:7. Upper School students typically attend 5 days per week.

Upper School Student Profile Grade 9: 121 students (121 boys); Grade 10: 106 students (106 boys); Grade 11: 103 students (103 boys); Grade 12: 88 students (88 boys).

Faculty School total: 117. In upper school: 36 men, 11 women; 31 have advanced degrees.

Subjects Offered Algebra, American history, American literature, animal behavior, art, astronomy, biology, calculus, ceramics, chemistry, Chinese, Chinese studies, drama, ecology, economics, economics and history, English, English literature, European history, fine arts, French, geology, geometry, German, government/civics, history, Latin, mathematics, music, photography, physical education, physics, physiology, science, social studies, Spanish, statistics, theater, trigonometry, world affairs, world history, world literature.

Graduation Requirements Arts and fine arts (art, music, dance, drama), English, foreign language, mathematics, physical education (includes health), science, social studies (includes history).

Special Academic Programs Honors section; independent study; term-away projects; academic accommodation for the gifted; remedial reading and/or remedial writing; remedial math.

College Admission Counseling 96 students graduated in 2011; 94 went to college, including Cornell University; Franklin & Marshall College; Penn State University Park; Princeton University; University of Pennsylvania; University of Pittsburgh. Other: 1 entered a postgraduate year, 1 had other specific plans. Mean SAT critical reading: 630, mean SAT math: 640, mean SAT writing: 640, mean combined SAT: 1910, mean composite ACT: 26. 41% scored over 600 on SAT critical reading, 48% scored over 600 on SAT math, 42% scored over 600 on SAT writing.

Student Life Upper grades have specified standards of dress, student council, honor system. Discipline rests equally with students and faculty.

Tuition and Aid Day student tuition: $31,800. Tuition installment plan (Insured Tuition Payment Plan, monthly payment plans, individually arranged payment plans). Merit scholarship grants, need-based scholarship grants available. In 2011–12, 32% of upper-school students received aid; total upper-school merit-scholarship money awarded: $20,000. Total amount of financial aid awarded in 2011–12: $2,614,756.

Admissions Traditional secondary-level entrance grade is 9. For fall 2011, 183 students applied for upper-level admission, 73 were accepted, 52 enrolled. ISEE, SSAT or Wechsler Intelligence Scale for Children required. Deadline for receipt of application materials: none. Application fee required: $50. Interview required.

Athletics Interscholastic: aquatics, baseball, basketball, crew, cross-country running, football, golf, ice hockey, indoor track, lacrosse, rowing, soccer, squash, swimming and diving, tennis, track and field, water polo, winter (indoor) track, wrestling; intramural: fitness, physical fitness, physical training, soccer, strength & conditioning, weight training. 6 PE instructors, 2 coaches, 2 athletic trainers.

Computers Computers are regularly used in art, English, history, mathematics, music, science classes. Computer network features include on-campus library services, online commercial services, Internet access. Computer access in designated common areas is available to students. Students grades are available online. The school has a published electronic and media policy.

Contact Mr. Henry D. Fairfax, Director of Admissions. 610-642-3020 Ext. 1923. Fax: 610-642-8724. E-mail: hfairfax@haverford.org. Web site: www.haverford.org.

HAWAIIAN MISSION ACADEMY

1438 Pensacola Street

Honolulu, Hawaii 96822

Head of School: Mr. Hugh P. Winn

General Information Coeducational boarding and day college-preparatory, general academic, arts, business, religious studies, bilingual studies, and technology school, affiliated with Seventh-day Adventist Church. Grades 9–12. Founded: 1895. Setting: urban. Students are housed in single-sex by floor dormitories. 4-acre campus. 4 buildings on campus. Approved or accredited by The Hawaii Council of Private Schools, Western Association of Schools and Colleges, and Hawaii Department of Education. Total enrollment: 118. Upper school average class size: 25. Upper school faculty-student ratio: 1:15. The average school day consists of 6 hours and 50 minutes.

Upper School Student Profile Grade 9: 30 students (16 boys, 14 girls); Grade 10: 34 students (20 boys, 14 girls); Grade 11: 34 students (20 boys, 14 girls); Grade 12: 22 students (8 boys, 14 girls). 20% of students are boarding students. 46% are state residents. 3 states are represented in upper school student body. 50% are international students. International students from China, Hong Kong, Japan, Macao, Republic of Korea, and Taiwan. 80% of students are Seventh-day Adventists.

Faculty School total: 13. In upper school: 8 men, 5 women; 9 have advanced degrees; 2 reside on campus.

Subjects Offered Algebra, anatomy and physiology, art, Bible, biology, business, business education, business skills, calculus, chemistry, choir, Christianity, community service, computer literacy, computer science, conceptual physics, concert choir, desktop publishing, digital art, economics, electives, English, English literature, ESL, family and consumer science, family living, general science, geometry, grammar, Hawaiian history, health, independent living, interactive media, journalism, keyboarding, lab science, library, Microsoft, personal finance, physical education, pre-algebra, pre-calculus, Spanish, student government, student publications, U.S. government, U.S. history, video film production, weight training, work experience, work-study, world history, yearbook.

Graduation Requirements Algebra, arts and fine arts (art, music, dance, drama), biology, chemistry, computer literacy, English, foreign language, geometry, Hawaiian history, keyboarding, physical education (includes health), physics, practical arts, religion (includes Bible studies and theology), social studies (includes history), U.S. government, work experience, world history, 25 hours of community service per year, 100 hours of work experience throughout the 4 years combined.

Special Academic Programs Honors section; ESL (8 students enrolled).

College Admission Counseling 33 students graduated in 2011; 30 went to college, including Kapiolani Community College; La Sierra University; Pacific Union College; University of Hawaii at Hilo; University of Hawaii at Manoa. Other: 3 had other specific plans. Mean SAT critical reading: 505, mean SAT math: 535.

Student Life Upper grades have uniform requirement, student council. Discipline rests primarily with faculty.

Tuition and Aid Day student tuition: $10,510; 7-day tuition and room/board: $9500. Tuition installment plan (Insured Tuition Payment Plan, monthly payment plans, individually arranged payment plans). Tuition reduction for siblings, need-based scholarship grants, paying campus jobs available. In 2011–12, 25% of upper-school students received aid.

Admissions Placement test and TOEFL required. Deadline for receipt of application materials: none. Application fee required: $25. Interview recommended.

Athletics Interscholastic: basketball (boys, girls), golf (b,g), volleyball (b,g). 3 PE instructors, 6 coaches.

Computers Computers are regularly used in desktop publishing, economics, graphic arts, journalism, keyboarding, media production, newspaper, publications, science, video film production, word processing, yearbook classes. Computer network features include on-campus library services, Internet access, wireless campus network. Students grades are available online.

Contact Mrs. Nenny Safotu, Registrar. 808-536-2207 Ext. 202. Fax: 808-524-3294. E-mail: registrar@hawaiianmissionacademy.org. Web site: www.hawaiianmissionacademy.org

HAWAII BAPTIST ACADEMY

2429 Pali Highway

Honolulu, Hawaii 96817

Head of School: Richard Bento

General Information Coeducational day college-preparatory and Christian education school, affiliated with Southern Baptist Convention. Grades K–12. Founded: 1949. Setting: urban. 13-acre campus. 6 buildings on campus. Approved or accredited by Association of Christian Schools International and Western Association of Schools and Colleges. Member of National Association of Independent Schools and Secondary School Admission Test Board. Endowment: $4.6 million. Total enrollment: 1,121. Upper school average class size: 18. Upper school faculty-student ratio: 1:11. There are 176 required school days per year for Upper School students. Upper School students typically attend 5 days per week. The average school day consists of 6 hours.

Upper School Student Profile Grade 9: 124 students (56 boys, 68 girls); Grade 10: 124 students (66 boys, 58 girls); Grade 11: 116 students (55 boys, 61 girls); Grade 12: 109 students (52 boys, 57 girls). 14% of students are Southern Baptist Convention.

Faculty School total: 80. In upper school: 19 men, 25 women; 25 have advanced degrees.

Subjects Offered Advanced Placement courses, algebra, American history, American history-AP, American literature, analytic geometry, ancient world history, art, Basic programming, Bible studies, biology, biology-AP, British literature, calculus-AP, ceramics, chemistry, chemistry-AP, Chinese, Christian education, Christian ethics, Christian studies, communication skills, computer applications, concert band, digital photography, drama, drama performance, drawing, economics, English, English language and composition-AP, English literature, English literature-AP, environmental science, film, film history, fine arts, forensics, French, geometry, handbells, Japanese, journalism, marine biology, mathematics, mechanical drawing, modern world history, music theory-AP, physical education, physics, physics-AP, political science, psychology, psychology-AP, religion, science, social studies, Spanish, speech, statistics, statistics-AP, trigonometry, world history, world literature, writing.

Graduation Requirements Algebra, ancient history, arts and fine arts (art, music, dance, drama), Bible studies, biology, communication skills, computer applications, economics, English, foreign language, mathematics, physical education (includes health), political science, science, social studies (includes history), U.S. history, world history.

Special Academic Programs Advanced Placement exam preparation; independent study.

College Admission Counseling 110 students graduated in 2011; all went to college, including Biola University; Creighton University; Pacific University; University of Hawaii at Manoa; University of Washington. Mean SAT critical reading: 552, mean SAT math: 603, mean SAT writing: 562, mean combined SAT: 1717, mean composite ACT: 24.

Student Life Upper grades have uniform requirement, student council. Discipline rests primarily with faculty. Attendance at religious services is required.

Summer Programs Remediation, enrichment, sports, art/fine arts, computer instruction programs offered; session focuses on academic/social preparation for entrance to regular school, instruction/remediation, and personal growth; held both on and off campus; held at various recreation sites; accepts boys and girls; open to students from other schools. 315 students usually enrolled. 2012 schedule: June 12 to July 10. Application deadline: May 11.

Tuition and Aid Day student tuition: $12,610. Guaranteed tuition plan. Tuition installment plan (Insured Tuition Payment Plan, monthly payment plans). Need-based scholarship grants available. In 2011–12, 13% of upper-school students received aid. Total amount of financial aid awarded in 2011–12: $229,635.

Admissions Traditional secondary-level entrance grade is 9. For fall 2011, 59 students applied for upper-level admission, 37 were accepted, 21 enrolled. Achievement tests and SSAT required. Deadline for receipt of application materials: January 31. Application fee required: $75. On-campus interview required.

Athletics Interscholastic: aquatics (boys, girls), baseball (b), basketball (b,g), bowling (b,g), canoeing/kayaking (b,g), cheering (g), cross-country running (b,g), diving (b,g), football (b), golf (b,g), judo (b,g), kayaking (b,g), riflery (b,g), soccer (b,g), softball (g), swimming and diving (b,g), tennis (b,g), track and field (b,g), volleyball (b,g), water polo (b,g), wrestling (b,g); coed interscholastic: canoeing/kayaking, cheering, golf, sailing. 3 PE instructors, 30 coaches, 2 athletic trainers.

Computers Computers are regularly used in digital applications, keyboarding, media production, newspaper, programming, word processing, yearbook classes. Computer resources include Internet access, Internet filtering or blocking technology. The school has a published electronic and media policy.

Contact Mrs. Katherine Lee, Director of Admissions. 808-595-7585. Fax: 808-564-0332. E-mail: klee@hba.net. Web site: www.hba.net.

HAWKEN SCHOOL

12465 County Line Road

PO Box 8002

Gates Mills, Ohio 44040-8002

Head of School: D. Scott Looney

General Information Coeducational day college-preparatory, arts, business, STEMM (Science, Technology, Engineering, Math, Medicine), and writing school. Grades PS–12. Founded: 1915. Setting: suburban. Nearest major city is Cleveland. 325-acre campus. 5 buildings on campus. Approved or accredited by Independent Schools Association of the Central States, Ohio Association of Independent Schools, and Ohio Department of Education. Member of National Association of Independent Schools. Endowment: $47.7 million. Total enrollment: 971. Upper school average class size: 15. Upper school faculty-student ratio: 1:9. Upper School students typically attend 5 days per week. The average school day consists of 4 hours and 33 minutes.

Upper School Student Profile Grade 9: 106 students (52 boys, 54 girls); Grade 10: 113 students (50 boys, 63 girls); Grade 11: 99 students (46 boys, 53 girls); Grade 12: 113 students (55 boys, 58 girls).

Faculty School total: 115. In upper school: 34 men, 23 women; 42 have advanced degrees.

Subjects Offered 20th century world history, accounting, acting, advanced chemistry, advanced math, Advanced Placement courses, advanced studio art-AP, African-American literature, algebra, American Civil War, American history, American history-AP, American literature, animal science, art, art appreciation, art history, band, Bible as literature, biology, botany, business, business mathematics, calculus, calculus-AP, ceramics, chemistry, chemistry-AP, Chinese, choir, choral music, chorus, Civil War, classical Greek literature, community service, computer applications, computer math, computer programming, computer science, computer science-AP, computer skills, concert band, creative dance, creative writing, dance, dance performance, drama, drawing, driver education, ecology, economics, economics and history, electronic music, English, English literature, English-AP, environmental science-AP, ethics, European history, field ecology, film, film studies, fine arts, first aid, French, French studies, French-AP, geography, geometry, government/civics, grammar, graphic design, health, history, history of jazz, history of rock and roll, Holocaust and other genocides, humanities, improvisation, Latin, Latin-AP, mathematics, mathematics-AP, music, music theory, outdoor education, painting, performing arts, philosophy, photography, physical education, physics, physics-AP, physiology, poetry, probability and statistics, qualitative analysis, science, science research, sculpture, senior project, social sciences, social studies, Spanish, Spanish literature-AP, speech, statistics-AP, strings, studio art-AP, swimming, theater, theater arts, theater design and production, theater production, trigonometry, U.S. history, U.S. history-AP, world history, world literature, World War I, World War II, writing.

Graduation Requirements Arts and fine arts (art, music, dance, drama), computer science, English, foreign language, history, mathematics, physical education (includes health), science. Community service is required.

Special Academic Programs Advanced Placement exam preparation; honors section; accelerated programs; independent study; term-away projects; study at local college for college credit; study abroad; academic accommodation for the gifted and the musically talented.

College Admission Counseling 93 students graduated in 2011; all went to college, including Case Western Reserve University; Miami University; Southern Methodist University; The Ohio State University; University of Michigan; University of Pennsylvania. Median SAT critical reading: 620, median SAT math: 640, median SAT writing: 630, median combined SAT: 1870, median composite ACT: 28. 60% scored over 600 on SAT critical reading, 67% scored over 600 on SAT math, 62% scored over 600 on SAT writing, 66% scored over 1800 on combined SAT, 72% scored over 26 on composite ACT.

Student Life Upper grades have specified standards of dress, student council, honor system. Discipline rests equally with students and faculty.

Summer Programs Remediation, enrichment, advancement, computer instruction programs offered; session focuses on credit, review, preview and enrichment in English, math, computer studies, and health; held on campus; accepts boys and girls; open to students from other schools. 133 students usually enrolled. 2012 schedule: June 11 to August 10. Application deadline: none.

Tuition and Aid Day student tuition: $25,101–$27,446. Tuition installment plan (Key Tuition Payment Plan, installment payment plan (60 percent by 8/15 and 40 percent by 1/15), AchieverLoans (Key Education Resources)). Merit scholarship grants, need-based scholarship grants, need-based loans available. In 2011–12, 36% of upper-school students received aid; total upper-school merit-scholarship money awarded: $131,000. Total amount of financial aid awarded in 2011–12: $5,000,000.

Admissions Traditional secondary-level entrance grade is 9. For fall 2011, 138 students applied for upper-level admission, 97 were accepted, 54 enrolled. ISEE required. Deadline for receipt of application materials: December 16. Application fee required: $25. On-campus interview required.

Athletics Interscholastic: baseball (boys), basketball (b,g), cross-country running (b,g), diving (b,g), field hockey (g), football (b), golf (b,g), lacrosse (b,g), soccer (b,g), softball (g), swimming and diving (b,g), tennis (b,g), track and field (b,g); intramural: basketball (b); coed intramural: dance, drill team, outdoor skills. 3 PE instructors, 33 coaches, 1 athletic trainer.

Computers Computers are regularly used in all classes. Computer network features include on-campus library services, Internet access, wireless campus network, Internet filtering or blocking technology. Campus intranet and student e-mail accounts are available to students. Students grades are available online. The school has a published electronic and media policy.

Contact Heather Daly, Director of Admission and Financial Assistance. 440-423-2955. Fax: 440-423-2994. E-mail: hdaly@hawken.edu. Web site: www.hawken.edu/.

HAWTHORNE CHRISTIAN ACADEMY

2000 Route 208

Hawthorne, New Jersey 07506

Head of School: Mr. Donald J. Klingen

General Information Coeducational day college-preparatory, arts, religious studies, technology, music, and missions school, affiliated with Christian faith, Christian faith. Grades PS–12. Founded: 1981. Setting: suburban. Nearest major city is New York, NY. 22-acre campus. 4 buildings on campus. Approved or accredited by Association of Christian Schools International, Middle States Association of Colleges and Schools, and New Jersey Department of Education. Total enrollment: 464. Upper school average class size: 21. Upper school faculty-student ratio: 1:7. There are 180 required school days per year for Upper School students. Upper School students typically attend 5 days per week. The average school day consists of 6 hours and 40 minutes.

Upper School Student Profile Grade 9: 30 students (15 boys, 15 girls); Grade 10: 46 students (21 boys, 25 girls); Grade 11: 37 students (22 boys, 15 girls); Grade 12: 33 students (17 boys, 16 girls). 100% of students are Christian faith, Christian.

Faculty School total: 60. In upper school: 10 men, 12 women; 6 have advanced degrees.

Subjects Offered Accounting, advanced computer applications, Advanced Placement courses, algebra, anatomy and physiology, art and culture, band, Basic programming, bell choir, Bible, biology, business applications, calculus, calculus-AP, chemistry, choir, choral music, chorus, composition, computer information systems, computer programming, computers, contemporary issues, creative writing, current events, drama, electives, English literature, English literature-AP, ensembles, foreign language, geometry, government, guidance, handbells, health, home economics, information technology, instrumental music, instruments, intro to computers, law, mathematics, music, music history, music theory, physical education, physical science, physics, politics, pre-calculus, psychology, Spanish, Spanish-AP, studio art, U.S. government, U.S. government and politics-AP, U.S. history-AP, video, visual arts, voice, Web site design, world history, yearbook.

Graduation Requirements Algebra, Bible, biology, chemistry, English literature, English literature-AP, geometry, intro to computers, mathematics, physical education (includes health), physical science, pre-calculus, Spanish, U.S. government, U.S. history, U.S. history-AP, world history, Christian service hours, Apologetics and Current Issues, specified number of Academic Elective Courses.

College Admission Counseling 45 students graduated in 2011; 27 went to college, including Liberty University; Montclair State University; New Jersey Institute of Technology; Philadelphia Biblical University; Ramapo College of New Jersey; William Paterson University of New Jersey. Other: 1 went to work. Mean SAT critical reading: 569, mean SAT math: 534, mean SAT writing: 601, mean combined SAT: 1103.

Student Life Upper grades have specified standards of dress, student council. Discipline rests primarily with faculty. Attendance at religious services is required.

Tuition and Aid Day student tuition: $10,331. Tuition installment plan (monthly payment plans). Tuition reduction for siblings, merit scholarship grants, need-based scholarship grants, pastoral discounts, teacher/employee discounts available. In 2011–12, 51% of upper-school students received aid; total upper-school merit-scholarship money awarded: $20,500. Total amount of financial aid awarded in 2011–12: $26,124.

Admissions Traditional secondary-level entrance grade is 9. Admissions testing, Otis-Lennon School Ability Test or WRAT required. Deadline for receipt of application materials: none. Application fee required: $100. On-campus interview required.

Athletics Interscholastic: baseball (boys), basketball (b,g), soccer (b,g), softball (g), strength & conditioning (b), volleyball (g); coed interscholastic: bowling, cross-country running, golf, track and field. 2 PE instructors.

Computers Computers are regularly used in business applications, computer applications, information technology, introduction to technology, lab/keyboard, library, technology, Web site design, yearbook classes. Computer network features include on-campus library services, Internet access, Internet filtering or blocking technology. Campus intranet is available to students. Students grades are available online. The school has a published electronic and media policy.

Contact Mrs. Judith De Boer, Admissions Coordinator. 973-423-3331 Ext. 261. Fax: 973-238-1718. E-mail: jdeboer@hca.org.

HAWTHORN SCHOOL FOR GIRLS

101 Scarsdale Road

North York, Ontario M3B 2R2, Canada

General Information Girls' day college-preparatory school, affiliated with Roman Catholic Church. Grades PS–12. Founded: 1989. Setting: urban. Nearest major city is Toronto, Canada. 1 building on campus. Approved or accredited by Canadian Educational Standards Institute, Conference of Independent Schools of Ontario, and Ontario Department of Education. Language of instruction: English. Total enrollment: 145.

Upper School Student Profile 75% of students are Roman Catholic.

Faculty School total: 40.

College Admission Counseling 5 students graduated in 2010; all went to college.

Student Life Upper grades have uniform requirement, student council, honor system. Discipline rests primarily with faculty.

Tuition and Aid Day student tuition: CAN$14,800. Need-based scholarship grants available.

Admissions Traditional secondary-level entrance grade is 7. Deadline for receipt of application materials: none. Application fee required: CAN$100. Interview required.

Computers Computer resources include Internet access. Computer access in designated common areas is available to students. The school has a published electronic and media policy.

Contact 416-444-3054. Fax: 416-449-2891. Web site: www.hawthornschool.com.

HEAD-ROYCE SCHOOL

4315 Lincoln Avenue

Oakland, California 94602

Head of School: Robert Lake

General Information Coeducational day college-preparatory, arts, technology, and STEM, robotics, Global Online Academy school. Grades K–12. Founded: 1887. Setting: urban. 14-acre campus. 8 buildings on campus. Approved or accredited by Western Association of Schools and Colleges and California Department of Education. Member of National Association of Independent Schools. Endowment: $15 million. Total enrollment: 832. Upper school average class size: 16. Upper school faculty-student ratio: 1:9. There are 175 required school days per year for Upper School students. Upper School students typically attend 5 days per week. The average school day consists of 7 hours.

Upper School Student Profile Grade 9: 86 students (46 boys, 40 girls); Grade 10: 92 students (51 boys, 41 girls); Grade 11: 80 students (41 boys, 39 girls); Grade 12: 82 students (38 boys, 44 girls).

Faculty School total: 95. In upper school: 24 men, 19 women; 29 have advanced degrees.

Subjects Offered Algebra, American history, American literature, art, art history, astronomy, biology, calculus, ceramics, chemistry, Chinese, community service, computer programming, computer science, creative writing, debate, drama, ecology, English, English literature, European history, expository writing, fine arts, French, geometry, graphic arts, health, history, journalism, Latin, marine biology, mathematics, music, neurobiology, photography, physical education, physics, psychology, science, social studies, Spanish, theater, trigonometry, typing, video, world history, world literature, writing.

Graduation Requirements Art history, arts and fine arts (art, music, dance, drama), computer science, English, foreign language, mathematics, physical education (includes health), science, social studies (includes history), 40 hours of community service.

Special Academic Programs 21 Advanced Placement exams for which test preparation is offered; honors section; independent study; term-away projects; study at local college for college credit; study abroad; academic accommodation for the gifted, the musically talented, and the artistically talented.

College Admission Counseling 84 students graduated in 2011; all went to college, including Princeton University; Stanford University; University of California, Davis; University of California, Los Angeles; University of Michigan; University of Pennsylvania. Mean SAT critical reading: 674, mean SAT math: 679, mean SAT writing: 701.

Student Life Upper grades have specified standards of dress, student council, honor system. Discipline rests primarily with faculty.

Summer Programs Remediation, enrichment, advancement programs offered; session focuses on sports and enrichment; held on campus; accepts boys and girls; open to students from other schools. 800 students usually enrolled. 2012 schedule: June 20 to July 29. Application deadline: February.

Tuition and Aid Day student tuition: $30,310. Tuition installment plan (SMART Tuition Payment Plan, monthly payment plans). Need-based scholarship grants, paying campus jobs, tuition remission for children of faculty and staff available. In 2011–12, 31% of upper-school students received aid. Total amount of financial aid awarded in 2011–12: $2,015,100.

Admissions Traditional secondary-level entrance grade is 9. For fall 2011, 186 students applied for upper-level admission, 82 were accepted, 29 enrolled. ISEE or SSAT required. Deadline for receipt of application materials: January 12. Application fee required: $100. On-campus interview required.

Athletics Interscholastic: baseball (boys), basketball (b,g), cross-country running (b,g), dance squad (g), golf (b,g), lacrosse (b), modern dance (g), outdoor education (b,g), physical fitness (b,g), soccer (b,g), softball (g), strength & conditioning (b,g), swimming and diving (b,g), tennis (b,g), volleyball (b,g), weight lifting (b,g), weight training (b,g); coed interscholastic: cross-country running, golf, outdoor education, physical fitness, strength & conditioning, swimming and diving; coed intramural: bicycling, dance, ultimate Frisbee. 6 PE instructors, 39 coaches.

Computers Computers are regularly used in all academic, English, graphics, mathematics, science, yearbook classes. Computer network features include on-campus library services, online commercial services, Internet access, wireless campus network, laptop carts, smartboards. Student e-mail accounts and computer access in designated common areas are available to students. Students grades are available online. The school has a published electronic and media policy.

Contact Mrs. Catherine Epstein, Director of Admissions and Financial Aid. 510-531-1300. Fax: 510-530-8329. E-mail: cepstein@headroyce.org. Web site: www.headroyce.org.

HEBREW ACADEMY

14401 Willow Lane

Huntington Beach, California 92647

Head of School: Dr. Megan Carlson

General Information Coeducational day college-preparatory, general academic, religious studies, and technology school, affiliated with Jewish faith. Boys grades N–8, girls grades N–12. Founded: 1969. Setting: suburban. 11-acre campus. 11 buildings on campus. Approved or accredited by Accrediting Commission for Schools and Western Association of Schools and Colleges. Total enrollment: 257. Upper school average class size: 10. Upper school faculty-student ratio: 1:4. There are 175 required school days per year for Upper School students. Upper School students typically attend 5 days per week. The average school day consists of 7 hours and 30 minutes.

Upper School Student Profile Grade 9: 9 students (9 girls); Grade 10: 4 students (4 girls); Grade 12: 1 student (1 girl). 100% of students are Jewish.

Faculty School total: 41. In upper school: 6 men, 12 women; 2 have advanced degrees.

Subjects Offered Algebra, American history, American literature, art history, biology, earth science, economics, English, English literature, geography, government/civics, grammar, Hebrew, history, mathematics, physical education, physics, physiology, psychology, religion, science, social sciences, social studies, theology, world cultures, world history, writing.

Graduation Requirements Computer science, English, foreign language, mathematics, physical education (includes health), religion (includes Bible studies and theology), science, social sciences, social studies (includes history).

Special Academic Programs International Baccalaureate program; 5 Advanced Placement exams for which test preparation is offered; honors section; independent study; remedial reading and/or remedial writing; remedial math; programs in general development for dyslexic students.

College Admission Counseling 15 students graduated in 2011; all went to college.

Student Life Upper grades have uniform requirement, student council. Discipline rests primarily with faculty. Attendance at religious services is required.

Tuition and Aid Day student tuition: $13,000. Guaranteed tuition plan. Tuition installment plan (monthly payment plans, individually arranged payment plans). Tuition reduction for siblings, need-based scholarship grants available. In 2011–12, 30% of upper-school students received aid. Total amount of financial aid awarded in 2011–12: $30,000.

Admissions Deadline for receipt of application materials: none. Application fee required: $100. On-campus interview required.

Athletics Interscholastic: aerobics/dance, aerobics/Nautilus, aquatics (b), archery (b), badminton, baseball (b), basketball (b), dance, jogging (b), physical fitness (b), soccer (b), softball (b), swimming and diving (b), volleyball. 1 PE instructor.

Computers Computers are regularly used in English, foreign language, science, technology classes. Computer network features include on-campus library services, online commercial services, Internet access, multimedia, including laser disks, digital cameras. Computer access in designated common areas is available to students.

Contact Mrs. Alex Greenberg, Director of Admissions. 714-898-0051 Ext. 284. Fax: 714-898-0633. E-mail: agreenberg@hebrewacademyhb.com. Web site: www.hebrewacademyhb.com.

HEBREW ACADEMY-THE FIVE TOWNS

635 Central Avenue

Cedarhurst, New York 11516

Head of School: Ms. Naomi Lippman

General Information Coeducational day college-preparatory, arts, business, and religious studies school, affiliated with Jewish faith. Grades 9–12. Founded: 1978. Setting: suburban. Nearest major city is New York. 1 building on campus. Approved or accredited by Middle States Association of Colleges and Schools, The College Board, and New York Department of Education. Languages of instruction: English and Hebrew. Total enrollment: 388. Upper school average class size: 20. The average school day consists of 9 hours and 15 minutes.

Upper School Student Profile 100% of students are Jewish.

Faculty School total: 60.

Subjects Offered Advanced Placement courses, arts, English, fine arts, foreign language, Jewish studies, Judaic studies, mathematics, physical education, religion, science, social sciences, social studies.

Graduation Requirements Arts and fine arts (art, music, dance, drama), English, foreign language, Judaic studies, mathematics, physical education (includes health), religion (includes Bible studies and theology), science, social sciences, social studies (includes history).

Special Academic Programs 11 Advanced Placement exams for which test preparation is offered; honors section; independent study; study abroad; academic accommodation for the artistically talented.

College Admission Counseling 95 students graduated in 2011; all went to college, including Barnard College; New York University; Queens College of the City University of New York; State University of New York at Binghamton; University of Maryland, College Park; Yeshiva University. Median SAT critical reading: 590, median SAT math: 610, median SAT writing: 570. 48% scored over 600 on SAT critical reading, 56% scored over 600 on SAT math, 41% scored over 600 on SAT writing.

Student Life Upper grades have specified standards of dress, student council, honor system. Discipline rests primarily with faculty. Attendance at religious services is required.

Tuition and Aid Tuition installment plan (monthly payment plans, individually arranged payment plans). Need-based scholarship grants available.

Admissions Traditional secondary-level entrance grade is 9. Board of Jewish Education Entrance Exam required. Deadline for receipt of application materials: March 15. Application fee required. On-campus interview required.

Athletics Interscholastic: baseball (boys, girls), basketball (b,g), field hockey (b), softball (b,g), tennis (b,g), volleyball (g); coed intramural: skiing (downhill). 2 PE instructors, 8 coaches.

Computers Computers are regularly used in computer applications classes. Computer resources include on-campus library services, online commercial services, Internet access, Internet filtering or blocking technology. Student e-mail accounts are available to students. The school has a published electronic and media policy.

Contact Ms. Naomi Lippman, Principal, General Studies. 516-569-3807. Fax: 516-374-5761. Web site: www.haftr.org.

HERITAGE CHRISTIAN ACADEMY

2003 McKnight Boulevard NE

Calgary, Alberta T2E 6L2, Canada

Head of School: Mrs. LaVerne Pue

General Information Coeducational day college-preparatory, general academic, arts, religious studies, bilingual studies, and technology school, affiliated with Christian faith, Evangelical faith. Grades K–12. Founded: 1979. Setting: urban. 10-acre campus. 1 building on campus. Approved or accredited by Association of Christian Schools International, Association of Independent Schools and Colleges of Alberta, and Alberta Department of Education. Language of instruction: English. Total enrollment: 568. Upper school average class size: 27. Upper school faculty-student ratio: 1:9. There are 200 required school days per year for Upper School students. Upper School students typically attend 5 days per week. The average school day consists of 7 hours.

Upper School Student Profile Grade 10: 31 students (13 boys, 18 girls); Grade 11: 29 students (16 boys, 13 girls); Grade 12: 34 students (20 boys, 14 girls). 100% of students are Christian, members of Evangelical faith.

Faculty School total: 34. In upper school: 5 men, 4 women; 2 have advanced degrees.

Subjects Offered Art, band, Bible, biology, career and personal planning, chemistry, choir, choral music, Christian education, computer applications, computer multimedia, creative writing, English, essential learning systems, French as a second language, health, language arts, mathematics, physical education, physics, psychology, religious studies, science, sewing, social studies, sports medicine, work experience.

Graduation Requirements Career and personal planning, English, mathematics, physical education (includes health), religious studies, science, social studies (includes history).

Special Academic Programs Independent study; remedial reading and/or remedial writing; remedial math; special instructional classes for deaf students, students with dyslexia addressed through IPPs and classroom accommodations.

College Admission Counseling 28 students graduated in 2011; 22 went to college, including Mount Royal University; The University of British Columbia; University of Calgary; University of Lethbridge; Wilfrid Laurier University. Other: 5 went to work, 1 had other specific plans.

Student Life Upper grades have uniform requirement, student council, honor system. Discipline rests primarily with faculty. Attendance at religious services is required.

Tuition and Aid Day student tuition: CAN$2895. Tuition installment plan (monthly payment plans, individually arranged payment plans). Tuition reduction for siblings available.

Admissions Traditional secondary-level entrance grade is 10. For fall 2011, 11 students applied for upper-level admission, 10 were accepted, 10 enrolled. CTBS (or similar from their school) required. Deadline for receipt of application materials: none. Application fee required: CAN$100. Interview required.

Athletics Interscholastic: badminton (boys, girls), basketball (b,g), cross-country running (b,g), floor hockey (b), golf (b,g), track and field (b,g), volleyball (b,g), wrestling (b,g); coed interscholastic: track and field; coed intramural: basketball, climbing, floor hockey, indoor soccer, indoor track & field, outdoor activities, physical fitness, project adventure, soccer, touch football, track and field, volleyball, wall climbing. 1 PE instructor.

Computers Computers are regularly used in animation, Bible studies, career education, data processing, English, graphics, information technology, keyboarding, mathematics, multimedia, photography, science, social studies classes. Computer network features include Internet access, Internet filtering or blocking technology. Student e-mail accounts are available to students. The school has a published electronic and media policy.

Contact Office. 403-219-3201. Fax: 403-219-3210. E-mail: heritage_info@pallisersd.ab.ca. Web site: www.hcacalgary.com.

HERITAGE CHRISTIAN SCHOOL

2850 Fourth Avenue

PO Box 400

Jordan, Ontario L0R 1S0, Canada

Head of School: Mr. A. Ben Harsevoort

General Information Coeducational day college-preparatory, general academic, arts, and religious studies school, affiliated with Reformed Church. Grades K–12. Founded: 1992. Setting: rural. Nearest major city is St. Catharines, Canada. 26-acre campus. 1 building on campus. Approved or accredited by Ontario Department of Education. Language of instruction: English. Total enrollment: 571. Upper school average class size: 50. Upper school faculty-student ratio: 1:15. There are 185 required school days per year for Upper School students. Upper School students typically attend 5 days per week. The average school day consists of 5 hours.

Upper School Student Profile Grade 9: 31 students (21 boys, 10 girls); Grade 10: 49 students (23 boys, 26 girls); Grade 11: 41 students (20 boys, 21 girls); Grade 12: 43 students (22 boys, 21 girls). 95% of students are Reformed.

Faculty School total: 30. In upper school: 11 men, 4 women; 4 have advanced degrees.

Subjects Offered 20th century American writers, 20th century physics, 20th century world history, advanced chemistry, advanced math, algebra, analysis and differential calculus, art, Bible, biology, bookkeeping, British literature, business mathematics, business studies, calculus, Canadian geography, Canadian history, Canadian law, Canadian literature, career education, chemistry, choral music, Christian and Hebrew scripture, Christian doctrine, Christian education, Christian ethics, Christian studies, Christian testament, Christianity, church history, civics, classical civilization, computer education, computer programming, computer skills, consumer mathematics, creative writing, culinary arts, drafting, English, English composition, English literature, entrepreneurship, environmental education, ethics, European civilization, European history, family studies, finite math, foods, foundations of civilization, French as a second language, general math, geography, geometry, grammar, health, history, honors algebra, honors English, honors geometry, honors world history, humanities, independent living, keyboarding, language and composition, language arts, law and the legal system, life science, literature, marketing, mathematics, media literacy, modern civilization, modern European history, modern Western civilization, music, music appreciation, novels, personal finance, physical education, physics, practicum, public speaking, religion and culture, religious education, religious studies, Shakespeare, society challenge and change, speech communications, technical drawing, vocal music, word processing, world civilizations, world literature, writing.

Graduation Requirements Ontario Secondary School Diploma requirements.

Special Academic Programs Independent study; remedial reading and/or remedial writing; remedial math.

College Admission Counseling 38 students graduated in 2011; 30 went to college, including Calvin College; Covenant College. Other: 8 went to work.

Student Life Upper grades have uniform requirement, student council. Discipline rests primarily with faculty. Attendance at religious services is required.

Tuition and Aid Day student tuition: CAN$12,500. Tuition installment plan (monthly payment plans).

Admissions Traditional secondary-level entrance grade is 9. Deadline for receipt of application materials: none. No application fee required. On-campus interview required.

Athletics Interscholastic: badminton (boys, girls), basketball (b,g), ice hockey (b), soccer (b,g), volleyball (b,g). 3 coaches.

Computers Computers are regularly used in accounting, business, economics, information technology, keyboarding, mathematics, newspaper, typing, yearbook classes. The school has a published electronic and media policy.

Contact Mrs. Mariam Sinke, Administrative Assistant. 905-562-7303 Ext. 221. Fax: 905-562-0020. E-mail: heritage@hcsjordan.ca. Web site: www.hcsjordan.ca.

THE HERITAGE SCHOOL

2093 Highway 29 North

Newnan, Georgia 30263

Head of School: Judith Griffith

General Information Coeducational day college-preparatory, arts, and technology school. Grades PK–12. Founded: 1970. Setting: suburban. Nearest major city is Atlanta. 62-acre campus. 10 buildings on campus. Approved or accredited by Georgia Independent School Association, Southern Association of Colleges and Schools, Southern Association of Independent Schools, and Georgia Department of Education. Member of National Association of Independent Schools. Endowment: $1.1 million. Total enrollment: 424. Upper school average class size: 18. Upper school faculty-student ratio: 1:7. There are 180 required school days per year for Upper School students. Upper School students typically attend 5 days per week.

Upper School Student Profile Grade 9: 41 students (29 boys, 12 girls); Grade 10: 41 students (25 boys, 16 girls); Grade 11: 42 students (20 boys, 22 girls); Grade 12: 20 students (13 boys, 7 girls).

Faculty School total: 49. In upper school: 5 men, 15 women; 3 have advanced degrees.

Subjects Offered Advanced Placement courses, algebra, American history, American literature, art, art history, biology, calculus, chemistry, computer applications, drama, earth science, economics, English, English literature, environmental science, European history, French, geography, geometry, government/civics, grammar, health, history, mathematics, music, physical education, public speaking, science, social sciences, social studies, Spanish, speech, theater, world history, world literature.

Graduation Requirements Arts and fine arts (art, music, dance, drama), computer science, electives, English, foreign language, mathematics, physical education (includes health), public speaking, science, social studies (includes history).

Special Academic Programs 16 Advanced Placement exams for which test preparation is offered; independent study.

College Admission Counseling 38 students graduated in 2010; 37 went to college, including Georgia Institute of Technology; Georgia Southern University; Mercer University; Savannah College of Art and Design; University of Georgia; Wake Forest University. Other: 1 entered military service. Mean SAT critical reading: 555, mean SAT math: 550, mean SAT writing: 525, mean combined SAT: 1620, mean composite ACT: 24.

Student Life Upper grades have specified standards of dress, student council, honor system. Discipline rests primarily with faculty.

Tuition and Aid Day student tuition: $6860–$12,980. Tuition installment plan (monthly payment plans). Tuition reduction for siblings, need-based scholarship grants available. In 2010–11, 20% of upper-school students received aid. Total amount of financial aid awarded in 2010–11: $175,000.

Admissions Traditional secondary-level entrance grade is 9. For fall 2010, 37 students applied for upper-level admission, 27 were accepted, 24 enrolled. Otis-Lennon School Ability Test required. Deadline for receipt of application materials: none. Application fee required: $50. On-campus interview required.

Athletics Interscholastic: aerobics/dance (girls), baseball (b), basketball (b,g), cheering (g), cross-country running (b,g), dance team (g), football (b), golf (b,g), soccer (b,g), softball (g), swimming and diving (b,g), tennis (b,g), weight training (b); intramural: cheering (g), football (b); coed interscholastic: physical fitness, skeet shooting; coed intramural: backpacking, basketball, canoeing/kayaking, climbing, equestrian sports, flag football, hiking/backpacking, juggling, kayaking, mountaineering, outdoor adventure, outdoor education, ropes courses, wilderness survival. 3 PE instructors, 1 athletic trainer.

Computers Computers are regularly used in college planning, creative writing, English, foreign language, publications, science, yearbook classes. Computer network features include on-campus library services, online commercial services, Internet access, wireless campus network, Internet filtering or blocking technology. Campus intranet, student e-mail accounts, and computer access in designated common areas are available to students. Students grades are available online. The school has a published electronic and media policy.

Contact Amy Riley, Advancement Director. 678-423-5393. Fax: 770-253-4850. E-mail: ariley@heritagehawks.org. Web site: www.heritagehawks.org.

THE HEWITT SCHOOL

45 East 75th Street

New York, New York 10021

Head of School: Ms. Joan Z. Lonergan

General Information Girls' day college-preparatory school. Grades K–12. Founded: 1920. Setting: urban. 1 building on campus. Approved or accredited by Middle States Association of Colleges and Schools, National Independent Private Schools Association, and New York State Association of Independent Schools. Member of National Association of Independent Schools and Secondary School Admission Test Board. Total enrollment: 498. Upper school average class size: 11. Upper school faculty-student ratio: 1:7. Upper School students typically attend 5 days per week. The average school day consists of 7 hours.

Upper School Student Profile Grade 9: 31 students (31 girls); Grade 10: 29 students (29 girls); Grade 11: 25 students (25 girls); Grade 12: 30 students (30 girls).

Faculty School total: 82. In upper school: 14 men, 16 women; 24 have advanced degrees.

Subjects Offered Algebra, American history, American literature, anatomy and physiology, art, biology, calculus, chemistry, computers, drama, earth science, English, English literature, European history, fine arts, French, genetics, geometry, history, Latin, mathematics, music, photography, physical education, physics, pre-calculus, science, Spanish, world history.

Graduation Requirements Creative arts, English, foreign language, history, mathematics, physical education (includes health), science, technology.

Special Academic Programs Advanced Placement exam preparation; honors section; independent study; term-away projects; study abroad.

College Admission Counseling 33 students graduated in 2010; 32 went to college, including Connecticut College; Cornell University; Duke University; Harvard University; Syracuse University; University of Michigan. Other: 1 had other specific plans.

Student Life Upper grades have uniform requirement, student council. Discipline rests primarily with faculty.

Tuition and Aid Day student tuition: $36,650. Guaranteed tuition plan. Tuition installment plan (Insured Tuition Payment Plan, Key Tuition Payment Plan, monthly payment plans). Need-based scholarship grants available. In 2010–11, 22% of upper-school students received aid. Total amount of financial aid awarded in 2010–11: $1,394,709.

Admissions Traditional secondary-level entrance grade is 9. ERB and ISEE required. Deadline for receipt of application materials: December 1. Application fee required: $60. On-campus interview required.

Athletics Interscholastic: badminton, basketball, cross-country running, soccer, swimming and diving, tennis, track and field, volleyball; intramural: badminton, basketball, crew, cross-country running, lacrosse, soccer, swimming and diving, tennis, track and field, volleyball. 4 PE instructors.

Computers Computers are regularly used in all academic, art, English, foreign language, history, humanities, mathematics, music, science classes. Computer network features include on-campus library services, online commercial services, Internet access, wireless campus network, Internet filtering or blocking technology. Student e-mail accounts are available to students. The school has a published electronic and media policy.

Contact Ms. Kathleen P. Kaminsky, Director of Admissions, Middle and Upper School. 212-288-1919. Fax: 212-472-7531. E-mail: kkaminsky@hewittschool.org. Web site: hewittschool.org.

HIGHLAND HALL WALDORF SCHOOL

17100 Superior Street

Northridge, California 91325

Head of School: Lynn Kern

General Information Coeducational day college-preparatory and arts school. Grades N–12. Founded: 1955. Setting: suburban. Nearest major city is Los Angeles. 11-acre campus. 4 buildings on campus. Approved or accredited by Association of Waldorf Schools of North America and Western Association of Schools and Colleges. Total enrollment: 296. Upper school average class size: 25. Upper school faculty-student ratio: 1:6. There are 170 required school days per year for Upper School students. Upper School students typically attend 5 days per week. The average school day consists of 7 hours and 10 minutes.

Upper School Student Profile Grade 9: 25 students (8 boys, 17 girls); Grade 10: 23 students (10 boys, 13 girls); Grade 11: 21 students (9 boys, 12 girls); Grade 12: 21 students (10 boys, 11 girls).

Faculty School total: 59. In upper school: 11 men, 15 women; 3 have advanced degrees.

Subjects Offered Algebra, American history, American literature, anatomy, ancient history, architecture, art, art history, astronomy, biology, bookbinding, botany, calculus, career/college preparation, cell biology, chemistry, choral music, chorus, clayworking, conflict resolution, CPR, creative writing, drama, drawing, earth science, economics, English, English literature, ethnic studies, European history, eurythmy, expository writing, geography, geology, geometry, German, government/civics, grammar, guidance, guitar, handbells, health, history, honors U.S. history, jazz ensemble, marine biology, mathematics, metalworking, music, music history, Native American history, orchestra, painting, physical education, physics, physiology, pre-algebra, pre-calculus, SAT preparation, sculpture, sewing, social studies, Spanish, speech, stained glass, stone carving, theater, trigonometry, woodworking, world history, world literature, writing, yearbook, zoology.

Graduation Requirements Ancient history, art, art history, crafts, earth science, economics, English, foreign language, government, history of music, human sexuality, mathematics, music, physical education (includes health), science, sculpture, society and culture, U.S. history, world history. Community service is required.

Special Academic Programs Independent study; study abroad.

College Admission Counseling 22 students graduated in 2011; 21 went to college, including Berklee College of Music; Lewis & Clark College; Marlboro College; Middlebury College; Sarah Lawrence College; Vassar College. Other: 1 went to work. Mean SAT critical reading: 645, mean SAT math: 550, mean composite ACT: 27. 50% scored over 600 on SAT critical reading, 60% scored over 600 on SAT math, 50% scored over 26 on composite ACT.

Student Life Upper grades have specified standards of dress, student council. Discipline rests primarily with faculty.

Tuition and Aid Day student tuition: $19,995. Tuition installment plan (Insured Tuition Payment Plan, FACTS Tuition Payment Plan, monthly payment plans). Need-based scholarship grants available. In 2011–12, 19% of upper-school students received aid. Total amount of financial aid awarded in 2011–12: $204,600.

Admissions Traditional secondary-level entrance grade is 9. For fall 2011, 28 students applied for upper-level admission, 22 were accepted, 9 enrolled. Essay, math and English placement tests and writing sample required. Deadline for receipt of application materials: January 31. Application fee required: $100. On-campus interview required.

Athletics Interscholastic: baseball (boys), basketball (b,g), softball (g), volleyball (b,g); coed interscholastic: soccer; coed intramural: golf. 2 PE instructors, 2 coaches.

Computers Computers are regularly used in library skills, newspaper, yearbook classes. Computer network features include on-campus library services, Internet access, wireless campus network.

Contact Lynn van Schilfgaarde, Enrollment Director. 818-349-1394 Ext. 211. Fax: 818-349-2390. E-mail: lvs@highlandhall.org. Web site: www.highlandhall.org.

HIGHROAD ACADEMY

46641 Chilliwack Central Road

Chilliwack, British Columbia V2P 1K3, Canada

Head of School: Mr. David Shinness

General Information college-preparatory and religious studies school, affiliated with Christian faith; primarily serves students with learning disabilities, individuals with Attention Deficit Disorder, individuals with emotional and behavioral problems, and dyslexic students. Founded: 1978. Setting: small town. Nearest major city is Vancouver, Canada. 45-acre campus. 1 building on campus. Approved or accredited by British Columbia Department of Education. Language of instruction: English. Total enrollment: 392. Upper school average class size: 25. Upper school faculty-student ratio: 1:10.

Upper School Student Profile Grade 6: 33 students (16 boys, 17 girls); Grade 7: 42 students (20 boys, 22 girls); Grade 8: 29 students (21 boys, 8 girls); Grade 9: 32 students (18 boys, 14 girls); Grade 10: 32 students (17 boys, 15 girls); Grade 11: 27 students (13 boys, 14 girls); Grade 12: 32 students (10 boys, 22 girls). 100% of students are Christian.

Faculty School total: 30. In upper school: 5 men, 5 women.

Graduation Requirements Bible.

Special Academic Programs Independent study; study at local college for college credit; ESL (25 students enrolled).

College Admission Counseling 32 students graduated in 2011; 12 went to college, including The University of British Columbia. Other: 6 went to work, 8 entered a postgraduate year, 6 had other specific plans.

Student Life Upper grades have uniform requirement, student council, honor system. Discipline rests primarily with faculty. Attendance at religious services is required.

Admissions Traditional secondary-level entrance grade is 10. Deadline for receipt of application materials: none. Application fee required: CAN$100. Interview required.

Athletics 1 PE instructor, 3 coaches.

Computers Computer network features include Internet access, wireless campus network, Internet filtering or blocking technology. Computer access in designated common areas is available to students. Students grades are available online.

Contact Mrs. Denise Kraubner, Office Manager. 604-792-4680. Fax: 604-792-2465. E-mail: dkraubner@highroadacademy.com. Web site: www.highroadacademy.com.

THE HILL CENTER, DURHAM ACADEMY

Durham, North Carolina

See Special Needs Schools section.

HILLCREST CHRISTIAN SCHOOL

384 Erbes Road

Thousand Oaks, California 91362

Head of School: Mr. Stephen Allen

General Information Coeducational day college-preparatory school, affiliated with Christian faith. Grades K–12. Founded: 1977. Setting: suburban. 4-acre campus. 7 buildings on campus. Approved or accredited by Association of Christian Schools International, Western Association of Schools and Colleges, and California Department of Education. Total enrollment: 288. Upper school average class size: 15. Upper school faculty-student ratio: 1:8. There are 179 required school days per year for Upper School students. Upper School students typically attend 5 days per week. The average school day consists of 6 hours and 30 minutes.

Upper School Student Profile Grade 9: 21 students (17 boys, 4 girls); Grade 10: 16 students (9 boys, 7 girls); Grade 11: 16 students (8 boys, 8 girls); Grade 12: 18 students (6 boys, 12 girls). 90% of students are Christian faith.

Faculty School total: 17. In upper school: 5 men, 7 women; 5 have advanced degrees.

Subjects Offered Algebra, American literature, anatomy and physiology, art, Bible, biology, British literature, British literature (honors), calculus, chemistry, computers, earth science, economics, film studies, French, geometry, health, Hebrew scripture, home economics, honors English, honors U.S. history, honors world history, introduction to literature, keyboarding, life science, marine biology, physical education, physics, pre-algebra, pre-calculus, Spanish, trigonometry, U.S. government, U.S. history, world history, world literature, yearbook.

Graduation Requirements Algebra, American literature, Bible, biology, British literature, chemistry, economics, electives, English, foreign language, geometry, introduction to literature, mathematics, physical education (includes health), physical science, U.S. government, U.S. history, world history, world literature, 20 hours of community service each year.

Special Academic Programs 3 Advanced Placement exams for which test preparation is offered; honors section; ESL (2 students enrolled).

College Admission Counseling 6 students graduated in 2011; all went to college, including Moorpark College; Westmont College. Mean SAT critical reading: 570, mean SAT math: 590. 10% scored over 600 on SAT critical reading, 10% scored over 600 on SAT math, 20% scored over 600 on SAT writing.

Student Life Upper grades have uniform requirement, student council, honor system. Discipline rests primarily with faculty. Attendance at religious services is required.

Tuition and Aid Day student tuition: $8980. Tuition installment plan (FACTS Tuition Payment Plan). Tuition reduction for siblings, need-based scholarship grants, tuition reduction for families of full-time pastors, tuition reduction for children of faculty and staff available. In 2011–12, 8% of upper-school students received aid. Total amount of financial aid awarded in 2011–12: $20,000.

Admissions Traditional secondary-level entrance grade is 9. For fall 2011, 11 students applied for upper-level admission, 9 were accepted, 9 enrolled. Admissions testing and Stanford Diagnostic Test required. Deadline for receipt of application materials: none. Application fee required: $100. On-campus interview required.

Athletics Interscholastic: baseball (boys), basketball (b,g), cheering (g), football (b), volleyball (g); coed interscholastic: golf; coed intramural: flag football. 2 PE instructors, 4 coaches.

Computers Computers are regularly used in all classes. Computer resources include on-campus library services, Internet access, wireless campus network, Internet filtering or blocking technology, computer lab. Computer access in designated common areas is available to students. Students grades are available online. The school has a published electronic and media policy.

Contact Mrs. Gail Matheson, Office Manager. 805-497-7501 Ext. 200. Fax: 805-494-9355. E-mail: gmatheson@hillcrestcs.org. Web site: www.hillcrestcs.org.

HILLCREST CHRISTIAN SCHOOL

4060 South Siwell Road

Jackson, Mississippi 39212

Head of School: Dr. Tom Prather

General Information Coeducational day college-preparatory, arts, business, religious studies, and technology school. Grades 1–12. Founded: 1971. Setting: urban. 36-acre campus. 5 buildings on campus. Approved or accredited by Association of Christian Schools International, Mississippi Private School Association, and Southern Association of Colleges and Schools. Total enrollment: 590. Upper school average class size: 15. Upper school faculty-student ratio: 1:11. There are 175 required school days per year for Upper School students. Upper School students typically attend 5 days per week. The average school day consists of 5 hours and 50 minutes.

Upper School Student Profile Grade 7: 35 students (17 boys, 18 girls); Grade 8: 53 students (29 boys, 24 girls); Grade 9: 59 students (25 boys, 34 girls); Grade 10: 31 students (13 boys, 18 girls); Grade 11: 39 students (26 boys, 13 girls); Grade 12: 39 students (17 boys, 22 girls).

Faculty School total: 63. In upper school: 12 men, 14 women; 11 have advanced degrees.

Subjects Offered Advanced biology, advanced math, Advanced Placement courses, algebra, American government, American history-AP, American literature, American literature-AP, anatomy and physiology, art, band, baseball, basketball, Bible, biology, biology-AP, British literature, business communications, calculus, chemistry, chemistry-AP, choir, choral music, comparative government and politics-AP, computer applications, computer graphics, critical writing, current events, desktop publishing, earth science, economics, electives, English, English language and composition-AP, English literature, English literature and composition-AP, geography, geometry, health, library assistant, life science, pre-algebra, reading/study skills, social studies, Spanish, sports, state history, transition mathematics, trigonometry, U.S. government, U.S. government and politics-AP, U.S. history, U.S. history-AP, world geography, world history.

Graduation Requirements Bible, electives, English, history, language, mathematics, science, must complete 10 community service hours per school year attended, must apply and be accepted to a college.

Special Academic Programs 7 Advanced Placement exams for which test preparation is offered; honors section; independent study; study at local college for college credit.

College Admission Counseling 31 students graduated in 2011; 30 went to college, including Hinds Community College; Holmes Community College; Mississippi College; Mississippi State University; University of Mississippi; University of Southern Mississippi. Other: 1 entered military service. Median composite ACT: 22. 3% scored over 26 on composite ACT.

Student Life Upper grades have uniform requirement, student council, honor system. Discipline rests primarily with faculty.

Tuition and Aid Day student tuition: $5628. Tuition installment plan (monthly payment plans). Tuition reduction for siblings, need-based scholarship grants available. In 2011–12, 8% of upper-school students received aid. Total amount of financial aid awarded in 2011–12: $42,824.

Admissions Traditional secondary-level entrance grade is 7. For fall 2011, 40 students applied for upper-level admission, 29 were accepted, 23 enrolled. Admissions testing and Stanford Achievement Test, Otis-Lennon School Ability Test required. Deadline for receipt of application materials: none. Application fee required: $50. Interview recommended.

Athletics Interscholastic: baseball (boys), basketball (b,g), cheering (g), drill team (g), football (b), golf (b), softball (g), weight lifting (b); intramural: basketball (b,g), football (b), softball (g); coed interscholastic: cross-country running, soccer, tennis; coed intramural: cross-country running, golf, tennis, track and field, weight lifting, weight training. 2 coaches.

Computers Computers are regularly used in computer applications, graphic design, yearbook classes. Computer resources include Internet access. Students grades are available online.

Contact Mrs. Melissa Jones, Director of Admissions. 601-372-0149 Ext. 300. Fax: 601-371-8061. E-mail: mjones@hillcrestchristian.org. Web site: www.hillcrestchristian.org.

HILLCREST SCHOOL

Midland, Texas

See Special Needs Schools section.

THE HILL SCHOOL

717 East High Street

Pottstown, Pennsylvania 19464-5791

Head of School: Mr. David R. Dougherty

General Information Coeducational boarding and day college-preparatory school, affiliated with Christian faith. Boarding grades 9–PG, day grades 9–12. Founded: 1851. Setting: small town. Nearest major city is Philadelphia. Students are housed in single-sex dormitories. 200-acre campus. 58 buildings on campus. Approved or accredited by Middle States Association of Colleges and Schools, The Association of Boarding Schools, and Pennsylvania Department of Education. Member of National Association of Independent Schools and Secondary School Admission Test Board. Endowment: $10 million. Total enrollment: 494. Upper school average class size: 13. Upper school faculty-student ratio: 1:7. Upper School students typically attend 6 days per week. The average school day consists of 5 hours and 33 minutes.

Upper School Student Profile Grade 9: 106 students (57 boys, 49 girls); Grade 10: 124 students (67 boys, 57 girls); Grade 11: 118 students (73 boys, 45 girls); Grade 12: 123 students (59 boys, 64 girls); Postgraduate: 23 students (21 boys, 2 girls). 80% of students are boarding students. 48% are state residents. 30 states are represented in upper school student body. 11% are international students. International students from China, Germany, Hong Kong, Republic of Korea, Spain, and Venezuela; 14 other countries represented in student body.

Faculty School total: 86. In upper school: 56 men, 30 women; 61 have advanced degrees; 80 reside on campus.

Subjects Offered Acting, advanced chemistry, advanced computer applications, advanced math, Advanced Placement courses, advanced studio art-AP, algebra, American Civil War, American history, American history-AP, American literature-AP, American studies, anatomy and physiology, Ancient Greek, ancient world history, art, art history, art-AP, arts, astronomy, athletic training, basic language skills, Basic programming, Bible studies, biochemistry, biology, biology-AP, boat building, botany, British literature-AP, calculus, calculus-AP, chamber groups, chemistry, chemistry-AP, Chinese, choral music, Christian ethics, Christian scripture, Christian testament, college admission preparation, college counseling, college placement, college planning, college writing, composition-AP, computer math, computer programming, computer science, computer science-AP, concert choir, creative writing, digital art, earth science, ecology, economics, economics-AP, English, English language and composition-AP, English literature, English literature and composition-AP, environmental science, European history, European history-AP, expository writing, French, French language-AP, French literature-AP, geography, geometry, German, government/civics, grammar, Greek, history, honors algebra, honors English, honors geometry, humanities, independent study, instrumental music, jazz band, journalism, lab science, Latin, Latin-AP, life issues, linear algebra, mathematics, music, oral communications, orchestra, participation in sports, photography, physics, physics-AP, pre-calculus, pre-college orientation, psychology, psychology-AP, radio broadcasting, religion, SAT/ACT preparation, science, sex education, sexuality, social studies, sociology, Spanish, speech, sports medicine, theater, theology, trigonometry, typing, U.S. history-AP, woodworking, world history, world literature.

Graduation Requirements Art, English, foreign language, mathematics, religion (includes Bible studies and theology), science, social studies (includes history).

Special Academic Programs Advanced Placement exam preparation; honors section; independent study; study abroad.

College Admission Counseling 130 students graduated in 2011; all went to college, including Brown University; Cornell University; Georgetown University; Trinity College; United States Naval Academy; University of Pennsylvania. Mean SAT critical reading: 625, mean SAT math: 633, mean SAT writing: 625, mean composite ACT: 26. 62% scored over 600 on SAT critical reading, 66% scored over 600 on SAT math, 53% scored over 26 on composite ACT.

Student Life Upper grades have specified standards of dress, student council, honor system. Discipline rests equally with students and faculty. Attendance at religious services is required.

Tuition and Aid Day student tuition: $32,800; 7-day tuition and room/board: $47,500. Tuition installment plan (Insured Tuition Payment Plan, monthly payment plans, individually arranged payment plans). Need-based scholarship grants available. In 2011–12, 38% of upper-school students received aid. Total amount of financial aid awarded in 2011–12: $4,800,000.

Admissions Traditional secondary-level entrance grade is 9. For fall 2011, 749 students applied for upper-level admission, 305 were accepted, 192 enrolled. ACT, ISEE, PSAT or SAT for applicants to grade 11 and 12, SSAT or TOEFL required. Deadline for receipt of application materials: January 31. Application fee required: $50. Interview required.

Athletics Interscholastic: baseball (boys), basketball (b,g), cross-country running (b,g), field hockey (g), football (b), ice hockey (b,g), indoor track (b,g), lacrosse (b,g), soccer (b,g), softball (g), squash (b,g), swimming and diving (b,g), tennis (b,g), water polo (b,g), winter (indoor) track (b,g), wrestling (b); coed interscholastic: diving, golf, track and field; coed intramural: aerobics, basketball, golf, martial arts, riflery, soccer, squash, strength & conditioning, tennis, volleyball, weight lifting. 2 coaches, 2 athletic trainers.

Computers Computers are regularly used in all classes. Computer network features include on-campus library services, online commercial services, Internet access, wireless campus network. Student e-mail accounts are available to students. The school has a published electronic and media policy.

Contact Mr. Thomas Eccleston, IV, Assistant Headmaster for Admission and External Affairs. 610-326-1000. Fax: 610-705-1753. E-mail: teccleston@thehill.org. Web site: www.thehill.org.

See Display on next page and Close-Up on page 632.

HILL SCHOOL OF FORT WORTH

4817 Odessa Avenue

Fort Worth, Texas 76133-1640

Head of School: Audrey Boda-Davis

General Information Coeducational day college-preparatory, general academic, arts, and technology school; primarily serves individuals with Attention Deficit Disorder and dyslexic students. Grades 1–12. Founded: 1973. Setting: suburban. 1 building on campus. Approved or accredited by Southern Association of Colleges and Schools and Texas Department of Education. Member of National Association of Independent Schools. Total enrollment: 169. Upper school average class size: 9. Upper school faculty-student ratio: 1:9. There are 175 required school days per year for Upper School students. Upper School students typically attend 5 days per week. The average school day consists of 6 hours and 30 minutes.

Faculty School total: 29. In upper school: 6 men, 13 women.

Special Academic Programs Special instructional classes for students with learning differences.

Student Life Upper grades have uniform requirement, student council, honor system. Discipline rests primarily with faculty.

Summer Programs Enrichment programs offered; held on campus; accepts boys and girls; open to students from other schools.

Tuition and Aid Tuition installment plan (The Tuition Plan).

Admissions Deadline for receipt of application materials: none. No application fee required. Interview required.

Athletics Interscholastic: basketball (boys, girls), football (b), track and field (b,g), volleyball (g).

Computers Computers are regularly used in all academic classes. Computer network features include on-campus library services, Internet access, wireless campus network, Internet filtering or blocking technology. Campus intranet and student e-mail accounts are available to students. Students grades are available online. The school has a published electronic and media policy.

Contact Judy King, Director of Admissions. 817-923-9482. E-mail: jking@hillschool.org. Web site: www.hillschool.org.

THE HILL TOP PREPARATORY SCHOOL

Rosemont, Pennsylvania

See Special Needs Schools section.

HILTON HEAD PREPARATORY SCHOOL

8 Fox Grape Road

Hilton Head Island, South Carolina 29928

Head of School: Dr. Anthony Kandel

General Information Coeducational day college-preparatory, arts, and technology school. Grades JK–12. Founded: 1965. Setting: small town. Nearest major city is Savannah, GA. 25-acre campus. 7 buildings on campus. Approved or accredited by South Carolina Independent School Association, Southern Association of Colleges and Schools, Southern Association of Independent Schools, The College Board, and South Carolina Department of Education. Member of National Association of Independent Schools and Secondary School Admission Test Board. Total enrollment: 439. Upper school average class size: 12. Upper school faculty-student ratio: 1:12.

Upper School Student Profile Grade 9: 47 students (22 boys, 25 girls); Grade 10: 45 students (22 boys, 23 girls); Grade 11: 43 students (23 boys, 20 girls); Grade 12: 45 students (27 boys, 18 girls).

Faculty School total: 66. In upper school: 14 men, 14 women; 12 have advanced degrees.

Subjects Offered Advanced studio art-AP, algebra, American literature-AP, art, biology-AP, British literature, calculus, calculus-AP, chemistry, chemistry-AP, Chinese, chorus, college counseling, community service, computer science-AP, computer studies, drama, English literature and composition-AP, geography, geometry, guidance, guitar, health education, history-AP, journalism, leadership and service, library, literature and composition-AP, marine biology, marine science, newspaper, peer counseling, performing arts, physical education, physical fitness, physics-AP, piano, pre-calculus, probability and statistics, SAT/ACT preparation, senior career experience, senior thesis, Spanish language-AP, Spanish-AP, statistics-AP, strings, student government, studio art, trigonometry, U.S. history, U.S. history-AP, visual and performing arts, world history, world literature, yearbook.

Graduation Requirements Arts and fine arts (art, music, dance, drama), computer literacy, English, foreign language, internship, mathematics, physical education (includes health), science, social studies (includes history), senior speech, 10 hours of community service per school year.

Special Academic Programs Advanced Placement exam preparation; honors section.

College Admission Counseling 42 students graduated in 2010; all went to college, including Clemson University; Dartmouth College; Furman University; Northwestern University; Notre Dame de Namur University; Wake Forest University. Median SAT critical reading: 612, median SAT math: 633, median SAT writing: 630.

Student Life Upper grades have specified standards of dress, student council, honor system. Discipline rests equally with students and faculty.

Tuition and Aid Day student tuition: $11,875–$15,295. Tuition installment plan (Insured Tuition Payment Plan, FACTS Tuition Payment Plan, monthly payment plans, individually arranged payment plans, bank-arranged plan, self-insured tuition refund plan). Tuition reduction for siblings, need-based scholarship grants, tuition discounts for children of faculty available. In 2010–11, 23% of upper-school students received aid. Total amount of financial aid awarded in 2010–11: $250,000.

Admissions Traditional secondary-level entrance grade is 9. For fall 2010, 25 students applied for upper-level admission, 20 were accepted, 17 enrolled. ERB, PSAT, PSAT or SAT, PSAT, SAT, or ACT for applicants to grade 11 and 12, SAT, school's own exam or writing sample required. Deadline for receipt of application materials: none. Application fee required: $75. Interview required.

Athletics Interscholastic: aerobics/dance (girls), baseball (b), basketball (b,g), cheering (g), dance team (g), football (b), running (b,g), soccer (b,g), swimming and diving (b,g), tennis (b,g), volleyball (g); intramural: aerobics/dance (g), basketball (b,g), dance team (g), soccer (b,g); coed interscholastic: aquatics, cross-country running, golf, running, swimming and diving; coed intramural: outdoor activities, physical fitness, strength & conditioning. 4 PE instructors, 4 coaches, 1 athletic trainer.

Computers Computers are regularly used in all academic, art, college planning, drawing and design, graphic arts, graphic design, library science, media arts, music, newspaper, photography, research skills, SAT preparation, senior seminar, speech, stock market, technical drawing, theater, theater arts, yearbook classes. Computer network features include on-campus library services, Internet access, wireless campus network, Internet filtering or blocking technology. Campus intranet is available to students. The school has a published electronic and media policy.

Contact Bobbie C. Somerville, Director of Admissions. 843-671-2286. Fax: 843-671-7624. E-mail: bsomerville@hhprep.org. Web site: www.hhprep.org.

THE HOCKADAY SCHOOL

11600 Welch Road

Dallas, Texas 75229-2999

Head of School: Kim Wargo

General Information Girls' boarding and day college-preparatory school. Boarding grades 8–12, day grades PK–12. Founded: 1913. Setting: suburban. Students are housed in single-sex dormitories. 100-acre campus. 12 buildings on campus. Approved or accredited by Independent Schools Association of the Southwest and The Association of Boarding Schools. Member of National Association of Independent Schools and Secondary School Admission Test Board. Endowment: $125.4 million. Total enrollment: 1,085. Upper school average class size: 15. Upper school faculty-student ratio: 1:14. There are 160 required school days per year for Upper School students. Upper School students typically attend 5 days per week. The average school day consists of 6 hours and 40 minutes.

Upper School Student Profile Grade 9: 116 students (116 girls); Grade 10: 124 students (124 girls); Grade 11: 117 students (117 girls); Grade 12: 120 students (120 girls). 15% of students are boarding students. 86% are state residents. 10 states are represented in upper school student body. 11% are international students. International students from China, Jamaica, Mexico, Nigeria, Republic of Korea, and Taiwan; 5 other countries represented in student body.

Faculty School total: 128. In upper school: 18 men, 41 women; 47 have advanced degrees.

Subjects Offered Acting, advanced math, advanced studio art-AP, algebra, American history, American history-AP, American literature, analytic geometry, anatomy, applied arts, applied music, art history, astronomy, athletics, audio visual/media, ballet, basketball, biology, biology-AP, body human, British literature, broadcast journalism, broadcasting, Broadway dance, calculus, calculus-AP, cell biology, ceramics, chemistry, chemistry-AP, college counseling, comparative religion, computer applications, computer science, computer science-AP, concert choir, consumer economics, CPR, creative writing, current events, dance, dance performance, debate, digital art, digital imaging, digital music, digital photography, directing, discrete mathematics, drawing and design, ecology, environmental systems, economics-AP, English, English literature, English literature and composition-AP, English-AP, environmental science, environmental science-AP, ESL, ESL, fencing, fine arts, finite math, first aid, French, French language-AP, French literature-AP, genetics, geometry, guitar, health, health and wellness, honors English, humanities, information technology, interdisciplinary studies, journalism, Latin, Latin-AP, madrigals, Mandarin, microbiology, modern European history-AP, newspaper, non-Western literature, orchestra, philosophy, photography, physical education, physical fitness, physics, physics-AP, piano, pre-calculus, printmaking, probability and statistics, psychology, psychology-AP, self-defense, senior internship, set design, short story, Spanish, Spanish language-AP, Spanish literature-AP, stagecraft, studio art, studio art-AP, swimming, technology, tennis, track and field, U.S. government, U.S. history, U.S. history-AP, voice, volleyball, Web site design, wellness, world history, yearbook.

Graduation Requirements Algebra, American literature, art history, audio visual/media, biology-AP, chemistry, computer literacy, computer skills, English, English literature, geometry, history of music, information technology, languages, physical education (includes health), physics, senior project, U.S. government, U.S. history, world history, One semester of History of Art and Music, 60 hours of community service.

Special Academic Programs Advanced Placement exam preparation; honors section; independent study; term-away projects; study abroad; ESL (12 students enrolled).

College Admission Counseling 122 students graduated in 2011; all went to college, including Cornell University; Georgetown University; Harvard University; Northwestern University; Stanford University; Vanderbilt University.

Student Life Upper grades have uniform requirement, student council, honor system. Discipline rests primarily with faculty.

Summer Programs Enrichment, advancement, ESL, sports, art/fine arts, computer instruction programs offered; session focuses on enrichment; held on campus; accepts boys and girls; open to students from other schools. 900 students usually enrolled. 2012 schedule: June 11 to July 20. Application deadline: none.

Tuition and Aid Day student tuition: $23,300–$23,925; 7-day tuition and room/board: $41,499–$46,258. Need-based scholarship grants, need-based financial aid available. In 2011–12, 22% of upper-school students received aid. Total amount of financial aid awarded in 2011–12: $1,851,800.

Admissions Traditional secondary-level entrance grade is 9. For fall 2011, 204 students applied for upper-level admission, 64 were accepted, 43 enrolled. Admissions testing required. Deadline for receipt of application materials: none. Application fee required: $175. Interview required.

Athletics Interscholastic: basketball, crew, cross-country running, fencing, field hockey, golf, independent competitive sports, jogging, lacrosse, rowing, running, soccer, softball, swimming and diving, tennis, track and field, volleyball, winter soccer; intramural: aerobics, aerobics/dance, aquatics, archery, ballet, basketball, cheering, cooperative games, dance, fitness, independent competitive sports, jogging, life saving, martial arts, modern dance, outdoor skills, physical fitness, physical training, project adventure, racquetball, ropes courses, running, self defense, strength & conditioning, swimming and diving, tennis, track and field, ultimate Frisbee, volleyball, weight lifting, weight training, yoga. 7 PE instructors, 5 coaches, 1 athletic trainer.

Computers Computers are regularly used in animation, art, computer applications, creative writing, dance, engineering, English, French, health, history, humanities, information technology, introduction to technology, journalism, Latin, mathematics, media, media production, media services, multimedia, music, newspaper, photography, photojournalism, psychology, publications, publishing, science, Spanish, technology, Web site design, yearbook classes. Computer network features include on-campus library services, online commercial services, Internet access, wireless campus network, Internet filtering or blocking technology. Campus intranet, student e-mail accounts, and computer access in designated common areas are available to students. Students grades are available online. The school has a published electronic and media policy.

Contact Jen Liggitt, Director of Admission. 214-363-6311. Fax: 214-265-1649. E-mail: admissions@mail.hockaday.org. Web site: www.hockaday.org.

See Display below and Close-Up on page 634.

HOLY CROSS HIGH SCHOOL

587 Oronoke Road

Waterbury, Connecticut 06708

Head of School: Mr. Timothy McDonald

General Information Coeducational day college-preparatory, arts, religious studies, and technology school, affiliated with Roman Catholic Church. Grades 9–12. Founded: 1968. Setting: suburban. 37-acre campus. 1 building on campus. Approved or accredited by Commission on Independent Schools, New England Association of Schools and Colleges, and Connecticut Department of Education. Total enrollment: 698. Upper school average class size: 21. Upper school faculty-student ratio: 1:15. There are 160 required school days per year for Upper School students. Upper School students typically attend 5 days per week. The average school day consists of 6 hours.

Upper School Student Profile Grade 9: 160 students (86 boys, 74 girls); Grade 10: 163 students (86 boys, 77 girls); Grade 11: 179 students (99 boys, 80 girls); Grade 12: 196 students (104 boys, 92 girls). 85% of students are Roman Catholic.

Faculty School total: 60. In upper school: 28 men, 32 women; 37 have advanced degrees.

Subjects Offered Advanced biology, advanced math, Advanced Placement courses, advanced studio art-AP, algebra, American history, American history-AP, American literature, American literature-AP, American studies, anatomy, anatomy and physiology, art, art-AP, arts, band, Basic programming, biology, biology-AP, British literature, British literature-AP, business, business law, calculus, calculus-AP, campus ministry, Catholic belief and practice, chamber groups, chemistry, chemistry-AP, choir, computer applications, computer programming, computer science, concert band, concert choir, CPR, creative writing, drama, driver education, economics, economics and history, English, English literature, English-AP, environmental science, French, geometry, history, mathematics, music, physical education, physics, physiology, psychology, religion, science, social studies, Spanish, statistics, theater, theology, trigonometry, word processing, world history, world literature.

Graduation Requirements English, foreign language, mathematics, physical education (includes health), religion (includes Bible studies and theology), science, social studies (includes history).

Special Academic Programs Advanced Placement exam preparation; honors section; independent study; study at local college for college credit.

College Admission Counseling 176 students graduated in 2011; 171 went to college, including Central Connecticut State University; Naugatuck Valley Community College; Southern Connecticut State University; University of Connecticut; Western Connecticut State University. Other: 3 went to work, 2 entered military service.

Student Life Upper grades have specified standards of dress, student council. Discipline rests primarily with faculty. Attendance at religious services is required.

Tuition and Aid Day student tuition: $9750. Tuition installment plan (monthly payment plans, individually arranged payment plans, Tuition Management Systems (TMS)). Merit scholarship grants, need-based scholarship grants available. In 2011–12, 30% of upper-school students received aid; total upper-school merit-scholarship money awarded: $135,000. Total amount of financial aid awarded in 2011–12: $550,000.

Admissions Traditional secondary-level entrance grade is 9. For fall 2011, 384 students applied for upper-level admission, 326 were accepted, 168 enrolled. ETS HSPT (closed) required. Deadline for receipt of application materials: none. Application fee required: $25.

Athletics Interscholastic: baseball (boys), basketball (b,g), cheering (g), cross-country running (b,g), diving (b,g), football (b), golf (b,g), gymnastics (g), lacrosse (b), soccer (b,g), softball (g), swimming and diving (b,g), tennis (b,g), track and field (b,g), volleyball (g), winter (indoor) track (b,g), wrestling (b); intramural: basketball (b), skiing (downhill) (b,g), weight lifting (b); coed intramural: bowling, table tennis, ultimate Frisbee, yoga. 4 PE instructors, 22 coaches, 1 athletic trainer.

Computers Computers are regularly used in accounting, business, computer applications, creative writing, English, foreign language, French, history, mathematics, music technology, psychology, religious studies, science, social sciences, social studies, Spanish, technology, theology, Web site design, word processing, writing, writing, yearbook classes. Computer network features include on-campus library services, online commercial services, Internet access, wireless campus network. Campus intranet and computer access in designated common areas are available to students. Students grades are available online.

Contact Mrs. Jodie LaCava McGarrity, Director of Admissions. 203-757-9248. Fax: 203-757-3423. E-mail: jmcgarrity@holycrosshs-ct.com. Web site: www.holycrosshs-ct.com.

HOLY CROSS HIGH SCHOOL

26-20 Francis Lewis Boulevard

Flushing, New York 11358

Head of School: Fr. Walter E. Jenkins, CSC

General Information Boys' day college-preparatory, arts, business, religious studies, and technology school, affiliated with Roman Catholic Church. Grades 9–12. Founded: 1955. Setting: urban. Nearest major city is New York. 1 building on campus. Approved or accredited by National Catholic Education Association and New York Department of Education. Upper school average class size: 29. There are 180 required school days per year for Upper School students. Upper School students typically attend 5 days per week. The average school day consists of 6 hours and 2 minutes.

Upper School Student Profile Grade 9: 240 students (240 boys); Grade 10: 230 students (230 boys); Grade 11: 220 students (220 boys); Grade 12: 210 students (210 boys). 70% of students are Roman Catholic.

Special Academic Programs Honors section; study at local college for college credit.

College Admission Counseling 212 students graduated in 2011; all went to college.

Student Life Upper grades have specified standards of dress, student council, honor system. Discipline rests primarily with faculty. Attendance at religious services is required.

Summer Programs Held on campus; accepts boys; open to students from other schools.

Tuition and Aid Day student tuition: $8125. Tuition installment plan (SMART Tuition Payment Plan). Tuition reduction for siblings, merit scholarship grants, need-based scholarship grants available.

Admissions Traditional secondary-level entrance grade is 9. No application fee required.

Athletics Interscholastic: baseball, basketball, bowling, cross-country running, football, golf, ice hockey, indoor track, soccer, tennis, winter (indoor) track. 3 PE instructors, 35 coaches.

Computers Computer network features include on-campus library services, online commercial services, Internet access. Student e-mail accounts are available to students. Students grades are available online. The school has a published electronic and media policy.

Contact Mr. Paul Gilvary, Director of Admissions. 718-886-7250 Ext. 525. Fax: 718-886-7257. E-mail: admissions@holycrosshs.org. Web site: www.holycrosshs.org.

HOLY GHOST PREPARATORY SCHOOL

2429 Bristol Pike

Bensalem, Pennsylvania 19020

Head of School: Rev. Jeffrey T. Duaime, CSSP

General Information Boys' day college-preparatory, arts, and technology school, affiliated with Roman Catholic Church. Grades 9–12. Founded: 1897. Setting: suburban. Nearest major city is Philadelphia. 53-acre campus. 4 buildings on campus. Approved or accredited by Middle States Association of Colleges and Schools, National Catholic Education Association, and Pennsylvania Association of Independent Schools. Member of National Association of Independent Schools. Endowment: $2 million. Total enrollment: 498. Upper school average class size: 17. Upper school faculty-student ratio: 1:11. The average school day consists of 6 hours and 30 minutes.

Upper School Student Profile Grade 9: 125 students (125 boys); Grade 10: 126 students (126 boys); Grade 11: 123 students (123 boys); Grade 12: 124 students (124 boys). 94% of students are Roman Catholic.

Faculty School total: 50. In upper school: 32 men, 18 women; 34 have advanced degrees.

Subjects Offered 3-dimensional art, Advanced Placement courses, advanced studio art-AP, algebra, American government, American history, American history-AP, American literature, analysis, anatomy and physiology, art, Bible, biology, biology-AP, calculus, calculus-AP, campus ministry, career/college preparation, careers, ceremonies of life, chemistry, Chinese history, choral music, church history, college admission preparation, college counseling, communication arts, communication skills, computer programming-AP, computer science, computer science-AP, creative writing, drama performance, earth science, economics, English, English language and composition-AP, English literature, English literature and composition-AP, environmental science, European history, European history-AP, film, fine arts, French, French language-AP, geometry, government and politics-AP, government/civics, health, history, journalism, language-AP, Latin, Latin-AP, mathematics, modern European history-AP, music, music theory-AP, oral communications, physical education, physics, public speaking, religion, science, sexuality, social studies, Spanish, Spanish language-AP, Spanish-AP, speech, statistics, trigonometry, U.S. history-AP, United States government-AP, world cultures, world history, world history-AP, world literature, writing, yearbook.

Graduation Requirements Arts and fine arts (art, music, dance, drama), computer science, English, foreign language, mathematics, physical education (includes health), religion (includes Bible studies and theology), science, social studies (includes history), summer reading. Community service is required.

Special Academic Programs Advanced Placement exam preparation; honors section; independent study; study abroad.

College Admission Counseling 126 students graduated in 2011; all went to college, including Boston College; Drexel University; Duquesne University; Saint Joseph's University; University of Pennsylvania; Villanova University. Median SAT critical reading: 610, median SAT math: 640.

Student Life Upper grades have specified standards of dress, student council, honor system. Discipline rests primarily with faculty.

Summer Programs Enrichment, advancement, sports, computer instruction programs offered; session focuses on entrance exam preparation; held on campus; accepts boys and girls; open to students from other schools. 100 students usually enrolled. 2012 schedule: June 29 to July 24. Application deadline: June 1.

Tuition and Aid Day student tuition: $16,000. Tuition installment plan (monthly payment plans, quarterly and semi-annual payment plans). Merit scholarship grants, need-based scholarship grants, music scholarships, minority scholarships, art scholarships available. In 2011–12, 35% of upper-school students received aid; total upper-school merit-scholarship money awarded: $1,000,000. Total amount of financial aid awarded in 2011–12: $1,000,000.

Admissions Traditional secondary-level entrance grade is 9. For fall 2011, 398 students applied for upper-level admission, 158 were accepted, 125 enrolled. High School Placement Test (closed version) from Scholastic Testing Service required. Deadline for receipt of application materials: December 12. Application fee required: $60. On-campus interview required.

Athletics Interscholastic: baseball, basketball, bowling, cross-country running, golf, ice hockey, indoor track & field, lacrosse, soccer, Special Olympics, swimming and diving, tennis, track and field; intramural: basketball, fitness walking, flag football, football, Frisbee, soccer, street hockey, tennis. 10 coaches, 1 athletic trainer.

Computers Computers are regularly used in college planning, English, foreign language, mathematics, programming, publications, science, speech, yearbook classes. Computer network features include on-campus library services, online commercial services, Internet access, wireless campus network, Internet filtering or blocking technology. Student e-mail accounts are available to students.
Contact Mr. Ryan T. Abramson, Director of Admissions. 215-639-0811. Fax: 215-639-4225. E-mail: rabramson@holyghostprep.org. Web site: www.holyghostprep.org.

HOLY INNOCENTS' EPISCOPAL SCHOOL

805 Mount Vernon Highway NW

Atlanta, Georgia 30327

Head of School: Mr. Eugene A. Bratek

General Information Coeducational day college-preparatory, arts, religious studies, and technology school, affiliated with Episcopal Church. Grades PS–12. Founded: 1959. Setting: suburban. 42-acre campus. 4 buildings on campus. Approved or accredited by Georgia Independent School Association, National Association of Episcopal Schools, Southern Association of Colleges and Schools, and Georgia Department of Education. Member of National Association of Independent Schools and Secondary School Admission Test Board. Endowment: $17 million. Total enrollment: 1,302. Upper school average class size: 14. Upper school faculty-student ratio: 1:7. There are 173 required school days per year for Upper School students. Upper School students typically attend 5 days per week. The average school day consists of 7 hours and 15 minutes.
Upper School Student Profile Grade 9: 119 students (64 boys, 55 girls); Grade 10: 120 students (56 boys, 64 girls); Grade 11: 105 students (53 boys, 52 girls); Grade 12: 100 students (43 boys, 57 girls). 26% of students are members of Episcopal Church.
Faculty School total: 180. In upper school: 29 men, 32 women; 45 have advanced degrees.
Subjects Offered 3-dimensional art, 3-dimensional design, advanced biology, advanced chemistry, advanced math, Advanced Placement courses, advanced studio art-AP, algebra, American government, American history, American history-AP, American literature, American literature-AP, anatomy, anatomy and physiology, ancient world history, applied music, art, art-AP, athletics, band, baseball, basketball, Bible, Bible studies, biology, biology-AP, calculus, calculus-AP, cheerleading, chemistry, chemistry-AP, choir, choral music, chorus, college counseling, college placement, community service, composition, computer animation, computer education, computer graphics, computer resources, computer science-AP, concert band, concert choir, creative writing, drama, drama performance, drawing and design, earth science, economics, electives, English, English composition, English language-AP, English literature, English literature AP, English AP, environmental studies, ethics, European history, European history-AP, fine arts, French, French language-AP, French AP, geometry, golf, government, government and politics-AP, government/civics, Greek, guidance, health and wellness, history, honors algebra, honors English, honors geometry, honors U.S. history, honors world history, human geography - AP, Jewish history, Jewish studies, language arts, Latin, Latin-AP, mathematics, New Testament, orchestra, peer counseling, performing arts, personal finance, photography, physical education, physics, physics-AP, pre-calculus, psychology, religion, religious studies, SAT preparation, SAT/ACT preparation, science, science project, sex education, social studies, Spanish, Spanish language-AP, speech and debate, sports, study skills, swimming, U.S. history, U.S. history-AP, visual arts, world history, writing workshop, yearbook.
Graduation Requirements Arts and fine arts (art, music, dance, drama), electives, English, foreign language, history, mathematics, physical education (includes health), physical fitness, religion (includes Bible studies and theology), science, 15 hours of community service each year, plus additional hours for NHS students.
Special Academic Programs Advanced Placement exam preparation; honors section; term-away projects; study abroad.
College Admission Counseling 90 students graduated in 2011; all went to college, including Auburn University; Clemson University; Georgia Institute of Technology; The University of Alabama; The University of North Carolina at Chapel Hill; University of Georgia. Mean SAT critical reading: 600, mean SAT math: 610, mean SAT writing: 620, mean composite ACT: 26.
Student Life Upper grades have uniform requirement, student council, honor system. Discipline rests primarily with faculty. Attendance at religious services is required.
Summer Programs Remediation, enrichment, advancement, sports, art/fine arts, computer instruction programs offered; session focuses on athletics, fine arts, and academics; held on campus; accepts boys and girls; open to students from other schools. 725 students usually enrolled. 2012 schedule: June 1 to August 14. Application deadline: February 12.
Tuition and Aid Day student tuition: $21,500. Tuition installment plan (Insured Tuition Payment Plan, FACTS Tuition Payment Plan, monthly payment plans). Need-based scholarship grants available. In 2011–12, 20% of upper-school students received aid. Total amount of financial aid awarded in 2011–12: $1,800,000.
Admissions Traditional secondary-level entrance grade is 9. For fall 2011, 116 students applied for upper-level admission, 59 were accepted, 33 enrolled. Essay, ISEE, mathematics proficiency exam, school's own test and SSAT required. Deadline for receipt of application materials: February 1. Application fee required: $95. Interview required.
Athletics Interscholastic: baseball (boys), basketball (b,g), cheering (g), cross-country running (b,g), equestrian sports (g), football (b), golf (b,g), lacrosse (b,g), physical fitness (b,g), physical training (b,g), soccer (b,g), softball (g), swimming and diving (b,g), tennis (b,g), track and field (b,g), volleyball (g), wrestling (b); intramural: combined training (b,g), fitness (b,g), ultimate Frisbee (b); coed intramural: combined training, fitness. 9 PE instructors, 120 coaches, 1 athletic trainer.
Computers Computers are regularly used in all academic classes. Computer network features include on-campus library services, Internet access, wireless campus network, Internet filtering or blocking technology, 1-to-1 student laptops (grades 5-12), two computer labs, and various individual classroom computers. Campus intranet and student e-mail accounts are available to students. Students grades are available online. The school has a published electronic and media policy.
Contact Mr. Chris Pomar, Director of Admissions. 404-255-4026. Fax: 404-847-1156. E-mail: chris.pomar@hies.org. Web site: www.hies.org.

HOLY NAMES ACADEMY

728 21st Avenue East

Seattle, Washington 98112

Head of School: Elizabeth Swift

General Information Girls' day college-preparatory school, affiliated with Roman Catholic Church. Grades 9–12. Founded: 1880. Setting: urban. Approved or accredited by Northwest Accreditation Commission, Pacific Northwest Association of Independent Schools, and Washington Department of Education. Member of National Association of Independent Schools. Upper school average class size: 14.
Upper School Student Profile 74% of students are Roman Catholic.
Student Life Attendance at religious services is required.
Tuition and Aid Day student tuition: $12,396. Financial aid available to upper-school students. In 2011–12, 31% of upper-school students received aid. Total amount of financial aid awarded in 2011–12: $1,005,360.
Admissions MAT 7 Metropolitan Achievement Test required. Deadline for receipt of application materials: January 12. Application fee required: $25.
Contact 206-323-4272. Web site: www.holynames-sea.org.

HOLYOKE CATHOLIC HIGH SCHOOL

134 Springfield Street

Chicopee, Massachusetts 01013

Head of School: Mrs. Theresa J. Kitchell

General Information Coeducational day college-preparatory and arts school, affiliated with Roman Catholic Church. Grades 9–12. Founded: 1963. Setting: small town. Nearest major city is Springfield. 2 buildings on campus. Approved or accredited by National Catholic Education Association, New England Association of Schools and Colleges, and Massachusetts Department of Education. Total enrollment: 301. Upper school average class size: 15. Upper school faculty-student ratio: 1:11. There are 180 required school days per year for Upper School students. Upper School students typically attend 5 days per week. The average school day consists of 6 hours.
Upper School Student Profile Grade 9: 73 students (30 boys, 43 girls); Grade 10: 72 students (31 boys, 41 girls); Grade 11: 85 students (35 boys, 50 girls); Grade 12: 71 students (32 boys, 39 girls). 88% of students are Roman Catholic.
Faculty School total: 28. In upper school: 12 men, 16 women; 19 have advanced degrees.
Subjects Offered Advanced biology, advanced math, algebra, American literature, American literature-AP, art, biology, calculus, calculus-AP, Catholic belief and practice, chemistry, English, English literature, environmental science, forensics, French, geometry, Latin, literature-AP, moral theology, multimedia design, performing arts, physics, pottery, pre-calculus, Spanish, studio art, The 20th Century, U.S. history, U.S. history-AP, Web site design, world civilizations, world history, world religions.
Graduation Requirements Electives, English, foreign language, internship, mathematics, religion (includes Bible studies and theology), science, social studies (includes history), U.S. literature, community service hours at each grade level, English research paper.
Special Academic Programs 5 Advanced Placement exams for which test preparation is offered; honors section; independent study; study at local college for college credit.
College Admission Counseling 84 students graduated in 2011; 80 went to college, including Framingham State University; Holyoke Community College; Springfield College; Westfield State University. Other: 2 went to work, 2 entered military service. Median SAT critical reading: 544, median SAT math: 517, median SAT writing: 536. 1% scored over 26 on composite ACT.
Student Life Upper grades have uniform requirement, student council. Discipline rests primarily with faculty. Attendance at religious services is required.
Tuition and Aid Day student tuition: $7500. Tuition installment plan (FACTS Tuition Payment Plan). Need-based scholarship grants available. In 2011–12, 25% of upper-school students received aid. Total amount of financial aid awarded in 2011–12: $174,000.

Admissions Traditional secondary-level entrance grade is 9. For fall 2011, 113 students applied for upper-level admission, 107 were accepted, 73 enrolled. Scholastic Testing Service High School Placement Test required. Deadline for receipt of application materials: none. Application fee required: $100. Interview required.

Athletics Interscholastic: baseball (boys), basketball (b,g), cheering (g), cross-country running (b,g), football (b), indoor track & field (b,g), lacrosse (b,g), soccer (b,g), softball (g), tennis (g), wrestling (b); coed interscholastic: Frisbee, golf, hiking/backpacking, outdoor adventure, skiing (downhill), swimming and diving; coed intramural: volleyball, weight training. 17 coaches.

Computers Computers are regularly used in multimedia classes. Computer network features include on-campus library services, Internet access, Internet filtering or blocking technology. Campus intranet and student e-mail accounts are available to students. Students grades are available online. The school has a published electronic and media policy.

Contact Mrs. Theresa Marie Zaborowski, Director of Admissions. 413-331-2480 Ext. 1132. Fax: 413-331-2708. E-mail: tzaborowski@gaels.org. Web site: www.gaels.org.

HOLY SAVIOR MENARD CATHOLIC HIGH SCHOOL

4603 Coliseum Boulevard

Alexandria, Louisiana 71303

Head of School: Mr. Joel Desselle

General Information Coeducational day college-preparatory and religious studies school, affiliated with Roman Catholic Church. Grades 7–12. Founded: 1930. Setting: suburban. 5-acre campus. 5 buildings on campus. Approved or accredited by National Catholic Education Association, Southern Association of Colleges and Schools, The College Board, and Louisiana Department of Education. Total enrollment: 480. Upper school average class size: 18. Upper school faculty-student ratio: 1:12. There are 178 required school days per year for Upper School students. Upper School students typically attend 5 days per week. The average school day consists of 7 hours and 15 minutes.

Upper School Student Profile Grade 9: 88 students (48 boys, 40 girls); Grade 10: 81 students (33 boys, 48 girls); Grade 11: 65 students (24 boys, 41 girls); Grade 12: 65 students (39 boys, 26 girls). 85% of students are Roman Catholic.

Faculty School total: 37. In upper school: 15 men, 19 women; 12 have advanced degrees.

Subjects Offered Advanced math, algebra, American history, anatomy and physiology, art, athletics, biology, biology-AP, British literature, British literature (honors), calculus-AP, campus ministry, Catholic belief and practice, cheerleading, chemistry, civics/free enterprise, computer applications, computer science, digital photography, English, English composition, English literature, English literature-AP, fine arts, French, general science, geometry, health, honors algebra, honors English, honors geometry, honors U.S. history, honors world history, journalism, language arts, moral reasoning, New Testament, newspaper, philosophy, physical education, physical science, physics, pre-algebra, pre-calculus, psychology, publications, reading/study skills, religion, sociology, Spanish, world geography, world history, yearbook.

Graduation Requirements Algebra, American history, arts and fine arts (art, music, dance, drama), biology, chemistry, civics/free enterprise, computer applications, English, foreign language, geometry, physical science, religion (includes Bible studies and theology), world history, 27 credits required.

Special Academic Programs 4 Advanced Placement exams for which test preparation is offered; honors section; independent study; study at local college for college credit.

College Admission Counseling 80 students graduated in 2011; 75 went to college, including Louisiana State University and Agricultural and Mechanical College; Louisiana Tech University; Millsaps College; Northwestern State University of Louisiana; Tulane University; University of Louisiana at Lafayette. Other: 3 went to work, 2 had other specific plans. Mean composite ACT: 23. 34% scored over 26 on composite ACT.

Student Life Upper grades have uniform requirement, student council, honor system. Discipline rests primarily with faculty. Attendance at religious services is required.

Summer Programs Remediation programs offered; session focuses on summer school for credit recovery; held on campus; accepts boys and girls; not open to students from other schools. 15 students usually enrolled. 2012 schedule: June 1 to June 30. Application deadline: May 31.

Tuition and Aid Day student tuition: $5500. Tuition installment plan (FACTS Tuition Payment Plan, monthly payment plans, individually arranged payment plans). Tuition reduction for siblings, merit scholarship grants, need-based scholarship grants available. In 2011–12, 9% of upper-school students received aid; total upper-school merit-scholarship money awarded: $5000. Total amount of financial aid awarded in 2011–12: $135,000.

Admissions Traditional secondary-level entrance grade is 9. For fall 2011, 36 students applied for upper-level admission, 36 were accepted, 36 enrolled. CTBS, Stanford Achievement Test, any other standardized test required. Deadline for receipt of application materials: March 15. Application fee required: $250. On-campus interview required.

Athletics Interscholastic: baseball (boys), basketball (b,g), cheering (g), cross-country running (b,g), danceline (g), football (b), golf (b,g), power lifting (b,g), running (b,g), soccer (b,g), softball (g), tennis (b,g), track and field (b,g); coed interscholastic: swimming and diving. 2 coaches.

Computers Computers are regularly used in computer applications, English, journalism, photography, publications, science, Web site design classes. Computer network features include on-campus library services, Internet access, wireless campus network, Internet filtering or blocking technology. Computer access in designated common areas is available to students. Students grades are available online.

Contact Mrs. Ashley Meadows, Guidance Secretary. 318-445-8233. Fax: 318-448-8170. E-mail: ameadows@holysaviormenard.com. Web site: www.holysaviormenard.com.

HOLY TRINITY DIOCESAN HIGH SCHOOL

98 Cherry Lane

Hicksville, New York 11801

Head of School: Mr. Gene Fennell

General Information Coeducational day college-preparatory school, affiliated with Roman Catholic Church. Grades 9–12. Founded: 1967. Setting: suburban. Nearest major city is New York. 1 building on campus. Approved or accredited by National Council for Private School Accreditation, New York State Board of Regents, The College Board, and New York Department of Education. Total enrollment: 1,496. Upper school average class size: 28.

Upper School Student Profile Grade 9: 382 students (190 boys, 192 girls); Grade 10: 389 students (185 boys, 204 girls); Grade 11: 340 students (137 boys, 203 girls); Grade 12: 385 students (157 boys, 228 girls). 90% of students are Roman Catholic.

Faculty School total: 110. In upper school: 43 men, 67 women; 91 have advanced degrees.

Subjects Offered Accounting, advanced math, Advanced Placement courses, American government, American history, American history-AP, American literature, American literature-AP, anatomy and physiology, architectural drawing, art, band, biology, biology-AP, British literature, British literature (honors), business law, calculus, calculus-AP, campus ministry, ceramics, chemistry, chemistry-AP, chorus, Christian scripture, Christian studies, Christian testament, comparative religion, composition, concert band, criminology, critical studies in film, dance, desktop publishing, earth science, economics, English, English composition, English language and composition-AP, English literature, English literature-AP, environmental science, film, food and nutrition, French, government and politics-AP, health, honors English, honors U.S. history, honors world history, intro to computers, jazz theory, keyboarding, literature and composition-AP, mathematics, music, performing arts, physical education, physics, physics-AP, pre-calculus, public speaking, religion, Spanish, Spanish language-AP, stagecraft, statistics, theater arts, theology, U.S. government and politics, U.S. government and politics-AP, U.S. history, U.S. history-AP, world wide web design.

Graduation Requirements Arts and fine arts (art, music, dance, drama), economics, English, foreign language, mathematics, physical education (includes health), religion (includes Bible studies and theology), science, U.S. government and politics.

Special Academic Programs Advanced Placement exam preparation; honors section; study at local college for college credit.

College Admission Counseling 431 students graduated in 2011; all went to college, including Adelphi University; Hofstra University; Nassau Community College; Stony Brook University, State University of New York. Mean SAT critical reading: 514, mean SAT math: 522, mean SAT writing: 520.

Student Life Upper grades have uniform requirement, student council. Discipline rests primarily with faculty.

Tuition and Aid Day student tuition: $7375. Tuition installment plan (monthly payment plans, individually arranged payment plans, 10-month tuition plan, 3-payment plan). Need-based scholarship grants available.

Admissions Traditional secondary-level entrance grade is 9. Catholic High School Entrance Examination required. Deadline for receipt of application materials: none. Application fee required. Interview recommended.

Athletics Interscholastic: badminton (girls), baseball (b), basketball (b,g), cheering (g), cross-country running (b,g), dance team (g), football (b), golf (b), gymnastics (g), indoor track (b,g), lacrosse (b,g), soccer (b,g), softball (g), swimming and diving (b,g), tennis (b,g), track and field (b,g), volleyball (b,g), weight lifting (b), weight training (b), winter (indoor) track (b,g), wrestling (b); intramural: physical training (b), weight training (b); coed interscholastic: bowling, fitness. 6 PE instructors, 1 athletic trainer.

Computers Computers are regularly used in college planning, computer applications, desktop publishing, drawing and design, economics, English, foreign language, graphic design, history, journalism, library, music technology, newspaper, occupational education, programming, research skills, SAT preparation, science, social studies, theater, Web site design, writing, yearbook classes. Computer network features include on-campus library services, Internet access, Internet filtering or blocking technology. Student e-mail accounts and computer access in designated common areas are available to students. Students grades are available online. The school has a published electronic and media policy.

Contact Admissions. 516-433-2900. Fax: 516-433-2827. E-mail: hths98@holytrinityhs.echalk.com. Web site: www.holytrinityhs.org.

HOLY TRINITY HIGH SCHOOL

1443 West Division Street

Chicago, Illinois 60642

Head of School: Mr. Timothy M. Bopp

General Information Coeducational day college-preparatory, arts, business, religious studies, bilingual studies, and technology school, affiliated with Roman Catholic Church. Grades 9–12. Founded: 1910. Setting: urban. 1 building on campus. Approved or accredited by North Central Association of Colleges and Schools and Illinois Department of Education. Total enrollment: 270. Upper school average class size: 20. Upper school faculty-student ratio: 1:12. There are 180 required school days per year for Upper School students. The average school day consists of 5 hours and 52 minutes.

Upper School Student Profile Grade 9: 63 students (35 boys, 28 girls); Grade 10: 58 students (31 boys, 27 girls); Grade 11: 79 students (49 boys, 30 girls); Grade 12: 70 students (40 boys, 30 girls). 40% of students are Roman Catholic.

Faculty School total: 28. In upper school: 12 men, 16 women; 14 have advanced degrees.

Subjects Offered Band, French.

Graduation Requirements Business, English, mathematics, modern languages, physical education (includes health), religion (includes Bible studies and theology), science, social studies (includes history), visual and performing arts.

Special Academic Programs Advanced Placement exam preparation; honors section; study at local college for college credit; remedial reading and/or remedial writing; ESL.

College Admission Counseling 65 students graduated in 2011; 64 went to college, including Brigham Young University; Knox College; Northeastern Illinois University; Northern Illinois University; Triton College; Western Illinois University. Other: 1 entered military service.

Student Life Upper grades have uniform requirement, student council, honor system. Discipline rests equally with students and faculty. Attendance at religious services is required.

Tuition and Aid Day student tuition: $6800. Tuition installment plan (monthly payment plans). Tuition reduction for siblings, merit scholarship grants, need-based scholarship grants available. In 2011–12, 95% of upper school students received aid; total upper-school merit-scholarship money awarded: $125,000. Total amount of financial aid awarded in 2011–12: $600,000.

Admissions Traditional secondary-level entrance grade is 9. For fall 2011, 195 students applied for upper-level admission, 176 were accepted, 84 enrolled. TerraNova required. Deadline for receipt of application materials: January 14. Application fee required: $25.

Athletics Interscholastic: baseball (boys), basketball (b,g), cross-country running (b,g), soccer (b,g), softball (g), track and field (b,g), volleyball (b,g); coed interscholastic: bowling, flag football; coed intramural: cheering, dance, dance team, fitness, physical fitness, weight lifting. 2 PE instructors, 4 coaches.

Computers Computers are regularly used in animation, business education, business skills, college planning, keyboarding classes. Computer network features include on-campus library services, Internet access, wireless campus network, Internet filtering or blocking technology. Computer access in designated common areas is available to students. The school has a published electronic and media policy.

Contact Ms. Samara Galvan, Admission Coordinator. 773-278-4212 Ext. 3025. Fax: 773-278-0144. E-mail: sglavan@holytrinity-hs.org. Web site: www.holytrinity-hs.org.

HOOSAC SCHOOL

PO Box 9

Hoosick, New York 12089

Head of School: Dean S. Foster

General Information Coeducational boarding and day college-preparatory and arts school, affiliated with Episcopal Church. Grades 8–PG. Founded: 1889. Setting: rural. Nearest major city is Albany. Students are housed in single-sex dormitories. 350-acre campus. 16 buildings on campus. Approved or accredited by Middle States Association of Colleges and Schools, National Association of Episcopal Schools, New York State Board of Regents, The Association of Boarding Schools, and New York Department of Education. Member of National Association of Independent Schools and Secondary School Admission Test Board. Endowment: $1.5 million. Total enrollment: 125. Upper school average class size: 8. Upper school faculty-student ratio: 1:5. Upper School students typically attend 6 days per week. The average school day consists of 6 hours and 15 minutes.

Upper School Student Profile Grade 8: 7 students (5 boys, 2 girls); Grade 9: 20 students (10 boys, 10 girls); Grade 10: 23 students (16 boys, 7 girls); Grade 11: 29 students (17 boys, 12 girls); Grade 12: 41 students (29 boys, 12 girls); Postgraduate: 5 students (5 boys). 90% of students are boarding students. 31% are state residents. 17 states are represented in upper school student body. 38% are international students. International students from Canada, China, Republic of Korea, Russian Federation, Rwanda, and Uruguay; 9 other countries represented in student body.

Faculty School total: 23. In upper school: 14 men, 9 women; 11 have advanced degrees; 15 reside on campus.

Subjects Offered Advertising design, algebra, American history, American literature, art, art history, astronomy, biology, British literature, calculus, calculus-AP, ceramics, chemistry, choral music, computer science, creative writing, criminology, dance, drama, driver education, earth science, English, English literature, English-AP, ESL, ethics, European history, expository writing, fine arts, French, French as a second language, geometry, government/civics, grammar, history, history-AP, Latin, marketing, mathematics, music, photography, physical education, physics, science, social studies, speech communications, theater, world history, world literature, writing.

Graduation Requirements Arts and fine arts (art, music, dance, drama), computer literacy, English, ethics, foreign language, mathematics, physical education (includes health), science, social studies (includes history), Ethics, public speaking.

Special Academic Programs 7 Advanced Placement exams for which test preparation is offered; honors section; accelerated programs; independent study; study at local college for college credit; academic accommodation for the musically talented and the artistically talented; remedial reading and/or remedial writing; remedial math; programs in English, mathematics, general development for dyslexic students; ESL (40 students enrolled).

College Admission Counseling 36 students graduated in 2011; all went to college, including Bentley University; Carnegie Mellon University; Cornell University; Gettysburg College; University of California, Berkeley; University of Michigan.

Student Life Upper grades have specified standards of dress, student council, honor system. Discipline rests primarily with faculty. Attendance at religious services is required.

Summer Programs ESL programs offered; session focuses on English as a second language; held on campus; accepts boys and girls; open to students from other schools. 35 students usually enrolled. 2012 schedule: June 24 to July 22.

Tuition and Aid Day student tuition: $17,000; 7-day tuition and room/board: $38,000. Tuition installment plan (Academic Management Services Plan, Key Tuition Payment Plan, monthly payment plans, individually arranged payment plans). Merit scholarship grants, need-based scholarship grants available. In 2011–12, 35% of upper-school students received aid. Total amount of financial aid awarded in 2011–12: $625,000.

Admissions Traditional secondary-level entrance grade is 9. For fall 2011, 198 students applied for upper-level admission, 108 were accepted, 56 enrolled. Deadline for receipt of application materials: none. Application fee required: $40. Interview required.

Athletics Interscholastic: baseball (boys), basketball (b,g), cross-country running (b,g), ice hockey (b), lacrosse (b,g); intramural: bicycling (b,g), flag football (b,g), floor hockey (b,g); coed intramural: aerobics/dance, alpine skiing, aquatics, backpacking, ball hockey, bowling, broomball, canoeing/kayaking, cooperative games, cross-country running, dance, deck hockey, fishing, freestyle skiing, golf, hiking/backpacking, indoor hockey, indoor soccer, life saving, mountain biking, outdoor activities, outdoor recreation, outdoor skills, physical fitness, physical training, weight training, whiffle ball, yoga. 1 PE instructor, 2 coaches.

Computers Computers are regularly used in computer applications, journalism, literary magazine, media arts, media production, multimedia, news writing, newspaper, photography, photojournalism classes. Computer network features include on-campus library services, Internet access, wireless campus network, Internet filtering or blocking technology. Campus intranet, student e-mail accounts, and computer access in designated common areas are available to students. Students grades are available online. The school has a published electronic and media policy.

Contact Mr. Michael S. Foster, Director of Admission and Residential Life. 800-822-0159. Fax: 518-686-3370. E-mail: admissions@hoosac.com. Web site: www.hoosac.com.

HOPKINS SCHOOL

986 Forest Road

New Haven, Connecticut 06515

Head of School: Ms. Barbara M. Riley

General Information Coeducational day college-preparatory school. Grades 7–12. Founded: 1660. Setting: urban. Nearest major city is New York, NY. 108-acre campus. 10 buildings on campus. Approved or accredited by New England Association of Schools and Colleges and Connecticut Department of Education. Member of National Association of Independent Schools. Endowment: $67.8 million. Total enrollment: 687. Upper school average class size: 12. Upper school faculty-student ratio: 1:6. There are 170 required school days per year for Upper School students. Upper School students typically attend 5 days per week. The average school day consists of 7 hours and 30 minutes.

Upper School Student Profile Grade 9: 137 students (67 boys, 70 girls); Grade 10: 138 students (64 boys, 74 girls); Grade 11: 133 students (72 boys, 61 girls); Grade 12: 122 students (63 boys, 59 girls).

Faculty School total: 126. In upper school: 53 men, 73 women; 97 have advanced degrees.

Subjects Offered African-American history, algebra, American history, American literature, anatomy and physiology, ancient history, art, art history, art history-AP, art-AP, Asian studies, biochemistry, biology, biology-AP, calculus, calculus-AP, ceramics, chemistry, chemistry-AP, chorus, classical music, computer math, computer programming, computer science, computer science-AP, creative writing, drama, earth science, economics, English, English literature, environmental science-AP, European history, expository writing, film, fine arts, French, French-AP, geometry, government/civics, Greek, history, Holocaust studies, HTML design, human geography - AP, human sexuality, Islamic history, Italian, jazz, Latin, Latin American history, Latin-AP, mathematics, military history, music, music theory, philosophy, photography, physics, physics-AP, politics, psychology, Russian history, Spanish, Spanish-AP, studio art, studio art-AP, theater, trigonometry, U.S. history-AP, urban studies, video, Web site design, woodworking, world history, world literature, writing.

Graduation Requirements Arts and fine arts (art, music, dance, drama), English, foreign language, mathematics, physical education (includes health), science, social studies (includes history), swimming, grade 12 community service project.

Special Academic Programs Advanced Placement exam preparation; honors section; independent study; term-away projects; study abroad.

College Admission Counseling 130 students graduated in 2011; all went to college, including Brown University; Georgetown University; Harvard University; Princeton University; Wesleyan University; Yale University. Mean SAT critical reading: 692, mean SAT math: 695, mean SAT writing: 705, mean combined SAT: 2092, mean composite ACT: 31.

Student Life Upper grades have specified standards of dress, student council, honor system. Discipline rests equally with students and faculty.

Summer Programs Remediation, enrichment, advancement, ESL, sports, art/fine arts, rigorous outdoor training, computer instruction programs offered; session focuses on academics and athletics; held on campus; accepts boys and girls; open to students from other schools. 220 students usually enrolled. 2012 schedule: June 25 to August 3. Application deadline: none.

Tuition and Aid Day student tuition: $32,100. Tuition installment plan (Academic Management Services Plan, Key Tuition Payment Plan). Need-based scholarship grants available. In 2011–12, 17% of upper-school students received aid. Total amount of financial aid awarded in 2011–12: $2,500,000.

Admissions Traditional secondary-level entrance grade is 9. For fall 2011, 245 students applied for upper-level admission, 134 were accepted, 73 enrolled. ISEE or SSAT required. Deadline for receipt of application materials: January 15. Application fee required: $75. On-campus interview required.

Athletics Interscholastic: baseball (boys), basketball (b,g), crew (b,g), cross-country running (b,g), diving (b,g), fencing (b,g), field hockey (g), football (b), independent competitive sports (b,g), indoor track (b), lacrosse (b,g), soccer (b,g), softball (g), squash (b,g), swimming and diving (b,g), tennis (b,g), track and field (b,g), volleyball (g), wrestling (b); intramural: independent competitive sports (b,g); coed interscholastic: aquatics, golf, independent competitive sports, skydiving, water polo, winter (indoor) track; coed intramural: aerobics, aerobics/dance, aerobics/Nautilus, ballet, basketball, climbing, cooperative games, dance, fencing, fitness, floor hockey, Frisbee, independent competitive sports, Nautilus, outdoor adventure, project adventure, ropes courses, running, soccer, swimming and diving, tennis, volleyball, weight lifting, weight training, wilderness, yoga. 5 coaches, 3 athletic trainers.

Computers Computers are regularly used in art, English, foreign language, history, mathematics, science classes. Computer network features include on-campus library services, Internet access, wireless campus network, Internet filtering or blocking technology. Campus intranet and student e-mail accounts are available to students. The school has a published electronic and media policy.

Contact Ms. Gena Eggert, Administrative Assistant to Director of Admissions. 203-397-1001 Ext. 211. Fax: 203-389-2249. E-mail: admissions@hopkins.edu. Web site: www.hopkins.edu.

HORIZON CHRISTIAN ACADEMY JUNIOR/SENIOR HIGH SCHOOL

5331 Mt. Alifan Drive

San Diego, California 92111

Head of School: Dr. F. Chapin Marsh III

General Information Coeducational day college-preparatory school, affiliated with Christian faith. Founded: 1992. Approved or accredited by Association of Christian Schools International, Western Association of Schools and Colleges, and California Department of Education. Upper school average class size: 25.

College Admission Counseling Colleges students went to include Biola University.

Student Life Upper grades have uniform requirement. Discipline rests primarily with faculty.

Admissions WRAT required. Application fee required: $350. On-campus interview required.

Athletics Interscholastic: baseball (boys, girls), basketball (b,g), cheering (g), cross-country running (b,g), curling (g), flag football (b), football (b), golf (b,g), soccer (b,g), surfing (b,g), volleyball (g), wilderness (b,g).

Contact Mrs. Katie Ramirez, Director of Admissions/Registrar. . 858-244-0376. E-mail: kramirez@horizonsd.org. Web site: www.horizonsd.org/jr_sr_high_school.asp.

THE HOTCHKISS SCHOOL

11 Interlaken Road

PO Box 800

Lakeville, Connecticut 06039

Head of School: Mr. Malcolm H. McKenzie

General Information Coeducational boarding and day college-preparatory school. Grades 9–PG. Founded: 1891. Setting: rural. Nearest major city is Hartford. Students are housed in single-sex dormitories. 810-acre campus. 80 buildings on campus. Approved or accredited by Connecticut Association of Independent Schools, New England Association of Schools and Colleges, The Association of Boarding Schools, and Connecticut Department of Education. Member of National Association of Independent Schools and Secondary School Admission Test Board. Endowment: $380.3 million. Total enrollment: 599. Upper school average class size: 12. Upper school faculty-student ratio: 1:6. There are 168 required school days per year for Upper School students. Upper School students typically attend 6 days per week. The average school day consists of 6 hours and 50 minutes.

Upper School Student Profile Grade 9: 103 students (48 boys, 55 girls); Grade 10: 152 students (70 boys, 82 girls); Grade 11: 166 students (80 boys, 86 girls); Grade 12: 160 students (77 boys, 83 girls); Postgraduate: 18 students (17 boys, 1 girl). 93% of students are boarding students. 19% are state residents. 40 states are represented in upper school student body. 18% are international students. International students from Canada, China, Colombia, Hong Kong, Republic of Korea, and Singapore; 21 other countries represented in student body.

Faculty School total: 115. In upper school: 63 men, 52 women; 91 have advanced degrees; 103 reside on campus.

Subjects Offered 3-dimensional design, acting, advanced math, Advanced Placement courses, advanced studio art-AP, algebra, American history, American history-AP, American literature, American studies, anatomy and physiology, Ancient Greek, ancient history, architecture, art, art history-AP, astronomy, bioethics, biology, biology-AP, calculus, calculus-AP, ceramics, chemistry, chemistry-AP, China/Japan history, Chinese, chorus, classics, college counseling, comparative government and politics-AP, computer programming, computer science, computer science-AP, conceptual physics, constitutional history of U.S., creative writing, dance, digital photography, discrete mathematics, drama, drawing, economics, economics-AP, English, English-AP, environmental science, environmental science-AP, ethics, European history, European history-AP, expository writing, fine arts, French, French language-AP, French literature-AP, geometry, German, history of music, Holocaust, humanities, independent study, jazz dance, jazz ensemble, Latin, Latin American history, Latin-AP, limnology, mathematics, music, music history, music technology, music theory, music theory-AP, musical productions, non-Western literature, orchestra, organic chemistry, philosophy, photography, physics, physics-AP, playwriting, pre-calculus, public speaking, religion, science, Spanish, Spanish language-AP, Spanish literature-AP, statistics-AP, studio art, theater, trigonometry, video, voice, world literature, writing.

Graduation Requirements American history, arts and fine arts (art, music, dance, drama), English, foreign language, mathematics, science.

Special Academic Programs Advanced Placement exam preparation; honors section; independent study; term-away projects; study abroad; academic accommodation for the gifted, the musically talented, and the artistically talented.

College Admission Counseling 170 students graduated in 2011; all went to college, including Bucknell University; Georgetown University; Harvard University; Hobart and William Smith Colleges; Princeton University; Yale University. Median SAT critical reading: 620, median SAT math: 640, median SAT writing: 630, median combined SAT: 1890, median composite ACT: 29. 61% scored over 600 on SAT critical reading, 70% scored over 600 on SAT math, 65% scored over 600 on SAT writing, 64% scored over 1800 on combined SAT, 75% scored over 26 on composite ACT.

Student Life Upper grades have specified standards of dress, student council. Discipline rests equally with students and faculty.

Summer Programs Art/fine arts programs offered; session focuses on chamber music, environmental studies; held on campus; accepts boys and girls; open to students from other schools. 92 students usually enrolled. 2012 schedule: July 1 to July 22. Application deadline: none.

Tuition and Aid Day student tuition: $38,650; 7-day tuition and room/board: $45,350. Tuition installment plan (Tuition Management Systems (formerly Key Tuition Plan)). Need-based scholarship grants, need-based loans available. In 2011–12, 37% of upper-school students received aid. Total amount of financial aid awarded in 2011–12: $8,282,237.

Admissions Traditional secondary-level entrance grade is 9. For fall 2011, 1,980 students applied for upper-level admission, 322 were accepted, 187 enrolled. ACT, ISEE, PSAT, SAT, or ACT for applicants to grade 11 and 12, SSAT or TOEFL required. Deadline for receipt of application materials: January 15. Application fee required: $65. Interview required.

Athletics Interscholastic: baseball (boys), basketball (b,g), cross-country running (b,g), diving (b,g), field hockey (g), football (b), golf (b,g), ice hockey (b,g), lacrosse (b,g), soccer (b,g), softball (g), squash (b,g), swimming and diving (b,g), tennis (b,g), touch football (b), track and field (b,g), volleyball (b,g), water polo (b), wrestling (b); coed interscholastic: Frisbee, sailing, ultimate Frisbee; coed intramural: aerobics, aerobics/Nautilus, ballet, basketball, canoeing/kayaking, climbing, combined training, dance, drill team, fitness, fitness walking, Frisbee, golf, hiking/backpacking, ice hockey, jogging, Nautilus, outdoor education, paddle tennis, physical fitness, physical training, rock climbing, running, squash, strength & conditioning, tennis, ultimate Frisbee, volleyball, walking, wall climbing, water polo, weight lifting, yoga. 2 coaches, 2 athletic trainers.

Computers Computers are regularly used in all academic classes. Computer network features include on-campus library services, online commercial services, Internet access, wireless campus network, Internet filtering or blocking technology. Campus intranet, student e-mail accounts, and computer access in designated common areas are available to students. Students grades are available online. The school has a published electronic and media policy.

Contact Ms. Rachael N. Beare, Dean of Admission and Financial Aid. 860-435-3102. Fax: 860-435-0042. E-mail: admission@hotchkiss.org. Web site: www.hotchkiss.org.

HOUGHTON ACADEMY

9790 Thayer Street

Houghton, New York 14744

Head of School: Mr. Scott Frazier and Mr. Dale Shatto

General Information Coeducational boarding and day college-preparatory, arts, religious studies, and ESL school, affiliated with Wesleyan Church. Boarding grades 9–PG, day grades 6–PG. Founded: 1883. Setting: rural. Nearest major city is Buffalo. Students are housed in single-sex dormitories and staff homes. 25-acre campus. 6 buildings on campus. Approved or accredited by Association of Christian Schools International, Middle States Association of Colleges and Schools, The Association of Boarding Schools, and New York Department of Education. Member of National Association of Independent Schools. Endowment: $90,000. Total enrollment: 142. Upper school average class size: 16. Upper school faculty-student ratio: 1:8. There are 177 required school days per year for Upper School students. Upper School students typically attend 5 days per week. The average school day consists of 6 hours and 30 minutes.

Upper School Student Profile Grade 9: 20 students (12 boys, 8 girls); Grade 10: 25 students (12 boys, 13 girls); Grade 11: 30 students (20 boys, 10 girls); Grade 12: 36 students (18 boys, 18 girls). 59% of students are boarding students. 42% are state residents. 2 states are represented in upper school student body. 57% are international students. International students from China, Nigeria, Republic of Korea, and Viet Nam; 5 other countries represented in student body. 25% of students are members of Wesleyan Church.

Faculty School total: 22. In upper school: 11 men, 11 women; 14 have advanced degrees; 3 reside on campus.

Subjects Offered Algebra, American history, American literature, art, band, Bible, Bible studies, biology, business, business skills, calculus, chemistry, chorus, community service, computer science, creative writing, desktop publishing, driver education, earth science, economics, English, English literature, environmental science, ESL, ethics, fine arts, geography, geometry, government/civics, grammar, history, home economics, industrial arts, international relations, mathematics, music, photography, physical education, physics, science, social sciences, social studies, Spanish, speech, trigonometry, word processing, world history, writing.

Graduation Requirements Arts and fine arts (art, music, dance, drama), Bible, electives, English, mathematics, physical education (includes health), science, social studies (includes history).

Special Academic Programs 4 Advanced Placement exams for which test preparation is offered; honors section; independent study; study at local college for college credit; ESL.

College Admission Counseling 43 students graduated in 2011; all went to college, including Drexel University; Grove City College; Houghton College; Michigan State University; State University of New York at Binghamton; Stony Brook University, State University of New York. Median SAT critical reading: 440, median SAT math: 660, median SAT writing: 520, median combined SAT: 1550, median composite ACT: 21. 11% scored over 600 on SAT critical reading, 67% scored over 600 on SAT math, 16% scored over 600 on SAT writing, 23% scored over 1800 on combined SAT, 13% scored over 26 on composite ACT.

Student Life Upper grades have specified standards of dress, student council. Discipline rests primarily with faculty. Attendance at religious services is required.

Tuition and Aid Tuition installment plan (FACTS Tuition Payment Plan). Need-based scholarship grants available. In 2011–12, 25% of upper-school students received aid. Total amount of financial aid awarded in 2011–12: $95,000.

Admissions Traditional secondary-level entrance grade is 9. For fall 2011, 121 students applied for upper-level admission, 68 were accepted, 36 enrolled. PSAT or SAT for applicants to grade 11 and 12, SLEP, SSAT or TOEFL required. Deadline for receipt of application materials: February 17. Application fee required: $50. Interview required.

Athletics Interscholastic: basketball (boys, girls), cheering (g), soccer (b), volleyball (g); intramural: badminton (b,g), basketball (b,g), floor hockey (b,g), golf (b,g), indoor soccer (b,g), paddle tennis (b,g), racquetball (b,g), skiing (downhill) (b,g), soccer (b,g), table tennis (b,g), tennis (b,g), volleyball (b,g); coed interscholastic: golf; coed intramural: badminton, ball hockey, indoor soccer, paddle tennis, skiing (downhill), softball, table tennis. 2 PE instructors, 9 coaches, 1 athletic trainer.

Computers Computers are regularly used in accounting, Bible studies, college planning, English, graphic design, keyboarding, mathematics, multimedia, SAT preparation, science, word processing, yearbook classes. Computer network features include on-campus library services, Internet access, Internet filtering or blocking technology, electronic access to Houghton College Library holdings. Computer access in designated common areas is available to students. Students grades are available online. The school has a published electronic and media policy.

Contact Mr. Ronald J. Bradbury, Director of Admissions. 585-567-8115. Fax: 585-567-8048. E-mail: admissions@houghtonacademy.org. Web site: www.houghtonacademy.org.

THE HOWARD SCHOOL

Atlanta, Georgia

See Special Needs Schools section.

THE HOWE SCHOOL

PO Box 240

Howe, Indiana 46746

Head of School: Mr. David Watson

General Information Coeducational boarding and day college-preparatory, religious studies, bilingual studies, Junior ROTC, and military school, affiliated with Episcopal Church. Grades 5–12. Founded: 1884. Setting: rural. Nearest major city is South Bend. Students are housed in single-sex dormitories. 100-acre campus. 15 buildings on campus. Approved or accredited by Independent Schools Association of the Central States, North Central Association of Colleges and Schools, The Association of Boarding Schools, and Indiana Department of Education. Member of National Association of Independent Schools. Total enrollment: 114. Upper school average class size: 10. Upper school faculty-student ratio: 1:9. There are 180 required school days per year for Upper School students. Upper School students typically attend 5 days per week. The average school day consists of 5 hours and 50 minutes.

Upper School Student Profile Grade 9: 14 students (14 boys); Grade 10: 22 students (18 boys, 4 girls); Grade 11: 31 students (24 boys, 7 girls); Grade 12: 22 students (18 boys, 4 girls). 99% of students are boarding students. 18% are state residents. 13 states are represented in upper school student body. 17% are international students. International students from Barbados, China, Republic of Korea, and Rwanda. 4% of students are members of Episcopal Church.

Faculty School total: 25. In upper school: 11 men, 9 women; 5 have advanced degrees; 6 reside on campus.

Subjects Offered Accounting, algebra, American history, American literature, band, biology, biology-AP, broadcasting, cabinet making, calculus, calculus-AP, chemistry, chemistry-AP, chorus, comparative religion, computer graphics, computer programming, drafting, economics, English, English language and composition-AP, English literature, environmental science, French, geography, geometry, German, government/civics, grammar, history, industrial arts, journalism, JROTC, leadership, mathematics, music, physical education, physics, pre-algebra, pre-calculus, religion, science, social studies, sociology, Spanish, speech, speech communications, trigonometry, world geography, world history, world literature, yearbook.

Graduation Requirements Computer education, English, foreign language, JROTC, leadership, mathematics, physical education (includes health), religion (includes Bible studies and theology), science, social studies (includes history).

Special Academic Programs Advanced Placement exam preparation; honors section; accelerated programs; study at local college for college credit; ESL (9 students enrolled).

College Admission Counseling 28 students graduated in 2010; 26 went to college, including Adrian College; Lake Superior State University; Michigan State University; Rose-Hulman Institute of Technology; The Citadel, The Military College of South Carolina; The College of Wooster. Other: 2 had other specific plans.

Student Life Upper grades have uniform requirement, student council, honor system. Discipline rests primarily with faculty. Attendance at religious services is required.

Tuition and Aid Day student tuition: $16,160; 7-day tuition and room/board: $26,800. Tuition installment plan (monthly payment plans). Tuition reduction for siblings, need-based scholarship grants available. In 2010–11, 38% of upper-school students received aid. Total amount of financial aid awarded in 2010–11: $187,865.

Admissions Traditional secondary-level entrance grade is 9. For fall 2010, 62 students applied for upper-level admission, 47 were accepted, 33 enrolled. OLSAT, Stanford Achievement Test and TOEFL or SLEP required. Deadline for receipt of application materials: none. Application fee required: $100. Interview recommended.

Athletics Interscholastic: baseball (boys), basketball (b,g), football (b), tennis (b,g), track and field (b,g), volleyball (g), wrestling (b); intramural: baseball (b), football (b), physical training (b), softball (b); coed interscholastic: basketball, golf, JROTC drill, riflery, soccer; coed intramural: basketball, horseback riding, physical fitness, soccer, swimming and diving, volleyball. 1 PE instructor, 1 coach.

Computers Computers are regularly used in English, foreign language, JROTC, mathematics, newspaper, science, yearbook classes. Computer network features include on-campus library services, Internet access, wireless campus network, Internet filtering or blocking technology, CAD, Microsoft Office. Campus intranet and student e-mail accounts are available to students. Students grades are available online.

Contact Mr. Charles Grady, Director of Admissions. 260-562-2131 Ext. 221. Fax: 260-562-3678. E-mail: cgrady@thehoweschool.org. Web site: www.thehoweschool.org.

HUMANEX ACADEMY

Englewood, Colorado

See Special Needs Schools section.

THE HUN SCHOOL OF PRINCETON

176 Edgerstoune Road

Princeton, New Jersey 08540

Head of School: Jonathan Brougham

General Information Coeducational boarding and day college-preparatory school. Boarding grades 9–PG, day grades 6–PG. Founded: 1914. Setting: small town. Nearest major city is New York, NY. Students are housed in single-sex dormitories. 45-acre campus. 7 buildings on campus. Approved or accredited by Middle States Association of Colleges and Schools, New Jersey Association of Independent Schools, and The Association of Boarding Schools. Member of National Association of Independent Schools and Secondary School Admission Test Board. Endowment: $12 million. Total enrollment: 597. Upper school average class size: 13. Upper school faculty-student ratio: 1:8.

Upper School Student Profile Grade 9: 106 students (56 boys, 50 girls); Grade 10: 128 students (73 boys, 55 girls); Grade 11: 134 students (84 boys, 50 girls); Grade 12: 121 students (75 boys, 46 girls); Postgraduate: 13 students (12 boys, 1 girl). 30% of students are boarding students. 14 states are represented in upper school student body. 13% are international students. International students from Bahrain, Republic of Korea, Russian Federation, Saudi Arabia, Taiwan, and Venezuela; 20 other countries represented in student body.

Faculty School total: 117. In upper school: 60 men, 57 women; 48 have advanced degrees; 29 reside on campus.

Subjects Offered 3-dimensional art, 3-dimensional design, advanced computer applications, Advanced Placement courses, advanced TOEFL/grammar, algebra, American government, American history, American history-AP, American literature, anatomy, architectural drawing, architecture, art, art history, art history-AP, astrophysics, biology, biology-AP, calculus, calculus-AP, ceramics, chemistry, chemistry-AP, chorus, community service, computer programming, computer science, drama, driver education, economics, engineering, English, English-AP, ESL, European history, fine arts, forensics, French, French-AP, geometry, government/civics, health, history, interdisciplinary studies, jazz band, Latin, Latin-AP, marine biology, mathematics, mechanical drawing, music, photography, physical education, physics, physics-AP, physiology, public speaking, science, social studies, Spanish, Spanish-AP, statistics-AP, television, theater, trigonometry, U.S. history-AP, video, video film production, world history.

Graduation Requirements Arts and fine arts (art, music, dance, drama), computer science, English, foreign language, health, history, mathematics, science, 10-20 hours of community service per year, summer reading, extra-curricular activities.

Special Academic Programs Advanced Placement exam preparation; honors section; academic accommodation for the gifted; ESL (35 students enrolled).

College Admission Counseling 151 students graduated in 2010; 149 went to college, including Boston University; Lehigh University; Penn State University Park; Princeton University; Syracuse University. Other: 2 entered military service. Median SAT critical reading: 590, median SAT math: 620, median SAT writing: 610, median composite ACT: 27.

Student Life Upper grades have specified standards of dress, student council, honor system. Discipline rests equally with students and faculty.

Tuition and Aid Day student tuition: $30,560; 7-day tuition and room/board: $44,420. Tuition installment plan (Academic Management Services Plan). Merit scholarship grants, need-based scholarship grants, prepGATE loans available. In 2010–11, 25% of upper-school students received aid; total upper-school merit-scholarship money awarded: $50,000. Total amount of financial aid awarded in 2010–11: $2,500,000.

Admissions Traditional secondary-level entrance grade is 9. PSAT or SAT for applicants to grade 11 and 12, SSAT or TOEFL required. Deadline for receipt of application materials: January 31. Application fee required: $50. Interview required.

Athletics Interscholastic: baseball (boys), basketball (b,g), crew (b,g), cross-country running (b,g), fencing (b,g), field hockey (g), football (b), lacrosse (b,g), soccer (b,g), softball (g), tennis (b,g); intramural: dance squad (g), soccer (b,g), weight training (b,g); coed interscholastic: golf, ice hockey, swimming and diving, track and field; coed intramural: aerobics/dance, aerobics/Nautilus, ballet, basketball, cross-country running, dance, fitness, flag football, Frisbee, jogging, Nautilus, paint ball, physical fitness, running, skiing (downhill), strength & conditioning, touch football, ultimate Frisbee, volleyball, weight lifting. 3 coaches, 1 athletic trainer.

Computers Computers are regularly used in all academic classes. Computer network features include on-campus library services, online commercial services, Internet access, wireless campus network, Internet filtering or blocking technology. Campus intranet and student e-mail accounts are available to students. The school has a published electronic and media policy.

Contact Mr. Steven C. Bristol, Director of Admissions. 609-921-7600. Fax: 609-279-9398. E-mail: admiss@hunschool.org. Web site: www.hunschool.org.

HUNTINGTON-SURREY SCHOOL

4804 Grover Avenue

Austin, Texas 78756

Head of School: Dr. Light Bailey German

General Information Coeducational day college-preparatory, arts, and writing, theater arts school. Grades 8–12. Founded: 1973. Setting: urban. 1 building on campus. Approved or accredited by Southern Association of Colleges and Schools and Texas Department of Education. Total enrollment: 36. Upper school average class size: 8. Upper school faculty-student ratio: 1:4. There are 160 required school days per year for Upper School students. Upper School students typically attend 5 days per week. The average school day consists of 4 hours and 45 minutes.

Upper School Student Profile Grade 9: 3 students (3 girls); Grade 10: 5 students (4 boys, 1 girl); Grade 11: 14 students (11 boys, 3 girls); Grade 12: 10 students (7 boys, 3 girls).

Faculty School total: 20. In upper school: 7 men, 13 women; 10 have advanced degrees.

Subjects Offered Algebra, art, biology, calculus, chemistry, college planning, comparative religion, creative drama, discrete mathematics, drama, ecology, environmental systems, English, film history, French, geometry, German, history, Latin, literature, math analysis, math review, mathematics, philosophy, physical science, physics, portfolio art, pre-algebra, pre-calculus, SAT preparation, senior science survey, social studies, Spanish, student publications, study skills, theater arts, trigonometry, U.S. history, work-study, world history, writing.

Graduation Requirements American literature, biology, British literature, mathematics, world history, world literature, writing, senior research project, school exit examinations: assertion with proof essay exam and mathematical competency exam, senior advisory course.

Special Academic Programs Accelerated programs; academic accommodation for the gifted.

College Admission Counseling 16 students graduated in 2011; 14 went to college, including Schreiner University; Southwestern University; St. Edward's University; Texas State University–San Marcos; Texas Tech University; The University of Texas at Austin. Other: 2 went to work. Median SAT critical reading: 540, median SAT math: 550, median SAT writing: 540, median combined SAT: 1630. 25% scored over 600 on SAT critical reading, 25% scored over 600 on SAT math, 25% scored over 600 on SAT writing, 25% scored over 1800 on combined SAT.

Student Life Upper grades have student council, honor system. Discipline rests primarily with faculty.

Summer Programs Remediation, enrichment, advancement programs offered; session focuses on one-on-one teaching, or small classes; held on campus; accepts boys and girls; open to students from other schools. 12 students usually enrolled. 2012 schedule: June 11 to July 27. Application deadline: May 7.

Tuition and Aid Day student tuition: $9000. Tuition installment plan (monthly payment plans).

Admissions Traditional secondary-level entrance grade is 9. For fall 2011, 11 students applied for upper-level admission, 9 were accepted, 9 enrolled. Deadline for receipt of application materials: none. No application fee required. On-campus interview required.

Computers Computers are regularly used in study skills, writing classes. Computer resources include study hall computers and printers (available for student use). Computer access in designated common areas is available to students.

Contact Ms. Johni Walker-Little, Assistant Director. 512-478-4743. Fax: 512-457-0235. Web site: www.huntingtonsurrey.com.

HYDE SCHOOL

PO Box 237

150 Route 169

Woodstock, Connecticut 06281

Head of School: Laura Gauld

General Information Coeducational boarding and day college-preparatory and general academic school. Grades 9–12. Founded: 1996. Setting: rural. Nearest major city is Providence, RI. Students are housed in single-sex dormitories. 120-acre campus. 7 buildings on campus. Approved or accredited by Association of Independent Schools in New England, New England Association of Schools and Colleges, The Association of Boarding Schools, and Connecticut Department of Education. Member of National Association of Independent Schools. Endowment: $8 million. Total enrollment: 178. Upper school average class size: 12. Upper school faculty-student ratio: 1:12.

Upper School Student Profile Grade 9: 9 students (8 boys, 1 girl); Grade 10: 28 students (18 boys, 10 girls); Grade 11: 52 students (36 boys, 16 girls); Grade 12: 60 students (38 boys, 22 girls); Postgraduate: 2 students (2 boys). 98% of students are boarding students. 24% are state residents. 21 states are represented in upper school student body. 21% are international students. International students from Canada, China, Japan, Nigeria, and Republic of Korea.

Faculty School total: 27. In upper school: 17 men, 10 women; 11 have advanced degrees; all reside on campus.

Subjects Offered 20th century history, advanced chemistry, Advanced Placement courses, algebra, athletics, biology, calculus, calculus-AP, character education, chemistry, English, English language and composition-AP, English language-AP, English literature, environmental science-AP, ethics, geometry, global issues, independent study, media arts, physics, pre-calculus, Spanish, Spanish-AP, sports, U.S. history, U.S. history-AP, wilderness education, wilderness experience.

Graduation Requirements Electives, English, foreign language, mathematics, science, social studies (includes history), Hyde's graduation requirements embody academic achievement and character development. Character growth is determined through an intense 40-hour, evaluation process involving all members of the senior class and faculty. All students make a speech at graduation representing their principles.

Special Academic Programs 5 Advanced Placement exams for which test preparation is offered; honors section; independent study; remedial reading and/or remedial writing; remedial math; ESL (6 students enrolled).

College Admission Counseling 47 students graduated in 2011; 44 went to college, including Abilene Christian University; Northeastern University; University of California, Berkeley; University of California, Santa Barbara. Other: 1 went to work, 1 entered military service, 1 entered a postgraduate year. Median SAT critical reading: 550, median SAT math: 525, median SAT writing: 530, median combined SAT: 1605, median composite ACT: 20.

Student Life Upper grades have specified standards of dress, honor system. Discipline rests equally with students and faculty.

Summer Programs Remediation, enrichment, sports, art/fine arts, rigorous outdoor training programs offered; session focuses on orientation for the fall and summer enrichment; held both on and off campus; held at Hyde's Wilderness Campus in Eustis, ME, and on Seguin Island off the coast of Maine; accepts boys and girls; open to students from other schools. 50 students usually enrolled. 2012 schedule: July 3 to July 31. Application deadline: none.

Tuition and Aid Day student tuition: $24,200; 5-day tuition and room/board: $46,700; 7-day tuition and room/board: $46,700. Tuition reduction for siblings, need-based scholarship grants available. In 2011–12, 25% of upper-school students received aid. Total amount of financial aid awarded in 2011–12: $258,000.

Admissions Traditional secondary-level entrance grade is 11. For fall 2011, 151 students applied for upper-level admission, 106 were accepted, 94 enrolled. Deadline for receipt of application materials: none. Application fee required: $100. Interview required.

Athletics Interscholastic: basketball (boys, girls), cross-country running (b,g), football (b), lacrosse (b,g), soccer (b,g), tennis (b,g), track and field (b,g), wrestling (b); coed interscholastic: equestrian sports, ropes courses, wrestling; coed intramural: backpacking, canoeing/kayaking, climbing, hiking/backpacking, outdoor adventure, outdoor skills, ropes courses, wilderness. 2 athletic trainers.

Computers Computer network features include on-campus library services, online commercial services, Internet access, Internet filtering or blocking technology. Student e-mail accounts are available to students. The school has a published electronic and media policy.

Contact Jason Warnick, Director of Admission. 860-963-4736. Fax: 860-928-0612. E-mail: jwarnick@hyde.edu. Web site: www.hyde.edu.

HYDE SCHOOL

616 High Street

Bath, Maine 04530

Head of School: Don MacMillan

General Information Coeducational boarding and day college-preparatory and arts school. Grades 9–12. Founded: 1966. Setting: small town. Nearest major city is Portland. Students are housed in single-sex dormitories. 145-acre campus. 32 buildings on campus. Approved or accredited by Association of Independent Schools in New England, Independent Schools of Northern New England, New England Association of Schools and Colleges, and The Association of Boarding Schools. Member of National Association of Independent Schools. Endowment: $16.5 million. Total enrollment: 143. Upper school average class size: 7. Upper school faculty-student ratio: 1:6. There are 191 required school days per year for Upper School students. Upper School students typically attend 6 days per week. The average school day consists of 7 hours.

Upper School Student Profile Grade 9: 7 students (3 boys, 4 girls); Grade 10: 20 students (15 boys, 5 girls); Grade 11: 52 students (38 boys, 14 girls); Grade 12: 46 students (24 boys, 22 girls); Postgraduate: 4 students (3 boys, 1 girl). 99% of students are boarding students. 21% are state residents. 27 states are represented in upper school student body. 21% are international students. International students from Canada, China, Democratic People's Republic of Korea, Rwanda, Spain, and United Kingdom; 7 other countries represented in student body.

Faculty School total: 23. In upper school: 12 men, 7 women; 16 have advanced degrees; 21 reside on campus.

Subjects Offered 20th century history, 3-dimensional design, acting, advanced biology, advanced chemistry, advanced math, Advanced Placement courses, advanced studio art-AP, advanced TOEFL/grammar, algebra, American government, American history, American history-AP, American literature-AP, ancient history, art, backpacking, band, biology, biology-AP, calculus, calculus-AP, chemistry, chemistry-AP, Chinese, college admission preparation, college counseling, college placement, college planning, college writing, communication skills, communications, comparative government and politics, comparative government and politics-AP, composition-AP, creative writing, early childhood, economics, English, European history, geometry, government, history, music, physical education, physics-AP, pre-calculus, public policy, religion and culture, Spanish, statistics, technical theater, U.S. history, U.S. history-AP.

Graduation Requirements Electives, English, foreign language, history, mathematics, science, Hyde's graduation requirements embody academic achievement and character development. Character growth is determined through an intense 40-hour, evaluation process involving all members of the senior class and faculty. All students make a speech at graduation representing their principles.

Special Academic Programs Honors section; independent study; study at local college for college credit; academic accommodation for the gifted, the musically talented, and the artistically talented; remedial reading and/or remedial writing; remedial math; programs in English, mathematics, general development for dyslexic students; ESL (18 students enrolled).

College Admission Counseling 53 students graduated in 2011; 51 went to college, including Brandeis University; Columbia University; Cornell University; Stanford University; Tufts University; United States Military Academy. Other: 1 went to work, 1 entered military service. Mean SAT critical reading: 530, mean SAT math: 520, mean SAT writing: 520, mean combined SAT: 1570, mean composite ACT: 21. 25% scored over 600 on SAT critical reading, 17% scored over 600 on SAT math, 14% scored over 600 on SAT writing, 18% scored over 1800 on combined SAT, 16% scored over 26 on composite ACT.

Student Life Upper grades have specified standards of dress, student council, honor system. Discipline rests equally with students and faculty.

Summer Programs Remediation, enrichment, advancement, sports, art/fine arts, rigorous outdoor training programs offered; session focuses on to offer a unique summer experience for teens; held both on and off campus; held at wilderness preserve in Eustis, ME and on Seguin Island off the coast of Maine and New York, NY, Washington DC, Philadelphia, PA; accepts boys and girls; open to students from other schools. 80 students usually enrolled. 2012 schedule: May 31 to August 31. Application deadline: none.

Tuition and Aid Day student tuition: $24,500; 7-day tuition and room/board: $46,200. Tuition installment plan (monthly payment plans, individually arranged payment plans). Tuition reduction for siblings, merit scholarship grants, need-based scholarship grants available. In 2011–12, 33% of upper-school students received aid. Total amount of financial aid awarded in 2011–12: $1,300,000.

Admissions Traditional secondary-level entrance grade is 9. For fall 2011, 137 students applied for upper-level admission, 83 were accepted, 68 enrolled. Deadline for receipt of application materials: none. Application fee required: $100. Interview required.

Athletics Interscholastic: basketball (boys, girls), crew (b,g), cross-country running (b,g), field hockey (g), football (b), lacrosse (b,g), rowing (b), soccer (b,g), swimming and diving (b,g), tennis (b,g), track and field (b,g), ultimate Frisbee (b); coed interscholastic: aerobics, aerobics/dance, aerobics/Nautilus, aquatics, climbing, dance, hiking/backpacking, indoor track, nordic skiing, rock climbing, ropes courses, wrestling; coed intramural: hiking/backpacking, kayaking, life saving, outdoor adventure, outdoor skills, physical fitness, physical training, project adventure, ropes courses, skateboarding, skiing (downhill), snowshoeing, strength & conditioning, ultimate Frisbee, walking, weight lifting, weight training, wilderness, wilderness survival. 8 coaches, 1 athletic trainer.

Computers Computer network features include on-campus library services, online commercial services, Internet access, wireless campus network, Internet filtering or blocking technology. Student e-mail accounts are available to students. The school has a published electronic and media policy.

Contact Wanda Smith, Admission Assistant. 207-443-7101. Fax: 207-442-9346. E-mail: wsmith@hyde.edu. Web site: www.hyde.edu.

HYMAN BRAND HEBREW ACADEMY OF GREATER KANSAS CITY

5801 West 115th Street

Overland Park, Kansas 66211

Head of School: Mr. Howard Haas

General Information Coeducational day college-preparatory, general academic, and religious studies school, affiliated with Jewish faith. Grades K–12. Founded: 1966. Setting: suburban. Nearest major city is Kansas City, MO. 32-acre campus. 1 building on campus. Approved or accredited by Independent Schools Association of the Central States. Languages of instruction: English and Hebrew. Endowment: $4.3 million. Total enrollment: 240. Upper school average class size: 11. Upper school faculty-student ratio: 1:5. There are 162 required school days per year for Upper School students. Upper School students typically attend 5 days per week. The average school day consists of 7 hours and 45 minutes.

Upper School Student Profile Grade 9: 10 students (4 boys, 6 girls); Grade 10: 17 students (8 boys, 9 girls); Grade 11: 11 students (7 boys, 4 girls); Grade 12: 9 students (5 boys, 4 girls). 100% of students are Jewish.
Faculty School total: 41. In upper school: 9 men, 9 women; 14 have advanced degrees.
Subjects Offered 3-dimensional design, algebra, American government, American history, American history-AP, American literature, anatomy and physiology, art, art history, Bible studies, biology, British literature, calculus-AP, chemistry, community service, computer applications, computer science, digital art, economics, English, English language and composition-AP, English literature, English literature and composition-AP, environmental science, ethics, European history, fine arts, geometry, health, Hebrew, Hebrew scripture, Holocaust seminar, Jewish studies, model United Nations, physical education, physics, statistics-AP, Talmud, trigonometry, U.S. government and politics-AP, world history, world literature, yearbook.
Graduation Requirements Arts and fine arts (art, music, dance, drama), English, foreign language, mathematics, physical education (includes health), religion (includes Bible studies and theology), science, social studies (includes history). Community service is required.
Special Academic Programs 6 Advanced Placement exams for which test preparation is offered; honors section; independent study; study at local college for college credit; academic accommodation for the gifted.
College Admission Counseling 15 students graduated in 2011; 12 went to college, including Clark University; Indiana University Bloomington; The George Washington University; The University of Kansas; Tulane University; Yeshiva University. Other: 3 entered a postgraduate year.
Student Life Upper grades have specified standards of dress, student council. Discipline rests primarily with faculty. Attendance at religious services is required.
Tuition and Aid Day student tuition: $6800. Tuition installment plan (FACTS Tuition Payment Plan). Need-based scholarship grants available. In 2011–12, 43% of upper-school students received aid. Total amount of financial aid awarded in 2011–12: $76,850.
Admissions Traditional secondary-level entrance grade is 9. For fall 2011, 3 students applied for upper-level admission, 3 were accepted, 3 enrolled. Writing sample required. Deadline for receipt of application materials: none. Application fee required: $50.
Athletics Interscholastic: basketball (boys, girls), soccer (b,g), tennis (b,g); coed interscholastic: cross-country running; coed intramural: tennis. 2 PE instructors, 6 coaches.
Computers Computers are regularly used in computer applications, desktop publishing, digital applications, economics, English, humanities, mathematics, newspaper, psychology, religious studies, science, social studies, writing, yearbook classes. Computer network features include on-campus library services, online commercial services, Internet access, wireless campus network. Student e-mail accounts and computer access in designated common areas are available to students. Students grades are available online. The school has a published electronic and media policy.
Contact Mrs. Tamara Lawson Schuster, Director of Admissions. 913-327-8135. Fax: 913-327-8180. E-mail: tschuster@hbha.edu. Web site: www.hbha.edu.

IDYLLWILD ARTS ACADEMY

52500 Temecula Road

PO Box 38

Idyllwild, California 92549

Head of School: Brian Cohen

General Information Coeducational boarding and day college-preparatory and arts school. Grades 9–PG. Founded: 1986. Setting: rural. Nearest major city is Los Angeles. Students are housed in single-sex dormitories. 205-acre campus. 44 buildings on campus. Approved or accredited by California Association of Independent Schools, The Association of Boarding Schools, Western Association of Schools and Colleges, and California Department of Education. Member of National Association of Independent Schools and Secondary School Admission Test Board. Endowment: $3 million. Total enrollment: 295. Upper school average class size: 16. Upper school faculty-student ratio: 1:12. Upper School students typically attend 6 days per week.
Upper School Student Profile Grade 9: 39 students (16 boys, 23 girls); Grade 10: 61 students (28 boys, 33 girls); Grade 11: 77 students (37 boys, 40 girls); Grade 12: 83 students (41 boys, 42 girls); Postgraduate: 4 students (2 boys, 2 girls). 92% of students are boarding students. 38% are state residents. 35 states are represented in upper school student body. 44% are international students. International students from Australia, China, Japan, Mexico, Republic of Korea, and Taiwan; 16 other countries represented in student body.
Faculty School total: 65. In upper school: 24 men, 20 women; 30 have advanced degrees; 23 reside on campus.
Subjects Offered 3-dimensional art, 3-dimensional design, acting, advanced math, algebra, American government, American history, American literature, anatomy, art, art history, audio visual/media, audition methods, ballet, biology, Broadway dance, calculus, career/college preparation, ceramics, chemistry, choir, choral music, choreography, computer graphics, computer science, creative writing, critical studies in film, dance, digital art, directing, drama, drawing and design, economics, English, English literature, ensembles, environmental science, ESL, fiction, film and literature, film and new technologies, film appreciation, film history, film studies, filmmaking, fine arts, French, geography, geometry, government/civics, grammar, history, illustration, improvisation, jazz dance, jazz ensemble, jazz theory, mathematics, multimedia, music, music theater, music theory, musical productions, musical theater dance, orchestra, performing arts, photography, physical education, physics, play production, playwriting and directing, poetry, pottery, printmaking, science, social sciences, social studies, Spanish, tap dance, technical theater, technology/design, theater, video film production, vocal music, voice and diction, voice ensemble, world history, world literature, writing.
Graduation Requirements Art, arts and fine arts (art, music, dance, drama), English, foreign language, mathematics, performing arts, physical education (includes health), science, social sciences, social studies (includes history).
Special Academic Programs Advanced Placement exam preparation; honors section; ESL (45 students enrolled).
College Admission Counseling 68 students graduated in 2011; 66 went to college, including California Institute of the Arts; New York University; The Johns Hopkins University; The Juilliard School; University of California, Los Angeles; University of Rochester. Other: 2 went to work.
Student Life Upper grades have student council. Discipline rests equally with students and faculty.
Summer Programs ESL, art/fine arts programs offered; session focuses on visual and performing arts; held on campus; accepts boys and girls; open to students from other schools. 600 students usually enrolled. 2012 schedule: July 10 to August 19. Application deadline: none.
Tuition and Aid Day student tuition: $36,000; 7-day tuition and room/board: $52,000. Tuition installment plan (Key Tuition Payment Plan, monthly payment plans, individually arranged payment plans, school's own payment plan). Need-based scholarship grants available. In 2011–12, 68% of upper-school students received aid. Total amount of financial aid awarded in 2011–12: $5,054,332.
Admissions Traditional secondary-level entrance grade is 10. For fall 2011, 400 students applied for upper-level admission, 400 were accepted, 295 enrolled. SLEP, SSAT or TOEFL required. Deadline for receipt of application materials: none. Application fee required: $50. Interview required.
Athletics Intramural: aerobics (boys, girls); coed intramural: aerobics, aerobics/dance, aerobics/Nautilus, ballet, basketball, bicycling, billiards, bowling, climbing, combined training, cooperative games, cross-country running, dance, fencing, fitness, Frisbee, hiking/backpacking, jogging, judo, martial arts, modern dance, mountain biking, outdoor activities, outdoor adventure, outdoor education, outdoor recreation, outdoors, physical fitness, physical training, rock climbing, soccer, swimming and diving, tennis, ultimate Frisbee, volleyball, walking, weight training, yoga. 1 PE instructor.
Computers Computers are regularly used in art, design, drafting, drawing and design, English, ESL, graphic design, media production, science classes. Computer resources include on-campus library services, Internet access, wireless campus network, Internet filtering or blocking technology. Computer access in designated common areas is available to students. Students grades are available online. The school has a published electronic and media policy.
Contact Mr. Marek Pramuka, Dean of Admission and Financial Aid. 951-659-2171 Ext. 2223. Fax: 951-659-3168. E-mail: admission@idyllwildarts.org. Web site: www.idyllwildarts.org.

See Display on next page and Close-Up on page 636.

IMMACULATA-LA SALLE HIGH SCHOOL

3601 South Miami Avenue

Miami, Florida 33133

Head of School: Sr. Kim Keraitis, FMA

General Information Coeducational day college-preparatory, arts, business, religious studies, and technology school, affiliated with Roman Catholic Church. Grades 9–12. Founded: 1958. Setting: urban. 13-acre campus. 7 buildings on campus. Approved or accredited by Southern Association of Colleges and Schools, The College Board, and Florida Department of Education. Endowment: $80,200. Total enrollment: 758. Upper school average class size: 24. Upper school faculty-student ratio: 1:15. There are 180 required school days per year for Upper School students. Upper School students typically attend 5 days per week. The average school day consists of 6 hours and 30 minutes.
Upper School Student Profile Grade 9: 187 students (70 boys, 117 girls); Grade 10: 203 students (73 boys, 130 girls); Grade 11: 183 students (67 boys, 116 girls); Grade 12: 185 students (52 boys, 133 girls). 95% of students are Roman Catholic.
Faculty School total: 59. In upper school: 22 men, 32 women; 22 have advanced degrees.
Subjects Offered Advanced Placement courses, African American studies, algebra, American history, American history-AP, analytic geometry, anatomy, art, automated accounting, band, Bible studies, biology, calculus, chemistry, Chinese, choral music, computer programming, computer programming-AP, computer science, desktop publishing, drama, economics, English, European history, fine arts, French, geometry, government/civics, health, history, humanities, Italian, marine biology, mathematics, music appreciation, physical education, physics, psychology, religion, science, social studies, sociology, Spanish, speech, trigonometry, U.S. government and politics-AP, world history.

Graduation Requirements Arts and fine arts (art, music, dance, drama), business skills (includes word processing), computer science, English, foreign language, mathematics, physical education (includes health), religion (includes Bible studies and theology), science, social studies (includes history), 20 hours of community service for each of the 4 years.

Special Academic Programs Advanced Placement exam preparation; honors section; independent study; study at local college for college credit; academic accommodation for the gifted.

College Admission Counseling 170 students graduated in 2011; all went to college, including Barry University; Florida International University; Florida State University; Miami Dade College; University of Central Florida; University of Miami. Mean SAT critical reading: 487, mean SAT math: 483, mean SAT writing: 488, mean combined SAT: 1458, mean composite ACT: 21. 13% scored over 600 on SAT critical reading, 11% scored over 600 on SAT math, 10% scored over 600 on SAT writing, 34% scored over 1800 on combined SAT, 18% scored over 26 on composite ACT.

Student Life Upper grades have uniform requirement, student council. Discipline rests equally with students and faculty. Attendance at religious services is required.

Summer Programs Remediation, enrichment programs offered; session focuses on remediation and enrichment; held on campus; accepts boys and girls; open to students from other schools. 150 students usually enrolled. 2012 schedule: June 18 to July 13. Application deadline: June 11.

Tuition and Aid Day student tuition: $11,000. Tuition installment plan (FACTS Tuition Payment Plan, monthly payment plans, individually arranged payment plans). Paying campus jobs available. In 2011–12, 11% of upper-school students received aid. Total amount of financial aid awarded in 2011–12: $165,000.

Admissions Traditional secondary-level entrance grade is 9. For fall 2011, 441 students applied for upper-level admission, 282 were accepted, 233 enrolled. Catholic High School Entrance Examination or PSAT and SAT for applicants to grade 11 and 12 required. Deadline for receipt of application materials: none. Application fee required: $500. On-campus interview required.

Athletics Interscholastic: baseball (boys), basketball (b,g), bicycling (b,g), cheering (g), cross-country running (b,g), dance team (g), football (b), lacrosse (b), soccer (b,g), softball (g), swimming and diving (b,g), tennis (b,g), track and field (b,g), trap and skeet (b,g), volleyball (g), weight training (b,g), winter soccer (b,g); intramural: football (b), volleyball (g); coed interscholastic: tennis, track and field; coed intramural: acrobics/dance, bicycling, dance, dance team, mountain biking, physical fitness, sailing, table tennis, weight training. 3 PE instructors, 15 coaches, 1 athletic trainer.

Computers Computers are regularly used in business, business applications, economics, French, journalism, mathematics, programming, science, technology, word processing, yearbook classes. Computer network features include on-campus library services, Internet access. Students grades are available online.

Contact Mrs. Nancy Ramirez, Admissions Director. 305-854-2334 Ext. 130. Fax: 305-858-5971. E-mail: admissions@ilsroyals.com. Web site: www.ilsroyals.com.

IMMACULATE CONCEPTION HIGH SCHOOL

258 South Main Street

Lodi, New Jersey 07644-2199

Head of School: Mr. Joseph Robert Azzolino

General Information Girls' day college-preparatory, arts, business, and religious studies school, affiliated with Roman Catholic Church. Grades 9–12. Founded: 1915. Setting: suburban. Nearest major city is Paterson. 3-acre campus. 1 building on campus. Approved or accredited by Middle States Association of Colleges and Schools, National Catholic Education Association, and New Jersey Department of Education. Total enrollment: 162. Upper school average class size: 17. Upper school faculty-student ratio: 1:10. There are 180 required school days per year for Upper School students. Upper School students typically attend 5 days per week. The average school day consists of 6 hours and 21 minutes.

Upper School Student Profile Grade 9: 45 students (45 girls); Grade 10: 39 students (39 girls); Grade 11: 40 students (40 girls); Grade 12: 38 students (38 girls). 85% of students are Roman Catholic.

Faculty School total: 16. In upper school: 3 men, 13 women.

Subjects Offered Advanced math, algebra, American government, American history, American history-AP, American literature, anatomy and physiology, art, Bible studies, biology, British literature, character education, chemistry, communications, computer graphics, computer skills, driver education, English, French, genetics, geometry, health and safety, honors algebra, honors English, honors geometry, honors U.S. history, lab science, musical productions, organic chemistry, performing arts, photography, physical education, physical science, pre-calculus, psychology, religious education, social psychology, Spanish, women in society, world cultures, writing.

Graduation Requirements English, foreign language, lab science, mathematics, physical education (includes health), religious studies, social studies (includes history). Community service is required.

Special Academic Programs 1 Advanced Placement exam for which test preparation is offered; honors section; study at local college for college credit.

College Admission Counseling 38 students graduated in 2011; 37 went to college, including Bergen Community College; Felician College; Ramapo College of New

Jersey; Rutgers, The State University of New Jersey, New Brunswick; Seton Hall University; William Paterson University of New Jersey. Other: 1 had other specific plans. Mean SAT critical reading: 500, mean SAT math: 450, mean SAT writing: 520, mean combined SAT: 1470.

Student Life Upper grades have uniform requirement, student council. Discipline rests primarily with faculty. Attendance at religious services is required.

Summer Programs Enrichment, advancement programs offered; session focuses on Jump Start Program for incoming freshmen; held on campus; accepts girls; not open to students from other schools. 15 students usually enrolled. 2012 schedule: August 6 to August 24. Application deadline: May 20.

Tuition and Aid Day student tuition: $8750. Tuition installment plan (FACTS Tuition Payment Plan, annual payment plan). Tuition reduction for siblings, merit scholarship grants, need-based scholarship grants available. In 2011–12, 27% of upper-school students received aid; total upper-school merit-scholarship money awarded: $54,500. Total amount of financial aid awarded in 2011–12: $73,250.

Admissions Traditional secondary-level entrance grade is 9. For fall 2011, 251 students applied for upper-level admission, 240 were accepted, 37 enrolled. Cooperative Entrance Exam (McGraw-Hill) required. Deadline for receipt of application materials: none. No application fee required. Interview recommended.

Athletics Interscholastic: basketball, cheering, cross-country running, soccer, softball, swimming and diving, tennis, volleyball; intramural: aerobics, basketball, fitness, fitness walking, floor hockey, physical fitness, physical training, tennis, volleyball, walking. 2 PE instructors, 12 coaches, 1 athletic trainer.

Computers Computers are regularly used in graphics, newspaper, photography, word processing, yearbook classes. Computer resources include Internet access, Internet filtering or blocking technology. Computer access in designated common areas is available to students. Students grades are available online. The school has a published electronic and media policy.

Contact Mrs. Sara Simon, Director of Enrollment Management. 973-773-2665. Fax: 973-614-0893. E-mail: ssimon@ichslodi.org. Web site: www.ichslodi.org.

IMMACULATE CONCEPTION SCHOOL

217 Cottage Hill Avenue

Elmhurst, Illinois 60126

Head of School: Pamela M. Levar

General Information Coeducational day college-preparatory, arts, and religious studies school, affiliated with Roman Catholic Church. Grades 9–12. Founded: 1936. Setting: suburban. Nearest major city is Chicago. 3 buildings on campus. Approved or accredited by North Central Association of Colleges and Schools and Illinois Department of Education. Member of National Association of Independent Schools. Total enrollment: 340. Upper school average class size: 18. Upper school faculty-student ratio: 1:12. There are 176 required school days per year for Upper School students. Upper School students typically attend 5 days per week. The average school day consists of 6 hours and 25 minutes.

Upper School Student Profile Grade 9: 85 students (36 boys, 49 girls); Grade 10: 86 students (51 boys, 35 girls); Grade 11: 82 students (40 boys, 42 girls); Grade 12: 87 students (44 boys, 43 girls). 89% of students are Roman Catholic.

Faculty School total: 28. In upper school: 11 men, 17 women; 14 have advanced degrees.

Subjects Offered 3-dimensional art, advanced chemistry, advanced math, algebra, American government, American history, anatomy and physiology, ancient world history, art, biology, biology-AP, British literature, business law, calculus, calculus-AP, campus ministry, career/college preparation, Catholic belief and practice, ceramics, chemistry, chemistry-AP, college counseling, computer applications, computer programming, constitutional history of U.S., consumer education, current events, drawing, ecology, environmental systems, economics, English, English-AP, environmental science, fitness, foreign language, French, geometry, government/civics, health education, honors algebra, honors English, honors geometry, honors U.S. history, humanities, keyboarding, library, musical theater, newspaper, painting, physical education, physics, pre-calculus, psychology, SAT/ACT preparation, sociology, Spanish, speech, student government, trigonometry, U.S. history-AP, yearbook.

Graduation Requirements Algebra, American government, American literature, anatomy and physiology, art, biology, British literature, calculus, Catholic belief and practice, chemistry, computer applications, constitutional history of U.S., consumer education, English, environmental science, foreign language, geometry, grammar, health, history, human biology, language and composition, mathematics, physical science, political science, pre-calculus, theology, trigonometry, U.S. history, world history, 40 hours of Christian service, attendance at retreat.

Special Academic Programs 5 Advanced Placement exams for which test preparation is offered; honors section; study at local college for college credit.

College Admission Counseling 85 students graduated in 2011; 84 went to college, including DePaul University; Illinois State University; Loyola University Chicago; Marquette University; St. Norbert College; University of Illinois at Urbana–Champaign. Other: 1 went to work.

Student Life Upper grades have uniform requirement, student council. Discipline rests primarily with faculty. Attendance at religious services is required.

Summer Programs Sports programs offered; session focuses on sports; held both on and off campus; held at Plunkett Field; accepts boys and girls; not open to students from other schools. 150 students usually enrolled. 2012 schedule: June 15 to July 28.

Tuition and Aid Day student tuition: $8700. Tuition installment plan (SMART Tuition Payment Plan). Tuition reduction for siblings, merit scholarship grants, need-based scholarship grants, merit scholarships (for placement test top scorers), externally funded scholarships (alumni, memorials), Catholic school teacher grants (1/3 reduction) available. In 2011–12, 33% of upper-school students received aid; total upper-school merit-scholarship money awarded: $15,000. Total amount of financial aid awarded in 2011–12: $150,000.

Admissions Traditional secondary-level entrance grade is 9. High School Placement Test (closed version) from Scholastic Testing Service required. Deadline for receipt of application materials: none. No application fee required.

Athletics Interscholastic: baseball (boys), basketball (b,g), bowling (b), cheering (g), cross-country running (b,g), dance team (g), football (b), lacrosse (b), pom squad (g), soccer (g), softball (g), track and field (b,g), volleyball (g), weight lifting (b), weight training (b,g), wrestling (b); coed interscholastic: fishing, golf, winter (indoor) track. 2 PE instructors, 38 coaches, 2 athletic trainers.

Computers Computers are regularly used in business applications, career exploration, college planning, computer applications, library, news writing, science, stock market, yearbook classes. Computer network features include on-campus library services, online commercial services, Internet access, Internet filtering or blocking technology. Computer access in designated common areas is available to students. Students grades are available online. The school has a published electronic and media policy.

Contact Mrs. Sarah Ford, Director of Admissions. 630-530-3484. Fax: 630-530-2290. E-mail: sford@ichsknights.org. Web site: www.ichsknights.org.

IMMACULATE HEART HIGH SCHOOL

625 East Magee Road

Oro Valley, Arizona 85704-7207

Head of School: Sr. Luisa Sanchez

General Information Coeducational day college-preparatory and religious studies school, affiliated with Roman Catholic Church. Grades 9–12. Founded: 1930. Setting: suburban. 5-acre campus. 2 buildings on campus. Approved or accredited by National Catholic Education Association, Western Catholic Education Association, and Arizona Department of Education. Total enrollment: 91. Upper school average class size: 10. Upper school faculty-student ratio: 1:10. There are 180 required school days per year for Upper School students. Upper School students typically attend 5 days per week. The average school day consists of 7 hours.

Upper School Student Profile Grade 9: 19 students (10 boys, 9 girls); Grade 10: 27 students (12 boys, 15 girls); Grade 11: 22 students (6 boys, 16 girls); Grade 12: 23 students (15 boys, 8 girls). 92% of students are Roman Catholic.

Faculty School total: 11. In upper school: 3 men, 8 women; 3 have advanced degrees.

Special Academic Programs International Baccalaureate program; Advanced Placement exam preparation; independent study; study at local college for college credit; ESL (3 students enrolled).

College Admission Counseling 14 students graduated in 2011; all went to college, including Arizona State University; Northern Arizona University; Pima Community College; The University of Arizona.

Student Life Upper grades have uniform requirement, student council, honor system. Discipline rests primarily with faculty. Attendance at religious services is required.

Tuition and Aid Day student tuition: $6400. Tuition installment plan (monthly payment plans). Tuition reduction for siblings, need-based scholarship grants available. In 2011–12, 45% of upper-school students received aid. Total amount of financial aid awarded in 2011–12: $121,000.

Admissions Traditional secondary-level entrance grade is 9. For fall 2011, 27 students applied for upper-level admission, 27 were accepted, 25 enrolled. Deadline for receipt of application materials: none. No application fee required. On-campus interview required.

Athletics Interscholastic: basketball (boys, girls), cheering (g), volleyball (g); coed interscholastic: bowling, cross-country running, golf, soccer, swimming and diving, tennis, track and field; coed intramural: billiards, bowling, skiing (downhill), table tennis. 1 PE instructor, 8 coaches.

Computers Computer network features include on-campus library services, Internet access, wireless campus network, Internet filtering or blocking technology, virtual high school courses for electives, homework online. Campus intranet, student e-mail accounts, and computer access in designated common areas are available to students. Students grades are available online. The school has a published electronic and media policy.

Contact Mr. Daniel Ethridge, Principal/Admissions. 520-297-2851. Fax: 520-797-7374. E-mail: danethridge@ihhschool.org. Web site: www.immaculateheartschool.com.

IMMACULATE HEART HIGH SCHOOL AND MIDDLE SCHOOL

5515 Franklin Avenue

Los Angeles, California 90028-5999

Head of School: Ms. Virginia Hurst

General Information Girls' day college-preparatory school, affiliated with Roman Catholic Church. Grades 6–12. Founded: 1906. Setting: urban. 7-acre campus. 7 buildings on campus. Approved or accredited by Western Association of Schools and Colleges and California Department of Education. Upper school average class size: 22. Upper school faculty-student ratio: 1:18.

Faculty School total: 47. In upper school: 35 have advanced degrees.

Student Life Upper grades have uniform requirement, student council, honor system. Discipline rests primarily with faculty. Attendance at religious services is required.

Admissions High School Placement Test (closed version) from Scholastic Testing Service required. Deadline for receipt of application materials: January 6. Application fee required: $50. On-campus interview required.

Contact Ms. Kristy Suzuki, Director of Admissions. 323-461-3651 Ext. 240. Fax: 323-462-0610. E-mail: knishina@immaculateheart.org. Web site: www.immaculateheart.org.

IMMANUEL CHRISTIAN HIGH SCHOOL

802 6th Avenue N

Lethbridge, Alberta T1H 0S1, Canada

Head of School: Mr. Rob van Spronsen

General Information Coeducational day college-preparatory, general academic, and religious studies school, affiliated with Christian Reformed Church, Reformed Church. Grades 7–12. Founded: 1962. Setting: urban. 4-acre campus. 1 building on campus. Approved or accredited by Christian Schools International and Alberta Department of Education. Language of instruction: English. Total enrollment: 228. Upper school average class size: 22. Upper school faculty-student ratio: 1:19. There are 188 required school days per year for Upper School students. Upper School students typically attend 5 days per week. The average school day consists of 5 hours and 30 minutes.

Upper School Student Profile 70% of students are members of Christian Reformed Church, Reformed.

Faculty School total: 18. In upper school: 10 men, 8 women; 4 have advanced degrees.

Subjects Offered Algebra, art, athletics, basketball, Bible, biology, business applications, calculus, career planning, carpentry, chemistry, choral music, Christian education, Christian ethics, Christian studies, computer applications, drama, English, first aid, food and nutrition, French as a second language, global issues, guidance, health, history, industrial arts, mathematics, science, social studies.

Graduation Requirements Alberta Learning requirements.

Special Academic Programs Independent study.

College Admission Counseling 41 students graduated in 2010; 18 went to college, including Calvin College; Dordt College; Redeemer University College; Trinity Western University; University of Alberta; University of Lethbridge. Other: 22 went to work.

Student Life Upper grades have specified standards of dress, student council, honor system. Discipline rests primarily with faculty. Attendance at religious services is required.

Tuition and Aid Day student tuition: CAN$6500–CAN$7200. Tuition installment plan (monthly payment plans, individually arranged payment plans). Tuition reduction for siblings available. In 2010–11, 0% of upper-school students received aid.

Admissions Traditional secondary-level entrance grade is 10. Deadline for receipt of application materials: none. No application fee required. Interview required.

Athletics Interscholastic: badminton (boys, girls), basketball (b,g), golf (b,g), running (b,g), track and field (b,g), volleyball (b,g); intramural: badminton (b,g), basketball (b,g), outdoor education (b,g), track and field (b,g), volleyball (b,g); coed interscholastic: badminton, cross-country running; coed intramural: badminton, outdoor education, scuba diving. 2 PE instructors.

Computers Computers are regularly used in all classes. Computer network features include on-campus library services, Internet access, wireless campus network, Internet filtering or blocking technology. Student e-mail accounts and computer access in designated common areas are available to students. Students grades are available online. The school has a published electronic and media policy.

Contact Mr. Rob van Spronsen, Principal. 403-328-4783. Fax: 403-327-6333. E-mail: rvanspronsen@immanuelcs.ca. Web site: ichs.icssa.ca.

INCARNATE WORD ACADEMY

609 Crawford

Houston, Texas 77002-3668

Head of School: Ms. Mary Getschow

General Information Girls' day college-preparatory, arts, and religious studies school, affiliated with Roman Catholic Church. Grades 9–12. Founded: 1873. Setting: urban. 2 buildings on campus. Approved or accredited by Southern Association of Colleges and Schools, Texas Catholic Conference, Texas Education Agency, and Texas Department of Education. Total enrollment: 272. Upper school average class size: 13. Upper school faculty-student ratio: 1:13. There are 180 required school days per year for Upper School students. Upper School students typically attend 5 days per week. The average school day consists of 7 hours.

Upper School Student Profile Grade 9: 82 students (82 girls); Grade 10: 69 students (69 girls); Grade 11: 72 students (72 girls); Grade 12: 51 students (51 girls). 85.7% of students are Roman Catholic.

Faculty School total: 26. In upper school: 6 men, 16 women; 15 have advanced degrees.

Subjects Offered Algebra, American government, American history, American history-AP, American literature, American literature-AP, art, biology, biology-AP, British literature, British literature-AP, calculus, chemistry, chemistry-AP, concert choir, drama, English composition, English literature, English literature and composition-AP, English literature-AP, English-AP, English/composition-AP, environmental science-AP, French, government and politics-AP, government-AP, health, history-AP, honors algebra, honors English, honors geometry, honors U.S. history, honors world history, Latin, literature and composition-AP, literature-AP, microeconomics, microeconomics-AP, newspaper, physical education, physics, pre-calculus, psychology, publications, SAT/ACT preparation, social studies, Spanish, Spanish language-AP, Spanish literature-AP, Spanish-AP, theater arts, theater production, theology, trigonometry, U.S. government and politics, U.S. government and politics-AP, U.S. history, U.S. history-AP, U.S. literature, United States government-AP, video and animation, Web site design, world geography, world history, world literature, world religions, world studies, world wide web design, World-Wide-Web publishing, yearbook.

Graduation Requirements 100 hours of community service.

Special Academic Programs Advanced Placement exam preparation; honors section; study at local college for college credit.

College Admission Counseling 54 students graduated in 2010; all went to college, including Baylor University; Texas A&M University; The University of Texas at Austin; University of Houston.

Student Life Upper grades have uniform requirement, student council, honor system. Discipline rests primarily with faculty. Attendance at religious services is required.

Tuition and Aid Day student tuition: $8600. Tuition installment plan (monthly payment plans). Merit scholarship grants, need-based scholarship grants, paying campus jobs available. In 2010–11, 30% of upper-school students received aid; total upper-school merit-scholarship money awarded: $43,850. Total amount of financial aid awarded in 2010–11: $119,606.

Admissions Traditional secondary-level entrance grade is 9. High School Placement Test (closed version) from Scholastic Testing Service or ISEE required. Deadline for receipt of application materials: January 15. Application fee required: $50. On-campus interview recommended.

Athletics Interscholastic: basketball, cheering, cross country running, dance, dance team, golf, running, soccer, softball, track and field, volleyball; intramural: fitness, physical fitness. 2 PE instructors, 6 coaches, 1 athletic trainer.

Computers Computers are regularly used in computer applications, economics, history, keyboarding, mathematics, research skills, science, social studies, technology, Web site design, yearbook classes. Computer network features include on-campus library services, online commercial services, Internet access, wireless campus network, Internet filtering or blocking technology. Students grades are available online. The school has a published electronic and media policy.

Contact Ms. Gianna Leggio, Director of Admissions. 713-227-3637 Ext. 117. Fax: 713-227-1014. E-mail: gleggio@incarnateword.org. Web site: www.incarnateword.org.

INDEPENDENT SCHOOL

8317 East Douglas

Wichita, Kansas 67207

Head of School: Dr. Mary Dickerson

General Information Coeducational day college-preparatory, arts, and technology school. Grades PK–12. Founded: 1980. Setting: suburban. 22-acre campus. 2 buildings on campus. Approved or accredited by Independent Schools Association of the Central States. Language of instruction: Spanish. Total enrollment: 547. Upper school average class size: 15. Upper school faculty-student ratio: 1:10. There are 170 required school days per year for Upper School students. Upper School students typically attend 5 days per week. The average school day consists of 7 hours.

Upper School Student Profile Grade 9: 48 students (22 boys, 26 girls); Grade 10: 45 students (27 boys, 18 girls); Grade 11: 60 students (39 boys, 21 girls); Grade 12: 45 students (23 boys, 22 girls).

Faculty School total: 26. In upper school: 16 men, 10 women; 19 have advanced degrees.
Subjects Offered 3-dimensional art, advanced math, Advanced Placement courses, algebra, American government, American history, American history-AP, American literature, anatomy and physiology, art, biology, biology-AP, British literature, British literature (honors), calculus, calculus-AP, ceramics, chemistry, chemistry-AP, choir, computer applications, computer art, debate, economics, engineering, English literature-AP, film and new technologies, foreign language, forensics, geometry, health, health and wellness, Latin, music, music theory-AP, music-AP, newspaper, physics, physics-AP, psychology, psychology-AP, Spanish, Spanish-AP, statistics-AP, theater, theater arts, trigonometry, U.S. government and politics-AP, Web site design, weight training, yearbook.
Graduation Requirements Algebra, American government, American history, American literature, arts and fine arts (art, music, dance, drama), biology, British literature, chemistry, computer applications, computer literacy, English, foreign language, geography, geometry, humanities, physical education (includes health), world history, world literature, 50 hours of community service.
Special Academic Programs Advanced Placement exam preparation; honors section; independent study; academic accommodation for the gifted, the musically talented, and the artistically talented.
College Admission Counseling 54 students graduated in 2011; all went to college, including Kansas State University; Oklahoma State University; The University of Kansas; Trinity University; University of Tulsa.
Student Life Upper grades have specified standards of dress, student council. Discipline rests primarily with faculty.
Summer Programs Enrichment, advancement, sports, art/fine arts, computer instruction programs offered; held on campus; accepts boys and girls; open to students from other schools.
Tuition and Aid Day student tuition: $9900. Tuition installment plan (monthly payment plans, individually arranged payment plans). Need-based scholarship grants available. In 2011–12, 23% of upper-school students received aid.
Admissions Traditional secondary-level entrance grade is 9. For fall 2011, 30 students applied for upper-level admission, 26 were accepted, 24 enrolled. Admissions testing, non-standardized placement tests and Otis-Lennon Ability or Stanford Achievement Test required. Deadline for receipt of application materials: none. Application fee required: $40. Interview recommended.
Athletics Interscholastic: baseball (boys), basketball (b,g), cheering (g), cross-country running (b,g), dance team (g), football (b), golf (b,g), soccer (b,g), softball (g), strength & conditioning (b,g), swimming and diving (b,g), tennis (b,g), track and field (b,g), volleyball (g), weight training (b,g), wrestling (b); coed interscholastic: strength & conditioning, weight training. 2 PE instructors, 5 coaches, 1 athletic trainer.
Computers Computers are regularly used in art, college planning, economics, English, humanities, introduction to technology, library, literary magazine, mathematics, newspaper, photography, publications, Web site design, yearbook classes. Computer network features include on-campus library services, Internet access, wireless campus network, Internet filtering or blocking technology, homework online. Students grades are available online. The school has a published electronic and media policy.
Contact Ms. Danielle T. Dankey, Director of Admissions. 316-686-0152 Ext. 405. Fax: 316-686-3918. E-mail: danielle.dankey@theindependentschool.com. Web site: www.theindependentschool.com.

INDIAN SPRINGS SCHOOL

190 Woodward Drive

Indian Springs, Alabama 35124

Head of School: Mr. Gareth Vaughan

General Information Coeducational boarding and day college-preparatory and arts school. Boarding grades 9–12, day grades 8–12. Founded: 1952. Setting: suburban. Nearest major city is Birmingham. Students are housed in single-sex dormitories. 350-acre campus. 38 buildings on campus. Approved or accredited by Southern Association of Colleges and Schools, Southern Association of Independent Schools, The Association of Boarding Schools, and Alabama Department of Education. Member of National Association of Independent Schools and Secondary School Admission Test Board. Endowment: $18 million. Total enrollment: 261. Upper school average class size: 12. Upper school faculty-student ratio: 1:7. There are 175 required school days per year for Upper School students. Upper School students typically attend 5 days per week. The average school day consists of 6 hours and 20 minutes.
Upper School Student Profile Grade 8: 30 students (15 boys, 15 girls); Grade 9: 51 students (28 boys, 23 girls); Grade 10: 57 students (29 boys, 28 girls); Grade 11: 60 students (29 boys, 31 girls); Grade 12: 63 students (29 boys, 34 girls). 32% of students are boarding students. 79% are state residents. 12 states are represented in upper school student body. 17% are international students. International students from Australia, China, Germany, Republic of Korea, Rwanda, and Spain; 13 other countries represented in student body.
Faculty School total: 43. In upper school: 20 men, 21 women; 34 have advanced degrees; 23 reside on campus.
Subjects Offered Advanced Placement courses, algebra, American history, American literature, art, art history, astronomy, athletics, biology, biology-AP, calculus, calculus-AP, ceramics, chemistry, chemistry-AP, Chinese, computer applications, computer multimedia, concert choir, constitutional law, contemporary issues, creative writing, drama, economics, economics-AP, English, English literature, English-AP, environmental science-AP, European history, expository writing, film studies, fine arts, French, French-AP, geology, geometry, government-AP, government/civics, history, jazz, jazz ensemble, keyboarding, Latin, Latin-AP, mathematics, music, painting, philosophy, photo shop, physical education, physical fitness, physics, play production, pre-calculus, science, Shakespeare, social studies, Spanish, Spanish-AP, statistics-AP, theater, trigonometry, U.S. government and politics-AP, world history, world literature, world religions, writing, yearbook.
Graduation Requirements Arts and fine arts (art, music, dance, drama), English, foreign language, mathematics, physical education (includes health), science, social studies (includes history), art or music history.
Special Academic Programs Advanced Placement exam preparation; independent study; academic accommodation for the gifted and the musically talented.
College Admission Counseling 73 students graduated in 2011; all went to college, including Emory University; Georgetown University; The Johns Hopkins University; The University of Alabama; University of Illinois at Urbana–Champaign. Mean SAT critical reading: 643, mean SAT math: 629, mean SAT writing: 633, mean composite ACT: 27.
Student Life Upper grades have student council, honor system. Discipline rests equally with students and faculty.
Summer Programs Remediation, enrichment, ESL, sports, art/fine arts programs offered; session focuses on middle school students; held on campus; accepts boys and girls; open to students from other schools. 2012 schedule: July 9 to August 3. Application deadline: June 7.
Tuition and Aid Day student tuition: $17,950; 5-day tuition and room/board: $32,000; 7-day tuition and room/board: $36,500. Tuition installment plan (FACTS Tuition Payment Plan, monthly payment plans). Need-based scholarship grants available. In 2011–12, 27% of upper-school students received aid. Total amount of financial aid awarded in 2011–12: $1,000,000.
Admissions Traditional secondary-level entrance grade is 9. For fall 2011, 205 students applied for upper-level admission, 111 were accepted, 84 enrolled. SSAT or TOEFL required. Deadline for receipt of application materials: January 31. Application fee required: $65. Interview required.
Athletics Interscholastic: baseball (boys), basketball (b,g), soccer (b,g), softball (g), tennis (b,g), volleyball (g); intramural: basketball (b,g), flag football (b), soccer (b,g); coed interscholastic: cross-country running, golf, ultimate Frisbee; coed intramural: aerobics, aerobics/Nautilus, outdoor activities, paint ball, physical fitness, strength & conditioning, table tennis, ultimate Frisbee, yoga. 2 PE instructors, 5 coaches, 1 athletic trainer.
Computers Computers are regularly used in all academic classes. Computer network features include on-campus library services, online commercial services, Internet access, wireless campus network, Internet filtering or blocking technology. Campus intranet, student e-mail accounts, and computer access in designated common areas are available to students. Students grades are available online.
Contact Mrs. Christine Copeland, Assistant Director of Admission and Financial Aid. 205-332-0582. Fax: 205-988-3797. E-mail: ccopeland@indiansprings.org. Web site: www.indiansprings.org.

INSTITUTE OF NOTRE DAME

901 Aisquith Street

Baltimore, Maryland 21202-5499

Head of School: Dr. Mary Funke

General Information Girls' day college-preparatory, arts, business, religious studies, bilingual studies, and technology school, affiliated with Roman Catholic Church. Grades 9–12. Founded: 1847. Setting: urban. 2-acre campus. 1 building on campus. Approved or accredited by Association of Independent Maryland Schools, Middle States Association of Colleges and Schools, and Maryland Department of Education. Endowment: $5 million. Total enrollment: 246. Upper school average class size: 18. Upper school faculty-student ratio: 1:12. There are 180 required school days per year for Upper School students. Upper School students typically attend 5 days per week. The average school day consists of 6 hours and 20 minutes.
Upper School Student Profile Grade 9: 103 students (103 girls); Grade 10: 89 students (89 girls); Grade 11: 89 students (89 girls); Grade 12: 66 students (66 girls). 70% of students are Roman Catholic.
Faculty School total: 27. In upper school: 5 men, 22 women; 20 have advanced degrees.
Subjects Offered Accounting, algebra, American history, American literature, anatomy, art, Bible studies, biology, business, calculus, chemistry, Christianity, computer applications, computer math, computer programming, computer science, creative writing, criminal justice, dance, design, drama, drawing, driver education, earth science, English, English literature, environmental science, finance, fine arts, French, freshman seminar, geography, geology, geometry, government/civics, health, history, journalism, Latin, marine biology, mathematics, music, music history, physical education, physics, physiology, psychology, religion, science, social studies, sociology, Spanish, speech, theater, theology, trigonometry, women's studies, world history, world literature.

Graduation Requirements Arts and fine arts (art, music, dance, drama), business skills (includes word processing), computer science, English, foreign language, mathematics, physical education (includes health), religion (includes Bible studies and theology), science, social studies (includes history), 80 hours of community service.
Special Academic Programs 10 Advanced Placement exams for which test preparation is offered; honors section; accelerated programs; independent study; study at local college for college credit; academic accommodation for the gifted; remedial reading and/or remedial writing; remedial math.
College Admission Counseling 65 students graduated in 2011; 64 went to college, including College of Notre Dame of Maryland; Loyola University Maryland; Stevenson University; Towson University; University of Maryland, Baltimore; University of Maryland, Baltimore County. Other: 1 entered military service.
Student Life Upper grades have uniform requirement, student council, honor system. Discipline rests primarily with faculty. Attendance at religious services is required.
Summer Programs Enrichment, sports, art/fine arts, rigorous outdoor training, computer instruction programs offered; session focuses on community; held both on and off campus; held at Patterson Park, Herring Run Park, and Meadowood Regional Park; accepts girls; open to students from other schools. 150 students usually enrolled. 2012 schedule: June to July. Application deadline: none.
Tuition and Aid Day student tuition: $12,500. Tuition installment plan (monthly payment plans). Tuition reduction for siblings, merit scholarship grants, need-based scholarship grants, paying campus jobs, bank loans available. In 2011–12, 49% of upper-school students received aid, total upper-school merit-scholarship money awarded: $180,000. Total amount of financial aid awarded in 2011–12: $400,000.
Admissions Traditional secondary-level entrance grade is 9. For fall 2011, 218 students applied for upper-level admission, 103 enrolled. Battery of testing done through outside agency or High School Placement Test required. Deadline for receipt of application materials: December 16. Application fee required: $30. On-campus interview required.
Athletics Interscholastic: aerobics/dance, badminton, basketball, cheering, crew, cross-country running, field hockey, golf, independent competitive sports, lacrosse, outdoor adventure, outdoors, physical training, pom squad, rowing, running, soccer, softball, strength & conditioning, swimming and diving, track and field, volleyball, winter (indoor) track, winter soccer; intramural: aerobics/dance, ballet, dance, dance squad, dance team, horseback riding, modern dance, outdoor adventure, self defense, weight training. 1 PE instructor, 16 coaches, 1 athletic trainer.
Computers Computers are regularly used in all academic classes. Computer network features include on-campus library services, online commercial services, Internet access, wireless campus network, Internet filtering or blocking technology. Campus intranet, student e-mail accounts, and computer access in designated common areas are available to students. Students grades are available online. The school has a published electronic and media policy.
Contact Mrs. Amy Hoey Conly, Director of Admissions. 410-522-7800 Ext. 220. Fax: 410-522-7810. E mail: aconly@indofmd.org. Web site: www.indofmd.org.

INTERLOCHEN ARTS ACADEMY

PO Box 199

4000 Highway M 137

Interlochen, Michigan 49643-0199

Head of School: Mr. Jeffrey S. Kimpton

General Information Coeducational boarding and day college-preparatory and arts school. Grades 9–PG. Founded: 1962. Setting: rural. Nearest major city is Traverse City. Students are housed in single-sex dormitories. 1,200-acre campus. 225 buildings on campus. Approved or accredited by North Central Association of Colleges and Schools and Michigan Department of Education. Member of National Association of Independent Schools and Secondary School Admission Test Board. Endowment: $55.8 million. Total enrollment: 474. Upper school average class size: 13. Upper school faculty-student ratio: 1:6. There are 151 required school days per year for Upper School students. Upper School students typically attend 5 days per week. The average school day consists of 6 hours and 40 minutes.
Upper School Student Profile Grade 9: 41 students (14 boys, 27 girls); Grade 10: 59 students (19 boys, 40 girls); Grade 11: 141 students (52 boys, 89 girls); Grade 12: 213 students (80 boys, 133 girls); Postgraduate: 20 students (10 boys, 10 girls). 96% of students are boarding students. 17% are state residents. 46 states are represented in upper school student body. 21% are international students. International students from Canada, China, Israel, Mexico, Republic of Korea, and Taiwan; 23 other countries represented in student body.
Faculty School total: 84. In upper school: 42 men, 42 women; 75 have advanced degrees; 21 reside on campus.
Subjects Offered Algebra, American history, American literature, art, ballet, ballet technique, biology, British literature, calculus, ceramics, chamber groups, chemistry, chemistry-AP, choir, choral music, choreography, civil war history, computer math, computer science, contemporary art, creative writing, current events, dance, dance performance, drafting, drama, dramatic arts, earth science, ecology, English, English literature, environmental science, European history, expository writing, film, fine arts, French, geometry, government/civics, health, history, mathematics, music, philosophy, photography, physical education, physics, science, social studies, Spanish, speech, statistics, theater, trigonometry, world history, world literature, writing.
Graduation Requirements Arts and fine arts (art, music, dance, drama), English, mathematics, physical education (includes health), science, social studies (includes history).
Special Academic Programs Advanced Placement exam preparation; accelerated programs; independent study; term-away projects; academic accommodation for the gifted, the musically talented, and the artistically talented; ESL (42 students enrolled).
College Admission Counseling 207 students graduated in 2011; 198 went to college, including Ball State University; Cleveland Institute of Music; DePaul University; Indiana University Bloomington; Oberlin College; University of Michigan. Other: 1 went to work, 5 entered a postgraduate year, 3 had other specific plans. Mean SAT critical reading: 607, mean SAT math: 571, mean SAT writing: 597, mean composite ACT: 25. 58% scored over 600 on SAT critical reading, 36% scored over 600 on SAT math, 53% scored over 600 on SAT writing, 33% scored over 26 on composite ACT.
Student Life Upper grades have uniform requirement, student council, honor system. Discipline rests primarily with faculty.
Summer Programs Art/fine arts programs offered; session focuses on fine and performing arts; held on campus; accepts boys and girls; open to students from other schools. 2,500 students usually enrolled. 2012 schedule: June 23 to August 6. Application deadline: February 1.
Tuition and Aid Day student tuition: $29,330; 7-day tuition and room/board: $46,540. Tuition installment plan (monthly payment plans, individually arranged payment plans, Sallie Mae, Your Tuition Solution, PrepGate). Merit scholarship grants, need-based scholarship grants available. In 2011–12, 80% of upper-school students received aid; total upper-school merit-scholarship money awarded: $1,029,500. Total amount of financial aid awarded in 2011–12: $9,400,000.
Admissions Traditional secondary-level entrance grade is 11. For fall 2011, 816 students applied for upper-level admission, 366 were accepted, 246 enrolled. Achievement tests, any standardized test, audition, essay, placement test or SSAT required. Deadline for receipt of application materials: none. Application fee required: $50. Interview recommended.
Athletics 1 PE instructor.
Computers Computers are regularly used in graphic arts, mathematics, music, science, video film production classes. Computer network features include on-campus library services, online commercial services, Internet access, wireless campus network. Campus intranet and student e-mail accounts are available to students. The school has a published electronic and media policy.
Contact Jim Bekkering, Director of Admission and Financial Aid. 231-276-7472. Fax: 231-276-7464. E-mail: admission@interlochen.org. Web site: www.interlochen.org.

INTERMOUNTAIN CHRISTIAN SCHOOL

6515 South Lion Lane

Salt Lake City, Utah 84121

Head of School: Adm. Layne Billings

General Information Coeducational day college-preparatory, general academic, arts, business, and religious studies school, affiliated with Evangelical Free Church of America, Christian faith. Grades PK–12. Founded: 1982. Setting: suburban. 6-acre campus. 1 building on campus. Approved or accredited by Association of Christian Schools International, Northwest Accreditation Commission, Northwest Association of Schools and Colleges, and Utah Department of Education. Endowment: $64,624. Total enrollment: 277. Upper school average class size: 17. Upper school faculty-student ratio: 1:7. There are 180 required school days per year for Upper School students. Upper School students typically attend 5 days per week. The average school day consists of 6 hours.
Upper School Student Profile Grade 9: 15 students (6 boys, 9 girls); Grade 10: 14 students (10 boys, 4 girls); Grade 11: 20 students (11 boys, 9 girls); Grade 12: 12 students (4 boys, 8 girls). 97% of students are members of Evangelical Free Church of America, Christian.
Faculty School total: 33. In upper school: 7 men, 10 women; 8 have advanced degrees.
Subjects Offered Advanced Placement courses, algebra, American government, American history, American literature, American literature-AP, art, ASB Leadership, athletics, baseball, basketball, bell choir, Bible, biology, calculus, career education, ceramics, chemistry, choir, chorus, Christian doctrine, church history, civics, community service, composition, computer programming, computer science, computer skills, concert band, concert bell choir, concert choir, current events, debate, drama, drama performance, economics, economics and history, electives, English, English literature-AP, environmental science-AP, European history, European literature, family and consumer science, finance, fine arts, food science, geometry, government, handbells, health, history, independent study, instrumental music, jazz band, jazz dance, keyboarding, leadership and service, Life of Christ, mathematics, peer ministry, physical education, physics, pre-algebra, pre-calculus, reading/study skills, science, senior seminar, sex education, social studies, Spanish, statistics, trigonometry, U.S. government, U.S. history, vocal ensemble, volleyball, world geography, world history.
Graduation Requirements Arts and fine arts (art, music, dance, drama), Bible, computer science, English, finance, foreign language, mathematics, physical education

(includes health), science, social studies (includes history), Class Trips. Community service is required.
Special Academic Programs 3 Advanced Placement exams for which test preparation is offered; honors section; study at local college for college credit.
College Admission Counseling 21 students graduated in 2011; 20 went to college, including Gonzaga University; Oklahoma State University; Salt Lake Community College; University of Oregon; University of Utah; Whitworth University. Other: 1 entered military service. Mean SAT critical reading: 569, mean SAT math: 559, mean SAT writing: 559, mean combined SAT: 1689, mean composite ACT: 26. 36% scored over 600 on SAT critical reading, 43% scored over 600 on SAT math, 36% scored over 600 on SAT writing, 36% scored over 1800 on combined SAT, 48% scored over 26 on composite ACT.
Student Life Upper grades have specified standards of dress, student council, honor system. Discipline rests primarily with faculty. Attendance at religious services is required.
Tuition and Aid Day student tuition: $6100. Tuition installment plan (Insured Tuition Payment Plan, monthly payment plans, discounted up-front tuition payment). Tuition reduction for siblings, need-based scholarship grants available. In 2011–12, 16% of upper-school students received aid. Total amount of financial aid awarded in 2011–12: $18,260.
Admissions Traditional secondary-level entrance grade is 9. For fall 2011, 7 students applied for upper-level admission, 7 were accepted, 7 enrolled. School's own test and TOEFL required. Deadline for receipt of application materials: none. Application fee required: $90. On-campus interview required.
Athletics Interscholastic: baseball (boys), basketball (b,g), golf (b,g), soccer (b,g), volleyball (g). 2 PE instructors, 4 coaches.
Computers Computers are regularly used in art, computer applications, English, history, mathematics, science, Spanish, technology, writing classes. Computer network features include Internet access, wireless campus network, Internet filtering or blocking technology. Computer access in designated common areas is available to students. Students grades are available online. The school has a published electronic and media policy.
Contact Eileen Rocco, Registrar. 801-942-8811. Fax: 801-942-8813. E-mail: rocco_e@slcics.org. Web site: www.slcics.org.

INTERNATIONAL COLLEGE SPAIN

Calle Vereda Norte, #3
La Moraleja
Madrid 28109, Spain

Head of School: Dr. Peter Southern

General Information Coeducational day college-preparatory and bilingual studies school. Grades PK–12. Founded: 1980. Setting: suburban. 3-hectare campus. 2 buildings on campus. Approved or accredited by International Baccalaureate Organization, Mennonite Schools Council, and New England Association of Schools and Colleges. Language of instruction: English. Total enrollment: 709. Upper school average class size: 18. Upper school faculty-student ratio: 1:9. There are 176 required school days per year for Upper School students. Upper School students typically attend 5 days per week. The average school day consists of 6 hours.
Upper School Student Profile Grade 6: 47 students (22 boys, 25 girls); Grade 7: 52 students (19 boys, 33 girls); Grade 8: 55 students (26 boys, 29 girls); Grade 9: 55 students (26 boys, 29 girls); Grade 10: 57 students (34 boys, 23 girls); Grade 11: 53 students (22 boys, 31 girls); Grade 12: 57 students (28 boys, 29 girls).
Faculty School total: 48. In upper school: 12 men, 27 women; 22 have advanced degrees.
Subjects Offered 20th century world history, advanced math, art, biology, chemistry, Danish, design, drama, Dutch, economics, English, English literature, European history, expressive arts, French, geography, global studies, history, humanities, information technology, interdisciplinary studies, International Baccalaureate courses, Italian, Japanese, mathematics, model United Nations, music, personal and social education, physical education, physics, science, social education, social studies, Spanish, Spanish literature, Swedish, technology, theory of knowledge, world literature.
Graduation Requirements English, foreign language, mathematics, science, social sciences, social studies (includes history), 90% minimum attendance, minimum average effort grade of satisfactory. Community service is required.
Special Academic Programs International Baccalaureate program; ESL (45 students enrolled).
College Admission Counseling 53 students graduated in 2010; 50 went to college, including Duke University; Northeastern University; The Johns Hopkins University. Other: 1 entered military service. 75% scored over 600 on SAT critical reading, 100% scored over 600 on SAT math.
Student Life Upper grades have specified standards of dress, student council. Discipline rests equally with students and faculty.
Tuition and Aid Day student tuition: €14,280–€14,970. Tuition installment plan (Insured Tuition Payment Plan). Tuition reduction for siblings, bursaries, merit scholarship grants, need-based scholarship grants available. In 2010–11, 4% of upper-school students received aid; total upper-school merit-scholarship money awarded: €20,613. Total amount of financial aid awarded in 2010–11: €39,000.
Admissions Traditional secondary-level entrance grade is 11. For fall 2010, 87 students applied for upper-level admission, 43 were accepted, 35 enrolled. Admissions testing and math and English placement tests required. Deadline for receipt of application materials: none. Application fee required: €550. On-campus interview recommended.
Athletics Interscholastic: basketball (boys, girls), cross-country running (b,g), soccer (b,g), volleyball (b,g); intramural: aerobics/dance (b,g), badminton (b,g), ballet (b,g), field hockey (b,g), gymnastics (b,g), physical fitness (b,g), soccer (b,g), softball (b,g), swimming and diving (b,g), table tennis (b,g), tennis (b,g), volleyball (b,g); coed interscholastic: track and field; coed intramural: alpine skiing, dance, fencing, golf, horseback riding, judo, martial arts, modern dance, skiing (downhill), snowboarding. 2 PE instructors, 2 coaches.
Computers Computers are regularly used in art, career education, career exploration, college planning, economics, English, ESL, information technology, mathematics, science classes. Computer network features include on-campus library services, online commercial services, Internet access, wireless campus network, Internet filtering or blocking technology. Campus intranet, student e-mail accounts, and computer access in designated common areas are available to students. Students grades are available online. The school has a published electronic and media policy.
Contact Mrs. Eunice Amondaray, Admissions Officer. 34-9-1-650-2398. Fax: 34-9-1-650-1035. E-mail: admissions@icsmadrid.org. Web site: www.icsmadrid.org.

INTERNATIONAL HIGH SCHOOL

150 Oak Street
San Francisco, California 94102

Head of School: Ms. Jane Camblin

General Information Coeducational day college-preparatory, arts, bilingual studies, and technology school. Grades PK–12. Founded: 1962. Setting: urban. 3-acre campus. 2 buildings on campus. Approved or accredited by Council of International Schools, French Ministry of Education, International Baccalaureate Organization, Western Association of Schools and Colleges, and California Department of Education. Member of National Association of Independent Schools, Secondary School Admission Test Board, and European Council of International Schools. Languages of instruction: English and French. Endowment: $4.9 million. Total enrollment: 1,009. Upper school average class size: 17. Upper school faculty-student ratio: 1:10. There are 165 required school days per year for Upper School students. The average school day consists of 7 hours.
Upper School Student Profile Grade 9: 90 students (39 boys, 51 girls); Grade 10: 81 students (35 boys, 46 girls); Grade 11: 78 students (33 boys, 45 girls); Grade 12: 80 students (35 boys, 45 girls).
Faculty School total: 139. In upper school: 33 men, 30 women; 35 have advanced degrees.
Subjects Offered Advanced chemistry, advanced math, algebra, American history, American literature, art, biology, calculus, chemistry, community service, computer science, creative writing, current events, drama, earth science, economics, English, English literature, environmental science, ESL, European history, expository writing, fine arts, French, geography, geometry, German, government/civics, history, International Baccalaureate courses, Mandarin, mathematics, music, philosophy, physical education, physics, science, social studies, Spanish, theater, theory of knowledge, trigonometry, world history, world literature, writing.
Graduation Requirements Arts and fine arts (art, music, dance, drama), English, foreign language, International Baccalaureate courses, mathematics, physical education (includes health), science, social studies (includes history), theory of knowledge, extended essay, 150 hours of CAS.
Special Academic Programs International Baccalaureate program; honors section; independent study; term-away projects; study abroad; academic accommodation for the gifted, the musically talented, and the artistically talented; ESL (12 students enrolled).
College Admission Counseling 94 students graduated in 2011; 93 went to college, including Boston University; McGill University; University of California, Berkeley; University of California, Davis; University of California, Santa Cruz; University of Southern California. Other: 1 had other specific plans. Mean SAT critical reading: 631, mean SAT math: 633, mean SAT writing: 645.
Student Life Upper grades have student council. Discipline rests equally with students and faculty.
Summer Programs Remediation, enrichment, advancement programs offered; session focuses on enrichment; held on campus; accepts boys and girls; open to students from other schools. 15 students usually enrolled.
Tuition and Aid Day student tuition: $31,270. Tuition installment plan (FACTS Tuition Payment Plan). Need-based scholarship grants, French bourse available. In 2011–12, 25% of upper-school students received aid. Total amount of financial aid awarded in 2011–12: $748,000.
Admissions Traditional secondary-level entrance grade is 9. For fall 2011, 355 students applied for upper-level admission, 195 were accepted, 58 enrolled. Any standardized test, SSAT or writing sample required. Deadline for receipt of application materials: January 12. Application fee required: $75. Interview required.
Athletics Interscholastic: baseball (boys, girls), basketball (b,g), football (b), soccer (b,g), volleyball (b,g); intramural: ballet (b,g), baseball (b), basketball (b,g), floor

hockey (b,g), soccer (b,g), softball (g), tennis (b,g), volleyball (b,g); coed interscholastic: badminton, cross-country running, swimming and diving, tennis, track and field; coed intramural: badminton, ballet, cross-country running, fencing, flagball, golf, handball, indoor hockey, outdoor activities, outdoor adventure, physical fitness, physical training, swimming and diving, water polo, weight training. 4 PE instructors, 8 coaches, 3 athletic trainers.

Computers Computers are regularly used in all academic classes. Computer network features include on-campus library services, online commercial services, Internet access, wireless campus network, video editing, Web page creation. Student e-mail accounts and computer access in designated common areas are available to students. The school has a published electronic and media policy.

Contact Ms. Erin Cronin, Associate Director of Admission. 415-558-2093. Fax: 415-558-2085. E-mail: erinc@internationalsf.org. Web site: www.internationalsf.org.

INTERNATIONAL SCHOOL BANGKOK

39/7 Soi Nichada Thani, Samakee Road

Pakkret 11120, Thailand

Head of School: Dr. William Gerritz

General Information Coeducational day college-preparatory, arts, and technology school. Grades PK–12. Founded: 1951. Setting: suburban. Nearest major city is Bangkok, Thailand. 37-acre campus. 2 buildings on campus. Approved or accredited by Western Association of Schools and Colleges and state department of education. Affiliate member of National Association of Independent Schools; member of European Council of International Schools. Language of instruction: English. Total enrollment: 1,840. Upper school average class size: 18. Upper school faculty-student ratio: 1:10. There are 183 required school days per year for Upper School students. Upper School students typically attend 5 days per week. The average school day consists of 6 hours.

Upper School Student Profile Grade 9: 185 students (93 boys, 92 girls); Grade 10: 162 students (83 boys, 79 girls); Grade 11: 178 students (100 boys, 78 girls); Grade 12: 178 students (77 boys, 101 girls).

Faculty School total: 229. In upper school: 50 men, 42 women; 70 have advanced degrees.

Subjects Offered 3-dimensional design, algebra, American history, American literature, art, art history, biology, business, business education, business studies, calculus, calculus-AP, ceramics, chemistry, choir, computer math, computer science, concert band, creative writing, dance, drama, drawing, drawing and design, Dutch, earth science, ecology, economics, economics and history, electives, English, English literature, environmental education, environmental science, environmental studies, ESL, European history, expository writing, fine arts, French, French studies, geography, geology, geometry, German, government/civics, health, history, humanities, industrial arts, Japanese, journalism, language arts, languages, mathematics, music, performing arts, philosophy, photography, physical education, physics, psychology, reading, science, social studies, sociology, Spanish, speech, statistics, Thai, theater, theory of knowledge, trigonometry, world history, world literature, writing.

Graduation Requirements Arts and fine arts (art, music, dance, drama), English, mathematics, physical education (includes health), science, social studies (includes history), community service hours, Senior Seminar, Global Citizenship Week, Thailand and Southeast Asia course. Community service is required.

Special Academic Programs International Baccalaureate program; Advanced Placement exam preparation; ESL.

College Admission Counseling 169 students graduated in 2011; 167 went to college, including Boston University; Northeastern University; Purdue University; University of Illinois at Urbana–Champaign; University of Southern California; University of Washington. Other: 1 entered military service, 1 had other specific plans.

Student Life Upper grades have uniform requirement, student council, honor system. Discipline rests primarily with faculty.

Summer Programs Remediation, enrichment, ESL, art/fine arts programs offered; held on campus; accepts boys and girls; open to students from other schools. 400 students usually enrolled. 2012 schedule: June 1 to July 27. Application deadline: June 3.

Tuition and Aid Day student tuition: 743,000 Thai bahts. Tuition installment plan (individually arranged payment plans).

Admissions Math and English placement tests and school's own exam required. Deadline for receipt of application materials: none. Application fee required: 4500 Thai bahts. On-campus interview required.

Athletics Interscholastic: aquatics (boys, girls), badminton (b,g), basketball (b,g), cross-country running (b,g), dance (b,g), rugby (b,g), running (b,g), soccer (b,g), softball (b,g), swimming and diving (b,g), tennis (b,g), track and field (b,g), volleyball (b,g); intramural: aquatics (b,g), badminton (b,g), basketball (b,g), cross-country running (b,g), dance (b,g), fencing (b), rugby (b,g), running (b,g), swimming and diving (b,g), track and field (b,g), volleyball (b,g); coed interscholastic: dance team. 5 PE instructors.

Computers Computers are regularly used in all academic classes. Computer network features include on-campus library services, Internet access, wireless campus network, Internet filtering or blocking technology. Campus intranet, student e-mail accounts, and computer access in designated common areas are available to students. Students grades are available online. The school has a published electronic and media policy.

Contact Ms. Wendy Van Bramer, Admissions Director. 662-963-5800. Fax: 662-960-4103. E-mail: register@isb.ac.th. Web site: www.isb.ac.th.

INTERNATIONAL SCHOOL HAMBURG

Hemmingstedter Weg 130

Hamburg 22609, Germany

Head of School: Mr. Andreas Swoboda

General Information Coeducational day college-preparatory, arts, and technology school. Grades PK–12. Founded: 1957. Setting: suburban. 3-acre campus. 1 building on campus. Approved or accredited by New England Association of Schools and Colleges. Language of instruction: English. Total enrollment: 694. Upper school average class size: 20. Upper school faculty-student ratio: 1:8. Upper School students typically attend 5 days per week.

Upper School Student Profile Grade 9: 69 students (43 boys, 26 girls); Grade 10: 51 students (29 boys, 22 girls); Grade 11: 46 students (25 boys, 21 girls); Grade 12: 47 students (22 boys, 25 girls).

Faculty School total: 85. In upper school: 47 men, 25 women; 25 have advanced degrees.

Subjects Offered Art, biology, chemistry, computer math, drama, English, ESL, European history, fine arts, French, geography, German, history, mathematics, model United Nations, music, photography, physical education, physics, science, social studies, Spanish, theater, theory of knowledge, world history.

Graduation Requirements Arts and fine arts (art, music, dance, drama), English, foreign language, mathematics, physical education (includes health), science, social studies (includes history).

Special Academic Programs International Baccalaureate program; ESL (80 students enrolled).

College Admission Counseling 50 students graduated in 2011; 45 went to college, including Columbia University; McGill University; University of Edinburgh; Yale University. Other: 1 entered military service, 3 had other specific plans.

Student Life Upper grades have student council. Discipline rests primarily with faculty.

Tuition and Aid Day student tuition: €14,250–€17,800. Tuition installment plan (2-payment plan). Financial aid available to upper-school students. In 2011–12, 1% of upper-school students received aid.

Admissions Traditional secondary-level entrance grade is 9. For fall 2011, 50 students applied for upper-level admission, 45 were accepted, 44 enrolled. ACT, CTBS, Stanford Achievement Test, any other standardized test or PSAT and SAT for applicants to grade 11 and 12 required. Deadline for receipt of application materials: none. Application fee required: €100. On-campus interview required.

Athletics Interscholastic: badminton (boys, girls), basketball (b,g), canoeing/kayaking (b,g), climbing (b,g), cross-country running (b,g), floor hockey (b,g), football (b,g), indoor hockey (b,g), indoor soccer (b,g), netball (b,g), physical training (b,g), rowing (b,g), running (b,g), sailing (b,g), soccer (b,g), tennis (b,g), track and field (b,g), volleyball (b,g); intramural: basketball (b,g), cross-country running (b,g), field hockey (b,g), football (b,g), soccer (b,g), tennis (b,g), track and field (b,g), volleyball (b,g); coed interscholastic: badminton, canoeing/kayaking, climbing, cross-country running, floor hockey, football, indoor hockey, indoor soccer, netball, running, sailing, soccer, tennis, track and field, volleyball; coed intramural: cross-country running, football, soccer, tennis, track and field, volleyball. 5 PE instructors, 4 coaches.

Computers Computers are regularly used in business studies, English, ESL, foreign language, French, geography, history, humanities, library, mathematics, music, science, Spanish, yearbook classes. Computer network features include on-campus library services, online commercial services, Internet access, wireless campus network, Internet filtering or blocking technology. Campus intranet and student e-mail accounts are available to students. Students grades are available online. The school has a published electronic and media policy.

Contact Catherine Bissonnet, Director of Admissions. 49-40-800050-133. Fax: 49-40-881-1405. E-mail: cbissonnet@ishamburg.org. Web site: www.ishamburg.org.

INTERNATIONAL SCHOOL MANILA

University Parkway

Fort Bonifacio

1634 Taguig City, Philippines

Head of School: Mr. David Toze

General Information Coeducational day college-preparatory, arts, business, bilingual studies, and technology school. Grades PS–12. Founded: 1920. Setting: urban. Nearest major city is Manila, Philippines. 7-hectare campus. 1 building on campus. Approved or accredited by Council of International Schools and Western Association of Schools and Colleges. Affiliate member of National Association of Independent Schools; member of Secondary School Admission Test Board. Language of instruction: English. Total enrollment: 1,966. Upper school average class size: 16. Upper school faculty-student ratio: 1:9. There are 181 required school days per year for Upper School students.

Upper School Student Profile Grade 6: 142 students (68 boys, 74 girls); Grade 7: 156 students (80 boys, 76 girls); Grade 8: 168 students (89 boys, 79 girls); Grade 9: 188 students (98 boys, 90 girls); Grade 10: 172 students (82 boys, 90 girls); Grade 11: 188 students (86 boys, 102 girls); Grade 12: 174 students (86 boys, 88 girls).

Faculty School total: 200. In upper school: 42 men, 38 women; 35 have advanced degrees.

Subjects Offered Acting, anthropology, art, athletic training, band, Basic programming, biology, business, calculus-AP, chemistry, Chinese, choir, college admission preparation, college awareness, college counseling, college placement, college planning, computer applications, computer graphics, computer literacy, computer multimedia, computer programming, computer science, creative writing, critical writing, dance, desktop publishing, digital photography, economics, economics and history, English, environmental science, ESL, film, filmmaking, foreign language, French, French as a second language, general science, geography, graphic design, health, health and wellness, health education, information technology, integrated mathematics, International Baccalaureate courses, international relations, Japanese, Japanese as Second Language, jazz band, leadership, math applications, math methods, mathematics, media studies, music, orchestra, parenting, peer counseling, personal fitness, Philippine culture, physical science, physics, political science, pre-calculus, programming, psychology, reading/study skills, remedial study skills, research, service learning/internship, sex education, Spanish, theater, theater arts, theory of knowledge, track and field, U.S. history, U.S. history-AP, video film production, visual and performing arts, visual arts, weight fitness, weight training, world history, world religions, writing.

Special Academic Programs International Baccalaureate program; Advanced Placement exam preparation; honors section; accelerated programs; independent study; ESL (166 students enrolled).

College Admission Counseling 166 students graduated in 2011; 161 went to college, including New York University; Penn State University Park; Purdue University; The University of British Columbia; University of California, Berkeley; University of Southern California. Other: 2 went to work, 3 had other specific plans. Mean SAT critical reading: 581, mean SAT math: 649, mean SAT writing: 603, mean combined SAT: 1832, mean composite ACT: 26.

Student Life Upper grades have uniform requirement, student council, honor system. Discipline rests equally with students and faculty.

Summer Programs ESL programs offered; session focuses on academics for ESL; held on campus; accepts boys and girls; open to students from other schools. 2012 schedule: June to July. Application deadline: none.

Tuition and Aid Day student tuition: $1997–$7280. Tuition installment plan (monthly payment plans, individually arranged payment plans, quarterly payment plan). Scholarships for low-income local students available.

Admissions Traditional secondary-level entrance grade is 9. For fall 2011, 273 students applied for upper-level admission, 170 were accepted, 148 enrolled. Deadline for receipt of application materials: none. Application fee required: $200. On-campus interview recommended.

Athletics Interscholastic: badminton (boys, girls), basketball (b,g), bowling (b,g), cheering (g), cross-country running (b,g), dance (b,g), golf (b,g), gymnastics (b,g), martial arts (b,g), rugby (b,g), soccer (b,g), softball (b,g), swimming and diving (b,g), table tennis (b,g), tennis (b,g), track and field (b,g), volleyball (b,g), wall climbing (b,g); intramural: rugby (b,g), wall climbing (b,g), water polo (b,g); coed interscholastic: wall climbing; coed intramural: volleyball, wall climbing. 4 PE instructors, 10 coaches.

Computers Computers are regularly used in art, English, foreign language, history, mathematics, music, science classes. Computer network features include on-campus library services, online commercial services, Internet access, wireless campus network, Internet filtering or blocking technology. Campus intranet and student e-mail accounts are available to students. Students grades are available online. The school has a published electronic and media policy.

Contact Stephanie Hagedorn, Director of Admissions and Advancement. 63-2-840-8488. Fax: 63-2-840-8489. E-mail: admission@ismanila.org. Web site: www.ismanila.org.

INTERNATIONAL SCHOOL OF AMSTERDAM

Sportlaan 45

Amstelveen 1185 TB, Netherlands

Head of School: Dr. Ed Greene

General Information Coeducational day college-preparatory, arts, bilingual studies, and technology school. Grades PS–12. Founded: 1964. Setting: suburban. Nearest major city is Amsterdam, Netherlands. 1-acre campus. 2 buildings on campus. Approved or accredited by New England Association of Schools and Colleges. Member of European Council of International Schools. Language of instruction: English. Total enrollment: 992. Upper school average class size: 20. Upper school faculty-student ratio: 1:5. There are 177 required school days per year for Upper School students. Upper School students typically attend 5 days per week. The average school day consists of 7 hours.

Upper School Student Profile Grade 9: 70 students (35 boys, 35 girls); Grade 10: 56 students (28 boys, 28 girls); Grade 11: 61 students (32 boys, 29 girls); Grade 12: 48 students (28 boys, 20 girls).

Faculty School total: 147. In upper school: 29 men, 42 women; 28 have advanced degrees.

Subjects Offered Addiction, advanced math, algebra, American literature, art, biology, calculus, chemistry, community service, computer programming, computer science, drama, Dutch, economics, English, English literature, ESL, European history, food science, French, geography, geometry, German, history, Japanese, mathematics, music, photography, physical education, physics, science, social sciences, social studies, Spanish, technology, theater, theory of knowledge, trigonometry, world history, world literature.

Graduation Requirements Arts, computer science, English, foreign language, mathematics, physical education (includes health), science, social sciences, social studies (includes history). Community service is required.

Special Academic Programs International Baccalaureate program; independent study; academic accommodation for the gifted, the musically talented, and the artistically talented; remedial reading and/or remedial writing; remedial math; programs in English, mathematics, general development for dyslexic students; ESL (26 students enrolled).

College Admission Counseling 44 students graduated in 2011; 36 went to college, including Stanford University; Webster University; Williams College. Other: 8 had other specific plans. Median SAT critical reading: 590, median SAT math: 630, median SAT writing: 600, median combined SAT: 1770. 45% scored over 600 on SAT critical reading, 55% scored over 600 on SAT math, 55% scored over 600 on SAT writing, 45% scored over 1800 on combined SAT.

Student Life Upper grades have specified standards of dress, student council, honor system. Discipline rests primarily with faculty.

Tuition and Aid Day student tuition: €20,800–€21,450. Tuition installment plan (monthly payment plans, individually arranged payment plans).

Admissions Traditional secondary-level entrance grade is 9. For fall 2011, 62 students applied for upper-level admission, 40 were accepted, 29 enrolled. Deadline for receipt of application materials: none. No application fee required. On-campus interview required.

Athletics Interscholastic: basketball (boys, girls), soccer (b,g), softball (b,g), swimming and diving (b,g), tennis (b,g), track and field (b,g), volleyball (g); coed intramural: aerobics, aerobics/dance, badminton, basketball, cricket, fitness, handball, hockey, netball, rugby, running, soccer, softball, tennis, track and field, volleyball. 7 PE instructors, 14 coaches, 14 athletic trainers.

Computers Computers are regularly used in art, drawing and design, English, foreign language, information technology, keyboarding, library, mathematics, music, science, yearbook classes. Computer network features include on-campus library services, online commercial services, Internet access, Internet filtering or blocking technology. Campus intranet and student e-mail accounts are available to students.

Contact Julia True, Director of Admissions. 31-20-347-1111. Fax: 31-20-347-1105. E-mail: admissions@isa.nl. Web site: www.isa.nl.

INTERNATIONAL SCHOOL OF ATHENS

Xenias and Artemidos Streets

PO Box 51051

Kifissia—Athens GR-145 10, Greece

Head of School: Mr. C. N. Dardoufas

General Information Coeducational day and distance learning college-preparatory and arts school. Grades N–12. Distance learning grades 9–12. Founded: 1972. Setting: suburban. Nearest major city is Athens, Greece. 2-acre campus. 1 building on campus. Approved or accredited by CITA (Commission on International and Trans-Regional Accreditation), Department of Defense Dependents Schools, International Baccalaureate Organization, and Middle States Association of Colleges and Schools. Language of instruction: English. Total enrollment: 358. Upper school average class size: 15. Upper school faculty-student ratio: 1:9. There are 174 required school days per year for Upper School students. Upper School students typically attend 5 days per week. The average school day consists of 6 hours.

Upper School Student Profile Grade 10: 35 students (20 boys, 15 girls); Grade 11: 31 students (20 boys, 11 girls); Grade 12: 57 students (33 boys, 24 girls).

Faculty School total: 69. In upper school: 13 men, 24 women; 24 have advanced degrees.

Subjects Offered American literature, Arabic, art, art history, biology, business studies, calculus, chemistry, drama, English, English literature, ESL, French, geography, Greek, history, information technology, mathematics, modern world history, music, physical education, physics, science, sociology, Spanish, studio art, theory of knowledge, world history, world literature, writing.

Graduation Requirements Art history, arts and fine arts (art, music, dance, drama), English, foreign language, history, information technology, mathematics, physical education (includes health), science, requirements for students in IB diploma program differ. Community service is required.

Special Academic Programs International Baccalaureate program; independent study; academic accommodation for the gifted; remedial reading and/or remedial

writing; remedial math; programs in English, mathematics, general development for dyslexic students; ESL.
Student Life Upper grades have uniform requirement, student council. Discipline rests primarily with faculty.
Tuition and Aid Day student tuition: €11,200–€12,350. Tuition installment plan (monthly payment plans, individually arranged payment plans). Tuition reduction for siblings, need-based scholarship grants, prepayment discount available.
Admissions Traditional secondary-level entrance grade is 10. For fall 2010, 22 students applied for upper-level admission, 19 were accepted, 17 enrolled. Math Placement Exam, Secondary Level English Proficiency or writing sample required. Deadline for receipt of application materials: none. Application fee required: €1200. On-campus interview required.
Athletics Interscholastic: basketball (boys, girls), cross-country running (b,g), jogging (b,g), soccer (b,g), track and field (b,g), volleyball (b,g); intramural: basketball (b,g), cross-country running (b,g), jogging (b,g), soccer (b,g), swimming and diving (b,g), volleyball (b,g); coed intramural: tennis, water volleyball. 4 PE instructors.
Computers Computers are regularly used in English, foreign language, information technology, library, mathematics, science, social studies, yearbook classes. Computer resources include on-campus library services, online commercial services, Internet access, wireless campus network, Internet filtering or blocking technology. Computer access in designated common areas is available to students.
Contact Ms. Helen Haniotakis, Admissions Officer. 30-210-623-3888. Fax: 30-210-623-3160. E-mail: chaniotaki@isa.edu.gr. Web site: www.isa.edu.gr/home.htm.

INTERNATIONAL SCHOOL OF BERNE

Mattenstrasse 3

Guemligen 3073, Switzerland

Head of School: Mr. Kevin Thomas Page

General Information Coeducational day college-preparatory school. Grades PK–12. Founded: 1961. Setting: suburban. Nearest major city is Berne, Switzerland. 1-hectare campus. 4 buildings on campus. Approved or accredited by International Baccalaureate Organization, New England Association of Schools and Colleges, and Swiss Federation of Private Schools. Language of instruction: English. Total enrollment: 246. Upper school average class size: 21. Upper school faculty-student ratio: 1:5. There are 180 required school days per year for Upper School students. Upper School students typically attend 5 days per week. The average school day consists of 6 hours.
Upper School Student Profile Grade 6: 21 students (14 boys, 7 girls); Grade 7: 21 students (10 boys, 11 girls); Grade 8: 20 students (13 boys, 7 girls); Grade 9: 21 students (10 boys, 11 girls); Grade 10: 22 students (11 boys, 11 girls); Grade 11: 28 students (17 boys, 11 girls); Grade 12: 19 students (12 boys, 7 girls).
Faculty School total: 42. In upper school: 16 men, 12 women; 19 have advanced degrees.
Subjects Offered Biology, chemistry, economics, English, English literature, ESL, European history, French, geography, German, history, mathematics, music, physical education, physics, science, technology, theater arts, visual arts, world history, world literature.
Graduation Requirements Biology, chemistry, economics, English, foreign language, French, geography, German, history, mathematics, music, physical education (includes health), physics, technology, theater arts, theory of knowledge, visual arts, extended essay, Creativity Action Service (CAS), Theory of Knowledge.
Special Academic Programs International Baccalaureate program; academic accommodation for the gifted; ESL (17 students enrolled).
College Admission Counseling 23 students graduated in 2010; 14 went to college, including Brown University; Northeastern University; University of California, Los Angeles. Other: 4 went to work, 5 had other specific plans. Mean SAT critical reading: 571, mean SAT math: 647, mean SAT writing: 581. 45% scored over 600 on SAT critical reading, 73% scored over 600 on SAT math, 45% scored over 600 on SAT writing, 45% scored over 1800 on combined SAT.
Student Life Upper grades have specified standards of dress, student council. Discipline rests primarily with faculty.
Tuition and Aid Day student tuition: 26,820 Swiss francs–30,140 Swiss francs. Tuition installment plan (monthly payment plans, individually arranged payment plans).
Admissions For fall 2010, 38 students applied for upper-level admission, 38 were accepted, 38 enrolled. Math and English placement tests required. Deadline for receipt of application materials: none. Application fee required: 250 Swiss francs. On-campus interview required.
Athletics Interscholastic: alpine skiing (boys, girls), basketball (b,g), cross-country running (b,g), indoor hockey (b,g), indoor soccer (b,g), running (b,g), skiing (downhill) (b,g), snowboarding (b,g), soccer (b,g), swimming and diving (b,g), track and field (b,g), volleyball (b,g); intramural: alpine skiing (b,g), basketball (b,g), cross-country running (b,g), ice skating (b,g), indoor hockey (b,g), indoor soccer (b,g), running (b,g), skiing (downhill) (b,g), snowboarding (b,g), soccer (b,g), swimming and diving (b,g), track and field (b,g), volleyball (b,g); coed interscholastic: alpine skiing, swimming and diving; coed intramural: alpine skiing, ice skating, swimming and diving. 1 PE instructor, 4 coaches.
Computers Computers are regularly used in English, French, information technology, library skills, mathematics, science classes. Computer network features include on-campus library services, online commercial services, Internet access, wireless campus network, Internet filtering or blocking technology. Student e-mail accounts and computer access in designated common areas are available to students. Students grades are available online. The school has a published electronic and media policy.
Contact Mr. Tobin Bechtel, Secondary School Principal. 41-(0) 31-951-23-58. Fax: 41-(0)31-951-1710. E-mail: tobin.bechtel@isberne.ch. Web site: www.isberne.ch.

THE INTERNATIONAL SCHOOL OF KUALA LUMPUR

Jalan Kolam Air

Ampang, Selangor 68000, Malaysia

Head of School: Mr. Paul B. Chmelik

General Information Coeducational day college-preparatory school. Grades PK–12. Founded: 1965. Setting: suburban. Nearest major city is Kuala Lumpur, Malaysia. 7-acre campus. 1 building on campus. Approved or accredited by Western Association of Schools and Colleges. Affiliate member of National Association of Independent Schools. Language of instruction: English. Total enrollment: 1,588. Upper school average class size: 20. Upper school faculty-student ratio: 1:9.
Upper School Student Profile Grade 9: 141 students (75 boys, 66 girls); Grade 10: 155 students (71 boys, 84 girls); Grade 11: 156 students (92 boys, 64 girls); Grade 12: 152 students (73 boys, 79 girls).
Faculty School total: 169. In upper school: 28 men, 22 women; 40 have advanced degrees.
Subjects Offered Advanced chemistry, advanced math, Advanced Placement courses, anthropology, applied arts, architecture, art, Asian history, biology, calculus-AP, ceramics, chemistry, computer multimedia, computer science, concert band, concert choir, economics, English, English literature, English-AP, environmental science, ESL, film studies, fine arts, French, graphic design, guitar, health, history, information technology, integrated mathematics, integrated science, International Baccalaureate courses, Japanese, jazz band, journalism, Korean, Malay, Mandarin, math analysis, mathematics, music theory, photography, physical education, physics, pre-calculus, psychology, science, Spanish, stagecraft, statistics-AP, theater, theory of knowledge, U.S. history-AP, vocal ensemble, world studies, world wide web design, yearbook.
Graduation Requirements Art, English, foreign language, health, mathematics, physical education (includes health), science, social studies (includes history).
Special Academic Programs International Baccalaureate program; Advanced Placement exam preparation; honors section; independent study; special instructional classes for students with mild learning disabilities; ESL (100 students enrolled).
College Admission Counseling 131 students graduated in 2010; 122 went to college, including McGill University; Northwestern University; Texas A&M University; The Ohio State University; The University of British Columbia; University of Victoria. Other: 2 went to work, 3 entered military service, 3 entered a postgraduate year, 1 had other specific plans. Mean SAT critical reading: 554, mean SAT math: 643, mean SAT writing: 553, mean combined SAT: 1750, mean composite ACT: 27. 37% scored over 600 on SAT critical reading, 73% scored over 600 on SAT math, 47% scored over 600 on SAT writing, 73% scored over 26 on composite ACT.
Student Life Upper grades have uniform requirement, student council, honor system. Discipline rests primarily with faculty.
Tuition and Aid Day student tuition: 64,600 Malaysian ringgits. Tuition installment plan (individually arranged payment plans). IB Scholarships to Malaysian students available.
Admissions Traditional secondary-level entrance grade is 9. For fall 2010, 95 students applied for upper-level admission, 93 were accepted, 93 enrolled. English for Non-native Speakers, Gates MacGinite Reading Tests or Math Placement Exam required. Deadline for receipt of application materials: none. Application fee required: 800 Malaysian ringgits.
Athletics Interscholastic: aerobics/dance (boys, girls), aquatics (b,g), badminton (b,g), basketball (b,g), climbing (b,g), cross-country running (b,g), dance (b,g), dance team (b,g), equestrian sports (b,g), golf (b,g), rugby (b), running (b,g), soccer (b,g), softball (b,g), swimming and diving (b,g), tennis (b,g), touch football (b,g), track and field (b,g), volleyball (b,g); intramural: aerobics/dance (b,g), aquatics (b,g), badminton (b,g), basketball (b,g), climbing (b,g), cooperative games (b,g), dance (b,g), fitness (b,g), Frisbee (b,g), judo (b,g), martial arts (b,g), outdoor education (b,g), paddle tennis (b,g), physical fitness (b,g), rock climbing (b,g), rugby (b), soccer (b,g), softball (b,g), swimming and diving (b,g), tennis (b,g), touch football (b,g), track and field (b,g), ultimate Frisbee (b,g), volleyball (b,g), water polo (b,g), water volleyball (b,g), weight training (b,g); coed interscholastic: aerobics/dance, aquatics, badminton, dance, dance team, swimming and diving, track and field, wall climbing; coed intramural: aerobics/dance, aquatics, badminton, baseball, basketball, climbing, cooperative games, Cosom hockey, dance, field hockey, fitness, floor hockey, football, golf, kickball, outdoor education, paddle tennis, physical fitness, rock climbing, self defense, soccer, softball, strength & conditioning, swimming and diving, touch football, track and field, ultimate Frisbee, wall climbing, weight training, yoga. 3 PE instructors, 2 coaches.
Computers Computers are regularly used in all academic, computer applications, graphic design, multimedia, newspaper, photography, programming, publications, video film production, Web site design, yearbook classes. Computer network features include

on-campus library services, online commercial services, Internet access, wireless campus network, Internet filtering or blocking technology, Microsoft Office. Campus intranet, student e-mail accounts, and computer access in designated common areas are available to students. The school has a published electronic and media policy.
Contact Ms. Amina O'Kane, Director of Admissions. 011-603-4259-5600 Ext. 5626. Fax: 011-603-4259-5738. E-mail: aokane@iskl.edu.my. Web site: www.iskl.edu.my.

THE INTERNATIONAL SCHOOL OF LONDON

139 Gunnersbury Avenue

London W3 8LG, United Kingdom

Head of School: Mr. Huw Davies

General Information Coeducational day college-preparatory school. Grades K–13. Founded: 1972. Setting: urban. 2 buildings on campus. Member of European Council of International Schools. Language of instruction: English. Total enrollment: 340. Upper school average class size: 18. Upper school faculty-student ratio: 1:8. Upper School students typically attend 5 days per week.
Upper School Student Profile Grade 11: 30 students (15 boys, 15 girls); Grade 12: 30 students (15 boys, 15 girls).
Faculty School total: 67. In upper school: 15 men, 16 women; 21 have advanced degrees.
Subjects Offered Art, economics, English, French, geography, history, languages, mathematics, music, physical education, science, social sciences, Spanish, world affairs.
Graduation Requirements Foreign language, mathematics, science, social sciences. Community service is required.
Special Academic Programs International Baccalaureate program; ESL (47 students enrolled).
College Admission Counseling 22 students graduated in 2011; all went to college, including University of London; University of Oxford.
Student Life Upper grades have student council. Discipline rests primarily with faculty.
Tuition and Aid Day student tuition: £19,500.
Admissions For fall 2011, 36 students applied for upper-level admission, 30 were accepted, 30 enrolled. Deadline for receipt of application materials: July 30. Application fee required: £150. Interview recommended.
Athletics Interscholastic: basketball (boys, girls), soccer (b); intramural: badminton (b,g), softball (b,g), swimming and diving (b,g), table tennis (b,g), tennis (b,g); coed interscholastic: soccer; coed intramural: softball, swimming and diving, table tennis, tennis. 2 PE instructors, 2 coaches.
Computers Computers are regularly used in English, foreign language, mathematics, science classes. Computer network features include on-campus library services, Internet access, wireless campus network, Internet filtering or blocking technology. Student e-mail accounts are available to students. The school has a published electronic and media policy.
Contact Mr. Yoel Gordon, Director of Admissions. 20-8992-5823. Fax: 44-8993-7012. E-mail: mail@islondon.com. Web site: www.islondon.com.

INTERNATIONAL SCHOOL OF ZUG AND LUZERN (ISZL)

Walterswil

Baar 6340, Switzerland

Head of School: Dominic Currer

General Information Coeducational day college-preparatory, International Baccalaureate (PYP, MYP, DP), and Advanced Placement school. Founded: 1961. Setting: small town. Nearest major city is Zurich, Switzerland. 5-hectare campus. 1 building on campus. Approved or accredited by International Baccalaureate Organization and The College Board. Member of European Council of International Schools. Language of instruction: English. Total enrollment: 1,189. Upper school average class size: 11. Upper school faculty-student ratio: 1:6. There are 180 required school days per year for Upper School students. Upper School students typically attend 5 days per week. The average school day consists of 7 hours.
Faculty School total: 200. In upper school: 16 men, 28 women.
Subjects Offered Art, art history-AP, biology, biology-AP, calculus-AP, chemistry, chemistry-AP, computer graphics, computer science-AP, dance, drama, English, English language and composition-AP, English literature and composition-AP, environmental science-AP, ESL, European history-AP, French, French language-AP, German, German-AP, human geography - AP, humanities, integrated mathematics, integrated science, macro/microeconomics-AP, music, physical education, physics, physics-AP, pre-calculus, studio art-AP, technology/design.
Graduation Requirements Art, art history-AP, biology-AP, calculus-AP, chemistry-AP, choir, college counseling, computer programming-AP, computer science-AP, computers, dance, drama, economics-AP, English, English language-AP, English literature-AP, environmental science-AP, ESL, European history-AP, foreign language, French, French language-AP, German, German-AP, health education, human geography - AP, International Baccalaureate courses, lab science, macro/microeconomics-AP, macroeconomics-AP, mathematics, model United Nations, modern European history-AP, music, physical education (includes health), physics-AP, pre-calculus, SAT/ACT preparation, social sciences, Spanish, studio art-AP, yearbook. Community service is required.
Special Academic Programs International Baccalaureate program; Advanced Placement exam preparation; accelerated programs; independent study; ESL (40 students enrolled).
College Admission Counseling 33 students graduated in 2010; 26 went to college, including Pace University; Pepperdine University; Stanford University; Villanova University; Yale University. Other: 3 entered a postgraduate year, 4 had other specific plans.
Student Life Upper grades have specified standards of dress, student council. Discipline rests primarily with faculty.
Tuition and Aid Day student tuition: 21,500 Swiss francs–32,000 Swiss francs. Tuition installment plan (monthly payment plans, individually arranged payment plans, semester payment plan). Discounts for children of staff and reciprocal arrangements with international primary school available.
Admissions English for Non-native Speakers or math and English placement tests required. Deadline for receipt of application materials: none. Application fee required: 5000 Swiss francs. Interview recommended.
Athletics Interscholastic: aerobics/dance (girls), alpine skiing (b,g), basketball (b,g), cross-country running (b,g), golf (b,g), indoor soccer (b,g), rugby (b), skiing (downhill) (b,g), soccer (b,g), swimming and diving (b,g), track and field (b,g), volleyball (b,g); intramural: alpine skiing (b,g), basketball (b,g), cross-country running (b,g), indoor soccer (b,g), soccer (b,g), track and field (b,g); coed interscholastic: canoeing/kayaking, climbing, softball; coed intramural: aerobics/dance, backpacking, badminton, ball hockey, bicycling, canoeing/kayaking, climbing, dance, field hockey, golf, hiking/backpacking, ice skating, kayaking, martial arts, mountain biking, outdoor activities, outdoor education, racquetball, rowing, running, sailing, skiing (downhill), snowboarding, soccer, softball, swimming and diving, tennis, walking, winter walking. 2 PE instructors, 2 coaches, 2 athletic trainers.
Computers Computers are regularly used in college planning classes. Computer network features include Internet access, Internet filtering or blocking technology. Campus intranet, student e-mail accounts, and computer access in designated common areas are available to students. The school has a published electronic and media policy.
Contact Urs Kappeler, Business Director. 41-41-768 2950. Fax: 41-41-768 2951. E-mail: urs.kappeler@iszl.ch. Web site: www.iszl.ch.

IOLANI SCHOOL

563 Kamoku Street

Honolulu, Hawaii 96826

Head of School: Dr. Val T. Iwashita

General Information Coeducational day college-preparatory, arts, and technology school, affiliated with Episcopal Church. Grades K–12. Founded: 1863. Setting: urban. 25-acre campus. 7 buildings on campus. Approved or accredited by National Association of Episcopal Schools, Western Association of Schools and Colleges, and Hawaii Department of Education. Member of National Association of Independent Schools and Secondary School Admission Test Board. Endowment: $100 million. Total enrollment: 1,867. Upper school average class size: 17. Upper school faculty-student ratio: 1:12. There are 178 required school days per year for Upper School students. Upper School students typically attend 5 days per week. The average school day consists of 6 hours.
Upper School Student Profile Grade 7: 181 students (84 boys, 97 girls); Grade 8: 196 students (99 boys, 97 girls); Grade 9: 244 students (120 boys, 124 girls); Grade 10: 242 students (113 boys, 129 girls); Grade 11: 233 students (109 boys, 124 girls); Grade 12: 230 students (114 boys, 116 girls).
Faculty School total: 185. In upper school: 63 men, 68 women; 90 have advanced degrees.
Subjects Offered 3-dimensional design, Advanced Placement courses, advanced studio art-AP, African American history, algebra, American history, American history-AP, American literature, American literature-AP, art, Asian studies, band, Basic programming, Bible, Bible studies, biology, biology-AP, British literature, calculus, calculus-AP, ceramics, chemistry, chemistry-AP, Chinese, chorus, computer programming, computer programming-AP, computer science, computer science-AP, conceptual physics, concert band, creative writing, dance, drama, earth science, economics, economics-AP, English, English as a foreign language, English language and composition-AP, English literature, English literature and composition-AP, English literature-AP, European history, European history-AP, expository writing, film and literature, fine arts, French, French language-AP, French literature-AP, geography, geometry, government-AP, government/civics, Hawaiian history, health, health education, history, Japanese, Japanese studies, jazz band, jazz ensemble, journalism, Latin, Latin-AP, leadership, macro/microeconomics-AP, macroeconomics-AP, Mandarin, marching band, mathematics, money management, music, newspaper, orchestra, photography, physical education, physics, physics-AP, pre-calculus, psychology, psychology-AP, religion, science, Shakespeare, social studies, Spanish, Spanish-AP, speech, statistics, statistics-AP, studio art-AP, theater, trigonometry, U.S. government and politics-AP, Web site design, world affairs, world history, world literature, writing.

Graduation Requirements Algebra, arts and fine arts (art, music, dance, drama), Bible, biology, chemistry, computer science, English, European history, foreign language, geometry, literature, physical education (includes health), physics, U.S. history.
Special Academic Programs Advanced Placement exam preparation; honors section; independent study; academic accommodation for the gifted, the musically talented, and the artistically talented; ESL (15 students enrolled).
College Admission Counseling 223 students graduated in 2010; all went to college, including Oregon State University; Santa Clara University; University of Hawaii at Manoa; University of Southern California; University of Washington.
Student Life Upper grades have specified standards of dress, student council. Discipline rests primarily with faculty. Attendance at religious services is required.
Tuition and Aid Day student tuition: $16,150. Tuition installment plan (monthly payment plans, semester and annual payment plans). Need-based scholarship grants available. In 2010–11, 12% of upper-school students received aid. Total amount of financial aid awarded in 2010–11: $3,000,500.
Admissions Traditional secondary-level entrance grade is 7. For fall 2010, 696 students applied for upper-level admission, 188 were accepted, 132 enrolled. SSAT required. Deadline for receipt of application materials: December 1. Application fee required: $125. On-campus interview recommended.
Athletics Interscholastic: aerobics/dance (girls), baseball (b), basketball (b,g), bowling (b,g), canoeing/kayaking (b,g), cheering (g), cross-country running (b,g), dance (b,g), dance team (g), diving (b,g), football (b), kayaking (b,g), modern dance (g), ocean paddling (b,g), soccer (b,g), softball (g), strength & conditioning (b,g), swimming and diving (b,g), tennis (b,g), track and field (b,g), volleyball (b,g), water polo (b,g), weight training (b,g), wrestling (b,g); coed interscholastic: ballet, golf, judo, tennis. 6 PE instructors, 170 coaches, 3 athletic trainers.
Computers Computers are regularly used in all academic classes. Computer network features include on-campus library services, online commercial services, Internet access, wireless campus network, Internet filtering or blocking technology. Student e-mail accounts and computer access in designated common areas are available to students. The school has a published electronic and media policy.
Contact Patricia N. Liu, Director of Admission. 808-943-2222. Fax: 808-943-2375. E-mail: admission@iolani.org. Web site: www.iolani.org.

IONA PREPARATORY SCHOOL

255 Wilmot Road

New Rochelle, New York 10804

Head of School: Br. Thomas Leto

General Information Boys' day college-preparatory, arts, religious studies, and technology school, affiliated with Roman Catholic Church. Grades 9–12. Founded: 1916. Setting: suburban. Nearest major city is New York. 29-acre campus. 3 buildings on campus. Approved or accredited by Christian Brothers Association, Middle States Association of Colleges and Schools, National Catholic Education Association, New York State Association of Independent Schools, and New York State Board of Regents. Member of National Association of Independent Schools. Endowment: $6 million. Total enrollment: 785. Upper school average class size: 26. Upper school faculty-student ratio: 1:13. There are 180 required school days per year for Upper School students. Upper School students typically attend 5 days per week. The average school day consists of 6 hours and 30 minutes.
Upper School Student Profile Grade 9: 213 students (213 boys); Grade 10: 195 students (195 boys); Grade 11: 188 students (188 boys); Grade 12: 189 students (189 boys). 87% of students are Roman Catholic.
Faculty School total: 67. In upper school: 47 men, 18 women; 65 have advanced degrees.
Subjects Offered Accounting, Advanced Placement courses, algebra, American history, American history-AP, American literature, anatomy, art, astronomy, biology, biology-AP, British literature, calculus, chemistry, chemistry-AP, communications, community service, composition-AP, computer programming, computer science, economics, English, English literature-AP, English/composition-AP, environmental science, European history, European history-AP, European literature, fine arts, French, French as a second language, geometry, government-AP, graphic design, health, health and safety, history, Italian, Latin, media, music, painting, physical education, physics, physiology, psychology, psychology-AP, religion, science, social sciences, social studies, Spanish, trigonometry, U.S. government and politics-AP, word processing, world literature, world religions.
Graduation Requirements Art, computer science, English, foreign language, mathematics, music, physical education (includes health), religion (includes Bible studies and theology), science, social studies (includes history), 75 hours of community service (senior year).
Special Academic Programs Advanced Placement exam preparation; honors section; study at local college for college credit; study abroad; academic accommodation for the gifted.
College Admission Counseling 168 students graduated in 2011; all went to college, including Boston College; Fairfield University; Fordham University; Iona College; Loyola University Maryland. Mean SAT critical reading: 610, mean SAT math: 620. 30% scored over 600 on SAT critical reading, 39% scored over 600 on SAT math.
Student Life Upper grades have specified standards of dress, student council, honor system. Discipline rests primarily with faculty. Attendance at religious services is required.
Tuition and Aid Day student tuition: $14,900. Tuition installment plan (monthly payment plans, individually arranged payment plans, 10-payment plan, semester payment plan). Merit scholarship grants, need-based scholarship grants available. In 2011–12, 31% of upper-school students received aid; total upper-school merit-scholarship money awarded: $187,000. Total amount of financial aid awarded in 2011–12: $325,000.
Admissions Traditional secondary-level entrance grade is 9. For fall 2011, 913 students applied for upper-level admission, 560 were accepted, 213 enrolled. Admissions testing, Catholic High School Entrance Examination, ISEE, SSAT, Test of Achievement and Proficiency or writing sample required. Deadline for receipt of application materials: none. No application fee required. Interview recommended.
Athletics Interscholastic: badminton, baseball, basketball, bowling, climbing, crew, cross-country running, diving, field hockey, flag football, football, golf, ice hockey, indoor track, indoor track & field, lacrosse, paint ball, physical fitness, rock climbing, running, soccer, swimming and diving, tennis, track and field, ultimate Frisbee, volleyball, weight lifting, weight training, winter (indoor) track, wrestling; intramural: baseball, basketball, climbing, fitness, flag football, floor hockey, Frisbee, physical fitness, physical training, rock climbing, soccer, strength & conditioning, tennis, volleyball, wall climbing, weight lifting. 3 PE instructors, 40 coaches, 1 athletic trainer.
Computers Computers are regularly used in all classes. Computer network features include on-campus library services, online commercial services, Internet access, wireless campus network, Internet filtering or blocking technology. Campus intranet and student e-mail accounts are available to students. The school has a published electronic and media policy.
Contact Mrs. Judy M. Musho, Director of Admissions. 914-632-0714 Ext. 215. Fax: 914-632-9760. E-mail: jmusho@ionaprep.org. Web site: www.ionaprep.org.

ISIDORE NEWMAN SCHOOL

1903 Jefferson Avenue

New Orleans, Louisiana 70115

Head of School: Dr. Thomas J. Locke

General Information Coeducational day college-preparatory school. Grades PK–12. Founded: 1903. Setting: urban. 11-acre campus. 10 buildings on campus. Approved or accredited by Independent Schools Association of the Southwest, Southern Association of Colleges and Schools, and Louisiana Department of Education. Member of National Association of Independent Schools. Endowment: $24 million. Total enrollment: 921. Upper school average class size: 16. Upper school faculty-student ratio: 1:17. There are 175 required school days per year for Upper School students. Upper School students typically attend 5 days per week. The average school day consists of 7 hours and 50 minutes.
Upper School Student Profile Grade 9: 73 students (41 boys, 32 girls); Grade 10: 70 students (44 boys, 26 girls); Grade 11: 83 students (52 boys, 31 girls); Grade 12: 80 students (50 boys, 30 girls).
Faculty School total: 117. In upper school: 19 men, 26 women.
Subjects Offered Advanced computer applications, Advanced Placement courses, algebra, American history, American history-AP, American literature, anatomy, art, art history, biology, biology-AP, calculus, calculus-AP, ceramics, chemistry, Chinese, choral music, chorus, civics, communications, computer science-AP, dance, drama, English, English literature, environmental science, European history-AP, film, film history, fine arts, French, French language-AP, French literature-AP, French-AP, genetics, geometry, government/civics, history, human development, humanities, Latin, Latin-AP, mathematics, modern European history, modern European history-AP, music, music theory, peer counseling, photojournalism, physical education, physics, physics-AP, physiology, science, sculpture, social studies, Spanish, Spanish language-AP, Spanish literature-AP, speech, statistics-AP, technical theater, theater, trigonometry, U.S. government and politics-AP, U.S. history, U.S. history-AP, world history.
Graduation Requirements Arts and fine arts (art, music, dance, drama), computer science, English, foreign language, mathematics, physical education (includes health), science, social studies (includes history), speech, senior Capstone Elective-one class each semester of senior year.
Special Academic Programs Advanced Placement exam preparation; honors section; independent study; term away projects.
College Admission Counseling 86 students graduated in 2010; all went to college, including Louisiana State University and Agricultural and Mechanical College; Loyola University New Orleans; Rhodes College; The University of Texas at Austin; Tulane University; University of Georgia.
Student Life Upper grades have specified standards of dress, student council, honor system. Discipline rests equally with students and faculty.
Tuition and Aid Day student tuition: $18,467. Tuition installment plan (Sallie Mae tuition loans). Need-based scholarship grants, Sallie Mae Loans available. In 2010–11, 25% of upper-school students received aid. Total amount of financial aid awarded in 2010–11: $847,872.
Admissions Traditional secondary-level entrance grade is 9. ERB (CTP-Verbal, Quantitative), ERB CTP III, independent norms, Individual IQ, Achievement and

behavior rating scale, ISEE, school's own test and writing sample required. Deadline for receipt of application materials: none. Application fee required: $35. Interview required.

Athletics Interscholastic: aquatics (boys, girls), baseball (b), basketball (b,g), cross-country running (b,g), football (b), golf (b,g), gymnastics (b,g), indoor track & field (b), soccer (b,g), softball (g), swimming and diving (b,g), tennis (b,g), track and field (b,g), volleyball (g); coed interscholastic: cheering. 16 coaches, 2 athletic trainers.

Computers Computers are regularly used in all academic classes. Computer network features include on-campus library services, online commercial services, Internet access, wireless campus network, Internet filtering or blocking technology. Campus intranet and student e-mail accounts are available to students. Students grades are available online. The school has a published electronic and media policy.

Contact Mrs. Ladd Sheets, Admission Assistant. 504-896-6323. Fax: 504-896-8597. E-mail: lsheets@newmanschool.org. Web site: www.newmanschool.org.

ISLAND SCHOOL

3-1875 Kaumualii Highway

Lihue, Hawaii 96766-9597

Head of School: Mr. Robert Springer

General Information Coeducational day college-preparatory, arts, bilingual studies, and technology school. Grades PK–12. Founded: 1977. Setting: small town. 38-acre campus. 11 buildings on campus. Approved or accredited by Academy of Orton-Gillingham Practitioners and Educators, The Hawaii Council of Private Schools, Western Association of Schools and Colleges, and Hawaii Department of Education. Endowment: $800,000. Total enrollment: 362. Upper school average class size: 15. Upper school faculty-student ratio: 1:11. There are 174 required school days per year for Upper School students. Upper School students typically attend 5 days per week. The average school day consists of 7 hours and 45 minutes.

Upper School Student Profile Grade 6: 27 students (11 boys, 16 girls); Grade 7: 40 students (17 boys, 23 girls); Grade 8: 34 students (18 boys, 16 girls); Grade 9: 30 students (18 boys, 12 girls); Grade 10: 23 students (8 boys, 15 girls); Grade 11: 34 students (11 boys, 23 girls); Grade 12: 23 students (10 boys, 13 girls).

Faculty School total: 46. In upper school: 6 men, 17 women; 9 have advanced degrees.

Subjects Offered Calculus, calculus-AP, chemistry, chemistry-AP, Chinese, intro to computers, introduction to literature, keyboarding, language structure, literature, marine ecology, marine science, mathematics, medieval history, medieval literature, microeconomics, modern Western civilization, modern world history, money management, music, news writing, organic gardening, performing arts, photo shop, photography, physical education, physical fitness, physics, physics-AP, poetry, pre-algebra, pre-calculus, religious studies, robotics, SAT/ACT preparation, scuba diving, sex education, Shakespeare, Shakespearean histories, short story, social studies, stagecraft, stock market, student government, theater, theater design and production, trigonometry, U.S. government, U.S. government and politics, U.S. government and politics-AP, U.S. history, U.S. literature, world history, world religions, world studies, world wide web design, writing, writing workshop, yearbook.

Graduation Requirements Drama, electives, English, foreign language, life skills, mathematics, music, physical education (includes health), science, social studies (includes history), visual arts.

Special Academic Programs 3 Advanced Placement exams for which test preparation is offered; honors section; independent study; study at local college for college credit; academic accommodation for the gifted.

College Admission Counseling 24 students graduated in 2010; all went to college, including Pepperdine University; University of Denver; University of Hawaii at Manoa. Mean SAT critical reading: 526, mean SAT math: 519, mean SAT writing: 511.

Student Life Upper grades have specified standards of dress, student council, honor system. Discipline rests primarily with faculty.

Tuition and Aid Day student tuition: $11,580. Tuition installment plan (FACTS Tuition Payment Plan). Need-based scholarship grants available. In 2010–11, 41% of upper-school students received aid. Total amount of financial aid awarded in 2010–11: $15,000.

Admissions Traditional secondary-level entrance grade is 9. For fall 2010, 100 students applied for upper-level admission, 65 were accepted, 55 enrolled. Admissions testing, any standardized test, essay, Math Placement Exam and Stanford Achievement Test required. Deadline for receipt of application materials: none. Application fee required: $40. Interview required.

Athletics Interscholastic: basketball (boys, girls), cross-country running (b,g), golf (b,g), marksmanship (b,g), riflery (b,g), soccer (b,g), swimming and diving (b,g), tennis (b,g), track and field (b,g), volleyball (b,g); intramural: basketball (b,g), cross-country running (b,g), physical fitness (b,g), physical training (b,g), scuba diving (b,g), soccer (b,g), softball (b,g), volleyball (b,g), weight lifting (b,g); coed interscholastic: riflery; coed intramural: baseball, basketball, combined training, dance, flag football, floor hockey, football, jogging, kickball, physical fitness, physical training, running, scuba diving, self defense, soccer, softball, volleyball, weight lifting, yoga. 1 PE instructor, 11 coaches.

Computers Computers are regularly used in business, data processing, desktop publishing, English, history, information technology, introduction to technology, mathematics classes. Computer network features include on-campus library services, Internet access, wireless campus network. Student e-mail accounts are available to students. Students grades are available online.

Contact Mr. Sean Magoun, Admission Director. 808-246-0233 Ext. 241. Fax: 808-245-6053. E-mail: sean@ischool.org. Web site: www.ischool.org.

JACK M. BARRACK HEBREW ACADEMY

272 South Bryn Mawr Avenue

Bryn Mawr, Pennsylvania 19010

Head of School: Mrs. Sharon P. Levin

General Information Coeducational day college-preparatory and religious studies school, affiliated with Jewish faith. Grades 6–12. Founded: 1946. Setting: suburban. Nearest major city is Philadelphia. 35-acre campus. 2 buildings on campus. Approved or accredited by Middle States Association of Colleges and Schools and Pennsylvania Department of Education. Member of National Association of Independent Schools. Languages of instruction: English and Hebrew. Endowment: $3.1 million. Total enrollment: 274. Upper school average class size: 16. Upper school faculty-student ratio: 1:15. There are 168 required school days per year for Upper School students. Upper School students typically attend 5 days per week. The average school day consists of 7 hours.

Upper School Student Profile Grade 9: 34 students (16 boys, 18 girls); Grade 10: 62 students (32 boys, 30 girls); Grade 11: 56 students (19 boys, 37 girls); Grade 12: 53 students (20 boys, 33 girls). 100% of students are Jewish.

Faculty School total: 53. In upper school: 17 men, 36 women; 40 have advanced degrees.

Subjects Offered Algebra, American history, American literature, art, astronomy, Bible studies, biology, calculus, chemistry, community service, computer math, computer programming, computer science, creative writing, earth science, English, English literature, environmental science, environmental science-AP, ethics, European history, French, geometry, government/civics, grammar, health, Hebrew, history, Jewish studies, Latin, mathematics, music, physical education, physics, public speaking, religion, science, social studies, Spanish, trigonometry, world history, writing.

Graduation Requirements English, foreign language, mathematics, physical education (includes health), religion (includes Bible studies and theology), science, social studies (includes history), senior community service project–150 hours in the senior year.

Special Academic Programs 8 Advanced Placement exams for which test preparation is offered; accelerated programs; independent study; term-away projects; study at local college for college credit; study abroad; academic accommodation for the gifted; remedial reading and/or remedial writing; remedial math; special instructional classes for deaf students.

College Admission Counseling 50 students graduated in 2011; all went to college, including Brandeis University; New York University; University of Maryland, College Park; University of Pennsylvania; University of Pittsburgh. Median SAT critical reading: 605, median SAT math: 642, median SAT writing: 605.

Student Life Upper grades have specified standards of dress, student council. Discipline rests primarily with faculty.

Tuition and Aid Day student tuition: $26,650. Tuition installment plan (Key Tuition Payment Plan, monthly payment plans, individually arranged payment plans). Merit scholarship grants, need-based scholarship grants available. In 2011–12, 48% of upper-school students received aid; total upper-school merit-scholarship money awarded: $151,200. Total amount of financial aid awarded in 2011–12: $1,483,690.

Admissions Traditional secondary-level entrance grade is 9. For fall 2011, 65 students applied for upper-level admission, 59 were accepted, 49 enrolled. ISEE required. Deadline for receipt of application materials: none. Application fee required: $75. On-campus interview required.

Athletics Interscholastic: baseball (boys), basketball (b,g), soccer (b,g), softball (g), tennis (b,g), track and field (g); intramural: basketball (b,g), field hockey (b,g), golf (b,g), lacrosse (g), running (b,g), soccer (b,g), squash (g), track and field (g), volleyball (b,g); coed interscholastic: cross-country running, soccer, swimming and diving. 2 PE instructors, 17 coaches.

Computers Computers are regularly used in foreign language, French, health, history, humanities, independent study, information technology, introduction to technology, journalism, keyboarding, Latin, library, literary magazine, mathematics, media production, multimedia, news writing, newspaper, photojournalism, programming, publications, remedial study skills, research skills, SAT preparation, science, social sciences, Spanish, study skills, technology, video film production, Web site design, word processing, writing, yearbook classes. Computer network features include on-campus library services, online commercial services, Internet access, wireless campus network, Internet filtering or blocking technology. Campus intranet, student e-mail accounts, and computer access in designated common areas are available to students. Students grades are available online. The school has a published electronic and media policy.

Contact Vivian Young, Director of Admissions. 610-922-2350. Fax: 610-922-2301. E-mail: vyoung@jbha.org. Web site: www.jbha.org.

JACKSON CHRISTIAN SCHOOL

832 Country Club Lane

Jackson, Tennessee 38305

Head of School: Dr. Rick Brooks

General Information Coeducational day college-preparatory, arts, religious studies, bilingual studies, and technology school, affiliated with Church of Christ. Grades JK–12. Founded: 1976. Setting: suburban. 30-acre campus. 6 buildings on campus. Approved or accredited by National Christian School Association, Southern Association of Colleges and Schools, and Tennessee Department of Education. Endowment: $875,000. Total enrollment: 857. Upper school average class size: 19. Upper school faculty-student ratio: 1:19. There are 180 required school days per year for Upper School students. Upper School students typically attend 5 days per week. The average school day consists of 6 hours.

Upper School Student Profile Grade 6: 86 students (39 boys, 47 girls); Grade 7: 72 students (41 boys, 31 girls); Grade 8: 58 students (30 boys, 28 girls); Grade 9: 79 students (40 boys, 39 girls); Grade 10: 60 students (28 boys, 32 girls); Grade 11: 77 students (38 boys, 39 girls); Grade 12: 70 students (40 boys, 30 girls). 34% of students are members of Church of Christ.

Faculty School total: 65. In upper school: 14 men, 24 women; 13 have advanced degrees.

Subjects Offered ACT preparation, advanced chemistry, advanced computer applications, advanced studio art-AP, algebra, American government, American history, anatomy and physiology, art, baseball, basketball, Bible, Bible studies, biology, calculus, chemistry, choir, chorus, current events, ecology, economics, English, English composition, geometry, government, government/civics, honors English, journalism, keyboarding, life science, physical education, physical science, physics, pre-calculus, psychology, Spanish, state history, theater, theater arts, trigonometry, U.S. government, U.S. history, word processing, world geography, world history.

Graduation Requirements 20th century world history, 3-dimensional art, 3-dimensional design, ACT preparation, arts and fine arts (art, music, dance, drama), English, foreign language, mathematics, physical education (includes health), religion (includes Bible studies and theology), science, social studies (includes history), must take the ACT test.

Special Academic Programs Honors section; study at local college for college credit, programs in English, mathematics for dyslexic students.

College Admission Counseling 81 students graduated in 2010; 79 went to college, including Freed-Hardeman University; Harding University; Jackson State Community College; Middle Tennessee State University; The University of Tennessee; Union University. Other: 2 went to work. Median composite ACT: 24. 35% scored over 26 on composite ACT.

Student Life Upper grades have uniform requirement, student council, honor system. Discipline rests primarily with faculty.

Tuition and Aid Day student tuition: $7200. Guaranteed tuition plan. Tuition installment plan (monthly payment plans, individually arranged payment plans, quarterly payment plan, semester payment plan, pay-in-full discount). Tuition reduction for siblings, need-based scholarship grants available. In 2010–11, 15% of upper-school students received aid. Total amount of financial aid awarded in 2010–11: $15,218.

Admissions Traditional secondary-level entrance grade is 9. For fall 2010, 40 students applied for upper-level admission, 32 were accepted, 31 enrolled. Math and English placement tests required. Deadline for receipt of application materials: none. Application fee required: $100. Interview required.

Athletics Interscholastic: baseball (boys), basketball (b,g), cheering (g), cross-country running (b,g), football (b), golf (b,g), soccer (b,g), softball (g), tennis (b,g), track and field (b,g); coed interscholastic: cheering. 3 PE instructors, 10 coaches.

Computers Computers are regularly used in business applications, computer applications, desktop publishing, library, multimedia, programming, science, Web site design classes. Computer network features include online commercial services, Internet access, wireless campus network, Internet filtering or blocking technology. Campus intranet, student e-mail accounts, and computer access in designated common areas are available to students. Students grades are available online.

Contact Chris Brush, Director of Admissions. 731-668-8055. Fax: 731-668-8055. E-mail: cbrush@jcseagles.org. Web site: www.jcseagles.org.

JACKSON PREPARATORY SCHOOL

3100 Lakeland Drive

Jackson, Mississippi 39232

Head of School: Susan R. Lindsay

General Information Coeducational day college-preparatory school. Grades 6–12. Founded: 1970. Setting: urban. 74-acre campus. 6 buildings on campus. Approved or accredited by Mississippi Private School Association, Southern Association of Colleges and Schools, Southern Association of Independent Schools, and The College Board. Member of National Association of Independent Schools. Endowment: $993,373. Total enrollment: 815. Upper school average class size: 16. Upper school faculty-student ratio: 1:13. There are 176 required school days per year for Upper School students. Upper School students typically attend 5 days per week. The average school day consists of 6 hours and 45 minutes.

Upper School Student Profile Grade 10: 137 students (74 boys, 63 girls); Grade 11: 126 students (67 boys, 59 girls); Grade 12: 135 students (63 boys, 72 girls).

Faculty School total: 90. In upper school: 26 men, 49 women; 42 have advanced degrees.

Subjects Offered Accounting, advanced chemistry, Advanced Placement courses, algebra, American government, American history, American history-AP, American literature, art, Asian studies, Bible as literature, biology, biology-AP, British literature, calculus, calculus-AP, chemistry, chemistry-AP, choral music, civics, classical studies, computer science, creative writing, debate, discrete mathematics, drama, driver education, earth science, economics, English, English literature, English literature-AP, European history, film, fine arts, finite math, French, geography, geometry, government-AP, government/civics, grammar, Greek, Greek culture, history, honors algebra, honors English, honors geometry, journalism, Latin, Latin-AP, mathematics, music, physical education, physics, physics-AP, pre-algebra, pre-calculus, science, social studies, Spanish, trigonometry, U.S. government, U.S. government and politics-AP, U.S. history, U.S. history-AP, world history, world literature.

Graduation Requirements Arts and fine arts (art, music, dance, drama), computer applications, English, foreign language, mathematics, science, social studies (includes history).

Special Academic Programs Advanced Placement exam preparation; honors section; academic accommodation for the gifted, the musically talented, and the artistically talented; programs in English, mathematics, general development for dyslexic students.

College Admission Counseling 122 students graduated in 2011; all went to college, including Louisiana State University in Shreveport; Mississippi State University; The University of Alabama; University of Mississippi. Mean SAT critical reading: 632, mean SAT math: 624, mean SAT writing: 614, mean composite ACT: 26.

Student Life Upper grades have uniform requirement, student council, honor system. Discipline rests primarily with faculty.

Summer Programs Remediation, enrichment, art/fine arts, computer instruction programs offered; session focuses on enrichment; held on campus; accepts boys and girls; open to students from other schools. 200 students usually enrolled. 2012 schedule: June 7 to July 16. Application deadline: May 1.

Tuition and Aid Day student tuition: $10,750. Tuition installment plan (monthly payment plans). Need-based scholarship grants available. In 2011–12, 12% of upper-school students received aid. Total amount of financial aid awarded in 2011–12: $195,000.

Admissions Traditional secondary-level entrance grade is 10. For fall 2011, 22 students applied for upper-level admission, 15 were accepted, 14 enrolled. Non-standardized placement tests and OLSAT, Stanford Achievement Test required. Deadline for receipt of application materials: none. Application fee required: $40. Interview required.

Athletics Interscholastic: baseball (boys), basketball (b,g), cheering (g), cross-country running (b,g), dance team (g), football (b), Frisbee (b), soccer (b,g), softball (g), swimming and diving (b,g), tennis (b,g), track and field (b,g), ultimate Frisbee (b); intramural: basketball (b,g), Frisbee (b), soccer (b,g), volleyball (b,g); coed interscholastic: cheering, golf. 4 coaches.

Computers Computers are regularly used in all classes. Computer network features include on-campus library services, online commercial services, Internet access, Electric Library, EBSCOhost®, GaleNet, Grolier Online, NewsBank, online subscription services. The school has a published electronic and media policy.

Contact Lesley W. Morton, Director of Admission. 601-932-8106 Ext. 1. Fax: 601-936-4068. E-mail: lmorton@jacksonprep.net. Web site: www.jacksonprep.net.

JESUIT COLLEGE PREPARATORY SCHOOL

12345 Inwood Road

Dallas, Texas 75244

Head of School: Mr. Tom Garrison

General Information Boys' day college-preparatory school, affiliated with Roman Catholic Church (Jesuit order). Grades 9–12. Founded: 1942. Setting: suburban. 27-acre campus. 2 buildings on campus. Approved or accredited by Jesuit Secondary Education Association, National Catholic Education Association, Southern Association of Colleges and Schools, Texas Catholic Conference, and Texas Department of Education. Endowment: $25.6 million. Total enrollment: 1,072. Upper school average class size: 17. Upper school faculty-student ratio: 1:11. There are 190 required school days per year for Upper School students. Upper School students typically attend 5 days per week. The average school day consists of 6 hours.

Upper School Student Profile Grade 9: 276 students (276 boys); Grade 10: 269 students (269 boys); Grade 11: 259 students (259 boys); Grade 12: 268 students (268 boys). 80.5% of students are Roman Catholic Church (Jesuit order).

Faculty School total: 115. In upper school: 85 men, 30 women; 56 have advanced degrees.

Subjects Offered Advanced chemistry, advanced computer applications, advanced math, American literature-AP, American studies, art, art appreciation, art-AP, arts, band, Bible, biology, biology-AP, British literature, British literature-AP, calculus, calculus-

AP, Catholic belief and practice, ceramics, chemistry, chemistry-AP, choir, Christian ethics, church history, civics, college counseling, community service, composition, composition-AP, computer applications, computer graphics, computer science, computer science-AP, contemporary issues, discrete mathematics, drama, drama performance, drama workshop, drawing, drawing and design, driver education, earth science, economics, economics-AP, English, English composition, English language and composition-AP, English language-AP, English literature, English literature and composition-AP, English literature-AP, English-AP, English/composition-AP, ethical decision making, European history, fine arts, French, French-AP, general science, geometry, government, government-AP, grammar, guitar, health, history, history-AP, honors algebra, honors English, honors geometry, honors U.S. history, honors world history, instrumental music, jazz band, journalism, Latin, literature and composition-AP, marching band, mathematics, mathematics-AP, microcomputer technology applications, music, music appreciation, musical productions, orchestra, peace and justice, peer ministry, performing arts, physical education, physics, physics-AP, pottery, prayer/spirituality, pre-calculus, psychology, public speaking, publications, religion, scripture, social studies, Spanish, Spanish language-AP, Spanish literature-AP, Spanish-AP, speech, speech and debate, speech and oral interpretations, statistics, student government, student publications, studio art, studio art-AP, symphonic band, theater, theology, U.S. government, U.S. government and politics-AP, U.S. history, U.S. history-AP, U.S. literature, world history, world history-AP.

Graduation Requirements Arts and fine arts (art, music, dance, drama), computer science, English, foreign language, mathematics, physical education (includes health), science, social studies (includes history), theology. Community service is required.

Special Academic Programs 18 Advanced Placement exams for which test preparation is offered; honors section; independent study; study at local college for college credit.

College Admission Counseling 248 students graduated in 2011; 246 went to college, including Saint Louis University; Southern Methodist University; Texas A&M University; Texas Christian University; The University of Alabama; The University of Texas at Austin. Other: 2 had other specific plans. Mean SAT critical reading: 598, mean SAT math: 618, mean SAT writing: 595.

Student Life Upper grades have specified standards of dress, student council, honor system. Discipline rests primarily with faculty. Attendance at religious services is required.

Summer Programs Remediation, enrichment, advancement, sports, art/fine arts, computer instruction programs offered; session focuses on youth recreation; held on campus; accepts boys and girls; open to students from other schools. 800 students usually enrolled. 2012 schedule: June 15 to July 10. Application deadline: May 30.

Tuition and Aid Day student tuition: $13,800. Tuition installment plan (FACTS Tuition Payment Plan). Merit scholarship grants, need-based scholarship grants, paying campus jobs available. In 2011–12, 25% of upper-school students received aid; total upper-school merit-scholarship money awarded: $56,000. Total amount of financial aid awarded in 2011–12: $1,233,850.

Admissions Traditional secondary-level entrance grade is 9. For fall 2011, 492 students applied for upper-level admission, 310 were accepted, 276 enrolled. ISEE required. Deadline for receipt of application materials: January 6. Application fee required: $75. Interview required.

Athletics Interscholastic: baseball, basketball, bowling, crew, cross-country running, diving, fencing, football, golf, ice hockey, lacrosse, power lifting, rugby, soccer, swimming and diving, tennis, track and field, water polo, wrestling; intramural: basketball, bicycling, broomball, flagball, floor hockey, indoor soccer, ultimate Frisbee, volleyball; coed interscholastic: cheering, drill team. 6 PE instructors, 30 coaches, 2 athletic trainers.

Computers Computers are regularly used in college planning, desktop publishing, digital applications, engineering, English, foreign language, graphic design, graphics, humanities, introduction to technology, journalism, literary magazine, mathematics, media production, multimedia, newspaper, programming, publications, science, social studies, technology, video film production, Web site design, writing, yearbook classes. Computer network features include on-campus library services, online commercial services, Internet access, wireless campus network, Internet filtering or blocking technology. Campus intranet, student e-mail accounts, and computer access in designated common areas are available to students. Students grades are available online. The school has a published electronic and media policy.

Contact Mrs. Susie Herrmann, Admissions Assistant. 972-387-8700 Ext. 453. Fax: 972-980-6707. E-mail: sherrmann@jesuitcp.org. Web site: www.jesuitcp.org.

JESUIT HIGH SCHOOL OF NEW ORLEANS

4133 Banks Street

New Orleans, Louisiana 70119-6883

Head of School: Rev. Raymond R. Fitzgerald, SJ

General Information Boys' day college-preparatory school, affiliated with Roman Catholic Church. Grades 8–12. Founded: 1847. Setting: urban. Nearest major city is Baton Rouge. 8-acre campus. 3 buildings on campus. Approved or accredited by Jesuit Secondary Education Association, National Catholic Education Association, Southern Association of Colleges and Schools, and Louisiana Department of Education. Endowment: $1.2 million. Total enrollment: 1,354. Upper school average class size: 22. Upper school faculty-student ratio: 1:22. There are 180 required school days per year for Upper School students. Upper School students typically attend 5 days per week. The average school day consists of 5 hours and 30 minutes.

Upper School Student Profile Grade 9: 292 students (292 boys); Grade 10: 270 students (270 boys); Grade 11: 261 students (261 boys); Grade 12: 266 students (266 boys). 87.4% of students are Roman Catholic.

Faculty School total: 110. In upper school: 73 men, 37 women; 59 have advanced degrees.

Subjects Offered Algebra, American history, American literature, analysis, art history, arts, band, Bible studies, biology, biology-AP, calculus, calculus-AP, chemistry, chemistry-AP, Christianity, church history, civics, community service, comparative government and politics-AP, computer applications, computer literacy, computer programming, computer science, creative writing, economics, English, English literature, English literature and composition-AP, environmental science, fine arts, French, French language-AP, geography, geometry, government/civics, grammar, Greek, health, history, JROTC, Latin, Latin-AP, law, mathematics, military history, military science, music, physical education, physical science, physics, physics-AP, politics, psychology, public speaking, religion, ROTC (for boys), SAT/ACT preparation, science, scripture, social studies, sociology, Spanish, Spanish language-AP, speech, study skills, theology, trigonometry, U.S. government and politics-AP, U.S. history-AP, Western civilization, world literature, writing.

Graduation Requirements Arts and fine arts (art, music, dance, drama), computer science, English, foreign language, mathematics, physical education (includes health), religion (includes Bible studies and theology), science, social sciences, social studies (includes history), speech. Community service is required.

Special Academic Programs Advanced Placement exam preparation; honors section.

College Admission Counseling 264 students graduated in 2011; 263 went to college, including Louisiana State University and Agricultural and Mechanical College; Loyola University New Orleans; The University of Alabama; University of Louisiana at Lafayette; Xavier University of Louisiana. Other: 1 had other specific plans. Median SAT critical reading: 640, median SAT math: 640, median SAT writing: 660, median combined SAT: 1940, median composite ACT: 27. 71% scored over 600 on SAT critical reading, 73% scored over 600 on SAT math, 71% scored over 600 on SAT writing, 64% scored over 1800 on combined SAT, 64% scored over 26 on composite ACT.

Student Life Upper grades have uniform requirement, student council, honor system. Discipline rests primarily with faculty. Attendance at religious services is required.

Summer Programs Enrichment programs offered; held on campus; accepts boys; not open to students from other schools. 120 students usually enrolled. 2012 schedule: June 4 to July 6. Application deadline: June 1.

Tuition and Aid Day student tuition: $7400. Tuition installment plan (monthly payment plans, individually arranged payment plans, monthly, quarterly as arranged with parents on an individual basis). Need-based scholarship grants, paying campus jobs available. In 2011–12, 10% of upper-school students received aid. Total amount of financial aid awarded in 2011–12: $523,900.

Admissions Traditional secondary-level entrance grade is 9. For fall 2011, 98 students applied for upper-level admission, 67 were accepted, 48 enrolled. High School Placement Test required. Deadline for receipt of application materials: January 7. Application fee required: $20.

Athletics Interscholastic: baseball, basketball, bowling, cross-country running, football, golf, in-line hockey, indoor track & field, JROTC drill, lacrosse, marksmanship, physical fitness, riflery, rugby, soccer, swimming and diving, tennis, track and field, wrestling; intramural: baseball, basketball, bicycling, bowling, cheering, flag football, football, Frisbee, golf, outdoors, paddle tennis, paint ball, touch football. 9 PE instructors, 41 coaches, 1 athletic trainer.

Computers Computers are regularly used in library skills, mathematics, reading, science, yearbook classes. Computer network features include on-campus library services, online commercial services, Internet access, Internet filtering or blocking technology. Computer access in designated common areas is available to students. The school has a published electronic and media policy.

Contact Mr. Jack S. Truxillo, Director of Admissions. 504-483-3936. Fax: 504-483-3942. E-mail: truxillo@jesuitnola.org. Web site: www.jesuitnola.org.

JESUIT HIGH SCHOOL OF TAMPA

4701 North Himes Avenue

Tampa, Florida 33614-6694

Head of School: Mr. Barry Neuburger

General Information Boys' day college-preparatory school, affiliated with Roman Catholic Church. Grades 9–12. Founded: 1899. Setting: urban. 40-acre campus. 9 buildings on campus. Approved or accredited by Jesuit Secondary Education Association, National Catholic Education Association, Southern Association of Colleges and Schools, and Florida Department of Education. Total enrollment: 733. Upper school average class size: 24. Upper school faculty-student ratio: 1:13. There are 175 required school days per year for Upper School students. Upper School students typically attend 5 days per week. The average school day consists of 7 hours and 23 minutes.

Upper School Student Profile Grade 9: 199 students (199 boys); Grade 10: 186 students (186 boys); Grade 11: 183 students (183 boys); Grade 12: 165 students (165 boys). 68% of students are Roman Catholic.
Faculty School total: 55. In upper school: 41 men, 14 women; 40 have advanced degrees.
Subjects Offered Algebra, American foreign policy, American government, American history, analytic geometry, anatomy, art, biology, calculus, calculus-AP, chemistry, chemistry-AP, chorus, computer science, economics, English, English language and composition-AP, English literature and composition-AP, ethics, European history, French, geometry, global studies, health, Latin, marine biology, math analysis, music, physical education, physics, physics-AP, physiology, pre-calculus, psychology, Spanish, Spanish language-AP, speech, studio art-AP, theology, trigonometry, U.S. government and politics-AP, U.S. history-AP, world history, world history-AP, writing.
Graduation Requirements Arts and fine arts (art, music, dance, drama), English, foreign language, mathematics, physical education (includes health), science, social studies (includes history), theology, 150 hours of community service (additional 20 hours for National Honor Society members).
Special Academic Programs 10 Advanced Placement exams for which test preparation is offered; honors section.
College Admission Counseling 151 students graduated in 2011; all went to college, including Florida Gulf Coast University; Florida State University; Georgia Institute of Technology; University of Florida; University of South Florida. Mean SAT critical reading: 600, mean SAT math: 617, mean SAT writing: 595, mean combined SAT: 1812, mean composite ACT: 27.
Student Life Upper grades have specified standards of dress, student council. Discipline rests primarily with faculty. Attendance at religious services is required.
Summer Programs Remediation programs offered; session focuses on remediation only; held on campus; accepts boys; not open to students from other schools. 2012 schedule: June 18 to July 20.
Tuition and Aid Day student tuition: $12,400. Tuition installment plan (FACTS Tuition Payment Plan). Need-based scholarship grants available. In 2011–12, 25% of upper-school students received aid. Total amount of financial aid awarded in 2011–12: $1,300,000.
Admissions Traditional secondary-level entrance grade is 9. For fall 2011, 358 students applied for upper-level admission, 263 were accepted, 199 enrolled. High School Placement Test (closed version) from Scholastic Testing Service required. Deadline for receipt of application materials: January 7. Application fee required: $50.
Athletics Interscholastic: baseball, basketball, bowling, cross-country running, diving, football, golf, lacrosse, soccer, swimming and diving, tennis, track and field, wrestling; intramural: basketball, football, Frisbee, ice hockey, sailing, softball, ultimate Frisbee. 2 PE instructors, 1 athletic trainer.
Computers Computer network features include on-campus library services, online commercial services, Internet access, Internet filtering or blocking technology. Campus intranet and computer access in designated common areas are available to students. Students grades are available online. The school has a published electronic and media policy.
Contact Mr. Steve Matesich, Director of Admissions. 813-877-5344 Ext. 509. Fax: 813-872-1853. E-mail: smatesich@jesuittampa.org. Web site: www.jesuittampa.org.

J. K. MULLEN HIGH SCHOOL

3601 South Lowell Boulevard

Denver, Colorado 80236

Head of School: Mrs. Linda Brady

General Information Coeducational day college-preparatory school, affiliated with Roman Catholic Church. Grades 9–12. Founded: 1931. Setting: suburban. 38-acre campus. 7 buildings on campus. Approved or accredited by Christian Brothers Association, North Central Association of Colleges and Schools, and Colorado Department of Education. Total enrollment: 1,010. Upper school average class size: 24. Upper school faculty-student ratio: 1:17.
Upper School Student Profile Grade 9: 265 students (143 boys, 122 girls); Grade 10: 250 students (115 boys, 135 girls); Grade 11: 250 students (123 boys, 127 girls); Grade 12: 245 students (116 boys, 129 girls). 70% of students are Roman Catholic.
Faculty School total: 60. In upper school: 32 men, 28 women; 40 have advanced degrees.
Subjects Offered 3-dimensional art, 3-dimensional design, accounting, advanced chemistry, advanced computer applications, advanced math, algebra, analysis and differential calculus, anatomy, art, Basic programming, Bible as literature, Bible studies, biology, British literature, British literature (honors), British literature-AP, business, calculus, calculus-AP, cartooning/animation, chemistry, choir, comparative religion, computer animation, computer applications, computer graphics, computer math, computer programming, computer science, computer-aided design, CPR, creative writing, debate, drafting, drama, ecology, economics, English, English literature, ethics, European history, expository writing, first aid, French, geography, geology, geometry, German, government, government/civics, grammar, health, history, history of the Catholic Church, honors algebra, honors English, honors geometry, honors U.S. history, honors world history, human relations, human sexuality, law studies, leadership, mathematics, mechanical drawing, music, mythology, philosophy, physical education, physical science, physics, physiology, pre-calculus, probability and statistics, psychology, religion, scripture, Shakespeare, social studies, Spanish, Spanish language-AP, Spanish literature-AP, speech, speech and debate, street law, student publications, theology, trigonometry, U.S. government, U.S. government and politics-AP, U.S. history, U.S. history-AP, U.S. literature, weight fitness, world geography, world history, world literature, writing.
Graduation Requirements English, foreign language, mathematics, physical education (includes health), religion (includes Bible studies and theology), science, social sciences, social studies (includes history), speech, 70 hours of community service.
Special Academic Programs Advanced Placement exam preparation; honors section; independent study; academic accommodation for the gifted; remedial reading and/or remedial writing.
College Admission Counseling 241 students graduated in 2010; all went to college, including Colorado School of Mines; Colorado State University; Creighton University; University of Colorado Boulder; University of Northern Colorado. Mean SAT critical reading: 568, mean SAT math: 555, mean composite ACT: 24.
Student Life Upper grades have uniform requirement, student council. Attendance at religious services is required.
Tuition and Aid Day student tuition: $9250. Tuition installment plan (monthly payment plans, individually arranged payment plans). Tuition reduction for siblings, merit scholarship grants, need-based scholarship grants available. In 2010–11, 33% of upper-school students received aid; total upper-school merit-scholarship money awarded: $30,000. Total amount of financial aid awarded in 2010–11: $808,000.
Admissions Traditional secondary-level entrance grade is 9. For fall 2010, 530 students applied for upper-level admission, 310 were accepted, 281 enrolled. High School Placement Test required. Deadline for receipt of application materials: none. No application fee required. On-campus interview required.
Athletics Interscholastic: baseball (boys), basketball (b,g), cheering (g), cross-country running (b,g), diving (b,g), football (b), golf (b,g), ice hockey (b,g), lacrosse (b,g), power lifting (b,g), running (b,g), soccer (b,g), softball (g), swimming and diving (b,g), tennis (b,g), track and field (b,g), volleyball (g), wrestling (b); intramural: bowling (b,g), skiing (downhill) (b,g), weight lifting (b,g).
Computers Computers are regularly used in art, English, foreign language, history, mathematics, science classes. Computer network features include on-campus library services, online commercial services, Internet access.
Contact Frank Cawley, Director of Admissions. 303-761-1764 Ext. 3304. Fax: 303-761-0502. E-mail: cawley@mullenhigh.com. Web site: www.mullenhigh.com.

JOHN BURROUGHS SCHOOL

755 South Price Road

St. Louis, Missouri 63124

Head of School: Andy Abbott

General Information Coeducational day college-preparatory school. Grades 7–12. Founded: 1923. Setting: suburban. 47-acre campus. 7 buildings on campus. Approved or accredited by Independent Schools Association of the Central States. Member of National Association of Independent Schools and Secondary School Admission Test Board. Endowment: $40.5 million. Total enrollment: 600. Upper school average class size: 13. Upper school faculty-student ratio: 1:7. There are 165 required school days per year for Upper School students. Upper School students typically attend 5 days per week. The average school day consists of 8 hours.
Upper School Student Profile Grade 9: 100 students (49 boys, 51 girls); Grade 10: 104 students (53 boys, 51 girls); Grade 11: 100 students (51 boys, 49 girls); Grade 12: 98 students (43 boys, 55 girls).
Faculty School total: 112. In upper school: 48 men, 59 women; 80 have advanced degrees.
Subjects Offered Acting, Advanced Placement courses, African American history, algebra, American history, American literature, Ancient Greek, ancient world history, applied arts, architectural drawing, art, art history, art history-AP, astronomy, bioethics, biology, biology-AP, calculus, calculus-AP, ceramics, chemistry, chemistry-AP, Chinese, choral music, chorus, classical language, community service, comparative religion, computer math, computer science, computer skills, computer-aided design, creative writing, dance, debate, drama, earth science, ecology, engineering, English, English literature, environmental science, environmental systems, expository writing, fine arts, finite math, foreign language, French, French language-AP, geology, geometry, German, global issues, global studies, Greek, Greek culture, health, history, home economics, honors English, industrial arts, jazz, jazz band, keyboarding, lab science, Latin, Latin-AP, mathematics, mechanical drawing, meteorology, model United Nations, music, orchestra, organic chemistry, personal finance, photography, physical education, physics, poetry, pre-algebra, pre-calculus, probability and statistics, psychology, public speaking, reading/study skills, religion, Russian, science, social sciences, social studies, Spanish, Spanish-AP, speech and debate, statistics, trigonometry, vocal music, word processing, world civilizations, world history, world literature, world religions, writing.
Graduation Requirements Arts and fine arts (art, music, dance, drama), English, foreign language, history, mathematics, performing arts, physical education (includes health), practical arts, science, Senior May project, Sophomore Diversity Seminar.

Special Academic Programs Advanced Placement exam preparation; honors section; independent study.

College Admission Counseling 103 students graduated in 2011; all went to college, including Dartmouth College; Indiana University Bloomington; Miami University; University of Missouri; Vanderbilt University; Washington University in St. Louis. Median SAT critical reading: 670, median SAT math: 700, median SAT writing: 690, median combined SAT: 2060, median composite ACT: 31. 86% scored over 600 on SAT critical reading, 86% scored over 600 on SAT math, 85% scored over 600 on SAT writing, 88% scored over 1800 on combined SAT, 93% scored over 26 on composite ACT.

Student Life Upper grades have student council, honor system. Discipline rests equally with students and faculty.

Tuition and Aid Day student tuition: $22,100. Tuition installment plan (monthly payment plans). Need-based scholarship grants, need-based loans available. In 2011–12, 21% of upper-school students received aid. Total amount of financial aid awarded in 2011–12: $1,956,000.

Admissions Traditional secondary-level entrance grade is 9. For fall 2011, 271 students applied for upper-level admission, 125 were accepted, 114 enrolled. SSAT required. Deadline for receipt of application materials: January 20. Application fee required: $40. On-campus interview required.

Athletics Interscholastic: baseball (boys), basketball (b,g), cheering (b,g), cross-country running (b,g), dance (g), dance squad (g), diving (b,g), field hockey (g), fitness (b,g), football (b), golf (b,g), ice hockey (b), independent competitive sports (b,g), lacrosse (b,g), modern dance (b,g), outdoor education (b,g), physical fitness (b,g), physical training (b,g), racquetball (b,g), socoer (b,g), swimming and diving (b,g), tennis (b,g), track and field (b,g), volleyball (g), water polo (b), wrestling (b), yoga (b,g); coed interscholastic: cheering, dance squad, ice hockey, outdoor education, physical fitness, physical training, yoga. 39 coaches, 1 athletic trainer.

Computers Computers are regularly used in all academic, animation, architecture, art, basic skills, cabinet making, college planning, current events, desktop publishing, drafting, drawing and design, industrial technology, keyboarding, lab/keyboard, library, library skills, media production, music, photography, photojournalism, remedial study skills, research skills, study skills, technical drawing, theater, video film production, Web site design, yearbook classes. Computer network features include on-campus library services, online commercial services, Internet access, wireless campus network, monitoring software. Campus intranet and computer access in designated common areas are available to students. The school has a published electronic and media policy.

Contact Caroline LaVigne, Director of Admissions and Tuition Aid. 314-993-4040. Fax: 314-567-2896. E-mail: clavigne@jburroughs.org. Web site: www.jburroughs.org.

THE JOHN COOPER SCHOOL

One John Cooper Drive

The Woodlands, Texas 77381

Head of School: Mr. Michael F. Maher

General Information Coeducational day college-preparatory, arts, and technology school. Grades PK–12. Founded: 1988. Setting: suburban. Nearest major city is Houston. 43-acre campus. 7 buildings on campus. Approved or accredited by Independent Schools Association of the Southwest. Member of National Association of Independent Schools. Endowment: $1.5 million. Total enrollment: 985. Upper school average class size: 16. Upper school faculty-student ratio: 1:12. There are 176 required school days per year for Upper School students. Upper School students typically attend 5 days per week. The average school day consists of 7 hours and 30 minutes.

Upper School Student Profile Grade 9: 92 students (43 boys, 49 girls); Grade 10: 82 students (39 boys, 43 girls); Grade 11: 81 students (39 boys, 42 girls); Grade 12: 84 students (42 boys, 42 girls).

Faculty School total: 110. In upper school: 10 men, 29 women; 31 have advanced degrees.

Subjects Offered 3-dimensional art, 3-dimensional design, acting, advanced chemistry, Advanced Placement courses, advanced studio art-AP, algebra, American history, American history-AP, American literature, anatomy and physiology, ancient history, ancient world history, art history, art history-AP, art-AP, athletics, band, biology, biology-AP, British literature, British literature (honors), business technology, calculus, calculus-AP, ceramics, character education, chemistry, chemistry-AP, choral music, college admission preparation, college counseling, college planning, comparative religion, computer art, computer information systems, computer programming, computer resources, computer science, computer science-AP, conceptual physics, concert band, concert choir, contemporary issues, creative dance, creative writing, dance, dance performance, digital imaging, digital photography, drama, drama performance, dramatic arts, drawing, economics, economics-AP, English, English literature and composition-AP, English literature-AP, environmental science, environmental studies, European history, European history-AP, filmmaking, fine arts, foreign language, French, French language-AP, French-AP, geometry, health, health and wellness, Holocaust, Holocaust studies, honors geometry, human anatomy, information technology, instrumental music, Latin, Latin-AP, linear algebra, literature-AP, modern European history-AP, modern political theory, musical theater, painting, photography, physical education, physics, physics-AP, pre-calculus, psychology, psychology-AP, Spanish, Spanish language-AP, Spanish-AP, speech, statistics-AP, student publications, symphonic band, theater, trigonometry, U.S. history-AP, video film production, volleyball, world history, world literature, world religions, yearbook.

Graduation Requirements Arts and fine arts (art, music, dance, drama), English, foreign language, mathematics, physical education (includes health), science, social studies (includes history).

Special Academic Programs 18 Advanced Placement exams for which test preparation is offered.

College Admission Counseling 81 students graduated in 2010; all went to college, including Baylor University; Columbia University; Louisiana State University and Agricultural and Mechanical College; Southern Methodist University; Texas Christian University; University of Chicago. Mean SAT critical reading: 661, mean SAT math: 674, mean SAT writing: 642, mean combined SAT: 1978, mean composite ACT: 28.

Student Life Upper grades have specified standards of dress, student council, honor system. Discipline rests primarily with faculty.

Tuition and Aid Day student tuition: $18,420. Tuition installment plan (monthly payment plans, 2-part , 4-part). Need-based scholarship grants available. In 2010–11, 12% of upper-school students received aid. Total amount of financial aid awarded in 2010–11: $306,970.

Admissions Traditional secondary-level entrance grade is 9. For fall 2010, 95 students applied for upper-level admission, 49 were accepted, 41 enrolled. CTP III, ISEE, Otis-Lennon School Ability Test or writing sample required. Deadline for receipt of application materials: none. Application fee required: $125. Interview required.

Athletics Interscholastic: baseball (boys), basketball (b,g), cross-country running (b,g), golf (b,g), softball (g), swimming and diving (b,g), tennis (b,g), track and field (b,g), volleyball (g), winter soccer (b,g). 7 PE instructors, 8 coaches, 1 athletic trainer.

Computers Computers are regularly used in all academic, art, computer applications, desktop publishing, drawing and design, foreign language, journalism, media production, music, publications, video film production, Web site design, yearbook classes. Computer network features include on-campus library services, online commercial services, Internet access, wireless campus network, Internet filtering or blocking technology. Campus intranet and computer access in designated common areas are available to students. Students grades are available online. The school has a published electronic and media policy.

Contact Mr. Craig Meredith, Director of Admission. 281-367-0900 Ext. 308. Fax: 281-298-5715. E-mail: cmeredith@johncooper.org. Web site: www.johncooper.org.

THE JOHN DEWEY ACADEMY

Great Barrington, Massachusetts

See Special Needs Schools section.

JOHN PAUL II CATHOLIC HIGH SCHOOL

5100 Terrebone Drive

Tallahassee, Florida 32311-7848

Head of School: Sr. Ellen Cronan

General Information Coeducational day college-preparatory and religious studies school, affiliated with Roman Catholic Church. Grades 9–12. Founded: 2001. Setting: suburban. 37-acre campus. 3 buildings on campus. Approved or accredited by Academy of Orton-Gillingham Practitioners and Educators, Accreditation Commission of the Texas Association of Baptist Schools, American Association of Christian Schools, Arizona Association of Independent Schools, Association for Experiential Education, Association of American Schools in South America, Association of Christian Schools International, Association of Colorado Independent Schools, Association of Independent Maryland Schools, Association of Independent Schools and Colleges of Alberta, Association of Independent Schools in New England, Association of Independent Schools of Florida, Association of Independent Schools of Greater Washington, Southern Association of Colleges and Schools, and Florida Department of Education. Total enrollment: 119. Upper school average class size: 12. Upper school faculty-student ratio: 1:8. There are 180 required school days per year for Upper School students. Upper School students typically attend 5 days per week. The average school day consists of 7 hours.

Upper School Student Profile Grade 9: 30 students (11 boys, 19 girls); Grade 10: 20 students (8 boys, 12 girls); Grade 11: 32 students (14 boys, 18 girls); Grade 12: 37 students (22 boys, 15 girls). 83% of students are Roman Catholic.

Faculty School total: 16. In upper school: 5 men, 11 women; 14 have advanced degrees.

Subjects Offered All academic, Bible, English language and composition-AP, English literature and composition-AP, history of the Catholic Church, Latin, music, Spanish, Spanish language-AP, strings.

Graduation Requirements Algebra, American government, American history, biology, Christian doctrine, economics, English, fitness, foreign language, health.

Special Academic Programs 6 Advanced Placement exams for which test preparation is offered; honors section; study at local college for college credit.

College Admission Counseling 21 students graduated in 2011; all went to college, including Florida State University; Georgia Institute of Technology; Mount St. Mary's University; Tallahassee Community College; University of South Florida. Mean SAT critical reading: 558, mean SAT math: 544, mean SAT writing: 535. 43% scored over 600 on SAT critical reading, 57% scored over 600 on SAT math.

Student Life Upper grades have uniform requirement, student council. Discipline rests primarily with faculty. Attendance at religious services is required.

Tuition and Aid Day student tuition: $8700. Tuition installment plan (FACTS Tuition Payment Plan). Need-based scholarship grants available. In 2011–12, 17% of upper-school students received aid. Total amount of financial aid awarded in 2011–12: $40,000.

Admissions Traditional secondary-level entrance grade is 9. Explore, High School Placement Test or High School Placement Test (closed version) from Scholastic Testing Service required. Deadline for receipt of application materials: none. Application fee required: $200. On-campus interview recommended.

Athletics Interscholastic: baseball (boys), basketball (b,g), cheering (g), cross-country running (b,g), football (b), golf (b), soccer (b,g), tennis (b,g), volleyball (g). 1 PE instructor, 8 coaches, 1 athletic trainer.

Computers Computers are regularly used in drawing and design, technology classes. Computer network features include on-campus library services, Internet access, Internet filtering or blocking technology. Student e-mail accounts are available to students. Students grades are available online. The school has a published electronic and media policy.

Contact Mrs. Sharon Strohl, Office Administrator. 850-201-5744. Fax: 850-205-3299. E-mail: sstrohl@jpiichs.org. Web site: www.jpiichs.org.

JOHN T. MORGAN ACADEMY

2901 West Dallas Avenue

PO Box 2650

Selma, Alabama 36702-2650

Head of School: Mr. Randy Skipper

General Information Coeducational day college-preparatory school. Grades K–12. Founded: 1965. Setting: small town. 5 buildings on campus. Approved or accredited by Southern Association of Colleges and Schools. Upper school average class size: 22. Upper school faculty-student ratio: 1:22. There are 178 required school days per year for Upper School students. Upper School students typically attend 5 days per week. The average school day consists of 6 hours.

Faculty School total: 36. In upper school: 5 men, 14 women; 4 have advanced degrees.

Subjects Offered World history.

Special Academic Programs Honors section.

College Admission Counseling 48 students graduated in 2011; all went to college, including The University of Alabama. Median composite ACT: 22.

Student Life Upper grades have uniform requirement, student council, honor system. Discipline rests primarily with faculty.

Tuition and Aid Day student tuition: $310. Tuition installment plan (monthly payment plans).

Admissions Traditional secondary-level entrance grade is 9. ACT required. Application fee required: $185. Interview required.

Athletics Interscholastic: baseball (boys), basketball (b,g), cheering (g), fitness (b,g), fitness walking (b,g), flag football (b,g), football (b), golf (b,g), physical fitness (b,g), running (b,g), scooter football (b), soccer (b,g), softball (g), strength & conditioning (b,g), tennis (b,g), track and field (b,g), volleyball (g), walking (b,g), weight lifting (b), weight training (b), whiffle ball (b,g), yoga (g); intramural: basketball (b,g), cooperative games (b,g), jogging (b,g), kickball (b,g), soccer (b,g), softball (g), tennis (b,g), touch football (b,g); coed interscholastic: golf, whiffle ball; coed intramural: cooperative games, jogging, jump rope, kickball. 2 PE instructors, 5 coaches.

Computers Computers are regularly used in computer applications classes. Computer resources include on-campus library services, Internet access, Internet filtering or blocking technology. Students grades are available online.

Contact Mrs. Tina P. Cox, Secretary. 334-375-1044. Fax: 334-875-4465. E-mail: tcox@morganacademy.com.

JOSEPHINUM ACADEMY

1501 North Oakley Boulevard

Chicago, Illinois 60622

Head of School: Mrs. Lourdes Weber

General Information Girls' day college-preparatory, arts, religious studies, and technology school, affiliated with Roman Catholic Church. Grades 9–12. Founded: 1890. Setting: urban. 2-acre campus. 1 building on campus. Approved or accredited by Network of Sacred Heart Schools, North Central Association of Colleges and Schools, and Illinois Department of Education. Endowment: $1.5 million. Total enrollment: 150. Upper school average class size: 18. Upper school faculty-student ratio: 1:9. There are 176 required school days per year for Upper School students. Upper School students typically attend 5 days per week. The average school day consists of 7 hours and 30 minutes.

Upper School Student Profile Grade 9: 50 students (50 girls); Grade 10: 40 students (40 girls); Grade 11: 30 students (30 girls); Grade 12: 30 students (30 girls). 50% of students are Roman Catholic.

Faculty School total: 18. In upper school: 4 men, 14 women; 11 have advanced degrees.

Subjects Offered Algebra, American literature, applied arts, art, Bible, biology, biology-AP, British literature, calculus-AP, chemistry, community service, computer education, constitutional history of U.S., consumer education, drama, English, English-AP, French, global studies, health, health and wellness, library research, peer counseling, physical education, scripture, senior project, social justice, softball, Spanish, Spanish-AP, U.S. history, volleyball, Web authoring, women's studies, world geography, world religions, yearbook.

Graduation Requirements Arts and fine arts (art, music, dance, drama), biology, college admission preparation, computer science, English, foreign language, mathematics, physical education (includes health), religion (includes Bible studies and theology), science, social sciences, social studies (includes history), technology, Senior capstone project. Community service is required.

Special Academic Programs Advanced Placement exam preparation; honors section; independent study; remedial reading and/or remedial writing; remedial math.

College Admission Counseling 30 students graduated in 2011; all went to college, including Carleton College; DePaul University; Grand Valley State University; Loyola University Chicago; University of Illinois at Chicago; University of Illinois at Urbana–Champaign.

Student Life Upper grades have uniform requirement, student council, honor system. Discipline rests primarily with faculty. Attendance at religious services is required.

Summer Programs Enrichment programs offered; session focuses on community service; held off campus; held at Sacred Heart schools; accepts girls; not open to students from other schools. 5 students usually enrolled.

Tuition and Aid Day student tuition: $4500. Tuition installment plan (monthly payment plans, individually arranged payment plans, Tuition Management Systems Plan). Tuition reduction for siblings, merit scholarship grants, need-based scholarship grants available. In 2011–12, 89% of upper-school students received aid; total upper-school merit-scholarship money awarded: $20,200. Total amount of financial aid awarded in 2011–12: $400,000.

Admissions Traditional secondary-level entrance grade is 9. For fall 2011, 97 students applied for upper-level admission, 84 were accepted, 50 enrolled. Catholic High School Entrance Examination required. Deadline for receipt of application materials: none. No application fee required. Interview recommended.

Athletics Interscholastic: basketball, soccer, softball, volleyball; intramural: cheering, fitness, football, track and field. 2 PE instructors, 5 coaches.

Computers Computers are regularly used in all academic, creative writing classes. Computer network features include Internet access, wireless campus network, Internet filtering or blocking technology. Student e-mail accounts are available to students. Students grades are available online. The school has a published electronic and media policy.

Contact Ms. Melissa Michaels, Admissions Director. 773-276-1261. Fax: 773-292-3963. E-mail: melissa.michaels@josephinum.org. Web site: www.josephinum.org.

THE JOURNEYS SCHOOL OF TETON SCIENCE SCHOOL

700 Coyote Canyon Road

Jackson, Wyoming 83001

Head of School: Mr. Nate McClennen

General Information Coeducational day college-preparatory school. Grades K–12. Founded: 2001. Setting: rural. 800-acre campus. 1 building on campus. Approved or accredited by Pacific Northwest Association of Independent Schools and Wyoming Department of Education. Upper school average class size: 7.

Special Academic Programs International Baccalaureate program.

Student Life Discipline rests equally with students and faculty.

Admissions No application fee required. Interview required.

Contact Tammie VanHolland, Director of Admissions. 307-734-3710. Fax: 307-733-3340. E-mail: tammie.vanholland@journeysschool.org.

THE JUDGE ROTENBERG EDUCATIONAL CENTER

Canton, Massachusetts

See Special Needs Schools section.

JUNIPERO SERRA HIGH SCHOOL

14830 South Van Ness Avenue

Gardena, California 90249

Head of School: Mr. Michael Wagner, JD

General Information Coeducational day college-preparatory, arts, and religious studies school, affiliated with Roman Catholic Church. Grades 9–12. Founded: 1950. Setting: urban. 24-acre campus. 10 buildings on campus. Approved or accredited by California Association of Independent Schools, National Catholic Education Association, Western Association of Schools and Colleges, Western Catholic Education Association, and California Department of Education. Member of Secondary School Admission Test Board. Endowment: $200,000. Total enrollment: 686. Upper school average class size: 26. Upper school faculty-student ratio: 1:25. There are 180 required school days per year for Upper School students. Upper School students typically attend 5 days per week. The average school day consists of 5 hours and 45 minutes.

Upper School Student Profile Grade 9: 210 students (146 boys, 64 girls); Grade 10: 191 students (120 boys, 71 girls); Grade 11: 133 students (76 boys, 57 girls); Grade 12: 152 students (87 boys, 65 girls). 45% of students are Roman Catholic.

Faculty School total: 36. In upper school: 22 men, 14 women; 25 have advanced degrees.

Subjects Offered Acting, advanced math, advanced studio art-AP, algebra, American history-AP, American literature, anatomy, biology, biology-AP, calculus-AP, chemistry, choir, computer science, drama, economics, English, English literature, English literature-AP, fine arts, geometry, government, journalism, mathematics, music, photography, physical education, physics, physiology, pre-calculus, religion, science, social studies, Spanish, Spanish-AP, theater, theology, U.S. history, world history, writing.

Graduation Requirements Arts and fine arts (art, music, dance, drama), computer science, English, foreign language, mathematics, physical education (includes health), religion (includes Bible studies and theology), science, social studies (includes history), completion of an SAT or ACT test preperation program, completion of 100 service hours, school does not accept D and F grades as passing. Community service is required.

Special Academic Programs Advanced Placement exam preparation; honors section; study at local college for college credit; academic accommodation for the gifted; remedial reading and/or remedial writing; remedial math.

College Admission Counseling 147 students graduated in 2011; all went to college, including California State University; El Camino College; Loyola Marymount University; University of California, Los Angeles. Mean SAT critical reading: 464, mean SAT math: 452, mean SAT writing: 455, mean composite ACT: 21. 10% scored over 600 on SAT critical reading, 10% scored over 600 on SAT math, 10% scored over 600 on SAT writing, 7% scored over 26 on composite ACT.

Student Life Upper grades have uniform requirement, student council, honor system. Discipline rests primarily with faculty. Attendance at religious services is required.

Summer Programs Remediation, enrichment, advancement, sports, art/fine arts, rigorous outdoor training, computer instruction programs offered; session focuses on advancement and remediation; held on campus; accepts boys and girls; open to students from other schools. 250 students usually enrolled. 2012 schedule: June 25 to July 30. Application deadline: June 16.

Tuition and Aid Day student tuition: $6400. Tuition installment plan (FACTS Tuition Payment Plan). Tuition reduction for siblings, merit scholarship grants, need-based scholarship grants available. In 2011–12, 60% of upper-school students received aid; total upper-school merit-scholarship money awarded: $35,000. Total amount of financial aid awarded in 2011–12: $500,000.

Admissions Traditional secondary-level entrance grade is 9. For fall 2011, 400 students applied for upper-level admission, 300 were accepted, 210 enrolled. High School Placement Test required. Deadline for receipt of application materials: none. Application fee required: $75. On-campus interview required.

Athletics Interscholastic: baseball (boys), basketball (b,g), cheering (g), cross-country running (b,g), football (b), golf (b,g), soccer (b,g), softball (g), tennis (b,g), track and field (b,g), volleyball (b,g), winter soccer (b,g), wrestling (b); coed interscholastic: swimming and diving, track and field; coed intramural: basketball, volleyball. 2 PE instructors, 23 coaches, 2 athletic trainers.

Computers Computers are regularly used in art, English, foreign language, history, mathematics, music, science classes. Computer network features include on-campus library services, Internet access, Internet filtering or blocking technology. Computer access in designated common areas is available to students. Students grades are available online. The school has a published electronic and media policy.

Contact Mr. John Posatko, Admissions Director. 310-324-6675 Ext. 1015. Fax: 310-352-4953. E-mail: jposatko@la-serrahs.org. Web site: www.serrahighschool.com.

JUNIPERO SERRA HIGH SCHOOL

451 West 20th Avenue

San Mateo, California 94403-1385

Head of School: Lars Lund

General Information Boys' day college-preparatory, arts, business, religious studies, and technology school, affiliated with Roman Catholic Church. Grades 9–12. Founded: 1944. Setting: suburban. Nearest major city is San Francisco. 13-acre campus. 9 buildings on campus. Approved or accredited by Western Association of Schools and Colleges. Endowment: $1.7 million. Total enrollment: 900. Upper school average class size: 27. Upper school faculty-student ratio: 1:27. There are 180 required school days per year for Upper School students. Upper School students typically attend 5 days per week. The average school day consists of 6 hours and 45 minutes.

Upper School Student Profile Grade 9: 230 students (230 boys); Grade 10: 215 students (215 boys); Grade 11: 230 students (230 boys); Grade 12: 225 students (225 boys). 75% of students are Roman Catholic.

Faculty School total: 69. In upper school: 54 men, 15 women; 32 have advanced degrees.

Subjects Offered Algebra, American history, American history-AP, American literature, architecture, art, art history-AP, astronomy, band, biology, biology-AP, business, calculus, calculus-AP, chemistry, college admission preparation, college counseling, college planning, community service, comparative government and politics-AP, computer programming, computer science, creative writing, drafting, drama, driver education, earth science, economics, electronics, English, English literature, English literature and composition-AP, English literature-AP, ethics, European history, fine arts, French, French language-AP, geography, geology, geometry, German, government and politics-AP, government/civics, grammar, graphic design, health, history, instrumental music, journalism, keyboarding, library skills, library studies, literature and composition-AP, mathematics, mechanical drawing, music, photography, physical education, physics, religion, science, social sciences, social studies, Spanish, Spanish language-AP, speech, statistics, student government, theater, trigonometry, U.S. government and politics-AP, U.S. history-AP, world history, writing.

Graduation Requirements Arts and fine arts (art, music, dance, drama), computer science, English, foreign language, literature, mathematics, physical education (includes health), political systems, religion (includes Bible studies and theology), science, social sciences, social studies (includes history). Community service is required.

Special Academic Programs Advanced Placement exam preparation; honors section; study at local college for college credit.

College Admission Counseling 225 students graduated in 2011; all went to college, including College of San Mateo; San Jose State University; Santa Clara University; University of California, Davis; University of Colorado Boulder; University of Oregon.

Student Life Upper grades have specified standards of dress, student council, honor system. Discipline rests primarily with faculty. Attendance at religious services is required.

Summer Programs Remediation, enrichment, advancement, sports, computer instruction programs offered; session focuses on enrichment and remediation; held on campus; accepts boys and girls; open to students from other schools. 460 students usually enrolled. 2012 schedule: June 18 to July 20. Application deadline: June 15.

Tuition and Aid Day student tuition: $16,320. Tuition installment plan (monthly payment plans, semester payment plan, annual payment plan, direct debit plan). Merit scholarship grants, need-based scholarship grants available. In 2011–12, 30% of upper-school students received aid; total upper-school merit-scholarship money awarded: $45,000. Total amount of financial aid awarded in 2011–12: $1,900,000.

Admissions Traditional secondary-level entrance grade is 9. For fall 2011, 475 students applied for upper-level admission, 325 were accepted, 230 enrolled. High School Placement Test required. Deadline for receipt of application materials: January 11. Application fee required: $90. On-campus interview required.

Athletics Interscholastic: baseball, basketball, crew, cross-country running, diving, football, golf, lacrosse, rowing, soccer, swimming and diving, tennis, track and field, volleyball, water polo, wrestling; intramural: basketball, bicycling, bowling, fishing, fitness, flag football, mountain biking, physical training, rock climbing, soccer, softball, strength & conditioning, surfing, touch football, weight lifting. 2 PE instructors, 48 coaches, 1 athletic trainer.

Computers Computers are regularly used in English, foreign language, history, library, library skills, mathematics, music, science, social sciences classes. Computer network features include on-campus library services, Internet access, wireless campus network. Student e-mail accounts are available to students. Students grades are available online. The school has a published electronic and media policy.

Contact Randy Vogel, Director of Admissions. 650-345-8242. Fax: 650-573-6638. E-mail: padres@serrahs.com. Web site: www.serrahs.com.

KALAMAZOO CHRISTIAN HIGH SCHOOL

2121 Stadium Drive

Kalamazoo, Michigan 49008-1692

Head of School: Ms. Linda Dahnke

General Information Coeducational day college-preparatory, general academic, arts, business, vocational, religious studies, bilingual studies, and technology school, affiliated with Christian Reformed Church, Reformed Church in America. Grades 9–12. Founded: 1877. Setting: urban. 3-acre campus. 1 building on campus. Approved or accredited by Christian Schools International, North Central Association of Colleges and Schools, and Michigan Department of Education. Endowment: $1 million. Total enrollment: 811. Upper school average class size: 22. Upper school faculty-student ratio: 1:11. There are 172 required school days per year for Upper School students. Upper School students typically attend 5 days per week. The average school day consists of 6 hours and 45 minutes.

Upper School Student Profile 50% of students are members of Christian Reformed Church, Reformed Church in America.

Faculty School total: 25. In upper school: 17 men, 8 women; 10 have advanced degrees.

Graduation Requirements 50 hours community service.

Special Academic Programs Advanced Placement exam preparation; honors section; study at local college for college credit.

College Admission Counseling 100 students graduated in 2010; 90 went to college, including Calvin College; Hope College; University of Michigan; Western Michigan University. Other: 2 entered military service. Median composite ACT: 24.

Student Life Upper grades have specified standards of dress, student council, honor system. Discipline rests primarily with faculty. Attendance at religious services is required.

Tuition and Aid Day student tuition: $8952. Tuition installment plan (FACTS Tuition Payment Plan, monthly payment plans, individually arranged payment plans). Tuition reduction for siblings, need-based scholarship grants available. In 2010–11, 50% of upper-school students received aid.

Admissions Traditional secondary-level entrance grade is 9. Deadline for receipt of application materials: none. Application fee required: $100. Interview required.

Athletics Interscholastic: baseball (boys), basketball (b,g), bowling (b,g), cheering (g), cross-country running (b,g), football (b), golf (b), hockey (b), physical fitness (b,g), soccer (b,g), softball (g), strength & conditioning (b,g), tennis (b,g), track and field (b,g), volleyball (g), weight lifting (b,g), weight training (b,g). 2 PE instructors, 32 coaches, 1 athletic trainer.

Computers Computers are regularly used in accounting, business, business applications, business skills, data processing, graphic arts, graphic design, keyboarding, lab/keyboard classes. Computer network features include on-campus library services, online commercial services, Internet access.

Contact Ms. Linda Dahnke, Principal. 269-381-2250 Ext. 220. Fax: 269-381-0319. E-mail: ldahnke@kcsa.org. Web site: www.kcsa.org.

KAPLAN COLLEGE PREPARATORY SCHOOL

4601 Sheridan Street

Suite 600

Hollywood, Florida 33021

Head of School: Miriam Rube

General Information Distance Learning only college-preparatory school. Distance learning grades 6–12. Founded: 2001. Setting: suburban. Nearest major city is Fort Lauderdale. Approved or accredited by Southern Association of Colleges and Schools, The College Board, and Florida Department of Education. Total enrollment: 256.

Upper School Student Profile Grade 9: 48 students (29 boys, 19 girls); Grade 10: 53 students (27 boys, 26 girls); Grade 11: 66 students (37 boys, 29 girls); Grade 12: 66 students (39 boys, 27 girls).

Faculty School total: 22. In upper school: 5 men, 17 women; 12 have advanced degrees.

Subjects Offered Advanced Placement courses, algebra, American government, American history, American history-AP, American literature, American literature-AP, art history, biology, biology-AP, business technology, chemistry, chemistry-AP, computer applications, earth and space science, economics, emerging technology, English, English language and composition-AP, English literature and composition-AP, English literature-AP, French, geometry, health, honors algebra, language, life management skills, marine science, mathematics, mathematics-AP, physical education, physical fitness, physics, pre-algebra, pre-calculus, psychology, SAT preparation, science, Spanish, U.S. government and politics-AP, U.S. history, world history, world literature.

Graduation Requirements American government, American history, American literature, biology, British literature, chemistry, economics, electives, English literature, foreign language, general science, life management skills, personal fitness, physical education (includes health), world history, world literature, the last six courses must be with KCPS for a Kaplan College Preparatory School diploma.

Special Academic Programs Advanced Placement exam preparation; honors section; accelerated programs; ESL.

College Admission Counseling 30 students graduated in 2010; 27 went to college, including Dartmouth College; Duke University; University of Miami; University of Michigan; University of South Carolina; Wake Forest University. Other: 1 went to work, 2 had other specific plans.

Student Life Upper grades have student council, honor system. Discipline rests primarily with faculty.

Tuition and Aid Tuition installment plan (monthly payment plans, individually arranged payment plans).

Admissions Traditional secondary-level entrance grade is 9. School placement exam required. Deadline for receipt of application materials: none. Application fee required: $100. Interview recommended.

Athletics 1 PE instructor.

Computers Computers are regularly used in all classes. Students grades are available online. The school has a published electronic and media policy.

Contact Alison Cohen, Registrar. 954-964-6502. Fax: 800-878-3152. E-mail: acohen2@kaplan.edu. Web site: www.kaplancollegepreparatory.com.

THE KARAFIN SCHOOL

Mount Kisco, New York

See Special Needs Schools section.

KAUAI CHRISTIAN ACADEMY

PO Box 1121

4000 Kilauea Road

Kilauea, Hawaii 96754

Head of School: Adm. Daniel A. Moore

General Information Coeducational day college preparatory, general academic, arts, religious studies, bilingual studies, and technology school, affiliated with Protestant-Evangelical faith, Christian faith. Grades PS–12. Founded: 1973. Setting: rural. Nearest major city is Lihue. 10-acre campus. 3 buildings on campus. Approved or accredited by American Association of Christian Schools and Hawaii Department of Education. Total enrollment: 79. Upper school average class size: 10. Upper school faculty-student ratio: 1:8. There are 171 required school days per year for Upper School students. Upper School students typically attend 5 days per week. The average school day consists of 6 hours and 30 minutes.

Upper School Student Profile Grade 7: 11 students (3 boys, 8 girls); Grade 8: 8 students (6 boys, 2 girls); Grade 9: 4 students (4 girls); Grade 11: 5 students (2 boys, 3 girls); Grade 12: 2 students (2 boys). 75% of students are Protestant-Evangelical faith, Christian faith.

Faculty School total: 9. In upper school: 5 men, 4 women; 3 have advanced degrees.

Subjects Offered Advanced math, agriculture, algebra, American government, American history, ancient history, art, arts, athletics, Basic programming, Bible, Bible as literature, Bible studies, biology, botany, calculus, chemistry, Christian and Hebrew scripture, economics, economics-AP, electives, English, English literature, English literature and composition-AP, family living, geography, geometry, government, history, Latin, music, physical science, pre-algebra, speech, world geography, world history.

Graduation Requirements Arts and fine arts (art, music, dance, drama), computer science, English, Latin, mathematics, science, social studies (includes history), speech, one year of Bible for each year enrolled.

Special Academic Programs Accelerated programs; independent study; remedial reading and/or remedial writing; remedial math.

College Admission Counseling 3 students graduated in 2011; 2 went to college, including Columbia International University; Montana State University. Other: 1 went to work. Median SAT critical reading: 570, median SAT math: 530, median SAT writing: 550, median combined SAT: 1705, median composite ACT: 24. 50% scored over 600 on SAT critical reading, 50% scored over 600 on SAT writing.

Student Life Upper grades have specified standards of dress, honor system. Discipline rests primarily with faculty.

Summer Programs Remediation, enrichment, advancement, art/fine arts, computer instruction programs offered; session focuses on enrichment; held on campus; accepts boys and girls; open to students from other schools. 2012 schedule: June 13 to July 8. Application deadline: May 31.

Tuition and Aid Day student tuition: $5875. Tuition installment plan (monthly payment plans, 10-month payment plan). Tuition reduction for siblings, need-based scholarship grants, paying campus jobs available. In 2011–12, 40% of upper-school students received aid. Total amount of financial aid awarded in 2011–12: $40,000.

Admissions Traditional secondary-level entrance grade is 7. For fall 2011, 12 students applied for upper-level admission, 12 were accepted, 12 enrolled. OLSAT, Stanford Achievement Test or Stanford Achievement Test, Otis-Lennon School Ability Test required. Deadline for receipt of application materials: none. Application fee required: $55. Interview recommended.

Computers Computers are regularly used in computer applications, typing classes. Computer network features include Internet access, wireless campus network, Internet filtering or blocking technology. Campus intranet and computer access in designated common areas are available to students.

Contact Adm. Daniel A. Moore, Principal. 808-828-0047. Fax: 808-828-1850. E-mail: dmoore@kcaschool.net. Web site: www.kcaschool.net.

KEITH COUNTRY DAY SCHOOL

1 Jacoby Place

Rockford, Illinois 61107

Head of School: Mr. Alan W. Gibby

General Information Coeducational day college-preparatory, arts, and technology school. Grades PK–12. Founded: 1916. Setting: suburban. Nearest major city is Chicago. 15-acre campus. 1 building on campus. Approved or accredited by Independent Schools Association of the Central States and Illinois Department of Education. Member of National Association of Independent Schools. Endowment: $985,000. Total enrollment: 290. Upper school average class size: 16. Upper school faculty-student ratio: 1:6. There are 176 required school days per year for Upper School students. Upper School students typically attend 5 days per week. The average school day consists of 7 hours and 15 minutes.

Upper School Student Profile Grade 9: 14 students (9 boys, 5 girls); Grade 10: 26 students (12 boys, 14 girls); Grade 11: 28 students (17 boys, 11 girls); Grade 12: 19 students (8 boys, 11 girls).

Faculty School total: 44. In upper school: 10 men, 17 women; 24 have advanced degrees.

Subjects Offered Advanced math, Advanced Placement courses, algebra, American history, American literature, Ancient Greek, art, arts, Bible as literature, biology, biology-AP, calculus, ceramics, chemistry, chemistry-AP, college counseling, community service, computer science, design, drama, drawing, economics, English, English literature, English-AP, environmental science, European history, fine arts, French, geography, geometry, government/civics, health, history, Latin, mathematics, music, painting, photography, physical education, physics, pre-calculus, research skills, science, social studies, speech, study skills, theater, trigonometry, world history, world literature.

Graduation Requirements Arts and fine arts (art, music, dance, drama), college counseling, computer science, English, foreign language, mathematics, physical education (includes health), research skills, science, senior project, social studies (includes history), speech, 90 hours of community service.

Special Academic Programs Advanced Placement exam preparation; honors section; study at local college for college credit; study abroad; academic accommodation for the gifted, the musically talented, and the artistically talented; remedial reading and/or remedial writing; programs in general development for dyslexic students.

College Admission Counseling 32 students graduated in 2011; 31 went to college, including Knox College; Purdue University; Saint Louis University; University of Chicago; University of Illinois at Urbana–Champaign; Yale University. Other: 1 went to work. Median SAT critical reading: 621, median SAT math: 634, median SAT writing: 589, median combined SAT: 1844, median composite ACT: 26. 60% scored over 600 on SAT critical reading, 60% scored over 600 on SAT math, 70% scored over 600 on SAT writing, 70% scored over 1800 on combined SAT, 73% scored over 26 on composite ACT.

Student Life Upper grades have specified standards of dress, student council, honor system. Discipline rests equally with students and faculty.

Summer Programs Enrichment, sports, art/fine arts programs offered; session focuses on sports skills camps, math camp, music camp; held on campus; accepts boys and girls; open to students from other schools. 65 students usually enrolled. 2012 schedule: June 10 to August 10.

Tuition and Aid Day student tuition: $14,200. Tuition installment plan (monthly payment plans, school's own payment plan). Tuition reduction for siblings, merit scholarship grants, need-based scholarship grants available. In 2011–12, 51% of upper-school students received aid; total upper-school merit-scholarship money awarded: $107,900. Total amount of financial aid awarded in 2011–12: $342,664.

Admissions Traditional secondary-level entrance grade is 9. For fall 2011, 25 students applied for upper-level admission, 24 were accepted, 9 enrolled. ERB, placement test and school's own exam required. Deadline for receipt of application materials: none. Application fee required: $50. On-campus interview required.

Athletics Interscholastic: basketball (boys, girls), physical fitness (b,g), soccer (b,g), tennis (b,g), volleyball (g); coed interscholastic: cross-country running, golf, table tennis; coed intramural: crew. 2 PE instructors, 6 coaches.

Computers Computers are regularly used in English, foreign language, history, mathematics, science, social studies, Spanish, writing, yearbook classes. Computer network features include on-campus library services, Internet access, wireless campus network, Internet filtering or blocking technology. Student e-mail accounts are available to students. Students grades are available online. The school has a published electronic and media policy.

Contact Marcia Aramovich, Director of Admissions. 815-399-8850 Ext. 144. Fax: 815-399-2470. E-mail: marcia.aramovich@keithschool.net. Web site: www.keithschool.com.

KENT PLACE SCHOOL

42 Norwood Avenue

Summit, New Jersey 07902-0308

Head of School: Mrs. Susan C. Bosland

General Information Coeducational day (boys' only in lower grades) college-preparatory school. Boys grades N–PK, girls grades N–12. Founded: 1894. Setting: suburban. Nearest major city is New York, NY. 25-acre campus. 6 buildings on campus. Approved or accredited by Middle States Association of Colleges and Schools and New Jersey Association of Independent Schools. Member of National Association of Independent Schools and Secondary School Admission Test Board. Endowment: $15 million. Total enrollment: 636. Upper school average class size: 16. Upper school faculty-student ratio: 1:7. There are 167 required school days per year for Upper School students. Upper School students typically attend 5 days per week. The average school day consists of 6 hours and 55 minutes.

Upper School Student Profile Grade 9: 69 students (69 girls); Grade 10: 78 students (78 girls); Grade 11: 67 students (67 girls); Grade 12: 63 students (63 girls).

Faculty School total: 119. In upper school: 7 men, 36 women; 35 have advanced degrees.

Subjects Offered Advanced Placement courses, algebra, American history, American history-AP, American literature, anatomy and physiology, art, art history-AP, biology, biology-AP, calculus, calculus-AP, ceramics, chemistry, chemistry-AP, computer literacy, computer programming-AP, computer science, creative writing, dance, drama, driver education, economics, English, English language-AP, English literature, English literature-AP, environmental science, environmental science-AP, European history, expository writing, fine arts, French, French language-AP, French literature-AP, geometry, government/civics, grammar, health, history, independent study, Latin, Latin-AP, macroeconomics-AP, mathematics, modern European history-AP, music, music theory-AP, photography, physical education, physics, science, social studies, Spanish, Spanish language-AP, Spanish literature-AP, statistics, statistics-AP, theater, trigonometry, world history.

Graduation Requirements Arts and fine arts (art, music, dance, drama), English, foreign language, history, mathematics, physical education (includes health), science.

Special Academic Programs 22 Advanced Placement exams for which test preparation is offered; independent study.

College Admission Counseling 62 students graduated in 2011; all went to college, including Boston College; Colgate University; Cornell University; Princeton University; University of Pennsylvania; Yale University.

Student Life Upper grades have specified standards of dress, student council, honor system. Discipline rests equally with students and faculty.

Tuition and Aid Day student tuition: $32,788. Tuition installment plan (Insured Tuition Payment Plan, Key Tuition Payment Plan, monthly payment plans). Need-based scholarship grants available. In 2011–12, 20% of upper-school students received aid. Total amount of financial aid awarded in 2011–12: $1,299,061.

Admissions Traditional secondary-level entrance grade is 9. ISEE or SSAT required. Deadline for receipt of application materials: January 6. Application fee required: $70. On-campus interview required.

Athletics Interscholastic: basketball, cross-country running, field hockey, indoor track, lacrosse, soccer, softball, swimming and diving, tennis, track and field, volleyball, winter (indoor) track; intramural: dance, fencing, modern dance, physical fitness, squash. 4 PE instructors, 19 coaches, 1 athletic trainer.

Computers Computers are regularly used in all classes. Computer network features include on-campus library services, online commercial services, Internet access, wireless campus network, Internet filtering or blocking technology. Campus intranet, student e-mail accounts, and computer access in designated common areas are available to students. The school has a published electronic and media policy.

Contact Mrs. Julia Wall, Director of Admission and Financial Aid. 908-273-0900 Ext. 254. Fax: 908-273-9390. E-mail: admission@kentplace.org. Web site: www.kentplace.org.

KENT SCHOOL

PO Box 2006

Kent, Connecticut 06757

Head of School: Rev. Richardson W. Schell

General Information Coeducational boarding and day college-preparatory, arts, religious studies, technology, and pre-engineering school, affiliated with Episcopal Church. Grades 9–PG. Founded: 1906. Setting: small town. Nearest major city is Hartford. Students are housed in single-sex dormitories. 1,200-acre campus. 17 buildings on campus. Approved or accredited by Association of Independent Schools in New England, Connecticut Association of Independent Schools, National Association of Episcopal Schools, New England Association of Schools and Colleges, New York State Association of Independent Schools, The Association of Boarding Schools, and Connecticut Department of Education. Member of National Association of Independent Schools and Secondary School Admission Test Board. Endowment: $73.5 million. Total enrollment: 560. Upper school average class size: 12. Upper school faculty-student ratio: 1:8.

Upper School Student Profile Grade 9: 70 students (35 boys, 35 girls); Grade 10: 147 students (70 boys, 77 girls); Grade 11: 155 students (80 boys, 75 girls); Grade 12:

188 students (98 boys, 90 girls). 90% of students are boarding students. 31% are state residents. 37 states are represented in upper school student body. 31% are international students. International students from Canada, China, Germany, Hong Kong, Republic of Korea, and Thailand; 44 other countries represented in student body.
Faculty School total: 73. In upper school: 43 men, 30 women; 55 have advanced degrees; 66 reside on campus.
Subjects Offered Advanced studio art-AP, African-American history, algebra, American history, American history-AP, American literature, architecture, art, art history-AP, Asian history, astronomy, Bible studies, biology, biology-AP, biotechnology, calculus, calculus-AP, ceramics, chemistry, chemistry-AP, Chinese, classical Greek literature, classical studies, composition-AP, computer math, computer programming, computer science, computer science-AP, digital imaging, drama, ecology, economics, English, English literature, English literature-AP, environmental science-AP, environmental studies, European history, European history-AP, expository writing, fine arts, French, French language-AP, French literature-AP, genetics, geology, geometry, German, German-AP, government and politics-AP, Greek, history, Latin, Latin American history, Latin-AP, law and the legal system, mathematics, meteorology, Middle Eastern history, modern European history-AP, music, music theory-AP, photography, physical education, physics, physics-AP, probability and statistics, psychology-AP, religion, science, sculpture, social studies, Spanish, Spanish language-AP, Spanish literature-AP, statistics-AP, theater, theology, trigonometry, U.S. government and politics-AP, world geography, world history, world literature.
Graduation Requirements Arts and fine arts (art, music, dance, drama), English, foreign language, history, mathematics, music, religion (includes Bible studies and theology), science, U.S. history.
Special Academic Programs 26 Advanced Placement exams for which test preparation is offered; honors section; independent study; academic accommodation for the gifted, the musically talented, and the artistically talented; ESL.
College Admission Counseling 171 students graduated in 2010; all went to college, including Boston University; Carnegie Mellon University; Colgate University; Cornell University; Princeton University; St. Lawrence University.
Student Life Upper grades have specified standards of dress, student council. Discipline rests equally with students and faculty. Attendance at religious services is required.
Tuition and Aid Day student tuition: $35,900; 7-day tuition and room/board: $45,300. Tuition installment plan (Key Tuition Payment Plan, monthly payment plans, individually arranged payment plans). Merit scholarship grants, need-based scholarship grants, need-based loans available. In 2010–11, 37% of upper-school students received aid. Total amount of financial aid awarded in 2010–11: $7,300,000.
Admissions Traditional secondary-level entrance grade is 9. For fall 2010, 1,200 students applied for upper-level admission, 450 were accepted, 190 enrolled. PSAT or SAT for applicants to grade 11 and 12, SSAT or TOEFL required. Deadline for receipt of application materials: January 15. Application fee required: $65. Interview required.
Athletics Interscholastic: baseball (boys), basketball (b,g), crew (b,g), cross-country running (b,g), diving (b,g), field hockey (g), football (b), golf (b,g), hockey (b,g), ice hockey (b,g), lacrosse (b,g), rowing (b,g), soccer (b,g), softball (g), squash (b,g), swimming and diving (b,g), tennis (b,g); intramural: basketball (b), crew (b,g), rowing (b,g); coed interscholastic: crew, dressage, equestrian sports, golf, horseback riding; coed intramural: aerobics/dance, aerobics/Nautilus, alpine skiing, ballet, bicycling, combined training, dance, dressage, equestrian sports, figure skating, fitness, hockey, horseback riding, ice skating, life saving, modern dance, mountain biking, physical fitness, physical training, ropes courses, sailing, skiing (downhill), snowboarding, soccer, squash, strength & conditioning, swimming and diving, tennis, ultimate Frisbee, weight training, yoga. 2 athletic trainers.
Computers Computers are regularly used in all academic, journalism, newspaper, yearbook classes. Computer network features include on-campus library services, online commercial services, Internet access, wireless campus network, all students receive a Tablet PC, students have online storage for schoolwork, Adobe Creative Suite, Autodesk, Mathcad and Microsoft Office Software for all students. Campus intranet, student e-mail accounts, and computer access in designated common areas are available to students. The school has a published electronic and media policy.
Contact Ms. Kathryn F. Sullivan, Director of Admissions. 860-927-6111. Fax: 860-927-6109. E-mail: admissions@kent-school.edu. Web site: www.kent-school.edu.

KENTUCKY COUNTRY DAY SCHOOL

4100 Springdale Road

Louisville, Kentucky 40241

Head of School: Mr. Bradley E. Lyman

General Information Coeducational day college-preparatory, arts, technology, honors program, independent study, and advanced programs for academically exceptional students school. Grades JK–12. Founded: 1972. Setting: suburban. 85-acre campus. 3 buildings on campus. Approved or accredited by Independent Schools Association of the Central States. Member of National Association of Independent Schools. Endowment: $10.3 million. Total enrollment: 947. Upper school average class size: 16. Upper school faculty-student ratio: 1:7. There are 170 required school days per year for Upper School students. Upper School students typically attend 5 days per week. The average school day consists of 7 hours and 5 minutes.
Upper School Student Profile Grade 9: 62 students (33 boys, 29 girls); Grade 10: 69 students (32 boys, 37 girls); Grade 11: 80 students (38 boys, 42 girls); Grade 12: 75 students (35 boys, 40 girls).
Faculty School total: 125. In upper school: 21 men, 19 women; 32 have advanced degrees.
Subjects Offered Algebra, American history, American literature, art, biology, calculus, ceramics, chemistry, collage and assemblage, communications, computer math, computer programming, computer science, drama, economics, English, English literature, European history, fine arts, French, geology, geometry, government/civics, history, humanities, instrumental music, Latin, law, mathematics, multimedia, music, physical education, physics, play production, psychology, psychology-AP, science, sculpture, senior internship, senior project, social sciences, social studies, Spanish, Spanish language-AP, speech, stagecraft, statistics, studio art-AP, technical theater, theater, trigonometry, U.S. government and politics-AP, U.S. history-AP.
Graduation Requirements Arts and fine arts (art, music, dance, drama), communications, English, foreign language, mathematics, physical education (includes health), science, social studies (includes history).
Special Academic Programs 20 Advanced Placement exams for which test preparation is offered; honors section; independent study; term-away projects; study abroad; academic accommodation for the gifted, the musically talented, and the artistically talented.
College Admission Counseling 81 students graduated in 2011; all went to college, including Furman University; Indiana University Bloomington; Kankakee Community College; Miami University; Northwestern University; University of Louisville. Median SAT critical reading: 600, median SAT math: 610, median SAT writing: 600, median combined SAT: 1860, median composite ACT: 27. 50% scored over 600 on SAT critical reading, 52% scored over 600 on SAT math, 52% scored over 600 on SAT writing, 54% scored over 1800 on combined SAT, 63% scored over 26 on composite ACT.
Student Life Upper grades have specified standards of dress, student council, honor system. Discipline rests equally with students and faculty.
Summer Programs Remediation, enrichment, advancement, sports, art/fine arts, rigorous outdoor training, computer instruction programs offered; session focuses on enrichment; held on campus; accepts boys and girls; open to students from other schools. 200 students usually enrolled. 2012 schedule: June 7 to August 20. Application deadline: none.
Tuition and Aid Day student tuition: $17,300. Tuition installment plan (FACTS Tuition Payment Plan). Merit scholarship grants, need-based scholarship grants available. In 2011–12, 24% of upper-school students received aid; total upper-school merit-scholarship money awarded: $37,850. Total amount of financial aid awarded in 2011–12: $857,811.
Admissions Traditional secondary-level entrance grade is 9. For fall 2011, 53 students applied for upper-level admission, 40 were accepted, 24 enrolled. ERB Reading and Math required. Deadline for receipt of application materials: none. Application fee required: $50. On-campus interview required.
Athletics Interscholastic: baseball (boys), basketball (b,g), cross-country running (b,g), diving (b,g), field hockey (g), football (b), golf (b,g), lacrosse (b,g), soccer (b,g), softball (g), swimming and diving (b,g), tennis (b,g), track and field (b,g), volleyball (g), winter (indoor) track (b,g); coed interscholastic: weight training; coed intramural: bowling, project adventure, ropes courses, weight lifting. 7 PE instructors, 86 coaches, 1 athletic trainer.
Computers Computers are regularly used in all classes. Computer network features include on-campus library services, online commercial services, Internet access, wireless campus network, Internet filtering or blocking technology. Campus intranet and student e-mail accounts are available to students. Students grades are available online. The school has a published electronic and media policy.
Contact Mr. Jeff Holbrook, Director of Admissions. 502-814-4375. Fax: 502-814-4381. E-mail: admissions@kcd.org. Web site: www.kcd.org.

KERR-VANCE ACADEMY

700 Vance Academy Road

Henderson, North Carolina 27537

Head of School: Mr. Paul Villatico

General Information Coeducational day college-preparatory school. Grades PK–12. Founded: 1968. Setting: rural. Nearest major city is Raleigh. 25-acre campus. 8 buildings on campus. Approved or accredited by Southern Association of Colleges and Schools and North Carolina Department of Education. Endowment: $40,000. Total enrollment: 472. Upper school average class size: 16. Upper school faculty-student ratio: 1:10. There are 180 required school days per year for Upper School students. Upper School students typically attend 5 days per week. The average school day consists of 6 hours.
Upper School Student Profile Grade 9: 32 students (20 boys, 12 girls); Grade 10: 40 students (16 boys, 24 girls); Grade 11: 30 students (17 boys, 13 girls); Grade 12: 45 students (25 boys, 20 girls).
Faculty School total: 41. In upper school: 5 men, 13 women; 12 have advanced degrees.
Subjects Offered Advanced Placement courses, algebra, American history, American literature, art, art history, biology, calculus, chemistry, computer programming, com-

puter science, creative writing, driver education, earth science, economics, English, English literature, environmental science, French, geography, geometry, government/civics, grammar, Latin, mathematics, music, physical education, physics, psychology, SAT/ACT preparation, science, social sciences, social studies, sociology, Spanish, speech, trigonometry, world history, world literature, writing.

Graduation Requirements Computer science, English, English composition, English literature, foreign language, mathematics, physical education (includes health), science, social sciences, social studies (includes history), writing. Community service is required.

Special Academic Programs International Baccalaureate program; Advanced Placement exam preparation; honors section.

College Admission Counseling 34 students graduated in 2011; all went to college, including East Carolina University; Meredith College; North Carolina State University; The University of North Carolina at Chapel Hill; The University of North Carolina at Greensboro; The University of North Carolina Wilmington. Mean SAT critical reading: 508, mean SAT math: 517, mean composite ACT: 25. 16% scored over 600 on SAT critical reading, 21% scored over 600 on SAT math, 33% scored over 26 on composite ACT.

Student Life Upper grades have specified standards of dress, student council. Discipline rests primarily with faculty.

Summer Programs Enrichment, advancement programs offered; session focuses on academic advancement; held on campus; accepts boys and girls; open to students from other schools. 50 students usually enrolled. 2012 schedule: July 10 to August 11. Application deadline: May 15.

Tuition and Aid Day student tuition: $8100. Tuition installment plan (monthly payment plans). Tuition reduction for siblings, need-based scholarship grants available. In 2011–12, 5% of upper-school students received aid. Total amount of financial aid awarded in 2011–12: $15,000.

Admissions Traditional secondary-level entrance grade is 9. Admissions testing or writing sample required. Deadline for receipt of application materials: none. Application fee required: $100. On-campus interview required.

Athletics Interscholastic: baseball (boys), basketball (b,g), cheering (g), cross-country running (b,g), golf (b), lacrosse (b), soccer (b,g), softball (g), tennis (b,g), track and field (b,g), volleyball (g), weight training (b,g), wrestling (b); intramural: soccer (b,g), weight lifting (b); coed intramural: swimming and diving, volleyball. 3 PE instructors, 7 coaches, 1 athletic trainer.

Computers Computers are regularly used in art, English, history, library, literary magazine, newspaper, programming, reading, research skills, SAT preparation, science, technology, writing, yearbook classes. Computer network features include on-campus library services, online commercial services, Internet access.

Contact Mrs. Rebecca W. Irvin, Admissions Coordinator. 252-492-0018. Fax: 252-438-4652. E-mail: rirvin@kerrvance.com. Web site: www.kerrvance.com.

THE KEW-FOREST SCHOOL

119-17 Union Turnpike

Forest Hills, New York 11375

Head of School: Mr. Mark P. Fish

General Information Coeducational day college-preparatory and arts school. Grades PK–12. Founded: 1918. Setting: urban. Nearest major city is New York. 1-acre campus. 1 building on campus. Approved or accredited by Middle States Association of Colleges and Schools, New York Department of Education, and New York Department of Education. Member of National Association of Independent Schools. Upper school average class size: 15. Upper school faculty-student ratio: 1:12. There are 162 required school days per year for Upper School students. Upper School students typically attend 5 days per week. The average school day consists of 6 hours.

Upper School Student Profile Grade 7: 17 students (7 boys, 10 girls); Grade 8: 21 students (11 boys, 10 girls); Grade 9: 16 students (4 boys, 12 girls); Grade 10: 30 students (16 boys, 14 girls); Grade 11: 17 students (9 boys, 8 girls); Grade 12: 33 students (14 boys, 19 girls).

Faculty School total: 34. In upper school: 14 men, 7 women; 14 have advanced degrees.

Subjects Offered Algebra, American history, ancient history, art, biology, biology-AP, calculus, calculus-AP, chemistry, English, English composition, English language and composition-AP, English literature, French, French-AP, geometry, health, history, honors geometry, Latin, Latin-AP, marine biology, modern European history, philosophy, physical education, physics, physics-AP, pre-calculus, Spanish, Spanish-AP, trigonometry, U.S. government and politics.

Graduation Requirements Art, English, history, history of the Catholic Church, mathematics, modern languages, music appreciation, physical education (includes health), science.

Special Academic Programs International Baccalaureate program; Advanced Placement exam preparation; academic accommodation for the gifted.

College Admission Counseling 25 students graduated in 2011; all went to college, including New York University. Median SAT critical reading: 520, median SAT math: 575, median SAT writing: 580. 25% scored over 600 on SAT critical reading, 40% scored over 600 on SAT math.

Student Life Upper grades have uniform requirement, student council, honor system. Discipline rests primarily with faculty.

Summer Programs Remediation, enrichment, advancement programs offered; session focuses on Summer Institute; held on campus; accepts boys and girls; open to students from other schools. 50 students usually enrolled. 2012 schedule: July 6 to August 15.

Tuition and Aid Day student tuition: $28,200. Tuition installment plan (FACTS Tuition Payment Plan, Tuition Management Systems Plan). Need-based scholarship grants available. In 2011–12, 25% of upper-school students received aid. Total amount of financial aid awarded in 2011–12: $900,000.

Admissions Traditional secondary-level entrance grade is 9. ISEE or SSAT required. Deadline for receipt of application materials: February 15. Application fee required: $75. On-campus interview required.

Athletics Interscholastic: basketball (boys, girls), cross-country running (b,g), soccer (b,g), tennis (b,g), volleyball (g); intramural: baseball (b), basketball (b,g), soccer (b,g), tennis (b,g); coed intramural: cross-country running, volleyball. 2 PE instructors, 5 coaches.

Computers Computers are regularly used in all academic classes. Computer network features include on-campus library services, Internet access, wireless campus network, Internet filtering or blocking technology. Students grades are available online.

Contact Mr. Rene A. Bolanos, Director of Admission. 718-268-4667 Ext. 125. Fax: 718-268-9121. E-mail: rbolanos@kewforest.org. Web site: www.kewforest.org.

KEY SCHOOL

Fort Worth, Texas

See Special Needs Schools section.

KILDONAN SCHOOL

Amenia, New York

See Special Needs Schools section.

KIMBALL UNION ACADEMY

PO Box 188

Main Street

Meriden, New Hampshire 03770

Head of School: Mr. Michael J. Schafer

General Information Coeducational boarding and day college-preparatory, arts, and environmental science school. Grades 9–PG. Founded: 1813. Setting: small town. Nearest major city is Boston, MA. Students are housed in single-sex dormitories. 1,300-acre campus. 35 buildings on campus. Approved or accredited by Independent Schools of Northern New England, New England Association of Schools and Colleges, The Association of Boarding Schools, The College Board, and New Hampshire Department of Education. Member of National Association of Independent Schools and Secondary School Admission Test Board. Endowment: $11 million. Total enrollment: 314. Upper school average class size: 12. Upper school faculty-student ratio: 1:9. There are 159 required school days per year for Upper School students. Upper School students typically attend 6 days per week. The average school day consists of 5 hours and 8 minutes.

Upper School Student Profile Grade 9: 56 students (32 boys, 24 girls); Grade 10: 77 students (41 boys, 36 girls); Grade 11: 91 students (61 boys, 30 girls); Grade 12: 83 students (43 boys, 40 girls); Postgraduate: 7 students (7 boys). 66% of students are boarding students. 34% are state residents. 18 states are represented in upper school student body. 25% are international students. International students from Canada, China, Germany, Mexico, Republic of Korea, and Spain; 11 other countries represented in student body.

Faculty School total: 47. In upper school: 32 men, 15 women; 33 have advanced degrees; 25 reside on campus.

Subjects Offered 3-dimensional design, acting, Advanced Placement courses, algebra, American history, American literature, anatomy, anthropology, architecture, art, art history, art history-AP, biology, biology-AP, calculus, calculus-AP, ceramics, chemistry, chemistry-AP, composition-AP, computer programming, creative writing, dance, digital photography, drama, driver education, English, English language and composition-AP, English literature, English literature and composition-AP, English-AP, environmental science, environmental science-AP, environmental studies, European history, fine arts, French, French language-AP, French literature-AP, geology, geometry, government/civics, grammar, health, history, history-AP, honors English, honors geometry, human geography - AP, independent study, international relations, jazz band, jazz ensemble, language-AP, Latin, Latin-AP, Mandarin, mathematical modeling, mathematics, modern European history-AP, modern world history, music, music history, music theory, music theory-AP, peer counseling, photo shop, photography, physics, physics-AP, physiology, playwriting, pottery, probability and statistics, programming, psychology, public speaking, science, social studies, Spanish, Spanish-AP, stagecraft, statistics-AP, student publications, studio art, studio art-AP, theater, theater arts, theater design and production, trigonometry, U.S. government, U.S. history, U.S. history-AP, video film production, visual arts, woodworking, world history, world literature, writing.

Graduation Requirements Art, English, foreign language, history, mathematics, science.

Special Academic Programs 19 Advanced Placement exams for which test preparation is offered; honors section; independent study; term-away projects; study abroad.

College Admission Counseling 99 students graduated in 2011; 94 went to college, including Boston University; Dartmouth College; Hobart and William Smith Colleges; Northeastern University; St. Lawrence University; Suffolk University. Other: 5 had other specific plans. Median SAT critical reading: 560, median SAT math: 570, median SAT writing: 560, median combined SAT: 1680, median composite ACT: 23. 27% scored over 600 on SAT critical reading, 41% scored over 600 on SAT math, 35% scored over 600 on SAT writing, 27% scored over 1800 on combined SAT, 21% scored over 26 on composite ACT.

Student Life Upper grades have specified standards of dress, student council, honor system. Discipline rests equally with students and faculty.

Summer Programs Enrichment, ESL, sports, art/fine arts programs offered; session focuses on environmental leadership (EE Just Institute) and ALPS (Accelerated Language Program) with Dartmouth College; held both on and off campus; held at Costa Rica; accepts boys and girls; open to students from other schools. 200 students usually enrolled. 2012 schedule: July 2 to July 30. Application deadline: April 15.

Tuition and Aid Day student tuition: $28,850, 7-day tuition and room/board: $45,990. Tuition installment plan (Insured Tuition Payment Plan, Academic Management Services Plan, Key Tuition Payment Plan, monthly payment plans). Need-based scholarship grants available. In 2011–12, 47% of upper-school students received aid. Total amount of financial aid awarded in 2011–12: $3,465,400.

Admissions Traditional secondary-level entrance grade is 9. For fall 2011, 382 students applied for upper-level admission, 288 were accepted, 130 enrolled. ACT, PSAT or SAT, SLEP, SSAT or TOEFL required. Deadline for receipt of application materials: February 1. Application fee required: $50. Interview required.

Athletics Interscholastic: alpine skiing (boys, girls), baseball (b), basketball (b,g), cross-country running (b,g), equestrian sports (b,g), field hockey (g), freestyle skiing (b,g), golf (b,g), hockey (b,g), horseback riding (b,g), ice hockey (b,g), lacrosse (b,g), nordic skiing (b,g), rugby (b), running (b,g), skiing (cross-country) (b,g), skiing (downhill) (b,g), snowboarding (b,g), soccer (b,g), softball (g), swimming and diving (b,g), tennis (b,g); coed interscholastic: bicycling, mountain biking; coed intramural: alpine skiing, backpacking, canoeing/kayaking, dance, equestrian sports, fitness, freestyle skiing, hiking/backpacking, modern dance, outdoor activities, physical fitness, rock climbing, squash, strength & conditioning, surfing, weight lifting, yoga. 1 coach, 2 athletic trainers.

Computers Computers are regularly used in architecture, literary magazine, theater arts, woodworking classes. Computer network features include on-campus library services, Internet access, wireless campus network, Internet filtering or blocking technology, computer music studio/audio recording. Campus intranet, student e-mail accounts, and computer access in designated common areas are available to students. Students grades are available online. The school has a published electronic and media policy.

Contact Mr. Rich Ryerson, Director of Admissions and Financial Aid. 603-469-2100. Fax: 603-469-2041. E-mail: admissions@kua.org. Web site: www.kua.org.

KING LOW HEYWOOD THOMAS

1450 Newfield Avenue
Stamford, Connecticut 06905

Head of School: Thomas B. Main

General Information Coeducational day college-preparatory and global studies, language distinctions, independent study school. Grades PK–12. Founded: 1865. Setting: suburban. Nearest major city is New York, NY. 40-acre campus. 4 buildings on campus. Approved or accredited by Connecticut Association of Independent Schools and New England Association of Schools and Colleges. Member of National Association of Independent Schools. Endowment: $18.1 million. Total enrollment: 684. Upper school average class size: 13. Upper school faculty-student ratio: 1:7. The average school day consists of 7 hours and 15 minutes.

Upper School Student Profile Grade 9: 78 students (42 boys, 36 girls); Grade 10: 85 students (49 boys, 36 girls); Grade 11: 85 students (45 boys, 40 girls); Grade 12: 66 students (42 boys, 24 girls).

Faculty School total: 105. In upper school: 22 men, 23 women; 37 have advanced degrees.

Subjects Offered Acting, advanced chemistry, advanced computer applications, advanced math, Advanced Placement courses, algebra, American history, ancient history, ancient world history, art, biology, calculus, calculus-AP, chemistry, chemistry-AP, Chinese, choral music, college counseling, college planning, computer multimedia, computer programming, creative writing, digital photography, economics, economics-AP, English, English language and composition-AP, English literature, English literature-AP, ethics, European history, European history-AP, expository writing, fine arts, French, French language-AP, general science, geometry, health, history, Holocaust, honors algebra, honors geometry, honors U.S. history, honors world history, independent study, introduction to theater, life skills, literature and composition-AP, macroeconomics-AP, mathematics, mathematics-AP, microeconomics-AP, model United Nations, modern European history-AP, modern languages, musical productions, musical theater, performing arts, philosophy, physics, physics-AP, play production, precalculus, SAT preparation, social studies, Spanish, Spanish language-AP, Spanish literature, Spanish literature-AP, statistics, statistics-AP, student government, student publications, studio art, theater arts, trigonometry, U.S. history-AP, U.S. literature, world history, writing workshop.

Graduation Requirements Arts and fine arts (art, music, dance, drama), English, ethics, foreign language, history, life skills, mathematics, science, sports, participation in one theater performance before graduation.

Special Academic Programs 19 Advanced Placement exams for which test preparation is offered; honors section; independent study; academic accommodation for the gifted, the musically talented, and the artistically talented.

College Admission Counseling 66 students graduated in 2011; 64 went to college, including Boston College; Bucknell University; Duke University; Loyola University Maryland; Syracuse University. Other: 2 entered a postgraduate year. Median SAT critical reading: 570, median SAT math: 610, median SAT writing: 610, median combined SAT: 1820, median composite ACT: 26. 47% scored over 600 on SAT critical reading, 58% scored over 600 on SAT math, 58% scored over 600 on SAT writing, 53% scored over 1800 on combined SAT, 50% scored over 26 on composite ACT.

Student Life Upper grades have specified standards of dress, student council, honor system. Discipline rests primarily with faculty.

Summer Programs Remediation, enrichment, advancement, sports, art/fine arts programs offered; session focuses on academics (grades 6-12), enrichment (elementary school), and sports (grades 4-8) enrichment; held on campus; accepts boys and girls; open to students from other schools. 200 students usually enrolled. 2012 schedule: June 18 to August 3. Application deadline: June 1.

Tuition and Aid Day student tuition: $33,800. Tuition installment plan (Key Tuition Payment Plan). Need-based scholarship grants available. In 2011–12, 12% of upper-school students received aid. Total amount of financial aid awarded in 2011–12: $933,795.

Admissions Traditional secondary-level entrance grade is 9. For fall 2011, 193 students applied for upper-level admission, 67 were accepted, 35 enrolled. ISEE, school's own test or SSAT required. Deadline for receipt of application materials: January 1. Application fee required: $75. On-campus interview required.

Athletics Interscholastic: baseball (boys), basketball (b,g), cross-country running (b,g), field hockey (g), football (b), golf (b,g), ice hockey (b), independent competitive sports (b,g), lacrosse (b,g), soccer (b,g), softball (g), squash (b,g), tennis (b,g), volleyball (g), intramural: dance (g), physical training (b,g); coed interscholastic: ice hockey, independent competitive sports, squash; coed intramural: aerobics/dance, dance, fitness, physical training, strength & conditioning, weight lifting, weight training. 27 coaches, 2 athletic trainers.

Computers Computers are regularly used in college planning, economics, English, ethics, foreign language, French, history, mathematics, science, technology, writing, yearbook classes. Computer network features include on-campus library services, online commercial services, Internet access, wireless campus network, Internet filtering or blocking technology. Campus intranet, student e-mail accounts, and computer access in designated common areas are available to students. The school has a published electronic and media policy.

Contact Carrie Salvatore, Director of Admission and Financial Aid. 203-322-3496 Ext. 352. Fax: 203-505-6288. E-mail: csalvatore@klht.org. Web site: www.klht.org.

THE KING'S ACADEMY

202 Smothers Road
Seymour, Tennessee 37865

Head of School: Mr. Walter Grubb

General Information Coeducational boarding and day and distance learning college-preparatory and religious studies school, affiliated with Southern Baptist Convention. Boarding grades 7–12, day grades K4–12. Distance learning grades 9–12. Founded: 1880. Setting: suburban. Nearest major city is Knoxville. Students are housed in single-sex dormitories. 67-acre campus. 8 buildings on campus. Approved or accredited by Southern Association of Colleges and Schools and Tennessee Department of Education. Total enrollment: 451. Upper school average class size: 14. Upper school faculty-student ratio: 1:14. There are 180 required school days per year for Upper School students. Upper School students typically attend 5 days per week. The average school day consists of 7 hours.

Upper School Student Profile Grade 9: 37 students (23 boys, 14 girls); Grade 10: 43 students (24 boys, 19 girls); Grade 11: 39 students (24 boys, 15 girls); Grade 12: 39 students (18 boys, 21 girls). 20% of students are boarding students. 79% are state residents. 3 states are represented in upper school student body. 28% are international students. International students from Bahamas, China, Iraq, Japan, Republic of Korea, and Thailand; 11 other countries represented in student body. 80% of students are Southern Baptist Convention.

Faculty School total: 40. In upper school: 10 men, 11 women; 11 have advanced degrees; 2 reside on campus.

Subjects Offered Advanced Placement courses, algebra, American history, anatomy, art, Bible studies, biology, calculus, chemistry, Chinese, choir, drama, economics, English, English-AP, ESL, fine arts, geometry, government/civics, grammar, health, health and wellness, history, keyboarding, mathematics, music, orchestra, physical education, physics, physiology, religion, science, social studies, Spanish, world history.
Graduation Requirements Arts and fine arts (art, music, dance, drama), computer science, English, foreign language, mathematics, religion (includes Bible studies and theology), science, social studies (includes history), wellness.
Special Academic Programs Advanced Placement exam preparation; honors section; independent study; study at local college for college credit; ESL (18 students enrolled).
College Admission Counseling 30 students graduated in 2011; 26 went to college, including Middle Tennessee State University; The University of Tennessee; University of Illinois at Urbana–Champaign; University of Minnesota, Twin Cities Campus; University of Mississippi; University of Washington. Other: 2 went to work, 1 entered military service.
Student Life Upper grades have uniform requirement, student council. Discipline rests primarily with faculty. Attendance at religious services is required.
Tuition and Aid Day student tuition: $5340–$6410; 5-day tuition and room/board: $15,510–$16,200; 7-day tuition and room/board: $22,020–$22,710. Tuition installment plan (monthly payment plans, individually arranged payment plans). Tuition reduction for siblings, need-based scholarship grants available. In 2011–12, 24% of upper-school students received aid. Total amount of financial aid awarded in 2011–12: $186,665.
Admissions Traditional secondary-level entrance grade is 9. For fall 2011, 36 students applied for upper-level admission, 31 were accepted, 25 enrolled. Deadline for receipt of application materials: none. Application fee required: $50. Interview recommended.
Athletics Interscholastic: baseball (boys), basketball (b,g), cheering (g), football (b), golf (b,g), soccer (b,g), tennis (b,g), volleyball (g), weight lifting (b,g), weight training (b,g); intramural: basketball (b,g), billiards (b,g), table tennis (b,g), tennis (b,g), volleyball (g), weight lifting (b,g), weight training (b,g); coed interscholastic: backpacking, bowling, cross-country running, rappelling, rock climbing, strength & conditioning, track and field; coed intramural: aerobics/Nautilus, canoeing/kayaking, cross-country running, fitness, outdoor education, physical fitness, physical training, rappelling, rock climbing, strength & conditioning, volleyball. 5 PE instructors, 30 coaches, 1 athletic trainer.
Computers Computers are regularly used in business applications, computer applications, keyboarding, yearbook classes. Computer network features include Internet access. Students grades are available online.
Contact Mrs. Janice Mink, Director of Admissions. 865-573-8321. Fax: 865-573-8323. E-mail: jmink@thekingsacademy.net. Web site: www.thekingsacademy.net.

KINGS CHRISTIAN SCHOOL

900 East D Street

Lemoore, California 93245

Head of School: Mr. Steven W. Reynolds

General Information Coeducational day college-preparatory, general academic, arts, business, religious studies, and technology school. Grades PK–12. Founded: 1979. Setting: small town. Nearest major city is Fresno. 17-acre campus. 12 buildings on campus. Approved or accredited by Association of Christian Schools International and Western Association of Schools and Colleges. Total enrollment: 294. Upper school average class size: 20. Upper school faculty-student ratio: 1:11. There are 180 required school days per year for Upper School students. Upper School students typically attend 5 days per week. The average school day consists of 6 hours and 45 minutes.
Upper School Student Profile Grade 9: 25 students (15 boys, 10 girls); Grade 10: 23 students (11 boys, 12 girls); Grade 11: 30 students (19 boys, 11 girls); Grade 12: 28 students (9 boys, 19 girls).
Faculty School total: 26. In upper school: 4 men, 6 women; 3 have advanced degrees.
Subjects Offered Accounting, advanced math, algebra, American government, art, auto mechanics, Bible studies, biology, business, calculus-AP, career education, chemistry, choir, chorus, community service, computer literacy, drama, drawing, driver education, economics, English, English literature-AP, finance, fine arts, geography, geometry, health, home economics, keyboarding, life skills, literature, mathematics, music, music theory, novels, physical education, physical science, physics, pre-algebra, religion, SAT preparation, science, Shakespeare, social sciences, social studies, Spanish, speech, U.S. history, weight training, word processing, yearbook.
Graduation Requirements Arts and fine arts (art, music, dance, drama), Bible studies, English, foreign language, mathematics, physical education (includes health), portfolio writing, science, social sciences, successfully pass Bible every year of attendance, proof of at least 9th grade proficiency (SAT Test).
Special Academic Programs 2 Advanced Placement exams for which test preparation is offered; honors section; accelerated programs; independent study; remedial reading and/or remedial writing; remedial math.
College Admission Counseling 26 students graduated in 2011; 25 went to college, including Azusa Pacific University; Biola University; California State University, Fresno; The Master's College and Seminary; Vanguard University of Southern California; West Hills Community College. Other: 1 went to work. Median SAT critical reading: 420, median SAT math: 470, median SAT writing: 410, median combined SAT: 1300. 15% scored over 600 on SAT critical reading, 8% scored over 600 on SAT math, 8% scored over 600 on SAT writing, 15% scored over 1800 on combined SAT.
Student Life Upper grades have specified standards of dress, student council. Discipline rests primarily with faculty.
Tuition and Aid Day student tuition: $5778. Tuition installment plan (monthly payment plans). Tuition reduction for siblings, need-based scholarship grants, paying campus jobs available. In 2011–12, 18% of upper-school students received aid. Total amount of financial aid awarded in 2011–12: $175,000.
Admissions Traditional secondary-level entrance grade is 9. For fall 2011, 19 students applied for upper-level admission, 16 were accepted, 15 enrolled. PSAT or Terra Nova-CTB required. Deadline for receipt of application materials: none. Application fee required: $150.
Athletics Interscholastic: baseball (boys), basketball (b,g), football (b), softball (g), track and field (b,g), volleyball (g); intramural: physical fitness (b,g), physical training (b,g), power lifting (b), strength & conditioning (b,g), track and field (b,g), weight training (b,g); coed interscholastic: cheering, cross-country running, track and field; coed intramural: badminton, fitness, Frisbee, physical fitness, strength & conditioning, track and field, volleyball. 5 PE instructors, 9 coaches, 2 athletic trainers.
Computers Computers are regularly used in Bible studies, college planning, English, introduction to technology, journalism, library skills, programming, SAT preparation, technical drawing, yearbook classes. Computer network features include on-campus library services, Internet access, wireless campus network, Internet filtering or blocking technology.
Contact Leslie Reynolds, Registrar. 559-924-8301 Ext. 107. Fax: 559-924-0607. E-mail: lreynolds@kcsnet.com. Web site: www.kcsnet.com.

KING'S-EDGEHILL SCHOOL

254 College Road

Windsor, Nova Scotia B0N 2T0, Canada

Head of School: Mr. Joseph Seagram

General Information Coeducational boarding and day college-preparatory school. Grades 6–12. Founded: 1788. Setting: small town. Nearest major city is Halifax, Canada. Students are housed in single-sex dormitories. 65-acre campus. 17 buildings on campus. Approved or accredited by California Association of Independent Schools and Nova Scotia Department of Education. Language of instruction: English. Total enrollment: 290. Upper school average class size: 15. Upper school faculty-student ratio: 1:10.
Upper School Student Profile Grade 10: 60 students (28 boys, 32 girls); Grade 11: 70 students (37 boys, 33 girls); Grade 12: 70 students (38 boys, 32 girls). 68% of students are boarding students. 55% are province residents. 13 provinces are represented in upper school student body. 30% are international students. International students from Germany, Hong Kong, Mexico, Republic of Korea, and Taiwan; 13 other countries represented in student body.
Faculty School total: 46. In upper school: 19 men, 23 women; 15 have advanced degrees; 22 reside on campus.
Subjects Offered Art, biology, calculus, chemistry, current events, drama, economics, English, French, geography, geology, history, mathematics, music, physics, political science, religion, science, social sciences, social studies, theater, theory of knowledge, world history.
Graduation Requirements English, foreign language, mathematics, science, social sciences, social studies (includes history).
Special Academic Programs International Baccalaureate program; honors section; term-away projects; study abroad; academic accommodation for the gifted; ESL (22 students enrolled).
College Admission Counseling 70 students graduated in 2011; all went to college, including Dalhousie University; McGill University; Queen's University at Kingston; The University of British Columbia; The University of Western Ontario; University of Toronto.
Student Life Upper grades have uniform requirement, student council, honor system. Discipline rests primarily with faculty. Attendance at religious services is required.
Tuition and Aid Day student tuition: CAN$15,050; 7-day tuition and room/board: CAN$35,750. Tuition installment plan (monthly payment plans, individually arranged payment plans). Bursaries, merit scholarship grants available. In 2011–12, 35% of upper-school students received aid. Total amount of financial aid awarded in 2011–12: CAN$900,000.
Admissions Traditional secondary-level entrance grade is 10. OLSAT and English Exam required. Deadline for receipt of application materials: none. Application fee required: CAN$100. Interview required.
Athletics Interscholastic: alpine skiing (boys, girls), aquatics (b,g), badminton (b,g), baseball (b,g), basketball (b,g), biathlon (b,g), bicycling (b,g), cross-country running (b,g), equestrian sports (b,g), fitness (b,g), Frisbee (b,g), golf (b,g), ice hockey (b,g), outdoor recreation (b,g), outdoor skills (b,g), physical fitness (b,g), rugby (b,g), skiing (cross-country) (b,g), skiing (downhill) (b,g), snowboarding (b,g), soccer (b,g), softball (b,g), table tennis (b,g), tennis (b,g), track and field (b,g), ultimate Frisbee (b,g), volleyball (b,g), weight lifting (b,g), wrestling (b,g); intramural: basketball (b,g), bicycling (b,g), cross-country running (b,g), golf (b,g), rugby (b,g), skiing (cross-country) (b,g), skiing (downhill) (b,g), snowboarding (b,g), soccer (b,g), softball (b,g), table tennis

(b,g), tennis (b,g), track and field (b,g), weight lifting (b,g), yoga (b,g); coed interscholastic: alpine skiing, aquatics, bicycling, equestrian sports, fitness, Frisbee, outdoor recreation, outdoor skills, physical fitness, table tennis; coed intramural: bowling, curling, field hockey, table tennis, yoga. 2 PE instructors, 30 coaches.
Computers Computers are regularly used in computer applications, English, foreign language, mathematics, music, science classes. Computer network features include on-campus library services, online commercial services, Internet access, Internet filtering or blocking technology. Campus intranet, student e-mail accounts, and computer access in designated common areas are available to students.
Contact Mr. Chris B. Strickey, Director of Admission. 902-798-2278. Fax: 902-798-2105. E-mail: strickey@kes.ns.ca. Web site: www.kes.ns.ca.

KING'S HIGH SCHOOL

19303 Fremont Avenue North
Seattle, Washington 98133

Head of School: Bob Ruhlman

General Information Coeducational day college-preparatory, arts, business, religious studies, and technology school, affiliated with Christian faith. Grades PK–12. Founded: 1950. Setting: suburban. 55-acre campus. 6 buildings on campus. Approved or accredited by Association of Christian Schools International, Northwest Association of Schools and Colleges, and Washington Department of Education. Total enrollment: 1,130. Upper school average class size: 25. Upper school faculty-student ratio: 1:15. There are 171 required school days per year for Upper School students. Upper School students typically attend 5 days per week. The average school day consists of 5 hours and 47 minutes.
Upper School Student Profile Grade 9: 127 students (58 boys, 69 girls); Grade 10: 113 students (61 boys, 52 girls); Grade 11: 120 students (62 boys, 58 girls); Grade 12: 111 students (52 boys, 59 girls). 80% of students are Christian faith.
Faculty School total: 89. In upper school: 11 men, 22 women; 20 have advanced degrees.
Subjects Offered Advanced Placement courses, algebra, American history, American literature, anatomy, anatomy and physiology, art, Bible, biology, business, calculus, calculus-AP, ceramics, chemistry, chemistry AP, choir, choral music, computer science, culinary arts, drama, earth science, English, English literature, English-AP, environmental science, European history, European history-AP, expository writing, fine arts, geography, geometry, health, history, history-AP, honors algebra, honors English, honors geometry, honors U.S. history, journalism, leadership, mathematics, music, orchestra, photography, physical education, physics, pre-calculus, psychology, religion, SAT preparation, science, social studies, Spanish, speech, theater, trigonometry, U.S. history, U.S. history-AP, video film production, vocal ensemble, vocal jazz, world history, writing.
Graduation Requirements Arts and fine arts (art, music, dance, drama), career and technology systems, computer science, English, foreign language, health education, mathematics, physical education (includes health), religion (includes Bible studies and theology), science, social studies (includes history), speech, senior thesis, senior project, senior retreat.
Special Academic Programs Advanced Placement exam preparation; honors section.
College Admission Counseling 102 students graduated in 2011; 100 went to college, including Central Washington University; Seattle Pacific University; University of Washington. Other: 2 went to work. Mean SAT critical reading: 546, mean SAT math: 587, mean SAT writing: 538, mean combined SAT: 1671, mean composite ACT: 24.
Student Life Upper grades have specified standards of dress, student council, honor system. Discipline rests primarily with faculty. Attendance at religious services is required.
Summer Programs Sports programs offered; session focuses on team and skill development; held both on and off campus; held at PLU, UW, WWU and NW Basketball Camps; accepts boys and girls; open to students from other schools. 30 students usually enrolled. 2012 schedule: June 14 to July 30. Application deadline: none.
Tuition and Aid Day student tuition: $10,660. Tuition installment plan (monthly payment plans). Tuition reduction for siblings, need-based scholarship grants, paying campus jobs available. In 2011–12, 16% of upper-school students received aid. Total amount of financial aid awarded in 2011–12: $572,000.
Admissions Traditional secondary-level entrance grade is 9. For fall 2011, 59 students applied for upper-level admission, 54 were accepted, 50 enrolled. Gates MacGinite Placement Test or TOEFL required. Deadline for receipt of application materials: none. Application fee required: $50. On-campus interview required.
Athletics Interscholastic: basketball (boys, girls), cross-country running (b,g), football (b), golf (b,g), soccer (b,g), track and field (b,g), volleyball (g); coed interscholastic: cheering, physical fitness, physical training, power lifting, strength & conditioning, weight training. 3 PE instructors, 26 coaches, 1 athletic trainer.
Computers Computers are regularly used in English, introduction to technology, journalism, keyboarding, media production, photography, science, study skills, technology, video film production, Web site design, yearbook classes. Computer network features include on-campus library services, online commercial services, Internet access, Internet filtering or blocking technology. Students grades are available online. The school has a published electronic and media policy.
Contact Leslie Young, Secondary Admissions Coordinator. 206-289-7783. Fax: 206-546-7214. E-mail: lyoung@crista.net. Web site: www.kingsschools.org.

KINGSHILL SCHOOL

St. Croix, Virgin Islands

See Special Needs Schools section.

KING'S RIDGE CHRISTIAN SCHOOL

2765 Bethany Bend
Alpharetta, Georgia 30004

Head of School: Mr. C. David Rhodes III

General Information Coeducational day college-preparatory school, affiliated with Christian faith. Grades K–12. Founded: 2001. Setting: suburban. Nearest major city is Atlanta. 70-acre campus. 3 buildings on campus. Approved or accredited by Georgia Accrediting Commission, Georgia Independent School Association, Southern Association of Colleges and Schools, and Southern Association of Independent Schools. Member of National Association of Independent Schools and Secondary School Admission Test Board. Total enrollment: 713. Upper school average class size: 12. Upper school faculty-student ratio: 1:8. There are 180 required school days per year for Upper School students. Upper School students typically attend 5 days per week. The average school day consists of 6 hours and 45 minutes.
Faculty School total: 120. In upper school: 12 men, 12 women; 14 have advanced degrees.
Subjects Offered Advanced Placement courses, algebra, American government, American history, art, astronomy, biology, calculus-AP, chemistry, Christian doctrine, Christian education, Christian ethics, civics, communication skills, computer programming, drama performance, drawing, English composition, English literature, European history, finance, French, geometry, honors algebra, honors English, honors geometry, honors U.S. history, Life of Christ, music composition, physical fitness, physics, public speaking, SAT preparation, Spanish, speech, statistics, studio art, video film production, yearbook.
Graduation Requirements 50 hours of community service between grades 9-12.
Special Academic Programs Advanced Placement exam preparation; honors section.
College Admission Counseling 16 students graduated in 2011; all went to college, including Auburn University; Georgia College & State University; Georgia Institute of Technology; Samford University; University of Georgia; University of Richmond.
Student Life Upper grades have uniform requirement, student council, honor system. Discipline rests primarily with faculty. Attendance at religious services is required.
Tuition and Aid Day student tuition: $14,643. Tuition installment plan (Insured Tuition Payment Plan, FACTS Tuition Payment Plan). Tuition reduction for siblings, need-based scholarship grants available. In 2011–12, 30% of upper-school students received aid.
Admissions SSAT, ERB, PSAT, SAT, PLAN or ACT required. Deadline for receipt of application materials: none. Application fee required: $75. Interview required.
Athletics Interscholastic: baseball (boys), basketball (b,g), cheering (g), football (b), lacrosse (b), soccer (b,g), softball (g), strength & conditioning (b), swimming and diving (b,g), tennis (b,g), volleyball (g); coed interscholastic: cross-country running, equestrian sports, golf, horseback riding, track and field; coed intramural: weight training. 3 PE instructors, 3 coaches.
Computers Computers are regularly used in all academic classes. Computer network features include online commercial services, Internet access, wireless campus network, Internet filtering or blocking technology, online collaboration of classroom activities. Campus intranet, student e-mail accounts, and computer access in designated common areas are available to students. Students grades are available online. The school has a published electronic and media policy.
Contact Lisa K. McGuire, Director of Admission/Marketing. 770-754-5738 Ext. 118. Fax: 770-754-5544. E-mail: lmcguire@kingsridgecs.org. Web site: www.kingsridgecs.org/.

KINGSWAY COLLEGE

1200 Leland Road
Oshawa, Ontario L1K 2H4, Canada

Head of School: Mr. Scott Bowes

General Information Coeducational boarding and day college-preparatory, general academic, religious studies, and bilingual studies school, affiliated with Seventh-day Adventists. Grades 9–12. Founded: 1903. Setting: small town. Nearest major city is Toronto, Canada. Students are housed in single-sex dormitories. 100-acre campus. 9 buildings on campus. Approved or accredited by Ontario Ministry of Education and

Ontario Department of Education. Language of instruction: English. Endowment: CAN$1.6 million. Total enrollment: 185. Upper school average class size: 25. Upper school faculty-student ratio: 1:11. There are 180 required school days per year for Upper School students. Upper School students typically attend 5 days per week. The average school day consists of 5 hours and 50 minutes.

Upper School Student Profile Grade 9: 40 students (19 boys, 21 girls); Grade 10: 51 students (22 boys, 29 girls); Grade 11: 50 students (27 boys, 23 girls); Grade 12: 44 students (27 boys, 17 girls). 45% of students are boarding students. 85% are province residents. 9 provinces are represented in upper school student body. 4% are international students. International students from Bahamas, Bermuda, Democratic People's Republic of Korea, Japan, United Kingdom, and United States. 90% of students are Seventh-day Adventists.

Faculty School total: 16. In upper school: 9 men, 7 women; 2 have advanced degrees; 8 reside on campus.

Subjects Offered Accounting, advanced chemistry, advanced computer applications, advanced math, algebra, American history, anthropology, band, biology, business studies, calculus, Canadian geography, Canadian history, Canadian law, career education, ceramics, chemistry, choir, civics, computer applications, computer information systems, computer programming, computer studies, concert band, English, English literature, ESL, French, healthful living, information processing, intro to computers, music, music performance, physical education, physics, psychology, religious education, science, sociology, U.S. history, visual arts, work-study, world civilizations, world religions.

Graduation Requirements Art, Canadian geography, Canadian history, careers, civics, English, French, mathematics, physical education (includes health), science, all students must take one religion course per year.

Special Academic Programs ESL (2 students enrolled).

College Admission Counseling 45 students graduated in 2010; 37 went to college, including Andrews University; McGill University; Southern Adventist University; University of Michigan; University of Toronto; Walla Walla University. Other: 1 entered military service, 2 had other specific plans.

Student Life Upper grades have specified standards of dress, student council. Discipline rests primarily with faculty. Attendance at religious services is required.

Tuition and Aid Day student tuition: CAN$9430; 7-day tuition and room/board: CAN$16,013. Tuition installment plan (monthly payment plans, individually arranged payment plans). Tuition reduction for siblings, merit scholarship grants, need-based scholarship grants, paying campus jobs available. In 2010–11, 45% of upper-school students received aid; total upper-school merit-scholarship money awarded: CAN$24,000. Total amount of financial aid awarded in 2010–11: CAN$156,000.

Admissions Traditional secondary-level entrance grade is 9. For fall 2010, 189 students applied for upper-level admission, 187 were accepted, 185 enrolled. Deadline for receipt of application materials: none. No application fee required. Interview recommended.

Athletics Interscholastic: basketball (boys, girls); intramural: basketball (b,g), flag football (b,g), floor hockey (b,g), ice hockey (b), indoor hockey (b,g), soccer (b,g), softball (b,g), volleyball (b,g); coed intramural: backpacking, badminton, bicycling, canoeing/kayaking, gymnastics, hiking/backpacking, outdoor education, roller skating, skiing (downhill), snowboarding, volleyball. 1 PE instructor.

Computers Computers are regularly used in accounting, business, career education, computer applications, data processing, English, ESL, history, programming, science, social sciences classes. Computer network features include Internet access, Internet filtering or blocking technology. Student e-mail accounts are available to students. Students grades are available online. The school has a published electronic and media policy.

Contact Ms. Remy Guenin, Director of Enrollment Services. 905-433-1144 Ext. 212. Fax: 905-433-1156. E-mail: gueninr@kingswaycollege.on.ca. Web site: www.kingswaycollege.on.ca.

KINGSWOOD-OXFORD SCHOOL

170 Kingswood Road

West Hartford, Connecticut 06119-1430

Head of School: Mr. Dennis Bisgaard

General Information Coeducational day college-preparatory school. Grades 6–12. Founded: 1909. Setting: suburban. Nearest major city is Hartford. 30-acre campus. 11 buildings on campus. Approved or accredited by New England Association of Schools and Colleges and Connecticut Department of Education. Member of National Association of Independent Schools and Secondary School Admission Test Board. Endowment: $25.7 million. Total enrollment: 496. Upper school average class size: 13. Upper school faculty-student ratio: 1:8. There are 160 required school days per year for Upper School students. Upper School students typically attend 5 days per week. The average school day consists of 7 hours.

Upper School Student Profile Grade 9: 74 students (30 boys, 44 girls); Grade 10: 95 students (50 boys, 45 girls); Grade 11: 76 students (41 boys, 35 girls); Grade 12: 101 students (46 boys, 55 girls).

Faculty School total: 53. In upper school: 27 men, 26 women; 33 have advanced degrees.

Subjects Offered Algebra, American history, American literature, art, art history-AP, band, biology, biology-AP, calculus, calculus-AP, chemistry, chemistry-AP, Chinese, Chinese studies, chorus, composition-AP, computer science, computer science-AP, concert band, concert choir, creative writing, digital music, digital photography, dramatic arts, drawing, economics, economics-AP, English, English language-AP, English literature, English literature-AP, environmental science, fine arts, forensics, French, French language-AP, geography, geometry, government/civics, jazz band, jazz ensemble, journalism, Latin, Latin-AP, marine biology, mathematics, media, music, orchestra, photography, physics, physics-AP, political science, public speaking, social studies, Spanish, Spanish language-AP, Spanish-AP, statistics, statistics-AP, theater, U.S. history-AP, visual arts, world history, world literature, writing.

Graduation Requirements Computer science, English, foreign language, mathematics, performing arts, science, social studies (includes history), technology, visual arts, participation on athletic teams, senior thesis in English, 30 hours of community service. Community service is required.

Special Academic Programs 17 Advanced Placement exams for which test preparation is offered; honors section; independent study; term-away projects; study at local college for college credit; study abroad.

College Admission Counseling 98 students graduated in 2011; all went to college, including Skidmore College; Syracuse University; Tufts University; Union College; University of Connecticut. Median SAT critical reading: 600, median SAT math: 605, median SAT writing: 620, median combined SAT: 1835, median composite ACT: 25.

Student Life Upper grades have specified standards of dress, student council, honor system. Discipline rests equally with students and faculty.

Tuition and Aid Day student tuition: $32,771. Tuition installment plan (Academic Management Services Plan). Merit scholarship grants, need-based scholarship grants available. In 2011–12, 35% of upper-school students received aid; total upper-school merit-scholarship money awarded: $276,500. Total amount of financial aid awarded in 2011–12: $2,300,000.

Admissions Traditional secondary-level entrance grade is 9. For fall 2011, 185 students applied for upper-level admission, 108 were accepted, 49 enrolled. SSAT required. Deadline for receipt of application materials: February 1. Application fee required: $55. On-campus interview required.

Athletics Interscholastic: alpine skiing (boys, girls), baseball (b), basketball (b,g), cross-country running (b,g), diving (b,g), field hockey (g), football (b), ice hockey (b,g), lacrosse (b,g), soccer (b,g), softball (g), squash (b,g), strength & conditioning (b,g), swimming and diving (b,g), tennis (b,g), track and field (b,g), volleyball (g); intramural: basketball (b,g), ice hockey (b), soccer (b,g), yoga (g); coed interscholastic: golf, skiing (downhill); coed intramural: strength & conditioning. 9 coaches, 2 athletic trainers.

Computers Computers are regularly used in English, foreign language, history, mathematics, music technology, photography, science classes. Computer resources include on-campus library services, Internet access, wireless campus network. Student e-mail accounts and computer access in designated common areas are available to students. Students grades are available online. The school has a published electronic and media policy.

Contact Mr. James E. O¿Donnell, Director of Enrollment Management. 860-727-5000. Fax: 860-236-3651. E-mail: odonnell.j@k-o.org. Web site: www.kingswoodoxford.org.

KIROV ACADEMY OF BALLET OF WASHINGTON, D.C.

4301 Harewood Road NE

Washington, District of Columbia 20017

Head of School: Mr. Michael Beard

General Information Coeducational boarding and day college-preparatory, arts, and classical ballet; Vaganova method school. Grades 6–12. Founded: 1990. Setting: urban. Students are housed in single-sex by floor dormitories. 3-acre campus. 1 building on campus. Approved or accredited by Middle States Association of Colleges and Schools and District of Columbia Department of Education. Total enrollment: 63. Upper school average class size: 10. Upper school faculty-student ratio: 1:8. There are 160 required school days per year for Upper School students. Upper School students typically attend 5 days per week. The average school day consists of 9 hours.

Upper School Student Profile Grade 6: 4 students (4 girls); Grade 7: 1 student (1 boy); Grade 8: 5 students (5 girls); Grade 9: 5 students (1 boy, 4 girls); Grade 10: 13 students (4 boys, 9 girls); Grade 11: 16 students (2 boys, 14 girls); Grade 12: 14 students (2 boys, 12 girls); Postgraduate: 4 students (2 boys, 2 girls). 90% of students are boarding students. 15 states are represented in upper school student body. International students from Italy, Japan, Mexico, Republic of Korea, and Taiwan.

Faculty School total: 9. In upper school: 3 men, 5 women; 6 have advanced degrees.

Subjects Offered 20th century physics, aesthetics, algebra, American government, American history, American literature, analytic geometry, anatomy, art history, ballet, ballet technique, biology, career planning, chemistry, dance, dance performance, English, ESL, European literature, French, health and wellness, mathematics, music appreciation, nutrition, personal finance, science, senior career experience, world history.

Special Academic Programs ESL (6 students enrolled).

College Admission Counseling 10 students graduated in 2010; 2 went to college, including Indiana University of Pennsylvania; New York University. Other: 8 went to work.
Student Life Upper grades have specified standards of dress, student council. Discipline rests primarily with faculty.
Tuition and Aid Tuition installment plan (monthly payment plans). Merit scholarship grants, paying campus jobs available.
Admissions Iowa Tests of Basic Skills required. Deadline for receipt of application materials: none. No application fee required. On-campus interview required.
Athletics Interscholastic: ballet (boys, girls), dance (b,g); intramural: ballet (b,g); coed interscholastic: ballet, dance; coed intramural: ballet.
Computers Computer network features include Internet access, wireless campus network, Internet filtering or blocking technology. Campus intranet and computer access in designated common areas are available to students. Students grades are available online.
Contact Ms. Rebecca Rorke, Director of Programs. 202-636-0635. Fax: 202-832-8995. E-mail: rorke@kirovacademydc.org. Web site: www.kirovacademydc.org.

LADYWOOD HIGH SCHOOL

14680 Newburgh Road
Livonia, Michigan 48154

Head of School: Mrs. Joan L Fitzgerald

General Information Girls' day college-preparatory, arts, business, and religious studies school, affiliated with Roman Catholic Church. Grades 9–12. Founded: 1950. Setting: suburban. Nearest major city is Detroit. 17-acre campus. 1 building on campus. Approved or accredited by National Catholic Education Association, North Central Association of Colleges and Schools, and Michigan Department of Education. Total enrollment: 316. Upper school average class size: 24. Upper school faculty-student ratio: 1:12. There are 179 required school days per year for Upper School students. Upper School students typically attend 5 days per week. The average school day consists of 5 hours and 30 minutes.
Upper School Student Profile Grade 9: 64 students (64 girls); Grade 10: 70 students (70 girls); Grade 11: 79 students (79 girls); Grade 12: 103 students (103 girls). 88% of students are Roman Catholic.
Faculty School total: 34. In upper school: 6 men, 24 women; 14 have advanced degrees.
Subjects Offered Accounting, advanced chemistry, algebra, American government, American history, American history-AP, American literature, anatomy and physiology, art, Asian history, Bible studies, biology, biology-AP, calculus, calculus-AP, career and personal planning, career exploration, career planning, Catholic belief and practice, ceramics, child development, choir, Christian and Hebrew scripture, college writing, composition, computer education, computer science, culinary arts, discrete mathematics, drama performance, drawing and design, economics, English, English composition, English literature and composition-AP, environmental science, environmental science-AP, film appreciation, food science, forensics, French, French language-AP, French-AP, geometry, global issues, graphic arts, health, history of the Catholic Church, independent living, Italian, keyboarding, language and composition, language arts, leadership and service, library assistant, life management skills, oil painting, orchestra, parent/child development, physical education, physics, poetry, prayer/spirituality, precalculus, probability and statistics, psychology, religion, scripture, sewing, short story, sociology, Spanish, Spanish language-AP, Spanish-AP, speech, studio art-AP, theater, theater arts, visual and performing arts, water color painting, world studies, writing, yearbook.
Graduation Requirements Algebra, American government, American history, American literature, arts and fine arts (art, music, dance, drama), athletic training, biology, British literature, Catholic belief and practice, chemistry, computer science, economics, English composition, foreign language, geometry, global studies, health education, keyboarding, literature, mathematics, physical education (includes health), religion (includes Bible studies and theology), science, social sciences, speech communications, world literature, service requirement for each grade level.
Special Academic Programs Advanced Placement exam preparation; study at local college for college credit.
College Admission Counseling 86 students graduated in 2011; all went to college, including Grand Valley State University; Michigan State University; University of Michigan–Dearborn; Wayne State University. Median composite ACT: 24. Mean SAT critical reading: 556, mean SAT math: 527, mean SAT writing: 543, mean combined SAT: 1626. 26% scored over 26 on composite ACT.
Student Life Upper grades have uniform requirement, student council, honor system. Discipline rests primarily with faculty. Attendance at religious services is required.
Tuition and Aid Day student tuition: $7650. Tuition installment plan (The Tuition Plan, monthly payment plans, individually arranged payment plans). Tuition reduction for siblings, merit scholarship grants, need-based scholarship grants available. In 2011–12, 14% of upper-school students received aid. Total amount of financial aid awarded in 2011–12: $135,000.
Admissions Traditional secondary-level entrance grade is 9. Catholic High School Entrance Examination required. Deadline for receipt of application materials: none. Application fee required: $300. Interview recommended.
Athletics Interscholastic: basketball, bowling, cheering, cross-country running, equestrian sports, field hockey, figure skating, flag football, golf, ice hockey, lacrosse, pom squad, skiing (downhill), snowboarding, soccer, softball, swimming and diving, tennis, track and field, volleyball; intramural: flag football. 1 PE instructor, 51 coaches, 1 athletic trainer.
Computers Computers are regularly used in accounting, computer applications, data processing, graphic design, keyboarding, Web site design, word processing, yearbook classes. Computer network features include on-campus library services, Internet access, Internet filtering or blocking technology. Campus intranet is available to students. Students grades are available online. The school has a published electronic and media policy.
Contact Mrs. Caryn Epps, Guidance Counselors. 734-591-5492 Ext. 227. Fax: 734-591-4214. E-mail: cepps@ladywood.org. Web site: www.ladywood.org.

LA JOLLA COUNTRY DAY SCHOOL

9490 Genesee Avenue
La Jolla, California 92037

Head of School: Mr. Christopher Schuck

General Information Coeducational day college-preparatory, arts, and technology school. Grades N 12. Founded: 1926. Setting: suburban. Nearest major city is San Diego. 24-acre campus. 8 buildings on campus. Approved or accredited by Western Association of Schools and Colleges and California Department of Education. Member of National Association of Independent Schools and Secondary School Admission Test Board. Endowment: $2.4 million. Total enrollment: 1,158. Upper school average class size: 16. Upper school faculty-student ratio: 1:15. There are 171 required school days per year for Upper School students. Upper School students typically attend 5 days per week. The average school day consists of 7 hours.
Upper School Student Profile Grade 9: 132 students (65 boys, 67 girls); Grade 10: 121 students (61 boys, 60 girls); Grade 11: 122 students (70 boys, 52 girls); Grade 12: 111 students (56 boys, 55 girls).
Faculty School total: 103. In upper school: 26 men, 24 women; 32 have advanced degrees.
Subjects Offered Advanced studio art-AP, algebra, Arabic, art, art history-AP, astronomy, biology, biology-AP, calculus-AP, chemistry, chemistry-AP, chorus, computer graphics, conceptual physics, dance, drama, economics, English, English language-AP, English literature, English literature and composition-AP, environmental science, European history, European history-AP, film studies, French, French literature-AP, French-AP, freshman seminar, geometry, government, government-AP, history of drama, honors algebra, honors geometry, independent study, instrumental music, journalism, linear algebra, madrigals, music appreciation, music-AP, neuroscience, performing arts, photography, physical education, physics, physics-AP, portfolio art, precalculus, programming, psychology, psychology-AP, Spanish, Spanish language-AP, Spanish literature-AP, Spanish-AP, speech, statistics-AP, strings, studio art, studio art-AP, technical theater, theater, theater arts, theater history, theater production, theory of knowledge, U.S. history-AP, women's studies, world cultures, writing.
Graduation Requirements Arts and fine arts (art, music, dance, drama), English, foreign language, mathematics, performing arts, physical education (includes health), science, senior project, social sciences, speech, 40 hours of community service.
Special Academic Programs Advanced Placement exam preparation; honors section; study abroad.
College Admission Counseling 113 students graduated in 2011; 111 went to college, including Boston University; Dartmouth College; Stanford University; The University of Arizona; University of California, San Diego; University of California, Santa Barbara. Other: 2 had other specific plans. Mean SAT critical reading: 600, mean SAT math: 600, mean SAT writing: 622.
Student Life Upper grades have specified standards of dress, student council. Discipline rests equally with students and faculty.
Summer Programs Remediation, enrichment, advancement, sports, art/fine arts, computer instruction programs offered; session focuses on academics, summer camp, sports camps; held on campus; accepts boys and girls; open to students from other schools. 300 students usually enrolled. 2012 schedule: June 22 to July 31. Application deadline: none.
Tuition and Aid Day student tuition: $26,635. Tuition installment plan (FACTS Tuition Payment Plan, monthly payment plans). Need-based scholarship grants available. In 2011–12, 54% of upper-school students received aid. Total amount of financial aid awarded in 2011–12: $2,316,168.
Admissions Traditional secondary-level entrance grade is 9. ERB (grade level), ISEE, TerraNova or writing sample required. Deadline for receipt of application materials: February 1. Application fee required: $125. On-campus interview required.
Athletics Interscholastic: aquatics (boys, girls), baseball (b), basketball (b,g), cheering (g), cross-country running (b,g), dance (b,g), fencing (b,g), football (b), golf (b,g), independent competitive sports (b,g), lacrosse (b,g), roller hockey (b), soccer (b,g), softball (g), swimming and diving (b,g), tennis (b,g), track and field (b,g), volleyball (b,g), water polo (b,g); coed interscholastic: physical fitness, physical training, strength & conditioning, surfing, ultimate Frisbee, weight lifting, weight training; coed intramural: dance team, outdoor education, snowboarding. 8 PE instructors, 50 coaches, 1 athletic trainer.

Computers Computers are regularly used in art, English, French, history, mathematics, science, Spanish, technology classes. Computer network features include on-campus library services, online commercial services, Internet access, wireless campus network, email connection from home. The school has a published electronic and media policy.

Contact Mr. Vincent Travaglione, Director of Admission. 858-453-3440 Ext. 117. Fax: 858-453-8210. E-mail: vtravaglione@ljcds.org. Web site: www.ljcds.org.

LAKEFIELD COLLEGE SCHOOL

4391 County Road, #29

Lakefield, Ontario K0L 2H0, Canada

Head of School: Mrs. Sarah J. McMahon

General Information Coeducational boarding and day college-preparatory, arts, technology, and distance learning, outdoor education program school, affiliated with Church of England (Anglican). Boarding grades 9–12, day grades 7–12. Founded: 1879. Setting: small town. Nearest major city is Toronto, Canada. Students are housed in single-sex dormitories. 315-acre campus. 25 buildings on campus. Approved or accredited by Canadian Association of Independent Schools, Canadian Educational Standards Institute, The Association of Boarding Schools, and Ontario Department of Education. Affiliate member of National Association of Independent Schools; member of Secondary School Admission Test Board. Language of instruction: English. Endowment: CAN$17 million. Total enrollment: 368. Upper school average class size: 16. Upper school faculty-student ratio: 1:7. The average school day consists of 5 hours.

Upper School Student Profile Grade 9: 66 students (34 boys, 32 girls); Grade 10: 85 students (51 boys, 34 girls); Grade 11: 98 students (50 boys, 48 girls); Grade 12: 98 students (45 boys, 53 girls). 74% of students are boarding students. 75% are province residents. 18 provinces are represented in upper school student body. 29% are international students. International students from Barbados, China, Germany, Saudi Arabia, U.S. Virgin Islands, and United States; 25 other countries represented in student body. 40% of students are members of Church of England (Anglican).

Faculty School total: 54. In upper school: 27 men, 26 women; 11 have advanced degrees; 23 reside on campus.

Subjects Offered Algebra, art, art history, biology, calculus, chemistry, computer science, creative writing, drama, driver education, earth science, economics, English, English literature, environmental science, fine arts, French, geography, geometry, government/civics, health, history, kinesiology, mathematics, music, outdoor education, physical education, physics, science, social studies, sociology, Spanish, theater, trigonometry, vocal music, world history, world literature.

Graduation Requirements English, foreign language, mathematics, physical education (includes health), science, social studies (includes history).

Special Academic Programs Advanced Placement exam preparation; honors section; accelerated programs; independent study; term-away projects; study at local college for college credit; study abroad; academic accommodation for the gifted, the musically talented, and the artistically talented.

College Admission Counseling 98 students graduated in 2011; 94 went to college, including McGill University; Queen's University at Kingston; The University of British Columbia; The University of Western Ontario; Trent University; University of Toronto. Other: 4 had other specific plans.

Student Life Upper grades have uniform requirement, student council, honor system. Discipline rests equally with students and faculty.

Summer Programs Session focuses on online courses for current students; held off campus; held at via distance learning; accepts boys and girls; not open to students from other schools. 100 students usually enrolled. 2012 schedule: June 22 to August 30.

Tuition and Aid Day student tuition: CAN$27,370; 7-day tuition and room/board: CAN$51,245. Tuition installment plan (Insured Tuition Payment Plan, monthly payment plans, individually arranged payment plans, 3-payment plans or custom payment plans if req'd). Bursaries, need-based scholarship grants available. In 2011–12, 33% of upper-school students received aid. Total amount of financial aid awarded in 2011–12: CAN$170,000.

Admissions Traditional secondary-level entrance grade is 9. For fall 2011, 231 students applied for upper-level admission, 192 were accepted, 118 enrolled. Otis-Lennon School Ability Test or SSAT required. Deadline for receipt of application materials: none. Application fee required: CAN$100. Interview required.

Athletics Interscholastic: alpine skiing (boys, girls), baseball (b), basketball (g), crew (g), cross-country running (b,g), field hockey (g), golf (b,g), hockey (b,g), ice hockey (b,g), nordic skiing (b,g), outdoor education (b,g), ropes courses (b,g), rowing (b,g), rugby (b,g), skiing (cross-country) (b,g), skiing (downhill) (b,g), snowboarding (b,g), soccer (b,g), softball (b); intramural: aerobics/dance (g), basketball (b,g), cross-country running (b,g), skiing (cross-country) (b,g); coed interscholastic: alpine skiing, cross-country running, equestrian sports, Frisbee, golf, hockey, horseback riding, ice hockey, nordic skiing, outdoor education, sailing, skiing (cross-country), skiing (downhill), snowboarding; coed intramural: aerobics/Nautilus, baseball, basketball, bicycling, canoeing/kayaking, climbing, cross-country running, dance, equestrian sports, fitness, ice hockey, kayaking, sailing, skiing (cross-country), skiing (downhill), softball.

Computers Computers are regularly used in art, English, foreign language, history, mathematics, music, science classes. Computer network features include on-campus library services, online commercial services, Internet access, Internet filtering or blocking technology. Student e-mail accounts are available to students. Students grades are available online. The school has a published electronic and media policy.

Contact Mrs. Barbara M. Rutherford, Assistant Director of Admissions. 705-652-3324 Ext. 345. Fax: 705-652-6320. E-mail: admissions@lcs.on.ca. Web site: www.lcs.on.ca.

LAKE FOREST ACADEMY

1500 West Kennedy Road

Lake Forest, Illinois 60045

Head of School: Dr. John Strudwick

General Information Coeducational boarding and day college-preparatory and arts school. Grades 9–12. Founded: 1857. Setting: suburban. Nearest major city is Chicago. Students are housed in single-sex dormitories. 160-acre campus. 30 buildings on campus. Approved or accredited by Independent Schools Association of the Central States, Midwest Association of Boarding Schools, The Association of Boarding Schools, The College Board, and Illinois Department of Education. Member of National Association of Independent Schools and Secondary School Admission Test Board. Endowment: $25.8 million. Total enrollment: 391. Upper school average class size: 12. Upper school faculty-student ratio: 1:7. The average school day consists of 7 hours.

Upper School Student Profile Grade 9: 80 students (48 boys, 32 girls); Grade 10: 104 students (56 boys, 48 girls); Grade 11: 108 students (60 boys, 48 girls); Grade 12: 94 students (52 boys, 42 girls); Postgraduate: 5 students (4 boys, 1 girl). 50% of students are boarding students. 71% are state residents. 20 states are represented in upper school student body. 30% are international students. International students from Canada, China, Germany, Republic of Korea, Taiwan, and Thailand; 30 other countries represented in student body.

Faculty School total: 69. In upper school: 36 men, 33 women; 46 have advanced degrees; 53 reside on campus.

Subjects Offered 20th century history, 20th century world history, 3-dimensional art, 3-dimensional design, acting, advanced chemistry, advanced computer applications, advanced math, Advanced Placement courses, advanced studio art-AP, algebra, American government, American history, American history-AP, American literature, American literature-AP, American studies, anatomy and physiology, anthropology, applied arts, applied music, art, art appreciation, art education, art history, art history-AP, art-AP, astronomy, bioethics, bioethics, DNA and culture, biology, biology-AP, calculus, calculus-AP, ceramics, chemistry, chemistry-AP, Chinese, choir, choral music, chorus, cinematography, comparative government and politics-AP, computer applications, computer graphics, computer information systems, computer programming, computer science, computer science-AP, creative writing, drama, ecology, English, English literature, environmental science, ESL, fine arts, French, geometry, health and wellness, history, journalism, Latin, Latin American literature, Latin-AP, literature and composition-AP, mathematics, music, mythology, photography, physics, poetry, pre-calculus, science, Shakespeare, social studies, Spanish, speech, statistics-AP, theater, U.S. government and politics-AP, world history.

Graduation Requirements Arts and fine arts (art, music, dance, drama), athletics, English, foreign language, mathematics, science, social studies (includes history). Community service is required.

Special Academic Programs Advanced Placement exam preparation; honors section; independent study; study abroad; academic accommodation for the gifted, the musically talented, and the artistically talented; ESL (16 students enrolled).

College Admission Counseling 105 students graduated in 2010; all went to college, including Duke University; Miami University; Northwestern University; University of Illinois at Urbana–Champaign; University of Michigan. Mean SAT critical reading: 580, mean SAT math: 640, mean SAT writing: 590, mean combined SAT: 1800, mean composite ACT: 27.

Student Life Upper grades have specified standards of dress, student council. Discipline rests equally with students and faculty.

Tuition and Aid Day student tuition: $31,000; 7-day tuition and room/board: $42,000. Tuition installment plan (FACTS Tuition Payment Plan). Merit scholarship grants, need-based scholarship grants available. In 2010–11, 30% of upper-school students received aid. Total amount of financial aid awarded in 2010–11: $3,100,000.

Admissions Traditional secondary-level entrance grade is 9. For fall 2010, 463 students applied for upper-level admission, 197 were accepted, 124 enrolled. SSAT or TOEFL required. Deadline for receipt of application materials: January 31. Application fee required: $50. Interview required.

Athletics Interscholastic: baseball (boys), basketball (b,g), cross-country running (b,g), field hockey (g), football (b), ice hockey (b,g), soccer (b,g), softball (g), swimming and diving (b,g), tennis (b,g), track and field (b,g), volleyball (b,g), wrestling (b); intramural: lacrosse (b,g); coed interscholastic: cheering, golf; coed intramural: bowling, dance, dance squad, fitness, martial arts, racquetball, sailing, squash, water polo, weight training, yoga. 3 coaches, 1 athletic trainer.

Computers Computers are regularly used in English, foreign language, history, mathematics, science classes. Computer network features include on-campus library services, online commercial services, Internet access, wireless campus network, Internet filtering or blocking technology, iPods, Smart Boards in classrooms. Campus intranet, student e-mail accounts, and computer access in designated common areas are available to students. The school has a published electronic and media policy.

Contact Admissions Office. 847-615-3267. Fax: 847-295-8149. E-mail: info@lfanet.org. Web site: www.lfanet.org.

LAKEHILL PREPARATORY SCHOOL

2720 Hillside Drive

Dallas, Texas 75214

Head of School: Roger L. Perry

General Information Coeducational day college-preparatory, arts, bilingual studies, and technology school. Grades K–12. Founded: 1971. Setting: urban. 23-acre campus. 4 buildings on campus. Approved or accredited by Independent Schools Association of the Southwest, Texas Private School Accreditation Commission, The College Board, and Texas Department of Education. Member of National Association of Independent Schools. Endowment: $200,000. Total enrollment: 400. Upper school average class size: 14. Upper school faculty-student ratio: 1:10. There are 175 required school days per year for Upper School students. Upper School students typically attend 5 days per week. The average school day consists of 7 hours and 30 minutes.

Upper School Student Profile Grade 9: 26 students (14 boys, 12 girls); Grade 10: 36 students (18 boys, 18 girls), Grade 11: 25 students (12 boys, 13 girls); Grade 12: 23 students (13 boys, 10 girls).

Faculty School total: 44. In upper school: 10 men, 13 women; 17 have advanced degrees.

Subjects Offered Advanced Placement courses, advanced studio art-AP, algebra, American history, American history-AP, American literature, art, art history, biology, calculus, calculus-AP, chemistry, college counseling, computer math, computer programming, computer programming-AP, computer science, digital photography, drama, earth science, economics, English, English language and composition-AP, English literature, environmental science-AP, European history, French, French language-AP, geography, geometry, government/civics, grammar, health, history, journalism, Latin, mathematics, music, music theater, physical education, physics, psychology, public speaking, publications, science, senior career experience, Shakespeare, social sciences, social studies, Spanish, Spanish language-AP, Spanish literature-AP, speech, statistics, theater, trigonometry, Western civilization, world history, world literature, writing.

Graduation Requirements Arts and fine arts (art, music, dance, drama), computer science, electives, English, foreign language, mathematics, physical education (includes health), science, social sciences, social studies (includes history), senior internship program.

Special Academic Programs Advanced Placement exam preparation; honors section; independent study; study abroad.

College Admission Counseling 32 students graduated in 2011; all went to college, including Brown University; Duke University; Morehouse College; Texas A&M University; Texas Christian University; Tufts University. Median SAT critical reading: 643, median SAT math: 594, median SAT writing: 604, median combined SAT: 1841, median composite ACT: 26.

Student Life Upper grades have specified standards of dress, student council, honor system. Discipline rests primarily with faculty.

Summer Programs Enrichment, sports, art/fine arts, computer instruction programs offered; session focuses on enrichment; held on campus; accepts boys and girls; open to students from other schools. 200 students usually enrolled. 2012 schedule: June 4 to July 27. Application deadline: May 15.

Tuition and Aid Day student tuition: $16,725. Tuition installment plan (monthly payment plans). Tuition reduction for siblings, need-based scholarship grants available. In 2011–12, 18% of upper-school students received aid.

Admissions Traditional secondary-level entrance grade is 9. ERB CTP IV, ISEE or Stanford Achievement Test required. Deadline for receipt of application materials: January 6. Application fee required: $150. On-campus interview recommended.

Athletics Interscholastic: baseball (boys), basketball (b,g), cheering (g), cross-country running (b,g), football (b), golf (b,g), jogging (b,g), rock climbing (b,g), softball (g), tennis (b,g), track and field (b,g), volleyball (g), weight training (b,g); coed interscholastic: tennis; coed intramural: bowling. 3 PE instructors, 12 coaches, 1 athletic trainer.

Computers Computers are regularly used in college planning, creative writing, English, graphic design, journalism, mathematics, science, speech, Web site design, word processing, writing, yearbook classes. Computer network features include on-campus library services, online commercial services, Internet access, wireless campus network, Internet filtering or blocking technology. Student e-mail accounts are available to students. Students grades are available online. The school has a published electronic and media policy.

Contact Holly Walker, Director of Admission. 214-826-2931. Fax: 214-826-4623. E-mail: hwalker@lakehillprep.org. Web site: www.lakehillprep.org.

LAKE MARY PREPARATORY SCHOOL

650 Rantoul Lane

Lake Mary, Florida 32746

Head of School: Dr. Spencer Taintor

General Information Coeducational boarding and day and distance learning college-preparatory, arts, business, and technology school. Boarding grades 7–12, day grades PK–12. Distance learning grade X. Founded: 1999. Setting: suburban. Nearest major city is Orlando. Students are housed in single-sex dormitories. 48-acre campus. 1 building on campus. Approved or accredited by Florida Council of Independent Schools and Florida Department of Education. Total enrollment: 644. Upper school average class size: 20. Upper school faculty-student ratio: 1:22. There are 180 required school days per year for Upper School students. Upper School students typically attend 5 days per week. The average school day consists of 7 hours and 30 minutes.

Upper School Student Profile Grade 6: 53 students (35 boys, 18 girls); Grade 7: 40 students (20 boys, 20 girls); Grade 8: 46 students (24 boys, 22 girls); Grade 9: 61 students (41 boys, 20 girls); Grade 10: 59 students (35 boys, 24 girls); Grade 11: 74 students (43 boys, 31 girls); Grade 12: 56 students (30 boys, 26 girls). 7% of students are boarding students. 93% are state residents. 2 states are represented in upper school student body. 7% are international students. International students from Brazil, China, Republic of Korea, Russian Federation, Turkey, and Viet Nam.

Faculty School total: 62. In upper school: 18 men, 21 women; 13 have advanced degrees; 8 reside on campus.

Subjects Offered .

Special Academic Programs Advanced Placement exam preparation; honors section; study abroad; ESL (52 students enrolled).

College Admission Counseling 52 students graduated in 2010; all went to college, including Florida State University; Penn State University Park; University of Central Florida; University of Florida; University of Miami. Median SAT critical reading: 490, median SAT math: 560, median SAT writing: 500, median combined SAT: 1050, median composite ACT: 23. 15% scored over 600 on SAT critical reading, 30% scored over 600 on SAT math, 10% scored over 600 on SAT writing, 18% scored over 1800 on combined SAT, 15% scored over 26 on composite ACT.

Student Life Upper grades have uniform requirement, student council, honor system. Discipline rests primarily with faculty.

Tuition and Aid Day student tuition: $11,950; 7-day tuition and room/board: $34,850. Tuition installment plan (monthly payment plans). Tuition reduction for siblings, need-based scholarship grants available. In 2010–11, 10% of upper-school students received aid.

Admissions Traditional secondary-level entrance grade is 9. ISEE required. Deadline for receipt of application materials: none. Application fee required: $100. Interview required.

Athletics Interscholastic: aerobics/dance (girls), aquatics (g), ballet (g), baseball (b), basketball (b,g), bowling (b), cheering (g), cross-country running (b,g), dance (b), dance squad (b), dance team (b), fitness (b,g), fitness walking (b,g), football (g), golf (b,g), gymnastics (b), jogging (b,g), lacrosse (g), physical fitness (b,g), physical training (b,g), pom squad (b), running (b,g), soccer (b,g), softball (b), strength & conditioning (b,g), swimming and diving (b), tennis (b,g), track and field (b,g), volleyball (b), winter soccer (b,g), yoga (b,g). 4 PE instructors, 22 coaches, 1 athletic trainer.

Computers Computers are regularly used in all academic classes. Computer network features include on-campus library services, Internet access, wireless campus network, Internet filtering or blocking technology. Students grades are available online. The school has a published electronic and media policy.

Contact Mrs. Laura Lykins, Director of Admissions. 407-805-0095 Ext. 105. Fax: 407-322-3872. E-mail: laura.lykins@lakemaryprep.com.

LAKE RIDGE ACADEMY

37501 Center Ridge Road

North Ridgeville, Ohio 44039

Head of School: Mrs. Carol L. Klimas

General Information Coeducational day college-preparatory, arts, technology, entrepreneurial studies, and environmental studies school. Grades K–12. Founded: 1963. Setting: suburban. Nearest major city is Cleveland. 88-acre campus. 12 buildings on campus. Approved or accredited by Independent Schools Association of the Central States and Ohio Department of Education. Member of National Association of Independent Schools. Endowment: $1.2 million. Total enrollment: 339. Upper school average class size: 12. Upper school faculty-student ratio: 1:8. There are 172 required school days per year for Upper School students. Upper School students typically attend 5 days per week. The average school day consists of 6 hours.

Upper School Student Profile Grade 9: 33 students (18 boys, 15 girls); Grade 10: 35 students (14 boys, 21 girls); Grade 11: 52 students (28 boys, 24 girls); Grade 12: 39 students (22 boys, 17 girls).

Faculty School total: 48. In upper school: 17 men, 28 women; 33 have advanced degrees.

Subjects Offered Algebra, American history, American literature, art, biology, biology-AP, calculus, calculus-AP, ceramics, chemistry, chemistry-AP, choir, computer applications, creative writing, design, digital imaging, discrete mathematics, ecology, environmental systems, economics, electronic publishing, English, English-AP, entrepreneurship, ethics, expository writing, fine arts, French, French-AP, functions, geometry, graphic arts, health, humanities, instrumental music, interactive media, journalism, literature, mathematics, music composition, music theory, physical education, physics, physics-AP, portfolio writing, pre-calculus, senior seminar, Shakespeare, social studies, Spanish, Spanish-AP, statistics, theater, U.S. history-AP, video film production, world civilizations, world history, world literature, writing.

Graduation Requirements Arts and fine arts (art, music, dance, drama), English, ethics, foreign language, mathematics, physical education (includes health), science, social studies (includes history), U.S. history.

Special Academic Programs Advanced Placement exam preparation; honors section; independent study; study at local college for college credit; academic accommodation for the gifted, the musically talented, and the artistically talented; programs in general development for dyslexic students; special instructional classes for deaf students; ESL (8 students enrolled).

College Admission Counseling 33 students graduated in 2010; all went to college, including Haverford College; Northwestern University; Ohio Wesleyan University; Purdue University; Rochester Institute of Technology; The George Washington University. Median SAT critical reading: 600, median SAT math: 630, median SAT writing: 600, median composite ACT: 26. 60% scored over 600 on SAT critical reading, 65% scored over 600 on SAT math, 40% scored over 600 on SAT writing, 50% scored over 1800 on combined SAT, 50% scored over 26 on composite ACT.

Student Life Upper grades have specified standards of dress, student council, honor system. Discipline rests primarily with faculty.

Tuition and Aid Day student tuition: $22,000–$24,250. Tuition installment plan (The Tuition Plan, Insured Tuition Payment Plan, monthly payment plans, individually arranged payment plans). Tuition reduction for siblings, merit scholarship grants, need-based scholarship grants available. In 2010–11, 50% of upper-school students received aid; total upper-school merit-scholarship money awarded: $472,095. Total amount of financial aid awarded in 2010–11: $841,475.

Admissions Traditional secondary-level entrance grade is 9. For fall 2010, 69 students applied for upper-level admission, 45 were accepted, 28 enrolled. CTBS, OLSAT, essay, ISEE, mathematics proficiency exam, school's own exam, TOEFL or SLEP and writing sample required. Deadline for receipt of application materials: none. Application fee required: $35. Interview required.

Athletics Interscholastic: baseball (boys), basketball (b,g), cross-country running (b,g), golf (b,g), indoor track & field (b), soccer (b,g), softball (g), tennis (b,g), track and field (b,g), volleyball (g), winter (indoor) track (b), wrestling (b); intramural: indoor soccer (b,g), strength & conditioning (b,g), winter soccer (b,g); coed intramural: backpacking, indoor soccer, outdoor adventure, outdoor recreation, physical fitness, physical training, strength & conditioning, ultimate Frisbee, weight lifting, weight training. 2 PE instructors, 12 coaches, 1 athletic trainer.

Computers Computers are regularly used in college planning, creative writing, drawing and design, English, foreign language, history, journalism, mathematics, media production, research skills, science classes. Computer network features include on-campus library services, online commercial services, Internet access, wireless campus network, Internet filtering or blocking technology. Campus intranet and student e-mail accounts are available to students. Students grades are available online. The school has a published electronic and media policy.

Contact Mrs. Edie Sweeterman, Associate Director of Admission. 440-327-1175 Ext. 106. Fax: 440-327-3641. E-mail: admission@lakeridgeacademy.org. Web site: www.lakeridgeacademy.org.

LAKESIDE SCHOOL

14050 First Avenue NE

Seattle, Washington 98125-3099

Head of School: Mr. Bernard Noe

General Information Coeducational day college-preparatory, arts, and technology school. Grades 5–12. Founded: 1919. Setting: urban. 34-acre campus. 19 buildings on campus. Approved or accredited by Northwest Association of Schools and Colleges, Pacific Northwest Association of Independent Schools, and Washington Department of Education. Member of National Association of Independent Schools. Endowment: $188.6 million. Total enrollment: 797. Upper school average class size: 16. Upper school faculty-student ratio: 1:9. There are 164 required school days per year for Upper School students. Upper School students typically attend 5 days per week. The average school day consists of 6 hours and 50 minutes.

Upper School Student Profile Grade 9: 135 students (65 boys, 70 girls); Grade 10: 128 students (65 boys, 63 girls); Grade 11: 143 students (72 boys, 71 girls); Grade 12: 132 students (67 boys, 65 girls).

Faculty School total: 92. In upper school: 33 men, 24 women; 44 have advanced degrees.

Subjects Offered Algebra, American history, American literature, art, biology, calculus, ceramics, chemistry, community service, computer programming, computer science, creative writing, drama, driver education, economics, English, English literature, environmental science, European history, expository writing, fine arts, French, geometry, government/civics, health, history, journalism, Latin, mathematics, music, outdoor education, philosophy, photography, physical education, physics, pre-calculus, science, social studies, Spanish, theater, trigonometry, world history, world literature, writing.

Graduation Requirements Arts, English, foreign language, history, mathematics, outdoor education, physical education (includes health), science. Community service is required.

Special Academic Programs Honors section; independent study; term-away projects; study abroad.

College Admission Counseling 127 students graduated in 2011; 125 went to college, including Columbia University; Stanford University; University of Southern California; University of Washington; Washington University in St. Louis; Whitman College. Other: 2 had other specific plans. Median SAT critical reading: 705, median SAT math: 720, median SAT writing: 690, median combined SAT: 2095, median composite ACT: 31.

Student Life Upper grades have student council, honor system. Discipline rests equally with students and faculty.

Summer Programs Enrichment, advancement, sports, art/fine arts, computer instruction programs offered; session focuses on Upper and Middle school classes, athletic camps, academic enrichment for public Middle School students; held on campus; accepts boys and girls; open to students from other schools. 590 students usually enrolled. 2012 schedule: June 25 to August 3. Application deadline: June 1.

Tuition and Aid Day student tuition: $26,200. Tuition installment plan (monthly payment plans). Need-based scholarship grants available. In 2011–12, 28% of upper-school students received aid. Total amount of financial aid awarded in 2011–12: $2,995,770.

Admissions Traditional secondary-level entrance grade is 9. For fall 2011, 362 students applied for upper-level admission, 71 were accepted, 57 enrolled. ISEE, PSAT or SAT for applicants to grade 11 and 12 or SSAT required. Deadline for receipt of application materials: January 26. Application fee required: $25. Interview required.

Athletics Interscholastic: baseball (boys), basketball (b,g), crew (b,g), cross-country running (b,g), diving (b,g), football (b), golf (b,g), lacrosse (b,g), soccer (b,g), softball (g), swimming and diving (b,g), tennis (b,g), track and field (b,g), volleyball (g); coed interscholastic: ultimate Frisbee, wrestling; coed intramural: outdoor education, skiing (cross-country), squash. 5 PE instructors, 71 coaches, 1 athletic trainer.

Computers Computers are regularly used in all academic classes. Computer network features include on-campus library services, online commercial services, Internet access, wireless campus network, Internet filtering or blocking technology, class schedule search, online course registration, online directory. Campus intranet, student e-mail accounts, and computer access in designated common areas are available to students. The school has a published electronic and media policy.

Contact Ms. Margaret Hardy, Admissions Associate. 206-368-3605. Fax: 206-440-2777. E-mail: admissions@lakesideschool.org. Web site: www.lakesideschool.org.

LA LUMIERE SCHOOL

6801 North Wilhelm Road

La Porte, Indiana 46350

Head of School: Michael H. Kennedy

General Information Coeducational boarding and day college-preparatory, arts, and religious studies school, affiliated with Roman Catholic Church. Boarding grades 9–PG, day grades 9–12. Founded: 1963. Setting: rural. Nearest major city is Chicago, IL. Students are housed in single-sex dormitories. 144-acre campus. 18 buildings on campus. Approved or accredited by Independent Schools Association of the Central States, Midwest Association of Boarding Schools, North Central Association of Colleges and Schools, and The Association of Boarding Schools. Member of National Association of Independent Schools. Total enrollment: 209. Upper school average class size: 12. Upper school faculty-student ratio: 1:8. The average school day consists of 7 hours and 30 minutes.

Upper School Student Profile Grade 9: 40 students (23 boys, 17 girls); Grade 10: 52 students (25 boys, 27 girls); Grade 11: 61 students (39 boys, 22 girls); Grade 12: 52 students (30 boys, 22 girls); Postgraduate: 2 students (2 boys). 35% of students are boarding students. 57% are state residents. 8 states are represented in upper school student body. 13% are international students. International students from China, Croatia, Iran, Republic of Korea, Serbia and Montenegro, and Spain; 3 other countries represented in student body. 40% of students are Roman Catholic.

Faculty School total: 27. In upper school: 14 men, 11 women; 13 have advanced degrees; 18 reside on campus.

Subjects Offered Advanced Placement courses, algebra, American history-AP, American literature, art, art history, biology, biology-AP, British literature, calculus, calculus-AP, chemistry, Christian and Hebrew scripture, college counseling, computer programming, conceptual physics, creative writing, drama, economics, English, English literature, English-AP, ESL, ethics, French, French-AP, geography, geometry, government/civics, graphic design, health, Latin, physics, physics-AP, pre-calculus, SAT/ACT preparation, Spanish, Spanish-AP, speech, study skills, trigonometry, U.S. history, U.S. history-AP, Web site design, world history, world literature, world religions.

Graduation Requirements American government, American history, American literature, arts and fine arts (art, music, dance, drama), Bible as literature, British literature, college writing, computer science, economics, electives, English, English composition, English literature, ethics, foreign language, government, health education, leadership, mathematics, public service, science, social studies (includes history), theology, U.S. history, world history. Community service is required.

Special Academic Programs Advanced Placement exam preparation; honors section; independent study; study at local college for college credit; academic accommodation for the gifted and the artistically talented; ESL (2 students enrolled).

College Admission Counseling 38 students graduated in 2010; all went to college, including DePaul University; Indiana University Bloomington; Loyola University Chicago; Michigan State University; Purdue University; University of Notre Dame. Mean SAT critical reading: 531, mean SAT math: 613, mean SAT writing: 522, mean composite ACT: 23.

Student Life Upper grades have uniform requirement, student council, honor system. Discipline rests primarily with faculty.

Tuition and Aid Day student tuition: $9495; 7-day tuition and room/board: $31,475. Tuition installment plan (Academic Management Services Plan, Key Tuition Payment Plan, FACTS Tuition Payment Plan, individually arranged payment plans). Tuition reduction for siblings, merit scholarship grants, need-based scholarship grants available. In 2010–11, 26% of upper-school students received aid; total upper-school merit-scholarship money awarded: $15,000. Total amount of financial aid awarded in 2010–11: $580,000.

Admissions Traditional secondary-level entrance grade is 9. For fall 2010, 127 students applied for upper-level admission, 71 were accepted, 59 enrolled. Achievement tests, English proficiency, ISEE, school's own exam or SLEP for foreign students required. Deadline for receipt of application materials: none. Application fee required: $50. Interview required.

Athletics Interscholastic: baseball (boys), basketball (b,g), football (b), golf (b,g), hockey (b), independent competitive sports (b,g), lacrosse (b), softball (g), tennis (b,g), track and field (b,g), volleyball (g); intramural: aerobics/dance (g), volleyball (b,g); coed interscholastic: cross-country running, running, soccer; coed intramural: aerobics/Nautilus, basketball, billiards, bowling, canoeing/kayaking, combined training, cooperative games, cross-country running, dance, fishing, fitness, flag football, floor hockey, Frisbee, hiking/backpacking, jogging, kayaking, martial arts, Nautilus, outdoor adventure, outdoor recreation, physical fitness, physical training, power lifting, ropes courses, skateboarding, strength & conditioning, table tennis, touch football, ultimate Frisbee, weight lifting, weight training, yoga. 10 coaches, 1 athletic trainer.

Computers Computers are regularly used in all academic, college planning, creative writing, programming, yearbook classes. Computer network features include on-campus library services, Internet access, wireless campus network, Internet filtering or blocking technology. Student e-mail accounts and computer access in designated common areas are available to students. Students grades are available online. The school has a published electronic and media policy.

Contact Ms. Mary C. O'Malley, Director of Admissions. 219-326-7450. Fax: 219-325-3185. E-mail: admissions@lalumiere.org. Web site: www.lalumiere.org.

LANCASTER MENNONITE HIGH SCHOOL

2176 Lincoln Highway East

Lancaster, Pennsylvania 17602

Head of School: Mr. Elvin Kennel

General Information Coeducational boarding and day college-preparatory, general academic, arts, vocational, religious studies, and agriculture school, affiliated with Mennonite Church. Boarding grades 9–12, day grades 6–12. Founded: 1942. Setting: suburban. Nearest major city is Philadelphia. Students are housed in coed dormitories and single-sex by wings. 100-acre campus. 9 buildings on campus. Approved or accredited by Mennonite Education Agency, Mennonite Schools Council, Middle States Association of Colleges and Schools, and Pennsylvania Department of Education. Endowment: $12 million. Total enrollment: 1,446. Upper school average class size: 18. Upper school faculty-student ratio: 1:15. There are 182 required school days per year for Upper School students. Upper School students typically attend 5 days per week. The average school day consists of 6 hours and 30 minutes.

Upper School Student Profile Grade 9: 162 students (92 boys, 70 girls); Grade 10: 153 students (71 boys, 82 girls); Grade 11: 183 students (99 boys, 84 girls); Grade 12: 150 students (70 boys, 80 girls). 8% of students are boarding students. 89% are state residents. 7 states are represented in upper school student body. 11% are international students. International students from China, Ethiopia, Ethiopia, Hong Kong, Republic of Korea, and Taiwan; 4 other countries represented in student body. 30% of students are Mennonite.

Faculty School total: 77. In upper school: 38 men, 37 women; 50 have advanced degrees; 4 reside on campus.

Subjects Offered 1 1/2 elective credits, 3-dimensional art, 3-dimensional design, accounting, advanced biology, advanced chemistry, advanced math, Advanced Placement courses, agriculture, American government, American history, American history-AP, art appreciation, athletics, band, baseball, basketball, bell choir, Bible, Bible as literature, Bible studies, biology, biology-AP, bowling, business, business mathematics, calculus, calculus-AP, career experience, career exploration, career/college preparation, chemistry, chemistry-AP, Chinese, choir, chorus, Christian doctrine, Christian education, Christian scripture, Christian studies, church history, communications, community service, comparative government and politics, comparative government and politics-AP, concert band, concert choir, creative writing, culinary arts, drama, drawing, driver education, ecology, electives, English, English composition, English language and composition-AP, entrepreneurship, environmental science, ESL, European history, family and consumer science, family living, family studies, fashion, foods, foreign language, French, German, guitar, health education, history, human development, instrumental music, jazz band, language arts, Life of Christ, literary magazine, literature-AP, music, music appreciation, music composition, music performance, music theory, music-AP, musical productions, newspaper, orchestra, painting, parent/child development, participation in sports, performing arts, photography, physical education, physics, physics-AP, psychology, psychology-AP, public speaking, science, senior project, small engine repair, sociology, softball, Spanish, Spanish language-AP, statistics, statistics-AP, strings, student government, student publications, tennis, track and field, U.S. history, U.S. history-AP, U.S. literature, visual and performing arts, visual arts, voice, volleyball, weight training, welding, wind ensemble, wind instruments, woodworking, world history, world history-AP, writing.

Graduation Requirements A certain amount of credits are needed in various academic areas.

Special Academic Programs Advanced Placement exam preparation; honors section; independent study; study at local college for college credit; academic accommodation for the musically talented; remedial reading and/or remedial writing; remedial math; special instructional classes for deaf students, blind students; ESL (40 students enrolled).

College Admission Counseling 174 students graduated in 2011; 121 went to college, including Eastern Mennonite University; Goshen College; Grove City College; Hesston College; Messiah College; Penn State University Park. Other: 28 went to work, 17 had other specific plans. Mean SAT critical reading: 542, mean SAT math: 537, mean SAT writing: 528, mean combined SAT: 1607.

Student Life Upper grades have specified standards of dress, student council. Discipline rests primarily with faculty. Attendance at religious services is required.

Summer Programs Enrichment, sports programs offered; held on campus; accepts boys and girls; open to students from other schools. 200 students usually enrolled. 2012 schedule: June to August. Application deadline: none.

Tuition and Aid Day student tuition: $7116; 5-day tuition and room/board: $10,881; 7-day tuition and room/board: $13,716. Tuition installment plan (monthly payment plans). Tuition reduction for siblings, merit scholarship grants, need-based scholarship grants, paying campus jobs available. In 2011–12, 40% of upper school students received aid; total upper-school merit-scholarship money awarded: $20,000. Total amount of financial aid awarded in 2011–12: $2,000,000.

Admissions Traditional secondary-level entrance grade is 9. For fall 2011, 391 students applied for upper-level admission, 375 were accepted, 349 enrolled. Deadline for receipt of application materials: none. Application fee required: $100. Interview recommended.

Athletics Interscholastic: ball hockey (girls), baseball (b), basketball (b,g), cross-country running (b,g), field hockey (g), golf (b), lacrosse (b), soccer (b,g), softball (g), tennis (b,g), track and field (b,g); coed interscholastic: baseball. 4 PE instructors, 20 coaches, 1 athletic trainer.

Computers Computers are regularly used in all academic classes. Computer network features include on-campus library services, Internet access, Internet filtering or blocking technology. Campus intranet and student e-mail accounts are available to students. Students grades are available online. The school has a published electronic and media policy.

Contact Christy L. Horst, Administrative Assistant for Admissions. 717-299-0436 Ext. 312. Fax: 717-299-0823. E-mail: horstcl@lancastermennonite.org. Web site: www.lancastermennonite.org.

LANDMARK CHRISTIAN ACADEMY

6502 Johnsontown Road

Louisville, Kentucky 40272

Head of School: Mr. Monte L. Ashworth

General Information Coeducational day college-preparatory and religious studies school, affiliated with Baptist Church. Grades K4–12. Founded: 1978. Setting: suburban. 5-acre campus. 1 building on campus. Approved or accredited by American Association of Christian Schools. Total enrollment: 130. Upper school average class size: 10. Upper school faculty-student ratio: 1:11. There are 177 required school days per year for Upper School students. Upper School students typically attend 5 days per week. The average school day consists of 6 hours and 50 minutes.

Upper School Student Profile Grade 9: 12 students (9 boys, 3 girls); Grade 10: 1 student (1 boy); Grade 11: 5 students (4 boys, 1 girl); Grade 12: 10 students (6 boys, 4 girls). 80% of students are Baptist.

Faculty School total: 13. In upper school: 3 men, 3 women; 2 have advanced degrees.

Subjects Offered Advanced math, algebra, American history, American literature, analytic geometry, ancient history, ancient world history, Bible, biology, business mathematics, chemistry, choir, computer technologies, consumer economics, consumer mathematics, economics, English composition, English literature, general science, geography, geometry, grammar, health, history, home economics, keyboarding, modern history, physical education, physics, pre-algebra, pre-calculus, speech, trigonometry, world geography, world history.

Graduation Requirements Bible, computers, English, foreign language, history, mathematics, science, social sciences.
College Admission Counseling 5 students graduated in 2011; 3 went to college, including Clearwater Christian College; Jefferson Community and Technical College. Other: 2 went to work. Median composite ACT: 23.
Student Life Upper grades have uniform requirement. Discipline rests primarily with faculty.
Tuition and Aid Day student tuition: $3250. Tuition installment plan (FACTS Tuition Payment Plan). Tuition reduction for siblings available.
Admissions Traditional secondary-level entrance grade is 9. For fall 2011, 3 students applied for upper-level admission, 3 were accepted, 3 enrolled. Math and English placement tests required. Deadline for receipt of application materials: none. Application fee required: $275. On-campus interview required.
Athletics Interscholastic: basketball (boys), soccer (b), track and field (b,g), volleyball (g). 1 PE instructor, 3 coaches.
Computers Computers are regularly used in computer applications, keyboarding, Spanish classes. The school has a published electronic and media policy.
Contact Mrs. Amy J. O'Brien, School Secretary. 502-933-3000. Fax: 502-933-5179. E-mail: LCAinfo@libcky.com. Web site: http://LCAky.com.

LANDMARK CHRISTIAN SCHOOL

50 South East Broad Street

Fairburn, Georgia 30213

Head of School: Mrs. Leanne Messer

General Information Coeducational day college-preparatory, arts, and religious studies school, affiliated with Christian faith, Protestant faith. Grades K4–12. Founded: 1989. Setting: suburban. Nearest major city is Atlanta. 60-acre campus. 4 buildings on campus. Approved or accredited by Southern Association of Colleges and Schools and Georgia Department of Education. Endowment: $130,000. Total enrollment: 805. Upper school average class size: 16. Upper school faculty-student ratio: 1:9. There are 175 required school days per year for Upper School students. Upper School students typically attend 5 days per week. The average school day consists of 7 hours and 15 minutes.
Upper School Student Profile Grade 9: 67 students (32 boys, 35 girls); Grade 10: 58 students (32 boys, 26 girls); Grade 11: 49 students (27 boys, 22 girls); Grade 12: 50 students (31 boys, 19 girls). 100% of students are Christian faith, Protestant.
Faculty School total: 77. In upper school: 11 men, 16 women; 14 have advanced degrees.
Subjects Offered Anatomy and physiology, art-AP, band, baseball, basketball, Bible, Bible studies, biology, biology-AP, calculus, calculus-AP, chamber groups, cheerleading, chemistry, chemistry-AP, choral music, chorus, composition, computer graphics, computer literacy, computer skills, computer studies, computer technologies, concert band, drama, drama performance, English, English language and composition-AP, English-AP, fine arts, history, keyboarding, music, music appreciation, physics, physics-AP, physiology, pre-algebra, pre-calculus, SAT preparation, SAT/ACT preparation, Spanish, Spanish language-AP, Spanish-AP, speech, swimming, tennis, U.S. history, U.S. history-AP, vocal ensemble, volleyball, World-Wide-Web publishing, writing, yearbook.
Special Academic Programs Advanced Placement exam preparation; honors section; academic accommodation for the gifted; remedial reading and/or remedial writing; remedial math; programs in English, mathematics, general development for dyslexic students.
College Admission Counseling 51 students graduated in 2011; all went to college, including Auburn University; Georgia State University; The University of Alabama; University of Georgia. Median SAT critical reading: 544, median SAT math: 550, median SAT writing: 535, median combined SAT: 1628, median composite ACT: 24. 25% scored over 600 on SAT critical reading, 28% scored over 600 on SAT math, 25% scored over 600 on SAT writing, 28% scored over 1800 on combined SAT, 41% scored over 26 on composite ACT.
Student Life Upper grades have uniform requirement, student council, honor system. Discipline rests equally with students and faculty. Attendance at religious services is required.
Summer Programs Computer instruction programs offered; held on campus; accepts boys and girls; not open to students from other schools. 20 students usually enrolled.
Tuition and Aid Day student tuition: $13,024. Tuition installment plan (monthly payment plans). Need-based scholarship grants available. In 2011–12, 11% of upper-school students received aid.
Admissions Traditional secondary-level entrance grade is 9. For fall 2011, 48 students applied for upper-level admission, 24 were accepted, 20 enrolled. Deadline for receipt of application materials: none. Application fee required: $100. On-campus interview required.
Athletics Interscholastic: baseball (boys), basketball (b,g), cheering (g), cross-country running (b,g), football (b), golf (b,g), physical training (b,g), soccer (b,g), softball (g), strength & conditioning (b,g), swimming and diving (b,g), tennis (b,g), track and field (b,g), volleyball (g), wrestling (b). 3 PE instructors, 36 coaches, 1 athletic trainer.
Computers Computers are regularly used in all academic classes. Computer network features include on-campus library services, Internet access, Internet filtering or blocking technology, class assignments available online. Computer access in designated common areas is available to students. Students grades are available online.
Contact Mrs. Tammy McCurry, Director of Admissions. 770-692-6767. Fax: 770-969-6551. E-mail: admissions@landmark-cs.org. Web site: www.landmarkchristianschool.org.

LANDMARK SCHOOL

Prides Crossing, Massachusetts

See Special Needs Schools section.

LANDON SCHOOL

6101 Wilson Lane

Bethesda, Maryland 20817

Head of School: Mr. David M. Armstrong

General Information Boys' day college-preparatory, arts, and music school. Grades 3–12. Founded: 1929. Setting: suburban. Nearest major city is Washington, DC. 75-acre campus. 13 buildings on campus. Approved or accredited by Association of Independent Maryland Schools, Middle States Association of Colleges and Schools, and Maryland Department of Education. Member of National Association of Independent Schools. Endowment: $10.4 million. Total enrollment: 691. Upper school average class size: 15. Upper school faculty-student ratio: 1:8. There are 170 required school days per year for Upper School students. Upper School students typically attend 5 days per week. The average school day consists of 7 hours and 10 minutes.
Upper School Student Profile Grade 9: 91 students (91 boys); Grade 10: 85 students (85 boys); Grade 11: 81 students (81 boys); Grade 12: 77 students (77 boys).
Faculty School total: 111. In upper school: 47 men, 15 women; 42 have advanced degrees.
Subjects Offered Acting, algebra, American Civil War, American foreign policy, American history, American literature, American studies, architecture, art, art history-AP, biology, biology-AP, calculus, calculus-AP, ceramics, chemistry, chemistry-AP, Chinese, Chinese history, classics, computer science, computer science-AP, conceptual physics, constitutional law, creative writing, digital art, drama, drawing, earth science, economics-AP, engineering, English, English literature, environmental science-AP, environmental studies, ethics, European history, expository writing, fine arts, foreign policy, forensics, French, French language-AP, French literature-AP, French studies, freshman foundations, geography, geology, geometry, government/civics, grammar, handbells, health, history, humanities, international relations, jazz band, journalism, justice seminar, Latin, mathematics, meteorology, Middle Eastern history, music, music history, music theory, music theory-AP, oceanography, painting, performing arts, photography, photojournalism, physical education, physics, physics-AP, pre-calculus, science, sculpture, senior project, Shakespeare, social studies, Spanish, Spanish language-AP, Spanish literature, statistics-AP, strings, technological applications, theater, trigonometry, typing, U.S. history, U.S. history-AP, world history, world literature, writing.
Graduation Requirements American Civil War, American government, arts and fine arts (art, music, dance, drama), biology, chemistry, English, ethics, foreign language, government, humanities, mathematics, music, physical education (includes health), pre-calculus, science, social studies (includes history), senior project and community service requirement, 2 year arts requirement.
Special Academic Programs Advanced Placement exam preparation; honors section; independent study; term-away projects; study abroad.
College Admission Counseling 82 students graduated in 2011; all went to college, including Dartmouth College; Davidson College; Tulane University; University of Maryland, College Park. Mean SAT critical reading: 619, mean SAT math: 640, mean SAT writing: 629, mean combined SAT: 1889, mean composite ACT: 27.
Student Life Upper grades have specified standards of dress, student council, honor system. Discipline rests equally with students and faculty.
Summer Programs Remediation, enrichment, advancement, art/fine arts programs offered; session focuses on enrichment, advancement, remediation, expanded time in art studios and music, and travel abroad; held both on and off campus; held at locations in France, China, Europe, Italy/Greece, and Spain; accepts boys and girls; open to students from other schools. 200 students usually enrolled. 2012 schedule: June 11 to July 27. Application deadline: none.
Tuition and Aid Day student tuition: $31,027. Tuition installment plan (2 payment plan (June and December), TADS plan). Need-based scholarship grants, 50% Tuition remission for faculty children available. In 2011–12, 22% of upper-school students received aid. Total amount of financial aid awarded in 2011–12: $1,443,680.
Admissions Traditional secondary-level entrance grade is 9. For fall 2011, 120 students applied for upper-level admission, 64 were accepted, 31 enrolled. ISEE or SSAT required. Deadline for receipt of application materials: January 31. Application fee required: $75. On-campus interview required.
Athletics Interscholastic: baseball, basketball, cross-country running, diving, fencing, football, golf, ice hockey, lacrosse, riflery, rugby, soccer, squash, strength & conditioning, swimming and diving, tennis, track and field, ultimate Frisbee, water polo, winter (indoor) track, wrestling; intramural: basketball, Frisbee, physical fitness,

softball, strength & conditioning, tennis, ultimate Frisbee, weight lifting. 13 coaches, 1 athletic trainer.

Computers Computers are regularly used in computer applications, photojournalism classes. Computer network features include on-campus library services, online commercial services, Internet access, wireless campus network, Internet filtering or blocking technology, password-accessed Web portals. Campus intranet, student e-mail accounts, and computer access in designated common areas are available to students. Students grades are available online. The school has a published electronic and media policy.

Contact Mr. George C. Mulligan, Director of Admissions. 301-320-1067. Fax: 301-320-1133. E-mail: george_mulligan@landon.net. Web site: www.landon.net.

LANSDALE CATHOLIC HIGH SCHOOL

700 Lansdale Avenue

Lansdale, Pennsylvania 19446-2995

Head of School: Mr. Timothy Quinn

General Information Coeducational day college-preparatory, general academic, and religious studies school, affiliated with Roman Catholic Church. Grades 9–12. Founded: 1949. Setting: suburban. Nearest major city is Philadelphia. 1 building on campus. Approved or accredited by Middle States Association of Colleges and Schools, National Catholic Education Association, and Pennsylvania Department of Education. Total enrollment: 785. Upper school average class size: 30. There are 190 required school days per year for Upper School students. Upper School students typically attend 5 days per week. The average school day consists of 6 hours and 45 minutes.

Upper School Student Profile Grade 9: 191 students (94 boys, 97 girls); Grade 10: 217 students (123 boys, 94 girls); Grade 11: 190 students (105 boys, 85 girls); Grade 12: 185 students (80 boys, 105 girls). 99% of students are Roman Catholic.

Faculty In upper school: 15 men, 15 women; 21 have advanced degrees.

Subjects Offered Algebra, American government, American history, American history-AP, American literature, analytic geometry, art, art history-AP, art-AP, band, Basic programming, biology-AP, business law, calculus, calculus-AP, career education, career planning, career/college preparation, Catholic belief and practice, chemistry, choir, chorus, church history, college counseling, college placement, college planning, composition-AP, computer education, computer programming, drama, English language and composition-AP, English literature and composition-AP, English literature-AP, English/composition-AP, environmental science, European history, European history AP, French, government and politics-AP, government-AP, health education, Italian, Latin, mathematics-AP, physical fitness, physical science, physics, pre-calculus, SAT/ACT preparation, Spanish, statistics, statistics-AP, student government, studio art, studio art-AP, The 20th Century, trigonometry, U.S. government and politics, U.S. government and politics-AP, U.S. history, U.S. history-AP, United States government-AP, Western civilization.

Graduation Requirements 30 hour service requirement by the middle of junior year.

Special Academic Programs 14 Advanced Placement exams for which test preparation is offered; honors section; study at local college for college credit.

College Admission Counseling 217 students graduated in 2011; 212 went to college, including Montgomery County Community College; Penn State University Park; Shippensburg University of Pennsylvania; Temple University. Other: 1 went to work, 2 had other specific plans.

Student Life Upper grades have uniform requirement, student council, honor system. Discipline rests primarily with faculty. Attendance at religious services is required.

Summer Programs Remediation, enrichment, advancement, sports, art/fine arts programs offered; held on campus; accepts boys and girls; open to students from other schools. 2012 schedule: June.

Tuition and Aid Tuition installment plan (monthly payment plans, individually arranged payment plans). Tuition reduction for siblings, merit scholarship grants, need-based scholarship grants, TAP Program available. In 2011–12, 20% of upper-school students received aid.

Admissions Traditional secondary-level entrance grade is 9. Deadline for receipt of application materials: none. Application fee required. Interview recommended.

Athletics Interscholastic: baseball (boys), basketball (b,g), cheering (g), cross-country running (b,g), dance squad (b,g), field hockey (g), football (b), golf (b,g), ice hockey (b,g), lacrosse (b,g), rugby (b,g), soccer (b,g), softball (g), swimming and diving (b,g), tennis (b,g), track and field (b,g), volleyball (g), weight lifting (b), winter (indoor) track (b,g); intramural: flag football (b), ice hockey (b,g); coed interscholastic: bowling, diving, indoor track, indoor track & field. 1 PE instructor, 1 athletic trainer.

Computers Computers are regularly used in all classes. Computer network features include on-campus library services, online commercial services, Internet access, wireless campus network, Internet filtering or blocking technology. Computer access in designated common areas is available to students. Students grades are available online. The school has a published electronic and media policy.

Contact Mr. James Casey, President. 215-362-6160 Ext. 133. Fax: 215-362-5746. E-mail: jcasey@lansdalecatholic.com. Web site: www.lansdalecatholic.com.

LA SALLE HIGH SCHOOL

3880 East Sierra Madre Boulevard

Pasadena, California 91107-1996

Head of School: Mr. Patrick Bonacci

General Information Coeducational day college-preparatory, arts, and religious studies school, affiliated with Roman Catholic Church. Grades 9–12. Founded: 1956. Setting: suburban. Nearest major city is Los Angeles. 10-acre campus. 3 buildings on campus. Approved or accredited by California Association of Independent Schools, Christian Brothers Association, Western Association of Schools and Colleges, Western Catholic Education Association, and California Department of Education. Total enrollment: 732. Upper school average class size: 26. Upper school faculty-student ratio: 1:11. There are 180 required school days per year for Upper School students. Upper School students typically attend 5 days per week. The average school day consists of 6 hours and 15 minutes.

Upper School Student Profile Grade 9: 184 students (96 boys, 88 girls); Grade 10: 169 students (84 boys, 85 girls); Grade 11: 181 students (93 boys, 88 girls); Grade 12: 198 students (98 boys, 100 girls). 66% of students are Roman Catholic.

Faculty School total: 71. In upper school: 43 men, 28 women; 42 have advanced degrees.

Subjects Offered 20th century history, acting, Advanced Placement courses, advanced studio art AP, algebra, American Civil War, American government, American literature-AP, ancient world history, art, art-AP, ASB Leadership, band, biology-AP, business law, calculus, calculus-AP, campus ministry, Catholic belief and practice, chemistry-AP, chorus, Christian and Hebrew scripture, church history, civics, classical civilization, community service, comparative religion, composition, composition-AP, computer applications, computer education, computer graphics, computer literacy, computer programming, concert choir, constitutional history of U.S., creative writing, dance, dance performance, digital photography, drama, dramatic arts, drawing, ecology, environmental systems, economics, economics-AP, education, electives, English, English composition, English language-AP, English literature, English literature and composition-AP, English-AP, fiction, film, fine arts, foreign language, French, general math, general science, geometry, government, government/civics, government/civics-AP, health and safety, health education, Hispanic literature, history, history-AP, honors algebra, honors English, honors U.S. history, honors world history, integrated mathematics, introduction to theater, jazz, jazz band, jazz dance, jazz ensemble, journalism, keyboarding, lab science, lab/keyboard, law and the legal system, leadership, leadership and service, mathematics, mathematics-AP, microbiology, modern European history-AP, musical productions, newspaper, photo shop, photography, physics, physics-AP, play production, pottery, pre-calculus, religion, religion and culture, religious studies, Roman civilization, science, social justice, Spanish, Spanish-AP, student government, studio art, studio art-AP, study skills, tap dance, technical theater, television, theater, theater arts, theater design and production, theater production, trigonometry, U.S. government, U.S. government and politics-AP, U.S. history, U.S. history-AP, U.S. literature, video communication, visual and performing arts, visual arts, wind instruments, world history, writing, yearbook.

Graduation Requirements Algebra, American literature, arts and fine arts (art, music, dance, drama), biology, campus ministry, chemistry, Christian and Hebrew scripture, Christian doctrine, church history, civics, computer literacy, economics, English, English composition, English literature, foreign language, geometry, integrated mathematics, physical education (includes health), physics, religious studies, U.S. history.

Special Academic Programs 14 Advanced Placement exams for which test preparation is offered; honors section.

College Admission Counseling 188 students graduated in 2011; all went to college, including California Polytechnic State University, San Luis Obispo; Loyola Marymount University; University of California, Berkeley; University of California, Riverside; University of California, Santa Barbara; University of Southern California. Median SAT critical reading: 580, median SAT math: 590, median SAT writing: 590, median combined SAT: 1780, median composite ACT: 24. 42% scored over 600 on SAT critical reading, 47% scored over 600 on SAT math, 48% scored over 600 on SAT writing, 44% scored over 1800 on combined SAT, 38% scored over 26 on composite ACT.

Student Life Upper grades have uniform requirement, student council, honor system. Discipline rests primarily with faculty. Attendance at religious services is required.

Summer Programs Remediation, enrichment, advancement, sports, art/fine arts, computer instruction programs offered; session focuses on academics and sports camps; held both on and off campus; held at Some students do classes online and Some students do classes at local Junior Colleges; accepts boys and girls; open to students from other schools. 460 students usually enrolled. 2012 schedule: June 11 to July 20. Application deadline: June 1.

Tuition and Aid Day student tuition: $13,920. Tuition installment plan (monthly payment plans, biannual). Merit scholarship grants, need-based scholarship grants available. In 2011–12, 40% of upper-school students received aid; total upper-school merit-scholarship money awarded: $80,000. Total amount of financial aid awarded in 2011–12: $1,250,000.

Admissions For fall 2011, 510 students applied for upper-level admission, 252 were accepted, 188 enrolled. STS required. Deadline for receipt of application materials: January 13. Application fee required: $80. Interview required.

Athletics Interscholastic: baseball (boys), basketball (b,g), cross-country running (b,g), equestrian sports (g), football (b), golf (b,g), soccer (b,g), softball (g), swimming and diving (b,g), tennis (b,g), track and field (b,g), volleyball (b,g), water polo (b,g); intramural: basketball (b,g), dance team (g), flag football (b); coed interscholastic: cheering, physical fitness, weight training; coed intramural: fitness, Frisbee, physical fitness, weight training. 2 PE instructors, 50 coaches, 2 athletic trainers.
Computers Computers are regularly used in all academic, computer applications, video film production classes. Computer resources include on-campus library services, online commercial services, Internet access. Campus intranet and computer access in designated common areas are available to students. Students grades are available online. The school has a published electronic and media policy.
Contact Ms. Teresa Ring, Admissions Secretary. 626-351-8951. Fax: 626-696-4411. E-mail: tring@lasallehs.org. Web site: www.lasallehs.org.

LA SCUOLA D'ITALIA GUGLIELMO MARCONI

12 East 96th Street

New York, New York 10128

Head of School: Prof. Anna Fiore

General Information Coeducational boarding and day and distance learning college-preparatory and bilingual studies school. Distance learning grade X. Founded: 1977. Setting: urban. Nearest major city is Manhattan. 1 building on campus. Approved or accredited by New York Department of Education. Languages of instruction: English and Italian. Total enrollment: 247. Upper school average class size: 10. There are 212 required school days per year for Upper School students. Upper School students typically attend 5 days per week.
Upper School Student Profile Grade 9: 13 students (6 boys, 7 girls); Grade 10: 10 students (6 boys, 4 girls); Grade 11: 7 students (2 boys, 5 girls); Grade 12: 13 students (6 boys, 7 girls).
Faculty School total: 43. In upper school: 4 men, 9 women; 13 have advanced degrees.
Special Academic Programs International Baccalaureate program; Advanced Placement exam preparation; honors section; study at local college for college credit; domestic exchange program; study abroad; remedial reading and/or remedial writing; remedial math; ESL (20 students enrolled).
College Admission Counseling 9 students graduated in 2011; all went to college.
Student Life Upper grades have uniform requirement, honor system. Discipline rests equally with students and faculty.
Admissions Traditional secondary-level entrance grade is 9. For fall 2011, 9 students applied for upper-level admission, 9 were accepted, 9 enrolled. Application fee required: $100. Interview required.
Athletics Coed Interscholastic: artistic gym, fencing, soccer. 2 PE instructors, 2 coaches, 2 athletic trainers.
Computers Computer network features include on-campus library services, Internet access, Internet filtering or blocking technology. Computer access in designated common areas is available to students. The school has a published electronic and media policy.
Contact Mrs. Pia Pedicini, Deputy Head of School/Director of Admissions. 212-369-3290. Fax: 212-369-1164. E-mail: secretary@lascuoladitalia.org. Web site: www.lascuoladitalia.org.

THE LATIN SCHOOL OF CHICAGO

59 West North Boulevard

Chicago, Illinois 60610-1492

Head of School: Randall Dunn

General Information Coeducational day college-preparatory school. Grades JK–12. Founded: 1888. Setting: urban. 1-acre campus. 1 building on campus. Approved or accredited by Independent Schools Association of the Central States and Illinois Department of Education. Member of National Association of Independent Schools and Secondary School Admission Test Board. Endowment: $23.6 million. Total enrollment: 1,110. Upper school average class size: 15. Upper school faculty-student ratio: 1:8. There are 165 required school days per year for Upper School students. Upper School students typically attend 5 days per week. The average school day consists of 6 hours and 30 minutes.
Upper School Student Profile Grade 9: 106 students (49 boys, 57 girls); Grade 10: 111 students (52 boys, 59 girls); Grade 11: 107 students (47 boys, 60 girls); Grade 12: 111 students (54 boys, 57 girls).
Faculty School total: 150. In upper school: 40 men, 37 women; 59 have advanced degrees.
Subjects Offered Advanced Placement courses, advanced studio art-AP, African studies, African-American literature, algebra, American history, American history-AP, American literature, anatomy, animal behavior, art, art history, Asian studies, astronomy, biochemistry, biology, biology-AP, calculus, calculus-AP, chemistry, chemistry-AP, chorus, community service, composition, computer graphics, computer programming, computer science, creative writing, dance, drama, ecology, electives, electronics, English, English literature, environmental science, environmental science-AP, ethics, European civilization, European history, fine arts, French, French language-AP, French literature-AP, geography, geometry, history, history of ideas, honors U.S. history, human relations, human sexuality, humanities, independent study, instrumental music, Latin, Latin American history, Latin American literature, Latin-AP, literature by women, Mandarin, mathematical modeling, mathematics, mathematics-AP, Middle East, Middle Eastern history, music theory, photography, physical education, physics, physics-AP, physiology, poetry, probability and statistics, psychology, religion, science, social studies, Spanish, Spanish language-AP, Spanish literature, Spanish literature-AP, speech, stage design, statistics, studio art-AP, theater, trigonometry, women's literature, world history, world literature, writing.
Graduation Requirements Arts and fine arts (art, music, dance, drama), English, ethics, foreign language, human relations, human sexuality, mathematics, performing arts, physical education (includes health), science, social studies (includes history), technology, one-week non-credit course each year, service learning requirement. Community service is required.
Special Academic Programs Advanced Placement exam preparation; honors section; independent study; study abroad; academic accommodation for the gifted; remedial reading and/or remedial writing; remedial math; programs in general development for dyslexic students.
College Admission Counseling 111 students graduated in 2011; 109 went to college, including Miami University; Northwestern University; Tufts University; University of Chicago; University of Wisconsin–Madison; Yale University. Other: 2 had other specific plans.
Student Life Upper grades have specified standards of dress, student council, honor system. Discipline rests equally with students and faculty.
Summer Programs Remediation, enrichment, advancement, sports, art/fine arts, rigorous outdoor training, computer instruction programs offered; session focuses on enrichment, remediation, sports, travel, and adventure; held both on and off campus; held at lakefront, city parks, wilderness experiences in the United States and abroad; accepts boys and girls; open to students from other schools. 180 students usually enrolled. 2012 schedule: June 11 to August 3. Application deadline: none.
Tuition and Aid Day student tuition: $27,985. Tuition installment plan (Insured Tuition Payment Plan, Key Tuition Payment Plan, FACTS Tuition Payment Plan, monthly payment plans, individually arranged payment plans). Need-based scholarship grants, need-based loans, middle-income loans, Key Education Achiever Loans available. In 2011–12, 20% of upper-school students received aid. Total amount of financial aid awarded in 2011–12: $1,999,129.
Admissions Traditional secondary-level entrance grade is 9. For fall 2011, 222 students applied for upper-level admission, 105 were accepted, 50 enrolled. ISEE required. Deadline for receipt of application materials: December 15. Application fee required: $80. On-campus interview required.
Athletics Interscholastic: aquatics (boys, girls), badminton (g), baseball (b), basketball (b,g), cross-country running (b,g), field hockey (g), golf (b,g), ice hockey (b,g), soccer (b,g), softball (g), swimming and diving (b,g), tennis (b,g), track and field (b,g), volleyball (b,g), water polo (b,g); intramural: life saving (b,g); coed intramural: dance, kayaking, outdoor activities, outdoor adventure, outdoor education, outdoor recreation, physical fitness, physical training, skiing (downhill). 6 PE instructors, 12 coaches, 2 athletic trainers.
Computers Computers are regularly used in art, English, foreign language, mathematics, science classes. Computer network features include on-campus library services, online commercial services, Internet access, wireless campus network. Campus intranet, student e-mail accounts, and computer access in designated common areas are available to students. The school has a published electronic and media policy.
Contact Frankie Brown, Director of Admissions and Financial Aid. 312-582-6060. Fax: 312-582-6061. E-mail: fbrown@latinschool.org. Web site: www.latinschool.org.

THE LAUREATE ACADEMY

Winnipeg, Manitoba, Canada

See Special Needs Schools section.

LAUREL SPRINGS SCHOOL

302 West El Paseo Road

Ojai, California 93023

Head of School: Marilyn Mosley

General Information Distance learning only college-preparatory, arts, vocational, technology, and distance learning school. Distance learning grades K–12. Founded: 1991. Setting: small town. Nearest major city is Los Angeles. 1 building on campus. Approved or accredited by Western Association of Schools and Colleges and California Department of Education. Total enrollment: 1,529. Upper school average class size: 1. Upper school faculty-student ratio: 1:1.
Faculty School total: 86. In upper school: 13 men, 51 women; 35 have advanced degrees.
Subjects Offered Algebra, American literature, art appreciation, art history, biology, biology-AP, British literature, British literature (honors), calculus, calculus-AP, career/college preparation, cartooning/animation, chemistry, chemistry-AP, college admission

preparation, college counseling, driver education, earth science, economics, electives, English composition, English language and composition-AP, English literature and composition-AP, environmental education, environmental studies, French, French-AP, geometry, German, health, history of music, honors algebra, honors English, honors geometry, honors U.S. history, honors world history, Latin, macroeconomics-AP, Mandarin, microeconomics-AP, music history, mythology, photo shop, physical education, physics, physics-AP, pre-calculus, psychology, psychology-AP, SAT/ACT preparation, Shakespeare, sociology, Spanish, Spanish language-AP, statistics-AP, trigonometry, U.S. government, U.S. government and politics-AP, U.S. history, U.S. history-AP, world cultures, world history, world literature.

Graduation Requirements Arts and fine arts (art, music, dance, drama), electives, English, foreign language, mathematics, physical education (includes health), science, social studies (includes history).

Special Academic Programs Advanced Placement exam preparation; honors section; accelerated programs; independent study; term-away projects; academic accommodation for the gifted, the musically talented, and the artistically talented; remedial reading and/or remedial writing; remedial math; programs in English, mathematics, general development for dyslexic students; special instructional classes for students needing customized learning options.

College Admission Counseling 102 students graduated in 2011; 94 went to college, including Middle Tennessee State University; New York University; Purdue University; University of California, Los Angeles; University of California, Santa Barbara; University of Southern California. Other: 8 had other specific plans. Mean SAT critical reading: 562, mean SAT math: 519, mean SAT writing: 547, mean composite ACT: 23.

Student Life Upper grades have student council, honor system. Discipline rests equally with students and faculty.

Summer Programs Enrichment, advancement, art/fine arts, computer instruction programs offered; session focuses on accelerated classes; held both on and off campus; held at individual homes of enrolled students; accepts boys and girls; open to students from other schools.

Tuition and Aid Tuition installment plan (monthly payment plans, individually arranged payment plans). Tuition reduction for siblings, need-based scholarship grants available.

Admissions Traditional secondary-level entrance grade is 9. Deadline for receipt of application materials: none. Application fee required: $250.

Computers Computers are regularly used in art, economics, English, foreign language, geography, health, history, independent study, information technology, language development, life skills, mathematics, psychology, SAT preparation, science, social studies, writing classes. Computer network features include on-campus library services, Internet access, 100 online courses. Students grades are available online.

Contact Admissions. 800-377-5890 Ext. 5502. Fax: 805-646-0186. Web site: www.laurelsprings.com.

LAUSANNE COLLEGIATE SCHOOL

1381 West Massey Road

Memphis, Tennessee 38120

Head of School: Mr. Stuart McCathie

General Information Coeducational day college-preparatory, arts, bilingual studies, technology, AP courses, honors curriculum, and sports education, electives school. Grades PK–12. Founded: 1926. Setting: suburban. 28-acre campus. 5 buildings on campus. Approved or accredited by National Independent Private Schools Association, Southern Association of Colleges and Schools, Southern Association of Independent Schools, and Tennessee Department of Education. Member of National Association of Independent Schools. Endowment: $700,000. Total enrollment: 809. Upper school average class size: 15. Upper school faculty-student ratio: 1:9. There are 175 required school days per year for Upper School students. Upper School students typically attend 5 days per week. The average school day consists of 6 hours and 30 minutes.

Upper School Student Profile Grade 9: 77 students (35 boys, 42 girls); Grade 10: 90 students (43 boys, 47 girls); Grade 11: 82 students (41 boys, 41 girls); Grade 12: 70 students (34 boys, 36 girls).

Faculty School total: 95. In upper school: 17 men, 17 women; 20 have advanced degrees.

Subjects Offered Acting, advanced math, algebra, American government, ancient world history, art, art-AP, biology, biology-AP, calculus, chemistry, choir, college admission preparation, comparative government and politics-AP, creative writing, economics, English, English-AP, French, French-AP, geometry, health and wellness, honors algebra, honors English, honors geometry, humanities, instrumental music, international studies, journalism, Latin, modern world history, photography, physical education, physical science, physics, physics-AP, play production, pre-calculus, public policy, short story, Spanish, Spanish-AP, statistics, U.S. history, U.S. history-AP, writing workshop.

Graduation Requirements Arts and fine arts (art, music, dance, drama), English, foreign language, mathematics, physical education (includes health), science, social studies (includes history).

Special Academic Programs International Baccalaureate program; 12 Advanced Placement exams for which test preparation is offered; honors section; independent study; academic accommodation for the gifted, the musically talented, and the artistically talented; ESL (35 students enrolled).

College Admission Counseling 79 students graduated in 2011; all went to college, including Dartmouth College; Northwestern University; Rhodes College; The University of Tennessee; University of Colorado Boulder; Wake Forest University. Mean SAT critical reading: 583, mean SAT math: 595, mean SAT writing: 578, mean combined SAT: 1756, mean composite ACT: 26.

Student Life Upper grades have specified standards of dress, student council, honor system. Discipline rests primarily with faculty.

Summer Programs Remediation, enrichment, advancement, sports, art/fine arts, computer instruction programs offered; session focuses on academics, athletics, and fun; held on campus; accepts boys and girls; open to students from other schools. 450 students usually enrolled. 2012 schedule: June 4 to August 3. Application deadline: none.

Tuition and Aid Day student tuition: $16,400. Tuition installment plan (monthly payment plans, Tuition Refund Plan (TRP)). Need-based scholarship grants, tuition remission for children of faculty available. In 2011–12, 18% of upper-school students received aid. Total amount of financial aid awarded in 2011–12: $494,108.

Admissions Traditional secondary-level entrance grade is 9. For fall 2011, 68 students applied for upper-level admission, 60 were accepted, 50 enrolled. ISEE required. Deadline for receipt of application materials: none. Application fee required: $75. Interview required.

Athletics Interscholastic: basketball (boys, girls), cheering (g), cross-country running (b,g), dance squad (g), dance team (g), golf (b,g), gymnastics (b,g), lacrosse (b,g), pom squad (g), soccer (b,g), softball (g), swimming and diving (b,g), tennis (b,g), track and field (b,g), volleyball (g); intramural: ballet (g), basketball (b,g), bowling (b,g), dance team (g), flag football (b,g), Frisbee (b,g), gymnastics (b,g), lacrosse (b,g), outdoor activities (b,g), physical fitness (b,g), soccer (b,g), strength & conditioning (b,g), tennis (b,g), track and field (b,g), ultimate Frisbee (b,g), volleyball (b,g), weight lifting (b,g); coed interscholastic: swimming and diving; coed intramural: basketball, bowling, flag football, Frisbee, lacrosse, martial arts, outdoor activities, physical fitness, soccer, strength & conditioning, tennis, track and field, ultimate Frisbee, volleyball, weight lifting, yoga. 30 coaches, 2 athletic trainers.

Computers Computers are regularly used in all academic, technology classes. Computer network features include on-campus library services, online commercial services, Internet access, wireless campus network, Internet filtering or blocking technology, homework assignments available online. Student e-mail accounts are available to students. Students grades are available online. The school has a published electronic and media policy.

Contact Mrs. Marcie Malin, Admission Coordinator. 901-474-1030. Fax: 901-474-1010. E-mail: mmalin@lausanneschool.com. Web site: www.lausanneschool.com.

LAWRENCE ACADEMY

Powderhouse Road

Groton, Massachusetts 01450

Head of School: Mr. Greg Foster

General Information Coeducational boarding and day college-preparatory, interdisciplinary ninth grade curriculum, and student-centered learning school. Grades 9–12. Founded: 1793. Setting: small town. Nearest major city is Boston. Students are housed in single-sex dormitories. 115-acre campus. 31 buildings on campus. Approved or accredited by Association of Independent Schools in New England, New England Association of Schools and Colleges, The Association of Boarding Schools, and Massachusetts Department of Education. Member of National Association of Independent Schools and Secondary School Admission Test Board. Endowment: $18 million. Total enrollment: 399. Upper school average class size: 12. Upper school faculty-student ratio: 1:5. Upper School students typically attend 5 days per week. The average school day consists of 6 hours and 20 minutes.

Upper School Student Profile Grade 9: 79 students (40 boys, 39 girls); Grade 10: 111 students (61 boys, 50 girls); Grade 11: 108 students (59 boys, 49 girls); Grade 12: 101 students (51 boys, 50 girls). 50% of students are boarding students. 60% are state residents. 21 states are represented in upper school student body. 13% are international students. International students from China, Germany, Kazakhstan, Republic of Korea, Russian Federation, and Spain; 15 other countries represented in student body.

Faculty School total: 83. In upper school: 44 men, 39 women; 50 have advanced degrees; 39 reside on campus.

Subjects Offered Advanced Placement courses, African-American literature, algebra, American history, anatomy, art, astronomy, biology, botany, calculus, calculus-AP, ceramics, chemistry, composition, creative writing, criminal justice, dance, drawing, ecology, electives, electronics, English, English literature, entomology, environmental science-AP, ESL, European history, fine arts, finite math, fractal geometry, French, government/civics, history, independent study, John F. Kennedy, Latin, Latin American literature, limnology, marine science, mathematics, microbiology, music, music composition, music technology, music theory, music-AP, ornithology, painting, photography, physics, playwriting, pre-calculus, psychology, scene study, science, sculpture, Shakespeare, social psychology, Spanish, studio art, theater, tropical biology, U.S. government and politics-AP, writing.

Graduation Requirements Arts and fine arts (art, music, dance, drama), English, foreign language, history, mathematics, science, Winterim participation.
Special Academic Programs Advanced Placement exam preparation; honors section; independent study; term-away projects; study abroad; academic accommodation for the musically talented and the artistically talented; special instructional classes for deaf students, blind students; ESL (20 students enrolled).
College Admission Counseling 91 students graduated in 2011; all went to college, including Boston College; Boston University; Colby College; Skidmore College; University of New Hampshire; University of Vermont. Median SAT critical reading: 560, median SAT math: 580, median SAT writing: 570. 34% scored over 600 on SAT critical reading, 46% scored over 600 on SAT math, 40% scored over 600 on SAT writing, 37% scored over 1800 on combined SAT.
Student Life Upper grades have specified standards of dress, student council, honor system. Discipline rests primarily with faculty.
Tuition and Aid Day student tuition: $38,770; 7-day tuition and room/board: $50,375. Tuition installment plan (Key Tuition Payment Plan, monthly payment plans). Need-based scholarship grants, need-based loans, prepGATE loans available. In 2011–12, 29% of upper-school students received aid. Total amount of financial aid awarded in 2011–12: $3,450,000.
Admissions Traditional secondary-level entrance grade is 9. For fall 2011, 682 students applied for upper-level admission, 252 were accepted, 141 enrolled. PSAT or SAT, SSAT or TOEFL required. Deadline for receipt of application materials: February 1. Application fee required: $50. Interview required.
Athletics Interscholastic: baseball (boys), basketball (b,g), cross-country running (b,g), field hockey (g), football (b), golf (b,g), ice hockey (b,g), lacrosse (b,g), soccer (b,g), softball (g), tennis (b,g), track and field (b,g), volleyball (g), wrestling (b); intramural: tennis (b,g); coed interscholastic: alpine skiing, independent competitive sports, mountain biking, skiing (downhill); coed intramural: dance, fitness, independent competitive sports, modern dance, outdoors, physical fitness, physical training, rappelling, skiing (downhill), snowboarding, strength & conditioning, volleyball, weight training, yoga. 5 coaches, 2 athletic trainers.
Computers Computers are regularly used in college planning, computer applications, ESL, library, media production, music, photography, SAT preparation, video film production, yearbook classes. Computer network features include on-campus library services, online commercial services, Internet access, wireless campus network, Internet filtering or blocking technology. Campus intranet, student e-mail accounts, and computer access in designated common areas are available to students. Students grades are available online. The school has a published electronic and media policy.
Contact Tony Hawgood, Director of Admissions. 978-448-6535. Fax: 978-448-1519. E-mail: admiss@lacademy.edu. Web site: www.lacademy.edu.

LAWRENCE SCHOOL

Sagamore Hills, Ohio

See Special Needs Schools section.

THE LAWRENCEVILLE SCHOOL

PO Box 6008

2500 Main Street

Lawrenceville, New Jersey 08648

Head of School: Elizabeth A. Duffy

General Information Coeducational boarding and day college-preparatory, arts, religious studies, and technology school. Grades 9–PG. Founded: 1810. Setting: small town. Nearest major city is Philadelphia, PA. Students are housed in single-sex dormitories. 700-acre campus. 39 buildings on campus. Approved or accredited by Middle States Association of Colleges and Schools, New Jersey Association of Independent Schools, The Association of Boarding Schools, and New Jersey Department of Education. Member of National Association of Independent Schools and Secondary School Admission Test Board. Endowment: $279. Total enrollment: 810. Upper school average class size: 12. Upper school faculty-student ratio: 1:8. Upper School students typically attend 6 days per week. The average school day consists of 7 hours.
Upper School Student Profile Grade 9: 144 students (71 boys, 73 girls); Grade 10: 221 students (113 boys, 108 girls); Grade 11: 216 students (113 boys, 103 girls); Grade 12: 214 students (118 boys, 96 girls); Postgraduate: 15 students (13 boys, 2 girls). 68% of students are boarding students. 45% are state residents. 32 states are represented in upper school student body. 15% are international students. International students from Canada, China, Hong Kong, Japan, Republic of Korea, and Saudi Arabia; 26 other countries represented in student body.
Faculty School total: 142. In upper school: 76 men, 66 women; 107 have advanced degrees.
Subjects Offered Acting, advanced chemistry, advanced computer applications, advanced studio art-AP, African-American literature, algebra, American Civil War, American foreign policy, American government, American history, American history-AP, American literature, American studies, architecture, art, art history, art history-AP, art-AP, arts, Asian history, astronomy, Basic programming, Bible, Bible studies, bioethics, bioethics, DNA and culture, biology, biology-AP, British literature, Buddhism, calculus, calculus-AP, Central and Eastern European history, ceramics, chamber groups, chemistry, chemistry-AP, China/Japan history, Chinese, Chinese studies, choir, chorus, Christian studies, Civil War, civil war history, classical Greek literature, classical language, comparative government and politics, conceptual physics, constitutional history of U.S., contemporary women writers, critical writing, dance, data analysis, design, digital applications, digital art, drama, dramatic arts, drawing, drawing and design, driver education, Eastern religion and philosophy, economics, electronic music, English, English literature, English literature-AP, English/composition-AP, environmental science, environmental studies, ethics, European history, European history-AP, European literature, evolution, field ecology, film and new technologies, film appreciation, filmmaking, foreign language, foreign policy, French, French language-AP, French literature-AP, French studies, French-AP, geometry, global science, Greek, health and wellness, Hebrew scripture, Hindi, historical foundations for arts, history of China and Japan, Holocaust, human biology, humanities, independent study, instruments, interdisciplinary studies, introduction to literature, introduction to theater, Irish literature, Irish studies, Islamic studies, Japanese, Japanese history, jazz, Jewish studies, John F. Kennedy, journalism, Latin, linear algebra, literature, medieval history, medieval literature, Middle East, Middle Eastern history, nature study, orchestra, organic chemistry, painting, participation in sports, personal development, philosophy, photography, physics, physics-AP, physiology, poetry, pre-algebra, pre-calculus, printmaking, probability and statistics, research seminar, robotics, science, set design, Shakespeare, short story, Southern literature, Spanish, Spanish language-AP, Spanish literature, studio art, the Presidency, the Sixties, theater, theater arts, U.S. constitutional history, U.S. government, U.S. government and politics, U.S. history, visual arts, water color painting, women in world history, world religions, world religions, writing.
Graduation Requirements Arts and fine arts (art, music, dance, drama), English, foreign language, interdisciplinary studies, mathematics, religion (includes Bible studies and theology), science, social sciences, social studies (includes history). Community service is required.
Special Academic Programs Honors section; independent study; term-away projects; study abroad.
College Admission Counseling 232 students graduated in 2010; 230 went to college, including Columbia College; New York University; Princeton University; University of Pennsylvania; Yale University. Other: 1 went to work, 1 entered a postgraduate year. Median SAT critical reading: 676, median SAT math: 697, median SAT writing: 687.
Student Life Upper grades have specified standards of dress, student council, honor system. Discipline rests equally with students and faculty.
Tuition and Aid Day student tuition: $38,050; 7-day tuition and room/board: $46,475. Tuition installment plan (one, two, and nine month installment plans are available). Need-based scholarship grants available. In 2010–11, 29% of upper-school students received aid. Total amount of financial aid awarded in 2010–11: $9,100,000.
Admissions Traditional secondary-level entrance grade is 9. For fall 2010, 1,929 students applied for upper-level admission, 244 enrolled. ISEE, PSAT and SAT for applicants to grade 11 and 12, SSAT or TOEFL or SLEP required. Deadline for receipt of application materials: January 31. Application fee required: $50. Interview required.
Athletics Interscholastic: baseball (boys), basketball (b,g), crew (b,g), cross-country running (b,g), fencing (b,g), field hockey (g), football (b), golf (b,g), hockey (b,g), ice hockey (b,g), indoor track (b,g), indoor track & field (b,g), lacrosse (b,g), rowing (b,g), soccer (b,g), softball (g), squash (b,g), swimming and diving (b,g), tennis (b,g), track and field (b,g), volleyball (b,g), water polo (b,g), winter (indoor) track (b,g); intramural: basketball (b,g), Frisbee (g), handball (b,g), team handball (b,g), ultimate Frisbee (g), weight lifting (b,g), weight training (b,g); coed interscholastic: wrestling; coed intramural: backpacking, bicycling, broomball, canoeing/kayaking, climbing, cricket, dance, fitness, hiking/backpacking, ice skating, kayaking, modern dance, Nautilus, outdoor activities, physical fitness, physical training, rock climbing, ropes courses, squash, strength & conditioning, wall climbing, yoga. 72 coaches, 4 athletic trainers.
Computers Computers are regularly used in art, English, mathematics, music, science, technology classes. Computer network features include on-campus library services, online commercial services, Internet access, wireless campus network, Internet filtering or blocking technology. Campus intranet, student e-mail accounts, and computer access in designated common areas are available to students. Students grades are available online. The school has a published electronic and media policy.
Contact Gregg W.M. Maloberti, Dean of Admission. 800-735-2030. Fax: 609-895-2217. E-mail: admissions@lawrenceville.org. Web site: www.lawrenceville.org.

See Display on next page and Close-Up on page 638.

LEE ACADEMY

415 Lee Drive

Clarksdale, Mississippi 38614

Head of School: Ricky Weiss

General Information Coeducational day college-preparatory, arts, and business school. Founded: 1970. Setting: small town. Nearest major city is Memphis, TN. 4 buildings on campus. Approved or accredited by Mississippi Private School Association, Southern Association of Colleges and Schools, and Mississippi Department of Education. Total enrollment: 357. Upper school average class size: 22. Upper school faculty-student ratio: 1:20. There are 185 required school days per year for Upper School students. Upper School students typically attend 5 days per week. The average school day consists of 6 hours and 30 minutes.

Upper School Student Profile Grade 6: 24 students (14 boys, 10 girls); Grade 7: 43 students (27 boys, 16 girls); Grade 8: 45 students (28 boys, 17 girls); Grade 9: 44 students (21 boys, 23 girls); Grade 10: 33 students (12 boys, 21 girls); Grade 11: 50 students (27 boys, 23 girls); Grade 12: 48 students (22 boys, 26 girls).

Faculty School total: 45. In upper school: 4 men, 15 women; 8 have advanced degrees.

Subjects Offered ACT preparation, American government, American history, ancient world history, art, athletics, baseball, basketball, Bible, biology, bookkeeping, business, business law, calculus, cheerleading, chemistry, choral music, computer applications, earth and space science, earth science, English, English composition, English literature, foreign language, geography, geometry, guidance, health, Spanish, speech, U.S. history, writing workshop, yearbook.

Graduation Requirements Math methods.

College Admission Counseling 43 students graduated in 2011; all went to college, including Mississippi State University; University of Mississippi.

Student Life Upper grades have uniform requirement, student council. Discipline rests primarily with faculty.

Tuition and Aid Day student tuition: $5000. Tuition installment plan (monthly payment plans). Tuition reduction for siblings, need-based scholarship grants available. In 2011–12, 15% of upper-school students received aid. Total amount of financial aid awarded in 2011–12: $35,000.

Admissions Traditional secondary-level entrance grade is 9. For fall 2011, 177 students applied for upper-level admission, 177 were accepted, 177 enrolled. Deadline for receipt of application materials: February 28. No application fee required.

Athletics Interscholastic: baseball (boys), basketball (b), cheering (g), football (b); coed interscholastic: cross-country running, golf, soccer. 1 PE instructor.

Computers Computer resources include on-campus library services. Computer access in designated common areas is available to students. Students grades are available online.

Contact Ricky Weiss, Headmaster. 662-627-7891. Fax: 662-627-7896. E-mail: leeoffice@acbleone.net.

LEHIGH VALLEY CHRISTIAN HIGH SCHOOL

330 Howertown Road

Catasauqua, Pennsylvania 18032

Head of School: Mr. Robert J. Brennan Jr.

General Information Coeducational day college-preparatory, general academic, arts, business, religious studies, and technology school, affiliated with Protestant-Evangelical faith. Grades 9–12. Founded: 1988. Setting: urban. Nearest major city is Allentown. 2-acre campus. 1 building on campus. Approved or accredited by Association of Christian Schools International, Middle States Association of Colleges and Schools, and Pennsylvania Department of Education. Total enrollment: 131. Upper school average class size: 20. Upper school faculty-student ratio: 1:11. There are 180 required school days per year for Upper School students. Upper School students typically attend 5 days per week. The average school day consists of 6 hours and 45 minutes.

Upper School Student Profile Grade 9: 38 students (25 boys, 13 girls); Grade 10: 28 students (9 boys, 19 girls); Grade 11: 27 students (7 boys, 20 girls); Grade 12: 38 students (18 boys, 20 girls). 90% of students are Protestant-Evangelical faith.

Faculty School total: 15. In upper school: 8 men, 7 women; 9 have advanced degrees.

Subjects Offered Accounting, Advanced Placement courses, algebra, American history, ancient world history, art, Bible, biology, biology-AP, calculus-AP, chemistry, chemistry AP, chorus, computer applications, economics, English, English language and composition-AP, English literature and composition-AP, geometry, government, health, history, keyboarding, physical education, physical science, physics, physics-AP, pre-algebra, pre-calculus, Spanish, state history, U.S. history, Western civilization, yearbook.

Graduation Requirements Algebra, American history, American literature, art, Bible, Bible studies, biology, British literature, chemistry, choir, civics, computer applications, English, foreign language, geometry, mathematics, physical education (includes health), physical science, science, social sciences, Western civilization, general lifestyle not harmful to the testimony of the school as a Christian institution, minimum one year of full-time enrollment in LVCH or another Christian high school.

Special Academic Programs Advanced Placement exam preparation; honors section; accelerated programs; independent study; study at local college for college credit; academic accommodation for the gifted; programs in English, mathematics, general development for dyslexic students; special instructional classes for students needing learning support; ESL (2 students enrolled).

College Admission Counseling 45 students graduated in 2011; all went to college, including Eastern University; Lehigh University; Liberty University; Moravian College; Penn State University Park; Philadelphia Biblical University. Mean SAT critical reading: 531, mean SAT math: 539, mean SAT writing: 521, mean combined SAT: 1591.

Student Life Upper grades have uniform requirement, student council. Discipline rests primarily with faculty.

Summer Programs Remediation, advancement programs offered; session focuses on make-up courses; held both on and off campus; held at students' homes (for independent credit); accepts boys and girls; not open to students from other schools. 5 students usually enrolled. 2012 schedule: June 18 to August 11.

Tuition and Aid Day student tuition: $8280. Tuition installment plan (FACTS Tuition Payment Plan, individually arranged payment plans). Tuition reduction for siblings, need-based scholarship grants available. In 2011–12, 34% of upper-school students received aid. Total amount of financial aid awarded in 2011–12: $2500.

Admissions Traditional secondary-level entrance grade is 9. For fall 2011, 50 students applied for upper-level admission, 50 were accepted, 49 enrolled. Achievement tests, Gates MacGinite Reading Tests or Wide Range Achievement Test required. Deadline for receipt of application materials: none. Application fee required: $250. On-campus interview required.

Athletics Interscholastic: baseball (boys), basketball (b,g), cheering (g), soccer (b,g), volleyball (g); coed interscholastic: track and field; coed intramural: fitness walking. 1 PE instructor, 10 coaches.

Computers Computers are regularly used in graphic arts, keyboarding, library, multimedia, science, technology, writing, yearbook classes. Computer network features include on-campus library services, Internet access, Internet filtering or blocking technology. Students grades are available online. The school has a published electronic and media policy.

Contact Dr. Alan H. Russell, Director of Admissions. 610-403-1000 Ext. 42. Fax: 610-403-1004. E-mail: a.russell@lvchs.org. Web site: www.lvchs.org.

LEHMAN HIGH SCHOOL

2400 Saint Mary Avenue

Sidney, Ohio 45365

Head of School: Mr. David Michael Barhorst

General Information Coeducational day and distance learning college-preparatory, arts, business, and religious studies school, affiliated with Roman Catholic Church. Grades 9–12. Distance learning grades 10–12. Founded: 1970. Setting: small town. Nearest major city is Dayton. 50-acre campus. 1 building on campus. Approved or accredited by North Central Association of Colleges and Schools, Ohio Catholic Schools Accreditation Association (OCSAA), and Ohio Department of Education. Endowment: $600,000. Total enrollment: 211. Upper school average class size: 15. Upper school faculty-student ratio: 1:15. There are 179 required school days per year for Upper School students. Upper School students typically attend 5 days per week. The average school day consists of 7 hours.

Upper School Student Profile Grade 9: 49 students (33 boys, 16 girls); Grade 10: 69 students (31 boys, 38 girls); Grade 11: 46 students (23 boys, 23 girls); Grade 12: 47 students (18 boys, 29 girls). 93% of students are Roman Catholic.

Faculty School total: 19. In upper school: 8 men, 11 women; 14 have advanced degrees.

Subjects Offered Accounting, algebra, American government, American literature, anatomy and physiology, art, art history, biology, biology-AP, British literature, British literature (honors), business, calculus, calculus-AP, ceramics, chemistry, chemistry-AP, choir, computer applications, concert band, earth science, English, English literature and composition-AP, environmental science, geography, geometry, government, health education, history of the Catholic Church, integrated science, intro to computers, Latin, moral theology, newspaper, painting, peace and justice, physical education, physics, pre-algebra, pre-calculus, psychology, sociology, Spanish, studio art, U.S. history, vocal music, weight fitness, world history, yearbook.

Graduation Requirements Biology, business, computer applications, electives, English composition, English literature, health education, mathematics, physical education (includes health), physical science, religion (includes Bible studies and theology), U.S. government, U.S. history, must attend a senior retreat.

Special Academic Programs Advanced Placement exam preparation; honors section; independent study; study at local college for college credit.

College Admission Counseling 60 students graduated in 2011; 53 went to college, including Miami University; The Ohio State University; University of Cincinnati; University of Dayton; Wright State University. Other: 1 went to work, 6 entered military service. Mean composite ACT: 23. 24% scored over 26 on composite ACT.

Student Life Upper grades have uniform requirement, student council, honor system. Discipline rests primarily with faculty. Attendance at religious services is required.

Tuition and Aid Day student tuition: $6960. Tuition installment plan (FACTS Tuition Payment Plan). Tuition reduction for siblings, need-based scholarship grants available. In 2011–12, 45% of upper-school students received aid. Total amount of financial aid awarded in 2011–12: $371,023.

Admissions Traditional secondary-level entrance grade is 9. For fall 2011, 3 students applied for upper-level admission, 3 were accepted, 3 enrolled. Achievement tests or any standardized test required. Deadline for receipt of application materials: none. Application fee required: $100. Interview recommended.

Athletics Interscholastic: baseball (boys), basketball (b,g), cheering (g), cross-country running (b,g), football (b), golf (b), soccer (b,g), softball (g), swimming and diving (b,g), tennis (b,g), track and field (b,g), volleyball (g), wrestling (b); intramural: strength & conditioning (b,g); coed intramural: indoor track. 41 coaches, 1 athletic trainer.

Computers Computers are regularly used in accounting, computer applications, newspaper, science, yearbook classes. Computer resources include on-campus library services, Internet access, wireless campus network, Internet filtering or blocking technology. Students grades are available online. The school has a published electronic and media policy.

Contact Mrs. Denise Stauffer, Principal. 937-498-1161 Ext. 115. Fax: 937-492-9877. E-mail: d.stauffer@lehmancatholic.com.

LE LYCÉE FRANCAIS DE LOS ANGELES

3261 Overland Avenue

Los Angeles, California 90034-3589

Head of School: Mrs. Clara-Lisa Kabbaz

General Information Coeducational day college-preparatory, general academic, arts, and bilingual studies school. Grades PS–12. Founded: 1964. Setting: suburban. Nearest major city is West Los Angeles. 12-acre campus. 1 building on campus. Approved or accredited by French Ministry of Education and Western Association of Schools and Colleges. Member of European Council of International Schools. Languages of instruction: English and French. Endowment: $400,000. Total enrollment: 729. Upper school average class size: 17. Upper school faculty-student ratio: 1:15. There are 170 required school days per year for Upper School students. Upper School students typically attend 5 days per week. The average school day consists of 7 hours and 45 minutes.

Upper School Student Profile Grade 9: 39 students (17 boys, 22 girls); Grade 10: 36 students (18 boys, 18 girls); Grade 11: 48 students (18 boys, 30 girls); Grade 12: 25 students (7 boys, 18 girls).

Faculty School total: 85. In upper school: 16 men, 26 women; 31 have advanced degrees.

Subjects Offered 20th century history, 3-dimensional art, Advanced Placement courses, algebra, American history, American literature, anatomy, Ancient Greek, art, arts, ballet, biology, calculus, calculus-AP, ceramics, chemistry, choir, computer programming, computer science, creative writing, dance, drama, earth science, economics, English, English language and composition-AP, English literature, environmental science, ESL, European history, expository writing, fencing, fine arts, French, French as a second language, French language-AP, French studies, gardening, geography, geology, geometry, German, government/civics, grammar, history, Latin, mathematics, microeconomics-AP, music, philosophy, photography, physical education, physics, pre-calculus, SAT preparation, science, social sciences, social studies, Spanish, sports, statistics, theater, theater arts, trigonometry, typing, U.S. history, volleyball, world history, world literature, writing, yoga.

Graduation Requirements Arts and fine arts (art, music, dance, drama), English, foreign language, mathematics, physical education (includes health), science, social sciences, social studies (includes history).

Special Academic Programs International Baccalaureate program; Advanced Placement exam preparation; honors section; remedial reading and/or remedial writing; remedial math; ESL (25 students enrolled).

College Admission Counseling 36 students graduated in 2011; all went to college, including Loyola Marymount University; New York University; University of California, Berkeley; University of California, Los Angeles; University of California, Santa Cruz; University of Southern California. Median SAT critical reading: 600, median SAT math: 590, median SAT writing: 600, median combined SAT: 1790, median composite ACT: 25.

Student Life Upper grades have uniform requirement, student council, honor system. Discipline rests primarily with faculty.

Summer Programs Session focuses on social activities, sports, foreign languages; held both on and off campus; held at field trips, local parks; accepts boys and girls; open to students from other schools. 2012 schedule: June 20 to July 29. Application deadline: April 1.

Tuition and Aid Day student tuition: $12,880–$20,350. Bursaries, merit scholarship grants, need-based scholarship grants available. In 2011–12, 12% of upper-school students received aid. Total amount of financial aid awarded in 2011–12: $63,000.

Admissions Traditional secondary-level entrance grade is 9. For fall 2011, 205 students applied for upper-level admission, 155 were accepted, 155 enrolled. School's own exam required. Deadline for receipt of application materials: February 28. Application fee required: $1000. Interview required.

Athletics Interscholastic: basketball (boys, girls), cheering (g), volleyball (b,g); intramural: ballet (g), baseball (g), fencing (b,g), outdoor activities (b,g), outdoor recreation (b,g), physical fitness (b,g); coed interscholastic: soccer; coed intramural: archery, martial arts. 6 PE instructors, 5 coaches, 4 athletic trainers.

Computers Computers are regularly used in English, foreign language, mathematics, science classes. Computer resources include on-campus library services, Internet access, wireless campus network, Internet filtering or blocking technology, Internet

Café. Computer access in designated common areas is available to students. The school has a published electronic and media policy.
Contact Mme. Sophie Darmon, Admissions. 310-836-3464 Ext. 315. Fax: 310-558-8069. E-mail: admissions@lyceela.org. Web site: www.LyceeLA.org.

LEO CATHOLIC HIGH SCHOOL

7901 South Sangamon Street
Chicago, Illinois 60620

Head of School: Mr. Philip G. Mesina

General Information Boys day college-preparatory and religious studies school, affiliated with Roman Catholic Church. Founded: 1926. Setting: urban. Students are housed in Male Only Day School. 1 building on campus. Approved or accredited by North Central Association of Colleges and Schools and Illinois Department of Education. Total enrollment: 141. Upper school average class size: 12. Upper school faculty-student ratio: 1:12. There are 178 required school days per year for Upper School students. Upper School students typically attend 5 days per week. The average school day consists of 7 hours.
Upper School Student Profile 10% of students are Roman Catholic.
Faculty School total: 13. In upper school: 9 men, 3 women; 4 have advanced degrees.
Subjects Offered ACT preparation, advanced biology, advanced chemistry, advanced computer applications, advanced math, African American history, African American studies, algebra, American Civil War, American government, American history, applied arts, applied music, art, art appreciation, art education, athletic training, athletics, band, baseball, Basic programming, basketball, Bible, Bible as literature, Bible studies, biology, Black history, bowling, business applications, calculus, campus ministry, career and personal planning, Catholic belief and practice, character education, chemistry, choir, choral music, church history, civics, civil rights, Civil War, civil war history, classics, college awareness, college counseling, college placement, college planning, college writing, comparative religion, composition, computer education, computer multimedia, computer skills, computers, consumer economics, consumer education, economics, English, environmental science, ethics, foreign language, geometry, golf, health education, history, honors algebra, honors English, honors U.S. history, honors world history, Internet, jazz band, journalism, library, music, public speaking, reading, religion and culture, science, social sciences, Spanish, sports conditioning, sports nutrition, student government, student publications, theology, track and field, trigonometry, typing, U.S. government, vocal music, word processing, yearbook.
Special Academic Programs Honors section.
Student Life Upper grades have uniform requirement, student council, honor system. Discipline rests primarily with faculty. Attendance at religious services is required.
Tuition and Aid Day student tuition: $7000. Tuition installment plan (monthly payment plans). Tuition reduction for siblings, need-based scholarship grants available.
Admissions ACT-Explore required. Deadline for receipt of application materials: none. No application fee required. Interview recommended.
Athletics Interscholastic: baseball (boys), basketball (b), bowling (b), cross-country running (b), football (b), indoor track & field (b), track and field (b); intramural: boxing (b), golf (b), physical fitness (b), physical training (b), weight training (b).
Computers Computers are regularly used in art, college planning, computer applications, economics, English, health, history, humanities, journalism, mathematics, music, newspaper, reading, religion, social sciences, Spanish, theology, word processing, yearbook classes. Computer network features include on-campus library services, Internet access, wireless campus network, Internet filtering or blocking technology. Computer access in designated common areas is available to students. Students grades are available online. The school has a published electronic and media policy.
Contact Mr. Michael Holmes, Director of Admissions. 773-224-9600 Ext. 212. Fax: 773-224-3856. E-mail: mholmes@leohighschool.org. Web site: www.leohighschool.org.

LEXINGTON CATHOLIC HIGH SCHOOL

2250 Clays Mill Road
Lexington, Kentucky 40503-1797

Head of School: Dr. Steven Angelucci

General Information Coeducational day college-preparatory and religious studies school, affiliated with Roman Catholic Church. Grades 9–12. Founded: 1823. Setting: urban. 7-acre campus. 3 buildings on campus. Approved or accredited by National Catholic Education Association, Southern Association of Colleges and Schools, and Kentucky Department of Education. Endowment: $600,000. Total enrollment: 807. Upper school average class size: 21. Upper school faculty-student ratio: 1:13. There are 177 required school days per year for Upper School students. Upper School students typically attend 5 days per week. The average school day consists of 7 hours and 15 minutes.
Upper School Student Profile 80% of students are Roman Catholic.
Faculty School total: 63. In upper school: 32 men, 31 women; 47 have advanced degrees.
Subjects Offered Accounting, advanced chemistry, Advanced Placement courses, advanced studio art-AP, algebra, American government, American history, American history-AP, American literature, anatomy and physiology, art, astronomy, band, Bible as literature, biology, biology-AP, British literature, British literature (honors), calculus, calculus-AP, Catholic belief and practice, ceramics, chemistry, chemistry-AP, choral music, Christian and Hebrew scripture, church history, comparative religion, computer applications, computer programming, creative writing, drama, economics, English-AP, ethics, film, French, French-AP, geography, geology, geometry, government and politics-AP, health, history of the Catholic Church, honors English, honors geometry, honors U.S. history, honors world history, humanities, introduction to literature, Latin, Latin-AP, physical education, physics, psychology, religious studies, sociology, Spanish, Spanish language-AP, U.S. government, U.S. government and politics-AP, U.S. history, U.S. history-AP, world history, world literature.
Graduation Requirements American history, American literature, arts and fine arts (art, music, dance, drama), biology, British literature, Catholic belief and practice, chemistry, Christian and Hebrew scripture, church history, comparative religion, computer applications, English, foreign language, mathematics, physical education (includes health), religion (includes Bible studies and theology), science, U.S. government, U.S. government and politics, U.S. history, world history.
Special Academic Programs 16 Advanced Placement exams for which test preparation is offered; honors section.
College Admission Counseling 202 students graduated in 2011; 200 went to college, including University of Kentucky. Mean SAT critical reading: 559, mean SAT math: 545, mean SAT writing: 539, mean composite ACT: 25.
Student Life Upper grades have uniform requirement, student council, honor system. Discipline rests primarily with faculty. Attendance at religious services is required.
Tuition and Aid Day student tuition: $7675. Tuition installment plan (monthly payment plans, individually arranged payment plans). Merit scholarship grants, need-based scholarship grants available. In 2011–12, 10% of upper-school students received aid; total upper-school merit-scholarship money awarded: $5000. Total amount of financial aid awarded in 2011–12: $450,000.
Admissions Traditional secondary-level entrance grade is 9. For fall 2011, 250 students applied for upper-level admission, 250 were accepted, 213 enrolled. Scholastic Testing Service High School Placement Test required. Deadline for receipt of application materials: none. Application fee required: $275.
Athletics Interscholastic: baseball (boys), basketball (b,g), cheering (g), cross-country running (b,g), dance team (g), diving (b,g), football (b), golf (b,g), ice hockey (b), power lifting (b), soccer (b,g), softball (g), swimming and diving (b,g), tennis (b,g), track and field (b,g), volleyball (g); intramural: basketball (b,g), flag football (g), lacrosse (b), physical training (b,g); coed interscholastic: bowling, ultimate Frisbee; coed intramural: hiking/backpacking, outdoor activities. 2 PE instructors, 2 athletic trainers.
Computers Computers are regularly used in all academic classes. Computer network features include on-campus library services, Internet access, wireless campus network. Computer access in designated common areas is available to students. Students grades are available online. The school has a published electronic and media policy.
Contact Ms. MIndy Towles, Admissions Director. 859-277-7183 Ext. 231. Fax: 859-276-5086. E-mail: mtowles@lexingtoncatholic.com. Web site: www.lexingtoncatholic.com.

LIBERTY CHRISTIAN SCHOOL

7661 Warner Avenue
Huntington Beach, California 92647

Head of School: Mrs. Teri Yates

General Information Coeducational day college-preparatory and religious studies school, affiliated with Protestant faith, Baptist Church. Grades K–12. Founded: 1970. Setting: suburban. Nearest major city is Los Angeles. 5-acre campus. 3 buildings on campus. Approved or accredited by Accrediting Commission for Schools, Western Association of Schools and Colleges, and California Department of Education. Total enrollment: 204. Upper school average class size: 20. Upper school faculty-student ratio: 1:6. There are 180 required school days per year for Upper School students. Upper School students typically attend 5 days per week. The average school day consists of 6 hours and 30 minutes.
Upper School Student Profile Grade 9: 31 students (19 boys, 12 girls); Grade 10: 23 students (11 boys, 12 girls); Grade 11: 19 students (11 boys, 8 girls); Grade 12: 20 students (11 boys, 9 girls). 90% of students are Protestant, Baptist.
Faculty School total: 25. In upper school: 8 men, 6 women; 3 have advanced degrees.
Subjects Offered American literature, U.S. government.
Graduation Requirements World cultures.
Special Academic Programs Advanced Placement exam preparation; honors section; independent study.
College Admission Counseling 29 students graduated in 2011; 25 went to college, including California State University, Long Beach; Golden West College; Orange Coast College; Point Loma Nazarene University. Other: 3 went to work, 1 entered military service.
Student Life Upper grades have specified standards of dress, student council, honor system. Discipline rests primarily with faculty.

Tuition and Aid Day student tuition: $8800. Tuition installment plan (SMART Tuition Payment Plan, monthly payment plans). Need-based scholarship grants available. In 2011–12, 60% of upper-school students received aid. Total amount of financial aid awarded in 2011–12: $300,000.

Admissions Traditional secondary-level entrance grade is 9. For fall 2011, 19 students applied for upper-level admission, 19 were accepted, 19 enrolled. Deadline for receipt of application materials: none. Application fee required: $400. On-campus interview required.

Athletics Interscholastic: baseball (boys), basketball (b,g), flag football (b), football (b), power lifting (b), softball (g), volleyball (g); intramural: flag football (g), power lifting (b). 1 PE instructor, 4 coaches.

Computers Computers are regularly used in media classes. Computer network features include on-campus library services, Internet access, wireless campus network. Computer access in designated common areas is available to students. Students grades are available online.

Contact Mrs. Julene Nye, Registrar. 714-842-5992 Ext. 2260. Fax: 714-848-7484. E-mail: jnye@libertychristian.org. Web site: www.libertychristian.org.

LICK-WILMERDING HIGH SCHOOL

755 Ocean Avenue

San Francisco, California 94112

Head of School: Dr. Albert M. Adams II

General Information Coeducational day college-preparatory, technology, performing arts, and visual arts school. Grades 9–12. Founded: 1895. Setting: urban. 4-acre campus. 6 buildings on campus. Approved or accredited by California Association of Independent Schools, Western Association of Schools and Colleges, and California Department of Education. Member of National Association of Independent Schools and Secondary School Admission Test Board. Endowment: $43 million. Total enrollment: 440. Upper school average class size: 15. Upper school faculty-student ratio: 1:9. Upper School students typically attend 5 days per week. The average school day consists of 7 hours and 30 minutes.

Upper School Student Profile Grade 9: 113 students (51 boys, 62 girls); Grade 10: 113 students (54 boys, 59 girls); Grade 11: 111 students (52 boys, 59 girls); Grade 12: 106 students (55 boys, 51 girls).

Faculty School total: 63. In upper school: 26 men, 35 women; 42 have advanced degrees.

Subjects Offered Acting, adolescent issues, advanced chemistry, advanced math, Advanced Placement courses, advanced studio art-AP, African-American literature, algebra, American history, American literature, anatomy and physiology, architectural drawing, architecture, art, biology, biology-AP, calculus, calculus-AP, chemistry, chemistry-AP, choral music, computer music, computer science, computer science-AP, creative writing, critical thinking, dance, digital imaging, drafting, drama, electronics, English, English literature, European history, fine arts, French, French language-AP, French literature-AP, French-AP, geometry, history, industrial arts, jazz band, jewelry making, journalism, mathematics, mechanical drawing, music, music theory-AP, music-AP, peer counseling, photography, physical education, physics, physics-AP, psychology, psychology-AP, science, social studies, Spanish, Spanish literature, Spanish-AP, stagecraft, statistics-AP, studio art-AP, technical arts, theater, trigonometry, U.S. history, woodworking, word processing, world history, world history-AP, world literature, writing, yoga.

Graduation Requirements Arts and fine arts (art, music, dance, drama), English, foreign language, mathematics, physical education (includes health), science, social studies (includes history), technical arts, technology/design, junior project with technical arts.

Special Academic Programs Advanced Placement exam preparation; honors section; independent study.

College Admission Counseling 101 students graduated in 2010; all went to college, including Cornell University; Occidental College; Stanford University; University of California, Berkeley; University of California, Los Angeles; Vassar College. Median SAT critical reading: 660, median SAT math: 680, median SAT writing: 700. 86% scored over 600 on SAT critical reading, 85% scored over 600 on SAT math, 89% scored over 600 on SAT writing.

Student Life Upper grades have student council. Discipline rests primarily with faculty.

Tuition and Aid Day student tuition: $34,395. Tuition installment plan (FACTS Tuition Payment Plan, 3- or 10-installment plans). Need-based scholarship grants available. In 2010–11, 42% of upper-school students received aid. Total amount of financial aid awarded in 2010–11: $4,300,000.

Admissions Traditional secondary-level entrance grade is 9. For fall 2010, 736 students applied for upper-level admission, 150 were accepted, 111 enrolled. ISEE or SSAT required. Deadline for receipt of application materials: January 14. Application fee required: $95. Interview required.

Athletics Interscholastic: baseball (boys), basketball (b,g), cross-country running (b,g), lacrosse (b,g), soccer (b,g), swimming and diving (b,g), tennis (b,g), track and field (b,g), volleyball (b,g); coed interscholastic: badminton, wrestling; coed intramural: dance, fitness, modern dance, physical fitness, rock climbing, ultimate Frisbee, yoga. 1 PE instructor, 25 coaches.

Computers Computers are regularly used in architecture, digital applications, drafting, history, journalism, library, literary magazine, mathematics, media, science, writing, yearbook classes. Computer network features include on-campus library services, online commercial services, Internet access, wireless campus network, Internet filtering or blocking technology. Campus intranet, student e-mail accounts, and computer access in designated common areas are available to students. Students grades are available online.

Contact Lisa Wu, Director of Admissions. 415-337-9990. Fax: 415-239-1230. E-mail: admissions@lwhs.org. Web site: www.lwhs.org.

LIFEGATE SCHOOL

1052 Fairfield Avenue

Eugene, Oregon 97402-2053

Head of School: Mr. Tom Gregersen

General Information Coeducational boarding and day and distance learning college-preparatory, general academic, arts, and religious studies school, affiliated with Church of Christ, Scientist. Grades 6–12. Distance learning grade X. Founded: 1994. Setting: suburban. 1-acre campus. 1 building on campus. Approved or accredited by Association of Christian Schools International, Northwest Association of Schools and Colleges, Texas Private School Accreditation Commission, and Oregon Department of Education. Total enrollment: 44. Upper school average class size: 8. Upper school faculty-student ratio: 1:10. Upper School students typically attend 5 days per week. The average school day consists of 7 hours.

Upper School Student Profile Grade 6: 5 students (4 boys, 1 girl); Grade 7: 4 students (2 boys, 2 girls); Grade 8: 5 students (2 boys, 3 girls); Grade 9: 7 students (4 boys, 3 girls); Grade 10: 10 students (5 boys, 5 girls); Grade 11: 9 students (4 boys, 5 girls); Grade 12: 6 students (3 boys, 3 girls). 100% are state residents. 50 states are represented in upper school student body. 95% of students are members of Church of Christ, Scientist.

Faculty School total: 16. In upper school: 5 men, 2 women; 5 have advanced degrees.

Subjects Offered Advanced biology, advanced chemistry, advanced math, Advanced Placement courses, algebra, American government, American history, ancient world history, art, band, Bible, Bible studies, biology, biology-AP, British literature (honors), British literature-AP, calculus, calculus-AP, career and personal planning, chemistry, computer applications, computer graphics, computer processing, cultural geography, drama, economics, English, English composition, English language and composition-AP, English literature-AP, geometry, health education, independent study, journalism, keyboarding, leadership, life skills, physical education, physical science, physics, pre-algebra, pre-calculus, reading/study skills, Spanish, world history, writing, yearbook.

Graduation Requirements Bible, English, government, history, keyboarding, life skills, mathematics, physical education (includes health), 25 hours of volunteer work per year.

Special Academic Programs Advanced Placement exam preparation; honors section; accelerated programs; independent study; academic accommodation for the gifted and the artistically talented; remedial reading and/or remedial writing; remedial math; programs in mathematics, general development for dyslexic students.

College Admission Counseling 12 students graduated in 2010; 9 went to college, including George Fox University; Georgia State University; Lane Community College; Oregon Institute of Technology; Oregon State University; University of Oregon. Other: 1 went to work, 2 entered military service.

Student Life Upper grades have specified standards of dress, student council. Discipline rests primarily with faculty. Attendance at religious services is required.

Tuition and Aid Day student tuition: $5550. Tuition installment plan (monthly payment plans). Tuition reduction for siblings, need-based scholarship grants available. In 2010–11, 14% of upper-school students received aid. Total amount of financial aid awarded in 2010–11: $50,000.

Admissions Traditional secondary-level entrance grade is 9. For fall 2010, 9 students applied for upper-level admission, 9 were accepted, 9 enrolled. Deadline for receipt of application materials: none. No application fee required. On-campus interview required.

Athletics Interscholastic: basketball (boys), outdoor activities (b,g), outdoor education (b,g), volleyball (g); coed interscholastic: track and field. 1 PE instructor, 1 coach.

Computers Computers are regularly used in desktop publishing, English, freshman foundations, lab/keyboard, media arts, Web site design, writing, yearbook classes. Computer network features include on-campus library services, Internet access, wireless campus network, Internet filtering or blocking technology. Campus intranet and student e-mail accounts are available to students. Students grades are available online.

Contact Ms. Donna Wickwire, Assistant Administrator. 541-689-5847. Fax: 541-689-6028. E-mail: donnaw@lifegatechristian.org. Web site: www.lifegatechristian.org.

LIGHTHOUSE CHRISTIAN SCHOOL

4290-50th Street

Sylvan Lake, Alberta T4S 0H3, Canada

Head of School: Dion Krause

General Information Coeducational day college-preparatory, general academic, arts, and religious studies school. Grades PK–12. Setting: small town. Nearest major city is Red Deer, Canada. Approved or accredited by Association of Christian Schools International and Alberta Department of Education. Language of instruction: English. Total enrollment: 84. Upper school faculty-student ratio: 1:15.

Upper School Student Profile Grade 10: 7 students (3 boys, 4 girls); Grade 11: 2 students (1 boy, 1 girl); Grade 12: 4 students (1 boy, 3 girls).

Faculty School total: 11. In upper school: 2 men, 9 women; 8 have advanced degrees.

Student Life Upper grades have specified standards of dress, honor system.

Tuition and Aid Tuition installment plan (individually arranged payment plans).

Admissions Traditional secondary-level entrance grade is 10. For fall 2011, 2 students applied for upper-level admission, 2 were accepted, 2 enrolled. Deadline for receipt of application materials: none. Application fee required. Interview required.

Athletics 1 PE instructor.

Contact Dion Krause, Principal. 403-887-2166. Fax: 403-887-5729. E-mail: lightca@telusplanet.net.

LIMA CENTRAL CATHOLIC HIGH SCHOOL

720 South Cable Road

Lima, Ohio 45805-3496

Head of School: Mr. Richard Mitterholzer

General Information Coeducational day college-preparatory and religious studies school, affiliated with Roman Catholic Church. Grades 9–12. Founded: 1956. Setting: small town. Nearest major city is Columbus. 78-acre campus. 2 buildings on campus. Approved or accredited by North Central Association of Colleges and Schools, Ohio Catholic Schools Accreditation Association (OCSAA), and Ohio Department of Education. Endowment: $4 million. Total enrollment: 350. Upper school average class size: 20. Upper school faculty-student ratio: 1:13. There are 178 required school days per year for Upper School students. Upper School students typically attend 5 days per week. The average school day consists of 6 hours.

Upper School Student Profile 80% of students are Roman Catholic.

Faculty School total: 30. In upper school: 16 men, 14 women; 15 have advanced degrees.

Subjects Offered Advanced Placement courses, arts, calculus-AP, chemistry, computer literacy, English, English-AP, German, health, Italian, mathematics, physical education, physics, pre-calculus, religion, science, social studies, Spanish, statistics-AP, Web site design, world history-AP.

Graduation Requirements Computer literacy, English, mathematics, physical education (includes health), religion (includes Bible studies and theology), science, social studies (includes history), requirements for academic and honors diplomas differ.

Special Academic Programs Advanced Placement exam preparation; honors section; study at local college for college credit.

College Admission Counseling 80 students graduated in 2010; 77 went to college, including The Ohio State University; University of Cincinnati; Wright State University; Xavier University. Other: 2 went to work, 1 had other specific plans. Mean composite ACT: 23.

Student Life Upper grades have uniform requirement, student council. Discipline rests primarily with faculty. Attendance at religious services is required.

Tuition and Aid Day student tuition: $4200. Tuition installment plan (FACTS Tuition Payment Plan, prepaid tuition through Union Bank). Merit scholarship grants, need-based scholarship grants available. In 2010–11, 35% of upper-school students received aid; total upper-school merit-scholarship money awarded: $10,000. Total amount of financial aid awarded in 2010–11: $75,000.

Admissions Traditional secondary-level entrance grade is 9. For fall 2010, 120 students applied for upper-level admission, 110 were accepted, 100 enrolled. ACT-Explore required. Deadline for receipt of application materials: none. Application fee required: $125. Interview recommended.

Athletics Interscholastic: aquatics (boys, girls), baseball (b), basketball (b,g), bowling (b,g), cross-country running (b,g), football (b), golf (b,g), soccer (b,g), softball (g), swimming and diving (b,g), track and field (b,g), volleyball (g), wrestling (b); intramural: bowling (b,g).

Computers Computer network features include Internet access.

Contact Mr. Robert Seggerson. 419-222-4276. Fax: 419-222-6933. Web site: www.lcchs.edu.

LINCOLN ACADEMY

81 Academy Hill

Newcastle, Maine 04553

Head of School: Mr. John B. Pinkerton

General Information Coeducational day college-preparatory, general academic, arts, business, vocational, technology, advanced placement, and world languages school. Grades 9–12. Founded: 1801. Setting: small town. Nearest major city is Portland. 85-acre campus. 4 buildings on campus. Approved or accredited by New England Association of Schools and Colleges and Maine Department of Education. Endowment: $5.5 million. Total enrollment: 547. Upper school average class size: 18. Upper school faculty-student ratio: 1:13. There are 176 required school days per year for Upper School students. Upper School students typically attend 5 days per week. The average school day consists of 6 hours and 40 minutes.

Faculty School total: 43.

Subjects Offered 20th century history, 20th century world history, 3-dimensional art, 3-dimensional design, accounting, acting, advanced biology, advanced chemistry, advanced math, Advanced Placement courses, advanced studio art-AP, algebra, American history, American history-AP, American literature, American literature-AP, architectural drawing, art and culture, art-AP, athletics, audio visual/media, auto mechanics, band, basic language skills, biology, biology-AP, bookkeeping, business, business skills, calculus, calculus-AP, career/college preparation, chemistry, chemistry-AP, chorus, computer skills, conceptual physics, concert band, concert choir, desktop publishing, developmental language skills, developmental math, drafting, drama, English composition, English language-AP, English literature-AP, English-AP, English/composition-AP, environmental science-AP, filmmaking, foreign language, French, French-AP, general math, geography, geometry, healthful living, history, history of rock and roll, honors algebra, honors English, honors geometry, honors U.S. history, honors world history, industrial arts, instrumental music, integrated physics, Italian, Japanese, jazz band, language arts, language development, marine science, mechanical drawing, music theory, music theory-AP, musical productions, performing arts, physical education, play production, play/screen writing, poetry, portfolio art, pre-algebra, pre-calculus, psychology, Russian, sculpture, social studies, Spanish, Spanish language-AP, studio art, technical drawing, technical education, U.S. history, U.S. history-AP, U.S. literature, visual and performing arts, work-study, world history, yearbook.

Graduation Requirements Job shadow experiences, community service.

Special Academic Programs 12 Advanced Placement exams for which test preparation is offered; honors section; independent study.

Student Life Upper grades have specified standards of dress, student council. Discipline rests primarily with faculty.

Tuition and Aid Day student tuition: $10,046.

Admissions Traditional secondary-level entrance grade is 9. Deadline for receipt of application materials: none. No application fee required. On-campus interview required.

Athletics Interscholastic: baseball (boys), basketball (b,g), cheering (g), cross-country running (b,g), field hockey (g), golf (b), lacrosse (b,g), soccer (b,g), softball (g), swimming and diving (b,g), tennis (b,g), track and field (b,g), wrestling (g); coed interscholastic: indoor track, Special Olympics; coed intramural: dance team, outdoor activities.

Computers Computers are regularly used in all classes. Computer network features include on-campus library services, online commercial services, Internet access, wireless campus network. Campus intranet, student e-mail accounts, and computer access in designated common areas are available to students. Students grades are available online. The school has a published electronic and media policy.

Contact Sarah Wills-Viega, Director of Counseling Services. 207-563-3596 Ext. 126. Fax: 207-563-3599. E-mail: wills-viega@lincolnacademy.org. Web site: www.lincolnacademy.org.

LINCOLN SCHOOL

301 Butler Avenue

Providence, Rhode Island 02906-5556

Head of School: Julia Russell Eells

General Information Coeducational day (boys' only in lower grades) college-preparatory, arts, and technology school, affiliated with Society of Friends. Boys grades N–PK, girls grades N–12. Founded: 1884. Setting: urban. 46-acre campus. 5 buildings on campus. Approved or accredited by Association of Independent Schools in New England, Friends Council on Education, New England Association of Schools and Colleges, and Rhode Island Department of Education. Member of National Association of Independent Schools and Secondary School Admission Test Board. Endowment: $7 million. Total enrollment: 352. Upper school average class size: 13. Upper school faculty-student ratio: 1:4. Upper School students typically attend 5 days per week. The average school day consists of 7 hours and 13 minutes.

Upper School Student Profile Grade 9: 44 students (44 girls); Grade 10: 40 students (40 girls); Grade 11: 33 students (33 girls); Grade 12: 48 students (48 girls). 1% of students are members of Society of Friends.

Faculty School total: 75. In upper school: 11 men, 35 women; 24 have advanced degrees.

Subjects Offered Algebra, American history, American literature, anatomy, Arabic, art, biology, biology-AP, calculus, calculus-AP, ceramics, chemistry, chemistry-AP, college awareness, community service, computer science, creative writing, dance, English, English literature, environmental science, ethics, European history, European history-AP, French, French-AP, geometry, health, history, Latin, music, photography, physical education, physics, pre-calculus, Spanish, Spanish language-AP, statistics-AP, theater, trigonometry, U.S. history-AP, visual literacy, women's studies, world history, world literature.

Graduation Requirements Arts and fine arts (art, music, dance, drama), college planning, computer science, English, ethics, foreign language, mathematics, physical education (includes health), science, social studies (includes history), senior service trip. Community service is required.

Special Academic Programs Advanced Placement exam preparation; honors section; independent study; term-away projects; study at local college for college credit; study abroad; programs in general development for dyslexic students.

College Admission Counseling 40 students graduated in 2011; all went to college, including Boston University; Brown University; Hobart and William Smith Colleges; Lehigh University; Trinity College; Vanderbilt University. Median SAT critical reading: 590, median SAT math: 570, median SAT writing: 609.

Student Life Upper grades have uniform requirement, student council, honor system. Discipline rests equally with students and faculty.

Tuition and Aid Day student tuition: $28,105. Tuition installment plan (FACTS Tuition Payment Plan, Tuition Management Systems Plan). Need-based scholarship grants available. In 2011–12, 39% of upper-school students received aid. Total amount of financial aid awarded in 2011–12: $2,000,000.

Admissions Traditional secondary-level entrance grade is 9. For fall 2011, 82 students applied for upper-level admission, 59 were accepted, 24 enrolled. ISEE or SSAT required. Deadline for receipt of application materials: February 15. Application fee required: $50. Interview required.

Athletics Interscholastic: basketball, crew, cross-country running, field hockey, lacrosse, soccer, squash, swimming and diving, tennis. 3 PE instructors, 17 coaches, 1 athletic trainer.

Computers Computers are regularly used in English, history, science classes. Computer network features include on-campus library services, Internet access, wireless campus network, Internet filtering or blocking technology. Student e-mail accounts and computer access in designated common areas are available to students. The school has a published electronic and media policy.

Contact Mrs. Diane Mota, Admission Office Administrative Assistant. 401-331-9696 Ext. 3157. Fax: 401-751-6670. E-mail: dmota@lincolnschool.org. Web site: www.lincolnschool.org.

LINDEN CHRISTIAN SCHOOL

877 Wilkes Avenue

Winnipeg, Manitoba R3P 1B8, Canada

Head of School: Mr. Robert Charach

General Information Coeducational day college-preparatory, arts, religious studies, and technology school, affiliated with Baptist Church. Grades 9–12. Founded: 1987. Setting: suburban. 1 building on campus. Approved or accredited by Association of Christian Schools International and Manitoba Department of Education. Language of instruction: English. Total enrollment: 887. Upper school average class size: 25. Upper school faculty-student ratio: 1:13.

Upper School Student Profile Grade 9: 78 students (38 boys, 40 girls); Grade 10: 62 students (19 boys, 43 girls); Grade 11: 68 students (37 boys, 31 girls); Grade 12: 66 students (33 boys, 33 girls).

Faculty School total: 61. In upper school: 14 men, 9 women.

Subjects Offered Choir, choral music, computer applications, computer information systems, computer science, computer studies, computer technologies, concert band, drama, dramatic arts, independent study, jazz band, jazz ensemble, leadership, leadership and service, music theater, religious studies, vocal jazz, voice ensemble.

Graduation Requirements Bible studies, English, mathematics, physical education (includes health), science, social studies (includes history).

Special Academic Programs Honors section; independent study.

College Admission Counseling 63 students graduated in 2011; 3 went to college, including Providence College; The University of Winnipeg; University of Manitoba. Other: 10 went to work, 50 entered a postgraduate year.

Student Life Upper grades have specified standards of dress, student council, honor system. Discipline rests primarily with faculty. Attendance at religious services is required.

Tuition and Aid Day student tuition: CAN$2940. Tuition installment plan (monthly payment plans). Tuition reduction for siblings, bursaries available. In 2011–12, 8% of upper-school students received aid.

Admissions Traditional secondary-level entrance grade is 9. PSAT required. Application fee required: CAN$25. Interview required.

Athletics Interscholastic: aerobics (boys, girls), badminton (b,g), baseball (b,g), basketball (b,g), bowling (b,g), broomball (b,g), climbing (b,g), cooperative games (b,g), cross-country running (b,g), curling (b,g), fitness (b,g), flag football (b,g), floor hockey (b,g), football (b,g), golf (b,g), life saving (b,g), physical fitness (b,g), soccer (b,g), track and field (b,g), volleyball (b,g); intramural: badminton (b,g), basketball (b,g), cross-country running (b,g), soccer (b,g), volleyball (b,g); coed interscholastic: aerobics, baseball, basketball, bowling, broomball, climbing, cooperative games, cross-country running, curling, fitness, football, golf, life saving, physical fitness, soccer, track and field, volleyball; coed intramural: basketball. 4 PE instructors.

Computers Computers are regularly used in all academic, art, Bible studies, career education, career exploration, Christian doctrine, college planning, creative writing, current events, data processing, desktop publishing, digital applications, drafting, drawing and design, ESL, geography, graphic arts, graphic design, health, history, independent study, information technology, lab/keyboard, learning cognition, library, library skills, life skills, literacy, mathematics, media, music, newspaper, photography, psychology, reading, religion, religious studies, research skills, science, social sciences, social studies, speech, study skills, technology, Web site design, word processing, writing, writing, yearbook classes. Computer network features include on-campus library services, Internet access, wireless campus network, Internet filtering or blocking technology. Student e-mail accounts are available to students. Students grades are available online. The school has a published electronic and media policy.

Contact Mrs. Terrie Bell, Registrar. 204-989-6739. Fax: 204-487-7068. E-mail: tbell@lindenchristian.org.

LINFIELD CHRISTIAN SCHOOL

31950 Pauba Road

Temecula, California 92592

Head of School: Karen Raftery

General Information Coeducational day college-preparatory, arts, religious studies, and technology school, affiliated with Christian faith. Grades K–12. Founded: 1936. Setting: suburban. Nearest major city is San Diego. 105-acre campus. 6 buildings on campus. Approved or accredited by Association of Christian Schools International, Western Association of Schools and Colleges, and California Department of Education. Total enrollment: 750. Upper school average class size: 20. Upper school faculty-student ratio: 1:14. There are 173 required school days per year for Upper School students. Upper School students typically attend 5 days per week. The average school day consists of 6 hours and 55 minutes.

Upper School Student Profile 70% of students are Christian faith.

Faculty School total: 54. In upper school: 9 men, 17 women; 8 have advanced degrees.

Subjects Offered Advanced math, algebra, American sign language, anatomy and physiology, art, ASB Leadership, athletics, band, Bible, biology, calculus-AP, career/college preparation, chemistry, chemistry-AP, choir, computers, economics, English, English-AP, European history-AP, film, filmmaking, French, freshman foundations, general science, geometry, government, government-AP, health, physical education, physics, pre-calculus, public policy, senior seminar, service learning/internship, Spanish, Spanish-AP, speech and debate, sports medicine, theater, U.S. history, U.S. history-AP, world history, world religions, yearbook.

Graduation Requirements Arts and fine arts (art, music, dance, drama), computer science, economics, English, foreign language, freshman foundations, government, mathematics, physical education (includes health), religion (includes Bible studies and theology), science, senior seminar, social sciences, social studies (includes history), speech and debate. Community service is required.

Special Academic Programs 12 Advanced Placement exams for which test preparation is offered; honors section.

College Admission Counseling 88 students graduated in 2010; all went to college, including Azusa Pacific University; California State University, San Marcos; University of California, Riverside; University of California, San Diego. Median SAT critical reading: 560, median SAT math: 540, median SAT writing: 520.

Student Life Upper grades have uniform requirement, student council, honor system. Discipline rests primarily with faculty. Attendance at religious services is required.

Tuition and Aid Day student tuition: $8580. Tuition installment plan (monthly payment plans). Merit scholarship grants, need-based scholarship grants available. In 2010–11, 30% of upper-school students received aid.

Admissions 3-R Achievement Test, SLEP and USC/UC Math Diagnostic Test required. Deadline for receipt of application materials: none. Application fee required: $50. On-campus interview required.

Athletics Interscholastic: baseball (boys), basketball (b,g), cheering (g), cross-country running (b,g), equestrian sports (g), football (b), soccer (b,g), softball (g), tennis (b,g), track and field (b,g), volleyball (g); intramural: volleyball (g); coed interscholastic: golf; coed intramural: cross-country running. 3 PE instructors, 16 coaches, 1 athletic trainer.

Computers Computers are regularly used in computer applications, keyboarding, science, senior seminar, yearbook classes. Computer network features include on-campus library services, Internet access, wireless campus network, Internet filtering or blocking technology. Computer access in designated common areas is available to students. Students grades are available online. The school has a published electronic and media policy.

Contact Mrs. Becky Swanson, Admissions Assistant. 951-676-8111 Ext. 1402. Fax: 951-695-1291. E-mail: bswanson@linfield.com. Web site: www.linfield.com.

THE LINSLY SCHOOL

60 Knox Lane

Wheeling, West Virginia 26003-6489

Head of School: Mr. Chad Barnett

General Information Coeducational boarding and day college-preparatory, arts, technology, and science, mathematics, humanities, foreign language school. Boarding grades 7–12, day grades 5–12. Founded: 1814. Setting: suburban. Nearest major city is Pittsburgh, PA. Students are housed in single-sex dormitories. 60-acre campus. 19 buildings on campus. Approved or accredited by Independent Schools Association of the Central States, North Central Association of Colleges and Schools, The Association of Boarding Schools, and West Virginia Department of Education. Member of National Association of Independent Schools. Endowment: $16 million. Total enrollment: 450. Upper school average class size: 15. Upper school faculty-student ratio: 1:9. There are 165 required school days per year for Upper School students. Upper School students typically attend 5 days per week. The average school day consists of 6 hours and 30 minutes.

Upper School Student Profile Grade 9: 80 students (49 boys, 31 girls); Grade 10: 71 students (36 boys, 35 girls); Grade 11: 69 students (38 boys, 31 girls); Grade 12: 76 students (44 boys, 32 girls). 32% of students are boarding students. 50% are state residents. 20 states are represented in upper school student body. 9% are international students. International students from Bahamas, Mexico, Republic of Korea, Saudi Arabia, South Africa, and Thailand; 15 other countries represented in student body.

Faculty School total: 51. In upper school: 23 men, 12 women; 26 have advanced degrees; 22 reside on campus.

Subjects Offered Algebra, American history, American literature, art, art history, biology, biology-AP, calculus-AP, character education, chemistry, chemistry-AP, Chinese, chorus, college counseling, communications, computer programming, computer science, concert band, contemporary issues, creative writing, drama, earth science, economics, English, English language-AP, English literature, English literature-AP, environmental science, expository writing, fine arts, French, geometry, German, government/civics, health, history, human geography - AP, humanities, Latin, mathematics, model United Nations, multimedia design, music, newspaper, physical education, physics, physics-AP, psychology, psychology-AP, science, social studies, Spanish, speech, statistics, technology/design, theater, U.S. history-AP, world history, writing, yearbook, zoology.

Graduation Requirements Arts and fine arts (art, music, dance, drama), computer science, English, foreign language, mathematics, physical education (includes health), science, social studies (includes history), Senior Research Essay.

Special Academic Programs 12 Advanced Placement exams for which test preparation is offered; academic accommodation for the gifted.

College Admission Counseling 60 students graduated in 2011; all went to college, including Duquesne University; Marshall University; New York University; Ohio University; West Virginia University. Mean SAT critical reading: 580, mean SAT math: 580, mean SAT writing: 570, mean combined SAT: 1730, mean composite ACT: 26.

Student Life Upper grades have uniform requirement, student council, honor system. Discipline rests primarily with faculty.

Summer Programs Enrichment, advancement, computer instruction programs offered; held on campus; accepts boys and girls; open to students from other schools. 100 students usually enrolled. 2012 schedule: June 12 to July 12. Application deadline: June 12.

Tuition and Aid Day student tuition: $14,280; 5-day tuition and room/board: $29,320; 7-day tuition and room/board: $29,320. Tuition installment plan (Academic Management Services Plan). Need-based scholarship grants available. In 2011–12, 40% of upper-school students received aid. Total amount of financial aid awarded in 2011–12: $900,000.

Admissions Traditional secondary-level entrance grade is 9. Otis-Lennon, Stanford Achievement Test or SSAT required. Deadline for receipt of application materials: January 31. No application fee required. Interview required.

Athletics Interscholastic: baseball (boys), basketball (b,g), cheering (g), cross-country running (b,g), diving (b,g), football (b), golf (b,g), ice hockey (b,g), lacrosse (b), soccer (b,g), softball (g), wrestling (b); intramural: flag football (b,g), floor hockey (b), football (b), hiking/backpacking (b,g), indoor soccer (b,g), indoor track (b,g), indoor track & field (b,g), life saving (b,g), mountain biking (b,g), outdoor activities (b,g), physical fitness (b,g), power lifting (b), rappelling (b,g), rock climbing (b,g), roller blading (b,g), ropes courses (b,g), running (b,g), street hockey (b); coed intramural: backpacking, badminton, bowling, canoeing/kayaking, climbing, combined training, cooperative games, cross-country running, fitness, Frisbee, ice skating, in-line skating, jogging, kayaking, kickball, life saving, mountain biking, Nautilus, physical fitness, physical training, rafting, rock climbing, ropes courses, running, scuba diving, soccer, softball. 4 PE instructors, 4 coaches, 1 athletic trainer.

Computers Computers are regularly used in economics, English, foreign language, humanities, journalism, mathematics, music, psychology, science classes. Computer network features include on-campus library services, online commercial services, Internet access, wireless campus network, Internet filtering or blocking technology. Student e-mail accounts are available to students. The school has a published electronic and media policy.

Contact Mr. Craig Tredenick, Director of Admissions. 304-233-1436. Fax: 304-234-4614. E-mail: admit@linsly.org. Web site: www.linsly.org.

See Display on next page and Close-Up on page 640.

LITTLE KESWICK SCHOOL

Keswick, Virginia

See Special Needs Schools section.

LODI ACADEMY

1230 South Central Avenue

Lodi, California 95242

Head of School: Mr. Doug Brown

General Information Coeducational day college-preparatory, general academic, arts, and religious studies school, affiliated with Seventh-day Adventist Church. Boys grade 9, girls grade 12. Founded: 1908. Setting: small town. Nearest major city is Sacramento. 30-acre campus. 9 buildings on campus. Approved or accredited by Western Association of Schools and Colleges and California Department of Education. Endowment: $1.1 million. Total enrollment: 101. Upper school average class size: 13. Upper school faculty-student ratio: 1:13. There are 180 required school days per year for Upper School students. Upper School students typically attend 5 days per week. The average school day consists of 6 hours and 40 minutes.

Upper School Student Profile Grade 9: 23 students (12 boys, 11 girls); Grade 10: 26 students (14 boys, 12 girls); Grade 11: 25 students (16 boys, 9 girls); Grade 12: 27 students (10 boys, 17 girls). 82% of students are Seventh-day Adventists.

Faculty School total: 13. In upper school: 7 men, 6 women; 6 have advanced degrees.

Subjects Offered Accounting, algebra, American history, American literature, art, auto mechanics, band, Bible, biology, chemistry, choir, chorus, computer applications, economics, English, English literature, general math, geography, geometry, government, health, life skills, music appreciation, physical education, physical science, physics, piano, pre-algebra, pre-calculus, Spanish, student publications, U.S. history, U.S. history-AP, work experience, world history, yearbook.

Graduation Requirements Algebra, American history, American literature, applied arts, arts and fine arts (art, music, dance, drama), Bible, biology, chemistry, computer applications, economics, English, English literature, geography, geometry, keyboarding, life skills, physical education (includes health), physical science, Spanish, U.S. government, U.S. history, work experience, world history, 100 hours of community service, 100 hours of paid work experience. Community service is required.

Special Academic Programs 2 Advanced Placement exams for which test preparation is offered.

College Admission Counseling 20 students graduated in 2011; 19 went to college, including La Sierra University; Pacific Union College; Walla Walla University. Other: 1 went to work. Median SAT critical reading: 510, median SAT math: 530, median SAT writing: 480, median combined SAT: 1614, median composite ACT: 26. 28% scored over 600 on SAT critical reading, 33.3% scored over 600 on SAT math, 22.2% scored over 600 on SAT writing, 17% scored over 1800 on combined SAT, 28.5% scored over 26 on composite ACT.

Student Life Upper grades have specified standards of dress, student council. Discipline rests equally with students and faculty. Attendance at religious services is required.

Tuition and Aid Day student tuition: $765. Tuition installment plan (monthly payment plans, individually arranged payment plans). Tuition reduction for siblings, merit scholarship grants, need-based scholarship grants, paying campus jobs available. In 2011–12, 30% of upper-school students received aid; total upper-school merit-scholarship money awarded: $7000. Total amount of financial aid awarded in 2011–12: $27,000.

Admissions Traditional secondary-level entrance grade is 9. Achievement tests or Iowa Tests of Basic Skills required. Deadline for receipt of application materials: none. Application fee required: $300. Interview required.

Athletics Interscholastic: basketball (boys, girls), flag football (b,g), soccer (g), volleyball (g); intramural: basketball (b,g), flag football (b,g), volleyball (g); coed interscholastic: golf. 1 PE instructor.

Computers Computers are regularly used in accounting, Bible studies, computer applications, English, mathematics classes. Computer network features include Internet access, Internet filtering or blocking technology. Student e-mail accounts and computer access in designated common areas are available to students. Students grades are available online. The school has a published electronic and media policy.

Contact Mrs. Dorene Hackett, Registrar. 209-369-2781 Ext. 102. Fax: 209-747-6689. E-mail: dorene@lodiacademy.net. Web site: www.lodiacademy.net.

LONG ISLAND LUTHERAN MIDDLE AND HIGH SCHOOL

131 Brookville Road

Brookville, New York 11545-3399

Head of School: Dr. David Hahn

General Information Coeducational day college-preparatory, arts, business, and religious studies school, affiliated with Lutheran Church. Grades 6–12. Founded: 1960. Setting: suburban. Nearest major city is New York. 32-acre campus. 6 buildings on campus. Approved or accredited by Evangelical Lutheran Church in America, Middle States Association of Colleges and Schools, US Department of State, and New York Department of Education. Endowment: $6 million. Total enrollment: 596. Upper school average class size: 18. Upper school faculty-student ratio: 1:9. There are 161 required school days per year for Upper School students. Upper School students typically attend 5 days per week. The average school day consists of 6 hours and 30 minutes.

Upper School Student Profile Grade 9: 92 students (47 boys, 45 girls); Grade 10: 102 students (53 boys, 49 girls); Grade 11: 112 students (67 boys, 45 girls); Grade 12: 102 students (56 boys, 46 girls). 33% of students are Lutheran.

Faculty School total: 58. In upper school: 20 men, 28 women; 45 have advanced degrees.

Subjects Offered Accounting, algebra, American history, American literature, anatomy, art, band, biology, biology-AP, business, business communications, business skills, calculus, calculus-AP, ceramics, choir, college planning, communication skills, computer programming, computer science, computer science-AP, creative writing, dance, decision making skills, driver education, earth science, economics-AP, English, English language-AP, English literature, English literature-AP, environmental science, ethics, European history, European history-AP, fine arts, French, French language-AP, freshman foundations, geography, geometry, government/civics, grammar, graphic arts, health, history, journalism, Mandarin, marketing, mathematics, multimedia, music, photography, physical education, physics, physics-AP, physiology, psychology, religion, social studies, Spanish, Spanish language-AP, theater, trigonometry, U.S. government and politics-AP, U.S. history-AP, video film production, word processing, world history, writing.

Graduation Requirements Arts and fine arts (art, music, dance, drama), business skills (includes word processing), computer science, English, foreign language, mathematics, physical education (includes health), religion (includes Bible studies and theology), science, social studies (includes history).

Special Academic Programs 14 Advanced Placement exams for which test preparation is offered; honors section; term-away projects; study at local college for college credit; ESL (7 students enrolled).

College Admission Counseling 102 students graduated in 2011; all went to college, including Fordham University; Hofstra University; New York University; Penn State University Park; State University of New York at Binghamton; Temple University. Mean SAT critical reading: 582, mean SAT math: 574, mean SAT writing: 576, mean combined SAT: 1732, mean composite ACT: 24. 25% scored over 26 on composite ACT.

Student Life Upper grades have uniform requirement, student council, honor system. Discipline rests primarily with faculty. Attendance at religious services is required.

Summer Programs Sports, art/fine arts, computer instruction programs offered; session focuses on sports, recreation, and education; held both on and off campus; held at local satellite facilities; accepts boys and girls; open to students from other schools. 5,000 students usually enrolled. 2012 schedule: June 25 to August 17. Application deadline: January.

Tuition and Aid Day student tuition: $10,050–$11,990. Tuition installment plan (monthly payment plans, school's own payment plan). Tuition reduction for siblings, merit scholarship grants, need-based scholarship grants available. In 2011–12, 30% of upper-school students received aid; total upper-school merit-scholarship money awarded: $10,000. Total amount of financial aid awarded in 2011–12: $325,000.

Admissions Traditional secondary-level entrance grade is 9. For fall 2011, 144 students applied for upper-level admission, 82 were accepted, 55 enrolled. Cognitive Abilities Test, Math Placement Exam and writing sample required. Deadline for receipt of application materials: none. Application fee required: $100. On-campus interview required.

Athletics Interscholastic: baseball (boys, girls), basketball (b), cheering (g), dance team (g), football (b), lacrosse (b,g), roller hockey (b), soccer (b,g), softball (g), tennis (b,g), volleyball (g), wrestling (b); intramural: dance team (g), flag football (b), horseback riding (b,g); coed interscholastic: cross-country running, golf, running, track and field, winter (indoor) track; coed intramural: bowling, equestrian sports, physical training, skiing (downhill). 3 PE instructors, 30 coaches.

Computers Computers are regularly used in accounting, art, business, business skills, college planning, design, English, graphic design, history, journalism, library skills, mathematics, science classes. Computer network features include on-campus library services, Internet access, wireless campus network, Internet filtering or blocking technology. Student e-mail accounts and computer access in designated common areas are available to students. Students grades are available online. The school has a published electronic and media policy.

Contact Barbara Ward, Director of Admissions. 516-626-1700 Ext. 546. Fax: 516-622-7459. E-mail: barbara.ward@luhi.org. Web site: www.luhi.org.

THE LOOMIS CHAFFEE SCHOOL

4 Batchelder Road

Windsor, Connecticut 06095

Head of School: Dr. Sheila Culbert

General Information Coeducational boarding and day college-preparatory and arts school. Grades 9–PG. Founded: 1914. Setting: rural. Nearest major city is Hartford. Students are housed in single-sex dormitories. 300-acre campus. 65 buildings on campus. Approved or accredited by New England Association of Schools and Colleges, The Association of Boarding Schools, and Connecticut Department of Education. Member of National Association of Independent Schools and Secondary School Admission Test Board. Endowment: $200 million. Total enrollment: 682. Upper school average class size: 12. Upper school faculty-student ratio: 1:5. There are 172 required school days per year for Upper School students. Upper School students typically attend 6 days per week. The average school day consists of 8 hours.

Upper School Student Profile Grade 9: 129 students (61 boys, 68 girls); Grade 10: 164 students (86 boys, 78 girls); Grade 11: 168 students (90 boys, 78 girls); Grade 12: 195 students (100 boys, 95 girls); Postgraduate: 26 students (22 boys, 4 girls). 60% of students are boarding students. 50% are state residents. 28 states are represented in upper school student body. 17% are international students. International students from Bermuda, Canada, China, Republic of Korea, Thailand, and Viet Nam; 29 other countries represented in student body.

Faculty School total: 160. In upper school: 75 men, 85 women; 110 have advanced degrees; 70 reside on campus.

Subjects Offered Algebra, American history, American literature, anatomy, art, art history, astronomy, biology, calculus, ceramics, chemistry, creative writing, dance, drama, ecology, economics, English, English literature, environmental science, ethics, European history, expository writing, fine arts, French, geometry, history, history of ideas, history of science, Latin, logic, Mandarin, mathematics, music, philosophy, photography, physical education, physics, physiology, religion, science, Spanish, statistics, theater, video film production, world history, world literature, writing.

Graduation Requirements Arts and fine arts (art, music, dance, drama), English, foreign language, history, mathematics, philosophy, physical education (includes health), science.

Special Academic Programs 19 Advanced Placement exams for which test preparation is offered; honors section; independent study; term-away projects; study at local college for college credit; study abroad.

College Admission Counseling 187 students graduated in 2011; 184 went to college, including Colgate University; Georgetown University; Hamilton College; Syracuse University; The George Washington University; Trinity College. Other: 2 had other specific plans. Mean SAT critical reading: 647, mean SAT math: 659, mean SAT writing: 649, mean combined SAT: 1306, mean composite ACT: 28.

Student Life Upper grades have specified standards of dress, student council. Discipline rests equally with students and faculty.

Summer Programs Enrichment programs offered; session focuses on communications—writing and speaking; held on campus; accepts boys and girls; open to students from other schools. 100 students usually enrolled. 2012 schedule: June 27 to August 1. Application deadline: June 27.

Tuition and Aid Day student tuition: $35,850; 7-day tuition and room/board: $47,100. Tuition installment plan (Insured Tuition Payment Plan, Key Tuition Payment Plan, monthly payment plans). Need-based scholarship grants, need-based loans available. In 2011–12, 34% of upper-school students received aid. Total amount of financial aid awarded in 2011–12: $7,700,000.

Admissions Traditional secondary-level entrance grade is 9. For fall 2011, 1,680 students applied for upper-level admission, 461 were accepted, 218 enrolled. ISEE, PSAT, SAT, SSAT or TOEFL required. Deadline for receipt of application materials: January 15. Application fee required: $75. Interview required.

Athletics Interscholastic: baseball (boys), basketball (b,g), cross-country running (b,g), field hockey (g), football (b), golf (b,g), ice hockey (b,g), lacrosse (b,g), soccer (b,g), softball (g), squash (b,g), swimming and diving (b,g), tennis (b,g), track and field (b,g), volleyball (g), water polo (b,g), wrestling (b); intramural: ice hockey (b,g), soccer (b,g), volleyball (b,g); coed interscholastic: alpine skiing, diving, skiing (downhill); coed intramural: aerobics, aerobics/dance, aerobics/Nautilus, backpacking, ballet, basketball, bicycling, canoeing/kayaking, climbing, dance, fencing, fitness, Frisbee, hiking/backpacking, jogging, kayaking, life saving, modern dance, mountain biking, Nautilus, outdoor activities, outdoor adventure, physical fitness, physical training, ropes courses, running, scuba diving, soccer, softball, squash, strength & conditioning, swimming and diving, tennis, ultimate Frisbee, weight training, yoga. 5 PE instructors, 2 athletic trainers.

Computers Computers are regularly used in all academic classes. Computer network features include on-campus library services, online commercial services, Internet access, wireless campus network. Campus intranet, student e-mail accounts, and computer access in designated common areas are available to students. Students grades are available online. The school has a published electronic and media policy.

Contact Mr. Erby Mitchell, Assistant Head of School for Enrollment. 860-687-6400. Fax: 860-298-8756. E-mail: erby_mitchell@loomis.org. Web site: www.loomis.org.

LORETTO ACADEMY

1300 Hardaway Street

El Paso, Texas 79903

Head of School: Sr. Mary E. (Buffy) Boesen, SL

General Information Coeducational day (boys' only in lower grades) college-preparatory, arts, religious studies, and technology school, affiliated with Roman Catholic Church. Boys grades PK–5, girls grades PK–12. Founded: 1923. Setting: urban. 17-acre campus. 3 buildings on campus. Approved or accredited by Southern Association of Colleges and Schools and Texas Catholic Conference. Endowment: $3.3 million. Total enrollment: 648. Upper school average class size: 20. Upper school faculty-student ratio: 1:20. There are 180 required school days per year for Upper School students. Upper School students typically attend 5 days per week. The average school day consists of 7 hours.

Upper School Student Profile 90% of students are Roman Catholic.

Faculty School total: 51. In upper school: 4 men, 22 women; 16 have advanced degrees.

Subjects Offered Acting, advanced math, Advanced Placement courses, algebra, American government, American history, anatomy and physiology, art, art appreciation, art-AP, arts, arts and crafts, Bible, biology, business mathematics, calculus, calculus-AP, chemistry, choir, choral music, Christian and Hebrew scripture, college writing, computer applications, computer programming, computer science, English, environmental science, fine arts, French, geology, geometry, government, government-AP, health, honors algebra, honors English, honors geometry, Internet, journalism, keyboarding, life issues, literature, literature-AP, mathematics, modern dance, moral theology, music appreciation, photo shop, physical education, physics, religion, science, social studies, Spanish, Spanish language-AP, Spanish-AP, speech, speech and debate, student government, study skills, technical writing, theater production, world geography, world history, world religions, yearbook, zoology.

Graduation Requirements Algebra, American government, arts and fine arts (art, music, dance, drama), biology, Christian and Hebrew scripture, Christian ethics, Christian studies, church history, computer science, economics, English, English composition, English literature, environmental science, foreign language, geography, lab/keyboard, life issues, mathematics, moral reasoning, physical education (includes health), physical science, psychology, religion (includes Bible studies and theology), science, social studies (includes history), speech communications, world geography, service learning .5 Credit, 4 credits of religion.

Special Academic Programs Advanced Placement exam preparation.

College Admission Counseling 81 students graduated in 2011; all went to college, including New Mexico State University; St. Edward's University; St. Mary's University; The University of Texas at El Paso; The University of Texas at San Antonio. Mean SAT critical reading: 502, mean SAT math: 475, mean SAT writing: 517. 17.1% scored over 600 on SAT critical reading, 11.8% scored over 600 on SAT math, 19.7% scored over 600 on SAT writing, 48.6% scored over 1800 on combined SAT, 10% scored over 26 on composite ACT.

Student Life Upper grades have uniform requirement, student council, honor system. Discipline rests primarily with faculty.

Summer Programs Remediation programs offered; session focuses on remediation; held on campus; accepts girls; not open to students from other schools. 25 students usually enrolled. 2012 schedule: June 1 to July 2.

Tuition and Aid Day student tuition: $6550. Tuition installment plan (FACTS Tuition Payment Plan). Tuition reduction for siblings, need-based scholarship grants, paying campus jobs, need-based financial aid available. In 2011–12, 27% of upper-school students received aid. Total amount of financial aid awarded in 2011–12: $220,000.

Admissions Traditional secondary-level entrance grade is 9. For fall 2011, 105 students applied for upper-level admission, 95 were accepted, 87 enrolled. Educational Development Series or High School Placement Test required. Deadline for receipt of application materials: none. Application fee required: $30. On-campus interview required.

Athletics Interscholastic: aquatics (girls), basketball (g), cheering (g), cross-country running (g), dance squad (g), dance team (g), golf (g), modern dance (g), soccer (g), softball (g), swimming and diving (g), tennis (g), track and field (g), volleyball (g). 2 PE instructors, 17 coaches.

Computers Computers are regularly used in all academic classes. Computer network features include on-campus library services, online commercial services, Internet access, Internet filtering or blocking technology. Computer access in designated common areas is available to students. Students grades are available online. The school has a published electronic and media policy.

Contact Mrs. Lily Miranda, Director of Admissions. 915-566-8400. Fax: 915-566-0636. E-mail: lmiranda@loretto.org. Web site: www.loretto.org.

LOS ANGELES BAPTIST MIDDLE SCHOOL/HIGH SCHOOL

9825 Woodley Avenue

North Hills, California 91343

Head of School: Mr. Walter Clarke

General Information Coeducational day college-preparatory, arts, religious studies, and technology school, affiliated with Baptist Church. Grades 6–12. Founded: 1962. Setting: suburban. Nearest major city is Los Angeles. 11-acre campus. 5 buildings on campus. Approved or accredited by Association of Christian Schools International and Western Association of Schools and Colleges. Total enrollment: 753. Upper school average class size: 30. Upper school faculty-student ratio: 1:22. There are 180 required school days per year for Upper School students. Upper School students typically attend 5 days per week. The average school day consists of 6 hours and 45 minutes.

Upper School Student Profile Grade 9: 117 students (50 boys, 67 girls); Grade 10: 110 students (58 boys, 52 girls); Grade 11: 143 students (67 boys, 76 girls); Grade 12: 105 students (54 boys, 51 girls).

Faculty School total: 38. In upper school: 16 men, 14 women; 29 have advanced degrees.

Subjects Offered 3-dimensional design, advanced computer applications, algebra, American history, American literature, analysis and differential calculus, anatomy and physiology, art, ASB Leadership, band, Bible studies, biology, biology-AP, calculus-AP, ceramics, chemistry, choir, choral music, Christian doctrine, Christian education, Christian ethics, computer applications, computer education, computer graphics, computer programming, computer science, computer skills, computer technologies, digital photography, drama, drama performance, earth science, economics, English, English literature, English-AP, expository writing, fine arts, French, French-AP, geography, geometry, government/civics, HTML design, intro to computers, jazz band, journalism, keyboarding, mathematics, music, photography, physical education, physics, physics-AP, practical arts, pre-calculus, psychology, psychology-AP, religion, science, social studies, Spanish, Spanish-AP, statistics, statistics-AP, studio art, theater arts, trigonometry, typing, U.S. history-AP, world history.

Graduation Requirements Arts and fine arts (art, music, dance, drama), English, foreign language, mathematics, physical education (includes health), practical arts, religion (includes Bible studies and theology), science, social studies (includes history).

Special Academic Programs Advanced Placement exam preparation; honors section; ESL (13 students enrolled).

College Admission Counseling 154 students graduated in 2011; 150 went to college, including California State University, Northridge; The Master's College and Seminary; University of California, Irvine; University of California, Los Angeles; University of Southern California. Other: 2 went to work, 1 entered military service, 1 had other specific plans. Median SAT critical reading: 560, median SAT math: 550, median SAT writing: 550, median combined SAT: 1645, median composite ACT: 24. 31.5% scored over 600 on SAT critical reading, 29.3% scored over 600 on SAT math, 31.5% scored over 600 on SAT writing, 29.3% scored over 1800 on combined SAT, 26.2% scored over 26 on composite ACT.

Student Life Upper grades have uniform requirement, student council, honor system. Discipline rests primarily with faculty. Attendance at religious services is required.

Summer Programs Remediation, advancement, sports, computer instruction programs offered; session focuses on remediation and enrichment; held both on and off campus; held at Internet based learning can be done from any computer.; accepts boys and girls; open to students from other schools. 350 students usually enrolled. 2012 schedule: June 1 to July 30.

Tuition and Aid Day student tuition: $8250. Tuition installment plan (FACTS Tuition Payment Plan, 2-semester payment plan, annual payment plan). Merit scholarship grants, need-based scholarship grants available. In 2011–12, 35% of upper-school students received aid. Total amount of financial aid awarded in 2011–12: $913,690.

Admissions Traditional secondary-level entrance grade is 9. For fall 2011, 62 students applied for upper-level admission, 49 were accepted, 46 enrolled. QUIC required. Deadline for receipt of application materials: August 1. Application fee required: $100. On-campus interview required.

Athletics Interscholastic: baseball (boys), basketball (b,g), cheering (g), cross-country running (b,g), football (b), golf (b), soccer (b,g), softball (g), tennis (g), track and field (b,g), volleyball (b,g). 1 PE instructor, 36 coaches.

Computers Computers are regularly used in animation, business applications, career technology, graphic design, graphics, introduction to technology, keyboarding, lab/keyboard, programming, technology, typing, Web site design, word processing classes. Computer network features include on-campus library services, Internet access, Internet filtering or blocking technology. The school has a published electronic and media policy.

Contact Mr. Jason French, Admissions/Recruitment Coordinator. 818-894-5742 Ext. 322. Fax: 818-892-5018. E-mail: jfrench@labaptist.org. Web site: www.labaptist.org/.

LOS ANGELES LUTHERAN HIGH SCHOOL

Now Concordia Jr/Sr High

13570 Eldridge Avenue

Sylmar, California 91342

Head of School: Mr. Edward R. Amey

General Information Coeducational day and distance learning college-preparatory, arts, and religious studies school, affiliated with Lutheran Church–Missouri Synod, Lutheran Church. Grades K–12. Distance learning grades 10–12. Founded: 1953. Setting: suburban. Nearest major city is Los Angeles. 4-acre campus. 3 buildings on campus. Approved or accredited by National Lutheran School Accreditation, Western Association of Schools and Colleges, and California Department of Education. Endowment: $450,000. Total enrollment: 440. Upper school average class size: 22. Upper school faculty-student ratio: 1:10. There are 180 required school days per year for Upper School students. Upper School students typically attend 5 days per week. The average school day consists of 6 hours and 30 minutes.

Upper School Student Profile Grade 9: 41 students (22 boys, 19 girls); Grade 10: 45 students (22 boys, 23 girls); Grade 11: 39 students (19 boys, 20 girls); Grade 12: 42 students (22 boys, 20 girls). 30% of students are Lutheran Church–Missouri Synod, Lutheran.

Faculty School total: 22. In upper school: 11 men, 11 women; 7 have advanced degrees.

Subjects Offered 3-dimensional art, Advanced Placement courses, algebra, American literature, American sign language, anatomy and physiology, ancient history, band, bell choir, Bible, Bible studies, biology, biology-AP, British literature (honors), business applications, business law, business mathematics, calculus, career/college preparation, chemistry, choir, choral music, Christian doctrine, Christian scripture, classical music, composition, concert band, drawing, economics, English literature, English-AP, ESL, ethics, family studies, film appreciation, geography, geometry, German, government, jazz, jazz band, journalism, Life of Christ, math analysis, music theory, painting, physics, psychology, Spanish, U.S. history, world history, yearbook.

Graduation Requirements Advanced math, algebra, American government, American history, American literature, analytic geometry, ancient world history, biology, British literature, career education, chemistry, Christian doctrine, Christian testament, comparative religion, composition, economics, English composition, English literature, geometry, government, keyboarding, physical education (includes health), religious education, Spanish, U.S. government, U.S. history, world history.

Special Academic Programs 6 Advanced Placement exams for which test preparation is offered; honors section; study at local college for college credit; academic accommodation for the gifted, the musically talented, and the artistically talented; ESL (25 students enrolled).

College Admission Counseling 39 students graduated in 2011; 37 went to college, including Berklee College of Music; California State Polytechnic University, Pomona; California State University, Northridge; Concordia University; University of California, Santa Barbara; University of Southern California. Other: 1 went to work, 1 entered military service.

Student Life Upper grades have uniform requirement, student council. Discipline rests primarily with faculty. Attendance at religious services is required.

Summer Programs Remediation, enrichment, ESL, sports programs offered; session focuses on mathematics and English; held on campus; accepts boys and girls; open to students from other schools. 25 students usually enrolled. 2012 schedule: July 7 to July 31. Application deadline: June 15.

Tuition and Aid Day student tuition: $7200. Tuition installment plan (SMART Tuition Payment Plan, monthly payment plans). Merit scholarship grants, need-based scholarship grants available. In 2011–12, 30% of upper-school students received aid; total upper-school merit-scholarship money awarded: $16,000. Total amount of financial aid awarded in 2011–12: $100,000.

Admissions Traditional secondary-level entrance grade is 9. For fall 2011, 43 students applied for upper-level admission, 40 were accepted, 37 enrolled. Achievement/Aptitude/Writing or placement test required. Deadline for receipt of application materials: none. Application fee required: $300. Interview required.

Athletics Interscholastic: baseball (boys), basketball (b,g), cheering (g), drill team (g), flag football (b), football (b), soccer (b), volleyball (b,g); intramural: aerobics (b,g), fitness (b,g), jogging (b,g), physical fitness (b,g), physical training (b,g), strength & conditioning (b), tennis (b,g), track and field (b,g), ultimate Frisbee (b,g), walking (b,g), weight training (b,g); coed interscholastic: flag football, soccer; coed intramural: golf. 4 PE instructors, 8 coaches.

Computers Computers are regularly used in business, business applications, college planning, computer applications, desktop publishing, digital applications, journalism, keyboarding, lab/keyboard, media production, religion, science, yearbook classes. Computer network features include on-campus library services, online commercial services, Internet access, Internet filtering or blocking technology. Students grades are available online. The school has a published electronic and media policy.

Contact Ms. Barbara Winslow, Admissions Counselor. 818-362-5861. Fax: 818-367-0043. E-mail: barbara.winslow@concordiaschoolsla.org. Web site: www.concordiahigh.org.

LOUISVILLE COLLEGIATE SCHOOL

2427 Glenmary Avenue

Louisville, Kentucky 40204

Head of School: Junius Scott Prince

General Information Coeducational day college-preparatory, arts, and technology school. Grades JK–12. Founded: 1915. Setting: urban. 24-acre campus. 2 buildings on campus. Approved or accredited by Independent Schools Association of the Central States. Member of National Association of Independent Schools and Secondary School Admission Test Board. Endowment: $5.7 million. Total enrollment: 693. Upper school average class size: 13. Upper school faculty-student ratio: 1:8.

Faculty School total: 80. In upper school: 12 men, 10 women; 20 have advanced degrees.

Subjects Offered Algebra, American history, American literature, ancient history, art, art history, biology, calculus, chemistry, Chinese, chorus, community service, composition, computer science, creative writing, discrete mathematics, drama, economics, English, English literature, ensembles, environmental science, European history, fine arts, French, geometry, German, history, mathematics, media, music, music history, physical education, physics, physiology, pre-calculus, science, social studies, Spanish, statistics, studio art, theater, trigonometry, world history, world literature, writing.

Graduation Requirements Arts and fine arts (art, music, dance, drama), English, foreign language, mathematics, physical education (includes health), science, social studies (includes history), senior symposium in leadership and service, individual and class service projects, senior speech.

Special Academic Programs Advanced Placement exam preparation; honors section; independent study; term-away projects; study abroad.

College Admission Counseling 53 students graduated in 2011; all went to college, including Centre College; Miami University; Northwestern University; Vanderbilt University; Wake Forest University. Median SAT critical reading: 623, median SAT math: 619, median SAT writing: 627, median combined SAT: 1869, median composite ACT: 27.

Student Life Upper grades have uniform requirement, student council, honor system. Discipline rests equally with students and faculty.

Summer Programs Enrichment, advancement, sports, art/fine arts, computer instruction programs offered; session focuses on educational enrichment and sports; held both on and off campus; held at Champion's Trace Athletic Fields; accepts boys and girls; open to students from other schools. 350 students usually enrolled. 2012 schedule: June 1 to July 31. Application deadline: none.

Tuition and Aid Day student tuition: $19,700. Tuition installment plan (The Tuition Plan, monthly payment plans, individually arranged payment plans). Merit scholarship grants, need-based scholarship grants available. In 2011–12, 28% of upper-school students received aid.

Admissions Traditional secondary-level entrance grade is 9. School's own exam and SSAT required. Deadline for receipt of application materials: none. Application fee required: $50. Interview required.

Athletics Interscholastic: basketball (boys, girls), crew (g), cross-country running (b,g), field hockey (g), golf (b,g), indoor track (b,g), lacrosse (b,g), rowing (b,g), soccer (b,g), softball (g), strength & conditioning (b,g), swimming and diving (b,g), tennis (b,g), track and field (b,g), winter (indoor) track (b,g); intramural: basketball (b,g), soccer (b,g), tennis (b,g); coed interscholastic: soccer, strength & conditioning; coed intramural: soccer. 4 PE instructors, 60 coaches, 1 athletic trainer.

Computers Computers are regularly used in art, English, foreign language, history, mathematics, science classes. Computer network features include on-campus library services, online commercial services, Internet access, wireless campus network, Internet filtering or blocking technology. Student e-mail accounts and computer access in designated common areas are available to students. Students grades are available online. The school has a published electronic and media policy.

Contact Lynne Age, Admission Office Administrative Assistant. 502-479-0378. Fax: 502-454-0549. E-mail: lynne_age@loucol.com. Web site: www.loucol.com.

LOUISVILLE HIGH SCHOOL

22300 Mulholland Drive

Woodland Hills, California 91364

Head of School: Mrs. Kathleen Vercillo

General Information Girls' day college-preparatory, arts, religious studies, and technology school, affiliated with Roman Catholic Church. Grades 9–12. Founded: 1960. Setting: suburban. Nearest major city is Tarzana. 17-acre campus. 7 buildings on campus. Approved or accredited by National Catholic Education Association, Western Association of Schools and Colleges, Western Catholic Education Association, and California Department of Education. Total enrollment: 428. Upper school average class size: 25. Upper school faculty-student ratio: 1:25. There are 180 required school days per year for Upper School students. Upper School students typically attend 5 days per week. The average school day consists of 6 hours.

Upper School Student Profile Grade 9: 111 students (111 girls); Grade 10: 122 students (122 girls); Grade 11: 115 students (115 girls); Grade 12: 80 students (80 girls). 78% of students are Roman Catholic.

Faculty School total: 35. In upper school: 7 men, 28 women; 24 have advanced degrees.

Subjects Offered Advanced Placement courses, advanced studio art-AP, algebra, American history, American literature, anatomy, art, Bible studies, biology, calculus, calculus-AP, campus ministry, ceramics, chemistry, computer science, creative writing, dance, drama, earth science, economics, English, English literature, European history, fine arts, French, geography, geometry, government/civics, grammar, history, journalism, law, mathematics, music, photography, physical education, physics, physiology, psychology, religion, science, social sciences, social studies, Spanish, speech, theater, trigonometry, video film production, Web site design, world history, world literature.

Graduation Requirements Arts and fine arts (art, music, dance, drama), biology, chemistry, computer science, economics, English, foreign language, mathematics, performing arts, physical education (includes health), religion (includes Bible studies and theology), science, social sciences, social studies (includes history), U.S. government, U.S. history, visual arts, world history. Community service is required.

Special Academic Programs Advanced Placement exam preparation.

College Admission Counseling 101 students graduated in 2011; all went to college, including California Polytechnic State University, San Luis Obispo; California State University, Northridge; Loyola Marymount University; New York University; University of California, Los Angeles; University of Oregon.

Student Life Upper grades have uniform requirement, student council, honor system. Discipline rests equally with students and faculty. Attendance at religious services is required.

Summer Programs Sports programs offered; session focuses on skill development; held both on and off campus; held at Los Angeles Pierce Community College and Balboa Park; accepts girls; open to students from other schools. 200 students usually enrolled. 2012 schedule: June 11 to July 27. Application deadline: May 25.

Tuition and Aid Day student tuition: $12,500. Tuition installment plan (FACTS Tuition Payment Plan). Merit scholarship grants, need-based scholarship grants available. In 2011–12, 40% of upper-school students received aid; total upper-school merit-scholarship money awarded: $72,000. Total amount of financial aid awarded in 2011–12: $623,000.

Admissions Traditional secondary-level entrance grade is 9. For fall 2011, 174 students applied for upper-level admission, 157 were accepted, 111 enrolled. High School Placement Test required. Deadline for receipt of application materials: January 25. Application fee required: $100. On-campus interview required.

Athletics Interscholastic: basketball, cross-country running, equestrian sports, field hockey, golf, soccer, softball, swimming and diving, tennis, track and field, volleyball, water polo; intramural: fitness walking, tennis, yoga. 2 PE instructors, 31 coaches, 1 athletic trainer.

Computers Computers are regularly used in all academic, college planning, computer applications, creative writing, economics, English, foreign language, French, graphic design, health, journalism, library, literary magazine, mathematics, media, media production, photography, religion, religious studies, science, social studies, Spanish, speech, technology, yearbook classes. Computer network features include on-campus library services, online commercial services, Internet access, wireless campus network, Internet filtering or blocking technology. Student e-mail accounts are available to students. Students grades are available online. The school has a published electronic and media policy.

Contact Mrs. Linda Klarin, Admissions Coordinator. 818-346-8812. Fax: 818-346-9483. E-mail: lklarin@louisvillehs.org. Web site: www.louisvillehs.org.

THE LOVETT SCHOOL

4075 Paces Ferry Road NW

Atlanta, Georgia 30327

Head of School: William S. Peebles

General Information Coeducational day college-preparatory school. Grades K–12. Founded: 1926. Setting: suburban. 100-acre campus. 8 buildings on campus. Approved or accredited by Southern Association of Colleges and Schools, Southern Association of Independent Schools, and Georgia Department of Education. Member of National Association of Independent Schools and Secondary School Admission Test Board. Endowment: $57.3 million. Total enrollment: 1,589. Upper school average class size: 13. Upper school faculty-student ratio: 1:7. There are 180 required school days per year for Upper School students. Upper School students typically attend 5 days per week. The average school day consists of 6 hours.

Upper School Student Profile Grade 9: 155 students (78 boys, 77 girls); Grade 10: 153 students (71 boys, 82 girls); Grade 11: 147 students (70 boys, 77 girls); Grade 12: 151 students (70 boys, 81 girls).

Faculty School total: 86. In upper school: 43 men, 43 women; 67 have advanced degrees.

Subjects Offered Advanced chemistry, advanced computer applications, advanced math, Advanced Placement courses, African American history, African history, African literature, African-American literature, algebra, American government, American history, American history-AP, American legal systems, American literature, ancient history, ancient world history, architecture, art, art history, Asian history, Asian studies, band, biology, botany, calculus, calculus-AP, career and personal planning, career/college preparation, ceramics, character education, chemistry, chorus, computer art, computer education, computer graphics, computer programming, computer science, creative writing, dance, debate, drama, driver education, earth science, ecology, economics, electronic music, English, English literature, English-AP, environmental science, ethics, European history, fiction, film history, fine arts, French, French language-AP, French literature-AP, French studies, French-AP, gender issues, genetics, geometry, German, history, human development, jazz dance, journalism, Latin, Latin-AP, leadership, marine biology, mathematics, medieval history, music theory, music theory-AP, newspaper, orchestra, painting, philosophy, photography, physical education, physics, portfolio art, pre-calculus, public speaking, religion, robotics, science, sculpture, social studies, Spanish, Spanish language-AP, Spanish literature-AP, speech, statistics, technical theater, theater, theater arts, trigonometry, U.S. government and politics-AP, video, Western civilization, Western philosophy, world cultures, world history, world literature, world religions, writing workshop, yearbook, zoology.

Graduation Requirements Algebra, American studies, arts and fine arts (art, music, dance, drama), biology, English, foreign language, geometry, history, mathematics, physical education (includes health), religion (includes Bible studies and theology), science, Western civilization.

Special Academic Programs Advanced Placement exam preparation; honors section; independent study; term-away projects; study abroad; academic accommodation for the gifted, the musically talented, and the artistically talented.

College Admission Counseling 139 students graduated in 2011; all went to college, including Auburn University; Georgia Institute of Technology; Samford University; Texas Christian University; The University of Alabama; University of Georgia.

Student Life Upper grades have uniform requirement, student council, honor system. Discipline rests primarily with faculty. Attendance at religious services is required.

Summer Programs Remediation, enrichment, advancement programs offered; session focuses on academic course work; held on campus; accepts boys and girls; open to students from other schools. 35 students usually enrolled. 2012 schedule: June 4 to July 20. Application deadline: June 1.

Tuition and Aid Day student tuition: $18,470–$22,020. Tuition installment plan (The Tuition Plan, Key Tuition Payment Plan, monthly payment plans, individually arranged payment plans, 1/2 paid in July and 1/2 paid in November). Need-based scholarship grants, local bank loans available. In 2011–12, 13% of upper-school students received aid. Total amount of financial aid awarded in 2011–12: $1,182,390.

Admissions Traditional secondary-level entrance grade is 9. SSAT required. Deadline for receipt of application materials: February 3. Application fee required: $75. On-campus interview required.

Athletics Interscholastic: artistic gym (girls), baseball (b), basketball (b,g), cheering (g), cross-country running (b,g), dance (g), diving (b,g), football (b), golf (b,g), gymnastics (g), lacrosse (b,g), modern dance (g), soccer (b,g), softball (g), swimming and diving (b,g), tennis (b,g), track and field (b,g), volleyball (g), wrestling (b); intramural: aerobics/dance (g), dance (g), in-line hockey (b), modern dance (g), roller hockey (b); coed intramural: backpacking, bicycling, bowling, canoeing/kayaking, climbing, fitness, flag football, Frisbee, hiking/backpacking, kayaking, mountain biking, outdoor activities, physical fitness, physical training, rappelling, rock climbing, ropes courses, strength & conditioning, ultimate Frisbee, wall climbing, weight lifting, weight training, yoga. 3 PE instructors, 26 coaches, 2 athletic trainers.

Computers Computers are regularly used in all academic classes. Computer network features include on-campus library services, online commercial services, Internet access, wireless campus network, Internet filtering or blocking technology, central file storage. Student e-mail accounts and computer access in designated common areas are available to students. Students grades are available online.

Contact Ms. Debbie Lange, Director of Admission. 404-262-3032. Fax: 404-479-8463. E-mail: dlange@lovett.org. Web site: www.lovett.org.

LOYOLA ACADEMY

1100 Laramie Avenue

Wilmette, Illinois 60091

Head of School: Rev. Patrick E. McGrath, SJ

General Information Coeducational day college-preparatory and comprehensive college preparation in the Jesuit tradition school, affiliated with Roman Catholic Church (Jesuit order). Grades 9–12. Founded: 1909. Setting: suburban. Nearest major city is Chicago. 26-acre campus. 1 building on campus. Approved or accredited by North Central Association of Colleges and Schools and Illinois Department of Education. Endowment: $40 million. Total enrollment: 2,000. Upper school average class size: 24. Upper school faculty-student ratio: 1:17. The average school day consists of 7 hours and 12 minutes.

Upper School Student Profile 88% of students are Roman Catholic Church (Jesuit order).

Faculty School total: 160. In upper school: 80 men, 70 women; 130 have advanced degrees.

Subjects Offered Advanced Placement courses, algebra, American history, American history-AP, American literature, American literature-AP, anatomy, Ancient Greek, art, art history, Asian history, band, biology, biology-AP, calculus, chemistry, chemistry-AP, Chinese, chorus, communications, computer math, computer programming, computer science, creative writing, dance, design, drama, drawing, earth science, economics, English, English literature, ethics, European history-AP, expository writing, fine arts, finite math, French, general science, genetics, geography, geometry, German, government and politics-AP, health, history, history-AP, humanities, instrumental music, justice seminar, keyboarding, Latin, literature, mathematics, music, musicianship, painting, physical education, physics, physics-AP, physiology, political science, psychology, psychology-AP, religious studies, science, sculpture, social studies, Spanish, Spanish-AP, speech, statistics, statistics-AP, theater, theology, theology and the arts, trigonometry, word processing, world history, world literature, writing.

Graduation Requirements Arts and fine arts (art, music, dance, drama), English, foreign language, mathematics, physical education (includes health), religion (includes Bible studies and theology), science, social studies (includes history), attendance at Freshman and Junior Retreats.

Special Academic Programs Advanced Placement exam preparation; honors section; independent study; study abroad; academic accommodation for the gifted; programs in English, mathematics, general development for dyslexic students; special instructional classes for students with mild learning challenges.

College Admission Counseling 479 students graduated in 2010; 478 went to college, including Boston College; DePaul University; Loyola University Chicago; Marquette University; University of Illinois; University of Notre Dame. Other: 1 went to work. Mean SAT critical reading: 569, mean SAT math: 579, mean composite ACT: 25. 27% scored over 600 on SAT critical reading, 29% scored over 600 on SAT math, 25% scored over 26 on composite ACT.

Student Life Upper grades have specified standards of dress, student council, honor system. Discipline rests primarily with faculty. Attendance at religious services is required.

Tuition and Aid Day student tuition: $12,500. Tuition installment plan (monthly payment plans, 1-, 2-, 4- and monthly payment plans). Need-based scholarship grants available. In 2010–11, 30% of upper-school students received aid. Total amount of financial aid awarded in 2010–11: $3,750,000.

Admissions Traditional secondary-level entrance grade is 9. For fall 2010, 920 students applied for upper-level admission, 700 were accepted, 535 enrolled. STS Examination required. Deadline for receipt of application materials: January 26. Application fee required: $25.

Athletics Interscholastic: baseball (boys), basketball (b,g), crew (b,g), cross-country running (b,g), diving (b,g), field hockey (g), football (b), golf (b,g), ice hockey (b,g), indoor track & field (b,g), lacrosse (b,g), rowing (b,g), soccer (b,g), softball (g), swimming and diving (b,g), tennis (b,g), track and field (b,g), volleyball (b,g), water polo (b,g), wrestling (b); intramural: cheering (g), dance (b,g), dance squad (g), dance team (g), drill team (g), modern dance (b,g), pom squad (g); coed interscholastic: bowling, sailing; coed intramural: aerobics, aerobics/dance, ballet, basketball, bicycling, billiards, bowling, canoeing/kayaking, climbing, fitness, Frisbee, golf, hiking/backpacking, kayaking, martial arts, mountain biking, outdoor education, physical fitness, scuba diving, skateboarding, skiing (downhill), snowboarding, strength & conditioning, table tennis, ultimate Frisbee, wall climbing, weight lifting, weight training, yoga. 6 PE instructors, 2 athletic trainers.

Computers Computers are regularly used in all academic classes. Computer network features include on-campus library services, Internet access, wireless campus network, Internet filtering or blocking technology. Campus intranet is available to students. Students grades are available online. The school has a published electronic and media policy.

Contact Mrs. Genevieve B. Atwood, Director of Admissions. 847-920-2480. Fax: 847-920-2552. E-mail: gatwood@loy.org. Web site: www.goramblers.org.

LOYOLA-BLAKEFIELD

PO Box 6819

Baltimore, Maryland 21285-6819

Head of School: Mr. Anthony I. Day

General Information Boys' day college-preparatory, arts, and religious studies school, affiliated with Roman Catholic Church. Grades 6–12. Founded: 1852. Setting: suburban. 60-acre campus. 7 buildings on campus. Approved or accredited by Association of Independent Maryland Schools and Jesuit Secondary Education Association. Endowment: $12.4 million. Total enrollment: 1,004. Upper school average class size: 19. Upper school faculty-student ratio: 1:11. There are 175 required school days per year for Upper School students. Upper School students typically attend 5 days per week. The average school day consists of 6 hours and 55 minutes.

Upper School Student Profile Grade 9: 191 students (191 boys); Grade 10: 184 students (184 boys); Grade 11: 183 students (183 boys); Grade 12: 183 students (183 boys). 80% of students are Roman Catholic.

Faculty School total: 88. In upper school: 55 men, 18 women; 60 have advanced degrees.

Subjects Offered Accounting, algebra, American government, American literature, American literature-AP, architecture, art, art history, band, biology, biology-AP, biotechnology, British literature, British literature (honors), calculus, calculus-AP, chemistry, chemistry-AP, Chesapeake Bay studies, chorus, civil war history, composition, composition-AP, computer graphics, computer science, concert band, drawing, driver education, engineering, English, English language-AP, English literature-AP, European history-AP, film studies, fine arts, forensics, French, French language-AP, German, German-AP, government and politics-AP, Greek, history, history of music, honors algebra, honors English, honors geometry, honors U.S. history, honors world history, instrumental music, jazz ensemble, journalism, Latin, Latin-AP, mathematics, music history, oil painting, painting, photography, physical education, physics, physics-AP, poetry, pre-calculus, psychology, public speaking, religion, science, Spanish, Spanish language-AP, statistics-AP, U.S. government and politics-AP, U.S. history, U.S. history-AP.

Graduation Requirements Arts and fine arts (art, music, dance, drama), computer science, English, foreign language, mathematics, physical education (includes health), religion (includes Bible studies and theology), science, social studies (includes history), 40 hours of Christian service.

Special Academic Programs Advanced Placement exam preparation; honors section; academic accommodation for the gifted, the musically talented, and the artistically talented; programs in English, mathematics, general development for dyslexic students.

College Admission Counseling 169 students graduated in 2011; 166 went to college, including College of Charleston; James Madison University; Loyola University Maryland; University of Maryland, College Park; University of South Carolina; Virginia Polytechnic Institute and State University. Other: 3 had other specific plans. Mean SAT critical reading: 610, mean SAT math: 615, mean SAT writing: 592.

Student Life Upper grades have specified standards of dress, student council, honor system. Discipline rests primarily with faculty. Attendance at religious services is required.

Summer Programs Remediation, enrichment, advancement, sports programs offered; held on campus; accepts boys and girls; open to students from other schools. 350 students usually enrolled. 2012 schedule: June 18 to July 20. Application deadline: none.

Tuition and Aid Day student tuition: $16,130. Tuition installment plan (Tuition Management Systems). Merit scholarship grants, need-based scholarship grants available. In 2011–12, 38% of upper-school students received aid; total upper-school merit-scholarship money awarded: $583,540. Total amount of financial aid awarded in 2011–12: $2,394,563.

Admissions Traditional secondary-level entrance grade is 9. For fall 2011, 284 students applied for upper-level admission, 249 were accepted, 117 enrolled. High School Placement Test or ISEE required. Deadline for receipt of application materials: December 15. No application fee required. On-campus interview required.

Athletics Interscholastic: baseball, basketball, cross-country running, diving, football, golf, ice hockey, indoor track & field, lacrosse, rugby, soccer, squash, swimming and diving, tennis, track and field, volleyball, water polo, winter (indoor) track, wrestling; intramural: basketball, flag football, indoor soccer, lacrosse, martial arts, rock climbing, tennis, ultimate Frisbee. 4 PE instructors, 30 coaches, 1 athletic trainer.

Computers Computers are regularly used in all classes. Computer network features include on-campus library services, online commercial services, Internet access, wireless campus network, Internet filtering or blocking technology. Campus intranet, student e-mail accounts, and computer access in designated common areas are available to students. Students grades are available online. The school has a published electronic and media policy.

Contact Ms. Paddy M. London, Admissions Assistant. 443-841-3680. Fax: 443-841-3105. E-mail: plondon@loyolablakefield.org. Web site: www.loyolablakefield.org.

LOYOLA SCHOOL

980 Park Avenue

New York, New York 10028-0020

Head of School: Mr. James F.X. Lyness

General Information Coeducational day college-preparatory school, affiliated with Roman Catholic Church (Jesuit order). Grades 9–12. Founded: 1900. Setting: urban. 2 buildings on campus. Approved or accredited by Jesuit Secondary Education Association, Middle States Association of Colleges and Schools, National Catholic Education Association, New York State Association of Independent Schools, and New York State Board of Regents. Member of National Association of Independent Schools. Total enrollment: 202. Upper school average class size: 17. Upper school faculty-student ratio: 1:9. There are 180 required school days per year for Upper School students. Upper School students typically attend 5 days per week. The average school day consists of 6 hours and 20 minutes.

Upper School Student Profile Grade 9: 49 students (25 boys, 24 girls); Grade 10: 45 students (20 boys, 25 girls); Grade 11: 53 students (25 boys, 28 girls); Grade 12: 55 students (24 boys, 31 girls). 85% of students are Roman Catholic Church (Jesuit order).

Faculty School total: 30. In upper school: 16 men, 14 women; 28 have advanced degrees.

Subjects Offered Advanced Placement courses, algebra, American government, American history, American literature, art, art history, biology, calculus, chemistry, chorus, college counseling, community service, comparative religion, computer programming, computer science, creative writing, death and loss, discrete mathematics, drama, economics, English, English literature, ethics, European history, expository writing, film, film history, fine arts, French, geometry, grammar, health, history, instrumental music, Italian, journalism, language-AP, Latin, mathematics, music history, philosophy, photography, physical education, physics, political science, pre-calculus, religion, science, social studies, Spanish, speech, statistics-AP, student government, student publications, theater, theology, trigonometry, world history, writing.

Graduation Requirements Art history, computer literacy, English, foreign language, guidance, mathematics, music history, physical education (includes health), science, social studies (includes history), speech, theology, Christian service program hours each year.

Special Academic Programs 9 Advanced Placement exams for which test preparation is offered; study at local college for college credit.

College Admission Counseling 55 students graduated in 2010; all went to college, including Cornell University; Fordham University; Georgetown University; Gettysburg College; Lafayette College; Northwestern University. Median SAT critical reading: 620, median SAT math: 600, median SAT writing: 630.

Student Life Upper grades have specified standards of dress, student council, honor system. Discipline rests primarily with faculty. Attendance at religious services is required.

Tuition and Aid Day student tuition: $28,000. Tuition installment plan (Academic Management Services Plan). Merit scholarship grants, need-based scholarship grants available. In 2010–11, 33% of upper-school students received aid; total upper-school merit-scholarship money awarded: $200,000. Total amount of financial aid awarded in 2010–11: $1,194,000.

Admissions Traditional secondary-level entrance grade is 9. ISEE, school's own exam or SSAT required. Deadline for receipt of application materials: November 19. Application fee required: $75. On-campus interview recommended.

Athletics Interscholastic: baseball (boys), basketball (b,g), cross-country running (b,g), soccer (b), softball (g), track and field (b,g), volleyball (g); intramural: basketball (b,g), dance (g); coed interscholastic: golf, physical fitness, soccer; coed intramural: Frisbee, hiking/backpacking, outdoor activities, outdoor adventure, paddle tennis, physical fitness, physical training, track and field. 1 PE instructor, 9 coaches.

Computers Computers are regularly used in all academic classes. Computer network features include on-campus library services, online commercial services, Internet access, wireless campus network, Internet filtering or blocking technology. Campus intranet, student e-mail accounts, and computer access in designated common areas are available to students. The school has a published electronic and media policy.

Contact Mr. Gabriel Rotman, Associate Director of Admissions. 646-346-8131. Fax: 646-346-8175. E-mail: grotman@loyola-nyc.org. Web site: www.loyola-nyc.org.

LUTHERAN HIGH SCHOOL

3960 Fruit Street

La Verne, California 91750

Head of School: Lance E. Ebel

General Information Coeducational day college-preparatory, general academic, arts, religious studies, and technology school, affiliated with Lutheran Church–Missouri Synod. Grades 9–12. Founded: 1973. Setting: suburban. Nearest major city is Los Angeles. 10-acre campus. 7 buildings on campus. Approved or accredited by Association of Christian Schools International, Lutheran School Accreditation Commission, National Lutheran School Accreditation, and Western Association of Schools and Colleges. Total enrollment: 130. Upper school average class size: 15. Upper school faculty-student ratio: 1:9. There are 180 required school days per year for Upper School students. Upper School students typically attend 5 days per week. The average school day consists of 6 hours and 40 minutes.

Upper School Student Profile Grade 9: 35 students (18 boys, 17 girls); Grade 10: 34 students (21 boys, 13 girls); Grade 11: 24 students (16 boys, 8 girls); Grade 12: 37 students (20 boys, 17 girls). 29% of students are Lutheran Church–Missouri Synod.

Faculty School total: 14. In upper school: 5 men, 9 women; 9 have advanced degrees.

Subjects Offered Advanced math, Advanced Placement courses, algebra, American government, American history, American history-AP, American literature, anatomy, anatomy and physiology, art, ASB Leadership, athletics, biology, biology-AP, British literature, calculus, calculus-AP, chemistry, choir, college counseling, community service, comparative religion, composition, computer literacy, computer programming, computer science, computer science-AP, computers, conceptual physics, drama, economics, English, English literature and composition-AP, English literature-AP, fine arts, geography, geometry, government, history-AP, honors algebra, honors English, honors geometry, honors U.S. history, honors world history, human anatomy, keyboarding, mathematics, naval science, NJROTC, physical education, physics, physics-AP, pre-calculus, psychology, religion, science, sign language, social sciences, social studies, Spanish, Spanish language-AP, theology, U.S. government, U.S. government and politics-AP, U.S. history-AP, word processing, world history, world literature, yearbook.

Graduation Requirements Arts and fine arts (art, music, dance, drama), business skills (includes word processing), computer science, English, foreign language, mathematics, physical education (includes health), religion (includes Bible studies and theology), science, social sciences, social studies (includes history), 24 hours per year of service to the community, senior project completion.

Special Academic Programs Advanced Placement exam preparation; honors section; accelerated programs; study at local college for college credit.

College Admission Counseling 31 students graduated in 2010; 30 went to college, including Azusa Pacific University; California State University, Fullerton; Columbia University; Concordia University; University of California, Berkeley. Other: 1 entered military service. Median SAT critical reading: 485, median SAT math: 495, median SAT writing: 515, median combined SAT: 1465. 18% scored over 600 on SAT critical reading, 14% scored over 600 on SAT math, 9% scored over 600 on SAT writing, 14% scored over 1800 on combined SAT.

Student Life Upper grades have specified standards of dress, student council, honor system. Discipline rests primarily with faculty. Attendance at religious services is required.

Tuition and Aid Day student tuition: $6200–$6950. Tuition installment plan (SMART Tuition Payment Plan, monthly payment plans, individually arranged payment plans, advance payment discounts, credit card payments). Tuition reduction for siblings, merit scholarship grants, need-based scholarship grants available. In 2010–11, 31% of upper-school students received aid; total upper-school merit-scholarship money awarded: $21,650. Total amount of financial aid awarded in 2010–11: $109,150.

Admissions Traditional secondary-level entrance grade is 9. High School Placement Test required. Deadline for receipt of application materials: none. Application fee required: $75. Interview required.

Athletics Interscholastic: aerobics/dance (girls), baseball (b), basketball (b,g), cheering (g), cross-country running (b,g), dance squad (g), dance team (g), drill team (b,g), football (b), golf (b,g), softball (g), volleyball (g), wrestling (b); coed interscholastic: golf, JROTC drill, soccer, track and field. 1 PE instructor, 20 coaches.

Computers Computers are regularly used in all academic, English, geography, history, information technology, mathematics, NJROTC, programming, science, Spanish, yearbook classes. Computer network features include online commercial services, Internet access, wireless campus network, Internet filtering or blocking technology. Campus intranet is available to students. Students grades are available online. The school has a published electronic and media policy.

Contact Kathy Johnson, Office Manager. 909-593-4494 Ext. 221. Fax: 909-596-3744. E-mail: kjohnson@lhslv.org. Web site: www.lhslv.org.

LUTHERAN HIGH SCHOOL

5555 South Arlington Avenue

Indianapolis, Indiana 46237-2366

Head of School: Mr. Michael Brandt

General Information Coeducational day college-preparatory, general academic, and religious studies school, affiliated with Lutheran Church–Missouri Synod. Grades 9–12. Founded: 1975. Setting: suburban. 14-acre campus. 1 building on campus. Approved or accredited by National Lutheran School Accreditation, North Central Association of Colleges and Schools, and Indiana Department of Education. Endowment: $600,000. Total enrollment: 235. Upper school average class size: 16. Upper school faculty-student ratio: 1:15. There are 180 required school days per year for Upper School students. Upper School students typically attend 5 days per week. The average school day consists of 8 hours and 15 minutes.

Upper School Student Profile Grade 9: 59 students (32 boys, 27 girls); Grade 10: 52 students (23 boys, 29 girls); Grade 11: 53 students (27 boys, 26 girls); Grade 12: 71 students (39 boys, 32 girls). 64% of students are Lutheran Church–Missouri Synod.

Faculty School total: 17. In upper school: 12 men, 5 women; 15 have advanced degrees.

Subjects Offered 3-dimensional art, Advanced Placement courses, advanced studio art-AP, algebra, American government, American history, American history-AP, American literature-AP, American sign language, anatomy, anatomy and physiology, art, art-AP, band, biology, biology-AP, calculus, calculus-AP, career experience, ceramics, chemistry, chemistry-AP, choir, chorus, Christian ethics, Christian scripture, Christian testament, computer information systems, computer programming, concert band, current events, desktop publishing, discrete mathematics, earth science, economics, English, English composition, English literature and composition-AP, English literature-AP, ethics, etymology, geography, geometry, German, health and wellness, honors algebra, humanities, integrated physics, math review, music theory, music theory-AP, New Testament, physical education, physical fitness, piano, pre-calculus, psychology, reading/study skills, sociology, Spanish, Spanish-AP, speech, statistics, studio art, U.S. government, U.S. history-AP, world history, world religions.

Graduation Requirements Arts and fine arts (art, music, dance, drama), biology, chemistry, Christian doctrine, Christian ethics, computer applications, economics, foreign language, geography, health and wellness, integrated physics, literature and composition-AP, New Testament, physical education (includes health), U.S. government, U.S. history, world religions.

Special Academic Programs 6 Advanced Placement exams for which test preparation is offered; honors section; independent study; study at local college for college credit; remedial reading and/or remedial writing; remedial math.

College Admission Counseling 68 students graduated in 2011; 67 went to college, including Ball State University; Indiana University Bloomington; Purdue University; University of Indianapolis; Valparaiso University. Other: 1 entered military service. Mean SAT critical reading: 515, mean SAT math: 550, mean SAT writing: 502, mean combined SAT: 1567, mean composite ACT: 23.

Student Life Upper grades have uniform requirement, student council. Discipline rests primarily with faculty. Attendance at religious services is required.

Tuition and Aid Day student tuition: $8900. Tuition installment plan (monthly payment plans, In Full, by semester, or through 10 month payment plan). Tuition reduction for siblings, need-based scholarship grants, paying campus jobs, Simply Giving (Thrivent), church worker grants available. In 2011–12, 30% of upper-school students received aid. Total amount of financial aid awarded in 2011–12: $160,000.

Admissions Traditional secondary-level entrance grade is 9. Math Placement Exam or SCAT required. Deadline for receipt of application materials: none. Application fee required: $250. On-campus interview required.

Athletics Interscholastic: baseball (boys), basketball (b,g), cross-country running (b,g), football (b), golf (b,g), soccer (b,g), softball (g), strength & conditioning (b,g), tennis (b,g), track and field (b,g), volleyball (b,g), weight lifting (b,g), weight training (b,g); intramural: basketball (b,g); coed interscholastic: cheering, physical fitness, weight training; coed intramural: bowling, fishing, football. 2 PE instructors, 22 coaches.

Computers Computers are regularly used in art, Bible studies, Christian doctrine, current events, desktop publishing, English, ethics, geography, health, history, mathematics, religious studies, science, social sciences, speech, yearbook classes. Computer network features include online commercial services, Internet access, wireless campus network, Internet filtering or blocking technology. Computer access in designated common areas is available to students. Students grades are available online. The school has a published electronic and media policy.

Contact Mrs. Christie Hampton, Director of Admissions. 317-787-5474 Ext. 218. Fax: 317-787-2794. E-mail: admissions@lhsi.org. Web site: www.lhsi.org.

LUTHERAN HIGH SCHOOL

12411 Wornall Road

Kansas City, Missouri 64145-1736

Head of School: Mr. Chris Domsch

General Information Coeducational day college-preparatory and religious studies school, affiliated with Lutheran Church–Missouri Synod. Grades 9–12. Founded: 1980. Setting: suburban. 29-acre campus. 1 building on campus. Approved or accredited by Missouri Independent School Association, National Lutheran School Accreditation, North Central Association of Colleges and Schools, and Missouri Department of Education. Endowment: $97,000. Total enrollment: 120. Upper school average class size: 15. Upper school faculty-student ratio: 1:12. There are 172 required school days per year for Upper School students. Upper School students typically attend 5 days per week. The average school day consists of 6 hours and 45 minutes.

Upper School Student Profile Grade 9: 41 students (30 boys, 11 girls); Grade 10: 19 students (6 boys, 13 girls); Grade 11: 27 students (19 boys, 8 girls); Grade 12: 32 students (17 boys, 15 girls). 80% of students are Lutheran Church–Missouri Synod.

Faculty School total: 14. In upper school: 5 men, 9 women; 5 have advanced degrees.

Subjects Offered Advanced math, algebra, American government, American literature, analysis, analytic geometry, anatomy and physiology, ancient world history, applied music, art, athletics, baseball, Basic programming, basketball, Bible studies, biology, biology-AP, calculus, cheerleading, chemistry, choir, Christian doctrine, Christian education, Christian ethics, Christian scripture, Christianity, church history, college counseling, communication skills, comparative religion, composition, contemporary art, earth science, English composition, English literature, geometry, government, graphic arts, health education, history, history of religion, instrumental music, Internet, Internet research, introduction to literature, keyboarding, Life of Christ, math analysis, New Testament, photography, physical education, physical science, physics, pre-algebra, psychology, sociology, Spanish, speech and oral interpretations, state history, statistics, student government, theater, theater production, track and field, trigonometry, U.S. government, volleyball, weightlifting.

Graduation Requirements Algebra, American government, American history, American literature, analytic geometry, art, arts and fine arts (art, music, dance, drama), Bible studies, biology, British literature, calculus, chemistry, church history, electives, geometry, health education, math analysis, modern world history, trigonometry, U.S. history.

Special Academic Programs Honors section; independent study; study at local college for college credit; remedial math.

College Admission Counseling 21 students graduated in 2010; 19 went to college, including Johnson County Community College; Kansas State University; Missouri State University; University of Central Missouri; University of Missouri. Other: 2 went to work. Mean SAT critical reading: 550, mean SAT math: 480, mean composite ACT: 24. 50% scored over 600 on SAT critical reading, 50% scored over 600 on SAT math, 25% scored over 26 on composite ACT.

Student Life Upper grades have specified standards of dress, student council, honor system. Discipline rests primarily with faculty.

Tuition and Aid Day student tuition: $6140–$9000. Tuition installment plan (monthly payment plans, individually arranged payment plans). Tuition reduction for siblings, need-based scholarship grants available. In 2010–11, 20% of upper-school students received aid. Total amount of financial aid awarded in 2010–11: $15,000.

Admissions Traditional secondary-level entrance grade is 9. For fall 2010, 120 students applied for upper-level admission, 120 were accepted, 120 enrolled. SLEP for foreign students required. Deadline for receipt of application materials: none. Application fee required: $275. On-campus interview required.

Athletics Interscholastic: baseball (boys), basketball (b,g), cheering (g), cross-country running (b,g), dance (g), dance team (g), fitness (b,g), golf (b), physical training (b,g), soccer (b,g), tennis (b,g), track and field (b,g), volleyball (g), weight lifting (b,g), weight training (b,g); coed intramural: basketball, bowling, golf, gymnastics, physical fitness, softball, volleyball, weight training. 2 coaches.

Computers Computers are regularly used in data processing, desktop publishing, journalism, photography, word processing classes. Computer network features include on-campus library services, Internet access, wireless campus network, Internet filtering or blocking technology. Student e-mail accounts are available to students. Students grades are available online. The school has a published electronic and media policy.

Contact Mrs. Paula Meier, Registrar. 816-241-5478. Fax: 816-876-2069. E-mail: pmeier@lhskc.com. Web site: www.lhskc.com.

LUTHERAN HIGH SCHOOL NORTH

5401 Lucas Hunt Road

St. Louis, Missouri 63121

Head of School: Mr. Timothy Brackman

General Information Coeducational day college-preparatory, arts, business, religious studies, bilingual studies, and technology school, affiliated with Lutheran Church. Grades 9–12. Founded: 1946. Setting: urban. 47-acre campus. 1 building on campus. Approved or accredited by Lutheran School Accreditation Commission, National Lutheran School Accreditation, North Central Association of Colleges and Schools, and Missouri Department of Education. Endowment: $5.8 million. Total enrollment: 314. Upper school average class size: 20. Upper school faculty-student ratio: 1:10. There are 176 required school days per year for Upper School students. Upper School students typically attend 5 days per week. The average school day consists of 6 hours and 20 minutes.

Upper School Student Profile Grade 9: 86 students (42 boys, 44 girls); Grade 10: 69 students (38 boys, 31 girls); Grade 11: 82 students (39 boys, 43 girls); Grade 12: 77 students (46 boys, 31 girls). 47% of students are Lutheran.

Faculty School total: 30. In upper school: 16 men, 14 women; 26 have advanced degrees.

Subjects Offered Accounting, advanced chemistry, Advanced Placement courses, algebra, American history, American history-AP, American literature, anatomy, art, Bible studies, biology, business, business law, business skills, calculus, calculus-AP, ceramics, chemistry, child development, choir, Christian doctrine, Christian education, Christian ethics, Christian scripture, Christian studies, Christianity, church history, computer applications, computer multimedia, computer science, concert band, concert choir, data analysis, design, drawing, drawing and design, economics, English, English composition, English literature, English literature-AP, entrepreneurship, European history, family and consumer science, fashion, fine arts, finite math, food and nutrition, foods, French, geography, geometry, government, government/civics, health education, history, human anatomy, keyboarding, literature-AP, Mandarin, marketing, mathematics, media studies, multimedia design, music, organic chemistry, painting, physical education, physics, physiology, practical arts, pre-calculus, printmaking, probability and statistics, psychology, religion, research, science, social studies, society and culture, Spanish, speech, statistics, student publications, theology, U.S. government, U.S. history-AP, world geography, world history, world literature, world religions, writing.

Graduation Requirements American history, arts and fine arts (art, music, dance, drama), English, mathematics, physical education (includes health), practical arts, religion (includes Bible studies and theology), science, social studies (includes history), Saved to Serve (community service hours).

Special Academic Programs Advanced Placement exam preparation; honors section; independent study; study at local college for college credit.

College Admission Counseling 93 students graduated in 2011; 91 went to college, including Ball State University; Southeast Missouri State University; Truman State University; University of Central Missouri; University of Missouri; University of Missouri–St. Louis. Other: 1 went to work. 50% scored over 26 on composite ACT.

Student Life Upper grades have uniform requirement, student council, honor system. Discipline rests primarily with faculty. Attendance at religious services is required.

Summer Programs Enrichment, sports programs offered; session focuses on fundamentals and enrichment; held on campus; accepts boys and girls; not open to students from other schools. 150 students usually enrolled. 2012 schedule: June 1 to July 31.

Tuition and Aid Day student tuition: $9525–$10,725. Tuition installment plan (FACTS Tuition Payment Plan, monthly payment plans, individually arranged payment plans, semester payment plan, full-year payment plan with discount). Tuition reduction for siblings, merit scholarship grants, need-based scholarship grants available. In 2011–12, 66% of upper-school students received aid; total upper-school merit-scholarship money awarded: $22,000. Total amount of financial aid awarded in 2011–12: $750,000.

Admissions Traditional secondary-level entrance grade is 9. For fall 2011, 97 students applied for upper-level admission, 93 were accepted, 86 enrolled. ACT-Explore required. Deadline for receipt of application materials: none. Application fee required: $250. Interview recommended.

Athletics Interscholastic: baseball (boys), basketball (b,g), cheering (g), cross-country running (b,g), dance squad (g), football (b), golf (b), pom squad (g), soccer (b,g), softball (g), tennis (b,g), track and field (b,g), volleyball (g). 2 PE instructors.

Computers Computers are regularly used in art, business education, English, history, mathematics, science, social studies, yearbook classes. Computer network features include on-campus library services, Internet access, wireless campus network, Internet filtering or blocking technology, Internet college work program. Campus intranet and computer access in designated common areas are available to students. Students grades are available online. The school has a published electronic and media policy.

Contact Karen Kersten, Records Clerk. 314-389-3100 Ext. 420. Fax: 314-389-3103. E-mail: kkersten@lhsn.org. Web site: www.lhsn.org.

LUTHERAN HIGH SCHOOL NORTHWEST

1000 Bagley Avenue

Rochester Hills, Michigan 48309

Head of School: Mr. Paul Looker

General Information Coeducational day college-preparatory and religious studies school, affiliated with Lutheran Church–Missouri Synod. Grades 9–12. Founded: 1978. Setting: suburban. Nearest major city is Detroit. 30-acre campus. 1 building on campus. Approved or accredited by National Lutheran School Accreditation, North Central Association of Colleges and Schools, and Michigan Department of Education. Endowment: $1 million. Total enrollment: 298. Upper school average class size: 25. Upper school faculty-student ratio: 1:15. There are 185 required school days per year for Upper School students. Upper School students typically attend 5 days per week. The average school day consists of 7 hours and 20 minutes.

Upper School Student Profile Grade 9: 71 students (31 boys, 40 girls); Grade 10: 82 students (43 boys, 39 girls); Grade 11: 78 students (40 boys, 38 girls); Grade 12: 67 students (35 boys, 32 girls). 75% of students are Lutheran Church–Missouri Synod.

Faculty School total: 20. In upper school: 12 men, 8 women; 15 have advanced degrees.

Subjects Offered Accounting, advanced chemistry, algebra, American history, American history-AP, art, audio visual/media, band, Basic programming, biology, biology-AP, bookkeeping, business, business mathematics, calculus, chemistry, chorus, computer science, drawing, drawing and design, Eastern world civilizations, economics, English, English-AP, geography, geometry, German, government/civics, graphic arts, law, mathematics, music, painting, physical education, physical science, physics-AP, psychology, Spanish, statistics-AP, theology, trigonometry, U.S. government and politics-AP, world history.

Graduation Requirements Arts and fine arts (art, music, dance, drama), English, mathematics, physical education (includes health), religion (includes Bible studies and theology), science, social sciences, social studies (includes history). Community service is required.

Special Academic Programs 7 Advanced Placement exams for which test preparation is offered; honors section; independent study; study at local college for college credit.

College Admission Counseling 66 students graduated in 2011; 65 went to college, including Central Michigan University; Concordia College; Michigan State University; Oakland University; University of Michigan; Western Michigan University. Other: 1 went to work. Median composite ACT: 24. 35% scored over 26 on composite ACT.

Student Life Upper grades have specified standards of dress, student council. Discipline rests primarily with faculty. Attendance at religious services is required.

Tuition and Aid Day student tuition: $7550. Tuition installment plan (monthly payment plans). Merit scholarship grants, need-based scholarship grants available. In 2011–12, 2% of upper-school students received aid; total upper-school merit-scholarship money awarded: $20,000. Total amount of financial aid awarded in 2011–12: $20,000.

Admissions Traditional secondary-level entrance grade is 9. For fall 2011, 298 students applied for upper-level admission, 298 were accepted, 298 enrolled. High School Placement Test required. Deadline for receipt of application materials: none. Application fee required: $350. On-campus interview required.

Athletics Interscholastic: baseball (boys), basketball (b,g), cheering (g), cross-country running (b,g), dance team (g), football (b), golf (b,g), hockey (b), soccer (b,g), softball (g), track and field (b,g), volleyball (g), wrestling (b); intramural: indoor soccer (b,g); coed intramural: badminton, fitness, physical fitness, physical training, tennis, weight training.

Computers Computers are regularly used in journalism, keyboarding, mathematics, media, research skills, word processing, yearbook classes. Computer network features include Internet access, wireless campus network, Internet filtering or blocking technology. Students grades are available online. The school has a published electronic and media policy.

Contact Mr. Paul Looker, Principal. 248-852-6677. Fax: 248-852-2667. E-mail: plooker@lhsa.com. Web site: www.lhnw.lhsa.com.

LUTHERAN HIGH SCHOOL OF HAWAII

1404 University Avenue

Honolulu, Hawaii 96822-2494

Head of School: Daryl S. Utsumi

General Information Coeducational day college-preparatory school, affiliated with Lutheran Church–Missouri Synod. Grades 9–12. Founded: 1988. Setting: urban. 1-acre campus. 3 buildings on campus. Approved or accredited by Lutheran School Accreditation Commission, The Hawaii Council of Private Schools, Western Association of Schools and Colleges, and Hawaii Department of Education. Member of Secondary School Admission Test Board. Endowment: $35,000. Total enrollment: 86. Upper school average class size: 12. Upper school faculty-student ratio: 1:7. There are 175 required school days per year for Upper School students. Upper School students typically attend 5 days per week. The average school day consists of 7 hours and 15 minutes.

Upper School Student Profile Grade 9: 9 students (4 boys, 5 girls); Grade 10: 25 students (13 boys, 12 girls); Grade 11: 22 students (12 boys, 10 girls); Grade 12: 30 students (17 boys, 13 girls). 13% of students are Lutheran Church–Missouri Synod.

Faculty School total: 14. In upper school: 5 men, 8 women; 4 have advanced degrees.

Subjects Offered 20th century history, 3-dimensional art, advanced math, Advanced Placement courses, algebra, American government, American history, American literature, analytic geometry, art, art-AP, Bible studies, biology, British literature, calculus, calculus-AP, chemistry, choir, computer applications, computer programming, computer science, concert band, consumer economics, drama, earth science, economics, English, English literature, European history, expository writing, fine arts, food and nutrition, geometry, government/civics, grammar, health, history, home economics, Japanese, journalism, keyboarding, life skills, marine biology, mathematics, music, oceanography, photography, physical education, physics, psychology, religion, science, social sciences, social studies, Spanish, speech, theater, world history, world literature.

Graduation Requirements Arts and fine arts (art, music, dance, drama), computer science, English, mathematics, physical education (includes health), religion (includes Bible studies and theology), science, social studies (includes history).

Special Academic Programs Advanced Placement exam preparation; honors section; study at local college for college credit; academic accommodation for the musically talented and the artistically talented.

College Admission Counseling 19 students graduated in 2011; 18 went to college, including Kapiolani Community College; University of Hawaii at Manoa. Other: 1 went to work. Median composite ACT: 23. Mean SAT critical reading: 525, mean SAT math: 530, mean SAT writing: 525. 10% scored over 600 on SAT critical reading, 15% scored over 600 on SAT math.

Student Life Upper grades have specified standards of dress, student council, honor system. Discipline rests primarily with faculty. Attendance at religious services is required.

Summer Programs Remediation, enrichment, advancement, sports, art/fine arts, computer instruction programs offered; held on campus; accepts boys and girls; open to students from other schools. 2012 schedule: June 12 to July 20.

Tuition and Aid Day student tuition: $8290–$10,250. Tuition installment plan (Insured Tuition Payment Plan). Tuition reduction for siblings, merit scholarship grants, need-based scholarship grants available. In 2011–12, 25% of upper-school students received aid; total upper-school merit-scholarship money awarded: $40,075. Total amount of financial aid awarded in 2011–12: $500,000.

Admissions Traditional secondary-level entrance grade is 9. For fall 2011, 45 students applied for upper-level admission, 43 were accepted, 16 enrolled. SSAT required. Deadline for receipt of application materials: none. Application fee required: $30. Interview recommended.

Athletics Interscholastic: baseball (boys), basketball (b,g), bowling (b,g), canoeing/kayaking (b,g), cross-country running (b,g), golf (b,g), judo (b,g), kayaking (b,g), paddling (b,g), soccer (b,g), softball (g), swimming and diving (b,g), tennis (b,g), track and field (b,g), volleyball (b,g), water polo (b,g), wrestling (b,g); coed interscholastic: cheering, football, gymnastics, sailing, strength & conditioning; coed intramural: dance. 1 PE instructor, 5 coaches, 1 athletic trainer.

Computers Computers are regularly used in art, desktop publishing, English, history, journalism, library, mathematics, newspaper, photography, photojournalism, science, yearbook classes. Computer network features include on-campus library services, Internet access, Internet filtering or blocking technology. Students grades are available online. The school has a published electronic and media policy.

Contact Lea Dominici, Admissions Officer. 808-949-5302. Fax: 808-947-3701. E-mail: office@lhshawaii.org. Web site: lhshawaii.org.

LUTHERAN HIGH SCHOOL OF SAN DIEGO

810 Buena Vista Way

Chula Vista, California 91910-6853

Head of School: Mr. Scott Dufresne

General Information Coeducational day and distance learning college-preparatory, arts, religious studies, and technology school, affiliated with Lutheran Church. Grades 9–12. Distance learning grades 9–12. Founded: 1975. Setting: urban. Nearest major city is San Diego. 9-acre campus. 6 buildings on campus. Approved or accredited by National Lutheran School Accreditation, Western Association of Schools and Colleges, and California Department of Education. Total enrollment: 75. Upper school average class size: 12. Upper school faculty-student ratio: 1:12. There are 180 required school days per year for Upper School students. Upper School students typically attend 5 days per week. The average school day consists of 6 hours and 30 minutes.

Upper School Student Profile Grade 9: 26 students (11 boys, 15 girls); Grade 10: 16 students (8 boys, 8 girls); Grade 11: 16 students (10 boys, 6 girls); Grade 12: 17 students (11 boys, 6 girls). 50% of students are Lutheran.

Faculty School total: 9. In upper school: 5 men, 4 women; 6 have advanced degrees.

Subjects Offered Accounting, acting, Advanced Placement courses, algebra, American government, American history, American literature, American literature-AP, analytic geometry, anatomy and physiology, applied arts, applied music, art, art appreciation, art history-AP, ASB Leadership, athletics, band, baseball, basketball, bell choir, Bible, biology, biology-AP, British literature, British literature-AP, calculus-AP, campus ministry, chemistry, choir, choral music, Christian education, Christian ethics, comparative religion, computer literacy, creative writing, drama, driver education, economics, English, English language and composition-AP, English language-AP, English literature and composition-AP, English literature-AP, English-AP, English/composition-AP, European history-AP, French, geometry, government, health education, history, music appreciation, physical education, physics, pre-calculus, softball, Spanish, Spanish language-AP, speech, student government, U.S. government and politics, yearbook.

Special Academic Programs Advanced Placement exam preparation.

College Admission Counseling 18 students graduated in 2011; 17 went to college, including Concordia University; Point Loma Nazarene University; San Diego State University; University of California, Irvine; University of California, Riverside. Other: 1 went to work. Mean SAT critical reading: 537, mean SAT math: 518, mean SAT writing: 540, mean combined SAT: 1595.

Student Life Upper grades have specified standards of dress, student council, honor system. Discipline rests primarily with faculty. Attendance at religious services is required.

Tuition and Aid Day student tuition: $8250. Tuition installment plan (monthly payment plans, individually arranged payment plans, Simply Giving—Thrivent Financial for Lutherans, Tuition Solution). Tuition reduction for siblings, merit scholarship grants, need-based scholarship grants available. In 2011–12, 31% of upper-school students received aid; total upper-school merit-scholarship money awarded: $8000. Total amount of financial aid awarded in 2011–12: $60,000.

Admissions Traditional secondary-level entrance grade is 9. Admissions testing required. Application fee required: $250. On-campus interview required.

Athletics Interscholastic: baseball (boys), basketball (b,g), cross-country running (b,g), football (b), softball (g), volleyball (g). 1 PE instructor, 10 coaches.

Computers Computer network features include on-campus library services, Internet access. Students grades are available online.

Contact Debbie Heien, Office Manager. 619-262-4444 Ext. 120. Fax: 619-872-0974. E-mail: debbie.heien@lhssd.org. Web site: www.lutheranhighsandiego.org.

LUTHERAN HIGH SCHOOL SOUTH

9515 Tesson Ferry Road

St. Louis, Missouri 63123-4317

Head of School: Mr. Brian Ryherd

General Information Coeducational day college-preparatory, arts, business, religious studies, and technology school, affiliated with Lutheran Church–Missouri Synod. Grades 9–12. Founded: 1957. Setting: suburban. 35-acre campus. 1 building on campus. Approved or accredited by National Lutheran School Accreditation, North Central Association of Colleges and Schools, and Missouri Department of Education. Endowment: $6.5 million. Total enrollment: 544. Upper school average class size: 21. Upper school faculty-student ratio: 1:14. There are 178 required school days per year for Upper School students. Upper School students typically attend 5 days per week. The average school day consists of 7 hours.

Upper School Student Profile Grade 9: 137 students (66 boys, 71 girls); Grade 10: 137 students (72 boys, 65 girls); Grade 11: 138 students (69 boys, 69 girls); Grade 12: 132 students (70 boys, 62 girls). 83% of students are Lutheran Church–Missouri Synod.

Faculty School total: 41. In upper school: 27 men, 14 women; 30 have advanced degrees.

Subjects Offered Accounting, algebra, American history, American history-AP, American literature, anatomy, art, art history, band, biology, biology-AP, business, business skills, calculus, calculus-AP, ceramics, chemistry, chorus, community service, composition, composition-AP, computer programming, computer science, consumer economics, creative writing, current events, drafting, drama, drawing, earth science, economics, English, English literature, English literature-AP, family studies, fine arts, food science, French, geography, geometry, German, government/civics, health, jazz, journalism, keyboarding, leadership, literature, mathematics, music history, music theory, nutrition, physical education, physics, physiology, psychology, reading, religion, robotics, science, sculpture, social sciences, sociology, Spanish, speech, technology, theater, theology, trigonometry, woodworking, world history, world literature, writing, yearbook.

Graduation Requirements Arts and fine arts (art, music, dance, drama), business skills (includes word processing), English, mathematics, physical education (includes health), religion (includes Bible studies and theology), science, social sciences, social studies (includes history), service component (30 hours per year).

Special Academic Programs Advanced Placement exam preparation; honors section; independent study; study at local college for college credit; remedial reading and/or remedial writing; remedial math; programs in English, mathematics, general development for dyslexic students.

College Admission Counseling 106 students graduated in 2010; all went to college, including Missouri State University; Saint Louis University; Southeast Missouri State University; Truman State University; University of Missouri; Webster University. Median composite ACT: 25. 33% scored over 26 on composite ACT.

Student Life Upper grades have uniform requirement, student council. Discipline rests primarily with faculty. Attendance at religious services is required.

Tuition and Aid Day student tuition: $10,425. Tuition installment plan (FACTS Tuition Payment Plan, monthly payment plans, individually arranged payment plans, 3% discount for paying in full by July 1 prior to the start of school). Tuition reduction for siblings, merit scholarship grants, need-based scholarship grants, paying campus jobs available. In 2010–11, 34% of upper-school students received aid; total upper-school merit-scholarship money awarded: $13,000. Total amount of financial aid awarded in 2010–11: $750,000.

Admissions Traditional secondary-level entrance grade is 9. For fall 2010, 159 students applied for upper-level admission, 157 were accepted, 137 enrolled. Explore required. Deadline for receipt of application materials: none. Application fee required: $250. On-campus interview required.

Athletics Interscholastic: baseball (boys), basketball (b,g), cheering (g), cross-country running (b,g), dance squad (g), diving (g), field hockey (g), football (b), golf (b,g), hockey (b), ice hockey (b), soccer (b,g), softball (g), swimming and diving (g), tennis (b,g), track and field (b,g), volleyball (g); coed intramural: bowling, table tennis, tennis. 1 PE instructor, 10 coaches, 1 athletic trainer.

Computers Computers are regularly used in accounting, drafting, drawing and design, English, industrial technology, journalism, keyboarding, mathematics, religion, science, social sciences classes. Computer network features include on-campus library services, online commercial services, Internet access, wireless campus network, Internet filtering or blocking technology. Student e-mail accounts and computer access in designated common areas are available to students. Students grades are available online. The school has a published electronic and media policy.

Contact Mrs. Jayne Lauer, Director of Recruitment and Public Relations. 314-631-1400 Ext. 426. Fax: 314-631-7762. E-mail: jlauer@lhssonline.org. Web site: www.lhssonline.org.

LUTHER COLLEGE HIGH SCHOOL

1500 Royal Street

Regina, Saskatchewan S4T 5A5, Canada

Head of School: Mr. Mark Anderson

General Information Coeducational boarding and day college-preparatory, general academic, arts, International Baccalaureate, and ESL school, affiliated with Lutheran Church. Grades 9–12. Founded: 1913. Setting: urban. Nearest major city is Winnipeg, MB, Canada. Students are housed in single-sex dormitories. 27-acre campus. 5 buildings on campus. Approved or accredited by Saskatchewan Department of Education. Language of instruction: English. Endowment: CAN$600,000. Total enrollment: 370. Upper school average class size: 22. Upper school faculty-student ratio: 1:16. There are 190 required school days per year for Upper School students. Upper School students typically attend 5 days per week. The average school day consists of 7 hours.

Upper School Student Profile 20% of students are boarding students. 84% are province residents. 5 provinces are represented in upper school student body. 16% are international students. International students from China, Germany, Hong Kong, Republic of Korea, Taiwan, and Thailand; 7 other countries represented in student body. 22% of students are Lutheran.

Faculty School total: 34. In upper school: 20 men, 14 women; 5 have advanced degrees; 1 resides on campus.

Subjects Offered Band, biology, calculus, chemistry, choir, Christian ethics, computer science, drama, English, ESL, French, German, handbells, history, information processing, International Baccalaureate courses, Latin, mathematics, music, orchestra, physical fitness, physics, psychology, science, video film production.

Graduation Requirements Christian ethics, English, mathematics, science, social studies (includes history).

Special Academic Programs International Baccalaureate program; independent study; study at local college for college credit; study abroad; academic accommodation for the gifted; ESL (15 students enrolled).

College Admission Counseling 115 students graduated in 2011; 98 went to college, including Queen's University at Kingston; University of Alberta; University of Regina; University of Saskatchewan; University of Toronto. Other: 10 went to work, 7 had other specific plans.

Student Life Upper grades have specified standards of dress, student council. Discipline rests primarily with faculty. Attendance at religious services is required.

Tuition and Aid Day student tuition: CAN$12,000; 7-day tuition and room/board: CAN$20,320. Tuition installment plan (monthly payment plans, individually arranged payment plans). Tuition reduction for siblings, bursaries, merit scholarship grants, need-based scholarship grants available. In 2011–12, 20% of upper-school students received aid; total upper-school merit-scholarship money awarded: CAN$30,000. Total amount of financial aid awarded in 2011–12: CAN$165,000.

Admissions Traditional secondary-level entrance grade is 9. For fall 2011, 134 students applied for upper-level admission, 118 were accepted, 118 enrolled. English entrance exam required. Deadline for receipt of application materials: none. Application fee required: CAN$300.

Athletics Interscholastic: badminton (boys, girls), baseball (b), basketball (b,g), bicycling (b,g), cheering (g), cross-country running (b,g), curling (b,g), football (b), golf (b,g), hockey (b,g), pom squad (g), rugby (b,g), soccer (b,g), softball (g), volleyball (g); intramural: basketball (b,g), floor hockey (b,g), soccer (b,g), volleyball (g); coed interscholastic: badminton, curling, pom squad, track and field; coed intramural: aerobics/dance, basketball, curling, floor hockey, football, outdoor education, table tennis, ultimate Frisbee. 2 PE instructors, 28 coaches, 2 athletic trainers.

Computers Computers are regularly used in all academic, yearbook classes. Computer network features include Internet access, wireless campus network, Internet filtering or blocking technology. Student e-mail accounts and computer access in designated common areas are available to students. Students grades are available online.

Contact Ms. Alanna Kalyniuk, Registrar. 306-791-9154. Fax: 306-359-6962. E-mail: lutherhs@luthercollege.edu. Web site: www.luthercollege.edu.

LUTHER HIGH SCHOOL NORTH

5700 West Berteau Avenue

Chicago, Illinois 60634

Head of School: Mr. Thomas E. Wiemann

General Information Coeducational day and distance learning college-preparatory, general academic, arts, business, religious studies, and technology school, affiliated with Lutheran Church–Missouri Synod, Evangelical Lutheran Church in America. Grades 9–12. Distance learning grades 10–12. Founded: 1909. Setting: urban. 10-acre campus. 1 building on campus. Approved or accredited by Evangelical Lutheran Church in America, National Lutheran School Accreditation, North Central Association of Colleges and Schools, and Illinois Department of Education. Endowment: $20,000. Total enrollment: 180. Upper school average class size: 16. Upper school faculty-student ratio: 1:16. There are 179 required school days per year for Upper School students. Upper School students typically attend 5 days per week. The average school day consists of 7 hours.

Upper School Student Profile Grade 9: 45 students (25 boys, 20 girls); Grade 10: 40 students (20 boys, 20 girls); Grade 11: 54 students (29 boys, 25 girls); Grade 12: 41 students (21 boys, 20 girls). 47% of students are Lutheran Church–Missouri Synod, Evangelical Lutheran Church in America.

Faculty School total: 17. In upper school: 7 men, 10 women; 14 have advanced degrees.

Subjects Offered 20th century history, 3-dimensional art, accounting, ACT preparation, advanced computer applications, algebra, American legal systems, anatomy, art, astronomy, band, biology, business, calculus, ceramics, chemistry, chorus, composition, computer science, crafts, drawing, economics, English, English-AP, fine arts, geography, geometry, German, government-AP, government/civics, health, keyboarding, law, mathematics, music, painting, photography, physical education, physics, physiology, psychology, public speaking, reading, science, sewing, social sciences, social studies, Spanish, study skills, theology, trigonometry, U.S. history, word processing.

Graduation Requirements Arts and fine arts (art, music, dance, drama), English, foreign language, mathematics, physical education (includes health), religion (includes Bible studies and theology), science, social sciences, social studies (includes history), word processing, summative portfolio demonstration of faculty selected, extra and co-curricular participation annually.

Special Academic Programs Advanced Placement exam preparation; honors section; accelerated programs; independent study; study at local college for college credit; academic accommodation for the gifted, the musically talented, and the artistically talented; remedial reading and/or remedial writing; remedial math; programs in general development for dyslexic students; special instructional classes for students with learning differences.

College Admission Counseling 54 students graduated in 2010; 48 went to college, including Concordia University; DePaul University; Northeastern Illinois University; University of Illinois at Chicago; University of Illinois at Urbana–Champaign; Valparaiso University. Other: 2 went to work, 2 entered military service, 2 had other specific plans. Median composite ACT: 23. 20% scored over 26 on composite ACT.

Student Life Upper grades have specified standards of dress, student council. Discipline rests primarily with faculty. Attendance at religious services is required.

Tuition and Aid Day student tuition: $7600. Tuition installment plan (Insured Tuition Payment Plan, Academic Management Services Plan, monthly payment plans, individually arranged payment plans). Tuition reduction for siblings, merit scholarship grants, need-based scholarship grants, paying campus jobs available. In 2010–11, 70% of upper-school students received aid; total upper-school merit-scholarship money awarded: $30,000.

Admissions Traditional secondary-level entrance grade is 9. For fall 2010, 75 students applied for upper-level admission, 64 were accepted, 62 enrolled. Admissions testing and Stanford Achievement Test, Otis-Lennon School Ability Test required. Deadline for receipt of application materials: none. Application fee required: $175. On-campus interview recommended.

Athletics Interscholastic: baseball (boys), basketball (b,g), cross-country running (b,g), football (b), indoor track & field (b,g), softball (g), track and field (b,g), volleyball (g); coed interscholastic: indoor track; coed intramural: bowling. 2 PE instructors, 10 coaches, 1 athletic trainer.

Computers Computers are regularly used in all academic classes. Computer network features include on-campus library services, online commercial services, Internet access, wireless campus network, Internet filtering or blocking technology, workshops for students and parents in technology. Student e-mail accounts and computer access in designated common areas are available to students. Students grades are available online. The school has a published electronic and media policy.
Contact Mr. Sam Radom, Admissions Assistant. 773-286-3600. Fax: 773-286-0304. E-mail: sradom@luthernorth.org. Web site: www.luthernorth.org.

THE LYCÉE INTERNATIONAL, AMERICAN SECTION

rue du Fer-a-Cheval

BP 70107

Saint-Germain-en-Laye Cedex 78101, France

Head of School: Mr. Sean Lynch

General Information Coeducational day college-preparatory and bilingual studies school. Grades PK–12. Founded: 1952. Setting: suburban. Nearest major city is Paris, France. 10-acre campus. 6 buildings on campus. Approved or accredited by French Ministry of Education and The College Board. Member of European Council of International Schools. Languages of instruction: English and French. Total enrollment: 705. Upper school average class size: 20. Upper school faculty-student ratio: 1:18. Upper School students typically attend 5 days per week. The average school day consists of 8 hours and 30 minutes.
Upper School Student Profile Grade 10: 63 students (27 boys, 36 girls); Grade 11: 54 students (19 boys, 35 girls); Grade 12: 55 students (19 boys, 36 girls).
Faculty School total: 20. In upper school: 5 men, 4 women; 6 have advanced degrees.
Subjects Offered Algebra, American history, American literature, art, biology, botany, calculus, chemistry, computer math, computer programming, computer science, drama, Dutch, economics, English, English literature, English-AP, European history, French, geography, geometry, German, grammar, Greek, health, history, Italian, Latin, mathematics, music, philosophy, physical education, physics, Russian, science, social sciences, social studies, Spanish, statistics, theater, trigonometry, world history, world literature, writing, zoology.
Graduation Requirements English, foreign language, French, mathematics, physical education (includes health), science, social sciences, social studies (includes history), examination (French Baccalaureate with International option).
Special Academic Programs Advanced Placement exam preparation; honors section.
College Admission Counseling 63 students graduated in 2010; all went to college, including Duke University; Harvard University; McGill University; New York University; Rhode Island School of Design; Tufts University. 73.4% scored over 600 on SAT critical reading, 73.4% scored over 600 on SAT math.
Student Life Upper grades have student council. Discipline rests primarily with faculty.
Tuition and Aid Day student tuition: €3250–€7500. Tuition installment plan (monthly payment plans). Tuition reduction for siblings, need-based scholarship grants available. In 2010–11, 5% of upper-school students received aid. Total amount of financial aid awarded in 2010–11: €30,000.
Admissions Traditional secondary-level entrance grade is 10. For fall 2010, 34 students applied for upper-level admission, 10 were accepted, 8 enrolled. Admissions testing required. Deadline for receipt of application materials: none. Application fee required: $250. On-campus interview recommended.
Athletics Intramural: badminton (boys, girls), basketball (b,g), climbing (b,g), judo (b), martial arts (b), rugby (b), soccer (b,g), tennis (b,g), track and field (b,g), volleyball (b,g), wall climbing (b,g); coed intramural: swimming and diving, table tennis. 9 PE instructors.
Computers Computers are regularly used in mathematics, technology classes. Computer resources include on-campus library services, Internet access.
Contact Mrs. Mary Friel, Director of Admissions. 33-1-34-51-90-92. Fax: 33-1 30 87 00 49. E-mail: admissions@americansection.org. Web site: www.americansection.org.

LYDIA PATTERSON INSTITUTE

517 South Florence Street

El Paso, Texas 79901-2998

Head of School: Mr. Hector Lachica

General Information Coeducational day college-preparatory, arts, religious studies, bilingual studies, and technology school, affiliated with United Methodist Church. Grades 9–12. Founded: 1913. Setting: urban. 1-acre campus. 5 buildings on campus. Approved or accredited by Southern Association of Colleges and Schools, University Senate of United Methodist Church, and Texas Department of Education. Languages of instruction: English and Spanish. Endowment: $5 million. Total enrollment: 399. Upper school average class size: 20. Upper school faculty-student ratio: 1:20. There are 183 required school days per year for Upper School students. Upper School students typically attend 5 days per week. The average school day consists of 6 hours and 45 minutes.
Upper School Student Profile Grade 9: 40 students (21 boys, 19 girls); Grade 10: 49 students (24 boys, 25 girls); Grade 11: 56 students (24 boys, 32 girls); Grade 12: 86 students (39 boys, 47 girls). 2% of students are United Methodist Church.
Faculty School total: 26. In upper school: 16 men, 10 women; 5 have advanced degrees.
Subjects Offered Computer science, economics, English, fine arts, foreign language, health, mathematics, physical education, religion, U.S. government, U.S. history, world geography, world history.
Graduation Requirements Arts and fine arts (art, music, dance, drama), computer science, economics, English, foreign language, mathematics, physical education (includes health), religion (includes Bible studies and theology), science, U.S. government, U.S. history, world history, world history, world geography.
Special Academic Programs International Baccalaureate program; Advanced Placement exam preparation; honors section; accelerated programs; independent study; study at local college for college credit; academic accommodation for the gifted; special instructional classes for deaf students; ESL (182 students enrolled).
College Admission Counseling 82 students graduated in 2010; 79 went to college, including El Paso Community College; MacMurray College; The University of Texas at El Paso. Other: 3 went to work. Median SAT critical reading: 400, median SAT math: 401, median SAT writing: 380, median combined SAT: 1170.
Student Life Upper grades have uniform requirement, student council. Discipline rests equally with students and faculty. Attendance at religious services is required.
Tuition and Aid Day student tuition: $2430. Tuition installment plan (monthly payment plans). Need-based scholarship grants available. In 2010–11, 30% of upper-school students received aid. Total amount of financial aid awarded in 2010–11: $157,950.
Admissions Traditional secondary-level entrance grade is 9. English entrance exam required. Deadline for receipt of application materials: none. Application fee required: $270. On-campus interview required.
Athletics Interscholastic: basketball (boys, girls), cross-country running (b,g), dance (b), soccer (b,g), track and field (b,g), volleyball (b,g), weight lifting (b,g); intramural: baseball (b), basketball (b,g), dance (b), soccer (b,g), track and field (b,g), volleyball (b,g); coed interscholastic: dance team. 2 PE instructors, 4 coaches.
Computers Computers are regularly used in yearbook classes. Computer network features include on-campus library services, online commercial services, Internet access, wireless campus network. Campus intranet and student e-mail accounts are available to students.
Contact Mr. Hector Lachica, Vice President for Academic Affairs. 915-533-8286 Ext. 20. Fax: 915-533-5236. E-mail: hlachica@lydiapattersoninstitute.org. Web site: www.lydiapattersoninstitute.org.

LYMAN WARD MILITARY ACADEMY

PO Box 550 P

174 Ward Circle

Camp Hill, Alabama 36850-0550

Head of School: Col. Albert W. Jenrette

General Information Boys' boarding and distance learning college-preparatory and military school, affiliated with Christian faith; primarily serves underachievers. Grades 6–12. Distance learning grades 11–12. Founded: 1898. Setting: small town. Nearest major city is Birmingham. Students are housed in single-sex dormitories. 300-acre campus. 23 buildings on campus. Approved or accredited by Southern Association of Colleges and Schools and Alabama Department of Education. Member of National Association of Independent Schools. Total enrollment: 115. Upper school average class size: 15. Upper school faculty-student ratio: 1:15. There are 180 required school days per year for Upper School students. Upper School students typically attend 5 days per week. The average school day consists of 7 hours.
Upper School Student Profile Grade 9: 20 students (20 boys); Grade 10: 20 students (20 boys); Grade 11: 20 students (20 boys); Grade 12: 25 students (25 boys). 100% of students are boarding students. 50% are state residents. 15 states are represented in upper school student body. 1% are international students. International students from Colombia, Germany, Guatemala, and Mexico; 4 other countries represented in student body. 85% of students are Christian faith.
Faculty School total: 14. In upper school: 8 men, 4 women; 6 have advanced degrees; 2 reside on campus.
Subjects Offered Advanced Placement courses, algebra, band, biology, chemistry, computers, economics, English, geometry, government, health, JROTC, physical science, physiology, pre-algebra, pre-calculus, reading, Spanish, trigonometry, U.S. history, world history.
Special Academic Programs Advanced Placement exam preparation; honors section; remedial reading and/or remedial writing; remedial math.
College Admission Counseling 26 students graduated in 2011; 15 went to college, including Auburn University; Clemson University; Florida State University; North Georgia College & State University; The Citadel, The Military College of South Carolina; The University of Alabama. Other: 5 went to work, 6 entered military service. 5%

scored over 600 on SAT critical reading, 5% scored over 600 on SAT math, 5% scored over 26 on composite ACT.

Student Life Upper grades have uniform requirement, student council, honor system. Discipline rests primarily with faculty. Attendance at religious services is required.

Summer Programs Remediation, enrichment, advancement, rigorous outdoor training programs offered; session focuses on leadership training through challenging exercises; held both on and off campus; held at Lake Martin, Natahalla River, and Mt. Cheaha; accepts boys; open to students from other schools. 25 students usually enrolled. 2012 schedule: June 16 to July 11. Application deadline: none.

Tuition and Aid 7-day tuition and room/board: $16,000. Tuition installment plan (monthly payment plans). Tuition reduction for siblings, merit scholarship grants, need-based scholarship grants available. In 2011–12, 10% of upper-school students received aid. Total amount of financial aid awarded in 2011–12: $50,000.

Admissions Traditional secondary-level entrance grade is 9. Star-9 required. Deadline for receipt of application materials: none. Application fee required: $250. Interview recommended.

Athletics Interscholastic: baseball, basketball, drill team, football, JROTC drill, marksmanship, riflery, soccer; intramural: aquatics, archery, basketball, billiards, canoeing/kayaking, cross-country running, drill team, fishing, fitness, flag football, football, Frisbee, hiking/backpacking, JROTC drill, life saving, marksmanship, outdoor activities, physical fitness, physical training, project adventure, rafting, rappelling, riflery, ropes courses, running, soccer, softball, strength & conditioning, swimming and diving, table tennis, tennis, ultimate Frisbee, volleyball. 2 PE instructors, 3 coaches, 1 athletic trainer.

Computers Computer resources include on-campus library services, Internet access, Internet filtering or blocking technology. Student e-mail accounts are available to students. The school has a published electronic and media policy.

Contact Maj. Joe C. Watson, Assistant to the President/Admissions. 256-896-4127. Fax: 256-896-4661. E-mail: info@lwma.org. Web site: www.lwma.org.

LYNDON INSTITUTE

PO Box 127

College Road

Lyndon Center, Vermont 05850-0127

General Information Coeducational boarding and day college-preparatory, general academic, arts, business, technology, and ESL school. Boarding grades 8–12, day grades 9–12. Founded: 1867. Setting: small town. Nearest major city is Burlington. Students are housed in single-sex dormitories. 150-acre campus. 27 buildings on campus. Approved or accredited by Independent Schools of Northern New England, New England Association of Schools and Colleges, The Association of Boarding Schools, and Vermont Department of Education. Endowment: $8 million. Total enrollment: 626. Upper school average class size: 16. Upper school faculty-student ratio: 1:10.

See Display on next page and Close-Up on page 642.

MacLACHLAN COLLEGE

337 Trafalgar Road

Oakville, Ontario L6J 3H3, Canada

Head of School: Mr. Michael Piening

General Information Coeducational day college-preparatory, arts, business, and technology school. Grades PK–12. Founded: 1978. Setting: suburban. Nearest major city is Toronto, Canada. 2-acre campus. 1 building on campus. Approved or accredited by Canadian Association of Independent Schools, Canadian Educational Standards Institute, Conference of Independent Schools of Ontario, Ontario Ministry of Education, and Ontario Department of Education. Language of instruction: English. Total enrollment: 344. Upper school average class size: 18. Upper school faculty-student ratio: 1:10. Upper School students typically attend 5 days per week. The average school day consists of 6 hours and 45 minutes.

Upper School Student Profile Grade 9: 28 students (17 boys, 11 girls); Grade 10: 36 students (21 boys, 15 girls); Grade 11: 37 students (21 boys, 16 girls); Grade 12: 32 students (23 boys, 9 girls).

Faculty School total: 30. In upper school: 2 men, 12 women; 7 have advanced degrees.

Subjects Offered 20th century history, accounting, algebra, band, business, business law, business mathematics, calculus, Canadian geography, Canadian history, Canadian law, Canadian literature, career education, chemistry, civics, computer multimedia, computer programming, computer science, drama, economics, English, environmental science, ESL, finite math, French, geography, geometry, health, history, law, marketing, mathematics, multimedia, physical education, physics, science, society challenge and change, TOEFL preparation, visual arts.

Graduation Requirements Arts, careers, civics, English, French, geography, history, mathematics, physical education (includes health), science, pass the grade 10 Ontario Literacy test, 40 hours of community service.

Special Academic Programs Advanced Placement exam preparation; accelerated programs; independent study; ESL (30 students enrolled).

College Admission Counseling 36 students graduated in 2011; they went to Carleton University; Ryerson University; The University of Western Ontario; University of Toronto; University of Waterloo; York University. Other: 36 entered a postgraduate year.

Student Life Upper grades have uniform requirement, student council, honor system. Discipline rests primarily with faculty.

Tuition and Aid Day student tuition: CAN$18,350. Tuition installment plan (monthly payment plans). Tuition reduction for siblings, bursaries available. In 2011–12, 1% of upper-school students received aid. Total amount of financial aid awarded in 2011–12: CAN$9000.

Admissions Traditional secondary-level entrance grade is 11. Deadline for receipt of application materials: none. Application fee required: CAN$250. Interview required.

Athletics Interscholastic: aerobics (boys), wrestling (b); intramural: ball hockey (b), baseball (b,g), basketball (b,g), flag football (b,g), floor hockey (b,g), soccer (b,g), softball (b,g), touch football (b,g), ultimate Frisbee (b,g), volleyball (b,g), wilderness survival (b,g); coed interscholastic: aerobics, archery, backpacking, badminton, ball hockey, baseball, basketball, bowling, canoeing/kayaking, cooperative games, cricket, cross-country running, curling, field hockey, fitness, fitness walking, flag football, flagball, floor hockey, football, golf, gymnastics, hiking/backpacking, ice skating, lacrosse, outdoor activities, outdoor adventure, outdoor education, physical fitness, racquetball, running, soccer, softball, touch football, ultimate Frisbee, volleyball, wilderness survival; coed intramural: football, hiking/backpacking, independent competitive sports. 2 PE instructors.

Computers Computers are regularly used in accounting, art, basic skills, business, business applications, business education, business studies, career education, career exploration, career technology, commercial art, computer applications, creative writing, data processing, design, desktop publishing, digital applications, economics, English, ESL, French, geography, graphic arts, health, history, humanities, information technology, library, mathematics, media arts, multimedia, music, programming, reading, research skills, science, theology, Web site design, wilderness education, writing, writing, yearbook classes. Computer network features include on-campus library services, Internet access, wireless campus network, Internet filtering or blocking technology. Campus intranet, student e-mail accounts, and computer access in designated common areas are available to students. The school has a published electronic and media policy.

Contact Ms. Nancy Norcross, Director of Admissions. 905-844-0372 Ext. 235. Fax: 905-844-9369. E-mail: nnorcross@maclachlan.ca. Web site: www.maclachlan.ca.

MADISON ACADEMY

325 Slaughter Road

Madison, Alabama 35758

Head of School: Dr. Robert F. Burton

General Information Coeducational day college-preparatory and religious studies school, affiliated with Church of Christ. Grades PS–12. Founded: 1955. Setting: suburban. Nearest major city is Huntsville. 160-acre campus. 5 buildings on campus. Approved or accredited by Southern Association of Colleges and Schools. Endowment: $1.2 million. Total enrollment: 900. Upper school average class size: 20. Upper school faculty-student ratio: 1:15.

Upper School Student Profile 35% of students are members of Church of Christ.

Faculty School total: 70. In upper school: 14 men, 20 women; 14 have advanced degrees.

Subjects Offered Accounting, advanced math, Alabama history and geography, algebra, American literature, anatomy, art, art history, arts, band, Bible studies, biology, calculus, calculus-AP, chemistry, choral music, chorus, Christian education, Christian ethics, Christian scripture, Christian studies, church history, community service, computer science, concert choir, consumer mathematics, creative writing, drama, earth science, economics, English, English literature, English/composition-AP, environmental science, European history, expository writing, French, general math, geography, geology, geometry, government/civics, health, human anatomy, journalism, keyboarding, music, photography, physical education, physical science, physics, physics-AP, physiology, pre-algebra, religion, Spanish, speech, studio art, trigonometry, U.S. government, U.S. government and politics, U.S. history, world geography, world history, world literature.

Graduation Requirements English, foreign language, mathematics, religion (includes Bible studies and theology), science, social sciences.

Special Academic Programs Honors section; accelerated programs; study at local college for college credit.

College Admission Counseling 70 students graduated in 2011; all went to college, including Abilene Christian University; Auburn University; Freed-Hardeman University; Lipscomb University; The University of Alabama. Mean composite ACT: 23.

Student Life Upper grades have uniform requirement, student council, honor system. Discipline rests primarily with faculty. Attendance at religious services is required.

Tuition and Aid Day student tuition: $4450. Tuition installment plan (monthly payment plans). Tuition reduction for siblings, need-based scholarship grants available. In 2011–12, 10% of upper-school students received aid. Total amount of financial aid awarded in 2011–12: $100,000.

Admissions Traditional secondary-level entrance grade is 9. For fall 2011, 100 students applied for upper-level admission, 50 were accepted, 41 enrolled. Stanford Achievement Test required. Deadline for receipt of application materials: none. Application fee required: $200. On-campus interview required.

Athletics Interscholastic: baseball (boys), basketball (b,g), cheering (g), football (b), golf (b), softball (g), volleyball (g). 3 PE instructors, 36 coaches, 1 athletic trainer.

Computers Computers are regularly used in art, foreign language, science classes. Computer network features include on-campus library services, Internet access.

Contact Dr. Michael Weimer, High School Principal. 256-971-1624. Fax: 256-971-1436. E-mail: mweimer@macademy.org. Web site: www.macademy.org.

MADISON-RIDGELAND ACADEMY

7601 Old Canton Road

Madison, Mississippi 39110

Head of School: Tommy Thompson

General Information Coeducational day college-preparatory school, affiliated with Christian faith. Grades 1–12. Founded: 1969. Setting: suburban. Nearest major city is Jackson. 25-acre campus. 6 buildings on campus. Approved or accredited by Mississippi Private School Association, Southern Association of Colleges and Schools, Southern Association of Independent Schools, and Mississippi Department of Education. Endowment: $1 million. Total enrollment: 906. Upper school average class size: 18. Upper school faculty-student ratio: 1:13. There are 180 required school days per year for Upper School students. Upper School students typically attend 5 days per week. The average school day consists of 7 hours and 15 minutes.

Upper School Student Profile Grade 9: 72 students (40 boys, 32 girls); Grade 10: 68 students (43 boys, 25 girls); Grade 11: 59 students (32 boys, 27 girls); Grade 12: 55 students (36 boys, 19 girls). 99% of students are Christian faith.

Faculty School total: 64. In upper school: 10 men, 48 women; 20 have advanced degrees.

Subjects Offered Accounting, algebra, American government, American history, American history-AP, anatomy and physiology, art, Bible, biology, biology-AP, chemistry, chemistry-AP, chorus, civics, communications, computer applications, computer programming, creative writing, debate, drama, driver education, economics, English, European history-AP, forensics, French, French-AP, geography, geometry, global studies, government, graphic arts, health, journalism, keyboarding, music, newspaper, physical fitness, physics, physics-AP, pre-calculus, probability and statistics, psychology, sociology, Spanish, Spanish-AP, speech, trigonometry, U.S. government and politics-AP, Web site design, world history, yearbook.

Graduation Requirements ACT preparation, advanced math, algebra, American government, biology, chemistry, civics, computer applications, economics, electives, English, foreign language, geometry, health, keyboarding, science, social studies (includes history).

Special Academic Programs Advanced Placement exam preparation; honors section; study at local college for college credit; academic accommodation for the gifted.

College Admission Counseling 56 students graduated in 2011; all went to college, including Belhaven University; Millsaps College; Mississippi College; Mississippi State University; University of Mississippi; University of Southern Mississippi. Median SAT critical reading: 705, median SAT math: 620, median composite ACT: 24. 100% scored over 600 on SAT critical reading, 100% scored over 600 on SAT math, 25% scored over 26 on composite ACT.

Student Life Upper grades have uniform requirement, student council, honor system. Discipline rests primarily with faculty. Attendance at religious services is required.

Summer Programs Enrichment, sports programs offered; held on campus; accepts boys and girls; open to students from other schools. 300 students usually enrolled. 2012 schedule: June 1 to July 30. Application deadline: May 15.

Tuition and Aid Day student tuition: $7680. Tuition installment plan (monthly payment plans, semiannual payment plan). Tuition reduction for siblings, merit scholarship grants, need-based scholarship grants available. In 2011–12, 3% of upper-school students received aid; total upper-school merit-scholarship money awarded: $21,300. Total amount of financial aid awarded in 2011–12: $170,000.

Admissions Traditional secondary-level entrance grade is 9. For fall 2011, 30 students applied for upper-level admission, 23 were accepted, 18 enrolled. Admissions testing, BASIS or Otis-Lennon Ability or Stanford Achievement Test required. Deadline for receipt of application materials: none. Application fee required: $35. On-campus interview required.

Athletics Interscholastic: aquatics (boys, girls), baseball (b), basketball (b,g), cheering (g), cross-country running (b,g), dance team (g), football (b), golf (b), soccer (b,g), softball (g), strength & conditioning (b,g), tennis (b,g), track and field (b,g), volleyball (g); coed interscholastic: aquatics, golf, tennis. 4 PE instructors, 12 coaches, 1 athletic trainer.

Computers Computers are regularly used in accounting, art, business applications, journalism, media, media services, Web site design classes. Computer network features include on-campus library services, Internet access, Internet filtering or blocking technology, Naviance (college guidance). Students grades are available online. The school has a published electronic and media policy.

Contact Mrs. Tammy Synder, Registrar. 601-856-4455. Fax: 601-853-3835. E-mail: tsnyder@mrapats.org. Web site: www.mrapats.com.

MAGNIFICAT HIGH SCHOOL

20770 Hilliard Boulevard

Rocky River, Ohio 44116

Head of School: Sr. Carol Anne Smith, HM

General Information Girls' day college-preparatory school, affiliated with Roman Catholic Church. Grades 9–12. Founded: 1955. Setting: suburban. Nearest major city is Cleveland. 20-acre campus. 1 building on campus. Approved or accredited by North Central Association of Colleges and Schools, Ohio Catholic Schools Accreditation Association (OCSAA), and Ohio Department of Education. Total enrollment: 800. Upper school average class size: 22. Upper school faculty-student ratio: 1:12. The average school day consists of 5 hours and 55 minutes.

Upper School Student Profile 93% of students are Roman Catholic.

Faculty School total: 77. In upper school: 4 men, 70 women; 42 have advanced degrees.

Subjects Offered Accounting, algebra, American literature, Arabic, art, art history, art history-AP, arts, band, biology, biology-AP, British literature, business, business technology, calculus-AP, chemistry, chemistry-AP, Chinese, choir, chorus, clayworking, comparative religion, computer applications, computer science-AP, CPR, dance, design, drama, drawing, earth science, economics, economics-AP, electives, English, film and literature, first aid, French, French-AP, geometry, government, health, keyboarding, life issues, mathematics, metalworking, modern languages, music, oral communications, orchestra, painting, photography, physical education, physics, pre-calculus, probability and statistics, programming, psychology, science, social studies, sociology, Spanish, Spanish-AP, statistics, statistics-AP, theology, trigonometry, U.S. history, U.S. history-AP, Web site design, world history, world history-AP, world literature, writing.

Graduation Requirements Art appreciation, electives, English, health education, keyboarding, mathematics, modern languages, physical education (includes health), science, social studies (includes history), theology, word processing, service requirements and senior Genesis Project.

Special Academic Programs 12 Advanced Placement exams for which test preparation is offered; honors section.

College Admission Counseling 205 students graduated in 2011; all went to college, including John Carroll University; Miami University; Ohio University; The Ohio State University; University of Cincinnati; University of Dayton. Mean SAT critical reading: 554, mean SAT math: 544, mean SAT writing: 557, mean composite ACT: 25.

Student Life Upper grades have uniform requirement, student council. Attendance at religious services is required.

Tuition and Aid Day student tuition: $10,900. Tuition installment plan (SMART Tuition Payment Plan). Merit scholarship grants, need-based scholarship grants available. In 2011–12, 46% of upper-school students received aid; total upper-school merit-scholarship money awarded: $82,500. Total amount of financial aid awarded in 2011–12: $900,000.

Admissions Traditional secondary-level entrance grade is 9. High School Placement Test (closed version) from Scholastic Testing Service required. Deadline for receipt of application materials: January 28. No application fee required.

Athletics Interscholastic: basketball, cross-country running, dance team, diving, field hockey, golf, gymnastics, lacrosse, soccer, softball, swimming and diving, tennis, track and field, volleyball. 3 PE instructors, 53 coaches, 1 athletic trainer.

Computers Computers are regularly used in all academic classes. Computer network features include on-campus library services, Internet access. Computer access in designated common areas is available to students. Students grades are available online. The school has a published electronic and media policy.

Contact Ms. Heather Schwager, Director of Admissions. 440-331-1572 Ext. 248. Fax: 440-331-7257. E-mail: hschwager@magnificaths.org. Web site: www.magnificaths.org.

MAHARISHI SCHOOL OF THE AGE OF ENLIGHTENMENT

804 Dr. Robert Keith Wallace Drive

Fairfield, Iowa 52556-2200

Head of School: Dr. Richard Beall

General Information Coeducational boarding and day college-preparatory, arts, Science of Creative Intelligence: the study of Natural Law, and Transcendental Meditation: Research in Consciousness school. Boarding grades 9–12, day grades PS–12. Founded: 1972. Setting: small town. Nearest major city is Iowa City. Students are housed in boarding students live with host families. 10-acre campus. 5 buildings on campus. Approved or accredited by Independent Schools Association of the Central States and Iowa Department of Education. Member of National Association of Independent Schools. Total enrollment: 204. Upper school average class size: 11. There are 186 required school days per year for Upper School students. Upper School students typically attend 5 days per week. The average school day consists of 9 hours.

Upper School Student Profile Grade 10: 26 students (15 boys, 11 girls); Grade 11: 20 students (13 boys, 7 girls); Grade 12: 15 students (9 boys, 6 girls).

Faculty School total: 54. In upper school: 11 men, 17 women; 12 have advanced degrees.

Subjects Offered Algebra, American government, American history, American literature, art, art history, basketball, British literature, business mathematics, chemistry, computer science, desktop publishing, digital photography, drama performance, driver education, economics, electives, environmental education, ESL, general math, integrated mathematics, photography, physical education, physiology, pre-calculus, Sanskrit, science project, senior thesis, track and field, Vedic science, vocal music, volleyball, world history, world literature, writing, yoga.

Graduation Requirements Art history, computer science, economics, electives, English, foreign language, mathematics, physical education (includes health), science, senior thesis, social studies (includes history), writing, Science of Creative Intelligence course, student etiquette.

Special Academic Programs Honors section; academic accommodation for the gifted, the musically talented, and the artistically talented; remedial reading and/or remedial writing; remedial math; ESL (15 students enrolled).

College Admission Counseling 20 students graduated in 2011; 19 went to college, including Chapman University; Georgetown University; Haverford College; Maharishi University of Management; The University of Iowa; University of California, Berkeley. Other: 1 had other specific plans. Median SAT critical reading: 620, median SAT math: 600, median SAT writing: 630, median combined SAT: 1880, median composite ACT: 29. 55% scored over 600 on SAT critical reading, 45% scored over 600 on SAT math, 64% scored over 600 on SAT writing, 55% scored over 1800 on combined SAT, 70% scored over 26 on composite ACT.

Student Life Upper grades have uniform requirement, student council. Discipline rests primarily with faculty.

Summer Programs Enrichment, ESL, sports, art/fine arts programs offered; session focuses on interscholastic sports, arts; held both on and off campus; held at neighboring schools and universities; accepts boys and girls; not open to students from other schools. 40 students usually enrolled. 2012 schedule: June 15 to August 15. Application deadline: June 12.

Tuition and Aid Day student tuition: $13,900. Tuition installment plan (two semester payments). Tuition reduction for siblings, need-based scholarship grants available. In 2011–12, 85% of upper-school students received aid.

Admissions Traditional secondary-level entrance grade is 10. For fall 2011, 18 students applied for upper-level admission, 18 were accepted, 18 enrolled. Deadline for receipt of application materials: none. No application fee required. Interview required.

Athletics Interscholastic: basketball (boys, girls), cheering (g), dance team (g), golf (b), indoor track & field (b,g), soccer (b), tennis (b,g), track and field (b,g), volleyball (g), winter (indoor) track (b,g); intramural: archery (b), badminton (b,g), ballet (g), baseball (b), basketball (b,g), canoeing/kayaking (b,g), dance (g), equestrian sports (g), fitness (b,g), fitness walking (g), handball (b,g), hiking/backpacking (b,g), jogging (b,g), life saving (b,g), modern dance (g), outdoor activities (b,g), outdoor recreation (b,g), physical fitness (b,g), physical training (b,g), running (b,g), strength & conditioning (b,g), table tennis (b,g), tennis (b,g), volleyball (g), wall climbing (b,g), winter (indoor) track (b,g), yoga (b,g). 3 PE instructors, 11 coaches.

Computers Computers are regularly used in business education, creative writing, desktop publishing, economics, English, ESL, geography, graphic design, history, independent study, library, library science, library skills, literacy, mathematics, multimedia, photography, programming, publications, science, senior seminar, social sciences, social studies, stock market, typing, video film production, writing classes. Computer network features include Internet access, Internet filtering or blocking technology, file and portfolio management. Campus intranet and computer access in designated common areas are available to students. Students grades are available online. The school has a published electronic and media policy.

Contact Ms. Noelle Boucherle, Director of Admissions. 641-472-9400 Ext. 5076. Fax: 641-472-1211. E-mail: nboucherle@msae.edu. Web site: www.maharishischooliowa.org.

MAINE CENTRAL INSTITUTE

295 Main Street

Pittsfield, Maine 04967

Head of School: Christopher Hopkins

General Information Coeducational boarding and day college-preparatory, general academic, arts, vocational, bilingual studies, technology, humanities, and mathematics, the sciences school. Grades 9–PG. Founded: 1866. Setting: small town. Nearest major city is Portland. Students are housed in single-sex dormitories and honors dorm is coed. 23-acre campus. Approved or accredited by Independent Schools of Northern New England, Massachusetts Department of Education, New England Association of Schools and Colleges, The Association of Boarding Schools, and Maine Department of Education. Member of National Association of Independent Schools and Secondary School Admission Test Board. Total enrollment: 464. Upper school average class size: 16. Upper school faculty-student ratio: 1:14. There are 175 required school days per year for Upper School students. Upper School students typically attend 5 days per week. The average school day consists of 7 hours and 15 minutes.

Upper School Student Profile Grade 9: 94 students (48 boys, 46 girls); Grade 10: 103 students (61 boys, 42 girls); Grade 11: 123 students (61 boys, 62 girls); Grade 12: 133 students (75 boys, 58 girls); Postgraduate: 11 students (11 boys). 71% are state residents. 11 states are represented in upper school student body. 85% are international students.

Faculty School total: 41. In upper school: 20 men, 21 women; 14 have advanced degrees; 25 reside on campus.

Subjects Offered Algebra, American history, American literature, anatomy, art, art-AP, Asian studies, astronomy, audio visual/media, ballet, biology, botany, calculus, calculus-AP, career exploration, chemistry, chemistry-AP, child development, civil rights, computer science, concert band, concert choir, contemporary issues, creative writing, drafting, drama, earth science, ecology, economics, electronic publishing, English, English literature, environmental science, ESL, ethics, fine arts, French, geology, geometry, government/civics, health, history, humanities, integrated science, jazz band, jazz dance, jazz ensemble, Latin, life management skills, literature-AP, mathematics, meteorology, music, music appreciation, music composition, music theory, personal finance, philosophy, photography, physical education, physics, physics-AP, piano, psychology, reading/study skills, SAT preparation, science, social sciences, social studies, sociology, Spanish, statistics, theater, trigonometry, video film production, Web site design, world history.

Graduation Requirements Arts and fine arts (art, music, dance, drama), computer skills, English, mathematics, physical education (includes health), science, senior project, social studies (includes history), Manson essay.

Special Academic Programs Advanced Placement exam preparation; honors section; accelerated programs; independent study; study at local college for college credit; study abroad; academic accommodation for the musically talented; remedial reading and/or remedial writing; remedial math; programs in English, mathematics, general development for dyslexic students; ESL (70 students enrolled).

College Admission Counseling 115 students graduated in 2011; 90 went to college, including Husson University; Maine Maritime Academy; University of Maine; University of Maine at Farmington; University of Southern Maine. Other: 15 went to work, 3 entered military service, 6 had other specific plans. Median SAT critical reading: 428, median SAT math: 444, median SAT writing: 442, median combined SAT: 1314.

Student Life Upper grades have specified standards of dress, student council, honor system. Discipline rests primarily with faculty.

Summer Programs ESL, art/fine arts programs offered; session focuses on basic ESL, summer ballet; held on campus; accepts boys and girls; open to students from other schools. 35 students usually enrolled. 2012 schedule: July to August. Application deadline: none.

Tuition and Aid Day student tuition: $10,000; 7-day tuition and room/board: $39,900. Tuition installment plan (Key Tuition Payment Plan, SMART Tuition Payment Plan, school's own payment plan). Merit scholarship grants, need-based scholarship grants available. In 2011–12, 25% of upper-school students received aid; total upper-school merit-scholarship money awarded: $24,430. Total amount of financial aid awarded in 2011–12: $705,450.

Admissions Traditional secondary-level entrance grade is 9. For fall 2011, 378 students applied for upper-level admission, 344 were accepted, 136 enrolled. Deadline for receipt of application materials: none. Application fee required: $50. Interview recommended.

Athletics Interscholastic: baseball (boys), basketball (b,g), field hockey (g), football (b), riflery (b,g); intramural: football (b); coed interscholastic: aerobics/dance, alpine skiing, ballet, cheering, cross-country running, dance, fencing, golf, modern dance, physical training; coed intramural: alpine skiing, backpacking, basketball, billiards, canoeing/kayaking, climbing, cooperative games, fencing, fishing, flagball, floor hockey, handball, outdoor activities, rafting. 1 PE instructor, 30 coaches, 1 athletic trainer.

Computers Computer network features include on-campus library services, Internet access, wireless campus network, Internet filtering or blocking technology. Student e-mail accounts are available to students. Students grades are available online.

Contact Mr. Clint M. Williams, Director of Admission. 207-487-2282 Ext. 128. Fax: 207-487-3512. E-mail: cwilliams@mci-school.org. Web site: www.mci-school.org.

See Display below and Close-Up on page 644.

MALDEN CATHOLIC HIGH SCHOOL

99 Crystal Street

Malden, Massachusetts 02148

Head of School: Mr. Edward Tyrrell

General Information Boys' day college-preparatory, arts, business, religious studies, bilingual studies, and technology school, affiliated with Roman Catholic Church; primarily serves students with learning disabilities and individuals with Attention Deficit Disorder. Grades 9–12. Founded: 1932. Setting: urban. Nearest major city is Boston. 15-acre campus. 1 building on campus. Approved or accredited by New England Association of Schools and Colleges and Massachusetts Department of Education.

Endowment: $2 million. Total enrollment: 700. Upper school average class size: 23. Upper school faculty-student ratio: 1:13. The average school day consists of 6 hours.

Upper School Student Profile Grade 9: 214 students (214 boys); Grade 10: 154 students (154 boys); Grade 11: 162 students (162 boys); Grade 12: 157 students (157 boys). 85% of students are Roman Catholic.

Faculty School total: 52. In upper school: 40 men, 12 women; 43 have advanced degrees.

Subjects Offered 20th century history, 3-dimensional art, accounting, advanced chemistry, advanced math, Advanced Placement courses, algebra, American government, American history-AP, American literature, ancient world history, art, art appreciation, art history, Asian history, athletics, basic language skills, Bible studies, biology, British literature, British literature (honors), British literature-AP, business, calculus-AP, campus ministry, Chinese history, Christian and Hebrew scripture, Christian testament, college admission preparation, community service, computer programming, computer skills, desktop publishing, English language and composition-AP, English-AP, European history, European history-AP, fine arts, foreign language, French, French language-AP, genetics, geometry, global studies, government, health and safety, honors algebra, honors English, honors geometry, honors U.S. history, honors world history, independent study, integrated science, language arts, leadership and service, library studies, marine biology, marine science, math analysis, modern European history, music appreciation, physical education, psychology, religion, SAT preparation, Spanish, Spanish language-AP, studio art, the Sixties, U.S. history, U.S. history-AP, world history, world history-AP.

Graduation Requirements Algebra, American literature, arts and fine arts (art, music, dance, drama), biology, British literature, Catholic belief and practice, chemistry, computer skills, foreign language, geometry, global studies, mathematics, physical education (includes health), religion (includes Bible studies and theology), science, social studies (includes history), Christian service.

Special Academic Programs 12 Advanced Placement exams for which test preparation is offered; honors section; independent study.

College Admission Counseling 175 students graduated in 2011; 170 went to college, including Assumption College; Boston College; Boston University; Merrimack College; Northeastern University; Salem State University. Other: 3 went to work, 2 entered military service.

Student Life Upper grades have specified standards of dress, student council, honor system. Discipline rests primarily with faculty. Attendance at religious services is required.

Summer Programs Enrichment, advancement, sports programs offered; session focuses on academic preparation/college preparation; held on campus; accepts boys and girls; open to students from other schools. 100 students usually enrolled. 2012 schedule: July 6 to July 28. Application deadline: July 1.

Tuition and Aid Day student tuition: $11,900. Tuition installment plan (FACTS Tuition Payment Plan, monthly payment plans). Merit scholarship grants, need-based scholarship grants, paying campus jobs available. In 2011–12, 40% of upper-school students received aid; total upper-school merit-scholarship money awarded: $300,000. Total amount of financial aid awarded in 2011–12: $300,000.

Admissions Traditional secondary-level entrance grade is 9. For fall 2011, 400 students applied for upper-level admission, 300 were accepted, 170 enrolled. Archdiocese of Boston High School entrance exam provided by STS required. Deadline for receipt of application materials: December 15. No application fee required. Interview recommended.

Athletics Interscholastic: baseball, basketball, cross-country running, football, golf, hockey, ice hockey, indoor track, indoor track & field, lacrosse, soccer, swimming and diving, tennis, track and field, winter (indoor) track, wrestling; intramural: alpine skiing, badminton, ball hockey, basketball, fitness, flag football, floor hockey, Frisbee, jogging, lacrosse, life saving, nordic skiing, physical fitness, physical training, rugby, skiing (downhill), snowboarding, strength & conditioning, table tennis, weight lifting, weight training. 2 PE instructors, 15 coaches, 1 athletic trainer.

Computers Computers are regularly used in all academic, basic skills, business applications, business studies, design, desktop publishing, graphic arts, graphic design, graphics, information technology, journalism, library, library skills, multimedia, news writing, photography, photojournalism, religion, study skills, technology, theology, Web site design, word processing classes. Computer network features include on-campus library services, online commercial services, Internet access, wireless campus network, Internet filtering or blocking technology. Students grades are available online. The school has a published electronic and media policy.

Contact Mr. Matthew O'Neil, Associate Director of Admissions. 781-475-5308. Fax: 781-397-0573. E-mail: oneilm@maldencatholic.org. Web site: www.maldencatholic.org.

MANHATTAN CHRISTIAN HIGH SCHOOL

8000 Churchill Road

Manhattan, Montana 59741

Head of School: Mr. Gary Kamps

General Information Coeducational day and distance learning college-preparatory, general academic, arts, business, religious studies, and technology school, affiliated with Christian Reformed Church, Christian faith. Grades PK–12. Distance learning grades 9–12. Founded: 1907. Setting: rural. Nearest major city is Bozeman. 20-acre campus. 1 building on campus. Approved or accredited by Christian Schools International, Office for Standards in Education (OFSTED), The College Board, home study, and Montana Department of Education. Endowment: $5 million. Total enrollment: 290. Upper school average class size: 15. Upper school faculty-student ratio: 1:10. There are 175 required school days per year for Upper School students. Upper School students typically attend 5 days per week. The average school day consists of 6 hours and 19 minutes.

Upper School Student Profile Grade 9: 11 students (5 boys, 6 girls); Grade 10: 21 students (15 boys, 6 girls); Grade 11: 19 students (9 boys, 10 girls); Grade 12: 36 students (21 boys, 15 girls). 50% of students are members of Christian Reformed Church, Christian faith.

Faculty School total: 17. In upper school: 4 men, 4 women; 2 have advanced degrees.

Subjects Offered Art, Bible studies, business, community service, English, general science, internship, mathematics, music, physical education, senior project, social studies, Spanish.

Graduation Requirements Arts and fine arts (art, music, dance, drama), business skills (includes word processing), English, mathematics, physical education (includes health), religion (includes Bible studies and theology), science, senior project, social studies (includes history), speech. Community service is required.

Special Academic Programs Advanced Placement exam preparation; honors section; independent study; term-away projects; study at local college for college credit; remedial reading and/or remedial writing; remedial math; programs in English, mathematics, general development for dyslexic students.

College Admission Counseling 17 students graduated in 2011; they went to Dordt College; Montana State University; The University of Montana Western. Mean composite ACT: 23.

Student Life Upper grades have specified standards of dress, student council, honor system. Discipline rests primarily with faculty. Attendance at religious services is required.

Tuition and Aid Day student tuition: $5500. Guaranteed tuition plan. Tuition installment plan (monthly payment plans, individually arranged payment plans). Tuition reduction for siblings, need-based scholarship grants available. In 2011–12, 80% of upper-school students received aid.

Admissions Traditional secondary-level entrance grade is 9. For fall 2011, 9 students applied for upper-level admission, 8 were accepted, 8 enrolled. Academic Profile Tests or any standardized test required. Deadline for receipt of application materials: none. Application fee required: $35. Interview required.

Athletics Interscholastic: baseball (boys), basketball (b,g), cheering (b,g), cross-country running (b,g), football (b), golf (b,g), track and field (b,g), volleyball (g). 1 PE instructor, 6 coaches, 2 athletic trainers.

Computers Computers are regularly used in business, English, science, senior seminar, social studies classes. Computer network features include on-campus library services, online commercial services, Internet access, Internet filtering or blocking technology. Student e-mail accounts are available to students. Students grades are available online. The school has a published electronic and media policy.

Contact Mrs. Gloria Veltkamp, Admissions Director. 406-282-7261. Fax: 406-282-7701. E-mail: gveltkamp@manhattanchristian.org. Web site: www.manhattanchristian.org.

MANLIUS PEBBLE HILL SCHOOL

5300 Jamesville Road

DeWitt, New York 13214

Head of School: Baxter F. Ball

General Information Coeducational day college-preparatory school. Grades PK–PG. Founded: 1869. Setting: suburban. Nearest major city is Syracuse. 25-acre campus. 10 buildings on campus. Approved or accredited by Middle States Association of Colleges and Schools. Member of National Association of Independent Schools. Endowment: $2.7 million. Total enrollment: 588. Upper school average class size: 13. Upper school faculty-student ratio: 1:6. There are 160 required school days per year for Upper School students. Upper School students typically attend 5 days per week. The average school day consists of 6 hours and 55 minutes.

Upper School Student Profile Grade 9: 51 students (25 boys, 26 girls); Grade 10: 61 students (29 boys, 32 girls); Grade 11: 63 students (29 boys, 34 girls); Grade 12: 75 students (32 boys, 43 girls).

Faculty School total: 81. In upper school: 20 men, 28 women; 25 have advanced degrees.

Subjects Offered 3-dimensional design, advanced chemistry, advanced math, Advanced Placement courses, advanced studio art-AP, algebra, American history, American history-AP, American literature, American literature-AP, ancient world history, art history, ballet, Basic programming, biology, biology-AP, calculus, calculus-AP, ceramics, chemistry, chemistry-AP, Chinese, college counseling, comedy, computer math, computer science, creative writing, drama, driver education, earth science, English, English literature, environmental science, European history, expository writing, fine arts, French, geometry, government/civics, health, information technology, Latin, literature, marketing, mathematics, music, philosophy, photography, physical education, physics, science, social studies, sociology, Spanish, statistics, theater, trigonometry, world history.

Graduation Requirements Arts and fine arts (art, music, dance, drama), computer science, electives, English, foreign language, health and wellness, history, mathematics, performing arts, physical education (includes health), science.

Special Academic Programs 18 Advanced Placement exams for which test preparation is offered; honors section; independent study; term-away projects; study at local college for college credit; study abroad; academic accommodation for the gifted; ESL (5 students enrolled).

College Admission Counseling 72 students graduated in 2010; 71 went to college, including Cornell University; Hamilton College; New York University; Princeton University; Syracuse University; Tufts University. Other: 1 had other specific plans. Mean SAT critical reading: 613, mean SAT math: 602, mean SAT writing: 616.

Student Life Upper grades have specified standards of dress, student council, honor system. Discipline rests primarily with faculty.

Tuition and Aid Day student tuition: $16,500–$17,875. Tuition installment plan (Insured Tuition Payment Plan, FACTS Tuition Payment Plan). Merit scholarship grants, need-based scholarship grants available. In 2010–11, 40% of upper-school students received aid; total upper-school merit-scholarship money awarded: $740,000. Total amount of financial aid awarded in 2010–11: $880,000.

Admissions Traditional secondary-level entrance grade is 9. For fall 2010, 54 students applied for upper-level admission, 44 were accepted, 30 enrolled. ERB or PSAT or SAT for applicants to grade 11 and 12 required. Deadline for receipt of application materials: none. Application fee required: $50. On-campus interview required.

Athletics Interscholastic: basketball (boys), diving (g), lacrosse (b,g), soccer (b,g), softball (g), swimming and diving (g), tennis (b,g), volleyball (g); intramural: lacrosse (g); coed interscholastic: alpine skiing, ballet, cheering, cross-country running, dance, equestrian sports, fitness, golf, indoor track, modern dance, outdoor education, skiing (downhill), snowboarding, strength & conditioning, track and field, winter (indoor) track; coed intramural: outdoor education, trap and skeet. 4 PE instructors, 9 coaches, 1 athletic trainer.

Computers Computers are regularly used in English, foreign language, graphic design, history, information technology, library skills, literary magazine, mathematics, newspaper, science, Web site design, yearbook classes. Computer network features include on-campus library services, online commercial services, Internet access, wireless campus network, Internet filtering or blocking technology. Campus intranet, student e-mail accounts, and computer access in designated common areas are available to students. The school has a published electronic and media policy.

Contact Lynne E. Allard, Director of Admission. 315-446-2452 Ext. 131. Fax: 315-446-2620. E-mail: lallard@mph.net. Web site: www.mph.net.

MAPLEBROOK SCHOOL

Amenia, New York

See Special Needs Schools section.

MARANATHA HIGH SCHOOL

169 South Saint John Avenue

Pasadena, California 91105

Head of School: Mr. Charles E. Crane

General Information Coeducational day college-preparatory, religious studies, and liberal arts school, affiliated with Christian faith. Grades 9–12. Founded: 1965. Setting: urban. Nearest major city is Los Angeles. 13-acre campus. 3 buildings on campus. Approved or accredited by Association of Christian Schools International, Western Association of Schools and Colleges, and California Department of Education. Endowment: $80,000. Total enrollment: 635. Upper school average class size: 20. Upper school faculty-student ratio: 1:12. There are 170 required school days per year for Upper School students. Upper School students typically attend 5 days per week. The average school day consists of 7 hours and 5 minutes.

Faculty School total: 52. In upper school: 26 men, 22 women; 27 have advanced degrees.

Subjects Offered Advanced math, algebra, American history, American history-AP, American literature, American sign language, anatomy and physiology, band, Bible, biology, biology-AP, calculus, calculus-AP, chemistry, chemistry-AP, choir, composition, computer animation, concert choir, drama performance, drawing, economics, English, English language-AP, English literature, English literature-AP, foreign language, French, freshman foundations, geometry, government, government-AP, honors algebra, honors English, honors U.S. history, jazz band, keyboarding, math analysis, performing arts, physical science, physics, physics-AP, psychology, Spanish, Spanish language-AP, Spanish-AP, sports medicine, studio art-AP, theater arts, U.S. government, work-study, world geography, world history.

Graduation Requirements English, foreign language, lab science, mathematics, performing arts, physical education (includes health), physical science, research, science, social sciences, visual arts, Bible must be taken every year student attends school. Community service is required.

Special Academic Programs Advanced Placement exam preparation; honors section; study at local college for college credit; academic accommodation for the artistically talented; remedial reading and/or remedial writing; remedial math; special instructional classes for students with learning difficulties and Attention Deficit Disorder.

College Admission Counseling 170 went to college, including Azusa Pacific University; California State Polytechnic University, Pomona; Citrus College; Pasadena City College; Point Loma Nazarene University; Vanguard University of Southern California.

Student Life Upper grades have uniform requirement, student council, honor system. Discipline rests primarily with faculty. Attendance at religious services is required.

Summer Programs Remediation, enrichment, advancement, sports, art/fine arts programs offered; session focuses on science and math; held on campus; accepts boys and girls; open to students from other schools. 140 students usually enrolled. 2012 schedule: June 18 to July 30. Application deadline: February 3.

Tuition and Aid Day student tuition: $16,750. Tuition installment plan (monthly payment plans, individually arranged payment plans). Merit scholarship grants, need-based scholarship grants available. In 2011–12, 25% of upper-school students received aid.

Admissions Traditional secondary-level entrance grade is 9. ISEE required. Deadline for receipt of application materials: none. Application fee required: $75. On-campus interview required.

Athletics Interscholastic: baseball (boys), basketball (b,g), cheering (g), cross-country running (b,g), diving (b,g), football (b), soccer (b,g), softball (g), swimming and diving (b,g), tennis (b,g), track and field (b,g), volleyball (b,g); coed interscholastic: golf; coed intramural: outdoor skills, wall climbing. 1 PE instructor, 27 coaches, 1 athletic trainer.

Computers Computers are regularly used in animation, career exploration, college planning, drafting, library, research skills, yearbook classes. Computer resources include on-campus library services, online commercial services, Internet access, eLibrary.

Contact Mrs. Debbie Middlebrook, Admissions Administrative Assistant. 626-817-4021. Fax: 626-817-4040. E-mail: d_middlebrook@mhs-hs.org. Web site: www.maranatha-hs.org.

MARET SCHOOL

3000 Cathedral Avenue NW

Washington, District of Columbia 20008

Head of School: Marjo Talbott

General Information Coeducational day college-preparatory, arts, and technology school. Grades K–12. Founded: 1911. Setting: urban. 7-acre campus. 6 buildings on campus. Approved or accredited by Association of Independent Maryland Schools, Association of Independent Schools of Greater Washington, Middle States Association of Colleges and Schools, and District of Columbia Department of Education. Member of National Association of Independent Schools and Secondary School Admission Test Board. Endowment: $19 million. Total enrollment: 635. Upper school average class size: 18. Upper school faculty-student ratio: 1:7. The average school day consists of 7 hours.

Upper School Student Profile Grade 9: 80 students (38 boys, 42 girls); Grade 10: 80 students (41 boys, 39 girls); Grade 11: 83 students (48 boys, 35 girls); Grade 12: 67 students (35 boys, 32 girls).

Faculty School total: 104. In upper school: 37 men, 67 women; 78 have advanced degrees.

Subjects Offered Acting, advanced computer applications, advanced studio art-AP, African-American literature, algebra, American history, American literature, anatomy, art, astronomy, biology, calculus-AP, ceramics, chemistry, civil rights, classical civilization, classical Greek literature, classical language, classics, computer graphics, computer math, computer programming, computer science, creative writing, drama, earth science, ecology, English, English literature, European history, film history, fine arts, French, gender issues, geometry, government/civics, history, humanities, Latin, marine biology, mathematics, music, photography, physical education, physics, physiology, psychology, science, Spanish, statistics, technology, trigonometry, world history, world literature, writing.

Graduation Requirements Arts and fine arts (art, music, dance, drama), English, foreign language, history, mathematics, music, performing arts, physical education (includes health), science, 15 hours of community service in grades 9 and 10, additional 15 hours in grades 11 and 12.

Special Academic Programs 16 Advanced Placement exams for which test preparation is offered; honors section; independent study; study at local college for college credit; study abroad; academic accommodation for the gifted, the musically talented, and the artistically talented.

College Admission Counseling 69 students graduated in 2011; 67 went to college, including Harvard University; Northwestern University; Pomona College; Tufts University; Washington University in St. Louis. Other: 2 entered a postgraduate year.

Student Life Upper grades have student council. Discipline rests primarily with faculty.

Summer Programs Advancement, sports, art/fine arts programs offered; session focuses on academics, athletics, and performing arts; held both on and off campus; held at locations in Honduras, Florida, France and China; accepts boys and girls; open to students from other schools. 100 students usually enrolled. 2012 schedule: June 15 to August 15. Application deadline: June 1.

Tuition and Aid Day student tuition: $31,670. Tuition installment plan (Key Tuition Payment Plan). Need-based scholarship grants available. In 2011–12, 24% of upper-school students received aid. Total amount of financial aid awarded in 2011–12: $2,800,000.

Admissions Traditional secondary-level entrance grade is 9. For fall 2011, 262 students applied for upper-level admission, 39 were accepted, 25 enrolled. ISEE, PSAT or SSAT required. Deadline for receipt of application materials: January 6. Application fee required: $65. On-campus interview required.

Athletics Interscholastic: baseball (boys), basketball (b,g), football (b), lacrosse (b,g), soccer (b,g), softball (g), tennis (b,g), volleyball (g), wrestling (b); intramural: ice hockey (b), squash (b,g); coed interscholastic: aerobics, cross-country running, diving, flag football, golf, independent competitive sports, martial arts, swimming and diving, track and field, ultimate Frisbee; coed intramural: indoor soccer, ultimate Frisbee, weight lifting, weight training, yoga. 6 PE instructors, 25 coaches, 1 athletic trainer.

Computers Computers are regularly used in graphic design, graphics, programming, publications, Web site design classes. Computer network features include on-campus library services, online commercial services, Internet access, wireless campus network, Internet filtering or blocking technology. Campus intranet and student e-mail accounts are available to students. Students grades are available online. The school has a published electronic and media policy.

Contact Annie M. Farquhar, Director of Admission and Financial Aid. 202-939-8814. Fax: 202-939-8845. E-mail: admissions@maret.org. Web site: www.maret.org.

MARIAN CENTRAL CATHOLIC HIGH SCHOOL

1001 McHenry Avenue

Woodstock, Illinois 60098

Head of School: Mr. Charles D. Rakers

General Information Coeducational day college-preparatory, arts, business, religious studies, bilingual studies, and technology school, affiliated with Roman Catholic Church. Grades 9–12. Founded: 1959. Setting: suburban. 42-acre campus. 1 building on campus. Approved or accredited by National Catholic Education Association, North Central Association of Colleges and Schools, and Illinois Department of Education. Endowment: $1.2 million. Total enrollment: 694. Upper school average class size: 24. Upper school faculty-student ratio: 1:17. There are 177 required school days per year for Upper School students. Upper School students typically attend 5 days per week. The average school day consists of 6 hours and 25 minutes.

Upper School Student Profile Grade 9: 192 students (108 boys, 84 girls); Grade 10: 167 students (84 boys, 83 girls); Grade 11: 166 students (91 boys, 75 girls); Grade 12: 169 students (88 boys, 81 girls). 89.5% of students are Roman Catholic.

Faculty School total: 52. In upper school: 26 men, 26 women; 37 have advanced degrees.

Subjects Offered Accounting, advanced biology, advanced chemistry, advanced math, Advanced Placement courses, algebra, American government, art, band, biology, business law, calculus, calculus-AP, chemistry, chemistry-AP, chorus, comparative government and politics-AP, composition, consumer economics, engineering, English, English composition, English literature-AP, first aid, French, general science, geography, geometry, global issues, government, health, honors algebra, honors English, honors geometry, honors U.S. history, information processing, integrated science, marketing, physical education, physical fitness, physical science, physics, pre-calculus, psychology, psychology-AP, publications, religious studies, Spanish, speech, theater, U.S. history, U.S. history-AP, world history, world history-AP.

Graduation Requirements Art, biology, consumer economics, electives, English, first aid, foreign language, government, mathematics, music, physical education (includes health), religious studies, science, U.S. history.

Special Academic Programs 7 Advanced Placement exams for which test preparation is offered; honors section; remedial reading and/or remedial writing; remedial math.

College Admission Counseling 193 students graduated in 2011; 188 went to college, including Illinois State University; Loyola University Chicago; Marquette University; Northern Illinois University; Saint Louis University; University of Illinois at Urbana–Champaign. Other: 4 entered military service, 1 had other specific plans. Mean composite ACT: 24. 32% scored over 26 on composite ACT.

Student Life Upper grades have uniform requirement, student council. Discipline rests primarily with faculty. Attendance at religious services is required.

Summer Programs Sports programs offered; session focuses on sports camps; held on campus; accepts boys and girls; open to students from other schools. 2012 schedule: June to August.

Tuition and Aid Day student tuition: $5570–$7450. Tuition installment plan (monthly payment plans, quarterly payment plan, semester payment plans, yearly payment plans). Tuition reduction for siblings, need-based scholarship grants, paying campus jobs available. In 2011–12, 20% of upper-school students received aid. Total amount of financial aid awarded in 2011–12: $294,625.

Admissions Traditional secondary-level entrance grade is 9. High School Placement Test (closed version) from Scholastic Testing Service required. Deadline for receipt of application materials: none. No application fee required.

Athletics Interscholastic: baseball (boys), basketball (b,g), cheering (g), cross-country running (b,g), dance team (g), football (b), golf (b,g), pom squad (g), soccer (b,g), softball (g), tennis (b,g), track and field (b,g), volleyball (g), wrestling (b); intramural: floor hockey (b,g); coed interscholastic: fencing, fishing. 3 PE instructors, 74 coaches, 1 athletic trainer.

Computers Computers are regularly used in information technology, publications classes. Computer resources include on-campus library services, online commercial services, Internet access, Internet filtering or blocking technology. Students grades are available online. The school has a published electronic and media policy.

Contact Mrs. Barbara Villont, Director of Curriculum and Technology. 815-338-4220 Ext. 105. Fax: 815-338-4253. E-mail: bvillont@marian.com. Web site: www.marian.com.

MARIAN HIGH SCHOOL

1311 South Logan Street

Mishawaka, Indiana 46544

Head of School: Carl Loesch

General Information Coeducational day college-preparatory, arts, business, vocational, religious studies, bilingual studies, and technology school, affiliated with Roman Catholic Church. Grades 9–12. Founded: 1965. Setting: suburban. 135-acre campus. 1 building on campus. Approved or accredited by North Central Association of Colleges and Schools, The College Board, and Indiana Department of Education. Total enrollment: 719. Upper school average class size: 27. Upper school faculty-student ratio: 1:24. There are 180 required school days per year for Upper School students. Upper School students typically attend 5 days per week. The average school day consists of 6 hours and 30 minutes.

Upper School Student Profile Grade 9: 199 students (89 boys, 110 girls); Grade 10: 182 students (102 boys, 80 girls); Grade 11: 172 students (86 boys, 86 girls); Grade 12: 166 students (82 boys, 84 girls). 83% of students are Roman Catholic.

Faculty School total: 48. In upper school: 18 men, 30 women; 22 have advanced degrees.

Subjects Offered 20th century history, 20th century physics, 20th century world history, 3-dimensional art, 3-dimensional design, accounting, acting, advanced chemistry, advanced computer applications, advanced math, algebra, alternative physical education, American government, American literature, analysis and differential calculus, analytic geometry, anatomy, ancient world history, art, art history, arts and crafts, arts appreciation, business law, calculus, Catholic belief and practice, chemistry, drama, drawing, drawing and design, economics, English composition, English literature-AP, environmental science, environmental studies, environmental systems, family and consumer science, family living, fashion, fine arts, food and nutrition, foods, French, French language-AP, general business, general math, geography, geometry, German, government and politics-AP, government-AP, government/civics, guidance, health, histology, honors world history, independent living, integrated science, keyboarding, Latin, Life of Christ, media, media arts, moral theology, music, music appreciation, nutrition, physics, physics-AP, pre-algebra, pre-calculus, psychology, religion, scripture, senior project, sewing, sociology, Spanish, Spanish language-AP, Spanish-AP, study skills, theology, U.S. government and politics-AP, U.S. history, U.S. history-AP, visual arts, vocal music, Western civilization.

Graduation Requirements Algebra, American government, American history, analytic geometry, arts and fine arts (art, music, dance, drama), biology, chemistry, computer information systems, computer skills, economics, English, English composition, English literature, French, keyboarding, languages, mathematics, science, scripture, writing, four years of theology.

Special Academic Programs Advanced Placement exam preparation; study at local college for college credit; remedial reading and/or remedial writing; remedial math.

College Admission Counseling 162 students graduated in 2011; 155 went to college, including Ball State University; DePaul University; Indiana University–Purdue University Fort Wayne; Indiana University Bloomington; Purdue University; University of Notre Dame. Other: 4 went to work, 1 entered military service, 2 had other specific plans. Mean SAT critical reading: 542, mean SAT math: 541, mean SAT writing: 537, mean composite ACT: 23.

Student Life Upper grades have specified standards of dress, student council, honor system. Discipline rests equally with students and faculty. Attendance at religious services is required.

Summer Programs Sports, art/fine arts, computer instruction programs offered; session focuses on enrichment; held on campus; accepts boys and girls; open to students from other schools. 2012 schedule: June 7 to July 2.

Tuition and Aid Day student tuition: $5575–$6575. Tuition installment plan (The Tuition Plan, FACTS Tuition Payment Plan, individually arranged payment plans). Tuition reduction for siblings, need-based loans available. In 2011–12, 45% of upper-school students received aid. Total amount of financial aid awarded in 2011–12: $350,000.

Admissions Traditional secondary-level entrance grade is 9. For fall 2011, 210 students applied for upper-level admission, 210 were accepted, 199 enrolled. High School Placement Test, Math Placement Exam or placement test required. Deadline for receipt of application materials: September 9. Application fee required: $100. Interview required.

Athletics Interscholastic: aerobics/dance (girls), aquatics (b,g), baseball (b), basketball (b,g), cheering (b,g), Cosom hockey (b), cross-country running (b,g), dance team (g), diving (b,g), flag football (g), football (b), golf (b,g), gymnastics (g), hockey (b), ice hockey (b), indoor hockey (b), lacrosse (b,g), power lifting (b,g), rugby (b), soccer (b,g), softball (g), swimming and diving (b,g), tennis (b,g), track and field (b,g), volleyball (g), weight training (b,g), wrestling (b,g); intramural: basketball (b), flag football (g), pom squad (g); coed interscholastic: cheering, wrestling; coed intramural: alpine skiing, bowling. 2 PE instructors, 42 coaches, 1 athletic trainer.

Computers Computers are regularly used in business education, business skills, career education, commercial art, economics, foreign language, graphic arts, history, library, media arts, occupational education, publications, religion, yearbook classes. Computer network features include on-campus library services, online commercial services, Internet access, Internet filtering or blocking technology. Students grades are available online. The school has a published electronic and media policy.

Contact Janet M. Hatfield, Dean. 574-259-5257. Fax: 574-258-7668. E-mail: jhatfield@marianhs.org. Web site: www.marianhs.org/.

MARIN ACADEMY

1600 Mission Avenue

San Rafael, California 94901-1859

Head of School: Travis Brownley

General Information Coeducational day college-preparatory, arts, technology, and outdoor education program school. Grades 9–12. Founded: 1971. Setting: suburban. Nearest major city is San Francisco. 10-acre campus. 11 buildings on campus. Approved or accredited by California Association of Independent Schools, The College Board, and Western Association of Schools and Colleges. Member of National Association of Independent Schools and Secondary School Admission Test Board. Endowment: $9.1 billion. Total enrollment: 406. Upper school average class size: 15. Upper school faculty-student ratio: 1:9. There are 180 required school days per year for Upper School students. Upper School students typically attend 5 days per week. The average school day consists of 6 hours and 45 minutes.

Upper School Student Profile Grade 9: 100 students (48 boys, 52 girls); Grade 10: 102 students (53 boys, 49 gjrls); Grade 11: 103 students (49 boys, 54 girls); Grade 12: 102 students (51 boys, 51 girls).

Faculty School total: 55. In upper school: 23 men, 32 women; 36 have advanced degrees.

Subjects Offered 20th century history, 20th century world history, 3-dimensional art, acting, adolescent issues, Advanced Placement courses, African history, algebra, American culture, American government, American history, American literature, American minority experience, American studies, ancient world history, art, Asian history, Asian literature, biology, British literature (honors), calculus, ceramics, chemistry, chorus, college counseling, community service, creative writing, dance, digital imaging, digital photography, English, English literature, environmental science, European history, fine arts, French, geology, geometry, government/civics, health, history, honors U.S. history, human development, Islamic history, Islamic studies, Japanese, journalism, Mandarin, mathematics, music, oceanography, photography, physical education, physics, pre-calculus, science, social studies, Spanish, theater, trigonometry, world cultures, world history-AP.

Graduation Requirements Arts and fine arts (art, music, dance, drama), English, foreign language, health and wellness, health education, mathematics, physical education (includes health), science, social studies (includes history), annual one-week experiential education course. Community service is required.

Special Academic Programs Advanced Placement exam preparation; honors section; independent study; term-away projects; study at local college for college credit; study abroad; academic accommodation for the gifted, the musically talented, and the artistically talented.

College Admission Counseling 99 students graduated in 2010; 92 went to college, including New York University; Oberlin College; Stanford University; University of California, Berkeley; University of California, Los Angeles; University of Southern California. Other: 1 had other specific plans. Median SAT critical reading: 670, median SAT math: 645, median SAT writing: 675, median combined SAT: 2000, median composite ACT: 28.

Student Life Upper grades have student council, honor system. Discipline rests primarily with faculty.

Tuition and Aid Day student tuition: $33,360. Tuition installment plan (Key Tuition Payment Plan). Need-based scholarship grants, need-based loans available. In 2010–11, 21% of upper-school students received aid. Total amount of financial aid awarded in 2010–11: $2,400,000.

Admissions Traditional secondary-level entrance grade is 9. For fall 2010, 470 students applied for upper-level admission, 170 were accepted, 100 enrolled. CTBS or ERB, ISEE, SSAT or Star-9 required. Deadline for receipt of application materials: January 13. Application fee required: $100. On-campus interview required.

Athletics Interscholastic: aquatics (boys, girls), baseball (b), basketball (b,g), combined training (b,g), cross-country running (b,g), fencing (b,g), golf (b,g), independent competitive sports (b,g), lacrosse (b), mountain biking (b,g), outdoor activities (b,g), rock climbing (b,g), sailing (b,g), soccer (b,g), softball (g), swimming and diving (b,g), tennis (b,g), track and field (b,g), volleyball (g), water polo (b,g); coed interscholastic: dance, golf; coed intramural: bicycling, climbing, fitness, flag football, Frisbee, hiking/backpacking, kayaking, martial arts, Nautilus, outdoor skills, physical fitness, rock climbing, scuba diving, ultimate Frisbee. 28 coaches, 1 athletic trainer.

Computers Computers are regularly used in art, English, foreign language, history, library skills, mathematics, music, photography, science, yearbook classes. Computer network features include on-campus library services, online commercial services, Internet access, wireless campus network, multimedia hardware and production applications. Student e-mail accounts and computer access in designated common areas are available to students.

Contact Dan Babior, Director of Admissions and Financial Aid. 415-453-4550 Ext. 216. Fax: 415-453-8905. E-mail: dbabior@ma.org. Web site: www.ma.org.

MARINE MILITARY ACADEMY

320 Iwo Jima Boulevard

Harlingen, Texas 78550

Head of School: Brig. Gen. Stephen A. Cheney, USMC-Retd.

General Information Boys' boarding college-preparatory, general academic, and military school. Grades 8–PG. Founded: 1965. Setting: small town. Students are housed in single-sex dormitories. 142-acre campus. 43 buildings on campus. Approved or accredited by Military High School and College Association, Southern Association of Colleges and Schools, Southern Association of Independent Schools, and Texas Department of Education. Endowment: $18 million. Total enrollment: 250. Upper school average class size: 12. Upper school faculty-student ratio: 1:12.

Upper School Student Profile Grade 8: 45 students (45 boys); Grade 9: 52 students (52 boys); Grade 10: 49 students (49 boys); Grade 11: 50 students (50 boys); Grade 12: 52 students (52 boys); Postgraduate: 2 students (2 boys). 100% of students are boarding students. 46% are state residents. 31 states are represented in upper school student body. 19% are international students. International students from China, Germany, Mexico, Panama, Russian Federation, and United Arab Emirates; 5 other countries represented in student body.

Faculty School total: 34. In upper school: 17 men, 17 women; 16 have advanced degrees; 20 reside on campus.

Subjects Offered Aerospace science, algebra, American history, band, biology, calculus, calculus-AP, chemistry, computer programming, computer science, economics, English, environmental science, French, French-AP, geography, geometry, German, German-AP, government/civics, history, journalism, JROTC, keyboarding, marine science, mathematics, military science, physics, physics-AP, political science, SAT preparation, science, social sciences, social studies, Spanish, Spanish-AP, speech, world history.

Graduation Requirements Business skills (includes word processing), computer science, English, foreign language, mathematics, military science, physical education (includes health), science, social sciences, social studies (includes history).

Special Academic Programs Advanced Placement exam preparation; honors section; study at local college for college credit; academic accommodation for the gifted; remedial math; ESL (34 students enrolled).

College Admission Counseling 54 students graduated in 2011; 53 went to college, including Texas A&M University; Texas Tech University; The Citadel, The Military College of South Carolina; United States Military Academy; United States Naval Academy; Virginia Military Institute. Other: 1 entered military service. 11.7% scored over 600 on SAT critical reading, 14% scored over 600 on SAT math.

Student Life Upper grades have uniform requirement, student council, honor system. Discipline rests equally with students and faculty.

Summer Programs ESL, sports, rigorous outdoor training programs offered; session focuses on leadership training; held on campus; accepts boys; open to students from other schools. 350 students usually enrolled. 2012 schedule: June 30 to July 28. Application deadline: none.

Tuition and Aid 7-day tuition and room/board: $33,000. Tuition installment plan (monthly payment plans, individually arranged payment plans, Chief Financial Officer authorization required). Tuition reduction for siblings, need-based scholarship grants available. In 2011–12, 12% of upper-school students received aid. Total amount of financial aid awarded in 2011–12: $300,000.

Admissions For fall 2011, 150 students applied for upper-level admission, 119 were accepted, 119 enrolled. Deadline for receipt of application materials: none. Application fee required: $100.

Athletics Interscholastic: baseball, basketball, boxing, cross-country running, diving, drill team, football, golf, JROTC drill, marksmanship, physical fitness, riflery, running, soccer, swimming and diving, tennis, track and field; intramural: baseball, basketball, boxing, climbing, fitness, flag football, football, kickball, martial arts, outdoor activities, paint ball, physical fitness, physical training, power lifting, racquetball, rappelling, rock climbing, running, sailing, scuba diving, soccer, softball, swimming and diving, track and field, volleyball, wall climbing, weight lifting, weight training. 15 coaches, 1 athletic trainer.

Computers Computers are regularly used in English, foreign language, mathematics, science, yearbook classes. Computer network features include on-campus library services, online commercial services, Internet access, Internet filtering or blocking technology. Student e-mail accounts and computer access in designated common areas are available to students. Students grades are available online.

Contact Mrs. Jay Perez, Admissions Officer. 956-423-6006 Ext. 251. Fax: 956-421-9273. E-mail: admissions@mma-tx.org. Web site: www.mma-tx.org.

THE MARIN SCHOOL

100 Ebbtide Avenue #300

Sausalito, California 94965

Head of School: Barbara Brown, EdD

General Information Coeducational day college-preparatory, arts, and film, technology, photography school. Grades 9–12. Founded: 1980. Setting: small town. Nearest major city is San Francisco. 2-acre campus. 4 buildings on campus. Approved or accredited by Western Association of Schools and Colleges and California Department of Education. Member of National Association of Independent Schools. Total enrollment: 100. Upper school average class size: 7. Upper school faculty-student ratio: 1:7. There are 174 required school days per year for Upper School students. Upper School students typically attend 5 days per week. The average school day consists of 6 hours.

Faculty School total: 17. In upper school: 12 men, 5 women; 14 have advanced degrees.

Subjects Offered Algebra, American literature, arts, biology, British literature (honors), calculus, chemistry, civics, community service, composition, drama, earth science, ecology, economics, English, environmental science, fine arts, general science, geography, geometry, health, life science, literature, mathematics, physics, pre-calculus, science, social sciences, social studies, Spanish, trigonometry, U.S. history, visual arts, Western civilization, women's literature.

Graduation Requirements Arts and fine arts (art, music, dance, drama), foreign language, mathematics, physical education (includes health), science, social sciences. Community service is required.

Special Academic Programs Honors section.

College Admission Counseling 25 students graduated in 2011; all went to college, including Bard College; Eugene Lang College The New School for Liberal Arts; Goucher College; Lewis & Clark College; Reed College; The Evergreen State College.

Student Life Upper grades have student council, honor system. Discipline rests primarily with faculty.

Tuition and Aid Day student tuition: $34,800. Tuition installment plan (FACTS Tuition Payment Plan). Need-based scholarship grants available. In 2011–12, 40% of upper-school students received aid.

Admissions ERB, SSAT, Star-9 or STS required. Deadline for receipt of application materials: none. No application fee required. On-campus interview required.

Athletics Coed Interscholastic: basketball, dance, indoor soccer, sailing, soccer; coed intramural: baseball, basketball, bicycling, fencing, mountain biking, sailing, soccer.

Computers Computers are regularly used in all classes. Computer network features include on-campus library services, online commercial services, Internet access, wireless campus network, Internet filtering or blocking technology. Campus intranet and student e-mail accounts are available to students. Students grades are available online. The school has a published electronic and media policy.

Contact Ms. Sierra Antonio, Admissions and Development Assistant. 415-339-9336 Ext. 142. E-mail: santonio@themarinschool.org. Web site: www.themarinschool.org.

MARION ACADEMY

1820 Prier Drive

Marion, Alabama 36756

Head of School: Mr. G. Travis Vaughn

General Information Coeducational day college-preparatory, general academic, arts, religious studies, bilingual studies, and technology school, affiliated with Christian faith. Grades K–12. Founded: 1987. Setting: small town. Nearest major city is Tuscaloosa. 5-acre campus. 1 building on campus. Approved or accredited by Southern Association of Colleges and Schools and Alabama Department of Education. Total enrollment: 84. Upper school average class size: 8. Upper school faculty-student ratio: 1:8. There are 180 required school days per year for Upper School students. Upper School students typically attend 5 days per week. The average school day consists of 6 hours and 30 minutes.

Upper School Student Profile Grade 7: 9 students (6 boys, 3 girls); Grade 8: 7 students (5 boys, 2 girls); Grade 9: 7 students (1 boy, 6 girls); Grade 10: 7 students (3 boys, 4 girls); Grade 11: 6 students (1 boy, 5 girls); Grade 12: 8 students (4 boys, 4 girls). 98% of students are Christian.

Faculty School total: 16. In upper school: 3 men, 5 women; 2 have advanced degrees.

Subjects Offered 20th century history, 20th century world history, advanced math, Alabama history and geography, algebra, American government, anatomy and physiology, art, athletics, basic language skills, Bible studies, biology, cheerleading, college planning, creative writing, drama, earth science, economics, English language and composition-AP, English language-AP, English literature, English literature and composition-AP, foreign language, general math, geography, government, grammar, health education, history, honors algebra, honors English, human anatomy, Internet, language, language and composition, language arts, library, math applications, math methods, math review, mathematics, mathematics-AP, physical education, SAT/ACT preparation, speech, U.S. government, U.S. history.

Student Life Upper grades have specified standards of dress, student council, honor system. Discipline rests primarily with faculty.

Tuition and Aid Guaranteed tuition plan.

Admissions Traditional secondary-level entrance grade is 9. Deadline for receipt of application materials: none. Application fee required. Interview required.

Athletics Interscholastic: baseball (boys), basketball (b,g), cheering (g), cross-country running (b,g), football (b), softball (g), track and field (b,g), volleyball (g); coed interscholastic: track and field. 1 PE instructor, 2 coaches.

Computers Computers are regularly used in career education, library skills classes. Computer network features include Internet access. Student e-mail accounts are available to students.

Contact Mrs. Margaret S. Hallmon, Secretary. 334-683-8204. Fax: 334-683-4938. E-mail: marionacademy@hotmail.com. Web site: www.marionacademy.org.

MARIST SCHOOL

3790 Ashford-Dunwoody Road NE

Atlanta, Georgia 30319-1899

Head of School: Rev. Joel M. Konzen, SM

General Information Coeducational day college-preparatory, arts, business, religious studies, and technology school, affiliated with Roman Catholic Church. Grades 7–12. Founded: 1901. Setting: suburban. 77-acre campus. 18 buildings on campus. Approved or accredited by Southern Association of Colleges and Schools, Southern Association of Independent Schools, and Georgia Department of Education. Member of National Association of Independent Schools and Secondary School Admission Test Board. Endowment: $16.5 million. Total enrollment: 1,079. Upper school average class size: 18. Upper school faculty-student ratio: 1:11. There are 174 required school days per year for Upper School students. Upper School students typically attend 5 days per week. The average school day consists of 5 hours and 30 minutes.

Upper School Student Profile Grade 7: 141 students (75 boys, 66 girls); Grade 8: 144 students (73 boys, 71 girls); Grade 9: 196 students (94 boys, 102 girls); Grade 10: 200 students (104 boys, 96 girls); Grade 11: 194 students (96 boys, 98 girls); Grade 12: 204 students (102 boys, 102 girls). 75% of students are Roman Catholic.

Faculty School total: 95. In upper school: 51 men, 44 women; 69 have advanced degrees.

Subjects Offered Algebra, American history, American literature, ancient history, art, art history, biology, business skills, calculus, ceramics, chemistry, community service, computer programming, computer science, creative writing, dance, drama, driver education, economics, English, English literature, European history, fine arts, French, general science, geography, geology, geometry, German, government/civics, health, history, humanities, journalism, Latin, mathematics, music, peace and justice, philosophy, photography, physical education, physics, religion, science, social studies, Spanish, speech, statistics, studio art, theater, theology, world history, world literature, world religions, writing.

Graduation Requirements Arts and fine arts (art, music, dance, drama), business skills (includes word processing), computer science, English, foreign language, mathematics, physical education (includes health), religion (includes Bible studies and theology), science, social studies (includes history), community service requirements in all grades. Community service is required.

Special Academic Programs Advanced Placement exam preparation; honors section; independent study.

College Admission Counseling 182 students graduated in 2011; 180 went to college, including Auburn University; Georgia Institute of Technology; The University of Alabama; University of Georgia; University of Notre Dame. Other: 1 entered a post-graduate year, 1 had other specific plans. 59% scored over 600 on SAT critical reading, 69% scored over 600 on SAT math, 63% scored over 600 on SAT writing, 69% scored over 1800 on combined SAT, 64% scored over 26 on composite ACT.

Student Life Upper grades have uniform requirement, student council, honor system. Discipline rests primarily with faculty. Attendance at religious services is required.

Summer Programs Enrichment, sports, art/fine arts programs offered; held on campus; accepts boys and girls; open to students from other schools.

Tuition and Aid Day student tuition: $15,850. Tuition installment plan (individually arranged payment plans, Tuition Management System). Need-based scholarship grants available. In 2011–12, 16% of upper-school students received aid. Total amount of financial aid awarded in 2011–12: $1,637,000.

Admissions Traditional secondary-level entrance grade is 7. SSAT required. Deadline for receipt of application materials: January 28. Application fee required: $75. On-campus interview required.

Athletics Interscholastic: baseball (boys), basketball (b,g), cheering (g), cross-country running (b,g), diving (b,g), football (b), golf (b,g), lacrosse (b,g), soccer (b,g), softball (g), swimming and diving (b,g), tennis (b,g), track and field (b,g), volleyball (g), weight lifting (b,g), wrestling (b); coed interscholastic: drill team; coed intramural: outdoor education, ultimate Frisbee. 6 PE instructors.

Computers Computers are regularly used in accounting, business applications, computer applications, drawing and design, English, foreign language, mathematics, music, science classes. Computer network features include on-campus library services, online

commercial services, Internet access, wireless campus network, Internet filtering or blocking technology. Student e-mail accounts and computer access in designated common areas are available to students. Students grades are available online. The school has a published electronic and media policy.
Contact Mr. Jim Byrne, Director of Admissions. 770-936-2214. Fax: 770-457-8402. E-mail: admissions@marist.com. Web site: www.marist.com.

MARLBOROUGH SCHOOL

250 South Rossmore Avenue

Los Angeles, California 90004

Head of School: Ms. Barbara E. Wagner

General Information Girls' day college-preparatory school. Grades 7–12. Founded: 1889. Setting: urban. 4-acre campus. 5 buildings on campus. Approved or accredited by Western Association of Schools and Colleges and California Department of Education. Member of National Association of Independent Schools. Endowment: $36.8 million. Total enrollment: 530. Upper school average class size: 12. Upper school faculty-student ratio: 1:8. There are 166 required school days per year for Upper School students. Upper School students typically attend 5 days per week. The average school day consists of 6 hours and 20 minutes.
Upper School Student Profile Grade 10: 92 students (92 girls); Grade 11: 91 students (91 girls); Grade 12: 91 students (91 girls).
Faculty School total: 77. In upper school: 20 men, 39 women; 47 have advanced degrees.
Subjects Offered Algebra, American literature, American studies, architecture, art history-AP, astronomy, athletic training, ballet technique, biology, biology-AP, calculus, calculus-AP, ceramics, chemistry, chemistry-AP, Chinese history, choral music, choreography, community service, computer programming, creative writing, dance, digital art, drawing, earth systems analysis, economics, English, English literature, English literature and composition-AP, environmental science, environmental science-AP, European history, European history-AP, French, French language-AP, gender issues, geometry, global studies, health, Hispanic literature, instrumental music, internship, journalism, Latin, Latin American literature, Latin-AP, linear algebra, Mandarin, metalworking, modern world history, music theory, newspaper, painting, photography, physical education, physics, physics-AP, political thought, psychology, research, robotics, Russian literature, sculpture, self-defense, social sciences, Spanish, Spanish language-AP, statistics, statistics-AP, studio art-AP, theater, trigonometry, U.S. history, U.S. history-AP, video and animation, world history, world history-AP, world literature, yearbook, yoga.
Graduation Requirements Arts and fine arts (art, music, dance, drama), English, foreign language, history, mathematics, science, social sciences.
Special Academic Programs 21 Advanced Placement exams for which test preparation is offered; honors section; independent study.
College Admission Counseling 84 students graduated in 2011; all went to college, including Carleton College; Columbia University; Stanford University; University of Pennsylvania; University of Southern California; Yale University.
Student Life Upper grades have uniform requirement, student council, honor system. Discipline rests equally with students and faculty.
Summer Programs Remediation, enrichment, advancement, sports, art/fine arts, computer instruction programs offered; held on campus; accepts boys and girls; open to students from other schools. 500 students usually enrolled. 2012 schedule: June 25 to July 27. Application deadline: June 1.
Tuition and Aid Day student tuition: $31,200. Tuition installment plan (FACTS Tuition Payment Plan, monthly payment plans). Need-based scholarship grants available. In 2011–12, 18% of upper-school students received aid.
Admissions ISEE required. Deadline for receipt of application materials: January 5. Application fee required: $150. On-campus interview required.
Athletics Interscholastic: basketball, cross-country running, equestrian sports, golf, independent competitive sports, soccer, softball, swimming and diving, tennis, track and field, volleyball, water polo. 7 PE instructors, 31 coaches, 1 athletic trainer.
Computers Computers are regularly used in all academic classes. Computer network features include on-campus library services, online commercial services, Internet access, wireless campus network, Internet filtering or blocking technology, videoconferencing. Student e-mail accounts are available to students. Students grades are available online. The school has a published electronic and media policy.
Contact Ms. Jeanette Woo Chitjian, Director of Admissions. 323-964-8450. Fax: 323-933-0542. E-mail: jeanette.woochitjian@marlboroughschool.org. Web site: www.marlboroughschool.org.

MARMION ACADEMY

1000 Butterfield Road

Aurora, Illinois 60502

Head of School: John K. Milroy

General Information Boys' day college-preparatory, business, religious studies, Junior ROTC, and LEAD (Leadership Education and Development) school, affiliated with Roman Catholic Church. Grades 9–12. Founded: 1933. Setting: suburban. Nearest major city is Chicago. 325-acre campus. 5 buildings on campus. Approved or accredited by National Catholic Education Association, North Central Association of Colleges and Schools, and Illinois Department of Education. Member of Secondary School Admission Test Board. Endowment: $9 million. Total enrollment: 499. Upper school average class size: 27. Upper school faculty-student ratio: 1:11. The average school day consists of 7 hours and 25 minutes.
Upper School Student Profile Grade 9: 113 students (113 boys); Grade 10: 125 students (125 boys); Grade 11: 118 students (118 boys); Grade 12: 143 students (143 boys). 88% of students are Roman Catholic.
Faculty School total: 50. In upper school: 40 men, 10 women; 31 have advanced degrees.
Subjects Offered 1 1/2 elective credits, accounting, algebra, American history, American literature, anatomy, art, astronomy, band, biology, biology-AP, botany, calculus, calculus-AP, chemistry, community service, computer science, computer science-AP, computer-aided design, creative writing, driver education, ecology, economics, English, English literature, English-AP, fine arts, French, general science, geometry, government/civics, history, history-AP, Italian, JROTC, Latin, leadership, leadership education training, mathematics, mathematics-AP, meteorology, music, philosophy, physical education, physics, physics-AP, physiology, psychology, religion, science, social sciences, social studies, sociology, Spanish, Spanish language-AP, theology, trigonometry, Western civilization, zoology.
Graduation Requirements Arts and fine arts (art, music, dance, drama), English, foreign language, JROTC, leadership education training, mathematics, music appreciation, physical education (includes health), religion (includes Bible studies and theology), science, social sciences, social studies (includes history). Community service is required.
Special Academic Programs Advanced Placement exam preparation; honors section; independent study; academic accommodation for the gifted.
College Admission Counseling 121 students graduated in 2010; all went to college, including Loyola University Chicago; Marquette University; Northern Illinois University; Saint Louis University; University of Illinois. Mean composite ACT: 25.
Student Life Upper grades have uniform requirement, student council. Discipline rests primarily with faculty. Attendance at religious services is required.
Tuition and Aid Day student tuition: $9100. Tuition installment plan (Tuition Management Systems). Merit scholarship grants, need-based scholarship grants, paying campus jobs available. In 2010–11, 30% of upper-school students received aid; total upper-school merit-scholarship money awarded: $144,000. Total amount of financial aid awarded in 2010–11: $323,000.
Admissions Traditional secondary-level entrance grade is 9. For fall 2010, 210 students applied for upper-level admission, 186 were accepted, 143 enrolled. High School Placement Test (closed version) from Scholastic Testing Service required. Deadline for receipt of application materials: none. Application fee required: $50. On-campus interview required.
Athletics Interscholastic: baseball, basketball, cross-country running, diving, football, golf, lacrosse, riflery, soccer, swimming and diving, tennis, track and field, wrestling; intramural: baseball, basketball, fencing, floor hockey, football, JROTC drill, outdoor activities, outdoors, soccer, swimming and diving, table tennis, tennis, volleyball, water polo, weight lifting. 2 PE instructors, 3 coaches, 1 athletic trainer.
Computers Computers are regularly used in design, science classes. Computer network features include on-campus library services, Internet access. The school has a published electronic and media policy.
Contact William J. Dickson Jr., Director of Admissions. 630-897-6936. Fax: 630-897-7086. Web site: www.marmion.org.

MARQUETTE UNIVERSITY HIGH SCHOOL

3401 West Wisconsin Avenue

Milwaukee, Wisconsin 53208

Head of School: Mr. Jeff Monday

General Information Boys' day college-preparatory school, affiliated with Roman Catholic Church. Grades 9–12. Founded: 1857. Setting: urban. 1 building on campus. Approved or accredited by National Catholic Education Association, North Central Association of Colleges and Schools, and Wisconsin Department of Education. Total enrollment: 1,067. Upper school average class size: 22. Upper school faculty-student ratio: 1:13. Upper School students typically attend 5 days per week.
Upper School Student Profile Grade 9: 278 students (278 boys); Grade 10: 272 students (272 boys); Grade 11: 267 students (267 boys); Grade 12: 250 students (250 boys). 85% of students are Roman Catholic.
Faculty School total: 86. In upper school: 57 men, 29 women; 64 have advanced degrees.
Subjects Offered Algebra, American history, American literature, architectural drawing, architecture, art, art-AP, Bible studies, biology, biology-AP, calculus, calculus-AP, ceramics, chemistry, chemistry-AP, choral music, computer math, computer programming, computer science, computer science-AP, creative writing, drama, driver education, economics, English, English language-AP, English literature, English literature-AP, ethics, European history, European history-AP, expository writing, geography, geometry, German, government/civics, grammar, graphic design, health, history, jazz

band, Latin, Latin-AP, macroeconomics-AP, mathematics, microeconomics-AP, music, philosophy, photography, physical education, physics, psychology, psychology-AP, religion, social studies, sociology, Spanish, Spanish language-AP, statistics-AP, studio art-AP, theology, trigonometry, U.S. government and politics-AP, U.S. history-AP, world history, world literature, World War I, World War II, writing.

Graduation Requirements Arts and fine arts (art, music, dance, drama), English, foreign language, mathematics, science, social studies (includes history), theology, retreats, community service hours. Community service is required.

Special Academic Programs Advanced Placement exam preparation; honors section.

College Admission Counseling 250 students graduated in 2010; 248 went to college, including Creighton University; Marquette University; Saint Louis University; University of Minnesota, Twin Cities Campus; University of Wisconsin–Madison; University of Wisconsin–Milwaukee. Other: 2 entered military service. Median composite ACT: 27. Mean SAT critical reading: 670, mean SAT math: 690.

Student Life Upper grades have specified standards of dress, student council, honor system. Discipline rests primarily with faculty.

Tuition and Aid Day student tuition: $9785. Tuition installment plan (monthly payment plans, prepaid tuition loan program). Need-based scholarship grants, paying campus jobs, state-sponsored voucher program available. In 2010–11, 27% of upper-school students received aid. Total amount of financial aid awarded in 2010–11: $1,400,000.

Admissions Traditional secondary-level entrance grade is 9. Essay and STS Educational Development Series required. Deadline for receipt of application materials: November 25. Application fee required: $25.

Athletics Interscholastic: baseball, basketball, cross-country running, diving, fitness, football, golf, hockey, ice hockey, indoor track, indoor track & field, lacrosse, physical fitness, physical training, power lifting, rugby, sailing, skiing (downhill), soccer, strength & conditioning, swimming and diving, tennis, track and field, volleyball, weight lifting, weight training, wrestling; intramural: basketball, bowling, soccer, softball, volleyball.

Computers Computers are regularly used in architecture, college planning, creative writing, data processing, desktop publishing, economics, English, graphic design, literary magazine, mathematics, music, newspaper, research skills, stock market, Web site design, word processing, writing, yearbook classes. Computer network features include on-campus library services, online commercial services, Internet access, Internet filtering or blocking technology, university and county library systems link. Student e-mail accounts are available to students.

Contact Mr. Casey Kowalewski, Director of Admissions. 414-933-7220 Ext. 3046. Fax: 414-937-6002. E-mail: admissions@muhs.edu. Web site: www.muhs.edu.

MARS HILL BIBLE SCHOOL

698 Cox Creek Parkway

Florence, Alabama 35630

Head of School: Dr. Kenny D. Barfield

General Information Coeducational day college-preparatory, arts, and religious studies school, affiliated with Church of Christ. Grades K–12. Founded: 1947. Setting: suburban. Nearest major city is Huntsville. 80-acre campus. 7 buildings on campus. Approved or accredited by National Christian School Association and Southern Association of Colleges and Schools. Endowment: $2.7 million. Total enrollment: 574. Upper school average class size: 22. Upper school faculty-student ratio: 1:14. There are 180 required school days per year for Upper School students. Upper School students typically attend 5 days per week. The average school day consists of 7 hours.

Upper School Student Profile Grade 9: 42 students (21 boys, 21 girls); Grade 10: 51 students (17 boys, 34 girls); Grade 11: 65 students (26 boys, 39 girls); Grade 12: 63 students (30 boys, 33 girls). 82% of students are members of Church of Christ.

Faculty School total: 42. In upper school: 11 men, 12 women; 14 have advanced degrees.

Subjects Offered ACT preparation, algebra, American government, American literature, American literature-AP, anatomy and physiology, ancient world history, band, Bible studies, biology, biology-AP, calculus, calculus-AP, chemistry, chorus, computer literacy, computer programming, computer science, concert band, concert choir, debate, drama, drama performance, driver education, ecology, economics, English, English composition, English literature, English literature and composition-AP, English literature-AP, ensembles, forensics, geometry, health, honors English, human anatomy, Internet research, jazz band, Life of Christ, marine biology, musical productions, physical education, physical science, physics, pre-algebra, pre-calculus, psychology, Spanish, speech, speech and debate, student government, student publications, U.S. history, U.S. history-AP, word processing, world geography, world history, yearbook.

Graduation Requirements Algebra, American government, American history, American literature, ancient world history, art, Bible, biology, British literature, chemistry, college writing, computer applications, computer literacy, economics, English composition, foreign language, geometry, health and wellness, introduction to literature, mathematics, physical education (includes health), physical science, science, social studies (includes history), speech communications. Community service is required.

Special Academic Programs 3 Advanced Placement exams for which test preparation is offered; honors section; independent study; study at local college for college credit; special instructional classes for students with learning disabilities, Attention Deficit Disorder, and dyslexia.

College Admission Counseling 48 students graduated in 2011; all went to college, including Auburn University; Freed-Hardeman University; Harding University; The University of Alabama; The University of Alabama at Birmingham; University of North Alabama. Median composite ACT: 25. 43% scored over 26 on composite ACT.

Student Life Upper grades have specified standards of dress, student council. Discipline rests primarily with faculty. Attendance at religious services is required.

Summer Programs Enrichment, sports, art/fine arts programs offered; session focuses on athletics, driver education, forensics, show choir, band; held on campus; accepts boys and girls; open to students from other schools. 200 students usually enrolled. 2012 schedule: June 1 to July 31. Application deadline: June 1.

Tuition and Aid Day student tuition: $5779. Tuition installment plan (FACTS Tuition Payment Plan, monthly payment plans). Tuition reduction for siblings, need-based scholarship grants available. In 2011–12, 20% of upper-school students received aid. Total amount of financial aid awarded in 2011–12: $150,000.

Admissions Traditional secondary-level entrance grade is 9. For fall 2011, 24 students applied for upper-level admission, 19 were accepted, 16 enrolled. Achievement tests, ACT-Explore, PSAT or Stanford Achievement Test required. Deadline for receipt of application materials: none. Application fee required: $100. Interview required.

Athletics Interscholastic: baseball (boys), basketball (b,g), cheering (g), cross-country running (b,g), football (b), golf (b,g), soccer (b,g), softball (g), tennis (b,g), track and field (b,g), volleyball (g); intramural: basketball (b,g). 3 PE instructors, 7 coaches.

Computers Computers are regularly used in all academic, Bible studies, English, history, remedial study skills, yearbook classes. Computer resources include on-campus library services, online commercial services, Internet access, wireless campus network, Internet filtering or blocking technology. Campus intranet and computer access in designated common areas are available to students. Students grades are available online. The school has a published electronic and media policy.

Contact Mrs. Jeannie Garrett, Director of Admissions. 256-767-1203 Ext. 2005. Fax: 256-767-6304. E-mail: jgarrett@mhbs.org. Web site: www.mhbs.org.

MARTIN LUTHER HIGH SCHOOL

60-02 Maspeth Avenue

Maspeth, New York 11378

Head of School: Randy Gast

General Information Coeducational day college-preparatory, arts, and business school, affiliated with Lutheran Church. Grades 9–12. Founded: 1960. Setting: urban. Nearest major city is New York. 1-acre campus. 1 building on campus. Approved or accredited by Middle States Association of Colleges and Schools and New York Department of Education. Endowment: $2.2 million. Total enrollment: 217. Upper school average class size: 22. Upper school faculty-student ratio: 1:12.

Upper School Student Profile Grade 6: 8 students (3 boys, 5 girls); Grade 7: 12 students (8 boys, 4 girls); Grade 8: 11 students (6 boys, 5 girls); Grade 9: 50 students (23 boys, 27 girls); Grade 10: 41 students (22 boys, 19 girls); Grade 11: 41 students (23 boys, 18 girls); Grade 12: 54 students (34 boys, 20 girls). 16% of students are Lutheran.

Faculty School total: 18. In upper school: 7 men, 11 women; 8 have advanced degrees.

Subjects Offered Algebra, American history, art, Bible studies, biology, business, business skills, calculus, chemistry, chemistry-AP, computer programming, computer science, drama, driver education, earth science, economics, English, English literature, English literature-AP, environmental science-AP, ethics, European history, fine arts, French, geography, geometry, German, government/civics, grammar, health, history, journalism, marine biology, mathematics, music, philosophy, photography, physical education, physics, psychology, religion, science, social studies, Spanish, Spanish-AP, speech, theater, theology, trigonometry, U.S. history-AP, world history.

Graduation Requirements Arts and fine arts (art, music, dance, drama), business skills (includes word processing), English, foreign language, mathematics, physical education (includes health), religion (includes Bible studies and theology), science, social studies (includes history), service hours.

Special Academic Programs Advanced Placement exam preparation; honors section; accelerated programs; independent study; study at local college for college credit; programs in general development for dyslexic students.

College Admission Counseling Colleges students went to include John Jay College of Criminal Justice of the City University of New York; Queens College of the City University of New York; St. Francis College; St. John's University; St. Joseph's College, New York. Other: 1 entered military service.

Student Life Upper grades have uniform requirement, student council. Discipline rests primarily with faculty. Attendance at religious services is required.

Summer Programs Remediation, computer instruction programs offered; held on campus; accepts boys and girls; open to students from other schools. 250 students usually enrolled. 2012 schedule: July 2 to August 16. Application deadline: none.

Tuition and Aid Day student tuition: $8000–$8300. Tuition installment plan (monthly payment plans). Tuition reduction for siblings, merit scholarship grants, need-based scholarship grants available. In 2011–12, 50% of upper-school students received aid; total upper-school merit-scholarship money awarded: $73,125. Total amount of financial aid awarded in 2011–12: $195,182.

Admissions Traditional secondary-level entrance grade is 9. School's own exam required. Deadline for receipt of application materials: none. Application fee required: $50. On-campus interview required.

Athletics Interscholastic: baseball (boys), basketball (b,g), cheering (g), cross-country running (b,g), fitness (b,g), soccer (b), softball (g), tennis (b,g), track and field (b,g), volleyball (g), wrestling (b,g); intramural: basketball (b,g), cross-country running (b,g), floor hockey (b,g), indoor hockey (b,g), soccer (b,g), weight lifting (b,g), wrestling (b); coed interscholastic: cheering, cross-country running, fitness, soccer; coed intramural: archery, badminton, cross-country running, fitness, handball, paddle tennis, racquetball, track and field, volleyball, wrestling. 3 PE instructors, 18 coaches.

Computers Computers are regularly used in business education, career education, Christian doctrine, history, keyboarding, newspaper, yearbook classes. Computer resources include on-campus library services, Internet access.

Contact Ms. Patricia Dee, Admissions Administrator. 718-894-4000 Ext. 122. Fax: 718-894-1469. E-mail: pdee@martinluthernyc.org. Web site: www.martinluthernyc.org.

THE MARVELWOOD SCHOOL

476 Skiff Mountain Road

PO Box 3001

Kent, Connecticut 06757-3001

Head of School: Mr. Arthur Goodearl

General Information Coeducational boarding and day college-preparatory, arts, technology, field science, and community service, ESL school; primarily serves students with learning disabilities, individuals with Attention Deficit Disorder, and dyslexic students. Grades 9–12. Founded: 1957. Setting: rural. Nearest major city is Hartford. Students are housed in single-sex dormitories. 83-acre campus. 10 buildings on campus. Approved or accredited by Connecticut Association of Independent Schools, New England Association of Schools and Colleges, The Association of Boarding Schools, and Connecticut Department of Education. Member of National Association of Independent Schools. Endowment: $1.6 million. Total enrollment: 165. Upper school average class size: 8. Upper school faculty-student ratio: 1:4. Upper School students typically attend 6 days per week. The average school day consists of 6 hours and 40 minutes.

Upper School Student Profile Grade 9: 20 students (12 boys, 8 girls); Grade 10: 40 students (25 boys, 15 girls); Grade 11: 55 students (37 boys, 18 girls); Grade 12: 37 students (21 boys, 16 girls). 94% of students are boarding students. 21% are state residents. 14 states are represented in upper school student body. 33% are international students. International students from China, Jamaica, Mexico, Republic of Korea, Spain, and United Kingdom; 7 other countries represented in student body.

Faculty School total: 48. In upper school: 19 men, 27 women; 24 have advanced degrees; 35 reside on campus.

Subjects Offered Algebra, American history, American literature, anatomy and physiology, art, art history, biology, calculus, ceramics, chemistry, chorus, college writing, community service, creative writing, drama, driver education, English, English literature, ESL, ethology, European history, film, fine arts, French, geography, geometry, history of China and Japan, limnology, mathematics, music, ornithology, photography, physics, pre-algebra, psychology, religion, SAT preparation, science, Shakespeare, social studies, Spanish, studio art, trigonometry, world cultures, world history, world literature.

Graduation Requirements Arts and fine arts (art, music, dance, drama), English, foreign language, mathematics, science, social studies (includes history), senior service project, daily participation in sports, weekly community service program.

Special Academic Programs Advanced Placement exam preparation; honors section; remedial reading and/or remedial writing; remedial math; programs in general development for dyslexic students; ESL (32 students enrolled).

College Admission Counseling 62 students graduated in 2011; 60 went to college, including Pace University; Savannah College of Art and Design; Syracuse University; University of Hartford; University of Wisconsin–Madison; Washington College. Other: 1 entered military service, 1 entered a postgraduate year. Median SAT critical reading: 458, median SAT math: 424, median SAT writing: 458.

Student Life Upper grades have uniform requirement, student council, honor system. Discipline rests primarily with faculty.

Summer Programs Remediation, enrichment, ESL, art/fine arts, computer instruction programs offered; session focuses on study skills; held on campus; accepts boys and girls; open to students from other schools. 30 students usually enrolled. 2012 schedule: July 5 to July 31. Application deadline: none.

Tuition and Aid Day student tuition: $30,000; 7-day tuition and room/board: $46,500. Tuition installment plan (Insured Tuition Payment Plan, Academic Management Services Plan, Key Tuition Payment Plan, individually arranged payment plans). Merit scholarship grants, need-based scholarship grants available. In 2011–12, 30% of upper-school students received aid; total upper-school merit-scholarship money awarded: $46,500. Total amount of financial aid awarded in 2011–12: $850,000.

Admissions Traditional secondary-level entrance grade is 9. For fall 2011, 257 students applied for upper-level admission, 168 were accepted, 58 enrolled. Deadline for receipt of application materials: none. Application fee required: $50. Interview required.

Athletics Interscholastic: baseball (boys), basketball (b,g), cross-country running (b,g), lacrosse (b), soccer (b,g), softball (g), tennis (b,g), volleyball (g), wrestling (b); intramural: lacrosse (g); coed interscholastic: alpine skiing, golf, skiing (downhill); coed intramural: bicycling, canoeing/kayaking, climbing, dance, fishing, fly fishing, Frisbee, hiking/backpacking, horseback riding, kayaking, mountain biking, mountaineering, outdoor activities, physical training, rock climbing, ropes courses, skiing (downhill), snowboarding, strength & conditioning, weight training, wilderness, wildernessways, yoga. 1 coach, 1 athletic trainer.

Computers Computers are regularly used in mathematics, newspaper, photography, science, writing classes. Computer network features include on-campus library services, Internet access, wireless campus network, Internet filtering or blocking technology. Campus intranet, student e-mail accounts, and computer access in designated common areas are available to students. The school has a published electronic and media policy.

Contact Mrs. Maureen Smith, Admissions Associate. 860-927-0047 Ext. 1005. Fax: 860-927-0021. E-mail: maureen.smith@marvelwood.org. Web site: www.marvelwood.org.

MARYKNOLL SCHOOL

1526 Alexander Street

Honolulu, Hawaii 96822

Head of School: Perry K. Martin

General Information Coeducational day college-preparatory school, affiliated with Roman Catholic Church. Grades K–12. Founded: 1927. Setting: urban. 3-acre campus. 3 buildings on campus. Approved or accredited by National Catholic Education Association, Western Association of Schools and Colleges, Western Catholic Education Association, and Hawaii Department of Education. Member of National Association of Independent Schools and Secondary School Admission Test Board. Endowment: $3.5 million. Total enrollment: 1,465. Upper school average class size: 18. Upper school faculty-student ratio: 1:11.

Upper School Student Profile Grade 6: 95 students (59 boys, 36 girls); Grade 7: 102 students (46 boys, 56 girls); Grade 8: 100 students (50 boys, 50 girls); Grade 9: 171 students (77 boys, 94 girls); Grade 10: 154 students (69 boys, 85 girls); Grade 11: 147 students (72 boys, 75 girls); Grade 12: 136 students (67 boys, 69 girls). 50% of students are Roman Catholic.

Faculty School total: 104. In upper school: 26 men, 28 women; 30 have advanced degrees.

Subjects Offered Adolescent issues, advanced chemistry, algebra, American literature, art, art history-AP, biology, biology-AP, biotechnology, calculus-AP, chemistry, chemistry-AP, college counseling, college placement, computer programming, creative writing, drawing, economics, English language and composition-AP, English literature and composition-AP, ethics, European history-AP, geography, geometry, global science, golf, government, government-AP, guitar, Hawaiian history, Hawaiian language, human development, Japanese, journalism, library assistant, marine science, media, mythology, novels, Pacific art, painting, philosophy, physical education, physics, physics-AP, poetry, pre-calculus, psychology, psychology-AP, religion, religious studies, research, Russian history, science fiction, senior project, Shakespeare, sociology, Spanish, speech, statistics, studio art-AP, theater, U.S. history, U.S. history-AP, Web site design, weight training, world history, world literature, yearbook.

Graduation Requirements Arts and fine arts (art, music, dance, drama), English, foreign language, mathematics, physical education (includes health), religion (includes Bible studies and theology), science, senior project, social sciences, social studies (includes history), portfolio of student works. Community service is required.

Special Academic Programs Advanced Placement exam preparation; honors section; independent study.

College Admission Counseling 125 students graduated in 2010; all went to college, including Loyola Marymount University; Santa Clara University; University of Hawaii at Manoa; University of San Francisco; University of Southern California; University of Washington.

Student Life Upper grades have uniform requirement, student council. Discipline rests equally with students and faculty. Attendance at religious services is required.

Tuition and Aid Day student tuition: $13,010. Tuition installment plan (Insured Tuition Payment Plan, monthly payment plans). Merit scholarship grants, need-based scholarship grants, paying campus jobs available. In 2010–11, 18% of upper-school students received aid; total upper-school merit-scholarship money awarded: $73,000. Total amount of financial aid awarded in 2010–11: $550,000.

Admissions Traditional secondary-level entrance grade is 9. PSAT or SSAT required. Deadline for receipt of application materials: December 15. Application fee required: $75. On-campus interview required.

Athletics Interscholastic: aerobics/dance (girls), baseball (b), basketball (b,g), bowling (b,g), canoeing/kayaking (b,g), cross-country running (b,g), dance (g), diving (b,g), football (b), golf (b,g), gymnastics (b,g), judo (b,g), kayaking (b,g), martial arts (b,g), ocean paddling (b,g), paddling (b,g), power lifting (b,g), riflery (b,g), sailing (b,g), soccer (b,g), softball (g), strength & conditioning (b,g), swimming and diving (b,g), tennis (b,g), track and field (b,g), volleyball (b,g), water polo (b,g), weight lifting (b,g), weight training (b,g), wrestling (b,g); intramural: basketball (b,g), volleyball (b,g); coed interscholastic: canoeing/kayaking, cheering, football, ocean paddling, paddling, strength & conditioning, weight training, wrestling; coed intramural: basketball, bowling, floor hockey. 4 PE instructors, 50 coaches, 2 athletic trainers.

Computers Computers are regularly used in English, foreign language, history, mathematics, science classes. Computer network features include on-campus library services, online commercial services, Internet access, wireless campus network, Internet filtering or blocking technology. Student e-mail accounts are available to students. The school has a published electronic and media policy.

Contact Mrs. Lori Carlos, Director of Admission. 808-952-7330. Fax: 808-952-7306. E-mail: admission@maryknollschool.org. Web site: www.maryknollschool.org.

MARYLAWN OF THE ORANGES

445 Scotland Road

South Orange, New Jersey 07079

Head of School: Dr. Christine H. Lopez

General Information Girls' day college-preparatory, arts, business, religious studies, bilingual studies, and technology school, affiliated with Roman Catholic Church. Grades 7–12. Founded: 1935. Setting: suburban. Nearest major city is Newark. 2 buildings on campus. Approved or accredited by Middle States Association of Colleges and Schools and New Jersey Department of Education. Total enrollment: 146. Upper school average class size: 15. Upper school faculty-student ratio: 1:15. There are 183 required school days per year for Upper School students. Upper School students typically attend 5 days per week. The average school day consists of 7 hours and 15 minutes.

Upper School Student Profile Grade 9: 29 students (29 girls); Grade 10: 22 students (22 girls); Grade 11: 34 students (34 girls); Grade 12: 35 students (35 girls). 25% of students are Roman Catholic.

Faculty School total: 22. In upper school: 7 men, 14 women; 8 have advanced degrees.

Subjects Offered Advanced chemistry, advanced math, algebra, American literature, anatomy and physiology, art, art history, athletics, biology, British literature (honors), calculus, campus ministry, career/college preparation, Catholic belief and practice, cheerleading, chemistry, choir, choral music, Christian ethics, Christian scripture, civics, classical studies, community service, constitutional law, dramatic arts, English, English-AP, fine arts, French, geometry, global studies, grammar, health education, honors algebra, honors English, honors geometry, honors U.S. history, Internet research, language arts, Latin, mathematics, moral theology, music theory, physical education, physics, pre-calculus, psychology, SAT/ACT preparation, social studies, Spanish, trigonometry, U.S. history, world history, world religions, yearbook.

Graduation Requirements Arts and fine arts (art, music, dance, drama), electives, English, foreign language, health education, mathematics, physical education (includes health), practical arts, religious studies, science, social studies (includes history), 20 hours of community service (sophomore year), 25 hours of community service (junior year), 40 hours of community service (senior year).

Special Academic Programs 1 Advanced Placement exam for which test preparation is offered; honors section; independent study; academic accommodation for the gifted, the musically talented, and the artistically talented; remedial reading and/or remedial writing; remedial math; ESL.

College Admission Counseling 41 students graduated in 2011; all went to college, including Johnson & Wales University; Kean University; Pace University; Rutgers, The State University of New Jersey, New Brunswick; Seton Hall University; Temple University. Median SAT critical reading: 450, median SAT math: 420, median SAT writing: 450. 10% scored over 600 on SAT critical reading, 2% scored over 600 on SAT math, 10% scored over 600 on SAT writing.

Student Life Upper grades have uniform requirement, student council. Discipline rests primarily with faculty. Attendance at religious services is required.

Summer Programs Remediation, enrichment, advancement, computer instruction programs offered; session focuses on prep and advancement for secondary school courses, make-up for failed classes; held on campus; accepts boys and girls; open to students from other schools. 75 students usually enrolled. 2012 schedule: June 27 to July 26. Application deadline: June 20.

Tuition and Aid Day student tuition: $8450. Tuition installment plan (monthly payment plans, Tuition Management Systems). Tuition reduction for siblings, merit scholarship grants, need-based scholarship grants available. In 2011–12, 45% of upper-school students received aid; total upper-school merit-scholarship money awarded: $20,000. Total amount of financial aid awarded in 2011–12: $111,850.

Admissions Traditional secondary-level entrance grade is 9. For fall 2011, 130 students applied for upper-level admission, 117 were accepted, 46 enrolled. Cooperative Entrance Exam (McGraw-Hill) required. Deadline for receipt of application materials: none. Application fee required: $125. On-campus interview recommended.

Athletics Interscholastic: basketball, cheering, dance, dance team, drill team, softball, track and field, volleyball; intramural: basketball, dance, fitness, physical fitness, soccer, softball, tennis, weight training. 1 PE instructor, 6 coaches.

Computers Computers are regularly used in all classes. Computer resources include on-campus library services, Internet access, wireless campus network, Internet filtering or blocking technology. Student e-mail accounts and computer access in designated common areas are available to students. Students grades are available online. The school has a published electronic and media policy.

Contact Ms. Fiana Muhlberger, Admissions Officer. 973-762-9222 Ext. 15. Fax: 973-378-7975. E-mail: fmuhlberger@marylawn.us. Web site: www.marylawn.us.

MARYMOUNT HIGH SCHOOL

10643 Sunset Boulevard

Los Angeles, California 90077

Head of School: Ms. Jacqueline Landry

General Information Girls' day college-preparatory, arts, and religious studies school, affiliated with Roman Catholic Church. Grades 9–12. Founded: 1923. Setting: suburban. 6-acre campus. 6 buildings on campus. Approved or accredited by National Catholic Education Association, The College Board, Western Association of Schools and Colleges, Western Catholic Education Association, and California Department of Education. Member of National Association of Independent Schools and Secondary School Admission Test Board. Endowment: $5.6 million. Total enrollment: 369. Upper school average class size: 15. Upper school faculty-student ratio: 1:7. There are 170 required school days per year for Upper School students. Upper School students typically attend 5 days per week. The average school day consists of 7 hours and 15 minutes.

Upper School Student Profile Grade 9: 91 students (91 girls), Grade 10: 90 students (90 girls); Grade 11: 98 students (98 girls); Grade 12: 90 students (90 girls). 68% of students are Roman Catholic.

Faculty School total: 51. In upper school: 13 men, 38 women; 42 have advanced degrees.

Subjects Offered Acting, advanced studio art-AP, aerobics, African literature, algebra, American history, American legal systems, American literature, anatomy, art, art history, art-AP, biology, biology-AP, British literature, calculus, calculus-AP, ceramics, chemistry, choir, Christian testament, community service, computer literacy, computer science, contemporary issues, dance, death and loss, design, drama, drawing, ecology, economics, English, English literature, environmental science, environmental science-AP, ethics, fencing, fine arts, French, French-AP, gender and religion, geography, geometry, government/civics, Hebrew scripture, human development, Japanese literature, jazz ensemble, journalism, language and composition, literary magazine, literature, literature-AP, music, musical productions, painting, peace studies, performing arts, photography, physical education, physics, physiology, pre-calculus, printmaking, psychology, religion, religious studies, robotics, science, self-defense, social justice, social studies, softball, Spanish, Spanish language-AP, Spanish literature-AP, speech, swimming, theology, trigonometry, U.S. government and politics-AP, U.S. history, U.S. history-AP, vocal music, volleyball, women's studies, world religions, writing.

Graduation Requirements Arts and fine arts (art, music, dance, drama), English, foreign language, mathematics, physical education (includes health), religion (includes Bible studies and theology), science, social studies (includes history), 100 hours of community service.

Special Academic Programs 17 Advanced Placement exams for which test preparation is offered; honors section; independent study.

College Admission Counseling 95 students graduated in 2011; all went to college, including Boston University; New York University; Santa Clara University; Southern Methodist University; University of Southern California; University of Washington. Mean SAT critical reading: 611, mean SAT math: 590, mean SAT writing: 661, mean combined SAT: 1862, mean composite ACT: 27.

Student Life Upper grades have uniform requirement, student council, honor system. Discipline rests equally with students and faculty. Attendance at religious services is required.

Summer Programs Remediation, enrichment, advancement, sports, art/fine arts, computer instruction programs offered; session focuses on enrichment, advancement; held on campus; accepts girls; open to students from other schools. 180 students usually enrolled. 2012 schedule: June 25 to July 27. Application deadline: May 25.

Tuition and Aid Day student tuition: $26,600. Tuition installment plan (FACTS Tuition Payment Plan). Merit scholarship grants, need-based scholarship grants available. In 2011–12, 25% of upper-school students received aid; total upper-school merit-scholarship money awarded: $12,000. Total amount of financial aid awarded in 2011–12: $1,125,000.

Admissions Traditional secondary-level entrance grade is 9. For fall 2011, 196 students applied for upper-level admission, 177 were accepted, 102 enrolled. ISEE required. Deadline for receipt of application materials: January 9. Application fee required: $100. On-campus interview required.

Athletics Interscholastic: basketball, cross-country running, equestrian sports, fencing, golf, soccer, softball, swimming and diving, tennis, track and field, volleyball, water polo; intramural: aerobics, aerobics/dance, archery, crew, dance, physical fitness, self defense, strength & conditioning. 1 PE instructor, 24 coaches, 1 athletic trainer.

Computers Computers are regularly used in all academic classes. Computer network features include on-campus library services, online commercial services, Internet access, wireless campus network, Internet filtering or blocking technology, one-to-one student laptop program, access to UCLA Library, Loyola Marymount University Library, 14 independent high school libraries. Campus intranet, student e-mail accounts, and computer access in designated common areas are available to students. Students grades are available online. The school has a published electronic and media policy.

Contact Mrs. Jessica E. Butler, Director of Admission. 310-472-1205 Ext. 220. Fax: 310-440-4316. E-mail: jbutler@mhs-la.org. Web site: www.mhs-la.org.

MARYMOUNT INTERNATIONAL SCHOOL

Via di Villa Lauchli 180

Rome 00191, Italy

Head of School: Ms. Maire McNamara

General Information Coeducational day college-preparatory school, affiliated with Roman Catholic Church. Grades PK–12. Founded: 1946. Setting: suburban. 16-acre campus. 3 buildings on campus. Approved or accredited by New England Association of Schools and Colleges. Member of European Council of International Schools. Language of instruction: English. Total enrollment: 655. Upper school average class size: 18. Upper school faculty-student ratio: 1:15. There are 170 required school days per year for Upper School students. Upper School students typically attend 5 days per week. The average school day consists of 6 hours and 45 minutes.

Upper School Student Profile Grade 9: 68 students (23 boys, 45 girls); Grade 10: 50 students (22 boys, 28 girls); Grade 11: 61 students (37 boys, 24 girls); Grade 12: 51 students (16 boys, 35 girls). 75% of students are Roman Catholic.

Faculty School total: 84. In upper school: 13 men, 34 women; 40 have advanced degrees.

Subjects Offered Algebra, American history, American literature, art, art history, art history-AP, biology, calculus, ceramics, chemistry, computer science, current events, drama, English, English literature, environmental science, ESL, European history, fine arts, French, geography, geometry, health, history, International Baccalaureate courses, international relations, Italian, Latin, mathematics, music, photography, physical education, physics, pre-calculus, psychology, religious education, science, social studies, Spanish, study skills, theater arts, theory of knowledge, trigonometry, world history.

Graduation Requirements Arts and fine arts (art, music, dance, drama), English, foreign language, mathematics, physical education (includes health), religion (includes Bible studies and theology), science, social studies (includes history).

Special Academic Programs International Baccalaureate program; ESL (40 students enrolled).

College Admission Counseling 46 students graduated in 2011; 44 went to college, including Boston University; New York University; Rensselaer Polytechnic Institute; The Johns Hopkins University; University of Southern California; University of Virginia. Other: 2 had other specific plans. Median SAT critical reading: 500, median SAT math: 500, median SAT writing: 520. 15% scored over 600 on SAT critical reading, 15% scored over 600 on SAT math, 15% scored over 600 on SAT writing.

Student Life Upper grades have specified standards of dress, student council, honor system. Discipline rests primarily with faculty. Attendance at religious services is required.

Tuition and Aid Day student tuition: €17,900.

Admissions Traditional secondary-level entrance grade is 9. For fall 2011, 57 students applied for upper-level admission, 44 were accepted, 36 enrolled. English proficiency or writing sample required. Deadline for receipt of application materials: none. Application fee required: €350. On-campus interview recommended.

Athletics Interscholastic: basketball (boys, girls), cheering (g), cross-country running (b,g), soccer (b,g), tennis (b,g), track and field (b,g), volleyball (b,g). 2 PE instructors, 9 coaches.

Computers Computers are regularly used in graphic arts classes. Computer network features include on-campus library services, Internet access, wireless campus network, Internet filtering or blocking technology, one to one lap top program in the middle school. Student e-mail accounts are available to students.

Contact Ms. Deborah Woods, Admissions Director. 39-063629101 Ext. 212. Fax: 39-36301738. E-mail: admissions@marymountrome.org. Web site: www.marymountrome.org.

MARYMOUNT INTERNATIONAL SCHOOL

George Road

Kingston upon Thames

Surrey KT2 7PE, United Kingdom

Head of School: Ms. Sarah Gallagher

General Information Girls' boarding and day college-preparatory, general academic, arts, religious studies, and International Baccalaureate school, affiliated with Roman Catholic Church. Grades 6–12. Founded: 1955. Setting: suburban. Nearest major city is London, United Kingdom. Students are housed in single-sex dormitories. 7-acre campus. 9 buildings on campus. Approved or accredited by Boarding Schools Association (UK), Department for Education and Skills (UK), Independent Schools Council (UK), International Baccalaureate Organization, and Middle States Association of Colleges and Schools. Member of Secondary School Admission Test Board. Language of instruction: English. Total enrollment: 212. Upper school average class size: 12. Upper school faculty-student ratio: 1:7. There are 176 required school days per year for Upper School students. Upper School students typically attend 5 days per week. The average school day consists of 7 hours and 30 minutes.

Upper School Student Profile Grade 9: 29 students (29 girls); Grade 10: 47 students (47 girls); Grade 11: 45 students (45 girls); Grade 12: 48 students (48 girls). 46% of students are boarding students. 41% are international students. International students from China, Germany, Japan, Republic of Korea, Spain, and United States; 40 other countries represented in student body. 37% of students are Roman Catholic.

Faculty School total: 44. In upper school: 11 men, 33 women; 20 have advanced degrees.

Subjects Offered Advanced biology, advanced chemistry, advanced math, algebra, art, biology, chemistry, Chinese, Chinese literature, drama, economics, English, English literature, ESL, European history, French, general science, geography, German, German literature, history, information technology, Japanese, Japanese literature, mathematics, music, personal and social education, physical education, physics, religion, Spanish, theater, theory of knowledge, world history, world literature.

Graduation Requirements English, foreign language, mathematics, physical education (includes health), religion (includes Bible studies and theology), science, social studies (includes history), IB Diploma requirements-3 Higher Level, 3 Standard Level courses, additional IB Diploma requirements—CAS program hours (Creativity, Action, Service), Theory of Knowledge Course, and Extended Essay.

Special Academic Programs International Baccalaureate program; honors section; independent study; ESL (32 students enrolled).

College Admission Counseling 57 students graduated in 2010; 53 went to college. Other: 4 had other specific plans.

Student Life Upper grades have uniform requirement, student council, honor system. Discipline rests primarily with faculty. Attendance at religious services is required.

Tuition and Aid Day student tuition: £15,950; 5-day tuition and room/board: £12,370; 7-day tuition and room/board: £11,070. Tuition installment plan (individually arranged payment plans, two semester payments, three term payments). Tuition reduction for siblings, bursaries, merit scholarship grants, need-based scholarship grants available. In 2010–11, 6% of upper-school students received aid. Total amount of financial aid awarded in 2010–11: £85,000.

Admissions Traditional secondary-level entrance grade is 11. For fall 2010, 94 students applied for upper-level admission, 72 were accepted, 58 enrolled. English proficiency, mathematics proficiency exam, school's own test or writing sample required. Deadline for receipt of application materials: none. Application fee required: £100. Interview recommended.

Athletics Interscholastic: badminton, basketball, fitness, soccer, softball, tennis, volleyball; intramural: aerobics/dance, badminton, basketball, dance, fencing, fitness, horseback riding, indoor soccer, modern dance, physical fitness, physical training, soccer, softball, strength & conditioning, tennis, volleyball, weight training. 3 PE instructors, 2 coaches.

Computers Computers are regularly used in all academic, information technology classes. Computer network features include on-campus library services, Internet access, wireless campus network, Internet filtering or blocking technology. Campus intranet, student e-mail accounts, and computer access in designated common areas are available to students. The school has a published electronic and media policy.

Contact Mr. Chris Hiscock, Marketing and Admissions Officer. 44-(0) 20 8949 0571. Fax: 44-(0) 20 8336 2485. E-mail: admissions@marymountlondon.com. Web site: www.marymountlondon.com.

MARYMOUNT SCHOOL

1026 Fifth Avenue

New York, New York 10028

General Information Coeducational day (boys' only in lower grades) college-preparatory, arts, religious studies, and technology school, affiliated with Roman Catholic Church. Boys grades N–PK, girls grades N–12. Founded: 1926. Setting: urban. 3 buildings on campus. Approved or accredited by New York State Association of Independent Schools. Member of National Association of Independent Schools. Endowment: $800,000. Total enrollment: 608. Upper school average class size: 15. Upper school faculty-student ratio: 1:6. The average school day consists of 7 hours and 30 minutes.

See Display on next page and Close-Up on page 646.

MARY STAR OF THE SEA HIGH SCHOOL

2500 North Taper Avenue

San Pedro, California 90731

Head of School: Ms. Rita Dever

General Information Coeducational day college-preparatory and religious studies school, affiliated with Roman Catholic Church. Grades 9–12. Founded: 1954. Setting: urban. 1-acre campus. 2 buildings on campus. Approved or accredited by Western Association of Schools and Colleges and California Department of Education. Total enrollment: 517. Upper school average class size: 25. Upper school faculty-student ratio: 1:17. There are 180 required school days per year for Upper School students. Upper School students typically attend 5 days per week. The average school day consists of 6 hours and 20 minutes.

Upper School Student Profile Grade 9: 120 students (63 boys, 57 girls); Grade 10: 137 students (76 boys, 61 girls); Grade 11: 132 students (62 boys, 70 girls); Grade 12: 120 students (63 boys, 57 girls). 96% of students are Roman Catholic.

Faculty School total: 31. In upper school: 19 men, 12 women; 27 have advanced degrees.

Subjects Offered Advanced Placement courses, algebra, American government, American literature, American literature-AP, anatomy and physiology, art, art history, biology, British literature, calculus, calculus-AP, chemistry, choir, consumer mathematics, economics, European history-AP, geometry, government, government-AP, health education, honors algebra, honors English, honors geometry, honors U.S. history, honors world history, human anatomy, Latin, marine biology, physics, pre-algebra, psychology, religion, Spanish, U.S. government and politics-AP, U.S. history, U.S. history-AP, Western civilization.

Graduation Requirements American literature, biology, British literature, chemistry, economics, English, foreign language, geography, geometry, government, religion (includes Bible studies and theology), world history, world literature, service hours.

Special Academic Programs Advanced Placement exam preparation; honors section.

College Admission Counseling 128 students graduated in 2011; 127 went to college, including California State University, Dominguez Hills; California State University, Fullerton; California State University, Long Beach; El Camino College; University of California, Irvine; University of California, San Diego. Other: 1 entered military service.

Student Life Upper grades have uniform requirement, student council. Discipline rests primarily with faculty. Attendance at religious services is required.

Summer Programs Remediation, art/fine arts programs offered; session focuses on remediation; held on campus; accepts boys and girls; open to students from other schools. 250 students usually enrolled. 2012 schedule: June 18 to July 20. Application deadline: June 15.

Tuition and Aid Day student tuition: $7300. Tuition installment plan (SMART Tuition Payment Plan). Tuition reduction for siblings, merit scholarship grants, need-based scholarship grants available. In 2011–12, 15% of upper-school students received aid. Total amount of financial aid awarded in 2011–12: $145,000.

Admissions Traditional secondary-level entrance grade is 9. Deadline for receipt of application materials: January 21. Application fee required: $75. Interview required.

Athletics Interscholastic: baseball (boys), basketball (b,g), cheering (g), cross-country running (b,g), dance squad (g), football (b), soccer (b,g), softball (g), track and field (b,g), volleyball (b,g); coed interscholastic: swimming and diving. 1 PE instructor, 20 coaches.

Computers Computer resources include on-campus library services, Internet access, wireless campus network, Internet filtering or blocking technology. Computer access in designated common areas is available to students. Students grades are available online. The school has a published electronic and media policy.

Contact Mrs. Nancy Phillips, Registrar. 310-547-1130. Fax: 310-547-1827. E-mail: nphillips@marystarhigh.com.

MARYVALE PREPARATORY SCHOOL

11300 Falls Road

Brooklandville, Maryland 21022

Head of School: Sr. Shawn Marie Maguire, SND

General Information Girls' day college-preparatory, arts, religious studies, bilingual studies, and technology school, affiliated with Roman Catholic Church. Grades 6–12. Founded: 1945. Setting: suburban. Nearest major city is Baltimore. 113-acre campus. 4 buildings on campus. Approved or accredited by Association of Independent Maryland Schools, Middle States Association of Colleges and Schools, National Catholic Education Association, and Maryland Department of Education. Member of National Association of Independent Schools. Endowment: $1 million. Total enrollment: 362. Upper school average class size: 15. Upper school faculty-student ratio: 1:8. Upper School students typically attend 5 days per week. The average school day consists of 6 hours.

Upper School Student Profile Grade 6: 23 students (23 girls); Grade 7: 32 students (32 girls); Grade 8: 27 students (27 girls); Grade 9: 70 students (70 girls); Grade 10: 64 students (64 girls); Grade 11: 67 students (67 girls); Grade 12: 79 students (79 girls). 80% of students are Roman Catholic.

Faculty School total: 50. In upper school: 5 men, 34 women; 27 have advanced degrees.

Subjects Offered Algebra, American history, American literature, anatomy and physiology, anthropology, art, art history, band, biology, biology-AP, British literature (honors), calculus, calculus-AP, chemistry, chorus, community service, computer science, digital photography, drama, economics, English, English literature, English literature-AP, English-AP, forensics, French, French-AP, geography, geometry, grammar, health, history, Holocaust, honors algebra, honors English, honors U.S. history, honors world history, journalism, keyboarding, Latin, literary magazine, marine biology, mathematics, model United Nations, music, newspaper, physical education, physics, piano, pre-algebra, pre-calculus, psychology, public speaking, religion, research, science, Shakespeare, social studies, Spanish, Spanish-AP, speech, statistics, theater, theology, trigonometry, U.S. history-AP, voice, Web site design, world history, world literature, writing, yearbook.

Graduation Requirements Arts and fine arts (art, music, dance, drama), computer science, English, foreign language, mathematics, physical education (includes health), religion (includes Bible studies and theology), science, social studies (includes history), 100 hours of community service.

Special Academic Programs Advanced Placement exam preparation; honors section; accelerated programs; study at local college for college credit.

College Admission Counseling 76 students graduated in 2010; 75 went to college, including Salisbury University; Towson University; University of Delaware; University of Maryland, Baltimore County; University of Maryland, College Park. Other: 1 entered military service. Mean SAT critical reading: 569, mean SAT math: 532, mean SAT writing: 602, mean combined SAT: 1703. 31% scored over 600 on SAT critical reading, 21% scored over 600 on SAT math, 43% scored over 600 on SAT writing, 30% scored over 1800 on combined SAT, 26% scored over 26 on composite ACT.

Student Life Upper grades have uniform requirement, student council, honor system. Discipline rests equally with students and faculty. Attendance at religious services is required.

Tuition and Aid Tuition installment plan (Academic Management Services Plan). Bursaries, need-based scholarship grants available. In 2010–11, 29% of upper-school students received aid. Total amount of financial aid awarded in 2010–11: $496,585.

Admissions Traditional secondary-level entrance grade is 9. For fall 2010, 152 students applied for upper-level admission, 119 were accepted, 42 enrolled. High School Placement Test required. Deadline for receipt of application materials: January 7. Application fee required: $50. On-campus interview required.

Athletics Interscholastic: basketball, cross-country running, field hockey, indoor soccer, indoor track, indoor track & field, lacrosse, physical fitness, soccer, softball, track and field, volleyball, winter soccer, yoga. 3 PE instructors, 26 coaches, 1 athletic trainer.

Computers Computers are regularly used in all academic classes. Computer network features include on-campus library services, online commercial services, Internet access, wireless campus network, Internet filtering or blocking technology. Student e-mail accounts and computer access in designated common areas are available to students. Students grades are available online. The school has a published electronic and media policy.

Contact Monica C. Graham, Director of Admissions. 410-560-3243. Fax: 410-561-1826. E-mail: grahamm@maryvale.com. Web site: www.maryvale.com.

THE MASTER'S SCHOOL

36 Westledge Road

West Simsbury, Connecticut 06092-9400

Head of School: Jon F. Holley

General Information Coeducational day college-preparatory, arts, religious studies, and technology school, affiliated with Christian faith. Grades PK–12. Founded: 1970. Setting: suburban. Nearest major city is Hartford. 76-acre campus. 10 buildings on campus. Approved or accredited by Association of Christian Schools International, Connecticut Association of Independent Schools, New England Association of Schools and Colleges, and Connecticut Department of Education. Endowment: $34,000. Total enrollment: 330. Upper school average class size: 15. Upper school faculty-student ratio: 1:7.

Upper School Student Profile Grade 9: 34 students (14 boys, 20 girls); Grade 10: 30 students (16 boys, 14 girls); Grade 11: 31 students (19 boys, 12 girls); Grade 12: 31 students (15 boys, 16 girls).

Faculty School total: 40. In upper school: 9 men, 12 women; 8 have advanced degrees.

Subjects Offered Advanced computer applications, advanced studio art-AP, algebra, American history, American literature, applied music, art, art history, Bible studies, biology, biology-AP, British literature, British literature (honors), calculus, calculus-AP, chemistry, chemistry-AP, chorus, civics, community service, computer applications, computer education, computer literacy, computer math, computer programming, computer skills, creative writing, earth science, English, English literature, English literature-AP, English-AP, ethics, expository writing, fine arts, French, geometry, grammar, health education, history, honors algebra, honors English, honors geometry, honors U.S. history, independent study, instrumental music, keyboarding, mathematics, music, music composition, philosophy, photography, physical education, physics, science, senior seminar, social studies, Spanish, theology, trigonometry, Western civilization, world history, world literature, writing workshop, yearbook.

Graduation Requirements Arts and fine arts (art, music, dance, drama), computer education, English, foreign language, mathematics, physical education (includes health), religion (includes Bible studies and theology), science, senior seminar, social studies (includes history).

Special Academic Programs Advanced Placement exam preparation; honors section; independent study; study at local college for college credit; academic accommodation for the gifted, the musically talented, and the artistically talented.

College Admission Counseling 33 students graduated in 2011; 30 went to college, including Boston College; Grove City College; Hofstra University; Houghton College; Messiah College; University of Connecticut. Other: 3 had other specific plans. Mean SAT critical reading: 545, mean SAT math: 543, mean SAT writing: 522.

Student Life Upper grades have specified standards of dress, student council, honor system. Discipline rests primarily with faculty. Attendance at religious services is required.

Summer Programs Enrichment, advancement, ESL, sports, art/fine arts, computer instruction programs offered; session focuses on academic enrichment and advancement for middle and secondary level students, sports clinics, art classes; held on campus; accepts boys and girls; open to students from other schools. 600 students usually enrolled. 2012 schedule: June 20 to August 12.

Tuition and Aid Day student tuition: $16,500. Tuition installment plan (FACTS Tuition Payment Plan, single payment plan). Tuition reduction for siblings, merit scholarship grants, need-based scholarship grants available. In 2011–12, 35% of upper-school students received aid; total upper-school merit-scholarship money awarded: $25,000. Total amount of financial aid awarded in 2011–12: $250,000.

Admissions Traditional secondary-level entrance grade is 9. For fall 2011, 165 students applied for upper-level admission, 85 were accepted, 72 enrolled. SLEP for foreign students and SSAT required. Deadline for receipt of application materials: none. Application fee required: $50. On-campus interview required.

Athletics Interscholastic: baseball (boys), basketball (b,g), lacrosse (b,g), soccer (b,g), softball (g), ultimate Frisbee (b,g), volleyball (g); intramural: ballet (g), dance (b); coed interscholastic: alpine skiing, Frisbee, golf, skiing (downhill); coed intramural: alpine skiing, cooperative games, fitness, nordic skiing, physical fitness, physical training, skiing (downhill), snowboarding, strength & conditioning, weight lifting, weight training. 3 PE instructors, 12 coaches, 1 athletic trainer.

Computers Computers are regularly used in career education, college planning, computer applications, data processing, desktop publishing, graphic design, keyboarding, mathematics, science, typing, Web site design, word processing, yearbook classes. Computer network features include on-campus library services, Internet access, Internet filtering or blocking technology, MS Office Suite, educational software, digital photography and darkroom facility. Students grades are available online. The school has a published electronic and media policy.

Contact Adm. Robin Egan, Director of Admissions. 860-651-9361 Ext. 5001. Fax: 860-651-9363. E-mail: regan@masterschool.org. Web site: www.masterschool.org.

THE MASTERS SCHOOL

49 Clinton Avenue

Dobbs Ferry, New York 10522

Head of School: Dr. Maureen Fonseca

General Information Coeducational boarding and day college-preparatory, arts, and technology school. Boarding grades 9–12, day grades 5–12. Founded: 1877. Setting: suburban. Nearest major city is New York. Students are housed in single-sex dormitories. 96-acre campus. 13 buildings on campus. Approved or accredited by Middle States Association of Colleges and Schools, New York State Association of Independent Schools, The Association of Boarding Schools, and New York Department of Education. Member of National Association of Independent Schools and Secondary School Admission Test Board. Endowment: $25.5 million. Total enrollment: 603. Upper school average class size: 14. Upper school faculty-student ratio: 1:8. Upper School students typically attend 5 days per week. The average school day consists of 6 hours.

Upper School Student Profile Grade 9: 90 students (37 boys, 53 girls); Grade 10: 122 students (55 boys, 67 girls); Grade 11: 110 students (48 boys, 62 girls); Grade 12: 116 students (57 boys, 59 girls). 40% of students are boarding students. 70% are state residents. 17 states are represented in upper school student body. 16% are international students. International students from China, Germany, Republic of Korea, Russian Federation, Switzerland, and Taiwan; 16 other countries represented in student body.

Faculty School total: 97. In upper school: 37 men, 50 women; 70 have advanced degrees; 60 reside on campus.

Subjects Offered Acting, algebra, American history, American literature, art history, biology, biology-AP, calculus, calculus-AP, ceramics, chemistry, chemistry-AP, computer math, computer programming, computer science, creative writing, dance, drama, driver education, earth science, electronics, English, English language-AP, English literature, English literature-AP, environmental science, ESL, ethics, European history, European history-AP, expository writing, fine arts, French, French language-AP, French literature-AP, geography, geometry, grammar, health, health and wellness, health education, jazz, jazz band, journalism, Latin, Latin-AP, mathematics, meteorology, music, music theory-AP, performing arts, photography, physical education, physics, physics-AP, pre-calculus, religion, science, senior thesis, social studies, Spanish, Spanish language-AP, Spanish literature-AP, speech, statistics, statistics-AP, studio art, studio art-AP, theater, trigonometry, U.S. history, U.S. history-AP, world history, world literature, world religions, writing, yearbook, yoga.

Graduation Requirements Arts and fine arts (art, music, dance, drama), computer science, English, foreign language, health, mathematics, physical education (includes health), public speaking, science, U.S. history, world history, world religions.

Special Academic Programs 19 Advanced Placement exams for which test preparation is offered; honors section; independent study; term-away projects; study at local college for college credit; study abroad; academic accommodation for the gifted, the musically talented, and the artistically talented; ESL (20 students enrolled).

College Admission Counseling 95 students graduated in 2011; all went to college, including Cornell University; Middlebury College; New York University; The Johns Hopkins University; University of Chicago; Williams College. Mean SAT critical reading: 660, mean SAT math: 630, mean SAT writing: 700, mean combined SAT:

1990. 61% scored over 600 on SAT critical reading, 57% scored over 600 on SAT math, 68% scored over 600 on SAT writing, 58% scored over 1800 on combined SAT.

Student Life Upper grades have specified standards of dress, student council. Discipline rests equally with students and faculty.

Tuition and Aid Day student tuition: $33,830; 7-day tuition and room/board: $47,780. Tuition installment plan (Insured Tuition Payment Plan, Key Tuition Payment Plan, monthly payment plans, individually arranged payment plans). Need-based scholarship grants available. In 2011–12, 25% of upper-school students received aid. Total amount of financial aid awarded in 2011–12: $4,000,000.

Admissions Traditional secondary-level entrance grade is 9. For fall 2011, 520 students applied for upper-level admission, 243 were accepted, 156 enrolled. ISEE, SSAT or TOEFL required. Deadline for receipt of application materials: February 1. Application fee required: $50. Interview required.

Athletics Interscholastic: baseball (boys), basketball (b,g), cross-country running (b,g), fencing (b,g), field hockey (g), lacrosse (b,g), soccer (b,g), softball (g), tennis (b,g), volleyball (g); coed interscholastic: dance, dance team, golf, indoor track, track and field; coed intramural: aerobics, aerobics/dance, aerobics/Nautilus, combined training, dance squad, dance team, fitness, Frisbee, martial arts, modern dance, outdoor activities, physical fitness, physical training, strength & conditioning, ultimate Frisbee, weight lifting, weight training, yoga. 2 PE instructors, 13 coaches, 1 athletic trainer.

Computers Computers are regularly used in computer applications, English, foreign language, graphic arts, graphic design, history, mathematics, newspaper, photography, programming, publications, science, senior seminar, study skills, video film production, Web site design, writing, yearbook classes. Computer network features include on-campus library services, online commercial services, Internet access, wireless campus network, Internet filtering or blocking technology. Student e-mail accounts and computer access in designated common areas are available to students. The school has a published electronic and media policy.

Contact Office of Admission. 914-479-6420. Fax: 914-693-7295. E-mail: admission@mastersny.org. Web site: www.mastersny.org.

MATIGNON HIGH SCHOOL

One Matignon Road

Cambridge, Massachusetts 02140

Head of School: Mr. Thomas F. Galligani

General Information Coeducational day college-preparatory, arts, business, religious studies, and technology school, affiliated with Roman Catholic Church. Grades 9–12. Founded: 1945. Setting: suburban. Nearest major city is Boston. 10-acre campus. 3 buildings on campus. Approved or accredited by Association of Independent Schools in New England, National Catholic Education Association, New England Association of Schools and Colleges, and Massachusetts Department of Education. Endowment: $253,000. Total enrollment: 442. Upper school average class size: 18. Upper school faculty-student ratio: 1:15. Upper School students typically attend 5 days per week. The average school day consists of 7 hours.

Upper School Student Profile Grade 9: 102 students (40 boys, 62 girls); Grade 10: 118 students (51 boys, 67 girls); Grade 11: 116 students (58 boys, 58 girls); Grade 12: 106 students (55 boys, 51 girls). 75% of students are Roman Catholic.

Faculty School total: 39. In upper school: 15 men, 24 women; 23 have advanced degrees.

Subjects Offered 3-dimensional art, 3-dimensional design, accounting, adolescent issues, Advanced Placement courses, algebra, American history, American literature, anatomy and physiology, art, art history, Bible studies, biology, calculus, chemistry, community service, computer science, drawing and design, economics, English, English literature, environmental science, fine arts, French, geometry, government/civics, grammar, health, history, Latin, law, mathematics, physical education, physics, psychology, religion, science, social sciences, social studies, Spanish, theology, trigonometry, world history, writing.

Graduation Requirements 20th century history, accounting, Advanced Placement courses, algebra, American history, anatomy and physiology, arts and fine arts (art, music, dance, drama), chemistry, computer science, English-AP, French, French-AP, geometry, health education, honors algebra, honors English, honors geometry, honors world history, Latin, law, physical education (includes health), psychology, religious studies, SAT preparation, senior internship, Spanish, Spanish-AP, U.S. history, U.S. history-AP, world cultures, world history, Christian service, forty-five hours of community service (before junior year).

Special Academic Programs Advanced Placement exam preparation; honors section; independent study; study at local college for college credit; study abroad; ESL (20 students enrolled).

College Admission Counseling 98 students graduated in 2011; 96 went to college, including Boston University; Northeastern University; Saint Anselm College; Suffolk University; University of Massachusetts Amherst; University of Massachusetts Boston. Other: 2 entered military service. Mean SAT critical reading: 529, mean SAT math: 550, mean SAT writing: 540, mean combined SAT: 1619. 21% scored over 600 on SAT critical reading, 23% scored over 600 on SAT math, 14% scored over 600 on SAT writing, 20% scored over 1800 on combined SAT.

Student Life Upper grades have uniform requirement, student council, honor system. Discipline rests primarily with faculty. Attendance at religious services is required.

Summer Programs Remediation, enrichment programs offered; held on campus; accepts boys and girls; open to students from other schools. 80 students usually enrolled. 2012 schedule: June 27 to August 12. Application deadline: none.

Tuition and Aid Day student tuition: $8600. Tuition installment plan (FACTS Tuition Payment Plan, monthly payment plans). Merit scholarship grants, need-based scholarship grants available. In 2011–12, 50% of upper-school students received aid; total upper-school merit-scholarship money awarded: $50,000. Total amount of financial aid awarded in 2011–12: $110,000.

Admissions Traditional secondary-level entrance grade is 9. For fall 2011, 430 students applied for upper-level admission, 320 were accepted, 102 enrolled. Catholic High School Entrance Examination, SSAT or TOEFL or SLEP required. Deadline for receipt of application materials: none. No application fee required. On-campus interview recommended.

Athletics Interscholastic: baseball (boys), basketball (b,g), cheering (g), cross-country running (b,g), football (b), golf (b,g), ice hockey (b,g), lacrosse (b,g), soccer (b,g), softball (g), swimming and diving (b,g), tennis (b,g), track and field (b,g), volleyball (g); intramural: aerobics/dance (b,g), dance (g), dance squad (g), dance team (g), figure skating (g), Frisbee (b,g), physical training (b,g), strength & conditioning (b,g), weight lifting (b,g), weight training (b,g); coed intramural: yoga. 1 PE instructor, 20 coaches, 1 athletic trainer.

Computers Computers are regularly used in all academic classes. Computer network features include on-campus library services, Internet access, wireless campus network, Internet filtering or blocking technology, all academic homework is provided online. Student e-mail accounts and computer access in designated common areas are available to students. Students grades are available online.

Contact Mr. Joseph A. DiSarcina, Principal. 617-876-1212 Ext. 14. Fax: 617-661-3905. E-mail: jdisarcina@matignon-hs.org. Web site: www.matignon-hs.org.

MAUI PREPARATORY ACADEMY

5095 Napilihau Street, #109B

PMB #186

Lahaina, Hawaii 96761

Head of School: Mr. George C. Baker

General Information Coeducational day college-preparatory school. Grades PK–12. Founded: 2005. Approved or accredited by Western Association of Schools and Colleges.

Subjects Offered Art, biology, calculus, chemistry, English, environmental science, foreign language, health, history, mathematics, physics, social studies, technology.

Graduation Requirements Science project.

Special Academic Programs Advanced Placement exam preparation.

Admissions ERB required.

Athletics Interscholastic: aquatics (boys, girls), canoeing/kayaking (b,g), cross-country running (b,g), golf (b), independent competitive sports (b,g), indoor track (b,g), ocean paddling (b,g), surfing (b,g), swimming and diving (b,g), tennis (b,g), track and field (b,g), volleyball (g); intramural: basketball (b,g), marksmanship (b,g), ropes courses (b,g), surfing (b,g), windsurfing (b,g); coed interscholastic: aquatics, canoeing/kayaking, cross-country running, independent competitive sports, indoor track, ocean paddling, surfing, swimming and diving, tennis, track and field; coed intramural: basketball, marksmanship, ropes courses, surfing, windsurfing.

Contact Mrs. Cathi Minami, Admissions Coordinator. 808-665-9966. Fax: 808-665-1075. E-mail: cminami@mauiprep.org.

MAUR HILL-MOUNT ACADEMY

1000 Green Street

Atchison, Kansas 66002

Head of School: Mr. Phil Baniewicz

General Information Coeducational boarding and day college-preparatory, arts, religious studies, bilingual studies, and English as a Second language school, affiliated with Roman Catholic Church. Grades 9–12. Founded: 1863. Setting: small town. Nearest major city is Kansas City, MO. Students are housed in single-sex dormitories. 90-acre campus. 7 buildings on campus. Approved or accredited by National Catholic Education Association, North Central Association of Colleges and Schools, The Association of Boarding Schools, and Kansas Department of Education. Member of Secondary School Admission Test Board. Total enrollment: 198. Upper school average class size: 17. Upper school faculty-student ratio: 1:9. There are 182 required school days per year for Upper School students. Upper School students typically attend 5 days per week. The average school day consists of 6 hours and 30 minutes.

Upper School Student Profile Grade 9: 53 students (29 boys, 24 girls); Grade 10: 45 students (24 boys, 21 girls); Grade 11: 56 students (32 boys, 24 girls); Grade 12: 54 students (27 boys, 27 girls). 40% of students are boarding students. 50% are state residents. 7 states are represented in upper school student body. 25% are international students. International students from China, Mexico, Republic of Korea, Saudi Arabia,

Sweden, and Taiwan; 5 other countries represented in student body. 65% of students are Roman Catholic.

Faculty School total: 21. In upper school: 13 men, 8 women; 11 have advanced degrees; 3 reside on campus.

Subjects Offered Algebra, American history, American literature, anatomy, art, basketball, Bible studies, biology, business, business skills, calculus, chemistry, computer math, computer programming, computer science, current events, drama, economics, English, English literature, ESL, ethics, fine arts, French, geography, geometry, government/civics, grammar, health, history, humanities, journalism, mathematics, music, photography, physical education, physics, physiology, psychology, religion, science, social sciences, social studies, sociology, Spanish, speech, theater, theology, trigonometry, typing, world history, world literature, writing.

Graduation Requirements Arts and fine arts (art, music, dance, drama), business skills (includes word processing), computer science, English, foreign language, mathematics, physical education (includes health), religion (includes Bible studies and theology), science, social sciences, social studies (includes history).

Special Academic Programs Honors section; study at local college for college credit; academic accommodation for the gifted; special instructional classes for students with Attention Deficit Disorder; ESL (19 students enrolled).

College Admission Counseling 57 students graduated in 2010; 56 went to college, including Benedictine College; Creighton University; Penn State University Park; Saint Louis University; The University of Kansas. Other: 1 went to work.

Student Life Upper grades have uniform requirement, student council, honor system. Discipline rests primarily with faculty. Attendance at religious services is required.

Tuition and Aid 5-day tuition and room/board: $16,000; 7-day tuition and room/board: $18,650. Tuition installment plan (FACTS Tuition Payment Plan, monthly payment plans, individually arranged payment plans). Tuition reduction for siblings, merit scholarship grants, need-based scholarship grants, paying campus jobs available. In 2010–11, 40% of upper-school students received aid. Total amount of financial aid awarded in 2010–11: $225,000.

Admissions Traditional secondary-level entrance grade is 10. For fall 2010, 134 students applied for upper-level admission, 65 were accepted, 54 enrolled. High School Placement Test required. Deadline for receipt of application materials: none. Application fee required: $50. Interview required.

Athletics Interscholastic: aquatics (girls), baseball (b), basketball (b,g), cheering (g), cross-country running (b,g), dance (g), dance squad (g), dance team (g), drill team (g), football (b), swimming and diving (g), tennis (b,g), track and field (b,g), volleyball (g); intramural: boxing (b), field hockey (b), fitness (b), flag football (b), floor hockey (b), football (b), running (b,g), skateboarding (b), skiing (downhill) (b,g), soccer (b,g), swimming and diving (b,g), touch football (b), track and field (b,g), weight lifting (b,g), weight training (b,g); coed interscholastic: golf, physical fitness, physical training, running, soccer, wrestling; coed intramural: baseball, basketball, bowling, Nautilus, physical fitness, physical training, roller blading, table tennis, tennis, volleyball, walking. 2 PE instructors, 10 coaches, 2 athletic trainers.

Computers Computer network features include on-campus library services, Internet access, Internet filtering or blocking technology. Students grades are available online.

Contact Mr. Deke Nolan, Admissions Director. 913-367-5482 Ext. 210. Fax: 913-367-5096. E-mail: admissions@mh-ma.com. Web site: www.mh-ma.com.

McDONOGH SCHOOL

8600 McDonogh Road

Owings Mills, Maryland 21117-0380

Head of School: Charles W. Britton

General Information Coeducational boarding and day college-preparatory school. Boarding grades 9–12, day grades K–12. Founded: 1873. Setting: suburban. Nearest major city is Baltimore. Students are housed in single-sex dormitories. 800-acre campus. 44 buildings on campus. Approved or accredited by Association of Independent Maryland Schools. Member of National Association of Independent Schools. Endowment: $83 million. Total enrollment: 1,296. Upper school average class size: 15. Upper school faculty-student ratio: 1:9. There are 169 required school days per year for Upper School students. Upper School students typically attend 5 days per week. The average school day consists of 6 hours and 10 minutes.

Upper School Student Profile Grade 9: 145 students (79 boys, 66 girls); Grade 10: 151 students (76 boys, 75 girls); Grade 11: 147 students (78 boys, 69 girls); Grade 12: 142 students (80 boys, 62 girls). 9% of students are boarding students. 98% are state residents. 3 states are represented in upper school student body. 1% are international students.

Faculty School total: 177. In upper school: 35 men, 48 women; 57 have advanced degrees; 32 reside on campus.

Subjects Offered 20th century American writers, acting, Advanced Placement courses, African history, African literature, African-American studies, algebra, American history, American history-AP, American literature, American literature-AP, anatomy, art, art history, art-AP, Asian studies, band, biology, biology-AP, botany, calculus, calculus-AP, ceramics, chemistry, chemistry-AP, Chesapeake Bay studies, classical Greek literature, composition-AP, computer animation, computer graphics, computer music, computer programming, computer science, computer science-AP, concert band, concert choir, creative writing, dance, drama, drawing, ecology, economics, economics-AP, electives, engineering, English, English composition, English literature, English literature and composition-AP, English literature-AP, English-AP, English/composition-AP, environmental science, environmental science-AP, ethics, European history, film, film and literature, fine arts, fitness, foreign language, French, French language-AP, French literature-AP, French-AP, genetics, geology, geometry, German, German-AP, government and politics-AP, government-AP, government/civics, health and wellness, history, history-AP, honors algebra, honors English, honors geometry, honors U.S. history, honors world history, jazz band, jazz dance, journalism, language-AP, languages, Latin, Latin American literature, linguistics, literature and composition-AP, literature by women, marine biology, mathematics, Middle Eastern history, music, music theory, music theory-AP, oceanography, photography, physical education, physical fitness, physics, poetry, pre-calculus, psychology, religion, Russian history, science, senior project, set design, Shakespeare, short story, Spanish, Spanish language-AP, Spanish literature, Spanish literature-AP, Spanish-AP, speech, speech communications, statistics-AP, tap dance, theater, trigonometry, U.S. government and politics-AP, U.S. history, U.S. history-AP, video, visual arts, Web site design, woodworking, world history, world history-AP, world religions, world wide web design, writing workshop, yearbook.

Graduation Requirements Arts and fine arts (art, music, dance, drama), English, foreign language, mathematics, physical education (includes health), science, senior project, social studies (includes history). Community service is required.

Special Academic Programs Advanced Placement exam preparation; honors section; independent study; term-away projects.

College Admission Counseling 138 students graduated in 2011; all went to college, including Bucknell University; College of Charleston; Cornell University; Franklin & Marshall College; University of Maryland, College Park; University of Pennsylvania. Mean SAT critical reading: 611, mean SAT math: 647, mean SAT writing: 620, mean combined SAT: 1878, mean composite ACT: 28.

Student Life Upper grades have uniform requirement, student council, honor system. Discipline rests primarily with faculty.

Summer Programs Enrichment, ESL, sports, art/fine arts, computer instruction programs offered; session focuses on recreation and sports camps; held both on and off campus; held at Gunpowder Falls State Park and Chesapeake Bay; accepts boys and girls; open to students from other schools. 1,800 students usually enrolled. 2012 schedule: June 18 to July 27. Application deadline: May 1.

Tuition and Aid Day student tuition: $23,370; 5-day tuition and room/board: $31,420. Tuition installment plan (Key Tuition Payment Plan, monthly payment plans, individually arranged payment plans). Need-based scholarship grants, need-based loans, middle-income loans available. In 2011–12, 24% of upper-school students received aid. Total amount of financial aid awarded in 2011–12: $2,415,935.

Admissions Traditional secondary-level entrance grade is 9. For fall 2011, 295 students applied for upper-level admission, 91 were accepted, 51 enrolled. ISEE required. Deadline for receipt of application materials: December 15. Application fee required: $50. On-campus interview required.

Athletics Interscholastic: aquatics (boys, girls), baseball (b), basketball (b,g), cross-country running (b,g), equestrian sports (b,g), field hockey (g), football (b), golf (b,g), indoor track & field (b,g), lacrosse (b,g), soccer (b,g), softball (g), swimming and diving (b,g), tennis (b,g), volleyball (g), water polo (b,g), winter (indoor) track (b,g), wrestling (b); coed interscholastic: cheering, equestrian sports, horseback riding, indoor track & field, squash, track and field; coed intramural: badminton, ballet, dance, fencing, fitness, squash, ultimate Frisbee. 14 PE instructors, 92 coaches, 2 athletic trainers.

Computers Computers are regularly used in all classes. Computer network features include on-campus library services, online commercial services, Internet access, wireless campus network, Internet filtering or blocking technology. Campus intranet, student e-mail accounts, and computer access in designated common areas are available to students. Students grades are available online. The school has a published electronic and media policy.

Contact Anita Hilson, Director of Admissions. 410-581-4719. Fax: 410-998-3537. E-mail: ahilson@mcdonogh.org. Web site: www.mcdonogh.org.

McGILL-TOOLEN CATHOLIC HIGH SCHOOL

1501 Old Shell Road

Mobile, Alabama 36604-2291

Head of School: Mrs. Michelle T. Haas

General Information Coeducational day college-preparatory, arts, religious studies, and technology school, affiliated with Roman Catholic Church. Grades 9–12. Founded: 1896. Setting: urban. 18-acre campus. 5 buildings on campus. Approved or accredited by Southern Association of Colleges and Schools and Alabama Department of Education. Total enrollment: 1,078. Upper school average class size: 21. Upper school faculty-student ratio: 1:14. There are 180 required school days per year for Upper School students. Upper School students typically attend 5 days per week. The average school day consists of 6 hours and 40 minutes.

Upper School Student Profile Grade 9: 266 students (132 boys, 134 girls); Grade 10: 278 students (141 boys, 137 girls); Grade 11: 301 students (144 boys, 157 girls); Grade 12: 233 students (123 boys, 110 girls). 90.4% of students are Roman Catholic.

Faculty School total: 79. In upper school: 36 men, 42 women; 51 have advanced degrees.
Subjects Offered 3-dimensional art, 3-dimensional design, ACT preparation, advanced biology, advanced chemistry, advanced math, Advanced Placement courses, American government, American history, American history-AP, American literature, analytic geometry, anatomy and physiology, athletic training, band, baseball, basketball, Bible studies, biology, biology-AP, British literature, British literature (honors), calculus, calculus-AP, campus ministry, Catholic belief and practice, ceramics, cheerleading, chemistry, chemistry-AP, choir, choral music, chorus, church history, conceptual physics, concert choir, current events, driver education, economics, English, English composition, English language and composition-AP, English-AP, French, geography, geometry, government, government and politics-AP, graphic design, health, health and wellness, history of the Catholic Church, honors algebra, honors English, honors geometry, honors U.S. history, honors world history, independent study, keyboarding, Latin, marine biology, modern European history-AP, modern world history, multimedia, music appreciation, painting, physical education, physical fitness, physics, physics-AP, pre-algebra, pre-calculus, psychology, reading, reading/study skills, softball, Spanish, Spanish language-AP, speech, studio art, studio art-AP, U.S. government, U.S. government and politics, U.S. government and politics-AP, U.S. history, U.S. history-AP, U.S. literature, video film production, vocal ensemble, volleyball, Web site design, weight fitness, weight training, world geography, world history, world history-AP, world literature, yearbook.
Graduation Requirements Electives, English, keyboarding, mathematics, physical education (includes health), religion (includes Bible studies and theology), science, social studies (includes history), must complete 1 cultural unit each semeseter enrolled at McGill-Toolen.
Special Academic Programs 14 Advanced Placement exams for which test preparation is offered; honors section; remedial reading and/or remedial writing; remedial math.
College Admission Counseling 239 students graduated in 2010; 220 went to college, including Auburn University; Louisiana State University and Agricultural and Mechanical College; Spring Hill College; The University of Alabama; University of South Alabama; University of Southern Mississippi. Other: 17 went to work, 2 entered military service. Median composite ACT: 23. 19% scored over 26 on composite ACT.
Student Life Upper grades have uniform requirement, student council. Discipline rests primarily with faculty. Attendance at religious services is required.
Tuition and Aid Day student tuition: $6000–$7200. Tuition installment plan (FACTS Tuition Payment Plan). Tuition reduction for siblings, merit scholarship grants, need-based scholarship grants available. In 2010–11, 25% of upper-school students received aid; total upper-school merit-scholarship money awarded: $25,000. Total amount of financial aid awarded in 2010–11: $335,000.
Admissions ACT-Explore required. Deadline for receipt of application materials: none. Application fee required: $100. On-campus interview recommended.
Athletics Interscholastic: baseball (boys), basketball (b,g), cheering (g), cross-country running (b,g), diving (b,g), football (b), golf (b,g), indoor track (g), soccer (b,g), softball (g), swimming and diving (b,g), tennis (b,g), track and field (b,g), volleyball (g); intramural: outdoor adventure (b,g), table tennis (b,g), ultimate Frisbee (b,g); coed intramural: hiking/backpacking. 4 PE instructors, 3 coaches, 1 athletic trainer.
Computers Computers are regularly used in current events, graphic design, keyboarding, reading, technology, video film production, Web site design, yearbook classes. Computer network features include on-campus library services, Internet access, wireless campus network, Internet filtering or blocking technology. Campus intranet is available to students. Students grades are available online. The school has a published electronic and media policy.
Contact Mr. Paul Knapstein, Director of Enrollment. 251-445-2934. Fax: 251-433-8356. E-mail: knapstp@mcgill-toolen.org.

MEADOWRIDGE SCHOOL

12224 240th Street

Maple Ridge, British Columbia V4R 1N1, Canada

Head of School: Mr. Hugh Burke

General Information Coeducational day college-preparatory, arts, and technology school. Grades JK–12. Founded: 1985. Setting: rural. Nearest major city is Vancouver, Canada. 16-acre campus. 1 building on campus. Approved or accredited by Canadian Association of Independent Schools, Canadian Educational Standards Institute, International Baccalaureate Organization, and British Columbia Department of Education. Language of instruction: English. Total enrollment: 511. Upper school average class size: 18. Upper school faculty-student ratio: 1:9. The average school day consists of 6 hours.
Upper School Student Profile Grade 8: 44 students (19 boys, 25 girls); Grade 9: 31 students (12 boys, 19 girls); Grade 10: 38 students (13 boys, 25 girls); Grade 11: 42 students (18 boys, 24 girls); Grade 12: 28 students (16 boys, 12 girls).
Faculty School total: 46. In upper school: 11 men, 9 women; 6 have advanced degrees.
Subjects Offered Accounting, Advanced Placement courses, art, biology, biology-AP, calculus, calculus-AP, career and personal planning, chemistry, comparative civilizations, computer science-AP, computer technologies, drama, English, English literature, English-AP, filmmaking, forensics, French, geography, history, humanities, marketing, mathematics, photography, physical education, physics, science, Spanish, weight training.
Graduation Requirements 3 provincially examinable courses.
Special Academic Programs International Baccalaureate program; study abroad; academic accommodation for the gifted.
College Admission Counseling 34 students graduated in 2010; all went to college, including McGill University; Queen's University at Kingston; Simon Fraser University; The University of British Columbia; University of Toronto; University of Victoria.
Student Life Upper grades have uniform requirement, student council, honor system. Discipline rests equally with students and faculty.
Tuition and Aid Day student tuition: CAN$13,800. Tuition installment plan (Insured Tuition Payment Plan, monthly payment plans). Tuition reduction for siblings, bursaries, merit scholarship grants available. In 2010–11, 1% of upper-school students received aid; total upper-school merit-scholarship money awarded: CAN$22,000.
Admissions Traditional secondary-level entrance grade is 8. For fall 2010, 39 students applied for upper-level admission, 28 were accepted, 26 enrolled. Admissions testing and writing sample required. Deadline for receipt of application materials: none. Application fee required: CAN$150. On-campus interview required.
Athletics Interscholastic: aerobics/dance (boys, girls), badminton (b,g), basketball (b,g), physical fitness (b,g), rugby (b,g), soccer (b,g), volleyball (b,g); intramural: aerobics/dance (b,g), basketball (b,g); coed interscholastic: aerobics/dance, cross-country running, flag football, outdoor activities, swimming and diving, track and field; coed intramural: aerobics/dance. 2 PE instructors.
Computers Computers are regularly used in information technology, journalism, video film production, yearbook classes. Computer network features include on-campus library services, Internet access, wireless campus network, Internet filtering or blocking technology. Student e-mail accounts and computer access in designated common areas are available to students.
Contact Ms. Christine Bickle, Director of Admissions. 604-476-3040. Fax: 604-467-4989. E-mail: christine.bickle@meadowridge.bc.ca. Web site: www.meadowridge.bc.ca.

THE MEADOWS SCHOOL

8601 Scholar Lane

Las Vegas, Nevada 89128-7302

Head of School: Mr. Henry L. Chanin

General Information Coeducational day college-preparatory, arts, technology, and debate, foreign languages school. Grades PK–12. Founded: 1981. Setting: suburban. 42-acre campus. 10 buildings on campus. Approved or accredited by CITA (Commission on International and Trans Regional Accreditation), Northwest Association of Schools and Colleges, Pacific Northwest Association of Independent Schools, and Nevada Department of Education. Member of National Association of Independent Schools and Secondary School Admission Test Board. Endowment: $12 million. Total enrollment: 900. Upper school average class size: 12. Upper school faculty-student ratio: 1:11. There are 180 required school days per year for Upper School students. Upper School students typically attend 5 days per week. The average school day consists of 7 hours.
Upper School Student Profile Grade 9: 77 students (35 boys, 42 girls); Grade 10: 81 students (37 boys, 44 girls); Grade 11: 67 students (32 boys, 35 girls); Grade 12: 70 students (34 boys, 36 girls).
Faculty School total: 89. In upper school: 18 men, 20 women; 26 have advanced degrees.
Subjects Offered 20th century American writers, 3-dimensional art, acting, advanced math, Advanced Placement courses, advanced studio art-AP, American literature, anatomy and physiology, anthropology, architectural drawing, architecture, art, art history, art history-AP, athletics, band, Basic programming, biology, biology-AP, British literature, British literature (honors), calculus, calculus-AP, ceramics, chemistry, chemistry-AP, choral music, chorus, comparative religion, composition, computer applications, computer graphics, computer literacy, computer programming, computer programming-AP, computer science, computer science-AP, concert choir, constitutional law, creative writing, dance, digital art, digital photography, drama, drama performance, drawing, drawing and design, economics, engineering, English, English composition, English language and composition-AP, English literature, English literature and composition-AP, European history, European history-AP, film studies, fine arts, finite math, foreign language, forensics, French, French language-AP, genetics, geometry, government-AP, health, honors English, honors geometry, honors U.S. history, honors world history, human anatomy, instrumental music, integrated mathematics, international affairs, international relations, journalism, keyboarding, Latin, Latin-AP, law, literature and composition-AP, macro/microeconomics-AP, money management, music theater, music theory-AP, organic chemistry, painting, philosophy, photography, physics, physics-AP, policy and value, pre-calculus, psychology-AP, sculpture, Shakespeare, social justice, social sciences, Spanish, Spanish language-AP, Spanish literature, Spanish literature-AP, Spanish-AP, speech, speech and debate, speech and oral interpretations, statistics, statistics-AP, studio art, studio art-AP, technical theater, technology, theater production, trigonometry, U.S. government, U.S. government and politics-AP, U.S. history, U.S. history-AP, yearbook.

Graduation Requirements American literature, ancient world history, arts and fine arts (art, music, dance, drama), biology, English, English composition, English literature, European history, foreign language, geometry, mathematics, physical education (includes health), physics, pre-calculus, science, social studies (includes history), technical skills, U.S. government, U.S. history, seniors have a 24-hour per semester community service requirement, grades 9-11 have a 16-hour per semester community service requirement.

Special Academic Programs 24 Advanced Placement exams for which test preparation is offered; honors section; academic accommodation for the gifted, the musically talented, and the artistically talented.

College Admission Counseling 44 students graduated in 2011; all went to college, including American University; Chapman University; Cornell University; University of California, San Diego; University of San Diego; University of Southern California. Median SAT critical reading: 680, median SAT math: 660, median SAT writing: 680, median combined SAT: 2020, median composite ACT: 29. 77% scored over 600 on SAT critical reading, 89% scored over 600 on SAT math, 91% scored over 600 on SAT writing, 82% scored over 1800 on combined SAT, 89% scored over 26 on composite ACT.

Student Life Upper grades have uniform requirement, student council, honor system. Discipline rests equally with students and faculty.

Summer Programs Enrichment, sports, art/fine arts programs offered; session focuses on enrichment; held on campus; accepts boys and girls; open to students from other schools. 50 students usually enrolled. 2012 schedule: June 11 to July 6. Application deadline: May 25.

Tuition and Aid Day student tuition: $20,450. Tuition installment plan (Insured Tuition Payment Plan, monthly payment plans, individually arranged payment plans, 2-payment plan, 70% by July 15 and 30% by February 15, 10 monthly payment plan using electronic withdrawal only). Need-based scholarship grants, need-based loans available. In 2011–12, 14% of upper-school students received aid. Total amount of financial aid awarded in 2011–12: $612,935.

Admissions Traditional secondary-level entrance grade is 9. ERB, ISEE, PSAT or SSAT required. Deadline for receipt of application materials: none. Application fee required: $100. On-campus interview required.

Athletics Interscholastic: baseball (boys), basketball (b,g), bowling (b,g), cheering (g), cross-country running (b,g), dance team (g), diving (b,g), football (b), softball (g), swimming and diving (b,g), tennis (b,g), track and field (b,g), volleyball (g), wrestling (b); coed interscholastic: golf, soccer. 1 PE instructor, 1 athletic trainer.

Computers Computers are regularly used in all academic, architecture, college planning, desktop publishing, English, foreign language, graphic design, history, independent study, information technology, introduction to technology, library, mathematics, music, news writing, photography, photojournalism, programming, publications, publishing, science, speech, technology, yearbook classes. Computer network features include on-campus library services, online commercial services, Internet access, wireless campus network, Internet filtering or blocking technology, Neon, SMART boards, three wireless mobile computer labs with notebook computers, course syllabus and homework for Upper and Middle School. Computer access in designated common areas is available to students. The school has a published electronic and media policy.

Contact 702-254-1610. Fax: 702-254-2452. Web site: www.themeadowsschool.org.

MEMORIAL HALL SCHOOL

5400 Mitchelldale, Ste. A-1

Houston, Texas 77092

Head of School: Rev. George C. Aurich

General Information Coeducational day college-preparatory, general academic, and bilingual studies school. Grades 4–12. Founded: 1966. Setting: urban. 1 building on campus. Approved or accredited by Southern Association of Colleges and Schools, Southern Association of Independent Schools, Texas Education Agency, and Texas Department of Education. Total enrollment: 80. Upper school average class size: 14. Upper school faculty-student ratio: 1:14. Upper School students typically attend 4 days per week. The average school day consists of 7 hours and 30 minutes.

Faculty School total: 11. In upper school: 4 men, 7 women; 3 have advanced degrees.

Subjects Offered Algebra, American history, art, biology, business mathematics, business skills, chemistry, computer science, economics, English, ESL, fine arts, geography, geometry, government/civics, health, history, journalism, mathematics, physical education, physics, psychology, science, social sciences, social studies, sociology, Spanish, trigonometry, world history.

Graduation Requirements Arts and crafts, arts and fine arts (art, music, dance, drama), business skills (includes word processing), computer science, English, foreign language, mathematics, physical education (includes health), science, social sciences, social studies (includes history), community service, foreign credit accepted upon completion.

Special Academic Programs Honors section; accelerated programs; independent study; study at local college for college credit; academic accommodation for the gifted; remedial reading and/or remedial writing; remedial math; programs in English, mathematics, general development for dyslexic students; special instructional classes for students with learning disabilities, Attention Deficit Disorder, and dyslexia; ESL (60 students enrolled).

College Admission Counseling 28 students graduated in 2010; all went to college, including Baylor University; Sam Houston State University; St. Thomas University; Texas A&M University; The University of Texas at Austin; University of Houston.

Student Life Upper grades have uniform requirement, student council, honor system. Discipline rests equally with students and faculty.

Tuition and Aid Day student tuition: $11,400. Tuition installment plan (Insured Tuition Payment Plan, monthly payment plans, individually arranged payment plans). Tuition reduction for siblings available. In 2010–11, 5% of upper-school students received aid.

Admissions Traditional secondary-level entrance grade is 9. Stanford Achievement Test required. Deadline for receipt of application materials: none. Application fee required: $300. Interview required.

Athletics Interscholastic: aerobics (boys, girls), aerobics/dance (b,g), fitness (b,g), fitness walking (b,g), jump rope (b,g), yoga (b,g); intramural: cheering (g); coed intramural: dance, outdoor activities, physical fitness. 2 PE instructors.

Computers Computers are regularly used in all academic, basic skills, foreign language classes. Computer network features include Internet access.

Contact Kimberly Smith, Coordinator. 713-688-5566. Fax: 713-956-9751. E-mail: memhallsch@aol.com. Web site: www.memorialhall.org.

MEMPHIS UNIVERSITY SCHOOL

6191 Park Avenue

Memphis, Tennessee 38119-5399

Head of School: Mr. Ellis L. Haguewood

General Information Boys' day college-preparatory school. Grades 7–12. Founded: 1893. Setting: suburban. 94-acre campus. 8 buildings on campus. Approved or accredited by Southern Association of Colleges and Schools, Southern Association of Independent Schools, and Tennessee Association of Independent Schools. Member of National Association of Independent Schools. Endowment: $21 million. Total enrollment: 660. Upper school average class size: 14. Upper school faculty-student ratio: 1:8. There are 176 required school days per year for Upper School students. Upper School students typically attend 5 days per week. The average school day consists of 7 hours.

Upper School Student Profile Grade 9: 128 students (128 boys); Grade 10: 114 students (114 boys); Grade 11: 129 students (129 boys); Grade 12: 85 students (85 boys).

Faculty School total: 75. In upper school: 47 men, 13 women; 41 have advanced degrees.

Subjects Offered Algebra, American government, American literature, art, art history, art history-AP, arts and crafts, Bible, biology, biology-AP, British literature, calculus, calculus-AP, chemistry, chemistry-AP, choral music, college counseling, college placement, comparative government and politics-AP, comparative religion, composition-AP, computer education, computer programming, computer science, computer science-AP, driver education, earth science, economics, economics and history, English, English composition, English literature, English literature and composition-AP, environmental science, ethics, ethics and responsibility, European history, European history-AP, expository writing, fine arts, foreign language, French, geometry, global studies, government and politics-AP, government/civics, grammar, health, history, humanities, introduction to theater, keyboarding, language and composition, Latin, library skills, literature, mathematics, music, music appreciation, music composition, music theory, physical education, physical science, physics, physics-AP, pre-algebra, pre-calculus, probability and statistics, psychology, religion, research skills, science, social sciences, social studies, Spanish, studio art, study skills, trigonometry, U.S. history, U.S. history-AP, United States government-AP, Western civilization, world history, writing.

Graduation Requirements Arts and fine arts (art, music, dance, drama), English, foreign language, mathematics, physical education (includes health), religion (includes Bible studies and theology), science, social sciences, social studies (includes history).

Special Academic Programs 18 Advanced Placement exams for which test preparation is offered; honors section; study abroad; remedial reading and/or remedial writing; remedial math.

College Admission Counseling 112 students graduated in 2011; all went to college, including Rhodes College; Southern Methodist University; The University of Alabama; The University of Tennessee; University of Mississippi; Vanderbilt University. Median composite ACT: 29. Mean SAT critical reading: 615, mean SAT math: 638, mean SAT writing: 614. 59% scored over 600 on SAT critical reading, 65% scored over 600 on SAT math, 61% scored over 600 on SAT writing, 61% scored over 1800 on combined SAT, 68% scored over 26 on composite ACT.

Student Life Upper grades have specified standards of dress, student council, honor system. Discipline rests primarily with faculty.

Summer Programs Remediation, enrichment, advancement, sports programs offered; session focuses on academics and athletics; held on campus; accepts boys and girls; open to students from other schools. 460 students usually enrolled. 2012 schedule: June 6 to July 29. Application deadline: none.

Tuition and Aid Day student tuition: $17,500. Tuition installment plan (FACTS Tuition Payment Plan, monthly payment plans, individually arranged payment plans).

Need-based scholarship grants available. In 2011–12, 31% of upper-school students received aid. Total amount of financial aid awarded in 2011–12: $1,300,000.
Admissions Traditional secondary-level entrance grade is 9. For fall 2011, 38 students applied for upper-level admission, 35 were accepted, 30 enrolled. ISEE required. Deadline for receipt of application materials: December 10. Application fee required: $50. On-campus interview recommended.
Athletics Interscholastic: baseball, basketball, cross-country running, football, golf, lacrosse, soccer, swimming and diving, tennis, track and field, trap and skeet, weight training, wrestling. 5 PE instructors, 9 coaches, 1 athletic trainer.
Computers Computers are regularly used in all academic, career exploration, college planning, graphic design, library science, newspaper, publications, yearbook classes. Computer network features include on-campus library services, online commercial services, Internet access, wireless campus network, Internet filtering or blocking technology. Campus intranet, student e-mail accounts, and computer access in designated common areas are available to students. Students grades are available online. The school has a published electronic and media policy.
Contact Mrs. Peggy E. Williamson, Director of Admissions. 901-260-1349. Fax: 901-260-1301. E-mail: peggy.williamson@musowls.org. Web site: www.musowls.org.

MENAUL SCHOOL

301 Menaul Boulevard NE

Albuquerque, New Mexico 87107

Head of School: Mr. Lindsey R. Gilbert Jr.

General Information Coeducational boarding and day college-preparatory and College Prep school, affiliated with Presbyterian Church. Boarding grades 9–12, day grades 6–12. Founded: 1896. Setting: urban. Students are housed in single-sex dormitories. 35-acre campus. 10 buildings on campus. Approved or accredited by Independent Schools Association of the Southwest, North Central Association of Colleges and Schools, The College Board, and New Mexico Department of Education. Endowment: $3.3 million. Total enrollment: 185. Upper school average class size: 12. Upper school faculty-student ratio: 1:9. There are 180 required school days per year for Upper School students. Upper School students typically attend 5 days per week. The average school day consists of 6 hours.
Upper School Student Profile 18% of students are boarding students. 9% are state residents. 3 states are represented in upper school student body. 19% are international students. International students from Belgium, China, and Viet Nam; 4 other countries represented in student body. 20% of students are Presbyterian.
Faculty School total: 25. In upper school: 13 men, 11 women, 16 have advanced degrees, 5 reside on campus.
Subjects Offered ACT preparation, Advanced Placement courses, algebra, American government, American history, American literature, art, arts and crafts, band, Bible studies, biology, calculus-AP, chemistry, clayworking, communications, computer graphics, computer programming, computer science, earth science, economics, English, English literature, English-AP, ethics, fine arts, geography, geometry, government/civics, history, Life of Christ, mathematics, music, Native American arts and crafts, physical education, physics, psychology, religion, science, social sciences, social studies, sociology, Spanish, theology, trigonometry, U.S. government and politics-AP, world history, world literature, writing, yearbook.
Graduation Requirements Arts and fine arts (art, music, dance, drama), communications, computer science, English, foreign language, mathematics, physical education (includes health), religion (includes Bible studies and theology), science, social sciences, social studies (includes history), 100 hours of community service.
Special Academic Programs Advanced Placement exam preparation; honors section; independent study; study at local college for college credit; academic accommodation for the gifted and the artistically talented; ESL (3 students enrolled).
College Admission Counseling 34 students graduated in 2011; all went to college, including New Mexico State University; University of New Mexico. 5% scored over 26 on composite ACT.
Student Life Upper grades have uniform requirement, student council, honor system. Discipline rests primarily with faculty. Attendance at religious services is required.
Summer Programs ESL programs offered; session focuses on ESL and International to U.S. transition; held both on and off campus; held at Albuquerque, Various locations in NM and Durango CO; accepts boys and girls; not open to students from other schools. 10 students usually enrolled. 2012 schedule: August 1 to August 15. Application deadline: February.
Tuition and Aid Day student tuition: $13,500; 5-day tuition and room/board: $29,000; 7-day tuition and room/board: $32,000. Tuition installment plan (FACTS Tuition Payment Plan). Need-based scholarship grants available. In 2011–12, 50% of upper-school students received aid. Total amount of financial aid awarded in 2011–12: $307,000.
Admissions Traditional secondary-level entrance grade is 9. Admissions testing, ERB, ISEE, SLEP for foreign students or SSAT required. Deadline for receipt of application materials: none. Application fee required: $35. Interview required.
Athletics Interscholastic: basketball (boys, girls), football (b), volleyball (g); intramural: football (b), lacrosse (b), soccer (b,g); coed interscholastic: golf, outdoor education, running, track and field; coed intramural: soccer. 2 PE instructors, 6 coaches, 1 athletic trainer.
Computers Computers are regularly used in art, college planning, English, graphics, history, mathematics, psychology, science, yearbook classes. Computer network features include on-campus library services, online commercial services, Internet access, wireless campus network, Internet filtering or blocking technology. Campus intranet and computer access in designated common areas are available to students. Students grades are available online. The school has a published electronic and media policy.
Contact Rebecca Toevs, Admission Assistant. 505-341-7250. Fax: 505-344-2517. E-mail: epaul@menaulschool.com. Web site: www.menaulschool.com.

MENLO SCHOOL

50 Valparaiso Avenue

Atherton, California 94027

Head of School: Norman M. Colb

General Information Coeducational day college-preparatory school. Grades 6–12. Founded: 1915. Setting: suburban. Nearest major city is San Jose. 35-acre campus. 23 buildings on campus. Approved or accredited by California Association of Independent Schools, Western Association of Schools and Colleges, and California Department of Education. Member of National Association of Independent Schools. Endowment: $22 million. Total enrollment: 810. Upper school average class size: 15. Upper school faculty-student ratio: 1:10. There are 170 required school days per year for Upper School students. Upper School students typically attend 5 days per week. The average school day consists of 7 hours.
Faculty School total: 86. In upper school: 29 men, 45 women; 58 have advanced degrees.
Subjects Offered 20th century American writers, advanced biology, advanced chemistry, advanced computer applications, advanced math, algebra, American history, American history-AP, American literature, American literature-AP, analytic geometry, anatomy and physiology, ancient world history, art, art history, art-AP, Asian studies, biology, biology-AP, British literature-AP, calculus, calculus-AP, chemistry, chemistry-AP, chorus, computer graphics, computer literacy, computer multimedia, computer programming, computer science, computer science-AP, creative writing, dance, debate, drama, earth science, economics, economics-AP, engineering, English, English language and composition-AP, English literature, English literature-AP, English-AP, environmental science, ethics, European history, European history-AP, film studies, fine arts, French, French as a second language, French language-AP, French literature-AP, French-AP, freshman seminar, geometry, government and politics-AP, history, honors English, honors geometry, honors U.S. history, intro to computers, Japanese, jazz band, jazz dance, jazz ensemble, journalism, Latin, Latin-AP, law, literature-AP, Mandarin, mathematics, mathematics-AP, methods of research, modern European history, modern world history, multimedia, music, music theory, music theory-AP, music-AP, musical productions, newspaper, orchestra, performing arts, philosophy, photography, physical education, physics, physics-AP, play production, poetry, pre-calculus, rhetoric, robotics, science, science fiction, science research, senior project, Shakespeare, society and culture, Spanish, Spanish language-AP, Spanish literature-AP, Spanish-AP, statistics, statistics-AP, student government, student publications, studio art, studio art-AP, swimming, U.S. government and politics-AP, U.S. history-AP, video film production, wellness, women's literature, world history, world religions, writing, yearbook.
Graduation Requirements Arts and fine arts (art, music, dance, drama), English, foreign language, mathematics, physical education (includes health), science, social studies (includes history), freshman seminar, Knight School, senior project (3-week project at the end of senior year). Community service is required.
Special Academic Programs Advanced Placement exam preparation; honors section; independent study.
College Admission Counseling 136 students graduated in 2010; 133 went to college, including Princeton University; Stanford University; University of California, Berkeley; University of California, Los Angeles; University of California, Santa Barbara; University of Southern California. Other: 1 entered a postgraduate year, 2 had other specific plans. Mean SAT critical reading: 655, mean SAT math: 681, mean SAT writing: 673. 74% scored over 600 on SAT critical reading, 88% scored over 600 on SAT math, 80% scored over 600 on SAT writing, 86% scored over 26 on composite ACT.
Student Life Upper grades have student council. Discipline rests equally with students and faculty.
Tuition and Aid Day student tuition: $33,600. Tuition installment plan (Key Tuition Payment Plan). Need-based scholarship grants, paying campus jobs available. In 2010–11, 20% of upper-school students received aid. Total amount of financial aid awarded in 2010–11: $4,200,000.
Admissions Traditional secondary-level entrance grade is 9. For fall 2010, 400 students applied for upper-level admission, 84 enrolled. ISEE, SSAT or TOEFL required. Deadline for receipt of application materials: January 13. Application fee required: $85. On-campus interview required.
Athletics Interscholastic: aerobics/dance (girls), baseball (b), basketball (b,g), cross-country running (b,g), dance (g), football (b), golf (b,g), lacrosse (b,g), soccer (b,g), softball (g), swimming and diving (b,g), tennis (b,g), track and field (b,g), volleyball (b,g), water polo (b,g); coed interscholastic: aerobics/dance, dance, martial arts. 67 coaches, 2 athletic trainers.

Computers Computers are regularly used in English, foreign language, history, journalism, mathematics, media arts, multimedia, newspaper, science, yearbook classes. Computer network features include on-campus library services, online commercial services, Internet access, wireless campus network, Internet filtering or blocking technology. Student e-mail accounts and computer access in designated common areas are available to students.

Contact Mary Emery, Admissions and Financial Aid Assistant. 650-330-2000 Ext. 2601. Fax: 650-330-2012. Web site: www.menloschool.org.

MERCHISTON CASTLE SCHOOL

Colinton

Edinburgh EH13 0PU, United Kingdom

Head of School: Mr. A.R. Hunter

General Information Boys' boarding and day college-preparatory, arts, business, religious studies, bilingual studies, and technology school, affiliated with Christian faith. Ungraded, ages 8–18. Founded: 1833. Setting: suburban. Students are housed in single-sex dormitories. 100-acre campus. 11 buildings on campus. Approved or accredited by Independent Schools Council (UK). Language of instruction: English. Upper school average class size: 9. Upper school faculty-student ratio: 1:9. The average school day consists of 9 hours.

Upper School Student Profile 66% of students are boarding students. 18% are international students. International students from China, France, Germany, Hong Kong, Russian Federation, and Spain; 13 other countries represented in student body. 50% of students are Christian faith.

Faculty School total: 64. In upper school: 38 men, 23 women; 37 have advanced degrees; 30 reside on campus.

Subjects Offered Algebra, art, biology, calculus, career education, chemistry, Chinese, computer science, creative writing, design, drama, economics, electronics, English, English as a foreign language, English literature, European history, French, geography, geometry, German, government/civics, grammar, history, Italian, Japanese, Latin, Mandarin, mathematics, music, physical education, physics, Portuguese, religion, Russian, science, social studies, Spanish, trigonometry, world history.

Graduation Requirements Any three A level courses.

Special Academic Programs Term-away projects; study abroad; academic accommodation for the gifted, the musically talented, and the artistically talented; remedial reading and/or remedial writing; remedial math; special instructional classes for deaf students, blind students; ESL (10 students enrolled).

College Admission Counseling 95 students graduated in 2011; 90 went to college. Other: 5 had other specific plans.

Student Life Upper grades have specified standards of dress, student council, honor system. Discipline rests equally with students and faculty.

Tuition and Aid Day student tuition: £11,625; 5-day tuition and room/board: £16,485; 7-day tuition and room/board: £16,485. Tuition reduction for siblings, bursaries, merit scholarship grants available. In 2011–12, 20% of upper-school students received aid.

Admissions Achievement/Aptitude/Writing, common entrance examinations and school's own exam required. Deadline for receipt of application materials: none. Application fee required: £100. Interview recommended.

Athletics Interscholastic: ball hockey (boys), basketball (b), cricket (b), cross-country running (b), curling (b), fencing (b), Fives (b), football (b), freestyle skiing (b), golf (b), hockey (b), horseback riding (b), riflery (b), rugby (b), sailing (b), scuba diving (b), skiing (cross-country) (b), skiing (downhill) (b), soccer (b), squash (b), swimming and diving (b), table tennis (b), tennis (b), track and field (b); intramural: archery (b), badminton (b), ball hockey (b), basketball (b), bicycling (b), canoeing/kayaking (b), cricket (b), cross-country running (b), curling (b), diving (b), fencing (b), Fives (b), football (b), freestyle skiing (b), golf (b), gymnastics (b), hockey (b), horseback riding (b), jogging (b), judo (b), life saving (b), marksmanship (b), martial arts (b), mountain biking (b), outdoor activities (b), outdoor education (b), outdoor skills (b), physical fitness (b), riflery (b), rock climbing (b), rugby (b), sailing (b), scuba diving (b), skiing (cross-country) (b), skiing (downhill) (b), soccer (b), squash (b), strength & conditioning (b), swimming and diving (b), table tennis (b), tennis (b), track and field (b), volleyball (b). 4 PE instructors, 2 coaches.

Computers Computers are regularly used in design, music classes. Computer network features include Internet access, wireless campus network. Campus intranet, student e-mail accounts, and computer access in designated common areas are available to students. The school has a published electronic and media policy.

Contact Mrs. Anne Rickard, Director of Admissions. 44-131-312-2201. Fax: 44-131-441 Ext. 6060. E-mail: admissions@merchiston.co.uk. Web site: www.merchiston.co.uk.

MERCY HIGH SCHOOL

1740 Randolph Road

Middletown, Connecticut 06457-5155

Head of School: Sr. Mary McCarthy, RSM

General Information Girls' day college-preparatory, arts, and religious studies school, affiliated with Roman Catholic Church. Grades 9–12. Founded: 1963. Setting: rural. Nearest major city is Hartford. 26-acre campus. 1 building on campus. Approved or accredited by National Catholic Education Association, New England Association of Schools and Colleges, and Connecticut Department of Education. Total enrollment: 651. Upper school average class size: 21. Upper school faculty-student ratio: 1:13. There are 172 required school days per year for Upper School students. Upper School students typically attend 5 days per week. The average school day consists of 6 hours and 30 minutes.

Upper School Student Profile Grade 9: 153 students (153 girls); Grade 10: 165 students (165 girls); Grade 11: 160 students (160 girls); Grade 12: 173 students (173 girls). 85% of students are Roman Catholic.

Faculty School total: 53. In upper school: 9 men, 44 women; 39 have advanced degrees.

Subjects Offered Accounting, advanced math, algebra, American government, American literature, American literature-AP, art, art history, arts and crafts, biology, biology-AP, business, calculus, calculus-AP, Catholic belief and practice, ceramics, chamber groups, chemistry, chemistry-AP, choir, chorus, civics, comparative government and politics, computer applications, concert band, concert choir, creative writing, drama workshop, drawing and design, English, English literature, English-AP, European history, expository writing, French, French language-AP, French literature-AP, French-AP, geometry, government/civics, grammar, health, history, honors algebra, honors English, honors geometry, honors U.S. history, honors world history, humanities, independent study, Italian, journalism, keyboarding, Latin, law, literature-AP, mathematics, modern history, music, musical theater, neuroscience, photography, physical education, physics, physics-AP, physiology, pottery, pre-algebra, pre-calculus, psychology, public speaking, religious studies, science, social studies, Spanish, Spanish language-AP, Spanish-AP, statistics, statistics-AP, theater arts, trigonometry, U.S. history, U.S. history-AP, wind ensemble, word processing, world history, world literature, world religions, writing.

Graduation Requirements Civics, computer applications, English, foreign language, mathematics, physical education (includes health), religion (includes Bible studies and theology), science, social studies (includes history), 100 hours of community service.

Special Academic Programs 12 Advanced Placement exams for which test preparation is offered; honors section; independent study; study at local college for college credit.

College Admission Counseling 170 students graduated in 2011; all went to college, including Central Connecticut State University; Eastern Connecticut State University; Quinnipiac University; Sacred Heart University; Salve Regina University; Southern Connecticut State University. Median SAT critical reading: 525, median SAT math: 510, median SAT writing: 530, median combined SAT: 1555, median composite ACT: 22. 21% scored over 600 on SAT critical reading, 16% scored over 600 on SAT math, 20% scored over 600 on SAT writing, 18% scored over 1800 on combined SAT, 15% scored over 26 on composite ACT.

Student Life Upper grades have uniform requirement, student council. Discipline rests primarily with faculty. Attendance at religious services is required.

Tuition and Aid Day student tuition: $10,350–$10,850. Tuition installment plan (FACTS Tuition Payment Plan, individually arranged payment plans). Tuition reduction for siblings, merit scholarship grants, need-based scholarship grants available.

Admissions Traditional secondary-level entrance grade is 9. For fall 2011, 300 students applied for upper-level admission, 279 were accepted, 174 enrolled. High School Placement Test (closed version) from Scholastic Testing Service required. Deadline for receipt of application materials: none. Application fee required: $50.

Athletics Interscholastic: basketball, cheering, cross-country running, diving, field hockey, golf, indoor track, lacrosse, soccer, softball, swimming and diving, tennis, track and field, volleyball; intramural: basketball, floor hockey, golf, soccer, tennis, volleyball. 1 PE instructor, 30 coaches, 1 athletic trainer.

Computers Computers are regularly used in accounting, all academic, computer applications, desktop publishing, journalism, photography, Web site design, word processing classes. Computer network features include on-campus library services, Internet access, Internet filtering or blocking technology. Campus intranet, student e-mail accounts, and computer access in designated common areas are available to students. Students grades are available online.

Contact Mrs. Diane Santostefano, Director of Admissions. 860-346-6659. Fax: 860-344-9887. E-mail: dsantostefano@mercyhigh.com. Web site: www.mercyhigh.com.

MERCY HIGH SCHOOL

1501 South 48th Street

Omaha, Nebraska 68106-2598

Head of School: Ms. Carolyn Jaworski

General Information Girls' day college-preparatory, general academic, arts, business, religious studies, and technology school, affiliated with Roman Catholic Church. Grades 9–12. Founded: 1955. Setting: urban. 2-acre campus. 1 building on campus. Approved or accredited by Mercy Secondary Education Association, National Catholic Education Association, North Central Association of Colleges and Schools, and Nebraska Department of Education. Total enrollment: 360. Upper school average class size: 20. Upper school faculty-student ratio: 1:12. There are 180 required school days per year for Upper School students. Upper School students typically attend 5 days per week. The average school day consists of 7 hours and 15 minutes.

Upper School Student Profile Grade 9: 118 students (118 girls); Grade 10: 89 students (89 girls); Grade 11: 109 students (109 girls); Grade 12: 76 students (76 girls). 90% of students are Roman Catholic.

Faculty School total: 33. In upper school: 6 men, 27 women; 20 have advanced degrees.

Subjects Offered Accounting, algebra, American government, American history, American history-AP, American literature, anatomy and physiology, art, ballet, biology, British literature, British literature-AP, business applications, calculus, calculus-AP, chemistry, chemistry-AP, child development, choir, computer education, consumer mathematics, culinary arts, debate, drama, drawing, ecology, English, French, general math, geometry, health, honors English, honors geometry, journalism, keyboarding, math review, moral theology, painting, participation in sports, peace and justice, physics, physics-AP, play production, pottery, pre-algebra, pre-calculus, psychology, social justice, Spanish, Spanish-AP, speech, speech and debate, sports medicine, stagecraft, statistics, theology, theology and the arts, trigonometry, U.S. government, U.S. history, U.S. history-AP, vocal music, world history, yearbook.

Graduation Requirements Advanced math, algebra, American government, anatomy and physiology, arts and fine arts (art, music, dance, drama), biology, chemistry, computer applications, debate, English, foreign language, geometry, mathematics, physical education (includes health), physics, social studies (includes history), speech, theology, U.S. history, world history, service hours.

Special Academic Programs 5 Advanced Placement exams for which test preparation is offered; honors section; study at local college for college credit; remedial reading and/or remedial writing; remedial math; programs in general development for dyslexic students; special instructional classes for deaf students, blind students, students with LD, ADD, emotional and behavioral problems.

College Admission Counseling 70 students graduated in 2011; 68 went to college, including Creighton University; University of Nebraska–Lincoln; University of Nebraska at Omaha. Other: 2 went to work.

Student Life Upper grades have uniform requirement, student council, honor system. Discipline rests primarily with faculty. Attendance at religious services is required.

Tuition and Aid Day student tuition: $8300. Tuition installment plan (individually arranged payment plans, each family has an individualized tuition based upon their income). Tuition reduction for siblings, merit scholarship grants, need-based scholarship grants, paying campus jobs available. In 2011–12, 85% of upper-school students received aid; total upper-school merit-scholarship money awarded: $100,000. Total amount of financial aid awarded in 2011–12: $1,000,000.

Admissions Traditional secondary-level entrance grade is 9. For fall 2011, 120 students applied for upper-level admission, 120 were accepted, 118 enrolled. STS Examination required. Deadline for receipt of application materials: March 31. Application fee required: $125. Interview required.

Athletics Interscholastic: aerobics, archery, badminton, ballet, basketball, bowling, cheering, cross-country running, dance squad, dance team, diving, fitness walking, golf, independent competitive sports, physical fitness, self defense, soccer, softball, strength & conditioning, swimming and diving, tennis, track and field, volleyball, weight training; intramural: indoor soccer. 2 PE instructors, 15 coaches, 1 athletic trainer.

Computers Computers are regularly used in accounting, business, business applications, business education, business studies, history, journalism, keyboarding, lab/keyboard, library, library skills, mathematics, music, photojournalism, publications, religion, science, yearbook classes. Computer network features include on-campus library services, online commercial services, Internet access, wireless campus network, Internet filtering or blocking technology. Student e-mail accounts and computer access in designated common areas are available to students. Students grades are available online. The school has a published electronic and media policy.

Contact Ms. Anne Zadina, Recruitment Director. 402-553-9424. Fax: 402-553-0394. E-mail: zadinaa@mercyhigh.org. Web site: www.mercyhigh.org.

MERCY HIGH SCHOOL COLLEGE PREPARATORY

3250 19th Avenue

San Francisco, California 94132-2000

Head of School: Dr. Dorothy McCrea

General Information Girls' day college-preparatory, arts, business, religious studies, and technology school, affiliated with Roman Catholic Church. Grades 9–12. Founded: 1952. Setting: urban. Nearest major city is Daly City. 6-acre campus. 2 buildings on campus. Approved or accredited by Western Association of Schools and Colleges, Western Catholic Education Association, and California Department of Education. Endowment: $2 million. Total enrollment: 442. Upper school average class size: 26. Upper school faculty-student ratio: 1:14. There are 180 required school days per year for Upper School students. Upper School students typically attend 5 days per week. The average school day consists of 7 hours and 5 minutes.

Upper School Student Profile Grade 9: 102 students (102 girls); Grade 10: 101 students (101 girls); Grade 11: 114 students (114 girls); Grade 12: 125 students (125 girls). 67.7% of students are Roman Catholic.

Faculty School total: 31. In upper school: 6 men, 25 women; 21 have advanced degrees.

Subjects Offered Algebra, American history, American literature, art, biology, business, calculus, ceramics, chemistry, chorus, computer applications, computer programming, creative writing, dance, drama, English, English literature, environmental science, ethnic studies, expository writing, French, geometry, government/civics, keyboarding, mathematics, physical education, physics, physics-AP, religious studies, social justice, social studies, Spanish, speech, statistics, theater, trigonometry, visual and performing arts, world history, world literature.

Graduation Requirements 50 volunteer hours and a senior culminating project, Intersession.

Special Academic Programs Advanced Placement exam preparation; honors section.

College Admission Counseling 126 students graduated in 2011; 125 went to college, including San Francisco State University; University of California, Davis; University of San Francisco. Other: 1 entered military service. Mean SAT critical reading: 486, mean SAT math: 485, mean SAT writing: 510, mean combined SAT: 1482, mean composite ACT: 21. 16% scored over 600 on SAT critical reading, 18% scored over 600 on SAT math, 25% scored over 600 on SAT writing, 16% scored over 1800 on combined SAT, 41% scored over 26 on composite ACT.

Student Life Upper grades have uniform requirement, student council, honor system. Discipline rests primarily with faculty. Attendance at religious services is required.

Summer Programs Enrichment programs offered; session focuses on pre-high program is enrichment only, secondary program is enrichment and remediation; held on campus; accepts boys and girls; open to students from other schools. 350 students usually enrolled. 2012 schedule: June 18 to July 13. Application deadline: June 14.

Tuition and Aid Day student tuition: $14,200. Tuition installment plan (FACTS Tuition Payment Plan, full payment, 10 months payment (July-April), semiannual payment (July & December)). Need-based scholarship grants available. In 2011–12, 40% of upper-school students received aid.

Admissions Traditional secondary-level entrance grade is 9. For fall 2011, 298 students applied for upper-level admission, 249 were accepted, 116 enrolled. High School Placement Test required. Deadline for receipt of application materials: none. Application fee required: $80. On-campus interview required.

Athletics Interscholastic: basketball, cross-country running, dance, dance squad, self defense, soccer, softball, swimming and diving, tennis, track and field, volleyball. 3 PE instructors, 19 coaches.

Computers Computers are regularly used in all academic classes. Computer network features include on-campus library services, Internet access, wireless campus network, Internet filtering or blocking technology, Hunter Systems. Campus intranet and computer access in designated common areas are available to students. Students grades are available online. The school has a published electronic and media policy.

Contact Liz Belonogoff, Admissions Director. 415-584-5929. Fax: 415-334-9726. E-mail: lbelonogoff@mercyhs.org. Web site: www.mercyhs.org.

MERCYHURST PREPARATORY SCHOOL

538 East Grandview Boulevard

Erie, Pennsylvania 16504-2697

Head of School: Mrs. Deborah A. Laughlin

General Information Coeducational day college-preparatory, arts, religious studies, and technology school, affiliated with Roman Catholic Church. Grades 9–12. Founded: 1926. Setting: urban. 5-acre campus. 1 building on campus. Approved or accredited by International Baccalaureate Organization, Middle States Association of Colleges and Schools, and Pennsylvania Department of Education. Total enrollment: 624. Upper school average class size: 25. Upper school faculty-student ratio: 1:13. There are 180 required school days per year for Upper School students. Upper School students typically attend 5 days per week. The average school day consists of 6 hours and 15 minutes.

Upper School Student Profile Grade 9: 124 students (38 boys, 86 girls); Grade 10: 175 students (85 boys, 90 girls); Grade 11: 177 students (65 boys, 112 girls); Grade 12: 152 students (50 boys, 102 girls). 81% of students are Roman Catholic.
Faculty School total: 51. In upper school: 19 men, 32 women; 19 have advanced degrees.
Subjects Offered Accounting, algebra, American Civil War, American government, American history, American literature, anatomy, art, art appreciation, art education, art history, astronomy, athletic training, ballet, biology, business skills, calculus, campus ministry, career exploration, ceramics, chemistry, chorus, Christian ethics, civil war history, communications, community service, computer applications, computer programming, computer science, creative arts, dance, digital photography, drama, drama performance, drawing, drawing and design, earth science, English, English literature, environmental science, ethics, European history, expository writing, fine arts, first aid, French, geology, geometry, government/civics, guitar, health, Hebrew scripture, history, Holocaust, humanities, Internet, journalism, keyboarding, leadership, mathematics, multimedia, music, music appreciation, music history, music theory-AP, musical productions, orchestra, painting, photography, physical education, physics, physiology, piano, psychology, public speaking, publications, reading/study skills, religion, SAT preparation, SAT/ACT preparation, science, senior internship, set design, social studies, Spanish, speech, speech and debate, study skills, tap dance, technical theater, technology/design, theater, theater arts, theology, theory of knowledge, trigonometry, typing, U.S. government, U.S. history, visual and performing arts, weight fitness, weightlifting, word processing, world cultures, world history, writing, yearbook.
Graduation Requirements Arts and fine arts (art, music, dance, drama), arts appreciation, business skills (includes word processing), computer science, creative arts, English, foreign language, health and wellness, mathematics, physical education (includes health), public speaking, religion (includes Bible studies and theology), science, social studies (includes history), technological applications, 25 service hours per year.
Special Academic Programs International Baccalaureate program; honors section; independent study; study at local college for college credit; academic accommodation for the gifted, the musically talented, and the artistically talented; remedial reading and/or remedial writing; remedial math; ESL (60 students enrolled).
College Admission Counseling 140 students graduated in 2011; 138 went to college, including Edinboro University of Pennsylvania; Gannon University; Indiana University of Pennsylvania; John Carroll University; Mercyhurst College; Penn State University Park. Other: 1 went to work, 1 entered military service.
Student Life Upper grades have uniform requirement, student council, honor system. Discipline rests primarily with faculty. Attendance at religious services is required.
Summer Programs Remediation, enrichment, advancement, art/fine arts, computer instruction programs offered; session focuses on enrichment; held on campus; accepts boys and girls; open to students from other schools. 130 students usually enrolled. 2012 schedule: June 18 to August 10. Application deadline: none.
Tuition and Aid Day student tuition: $7300. Tuition installment plan (FACTS Tuition Payment Plan). Merit scholarship grants, need-based scholarship grants, creative arts scholarships, alumni scholarships, endowment scholarships available. In 2011–12, 51% of upper-school students received aid; total upper-school merit-scholarship money awarded: $89,950. Total amount of financial aid awarded in 2011–12: $578,050.
Admissions Traditional secondary-level entrance grade is 9. For fall 2011, 277 students applied for upper-level admission, 234 were accepted, 121 enrolled. Achievement tests, ACT, High School Placement Test or Iowa Tests of Basic Skills required. Deadline for receipt of application materials: none. Application fee required: $10.
Athletics Interscholastic: ballet (girls), baseball (b), basketball (b,g), bowling (g), cheering (g), crew (b,g), cross-country running (b,g), football (b), golf (b,g), modern dance (g), rowing (b,g), skiing (downhill) (g), soccer (b,g), softball (g), swimming and diving (b,g), tennis (b,g), track and field (b,g), volleyball (g); coed interscholastic: tennis, weight training; coed intramural: weight lifting, weight training. 2 PE instructors, 40 coaches, 1 athletic trainer.
Computers Computers are regularly used in college planning, data processing, design, desktop publishing, English, foreign language, graphic design, history, journalism, mathematics, media, newspaper, photography, photojournalism, programming, publications, publishing, SAT preparation, science, typing, Web site design, word processing, writing, yearbook classes. Computer network features include on-campus library services, online commercial services, Internet access, wireless campus network, Internet filtering or blocking technology. Campus intranet is available to students. Students grades are available online. The school has a published electronic and media policy.
Contact Mrs. Marcia E. DiTullio, Administrative Assistant. 814-824-2323. Fax: 814-824-2116. E-mail: mditullio@mpslakers.com. Web site: www.mpslakers.com.

MERCY VOCATIONAL HIGH SCHOOL

2900 West Hunting Park Avenue

Philadelphia, Pennsylvania 19129

Head of School: Sr. Rosemary Herron, RSM

General Information Coeducational day college-preparatory and vocational school, affiliated with Roman Catholic Church. Grades 9–12. Founded: 1950. Setting: urban. 2 buildings on campus. Approved or accredited by Middle States Association of Colleges and Schools and Pennsylvania Department of Education. Upper school average class size: 26. Upper school faculty-student ratio: 1:16. There are 180 required school days per year for Upper School students. Upper School students typically attend 5 days per week. The average school day consists of 7 hours and 5 minutes.
Upper School Student Profile Grade 9: 125 students (71 boys, 54 girls); Grade 10: 89 students (50 boys, 39 girls); Grade 11: 90 students (50 boys, 40 girls); Grade 12: 78 students (37 boys, 41 girls).
Faculty School total: 38. In upper school: 14 men, 24 women.
Graduation Requirements ACT preparation, Community Service.
Special Academic Programs Remedial reading and/or remedial writing.
College Admission Counseling 75 students graduated in 2010.
Student Life Upper grades have uniform requirement, student council, honor system. Discipline rests primarily with faculty. Attendance at religious services is required.
Tuition and Aid Tuition installment plan (SMART Tuition Payment Plan). Need-based scholarship grants available. In 2010–11, 74% of upper-school students received aid.
Admissions Traditional secondary-level entrance grade is 9. For fall 2010, 179 students applied for upper-level admission, 125 were accepted, 125 enrolled. School's own test required. Deadline for receipt of application materials: none. No application fee required.
Athletics Interscholastic: baseball (boys), basketball (b,g), biathlon (g), cheering (g), cross-country running (b,g), soccer (b,g), softball (g), track and field (b,g); intramural: weight lifting (b), weight training (b). 1 PE instructor, 6 coaches.
Computers Computers are regularly used in aerospace science, animation, architecture, art, aviation, classics, commercial art, dance, design, desktop publishing, desktop publishing, ESL, digital applications, drafting, drawing and design, economics, engineering, ESL, ethics, foreign language, French, French as a second language, freshman foundations, geography, graphic arts, graphic design, graphics, historical foundations for arts, human geography - AP, humanities, independent study, journalism, JROTC, language development, Latin, learning cognition, library, library science, literacy, literary magazine, media, media arts, media production, media services, mentorship program, multimedia, music, music technology, news writing, newspaper, NJROTC, occupational education, philosophy, photography, photojournalism, programming, psychology, publications, publishing, SAT preparation, senior seminar, Spanish, speech, stock market, technical drawing, theater, theater arts, typing, video film production, Web site design, wilderness education classes. Computer network features include wireless campus network, Internet filtering or blocking technology. Campus intranet and student e-mail accounts are available to students. Students grades are available online.
Contact Director of Admissions. 215-226-1225 Ext. 115. Fax: 215-228-6337. E-mail: wdonahue@mercyvhs.org. Web site: www.mercyvocational.org.

MERION MERCY ACADEMY

511 Montgomery Avenue

Merion Station, Pennsylvania 19066

Head of School: Sr. Barbara Buckley

General Information Girls' day college-preparatory, arts, and religious studies school, affiliated with Roman Catholic Church. Grades 9–12. Founded: 1884. Setting: suburban. Nearest major city is Philadelphia. 35-acre campus. 7 buildings on campus. Approved or accredited by Middle States Association of Colleges and Schools. Endowment: $350,000. Total enrollment: 482. Upper school average class size: 17. Upper school faculty-student ratio: 1:9.
Upper School Student Profile Grade 9: 123 students (123 girls); Grade 10: 116 students (116 girls); Grade 11: 125 students (125 girls); Grade 12: 118 students (118 girls). 90% of students are Roman Catholic.
Faculty School total: 53. In upper school: 6 men, 47 women; 41 have advanced degrees.
Subjects Offered Algebra, American history, American literature, art, art history, biology, business, calculus, chemistry, computer programming, creative writing, drama, economics, English, English literature, environmental science, European history, fine arts, French, geometry, government/civics, grammar, health, history, journalism, Latin, mathematics, music, music history, physical education, physics, physiology, psychology, religion, science, social studies, Spanish, speech, theater, theology, trigonometry, women's studies, world history, world literature, writing.
Graduation Requirements Arts and fine arts (art, music, dance, drama), English, foreign language, mathematics, physical education (includes health), religion (includes Bible studies and theology), science, social studies (includes history).
Special Academic Programs Advanced Placement exam preparation; honors section; study at local college for college credit; academic accommodation for the gifted, the musically talented, and the artistically talented; remedial reading and/or remedial writing; remedial math.
College Admission Counseling 116 students graduated in 2011; all went to college, including Boston College; Georgetown University; Penn State University Park; Saint Joseph's University; The University of Scranton; Villanova University. Mean SAT critical reading: 601, mean SAT math: 573, mean SAT writing: 620.
Student Life Upper grades have uniform requirement, student council, honor system. Discipline rests primarily with faculty. Attendance at religious services is required.

Summer Programs Enrichment, advancement, sports, art/fine arts programs offered; session focuses on enrichment; held on campus; accepts boys and girls; open to students from other schools. 150 students usually enrolled. 2012 schedule: June 11 to August 5. Application deadline: May 1.

Tuition and Aid Day student tuition: $14,900. Tuition installment plan (The Tuition Plan, monthly payment plans, 2 equal payments plan). Tuition reduction for siblings, merit scholarship grants, need-based scholarship grants, middle-income loans, alumnae, Mercy, and music scholarships available. In 2011–12, 36% of upper-school students received aid; total upper-school merit-scholarship money awarded: $452,150. Total amount of financial aid awarded in 2011–12: $857,600.

Admissions Traditional secondary-level entrance grade is 9. For fall 2011, 300 students applied for upper-level admission, 180 were accepted, 123 enrolled. High School Placement Test required. Deadline for receipt of application materials: November 15. Application fee required: $30. On-campus interview required.

Athletics Interscholastic: basketball, cheering, crew, cross-country running, field hockey, golf, lacrosse, soccer, softball, swimming and diving, tennis, track and field, volleyball, winter (indoor) track; intramural: basketball, dance, tennis. 2 PE instructors, 19 coaches, 1 athletic trainer.

Computers Computers are regularly used in all academic classes. Computer network features include on-campus library services, online commercial services, Internet access, wireless campus network, Internet filtering or blocking technology. Student e-mail accounts and computer access in designated common areas are available to students.

Contact Eileen Killeen, Director of Admissions. 610-664-6655 Ext. 116. Fax: 610-664-6322. E-mail: ekilleen@merion-mercy.com. Web site: www.merion-mercy.com.

MESA GRANDE SEVENTH-DAY ACADEMY

975 South Fremont Street

Calimesa, California 92320

Head of School: Alfred J. Riddle

General Information Coeducational day college-preparatory, arts, religious studies, and technology school, affiliated with Seventh-day Adventists, Christian faith. Grades K–12. Founded: 1928. Setting: rural. Nearest major city is San Bernardino. 14-acre campus. 3 buildings on campus. Approved or accredited by Western Association of Schools and Colleges and California Department of Education. Endowment: $650,000. Total enrollment: 264. Upper school average class size: 30. Upper school faculty-student ratio: 1:10. There are 180 required school days per year for Upper School students. Upper School students typically attend 5 days per week. The average school day consists of 8 hours.

Upper School Student Profile Grade 9: 31 students (17 boys, 14 girls); Grade 10: 31 students (17 boys, 14 girls), Grade 11: 32 students (16 boys, 16 girls); Grade 12: 29 students (17 boys, 12 girls). 90% of students are Seventh-day Adventists, Christian.

Faculty School total: 23. In upper school: 6 men, 8 women; 8 have advanced degrees.

Subjects Offered Algebra, American literature, arts, ASB Leadership, auto mechanics, bell choir, biology, British literature, career education, chemistry, choral music, community service, composition, computer applications, computer-aided design, computers, concert choir, desktop publishing, drama, economics, economics and history, English, English composition, family living, fine arts, geometry, government/civics, graphic arts, handbells, health, instrumental music, keyboarding, lab science, marine biology, mathematics, music composition, music theory, physical education, physical science, physics, pre-calculus, relationships, religion, religious education, science, social sciences, social studies, Spanish, U.S. government, U.S. history, video film production, world history, world literature, yearbook.

Graduation Requirements Algebra, American government, applied skills, arts and fine arts (art, music, dance, drama), biology, British literature, career education, chemistry, computer education, computer technologies, economics, English, English composition, family living, industrial technology, keyboarding, mathematics, modern languages, physical education (includes health), physical fitness, physical science, physics, religious studies, science, social studies (includes history), Spanish, technical skills, work experience, community service.

College Admission Counseling 46 students graduated in 2011; 43 went to college, including La Sierra University; Pacific Union College; Southern Adventist University; University of California, Irvine; University of California, Los Angeles; Walla Walla University. Other: 2 went to work, 1 entered military service.

Student Life Upper grades have uniform requirement, student council, honor system. Discipline rests primarily with faculty. Attendance at religious services is required.

Summer Programs Sports programs offered; held both on and off campus; held at Drayson Center, Loma Linda, CA; accepts boys and girls; open to students from other schools. 50 students usually enrolled. 2012 schedule: June 8 to August 3. Application deadline: May 5.

Tuition and Aid Day student tuition: $7980. Tuition installment plan (monthly payment plans, individually arranged payment plans). Need-based scholarship grants, need-based loans, middle-income loans available. In 2011–12, 25% of upper-school students received aid. Total amount of financial aid awarded in 2011–12: $35,000.

Admissions Traditional secondary-level entrance grade is 9. For fall 2011, 30 students applied for upper-level admission, 28 were accepted, 28 enrolled. Any standardized test, ITBS-TAP or Math Placement Exam required. Deadline for receipt of application materials: none. Application fee required: $50. On-campus interview required.

Athletics Interscholastic: baseball (boys), basketball (b,g), flag football (b,g), softball (g), volleyball (b,g); coed interscholastic: cross-country running, golf, physical fitness, weight lifting. 3 PE instructors, 12 coaches, 2 athletic trainers.

Computers Computers are regularly used in art, design, graphic design, library skills, science, technical drawing, technology, typing, video film production, writing, yearbook classes. Computer network features include on-campus library services, online commercial services, Internet access, wireless campus network, Internet filtering or blocking technology. Student e-mail accounts and computer access in designated common areas are available to students. Students grades are available online. The school has a published electronic and media policy.

Contact Lois M. Myhre, Admissions Office. 909-795-1112 Ext. 257. Fax: 909-795-1653. E-mail: lois.myhre@mgak-12.org. Web site: www.mesagrandeacademy.org.

THE MIAMI VALLEY SCHOOL

5151 Denise Drive

Dayton, Ohio 45429

Head of School: Peter B. Benedict II

General Information Coeducational day college-preparatory, arts, religious studies, and technology school. Grades PK–12. Founded: 1964. Setting: suburban. 22-acre campus. 3 buildings on campus. Approved or accredited by Independent Schools Association of the Central States, Ohio Association of Independent Schools, and Ohio Department of Education. Member of National Association of Independent Schools. Endowment: $2.1 million. Total enrollment: 439. Upper school average class size: 16. Upper school faculty-student ratio: 1:9. Upper School students typically attend 5 days per week. The average school day consists of 7 hours and 15 minutes.

Faculty School total: 82. In upper school: 13 men, 12 women; 21 have advanced degrees.

Subjects Offered Algebra, American history, American literature, anatomy, art, art history, biology, calculus, ceramics, chemistry, Chinese, Chinese history, community service, computer programming, computer science, creative writing, drama, earth science, ecology, economics, English, English literature, environmental science, European history, fine arts, French, gender issues, genetics, geology, geometry, government/civics, grammar, health, history, instrumental music, journalism, Latin, marine biology, mathematics, microbiology, music, philosophy, photography, physical education, physics, physiology, psychology, religion, science, social sciences, social studies, sociology, Spanish, speech, statistics, theater, trigonometry, word processing, world history, world literature, writing.

Graduation Requirements Alternative physical education, arts and fine arts (art, music, dance, drama), English, foreign language, mathematics, science, social sciences, social studies (includes history), Immersion Term. Community service is required.

Special Academic Programs Advanced Placement exam preparation; honors section; independent study; study at local college for college credit; study abroad; academic accommodation for the gifted, the musically talented, and the artistically talented.

College Admission Counseling 55 students graduated in 2010; all went to college, including Dartmouth College; Duke University; Emory University, Oxford College; Haverford College; The George Washington University; Vanderbilt University. Mean SAT critical reading: 625, mean SAT math: 608, mean SAT writing: 623, mean composite ACT: 26.

Student Life Upper grades have specified standards of dress, student council, honor system. Discipline rests equally with students and faculty.

Tuition and Aid Day student tuition: $17,400. Tuition installment plan (FACTS Tuition Payment Plan). Merit scholarship grants, need-based scholarship grants available. In 2010–11, 36% of upper-school students received aid; total upper-school merit-scholarship money awarded: $60,000. Total amount of financial aid awarded in 2010–11: $500,000.

Admissions Traditional secondary-level entrance grade is 9. For fall 2010, 30 students applied for upper-level admission, 25 were accepted, 23 enrolled. Achievement/Aptitude/Writing, school's own test, SSAT, Stanford Achievement Test, Otis-Lennon School Ability Test, TOEFL or SLEP or writing sample required. Deadline for receipt of application materials: February 15. Application fee required: $70. On-campus interview required.

Athletics Interscholastic: baseball (boys), basketball (b,g), cheering (g), lacrosse (b,g), soccer (b,g), softball (g), strength & conditioning (b,g), tennis (b,g), track and field (b,g), volleyball (g), weight training (b,g), wrestling (b); coed interscholastic: cross-country running, golf, running, squash, swimming and diving; coed intramural: crew. 2 PE instructors, 25 coaches, 1 athletic trainer.

Computers Computers are regularly used in literary magazine, mathematics, media production, multimedia, music technology, newspaper, photography, programming, science, social sciences, technology, yearbook classes. Computer network features include on-campus library services, online commercial services, Internet access, wireless campus network, Internet filtering or blocking technology. Campus intranet and student e-mail accounts are available to students. Students grades are available online. The school has a published electronic and media policy.

Contact Mr. C.S. Adams III, Director of Enrollment and Financial Aid. 937-434-4444 Ext. 125. Fax: 937-434-1033. E-mail: trey.adams@mvschool.com. Web site: www.mvschool.com.

MIDDLESEX SCHOOL

1400 Lowell Road

Concord, Massachusetts 01742

Head of School: Kathleen C. Giles

General Information Coeducational boarding and day college-preparatory and arts school. Grades 9–12. Founded: 1901. Setting: suburban. Nearest major city is Boston. Students are housed in single-sex dormitories. 350-acre campus. 31 buildings on campus. Approved or accredited by New England Association of Schools and Colleges. Member of National Association of Independent Schools and Secondary School Admission Test Board. Endowment: $160 million. Total enrollment: 372. Upper school average class size: 12. Upper school faculty-student ratio: 1:6. There are 178 required school days per year for Upper School students. Upper School students typically attend 6 days per week. The average school day consists of 7 hours and 7 minutes.

Upper School Student Profile Grade 9: 78 students (40 boys, 38 girls); Grade 10: 92 students (48 boys, 44 girls); Grade 11: 99 students (43 boys, 56 girls); Grade 12: 103 students (52 boys, 51 girls). 67% of students are boarding students. 56% are state residents. 33 states are represented in upper school student body. 9% are international students. International students from Bermuda, Canada, China, Japan, Republic of Korea, and Switzerland; 9 other countries represented in student body.

Faculty School total: 63. In upper school: 35 men, 28 women; 44 have advanced degrees; 52 reside on campus.

Subjects Offered Acting, advanced biology, advanced chemistry, advanced computer applications, Advanced Placement courses, advanced studio art-AP, African American history, African history, African-American history, algebra, American literature, analytic geometry, art, art history, art history-AP, art-AP, Asian literature, astronomy, biology, biology-AP, British literature, calculus, calculus-AP, ceramics, chemistry, chemistry-AP, Chinese, classical Greek literature, computer programming, computer programming-AP, computer science, computer science-AP, creative writing, discrete mathematics, DNA, drama, economics, economics-AP, English, English literature, English literature and composition-AP, environmental science, environmental science-AP, ethics, European history, European history-AP, finite math, forensics, French, French language-AP, French literature-AP, geometry, Greek, history, history of jazz, Holocaust studies, independent study, jazz band, Latin, Latin American history, marine studies, mathematics, media, Middle East, Middle Eastern history, model United Nations, music, music theory, music theory-AP, philosophy, photography, physics, physics-AP, political science, religion, Shakespeare, Spanish, Spanish language-AP, Spanish literature-AP, statistics, statistics-AP, studio art-AP, theater, trigonometry, U.S. government and politics-AP, U.S. history, U.S. history-AP, video film production, Vietnam history, Vietnam War, vocal ensemble, women in world history, woodworking, world history, writing, writing workshop.

Graduation Requirements Algebra, analytic geometry, arts, English, English literature and composition-AP, European history, foreign language, geometry, science, trigonometry, U.S. history, completion of a wooden plaque.

Special Academic Programs 22 Advanced Placement exams for which test preparation is offered; honors section; independent study; academic accommodation for the gifted.

College Admission Counseling 85 students graduated in 2011; all went to college, including College of the Holy Cross; Dartmouth College; Harvard University; Massachusetts Institute of Technology; Middlebury College; Wesleyan University. Median SAT critical reading: 670, median SAT math: 670, median SAT writing: 700, median combined SAT: 2040, median composite ACT: 29. 86% scored over 600 on SAT critical reading, 87% scored over 600 on SAT math, 91% scored over 600 on SAT writing, 92% scored over 1800 on combined SAT, 76% scored over 26 on composite ACT.

Student Life Upper grades have specified standards of dress, student council, honor system. Discipline rests equally with students and faculty.

Summer Programs Art/fine arts programs offered; session focuses on arts; held on campus; accepts boys and girls; open to students from other schools. 180 students usually enrolled. 2012 schedule: June 27 to August 30.

Tuition and Aid Day student tuition: $38,710; 7-day tuition and room/board: $48,390. Guaranteed tuition plan. Tuition installment plan (Insured Tuition Payment Plan, monthly payment plans, semiannual payment plan). Need-based scholarship grants, need-based loans available. In 2011–12, 30% of upper-school students received aid. Total amount of financial aid awarded in 2011–12: $4,100,000.

Admissions Traditional secondary-level entrance grade is 9. For fall 2011, 1,020 students applied for upper-level admission, 97 enrolled. ISEE, SSAT or TOEFL required. Deadline for receipt of application materials: January 15. Application fee required: $50. Interview recommended.

Athletics Interscholastic: alpine skiing (boys, girls), baseball (b), basketball (b,g), crew (b,g), cross-country running (b,g), field hockey (g), football (b), ice hockey (b,g), lacrosse (b,g), skiing (downhill) (b,g), soccer (b,g), softball (g), squash (b,g), tennis (b,g), wrestling (b); coed interscholastic: golf, track and field; coed intramural: dance, fitness, physical training, squash, strength & conditioning, yoga. 1 PE instructor, 18 coaches, 2 athletic trainers.

Computers Computers are regularly used in all classes. Computer network features include on-campus library services, online commercial services, Internet access, wireless campus network, Internet filtering or blocking technology. Campus intranet, student e-mail accounts, and computer access in designated common areas are available to students. Students grades are available online. The school has a published electronic and media policy.

Contact Douglas C. Price, Director of Admissions. 978-371-6524. Fax: 978-402-1400. E-mail: admissions@mxschool.edu. Web site: www.mxschool.edu.

MIDLAND SCHOOL

PO Box 8

5100 Figueroa Mountain Road

Los Olivos, California 93441

Head of School: Will Graham

General Information Coeducational boarding college-preparatory and environmental studies school. Grades 9–12. Founded: 1932. Setting: rural. Nearest major city is Santa Barbara. Students are housed in single-sex cabins. 2,860-acre campus. Approved or accredited by California Association of Independent Schools, The Association of Boarding Schools, The College Board, US Department of State, and Western Association of Schools and Colleges. Member of National Association of Independent Schools and Secondary School Admission Test Board. Endowment: $10 million. Total enrollment: 82. Upper school average class size: 10. Upper school faculty-student ratio: 1:5. Upper School students typically attend 6 days per week.

Upper School Student Profile Grade 9: 21 students (9 boys, 12 girls); Grade 10: 14 students (3 boys, 11 girls); Grade 11: 24 students (14 boys, 10 girls); Grade 12: 23 students (8 boys, 15 girls). 100% of students are boarding students. 70% are state residents. 10 states are represented in upper school student body. 10% are international students. International students from China, Hong Kong, and Republic of Korea.

Faculty School total: 23. In upper school: 14 men, 9 women; 9 have advanced degrees; 20 reside on campus.

Subjects Offered 3-dimensional art, adolescent issues, advanced chemistry, advanced math, agroecology, algebra, American history, American literature, American studies, anthropology, backpacking, basketball, biology, ceramics, character education, chemistry, Chinese history, clayworking, community service, composition, creative writing, drama, economics, environmental education, environmental studies, equestrian sports, film and literature, foreign language, gardening, geology, geometry, health education, human sexuality, hydrology, integrated science, land and ranch management, leadership, literature by women, metalworking, music, painting, physics, pre-calculus, senior project, senior seminar, senior thesis, sex education, Spanish, Spanish literature, statistics, U.S. history, utopia, volleyball, wilderness education, wilderness experience, world studies.

Graduation Requirements Arts and fine arts (art, music, dance, drama), English, foreign language, history, mathematics, science, senior thesis, independent senior thesis.

Special Academic Programs Honors section; independent study.

College Admission Counseling 22 students graduated in 2011; 19 went to college. Other: 3 entered a postgraduate year.

Student Life Upper grades have student council, honor system. Discipline rests equally with students and faculty.

Tuition and Aid 7-day tuition and room/board: $38,600. Need-based scholarship grants available. In 2011–12, 53% of upper-school students received aid. Total amount of financial aid awarded in 2011–12: $1,000,000.

Admissions Traditional secondary-level entrance grade is 9. For fall 2011, 58 students applied for upper-level admission, 50 were accepted, 31 enrolled. SSAT or TOEFL or SLEP required. Deadline for receipt of application materials: February 15. Application fee required: $30. Interview required.

Athletics Interscholastic: cross-country running (boys, girls), lacrosse (b,g), soccer (b,g), volleyball (g); intramural: table tennis (b,g); coed interscholastic: basketball; coed intramural: backpacking, bicycling, dance, equestrian sports, hiking/backpacking, horseback riding, mountain biking, outdoor adventure, outdoor education, outdoor skills, surfing, touch football, ultimate Frisbee, yoga.

Computers Computer network features include on-campus library services, Internet access, Internet filtering or blocking technology. Student e-mail accounts are available to students. The school has a published electronic and media policy.

Contact Amy E. Graham, Director of Admissions and Financial Aid. 805-688-5114 Ext. 114. Fax: 805-686-2470. E-mail: admissions@midland-school.org. Web site: www.midland-school.org.

MID-PACIFIC INSTITUTE

2445 Kaala Street

Honolulu, Hawaii 96822-2299

Head of School: Mr. Joe C. Rice

General Information Coeducational day college-preparatory, arts, bilingual studies, technology, and International Baccalaureate school, affiliated with United Church of

Christ. Grades K–12. Founded: 1908. Setting: urban. 38-acre campus. 31 buildings on campus. Approved or accredited by International Baccalaureate Organization and Western Association of Schools and Colleges. Member of National Association of Independent Schools and Secondary School Admission Test Board. Total enrollment: 1,550. Upper school average class size: 20. Upper school faculty-student ratio: 1:20. Upper School students typically attend 5 days per week. The average school day consists of 6 hours and 15 minutes.

Faculty School total: 171. In upper school: 20 have advanced degrees.

Subjects Offered Algebra, American history, American literature, art, art history, astronomy, ballet, band, biology, business skills, calculus, career education, ceramics, chemistry, computer programming, computer science, creative writing, dance, debate, drama, drawing, economics, English, English literature, ESL, film, fine arts, first aid, French, general science, geography, geometry, Hawaiian history, health, history, instrumental music, Japanese, Latin, law, mathematics, oceanography, oral communications, painting, philosophy, photography, physical education, physics, printmaking, psychology, religion, science, sculpture, social sciences, social studies, Spanish, speech, swimming, swimming competency, technological applications, technology, theater, video, weight training, world history, world literature, writing.

Graduation Requirements Arts and fine arts (art, music, dance, drama), business skills (includes word processing), career education, computer science, English, foreign language, mathematics, oral communications, physical education (includes health), religion (includes Bible studies and theology), science, social sciences, social studies (includes history), speech, swimming competency.

Special Academic Programs International Baccalaureate program; Advanced Placement exam preparation; honors section; study at local college for college credit; academic accommodation for the gifted and the artistically talented; ESL (41 students enrolled).

College Admission Counseling 200 students graduated in 2011; all went to college, including Oregon State University; Seattle University; University of Hawaii at Manoa; University of Oregon; University of Southern California.

Student Life Upper grades have specified standards of dress, student council, honor system. Discipline rests primarily with faculty. Attendance at religious services is required.

Summer Programs Enrichment, advancement, ESL, art/fine arts, computer instruction programs offered; session focuses on physical fitness and skills; held on campus; accepts boys and girls; open to students from other schools. 1,200 students usually enrolled. 2012 schedule: June 5 to July 26. Application deadline: April 5.

Tuition and Aid Day student tuition: $17,600. Tuition installment plan (FACTS Tuition Payment Plan, monthly payment plans, semiannual payment plan). Merit scholarship grants, need-based scholarship grants, paying campus jobs, tuition reduction for children of employees available. In 2011–12, 17% of upper-school students received aid. Total amount of financial aid awarded in 2011–12: $2,900,000.

Admissions Traditional secondary-level entrance grade is 9. For fall 2011, 700 students applied for upper-level admission, 220 were accepted, 150 enrolled. SAT, SSAT and TOEFL required. Deadline for receipt of application materials: December 1. Application fee required: $100. Interview required.

Athletics Interscholastic: aquatics (boys, girls), baseball (b), basketball (b,g), bowling (b,g), canoeing/kayaking (b,g), cheering (g), cross-country running (b,g), football (b), golf (b,g), gymnastics (g), independent competitive sports (b,g), kayaking (b,g), ocean paddling (b,g), physical fitness (b,g), physical training (b,g), riflery (b,g), soccer (b,g), softball (g), strength & conditioning (b,g), surfing (b,g), swimming and diving (b,g), tennis (b,g), track and field (b,g), volleyball (b,g), water polo (b,g), wrestling (b,g); intramural: badminton (b,g), weight lifting (b,g), weight training (b,g); coed interscholastic: fitness, modern dance; coed intramural: badminton. 6 PE instructors, 25 coaches, 2 athletic trainers.

Computers Computers are regularly used in English, foreign language, mathematics, media arts, science classes. Computer network features include on-campus library services, online commercial services, Internet access, wireless campus network, Internet filtering or blocking technology. Campus intranet, student e-mail accounts, and computer access in designated common areas are available to students. Students grades are available online. The school has a published electronic and media policy.

Contact Ms. Heidi Bow, Admissions Assistant. 808-973-5005. Fax: 808-973-5099. E-mail: admissions@midpac.edu. Web site: www.midpac.edu.

MILLBROOK SCHOOL

131 Millbrook School Road

Millbrook, New York 12545

Head of School: Mr. Drew Casertano

General Information Coeducational boarding and day college-preparatory, arts, environmental stewardship, and community service school. Grades 9–12. Founded: 1931. Setting: rural. Nearest major city is New York. Students are housed in single-sex dormitories. 800-acre campus. 40 buildings on campus. Approved or accredited by The Association of Boarding Schools and New York Department of Education. Member of National Association of Independent Schools and Secondary School Admission Test Board. Endowment: $24 million. Total enrollment: 272. Upper school average class size: 14. Upper school faculty-student ratio: 1:5. There are 179 required school days per year for Upper School students. Upper School students typically attend 6 days per week. The average school day consists of 7 hours.

Upper School Student Profile Grade 9: 40 students (18 boys, 22 girls); Grade 10: 77 students (43 boys, 34 girls); Grade 11: 75 students (38 boys, 37 girls); Grade 12: 75 students (45 boys, 30 girls); Postgraduate: 5 students (3 boys, 2 girls). 80% of students are boarding students. 40% are state residents. 22 states are represented in upper school student body. 15% are international students. International students from Canada, China, Ghana, Republic of Korea, Venezuela, and Viet Nam; 6 other countries represented in student body.

Faculty School total: 55. In upper school: 25 men, 30 women; 30 have advanced degrees; 45 reside on campus.

Subjects Offered Acting, advanced biology, advanced chemistry, advanced math, Advanced Placement courses, advanced studio art-AP, aesthetics, algebra, American history, American literature, ancient history, ancient world history, animal behavior, animal science, anthropology, art, art history, astronomy, biology, calculus, calculus-AP, ceramics, chemistry, choral music, constitutional law, creative writing, dance, dance performance, digital photography, drama, drama performance, drawing, ecology, English, English language-AP, English literature, English-AP, environmental science, European history, fine arts, forensics, French, French language-AP, French-AP, geometry, global studies, history, honors English, honors geometry, human biology, human development, independent study, instrumental music, jazz band, jazz ensemble, journalism, Mandarin, mathematics, medieval history, Middle Eastern history, music, music appreciation, music history, painting, philosophy, photography, physics, pre-calculus, psychology, science, senior project, social sciences, social studies, Spanish, Spanish-AP, studio art, study skills, theater, trigonometry, world history.

Graduation Requirements Biology, English, foreign language, history, mathematics, science, visual and performing arts, Culminating Experience for Seniors.

Special Academic Programs 8 Advanced Placement exams for which test preparation is offered; honors section; independent study; term-away projects; study abroad.

College Admission Counseling 65 students graduated in 2011; 60 went to college, including Barnard College; Cornell University; Dickinson College; Hamilton College; Kenyon College; Wake Forest University. Other: 2 entered a postgraduate year, 3 had other specific plans. Mean SAT critical reading: 576, mean SAT math: 578, mean SAT writing: 586, mean combined SAT: 1740, mean composite ACT: 23.

Student Life Upper grades have specified standards of dress, student council, honor system. Discipline rests equally with students and faculty.

Tuition and Aid Day student tuition: $34,500; 7-day tuition and room/board: $46,950. Tuition installment plan (individually arranged payment plans, Tuition Management Services). Need-based scholarship grants, need-based loans available. In 2011–12, 27% of upper-school students received aid. Total amount of financial aid awarded in 2011–12: $2,148,000.

Admissions Traditional secondary-level entrance grade is 9. For fall 2011, 545 students applied for upper-level admission, 270 were accepted, 96 enrolled. ISEE, PSAT or SAT for applicants to grade 11 and 12, SSAT, TOEFL or writing sample required. Deadline for receipt of application materials: January 15. Application fee required: $50. Interview required.

Athletics Interscholastic: baseball (boys), basketball (b,g), cross-country running (b,g), field hockey (g), ice hockey (b,g), lacrosse (b,g), soccer (b,g), softball (g), squash (b,g), tennis (b,g); coed interscholastic: golf; coed intramural: aerobics/dance, aerobics/Nautilus, alpine skiing, badminton, bicycling, dance, equestrian sports, fitness, hiking/backpacking, horseback riding, modern dance, outdoor education, physical training, running, skiing (downhill), snowboarding, strength & conditioning, weight training, yoga. 1 coach, 1 athletic trainer.

Computers Computers are regularly used in foreign language, history, journalism, mathematics, photography, science, study skills, video film production, yearbook classes. Computer network features include on-campus library services, online commercial services, Internet access, wireless campus network, Internet filtering or blocking technology. Campus intranet, student e-mail accounts, and computer access in designated common areas are available to students. Students grades are available online. The school has a published electronic and media policy.

Contact Mrs. Wendy Greenfield, Admission Office Assistant. 845-677-8261 Ext. 138. Fax: 845-677-1265. E-mail: admissions@millbrook.org. Web site: www.millbrook.org.

MILLER SCHOOL

1000 Samuel Miller Loop

Charlottesville, Virginia 22903-9328

Head of School: Mr. Rick France

General Information Coeducational boarding and day college-preparatory and arts school. Grades 8–12. Founded: 1878. Setting: rural. Students are housed in single-sex dormitories. 1,600-acre campus. 6 buildings on campus. Approved or accredited by The Association of Boarding Schools and Virginia Association of Independent Schools. Member of National Association of Independent Schools. Endowment: $14 million. Total enrollment: 145. Upper school average class size: 10. Upper school faculty-student ratio: 1:6. Upper School students typically attend 5 days per week.

Upper School Student Profile Grade 9: 27 students (17 boys, 10 girls); Grade 10: 28 students (15 boys, 13 girls); Grade 11: 40 students (26 boys, 14 girls); Grade 12: 40 students (16 boys, 24 girls); Postgraduate: 1 student (1 boy). 68% of students are boarding students. 55% are state residents. 9 states are represented in upper school student body. 26% are international students. International students from China, France, Republic of Korea, Spain, Taiwan, and Viet Nam.

Faculty School total: 26. In upper school: 15 men, 11 women; 19 have advanced degrees; 23 reside on campus.

Subjects Offered Algebra, American government, American literature, ancient history, art, arts, baseball, basketball, biology, calculus, calculus-AP, carpentry, chemistry, civics, CPR, creative writing, drama performance, driver education, earth science, economics, economics and history, electives, English, English composition, English language and composition-AP, English language-AP, English literature, English literature and composition-AP, English literature-AP, English-AP, English/composition-AP, environmental science, environmental science-AP, environmental studies, environmental systems, ESL, European history, European history-AP, fine arts, fitness, foreign language, French, French language-AP, French literature-AP, French studies, French-AP, geography, geometry, government, government and politics-AP, government-AP, government/civics, history-AP, independent study, instrumental music, Latin, macroeconomics-AP, mathematics-AP, modern European history, modern European history-AP, music, music performance, musical productions, musical theater, participation in sports, photography, physical education, physical fitness, physical science, physics, poetry, pre-algebra, pre-calculus, reading/study skills, Spanish, Spanish language-AP, Spanish literature-AP, Spanish-AP, sports conditioning, statistics, student government, studio art, studio art-AP, study skills, tennis, trigonometry, U.S. government, U.S. government and politics-AP, U.S. history, U.S. history-AP, visual arts, volleyball, woodworking, wrestling, yearbook.

Graduation Requirements Arts and fine arts (art, music, dance, drama), English, foreign language, mathematics, physical education (includes health), science, social studies (includes history). Community service is required.

Special Academic Programs Advanced Placement exam preparation; honors section; accelerated programs; independent study; academic accommodation for the gifted, the musically talented, and the artistically talented; ESL (8 students enrolled).

College Admission Counseling 42 students graduated in 2011; 40 went to college, including Duke University; James Madison University; Longwood University; Penn State University Park; University of Virginia; Virginia Polytechnic Institute and State University. Mean SAT critical reading: 561, mean SAT math: 568, mean SAT writing: 542. 35% scored over 600 on SAT critical reading, 35% scored over 600 on SAT math.

Student Life Upper grades have specified standards of dress, student council, honor system. Discipline rests equally with students and faculty.

Tuition and Aid Day student tuition: $15,865; 5-day tuition and room/board: $33,165; 7-day tuition and room/board: $36,980. Tuition installment plan (Insured Tuition Payment Plan, FACTS Tuition Payment Plan, individually arranged payment plans). Tuition reduction for siblings, need-based scholarship grants available. In 2011–12, 33% of upper-school students received aid. Total amount of financial aid awarded in 2011–12: $525,000.

Admissions Traditional secondary-level entrance grade is 9. For fall 2011, 130 students applied for upper-level admission, 94 were accepted, 58 enrolled. ACT, California Achievement Test, Iowa Tests of Basic Skills, PSAT or SAT, SSAT, Stanford Achievement Test or TOEFL or SLEP required. Deadline for receipt of application materials: none. Application fee required: $50. Interview required.

Athletics Interscholastic: badminton (boys, girls), baseball (b), basketball (b,g), cross-country running (b,g), lacrosse (b), mountain biking (b,g), outdoor activities (b,g), skiing (downhill) (b,g), snowboarding (b,g), soccer (b,g), tennis (b,g), volleyball (g), wrestling (b); coed interscholastic: equestrian sports, golf, horseback riding; coed intramural: basketball, bicycling, canoeing/kayaking, cross-country running, fishing, fitness, Frisbee, hiking/backpacking, indoor soccer, jogging, mountain biking, outdoor activities, paint ball, physical fitness, physical training, power lifting, running, skateboarding, soccer, softball, street hockey, strength & conditioning, swimming and diving, table tennis, tennis, touch football, ultimate Frisbee, volleyball, walking, weight lifting, weight training. 5 coaches, 1 athletic trainer.

Computers Computers are regularly used in English, foreign language, history, mathematics, science classes. Computer network features include on-campus library services, online commercial services, Internet access, wireless campus network, Internet filtering or blocking technology. Campus intranet and student e-mail accounts are available to students. The school has a published electronic and media policy.

Contact Ms. Dee Gregory, Assistant Director of Admissions. 434-823-4805 Ext. 248. Fax: 434-205-5007. E-mail: dgregory@millerschool.org. Web site: www.millerschool.org.

MILL SPRINGS ACADEMY

Alpharetta, Georgia

See Special Needs Schools section.

MILTON ACADEMY

170 Centre Street

Milton, Massachusetts 02186

Head of School: Todd Bland

General Information Coeducational boarding and day college-preparatory school. Boarding grades 9–12, day grades K–12. Founded: 1798. Setting: suburban. Nearest major city is Boston. Students are housed in single-sex dormitories. 125-acre campus. 25 buildings on campus. Approved or accredited by Association of Independent Schools in New England, New England Association of Schools and Colleges, The Association of Boarding Schools, and Massachusetts Department of Education. Member of National Association of Independent Schools and Secondary School Admission Test Board. Endowment: $167 million. Total enrollment: 980. Upper school average class size: 14. Upper school faculty-student ratio: 1:5. There are 162 required school days per year for Upper School students. Upper School students typically attend 5 days per week. The average school day consists of 7 hours.

Upper School Student Profile 50% of students are boarding students. 64% are state residents. 26 states are represented in upper school student body. 13% are international students. International students from Hong Kong, Jamaica, Japan, Malaysia, Republic of Korea, and Taiwan; 18 other countries represented in student body.

Faculty School total: 180. In upper school: 62 men, 65 women; 99 have advanced degrees; 102 reside on campus.

Subjects Offered Algebra, American history, American literature, anatomy, architecture, art, art history, astronomy, biology, calculus, ceramics, chemistry, Chinese, computer math, computer programming, computer science, creative writing, current events, dance, drama, earth science, economics, English, English literature, ethics, European history, expository writing, fine arts, French, geography, geometry, government/civics, grammar, Greek, health, history, Latin, mathematics, music, philosophy, photography, physical education, physics, physiology, psychology, religion, science, social studies, sociology, Spanish, speech, statistics, theater, trigonometry, world history, world literature, writing.

Graduation Requirements Arts and fine arts (art, music, dance, drama), current events, English, foreign language, leadership, mathematics, physical education (includes health), public speaking, science, social studies (includes history).

Special Academic Programs Advanced Placement exam preparation; honors section; independent study; term-away projects; study abroad; academic accommodation for the gifted, the musically talented, and the artistically talented.

College Admission Counseling 164 students graduated in 2011; all went to college, including Boston College; Brown University; Columbia University; Georgetown University; Harvard University; Tufts University. Mean SAT critical reading: 680, mean SAT math: 692, mean SAT writing: 693.

Student Life Upper grades have student council, honor system. Discipline rests equally with students and faculty.

Tuition and Aid Day student tuition: $37,530; 7-day tuition and room/board: $45,720. Tuition installment plan (The Tuition Management Systems (TMS)). Need-based scholarship grants available. In 2011–12, 32% of upper-school students received aid. Total amount of financial aid awarded in 2011–12: $7,169,420.

Admissions Traditional secondary-level entrance grade is 9. For fall 2011, 1,100 students applied for upper-level admission, 275 were accepted, 165 enrolled. ISEE, PSAT, SAT, SSAT or TOEFL required. Deadline for receipt of application materials: January 15. Application fee required: $50. Interview required.

Athletics Interscholastic: baseball (boys), basketball (b,g), cross-country running (b,g), field hockey (g), football (b), ice hockey (b,g), lacrosse (b,g), soccer (b,g), softball (g), squash (b,g), tennis (b,g), track and field (b,g), volleyball (g); intramural: basketball (b,g), soccer (b,g), strength & conditioning (b,g); coed interscholastic: alpine skiing, diving, golf, sailing, skiing (downhill), swimming and diving, wrestling; coed intramural: climbing, outdoor activities, outdoor education, project adventure, rock climbing, skiing (downhill), squash, tennis, ultimate Frisbee, yoga. 6 PE instructors, 107 coaches, 3 athletic trainers.

Computers Computers are regularly used in mathematics, science classes. Computer network features include on-campus library services, online commercial services, Internet access, wireless campus network, Internet filtering or blocking technology. Student e-mail accounts and computer access in designated common areas are available to students.

Contact Mrs. Patricia Finn, Admission Assistant. 617-898-2227. Fax: 617-898-1701. E-mail: admissions@milton.edu. Web site: www.milton.edu.

See Display on next page and Close-Up on page 648.

MISS EDGAR'S AND MISS CRAMP'S SCHOOL

525 Mount Pleasant Avenue

Montreal, Quebec H3Y 3H6, Canada

Head of School: Ms. Katherine Nikidis

General Information Girls' day college-preparatory, arts, bilingual studies, and technology school. Grades K–11. Founded: 1909. Setting: urban. 4-acre campus. 1 building on campus. Approved or accredited by Canadian Association of Independent Schools, Quebec Association of Independent Schools, and Quebec Department of Education. Affiliate member of National Association of Independent Schools; member of Secondary School Admission Test Board. Languages of instruction: English and French. Total enrollment: 335. Upper school average class size: 19. Upper school faculty-student ratio: 1:9. There are 180 required school days per year for Upper School students. Upper School students typically attend 5 days per week. The average school day consists of 5 hours.

Upper School Student Profile Grade 9: 39 students (39 girls); Grade 10: 40 students (40 girls); Grade 11: 36 students (36 girls).

Faculty School total: 40. In upper school: 3 men, 15 women; 8 have advanced degrees.

Subjects Offered Art, art history, biology, calculus, career exploration, chemistry, computer science, creative writing, drama, ecology, economics, English, environmental science, European history, French, geography, history, mathematics, media, music, physical education, physics, science, social studies, Spanish, theater, women's studies, world history.

Graduation Requirements English, foreign language, mathematics, science, social studies (includes history).

Special Academic Programs 2 Advanced Placement exams for which test preparation is offered; honors section.

College Admission Counseling 36 students graduated in 2011; all went to college, including John Abbott College; Lower Canada College; Marianopolis College.

Student Life Upper grades have uniform requirement, student council, honor system. Discipline rests primarily with faculty.

Tuition and Aid Day student tuition: CAN$15,000. Tuition installment plan (individually arranged payment plans). Bursaries, merit scholarship grants available. In 2011–12, 18% of upper-school students received aid; total upper-school merit-scholarship money awarded: CAN$80,000. Total amount of financial aid awarded in 2011–12: CAN$105,000.

Admissions Traditional secondary-level entrance grade is 9. For fall 2011, 22 students applied for upper-level admission, 15 were accepted, 8 enrolled. CCAT, SSAT or writing sample required. Deadline for receipt of application materials: none. Application fee required: CAN$50. On-campus interview required.

Athletics Interscholastic: badminton, basketball, cross-country running, golf, hockey, ice hockey, running, soccer, swimming and diving, tennis, touch football, track and field, volleyball; intramural: badminton, baseball, basketball, crew, cross-country running, curling, dance, field hockey, gymnastics, ice hockey, outdoor adventure, outdoor education, outdoor skills, physical fitness, rugby, running, skiing (cross-country), soccer, softball, touch football, track and field, volleyball. 3 PE instructors, 11 coaches.

Computers Computers are regularly used in art, English, French, history, newspaper, writing, yearbook classes. Computer network features include on-campus library services, Internet access, wireless campus network, Internet filtering or blocking technology. Campus intranet, student e-mail accounts, and computer access in designated common areas are available to students. The school has a published electronic and media policy.

Contact Ms. Carla Bolsius, Admissions Coordinator. 514-935-6357 Ext. 254. Fax: 514-935-1099. E-mail: bolsiusc@ecs.qc.ca. Web site: www.ecs.qc.ca.

MISS HALL'S SCHOOL

492 Holmes Road

Pittsfield, Massachusetts 01201

Head of School: Ms. Jeannie Norris

General Information Girls' boarding and day college-preparatory, arts, technology, community service, and leadership development school. Grades 9–12. Founded: 1898. Setting: suburban. Nearest major city is Albany, NY. Students are housed in single-sex dormitories. 80-acre campus. 9 buildings on campus. Approved or accredited by Association of Independent Schools in New England, New England Association of Schools and Colleges, The Association of Boarding Schools, and Massachusetts Department of Education. Member of National Association of Independent Schools and Secondary School Admission Test Board. Endowment: $16 million. Total enrollment: 180. Upper school average class size: 10. Upper school faculty-student ratio: 1:5.

Upper School Student Profile Grade 9: 50 students (50 girls); Grade 10: 50 students (50 girls); Grade 11: 40 students (40 girls); Grade 12: 40 students (40 girls). 75% of students are boarding students. 34% are state residents. 20 states are represented in upper school student body. 30% are international students. International students from China, Germany, Republic of Korea, Taiwan, and Viet Nam; 14 other countries represented in student body.

Faculty School total: 36. In upper school: 8 men, 28 women; 26 have advanced degrees; 16 reside on campus.

Subjects Offered Advanced Placement courses, algebra, American government, American history, American literature, anatomy, art, art history, biology, business skills, calculus, ceramics, chamber groups, chemistry, college counseling, community service, computer science, CPR, dance, drama, drawing, driver education, ecology, economics, English, English literature, English-AP, environmental science, ESL, ethics, ethics and responsibility, European history, European history-AP, expressive arts, fine arts, forensics, French, geometry, government/civics, health, history, Latin, mathematics, music, music history, painting, photography, physics, physiology, political science, psychology, science, social studies, Spanish, theater, trigonometry, world cultures, world history.

Graduation Requirements Arts and fine arts (art, music, dance, drama), English, foreign language, history, mathematics, physical education (includes health), science. Community service is required.

Special Academic Programs Advanced Placement exam preparation; honors section; independent study; academic accommodation for the gifted, the musically talented, and the artistically talented; special instructional classes for students with mild learning disabilities and Attention Deficit Disorder; ESL (20 students enrolled).

College Admission Counseling 44 students graduated in 2011; all went to college, including New York University; St. Lawrence University; University of Illinois at Urbana–Champaign; University of Vermont.

Student Life Upper grades have specified standards of dress, student council, honor system. Discipline rests equally with students and faculty.

Tuition and Aid Day student tuition: $29,015; 7-day tuition and room/board: $46,970. Tuition installment plan (Insured Tuition Payment Plan, Academic Management Services Plan, Key Tuition Payment Plan, monthly payment plans, individually arranged payment plans). Merit scholarship grants, need-based scholarship grants available. In 2011–12, 48% of upper-school students received aid; total upper-school merit-scholarship money awarded: $275,000. Total amount of financial aid awarded in 2011–12: $2,500,000.

Admissions Traditional secondary-level entrance grade is 9. For fall 2011, 250 students applied for upper-level admission, 122 were accepted, 70 enrolled. PSAT, SAT, SSAT or TOEFL required. Deadline for receipt of application materials: February 15. Application fee required: $50. Interview required.

Athletics Interscholastic: alpine skiing, basketball, cross-country running, field hockey, lacrosse, skiing (downhill), soccer, softball, tennis, volleyball; intramural: aerobics, aerobics/dance, alpine skiing, dance, equestrian sports, fitness, jogging, modern dance, outdoor activities, outdoor education, outdoor skills, physical fitness, rock climbing, ropes courses, running, skiing (cross-country), skiing (downhill), snowboarding, tennis, walking, wall climbing, wilderness, yoga. 3 coaches, 1 athletic trainer.

Computers Computers are regularly used in computer applications, English, foreign language, history, music, newspaper, photography, science, yearbook classes. Computer network features include on-campus library services, online commercial services, Internet access, wireless campus network. Student e-mail accounts and computer access in designated common areas are available to students. The school has a published electronic and media policy.

Contact Ms. Julie Bradley, Director of Admission. 413-499-1300. Fax: 413-448-2994. E-mail: info@misshalls.org. Web site: www.misshalls.org.

MISSOURI MILITARY ACADEMY

204 Grand Avenue

Mexico, Missouri 65265

Head of School: Maj. Gen. Robert M. Flanagan

General Information Boys' boarding and day college-preparatory, technology, ESL, military science, and military school, affiliated with Christian faith; primarily serves individuals with Attention Deficit Disorder. Boarding grades 6–PG, day grades 6–12. Founded: 1889. Setting: small town. Nearest major city is St. Louis. Students are housed in single-sex dormitories. 288-acre campus. 19 buildings on campus. Approved or accredited by Independent Schools Association of the Central States and The Association of Boarding Schools. Member of National Association of Independent Schools and Secondary School Admission Test Board. Endowment: $39 million. Total enrollment: 232. Upper school average class size: 10. Upper school faculty-student ratio: 1:11. There are 175 required school days per year for Upper School students. Upper School students typically attend 5 days per week. The average school day consists of 5 hours and 50 minutes.

Upper School Student Profile Grade 9: 55 students (55 boys); Grade 10: 52 students (52 boys); Grade 11: 53 students (53 boys); Grade 12: 50 students (50 boys). 100% of students are boarding students. 20% are state residents. 30 states are represented in upper school student body. International students from Canada, China, Mexico, Republic of Korea, Russian Federation, and Taiwan; 10 other countries represented in student body.

Faculty School total: 47. In upper school: 27 men, 7 women; 27 have advanced degrees; 5 reside on campus.

Subjects Offered Algebra, American literature, art, biology, broadcasting, business, business skills, calculus, chemistry, computer science, drama, economics, English, ESL, fine arts, French, geography, geometry, government/civics, history, honors algebra, honors English, honors U.S. history, humanities, instrumental music, Internet, jazz band, journalism, JROTC or LEAD (Leadership Education and Development), keyboarding, languages, Latin American studies, leadership, literary magazine, marching band, mathematics, military science, music, newspaper, physical education, physical science, physics, physics-AP, psychology, science, social studies, sociology, Spanish, speech, statistics, student government, student publications, swimming, theater, track and field, typing, U.S. government, U.S. history, vocal ensemble, vocal music, world history, wrestling, writing, yearbook.

Graduation Requirements Arts and fine arts (art, music, dance, drama), business skills (includes word processing), computer science, English, foreign language, JROTC, mathematics, physical education (includes health), science, social studies (includes history), 20 hours of community service per school year.

Special Academic Programs 9 Advanced Placement exams for which test preparation is offered; honors section; independent study; study at local college for college credit; academic accommodation for the gifted, the musically talented, and the artistically talented; remedial reading and/or remedial writing; remedial math; special instructional classes for students with Attention Deficit Disorder; ESL (33 students enrolled).

College Admission Counseling 52 students graduated in 2011; all went to college, including Saint Louis University; Texas A&M University; The University of Arizona; The University of Texas at Austin; University of Miami; University of Missouri. Median SAT critical reading: 467, median SAT math: 547, median combined SAT: 1016, median composite ACT: 21.

Student Life Upper grades have uniform requirement, student council, honor system. Discipline rests equally with students and faculty. Attendance at religious services is required.

Summer Programs Remediation, enrichment, ESL, sports, rigorous outdoor training programs offered; session focuses on academics and leadership; held both on and off campus; held at Water Park in Jefferson City, MO and Courtois River for float/canoe trips; accepts boys and girls; open to students from other schools. 70 students usually enrolled. 2012 schedule: June 24 to July 21. Application deadline: June 15.

Tuition and Aid Day student tuition: $8750; 7-day tuition and room/board: $29,400. Guaranteed tuition plan. Tuition installment plan (individually arranged payment plans, school's own payment plan). Tuition reduction for siblings, merit scholarship grants, need-based scholarship grants, need-based loans available. In 2011–12, 30% of upper-school students received aid. Total amount of financial aid awarded in 2011–12: $750,000.

Admissions Traditional secondary-level entrance grade is 9. For fall 2011, 250 students applied for upper-level admission, 147 were accepted, 135 enrolled. Deadline for receipt of application materials: none. Application fee required: $100. Interview required.

Athletics Interscholastic: aquatics, baseball, basketball, cross-country running, drill team, football, golf, JROTC drill, marksmanship, outdoor activities, riflery, soccer, swimming and diving, tennis, track and field, weight training, wrestling; intramural: aquatics, basketball, canoeing/kayaking, equestrian sports, fishing, fitness, fitness walking, flag football, horseback riding, indoor track, marksmanship, martial arts, outdoor activities, outdoor recreation, outdoor skills, paint ball, physical fitness, physical training, rappelling, riflery, roller blading, ropes courses, running, soccer, softball, strength & conditioning, swimming and diving, table tennis, tennis, touch football, track and field, volleyball, weight lifting, weight training, winter (indoor) track, wrestling. 12 coaches, 1 athletic trainer.

Computers Computers are regularly used in business, English, history, journalism, library, mathematics, newspaper, science, yearbook classes. Computer network features include on-campus library services, online commercial services, Internet access, wireless campus network, Internet filtering or blocking technology. Campus intranet, student e-mail accounts, and computer access in designated common areas are available to students. Students grades are available online. The school has a published electronic and media policy.

Contact Lt. Col. Roger L. Hill, Director of Admissions. 573-581-1776 Ext. 323. Fax: 573-581-0081. E-mail: roger.hill@missourimilitaryacademy.org. Web site: www.MissouriMilitaryAcademy.org.

MISS PORTER'S SCHOOL

60 Main Street

Farmington, Connecticut 06032

Head of School: Dr. Katherine G. Windsor

General Information Girls' boarding and day college-preparatory and arts school. Grades 9–12. Founded: 1843. Setting: suburban. Nearest major city is Hartford. Students are housed in single-sex dormitories. 50-acre campus. 56 buildings on campus. Approved or accredited by New England Association of Schools and Colleges and Connecticut Department of Education. Member of National Association of Independent Schools and Secondary School Admission Test Board. Endowment: $100 million. Upper school average class size: 11. Upper school faculty-student ratio: 1:8.

Upper School Student Profile Grade 9: 73 students (73 girls); Grade 10: 85 students (85 girls); Grade 11: 82 students (82 girls); Grade 12: 91 students (91 girls). 67% of students are boarding students. 54% are state residents. 25 states are represented in upper school student body. 11% are international students. International students from China, Hong Kong, and Republic of Korea; 15 other countries represented in student body.

Faculty School total: 52. In upper school: 20 men, 32 women; 33 have advanced degrees; 28 reside on campus.

Subjects Offered Acting, advanced chemistry, advanced computer applications, advanced math, Advanced Placement courses, advanced studio art-AP, African history, algebra, American history, American literature, anatomy and physiology, aquatics, area studies, art history, art history-AP, arts, astronomy, athletics, ballet, biology, biology-AP, British literature, calculus, calculus-AP, career/college preparation, ceramics, chemistry, chemistry-AP, Chinese, Chinese history, classical language, college counseling, college planning, community service, computer applications, computer graphics, computer programming, computer science, creative writing, dance, dance performance, desktop publishing, drama, drama performance, economics, economics and history, engineering, English, English literature, environmental science, environmental science-AP, ethical decision making, ethics, European history, European history-AP, experiential education, expository writing, fitness, foreign language, forensics, French, French language-AP, French literature-AP, geometry, global issues, golf, graphic design, health and wellness, history, honors geometry, human rights, international relations, intro to computers, Japanese history, jazz, jewelry making, languages, Latin, Latin American literature, Latin-AP, leadership, mathematics, Middle Eastern history, model United Nations, modern dance, modern European history-AP, multicultural literature, music, music history, music performance, music theory, participation in sports, performing arts, personal finance, photography, physics, physics-AP, pre-calculus, printmaking, psychology, public speaking, science, Shakespeare, social studies, Spanish, Spanish language-AP, Spanish literature-AP, sports, squash, statistics, statistics-AP, student government, studio art, studio art-AP, swimming, swimming test, tennis, textiles, theater, trigonometry, U.S. history, U.S. history-AP, video film production, visual arts, vocal music, Web site design, Western civilization, writing, yoga.

Graduation Requirements Arts and fine arts (art, music, dance, drama), athletics, computer science, English, experiential education, foreign language, leadership, mathematics, science, social studies (includes history). Community service is required.

Special Academic Programs 26 Advanced Placement exams for which test preparation is offered; honors section; independent study; term-away projects; study abroad; ESL.

College Admission Counseling 87 students graduated in 2011; all went to college, including Cornell University; Gettysburg College; Hobart and William Smith Colleges; Northeastern University; University of Pennsylvania; Yale University. Mean SAT critical reading: 627, mean SAT math: 636, mean SAT writing: 633, mean combined SAT: 1896.

Student Life Upper grades have specified standards of dress, student council, honor system. Discipline rests equally with students and faculty.

Summer Programs Enrichment, advancement, art/fine arts programs offered; session focuses on Model UN, leadership, held on campus; accepts girls; open to students from other schools. 60 students usually enrolled. Application deadline: none.

Tuition and Aid Day student tuition: $36,850; 7-day tuition and room/board: $46,650. Tuition installment plan (monthly payment plans, individually arranged payment plans). Merit scholarship grants, need-based scholarship grants available. In 2011–12, 34% of upper-school students received aid. Total amount of financial aid awarded in 2011–12: $3,300,000.

Admissions Traditional secondary-level entrance grade is 9. For fall 2011, 456 students applied for upper-level admission, 199 were accepted, 109 enrolled. ISEE, PSAT and SAT for applicants to grade 11 and 12, SSAT or TOEFL required. Deadline for receipt of application materials: January 15. Application fee required: $50. Interview required.

Athletics Interscholastic: alpine skiing, badminton, basketball, crew, cross-country running, dance, diving, equestrian sports, field hockey, golf, horseback riding, independent competitive sports, lacrosse, skiing (downhill), soccer, softball, squash, swimming and diving, tennis, track and field, ultimate Frisbee, volleyball; intramural: aerobics, aerobics/Nautilus, ballet, climbing, dance, equestrian sports, fencing, fitness, fitness walking, golf, horseback riding, jogging, life saving, martial arts, modern dance, physical fitness, self defense, skiing (downhill), snowboarding, squash, strength & conditioning, swimming and diving, tennis, walking, wall climbing, yoga.

Computers Computers are regularly used in computer applications, desktop publishing, graphic design, graphics, introduction to technology, publications, Web site design classes. Computer network features include on-campus library services, online commercial services, Internet access, wireless campus network, Internet filtering or blocking technology. Campus intranet, student e-mail accounts, and computer access in designated common areas are available to students. Students grades are available online. The school has a published electronic and media policy.

Contact Liz Schmitt, Director of Admission. 860-409-3530. Fax: 860-409-3531. E-mail: liz_schmitt@missporters.org. Web site: www.porters.org.

MMI PREPARATORY SCHOOL

154 Centre Street

Freeland, Pennsylvania 18224

Head of School: Mr. Thomas G. Hood

General Information Coeducational day college-preparatory, arts, and technology school. Grades 6–12. Founded: 1879. Setting: small town. Nearest major city is Hazleton. 20-acre campus. 1 building on campus. Approved or accredited by Middle States Association of Colleges and Schools and Pennsylvania Department of Education. Member of National Association of Independent Schools. Endowment: $17 million. Total enrollment: 248. Upper school average class size: 16. Upper school faculty-student ratio: 1:11. There are 177 required school days per year for Upper School students. Upper School students typically attend 5 days per week. The average school day consists of 6 hours and 30 minutes.

Upper School Student Profile Grade 9: 44 students (25 boys, 19 girls); Grade 10: 36 students (17 boys, 19 girls); Grade 11: 44 students (19 boys, 25 girls); Grade 12: 38 students (24 boys, 14 girls).

Faculty School total: 27. In upper school: 11 men, 16 women; 19 have advanced degrees.

Subjects Offered Algebra, American history, American literature, anatomy, anthropology, art, art-AP, biology, biology-AP, calculus, chemistry, chemistry-AP, Chinese, computer programming, computer programming-AP, computer science, consumer education, creative writing, earth science, economics, English, English language and composition-AP, English literature, English literature and composition-AP, environmental science, European history, European history-AP, expository writing, fine arts, geography, geometry, German, government/civics, grammar, health, history, keyboarding, Latin, mathematics, music, physical education, physics, physics-AP, physiology, psychology, science, social studies, Spanish, speech, statistics, trigonometry, world history, world literature.

Graduation Requirements Analysis and differential calculus, arts and fine arts (art, music, dance, drama), college counseling, computer science, consumer education, economics, English, foreign language, mathematics, physical education (includes health), science, social studies (includes history), speech, independent research project presentation every spring, public speaking assembly project every year.

Special Academic Programs 9 Advanced Placement exams for which test preparation is offered; honors section; independent study; study at local college for college credit; academic accommodation for the gifted; special instructional classes for blind students.

College Admission Counseling 39 students graduated in 2011; all went to college, including Carnegie Mellon University; New York University; Penn State University Park; Saint Joseph's University; Temple University; The University of Scranton. Mean SAT critical reading: 610, mean SAT math: 620, mean SAT writing: 613, mean combined SAT: 1843.

Student Life Upper grades have specified standards of dress, student council, honor system. Discipline rests primarily with faculty.

Summer Programs Remediation, enrichment, advancement, computer instruction programs offered; session focuses on academics; held on campus; accepts boys and girls; open to students from other schools. 100 students usually enrolled. 2012 schedule: June 6 to July 8. Application deadline: May 15.

Tuition and Aid Day student tuition: $12,625. Tuition installment plan (monthly payment plans). Merit scholarship grants, need-based scholarship grants, paying campus jobs available. In 2011–12, 60% of upper-school students received aid; total upper-school merit-scholarship money awarded: $56,950. Total amount of financial aid awarded in 2011–12: $893,050.

Admissions Traditional secondary-level entrance grade is 9. For fall 2011, 35 students applied for upper-level admission, 23 were accepted, 13 enrolled. Cognitive Abilities Test and Iowa Tests of Basic Skills required. Deadline for receipt of application materials: none. Application fee required: $25. On-campus interview required.

Athletics Interscholastic: baseball (boys), basketball (b,g), cross-country running (b,g), soccer (b,g), softball (g), tennis (b,g), volleyball (g); intramural: bowling (b,g); coed interscholastic: golf; coed intramural: skiing (downhill), snowboarding. 2 PE instructors.

Computers Computers are regularly used in all classes. Computer network features include on-campus library services, Internet access, Internet filtering or blocking technology. Computer access in designated common areas is available to students. Students grades are available online. The school has a published electronic and media policy.

Contact Aprilaurie Whitley, Director of Admissions and Financial Aid. 570-636-1108 Ext. 136. Fax: 570-636-0742. E-mail: awhitley@mmiprep.org. Web site: www.mmiprep.org.

MONSIGNOR DONOVAN HIGH SCHOOL

711 Hooper Avenue

Toms River, New Jersey 08753

Head of School: Edward Gere

General Information Coeducational day college-preparatory school, affiliated with Roman Catholic Church. Grades 9–12. Founded: 1962. Setting: suburban. 1 building on campus. Approved or accredited by Middle States Association of Colleges and Schools, National Catholic Education Association, and New Jersey Department of Education. Total enrollment: 787. Upper school average class size: 30. Upper school faculty-student ratio: 1:15.

Upper School Student Profile Grade 9: 178 students (78 boys, 100 girls); Grade 10: 186 students (91 boys, 95 girls); Grade 11: 212 students (99 boys, 113 girls); Grade 12: 211 students (105 boys, 106 girls). 85% of students are Roman Catholic.

Faculty School total: 60. In upper school: 28 men, 32 women.

Special Academic Programs Advanced Placement exam preparation; honors section; independent study; study at local college for college credit; academic accommodation for the gifted, the musically talented, and the artistically talented; remedial reading and/or remedial writing; remedial math.

College Admission Counseling 218 students graduated in 2011; 216 went to college. Other: 1 went to work, 1 entered military service.

Student Life Upper grades have uniform requirement, student council, honor system. Discipline rests equally with students and faculty. Attendance at religious services is required.

Tuition and Aid Day student tuition: $10,525. Tuition installment plan (SMART Tuition Payment Plan, monthly payment plans). Merit scholarship grants, need-based scholarship grants, paying campus jobs available. In 2011–12, 20% of upper-school students received aid. Total amount of financial aid awarded in 2011–12: $400,000.

Admissions Traditional secondary-level entrance grade is 9. High School Placement Test (closed version) from Scholastic Testing Service or Scholastic Testing Service High School Placement Test required. Deadline for receipt of application materials: October 31. Application fee required: $50. On-campus interview recommended.

Athletics Interscholastic: baseball (boys), cheering (g), football (b), golf (b), ice hockey (b), lacrosse (g), softball (g), wrestling (b); coed interscholastic: basketball, bowling, cross-country running, dance, hiking/backpacking, sailing, skiing (cross-country), snowboarding, soccer, strength & conditioning, surfing, swimming and diving, tennis, weight lifting, weight training. 5 PE instructors, 22 coaches, 1 athletic trainer.

Computers Computers are regularly used in all academic classes. Computer network features include on-campus library services, Internet access, wireless campus network, Internet filtering or blocking technology. Student e-mail accounts are available to students. Students grades are available online.

Contact Mrs. Carol A. Gaspartich, Registrar. 732-349-8801 Ext. 2426. Fax: 732-505-8014. E-mail: cgaspartich@mondonhs.com. Web site: www.mondonhs.com.

MONTCLAIR COLLEGE PREPARATORY SCHOOL

8071 Sepulveda Boulevard

Van Nuys, California 91402-4420

Head of School: Mr. Mark Simpson

General Information Coeducational boarding and day college-preparatory, arts, and technology school. Grades 7–12. Founded: 1956. Setting: urban. Nearest major city is Los Angeles. Students are housed in coed dormitories. 5-acre campus. 5 buildings on campus. Approved or accredited by Western Association of Schools and Colleges. Total enrollment: 254. Upper school average class size: 20. Upper school faculty-student ratio: 1:15. Upper School students typically attend 5 days per week. The average school day consists of 6 hours and 30 minutes.

Upper School Student Profile 5% of students are boarding students. 5% are international students. International students from Cameroon, China, Japan, Republic of Korea, and Taiwan; 1 other country represented in student body.

Faculty School total: 45. In upper school: 23 men, 22 women; 12 have advanced degrees; 2 reside on campus.

Subjects Offered Advanced Placement courses.

Graduation Requirements Arts and fine arts (art, music, dance, drama), computer science, English, foreign language, lab science, mathematics, U.S. government, U.S. history.

Special Academic Programs Advanced Placement exam preparation; honors section; independent study; study at local college for college credit; ESL (64 students enrolled).

College Admission Counseling 78 students graduated in 2010; 75 went to college, including Loyola Marymount University; San Francisco State University; University of California, Berkeley; University of California, Los Angeles; University of California, Santa Barbara. Other: 3 had other specific plans.

Student Life Upper grades have uniform requirement, student council, honor system. Discipline rests primarily with faculty.

Tuition and Aid Day student tuition: $15,000; 7-day tuition and room/board: $39,950. Tuition installment plan (monthly payment plans, 1- and 2-payment plans). Limited need-based financial aid available. In 2010–11, 8% of upper-school students received aid. Total amount of financial aid awarded in 2010–11: $250,000.

Admissions Traditional secondary-level entrance grade is 9. For fall 2010, 150 students applied for upper-level admission, 100 were accepted, 50 enrolled. ISEE or school's own exam required. Deadline for receipt of application materials: none. Application fee required: $100.

Athletics Interscholastic: baseball (boys), basketball (b,g), cross-country running (b,g), flag football (b), football (b), golf (b,g), soccer (b,g), softball (g), volleyball (b,g); coed interscholastic: cheering, cross-country running, golf, horseback riding, tennis; coed intramural: alpine skiing, badminton, dance, dance squad, dance team, skiing (downhill), snowboarding, surfing, weight lifting. 2 PE instructors, 10 coaches, 1 athletic trainer.

Computers Computers are regularly used in all academic, desktop publishing classes. Computer network features include Internet access, wireless campus network, Internet filtering or blocking technology. Campus intranet and computer access in designated common areas are available to students. Students grades are available online.

Contact Mrs. Kandice Neumann, Director of Admissions. 818-787-5290 Ext. 10. Fax: 818-786-3382. E-mail: kneumann@montclairprep.com. Web site: www.montclairprep.org.

MONTCLAIR KIMBERLEY ACADEMY

201 Valley Road

Montclair, New Jersey 07042

Head of School: Mr. Thomas W. Nammack

General Information Coeducational day college-preparatory, arts, and technology school. Grades PK–12. Founded: 1887. Setting: suburban. Nearest major city is New York, NY. 28-acre campus. 1 building on campus. Approved or accredited by Middle States Association of Colleges and Schools and National Lutheran School Accreditation. Member of National Association of Independent Schools and Secondary School Admission Test Board. Endowment: $12 million. Total enrollment: 1,043. Upper school average class size: 12. Upper school faculty-student ratio: 1:6. Upper School students typically attend 5 days per week. The average school day consists of 6 hours and 30 minutes.

Upper School Student Profile Grade 9: 108 students (56 boys, 52 girls); Grade 10: 117 students (56 boys, 61 girls); Grade 11: 108 students (59 boys, 49 girls); Grade 12: 101 students (63 boys, 38 girls).

Faculty School total: 73. In upper school: 40 men, 33 women; 64 have advanced degrees.

Subjects Offered Acting, advanced chemistry, advanced math, algebra, American history, American literature, architecture, art, astronomy, biology, biology-AP, British literature, calculus, calculus-AP, chemistry, chemistry-AP, Chinese, chorus, communications, concert band, creative writing, dance, digital photography, drama, driver education, ecology, economics, economics-AP, English, English literature, environmental science, ethics, European history, expository writing, fine arts, French, French language-AP, French literature-AP, geometry, government/civics, health, history, Latin, mathematics, music, photography, physical education, physics, physics-AP, post-calculus, Spanish, Spanish language-AP, Spanish literature-AP, statistics-AP, theater, trigonometry, world history, world literature, world wide web design, writing.

Graduation Requirements Art, arts and fine arts (art, music, dance, drama), English, foreign language, history, mathematics, music, physical education (includes health), science, swimming, citizenship.

Special Academic Programs Advanced Placement exam preparation; honors section; independent study; term-away projects; study abroad; academic accommodation for the gifted.

College Admission Counseling 105 students graduated in 2011; 104 went to college, including Georgetown University; Lafayette College; New York University; Penn State University Park; Princeton University; The George Washington University. Other: 1 entered a postgraduate year. Mean SAT critical reading: 630, mean SAT math: 647. 60% scored over 600 on SAT critical reading, 65% scored over 600 on SAT math.

Student Life Upper grades have specified standards of dress, student council, honor system. Discipline rests equally with students and faculty.

Summer Programs Enrichment, advancement, sports, art/fine arts, computer instruction programs offered; held on campus; accepts boys and girls; open to students from other schools. 250 students usually enrolled. 2012 schedule: June 27 to August 5. Application deadline: none.

Tuition and Aid Day student tuition: $30,900. Tuition installment plan (Insured Tuition Payment Plan, monthly payment plans, individually arranged payment plans). Need-based scholarship grants available. In 2011–12, 15% of upper-school students received aid. Total amount of financial aid awarded in 2011–12: $1,281,308.

Admissions Traditional secondary-level entrance grade is 9. ISEE or SSAT required. Deadline for receipt of application materials: January 31. Application fee required: $50. On-campus interview required.

Athletics Interscholastic: baseball (boys), basketball (b,g), cheering (g), cross-country running (b,g), dance (b,g), dance team (b,g), fencing (b,g), field hockey (g), football (b), ice hockey (b), lacrosse (b,g), outdoor activities (b,g), physical fitness (b,g), soccer (b,g), softball (g), swimming and diving (b,g), tennis (b,g), track and field (b,g), volleyball (g), winter (indoor) track (b,g), wrestling (b); coed interscholastic: golf. 5 PE instructors, 9 coaches, 2 athletic trainers.

Computers Computer network features include on-campus library services, online commercial services, Internet access, wireless campus network, Internet filtering or blocking technology, 1:1 laptop school, community Intranet. Campus intranet and student e-mail accounts are available to students. The school has a published electronic and media policy.

Contact Sarah Rowland, Director of Admissions and Financial Aid. 973-509-7930. Fax: 973-509-4526. E-mail: srowland@mka.org. Web site: www.mka.org.

MONTEREY BAY ACADEMY

783 San Andreas Road

La Selva Beach, California 95076-1907

Head of School: Mr. Timothy Kubrock

General Information Coeducational boarding and day college-preparatory and religious studies school, affiliated with Seventh-day Adventist Church. Grades 9–12. Founded: 1949. Setting: rural. Nearest major city is San Jose. Students are housed in single-sex dormitories. 379-acre campus. 12 buildings on campus. Approved or accredited by Western Association of Schools and Colleges and California Department of Education. Total enrollment: 211. Upper school average class size: 20. Upper school faculty-student ratio: 1:13. There are 180 required school days per year for Upper School students. Upper School students typically attend 5 days per week. The average school day consists of 7 hours.

Upper School Student Profile Grade 9: 29 students (14 boys, 15 girls); Grade 10: 45 students (27 boys, 18 girls); Grade 11: 70 students (34 boys, 36 girls); Grade 12: 67 students (37 boys, 30 girls). 75% of students are boarding students. 75% are state residents. 7 states are represented in upper school student body. 10% are international students. International students from China, Germany, Hong Kong, Japan, Republic of Korea, and Russian Federation. 80% of students are Seventh-day Adventists.

Faculty School total: 16. In upper school: 12 men, 4 women; 7 have advanced degrees; all reside on campus.

Subjects Offered Accounting, Advanced Placement courses, algebra, American literature, biology, calculus, chemistry, choir, Christianity, computer applications, computer literacy, drama, economics, English, English language and composition-AP, geography, geometry, graphics, health, instrumental music, keyboarding, marine biology, photography, physical education, physical science, physics, physiology, piano, pre-algebra, pre-calculus, religion, Spanish, statistics, technology, typing, U.S. government, U.S. history, U.S. history-AP, voice, weight training, woodworking, world history.

Graduation Requirements Arts and fine arts (art, music, dance, drama), business skills (includes word processing), computer science, English, life skills, mathematics, physical education (includes health), science, social studies (includes history), work experience, religious studies for each year in a Seventh-day Adventist School.

Special Academic Programs Advanced Placement exam preparation; ESL (15 students enrolled).

College Admission Counseling 51 students graduated in 2010; 47 went to college, including La Sierra University; Pacific Union College; Southern Adventist University; University of California System; Walla Walla University. Other: 3 went to work, 1 entered military service.

Student Life Upper grades have specified standards of dress, student council. Discipline rests primarily with faculty. Attendance at religious services is required.

Tuition and Aid Day student tuition: $8600–$10,100; 7-day tuition and room/board: $14,700–$23,050. Tuition installment plan (monthly payment plans). Need-based scholarship grants, paying campus jobs available. In 2010–11, 30% of upper-school students received aid. Total amount of financial aid awarded in 2010–11: $300,000.

Admissions Traditional secondary-level entrance grade is 9. For fall 2010, 225 students applied for upper-level admission, 220 were accepted, 211 enrolled. TOEFL required. Deadline for receipt of application materials: July 15. Application fee required: $50. Interview recommended.

Athletics Interscholastic: basketball (boys, girls), flag football (b,g), softball (b,g), volleyball (b,g). 2 PE instructors, 7 coaches.

Computers Computers are regularly used in accounting, mathematics, science, typing, yearbook classes. Computer resources include Internet access, Internet filtering or blocking technology. Students grades are available online. The school has a published electronic and media policy.

Contact Ms. Donna J. Baerg, Vice Principal for Academic Affairs. 831-728-1481 Ext. 1218. Fax: 831-728-1485. E-mail: academics@montereybayacademy.org. Web site: www.montereybayacademy.org.

MONTE VISTA CHRISTIAN SCHOOL

2 School Way

Watsonville, California 95076

Head of School: Mr. Stephen Sharp

General Information Coeducational boarding and day college-preparatory, arts, religious studies, technology, and ESL school, affiliated with Christian faith. Boarding grades 9–12, day grades 6–12. Founded: 1926. Setting: rural. Nearest major city is San Jose. Students are housed in single-sex dormitories. 100-acre campus. 27 buildings on campus. Approved or accredited by Association of Christian Schools International, The Association of Boarding Schools, and Western Association of Schools and Colleges. Endowment: $1 million. Total enrollment: 808. Upper school average class size: 17. Upper school faculty-student ratio: 1:9. There are 180 required school days per year for Upper School students. Upper School students typically attend 5 days per week. The average school day consists of 7 hours and 5 minutes.

Upper School Student Profile Grade 9: 150 students (75 boys, 75 girls); Grade 10: 153 students (75 boys, 78 girls); Grade 11: 145 students (75 boys, 70 girls); Grade 12: 150 students (73 boys, 77 girls). 22% of students are boarding students. 80% are state residents. 1 state is represented in upper school student body. 20% are international students. International students from China, Hong Kong, Japan, Republic of Korea, Taiwan, and Thailand; 4 other countries represented in student body. 80% of students are Christian faith.

Faculty School total: 68. In upper school: 23 men, 23 women; 15 have advanced degrees; 15 reside on campus.

Subjects Offered 3-dimensional art, 3-dimensional design, advanced chemistry, advanced computer applications, advanced TOEFL/grammar, algebra, American government, American literature, anatomy, art, ASB Leadership, auto mechanics, band, basic skills, Bible studies, biology, biology-AP, calculus, calculus-AP, calligraphy, campus ministry, career/college preparation, carpentry, ceramics, chemistry, chemistry-AP, choir, choral music, Christian doctrine, Christian ethics, Christian scripture, Christian studies, Christianity, computer applications, computer education, computer graphics, computer literacy, computer science, computer skills, culinary arts, desktop publishing, digital imaging, drafting, drama, drama performance, drawing, drawing and design, earth science, economics, English, English literature, English-AP, environmental science, equestrian sports, ESL, European history-AP, fine arts, French, geology, geometry, government/civics, grammar, guitar, health, history, honors algebra, honors English, honors geometry, honors world history, human anatomy, industrial arts, Japanese, keyboarding, learning lab, marine biology, mathematics, music, orchestra, photography, physical education, physics, physiology, pre-calculus, psychology, religion, SAT preparation, science, social studies, Spanish, statistics-AP, student government, trigonometry, U.S. government and politics-AP, U.S. history, U.S. history-AP, vocal music, Web site design, woodworking, world history, world literature, wrestling, yearbook.

Graduation Requirements American government, arts and fine arts (art, music, dance, drama), Bible, biology, computer science, economics, English, foreign language, geometry, health education, keyboarding, mathematics, physical education (includes health), science, U.S. history, world history.

Special Academic Programs Advanced Placement exam preparation; honors section; special instructional classes for students with mild learning differences; ESL (12 students enrolled).

College Admission Counseling 138 students graduated in 2010; 136 went to college, including University of California, Berkeley; University of California, Davis; University of California, Los Angeles; University of California, San Diego; University of Wisconsin–Madison. Other: 2 went to work. Median SAT critical reading: 513, median SAT math: 571, median SAT writing: 528, median composite ACT: 23.

Student Life Upper grades have specified standards of dress, student council. Discipline rests primarily with faculty. Attendance at religious services is required.

Tuition and Aid Day student tuition: $8700; 7-day tuition and room/board: $34,550–$35,330. Tuition installment plan (FACTS Tuition Payment Plan, individually arranged payment plans, three payments (enrollment, 7/1 and 12/1)). Tuition reduction for siblings, need-based scholarship grants available. In 2010–11, 5% of upper-school students received aid. Total amount of financial aid awarded in 2010–11: $500,000.

Admissions Traditional secondary-level entrance grade is 9. SSAT or TOEFL required. Deadline for receipt of application materials: February 15. Application fee required: $80. Interview required.

Athletics Interscholastic: baseball (boys), basketball (b,g), cheering (g), cross-country running (b,g), football (b), golf (b,g), soccer (b,g), softball (g), swimming and diving (b,g), tennis (b,g), track and field (b,g), volleyball (b,g), wrestling (b); intramural: baseball (b), basketball (b,g), cross-country running (b,g), equestrian sports (b,g), field hockey (b,g), football (b), golf (b,g), soccer (b,g), swimming and diving (b,g), tennis (b,g), track and field (b,g), volleyball (b,g), weight lifting (b,g), wrestling (b); coed interscholastic: aquatics, diving, drill team, horseback riding. 6 PE instructors, 14 coaches, 2 athletic trainers.

Computers Computers are regularly used in desktop publishing, ESL, foreign language, mathematics, writing classes. Computer network features include on-campus library services, Internet access, wireless campus network, Internet filtering or blocking technology, iPads. Student e-mail accounts and computer access in designated common areas are available to students. Students grades are available online. The school has a published electronic and media policy.

Contact Mr. Peter C. Gieseke, Director of Admission. 831-722-8178 Ext. 194. Fax: 831-722-0361. E-mail: petergieseke@mvcs.com. Web site: mvcs.org.

MONTGOMERY BELL ACADEMY

4001 Harding Road

Nashville, Tennessee 37205

Head of School: Bradford Gioia

General Information Boys' day college-preparatory and arts school. Grades 7–12. Founded: 1867. Setting: urban. 43-acre campus. 10 buildings on campus. Approved or accredited by National Association of Episcopal Schools, Southern Association of Colleges and Schools, Southern Association of Independent Schools, and Tennessee Association of Independent Schools. Member of National Association of Independent Schools and Secondary School Admission Test Board. Endowment: $56.2 million. Total enrollment: 715. Upper school average class size: 14. Upper school faculty-student ratio: 1:8. There are 180 required school days per year for Upper School students. Upper School students typically attend 5 days per week. The average school day consists of 7 hours and 20 minutes.

Upper School Student Profile Grade 9: 123 students (123 boys); Grade 10: 117 students (117 boys); Grade 11: 127 students (127 boys); Grade 12: 119 students (119 boys).

Faculty School total: 90. In upper school: 67 men, 21 women; 71 have advanced degrees.

Subjects Offered Advanced Placement courses, algebra, American history, American history-AP, American literature, American literature-AP, art, art history, art history-AP, biology, biology-AP, calculus, calculus-AP, chemistry, chemistry-AP, Chinese, computer programming, computer science, computer science-AP, drama, earth science, economics, English, English literature, environmental science-AP, European history, European history-AP, fine arts, French, French language-AP, French literature-AP, French-AP, geography, geology, geometry, German, German-AP, government/civics, grammar, Greek, history, Latin, Latin-AP, mathematics, music, music history, music theory, music theory-AP, physical education, physics, physics-AP, science, social studies, Spanish, Spanish-AP, speech, statistics, statistics-AP, theater, trigonometry, U.S. government and politics-AP, U.S. history-AP, world history, world history-AP, writing.

Graduation Requirements Arts and fine arts (art, music, dance, drama), English, foreign language, mathematics, physical education (includes health), science, social studies (includes history).

Special Academic Programs Advanced Placement exam preparation; honors section; term-away projects; study abroad.

College Admission Counseling Colleges students went to include Auburn University; The University of Alabama; The University of Tennessee; University of Georgia; University of Mississippi; Vanderbilt University. Mean SAT critical reading: 634, mean SAT math: 668, mean SAT writing: 651, mean combined SAT: 1953, mean composite ACT: 29.

Student Life Upper grades have specified standards of dress, student council, honor system. Discipline rests primarily with faculty.

Summer Programs Remediation, enrichment, sports, rigorous outdoor training, computer instruction programs offered; held both on and off campus; held at Long Mountain, TN; accepts boys and girls; open to students from other schools. 800 students usually enrolled. 2012 schedule: June 1 to July 31.

Tuition and Aid Day student tuition: $20,425. Tuition installment plan (monthly payment plans, Dewar Tuition Refund Plan). Need-based scholarship grants available. In 2011–12, 23% of upper-school students received aid. Total amount of financial aid awarded in 2011–12: $1,632,000.

Admissions Traditional secondary-level entrance grade is 9. For fall 2011, 75 students applied for upper-level admission, 39 were accepted, 28 enrolled. ISEE required. Deadline for receipt of application materials: February 1. Application fee required: $50. On-campus interview required.

Athletics Interscholastic: baseball, basketball, bowling, crew, cross-country running, diving, football, Frisbee, golf, hockey, ice hockey, lacrosse, riflery, rock climbing, rowing, soccer, swimming and diving, track and field, ultimate Frisbee, wrestling; intramural: backpacking, baseball, basketball, cheering, climbing, crew, cricket, fencing, flag football, football, Frisbee, hiking/backpacking, independent competitive sports, outdoor activities, paddle tennis, running, soccer, strength & conditioning, table tennis, track and field, weight training, yoga. 2 PE instructors, 6 coaches, 2 athletic trainers.

Computers Computers are regularly used in all academic classes. Computer network features include on-campus library services, online commercial services, Internet access, wireless campus network, Internet filtering or blocking technology. Student e-mail accounts are available to students. Students grades are available online.

Contact Mr. Greg Ferrell, Director, Admission and Financial Aid. 615-369-5311 Ext. 251. Fax: 615-297-0271. E-mail: greg.ferrell@montgomerybell.edu. Web site: www.montgomerybell.com.

MOORESTOWN FRIENDS SCHOOL

110 East Main Street

Moorestown, New Jersey 08057

Head of School: Mr. Laurence Van Meter

General Information Coeducational day college-preparatory, arts, religious studies, and technology school, affiliated with Society of Friends. Grades PS–12. Founded: 1785. Setting: suburban. Nearest major city is Philadelphia, PA. 48-acre campus. 9 buildings on campus. Approved or accredited by Middle States Association of Colleges and Schools and New Jersey Department of Education. Member of National Association of Independent Schools. Endowment: $7.9 million. Total enrollment: 713. Upper school average class size: 18. Upper school faculty-student ratio: 1:9. There are 170 required school days per year for Upper School students. Upper School students typically attend 5 days per week.

Upper School Student Profile Grade 9: 76 students (38 boys, 38 girls); Grade 10: 71 students (34 boys, 37 girls); Grade 11: 70 students (28 boys, 42 girls); Grade 12: 72 students (32 boys, 40 girls). 3% of students are members of Society of Friends.

Faculty School total: 88. In upper school: 24 men, 42 women; 42 have advanced degrees.

Subjects Offered Algebra, American history, American literature, art, art history, biology, calculus, ceramics, chemistry, Chinese, community service, computer programming, computer science, creative writing, drama, driver education, earth science, economics, English, English literature, environmental science, ethics, European history, expository writing, fine arts, French, geometry, government/civics, grammar, health, history, mathematics, music, philosophy, photography, physical education, physics, psychology, religion, science, social studies, Spanish, theater, trigonometry, world history, writing.

Graduation Requirements Arts and fine arts (art, music, dance, drama), English, foreign language, mathematics, physical education (includes health), science, senior project, social studies (includes history). Community service is required.

Special Academic Programs Advanced Placement exam preparation; honors section; independent study; term-away projects; study abroad.

College Admission Counseling 74 students graduated in 2011; all went to college, including Cornell University; Emory University; Penn State University Park; Rutgers, The State University of New Jersey, New Brunswick; Swarthmore College; The Johns Hopkins University. Mean SAT critical reading: 628, mean SAT math: 641, mean SAT writing: 644, mean combined SAT: 1913.

Student Life Upper grades have specified standards of dress, student council, honor system. Discipline rests primarily with faculty. Attendance at religious services is required.

Tuition and Aid Day student tuition: $22,350. Tuition installment plan (Academic Management Services Plan, Tuition Refund Plan). Need-based scholarship grants, need-based loans, tuition reduction for children of faculty and staff available. In 2011–12, 15% of upper-school students received aid. Total amount of financial aid awarded in 2011–12: $1,550,300.

Admissions Traditional secondary-level entrance grade is 9. For fall 2011, 74 students applied for upper-level admission, 42 were accepted, 33 enrolled. ERB CTP required. Deadline for receipt of application materials: none. Application fee required: $45. On-campus interview required.

Athletics Interscholastic: baseball (boys), basketball (b,g), crew (b,g), cross-country running (b,g), fencing (b,g), field hockey (g), independent competitive sports (b,g), lacrosse (g), physical training (b,g), soccer (b,g), swimming and diving (b,g), tennis (b,g); intramural: floor hockey (b), roller hockey (b), street hockey (b), weight training (b,g); coed interscholastic: golf. 5 PE instructors, 24 coaches, 1 athletic trainer.

Computers Computers are regularly used in English, foreign language, mathematics, music, science classes. Computer network features include on-campus library services, Internet access, wireless campus network, Internet filtering or blocking technology. Campus intranet, student e-mail accounts, and computer access in designated common areas are available to students. Students grades are available online.

Contact Karin B. Miller, Director of Admission and Financial Aid. 856-235-2900 Ext. 227. Fax: 856-235-6684. E-mail: kmiller@mfriends.org. Web site: www.mfriends.org.

MOOSEHEART HIGH SCHOOL

255 James J. Davis Drive

Mooseheart, Illinois 60539

Head of School: Mr. Gary Lee Urwiler

General Information Coeducational boarding and day college-preparatory, general academic, arts, business, vocational, religious studies, bilingual studies, technology, nursing, and cosmetology school, affiliated with Protestant faith, Roman Catholic Church; primarily serves underachievers and students in dysfunctional family situations. Grades K–12. Founded: 1913. Setting: small town. Nearest major city is Aurora. Students are housed in family homes. 1,000-acre campus. 40 buildings on campus. Approved or accredited by North Central Association of Colleges and Schools and Illinois Department of Education. Total enrollment: 210. Upper school average class size: 13. Upper school faculty-student ratio: 1:6. There are 176 required school days per year for Upper School students. Upper School students typically attend 5 days per week. The average school day consists of 6 hours and 45 minutes.

Upper School Student Profile Grade 9: 28 students (19 boys, 9 girls); Grade 10: 32 students (24 boys, 8 girls); Grade 11: 41 students (27 boys, 14 girls); Grade 12: 19 students (10 boys, 9 girls). 95% of students are Protestant, Roman Catholic.

Faculty School total: 45. In upper school: 9 men, 11 women; 5 have advanced degrees.

Special Academic Programs Independent study; remedial reading and/or remedial writing; remedial math.

College Admission Counseling 26 students graduated in 2011.

Student Life Upper grades have specified standards of dress, student council, honor system. Discipline rests primarily with faculty. Attendance at religious services is required.

Summer Programs Remediation, sports programs offered; session focuses on recreation; held on campus; accepts boys and girls; not open to students from other schools. 221 students usually enrolled. 2012 schedule: June 14 to August 13. Application deadline: none.

Admissions Traditional secondary-level entrance grade is 9. Mathematics proficiency exam required. Deadline for receipt of application materials: March. No application fee required. Interview recommended.

Athletics Interscholastic: basketball (boys, girls), drill team (b,g), football (b), JROTC drill (b,g), track and field (b,g), volleyball (g), wrestling (b); intramural: aerobics (b), aerobics/dance (g). 2 PE instructors, 10 coaches.

Computers Computers are regularly used in word processing classes. Computer resources include on-campus library services, Internet access, wireless campus network, Internet filtering or blocking technology. Campus intranet and computer access in designated common areas are available to students. The school has a published electronic and media policy.

Contact Kyle Rife, Director of Admission. 630-906-3631 Ext. 3631. Fax: 630-906-3634 Ext. 3634. E-mail: krife@mooseheart.org.

MORAVIAN ACADEMY

4313 Green Pond Road

Bethlehem, Pennsylvania 18020

Head of School: George N. King Jr.

General Information Coeducational day college-preparatory school, affiliated with Moravian Church. Grades PK–12. Founded: 1742. Setting: rural. Nearest major city is Philadelphia. 120-acre campus. 8 buildings on campus. Approved or accredited by Middle States Association of Colleges and Schools, Pennsylvania Association of Independent Schools, and Pennsylvania Department of Education. Member of National Association of Independent Schools and Secondary School Admission Test Board. Endowment: $15.3 million. Total enrollment: 779. Upper school average class size: 15. Upper school faculty-student ratio: 1:7. There are 173 required school days per year for Upper School students. Upper School students typically attend 5 days per week. The average school day consists of 7 hours and 15 minutes.

Upper School Student Profile Grade 9: 67 students (33 boys, 34 girls); Grade 10: 79 students (38 boys, 41 girls); Grade 11: 75 students (34 boys, 41 girls); Grade 12: 63 students (21 boys, 42 girls).

Faculty School total: 99. In upper school: 20 men, 22 women; 40 have advanced degrees.

Subjects Offered Acting, advanced biology, advanced chemistry, Advanced Placement courses, algebra, American history, American history-AP, American literature, anatomy, ancient history, ancient world history, art, bell choir, biology, biology-AP, botany, calculus, calculus-AP, ceramics, chemistry, chemistry-AP, Chinese, Chinese history, community service, drama, drawing, driver education, ecology, economics, English, English language-AP, English literature, English literature-AP, environmental science, environmental science-AP, ethics, European history, European history-AP, film, fine arts, French, French language-AP, geometry, government, health, history, honors geometry, Latin American history, mathematics, Middle East, music, painting, photography, physical education, physics, playwriting, poetry, probability and statistics, religion, science, short story, Spanish, Spanish language-AP, statistics, statistics-AP, theater, trigonometry, U.S. history-AP, woodworking, world history, world literature, zoology.

Graduation Requirements Arts and fine arts (art, music, dance, drama), English, foreign language, mathematics, physical education (includes health), religion (includes Bible studies and theology), science, social studies (includes history), service project.

Special Academic Programs 12 Advanced Placement exams for which test preparation is offered; honors section; independent study; study at local college for college credit.

College Admission Counseling 70 students graduated in 2011; 69 went to college, including Bucknell University; Cornell University; Lehigh University; Villanova University; Wellesley College; Yale University. Other: 1 had other specific plans. Mean SAT critical reading: 656, mean SAT math: 658, mean SAT writing: 655.

Student Life Upper grades have specified standards of dress, student council. Discipline rests equally with students and faculty. Attendance at religious services is required.

Summer Programs Enrichment, sports, art/fine arts programs offered; session focuses on enrichment; held on campus; accepts boys and girls; open to students from other schools. 2012 schedule: June 11 to August 3.

Tuition and Aid Day student tuition: $22,540. Tuition installment plan (monthly payment plans). Need-based scholarship grants available. In 2011–12, 25% of upper-school students received aid. Total amount of financial aid awarded in 2011–12: $1,006,630.

Admissions Traditional secondary-level entrance grade is 9. For fall 2011, 57 students applied for upper-level admission, 47 were accepted, 30 enrolled. ERB and Otis-Lennon School Ability Test required. Deadline for receipt of application materials: none. Application fee required: $65. On-campus interview required.

Athletics Interscholastic: baseball (boys), basketball (b,g), field hockey (g), football (b), lacrosse (b), soccer (b,g), softball (g), tennis (b,g), track and field (b,g), volleyball (g), wrestling (b); coed interscholastic: cross-country running, golf, swimming and diving. 3 PE instructors, 15 coaches, 1 athletic trainer.

Computers Computers are regularly used in all academic, art, English, foreign language, history, mathematics, music, science classes. Computer resources include on-campus library services, Internet access, wireless campus network. Computer access in designated common areas is available to students. The school has a published electronic and media policy.

Contact Daniel Axford, Director of Upper School Admissions. 610-691-1600. Fax: 610-691-3354. E-mail: daxford@moravianacademy.org. Web site: www.moravianacademy.org.

See Display on next page and Close-Up on page 650.

MOREAU CATHOLIC HIGH SCHOOL

27170 Mission Boulevard

Hayward, California 94544

Head of School: Mr. Terry Lee

General Information Coeducational day college-preparatory, arts, business, religious studies, and technology school, affiliated with Roman Catholic Church. Grades 9–12. Founded: 1965. Setting: suburban. Nearest major city is Oakland. 14-acre campus. 6 buildings on campus. Approved or accredited by National Catholic Education Association, Western Association of Schools and Colleges, Western Catholic Education Association, and California Department of Education. Endowment: $2.5 million. Total enrollment: 896. Upper school average class size: 24. Upper school faculty-student ratio: 1:18. There are 186 required school days per year for Upper School students. Upper School students typically attend 5 days per week. The average school day consists of 6 hours and 35 minutes.

Upper School Student Profile Grade 9: 243 students (106 boys, 137 girls); Grade 10: 212 students (112 boys, 100 girls); Grade 11: 208 students (109 boys, 99 girls); Grade 12: 229 students (125 boys, 104 girls). 74% of students are Roman Catholic.

Faculty School total: 69. In upper school: 29 men, 25 women; 27 have advanced degrees.

Subjects Offered Advanced Placement courses, aerobics, algebra, American Civil War, American history, American literature, anatomy, art, art history, ASB Leadership, astronomy, athletics, biology, biology-AP, business, business law, business skills, calculus, calculus-AP, campus ministry, ceramics, cheerleading, chemistry, choral music, Christian ethics, Christian scripture, Christianity, church history, community service, computer education, computer math, computer programming, computer science, concert band, creative writing, drafting, drama, drama performance, driver education, earth science, economics, electronics, engineering, English, English literature, English/composition-AP, ethics, ethics and responsibility, European history, expository writing, fine arts, French, French-AP, geometry, government-AP, government/civics, grammar, health, health education, history, history of the Catholic Church, home economics, honors algebra, honors English, honors geometry, honors U.S. history, honors world history, human biology, instrumental music, jazz band, jazz ensemble, journalism, marching band, mathematics, mechanical drawing, media studies, moral and social development, moral theology, music, music appreciation, newspaper, physical education, physics, physics-AP, physiology, psychology, religion, science, sculpture, social sciences, social studies, Spanish, Spanish language-AP, speech, sports medicine, sports science, student government, student publications, symphonic band, the Sixties, theater, theology, trigonometry, typing, U.S. government, U.S. government and politics-AP, U.S. history, U.S. history-AP, weight training, world history, world literature, writing, yearbook.

Graduation Requirements Arts and fine arts (art, music, dance, drama), computer science, English, foreign language, mathematics, physical education (includes health), religion (includes Bible studies and theology), science, social sciences, social studies (includes history). Community service is required.

Special Academic Programs Advanced Placement exam preparation; honors section; special instructional classes for Saints and Scholars program for students with documented learning disabilities who require accommodations.

College Admission Counseling 229 students graduated in 2011; all went to college, including California State University; Saint Mary's College of California; Santa Clara University; Stanford University; University of California, Berkeley; University of San Francisco. Mean SAT critical reading: 555, mean SAT math: 559, mean composite ACT: 23.

Student Life Upper grades have specified standards of dress, student council, honor system. Discipline rests primarily with faculty. Attendance at religious services is required.

Summer Programs Remediation, enrichment, sports programs offered; session focuses on enrichment and remediation; held on campus; accepts boys and girls; open to students from other schools. 2012 schedule: June 18 to July 20. Application deadline: June 8.

Tuition and Aid Day student tuition: $13,356. Tuition installment plan (monthly payment plans). Merit scholarship grants, need-based scholarship grants available. In 2011–12, 37% of upper-school students received aid. Total amount of financial aid awarded in 2011–12: $1,400,000.

Admissions Traditional secondary-level entrance grade is 9. Scholastic Testing Service High School Placement Test required. Deadline for receipt of application materials: January 6. Application fee required: $90. On-campus interview required.

Athletics Interscholastic: aquatics (boys, girls), badminton (b,g), baseball (b), basketball (b,g), cheering (g), cross-country running (b,g), dance squad (g), football (b), golf (b,g), soccer (b,g), softball (g), swimming and diving (b,g), tennis (b,g), track and field (b,g), volleyball (b,g); intramural: lacrosse (g); coed interscholastic: aerobics/

dance, modern dance; coed intramural: equestrian sports, skiing (downhill), strength & conditioning. 5 PE instructors, 50 coaches, 1 athletic trainer.

Computers Computers are regularly used in career exploration, college planning, English, foreign language, history, journalism, keyboarding, mathematics, newspaper, religious studies, science, Spanish, technology, theology, writing, yearbook classes. Computer network features include on-campus library services, online commercial services, Internet access, wireless campus network, PowerSchool grade program, 1:1 student laptop program (every student at Moreau has a laptop). Campus intranet, student e-mail accounts, and computer access in designated common areas are available to students. Students grades are available online. The school has a published electronic and media policy.

Contact Patricia Bevilacqua, Admissions Assistant. 510-881-4320. Fax: 510-582-8405. E-mail: admissions@moreaucatholic.org. Web site: www.moreaucatholic.org.

MORRISTOWN-BEARD SCHOOL

70 Whippany Road

Morristown, New Jersey 07960

Head of School: Mr. Peter Caldwell

General Information Coeducational day college-preparatory and arts school. Grades 6–12. Founded: 1891. Setting: suburban. Nearest major city is New York, NY. 22-acre campus. 11 buildings on campus. Approved or accredited by Middle States Association of Colleges and Schools and New Jersey Department of Education. Member of National Association of Independent Schools and Secondary School Admission Test Board. Endowment: $11 million. Total enrollment: 547. Upper school average class size: 12. Upper school faculty-student ratio: 1:7. There are 160 required school days per year for Upper School students. Upper School students typically attend 5 days per week. The average school day consists of 7 hours.

Upper School Student Profile Grade 9: 102 students (58 boys, 44 girls); Grade 10: 98 students (54 boys, 44 girls); Grade 11: 97 students (48 boys, 49 girls); Grade 12: 99 students (51 boys, 48 girls).

Faculty School total: 94. In upper school: 33 men, 37 women; 40 have advanced degrees.

Subjects Offered 20th century history, acting, advanced chemistry, advanced math, Advanced Placement courses, advanced studio art-AP, African history, African literature, African studies, algebra, American history, American legal systems, American studies, anatomy and physiology, ancient world history, architecture, art, art history, Asian studies, astronomy, astrophysics, Bible as literature, biology, biology-AP, calculus, calculus-AP, career exploration, ceramics, chemistry, chemistry-AP, choir, chorus, community service, computer programming, computer science, computer science-AP, computer skills, computer studies, constitutional law, creative writing, dance, drama, drawing, earth science, ecology, engineering, English, English-AP, fine arts, French, geometry, health, instrumental music, journalism, Latin, Middle Eastern history, mythology, nature writers, painting, photography, physical education, physical science, physics, physics-AP, public speaking, regional literature, rite of passage, Spanish, Spanish-AP, speech, statistics, statistics-AP, studio art-AP, the comic tradition, theater, trigonometry, U.S. history-AP, women in literature, world history.

Graduation Requirements Arts and fine arts (art, music, dance, drama), English, foreign language, mathematics, physical education (includes health), science, service learning/internship, social studies (includes history). Community service is required.

Special Academic Programs 13 Advanced Placement exams for which test preparation is offered; honors section; independent study; term-away projects; study abroad.

College Admission Counseling 92 students graduated in 2011; 90 went to college, including Boston University; Bucknell University; Emory University; New York University; Northeastern University; Syracuse University. Other: 1 entered a postgraduate year, 1 had other specific plans. Mean SAT critical reading: 571, mean SAT math: 607, mean SAT writing: 592, mean composite ACT: 26.

Student Life Upper grades have specified standards of dress, student council, honor system. Discipline rests equally with students and faculty.

Summer Programs Enrichment, advancement, sports, art/fine arts, computer instruction programs offered; session focuses on traditional day camp; held on campus; accepts boys and girls; open to students from other schools. 700 students usually enrolled. 2012 schedule: June 25 to August 3.

Tuition and Aid Day student tuition: $31,850. Tuition installment plan (Tuition Management Systems). Merit scholarship grants, need-based scholarship grants available. In 2011–12, 13% of upper-school students received aid; total upper-school merit-scholarship money awarded: $85,500. Total amount of financial aid awarded in 2011–12: $1,800,000.

Admissions Traditional secondary-level entrance grade is 9. For fall 2011, 406 students applied for upper-level admission, 194 were accepted, 121 enrolled. ISEE or SSAT required. Deadline for receipt of application materials: February 6. Application fee required: $55. On-campus interview required.

Athletics Interscholastic: baseball (boys), basketball (b,g), field hockey (g), football (b), ice hockey (b,g), lacrosse (b,g), skiing (downhill) (b,g), soccer (b,g), softball (g), swimming and diving (b,g), tennis (b,g), track and field (b,g), volleyball (g); coed interscholastic: alpine skiing, cross-country running, dance, golf, swimming and diving, track and field, yoga; coed intramural: dance, fitness, physical fitness, strength & conditioning. 4 PE instructors, 3 coaches, 1 athletic trainer.

Computers Computers are regularly used in architecture, art, English, foreign language, history, mathematics, music, science classes. Computer network features include

on-campus library services, online commercial services, Internet access, wireless campus network, Internet filtering or blocking technology, Jstor, Jerseycat. Student e-mail accounts are available to students. Students grades are available online. The school has a published electronic and media policy.
Contact Mrs. Barbara Luperi, Admission Assistant. 973-539-3032. Fax: 973-539-1590. E-mail: bluperi@mbs.net. Web site: www.mbs.net.

MOTHER MCAULEY HIGH SCHOOL

3737 West 99th Street

Chicago, Illinois 60655-3133

Head of School: Dr. Christine M. Melone

General Information Girls' day college-preparatory, arts, religious studies, and technology school, affiliated with Roman Catholic Church. Grades 9–12. Founded: 1846. Setting: urban. 21-acre campus. 2 buildings on campus. Approved or accredited by Mercy Secondary Education Association, National Catholic Education Association, North Central Association of Colleges and Schools, The College Board, and Illinois Department of Education. Endowment: $2 million. Total enrollment: 1,362. Upper school average class size: 25. Upper school faculty-student ratio: 1:17. There are 180 required school days per year for Upper School students. Upper School students typically attend 5 days per week. The average school day consists of 6 hours and 30 minutes.
Upper School Student Profile Grade 9: 314 students (314 girls); Grade 10: 292 students (292 girls); Grade 11: 334 students (334 girls); Grade 12: 317 students (317 girls). 87% of students are Roman Catholic.
Faculty School total: 92. In upper school: 12 men, 80 women; 56 have advanced degrees.
Subjects Offered Anatomy and physiology, art history, art history-AP, calculus-AP, ceramics, chemistry-AP, English, English literature, English literature and composition-AP, European history-AP, first aid, French, French-AP, general science, geography, geometry, geometry with art applications, global issues, graphic design, history of the Catholic Church, honors algebra, honors English, honors geometry, honors U.S. history, honors world history, introduction to theater, journalism, Latin, Latin-AP, Life of Christ, marching band, media literacy, music appreciation, newspaper, orchestra, painting, photography, physical education, physics, play production, scripture, Spanish, Spanish-AP, speech, studio art, studio art-AP, theater, theology, U.S. history, U.S. history-AP, U.S. literature, Web site design, wind ensemble, world history, world history-AP, yearbook.
Graduation Requirements Art history, English, lab science, language, mathematics, music, physical education (includes health), social sciences, speech, technology, theology.
Special Academic Programs Advanced Placement exam preparation; honors section; study at local college for college credit.
College Admission Counseling 370 students graduated in 2011; 317 went to college, including Eastern Illinois University; Illinois State University; Loyola University Chicago; University of Illinois at Chicago; University of Illinois at Urbana–Champaign. Mean composite ACT: 23.
Student Life Upper grades have uniform requirement, student council. Discipline rests primarily with faculty. Attendance at religious services is required.
Summer Programs Remediation, enrichment, advancement, sports, art/fine arts, computer instruction programs offered; session focuses on academics; held on campus; accepts girls; open to students from other schools. 200 students usually enrolled. 2012 schedule: June 11 to July 27. Application deadline: June 8.
Tuition and Aid Day student tuition: $8900. Tuition installment plan (monthly payment plans, individually arranged payment plans). Tuition reduction for siblings, merit scholarship grants, need-based scholarship grants, paying campus jobs available. In 2011–12, 30% of upper-school students received aid; total upper-school merit-scholarship money awarded: $30,000. Total amount of financial aid awarded in 2011–12: $900,000.
Admissions Traditional secondary-level entrance grade is 9. For fall 2011, 383 students applied for upper-level admission, 380 were accepted, 314 enrolled. High School Placement Test required. Deadline for receipt of application materials: August 10. Application fee required: $150.
Athletics Interscholastic: basketball, bowling, cross-country running, diving, golf, independent competitive sports, lacrosse, sailing, soccer, softball, swimming and diving, tennis, track and field, volleyball, water polo; intramural: aerobics, basketball, bowling, flag football, Frisbee, softball, touch football, ultimate Frisbee, volleyball. 2 PE instructors, 20 coaches, 1 athletic trainer.
Computers Computers are regularly used in accounting, art, basic skills, business education, drafting, drawing and design, English, foreign language, French, graphics, journalism, Latin, mathematics, music, newspaper, photography, science, social sciences, Spanish, theater, Web site design, writing, yearbook classes. Computer network features include on-campus library services, Internet access, wireless campus network, Internet filtering or blocking technology. Student e-mail accounts and computer access in designated common areas are available to students. Students grades are available online. The school has a published electronic and media policy.
Contact Mrs. Kathryn Klyczek, Director of Admissions and Financial Aid. 773-881-6534. Fax: 773-429-4235. E-mail: kklyczek@mothermcauley.org. Web site: www.mothermcauley.org.

MOUNT CARMEL HIGH SCHOOL

6410 South Dante

Chicago, Illinois 60637

Head of School: Rev. Carl J. Markelz, O. Carm.

General Information Boys' day college-preparatory, arts, business, religious studies, and technology school, affiliated with Roman Catholic Church. Grades 9–12. Founded: 1900. Setting: urban. 3-acre campus. 5 buildings on campus. Approved or accredited by National Catholic Education Association, North Central Association of Colleges and Schools, The College Board, and Illinois Department of Education. Endowment: $5.1 million. Total enrollment: 790. Upper school average class size: 25. Upper school faculty-student ratio: 1:19. There are 176 required school days per year for Upper School students. Upper School students typically attend 5 days per week. The average school day consists of 6 hours and 15 minutes.
Upper School Student Profile Grade 9: 194 students (194 boys); Grade 10: 201 students (201 boys); Grade 11: 202 students (202 boys); Grade 12: 193 students (193 boys). 89% of students are Roman Catholic.
Faculty School total: 59. In upper school: 42 men, 11 women; 44 have advanced degrees.
Subjects Offered Art appreciation, art history, business, computer science, economics, English, French, general science, geography, government/civics, health, history of music, Latin, mathematics, physical education, psychology, religion, science, social sciences, social studies, Spanish, speech, theology.
Graduation Requirements Computer science, English, foreign language, mathematics, physical education (includes health), religion (includes Bible studies and theology), science, social sciences, social studies (includes history). Community service is required.
Special Academic Programs Advanced Placement exam preparation; honors section; remedial reading and/or remedial writing; remedial math.
College Admission Counseling 195 students graduated in 2010; 191 went to college, including DePaul University; Eastern Illinois University; Marquette University; Northern Illinois University; University of Illinois; University of Illinois at Chicago. Other: 1 went to work, 1 entered military service, 2 entered a postgraduate year. Mean SAT critical reading: 556, mean SAT math: 528, mean SAT writing: 569, mean combined SAT: 1654, mean composite ACT: 22. 35% scored over 600 on SAT critical reading, 35% scored over 600 on SAT math, 35% scored over 600 on SAT writing, 35% scored over 1800 on combined SAT, 14% scored over 26 on composite ACT.
Student Life Upper grades have specified standards of dress, student council. Discipline rests primarily with faculty. Attendance at religious services is required.
Tuition and Aid Day student tuition: $8600. Tuition installment plan (The Tuition Plan, FACTS Tuition Payment Plan). Tuition reduction for siblings, bursaries, merit scholarship grants, need-based scholarship grants, paying campus jobs available. In 2010–11, 33% of upper-school students received aid; total upper-school merit-scholarship money awarded: $100,000. Total amount of financial aid awarded in 2010–11: $500,000.
Admissions Traditional secondary-level entrance grade is 9. For fall 2010, 279 students applied for upper-level admission, 264 were accepted, 195 enrolled. ACT-Explore required. Deadline for receipt of application materials: none. Application fee required: $300. Interview recommended.
Athletics Interscholastic: baseball, basketball, bowling, cross-country running, football, golf, ice hockey, lacrosse, rugby, soccer, swimming and diving, tennis, track and field, volleyball, water polo, weight training, wrestling; intramural: basketball, football, soccer, softball, volleyball, weight lifting. 3 PE instructors, 27 coaches, 1 athletic trainer.
Computers Computers are regularly used in art, business, business education, college planning, data processing, desktop publishing, economics, English, foreign language, geography, graphic design, humanities, journalism, library, mathematics, psychology, science, technology classes. Computer network features include on-campus library services, Internet access, numerous databases, word processing, PowerPoint, spreadsheet training.
Contact Mr. John Stimler, Principal. 773-324-1020 Ext. 272. Fax: 773-324-9235. E-mail: jstimler@mchs.org. Web site: www.mchs.org.

MT. DE SALES ACADEMY

851 Orange Street

Macon, Georgia 31201

Head of School: Mr. David Held

General Information Coeducational day college-preparatory, arts, and technology school, affiliated with Roman Catholic Church. Grades 6–12. Founded: 1876. Setting: urban. 10 buildings on campus. Approved or accredited by Georgia Independent School Association, Mercy Secondary Education Association, Southern Association of Colleges and Schools, Southern Association of Independent Schools, and Georgia Department of Education. Endowment: $400,000. Total enrollment: 656. Upper school average class size: 17. Upper school faculty-student ratio: 1:10. There are 180 required

school days per year for Upper School students. Upper School students typically attend 5 days per week. The average school day consists of 7 hours.

Upper School Student Profile Grade 6: 43 students (23 boys, 20 girls); Grade 7: 91 students (41 boys, 50 girls); Grade 8: 77 students (41 boys, 36 girls); Grade 9: 123 students (50 boys, 73 girls); Grade 10: 112 students (51 boys, 61 girls); Grade 11: 108 students (58 boys, 50 girls); Grade 12: 102 students (47 boys, 55 girls). 42% of students are Roman Catholic.

Faculty School total: 68. In upper school: 34 men, 34 women; 41 have advanced degrees.

Subjects Offered 20th century world history, advanced biology, advanced chemistry, advanced computer applications, advanced math, Advanced Placement courses, advanced studio art-AP, African American studies, algebra, American Civil War, American government, American history, American history-AP, American literature, American literature-AP, anatomy and physiology, art history-AP, astronomy, athletic training, band, biology, biology-AP, British literature, calculus, calculus-AP, chemistry, chemistry-AP, choral music, chorus, Christian education, Christian scripture, computer applications, computer multimedia, computer programming-AP, drawing and design, economics, English, English language and composition-AP, English literature and composition-AP, European history-AP, forensics, French, government, government and politics-AP, health, Holocaust studies, honors algebra, honors English, honors geometry, New Testament, physical education, physics-AP, portfolio art, pre-calculus, programming, psychology, psychology-AP, Spanish-AP, speech, statistics, statistics-AP, studio art, U.S. government, U.S. government and politics-AP, U.S. history, U.S. history-AP, visual arts, World War II, yearbook.

Special Academic Programs Honors section.

College Admission Counseling 101 students graduated in 2010; all went to college, including Georgia Institute of Technology; Georgia Southern University; Macon State College; University of Georgia. Mean SAT critical reading: 670, mean SAT math: 660, mean SAT writing: 650, mean combined SAT: 1980.

Student Life Upper grades have specified standards of dress, student council, honor system. Discipline rests primarily with faculty. Attendance at religious services is required.

Tuition and Aid Tuition installment plan (FACTS Tuition Payment Plan). Merit scholarship grants, need-based scholarship grants available. In 2010–11, 30% of upper-school students received aid; total upper-school merit-scholarship money awarded: $122,000. Total amount of financial aid awarded in 2010–11: $813,771.

Admissions Traditional secondary-level entrance grade is 9. For fall 2010, 214 students applied for upper-level admission, 174 were accepted, 132 enrolled. Stanford Achievement Test or Terra Nova-CTB required. Deadline for receipt of application materials: none. Application fee required: $50.

Athletics Interscholastic: baseball (boys), basketball (b,g), cheering (g), cross-country running (b,g), dance team (g), fitness (b,g), football (b), physical fitness (b,g), physical training (b,g), soccer (b,g), softball (g), swimming and diving (b,g), track and field (b,g), weight training (b,g).

Computers Computers are regularly used in all classes. Computer network features include on-campus library services, Internet access, wireless campus network. Campus intranet and student e-mail accounts are available to students. Students grades are available online. The school has a published electronic and media policy.

Contact 912-751-3240. Fax: 912-751-3241. Web site: www.mountdesales.net.

MOUNT MERCY ACADEMY

88 Red Jacket Parkway

Buffalo, New York 14220

Head of School: Mrs. Paulette C. Gaske

General Information Girls' day college-preparatory, arts, and religious studies school, affiliated with Roman Catholic Church. Grades 9–12. Founded: 1904. Setting: urban. 2 buildings on campus. Approved or accredited by Middle States Association of Colleges and Schools and New York Department of Education. Total enrollment: 273. Upper school average class size: 20. Upper school faculty-student ratio: 1:20. There are 180 required school days per year for Upper School students. Upper School students typically attend 5 days per week. The average school day consists of 6 hours and 43 minutes.

Upper School Student Profile Grade 9: 75 students (75 girls); Grade 10: 54 students (54 girls); Grade 11: 76 students (76 girls); Grade 12: 68 students (68 girls). 97% of students are Roman Catholic.

Faculty School total: 39. In upper school: 6 men, 30 women.

Special Academic Programs Advanced Placement exam preparation; honors section; independent study.

College Admission Counseling 108 students graduated in 2010; 97 went to college. Other: 1 entered military service.

Student Life Upper grades have uniform requirement, student council, honor system. Discipline rests equally with students and faculty. Attendance at religious services is required.

Tuition and Aid Day student tuition: $7800. Tuition installment plan (FACTS Tuition Payment Plan). Tuition reduction for siblings, merit scholarship grants, need-based scholarship grants, paying campus jobs available.

Admissions Admissions testing or High School Placement Test (closed version) from Scholastic Testing Service required. Deadline for receipt of application materials: none. Application fee required: $20. On-campus interview required.

Athletics Interscholastic: aquatics, basketball, bowling, cross-country running, golf, lacrosse, modern dance, skiing (downhill), soccer, softball, swimming and diving, tennis, volleyball. 2 PE instructors, 13 coaches.

Computers Computers are regularly used in art, business, desktop publishing, keyboarding, study skills, yearbook classes. Computer network features include on-campus library services, Internet access, wireless campus network, Internet filtering or blocking technology. Campus intranet, student e-mail accounts, and computer access in designated common areas are available to students. Students grades are available online. The school has a published electronic and media policy.

Contact Mrs. Jeanne Burvid, Director of Admissions. 716-825-8796 Ext. 511. Fax: 716-825-0976. E-mail: jburvid@mtmercy.org. Web site: www.mtmercy.org.

MOUNT MICHAEL BENEDICTINE SCHOOL

22520 Mount Michael Road

Elkhorn, Nebraska 68022-3400

Head of School: Dr. David Peters

General Information Boys' boarding and day college-preparatory, arts, religious studies, and technology school, affiliated with Roman Catholic Church. Grades 9–12. Founded: 1970. Setting: suburban. Nearest major city is Omaha. Students are housed in single-sex dormitories and private homes. 440-acre campus. 1 building on campus. Approved or accredited by National Catholic Education Association, North Central Association of Colleges and Schools, The College Board, and Nebraska Department of Education. Endowment: $2.7 million. Total enrollment: 220. Upper school average class size: 15. Upper school faculty-student ratio: 1:10. There are 180 required school days per year for Upper School students. Upper School students typically attend 5 days per week. The average school day consists of 7 hours and 25 minutes.

Upper School Student Profile Grade 9: 64 students (64 boys); Grade 10: 56 students (56 boys); Grade 11: 42 students (42 boys); Grade 12: 58 students (58 boys). 65% of students are boarding students. 85% are state residents. 6 states are represented in upper school student body. 12% are international students. International students from China, Republic of Korea, Rwanda, and Viet Nam. 84% of students are Roman Catholic.

Faculty School total: 29. In upper school: 22 men, 7 women; 19 have advanced degrees; 6 reside on campus.

Subjects Offered Accounting, Advanced Placement courses, algebra, American history, American history-AP, American literature, architectural drawing, art, band, Basic programming, basketball, bioethics, DNA and culture, biology, biology-AP, business, business skills, calculus-AP, ceramics, chemistry, chemistry-AP, chorus, Christian doctrine, Christian ethics, Christian scripture, Christianity, community service, computer programming, computer science, critical writing, drafting, drama, economics, English, English language-AP, English literature, English literature and composition-AP, European history, European history-AP, French, French language-AP, geography, geometry, government/civics, health education, Hebrew scripture, history of the Catholic Church, journalism, keyboarding, Latin, math applications, mathematics, music, physical education, physics, physics-AP, psychology-AP, reading, science, social sciences, social studies, Spanish, speech, theater, theology, trigonometry, weight training, Western civilization, world religions, wrestling, writing, yearbook.

Graduation Requirements Advanced math, algebra, American government, American history, anatomy and physiology, biology, biology-AP, career/college preparation, chemistry, Christian studies, computer science, economics, economics and history, English, foreign language, geometry, government, mathematics, physical education (includes health), physics, pre-calculus, social studies (includes history), speech, Western civilization, world cultures, world religions, service hours requirement. Community service is required.

Special Academic Programs 11 Advanced Placement exams for which test preparation is offered; honors section; independent study; study at local college for college credit.

College Admission Counseling 46 students graduated in 2011; all went to college, including Benedictine College; Saint John's University; University of Nebraska–Lincoln; University of Nebraska at Omaha. Median SAT critical reading: 650, median SAT math: 750, median SAT writing: 710, median combined SAT: 2040, median composite ACT: 29. 75% scored over 600 on SAT critical reading, 100% scored over 600 on SAT math, 81% scored over 600 on SAT writing, 88% scored over 1800 on combined SAT, 70% scored over 26 on composite ACT.

Student Life Upper grades have specified standards of dress, student council, honor system. Discipline rests primarily with faculty. Attendance at religious services is required.

Tuition and Aid Day student tuition: $10,245–$10,550; 5-day tuition and room/board: $15,255–$15,560; 7-day tuition and room/board: $20,565–$20,870. Tuition installment plan (FACTS Tuition Payment Plan). Tuition reduction for siblings, bursaries, merit scholarship grants, need-based loans, paying campus jobs available. In 2011–12, 53% of upper-school students received aid; total upper-school merit-scholarship money awarded: $19,097. Total amount of financial aid awarded in 2011–12: $611,812.

Admissions Traditional secondary-level entrance grade is 9. For fall 2011, 81 students applied for upper-level admission, 71 were accepted, 64 enrolled. California Achievement Test, Explore, High School Placement Test, Iowa Tests of Basic Skills, Stanford Achievement Test or TOEFL required. Deadline for receipt of application materials: July 1. Application fee required: $25. Interview required.
Athletics Interscholastic: baseball, basketball, bowling, cheering, cross-country running, diving, football, golf, soccer, swimming and diving, tennis, trap and skeet, wrestling; intramural: ball hockey, basketball, flag football, floor hockey, physical fitness, physical training, soccer, strength & conditioning, ultimate Frisbee, weight lifting, weight training. 1 PE instructor, 22 coaches, 2 athletic trainers.
Computers Computers are regularly used in architecture, career education, career exploration, career technology, college planning, drafting, economics, French, geography, history, journalism, keyboarding, library, mathematics, newspaper, science, Spanish, stock market, Web site design, yearbook classes. Computer network features include on-campus library services, online commercial services, Internet access, wireless campus network, Internet filtering or blocking technology. Campus intranet, student e-mail accounts, and computer access in designated common areas are available to students. Students grades are available online. The school has a published electronic and media policy.
Contact Mr. Eric Crawford, Director of Admissions. 402-253-0946. Fax: 402-289-4539. E-mail: ecrawford@mountmichael.org. Web site: www.mountmichaelhs.com.

MOUNT SAINT CHARLES ACADEMY

800 Logee Street
Woonsocket, Rhode Island 02895-5599

Head of School: Mr. Herve E. Richer Jr.

General Information Coeducational day college-preparatory, arts, and religious studies school, affiliated with Roman Catholic Church. Grades 7–12. Founded: 1924. Setting: suburban. Nearest major city is Providence. 22-acre campus. 2 buildings on campus. Approved or accredited by New England Association of Schools and Colleges and Rhode Island Department of Education. Total enrollment: 874. Upper school average class size: 25. Upper school faculty-student ratio: 1:18. There are 180 required school days per year for Upper School students. The average school day consists of 6 hours and 15 minutes.
Upper School Student Profile Grade 7: 80 students (29 boys, 51 girls); Grade 8: 83 students (46 boys, 37 girls); Grade 9: 154 students (82 boys, 72 girls); Grade 10: 187 students (76 boys, 111 girls); Grade 11: 174 students (74 boys, 100 girls); Grade 12: 196 students (90 boys, 106 girls). 85% of students are Roman Catholic.
Faculty School total: 55. In upper school: 26 men, 26 women, 30 have advanced degrees.
Subjects Offered Advanced computer applications, algebra, American literature, architecture, art, art-AP, band, biology, biology-AP, British literature, calculus, calculus-AP, chemistry, chorus, computer science, creative writing, dance, drama, economics, English, English language and composition-AP, English literature, English literature and composition-AP, English literature-AP, environmental science, environmental science-AP, European history, European history-AP, fine arts, forensics, French, geography, geometry, government, government and politics-AP, government/civics, handbells, health education, history, history of the Catholic Church, honors U.S. history, honors world history, jazz band, mathematics, mathematics-AP, modern European history, music, music theory-AP, physical education, physics, physiology, psychology, psychology-AP, religion, science, social studies, Spanish, theater, trigonometry, U.S. history, U.S. history-AP, world history, world literature, writing, yearbook.
Graduation Requirements Arts and fine arts (art, music, dance, drama), computer science, English, foreign language, mathematics, physical education (includes health), religion (includes Bible studies and theology), science, social studies (includes history).
Special Academic Programs 14 Advanced Placement exams for which test preparation is offered; honors section; study at local college for college credit.
College Admission Counseling 176 students graduated in 2011; 174 went to college. Other: 1 entered military service, 1 entered a postgraduate year.
Student Life Upper grades have uniform requirement, student council. Discipline rests primarily with faculty. Attendance at religious services is required.
Summer Programs Sports, art/fine arts programs offered; session focuses on fine arts, soccer, hockey, basketball; held on campus; accepts boys and girls; open to students from other schools. 220 students usually enrolled. 2012 schedule: July. Application deadline: none.
Tuition and Aid Day student tuition: $10,900. Tuition installment plan (FACTS Tuition Payment Plan, full payment discount plan). Need-based scholarship grants available. In 2011–12, 30% of upper-school students received aid. Total amount of financial aid awarded in 2011–12: $700,000.
Admissions Traditional secondary-level entrance grade is 7. For fall 2011, 275 students applied for upper-level admission, 225 were accepted, 160 enrolled. Diocesan Entrance Exam, ISEE, SAS, STS-HSPT, SSAT or STS required. Deadline for receipt of application materials: none. Application fee required: $25.
Athletics Interscholastic: baseball (boys), basketball (b,g), cross-country running (b,g), gymnastics (g), ice hockey (b,g), indoor track (b,g), lacrosse (b,g), sailing (b,g), soccer (b,g), softball (g), swimming and diving (b,g), tennis (b,g), track and field (b,g), volleyball (b,g), winter (indoor) track (b,g); intramural: aerobics/dance (g), basketball (b,g), dance (g); coed interscholastic: cheering, golf; coed intramural: billiards, bowling, dance team, flag football, indoor soccer, lacrosse, physical training, soccer, strength & conditioning, touch football. 4 PE instructors, 15 coaches, 1 athletic trainer.
Computers Computers are regularly used in accounting, architecture, art, computer applications, desktop publishing, graphic design, science, yearbook classes. Computer network features include on-campus library services, online commercial services, Internet access, Internet filtering or blocking technology, college/financial aid searches. Campus intranet, student e-mail accounts, and computer access in designated common areas are available to students. Students grades are available online. The school has a published electronic and media policy.
Contact Joseph J. O'Neill Jr., Registrar/Director of Admissions. 401-769-0310 Ext. 137. Fax: 401-762-2327. E-mail: admissions@mountsaintcharles.org. Web site: www.mountsaintcharles.org.

MT. SAINT DOMINIC ACADEMY

3 Ryerson Avenue
Caldwell, New Jersey 07006

Head of School: Sr. Frances Sullivan, OP

General Information Girls' day college-preparatory, arts, religious studies, and technology school, affiliated with Roman Catholic Church. Grades 9–12. Founded: 1892. Setting: suburban. Nearest major city is Newark. 70-acre campus. 3 buildings on campus. Approved or accredited by Middle States Association of Colleges and Schools, New Jersey Association of Independent Schools, and New Jersey Department of Education. Endowment: $1.5 million. Total enrollment: 315. Upper school average class size: 12. Upper school faculty-student ratio: 1:12. There are 180 required school days per year for Upper School students. Upper School students typically attend 5 days per week. The average school day consists of 6 hours.
Upper School Student Profile Grade 9: 98 students (98 girls); Grade 10: 65 students (65 girls); Grade 11: 86 students (86 girls); Grade 12: 66 students (66 girls). 88% of students are Roman Catholic.
Faculty School total: 39. In upper school: 5 men, 34 women; 16 have advanced degrees.
Subjects Offered Advanced math, advanced studio art-AP, algebra, American history-AP, American literature, American literature-AP, anatomy and physiology, art, Bible studies, biology, biology-AP, British literature, British literature (honors), calculus, calculus-AP, Catholic belief and practice, chemistry, choir, college counseling, college placement, college planning, communication skills, composition, composition-AP, computer applications, computer science, computer skills, computer technologies, concert choir, contemporary history, creative arts, creative writing, dance, debate, desktop publishing, digital photography, drama, drama workshop, drawing and design, driver education, ecology, environmental systems, English, English language and composition-AP, English literature, English literature and composition-AP, environmental science, forensics, French, geometry, health, history, Holocaust studies, literature, mathematics, music, photography, physical education, physics, pre-calculus, psychology, public speaking, religion, SAT preparation, science, Spanish, studio art-AP, U.S. history, U.S. history-AP, U.S. literature, word processing, world history, world literature, world wide web design.
Graduation Requirements 4 years of community service.
Special Academic Programs Advanced Placement exam preparation; honors section; independent study; academic accommodation for the gifted, the musically talented, and the artistically talented.
College Admission Counseling 99 students graduated in 2010; 96 went to college, including Loyola University Maryland; Montclair State University; Ramapo College of New Jersey; Rutgers, The State University of New Jersey, New Brunswick; Seton Hall University. Median SAT critical reading: 557, median SAT math: 541, median SAT writing: 573. 19% scored over 600 on SAT critical reading, 21% scored over 600 on SAT math, 18% scored over 600 on SAT writing.
Student Life Upper grades have uniform requirement, student council, honor system. Discipline rests primarily with faculty. Attendance at religious services is required.
Tuition and Aid Day student tuition: $14,150. Tuition installment plan (individually arranged payment plans, one payment in full, or otherwise monthly, quarterly, or semi-annually). Tuition reduction for siblings, merit scholarship grants, need-based scholarship grants available. In 2010–11, 16% of upper-school students received aid; total upper-school merit-scholarship money awarded: $95,000. Total amount of financial aid awarded in 2010–11: $192,000.
Admissions Traditional secondary-level entrance grade is 9. For fall 2010, 215 students applied for upper-level admission, 211 were accepted, 99 enrolled. Cooperative Entrance Exam (McGraw-Hill) required. Deadline for receipt of application materials: December 15. Application fee required: $40.
Athletics Interscholastic: aerobics/dance, aquatics, basketball, cross-country running, golf, indoor track, indoor track & field, lacrosse, soccer, softball, swimming and diving, tennis, track and field, volleyball; intramural: ballet, cheering, dance, dance squad, dance team, field hockey, modern dance. 1 PE instructor, 20 coaches, 1 athletic trainer.
Computers Computers are regularly used in English, foreign language, history, mathematics, music, science classes. Computer network features include on-campus library services, online commercial services, Internet access, wireless campus network, Internet filtering or blocking technology. Student e-mail accounts are available to stu-

dents. Students grades are available online. The school has a published electronic and media policy.

Contact Maryann Feuerstein, Director of Admission. 973-226-0660 Ext. 1114. Fax: 973-226-2135. E-mail: mfeuerstein@msdacademy.org. Web site: www.msdacademy.org.

MOUNT SAINT JOSEPH ACADEMY

120 West Wissahickon Avenue

Flourtown, Pennsylvania 19031

Head of School: Sr. Kathleen Brabson, SSJ

General Information Girls' day college-preparatory school, affiliated with Roman Catholic Church. Grades 9–12. Founded: 1858. Setting: suburban. Nearest major city is Philadelphia. 78-acre campus. 1 building on campus. Approved or accredited by Middle States Association of Colleges and Schools, National Catholic Education Association, Pennsylvania Association of Independent Schools, and Pennsylvania Department of Education. Member of National Association of Independent Schools. Endowment: $3 million. Total enrollment: 560. Upper school average class size: 19. Upper school faculty-student ratio: 1:10. There are 180 required school days per year for Upper School students. Upper School students typically attend 5 days per week. The average school day consists of 6 hours and 45 minutes.

Upper School Student Profile Grade 9: 138 students (138 girls); Grade 10: 138 students (138 girls); Grade 11: 142 students (142 girls); Grade 12: 142 students (142 girls). 95% of students are Roman Catholic.

Faculty School total: 61. In upper school: 14 men, 47 women; 41 have advanced degrees.

Subjects Offered Accounting, algebra, American history, American history-AP, American literature, American studies, art, art history, astronomy, biochemistry, biology, calculus, calculus-AP, chemistry, chorus, communications, computer science, design, desktop publishing, drama, drawing, economics, English, English literature, English literature-AP, ethics, European history, film, fine arts, French, French-AP, geography, geometry, government/civics, health, history, human sexuality, instrumental music, journalism, keyboarding, Latin, literature, mathematics, music, music-AP, painting, physical education, physics, physics-AP, physiology, pre-calculus, psychology, religion, science, social studies, Spanish, Spanish-AP, speech, technology, theater, theology, trigonometry, word processing, world history, world literature, writing.

Graduation Requirements Arts and fine arts (art, music, dance, drama), computer science, English, foreign language, mathematics, physical education (includes health), religion (includes Bible studies and theology), science, social studies (includes history).

Special Academic Programs 13 Advanced Placement exams for which test preparation is offered; honors section; independent study; study at local college for college credit; academic accommodation for the gifted, the musically talented, and the artistically talented.

College Admission Counseling 145 students graduated in 2011; all went to college, including Drexel University; Fordham University; Penn State University Park; Saint Joseph's University; University of Delaware; Villanova University. Mean SAT critical reading: 632, mean SAT math: 610, mean SAT writing: 655, mean combined SAT: 1897. 65% scored over 600 on SAT critical reading, 52% scored over 600 on SAT math, 70% scored over 600 on SAT writing, 61% scored over 1800 on combined SAT.

Student Life Upper grades have uniform requirement, student council, honor system. Discipline rests primarily with faculty. Attendance at religious services is required.

Tuition and Aid Day student tuition: $13,800. Tuition installment plan (Higher Education Service, Inc., semester payment plan). Tuition reduction for siblings, merit scholarship grants, need-based scholarship grants available. In 2011–12, 19% of upper-school students received aid; total upper-school merit-scholarship money awarded: $391,400. Total amount of financial aid awarded in 2011–12: $706,460.

Admissions Traditional secondary-level entrance grade is 9. For fall 2011, 285 students applied for upper-level admission, 138 enrolled. High School Placement Test, SAS, STS-HSPT or school's own test required. Deadline for receipt of application materials: October 28. Application fee required: $75.

Athletics Interscholastic: basketball, crew, cross-country running, diving, field hockey, golf, indoor track, lacrosse, soccer, softball, swimming and diving, tennis, track and field, volleyball. 2 PE instructors, 24 coaches, 1 athletic trainer.

Computers Computers are regularly used in art, business studies, career exploration, college planning, commercial art, computer applications, desktop publishing, English, foreign language, graphic design, history, mathematics, music, science, theater arts, writing, writing, yearbook classes. Computer network features include on-campus library services, online commercial services, Internet access, wireless campus network, Internet filtering or blocking technology, video conferencing, SmartBoards. Campus intranet, student e-mail accounts, and computer access in designated common areas are available to students. Students grades are available online. The school has a published electronic and media policy.

Contact Ms. Carol Finney, Director of Admissions. 215-233-9133. Fax: 215-233-5887. E-mail: cfinney@msjacad.org. Web site: www.msjacad.org.

MPS ETOBICOKE

30 Barrhead Crescent

Toronto, Ontario M9W 3Z7, Canada

Head of School: Mrs. Gabrielle Bush

General Information Coeducational day college-preparatory, arts, business, and technology school. Grades JK–12. Founded: 1977. Setting: urban. 1 building on campus. Approved or accredited by Ontario Ministry of Education and Ontario Department of Education. Language of instruction: English. Total enrollment: 318. Upper school average class size: 18. Upper school faculty-student ratio: 1:14. There are 192 required school days per year for Upper School students. Upper School students typically attend 5 days per week. The average school day consists of 6 hours and 30 minutes.

Upper School Student Profile Grade 9: 29 students (17 boys, 12 girls); Grade 10: 23 students (14 boys, 9 girls); Grade 11: 35 students (25 boys, 10 girls); Grade 12: 48 students (31 boys, 17 girls).

Faculty School total: 37. In upper school: 9 men, 7 women; 5 have advanced degrees.

Subjects Offered Accounting, anthropology, biology, Canadian geography, Canadian history, Canadian law, chemistry, civics, communications, data processing, discrete mathematics, dramatic arts, English, film, French, functions, geometry, healthful living, information technology, learning strategies, mathematics, organizational studies, personal finance, physics, psychology, reading, science, society challenge and change, sociology, visual arts, world history, writing.

Graduation Requirements English, Ontario Ministry of Education requirements.

Special Academic Programs ESL (15 students enrolled).

College Admission Counseling 36 students graduated in 2011; 35 went to college, including McMaster University; Ryerson University; University of Guelph; University of Ottawa; University of Toronto; York University. Other: 1 went to work.

Student Life Upper grades have uniform requirement, student council, honor system. Discipline rests primarily with faculty.

Summer Programs Remediation, enrichment, advancement, ESL, sports, art/fine arts, computer instruction programs offered; session focuses on academics; held on campus; accepts boys and girls; open to students from other schools. 100 students usually enrolled. 2012 schedule: July 2 to July 31. Application deadline: June 25.

Tuition and Aid Day student tuition: CAN$13,500. Tuition installment plan (individually arranged payment plans, MPS Payment Plan). Tuition reduction for siblings available.

Admissions Traditional secondary-level entrance grade is 9. For fall 2011, 20 students applied for upper-level admission, 20 were accepted, 20 enrolled. Admissions testing required. Deadline for receipt of application materials: October 31. No application fee required. Interview required.

Athletics Interscholastic: baseball (boys, girls), basketball (b,g), flag football (b,g), football (b), indoor track & field (b,g), running (b,g), soccer (b,g), swimming and diving (b,g), track and field (b,g), volleyball (b,g); intramural: basketball (b,g), flag football (b,g), floor hockey (b,g), Frisbee (b,g), indoor hockey (b,g), physical fitness (b,g), rhythmic gymnastics (b,g), running (b,g), soccer (b,g), swimming and diving (b,g), touch football (b,g), track and field (b,g), ultimate Frisbee (b,g), volleyball (b,g), winter (indoor) track (b,g), winter soccer (b,g); coed interscholastic: aquatics, bowling, cross-country running, field hockey, flag football; coed intramural: badminton, baseball, basketball, bowling, cooperative games, cross-country running, flag football, table tennis, tennis. 2 PE instructors, 12 coaches.

Computers Computers are regularly used in art, business education, computer applications, graphic arts, media arts, photography classes. Computer resources include Internet access, Internet filtering or blocking technology. The school has a published electronic and media policy.

Contact Mrs. Gabrielle Bush, Director. 416-745-1328. Fax: 416-745-4168. E-mail: gbushmps@rogers.com. Web site: www.mpsetobicoke.com.

MU HIGH SCHOOL

136 Clark Hall

Columbia, Missouri 65211

Head of School: Ms. Kristi D. Smalley

General Information Coeducational day college-preparatory, general academic, and distance learning school. Grades 9–12. Founded: 1999. Setting: small town. Nearest major city is St. Louis. Approved or accredited by Missouri Independent School Association and North Central Association of Colleges and Schools.

Subjects Offered 20th century American writers, 20th century physics, 20th century world history, 3-dimensional art, accounting, adolescent issues, advanced math, Advanced Placement courses, aerospace science, African-American literature, algebra, American history, ancient world history, art, art appreciation, astronomy, basic language skills, Basic programming, biology, business applications, business mathematics, business skills, business studies, career exploration, career planning, career/college preparation, careers, character education, chemistry, child development, civics, college planning, communication arts, comparative politics, comparative religion, computer applications, computer literacy, computer programming, conservation, consumer education, consumer mathematics, contemporary history, contemporary issues, contemporary math, creative writing, decision making skills, economics, English, English literature and composition-AP, entrepreneurship, environmental science, European literature, family and consumer science, family living, family studies, female experience in America, fiction, film and literature, fitness, food and nutrition, French, general science, geography, geology, geometry, German, government, grammar, health and wellness, history, independent study, integrated mathematics, interpersonal skills, Japanese, keyboarding, language, language arts, Latin, law and the legal system, literature, literature by women, math applications, mathematics, media studies, medieval history, modern history, modern world history, music appreciation, mythology, newspaper, North American literature, novels, parent/child development, personal and social education, personal development, personal fitness, personal money management, photography, poetry, political science, pre-algebra, pre-calculus, psychology, reading/study skills, religious studies, science fiction, Shakespeare, short story, skills for success, social studies, sociology, Spanish, state history, statistics, study skills, trigonometry, U.S. constitutional history, U.S. government and politics, U.S. literature, women's literature, world geography, world religions, writing.

Graduation Requirements Missouri Department of Elementary and Secondary Education requirements.

Special Academic Programs Advanced Placement exam preparation; accelerated programs; independent study; study at local college for college credit; academic accommodation for the gifted; remedial reading and/or remedial writing.

College Admission Counseling 69 students graduated in 2011.

Admissions Deadline for receipt of application materials: none. Application fee required: $25.

Computers Computers are regularly used in accounting, art, business, business applications, business education, business skills, business studies, career education, career exploration, classics, college planning, computer applications, creative writing, current events, digital applications, economics, English, foreign language, French, French as a second language, geography, health, historical foundations for arts, history, humanities, independent study, information technology, journalism, keyboarding, language development, Latin, life skills, mathematics, media, music, news writing, occupational education, photography, programming, psychology, reading, religious studies, research skills, science, social sciences, social studies, Spanish, study skills, theater, theater arts, typing, writing, writing classes. Computer resources include INET Library, Britannica Online School Edition, course access. Computer access in designated common areas is available to students. Students grades are available online. The school has a published electronic and media policy.

Contact Alicia Bixby, Counselor. 800-609-3727. Fax: 573-882-6808. E-mail: cdis@missouri.edu. Web site: cdis.missouri.edu/.

MUNICH INTERNATIONAL SCHOOL

Schloss Buchhof

Starnberg D-82319, Germany

Head of School: Simon Taylor

General Information Coeducational day college-preparatory, arts, business, bilingual studies, and technology school. Grades PK–12. Founded: 1966. Setting: rural. Nearest major city is Munich, Germany. 26-acre campus. 5 buildings on campus. Approved or accredited by Council of International Schools, International Baccalaureate Organization, and New England Association of Schools and Colleges. Affiliate member of National Association of Independent Schools; member of Secondary School Admission Test Board and European Council of International Schools. Language of instruction: English. Total enrollment: 1,212. Upper school average class size: 21. Upper school faculty-student ratio: 1:6. There are 185 required school days per year for Upper School students. Upper School students typically attend 5 days per week. The average school day consists of 6 hours and 55 minutes.

Upper School Student Profile Grade 9: 108 students (49 boys, 59 girls); Grade 10: 110 students (54 boys, 56 girls); Grade 11: 105 students (48 boys, 57 girls); Grade 12: 97 students (50 boys, 47 girls).

Faculty School total: 161. In upper school: 26 men, 45 women; 33 have advanced degrees.

Subjects Offered Adolescent issues, algebra, art, biology, business, calculus, chemistry, computer science, computer-aided design, design, drama, Dutch, earth science, economics, English, English literature, ESL, European history, film studies, fine arts, French, geography, geometry, German, grammar, health, health education, history, home economics, information technology, instrumental music, integrated mathematics, International Baccalaureate courses, Japanese, journalism, lab/keyboard, library skills, math methods, mathematics, model United Nations, music, personal and social education, physical education, physics, Russian, SAT preparation, science, senior thesis, social sciences, social studies, Spanish, speech and debate, student government, Swedish, technology/design, theater, theory of knowledge, trigonometry, world history, world literature, writing, yearbook.

Graduation Requirements Arts and fine arts (art, music, dance, drama), English, foreign language, mathematics, philosophy, physical education (includes health), science, social sciences, social studies (includes history), theory of knowledge, extended essay, community service. Community service is required.

Special Academic Programs International Baccalaureate program; academic accommodation for the gifted; remedial math; ESL (18 students enrolled).

College Admission Counseling 90 students graduated in 2011; 52 went to college, including Boston University; Brown University; Cornell University; Georgetown University; Queen's University at Kingston; Stanford University. Other: 2 went to work, 3 entered a postgraduate year, 33 had other specific plans. Mean SAT critical reading: 571, mean SAT math: 620, mean SAT writing: 586, mean combined SAT: 1777, mean composite ACT: 25. 44% scored over 600 on SAT critical reading, 66% scored over 600 on SAT math, 61% scored over 600 on SAT writing, 50% scored over 1800 on combined SAT, 58% scored over 26 on composite ACT.

Student Life Upper grades have specified standards of dress, student council, honor system. Discipline rests primarily with faculty.

Summer Programs Sports, rigorous outdoor training programs offered; held both on and off campus; held at Lake Garda (Italy); accepts boys and girls; open to students from other schools. 2012 schedule: July 1 to July 15. Application deadline: May 31.

Tuition and Aid Day student tuition: €17,400. Tuition installment plan (monthly payment plans, individually arranged payment plans). Tuition reduction for siblings, need-based tuition remission for current students available. In 2011–12, 1% of upper-school students received aid. Total amount of financial aid awarded in 2011–12: €31,326.

Admissions Traditional secondary-level entrance grade is 9. For fall 2011, 98 students applied for upper-level admission, 64 were accepted, 50 enrolled. English for Non-native Speakers, Math Placement Exam or Secondary Level English Proficiency required. Deadline for receipt of application materials: none. Application fee required: €100. On-campus interview recommended.

Athletics Interscholastic: alpine skiing (boys, girls), basketball (b,g), cross-country running (b,g), freestyle skiing (b,g), golf (b,g), rugby (b), skiing (downhill) (b,g), soccer (b,g), softball (g), swimming and diving (b,g), tennis (b,g), track and field (b,g), volleyball (b,g); intramural: badminton (b,g), ballet (b,g), basketball (b,g), canoeing/kayaking (b,g), climbing (b,g), cross-country running (b,g), dance (b,g), gymnastics (b,g), outdoor skills (b,g), soccer (b,g), strength & conditioning (b,g), swimming and diving (b,g), table tennis (b,g), tennis (b,g), track and field (b,g), volleyball (b,g), wall climbing (b,g); coed interscholastic: alpine skiing, cross-country running, golf, skiing (downhill), swimming and diving, tennis, track and field; coed intramural: ballet, canoeing/kayaking, climbing, dance, gymnastics, outdoor skills, swimming and diving, wall climbing. 5 PE instructors, 10 coaches.

Computers Computers are regularly used in all academic, current events, library skills, newspaper, research skills, yearbook classes. Computer network features include on-campus library services, Internet access, wireless campus network, Internet filtering or blocking technology. Campus intranet and student e-mail accounts are available to students. Students grades are available online. The school has a published electronic and media policy.

Contact Ms. Manuela Black, Director of Admissions. 49-8151-366 Ext. 120. Fax: 49-8151-366 Ext. 129. E-mail: admissions@mis-munich.de. Web site: www.mis-munich.de.

See Display on next page and Close-Up on page 652.

NASHVILLE CHRISTIAN SCHOOL

7555 Sawyer Brown Road

Nashville, Tennessee 37221

Head of School: Mrs. Connie Jo Shelton

General Information Coeducational day college-preparatory, arts, and religious studies school, affiliated with Christian faith, Church of Christ. Grades K–12. Founded: 1971. Setting: suburban. 45-acre campus. 2 buildings on campus. Approved or accredited by National Christian School Association, Southern Association of Colleges and Schools, and Tennessee Department of Education. Total enrollment: 483. Upper school average class size: 18. Upper school faculty-student ratio: 1:18. There are 176 required school days per year for Upper School students. Upper School students typically attend 5 days per week. The average school day consists of 7 hours and 15 minutes.

Upper School Student Profile Grade 9: 66 students (33 boys, 33 girls); Grade 10: 39 students (22 boys, 17 girls); Grade 11: 35 students (17 boys, 18 girls); Grade 12: 41 students (25 boys, 16 girls). 60% of students are Christian, members of Church of Christ.

Faculty School total: 40. In upper school: 12 men, 9 women; 15 have advanced degrees.

Subjects Offered Advanced Placement courses, algebra, American history, art, Bible, Bible studies, biology, calculus, chemistry, chorus, computer science, economics, English, fine arts, general science, geometry, government/civics, health, journalism, keyboarding, Latin, Mandarin, mathematics, music, physical education, physical science, physics, pre-algebra, pre-calculus, science, social sciences, social studies, Spanish, speech.

Graduation Requirements American history, American history-AP, arts and fine arts (art, music, dance, drama), Bible, computer science, English, foreign language, mathematics, physical education (includes health), science, social sciences, social studies (includes history).

Special Academic Programs Advanced Placement exam preparation; honors section; independent study; study at local college for college credit; remedial reading and/or remedial writing; remedial math; programs in English, mathematics, general development for dyslexic students; special instructional classes for students with Attention Deficit Disorder.

College Admission Counseling 48 students graduated in 2010; 45 went to college, including Belmont University; Lipscomb University; Middle Tennessee State University; Tennessee Technological University; The University of Tennessee at Chattanooga; Western Kentucky University. Other: 2 went to work, 1 entered military service.

Student Life Upper grades have uniform requirement, student council, honor system. Discipline rests primarily with faculty. Attendance at religious services is required.

Tuition and Aid Day student tuition: $7790. Guaranteed tuition plan. Tuition installment plan (SMART Tuition Payment Plan). Tuition reduction for siblings, need-based scholarship grants, paying campus jobs available. In 2010–11, 3% of upper-school students received aid. Total amount of financial aid awarded in 2010–11: $3000.

Admissions Traditional secondary-level entrance grade is 9. For fall 2010, 30 students applied for upper-level admission, 29 were accepted, 28 enrolled. Stanford Diagnostic Test required. Deadline for receipt of application materials: none. Application fee required: $100. Interview required.

Athletics Interscholastic: baseball (boys), basketball (b,g), bowling (b,g), cheering (g), cross-country running (b,g), football (b), golf (b,g), riflery (b,g), soccer (g), softball (g), strength & conditioning (b,g), track and field (b,g), volleyball (g), weight lifting (b,g), weight training (b,g), wrestling (b); intramural: aerobics/dance (g); coed interscholastic: fitness, physical fitness, physical training. 2 PE instructors, 6 coaches, 1 athletic trainer.

Computers Computers are regularly used in all academic classes. Computer network features include on-campus library services, Internet access, wireless campus network, Internet filtering or blocking technology. Student e-mail accounts and computer access in designated common areas are available to students. Students grades are available online.

Contact Mr. Phillip Montgomery, Director of Admissions. 615-356-5600 Ext. 117. Fax: 615-352-1324. E-mail: montgomeryp@nashvillechristian.org. Web site: www.nashvillechristian,org.

NATIONAL HIGH SCHOOL

6685 Peachtree Industrial Boulevard

Atlanta, Georgia 30360

Head of School: Alex Mithani

General Information Distance learning only college-preparatory, general academic, arts, and business school. Distance learning grades 9–12. Founded: 2000. Setting: urban. 1 building on campus. Approved or accredited by CITA (Commission on International and Trans-Regional Accreditation), Southern Association of Colleges and Schools, and Georgia Department of Education. Total enrollment: 396. Upper school faculty-student ratio: 1:10.

Faculty School total: 64.

Subjects Offered 1 1/2 elective credits, advanced biology, advanced chemistry, advanced computer applications, advanced math, Advanced Placement courses, American history, American history-AP, American literature, American literature-AP, biology, biology-AP, British literature, chemistry, chemistry-AP, electives, English, French, general math, geography, geometry, German, health, keyboarding, language arts, mathematical modeling, physical education, physical science, physics, physics-AP, pre-algebra, pre-calculus, U.S. history, world geography.

Graduation Requirements Algebra, American government, American history, American literature, biology, chemistry, earth science, economics and history, electives, English, English literature, foreign language, geography, geometry, grammar, history, physical fitness, physical science, physics, pre-calculus, U.S. government, U.S. history, world history, world literature, two elective credits.

Special Academic Programs Advanced Placement exam preparation; honors section; accelerated programs; academic accommodation for the gifted, the musically talented, and the artistically talented; remedial reading and/or remedial writing; remedial math.

Student Life Upper grades have student council, honor system. Discipline rests primarily with faculty.

Tuition and Aid Guaranteed tuition plan. Tuition installment plan (The Tuition Plan).

Admissions Traditional secondary-level entrance grade is 11. Admissions testing required. Deadline for receipt of application materials: none. No application fee required. Interview required.

Computers Computers are regularly used in all classes. Computer resources include Internet access, wireless campus network, Internet filtering or blocking technology. Campus intranet and student e-mail accounts are available to students. Students grades are available online. The school has a published electronic and media policy.

Contact Ms. Dona Mathews, Director of Admissions. 404-214-6014 Ext. 6010. Fax: 678-387-5289. E-mail: dmathews@nationalhighschool.com. Web site: www.nationalhighschool.com.

NATIVITY B.V.M. HIGH SCHOOL

One Lawtons Hill

Pottsville, Pennsylvania 17901

Head of School: Mrs. Lynn Sabol

General Information Coeducational day college-preparatory and general academic school, affiliated with Roman Catholic Church. Founded: 1955. Setting: small town. 1 building on campus. Approved or accredited by Middle States Association of Colleges and Schools and Pennsylvania Department of Education. Total enrollment: 189. Upper school average class size: 200. Upper school faculty-student ratio: 1:10. There are 180 required school days per year for Upper School students. Upper School students typically attend 5 days per week. The average school day consists of 6 hours and 20 minutes.

Upper School Student Profile Grade 9: 39 students (21 boys, 18 girls); Grade 10: 48 students (22 boys, 26 girls); Grade 11: 41 students (21 boys, 20 girls); Grade 12: 61 students (35 boys, 26 girls). 75% of students are Roman Catholic.

Faculty School total: 21. In upper school: 13 men, 7 women; 6 have advanced degrees.

Special Academic Programs 3 Advanced Placement exams for which test preparation is offered; honors section; independent study; study at local college for college credit; academic accommodation for the gifted.

College Admission Counseling 43 students graduated in 2011; 40 went to college. Other: 2 went to work, 1 had other specific plans.

Student Life Upper grades have uniform requirement, student council, honor system. Discipline rests primarily with faculty. Attendance at religious services is required.

Tuition and Aid Day student tuition: $4750. Tuition installment plan (monthly payment plans, individually arranged payment plans). Tuition reduction for siblings, merit scholarship grants, need-based scholarship grants available. In 2011–12, 65% of upper-school students received aid. Total amount of financial aid awarded in 2011–12: $155,000.

Admissions Traditional secondary-level entrance grade is 9. For fall 2011, 55 students applied for upper-level admission, 55 were accepted, 53 enrolled. Deadline for receipt of application materials: none. Application fee required: $50. Interview recommended.

Athletics Interscholastic: baseball (boys, girls), basketball (b,g), cheering (g), cross-country running (b,g), football (b), golf (b,g), soccer (b,g), softball (g), strength & conditioning (b,g), track and field (b,g), volleyball (g), weight lifting (b). 1 PE instructor, 40 coaches, 1 athletic trainer.

Computers The school has a published electronic and media policy.

Contact Mr. Robert Beruck, Guidance Counselor. 570-622-8110. Fax: 570-622-0454. E-mail: rberuck@nativitybvm.net.

NAVAJO PREPARATORY SCHOOL, INC.

1220 West Apache Street

Farmington, New Mexico 87401

Head of School: Mr. John C. Tohtsoni Jr.

General Information Coeducational boarding and day college-preparatory, arts, and bilingual studies school. Grades 9–12. Founded: 1991. Setting: suburban. Nearest major city is Albuquerque. Students are housed in single-sex dormitories. 84-acre campus. 12 buildings on campus. Approved or accredited by National Council for Nonpublic Schools, North Central Association of Colleges and Schools, and New Mexico Department of Education. Upper school average class size: 10. Upper school faculty-student ratio: 1:15. There are 181 required school days per year for Upper School students. Upper School students typically attend 5 days per week. The average school day consists of 7 hours.

Upper School Student Profile Grade 9: 52 students (19 boys, 33 girls); Grade 10: 49 students (19 boys, 30 girls); Grade 11: 40 students (19 boys, 21 girls); Grade 12: 42 students (14 boys, 28 girls). 65% of students are boarding students. 60% are state residents. 6 states are represented in upper school student body.

Faculty School total: 19. In upper school: 10 men, 9 women; 16 have advanced degrees.

Graduation Requirements Navajo language, Navajo history, Navajo culture.

College Admission Counseling 39 students graduated in 2010; 36 went to college, including Fort Lewis College; San Juan College; The University of Arizona; University of New Mexico; Whittier College. Other: 2 went to work, 1 entered military service.

Student Life Upper grades have specified standards of dress, student council, honor system. Discipline rests primarily with faculty.

Tuition and Aid Tuition installment plan (SMART Tuition Payment Plan). Merit scholarship grants available.

Admissions ACT-Explore required. Deadline for receipt of application materials: none. Application fee required: $20. Interview required.

Athletics Interscholastic: baseball (boys, girls), basketball (b,g), cheering (b,g), cross-country running (b,g), football (b,g), golf (b,g), softball (b,g), volleyball (b,g). 1 PE instructor, 19 coaches.

Computers Computer network features include on-campus library services, Internet access, wireless campus network. Student e-mail accounts are available to students. The school has a published electronic and media policy.

Contact Ms. Sandra Westbrook, Admissions. 505-326-6571 Ext. 129. Fax: 505-564-8099. E-mail: sandra.westbrook@bie.edu. Web site: www.navajoprep.com.

NAZARETH ACADEMY

1209 West Ogden Avenue

LaGrange Park, Illinois 60526

Head of School: Mrs. Deborah A. Tracy

General Information Coeducational day college-preparatory school, affiliated with Roman Catholic Church. Grades 9–12. Founded: 1900. Setting: suburban. Nearest major city is Chicago. 15-acre campus. 2 buildings on campus. Approved or accredited by North Central Association of Colleges and Schools and Illinois Department of Education. Total enrollment: 824. Upper school average class size: 24. Upper school faculty-student ratio: 1:18. There are 180 required school days per year for Upper School students. Upper School students typically attend 5 days per week. The average school day consists of 7 hours.

Upper School Student Profile Grade 9: 222 students (119 boys, 103 girls); Grade 10: 212 students (100 boys, 112 girls); Grade 11: 203 students (102 boys, 101 girls); Grade 12: 187 students (96 boys, 91 girls). 90% of students are Roman Catholic.

Faculty School total: 47. In upper school: 19 men, 28 women; 40 have advanced degrees.

Subjects Offered 3-dimensional design, acting, algebra, American government, American literature, art, biology, biology-AP, calculus-AP, chemistry, chemistry-AP, computer programming, computer science-AP, concert band, concert choir, creative writing, drawing and design, economics, English, English language and composition-AP, English literature and composition-AP, environmental science, French, geometry, health, Italian, journalism, music theory, photography, physical education, physics, physics-AP, pre-calculus, psychology, religion, scripture, Spanish, speech, studio art, theater, trigonometry, U.S. history, U.S. history-AP, Western civilization, wind ensemble, world history, world literature, world religions.

Graduation Requirements Advanced math, algebra, American literature, arts and fine arts (art, music, dance, drama), biology, chemistry, church history, English, foreign language, geometry, physical education (includes health), physics, religion (includes Bible studies and theology), scripture, U.S. history, Western civilization, world literature, world religions, world studies, service hours, off-campus retreat for juniors.

Special Academic Programs 11 Advanced Placement exams for which test preparation is offered; honors section.

College Admission Counseling 172 students graduated in 2011; 171 went to college, including Loyola University Chicago; Marquette University; Northwestern University; University of Illinois at Chicago; University of Illinois at Urbana–Champaign; University of Notre Dame. Other: 1 entered military service. Median composite ACT: 25. 34% scored over 26 on composite ACT.

Student Life Upper grades have uniform requirement, student council, honor system. Discipline rests primarily with faculty. Attendance at religious services is required.

Summer Programs Enrichment, sports, art/fine arts programs offered; session focuses on athletic camps; held on campus; accepts boys and girls; open to students from other schools.

Tuition and Aid Day student tuition: $1038. Tuition installment plan (monthly payment plans). Tuition reduction for siblings, merit scholarship grants, need-based scholarship grants available. In 2011–12, 22% of upper-school students received aid; total upper-school merit-scholarship money awarded: $40,000. Total amount of financial aid awarded in 2011–12: $300,000.

Admissions Traditional secondary-level entrance grade is 9. For fall 2011, 350 students applied for upper-level admission, 222 enrolled. High School Placement Test (closed version) from Scholastic Testing Service required. Deadline for receipt of application materials: June 30. No application fee required.

Athletics Interscholastic: baseball (boys), basketball (b,g), cheering (g), cross-country running (b,g), football (b), golf (b,g), hockey (b), lacrosse (b,g), pom squad (g), soccer (b,g), softball (g), swimming and diving (g), tennis (b,g), track and field (b,g), volleyball (b,g), wrestling (b). 2 PE instructors, 1 coach, 1 athletic trainer.

Computers Computers are regularly used in English, foreign language, history, mathematics, science classes. Computer network features include on-campus library services, Internet access, wireless campus network, Internet filtering or blocking technology. Students grades are available online. The school has a published electronic and media policy.

Contact Mr. John Bonk, Recruitment Director. 708-387-8538. Fax: 708-354-0109. E-mail: jbonk@nazarethacademy.com. Web site: www.nazarethacademy.com.

NEBRASKA CHRISTIAN SCHOOLS

1847 Inskip Avenue

Central City, Nebraska 68826

Head of School: Mr. Josh Cumpston

General Information Coeducational boarding and day college-preparatory school, affiliated with Protestant-Evangelical faith. Boarding grades 7–12, day grades K–12. Founded: 1959. Setting: rural. Nearest major city is Lincoln. Students are housed in single-sex dormitories. 27-acre campus. 7 buildings on campus. Approved or accredited by Association of Christian Schools International and Nebraska Department of Education. Endowment: $35,000. Total enrollment: 210. Upper school average class size: 20. Upper school faculty-student ratio: 1:10. There are 155 required school days per year for Upper School students. Upper School students typically attend 4 days per week. The average school day consists of 8 hours.

Upper School Student Profile Grade 9: 29 students (15 boys, 14 girls); Grade 10: 30 students (11 boys, 19 girls); Grade 11: 36 students (16 boys, 20 girls); Grade 12: 28 students (17 boys, 11 girls). 38% of students are boarding students. 72% are state residents. 2 states are represented in upper school student body. 28% are international students. International students from China, Hong Kong, Republic of Korea, Taiwan, Thailand, and Viet Nam; 2 other countries represented in student body. 90% of students are Protestant-Evangelical faith.

Faculty School total: 18. In upper school: 13 men, 5 women; 5 have advanced degrees; 5 reside on campus.

Subjects Offered Accounting, advanced math, algebra, American government, American history, American literature, anatomy and physiology, ancient world history, art, band, Bible, biology, business, business law, chemistry, choir, Christian doctrine, Christian ethics, Christian studies, composition, computer applications, computer programming, concert band, consumer mathematics, creation science, desktop publishing, economics, English, English composition, ESL, family living, fitness, general math, geography, geometry, health and safety, history, keyboarding, lab science, language arts, Life of Christ, life science, literature, mathematics, music, music theory, physical education, physical fitness, physical science, physics, pre-calculus, science, science project, social studies, Spanish, speech, trigonometry, vocal ensemble, vocal music, Web site design, word processing, world geography, world history, writing, yearbook.

Graduation Requirements Algebra, American government, American history, American literature, art, Bible, biology, Christian doctrine, economics, English, family living, geometry, history, keyboarding, Life of Christ, physical education (includes health), physical science, world history.

Special Academic Programs Independent study; study at local college for college credit; ESL (16 students enrolled).

College Admission Counseling 27 students graduated in 2011; 22 went to college, including Northwestern College; Parsons The New School for Design; Stony Brook University, State University of New York; University of Nebraska–Lincoln; University of Nebraska at Kearney; University of Nebraska at Omaha. Other: 4 went to work, 1 entered military service. Median composite ACT: 25. 27% scored over 26 on composite ACT.

Student Life Upper grades have specified standards of dress, student council, honor system. Discipline rests primarily with faculty. Attendance at religious services is required.

Tuition and Aid Day student tuition: $5000; 5-day tuition and room/board: $8000; 7-day tuition and room/board: $24,950. Guaranteed tuition plan. Tuition installment plan (FACTS Tuition Payment Plan, individually arranged payment plans). Tuition reduction for siblings, merit scholarship grants, need-based scholarship grants available. In 2011–12, 33% of upper-school students received aid. Total amount of financial aid awarded in 2011–12: $180,000.

Admissions Traditional secondary-level entrance grade is 9. For fall 2011, 21 students applied for upper-level admission, 15 were accepted, 15 enrolled. SLEP for foreign students or TOEFL or SLEP required. Deadline for receipt of application materials: none. Application fee required: $300. Interview recommended.

Athletics Interscholastic: basketball (boys, girls), cross-country running (b,g), football (b), track and field (b,g), volleyball (g), wrestling (b). 2 PE instructors, 7 coaches.

Computers Computers are regularly used in business applications, desktop publishing, programming, Web site design, yearbook classes. Computer network features include Internet access, wireless campus network, Internet filtering or blocking technology. Students grades are available online.

Contact Mr. Larry Hoff, Director, International Programs. 308-946-3836. Fax: 308-946-3837. E-mail: lhoff@nebraskachristian.org. Web site: www.nebraskachristian.org.

NERINX HALL

530 East Lockwood Avenue

Webster Groves, Missouri 63119

Head of School: Sr. Barbara Roche, SL

General Information Girls' day college-preparatory and arts school, affiliated with Roman Catholic Church. Grades 9–12. Founded: 1924. Setting: suburban. Nearest major city is St. Louis. 12-acre campus. 4 buildings on campus. Approved or accredited by National Catholic Education Association, North Central Association of Colleges and Schools, and Missouri Department of Education. Endowment: $3.7 million. Total enrollment: 627. Upper school average class size: 20. Upper school faculty-student ratio: 1:12. There are 176 required school days per year for Upper School students. Upper School students typically attend 5 days per week. The average school day consists of 6 hours and 25 minutes.

Upper School Student Profile Grade 9: 149 students (149 girls); Grade 10: 166 students (166 girls); Grade 11: 156 students (156 girls); Grade 12: 156 students (156 girls). 91% of students are Roman Catholic.

Faculty School total: 53. In upper school: 12 men, 41 women; 42 have advanced degrees.

Subjects Offered Acting, advanced math, American government, American history, American literature, anatomy, anthropology, art, astronomy, athletics, biology, business, calculus, ceramics, chemistry, computer applications, computer graphics, conceptual physics, creative writing, death and loss, desktop publishing, drawing and design, Eastern world civilizations, economics, English composition, English literature, film appreciation, French, geology, German, graphics, health, history, Holocaust, honors algebra, honors English, honors geometry, honors U.S. history, instrumental music, jazz band, keyboarding, lab science, Latin, media, Middle East, model United Nations, multimedia, orchestra, painting, performing arts, personal finance, physics, pre-calculus, psychology, public speaking, religious education, Spanish, theology, Web site design, Western civilization.

Graduation Requirements Algebra, arts and fine arts (art, music, dance, drama), biology, chemistry, computer applications, foreign language, geometry, physical education (includes health), physical fitness, physics, public speaking, theology, U.S. government and politics, U.S. history, U.S. literature, world history, writing. Community service is required.

Special Academic Programs 9 Advanced Placement exams for which test preparation is offered; honors section; study at local college for college credit.

College Admission Counseling 150 students graduated in 2011; all went to college, including Missouri State University; Rockhurst University; Saint Louis University; The University of Kansas; Truman State University; University of Missouri. Mean composite ACT: 27.

Student Life Upper grades have uniform requirement, student council, honor system. Discipline rests primarily with faculty. Attendance at religious services is required.

Summer Programs Advancement programs offered; session focuses on advancement; held on campus; accepts girls; not open to students from other schools. 175 students usually enrolled.

Tuition and Aid Day student tuition: $10,800. Tuition installment plan (individually arranged payment plans). Tuition reduction for siblings, need-based scholarship grants, paying campus jobs available. In 2011–12, 28% of upper-school students received aid. Total amount of financial aid awarded in 2011–12: $505,000.

Admissions Traditional secondary-level entrance grade is 9. For fall 2011, 167 students applied for upper-level admission, 158 were accepted, 149 enrolled. Any standardized test or CTBS (or similar from their school) required. Deadline for receipt of application materials: November 21. Application fee required: $10. On-campus interview required.

Athletics Interscholastic: basketball, cross-country running, diving, field hockey, golf, lacrosse, racquetball, soccer, softball, swimming and diving, tennis, track and field, volleyball. 3 PE instructors, 25 coaches.

Computers Computers are regularly used in graphics, humanities, mathematics, science, speech, writing, writing classes. Computer network features include on-campus library services, Internet access, wireless campus network, Internet filtering or blocking technology. Student e-mail accounts are available to students. Students grades are available online. The school has a published electronic and media policy.

Contact Mrs. Mary Ann Gentry. 314-968-1505 Ext. 151. Fax: 314-968-0604. E-mail: mgentry@nerinxhs.org. Web site: www.nerinxhs.org.

NEUCHÂTEL JUNIOR COLLEGE

Cret-Taconnet 4

Neuchâtel 2002, Switzerland

Head of School: Mr. Bill Boyer

General Information Coeducational boarding college-preparatory, arts, business, bilingual studies, and international development school. Grade 12. Founded: 1956. Setting: urban. Nearest major city is Berne, Switzerland. Students are housed in homes of host families. 1-acre campus. 3 buildings on campus. Approved or accredited by Canadian Association of Independent Schools, Canadian Educational Standards Institute, and state department of education. Languages of instruction: English and French. Endowment: CAN$440,000. Total enrollment: 56. Upper school average class size: 15. Upper school faculty-student ratio: 1:10. Upper School students typically attend 5 days per week. The average school day consists of 5 hours and 15 minutes.

Upper School Student Profile Grade 12: 41 students (15 boys, 26 girls); Postgraduate: 15 students (6 boys, 9 girls). 100% of students are boarding students. 4% are international students. International students from Canada, France, Germany, Japan, United Kingdom, and United States; 1 other country represented in student body.

Faculty School total: 9. In upper school: 3 men, 6 women; 6 have advanced degrees; 1 resides on campus.

Subjects Offered 20th century world history, advanced chemistry, advanced math, Advanced Placement courses, advanced studio art-AP, algebra, analysis and differential calculus, ancient world history, applied arts, art, art history, art history-AP, athletics, biology, biology-AP, British history, calculus, calculus-AP, Canadian history, Canadian law, Canadian literature, chemistry, chemistry-AP, classical civilization, comparative government and politics-AP, comparative politics, debate, dramatic arts, earth science, economics, economics-AP, English, English language and composition-AP, English literature-AP, environmental science, European history, European history-AP, finite math, French as a second language, French language-AP, French literature-AP, German-AP, government and politics-AP, human geography - AP, law, personal and social education, physics, physics-AP, public speaking, studio art-AP, United Nations and international issues, world history-AP, world issues.

Graduation Requirements Minimum of 6 senior year university prep level courses.

Special Academic Programs 8 Advanced Placement exams for which test preparation is offered; study abroad.
College Admission Counseling 83 students graduated in 2011; 81 went to college, including Dalhousie University; Harvard University; McGill University; Queen's University at Kingston; The University of Western Ontario; University of Toronto. Other: 2 had other specific plans.
Student Life Upper grades have specified standards of dress, student council, honor system. Discipline rests primarily with faculty.
Tuition and Aid 7-day tuition and room/board: 47,000 Swiss francs. Bursaries available. In 2011–12, 11% of upper-school students received aid. Total amount of financial aid awarded in 2011–12: 90,000 Swiss francs.
Admissions Traditional secondary-level entrance grade is 12. For fall 2011, 72 students applied for upper-level admission, 56 were accepted, 56 enrolled. Deadline for receipt of application materials: January 16. Application fee required: CAN$175. Interview recommended.
Athletics Interscholastic: field hockey (boys, girls), rugby (b,g), soccer (b,g); intramural: hockey (b,g), ice hockey (b,g), indoor hockey (b,g), rugby (b,g), soccer (b,g); coed interscholastic: alpine skiing, aquatics, snowboarding, swimming and diving; coed intramural: alpine skiing, aquatics, basketball, bicycling, cross-country running, curling, floor hockey, jogging, sailing, snowboarding, volleyball.
Computers Computer network features include on-campus library services, Internet access, wireless campus network. Student e-mail accounts are available to students. The school has a published electronic and media policy.
Contact Ms. Anne Hamilton, Admission Officer. 416-368-8169 Ext. 222. Fax: 416-368-0956. E-mail: admissions@neuchatel.org. Web site: www.njc.ch.

NEWARK ACADEMY

91 South Orange Avenue

Livingston, New Jersey 07039-4989

Head of School: M. Donald M. Austin

General Information Coeducational day college-preparatory, arts, technology, and International Baccalaureate school. Grades 6–12. Founded: 1774. Setting: suburban. Nearest major city is Morristown. 68-acre campus. 1 building on campus. Approved or accredited by Middle States Association of Colleges and Schools, New Jersey Association of Independent Schools, and New Jersey Department of Education. Member of National Association of Independent Schools and Secondary School Admission Test Board. Endowment: $20.1 million. Total enrollment: 568. Upper school average class size: 13. Upper school faculty-student ratio: 1:12. There are 165 required school days per year for Upper School students. Upper School students typically attend 5 days per week. The average school day consists of 6 hours.
Upper School Student Profile Grade 9: 101 students (52 boys, 49 girls); Grade 10: 102 students (49 boys, 53 girls); Grade 11: 103 students (52 boys, 51 girls); Grade 12: 93 students (47 boys, 46 girls).
Faculty School total: 84. In upper school: 38 men, 34 women; 72 have advanced degrees.
Subjects Offered Accounting, acting, advanced biology, advanced chemistry, advanced computer applications, advanced math, Advanced Placement courses, advanced studio art-AP, algebra, American history, American literature, anatomy, art, art history, arts, biology, botany, calculus, ceramics, chemistry, chorus, community service, computer programming, computer science, creative writing, drama, driver education, ecology, economics, English, English literature, European history, film studies, filmmaking, finance, fine arts, French, geometry, government/civics, grammar, health, history, history-AP, Holocaust studies, honors algebra, honors geometry, humanities, International Baccalaureate courses, jazz band, leadership, Mandarin, mathematics, mechanical drawing, model United Nations, modern dance, money management, music, musical theater, newspaper, oil painting, participation in sports, peer counseling, philosophy, physical education, physical science, physics, play production, playwriting and directing, poetry, political science, pottery, pre-algebra, pre-calculus, probability and statistics, SAT/ACT preparation, science, Spanish, theater, theory of knowledge, trigonometry, world history, world literature, writing.
Graduation Requirements Arts and fine arts (art, music, dance, drama), computer science, English, foreign language, mathematics, physical education (includes health), science, social studies (includes history), 40-hour senior service project, community service.
Special Academic Programs International Baccalaureate program; 4 Advanced Placement exams for which test preparation is offered; honors section; accelerated programs; independent study; term-away projects; study abroad; academic accommodation for the gifted, the musically talented, and the artistically talented.
College Admission Counseling 98 students graduated in 2011; 97 went to college, including Cornell University; Harvard University; New York University; The George Washington University; University of Pennsylvania; Williams College. Other: 1 had other specific plans. Median SAT critical reading: 657, median SAT math: 678, median SAT writing: 681, median combined SAT: 2016, median composite ACT: 30.
Student Life Upper grades have specified standards of dress, student council, honor system. Discipline rests primarily with faculty.
Summer Programs Remediation, enrichment, advancement, ESL, sports, art/fine arts, computer instruction programs offered; session focuses on enrichment and advancement; held on campus; accepts boys and girls; open to students from other schools. 850 students usually enrolled. 2012 schedule: June 27 to August 5. Application deadline: May 1.
Tuition and Aid Day student tuition: $30,215. Tuition installment plan (Insured Tuition Payment Plan, Key Tuition Payment Plan, monthly payment plans, individually arranged payment plans). Need-based scholarship grants available. In 2011–12, 18% of upper-school students received aid. Total amount of financial aid awarded in 2011–12: $1,788,634.
Admissions Traditional secondary-level entrance grade is 9. For fall 2011, 534 students applied for upper-level admission, 100 were accepted, 55 enrolled. ISEE or SSAT required. Deadline for receipt of application materials: December 9. Application fee required: $65. On-campus interview required.
Athletics Interscholastic: baseball (boys), basketball (b,g), cross-country running (b,g), fencing (b,g), field hockey (g), football (b), golf (b,g), lacrosse (b,g), running (b,g), skiing (downhill) (b,g), soccer (b,g), softball (g), swimming and diving (b,g), tennis (b,g), track and field (b,g), volleyball (g), wrestling (b); intramural: aerobics/dance (b,g), aerobics/Nautilus (b,g), baseball (b), basketball (b,g), bicycling (b,g), cross-country running (b,g), dance (b,g), dance team (b,g), field hockey (g), fitness (b,g), football (b), golf (b,g), hockey (b), ice hockey (b), lacrosse (b,g), modern dance (b,g), soccer (b,g), softball (g), swimming and diving (b,g), tennis (b,g), track and field (b,g), volleyball (g), weight lifting (b,g), wrestling (b), yoga (b,g); coed intramural: aerobics/dance, aerobics/Nautilus, bicycling, cricket, dance, dance team, fitness, modern dance, mountain biking, skiing (downhill), table tennis, ultimate Frisbee, weight lifting, yoga. 5 PE instructors, 10 coaches, 1 athletic trainer.
Computers Computers are regularly used in all academic classes. Computer network features include on-campus library services, online commercial services, Internet access, wireless campus network, Internet filtering or blocking technology. Student e-mail accounts are available to students. Students grades are available online. The school has a published electronic and media policy.
Contact Ms. Imaani F. Sanders, Admission Office Manager. 973-992-7000 Ext. 323. Fax: 973-488-0040. E-mail: Isanders@newarka.edu. Web site: www.newarka.edu.

NEW COVENANT ACADEMY

3304 South Cox Road

Springfield, Missouri 65807

Head of School: Mr. Matt Searson

General Information Coeducational day college-preparatory, arts, business, religious studies, technology, and science, math, foreign language, language arts school, affiliated with Christian faith. Grades JK–12. Founded: 1979. Setting: suburban. 22-acre campus. 1 building on campus. Approved or accredited by Association of Christian Schools International and North Central Association of Colleges and Schools. Total enrollment: 342. Upper school faculty-student ratio: 1:10. There are 167 required school days per year for Upper School students. Upper School students typically attend 5 days per week. The average school day consists of 7 hours and 30 minutes.
Upper School Student Profile 99% of students are Christian.
Faculty School total: 30. In upper school: 5 men, 7 women.
Subjects Offered Advanced math, algebra, American government, American history, American literature, anatomy and physiology, ancient world history, art, athletics, Bible, biology, British literature, business, calculus, chemistry, Christianity, comparative government and politics, computer processing, computer technologies, computers, concert choir, economics, English, English composition, geology, geometry, health, history, independent study, Life of Christ, literature, mathematics, music appreciation, New Testament, oceanography, physical education, physics, pre-algebra, robotics, science, scripture, Spanish, trigonometry, world history, yearbook.
Special Academic Programs Independent study; study at local college for college credit.
College Admission Counseling 34 students graduated in 2011; all went to college.
Student Life Upper grades have specified standards of dress, student council, honor system. Discipline rests primarily with faculty. Attendance at religious services is required.
Tuition and Aid Guaranteed tuition plan. Tuition installment plan (monthly payment plans, individually arranged payment plans). Need-based scholarship grants available.
Admissions Otis-Lennon School Ability Test, SLEP for foreign students or Stanford Achievement Test required. Deadline for receipt of application materials: none. Application fee required: $50. Interview required.
Athletics Interscholastic: basketball (boys, girls), cheering (g), golf (b), soccer (b,g), track and field (b,g), volleyball (g); coed interscholastic: golf. 2 PE instructors, 11 coaches.
Computers Computers are regularly used in computer applications, journalism, technology, word processing, yearbook classes. Computer network features include Internet access, Internet filtering or blocking technology. Student e-mail accounts and computer access in designated common areas are available to students. Students grades are available online.
Contact Mrs. Delana Reynolds, Admissions Officer. 417-887-9848 Ext. 3. Fax: 417-887-2419. E-mail: dreynolds@newcovenant.net. Web site: www.newcovenant.net.

NEW ENGLISH SCHOOL

PO Box 6156

Hawalli 32036, Kuwait

Head of School: Dr. Ziad S. Rajab

General Information Coeducational day college-preparatory, arts, business, bilingual studies, and technology school. Grades K–13. Founded: 1969. Setting: urban. Nearest major city is Kuwait City, Kuwait. 1-hectare campus. 5 buildings on campus. Approved or accredited by Kuwait Ministry of Education. Language of instruction: English. Total enrollment: 2,249. Upper school average class size: 25. Upper school faculty-student ratio: 1:12. There are 175 required school days per year for Upper School students. Upper School students typically attend 5 days per week. The average school day consists of 6 hours and 30 minutes.

Upper School Student Profile Grade 6: 150 students (89 boys, 61 girls); Grade 7: 167 students (92 boys, 75 girls); Grade 8: 204 students (122 boys, 82 girls); Grade 9: 218 students (114 boys, 104 girls); Grade 10: 238 students (141 boys, 97 girls); Grade 11: 254 students (146 boys, 108 girls); Grade 12: 103 students (63 boys, 40 girls); Grade 13: 25 students (13 boys, 12 girls).

Faculty School total: 215. In upper school: 48 men, 43 women; 10 have advanced degrees.

Subjects Offered Accounting, advanced math, art, biology, business studies, chemistry, computer science, drama, economics, French, geography, history, information technology, mathematics, music, physical education.

Special Academic Programs ESL (60 students enrolled).

College Admission Counseling 225 students graduated in 2010.

Student Life Upper grades have uniform requirement. Discipline rests primarily with faculty.

Tuition and Aid Day student tuition: 1400 Kuwaiti dinars–3570 Kuwaiti dinars.

Admissions Traditional secondary-level entrance grade is 7. For fall 2010, 400 students applied for upper-level admission, 250 were accepted, 250 enrolled. School's own exam required. Application fee required: 10 Kuwaiti dinars. Interview required.

Athletics Interscholastic: netball (girls); intramural: netball (g); coed interscholastic: basketball, cricket, football, track and field; coed intramural: badminton, ball hockey, basketball, cricket, football, gymnastics, hockey, outdoor adventure, paint ball, sailing, table tennis, tennis, track and field, walking, yoga.

Computers Computer network features include on-campus library services, Internet access.

Contact Ms. Hasmiq Hagop, Admissions. 965-25318061. Fax: 965-25319924. E-mail: hagop@neskt.com. Web site: www.neskt.com.

THE NEWMAN SCHOOL

247 Marlborough Street

Boston, Massachusetts 02116

General Information Coeducational day college-preparatory and ESL school. Grades 9–PG. Founded: 1945. Setting: urban. 2 buildings on campus. Approved or accredited by Association of Independent Schools in New England, New England Association of Schools and Colleges, and Massachusetts Department of Education. Member of Secondary School Admission Test Board. Total enrollment: 230. Upper school average class size: 14. Upper school faculty-student ratio: 1:14.

See Display on this page and Close-Up on page 654.

NEW TRIBES MISSION ACADEMY

PO Box 707

Durham, Ontario N0G 1R0, Canada

Head of School: Helmut Penner

General Information Coeducational day college-preparatory school, affiliated with Baptist Bible Fellowship, Brethren Church. Boys grades K–11, girls grades K–9. Founded: 1992. Setting: small town. 1-acre campus. 1 building on campus. Approved or accredited by Association of Christian Schools International. Language of instruction: English. Total enrollment: 21. Upper school average class size: 5. Upper school faculty-student ratio: 1:3. There are 172 required school days per year for Upper School students. Upper School students typically attend 5 days per week. The average school day consists of 6 hours.

Upper School Student Profile Grade 9: 2 students (1 boy, 1 girl); Grade 10: 1 student (1 boy); Grade 11: 1 student (1 boy). 80% of students are Baptist Bible Fellowship, Brethren.

Faculty School total: 8. In upper school: 3 men, 3 women.

Subjects Offered Algebra, Bible studies, biology, computer applications, English language and composition-AP, French, history, literature, physical education.

Graduation Requirements Advanced math, algebra, Bible studies, biology, Canadian geography, Canadian history, chemistry, computer skills, consumer mathematics, English, English language and composition-AP, English literature and composition-AP, French, history, mathematics, physical education (includes health), physics, science.

Student Life Upper grades have specified standards of dress. Discipline rests equally with students and faculty.

Tuition and Aid Day student tuition: CAN$1200. Tuition installment plan (monthly payment plans).

Admissions For fall 2011, 1 student applied for upper-level admission, 1 was accepted, 1 enrolled. CAT or SAT required. Deadline for receipt of application materials: August 29. No application fee required. Interview recommended.

Athletics Coed Intramural: archery, badminton, ball hockey, basketball, flag football, floor hockey, Frisbee, indoor soccer, soccer, softball, table tennis, tennis, track and field, volleyball. 1 PE instructor.

Computers Computer access in designated common areas is available to students.

Contact Helmut Penner, Principal. 519-369-2622. Fax: 519-369-5828. E-mail: academy@canada.ntm.org.

NIAGARA CHRISTIAN COMMUNITY OF SCHOOLS

2619 Niagara Boulevard
Fort Erie, Ontario L2A 5M4, Canada

Head of School: Mr. Mark Thiessen

General Information Coeducational boarding and day college-preparatory, general academic, arts, business, and religious studies school, affiliated with Brethren in Christ Church. Boarding grades 9–12, day grades JK–12. Founded: 1932. Setting: rural. Nearest major city is Niagara Falls, Canada. Students are housed in single-sex dormitories. 121-acre campus. 16 buildings on campus. Approved or accredited by Ontario Department of Education. Language of instruction: English. Total enrollment: 254. Upper school average class size: 17. Upper school faculty-student ratio: 1:17. There are 170 required school days per year for Upper School students. Upper School students typically attend 5 days per week. The average school day consists of 7 hours.

Upper School Student Profile Grade 9: 16 students (9 boys, 7 girls); Grade 10: 44 students (25 boys, 19 girls); Grade 11: 41 students (20 boys, 21 girls); Grade 12: 78 students (51 boys, 27 girls). 70% of students are boarding students. 25% are province residents. 2 provinces are represented in upper school student body. 75% are international students. International students from Cayman Islands, Hong Kong, Japan, Mexico, Republic of Korea, and Taiwan; 4 other countries represented in student body. 17% of students are Brethren in Christ Church.

Faculty School total: 24. In upper school: 11 men, 13 women; 4 have advanced degrees; 1 resides on campus.

Subjects Offered 20th century world history, accounting, advanced chemistry, advanced computer applications, advanced math, Advanced Placement courses, advanced TOEFL/grammar, algebra, analysis and differential calculus, analysis of data, analytic geometry, anatomy, anthropology, art, art history, athletics, Bible, biology, biology-AP, business, business applications, business education, business mathematics, business technology, calculus, calculus-AP, Canadian geography, Canadian history, Canadian literature, career education, chemistry, choir, civics, computer applications, computer programming, concert choir, CPR, data processing, discrete mathematics, dramatic arts, early childhood, economics, English, English literature, ESL, European history, exercise science, family studies, French as a second language, general math, geography, geometry, guidance, health education, history, information technology, instrumental music, integrated science, international affairs, Italian, leadership education training, Life of Christ, mathematics, media studies, modern world history, music, parenting, physical education, physics, politics, pre-calculus, science, Spanish, TOEFL preparation, world history, world history-AP, world issues, world religions, writing, writing.

Special Academic Programs International Baccalaureate program; independent study; special instructional classes for students with learning disabilities; ESL (125 students enrolled).

College Admission Counseling 64 students graduated in 2011; 60 went to college, including Brock University; McMaster University; The University of Western Ontario; University of Toronto; University of Waterloo; Wilfrid Laurier University. Other: 4 had other specific plans.

Student Life Upper grades have uniform requirement, student council, honor system. Discipline rests primarily with faculty. Attendance at religious services is required.

Summer Programs ESL programs offered; session focuses on ESL; held on campus; accepts boys and girls; not open to students from other schools. 80 students usually enrolled. 2012 schedule: July 11 to August 31. Application deadline: none.

Tuition and Aid Day student tuition: CAN$8495; 5-day tuition and room/board: CAN$10,450; 7-day tuition and room/board: CAN$18,995. Tuition installment plan (monthly payment plans, individually arranged payment plans, quarterly payment plan). Tuition reduction for siblings, bursaries, merit scholarship grants, need-based scholarship grants, paying campus jobs available. In 2011–12, 30% of upper-school students received aid; total upper-school merit-scholarship money awarded: CAN$50,000. Total amount of financial aid awarded in 2011–12: CAN$400,000.

Admissions Traditional secondary-level entrance grade is 9. For fall 2011, 70 students applied for upper-level admission, 58 were accepted, 56 enrolled. Admissions testing and English proficiency required. Deadline for receipt of application materials: none. Application fee required: CAN$100. Interview required.

Athletics Interscholastic: badminton (boys, girls), basketball (b,g), cross-country running (b,g), golf (b), hockey (b,g), ice hockey (b,g), soccer (b,g), track and field (b,g); intramural: basketball (b,g), indoor soccer (b,g); coed interscholastic: badminton; coed intramural: aerobics, alpine skiing, aquatics, badminton, ball hockey, baseball, bowling, canoeing/kayaking, cross-country running, fitness, fitness walking, floor hockey, golf, ice skating, skiing (downhill), soccer. 1 PE instructor, 1 coach.

Computers Computers are regularly used in accounting, all academic, business, data processing, economics, ESL, mathematics, science, yearbook classes. Computer network features include on-campus library services, Internet access, wireless campus network, Internet filtering or blocking technology. Computer access in designated common areas is available to students. Students grades are available online. The school has a published electronic and media policy.

Contact Mr. Tom Auld, Director of Student Life. 905-871-6980 Ext. 2280. Fax: 905-871-9260. E-mail: tomauld@niagaracc.com. Web site: www.niagaracc.com.

NICHOLS SCHOOL

1250 Amherst Street
Buffalo, New York 14216

Head of School: Richard C. Bryan Jr.

General Information Coeducational day college-preparatory, arts, and technology school. Grades 5–12. Founded: 1892. Setting: urban. 30-acre campus. 8 buildings on campus. Approved or accredited by New York Department of Education and New York Department of Education. Member of National Association of Independent Schools. Endowment: $25 million. Total enrollment: 582. Upper school average class size: 14. Upper school faculty-student ratio: 1:8. Upper School students typically attend 5 days per week. The average school day consists of 7 hours.

Upper School Student Profile Grade 9: 92 students (53 boys, 39 girls); Grade 10: 112 students (62 boys, 50 girls); Grade 11: 101 students (48 boys, 53 girls); Grade 12: 84 students (37 boys, 47 girls).

Faculty School total: 77. In upper school: 26 men, 22 women; 36 have advanced degrees.

Subjects Offered Algebra, American history, American literature, anatomy, art, art history, biology, calculus, chemistry, Chinese, community service, computer graphics, computer math, computer programming, computer science, creative writing, dance, drama, driver education, earth science, economics, English, English literature, environmental science, European history, expository writing, fine arts, French, geology, geometry, government/civics, history, Latin, mathematics, music, photography, physical education, physics, science, social studies, Spanish, speech, theater, trigonometry, world history, world literature.

Graduation Requirements Arts and fine arts (art, music, dance, drama), English, foreign language, mathematics, physical education (includes health), science, social studies (includes history).

Special Academic Programs Advanced Placement exam preparation; honors section; independent study; study abroad.

College Admission Counseling 103 students graduated in 2011; 101 went to college, including Boston College; Canisius College; Hobart and William Smith Colleges; Niagara University; The George Washington University; University at Buffalo, the State University of New York. Other: 1 entered a postgraduate year, 1 had other specific plans. Median SAT critical reading: 550, median SAT math: 580, median SAT writing: 560. 46% scored over 600 on SAT critical reading, 56% scored over 600 on SAT math, 42% scored over 600 on SAT writing.

Student Life Upper grades have specified standards of dress, student council, honor system. Discipline rests equally with students and faculty.

Summer Programs Remediation, enrichment, advancement, art/fine arts programs offered; session focuses on academic enrichment; held on campus; accepts boys and girls; open to students from other schools. 68 students usually enrolled. 2012 schedule: June 15 to August 15. Application deadline: none.

Tuition and Aid Day student tuition: $17,700–$19,400. Tuition installment plan (Insured Tuition Payment Plan, monthly payment plans). Need-based scholarship grants available. In 2011–12, 30% of upper-school students received aid. Total amount of financial aid awarded in 2011–12: $1,720,000.

Admissions Traditional secondary-level entrance grade is 9. For fall 2011, 238 students applied for upper-level admission, 220 were accepted, 136 enrolled. Otis-Lennon and 2 sections of ERB required. Deadline for receipt of application materials: none. Application fee required: $50. On-campus interview required.

Athletics Interscholastic: baseball (boys), basketball (b,g), crew (b,g), cross-country running (b,g), field hockey (g), football (b), golf (b,g), hockey (b,g), ice hockey (b,g), lacrosse (b,g), soccer (b,g), softball (g), squash (b,g), tennis (b,g), volleyball (g), wrestling (b); coed interscholastic: aerobics, aerobics/dance, dance, modern dance; coed intramural: aerobics/dance. 21 coaches, 1 athletic trainer.

Computers Computers are regularly used in art, library skills, newspaper, photography, science, technology, yearbook classes. Computer network features include on-campus library services, online commercial services, Internet access. Student e-mail accounts are available to students. The school has a published electronic and media policy.

Contact Mrs. Heather Newton, Director of Admissions. 716-332-6325. Fax: 716-875-6474. E-mail: hnewton@nicholsschool.org. Web site: www.nicholsschool.org.

NOBLE ACADEMY

Greensboro, North Carolina

See Special Needs Schools section.

NOBLE AND GREENOUGH SCHOOL

10 Campus Drive

Dedham, Massachusetts 02026-4099

Head of School: Mr. Robert P. Henderson Jr.

General Information Coeducational boarding and day college-preparatory school. Boarding grades 9–12, day grades 7–12. Founded: 1866. Setting: suburban. Nearest major city is Boston. Students are housed in single-sex dormitories. 187-acre campus. 12 buildings on campus. Approved or accredited by Association of Independent Schools in New England, New England Association of Schools and Colleges, The College Board, and Massachusetts Department of Education. Member of National Association of Independent Schools and Secondary School Admission Test Board. Endowment: $101 million. Total enrollment: 589. Upper school average class size: 14. Upper school faculty-student ratio: 1:7. There are 162 required school days per year for Upper School students. Upper School students typically attend 5 days per week. The average school day consists of 7 hours and 5 minutes.

Upper School Student Profile Grade 9: 114 students (54 boys, 60 girls); Grade 10: 122 students (68 boys, 54 girls); Grade 11: 124 students (59 boys, 65 girls); Grade 12: 107 students (57 boys, 50 girls). 8% of students are boarding students. 99% are state residents. 5 states are represented in upper school student body.

Faculty School total: 114. In upper school: 58 men, 56 women; 31 reside on campus.

Subjects Offered 20th century history, Advanced Placement courses, African-American literature, algebra, American history, American literature, anatomy, ancient history, art, art history, astronomy, biology, calculus, ceramics, chemistry, community service, computer programming, computer science, concert band, creative writing, drama, drawing, earth science, ecology, economics, English, English literature, environmental science, ethics, European history, expository writing, fine arts, French, genetics, geography, geometry, government/civics, grammar, health, history, independent study, Japanese, journalism, Latin, Latin American history, marine biology, mathematics, music, painting, philosophy, photography, physics, physiology, printmaking, psychology, Roman civilization, science, senior internship, senior project, social studies, Spanish, speech, statistics, theater, trigonometry, Vietnam, world history, world literature, writing.

Graduation Requirements Arts and fine arts (art, music, dance, drama), computer science, English, foreign language, mathematics, performing arts, physical education (includes health), science, social studies (includes history), 80 hours of community service must be completed.

Special Academic Programs Advanced Placement exam preparation; honors section; independent study; term-away projects; study abroad; academic accommodation for the gifted, the musically talented, and the artistically talented.

College Admission Counseling 118 students graduated in 2011; all went to college, including Boston College; Brown University; Dartmouth College; Duke University; Harvard University; Princeton University. 72% scored over 600 on SAT critical reading, 75% scored over 600 on SAT math, 80% scored over 600 on SAT writing.

Student Life Upper grades have specified standards of dress, student council, honor system. Discipline rests equally with students and faculty.

Tuition and Aid Day student tuition: $37,300; 5-day tuition and room/board: $42,500. Tuition installment plan (Tuition Management Systems). Need-based scholarship grants, need-based loans available. In 2011–12, 20% of upper-school students received aid. Total amount of financial aid awarded in 2011–12: $3,077,675.

Admissions Traditional secondary-level entrance grade is 9. For fall 2011, 497 students applied for upper-level admission, 124 were accepted, 64 enrolled. ISEE or SSAT required. Deadline for receipt of application materials: January 15. Application fee required: $50. On-campus interview required.

Athletics Interscholastic: baseball (boys), basketball (b,g), crew (b,g), cross-country running (b,g), field hockey (g), football (b); coed intramural: aerobics/dance, dance. 12 coaches, 2 athletic trainers.

Computers Computers are regularly used in English, foreign language, history, journalism, Latin, mathematics, music, science classes. Computer network features include on-campus library services, online commercial services, Internet access, Internet filtering or blocking technology, NoblesNet (first class e-mail and bulletin board with electronic conferencing capability), wireless iBooks. Campus intranet, student e-mail accounts, and computer access in designated common areas are available to students. The school has a published electronic and media policy.

Contact Ms. Jennifer Hines, Dean of Enrollment Management. 781-320-7100. Fax: 781-320-1329. E-mail: admission@nobles.edu. Web site: www.nobles.edu.

THE NORA SCHOOL

955 Sligo Avenue

Silver Spring, Maryland 20910

Head of School: David E. Mullen

General Information Coeducational day college-preparatory, arts, and technology school. Grades 9–12. Founded: 1964. Setting: urban. Nearest major city is Washington, DC. 1-acre campus. 1 building on campus. Approved or accredited by Association of Independent Schools of Greater Washington, Middle States Association of Colleges and Schools, and Maryland Department of Education. Endowment: $208,000. Total enrollment: 60. Upper school average class size: 8. Upper school faculty-student ratio: 1:6. There are 175 required school days per year for Upper School students. Upper School students typically attend 5 days per week. The average school day consists of 5 hours and 35 minutes.

Upper School Student Profile Grade 9: 12 students (9 boys, 3 girls); Grade 10: 9 students (6 boys, 3 girls); Grade 11: 18 students (11 boys, 7 girls); Grade 12: 19 students (9 boys, 10 girls).

Faculty School total: 10. In upper school: 8 men, 2 women; all have advanced degrees.

Subjects Offered African-American literature, algebra, American literature, American studies, art, art history, astronomy, biology, British literature, calculus, ceramics, chemistry, college writing, community service, computer graphics, conceptual physics, conflict resolution, crafts, creative writing, English composition, environmental science, expository writing, film and literature, forensics, geography, geometry, German, graphic design, illustration, integrated science, peace studies, peer counseling, photo shop, photography, physical education, physics, political science, pre-algebra, pre-calculus, psychology, sculpture, Shakespeare, social justice, Spanish, street law, studio art, trigonometry, U.S. history, wilderness education, women's literature, world history, world religions, writing.

Graduation Requirements Arts and fine arts (art, music, dance, drama), English, foreign language, lab science, mathematics, personal fitness, science, social studies (includes history), sports, U.S. history, wilderness education, writing, graduation portfolio. Community service is required.

Special Academic Programs Independent study; term-away projects; study at local college for college credit; academic accommodation for the gifted and the artistically talented; remedial reading and/or remedial writing; remedial math; programs in English, mathematics, general development for dyslexic students; special instructional classes for students with Attention Deficit Disorder and learning disabilities, students who have been unsuccessful in a traditional learning environment.

College Admission Counseling 15 students graduated in 2011; all went to college, including Dickinson College; Drew University; Florida Gulf Coast University; Goucher College; Loyola University Maryland; Mount Holyoke College.

Student Life Upper grades have student council. Discipline rests primarily with faculty.

Tuition and Aid Day student tuition: $23,650. Tuition installment plan (Key Tuition Payment Plan, monthly payment plans, individually arranged payment plans). Need-based scholarship grants, Black Student Fund, Latino Student Fund, Washington Scholarship Fund available. In 2011–12, 18% of upper-school students received aid. Total amount of financial aid awarded in 2011–12: $115,000.

Admissions Traditional secondary-level entrance grade is 9. For fall 2011, 41 students applied for upper-level admission, 29 were accepted, 19 enrolled. Writing sample required. Deadline for receipt of application materials: none. Application fee required: $75. On-campus interview required.

Athletics Interscholastic: basketball (boys, girls); intramural: cheering (g); coed interscholastic: soccer, softball; coed intramural: alpine skiing, backpacking, bicycling, bowling, canoeing/kayaking, climbing, cooperative games, hiking/backpacking, ice skating, kayaking, outdoor activities, outdoor adventure, rafting, rock climbing, ropes courses, skiing (downhill), table tennis, tennis, volleyball, wilderness. 2 coaches.

Computers Computers are regularly used in art, college planning, creative writing, design, drawing and design, English, graphic arts, graphic design, independent study, literary magazine, mathematics, photography, SAT preparation, writing, writing, yearbook classes. Computer network features include on-campus library services, online commercial services, Internet access, wireless campus network, Internet filtering or blocking technology. Students grades are available online. The school has a published electronic and media policy.

Contact Janette Patterson, Director of Admissions. 301-495-6672. Fax: 301-495-7829. E-mail: janette@nora-school.org. Web site: www.nora-school.org.

NORFOLK ACADEMY

1585 Wesleyan Drive

Norfolk, Virginia 23502

Head of School: Mr. Dennis G. Manning

General Information Coeducational day college-preparatory school. Grades 1–12. Founded: 1728. Setting: suburban. 70-acre campus. 14 buildings on campus. Approved or accredited by Southern Association of Colleges and Schools, Virginia Association of Independent Schools, and Virginia Department of Education. Member of National Association of Independent Schools. Endowment: $3.7 million. Total enrollment: 1,229. Upper school average class size: 15. Upper school faculty-student ratio: 1:10.

There are 175 required school days per year for Upper School students. Upper School students typically attend 5 days per week. The average school day consists of 7 hours.
Upper School Student Profile Grade 10: 131 students (62 boys, 69 girls); Grade 11: 122 students (67 boys, 55 girls); Grade 12: 117 students (61 boys, 56 girls).
Faculty School total: 124. In upper school: 39 men, 13 women; 32 have advanced degrees.
Subjects Offered Algebra, American history, American literature, art, art history, band, biology, calculus, chemistry, chorus, computer math, computer programming, computer science, dance, driver education, economics, English, English literature, environmental science, European history, film studies, fine arts, French, geography, geometry, German, government/civics, health, history, instrumental music, Italian, Latin, mathematics, music, music history, music theory, physical education, physics, science, social studies, Spanish, speech, statistics, studio art, theater arts, world history.
Graduation Requirements Arts and fine arts (art, music, dance, drama), English, foreign language, mathematics, physical education (includes health), science, social studies (includes history), 8-minute senior speech, seminar program. Community service is required.
Special Academic Programs Advanced Placement exam preparation; study abroad; academic accommodation for the gifted, the musically talented, and the artistically talented.
College Admission Counseling 115 students graduated in 2011; all went to college, including Hampden-Sydney College; James Madison University; The College of William and Mary; University of Virginia; Virginia Polytechnic Institute and State University. Mean SAT critical reading: 641, mean SAT math: 661, mean SAT writing: 627.
Student Life Upper grades have specified standards of dress, student council, honor system. Discipline rests primarily with students.
Summer Programs Enrichment, advancement, sports, art/fine arts programs offered; session focuses on academics and athletics; held both on and off campus; held at Surfing camp located at beach and Business internships; accepts boys and girls; open to students from other schools. 500 students usually enrolled. 2012 schedule: June 18 to July 27.
Tuition and Aid Day student tuition: $20,500. Tuition installment plan (Key Tuition Payment Plan, monthly payment plans). Need-based scholarship grants available. In 2011–12, 20% of upper-school students received aid.
Admissions Traditional secondary-level entrance grade is 10. For fall 2011, 19 students applied for upper-level admission, 6 were accepted, 4 enrolled. ERB Achievement Test, ERB CTP IV and Otis-Lennon School Ability Test required. Deadline for receipt of application materials: January 28. Application fee required: $35. Interview required.
Athletics Interscholastic: baseball (boys), basketball (b,g), cheering (g), crew (b,g), cross-country running (b,g), diving (b,g), field hockey (g), football (b), golf (b,g), indoor track (b,g), lacrosse (b,g), sailing (b,g), soccer (b,g), softball (g), swimming and diving (b,g), tennis (b,g), track and field (b,g), volleyball (g), winter (indoor) track (b,g), wrestling (b); intramural: dance (g), dance team (g). 2 PE instructors, 2 coaches, 3 athletic trainers.
Computers Computers are regularly used in all academic classes. Computer network features include on-campus library services, Internet access, wireless campus network, Internet filtering or blocking technology, online library resources, video production, curriculum-based software, desktop publishing, campus-wide media distribution system. Campus intranet, student e-mail accounts, and computer access in designated common areas are available to students. The school has a published electronic and media policy.
Contact Mr. James H. Lasley Jr., Director of Admissions. 757-455-5582 Ext. 5337. Fax: 757-455-3199. E-mail: jlasley@norfolkacademy.org. Web site: www.norfolkacademy.org.

NORTH CATHOLIC HIGH SCHOOL

1400 Troy Hill Road

Pittsburgh, Pennsylvania 15212

Head of School: Mr. Michael Pendred II

General Information Coeducational day college-preparatory school, affiliated with Roman Catholic Church. Grades 9–12. Founded: 1939. Setting: urban. 2 buildings on campus. Approved or accredited by Middle States Association of Colleges and Schools and Pennsylvania Department of Education. Total enrollment: 250. Upper school average class size: 20. There are 180 required school days per year for Upper School students. Upper School students typically attend 5 days per week. The average school day consists of 6 hours and 30 minutes.
Upper School Student Profile 95% of students are Roman Catholic.
Faculty School total: 20. In upper school: 10 men, 7 women.
Special Academic Programs Advanced Placement exam preparation; honors section; independent study; study at local college for college credit; academic accommodation for the gifted; remedial reading and/or remedial writing.
College Admission Counseling 60 students graduated in 2011; 59 went to college. Other: 1 entered military service.
Student Life Upper grades have uniform requirement, student council, honor system. Discipline rests primarily with faculty. Attendance at religious services is required.
Tuition and Aid Day student tuition: $8635. Tuition installment plan (SMART Tuition Payment Plan). Need-based scholarship grants available. In 2011–12, 80% of upper-school students received aid.
Admissions Iowa Tests of Basic Skills required. Deadline for receipt of application materials: none. Application fee required: $35.
Athletics Interscholastic: baseball (boys), basketball (b,g), cheering (g), football (b), softball (g), strength & conditioning (b,g), volleyball (g), weight lifting (b), weight training (b); coed interscholastic: crew, golf, soccer. 2 PE instructors, 9 coaches, 1 athletic trainer.
Computers Computer network features include Internet access, wireless campus network, Internet filtering or blocking technology. Computer access in designated common areas is available to students. Students grades are available online.
Contact Ms. Maura A. DeRiggi, Director of Admissions. 412-321-4823 Ext. 127. Fax: 412-321-0599. E-mail: deriggim@north-catholic.org. Web site: www.north-catholic.org.

NORTH COBB CHRISTIAN SCHOOL

4500 Lakeview Drive

Kennesaw, Georgia 30144

Head of School: Mr. Todd Clingman

General Information Coeducational day college-preparatory, arts, business, and religious studies school, affiliated with Christian faith. Grades PK–12. Founded: 1983. Setting: suburban. Nearest major city is Atlanta. 25-acre campus. 3 buildings on campus. Approved or accredited by Association of Christian Schools International, Georgia Accrediting Commission, and Southern Association of Colleges and Schools. Endowment: $102,225. Total enrollment: 841. Upper school average class size: 13. Upper school faculty-student ratio: 1:10. There are 180 required school days per year for Upper School students. Upper School students typically attend 5 days per week. The average school day consists of 7 hours.
Upper School Student Profile Grade 9: 64 students (38 boys, 26 girls); Grade 10: 55 students (31 boys, 24 girls); Grade 11: 72 students (33 boys, 39 girls); Grade 12: 54 students (28 boys, 26 girls). 95% of students are Christian.
Faculty School total: 75. In upper school: 11 men, 17 women; 10 have advanced degrees.
Subjects Offered Acting, Advanced Placement courses, algebra, American literature, analysis, analysis and differential calculus, anatomy and physiology, band, Bible, Bible studies, biology, British literature, British literature (honors), British literature-AP, calculus, calculus-AP, chemistry, choral music, composition, computer graphics, computer programming, computer skills, computer technology certification, computers, concert band, concert choir, dance, desktop publishing, drama, ecology, economics, economics-AP, electives, English, English literature-AP, English-AP, English/composition-AP, fine arts, French, French-AP, geometry, government, graphic arts, health, honors algebra, honors geometry, honors U.S. history, HTML design, instrumental music, journalism, keyboarding, leadership, life management skills, literature, marching band, math analysis, physical education, physical science, physics, psychology, Spanish, Spanish-AP, statistics, student government, theater, trigonometry, U.S. government, U.S. government and politics-AP, U.S. history, U.S. history-AP, U.S. literature, weight training, word processing, world governments, world history, world history-AP, world literature, world wide web design.
Graduation Requirements Arts and fine arts (art, music, dance, drama), Bible, computers, electives, English, foreign language, mathematics, physical education (includes health), science, social studies (includes history), community service, leadership practicum. Community service is required.
Special Academic Programs Advanced Placement exam preparation; honors section; study at local college for college credit; academic accommodation for the musically talented and the artistically talented.
College Admission Counseling 70 students graduated in 2011; all went to college, including Covenant College; Georgia College & State University; Georgia State University; Kennesaw State University; University of Georgia; Young Harris College. Median SAT critical reading: 570, median SAT math: 550, median SAT writing: 530, median combined SAT: 1570, median composite ACT: 24. 39% scored over 600 on SAT critical reading, 43% scored over 600 on SAT math, 22% scored over 600 on SAT writing, 35% scored over 1800 on combined SAT, 60% scored over 26 on composite ACT.
Student Life Upper grades have specified standards of dress, student council. Discipline rests primarily with faculty. Attendance at religious services is required.
Summer Programs Remediation, enrichment, sports, art/fine arts, computer instruction programs offered; session focuses on advancing skills and pleasure; held both on and off campus; held at other college campus for sports purposes; accepts boys and girls; open to students from other schools. 125 students usually enrolled. 2012 schedule: June 4 to July 27. Application deadline: May 1.
Tuition and Aid Day student tuition: $10,995–$11,545. Tuition installment plan (FACTS Tuition Payment Plan). Tuition reduction for siblings, need-based scholarship grants available. In 2011–12, 30% of upper-school students received aid. Total amount of financial aid awarded in 2011–12: $270,000.
Admissions Traditional secondary-level entrance grade is 9. For fall 2011, 36 students applied for upper-level admission, 25 were accepted, 21 enrolled. Otis-Lennon,

Stanford Achievement Test required. Deadline for receipt of application materials: none. Application fee required: $100. Interview required.
Athletics Interscholastic: aerobics (boys, girls), aerobics/dance (g), ballet (g), baseball (b), basketball (b,g), cheering (g), cross-country running (b,g), dance (g), equestrian sports (b,g), football (b), physical fitness (b,g), soccer (b,g), softball (g), swimming and diving (b,g), tennis (b,g), track and field (b,g), volleyball (g); coed interscholastic: aquatics, archery, golf, strength & conditioning, weight training. 6 PE instructors, 6 coaches, 2 athletic trainers.
Computers Computers are regularly used in art, basic skills, desktop publishing, drawing and design, graphic arts, graphic design, keyboarding, library skills, media production, video film production, word processing, yearbook classes. Computer network features include on-campus library services, Internet access, wireless campus network. Computer access in designated common areas is available to students. Students grades are available online. The school has a published electronic and media policy.
Contact Mrs. Joan Carver, Admissions Assistant. 770-975-0252 Ext. 501. Fax: 770-874-9978. E-mail: jcarver@ncchristian.org. Web site: www.ncchristian.org.

NORTH COUNTRY SCHOOL

Lake Placid, New York

See Junior Boarding Schools section.

NORTH SHORE COUNTRY DAY SCHOOL

310 Green Bay Road

Winnetka, Illinois 60093-4094

Head of School: Mr. Tom Doar III

General Information Coeducational day college-preparatory, arts, technology, global, and service-learning school. Grades PK–12. Founded: 1919. Setting: suburban. Nearest major city is Chicago. 16-acre campus. 6 buildings on campus. Approved or accredited by Independent Schools Association of the Central States and Illinois Department of Education. Member of National Association of Independent Schools and Secondary School Admission Test Board. Endowment: $17 million. Total enrollment: 500. Upper school average class size: 14. Upper school faculty-student ratio: 1:8. Upper School students typically attend 5 days per week.
Upper School Student Profile Grade 9: 51 students (23 boys, 28 girls); Grade 10: 51 students (28 boys, 23 girls); Grade 11: 51 students (27 boys, 24 girls); Grade 12: 47 students (24 boys, 23 girls).
Faculty School total: 80. In upper school: 27 men, 35 women; 42 have advanced degrees.
Subjects Offered Algebra, American history, American literature, anatomy, art, art history, Asian studies, biology, biology-AP, calculus, calculus-AP, ceramics, chemistry, chemistry-AP, computer math, computer programming, computer science, creative writing, drama, earth science, ecology, economics, English, English literature, English-AP, environmental science, European history, expository writing, fine arts, French, French-AP, geography, geometry, government/civics, grammar, industrial arts, journalism, Mandarin, marine biology, mathematics, music, photography, physical education, physics, physics-AP, science, social studies, Spanish, Spanish-AP, speech, statistics, statistics-AP, technology, theater, trigonometry, U.S. history-AP, world history, world literature, writing.
Graduation Requirements Arts and fine arts (art, music, dance, drama), computer science, English, foreign language, mathematics, physical education (includes health), physical fitness, science, service learning/internship, social studies (includes history), technology, one stage performance in four years, completion of senior service project in May, completion of one-week community service project in four years.
Special Academic Programs Advanced Placement exam preparation; independent study; term-away projects; study at local college for college credit; study abroad.
College Admission Counseling 43 students graduated in 2010; all went to college, including Claremont McKenna College; Rice University; University of Michigan; Vanderbilt University.
Student Life Upper grades have specified standards of dress, student council, honor system. Discipline rests primarily with faculty.
Tuition and Aid Day student tuition: $22,422–$23,485. Tuition installment plan (Insured Tuition Payment Plan, Key Tuition Payment Plan, monthly payment plans, individually arranged payment plans, trimester payment plan). Merit scholarship grants, need-based scholarship grants, need-based loans, middle-income loans available. In 2010–11, 15% of upper-school students received aid. Total amount of financial aid awarded in 2010–11: $1,000,000.
Admissions Traditional secondary-level entrance grade is 9. ERB and writing sample required. Deadline for receipt of application materials: March 1. Application fee required: $50. On-campus interview required.
Athletics Interscholastic: baseball (boys), basketball (b,g), cross-country running (b,g), field hockey (g), football (b), golf (b,g), indoor track & field (b,g), soccer (b,g), tennis (b,g), track and field (b,g), volleyball (g); intramural: physical training (b,g), weight lifting (b,g); coed intramural: dance, sailing. 4 PE instructors, 24 coaches, 1 athletic trainer.
Computers Computers are regularly used in accounting, all academic classes. Computer network features include on-campus library services, online commercial services, Internet access, wireless campus network, Internet filtering or blocking technology. Campus intranet and student e-mail accounts are available to students. The school has a published electronic and media policy.
Contact Ms. Hannah Ruddock, Admissions Associate. 847-441-3313. Fax: 847-446-0675. E-mail: hruddock@nscds.org. Web site: www.nscds.org.

NORTH TORONTO CHRISTIAN SCHOOL

255 Yorkland Boulevard

Toronto, Ontario M2J 1S3, Canada

Head of School: Mr. Michael Broomer

General Information Coeducational day college-preparatory school, affiliated with Protestant-Evangelical faith. Grades JK–12. Founded: 1981. Setting: urban. 6-acre campus. 1 building on campus. Approved or accredited by Association of Christian Schools International and Ontario Department of Education. Language of instruction: English. Total enrollment: 504. Upper school average class size: 25. Upper school faculty-student ratio: 1:15. There are 184 required school days per year for Upper School students. Upper School students typically attend 5 days per week. The average school day consists of 6 hours.
Faculty School total: 31. In upper school: 12 men, 11 women; 8 have advanced degrees.
Subjects Offered Accounting, biology, business, calculus, Canadian geography, Canadian law, career exploration, chemistry, civics, computer applications, discrete mathematics, economics, English, environmental studies, French, functions, geography, geometry, healthful living, information technology, instrumental music, marketing, physics, visual arts, world history, world issues, world religions.
Special Academic Programs Independent study; ESL (12 students enrolled).
College Admission Counseling 63 students graduated in 2011; 59 went to college, including Brock University; McMaster University; Queen's University at Kingston; The University of Western Ontario; University of Toronto; York University. Other: 4 had other specific plans.
Student Life Upper grades have uniform requirement. Discipline rests primarily with faculty. Attendance at religious services is required.
Tuition and Aid Day student tuition: CAN$6576. Tuition installment plan (monthly payment plans, individually arranged payment plans). Tuition reduction for siblings, bursaries available.
Admissions Traditional secondary-level entrance grade is 9. Deadline for receipt of application materials: none. Application fee required: CAN$150. On-campus interview required.
Athletics Interscholastic: rugby (girls); coed interscholastic: aquatics, badminton, ball hockey, basketball, cross-country running, golf, soccer, softball, squash, swimming and diving, table tennis, tennis, track and field, volleyball, wrestling; coed intramural: alpine skiing, canoeing/kayaking, diving, fitness, floor hockey, judo, kayaking, outdoor education, outdoor skills, street hockey, water polo. 5 PE instructors.
Computers Computers are regularly used in business applications, information technology, introduction to technology, keyboarding, mathematics, programming, science, typing, word processing classes. Computer network features include Internet access. The school has a published electronic and media policy.
Contact Mr. Gordon Cooke, Administrator. 416-491-7667. Fax: 416-491-3806. E-mail: admin@ntcs.on.ca. Web site: www.ntcs.on.ca.

NORTHWEST ACADEMY

1130 Southwest Main Street

Portland, Oregon 97205

Head of School: Mary Vinton Folberg

General Information Coeducational day college-preparatory and arts school. Grades 6–12. Founded: 1996. Setting: urban. 4 buildings on campus. Approved or accredited by Northwest Accreditation Commission, Pacific Northwest Association of Independent Schools, and Oregon Department of Education. Member of National Association of Independent Schools. Total enrollment: 137. Upper school average class size: 15. Upper school faculty-student ratio: 1:7. Upper School students typically attend 5 days per week. The average school day consists of 6 hours and 30 minutes.
Upper School Student Profile Grade 9: 20 students (9 boys, 11 girls); Grade 10: 15 students (6 boys, 9 girls); Grade 11: 13 students (5 boys, 8 girls); Grade 12: 15 students (7 boys, 8 girls).
Faculty School total: 31. In upper school: 12 men, 16 women; 11 have advanced degrees.
Subjects Offered 20th century history, acting, algebra, anatomy and physiology, animation, art history, ballet, biology, calculus, career/college preparation, chamber groups, chemistry, comparative government and politics, comparative politics, comparative religion, computer animation, computer literacy, computer music, creative writing, critical thinking, dance performance, desktop publishing, digital art, drama workshop, drawing, earth and space science, ecology, environmental systems, English literature,

European civilization, film studies, French, geometry, history of music, Holocaust studies, human anatomy, humanities, illustration, independent study, internship, introduction to digital multitrack recording techniques, jazz band, jazz dance, jazz ensemble, journalism, keyboarding, martial arts, media arts, medieval/Renaissance history, multimedia design, music composition, music history, music performance, musical theater, painting, photo shop, physics, play/screen writing, political systems, pre-calculus, printmaking, senior thesis, Shakespeare, social sciences, Spanish, student publications, tap dance, theater, trigonometry, U.S. government and politics, U.S. history, video film production, visual arts, vocal ensemble, vocal jazz, world cultures, world history, world wide web design, writing.

Graduation Requirements 4 years of English/humanities, senior thesis seminar, 3 years of both math and science, 2 years of foreign language, 7 units of credit of arts electives, community service, computer literacy, PE.

Special Academic Programs Accelerated programs; independent study; study at local college for college credit; academic accommodation for the gifted, the musically talented, and the artistically talented.

College Admission Counseling 9 students graduated in 2011; all went to college, including Duke University; Goucher College; The College of Wooster.

Student Life Upper grades have student council, honor system. Discipline rests primarily with faculty.

Tuition and Aid Day student tuition: $18,250. Tuition installment plan (FACTS Tuition Payment Plan). Need-based scholarship grants available. In 2011–12, 28% of upper-school students received aid.

Admissions Traditional secondary-level entrance grade is 9. For fall 2011, 75 students applied for upper-level admission, 70 were accepted, 55 enrolled. Admissions testing, placement test and writing sample required. Deadline for receipt of application materials: February 1. Application fee required: $100. Interview required.

Athletics Coed Intramural: aerobics/dance, artistic gym, ballet, cooperative games, dance, modern dance, tai chi, yoga.

Computers Computers are regularly used in all academic classes. Computer network features include Internet access, wireless campus network, film and audio editing, sound design, animation, Flash. Campus intranet and computer access in designated common areas are available to students. The school has a published electronic and media policy.

Contact Lainie Keslin Ettinger, Director of Admissions. 503-223-3367 Ext. 104. Fax: 503-402-1043. E-mail: lettinger@nwacademy.org. Web site: www.nwacademy.org.

NORTHWEST CATHOLIC HIGH SCHOOL

29 Wampanoag Drive

West Hartford, Connecticut 06117

Head of School: Mrs. Margaret Williamson

General Information Coeducational day college-preparatory school, affiliated with Roman Catholic Church. Grades 9–12. Founded: 1961. Setting: suburban. Nearest major city is Hartford. 1 building on campus. Approved or accredited by New England Association of Schools and Colleges and Connecticut Department of Education. Total enrollment: 643. Upper school average class size: 18. Upper school faculty-student ratio: 1:12. There are 180 required school days per year for Upper School students. Upper School students typically attend 5 days per week. The average school day consists of 6 hours and 18 minutes.

Upper School Student Profile Grade 9: 166 students (91 boys, 75 girls); Grade 10: 142 students (63 boys, 79 girls); Grade 11: 172 students (87 boys, 85 girls); Grade 12: 163 students (71 boys, 92 girls). 80% of students are Roman Catholic.

Faculty School total: 56. In upper school: 25 men, 31 women; 42 have advanced degrees.

Subjects Offered Biology-AP, calculus-AP, chemistry-AP, computer science-AP, English language and composition-AP, English literature and composition-AP, French language-AP, Latin-AP, music theory-AP, physics-AP, Spanish-AP, statistics-AP, studio art-AP, U.S. government and politics-AP, U.S. history-AP.

Graduation Requirements Arts and fine arts (art, music, dance, drama), English, foreign language, health education, mathematics, physical education (includes health), religion (includes Bible studies and theology), science, social studies (includes history), 25 hours of community service.

Special Academic Programs 15 Advanced Placement exams for which test preparation is offered; honors section; study at local college for college credit.

College Admission Counseling 130 students graduated in 2011; 128 went to college. Other: 1 entered a postgraduate year, 1 had other specific plans. Mean SAT critical reading: 540, mean SAT math: 560, mean SAT writing: 548.

Student Life Upper grades have uniform requirement, student council, honor system. Discipline rests primarily with faculty. Attendance at religious services is required.

Tuition and Aid Day student tuition: $12,760. Tuition installment plan (monthly payment plans). Tuition reduction for siblings, merit scholarship grants, need-based scholarship grants available. Total amount of financial aid awarded in 2011–12: $1,300,000.

Admissions Traditional secondary-level entrance grade is 9. High School Placement Test required. Deadline for receipt of application materials: March. Application fee required: $25.

Athletics Interscholastic: baseball (boys), basketball (b,g), cheering (g), cross-country running (b,g), field hockey (g), golf (b,g), ice hockey (b), indoor track & field (b,g), lacrosse (b,g), soccer (b,g), softball (g), tennis (b,g), track and field (b,g), volleyball (g), winter (indoor) track (b,g); intramural: basketball (b,g); coed interscholastic: diving, football, swimming and diving; coed intramural: canoeing/kayaking, dance team, flag football, indoor soccer, outdoor adventure, rappelling, rock climbing, scuba diving, skiing (downhill), snowboarding, strength & conditioning, ultimate Frisbee, weight training, whiffle ball. 1 PE instructor, 1 athletic trainer.

Computers Computers are regularly used in all academic classes. Computer network features include on-campus library services, Internet access, Internet filtering or blocking technology. Student e-mail accounts and computer access in designated common areas are available to students. Students grades are available online. The school has a published electronic and media policy.

Contact Mrs. Nancy Scully Bannon, Director of Admissions. 860-236-4221 Ext. 124. Fax: 860-570-0080. E-mail: nbannon@nwcath.org. Web site: www.northwestcatholic.org.

THE NORTHWEST SCHOOL

1415 Summit Avenue

Seattle, Washington 98122

Head of School: Ellen Taussig

General Information Coeducational boarding and day college-preparatory, arts, and ESL school. Boarding grades 9–12, day grades 6–12. Founded: 1978. Setting: urban. Students are housed in coed dormitories. 1-acre campus. 4 buildings on campus. Approved or accredited by Northwest Accreditation Commission, Pacific Northwest Association of Independent Schools, and Washington Department of Education. Member of National Association of Independent Schools. Endowment: $788,915. Total enrollment: 462. Upper school average class size: 16. Upper school faculty-student ratio: 1:9. There are 168 required school days per year for Upper School students. Upper School students typically attend 5 days per week. The average school day consists of 7 hours and 20 minutes.

Upper School Student Profile Grade 9: 71 students (38 boys, 33 girls); Grade 10: 85 students (47 boys, 38 girls); Grade 11: 90 students (41 boys, 49 girls); Grade 12: 80 students (42 boys, 38 girls). 11% of students are boarding students. 79% are state residents. 1 state is represented in upper school student body. 21% are international students. International students from China, Japan, Republic of Korea, Spain, Taiwan, and Thailand; 3 other countries represented in student body.

Faculty School total: 70. In upper school: 21 men, 33 women; 36 have advanced degrees.

Subjects Offered Advanced chemistry, algebra, astronomy, biology, calculus, ceramics, chemistry, Chinese, chorus, computer skills, contemporary problems, dance, drama, drawing, earth science, English, ESL, evolution, fiber arts, film, fine arts, French, geometry, health, history, humanities, illustration, improvisation, jazz dance, jazz ensemble, journalism, life science, literature, math analysis, mathematics, mentorship program, musical theater, orchestra, outdoor education, painting, performing arts, philosophy, photography, physical education, physical science, physics, play production, pre-algebra, pre-calculus, printmaking, Spanish, statistics, strings, textiles, theater, trigonometry, U.S. government and politics, U.S. history, visual arts, Washington State and Northwest History, water color painting, wilderness education, world history, writing.

Graduation Requirements English, foreign language, history, humanities, mathematics, physical education (includes health), science, senior project, social studies (includes history), visual and performing arts, participation in environmental maintenance program.

Special Academic Programs ESL (42 students enrolled).

College Admission Counseling 87 students graduated in 2010; 83 went to college, including Cornish College of the Arts; Oberlin College; University of California, Berkeley; University of Southern California; University of Washington; Whitman College. Other: 2 went to work, 2 had other specific plans.

Student Life Upper grades have honor system. Discipline rests primarily with faculty.

Tuition and Aid Day student tuition: $27,405; 7-day tuition and room/board: $38,975. Tuition installment plan (school's own payment plan). Need-based scholarship grants available. In 2010–11, 18% of upper-school students received aid. Total amount of financial aid awarded in 2010–11: $1,180,555.

Admissions Traditional secondary-level entrance grade is 9. For fall 2010, 226 students applied for upper-level admission, 127 were accepted, 50 enrolled. ISEE or TOEFL required. Deadline for receipt of application materials: January 13. Application fee required: $65. Interview required.

Athletics Interscholastic: basketball (boys, girls), cross-country running (b,g), soccer (b,g), track and field (b,g), ultimate Frisbee (b,g), volleyball (g); coed intramural: fitness, hiking/backpacking, outdoor education, physical fitness, rock climbing, ropes courses, skiing (cross-country), skiing (downhill). 2 PE instructors, 20 coaches.

Computers Computers are regularly used in art, English, ESL, foreign language, graphic design, health, history, humanities, journalism, library, mathematics, music, science, social studies, theater, video film production, writing, yearbook classes. Computer network features include on-campus library services, Internet access, wireless campus network, ProQuest, ABC-Cleo, JSTOR, eLibrary, CultureGrams, World Con-

flicts and Online Encyclopedias. Computer access in designated common areas is available to students. The school has a published electronic and media policy.
Contact Anne Smith, Director of Admissions. 206-682-7309. Fax: 206-467-7353. E-mail: anne.smith@northwestschool.org. Web site: www.northwestschool.org.

NORTHWEST YESHIVA HIGH SCHOOL

5017 90th Avenue Southeast

Mercer Island, Washington 98040

Head of School: Rabbi Bernie Fox

General Information Coeducational day college-preparatory and religious studies school, affiliated with Jewish faith. Grades 9–12. Founded: 1974. Setting: suburban. Nearest major city is Seattle. 2-acre campus. 3 buildings on campus. Approved or accredited by Northwest Association of Schools and Colleges and Washington Department of Education. Languages of instruction: English and Hebrew. Endowment: $1.2 million. Total enrollment: 87. Upper school average class size: 12. Upper school faculty-student ratio: 1:4. There are 180 required school days per year for Upper School students. Upper School students typically attend 5 days per week. The average school day consists of 7 hours.
Upper School Student Profile Grade 9: 23 students (13 boys, 10 girls); Grade 10: 20 students (11 boys, 9 girls); Grade 11: 21 students (12 boys, 9 girls); Grade 12: 23 students (12 boys, 11 girls). 100% of students are Jewish.
Faculty School total: 24. In upper school: 15 men, 9 women; 12 have advanced degrees.
Subjects Offered 20th century history, algebra, American legal systems, art, art history, biology, calculus, chemistry, college admission preparation, college counseling, drama, economics, English, film appreciation, fine arts, geometry, Hebrew, Hebrew scripture, integrated mathematics, Jewish history, Judaic studies, lab science, language arts, modern Western civilization, newspaper, philosophy, physical education, physics, prayer/spirituality, pre-algebra, pre-calculus, psychology, Rabbinic literature, religious studies, Spanish, Talmud, U.S. government, U.S. history, U.S. literature, Western civilization, world history, writing, yearbook.
Graduation Requirements Advanced math, arts and fine arts (art, music, dance, drama), biology, conceptual physics, Hebrew, integrated mathematics, Judaic studies, language arts, physics, Spanish, Talmud, U.S. government, U.S. history, world history. Community service is required.
Special Academic Programs Independent study; academic accommodation for the gifted; remedial reading and/or remedial writing; remedial math; special instructional classes for deaf students; ESL (1 student enrolled).
College Admission Counseling 16 students graduated in 2011; 10 went to college, including Brandeis University; University of Washington; Yeshiva University. Other: 6 had other specific plans. Median SAT critical reading: 620, median SAT math: 620, median SAT writing: 630, median combined SAT: 1870. 53% scored over 600 on SAT critical reading, 67% scored over 600 on SAT math, 60% scored over 600 on SAT writing, 53% scored over 1800 on combined SAT.
Student Life Upper grades have specified standards of dress, student council, honor system. Discipline rests primarily with faculty. Attendance at religious services is required.
Tuition and Aid Day student tuition: $14,175. Tuition installment plan (monthly payment plans, individually arranged payment plans). Need-based scholarship grants available. In 2011–12, 50% of upper-school students received aid. Total amount of financial aid awarded in 2011–12: $465,591.
Admissions Traditional secondary-level entrance grade is 9. Deadline for receipt of application materials: none. Application fee required: $250. Interview required.
Athletics Interscholastic: basketball (boys, girls), cross-country running (b,g), golf (b,g), volleyball (g); coed interscholastic: cross-country running, softball. 5 PE instructors, 5 coaches.
Computers Computer network features include Internet access. Student e-mail accounts are available to students.
Contact Mr. Ian Weiner, Director of Student Services. 206-232-5272. Fax: 206-232-2711. E-mail: iw@nyhs.net. Web site: www.nyhs.net.

NORTHWOOD SCHOOL

PO Box 1070

92 Northwood Road

Lake Placid, New York 12946

Head of School: Edward M. Good

General Information Coeducational boarding and day college-preparatory and arts school. Grades 9–PG. Founded: 1905. Setting: small town. Nearest major city is Albany. Students are housed in single-sex dormitories. 80-acre campus. 8 buildings on campus. Approved or accredited by New York State Association of Independent Schools and The Association of Boarding Schools. Member of National Association of Independent Schools and Secondary School Admission Test Board. Endowment: $8 million. Total enrollment: 182. Upper school average class size: 9. Upper school faculty-student ratio: 1:6. There are 180 required school days per year for Upper School students. Upper School students typically attend 5 days per week. The average school day consists of 7 hours.
Upper School Student Profile Grade 9: 17 students (8 boys, 9 girls); Grade 10: 48 students (30 boys, 18 girls); Grade 11: 58 students (38 boys, 20 girls); Grade 12: 59 students (38 boys, 21 girls). 79% of students are boarding students. 39% are state residents. 19 states are represented in upper school student body. 36% are international students. International students from Canada, China, Finland, Mexico, Republic of Korea, and Spain; 6 other countries represented in student body.
Faculty School total: 33. In upper school: 22 men, 8 women; 15 have advanced degrees; 17 reside on campus.
Subjects Offered Algebra, American history, American literature, art, biology, calculus, ceramics, chemistry, computer science, drama, earth science, English, English literature, ensembles, environmental science, expository writing, fiber arts, French, geography, geology, geometry, government/civics, great issues, health, history, journalism, mathematics, music, photography, physical education, physics, psychology, SAT preparation, science, social studies, sociology, Spanish, theater, trigonometry, world history.
Graduation Requirements Arts and fine arts (art, music, dance, drama), English, foreign language, mathematics, physical education (includes health), science, social studies (includes history).
Special Academic Programs 5 Advanced Placement exams for which test preparation is offered; honors section; independent study; remedial reading and/or remedial writing; ESL (25 students enrolled).
College Admission Counseling 69 students graduated in 2011; 60 went to college, including Clarkson University; New York University; Penn State University Park; Skidmore College; St. Lawrence University; Syracuse University. Other: 3 entered a postgraduate year, 6 had other specific plans. Median SAT critical reading: 520, median SAT math: 500, median SAT writing: 510.
Student Life Upper grades have specified standards of dress, student council, honor system. Discipline rests primarily with faculty.
Tuition and Aid Day student tuition: $25,450; 7-day tuition and room/board: $44,425. Tuition installment plan (The Tuition Plan). Need-based scholarship grants available. In 2011–12, 56% of upper-school students received aid.
Admissions Traditional secondary-level entrance grade is 11. For fall 2011, 255 students applied for upper-level admission, 163 were accepted, 99 enrolled. Any standardized test or TOEFL or SLEP required. Deadline for receipt of application materials: none. Application fee required: $50. Interview required.
Athletics Interscholastic: crew (boys, girls), hockey (b,g), ice hockey (b,g), ice skating (b,g), lacrosse (b,g), nordic skiing (b,g), ski jumping (b,g), skiing (downhill) (b,g), soccer (b,g), telemark skiing (b,g), tennis (b,g); intramural: hockey (b,g), ice hockey (b,g), ice skating (b,g), skiing (downhill) (b,g), snowboarding (b,g); coed interscholastic: alpine skiing, figure skating, fitness, freestyle skiing, golf, nordic skiing, skiing (cross-country), snowboarding, telemark skiing; coed intramural: alpine skiing, backpacking, bicycling, canoeing/kayaking, climbing, combined training, cross-country running, figure skating, fishing, fitness, fly fishing, freestyle skiing, golf, hiking/backpacking, jogging, kayaking, luge, mountain biking, mountaineering, nordic skiing, outdoor adventure, physical training, rafting, rappelling, rock climbing, ropes courses, rowing, running, skiing (cross-country), skiing (downhill), snowboarding, street hockey, strength & conditioning, tennis, walking, wall climbing, weight training, wilderness, wilderness survival, wildernessways, winter walking. 1 coach, 1 athletic trainer.
Computers Computers are regularly used in English, foreign language, history, mathematics, science classes. Computer network features include on-campus library services, online commercial services, Internet access, wireless campus network, Internet filtering or blocking technology. Students grades are available online. The school has a published electronic and media policy.
Contact Timothy Weaver, Director of Admissions. 518-523-3382 Ext. 205. Fax: 518-523-3405. E-mail: weavert@northwoodschool.com. Web site: www.northwoodschool.com.

See Display on next page and Close-Up on page 656.

THE NORWICH FREE ACADEMY

305 Broadway

Norwich, Connecticut 06360

Head of School: Mr. David J Klein

General Information Coeducational day college-preparatory, general academic, arts, business, vocational, bilingual studies, and technology school. Grades 9–12. Founded: 1856. Setting: suburban. 15-acre campus. 11 buildings on campus. Approved or accredited by New England Association of Schools and Colleges and Connecticut Department of Education. Member of National Association of Independent Schools. Total enrollment: 2,315. Upper school average class size: 24. Upper school faculty-student ratio: 1:22. There are 181 required school days per year for Upper School students. Upper School students typically attend 5 days per week. The average school day consists of 7 hours.
Faculty School total: 171. In upper school: 66 men, 105 women.
Special Academic Programs 20 Advanced Placement exams for which test preparation is offered; honors section; study at local college for college credit; remedial

reading and/or remedial writing; remedial math; special instructional classes for students with learning disabilities, Attention Deficit Disorder, emotional and behavioral problems, and dyslexia; ESL (90 students enrolled).

College Admission Counseling 533 students graduated in 2011; 444 went to college. Other: 30 went to work, 10 entered military service, 33 entered a postgraduate year, 16 had other specific plans. Mean SAT critical reading: 513, mean SAT math: 513, mean SAT writing: 502, mean composite ACT: 24.

Student Life Upper grades have specified standards of dress, student council, honor system. Discipline rests primarily with faculty.

Summer Programs Remediation, enrichment, ESL, sports programs offered; held on campus; accepts boys and girls; open to students from other schools. 250 students usually enrolled. 2012 schedule: July 1 to July 29. Application deadline: June 1.

Tuition and Aid Day student tuition: $11,400.

Admissions Traditional secondary-level entrance grade is 9. ACT-Explore required. Deadline for receipt of application materials: none. No application fee required. Interview required.

Athletics Interscholastic: baseball (boys), basketball (b,g), cheering (b,g), cross-country running (b,g), fencing (b,g), field hockey (g), football (b), golf (b,g), gymnastics (g), hockey (b), ice hockey (b), indoor track (b,g), indoor track & field (b,g), lacrosse (b,g), running (b,g), soccer (b,g), softball (g), Special Olympics (b,g), swimming and diving (b,g), tennis (b,g), track and field (b,g), volleyball (b,g), winter (indoor) track (b,g), wrestling (b); intramural: skiing (downhill) (b,g), snowboarding (b,g); coed interscholastic: drill team; coed intramural: dance, dance team, physical fitness, weight lifting, weight training. 4 PE instructors, 25 coaches, 5 athletic trainers.

Computers Computer network features include on-campus library services, Internet access, Internet filtering or blocking technology. The school has a published electronic and media policy.

Contact Mrs. Jeanne M. Elliott, Director of Guidance. 860-425-5601. Fax: 860-889-7124. E-mail: elliottj@norwichfreeacademy.com. Web site: www.norwichfreeacademy.com.

NOTRE DAME ACADEMY

2851 Overland Avenue

Los Angeles, California 90064

Head of School: Mrs. Joan Gumaer Tyhurst

General Information Girls' day college-preparatory, arts, religious studies, technology, and athletics school, affiliated with Roman Catholic Church. Grades 9–12. Founded: 1949. Setting: urban. 1 building on campus. Approved or accredited by Western Association of Schools and Colleges, Western Catholic Education Association, and California Department of Education. Total enrollment: 400. Upper school average class size: 23. Upper school faculty-student ratio: 1:13.

Upper School Student Profile 86% of students are Roman Catholic.

Faculty School total: 31. In upper school: 7 men, 24 women.

Subjects Offered Advanced studio art-AP, algebra, American history, art, art history-AP, athletic training, biology, biology-AP, calculus, calculus-AP, campus ministry, chemistry, chemistry-AP, choir, Christian and Hebrew scripture, community service, computer science, dance, design, digital photography, drama, drama performance, economics, English, English language and composition-AP, English literature and composition-AP, French, French-AP, geometry, government and politics-AP, government/civics, health, history, honors geometry, Japanese, law, leadership, photography, physical education, physics, pre-calculus, psychology, psychology-AP, religion, Spanish, Spanish language-AP, speech and oral interpretations, statistics, trigonometry, U.S. government and politics-AP, U.S. history-AP, world civilizations, world history-AP.

Graduation Requirements Arts and fine arts (art, music, dance, drama), computer science, English, foreign language, mathematics, physical education (includes health), religion (includes Bible studies and theology), science, social studies (includes history), speech. Community service is required.

Special Academic Programs 14 Advanced Placement exams for which test preparation is offered; honors section.

College Admission Counseling 99 students graduated in 2011; all went to college, including California State Polytechnic University, Pomona; Cornell University; Loyola Marymount University; University of California, Irvine; University of California, Los Angeles; University of Southern California. Mean SAT critical reading: 571, mean SAT math: 552, mean SAT writing: 597, mean combined SAT: 1720.

Student Life Upper grades have uniform requirement, student council, honor system. Discipline rests primarily with faculty. Attendance at religious services is required.

Summer Programs Remediation, enrichment, advancement, sports, art/fine arts, computer instruction programs offered; session focuses on academic advancement, required prerequisites, enrichment; held both on and off campus; held at various athletic facilities; accepts boys and girls; open to students from other schools. 300 students usually enrolled. 2012 schedule: June 11 to July 13. Application deadline: May.

Tuition and Aid Day student tuition: $10,950. Tuition installment plan (FACTS Tuition Payment Plan, monthly payment plans, quarterly and semester payment plans). Merit scholarship grants, need-based scholarship grants, paying campus jobs available. In 2011–12, 29% of upper school students received aid.

Admissions Traditional secondary-level entrance grade is 9. For fall 2011, 230 students applied for upper-level admission, 107 enrolled. High School Placement Test (closed version) from Scholastic Testing Service required. Deadline for receipt of application materials: January 6. Application fee required: $75. On-campus interview required.
Athletics Interscholastic: basketball, cross-country running, dance, soccer, softball, swimming and diving, track and field, volleyball. 1 PE instructor, 19 coaches, 1 athletic trainer.
Computers Computers are regularly used in all academic, computer applications, design, journalism, photography, yearbook classes. Computer network features include on-campus library services, online commercial services, Internet access, wireless campus network, Internet filtering or blocking technology. Student e-mail accounts and computer access in designated common areas are available to students. Students grades are available online. The school has a published electronic and media policy.
Contact Ms. Brigid Williams, Director of Admissions. 310-839-5289 Ext. 218. Fax: 310-839-7957. E-mail: bwilliams@ndala.com. Web site: www.ndala.com.

NOTRE DAME COLLEGE PREP

7655 West Dempster Street

Niles, Illinois 60714-2098

Head of School: Mr. Daniel Tully

General Information Boys' day college-preparatory, arts, business, religious studies, and technology school, affiliated with Roman Catholic Church. Grades 9–12. Founded: 1955. Setting: suburban. Nearest major city is Chicago. 28-acre campus. 1 building on campus. Approved or accredited by National Catholic Education Association, North Central Association of Colleges and Schools, and Illinois Department of Education. Endowment: $1.2 million. Total enrollment: 802. Upper school average class size: 17. Upper school faculty-student ratio: 1:17. There are 174 required school days per year for Upper School students. Upper School students typically attend 5 days per week. The average school day consists of 6 hours and 50 minutes.
Upper School Student Profile Grade 9: 205 students (205 boys); Grade 10: 202 students (202 boys); Grade 11: 172 students (172 boys); Grade 12: 223 students (223 boys). 87% of students are Roman Catholic.
Faculty School total: 57. In upper school: 31 men, 26 women; 33 have advanced degrees.
Subjects Offered 3-dimensional art, accounting, advanced biology, advanced chemistry, advanced math, algebra, American literature, art, art history, art history-AP, band, Bible as literature, Bible studies, bioethics, biology, biology-AP, British literature, British literature (honors), calculus, calculus-AP, Catholic belief and practice, chemistry, chemistry-AP, choir, comedy, computer literacy, computer programming, concert band, contemporary history, creative writing, drama, dramatic arts, economics, English, English-AP, environmental science, ESL, ethics, European history-AP, film appreciation, fine arts, geography, geometry, government-AP, health, history, honors algebra, honors English, honors geometry, Italian, jazz, jazz band, journalism, Latin, Latin-AP, leadership, mathematics, music, music appreciation, music theory, philosophy, physical education, physics, pre-calculus, psychology, reading/study skills, religion, social studies, sociology, Spanish, Spanish-AP, speech, statistics, studio art-AP, theology, trigonometry, U.S. history, U.S. history-AP, Web site design, weight training, weightlifting, Western civilization, world literature, world religions.
Graduation Requirements Algebra, arts and fine arts (art, music, dance, drama), biology, computer literacy, English, foreign language, geometry, mathematics, physical education (includes health), religion (includes Bible studies and theology), science, social studies (includes history), U.S. history, Western civilization, four years of religious retreats and community services.
Special Academic Programs 11 Advanced Placement exams for which test preparation is offered; honors section; study at local college for college credit; academic accommodation for the gifted; remedial reading and/or remedial writing; remedial math; special instructional classes for remedial religion, science and social studies; ESL.
College Admission Counseling 210 students graduated in 2011; 203 went to college, including DePaul University; Illinois State University; Marquette University; The University of Iowa; University of Illinois at Chicago; University of Illinois at Urbana–Champaign. Other: 3 went to work, 2 entered military service, 2 had other specific plans. Mean composite ACT: 24. 30% scored over 26 on composite ACT.
Student Life Upper grades have specified standards of dress, student council, honor system. Discipline rests primarily with faculty. Attendance at religious services is required.
Summer Programs Remediation, sports, art/fine arts, computer instruction programs offered; session focuses on remediation/make up; held on campus; accepts boys and girls; open to students from other schools. 200 students usually enrolled. 2012 schedule: May 29 to July 27.
Tuition and Aid Day student tuition: $9300. Tuition installment plan (The Tuition Plan, monthly payment plans). Tuition reduction for siblings, merit scholarship grants, need-based scholarship grants, paying campus jobs available. In 2011–12, 32% of upper-school students received aid; total upper-school merit-scholarship money awarded: $80,000. Total amount of financial aid awarded in 2011–12: $3,600,000.
Admissions Traditional secondary-level entrance grade is 9. For fall 2011, 238 students applied for upper-level admission, 232 were accepted, 205 enrolled. ACT-Explore or TOEFL or SLEP required. Deadline for receipt of application materials: June 1. Application fee required: $25. Interview recommended.
Athletics Interscholastic: baseball, basketball, bowling, cross-country running, diving, football, golf, ice hockey, lacrosse, soccer, swimming and diving, tennis, track and field, volleyball, wrestling; intramural: baseball, basketball, boxing, combined training, flag football, floor hockey, football, lacrosse, outdoor adventure, paddle tennis, physical fitness, softball, table tennis, ultimate Frisbee, volleyball, weight lifting, weight training, wrestling. 4 PE instructors, 25 coaches, 1 athletic trainer.
Computers Computers are regularly used in accounting, art, computer applications, English, geography, health, history, science, Web site design classes. Computer network features include on-campus library services, Internet access, Internet filtering or blocking technology, college search and scholarships. Computer access in designated common areas is available to students. Students grades are available online. The school has a published electronic and media policy.
Contact Mr. Paul W. Tokarz, Director of Enrollment. 847-779-8616. Fax: 847-965-2975. E-mail: ptokarz@nddons.org. Web site: www.nddons.org.

NOTRE DAME HIGH SCHOOL

596 South Second Street

San Jose, California 95112

Head of School: Mrs. Mary Elizabeth Riley

General Information Girls' day college-preparatory, arts, religious studies, and technology school, affiliated with Roman Catholic Church. Grades 9–12. Founded: 1851. Setting: urban. 2-acre campus. 4 buildings on campus. Approved or accredited by Western Association of Schools and Colleges, Western Catholic Education Association, and California Department of Education. Total enrollment: 620. Upper school average class size: 27. Upper school faculty-student ratio: 1:13. There are 173 required school days per year for Upper School students. Upper School students typically attend 5 days per week. The average school day consists of 6 hours.
Upper School Student Profile Grade 9: 155 students (155 girls); Grade 10: 168 students (168 girls); Grade 11: 146 students (146 girls); Grade 12: 151 students (151 girls). 66% of students are Roman Catholic.
Faculty School total: 46. In upper school: 5 men, 41 women; 37 have advanced degrees.
Subjects Offered Advanced biology, advanced chemistry, Advanced Placement courses, algebra, art, ASB Leadership, athletics, Basic programming, biology, biology-AP, calculus, calculus-AP, campus ministry, ceramics, chemistry, Christian and Hebrew scripture, computer programming, computer science, creative writing, dance, decision making skills, digital photography, drama, drama performance, economics, English, English language and composition-AP, English literature, English literature and composition-AP, environmental science-AP, film and literature, fine arts, French, French language-AP, French literature-AP, geography, geometry, global studies, government/civics, healthful living, honors algebra, honors English, honors geometry, honors U.S. history, honors world history, journalism, library research, library skills, mathematics, modern world history, moral and social development, musical theater, painting, peer counseling, peer ministry, philosophy, photography, physical education, physical fitness, physics, post-calculus, pre-calculus, psychology, psychology-AP, public speaking, religion, research skills, robotics, science, service learning/internship, social justice, social psychology, social studies, Spanish, Spanish language-AP, Spanish literature-AP, speech and debate, statistics, study skills, theater, trigonometry, U.S. government, U.S. government and politics-AP, U.S. history, U.S. history-AP, video film production, Web site design, women in society, world history, world history-AP, world religions, yearbook.
Graduation Requirements Arts and fine arts (art, music, dance, drama), computer science, English, foreign language, mathematics, physical education (includes health), religion (includes Bible studies and theology), science, social studies (includes history), community service learning program.
Special Academic Programs 10 Advanced Placement exams for which test preparation is offered; honors section; independent study; study at local college for college credit.
College Admission Counseling 148 students graduated in 2010; all went to college, including Loyola Marymount University; Saint Mary's College of California; San Jose State University; Santa Clara University; University of California, Davis; University of San Francisco. Median SAT critical reading: 570, median SAT math: 575, median SAT writing: 580. 41% scored over 600 on SAT critical reading, 43% scored over 600 on SAT math, 45% scored over 600 on SAT writing.
Student Life Upper grades have uniform requirement, student council, honor system. Discipline rests primarily with faculty. Attendance at religious services is required.
Tuition and Aid Day student tuition: $14,250. Tuition installment plan (FACTS Tuition Payment Plan, monthly payment plans, annual payment plan, 2-payment plan). Merit scholarship grants, need-based scholarship grants, paying campus jobs, individual sponsored grants available. In 2010–11, 22% of upper-school students received aid; total upper-school merit-scholarship money awarded: $6600. Total amount of financial aid awarded in 2010–11: $700,000.

Admissions Traditional secondary-level entrance grade is 9. For fall 2010, 388 students applied for upper-level admission, 273 were accepted, 155 enrolled. High School Placement Test required. Deadline for receipt of application materials: January 26. Application fee required: $60.

Athletics Interscholastic: basketball, cross-country running, golf, lacrosse, soccer, softball, swimming and diving, tennis, track and field, volleyball; intramural: badminton, basketball, volleyball. 1 PE instructor, 25 coaches, 1 athletic trainer.

Computers Computers are regularly used in all academic, English, foreign language, history, mathematics, science classes. Computer network features include on-campus library services, online commercial services, Internet access, wireless campus network, Internet filtering or blocking technology. Student e-mail accounts are available to students. Students grades are available online. The school has a published electronic and media policy.

Contact Ms. Diana Hernandez, Director of Admissions. 408-294-1113. Fax: 408-293-9779. E-mail: dhernandez@ndsj.org. Web site: ndsj.org.

NOTRE DAME HIGH SCHOOL

601 Lawrence Road

Lawrenceville, New Jersey 08648

Head of School: Mr. Barry Edward Breen and Ms. Mary Liz Ivins

General Information Coeducational day college-preparatory school, affiliated with Roman Catholic Church. Grades 9–12. Founded: 1957. Setting: suburban. Nearest major city is Trenton. 100-acre campus. 1 building on campus. Approved or accredited by Middle States Association of Colleges and Schools, National Catholic Education Association, and New Jersey Department of Education. Total enrollment: 1,266. Upper school average class size: 24. Upper school faculty-student ratio: 1:23. There are 180 required school days per year for Upper School students. Upper School students typically attend 5 days per week. The average school day consists of 6 hours and 30 minutes.

Upper School Student Profile Grade 9: 327 students (168 boys, 159 girls); Grade 10: 333 students (170 boys, 163 girls); Grade 11: 288 students (156 boys, 132 girls); Grade 12: 318 students (177 boys, 141 girls). 88% of students are Roman Catholic.

Faculty School total: 96. In upper school: 35 men, 61 women; 42 have advanced degrees.

Subjects Offered 20th century history, 3-dimensional art, 3-dimensional design, accounting, acting, advanced chemistry, advanced computer applications, advanced math, Advanced Placement courses, algebra, American history, American history-AP, American literature, ancient world history, applied music, art, art and culture, athletics, Basic programming, Bible studies, biology, biology-AP, British literature, business, business applications, business studies, calculus, calculus-AP, Catholic belief and practice, ceramics, chemistry, chemistry-AP, choir, Christian doctrine, comparative religion, computer applications, computer science, concert band, concert choir, constitutional law, contemporary issues, creative writing, dance, dance performance, discrete mathematics, drama, driver education, ecology, environmental systems, economics, English, English composition, English literature-AP, environmental science-AP, etymology, European history-AP, film studies, first aid, French, geometry, German, German literature, health education, honors algebra, honors English, honors world history, Italian, Japanese, journalism, language-AP, Latin, law, leadership and service, leadership education training, literature-AP, madrigals, math review, peer ministry, philosophy, photography, physical education, physics, physics-AP, piano, portfolio art, pre-algebra, pre-calculus, probability and statistics, psychology, psychology-AP, public speaking, reading/study skills, SAT preparation, scripture, senior internship, senior project, sociology, Spanish, Spanish literature, speech and debate, sports medicine, U.S. government, U.S. government and politics-AP, U.S. literature, women spirituality and faith, world history, world literature, writing.

Graduation Requirements Biology, English, foreign language, integrated technology fundamentals, lab science, mathematics, physical education (includes health), religion (includes Bible studies and theology), U.S. history, world history, service-learning. Community service is required.

Special Academic Programs 14 Advanced Placement exams for which test preparation is offered; honors section; independent study; study at local college for college credit; remedial reading and/or remedial writing; remedial math.

College Admission Counseling 315 students graduated in 2010; 312 went to college, including Duquesne University; Penn State University Park; Rutgers, The State University of New Jersey, New Brunswick; Saint Joseph's University; The College of New Jersey. Other: 1 went to work, 2 entered military service. Mean SAT critical reading: 556, mean SAT math: 557, mean SAT writing: 554, mean combined SAT: 1667. 30% scored over 600 on SAT critical reading, 34% scored over 600 on SAT math, 28% scored over 600 on SAT writing, 26% scored over 1800 on combined SAT.

Student Life Upper grades have uniform requirement, student council, honor system. Discipline rests primarily with faculty. Attendance at religious services is required.

Tuition and Aid Day student tuition: $9900. Tuition installment plan (Tuition Management Systems Plan). Tuition reduction for siblings, need-based scholarship grants available. In 2010–11, 10% of upper-school students received aid. Total amount of financial aid awarded in 2010–11: $180,000.

Admissions Traditional secondary-level entrance grade is 9. For fall 2010, 500 students applied for upper-level admission, 400 were accepted, 327 enrolled. Scholastic Testing Service High School Placement Test required. Deadline for receipt of application materials: November 30. Application fee required: $50. On-campus interview required.

Athletics Interscholastic: baseball (boys), basketball (b,g), cheering (g), cross-country running (b,g), dance (b,g), field hockey (g), football (b), golf (b,g), ice hockey (b), indoor track (b,g), lacrosse (b,g), soccer (b,g), softball (g), swimming and diving (b,g), tennis (b,g), track and field (b,g), winter (indoor) track (b,g), wrestling (b); intramural: touch football (g), volleyball (b,g); coed interscholastic: cheering, diving, fitness, strength & conditioning; coed intramural: Frisbee, outdoor activities, outdoor recreation, physical fitness, ultimate Frisbee, volleyball, weight lifting, weight training. 9 PE instructors, 65 coaches, 1 athletic trainer.

Computers Computers are regularly used in all academic classes. Computer network features include on-campus library services, online commercial services, Internet access, wireless campus network, Internet filtering or blocking technology. Campus intranet and computer access in designated common areas are available to students. Students grades are available online. The school has a published electronic and media policy.

Contact Ms. Peggy Miller, Director of Enrollment Management. 609-882-7900 Ext. 139. Fax: 609-882-6599. E-mail: miller@ndnj.org. Web site: www.ndnj.org.

NOTRE DAME HIGH SCHOOL

2701 Vermont Avenue

Chattanooga, Tennessee 37404

Head of School: Mr. Perry L. Storey

General Information Coeducational day college-preparatory, arts, religious studies, technology, and Microsoft IT Academy Certification school, affiliated with Roman Catholic Church. Grades 9–12. Founded: 1876. Setting: urban. 22-acre campus. 3 buildings on campus. Approved or accredited by Southern Association of Colleges and Schools and Tennessee Department of Education. Endowment: $750,000. Total enrollment: 407. Upper school average class size: 18. Upper school faculty-student ratio: 1:10. There are 180 required school days per year for Upper School students. Upper School students typically attend 5 days per week. The average school day consists of 5 hours and 50 minutes.

Upper School Student Profile Grade 9: 115 students (57 boys, 58 girls); Grade 10: 82 students (42 boys, 40 girls); Grade 11: 107 students (49 boys, 58 girls); Grade 12: 103 students (54 boys, 49 girls). 77% of students are Roman Catholic.

Faculty School total: 40. In upper school: 15 men, 25 women; 30 have advanced degrees.

Subjects Offered 3-dimensional art, ACT preparation, Advanced Placement courses, algebra, American history-AP, American literature, anatomy, anatomy and physiology, art-AP, band, biology, biology-AP, British literature, calculus, Catholic belief and practice, chemistry, choir, civics, conceptual physics, creative dance, criminal justice, drama, economics, electives, English composition, English literature, English-AP, environmental science-AP, European history-AP, foreign language, French, geometry, German, government, government/civics, health and wellness, history-AP, honors algebra, honors English, honors geometry, honors U.S. history, honors world history, Latin, physics, religion, Spanish, U.S. government and politics-AP, weight training, wellness, world geography, world history, world history-AP, writing, yoga.

Special Academic Programs Advanced Placement exam preparation; honors section; independent study; study at local college for college credit.

College Admission Counseling 126 students graduated in 2011; 125 went to college, including Auburn University; Middle Tennessee State University; The University of Tennessee; The University of Tennessee at Chattanooga; University of Georgia. Other: 1 had other specific plans.

Student Life Upper grades have uniform requirement, student council, honor system. Discipline rests primarily with faculty. Attendance at religious services is required.

Summer Programs Enrichment, sports, art/fine arts programs offered; session focuses on enrichment; held both on and off campus; held at various sites in Chattanooga; accepts boys and girls; open to students from other schools. 250 students usually enrolled. 2012 schedule: June 4 to July 27. Application deadline: April 1.

Tuition and Aid Day student tuition: $9150–$11,754. Tuition installment plan (Insured Tuition Payment Plan, FACTS Tuition Payment Plan, monthly payment plans, individually arranged payment plans). Tuition reduction for siblings, need-based scholarship grants available. In 2011–12, 30% of upper-school students received aid. Total amount of financial aid awarded in 2011–12: $378,271.

Admissions Traditional secondary-level entrance grade is 9. ACT-Explore required. Deadline for receipt of application materials: none. Application fee required: $100. On-campus interview required.

Athletics Interscholastic: aerobics/dance (girls), baseball (b), basketball (b,g), bowling (b,g), cross-country running (b,g), dance (g), dance squad (g), dance team (g), diving (b,g), football (b), golf (b,g), modern dance (g), physical training (b,g), running (b,g), soccer (b,g), softball (g), swimming and diving (b,g), tennis (b,g), track and field (b,g), volleyball (g), weight training (b,g), wrestling (b); intramural: aerobics/dance (g), cheering (g), indoor soccer (b), indoor track (b,g), lacrosse (b,g); coed interscholastic: cheering, yoga; coed intramural: backpacking, canoeing/kayaking, climbing, crew, hiking/backpacking, kayaking, mountaineering, outdoors, rafting, rappelling, rock climbing, rowing, skiing (downhill), snowboarding, wall climbing. 5 PE instructors, 30 coaches, 2 athletic trainers.

Computers Computers are regularly used in information technology classes. Computer network features include on-campus library services, Internet access, wireless campus network, Internet filtering or blocking technology, language software labs, Microsoft IT Academy Training. Student e-mail accounts and computer access in designated common areas are available to students. Students grades are available online. The school has a published electronic and media policy.

Contact Ms. Jenny Rittgers, Admissions Director. 423-624-4618 Ext. 1004. Fax: 423-624-4621. E-mail: admissions@myndhs.com. Web site: www.myndhs.com.

NOTRE DAME JUNIOR/SENIOR HIGH SCHOOL

60 Spangenburg Avenue

East Stroudsburg, Pennsylvania 18301-2799

Head of School: Mr. Jeffrey Neill Lyons

General Information Coeducational day college-preparatory, arts, and religious studies school, affiliated with Roman Catholic Church. Grades 7–12. Founded: 1967. Setting: suburban. 40-acre campus. 4 buildings on campus. Approved or accredited by Middle States Association of Colleges and Schools, National Catholic Education Association, and Pennsylvania Department of Education. Total enrollment: 233. Upper school average class size: 25. Upper school faculty-student ratio: 1:15. There are 180 required school days per year for Upper School students. Upper School students typically attend 5 days per week. The average school day consists of 6 hours and 30 minutes.

Upper School Student Profile Grade 7: 22 students (7 boys, 15 girls); Grade 8: 40 students (19 boys, 21 girls); Grade 9: 32 students (14 boys, 18 girls); Grade 10: 45 students (20 boys, 25 girls); Grade 11: 49 students (22 boys, 27 girls); Grade 12: 45 students (20 boys, 25 girls). 88% of students are Roman Catholic.

Faculty School total: 25. In upper school: 9 men, 16 women; 12 have advanced degrees.

Graduation Requirements Lab/keyboard, mathematics, moral theology, physical education (includes health), physical science, religion (includes Bible studies and theology), senior project, U.S. history, U.S. literature, word processing, world cultures, world religions.

Special Academic Programs Advanced Placement exam preparation; honors section; study at local college for college credit.

College Admission Counseling 58 students graduated in 2011; 57 went to college, including Marywood University; Mount St. Mary's University; Penn State University Park; Saint Joseph's University; Temple University; The University of Scranton. Other: 1 went to work. Median SAT critical reading: 500, median SAT math: 460, median SAT writing: 500, median combined SAT: 1460. 10% scored over 600 on SAT critical reading, 15% scored over 600 on SAT math, 10% scored over 600 on SAT writing, 25% scored over 1800 on combined SAT.

Student Life Upper grades have uniform requirement, student council. Discipline rests primarily with faculty. Attendance at religious services is required.

Tuition and Aid Tuition installment plan (FACTS Tuition Payment Plan). Tuition reduction for siblings, need-based scholarship grants available. In 2011–12, 30% of upper-school students received aid.

Admissions Traditional secondary-level entrance grade is 7. Achievement tests or TerraNova required. Deadline for receipt of application materials: May 1. No application fee required. Interview required.

Athletics Interscholastic: baseball (boys), basketball (b,g), cheering (g), field hockey (g), soccer (b,g), softball (g), swimming and diving (b,g), tennis (b,g), winter soccer (b,g); coed interscholastic: golf, soccer; coed intramural: cross-country running, indoor soccer, jogging, strength & conditioning. 2 PE instructors, 15 coaches, 1 athletic trainer.

Computers Computer network features include on-campus library services, Internet access, Internet filtering or blocking technology. The school has a published electronic and media policy.

Contact Mr. Jeffrey Neill Lyons, Principal. 570-421-0466. Fax: 570-476-0629. E-mail: principal@ndhigh.org. Web site: www.ndhigh.org.

OAKCREST SCHOOL

850 Balls Hill Road

McLean, Virginia 22101

Head of School: Ms. Ellen M. Cavanagh

General Information Girls' day college-preparatory school. Grades 6–12. Founded: 1976. Setting: urban. Approved or accredited by Virginia Department of Education. Total enrollment: 187. Upper school average class size: 14.

Upper School Student Profile Grade 6: 19 students (19 girls); Grade 7: 25 students (25 girls); Grade 8: 23 students (23 girls); Grade 9: 31 students (31 girls); Grade 10: 31 students (31 girls); Grade 11: 28 students (28 girls); Grade 12: 31 students (31 girls).

College Admission Counseling 23 students graduated in 2010; all went to college. Mean SAT critical reading: 660, mean SAT math: 597, mean SAT writing: 640, mean combined SAT: 1897, mean composite ACT: 24.

Tuition and Aid Tuition installment plan (SMART Tuition Payment Plan).

Admissions Deadline for receipt of application materials: February 1. Application fee required: $50. Interview required.

Contact Mrs. Terri Collins, Director of Admission. 703-790-5450. Fax: 703-790-5380. E-mail: admissions@oakcrest.org. Web site: www.oakcrest.org.

OAK GROVE SCHOOL

220 West Lomita Avenue

Ojai, California 93023

Head of School: Meredy Benson Rice

General Information Coeducational boarding and day college-preparatory and arts school. Boarding grades 7–12, day grades PK–12. Founded: 1975. Setting: small town. Nearest major city is Los Angeles. Students are housed in coed dormitories. 150-acre campus. 6 buildings on campus. Approved or accredited by California Association of Independent Schools, The Association of Boarding Schools, Western Association of Schools and Colleges, and California Department of Education. Member of National Association of Independent Schools and Secondary School Admission Test Board. Endowment: $900,000. Total enrollment: 197. Upper school average class size: 15. Upper school faculty-student ratio: 1:7. There are 170 required school days per year for Upper School students. Upper School students typically attend 5 days per week. The average school day consists of 8 hours and 30 minutes.

Upper School Student Profile Grade 9: 18 students (9 boys, 9 girls); Grade 10: 8 students (3 boys, 5 girls); Grade 11: 9 students (4 boys, 5 girls); Grade 12: 10 students (4 boys, 6 girls). 35% of students are boarding students. 83% are state residents. 2 states are represented in upper school student body. 23% are international students. International students from China, India, Japan, Mexico, Republic of Korea, and Viet Nam.

Faculty School total: 35. In upper school: 6 men, 5 women; 5 have advanced degrees; 2 reside on campus.

Subjects Offered Algebra, American history, American literature, anatomy, art, art history, biology, calculus, ceramics, chemistry, communications, community service, comparative religion, computer science, drama, earth science, economics, English, English literature, ethics, film and new technologies, fine arts, gardening, geography, geometry, global studies, history, horticulture, human development, inquiry into relationship, mathematics, music, permaculture, photography, physical education, physics, relationships, religion and culture, science, social studies, Spanish, studio art, theater, world cultures, world history, world literature.

Graduation Requirements Algebra, American history, arts and fine arts (art, music, dance, drama), backpacking, biology, chemistry, college admission preparation, comparative religion, economics and history, English, ethics and responsibility, foreign language, geometry, mathematics, science, social studies (includes history), Spanish, world religions, participation in camping and travel programs and sports, one year of visual and performing arts. Community service is required.

Special Academic Programs 3 Advanced Placement exams for which test preparation is offered; honors section; ESL (4 students enrolled).

College Admission Counseling 12 students graduated in 2011; 11 went to college, including California Institute of the Arts; New York University; Pace University; The Colorado College; University of California, Berkeley. Other: 1 had other specific plans. Mean SAT critical reading: 627, mean SAT math: 580, mean SAT writing: 617. 57% scored over 600 on SAT critical reading, 28% scored over 600 on SAT math, 42% scored over 600 on SAT writing.

Student Life Upper grades have student council, honor system. Discipline rests equally with students and faculty.

Summer Programs ESL programs offered; held on campus; accepts boys and girls; open to students from other schools. 15 students usually enrolled. 2012 schedule: July to August. Application deadline: June.

Tuition and Aid Day student tuition: $15,650; 7-day tuition and room/board: $37,900. Tuition installment plan (FACTS Tuition Payment Plan, annual and semi-annual payment plans). Need-based scholarship grants, African-American scholarships available. In 2011–12, 40% of upper-school students received aid. Total amount of financial aid awarded in 2011–12: $60,000.

Admissions Traditional secondary-level entrance grade is 9. For fall 2011, 31 students applied for upper-level admission, 22 were accepted, 8 enrolled. SSAT or TOEFL or SLEP required. Deadline for receipt of application materials: none. Application fee required: $50. Interview required.

Athletics Interscholastic: soccer (boys, girls), volleyball (b,g); intramural: equestrian sports (g), soccer (b,g), volleyball (b,g); coed intramural: backpacking, fitness, hiking/backpacking, outdoor activities, outdoor education, outdoor skills, physical fitness, ropes courses, skiing (downhill), table tennis, tennis, wilderness. 1 PE instructor, 3 coaches.

Computers Computers are regularly used in art, ESL, graphic arts, history, independent study, library, mathematics, multimedia, photography, SAT preparation, science, technology, typing, writing, yearbook classes. Computer network features include on-campus library services, online commercial services, Internet access, wireless campus network, Internet filtering or blocking technology. Computer access in designated common areas is available to students.

Contact Joy Maguire-Parsons, Director of Admissions. 805-646-8236 Ext. 109. Fax: 805-646-6509. E-mail: enroll@oakgroveschool.com. Web site: www.oakgroveschool.com.

OAK HILL ACADEMY

2635 Oak Hill Road

Mouth of Wilson, Virginia 24363

Head of School: Dr. Michael D. Groves

General Information Coeducational boarding and day college-preparatory, general academic, dual-credit courses, and honors classes school, affiliated with Baptist Church. Grades 8–12. Founded: 1878. Setting: rural. Nearest major city is Charlotte, NC. Students are housed in single-sex dormitories. 300-acre campus. 22 buildings on campus. Approved or accredited by Southern Association of Colleges and Schools, Southern Association of Independent Schools, The Association of Boarding Schools, and Virginia Department of Education. Member of Secondary School Admission Test Board. Endowment: $1.9 million. Total enrollment: 122. Upper school average class size: 10. Upper school faculty-student ratio: 1:10. There are 180 required school days per year for Upper School students. Upper School students typically attend 6 days per week. The average school day consists of 7 hours.

Upper School Student Profile Grade 8: 3 students (2 boys, 1 girl); Grade 9: 16 students (9 boys, 7 girls); Grade 10: 19 students (13 boys, 6 girls); Grade 11: 38 students (23 boys, 15 girls); Grade 12: 46 students (25 boys, 21 girls). 98% of students are boarding students. 17% are state residents. 24 states are represented in upper school student body. 22% are international students. International students from Bahamas, Canada, China, France, Republic of Korea, and Senegal; 7 other countries represented in student body. 18% of students are Baptist.

Faculty School total: 20. In upper school: 8 men, 10 women; 14 have advanced degrees; 11 reside on campus.

Subjects Offered Advanced math, algebra, anatomy and physiology, art, art history, Bible as literature, biology, business, business mathematics, calculus, chemistry, choir, computer programming, creative writing, desktop publishing, digital photography, earth science, English, environmental science, equine science, fine arts, geometry, health, honors algebra, honors English, honors geometry, honors U.S. history, honors world history, instrumental music, intro to computers, keyboarding, mathematics, Microsoft, modern world history, physical education, physics, psychology, reading/study skills, religion, science, social sciences, social studies, Spanish, study skills, trigonometry, U.S. government, U.S. history, world geography, world history, world religions, world studies, yearbook.

Graduation Requirements Arts and fine arts (art, music, dance, drama), computer science, English, foreign language, mathematics, physical education (includes health), religion (includes Bible studies and theology), science, social sciences, social studies (includes history).

Special Academic Programs Honors section; study at local college for college credit; remedial reading and/or remedial writing; special instructional classes for students with Attention Deficit Disorder; ESL (18 students enrolled).

College Admission Counseling 50 students graduated in 2011; 46 went to college, including George Mason University; Indiana University Bloomington; The University of Arizona; The University of Iowa; University of Illinois at Urbana–Champaign; University of Kentucky. Other: 1 entered military service, 3 had other specific plans. Median SAT critical reading: 480, median SAT math: 470. 10% scored over 600 on SAT critical reading, 5% scored over 600 on SAT math, 5% scored over 26 on composite ACT.

Student Life Upper grades have uniform requirement, student council, honor system. Discipline rests primarily with faculty. Attendance at religious services is required.

Summer Programs Remediation, advancement programs offered; session focuses on advancement and remediation; held on campus; accepts boys and girls; open to students from other schools. 50 students usually enrolled. 2012 schedule: June 18 to July 21. Application deadline: none.

Tuition and Aid Day student tuition: $9000; 7-day tuition and room/board: $28,700. Tuition installment plan (monthly payment plans, individually arranged payment plans, 12-month interest-free payment plan for those students accepted by June 1). Tuition reduction for siblings, need-based scholarship grants available. In 2011–12, 30% of upper-school students received aid. Total amount of financial aid awarded in 2011–12: $370,000.

Admissions Traditional secondary-level entrance grade is 11. For fall 2011, 69 students applied for upper-level admission, 54 were accepted, 41 enrolled. TOEFL or SLEP required. Deadline for receipt of application materials: none. Application fee required: $50. On-campus interview recommended.

Athletics Interscholastic: baseball (boys), basketball (b,g), cheering (g), tennis (b,g), volleyball (g); intramural: baseball (b), basketball (b,g), billiards (b,g), bowling (b,g), canoeing/kayaking (b,g), equestrian sports (b,g), fishing (b), golf (b,g), hiking/backpacking (b,g), horseback riding (b,g), jogging (b,g), Nautilus (b,g), outdoor recreation (b,g), running (b,g), softball (g), strength & conditioning (b,g), table tennis (b,g), tennis (b,g), walking (g), weight lifting (b,g); coed interscholastic: cross-country running, soccer, track and field; coed intramural: aquatics, fitness walking, flag football, paint ball, skiing (downhill), snowboarding, soccer, swimming and diving, ultimate Frisbee, volleyball, yoga. 1 PE instructor, 1 coach, 1 athletic trainer.

Computers Computers are regularly used in all academic, business education, creative writing, desktop publishing, English, ESL, mathematics, science, yearbook classes. Computer resources include on-campus library services, Internet access, wireless campus network, Internet filtering or blocking technology. Student e-mail accounts are available to students. Students grades are available online. The school has a published electronic and media policy.

Contact Mr. Michael Rodgers, Director of Admissions. 276-579-2619. Fax: 276-579-4722. E-mail: mrodgers@oak-hill.net. Web site: www.oak-hill.net.

OAK HILL SCHOOL

86397 Eldon Schafer Drive

Eugene, Oregon 97405-9647

Head of School: Bob Sarkisian

General Information Coeducational day college-preparatory, arts, and technology school. Grades K–12. Founded: 1994. Setting: small town. 72-acre campus. 2 buildings on campus. Approved or accredited by Northwest Association of Schools and Colleges, Pacific Northwest Association of Independent Schools, and Oregon Department of Education. Member of National Association of Independent Schools. Total enrollment: 151. Upper school average class size: 10. Upper school faculty-student ratio: 1:10. There are 175 required school days per year for Upper School students. Upper School students typically attend 5 days per week. The average school day consists of 7 hours.

Faculty School total: 26. In upper school: 5 men, 9 women; 9 have advanced degrees.

Subjects Offered Acting, advanced math, algebra, American literature, analytic geometry, anatomy, art, arts, band, calculus-AP, ceramics, chemistry, comparative government and politics, composition, computer education, drama performance, drawing and design, economics, English composition, English literature, English literature-AP, fitness, French, geometry, health education, history, independent study, Latin, outdoor education, physical education, pre-calculus, probability and statistics, Spanish, Spanish language-AP, Spanish literature-AP, speech communications, theater arts, U.S. government and politics, U.S. history, world history, writing.

Graduation Requirements American government, American history, arts, computer skills, economics, English, English composition, foreign language, French, lab science, mathematics, physical education (includes health), science, Spanish, world history, 70 community service hours.

Special Academic Programs Advanced Placement exam preparation; honors section; academic accommodation for the gifted.

College Admission Counseling 6 students graduated in 2011; all went to college, including Savannah College of Art and Design; Southern Oregon University; University of California, San Diego; University of Oregon; Willamette University. Median SAT critical reading: 560, median SAT math: 610. 27% scored over 600 on SAT critical reading, 27% scored over 600 on SAT math.

Student Life Upper grades have specified standards of dress, student council, honor system. Discipline rests equally with students and faculty.

Tuition and Aid Day student tuition: $15,000. Tuition installment plan (monthly payment plans). Merit scholarship grants, need-based scholarship grants available. In 2011–12, 50% of upper-school students received aid.

Admissions Traditional secondary-level entrance grade is 9. Comprehensive educational evaluation required. Deadline for receipt of application materials: February 15. Application fee required: $100. Interview required.

Athletics Interscholastic: basketball (boys); intramural: basketball (g), volleyball (g); coed interscholastic: cross-country running, indoor track & field, running, track and field; coed intramural: golf, outdoor education, physical training, strength & conditioning. 1 PE instructor, 1 coach.

Computers Computers are regularly used in desktop publishing, graphic arts, graphic design, information technology, introduction to technology, multimedia, publications, technology, Web site design, writing classes. Computer network features include Internet access, wireless campus network, Internet filtering or blocking technology, online homework calendars for each upper school class. Campus intranet, student e-mail accounts, and computer access in designated common areas are available to students. The school has a published electronic and media policy.

Contact Lauren Moody, Admissions Director. 541-744-0954. Fax: 541-741-6968. E-mail: admission@oakhillschool.com. Web site: oakhillschool.net.

OAK KNOLL SCHOOL OF THE HOLY CHILD

44 Blackburn Road

Summit, New Jersey 07901

Head of School: Timothy J. Saburn

General Information Girls' day college-preparatory, arts, and religious studies school, affiliated with Roman Catholic Church. Grades K–12. Founded: 1924. Setting: suburban. Nearest major city is New York, NY. 11-acre campus. 4 buildings on campus. Approved or accredited by Middle States Association of Colleges and Schools and New Jersey Department of Education. Member of National Association of Independent Schools and Secondary School Admission Test Board. Endowment: $8.5 million. Total enrollment: 544. Upper school average class size: 15. Upper school faculty-student ratio: 1:8.

Upper School Student Profile Grade 7: 35 students (35 girls); Grade 8: 38 students (38 girls); Grade 9: 63 students (63 girls); Grade 10: 63 students (63 girls); Grade 11: 52 students (52 girls); Grade 12: 63 students (63 girls). 86% of students are Roman Catholic.

Faculty School total: 72. In upper school: 5 men, 47 women; 38 have advanced degrees.

Subjects Offered 20th century American writers, addiction, adolescent issues, advanced studio art-AP, African American studies, African-American literature, algebra, alternative physical education, American history, American literature, American studies, anatomy, ancient world history, art, art appreciation, Asian studies, ballet, Basic programming, Bible studies, biology, biology-AP, British literature, calculus, calculus-AP, calligraphy, campus ministry, career/college preparation, Catholic belief and practice, chemistry, chemistry-AP, Christian and Hebrew scripture, church history, college counseling, computer graphics, computer literacy, computer programming-AP, computer science, computer science-AP, concert choir, creative writing, dance, dance performance, decision making skills, desktop publishing, digital photography, driver education, engineering, English, English literature, English literature-AP, English-AP, ensembles, ethics, ethnic studies, European history, European history-AP, expository writing, fine arts, French, French-AP, genetics, geometry, health and wellness, history, Latin, leadership and service, marine science, mathematics, modern world history, music, Native American history, oceanography, peer ministry, physical education, physics, physics-AP, physiology, pre-calculus, probability and statistics, psychology, SAT preparation, science, social psychology, Spanish, Spanish-AP, studio art-AP, theology, trigonometry, U.S. history-AP, word processing, world history, world literature, writing.

Graduation Requirements Arts and fine arts (art, music, dance, drama), computer science, English, foreign language, mathematics, physical education (includes health), religion (includes Bible studies and theology), science, U.S. history, world history.

Special Academic Programs Advanced Placement exam preparation; honors section; independent study.

College Admission Counseling 63 students graduated in 2010; all went to college, including Boston College; Colgate University; Georgetown University; Princeton University; University of Notre Dame; Villanova University. Mean SAT critical reading: 615, mean SAT math: 624, mean SAT writing: 656.

Student Life Upper grades have uniform requirement, student council. Discipline rests primarily with faculty. Attendance at religious services is required.

Tuition and Aid Day student tuition: $30,800. Tuition installment plan (Key Tuition Payment Plan). Merit scholarship grants, need-based scholarship grants available. In 2010–11, 16% of upper-school students received aid; total upper-school merit-scholarship money awarded: $98,600. Total amount of financial aid awarded in 2010–11: $1,400,000.

Admissions Traditional secondary-level entrance grade is 9. For fall 2010, 107 students applied for upper-level admission, 84 were accepted, 44 enrolled. ISEE required. Deadline for receipt of application materials: January 26. Application fee required: $50. Interview required.

Athletics Interscholastic: basketball, cross-country running, fencing, field hockey, golf, lacrosse, soccer, softball, swimming and diving, tennis, track and field, volleyball, winter (indoor) track; intramural: dance squad, deck hockey, fitness, yoga. 3 PE instructors, 14 coaches, 1 athletic trainer.

Computers Computers are regularly used in all academic classes. Computer network features include on-campus library services, Internet access, wireless campus network, campus-wide laptop program grades 7-12. Campus intranet, student e-mail accounts, and computer access in designated common areas are available to students. Students grades are available online. The school has a published electronic and media policy.

Contact Suzanne Kimm Lewis, Admissions Director. 908-522-8109. Fax: 908-277-1838. E-mail: okadmissions@oakknoll.org. Web site: www.oakknoll.org.

THE OAKLAND SCHOOL

362 McKee Place

Pittsburgh, Pennsylvania 15213

Head of School: Mr. Jack C. King

General Information Coeducational day college-preparatory and arts school. Grades 8–12. Founded: 1982. Setting: urban. 1 building on campus. Approved or accredited by Pennsylvania Department of Education. Candidate for accreditation by Middle States Association of Colleges and Schools. Total enrollment: 55. Upper school average class size: 6. Upper school faculty-student ratio: 1:6. There are 180 required school days per year for Upper School students. Upper School students typically attend 5 days per week. The average school day consists of 5 hours and 30 minutes.

Upper School Student Profile Grade 8: 2 students (1 boy, 1 girl); Grade 9: 11 students (5 boys, 6 girls); Grade 10: 13 students (5 boys, 8 girls); Grade 11: 16 students (8 boys, 8 girls); Grade 12: 13 students (6 boys, 7 girls).

Faculty School total: 10. In upper school: 3 men, 7 women; 5 have advanced degrees.

Subjects Offered Advanced math, algebra, American history, American literature, art, art history, biology, business skills, calculus, chemistry, computer math, computer science, creative writing, drama, earth science, ecology, economics, English, English literature, environmental science, ESL, expository writing, fine arts, French, geography, geometry, German, government/civics, history, mathematics, physical education, physics, pre-calculus, psychology, SAT/ACT preparation, science, social studies, Spanish, speech, trigonometry, world history, world literature, writing.

Graduation Requirements Arts and fine arts (art, music, dance, drama), computer literacy, English, mathematics, physical education (includes health), science, social studies (includes history), community service.

Special Academic Programs Honors section; accelerated programs; independent study; study at local college for college credit; academic accommodation for the gifted and the artistically talented; remedial reading and/or remedial writing; remedial math; ESL (2 students enrolled).

College Admission Counseling 12 students graduated in 2011; 9 went to college, including University of Pittsburgh. Other: 2 entered military service, 1 had other specific plans. Mean SAT critical reading: 530, mean SAT math: 512, mean SAT writing: 550.

Student Life Upper grades have student council. Discipline rests primarily with faculty.

Tuition and Aid Day student tuition: $9700. Tuition installment plan (monthly payment plans, individually arranged payment plans, quarterly payment plan, semi-annual payment plan). Tuition reduction for siblings, merit scholarship grants, need-based scholarship grants available. In 2011–12, 25% of upper-school students received aid. Total amount of financial aid awarded in 2011–12: $40,000.

Admissions Traditional secondary-level entrance grade is 10. For fall 2011, 30 students applied for upper-level admission, 26 were accepted, 21 enrolled. WRAT required. Deadline for receipt of application materials: none. Application fee required: $100. On-campus interview required.

Athletics Intramural: aerobics/dance (girls), dance (g); coed intramural: baseball, basketball, bicycling, billiards, bowling, cooperative games, cross-country running, fitness, fitness walking, flag football, Frisbee, golf, hiking/backpacking, ice skating, jogging, jump rope, kickball, martial arts, racquetball, running, skateboarding, skiing (cross-country), skiing (downhill), snowboarding, softball, swimming and diving, tai chi, tennis, volleyball, walking. 1 PE instructor.

Computers Computers are regularly used in all academic classes. Computer network features include Internet access, wireless campus network. Student e-mail accounts and computer access in designated common areas are available to students. Students grades are available online.

Contact Admissions Desk. 412-621-7878. Fax: 412-621-7881. E-mail: oschool@stargate.net. Web site: www.theoaklandschool.org.

OAKLAND SCHOOL

Keswick, Virginia

See Special Needs Schools section.

OAK MOUNTAIN ACADEMY

222 Cross Plains Road

Carrollton, Georgia 30116

Head of School: Mrs. Paula J. Gillispie

General Information Coeducational day college-preparatory school, affiliated with Christian faith. Grades K4–12. Founded: 1962. Setting: small town. Nearest major city is Atlanta. 88-acre campus. 2 buildings on campus. Approved or accredited by Georgia Accrediting Commission, Southern Association of Colleges and Schools, and Georgia Department of Education. Total enrollment: 191. Upper school average class size: 10. Upper school faculty-student ratio: 1:5. There are 180 required school days per year for Upper School students. Upper School students typically attend 5 days per week. The average school day consists of 7 hours and 15 minutes.

Upper School Student Profile Grade 6: 6 students (1 boy, 5 girls); Grade 7: 10 students (6 boys, 4 girls); Grade 8: 20 students (7 boys, 13 girls); Grade 9: 18 students (7 boys, 11 girls); Grade 10: 17 students (7 boys, 10 girls); Grade 11: 17 students (10 boys, 7 girls); Grade 12: 17 students (9 boys, 8 girls).

Faculty School total: 28. In upper school: 5 men, 6 women; 8 have advanced degrees.

Subjects Offered Advanced math, Advanced Placement courses, algebra, American government, American history, American literature, anatomy, ancient world history, art, athletic training, athletics, Bible, biology, biology-AP, calculus, calculus-AP, chemistry, chemistry-AP, chorus, college counseling, community service, computer graphics, computer science, discrete mathematics, drama, economics, electives, English composition, English language-AP, English literature, English literature-AP, English-AP, expository writing, geometry, government, graphic arts, guidance, independent study, Latin, modern civilization, music, physical fitness, physical science, physics, pre-calculus, public speaking, research skills, senior internship, senior project, Spanish, statistics, student government, U.S. history, U.S. history-AP, world literature, yearbook.

Graduation Requirements Algebra, ancient world history, Bible, biology, calculus, chemistry, economics, electives, English, foreign language, geometry, modern civilization, physical education (includes health), physical science, public speaking, senior internship, senior project, U.S. government, U.S. history, senior project, including research paper, oral presentation, creating a product and 50-hour internship. Community service is required.

Special Academic Programs 5 Advanced Placement exams for which test preparation is offered; honors section; independent study; study at local college for college credit.

College Admission Counseling 17 students graduated in 2010; all went to college, including Georgia College & State University; Samford University; University of Georgia; University of West Georgia; Vanderbilt University. Median SAT critical reading: 540, median SAT math: 620, median SAT writing: 580, median combined SAT: 1760, median composite ACT: 27. 41% scored over 600 on SAT critical reading, 65% scored over 600 on SAT math, 47% scored over 600 on SAT writing, 47% scored over 1800 on combined SAT, 67% scored over 26 on composite ACT.

Student Life Upper grades have specified standards of dress, student council, honor system. Discipline rests primarily with faculty.

Tuition and Aid Day student tuition: $10,848. Tuition installment plan (monthly payment plans, three payment plan). Tuition reduction for siblings, need-based scholarship grants available. In 2010–11, 15% of upper-school students received aid. Total amount of financial aid awarded in 2010–11: $38,000.

Admissions Traditional secondary-level entrance grade is 9. For fall 2010, 18 students applied for upper-level admission, 11 were accepted, 11 enrolled. Deadline for receipt of application materials: none. Application fee required: $75. Interview required.

Athletics Interscholastic: baseball (boys), basketball (b,g), cheering (b,g), cross-country running (b,g), running (b,g), soccer (b,g), softball (g), swimming and diving (b,g), tennis (b,g), volleyball (g), weight training (b,g); coed interscholastic: golf. 2 PE instructors, 6 coaches.

Computers Computers are regularly used in Bible studies, college planning, English, foreign language, graphic arts, independent study, lab/keyboard, Latin, programming, religion, science, senior seminar, Spanish, yearbook classes. Computer network features include on-campus library services, online commercial services, Internet access, Internet filtering or blocking technology. Student e-mail accounts and computer access in designated common areas are available to students. Students grades are available online. The school has a published electronic and media policy.

Contact Mrs. Kristen Glauner, Director of Admissions. 770-834-6651. Fax: 770-834-6785. E-mail: kristenglauner@oakmountain.us. Web site: www.oakmountain.us.

OAK RIDGE MILITARY ACADEMY

2317 Oak Ridge Road

PO Box 498

Oak Ridge, North Carolina 27310

Head of School: Mr. David Johnson

General Information Coeducational boarding and day college-preparatory, leadership, and military school. Grades 7–12. Founded: 1852. Setting: small town. Nearest major city is Greensboro. Students are housed in single-sex dormitories. 101-acre campus. 22 buildings on campus. Approved or accredited by Southern Association of Colleges and Schools, Southern Association of Independent Schools, and North Carolina Department of Education. Member of National Association of Independent Schools. Total enrollment: 65. Upper school average class size: 8. Upper school faculty-student ratio: 1:11. Upper School students typically attend 5 days per week. The average school day consists of 7 hours.

Upper School Student Profile 84% of students are boarding students. 49% are state residents. 16 states are represented in upper school student body. 14% are international students. International students from Bermuda, China, Honduras, Mexico, Philippines, and Republic of Korea; 4 other countries represented in student body.

Faculty School total: 25. In upper school: 12 men, 13 women; 8 have advanced degrees; 9 reside on campus.

Subjects Offered Algebra, American history, American literature, biology, calculus, chemistry, college writing, computer math, computer science, creative writing, driver education, earth science, English, English literature, environmental science, ESL, French, geometry, German, government/civics, grammar, health, JROTC, JROTC or LEAD (Leadership Education and Development), mathematics, military science, music, physical education, physics, SAT preparation, science, social studies, Spanish, trigonometry, world history, writing.

Graduation Requirements Computer science, English, foreign language, mathematics, physical education (includes health), ROTC, SAT preparation, science, social studies (includes history), writing, complete three college applications, 20 hours of community service.

Special Academic Programs Honors section; accelerated programs; study at local college for college credit; academic accommodation for the gifted; special instructional classes for students with Attention Deficit Disorder and Attention Deficit Hyperactivity Disorder; ESL (6 students enrolled).

College Admission Counseling 28 students graduated in 2011; 27 went to college, including Appalachian State University; East Carolina University; North Carolina State University; The Citadel, The Military College of South Carolina; The University of North Carolina at Chapel Hill; The University of North Carolina at Charlotte. Other: 1 entered military service.

Student Life Upper grades have uniform requirement, student council, honor system. Discipline rests equally with students and faculty. Attendance at religious services is required.

Summer Programs Remediation, enrichment, advancement, ESL programs offered; session focuses on leadership, adventure, academics, confidence building; held both on and off campus; held at Carowinds, Wet and Wild and white water rafting in WV; accepts boys and girls; open to students from other schools. 200 students usually enrolled. 2012 schedule: June 24 to August 5. Application deadline: June 1.

Tuition and Aid Day student tuition: $12,815; 5-day tuition and room/board: $22,195; 7-day tuition and room/board: $25,095. Tuition installment plan (Key Tuition Payment Plan, SMART Tuition Payment Plan, monthly payment plans). Tuition reduction for siblings, merit scholarship grants, USS Education Loan Program available. In 2011–12, 24% of upper-school students received aid.

Admissions Traditional secondary-level entrance grade is 10. Deadline for receipt of application materials: none. Application fee required: $200. Interview recommended.

Athletics Interscholastic: baseball (boys), basketball (b,g), football (b), golf (b), soccer (b,g), swimming and diving (b,g), tennis (b), track and field (b,g), volleyball (g), wrestling (b); intramural: basketball (b,g), flag football (b), outdoor adventure (b,g), paint ball (b,g), rappelling (b,g), scuba diving (b,g), skydiving (b,g), strength & conditioning (b,g), weight lifting (b,g); coed interscholastic: cross-country running, drill team, JROTC drill, marksmanship, riflery, swimming and diving, track and field; coed intramural: outdoor adventure, paint ball, pistol, rappelling, scuba diving, skydiving, softball, strength & conditioning, weight lifting. 1 PE instructor, 10 coaches, 1 athletic trainer.

Computers Computers are regularly used in English, mathematics, science classes. Computer resources include on-campus library services, Internet access.

Contact Mr. Bob Lipke, Director of Admissions. 336-643-4131 Ext. 196. Fax: 336-643-1797. E-mail: blipke@ormila.com. Web site: www.oakridgemilitary.com.

THE OAKRIDGE SCHOOL

5900 West Pioneer Parkway

Arlington, Texas 76013-2899

Head of School: Mr. Jonathan Kellam

General Information Coeducational day college-preparatory, arts, and technology school. Grades PS–12. Founded: 1979. Setting: suburban. 90-acre campus. 6 buildings on campus. Approved or accredited by Independent Schools Association of the Southwest and Texas Department of Education. Member of National Association of Independent Schools. Total enrollment: 876. Upper school average class size: 16. Upper school faculty-student ratio: 1:10. There are 176 required school days per year for Upper School students. Upper School students typically attend 5 days per week. The average school day consists of 7 hours and 30 minutes.

Faculty School total: 80. In upper school: 14 men, 13 women; 23 have advanced degrees.

Subjects Offered 3-dimensional art, acting, Advanced Placement courses, advanced studio art-AP, algebra, American history, American history-AP, American literature, anatomy, ancient world history, anthropology, archaeology, art, art history-AP, athletics, biology, British literature, calculus, calculus-AP, chemistry, chemistry-AP, Chinese, choir, choral music, classical civilization, college admission preparation, college counseling, college writing, community service, comparative religion, composition-AP, computer animation, computer applications, computer art, computer graphics, computer information systems, computer literacy, computer multimedia, computer processing, computer programming-AP, computer science-AP, computer skills, concert choir, creative writing, current events, desktop publishing, digital applications, digital art, digital imaging, digital music, digital photography, discrete mathematics, drafting, drama, drama performance, drama workshop, dramatic arts, drawing, drawing and design, economics, economics and history, English, English language and composition-AP, English literature and composition-AP, environmental science-AP, European civilization, European history-AP, expository writing, film and literature, fine arts, fractal geometry, French, French language-AP, French-AP, geometry, golf, government, government and politics-AP, government-AP, government/civics, graphic arts, graphic design, graphics, health, honors algebra, honors English, honors geometry, honors world history, human biology, independent study, keyboarding, language and composition, language arts, Latin, literature and composition-AP, media literacy, modern European history-AP, modern world history, music theory, music theory-AP, musical productions, organic chemistry, physics, physics-AP, play production, poetry, portfolio art, portfolio writing, pre-algebra, pre-calculus, printmaking, probability and statistics, programming, public service, public speaking, reading/study skills, SAT preparation, SAT/ACT preparation, Spanish, Spanish-AP, strings, theater, track and field, U.S. government, U.S. government and politics, U.S. government and politics-AP, U.S. history, U.S. history-AP, United States government-AP, video, video and animation, video communication, video film production, visual and performing arts, voice, voice ensemble, Web site design, weightlifting, world history.

Graduation Requirements Arts and fine arts (art, music, dance, drama), English, foreign language, mathematics, physical education (includes health), science, social studies (includes history), participation in six seasons of athletics. Community service is required.

Special Academic Programs Advanced Placement exam preparation; honors section; independent study; study at local college for college credit; study abroad; academic accommodation for the gifted, the musically talented, and the artistically talented.

College Admission Counseling 74 students graduated in 2011; all went to college, including Texas A&M University; Texas Christian University; Texas Tech University; The University of Texas at Austin; University of Notre Dame; University of Oklahoma. Mean SAT critical reading: 602, mean SAT math: 627, mean SAT writing: 591, mean combined SAT: 1820, mean composite ACT: 27.

Student Life Upper grades have uniform requirement, student council, honor system. Discipline rests primarily with faculty.

Summer Programs Remediation, enrichment, advancement, sports, art/fine arts, rigorous outdoor training, computer instruction programs offered; session focuses on enrichment; held both on and off campus; held at museums and recreational facilities; accepts boys and girls; open to students from other schools. 200 students usually enrolled. 2012 schedule: June 6 to July 15. Application deadline: none.

Tuition and Aid Day student tuition: $17,090. Tuition installment plan (FACTS Tuition Payment Plan, early discount option). Need-based scholarship grants available.

Admissions Traditional secondary-level entrance grade is 9. ERB Reading and Math, ISEE or Otis-Lennon School Ability Test required. Deadline for receipt of application materials: March 1. Application fee required: $65. Interview required.

Athletics Interscholastic: ball hockey (girls), baseball (b), basketball (b,g), cheering (g), cross-country running (b,g), field hockey (g), football (b), golf (b,g), physical fitness (b,g), physical training (b,g), power lifting (b), soccer (b,g), softball (g), strength & conditioning (b,g), tennis (b,g), track and field (b,g), volleyball (g), weight lifting (b), winter soccer (b,g), wrestling (b); intramural: strength & conditioning (b,g), weight training (b); coed interscholastic: aquatics; coed intramural: fitness, fitness walking, judo, outdoor activities, physical fitness, physical training, running, winter walking. 5 PE instructors, 10 coaches, 1 athletic trainer.

Computers Computers are regularly used in art, English, foreign language, history, mathematics, programming, science, stock market, technology, video film production, Web site design, writing, yearbook classes. Computer network features include on-campus library services, online commercial services, Internet access, wireless campus network, Internet filtering or blocking technology. Campus intranet, student e-mail accounts, and computer access in designated common areas are available to students. Students grades are available online. The school has a published electronic and media policy.

Contact Dr. Jerry A. Davis Jr., Director of Admissions. 817-451-4994 Ext. 2708. Fax: 817-457-6681. E-mail: jadavis@theoakridgeschool.org. Web site: www.theoakridgeschool.org.

OJAI VALLEY SCHOOL

723 El Paseo Road

Ojai, California 93023

Head of School: Mr. Michael J. Hall-Mounsey

General Information Coeducational boarding and day college-preparatory, arts, and technology school; primarily serves students with learning disabilities, individuals with Attention Deficit Disorder, and dyslexic students. Boarding grades 3–12, day grades PK–12. Founded: 1911. Setting: rural. Nearest major city is Los Angeles. Students are housed in single-sex dormitories. 200-acre campus. 13 buildings on campus. Approved or accredited by California Association of Independent Schools, The Association of Boarding Schools, Western Association of Schools and Colleges, and California Department of Education. Member of National Association of Independent Schools and Secondary School Admission Test Board. Endowment: $1 million. Total enrollment: 291. Upper school average class size: 12. Upper school faculty-student ratio: 1:6.

Upper School Student Profile Grade 9: 30 students (18 boys, 12 girls); Grade 10: 27 students (11 boys, 16 girls); Grade 11: 30 students (21 boys, 9 girls); Grade 12: 26 students (15 boys, 11 girls). 74% of students are boarding students. 51% are state residents. 6 states are represented in upper school student body. 49% are international students. International students from China, Japan, Mexico, Republic of Korea, Taiwan, and Thailand; 3 other countries represented in student body.

Faculty School total: 54. In upper school: 11 men, 12 women; 10 have advanced degrees; 10 reside on campus.

Subjects Offered 20th century history, algebra, American history, American literature, art, art history, biology, biology-AP, calculus-AP, chemistry, chemistry-AP, community service, computer science, conceptual physics, creative writing, drama, ecology, economics, English, English literature, English-AP, environmental science, equestrian sports, ESL, fine arts, geography, geometry, government/civics, grammar, history, honors English, humanities, independent study, mathematics, music, music theory-AP, photography, physical education, physics, psychology, science, social studies, Spanish, Spanish-AP, speech, statistics, studio art, studio art-AP, theater, trigonometry, wilderness education, world history, writing.

Graduation Requirements Arts and fine arts (art, music, dance, drama), economics, English, foreign language, government, mathematics, science, social studies (includes history).

Special Academic Programs 11 Advanced Placement exams for which test preparation is offered; honors section; accelerated programs; independent study; study abroad; academic accommodation for the gifted and the artistically talented; remedial reading and/or remedial writing; remedial math; ESL (12 students enrolled).

College Admission Counseling 27 students graduated in 2011; all went to college, including Boston University; New York University; The Johns Hopkins University; University of California, Riverside; University of California, Santa Barbara. Median SAT critical reading: 540, median SAT math: 625, median SAT writing: 585, median combined SAT: 1750. 25% scored over 600 on SAT math.

Student Life Upper grades have specified standards of dress, student council, honor system. Discipline rests equally with students and faculty.

Summer Programs Remediation, enrichment, advancement, ESL, art/fine arts, computer instruction programs offered; session focuses on academic and course credit; held on campus; accepts boys and girls; open to students from other schools. 300 students usually enrolled. 2012 schedule: June 20 to July 31. Application deadline: none.

Tuition and Aid Day student tuition: $19,500; 7-day tuition and room/board: $45,500. Tuition installment plan (individually arranged payment plans). Need-based scholarship grants, need-based loans available. In 2011–12, 15% of upper-school students received aid. Total amount of financial aid awarded in 2011–12: $282,105.

Admissions Traditional secondary-level entrance grade is 9. For fall 2011, 143 students applied for upper-level admission, 66 were accepted, 35 enrolled. Any standardized test, SSAT or TOEFL required. Deadline for receipt of application materials: none. Application fee required: $50. Interview required.

Athletics Interscholastic: baseball (boys), basketball (b,g), cross-country running (b,g), dressage (b,g), football (b), lacrosse (b,g), soccer (b,g), volleyball (b,g); coed interscholastic: equestrian sports, golf, track and field; coed intramural: backpacking, basketball, bicycling, climbing, cross-country running, equestrian sports, fencing, fitness, fitness walking, golf, hiking/backpacking, horseback riding, kayaking, martial arts, mountain biking, outdoor education, physical fitness, rappelling, rock climbing, ropes courses, surfing, swimming and diving, weight training, yoga. 2 PE instructors, 2 coaches, 2 athletic trainers.

Computers Computers are regularly used in economics, English, ESL, geography, history, humanities, journalism, mathematics, music, photography, SAT preparation, science, social sciences, yearbook classes. Computer resources include on-campus library services, online commercial services, Internet access, wireless campus network, Internet filtering or blocking technology. The school has a published electronic and media policy.

Contact Ms. Tracy Wilson, Director of Admission. 805-646-1423. Fax: 805-646-0362. E-mail: admission@ovs.org. Web site: www.ovs.org.

OLDENBURG ACADEMY

1 Twister Circle

Oldenburg, Indiana 47036

Head of School: Sr. Therese Gillman, OSF

General Information Coeducational day college-preparatory, arts, and religious studies school, affiliated with Roman Catholic Church. Grades 9–12. Founded: 1852. Setting: small town. Nearest major city is Cincinnati, OH. 23-acre campus. 3 buildings on campus. Approved or accredited by North Central Association of Colleges and Schools and Indiana Department of Education. Total enrollment: 209. Upper school average class size: 15. Upper school faculty-student ratio: 1:12. There are 180 required school days per year for Upper School students. The average school day consists of 6 hours.

Upper School Student Profile Grade 9: 38 students (12 boys, 26 girls); Grade 10: 71 students (32 boys, 39 girls); Grade 11: 44 students (15 boys, 29 girls); Grade 12: 55 students (23 boys, 32 girls). 80% of students are Roman Catholic.

Faculty School total: 18. In upper school: 5 men, 13 women; 13 have advanced degrees.

Graduation Requirements 40 hours of community service.

Special Academic Programs Advanced Placement exam preparation; honors section.

College Admission Counseling Colleges students went to include Butler University; Indiana University Bloomington; Purdue University.

Student Life Upper grades have uniform requirement, student council, honor system. Discipline rests primarily with faculty. Attendance at religious services is required.

Tuition and Aid Day student tuition: $6700. Tuition installment plan (FACTS Tuition Payment Plan). Tuition reduction for siblings, merit scholarship grants, need-based scholarship grants available. In 2010–11, 35% of upper-school students received aid. Total amount of financial aid awarded in 2010–11: $60,000.

Admissions Traditional secondary-level entrance grade is 9. High School Placement Test (closed version) from Scholastic Testing Service required. Deadline for receipt of application materials: none. Application fee required: $350. Interview recommended.

Athletics Interscholastic: baseball (boys), basketball (b,g), cheering (g), cross-country running (b,g), dance team (g), wrestling (b). 1 PE instructor, 9 coaches.

Computers Computers are regularly used in all academic classes. Computer network features include on-campus library services, Internet access, wireless campus network, Internet filtering or blocking technology. Student e-mail accounts and computer access in designated common areas are available to students. Students grades are available online. The school has a published electronic and media policy.

Contact Mrs. Bettina Rose, Principal. 812-934-4440 Ext. 223. Fax: 812-934-4838. E-mail: brose@oldenburgacademy.org.

THE OLIVERIAN SCHOOL

Haverhill, New Hampshire

See Special Needs Schools section.

THE O'NEAL SCHOOL

3300 Airport Road

PO Box 290

Southern Pines, North Carolina 28388-0290

Head of School: Mr. Alan Barr

General Information Coeducational day college-preparatory school. Grades PK–12. Founded: 1971. Setting: small town. Nearest major city is Raleigh. 40-acre campus. 3 buildings on campus. Approved or accredited by Southern Association of Colleges and Schools, Southern Association of Independent Schools, and North Carolina Department of Education. Member of National Association of Independent Schools. Endowment: $1.4 million. Total enrollment: 430. Upper school average class size: 15. Upper school faculty-student ratio: 1:12. There are 175 required school days per year for Upper School students. Upper School students typically attend 5 days per week. The average school day consists of 7 hours.

Upper School Student Profile Grade 9: 44 students (19 boys, 25 girls); Grade 10: 38 students (17 boys, 21 girls); Grade 11: 42 students (16 boys, 26 girls); Grade 12: 34 students (14 boys, 20 girls).

Faculty School total: 54. In upper school: 6 men, 10 women; 7 have advanced degrees.

Subjects Offered Algebra, American history, American literature, art, art history, art history-AP, biology, biology-AP, calculus-AP, chemistry, community service, computer science, creative writing, drama, economics, English, English language-AP, English literature, English literature-AP, environmental science, environmental science-AP, European history, European history-AP, expository writing, film, fine arts, French, geometry, government-AP, jazz band, Latin, mathematics, music, philosophy, photography, physical education, physics-AP, political science, pottery, pre-calculus, science, social studies, Spanish, statistics-AP, U.S. history-AP, world history, world literature, yearbook.

Graduation Requirements Arts and fine arts (art, music, dance, drama), English, foreign language, mathematics, physical education (includes health), science, social studies (includes history), 36 hours of community service.

Special Academic Programs 13 Advanced Placement exams for which test preparation is offered; independent study; study at local college for college credit.

College Admission Counseling 43 students graduated in 2011; 41 went to college, including Appalachian State University; Belmont University; Elon University; North Carolina State University; The University of North Carolina at Chapel Hill; The University of North Carolina Wilmington. Other: 1 went to work, 1 had other specific plans. Median SAT critical reading: 570, median SAT math: 610, median SAT writing: 590, median combined SAT: 1770. 50% scored over 600 on SAT critical reading, 45% scored over 600 on SAT math, 48% scored over 600 on SAT writing, 45% scored over 1800 on combined SAT, 57% scored over 26 on composite ACT.

Student Life Upper grades have specified standards of dress, student council, honor system. Discipline rests primarily with faculty.

Tuition and Aid Day student tuition: $15,200. Tuition installment plan (Insured Tuition Payment Plan, monthly payment plans, individually arranged payment plans). Merit scholarship grants, need-based scholarship grants available. In 2011–12, 31% of upper-school students received aid; total upper-school merit-scholarship money awarded: $45,600. Total amount of financial aid awarded in 2011–12: $413,315.

Admissions Traditional secondary-level entrance grade is 9. For fall 2011, 45 students applied for upper-level admission, 35 were accepted, 28 enrolled. Admissions testing, essay, OLSAT, Stanford Achievement Test, PSAT and SAT for applicants to grade 11 and 12, WRAT or writing sample required. Deadline for receipt of application materials: none. Application fee required: $75. On-campus interview required.

Athletics Interscholastic: baseball (boys), basketball (b,g), cheering (g), cross-country running (b,g), soccer (b,g), swimming and diving (b,g), tennis (b,g), track and field (b,g), volleyball (g); intramural: cheering (g); coed interscholastic: golf; coed intramural: martial arts. 2 PE instructors, 2 coaches.

Computers Computers are regularly used in all academic classes. Computer network features include on-campus library services, Internet access, wireless campus network, Internet filtering or blocking technology, EBSCO, World Book Online. Student e-mail accounts and computer access in designated common areas are available to students. The school has a published electronic and media policy.

Contact Mrs. Alice Droppers, Director of Admissions and Financial Aid. 910-692-6920 Ext. 103. Fax: 910-692-6930. E-mail: adroppers@onealschool.org. Web site: www.onealschool.org.

ONEIDA BAPTIST INSTITUTE

11 Mulberry Street

Oneida, Kentucky 40972

Head of School: Dr. W.F. Underwood

General Information Coeducational boarding and day college-preparatory, general academic, arts, vocational, religious studies, bilingual studies, and agriculture school, affiliated with Southern Baptist Convention. Grades 6–12. Founded: 1899. Setting: rural. Nearest major city is Lexington. Students are housed in single-sex dormitories. 200-acre campus. 15 buildings on campus. Approved or accredited by The Kentucky Non-Public School Commission, The National Non-Public School Commission, and Kentucky Department of Education. Endowment: $15 million. Total enrollment: 300. Upper school average class size: 11. Upper school faculty-student ratio: 1:11. There are 174 required school days per year for Upper School students. Upper School students typically attend 5 days per week. The average school day consists of 6 hours.

Upper School Student Profile Grade 9: 44 students (23 boys, 21 girls); Grade 10: 54 students (30 boys, 24 girls); Grade 11: 62 students (34 boys, 28 girls); Grade 12: 65 students (32 boys, 33 girls). 84% of students are boarding students. 65% are state residents. 20 states are represented in upper school student body. 20% are international students. International students from China, Ethiopia, Japan, Nigeria, Republic of Korea, and Thailand; 4 other countries represented in student body. 25% of students are Southern Baptist Convention.

Faculty School total: 38. In upper school: 16 men, 13 women; 10 have advanced degrees; all reside on campus.

Subjects Offered Agriculture, algebra, art, auto mechanics, band, Bible, biology, biology-AP, calculus-AP, chemistry, child development, choir, commercial art, computers, cultural geography, drama, earth and space science, English, English-AP, ESL, foods, geography, geometry, government, government-AP, guitar, health, language arts, life skills, literature, mathematics, physical education, physical science, piano, pre-calculus, psychology, social sciences, Spanish, stagecraft, U.S. history, U.S. history-AP, world history.

Graduation Requirements Arts and fine arts (art, music, dance, drama), Bible, computer literacy, English, foreign language, mathematics, physical education (includes health), science, social studies (includes history), field placement.

Special Academic Programs 5 Advanced Placement exams for which test preparation is offered; independent study; remedial reading and/or remedial writing; remedial math; ESL (28 students enrolled).

College Admission Counseling 53 students graduated in 2011; 45 went to college, including Berea College; Lindsey Wilson College; Union College; University of Kentucky; University of the Cumberlands. Other: 5 went to work.

Student Life Upper grades have specified standards of dress. Discipline rests primarily with faculty. Attendance at religious services is required.

Summer Programs Remediation, enrichment, advancement, ESL programs offered; session focuses on remediation and make-up courses; held on campus; accepts boys and girls; open to students from other schools. 125 students usually enrolled. 2012 schedule: June 10 to July 20. Application deadline: none.

Tuition and Aid 7-day tuition and room/board: $5150–$10,200. Tuition installment plan (monthly payment plans). Need-based scholarship grants available. In 2011–12, 100% of upper-school students received aid.

Admissions Traditional secondary-level entrance grade is 9. Deadline for receipt of application materials: none. Application fee required: $35. On-campus interview required.

Athletics Interscholastic: baseball (boys), basketball (b,g), cheering (g), cross-country running (b,g), softball (g), swimming and diving (b,g), tennis (b,g), track and field (b,g), volleyball (g); coed interscholastic: soccer.

Computers Computers are regularly used in commercial art classes. Computer resources include Internet access, Internet filtering or blocking technology. The school has a published electronic and media policy.

Contact Admissions. 606-847-4111 Ext. 233. Fax: 606-847-4496. E-mail: admissions@oneidaschool.org. Web site: www.oneidaschool.org.

ORANGEWOOD CHRISTIAN SCHOOL

1300 West Maitland Boulevard

Maitland, Florida 32751

Head of School: Mrs. LuAnne Schendel

General Information Coeducational day college-preparatory, arts, and technology school, affiliated with Presbyterian Church in America, Christian faith. Grades K–12. Founded: 1980. Setting: suburban. Nearest major city is Orlando. 2 buildings on campus. Approved or accredited by Association of Christian Schools International, Christian Schools of Florida, National Council for Private School Accreditation, and Southern Association of Colleges and Schools. Total enrollment: 711. Upper school average class size: 14. Upper school faculty-student ratio: 1:11. The average school day consists of 7 hours.

Upper School Student Profile 100% of students are Presbyterian Church in America, Christian.

Faculty School total: 65. In upper school: 13 men, 12 women; 14 have advanced degrees.

Subjects Offered Advanced Placement courses, algebra, American culture, American government, American history, American history-AP, anatomy and physiology, art, art-AP, astronomy, Bible, biology, biology-AP, calculus-AP, career exploration, ceramics, chemistry, choir, commercial art, computer applications, computer graphics, creative writing, drama, drawing, economics, English, English language and composition-AP, English literature and composition-AP, environmental science, foreign language, geometry, graphic design, honors algebra, honors English, honors geometry, honors U.S. history, honors world history, Latin, life management skills, marine science, meteorology, oceanography, painting, personal fitness, photography, physics, physics-AP, pre-calculus, psychology, SAT preparation, sculpture, senior seminar, Spanish, Spanish language-AP, speech, studio art-AP, television, trigonometry, weight training, world geography, world history, world religions, yearbook.

Graduation Requirements Algebra, American government, American history, arts and fine arts (art, music, dance, drama), Bible, biology, computer applications, economics, electives, English, foreign language, life management skills, mathematics, personal fitness, physical education (includes health), science, senior seminar, world history.

Special Academic Programs Advanced Placement exam preparation; honors section; accelerated programs; independent study; study at local college for college credit.

College Admission Counseling 60 students graduated in 2010; all went to college, including Covenant College; Florida State University; Palm Beach Atlantic University; University of Central Florida; University of Florida; University of North Florida. Median SAT critical reading: 550, median SAT math: 550. 32% scored over 600 on SAT critical reading, 27% scored over 600 on SAT math.

Student Life Upper grades have specified standards of dress, student council, honor system. Discipline rests primarily with faculty. Attendance at religious services is required.

Tuition and Aid Day student tuition: $8280. Tuition installment plan (SMART Tuition Payment Plan, 4% discount if paid in full). Tuition reduction for siblings, need-based scholarship grants available. In 2010–11, 10% of upper-school students received aid. Total amount of financial aid awarded in 2010–11: $91,461.

Admissions Traditional secondary-level entrance grade is 9. For fall 2010, 28 students applied for upper-level admission, 23 were accepted, 21 enrolled. Admissions testing or Iowa Tests of Basic Skills required. Deadline for receipt of application materials: none. Application fee required: $100. Interview required.

Athletics Interscholastic: baseball (boys), basketball (b,g), cheering (g), cross-country running (b,g), flag football (b), football (b), golf (b), physical fitness (b,g), physical training (b,g), soccer (b,g), softball (g), strength & conditioning (b,g), swimming and diving (g), tennis (b,g), track and field (b,g), volleyball (g), weight training (b,g), wrestling (b); coed intramural: bowling, sailing, table tennis, ultimate Frisbee. 2 PE instructors, 8 coaches, 2 athletic trainers.

Computers Computers are regularly used in all classes. Computer network features include on-campus library services, Internet access, wireless campus network, Internet filtering or blocking technology. Campus intranet, student e-mail accounts, and computer access in designated common areas are available to students. Students grades are available online. The school has a published electronic and media policy.

Contact Mrs. Joyce McDonald, Director of Admissions. 407-339-0223. Fax: 407-339-4148. E-mail: jmcdonald@orangewoodchristian.org. Web site: www.orangewoodchristian.org.

OREGON EPISCOPAL SCHOOL

6300 Southwest Nicol Road

Portland, Oregon 97223-7566

Head of School: Mrs. Mo Copeland

General Information Coeducational boarding and day college-preparatory, arts, religious studies, technology, and science school, affiliated with Episcopal Church. Boarding grades 9–12, day grades PK–12. Founded: 1869. Setting: suburban. Students are housed in single-sex dormitories. 59-acre campus. 9 buildings on campus. Approved or accredited by National Association of Episcopal Schools, Northwest Association of Schools and Colleges, Pacific Northwest Association of Independent Schools, and Oregon Department of Education. Member of National Association of Independent Schools and Secondary School Admission Test Board. Endowment: $22.1 million. Total enrollment: 845. Upper school average class size: 14. Upper school faculty-student ratio: 1:7. There are 175 required school days per year for Upper School students. Upper School students typically attend 5 days per week. The average school day consists of 7 hours.

Upper School Student Profile Grade 9: 75 students (35 boys, 40 girls); Grade 10: 84 students (45 boys, 39 girls); Grade 11: 70 students (32 boys, 38 girls); Grade 12: 75 students (41 boys, 34 girls); Postgraduate: 1 student (1 boy). 19% of students are boarding students. 79% are state residents. 4 states are represented in upper school student body. 16% are international students. International students from China, Hong Kong, Republic of Korea, Rwanda, Taiwan, and Thailand; 5 other countries represented in student body. 10% of students are members of Episcopal Church.

Faculty School total: 127. In upper school: 26 men, 29 women; 40 have advanced degrees; 7 reside on campus.

Subjects Offered Advanced chemistry, advanced math, Advanced Placement courses, algebra, American history, American literature, American studies, anatomy, anatomy and physiology, Arabic studies, art, Asian history, astronomy, athletic training, Basic programming, biology, Buddhism, calculus, calculus-AP, ceramics, chemistry, Chinese, chorus, Christian studies, Christianity, college counseling, college planning, college writing, community service, computer graphics, computer science, computer science-AP, constitutional law, creative writing, dance, debate, discrete mathematics, drama, drawing, driver education, East Asian history, ecology, electronics, engineering, English, English literature, environmental science, ESL, ESL, European history, fencing, film, film and literature, filmmaking, fine arts, finite math, foreign language, foreign policy, French, French language-AP, French-AP, freshman seminar, functions, gardening, geology, geometry, graphic arts, graphic design, graphics, health, health and wellness, history, history of China and Japan, history of ideas, history of rock and roll, history-AP, human anatomy, human relations, human sexuality, humanities, independent study, international affairs, international relations, jazz band, jazz dance, jazz ensemble, journalism, literature, marine biology, marine ecology, mathematics, mathematics-AP, microbiology, model United Nations, modern Chinese history, music, music history, music technology, musical productions, musical theater, newspaper, painting, personal finance, personal fitness, philosophy, photography, photojournalism, physical education, physical fitness, physics, playwriting and directing, poetry, pre-algebra, pre-calculus, psychology, psychology-AP, religion, religion and culture, research, science, science project, science research, service learning/internship, sex education, sexuality, Shakespeare, social studies, Spanish, Spanish language-AP, Spanish literature, Spanish-AP, speech, stagecraft, statistics, statistics-AP, tennis, theater, theater design and production, theology, track and field, trigonometry, U.S. history, U.S. history-AP, urban studies, video and animation, video film production, visual arts, vocal ensemble, vocal music, weight training, weightlifting, wellness, wilderness education, wilderness experience, world history, world literature, world religions, world religions, world wide web design, yearbook, yoga, zoology.

Graduation Requirements Arts and fine arts (art, music, dance, drama), electives, English, foreign language, health education, humanities, mathematics, philosophy, physical education (includes health), religion (includes Bible studies and theology), science, U.S. history, Winterim, College Decisions (for juniors), 120 hours of service learning.

Special Academic Programs Advanced Placement exam preparation; honors section; independent study; term-away projects; study abroad; academic accommodation for the gifted; ESL (9 students enrolled).

College Admission Counseling 78 students graduated in 2011; 77 went to college, including Boston University; Carleton College; Stanford University; University of Oregon; University of Southern California; University of Washington. Other: 1 had other specific plans. Median SAT critical reading: 658, median SAT math: 673, median SAT writing: 679, median combined SAT: 2010, median composite ACT: 28. 76% scored over 600 on SAT critical reading, 74% scored over 600 on SAT math, 82% scored over 600 on SAT writing, 92% scored over 1800 on combined SAT, 66% scored over 26 on composite ACT.

Student Life Upper grades have specified standards of dress, student council. Discipline rests equally with students and faculty. Attendance at religious services is required.

Summer Programs Remediation, enrichment, advancement, sports, art/fine arts, computer instruction programs offered; session focuses on a variety of academic, sports, and artistic enrichment programs; held on campus; accepts boys and girls; open to students from other schools. 1,000 students usually enrolled. 2012 schedule: June 17 to August 21.

Tuition and Aid Day student tuition: $24,230; 7-day tuition and room/board: $46,280. Tuition installment plan (Insured Tuition Payment Plan, monthly payment plans). Need-based scholarship grants available. In 2011–12, 19% of upper-school students received aid. Total amount of financial aid awarded in 2011–12: $400,000.

Admissions Traditional secondary-level entrance grade is 9. For fall 2011, 184 students applied for upper-level admission, 73 were accepted, 40 enrolled. SSAT or TOEFL required. Deadline for receipt of application materials: January 30. Application fee required: $75. Interview required.

Athletics Interscholastic: alpine skiing (boys, girls), basketball (b,g), cross-country running (b,g), fencing (b,g), golf (b,g), lacrosse (b,g), skiing (downhill) (b,g), soccer (b,g), tennis (b,g), track and field (b,g), volleyball (g); intramural: backpacking (b,g), dance (b,g), hiking/backpacking (b,g), outdoor activities (b,g), snowboarding (b,g), yoga (b,g); coed intramural: outdoor education, physical fitness, physical training, rock climbing, ropes courses. 2 PE instructors, 22 coaches, 1 athletic trainer.

Computers Computers are regularly used in art, English, foreign language, history, humanities, independent study, mathematics, music, philosophy, religion, science, social sciences, technology classes. Computer network features include on-campus library services, online commercial services, Internet access, wireless campus network, Internet filtering or blocking technology. Campus intranet, student e-mail accounts, and computer access in designated common areas are available to students. Students grades are available online. The school has a published electronic and media policy.

Contact Ms. Jen Bash, Admissions Associate. 503-768-3115. Fax: 503-768-3140. E-mail: admit@oes.edu. Web site: www.oes.edu.

ORINDA ACADEMY

19 Altarinda Road

Orinda, California 94563-2602

Head of School: Ron Graydon

General Information Coeducational day college-preparatory, general academic, arts, and technology school. Grades 7–12. Founded: 1982. Setting: suburban. Nearest major city is Walnut Creek. 1-acre campus. 2 buildings on campus. Approved or accredited by East Bay Independent Schools Association, The College Board, and Western Association of Schools and Colleges. Total enrollment: 81. Upper school average class size: 10. Upper school faculty-student ratio: 1:9. There are 175 required school days per year for Upper School students. Upper School students typically attend 5 days per week. The average school day consists of 6 hours and 30 minutes.

Upper School Student Profile Grade 9: 17 students (9 boys, 8 girls); Grade 10: 27 students (14 boys, 13 girls); Grade 11: 14 students (10 boys, 4 girls); Grade 12: 15 students (8 boys, 7 girls).

Faculty School total: 17. In upper school: 7 men, 9 women; 9 have advanced degrees.

Subjects Offered Algebra, American history, American literature, art, basketball, biology, British literature, calculus, chemistry, chorus, community service, computer graphics, computer literacy, computer multimedia, computer music, computer processing, computer programming, contemporary issues, creative writing, dance, drama, earth science, economics, English, English literature, English literature and composition-AP, ensembles, environmental science, ESL, European history, film history, fine arts, French, geography, geometry, government/civics, health, history, history of music, introduction to theater, journalism, keyboarding, mathematics, music, music performance, musical productions, performing arts, physical education, physics, science, social studies, Spanish, Spanish language-AP, theater, trigonometry, visual arts, women's literature, yearbook.

Graduation Requirements Algebra, biology, civics, composition, economics, English, foreign language, geometry, physical education (includes health), science, trigonometry, U.S. history, visual and performing arts. Community service is required.

Special Academic Programs 2 Advanced Placement exams for which test preparation is offered; honors section; accelerated programs; academic accommodation for the gifted; ESL (2 students enrolled).

College Admission Counseling 15 students graduated in 2011; 14 went to college, including Humboldt State University; San Francisco State University; San Jose State University; University of California, Davis; University of the Pacific; Willamette University. Other: 1 had other specific plans. Mean SAT critical reading: 548, mean SAT math: 534, mean SAT writing: 551, mean combined SAT: 1634, mean composite ACT: 27. 17% scored over 600 on SAT critical reading, 17% scored over 600 on SAT math, 17% scored over 600 on SAT writing, 17% scored over 1800 on combined SAT, 100% scored over 26 on composite ACT.

Student Life Upper grades have specified standards of dress, student council, honor system. Discipline rests primarily with faculty.

Summer Programs Remediation, enrichment, advancement programs offered; session focuses on academics; held on campus; accepts boys and girls; open to students from other schools. 50 students usually enrolled. 2012 schedule: June 18 to August 3. Application deadline: none.

Tuition and Aid Day student tuition: $28,975. Tuition installment plan (FACTS Tuition Payment Plan). Tuition reduction for siblings, need-based scholarship grants available. In 2011–12, 25% of upper-school students received aid. Total amount of financial aid awarded in 2011–12: $300,000.

Admissions Traditional secondary-level entrance grade is 9. For fall 2011, 60 students applied for upper-level admission, 23 were accepted, 13 enrolled. ISEE or SSAT required. Deadline for receipt of application materials: January 12. Application fee required: $75. On-campus interview required.

Athletics Interscholastic: baseball (boys), basketball (b,g); coed interscholastic: soccer; coed intramural: soccer, softball. 1 PE instructor, 1 coach.

Computers Computers are regularly used in English, journalism, social sciences, typing, writing, yearbook classes. Computer network features include Internet access, Internet filtering or blocking technology. Student e-mail accounts are available to students. The school has a published electronic and media policy.

Contact Laurel Evans, Admissions Assistant. 925-250-7659 Ext. 305. Fax: 925-254-4768. E-mail: laurel@orindaacademy.org. Web site: www.orindaacademy.org.

THE ORME SCHOOL

HC 63, Box 3040

Mayer, Arizona 86333

Head of School: Mr. KC Cassell

General Information Coeducational boarding and day college-preparatory, arts, bilingual studies, ESL program, and horsemanship school. Boarding grades 8–PG, day grades 1–PG. Founded: 1929. Setting: rural. Nearest major city is Phoenix. Students are housed in single-sex dormitories. 360-acre campus. 30 buildings on campus. Approved or accredited by Arizona Association of Independent Schools, North Central Association of Colleges and Schools, The Association of Boarding Schools, and Arizona Department of Education. Member of National Association of Independent Schools and Secondary School Admission Test Board. Endowment: $1 million. Total enrollment: 124. Upper school average class size: 12. Upper school faculty-student ratio: 1:6. There are 179 required school days per year for Upper School students. Upper School students typically attend 5 days per week. The average school day consists of 7 hours.

Upper School Student Profile Grade 9: 16 students (10 boys, 6 girls); Grade 10: 28 students (16 boys, 12 girls); Grade 11: 36 students (13 boys, 23 girls); Grade 12: 34 students (21 boys, 13 girls). 80% of students are boarding students. 60% are state residents. 15 states are represented in upper school student body. 30% are international students. International students from China, Germany, Hong Kong, Republic of Korea, Taiwan, and Turkey; 5 other countries represented in student body.

Faculty School total: 25. In upper school: 10 men, 12 women; 15 have advanced degrees; 20 reside on campus.

Subjects Offered Advanced Placement courses, advanced TOEFL/grammar, algebra, American history, American history-AP, American literature, American literature-AP, ancient world history, art, art history, astronomy, band, biology, British literature (honors), calculus, calculus-AP, ceramics, chemistry, choir, college admission preparation, college counseling, community service, computer programming, computer science, creative writing, drama, drama performance, ecology, English, English language and composition-AP, English literature, English literature and composition-AP, European history, European history-AP, fine arts, French, geography, geology, geometry, government, grammar, history, history of music, honors English, honors U.S. history, humanities, Latin, mathematics, music, performing arts, photography, physics, physics-AP, psychology, science, social sciences, social studies, Spanish, statistics-AP, student government, theater, trigonometry, U.S. history, U.S. history-AP, weightlifting, world cultures, world history, world literature, writing.

Graduation Requirements Arts and fine arts (art, music, dance, drama), computer science, English, foreign language, humanities, mathematics, science, social sciences, social studies (includes history), students must participate in annual outdoor programs such as Fall outing and Caravan. Community service is required.

Special Academic Programs Advanced Placement exam preparation; honors section; independent study; remedial reading and/or remedial writing; remedial math; programs in English, mathematics, general development for dyslexic students; ESL (27 students enrolled).

College Admission Counseling 33 students graduated in 2010; 32 went to college, including Arizona State University; Boston University; Columbia University; Cornell University; Dartmouth College; Northern Arizona University. Other: 1 went to work. Mean SAT critical reading: 500, mean SAT math: 533, mean SAT writing: 495, mean combined SAT: 1528, mean composite ACT: 21. 19% scored over 600 on SAT critical reading, 12% scored over 1800 on combined SAT, 9% scored over 26 on composite ACT.

Student Life Upper grades have specified standards of dress, student council, honor system. Discipline rests equally with students and faculty.

Tuition and Aid Day student tuition: $18,900; 5-day tuition and room/board: $26,290; 7-day tuition and room/board: $37,900. Tuition installment plan (monthly payment plans, individually arranged payment plans). Tuition reduction for siblings, need-based scholarship grants, need-based loans available. In 2010–11, 31% of upper-school students received aid. Total amount of financial aid awarded in 2010–11: $1,400,000.

Admissions Traditional secondary-level entrance grade is 9. For fall 2010, 91 students applied for upper-level admission, 66 were accepted, 33 enrolled. PSAT and SAT for applicants to grade 11 and 12 or TOEFL or SLEP required. Deadline for receipt of application materials: February 15. Application fee required: $50. Interview required.

Athletics Interscholastic: baseball (boys), basketball (b,g), cheering (g), cross-country running (b,g), equestrian sports (b,g), football (b), pom squad (g), rodeo (b,g), softball (g), tennis (b,g), track and field (b,g), volleyball (g); intramural: aerobics/dance (g), climbing (b,g), fitness (b,g), physical training (b,g), rappelling (b,g), rock climbing (b,g), rodeo (b,g), strength & conditioning (b,g), tennis (b,g), wall climbing (b,g), weight lifting (b,g), weight training (b,g), wilderness (b,g), wilderness survival (b,g), wrestling (b); coed interscholastic: equestrian sports, horseback riding, rodeo; coed intramural: backpacking, climbing, fitness, fitness walking, hiking/backpacking, horseback riding, mountain biking, mountaineering, outdoor activities, outdoor adventure, outdoor recreation, outdoor skills, outdoors, physical training, power lifting, rappelling, rock climbing, rodeo, skiing (downhill), snowboarding, soccer, strength & conditioning, walking, wall climbing, weight lifting, weight training, wilderness, wilderness survival.

Computers Computers are regularly used in all academic classes. Computer network features include on-campus library services, Internet access, wireless campus network, Internet filtering or blocking technology. Campus intranet and computer access in designated common areas are available to students. Students grades are available online. The school has a published electronic and media policy.

Contact Mrs. Johanna Hendrikse, Assistant Director of Admissions. 928-632-7601 Ext. 2224. Fax: 928-632-7605. E-mail: jhendrikse@ormeschool.org. Web site: www.ormeschool.org.

OUR LADY ACADEMY

222 South Beach Boulevard

Bay St. Louis, Mississippi 38520-4320

Head of School: Mrs. Tiffany Lindmark

General Information Girls' day and distance learning college-preparatory and religious studies school, affiliated with Roman Catholic Church. Grades 7–12. Distance learning grades 10–12. Founded: 1971. Setting: small town. Nearest major city is New Orleans, LA. 3-acre campus. 4 buildings on campus. Approved or accredited by Mercy Secondary Education Association, National Catholic Education Association, and Southern Association of Colleges and Schools. Endowment: $2 million. Total enrollment: 220. Upper school average class size: 22. Upper school faculty-student ratio: 1:13. There are 150 required school days per year for Upper School students. Upper School students typically attend 5 days per week. The average school day consists of 7 hours.

Upper School Student Profile Grade 9: 40 students (40 girls); Grade 10: 35 students (35 girls); Grade 11: 50 students (50 girls); Grade 12: 25 students (25 girls). 85% of students are Roman Catholic.

Faculty School total: 20. In upper school: 1 man, 19 women; 8 have advanced degrees.

Subjects Offered Advanced biology, advanced math, aquatics, band, Catholic belief and practice, choral music, Christian ethics, Christian studies, English composition, English literature, European history-AP, fine arts, integrated science, Latin, learning strategies, minority studies, moral reasoning, mythology, oral communications, physics, physiology, scripture, theater, theater arts, U.S. government, world religions.

Graduation Requirements Art, computers, English, foreign language, mathematics, physical education (includes health), religious studies, science, social sciences.

Special Academic Programs 10 Advanced Placement exams for which test preparation is offered; honors section; independent study; programs in English, general development for dyslexic students; ESL (3 students enrolled).

College Admission Counseling 45 students graduated in 2011; 37 went to college, including Louisiana State University and Agricultural and Mechanical College; Mississippi State University; University of Mississippi; University of South Alabama; University of Southern Mississippi. Median composite ACT: 25. 33% scored over 26 on composite ACT.

Student Life Upper grades have uniform requirement, student council, honor system. Discipline rests primarily with faculty. Attendance at religious services is required.

Tuition and Aid Day student tuition: $5200. Tuition installment plan (The Tuition Plan, monthly payment plans, individually arranged payment plans). Need-based scholarship grants available. In 2011–12, 8% of upper-school students received aid. Total amount of financial aid awarded in 2011–12: $40,000.

Admissions Traditional secondary-level entrance grade is 9. For fall 2011, 47 students applied for upper-level admission, 40 were accepted, 40 enrolled. CTBS, Stanford Achievement Test, any other standardized test, Metropolitan Achievement Short Form and Stanford Achievement Test required. Deadline for receipt of application materials: none. No application fee required. On-campus interview required.

Athletics Interscholastic: basketball, cheering, cross-country running, dance squad, drill team, sailing, soccer, softball, track and field, volleyball; coed interscholastic: swimming and diving, tennis. 1 PE instructor, 8 coaches, 1 athletic trainer.

Computers Computers are regularly used in accounting, business, college planning, creative writing, desktop publishing, English, foreign language, keyboarding, library science, newspaper, typing, Web site design, word processing, writing, yearbook classes. Computer network features include Internet access, wireless campus network, Internet filtering or blocking technology. Campus intranet and computer access in designated common areas are available to students. Students grades are available online. The school has a published electronic and media policy.

Contact Mrs. Tiffany Lindmark, Principal. 228-467-7048 Ext. 12. Fax: 228-467-1666. E-mail: tiffany.lindmark@ourladyacademy.com. Web site: www.ourladyacademy.com.

OUR LADY OF MERCY ACADEMY

1001 Main Road

Newfield, New Jersey 08344

Head of School: Sr. Grace Marie Scandale

General Information Girls' day college-preparatory, arts, religious studies, bilingual studies, and technology school, affiliated with Roman Catholic Church. Grades 9–12. Founded: 1962. Setting: rural. Nearest major city is Vineland. 58-acre campus. 2 buildings on campus. Approved or accredited by Middle States Association of Colleges and Schools and National Catholic Education Association. Endowment: $250,000. Total enrollment: 147. Upper school average class size: 20. Upper school faculty-student ratio: 1:11. There are 180 required school days per year for Upper School students. Upper School students typically attend 5 days per week. The average school day consists of 6 hours and 30 minutes.

Upper School Student Profile Grade 9: 32 students (32 girls); Grade 10: 45 students (45 girls); Grade 11: 35 students (35 girls); Grade 12: 35 students (35 girls); Postgraduate: 147 students (147 girls). 90% of students are Roman Catholic.

Faculty School total: 22. In upper school: 22 women; 10 have advanced degrees.

Subjects Offered Algebra, American history, American literature, art, biology, botany, British literature (honors), career and personal planning, Catholic belief and practice, chemistry, choral music, chorus, Christian ethics, Christian scripture, Christian testament, Christianity, college counseling, computer technologies, CPR, current events, death and loss, driver education, economics, electronic publishing, English literature, first aid, food and nutrition, French, graphic design, honors algebra, honors geometry, horticulture, Middle Eastern history, physics, pre-calculus, probability and statistics, psychology, publications, religion, remedial/makeup course work, social justice, sociology, technology, Western civilization.

Graduation Requirements Algebra, biology, chemistry, English, geometry, physical education (includes health), religion (includes Bible studies and theology), technology, U.S. history, Western civilization.

College Admission Counseling 50 students graduated in 2011; all went to college, including La Salle University; Rutgers, The State University of New Jersey, New Brunswick; Saint Joseph's University; Seton Hall University; University of Pennsylvania.

Student Life Upper grades have uniform requirement, student council, honor system. Discipline rests primarily with faculty. Attendance at religious services is required.

Tuition and Aid Day student tuition: $9544. Tuition installment plan (SMART Tuition Payment Plan, monthly payment plans, individually arranged payment plans). Tuition reduction for siblings, merit scholarship grants, need-based scholarship grants, paying campus jobs available. In 2011–12, 15% of upper-school students received aid; total upper-school merit-scholarship money awarded: $34,500. Total amount of financial aid awarded in 2011–12: $48,000.

Admissions Traditional secondary-level entrance grade is 9. For fall 2011, 62 students applied for upper-level admission, 50 were accepted, 32 enrolled. High School Placement Test (closed version) from Scholastic Testing Service required. Deadline for receipt of application materials: none. Application fee required: $200.

Athletics Interscholastic: basketball, cheering, crew, cross-country running, lacrosse, running, soccer, softball, strength & conditioning, swimming and diving, tennis, track and field, volleyball; intramural: badminton, basketball, flag football, golf, gymnastics, physical fitness, soccer, softball, synchronized swimming, volleyball. 2 PE instructors, 12 coaches.

Computers Computers are regularly used in all academic, career exploration, college planning, creative writing, graphic design, graphics, library, library skills, photography, publications, research skills, technology, typing, Web site design, word processing, yearbook classes. Computer network features include on-campus library services, online commercial services, Internet access, wireless campus network, Internet filtering or blocking technology. Students grades are available online. The school has a published electronic and media policy.

Contact Sr. Grace Marie Scandale, Principal. 856-697-2008. Fax: 856-697-2887. E-mail: srgrace@olmanj.org. Web site: www.olmanj.org.

OUR LADY OF MERCY HIGH SCHOOL

1437 Blossom Road

Rochester, New York 14610

Head of School: Mr. Terence Quinn

General Information Girls' day college-preparatory, arts, business, religious studies, and technology school, affiliated with Roman Catholic Church. Grades 7–12. Founded: 1928. Setting: suburban. 1 building on campus. Approved or accredited by Mercy Secondary Education Association, Middle States Association of Colleges and Schools, National Catholic Education Association, and New York State Board of Regents. Total enrollment: 691. Upper school average class size: 22. Upper school faculty-student ratio: 1:11. There are 177 required school days per year for Upper School students. Upper School students typically attend 5 days per week. The average school day consists of 6 hours and 35 minutes.

Upper School Student Profile Grade 9: 120 students (120 girls); Grade 10: 144 students (144 girls); Grade 11: 147 students (147 girls); Grade 12: 143 students (143 girls). 78% of students are Roman Catholic.

Faculty School total: 61. In upper school: 14 men, 47 women.

Subjects Offered Accounting, algebra, American history, American history-AP, American literature, art, biology, biology-AP, business, calculus-AP, ceramics, chemistry, chemistry-AP, creative writing, drama, earth science, economics, English, English literature, English literature-AP, entrepreneurship, European history-AP, finance, French, French-AP, geometry, government/civics, health, Latin, Latin-AP, mathematics, music, orchestra, photography, physical education, physics, physics-AP, prayer/spirituality, pre-calculus, psychology, psychology-AP, science, scripture, social justice, Spanish, Spanish-AP, speech, studio art, theater, theater arts, theology, world history, world history-AP, world literature, writing.

Graduation Requirements Arts and fine arts (art, music, dance, drama), English, foreign language, mathematics, physical education (includes health), science, social studies (includes history), theology.

Special Academic Programs 12 Advanced Placement exams for which test preparation is offered; honors section; study at local college for college credit; ESL.

College Admission Counseling 125 students graduated in 2011; all went to college, including Nazareth College of Rochester; Rochester Institute of Technology; University of Rochester. Mean SAT critical reading: 564, mean SAT math: 555, mean SAT writing: 600. 39% scored over 26 on composite ACT.

Student Life Upper grades have specified standards of dress, student council, honor system. Discipline rests primarily with faculty. Attendance at religious services is required.
Summer Programs Remediation, sports, art/fine arts, computer instruction programs offered; held on campus; accepts girls; open to students from other schools.
Tuition and Aid Day student tuition: $8100. Tuition installment plan (monthly payment plans, individually arranged payment plans, 2-payment plan). Merit scholarship grants, need-based scholarship grants available. In 2011–12, 20% of upper-school students received aid; total upper-school merit-scholarship money awarded: $1,200,000. Total amount of financial aid awarded in 2011–12: $1,200,000.
Admissions Traditional secondary-level entrance grade is 9. For fall 2011, 103 students applied for upper-level admission, 88 were accepted, 55 enrolled. Educational Development Series, High School Placement Test (closed version) from Scholastic Testing Service or Scholastic Testing Service High School Placement Test required. Deadline for receipt of application materials: none. Application fee required: $200. On-campus interview recommended.
Athletics Interscholastic: basketball, bowling, cheering, crew, cross-country running, diving, golf, indoor track, lacrosse, sailing, skiing (downhill), soccer, softball, swimming and diving, tennis, track and field, volleyball. 3 PE instructors, 12 coaches, 1 athletic trainer.
Computers Computers are regularly used in accounting, all academic, business, business education, career exploration, college planning, English, keyboarding, library skills, literary magazine, mathematics, newspaper, photography, publications, research skills, science, technology, yearbook classes. Computer resources include on-campus library services, Internet access. The school has a published electronic and media policy.
Contact Mary Elizabeth McCahill, Director of Admissions. 585-288-7120 Ext. 310. Fax: 585-288-7966. E-mail: mmccahill@mercyhs.com. Web site: www.mercyhs.com.

OUT-OF-DOOR ACADEMY

5950 Deer Drive

Sarasota, Florida 34240

Head of School: Mr. David Mahler

General Information Coeducational day college-preparatory school. Grades PK–12. Founded: 1924. Setting: suburban. Nearest major city is Tampa. 85-acre campus. 9 buildings on campus. Approved or accredited by Florida Council of Independent Schools. Member of National Association of Independent Schools. Endowment: $7.5 million. Total enrollment: 615. Upper school average class size: 16. Upper school faculty-student ratio: 1:13. There are 172 required school days per year for Upper School students. Upper School students typically attend 5 days per week. The average school day consists of 7 hours.
Upper School Student Profile Grade 9: 64 students (27 boys, 37 girls); Grade 10: 57 students (28 boys, 29 girls); Grade 11: 53 students (21 boys, 32 girls); Grade 12: 56 students (32 boys, 24 girls).
Faculty School total: 75. In upper school: 13 men, 19 women; 18 have advanced degrees.
Subjects Offered Advanced Placement courses, advanced studio art-AP, algebra, American history-AP, art history, biology, biology-AP, British literature, calculus, calculus-AP, chemistry, chemistry-AP, college counseling, computers, drama, drama performance, dramatic arts, English, English composition, English language and composition-AP, English literature, English literature and composition-AP, English-AP, European history-AP, expository writing, French, French language-AP, geometry, graphic design, health and wellness, history-AP, honors algebra, honors geometry, Latin, Latin-AP, literature, literature and composition-AP, music, newspaper, photography, portfolio art, Spanish, Spanish language-AP, studio art, studio art-AP, U.S. government, U.S. history, U.S. history-AP, women's studies, world cultures, world literature, world studies, yearbook, zoology.
Graduation Requirements Arts and fine arts (art, music, dance, drama), electives, English, foreign language, health, history, mathematics, performing arts, personal fitness, science. Community service is required.
Special Academic Programs 21 Advanced Placement exams for which test preparation is offered; honors section; independent study.
College Admission Counseling 53 students graduated in 2011; all went to college, including Colgate University; New York University; Syracuse University; Trinity College; Vanderbilt University. Mean SAT critical reading: 622, mean SAT math: 618, mean SAT writing: 613, mean combined SAT: 1854. 59% scored over 600 on SAT critical reading, 59% scored over 600 on SAT math, 61% scored over 600 on SAT writing, 61% scored over 1800 on combined SAT.
Student Life Upper grades have specified standards of dress, student council, honor system. Discipline rests equally with students and faculty.
Summer Programs Enrichment, sports, art/fine arts programs offered; held on campus; accepts boys and girls; open to students from other schools. 150 students usually enrolled. 2012 schedule: June 4 to August 10. Application deadline: May.
Tuition and Aid Day student tuition: $18,460. Tuition installment plan (FACTS Tuition Payment Plan). Need-based scholarship grants, faculty/staff tuition remission available. In 2011–12, 28% of upper-school students received aid. Total amount of financial aid awarded in 2011–12: $650,465.
Admissions Traditional secondary-level entrance grade is 9. For fall 2011, 67 students applied for upper-level admission, 41 were accepted, 35 enrolled. ERB or SSAT required. Deadline for receipt of application materials: March 2. Application fee required: $100. Interview required.
Athletics Interscholastic: baseball (boys), basketball (b,g), cheering (g), cross-country running (b,g), football (b), golf (b,g), independent competitive sports (b,g), lacrosse (b,g), soccer (b,g), softball (g), swimming and diving (b,g), tennis (b,g), track and field (b,g), volleyball (g); intramural: fitness (b,g); coed interscholastic: sailing; coed intramural: physical fitness, physical training, strength & conditioning, weight training. 3 PE instructors, 21 coaches, 1 athletic trainer.
Computers Computers are regularly used in computer applications, English, foreign language, French, graphic design, history, Latin, mathematics, newspaper, science, senior seminar, social studies, Spanish, yearbook classes. Computer network features include on-campus library services, online commercial services, Internet access, wireless campus network, Internet filtering or blocking technology, digital video production. Campus intranet and computer access in designated common areas are available to students. Students grades are available online. The school has a published electronic and media policy.
Contact Mr. Jamie Carver, Director of Middle and Upper School Admissions. 941-554-5954. Fax: 941-907-1251. E-mail: jcarver@oda.edu. Web site: www.oda.edu.

THE OVERLAKE SCHOOL

20301 Northeast 108th Street

Redmond, Washington 98053

Head of School: Francisco J. Grijalva, EdD

General Information Coeducational day college-preparatory and arts school. Grades 5–12. Founded: 1967. Setting: rural. Nearest major city is Seattle. 75-acre campus. 22 buildings on campus. Approved or accredited by Northwest Accreditation Commission, Pacific Northwest Association of Independent Schools, The College Board, and Washington Department of Education. Member of National Association of Independent Schools. Endowment: $15 million. Total enrollment: 535. Upper school average class size: 13. Upper school faculty-student ratio: 1:9. There are 173 required school days per year for Upper School students. Upper School students typically attend 5 days per week. The average school day consists of 6 hours.
Upper School Student Profile Grade 9: 80 students (43 boys, 37 girls); Grade 10: 77 students (36 boys, 41 girls); Grade 11: 70 students (38 boys, 32 girls); Grade 12: 75 students (47 boys, 28 girls).
Faculty School total: 64. In upper school: 17 men, 23 women; 38 have advanced degrees.
Subjects Offered African studies, algebra, American history, American history-AP, American literature, art-AP, bioethics, biology-AP, botany, calculus, calculus-AP, ceramics, chamber groups, chemistry-AP, Chinese, chorus, community service, comparative religion, computer programming, computer science, concert band, constitutional law, creative writing, dance, drama, drawing, economics, economics and history, English, English literature, English-AP, environmental science, ethics, European history-AP, European literature, film, fine arts, French, French-AP, geometry, global issues, graphic design, Holocaust and other genocides, integrated science, Japanese, jazz band, journalism, lab science, Latin, Latin American literature, Latin-AP, life skills, literature, math review, mathematics, metalworking, Middle East, music, music theater, outdoor education, painting, performing arts, photography, physical education, physics, physics-AP, pre-calculus, printmaking, psychology, science, social studies, Spanish, Spanish-AP, stagecraft, statistics, studio art, study skills, theater, video film production, Vietnam history, Vietnam War, woodworking, world history, world literature, World-Wide-Web publishing, yearbook.
Graduation Requirements Arts and fine arts (art, music, dance, drama), English, foreign language, history, lab science, mathematics, outdoor education, physical education (includes health), senior project, annual Project Week, 3 co-curricular activities, 15 hours of community service per year (60 total).
Special Academic Programs 14 Advanced Placement exams for which test preparation is offered; honors section; independent study; term-away projects; study abroad; academic accommodation for the gifted, the musically talented, and the artistically talented.
College Admission Counseling 69 students graduated in 2011; 68 went to college, including Santa Clara University; University of Puget Sound; University of Southern California; University of Washington; Western Washington University; Whitman College. Other: 1 had other specific plans. Median composite ACT: 29. Mean SAT critical reading: 644, mean SAT math: 665, mean SAT writing: 643, mean combined SAT: 1952. 79% scored over 600 on SAT critical reading, 85% scored over 600 on SAT math, 67% scored over 600 on SAT writing, 100% scored over 26 on composite ACT.
Student Life Upper grades have student council. Discipline rests equally with students and faculty.
Summer Programs Sports programs offered; session focuses on skill-building sports camps; held on campus; accepts boys and girls; not open to students from other schools. 75 students usually enrolled. 2012 schedule: August 1 to August 15. Application deadline: June 30.
Tuition and Aid Day student tuition: $25,602. Tuition installment plan (Insured Tuition Payment Plan, monthly payment plans). Need-based scholarship grants, 50%

tuition remission for faculty and staff, Malone Scholarship, Gibson Scholarship available. In 2011–12, 18% of upper-school students received aid. Total amount of financial aid awarded in 2011–12: $675,904.

Admissions Traditional secondary-level entrance grade is 9. For fall 2011, 72 students applied for upper-level admission, 31 were accepted, 21 enrolled. ISEE required. Deadline for receipt of application materials: January 12. Application fee required: $60. Interview required.

Athletics Interscholastic: baseball (boys), basketball (b,g), cross-country running (b,g), golf (b,g), lacrosse (b,g), outdoor education (b,g), physical fitness (b,g), rock climbing (b,g), ropes courses (b,g), soccer (b,g), tennis (b,g), ultimate Frisbee (b), volleyball (g); intramural: baseball (b), basketball (b,g), cross-country running (b,g), lacrosse (b,g), outdoor education (b,g), physical fitness (b,g), rock climbing (b,g), ropes courses (b,g), skiing (downhill) (b,g), soccer (b,g), strength & conditioning (b,g), tennis (b,g), volleyball (b,g), weight lifting (b,g), weight training (b,g); coed interscholastic: outdoor education, rock climbing, ropes courses, squash, tennis; coed intramural: backpacking, basketball, bicycling, canoeing/kayaking, climbing, cross-country running, dance, golf, hiking/backpacking, kayaking, mountain biking, mountaineering, outdoor activities, outdoor education, outdoor skills, rafting, rock climbing, ropes courses, skiing (downhill), snowshoeing, table tennis, tennis, ultimate Frisbee, wall climbing, wilderness. 4 PE instructors, 45 coaches, 2 athletic trainers.

Computers Computers are regularly used in all classes. Computer network features include on-campus library services, online commercial services, Internet access, wireless campus network. Campus intranet and computer access in designated common areas are available to students. The school has a published electronic and media policy.

Contact Lori Maughan, Director of Admission. 425-868-1000. Fax: 425-868-5771. E-mail: lmaughan@overlake.org. Web site: www.overlake.org.

THE OXFORD ACADEMY

1393 Boston Post Road

Westbrook, Connecticut 06498-0685

Head of School: Philip B. Cocchiola

General Information Boys' boarding college-preparatory, general academic, arts, bilingual studies, and ESL school. Grades 9–PG. Founded: 1906. Setting: small town. Nearest major city is New Haven. Students are housed in single-sex dormitories. 13-acre campus. 8 buildings on campus. Approved or accredited by Connecticut Association of Independent Schools, New England Association of Schools and Colleges, The Association of Boarding Schools, and Connecticut Department of Education. Member of National Association of Independent Schools and Secondary School Admission Test Board. Endowment: $250,000. Total enrollment: 38. Upper school average class size: 1. Upper school faculty-student ratio: 1:1.

Upper School Student Profile Grade 9: 4 students (4 boys); Grade 10: 5 students (5 boys); Grade 11: 10 students (10 boys); Grade 12: 17 students (17 boys). 100% of students are boarding students. 35% are state residents. 8 states are represented in upper school student body. 33% are international students. International students from Bahamas, Bermuda, France, Mexico, Republic of Korea, and Saudi Arabia.

Faculty School total: 22. In upper school: 15 men, 7 women; 10 have advanced degrees; 12 reside on campus.

Subjects Offered Algebra, American history, American literature, anatomy, astronomy, biology, botany, calculus, chemistry, creative writing, earth science, ecology, economics, English, English literature, environmental science, ESL, European history, expository writing, French, geography, geology, geometry, German, government/civics, grammar, history, Latin, marine biology, mathematics, oceanography, paleontology, philosophy, physical education, physics, physiology, psychology, science, social studies, sociology, Spanish, study skills, trigonometry, world history, world literature, writing, zoology.

Graduation Requirements English, foreign language, mathematics, science, social studies (includes history). Community service is required.

Special Academic Programs Advanced Placement exam preparation; honors section; accelerated programs; independent study; academic accommodation for the gifted; remedial reading and/or remedial writing; remedial math; special instructional classes for students with mild ADD and learning differences; ESL (6 students enrolled).

College Admission Counseling 17 students graduated in 2010; all went to college, including Bucknell University; Georgia Southern University; Lynn University; Rhode Island School of Design; Suffolk University; Wheaton College. 20% scored over 600 on SAT critical reading, 20% scored over 600 on SAT math, 20% scored over 600 on SAT writing.

Student Life Upper grades have specified standards of dress, student council, honor system. Discipline rests equally with students and faculty.

Tuition and Aid 7-day tuition and room/board: $52,474. Tuition installment plan (monthly payment plans, individually arranged payment plans).

Admissions For fall 2010, 22 students applied for upper-level admission, 19 were accepted, 13 enrolled. SLEP for foreign students, Stanford Achievement Test, Otis-Lennon School Ability Test, TOEFL, WISC or WAIS or Woodcock-Johnson required. Deadline for receipt of application materials: none. Application fee required: $65. Interview recommended.

Athletics Interscholastic: basketball, soccer, tennis; intramural: basketball, flag football, Frisbee, hiking/backpacking, paint ball, power lifting, roller blading, strength & conditioning, table tennis, weight lifting, weight training. 6 coaches.

Computers Computers are regularly used in mathematics classes. Computer network features include Internet access. Student e-mail accounts are available to students. The school has a published electronic and media policy.

Contact Mrs. Patricia Davis, Director of Admissions. 860-399-6247 Ext. 100. Fax: 860-399-6805. E-mail: admissions@oxfordacademy.net. Web site: www.oxfordacademy.net.

See Display on next page and Close-Up on page 658.

PACIFIC CREST COMMUNITY SCHOOL

116 Northeast 29th Street

Portland, Oregon 97232

Head of School: Becky Lukens

General Information Coeducational day college-preparatory and arts school. Grades 6–12. Founded: 1993. Setting: urban. 1 building on campus. Approved or accredited by Northwest Accreditation Commission, Northwest Association of Schools and Colleges, and Oregon Department of Education. Total enrollment: 80. Upper school average class size: 10. Upper school faculty-student ratio: 1:9. There are 180 required school days per year for Upper School students. Upper School students typically attend 5 days per week. The average school day consists of 6 hours.

Faculty School total: 10. In upper school: 4 men, 6 women; 9 have advanced degrees.

Graduation Requirements Senior seminar/dissertation.

Special Academic Programs Independent study; study at local college for college credit; academic accommodation for the gifted.

College Admission Counseling 13 students graduated in 2011; 10 went to college. Other: 3 had other specific plans.

Student Life Discipline rests equally with students and faculty.

Tuition and Aid Day student tuition: $11,000. Tuition installment plan (monthly payment plans). Need-based scholarship grants available. In 2011–12, 15% of upper-school students received aid. Total amount of financial aid awarded in 2011–12: $50,000.

Admissions Traditional secondary-level entrance grade is 9. For fall 2011, 17 students applied for upper-level admission, 17 were accepted, 17 enrolled. Deadline for receipt of application materials: none. Application fee required: $100. Interview required.

Athletics Coed Intramural: artistic gym, basketball, bicycling, bowling, canoeing/kayaking, hiking/backpacking, outdoor adventure, outdoor education, outdoor skills, rock climbing, running, skiing (cross-country). 2 PE instructors.

Computers Computer network features include Internet access, wireless campus network. Student e-mail accounts are available to students.

Contact Jenny Osborne, Co-Director. 503-234-2826. Fax: 503-234-3186. E-mail: Jenny@pcrest.org. Web site: www.pcrest.org.

PACIFIC HILLS SCHOOL

8628 Holloway Drive

West Hollywood, California 90069

Head of School: Dr. Peter Temes

General Information Coeducational day college-preparatory school. Grades 6–12. Founded: 1983. Setting: urban. Nearest major city is Beverly Hills. 2-acre campus. 2 buildings on campus. Approved or accredited by Western Association of Schools and Colleges and California Department of Education. Member of National Association of Independent Schools. Total enrollment: 207. Upper school average class size: 15. Upper school faculty-student ratio: 1:10. There are 175 required school days per year for Upper School students. Upper School students typically attend 5 days per week. The average school day consists of 6 hours and 35 minutes.

Upper School Student Profile Grade 9: 23 students (13 boys, 10 girls); Grade 10: 41 students (22 boys, 19 girls); Grade 11: 35 students (23 boys, 12 girls); Grade 12: 51 students (33 boys, 18 girls).

Faculty School total: 27. In upper school: 16 men, 11 women; 9 have advanced degrees.

Subjects Offered Advanced Placement courses, aerobics, algebra, American history, American literature, anatomy, art, biology, calculus-AP, cheerleading, chemistry, computers, economics, English, English literature, film, French, geometry, government, human development, music, newspaper, photography, physical education, physics, precalculus, Spanish, speech, theater arts, yearbook.

Graduation Requirements Arts and fine arts (art, music, dance, drama), English, foreign language, mathematics, outdoor education, physical education (includes health), science, social sciences, social studies (includes history). Community service is required.

Special Academic Programs 9 Advanced Placement exams for which test preparation is offered; honors section.

College Admission Counseling 32 students graduated in 2011; all went to college, including California State University, Northridge; Loyola Marymount University, University of California, Irvine; University of California, Los Angeles; University of California, San Diego; University of Southern California. Mean SAT critical reading: 525, mean SAT math: 510, mean SAT writing: 532. 17% scored over 600 on SAT critical reading, 15% scored over 600 on SAT math, 15% scored over 600 on SAT writing.

Student Life Upper grades have specified standards of dress, student council, honor system. Discipline rests primarily with faculty.

Summer Programs Remediation, enrichment programs offered; session focuses on remediation; held on campus; accepts boys and girls; open to students from other schools. 185 students usually enrolled. 2012 schedule: June 21 to July 29. Application deadline: none.

Tuition and Aid Day student tuition: $20,950. Tuition installment plan (Insured Tuition Payment Plan, monthly payment plans, individually arranged payment plans). Tuition reduction for siblings, need-based scholarship grants, need-based loans available. In 2011–12, 52% of upper-school students received aid.

Admissions Traditional secondary-level entrance grade is 9. For fall 2011, 118 students applied for upper-level admission, 61 were accepted, 54 enrolled. CTBS (or similar from their school), ERB or ISEE required. Deadline for receipt of application materials: none. Application fee required: $100. On-campus interview required.

Athletics Interscholastic: baseball (boys), basketball (b,g), cheering (g), flag football (b), softball (g), volleyball (b,g); coed interscholastic: cross-country running, dance team, outdoor education, soccer, track and field. 3 PE instructors, 7 coaches.

Computers Computers are regularly used in graphic design, journalism, yearbook classes. Computer network features include Internet access, wireless campus network, Internet filtering or blocking technology. Computer access in designated common areas is available to students. Students grades are available online. The school has a published electronic and media policy.

Contact Ms. Lynne Bradshaw, Admissions Assistant. 310-276-3068 Ext. 112. Fax: 310-657-3831. E-mail: lbradshaw@phschool.org. Web site: www.phschool.org.

PADUA FRANCISCAN HIGH SCHOOL

6740 State Road

Parma, Ohio 44134-4598

Head of School: Mr. David Stec

General Information Coeducational day college-preparatory, arts, business, religious studies, and technology school, affiliated with Roman Catholic Church; primarily serves students with learning disabilities and dyslexic students. Grades 9–12. Founded: 1961. Setting: suburban. Nearest major city is Cleveland. 40-acre campus. 1 building on campus. Approved or accredited by North Central Association of Colleges and Schools, Ohio Catholic Schools Accreditation Association (OCSAA), and Ohio Department of Education. Endowment: $1.5 million. Total enrollment: 837. Upper school average class size: 25. Upper school faculty-student ratio: 1:19. There are 179 required school days per year for Upper School students. Upper School students typically attend 5 days per week. The average school day consists of 6 hours and 30 minutes.

Upper School Student Profile Grade 9: 220 students (122 boys, 98 girls); Grade 10: 181 students (96 boys, 85 girls); Grade 11: 208 students (111 boys, 97 girls); Grade 12: 228 students (105 boys, 123 girls). 90% of students are Roman Catholic.

Faculty School total: 60. In upper school: 27 men, 31 women; 30 have advanced degrees.

Subjects Offered Accounting, algebra, American government, art appreciation, biology-AP, business, calculus-AP, chemistry, child development, Christian ethics, church history, computers, concert band, concert choir, consumer economics, current events, design, drawing, earth science, economics, English, English language-AP, ensembles, fitness, food and nutrition, French, French-AP, geography, geometry, German, German-AP, honors algebra, honors English, honors geometry, honors U.S. history, integrated science, interior design, Italian, Latin, Latin-AP, marching band, marketing, math analysis, music appreciation, music theory, orchestra, painting, photography, physics, pre-calculus, programming, psychology, social issues, social justice, sociology, Spanish, Spanish-AP, stagecraft, symphonic band, theater, trigonometry, U.S. history, U.S. history-AP, world cultures, world history.

Graduation Requirements Arts and fine arts (art, music, dance, drama), computer science, English, foreign language, lab science, mathematics, physical education (includes health), social studies (includes history), theology, four years of service projects.

Special Academic Programs Advanced Placement exam preparation; honors section; accelerated programs; study at local college for college credit; study abroad; remedial reading and/or remedial writing; remedial math; programs in English, mathematics for dyslexic students; special instructional classes for students with learning disabilities.

College Admission Counseling 202 students graduated in 2011; 198 went to college, including Bowling Green State University; Kent State University; Miami University; The University of Akron; The University of Toledo; University of Dayton. Other: 2 went to work, 2 entered military service. Median SAT critical reading: 537, median SAT math: 530, median composite ACT: 23.

Student Life Upper grades have specified standards of dress, student council, honor system. Discipline rests primarily with faculty. Attendance at religious services is required.

Summer Programs Enrichment, sports, art/fine arts, computer instruction programs offered; session focuses on introducing students to school, programs, coaches, and other students; held on campus; accepts boys and girls; open to students from other schools. 175 students usually enrolled. 2012 schedule: June 18 to June 22. Application deadline: May 18.

Tuition and Aid Day student tuition: $8975. Tuition installment plan (monthly payment plans, individually arranged payment plans). Tuition reduction for siblings, merit scholarship grants, need-based scholarship grants, paying campus jobs available. In 2011–12, 48% of upper-school students received aid; total upper-school merit-scholarship money awarded: $181,000. Total amount of financial aid awarded in 2011–12: $12,500,000.

Admissions Traditional secondary-level entrance grade is 9. For fall 2011, 250 students applied for upper-level admission, 240 were accepted, 220 enrolled. STS required. Deadline for receipt of application materials: January 27. Application fee required: $100.

Athletics Interscholastic: aquatics (boys, girls), baseball (b), basketball (b,g), cheering (g), combined training (b,g), cross-country running (b,g), dance team (g), diving (b,g), football (b), golf (b,g), hockey (b), ice hockey (b), lacrosse (b), physical fitness (b,g), soccer (b,g), softball (g), strength & conditioning (b,g), swimming and diving (b,g), tennis (g), track and field (b,g), volleyball (g), wrestling (b); intramural: basketball (b), flag football (b), football (b), freestyle skiing (b,g), golf (g), gymnastics (g), power lifting (b), touch football (b), weight lifting (b), weight training (b,g), winter soccer (b), yoga (b); coed interscholastic: figure skating, fitness; coed intramural: alpine skiing, backpacking, canoeing/kayaking, fishing, hiking/backpacking, skiing (downhill), snowboarding, wilderness, wilderness survival, wildernessways. 3 PE instructors, 30 coaches, 5 athletic trainers.

Computers Computers are regularly used in all academic classes. Computer network features include on-campus library services, online commercial services, Internet access, wireless campus network. Computer access in designated common areas is available to students. Students grades are available online. The school has a published electronic and media policy.

Contact Mrs. Nancy Hodas, Admissions Coordinator. 440-845-2444 Ext. 112. Fax: 440-845-5710. E-mail: nhodas@paduafranciscan.com. Web site: www.paduafranciscan.com.

THE PAIDEIA SCHOOL

1509 Ponce de Leon Avenue

Atlanta, Georgia 30307

Head of School: Paul F. Bianchi

General Information Coeducational day college-preparatory, arts, and technology school. Grades PK–12. Founded: 1971. Setting: urban. 28-acre campus. 13 buildings on campus. Approved or accredited by Georgia Independent School Association, Southern Association of Colleges and Schools, Southern Association of Independent Schools, and Georgia Department of Education. Endowment: $10.8 million. Total enrollment: 975. Upper school average class size: 12. Upper school faculty-student ratio: 1:9. There are 179 required school days per year for Upper School students. Upper School students typically attend 5 days per week. The average school day consists of 6 hours and 45 minutes.

Upper School Student Profile Grade 9: 102 students (55 boys, 47 girls); Grade 10: 108 students (53 boys, 55 girls); Grade 11: 107 students (48 boys, 59 girls); Grade 12: 98 students (51 boys, 47 girls).

Faculty School total: 135. In upper school: 33 men, 33 women; 55 have advanced degrees.

Subjects Offered African-American history, algebra, American culture, American government, American history, American literature, anatomy, archaeology, art, art history, Asian history, Asian studies, auto mechanics, bioethics, biology, biology-AP, calculus, ceramics, chemistry, chemistry-AP, chorus, community service, comparative religion, computer programming, creative writing, drama, drawing, ecology, environmental systems, economics, English, English literature, environmental science, ethics, European history-AP, expository writing, fine arts, forensics, French, French studies, geography, geology, geometry, government/civics, health, history, humanities, jazz, journalism, literature, mathematics, medieval history, organic chemistry, photography, physical education, physics, physics-AP, physiology, poetry, pre-calculus, psychology, psychology-AP, Shakespeare, social studies, sociology, Spanish, Spanish literature, speech, statistics, statistics-AP, theater, trigonometry, U.S. history, Web site design, weight training, women's health, women's studies, world history, world literature, writing.

Graduation Requirements Arts and fine arts (art, music, dance, drama), English, foreign language, mathematics, physical education (includes health), science, social studies (includes history). Community service is required.

Special Academic Programs 11 Advanced Placement exams for which test preparation is offered; honors section; independent study.

College Admission Counseling 95 students graduated in 2011; 94 went to college, including Eckerd College; Elon University; Emory University; University of Georgia. Other: 1 entered a postgraduate year.

Student Life Upper grades have student council, honor system. Discipline rests equally with students and faculty.

Summer Programs Enrichment programs offered; session focuses on two-week Urban Institute for students in grades 10-12; held both on and off campus; held at various government buildings around Atlanta; accepts boys and girls; open to students from other schools. 12 students usually enrolled. 2012 schedule: June 11 to June 22. Application deadline: March 6.

Tuition and Aid Day student tuition: $19,563. Tuition installment plan (bank-arranged tuition loan program). Need-based tuition assistance available. In 2011–12, 18% of upper-school students received aid. Total amount of financial aid awarded in 2011–12: $1,156,509.

Admissions Traditional secondary-level entrance grade is 9. Deadline for receipt of application materials: February 1. Application fee required: $75. On-campus interview required.

Athletics Interscholastic: baseball (boys), basketball (b,g), cross-country running (b,g), diving (b,g), soccer (b,g), softball (g), swimming and diving (b,g), tennis (b,g), track and field (b,g), ultimate Frisbee (b,g), volleyball (g); coed interscholastic: golf, ultimate Frisbee; coed intramural: aerobics, basketball, bicycling, bowling, fitness, flag football, hiking/backpacking, lacrosse, outdoor education, soccer, softball, tai chi, ultimate Frisbee, yoga. 2 PE instructors, 1 athletic trainer.

Computers Computers are regularly used in art, English, foreign language, graphic arts, history, journalism, mathematics, music, science classes. Computer network features include on-campus library services, Internet access, wireless campus network, Internet filtering or blocking technology, technology assistant program, computer borrowing program for students, technology courses. Campus intranet, student e-mail accounts, and computer access in designated common areas are available to students. The school has a published electronic and media policy.

Contact Admissions Office. 404-270-2312. Fax: 404-270-2312. E-mail: admissions@paideiaschool.org. Web site: www.paideiaschool.org.

PALMA SCHOOL

919 Iverson Street

Salinas, California 93901

Head of School: Br. Patrick D. Dunne, CFC

General Information Boys' day college-preparatory and religious studies school, affiliated with Roman Catholic Church. Grades 7–12. Founded: 1951. Setting: suburban. Nearest major city is San Jose. 25-acre campus. 16 buildings on campus. Approved or accredited by Western Association of Schools and Colleges, Western Catholic Education Association, and California Department of Education. Endowment: $200,000. Total enrollment: 534. Upper school average class size: 25. Upper school faculty-student ratio: 1:15. Upper School students typically attend 5 days per week.

Upper School Student Profile Grade 9: 116 students (116 boys); Grade 10: 102 students (102 boys); Grade 11: 107 students (107 boys); Grade 12: 77 students (77 boys). 69% of students are Roman Catholic.

Faculty School total: 31. In upper school: 26 men, 5 women; 19 have advanced degrees.

Subjects Offered Algebra, American history, American literature, anatomy, art, art history, band, biology, business, calculus, calculus-AP, chemistry, Chinese, Christian and Hebrew scripture, church history, civics, community service, computer applications, computer art, computer math, computer multimedia, computer programming, computer programming-AP, computer science, computer-aided design, creative writing, debate, digital art, driver education, earth science, economics, English, English language and composition-AP, English literature, English literature-AP, ethics, European history, European history-AP, expository writing, film, film studies, fine arts, French, geography, geometry, government/civics, grammar, health, health education, history, honors algebra, honors geometry, Japanese, jazz ensemble, journalism, Latin, mathematics, music, participation in sports, physical education, physical science, physics, pre-calculus, psychology, religion, Russian, Russian literature, science, social studies, Spanish, Spanish language-AP, speech, statistics-AP, student government, theology, trigonometry, typing, U.S. government and politics-AP, U.S. history-AP, video film production, world history, world literature, world religions, writing.

Graduation Requirements Advanced biology, arts and fine arts (art, music, dance, drama), English, foreign language, mathematics, physical education (includes health), religion (includes Bible studies and theology), science, social studies (includes history), religious retreat (8th, 9th, 10th grades), 60 hours of community service, Must take the ACT College Entrance Exam.

Special Academic Programs Advanced Placement exam preparation; honors section; study at local college for college credit.

College Admission Counseling 115 students graduated in 2011; 111 went to college, including California Polytechnic State University, San Luis Obispo; California State University, Fresno; California State University, Monterey Bay; Saint Mary's College of California; Santa Clara University; University of California, Davis. Other: 2 went to work, 2 entered military service.

Student Life Upper grades have specified standards of dress, student council, honor system. Discipline rests primarily with faculty. Attendance at religious services is required.

Summer Programs Remediation, enrichment, advancement programs offered; session focuses on remediation and advancement; held on campus; accepts boys and girls; open to students from other schools. 150 students usually enrolled. 2012 schedule: June 15 to July 25. Application deadline: March 1.

Tuition and Aid Day student tuition: $9900. Tuition installment plan (Insured Tuition Payment Plan, monthly payment plans, 2-payment plan). Merit scholarship grants, need-based scholarship grants available. In 2011–12, 15% of upper-school students received aid. Total amount of financial aid awarded in 2011–12: $229,000.

Admissions Traditional secondary-level entrance grade is 9. For fall 2011, 65 students applied for upper-level admission, 45 were accepted, 40 enrolled. ETS high school placement exam required. Deadline for receipt of application materials: none. Application fee required: $75. On-campus interview required.

Athletics Interscholastic: baseball, basketball, cross-country running, diving, football, golf, soccer, swimming and diving, track and field, volleyball, water polo, wrestling; intramural: basketball, indoor soccer. 4 PE instructors, 15 coaches, 1 athletic trainer.

Computers Computers are regularly used in art, economics, English, foreign language, history, mathematics, multimedia, music, newspaper, photography, science, social sciences, video film production, writing, yearbook classes. Computer network features include on-campus library services, online commercial services, Internet access, wireless campus network, Internet filtering or blocking technology. Computer access in designated common areas is available to students. Students grades are available online. The school has a published electronic and media policy.

Contact Mr. Chris Dalman, Director of Admissions. 831-422-6391. Fax: 831-422-5065. E-mail: dalman@palmahs.org. Web site: www.palmahs.org.

PARADISE ADVENTIST ACADEMY

5699 Academy Drive

PO Box 2169

Paradise, California 95969

Head of School: Mr. Lance Taggart

General Information Coeducational day college-preparatory school, affiliated with Seventh-day Adventists. Grades K–12. Founded: 1908. Setting: small town. Nearest major city is Sacramento. 12-acre campus. 6 buildings on campus. Approved or accredited by Western Association of Schools and Colleges and California Department of Education. Endowment: $200,000. Total enrollment: 182. Upper school average class size: 20. Upper school faculty-student ratio: 1:8. There are 180 required school days per year for Upper School students. Upper School students typically attend 5 days per week. The average school day consists of 8 hours and 5 minutes.

Upper School Student Profile Grade 9: 25 students (11 boys, 14 girls); Grade 10: 20 students (12 boys, 8 girls); Grade 11: 22 students (13 boys, 9 girls); Grade 12: 21 students (9 boys, 12 girls). 80% of students are Seventh-day Adventists.

Faculty School total: 20. In upper school: 7 men, 3 women; 6 have advanced degrees.

Subjects Offered Advanced biology, advanced computer applications, advanced math, algebra, American government, American history, auto mechanics, band, basketball, Bible, biology, career education, carpentry, chemistry, choir, computer applications, computers, drama, earth science, English, geometry, health, keyboarding, military history, physical education, physical science, physics, pre-algebra, pre-calculus, Spanish, speech, U.S. government, U.S. history, volleyball, weightlifting, woodworking, world history, yearbook.

Graduation Requirements Advanced computer applications, algebra, American government, American history, arts and fine arts (art, music, dance, drama), Bible, biology, career and personal planning, career education, chemistry, computer literacy, electives, English, keyboarding, languages, life skills, physical education (includes health), physics, Spanish, world history, 100 hours of community service, 20 credits of fine arts, career development portfolio.

Special Academic Programs Accelerated programs; independent study.

College Admission Counseling 18 students graduated in 2011; all went to college, including Azusa Pacific University; Pacific Union College; Southern Adventist University; Walla Walla University. Median SAT critical reading: 555, median SAT math: 600, median SAT writing: 590, median combined SAT: 1745, median composite ACT: 24. 33% scored over 600 on SAT critical reading, 58% scored over 600 on SAT math, 42% scored over 600 on SAT writing, 42% scored over 1800 on combined SAT, 40% scored over 26 on composite ACT.

Student Life Upper grades have specified standards of dress, student council. Discipline rests primarily with faculty. Attendance at religious services is required.

Summer Programs Sports programs offered; session focuses on basketball; held on campus; accepts boys and girls; open to students from other schools. 20 students usually enrolled. 2012 schedule: June 18 to June 22. Application deadline: June 18.

Tuition and Aid Day student tuition: $8180. Tuition installment plan (monthly payment plans, individually arranged payment plans, By semester or year-$50 off, 10 or 12 month plan, Automatic Bank withdrawal). Tuition reduction for siblings, need-based scholarship grants, paying campus jobs available. In 2011–12, 25% of upper-school students received aid. Total amount of financial aid awarded in 2011–12: $50,000.

Admissions Traditional secondary-level entrance grade is 9. For fall 2011, 8 students applied for upper-level admission, 8 were accepted, 8 enrolled. Any standardized test required. Deadline for receipt of application materials: August 17. Application fee required: $50. Interview required.

Athletics Interscholastic: basketball (boys, girls), football (b,g), soccer (b), volleyball (g). 1 PE instructor, 2 coaches.

Computers Computers are regularly used in all academic classes. Computer network features include on-campus library services, Internet access, wireless campus network, Internet filtering or blocking technology. Campus intranet, student e-mail accounts, and computer access in designated common areas are available to students. Students grades are available online. The school has a published electronic and media policy.

Contact Mrs. Brenda Muth, Registrar. 530-877-6540 Ext. 3010. Fax: 530-877-0870. E-mail: bmuth@mypaa.net. Web site: www.mypaa.net.

THE PARK SCHOOL OF BALTIMORE

2425 Old Court Road

P.O. Box 8200

Brooklandville, Maryland 21022

Head of School: Mr. Daniel Paradis

General Information Coeducational day college-preparatory school. Grades PK–12. Founded: 1912. Setting: suburban. Nearest major city is Baltimore. 100-acre campus. 4 buildings on campus. Approved or accredited by Association of Independent Maryland Schools and Maryland Department of Education. Member of National Association of Independent Schools. Endowment: $24.2 million. Total enrollment: 863. Upper school average class size: 15. Upper school faculty-student ratio: 1:7. There are 170 required school days per year for Upper School students. Upper School students typically attend 5 days per week. The average school day consists of 4 hours and 30 minutes.

Upper School Student Profile Grade 9: 88 students (46 boys, 42 girls); Grade 10: 82 students (38 boys, 44 girls); Grade 11: 81 students (33 boys, 48 girls); Grade 12: 82 students (38 boys, 44 girls).

Faculty School total: 121. In upper school: 27 men, 22 women; 36 have advanced degrees.

Subjects Offered 20th century history, 20th century world history, 3 dimensional art, 3-dimensional design, acting, advanced biology, advanced chemistry, advanced computer applications, advanced math, advanced studio art-AP, African-American literature, algebra, American history, American literature, American studies, analysis and differential calculus, analytic geometry, ancient world history, animal behavior, art, art history, astronomy, Bible as literature, biology, botany, British literature, calculus, calculus-AP, ceramics, chamber groups, chemistry, Chesapeake Bay studies, Chinese, choral music, chorus, civil rights, computer graphics, computer science, contemporary history, creative writing, criminal justice, design, drama, drama performance, drawing, earth science, ecology, economics, English, English literature, environmental science, environmental studies, equality and freedom, European history, expository writing, film studies, fine arts, food science, foreign language, forensics, French, French studies, genetics, geometry, global studies, government/civics, health, health and wellness, history, history of science, jazz ensemble, Latin American history, Latin American literature, marine biology, mathematics, mechanical drawing, music, music technology, music theory, musical theater, newspaper, painting, philosophy, photography, physical education, physics, science, sculpture, short story, social studies, Spanish, Spanish literature, technical theater, theater design and production, trigonometry, woodworking, world history, world literature, writing, yearbook.

Graduation Requirements Arts and fine arts (art, music, dance, drama), electives, English, foreign language, history, mathematics, physical education (includes health), science.

Special Academic Programs 14 Advanced Placement exams for which test preparation is offered; independent study; term-away projects; academic accommodation for the gifted, the musically talented, and the artistically talented.

College Admission Counseling 82 students graduated in 2011; 81 went to college, including American University; New York University; The Johns Hopkins University; University of Maryland, College Park; University of Pennsylvania; Washington University in St. Louis. Other: 1 had other specific plans. 78% scored over 600 on SAT critical reading, 75% scored over 600 on SAT math, 75% scored over 600 on SAT writing, 75% scored over 1800 on combined SAT, 79% scored over 26 on composite ACT.

Student Life Upper grades have student council. Discipline rests equally with students and faculty.

Tuition and Aid Day student tuition: $24,270. Tuition installment plan (The Tuition Plan, Insured Tuition Payment Plan, monthly payment plans). Need-based scholarship grants available. In 2011–12, 21% of upper-school students received aid. Total amount of financial aid awarded in 2011–12: $1,292,085.

Admissions Traditional secondary-level entrance grade is 9. For fall 2011, 90 students applied for upper-level admission, 64 were accepted, 28 enrolled. ISEE required. Deadline for receipt of application materials: January 1. Application fee required: $50. Interview required.

Athletics Interscholastic: baseball (boys), basketball (b,g), cross-country running (b,g), field hockey (g), indoor soccer (g), lacrosse (b,g), soccer (b,g), softball (g), squash (b,g), tennis (b,g), winter soccer (g); coed intramural: climbing, Frisbee, strength & conditioning, ultimate Frisbee, wall climbing, yoga. 3 PE instructors, 30 coaches, 1 athletic trainer.

Computers Computers are regularly used in art, computer applications, creative writing, desktop publishing, English, foreign language, French, graphic design, history, journalism, library skills, mathematics, media production, music, music technology, news writing, newspaper, photojournalism, programming, publications, science, Spanish, theater, theater arts, video film production, woodworking, writing, writing, yearbook classes. Computer network features include on-campus library services, online commercial services, Internet access, wireless campus network, Internet filtering or blocking technology, access to course materials and assignments through faculty Web pages and wikis, discounted software purchase plan. Campus intranet, student e-mail accounts, and computer access in designated common areas are available to students. Students grades are available online. The school has a published electronic and media policy.

Contact Rachel Hockett, Admission Receptionist. 410-339-4130. Fax: 410-339-4127. E-mail: admission@parkschool.net. Web site: www.parkschool.net.

THE PARK SCHOOL OF BUFFALO

4625 Harlem Road

Snyder, New York 14226

Head of School: Christopher J. Lauricella

General Information Coeducational day college-preparatory and arts school. Grades N–12. Founded: 1912. Setting: suburban. Nearest major city is Buffalo. 34-acre campus. 15 buildings on campus. Approved or accredited by National Independent Private Schools Association, New York Department of Education, New York State Association of Independent Schools, and New York Department of Education. Member of National Association of Independent Schools. Endowment: $1.3 million. Total enrollment: 242. Upper school average class size: 14. Upper school faculty-student ratio: 1:8. There are 166 required school days per year for Upper School students. Upper School students typically attend 5 days per week. The average school day consists of 7 hours.

Upper School Student Profile Grade 9: 20 students (11 boys, 9 girls); Grade 10: 21 students (9 boys, 12 girls); Grade 11: 32 students (15 boys, 17 girls); Grade 12: 33 students (14 boys, 19 girls).

Faculty School total: 39. In upper school: 11 men, 13 women; 20 have advanced degrees.

Subjects Offered Advanced studio art-AP, algebra, American history, American history-AP, American literature, American literature-AP, art, band, biology, biology-AP, calculus, calculus-AP, ceramics, chemistry, chorus, college admission preparation, college counseling, community service, computer applications, computer programming, critical thinking, drama, drawing, economics, English, environmental science, fine arts, forensics, French, French language-AP, freshman seminar, geometry, government/civics, health, junior and senior seminars, marine biology, media, media production, metalworking, music, orchestra, organic chemistry, photography, physical education, physics, senior project, senior seminar, senior thesis, Spanish, Spanish-AP, studio art-AP, trigonometry, U.S. government and politics-AP, woodworking, world history, yearbook.

Graduation Requirements Arts and fine arts (art, music, dance, drama), computer science, English, foreign language, mathematics, physical education (includes health), science, senior project, senior thesis, social sciences, social studies (includes history). Community service is required.

Special Academic Programs Advanced Placement exam preparation; honors section; accelerated programs; independent study; study at local college for college credit; study abroad; academic accommodation for the gifted; ESL (13 students enrolled).

College Admission Counseling 34 students graduated in 2010; all went to college, including Bard College; Bowdoin College; Purchase College, State University of New York; Purdue University; The George Washington University; University of Toronto. Median SAT critical reading: 587, median SAT math: 581, median SAT writing: 577, median combined SAT: 1968, median composite ACT: 25. 48% scored over 600 on SAT critical reading, 40% scored over 600 on SAT math, 44% scored over 600 on SAT writing, 44% scored over 1800 on combined SAT, 50% scored over 26 on composite ACT.

Student Life Upper grades have specified standards of dress, student council, honor system. Discipline rests equally with students and faculty.

Tuition and Aid Day student tuition: $16,700–$17,750. Tuition installment plan (Insured Tuition Payment Plan, FACTS Tuition Payment Plan). Tuition reduction for siblings, merit scholarship grants, need-based scholarship grants available. In 2010–11, 59% of upper-school students received aid; total upper-school merit-scholarship money awarded: $35,500. Total amount of financial aid awarded in 2010–11: $900,000.

Admissions Traditional secondary-level entrance grade is 9. For fall 2010, 56 students applied for upper-level admission, 26 were accepted, 25 enrolled. ERB Reading and Math, Otis-Lennon School Ability Test or TOEFL required. Deadline for receipt of application materials: none. Application fee required: $50. Interview required.

Athletics Interscholastic: basketball (boys, girls), bowling (b,g), golf (b), lacrosse (b), soccer (b,g), softball (g), tennis (b,g); coed intramural: aerobics, badminton, ball hockey, bicycling, cooperative games, cross-country running, fishing, fitness, flag football, floor hockey, Frisbee, hiking/backpacking, indoor soccer, outdoor activities, outdoor adventure, outdoor education, outdoor recreation, outdoor skills, outdoors, physical fitness, running, skiing (downhill), snowboarding, snowshoeing, soccer, strength & conditioning, weight lifting, weight training, winter walking, yoga. 2 PE instructors, 14 coaches.

Computers Computers are regularly used in creative writing, current events, data processing, English, graphic arts, independent study, mathematics, media, media arts, media services, newspaper, photography, science, word processing, yearbook classes. Computer network features include on-campus library services, online commercial services, Internet access, wireless campus network, Internet filtering or blocking technology. Campus intranet, student e-mail accounts, and computer access in designated common areas are available to students. Students grades are available online. The school has a published electronic and media policy.

Contact Jennifer A. Brady, Director of Admissions. 716-839-1242 Ext. 107. Fax: 716-408-9511. E-mail: jbrady@theparkschool.org. Web site: www.theparkschool.org.

THE PATHWAY SCHOOL

Norristown, Pennsylvania

See Special Needs Schools section.

PEDDIE SCHOOL

201 South Main Street

Hightstown, New Jersey 08520

Head of School: John F. Green

General Information Coeducational boarding and day college-preparatory, arts, and technology school. Grades 9–PG. Founded: 1864. Setting: small town. Nearest major city is Princeton. Students are housed in single-sex dormitories. 230-acre campus. 53 buildings on campus. Approved or accredited by Middle States Association of Colleges and Schools, The Association of Boarding Schools, and New Jersey Department of Education. Member of National Association of Independent Schools and Secondary School Admission Test Board. Endowment: $278 million. Total enrollment: 550. Upper school average class size: 12. Upper school faculty-student ratio: 1:6. Upper School students typically attend 6 days per week. The average school day consists of 7 hours.

Upper School Student Profile Grade 9: 116 students (57 boys, 59 girls); Grade 10: 132 students (68 boys, 64 girls); Grade 11: 148 students (75 boys, 73 girls); Grade 12: 146 students (75 boys, 71 girls); Postgraduate: 15 students (11 boys, 4 girls). 62% of students are boarding students. 22 states are represented in upper school student body. 11% are international students. International students from China, Hong Kong, Japan, Republic of Korea, Thailand, and United Kingdom; 24 other countries represented in student body.

Faculty School total: 94. In upper school: 45 men, 35 women; 75 have advanced degrees; 72 reside on campus.

Subjects Offered Acting, African studies, algebra, American history, American literature, American studies, anatomy, architecture, art, art history, art history-AP, Asian studies, astronomy, Bible studies, biology, biology-AP, calculus, calculus-AP, chemistry, Chinese, comedy, comparative religion, computer programming, computer science, creative writing, debate, digital imaging, DNA, DNA science lab, drama, earth science, ecology, economics, English, English literature, environmental science, environmental science-AP, European history, European history-AP, expository writing, film history, fine arts, forensics, French, French language-AP, French literature-AP, geometry, global issues, global science, government/civics, health, history, information technology, Latin, Latin-AP, mathematics, Middle East, music, music theory-AP, neuroscience, philosophy, photography, physical education, physics, physics-AP, psychology, psychology-AP, robotics, science, Shakespeare, social studies, Spanish, Spanish language-AP, Spanish literature-AP, speech, statistics, statistics-AP, studio art-AP, theater, trigonometry, U.S. history, U.S. history-AP, video film production, world history, world literature, World War I, World War II, writing.

Graduation Requirements Arts and fine arts (art, music, dance, drama), computer science, English, foreign language, history, mathematics, physical education (includes health), science. Community service is required.

Special Academic Programs Advanced Placement exam preparation; honors section; independent study; term-away projects; study abroad.

College Admission Counseling 140 students graduated in 2011; all went to college, including Carnegie Mellon University; Cornell University; Georgetown University; The George Washington University; University of Pennsylvania; University of Richmond.

Student Life Upper grades have specified standards of dress, student council. Discipline rests primarily with faculty.

Summer Programs Enrichment, advancement, sports, art/fine arts programs offered; session focuses on enrichment; held on campus; accepts boys and girls; open to students from other schools. 175 students usually enrolled. 2012 schedule: June 21 to August 2. Application deadline: none.

Tuition and Aid Day student tuition: $35,000; 7-day tuition and room/board: $45,000. Tuition installment plan (Academic Management Services Plan, monthly payment plans, individually arranged payment plans). Merit scholarship grants, need-based scholarship grants, need-based loans available. In 2011–12, 40% of upper-school students received aid; total upper-school merit-scholarship money awarded: $70,000. Total amount of financial aid awarded in 2011–12: $5,000,000.

Admissions Traditional secondary-level entrance grade is 9. For fall 2011, 1,561 students applied for upper-level admission, 305 were accepted, 167 enrolled. ISEE or SSAT required. Deadline for receipt of application materials: January 15. Application fee required: $50. Interview required.

Athletics Interscholastic: baseball (boys), basketball (b,g), crew (b,g), cross-country running (b,g), diving (b,g), field hockey (g), fitness (b,g), football (b), golf (b,g), indoor track & field (b,g), lacrosse (b,g), soccer (b,g), softball (g), strength & conditioning (b,g), swimming and diving (b,g), tennis (b,g), track and field (b,g), winter (indoor) track (b,g), wrestling (b), yoga (b,g); intramural: weight lifting (b,g), weight training (b,g); coed intramural: bicycling, bowling, softball. 9 coaches, 3 athletic trainers.

Computers Computers are regularly used in English, foreign language, history, mathematics, science classes. Computer network features include on-campus library services, online commercial services, Internet access, wireless campus network, Internet filtering or blocking technology, NewsBank, Britannica, GaleNet, Electric Library. Student e-mail accounts are available to students. Students grades are available online. The school has a published electronic and media policy.

Contact Raymond H. Cabot, Director of Admissions. 609-944-7501. Fax: 609-944-7901. E-mail: admission@peddie.org. Web site: www.peddie.org.

PENINSULA CATHOLIC HIGH SCHOOL

600 Harpersville Road

Newport News, Virginia 23601-1813

Head of School: Dr. Francine Gagne

General Information Coeducational day college-preparatory, arts, religious studies, and technology school, affiliated with Roman Catholic Church. Grades 8–12. Founded: 1903. Setting: suburban. Nearest major city is Newport News/Norfolk. 15-acre campus. 1 building on campus. Approved or accredited by National Catholic Education Association, Southern Association of Colleges and Schools, and Virginia Department of Education. Endowment: $180,000. Total enrollment: 305. Upper school average class size: 18. Upper school faculty-student ratio: 1:16. There are 183 required school days per year for Upper School students. Upper School students typically attend 5 days per week. The average school day consists of 6 hours.

Upper School Student Profile Grade 8: 26 students (12 boys, 14 girls); Grade 9: 101 students (48 boys, 53 girls); Grade 10: 66 students (25 boys, 41 girls); Grade 11: 79 students (39 boys, 40 girls); Grade 12: 66 students (28 boys, 38 girls). 75% of students are Roman Catholic.

Faculty School total: 29. In upper school: 10 men, 18 women; 20 have advanced degrees.

Subjects Offered 20th century American writers, 20th century history, 20th century world history, advanced chemistry, advanced math, algebra, American Civil War, American foreign policy, American government, American history, American history-AP, American literature, American literature-AP, analysis and differential calculus, anatomy and physiology, art, Bible as literature, Bible studies, biology, biology-AP, calculus, calculus-AP, campus ministry, Christian ethics, Christian testament, church history, college admission preparation, college placement, college planning, college writing, drama, driver education, English, English composition, English language and composition-AP, English language-AP, English literature, English literature and composition-AP, English-AP, foreign language, French, geography, geology, geometry, German, government, history, history of the Catholic Church, honors algebra, honors English, honors U.S. history, keyboarding, studio art-AP, U.S. government and politics-AP.

Graduation Requirements Arts and fine arts (art, music, dance, drama), English, foreign language, mathematics, physical education (includes health), religion (includes Bible studies and theology), science, social studies (includes history).

Special Academic Programs Advanced Placement exam preparation; honors section.

College Admission Counseling 70 students graduated in 2010; all went to college, including James Madison University; Longwood University; Old Dominion University; The College of William and Mary; University of Virginia; Virginia Polytechnic Institute and State University. Mean SAT critical reading: 543, mean SAT math: 537, mean SAT writing: 539.

Student Life Upper grades have uniform requirement, student council, honor system. Discipline rests primarily with faculty. Attendance at religious services is required.

Tuition and Aid Day student tuition: $8540. Tuition installment plan (FACTS Tuition Payment Plan). Tuition reduction for siblings, need-based scholarship grants available. In 2010–11, 25% of upper-school students received aid.

Admissions Traditional secondary-level entrance grade is 9. High School Placement Test (closed version) from Scholastic Testing Service or placement test required. Deadline for receipt of application materials: none. Application fee required: $100. Interview recommended.

Athletics Interscholastic: baseball (boys), basketball (b,g), cross-country running (b,g), soccer (b,g), softball (g), swimming and diving (b,g), tennis (b,g), track and field (b,g), volleyball (b,g), wrestling (b); coed interscholastic: cheering, golf. 2 PE instructors, 1 athletic trainer.

Computers Computers are regularly used in journalism, programming, yearbook classes. Computer resources include on-campus library services, Internet access.

Contact Mrs. Christine Miller, Guidance Counselor. 757-596-7247 Ext. 14. Fax: 757-591-9718. E-mail: guidance@peninsulacatholic.com. Web site: www.peninsulacatholic.com.

THE PENNINGTON SCHOOL

112 West Delaware Avenue

Pennington, New Jersey 08534-1601

General Information Coeducational boarding and day college-preparatory and arts school, affiliated with Methodist Church; primarily serves students with learning disabilities and dyslexic students. Boarding grades 7–12, day grades 6–12. Founded: 1838. Setting: small town. Nearest major city is Philadelphia, PA. Students are housed in single-sex by floor dormitories and single-sex dormitories. 54-acre campus. 17 buildings on campus. Approved or accredited by Middle States Association of Colleges and Schools, National Independent Private Schools Association, New Jersey Association of Independent Schools, The Association of Boarding Schools, The College Board, University Senate of United Methodist Church, and New Jersey Department of Education. Member of National Association of Independent Schools and Secondary School Admission Test Board. Endowment: $24.5 million. Total enrollment: 485. Upper school average class size: 13. Upper school faculty-student ratio: 1:8. Upper School students typically attend 5 days per week.

See Display on next page and Close-Up on page 660.

PENSACOLA CATHOLIC HIGH SCHOOL

3043 West Scott Street

Pensacola, Florida 32505

Head of School: Sr. Kierstin Martin

General Information Coeducational day college-preparatory and technology school, affiliated with Roman Catholic Church. Grades 9–12. Founded: 1941. Setting: urban. 25-acre campus. 5 buildings on campus. Approved or accredited by Southern Association of Colleges and Schools. Total enrollment: 571. Upper school average class size: 22. Upper school faculty-student ratio: 1:18.

Upper School Student Profile Grade 9: 164 students (92 boys, 72 girls); Grade 10: 146 students (83 boys, 63 girls); Grade 11: 128 students (66 boys, 62 girls); Grade 12: 133 students (72 boys, 61 girls). 70% of students are Roman Catholic.

Faculty School total: 50. In upper school: 15 men, 35 women; 15 have advanced degrees.

Subjects Offered Advanced math, Advanced Placement courses, algebra, American government, American history, American history-AP, American literature, analysis and differential calculus, analytic geometry, anatomy and physiology, art, art appreciation, arts and crafts, athletics, band, baseball, basketball, Bible, Bible studies, biology, botany, British literature, broadcast journalism, business law, calculus, calculus-AP, campus ministry, Catholic belief and practice, chemistry, Christian ethics, Christian scripture, Christian studies, Christian testament, church history, civics, college counseling, comparative religion, composition, composition-AP, computer applications, computer graphics, consumer mathematics, CPR, creative arts, criminal justice, desktop publishing, digital photography, drawing, earth science, economics, electives, English, English composition, English language and composition-AP, English literature, English literature and composition-AP, environmental science, fabric arts, film appreciation, film history, filmmaking, foreign language, French, general science, genetics, geography, geometry, government, government-AP, grammar, graphic arts, guidance, health education, history, history of the Catholic Church, honors algebra, honors English, honors geometry, honors U.S. history, honors world history, human sexuality, journalism, keyboarding, lab science, library, library assistant, Life of Christ, literature and composition-AP, marine biology, music appreciation, music history, physical education, physical science, physics, pottery, pre-algebra, pre-calculus, probability and statistics, reading, religion, sex education, social studies, Spanish, student government, student publications, telecommunications and the Internet, television, the Web, trigonometry, U.S. government, U.S. government and politics-AP, U.S. history, U.S. literature, vocal music, weight training, Western civilization, world geography, world history, world religions.

Special Academic Programs Advanced Placement exam preparation; honors section; study at local college for college credit; academic accommodation for the gifted; remedial reading and/or remedial writing; remedial math; programs in English, mathematics, general development for dyslexic students; special instructional classes for deaf students, blind students.

College Admission Counseling 120 students graduated in 2010; 117 went to college, including Florida State University; Mississippi State University; Pensacola State College; The University of Alabama; University of Florida. Other: 2 entered military service, 1 had other specific plans. Mean SAT critical reading: 512, mean SAT math: 535, mean SAT writing: 511, mean combined SAT: 1557, mean composite ACT: 23.

Student Life Upper grades have specified standards of dress, student council. Discipline rests primarily with faculty. Attendance at religious services is required.

Tuition and Aid Tuition reduction for siblings, need-based scholarship grants available.

Admissions Traditional secondary-level entrance grade is 9. ETS high school placement exam required. Deadline for receipt of application materials: none. Application fee required. On-campus interview required.

Athletics Interscholastic: baseball (boys), basketball (b,g), cheering (b,g), golf (b,g), physical training (b), soccer (b,g), softball (g), swimming and diving (b,g), wrestling (b).

Computers Computers are regularly used in Bible studies, computer applications, creative writing, desktop publishing, foreign language, French, geography, graphic design, history, independent study, keyboarding, mathematics, publications, reading, religion, science, social studies, Spanish, stock market, study skills, video film production, Web site design, word processing, yearbook classes. Computer network features include on-campus library services, online commercial services, Internet access, wireless campus network, Internet filtering or blocking technology. Student e-mail accounts and computer access in designated common areas are available to students. Students grades are available online. The school has a published electronic and media policy.

Contact Mary Kyte, Senior Guidance Counselor. 850-436-6400 Ext. 119. Fax: 850-436-6405. E-mail: mkyte@pensacolachs.org. Web site: www.pensacolachs.org.

PEOPLES CHRISTIAN ACADEMY

245 Renfrew Drive

Markham, Ontario L3R 6G3, Canada

Head of School: Mr. Reg Andrews

General Information Coeducational day college-preparatory and religious studies school, affiliated with Christian faith. Grades JK–12. Founded: 1971. Setting: urban. Nearest major city is Toronto, Canada. 5-acre campus. 1 building on campus. Approved or accredited by Association of Christian Schools International, Christian Schools International, Ontario Ministry of Education, and Ontario Department of Education. Language of instruction: English. Endowment: CAN$15,000. Total enrollment: 339. Upper school average class size: 20. Upper school faculty-student ratio: 1:10. There are 176 required school days per year for Upper School students. Upper School students typically attend 5 days per week. The average school day consists of 7 hours.

Upper School Student Profile Grade 7: 30 students (12 boys, 18 girls); Grade 8: 34 students (17 boys, 17 girls); Grade 9: 28 students (13 boys, 15 girls); Grade 10: 21 students (15 boys, 6 girls); Grade 11: 31 students (16 boys, 15 girls); Grade 12: 34 students (20 boys, 14 girls). 85% of students are Christian.

Faculty School total: 36. In upper school: 9 men, 13 women; 4 have advanced degrees.

Subjects Offered Accounting, Bible, biology, calculus, Canadian geography, Canadian history, Canadian law, careers, chemistry, civics, discrete mathematics, dramatic arts, economics, English, exercise science, family studies, French, functions, geography, geometry, health education, healthful living, ideas, information technology, instrumental music, journalism, keyboarding, literature, mathematics, media arts, organizational studies, philosophy, physical education, physics, psychology, science, sociology, visual arts, vocal music, world history, world religions, writing.

Graduation Requirements Arts, Canadian geography, Canadian history, careers, civics, English, French as a second language, mathematics, physical education (includes health), science, must complete Bible course curriculum for all grades.

College Admission Counseling 42 students graduated in 2011; 40 went to college, including McMaster University; The University of Western Ontario; University of Guelph; University of Toronto; Wilfrid Laurier University; York University. Other: 2 had other specific plans.

Student Life Upper grades have uniform requirement, student council, honor system. Discipline rests primarily with faculty. Attendance at religious services is required.

Tuition and Aid Day student tuition: CAN$9300. Tuition installment plan (monthly payment plans). Tuition reduction for siblings, bursaries, need-based scholarship grants, alumni scholarships, prepayment tuition reduction available. In 2011–12, 2% of upper-school students received aid. Total amount of financial aid awarded in 2011–12: CAN$30,000.

Admissions Traditional secondary-level entrance grade is 9. For fall 2011, 15 students applied for upper-level admission, 10 were accepted, 10 enrolled. CTBS (or similar from their school) required. Deadline for receipt of application materials: none. Application fee required: CAN$295. Interview required.

Athletics Interscholastic: badminton (boys, girls), baseball (b,g), basketball (b,g), cross-country running (b,g), running (b,g), track and field (b,g), volleyball (b,g); intramural: badminton (b,g), basketball (b,g), cross-country running (b,g), floor hockey (b,g), running (b,g); coed interscholastic: badminton, baseball, basketball, cross-country running, running, swimming and diving, track and field; coed intramural: badminton, basketball, cross-country running, floor hockey, running, volleyball. 2 PE instructors.

Computers Computers are regularly used in business studies, drawing and design, graphics, information technology, introduction to technology, journalism, mathematics, yearbook classes. Computer network features include Internet access, Internet filtering or blocking technology. The school has a published electronic and media policy.

Contact School Office. 416-733-2010 Ext. 303. Fax: 416-733-2011. E-mail: admissions@pca.ca. Web site: www.pca.ca.

THE PHELPS SCHOOL

583 Sugartown Road

Malvern, Pennsylvania 19355

Head of School: Mr. Michael J. Reardon

General Information Boys' boarding and day college-preparatory, general academic, academic support program, and ESL program school; primarily serves underachievers. Grades 7–PG. Founded: 1946. Setting: suburban. Nearest major city is Philadelphia. Students are housed in single-sex dormitories. 75-acre campus. 18 buildings on campus. Approved or accredited by Academy of Orton-Gillingham Practitioners and Educators, Middle States Association of Colleges and Schools, Pennsylvania Association of Independent Schools, The Association of Boarding Schools, and Pennsylvania Department of Education. Total enrollment: 138. Upper school average class size: 7. Upper school faculty-student ratio: 1:5.

Upper School Student Profile Grade 7: 3 students (3 boys); Grade 8: 6 students (6 boys); Grade 9: 22 students (22 boys); Grade 10: 33 students (33 boys); Grade 11: 34 students (34 boys); Grade 12: 31 students (31 boys); Postgraduate: 9 students (9 boys). 87% of students are boarding students. 39% are state residents. 16 states are represented in upper school student body. 41% are international students. International students from China, Lithuania, Republic of Korea, Spain, Sweden, and Taiwan; 14 other countries represented in student body.

Faculty School total: 28. In upper school: 20 men, 8 women; 9 have advanced degrees; 24 reside on campus.

Subjects Offered Algebra, American history, art, biology, calculus, calculus-AP, chemistry, college admission preparation, earth science, English, environmental science, ESL, fitness, general math, geometry, government, health, learning strategies, mathematics, participation in sports, photography, physical education, physical science, physics, pre-algebra, pre-calculus, psychology, reading, reading/study skills, remedial study skills, SAT preparation, scuba diving, shop, Spanish, study skills, weight training, world history, yearbook.

Graduation Requirements English, mathematics, physical education (includes health), science, social studies (includes history). Community service is required.

Special Academic Programs Advanced Placement exam preparation; independent study; academic accommodation for the gifted, the musically talented, and the artistically talented; remedial reading and/or remedial writing; remedial math; programs in English, mathematics, general development for dyslexic students; ESL (42 students enrolled).

College Admission Counseling 44 students graduated in 2010; 43 went to college, including College of Charleston; Drexel University; Lynn University; Rochester Institute of Technology; University of Oregon; University of Rochester. Other: 1 went to work.

Student Life Upper grades have specified standards of dress, student council. Discipline rests primarily with faculty.

Tuition and Aid Day student tuition: $21,250; 5-day tuition and room/board: $36,200; 7-day tuition and room/board: $40,200. Tuition installment plan (individually arranged payment plans). Tuition reduction for siblings, need-based scholarship grants available. In 2010–11, 36% of upper-school students received aid. Total amount of financial aid awarded in 2010–11: $1,193,650.

Admissions Traditional secondary-level entrance grade is 7. For fall 2010, 156 students applied for upper-level admission, 110 were accepted, 65 enrolled. Deadline for receipt of application materials: none. Application fee required: $50. Interview required.

Athletics Interscholastic: baseball, basketball, cross-country running, golf, lacrosse, roller hockey, soccer, street hockey, tennis; intramural: bowling, climbing, fitness, flag football, Frisbee, golf, horseback riding, in-line skating, independent competitive sports, indoor soccer, martial arts, physical fitness, rock climbing, roller blading, ropes courses, scuba diving, softball, strength & conditioning, tennis, volleyball, wall climbing, weight lifting, weight training, winter soccer. 3 PE instructors.

Computers Computers are regularly used in all classes. Computer network features include Internet access, wireless campus network, Internet filtering or blocking technology, all students are provided a laptop with the option to buy. Campus intranet, student e-mail accounts, and computer access in designated common areas are available to students. Students grades are available online. The school has a published electronic and media policy.

Contact Mrs. Julie Wells Romain, Assistant Director of Admissions. 610-644-1754. Fax: 610-644-6679. E-mail: admis@thephelpsschool.org. Web site: www.thephelpsschool.org.

PHILADELPHIA-MONTGOMERY CHRISTIAN ACADEMY

35 Hillcrest Avenue

Erdenheim, Pennsylvania 19038

Head of School: Mr. Donald B. Beebe

General Information Coeducational day college-preparatory, arts, religious studies, and bilingual studies school, affiliated with Christian faith. Grades PK–12. Founded: 1943. Setting: suburban. Nearest major city is Philadelphia. 1-acre campus. 1 building on campus. Approved or accredited by Christian Schools International and Middle States Association of Colleges and Schools. Endowment: $150,205. Total enrollment: 298. Upper school average class size: 18. Upper school faculty-student ratio: 1:10. There are 178 required school days per year for Upper School students. Upper School students typically attend 5 days per week. The average school day consists of 6 hours and 50 minutes.

Upper School Student Profile Grade 9: 25 students (13 boys, 12 girls); Grade 10: 37 students (20 boys, 17 girls); Grade 11: 18 students (10 boys, 8 girls); Grade 12: 38 students (21 boys, 17 girls). 99% of students are Christian.

Faculty School total: 35. In upper school: 11 men, 8 women; 10 have advanced degrees.

Subjects Offered Algebra, American history, American literature, art, art history, biology, calculus, ceramics, chemistry, creative writing, drama, English, English literature, ethics, European history, fine arts, geography, geometry, German, government/civics, grammar, health, history, mathematics, music, physical education, physics, religion, science, social studies, sociology, Spanish, theater, trigonometry, typing, world history, writing.

Graduation Requirements Arts and fine arts (art, music, dance, drama), Bible, English, mathematics, physical education (includes health), science, social studies (includes history).

Special Academic Programs 4 Advanced Placement exams for which test preparation is offered; honors section; academic accommodation for the gifted, the musically talented, and the artistically talented.

College Admission Counseling 37 students graduated in 2011; 36 went to college, including Drexel University; Eastern University; Liberty University; Penn State University Park; Temple University; University of Pittsburgh. Other: 1 went to work. Mean SAT critical reading: 548, mean SAT math: 562, mean SAT writing: 538. 34% scored over 600 on SAT critical reading, 34% scored over 600 on SAT math, 26% scored over 600 on SAT writing.

Student Life Upper grades have uniform requirement, student council. Discipline rests primarily with faculty. Attendance at religious services is required.

Tuition and Aid Day student tuition: $11,765. Tuition installment plan (FACTS Tuition Payment Plan). Tuition reduction for siblings, need-based scholarship grants available. In 2011–12, 50% of upper-school students received aid. Total amount of financial aid awarded in 2011–12: $500,000.

Admissions Traditional secondary-level entrance grade is 9. For fall 2011, 19 students applied for upper-level admission, 16 were accepted, 15 enrolled. Iowa Tests of Basic Skills required. Deadline for receipt of application materials: February 6. Application fee required: $100. On-campus interview required.

Athletics Interscholastic: baseball (boys), basketball (b,g), soccer (b,g), softball (g), tennis (b,g), track and field (b,g), wrestling (b); coed interscholastic: cross-country running. 2 PE instructors.

Computers Computers are regularly used in art, English, mathematics classes. Computer resources include on-campus library services, Internet access, Internet filtering or blocking technology, online college search. The school has a published electronic and media policy.

Contact Rosanna Lu, Admissions and Marketing Manager. 215-233-0782 Ext. 408. Fax: 215-233-0829. E-mail: admissions@phil-mont.com. Web site: www.phil-mont.com.

PHILLIPS ACADEMY (ANDOVER)

180 Main Street

Andover, Massachusetts 01810-4161

Head of School: Barbara L. Chase

General Information Coeducational boarding and day college-preparatory school. Grades 9–PG. Founded: 1778. Setting: suburban. Nearest major city is Boston. Students are housed in single-sex dormitories and 9th graders housed separately from other students. 500-acre campus. 160 buildings on campus. Approved or accredited by New England Association of Schools and Colleges and The Association of Boarding Schools. Member of National Association of Independent Schools and Secondary School Admission Test Board. Endowment: $850 million. Total enrollment: 1,105. Upper school average class size: 13. Upper school faculty-student ratio: 1:5. There are 157 required school days per year for Upper School students. Upper School students typically attend 5 days per week. The average school day consists of 8 hours.

Upper School Student Profile Grade 9: 214 students (108 boys, 106 girls); Grade 10: 283 students (145 boys, 138 girls); Grade 11: 294 students (145 boys, 149 girls); Grade 12: 279 students (132 boys, 147 girls); Postgraduate: 35 students (24 boys, 11 girls). 74% of students are boarding students. 41% are state residents. 46 states are represented in upper school student body. 16% are international students. International students from Canada, China, Hong Kong, Republic of Korea, Thailand, and United Kingdom; 30 other countries represented in student body.

Faculty School total: 207. In upper school: 99 men, 108 women; 165 have advanced degrees; 190 reside on campus.

Subjects Offered Algebra, American history, American literature, ancient history, animal behavior, animation, Arabic, Arabic studies, architecture, art, art history, astronomy, band, Bible studies, biology, calculus, ceramics, chamber groups, chemistry, Chinese, chorus, computer graphics, computer programming, computer science, creative writing, dance, drama, drawing, driver education, ecology, economics, English, English literature, environmental science, ethics, European history, expository writing, film, fine arts, French, geology, geometry, German, government/civics, grammar, Greek, health, history, international relations, Japanese, jazz, Latin, Latin American studies, life issues, literature, mathematics, Middle Eastern history, music, mythology, oceanography, painting, philosophy, photography, physical education, physics, physiology, printmaking, psychology, religion, Russian, Russian studies, science, sculpture, social sciences, social studies, sociology, Spanish, speech, swimming, theater, trigonometry, video, world history, writing.

Graduation Requirements Arts and fine arts (art, music, dance, drama), English, foreign language, history, life issues, mathematics, philosophy, physical education (includes health), religion (includes Bible studies and theology), science, social sciences, swimming test.

Special Academic Programs Advanced Placement exam preparation; honors section; independent study; term-away projects; study abroad; academic accommodation for the gifted, the musically talented, and the artistically talented; programs in English, mathematics, general development for dyslexic students; special instructional classes for deaf students, blind students.

College Admission Counseling 329 students graduated in 2011; 320 went to college, including Columbia University; Cornell University; Harvard University; Stanford University; University of Southern California; Yale University. Other: 9 had other specific plans. Mean SAT critical reading: 686, mean SAT math: 697, mean SAT writing: 684.

Student Life Upper grades have student council, honor system. Discipline rests primarily with faculty.

Summer Programs Remediation, enrichment, advancement, ESL, art/fine arts, computer instruction programs offered; session focuses on academics; held both on and off campus; held at Colorado; accepts boys and girls; open to students from other schools. 550 students usually enrolled. 2012 schedule: June 26 to August 1. Application deadline: none.

Tuition and Aid Day student tuition: $32,850; 7-day tuition and room/board: $42,350. Tuition installment plan (individually arranged payment plans, The Andover Plan). Need-based scholarship grants, middle-income loans available. In 2011–12, 46% of upper-school students received aid. Total amount of financial aid awarded in 2011–12: $17,015,000.

Admissions For fall 2011, 3,186 students applied for upper-level admission, 458 were accepted, 361 enrolled. ISEE or SSAT required. Deadline for receipt of application materials: February 1. Application fee required: $40. Interview required.

Athletics Interscholastic: baseball (boys), basketball (b,g), bicycling (b,g), crew (b,g), cross-country running (b,g), diving (b,g), field hockey (g), football (b), golf (b,g), ice hockey (b,g), indoor track & field (b,g), lacrosse (b,g), nordic skiing (b,g), skiing (cross-country) (b,g), soccer (b,g), softball (g), squash (b,g), swimming and diving (b,g), tennis (b,g), track and field (b,g), volleyball (b,g), water polo (b,g), winter (indoor) track (b,g), wrestling (b); intramural: aerobics/dance (b,g), backpacking (b,g), basketball (b,g), crew (b,g), martial arts (b,g), physical fitness (b,g), physical training (b,g); coed interscholastic: bicycling, Frisbee, golf, ultimate Frisbee, wrestling; coed intramural: badminton, ballet, canoeing/kayaking, cheering, cross-country running, dance, fencing, fitness, fitness walking, hiking/backpacking, martial arts, modern dance, outdoor adventure, outdoor education, physical fitness, physical training, rappelling, rock climbing, ropes courses, soccer, softball, strength & conditioning, tennis, wall climbing. 7 PE instructors, 25 coaches, 3 athletic trainers.

Computers Computers are regularly used in animation, architecture, art, classics, computer applications, digital applications, English, foreign language, history, mathematics, music, photography, psychology, religious studies, science, theater, video film production classes. Computer network features include on-campus library services, online commercial services, Internet access, wireless campus network. Campus intranet and student e-mail accounts are available to students. The school has a published electronic and media policy.

Contact Jane F. Fried, Dean of Admission. 978-749-4050. Fax: 978-749-4068. E-mail: admissions@andover.edu. Web site: www.andover.edu.

PHILLIPS EXETER ACADEMY

20 Main Street

Exeter, New Hampshire 03833-2460

Head of School: Mr. Thomas E. Hassan

General Information Coeducational boarding and day college-preparatory school. Grades 9–PG. Founded: 1781. Setting: small town. Nearest major city is Boston, MA. Students are housed in single-sex dormitories. 670-acre campus. 130 buildings on campus. Approved or accredited by Association of Independent Schools in New England, New England Association of Schools and Colleges, and The Association of Boarding Schools. Member of National Association of Independent Schools and Secondary School Admission Test Board. Endowment: $969.1 million. Upper school average class size: 12. Upper school faculty-student ratio: 1:5.

Upper School Student Profile 80% of students are boarding students. 45 states are represented in upper school student body. 10% are international students.

Faculty School total: 209. In upper school: 103 men, 106 women.

Subjects Offered Algebra, American history, American literature, anatomy, anthropology, Arabic, archaeology, architecture, art, art history, astronomy, biology, botany, calculus, ceramics, chemistry, Chinese, classics, computer programming, computer science, creative writing, dance, discrete mathematics, drama, driver education, ecology, economics, electronics, English, English literature, environmental science, ethics, European history, evolution, existentialism, expository writing, film, fine arts, French, genetics, geology, geometry, German, Greek, health, history, Italian, Japanese, Latin, linear algebra, logic, marine biology, mathematics, music, music composition, ornithology, philosophy, photography, physical education, physics, physiology, psychology, religion, Russian, science, sculpture, Spanish, statistics, theater, trigonometry, world literature, writing, Zen Buddhism.

Graduation Requirements American history, art, biology, computer science, English, foreign language, mathematics, physical education (includes health), physical science, religion (includes Bible studies and theology), science.

Special Academic Programs Advanced Placement exam preparation; honors section; independent study; term-away projects; study abroad; academic accommodation for the gifted, the musically talented, and the artistically talented.

College Admission Counseling Colleges students went to include Harvard University; New York University; Stanford University; The George Washington University; The Johns Hopkins University; University of Pennsylvania.

Student Life Upper grades have specified standards of dress, student council, honor system. Discipline rests primarily with faculty.

Summer Programs Enrichment programs offered; session focuses on academic enrichment; held on campus; accepts boys and girls; open to students from other schools. 700 students usually enrolled. 2012 schedule: July 1 to August 4. Application deadline: none.

Tuition and Aid Day student tuition: $32,470; 7-day tuition and room/board: $41,800. Tuition installment plan (Academic Management Services Plan, Tuition Management Systems Plan). Need-based scholarship grants available. In 2011–12, 47% of upper-school students received aid. Total amount of financial aid awarded in 2011–12: $15,635,367.

Admissions Traditional secondary-level entrance grade is 9. PSAT or SAT, SSAT or TOEFL required. Deadline for receipt of application materials: January 15. Application fee required: $50. Interview required.

Athletics Interscholastic: baseball (boys), basketball (b,g), crew (b,g), cross-country running (b,g), field hockey (g), football (b), golf (b,g), ice hockey (b,g), lacrosse (b,g), soccer (b,g), softball (g), squash (b,g), swimming and diving (b,g), tennis (b,g), track and field (b,g), volleyball (g), water polo (b,g), wrestling (b); coed interscholastic: bicycling, winter (indoor) track.

Computers Computers are regularly used in computer applications, foreign language, mathematics, science classes. Computer network features include on-campus library services, Internet access, Internet filtering or blocking technology. Campus intranet and student e-mail accounts are available to students.

Contact Mr. Michael Gary, Director of Admissions. 603-777-3437. Fax: 603-777-4399. E-mail: admit@exeter.edu. Web site: www.exeter.edu.

PHOENIX CHRISTIAN UNIFIED SCHOOLS

1751 West Indian School Road

Phoenix, Arizona 85015

Head of School: Mr. James H. Koan II

General Information Coeducational day college-preparatory, general academic, religious studies, and AP/Honors school, affiliated with Christian faith. Grades PS–12. Founded: 1949. Setting: suburban. 12-acre campus. 10 buildings on campus. Approved or accredited by Association of Christian Schools International, North Central Association of Colleges and Schools, and Arizona Department of Education. Total enrollment: 476. Upper school average class size: 20. Upper school faculty-student ratio: 1:20. There are 180 required school days per year for Upper School students. Upper School students typically attend 5 days per week. The average school day consists of 6 hours and 40 minutes.

Upper School Student Profile Grade 6: 17 students (10 boys, 7 girls); Grade 7: 35 students (13 boys, 22 girls); Grade 8: 40 students (19 boys, 21 girls); Grade 9: 61 students (31 boys, 30 girls); Grade 10: 39 students (21 boys, 18 girls); Grade 11: 57 students (30 boys, 27 girls); Grade 12: 64 students (31 boys, 33 girls).

Faculty School total: 43. In upper school: 12 men, 14 women.

Subjects Offered Advanced computer applications, algebra, American literature, American literature-AP, anatomy, art, arts, band, Bible, biology, biology-AP, calculus, calculus-AP, career and personal planning, chemistry, choir, choral music, computer applications, computers, creative writing, culinary arts, drama, drama performance,

drawing, economics, English, English literature, English literature-AP, English-AP, geometry, government, government-AP, home economics, instrumental music, integrated science, internship, intro to computers, language-AP, library, literature, literature-AP, marching band, photography, physical education, physics, pre-algebra, precalculus, psychology, religious education, sociology, Spanish, Spanish language-AP, statistics, student government, study skills, U.S. government, U.S. history, U.S. history-AP, Web site design, world history, yearbook.
Graduation Requirements Advanced math, Advanced Placement courses, algebra, American literature, arts and fine arts (art, music, dance, drama), biology, British literature, chemistry, computer education, economics, English, English composition, English literature, foreign language, geometry, government, integrated science, pre-calculus, religious studies, study skills, U.S. history, world history, world literature.
Special Academic Programs Advanced Placement exam preparation; honors section; independent study; study at local college for college credit; ESL (12 students enrolled).
College Admission Counseling 58 students graduated in 2010; 49 went to college, including Arizona State University; Glendale Community College; Grand Canyon University; Northern Arizona University; The University of Arizona. Other: 1 entered military service, 4 entered a postgraduate year, 1 had other specific plans. Mean SAT critical reading: 544, mean SAT math: 544, mean SAT writing: 532.
Student Life Upper grades have uniform requirement, student council. Discipline rests primarily with faculty. Attendance at religious services is required.
Tuition and Aid Day student tuition: $8560. Tuition installment plan (monthly payment plans, individually arranged payment plans). Tuition reduction for siblings, need-based scholarship grants available.
Admissions Traditional secondary-level entrance grade is 9. Achievement tests or any standardized test required. Deadline for receipt of application materials: none. Application fee required: $200. Interview required.
Athletics Interscholastic: baseball (boys), basketball (b,g), cheering (g), drill team (g), football (b), softball (g), volleyball (g), wrestling (b); coed interscholastic: cross-country running, diving, golf, soccer, swimming and diving, tennis, track and field, weight lifting, weight training. 24 coaches.
Computers Computers are regularly used in career exploration, college planning, computer applications, keyboarding, library, media services, Web site design, yearbook classes. Computer resources include on-campus library services, Internet access, Internet filtering or blocking technology. Campus intranet and computer access in designated common areas are available to students. Students grades are available online. The school has a published electronic and media policy.
Contact Mrs. Nancy L. Smith, Student Recruitment Coordinator. 602-265-4707 Ext. 221. Fax: 602-277-7170. E-mail: nsmith@phoenixchristian.org. Web site: www.phoenixchristian.org.

PHOENIX COUNTRY DAY SCHOOL

3901 East Stanford Drive

Paradise Valley, Arizona 85253

Head of School: Mr. Andrew Rodin

General Information Coeducational day college-preparatory, arts, performing and studio arts, extensive athletics, and community service, global citizenship, and travel school. Grades PK–12. Founded: 1961. Setting: suburban. Nearest major city is Phoenix. 40-acre campus. 8 buildings on campus. Approved or accredited by Independent Schools Association of the Southwest, National Independent Private Schools Association, and North Central Association of Colleges and Schools. Member of National Association of Independent Schools. Endowment: $13.3 million. Total enrollment: 722. Upper school average class size: 15. Upper school faculty-student ratio: 1:7. There are 168 required school days per year for Upper School students. Upper School students typically attend 5 days per week. The average school day consists of 5 hours.
Upper School Student Profile Grade 9: 60 students (26 boys, 34 girls); Grade 10: 59 students (22 boys, 37 girls); Grade 11: 66 students (26 boys, 40 girls); Grade 12: 58 students (27 boys, 31 girls).
Faculty School total: 90. In upper school: 22 men, 13 women; 27 have advanced degrees.
Subjects Offered Acting, advanced biology, advanced chemistry, advanced math, Advanced Placement courses, African-American literature, algebra, American government, American history, American history-AP, American literature, anatomy, anatomy and physiology, anthropology, art, art history, art history-AP, astronomy, band, baseball, basketball, biology, biology-AP, British literature, calculus, calculus-AP, ceramics, chemistry, chemistry-AP, Chinese, Chinese studies, choir, chorus, computer programming, computer science, creative writing, digital photography, directing, discrete mathematics, drawing, ecology, English, English composition, English literature, environmental science, environmental science-AP, ethics, European history, evolution, fine arts, French, French-AP, geography, geology, geometry, government/civics, history, Holocaust studies, jazz band, journalism, Latin, Latin American literature, Latin-AP, literature, Mandarin, marine biology, mathematics, music, oceanography, orchestra, painting, photography, physical education, physics, physics-AP, physiology, pre-calculus, probability and statistics, psychology, scene study, science, Shakespeare, social sciences, social studies, Spanish, Spanish-AP, speech, statistics, statistics-AP, theater, theater arts, trigonometry, world history, world literature, world religions.
Graduation Requirements Advanced biology, American history, American literature, ancient world history, arts and fine arts (art, music, dance, drama), biology, chemistry, English, foreign language, mathematics, physical education (includes health), physics, science, U.S. history, Western civilization, world history, 40 hours of community service.
Special Academic Programs 15 Advanced Placement exams for which test preparation is offered; honors section; independent study; study abroad.
College Admission Counseling 57 students graduated in 2011; all went to college, including Arizona State University; Duke University; Pomona College; Texas Christian University; Tulane University; Yale University. Median SAT critical reading: 680, median SAT math: 670, median SAT writing: 680, median combined SAT: 2020, median composite ACT: 30. 76% scored over 600 on SAT critical reading, 89% scored over 600 on SAT math, 82% scored over 600 on SAT writing, 89% scored over 1800 on combined SAT, 86% scored over 26 on composite ACT.
Student Life Upper grades have specified standards of dress, student council, honor system. Discipline rests primarily with faculty.
Summer Programs Enrichment, advancement, sports, art/fine arts, computer instruction programs offered; session focuses on academics/sports camp/arts program; held on campus; accepts boys and girls; open to students from other schools. 500 students usually enrolled. 2012 schedule: June 4 to July 13. Application deadline: none.
Tuition and Aid Day student tuition: $22,100. Tuition installment plan (Insured Tuition Payment Plan, monthly payment plans, individually arranged payment plans, 10 months, quarterly, semiannual, and yearly payment plans). Need-based scholarship grants available. In 2011–12, 26% of upper-school students received aid. Total amount of financial aid awarded in 2011–12: $1,016,600.
Admissions Traditional secondary-level entrance grade is 9. For fall 2011, 82 students applied for upper-level admission, 45 were accepted, 31 enrolled. Achievement/Aptitude/Writing, ERB CTP IV, Math Placement Exam, Otis-Lennon IQ and writing sample required. Deadline for receipt of application materials: March 1. Application fee required: $100. Interview required.
Athletics Interscholastic: baseball (boys), basketball (b,g), cheering (g), diving (b,g), flag football (b), golf (b,g), lacrosse (b,g), soccer (b,g), softball (g), winter soccer (g); intramural: archery (b,g), badminton (b,g), basketball (b,g), lacrosse (b,g), outdoor education (b,g), outdoor recreation (b,g), physical fitness (b,g), softball (g), strength & conditioning (b,g), yoga (b,g); coed interscholastic: cheering, diving, swimming and diving, tennis, volleyball; coed intramural: basketball, cross-country running, flag football, golf, running, soccer, swimming and diving, tennis, volleyball, winter soccer. 5 PE instructors, 23 coaches, 1 athletic trainer.
Computers Computers are regularly used in art, college planning, creative writing, data processing, desktop publishing, economics, engineering, English, foreign language, French, history, humanities, independent study, information technology, keyboarding, library, library skills, literary magazine, mathematics, news writing, newspaper, photography, programming, publications, research skills, science, social sciences, social studies, Spanish, stock market, Web site design, writing, yearbook classes. Computer network features include on-campus library services, online commercial services, Internet access, wireless campus network, Internet filtering or blocking technology. Campus intranet, student e-mail accounts, and computer access in designated common areas are available to students. Students grades are available online. The school has a published electronic and media policy.
Contact Sandy Orrick, Admissions Assistant. 602-955-8200 Ext. 2255. Fax: 602-381-4554. E-mail: sandy.orrick@pcds.org. Web site: www.pcds.org.

PICKENS ACADEMY

225 Ray Bass Road

Carrollton, Alabama 35447

Head of School: Mr. Brach White

General Information Coeducational day college-preparatory and general academic school. Grades K4–12. Founded: 1970. Setting: rural. Nearest major city is Tuscaloosa. 3 buildings on campus. Approved or accredited by Distance Education and Training Council, Southern Association of Colleges and Schools, and Alabama Department of Education. Total enrollment: 247. Upper school average class size: 25. Upper school faculty-student ratio: 1:20. There are 180 required school days per year for Upper School students. Upper School students typically attend 5 days per week. The average school day consists of 7 hours.
Upper School Student Profile Grade 7: 27 students (10 boys, 17 girls); Grade 8: 15 students (7 boys, 8 girls); Grade 9: 25 students (13 boys, 12 girls); Grade 10: 16 students (6 boys, 10 girls); Grade 11: 32 students (13 boys, 19 girls); Grade 12: 18 students (10 boys, 8 girls).
Faculty School total: 21. In upper school: 5 men, 16 women; 8 have advanced degrees.
Subjects Offered 20th century history, 20th century world history, advanced chemistry, advanced computer applications, advanced math, Alabama history and geography, algebra, American democracy, American government, American history, American literature, anatomy and physiology, ancient history, ancient world history, applied music, art, band, baseball, basketball, biology, British literature, business mathematics, calculus, career/college preparation, cheerleading, chemistry, civics, college admission

preparation, composition, computer literacy, consumer economics, CPR, creative writing, desktop publishing, economics, English composition, English literature, environmental science, family and consumer science, French, geography, government, grammar, health education, history, keyboarding, land management, leadership education training, library assistant, Microsoft, music, music appreciation, physical education, physical science, physics, research skills, science, student government, trigonometry, U.S. government and politics, Web site design, weight training, weightlifting.

Graduation Requirements 20th century world history, advanced math, American government, American history, anatomy and physiology, calculus, economics, English, English composition, English literature, physics, research skills, trigonometry.

Special Academic Programs Honors section; study at local college for college credit.

College Admission Counseling 24 students graduated in 2011; 22 went to college, including Auburn University; Mississippi State University; The University of Alabama. Other: 1 went to work, 1 entered military service. Median composite ACT: 21. 8% scored over 26 on composite ACT.

Student Life Upper grades have specified standards of dress, student council. Discipline rests primarily with faculty.

Tuition and Aid Day student tuition: $3000. Guaranteed tuition plan. Tuition installment plan (Insured Tuition Payment Plan, monthly payment plans).

Admissions Traditional secondary-level entrance grade is 9. PSAT or Stanford Achievement Test, Otis-Lennon School Ability Test required. Deadline for receipt of application materials: none. No application fee required. On-campus interview required.

Athletics Interscholastic: baseball (boys), basketball (b,g), cheering (g), cross-country running (b,g), danceline (g), football (b), golf (b,g), softball (g), volleyball (g), weight lifting (b,g); coed interscholastic: tennis, track and field. 1 PE instructor, 2 coaches.

Computers Computers are regularly used in all academic classes. Computer network features include on-campus library services, Internet access, Internet filtering or blocking technology. Student e-mail accounts are available to students. Students grades are available online. The school has a published electronic and media policy.

Contact Admissions. 205-367-8144. Fax: 205-367-8145. Web site: www.pickensacademy.com.

PICKERING COLLEGE

16945 Bayview Avenue

Newmarket, Ontario L3Y 4X2, Canada

Head of School: Mr. Peter C. Sturrup

General Information Coeducational boarding and day college-preparatory, arts, technology, film studies and radio station, and leadership school. Boarding grades 7–12, day grades JK–12. Founded: 1842. Setting: suburban. Nearest major city is Toronto, Canada. Students are housed in single-sex dormitories. 42-acre campus. 6 buildings on campus. Approved or accredited by Canadian Association of Independent Schools, Canadian Educational Standards Institute, National Independent Private Schools Association, Ontario Ministry of Education, The Association of Boarding Schools, and Ontario Department of Education. Affiliate member of National Association of Independent Schools; member of Secondary School Admission Test Board. Language of instruction: English. Total enrollment: 373. Upper school average class size: 18. Upper school faculty-student ratio: 1:9. There are 164 required school days per year for Upper School students. Upper School students typically attend 5 days per week. The average school day consists of 8 hours.

Upper School Student Profile Grade 9: 42 students (26 boys, 16 girls); Grade 10: 54 students (32 boys, 22 girls); Grade 11: 57 students (31 boys, 26 girls); Grade 12: 65 students (32 boys, 33 girls). 40% of students are boarding students. 60% are province residents. 40% are international students. International students from Barbados, China, Germany, Japan, Mexico, and Russian Federation; 20 other countries represented in student body.

Faculty School total: 42. In upper school: 17 men, 12 women; 7 have advanced degrees; 15 reside on campus.

Subjects Offered Algebra, art, art history, biology, business, business skills, business studies, calculus, Canadian geography, Canadian history, careers, chemistry, community service, computer applications, computer multimedia, computer programming, computer science, concert band, creative writing, drama, dramatic arts, economics, English, English composition, English literature, entrepreneurship, environmental science, ESL, experiential education, family studies, filmmaking, fine arts, finite math, French, geography, geometry, government/civics, guitar, health, health education, history, instrumental music, jazz band, law, leadership, literature, Mandarin, mathematics, media studies, music, physical education, physics, politics, science, social sciences, social studies, Spanish, theater, video film production, visual arts, vocal music, world history.

Graduation Requirements English, 60 hours of community service completed over 4 years before graduation.

Special Academic Programs Independent study; ESL (25 students enrolled).

College Admission Counseling 60 students graduated in 2011; 58 went to college, including Dalhousie University; McGill University; Queen's University at Kingston; The University of Western Ontario; University of Toronto; University of Waterloo. Other: 1 entered military service, 1 had other specific plans.

Student Life Upper grades have uniform requirement, student council, honor system. Discipline rests equally with students and faculty.

Summer Programs ESL programs offered; session focuses on ESL Summer Camp; held on campus; accepts boys and girls; open to students from other schools. 60 students usually enrolled. 2012 schedule: June 25 to August 17. Application deadline: May.

Tuition and Aid Day student tuition: CAN$18,220–CAN$21,905; 7-day tuition and room/board: CAN$45,430–CAN$47,550. Tuition installment plan (Insured Tuition Payment Plan, monthly payment plans). Tuition reduction for siblings, bursaries, merit scholarship grants, need-based scholarship grants available. In 2011–12, 4% of upper-school students received aid; total upper-school merit-scholarship money awarded: CAN$13,000. Total amount of financial aid awarded in 2011–12: CAN$112,000.

Admissions Traditional secondary-level entrance grade is 9. For fall 2011, 109 students applied for upper-level admission, 52 enrolled. CAT, International English Language Test, SLEP for foreign students, SSAT or TOEFL required. Deadline for receipt of application materials: none. Application fee required: CAN$200. Interview required.

Athletics Interscholastic: badminton (boys, girls), basketball (b,g), cross-country running (b,g), figure skating (b,g), hockey (b), horseback riding (b,g), ice hockey (b), ice skating (b,g), rugby (b,g), skiing (downhill) (b,g), snowboarding (b,g), softball (b,g), swimming and diving (b,g), tennis (b,g), track and field (b,g), volleyball (b,g); intramural: badminton (b,g), ball hockey (b,g), combined training (b,g), figure skating (b,g), floor hockey (b,g), hockey (b,g), horseback riding (b,g), ice skating (b,g), outdoor activities (b,g), outdoor adventure (b,g), outdoor recreation (b,g), paddle tennis (b,g), physical training (b,g), running (b,g), skiing (downhill) (b,g), strength & conditioning (b,g), swimming and diving (b,g), tennis (b,g), track and field (b,g), volleyball (b,g); coed interscholastic: alpine skiing, aquatics, badminton, cross-country running, equestrian sports, figure skating, hockey, horseback riding, ice hockey, ice skating, mountain biking, skiing (downhill), snowboarding, swimming and diving, tennis, track and field; coed intramural: ball hockey, basketball, bowling, broomball, cooperative games, cross-country running, dance squad, equestrian sports, figure skating, fitness, floor hockey, Frisbee, golf, hockey, horseback riding, ice skating, indoor soccer, mountain biking, outdoor adventure, outdoor education, paint ball, rock climbing, skiing (downhill), strength & conditioning, swimming and diving, table tennis, tennis, touch football, track and field, volleyball, wilderness survival. 3 PE instructors, 2 coaches, 1 athletic trainer.

Computers Computers are regularly used in all classes. Computer network features include on-campus library services, Internet access, wireless campus network, Internet filtering or blocking technology. Student e-mail accounts are available to students. Students grades are available online. The school has a published electronic and media policy.

Contact Ms. Susan Hundert, Admission Associate. 905-895-1700 Ext. 259. Fax: 905-895-1306. E-mail: admission@pickeringcollege.on.ca. Web site: www.pickeringcollege.on.ca.

PIC RIVER PRIVATE HIGH SCHOOL

21 Rabbit Drive

PO Box 216

Heron Bay, Ontario P0T 1R0, Canada

Head of School: Mrs. Lisa Michano-Courchene

General Information Coeducational day college-preparatory school, affiliated with Roman Catholic Church. Grades K–12. Founded: 1993. Setting: small town. Nearest major city is Thunder Bay, Canada. 2-acre campus. 1 building on campus. Approved or accredited by Ontario Department of Education. Language of instruction: English. Upper school average class size: 22. Upper school faculty-student ratio: 1:10. There are 194 required school days per year for Upper School students. Upper School students typically attend 5 days per week. The average school day consists of 3 hours.

Upper School Student Profile 100% of students are Roman Catholic.

Faculty School total: 1. In upper school: 1 man.

Student Life Discipline rests primarily with faculty.

Admissions No application fee required.

Computers Computer network features include on-campus library services, Internet access, Internet filtering or blocking technology. Campus intranet and student e-mail accounts are available to students.

Contact Mr. Douglas L. Vollett, Teacher. 807-229-3726. Fax: 807-229-1944. E-mail: dvollett@picriver.com.

PIEDMONT ACADEMY

PO Box 231

126 Highway 212 West

Monticello, Georgia 31064

Head of School: Mr. Tony Tanner

General Information Coeducational day college-preparatory, arts, business, vocational, religious studies, bilingual studies, technology, and dual enrollment with Georgia Military College school, affiliated with Protestant faith. Grades PK–12. Founded: 1970.

Setting: small town. Nearest major city is Atlanta. 25-acre campus. 8 buildings on campus. Approved or accredited by Georgia Accrediting Commission and Georgia Independent School Association. Total enrollment: 314. Upper school average class size: 17. Upper school faculty-student ratio: 1:13. There are 180 required school days per year for Upper School students. Upper School students typically attend 5 days per week. The average school day consists of 7 hours.

Upper School Student Profile Grade 6: 29 students (16 boys, 13 girls); Grade 7: 23 students (15 boys, 8 girls); Grade 8: 28 students (18 boys, 10 girls); Grade 9: 33 students (11 boys, 22 girls); Grade 10: 18 students (4 boys, 14 girls); Grade 11: 18 students (14 boys, 4 girls); Grade 12: 26 students (14 boys, 12 girls). 98% of students are Protestant.

Faculty School total: 31. In upper school: 6 men, 15 women; 15 have advanced degrees.

Subjects Offered Advanced chemistry, advanced computer applications, advanced math, algebra, American government, American history, American history-AP, anatomy and physiology, band, biology, business law, calculus, calculus-AP, chemistry, chemistry-AP, civics, computer science, computer science-AP, computers, concert band, concert choir, consumer economics, consumer law, economics, English, English-AP, geometry, government and politics-AP, government-AP, government/civics, grammar, health education, honors algebra, honors English, honors geometry, Internet, intro to computers, keyboarding, language arts, leadership and service, literature, mathematics, performing arts, personal finance, physical fitness, physical science, physics, pre-calculus, science, sociology, Spanish, student government, wind instruments, world history, yearbook.

Graduation Requirements Algebra, American government, American literature, biology, calculus, chemistry, civics, English composition, English literature, geometry, government, grammar, history, keyboarding, mathematics, physical education (includes health), physical science, science, Spanish.

Special Academic Programs Study at local college for college credit.

College Admission Counseling 25 students graduated in 2010; all went to college, including Georgia Perimeter College; North Georgia College & State University; University of Georgia.

Student Life Upper grades have uniform requirement, student council, honor system. Discipline rests primarily with faculty.

Tuition and Aid Day student tuition: $6000. Guaranteed tuition plan. Tuition installment plan (monthly payment plans, individually arranged payment plans). Tuition reduction for siblings, need-based scholarship grants available. In 2010–11, 10% of upper-school students received aid. Total amount of financial aid awarded in 2010–11: $25,000.

Admissions For fall 2010, 45 students applied for upper-level admission, 37 were accepted, 37 enrolled. OLSAT, Stanford Achievement Test required. Deadline for receipt of application materials: February 1. Application fee required: $75. Interview required.

Athletics Interscholastic: baseball (boys), basketball (b,g), cheering (b,g), fitness (b,g), flag football (b,g), football (b), golf (b,g), power lifting (b,g), soccer (b,g), softball (g), strength & conditioning (b,g), tennis (b,g), weight lifting (b,g), weight training (b,g), wrestling (b,g); coed interscholastic: track and field; coed intramural: flag football. 6 PE instructors, 10 coaches.

Computers Computers are regularly used in all academic classes. Computer network features include on-campus library services, online commercial services, Internet access, wireless campus network, Internet filtering or blocking technology. Campus intranet is available to students. Students grades are available online. The school has a published electronic and media policy.

Contact Judy M. Nelson, Director of Admissions/Public and Alumni Relations. 706-468-8818 Ext. 19. Fax: 706-468-2409. E-mail: judy_nelson@piedmontacademy.com. Web site: www.piedmontacademy.com.

PINECREST ACADEMY

955 Peachtree Parkway

Cumming, Georgia 30041

Head of School: Fr. Robert Presutti, LC,, PhD

General Information Coeducational day college-preparatory and technology school, affiliated with Roman Catholic Church. Grades PK–12. Founded: 1993. Setting: suburban. Nearest major city is Atlanta. 70-acre campus. 4 buildings on campus. Approved or accredited by Georgia Accrediting Commission, Georgia Independent School Association, National Catholic Education Association, Southern Association of Colleges and Schools, and Georgia Department of Education. Member of National Association of Independent Schools. Total enrollment: 830. Upper school average class size: 17. Upper school faculty-student ratio: 1:10. There are 180 required school days per year for Upper School students. Upper School students typically attend 5 days per week. The average school day consists of 7 hours and 30 minutes.

Upper School Student Profile Grade 6: 62 students (33 boys, 29 girls); Grade 7: 76 students (44 boys, 32 girls); Grade 8: 70 students (35 boys, 35 girls); Grade 9: 70 students (28 boys, 42 girls); Grade 10: 59 students (32 boys, 27 girls); Grade 11: 52 students (24 boys, 28 girls); Grade 12: 54 students (21 boys, 33 girls). 88% of students are Roman Catholic.

Faculty School total: 83. In upper school: 16 men, 29 women; 31 have advanced degrees.

Subjects Offered Advanced Placement courses.

Special Academic Programs 10 Advanced Placement exams for which test preparation is offered.

College Admission Counseling 44 students graduated in 2011; all went to college, including Emory University; Georgia Institute of Technology; University of Georgia.

Student Life Upper grades have uniform requirement, student council, honor system. Discipline rests primarily with faculty. Attendance at religious services is required.

Tuition and Aid Tuition reduction for siblings, need-based scholarship grants available.

Admissions Traditional secondary-level entrance grade is 9. Admissions testing, English for Non-native Speakers, PSAT, SLEP for foreign students, SSAT or TOEFL required. Deadline for receipt of application materials: none. Application fee required: $150. Interview required.

Athletics Interscholastic: baseball (boys), basketball (b,g), cheering (g), cross-country running (b,g), equestrian sports (g), football (b), soccer (b,g), softball (g), swimming and diving (b,g); intramural: baseball (b), basketball (b,g), cross-country running (b,g), dance squad (g), football (b), running (b,g), soccer (b,g), softball (b,g). 3 PE instructors, 13 coaches.

Computers Computer resources include on-campus library services, online commercial services, Internet access, wireless campus network, Internet filtering or blocking technology. Campus intranet and computer access in designated common areas are available to students. Students grades are available online. The school has a published electronic and media policy.

Contact Ms. Melissa McWaters, Admissions Assistant. 770-888-4477 Ext. 245. Fax: 770-886-5584. E-mail: mmcwaters@pinecrestacademy.org. Web site: www.pinecrestacademy.org/.

PINE CREST SCHOOL

1501 Northeast 62nd Street

Fort Lauderdale, Florida 33334-5116

Head of School: Dr. Dana Markham

General Information Coeducational day college-preparatory school. Grades PK–12. Founded: 1934. Setting: urban. 49-acre campus. 22 buildings on campus. Approved or accredited by Florida Council of Independent Schools, Southern Association of Colleges and Schools, and Southern Association of Independent Schools. Member of National Association of Independent Schools and Secondary School Admission Test Board. Endowment: $36.2 million. Total enrollment: 1,755. Upper school average class size: 17. Upper school faculty-student ratio: 1:10.

Upper School Student Profile Grade 9: 214 students (98 boys, 116 girls); Grade 10: 200 students (107 boys, 93 girls); Grade 11: 185 students (97 boys, 88 girls); Grade 12: 207 students (101 boys, 106 girls).

Faculty School total: 219. In upper school: 42 men, 59 women.

Subjects Offered Algebra, American history, art, art history, ballet, band, biology, calculus, ceramics, chemistry, Chinese, chorus, comparative government and politics-AP, computer graphics, computer programming, computer science, dance, drama, economics, English, environmental science, ethics, European history, fine arts, forensics, French, geometry, German, government/civics, history, mathematics, music, orchestra, photography, physical education, physics, psychology, Spanish, speech, statistics.

Graduation Requirements Arts and fine arts (art, music, dance, drama), English, ethics, foreign language, humanities, mathematics, physical education (includes health), science, social studies (includes history), speech.

Special Academic Programs Advanced Placement exam preparation; honors section; ESL (12 students enrolled).

College Admission Counseling 208 students graduated in 2011; all went to college, including Florida State University; Northwestern University; University of Florida; University of Miami; University of Pennsylvania; Vanderbilt University. Median SAT critical reading: 670, median SAT math: 680, median SAT writing: 670, median combined SAT: 2020, median composite ACT: 30.

Student Life Upper grades have uniform requirement, student council, honor system. Discipline rests primarily with faculty.

Summer Programs Enrichment, advancement, sports programs offered; session focuses on competitive swimming, dance, summer school (grades 9-12); held on campus; accepts boys and girls; open to students from other schools. 300 students usually enrolled. 2012 schedule: June to July. Application deadline: none.

Tuition and Aid Day student tuition: $23,560. Tuition installment plan (The Tuition Refund Plan). Need-based scholarship grants available. In 2011–12, 18% of upper-school students received aid. Total amount of financial aid awarded in 2011–12: $1,888,380.

Admissions Traditional secondary-level entrance grade is 9. For fall 2011, 187 students applied for upper-level admission, 114 were accepted, 76 enrolled. SSAT required. Deadline for receipt of application materials: none. Application fee required: $100. Interview required.

Athletics Interscholastic: aquatics (boys, girls), baseball (b), basketball (b,g), crew (b,g), cross-country running (b,g), diving (b,g), football (b), golf (b,g), lacrosse (b,g), physical fitness (b,g), soccer (b,g), softball (g), strength & conditioning (b,g), swimming and diving (b,g), tennis (b,g), track and field (b,g), volleyball (b,g), weight lifting (b,g); intramural: aquatics (b,g), swimming and diving (b,g); coed interscholastic: ballet, cheering; coed intramural: ballet, physical training, strength & conditioning. 8 PE instructors, 1 athletic trainer.

Computers Computer network features include on-campus library services, online commercial services, Internet access, wireless campus network, Internet filtering or blocking technology, laptop program (grades 6-12), SmartBoards in classrooms. Campus intranet and student e-mail accounts are available to students. Students grades are available online. The school has a published electronic and media policy.

Contact Mrs. Elena Del Alamo, Director of Admission and Financial Aid. 954-492-4103. Fax: 954-492-4188. E-mail: pcadmit@pinecrest.edu. Web site: www.pinecrest.edu.

PINEHURST SCHOOL

St. Catharines, Ontario, Canada

See Special Needs Schools section.

THE PINE SCHOOL

12350 SE Federal Highway

Hobe Sound, Florida 33455

Head of School: Mr. Stephen M. Mandell

General Information Coeducational day college-preparatory school. Founded: 1969. Setting: small town. Nearest major city is West Palm Beach. Approved or accredited by Florida Department of Education. Member of National Association of Independent Schools. Upper school average class size: 9. Upper school faculty-student ratio: 1:9. Upper School students typically attend 5 days per week.

Special Academic Programs Advanced Placement exam preparation; honors section; study abroad.

Student Life Upper grades have uniform requirement, student council, honor system. Discipline rests primarily with faculty.

Tuition and Aid Financial aid available to upper-school students. In 2011–12, 29% of upper-school students received aid. Total amount of financial aid awarded in 2011–12: $1,000,000.

Admissions Deadline for receipt of application materials: none. Application fee required: $60. Interview required.

Computers Computer network features include on-campus library services, Internet access, wireless campus network, Internet filtering or blocking technology. Student e-mail accounts and computer access in designated common areas are available to students. Students grades are available online. The school has a published electronic and media policy.

Contact 772-675-7005. Web site: www.thepineschool.org.

THE PINGREE SCHOOL

537 Highland Street

South Hamilton, Massachusetts 01982

Head of School: Dr. Timothy M. Johnson

General Information Coeducational day college-preparatory school. Grades 9–12. Founded: 1961. Setting: suburban. Nearest major city is Boston. 100-acre campus. 2 buildings on campus. Approved or accredited by Association of Independent Schools in New England, National Independent Private Schools Association, and New England Association of Schools and Colleges. Member of National Association of Independent Schools and Secondary School Admission Test Board. Endowment: $11 million. Total enrollment: 340. Upper school average class size: 15. Upper school faculty-student ratio: 1:7. There are 162 required school days per year for Upper School students. Upper School students typically attend 5 days per week. The average school day consists of 8 hours.

Upper School Student Profile Grade 9: 80 students (39 boys, 41 girls); Grade 10: 93 students (40 boys, 53 girls); Grade 11: 89 students (37 boys, 52 girls); Grade 12: 79 students (38 boys, 41 girls).

Faculty School total: 57. In upper school: 20 men, 34 women; 42 have advanced degrees.

Subjects Offered Algebra, American history, American literature, American studies, art, art history, astronomy, biology, calculus, ceramics, chemistry, computer programming, computer science, creative writing, dance, drama, driver education, earth science, ecology, economics, English, English literature, European history, fine arts, French, geometry, history, Latin, mathematics, music, oceanography, philosophy, photography, physics, psychology, Russian literature, science, social studies, Spanish, theater, trigonometry, writing.

Graduation Requirements Arts and fine arts (art, music, dance, drama), English, foreign language, mathematics, science, social studies (includes history), 50 hours of community service, senior projects.

Special Academic Programs Advanced Placement exam preparation; honors section; independent study; term-away projects.

College Admission Counseling 86 students graduated in 2011; 85 went to college, including Bentley University; Boston College; Boston University; Lafayette College; St. Lawrence University. Other: 1 entered military service. Median SAT critical reading: 610, median SAT math: 620, median SAT writing: 630, median combined SAT: 1860, median composite ACT: 27. 60% scored over 600 on SAT critical reading, 63% scored over 600 on SAT math, 63% scored over 600 on SAT writing, 60% scored over 1800 on combined SAT, 27% scored over 26 on composite ACT.

Student Life Upper grades have specified standards of dress, student council, honor system. Discipline rests equally with students and faculty.

Tuition and Aid Day student tuition: $34,750. Tuition installment plan (Academic Management Services Plan). Merit scholarship grants, need-based scholarship grants, need-based loans available. In 2011–12, 25% of upper-school students received aid; total upper-school merit-scholarship money awarded: $100,000. Total amount of financial aid awarded in 2011–12: $1,310,000.

Admissions Traditional secondary-level entrance grade is 9. For fall 2011, 379 students applied for upper-level admission, 208 were accepted, 77 enrolled. ISEE or SSAT required. Deadline for receipt of application materials: January 15. Application fee required: $50. On-campus interview required.

Athletics Interscholastic: baseball (boys), basketball (b,g), cross-country running (b,g), field hockey (g), football (b), golf (b,g), ice hockey (b,g), lacrosse (b,g), running (b,g), soccer (b,g), softball (g), swimming and diving (b,g), tennis (b,g), volleyball (g); coed interscholastic: Frisbee, sailing, ultimate Frisbee; coed intramural: dance, fitness, golf, hiking/backpacking, modern dance, mountaineering, outdoor adventure, outdoor education, outdoor skills, physical fitness, physical training, skiing (downhill), strength & conditioning, weight lifting, weight training, wilderness. 24 coaches, 2 athletic trainers.

Computers Computers are regularly used in college planning, computer applications, desktop publishing, digital applications, drawing and design, English, foreign language, graphic arts, graphic design, independent study, information technology, mathematics, programming, publications, science, technology, Web site design, word processing, writing, yearbook classes. Computer network features include on-campus library services, online commercial services, Internet access, Internet filtering or blocking technology. Student e-mail accounts are available to students. Students grades are available online.

Contact Mrs. Jody MacWhinnie, Admission Office Coordinator. 978-468-4415 Ext. 262. Fax: 978-468-3758. E-mail: jmacwhinnie@pingree.org. Web site: www.pingree.org.

THE PINGRY SCHOOL

Martinsville Road

PO Box 366

Martinsville, New Jersey 08836

Head of School: Mr. Nathaniel Conard

General Information Coeducational day college-preparatory and arts school. Grades K–12. Founded: 1861. Setting: suburban. Nearest major city is New York, NY. 240-acre campus. 1 building on campus. Approved or accredited by Middle States Association of Colleges and Schools and New Jersey Department of Education. Member of National Association of Independent Schools. Endowment: $60 million. Total enrollment: 1,079. Upper school average class size: 14. Upper school faculty-student ratio: 1:8. There are 168 required school days per year for Upper School students. Upper School students typically attend 5 days per week. The average school day consists of 6 hours and 15 minutes.

Upper School Student Profile Grade 9: 147 students (75 boys, 72 girls); Grade 10: 137 students (72 boys, 65 girls); Grade 11: 133 students (70 boys, 63 girls); Grade 12: 131 students (71 boys, 60 girls).

Faculty School total: 120. In upper school: 47 men, 37 women; 61 have advanced degrees.

Subjects Offered Algebra, American literature, analysis, analysis and differential calculus, anatomy, architecture, art, art history-AP, biology, biology-AP, brass choir, calculus, chemistry, chemistry-AP, Chinese, clayworking, comparative cultures, computer science-AP, creative writing, drafting, drama, driver education, English, ethics, European literature, filmmaking, French, French-AP, geometry, German, German-AP, Greek drama, health, jazz band, jewelry making, Latin, literature by women, macro/microeconomics-AP, macroeconomics-AP, modern European history, music theory, mythology, orchestra, painting, peer counseling, photography, physics, physics-AP, physiology, psychology, psychology-AP, sculpture, Shakespeare, Spanish, Spanish-AP, studio art-AP, trigonometry, U.S. government and politics-AP, U.S. history-AP, wind ensemble, world literature, yearbook.

Graduation Requirements Arts and fine arts (art, music, dance, drama), English, foreign language, mathematics, physical education (includes health), science, social studies (includes history). Community service is required.

Special Academic Programs 20 Advanced Placement exams for which test preparation is offered; honors section; independent study; term-away projects; study abroad; academic accommodation for the gifted.

College Admission Counseling 131 students graduated in 2011; 126 went to college, including Boston College; Cornell University; Georgetown University; Hamilton College; Princeton University; University of Pennsylvania. Other: 2 entered a postgraduate year, 3 had other specific plans. Mean SAT critical reading: 686, mean SAT math: 693, mean SAT writing: 698, mean composite ACT: 30.

Student Life Upper grades have specified standards of dress, student council, honor system. Discipline rests equally with students and faculty.

Summer Programs Enrichment, sports programs offered; session focuses on enrichment, writing, and study skills; held on campus; accepts boys and girls; open to students from other schools. 30 students usually enrolled. 2012 schedule: June 27 to August 5.

Tuition and Aid Day student tuition: $25,670–$30,225. Tuition installment plan (individually arranged payment plans, My Tuition Solutions). Need-based scholarship grants available. In 2011–12, 15% of upper-school students received aid. Total amount of financial aid awarded in 2011–12: $199,259.

Admissions Traditional secondary-level entrance grade is 9. For fall 2011, 288 students applied for upper-level admission, 131 were accepted, 102 enrolled. ERB, ISEE, SSAT or Wechsler Intelligence Scale for Children required. Deadline for receipt of application materials: January 3. Application fee required: $75. On-campus interview required.

Athletics Interscholastic: alpine skiing (boys, girls), baseball (b), basketball (b,g), cross-country running (b,g), fencing (b,g), field hockey (g), football (b), golf (b,g), ice hockey (b,g), indoor track & field (b,g), lacrosse (b,g), skiing (downhill) (b,g), soccer (b,g), softball (g), squash (b,g), swimming and diving (b,g), tennis (b,g), track and field (b,g), wrestling (b); intramural: fitness (b,g), yoga (b,g); coed interscholastic: dance, physical fitness, physical training, water polo. 3 PE instructors, 15 coaches, 1 athletic trainer.

Computers Computers are regularly used in all academic classes. Computer network features include on-campus library services, online commercial services, Internet access, wireless campus network, Internet filtering or blocking technology. Campus intranet, student e-mail accounts, and computer access in designated common areas are available to students. The school has a published electronic and media policy.

Contact Ms. Samantha Paladini, Admission Coordinator. 908-647-5555 Ext. 1228. Fax: 908-647-4395. E-mail: spaladini@pingry.org. Web site: www.pingry.org.

PIONEER VALLEY CHRISTIAN SCHOOL

965 Plumtree Road

Springfield, Massachusetts 01119

Head of School: Mr. Timothy L. Duff

General Information Coeducational day college-preparatory, religious studies, bilingual studies, and technology school, affiliated with Protestant faith, Evangelical faith. Grades PS–12. Founded: 1972. Setting: suburban. 25-acre campus. 1 building on campus. Approved or accredited by Association of Christian Schools International, New England Association of Schools and Colleges, and Massachusetts Department of Education. Total enrollment: 270. Upper school average class size: 22. Upper school faculty-student ratio: 1:5. There are 181 required school days per year for Upper School students. Upper School students typically attend 5 days per week. The average school day consists of 6 hours and 40 minutes.

Upper School Student Profile Grade 9: 20 students (13 boys, 7 girls); Grade 10: 14 students (5 boys, 9 girls); Grade 11: 23 students (11 boys, 12 girls); Grade 12: 32 students (16 boys, 16 girls). 95% of students are Protestant, members of Evangelical faith.

Faculty School total: 32. In upper school: 5 men, 13 women; 11 have advanced degrees.

Subjects Offered Advanced math, algebra, American literature, American literature-AP, anatomy, art, athletics, baseball, basketball, bell choir, Bible studies, biology, British literature, British literature-AP, calculus-AP, chemistry, choir, choral music, Christian education, drama, economics, English, English-AP, French, geometry, government, history, instrumental music, music, physical education, physical science, physics, pre-algebra, sociology, softball, Spanish, speech, sports, technology, tennis, U.S. history, volleyball, weight training, Western civilization, world history, yearbook.

Graduation Requirements Algebra, American literature, arts and fine arts (art, music, dance, drama), Bible, biology, British literature, economics, English, foreign language, government, physical education (includes health), physical science, sociology, speech, U.S. history, Christian/community service hours.

Special Academic Programs Advanced Placement exam preparation; honors section; remedial reading and/or remedial writing; remedial math; programs in English, mathematics, general development for dyslexic students; special instructional classes for students with learning disabilities, Attention Deficit Disorder, and dyslexia.

College Admission Counseling 21 students graduated in 2011; all went to college, including Gordon College; Holyoke Community College; Liberty University; Springfield College. Median SAT critical reading: 530, median SAT math: 490, median SAT writing: 495, median composite ACT: 20.

Student Life Upper grades have uniform requirement, honor system. Discipline rests primarily with faculty. Attendance at religious services is required.

Tuition and Aid Day student tuition: $9900. Tuition installment plan (monthly payment plans, Electronic Funds Transfer, weekly, biweekly, monthly). Need-based scholarship grants, need-based financial aid and scholarship available. In 2011–12, 45% of upper-school students received aid. Total amount of financial aid awarded in 2011–12: $80,400.

Admissions Traditional secondary-level entrance grade is 9. For fall 2011, 14 students applied for upper-level admission, 11 were accepted, 11 enrolled. Admissions testing required. Deadline for receipt of application materials: none. Application fee required: $80. Interview required.

Athletics Interscholastic: baseball (boys), basketball (b,g), softball (g), tennis (b,g), volleyball (g); intramural: soccer (b,g); coed interscholastic: soccer, weight training; coed intramural: combined training, golf, physical training, soccer, strength & conditioning. 2 PE instructors, 12 coaches.

Computers Computers are regularly used in all academic classes. Computer network features include Internet access, Internet filtering or blocking technology, homework assignments available online.

Contact Mr. Pat Sterlacci, Director of Admissions. 413-782-8031. Fax: 413-782-8033. E-mail: psterlacci@pvcs.org. Web site: www.pvcs.org.

POLYTECHNIC SCHOOL

1030 East California Boulevard

Pasadena, California 91106-4099

Head of School: Mrs. Deborah E. Reed

General Information Coeducational day college-preparatory school. Grades K–12. Founded: 1907. Setting: suburban. 15-acre campus. 7 buildings on campus. Approved or accredited by California Association of Independent Schools, The College Board, Western Association of Schools and Colleges, and California Department of Education. Member of National Association of Independent Schools. Endowment: $47 million. Total enrollment: 860. Upper school average class size: 17. Upper school faculty-student ratio: 1:17. Upper School students typically attend 5 days per week. The average school day consists of 7 hours.

Upper School Student Profile Grade 9: 99 students (49 boys, 50 girls); Grade 10: 93 students (43 boys, 50 girls); Grade 11: 91 students (52 boys, 39 girls); Grade 12: 91 students (45 boys, 46 girls).

Faculty School total: 99. In upper school: 12 men, 25 women; 28 have advanced degrees.

Subjects Offered Acting, algebra, American history, American history-AP, analytic geometry, art history, athletics, audio visual/media, Basic programming, batik, biology, biology-AP, calculus, calculus-AP, ceramics, chamber groups, chemistry, chemistry-AP, choral music, communications, computer art, computer science, constitutional law, data analysis, drama, drama performance, drawing, East Asian history, economics, English, English language and composition-AP, English literature and composition-AP, ensembles, ethics, filmmaking, French, French literature-AP, functions, geometry, guitar, improvisation, jazz dance, jazz ensemble, Latin, Latin-AP, madrigals, math analysis, mathematical modeling, music history, music theory, musical productions, musical theater, orchestra, painting, photography, physical science, physics, physics-AP, Roman civilization, sculpture, silk screening, society, Spanish, Spanish literature-AP, statistics, tap dance, technical theater, theater, theater design and production, theater history, trigonometry, U.S. government and politics, U.S. history-AP, Vietnam War, visual arts, Western civilization, woodworking, world cultures, world religions.

Special Academic Programs 12 Advanced Placement exams for which test preparation is offered; honors section; independent study; study abroad.

College Admission Counseling 92 students graduated in 2010; all went to college, including Dartmouth College; Harvard University; Princeton University; University of California, Berkeley; University of Southern California; Wesleyan University.

Student Life Upper grades have specified standards of dress, student council, honor system. Discipline rests equally with students and faculty.

Tuition and Aid Day student tuition: $26,600. Tuition installment plan (monthly payment plans). Need-based scholarship grants available. In 2010–11, 20% of upper-school students received aid. Total amount of financial aid awarded in 2010–11: $2,800,000.

Admissions Traditional secondary-level entrance grade is 9. For fall 2010, 202 students applied for upper-level admission, 52 were accepted, 38 enrolled. ISEE required. Deadline for receipt of application materials: January 8. Application fee required: $100. On-campus interview required.

Athletics Interscholastic: aquatics (boys, girls), baseball (b), basketball (b,g), cross-country running (b,g), diving (b,g), golf (b,g), soccer (b,g), softball (g), swimming and diving (b,g), tennis (b,g), track and field (b,g), volleyball (b,g), water polo (b,g); coed interscholastic: badminton, dance squad, equestrian sports, fencing, football, outdoor education, physical fitness, physical training, strength & conditioning, weight lifting, weight training, yoga. 3 PE instructors, 27 coaches, 2 athletic trainers.

Computers Computers are regularly used in all classes. Computer network features include on-campus library services, Internet access, Internet filtering or blocking technology. Student e-mail accounts are available to students.

Contact Ms. Sally Jeanne McKenna, Director of Admissions. 626-396-6300. Fax: 626-396-6591. E-mail: sjmckenna@polytechnic.org. Web site: www.polytechnic.org.

POPE JOHN XXIII REGIONAL HIGH SCHOOL

28 Andover Road

Sparta, New Jersey 07871

Head of School: Mrs. Gloria Shope

General Information Coeducational day college-preparatory, arts, business, religious studies, and technology school, affiliated with Roman Catholic Church. Grades 8–12. Founded: 1956. Setting: suburban. Nearest major city is New York, NY. 15-acre campus. 1 building on campus. Approved or accredited by Department of Defense Dependents Schools and New Jersey Department of Education. Total enrollment: 974. Upper school average class size: 20. Upper school faculty-student ratio: 1:13. There are 180 required school days per year for Upper School students. Upper School students typically attend 5 days per week. The average school day consists of 5 hours and 42 minutes.

Upper School Student Profile Grade 8: 39 students (23 boys, 16 girls); Grade 9: 232 students (133 boys, 99 girls); Grade 10: 211 students (100 boys, 111 girls); Grade 11: 236 students (125 boys, 111 girls); Grade 12: 256 students (131 boys, 125 girls). 80% of students are Roman Catholic.

Faculty School total: 78. In upper school: 36 men, 42 women; 35 have advanced degrees.

Subjects Offered Advanced chemistry, advanced computer applications, advanced math, Advanced Placement courses, algebra, American literature, American studies, anatomy and physiology, art, biology, biology-AP, British literature, business, business law, calculus, calculus-AP, chemistry, chemistry-AP, choral music, computer literacy, computer science, computer science-AP, conceptual physics, concert choir, earth science, economics, English, English language-AP, English literature, English literature and composition-AP, environmental science, environmental science-AP, European history-AP, fine arts, French, French-AP, geometry, German, global issues, government and politics-AP, graphic arts, health and safety, history-AP, honors algebra, honors English, honors geometry, honors U.S. history, honors world history, Italian, Japanese, jazz band, journalism, lab science, Latin, macroeconomics-AP, microeconomics-AP, modern politics, music theory, physical education, physics, physics-AP, pre-calculus, psychology, public speaking, reading/study skills, robotics, Spanish, Spanish language-AP, statistics, statistics-AP, theater arts, theology, U.S. government, U.S. government and politics-AP, U.S. history, U.S. history-AP, world cultures, world history-AP, writing, zoology.

Graduation Requirements Arts and fine arts (art, music, dance, drama), English, foreign language, health and safety, mathematics, science, social studies (includes history), theology, 60 hours of community service (15 hours per year).

Special Academic Programs Honors section; ESL (26 students enrolled).

College Admission Counseling 230 students graduated in 2011; 228 went to college, including High Point University; Manhattan College; Seton Hall University; Susquehanna University; The Catholic University of America; The College of New Jersey. Other: 1 went to work, 1 had other specific plans. Mean SAT critical reading: 536, mean SAT math: 541, mean SAT writing: 532, mean combined SAT: 1609.

Student Life Upper grades have uniform requirement, student council. Discipline rests primarily with faculty. Attendance at religious services is required.

Summer Programs Remediation, enrichment, sports programs offered; session focuses on sports; held on campus; accepts boys and girls; open to students from other schools. 200 students usually enrolled.

Tuition and Aid Day student tuition: $13,500. Guaranteed tuition plan. Tuition installment plan (SMART Tuition Payment Plan). Need-based scholarship grants available.

Admissions Traditional secondary-level entrance grade is 9. CTB/McGraw-Hill/Macmillan Co-op Test, Math Placement Exam, placement test and writing sample required. Deadline for receipt of application materials: none. No application fee required.

Athletics Interscholastic: baseball (boys), basketball (b,g), cheering (g), cross-country running (b,g), field hockey (g), football (b), ice hockey (b), indoor track & field (b,g), lacrosse (b,g), running (b,g), skiing (downhill) (b,g), softball (g), swimming and diving (b,g), tennis (b,g), track and field (b,g), volleyball (b,g), winter (indoor) track (b,g), wrestling (b); coed interscholastic: golf.

Computers Computers are regularly used in graphic arts, programming classes. Computer network features include Internet access, Internet filtering or blocking technology, Naviance Succeed. The school has a published electronic and media policy.

Contact Mrs. Anne Kaiser, Administrative Assistant for Admissions. 973-729-6125 Ext. 255. Fax: 973-729-4536. E-mail: annekaiser@popejohn.org. Web site: www.popejohn.org.

PORTER-GAUD SCHOOL

300 Albemarle Road

Charleston, South Carolina 29407

Head of School: Mr. David DuBose Egleston Jr.

General Information Coeducational day college-preparatory, arts, religious studies, and technology school, affiliated with Christian faith, Episcopal Church. Grades 1–12. Founded: 1867. Setting: suburban. 80-acre campus. 7 buildings on campus. Approved or accredited by National Association of Episcopal Schools, South Carolina Independent School Association, Southern Association of Colleges and Schools, Southern Association of Independent Schools, and South Carolina Department of Education. Member of National Association of Independent Schools. Endowment: $10 million. Total enrollment: 903. Upper school average class size: 15. Upper school faculty-student ratio: 1:15. There are 175 required school days per year for Upper School students. Upper School students typically attend 5 days per week. The average school day consists of 6 hours.

Upper School Student Profile Grade 9: 89 students (55 boys, 34 girls); Grade 10: 85 students (54 boys, 31 girls); Grade 11: 81 students (47 boys, 34 girls); Grade 12: 85 students (57 boys, 28 girls); Postgraduate: 340 students (213 boys, 127 girls). 80% of students are Christian, members of Episcopal Church.

Faculty School total: 95. In upper school: 15 men, 25 women; 30 have advanced degrees.

Subjects Offered Advanced Placement courses, algebra, American history, American literature, art, art history, art-AP, biology, calculus, chemistry, computer programming, computer science, drama, economics, English, English literature, ethics, European history, expository writing, fine arts, French, geometry, government/civics, health, Latin, music, music appreciation, music theory-AP, physical education, physics, pre-calculus, Spanish, world history, world literature.

Graduation Requirements Algebra, American literature, art education, arts and fine arts (art, music, dance, drama), biology, chemistry, computer science, English, English composition, English literature, European history, foreign language, geometry, physical education (includes health), physics, pre-calculus, religion (includes Bible studies and theology), trigonometry, U.S. history, world history.

Special Academic Programs 17 Advanced Placement exams for which test preparation is offered; honors section; independent study.

College Admission Counseling 94 students graduated in 2011; all went to college, including Clemson University; College of Charleston; The University of North Carolina at Chapel Hill; University of Georgia; University of Virginia. Mean SAT critical reading: 626, mean SAT math: 612, mean SAT writing: 635, mean combined SAT: 1873, mean composite ACT: 27.

Student Life Upper grades have uniform requirement, student council, honor system. Discipline rests equally with students and faculty. Attendance at religious services is required.

Tuition and Aid Day student tuition: $18,610. Tuition installment plan (monthly payment plans, individually arranged payment plans, 60/40 payment plan). Need-based scholarship grants available. In 2011–12, 20% of upper-school students received aid. Total amount of financial aid awarded in 2011–12: $467,620.

Admissions Traditional secondary-level entrance grade is 9. For fall 2011, 60 students applied for upper-level admission, 53 were accepted, 33 enrolled. ISEE required. Deadline for receipt of application materials: January 30. Application fee required: $75. Interview required.

Athletics Interscholastic: baseball (boys), basketball (b,g), football (b), ice hockey (b), lacrosse (b), physical training (b,g), soccer (b,g), swimming and diving (b,g), tennis (b,g), track and field (b,g), volleyball (g), weight lifting (b,g), weight training (b,g); intramural: basketball (b,g), Frisbee (b,g), lacrosse (b); coed interscholastic: cheering, cross-country running, golf, Nautilus, sailing, strength & conditioning; coed intramural: Frisbee, ultimate Frisbee. 4 PE instructors, 26 coaches, 1 athletic trainer.

Computers Computers are regularly used in English, foreign language, history, mathematics, music, programming, science, video film production, yearbook classes. Computer network features include on-campus library services, Internet access, wireless campus network, Internet filtering or blocking technology, 4 year Computer Science degree with college credit earned. Campus intranet, student e-mail accounts, and computer access in designated common areas are available to students. Students grades are available online. The school has a published electronic and media policy.

Contact Mrs. Eleanor W. Hurtes, Director of Admissions. 843-402-4775. Fax: 843-556-7404. E-mail: eleanor.hurtes@portergaud.edu. Web site: www.portergaud.edu.

PORTSMOUTH ABBEY SCHOOL

285 Cory's Lane

Portsmouth, Rhode Island 02871

Head of School: Dr. James De Vecchi

General Information Coeducational boarding and day college-preparatory, arts, religious studies, and music, classics, humanities school, affiliated with Roman Catholic Church. Grades 9–12. Founded: 1926. Setting: small town. Nearest major city is Providence. Students are housed in single-sex dormitories. 500-acre campus. 36 buildings on campus. Approved or accredited by Association of Independent Schools in New England, National Independent Private Schools Association, New England Association of Schools and Colleges, and The Association of Boarding Schools. Member of National Association of Independent Schools and Secondary School Admission Test Board. Endowment: $30 million. Total enrollment: 373. Upper school average class size: 13. Upper school faculty-student ratio: 1:8. There are 180 required school days per year for Upper School students. Upper School students typically attend 6 days per week. The average school day consists of 7 hours.

Upper School Student Profile Grade 9: 62 students (34 boys, 28 girls); Grade 10: 86 students (42 boys, 44 girls); Grade 11: 102 students (53 boys, 49 girls); Grade 12: 105 students (47 boys, 58 girls). 70% of students are boarding students. 41% are state residents. 23 states are represented in upper school student body. 11% are international students. International students from Canada, Dominican Republic, Germany, Guatemala, Republic of Korea, and Spain; 11 other countries represented in student body. 62% of students are Roman Catholic.

Faculty School total: 45. In upper school: 30 men, 15 women; 41 have advanced degrees; 34 reside on campus.

Subjects Offered Algebra, American literature, art, art history, art history-AP, art-AP, biology, biology-AP, calculus, calculus-AP, chemistry, chemistry-AP, Chinese, Christian doctrine, Christian ethics, church history, computer programming, computer programming-AP, computer science, computer science-AP, drama, economics, English, English language and composition-AP, English literature, English literature and composition-AP, ethics, European history, European history-AP, fine arts, French, French language-AP, French literature-AP, geometry, government/civics, Greek, health, history, history-AP, humanities, international relations, Latin, Latin-AP, Mandarin, marine biology, mathematics, mathematics-AP, modern European history, modern European history-AP, music, music appreciation, music composition, music history, music theory, music theory-AP, philosophy, photography, physical education, physics, physics-AP, physiology, political science, probability and statistics, religion, science, social sciences, Spanish, Spanish language-AP, Spanish literature-AP, statistics-AP, studio art-AP, theater, theology, trigonometry, U.S. history, U.S. history-AP, world history, writing workshop.

Graduation Requirements Arts and fine arts (art, music, dance, drama), English, foreign language, history, Latin, mathematics, religion (includes Bible studies and theology), science, humanities.

Special Academic Programs Advanced Placement exam preparation; honors section; independent study; academic accommodation for the gifted.

College Admission Counseling 101 students graduated in 2010; all went to college, including Boston College; Cornell University; Georgetown University; New York University; Northeastern University; The Catholic University of America. Median SAT critical reading: 600, median SAT math: 590, median SAT writing: 600, median combined SAT: 1830. 50% scored over 600 on SAT critical reading, 54% scored over 600 on SAT math, 44% scored over 600 on SAT writing, 46% scored over 1800 on combined SAT, 32% scored over 26 on composite ACT.

Student Life Upper grades have specified standards of dress, student council, honor system. Discipline rests primarily with faculty. Attendance at religious services is required.

Tuition and Aid Day student tuition: $30,680; 7-day tuition and room/board: $44,850. Tuition installment plan (monthly payment plans, individually arranged payment plans, Tuition Management Systems Plan). Merit scholarship grants, need-based scholarship grants available. In 2010–11, 35% of upper-school students received aid; total upper-school merit-scholarship money awarded: $180,000. Total amount of financial aid awarded in 2010–11: $3,000,000.

Admissions Traditional secondary-level entrance grade is 9. For fall 2010, 380 students applied for upper-level admission, 215 were accepted, 108 enrolled. PSAT or SAT for applicants to grade 11 and 12, SSAT and SSAT or WISC III required. Deadline for receipt of application materials: January 31. Application fee required: $50. Interview required.

Athletics Interscholastic: baseball (boys), basketball (b,g), cross-country running (b,g), field hockey (g), football (b), golf (b,g), ice hockey (b,g), lacrosse (b,g), soccer (b,g), softball (g), squash (b,g), swimming and diving (b,g), track and field (b,g); coed interscholastic: cross-country running, sailing, tennis, track and field, weight training; coed intramural: ballet, dance, equestrian sports, fitness, horseback riding, modern dance. 2 athletic trainers.

Computers Computers are regularly used in science classes. Computer network features include on-campus library services, Internet access, wireless campus network. Student e-mail accounts are available to students.

Contact Mrs. Ann Motta, Admissions Coordinator. 401-643-1248. Fax: 401-643-1355. E-mail: admissions@portsmouthabbey.org. Web site: www.portsmouthabbey.org.

PORTSMOUTH CHRISTIAN ACADEMY

20 Seaborne Drive

Dover, New Hampshire 03820

Head of School: Mr. Brian Bell

General Information Coeducational day college-preparatory, arts, religious studies, technology, science/mathematics, and communication school, affiliated with Christian faith. Grades K–12. Founded: 1979. Setting: rural. Nearest major city is Portsmouth. 50-acre campus. 3 buildings on campus. Approved or accredited by Association of Christian Schools International, New England Association of Schools and Colleges, and New Hampshire Department of Education. Total enrollment: 617. Upper school average class size: 17. Upper school faculty-student ratio: 1:13. There are 180 required school days per year for Upper School students. Upper School students typically attend 5 days per week. The average school day consists of 7 hours and 5 minutes.

Upper School Student Profile Grade 9: 46 students (21 boys, 25 girls); Grade 10: 51 students (25 boys, 26 girls); Grade 11: 36 students (21 boys, 15 girls); Grade 12: 48 students (15 boys, 33 girls). 70% of students are Christian faith.

Faculty School total: 71. In upper school: 11 men, 13 women; 14 have advanced degrees.

Subjects Offered 20th century American writers, 20th century history, 3-dimensional art, 3-dimensional design, ACT preparation, advanced chemistry, advanced computer applications, advanced math, Advanced Placement courses, advanced studio art-AP, African drumming, algebra, alternative physical education, American history, American literature, American literature-AP, analysis and differential calculus, anatomy and physiology, applied music, art, art appreciation, art education, art history, art history-AP, arts appreciation, athletic training, athletics, band, baseball, basketball, Bible, Bible studies, biochemistry, biology, British literature, British literature (honors), calculus, calculus-AP, chemistry, chemistry-AP, choir, choral music, chorus, Christian doctrine, Christian education, Christian ethics, Christian scripture, Christian studies, Christian testament, Christianity, church history, civics, college admission preparation, college awareness, college counseling, college placement, college planning, college writing, comparative religion, composition, composition-AP, computer applications, computer education, computer graphics, computer processing, computer resources, computer skills, computer-aided design, contemporary issues, current history, digital photography, drama, drama performance, drama workshop, drawing, economics, economics and history, English, English composition, English language and composition-AP, English literature and composition-AP, English literature-AP, environmental science, European history, film and literature, foreign language, French, French language-AP, French studies, geometry, government, government/civics, guitar, health, health and wellness, honors algebra, honors English, honors geometry, instrumental music, jazz band, law studies, literature, literature and composition-AP, literature-AP, marine science, math review, mathematics, microbiology, modern history, music, music appreciation, musical productions, musical theater, New Testament, novels, performing arts, photography, physics, physics-AP, political economy, pre-calculus, religion and culture, rhetoric, SAT preparation, SAT/ACT preparation, Shakespeare, Spanish, Spanish language-AP, Spanish-AP, student government, symphonic band, theater arts, theology, U.S. history, U.S. literature, world history, World War II, writing, writing workshop, yearbook.

Graduation Requirements 20th century history, algebra, arts and fine arts (art, music, dance, drama), biology, chemistry, comparative cultures, composition, computer skills, foreign language, geometry, physical education (includes health), physical science, U.S. history, writing, one Bible course for each year of Upper School attendance, service hours.

Special Academic Programs Advanced Placement exam preparation; honors section; accelerated programs; independent study; study at local college for college credit; academic accommodation for the gifted and the musically talented; special instructional classes for students with Attention Deficit Disorder and dyslexia.

College Admission Counseling 47 students graduated in 2010; 44 went to college, including Pepperdine University; Rochester Institute of Technology; Seattle Pacific University; Texas A&M University; University of Massachusetts Amherst; University of New Hampshire. Other: 3 had other specific plans. Mean SAT critical reading: 562, mean SAT math: 536, mean SAT writing: 551.

Student Life Upper grades have specified standards of dress, student council, honor system. Discipline rests primarily with faculty.

Tuition and Aid Day student tuition: $9350. Tuition installment plan (FACTS Tuition Payment Plan). Tuition reduction for siblings, merit scholarship grants, need-based scholarship grants available. In 2010–11, 20% of upper-school students received aid. Total amount of financial aid awarded in 2010–11: $165,000.

Admissions Traditional secondary-level entrance grade is 9. Achievement tests, PSAT or SAT, PSAT or SAT for applicants to grade 11 and 12, PSAT, SAT, or ACT for applicants to grade 11 and 12, SAT, standardized test scores, Stanford Achievement Test, Test of Achievement and Proficiency, TOEFL, TOEFL or SLEP or writing sample required. Deadline for receipt of application materials: none. Application fee required: $100. Interview required.

Athletics Interscholastic: baseball (boys), basketball (b,g), cross-country running (b,g), indoor track & field (b,g), soccer (b,g), softball (g), tennis (b,g), track and field (b,g), volleyball (g), winter (indoor) track (b,g); intramural: golf (b,g), skiing (cross-country) (b,g); coed interscholastic: alpine skiing, cross-country running, fitness, indoor track & field, winter (indoor) track. 1 PE instructor, 14 coaches.

Computers Computers are regularly used in art, Bible studies, career education, Christian doctrine, classics, college planning, desktop publishing, economics, English, foreign language, graphic design, history, humanities, independent study, library, library skills, mathematics, media arts, photography, religion, religious studies, SAT preparation, science, social studies, writing, yearbook classes. Computer network features include on-campus library services, online commercial services, Internet access, Internet filtering or blocking technology. Computer access in designated common areas is available to students. Students grades are available online. The school has a published electronic and media policy.

Contact Mrs. Diane Sipp, Director of Admissions. 603-742-3617 Ext. 116. Fax: 603-750-0490. E-mail: dsipp@pcaschool.org. Web site: www.pcaschool.org.

THE POTOMAC SCHOOL

1301 Potomac School Road

McLean, Virginia 22101

Head of School: Geoffrey Jones

General Information Coeducational day college-preparatory and liberal arts, arts, athletics, and character education school. Grades K–12. Founded: 1904. Setting: suburban. Nearest major city is Washington, DC. 90-acre campus. Approved or accredited by Association of Independent Schools of Greater Washington and Virginia Association of Independent Schools. Member of National Association of Independent Schools and Secondary School Admission Test Board. Endowment: $28 million. Total enrollment: 1,007. Upper school average class size: 14. Upper school faculty-student ratio: 1:6.

Upper School Student Profile Grade 9: 109 students (54 boys, 55 girls); Grade 10: 93 students (48 boys, 45 girls); Grade 11: 102 students (54 boys, 48 girls); Grade 12: 106 students (52 boys, 54 girls).

Faculty School total: 150. In upper school: 27 men, 34 women; 45 have advanced degrees.

Subjects Offered 20th century American writers, 20th century history, 20th century world history, 3-dimensional art, 3-dimensional design, acting, advanced computer applications, advanced math, Advanced Placement courses, advanced studio art-AP, African history, African-American literature, African-American studies, algebra, American foreign policy, American literature, ancient history, art, art history, Asian studies, band, bell choir, Bible as literature, bioethics, biology, British literature, calculus, calculus-AP, cell biology, ceramics, chamber groups, character education, chemistry, chemistry-AP, Chinese history, choral music, civil war history, community service, comparative religion, computer programming, computer programming-AP, computer science, conceptual physics, concert band, creative writing, debate, directing, drama, drama performance, drawing and design, economics and history, engineering, English, English literature, environmental science, European history, expository writing, film and literature, fine arts, French, French language-AP, French literature-AP, functions, geometry, global studies, government/civics, handbells, Harlem Renaissance, historical research, history of jazz, history of music, independent study, jazz band, Latin, Latin American history, Latin-AP, leadership, literary magazine, madrigals, mathematics, medieval history, Middle Eastern history, model United Nations, modern European history, music, music composition, music theory-AP, newspaper, painting, performing arts, photography, physical education, physics, physics-AP, portfolio art, pre-calculus, robotics, science, science and technology, sculpture, senior project, Shakespeare, short story, Spanish, Spanish language-AP, Spanish literature-AP, stagecraft, statistics-AP, strings, student government, studio art-AP, theater arts, trigonometry, U.S. government and politics, U.S. history-AP, vocal music, World War II, yearbook.

Graduation Requirements Arts and fine arts (art, music, dance, drama), English, ethics, foreign language, history, mathematics, physical education (includes health), science, senior project, month-long senior project.

Special Academic Programs Advanced Placement exam preparation; honors section; independent study.

College Admission Counseling 98 students graduated in 2011; 96 went to college, including Columbia University; Cornell University; Georgetown University; Southern Methodist University; University of Virginia; Villanova University. Median SAT critical reading: 690, median SAT math: 700.

Student Life Upper grades have specified standards of dress, student council, honor system. Discipline rests equally with students and faculty.

Summer Programs Enrichment, advancement, sports, art/fine arts programs offered; session focuses on academics and enrichment; held on campus; accepts boys and girls; open to students from other schools. 2012 schedule: June 27 to August 19. Application deadline: none.

Tuition and Aid Day student tuition: $28,915. Tuition installment plan (Insured Tuition Payment Plan, monthly payment plans). Need-based scholarship grants available. In 2011–12, 15% of upper-school students received aid. Total amount of financial aid awarded in 2011–12: $1,293,670.

Admissions Traditional secondary-level entrance grade is 9. ISEE or SSAT required. Deadline for receipt of application materials: January 10. Application fee required: $65. On-campus interview required.

Athletics Interscholastic: baseball (boys), basketball (b,g), cross-country running (b,g), field hockey (g), football (b), lacrosse (b,g), soccer (b,g), softball (g), squash (b,g), tennis (b,g), track and field (b,g), wrestling (b); intramural: weight lifting (b,g); coed interscholastic: golf, ice hockey, swimming and diving, winter (indoor) track; coed intramural: canoeing/kayaking, fitness, hiking/backpacking, ice hockey, outdoor education, physical fitness, physical training, sailing, strength & conditioning, weight training. 5 PE instructors, 33 coaches, 2 athletic trainers.

Computers Computers are regularly used in all academic, computer applications, drawing and design, independent study, literary magazine, newspaper, photography, programming, yearbook classes. Computer network features include on-campus library services, online commercial services, Internet access, wireless campus network, Internet filtering or blocking technology, ebooks. Campus intranet and student e-mail accounts are available to students. The school has a published electronic and media policy.

Contact Leslie Vorndran, Admission Services Coordinator. 703-749-6313. Fax: 703-356-1764. Web site: www.potomacschool.org.

POUGHKEEPSIE DAY SCHOOL

260 Boardman Road

Poughkeepsie, New York 12603

Head of School: Josie Holford

General Information Coeducational day college-preparatory and arts school. Grades PK–12. Founded: 1934. Setting: suburban. Nearest major city is New York. 35-acre campus. 2 buildings on campus. Approved or accredited by New York State Association of Independent Schools and New York Department of Education. Member of National Association of Independent Schools. Endowment: $4.1 million. Total enrollment: 290. Upper school average class size: 12. Upper school faculty-student ratio: 1:7. There are 165 required school days per year for Upper School students. Upper School students typically attend 5 days per week. The average school day consists of 7 hours.

Upper School Student Profile Grade 9: 27 students (14 boys, 13 girls); Grade 10: 21 students (11 boys, 10 girls); Grade 11: 21 students (6 boys, 15 girls); Grade 12: 26 students (11 boys, 15 girls).

Faculty School total: 44. In upper school: 5 men, 12 women; 13 have advanced degrees.

Subjects Offered 3-dimensional art, acting, advanced math, Advanced Placement courses, African drumming, algebra, American literature, American literature-AP, analysis and differential calculus, analytic geometry, anatomy, anatomy and physiology, ancient history, ancient world history, art history, arts, Basic programming, bioethics, biology, calculus, calculus-AP, chamber groups, chemistry, collage and assemblage, college admission preparation, college planning, community service, computer programming, computer science, computer-aided design, conflict resolution, contemporary art, creative arts, creative drama, creative writing, decision making skills, desktop publishing, digital art, digital photography, discrete mathematics, drama, drama performance, drawing, ecology, economics, English, English literature, English literature-AP, English-AP, ensembles, European civilization, European history, fiction, filmmaking, fine arts, French, French language-AP, French-AP, geology, geometry, guitar, history, Holocaust and other genocides, Holocaust studies, independent study, instrumental music, integrated arts, interdisciplinary studies, Islamic studies, jazz band, jazz ensemble, lab science, leadership, life saving, life skills, linear algebra, literary magazine, literature, literature-AP, mathematics, modern European history, multicultural literature, multicultural studies, music, music appreciation, music composition, music performance, music theory, music theory-AP, musical productions, oil painting, painting, peer counseling, performing arts, photography, physical education, physical science, physics, physiology, play production, playwriting and directing, pre-calculus, printmaking, probability and statistics, religion and culture, SAT preparation, science, senior internship, service learning/internship, social issues, social studies, Spanish, Spanish language-AP, Spanish-AP, stained glass, statistics, strings, studio art, theater arts, theater production, trigonometry, U.S. history, video film production, visual arts, voice ensemble, Web site design, Western civilization, wind ensemble, writing workshop, yearbook, zoology.

Graduation Requirements Algebra, arts, biology, chemistry, classical Greek literature, college planning, electives, English, English literature, foreign language, geometry, interdisciplinary studies, life skills, mathematics, music, performing arts, physical education (includes health), physics, physiology, pre-calculus, SAT preparation, senior internship, senior thesis, trigonometry, visual arts, four-week off-campus senior internship. Community service is required.

Special Academic Programs Advanced Placement exam preparation; honors section; independent study; term-away projects; study at local college for college credit; academic accommodation for the gifted, the musically talented, and the artistically talented.

College Admission Counseling 19 students graduated in 2010; 17 went to college, including Barnard College; Clark University; Hampshire College; Smith College; Stanford University; The Johns Hopkins University. Other: 2 entered a postgraduate year. Mean SAT critical reading: 660, mean SAT math: 600, mean SAT writing: 640, mean combined SAT: 1900. 79% scored over 600 on SAT critical reading, 53% scored over 600 on SAT math, 63% scored over 600 on SAT writing, 74% scored over 1800 on combined SAT.

Student Life Upper grades have student council, honor system. Discipline rests primarily with faculty.

Tuition and Aid Day student tuition: $21,675. Tuition installment plan (FACTS Tuition Payment Plan, The Tuition Refund Plan). Need-based scholarship grants, tuition reduction for children of full-time faculty and staff available. In 2010–11, 34% of upper-school students received aid. Total amount of financial aid awarded in 2010–11: $281,560.

Admissions Traditional secondary-level entrance grade is 9. For fall 2010, 27 students applied for upper-level admission, 17 were accepted, 15 enrolled. School's own exam required. Deadline for receipt of application materials: January 15. Application fee required: $50. On-campus interview required.

Athletics Interscholastic: baseball (boys), basketball (b,g), cross-country running (b,g), soccer (b,g), softball (g); intramural: basketball (b,g), softball (g); coed interscholastic: cross-country running, Frisbee, soccer, ultimate Frisbee; coed intramural: alpine skiing, basketball, bicycling, cooperative games, cross-country running, dance, figure skating, fitness, fitness walking, Frisbee, hiking/backpacking, ice skating, jogging, life saving, outdoor education, outdoor skills, skiing (downhill), snowboarding, soccer, swimming and diving, tennis, ultimate Frisbee, volleyball, walking, yoga. 2 PE instructors, 5 coaches.

Computers Computers are regularly used in all academic, college planning, desktop publishing, journalism, library skills, literary magazine, media, music, newspaper, photography, photojournalism, programming, SAT preparation, video film production, Web site design, yearbook classes. Computer network features include on-campus library services, online commercial services, Internet access, wireless campus network, EBSCOhost®, Maps101, Web Feet Guides, Gale databases, ProQuest, unitedstreaming, Britannica Online, World Book Online, Grolier Online. Campus intranet, student e-mail accounts, and computer access in designated common areas are available to students. The school has a published electronic and media policy.

Contact Tammy Reilly, Admissions Assistant. 845-462-7600 Ext. 201. Fax: 845-462-7602. E-mail: treilly@poughkeepsieday.org. Web site: www.poughkeepsieday.org/.

POWERS CATHOLIC HIGH SCHOOL

G-2040 West Carpenter Road

Flint, Michigan 48505-1028

Head of School: Mr. Thomas H. Furnas

General Information Coeducational day college-preparatory, arts, and religious studies school, affiliated with Roman Catholic Church. Grades 9–12. Founded: 1970. Setting: urban. 67-acre campus. 1 building on campus. Approved or accredited by National Catholic Education Association, North Central Association of Colleges and Schools, and Michigan Department of Education. Endowment: $3 million. Total enrollment: 542. Upper school average class size: 25. Upper school faculty-student ratio: 1:19. There are 188 required school days per year for Upper School students. Upper School students typically attend 5 days per week. The average school day consists of 6 hours and 40 minutes.

Upper School Student Profile Grade 9: 149 students (72 boys, 77 girls); Grade 10: 118 students (60 boys, 58 girls); Grade 11: 128 students (77 boys, 51 girls); Grade 12: 147 students (65 boys, 82 girls). 75% of students are Roman Catholic.

Faculty School total: 29. In upper school: 10 men, 19 women; 20 have advanced degrees.

Subjects Offered Art, art-AP, biology, biology-AP, calculus-AP, ceramics, chemistry, choir, computer skills, concert band, drafting, economics, English, English literature and composition-AP, European history-AP, French, geometry, government, government-AP, health, honors algebra, honors English, honors geometry, integrated science, interdisciplinary studies, macroeconomics-AP, marching band, math analysis, math applications, mechanical drawing, physics, pre-algebra, pre-calculus, psychology, psychology-AP, public speaking, religion, social justice, Spanish, state history, studio art-AP, theology, trigonometry, U.S. history, wind ensemble, world geography, world history, world religions, yearbook.

Graduation Requirements American history, English, government, health, mathematics, science, theology, world history, 40 hours of community service.

Special Academic Programs 8 Advanced Placement exams for which test preparation is offered; honors section; remedial reading and/or remedial writing; remedial math.

College Admission Counseling 133 students graduated in 2011; 130 went to college, including Central Michigan University; Grand Valley State University; Michigan State University; Saginaw Valley State University; University of Michigan. Other: 1 went to work, 2 had other specific plans. Mean composite ACT: 22.

Student Life Upper grades have specified standards of dress, student council. Discipline rests primarily with faculty. Attendance at religious services is required.

Tuition and Aid Day student tuition: $7800. Tuition installment plan (monthly payment plans, individually arranged payment plans). Tuition reduction for siblings, need-based scholarship grants available. In 2011–12, 33% of upper-school students received aid. Total amount of financial aid awarded in 2011–12: $450,300.

Admissions Traditional secondary-level entrance grade is 9. ACT-Explore required. Deadline for receipt of application materials: none. Application fee required: $50. Interview required.

Athletics Interscholastic: alpine skiing (boys, girls), baseball (b), basketball (b,g), bowling (b,g), cross-country running (b,g), dance squad (g), dance team (g), diving (b,g), football (b), golf (b,g), ice hockey (b), lacrosse (b,g), skiing (downhill) (b,g), soccer (b,g), softball (g), swimming and diving (b,g), tennis (b,g), track and field (b,g), volleyball (g), wrestling (b); coed interscholastic: cheering, equestrian sports, indoor track, power lifting, skeet shooting, strength & conditioning, weight lifting; coed intramural: ultimate Frisbee, weight training. 2 PE instructors.

Computers Computers are regularly used in accounting, business applications, drafting, graphic design, keyboarding, yearbook classes. Computer resources include on-campus library services, Internet access, wireless campus network, Internet filtering or blocking technology. Computer access in designated common areas is available to students. Students grades are available online. The school has a published electronic and media policy.

Contact Ms. Sally Bartos, Assistant Principal for Instruction. 810-591-4741. Fax: 810-591-0383. E-mail: sbartos@powerscatholic.org. Web site: www.powerscatholic.org.

THE PRAIRIE SCHOOL

4050 Lighthouse Drive

Racine, Wisconsin 53402

Head of School: Mr. Wm. Mark H. Murphy

General Information Coeducational day college-preparatory, arts, and technology school. Grades PK–12. Founded: 1965. Setting: small town. Nearest major city is Milwaukee. 33-acre campus. 2 buildings on campus. Approved or accredited by Independent Schools Association of the Central States and Wisconsin Department of Education. Member of National Association of Independent Schools. Endowment: $38 million. Total enrollment: 687. Upper school average class size: 17. Upper school faculty-student ratio: 1:17. There are 175 required school days per year for Upper School students. Upper School students typically attend 5 days per week. The average school day consists of 7 hours.

Upper School Student Profile Grade 9: 67 students (34 boys, 33 girls); Grade 10: 60 students (24 boys, 36 girls); Grade 11: 63 students (34 boys, 29 girls); Grade 12: 75 students (38 boys, 37 girls).

Faculty School total: 75. In upper school: 19 men, 15 women; 18 have advanced degrees.

Subjects Offered Algebra, American history, American history-AP, American literature, anatomy and physiology, art, athletic training, biology, biology-AP, calculus, calculus-AP, ceramics, chemistry, chemistry-AP, Chinese, choir, community service, computer science, CPR, creative writing, dance, digital imaging, drama, drawing and design, earth and space science, ecology, economics, English, English literature, English-AP, environmental science, environmental science-AP, European history, European history-AP, film studies, fine arts, French, French language-AP, geometry, glassblowing, government/civics, health, history, international relations, jazz ensemble, mathematics, multicultural literature, music, music theory-AP, orchestra, philosophy, photography, physical education, physics, physics-AP, pre-calculus, probability and statistics, public speaking, science, social studies, Spanish, Spanish language-AP, speech, statistics, statistics-AP, study skills, theater, trigonometry, Western literature, world geography, world history, world literature, writing.

Graduation Requirements Arts and fine arts (art, music, dance, drama), English, foreign language, mathematics, physical education (includes health), science, social studies (includes history), study skills, spring Interim program (including on-campus seminars, community service, off-campus internships), 100-hour service requirement.

Special Academic Programs 14 Advanced Placement exams for which test preparation is offered; honors section; independent study; term-away projects; academic accommodation for the gifted, the musically talented, and the artistically talented; remedial reading and/or remedial writing; special instructional classes for blind students; ESL (2 students enrolled).

College Admission Counseling 72 students graduated in 2011; all went to college, including Marquette University; The University of Tampa; University of Denver; University of Minnesota, Twin Cities Campus; University of Wisconsin–Madison; University of Wisconsin–Milwaukee. Median SAT math: 595, median SAT writing: 590, median combined SAT: 1185, median composite ACT: 27.

Student Life Upper grades have specified standards of dress, student council, honor system. Discipline rests primarily with faculty.

Summer Programs Enrichment, ESL, art/fine arts, computer instruction programs offered; session focuses on enrichment and athletics; held on campus; accepts boys and girls; open to students from other schools. 200 students usually enrolled. 2012 schedule: June 18 to August 10. Application deadline: May.

Tuition and Aid Day student tuition: $14,040. Tuition installment plan (FACTS Tuition Payment Plan). Tuition reduction for siblings, merit scholarship grants, need-based scholarship grants available. In 2011–12, 43% of upper-school students received aid; total upper-school merit-scholarship money awarded: $98,000. Total amount of financial aid awarded in 2011–12: $120,000.

Admissions Traditional secondary-level entrance grade is 9. For fall 2011, 35 students applied for upper-level admission, 26 were accepted, 16 enrolled. Admissions testing, school's own exam or TerraNova required. Deadline for receipt of application materials: none. Application fee required: $50. On-campus interview required.

Athletics Interscholastic: baseball (boys), basketball (b,g), soccer (b,g), tennis (b,g), volleyball (g); coed interscholastic: cross-country running, golf, modern dance, outdoor activities, track and field. 7 PE instructors, 13 coaches, 1 athletic trainer.

Computers Computers are regularly used in all academic classes. Computer network features include on-campus library services, Internet access, wireless campus network, Internet filtering or blocking technology. Campus intranet, student e-mail accounts, and computer access in designated common areas are available to students. Students grades are available online. The school has a published electronic and media policy.

Contact Ms. Molly Lofquist Johnson, Director of Admissions. 262-260-4393. Fax: 262-260-3790. E-mail: mlofquist@prairieschool.com. Web site: www.prairieschool.com.

PRESBYTERIAN PAN AMERICAN SCHOOL

PO Box 1578

223 North FM Road 772

Kingsville, Texas 78364-1578

Head of School: Dr. James H. Matthews

General Information Coeducational boarding and day and distance learning college-preparatory school, affiliated with Presbyterian Church (U.S.A.). Grades 9–12. Distance learning grades 9–12. Founded: 1912. Setting: rural. Nearest major city is Corpus Christi. Students are housed in single-sex dormitories. 670-acre campus. 22 buildings on campus. Approved or accredited by Southern Association of Colleges and Schools, Texas Private School Accreditation Commission, and Texas Department of Education. Endowment: $5.3 million. Total enrollment: 158. Upper school average class size: 18. Upper school faculty-student ratio: 1:9. There are 180 required school days per year for Upper School students. Upper School students typically attend 5 days per week. The average school day consists of 8 hours.

Upper School Student Profile Grade 9: 29 students (14 boys, 15 girls); Grade 10: 48 students (24 boys, 24 girls); Grade 11: 30 students (12 boys, 18 girls); Grade 12: 41 students (22 boys, 19 girls); Grade 13: 4 students (2 boys, 2 girls). 100% of students are boarding students. 6% are state residents. 2 states are represented in upper school student body. 94% are international students. International students from China, Costa Rica, Democratic People's Republic of Korea, Mexico, Rwanda, and Spain; 2 other countries represented in student body. 40% of students are Presbyterian Church (U.S.A.).

Faculty School total: 17. In upper school: 5 men, 11 women; 5 have advanced degrees; 3 reside on campus.

Subjects Offered Acting, algebra, American history, American literature, art, arts, Bible studies, biology, calculus, chemistry, computer science, English, English literature, ESL, fine arts, geography, geometry, government/civics, health, history, mathematics, music, physical education, physics, pre-calculus, religion, science, social sciences, social studies, Spanish, speech, trigonometry, world history, world literature, writing.

Graduation Requirements Arts and fine arts (art, music, dance, drama), career exploration, economics, English, foreign language, mathematics, religion (includes Bible studies and theology), science, social sciences, social studies (includes history), TOEFL score of 550, or SAT Reading of 550.

Special Academic Programs Study at local college for college credit; ESL (59 students enrolled).

College Admission Counseling 30 students graduated in 2011; all went to college, including Schreiner University; Texas A&M University; The University of Texas at Austin; The University of Texas at San Antonio; University of Houston. Median SAT critical reading: 400, median SAT math: 440, median SAT writing: 420. 3% scored over 600 on SAT critical reading, 3% scored over 600 on SAT math.

Student Life Upper grades have specified standards of dress, student council, honor system. Discipline rests primarily with faculty. Attendance at religious services is required.

Tuition and Aid Day student tuition: $8500; 7-day tuition and room/board: $15,000. Guaranteed tuition plan. Tuition installment plan (monthly payment plans, individually arranged payment plans, quarterly payment plan, semester payment plan). Tuition reduction for siblings, merit scholarship grants, need-based scholarship grants, need-based financial aid, discounts tied to enrollment referred by current student families available. In 2011–12, 89% of upper-school students received aid. Total amount of financial aid awarded in 2011–12: $907,340.

Admissions Traditional secondary-level entrance grade is 9. For fall 2011, 112 students applied for upper-level admission, 81 were accepted, 67 enrolled. Secondary Level English Proficiency and TOEFL required. Deadline for receipt of application materials: none. Application fee required: $75. Interview recommended.

Athletics Interscholastic: baseball (boys), basketball (b,g), cheering (g), cross-country running (b,g), soccer (b), track and field (b,g), volleyball (g); intramural: billiards (b), jogging (b,g), life saving (b,g), paddle tennis (b,g), physical fitness (b,g), strength & conditioning (b), table tennis (b,g), tennis (b,g), walking (b,g), winter walking (b,g); coed intramural: aquatics, fitness walking, jogging, life saving, paddle tennis, table tennis, walking, winter walking. 2 PE instructors, 5 coaches, 1 athletic trainer.

Computers Computers are regularly used in all academic, English, ESL, mathematics, publications, yearbook classes. Computer resources include on-campus library services, Internet access, Internet filtering or blocking technology. Campus intranet and computer access in designated common areas are available to students. Students grades are available online. The school has a published electronic and media policy.

Contact Joe L. Garcia, Director of Admission/Registrar. 361-592-4307. Fax: 361-592-6126. E-mail: jlgarcia@ppas.org. Web site: www.ppas.org.

See Display below and Close-Up on page 662.

PRESTONWOOD CHRISTIAN ACADEMY

6801 West Park Boulevard

Plano, Texas 75093

Head of School: Dr. Larry Taylor

General Information Coeducational day and distance learning college-preparatory and Bible courses school, affiliated with Southern Baptist Convention. Grades PK–12.

Distance learning grades 6–12. Founded: 1997. Setting: suburban. Nearest major city is Dallas. 44-acre campus. 2 buildings on campus. Approved or accredited by Southern Association of Colleges and Schools and Texas Department of Education. Total enrollment: 1,439. Upper school average class size: 18. Upper school faculty-student ratio: 1:11. There are 172 required school days per year for Upper School students. Upper School students typically attend 5 days per week. The average school day consists of 7 hours and 35 minutes.

Upper School Student Profile Grade 9: 108 students (43 boys, 65 girls); Grade 10: 123 students (63 boys, 60 girls); Grade 11: 112 students (60 boys, 52 girls); Grade 12: 124 students (62 boys, 62 girls). 66% of students are Southern Baptist Convention.

Faculty School total: 111. In upper school: 18 men, 23 women; 20 have advanced degrees.

Subjects Offered 20th century history, 20th century physics, advanced chemistry, advanced math, Advanced Placement courses, algebra, American history-AP, American literature, anatomy and physiology, art, art-AP, band, Bible, biology, biology-AP, British literature, calculus-AP, ceramics, chemistry, choir, Christian doctrine, computer applications, conceptual physics, debate, drama, drawing, economics, ethics, fine arts, fitness, geometry, government, government-AP, health, honors algebra, honors English, honors geometry, honors U.S. history, honors world history, internship, language-AP, leadership education training, learning lab, literature-AP, logic, multimedia, multimedia design, newspaper, painting, performing arts, personal fitness, philosophy, photo shop, physical fitness, physics, physics-AP, pre-calculus, printmaking, sculpture, service learning/internship, Spanish, Spanish-AP, speech, statistics, student government, studio art, U.S. government and politics-AP, U.S. history, Web site design, Western literature, world history, world religions, yearbook.

Graduation Requirements 1 1/2 elective credits, algebra, arts and fine arts (art, music, dance, drama), Bible, biology, British literature, chemistry, Christian doctrine, computer applications, economics, English, English literature, ethics, foreign language, geometry, government, mathematics, philosophy, physical education (includes health), physics, speech, U.S. history, Western literature, world history, mission trip.

Special Academic Programs Advanced Placement exam preparation; honors section; academic accommodation for the gifted.

College Admission Counseling 121 students graduated in 2011; 120 went to college, including Baylor University; Oklahoma State University; Southern Methodist University; Texas Tech University; University of Arkansas; University of Oklahoma. Other: 1 entered military service. Median SAT critical reading: 549, median SAT math: 537, median SAT writing: 550, median combined SAT: 1086, median composite ACT: 25. 30% scored over 600 on SAT critical reading, 26% scored over 600 on SAT math, 32% scored over 600 on SAT writing, 27% scored over 1800 on combined SAT, 40% scored over 26 on composite ACT.

Student Life Upper grades have uniform requirement, student council, honor system. Discipline rests primarily with faculty.

Summer Programs Remediation, enrichment, advancement, sports, art/fine arts, rigorous outdoor training, computer instruction programs offered; held on campus; accepts boys and girls; open to students from other schools. 800 students usually enrolled. 2012 schedule: June 1 to August 5. Application deadline: May 1.

Tuition and Aid Day student tuition: $15,500–$15,980. Tuition installment plan (FACTS Tuition Payment Plan, monthly payment plans, individually arranged payment plans). Tuition reduction for siblings, need-based scholarship grants available. In 2011–12, 24% of upper-school students received aid. Total amount of financial aid awarded in 2011–12: $806,285.

Admissions Traditional secondary-level entrance grade is 9. For fall 2011, 106 students applied for upper-level admission, 81 were accepted, 68 enrolled. ISEE or Stanford Achievement Test required. Deadline for receipt of application materials: none. Application fee required: $100. Interview required.

Athletics Interscholastic: baseball (boys), basketball (b,g), cheering (g), cross-country running (b,g), drill team (g), football (b), golf (b,g), soccer (b,g), softball (g), swimming and diving (b,g), tennis (b,g), track and field (b,g), volleyball (g). 42 coaches.

Computers Computers are regularly used in all academic, technology classes. Computer network features include on-campus library services, Internet access, wireless campus network, Internet filtering or blocking technology. Students grades are available online. The school has a published electronic and media policy.

Contact Mrs. Marsha Backof, Admissions Assistant. 972-930-4010. Fax: 972-930-4008. E-mail: mbackof@prestonwoodchristian.org. Web site: www.prestonwoodchristian.org.

PROFESSIONAL CHILDREN'S SCHOOL

132 West 60th Street

New York, New York 10023

Head of School: Dr. James Dawson

General Information Coeducational day college-preparatory school. Grades 6–12. Founded: 1914. Setting: urban. 1 building on campus. Approved or accredited by New York State Association of Independent Schools. Member of National Association of Independent Schools. Endowment: $2.7 million. Total enrollment: 198. Upper school average class size: 10. Upper school faculty-student ratio: 1:8. There are 163 required school days per year for Upper School students. Upper School students typically attend 5 days per week. The average school day consists of 7 hours.

Upper School Student Profile Grade 9: 25 students (8 boys, 17 girls); Grade 10: 32 students (10 boys, 22 girls); Grade 11: 49 students (12 boys, 37 girls); Grade 12: 53 students (16 boys, 37 girls).

Faculty School total: 29. In upper school: 10 men, 15 women; 24 have advanced degrees.

Subjects Offered Advanced math, algebra, American government, American history, biology, calculus, chemistry, chorus, computer education, constitutional history of U.S., constitutional law, creative writing, drama, English, English literature, environmental science, ESL, foreign language, French, general math, geometry, health education, introduction to literature, keyboarding, library research, library skills, physical education, physics, pre-algebra, pre-calculus, Spanish, studio art, U.S. government, U.S. history.

Graduation Requirements Art, English, foreign language, health, history, mathematics, science.

Special Academic Programs ESL (20 students enrolled).

College Admission Counseling 38 students graduated in 2011; 32 went to college, including Columbia University; Eugene Lang College The New School for Liberal Arts; Fordham University; New York University; Pace University; Princeton University. Other: 4 went to work, 2 had other specific plans.

Student Life Upper grades have student council, honor system. Discipline rests primarily with faculty.

Tuition and Aid Day student tuition: $32,250. Tuition installment plan (Tuition Management Systems). Need-based scholarship grants available. In 2011–12, 28% of upper-school students received aid. Total amount of financial aid awarded in 2011–12: $692,500.

Admissions Traditional secondary-level entrance grade is 9. For fall 2011, 117 students applied for upper-level admission, 90 were accepted, 64 enrolled. ERB, ISEE, SSAT or Stanford Achievement Test required. Deadline for receipt of application materials: none. Application fee required: $75. On-campus interview recommended.

Athletics 1 PE instructor.

Computers Computers are regularly used in all academic classes. Computer network features include on-campus library services, Internet access, wireless campus network, Internet filtering or blocking technology. Student e-mail accounts are available to students. The school has a published electronic and media policy.

Contact Sherrie A. Hinkle, Director of Admissions. 212-582-3116 Ext. 112. Fax: 212-307-6542. E-mail: info@pcs-nyc.org. Web site: www.pcs-nyc.org.

THE PROUT SCHOOL

4640 Tower Hill Road

Wakefield, Rhode Island 02879

Head of School: Mr. Gary Delneo

General Information Coeducational day college-preparatory, arts, religious studies, and technology school, affiliated with Roman Catholic Church. Grades 9–12. Founded: 1966. Setting: small town. Nearest major city is Providence. 25-acre campus. 1 building on campus. Approved or accredited by International Baccalaureate Organization, New England Association of Schools and Colleges, Rhode Island State Certified Resource Progam, and Rhode Island Department of Education. Total enrollment: 640. Upper school average class size: 21. Upper school faculty-student ratio: 1:18. There are 182 required school days per year for Upper School students. Upper School students typically attend 5 days per week. The average school day consists of 6 hours and 30 minutes.

Upper School Student Profile 75% of students are Roman Catholic.

Faculty School total: 53. In upper school: 25 men, 28 women; 40 have advanced degrees.

Subjects Offered Acting, American literature, anatomy and physiology, art education, art history, athletic training, ballet, ballet technique, band, biology, calculus, chemistry, Chinese, choir, chorus, Christian doctrine, Christian education, Christian ethics, Christian scripture, Christian studies, Christianity, church history, clayworking, college planning, college writing, community service, comparative religion, computer applications, computer art, computer education, computer graphics, computer multimedia, computer programming, computer science, computer skills, computer studies, contemporary history, contemporary issues, costumes and make-up, CPR, creative dance, creative drama, creative thinking, critical studies in film, critical writing, dance performance, drama performance, drama workshop, dramatic arts, drawing, drawing and design, earth science, economics, economics and history, English, English composition, English literature, environmental science, environmental studies, first aid, fitness, food and nutrition, foreign language, French, general science, government, graphic arts, graphic design, health, health and wellness, history, history of the Catholic Church, honors English, honors U.S. history, honors world history, human anatomy, instruments, introduction to theater, Italian, jazz band, keyboarding, lab science, language, language and composition, law and the legal system, life science, marine science, mathematics, modern history, music performance, music theater, musical theater, musical theater dance, oceanography, personal fitness, physical fitness, physics, play production, portfolio art, pre-calculus, public service, religion, religion and culture, religious education, religious studies, scene study, science, science research, scripture, set design, Spanish, sports nutrition, stage and body movement, stage design, theater,

theater arts, theater design and production, theater history, visual and performing arts, yearbook.

Graduation Requirements Computers, English, foreign language, health education, history, lab science, mathematics, oceanography, physical education (includes health), religion (includes Bible studies and theology), science.

Special Academic Programs International Baccalaureate program; Advanced Placement exam preparation; honors section.

College Admission Counseling 158 students graduated in 2010; 152 went to college, including Coker College; Johnson & Wales University; Providence College; Salve Regina University; University of New Hampshire; University of Rhode Island. Other: 1 went to work, 2 entered military service, 3 entered a postgraduate year.

Student Life Upper grades have uniform requirement, student council, honor system. Discipline rests primarily with faculty. Attendance at religious services is required.

Tuition and Aid Day student tuition: $10,750. Tuition installment plan (FACTS Tuition Payment Plan). Tuition reduction for siblings, need-based scholarship grants available. In 2010–11, 28% of upper-school students received aid. Total amount of financial aid awarded in 2010–11: $225,000.

Admissions Traditional secondary-level entrance grade is 9. For fall 2010, 310 students applied for upper-level admission, 228 were accepted, 167 enrolled. Admissions testing and essay required. Deadline for receipt of application materials: December 22. Application fee required: $25.

Athletics Interscholastic: baseball (boys), basketball (b,g), cheering (g), cross-country running (b,g), gymnastics (g), lacrosse (b,g), soccer (b,g), softball (g), swimming and diving (b,g), tennis (b,g), track and field (b,g), volleyball (g); intramural: dance (g), outdoor recreation (b,g); coed interscholastic: aquatics, golf, ice hockey; coed intramural: aerobics, aerobics/dance, ballet, bicycling, fitness, outdoor recreation, sailing, strength & conditioning, table tennis, weight lifting, weight training. 3 PE instructors, 14 coaches.

Computers Computers are regularly used in all academic classes. Computer resources include on-campus library services, Internet access, Internet filtering or blocking technology. Computer access in designated common areas is available to students. The school has a published electronic and media policy.

Contact Ms. Kristen Need, Director of Admissions. 401-789-9262 Ext. 515. Fax: 401-782-2262. E-mail: kneed@theproutschool.org. Web site: www.theproutschool.org.

PROVIDENCE CATHOLIC SCHOOL, THE COLLEGE PREPARATORY SCHOOL FOR GIRLS GRADES 6-12

1215 North St. Mary's

San Antonio, Texas 78215-1787

Head of School: Ms. Alicia Garcia

General Information Girls' day college-preparatory, arts, and religious studies school, affiliated with Roman Catholic Church. Grades 6–12. Founded: 1951. Setting: urban. 3-acre campus. 4 buildings on campus. Approved or accredited by Southern Association of Colleges and Schools, Southern Association of Independent Schools, Texas Catholic Conference, and Texas Education Agency. Total enrollment: 346. Upper school average class size: 22. Upper school faculty-student ratio: 1:11. There are 186 required school days per year for Upper School students. Upper School students typically attend 5 days per week. The average school day consists of 7 hours.

Upper School Student Profile Grade 9: 49 students (49 girls); Grade 10: 50 students (50 girls); Grade 11: 57 students (57 girls); Grade 12: 50 students (50 girls). 80% of students are Roman Catholic.

Faculty School total: 34. In upper school: 5 men, 26 women; 28 have advanced degrees.

Subjects Offered Acting, advanced biology, advanced chemistry, advanced math, Advanced Placement courses, aerobics, algebra, American history, American history-AP, American literature, American literature-AP, anatomy, ancient world history, art, athletics, audio visual/media, band, biology, biology-AP, British literature, British literature-AP, broadcast journalism, broadcasting, calculus-AP, career education internship, Catholic belief and practice, cheerleading, chemistry, choir, choral music, church history, composition-AP, computer information systems, concert band, concert choir, conflict resolution, creative writing, dance, dance performance, desktop publishing, drama, drama performance, drama workshop, economics, English, English language and composition-AP, English language-AP, English literature, English literature and composition-AP, English literature-AP, English-AP, film, fitness, foreign language, French, geography, government, government and politics-AP, history, history-AP, human anatomy, jazz band, journalism, JROTC, JROTC or LEAD (Leadership Education and Development), Latin, law, leadership, literature and composition-AP, music theory, newspaper, peer ministry, personal fitness, photography, photojournalism, physical education, physical fitness, physical science, physics, play production, psychology, social justice, sociology, softball, Spanish, Spanish language-AP, Spanish-AP, speech, sports, statistics-AP, student government, student publications, swimming, swimming competency, tennis, Texas history, the Web, theater, theater arts, theater design and production, theater production, theology, track and field, U.S. government and politics, U.S. government and politics-AP, U.S. history, U.S. history-AP, volleyball, Web site design, world geography, world history, yearbook.

Graduation Requirements All academic, 100 hours of community service completed by grade 12, senior retreat participation.

Special Academic Programs International Baccalaureate program; 13 Advanced Placement exams for which test preparation is offered; honors section; independent study; study at local college for college credit.

College Admission Counseling 42 students graduated in 2011; all went to college, including St. Mary's University; Texas A&M University; The University of Texas at Austin; The University of Texas at San Antonio; University of the Incarnate Word.

Student Life Upper grades have uniform requirement, student council, honor system. Discipline rests primarily with faculty. Attendance at religious services is required.

Summer Programs Remediation, enrichment, advancement, sports, art/fine arts, computer instruction programs offered; session focuses on getting ahead (improvement); held on campus; accepts girls; open to students from other schools. 100 students usually enrolled. 2012 schedule: June 6 to July 14. Application deadline: May 25.

Tuition and Aid Day student tuition: $7035. Tuition installment plan (monthly payment plans, Middle School Tuition $4,202). Tuition reduction for siblings, merit scholarship grants, need-based scholarship grants available. In 2011–12, 20% of upper-school students received aid; total upper-school merit-scholarship money awarded: $55,500. Total amount of financial aid awarded in 2011–12: $200,000.

Admissions Traditional secondary-level entrance grade is 9. High School Placement Test or QUIC required. Deadline for receipt of application materials: none. No application fee required. On-campus interview recommended.

Athletics Interscholastic: aerobics, aerobics/dance, basketball, bowling, cheering, cross-country running, dance, dance team, drill team, JROTC drill, physical fitness, physical training, running, soccer, softball, tennis, track and field, volleyball, weight training, winter soccer; coed interscholastic: aquatics. 2 PE instructors, 7 coaches, 1 athletic trainer.

Computers Computers are regularly used in desktop publishing, journalism, newspaper, Web site design, yearbook classes. Computer network features include on-campus library services, online commercial services, Internet access, Internet filtering or blocking technology, online classrooms. Campus intranet and student e-mail accounts are available to students. Students grades are available online. The school has a published electronic and media policy.

Contact Mrs. Nora Walsh, Enrollment Director. 210-224-6651 Ext. 210. Fax: 210-224-6214. E-mail: nwalsh@providencehs.net. Web site: www.providencehs.net.

PROVIDENCE CHRISTIAN SCHOOL

P.O. Box 240

Monarch, Alberta T0L 1M0, Canada

Head of School: Mr. Chris Heikoop

General Information Coeducational day college-preparatory, general academic, and religious studies school, affiliated with Calvinist faith, Reformed Church. Grades K–12. Founded: 1994. Setting: rural. Nearest major city is Lethbridge, Canada. 5-acre campus. 1 building on campus. Approved or accredited by Alberta Department of Education. Language of instruction: English. Total enrollment: 120. Upper school average class size: 12. Upper school faculty-student ratio: 1:11. There are 180 required school days per year for Upper School students. Upper School students typically attend 4 days per week. The average school day consists of 6 hours and 25 minutes.

Upper School Student Profile Grade 10: 7 students (2 boys, 5 girls); Grade 11: 6 students (2 boys, 4 girls); Grade 12: 8 students (4 boys, 4 girls). 90% of students are Calvinist, Reformed.

Faculty School total: 10. In upper school: 3 men, 2 women.

Subjects Offered Accounting, advanced biology, advanced math, Bible, Bible studies, bookkeeping, business applications, business education, business law, business studies, career and personal planning, career and technology systems, Christian doctrine, Christian scripture, church history, civil rights, computer technologies, critical thinking, English, ESL, finance, first aid, French, general science, health education, human sexuality, information processing, information technology, integrated mathematics, integrated physics, integrated science, keyboarding, language arts, library, life skills, mathematics, music, music appreciation, participation in sports, personal finance, physics, reading, religious education, science project, sewing, sex education, social studies, sports, Web site design.

Graduation Requirements Alberta Ministry of Education requirements.

Special Academic Programs International Baccalaureate program; ESL (6 students enrolled).

College Admission Counseling 6 students graduated in 2011; 1 went to college. Other: 3 went to work, 2 entered a postgraduate year.

Student Life Upper grades have specified standards of dress, student council, honor system. Discipline rests primarily with faculty. Attendance at religious services is required.

Tuition and Aid Day student tuition: CAN$5100. Tuition installment plan (The Tuition Plan). Tuition reduction for siblings available.

Admissions Traditional secondary-level entrance grade is 10. For fall 2011, 21 students applied for upper-level admission, 21 were accepted, 21 enrolled. Deadline for receipt of application materials: September 30. No application fee required. Interview required.

Athletics 2 PE instructors.
Computers Computers are regularly used in all classes. Computer network features include Internet access, wireless campus network, Internet filtering or blocking technology. The school has a published electronic and media policy.
Contact Mr. Chris Heikoop, Principal. 403-381-4418. Fax: 403-381-4428. E-mail: principal@pcsmonarch.com. Web site: www.pcsmonarch.com/.

PROVIDENCE COUNTRY DAY SCHOOL

660 Waterman Avenue

East Providence, Rhode Island 02914-1724

Head of School: Mr. Vince Watchorn

General Information Coeducational day college-preparatory and arts school. Grades 6–12. Founded: 1923. Setting: suburban. Nearest major city is Providence. 18-acre campus. 6 buildings on campus. Approved or accredited by Association of Independent Schools in New England, New England Association of Schools and Colleges, The College Board, and Rhode Island Department of Education. Member of National Association of Independent Schools and Secondary School Admission Test Board. Endowment: $1.5 million. Total enrollment: 216. Upper school average class size: 12. Upper school faculty-student ratio: 1:7. The average school day consists of 6 hours and 50 minutes.
Upper School Student Profile Grade 9: 39 students (24 boys, 15 girls); Grade 10: 42 students (24 boys, 18 girls); Grade 11: 48 students (32 boys, 16 girls); Grade 12: 50 students (34 boys, 16 girls).
Faculty School total: 34. In upper school: 16 men, 15 women; 19 have advanced degrees.
Subjects Offered Advanced Placement courses, algebra, American government, American history, American history-AP, American literature, ancient history, art, art history-AP, Asian studies, Bible as literature, bioethics, biology, biology-AP, British literature, calculus, calculus-AP, ceramics, chemistry, choir, computer graphics, conceptual physics, creative writing, drama, earth science, electives, English, English literature, English literature-AP, environmental science, European civilization, European history, expository writing, fine arts, foreign language, forensics, French, geography, geometry, government/civics, graphic design, health, history, independent study, jazz ensemble, journalism, Latin, mathematics, media production, modern European history, music, performing arts, photography, physical education, physics, pottery, pre-algebra, pre-calculus, public speaking, science, senior internship, social studies, Spanish, Spanish language-AP, studio art, theater, trigonometry, U.S. government and politics-AP, visual arts, world history, writing.
Graduation Requirements Arts and fine arts (art, music, dance, drama), English, foreign language, history, mathematics, physical education (includes health), science, senior independent project, community service hours.
Special Academic Programs 8 Advanced Placement exams for which test preparation is offered; honors section; independent study; term-away projects; study abroad; academic accommodation for the gifted, the musically talented, and the artistically talented.
College Admission Counseling 45 students graduated in 2011; 43 went to college, including Boston College; Merrimack College; Providence College; The George Washington University; Union College; University of Rhode Island. Other: 2 entered a postgraduate year. Mean SAT critical reading: 565, mean SAT math: 557, mean SAT writing: 566.
Student Life Upper grades have specified standards of dress, student council, honor system. Discipline rests primarily with faculty.
Summer Programs Sports, art/fine arts programs offered; held on campus; accepts boys and girls; not open to students from other schools.
Tuition and Aid Day student tuition: $28,400–$28,900. Tuition installment plan (SMART Tuition Payment Plan, monthly payment plans). Need-based scholarship grants available. In 2011–12, 41% of upper-school students received aid. Total amount of financial aid awarded in 2011–12: $1,500,000.
Admissions Traditional secondary-level entrance grade is 9. For fall 2011, 93 students applied for upper-level admission, 70 were accepted, 29 enrolled. ISEE or SSAT required. Deadline for receipt of application materials: February 1. Application fee required: $55. On-campus interview required.
Athletics Interscholastic: baseball (boys), basketball (b,g), cross-country running (b,g), football (b), golf (b,g), ice hockey (b), indoor track & field (b,g), lacrosse (b,g), sailing (b,g), soccer (b,g), swimming and diving (b,g), tennis (b,g), track and field (b,g), winter (indoor) track (b,g), wrestling (b); coed interscholastic: physical fitness, yoga; coed intramural: strength & conditioning, weight training. 2 PE instructors, 8 coaches, 1 athletic trainer.
Computers Computers are regularly used in art, English, foreign language, history, mathematics, music, science classes. Computer network features include on-campus library services, online commercial services, Internet access, Internet filtering or blocking technology. Campus intranet, student e-mail accounts, and computer access in designated common areas are available to students. The school has a published electronic and media policy.
Contact Ms. Ashley E. Randlett, Director of Admissions and Financial Aid. 401-438-5170 Ext. 102. Fax: 401-435-4514. E-mail: randlett@providencecountryday.org. Web site: www.providencecountryday.org.

PROVIDENCE DAY SCHOOL

5800 Sardis Road

Charlotte, North Carolina 28270

Head of School: Dr. Glyn Cowlishaw

General Information Coeducational day college-preparatory and global studies diploma program school. Grades PK–12. Founded: 1971. Setting: suburban. 44-acre campus. 18 buildings on campus. Approved or accredited by Southern Association of Colleges and Schools, Southern Association of Independent Schools, and North Carolina Department of Education. Member of National Association of Independent Schools. Endowment: $4 million. Total enrollment: 1,501. Upper school average class size: 18. Upper school faculty-student ratio: 1:12. There are 177 required school days per year for Upper School students. Upper School students typically attend 5 days per week. The average school day consists of 7 hours and 10 minutes.
Upper School Student Profile Grade 9: 148 students (76 boys, 72 girls); Grade 10: 129 students (68 boys, 61 girls); Grade 11: 120 students (55 boys, 65 girls); Grade 12: 137 students (81 boys, 56 girls).
Faculty School total: 148. In upper school: 46 men, 34 women; 56 have advanced degrees.
Subjects Offered 3-dimensional design, accounting, African-American history, algebra, American history, American literature, art, art history-AP, Asian history, band, biology, biology-AP, calculus-AP, chemistry, chemistry-AP, chorus, Civil War, composition, computer graphics, computer programming, computer science, computer science-AP, drama, economics, English, English literature, English-AP, environmental science, environmental science-AP, fine arts, French, French-AP, geometry, German, German-AP, government-AP, government/civics, health, history, history-AP, instrumental music, international relations, journalism, Judaic studies, keyboarding, Latin, Latin-AP, literature, Mandarin, mathematics, music-AP, photography, physical education, physical science, physics, physics-AP, political science, pre-calculus, psychology, science, set design, social studies, Spanish, Spanish-AP, sports medicine, statistics-AP, theater, word processing, world history, writing, yearbook.
Graduation Requirements Arts and fine arts (art, music, dance, drama), computer science, English, foreign language, mathematics, physical education (includes health), science, social studies (includes history), Global Studies Diploma.
Special Academic Programs 24 Advanced Placement exams for which test preparation is offered; honors section; accelerated programs; domestic exchange program; study abroad; academic accommodation for the gifted, the musically talented, and the artistically talented.
College Admission Counseling 118 students graduated in 2011; all went to college, including Appalachian State University; Duke University; North Carolina State University; The University of North Carolina at Chapel Hill; University of Virginia; Wake Forest University. Median SAT critical reading: 650, median SAT math: 660, median SAT writing: 650, median combined SAT: 1960, median composite ACT: 28. 73% scored over 600 on SAT critical reading, 80% scored over 600 on SAT math, 71% scored over 600 on SAT writing, 73% scored over 1800 on combined SAT.
Student Life Upper grades have specified standards of dress, student council, honor system. Discipline rests equally with students and faculty.
Summer Programs Remediation, enrichment, advancement, sports, art/fine arts, computer instruction programs offered; session focuses on academics, enrichment; held both on and off campus; held at various parks, recreation centers, museums; accepts boys and girls; open to students from other schools. 2,500 students usually enrolled. 2012 schedule: June 7 to August 6. Application deadline: none.
Tuition and Aid Day student tuition: $20,730. Tuition installment plan (Academic Management Services Plan, monthly payment plans). Need-based scholarship grants available. In 2011–12, 14% of upper-school students received aid. Total amount of financial aid awarded in 2011–12: $1,056,585.
Admissions Traditional secondary-level entrance grade is 9. For fall 2011, 113 students applied for upper-level admission, 65 were accepted, 39 enrolled. Cognitive Abilities Test, ERB CTP IV, ISEE, SSAT, ERB, PSAT, SAT, PLAN or ACT or Woodcock-Johnson Educational Evaluation, WISC III required. Deadline for receipt of application materials: January 15. Application fee required: $90. On-campus interview required.
Athletics Interscholastic: aerobics/dance (girls), baseball (b), basketball (b,g), cheering (g), cross-country running (b,g), dance squad (g), field hockey (g), football (b), golf (b,g), lacrosse (b,g), soccer (b,g), softball (g), swimming and diving (b,g), tennis (b,g), track and field (b,g), volleyball (g), wrestling (b); intramural: indoor hockey (b,g), indoor soccer (b,g), Newcombe ball (b,g), physical fitness (b,g), pillo polo (b,g), soccer (b,g), softball (b,g), strength & conditioning (b,g), volleyball (b,g); coed intramural: indoor hockey, indoor soccer, Newcombe ball, physical fitness, pillo polo, soccer, softball, strength & conditioning, tennis, volleyball. 4 PE instructors, 36 coaches, 2 athletic trainers.
Computers Computers are regularly used in English, mathematics, science, technology, word processing classes. Computer network features include on-campus library services, online commercial services, Internet access, wireless campus network, Internet filtering or blocking technology, wireless iBook lab available for individual student check-out, ipads. Student e-mail accounts and computer access in designated common areas are available to students. Students grades are available online. The school has a published electronic and media policy.

Contact Mrs. Carissa Goddard, Admissions Assistant. 704-887-7040. Fax: 704-887-7520 Ext. 7041. E-mail: carissa.goddard@providenceday.org. Web site: www.providenceday.org.

PROVIDENCE HIGH SCHOOL

511 South Buena Vista Street

Burbank, California 91505-4865

Head of School: Mr. Joe Sciuto

General Information Coeducational day college-preparatory, arts, religious studies, and technology school, affiliated with Roman Catholic Church. Grades 9–12. Founded: 1955. Setting: urban. Nearest major city is Los Angeles. 4-acre campus. 6 buildings on campus. Approved or accredited by National Catholic Education Association, The College Board, Western Association of Schools and Colleges, Western Catholic Education Association, and California Department of Education. Endowment: $1.4 million. Total enrollment: 401. Upper school average class size: 22. Upper school faculty-student ratio: 1:12. There are 183 required school days per year for Upper School students. Upper School students typically attend 5 days per week. The average school day consists of 6 hours.

Upper School Student Profile Grade 9: 129 students (55 boys, 74 girls); Grade 10: 81 students (36 boys, 45 girls); Grade 11: 92 students (49 boys, 43 girls); Grade 12: 99 students (52 boys, 47 girls). 72% of students are Roman Catholic.

Faculty School total: 48. In upper school: 19 men, 29 women; 29 have advanced degrees.

Subjects Offered 3-dimensional art, accounting, advanced computer applications, Advanced Placement courses, advanced studio art-AP, algebra, American history, American history-AP, American literature, American literature-AP, Basic programming, Bible studies, biology, biology-AP, calculus, calculus-AP, Catholic belief and practice, ceramics, chemistry, chorus, church history, community service, computer animation, computer art, computer programming, computer science, digital photography, drama, economics, economics-AP, English, English literature, English literature and composition-AP, environmental science, ethics, film, fine arts, French, geometry, graphic arts, health, history, journalism, language-AP, Latin, law, mathematics, media studies, music, photography, physical education, physics, physics-AP, pre-calculus, psychology, psychology-AP, religion, robotics, science, social studies, Spanish, Spanish-AP, theater, trigonometry, U.S. government, U.S. government and politics-AP, U.S. history-AP, United States government-AP, video, video and animation, video film production, visual and performing arts, volleyball, world cultures, world geography, world history, world religions, world religions, writing, yearbook, yoga.

Graduation Requirements American government, American history, American literature, art, biology, British literature, chemistry, comparative religion, computer science, cultural geography, economics, electives, English, ethics, foreign language, mathematics, physical education (includes health), religion (includes Bible studies and theology), science, social studies (includes history), world literature, completion of Christian Service hours.

Special Academic Programs 11 Advanced Placement exams for which test preparation is offered; honors section; academic accommodation for the musically talented and the artistically talented.

College Admission Counseling 96 students graduated in 2011; 93 went to college, including California State Polytechnic University, Pomona; California State University, Northridge; Loyola Marymount University; Pasadena City College; Santa Monica College; University of California, Los Angeles. Other: 3 had other specific plans. Median SAT critical reading: 530, median SAT math: 525, median SAT writing: 537, median composite ACT: 23.

Student Life Upper grades have uniform requirement, student council. Discipline rests equally with students and faculty. Attendance at religious services is required.

Summer Programs Remediation, enrichment, advancement, sports, art/fine arts, computer instruction programs offered; session focuses on enrichment, remediation, and extracurricular activities; held on campus; accepts boys and girls; open to students from other schools. 250 students usually enrolled. 2012 schedule: July 2 to July 27. Application deadline: June 15.

Tuition and Aid Day student tuition: $10,880. Tuition installment plan (The Tuition Plan, 1-payment plan: payment in full due July 1st, 2-payment plan-60% due July 1st, 40% due January 1st, 10-payment plan: monthly beginning July 1, ending April 1). Tuition reduction for siblings, merit scholarship grants, need-based scholarship grants, PSJMC Employee Discount available. In 2011–12, 30% of upper-school students received aid; total upper-school merit-scholarship money awarded: $99,800. Total amount of financial aid awarded in 2011–12: $276,600.

Admissions Traditional secondary-level entrance grade is 9. Admissions testing or High School Placement Test (closed version) from Scholastic Testing Service required. Deadline for receipt of application materials: January 12. Application fee required: $65. On-campus interview recommended.

Athletics Interscholastic: baseball (boys), basketball (b,g), combined training (b), cross-country running (b,g), fitness (b,g), golf (b), physical fitness (b,g), soccer (b,g), softball (g), strength & conditioning (b,g), volleyball (b,g), weight training (b); coed interscholastic: cheering, cross-country running, dance team, track and field, yoga; coed intramural: kickball, volleyball. 2 PE instructors, 23 coaches.

Computers Computers are regularly used in accounting, animation, computer applications, desktop publishing, digital applications, information technology, journalism, library, literary magazine, media, media production, newspaper, photography, publications, video film production, Web site design, word processing, writing, yearbook classes. Computer network features include on-campus library services, online commercial services, Internet access, wireless campus network, Microsoft Office Suite XP Professional, extranet portal. Student e-mail accounts are available to students. Students grades are available online. The school has a published electronic and media policy.

Contact Mrs. Judy Umeck, Director of Admissions. 818-846-8141 Ext. 501. Fax: 818-843-8421. E-mail: judy.umeck@providencehigh.org. Web site: www.providencehigh.org.

PUNAHOU SCHOOL

1601 Punahou Street

Honolulu, Hawaii 96822

Head of School: Dr. James K. Scott

General Information Coeducational day college-preparatory, arts, bilingual studies, and technology school. Grades K–12. Founded: 1841. Setting: urban. 76-acre campus. 21 buildings on campus. Approved or accredited by Western Association of Schools and Colleges. Member of National Association of Independent Schools and Secondary School Admission Test Board. Endowment: $171.7 million. Total enrollment: 3,743. Upper school average class size: 21. Upper school faculty-student ratio: 1:11. There are 165 required school days per year for Upper School students. Upper School students typically attend 5 days per week. The average school day consists of 7 hours.

Upper School Student Profile Grade 9: 425 students (207 boys, 218 girls); Grade 10: 441 students (208 boys, 233 girls); Grade 11: 421 students (200 boys, 221 girls); Grade 12: 427 students (214 boys, 213 girls).

Faculty School total: 328. In upper school: 68 men, 91 women; 133 have advanced degrees.

Subjects Offered 20th century history, acting, Advanced Placement courses, advanced studio art-AP, algebra, American culture, American literature, American studies, anatomy and physiology, anthropology, Asian history, astronomy, ballet, Bible as literature, bioethics, biology, biology-AP, British literature, Buddhism, business studies, calculus, calculus-AP, career/college preparation, ceramics, chamber groups, character education, chemistry, chemistry-AP, child development, choir, choral music, chorus, clayworking, college admission preparation, college counseling, college planning, college writing, community garden, composition, computer science, computer science-AP, concert band, contemporary issues, CPR, creative writing, dance, digital art, drama performance, drawing, driver education, early childhood, economics, English, English composition, environmental science, environmental science-AP, European history, European history-AP, film and literature, French, French language-AP, French studies, geometry, glassblowing, government and politics-AP, guidance, guitar, Hawaiian history, Hawaiian language, history of jazz, humanities, independent study, integrated science, Japanese, Japanese history, jewelry making, journalism, JROTC or LEAD (Leadership Education and Development), law, Mandarin, marching band, marine biology, mechanical drawing, medieval history, money management, music theory, oceanography, painting, peer counseling, photography, physical education, physics, physics-AP, pre-calculus, psychology, psychology-AP, religion, robotics, sculpture, Shakespeare, social studies, Spanish, Spanish-AP, sports psychology, statistics-AP, studio art, studio art-AP, symphonic band, technical theater, theater design and production, trigonometry, U.S. government and politics-AP, U.S. history, U.S. history-AP, video, video film production, Western literature, wind ensemble, world civilizations, world literature, writing, yoga.

Graduation Requirements Electives, English, foreign language, mathematics, physical education (includes health), science, social studies (includes history), visual and performing arts, seniors are required to take a CapSeeds course that combines economics and community service, one course with the Spiritual, Ethical, Community Responsibility (SECR) designation.

Special Academic Programs 13 Advanced Placement exams for which test preparation is offered; honors section; independent study; study abroad.

College Admission Counseling 429 students graduated in 2011; 419 went to college, including Boston University; Creighton University; Santa Clara University; Seattle University; University of Hawaii at Manoa; University of Southern California. Other: 3 went to work, 7 had other specific plans. Median SAT critical reading: 610, median SAT math: 670, median SAT writing: 620, median combined SAT: 1890. 55% scored over 600 on SAT critical reading, 77% scored over 600 on SAT math, 61% scored over 600 on SAT writing, 66% scored over 1800 on combined SAT.

Student Life Upper grades have specified standards of dress, student council, honor system. Discipline rests primarily with faculty. Attendance at religious services is required.

Summer Programs Enrichment, advancement, sports, art/fine arts programs offered; session focuses on enrichment and graduation credit; held both on and off campus; held at Japan, Costa Rica, China; accepts boys and girls; not open to students from other schools. 1,400 students usually enrolled. 2012 schedule: June 12 to July 20. Application deadline: April 27.

Tuition and Aid Day student tuition: $18,450. Tuition installment plan (Insured Tuition Payment Plan, monthly payment plans, semester payment plan; annual payment plan). Merit scholarship grants, need-based scholarship grants available. In 2011–12, 50% of upper-school students received aid; total upper-school merit-scholarship money awarded: $221,400. Total amount of financial aid awarded in 2011–12: $2,201,900.

Admissions Traditional secondary-level entrance grade is 9. For fall 2011, 424 students applied for upper-level admission, 139 were accepted, 92 enrolled. SAT or SSAT required. Deadline for receipt of application materials: December 1. Application fee required: $125. Interview required.

Athletics Interscholastic: baseball (boys), basketball (b,g), bowling (b,g), canoeing/kayaking (b,g), cheering (g), cross-country running (b,g), football (b), golf (b,g), judo (b,g), kayaking (b,g), paddling (b,g), riflery (b,g), sailing (b,g), soccer (b,g), softball (g), swimming and diving (b,g), tennis (b,g), track and field (b,g), volleyball (b,g), water polo (b,g), wrestling (b,g); coed interscholastic: canoeing/kayaking, paddling. 4 PE instructors, 200 coaches, 4 athletic trainers.

Computers Computers are regularly used in all academic classes. Computer network features include on-campus library services, online commercial services, Internet access, wireless campus network, Internet filtering or blocking technology. Campus intranet, student e-mail accounts, and computer access in designated common areas are available to students. The school has a published electronic and media policy.

Contact Mrs. Betsy S. Hata, Director of Admission and Financial Aid. 808-944-5714. Fax: 808-943-3602. E-mail: admission@punahou.edu. Web site: www.punahou.edu.

QUEEN MARGARET'S SCHOOL

660 Brownsey Avenue

Duncan, British Columbia V9L 1C2, Canada

Head of School: Mrs. Wilma Jamieson

General Information Girls' boarding and coeducational day college-preparatory, arts, technology, equestrian studies, and pre-engineering and sciences school, affiliated with Anglican Church of Canada. Boarding girls grades 6–12, day boys grades PS–8, day girls grades PS–12. Founded: 1921. Setting: small town. Nearest major city is Victoria, Canada. Students are housed in single-sex dormitories. 27-acre campus. 8 buildings on campus. Approved or accredited by Canadian Association of Independent Schools, Canadian Educational Standards Institute, The Association of Boarding Schools, and British Columbia Department of Education. Affiliate member of National Association of Independent Schools; member of Secondary School Admission Test Board and Canadian Association of Independent Schools. Language of instruction: English. Endowment: CAN$500,000. Total enrollment: 302. Upper school average class size: 16. Upper school faculty student ratio: 1:8. There are 168 required school days per year for Upper School students. Upper School students typically attend 5 days per week. The average school day consists of 7 hours.

Upper School Student Profile Grade 8: 22 students (5 boys, 17 girls); Grade 9: 24 students (24 girls); Grade 10: 37 students (37 girls); Grade 11: 36 students (36 girls); Grade 12: 33 students (33 girls). 56% of students are boarding students. 49% are province residents. 7 provinces are represented in upper school student body. 41% are international students. International students from China, Hong Kong, Mexico, Republic of Korea, Taiwan, and United States; 14 other countries represented in student body.

Faculty School total: 40. In upper school: 4 men, 18 women; 9 have advanced degrees; 4 reside on campus.

Subjects Offered Advanced math, algebra, all academic, animal husbandry, animal science, applied skills, art, biology, business education, business skills, calculus, Canadian history, career and personal planning, career exploration, chemistry, chorus, college planning, computer science, creative writing, drama, English, English literature, equestrian sports, equine management, equine science, equitation, ESL, fine arts, French, geography, geometry, grammar, health, history, home economics, instrumental music, international relations, international studies, Japanese, journalism, mathematics, photography, physical education, physics, science, social studies, speech, sports, sports psychology, theater, TOEFL preparation, trigonometry, visual arts, world history, writing.

Graduation Requirements Arts and fine arts (art, music, dance, drama), career and personal planning, computer science, English, foreign language, mathematics, physical education (includes health), science, social studies (includes history). Community service is required.

Special Academic Programs Independent study; study at local college for college credit; academic accommodation for the gifted, the musically talented, and the artistically talented; ESL (40 students enrolled).

College Admission Counseling 23 students graduated in 2011; 21 went to college, including McGill University; Queen's University at Kingston; Savannah College of Art and Design; The University of British Columbia; University of Ottawa; University of Toronto. Other: 2 had other specific plans.

Student Life Upper grades have uniform requirement, student council, honor system. Discipline rests primarily with faculty. Attendance at religious services is required.

Summer Programs Enrichment, ESL, sports programs offered; session focuses on ESL group camps, equestrian riding, and pre-vet camp; held on campus; accepts boys and girls; open to students from other schools. 25 students usually enrolled. 2012 schedule: July 6 to August 29. Application deadline: May 15.

Tuition and Aid Day student tuition: CAN$8200–CAN$12,450; 5-day tuition and room/board: CAN$29,800; 7-day tuition and room/board: CAN$32,600–CAN$43,700. Tuition installment plan (Insured Tuition Payment Plan, monthly payment plans, individually arranged payment plans). Tuition reduction for siblings, bursaries, merit scholarship grants, Tuition reduction for children of staff available. In 2011–12, 30% of upper-school students received aid; total upper-school merit-scholarship money awarded: CAN$50,000. Total amount of financial aid awarded in 2011–12: CAN$150,000.

Admissions Traditional secondary-level entrance grade is 8. Otis-Lennon School Ability Test, SLEP or Stanford Achievement Test required. Deadline for receipt of application materials: none. Application fee required: CAN$200. Interview required.

Athletics Interscholastic: aquatics (girls), badminton (g), basketball (g), canoeing/kayaking (g), dressage (g), equestrian sports (g), field hockey (g), golf (g), hockey (g), horseback riding (g), running (g), soccer (g), tennis (g), track and field (g), volleyball (g); intramural: aerobics (g), aerobics/dance (g), ballet (g), field hockey (g), flag football (g), lacrosse (g), modern dance (g), rafting (g), rappelling (g), rowing (g), sailing (g), scuba diving (g), sea rescue (g), surfing (g), ultimate Frisbee (g), volleyball (g), yoga (g); coed intramural: alpine skiing, aquatics, archery, backpacking, ball hockey, baseball, basketball, bowling, canoeing/kayaking, climbing, cooperative games, cross-country running, curling, dance, dressage, equestrian sports, figure skating, fitness, floor hockey, freestyle skiing, Frisbee, golf, gymnastics, hiking/backpacking, hockey, horseback riding, indoor hockey, indoor soccer, jogging, jump rope, kayaking, nordic skiing, ocean paddling, outdoor activities, outdoor adventure, outdoor education, outdoor recreation, outdoor skills, outdoors, paddling, physical fitness, physical training, rock climbing, rugby, running, skiing (downhill), snowboarding, soccer, softball, street hockey, swimming and diving, tennis, track and field. 2 PE instructors, 2 coaches, 2 athletic trainers.

Computers Computers are regularly used in all academic, career education, career exploration, college planning, creative writing, English, ESL, French, information technology, introduction to technology, journalism, mathematics, media arts, media production, science, social sciences, technology classes. Computer network features include on-campus library services, Internet access, wireless campus network, Internet filtering or blocking technology. Campus intranet and student e-mail accounts are available to students. The school has a published electronic and media policy.

Contact Admissions Coordinator. 250-746-4185. Fax: 250-746-4187. E-mail: admissions@qms.bc.ca. Web site: www.qms.bc.ca.

QUEEN OF PEACE HIGH SCHOOL

191 Rutherford Place

North Arlington, New Jersey 07031-6091

Head of School: Br. Larry Lavallee, FMS

General Information Coeducational day college-preparatory, arts, business, religious studies, and technology school, affiliated with Roman Catholic Church. Grades 9–12. Founded: 1930. Setting: suburban. Nearest major city is Newark. 3 buildings on campus. Approved or accredited by Christian Brothers Association, Middle States Association of Colleges and Schools, and New Jersey Department of Education. Endowment: $2 million. Total enrollment: 525. Upper school average class size: 20. Upper school faculty-student ratio: 1:15. There are 180 required school days per year for Upper School students. Upper School students typically attend 5 days per week. The average school day consists of 6 hours and 35 minutes.

Upper School Student Profile Grade 9: 115 students (62 boys, 53 girls); Grade 10: 108 students (54 boys, 54 girls); Grade 11: 128 students (56 boys, 72 girls); Grade 12: 174 students (74 boys, 100 girls). 90% of students are Roman Catholic.

Faculty School total: 44. In upper school: 20 men, 24 women; 28 have advanced degrees.

Subjects Offered Accounting, adolescent issues, advanced chemistry, advanced computer applications, advanced math, algebra, American history, American history-AP, American literature, anatomy and physiology, area studies, art, art appreciation, biology, British literature, British literature (honors), business applications, business technology, calculus, calculus-AP, campus ministry, career education, chemistry, Christian and Hebrew scripture, computer applications, computer graphics, computer programming, contemporary issues, drama, driver education, English, English-AP, ESL, European history, French, general science, geometry, history-AP, honors algebra, honors English, honors geometry, honors U.S. history, honors world history, introduction to technology, keyboarding, modern European history, music appreciation, physical education, physics, pre-calculus, psychology, religion, religious studies, Spanish, speech, trigonometry, U.S. history, U.S. history-AP, Western civilization, writing.

Special Academic Programs Advanced Placement exam preparation; honors section; study at local college for college credit; remedial reading and/or remedial writing; remedial math; ESL (14 students enrolled).

College Admission Counseling 171 students graduated in 2010; 168 went to college, including Caldwell College; Kean University; Montclair State University; Rutgers, The State University of New Jersey, New Brunswick; Seton Hall University; William Paterson University of New Jersey. Other: 1 went to work, 2 entered military service.

Student Life Upper grades have uniform requirement, student council. Discipline rests primarily with faculty. Attendance at religious services is required.

Tuition and Aid Day student tuition: $8250. Tuition installment plan (monthly payment plans, individually arranged payment plans, plans vary depending upon family needs/abilities). Tuition reduction for siblings, merit scholarship grants, need-based scholarship grants, limited financial aid available. In 2010–11, 20% of upper-school students received aid; total upper-school merit-scholarship money awarded: $100,000.
Admissions Traditional secondary-level entrance grade is 9. For fall 2010, 505 students applied for upper-level admission, 260 were accepted, 115 enrolled. CTB/McGraw-Hill/Macmillan Co-op Test required. Deadline for receipt of application materials: none. No application fee required.
Athletics Interscholastic: baseball (boys), basketball (b,g), cheering (g), cross-country running (b,g), football (b), indoor track (b,g), soccer (b,g), softball (g), tennis (b,g), track and field (b,g), volleyball (g), wrestling (b); intramural: roller hockey (b), skiing (downhill) (b), snowboarding (b), street hockey (b), strength & conditioning (b), weight training (b,g); coed interscholastic: bowling, dance team, golf, riflery; coed intramural: aerobics/dance, alpine skiing, ball hockey, dance team, fitness, floor hockey, freestyle skiing, in-line hockey, strength & conditioning. 3 PE instructors, 53 coaches, 1 athletic trainer.
Computers Computers are regularly used in accounting, animation, business applications, career exploration, college planning, computer applications, creative writing, current events, English, foreign language, French, graphic arts, graphic design, introduction to technology, keyboarding, library, literary magazine, mathematics, newspaper, remedial study skills, Spanish, study skills, technology, word processing, yearbook classes. Computer network features include on-campus library services, online commercial services, Internet access, wireless campus network, Internet filtering or blocking technology, parent computer access to daily grading system. Computer access in designated common areas is available to students. Students grades are available online. The school has a published electronic and media policy.
Contact Mr. Edmund G. McKeown, Admissions Director. 201-998-8227 Ext. 30. Fax: 201-998-3040. E-mail: admissions@qphs.org. Web site: www.qphs.org.

QUINTE CHRISTIAN HIGH SCHOOL

138 Wallbridge-Loyalist Road

RR 2

Belleville, Ontario K8N 4Z2, Canada

Head of School: Mr. Johan Cooke

General Information Coeducational day college-preparatory, general academic, arts, business, vocational, religious studies, bilingual studies, and technology school, affiliated with Christian faith, Protestant faith. Grades 9–12. Founded: 1977. Setting: suburban. Nearest major city is Toronto, Canada. 25-acre campus. 1 building on campus. Approved or accredited by Christian Schools International, Ontario Ministry of Education, and Ontario Department of Education. Language of instruction: English. Total enrollment: 161. Upper school average class size: 15. Upper school faculty-student ratio: 1:15. There are 176 required school days per year for Upper School students. Upper School students typically attend 5 days per week. The average school day consists of 6 hours and 10 minutes.
Upper School Student Profile Grade 9: 36 students (22 boys, 14 girls); Grade 10: 35 students (16 boys, 19 girls); Grade 11: 37 students (13 boys, 24 girls); Grade 12: 45 students (25 boys, 20 girls). 90% of students are Christian, Protestant.
Faculty School total: 16. In upper school: 9 men, 7 women; 2 have advanced degrees.
Subjects Offered Accounting, art, Bible, biology, calculus, careers, chemistry, Christian education, civics, computers, drama, English, English literature, ESL, French, geography, history, law, leadership education training, mathematics, mathematics-AP, media, music, peer counseling, physical education, physics, religious education, science, shop, society challenge and change, technical education, transportation technology, world issues, world religions.
Graduation Requirements Accounting, applied arts, careers, Christian education, civics, computers, English, French, geography, mathematics, physical education (includes health), religious education, science, social studies (includes history), world religions, Ontario Christian School diploma requirements.
Special Academic Programs Special instructional classes for students with learning disabilities.
College Admission Counseling 39 students graduated in 2011; 20 went to college, including Calvin College; Dordt College; Queen's University at Kingston; Redeemer University College; University of Guelph; University of Waterloo. 100% scored over 26 on composite ACT.
Student Life Upper grades have specified standards of dress, student council, honor system. Discipline rests primarily with faculty. Attendance at religious services is required.
Tuition and Aid Day student tuition: CAN$12,200. Tuition installment plan (monthly payment plans, individually arranged payment plans). Tuition reduction for siblings, need-based scholarship grants available. In 2011–12, 18% of upper-school students received aid.
Admissions Traditional secondary-level entrance grade is 9. Deadline for receipt of application materials: March 31. Application fee required: CAN$250. Interview required.
Athletics Interscholastic: badminton (boys, girls), basketball (b,g), cross-country running (b,g), track and field (b,g), volleyball (b,g); coed interscholastic: badminton; coed intramural: badminton, basketball, fitness walking, indoor soccer, physical training, volleyball. 3 PE instructors.
Computers Computers are regularly used in all classes. Computer network features include on-campus library services, Internet access, wireless campus network, Internet filtering or blocking technology. Campus intranet, student e-mail accounts, and computer access in designated common areas are available to students. The school has a published electronic and media policy.
Contact Mrs. Hermien Hogewoning, Administrative Assistant. 613-968-7870. Fax: 613-968-7970. E-mail: admin@qchs.ca. Web site: www.qchs.ca.

RABBI ALEXANDER S. GROSS HEBREW ACADEMY

2425 Pine Tree Drive

Miami Beach, Florida 33140

Head of School: Dr. Roni Raab

General Information Coeducational day college-preparatory, general academic, religious studies, and technology school, affiliated with Jewish faith. Grades N–12. Founded: 1948. Setting: urban. 4-acre campus. 1 building on campus. Approved or accredited by Massachusetts Office of Child Care Services, Southern Association of Colleges and Schools, and Florida Department of Education. Member of Secondary School Admission Test Board. Languages of instruction: English and Hebrew. Endowment: $650,000. Total enrollment: 468. Upper school average class size: 18. Upper school faculty-student ratio: 1:4.
Upper School Student Profile Grade 9: 45 students (20 boys, 25 girls); Grade 10: 38 students (20 boys, 18 girls); Grade 11: 32 students (15 boys, 17 girls); Grade 12: 40 students (20 boys, 20 girls). 100% of students are Jewish.
Faculty School total: 70. In upper school: 21 men, 18 women; 23 have advanced degrees.
Subjects Offered Algebra, audio visual/media, Bible studies, biology, biology-AP, calculus, calculus-AP, chemistry, chemistry-AP, computers, economics, English, English-AP, environmental science, geometry, Jewish studies, life science, physical education, physics, political science, pre-calculus, SAT preparation, social studies, Spanish, Talmud, technology.
Graduation Requirements Arts and fine arts (art, music, dance, drama), business skills (includes word processing), computer science, English, foreign language, mathematics, physical education (includes health), religion (includes Bible studies and theology), science, social sciences, social studies (includes history). Community service is required.
Special Academic Programs 7 Advanced Placement exams for which test preparation is offered; honors section; independent study; study at local college for college credit; academic accommodation for the gifted; ESL (3 students enrolled).
College Admission Counseling 57 students graduated in 2011; 56 went to college, including Florida International University; Florida State University; University of Florida; University of Maryland, College Park; Yeshiva University. Other: 1 went to work. Mean SAT critical reading: 544, mean SAT math: 542, mean SAT writing: 521, mean combined SAT: 1607, mean composite ACT: 23.
Student Life Upper grades have specified standards of dress, student council, honor system. Discipline rests primarily with faculty. Attendance at religious services is required.
Tuition and Aid Day student tuition: $14,000. Tuition installment plan (monthly payment plans, individually arranged payment plans). Tuition reduction for siblings, need-based scholarship grants available. In 2011–12, 46% of upper-school students received aid. Total amount of financial aid awarded in 2011–12: $300,000.
Admissions Traditional secondary-level entrance grade is 9. For fall 2011, 40 students applied for upper-level admission, 33 were accepted, 30 enrolled. SSAT required. Deadline for receipt of application materials: none. No application fee required. On-campus interview required.
Athletics Interscholastic: basketball (boys, girls), soccer (b), tennis (b,g), volleyball (g); intramural: basketball (b,g), soccer (b), tennis (b,g), volleyball (g). 2 PE instructors, 3 coaches.
Computers Computers are regularly used in English, mathematics, religion, science classes. Computer network features include Internet access. Student e-mail accounts are available to students.
Contact Mrs. Dara Lieber, Assistant Principal. 305-532-6421 Ext. 217. Fax: 305-604-0011. E-mail: dlieber@rasg.org. Web site: www.rasg.org.

RANDOLPH-MACON ACADEMY

200 Academy Drive

Front Royal, Virginia 22630

Head of School: Maj. Gen. Henry M. Hobgood

General Information Coeducational boarding and day college-preparatory, religious studies, technology, Air Force Junior ROTC, ESL, and military school, affiliated with Methodist Church. Grades 6–PG. Founded: 1892. Setting: small town. Nearest major city is Washington, DC. Students are housed in single-sex dormitories. 135-acre campus. 9 buildings on campus. Approved or accredited by Southern Association of Colleges and Schools, The Association of Boarding Schools, University Senate of United Methodist Church, Virginia Association of Independent Schools, and Virginia Department of Education. Member of National Association of Independent Schools. Endowment: $3.8 million. Total enrollment: 367. Upper school average class size: 15. Upper school faculty-student ratio: 1:9. Upper School students typically attend 5 days per week. The average school day consists of 7 hours.

Upper School Student Profile Grade 9: 53 students (37 boys, 16 girls); Grade 10: 79 students (50 boys, 29 girls); Grade 11: 77 students (52 boys, 25 girls); Grade 12: 82 students (60 boys, 22 girls); Postgraduate: 3 students (3 boys). 85% of students are boarding students. 45% are state residents. 22 states are represented in upper school student body. 25% are international students. International students from China, Democratic People's Republic of Korea, Nigeria, Russian Federation, Saudi Arabia, and Viet Nam; 8 other countries represented in student body. 11% of students are Methodist.

Faculty School total: 39. In upper school: 23 men, 9 women; 18 have advanced degrees; 15 reside on campus.

Subjects Offered Advanced math, aerospace science, algebra, American government, American history, American history-AP, American literature, American literature-AP, anatomy, anatomy and physiology, art, art history-AP, Asian history, aviation, band, Bible studies, biology, biology-AP, British literature, calculus, calculus-AP, career education, chemistry, chorus, college counseling, comparative religion, composition-AP, computer applications, computer literacy, conceptual physics, concert band, concert choir, critical thinking, desktop publishing, discrete mathematics, drama, English, English composition, English literature, English literature and composition-AP, English-AP, epic literature, ESL, European history-AP, flight instruction, geometry, German, German-AP, government/civics, handbells, history, honors algebra, honors English, honors geometry, honors U.S. history, independent study, journalism, JROTC, keyboarding, life management skills, mathematics, music, music appreciation, New Testament, personal finance, personal fitness, photography, physical education, physics, physics-AP, physiology, pre-algebra, pre-calculus, psychology, religion, SAT preparation, science, senior seminar, Shakespeare, social studies, Spanish, Spanish literature-AP, speech and debate, statistics-AP, studio art, theater arts, trigonometry, U.S. government, U.S. history, world history, yearbook.

Graduation Requirements Aerospace science, arts and fine arts (art, music, dance, drama), computer science, English, foreign language, mathematics, physical education (includes health), religion (includes Bible studies and theology), science, social studies (includes history), Air Force Junior ROTC for each year student is enrolled.

Special Academic Programs Advanced Placement exam preparation; honors section; independent study; study at local college for college credit; study abroad; academic accommodation for the gifted; ESL (18 students enrolled).

College Admission Counseling 73 students graduated in 2011; all went to college, including James Madison University; Norwich University; Penn State University Park; United States Air Force Academy; University of California, Berkeley; Virginia Commonwealth University. Median SAT critical reading: 510, median SAT math: 565, median SAT writing: 525, median combined SAT: 1625, median composite ACT: 21. 25% scored over 600 on SAT critical reading, 30% scored over 600 on SAT math, 16% scored over 600 on SAT writing, 22% scored over 1800 on combined SAT, 13% scored over 26 on composite ACT.

Student Life Upper grades have uniform requirement, student council, honor system. Discipline rests equally with students and faculty. Attendance at religious services is required.

Summer Programs Remediation, enrichment, advancement, ESL, art/fine arts, computer instruction programs offered; session focuses on remediation, new courses, ESL, flight, college counseling; held on campus; accepts boys and girls; open to students from other schools. 180 students usually enrolled. 2012 schedule: June 24 to July 20. Application deadline: June 22.

Tuition and Aid Day student tuition: $15,342; 7-day tuition and room/board: $30,977. Tuition installment plan (monthly payment plans, 2-payment plan). Tuition reduction for siblings, merit scholarship grants, need-based scholarship grants, paying campus jobs, Methodist Church scholarships available. In 2011–12, 19% of upper-school students received aid; total upper-school merit-scholarship money awarded: $20,000. Total amount of financial aid awarded in 2011–12: $460,000.

Admissions Traditional secondary-level entrance grade is 9. For fall 2011, 191 students applied for upper-level admission, 181 were accepted, 134 enrolled. Any standardized test or SSAT required. Deadline for receipt of application materials: none. Application fee required: $75. Interview required.

Athletics Interscholastic: baseball (boys), basketball (b,g), cross-country running (b,g), football (b), lacrosse (b), soccer (b,g), softball (g), swimming and diving (b,g), tennis (b,g), track and field (b,g), volleyball (b,g), wrestling (b); intramural: basketball (b,g), horseback riding (g), independent competitive sports (b,g), soccer (b,g), softball (g), strength & conditioning (b,g), swimming and diving (b,g), tennis (b,g), track and field (b,g), volleyball (b,g); coed interscholastic: cheering, drill team, golf, JROTC drill; coed intramural: golf, horseback riding, indoor soccer, jogging, JROTC drill, outdoor activities, outdoor recreation, physical fitness, soccer, strength & conditioning, swimming and diving, table tennis, volleyball, weight lifting, weight training. 2 PE instructors, 1 athletic trainer.

Computers Computers are regularly used in aerospace science, aviation, English, ESL, foreign language, independent study, mathematics, science, yearbook classes. Computer network features include on-campus library services, online commercial services, Internet access, Internet filtering or blocking technology. Campus intranet and student e-mail accounts are available to students. Students grades are available online. The school has a published electronic and media policy.

Contact Mrs. Paula Brady, Admission Coordinator. 540-636-5484. Fax: 540-636-5419. E-mail: pbrady@rma.edu. Web site: www.rma.edu.

RANDOLPH SCHOOL

1005 Drake Avenue SE

Huntsville, Alabama 35802

Head of School: Dr. Byron C. Hulsey

General Information Coeducational day college-preparatory and arts school. Grades K–12. Founded: 1959. Setting: suburban. 67-acre campus. 3 buildings on campus. Approved or accredited by Southern Association of Colleges and Schools, Southern Association of Independent Schools, and The College Board. Member of National Association of Independent Schools. Endowment: $12 million. Total enrollment: 939. Upper school average class size: 13. Upper school faculty-student ratio: 1:10. The average school day consists of 7 hours.

Faculty School total: 102. In upper school: 13 men, 20 women; 21 have advanced degrees.

Subjects Offered 3-dimensional art, acting, algebra, American history, American history-AP, American literature, anatomy, art, art-AP, band, biology, biology-AP, calculus, calculus-AP, ceramics, chemistry, chemistry-AP, comparative government and politics-AP, computer math, concert choir, consumer economics, creative writing, drama, drama workshop, economics, English, English literature, English-AP, environmental science, European history, European history-AP, film appreciation, filmmaking, fine arts, forensics, French, French-AP, geometry, history, Homeric Greek, journalism, Latin, marine biology, mathematics, music, music theory-AP, physical education, physics, physics-AP, physiology, psychology, science, social studies, Southern literature, Spanish, Spanish-AP, speech, stage design, stagecraft, student publications, studio art-AP, theater, trigonometry, U.S. government and politics-AP, U.S. history-AP, world history, world history-AP, world literature, writing, yearbook.

Graduation Requirements Algebra, American literature, arts and fine arts (art, music, dance, drama), biology, British literature, chemistry, computer science, English, European history, foreign language, geometry, literature, mathematics, science, social studies (includes history), world literature.

Special Academic Programs 12 Advanced Placement exams for which test preparation is offered; honors section; independent study; study at local college for college credit.

College Admission Counseling 61 students graduated in 2010; all went to college, including Auburn University; Birmingham-Southern College; Sewanee: The University of the South; The University of Alabama; The University of Alabama at Birmingham; Vanderbilt University. Median SAT critical reading: 640, median SAT math: 670, median SAT writing: 640, median combined SAT: 1940, median composite ACT: 29. 65% scored over 600 on SAT critical reading, 72% scored over 600 on SAT math, 63% scored over 600 on SAT writing, 77% scored over 1800 on combined SAT, 67% scored over 26 on composite ACT.

Student Life Upper grades have specified standards of dress, student council, honor system. Discipline rests primarily with faculty.

Tuition and Aid Day student tuition: $11,850–$14,785. Tuition installment plan (Insured Tuition Payment Plan, 2- and 10-payment plans). Merit scholarship grants, need-based scholarship grants available. In 2010–11, 4% of upper-school students received aid; total upper-school merit-scholarship money awarded: $21,932. Total amount of financial aid awarded in 2010–11: $88,875.

Admissions Traditional secondary-level entrance grade is 9. For fall 2010, 31 students applied for upper-level admission, 19 were accepted, 15 enrolled. ERB, ISEE or writing sample required. Deadline for receipt of application materials: none. Application fee required: $75. On-campus interview required.

Athletics Interscholastic: baseball (boys), basketball (b,g), cheering (g), cross-country running (b,g), diving (b,g), football (b), golf (b,g), indoor track & field (b,g), physical fitness (b,g), physical training (b,g), soccer (b,g), softball (g), swimming and diving (b,g), tennis (b,g), track and field (b,g), volleyball (g), winter (indoor) track (b,g); coed interscholastic: diving; coed intramural: flag football. 6 PE instructors, 5 coaches, 1 athletic trainer.

Computers Computers are regularly used in all academic classes. Computer network features include on-campus library services, online commercial services, Internet access, wireless campus network, Internet filtering or blocking technology, laptops. Campus intranet, student e-mail accounts, and computer access in designated common areas are available to students. Students grades are available online. The school has a published electronic and media policy.

Contact Glynn Below, Director of Admissions. 256-799-6104. Fax: 256-881-1784. E-mail: gbelow@randolphschool.net. Web site: www.randolphschool.net.

RANNEY SCHOOL

235 Hope Road

Tinton Falls, New Jersey 07724

Head of School: Dr. Lawrence S. Sykoff

General Information Coeducational day college-preparatory school. Grades N–12. Founded: 1960. Setting: suburban. Nearest major city is New York, NY. 60-acre campus. 3 buildings on campus. Approved or accredited by Middle States Association of Colleges and Schools and New Jersey Department of Education. Member of National Association of Independent Schools and Secondary School Admission Test Board. Total enrollment: 821. Upper school average class size: 15. Upper school faculty-student ratio: 1:9.

Upper School Student Profile Grade 9: 78 students (29 boys, 49 girls); Grade 10: 61 students (30 boys, 31 girls); Grade 11: 52 students (27 boys, 25 girls); Grade 12: 62 students (32 boys, 30 girls).

Faculty School total: 94.

Subjects Offered ACT preparation, Advanced Placement courses, algebra, American history, American literature, anatomy and physiology, art, art history, art history-AP, astronomy, biology, biology-AP, British literature (honors), calculus, calculus-AP, ceramics, chemistry, chemistry-AP, computer programming, computer science, computer science-AP, ecology, environmental systems, economics, economics-AP, English, English language-AP, English literature, English literature-AP, environmental science, environmental science-AP, ethics, European history, European history-AP, fine arts, French, French-AP, geometry, government, government and politics-AP, grammar, health, history, honors English, honors geometry, journalism, macro/microeconomics-AP, macroeconomics-AP, Mandarin, marine biology, mathematics, music, music history, music theory-AP, music-AP, physical education, physics, SAT preparation, science, senior internship, senior thesis, Spanish, Spanish language-AP, strings, studio art, studio art-AP, theater arts, world history, world history-AP, world literature, writing.

Graduation Requirements Arts and fine arts (art, music, dance, drama), English, foreign language, history, mathematics, physical education (includes health), science.

Special Academic Programs 19 Advanced Placement exams for which test preparation is offered; honors section.

College Admission Counseling 56 students graduated in 2011; all went to college, including Cornell University; Franklin & Marshall College; Georgetown University; New York University; The George Washington University; University of Notre Dame. Mean SAT critical reading: 626, mean SAT math: 621, mean SAT writing: 638, mean combined SAT: 1884.

Student Life Upper grades have specified standards of dress, student council, honor system. Discipline rests equally with students and faculty.

Summer Programs Enrichment, sports, art/fine arts, computer instruction programs offered; session focuses on mathematics and English; held on campus; accepts boys and girls; open to students from other schools. 200 students usually enrolled. 2012 schedule: July 1 to August 23. Application deadline: March 30.

Tuition and Aid Day student tuition: $21,650–$24,100. Tuition installment plan (Tuiton Management Systems (TMS)). Need-based scholarship grants, reduced tuition for children of employees available. In 2011–12, 6% of upper-school students received aid. Total amount of financial aid awarded in 2011–12: $139,000.

Admissions Traditional secondary-level entrance grade is 9. For fall 2011, 57 students applied for upper-level admission, 43 were accepted, 26 enrolled. ERB required. Deadline for receipt of application materials: none. Application fee required: $75. On-campus interview required.

Athletics Interscholastic: baseball (boys), basketball (b,g), cheering (g), field hockey (g), lacrosse (b,g), soccer (b,g), softball (g), tennis (b,g); coed interscholastic: aquatics, crew, cross-country running, golf, swimming and diving, track and field; coed intramural: aquatics, climbing, crew, dance team, fencing, fishing, fitness, ropes courses, running, squash, strength & conditioning, weight training. 6 PE instructors, 18 coaches, 1 athletic trainer.

Computers Computers are regularly used in all academic classes. Computer network features include on-campus library services, Internet access, wireless campus network, Internet filtering or blocking technology, 1:1 laptop program in grades 6-12. Campus intranet, student e-mail accounts, and computer access in designated common areas are available to students. The school has a published electronic and media policy.

Contact Joseph M. Tweed, Director of Admissions and Financial Aid. 732-542-4777 Ext. 1107. Fax: 732-460-1078. E-mail: jtweed@ranneyschool.org. Web site: www.ranneyschool.org.

See Display below and Close-Up on page 664.

RANSOM EVERGLADES SCHOOL

3575 Main Highway

Miami, Florida 33133

Head of School: Mrs. Ellen Y. Moceri

General Information Coeducational day college-preparatory school. Grades 6–12. Founded: 1903. Setting: urban. 11-acre campus. 19 buildings on campus. Approved or accredited by Southern Association of Colleges and Schools, Southern Association of Independent Schools, and Florida Department of Education. Member of National Association of Independent Schools and Secondary School Admission Test Board. Endowment: $23.2 million. Total enrollment: 1,079. Upper school average class size:

14. Upper school faculty-student ratio: 1:10. There are 175 required school days per year for Upper School students. Upper School students typically attend 5 days per week. The average school day consists of 7 hours and 30 minutes.
Upper School Student Profile Grade 9: 154 students (73 boys, 81 girls); Grade 10: 158 students (79 boys, 79 girls); Grade 11: 153 students (84 boys, 69 girls); Grade 12: 142 students (64 boys, 78 girls).
Faculty School total: 96. In upper school: 29 men, 26 women; 40 have advanced degrees.
Subjects Offered Advanced Placement courses, algebra, American history, American history-AP, American literature, anatomy and physiology, art, art history, art history-AP, Asian studies, astronomy, band, biology, calculus, calculus-AP, ceramics, chemistry, chemistry-AP, Chinese, choir, chorus, college counseling, comparative government and politics-AP, computer math, computer programming, computer science, computer science-AP, computer-aided design, concert band, creative writing, dance, dance performance, debate, digital photography, drama, earth science, ecology, economics, economics-AP, engineering, English, English literature, English literature and composition-AP, English-AP, environmental science, environmental science-AP, environmental studies, ethical decision making, ethics, ethics and responsibility, European history, European history-AP, experiential education, fine arts, French, French language-AP, French-AP, geography, geology, geometry, government and politics-AP, government/civics, grammar, graphic design, guitar, health, health and wellness, history, history-AP, human anatomy, interdisciplinary studies, jazz ensemble, journalism, macro/microeconomics-AP, macroeconomics-AP, Mandarin, marine biology, mathematics, mathematics-AP, music, music theory, music theory-AP, music-AP, mythology, philosophy, photography, physical education, physics, physics-AP, probability and statistics, psychology, psychology-AP, robotics, science, sculpture, social studies, sociology, Spanish, Spanish language-AP, Spanish literature-AP, speech, speech and debate, statistics, statistics-AP, theater, theory of knowledge, trigonometry, U.S. government and politics-AP, U.S. history, U.S. history-AP, world history, world history-AP, world literature, writing, yearbook.
Graduation Requirements Arts and fine arts (art, music, dance, drama), computer science, English, foreign language, mathematics, physical education (includes health), science, social studies (includes history).
Special Academic Programs 21 Advanced Placement exams for which test preparation is offered; honors section.
College Admission Counseling 141 students graduated in 2011; all went to college, including Georgetown University; New York University; Tufts University; University of Miami; University of Michigan; Vanderbilt University. Median SAT critical reading: 660, median SAT math: 690, median SAT writing: 680, median combined SAT: 2020, median composite ACT: 30.
Student Life Upper grades have specified standards of dress, student council, honor system. Discipline rests primarily with faculty.
Summer Programs Enrichment, advancement, computer instruction programs offered; session focuses on enrichment to reinforce basic skills and advancement for credit; held on campus; accepts boys and girls; open to students from other schools. 130 students usually enrolled. 2012 schedule: June 11 to July 20. Application deadline: June 6.
Tuition and Aid Day student tuition: $26,560. Tuition installment plan (monthly payment plans, 60%/40% payment plan). Need-based scholarship grants available. In 2011–12, 16% of upper-school students received aid. Total amount of financial aid awarded in 2011–12: $3,643,980.
Admissions Traditional secondary-level entrance grade is 9. For fall 2011, 144 students applied for upper-level admission, 23 were accepted, 15 enrolled. SSAT required. Deadline for receipt of application materials: December 1. Application fee required: $100. On-campus interview required.
Athletics Interscholastic: baseball (boys), basketball (b,g), canoeing/kayaking (b,g), cheering (g), crew (b,g), cross-country running (b,g), dance (g), dance team (g), football (b), golf (b,g), kayaking (b,g), lacrosse (b), physical training (b,g), sailing (b,g), soccer (b,g), softball (g), swimming and diving (b,g), tennis (b,g), track and field (b,g), volleyball (b,g), water polo (b,g), wrestling (b); coed interscholastic: crew, kayaking, sailing. 4 PE instructors, 80 coaches, 2 athletic trainers.
Computers Computers are regularly used in all classes. Computer network features include on-campus library services, online commercial services, Internet access, wireless campus network, Internet filtering or blocking technology. Student e-mail accounts and computer access in designated common areas are available to students. Students grades are available online. The school has a published electronic and media policy.
Contact Amy Sayfie, Director of Admission. 305-250-6875. Fax: 305-854-1846. E-mail: asayfie@ransomeverglades.org. Web site: www.ransomeverglades.org.

RAVENSCROFT SCHOOL

7409 Falls of the Neuse Road

Raleigh, North Carolina 27615

Head of School: Mrs. Doreen C. Kelly

General Information Coeducational day college-preparatory, arts, and technology school. Grades PK–12. Founded: 1862. Setting: suburban. 127-acre campus. 13 buildings on campus. Approved or accredited by Southern Association of Colleges and Schools, Southern Association of Independent Schools, and North Carolina Department of Education. Member of National Association of Independent Schools. Endowment: $15 million. Total enrollment: 1,237. Upper school average class size: 13. Upper school faculty-student ratio: 1:8. There are 179 required school days per year for Upper School students. Upper School students typically attend 5 days per week. The average school day consists of 7 hours and 10 minutes.
Upper School Student Profile Grade 9: 118 students (53 boys, 65 girls); Grade 10: 119 students (64 boys, 55 girls); Grade 11: 106 students (56 boys, 50 girls); Grade 12: 114 students (64 boys, 50 girls).
Faculty School total: 187. In upper school: 25 men, 30 women; 42 have advanced degrees.
Subjects Offered Advanced Placement courses, algebra, American history, American literature, anatomy, art, art history, astronomy, biology, biotechnology, calculus, chemistry, computer programming, computer science, discrete mathematics, drama, economics, engineering, English, English literature, environmental science, environmental science-AP, European history, expository writing, fine arts, French, geometry, government/civics, Greek, health, history, journalism, Latin, mathematics, music, photography, physical education, physics, psychology, science, social sciences, social studies, Spanish, speech, sports medicine, stagecraft, statistics-AP, theater, world history, writing.
Graduation Requirements Arts and fine arts (art, music, dance, drama), composition, English, foreign language, mathematics, physical education (includes health), science, social sciences, social studies (includes history). Community service is required.
Special Academic Programs 24 Advanced Placement exams for which test preparation is offered; honors section; independent study; term-away projects; study at local college for college credit; study abroad; academic accommodation for the gifted, the musically talented, and the artistically talented.
College Admission Counseling 103 students graduated in 2011; all went to college, including Clemson University; North Carolina State University; The University of North Carolina at Chapel Hill; The University of North Carolina Wilmington; University of Mississippi; University of South Carolina. Median SAT critical reading: 640, median SAT math: 650, median SAT writing: 650, median combined SAT: 1930, median composite ACT: 27. 58% scored over 600 on SAT critical reading, 74% scored over 600 on SAT math, 71% scored over 600 on SAT writing, 73% scored over 1800 on combined SAT, 51% scored over 26 on composite ACT.
Student Life Upper grades have specified standards of dress, student council, honor system. Discipline rests equally with students and faculty.
Summer Programs Enrichment, advancement, sports, art/fine arts, computer instruction programs offered; session focuses on enrichment; held on campus; accepts boys and girls; open to students from other schools. 2,000 students usually enrolled. 2012 schedule: June 11 to August 10. Application deadline: none.
Tuition and Aid Day student tuition: $18,750. Tuition installment plan (individually arranged payment plans). Merit scholarship grants, need-based scholarship grants, need-based loans available. In 2011–12, 7% of upper-school students received aid.
Admissions Traditional secondary-level entrance grade is 9. ERB and SSAT required. Deadline for receipt of application materials: none. Application fee required: $70. On-campus interview required.
Athletics Interscholastic: baseball (boys), basketball (b,g), cheering (g), cross-country running (b,g), dance squad (g), field hockey (g), fitness (b,g), football (b), golf (b,g), lacrosse (b,g), physical training (b,g), soccer (b,g), softball (g), strength & conditioning (b,g), swimming and diving (b,g), tennis (b,g), track and field (b,g), volleyball (g), weight training (b,g), wrestling (b); intramural: baseball (b), basketball (b,g), cheering (g), dance team (g), football (b,g), lacrosse (b), soccer (b,g), softball (g), strength & conditioning (b,g), swimming and diving (b,g), tennis (b,g), track and field (b,g), volleyball (g), wrestling (b); coed interscholastic: life saving. 10 PE instructors, 68 coaches, 2 athletic trainers.
Computers Computers are regularly used in economics, English, foreign language, history, mathematics, science, social studies, writing classes. Computer network features include on-campus library services, online commercial services, Internet access, wireless campus network, Internet filtering or blocking technology. Campus intranet, student e-mail accounts, and computer access in designated common areas are available to students. Students grades are available online. The school has a published electronic and media policy.
Contact Mrs. Pamela J. Jamison, Director of Admissions. 919-847-0900 Ext. 2226. Fax: 919-846-2371. E-mail: admissions@ravenscroft.org. Web site: www.ravenscroft.org.

REALMS OF INQUIRY

1140 South 900 East

Salt Lake City, Utah 84105

Head of School: Jochen Schmidt

General Information Coeducational day college-preparatory, general academic, arts, bilingual studies, and outdoor education school; primarily serves underachievers and gifted students. Grades 7–12. Founded: 1972. Setting: urban. 1-acre campus. 1 building on campus. Approved or accredited by Northwest Accreditation Commission and Utah Department of Education. Total enrollment: 22. Upper school average class size: 8.

Upper school faculty-student ratio: 1:10. There are 180 required school days per year for Upper School students. Upper School students typically attend 5 days per week. The average school day consists of 6 hours and 15 minutes.
Upper School Student Profile Grade 9: 1 student (1 boy); Grade 10: 3 students (2 boys, 1 girl); Grade 11: 4 students (3 boys, 1 girl); Grade 12: 5 students (3 boys, 2 girls).
Faculty School total: 5. In upper school: 3 men, 1 woman; 1 has an advanced degree.
Subjects Offered Algebra, art, band, biology, calculus, chemistry, computer literacy, drama, earth science, English, French, geometry, history, life skills, outdoor education, photography, physical education, physics, pre-calculus, Spanish, writing.
Graduation Requirements Arts and fine arts (art, music, dance, drama), computer science, English, foreign language, mathematics, outdoor education, physical education (includes health), science, social sciences, social studies (includes history), 30 volunteer service hours per year.
Special Academic Programs Accelerated programs; independent study; study at local college for college credit; study abroad; academic accommodation for the gifted, the musically talented, and the artistically talented; programs in English, mathematics, general development for dyslexic students.
College Admission Counseling 4 students graduated in 2011; 3 went to college, including University of Utah; Westminster College. Other: 1 had other specific plans. Median SAT critical reading: 690, median SAT math: 640, median SAT writing: 670, median combined SAT: 2000, median composite ACT: 28. 100% scored over 600 on SAT critical reading, 100% scored over 600 on SAT math, 100% scored over 600 on SAT writing, 100% scored over 1800 on combined SAT, 100% scored over 26 on composite ACT.
Student Life Upper grades have student council, honor system. Discipline rests equally with students and faculty.
Summer Programs Rigorous outdoor training programs offered; session focuses on climbing, rafting, wilderness skills; held both on and off campus; held at various locations; accepts boys and girls; open to students from other schools. 10 students usually enrolled.
Tuition and Aid Day student tuition: $16,210. Tuition installment plan (monthly payment plans). Tuition reduction for siblings, need-based scholarship grants available. In 2011–12, 40% of upper-school students received aid. Total amount of financial aid awarded in 2011–12: $40,000.
Admissions Traditional secondary-level entrance grade is 9. Admissions testing, WISC-III and Woodcock-Johnson, WISC/Woodcock-Johnson or Woodcock-Johnson required. Deadline for receipt of application materials: none. Application fee required: $25. On-campus interview required.
Athletics Coed Intramural: alpine skiing, aquatics, backpacking, basketball, bicycling, bowling, canoeing/kayaking, climbing, combined training, cooperative games, fitness, fitness walking, flag football, freestyle skiing, Frisbee, hiking/backpacking, ice skating, indoor soccer, jogging, jump rope, kayaking, kickball, life saving, martial arts, mountain biking, mountaineering, nordic skiing, outdoor activities, outdoor adventure, outdoor education, outdoor recreation, outdoor skills, outdoors, paint ball, physical fitness, physical training, project adventure, rafting, rappelling, rock climbing, ropes courses, running, scuba diving, skateboarding, ski jumping, skiing (cross-country), skiing (downhill), snowboarding, snowshoeing, soccer, softball, speleology, strength & conditioning, swimming and diving, telemark skiing, touch football, ultimate Frisbee, volleyball, walking, wall climbing, weight lifting, weight training, wilderness, wilderness survival, wildernessways, winter walking, yoga.
Computers Computers are regularly used in all academic, English, foreign language, history, mathematics, science classes. Computer network features include on-campus library services, Internet access, wireless campus network. Computer access in designated common areas is available to students. Students grades are available online. The school has a published electronic and media policy.
Contact Front Desk. 801-467-5911. Fax: 801-467-5932. E-mail: frontdesk@realmsofinquiry.org. Web site: www.realmsofinquiry.org.

THE RECTORY SCHOOL

Pomfret, Connecticut

See Junior Boarding Schools section.

REDWOOD ADVENTIST ACADEMY

385 Mark West Springs Road

Santa Rosa, California 95404

Head of School: Mr. Robert Fenderson

General Information Coeducational day college-preparatory school, affiliated with Seventh-day Adventists. Grades K–12. Founded: 1931. Setting: suburban. Nearest major city is San Francisco. 10-acre campus. 3 buildings on campus. Approved or accredited by Board of Regents, General Conference of Seventh-day Adventists, Western Association of Schools and Colleges, and California Department of Education. Total enrollment: 107. Upper school average class size: 18. Upper school faculty-student ratio: 1:6. There are 180 required school days per year for Upper School students. Upper School students typically attend 5 days per week. The average school day consists of 7 hours and 45 minutes.
Upper School Student Profile Grade 9: 13 students (5 boys, 8 girls); Grade 10: 7 students (3 boys, 4 girls); Grade 11: 11 students (6 boys, 5 girls); Grade 12: 8 students (3 boys, 5 girls). 81% of students are Seventh-day Adventists.
Faculty School total: 12. In upper school: 5 men, 2 women; 2 have advanced degrees.
Subjects Offered All academic.
Graduation Requirements Engineering.
Special Academic Programs Accelerated programs; study at local college for college credit.
College Admission Counseling 15 students graduated in 2010; 13 went to college, including La Sierra University; Pacific Union College; University of California, Davis; Walla Walla University. Other: 1 went to work.
Student Life Upper grades have specified standards of dress, student council, honor system. Discipline rests primarily with faculty.
Tuition and Aid Day student tuition: $9500. Tuition reduction for siblings, need-based scholarship grants, paying campus jobs available. In 2010–11, 24% of upper-school students received aid. Total amount of financial aid awarded in 2010–11: $50,000.
Admissions Traditional secondary-level entrance grade is 9. For fall 2010, 4 students applied for upper-level admission, 4 were accepted, 4 enrolled. TOEFL or WRAT required. Deadline for receipt of application materials: none. Application fee required: $30. Interview recommended.
Athletics Interscholastic: basketball (boys, girls), flag football (b,g), softball (b,g), volleyball (g); intramural: outdoor education (b,g), physical fitness (b,g). 1 PE instructor.
Computers Computers are regularly used in computer applications, desktop publishing, keyboarding, life skills, mathematics, Spanish, video film production, word processing, yearbook classes. Computer network features include Internet access, wireless campus network, Internet filtering or blocking technology. Computer access in designated common areas is available to students. Students grades are available online. The school has a published electronic and media policy.
Contact Mrs. Glenda Purdy, Registrar. 707-545-1697 Ext. 45. Fax: 707-545-8020. E-mail: glendapurdy@gmail.com. Web site: www.redwoodaa.com.

REDWOOD CHRISTIAN SCHOOLS

4200 James Avenue

Castro Valley, California 94546

Head of School: Mr. Bruce D. Johnson

General Information Coeducational day college-preparatory and religious studies school, affiliated with Christian faith. Grades K–12. Founded: 1970. Setting: urban. Nearest major city is Oakland. 10-acre campus. 11 buildings on campus. Approved or accredited by Association of Christian Schools International, Western Association of Schools and Colleges, and California Department of Education. Total enrollment: 648. Upper school average class size: 18. Upper school faculty-student ratio: 1:10. There are 175 required school days per year for Upper School students. Upper School students typically attend 5 days per week. The average school day consists of 6 hours and 50 minutes.
Upper School Student Profile Grade 6: 40 students (24 boys, 16 girls); Grade 7: 54 students (28 boys, 26 girls); Grade 8: 56 students (30 boys, 26 girls); Grade 9: 66 students (38 boys, 28 girls); Grade 10: 67 students (38 boys, 29 girls); Grade 11: 60 students (30 boys, 30 girls); Grade 12: 67 students (41 boys, 26 girls). 50% of students are Christian.
Faculty School total: 27. In upper school: 16 men, 11 women; 9 have advanced degrees.
Subjects Offered Advanced math, Advanced Placement courses, algebra, art, athletics, band, baseball, basketball, Bible studies, biology, chemistry, choir, computer literacy, concert band, drama, economics, English, European history-AP, fitness, geometry, honors English, keyboarding, macro/microeconomics-AP, physical education, physical science, physics, softball, Spanish, speech, track and field, trigonometry, U.S. government, U.S. history, vocal music, woodworking, world history, world history-AP, yearbook.
Graduation Requirements Arts and fine arts (art, music, dance, drama), Bible, computer literacy, electives, English, foreign language, mathematics, physical education (includes health), science, speech, world history.
Special Academic Programs Advanced Placement exam preparation; honors section; study at local college for college credit; remedial reading and/or remedial writing; remedial math; programs in English, mathematics, general development for dyslexic students; ESL (30 students enrolled).
College Admission Counseling 56 students graduated in 2011; 54 went to college, including Azusa Pacific University; California State University, East Bay; Seattle Pacific University; Simpson University; University of California, Davis; University of California, Irvine. Other: 2 went to work. Mean SAT critical reading: 610, mean SAT math: 627, mean SAT writing: 603, mean combined SAT: 1840. 50% scored over 600 on SAT critical reading, 52% scored over 600 on SAT math, 55% scored over 600 on SAT writing, 52% scored over 1800 on combined SAT.
Student Life Upper grades have specified standards of dress, student council, honor system. Discipline rests primarily with faculty.
Tuition and Aid Day student tuition: $10,362. Tuition installment plan (monthly payment plans, individually arranged payment plans). Tuition reduction for siblings,

merit scholarship grants, need-based scholarship grants, paying campus jobs available. In 2011–12, 65% of upper-school students received aid; total upper-school merit-scholarship money awarded: $356,524. Total amount of financial aid awarded in 2011–12: $356,524.

Admissions Traditional secondary-level entrance grade is 9. For fall 2011, 76 students applied for upper-level admission, 74 were accepted, 58 enrolled. Stanford Achievement Test required. Deadline for receipt of application materials: none. Application fee required: $125. On-campus interview required.

Athletics Interscholastic: baseball (boys), basketball (b,g), cross-country running (b,g), soccer (b,g), softball (g), tennis (b,g), track and field (b,g), volleyball (b,g). 2 PE instructors, 1 coach.

Computers Computers are regularly used in computer applications, keyboarding, yearbook classes. Computer network features include on-campus library services, Internet access. Campus intranet is available to students. Students grades are available online. The school has a published electronic and media policy.

Contact Mrs. Deborah Wright, Administrative Assistant. 510-889-7526. Fax: 510-881-0127. E-mail: deborahwright@rcs.edu. Web site: www.rcs.edu.

REGIS HIGH SCHOOL

55 East 84th Street

New York, New York 10028-0884

Head of School: Dr. Gary J. Tocchet

General Information Boys' day college-preparatory school, affiliated with Roman Catholic Church. Grades 9–12. Founded: 1914. Setting: urban. 3-acre campus. 1 building on campus. Approved or accredited by Jesuit Secondary Education Association, Middle States Association of Colleges and Schools, and New York Department of Education. Total enrollment: 530. Upper school average class size: 14. Upper school faculty-student ratio: 1:15. There are 180 required school days per year for Upper School students. Upper School students typically attend 5 days per week. The average school day consists of 6 hours and 50 minutes.

Upper School Student Profile Grade 9: 136 students (136 boys); Grade 10: 133 students (133 boys); Grade 11: 133 students (133 boys); Grade 12: 128 students (128 boys). 100% of students are Roman Catholic.

Faculty School total: 61. In upper school: 41 men, 20 women; 57 have advanced degrees.

Subjects Offered Algebra, American history, American literature, art, art history, band, biology, calculus, chemistry, Chinese, computer programming, computer science, creative writing, drama, driver education, economics, English, English literature, ethics, European history, expository writing, film, French, geometry, German, health, history, Latin, mathematics, music, physical education, physics, psychology, social studies, Spanish, speech, statistics, theater, theology, trigonometry, writing.

Graduation Requirements Art, computer literacy, English, foreign language, history, mathematics, music, physical education (includes health), science, theology, Christian service program.

Special Academic Programs 14 Advanced Placement exams for which test preparation is offered; independent study; study abroad.

College Admission Counseling 135 students graduated in 2011; all went to college, including Boston College; College of the Holy Cross; Cornell University; Fordham University; Georgetown University; Villanova University. Mean SAT critical reading: 713, mean SAT math: 713, mean SAT writing: 719, mean combined SAT: 2145.

Student Life Upper grades have specified standards of dress, student council. Discipline rests primarily with faculty. Attendance at religious services is required.

Tuition and Aid Tuition-free school available.

Admissions Traditional secondary-level entrance grade is 9. For fall 2011, 795 students applied for upper-level admission, 143 were accepted, 136 enrolled. Admissions testing required. Deadline for receipt of application materials: October 21. Application fee required: $50. On-campus interview required.

Athletics Interscholastic: baseball, basketball, cross-country running, volleyball; intramural: basketball, flag football, floor hockey, indoor hockey, indoor soccer. 2 PE instructors, 10 coaches.

Computers Computers are regularly used in all academic classes. Computer network features include on-campus library services, Internet access, wireless campus network, Internet filtering or blocking technology. Campus intranet, student e-mail accounts, and computer access in designated common areas are available to students.

Contact Mr. Eric P. DiMichele, Director of Admissions. 212-288-1100 Ext. 2057. Fax: 212-794-1221. E-mail: edimiche@regis-nyc.org. Web site: www.regis-nyc.org.

REITZ MEMORIAL HIGH SCHOOL

1500 Lincoln Avenue

Evansville, Indiana 47714

Head of School: Cynthia Schneider

General Information Coeducational day college-preparatory, arts, business, religious studies, and technology school, affiliated with Roman Catholic Church. Grades 9–12. Founded: 1925. Setting: urban. Nearest major city is Indianapolis. 2 buildings on campus. Approved or accredited by National Catholic Education Association, North Central Association of Colleges and Schools, The College Board, and Indiana Department of Education. Total enrollment: 781. Upper school average class size: 25. Upper school faculty-student ratio: 1:14. There are 180 required school days per year for Upper School students. Upper School students typically attend 5 days per week. The average school day consists of 7 hours and 15 minutes.

Upper School Student Profile Grade 9: 176 students (92 boys, 84 girls); Grade 10: 211 students (107 boys, 104 girls); Grade 11: 204 students (110 boys, 94 girls); Grade 12: 190 students (93 boys, 97 girls). 85% of students are Roman Catholic.

Faculty School total: 52. In upper school: 17 men, 35 women; 37 have advanced degrees.

Subjects Offered 20th century American writers, 20th century history, 3-dimensional art, accounting, advanced biology, advanced chemistry, advanced computer applications, Advanced Placement courses, algebra, American government, American history, American literature, anatomy, anatomy and physiology, anthropology, applied music, art, art appreciation, art history, band, Basic programming, biology, biology-AP, botany, British literature, business, business communications, business law, business skills, calculus, calculus-AP, Catholic belief and practice, ceramics, chemistry, chemistry-AP, choir, choral music, chorus, church history, commercial art, composition, computer applications, computer programming, computer skills, concert band, concert choir, consumer economics, current events, digital photography, dramatic arts, drawing, drawing and design, driver education, earth and space science, earth science, ecology, environmental systems, English, English composition, English literature and composition-AP, English-AP, entomology, environmental science, environmental studies, etymology, fitness, foreign language, forensics, French, French language-AP, French-AP, geometry, German, government, grammar, guitar, health and wellness, history of the Catholic Church, honors algebra, honors English, honors geometry, honors U.S. history, honors world history, instrumental music, integrated physics, jewelry making, journalism, keyboarding, law, law and the legal system, library assistant, Life of Christ, literary genres, literature, marching band, media arts, moral theology, music appreciation, music composition, music history, New Testament, newspaper, oil painting, orchestra, painting, peace and justice, personal finance, photography, physical education, physics, physics-AP, physiology, piano, play production, portfolio art, prayer/spirituality, pre-calculus, printmaking, psychology, publications, SAT/ACT preparation, social justice, sociology, Spanish, Spanish language-AP, Spanish-AP, sports conditioning, state history, studio art, theater, theater arts, theater design and production, theology, trigonometry, U.S. history, Web site design, weight fitness, weight training, world history, world history-AP, yearbook.

Graduation Requirements Service hours.

Special Academic Programs 8 Advanced Placement exams for which test preparation is offered; honors section; study at local college for college credit.

College Admission Counseling 184 students graduated in 2011; 171 went to college, including Indiana University Bloomington; Purdue University; University of Evansville; University of Kentucky; University of Mississippi; Western Kentucky University. Other: 3 went to work, 3 entered military service, 7 entered a postgraduate year. Mean SAT critical reading: 522, mean SAT math: 540, mean SAT writing: 526, mean combined SAT: 1588, mean composite ACT. 24.

Student Life Upper grades have uniform requirement, student council. Discipline rests primarily with faculty. Attendance at religious services is required.

Summer Programs Remediation, sports programs offered; held both on and off campus; held at city-owned local schools and fields; accepts boys and girls; open to students from other schools. 400 students usually enrolled. 2012 schedule: May 26 to July 31.

Tuition and Aid Day student tuition: $4500–$7050. Tuition installment plan (monthly payment plans, ETFCU Loans). Tuition reduction for siblings, need-based scholarship grants, need-based loans available. In 2011–12, 12% of upper-school students received aid. Total amount of financial aid awarded in 2011–12: $264,840.

Admissions Traditional secondary-level entrance grade is 9. For fall 2011, 781 students applied for upper-level admission, 781 were accepted, 781 enrolled. ACT-Explore required. Deadline for receipt of application materials: none. Application fee required: $180.

Athletics Interscholastic: baseball (boys), basketball (b,g), cheering (g), dance squad (g), dance team (g), diving (b,g), drill team (g), football (b), golf (b,g), soccer (b,g), softball (g), swimming and diving (b,g), tennis (b,g), track and field (b,g), volleyball (g), weight training (b), wrestling (b); intramural: bowling (b,g), lacrosse (b,g), paint ball (b); coed interscholastic: cross-country running; coed intramural: ice hockey, table tennis. 4 PE instructors, 1 athletic trainer.

Computers Computers are regularly used in all classes. Computer network features include on-campus library services, Internet access, wireless campus network, Internet filtering or blocking technology. Campus intranet and computer access in designated common areas are available to students. Students grades are available online. The school has a published electronic and media policy.

Contact Mrs. Lisa Popham, Assistant Principal. 812-476-4973 Ext. 205. Fax: 812-474-2942. E-mail: lisapopham@reitzmemorial.org. Web site: www.reitzmemorial.org.

REJOICE CHRISTIAN SCHOOLS

12200 East 86th Street North

Owasso, Oklahoma 74055

Head of School: Dr. Craig D. Shaw

General Information Coeducational day college-preparatory school, affiliated with Free Will Baptist Church. Grades P3–12. Founded: 1992. Setting: suburban. Nearest major city is Tulsa. 1 building on campus. Approved or accredited by Association of Christian Schools International and Oklahoma Department of Education. Total enrollment: 713. Upper school average class size: 12. Upper school faculty-student ratio: 1:12.

Upper School Student Profile Grade 6: 36 students (14 boys, 22 girls); Grade 7: 40 students (17 boys, 23 girls); Grade 8: 37 students (20 boys, 17 girls); Grade 9: 35 students (14 boys, 21 girls); Grade 10: 17 students (8 boys, 9 girls); Grade 11: 17 students (10 boys, 7 girls); Grade 12: 15 students (9 boys, 6 girls). 30% of students are Free Will Baptist Church.

Faculty School total: 22. In upper school: 5 men, 17 women; 8 have advanced degrees.

Subjects Offered Advanced biology, advanced chemistry, Advanced Placement courses, algebra, American democracy, American government, American history, American history-AP, anatomy, anatomy and physiology, art, art appreciation, art education, art history, athletic training, athletics, band, basketball, Bible, Bible studies, biology, biology-AP, business, business education, calculus, calculus-AP, cheerleading, chemistry, chemistry-AP, choir, chorus, Christian education, civics, computer skills, electives, English, English language-AP, English literature and composition-AP, English literature-AP, English-AP, English/composition-AP, fitness, general business, general math, geography, geometry, golf, government, government and politics-AP, government-AP, government/civics, government/civics-AP, history, honors algebra, honors English, honors geometry, honors U.S. history, honors world history, journalism, language, language arts, library, mathematics, mathematics-AP, media, music, novels, physical education, physical fitness, physical science, pre-algebra, pre-calculus, Spanish, Spanish language-AP, speech, speech and debate, sports, sports conditioning, state history, technology, track and field, trigonometry, U.S. government, U.S. government and politics-AP, U.S. history, U.S. history-AP, weight training, world history, world history-AP, yearbook.

Special Academic Programs Honors section; study at local college for college credit.

Student Life Upper grades have student council, honor system. Discipline rests primarily with faculty.

Tuition and Aid Tuition installment plan (SMART Tuition Payment Plan, monthly payment plans). Need-based scholarship grants available.

Admissions Gates MacGinite Reading Tests, Gates MacGinite Reading/Key Math or Stanford Achievement Test required. Deadline for receipt of application materials: none. Application fee required: $160. Interview required.

Athletics Interscholastic: basketball (boys, girls), cheering (g), cross-country running (b,g), fitness (b,g), flag football (b,g), football (b), golf (b,g), jogging (b,g), outdoor activities (b,g), outdoor recreation (b,g), physical fitness (b,g), physical training (b,g), ropes courses (b,g), running (b,g), strength & conditioning (b,g), track and field (b,g), volleyball (g), weight lifting (b), weight training (b,g). 2 PE instructors, 15 coaches, 2 athletic trainers.

Computers Computers are regularly used in English, journalism, library, media, newspaper, yearbook classes. Computer network features include on-campus library services, Internet access, wireless campus network, Internet filtering or blocking technology. Campus intranet is available to students. Students grades are available online. The school has a published electronic and media policy.

Contact Mrs. Julie Long, High School Registrar. 918-516-0050. Fax: 918-516-0299. E-mail: jlong@rejoiceschool.com. Web site: www.rejoiceschool.com.

RIDLEY COLLEGE

2 Ridley Road

St. Catharines, Ontario L2R7C3, Canada

Head of School: Mr. Jonathan Leigh

General Information Coeducational boarding and day college-preparatory, arts, business, and technology school, affiliated with Church of England (Anglican). Boarding grades 5–PG, day grades JK–PG. Founded: 1889. Setting: suburban. Nearest major city is Buffalo, NY. Students are housed in single-sex dormitories. 100-acre campus. 13 buildings on campus. Approved or accredited by Canadian Association of Independent Schools, Canadian Educational Standards Institute, Conference of Independent Schools of Ontario, The Association of Boarding Schools, and Ontario Department of Education. Affiliate member of National Association of Independent Schools; member of Secondary School Admission Test Board. Language of instruction: English. Endowment: CAN$25 million. Total enrollment: 591. Upper school average class size: 17. Upper school faculty-student ratio: 1:7. There are 222 required school days per year for Upper School students. Upper School students typically attend 6 days per week. The average school day consists of 6 hours.

Upper School Student Profile Grade 9: 69 students (39 boys, 30 girls); Grade 10: 91 students (48 boys, 43 girls); Grade 11: 111 students (70 boys, 41 girls); Grade 12: 139 students (67 boys, 72 girls); Postgraduate: 6 students (6 boys). 61% of students are boarding students. 62% are province residents. 17 provinces are represented in upper school student body. 36% are international students. International students from China, Germany, Hong Kong, Mexico, Republic of Korea, and United States; 25 other countries represented in student body. 20% of students are members of Church of England (Anglican).

Faculty School total: 70. In upper school: 40 men, 30 women; 27 have advanced degrees; 40 reside on campus.

Subjects Offered Accounting, Advanced Placement courses, algebra, American history, anthropology, art, art history, biology, business mathematics, business skills, calculus, Canadian history, Canadian law, chemistry, computer programming, computer science, creative writing, drafting, drama, dramatic arts, driver education, economics, English, English literature, ESL, fine arts, French, geography, German, kinesiology, Latin, Mandarin, mathematics, music, physical education, physics, science, social sciences, social studies, Spanish, theater, world history.

Graduation Requirements Arts and fine arts (art, music, dance, drama), business skills (includes word processing), English, foreign language, mathematics, physical education (includes health), science, social sciences, social studies (includes history).

Special Academic Programs 12 Advanced Placement exams for which test preparation is offered; honors section; independent study; study abroad; academic accommodation for the musically talented and the artistically talented; ESL (20 students enrolled).

College Admission Counseling 150 students graduated in 2011; 140 went to college, including Brock University; Queen's University at Kingston; The University of British Columbia; The University of Western Ontario; University of Toronto; University of Waterloo. Other: 4 entered a postgraduate year, 6 had other specific plans. Mean SAT critical reading: 570, mean SAT math: 590.

Student Life Upper grades have uniform requirement, student council, honor system. Discipline rests primarily with faculty. Attendance at religious services is required.

Tuition and Aid Day student tuition: CAN$26,200; 5-day tuition and room/board: CAN$34,500; 7-day tuition and room/board: CAN$46,250. Tuition installment plan (monthly payment plans, individually arranged payment plans). Bursaries, merit scholarship grants, need-based scholarship grants, need-based loans available. In 2011–12, 38% of upper-school students received aid; total upper-school merit-scholarship money awarded: CAN$300,000. Total amount of financial aid awarded in 2011–12: CAN$3,000,000.

Admissions Traditional secondary-level entrance grade is 9. For fall 2011, 287 students applied for upper-level admission, 203 were accepted, 138 enrolled. Deadline for receipt of application materials: none. Application fee required: CAN$150. Interview required.

Athletics Interscholastic: aerobics/dance (girls), artistic gym (g), baseball (b,g), basketball (b,g), crew (b,g), cross-country running (b,g), dance (g), dance squad (g), dance team (g), field hockey (g), fitness walking (g), gymnastics (g), hockey (b,g), ice hockey (b,g), rowing (b,g), rugby (b,g), running (b,g), soccer (b,g), softball (b,g), squash (b,g), swimming and diving (b,g), tennis (b,g), track and field (b,g), volleyball (g); intramural: aerobics (g), aerobics/dance (g), ball hockey (b), ballet (g), Cosom hockey (g), hockey (b,g), ice hockey (b,g), running (b,g); coed interscholastic: golf, tennis; coed intramural: alpine skiing, aquatics, backpacking, badminton, baseball, basketball, bicycling, bowling, canoeing/kayaking, climbing, cooperative games, curling, drill team, equestrian sports, fencing, fitness, Frisbee, golf, hiking/backpacking, horseback riding, ice skating, jogging, life saving, martial arts, modern dance, outdoor activities, outdoor education, outdoor recreation, outdoor skills, physical fitness, physical training, power lifting, racquetball, rock climbing, ropes courses, sailing, scuba diving, self defense, skiing (cross-country), skiing (downhill), snowboarding, snowshoeing, soccer, softball, squash, strength & conditioning, swimming and diving, table tennis, tennis, track and field, trap and skeet, ultimate Frisbee, volleyball, walking, wall climbing, weight lifting, weight training, yoga. 8 coaches, 3 athletic trainers.

Computers Computers are regularly used in all academic classes. Computer network features include on-campus library services, online commercial services, Internet access, wireless campus network, Internet filtering or blocking technology. Student e-mail accounts are available to students. Students grades are available online. The school has a published electronic and media policy.

Contact Mrs. Stephanie Park, Admissions Administrative Assistant. 905-684-1889 Ext. 2207. Fax: 905-684-8875. E-mail: admissions@ridleycollege.com. Web site: www.ridleycollege.com.

See Display on next page and Close-Up on page 666.

RINCON VALLEY CHRISTIAN SCHOOL

4585 Badger Road

Santa Rosa, California 95409

Head of School: Mr. Brent Mitten

General Information Coeducational day college-preparatory school. Founded: 1970. Setting: suburban. Approved or accredited by Association of Christian Schools International, Western Association of Schools and Colleges, and California Department of Education. Total enrollment: 270.

College Admission Counseling 29 students graduated in 2011; all went to college.

Tuition and Aid Day student tuition: $7620.

Admissions Any standardized test required. Deadline for receipt of application materials: none. Application fee required: $25. Interview required.

Contact Carol MacLeod, Registrar. 707-539-1486. Fax: 707-539-1493. E-mail: registrar@rvchristian.org. Web site: www.rvchristian.org.

RIO HONDO PREPARATORY SCHOOL

5150 Farna Avenue

PO Box 662080

Arcadia, California 91066-2080

Head of School: Mrs. Leslie Orsburn

General Information Coeducational day college-preparatory and arts school. Grades 6–12. Founded: 1964. Setting: suburban. Nearest major city is Los Angeles. 6-acre campus. 5 buildings on campus. Approved or accredited by Western Association of Schools and Colleges and California Department of Education. Total enrollment: 187. Upper school average class size: 24. Upper school faculty-student ratio: 1:4. Upper School students typically attend 5 days per week. The average school day consists of 6 hours.

Upper School Student Profile Grade 6: 16 students (10 boys, 6 girls); Grade 7: 26 students (17 boys, 9 girls); Grade 8: 19 students (10 boys, 9 girls); Grade 9: 34 students (17 boys, 17 girls); Grade 10: 25 students (16 boys, 9 girls); Grade 11: 22 students (11 boys, 11 girls); Grade 12: 19 students (8 boys, 11 girls).

Faculty School total: 28. In upper school: 13 men, 9 women; 4 have advanced degrees.

Subjects Offered Advanced biology, Advanced Placement courses, algebra, American history, American history-AP, American literature, art, art appreciation, astronomy, athletics, band, baseball, basketball, bell choir, biology, biology-AP, calculus, calculus-AP, chemistry, chorus, college planning, comparative government and politics-AP, computer applications, driver education, earth science, economics, English, English literature, English literature and composition-AP, ESL, European history, fine arts, geology, geometry, government/civics, history, instrumental music, Internet research, Latin, mathematics, music, physical education, physics, physiology, psychology, psychology-AP, reading, science, social studies, softball, Spanish, statistics, theater production, travel, world history, yearbook.

Graduation Requirements Arts and fine arts (art, music, dance, drama), English, foreign language, mathematics, physical education (includes health), science, social studies (includes history), participation in one school summer tour (U.S. or Europe).

Special Academic Programs Advanced Placement exam preparation; honors section; study abroad; ESL (3 students enrolled).

College Admission Counseling 19 students graduated in 2010; all went to college, including California State Polytechnic University, Pomona; California State University, Fullerton; California State University, Long Beach; Citrus College; Pasadena City College; Penn State University Park. Median composite ACT: 20. Mean SAT critical reading: 457, mean SAT math: 517, mean SAT writing: 458, mean combined SAT: 1432.

Student Life Upper grades have uniform requirement, student council, honor system. Discipline rests equally with students and faculty.

Tuition and Aid Day student tuition: $8175. Tuition installment plan (individually arranged payment plans). Tuition reduction for siblings, need-based scholarship grants available. In 2010–11, 20% of upper-school students received aid.

Admissions Traditional secondary-level entrance grade is 9. Iowa Tests of Basic Skills required. Deadline for receipt of application materials: April 1. Application fee required: $25. On-campus interview required.

Athletics Interscholastic: baseball (boys), basketball (b,g), cheering (g), football (b), soccer (b,g), softball (g). 2 PE instructors, 5 coaches, 1 athletic trainer.

Computers Computers are regularly used in design, English, ESL, history, keyboarding, mathematics, science, word processing, writing, yearbook classes. Computer network features include on-campus library services, Internet access, wireless campus network, Internet filtering or blocking technology. Students grades are available online.

Contact Dina Loomis, Admissions Office. 626-444-9531. Fax: 626-442-1113. Web site: www.rhprep.org.

RIPON CHRISTIAN SCHOOLS

435 North Maple Avenue

Ripon, California 95366

Head of School: Mrs. Mary Ann Sybesma

General Information Coeducational day college-preparatory, arts, business, vocational, religious studies, and technology school, affiliated with Calvinist faith; primarily serves students with learning disabilities. Grades K–12. Founded: 1946. Setting: small town. Nearest major city is San Francisco. 34-acre campus. 5 buildings on campus. Approved or accredited by Association of Christian Schools International, Christian Schools International, Western Association of Schools and Colleges, and California Department of Education. Endowment: $2.5 million. Total enrollment: 659. Upper school average class size: 22. Upper school faculty-student ratio: 1:18. There are 175 required school days per year for Upper School students. Upper School students typically attend 5 days per week. The average school day consists of 6 hours and 40 minutes.

Upper School Student Profile 50% of students are Calvinist.

Faculty School total: 47. In upper school: 10 men, 11 women; 10 have advanced degrees.

Subjects Offered 20th century American writers, accounting, advanced computer applications, algebra, American history, anatomy and physiology, animal science, art, band, Bible studies, biology, business, business mathematics, calculus, calculus-AP, ceramics, chemistry, choir, computer applications, computer education, computer science, computer-aided design, drafting, English, English language and composition-AP, English literature and composition-AP, environmental education, environmental science, ethics, family living, fine arts, geography, geometry, government/civics, grammar, health, history, keyboarding, leadership, life skills, mathematics, music, physical education, physics, psychology, science, social sciences, social studies, Spanish, Spanish-AP, U.S. history-AP, weightlifting, welding, woodworking, world history, yearbook.

Graduation Requirements Computer science, English, mathematics, physical education (includes health), religion (includes Bible studies and theology), science, social sciences, social studies (includes history), 10 service hours per semester are required of all students.

Special Academic Programs 4 Advanced Placement exams for which test preparation is offered; independent study; academic accommodation for the musically talented and the artistically talented; remedial math.

College Admission Counseling 55 students graduated in 2011; 52 went to college, including Azusa Pacific University; California Polytechnic State University, San Luis Obispo; California State University, Stanislaus; Dordt College; Modesto Junior College; Trinity Christian College. Other: 1 went to work, 2 entered military service.

Student Life Upper grades have specified standards of dress, student council. Discipline rests primarily with faculty. Attendance at religious services is required.

Tuition and Aid Day student tuition: $8150. Tuition installment plan (FACTS Tuition Payment Plan, individually arranged payment plans, 1-payment plan, biannual payment plan, quarterly payment plan). Tuition reduction for siblings, need-based scholarship grants, need-based financial assistance, TRIP program available. In 2011–12, 10% of upper-school students received aid. Total amount of financial aid awarded in 2011–12: $20,000.

Admissions Traditional secondary-level entrance grade is 9. For fall 2011, 16 students applied for upper-level admission, 14 were accepted, 14 enrolled. Kaufman Test of Educational Achievement or Woodcock-Johnson required. Deadline for receipt of application materials: none. No application fee required. On-campus interview required.

Athletics Interscholastic: baseball (boys), basketball (b,g), football (b), golf (b,g), physical fitness (b,g), physical training (b,g), soccer (b,g), softball (g), tennis (b,g), volleyball (g), weight training (b,g); intramural: indoor soccer (b); coed interscholastic: tennis; coed intramural: tennis. 2 PE instructors, 15 coaches.

Computers Computers are regularly used in business skills classes. Computer network features include on-campus library services, Internet access, wireless campus network, Internet filtering or blocking technology. Students grades are available online. The school has a published electronic and media policy.

Contact Mrs. Mary Ann Sybesma, Principal. 209-599-2155. Fax: 209-599-2170. E-mail: msybesma@rcschools.com. Web site: www.rcschools.com.

RIVERDALE COUNTRY SCHOOL

5250 Fieldston Road

Bronx, New York 10471-2999

Head of School: Dominic A.A. Randolph

General Information Coeducational day college-preparatory school. Grades PK–12. Founded: 1907. Setting: suburban. Nearest major city is New York. 27-acre campus. 9 buildings on campus. Approved or accredited by New York Department of Education. Member of National Association of Independent Schools and Secondary School Admission Test Board. Endowment: $56 million. Total enrollment: 1,138. Upper school average class size: 16. Upper school faculty-student ratio: 1:8. Upper School students typically attend 5 days per week.

Faculty School total: 185.

Subjects Offered Algebra, American literature, anatomy, art, art history, biology, calculus, ceramics, chemistry, community service, computer math, computer programming, computer science, creative writing, drama, driver education, earth science, ecology, economics, English, English literature, environmental science, European history, expository writing, fine arts, French, geology, geometry, government/civics, grammar, health, history, history of science, introduction to liberal studies, Japanese, journalism, Latin, Mandarin, marine biology, mathematics, music, oceanography, philosophy, photography, physical education, physics, psychology, science, social studies, Spanish, speech, statistics, theater, theory of knowledge, trigonometry, world history, writing.

Graduation Requirements American studies, arts and fine arts (art, music, dance, drama), computer science, English, foreign language, mathematics, physical education (includes health), science, social studies (includes history), integrated liberal studies. Community service is required.

Special Academic Programs Honors section; independent study; term-away projects; study abroad; academic accommodation for the gifted, the musically talented, and the artistically talented.

College Admission Counseling 117 students graduated in 2011; all went to college, including Cornell University; Dartmouth College; Duke University; Harvard University; Stanford University; Yale University.

Student Life Upper grades have student council, honor system. Discipline rests equally with students and faculty.

Summer Programs Enrichment programs offered; session focuses on science research; held on campus; accepts boys and girls; not open to students from other schools.

Tuition and Aid Day student tuition: $40,450. Tuition installment plan (monthly payment plans). Need-based scholarship grants available. In 2011–12, 20% of upper-school students received aid.

Admissions Traditional secondary-level entrance grade is 9. ISEE or SSAT required. Deadline for receipt of application materials: November 15. Application fee required: $60. On-campus interview required.

Athletics Interscholastic: baseball (boys), basketball (b,g), field hockey (g), football (b), gymnastics (g), lacrosse (b,g), soccer (b,g), softball (g), tennis (b,g), volleyball (g), wrestling (b); intramural: baseball (b), basketball (b,g), field hockey (g), football (b), gymnastics (g), lacrosse (b,g), soccer (b,g), softball (g), tennis (b,g), volleyball (g), wrestling (b); coed interscholastic: cross-country running, fencing, golf, squash, swimming and diving, track and field, ultimate Frisbee; coed intramural: cross-country running, dance, fencing, fitness, physical fitness, squash, swimming and diving, tennis, track and field, ultimate Frisbee, yoga. 7 PE instructors, 31 coaches, 1 athletic trainer.

Computers Computers are regularly used in art, English, foreign language, history, mathematics, music, science classes. Computer network features include on-campus library services, online commercial services, Internet access, wireless campus network, Internet filtering or blocking technology, off-campus email, off-campus library services. Student e-mail accounts and computer access in designated common areas are available to students. The school has a published electronic and media policy.

Contact Jenna Rogers King, Director of Middle and Upper School Admission. 718-519-2715. Fax: 718-519-2793. E-mail: jrking@riverdale.edu. Web site: www.riverdale.edu.

RIVERFIELD ACADEMY

115 Wood Street

Rayville, Louisiana 71269

Head of School: Marie D. Miller

General Information Coeducational day college-preparatory school. Founded: 1970. Setting: small town. Nearest major city is Monroe. 15-acre campus. 5 buildings on campus. Approved or accredited by Louisiana Department of Education. Language of instruction: Spanish. Total enrollment: 280. Upper school faculty-student ratio: 1:10. There are 180 required school days per year for Upper School students. Upper School students typically attend 5 days per week. The average school day consists of 7 hours and 10 minutes.

Upper School Student Profile Grade 6: 18 students (12 boys, 6 girls); Grade 7: 15 students (10 boys, 5 girls); Grade 8: 27 students (9 boys, 18 girls); Grade 9: 23 students (10 boys, 13 girls); Grade 10: 34 students (18 boys, 16 girls); Grade 11: 23 students (12 boys, 11 girls); Grade 12: 22 students (11 boys, 11 girls).

Faculty School total: 25. In upper school: 5 men, 5 women; 5 have advanced degrees.

Special Academic Programs International Baccalaureate program.

College Admission Counseling 34 students graduated in 2010; 32 went to college. Other: 2 went to work.

Student Life Upper grades have specified standards of dress, student council. Discipline rests primarily with faculty.

Admissions For fall 2010, 149 students applied for upper-level admission, 14 were accepted, 14 enrolled. Deadline for receipt of application materials: August 16. No application fee required. Interview recommended.

Athletics Interscholastic: baseball (boys), basketball (b), softball (g), tennis (b,g). 4 PE instructors, 4 coaches, 1 athletic trainer.

Computers Computer network features include on-campus library services, Internet access, wireless campus network. Campus intranet and computer access in designated common areas are available to students.

Contact Karen Smith, Secretary. 318-728-3281. Fax: 318-728-3285. Web site: riverfieldacademy.net.

RIVERMONT COLLEGIATE

1821 Sunset Drive

Bettendorf, Iowa 52722

Head of School: Mr. Richard E. St. Laurent

General Information Coeducational day college-preparatory, arts, and technology school. Grades PS–12. Founded: 1884. Setting: suburban. Nearest major city is Davenport. 16-acre campus. 4 buildings on campus. Approved or accredited by Independent

Schools Association of the Central States and Iowa Department of Education. Member of National Association of Independent Schools and Secondary School Admission Test Board. Total enrollment: 192. Upper school average class size: 9. Upper school faculty-student ratio: 1:2. Upper School students typically attend 5 days per week.

Faculty School total: 31. In upper school: 4 men, 14 women; 6 have advanced degrees.

Subjects Offered Acting, advanced chemistry, advanced math, Advanced Placement courses, algebra, animation, art, arts, band, basketball, biology, biology-AP, calculus, calculus-AP, character education, cheerleading, chemistry, chemistry-AP, Chinese, choir, choral music, chorus, college counseling, college writing, computer animation, computer graphics, computer multimedia, computer programming, computer science, concert band, concert choir, creative drama, creative writing, desktop publishing, digital photography, drama, drama performance, drama workshop, dramatic arts, drawing, drawing and design, earth science, economics, English, English language and composition-AP, English literature, English literature and composition-AP, English-AP, environmental science-AP, fine arts, foreign language, French, French language-AP, French literature-AP, French-AP, geography, geometry, global science, government/civics, guidance, health, health education, Hispanic literature, history, history-AP, honors algebra, honors English, HTML design, human biology, humanities, independent study, instrumental music, Latin, Latin American literature, life science, literature and composition-AP, macro/microeconomics-AP, mathematics, media, media arts, microeconomics, Middle East, model United Nations, multimedia, multimedia design, music, music theater, musical productions, musical theater, oral communications, performing arts, photography, physical education, physical fitness, physics, physics-AP, play production, pre-algebra, pre-calculus, probability and statistics, psychology, psychology-AP, public speaking, science, science project, science research, senior career experience, senior internship, senior project, service learning/internship, social studies, Spanish, Spanish language-AP, Spanish literature, Spanish literature-AP, Spanish-AP, speech, speech and debate, stage design, statistics-AP, studio art, symphonic band, theater, theater arts, theater design and production, theater production, U.S. government, U.S. government and politics, U.S. government and politics-AP, U.S. history, U.S. history-AP, United States government-AP, visual and performing arts, visual arts, vocal ensemble, voice, Web site design, wilderness education, wilderness experience, wind ensemble, wind instruments, world history, world history-AP, writing, yearbook.

Graduation Requirements Senior Project/Internship, Junior Service Project.

Special Academic Programs Advanced Placement exam preparation; honors section; independent study; study at local college for college credit; academic accommodation for the gifted, the musically talented, and the artistically talented.

College Admission Counseling 11 students graduated in 2011; they went to Case Western Reserve University; Philadelphia Biblical University; Pratt Institute; The University of Iowa; University of Illinois at Urbana–Champaign; University of Miami.

Student Life Upper grades have specified standards of dress, student council, honor system. Discipline rests primarily with faculty.

Summer Programs Enrichment, advancement, sports, art/fine arts, computer instruction programs offered; session focuses on enrichment; held on campus; accepts boys and girls; open to students from other schools. 80 students usually enrolled.

Tuition and Aid Tuition installment plan (Insured Tuition Payment Plan, monthly payment plans, individually arranged payment plans). Tuition reduction for siblings, merit scholarship grants, need-based scholarship grants available.

Admissions Otis-Lennon Ability or Stanford Achievement Test, Otis-Lennon School Ability Test, Otis-Lennon School Ability Test, ERB CPT III, Otis-Lennon School Ability Test/writing sample, Otis-Lennon, Stanford Achievement Test, Wide Range Achievement Test or WRAT required. Deadline for receipt of application materials: none. Application fee required: $50. Interview required.

Athletics Interscholastic: basketball (boys, girls), cheering (g), cross-country running (b,g), running (b,g), track and field (b,g), volleyball (g); intramural: basketball (b,g), cheering (g), cross-country running (b,g), running (b,g), track and field (b,g), volleyball (g). 1 PE instructor, 4 coaches.

Computers Computer network features include on-campus library services, online commercial services, Internet access, wireless campus network, Internet filtering or blocking technology. Campus intranet and student e-mail accounts are available to students. Students grades are available online. The school has a published electronic and media policy.

Contact Mrs. Brittany A. Marietta, Director of Admission/Marketing Coordinator. 563-359-1366 Ext. 302. Fax: 563-359-7576. E-mail: marietta@rvmt.org. Web site: www.rvmt.org.

RIVERSIDE MILITARY ACADEMY

2001 Riverside Drive

Gainesville, Georgia 30501

Head of School: Dr. James H. Benson, Col., USMC-Retd.

General Information Boys' boarding and day college-preparatory, arts, technology, JROTC (grades 9-12), and military school, affiliated with Christian faith. Grades 7–12. Founded: 1907. Setting: suburban. Nearest major city is Atlanta. Students are housed in single-sex dormitories. 206-acre campus. 9 buildings on campus. Approved or accredited by Southern Association of Colleges and Schools, Southern Association of Independent Schools, and Georgia Department of Education. Member of National Association of Independent Schools. Endowment: $53 million. Total enrollment: 349. Upper school average class size: 14. Upper school faculty-student ratio: 1:14. There are 180 required school days per year for Upper School students. Upper School students typically attend 5 days per week. The average school day consists of 5 hours and 45 minutes.

Upper School Student Profile Grade 9: 52 students (52 boys); Grade 10: 58 students (58 boys); Grade 11: 97 students (97 boys); Grade 12: 93 students (93 boys). 90% of students are boarding students. 60% are state residents. 30 states are represented in upper school student body. 29% are international students. International students from Bahamas, Canada, Dominican Republic, Mexico, Republic of Korea, and Taiwan; 8 other countries represented in student body. 80% of students are Christian faith.

Faculty School total: 45. In upper school: 35 men, 10 women; 30 have advanced degrees; 20 reside on campus.

Subjects Offered Algebra, American literature, art, art appreciation, band, biology, biology-AP, calculus, calculus-AP, ceramics, chemistry, chemistry-AP, chorus, computer applications, computer education, computer programming, computer science, computer skills, computer studies, computer technologies, desktop publishing, drama, drawing, earth science, economics, English, English composition, English literature, English/composition-AP, ESL, ethics, European history, fine arts, geography, geometry, German, government/civics, grammar, health, history-AP, honors English, honors geometry, honors U.S. history, honors world history, JROTC, keyboarding, Latin, leadership, mathematics, military science, modern world history, music, music technology, music theory, painting, physical education, physics, physics-AP, pre-algebra, pre-calculus, science, social studies, Spanish, statistics, swimming, theater, U.S. government, U.S. government and politics-AP, U.S. history, U.S. history-AP, U.S. literature, visual arts, weight training, world geography, world history, world history-AP, world literature, yearbook.

Graduation Requirements Arts and fine arts (art, music, dance, drama), computer science, electives, English, foreign language, JROTC, lab science, mathematics, military science, physical education (includes health), science, social studies (includes history).

Special Academic Programs 8 Advanced Placement exams for which test preparation is offered; honors section; independent study; special instructional classes for Attention Deficit Hyperactivity Disorder, Attention Deficit Disorder; ESL (24 students enrolled).

College Admission Counseling 57 students graduated in 2011; 54 went to college, including Clemson University; Georgia Institute of Technology; The Citadel, The Military College of South Carolina; The University of Alabama; University of California, Los Angeles; University of Georgia. Other: 3 entered military service. Median SAT critical reading: 463, median SAT math: 469, median SAT writing: 434, median combined SAT: 1366, median composite ACT: 19.

Student Life Upper grades have uniform requirement, student council, honor system. Discipline rests equally with students and faculty. Attendance at religious services is required.

Summer Programs Remediation, enrichment, advancement, ESL, sports, art/fine arts, rigorous outdoor training, computer instruction programs offered; session focuses on academics; held on campus; accepts boys; open to students from other schools. 120 students usually enrolled. 2012 schedule: June 17 to July 14. Application deadline: none.

Tuition and Aid Day student tuition: $17,150; 7-day tuition and room/board: $28,600. Tuition installment plan (Key Tuition Payment Plan, FACTS Tuition Payment Plan, monthly payment plans). Need-based scholarship grants available.

Admissions Traditional secondary-level entrance grade is 9. Any standardized test required. Deadline for receipt of application materials: none. Application fee required: $100. Interview required.

Athletics Interscholastic: aquatics, baseball, basketball, cross-country running, drill team, football, golf, JROTC drill, lacrosse, marksmanship, riflery, soccer, swimming and diving, tennis, track and field, wrestling; intramural: aquatics, backpacking, baseball, basketball, billiards, canoeing/kayaking, cheering, climbing, combined training, crew, cross-country running, fencing, fishing, fitness, flag football, football, hiking/backpacking, indoor soccer, indoor track, indoor track & field, jogging, kayaking, marksmanship, mountaineering, outdoor activities, paddle tennis, paint ball, physical fitness, physical training, rafting, rappelling, rock climbing, ropes courses, rowing, running, skateboarding, soccer, softball, strength & conditioning, swimming and diving, table tennis, tennis, volleyball, wall climbing, water polo, water volleyball, weight lifting, weight training, wilderness. 5 PE instructors, 20 coaches, 1 athletic trainer.

Computers Computers are regularly used in college planning, desktop publishing, English, ESL, foreign language, library, mathematics, multimedia, music, SAT preparation, science, Spanish, technology, theater, yearbook classes. Computer network features include on-campus library services, Internet access, wireless campus network, Internet filtering or blocking technology. Campus intranet, student e-mail accounts, and computer access in designated common areas are available to students. Students grades are available online. The school has a published electronic and media policy.

Contact Admissions Office. 800-462-2338. Fax: 678-291-3364. E-mail: apply@riversidemilitary.com. Web site: www.riversidemilitary.com.

THE RIVERS SCHOOL

333 Winter Street

Weston, Massachusetts 02493-1040

Head of School: Thomas P. Olverson

General Information Coeducational day college-preparatory and arts school. Grades 6–12. Founded: 1915. Setting: suburban. Nearest major city is Boston. 53-acre campus. 8 buildings on campus. Approved or accredited by Association of Independent Schools in New England and New England Association of Schools and Colleges. Member of National Association of Independent Schools and Secondary School Admission Test Board. Endowment: $18.9 million. Total enrollment: 469. Upper school average class size: 12. Upper school faculty-student ratio: 1:6. Upper School students typically attend 5 days per week. The average school day consists of 7 hours and 15 minutes.

Upper School Student Profile Grade 9: 87 students (46 boys, 41 girls); Grade 10: 93 students (55 boys, 38 girls); Grade 11: 82 students (42 boys, 40 girls); Grade 12: 88 students (45 boys, 43 girls).

Faculty School total: 86. In upper school: 43 men, 43 women; 54 have advanced degrees.

Subjects Offered Advanced Placement courses, algebra, American history, American literature, art, art history, art history-AP, astronomy, biochemistry, biology, biology-AP, calculus, calculus-AP, ceramics, chamber groups, chemistry, chemistry-AP, chorus, civil rights, Civil War, computer graphics, computer science, computer science-AP, creative writing, drama, earth science, economics-AP, English, English language and composition-AP, English literature, English literature and composition-AP, environmental science-AP, European history, expository writing, film studies, filmmaking, fine arts, French, French-AP, geography, geometry, history, Holocaust, jazz band, journalism, kinesiology, Latin, Latin-AP, Mandarin, mathematics, modern European history-AP, music, photography, physics, physics-AP, playwriting, science, Spanish, Spanish-AP, statistics-AP, the Presidency, theater, theater arts, trigonometry, U.S. history-AP, world history, world literature.

Graduation Requirements Algebra, athletics, English, foreign language, geometry, history, mathematics, modern European history, science, U.S. history, visual and performing arts, participation in athletics. Community service is required.

Special Academic Programs Advanced Placement exam preparation; honors section; independent study; study at local college for college credit.

College Admission Counseling 84 students graduated in 2011; all went to college, including Babson College; Brown University; Bucknell University; Colby College; Colgate University; Lehigh University. Median SAT critical reading: 650, median SAT math: 690, median SAT writing: 680, median combined SAT: 2000. 82% scored over 600 on SAT critical reading, 75% scored over 600 on SAT math, 76% scored over 600 on SAT writing, 82% scored over 1800 on combined SAT.

Student Life Upper grades have specified standards of dress, student council, honor system. Discipline rests primarily with faculty.

Tuition and Aid Day student tuition: $36,950. Tuition installment plan (Academic Management Services Plan, Key Tuition Payment Plan, monthly payment plans). Need-based scholarship grants available. In 2011–12, 31% of upper-school students received aid. Total amount of financial aid awarded in 2011–12: $3,304,050.

Admissions Traditional secondary-level entrance grade is 9. For fall 2011, 318 students applied for upper-level admission, 137 were accepted, 66 enrolled. ISEE or SSAT required. Deadline for receipt of application materials: February 1. Application fee required: $40. On-campus interview required.

Athletics Interscholastic: alpine skiing (boys, girls), baseball (b), basketball (b,g), cross-country running (b,g), field hockey (g), football (b), ice hockey (b,g), lacrosse (b,g), skiing (downhill) (b,g), soccer (b,g), softball (g), strength & conditioning (b,g), tennis (b,g); intramural: basketball (b,g), tennis (g); coed interscholastic: fitness, physical training, track and field, weight lifting, weight training; coed intramural: strength & conditioning. 4 coaches, 2 athletic trainers.

Computers Computers are regularly used in art, aviation, English, foreign language, history, humanities, language development, mathematics, newspaper, publications, science, writing, yearbook classes. Computer network features include on-campus library services, online commercial services, Internet access, wireless campus network, Internet filtering or blocking technology, language lab. Campus intranet, student e-mail accounts, and computer access in designated common areas are available to students. Students grades are available online. The school has a published electronic and media policy.

Contact Gillian Lloyd, Director of Admissions. 781-235-9300. Fax: 781-239-3614. E-mail: g.lloyd@rivers.org. Web site: www.rivers.org.

RIVERSTONE INTERNATIONAL SCHOOL

55213 Warm Springs Avenue

Boise, Idaho 83716

Head of School: Mr. Andrew Derry

General Information Coeducational day college-preparatory school. Grades PS–12. Founded: 1997. Setting: suburban. 14-acre campus. 1 building on campus. Approved or accredited by International Baccalaureate Organization, Northwest Association of Schools and Colleges, Pacific Northwest Association of Independent Schools, Western Catholic Education Association, and Idaho Department of Education. Total enrollment: 314. Upper school average class size: 12. Upper school faculty-student ratio: 1:6. There are 169 required school days per year for Upper School students. Upper School students typically attend 5 days per week. The average school day consists of 7 hours and 20 minutes.

Upper School Student Profile Grade 9: 20 students (12 boys, 8 girls); Grade 10: 21 students (9 boys, 12 girls); Grade 11: 35 students (22 boys, 13 girls); Grade 12: 31 students (21 boys, 10 girls).

Faculty School total: 45. In upper school: 8 men, 14 women; 12 have advanced degrees.

Graduation Requirements Art, English, foreign language, history, mathematics, science.

Special Academic Programs International Baccalaureate program; independent study; study abroad; ESL (15 students enrolled).

College Admission Counseling 22 students graduated in 2010; all went to college, including Barnard College; Brown University; Colby College; Smith College; Stanford University; Whitman College. Median SAT critical reading: 660, median SAT math: 620, median SAT writing: 650, median combined SAT: 1940. 82% scored over 600 on SAT critical reading, 64% scored over 600 on SAT math, 73% scored over 600 on SAT writing, 73% scored over 1800 on combined SAT.

Student Life Upper grades have specified standards of dress, student council, honor system. Discipline rests equally with students and faculty.

Tuition and Aid Day student tuition: $14,550. Tuition installment plan (monthly payment plans). Need-based scholarship grants available. In 2010–11, 20% of upper-school students received aid.

Admissions Traditional secondary-level entrance grade is 9. For fall 2010, 43 students applied for upper-level admission, 30 were accepted, 18 enrolled. Deadline for receipt of application materials: none. Application fee required: $75. Interview required.

Athletics Interscholastic: volleyball (girls); intramural: fitness (g); coed interscholastic: alpine skiing, basketball, indoor soccer, nordic skiing, skiing (cross-country), skiing (downhill), snowboarding; coed intramural: backpacking, golf, hiking/backpacking, ice skating, kayaking, lacrosse, nordic skiing, outdoor activities, outdoor education, outdoor skills, physical fitness, rafting, rock climbing, ropes courses, running, skiing (cross-country), skiing (downhill), snowboarding, snowshoeing, soccer. 1 PE instructor, 3 coaches.

Computers Computers are regularly used in art, college planning, data processing, English, ESL, foreign language, French, history, lab/keyboard, music, research skills, Spanish, writing, yearbook classes. Computer network features include online commercial services, Internet access, wireless campus network. The school has a published electronic and media policy.

Contact Ms. Rachel Pusch, Director of Admissions and Marketing. 208-424-5000 Ext. 2104. Fax: 208-424-0033. E-mail: rpusch@riverstoneschool.org. Web site: www.riverstoneschool.org.

ROBERT LAND ACADEMY

Wellandport, Ontario, Canada

See Special Needs Schools section.

ROBERT LOUIS STEVENSON SCHOOL

New York, New York

See Special Needs Schools section.

ROBINSON SCHOOL

5 Nairn Street

San Juan, Puerto Rico 00907

Head of School: Dr. Nan Wodarz, EdD

General Information Coeducational boarding and day and distance learning college-preparatory, arts, religious studies, bilingual studies, technology, and music/drama school, affiliated with United Methodist Church. Boarding grades 7–12, day grades PK–12. Distance learning grades 11–12. Founded: 1902. Setting: urban. Nearest major city is San Juan/Carolina/Bayamon, Puerto Rico. Students are housed in coed dormitories. 5-acre campus. 1 building on campus. Approved or accredited by Middle States Association of Colleges and Schools, The College Board, and Puerto Rico Department of Education. Member of National Association For Equal Opportunity in Higher Education's (NAFEO) historically/predominantly black colleges and universities (HBCU). Languages of instruction: English and Spanish. Total enrollment: 604. Upper school average class size: 18. Upper school faculty-student ratio: 1:18. There are 168 required school days per year for Upper School students. Upper School students typically attend 5 days per week. The average school day consists of 7 hours and 30 minutes.

Upper School Student Profile Grade 7: 45 students (24 boys, 21 girls); Grade 8: 49 students (33 boys, 16 girls); Grade 9: 68 students (45 boys, 23 girls); Grade 10: 54 students (29 boys, 25 girls); Grade 11: 42 students (27 boys, 15 girls); Grade 12: 47 students (21 boys, 26 girls). 2% of students are United Methodist Church.

Faculty School total: 84. In upper school: 16 men, 27 women; 12 have advanced degrees; 2 reside on campus.
Subjects Offered Algebra, art, biology, biology-AP, calculus, chemistry, computer science, economics, English, English literature, English-AP, general science, geometry, health, history-AP, journalism, mathematics, music, physical education, physical science, physics, physics-AP, pre-calculus, Puerto Rican history, religion, SAT preparation, social studies, Spanish, Spanish-AP, writing.
Graduation Requirements Computers, electives, English, mathematics, physical education (includes health), religion (includes Bible studies and theology), science, social studies (includes history), Spanish.
Special Academic Programs Advanced Placement exam preparation; honors section; independent study; domestic exchange program; academic accommodation for the gifted; remedial reading and/or remedial writing; remedial math; programs in English, mathematics, general development for dyslexic students; special instructional classes for students with specific learning disabilities.
College Admission Counseling 37 students graduated in 2010; all went to college, including Boston College; Boston University; Manhattanville College; Syracuse University; University of Florida; University of Miami. Median SAT critical reading: 550, median SAT math: 535.
Student Life Upper grades have uniform requirement, student council, honor system. Discipline rests primarily with faculty. Attendance at religious services is required.
Tuition and Aid Tuition installment plan (monthly payment plans, individually arranged payment plans, annual and semi-annual payment plans, Semi-annually and anually). Tuition reduction for siblings, need-based scholarship grants available. In 2010–11, 11% of upper-school students received aid. Total amount of financial aid awarded in 2010–11: $78,820.
Admissions For fall 2010, 47 students applied for upper-level admission, 38 were accepted, 35 enrolled. Achievement tests, Iowa Tests of Basic Skills, Math Placement Exam, Otis-Lennon Mental Ability Test or PSAT required. Deadline for receipt of application materials: none. No application fee required. On-campus interview required.
Athletics Interscholastic: aquatics (boys, girls), basketball (b,g), cross-country running (b,g), indoor soccer (b,g), running (b,g), soccer (b,g), swimming and diving (b,g), track and field (b,g), volleyball (b,g); intramural: combined training (b,g), cooperative games (b,g), fitness (b,g), flag football (b,g), floor hockey (b,g), gymnastics (b,g), handball (b,g), indoor soccer (b,g), jogging (b,g), jump rope (b,g), kickball (b,g), outdoor recreation (b,g), physical fitness (b,g), physical training (b,g), running (b,g), soccer (b,g), strength & conditioning (b,g), table tennis (b,g), volleyball (b,g); coed interscholastic: soccer; coed intramural: basketball, combined training, cooperative games, fitness, flag football, floor hockey, gymnastics, handball, horseshoes, indoor soccer, jogging, jump rope, kickball, outdoor recreation, paddling, physical fitness, physical training, running, soccer, strength & conditioning, table tennis, tennis, volleyball. 4 PE instructors, 4 coaches, 4 athletic trainers.
Computers Computers are regularly used in English, mathematics, science classes. Computer network features include on-campus library services, Internet access. The school has a published electronic and media policy.
Contact Admissions Officer. 787-999-4604 Ext. 4618. Fax: 787-999-4618. E-mail: mtorres1@robinsonschool.org. Web site: www.robinsonschool.org.

ROCKLAND COUNTRY DAY SCHOOL

34 Kings Highway

Congers, New York 10920-2253

Head of School: Dr. Brian Mahoney

General Information Coeducational day college-preparatory and arts school. Grades PK–12. Founded: 1959. Setting: suburban. Nearest major city is New York. 20-acre campus. 5 buildings on campus. Approved or accredited by New York State Association of Independent Schools and New York Department of Education. Member of National Association of Independent Schools. Total enrollment: 130. Upper school average class size: 14. Upper school faculty-student ratio: 1:8. There are 163 required school days per year for Upper School students. Upper School students typically attend 5 days per week. The average school day consists of 5 hours and 2 minutes.
Upper School Student Profile Grade 9: 9 students (3 boys, 6 girls); Grade 10: 20 students (9 boys, 11 girls); Grade 11: 14 students (8 boys, 6 girls); Grade 12: 18 students (10 boys, 8 girls).
Faculty School total: 31. In upper school: 10 men, 11 women; 8 have advanced degrees.
Subjects Offered Algebra, American history, American literature, art, art history, band, biology, biology-AP, calculus, calculus-AP, career exploration, ceramics, chemistry, chorus, college admission preparation, college counseling, college placement, community service, computers, creative arts, creative writing, dance, debate, digital photography, drama, drama performance, dramatic arts, drawing, earth science, economics, electives, English, English literature, English-AP, environmental science, environmental studies, European history, European history-AP, fine arts, forensics, French, French-AP, gardening, geometry, global studies, guitar, health, health education, history, honors English, humanities, independent study, instrumental music, internship, jazz ensemble, lab science, language-AP, literature-AP, madrigals, mathematics, mathematics-AP, modern European history-AP, music, music theory-AP, painting, performing arts, philosophy, photography, photojournalism, physical education, physics, physics-AP, pre-algebra, pre-calculus, science, social studies, Spanish, Spanish-AP, student government, studio art, theater, theater arts, U.S. history-AP, visual arts, voice ensemble, world history, world literature, writing, yearbook.
Graduation Requirements Arts and fine arts (art, music, dance, drama), computer science, English, experiential education, foreign language, mathematics, music, physical education (includes health), science, social studies (includes history), WISE Program, off-campus senior independent senior project. Community service is required.
Special Academic Programs 15 Advanced Placement exams for which test preparation is offered; honors section; independent study; study at local college for college credit; academic accommodation for the gifted, the musically talented, and the artistically talented.
College Admission Counseling 15 students graduated in 2010; all went to college, including Boston University; Ithaca College; New York University; Purchase College, State University of New York; Quinnipiac University; Smith College. Median SAT critical reading: 580, median SAT math: 550, median SAT writing: 560, median combined SAT: 1690.
Student Life Upper grades have specified standards of dress, student council, honor system. Discipline rests primarily with faculty.
Tuition and Aid Day student tuition: $14,900–$29,475. Tuition installment plan (Insured Tuition Payment Plan, monthly payment plans, individually arranged payment plans). Tuition reduction for siblings, need-based scholarship grants available. In 2010–11, 33% of upper-school students received aid. Total amount of financial aid awarded in 2010–11: $360,930.
Admissions Traditional secondary-level entrance grade is 9. For fall 2010, 20 students applied for upper-level admission, 12 were accepted, 4 enrolled. Any standardized test and writing sample required. Deadline for receipt of application materials: none. Application fee required: $50. Interview required.
Athletics Interscholastic: basketball (boys, girls), cheering (g); intramural: cheering (g); coed interscholastic: aerobics/dance, soccer; coed intramural: bowling, dance, golf, lacrosse, tennis. 1 PE instructor.
Computers Computers are regularly used in art, desktop publishing, English, foreign language, history, humanities, keyboarding, lab/keyboard, mathematics, newspaper, photography, research skills, science, video film production, word processing, yearbook classes. Computer network features include online commercial services, Internet access, wireless campus network, Internet filtering or blocking technology, E-Library. The school has a published electronic and media policy.
Contact Ms. Lorraine Greenwell, Admissions Director. 845-268-6802 Ext. 201. Fax: 845-268-4644. E-mail: lgreenwell@rocklandcds.org. Web site: www.rocklandcds.org.

ROCK POINT SCHOOL

1 Rock Point Road

Burlington, Vermont 05408

Head of School: C.J. Spirito

General Information Coeducational boarding and day college-preparatory and arts school, affiliated with Episcopal Church. Grades 9–12. Founded: 1928. Setting: small town. Students are housed in single-sex by floor dormitories. 130-acre campus. 3 buildings on campus. Approved or accredited by Association of Independent Schools in New England, Independent Schools of Northern New England, National Association of Episcopal Schools, New England Association of Schools and Colleges, The Association of Boarding Schools, and Vermont Department of Education. Member of National Association of Independent Schools. Endowment: $2.5 million. Total enrollment: 29. Upper school average class size: 10. Upper school faculty-student ratio: 1:5. There are 167 required school days per year for Upper School students. Upper School students typically attend 5 days per week. The average school day consists of 6 hours and 45 minutes.
Upper School Student Profile Grade 9: 4 students (2 boys, 2 girls); Grade 10: 6 students (4 boys, 2 girls); Grade 11: 7 students (4 boys, 3 girls); Grade 12: 12 students (6 boys, 6 girls). 80% of students are boarding students. 15% are state residents. 9 states are represented in upper school student body. 7% are international students. International students from India and United Kingdom. 12% of students are members of Episcopal Church.
Faculty School total: 9. In upper school: 2 men, 6 women; 3 have advanced degrees.
Subjects Offered Algebra, American history, American literature, ancient history, animation, art, art history, biology, calculus, chemistry, community service, creative thinking, critical thinking, drawing, earth science, English, geometry, health, historical foundations for arts, history, mathematics, painting, photography, physical education, poetry, portfolio art, pre-calculus, science, stained glass, Western civilization, world history, world literature.
Graduation Requirements Art, art history, English, history, mathematics, physical education (includes health), science. Community service is required.
Special Academic Programs Independent study; term-away projects; study at local college for college credit; special instructional classes for students who need structure and personal attention; ESL.
College Admission Counseling 8 students graduated in 2011; 7 went to college, including Roger Williams University. Other: 1 went to work. Median SAT critical reading: 540, median SAT math: 490, median SAT writing: 490, median combined SAT:

1500. 29% scored over 600 on SAT critical reading, 14% scored over 600 on SAT math, 14% scored over 600 on SAT writing, 29% scored over 1800 on combined SAT.

Student Life Upper grades have specified standards of dress. Discipline rests primarily with faculty.

Summer Programs Remediation, art/fine arts programs offered; session focuses on strengthen learning skills, earn credits, and have fun in Vermont; held both on and off campus; held at day trips outside into Burlington Vermont, throughout the State, and beyond; accepts boys and girls; open to students from other schools. 10 students usually enrolled. 2012 schedule: July 8 to August 18. Application deadline: June 30.

Tuition and Aid Day student tuition: $26,500; 7-day tuition and room/board: $51,000. Tuition installment plan (individually arranged payment plans, deposit and two installment plan (September 1 and December 1);, other specially created plans with a family.). Need-based scholarship grants available. In 2011–12, 31% of upper-school students received aid. Total amount of financial aid awarded in 2011–12: $150,000.

Admissions Traditional secondary-level entrance grade is 10. For fall 2011, 20 students applied for upper-level admission, 17 were accepted, 15 enrolled. Essay or writing sample required. Deadline for receipt of application materials: none. Application fee required. On-campus interview required.

Athletics Coed Interscholastic: basketball; coed intramural: alpine skiing, backpacking, ball hockey, basketball, bicycling, billiards, broomball, climbing, cooperative games, fitness, fitness walking, Frisbee, hiking/backpacking, jogging, kickball, martial arts, outdoor activities, outdoor adventure, outdoor recreation, physical fitness, physical training, rock climbing, ropes courses, running, skateboarding, skiing (downhill), snowboarding, soccer, softball, touch football, ultimate Frisbee, walking, weight lifting, winter walking, yoga. 7 PE instructors.

Computers Computers are regularly used in all academic, animation, art, college planning, creative writing, media, music, photography, video film production, word processing classes. Computer network features include Internet access, Internet filtering or blocking technology. Student e-mail accounts are available to students.

Contact Hillary Kramer, Director of Admissions. 802-863-1104 Ext. 12. Fax: 802-863-6628. E-mail: hkramer@rockpoint.org. Web site: www.rockpoint.org.

THE ROEPER SCHOOL

41190 Woodward Avenue

Bloomfield Hills, Michigan 48304

Head of School: Philip Deely

General Information Coeducational day college-preparatory school. Grades PK–12. Founded: 1941. Setting: urban. Nearest major city is Birmingham. 1-acre campus. 1 building on campus. Approved or accredited by Independent Schools Association of the Central States. Member of National Association of Independent Schools. Endowment: $6 million. Total enrollment: 551. Upper school average class size: 14. Upper school faculty-student ratio: 1:6. There are 165 required school days per year for Upper School students. Upper School students typically attend 5 days per week. The average school day consists of 7 hours and 10 minutes.

Upper School Student Profile Grade 9: 44 students (29 boys, 15 girls); Grade 10: 52 students (24 boys, 28 girls); Grade 11: 47 students (29 boys, 18 girls); Grade 12: 48 students (23 boys, 25 girls).

Faculty School total: 90. In upper school: 14 men, 24 women; 21 have advanced degrees.

Subjects Offered Algebra, American history, American literature, art, art history, biology, calculus, chemistry, computer programming, creative writing, dance, drama, English, English literature, European history, fine arts, French, geometry, government/civics, health, history, journalism, Latin, mathematics, music, philosophy, photography, physical education, physics, science, social studies, Spanish, speech, statistics, theater, trigonometry, world history, world literature, writing.

Graduation Requirements Arts and fine arts (art, music, dance, drama), computer science, English, foreign language, government, health, mathematics, science, social studies (includes history).

Special Academic Programs 13 Advanced Placement exams for which test preparation is offered; independent study; academic accommodation for the gifted, the musically talented, and the artistically talented; programs in English, mathematics, general development for dyslexic students.

College Admission Counseling 49 students graduated in 2011; all went to college, including Kalamazoo College; Northwestern University; University of Chicago; University of Michigan; Western Michigan University.

Student Life Upper grades have student council, honor system. Discipline rests primarily with faculty.

Summer Programs Art/fine arts programs offered; session focuses on theater; held on campus; accepts boys and girls; open to students from other schools. 75 students usually enrolled. 2012 schedule: June 20 to August 12.

Tuition and Aid Day student tuition: $22,250. Tuition installment plan (FACTS Tuition Payment Plan, individually arranged payment plans). Need-based scholarship grants available. In 2011–12, 31% of upper-school students received aid. Total amount of financial aid awarded in 2011–12: $384,375.

Admissions Traditional secondary-level entrance grade is 9. For fall 2011, 31 students applied for upper-level admission, 29 were accepted, 16 enrolled. Individual IQ required. Deadline for receipt of application materials: none. Application fee required: $75. On-campus interview required.

Athletics Interscholastic: baseball (boys), basketball (b,g), cross-country running (b,g), golf (b,g), physical training (b,g), soccer (b,g), strength & conditioning (b,g), track and field (b,g), volleyball (g), weight lifting (b,g); intramural: indoor soccer (b,g); coed intramural: physical training, strength & conditioning, weight lifting. 4 PE instructors, 30 coaches.

Computers Computers are regularly used in English, journalism, library, mathematics, publishing, science, yearbook classes. Computer network features include on-campus library services, online commercial services, Internet access. Student e-mail accounts and computer access in designated common areas are available to students. Students grades are available online.

Contact Lori Zinser, Director of Admissions. 248-203-7302. Fax: 248-203-7310. E-mail: lori.zinser@roeper.org. Web site: www.roeper.org.

ROLAND PARK COUNTRY SCHOOL

5204 Roland Avenue

Baltimore, Maryland 21210

Head of School: Mrs. Jean Waller Brune

General Information Girls' day and distance learning college-preparatory and arts school. Grades K–12. Distance learning grades 9–12. Founded: 1901. Setting: suburban. 21-acre campus. 1 building on campus. Approved or accredited by Association of Independent Maryland Schools. Member of National Association of Independent Schools and Secondary School Admission Test Board. Endowment: $46.4 million. Total enrollment: 650. Upper school average class size: 14. Upper school faculty-student ratio: 1:7. There are 171 required school days per year for Upper School students. Upper School students typically attend 5 days per week. The average school day consists of 7 hours and 45 minutes.

Upper School Student Profile Grade 9: 74 students (74 girls); Grade 10: 71 students (71 girls); Grade 11: 80 students (80 girls); Grade 12: 62 students (62 girls).

Faculty School total: 100. In upper school: 8 men, 40 women; 40 have advanced degrees.

Subjects Offered 3-dimensional art, advanced biology, advanced chemistry, advanced math, Advanced Placement courses, advanced studio art-AP, algebra, American history-AP, American literature, American literature-AP, anatomy, ancient world history, Arabic, archaeology, art, art history, art history-AP, astronomy, biology, biology-AP, calculus, calculus-AP, ceramics, chemistry, chemistry-AP, Chesapeake Bay studies, Chinese, community service, computer programming, computer science, creative writing, dance, drama, ecology, economics, engineering, English, English language-AP, English literature, English literature-AP, English-AP, environmental science, environmental studies, European civilization, European history, European history-AP, French, French language-AP, French literature-AP, geometry, German, government/civics, Greek, health, integrated mathematics, Latin, music, philosophy, photography, physical education, physics, physiology, religion, Russian, science, social studies, Spanish, speech, statistics, theater, trigonometry, world history.

Graduation Requirements Adolescent issues, arts and fine arts (art, music, dance, drama), biology, chemistry, English, foreign language, history, mathematics, physical education (includes health), physics, public speaking, science. Community service is required.

Special Academic Programs Advanced Placement exam preparation; honors section; independent study; term-away projects; study abroad.

College Admission Counseling 76 students graduated in 2011; all went to college, including Carnegie Mellon University; The George Washington University; The Johns Hopkins University; The University of North Carolina at Chapel Hill; University of Maryland, College Park; University of Pennsylvania. Mean SAT critical reading: 563, mean SAT math: 567, mean SAT writing: 589, mean combined SAT: 1719, mean composite ACT: 26. 41% scored over 600 on SAT critical reading, 48% scored over 600 on SAT math, 63% scored over 600 on SAT writing, 49% scored over 1800 on combined SAT, 50% scored over 26 on composite ACT.

Student Life Upper grades have uniform requirement, student council, honor system. Discipline rests equally with students and faculty.

Summer Programs Remediation, enrichment, advancement, sports, art/fine arts programs offered; session focuses on summer camp, arts, some academics; held both on and off campus; held at off-site pool and venues for outdoor education programs and various sites around Baltimore for art projects; accepts boys and girls; open to students from other schools. 657 students usually enrolled. 2012 schedule: June 11 to August 31. Application deadline: none.

Tuition and Aid Day student tuition: $23,335. Tuition installment plan (FACTS Tuition Payment Plan, individually arranged payment plans). Need-based scholarship grants, paying campus jobs available. In 2011–12, 26% of upper-school students received aid.

Admissions Traditional secondary-level entrance grade is 9. For fall 2011, 90 students applied for upper-level admission, 61 were accepted, 26 enrolled. CTP, ERB CTP IV or ISEE required. Deadline for receipt of application materials: January 15. Application fee required: $50. Interview required.

Athletics Interscholastic: badminton, basketball, crew, cross-country running, field hockey, golf, independent competitive sports, indoor soccer, indoor track, lacrosse, soccer, softball, squash, swimming and diving, tennis, volleyball, winter (indoor) track, winter soccer; intramural: dance, fitness, modern dance, outdoor education, physical fitness, rock climbing, strength & conditioning. 7 PE instructors, 1 athletic trainer.

Computers Computers are regularly used in all classes. Computer network features include on-campus library services, online commercial services, Internet access, wireless campus network, Internet filtering or blocking technology, online database. Campus intranet, student e-mail accounts, and computer access in designated common areas are available to students. Students grades are available online. The school has a published electronic and media policy.

Contact Peggy Wolf, Director of Admissions. 410-323-5500. Fax: 410-323-2164. E-mail: admissions@rpcs.org. Web site: www.rpcs.org.

ROLLING HILLS PREPARATORY SCHOOL

One Rolling Hills Prep Way

San Pedro, California 90732

Head of School: Peter McCormack

General Information Coeducational day college-preparatory, arts, and technology school. Grades 6–12. Founded: 1981. Setting: suburban. Nearest major city is Los Angeles. 21-acre campus. 20 buildings on campus. Approved or accredited by Western Association of Schools and Colleges and California Department of Education. Member of National Association of Independent Schools. Total enrollment: 235. Upper school average class size: 16. Upper school faculty-student ratio: 1:9. There are 180 required school days per year for Upper School students. Upper School students typically attend 5 days per week. The average school day consists of 6 hours.

Upper School Student Profile Grade 9: 32 students (16 boys, 16 girls); Grade 10: 36 students (21 boys, 15 girls); Grade 11: 47 students (26 boys, 21 girls); Grade 12: 46 students (28 boys, 18 girls).

Faculty School total: 37. In upper school: 6 men, 21 women; 14 have advanced degrees.

Subjects Offered Algebra, American history, American literature, American sign language, anatomy, art, biology, calculus, ceramics, chemistry, Chinese, computer science, creative writing, drama, economics, English, English literature, European history, fine arts, French, geography, geometry, government/civics, history, mathematics, music, photography, physical education, physics, pre-calculus, robotics, science, social studies, Spanish, speech, statistics, theater, trigonometry, world history.

Graduation Requirements Arts and fine arts (art, music, dance, drama), English, foreign language, mathematics, outdoor education, physical education (includes health), science, social studies (includes history), two-week senior internship, senior speech.

Special Academic Programs 10 Advanced Placement exams for which test preparation is offered; honors section; independent study; academic accommodation for the gifted; programs in general development for dyslexic students; ESL (16 students enrolled).

College Admission Counseling 33 students graduated in 2011; 32 went to college, including Hampshire College; Skidmore College; University of California, Berkeley; University of California, Los Angeles; University of California, Santa Barbara; University of Southern California. Other: 1 had other specific plans. Mean SAT critical reading: 590, mean SAT math: 590, mean SAT writing: 610. 45% scored over 600 on SAT critical reading, 40% scored over 600 on SAT math, 45% scored over 600 on SAT writing.

Student Life Upper grades have specified standards of dress, student council, honor system. Discipline rests primarily with faculty.

Summer Programs Enrichment, art/fine arts programs offered; session focuses on algebra and photography; held on campus; accepts boys and girls; open to students from other schools. 30 students usually enrolled. 2012 schedule: June 26 to August 28. Application deadline: June 1.

Tuition and Aid Day student tuition: $23,650. Tuition installment plan (Insured Tuition Payment Plan, Key Tuition Payment Plan, monthly payment plans). Merit scholarship grants, need-based scholarship grants available. In 2011–12, 35% of upper-school students received aid. Total amount of financial aid awarded in 2011–12: $550,000.

Admissions Traditional secondary-level entrance grade is 9. For fall 2011, 21 students applied for upper-level admission, 14 were accepted, 8 enrolled. ISEE or SLEP for foreign students required. Deadline for receipt of application materials: none. Application fee required: $150. Interview required.

Athletics Interscholastic: baseball (boys), basketball (b,g), cheering (g), football (b), soccer (b,g), softball (g), track and field (g), volleyball (b,g); intramural: cheering (g), dance (g); coed interscholastic: cross-country running, golf, roller hockey, running, track and field; coed intramural: backpacking, climbing, fitness, hiking/backpacking, outdoor education, physical fitness, rock climbing, ropes courses. 4 PE instructors, 10 coaches, 1 athletic trainer.

Computers Computers are regularly used in English, foreign language, history, mathematics, photography, science classes. Computer network features include on-campus library services, Internet access, wireless campus network. The school has a published electronic and media policy.

Contact Bryonna Fisco, Director of Admission. 310-791-1101 Ext. 148. Fax: 310-373-4931. E-mail: bfisco@rollinghillsprep.org. Web site: www.rollinghillsprep.org.

RON PETTIGREW CHRISTIAN SCHOOL

1761 110th Avenue

Dawson Creek, British Columbia V1G 4X4, Canada

Head of School: Phyllis L. Roch

General Information Coeducational day college-preparatory and general academic school, affiliated with Christian faith. Grades K–12. Founded: 1989. Setting: small town. Nearest major city is Prince George, Canada. 1-acre campus. 1 building on campus. Approved or accredited by Association of Christian Schools International and British Columbia Department of Education. Language of instruction: English. Total enrollment: 88. Upper school faculty-student ratio: 1:5.

Upper School Student Profile 76% of students are Christian faith.

Faculty School total: 6. In upper school: 2 men, 4 women.

College Admission Counseling 2 students graduated in 2010. Other: 2 went to work.

Student Life Upper grades have uniform requirement, student council, honor system. Discipline rests primarily with faculty. Attendance at religious services is required.

Admissions No application fee required. Interview required.

Computers Computer network features include Internet access, wireless campus network, Internet filtering or blocking technology.

Contact Phyllis L. Roch, Head of School. 250-782-4580. Fax: 250-782-9805. E-mail: rpcs@pris.ca.

ROSSEAU LAKE COLLEGE

1967 Bright Street

Rosseau, Ontario P0C 1J0, Canada

Head of School: Mr. Lance Postma

General Information Coeducational boarding and day college-preparatory, arts, business, and technology school. Grades 7–12. Founded: 1967. Setting: rural. Nearest major city is Toronto, Canada. Students are housed in single-sex dormitories. 53-acre campus. 13 buildings on campus. Approved or accredited by Canadian Association of Independent Schools, Canadian Educational Standards Institute, The Association of Boarding Schools, and Ontario Department of Education. Languages of instruction: English and French. Endowment: CAN$100,000. Total enrollment: 81. Upper school average class size: 12. Upper school faculty-student ratio: 1:6. There are 176 required school days per year for Upper School students. Upper School students typically attend 5 days per week. The average school day consists of 5 hours and 30 minutes.

Upper School Student Profile Grade 9: 14 students (5 boys, 9 girls); Grade 10: 18 students (10 boys, 8 girls); Grade 11: 14 students (12 boys, 2 girls); Grade 12: 18 students (12 boys, 6 girls). 45% of students are boarding students. 80% are province residents. 2 provinces are represented in upper school student body. 20% are international students. International students from China, Democratic People's Republic of Korea, Japan, Mexico, Nigeria, and Spain; 4 other countries represented in student body.

Faculty School total: 19. In upper school: 8 men, 11 women; 5 have advanced degrees; 11 reside on campus.

Subjects Offered Accounting, algebra, art, art history, biology, business, calculus, Canadian law, career and personal planning, chemistry, civics, computer programming, computer science, data analysis, economics, English, entrepreneurship, ESL, European history, experiential education, fine arts, French, geography, geometry, health, history, information technology, marketing, mathematics, music, outdoor education, physical education, physics, political science, science, social sciences, trigonometry, visual arts, world governments, writing.

Graduation Requirements Arts and fine arts (art, music, dance, drama), business skills (includes word processing), career planning, civics, computer science, English, foreign language, mathematics, physical education (includes health), science, social studies (includes history).

Special Academic Programs Accelerated programs; independent study; term-away projects; study abroad; academic accommodation for the gifted; remedial reading and/or remedial writing; remedial math; ESL (18 students enrolled).

College Admission Counseling 16 students graduated in 2011; all went to college, including McMaster University; Queen's University at Kingston; The University of Western Ontario; University of Guelph; University of Toronto; York University.

Student Life Upper grades have uniform requirement, student council, honor system. Discipline rests primarily with faculty.

Summer Programs Remediation, enrichment, advancement programs offered; session focuses on academics; held on campus; accepts boys and girls; open to students from other schools. 10 students usually enrolled. 2012 schedule: July 1 to July 30. Application deadline: June 15.

Tuition and Aid Day student tuition: CAN$17,700; 7-day tuition and room/board: CAN$40,500. Tuition installment plan (monthly payment plans, individually arranged payment plans). Merit scholarship grants, need-based scholarship grants available. In 2011–12, 10% of upper-school students received aid; total upper-school merit-scholarship money awarded: CAN$40,000. Total amount of financial aid awarded in 2011–12: CAN$160,000.

Admissions Traditional secondary-level entrance grade is 9. Admissions testing and English Composition Test for ESL students required. Deadline for receipt of application materials: none. Application fee required: CAN$150. Interview required.

Athletics Interscholastic: baseball (boys), basketball (b,g), cross-country running (b,g), field hockey (g), hockey (b), ice hockey (b), mountain biking (b,g), nordic skiing (b,g), rugby (b), running (b,g), skiing (cross-country) (b,g), snowboarding (b,g), soccer (b,g), softball (b), swimming and diving (b,g), tennis (b,g), track and field (b,g), volleyball (b,g); intramural: alpine skiing (b,g), baseball (b), basketball (b,g), cross-country running (b,g), field hockey (g), hockey (b,g), ice hockey (b,g), rugby (b), running (b,g), skiing (cross-country) (b,g), snowboarding (b,g); coed interscholastic: bicycling, canoeing/kayaking, climbing, golf, kayaking, mountain biking, nordic skiing, running, skiing (cross-country), skiing (downhill), snowboarding, softball, track and field; coed intramural: aerobics, aerobics/dance, aquatics, backpacking, ball hockey, baseball, basketball, bicycling, bowling, broomball, canoeing/kayaking, climbing, combined training, cooperative games, Cosom hockey, cross-country running, equestrian sports, fishing, fitness, fitness walking, flag football, floor hockey, fly fishing, freestyle skiing, Frisbee, golf, hiking/backpacking, horseback riding, ice skating, indoor hockey, indoor soccer, jogging, kayaking, life saving, mountain biking, mountaineering, nordic skiing, outdoor activities, paddle tennis, paddling, physical fitness, physical training, rappelling, rock climbing, ropes courses, sailboarding, sailing, scuba diving, skateboarding, skiing (cross-country), skiing (downhill), snowboarding, snowshoeing, soccer, softball, squash, street hockey, strength & conditioning, swimming and diving, table tennis, tennis, track and field, triathlon, ultimate Frisbee, volleyball, walking, wall climbing, water skiing, weight lifting, weight training, wilderness, wilderness survival, wildernessways, windsurfing, winter walking, yoga. 2 PE instructors, 2 coaches.

Computers Computers are regularly used in geography, graphic arts, information technology classes. Computer network features include on-campus library services, Internet access, wireless campus network, Internet filtering or blocking technology. Campus intranet, student e-mail accounts, and computer access in designated common areas are available to students. The school has a published electronic and media policy.

Contact Ms. Lynda Marshall, Director of Admissions. 705-732-4351 Ext. 12. Fax: 705-732-6319. E-mail: lynda.marshall@rlc.on.ca. Web site: www.rosseaulakecollege.com.

ROSS SCHOOL

18 Goodfriend Drive

East Hampton, New York 11937

Head of School: Michele Claeys

General Information Coeducational boarding and day college-preparatory, globally-focused, integrated curriculum, and ELL curriculum school. Boarding grades 7–12, day grades N–12. Founded: 1991. Setting: small town. Nearest major city is New York. Students are housed in single-sex dormitories. 100-acre campus. 7 buildings on campus. Approved or accredited by Middle States Association of Colleges and Schools and New York Department of Education. Member of National Association of Independent Schools and Secondary School Admission Test Board. Upper school average class size: 15. Upper school faculty-student ratio: 1:7. There are 164 required school days per year for Upper School students. Upper School students typically attend 5 days per week. The average school day consists of 7 hours and 25 minutes.

Upper School Student Profile 35% of students are boarding students. 6 states are represented in upper school student body. International students from Brazil, China, Germany, Republic of Korea, and Taiwan; 6 other countries represented in student body.

Faculty School total: 94. In upper school: 27 reside on campus.

Subjects Offered Advanced biology, advanced chemistry, advanced math, art history, athletics, Chinese, college counseling, computer multimedia, English literature, ESL, French, health and wellness, independent study, jazz band, media studies, model United Nations, music, philosophy, physics, SAT preparation, senior internship, senior project, Spanish, theater arts, United Nations and international issues, visual arts, world history.

Graduation Requirements 30 hours of community service.

Special Academic Programs 9 Advanced Placement exams for which test preparation is offered; honors section; independent study; term-away projects; ESL (30 students enrolled).

College Admission Counseling 59 students graduated in 2011; all went to college, including American University; Bard College; Boston University; New York University; Roger Williams University; Wesleyan University.

Student Life Upper grades have uniform requirement, student council, honor system. Discipline rests primarily with faculty.

Summer Programs ESL, sports, art/fine arts programs offered; session focuses on sports and fine arts; held on campus; accepts boys and girls; open to students from other schools. 2012 schedule: June 25 to August 17. Application deadline: none.

Tuition and Aid Day student tuition: $31,100; 5-day tuition and room/board: $45,600. Tuition installment plan (monthly payment plans). Tuition reduction for siblings, need-based scholarship grants available. In 2011–12, 45% of upper-school students received aid.

Admissions Traditional secondary-level entrance grade is 9. Any standardized test required. Deadline for receipt of application materials: January 31. Application fee required: $50. Interview required.

Athletics Interscholastic: baseball (boys), basketball (b,g), lacrosse (b,g), soccer (b,g), softball (g), tennis (b,g), track and field (b,g), volleyball (b,g); coed interscholastic: cheering, golf, sailing; coed intramural: dance, fitness, kayaking, modern dance, mountain biking, sailing, surfing, tai chi, yoga.

Computers Computers are regularly used in all classes. Computer network features include on-campus library services, online commercial services, Internet access, wireless campus network, Internet filtering or blocking technology. Campus intranet and student e-mail accounts are available to students. Students grades are available online. The school has a published electronic and media policy.

Contact Ms. Kristen Kaschub, Director of International Recruitment. 631-907-5205. Fax: 631-907-5563. E-mail: kkaschub@ross.org. Web site: www.ross.org.

ROTHESAY NETHERWOOD SCHOOL

40 College Hill Road

Rothesay, New Brunswick E2E 5H1, Canada

Head of School: Mr. Paul G. Kitchen

General Information Coeducational boarding and day college-preparatory, arts, and technology school, affiliated with Anglican Church of Canada. Grades 6–12. Founded: 1877. Setting: small town. Nearest major city is Saint John, Canada. Students are housed in single-sex dormitories. 180-acre campus. 26 buildings on campus. Approved or accredited by Canadian Association of Independent Schools, Conference of Independent Schools of Ontario, International Baccalaureate Organization, The Association of Boarding Schools, and New Brunswick Department of Education. Affiliate member of National Association of Independent Schools. Languages of instruction: English and French. Endowment: CAN$3.1 million. Total enrollment: 270. Upper school average class size: 16. Upper school faculty-student ratio: 1:8. There are 176 required school days per year for Upper School students. Upper School students typically attend 5 days per week. The average school day consists of 7 hours and 45 minutes.

Upper School Student Profile Grade 9: 38 students (24 boys, 14 girls); Grade 10: 36 students (21 boys, 15 girls); Grade 11: 74 students (45 boys, 29 girls); Grade 12: 60 students (24 boys, 36 girls). 58% of students are boarding students. 66% are province residents. 9 provinces are represented in upper school student body. 17% are international students. International students from Bermuda, China, Dominica, Germany, Jamaica, and Mexico; 4 other countries represented in student body. 30% of students are members of Anglican Church of Canada.

Faculty School total: 34. In upper school: 19 men, 15 women; 6 have advanced degrees; 19 reside on campus.

Subjects Offered Advanced chemistry, art, art history, biology, Canadian history, chemistry, computer programming, computer science, CPR, digital art, drama, driver education, English, English literature, ESL, European history, fine arts, French, geography, geometry, health, history, information technology, International Baccalaureate courses, leadership, math applications, mathematics, music, outdoor education, physical education, physics, science, social studies, Spanish, theater arts, world history, writing.

Graduation Requirements Arts and fine arts (art, music, dance, drama), computer science, English, foreign language, mathematics, physical education (includes health), science, social sciences, social studies (includes history), IB Theory of Knowledge, IB designation CAS hours (creativity, action, service), Extended Essay, Outward Bound adventure.

Special Academic Programs International Baccalaureate program; honors section; independent study; term-away projects; study at local college for college credit; academic accommodation for the gifted, the musically talented, and the artistically talented; ESL (10 students enrolled).

College Admission Counseling 48 students graduated in 2011; all went to college, including Acadia University; Dalhousie University; Mount Allison University; Queen's University at Kingston; St. Francis Xavier University; University of Toronto.

Student Life Upper grades have uniform requirement, student council, honor system. Discipline rests primarily with faculty. Attendance at religious services is required.

Tuition and Aid Day student tuition: CAN$19,270; 7-day tuition and room/board: CAN$39,620. Tuition installment plan (monthly payment plans, individually arranged payment plans). Tuition reduction for siblings, bursaries, merit scholarship grants, need-based scholarship grants available. In 2011–12, 32% of upper-school students received aid; total upper-school merit-scholarship money awarded: CAN$132,000. Total amount of financial aid awarded in 2011–12: CAN$667,845.

Admissions Traditional secondary-level entrance grade is 9. For fall 2011, 91 students applied for upper-level admission, 82 were accepted, 63 enrolled. School's own exam required. Deadline for receipt of application materials: none. Application fee required: CAN$100. Interview required.

Athletics Interscholastic: badminton (boys, girls), basketball (b,g), crew (b,g), cross-country running (b,g), field hockey (g), ice hockey (b,g), rowing (b,g), rugby (b,g), running (b,g), soccer (b,g), squash (b,g), tennis (b,g), track and field (b,g), volleyball (b,g); intramural: aerobics (g), badminton (b,g), cross-country running (b,g), golf (b,g), ice hockey (b,g), indoor soccer (b), squash (b,g), tennis (b,g), track and field (b,g), yoga (g); coed interscholastic: badminton, crew, cross-country running, ice hockey, rowing, tennis, track and field; coed intramural: backpacking, badminton, bicycling, billiards, broomball, canoeing/kayaking, climbing, cooperative games, cross-country running, fitness, fitness walking, floor hockey, golf, hiking/backpacking, ice hockey, ice skating, indoor soccer, jogging, kayaking, mountain biking, outdoor activities, outdoor edu-

cation, physical fitness, physical training, rock climbing, running, skiing (cross-country), skiing (downhill), snowboarding, snowshoeing, squash, street hockey, strength & conditioning, tennis, track and field, ultimate Frisbee, volleyball, walking, wall climbing, weight training. 5 PE instructors, 1 coach.
Computers Computers are regularly used in all classes. Computer network features include on-campus library services, Internet access, wireless campus network, Internet filtering or blocking technology, Web site for each academic course, informative, interactive online community for parents, teachers, and students. Campus intranet and student e-mail accounts are available to students. Students grades are available online. The school has a published electronic and media policy.
Contact Mrs. Elizabeth Kitchen, Associate Director of Admission. 506-848-0866. Fax: 506-848-0851. E-mail: Elizabeth.Kitchen@rns.cc. Web site: www.rns.cc.

ROTTERDAM INTERNATIONAL SECONDARY SCHOOL, WOLFERT VAN BORSELEN

Bentincklaan 294

Rotterdam 3039 KK, Netherlands

Head of School: Ms. Jane Forrest

General Information Coeducational day college-preparatory, bilingual studies, and languages school. Grades 6–12. Founded: 1988. Setting: urban. 2-hectare campus. 1 building on campus. Approved or accredited by International Baccalaureate Organization, New England Association of Schools and Colleges, and state department of education. Language of instruction: English. Total enrollment: 193. Upper school average class size: 15. Upper school faculty-student ratio: 1:10. There are 190 required school days per year for Upper School students. Upper School students typically attend 5 days per week. The average school day consists of 6 hours.
Upper School Student Profile Grade 6: 18 students (12 boys, 6 girls); Grade 7: 20 students (8 boys, 12 girls); Grade 8: 23 students (13 boys, 10 girls); Grade 9: 29 students (21 boys, 8 girls); Grade 10: 27 students (16 boys, 11 girls); Grade 11: 30 students (14 boys, 16 girls); Grade 12: 46 students (24 boys, 22 girls).
Faculty School total: 32. In upper school: 8 men, 18 women; 16 have advanced degrees.
Special Academic Programs International Baccalaureate program; ESL.
College Admission Counseling 31 students graduated in 2010; 20 went to college. Other: 1 entered military service, 10 had other specific plans.
Student Life Upper grades have student council. Discipline rests primarily with faculty.
Tuition and Aid Day student tuition: €5800–€7500. Tuition installment plan (monthly payment plans, eight yearly payments).
Admissions Admissions testing required. Deadline for receipt of application materials: none. Application fee required: €250. On-campus interview required.
Athletics Coed Interscholastic: basketball, soccer; coed intramural: baseball, basketball, bicycling, rowing, soccer, tai chi, track and field, volleyball. 4 PE instructors.
Computers Computers are regularly used in all academic classes. Computer network features include online commercial services, Internet access. Student e-mail accounts are available to students. Students grades are available online. The school has a published electronic and media policy.
Contact Alexa Nijpels, Admissions Officer. 31-10 890 7745. Fax: 31-10 8907755. E-mail: info.riss@wolfert.nl. Web site: www.wolfert.nl/riss/.

ROWLAND HALL

843 South Lincoln Street

Salt Lake City, Utah 84102

Head of School: Mr. Alan C. Sparrow

General Information Coeducational day college-preparatory school. Grades PK–12. Founded: 1867. Setting: urban. 4-acre campus. 1 building on campus. Approved or accredited by National Association of Episcopal Schools, Northwest Accreditation Commission, Northwest Association of Schools and Colleges, Pacific Northwest Association of Independent Schools, The College Board, and Utah Department of Education. Member of National Association of Independent Schools. Endowment: $4 million. Total enrollment: 1,001. Upper school average class size: 16. Upper school faculty-student ratio: 1:8. There are 170 required school days per year for Upper School students. Upper School students typically attend 5 days per week. The average school day consists of 5 hours and 16 minutes.
Upper School Student Profile Grade 9: 70 students (34 boys, 36 girls); Grade 10: 73 students (42 boys, 31 girls); Grade 11: 86 students (43 boys, 43 girls); Grade 12: 67 students (28 boys, 39 girls).
Faculty School total: 38. In upper school: 19 men, 19 women; 28 have advanced degrees.
Subjects Offered Adolescent issues, algebra, biology, biology-AP, calculus, calculus-AP, ceramics, chemistry, chemistry-AP, Chinese, chorus, computer graphics, creative writing, dance, debate, drama, English, English language and composition-AP, English literature and composition-AP, environmental science, ethics, European history-AP, French, French language-AP, French literature-AP, geometry, graphic arts, graphic design, history, human development, jazz band, Latin, Latin-AP, math applications, modern European history-AP, music theory, newspaper, orchestra, photography, physical education, physics, physics-AP, political science, pre-calculus, psychology-AP, Spanish, Spanish-AP, statistics-AP, studio art, studio art-AP, theater, trigonometry, U.S. history, U.S. history-AP, Web site design, weight training, Western civilization, world cultures, world religions, yearbook.
Graduation Requirements American history, arts and fine arts (art, music, dance, drama), biology, chemistry, English, ethics, foreign language, health education, mathematics, physical education (includes health), physics, science, social studies (includes history), world religions.
Special Academic Programs 17 Advanced Placement exams for which test preparation is offered; honors section; independent study.
College Admission Counseling 63 students graduated in 2011; 60 went to college, including Bates College; St. Olaf College; Trinity University; University of Utah; Wesleyan University; Whitman College. Other: 3 had other specific plans. Median SAT critical reading: 620, median SAT math: 620, median SAT writing: 610, median combined SAT: 1830, median composite ACT: 28. 57% scored over 600 on SAT critical reading, 61% scored over 600 on SAT math, 57% scored over 600 on SAT writing, 57% scored over 1800 on combined SAT, 60% scored over 26 on composite ACT.
Student Life Upper grades have specified standards of dress, student council, honor system. Discipline rests equally with students and faculty.
Summer Programs Enrichment, advancement, sports, art/fine arts, computer instruction programs offered; session focuses on advancement and elective courses; held on campus; accepts boys and girls; open to students from other schools. 60 students usually enrolled. 2012 schedule: June 18 to July 27. Application deadline: none.
Tuition and Aid Day student tuition: $17,010. Tuition installment plan (monthly payment plans, individually arranged payment plans, 2-installment plan). Merit scholarship grants, need-based scholarship grants, Ethnic/Racial Diversity scholarship grants, Malone Family Foundation Academically Talented/Need Based Scholarships available. In 2011–12, 18% of upper-school students received aid; total upper-school merit-scholarship money awarded: $54,500. Total amount of financial aid awarded in 2011–12: $467,658.
Admissions Traditional secondary-level entrance grade is 9. For fall 2011, 49 students applied for upper-level admission, 39 were accepted, 31 enrolled. ACT-Explore, ERB CTP IV, ISEE, TOEFL or writing sample required. Deadline for receipt of application materials: March 1. Application fee required: $50. Interview recommended.
Athletics Interscholastic: baseball (boys), basketball (b,g), golf (b,g), skiing (downhill) (b,g), soccer (b,g), softball (g), swimming and diving (b,g), tennis (b,g), volleyball (g); intramural: alpine skiing (b,g), skiing (downhill) (b,g); coed interscholastic: cross-country running, dance, modern dance, physical fitness, physical training, ropes courses, strength & conditioning; coed intramural: climbing, deck hockey, hiking/backpacking, mountain biking, outdoor activities, outdoor education, rock climbing, skiing (cross-country), snowboarding, swimming and diving, telemark skiing, track and field, weight training, yoga. 6 PE instructors, 22 coaches, 1 athletic trainer.
Computers Computers are regularly used in desktop publishing, graphic design, yearbook classes. Computer network features include on-campus library services, Internet access, wireless campus network, Internet filtering or blocking technology, all students have their own laptop computer. Campus intranet, student e-mail accounts, and computer access in designated common areas are available to students. Students grades are available online. The school has a published electronic and media policy.
Contact Karen Hyde, Director of Admission. 801-924-5940. Fax: 801-355-0474. E-mail: karenhyde@rowlandhall.org. Web site: www.rowlandhall.org.

THE ROXBURY LATIN SCHOOL

101 St. Theresa Avenue

West Roxbury, Massachusetts 02132

Head of School: Mr. Kerry Paul Brennan

General Information Boys' day college-preparatory school. Grades 7–12. Founded: 1645. Setting: urban. Nearest major city is Boston. 117-acre campus. 10 buildings on campus. Approved or accredited by Association of Independent Schools in New England, Headmasters' Conference, and New England Association of Schools and Colleges. Member of National Association of Independent Schools and Secondary School Admission Test Board. Endowment: $116 million. Total enrollment: 297. Upper school average class size: 13. Upper school faculty-student ratio: 1:8. There are 176 required school days per year for Upper School students. Upper School students typically attend 5 days per week. The average school day consists of 6 hours and 30 minutes.
Upper School Student Profile Grade 7: 43 students (43 boys); Grade 8: 43 students (43 boys); Grade 9: 56 students (56 boys); Grade 10: 52 students (52 boys); Grade 11: 51 students (51 boys); Grade 12: 52 students (52 boys).
Faculty School total: 39. In upper school: 34 men, 5 women; 30 have advanced degrees.
Subjects Offered Advanced biology, advanced chemistry, advanced math, advanced studio art-AP, algebra, American Civil War, American government, American history, American literature, American studies, analysis, analytic geometry, Ancient Greek, ancient history, ancient world history, art, art history, arts, biology, calculus, calculus-AP, chemistry, classical Greek literature, classical language, college counseling, college

placement, computer science, computer science-AP, creative writing, design, drama, earth science, economics, English, English literature, European history, expository writing, fine arts, French, French language-AP, geometry, global studies, government/civics, grammar, history, Indian studies, Latin, Latin-AP, life science, macro/microeconomics-AP, mathematics, Middle East, model United Nations, music, music theory-AP, personal development, photography, physical education, physical science, physics, pre-algebra, science, senior project, Spanish, Spanish language-AP, statistics-AP, studio art, theater, trigonometry, U.S. government and politics-AP, U.S. history, visual arts, water color painting, Western civilization, world history, writing.

Graduation Requirements Arts, English, foreign language, history, Latin, mathematics, science, U.S. history, Western civilization, independent senior project.

Special Academic Programs Advanced Placement exam preparation; honors section; independent study; academic accommodation for the gifted, the musically talented, and the artistically talented.

College Admission Counseling 51 students graduated in 2011; 50 went to college, including Bowdoin College; Columbia University; Dartmouth College; Harvard University; Princeton University; Vanderbilt University. Other: 1 had other specific plans. Median SAT critical reading: 730, median SAT math: 755, median SAT writing; 750, median combined SAT: 2250. 94% scored over 600 on SAT critical reading, 96% scored over 600 on SAT math, 96% scored over 600 on SAT writing, 96% scored over 1800 on combined SAT.

Student Life Upper grades have specified standards of dress, student council, honor system. Discipline rests equally with students and faculty.

Summer Programs Enrichment, sports, computer instruction programs offered; held on campus; accepts boys and girls; open to students from other schools.

Tuition and Aid Day student tuition: $22,300. Tuition installment plan (Insured Tuition Payment Plan, Key Tuition Payment Plan, 2-payment plan). Need-based scholarship grants available. In 2011–12, 40% of upper-school students received aid. Total amount of financial aid awarded in 2011–12: $1,918,630.

Admissions Traditional secondary-level entrance grade is 7. For fall 2011, 450 students applied for upper-level admission, 65 were accepted, 57 enrolled. ISEE or SSAT required. Deadline for receipt of application materials: January 6. No application fee required. On-campus interview required.

Athletics Interscholastic: baseball, basketball, cross-country running, football, ice hockey, lacrosse, soccer, tennis, track and field, wrestling. 1 PE instructor, 11 coaches, 1 athletic trainer.

Computers Computers are regularly used in all academic, desktop publishing, literary magazine, newspaper, yearbook classes. Computer network features include on-campus library services, online commercial services, Internet access, wireless campus network, Internet filtering or blocking technology. Campus intranet, student e-mail accounts, and computer access in designated common areas are available to students. The school has a published electronic and media policy.

Contact Ms. Lindsay Schuyler, Assistant Director of Admission. 617-325-4920. Fax: 617-325-3585. E-mail: admission@roxburylatin.org. Web site: www.roxburylatin.org.

ROYAL CANADIAN COLLEGE

8610 Ash Street

Vancouver, British Columbia V6P 3M2, Canada

Head of School: Mr. Howard H. Jiang

General Information Coeducational day college-preparatory and general academic school. Grades 8–12. Founded: 1989. Setting: suburban. 1-acre campus. 1 building on campus. Approved or accredited by British Columbia Department of Education. Language of instruction: English. Total enrollment: 70. Upper school average class size: 20. Upper school faculty-student ratio: 1:15. There are 197 required school days per year for Upper School students. Upper School students typically attend 5 days per week. The average school day consists of 5 hours and 30 minutes.

Upper School Student Profile Grade 10: 18 students (9 boys, 9 girls); Grade 11: 22 students (13 boys, 9 girls); Grade 12: 30 students (18 boys, 12 girls).

Faculty School total: 6. In upper school: 5 men, 1 woman; 1 has an advanced degree.

Subjects Offered Accounting, applied skills, biology, calculus, Canadian geography, Canadian history, career planning, chemistry, communications, computer science, computer science-AP, drama, economics, English, ESL, fine arts, general science, geography, history, information technology, Mandarin, mathematics, physical education, physics, pre-calculus, social sciences, world history, writing.

Graduation Requirements Applied skills, arts and fine arts (art, music, dance, drama), career and personal planning, language arts, mathematics, science, social studies (includes history).

Special Academic Programs ESL (10 students enrolled).

College Admission Counseling 27 students graduated in 2011; 26 went to college, including Simon Fraser University; The University of British Columbia; University of Alberta; University of Toronto; University of Victoria. Other: 1 had other specific plans.

Student Life Upper grades have student council, honor system. Discipline rests primarily with faculty.

Summer Programs ESL programs offered; session focuses on learning survival English conversational skills, and Canadian cultural experience; held on campus; accepts boys and girls; open to students from other schools. 30 students usually enrolled. 2012 schedule: July 2 to August 24. Application deadline: May 31.

Tuition and Aid Day student tuition: CAN$13,500. Merit scholarship grants available. In 2011–12, 5% of upper-school students received aid; total upper-school merit-scholarship money awarded: CAN$10,000.

Admissions Traditional secondary-level entrance grade is 11. For fall 2011, 31 students applied for upper-level admission, 26 were accepted, 26 enrolled. English language required. Deadline for receipt of application materials: none. Application fee required: CAN$200. Interview recommended.

Athletics Intramural: badminton (boys, girls), baseball (b,g), basketball (b,g), soccer (b,g), ultimate Frisbee (b,g); coed intramural: badminton, baseball, soccer, ultimate Frisbee. 1 PE instructor.

Computers Computers are regularly used in accounting, career exploration, English, information technology, programming, science, social studies classes. Computer network features include Internet access, wireless campus network, Internet filtering or blocking technology. Computer access in designated common areas is available to students.

Contact Mr. Jeffry Yip, Senior Administrator. 604-738-2221. Fax: 604-738-2282. E-mail: info@royalcanadiancollege.com. Web site: www.royalcanadiancollege.com.

ROYCEMORE SCHOOL

640 Lincoln Street

Evanston, Illinois 60201

Head of School: Mr. Joseph A. Becker

General Information Coeducational day college-preparatory and arts school. Grades PK–12. Founded: 1915. Setting: suburban. Nearest major city is Chicago. 1-acre campus. 1 building on campus. Approved or accredited by Independent Schools Association of the Central States and Illinois Department of Education. Member of National Association of Independent Schools. Endowment: $1 million. Total enrollment: 262. Upper school average class size: 9. Upper school faculty-student ratio: 1:5. There are 165 required school days per year for Upper School students. Upper School students typically attend 5 days per week. The average school day consists of 7 hours.

Upper School Student Profile Grade 9: 14 students (7 boys, 7 girls); Grade 10: 19 students (11 boys, 8 girls); Grade 11: 33 students (18 boys, 15 girls); Grade 12: 27 students (18 boys, 9 girls).

Faculty School total: 37. In upper school: 5 men, 15 women; 14 have advanced degrees.

Subjects Offered African-American literature, algebra, American literature, art, biology, biology-AP, calculus-AP, chemistry, choir, comedy, composition, drawing, English language and composition-AP, English literature, environmental science, European history-AP, French, French-AP, geometry, government/civics, human development, independent study, international relations, introduction to theater, literature-AP, microeconomics, modern European history, music composition, music history, music theory, music theory-AP, mythology, painting, physical education, physics, physics-AP, pottery, public speaking, sculpture, society, politics and law, sociology, Spanish, Spanish-AP, studio art-AP, trigonometry, U.S. history, U.S. history-AP, world history, world literature, world religions, yearbook.

Graduation Requirements Arts and fine arts (art, music, dance, drama), English, foreign language, mathematics, physical education (includes health), science, social studies (includes history), participation in a 2-week January short-term project each year.

Special Academic Programs 10 Advanced Placement exams for which test preparation is offered; accelerated programs; independent study; study at local college for college credit.

College Admission Counseling 16 students graduated in 2010; all went to college, including Columbia University; DePaul University; Purdue University; The George Washington University; University of Illinois at Urbana–Champaign. Median SAT critical reading: 560, median SAT math: 650, median SAT writing: 620, median combined SAT: 1830, median composite ACT: 24. 44% scored over 600 on SAT critical reading, 67% scored over 600 on SAT math, 56% scored over 600 on SAT writing, 56% scored over 1800 on combined SAT, 46% scored over 26 on composite ACT.

Student Life Upper grades have specified standards of dress, student council, honor system. Discipline rests primarily with faculty.

Tuition and Aid Day student tuition: $22,810. Tuition installment plan (individually arranged payment plans, semiannual payment plan, 9-month payment plan). Merit scholarship grants, need-based scholarship grants, discounts for children of Northwestern University and NorthShore University, HealthSystem employees available. In 2010–11, 57% of upper-school students received aid; total upper-school merit-scholarship money awarded: $123,000. Total amount of financial aid awarded in 2010–11: $620,400.

Admissions Traditional secondary-level entrance grade is 9. For fall 2010, 28 students applied for upper-level admission, 20 were accepted, 15 enrolled. Any standardized test or writing sample required. Deadline for receipt of application materials: none. Application fee required: $75. Interview required.

Athletics Interscholastic: basketball (boys, girls), volleyball (g); intramural: softball (b), strength & conditioning (b), volleyball (b); coed interscholastic: soccer; coed intramural: gymnastics, table tennis. 3 PE instructors, 2 coaches.

Computers Computers are regularly used in all academic classes. Computer network features include on-campus library services, Internet access, wireless campus network. The school has a published electronic and media policy.

Contact Ms. Jessica Acee, Director of Admissions. 847-866-6055. Fax: 847-866-6545. E-mail: jacee@roycemoreschool.org. Web site: www.roycemoreschool.org.

RUMSEY HALL SCHOOL

Washington Depot, Connecticut

See Junior Boarding Schools section.

RUNDLE COLLEGE

4411 Manitoba Road SE

Calgary, Alberta T2G 4B9, Canada

Head of School: Mtro. David Hauk

General Information Coeducational day college-preparatory, arts, business, bilingual studies, and technology school. Grades PK–12. Approved or accredited by Association of Independent Schools and Colleges of Alberta. Language of instruction: English. Total enrollment: 783. Upper school average class size: 14.

Upper School Student Profile Grade 10: 83 students (43 boys, 40 girls); Grade 11: 82 students (43 boys, 39 girls); Grade 12: 80 students (36 boys, 44 girls).

Subjects Offered Accounting, art, band, biology, calculus, chemistry, computer science, drama, English, French, general science, mathematics, physical education, physics, science, social studies, Spanish, theater.

Graduation Requirements Career and personal planning, English, mathematics, physical education (includes health), science, social sciences.

Special Academic Programs Honors section; study abroad.

College Admission Counseling 80 students graduated in 2011; 78 went to college, including The University of British Columbia; The University of Western Ontario; University of Alberta; University of Calgary; University of Victoria; University of Waterloo. Other: 2 had other specific plans.

Tuition and Aid Day student tuition: CAN$12,000. Tuition installment plan (monthly payment plans). Bursaries, merit scholarship grants available. In 2011–12, 1% of upper-school students received aid; total upper-school merit-scholarship money awarded: CAN$24,000. Total amount of financial aid awarded in 2011–12: CAN$24,000.

Admissions Traditional secondary-level entrance grade is 10. For fall 2011, 50 students applied for upper-level admission, 25 were accepted, 20 enrolled. Achievement tests and SSAT or WISC III required. Deadline for receipt of application materials: none. Application fee required: CAN$100. On-campus interview required.

Athletics Interscholastic: badminton (boys, girls), basketball (b,g), cross-country running (b,g), curling (b,g), dance squad (b,g), flag football (b,g), floor hockey (b,g), football (b), golf (b,g), rugby (b,g), soccer (b,g), track and field (b,g), volleyball (b,g), wrestling (b,g); intramural: aerobics (g), badminton (b,g), dance (g), football (b); coed interscholastic: badminton, softball; coed intramural: badminton, baseball, basketball, cross-country running, flag football, football, lacrosse, outdoor recreation, skiing (downhill), soccer, table tennis, track and field, volleyball, weight lifting, wrestling. 4 PE instructors.

Computers Computers are regularly used in all classes. Computer network features include Internet access, wireless campus network, Web page hosting, multimedia productions, streaming video student news. Student e-mail accounts are available to students. The school has a published electronic and media policy.

Contact Nicola Spencer, Associate Director of Admissions. 403-291-3866 Ext. 106. Fax: 403-291-5458. E-mail: spencer@rundle.ab.ca. Web site: www.rundle.ab.ca.

RYE COUNTRY DAY SCHOOL

Cedar Street

Rye, New York 10580-2034

Head of School: Mr. Scott A. Nelson

General Information Coeducational day college-preparatory, arts, and technology school. Grades PK–12. Founded: 1869. Setting: suburban. Nearest major city is New York. 30-acre campus. 8 buildings on campus. Approved or accredited by New York Department of Education. Member of National Association of Independent Schools and Secondary School Admission Test Board. Endowment: $29 million. Total enrollment: 886. Upper school average class size: 13. Upper school faculty-student ratio: 1:7. There are 165 required school days per year for Upper School students. Upper School students typically attend 5 days per week. The average school day consists of 6 hours and 50 minutes.

Upper School Student Profile Grade 9: 102 students (44 boys, 58 girls); Grade 10: 106 students (60 boys, 46 girls); Grade 11: 87 students (43 boys, 44 girls); Grade 12: 98 students (46 boys, 52 girls).

Faculty School total: 125. In upper school: 21 men, 28 women; 49 have advanced degrees.

Subjects Offered 20th century history, algebra, American history, American history-AP, American literature, American literature-AP, art, art history, art history-AP, art-AP, astronomy, biology, biology-AP, calculus, calculus-AP, ceramics, chemistry, chemistry-AP, chorus, classics, computer music, computer programming, computer science-AP, computer-aided design, CPR, creative writing, dance, drama, driver education, economics, English, English literature, English literature-AP, English-AP, environmental science, environmental science-AP, European history, European history-AP, expository writing, fencing, fine arts, forensics, French, French-AP, geometry, government, government and politics-AP, government-AP, Greek, health, history, honors English, honors geometry, independent study, instrumental music, interdisciplinary studies, jazz band, Latin, Latin-AP, Mandarin, mathematics, mechanical drawing, modern European history-AP, music, music theory-AP, oceanography, philosophy, photography, physical education, physics, physics-AP, psychology, psychology-AP, science, social studies, Spanish, Spanish-AP, speech, squash, statistics-AP, studio art-AP, The 20th Century, the Sixties, theater, theater arts, trigonometry, U.S. government and politics-AP, U.S. history, U.S. history-AP, U.S. literature, weight training, wind ensemble, world civilizations, writing.

Graduation Requirements Arts and fine arts (art, music, dance, drama), English, foreign language, life management skills, mathematics, physical education (includes health), science, social studies (includes history).

Special Academic Programs 26 Advanced Placement exams for which test preparation is offered; honors section; independent study; academic accommodation for the gifted; special instructional classes for deaf students.

College Admission Counseling 97 students graduated in 2011; all went to college, including Boston University; Lehigh University; Syracuse University; University of Michigan; University of Pennsylvania. Mean SAT critical reading: 667, mean SAT math: 674, mean SAT writing: 695, mean combined SAT: 2039, mean composite ACT: 30.

Student Life Upper grades have student council. Discipline rests primarily with faculty.

Summer Programs Remediation, enrichment, advancement, ESL, sports, art/fine arts, computer instruction programs offered; session focuses on remediation; held on campus; accepts boys and girls; open to students from other schools. 100 students usually enrolled. 2012 schedule: June 25 to August 3. Application deadline: June 1.

Tuition and Aid Day student tuition: $32,800. Tuition installment plan (monthly payment plans, individually arranged payment plans). Need-based scholarship grants available. In 2011–12, 19% of upper-school students received aid. Total amount of financial aid awarded in 2011–12: $2,300,000.

Admissions Traditional secondary-level entrance grade is 9. For fall 2011, 226 students applied for upper-level admission, 52 were accepted, 35 enrolled. ISEE or SSAT required. Deadline for receipt of application materials: December 15. Application fee required: $75. On-campus interview required.

Athletics Interscholastic: baseball (boys), basketball (b,g), cross-country running (b,g), fencing (b,g), field hockey (g), football (b), golf (b,g), ice hockey (b,g), lacrosse (b,g), sailing (b,g), soccer (b,g), softball (g), squash (b,g), tennis (b,g), track and field (b,g), wrestling (b); intramural: basketball (b), fitness (b,g), physical fitness (b,g), physical training (b,g), squash (b,g), strength & conditioning (b,g), tennis (b,g), ultimate Frisbee (b), weight training (b,g), wrestling (b); coed intramural: aerobics, aerobics/dance, ballet, cross-country running, dance, dance squad, fitness, ice skating, jogging, modern dance, running, squash, yoga. 4 PE instructors, 19 coaches, 2 athletic trainers.

Computers Computers are regularly used in art, classics, English, foreign language, history, mathematics, music, photography, publishing, science, technology, yearbook classes. Computer network features include on-campus library services, online commercial services, Internet access, wireless campus network, Internet filtering or blocking technology. Campus intranet and student e-mail accounts are available to students. Students grades are available online. The school has a published electronic and media policy.

Contact Mr. Matthew J.M. Suzuki, Director of Admissions. 914-925-4513. Fax: 914-921-2147. E-mail: matt_suzuki@ryecountryday.org. Web site: www.ryecountryday.org.

See Display on next page and Close-Up on page 668.

SACRAMENTO ADVENTIST ACADEMY

5601 Winding Way

Carmichael, California 95608-1298

Head of School: John Soule

General Information Coeducational day college-preparatory, general academic, arts, business, vocational, religious studies, bilingual studies, and technology school, affiliated with Seventh-day Adventist Church. Grades K–12. Founded: 1957. Setting: suburban. Nearest major city is Sacramento. 36-acre campus. 5 buildings on campus. Approved or accredited by Board of Regents, General Conference of Seventh-day Adventists, National Council for Private School Accreditation, Western Association of Schools and Colleges, and California Department of Education. Total enrollment: 222. Upper school average class size: 29. Upper school faculty-student ratio: 1:12. There are 180 required school days per year for Upper School students. Upper School students typically attend 5 days per week. The average school day consists of 7 hours and 15 minutes.

Upper School Student Profile 96% of students are Seventh-day Adventists.

Faculty School total: 25. In upper school: 8 men, 4 women; 4 have advanced degrees.

Subjects Offered Accounting, advanced math, Advanced Placement courses, algebra, art, band, Bible, biology, biology-AP, business technology, calculus-AP, chemistry, choir, computer applications, computer education, conceptual physics, concert band, consumer mathematics, driver education, economics, English, English composition, English language and composition-AP, geometry, graphic design, handbells, health, health education, keyboarding, life skills, microcomputer technology applications, photography, physical education, physics, public speaking, religion, softball, Spanish, Spanish-AP, speech, technical skills, U.S. government, U.S. history, word processing, world history, world history-AP, World War I.

Graduation Requirements Arts and fine arts (art, music, dance, drama), biology, computer applications, economics, English, keyboarding, life skills, mathematics, physical education (includes health), religion (includes Bible studies and theology), science, U.S. government, U.S. history, 100 hours of documented work experience, 25 hours of documented community service per year of attendance.

Special Academic Programs 4 Advanced Placement exams for which test preparation is offered; honors section; accelerated programs; study at local college for college credit; remedial math.

College Admission Counseling 27 students graduated in 2011; 24 went to college, including American River College; La Sierra University; Pacific Union College; Sierra College; Walla Walla University. Other: 2 went to work, 1 entered military service. Mean SAT critical reading: 559, mean SAT math: 566, mean composite ACT: 23. 22% scored over 600 on SAT critical reading, 44% scored over 600 on SAT math, 45% scored over 26 on composite ACT.

Student Life Upper grades have specified standards of dress, student council. Discipline rests primarily with faculty.

Tuition and Aid Day student tuition: $5160–$9370. Tuition installment plan (monthly payment plans, individually arranged payment plans). Tuition reduction for siblings, paying campus jobs, academy day scholarships available. In 2011–12, 5% of upper-school students received aid. Total amount of financial aid awarded in 2011–12: $10,000.

Admissions Traditional secondary-level entrance grade is 9. Deadline for receipt of application materials: none. Application fee required: $25. Interview required.

Athletics Interscholastic: baseball (girls), basketball (b,g), flag football (b,g), golf (b), softball (b,g), volleyball (g). 1 PE instructor, 1 coach.

Computers Computers are regularly used in accounting, business applications, English, history, keyboarding, religion, word processing classes. Computer network features include on-campus library services, online commercial services, Internet access.

Contact Mrs. Sheri Miller, Registrar/Guidance Counselor. 916-481-2300 Ext. 102. Fax: 916-481-7426. E-mail: smiller@sacaa.org. Web site: www.sacaa.org.

SACRAMENTO COUNTRY DAY SCHOOL

2636 Latham Drive
Sacramento, California 95864-7198

Head of School: Stephen T. Repsher

General Information Coeducational day college-preparatory, arts, and technology school. Grades PK–12. Founded: 1964. Setting: suburban. 12-acre campus. 8 buildings on campus. Approved or accredited by California Association of Independent Schools and Western Association of Schools and Colleges. Member of National Association of Independent Schools. Endowment: $2 million. Total enrollment: 468. Upper school average class size: 12. Upper school faculty-student ratio: 1:9. There are 175 required school days per year for Upper School students. Upper School students typically attend 5 days per week. The average school day consists of 6 hours and 25 minutes.

Upper School Student Profile Grade 9: 30 students (16 boys, 14 girls); Grade 10: 26 students (13 boys, 13 girls); Grade 11: 41 students (23 boys, 18 girls); Grade 12: 34 students (19 boys, 15 girls).

Faculty School total: 65. In upper school: 18 men, 10 women; 19 have advanced degrees.

Subjects Offered Acting, algebra, American history, American literature, ancient history, ancient/medieval philosophy, art, art history, art history-AP, art-AP, band, biology, biology-AP, British literature, calculus, calculus-AP, ceramics, chamber groups, chemistry, chemistry-AP, community service, computer skills, computer technologies, concert band, creative writing, digital imaging, digital music, drama, drama performance, drawing, earth science, economics, English, English literature, European history, fine arts, French, French-AP, geography, geometry, government/civics, grammar, history, international relations, jazz band, journalism, language and composition, Latin, Latin-AP, mathematics, newspaper, nutrition, orchestra, physical education, physics, physics-AP, physiology, pre-calculus, public speaking, science, social studies, Spanish, Spanish-AP, speech, studio art, studio art-AP, technology/design, theater, trigonometry, U.S. history, U.S. history-AP, world history, world literature, writing.

Graduation Requirements Arts and fine arts (art, music, dance, drama), computer science, electives, English, foreign language, history, mathematics, physical education (includes health), science, 40-hour senior project. Community service is required.
Special Academic Programs Advanced Placement exam preparation; independent study; study at local college for college credit; ESL (5 students enrolled).
College Admission Counseling 36 students graduated in 2011; all went to college, including California State Polytechnic University, Pomona; Occidental College; Santa Clara University; University of California, San Diego; University of California, Santa Cruz; University of Puget Sound. Median SAT critical reading: 622, median SAT math: 619, median SAT writing: 638, median combined SAT: 1879.
Student Life Upper grades have specified standards of dress, student council, honor system. Discipline rests primarily with faculty.
Tuition and Aid Day student tuition: $20,230. Tuition installment plan (Insured Tuition Payment Plan, monthly payment plans, individually arranged payment plans). Need-based scholarship grants available. In 2011–12, 27% of upper-school students received aid. Total amount of financial aid awarded in 2011–12: $447,850.
Admissions Traditional secondary-level entrance grade is 9. For fall 2011, 28 students applied for upper-level admission, 17 were accepted, 16 enrolled. ERB, Otis-Lennon Mental Ability Test and writing sample required. Deadline for receipt of application materials: none. Application fee required: $25. Interview required.
Athletics Interscholastic: baseball (boys), basketball (b,g), flag football (b), lacrosse (b), soccer (b,g), softball (g), swimming and diving (b,g), track and field (b,g), volleyball (b,g); coed interscholastic: cross-country running, golf, skiing (downhill), snowboarding, tennis, wrestling. 3 PE instructors, 14 coaches.
Computers Computers are regularly used in all academic classes. Computer network features include on-campus library services, online commercial services, Internet access, Internet filtering or blocking technology. Campus intranet and student e-mail accounts are available to students. The school has a published electronic and media policy.
Contact Lonna Bloedau, Director of Admission. 916-481-8811. Fax: 916-481-6016. E-mail: lbloedau@saccds.org. Web site: www.saccds.org.

SACRED HEART ACADEMY

3175 Lexington Road
Louisville, Kentucky 40206

Head of School: Dr. Beverly McAuliffe, EdD

General Information Girls' day college-preparatory, arts, religious studies, and technology school, affiliated with Roman Catholic Church. Grades 9–12. Founded: 1877. Setting: suburban. 46-acre campus. 2 buildings on campus. Approved or accredited by Southern Association of Colleges and Schools and Kentucky Department of Education. Upper school average class size: 21. Upper school faculty-student ratio: 1:15.
Upper School Student Profile 87% of students are Roman Catholic.
Faculty School total: 87. In upper school: 9 men, 78 women; 48 have advanced degrees.
Subjects Offered Algebra, American history, American literature, anatomy, art, art history, Bible studies, biology, business, business law, calculus, ceramics, chemistry, computer graphics, computer programming, computer science, creative writing, drama, economics, English, English literature, environmental science, ethics, European history, French, geography, geometry, German, government/civics, grammar, health, history, home economics, journalism, Latin, marketing, mathematics, music, nutrition, physical education, physics, physiology, psychology, religion, science, social studies, sociology, Spanish, speech, statistics, theater, theology, trigonometry, video, world history, world literature, writing.
Graduation Requirements Computer science, English, foreign language, mathematics, physical education (includes health), religion (includes Bible studies and theology), science, social studies (includes history).
Special Academic Programs Advanced Placement exam preparation; honors section; independent study; study at local college for college credit; academic accommodation for the gifted, the musically talented, and the artistically talented.
College Admission Counseling Colleges students went to include Bellarmine University; Miami University; Saint Louis University; University of Kentucky; University of Louisville; Xavier University.
Student Life Upper grades have uniform requirement, student council. Discipline rests primarily with faculty. Attendance at religious services is required.
Tuition and Aid Day student tuition: $5035. Merit scholarship grants, need-based scholarship grants, paying campus jobs available. In 2010–11, 86% of upper-school students received aid; total upper-school merit-scholarship money awarded: $10,500.
Admissions High School Placement Test required. Deadline for receipt of application materials: none. No application fee required. On-campus interview required.
Athletics Interscholastic: basketball, cross-country running, diving, field hockey, golf, soccer, softball, swimming and diving, tennis, track and field, volleyball; intramural: basketball, volleyball. 1 PE instructor, 14 coaches, 1 athletic trainer.
Computers Computers are regularly used in English, mathematics classes. Computer network features include on-campus library services, Internet access, Internet filtering or blocking technology, America Online. Student e-mail accounts and computer access in designated common areas are available to students. Students grades are available online.
Contact Dean of Studies. 502-897-6097. Fax: 502-896-3935. Web site: www.sacredheartschools.org.

SACRED HEART/GRIFFIN HIGH SCHOOL

1200 West Washington
Springfield, Illinois 62702-4794

Head of School: Sr. Margaret Joanne Grueter, OP

General Information Coeducational day college-preparatory, arts, business, vocational, religious studies, and technology school, affiliated with Roman Catholic Church. Grades 9–12. Founded: 1895. Setting: urban. 13-acre campus. 2 buildings on campus. Approved or accredited by National Catholic Education Association, North Central Association of Colleges and Schools, and Illinois Department of Education. Endowment: $8 million. Total enrollment: 774. Upper school average class size: 20. Upper school faculty-student ratio: 1:17. There are 181 required school days per year for Upper School students. Upper School students typically attend 5 days per week. The average school day consists of 6 hours and 30 minutes.
Upper School Student Profile Grade 9: 200 students (104 boys, 96 girls); Grade 10: 218 students (127 boys, 91 girls); Grade 11: 162 students (83 boys, 79 girls); Grade 12: 194 students (91 boys, 103 girls). 92% of students are Roman Catholic.
Faculty School total: 60. In upper school: 20 men, 40 women; 25 have advanced degrees.
Subjects Offered Advanced biology.
Graduation Requirements 80 hours of service to community or approved organizations.
Special Academic Programs 8 Advanced Placement exams for which test preparation is offered; honors section; domestic exchange program; academic accommodation for the gifted, the musically talented, and the artistically talented.
College Admission Counseling 199 students graduated in 2011; 195 went to college. Other: 2 entered military service, 2 had other specific plans. Median SAT critical reading: 583, median SAT math: 615, median SAT writing: 596, median composite ACT: 24.
Student Life Upper grades have specified standards of dress, student council, honor system. Discipline rests primarily with faculty. Attendance at religious services is required.
Summer Programs Enrichment, advancement, sports programs offered; session focuses on physical education and health; held on campus; accepts boys and girls; open to students from other schools. 300 students usually enrolled. 2012 schedule: May 26 to July 3. Application deadline: April 15.
Tuition and Aid Day student tuition: $6975. Tuition installment plan (FACTS Tuition Payment Plan, individually arranged payment plans). Tuition reduction for siblings, merit scholarship grants, need-based scholarship grants available. In 2011–12, 33% of upper-school students received aid; total upper-school merit-scholarship money awarded: $7000. Total amount of financial aid awarded in 2011–12: $442,207.
Admissions Traditional secondary-level entrance grade is 9. For fall 2011, 200 students applied for upper-level admission, 200 were accepted, 200 enrolled. Explore required. Deadline for receipt of application materials: none. Application fee required: $150. Interview recommended.
Athletics Interscholastic: aquatics (boys, girls), baseball (b), basketball (b,g), cheering (g), cross-country running (b,g), diving (b,g), football (b), golf (b,g), hockey (b), pom squad (g), soccer (b,g), softball (g), tennis (b,g), track and field (b,g), volleyball (g). 1 PE instructor, 3 coaches, 1 athletic trainer.
Computers Computers are regularly used in all academic classes. Computer resources include on-campus library services, Internet access, wireless campus network, Internet filtering or blocking technology. Students grades are available online. The school has a published electronic and media policy.
Contact Erica Cusumano, Marketing/Alumni Coordinator. 217-787-9732. Fax: 217-726-9791. E-mail: Cusumano@shg.org. Web site: www.shg.org.

SACRED HEART SCHOOL OF HALIFAX

5820 Spring Garden Road
Halifax, Nova Scotia B3H 1X8, Canada

Head of School: Ms. Patricia Donnelly

General Information Coeducational day college-preparatory and religious studies school, affiliated with Roman Catholic Church. Grades K–12. Founded: 1849. Setting: urban. 1 building on campus. Approved or accredited by Canadian Association of Independent Schools and Nova Scotia Department of Education. Language of instruction: English. Total enrollment: 485. Upper school average class size: 18. Upper school faculty-student ratio: 1:15. There are 175 required school days per year for Upper School students. Upper School students typically attend 5 days per week. The average school day consists of 7 hours.
Upper School Student Profile Grade 7: 60 students (18 boys, 42 girls); Grade 8: 55 students (17 boys, 38 girls); Grade 9: 54 students (22 boys, 32 girls); Grade 10: 38 students (11 boys, 27 girls); Grade 11: 37 students (7 boys, 30 girls); Grade 12: 41 students (10 boys, 31 girls). 60% of students are Roman Catholic.

Faculty School total: 65. In upper school: 1 man, 23 women; 11 have advanced degrees.
Subjects Offered 20th century history, 20th century world history, algebra, art, Bible studies, biology, calculus, Canadian history, chemistry, creative writing, earth science, economics, English, English literature, environmental science, European history, expository writing, French, geography, geometry, government/civics, grammar, health, history, mathematics, music, physical education, physics, religion, science, social studies, sociology, Spanish, theater, trigonometry, world history, writing.
Graduation Requirements Arts and fine arts (art, music, dance, drama), English, foreign language, history, mathematics, physical education (includes health), religion (includes Bible studies and theology), science. Community service is required.
Special Academic Programs 8 Advanced Placement exams for which test preparation is offered; honors section; domestic exchange program (with Network of Sacred Heart Schools); study abroad; ESL (19 students enrolled).
College Admission Counseling 41 students graduated in 2011; 39 went to college, including Acadia University; Carleton University; Dalhousie University; Mount Allison University; Saint Mary's University; St. Francis Xavier University. Other: 2 had other specific plans.
Student Life Upper grades have uniform requirement, student council, honor system. Discipline rests primarily with faculty. Attendance at religious services is required.
Summer Programs Remediation, enrichment programs offered; session focuses on French remediation, debate; held on campus; accepts boys and girls; open to students from other schools. 45 students usually enrolled. Application deadline: none.
Tuition and Aid Day student tuition: CAN$12,336. Tuition installment plan (monthly payment plans, individually arranged payment plans). Tuition reduction for siblings, bursaries, merit scholarship grants, need-based scholarship grants available. In 2011–12, 12% of upper-school students received aid; total upper-school merit-scholarship money awarded: CAN$106,000. Total amount of financial aid awarded in 2011–12: CAN$138,000.
Admissions Traditional secondary-level entrance grade is 7. For fall 2011, 53 students applied for upper-level admission, 52 were accepted, 50 enrolled. Otis-Lennon School Ability Test and school's own test required. Deadline for receipt of application materials: none. Application fee required: CAN$100. On-campus interview required.
Athletics Interscholastic: aquatics (girls), badminton (b,g), basketball (b,g), cross-country running (b,g), field hockey (g), ice hockey (b), soccer (b,g), swimming and diving (b,g), tennis (g), volleyball (g); intramural: alpine skiing (b,g), badminton (b,g), basketball (b,g), cross-country running (b,g), curling (g), fitness walking (g), jogging (b,g), running (b,g), skiing (downhill) (b,g), soccer (b,g), swimming and diving (b), tennis (g), track and field (g), volleyball (g). 3 PE instructors.
Computers Computer network features include on-campus library services, Internet access, wireless campus network, Internet filtering or blocking technology. Campus intranet and student e-mail accounts are available to students. The school has a published electronic and media policy.
Contact Ms. Pauline Scott, Principal, Sacred Heart High School. 902-422-4459 Ext. 209. Fax: 902-423-7691. E-mail: pscott@shsh.ca. Web site: www.sacredheartschool.ns.ca.

SADDLEBACK VALLEY CHRISTIAN SCHOOL

26333 Oso Road

San Juan Capistrano, California 92675

Head of School: Mr. Edward Carney

General Information Coeducational day college-preparatory, general academic, arts, religious studies, and technology school, affiliated with Christian faith. Grades PK–12. Founded: 1997. Setting: suburban. Nearest major city is Irvine/Anaheim. 69-acre campus. 6 buildings on campus. Approved or accredited by Association of Christian Schools International, Western Association of Schools and Colleges, and California Department of Education. Total enrollment: 855. Upper school average class size: 20. Upper school faculty-student ratio: 1:15. There are 180 required school days per year for Upper School students. Upper School students typically attend 5 days per week. The average school day consists of 6 hours and 35 minutes.
Upper School Student Profile Grade 9: 100 students (58 boys, 42 girls); Grade 10: 92 students (45 boys, 47 girls); Grade 11: 79 students (40 boys, 39 girls); Grade 12: 67 students (30 boys, 37 girls). 75% of students are Christian faith.
Faculty School total: 75. In upper school: 10 men, 22 women; 9 have advanced degrees.
Subjects Offered 1 1/2 elective credits, algebra, American history, American history-AP, American literature, American sign language, anatomy and physiology, applied arts, art, art history-AP, ASB Leadership, athletic training, Bible, Bible as literature, biology, biology-AP, British literature, business mathematics, calculus-AP, chemistry, computers, concert choir, debate, drama, English language and composition-AP, English literature and composition-AP, environmental science, ESL, geography, geometry, government and politics-AP, history, honors English, music, musical theater, oceanography, psychology-AP, public speaking, religious studies, science, senior project, Spanish, Spanish language-AP, speech and debate, sports, statistics-AP, studio art-AP, trigonometry, U.S. government and politics, U.S. government and politics-AP, U.S. history, U.S. history-AP, visual and performing arts, world history, world literature, world religions, yearbook.
Graduation Requirements Algebra, American history, American literature, anatomy and physiology, art, Bible, biology, British literature, earth science, English, English literature, foreign language, geometry, history, life science, physical education (includes health), physical science, science, senior project, Spanish, speech, trigonometry, U.S. history, visual arts, world history, Senior Project required for seniors to graduate.
Special Academic Programs 11 Advanced Placement exams for which test preparation is offered; honors section; independent study; study at local college for college credit; study abroad; remedial reading and/or remedial writing; remedial math; programs in English, mathematics, general development for dyslexic students; special instructional classes for students with learning disabilities; ESL (24 students enrolled).
College Admission Counseling 72 students graduated in 2011; 65 went to college, including Biola University; California Polytechnic State University, San Luis Obispo; Point Loma Nazarene University; University of California, Los Angeles; Vanguard University of Southern California. Other: 7 went to work. Median SAT critical reading: 540, median SAT math: 540, median SAT writing: 540, median combined SAT: 1620, median composite ACT: 22. 32% scored over 600 on SAT critical reading, 21% scored over 600 on SAT math, 32% scored over 600 on SAT writing, 26% scored over 1800 on combined SAT, 27% scored over 26 on composite ACT.
Student Life Upper grades have uniform requirement, student council, honor system. Discipline rests primarily with faculty. Attendance at religious services is required.
Summer Programs Remediation programs offered; session focuses on make-up of school work; held on campus; accepts boys and girls; not open to students from other schools. 10 students usually enrolled. 2012 schedule: June 20 to July 31. Application deadline: June 5.
Tuition and Aid Day student tuition: $8500. Tuition installment plan (monthly payment plans). Tuition reduction for siblings, merit scholarship grants, need-based scholarship grants available. In 2011–12, 25% of upper-school students received aid; total upper-school merit-scholarship money awarded: $175,000. Total amount of financial aid awarded in 2011–12: $175,000.
Admissions Traditional secondary-level entrance grade is 9. For fall 2011, 70 students applied for upper-level admission, 65 were accepted, 60 enrolled. Placement test required. Deadline for receipt of application materials: none. Application fee required: $200. Interview required.
Athletics Interscholastic: baseball (boys), basketball (b,g), cheering (g), cross-country running (b,g), football (b), golf (b,g), soccer (b,g), softball (g), swimming and diving (b,g), tennis (g), track and field (b,g), volleyball (b,g); intramural: equestrian sports (g); coed interscholastic: dance team. 5 PE instructors, 15 coaches, 4 athletic trainers.
Computers Computers are regularly used in computer applications classes. Computer network features include Internet access, Internet filtering or blocking technology. Student e-mail accounts are available to students. Students grades are available online. The school has a published electronic and media policy.
Contact Mrs. Denise Karlsen, Registrar. 949-443-4050. Fax: 949-443-3941 Ext. 1201. E-mail: denisek@svcschools.org. Web site: www.svcschools.org.

SADDLEBROOK PREPARATORY SCHOOL

5700 Saddlebrook Way

Wesley Chapel, Florida 33543

Head of School: Mr. Larry W. Robison

General Information Coeducational boarding and day college-preparatory school. Boarding grades 6–12, day grades 3–12. Founded: 1993. Setting: suburban. Nearest major city is Tampa. Students are housed in single-sex dormitories. 50-acre campus. 8 buildings on campus. Approved or accredited by Southern Association of Colleges and Schools and Florida Department of Education. Total enrollment: 97. Upper school average class size: 9. Upper school faculty-student ratio: 1:9. There are 175 required school days per year for Upper School students. Upper School students typically attend 5 days per week. The average school day consists of 7 hours and 15 minutes.
Upper School Student Profile Grade 9: 18 students (11 boys, 7 girls); Grade 10: 12 students (8 boys, 4 girls); Grade 11: 18 students (13 boys, 5 girls); Grade 12: 32 students (24 boys, 8 girls); Postgraduate: 3 students (3 boys). 66% of students are boarding students. 17% are state residents. 11 states are represented in upper school student body. 61% are international students. International students from Bahamas, Brazil, China, Germany, Mexico, and Republic of Korea; 17 other countries represented in student body.
Faculty School total: 14. In upper school: 4 men, 8 women; 5 have advanced degrees; 1 resides on campus.
Subjects Offered Algebra, American government, American history, biology, calculus, chemistry, economics, English, geometry, marine biology, physical science, physics, pre-algebra, pre-calculus, SAT preparation, Spanish, world geography, world history.
Graduation Requirements Algebra, American history, English, geometry, mathematics, physical education (includes health), science, social studies (includes history), world history.
Special Academic Programs ESL (14 students enrolled).
College Admission Counseling 15 students graduated in 2011; 13 went to college, including Babson College; Syracuse University; The University of Tampa; University

of Arkansas; University of Richmond; University of South Florida. Other: 2 entered a postgraduate year.

Student Life Upper grades have uniform requirement, student council, honor system. Discipline rests primarily with faculty.

Summer Programs Remediation, advancement, ESL programs offered; session focuses on academics; held on campus; accepts boys and girls; open to students from other schools. 10 students usually enrolled. 2012 schedule: June 11 to August 3. Application deadline: May 25.

Tuition and Aid Day student tuition: $16,885; 7-day tuition and room/board: $32,885. Tuition installment plan (individually arranged payment plans). Tuition reduction for siblings available.

Admissions Traditional secondary-level entrance grade is 12. For fall 2011, 45 students applied for upper-level admission, 40 were accepted, 29 enrolled. Deadline for receipt of application materials: none. Application fee required: $50. Interview recommended.

Athletics Interscholastic: golf (boys, girls). 27 coaches, 3 athletic trainers.

Computers Computers are regularly used in English, foreign language, history, mathematics, science classes. Computer network features include on-campus library services, online commercial services, Internet access, wireless campus network, Internet filtering or blocking technology, RenWeb. Student e-mail accounts and computer access in designated common areas are available to students. Students grades are available online. The school has a published electronic and media policy.

Contact Ms. Donna Claggett, Administrative Manager. 813-907-4525. Fax: 813-991-4713. E-mail: dclaggett@saddlebrookresort.com. Web site: www.saddlebrookprep.com.

SAGE HILL SCHOOL

20402 Newport Coast Drive

Newport Coast, California 92657-0300

Head of School: Mr. Gordon McNeill

General Information Coeducational day college-preparatory and arts school. Grades 9–12. Founded: 2000. Setting: suburban. Nearest major city is Newport Beach. 30-acre campus. 6 buildings on campus. Approved or accredited by Western Association of Schools and Colleges and California Department of Education. Member of National Association of Independent Schools. Endowment: $8 million. Total enrollment: 443. Upper school average class size: 15. Upper school faculty-student ratio: 1:10. There are 170 required school days per year for Upper School students. Upper School students typically attend 5 days per week. The average school day consists of 7 hours.

Upper School Student Profile Grade 9: 113 students (54 boys, 59 girls); Grade 10: 113 students (53 boys, 60 girls); Grade 11: 119 students (49 boys, 70 girls); Grade 12: 98 students (48 boys, 50 girls).

Faculty School total: 46. In upper school: 22 men, 24 women; 26 have advanced degrees.

Subjects Offered Algebra, art, art history, art history-AP, art-AP, biology, biology-AP, calculus, calculus-AP, chemistry, chemistry-AP, Chinese, computer science-AP, dance, dance performance, digital art, economics, English, English-AP, environmental science-AP, European history, European history-AP, forensics, French, geometry, Latin, marine science, music, music theory-AP, physical science, physics-AP, pre-calculus, Spanish, Spanish-AP, statistics, statistics-AP, studio art-AP, theater, U.S. history, U.S. history-AP, United States government-AP.

Graduation Requirements Arts, English, history, languages, mathematics, physical education (includes health), science.

Special Academic Programs 19 Advanced Placement exams for which test preparation is offered; honors section; independent study; academic accommodation for the gifted, the musically talented, and the artistically talented.

College Admission Counseling 113 students graduated in 2011; 111 went to college, including Boston University; Emory University; New York University; Southern Methodist University; Stanford University; University of Southern California. Other: 2 had other specific plans. Mean combined SAT: 1969.

Student Life Upper grades have specified standards of dress, student council, honor system. Discipline rests equally with students and faculty.

Summer Programs Remediation, enrichment, advancement, sports, art/fine arts programs offered; session focuses on academics; held on campus; accepts boys and girls; open to students from other schools. 200 students usually enrolled. 2012 schedule: June to July.

Tuition and Aid Day student tuition: $29,140. Tuition installment plan (Insured Tuition Payment Plan, monthly payment plans). Need-based scholarship grants available. In 2011–12, 15% of upper-school students received aid. Total amount of financial aid awarded in 2011–12: $1,783,170.

Admissions Traditional secondary-level entrance grade is 9. For fall 2011, 288 students applied for upper-level admission, 218 were accepted, 139 enrolled. ISEE required. Deadline for receipt of application materials: February 15. Application fee required: $100. On-campus interview required.

Athletics Interscholastic: baseball (boys), basketball (b,g), cross-country running (b,g), diving (b,g), football (b), golf (b,g), lacrosse (b,g), soccer (b,g), softball (g), swimming and diving (b,g), tennis (b,g), track and field (b,g), volleyball (b,g), water polo (b). 36 coaches, 1 athletic trainer.

Computers Computers are regularly used in computer applications, digital applications, video film production classes. Computer network features include on-campus library services, online commercial services, Internet access, wireless campus network, Internet filtering or blocking technology. Student e-mail accounts and computer access in designated common areas are available to students. Students grades are available online. The school has a published electronic and media policy.

Contact Ms. Elaine Mijalis-Kahn, Director of Admission and Financial Aid. 949-219-1337. Fax: 949-219-1399. E-mail: mijaliskahne@sagehillschool.org. Web site: www.sagehillschool.org.

SAGE RIDGE SCHOOL

2515 Crossbow Court

Reno, Nevada 89511

Head of School: Mr. Daryl DiBitonto

General Information Coeducational day college-preparatory, arts, and technology school. Grades 5–12. Founded: 1997. Setting: suburban. 44-acre campus. 2 buildings on campus. Approved or accredited by Pacific Northwest Association of Independent Schools and Nevada Department of Education. Total enrollment: 224. Upper school average class size: 14. Upper school faculty-student ratio: 1:6. There are 180 required school days per year for Upper School students. Upper School students typically attend 5 days per week. The average school day consists of 7 hours and 10 minutes.

Upper School Student Profile Grade 9: 15 students (7 boys, 8 girls); Grade 10: 25 students (14 boys, 11 girls); Grade 11: 16 students (10 boys, 6 girls); Grade 12: 20 students (8 boys, 12 girls).

Faculty School total: 30. In upper school: 8 men, 5 women; 9 have advanced degrees.

Subjects Offered Advanced chemistry, algebra, American history-AP, American literature, American literature-AP, analytic geometry, anatomy and physiology, ancient world history, art history, biology, biology-AP, British literature, British literature-AP, calculus, calculus-AP, ceramics, chemistry, choir, classical language, college counseling, conceptual physics, creative writing, debate, drama performance, electives, English language and composition-AP, English language-AP, English literature and composition-AP, English literature-AP, European history, European literature, foreign language, geometry, honors algebra, honors English, lab science, language-AP, Latin, Latin-AP, medieval history, modern European history, music history, music performance, music theory, outdoor education, philosophy, physical education, physical fitness, physics, playwriting and directing, poetry, pre-algebra, pre-calculus, probability and statistics, public speaking, senior internship, senior seminar, senior thesis, Spanish, Spanish language-AP, Spanish literature, Spanish literature-AP, Spanish-AP, statistics, studio art, studio art-AP, theater, theater arts, theater history, theory of knowledge, trigonometry, U.S. government and politics-AP, U.S. history, U.S. history-AP, Western literature, world history.

Graduation Requirements 20th century world history, algebra, American history, American literature, analytic geometry, ancient world history, art history, biology, British literature, chemistry, conceptual physics, English composition, European history, foreign language, history of music, modern European history, music, outdoor education, participation in sports, pre-calculus, public speaking, science, senior internship, senior thesis, speech, theater history, trigonometry, U.S. history, 15 hours of community service per year, senior thesis and senior internship, two mini-semester seminars per year.

Special Academic Programs 16 Advanced Placement exams for which test preparation is offered; honors section; independent study; academic accommodation for the gifted.

College Admission Counseling 18 students graduated in 2011; all went to college, including Bentley University; Tulane University; University of Chicago. Mean SAT critical reading: 612, mean SAT math: 660, mean SAT writing: 636, mean combined SAT: 1907, mean composite ACT: 27.

Student Life Upper grades have uniform requirement, student council, honor system. Discipline rests equally with students and faculty.

Summer Programs Enrichment, art/fine arts programs offered; session focuses on enrichment for middle school students; held on campus; accepts boys and girls; open to students from other schools. 150 students usually enrolled. 2012 schedule: July 12 to July 30.

Tuition and Aid Day student tuition: $18,300. Tuition installment plan (Insured Tuition Payment Plan). Need-based scholarship grants available. In 2011–12, 13% of upper-school students received aid. Total amount of financial aid awarded in 2011–12: $176,225.

Admissions Traditional secondary-level entrance grade is 9. For fall 2011, 12 students applied for upper-level admission, 10 were accepted, 8 enrolled. ERB required. Deadline for receipt of application materials: none. Application fee required: $50. Interview required.

Athletics Interscholastic: alpine skiing (boys, girls), basketball (b,g), cross-country running (b,g), golf (b), skiing (downhill) (b,g), track and field (b,g), volleyball (g), wrestling (b,g); intramural: alpine skiing (b,g), basketball (b,g), cross-country running (b,g), golf (b,g), skiing (downhill) (b,g), swimming and diving (b,g), track and field (b,g), volleyball (g); coed intramural: bicycling, Frisbee, lacrosse, outdoor education, ropes courses, soccer. 2 PE instructors, 12 coaches.

Computers Computers are regularly used in art, classics, college planning, current events, English, foreign language, history, humanities, independent study, Latin, literary magazine, mathematics, newspaper, publications, SAT preparation, science, senior seminar, social sciences, social studies, Spanish, speech, word processing, writing, yearbook classes. Computer network features include on-campus library services, online commercial services, Internet access, wireless campus network, Internet filtering or blocking technology. Student e-mail accounts are available to students. Students grades are available online.

Contact Mrs. Laurice Antoun-Becker, Director of Admission. 775-852-6222 Ext. 509. Fax: 775-852-6228. E-mail: LBecker@sageridge.org. Web site: www.sageridge.org.

ST. AGNES ACADEMY

9000 Bellaire Boulevard

Houston, Texas 77036

Head of School: Sr. Jane Meyer

General Information Girls' day college-preparatory, arts, business, religious studies, and technology school, affiliated with Roman Catholic Church. Grades 9–12. Founded: 1906. Setting: urban. 33-acre campus. 3 buildings on campus. Approved or accredited by Southern Association of Colleges and Schools and Texas Department of Education. Endowment: $6 million. Total enrollment: 871. Upper school average class size: 22. Upper school faculty-student ratio: 1:15. There are 180 required school days per year for Upper School students. Upper School students typically attend 5 days per week. The average school day consists of 6 hours and 5 minutes.

Upper School Student Profile Grade 9: 237 students (237 girls); Grade 10: 217 students (217 girls); Grade 11: 210 students (210 girls); Grade 12: 207 students (207 girls). 78% of students are Roman Catholic.

Faculty School total: 80. In upper school: 18 men, 62 women; 51 have advanced degrees.

Subjects Offered Accounting, acting, algebra, American history, American literature, art, art history, biology, business law, business skills, calculus, chemistry, community service, computer programming, computer science, creative writing, dance, digital photography, drama, economics, English, English literature, European history, fine arts, French, geology, geometry, government/civics, health, history, integrated physics, journalism, keyboarding, Latin, marine biology, mathematics, music, philosophy, photography, physical education, physics, physiology, psychology, religion, science, social sciences, social studies, Spanish, speech, theater, theology, trigonometry, video film production, world history, world literature.

Graduation Requirements Arts and fine arts (art, music, dance, drama), computer science, electives, English, foreign language, mathematics, physical education (includes health), religion (includes Bible studies and theology), science, social sciences, social studies (includes history), speech, 100 hours of community service.

Special Academic Programs Advanced Placement exam preparation; honors section; independent study.

College Admission Counseling 209 students graduated in 2011; all went to college, including Louisiana State University and Agricultural and Mechanical College; St. Edward's University; Texas A&M University; The University of Texas at Austin; The University of Texas at San Antonio. Mean SAT critical reading: 620, mean SAT math: 620, mean composite ACT: 26. 56% scored over 600 on SAT critical reading, 58% scored over 600 on SAT math, 50% scored over 26 on composite ACT.

Student Life Upper grades have uniform requirement, student council, honor system. Discipline rests primarily with faculty. Attendance at religious services is required.

Summer Programs Remediation, art/fine arts, computer instruction programs offered; session focuses on remediation and elective credit; held on campus; accepts girls; not open to students from other schools. 100 students usually enrolled. 2012 schedule: June to June.

Tuition and Aid Day student tuition: $13,600. Tuition installment plan (plans arranged through local bank). Merit scholarship grants, need-based scholarship grants available. In 2011–12, 30% of upper-school students received aid; total upper-school merit-scholarship money awarded: $24,000. Total amount of financial aid awarded in 2011–12: $800,000.

Admissions Traditional secondary-level entrance grade is 9. For fall 2011, 507 students applied for upper-level admission, 319 were accepted, 237 enrolled. ISEE required. Deadline for receipt of application materials: January 15. Application fee required: $50. On-campus interview required.

Athletics Interscholastic: aquatics, basketball, cheering, cross-country running, dance team, diving, field hockey, golf, lacrosse, soccer, softball, swimming and diving, tennis, track and field, volleyball, water polo, winter soccer; intramural: badminton, floor hockey, volleyball. 4 PE instructors, 6 coaches, 1 athletic trainer.

Computers Computers are regularly used in all classes. Computer network features include on-campus library services, online commercial services, Internet access, wireless campus network, Internet filtering or blocking technology. Campus intranet and student e-mail accounts are available to students. Students grades are available online. The school has a published electronic and media policy.

Contact Erin Hoover, Assistant Director of Admission. 713-219-5400. Fax: 713-219-5499. E-mail: ehoover@st-agnes.org. Web site: www.st-agnes.org.

SAINT AGNES BOYS HIGH SCHOOL

555 West End Avenue

New York, New York 10024

Head of School: Robert J. Conte

General Information Boys' day college-preparatory and religious studies school, affiliated with Roman Catholic Church. Grades 9–12. Founded: 1892. Setting: urban. 1 building on campus. Approved or accredited by Middle States Association of Colleges and Schools, New York State Board of Regents, New York State University, and New York Department of Education. Language of instruction: Spanish. Upper school average class size: 25. Upper school faculty-student ratio: 1:16. There are 180 required school days per year for Upper School students. Upper School students typically attend 5 days per week. The average school day consists of 6 hours and 6 minutes.

Upper School Student Profile Grade 9: 70 students (70 boys); Grade 10: 60 students (60 boys); Grade 11: 70 students (70 boys); Grade 12: 55 students (55 boys). 85% of students are Roman Catholic.

Faculty School total: 25. In upper school: 18 men, 7 women; 20 have advanced degrees.

Special Academic Programs 3 Advanced Placement exams for which test preparation is offered; honors section.

College Admission Counseling 71 students graduated in 2011; all went to college, including Hunter College of the City University of New York; Manhattan College; St. John's University; State University of New York at Binghamton. Mean SAT critical reading: 450, mean SAT math: 450.

Student Life Upper grades have specified standards of dress. Discipline rests primarily with faculty. Attendance at religious services is required.

Summer Programs Remediation programs offered; session focuses on remediation; held on campus; accepts boys and girls; open to students from other schools. 200 students usually enrolled. 2012 schedule: July 5 to August 15.

Tuition and Aid Day student tuition: $5350. Tuition installment plan (monthly payment plans). Need-based scholarship grants available. In 2011–12, 60% of upper-school students received aid.

Admissions Traditional secondary-level entrance grade is 9. For fall 2011, 390 students applied for upper-level admission, 280 were accepted, 70 enrolled. Cooperative Entrance Exam (McGraw-Hill) required. Deadline for receipt of application materials: none. No application fee required. Interview recommended.

Athletics Interscholastic: baseball, basketball, bowling, cross-country running, soccer; intramural: basketball, floor hockey, table tennis, volleyball. 1 PE instructor, 5 coaches.

Computers Computer network features include on-campus library services, Internet access. The school has a published electronic and media policy.

Contact Principal. 212-873-9100. Fax: 212-873-9292. Web site: www.staghs.org.

ST. ALBANS SCHOOL

Mount Saint Alban

Washington, District of Columbia 20016

Head of School: Mr. Vance Wilson

General Information Boys' boarding and day college-preparatory school, affiliated with Episcopal Church. Boarding grades 9–12, day grades 4–12. Founded: 1909. Setting: urban. Students are housed in single-sex dormitories. 54-acre campus. 7 buildings on campus. Approved or accredited by Association of Independent Maryland Schools, Association of Independent Schools of Greater Washington, The Association of Boarding Schools, and District of Columbia Department of Education. Member of National Association of Independent Schools and Secondary School Admission Test Board. Endowment: $51.3 million. Total enrollment: 578. Upper school average class size: 13. Upper school faculty-student ratio: 1:7. There are 170 required school days per year for Upper School students. Upper School students typically attend 5 days per week.

Upper School Student Profile Grade 9: 77 students (77 boys); Grade 10: 76 students (76 boys); Grade 11: 81 students (81 boys); Grade 12: 78 students (78 boys). 9% of students are boarding students. 40% are state residents. 6 states are represented in upper school student body. 2% are international students. International students from Bulgaria, China, Lithuania, Mexico, and Republic of Korea; 5 other countries represented in student body. 20% of students are members of Episcopal Church.

Faculty School total: 90. In upper school: 50 men, 19 women; 39 have advanced degrees; 4 reside on campus.

Subjects Offered Advanced Placement courses, algebra, American history, American literature, art, art history, Bible studies, biology, calculus, ceramics, chemistry, Chinese, community service, computer math, computer programming, computer science, creative writing, dance, drama, earth science, economics, English, English literature, ethics, European history, expository writing, fine arts, French, geography, geometry, government/civics, Greek, history, Japanese, Latin, marine biology, mathematics, music, photography, physical education, physics, religion, science, social studies, Spanish, speech, theater.

Graduation Requirements American history, ancient history, arts and fine arts (art, music, dance, drama), English, ethics, foreign language, mathematics, physical education (includes health), science, participation in athletic program. Community service is required.

Special Academic Programs Advanced Placement exam preparation; honors section; independent study; term-away projects; study abroad.
College Admission Counseling 82 students graduated in 2011; all went to college, including Amherst College; Bowdoin College; Georgetown University; Harvard University; The College of William and Mary; University of Michigan.
Student Life Upper grades have specified standards of dress, student council, honor system. Discipline rests equally with students and faculty. Attendance at religious services is required.
Summer Programs Remediation, enrichment, advancement, ESL, sports, art/fine arts, rigorous outdoor training, computer instruction programs offered; session focuses on academics and day camp; held on campus; accepts boys and girls; open to students from other schools. 1,500 students usually enrolled. 2012 schedule: June 7 to August 21. Application deadline: none.
Tuition and Aid Day student tuition: \$35,723; 7-day tuition and room/board: \$50,532. Tuition installment plan (Insured Tuition Payment Plan, monthly payment plans, individually arranged payment plans). Need-based scholarship grants, need-based loans available. In 2011–12, 27% of upper-school students received aid. Total amount of financial aid awarded in 2011–12: \$2,313,228.
Admissions Traditional secondary-level entrance grade is 9. For fall 2011, 115 students applied for upper-level admission, 41 were accepted, 20 enrolled. ISEE or SSAT required. Deadline for receipt of application materials: January 6. Application fee required: \$80. Interview required.
Athletics Interscholastic: aquatics, baseball, basketball, canoeing/kayaking, climbing, crew, cross-country running, diving, football, golf, ice hockey, independent competitive sports, indoor soccer, indoor track, indoor track & field, kayaking, lacrosse, rappelling, rock climbing, soccer, swimming and diving, tennis, track and field, wall climbing, weight training, winter (indoor) track, winter soccer, wrestling; intramural: aquatics, basketball, combined training, dance, fitness, indoor soccer, outdoor activities, physical training, tennis, track and field, yoga. 5 coaches, 2 athletic trainers.
Computers Computers are regularly used in mathematics, programming, science classes. Computer network features include on-campus library services, online commercial services, Internet access, wireless campus network. Campus intranet and student e-mail accounts are available to students. The school has a published electronic and media policy.
Contact Mr. Kyle Slatery, Admissions and Financial Aid Coordinator. 202-537-6440. Fax: 202-537-2225. E-mail: kslatery@cathedral.org. Web site: www.stalbansschool.org/.

ST. ANDREW'S COLLEGE

15800 Yonge Street

Aurora, Ontario L4G 3H7, Canada

Head of School: Mr. Kevin R. McHenry

General Information Boys' boarding and day college-preparatory, arts, business, and technology school. Grades 6–12. Founded: 1899. Setting: small town. Nearest major city is Toronto, Canada. Students are housed in single-sex dormitories. 110-acre campus. 24 buildings on campus. Approved or accredited by Canadian Association of Independent Schools, Canadian Educational Standards Institute, Conference of Independent Schools of Ontario, Ontario Ministry of Education, The Association of Boarding Schools, and Ontario Department of Education. Affiliate member of National Association of Independent Schools; member of Secondary School Admission Test Board. Language of instruction: English. Endowment: CAN\$22.7 million. Total enrollment: 591. Upper school average class size: 17. Upper school faculty-student ratio: 1:9. Upper School students typically attend 5 days per week. The average school day consists of 5 hours and 20 minutes.
Upper School Student Profile Grade 9: 106 students (106 boys); Grade 10: 93 students (93 boys); Grade 11: 145 students (145 boys); Grade 12: 114 students (114 boys). 52% of students are boarding students. 82% are province residents. 8 provinces are represented in upper school student body. 16% are international students. International students from China, Hong Kong, Jamaica, Mexico, Republic of Korea, and Taiwan; 18 other countries represented in student body.
Faculty School total: 66. In upper school: 43 men, 8 women; 15 have advanced degrees; 23 reside on campus.
Subjects Offered Accounting, Advanced Placement courses, algebra, American history, art, biology, business, calculus, chemistry, communications, community service, computer science, creative writing, drama, economics, English, English literature, environmental science, fine arts, French, geography, geometry, health, history, mathematics, music, physical education, physics, physiology, science, social sciences, social studies, sociology, Spanish, statistics, world history, world religions.
Graduation Requirements Arts, arts and fine arts (art, music, dance, drama), business, careers, civics, computer science, dance, drama, English, foreign language, French, geography, health education, history, mathematics, physical education (includes health), science, science and technology, social sciences. Community service is required.
Special Academic Programs 10 Advanced Placement exams for which test preparation is offered; honors section; accelerated programs; independent study; term-away projects; study abroad; ESL (16 students enrolled).
College Admission Counseling 119 students graduated in 2011; all went to college, including McGill University; Queen's University at Kingston; The University of British Columbia; The University of Western Ontario; University of Toronto; University of Waterloo.
Student Life Upper grades have uniform requirement, student council, honor system. Discipline rests equally with students and faculty. Attendance at religious services is required.
Summer Programs ESL, sports, art/fine arts programs offered; session focuses on Scottish music (piping and drumming), sports/arts camps, leadership camps, academics; held on campus; accepts boys and girls; open to students from other schools. 1,200 students usually enrolled. 2012 schedule: June 20 to August 10. Application deadline: none.
Tuition and Aid Day student tuition: CAN\$27,730; 5-day tuition and room/board: CAN\$44,616; 7-day tuition and room/board: CAN\$44,616. Tuition installment plan (monthly payment plans, one-time payment, three installments plan). Bursaries, merit scholarship grants, need-based scholarship grants available. In 2011–12, 21% of upper-school students received aid; total upper-school merit-scholarship money awarded: CAN\$263,000. Total amount of financial aid awarded in 2011–12: CAN\$1,944,330.
Admissions Traditional secondary-level entrance grade is 9. For fall 2011, 166 students applied for upper-level admission, 138 were accepted, 109 enrolled. CAT, SLEP, SSAT or TOEFL required. Deadline for receipt of application materials: none. Application fee required: CAN\$150. Interview required.
Athletics Interscholastic: alpine skiing, aquatics, badminton, baseball, basketball, biathlon, cricket, cross-country running, curling, fencing, football, golf, ice hockey, indoor track, indoor track & field, lacrosse, marksmanship, nordic skiing, rugby, running, skiing (cross-country), skiing (downhill), soccer, softball, squash, swimming and diving, table tennis, tennis, track and field, triathlon, volleyball, winter (indoor) track; intramural: aquatics, archery, backpacking, badminton, ball hockey, baseball, basketball, canoeing/kayaking, climbing, cooperative games, cross-country running, curling, fencing, fitness, flag football, floor hockey, football, Frisbee, golf, hiking/backpacking, ice hockey, ice skating, jogging, lacrosse, marksmanship, mountain biking, nordic skiing, outdoor activities, outdoor education, outdoor skills, physical fitness, rock climbing, ropes courses, running, scuba diving, self defense, skiing (cross-country), skiing (downhill), snowboarding, soccer, softball, squash, strength & conditioning, swimming and diving, table tennis, tennis, touch football, track and field, triathlon, ultimate Frisbee, volleyball, wall climbing, water polo, weight training, wilderness survival. 7 athletic trainers.
Computers Computers are regularly used in all academic classes. Computer network features include on-campus library services, online commercial services, Internet access, wireless campus network, Internet filtering or blocking technology. The school has a published electronic and media policy.
Contact Mrs. Natascia Stewart, Admission Associate. 905-727-3178 Ext. 303. Fax: 905-727-9032. E-mail: admission@sac.on.ca. Web site: www.sac.on.ca.

ST. ANDREW'S PRIORY SCHOOL

224 Queen Emma Square

Honolulu, Hawaii 96813

Head of School: Ms. Sandra J. Theunick

General Information Girls' day college-preparatory, arts, and technology school, affiliated with Episcopal Church. Grades K–12. Founded: 1867. Setting: urban. 3-acre campus. 7 buildings on campus. Approved or accredited by National Association of Episcopal Schools, The College Board, The Hawaii Council of Private Schools, Western Association of Schools and Colleges, and Hawaii Department of Education. Member of National Association of Independent Schools and Secondary School Admission Test Board. Endowment: \$3.2 million. Total enrollment: 401. Upper school average class size: 12. Upper school faculty-student ratio: 1:8. There are 175 required school days per year for Upper School students. Upper School students typically attend 5 days per week. The average school day consists of 7 hours and 15 minutes.
Upper School Student Profile Grade 9: 26 students (26 girls); Grade 10: 32 students (32 girls); Grade 11: 40 students (40 girls); Grade 12: 25 students (25 girls). 15% of students are members of Episcopal Church.
Faculty School total: 55. In upper school: 13 men, 25 women; 27 have advanced degrees.
Subjects Offered Algebra, American government, American history, American literature, ancient history, applied arts, applied music, art, art history, Asian studies, Bible studies, biology, biology-AP, British literature, British literature-AP, calculus, calculus-AP, ceramics, chemistry, chemistry-AP, choir, college counseling, college placement, community service, competitive science projects, computer art, computer education, computer graphics, computer literacy, computer multimedia, computer programming, computer science, computer technology certification, creative writing, drama, economics, economics and history, English, English literature, English literature-AP, ESL, European history, expository writing, fine arts, French, geography, geometry, government/civics, grammar, guidance, handbells, Hawaiian history, Hawaiian language, health, history, honors U.S. history, humanities, Japanese, journalism, Latin, leadership, life skills, mathematics, mechanical drawing, medieval history, microbiology, modern world history, music, Pacific Island studies, photography, physical education, physics, physics-AP, physiology, Polynesian dance, pre-algebra, pre-calculus, psychology,

religion, science, science research, social sciences, social studies, sociology, Spanish, Spanish-AP, speech, speech communications, theater, theology, trigonometry, U.S. history-AP, United States government-AP, video and animation, visual and performing arts, wind ensemble, women's studies, world civilizations, world history, world literature, world wide web design, writing workshop, yearbook.

Graduation Requirements Advanced Placement courses, arts and fine arts (art, music, dance, drama), computer science, English, foreign language, Hawaiian history, mathematics, physical education (includes health), religion (includes Bible studies and theology), science, science research, social sciences, social studies (includes history), speech, technological applications. Community service is required.

Special Academic Programs 8 Advanced Placement exams for which test preparation is offered; honors section; independent study; study at local college for college credit; academic accommodation for the musically talented and the artistically talented; ESL (10 students enrolled).

College Admission Counseling 41 students graduated in 2011; all went to college, including American University; Barnard College; The George Washington University; University of California, Berkeley; University of Hawaii at Manoa; Vassar College.

Student Life Upper grades have uniform requirement, student council, honor system. Discipline rests primarily with faculty. Attendance at religious services is required.

Summer Programs Remediation, enrichment, advancement, ESL, sports, art/fine arts, rigorous outdoor training, computer instruction programs offered; session focuses on academics, arts, sports, leadership; held on campus; accepts boys and girls; open to students from other schools. 500 students usually enrolled. 2012 schedule: June 12 to July 20. Application deadline: May 1.

Tuition and Aid Day student tuition: $15,000. Tuition installment plan (SMART Tuition Payment Plan, monthly payment plans, individually arranged payment plans). Tuition reduction for siblings, merit scholarship grants, need-based scholarship grants, middle-income loans available. In 2011–12, 32% of upper-school students received aid; total upper-school merit-scholarship money awarded: $139,500. Total amount of financial aid awarded in 2011–12: $491,650.

Admissions Traditional secondary-level entrance grade is 9. PSAT or SAT for applicants to grade 11 and 12 or SSAT required. Deadline for receipt of application materials: none. Application fee required: $50. On-campus interview required.

Athletics Interscholastic: basketball, bowling, canoeing/kayaking, cheering, cross-country running, dance team, diving, drill team, golf, gymnastics, martial arts, ocean paddling, sailing, soccer, softball, swimming and diving, tennis, track and field, volleyball, water polo, wrestling; intramural: aerobics/dance, badminton, dance squad, drill team, fitness, flag football, jogging, outdoor activities, outdoor adventure, physical fitness, ropes courses, self defense, strength & conditioning, tai chi, weight training, windsurfing. 4 PE instructors, 18 coaches.

Computers Computers are regularly used in animation, art, college planning, English, ESL, foreign language, graphic design, history, humanities, independent study, library, literary magazine, mathematics, media arts, music, newspaper, photojournalism, psychology, religion, science, speech, technology, writing, yearbook classes. Computer network features include on-campus library services, online commercial services, Internet access, wireless campus network, Internet filtering or blocking technology. Campus intranet and student e-mail accounts are available to students. Students grades are available online. The school has a published electronic and media policy.

Contact Ms. Sue Ann Wargo, Director of Admissions. 808-532-2418. Fax: 808-531-8426. E-mail: sawargo@priory.net. Web site: www.priory.net.

ST. ANDREW'S REGIONAL HIGH SCHOOL

880 Mckenzie Avenue

Victoria, British Columbia V8X 3G5, Canada

Head of School: Mr. Andrew Keleher

General Information Coeducational day college-preparatory, general academic, and religious studies school, affiliated with Roman Catholic Church. Grades 8–12. Founded: 1983. Setting: urban. 2-acre campus. 1 building on campus. Approved or accredited by British Columbia Department of Education. Language of instruction: English. Upper school average class size: 24. Upper school faculty-student ratio: 1:14. There are 178 required school days per year for Upper School students. Upper School students typically attend 5 days per week. The average school day consists of 5 hours.

Upper School Student Profile 65% of students are Roman Catholic.

Faculty School total: 34. In upper school: 16 men, 15 women; 11 have advanced degrees.

Subjects Offered Religious education, yoga.

Graduation Requirements Religious studies.

Special Academic Programs Honors section.

College Admission Counseling 103 students graduated in 2011. Other: 10 went to work, 90 entered a postgraduate year, 3 had other specific plans.

Student Life Upper grades have uniform requirement, student council, honor system. Discipline rests primarily with faculty. Attendance at religious services is required.

Tuition and Aid Tuition reduction for siblings, bursaries available.

Admissions Deadline for receipt of application materials: February 28. Application fee required: CAN$50. Interview required.

Athletics Interscholastic: badminton (boys, girls), basketball (b,g), bicycling (b,g), cross-country running (b,g); intramural: basketball (b,g); coed interscholastic: aquatics; coed intramural: dance team, floor hockey, indoor soccer.

Computers Computers are regularly used in business education, career education, computer applications, digital applications, photography classes. Computer resources include on-campus library services, Internet access, Internet filtering or blocking technology. The school has a published electronic and media policy.

Contact Diane Chimich, Vice Principal. 250-479-1414. Fax: 250-479-5356. E-mail: dchimich@cisdv.bc.ca. Web site: www.standrewshigh.ca/.

ST. ANDREW'S SCHOOL

350 Noxontown Road

Middletown, Delaware 19709

Head of School: Daniel T. Roach

General Information Coeducational boarding college-preparatory, arts, and religious studies school, affiliated with Episcopal Church. Grades 9–12. Founded: 1929. Setting: small town. Nearest major city is Wilmington. Students are housed in single-sex dormitories. 2,200-acre campus. 16 buildings on campus. Approved or accredited by Middle States Association of Colleges and Schools, National Association of Episcopal Schools, The Association of Boarding Schools, The College Board, and Delaware Department of Education. Member of National Association of Independent Schools and Secondary School Admission Test Board. Endowment: $170 million. Total enrollment: 297. Upper school average class size: 11. Upper school faculty-student ratio: 1:5.

Upper School Student Profile Grade 9: 65 students (33 boys, 32 girls); Grade 10: 72 students (38 boys, 34 girls); Grade 11: 77 students (42 boys, 35 girls); Grade 12: 83 students (43 boys, 40 girls). 100% of students are boarding students. 12% are state residents. 26 states are represented in upper school student body. 14% are international students. International students from Bermuda, China, India, Italy, Republic of Korea, and Viet Nam; 8 other countries represented in student body. 30% of students are members of Episcopal Church.

Faculty School total: 60. In upper school: 35 men, 25 women; 52 have advanced degrees.

Subjects Offered 20th century world history, acting, advanced chemistry, advanced math, algebra, American history, American literature, art, art history, art history-AP, Asian history, biology, calculus, calculus-AP, ceramics, chemistry, Chinese, choir, choral music, college counseling, comparative religion, computer literacy, computer programming, concert choir, creative writing, digital music, drama, drawing, driver education, East Asian history, English, English literature, English literature-AP, environmental science, ethics, European history, European history-AP, film, film studies, fine arts, French, French literature-AP, geometry, Greek, history, honors geometry, improvisation, Islamic history, Latin, Latin-AP, mathematics, Middle Eastern history, modern European history, music, music theory, organic chemistry, painting, philosophy, photography, physics, physics-AP, poetry, pottery, psychology, religion, religious studies, science, science research, Spanish, Spanish literature-AP, speech, statistics-AP, theater, trigonometry, U.S. history, Western religions.

Graduation Requirements Arts and fine arts (art, music, dance, drama), English, foreign language, history, mathematics, religion (includes Bible studies and theology), science.

Special Academic Programs Honors section; independent study; academic accommodation for the gifted, the musically talented, and the artistically talented.

College Admission Counseling 68 students graduated in 2011; all went to college, including Davidson College; University of Delaware; University of Virginia; Vassar College; Williams College. Mean SAT critical reading: 629, mean SAT math: 651, mean SAT writing: 625.

Student Life Upper grades have specified standards of dress, student council, honor system. Discipline rests equally with students and faculty. Attendance at religious services is required.

Tuition and Aid 7-day tuition and room/board: $47,000. Tuition installment plan (Key Tuition Payment Plan, monthly payment plans). Need-based scholarship grants available. In 2011–12, 46% of upper-school students received aid. Total amount of financial aid awarded in 2011–12: $4,950,000.

Admissions Traditional secondary-level entrance grade is 9. For fall 2011, 450 students applied for upper-level admission, 125 were accepted, 77 enrolled. ISEE, SSAT or TOEFL required. Deadline for receipt of application materials: January 15. Application fee required: $50. On-campus interview required.

Athletics Interscholastic: aquatics (boys, girls), baseball (b), basketball (b,g), crew (b,g), cross-country running (b,g), field hockey (g), football (b), lacrosse (b,g), rowing (b,g), soccer (b,g), squash (b,g), swimming and diving (b,g), tennis (b,g), volleyball (g), wrestling (b); coed intramural: aerobics, aerobics/dance, canoeing/kayaking, dance, fencing, fishing, fitness, Frisbee, indoor soccer, kayaking, outdoors, paddle tennis, physical training, rowing, sailboarding, sailing, weight lifting, weight training, windsurfing, yoga. 1 athletic trainer.

Computers Computers are regularly used in English, foreign language, history, mathematics, science classes. Computer network features include on-campus library services, online commercial services, Internet access, Internet filtering or blocking technology. Campus intranet, student e-mail accounts, and computer access in designated common areas are available to students. The school has a published electronic and media policy.

Contact Louisa H. Zendt, Director of Admission. 302-285-4230. Fax: 302-378-7120. E-mail: lzendt@standrews-de.org. Web site: www.standrews-de.org.

ST. ANDREW'S SCHOOL

63 Federal Road

Barrington, Rhode Island 02806

Head of School: Mr. John D. Martin

General Information Coeducational boarding and day college-preparatory and arts school. Boarding grades 9–12, day grades 3–12. Founded: 1893. Setting: suburban. Nearest major city is Providence. Students are housed in single-sex dormitories. 100-acre campus. 33 buildings on campus. Approved or accredited by Massachusetts Department of Education, National Association of Episcopal Schools, New England Association of Schools and Colleges, Rhode Island State Certified Resource Progam, The Association of Boarding Schools, and Rhode Island Department of Education. Member of National Association of Independent Schools and Secondary School Admission Test Board. Endowment: $17.3 million. Total enrollment: 218. Upper school average class size: 12. Upper school faculty-student ratio: 1:5. There are 150 required school days per year for Upper School students. Upper School students typically attend 5 days per week. The average school day consists of 8 hours.

Upper School Student Profile Grade 9: 39 students (25 boys, 14 girls); Grade 10: 47 students (31 boys, 16 girls); Grade 11: 47 students (32 boys, 15 girls); Grade 12: 40 students (24 boys, 16 girls). 27% of students are boarding students. 61% are state residents. 7 states are represented in upper school student body. 18% are international students. International students from China, France, Greece, India, Republic of Korea, and Taiwan; 2 other countries represented in student body.

Faculty School total: 49. In upper school: 20 men, 20 women; 24 have advanced degrees; 22 reside on campus.

Subjects Offered Advanced biology, Advanced Placement courses, algebra, American history, ancient history, art, astronomy, biology, calculus, calculus-AP, ceramics, chemistry, chorus, college counseling, computer applications, creative writing, digital applications, digital photography, drawing, English, environmental science, ESL, European history, French, geometry, honors world history, human anatomy, humanities, jewelry making, lab science, music history, music theory, music theory-AP, oceanography, oral communications, physical education, physics, physics-AP, pre-calculus, printmaking, probability and statistics, remedial study skills, SAT preparation, Spanish, statistics-AP, studio art, study skills, technical theater, theater, TOEFL preparation, trigonometry, water color painting, yearbook.

Graduation Requirements Arts and fine arts (art, music, dance, drama), English, mathematics, physical education (includes health), science, social studies (includes history), community service.

Special Academic Programs Advanced Placement exam preparation; honors section; independent study; remedial reading and/or remedial writing; programs in English for dyslexic students; special instructional classes for students with mild language-based learning disabilities, students with attention/organizational issues (ADHD); ESL (24 students enrolled).

College Admission Counseling 39 students graduated in 2011; 37 went to college, including Brandeis University; Holy Cross College; Northeastern University; Penn State University Park; Syracuse University; University of Illinois at Chicago. Other: 2 entered military service. Median SAT critical reading: 459, median SAT math: 540, median SAT writing: 470, median combined SAT: 1469. 16% scored over 600 on SAT critical reading, 42% scored over 600 on SAT math, 10% scored over 600 on SAT writing, 21% scored over 1800 on combined SAT.

Student Life Upper grades have specified standards of dress, student council. Discipline rests primarily with faculty.

Summer Programs Remediation, enrichment, advancement, ESL, sports, art/fine arts, rigorous outdoor training, computer instruction programs offered; session focuses on skills development; held on campus; accepts boys and girls; open to students from other schools. 1,200 students usually enrolled. 2012 schedule: June 25 to August 16. Application deadline: June 15.

Tuition and Aid Day student tuition: $28,650; 7-day tuition and room/board: $44,700. Tuition installment plan (Key Tuition Payment Plan). Need-based scholarship grants, need-based loans available. In 2011–12, 48% of upper-school students received aid. Total amount of financial aid awarded in 2011–12: $2,173,820.

Admissions Traditional secondary-level entrance grade is 9. For fall 2011, 252 students applied for upper-level admission, 111 were accepted, 58 enrolled. Any standardized test required. Deadline for receipt of application materials: January 15. Application fee required: $50. Interview required.

Athletics Interscholastic: basketball (boys, girls), cross-country running (b,g), golf (b), lacrosse (b,g), soccer (b,g), tennis (b,g); coed interscholastic: soccer; coed intramural: badminton, ball hockey, basketball, bicycling, billiards, bocce, cooperative games, croquet, dance, fitness, fitness walking, flag football, floor hockey, Frisbee, horseshoes, jogging, physical fitness, project adventure, ropes courses, running, soccer, strength & conditioning, tennis, touch football, ultimate Frisbee, walking, weight lifting, weight training, yoga. 1 PE instructor, 20 coaches, 1 athletic trainer.

Computers Computers are regularly used in all academic, computer applications, library skills, multimedia, photography, SAT preparation, yearbook classes. Computer network features include on-campus library services, Internet access, wireless campus network, Internet filtering or blocking technology, NetClassroom is available for parents and students. Campus intranet, student e-mail accounts, and computer access in designated common areas are available to students. Students grades are available online. The school has a published electronic and media policy.

Contact Mary Bishop, Administrative Assistant to Admissions. 401-246-1230 Ext. 3025. Fax: 401-246-0510. E-mail: mbishop@standrews-ri.org. Web site: www.standrews-ri.org.

See Display on next page and Close-Up on page 670.

ST. ANDREW'S–SEWANEE SCHOOL

290 Quintard Road

Sewanee, Tennessee 37375-3000

Head of School: Rev. John T. Thomas

General Information Coeducational boarding and day college-preparatory, arts, and science school, affiliated with Episcopal Church. Boarding grades 9–12, day grades 6–12. Founded: 1868. Setting: small town. Nearest major city is Chattanooga. Students are housed in single-sex dormitories. 550-acre campus. 19 buildings on campus. Approved or accredited by National Association of Episcopal Schools, Southern Association of Colleges and Schools, Southern Association of Independent Schools, The Association of Boarding Schools, and Tennessee Department of Education. Member of National Association of Independent Schools and Secondary School Admission Test Board. Endowment: $11.5 million. Total enrollment: 255. Upper school average class size: 14. Upper school faculty-student ratio: 1:4. There are 168 required school days per year for Upper School students. Upper School students typically attend 5 days per week. The average school day consists of 4 hours and 30 minutes.

Upper School Student Profile Grade 9: 39 students (27 boys, 12 girls); Grade 10: 59 students (16 boys, 43 girls); Grade 11: 42 students (26 boys, 16 girls); Grade 12: 47 students (21 boys, 26 girls). 45% of students are boarding students. 66% are state residents. 15 states are represented in upper school student body. 20% are international students. International students from China, Denmark, Germany, Republic of Korea, Spain, and Taiwan; 7 other countries represented in student body. 36% of students are members of Episcopal Church.

Faculty School total: 47. In upper school: 21 men, 21 women; 29 have advanced degrees, 28 reside on campus.

Subjects Offered 20th century history, acting, adolescent issues, advanced biology, advanced chemistry, advanced TOEFL/grammar, African history, African-American literature, algebra, American biography, American history, American literature, American studies, art, Asian history, band, biology, British literature, calculus, chamber groups, chemistry, Chinese, choir, civil rights, college counseling, community service, comparative religion, creative writing, drama, dramatic arts, ecology, emergency medicine, English, English literature, environmental systems, ESL, filmmaking, fine arts, French, general science, geometry, history, Holocaust, humanities, Latin, literature, mathematics, minority studies, music, philosophy, physical education, physics, pottery, pre-algebra, religion, religion and culture, religious studies, science, social studies, Southern literature, Spanish, statistics, theater, trigonometry, world history, yearbook.

Graduation Requirements Arts and fine arts (art, music, dance, drama), English, foreign language, mathematics, physical education (includes health), religion (includes Bible studies and theology), science, social studies (includes history), senior lecture series, creedal statement. Community service is required.

Special Academic Programs Advanced Placement exam preparation; independent study; term-away projects; study at local college for college credit; study abroad; academic accommodation for the gifted, the musically talented, and the artistically talented; remedial reading and/or remedial writing; remedial math; ESL (17 students enrolled).

College Admission Counseling 46 students graduated in 2011; 41 went to college, including Boston University; Eckerd College; Emory University; Middle Tennessee State University; Sewanee: The University of the South; Tennessee Technological University. Other: 2 went to work, 3 had other specific plans.

Student Life Upper grades have specified standards of dress, student council, honor system. Discipline rests equally with students and faculty. Attendance at religious services is required.

Tuition and Aid Day student tuition: $15,865–$16,040; 7-day tuition and room/board: $38,475–$39,475. Tuition installment plan (monthly payment plans). Merit scholarship grants, need-based scholarship grants available. In 2011–12, 51% of upper-school students received aid; total upper-school merit-scholarship money awarded: $202,983. Total amount of financial aid awarded in 2011–12: $1,499,125.

Admissions Traditional secondary-level entrance grade is 9. For fall 2011, 132 students applied for upper-level admission, 109 were accepted, 75 enrolled. SLEP, TOEFL or writing sample required. Deadline for receipt of application materials: none. Application fee required: $50. Interview required.

Athletics Interscholastic: baseball (boys), basketball (b,g), cross-country running (b,g), football (b), soccer (b,g), softball (g), swimming and diving (b,g), tennis (b,g), track and field (b,g), volleyball (g), wrestling (b,g); intramural: aerobics (g), ballet (g);

coed interscholastic: bicycling, diving, Frisbee, golf, mountain biking, rock climbing, ultimate Frisbee; coed intramural: aerobics/dance, backpacking, bicycling, billiards, canoeing/kayaking, climbing, combined training, dance, dance team, equestrian sports, fishing, fitness, flag football, hiking/backpacking, horseback riding, independent competitive sports, kayaking, modern dance, mountain biking, mountaineering, outdoor activities, outdoor adventure, outdoor education, outdoor recreation, outdoor skills, outdoors, paint ball, physical fitness, physical training, rafting, rappelling, rock climbing, ropes courses, running, soccer, strength & conditioning, table tennis, tennis, touch football, triathlon, walking, wall climbing, weight training, wilderness, wilderness survival, yoga. 2 PE instructors, 7 coaches, 1 athletic trainer.

Computers Computers are regularly used in art, English, foreign language, history, introduction to technology, mathematics, SAT preparation, science, yearbook classes. Computer network features include on-campus library services, online commercial services, Internet access, wireless campus network, Internet filtering or blocking technology, access to University of the South technology facilities. Student e-mail accounts and computer access in designated common areas are available to students. Students grades are available online.

Contact Ms. Anne Chenoweth, Director of Admission and Financial Aid. 931-598-5651 Ext. 2117. Fax: 931-463-2121. E-mail: admission@sasweb.org. Web site: www.sasweb.org.

ST. ANNE'S–BELFIELD SCHOOL

2132 Ivy Road

Charlottesville, Virginia 22903

Head of School: Mr. David S. Lourie

General Information Coeducational boarding and day college-preparatory, arts, religious studies, and ESL school, affiliated with Christian faith. Boarding grades 9–12, day grades PK–12. Founded: 1910. Setting: small town. Nearest major city is Washington, DC. Students are housed in coed dormitories. 49-acre campus. 7 buildings on campus. Approved or accredited by The Association of Boarding Schools and Virginia Association of Independent Schools. Member of National Association of Independent Schools and Secondary School Admission Test Board. Endowment: $21.5 million. Total enrollment: 892. Upper school average class size: 13. Upper school faculty-student ratio: 1:8. There are 180 required school days per year for Upper School students. Upper School students typically attend 5 days per week. The average school day consists of 7 hours and 35 minutes.

Upper School Student Profile Grade 9: 80 students (40 boys, 40 girls); Grade 10: 75 students (44 boys, 31 girls); Grade 11: 89 students (58 boys, 31 girls); Grade 12: 89 students (41 boys, 48 girls). 18% of students are boarding students. 87% are state residents. 7 states are represented in upper school student body. 9% are international students. International students from China, Italy, Morocco, Republic of Korea, South Africa, and Taiwan; 17 other countries represented in student body.

Faculty School total: 100. In upper school: 19 men, 21 women; 32 have advanced degrees; 6 reside on campus.

Subjects Offered Algebra, art, art history, biology, biology-AP, calculus-AP, ceramics, chemistry, chemistry-AP, choir, Civil War, conceptual physics, drama, economics, English, environmental science-AP, ESL, French, French language-AP, French literature-AP, geometry, honors algebra, honors geometry, human development, humanities, Latin, Latin-AP, model United Nations, modern European history-AP, modern world history, music theory, music theory-AP, orchestra, photography, physics, physics-AP, pre-calculus, religion, sculpture, Shakespeare, short story, Spanish, Spanish language-AP, Spanish literature-AP, statistics, statistics-AP, theology, trigonometry, U.S. history, U.S. history-AP, video, world history, World War II, writing workshop.

Graduation Requirements Art, English, foreign language, history, mathematics, physical education (includes health), religion (includes Bible studies and theology), science. Community service is required.

Special Academic Programs Advanced Placement exam preparation; honors section; independent study; study at local college for college credit; ESL (12 students enrolled).

College Admission Counseling 76 students graduated in 2011; 75 went to college, including James Madison University; Lynchburg College; The College of William and Mary; University of Mary Washington; University of Virginia; Virginia Commonwealth University. Other: 1 had other specific plans. Median SAT critical reading: 630, median SAT math: 620. Mean SAT writing: 622. 59% scored over 600 on SAT critical reading, 57% scored over 600 on SAT math, 68% scored over 600 on SAT writing, 72% scored over 1800 on combined SAT.

Student Life Upper grades have uniform requirement, student council, honor system. Discipline rests primarily with faculty. Attendance at religious services is required.

Summer Programs Remediation, enrichment, sports programs offered; session focuses on academic enrichment and remediation through 8th grade; held on campus; accepts boys and girls; open to students from other schools. 350 students usually enrolled. 2012 schedule: June 15 to July 31. Application deadline: none.

Tuition and Aid Day student tuition: $21,000; 5-day tuition and room/board: $34,600–$334,600; 7-day tuition and room/board: $44,000. Tuition installment plan (The Tuition Plan, Insured Tuition Payment Plan, FACTS Tuition Payment Plan, Your Tuition Solution). Need-based scholarship grants, need-based financial aid available. In 2011–12, 36% of upper-school students received aid. Total amount of financial aid awarded in 2011–12: $1,633,575.

Admissions Traditional secondary-level entrance grade is 9. For fall 2011, 104 students applied for upper-level admission, 60 were accepted, 45 enrolled. ERB verbal, ERB math, SSAT, TOEFL or writing sample required. Deadline for receipt of application materials: February 20. Application fee required: $30. Interview recommended.
Athletics Interscholastic: baseball (boys), basketball (b,g), cross-country running (b,g), field hockey (g), football (b), golf (b,g), lacrosse (b,g), soccer (b,g), softball (g), squash (b,g), swimming and diving (b,g), tennis (b,g), track and field (b,g), volleyball (g), wrestling (b); coed interscholastic: cross-country running, golf, squash, swimming and diving, track and field; coed intramural: aerobics, aerobics/dance, dance, fitness, physical fitness, yoga. 6 PE instructors, 8 coaches, 2 athletic trainers.
Computers Computers are regularly used in all academic classes. Computer network features include on-campus library services, online commercial services, Internet access, wireless campus network. Computer access in designated common areas is available to students. Students grades are available online. The school has a published electronic and media policy.
Contact Mrs. Stacey Gearhart, Assistant Director of Admission for Grades 5-12. 434-296-5106. Fax: 434-979-1486. E-mail: sgearhart@stab.org. Web site: www.stab.org.

ST. ANN'S ACADEMY

205 Columbia Street

Kamloops, British Columbia V2C 2S7, Canada

Head of School: Mr. Shawn Chisholm

General Information Coeducational day college-preparatory, general academic, arts, and religious studies school, affiliated with Roman Catholic Church. Grades K–12. Founded: 1880. Setting: urban. Nearest major city is Vancouver, Canada. 10-acre campus. 3 buildings on campus. Approved or accredited by Canadian Association of Independent Schools, Christian Brothers Association, North Central Association of Colleges and Schools, and British Columbia Department of Education. Language of instruction: English. Total enrollment: 528. Upper school average class size: 24. Upper school faculty-student ratio: 1:24. There are 181 required school days per year for Upper School students. Upper School students typically attend 5 days per week. The average school day consists of 5 hours.
Upper School Student Profile 80% of students are Roman Catholic.
Faculty School total: 33. In upper school: 11 men, 7 women; 6 have advanced degrees.
Subjects Offered All academic.
Special Academic Programs Independent study; remedial reading and/or remedial writing; remedial math; ESL (11 students enrolled).
College Admission Counseling 72 students graduated in 2010; 64 went to college, including The University of British Columbia. Other: 7 went to work, 1 had other specific plans.
Student Life Upper grades have specified standards of dress, student council, honor system. Discipline rests primarily with faculty. Attendance at religious services is required.
Tuition and Aid Day student tuition: CAN$9000. Tuition reduction for siblings, merit scholarship grants available. In 2010–11, 12% of upper-school students received aid; total upper-school merit-scholarship money awarded: CAN$3000. Total amount of financial aid awarded in 2010–11: CAN$30,000.
Admissions For fall 2010, 26 students applied for upper-level admission, 19 were accepted, 19 enrolled. English Composition Test for ESL students required. Deadline for receipt of application materials: none. No application fee required. Interview required.
Athletics Interscholastic: badminton (boys, girls), basketball (b,g), bicycling (b,g), bowling (g), cross-country running (b,g), flag football (b,g), football (b,g), golf (b,g), rugby (g), snowboarding (b,g), soccer (b,g), track and field (b,g), volleyball (b,g); intramural: track and field (b,g); coed interscholastic: aquatics. 3 PE instructors, 5 coaches.
Computers Computers are regularly used in mathematics classes. Computer network features include on-campus library services, online commercial services, Internet access, Internet filtering or blocking technology. The school has a published electronic and media policy.
Contact Mr. Shawn Chisholm, Principal. 250-372-5452 Ext. 222. Fax: 250-372-5257. E-mail: principal@stannsacademy.bc.ca.

ST. ANTHONY CATHOLIC HIGH SCHOOL

3200 McCullough Avenue

San Antonio, Texas 78212-3099

Head of School: Mr. Rene Escobedo

General Information Coeducational boarding and day and distance learning college-preparatory, arts, religious studies, technology, AP Dual Credit, and college course credit school, affiliated with Roman Catholic Church. Grades 9–12. Distance learning grades 9–12. Founded: 1905. Setting: urban. Students are housed in single-sex by floor dormitories. 14-acre campus. 5 buildings on campus. Approved or accredited by National Catholic Education Association, Southern Association of Colleges and Schools, Texas Catholic Conference, The College Board, and Texas Department of Education. Total enrollment: 402. Upper school average class size: 19. Upper school faculty-student ratio: 1:12. There are 180 required school days per year for Upper School students. Upper School students typically attend 5 days per week. The average school day consists of 7 hours.
Upper School Student Profile Grade 9: 89 students (50 boys, 39 girls); Grade 10: 108 students (65 boys, 43 girls); Grade 11: 91 students (52 boys, 39 girls); Grade 12: 112 students (71 boys, 41 girls). 5% of students are boarding students. 8 states are represented in upper school student body. 100% are international students. International students from China, Japan, Mexico, Republic of Korea, Spain, and Viet Nam; 1 other country represented in student body. 85% of students are Roman Catholic.
Faculty School total: 36. In upper school: 16 men, 19 women; 16 have advanced degrees.
Subjects Offered Advanced biology, advanced chemistry, advanced math, Advanced Placement courses, algebra, anatomy and physiology, art, athletics, band, Bible studies, biology, calculus, Catholic belief and practice, chemistry, chemistry-AP, choir, computer graphics, computer literacy, dance, drama, economics, English, English language and composition-AP, English literature, English literature and composition-AP, environmental science, environmental science-AP, ESL, film appreciation, geology, geometry, government, graphic arts, graphic design, health, history, history of the Catholic Church, honors algebra, Japanese, jazz band, keyboarding, Latin, mathematical modeling, media literacy, meteorology, moral theology, oceanography, photography, photojournalism, physical education, physics, physics-AP, pre-calculus, psychology, robotics, sexuality, sociology, Spanish, Spanish AP, speech, theater, theater arts, theology, trigonometry, U.S. government, U.S. history, U.S. history-AP, world history, world history-AP, world religions, writing, yearbook.
Graduation Requirements Arts and fine arts (art, music, dance, drama), computer applications, economics, English, foreign language, government, mathematics, physical education (includes health), religion (includes Bible studies and theology), science, speech, U.S. history, world history.
Special Academic Programs Advanced Placement exam preparation; honors section; independent study; study at local college for college credit; study abroad; academic accommodation for the gifted; ESL (34 students enrolled).
College Admission Counseling 106 students graduated in 2011; all went to college, including Southern Methodist University; St. Mary's University; Texas A&M University; Texas State University–San Marcos; The University of Texas at San Antonio; University of the Incarnate Word.
Student Life Upper grades have uniform requirement, student council, honor system. Discipline rests primarily with faculty. Attendance at religious services is required.
Summer Programs Remediation, enrichment, advancement, sports, art/fine arts, computer instruction programs offered; session focuses on enrichment/advancement; held both on and off campus; held at Incarnate Word High School; accepts boys and girls; open to students from other schools. 200 students usually enrolled. 2012 schedule: June 1 to June 29. Application deadline: May 30.
Tuition and Aid Day student tuition: $7600; 7-day tuition and room/board: $14,000. Tuition installment plan (monthly payment plans). Tuition reduction for siblings, merit scholarship grants, need-based scholarship grants available. In 2011–12, 35% of upper-school students received aid; total upper-school merit-scholarship money awarded: $5000. Total amount of financial aid awarded in 2011–12: $185,000.
Admissions Traditional secondary-level entrance grade is 9. For fall 2011, 422 students applied for upper-level admission, 402 were accepted, 402 enrolled. High School Placement Test required. Deadline for receipt of application materials: none. No application fee required. Interview required.
Athletics Interscholastic: baseball (boys), basketball (b,g), cheering (g), dance team (g), football (b), lacrosse (b), soccer (b,g), softball (g), swimming and diving (b,g), tennis (b,g), volleyball (g), wrestling (b); coed interscholastic: cross-country running, golf, track and field. 2 PE instructors, 32 coaches, 1 athletic trainer.
Computers Computers are regularly used in all academic classes. Computer network features include on-campus library services, Internet access, wireless campus network, Internet filtering or blocking technology. Students grades are available online. The school has a published electronic and media policy.
Contact Mr. Alejandro Calderon, Director of Enrollment. 210-832-5632. Fax: 210-832-5633. E-mail: sachs@uiwtx.edu. Web site: www.sachs.org.

SAINT ANTHONY HIGH SCHOOL

620 Olive Avenue

Long Beach, California 90802

Head of School: Mr. Mike Schabert

General Information Coeducational day college-preparatory, arts, business, religious studies, and technology school, affiliated with Roman Catholic Church. Grades 9–12. Founded: 1920. Setting: urban. 15-acre campus. 5 buildings on campus. Approved or accredited by National Catholic Education Association, Western Association of Schools and Colleges, Western Catholic Education Association, and California Department of Education. Total enrollment: 440. Upper school average class size: 25. Upper school faculty-student ratio: 1:15. There are 180 required school days per year for Upper School students. Upper School students typically attend 5 days per week. The average school day consists of 7 hours and 15 minutes.
Upper School Student Profile 80% of students are Roman Catholic.

Faculty School total: 29. In upper school: 14 men, 10 women; 23 have advanced degrees.

Subjects Offered Algebra, American history, American history-AP, American literature-AP, anatomy and physiology, art, ASB Leadership, band, Bible studies, biology, biology-AP, British literature, calculus, calculus-AP, campus ministry, career/college preparation, Catholic belief and practice, chemistry, chemistry-AP, choir, church history, civics, college admission preparation, college awareness, college counseling, comparative religion, computer resources, computer technologies, constitutional history of U.S., drama, economics, economics-AP, English, English literature-AP, English-AP, environmental science-AP, ethics, fine arts, geometry, government, government-AP, government/civics, health, health education, history, honors English, honors geometry, honors U.S. history, honors world history, jazz band, leadership, leadership and service, Life of Christ, literature and composition-AP, macroeconomics-AP, marching band, marine science, mathematics, mathematics-AP, music, music appreciation, musical productions, New Testament, peace and justice, physical education, physics, physics-AP, play production, prayer/spirituality, pre-algebra, pre-calculus, religion, religious studies, SAT/ACT preparation, science, social justice, social sciences, social studies, Spanish, Spanish-AP, student government, theater, U.S. government, U.S. history-AP, world history, world history-AP, world religions, yearbook.

Graduation Requirements Arts and fine arts (art, music, dance, drama), English, foreign language, mathematics, physical education (includes health), religion (includes Bible studies and theology), science, social sciences, social studies (includes history), Christian service hours. Community service is required.

Special Academic Programs Advanced Placement exam preparation; honors section; academic accommodation for the gifted and the artistically talented; remedial reading and/or remedial writing; remedial math.

College Admission Counseling 66 students graduated in 2011; all went to college, including California State University, Dominguez Hills; California State University, Long Beach; Loyola Marymount University; University of California, Irvine; University of California, Los Angeles; University of California, San Diego. Mean SAT critical reading: 471, mean SAT math: 445, mean SAT writing: 451, mean combined SAT: 1367. 7% scored over 600 on SAT critical reading, 5% scored over 600 on SAT math, 4% scored over 600 on SAT writing, 4% scored over 1800 on combined SAT.

Student Life Upper grades have uniform requirement, student council, honor system. Discipline rests primarily with faculty. Attendance at religious services is required.

Summer Programs Remediation, sports programs offered; session focuses on remediation/make-up; held both on and off campus; held at Clark Field; accepts boys and girls; open to students from other schools.

Tuition and Aid Day student tuition: $6100. Tuition installment plan (SMART Tuition Payment Plan, monthly payment plans, individually arranged payment plans). Tuition reduction for siblings, merit scholarship grants, need-based scholarship grants available. In 2011–12, 60% of upper-school students received aid.

Admissions Traditional secondary-level entrance grade is 9. For fall 2011, 250 students applied for upper-level admission, 90 enrolled. High School Placement Test required. Deadline for receipt of application materials: none. Application fee required: $50. On-campus interview required.

Athletics Interscholastic: baseball (boys), basketball (b,g), cheering (g), cross-country running (b,g), dance squad (g), football (b), golf (b,g), independent competitive sports (b,g), power lifting (b,g), running (b,g), soccer (b,g), softball (g), strength & conditioning (b,g), track and field (b,g), volleyball (b,g), weight training (b,g); coed interscholastic: aquatics, cheering, diving; coed intramural: fitness, physical fitness, roller blading, roller hockey, running, tennis. 28 coaches, 1 athletic trainer.

Computers Computers are regularly used in aerospace science, all academic, aviation, basic skills, Bible studies, business, career education, Christian doctrine, college planning, creative writing, current events, design, drawing and design, economics, English, foreign language, graphic arts, graphic design, graphics, historical foundations for arts, history, journalism, keyboarding, library, mathematics, media, media arts, media production, media services, mentorship program, multimedia, news writing, newspaper, photojournalism, publications, publishing, religion, religious studies, remedial study skills, research skills, SAT preparation, science, technology, theater arts, word processing, writing, writing, yearbook classes. Computer network features include on-campus library services, online commercial services, Internet access, wireless campus network, Internet filtering or blocking technology, fiber optic, multimedia laboratory. Campus intranet and computer access in designated common areas are available to students. Students grades are available online. The school has a published electronic and media policy.

Contact Ms. Beatriz McGuiness, Registrar. 562-435-4496 Ext. 1214. Fax: 562-437-3055. E-mail: beatriz.mcguiness@longbeachsaints.org. Web site: www.longbeachsaints.org.

SAINT ANTHONY HIGH SCHOOL

304 East Roadway Avenue

Effingham, Illinois 62401

Head of School: Mr. Ron Niebrugge

General Information Coeducational day college-preparatory, arts, business, religious studies, bilingual studies, and technology school, affiliated with Roman Catholic Church. Grades 9–12. Setting: small town. Nearest major city is St. Louis, MO. 1 building on campus. Approved or accredited by Illinois Department of Education. Total enrollment: 190. Upper school average class size: 20. Upper school faculty-student ratio: 1:10. There are 176 required school days per year for Upper School students. Upper School students typically attend 5 days per week. The average school day consists of 5 hours and 42 minutes.

Upper School Student Profile Grade 9: 48 students (27 boys, 21 girls); Grade 10: 38 students (22 boys, 16 girls); Grade 11: 51 students (23 boys, 28 girls); Grade 12: 52 students (32 boys, 20 girls). 97% of students are Roman Catholic.

Faculty School total: 21. In upper school: 6 men, 15 women; 8 have advanced degrees.

Subjects Offered Accounting, advanced math, algebra, American government, anatomy, art appreciation, band, biology, British literature, calculus-AP, career exploration, Catholic belief and practice, ceramics, chemistry, chorus, communications, composition, computer applications, conceptual physics, concert band, consumer education, criminal justice, current events, drawing, earth science, English literature, English-AP, environmental science, finite math, forensics, general math, geography, geometry, health, microbiology, music appreciation, physical education, physical science, physics, pre-algebra, psychology, publications, Spanish, statistics-AP, U.S. history, world history, world wide web design.

Graduation Requirements American government, arts and fine arts (art, music, dance, drama), computer science, consumer education, English, mathematics, physical education (includes health), religion (includes Bible studies and theology), science, social sciences, speech, U.S. history, world history.

Special Academic Programs International Baccalaureate program; 3 Advanced Placement exams for which test preparation is offered; independent study; study at local college for college credit; remedial math; special instructional classes for deaf students.

College Admission Counseling 53 students graduated in 2011; 51 went to college, including Eastern Illinois University; Southern Illinois University Edwardsville; University of Illinois at Urbana–Champaign. Other: 1 went to work, 1 entered military service. Median composite ACT: 23.

Student Life Upper grades have specified standards of dress, student council. Discipline rests primarily with faculty. Attendance at religious services is required.

Tuition and Aid Tuition installment plan (monthly payment plans). Need-based scholarship grants available.

Admissions Traditional secondary-level entrance grade is 9. Deadline for receipt of application materials: none. No application fee required.

Athletics Interscholastic: baseball (boys), basketball (b,g), bowling (b,g), cheering (g), dance team (g), golf (b,g), soccer (b,g), softball (g), tennis (b,g), track and field (b,g), volleyball (g), wrestling (b); coed interscholastic: cross-country running. 2 PE instructors, 19 coaches.

Computers Computers are regularly used in drafting, publications, yearbook classes. Computer network features include on-campus library services, Internet access, Internet filtering or blocking technology. Student e-mail accounts are available to students. Students grades are available online. The school has a published electronic and media policy.

Contact Mr. Ron Niebrugge, Principal. 217-342-6969. Fax: 217-342-6997. E-mail: rniebrugge@stanthony.com. Web site: www.stanthony.com.

ST. ANTHONY'S JUNIOR-SENIOR HIGH SCHOOL

1618 Lower Main Street

Wailuku, Hawaii 96793

Head of School: Mrs. Patricia Rickard

General Information Coeducational day college-preparatory, general academic, arts, religious studies, and technology school, affiliated with Roman Catholic Church. Grades 7–12. Founded: 1848. Setting: small town. 15-acre campus. 13 buildings on campus. Approved or accredited by National Catholic Education Association, Western Association of Schools and Colleges, and Hawaii Department of Education. Member of National Association of Independent Schools. Endowment: $216,177. Total enrollment: 140. Upper school average class size: 22. Upper school faculty-student ratio: 1:10. There are 180 required school days per year for Upper School students. Upper School students typically attend 5 days per week. The average school day consists of 6 hours and 45 minutes.

Upper School Student Profile Grade 9: 32 students (22 boys, 10 girls); Grade 10: 22 students (10 boys, 12 girls); Grade 11: 26 students (11 boys, 15 girls); Grade 12: 35 students (22 boys, 13 girls). 65% of students are Roman Catholic.

Faculty School total: 20. In upper school: 8 men, 12 women; 8 have advanced degrees.

Subjects Offered Advanced math, American government, American history, American history-AP, American literature, American literature-AP, anatomy and physiology, applied arts, art, athletic training, athletics, baseball, basic skills, basketball, Bible, Bible as literature, Bible studies, biology, bowling, British literature, British literature-AP, business, calculus, calculus-AP, campus ministry, chemistry, college counseling, college planning, computer education, computer graphics, computer literacy, computer skills, computer technologies, computer technology certification, computer tools, computer-aided design, computers, creative arts, dance, drama, drama performance, drama workshop, dramatic arts, drawing, drawing and design, driver education, electives, English, English language and composition-AP, English language-AP, English literature, English literature and composition-AP, English-AP, environmental science, environmental science-AP, foreign language, health, keyboarding, mathematics, music, physical education, Polynesian dance, pre-algebra, pre-calculus, religion, religious studies, robotics, SAT preparation, SAT/ACT preparation, science, social studies, sports medicine, standard curriculum, technology, U.S. government and politics-AP, U.S. history-AP, world geography, writing, writings, yearbook.

Graduation Requirements Art, English, languages, mathematics, physical education (includes health), religion (includes Bible studies and theology), science, social studies (includes history), technology.

Special Academic Programs 6 Advanced Placement exams for which test preparation is offered; honors section; study at local college for college credit.

College Admission Counseling 34 students graduated in 2011; all went to college, including Oregon State University; Pepperdine University; University of California, Santa Cruz; University of Hawaii at Manoa; University of Portland. 50% scored over 600 on SAT critical reading, 50% scored over 600 on SAT math, 50% scored over 600 on SAT writing, 50% scored over 1800 on combined SAT, 50% scored over 26 on composite ACT.

Student Life Upper grades have uniform requirement, student council. Discipline rests primarily with faculty. Attendance at religious services is required.

Summer Programs Remediation, enrichment programs offered; session focuses on remediation; held on campus; accepts boys and girls; open to students from other schools. 100 students usually enrolled. 2012 schedule: June 13 to July 15. Application deadline: June 1.

Tuition and Aid Day student tuition: $7500–$10,300. Tuition installment plan (FACTS Tuition Payment Plan). Merit scholarship grants, need-based scholarship grants, need-based loans available. In 2011–12, 50% of upper-school students received aid.

Admissions Traditional secondary-level entrance grade is 9. For fall 2011, 40 students applied for upper-level admission, 36 were accepted, 36 enrolled. Achievement tests or Educational Development Series required. Deadline for receipt of application materials: none. Application fee required: $300. Interview required.

Athletics Interscholastic: aquatics (boys, girls), baseball (b), basketball (b), bowling (b,g), canoeing/kayaking (b,g), cross-country running (b,g), curling (g), drill team (b,g), football (b), golf (b,g), judo (b,g), ocean paddling (b,g), paddling (b,g), racquetball (b,g), riflery (b,g), running (b,g), soccer (b,g), softball (g), strength & conditioning (b,g), surfing (b,g), swimming and diving (b,g), tennis (b,g), track and field (b,g), volleyball (g), weight lifting (b,g), weight training (b,g), wrestling (b,g); intramural: basketball (b,g), flag football (b,g); coed interscholastic: cheering, flag football, paddling, racquetball; coed intramural: flag football. 2 PE instructors, 36 coaches, 1 athletic trainer.

Computers Computers are regularly used in all classes. Computer network features include on-campus library services, Internet access, Internet filtering or blocking technology. Student e-mail accounts and computer access in designated common areas are available to students. Students grades are available online. The school has a published electronic and media policy.

Contact Mrs. Cindy Martin, Guidance/College Counselor. 808-244-4190 Ext. 224. Fax: 808-242-8081. E-mail: cmartin@sasmaui.org. Web site: www.sasmaui.org.

SAINT AUGUSTINE PREPARATORY SCHOOL

611 Cedar Avenue

PO Box 279

Richland, New Jersey 08350

Head of School: Rev. Francis J. Horn, OSA

General Information Boys' day college-preparatory and religious studies school, affiliated with Roman Catholic Church. Grades 9–12. Founded: 1959. Setting: rural. Nearest major city is Vineland. 120-acre campus. 4 buildings on campus. Approved or accredited by Middle States Association of Colleges and Schools, National Catholic Education Association, and New Jersey Department of Education. Member of National Association of Independent Schools. Endowment: $250,000. Total enrollment: 682. Upper school average class size: 17. Upper school faculty-student ratio: 1:13. There are 180 required school days per year for Upper School students. Upper School students typically attend 5 days per week. The average school day consists of 6 hours and 8 minutes.

Upper School Student Profile Grade 9: 195 students (195 boys); Grade 10: 167 students (167 boys); Grade 11: 173 students (173 boys); Grade 12: 147 students (147 boys). 79% of students are Roman Catholic.

Faculty School total: 57. In upper school: 42 men, 15 women; 20 have advanced degrees.

Subjects Offered 20th century history, accounting, Advanced Placement courses, advanced studio art-AP, algebra, American literature, anatomy and physiology, ancient world history, Arabic, Arabic studies, art, band, Bible, biology, biology-AP, British literature, British literature (honors), calculus, calculus-AP, Catholic belief and practice, chemistry, chemistry-AP, choir, Christian and Hebrew scripture, Christian doctrine, Christian ethics, church history, classical language, college counseling, college planning, community service, comparative religion, computer applications, computer programming, computer science, computer science-AP, computer-aided design, concert choir, constitutional law, culinary arts, drama, drama performance, driver education, engineering, English, English composition, English literature, English literature-AP, environmental education, ethics and responsibility, European history, European history-AP, finance, French, geometry, German, grammar, guitar, history, history of the Catholic Church, history-AP, honors algebra, honors English, honors geometry, honors U.S. history, independent study, Italian, jazz band, jazz ensemble, lab science, language-AP, Latin, marine biology, mathematics-AP, model United Nations, moral theology, music theory, music theory-AP, peer ministry, philosophy, physical education, physics, physics-AP, political science, pre-calculus, psychology, psychology-AP, public speaking, religion, religious studies, SAT preparation, scripture, service learning/internship, social skills, sociology, Spanish, Spanish language-AP, Spanish literature-AP, Spanish-AP, statistics-AP, studio art, travel, U.S. history-AP, vocal music, Web site design, world cultures, world religions, writing.

Graduation Requirements Electives, English, foreign language, lab science, mathematics, religion (includes Bible studies and theology), science, service learning/internship, U.S. history, world cultures, social service project (approximately 100 hours), retreat experiences, third semester experiences.

Special Academic Programs 18 Advanced Placement exams for which test preparation is offered; honors section; independent study; study at local college for college credit; study abroad; programs in general development for dyslexic students.

College Admission Counseling 175 students graduated in 2011; 171 went to college, including La Salle University; Rutgers, The State University of New Jersey, Newark; Saint Joseph's University; Villanova University. Other: 4 had other specific plans. Mean SAT critical reading: 562, mean SAT math: 593, mean SAT writing: 562, mean combined SAT: 1717.

Student Life Upper grades have uniform requirement, student council, honor system. Discipline rests primarily with faculty. Attendance at religious services is required.

Summer Programs Enrichment, advancement, sports, art/fine arts, rigorous outdoor training, computer instruction programs offered; session focuses on academic enrichment, community relations, sports camps; held both on and off campus; held at crew camp on nearby lake; accepts boys and girls; open to students from other schools. 656 students usually enrolled. 2012 schedule: June 20 to August 5. Application deadline: May 15.

Tuition and Aid Day student tuition: $13,650. Tuition installment plan (FACTS Tuition Payment Plan, individually arranged payment plans, credit card payment; discount for pre-payment). Merit scholarship grants, need-based scholarship grants available. In 2011–12, 30% of upper-school students received aid; total upper-school merit-scholarship money awarded: $75,000. Total amount of financial aid awarded in 2011–12: $1,010,000.

Admissions Traditional secondary-level entrance grade is 9. For fall 2011, 308 students applied for upper-level admission, 210 were accepted, 195 enrolled. School's own exam required. Deadline for receipt of application materials: December 20. Application fee required: $75. On-campus interview recommended.

Athletics Interscholastic: baseball, basketball, bowling, crew, cross-country running, fencing, football, golf, ice hockey, indoor track, lacrosse, rowing, rugby, sailing, soccer, swimming and diving, tennis, track and field, volleyball, winter (indoor) track, wrestling; intramural: basketball, ultimate Frisbee, weight training. 2 PE instructors, 11 coaches, 1 athletic trainer.

Computers Computers are regularly used in all academic, art, career education, design classes. Computer network features include on-campus library services, online commercial services, Internet access, wireless campus network, Internet filtering or blocking technology, syllabus, current grades, and assignments available online for all courses. Computer access in designated common areas is available to students. Students grades are available online. The school has a published electronic and media policy.

Contact Mrs. Linda Pine, Director of Admissions. 856-697-2600 Ext. 112. Fax: 856-697-8389. E-mail: mrs.pine@hermits.com. Web site: www.hermits.com.

SAINT BASIL ACADEMY

711 Fox Chase Road

Jenkintown, Pennsylvania 19046

Head of School: Sr. Carla Hern?ez

General Information Girls' day college-preparatory, arts, business, religious studies, bilingual studies, and technology school, affiliated with Roman Catholic Church. Grades 9–12. Founded: 1931. Setting: suburban. Nearest major city is Philadelphia. 28-acre campus. 1 building on campus. Approved or accredited by Middle States Association of Colleges and Schools and Pennsylvania Department of Education. Endowment: $350,000. Total enrollment: 324. Upper school average class size: 18. Upper school faculty-student ratio: 1:10. There are 180 required school days per year for Upper School students. Upper School students typically attend 5 days per week. The average school day consists of 6 hours and 30 minutes.

Upper School Student Profile Grade 9: 71 students (71 girls); Grade 10: 83 students (83 girls); Grade 11: 79 students (79 girls); Grade 12: 91 students (91 girls). 96% of students are Roman Catholic.

Faculty School total: 36. In upper school: 9 men, 25 women; 22 have advanced degrees.

Subjects Offered Accounting, advanced biology, algebra, American history, American history-AP, American literature, anatomy, art, band, biology, British literature, business, calculus-AP, chemistry, Christian and Hebrew scripture, computer applications, concert choir, creative writing, desktop publishing, digital applications, economics, English, English language-AP, English literature, English literature-AP, ensembles, environmental science, European history, fine arts, French, French literature-AP, geometry, German, government/civics, guitar, health, Hebrew scripture, history, honors algebra, honors English, honors geometry, Italian, journalism, keyboarding, Latin, mathematics, music, physical education, physics, pre-calculus, probability and statistics, psychology, religion, religious studies, SAT preparation, science, Shakespeare, social studies, sociology, Spanish, Spanish literature-AP, Spanish-AP, statistics, trigonometry, U.S. government and politics-AP, U.S. history, U.S. history-AP, Ukrainian, world cultures, world history.

Graduation Requirements Arts and fine arts (art, music, dance, drama), English, foreign language, keyboarding, mathematics, physical education (includes health), religion (includes Bible studies and theology), science, social studies (includes history). Community service is required.

Special Academic Programs Advanced Placement exam preparation; honors section; study at local college for college credit.

College Admission Counseling 102 students graduated in 2011; all went to college, including Drexel University; La Salle University; Penn State University Park; Saint Joseph's University; Temple University; West Chester University of Pennsylvania. Mean SAT critical reading: 576, mean SAT math: 550, mean SAT writing: 600, mean combined SAT: 1726, mean composite ACT: 24.

Student Life Upper grades have uniform requirement, student council, honor system. Discipline rests primarily with faculty. Attendance at religious services is required.

Summer Programs Enrichment, sports programs offered; session focuses on sports camps, enrichment programs; held on campus; accepts girls; open to students from other schools. 50 students usually enrolled. 2012 schedule: June 15 to June 30. Application deadline: May 31.

Tuition and Aid Tuition installment plan (monthly payment plans, 2-installments (pay 1/2 tuition July 15, 1/2 tuition November 15), first installment (due July 15 (3 months), 7 installments (pay Oct. 15-April 15)). Tuition reduction for siblings, merit scholarship grants, need-based scholarship grants, Ellis Grant for children of single parents living in Philadelphia, BLOCS scholarships and foundations available. In 2011–12, 20% of upper-school students received aid; total upper-school merit-scholarship money awarded: $193,925. Total amount of financial aid awarded in 2011–12: $268,175.

Admissions Traditional secondary-level entrance grade is 9. For fall 2011, 162 students applied for upper-level admission, 71 enrolled. High School Placement Test required. Deadline for receipt of application materials: October 24. Application fee required: $40.

Athletics Interscholastic: basketball, cheering, cross-country running, field hockey, indoor track, lacrosse, soccer, softball, tennis, track and field, volleyball, winter (indoor) track. 1 PE instructor, 25 coaches.

Computers Computers are regularly used in accounting, computer applications, creative writing, desktop publishing, digital applications, economics, journalism, keyboarding, science classes. Computer network features include Internet access, wireless campus network, Internet filtering or blocking technology, student accessible server storage space, on-campus and Web-based library services (catalog and book request). Student e-mail accounts are available to students. The school has a published electronic and media policy.

Contact Mrs. Maureen Walsh, Director of Admissions. 215-885-6952. Fax: 215-885-0395. E-mail: mwalsh@stbasilacademy.org. Web site: www.stbasilacademy.org.

ST. BENEDICT AT AUBURNDALE

8250 Varnavas Drive

Cordova, Tennessee 38016

Head of School: Mr. George D. Valadie

General Information Coeducational day college-preparatory, arts, business, religious studies, bilingual studies, and technology school, affiliated with Roman Catholic Church. Grades 9–12. Founded: 1966. Setting: suburban. Nearest major city is Memphis. 40-acre campus. 1 building on campus. Approved or accredited by National Catholic Education Association, Southern Association of Colleges and Schools, and Tennessee Department of Education. Endowment: $100,000. Total enrollment: 982. Upper school average class size: 26. Upper school faculty-student ratio: 1:16. There are 186 required school days per year for Upper School students. Upper School students typically attend 5 days per week. The average school day consists of 7 hours and 15 minutes.

Upper School Student Profile Grade 9: 254 students (110 boys, 144 girls); Grade 10: 255 students (125 boys, 130 girls); Grade 11: 245 students (110 boys, 135 girls); Grade 12: 228 students (102 boys, 126 girls). 85% of students are Roman Catholic.

Faculty School total: 65. In upper school: 15 men, 50 women; 40 have advanced degrees.

Subjects Offered Accounting, algebra, American government, American history, American history-AP, American literature-AP, anatomy and physiology, applied music, art, art appreciation, art education, art history, art-AP, astronomy, band, biology, calculus, calculus-AP, Catholic belief and practice, chemistry, choir, choral music, choreography, chorus, church history, cinematography, clayworking, comparative religion, composition-AP, computer graphics, computer multimedia, computers, creative writing, dance, digital art, digital photography, drama, drama performance, drawing, driver education, ecology, economics, economics-AP, English, English language-AP, English literature-AP, English-AP, English/composition-AP, etymology, European history, film, filmmaking, fine arts, first aid, fitness, forensics, French, French-AP, general business, geometry, German, government, government-AP, graphic arts, graphic design, health and wellness, health education, history, history of the Catholic Church, history-AP, honors algebra, honors English, honors geometry, honors U.S. history, human anatomy, human biology, instrumental music, internship, jazz band, jazz dance, journalism, keyboarding, lab/keyboard, Latin, literature-AP, macroeconomics-AP, marketing, modern history, music appreciation, music history, music theory, newspaper, performing arts, personal finance, photography, physical education, physical science, physics, play production, pre-algebra, pre-calculus, psychology, religion, set design, sociology, Spanish, Spanish-AP, speech, sports conditioning, stage design, statistics-AP, student publications, U.S. government and politics-AP, U.S. history-AP, world geography, world history, yearbook.

Graduation Requirements Arts and fine arts (art, music, dance, drama), economics, English, foreign language, government, mathematics, physical education (includes health), religion (includes Bible studies and theology), science, social studies (includes history), technology, theology.

Special Academic Programs 10 Advanced Placement exams for which test preparation is offered; study at local college for college credit; academic accommodation for the gifted, the musically talented, and the artistically talented; remedial reading and/or remedial writing; remedial math; programs in English, mathematics, general development for dyslexic students; special instructional classes for students with diagnosed learning disabilities and Attention Deficit Disorder.

College Admission Counseling 239 students graduated in 2011; 238 went to college, including Christian Brothers University; Middle Tennessee State University; Mississippi State University; The University of Alabama; The University of Tennessee; University of Memphis. Other: 1 entered military service. Mean SAT critical reading: 570, mean SAT math: 560, mean composite ACT: 24. 38% scored over 600 on SAT critical reading, 37% scored over 600 on SAT math, 30% scored over 26 on composite ACT.

Student Life Upper grades have uniform requirement, student council, honor system. Discipline rests primarily with faculty. Attendance at religious services is required.

Summer Programs Remediation, enrichment programs offered; session focuses on enrichment for math and language; held on campus; accepts boys and girls; not open to students from other schools. 30 students usually enrolled. 2012 schedule: July 5 to July 29. Application deadline: none.

Tuition and Aid Day student tuition: $8000. Tuition installment plan (FACTS Tuition Payment Plan, monthly payment plans, individually arranged payment plans). Merit scholarship grants, need-based scholarship grants available. In 2011–12, 4% of upper-school students received aid; total upper-school merit-scholarship money awarded: $30,000. Total amount of financial aid awarded in 2011–12: $35,000.

Admissions Traditional secondary-level entrance grade is 9. For fall 2011, 287 students applied for upper-level admission, 280 were accepted, 273 enrolled. High School Placement Test required. Deadline for receipt of application materials: none. Application fee required: $75. Interview required.

Athletics Interscholastic: baseball (boys), basketball (b,g), bowling (b,g), cheering (g), cross-country running (b,g), dance (g), dance squad (g), dance team (g), football (b), Frisbee (b,g), golf (b,g), lacrosse (b,g), pom squad (g), soccer (b,g), softball (g), strength & conditioning (b), swimming and diving (b,g), tennis (b,g), track and field (b,g), volleyball (g), weight lifting (b), weight training (b), wrestling (b); coed intramural: Frisbee. 4 PE instructors, 17 coaches, 1 athletic trainer.

Computers Computers are regularly used in all academic, art, business, commercial art, current events, dance, design, desktop publishing, economics, French, graphic arts, graphic design, health, history, journalism, lab/keyboard, Latin, mathematics, music, newspaper, photography, psychology, publications, religion, science, social sciences, social studies, Spanish, speech, study skills, technology, theater, theater arts, theology, Web site design, writing, yearbook classes. Computer network features include on-campus library services, Internet access, wireless campus network, Internet filtering or blocking technology. Students grades are available online. The school has a published electronic and media policy.

Contact Mrs. Ann O'Leary, Director of Admissions. 901-260-2875. Fax: 901-260-2850. E-mail: olearya@sbaeagles.org. Web site: www.sbaeagles.org.

ST. BENEDICT'S PREPARATORY SCHOOL

520 Dr. Martin Luther King, Jr. Boulevard

Newark, New Jersey 07102-1314

Head of School: Rev. Edwin D. Leahy, OSB

General Information Boys' day college-preparatory school, affiliated with Roman Catholic Church. Grades 7–12. Founded: 1868. Setting: urban. 12-acre campus. 15 buildings on campus. Approved or accredited by Middle States Association of Colleges and Schools, New Jersey Association of Independent Schools, and New Jersey Department of Education. Endowment: $28 million. Total enrollment: 562. Upper school average class size: 20. Upper school faculty-student ratio: 1:11. Upper School students typically attend 5 days per week. The average school day consists of 6 hours.

Upper School Student Profile Grade 9: 132 students (132 boys); Grade 10: 118 students (118 boys); Grade 11: 116 students (116 boys); Grade 12: 109 students (109 boys). 40% of students are Roman Catholic.

Faculty School total: 55. In upper school: 44 men, 8 women; 40 have advanced degrees.

Subjects Offered Algebra, American history, American literature, architecture, art, astronomy, Bible studies, biology, Black history, calculus, chemistry, computer science, creative writing, drama, economics, English, English literature, ESL, European history, French, geometry, health, Hispanic literature, history, Latin, mathematics, mechanical drawing, music, physical education, physics, religion, social studies, sociology, Spanish, theater, trigonometry, world history.

Graduation Requirements English, foreign language, mathematics, physical education (includes health), religion (includes Bible studies and theology), science, social studies (includes history), spring projects, summer phase courses.

Special Academic Programs Term-away projects; domestic exchange program (with The Network Program Schools); remedial reading and/or remedial writing; remedial math; ESL (20 students enrolled).

College Admission Counseling 119 students graduated in 2011; 115 went to college, including Boston College; College of the Holy Cross; Rutgers, The State University of New Jersey, Newark; Saint John's University; Saint Peter's College; University of Notre Dame. Other: 2 went to work, 2 entered military service. Mean SAT critical reading: 468, mean SAT math: 492, mean SAT writing: 476, mean combined SAT: 1436.

Student Life Upper grades have uniform requirement, student council, honor system. Discipline rests equally with students and faculty. Attendance at religious services is required.

Summer Programs Remediation, enrichment, ESL, art/fine arts, computer instruction programs offered; session focuses on enrichment or remedial academic courses as appropriate; held on campus; accepts boys; not open to students from other schools. 565 students usually enrolled. 2012 schedule: July 30 to August 31.

Tuition and Aid Day student tuition: $8500. Tuition installment plan (FACTS Tuition Payment Plan). Need-based scholarship grants available. In 2011–12, 75% of upper-school students received aid. Total amount of financial aid awarded in 2011–12: $1,908,723.

Admissions For fall 2011, 365 students applied for upper-level admission, 281 were accepted, 175 enrolled. Deadline for receipt of application materials: December 31. No application fee required. On-campus interview required.

Athletics Interscholastic: baseball, basketball, cross-country running, fencing, golf, indoor track & field, soccer, swimming and diving, tennis, track and field, water polo, winter (indoor) track, wrestling; intramural: basketball, flag football, floor hockey, hiking/backpacking, life saving, outdoor adventure, outdoor skills, physical training, soccer, swimming and diving, weight lifting. 2 PE instructors, 20 coaches.

Computers Computers are regularly used in English, information technology, journalism, science classes. Computer network features include on-campus library services, online commercial services, Internet access, wireless campus network, Internet filtering or blocking technology. Student e-mail accounts are available to students. The school has a published electronic and media policy.

Contact Ms. Doris Lamourt, Admissions Administrative Assistant. 973-792-5744. Fax: 973-792-5706. E-mail: DLamourt@sbp.org. Web site: www.sbp.org.

ST. BERNARD HIGH SCHOOL

1593 Norwich-New London Turnpike

Uncasville, Connecticut 06382

Head of School: Mr. Thomas J. Doherty III

General Information Coeducational day college-preparatory school, affiliated with Roman Catholic Church. Grades 6–12. Founded: 1956. Setting: suburban. Nearest major city is Hartford. 113-acre campus. 1 building on campus. Approved or accredited by New England Association of Schools and Colleges and Connecticut Department of Education. Total enrollment: 373. Upper school average class size: 20. There are 177 required school days per year for Upper School students. Upper School students typically attend 5 days per week. The average school day consists of 6 hours.

Upper School Student Profile Grade 9: 66 students (26 boys, 40 girls); Grade 10: 61 students (34 boys, 27 girls); Grade 11: 81 students (42 boys, 39 girls); Grade 12: 74 students (33 boys, 41 girls). 80% of students are Roman Catholic.

Faculty School total: 33. In upper school: 19 men, 12 women; 21 have advanced degrees.

Subjects Offered 3-dimensional art, accounting, acting, algebra, anatomy and physiology, athletic training, biology, biology-AP, calculus, calculus-AP, chemistry, chemistry-AP, Christian doctrine, Christian ethics, Christian scripture, church history, conceptual physics, concert band, concert choir, creative writing, design, drawing and design, economics, English, English literature and composition-AP, environmental science, European history-AP, fine arts, forensics, French, French-AP, geometry, global issues, health, honors algebra, honors English, honors geometry, honors U.S. history, honors world history, integrated science, intro to computers, modern world history, moral theology, music, music theory, music theory-AP, Native American studies, nutrition, organic chemistry, painting, peace and justice, peer counseling, peer ministry, performing arts, personal finance, personal fitness, philosophy, photography, physical education, physics, pottery, pre-algebra, pre-calculus, printmaking, psychology-AP, public speaking, religious studies, scripture, sociology, Spanish, Spanish-AP, sports conditioning, sports nutrition, statistics, street law, strings, studio art, technology, theater arts, U.S. history, U.S. history-AP, world history.

Graduation Requirements Art, biology, chemistry, English, health education, history, intro to computers, mathematics, physical education (includes health), theology, U.S. history, world history, all students are required to complete 100 hours of community service prior to high school graduation.

Special Academic Programs Honors section; study at local college for college credit; ESL (6 students enrolled).

College Admission Counseling 74 students graduated in 2011; 72 went to college, including Keene State College; Providence College; Roger Williams University; Saint Michael's College; University of Connecticut; Worcester Polytechnic Institute. Other: 2 entered military service. Mean SAT critical reading: 546, mean SAT math: 518, mean SAT writing: 533.

Student Life Upper grades have uniform requirement, student council, honor system. Discipline rests primarily with faculty. Attendance at religious services is required.

Summer Programs Art/fine arts, computer instruction programs offered; held on campus; accepts boys and girls; not open to students from other schools. 2012 schedule: June to August.

Tuition and Aid Day student tuition: $10,500. Tuition installment plan (SMART Tuition Payment Plan, FACTS Tuition Payment Plan, monthly payment plans, individually arranged payment plans). Tuition reduction for siblings, merit scholarship grants, need-based scholarship grants available. In 2011–12, 32% of upper-school students received aid; total upper-school merit-scholarship money awarded: $166,050. Total amount of financial aid awarded in 2011–12: $354,257.

Admissions Traditional secondary-level entrance grade is 9. For fall 2011, 123 students applied for upper-level admission, 96 were accepted, 66 enrolled. Scholastic Testing Service required. Deadline for receipt of application materials: January 15. No application fee required. On-campus interview recommended.

Athletics Interscholastic: baseball (boys), basketball (b,g), cheering (g), cross-country running (b,g), diving (b,g), fencing (b,g), football (b), golf (b,g), ice hockey (b), indoor track & field (b,g), lacrosse (b,g), physical fitness (b,g), soccer (b,g), softball (g), swimming and diving (b,g), tennis (b,g), track and field (b,g), wrestling (b,g); coed interscholastic: cheering, cross-country running, fencing, golf, physical fitness, soccer, swimming and diving, wrestling; coed intramural: skiing (cross-country), skiing (downhill), snowboarding, strength & conditioning, volleyball, weight training. 2 PE instructors, 50 coaches, 1 athletic trainer.

Computers Computers are regularly used in computer applications, design classes. Computer resources include on-campus library services, Internet access, wireless campus network, Internet filtering or blocking technology. Campus intranet, student e-mail accounts, and computer access in designated common areas are available to students. Students grades are available online. The school has a published electronic and media policy.

Contact Mrs. Cathy Brown, Director of Admissions. 860-848-1271 Ext. 108. Fax: 860-848-1274. E-mail: Admissions@Saint-Bernard.com. Web site: www.saint-bernard.com.

ST. BERNARD'S CATHOLIC SCHOOL

222 Dollison Street

Eureka, California 95501

Head of School: Mr. David Sharp

General Information Coeducational boarding and day college-preparatory and religious studies school, affiliated with Roman Catholic Church. Boarding grades 9–12, day grades PK–12. Founded: 1912. Setting: small town. Nearest major city is San Francisco. 5-acre campus. 4 buildings on campus. Approved or accredited by National Catholic Education Association, Western Association of Schools and Colleges, Western Catholic Education Association, and California Department of Education. Endowment: $63,000. Total enrollment: 300. Upper school average class size: 20. Upper school faculty-student ratio: 1:12. There are 162 required school days per year for Upper School students. Upper School students typically attend 5 days per week. The average school day consists of 6 hours.

Upper School Student Profile 25% of students are boarding students. 75% are state residents. 25% are international students. International students from China, Republic of Korea, and Viet Nam. 35% of students are Roman Catholic.

Faculty School total: 20. In upper school: 9 men, 11 women; 5 have advanced degrees.

Subjects Offered Arts, community service, English, fine arts, mathematics, physical education, religion, science, social studies.

Graduation Requirements Arts and fine arts (art, music, dance, drama), English, foreign language, mathematics, physical education (includes health), science, social studies (includes history), theology, follow the University of California requirements (250 units). Community service is required.

Special Academic Programs Advanced Placement exam preparation; honors section; remedial reading and/or remedial writing; remedial math; special instructional classes for students with learning disabilities.

College Admission Counseling 44 students graduated in 2011; 43 went to college, including College of the Redwoods; Humboldt State University; Pacific University;

Sonoma State University; University of California, San Diego; University of San Francisco. Other: 1 entered military service.
Student Life Upper grades have specified standards of dress, student council. Discipline rests equally with students and faculty. Attendance at religious services is required.
Summer Programs Remediation programs offered; session focuses on make-up; held on campus; accepts boys and girls; open to students from other schools. 10 students usually enrolled. 2012 schedule: June 16 to July 23. Application deadline: June 6.
Tuition and Aid Day student tuition: $6300. Tuition installment plan (monthly payment plans, individually arranged payment plans, 3% reduction if paid in full by July 10). Tuition reduction for siblings, merit scholarship grants, need-based scholarship grants, paying campus jobs available. In 2011–12, 47% of upper-school students received aid; total upper-school merit-scholarship money awarded: $2500. Total amount of financial aid awarded in 2011–12: $55,000.
Admissions Traditional secondary-level entrance grade is 9. Admissions testing required. Deadline for receipt of application materials: none. Application fee required: $40. Interview required.
Athletics Interscholastic: baseball (boys), basketball (b,g), football (b), golf (b,g), soccer (b,g), softball (g), tennis (b,g), volleyball (g), wrestling (b); intramural: cheering (g); coed interscholastic: track and field. 1 PE instructor, 15 coaches, 1 athletic trainer.
Computers Computers are regularly used in graphic design, journalism, yearbook classes. Computer network features include on-campus library services, Internet access, wireless campus network, Internet filtering or blocking technology. Students grades are available online. The school has a published electronic and media policy.
Contact Mrs. Shirley Sobol, Domestic Admissions. 707-443-2735 Ext. 115. Fax: 707-443-4723. E-mail: sobol@saintbernards.us. Web site: www.saintbernards.us/.

ST. BRENDAN HIGH SCHOOL

2950 Southwest 87th Avenue

Miami, Florida 33165-3295

Head of School: Br. Felix Elardo

General Information Coeducational day college-preparatory, general academic, arts, business, religious studies, bilingual studies, and technology school, affiliated with Roman Catholic Church. Grades 9–12. Founded: 1975. Setting: urban. 34-acre campus. 3 buildings on campus. Approved or accredited by Southern Association of Colleges and Schools and Florida Department of Education. Total enrollment: 1,181. Upper school average class size: 28. Upper school faculty-student ratio: 1:15. There are 180 required school days per year for Upper School students. Upper School students typically attend 5 days per week. The average school day consists of 6 hours and 45 minutes.
Upper School Student Profile Grade 9: 262 students (59 boys, 203 girls); Grade 10: 299 students (73 boys, 226 girls); Grade 11: 297 students (83 boys, 214 girls); Grade 12: 269 students (78 boys, 191 girls). 98% of students are Roman Catholic.
Faculty School total: 95. In upper school: 27 men, 68 women; 50 have advanced degrees.
Graduation Requirements Students must complete 100 community service hours in their four years of high school.
Special Academic Programs 10 Advanced Placement exams for which test preparation is offered; honors section; study at local college for college credit; academic accommodation for the gifted; remedial reading and/or remedial writing.
College Admission Counseling 284 students graduated in 2011; 282 went to college, including Florida International University; Florida State University; Miami Dade College; University of Florida; University of Miami. Other: 2 entered military service. Median composite ACT: 20. 10% scored over 26 on composite ACT.
Student Life Upper grades have uniform requirement, student council, honor system. Discipline rests primarily with faculty. Attendance at religious services is required.
Summer Programs Remediation, advancement, computer instruction programs offered; held on campus; accepts boys and girls; open to students from other schools. 100 students usually enrolled. 2012 schedule: June 12 to June 29. Application deadline: June 11.
Tuition and Aid Tuition installment plan (FACTS Tuition Payment Plan, monthly payment plans). Need-based scholarship grants, paying campus jobs available. In 2011–12, 15% of upper-school students received aid.
Admissions Traditional secondary-level entrance grade is 9. For fall 2011, 550 students applied for upper-level admission, 400 were accepted, 400 enrolled. Catholic High School Entrance Examination or placement test required. Deadline for receipt of application materials: January 21. Application fee required: $50.
Athletics Interscholastic: baseball (boys, girls), basketball (b,g), cheering (g), cross-country running (b,g), dance team (g), soccer (b,g), softball (g), swimming and diving (b,g), tennis (b,g), track and field (b,g), volleyball (g). 3 PE instructors, 17 coaches.
Computers Computers are regularly used in business, computer applications, graphic design, mathematics, media arts, media production, newspaper, programming, reading, remedial study skills, research skills, science, speech, Web site design, word processing, yearbook classes. Computer network features include on-campus library services, Internet access, wireless campus network, Internet filtering or blocking technology. Computer access in designated common areas is available to students. Students grades are available online. The school has a published electronic and media policy.
Contact Melissa Ferrer, Director of Admissions. 305-223-5181 Ext. 578. Fax: 305-220-7434. E-mail: cbarket@stbhs.org. Web site: www.stbhs.org.

ST. CATHERINE'S ACADEMY

Anaheim, California

See Junior Boarding Schools section.

ST. CATHERINE'S SCHOOL

6001 Grove Avenue

Richmond, Virginia 23226

Head of School: Laura J. Fuller

General Information Girls' day college-preparatory school, affiliated with Episcopal Church. Grades JK–12. Founded: 1890. Setting: suburban. Nearest major city is Washington, DC. 17-acre campus. 22 buildings on campus. Approved or accredited by Virginia Association of Independent Schools and Virginia Department of Education. Member of National Association of Independent Schools and Secondary School Admission Test Board. Endowment: $535 million. Total enrollment: 909. Upper school average class size: 16.
Upper School Student Profile Grade 9: 78 students (78 girls); Grade 10: 76 students (76 girls); Grade 11: 65 students (65 girls); Grade 12: 59 students (59 girls). 46% of students are members of Episcopal Church.
Faculty School total: 127. In upper school: 18 men, 27 women; 34 have advanced degrees.
Subjects Offered Acting, adolescent issues, advanced chemistry, advanced computer applications, advanced math, African-American literature, algebra, American government, American history, American history-AP, American literature, ancient history, architecture, art, art and culture, art history, art history-AP, band, Bible, biology, British literature-AP, calculus, calculus-AP, ceramics, chamber groups, chemistry, chemistry-AP, Chinese, choir, choral music, choreography, chorus, comparative government and politics-AP, comparative religion, computer applications, computer math, computer programming, computer science, computer science-AP, constitutional law, creative writing, dance, dance performance, desktop publishing, drama, driver education, economics, economics-AP, English, English language and composition-AP, English literature, English literature and composition-AP, environmental science, environmental science-AP, ethics, ethics and responsibility, European history, expository writing, film and literature, fine arts, French, French language-AP, French literature-AP, gender issues, geography, geometry, government and politics-AP, government/civics, grammar, Greek, guitar, health and wellness, health education, history, history of jazz, honors algebra, honors English, honors geometry, independent study, Latin, Latin-AP, macro/microeconomics-AP, mathematics, modern dance, moral and social development, moral theology, music, music history, music theory, music theory-AP, orchestra, painting, performing arts, philosophy, photography, physical education, physical fitness, physics, physics-AP, playwriting and directing, portfolio art, post-calculus, pre-calculus, printmaking, regional literature, religion, rhetoric, robotics, science, sculpture, short story, social studies, Southern literature, Spanish, Spanish language-AP, Spanish literature, Spanish literature-AP, speech, speech communications, statistics, statistics-AP, theater, theater arts, theology, trigonometry, U.S. government and politics-AP, Vietnam, world cultures, world geography, world history, world literature, writing.
Graduation Requirements Arts and fine arts (art, music, dance, drama), computer science, English, foreign language, mathematics, physical education (includes health), religion (includes Bible studies and theology), science, social sciences, social studies (includes history), Community Service reuirement.
Special Academic Programs Advanced Placement exam preparation; honors section; independent study; term-away projects; study abroad.
College Admission Counseling 60 students graduated in 2010; all went to college, including James Madison University; The College of William and Mary; Tulane University; University of Virginia; Vanderbilt University; Virginia Polytechnic Institute and State University. Median SAT math: 640, median SAT writing: 660, median combined SAT: 1930, median composite ACT: 26. Mean SAT critical reading: 636. 72% scored over 600 on SAT critical reading, 66.7% scored over 600 on SAT math, 82.5% scored over 600 on SAT writing, 77.2% scored over 1800 on combined SAT, 60% scored over 26 on composite ACT.
Student Life Upper grades have specified standards of dress, student council, honor system. Discipline rests equally with students and faculty. Attendance at religious services is required.
Tuition and Aid Day student tuition: $15,400–$20,340. Tuition installment plan (monthly payment plans, Tuition Management Systems Plan). Need-based scholarship grants available. In 2010–11, 13% of upper-school students received aid. Total amount of financial aid awarded in 2010–11: $448,800.
Admissions Traditional secondary-level entrance grade is 9. SSAT, TOEFL and TOEFL or SLEP required. Deadline for receipt of application materials: none. Application fee required: $50. Interview required.
Athletics Interscholastic: basketball, cross-country running, diving, field hockey, golf, indoor track, indoor track & field, lacrosse, soccer, softball, squash, swimming and diving, tennis, track and field, volleyball, winter (indoor) track; intramural: aerobics,

aerobics/dance, aerobics/Nautilus, aquatics, ballet, basketball, canoeing/kayaking, climbing, dance, equestrian sports, field hockey, golf, lacrosse, martial arts, modern dance, physical fitness, physical training, soccer, softball, strength & conditioning, swimming and diving, tennis, track and field, volleyball, weight lifting, weight training, wilderness, yoga; coed interscholastic: indoor track & field, track and field; coed intramural: aerobics/dance, backpacking, ballet, canoeing/kayaking, climbing, dance, modern dance, outdoor adventure, wilderness. 3 PE instructors, 50 coaches, 2 athletic trainers.

Computers Computers are regularly used in all classes. Computer network features include on-campus library services, online commercial services, Internet access, wireless campus network. Campus intranet and student e-mail accounts are available to students. Students grades are available online. The school has a published electronic and media policy.

Contact Jennifer Cullinan, Director of Admissions. 804-288-2804. Fax: 804-285-8169. E-mail: jcullinan@st.catherines.org. Web site: www.st.catherines.org.

ST. CECILIA ACADEMY

4210 Harding Road

Nashville, Tennessee 37205

Head of School: Sr. Mary Thomas, OP

General Information Girls' day college-preparatory, arts, religious studies, and technology school, affiliated with Roman Catholic Church. Grades 9–12. Founded: 1860. Setting: suburban. 83-acre campus. 6 buildings on campus. Approved or accredited by National Catholic Education Association, Southern Association of Colleges and Schools, Southern Association of Independent Schools, Tennessee Association of Independent Schools, The College Board, and Tennessee Department of Education. Total enrollment: 257. Upper school average class size: 14. Upper school faculty-student ratio: 1:9. There are 180 required school days per year for Upper School students. Upper School students typically attend 5 days per week. The average school day consists of 7 hours.

Upper School Student Profile Grade 9: 59 students (59 girls); Grade 10: 71 students (71 girls); Grade 11: 71 students (71 girls); Grade 12: 56 students (56 girls). 70% of students are Roman Catholic.

Faculty School total: 32. In upper school: 4 men, 28 women; 21 have advanced degrees.

Subjects Offered Algebra, American history-AP, American literature, anatomy and physiology, biology, biology-AP, British literature, calculus, calculus-AP, Catholic belief and practice, chamber groups, chemistry, chemistry-AP, chorus, church history, computer programming, computer science, current events, dance, drawing, economics, economics and history, English literature, English-AP, ethics, European civilization, European history, European history-AP, fine arts, French, French language-AP, geometry, German, German-AP, government, government/civics, Internet research, journalism, Latin, microcomputer technology applications, moral theology, music, music appreciation, music theory, natural history, photography, physical education, physics, physics-AP, religion, scripture, Spanish language-AP, Spanish-AP, speech, studio art-AP, tap dance, theology, trigonometry, U.S. history, U.S. history-AP, visual and performing arts, visual arts, world history, yearbook.

Graduation Requirements Arts and fine arts (art, music, dance, drama), computer science, English, foreign language, history, mathematics, physical education (includes health), religion (includes Bible studies and theology), science.

Special Academic Programs Advanced Placement exam preparation; honors section; study at local college for college credit; academic accommodation for the gifted, the musically talented, and the artistically talented.

College Admission Counseling 53 students graduated in 2010; all went to college. Mean SAT critical reading: 601, mean SAT math: 540, mean SAT writing: 601, mean composite ACT: 26.

Student Life Upper grades have uniform requirement, student council, honor system. Discipline rests primarily with faculty. Attendance at religious services is required.

Tuition and Aid Day student tuition: $14,200. Tuition installment plan (Tuition Management Systems Plan). Need-based scholarship grants available. In 2010–11, 42% of upper-school students received aid. Total amount of financial aid awarded in 2010–11: $650,000.

Admissions Traditional secondary-level entrance grade is 9. For fall 2010, 117 students applied for upper-level admission, 90 were accepted, 60 enrolled. High School Placement Test and ISEE required. Deadline for receipt of application materials: January 10. Application fee required: $60. Interview required.

Athletics Interscholastic: aquatics, basketball, bowling, cross-country running, diving, golf, running, soccer, softball, swimming and diving, tennis, track and field, volleyball; intramural: dance, dance team, independent competitive sports, lacrosse, modern dance, physical training, self defense, strength & conditioning, weight lifting, weight training. 1 PE instructor, 16 coaches, 1 athletic trainer.

Computers Computers are regularly used in art, English, foreign language, history, journalism, mathematics, newspaper, publications, science, Spanish, writing classes. Computer network features include on-campus library services, online commercial services, Internet access, Internet filtering or blocking technology. Students grades are available online. The school has a published electronic and media policy.

Contact Mrs. Betty Bader, Director of Admissions. 615-298-4525 Ext. 377. Fax: 615-783-0561. E-mail: admissions@stcecilia.edu. Web site: www.stcecilia.edu.

SAINT CECILIA HIGH SCHOOL

521 North Kansas Avenue

Hastings, Nebraska 68901-7594

Head of School: Rev. Fr. Troy J. Schweiger

General Information Coeducational day and distance learning college-preparatory, arts, business, vocational, religious studies, and technology school, affiliated with Roman Catholic Church. Grades 6–12. Distance learning grades 11–12. Founded: 1912. Setting: small town. Nearest major city is Lincoln. 1-acre campus. 2 buildings on campus. Approved or accredited by National Catholic Education Association, North Central Association of Colleges and Schools, and Nebraska Department of Education. Endowment: $1 million. Total enrollment: 262. Upper school average class size: 20. Upper school faculty-student ratio: 1:5. There are 178 required school days per year for Upper School students. Upper School students typically attend 5 days per week. The average school day consists of 6 hours and 16 minutes.

Upper School Student Profile Grade 9: 36 students (20 boys, 16 girls); Grade 10: 38 students (17 boys, 21 girls); Grade 11: 43 students (17 boys, 26 girls); Grade 12: 43 students (27 boys, 16 girls). 98% of students are Roman Catholic.

Faculty School total: 32. In upper school: 12 men, 20 women; 15 have advanced degrees.

Subjects Offered Accounting, aerospace education, algebra, American history, American literature-AP, art history, automated accounting, band, Basic programming, biology, business law, business mathematics, calculus-AP, career education, Catholic belief and practice, chemistry, chorus, computer applications, computer programming, computer technology certification, computer-aided design, consumer economics, drafting, drawing, driver education, economics, English, environmental science, ESL, family and consumer science, fashion, fine arts, foods, geometry, health, history of the Catholic Church, instrumental music, interior design, Internet, introduction to technology, jazz band, language arts, library skills, Life of Christ, marketing, music, musical productions, newspaper, painting, peace and justice, physical education, physics, play production, portfolio art, pre-calculus, probability and statistics, psychology, religion, science, science project, sculpture, social sciences, social studies, sociology, Spanish, Spanish literature, speech, statistics, textiles, theater arts, TOEFL preparation, trigonometry, U.S. government, video film production, vocational arts, weight training, world history, yearbook.

Graduation Requirements Algebra, American government, American history, American literature, arts and fine arts (art, music, dance, drama), British literature, career education, computer skills, economics, English, foreign language, mathematics, physical education (includes health), practical arts, religion (includes Bible studies and theology), science, social studies (includes history), speech, vocational arts, vocational-technical courses, 50-60 volunteer service hours.

Special Academic Programs 1 Advanced Placement exam for which test preparation is offered; honors section; independent study; study at local college for college credit; remedial reading and/or remedial writing; remedial math; special instructional classes for students with learning disabilities and Attention Deficit Disorder; ESL (24 students enrolled).

College Admission Counseling 44 students graduated in 2010; 43 went to college, including Benedictine College; Creighton University; Doane College; University of Nebraska–Lincoln; University of Nebraska at Kearney; University of Nebraska at Omaha. Other: 1 went to work. Median SAT critical reading: 550, median SAT math: 650, median SAT writing: 420, median combined SAT: 1200, median composite ACT: 22. 1% scored over 600 on SAT math, 18% scored over 26 on composite ACT.

Student Life Upper grades have uniform requirement, student council, honor system. Discipline rests primarily with faculty. Attendance at religious services is required.

Tuition and Aid Day student tuition: $1375. Guaranteed tuition plan. Tuition installment plan (monthly payment plans, individually arranged payment plans, automatic bank draft). Tuition reduction for siblings, merit scholarship grants, scrip participation program, tuition assistance with parish pastors, parish pastor will pay or match family contribution to reach the total tuition available. In 2010–11, 16% of upper-school students received aid; total upper-school merit-scholarship money awarded: $8000. Total amount of financial aid awarded in 2010–11: $8000.

Admissions ACT, ACT-Explore, English proficiency, PSAT, Terra Nova-CTB, TOEFL or writing sample required. Deadline for receipt of application materials: none. No application fee required. Interview required.

Athletics Interscholastic: aerobics/dance (girls), basketball (b,g), bowling (b,g), cheering (g), dance (g), dance team (g), drill team (g), football (b), golf (b,g), running (b,g), tennis (g), volleyball (g), wrestling (b); intramural: dance team (g), drill team (g), power lifting (b); coed interscholastic: track and field; coed intramural: badminton, bowling, juggling, jump rope, life saving, physical fitness, physical training, weight lifting, weight training. 2 PE instructors, 2 athletic trainers.

Computers Computers are regularly used in accounting, business, career education, career exploration, career technology, Christian doctrine, college planning, computer applications, desktop publishing, ESL, drafting, drawing and design, English, ESL, foreign language, graphic design, graphics, health, journalism, keyboarding, mathematics, media production, music, newspaper, reading, science, Spanish, speech, video

film production, vocational-technical courses, Web site design, word processing, writing, writing, yearbook classes. Computer network features include on-campus library services, online commercial services, Internet access, wireless campus network, Internet filtering or blocking technology, SmartBoards. Student e-mail accounts and computer access in designated common areas are available to students. Students grades are available online. The school has a published electronic and media policy.
Contact Mrs. Marie K. Butler, Assistant Super/Curriculum Director. 402-462-2105. Fax: 402-462-2106. E-mail: mbutler@esu9.org. Web site: www.hastingscatholicschools.org.

ST. CHRISTOPHER'S SCHOOL

711 St. Christopher's Road

Richmond, Virginia 23226

Head of School: Mr. Charles M. Stillwell

General Information Boys' day college-preparatory school, affiliated with Episcopal Church. Grades JK–12. Founded: 1911. Setting: suburban. 46-acre campus. 9 buildings on campus. Approved or accredited by National Association of Episcopal Schools and Virginia Association of Independent Schools. Member of National Association of Independent Schools and Secondary School Admission Test Board. Endowment: $61.6 million. Total enrollment: 956. Upper school average class size: 15. Upper school faculty-student ratio: 1:6. Upper School students typically attend 5 days per week. The average school day consists of 7 hours and 30 minutes.
Upper School Student Profile Grade 9: 86 students (86 boys); Grade 10: 65 students (65 boys); Grade 11: 67 students (67 boys); Grade 12: 75 students (75 boys). 45% of students are members of Episcopal Church.
Faculty School total: 157. In upper school: 32 men, 17 women; 32 have advanced degrees.
Subjects Offered Algebra, American history, American literature, ancient history, architecture, art, art history, astronomy, Bible studies, biology, calculus, ceramics, chemistry, Chinese, community service, computer math, computer programming, computer science, creative thinking, creative writing, dance, drama, driver education, ecology, economics, English, English literature, environmental science, ethics, European history, expository writing, fine arts, French, geography, geology, geometry, government/civics, grammar, Greek, health, history, industrial arts, journalism, Latin, mathematics, music, philosophy, photography, physics, public speaking, religion, science, social studies, Spanish, speech, statistics, theater, theology, trigonometry, typing, woodworking, writing.
Graduation Requirements 1 1/2 elective credits, algebra, American history, American literature, ancient history, arts and fine arts (art, music, dance, drama), biology, British literature, chemistry, church history, computer science, English, English literature, European history, foreign language, geometry, physical education (includes health), physics, public speaking, religion (includes Bible studies and theology), speech, U.S. history. Community service is required.
Special Academic Programs 20 Advanced Placement exams for which test preparation is offered; honors section; independent study; academic accommodation for the gifted, the musically talented, and the artistically talented.
College Admission Counseling 73 students graduated in 2011; all went to college, including Hampden-Sydney College; Sewanee: The University of the South; The College of William and Mary; University of Virginia; Virginia Polytechnic Institute and State University; Washington and Lee University.
Student Life Upper grades have specified standards of dress, student council, honor system. Discipline rests equally with students and faculty. Attendance at religious services is required.
Summer Programs Advancement programs offered; session focuses on enrichment, sports, day camp, leadership; held on campus; accepts boys and girls; open to students from other schools. 750 students usually enrolled. 2012 schedule: June 20 to July 29. Application deadline: none.
Tuition and Aid Day student tuition: $21,835. Tuition installment plan (Academic Management Services Plan, monthly payment plans, individually arranged payment plans, Tuition Refund Plan). Merit scholarship grants, need-based scholarship grants available. In 2011–12, 27% of upper-school students received aid; total upper-school merit-scholarship money awarded: $3000. Total amount of financial aid awarded in 2011–12: $783,200.
Admissions Traditional secondary-level entrance grade is 9. For fall 2011, 56 students applied for upper-level admission, 36 were accepted, 19 enrolled. SSAT and writing sample required. Deadline for receipt of application materials: none. Application fee required: $50. On-campus interview required.
Athletics Interscholastic: baseball, basketball, cross-country running, diving, football, golf, indoor soccer, indoor track & field, lacrosse, sailing, soccer, squash, strength & conditioning, swimming and diving, tennis, track and field, weight lifting, weight training, winter (indoor) track, wrestling; coed interscholastic: canoeing/kayaking, climbing, dance, martial arts, outdoor adventure, rappelling. 5 coaches, 2 athletic trainers.
Computers Computers are regularly used in computer applications, desktop publishing, digital applications, English, foreign language, health, history, journalism, literary magazine, mathematics, music, photography, publications, science classes. Computer network features include on-campus library services, online commercial services, Internet access, wireless campus network, Internet filtering or blocking technology. Student e-mail accounts and computer access in designated common areas are available to students. Students grades are available online. The school has a published electronic and media policy.
Contact Cary C. Mauck, Director of Admission. 804-282-3185 Ext. 2388. Fax: 804-673-6632. E-mail: mauckc@stcva.org. Web site: www.stchristophers.com.

SAINT CLEMENT ACADEMY

88 Main St

Ottawa, Ontario K1S 1C2, Canada

Head of School: Mrs. Beryl Devine

General Information Coeducational day college-preparatory school, affiliated with Roman Catholic Church. Grades 7–12. Founded: 1996. Setting: urban. Approved or accredited by Ontario Department of Education. Language of instruction: English. Total enrollment: 20. Upper school average class size: 9. Upper school faculty-student ratio: 1:3. There are 181 required school days per year for Upper School students. Upper School students typically attend 5 days per week. The average school day consists of 6 hours.
Upper School Student Profile Grade 9: 4 students (2 boys, 2 girls); Grade 10: 2 students (1 boy, 1 girl); Grade 11: 5 students (2 boys, 3 girls); Grade 12: 2 students (1 boy, 1 girl). 100% of students are Roman Catholic.
Faculty School total: 15. In upper school: 7 men, 4 women; 9 have advanced degrees.
Subjects Offered Advanced math, algebra, arts and crafts, calculus, Canadian geography, Canadian history, Catholic belief and practice, chemistry, choir, church history, English literature and composition-AP, French, French as a second language, geometry, Greek, history, Latin, mathematics, music history, music theory, physical education, science, world history.
Graduation Requirements Biology, calculus, chemistry, church history, English, French, French as a second language, Greek, Latin, mathematics, music history, music theory, physics, religion (includes Bible studies and theology).
Special Academic Programs Honors section; ESL.
College Admission Counseling 4 students graduated in 2011; all went to college.
Student Life Upper grades have uniform requirement, honor system. Discipline rests primarily with faculty. Attendance at religious services is required.
Tuition and Aid Day student tuition: CAN$3700. Tuition installment plan (full payment in advance, 5-month payment plan). Tuition reduction for siblings available.
Admissions Traditional secondary-level entrance grade is 9. Canadian Standardized Test required. Deadline for receipt of application materials: April 1. No application fee required. On-campus interview required.
Athletics Coed Intramural: fitness, Frisbee, independent competitive sports, paddle tennis, physical training, running, soccer, tennis, touch football, track and field, volleyball. 2 PE instructors.
Computers Computer resources include Internet access, word processing, encyclopedia.
Contact Mrs. Beryl Devine, Headmistress. 613-236-7231. Fax: 613-236-9159. E-mail: st.clementacademy@bellnet.ca.

ST. CLEMENT'S SCHOOL

21 St. Clements Avenue

Toronto, Ontario M4R 1G8, Canada

Head of School: Ms. Martha Perry

General Information Girls' day college-preparatory, arts, business, and technology school, affiliated with Anglican Church of Canada. Grades 1–12. Founded: 1901. Setting: urban. 1-acre campus. 1 building on campus. Approved or accredited by Canadian Association of Independent Schools, Canadian Educational Standards Institute, Conference of Independent Schools of Ontario, and Ontario Department of Education. Affiliate member of National Association of Independent Schools; member of Secondary School Admission Test Board. Language of instruction: English. Total enrollment: 473. Upper school average class size: 16. Upper school faculty-student ratio: 1:7. Upper School students typically attend 5 days per week.
Upper School Student Profile Grade 10: 60 students (60 girls); Grade 11: 60 students (60 girls); Grade 12: 60 students (60 girls).
Faculty School total: 62. In upper school: 7 men, 43 women; 20 have advanced degrees.
Subjects Offered Accounting, Advanced Placement courses, algebra, Ancient Greek, ancient world history, art, art history-AP, art-AP, band, biology, biology-AP, business, business studies, calculus, calculus-AP, Canadian geography, Canadian history, Canadian law, Canadian literature, career and personal planning, career education, character education, chemistry, chemistry-AP, civics, classics, college admission preparation, communication arts, computer science, creative writing, dance, data processing, design, drama, economics, economics-AP, English, English language-AP, English literature, English literature and composition-AP, environmental science, environmental science-AP, European history, European history-AP, exercise science, film studies, fine arts, finite math, French, French-AP, geography, geometry, grammar, graphic design,

guidance, health, history, history-AP, human geography - AP, instrumental music, interdisciplinary studies, jazz ensemble, keyboarding, kinesiology, language and composition, language arts, Latin, Latin-AP, law, leadership and service, library, macro/microeconomics-AP, Mandarin, mathematics, modern Western civilization, music, music theory-AP, musical theater, philosophy, photography, physical education, physics, physics-AP, physiology, religion, science, social sciences, social studies, Spanish, Spanish-AP, statistics-AP, studio art-AP, theater, trigonometry, U.S. history-AP, Western civilization, world history, world issues, writing workshop.

Graduation Requirements Arts, business skills (includes word processing), career/college preparation, civics, computer science, English, foreign language, geography, mathematics, physical education (includes health), science, social studies (includes history).

Special Academic Programs 20 Advanced Placement exams for which test preparation is offered; independent study; academic accommodation for the gifted.

College Admission Counseling 57 students graduated in 2011; all went to college, including Dalhousie University; McGill University; Queen's University at Kingston; The University of British Columbia; The University of Western Ontario; University of Toronto.

Student Life Upper grades have uniform requirement, student council, honor system. Discipline rests equally with students and faculty. Attendance at religious services is required.

Summer Programs Advancement, art/fine arts programs offered; session focuses on cooperative program and summer school credit courses; held both on and off campus; held at Europe; accepts boys and girls; open to students from other schools. 15 students usually enrolled. 2012 schedule: June 20 to July 22. Application deadline: May.

Tuition and Aid Day student tuition: CAN$24,150. Tuition installment plan (monthly payment plans, individually arranged payment plans). Bursaries, merit scholarship grants, need-based scholarship grants available. In 2011–12, 8% of upper-school students received aid.

Admissions SSAT required. Deadline for receipt of application materials: December 16. Application fee required: CAN$150. Interview required.

Athletics Interscholastic: alpine skiing, badminton, basketball, cross-country running, dance, dance team, equestrian sports, field hockey, hockey, ice hockey, nordic skiing, running, skiing (downhill), soccer, softball, swimming and diving, tennis, track and field, volleyball; intramural: aerobics, aerobics/dance, backpacking, badminton, basketball, bocce, canoeing/kayaking, cooperative games, cross-country running, dance, dance team, field hockey, fitness, floor hockey, hiking/backpacking, indoor soccer, jogging, life saving, outdoor education, paddle tennis, running, soccer, softball, swimming and diving, table tennis, tennis, track and field, ultimate Frisbee, volleyball, wilderness survival, yoga. 5 PE instructors, 12 coaches.

Computers Computers are regularly used in all academic classes. Computer network features include on-campus library services, online commercial services, Internet access, wireless campus network, Internet filtering or blocking technology. Campus intranet, student e-mail accounts, and computer access in designated common areas are available to students. The school has a published electronic and media policy.

Contact Mrs. Jennifer Gray, Director of Admissions. 416-483-4414 Ext. 2227. Fax: 416-483-8242. E-mail: jgray@scs.on.ca. Web site: www.scs.on.ca.

ST. CROIX COUNTRY DAY SCHOOL

RR #1, Box 6199

Kingshill, Virgin Islands 00850-9807

Head of School: Mr. William D. Sinfield

General Information Coeducational day college-preparatory and technology school. Grades N–12. Founded: 1964. Setting: rural. Nearest major city is Christiansted, U.S. Virgin Islands. 25-acre campus. 6 buildings on campus. Approved or accredited by Middle States Association of Colleges and Schools and Virgin Islands Department of Education. Member of National Association of Independent Schools. Endowment: $574,000. Total enrollment: 413. Upper school average class size: 14. Upper school faculty-student ratio: 1:12. Upper School students typically attend 5 days per week. The average school day consists of 7 hours.

Upper School Student Profile Grade 9: 41 students (17 boys, 24 girls); Grade 10: 32 students (18 boys, 14 girls); Grade 11: 34 students (20 boys, 14 girls); Grade 12: 37 students (19 boys, 18 girls).

Faculty School total: 51. In upper school: 6 men, 17 women; 11 have advanced degrees.

Subjects Offered Algebra, American history, American literature, art, art history, arts, band, biology, calculus, ceramics, chemistry, chorus, community service, computer programming, computer science, creative writing, current events, dance, drama, earth science, ecology, economics, electronics, English, English literature, film, fine arts, French, geometry, government/civics, health, history, journalism, keyboarding, marine biology, mathematics, music, Native American studies, photography, physical education, physical science, physics, pre-calculus, psychology, public speaking, science, social studies, sociology, Spanish, statistics, swimming, theater, trigonometry, world history.

Graduation Requirements Arts and fine arts (art, music, dance, drama), computer science, English, foreign language, mathematics, physical education (includes health), science, social studies (includes history), swimming, typing. Community service is required.

Special Academic Programs Advanced Placement exam preparation.

College Admission Counseling 44 students graduated in 2011; all went to college, including Michigan Technological University; University of Pennsylvania; University of Pittsburgh; Vassar College. Median SAT critical reading: 520, median SAT math: 540, median composite ACT: 22. 35% scored over 600 on SAT critical reading, 25% scored over 600 on SAT math, 19% scored over 26 on composite ACT.

Student Life Upper grades have specified standards of dress, student council, honor system. Discipline rests primarily with faculty.

Tuition and Aid Day student tuition: $14,000. Tuition installment plan (monthly payment plans, individually arranged payment plans, semiannual and annual payment plans). Merit scholarship grants, need-based scholarship grants available. In 2011–12, 33% of upper-school students received aid; total upper-school merit-scholarship money awarded: $42,500. Total amount of financial aid awarded in 2011–12: $265,550.

Admissions Traditional secondary-level entrance grade is 9. For fall 2011, 25 students applied for upper-level admission, 10 were accepted, 10 enrolled. Essay and Test of Achievement and Proficiency required. Deadline for receipt of application materials: none. Application fee required: $150. On-campus interview required.

Athletics Interscholastic: baseball (boys), basketball (b,g), football (b), softball (g), tennis (b,g), volleyball (b,g); intramural: volleyball (b,g); coed interscholastic: aerobics, aquatics, basketball, cross-country running, sailing, soccer; coed intramural: basketball, soccer, ultimate Frisbee. 3 PE instructors, 7 coaches.

Computers Computers are regularly used in mathematics, music, science, yearbook classes. Computer network features include on-campus library services, online commercial services, Internet access. The school has a published electronic and media policy.

Contact Mrs. Alma V. Castro-Nieves, Registrar. 340-778-1974 Ext. 2108. Fax: 340-779-3331. E-mail: anieves@stxcountryday.com. Web site: www.stxcountryday.com.

ST. CROIX SCHOOLS

1200 Oakdale Avenue

West St. Paul, Minnesota 55118

Head of School: Dr. Gene Pfeifer

General Information Coeducational boarding and day college-preparatory, general academic, arts, business, vocational, religious studies, bilingual studies, technology, and ESL school, affiliated with Wisconsin Evangelical Lutheran Synod, Christian faith. Grades 6–12. Founded: 1958. Setting: suburban. Nearest major city is St. Paul. Students are housed in single-sex dormitories. 30-acre campus. 3 buildings on campus. Approved or accredited by Minnesota Department of Education. Endowment: $1.6 million. Total enrollment: 500. Upper school average class size: 21. Upper school faculty-student ratio: 1:15. There are 176 required school days per year for Upper School students. Upper School students typically attend 5 days per week. The average school day consists of 5 hours and 30 minutes.

Upper School Student Profile Grade 9: 110 students (52 boys, 58 girls); Grade 10: 110 students (57 boys, 53 girls); Grade 11: 110 students (56 boys, 54 girls); Grade 12: 110 students (53 boys, 57 girls). 30% of students are boarding students. 74% are state residents. 7 states are represented in upper school student body. 22% are international students. International students from China, Japan, Republic of Korea, Taiwan, Thailand, and Viet Nam; 6 other countries represented in student body. 67% of students are Wisconsin Evangelical Lutheran Synod, Christian.

Faculty School total: 32. In upper school: 21 men, 11 women; 18 have advanced degrees; 4 reside on campus.

Subjects Offered Accounting, advanced biology, advanced chemistry, advanced math, Advanced Placement courses, algebra, American history, American literature, applied skills, art, band, Bible studies, biology, biology-AP, business skills, calculus, chemistry, choir, chorus, computer programming, computer science, drama, economics, English, English literature, environmental science, general science, geography, geology, geometry, German, home economics, keyboarding, Latin, literature, Mandarin, mathematics, music, physical education, physics, pre-algebra, reading, religion, science, social sciences, social studies, Spanish, speech, trigonometry, world history, writing.

Graduation Requirements Algebra, arts and fine arts (art, music, dance, drama), biology, chemistry, English, English composition, English literature, foreign language, geometry, government, grammar, literature, physical education (includes health), physics, religion (includes Bible studies and theology), science, social studies (includes history), speech, world geography.

Special Academic Programs 11 Advanced Placement exams for which test preparation is offered; honors section; independent study; academic accommodation for the gifted, the musically talented, and the artistically talented; remedial reading and/or remedial writing; remedial math; programs in English for dyslexic students; special instructional classes for students with learning disabilities; ESL (30 students enrolled).

College Admission Counseling 110 students graduated in 2011; 106 went to college, including Bethany Lutheran College; Martin Luther College; Minnesota State University Mankato; University of Minnesota, Twin Cities Campus; University of Wisconsin–Madison. Other: 1 went to work, 3 entered military service.

Student Life Upper grades have specified standards of dress, student council, honor system. Discipline rests equally with students and faculty.

Summer Programs ESL, sports programs offered; session focuses on ESL and activities, and a variety of sports camps; held on campus; accepts boys and girls; open to students from other schools. 80 students usually enrolled. 2012 schedule: July 16 to August 3. Application deadline: June 1.
Tuition and Aid 7-day tuition and room/board: $25,200. Tuition installment plan (SMART Tuition Payment Plan). Merit scholarship grants, need-based scholarship grants available. In 2011–12, 35% of upper-school students received aid; total upper-school merit-scholarship money awarded: $28,000. Total amount of financial aid awarded in 2011–12: $446,000.
Admissions Traditional secondary-level entrance grade is 9. For fall 2011, 163 students applied for upper-level admission, 124 were accepted, 100 enrolled. Secondary Level English Proficiency or writing sample required. Deadline for receipt of application materials: none. Application fee required: $100. Interview recommended.
Athletics Interscholastic: baseball (boys), basketball (b,g), bowling (b,g), cheering (g), cross-country running (b,g), dance team (g), football (b), golf (b,g), hockey (b,g), ice hockey (b,g), softball (g), swimming and diving (b,g), tennis (b,g), track and field (b,g), volleyball (g), wrestling (b); intramural: basketball (b,g); coed intramural: alpine skiing, ball hockey, basketball, bowling, cheering, cross-country running, dance team, flag football, floor hockey, Frisbee, jogging, juggling, kickball, physical fitness, physical training, power lifting, skiing (downhill), snowboarding, softball, swimming and diving, table tennis, tennis, track and field, ultimate Frisbee, volleyball, weight lifting, weight training, whiffle ball. 3 PE instructors, 7 coaches, 2 athletic trainers.
Computers Computers are regularly used in accounting, computer applications, desktop publishing, economics, keyboarding, media production, yearbook classes. Computer network features include on-campus library services, online commercial services, Internet access, wireless campus network, Internet filtering or blocking technology. Computer access in designated common areas is available to students. Students grades are available online. The school has a published electronic and media policy.
Contact Mr. Jeff Lemke, Admissions Director. 651-455-1521. Fax: 651-451-3968. E-mail: international@stcroixschools.org. Web site: www.stcroixschools.org.

ST. DAVID'S SCHOOL

3400 White Oak Road
Raleigh, North Carolina 27609

Head of School: Mr. Kevin J. Lockerbie

General Information Coeducational day college-preparatory, arts, religious studies, and technology school, affiliated with Episcopal Church, Christian faith. Grades K–12. Founded: 1972. Setting: suburban. 15-acre campus. 7 buildings on campus. Approved or accredited by National Association of Episcopal Schools, North Carolina Association of Independent Schools, Southern Association of Colleges and Schools, Southern Association of Independent Schools, and North Carolina Department of Education. Member of Secondary School Admission Test Board. Endowment: $1.6 million. Total enrollment: 611. Upper school average class size: 12. Upper school faculty-student ratio: 1:7. There are 180 required school days per year for Upper School students. Upper School students typically attend 5 days per week. The average school day consists of 7 hours and 15 minutes.
Upper School Student Profile Grade 9: 55 students (25 boys, 30 girls); Grade 10: 50 students (27 boys, 23 girls); Grade 11: 46 students (29 boys, 17 girls); Grade 12: 44 students (30 boys, 14 girls).
Faculty School total: 69. In upper school: 17 men, 14 women; 24 have advanced degrees.
Subjects Offered Algebra, American history, American literature, art, Bible, biology, biology-AP, calculus, calculus-AP, ceramics, chemistry, chemistry-AP, choir, composition, computer programming, computer-aided design, drama, drawing, earth science, English, English literature, English literature-AP, English/composition-AP, European history, European history-AP, French, French language-AP, geography, geometry, Greek, Latin, Latin-AP, mathematics, media production, music theory-AP, philosophy, physical education, physical science, physics, physics-AP, psychology-AP, public speaking, robotics, science, social studies, Spanish, Spanish-AP, statistics-AP, studio art, studio art-AP, theater, U.S. history-AP, Web site design, wind ensemble, world history, world literature.
Graduation Requirements English, foreign language, mathematics, physical education (includes health), religion (includes Bible studies and theology), science, social studies (includes history), 80 hours of community service, Senior Seminar.
Special Academic Programs Advanced Placement exam preparation; honors section; independent study.
College Admission Counseling 60 students graduated in 2010; all went to college, including Appalachian State University; Elon University; North Carolina State University; The University of North Carolina at Chapel Hill; Vanderbilt University; Wake Forest University. Mean SAT critical reading: 600, mean SAT math: 589, mean SAT writing: 599, mean combined SAT: 1788, mean composite ACT: 25.
Student Life Upper grades have specified standards of dress, student council, honor system. Discipline rests equally with students and faculty. Attendance at religious services is required.
Tuition and Aid Day student tuition: $15,900. Tuition installment plan (Insured Tuition Payment Plan, monthly payment plans, 10-month payment plan). Need-based scholarship grants available.
Admissions Traditional secondary-level entrance grade is 9. For fall 2010, 35 students applied for upper-level admission, 31 were accepted, 23 enrolled. ISEE and writing sample required. Deadline for receipt of application materials: February 21. Application fee required: $75. On-campus interview required.
Athletics Interscholastic: baseball (boys, girls), basketball (b,g), cheering (g), cross-country running (b,g), football (b), indoor track & field (b,g), lacrosse (b), soccer (b,g), softball (g), tennis (b,g), track and field (b,g), volleyball (g), winter (indoor) track (b,g), wrestling (b); intramural: basketball (b,g), soccer (b,g); coed interscholastic: golf, swimming and diving. 5 PE instructors, 5 coaches, 1 athletic trainer.
Computers Computers are regularly used in all academic classes. Computer network features include on-campus library services, Internet access. Computer access in designated common areas is available to students. Students grades are available online. The school has a published electronic and media policy.
Contact Mrs. Teresa Wilson, Director of Admissions. 919-782-3331 Ext. 230. Fax: 919-232-5053. E-mail: twilson@sdsw.org. Web site: www.sdsw.org.

SAINT DOMINIC ACADEMY

Bishop Joseph OSB Boulevard
121 Gracelawn Road
Auburn, Maine 04210

Head of School: Mr. Donald Fournier

General Information Coeducational day and distance learning college-preparatory, arts, business, and religious studies school, affiliated with Roman Catholic Church. Grades 9–12. Distance learning grades 11–12. Founded: 1941. Setting: suburban. 70-acre campus. 1 building on campus. Approved or accredited by Maine Department of Education. Total enrollment: 598. Upper school average class size: 17. Upper school faculty-student ratio: 1:12. There are 175 required school days per year for Upper School students. Upper School students typically attend 5 days per week. The average school day consists of 6 hours and 15 minutes.
Upper School Student Profile Grade 9: 50 students (30 boys, 20 girls); Grade 10: 58 students (28 boys, 30 girls); Grade 11: 78 students (41 boys, 37 girls); Grade 12: 56 students (29 boys, 27 girls). 70% of students are Roman Catholic.
Faculty School total: 25. In upper school: 10 men, 15 women.
Special Academic Programs International Baccalaureate program; Advanced Placement exam preparation; honors section; independent study.
College Admission Counseling 53 students graduated in 2011; 50 went to college. Other: 2 went to work, 1 entered military service. Median SAT critical reading: 542, median SAT math: 534, median SAT writing: 524, median combined SAT: 1600.
Student Life Upper grades have specified standards of dress, student council, honor system. Discipline rests primarily with faculty. Attendance at religious services is required.
Tuition and Aid Day student tuition: $9075. Tuition installment plan (FACTS Tuition Payment Plan). Merit scholarship grants, need-based scholarship grants available. In 2011–12, 33% of upper-school students received aid.
Admissions Traditional secondary-level entrance grade is 9. Scholastic Testing Service High School Placement Test required. Deadline for receipt of application materials: none. Application fee required: $50. On-campus interview required.
Athletics Interscholastic: baseball (boys), basketball (b,g), field hockey (g), hockey (b,g), indoor hockey (b,g); coed interscholastic: aquatics, cheering, cross-country running, dance team, golf. 1 PE instructor, 30 coaches.
Computers Computer network features include on-campus library services, online commercial services, Internet access, Internet filtering or blocking technology. Campus intranet, student e-mail accounts, and computer access in designated common areas are available to students. Students grades are available online. The school has a published electronic and media policy.
Contact Mr. James Boulet, Director of Admissions. 207-782-6911 Ext. 2110. Fax: 207-795-6439. E-mail: james.boulet@portlanddiocese.org. Web site: www.st-dominic.net.

SAINT EDWARD'S SCHOOL

1895 Saint Edward's Drive
Vero Beach, Florida 32963

Head of School: Mr. Michael J. Mersky

General Information Coeducational day college-preparatory, technology, and Advanced Placement school, affiliated with Episcopal Church. Grades PK–12. Founded: 1965. Setting: suburban. Nearest major city is West Palm Beach. 33-acre campus. 12 buildings on campus. Approved or accredited by Florida Council of Independent Schools, National Association of Episcopal Schools, Southern Association of Colleges and Schools, and The College Board. Member of National Association of Independent Schools and Secondary School Admission Test Board. Endowment: $4 million. Total enrollment: 500. Upper school average class size: 12. Upper school faculty-student ratio: 1:7. There are 175 required school days per year for Upper School students. Upper School students typically attend 5 days per week. The average school day consists of 5 hours and 45 minutes.

Upper School Student Profile Grade 9: 57 students (32 boys, 25 girls); Grade 10: 51 students (23 boys, 28 girls); Grade 11: 46 students (22 boys, 24 girls); Grade 12: 70 students (32 boys, 38 girls).

Faculty School total: 62. In upper school: 12 men, 16 women; 20 have advanced degrees.

Subjects Offered Advanced Placement courses, algebra, American history, American literature, anatomy and physiology, art, band, biology, biology-AP, calculus, calculus-AP, chemistry, chemistry-AP, Chinese, choir, choral music, chorus, Christian ethics, computer science-AP, concert band, concert choir, contemporary issues, contemporary studies, drama, economics, economics-AP, English, English as a foreign language, English language and composition-AP, English literature and composition-AP, ethics, fine arts, geometry, global studies, government, government-AP, graphic design, health and wellness, honors algebra, honors English, honors geometry, human geography - AP, instrumental music, Internet research, Mandarin, marine biology, mathematics, model United Nations, modern European history-AP, music, music theory-AP, performing arts, physical education, physical fitness, physics, physics-AP, pre-calculus, psychology, religion, science, senior internship, senior project, social sciences, social studies, sociology, Spanish, Spanish language-AP, statistics-AP, theater arts, U.S. government and politics-AP, U.S. history-AP, world history, world history-AP.

Graduation Requirements Arts and fine arts (art, music, dance, drama), English, foreign language, mathematics, physical education (includes health), religion (includes Bible studies and theology), science, social sciences, social studies (includes history), 25 hours of community service each year of high school.

Special Academic Programs Advanced Placement exam preparation; honors section; independent study; study at local college for college credit; study abroad; academic accommodation for the gifted, the musically talented, and the artistically talented; ESL (10 students enrolled).

College Admission Counseling 62 students graduated in 2011; all went to college, including Florida State University; New York University; The University of Alabama at Birmingham; University of Colorado Boulder; University of Florida; University of Miami. Mean SAT critical reading: 599, mean SAT math: 611, mean SAT writing: 596, mean combined SAT: 1807, mean composite ACT: 26. 53% scored over 600 on SAT critical reading, 58% scored over 600 on SAT math, 53% scored over 600 on SAT writing, 58% scored over 1800 on combined SAT, 57% scored over 26 on composite ACT.

Student Life Upper grades have specified standards of dress, student council, honor system. Discipline rests primarily with faculty. Attendance at religious services is required.

Summer Programs Remediation, enrichment, sports, art/fine arts, computer instruction programs offered; session focuses on enrichment, water activities, sports, study skills; held both on and off campus; held at Waterfront Indian River Lagoon; accepts boys and girls; open to students from other schools. 870 students usually enrolled. 2012 schedule: June 4 to August 17. Application deadline: none.

Tuition and Aid Day student tuition: $5800–$23,900. Tuition installment plan (FACTS Tuition Payment Plan, 1-, 2-, and 10-payment plans). Need-based scholarship grants available. In 2011–12, 32% of upper-school students received aid. Total amount of financial aid awarded in 2011–12: $889,050.

Admissions Traditional secondary-level entrance grade is 9. For fall 2011, 52 students applied for upper-level admission, 37 were accepted, 22 enrolled. ACT, PSAT, SAT or SSAT required. Deadline for receipt of application materials: February 15. Application fee required: $50. Interview recommended.

Athletics Interscholastic: baseball (boys), basketball (b,g), cheering (g), crew (b,g), cross-country running (b,g), football (b), golf (b,g), independent competitive sports (b,g), lacrosse (b,g), soccer (b,g), swimming and diving (b,g), tennis (b,g), volleyball (g), weight lifting (b,g); intramural: baseball (b), basketball (b,g), cheering (g), cross-country running (b,g), flagball (b), football (b), golf (b,g), lacrosse (b,g), physical fitness (b,g), sailing (b,g), soccer (b,g), tennis (b,g), volleyball (g); coed interscholastic: aquatics, swimming and diving; coed intramural: aquatics, outdoor education, physical fitness, soccer, softball. 4 PE instructors, 14 coaches, 1 athletic trainer.

Computers Computers are regularly used in all academic classes. Computer network features include on-campus library services, online commercial services, Internet access, wireless campus network, Internet filtering or blocking technology, issuance of tablet technology to all students in grades 6-12, electronic submission of homework, class assignments and homework available online. Campus intranet and student e-mail accounts are available to students. Students grades are available online. The school has a published electronic and media policy.

Contact Ms. Peggy Anderson, Director of Admission. 772-492-2364. Fax: 772-231-2427. E-mail: panderson@steds.org. Web site: www.steds.org.

SAINT ELIZABETH HIGH SCHOOL

1530 34th Avenue

Oakland, California 94601

Head of School: Sr. Mary Liam Brock, OP

General Information Coeducational day college-preparatory, arts, and religious studies school, affiliated with Roman Catholic Church. Grades 9–12. Founded: 1921. Setting: urban. Nearest major city is Berkeley. 2-acre campus. 1 building on campus. Approved or accredited by National Catholic Education Association, Western Association of Schools and Colleges, and California Department of Education. Endowment: $250,000. Total enrollment: 165. Upper school average class size: 16. Upper school faculty-student ratio: 1:15. There are 180 required school days per year for Upper School students. Upper School students typically attend 5 days per week. The average school day consists of 6 hours and 48 minutes.

Upper School Student Profile Grade 9: 48 students (29 boys, 19 girls); Grade 10: 42 students (23 boys, 19 girls); Grade 11: 33 students (19 boys, 14 girls); Grade 12: 42 students (19 boys, 23 girls). 79% of students are Roman Catholic.

Faculty School total: 17. In upper school: 9 men, 8 women; 14 have advanced degrees.

Subjects Offered Advanced math, algebra, American literature, American literature-AP, anatomy and physiology, art and culture, biology, business mathematics, calculus-AP, Catholic belief and practice, chemistry, Christian and Hebrew scripture, Christian testament, civics, composition, computer applications, computer graphics, computer literacy, creative writing, drawing and design, economics, economics and history, English, English literature and composition-AP, geometry, journalism, learning strategies, moral and social development, physical education, physical science, physics, pre-algebra, precalculus, psychology, social justice, Spanish, Spanish language-AP, Spanish literature-AP, speech, speech communications, trigonometry, U.S. history, world cultures, world geography, world history, world religions.

Graduation Requirements Arts and fine arts (art, music, dance, drama), electives, English, foreign language, mathematics, physical education (includes health), religious studies, science, social sciences, 100 hours of community service.

Special Academic Programs 3 Advanced Placement exams for which test preparation is offered; honors section; remedial reading and/or remedial writing; remedial math; programs in English, mathematics for dyslexic students; special instructional classes for students with learning disabilities, Attention Deficit Disorder, dyslexia, and emotional and behavioral problems.

College Admission Counseling 36 students graduated in 2011; all went to college, including California State University, East Bay; San Francisco State University; San Jose State University; University of California, Berkeley.

Student Life Upper grades have specified standards of dress, honor system. Discipline rests primarily with faculty. Attendance at religious services is required.

Summer Programs Remediation programs offered; session focuses on academics; held on campus; accepts boys and girls; not open to students from other schools. 25 students usually enrolled. 2012 schedule: June 16 to July 15. Application deadline: June 1.

Tuition and Aid Day student tuition: $10,700. Tuition reduction for siblings, merit scholarship grants, need-based scholarship grants available. In 2011–12, 90% of upper-school students received aid; total upper-school merit-scholarship money awarded: $56,000. Total amount of financial aid awarded in 2011–12: $980,000.

Admissions Traditional secondary-level entrance grade is 9. For fall 2011, 83 students applied for upper-level admission, 68 were accepted, 46 enrolled. High School Placement Test required. Deadline for receipt of application materials: none. Application fee required: $75. Interview required.

Athletics Interscholastic: baseball (boys), basketball (b,g), football (b), soccer (b,g), softball (g), track and field (b,g), volleyball (b,g). 1 PE instructor, 5 coaches.

Computers Computer network features include on-campus library services, Internet access, wireless campus network, Internet filtering or blocking technology. Students grades are available online. The school has a published electronic and media policy.

Contact Lisseth Aguilar, Secretary. 510-532-8947. Fax: 510-532-9754. E-mail: laguilar@stliz-hs.org. Web site: www.stliz-hs.org.

ST. FRANCIS DE SALES HIGH SCHOOL

2323 West Bancroft Street

Toledo, Ohio 43607

Head of School: Mr. Eric J. Smola

General Information Boys' day college-preparatory, religious studies, AP courses, and community service school, affiliated with Roman Catholic Church. Grades 9–12. Founded: 1955. Setting: urban. Nearest major city is Cleveland. 25-acre campus, 1 building on campus. Approved or accredited by Ohio Catholic Schools Accreditation Association (OCSAA) and Ohio Department of Education. Endowment: $7.2 million. Total enrollment: 629. Upper school average class size: 24. Upper school faculty-student ratio: 1:14. There are 180 required school days per year for Upper School students. Upper School students typically attend 5 days per week. The average school day consists of 6 hours and 30 minutes.

Upper School Student Profile Grade 9: 183 students (183 boys); Grade 10: 169 students (169 boys); Grade 11: 127 students (127 boys); Grade 12: 150 students (150 boys). 72% of students are Roman Catholic.

Faculty School total: 61. In upper school: 47 men, 14 women; 37 have advanced degrees.

Subjects Offered Advanced Placement courses, advanced studio art-AP, algebra, American history, American history-AP, American literature, American literature-AP, anatomy, animation, art, biology, biology-AP, British literature, calculus, calculus-AP, ceramics, chemistry, chemistry-AP, Chinese, chorus, church history, community service, computer programming, computer science, creative writing, criminal justice, drawing, economics, English literature, English-AP, environmental science, expository writing, French, French-AP, geometry, government/civics, grammar, graphic design, health, Latin, Latin-AP, macroeconomics-AP, math analysis, mathematics, microeconomics-AP, military history, music, New Testament, physical education, physical science, physics, physics-AP, pre-algebra, pre-calculus, psychology, psychology-AP, public speaking, science, social justice, social studies, Spanish, Spanish-AP, statistics, theology, trigonometry, U.S. government, U.S. government and politics-AP, U.S. history-AP, Web site design, world geography, world history, yearbook.

Graduation Requirements Art, computer science, English, foreign language, mathematics, physical education (includes health), religion (includes Bible studies and theology), science, social studies (includes history), participation in religious retreats four of 4 years. Community service is required.

Special Academic Programs Advanced Placement exam preparation; honors section; study at local college for college credit.

College Admission Counseling 136 students graduated in 2011; all went to college, including Bowling Green State University; Miami University; The Ohio State University; The University of Toledo; University of Michigan; Xavier University. Mean SAT critical reading: 531, mean SAT math: 547, mean SAT writing: 503, mean composite ACT: 23.

Student Life Upper grades have specified standards of dress, student council. Discipline rests primarily with faculty. Attendance at religious services is required.

Summer Programs Enrichment programs offered; session focuses on mathematics, English, reading; held on campus; accepts boys; not open to students from other schools. 100 students usually enrolled. 2012 schedule: June 14 to July 3. Application deadline: June 1.

Tuition and Aid Day student tuition: $9240. Tuition installment plan (monthly payment plans, quarterly payment plan). Tuition reduction for siblings, merit scholarship grants, need-based scholarship grants, paying campus jobs available. In 2011–12, 66% of upper-school students received aid; total upper-school merit-scholarship money awarded: $437,959. Total amount of financial aid awarded in 2011–12: $1,672,600.

Admissions Traditional secondary-level entrance grade is 9. For fall 2011, 241 students applied for upper-level admission, 207 were accepted, 196 enrolled. STS required. Deadline for receipt of application materials: none. No application fee required. On-campus interview required.

Athletics Interscholastic: baseball, basketball, bowling, crew, cross-country running, diving, football, golf, ice hockey, lacrosse, soccer, swimming and diving, tennis, track and field, water polo, winter (indoor) track, wrestling; intramural: basketball, football. 2 PE instructors, 36 coaches, 1 athletic trainer.

Computers Computers are regularly used in animation, art, desktop publishing, English, mathematics, science, Web site design classes. Computer network features include Internet access, Internet filtering or blocking technology. Student e-mail accounts and computer access in designated common areas are available to students. Students grades are available online. The school has a published electronic and media policy.

Contact Mrs. Jacqueline VanDemark, Administrative Assistant. 419-531-1618. Fax: 419-531-9740. E-mail: jvandemark@sfstoledo.org. Web site: www.sfstoledo.org.

SAINT FRANCIS GIRLS HIGH SCHOOL

5900 Elvas Avenue

Sacramento, California 95819

Head of School: Mrs. Marion L. Bishop

General Information Girls' day college-preparatory, arts, and religious studies school, affiliated with Roman Catholic Church. Grades 9–12. Founded: 1940. Setting: urban. 11 buildings on campus. Approved or accredited by Western Association of Schools and Colleges, Western Catholic Education Association, and California Department of Education. Total enrollment: 1,139. Upper school average class size: 24. Upper school faculty-student ratio: 1:15. Upper School students typically attend 5 days per week.

Upper School Student Profile Grade 9: 299 students (299 girls); Grade 10: 277 students (277 girls); Grade 11: 279 students (279 girls); Grade 12: 284 students (284 girls). 73% of students are Roman Catholic.

Faculty School total: 77. In upper school: 20 men, 57 women; 59 have advanced degrees.

Subjects Offered Acting, advanced biology, advanced chemistry, advanced computer applications, advanced math, Advanced Placement courses, advanced studio art-AP, algebra, American government, American history, American history-AP, American literature, anatomy and physiology, art, art history-AP, biology, biology-AP, biotechnology, calculus, calculus-AP, chemistry, chemistry-AP, choir, Christian ethics, church history, civics, computer education, computer multimedia, computer science-AP, dance, drawing, economics, English literature and composition-AP, equality and freedom, ethics, film and literature, fitness, French, French literature-AP, French-AP, geography, geometry, health, Hebrew scripture, integrated science, Italian, jazz, Latin, model United Nations, orchestra, painting, philosophy, physics, prayer/spirituality, pre-calculus, robotics, sculpture, self-defense, Spanish, Spanish language-AP, Spanish literature-AP, speech, statistics, studio art-AP, U.S. government and politics-AP, U.S. history, U.S. history-AP, world history, world religions, yearbook, yoga.

Special Academic Programs 13 Advanced Placement exams for which test preparation is offered; honors section.

College Admission Counseling 262 students graduated in 2010; 260 went to college, including California Polytechnic State University, San Luis Obispo; California State University, Chico; California State University, Sacramento; Saint Mary's College of California; San Francisco State University; University of Oregon. Other: 2 had other specific plans. Mean SAT critical reading: 566, mean SAT math: 543, mean SAT writing: 588, mean composite ACT: 24.

Student Life Upper grades have uniform requirement, student council, honor system. Discipline rests primarily with faculty. Attendance at religious services is required.

Tuition and Aid Day student tuition: $11,100. Tuition installment plan (monthly payment plans). Need-based scholarship grants available. In 2010–11, 15% of upper-school students received aid. Total amount of financial aid awarded in 2010–11: $1,000,000.

Admissions Traditional secondary-level entrance grade is 9. CTBS (or similar from their school) required. Deadline for receipt of application materials: January 28. No application fee required. Interview required.

Athletics Interscholastic: basketball, cheering, cross-country running, golf, lacrosse, soccer, softball, swimming and diving, tennis, track and field, volleyball, water polo. 4 PE instructors, 45 coaches, 2 athletic trainers.

Computers Computer resources include on-campus library services, Internet access, wireless campus network, Internet filtering or blocking technology. Student e-mail accounts and computer access in designated common areas are available to students. Students grades are available online. The school has a published electronic and media policy.

Contact Mrs. Moira O'Brien, Director of Admissions. 916-727-5095. E-mail: mobrien@stfrancishs.org. Web site: www.stfrancishs.org.

SAINT FRANCIS HIGH SCHOOL

200 Foothill Boulevard

La Canada Flintridge, California 91011

Head of School: Mr. Thomas G. Moran

General Information Boys' day college-preparatory and religious studies school, affiliated with Roman Catholic Church. Grades 9–12. Founded: 1946. Setting: suburban. Nearest major city is Los Angeles. 19-acre campus. 5 buildings on campus. Approved or accredited by Western Association of Schools and Colleges and Western Catholic Education Association. Total enrollment: 658. Upper school average class size: 28. Upper school faculty-student ratio: 1:15. There are 182 required school days per year for Upper School students. Upper School students typically attend 5 days per week. The average school day consists of 6 hours.

Upper School Student Profile Grade 9: 173 students (173 boys); Grade 10: 175 students (175 boys); Grade 11: 144 students (144 boys); Grade 12: 166 students (166 boys). 70% of students are Roman Catholic.

Faculty School total: 48. In upper school: 38 men, 10 women; 20 have advanced degrees.

Subjects Offered Advanced Placement courses, English, fine arts, foreign language, health, history, mathematics, physical education, religion, science, social sciences, technology.

Graduation Requirements Arts and fine arts (art, music, dance, drama), English, foreign language, mathematics, physical education (includes health), religion (includes Bible studies and theology), science, social sciences, technology, Christian service hours, retreat each year of attendance. Community service is required.

Special Academic Programs Advanced Placement exam preparation; honors section.

College Admission Counseling 166 students graduated in 2011; 163 went to college, including California State University, Northridge; Loyola Marymount University; Santa Clara University; University of California, Irvine. Other: 3 entered a postgraduate year. Mean SAT critical reading: 561, mean SAT math: 557, mean SAT writing: 538, mean composite ACT: 23.

Student Life Upper grades have specified standards of dress, student council. Discipline rests primarily with faculty. Attendance at religious services is required.

Summer Programs Remediation, enrichment, sports programs offered; session focuses on remediation and enrichment; held on campus; accepts boys and girls; open to students from other schools. 450 students usually enrolled. 2012 schedule: June 25 to July 27. Application deadline: June 18.

Tuition and Aid Day student tuition: $11,800. Tuition installment plan (FACTS Tuition Payment Plan, monthly payment plans). Merit scholarship grants, need-based scholarship grants available. In 2011–12, 20% of upper-school students received aid; total upper-school merit-scholarship money awarded: $35,000. Total amount of financial aid awarded in 2011–12: $450,000.

Admissions Traditional secondary-level entrance grade is 9. For fall 2011, 402 students applied for upper-level admission, 220 were accepted, 173 enrolled. High School Placement Test required. Deadline for receipt of application materials: January 25. Application fee required: $75. On-campus interview required.

Athletics Interscholastic: baseball, basketball, cross-country running, football, golf, soccer, tennis, track and field, volleyball. 3 PE instructors, 14 coaches, 1 athletic trainer.

Computers Computers are regularly used in all academic, yearbook classes. Computer network features include on-campus library services, Internet access, wireless campus network, Internet filtering or blocking technology. Students grades are available online. The school has a published electronic and media policy.

Contact Mrs. Stephanie Martinez, Registrar. 818-790-0325 Ext. 502. Fax: 818-790-5542. E-mail: martinezs@sfhs.net. Web site: www.sfhs.net.

SAINT FRANCIS SCHOOL

2707 Pamoa Road

Honolulu, Hawaii 96822

Head of School: Sr. Joan of Arc Souza

General Information Coeducational day college-preparatory, arts, religious studies, bilingual studies, technology, and ESL school, affiliated with Roman Catholic Church. Boys grades K–11, girls grades K–12. Founded: 1924. Setting: suburban. 11-acre campus. 9 buildings on campus. Approved or accredited by Western Association of Schools and Colleges, Western Catholic Education Association, and Hawaii Department of Education. Member of National Association of Independent Schools. Total enrollment: 445. Upper school average class size: 20. Upper school faculty-student ratio: 1:20. There are 180 required school days per year for Upper School students. Upper School students typically attend 5 days per week. The average school day consists of 6 hours and 30 minutes.

Upper School Student Profile Grade 9: 75 students (47 boys, 28 girls); Grade 10: 71 students (43 boys, 28 girls); Grade 11: 79 students (59 boys, 20 girls); Grade 12: 41 students (41 girls). 60% of students are Roman Catholic.

Faculty School total: 46. In upper school: 13 men, 33 women; 21 have advanced degrees.

Subjects Offered Algebra, American history, American literature, American sign language, ancient history, art, band, Bible studies, biology, biology-AP, calculus-AP, Catholic belief and practice, ceramics, chemistry, choir, chorus, cinematography, college admission preparation, college counseling, college planning, computer literacy, computer technologies, creative writing, earth science, English, English language and composition-AP, English literature, English literature and composition-AP, environmental science, ESL, fine arts, geography, geometry, government-AP, government/civics, grammar, health, history, humanities, Japanese, journalism, keyboarding, mathematics, medieval/Renaissance history, music, newspaper, NJROTC, oral communications, physical education, physical science, physics, pre-algebra, pre-calculus, psychology, religion, SAT preparation, science, social studies, Spanish, Spanish language-AP, speech, theater, TOEFL preparation, trigonometry, U.S. history-AP, world history, world literature, world religions, writing, yearbook.

Graduation Requirements Algebra, American history, American literature, arts and fine arts (art, music, dance, drama), biology, chemistry, computer applications, computer skills, English, foreign language, humanities, keyboarding, mathematics, physical education (includes health), religion (includes Bible studies and theology), science, social studies (includes history), U.S. history, 100 hours of community service. Community service is required.

Special Academic Programs 7 Advanced Placement exams for which test preparation is offered; honors section; independent study; study at local college for college credit; ESL (15 students enrolled).

College Admission Counseling 56 students graduated in 2011; 53 went to college, including Chaminade University of Honolulu; Hawai`i Pacific University; Seattle University; Southern Oregon University; University of Hawaii at Manoa; University of Oregon. Other: 3 went to work.

Student Life Upper grades have uniform requirement, student council, honor system. Discipline rests primarily with faculty. Attendance at religious services is required.

Summer Programs Remediation, enrichment, advancement, ESL, computer instruction programs offered; session focuses on enrichment and advancement; held on campus; accepts boys and girls; open to students from other schools. 150 students usually enrolled. 2012 schedule: June 7 to July 7. Application deadline: May 20.

Tuition and Aid Day student tuition: $8600. Tuition installment plan (FACTS Tuition Payment Plan, monthly payment plans, individually arranged payment plans, semiannual payment plan). Tuition reduction for siblings, merit scholarship grants, need-based scholarship grants, alumni scholarships, Support A Student Scholarships, Alverna Scholarships available. In 2011–12, 38% of upper-school students received aid; total upper-school merit-scholarship money awarded: $173,000. Total amount of financial aid awarded in 2011–12: $317,000.

Admissions Traditional secondary-level entrance grade is 9. For fall 2011, 291 students applied for upper-level admission, 227 were accepted, 137 enrolled. School placement exam or SSAT required. Deadline for receipt of application materials: none. Application fee required: $40. Interview required.

Athletics Interscholastic: baseball (boys), basketball (b,g), bowling (g), canoeing/kayaking (b,g), cheering (b,g), football (b), ocean paddling (g), paddling (g), riflery (b,g), running (g), soccer (g), softball (g), swimming and diving (b,g), tennis (b,g), track and field (b,g), volleyball (g), water polo (g), wrestling (b,g); coed interscholastic: cross-country running, golf, JROTC drill, weight training. 2 PE instructors, 36 coaches, 1 athletic trainer.

Computers Computers are regularly used in art, English, foreign language, mathematics, music, newspaper, religion, science, social studies, yearbook classes. Computer network features include on-campus library services, Internet access, wireless campus network, Internet filtering or blocking technology. Computer access in designated common areas is available to students. Students grades are available online. The school has a published electronic and media policy.

Contact Karen Curry, Director of Admissions. 808-988-4111 Ext. 712. Fax: 808-988-5497. E-mail: kcurry@stfrancis-oahu.org. Web site: www.stfrancis-oahu.org.

ST. GEORGE'S INDEPENDENT SCHOOL

1880 Wolf River Road

Collierville, Tennessee 38017

Head of School: Mr. William W. Taylor

General Information Coeducational day college-preparatory school, affiliated with Christian faith. Grades PK–12. Founded: 1959. Setting: suburban. Nearest major city is Memphis. 250-acre campus. 5 buildings on campus. Approved or accredited by Southern Association of Colleges and Schools, Southern Association of Independent Schools, and Tennessee Association of Independent Schools. Member of National Association of Independent Schools. Endowment: $3.2 million. Total enrollment: 1,207. Upper school average class size: 19. Upper school faculty-student ratio: 1:7. There are 175 required school days per year for Upper School students. Upper School students typically attend 5 days per week. The average school day consists of 7 hours and 18 minutes.

Upper School Student Profile Grade 9: 89 students (48 boys, 41 girls); Grade 10: 86 students (43 boys, 43 girls); Grade 11: 91 students (47 boys, 44 girls); Grade 12: 102 students (45 boys, 57 girls).

Faculty School total: 126. In upper school: 22 men, 22 women; 31 have advanced degrees.

Subjects Offered Algebra, American literature, astronomy, band, biology, biology-AP, calculus, calculus-AP, chemistry, chemistry-AP, chorus, computer programming, drawing, English, English language and composition-AP, English literature and composition-AP, environmental science, ethics, European history-AP, European literature, film, French, French language-AP, geometry, global studies, government/civics, honors algebra, honors geometry, human anatomy, independent study, journalism, Latin, Latin-AP, painting, philosophy, photography, physics, physics-AP, pottery, pre-calculus, printmaking, psychology, religion, short story, social justice, Southern literature, Spanish, Spanish language-AP, statistics-AP, theater, trigonometry, U.S. history, U.S. history-AP, visual arts, wellness, world history, world history-AP.

Graduation Requirements Art, electives, English, history, independent study, language, mathematics, religion (includes Bible studies and theology), science, wellness, senior independent study, senior Global Challenge.

Special Academic Programs Advanced Placement exam preparation; honors section; independent study.

College Admission Counseling 89 students graduated in 2011; all went to college, including Mississippi State University; Southern Methodist University; The University of Alabama; The University of Tennessee; University of Arkansas; University of Mississippi. Mean SAT critical reading: 621, mean SAT math: 615, mean SAT writing: 616, mean combined SAT: 1852, mean composite ACT: 27.

Student Life Upper grades have specified standards of dress, student council, honor system. Discipline rests equally with students and faculty. Attendance at religious services is required.

Summer Programs Remediation, enrichment, advancement, sports, art/fine arts, computer instruction programs offered; session focuses on enrichment; held on campus; accepts boys and girls; open to students from other schools. 2012 schedule: June to August. Application deadline: June.

Tuition and Aid Day student tuition: $15,800. Tuition installment plan (individually arranged payment plans, One payment per year, two payments per year, and four payments per year.). Need-based scholarship grants available. In 2011–12, 14% of upper-school students received aid. Total amount of financial aid awarded in 2011–12: $305,421.

Admissions Traditional secondary-level entrance grade is 9. For fall 2011, 30 students applied for upper-level admission, 22 were accepted, 16 enrolled. Admissions testing or ISEE required. Deadline for receipt of application materials: none. Application fee required: $50. Interview required.

Athletics Interscholastic: baseball (boys), basketball (b,g), cheering (g), cross-country running (b,g), football (b), golf (b,g), lacrosse (b,g), pom squad (g), soccer (b,g), softball (g), tennis (b,g), track and field (b,g), volleyball (g), wrestling (b); coed interscholastic: swimming and diving. 5 PE instructors, 9 coaches, 2 athletic trainers.

Computers Computers are regularly used in all classes. Computer network features include on-campus library services, Internet access, wireless campus network, Internet filtering or blocking technology. Campus intranet, student e-mail accounts, and computer access in designated common areas are available to students. Students grades are available online. The school has a published electronic and media policy.

Contact Mrs. Jennifer Taylor, Director of Admission. 901-457-2000. Fax: 901-457-2111. E-mail: jtaylor@sgis.org. Web site: www.sgis.org.

ST. GEORGE'S SCHOOL

372 Purgatory Road

Middletown, Rhode Island 02842-5984

Head of School: Eric F. Peterson

General Information Coeducational boarding and day college-preparatory, arts, religious studies, technology, and marine sciences school, affiliated with Episcopal Church. Grades 9–12. Founded: 1896. Setting: suburban. Nearest major city is Providence. Students are housed in single-sex dormitories. 150-acre campus. 47 buildings on campus. Approved or accredited by Association of Independent Schools in New England, National Association of Episcopal Schools, New England Association of Schools and Colleges, The Association of Boarding Schools, and Rhode Island Department of Education. Member of National Association of Independent Schools and Secondary School Admission Test Board. Endowment: $92.8 million. Total enrollment: 367. Upper school average class size: 11. Upper school faculty-student ratio: 1:6. Upper School students typically attend 6 days per week. The average school day consists of 6 hours and 50 minutes.

Upper School Student Profile Grade 9: 75 students (36 boys, 39 girls); Grade 10: 99 students (54 boys, 45 girls); Grade 11: 97 students (41 boys, 56 girls); Grade 12: 93 students (41 boys, 52 girls). 80% of students are boarding students. 34% are state residents. 27 states are represented in upper school student body. 15% are international students. International students from Bermuda, China, Republic of Korea, and Thailand; 13 other countries represented in student body.

Faculty School total: 68. In upper school: 39 men, 29 women; 53 have advanced degrees; 56 reside on campus.

Subjects Offered 3-dimensional art, 3-dimensional design, acting, advanced biology, advanced chemistry, advanced computer applications, advanced math, Advanced Placement courses, advanced studio art-AP, African American history, African American studies, algebra, American history, American history-AP, American literature, American literature-AP, American studies, analytic geometry, architectural drawing, architecture, art, art history, art-AP, Asian studies, Bible, Bible as literature, Bible studies, biology, biology-AP, calculus, calculus-AP, ceramics, chemistry, chemistry-AP, Chinese, computer graphics, computer math, computer programming, computer science, computer science-AP, creative writing, dance, DNA, drama, dramatic arts, drawing, ecology, economics, economics-AP, English, English language and composition-AP, English literature, English literature-AP, environmental science, environmental science-AP, ethics, European history, European history-AP, expository writing, fine arts, French, French language-AP, geometry, global studies, government/civics, grammar, health, history, journalism, Latin, Latin-AP, law, logic, macro/microeconomics-AP, Mandarin, marine biology, mathematics, microbiology, music, music theory-AP, navigation, oceanography, philosophy, photography, physics, physics-AP, psychology, public speaking, religion, robotics, science, sculpture, social studies, Spanish, Spanish language-AP, Spanish literature-AP, statistics, studio art-AP, theater, theology, trigonometry, U.S. government and politics-AP, veterinary science, world history, world history-AP, world literature, writing.

Graduation Requirements Arts and fine arts (art, music, dance, drama), computer science, English, foreign language, mathematics, physical education (includes health), religion (includes Bible studies and theology), science, social studies (includes history).

Special Academic Programs Advanced Placement exam preparation; honors section; independent study; term-away projects; study abroad; academic accommodation for the gifted, the musically talented, and the artistically talented.

College Admission Counseling 89 students graduated in 2010; all went to college, including Cornell University; Hamilton College; Lehigh University; The Colorado College; The George Washington University; Trinity College. Mean SAT critical reading: 626, mean SAT math: 651, mean SAT writing: 628, mean combined SAT: 1905.

Student Life Upper grades have specified standards of dress, student council, honor system. Discipline rests primarily with faculty. Attendance at religious services is required.

Tuition and Aid Day student tuition: $31,000; 7-day tuition and room/board: $45,000. Tuition installment plan (Insured Tuition Payment Plan, Academic Management Services Plan, Key Tuition Payment Plan, monthly payment plans, individually arranged payment plans). Need-based scholarship grants, need-based loans, middle-income loans available. In 2010–11, 30% of upper-school students received aid.

Admissions Traditional secondary-level entrance grade is 9. For fall 2010, 676 students applied for upper-level admission, 235 were accepted, 111 enrolled. ISEE, PSAT, SSAT or TOEFL required. Deadline for receipt of application materials: February 1. Application fee required: $50. Interview required.

Athletics Interscholastic: baseball (boys), basketball (b,g), cross-country running (b,g), field hockey (g), football (b), hockey (b,g), ice hockey (b,g), lacrosse (b,g), sailing (b,g), soccer (b,g), softball (g), squash (b,g), swimming and diving (b,g), tennis (b,g), track and field (b,g); coed interscholastic: dance, sailing; coed intramural: aerobics/dance, dance, modern dance, mountain biking, Nautilus, soccer, softball, squash, strength & conditioning. 2 coaches, 3 athletic trainers.

Computers Computers are regularly used in art, English, foreign language, history, mathematics, music, religion, science, theater classes. Computer network features include on-campus library services, online commercial services, Internet access, wireless campus network, Internet filtering or blocking technology, scanners, digital cameras, and access to printers. Campus intranet, student e-mail accounts, and computer access in designated common areas are available to students. Students grades are available online. The school has a published electronic and media policy.

Contact James A. Hamilton, Director of Admission. 401-842-6600. Fax: 401-842-6696. E-mail: admission@stgeorges.edu. Web site: www.stgeorges.edu.

ST. GEORGE'S SCHOOL

4175 West 29th Avenue

Vancouver, British Columbia V6S 1V1, Canada

Head of School: Dr. Tom Matthews

General Information Boys' boarding and day college-preparatory, arts, bilingual studies, and technology school. Boarding grades 7–12, day grades 1–12. Founded: 1930. Setting: suburban. Students are housed in single-sex dormitories. 27-acre campus. 2 buildings on campus. Approved or accredited by Canadian Association of Independent Schools, The Association of Boarding Schools, and British Columbia Department of Education. Affiliate member of National Association of Independent Schools; member of Secondary School Admission Test Board. Language of instruction: English. Total enrollment: 1,157. Upper school average class size: 19. Upper school faculty-student ratio: 1:10.

Upper School Student Profile Grade 8: 144 students (144 boys); Grade 9: 149 students (149 boys); Grade 10: 157 students (157 boys); Grade 11: 156 students (156 boys); Grade 12: 155 students (155 boys). 18% of students are boarding students. 91% are province residents. 9 provinces are represented in upper school student body. 9% are international students. International students from Germany, Hong Kong, Mexico, Republic of Korea, Taiwan, and United States; 4 other countries represented in student body.

Faculty School total: 130. In upper school: 63 men, 23 women; 35 have advanced degrees; 9 reside on campus.

Subjects Offered Advanced chemistry, advanced computer applications, advanced math, algebra, analysis and differential calculus, applied arts, applied music, applied skills, architecture, art, art history, art history-AP, biology, biology-AP, business, business skills, calculus, calculus-AP, Canadian geography, Canadian history, Canadian literature, career and personal planning, ceramics, chemistry, chemistry-AP, comparative government and politics-AP, computer graphics, computer programming, computer programming-AP, computer science, computer science-AP, creative writing, critical thinking, debate, drama, drama performance, dramatic arts, earth science, economics, economics-AP, English, English literature, English literature-AP, environmental science, European history, expository writing, film, fine arts, French, French-AP, geography, geology, geometry, German, German-AP, government/civics, grammar, history, industrial arts, introduction to theater, Japanese, journalism, Latin, Latin-AP, law, library, Mandarin, mathematics, mathematics-AP, music, music-AP, performing arts, photography, physical education, physical fitness, physics, physics-AP, psychology, psychology-AP, science, social studies, society, politics and law, Spanish, Spanish-AP, speech and debate, studio art, studio art-AP, technical theater, theater, trigonometry, typing, U.S. history-AP, United States government-AP, Western civilization, world history, world literature, writing.

Graduation Requirements Arts and fine arts (art, music, dance, drama), business skills (includes word processing), English, foreign language, mathematics, physical education (includes health), science, social studies (includes history).

Special Academic Programs Advanced Placement exam preparation; honors section; remedial reading and/or remedial writing.

College Admission Counseling 155 students graduated in 2010; 152 went to college, including McGill University; Queen's University at Kingston; The University of British Columbia; The University of Western Ontario; University of Toronto; University of Victoria.

Student Life Upper grades have uniform requirement, student council, honor system. Discipline rests primarily with faculty.

Tuition and Aid Day student tuition: CAN$15,355–CAN$46,000; 7-day tuition and room/board: CAN$37,470–CAN$46,000. Tuition installment plan (monthly payment plans, individually arranged payment plans, term payment plan, one-time payment plan). Tuition reduction for siblings, bursaries, merit scholarship grants, need-based scholarship grants available. In 2010–11, 12% of upper-school students received aid; total upper-school merit-scholarship money awarded: CAN$75,000. Total amount of financial aid awarded in 2010–11: CAN$800,000.

Admissions Traditional secondary-level entrance grade is 8. For fall 2010, 250 students applied for upper-level admission, 90 were accepted, 50 enrolled. School's own exam and SSAT required. Deadline for receipt of application materials: February 10. Application fee required: CAN$200. Interview required.

Athletics Interscholastic: badminton, basketball, cricket, cross-country running, field hockey, golf, ice hockey, rowing, rugby, soccer, swimming and diving, tennis, track and field, triathlon, volleyball, water polo; intramural: badminton, ball hockey, basketball, bicycling, canoeing/kayaking, cross-country running, flag football, floor hockey, ice hockey, martial arts, outdoor education, outdoor recreation, physical fitness, rugby, running, sailing, skiing (downhill), soccer, softball, squash, swimming and diving, table tennis, tennis, track and field, ultimate Frisbee, volleyball, water polo, weight lifting. 4 PE instructors, 8 coaches.

Computers Computers are regularly used in desktop publishing, history, information technology, mathematics, media, publications, science, technology classes. Computer network features include on-campus library services, online commercial services, Internet access. The school has a published electronic and media policy.

Contact Mr. Lindsay Thierry, Director of Admissions and Residential Life. 604-221-3881. Fax: 604-224-5820. E-mail: lthierry@stgeorges.bc.ca. Web site: www.stgeorges.bc.ca.

ST. GEORGE'S SCHOOL OF MONTREAL

3100 The Boulevard

Montreal, Quebec H3Y 1R9, Canada

Head of School: Mr. James A. Officer

General Information Coeducational day college-preparatory, arts, bilingual studies, and technology school. Grades K–11. Founded: 1930. Setting: urban. 2-acre campus. 1 building on campus. Approved or accredited by Canadian Association of Independent Schools, Quebec Association of Independent Schools, and Quebec Department of Education. Affiliate member of National Association of Independent Schools. Languages of instruction: English and French. Total enrollment: 442. Upper school average class size: 17. Upper school faculty-student ratio: 1:17. There are 181 required school days per year for Upper School students. Upper School students typically attend 5 days per week. The average school day consists of 6 hours and 55 minutes.

Upper School Student Profile Grade 7: 40 students (25 boys, 15 girls); Grade 8: 50 students (34 boys, 16 girls); Grade 9: 55 students (29 boys, 26 girls); Grade 10: 40 students (23 boys, 17 girls); Grade 11: 62 students (26 boys, 36 girls).

Faculty School total: 38. In upper school: 14 men, 24 women; 17 have advanced degrees.

Subjects Offered Advanced math, Advanced Placement courses, algebra, art, art history, art-AP, biology, calculus, Canadian history, chemistry, computer art, computer programming, creative writing, dance, debate, drama, earth science, ecology, economics, English, English literature, English AP, environmental science, expository writing, film, fine arts, French, French as a second language, French studies, French AP, general math, general science, geography, government/civics, Internet research, leadership, library research, mathematics, media, moral and social development, moral reasoning, music, music appreciation, musical productions, outdoor education, performing arts, physical education, physics, pre-calculus, psychology, science, science project, set design, social studies, theater, writing.

Graduation Requirements Art, economics, electives, English, ethics, French as a second language, mathematics, physical education (includes health), science, social studies (includes history), community service learning.

Special Academic Programs 4 Advanced Placement exams for which test preparation is offered; honors section; independent study; academic accommodation for the gifted, the musically talented, and the artistically talented; remedial reading and/or remedial writing; remedial math; ESL (7 students enrolled).

College Admission Counseling 58 students graduated in 2011; all went to college.

Student Life Upper grades have specified standards of dress, student council. Discipline rests primarily with faculty.

Tuition and Aid Guaranteed tuition plan. Tuition installment plan (monthly payment plans). Tuition reduction for siblings, need-based scholarship grants available.

Admissions Traditional secondary-level entrance grade is 7. For fall 2011, 24 students applied for upper-level admission, 24 were accepted, 24 enrolled. Academic Profile Tests or battery of testing done through outside agency required. Deadline for receipt of application materials: none. Application fee required. Interview required.

Athletics Interscholastic: badminton (boys, girls), basketball (b,g), cross-country running (b,g), flag football (g), football (b), golf (b,g), rugby (b), running (b,g), soccer (b,g), swimming and diving (b,g), tennis (b,g), track and field (b,g); intramural: badminton (b,g); coed interscholastic: aquatics, independent competitive sports, indoor soccer, jogging; coed intramural: aerobics, alpine skiing, aquatics, ball hockey, baseball, basketball, bicycling, canoeing/kayaking, Circus, climbing, cooperative games, Cosom hockey, cross-country running, curling, dance, fencing, fitness, fitness walking, floor hockey, ice hockey, indoor soccer, jogging, lacrosse, life saving, martial arts, outdoor recreation, physical fitness, scuba diving, self defense, skiing (cross-country), soccer, squash, track and field, volleyball, wall climbing, yoga. 3 PE instructors, 5 coaches.

Computers Computers are regularly used in all classes. Computer network features include wireless campus network, Internet filtering or blocking technology. Campus intranet and student e-mail accounts are available to students. The school has a published electronic and media policy.

Contact Ms. Kathay Carson, Director of High School Admissions. 514-904-0542. Fax: 514-933-3621. E-mail: kathay.carson@stgeorges.qc.ca. Web site: www.stgeorges.qc.ca.

ST. GREGORY COLLEGE PREPARATORY SCHOOL

3231 North Craycroft Road

Tucson, Arizona 85712

Head of School: Mr. Jonathan Martin

General Information Coeducational day college-preparatory and arts school. Grades 6–12. Founded: 1980. Setting: suburban. 40-acre campus. 9 buildings on campus. Approved or accredited by Independent Schools Association of the Southwest, The College Board, and Arizona Department of Education. Member of National Association of Independent Schools and Secondary School Admission Test Board. Total enrollment: 305. Upper school average class size: 16. Upper school faculty-student ratio: 1:9. Upper School students typically attend 5 days per week. The average school day consists of 7 hours and 30 minutes.

Upper School Student Profile Grade 9: 38 students (20 boys, 18 girls); Grade 10: 59 students (32 boys, 27 girls); Grade 11: 51 students (26 boys, 25 girls); Grade 12: 29 students (16 boys, 13 girls).

Faculty School total: 34. In upper school: 11 men, 12 women; 17 have advanced degrees.

Subjects Offered Advanced studio art-AP, algebra, American history, American literature, anatomy and physiology, ancient world history, art, art history, band, biology, biology-AP, calculus, ceramics, chemistry, chemistry-AP, choir, chorus, college counseling, college placement, community service, comparative government and politics-AP, computer programming, creative writing, drama, earth science, ecology, economics, English, English literature, English-AP, ethics, European history, European history-AP, expository writing, fine arts, finite math, French, French language-AP, French-AP, geography, geology, geometry, government and politics-AP, government/civics, government/civics-AP, grammar, history, history of drama, history of music, humanities, independent study, jazz band, journalism, Latin, Latin-AP, literature, marine biology, mathematics, music, music theory, music theory-AP, newspaper, photography, physical education, physical science, physics, pre-calculus, religion, SAT preparation, science, social studies, Spanish, Spanish language-AP, Spanish-AP, speech, stage design, stagecraft, studio art-AP, theater, trigonometry, U.S. government and politics-AP, U.S. history-AP, world history, writing.

Graduation Requirements Arts and fine arts (art, music, dance, drama), English, foreign language, history, humanities, mathematics, science, senior internships. Community service is required.

Special Academic Programs Advanced Placement exam preparation; honors section; accelerated programs; independent study, term-away projects; study at local college for college credit; academic accommodation for the gifted, the musically talented, and the artistically talented.

College Admission Counseling 35 students graduated in 2011; all went to college, including Cornell University; Emory University; The University of Arizona; University of Pennsylvania; University of Southern California. Mean SAT critical reading: 573, mean SAT math: 590, mean composite ACT: 26.

Student Life Upper grades have specified standards of dress, student council, honor system. Discipline rests primarily with faculty.

Tuition and Aid Day student tuition: $15,950. Tuition installment plan (monthly payment plans, 2- and 10-payment plans). Need-based scholarship grants available. In 2011–12, 42% of upper-school students received aid. Total amount of financial aid awarded in 2011–12: $1,230,000.

Admissions Traditional secondary-level entrance grade is 9. ERB CTP IV and writing sample required. Deadline for receipt of application materials: February. Application fee required: $45. Interview recommended.

Athletics Interscholastic: baseball (boys), basketball (b,g), golf (b,g), soccer (b,g), softball (g), swimming and diving (b,g), tennis (b,g), volleyball (b,g); intramural: touch football (b); coed interscholastic: cross-country running, hiking/backpacking, outdoor education, ropes courses, strength & conditioning; coed intramural: basketball, cooperative games, cross-country running, dance, flag football, football, hiking/backpacking, outdoor education, outdoor recreation, outdoor skills, physical training, ropes courses, strength & conditioning, volleyball, weight training, yoga. 3 PE instructors, 12 coaches, 1 athletic trainer.

Computers Computers are regularly used in English, foreign language, history, journalism, mathematics, newspaper, photography, science classes. Computer network features include on-campus library services, online commercial services, Internet access, wireless campus network, Internet filtering or blocking technology. Campus intranet, student e-mail accounts, and computer access in designated common areas are available to students. Students grades are available online. The school has a published electronic and media policy.

Contact Director of Admissions. 520-327-6395 Ext. 209. Fax: 520-327-8276. E-mail: admissions@stgregoryschool.org. Web site: www.stgregoryschool.org.

ST. JOHN'S NORTHWESTERN MILITARY ACADEMY

1101 Genesee Street

Delafield, Wisconsin 53018-1498

Head of School: Mr. Jack H. Albert Jr.

General Information Boys' boarding and day college-preparatory, arts, business, and military school, affiliated with Episcopal Church. Boarding grades 7–PG, day grades 6–PG. Founded: 1884. Setting: small town. Nearest major city is Milwaukee. Students are housed in single-sex dormitories. 110-acre campus. 15 buildings on campus. Approved or accredited by Independent Schools Association of the Central States, Midwest Association of Boarding Schools, National Association of Episcopal Schools, North Central Association of Colleges and Schools, The Association of Boarding Schools, and Wisconsin Department of Education. Member of National Association of Independent Schools and Secondary School Admission Test Board. Endowment: $6.5 million. Total enrollment: 300. Upper school average class size: 12. Upper school faculty-student ratio: 1:12.

Upper School Student Profile Grade 9: 56 students (56 boys); Grade 10: 63 students (63 boys); Grade 11: 51 students (51 boys); Grade 12: 55 students (55 boys); Postgraduate: 14 students (14 boys). 98% of students are boarding students. 22% are state residents. 22 states are represented in upper school student body. 28% are international students. International students from Canada, China, Mexico, Nicaragua, Republic of Korea, and Thailand; 6 other countries represented in student body. 4% of students are members of Episcopal Church.

Faculty School total: 40. In upper school: 34 men, 6 women; 16 have advanced degrees; 12 reside on campus.

Subjects Offered Advanced math, algebra, American government, American literature, art, aviation, band, biology, British literature, calculus, ceramics, chemistry, choir, Christianity, computer programming, computer science, current events, drama, driver education, earth science, economics, English, entrepreneurship, environmental science, ESL, geography, geometry, German, government/civics, grammar, health, history, honors English, honors U.S. history, journalism, JROTC, mathematics, music, physical science, physics, psychology, reading, science, social studies, sociology, Spanish, statistics, strings, trigonometry, U.S. history, world geography, world history, world literature.

Graduation Requirements Advanced math, algebra, American government, American literature, arts and fine arts (art, music, dance, drama), biology, British literature, chemistry, computer science, electives, foreign language, geometry, introduction to literature, JROTC, physical science, U.S. history, world history, world literature. Community service is required.

Special Academic Programs Honors section; independent study; study at local college for college credit; ESL (10 students enrolled).

College Admission Counseling 56 students graduated in 2010; all went to college, including DePaul University; Embry-Riddle Aeronautical University–Daytona; Marquette University; Purdue University; University of Illinois at Urbana–Champaign; University of Wisconsin–Madison.

Student Life Upper grades have uniform requirement, student council, honor system. Discipline rests primarily with faculty. Attendance at religious services is required.

Tuition and Aid 7-day tuition and room/board: $31,000. Tuition installment plan (Key Tuition Payment Plan, FACTS Tuition Payment Plan, TeriPlease Tuition Payment Plans). Tuition reduction for siblings, merit scholarship grants, need-based scholarship grants, tuition remission for children of employees, endowed scholarships, alumni scholarships available. In 2010–11, 29% of upper-school students received aid; total upper-school merit-scholarship money awarded: $113,500. Total amount of financial aid awarded in 2010–11: $950,000.

Admissions Traditional secondary-level entrance grade is 9. For fall 2010, 430 students applied for upper-level admission, 236 were accepted, 125 enrolled. Kuhlmann-Anderson, SSAT or TOEFL required. Deadline for receipt of application materials: none. Application fee required: $100. On-campus interview required.

Athletics Interscholastic: archery, baseball, basketball, cross-country running, equestrian sports, football, golf, hockey, ice hockey, lacrosse, scuba diving; intramural: billiards, fishing, handball. 2 PE instructors.

Computers Computers are regularly used in all academic classes. Computer network features include on-campus library services, Internet access, Internet filtering or blocking technology. Campus intranet and student e-mail accounts are available to students. Students grades are available online. The school has a published electronic and media policy.

Contact Duane E. Rutherford, Director of Enrollment Services. 262-646-7122. Fax: 262-646-7128. E-mail: admissions@sjnma.org. Web site: www.sjnma.org.

ST. JOHN'S PREPARATORY SCHOOL

72 Spring Street

Danvers, Massachusetts 01923

Head of School: Dr. Edward P. Hardiman

General Information Boys' day college-preparatory, arts, religious studies, and technology school, affiliated with Roman Catholic Church. Grades 9–12. Founded: 1907. Setting: suburban. Nearest major city is Boston. 175-acre campus. 9 buildings on campus. Approved or accredited by National Catholic Education Association and New England Association of Schools and Colleges. Member of National Association of Independent Schools. Endowment: $9 million. Total enrollment: 1,200. Upper school average class size: 19. Upper school faculty-student ratio: 1:11. There are 161 required school days per year for Upper School students. Upper School students typically attend 5 days per week. The average school day consists of 6 hours and 9 minutes.

Upper School Student Profile Grade 9: 300 students (300 boys); Grade 10: 300 students (300 boys); Grade 11: 300 students (300 boys); Grade 12: 300 students (300 boys). 70% of students are Roman Catholic.

Faculty School total: 111. In upper school: 67 men, 40 women; 86 have advanced degrees.

Subjects Offered Accounting, acting, algebra, American history, American history-AP, American literature, anatomy and physiology, art, biology, biology-AP, business, calculus, calculus-AP, ceramics, chemistry, chemistry-AP, Chinese, chorus, computer programming, computer science, computer science-AP, desktop publishing, drama, driver education, economics, economics-AP, English, English literature, English-AP, environmental science, environmental studies, ethics, European history, European history-AP, geometry, German, German-AP, government/civics, Latin, Latin-AP, mathematics, music, neuroscience, physical education, physics, physics-AP, religion, robotics, science, sculpture, social studies, society, politics and law, Spanish, Spanish-AP, statistics, statistics-AP, studio art, technology, trigonometry, U.S. government and politics-AP, U.S. history-AP, video, world history, world religions.

Graduation Requirements Arts and fine arts (art, music, dance, drama), English, foreign language, mathematics, physical education (includes health), religion (includes Bible studies and theology), science, social studies (includes history).

Special Academic Programs Advanced Placement exam preparation; honors section; independent study; study abroad; academic accommodation for the gifted, the musically talented, and the artistically talented.

College Admission Counseling 332 students graduated in 2011; 326 went to college, including Boston College; College of the Holy Cross; Fairfield University; Northeastern University; University of Massachusetts Amherst; University of Vermont. Mean SAT critical reading: 591, mean SAT math: 613, mean SAT writing: 597.

Student Life Upper grades have specified standards of dress, student council. Discipline rests primarily with faculty. Attendance at religious services is required.

Summer Programs Enrichment, advancement, sports, art/fine arts, computer instruction programs offered; session focuses on academic enrichment, study skills, arts, and fitness; held on campus; accepts boys and girls; open to students from other schools.

Tuition and Aid Day student tuition: $18,695. Tuition installment plan (monthly payment plans). Merit scholarship grants, need-based scholarship grants available. In 2011–12, 28% of upper-school students received aid. Total amount of financial aid awarded in 2011–12: $2,800,000.

Admissions Traditional secondary-level entrance grade is 9. SSAT or STS, Diocese Test required. Deadline for receipt of application materials: December 15. No application fee required.

Athletics Interscholastic: alpine skiing, baseball, basketball, cross-country running, fencing, football, Frisbee, golf, hockey, ice hockey, indoor track, lacrosse, rugby, sailing, skiing (downhill), soccer, swimming and diving, tennis, track and field, ultimate Frisbee, volleyball, water polo, winter (indoor) track, wrestling; intramural: baseball, basketball, bicycling, bocce, bowling, boxing, climbing, combined training, cooperative games, crew, flag football, floor hockey, Frisbee, golf, ice hockey, martial arts, mountain biking, Nautilus, physical fitness, rowing, sailing, skiing (downhill), snowboarding, strength & conditioning, surfing, table tennis, tennis, touch football, ultimate Frisbee, volleyball, weight lifting, weight training, whiffle ball. 2 PE instructors, 57 coaches, 2 athletic trainers.

Computers Computers are regularly used in all academic, career exploration, college planning, research skills classes. Computer network features include on-campus library services, Internet access, wireless campus network, Internet filtering or blocking technology, student access to 300 computer workstations. Student e-mail accounts are available to students. Students grades are available online. The school has a published electronic and media policy.

Contact Ms. Maureen Ward, Admissions Assistant. 978-624-1301. Fax: 978-624-1315. E-mail: mward@stjohnsprep.org. Web site: www.stjohnsprep.org.

SAINT JOHN'S PREPARATORY SCHOOL

Box 4000

2280 Watertower Road

Collegeville, Minnesota 56321

Head of School: Fr. Timothy Backous, OSB

General Information Coeducational boarding and day college-preparatory, arts, religious studies, bilingual studies, and theatre school, affiliated with Roman Catholic Church. Boarding grades 9–PG, day grades 6–PG. Founded: 1857. Setting: rural. Nearest major city is St. Cloud. Students are housed in single-sex dormitories. 2,700-acre campus. 23 buildings on campus. Approved or accredited by Independent Schools Association of the Central States, Midwest Association of Boarding Schools, The Association of Boarding Schools, and Minnesota Department of Education. Member of National Association of Independent Schools. Endowment: $9 million. Total enrollment: 313. Upper school average class size: 16. Upper school faculty-student ratio: 1:10. There are 172 required school days per year for Upper School students. Upper School students typically attend 5 days per week. The average school day consists of 5 hours and 35 minutes.

Upper School Student Profile Grade 9: 63 students (39 boys, 24 girls); Grade 10: 60 students (28 boys, 32 girls); Grade 11: 56 students (31 boys, 25 girls); Grade 12: 52 students (28 boys, 24 girls). 37% of students are boarding students. 62% are state residents. 6 states are represented in upper school student body. 25% are international students. International students from Austria, Chile, China, Mexico, Republic of Korea, and Taiwan; 13 other countries represented in student body. 50% of students are Roman Catholic.

Faculty School total: 34. In upper school: 18 men, 16 women; 24 have advanced degrees.

Subjects Offered 3-dimensional design, advanced chemistry, Advanced Placement courses, algebra, American history, American literature, art, art history, band, Bible studies, biology, biology-AP, British literature, calculus, ceramics, chemistry, Chinese, choir, civics, conceptual physics, creative writing, current events, drawing, driver education, earth science, economics, English, English literature, English-AP, environmental science-AP, ESL, European history, fine arts, geometry, German, government/civics, health, history, International Baccalaureate courses, mathematics, music, orchestra, photography, physical education, physics, pre-calculus, religion, science, social studies, Spanish, speech, statistics, theology, trigonometry, world history, world literature, writing.

Graduation Requirements Yiddish.

Special Academic Programs International Baccalaureate program; Advanced Placement exam preparation; honors section; independent study; term-away projects; study at local college for college credit; study abroad; academic accommodation for the gifted, the musically talented, and the artistically talented; ESL (23 students enrolled).

College Admission Counseling 62 students graduated in 2011; 60 went to college, including Carleton College; College of Saint Benedict; St. John's University; University of Minnesota, Twin Cities Campus; University of Portland. Other: 2 went to work. Mean SAT critical reading: 713, mean SAT math: 685, mean SAT writing: 672, mean combined SAT: 2070, mean composite ACT: 27.

Student Life Upper grades have specified standards of dress, student council, honor system. Discipline rests primarily with faculty. Attendance at religious services is required.

Summer Programs Enrichment, advancement, art/fine arts programs offered; session focuses on fun camp experiences; held on campus; accepts boys and girls; open to students from other schools. 1,000 students usually enrolled. 2012 schedule: June 14 to August 6. Application deadline: June 1.

Tuition and Aid Day student tuition: $13,999; 5-day tuition and room/board: $28,861; 7-day tuition and room/board: $32,248. Tuition installment plan (monthly payment plans, individually arranged payment plans, semester payment plan). Merit scholarship grants, need-based scholarship grants, paying campus jobs available. In 2011–12, 46% of upper-school students received aid; total upper-school merit-scholarship money awarded: $31,350. Total amount of financial aid awarded in 2011–12: $725,000.

Admissions Traditional secondary-level entrance grade is 9. For fall 2011, 122 students applied for upper-level admission, 72 were accepted, 56 enrolled. SLEP required. Deadline for receipt of application materials: none. Application fee required: $25. Interview required.

Athletics Interscholastic: alpine skiing (boys, girls), aquatics (g), baseball (b), basketball (b,g), cross-country running (b,g), diving (g), football (b), gymnastics (g), ice hockey (b,g), indoor track & field (b,g), nordic skiing (b,g), soccer (b,g), softball (g), swimming and diving (g), tennis (b,g), track and field (b,g); intramural: aerobics (g), aerobics/dance (g), dance (g), figure skating (g), golf (b,g), ice skating (g); coed intramural: bicycling, canoeing/kayaking, cross-country running, fitness, fitness walking, flag football, floor hockey, Frisbee, indoor soccer, mountain biking, nordic skiing, physical fitness, physical training, racquetball, rock climbing, roller blading, skiing (cross-country), skiing (downhill), soccer, strength & conditioning, swimming and diving, ultimate Frisbee, volleyball, walking, wall climbing, wallyball, weight lifting, weight training, winter (indoor) track, winter soccer, winter walking, yoga. 1 PE instructor, 21 coaches.

Computers Computers are regularly used in English, science classes. Computer network features include on-campus library services, Internet access, Internet filtering or blocking technology. Student e-mail accounts and computer access in designated common areas are available to students. Students grades are available online. The school has a published electronic and media policy.

Contact Jennine Klosterman, Director of Admissions. 320-363-3321. Fax: 320-363-3322. E-mail: jklosterman@csbsju.edu. Web site: www.sjprep.net.

ST. JOHN'S-RAVENSCOURT SCHOOL

400 South Drive

Winnipeg, Manitoba R3T 3K5, Canada

Head of School: Dr. Stephen Johnson

General Information Coeducational boarding and day college-preparatory school. Boarding grades 8–12, day grades K–12. Founded: 1820. Setting: suburban. Students are housed in single-sex dormitories. 23-acre campus. 6 buildings on campus. Approved or accredited by Canadian Association of Independent Schools, Canadian Educational Standards Institute, The Association of Boarding Schools, and Manitoba Department of Education. Language of instruction: English. Endowment: CAN$8.3 million. Total enrollment: 830. Upper school average class size: 20. Upper school faculty-student ratio: 1:9. There are 172 required school days per year for Upper School students.

Upper School Student Profile Grade 9: 87 students (53 boys, 34 girls); Grade 10: 91 students (48 boys, 43 girls); Grade 11: 102 students (55 boys, 47 girls); Grade 12: 94 students (62 boys, 32 girls). 4% of students are boarding students. 97% are province residents. 3 provinces are represented in upper school student body. 2% are international students. International students from China, Democratic People's Republic of Korea, Germany, Hong Kong, Taiwan, and United States; 2 other countries represented in student body.

Faculty School total: 78. In upper school: 25 men, 23 women; 13 have advanced degrees; 4 reside on campus.

Subjects Offered Advanced Placement courses, algebra, American history, animation, art, biology, biology-AP, calculus, calculus-AP, Canadian geography, Canadian history, chemistry, chemistry-AP, computer science, debate, drama, driver education, economics, English, English literature, European history, European history-AP, French, French-AP, geography, geometry, history, information technology, law, linear algebra, mathematics, music, physical education, physics, physics-AP, pre-calculus, psychology, psychology-AP, science, social studies, Spanish, theater, visual arts, Web site design, world issues.

Graduation Requirements Canadian geography, Canadian history, computer science, English, French, geography, history, mathematics, physical education (includes health), pre-calculus, science, social sciences.

Special Academic Programs Advanced Placement exam preparation; honors section; independent study; study at local college for college credit; ESL (27 students enrolled).

College Admission Counseling 86 students graduated in 2011; all went to college, including McGill University; Queen's University at Kingston; The University of British Columbia; The University of Western Ontario; University of Manitoba; University of Toronto.

Student Life Upper grades have uniform requirement, student council, honor system. Discipline rests equally with students and faculty.

Tuition and Aid Day student tuition: CAN$16,280; 7-day tuition and room/board: CAN$33,620–CAN$43,870. Tuition installment plan (monthly payment plans, individually arranged payment plans). Bursaries, merit scholarship grants available. In 2011–12, 21% of upper-school students received aid; total upper-school merit-scholarship money awarded: CAN$95,000. Total amount of financial aid awarded in 2011–12: CAN$262,250.

Admissions Traditional secondary-level entrance grade is 9. For fall 2011, 72 students applied for upper-level admission, 47 were accepted, 39 enrolled. Otis-Lennon School Ability Test, school's own exam or TOEFL or SLEP required. Deadline for receipt of application materials: none. Application fee required: CAN$125. Interview recommended.

Athletics Interscholastic: aerobics (boys, girls), badminton (b,g), basketball (b,g), cross-country running (b,g), Frisbee (b,g), golf (b), hockey (b,g), ice hockey (b,g), indoor track (b,g), indoor track & field (b,g), lacrosse (b,g); intramural: badminton (b,g), basketball (b,g), cross-country running (b,g), dance (b,g), hockey (b,g); coed interscholastic: badminton, Frisbee, physical fitness; coed intramural: badminton, flag football, floor hockey. 6 PE instructors.

Computers Computers are regularly used in business skills, career exploration, college planning, creative writing, English, history, library skills, newspaper, science, social studies, yearbook classes. Computer network features include on-campus library services, Internet access, wireless campus network, Internet filtering or blocking technology, EBSCO. Campus intranet and student e-mail accounts are available to students. The school has a published electronic and media policy.

Contact Mrs. Lisa Kachulak-Babey, Director of Admissions and Communications. 204-477-2400. Fax: 204-477-2429. E-mail: admissions@sjr.mb.ca. Web site: www.sjr.mb.ca.

ST. JOSEPH ACADEMY

155 State Road 207

St. Augustine, Florida 32084

Head of School: Mr. Michael H. Heubeck

General Information Coeducational day college-preparatory, arts, religious studies, and technology school, affiliated with Roman Catholic Church. Grades 9–12. Founded: 1866. Setting: suburban. 33-acre campus. 13 buildings on campus. Approved or accredited by Southern Association of Colleges and Schools and Florida Department of Education. Total enrollment: 260. Upper school average class size: 14. Upper school faculty-student ratio: 1:11. There are 184 required school days per year for Upper School students. Upper School students typically attend 5 days per week. The average school day consists of 5 hours and 6 minutes.

Upper School Student Profile Grade 9: 58 students (26 boys, 32 girls); Grade 10: 74 students (36 boys, 38 girls); Grade 11: 72 students (32 boys, 40 girls); Grade 12: 56 students (27 boys, 29 girls). 84% of students are Roman Catholic.

Faculty School total: 24. In upper school: 12 men, 12 women; 10 have advanced degrees.

Subjects Offered Advanced computer applications, advanced math, Advanced Placement courses, advanced studio art-AP, algebra, American government, American history, American sign language, anatomy and physiology, ancient world history, applied arts, art, art history, Bible studies, biology, calculus-AP, career education, career exploration, career planning, Catholic belief and practice, chemistry, Christianity, church history, clayworking, college counseling, college placement, college planning, community service, computer applications, computer education, computer skills, costumes and make-up, creative drama, drama, drama performance, drama workshop, drawing, English, English composition, English language-AP, environmental science, government, history of the Catholic Church, honors algebra, honors English, honors geometry, honors U.S. history, honors world history, integrated mathematics, Internet research, life management skills, marine biology, Microsoft, moral theology, peer ministry, personal fitness, physical education, physics, play production, playwriting and directing, portfolio art, pottery, pre-algebra, pre-calculus, psychology, religious education, senior career experience, Shakespeare, Spanish, Spanish language-AP, Spanish literature-AP, theology, U.S. history, weight training.

Graduation Requirements Advanced Placement courses, career/college preparation, Catholic belief and practice, college writing, computer literacy, dramatic arts, economics, English, environmental science, foreign language, government, mathematics, physical education (includes health), religion (includes Bible studies and theology), social studies (includes history), theology.

Special Academic Programs Advanced Placement exam preparation; study at local college for college credit; academic accommodation for the gifted and the artistically talented; special instructional classes for students with Attention Deficit Disorder.

College Admission Counseling 74 students graduated in 2011; all went to college, including Florida Atlantic University; University of Central Florida; University of Florida; University of North Florida.

Student Life Upper grades have uniform requirement, student council, honor system. Discipline rests primarily with faculty. Attendance at religious services is required.

Summer Programs Sports programs offered; session focuses on football conditioning, weight training, basketball clinics and tournaments; held on campus; accepts boys and girls; not open to students from other schools. 104 students usually enrolled. 2012 schedule: June 1 to July 30.

Tuition and Aid Day student tuition: $7665–$9780. Tuition installment plan (FACTS Tuition Payment Plan). Need-based scholarship grants available. In 2011–12, 42% of upper-school students received aid. Total amount of financial aid awarded in 2011–12: $119,467.

Admissions Traditional secondary-level entrance grade is 9. For fall 2011, 63 students applied for upper-level admission, 58 were accepted, 58 enrolled. ACT-Explore, Iowa Tests of Basic Skills, Iowa Tests of Basic Skills-Grades 7-8, Archdiocese HSEPT-Grade 9, PSAT or SAT required. Deadline for receipt of application materials: none. Application fee required: $580. Interview required.

Athletics Interscholastic: baseball (boys), basketball (b,g), cheering (g), cross-country running (b,g), flag football (g), football (b), golf (b,g), physical fitness (b,g), physical training (b,g), soccer (b,g), softball (g), swimming and diving (b,g), tennis (b,g), track and field (b,g), volleyball (g), weight training (b), winter soccer (b,g), wrestling (b). 1 PE instructor, 3 coaches, 2 athletic trainers.

Computers Computers are regularly used in all academic classes. Computer network features include on-campus library services, Internet access, Internet filtering or blocking technology. Students grades are available online. The school has a published electronic and media policy.

Contact Mr. Patrick M. Keane, Director of Admissions. 904-824-0431 Ext. 305. Fax: 904-824-4412. E-mail: admissions@sjaweb.org. Web site: www.sjaweb.org.

SAINT JOSEPH ACADEMY HIGH SCHOOL

3430 Rocky River Drive

Cleveland, Ohio 44111

Head of School: Dr. Jim Cantwell

General Information Girls' day college-preparatory, technology, pre-engineering, and Mandarin school, affiliated with Roman Catholic Church. Grades 9–12. Founded: 1890. Setting: urban. 44-acre campus. 2 buildings on campus. Approved or accredited by North Central Association of Colleges and Schools, Ohio Catholic Schools Accreditation Association (OCSAA), and Ohio Department of Education. Endowment: $3.5 million. Total enrollment: 650. Upper school average class size: 23. Upper school faculty-student ratio: 1:12. The average school day consists of 7 hours.

Upper School Student Profile Grade 9: 166 students (166 girls); Grade 10: 170 students (170 girls); Grade 11: 169 students (169 girls); Grade 12: 145 students (145 girls). 90% of students are Roman Catholic.

Faculty School total: 63. In upper school: 15 men, 48 women; 38 have advanced degrees.

Graduation Requirements 4 credits of Theology.

Special Academic Programs 7 Advanced Placement exams for which test preparation is offered; honors section; independent study; study abroad.

College Admission Counseling 145 students graduated in 2010; 138 went to college, including Cleveland State University; John Carroll University; Kent State University; Miami University; Ohio University; University of Dayton. Other: 7 went to work. Mean SAT critical reading: 540, mean SAT math: 521, mean SAT writing: 528, mean combined SAT: 1589, mean composite ACT: 23.

Student Life Upper grades have uniform requirement, student council, honor system. Discipline rests primarily with faculty. Attendance at religious services is required.

Tuition and Aid Day student tuition: $9575. Tuition installment plan (monthly payment plans). Merit scholarship grants, need-based scholarship grants, need-based loans, paying campus jobs available. In 2010–11, 60% of upper-school students received aid; total upper-school merit-scholarship money awarded: $130,000. Total amount of financial aid awarded in 2010–11: $850,000.

Admissions Traditional secondary-level entrance grade is 9. For fall 2010, 200 students applied for upper-level admission, 195 were accepted, 175 enrolled. ACT-Explore required. Deadline for receipt of application materials: January 28. No application fee required. Interview required.

Athletics Interscholastic: basketball, cheering, cross-country running, diving, golf, rugby, soccer, softball, swimming and diving, tennis, track and field, volleyball; intramural: alpine skiing, dance team, physical fitness, strength & conditioning. 2 PE instructors, 14 coaches.

Computers Computer network features include on-campus library services, Internet access, wireless campus network, Internet filtering or blocking technology. Student e-mail accounts and computer access in designated common areas are available to students. Students grades are available online. The school has a published electronic and media policy.

Contact Ms. Diane Marie Kanney, Director of Admissions. 216-251-4868 Ext. 220. Fax: 216-251-5809. E-mail: admissions@sja1890.org. Web site: www.sja1890.org.

ST. JOSEPH HIGH SCHOOL

4120 Bradley Road

Santa Maria, California 93455

Head of School: Mr. Joseph Thomas Myers

General Information Coeducational day college-preparatory, arts, religious studies, and technology school, affiliated with Roman Catholic Church. Grades 9–12. Founded: 1964. Setting: suburban. 15-acre campus. 8 buildings on campus. Approved or accredited by National Catholic Education Association, Western Association of Schools and Colleges, and Western Catholic Education Association. Endowment: $3.6 million. Total enrollment: 561. Upper school average class size: 25. Upper school faculty-student ratio: 1:19. There are 180 required school days per year for Upper School students. Upper School students typically attend 5 days per week. The average school day consists of 5 hours and 45 minutes.

Upper School Student Profile Grade 9: 139 students (64 boys, 75 girls); Grade 10: 159 students (77 boys, 82 girls); Grade 11: 118 students (55 boys, 63 girls); Grade 12: 190 students (91 boys, 99 girls). 66% of students are Roman Catholic.

Faculty School total: 36. In upper school: 15 men, 21 women; 16 have advanced degrees.

Subjects Offered Art, biology, biology-AP, computer literacy, economics, English literature, English literature-AP, ethics, European history-AP, French, general science, grammar, Hebrew scripture, keyboarding, language and composition, marine science, New Testament, painting, peace and justice, physical science, physics, pre-algebra, psychology, remedial study skills, scripture, sculpture, sociology, Spanish, Spanish language-AP, speech, U.S. government, U.S. history, U.S. history-AP, U.S. literature, weight training, Western civilization.

Graduation Requirements Arts and fine arts (art, music, dance, drama), Catholic belief and practice, Christian and Hebrew scripture, Christian doctrine, Christian ethics, church history, civics, communication arts, composition, computer skills, economics, English, English literature, ethics, foreign language, health, history, human biology, introduction to literature, keyboarding, language structure, life science, literature, mathematics, religion (includes Bible studies and theology), science, U.S. government, Western civilization, world geography.

Special Academic Programs Remedial reading and/or remedial writing; remedial math.

College Admission Counseling 132 students graduated in 2010; all went to college, including California Polytechnic State University, San Luis Obispo; Loyola Marymount University; Santa Clara University; University of California, Santa Barbara. Mean SAT critical reading: 532, mean SAT math: 533, mean SAT writing: 538. 22% scored over 600 on SAT critical reading, 28% scored over 600 on SAT math, 22% scored over 600 on SAT writing.

Student Life Upper grades have specified standards of dress, student council. Discipline rests primarily with faculty. Attendance at religious services is required.

Tuition and Aid Day student tuition: $7350. Tuition installment plan (monthly payment plans). Tuition reduction for siblings, merit scholarship grants, need-based scholarship grants, paying campus jobs available. In 2010–11, 30% of upper-school students received aid; total upper-school merit-scholarship money awarded: $12,000. Total amount of financial aid awarded in 2010–11: $310,000.

Admissions Traditional secondary-level entrance grade is 9. For fall 2010, 158 students applied for upper-level admission, 154 were accepted, 139 enrolled. High School Placement Test required. Deadline for receipt of application materials: February 5. Application fee required: $50.

Athletics Interscholastic: baseball (boys), basketball (b,g), cross-country running (b,g), football (b), golf (b,g), soccer (b,g), softball (g), swimming and diving (b,g), tennis (b,g), track and field (b,g), volleyball (b,g), water polo (b,g); intramural: dance team (g), flag football (g); coed interscholastic: cheering, wrestling; coed intramural: basketball. 3 PE instructors, 35 coaches, 1 athletic trainer.

Computers Computers are regularly used in computer applications, economics, English, history, keyboarding, mathematics, religion, Spanish, theology, yearbook classes. Computer network features include on-campus library services, online commercial services, Internet access, wireless campus network, Internet filtering or blocking technology. Computer access in designated common areas is available to students. Students grades are available online. The school has a published electronic and media policy.

Contact Joanne Poloni, Director of Admissions. 805-937-2038 Ext. 114. Fax: 805-937-4248. E-mail: poloni@sjhsknights.com. Web site: www.sjhsknights.com.

SAINT JOSEPH HIGH SCHOOL

10900 West Cermak Road

Westchester, Illinois 60154-4299

Head of School: Mr. Ronald Hoover

General Information Coeducational day college-preparatory, arts, business, vocational, religious studies, bilingual studies, and technology school, affiliated with Roman Catholic Church. Grades 9–12. Founded: 1960. Setting: suburban. Nearest major city is Chicago. 21-acre campus. 2 buildings on campus. Approved or accredited by Christian Brothers Association, North Central Association of Colleges and Schools, and Illinois Department of Education. Total enrollment: 605. Upper school average class size: 25. Upper school faculty-student ratio: 1:20. There are 176 required school days per year for Upper School students. Upper School students typically attend 5 days per week. The average school day consists of 6 hours and 30 minutes.

Upper School Student Profile Grade 9: 172 students (88 boys, 84 girls); Grade 10: 130 students (71 boys, 59 girls); Grade 11: 153 students (90 boys, 63 girls); Grade 12: 150 students (94 boys, 56 girls). 39% of students are Roman Catholic.

Faculty School total: 49. In upper school: 31 men, 18 women; 27 have advanced degrees.

Subjects Offered Accounting, ACT preparation, acting, advanced studio art-AP, algebra, American foreign policy, American history, anatomy and physiology, art, band, biology, business law, calculus, calculus-AP, ceramics, chemistry, Christian ethics, computer applications, computer graphics, computer programming, computer science-AP, computer-aided design, concert band, concert choir, consumer economics, creative writing, current events, digital photography, economics, English, English-AP, environmental science, European history-AP, film studies, fine arts, French, geography, geometry, graphic arts, health, human biology, internship, Italian, jazz band, journalism, Mandarin, marching band, marketing, men's studies, moral and social development, music appreciation, peace and justice, peer ministry, photography, physical education, physics, physics-AP, pre-algebra, pre-calculus, reading, reading/study skills, sociology, Spanish, Spanish-AP, speech, sports conditioning, sports medicine, studio art, studio art-AP, theater production, U.S. history, video and animation, video film production, Web site design, women spirituality and faith, world cultures, world religions.

Graduation Requirements Arts and fine arts (art, music, dance, drama), computer applications, economics, English, foreign language, mathematics, physical education (includes health), religion (includes Bible studies and theology), science, social studies (includes history), each student must complete 40 community service hours.

Special Academic Programs 7 Advanced Placement exams for which test preparation is offered; honors section; study at local college for college credit; academic accommodation for the gifted, the musically talented, and the artistically talented; remedial reading and/or remedial writing; remedial math.

College Admission Counseling 182 students graduated in 2011; 172 went to college, including Dominican University; Illinois State University; Lewis University; Loyola University Chicago; Northern Illinois University; University of Illinois at Urbana–Champaign. Other: 7 went to work, 1 entered military service, 2 had other specific plans. Median composite ACT: 22. 14% scored over 26 on composite ACT.

Student Life Upper grades have uniform requirement, student council, honor system. Discipline rests primarily with faculty. Attendance at religious services is required.

Summer Programs Remediation, enrichment, advancement, sports, art/fine arts, computer instruction programs offered; session focuses on remediation; held on campus; accepts boys and girls; open to students from other schools. 200 students usually enrolled. 2012 schedule: June 15 to July 25. Application deadline: May 31.

Tuition and Aid Day student tuition: $8800. Tuition installment plan (monthly payment plans, individually arranged payment plans, based on parents income special arrangements are made with income tax return). Tuition reduction for siblings, merit scholarship grants, need-based scholarship grants, paying campus jobs available. In 2011–12, 57% of upper-school students received aid; total upper-school merit-scholarship money awarded: $95,000. Total amount of financial aid awarded in 2011–12: $800,000.

Admissions Traditional secondary-level entrance grade is 9. For fall 2011, 200 students applied for upper-level admission, 200 were accepted, 186 enrolled. Explore required. Deadline for receipt of application materials: none. Application fee required: $300. Interview required.

Athletics Interscholastic: aerobics/dance (girls), baseball (b), basketball (b,g), bowling (b,g), boxing (b), cheering (g), cross-country running (b,g), dance team (g), football (b), golf (b,g), hockey (g), soccer (b,g), softball (g), strength & conditioning (b,g), tennis (b,g), track and field (b,g), volleyball (b,g), wrestling (b). 2 PE instructors, 30 coaches, 1 athletic trainer.

Computers Computers are regularly used in business applications, computer applications, current events, desktop publishing, drafting, economics, English, French, geography, graphic arts, graphic design, health, history, journalism, mathematics, music, newspaper, photography, reading, religion, science, social studies, Spanish, speech, technology, theater arts, video film production, writing, yearbook classes. Computer network features include on-campus library services, online commercial services, Internet access, wireless campus network, Internet filtering or blocking technology, all students have a laptop computer with wireless access to the Internet, anywhere on campus. Campus intranet and student e-mail accounts are available to students. Students grades are available online. The school has a published electronic and media policy.

Contact Ms. Tricia Devereux, Director of Student Accounts and Admissions. 708-562-4433 Ext. 166. Fax: 708-562-4459. E-mail: tdevereux@stjoeshs.org.

SAINT JOSEPH HIGH SCHOOL

328 Vine Street

Hammonton, New Jersey 08037

Head of School: Mrs. Lynn Domenico

General Information Coeducational day college-preparatory, arts, religious studies, technology, and global studies/distance learning school, affiliated with Roman Catholic Church. Grades 9–12. Founded: 1939. Setting: small town. Nearest major city is Philadelphia, PA. 7-acre campus. 2 buildings on campus. Approved or accredited by Middle States Association of Colleges and Schools and New Jersey Department of Education. Total enrollment: 380. Upper school average class size: 25. Upper school faculty-student ratio: 1:17. There are 180 required school days per year for Upper School students. Upper School students typically attend 5 days per week. The average school day consists of 5 hours and 30 minutes.

Upper School Student Profile Grade 9: 96 students (57 boys, 39 girls); Grade 10: 92 students (39 boys, 53 girls), Grade 11: 100 students (51 boys, 49 girls); Grade 12: 98 students (52 boys, 46 girls). 90% of students are Roman Catholic.

Faculty School total: 33. In upper school: 12 men, 15 women; 12 have advanced degrees.

Subjects Offered Advanced Placement courses, algebra, American history, American history-AP, American literature-AP, anatomy and physiology, biology, biology-AP, British literature, British literature (honors), business law, business technology, calculus, calculus-AP, chemistry, chemistry-AP, choral music, Christian doctrine, Christian scripture, church history, community service, composition-AP, computer applications, creative writing, desktop publishing, earth science, economics, English, English composition, English language and composition-AP, English literature and composition-AP, environmental science, European history, finite math, foreign language, forensics, French, geometry, global studies, health, health education, history, honors algebra, honors English, honors geometry, honors U.S. history, honors world history, lab science, Latin, music, physical education, physical science, physics, pre-calculus, psychology, religion, religious education, SAT preparation, Spanish, statistics, theater arts, U.S. history, U.S. history-AP, world cultures, world history.

Graduation Requirements 20th century history, algebra, American history, American literature, biology, British literature, chemistry, church history, computer education, driver education, English, English literature, European history, geometry, health, history of the Catholic Church, lab science, languages, mathematics, religious education, science, social studies (includes history), theology, U.S. history, world cultures. Community service is required.

Special Academic Programs Academic accommodation for the gifted; remedial reading and/or remedial writing; programs in English, mathematics, general development for dyslexic students.

College Admission Counseling 98 students graduated in 2011; 96 went to college, including Penn State University Park; Widener University. Other: 1 went to work, 1 entered military service. Median SAT critical reading: 500, median SAT math: 490, median SAT writing: 450, median combined SAT: 1440. 4% scored over 600 on SAT critical reading, 11% scored over 600 on SAT math, 3% scored over 600 on SAT writing, 1% scored over 1800 on combined SAT.

Student Life Upper grades have uniform requirement, student council, honor system. Discipline rests primarily with faculty. Attendance at religious services is required.

Summer Programs Remediation, enrichment programs offered; session focuses on jump starting the high school experience and enhancing the school year; held on campus; accepts boys and girls; open to students from other schools. 120 students usually enrolled. 2012 schedule: July 10 to August 18. Application deadline: June 1.

Tuition and Aid Day student tuition: $7650. Tuition installment plan (SMART Tuition Payment Plan). Tuition reduction for siblings, merit scholarship grants, need-based scholarship grants available. In 2011–12, 20% of upper-school students received aid; total upper-school merit-scholarship money awarded: $10,000. Total amount of financial aid awarded in 2011–12: $50,000.

Admissions Traditional secondary-level entrance grade is 9. For fall 2011, 400 students applied for upper-level admission, 304 were accepted, 96 enrolled. Admissions testing, CAT, Catholic High School Entrance Examination, CTBS, Stanford Achievement Test, any other standardized test, Iowa Tests of Basic Skills, Stanford Achievement Test, STS Examination or Terra Nova-CTB required. Deadline for receipt of application materials: none. Application fee required: $200. Interview recommended.

Athletics Interscholastic: baseball (boys, girls), basketball (b,g), bowling (b,g), cheering (b,g), cross-country running (b,g), dance (g), field hockey (g), football (b), golf (b,g), gymnastics (g), ice hockey (b), ice skating (g), indoor track (b,g), indoor track & field (b,g), lacrosse (b,g), physical training (b,g), power lifting (b,g), soccer (b,g), softball (g), swimming and diving (g), track and field (b,g), volleyball (g), weight lifting (b,g), weight training (b,g), winter (indoor) track (b,g), wrestling (b); coed interscholastic: bowling; coed intramural: bowling, snowboarding, weight training. 3 PE instructors, 43 coaches, 1 athletic trainer.

Computers Computers are regularly used in business applications, desktop publishing classes. Computer network features include on-campus library services, Internet access, wireless campus network, Internet filtering or blocking technology. Campus intranet and student e-mail accounts are available to students. Students grades are available online. The school has a published electronic and media policy.

Contact Mr. Renee DeFinis, Administrative Assistant to the Principal. 609-561-8700. Fax: 609-561-8701. E-mail: rdefinis@stjoek12.org. Web site: www.stjoek12.org.

SAINT JOSEPH HIGH SCHOOL

2401 69th Street

Kenosha, Wisconsin 53143

Head of School: Mr. Edward Kovochich

General Information Coeducational day college-preparatory, general academic, arts, religious studies, and technology school, affiliated with Roman Catholic Church. Grades 6–12. Founded: 1957. Setting: suburban. Nearest major city is Milwaukee. 1 building on campus. Approved or accredited by North Central Association of Colleges and Schools and Wisconsin Department of Education. Endowment: $100,000. Total enrollment: 654. Upper school average class size: 20. Upper school faculty-student ratio: 1:20. There are 180 required school days per year for Upper School students. Upper School students typically attend 5 days per week. The average school day consists of 7 hours.

Upper School Student Profile Grade 6: 40 students (19 boys, 21 girls); Grade 7: 45 students (27 boys, 18 girls); Grade 8: 70 students (33 boys, 37 girls); Grade 9: 85 students (42 boys, 43 girls); Grade 10: 82 students (39 boys, 43 girls); Grade 11: 72 students (44 boys, 28 girls); Grade 12: 53 students (26 boys, 27 girls). 80% of students are Roman Catholic.

Faculty School total: 34. In upper school: 11 men, 19 women; 12 have advanced degrees.

Subjects Offered Algebra, American government, anatomy and physiology, architecture, art, band, biology, biology-AP, calculus-AP, ceramics, chemistry, chemistry-AP, choir, Christian scripture, computer applications, computers, consumer mathematics, creative writing, critical writing, drafting, drama, drawing, economics, English, English-AP, film, French, geometry, health, Hebrew scripture, Italian, journalism, keyboarding, mathematics, microeconomics-AP, newspaper, photography, physical education, physical science, physics-AP, pre-algebra, pre-calculus, psychology, reading/study skills, science, social studies, Spanish, speech, statistics, studio art, theater, theology, trigonometry, U.S. history, world history, world religions, yearbook.

Graduation Requirements Arts and fine arts (art, music, dance, drama), computers, electives, English, mathematics, physical education (includes health), religion (includes Bible studies and theology), science, social studies (includes history).

Special Academic Programs Advanced Placement exam preparation; honors section; study at local college for college credit.

College Admission Counseling 79 students graduated in 2010; 75 went to college, including Marquette University; University of Wisconsin–Madison; University of Wisconsin–Milwaukee. Other: 4 went to work. Mean composite ACT: 23. 25% scored over 26 on composite ACT.

Student Life Upper grades have specified standards of dress, student council, honor system. Discipline rests primarily with faculty. Attendance at religious services is required.

Tuition and Aid Day student tuition: $6650–$7150. Tuition installment plan (monthly payment plans, individually arranged payment plans, Tuition Management Systems). Tuition reduction for siblings, merit scholarship grants, need-based scholarship grants available. In 2010–11, 50% of upper-school students received aid; total upper-school merit-scholarship money awarded: $45,000. Total amount of financial aid awarded in 2010–11: $150,000.

Admissions Traditional secondary-level entrance grade is 9. For fall 2010, 110 students applied for upper-level admission, 105 were accepted, 89 enrolled. ACT-Explore or admissions testing required. Deadline for receipt of application materials: none. Application fee required: $100.

Athletics Interscholastic: baseball (boys), basketball (b,g), cheering (b,g), cross-country running (b,g), football (b), golf (b,g), soccer (b,g), softball (g), tennis (b,g), track and field (b,g), volleyball (g), wrestling (b); coed intramural: bowling, weight lifting, weight training. 2 PE instructors, 15 coaches, 1 athletic trainer.

Computers Computers are regularly used in all classes. Computer network features include Internet access, wireless campus network, Internet filtering or blocking technology. Campus intranet is available to students. Students grades are available online.

Contact Mrs. Wanda Jaraczewski, Director of Admissions. 262-654-8651 Ext. 104. Fax: 262-654-1615. E-mail: wjaraczewski@kenoshastjoseph.com. Web site: www.kenoshastjoseph.com.

SAINT JOSEPH JUNIOR-SENIOR HIGH SCHOOL

1000 Ululani Street

Hilo, Hawaii 96720

Head of School: Ms. Victoria Torcolini

General Information Coeducational day college-preparatory, arts, religious studies, and technology school, affiliated with Roman Catholic Church. Grades 7–12. Founded: 1948. Setting: urban. 14-acre campus. 3 buildings on campus. Approved or accredited by The Hawaii Council of Private Schools, Western Association of Schools and Colleges, Western Catholic Education Association, and Hawaii Department of Education. Member of National Association of Independent Schools. Total enrollment: 193. Upper school average class size: 18. Upper school faculty-student ratio: 1:12. There are 176 required school days per year for Upper School students. Upper School students typically attend 5 days per week. The average school day consists of 5 hours and 25 minutes.

Upper School Student Profile 55% of students are Roman Catholic.

Faculty School total: 32. In upper school: 8 men, 8 women; 6 have advanced degrees.

Subjects Offered Advanced Placement courses, algebra, American history, American literature, art, astronomy, biology, British literature, British literature-AP, calculus, calculus-AP, chemistry, composition-AP, computer science, concert band, creative writing, criminal justice, cultural geography, drama, earth science, English, English literature, European history, European history-AP, expository writing, fine arts, geometry, government and politics-AP, government/civics, Hawaiian history, history, Japanese, JROTC, life skills, marine biology, marine science, mathematics, music, physical education, physics, physiology, psychology, religion, science, senior project, social studies, sociology, Spanish, speech, theology, trigonometry, typing, world history, world literature, yearbook.

Graduation Requirements Arts and fine arts (art, music, dance, drama), English, foreign language, mathematics, physical education (includes health), religion (includes Bible studies and theology), science, social studies (includes history).

Special Academic Programs Advanced Placement exam preparation; honors section; independent study; study at local college for college credit; academic accommodation for the gifted; remedial math; ESL (6 students enrolled).

College Admission Counseling 28 students graduated in 2011; 27 went to college, including Chaminade University of Honolulu; The George Washington University; University of Alaska Anchorage; University of California, Davis; University of Hawaii at Hilo; University of Hawaii at Manoa. Other: 1 had other specific plans. Median SAT critical reading: 510, median SAT math: 489, median composite ACT: 21.

Student Life Upper grades have uniform requirement, student council, honor system. Discipline rests primarily with faculty. Attendance at religious services is required.

Summer Programs Enrichment, sports, art/fine arts, computer instruction programs offered; session focuses on SAT/ACT preparation, enrichment; held on campus; accepts boys and girls; open to students from other schools. 35 students usually enrolled. 2012 schedule: May 15 to June 21. Application deadline: May 1.

Tuition and Aid Day student tuition: $8000. Tuition installment plan (FACTS Tuition Payment Plan, individually arranged payment plans). Tuition reduction for siblings, need-based scholarship grants, paying campus jobs available. In 2011–12, 45% of upper-school students received aid. Total amount of financial aid awarded in 2011–12: $225,000.

Admissions For fall 2011, 43 students applied for upper-level admission, 36 were accepted. 3-R Achievement Test and English proficiency required. Deadline for receipt of application materials: none. Application fee required: $25. Interview required.

Athletics Interscholastic: aquatics (girls), basketball (b,g), bowling (b,g), cheering (g), cross-country running (b,g), golf (g), paddling (b,g), riflery (b,g), running (b), soccer (b,g), swimming and diving (b,g), tennis (b,g), track and field (b), volleyball (b,g); coed interscholastic: paddling. 1 PE instructor.

Computers Computers are regularly used in college planning, creative writing, data processing, desktop publishing, ESL, English, ESL, foreign language, geography, graphic arts, graphic design, graphics, health, history, keyboarding, lab/keyboard, library, life skills, mathematics, newspaper, publications, science, technology, typing, word processing, writing, writing, yearbook classes. Computer network features include on-campus library services, Internet access, wireless campus network, Internet filtering or blocking technology, State of Hawaii's College and Career Information Delivery System. Student e-mail accounts are available to students. Students grades are available online.

Contact Mrs. Rachel Dawson, Registrar. 808-935-4936 Ext. 226. Fax: 808-969-9019. Web site: www.sjshilo.org.

ST. JOSEPH'S ACADEMY

3015 Broussard Street

Baton Rouge, Louisiana 70808

Head of School: Mrs. Linda Fryoux Harvison

General Information Girls' day college-preparatory, arts, religious studies, and technology school, affiliated with Roman Catholic Church. Grades 9–12. Founded: 1868. Setting: urban. 14-acre campus. 7 buildings on campus. Approved or accredited by National Catholic Education Association, Southern Association of Colleges and Schools, Southern Association of Independent Schools, and Louisiana Department of Education. Endowment: $3.6 million. Total enrollment: 976. Upper school average class size: 23. Upper school faculty-student ratio: 1:14. There are 179 required school days per year for Upper School students. Upper School students typically attend 5 days per week. The average school day consists of 7 hours and 15 minutes.

Upper School Student Profile Grade 9: 255 students (255 girls); Grade 10: 253 students (253 girls); Grade 11: 251 students (251 girls); Grade 12: 217 students (217 girls). 96% of students are Roman Catholic.

Faculty School total: 71. In upper school: 10 men, 61 women; 37 have advanced degrees.

Subjects Offered Accounting, acting, advanced chemistry, advanced computer applications, advanced math, Advanced Placement courses, algebra, American history, American history-AP, American literature, American literature-AP, analysis, analysis and differential calculus, art, art appreciation, band, Basic programming, biology, biology-AP, business law, calculus-AP, campus ministry, Catholic belief and practice, chemistry, child development, choir, choral music, chorus, Christian and Hebrew scripture, church history, civics, civics/free enterprise, computer applications, computer information systems, computer multimedia, computer programming, computer technologies, computer technology certification, CPR, critical studies in film, dance, desktop publishing, drama, drama performance, economics, English, English literature-AP, English-AP, entrepreneurship, environmental science, European history-AP, family and consumer science, film and literature, fine arts, foreign language, French, French as a second language, geometry, grammar, health, health and safety, health education, Hebrew scripture, honors algebra, honors English, honors geometry, human sexuality, independent study, information technology, Latin, marching band, media arts, media production, music, novels, physical education, physical fitness, physics, poetry, pre-calculus, public speaking, religion, research, Shakespeare, social justice, Spanish, speech, speech communications, technology, the Web, transition mathematics, U.S. history, U.S. history-AP, U.S. literature, visual arts, vocal ensemble, vocal music, Web authoring, Web site design, world history-AP.

Graduation Requirements Advanced math, algebra, American history, arts and fine arts (art, music, dance, drama), biology, chemistry, civics, computer applications, English, foreign language, geometry, physical education (includes health), physical science, physics, religion (includes Bible studies and theology), world history, service hours.

Special Academic Programs Advanced Placement exam preparation; honors section; independent study; study at local college for college credit.

College Admission Counseling 221 students graduated in 2011; all went to college, including Auburn University; Louisiana State University and Agricultural and Mechanical College; Louisiana Tech University; Loyola University New Orleans; The University of Alabama; University of Louisiana at Lafayette. 69% scored over 26 on composite ACT.

Student Life Upper grades have uniform requirement, student council, honor system. Discipline rests primarily with faculty. Attendance at religious services is required.

Summer Programs Computer instruction programs offered; session focuses on computer orientation for incoming 9th grade students; held on campus; accepts girls; not open to students from other schools. 254 students usually enrolled. 2012 schedule: June 1 to June 30. Application deadline: March 16.

Tuition and Aid Day student tuition: $9420. Tuition installment plan (monthly debit plan). Need-based scholarship grants available. In 2011–12, 6% of upper-school students received aid. Total amount of financial aid awarded in 2011–12: $350,000.

Admissions Traditional secondary-level entrance grade is 9. For fall 2011, 302 students applied for upper-level admission, 268 were accepted, 255 enrolled. ACT-Explore required. Deadline for receipt of application materials: November 18. Application fee required: $45. On-campus interview required.

Athletics Interscholastic: ballet, basketball, bowling, cheering, cross-country running, dance squad, golf, gymnastics, indoor track, modern dance, physical fitness, physical training, rodeo, running, soccer, softball, strength & conditioning, swimming and diving, tennis, track and field, triathlon, volleyball, weight training, winter (indoor) track, winter soccer; coed intramural: volleyball. 6 PE instructors, 9 coaches, 1 athletic trainer.

Computers Computers are regularly used in all classes. Computer network features include on-campus library services, online commercial services, Internet access, wireless campus network, Internet filtering or blocking technology, administrative software/grading/scheduling. Student e-mail accounts are available to students. Students grades are available online. The school has a published electronic and media policy.

Contact Mrs. Kathy Meares, Assistant Principal of Records. 225-388-2213. Fax: 225-344-5714. E-mail: mearesk@sjabr.org. Web site: www.sjabr.org.

ST. JOSEPH'S CATHOLIC SCHOOL

100 St. Joseph's Drive

Greenville, South Carolina 29607

Head of School: Mr. Keith F. Kiser

General Information Coeducational day college-preparatory school, affiliated with Roman Catholic Church. Grades 6–12. Founded: 1993. Setting: suburban. 36-acre campus. 3 buildings on campus. Approved or accredited by South Carolina Department of Education. Total enrollment: 611. Upper school average class size: 17. Upper school faculty-student ratio: 1:12. Upper School students typically attend 5 days per week. The average school day consists of 7 hours and 10 minutes.

Upper School Student Profile Grade 9: 102 students (53 boys, 49 girls); Grade 10: 104 students (51 boys, 53 girls); Grade 11: 78 students (36 boys, 42 girls); Grade 12: 71 students (33 boys, 38 girls). 74% of students are Roman Catholic.

Faculty School total: 55. In upper school: 17 men, 21 women; 17 have advanced degrees.

Subjects Offered Algebra, American history, American literature, art, arts appreciation, bell choir, biology, biology-AP, calculus-AP, chemistry, chemistry-AP, chorus, Christian doctrine, Christian ethics, church history, composition, computer applications, computer graphics, dance, drama workshop, drawing, economics, economics-AP, English literature and composition-AP, English-AP, ensembles, European history, European history-AP, European literature, exercise science, film studies, fine arts, forensics, French, geometry, government, government-AP, honors algebra, honors English, honors geometry, human movement and its application to health, Latin, literature, medieval/Renaissance history, moral theology, newspaper, personal money management, physical education, physics, physics-AP, pre-calculus, science fiction, Shakespeare, Spanish, Spanish-AP, speech, statistics-AP, strings, theater arts, theater production, U.S. history, U.S. history-AP, yearbook.

Graduation Requirements 65 hours of community service.

Special Academic Programs Advanced Placement exam preparation; honors section.

College Admission Counseling 76 students graduated in 2011; all went to college, including Clemson University; College of Charleston; Furman University; The University of Alabama; University of South Carolina. Median SAT critical reading: 615, median SAT math: 611, median SAT writing: 598, median combined SAT: 1824, median composite ACT: 27.

Student Life Upper grades have uniform requirement, student council, honor system. Discipline rests primarily with faculty. Attendance at religious services is required.

Summer Programs Sports, art/fine arts programs offered; held on campus; accepts boys and girls; open to students from other schools.

Tuition and Aid Day student tuition: $8790. Tuition installment plan (monthly payment plans, yearly payment plan, semiannual payment plan). Tuition reduction for siblings, merit scholarship grants, need-based scholarship grants, tuition reduction for staff available. In 2011–12, 35% of upper-school students received aid; total upper-school merit-scholarship money awarded: $36,633. Total amount of financial aid awarded in 2011–12: $376,126.

Admissions Traditional secondary-level entrance grade is 9. For fall 2011, 67 students applied for upper-level admission, 51 were accepted, 37 enrolled. High School Placement Test (closed version) from Scholastic Testing Service required. Deadline for receipt of application materials: May 31. Application fee required: $125. On-campus interview required.

Athletics Interscholastic: baseball (boys), basketball (b,g), cheering (g), cross-country running (b,g), football (b), golf (b), soccer (b,g), softball (g), swimming and diving (b,g), tennis (b,g), volleyball (g), wrestling (b); intramural: basketball (b,g), flag football (b), Frisbee (b,g), soccer (b,g), volleyball (g); coed interscholastic: golf; coed intramural: dance, weight training.

Computers Computers are regularly used in computer applications, graphic design, keyboarding, programming, yearbook classes. Computer network features include Internet access.

Contact Mrs. Barbara L. McGrath, Director of Admissions. 864-234-9009 Ext. 104. Fax: 864-234-5516. E-mail: bmcgrath@sjcatholicschool.org. Web site: www.sjcatholicschool.org.

SAINT JOSEPH'S HIGH SCHOOL

145 Plainfield Avenue

Metuchen, New Jersey 08840

Head of School: Mr. John A. Anderson '70

General Information Boys' day college-preparatory, arts, religious studies, and technology school, affiliated with Roman Catholic Church. Grades 9–12. Founded: 1961. Setting: suburban. Nearest major city is New York, NY. 68-acre campus. 8 buildings on campus. Approved or accredited by Middle States Association of Colleges and Schools, National Catholic Education Association, and New Jersey Department of Education. Endowment: $2 million. Total enrollment: 761. Upper school average class size: 24. Upper school faculty-student ratio: 1:16. There are 170 required school days per year for Upper School students. Upper School students typically attend 5 days per week. The average school day consists of 6 hours and 12 minutes.

Upper School Student Profile Grade 9: 181 students (181 boys); Grade 10: 200 students (200 boys); Grade 11: 210 students (210 boys); Grade 12: 170 students (170 boys). 75% of students are Roman Catholic.

Faculty School total: 68. In upper school: 44 men, 24 women; 44 have advanced degrees.

Subjects Offered Accounting, acting, Advanced Placement courses, algebra, American Civil War, American government, American history, American literature, art, arts, astronomy, biology, biology-AP, calculus, calculus-AP, campus ministry, career education, Catholic belief and practice, chemistry, chemistry-AP, Christian ethics, Christian scripture, Christian studies, Christianity, church history, computer animation, computer applications, computer programming, computer science, computer science-AP, desktop publishing, discrete mathematics, driver education, English, English literature, English-AP, European history, European history-AP, French, French as a second language, French-AP, geometry, German, German literature, guitar, health, history, lab science, Latin, mathematics, mathematics-AP, meteorology, music, personal finance, photo shop, photography, physical education, physics, physics-AP, pre-calculus, public speaking, religion, social studies, Spanish, Spanish-AP, technical drawing, theology, U.S. government and politics-AP, U.S. history-AP, Web site design, world history, world literature, writing.

Graduation Requirements Arts and fine arts (art, music, dance, drama), career education, computer science, English, foreign language, lab science, mathematics, physical education (includes health), religion (includes Bible studies and theology), science, social studies (includes history). Community service is required.

Special Academic Programs 33 Advanced Placement exams for which test preparation is offered; honors section; independent study; study at local college for college credit; academic accommodation for the gifted.

College Admission Counseling 184 students graduated in 2011; all went to college, including Penn State University Park; Rutgers, The State University of New Jersey, Rutgers College; Saint Joseph's University; Seton Hall University; The College of New Jersey; University of Notre Dame. Mean SAT critical reading: 551, mean SAT math: 587, mean SAT writing: 551.

Student Life Upper grades have specified standards of dress, student council, honor system. Discipline rests primarily with faculty. Attendance at religious services is required.

Summer Programs Remediation, enrichment, advancement, sports, computer instruction programs offered; session focuses on remediation and enrichment; held on campus; accepts boys and girls; open to students from other schools. 205 students usually enrolled. 2012 schedule: June to July. Application deadline: June.

Tuition and Aid Day student tuition: $113,000. Tuition installment plan (FACTS Tuition Payment Plan, monthly payment plans, individually arranged payment plans). Merit scholarship grants, need-based scholarship grants available. In 2011–12, 10% of upper-school students received aid; total upper-school merit-scholarship money awarded: $150,000. Total amount of financial aid awarded in 2011–12: $250,000.

Admissions Traditional secondary-level entrance grade is 9. For fall 2011, 400 students applied for upper-level admission, 280 were accepted, 225 enrolled. High School Placement Test required. Deadline for receipt of application materials: none. No application fee required. On-campus interview recommended.

Athletics Interscholastic: baseball, basketball, bowling, cross-country running, football, golf, ice hockey, indoor track & field, lacrosse, soccer, swimming and diving, tennis, track and field, volleyball, winter (indoor) track; intramural: crew, flag football, Frisbee, skiing (downhill), snowboarding, strength & conditioning, ultimate Frisbee, volleyball, weight lifting, weight training. 3 PE instructors, 41 coaches, 1 athletic trainer.

Computers Computers are regularly used in animation, computer applications, desktop publishing, desktop publishing, ESL, drawing and design, graphic design, graphics, journalism, lab/keyboard, mathematics, news writing, newspaper, photography, publications, publishing, science, technical drawing, technology, Web site design, word processing, yearbook classes. Computer network features include on-campus library services, online commercial services, Internet access, Internet filtering or blocking technology. Students grades are available online. The school has a published electronic and media policy.

Contact Mr. Thomas Bacsik '06, Admissions Director. 732-549-7600 Ext. 221. Fax: 732-549-0282. E-mail: admissions@stjoes.org. Web site: www.stjoes.org.

ST. JOSEPH'S PREPARATORY SCHOOL

1733 Girard Avenue

Philadelphia, Pennsylvania 19130

Head of School: Rev. George W. Bur, SJ

General Information Boys' day college-preparatory, arts, and religious studies school, affiliated with Roman Catholic Church. Grades 9–12. Founded: 1851. Setting: urban. 7-acre campus. 3 buildings on campus. Approved or accredited by Jesuit Secondary Education Association, Middle States Association of Colleges and Schools, National Catholic Education Association, and Pennsylvania Department of Education. Member of National Association of Independent Schools. Endowment: $9 million. Total enrollment: 993. Upper school average class size: 22. Upper school faculty-student ratio: 1:16. Upper School students typically attend 5 days per week. The average school day consists of 6 hours.

Upper School Student Profile Grade 9: 257 students (257 boys); Grade 10: 262 students (262 boys); Grade 11: 243 students (243 boys); Grade 12: 231 students (231 boys). 95% of students are Roman Catholic.

Faculty School total: 75. In upper school: 60 men, 15 women; 65 have advanced degrees.

Subjects Offered Algebra, American history, American literature, anatomy, archaeology, art, biology, business, calculus, chemistry, classics, computer math, computer programming, computer science, driver education, earth science, economics, English, English literature, environmental science, ethics, European history, fine arts, French, geometry, German, government/civics, Greek, history, Latin, Mandarin, marine biology, mathematics, photography, physical education, physics, physiology, religion, science, social sciences, social studies, Spanish, speech, trigonometry, world history, world literature.

Graduation Requirements Arts and fine arts (art, music, dance, drama), classics, computer science, English, foreign language, mathematics, physical education (includes health), religion (includes Bible studies and theology), science, social sciences, social studies (includes history), Christian service hours in junior and senior year.

Special Academic Programs International Baccalaureate program; 17 Advanced Placement exams for which test preparation is offered; honors section; accelerated programs; independent study; study at local college for college credit; study abroad; academic accommodation for the gifted, the musically talented, and the artistically talented.

College Admission Counseling 235 students graduated in 2011; 234 went to college, including Fordham University; Georgetown University; Penn State University Park; Saint Joseph's University; Temple University; University of Pennsylvania. Other: 1 entered a postgraduate year. Mean SAT critical reading: 617, mean SAT math: 612, mean SAT writing: 598, mean combined SAT: 1827. 55% scored over 600 on SAT critical reading, 55% scored over 600 on SAT math, 55% scored over 600 on SAT writing, 55% scored over 1800 on combined SAT.

Student Life Upper grades have specified standards of dress, student council. Discipline rests primarily with faculty. Attendance at religious services is required.

Summer Programs Remediation, enrichment, art/fine arts programs offered; session focuses on pre-8th grade enrichment; held on campus; accepts boys and girls; open to students from other schools. 500 students usually enrolled. 2012 schedule: June 25 to July 25. Application deadline: none.

Tuition and Aid Day student tuition: $18,475. Tuition installment plan (monthly payment plans). Tuition reduction for siblings, merit scholarship grants, need-based scholarship grants, need-based loans, middle-income loans, paying campus jobs available. In 2011–12, 35% of upper-school students received aid; total upper-school merit-scholarship money awarded: $500,000. Total amount of financial aid awarded in 2011–12: $2,000,000.

Admissions Traditional secondary-level entrance grade is 9. For fall 2011, 645 students applied for upper-level admission, 310 were accepted, 258 enrolled. 3-R Achievement Test, High School Placement Test or High School Placement Test (closed version) from Scholastic Testing Service required. Deadline for receipt of application materials: November 18. Application fee required: $75. On-campus interview recommended.

Athletics Interscholastic: baseball, basketball, bowling, crew, cross-country running, football, Frisbee, golf, ice hockey, indoor track & field, lacrosse, rowing, rugby, soccer, squash, swimming and diving, tennis, track and field, ultimate Frisbee, winter (indoor) track, wrestling; intramural: basketball, flag football, juggling, martial arts, table tennis, volleyball, water polo. 35 coaches, 1 athletic trainer.

Computers Computers are regularly used in English, mathematics, science classes. Computer network features include on-campus library services, online commercial services, Internet access, wireless campus network, Internet filtering or blocking technology. Student e-mail accounts and computer access in designated common areas are available to students. Students grades are available online. The school has a published electronic and media policy.

Contact Jason M. Zazyczny, Director of Admission. 215-978-1958. Fax: 215-978-1920. E-mail: jzazyczny@sjprep.org. Web site: www.sjprep.org.

ST. JUDE'S SCHOOL

888 Trillium Drive

Kitchener, Ontario N2R 1K4, Canada

Head of School: Mr. Frederick T. Gore

General Information Coeducational day college-preparatory, arts, and bright learning disabled school; primarily serves underachievers, students with learning disabilities, individuals with Attention Deficit Disorder, and dyslexic students. Grades 1–12. Founded: 1982. Setting: small town. Nearest major city is Toronto, Canada. 10-acre campus. 1 building on campus. Approved or accredited by Ontario Ministry of Education and Ontario Department of Education. Language of instruction: English. Total enrollment: 30. Upper school average class size: 6. Upper school faculty-student ratio: 1:6. There are 200 required school days per year for Upper School students. Upper School students typically attend 5 days per week. The average school day consists of 7 hours.

Upper School Student Profile Grade 10: 2 students (2 boys); Grade 11: 1 student (1 boy).

Faculty School total: 6. In upper school: 3 men, 3 women; 3 have advanced degrees.
Subjects Offered 20th century history, 20th century physics, 20th century world history, accounting, acting, adolescent issues, advanced chemistry, advanced math, algebra, analytic geometry, ancient history, ancient world history, ancient/medieval philosophy, anthropology, applied arts, art, art appreciation, art education, art history, basic skills, biology, bookkeeping, business education, business law, business mathematics, business studies, calculus, Canadian history, Canadian law, Canadian literature, career and personal planning, career education, chemistry, civics, college counseling, communication skills, computer literacy, computer science, computer skills, computer studies, discrete mathematics, dramatic arts, drawing and design, earth and space science, ecology, ecology, environmental systems, economics, economics and history, English, English literature, environmental studies, ESL, family studies, fencing, finite math, general science, geography, health, health education, history, honors algebra, honors English, honors geometry, independent study, intro to computers, keyboarding, law, law studies, marketing, media studies, modern Western civilization, modern world history, philosophy, physical education, physical fitness, remedial study skills, remedial/makeup course work, science, science and technology, society, politics and law, sociology, Spanish, study skills, visual arts, Western philosophy, world issues.
Graduation Requirements Ontario requirements.
Special Academic Programs Remedial reading and/or remedial writing; remedial math; programs in English, mathematics, general development for dyslexic students; special instructional classes for students with learning disabilities, Attention Deficit Disorder, and dyslexia; ESL (2 students enrolled).
College Admission Counseling 5 students graduated in 2011; all went to college, including University of Waterloo; Wilfrid Laurier University.
Student Life Upper grades have uniform requirement, student council, honor system. Discipline rests primarily with faculty.
Summer Programs Session focuses on English and math; held on campus; accepts boys and girls; open to students from other schools. 15 students usually enrolled. 2012 schedule: July 1 to July 30. Application deadline: June 1.
Tuition and Aid Day student tuition: CAN$16,900. Tuition installment plan (monthly payment plans, individually arranged payment plans).
Admissions For fall 2011, 5 students applied for upper-level admission, 5 were accepted, 5 enrolled. Academic Profile Tests, achievement tests, Woodcock Reading Mastery Key Math and Woodcock-Johnson Educational Evaluation, WISC III required. Deadline for receipt of application materials: none. No application fee required. Interview required.
Athletics Interscholastic: synchronized swimming (girls); coed interscholastic: basketball, bowling, cross-country running, fencing, golf; coed intramural: badminton, ball hockey, baseball, basketball, bowling, cross-country running, curling, fencing, fitness, floor hockey, golf, martial arts. 2 PE instructors.
Computers Computers are regularly used in all classes. Computer network features include Internet access, Internet filtering or blocking technology.
Contact Frederick T. Gore, Director of Education. 519-888-0807. Fax: 519-888-0316. E-mail: director@stjudes.com. Web site: www.stjudes.com.

SAINT LUCY'S PRIORY HIGH SCHOOL

655 West Sierra Madre Avenue

Glendora, California 91741-1997

Head of School: Sr. Monica Collins, OSB

General Information Girls' day college-preparatory, arts, religious studies, and technology school, affiliated with Roman Catholic Church. Grades 9–12. Founded: 1962. Setting: suburban. Nearest major city is Pasadena. 14-acre campus. 4 buildings on campus. Approved or accredited by The College Board, Western Association of Schools and Colleges, Western Catholic Education Association, and California Department of Education. Endowment: $2 million. Total enrollment: 696. Upper school average class size: 20. Upper school faculty-student ratio: 1:20. There are 182 required school days per year for Upper School students. Upper School students typically attend 5 days per week. The average school day consists of 6 hours and 45 minutes.
Upper School Student Profile Grade 9: 165 students (165 girls); Grade 10: 187 students (187 girls); Grade 11: 170 students (170 girls); Grade 12: 174 students (174 girls). 80% of students are Roman Catholic.
Faculty School total: 38. In upper school: 6 men, 31 women; 15 have advanced degrees.
Subjects Offered Adolescent issues, advanced math, algebra, art, art appreciation, ASB Leadership, athletics, Bible studies, biology, biology-AP, calculus, calculus-AP, calligraphy, chemistry, child development, Christian ethics, Christian scripture, church history, commercial art, computer art, creative dance, creative writing, dance, drama, drawing, early childhood, economics, English, English language and composition-AP, English literature, English literature-AP, ethics, European history-AP, film studies, French, geometry, health, health education, Hebrew scripture, journalism, kinesiology, library assistant, literary magazine, mechanical drawing, media arts, meditation, modern European history-AP, moral and social development, moral theology, musical productions, painting, physical education, physical science, physics, physiology, psychology, religion, sculpture, sewing, Spanish, Spanish-AP, theater production, trigonometry, U.S. government, U.S. government and politics-AP, U.S. history, U.S. history-AP, voice, world history, yearbook.
Graduation Requirements Arts and fine arts (art, music, dance, drama), English, foreign language, mathematics, physical education (includes health), religion (includes Bible studies and theology), science, social sciences, social studies (includes history).
Special Academic Programs Advanced Placement exam preparation; honors section.
College Admission Counseling 195 students graduated in 2010; all went to college, including Azusa Pacific University; California State Polytechnic University, Pomona; Loyola Marymount University; Mount St. Mary's College; University of California, Irvine; University of California, Riverside. Mean SAT critical reading: 564, mean SAT math: 532, mean SAT writing: 562, mean composite ACT: 25. 40% scored over 600 on SAT critical reading, 20% scored over 600 on SAT math, 35% scored over 600 on SAT writing, 46% scored over 26 on composite ACT.
Student Life Upper grades have uniform requirement, student council. Discipline rests equally with students and faculty. Attendance at religious services is required.
Tuition and Aid Day student tuition: $7100. Tuition installment plan (monthly payment plans, individually arranged payment plans, quarterly payment plan). Tuition reduction for siblings, merit scholarship grants, need-based scholarship grants available. In 2010–11, 5% of upper-school students received aid; total upper-school merit-scholarship money awarded: $15,000. Total amount of financial aid awarded in 2010–11: $90,000.
Admissions STS required. Deadline for receipt of application materials: January 21. Application fee required: $75. On-campus interview required.
Athletics Interscholastic: basketball, cross-country running, drill team, soccer, softball, swimming and diving, tennis, track and field, volleyball, water polo; intramural: badminton, basketball, cheering, dance squad, dance team, physical fitness, soccer, softball. 2 PE instructors, 36 coaches, 1 athletic trainer.
Computers Computers are regularly used in art, drawing and design, English, graphic arts, history, journalism, literary magazine, mathematics, media production, music, psychology, science, yearbook classes. Computer resources include Internet access, wireless campus network, Internet filtering or blocking technology. Campus intranet and computer access in designated common areas are available to students. Students grades are available online.
Contact Mrs. Irma Esparza, Secretary. 626-335-3322. Fax: 626-335-4373. Web site: www.stlucys.com.

ST. MARGARET'S EPISCOPAL SCHOOL

31641 La Novia Avenue

San Juan Capistrano, California 92675

Head of School: Mr. Marcus D. Hurlbut

General Information Coeducational day college preparatory, arts, religious studies, and technology school, affiliated with Episcopal Church. Grades PS–12. Founded: 1979. Setting: suburban. Nearest major city is Los Angeles/San Diego. 21-acre campus. 6 buildings on campus. Approved or accredited by California Association of Independent Schools, National Association of Episcopal Schools, Western Association of Schools and Colleges, and California Department of Education. Member of National Association of Independent Schools. Endowment: $2.4 million. Total enrollment: 1,228. Upper school average class size: 14. Upper school faculty-student ratio: 1:7. There are 176 required school days per year for Upper School students. Upper School students typically attend 5 days per week. The average school day consists of 7 hours and 15 minutes.
Upper School Student Profile Grade 9: 105 students (57 boys, 48 girls); Grade 10: 114 students (52 boys, 62 girls); Grade 11: 108 students (50 boys, 58 girls); Grade 12: 104 students (51 boys, 53 girls). 13% of students are members of Episcopal Church.
Faculty School total: 62. In upper school: 20 men, 21 women; 23 have advanced degrees.
Subjects Offered Algebra, American history, American literature, anatomy and physiology, anthropology, art, art history, art history-AP, art-AP, astronomy, Bible studies, biology, biology-AP, calculus, calculus-AP, chemistry, chemistry-AP, Chinese, community service, computer math, computer programming, computer science, computer science-AP, creative writing, drama, economics, English, English language and composition-AP, English language-AP, English literature, English literature and composition-AP, environmental science, environmental science-AP, ethics, European history, expository writing, fine arts, French, French language-AP, French literature-AP, French-AP, geography, geometry, government-AP, government/civics, history, history-AP, human development, Japanese, Japanese literature, journalism, Latin, Latin-AP, marine science, mathematics, music, music theory-AP, philosophy, physical education, physics, physics-AP, religion, science, social sciences, social studies, Spanish, Spanish language-AP, Spanish literature-AP, Spanish-AP, speech, statistics-AP, theater, trigonometry, world history, world history-AP, world literature, world religions, writing.
Graduation Requirements Arts and fine arts (art, music, dance, drama), computer science, English, foreign language, mathematics, physical education (includes health), religion (includes Bible studies and theology), science, social sciences, social studies (includes history). Community service is required.
Special Academic Programs Advanced Placement exam preparation; honors section; independent study; academic accommodation for the gifted, the musically talented, and the artistically talented.

College Admission Counseling 96 students graduated in 2010; all went to college, including New York University; Northwestern University; Pitzer College; University of California, Berkeley; University of Southern California; University of Washington. Mean SAT critical reading: 610, mean SAT math: 621, mean SAT writing: 638, mean combined SAT: 1869, mean composite ACT: 27.

Student Life Upper grades have specified standards of dress, student council, honor system. Discipline rests equally with students and faculty. Attendance at religious services is required.

Tuition and Aid Day student tuition: $22,100. Tuition installment plan (monthly payment plans). Need-based scholarship grants available. In 2010–11, 26% of upper-school students received aid. Total amount of financial aid awarded in 2010–11: $1,929,690.

Admissions Traditional secondary-level entrance grade is 9. For fall 2010, 62 students applied for upper-level admission, 54 were accepted, 42 enrolled. ISEE required. Deadline for receipt of application materials: February 1. Application fee required: $75. Interview required.

Athletics Interscholastic: aquatics (boys, girls), basketball (b,g), cheering (g), cross-country running (b,g), equestrian sports (b,g), football (b), golf (b,g), lacrosse (b,g), soccer (b,g), swimming and diving (b,g), tennis (b,g), track and field (b,g), volleyball (b,g); coed interscholastic: baseball. 1 PE instructor, 7 coaches, 1 athletic trainer.

Computers Computers are regularly used in English, foreign language, history, mathematics, science, technology classes. Computer network features include on-campus library services, Internet access, wireless campus network, Internet filtering or blocking technology. Campus intranet, student e-mail accounts, and computer access in designated common areas are available to students. Students grades are available online. The school has a published electronic and media policy.

Contact Mrs. Phoebe F. Larson, Director of Admission and Financial Aid. 949-661-0108 Ext. 251. Fax: 949-240-1748. E-mail: phoebe.larson@smes.org. Web site: www.smes.org.

ST. MARGARET'S SCHOOL

444 Water Lane

PO Box 158

Tappahannock, Virginia 22560

Head of School: Margaret R. Broad

General Information Girls' boarding and day college-preparatory, arts, and religious studies school, affiliated with Episcopal Church. Grades 8–12. Founded: 1921. Setting: small town. Nearest major city is Richmond. Students are housed in single-sex dormitories. 51-acre campus. 9 buildings on campus. Approved or accredited by Southern Association of Colleges and Schools, Virginia Association of Independent Schools, and Virginia Department of Education. Member of National Association of Independent Schools and Secondary School Admission Test Board. Endowment: $5.7 million. Total enrollment: 123. Upper school average class size: 8. Upper school faculty-student ratio: 1:6.

Upper School Student Profile Grade 8: 11 students (11 girls); Grade 9: 24 students (24 girls); Grade 10: 31 students (31 girls); Grade 11: 24 students (24 girls); Grade 12: 33 students (33 girls). 80% of students are boarding students. 39% are state residents. 13 states are represented in upper school student body. 28% are international students. International students from China, Japan, Mexico, Republic of Korea, and Viet Nam; 5 other countries represented in student body. 25% of students are members of Episcopal Church.

Faculty School total: 34. In upper school: 8 men, 22 women; 16 have advanced degrees; 30 reside on campus.

Subjects Offered Algebra, American literature, anatomy and physiology, ancient history, art, art history, biology, biology-AP, British literature, calculus, calculus-AP, ceramics, chemistry, chorus, community service, computer science, conceptual physics, creative writing, drama, driver education, ecology, English, English-AP, ESL, European history, finance, fine arts, French, French-AP, geography, geometry, government/civics, health, history, history-AP, illustration, journalism, Latin, leadership, mathematics, music, music history, painting, photography, physical education, physics, piano, pre-algebra, religion, science, social studies, Spanish, U.S. government, world history, world literature, writing.

Graduation Requirements Arts and fine arts (art, music, dance, drama), computer science, English, foreign language, history, mathematics, physical education (includes health), religion (includes Bible studies and theology), science. Community service is required.

Special Academic Programs Advanced Placement exam preparation; honors section; independent study; study abroad; ESL (29 students enrolled).

College Admission Counseling 33 students graduated in 2010; 32 went to college, including Longwood University; Michigan State University; Randolph-Macon College; Rhode Island School of Design; University of Richmond. Other: 1 had other specific plans. Mean SAT critical reading: 533, mean SAT math: 573, mean SAT writing: 563, mean combined SAT: 1669.

Student Life Upper grades have uniform requirement, student council, honor system. Discipline rests equally with students and faculty. Attendance at religious services is required.

Tuition and Aid Day student tuition: $16,800; 7-day tuition and room/board: $43,200. Tuition installment plan (monthly payment plans, Pay in Full, 10-Month Plan). Need-based scholarship grants available. In 2010–11, 37% of upper-school students received aid. Total amount of financial aid awarded in 2010–11: $949,000.

Admissions Traditional secondary-level entrance grade is 9. For fall 2010, 86 students applied for upper-level admission, 75 were accepted, 46 enrolled. SSAT required. Deadline for receipt of application materials: none. Application fee required: $40. On-campus interview required.

Athletics Interscholastic: basketball, crew, cross-country running, field hockey, golf, indoor track & field, lacrosse, soccer, softball, swimming and diving, tennis, volleyball; intramural: ballet, canoeing/kayaking, crew, dance, fitness, fitness walking, horseback riding, kayaking, modern dance, outdoor activities, strength & conditioning, tennis, ultimate Frisbee, walking, weight training, yoga. 1 PE instructor, 7 coaches, 1 athletic trainer.

Computers Computers are regularly used in English, foreign language, history, journalism, science, yearbook classes. Computer network features include on-campus library services, online commercial services, Internet access, wireless campus network, Internet filtering or blocking technology. Campus intranet, student e-mail accounts, and computer access in designated common areas are available to students. The school has a published electronic and media policy.

Contact Kimberly McDowell, Assistant Head, External Affairs/Director of Admission. 804-443-3357. Fax: 804-443-6781. E-mail: admit@sms.com. Web site: www.sms.org.

ST. MARK'S HIGH SCHOOL

2501 Pike Creek Road

Wilmington, Delaware 19808

Head of School: Mark J. Freund

General Information Coeducational day college-preparatory, arts, business, religious studies, and technology school, affiliated with Roman Catholic Church. Grades 9–12. Founded: 1969. Setting: suburban. Nearest major city is Philadelphia, PA. 60-acre campus. 1 building on campus. Approved or accredited by Middle States Association of Colleges and Schools, National Catholic Education Association, and Delaware Department of Education. Member of National Association of Independent Schools. Endowment: $3 million. Total enrollment: 1,100. Upper school average class size: 24. Upper school faculty-student ratio: 1:11. There are 180 required school days per year for Upper School students. Upper School students typically attend 5 days per week. The average school day consists of 6 hours and 25 minutes.

Upper School Student Profile Grade 9: 245 students (125 boys, 120 girls); Grade 10: 260 students (135 boys, 125 girls); Grade 11: 300 students (160 boys, 140 girls); Grade 12: 295 students (140 boys, 155 girls). 80% of students are Roman Catholic.

Faculty School total: 105. In upper school: 47 men, 58 women; 60 have advanced degrees.

Subjects Offered Advanced Placement courses, art, business, computer science, drama, driver education, English, family and consumer science, fine arts, French, general science, German, history, Italian, mathematics, media, music, physical education, reading, religion, science, social studies, Spanish, theater.

Graduation Requirements Arts and fine arts (art, music, dance, drama), English, health education, mathematics, physical education (includes health), religion (includes Bible studies and theology), science, social studies (includes history).

Special Academic Programs 22 Advanced Placement exams for which test preparation is offered; honors section; study at local college for college credit; study abroad; academic accommodation for the gifted; remedial reading and/or remedial writing; remedial math; programs in general development for dyslexic students; special instructional classes for deaf students, blind students, students with learning challenges.

College Admission Counseling 341 students graduated in 2011; 334 went to college, including Neumann University; Penn State University Park; Towson University; University of Delaware; University of Maryland, College Park; West Chester University of Pennsylvania. Other: 6 went to work, 1 entered military service. Median SAT critical reading: 530, median SAT math: 520, median SAT writing: 520, median combined SAT: 1600, median composite ACT: 23. 28% scored over 600 on SAT critical reading, 25% scored over 600 on SAT math, 21% scored over 600 on SAT writing, 22% scored over 1800 on combined SAT, 29% scored over 26 on composite ACT.

Student Life Upper grades have uniform requirement, student council. Discipline rests primarily with faculty. Attendance at religious services is required.

Summer Programs Remediation programs offered; session focuses on skill development and remediation; held on campus; accepts boys and girls; open to students from other schools. 30 students usually enrolled. 2012 schedule: June to July. Application deadline: none.

Tuition and Aid Day student tuition: $9900. Tuition installment plan (monthly payment plans). Merit scholarship grants, need-based scholarship grants, full academic scholarships for gifted students available. In 2011–12, 25% of upper-school students received aid; total upper-school merit-scholarship money awarded: $50,000. Total amount of financial aid awarded in 2011–12: $1,000,000.

Admissions Traditional secondary-level entrance grade is 9. For fall 2011, 380 students applied for upper-level admission, 375 were accepted, 275 enrolled. High School

Placement Test or STS required. Deadline for receipt of application materials: none. Application fee required: $100.

Athletics Interscholastic: baseball (boys), basketball (b,g), cheering (g), crew (b,g), cross-country running (b,g), dance team (g), field hockey (g), football (b), ice hockey (b), indoor track & field (b,g), lacrosse (b,g), soccer (b,g), softball (g), swimming and diving (b,g), tennis (b,g), track and field (b,g), volleyball (b,g), wrestling (b); coed interscholastic: golf; coed intramural: bowling, Frisbee, ultimate Frisbee. 4 PE instructors, 6 coaches, 1 athletic trainer.

Computers Computers are regularly used in all classes. Computer network features include on-campus library services, online commercial services, Internet access, wireless campus network, Internet filtering or blocking technology, PowerSchool system for parents to monitor child's progress. Campus intranet is available to students. Students grades are available online. The school has a published electronic and media policy.

Contact Mrs. Clarice G. Kwasnieski, Director of Admissions. 302-757-8723. Fax: 302-738-5132. E-mail: ckwasnieski@stmarkshs.net. Web site: www.stmarkshs.net.

SAINT MARK'S SCHOOL

25 Marlborough Road

Southborough, Massachusetts 01772

Head of School: Mr. John Warren

General Information Coeducational boarding and day college-preparatory, arts, religious studies, technology, and classics, math school, affiliated with Episcopal Church. Grades 9–12. Founded: 1865. Setting: suburban. Nearest major city is Boston. Students are housed in single-sex dormitories. 250-acre campus. 15 buildings on campus. Approved or accredited by New England Association of Schools and Colleges and Massachusetts Department of Education. Member of National Association of Independent Schools and Secondary School Admission Test Board. Endowment: $108 million. Total enrollment: 340. Upper school average class size: 12. Upper school faculty-student ratio: 1:5. There are 160 required school days per year for Upper School students. Upper School students typically attend 6 days per week. The average school day consists of 5 hours and 40 minutes.

Upper School Student Profile Grade 9: 73 students (41 boys, 32 girls); Grade 10: 88 students (45 boys, 43 girls); Grade 11: 86 students (47 boys, 39 girls); Grade 12: 93 students (53 boys, 40 girls). 78% of students are boarding students. 58% are state residents. 17 states are represented in upper school student body. 18% are international students. International students from Canada, China, Japan, Republic of Korea, Saudi Arabia, and Taiwan; 10 other countries represented in student body. 30% of students are members of Episcopal Church.

Faculty School total: 75. In upper school: 41 men, 34 women; 52 have advanced degrees; all reside on campus.

Subjects Offered 20th century history, Advanced Placement courses, algebra, American history, American literature, art, art history, biology, calculus, ceramics, chemistry, civil war history, computer math, computer science, computer science-AP, computer skills, computer studies, constitutional history of U.S., creative writing, DNA, drama, drama workshop, earth science, Eastern religion and philosophy, English, English literature, environmental science, ethics, European history, expository writing, fine arts, French, geography, geometry, German, government/civics, Greek, history, Latin, Latin-AP, logic, mathematics, music, music history, music theory, music theory-AP, music-AP, photography, physics, physiology, psychology, religion, science, social studies, Spanish, Spanish language-AP, Spanish literature, Spanish literature-AP, statistics, studio art, studio art-AP, theater, trigonometry, world history, world literature.

Graduation Requirements Arts and fine arts (art, music, dance, drama), English, foreign language, mathematics, religion (includes Bible studies and theology), science, social studies (includes history).

Special Academic Programs 23 Advanced Placement exams for which test preparation is offered; honors section; independent study; term-away projects; study abroad; academic accommodation for the gifted, the musically talented, and the artistically talented.

College Admission Counseling 86 students graduated in 2010; all went to college, including Colby College; Georgetown University; Massachusetts Institute of Technology; Tufts University; University of Pennsylvania; Villanova University. Median SAT critical reading: 635, median SAT math: 680, median SAT writing: 655, median combined SAT: 1970.

Student Life Upper grades have specified standards of dress, student council, honor system. Discipline rests equally with students and faculty. Attendance at religious services is required.

Tuition and Aid Day student tuition: $36,000; 7-day tuition and room/board: $45,100. Tuition installment plan (Key Tuition Payment Plan, monthly payment plans). Need-based scholarship grants available. In 2010–11, 28% of upper-school students received aid. Total amount of financial aid awarded in 2010–11: $3,500,000.

Admissions Traditional secondary-level entrance grade is 9. For fall 2010, 654 students applied for upper-level admission, 252 were accepted, 106 enrolled. SSAT and TOEFL required. Deadline for receipt of application materials: January 31. Application fee required: $50. Interview required.

Athletics Interscholastic: baseball (boys), basketball (b,g), crew (b,g), cross-country running (b,g), field hockey (g), Fives (b), football (b), golf (b,g), ice hockey (b,g), lacrosse (b,g), soccer (b,g), softball (g), squash (b,g), tennis (b,g), volleyball (g), wrestling (b); intramural: aerobics/dance (g), volleyball (b,g), weight lifting (b,g); coed interscholastic: dance; coed intramural: aerobics, aerobics/Nautilus, billiards, outdoor activities, yoga. 15 coaches, 2 athletic trainers.

Computers Computers are regularly used in English, foreign language, mathematics, science classes. Computer network features include on-campus library services, Internet access, wireless campus network, Internet filtering or blocking technology. Student e-mail accounts and computer access in designated common areas are available to students. The school has a published electronic and media policy.

Contact Anne E. Behnke, Director of Admission. 508-786-6000. Fax: 508-786-6120. E-mail: annebehnke@stmarksschool.org. Web site: www.stmarksschool.org.

ST. MARK'S SCHOOL OF TEXAS

10600 Preston Road

Dallas, Texas 75230-4000

Head of School: Mr. Arnold E. Holtberg

General Information Boys' day college-preparatory, arts, technology, and advanced placement school. Grades 1–12. Founded: 1906. Setting: urban. 40-acre campus. 13 buildings on campus. Approved or accredited by Independent Schools Association of the Southwest. Member of National Association of Independent Schools and Secondary School Admission Test Board. Endowment: $106.8 million. Total enrollment: 852. Upper school average class size: 14. Upper school faculty-student ratio: 1:8. There are 172 required school days per year for Upper School students. Upper School students typically attend 5 days per week. The average school day consists of 7 hours and 55 minutes.

Upper School Student Profile Grade 9: 96 students (96 boys); Grade 10: 94 students (94 boys); Grade 11: 94 students (94 boys); Grade 12: 90 students (90 boys).

Faculty School total: 104. In upper school: 39 men, 19 women; 50 have advanced degrees.

Subjects Offered 3-dimensional art, acting, algebra, American history-AP, ancient world history, art, art history, astronomy, Basic programming, biology, biology-AP, calculus, calculus-AP, ceramics, chemistry, chemistry-AP, Chinese, choir, community service, computer programming, computer science, computer science-AP, concert band, creative writing, digital art, digital photography, DNA, DNA science lab, drama, drama workshop, economics, economics-AP, English, English literature and composition-AP, English literature-AP, environmental science-AP, European history, European history-AP, fine arts, geology, geometry, German-AP, history, honors English, honors geometry, independent study, Japanese, journalism, Latin, Latin-AP, macroeconomics-AP, mathematics, microeconomics-AP, modern European history-AP, modern world history, music, photography, physical education, physics, physics-AP, pottery, psychology, science, senior project, Spanish, Spanish language-AP, Spanish literature-AP, statistics-AP, studio art-AP, theater, trigonometry, U.S. history, video film production, woodworking, world history, world religions.

Graduation Requirements Arts and fine arts (art, music, dance, drama), English, foreign language, mathematics, physical education (includes health), science, social studies (includes history), senior exhibition. Community service is required.

Special Academic Programs Advanced Placement exam preparation; honors section; independent study; term-away projects; academic accommodation for the gifted.

College Admission Counseling 83 students graduated in 2011; all went to college, including Duke University; Southern Methodist University; Texas A&M University; The University of Texas at Austin; University of Pennsylvania; University of Southern California. Median SAT critical reading: 690, median SAT math: 740, median SAT writing: 670, median combined SAT: 2130, median composite ACT: 32. 81% scored over 600 on SAT critical reading, 94% scored over 600 on SAT math, 76% scored over 600 on SAT writing, 87% scored over 1800 on combined SAT, 97% scored over 26 on composite ACT.

Student Life Upper grades have uniform requirement, student council, honor system. Discipline rests primarily with faculty. Attendance at religious services is required.

Tuition and Aid Day student tuition: $23,636–$25,186. Tuition installment plan (Insured Tuition Payment Plan, individually arranged payment plans, financial aid student monthly payment plan). Need-based scholarship grants, tuition remission for sons of faculty and staff, need-based middle-income financial aid available. In 2011–12, 17% of upper-school students received aid. Total amount of financial aid awarded in 2011–12: $1,194,576.

Admissions Traditional secondary-level entrance grade is 9. For fall 2011, 103 students applied for upper-level admission, 13 were accepted, 10 enrolled. ISEE required. Deadline for receipt of application materials: January 9. Application fee required: $125. Interview required.

Athletics Interscholastic: backpacking, baseball, basketball, cheering, climbing, crew, cross-country running, diving, fencing, football, golf, hiking/backpacking, hockey, ice hockey, lacrosse, outdoor education, outdoor skills, physical fitness, physical training, soccer, strength & conditioning, swimming and diving, tennis, track and field, volleyball, wall climbing, water polo, weight training, wilderness, winter soccer, wrestling; intramural: basketball, bicycling, cooperative games, cross-country running, fitness, flag football, floor hockey, jump rope, kickball, lacrosse, physical fitness, physical training, soccer, softball, swimming and diving, table tennis, team handball, tennis, track and field, volleyball, water polo, weight training, winter soccer, wrestling. 8 PE instructors, 9 coaches, 2 athletic trainers.

Computers Computers are regularly used in English, foreign language, humanities, mathematics, science classes. Computer network features include on-campus library services, online commercial services, Internet access, wireless campus network, Internet filtering or blocking technology. Student e-mail accounts are available to students. The school has a published electronic and media policy.

Contact Mr. David P. Baker, Director of Admission and Financial Aid. 214-346-8700. Fax: 214-346-8701. E-mail: admission@smtexas.org. Web site: www.smtexas.org.

See Display below and Close-Up on page 672.

ST. MARTIN'S EPISCOPAL SCHOOL

225 Green Acres Road

Metairie, Louisiana 70003

Head of School: Rev. Dr. Walter J. Baer

General Information Coeducational day college-preparatory school, affiliated with Episcopal Church. Grades PK–12. Founded: 1947. Setting: suburban. Nearest major city is New Orleans. 18-acre campus. 13 buildings on campus. Approved or accredited by Independent Schools Association of the Southwest, National Association of Episcopal Schools, Southern Association of Colleges and Schools, Southwest Association of Episcopal Schools, The College Board, and Louisiana Department of Education. Member of National Association of Independent Schools. Endowment: $6.4 million. Total enrollment: 515. Upper school average class size: 17. Upper school faculty-student ratio: 1:8. There are 180 required school days per year for Upper School students. Upper School students typically attend 5 days per week. The average school day consists of 5 hours and 30 minutes.

Upper School Student Profile Grade 9: 54 students (32 boys, 22 girls); Grade 10: 66 students (34 boys, 32 girls); Grade 11: 61 students (34 boys, 27 girls); Grade 12: 54 students (32 boys, 22 girls). 11.2% of students are members of Episcopal Church.

Faculty School total: 67. In upper school: 14 men, 19 women; 23 have advanced degrees.

Subjects Offered Advanced chemistry, advanced math, Advanced Placement courses, advanced studio art-AP, algebra, American history, American history-AP, American literature, American literature-AP, art, art history, band, baseball, basketball, bell choir, Bible studies, biology, biology-AP, calculus, calculus-AP, career education internship, career/college preparation, ceramics, cheerleading, chemistry, chemistry-AP, Chinese studies, chorus, civics, college counseling, community garden, community service, computer literacy, creative writing, digital photography, drama, earth science, economics, economics and history, economics-AP, English, English language and composition-AP, English literature, English literature and composition-AP, English literature-AP, environmental science, ethics, European history-AP, film studies, fine arts, French, French-AP, geography, geology, geometry, grammar, history-AP, honors algebra, honors English, honors geometry, humanities, internship, jazz ensemble, journalism, lab science, Latin, Latin-AP, life management skills, life skills, literary magazine, Mandarin, mathematics, Middle East, model United Nations, music, music appreciation, musical productions, newspaper, philosophy, physical education, physics, pre-algebra, publications, religion, SAT preparation, science, scripture, senior internship, social studies, softball, Southern literature, Spanish, Spanish-AP, speech, statistics-AP, student government, studio art, studio art-AP, swimming, tennis, theater, theater design and production, theology, track and field, trigonometry, U.S. history-AP, volleyball, world history, world literature, world religions, writing.

Graduation Requirements Arts and fine arts (art, music, dance, drama), electives, English, foreign language, life skills, mathematics, physical education (includes health), religion (includes Bible studies and theology), science, senior internship, social studies (includes history), senior intern program, 50 hours of community service.

Special Academic Programs 10 Advanced Placement exams for which test preparation is offered; honors section; independent study.

College Admission Counseling 42 students graduated in 2011; all went to college, including Harvard University; Louisiana State University and Agricultural and Mechanical College; Loyola University New Orleans; Princeton University; The University of Texas at Austin; Tulane University. Median SAT critical reading: 560, median SAT math: 590, median SAT writing: 585, median combined SAT: 1720, median composite ACT: 26. 35% scored over 600 on SAT critical reading, 47.5% scored over 600 on SAT math, 45% scored over 600 on SAT writing, 42.5% scored over 1800 on combined SAT, 48.8% scored over 26 on composite ACT.

Student Life Upper grades have specified standards of dress, student council, honor system. Discipline rests primarily with faculty. Attendance at religious services is required.

Summer Programs Remediation, enrichment, advancement, sports, art/fine arts, computer instruction programs offered; session focuses on academics, athletics, creative arts, and enrichment; held on campus; accepts boys and girls; open to students from other schools. 477 students usually enrolled. 2012 schedule: June 1 to August 7. Application deadline: May 15.

Tuition and Aid Day student tuition: $17,750. Tuition installment plan (local bank-arranged plan). Merit scholarship grants, need-based scholarship grants available. In 2011–12, 36% of upper-school students received aid; total upper-school merit-scholarship money awarded: $214,250. Total amount of financial aid awarded in 2011–12: $700,925.

Admissions Traditional secondary-level entrance grade is 9. For fall 2011, 33 students applied for upper-level admission, 29 were accepted, 17 enrolled. CTP, ISEE, WISC III or other aptitude measures; standardized achievement test or writing sample required.

Deadline for receipt of application materials: none. Application fee required: $50. On-campus interview required.

Athletics Interscholastic: baseball (boys), basketball (b,g), cheering (b,g), cross-country running (b,g), flag football (b), football (b), golf (b,g), running (b,g), soccer (b,g), softball (g), swimming and diving (b,g), tennis (b,g), track and field (b,g), volleyball (g); intramural: basketball (b,g), cheering (b,g), cross-country running (b,g), golf (b,g), ropes courses (b,g), running (b,g), soccer (b,g), swimming and diving (b,g), tennis (b,g), track and field (b,g), volleyball (g); coed interscholastic: cheering; coed intramural: cheering. 5 PE instructors, 4 coaches, 1 athletic trainer.

Computers Computers are regularly used in all academic classes. Computer network features include on-campus library services, online commercial services, Internet access, wireless campus network, Internet filtering or blocking technology, VPN for teachers, staff, and students. Campus intranet, student e-mail accounts, and computer access in designated common areas are available to students. Students grades are available online. The school has a published electronic and media policy.

Contact Mrs. Mary White, Assistant Director of Admission. 504-736-9918. Fax: 504-736-8802. E-mail: mary.white@stmsaints.com. Web site: www.stmsaints.com.

SAINT MARY'S COLLEGE HIGH SCHOOL

1294 Albina Avenue

Peralta Park

Berkeley, California 94706

Head of School: Dr. Peter Imperial

General Information Coeducational day college-preparatory school, affiliated with Roman Catholic Church. Grades 9–12. Founded: 1863. Setting: urban. Nearest major city is Oakland. 13-acre campus. 9 buildings on campus. Approved or accredited by National Catholic Education Association, Western Association of Schools and Colleges, and Western Catholic Education Association. Endowment: $4.2 million. Total enrollment: 625. Upper school average class size: 28. Upper school faculty-student ratio: 1:16. There are 180 required school days per year for Upper School students. Upper School students typically attend 5 days per week. The average school day consists of 6 hours and 50 minutes.

Upper School Student Profile Grade 9: 160 students (79 boys, 81 girls); Grade 10: 165 students (86 boys, 79 girls); Grade 11: 146 students (65 boys, 81 girls); Grade 12: 148 students (73 boys, 75 girls). 51% of students are Roman Catholic.

Faculty School total: 44. In upper school: 26 men, 16 women; 26 have advanced degrees.

Subjects Offered Algebra, American history, American literature, art, band, biology, biology-AP, calculus-AP, chemistry, chorus, conceptual physics, concert band, dance, diversity studies, economics, English, English language and composition-AP, English literature, English literature and composition-AP, finite math, forensics, French, French language-AP, geometry, government-AP, government/civics, graphic design, health education, jazz band, math analysis, mathematics, philosophy, photography, physical education, physics, physics-AP, psychology, religion, scripture, Spanish, Spanish language-AP, sports medicine, studio art-AP, theater, trigonometry, U.S. government and politics-AP, U.S. history-AP, world history, world history-AP, world religions, world religions, yearbook.

Graduation Requirements Electives, English, foreign language, health and wellness, lab science, mathematics, physical education (includes health), religious studies, U.S. history, visual and performing arts, world history, service learning, enrichment week mini-course (once a year).

Special Academic Programs 13 Advanced Placement exams for which test preparation is offered; honors section.

College Admission Counseling 146 students graduated in 2011; 142 went to college, including California State University, Monterey Bay; California State University, Sacramento; Saint Mary's College of California; San Francisco State University; University of California, Berkeley; University of California, Santa Cruz. Other: 4 had other specific plans.

Student Life Upper grades have specified standards of dress, student council, honor system. Discipline rests primarily with faculty. Attendance at religious services is required.

Summer Programs Remediation programs offered; held on campus; accepts boys and girls; not open to students from other schools. 50 students usually enrolled.

Tuition and Aid Day student tuition: $17,500. Tuition installment plan (monthly payment plans). Merit scholarship grants, need-based scholarship grants available. In 2011–12, 42% of upper-school students received aid; total upper-school merit-scholarship money awarded: $10,000. Total amount of financial aid awarded in 2011–12: $2,220,840.

Admissions Traditional secondary-level entrance grade is 9. For fall 2011, 413 students applied for upper-level admission, 327 were accepted, 167 enrolled. High School Placement Test and writing sample required. Deadline for receipt of application materials: January 5. Application fee required: $85. Interview required.

Athletics Interscholastic: baseball (boys), basketball (b,g), cross-country running (b,g), football (b), golf (b,g), lacrosse (b), soccer (b,g), softball (g), tennis (b,g), track and field (b,g), volleyball (b,g); coed interscholastic: cheering, diving, swimming and diving; coed intramural: basketball. 1 PE instructor, 45 coaches, 1 athletic trainer.

Computers Computers are regularly used in all academic, art, college planning, graphic arts, yearbook classes. Computer network features include on-campus library services, online commercial services, Internet access, wireless campus network, Internet filtering or blocking technology. Student e-mail accounts are available to students. Students grades are available online. The school has a published electronic and media policy.

Contact Lawrence Puck, Director of Admissions. 510-559-6235. Fax: 510-559-6277. E-mail: lpuck@stmchs.org. Web site: www.saintmaryschs.org.

ST. MARY'S EPISCOPAL SCHOOL

60 Perkins Extended

Memphis, Tennessee 38117-3199

Head of School: Ms. Marlene R. Shaw

General Information Girls' day college-preparatory, arts, religious studies, technology, and global issues school, affiliated with Episcopal Church. Grades PK–12. Founded: 1847. Setting: urban. 25-acre campus. 8 buildings on campus. Approved or accredited by National Association of Episcopal Schools, Southern Association of Colleges and Schools, Southern Association of Independent Schools, The College Board, and Tennessee Department of Education. Member of National Association of Independent Schools. Endowment: $17.5 million. Total enrollment: 845. Upper school average class size: 13. Upper school faculty-student ratio: 1:13. There are 175 required school days per year for Upper School students. Upper School students typically attend 5 days per week. The average school day consists of 6 hours and 40 minutes.

Upper School Student Profile Grade 9: 53 students (53 girls); Grade 10: 57 students (57 girls); Grade 11: 64 students (64 girls); Grade 12: 60 students (60 girls). 15% of students are members of Episcopal Church.

Faculty School total: 105. In upper school: 9 men, 25 women; 27 have advanced degrees.

Subjects Offered Algebra, anatomy and physiology, art history, art history-AP, biology, biology-AP, calculus, calculus-AP, chamber groups, chemistry, chemistry-AP, choir, comparative religion, economics, English, English language and composition-AP, English literature and composition-AP, ethics, French, French-AP, geography, geometry, global issues, guitar, health, humanities, instrumental music, Latin, Latin-AP, Mandarin, microbiology, music theory-AP, performing arts, physical education, physics, physics-AP, pre-calculus, psychology, religion, robotics, Spanish, Spanish-AP, speech, studio art, studio art-AP, technology, theater, U.S. government, U.S. history, U.S. history-AP, wind ensemble, world history, world history-AP.

Graduation Requirements 1 1/2 elective credits, algebra, arts and fine arts (art, music, dance, drama), biology, calculus, chemistry, English, English language-AP, English literature-AP, foreign language, geometry, physical education (includes health), physics, pre calculus, religion (includes Bible studies and theology), social studies (includes history), U.S. history, world history.

Special Academic Programs 15 Advanced Placement exams for which test preparation is offered; honors section; independent study; academic accommodation for the gifted, the musically talented, and the artistically talented.

College Admission Counseling 59 students graduated in 2011; all went to college, including Samford University; The University of Tennessee; University of Mississippi; University of Virginia; Vanderbilt University; Washington and Lee University. Median SAT critical reading: 680, median SAT math: 650, median SAT writing: 710, median combined SAT: 2020, median composite ACT: 31. 64% scored over 600 on SAT critical reading, 64% scored over 600 on SAT math, 75% scored over 600 on SAT writing, 68% scored over 1800 on combined SAT, 76% scored over 26 on composite ACT.

Student Life Upper grades have specified standards of dress, student council, honor system. Discipline rests equally with students and faculty. Attendance at religious services is required.

Summer Programs Enrichment, sports, art/fine arts programs offered; session focuses on summer enrichment; held both on and off campus; held at predominantly held on the school campus. Swimming component at a neighborhood pool; accepts boys and girls; open to students from other schools. 578 students usually enrolled. 2012 schedule: June 6 to August 12. Application deadline: none.

Tuition and Aid Day student tuition: $17,010. Tuition installment plan (monthly payment plans, credit card payment). Need-based scholarship grants, discounts for children of faculty, staff, and clergy available. In 2011–12, 20% of upper-school students received aid. Total amount of financial aid awarded in 2011–12: $318,600.

Admissions Traditional secondary-level entrance grade is 9. For fall 2011, 23 students applied for upper-level admission, 19 were accepted, 7 enrolled. ISEE and writing sample required. Deadline for receipt of application materials: none. Application fee required: $75. On-campus interview required.

Athletics Interscholastic: basketball, bowling, cross-country running, dance team, golf, lacrosse, soccer, softball, swimming and diving, tennis, track and field, volleyball. 1 PE instructor, 7 coaches, 1 athletic trainer.

Computers Computers are regularly used in all academic, career exploration, college planning, creative writing, library, literary magazine, music, newspaper, research skills, SAT preparation, speech, theater arts, yearbook classes. Computer network features include on-campus library services, Internet access, wireless campus network, Internet filtering or blocking technology, online database services for research available at school and at home. Campus intranet, student e-mail accounts, and computer access in designated common areas are available to students. Students grades are available online. The school has a published electronic and media policy.

Contact Ms. Nicole Hernandez, Director of Admission and Financial Aid. 901-537-1405. Fax: 901-685-1098. E-mail: nhernandez@stmarysschool.org. Web site: www.stmarysschool.org.

SAINT MARY'S HALL

9401 Starcrest Drive

San Antonio, Texas 78217

Head of School: Mr. Bob Windham

General Information Coeducational day college-preparatory and arts school. Grades PK–12. Founded: 1879. Setting: suburban. 60-acre campus. 14 buildings on campus. Approved or accredited by Independent Schools Association of the Southwest. Member of National Association of Independent Schools and Secondary School Admission Test Board. Endowment: $31.7 million. Total enrollment: 990. Upper school average class size: 15. Upper school faculty-student ratio: 1:6. There are 173 required school days per year for Upper School students. Upper School students typically attend 5 days per week. The average school day consists of 7 hours and 15 minutes.

Upper School Student Profile Grade 9: 94 students (47 boys, 47 girls); Grade 10: 104 students (44 boys, 60 girls); Grade 11: 94 students (47 boys, 47 girls); Grade 12: 93 students (40 boys, 53 girls).

Faculty School total: 102. In upper school: 29 men, 20 women; 37 have advanced degrees.

Subjects Offered 3-dimensional art, Advanced Placement courses, algebra, American history-AP, American literature, anatomy and physiology, art, art history, art history-AP, art-AP, athletic training, ballet, baseball, basketball, biology, biology-AP, British literature, calculus, calculus-AP, cell biology, ceramics, chemistry, chemistry-AP, choir, college counseling, composition, computer science, computer science-AP, concert choir, creative writing, dance, digital photography, directing, drama, drawing, drawing and design, economics, economics-AP, English language and composition-AP, English literature and composition-AP, environmental science-AP, European history, European history-AP, fitness, French, French language-AP, genetics, geology, geometry, golf, government/civics, great books, guitar, health, human geography - AP, jazz band, Latin, Latin-AP, literary magazine, marine biology, model United Nations, music theory, painting, photography, physical education, physics, physics-AP, piano, pre-calculus, religious studies, science research, sculpture, set design, softball, Spanish, Spanish language-AP, Spanish literature-AP, speech, statistics-AP, swimming, technical theater, tennis, track and field, U.S. history, voice, volleyball, Web site design, world geography, world history, world literature, world religions, yearbook, zoology.

Graduation Requirements Arts and fine arts (art, music, dance, drama), athletics, electives, English, foreign language, mathematics, physical education (includes health), science, social studies (includes history), 40 hours of community service.

Special Academic Programs 25 Advanced Placement exams for which test preparation is offered; honors section; independent study; study abroad.

College Admission Counseling 79 students graduated in 2011; all went to college, including Harvard University; Southern Methodist University; The University of Texas at Austin; Trinity University; University of Southern California; Vanderbilt University. Median SAT critical reading: 630, median SAT math: 644, median SAT writing: 651.

Student Life Upper grades have uniform requirement, student council, honor system. Discipline rests primarily with faculty. Attendance at religious services is required.

Summer Programs Enrichment, sports, art/fine arts, computer instruction programs offered; held on campus; accepts boys and girls; open to students from other schools. 837 students usually enrolled. 2012 schedule: June 1 to August 5. Application deadline: May 13.

Tuition and Aid Day student tuition: $20,435. Tuition installment plan (monthly payment plans, individually arranged payment plans, full-year payment plan, 2-payment plan, monthly payment plan). Merit scholarship grants, need-based scholarship grants available. In 2011–12, 22% of upper-school students received aid; total upper-school merit-scholarship money awarded: $538,960. Total amount of financial aid awarded in 2011–12: $621,990.

Admissions Traditional secondary-level entrance grade is 9. For fall 2011, 133 students applied for upper-level admission, 79 were accepted, 47 enrolled. ISEE required. Deadline for receipt of application materials: November 14. Application fee required: $50. Interview required.

Athletics Interscholastic: ballet (boys, girls), baseball (b), basketball (b,g), cheering (g), dance (b,g), field hockey (g), fitness (b,g), football (b), golf (b,g), independent competitive sports (b,g), lacrosse (b), soccer (b,g), softball (g), volleyball (b,g); coed interscholastic: cross-country running, physical fitness, physical training, strength & conditioning, tennis, track and field, weight training. 14 coaches, 2 athletic trainers.

Computers Computers are regularly used in media arts classes. Computer network features include on-campus library services, Internet access, wireless campus network, Internet filtering or blocking technology, SmartBoards. Student e-mail accounts are available to students. Students grades are available online. The school has a published electronic and media policy.

Contact Mrs. Julie Hellmund, Director of Admission. 210-483-9234. Fax: 210-655-5211. E-mail: jhellmund@smhall.org. Web site: www.smhall.org.

SAINT MARY'S HIGH SCHOOL

2525 North Third Street

Phoenix, Arizona 85004

Head of School: Mrs. Suzanne M. Fessler

General Information Coeducational day college-preparatory, general academic, arts, and religious studies school, affiliated with Roman Catholic Church. Grades 9–12. Founded: 1917. Setting: urban. 6-acre campus. 5 buildings on campus. Approved or accredited by North Central Association of Colleges and Schools, Western Catholic Education Association, and Arizona Department of Education. Endowment: $1 million. Total enrollment: 501. Upper school average class size: 27. Upper school faculty-student ratio: 1:17. There are 180 required school days per year for Upper School students. Upper School students typically attend 5 days per week. The average school day consists of 6 hours and 45 minutes.

Upper School Student Profile Grade 9: 137 students (70 boys, 67 girls); Grade 10: 113 students (44 boys, 69 girls); Grade 11: 134 students (61 boys, 73 girls); Grade 12: 117 students (65 boys, 52 girls). 80% of students are Roman Catholic.

Faculty School total: 32. In upper school: 13 men, 19 women; 23 have advanced degrees.

Subjects Offered Advanced Placement courses, algebra, American government, American history, American history-AP, American literature, art, band, biology, British literature, British literature (honors), calculus-AP, Catholic belief and practice, chemistry, chorus, Christian and Hebrew scripture, composition, computer graphics, conceptual physics, dance, drama, economics, electives, English, English composition, English language and composition-AP, English literature, English literature and composition-AP, fine arts, foreign language, French, geometry, health, history, history of the Catholic Church, honors algebra, honors English, honors geometry, honors U.S. history, intro to computers, journalism, Life of Christ, personal finance, physical education, physical science, physics, prayer/spirituality, pre-algebra, pre-calculus, religious education, remedial study skills, social studies, Spanish, Spanish language-AP, standard curriculum, state government, state history, theology, trigonometry, U.S. government and politics-AP, world geography, world history, world religions, yearbook.

Graduation Requirements Advanced math, algebra, American government, American history, American literature, anatomy and physiology, arts and fine arts (art, music, dance, drama), biology, British literature, Catholic belief and practice, chemistry, Christian and Hebrew scripture, composition, economics, electives, English, foreign language, geometry, health education, history of the Catholic Church, language and composition, physical education (includes health), physics, pre-calculus, theology, trigonometry, world history, world literature, 90 hours of Christian community service, 4 credtis of Catholic Theology courses.

Special Academic Programs 6 Advanced Placement exams for which test preparation is offered; honors section; study at local college for college credit; remedial reading and/or remedial writing; remedial math.

College Admission Counseling 162 students graduated in 2011; 156 went to college, including Arizona State University; Grand Canyon University; Northern Arizona University; The University of Arizona. Other: 4 went to work, 2 entered military service. Mean SAT critical reading: 473, mean SAT math: 467, mean SAT writing: 453, mean composite ACT: 21. 7% scored over 600 on SAT critical reading, 9% scored over 600 on SAT math, 4% scored over 600 on SAT writing, 11% scored over 26 on composite ACT.

Student Life Upper grades have uniform requirement, student council. Discipline rests primarily with faculty. Attendance at religious services is required.

Summer Programs Remediation, enrichment, advancement, sports, art/fine arts programs offered; session focuses on high school preparation for incoming freshmen; held on campus; accepts boys and girls; open to students from other schools. 200 students usually enrolled. 2012 schedule: June 5 to July 13. Application deadline: May 11.

Tuition and Aid Day student tuition: $8715–$11,235. Tuition installment plan (FACTS Tuition Payment Plan, monthly payment plans, individually arranged payment plans, quarterly and semester payment plans). Need-based scholarship grants, paying campus jobs available. In 2011–12, 70% of upper-school students received aid. Total amount of financial aid awarded in 2011–12: $1,500,000.

Admissions Traditional secondary-level entrance grade is 9. For fall 2011, 150 students applied for upper-level admission, 145 were accepted, 140 enrolled. High School Placement Test required. Deadline for receipt of application materials: none. Application fee required: $300. On-campus interview required.

Athletics Interscholastic: baseball (boys), basketball (b,g), cheering (g), football (b), golf (b,g), physical fitness (b,g), pom squad (g), soccer (b,g), softball (g), strength & conditioning (b,g), tennis (b,g), volleyball (b,g), weight training (b,g), winter soccer (b,g); intramural: dance (g); coed interscholastic: cross-country running, physical fitness, strength & conditioning, swimming and diving, track and field, weight training; coed intramural: bowling. 3 PE instructors, 20 coaches, 1 athletic trainer.

Computers Computers are regularly used in computer applications, graphics, journalism, newspaper, Web site design, yearbook classes. Computer resources include on-campus library services, Internet access, Internet filtering or blocking technology. Students grades are available online. The school has a published electronic and media policy.

Contact Mr. Robert D. Rogers. 602-251-2515. Fax: 602-251-2595. E-mail: rrogers@smknights.org. Web site: www.smknights.org.

SAINT MARY'S HIGH SCHOOL

113 Duke of Gloucester Street

Annapolis, Maryland 21401

Head of School: Mr. Richard Bayhan

General Information Coeducational day college-preparatory, arts, religious studies, bilingual studies, and technology school, affiliated with Roman Catholic Church. Grades 9–12. Founded: 1946. Setting: small town. 5-acre campus. 3 buildings on campus. Approved or accredited by Southern Association of Independent Schools and Maryland Department of Education. Total enrollment: 480. Upper school average class size: 25. Upper school faculty-student ratio: 1:15. Upper School students typically attend 5 days per week. The average school day consists of 6 hours and 25 minutes.

Upper School Student Profile 80% of students are Roman Catholic.

Faculty School total: 41. In upper school: 17 men, 24 women.

Subjects Offered Accounting, algebra, American government, American literature, art, art history, art history-AP, biology, biology-AP, British literature, calculus-AP, Catholic belief and practice, chemistry, chemistry-AP, Christian scripture, Christianity, cinematography, computer applications, creative writing, current events, drama, economics, environmental science, European history-AP, fiction, forensics, French, geography, geometry, health, integrated mathematics, interdisciplinary studies, Irish literature, Latin, literature and composition-AP, math analysis, mathematics, mechanical drawing, microbiology, musical theater, peace and justice, physical education, physical science, physics, physics-AP, pre-calculus, psychology, public speaking, relationships, religion, religion and culture, senior project, Shakespeare, social justice, sociology, Spanish, sports conditioning, studio art, trigonometry, U.S. government and politics-AP, U.S. history, U.S. history-AP, weight training, world arts, world history, world literature, writing, zoology.

Graduation Requirements Arts and fine arts (art, music, dance, drama), computers, English, foreign language, mathematics, physical education (includes health), religion (includes Bible studies and theology), science, social studies (includes history).

Special Academic Programs Advanced Placement exam preparation; honors section; study at local college for college credit; study abroad; academic accommodation for the gifted.

College Admission Counseling 130 students graduated in 2011; all went to college, including United States Naval Academy; University of Maryland, College Park; Washington College. Mean combined SAT: 1675.

Student Life Upper grades have uniform requirement, student council, honor system. Discipline rests primarily with faculty. Attendance at religious services is required.

Tuition and Aid Day student tuition: $13,200. Tuition installment plan (monthly payment plans). Merit scholarship grants, need-based scholarship grants available. In 2011–12, 25% of upper-school students received aid; total upper-school merit-scholarship money awarded: $30,000. Total amount of financial aid awarded in 2011–12: $250,000.

Admissions Traditional secondary-level entrance grade is 9. For fall 2011, 265 students applied for upper-level admission, 175 were accepted, 110 enrolled. High School Placement Test required. Deadline for receipt of application materials: January 6. Application fee required: $75.

Athletics Interscholastic: baseball (boys), basketball (b,g), cross-country running (b,g), dance team (g), field hockey (g), football (b), golf (b,g), lacrosse (b,g), soccer (b,g), swimming and diving (b,g), tennis (b,g), track and field (b,g), volleyball (g), wrestling (b); intramural: crew (g); coed interscholastic: weight training; coed intramural: dance team, fishing, Frisbee, sailing, yoga. 2 PE instructors, 56 coaches, 1 athletic trainer.

Computers Computers are regularly used in all classes. Computer network features include on-campus library services, online commercial services, Internet access, wireless campus network. The school has a published electronic and media policy.

Contact Mrs. Chrissie Chomo, Director of Admissions. 410-990-4236. Fax: 410-269-7843. E-mail: cchomo@stmarysannapolis.org. Web site: www.stmarysannapolis.org.

ST. MARY'S PREPARATORY SCHOOL

3535 Indian Trail

Orchard Lake, Michigan 48324

Head of School: James Glowacki

General Information Boys' boarding and day college-preparatory school, affiliated with Roman Catholic Church; primarily serves students with learning disabilities and individuals with Attention Deficit Disorder. Grades 9–12. Founded: 1885. Setting: suburban. Nearest major city is Detroit. Students are housed in single-sex dormitories. 80-acre campus. 12 buildings on campus. Approved or accredited by Michigan Association of Non-Public Schools and Michigan Department of Education. Total enrollment: 480. Upper school average class size: 18. Upper school faculty-student ratio: 1:10. There are 185 required school days per year for Upper School students. Upper School students typically attend 5 days per week. The average school day consists of 7 hours.

Upper School Student Profile Grade 9: 122 students (122 boys); Grade 10: 123 students (123 boys); Grade 11: 102 students (102 boys); Grade 12: 126 students (126 boys). 15% of students are boarding students. 80% are state residents. 5 states are represented in upper school student body. 15% are international students. International students from Brazil, China, Poland, Republic of Korea, Russian Federation, and Taiwan. 80% of students are Roman Catholic.

Faculty School total: 58. In upper school: 43 men, 15 women; 16 have advanced degrees; 6 reside on campus.

Subjects Offered Algebra, American history, American literature, art, band, Bible studies, biology, business, business skills, calculus, chemistry, Chinese, computer programming, computer science, creative writing, drafting, driver education, earth science, ecology, economics, English, English literature, expository writing, fine arts, French, geometry, government/civics, grammar, health, history, journalism, law, mathematics, music technology, mythology, physical education, physics, Polish, psychology, religion, robotics, science, social sciences, social studies, Spanish, speech, theology, trigonometry, world history, writing.

Graduation Requirements Arts and fine arts (art, music, dance, drama), business skills (includes word processing), computer science, English, foreign language, mathematics, physical education (includes health), religion (includes Bible studies and theology), science, social sciences, social studies (includes history).

Special Academic Programs Advanced Placement exam preparation; honors section; study at local college for college credit; academic accommodation for the musically talented and the artistically talented; programs in general development for dyslexic students; special instructional classes for students with learning disabilities, Attention Deficit Disorder, and dyslexia; ESL (60 students enrolled).

College Admission Counseling 115 students graduated in 2011; 114 went to college, including Michigan State University; Oakland University; University of Detroit Mercy; University of Michigan; Wayne State University; Western Michigan University. Other: 1 entered military service. Median SAT critical reading: 503, median SAT math: 600, median SAT writing: 510, median combined SAT: 1613, median composite ACT: 25. 5% scored over 600 on SAT critical reading, 15% scored over 600 on SAT math, 40% scored over 26 on composite ACT.

Student Life Upper grades have specified standards of dress, student council, honor system. Discipline rests primarily with faculty. Attendance at religious services is required.

Summer Programs Remediation, sports programs offered; session focuses on football, basketball, and lacrosse; held on campus; accepts boys and girls; open to students from other schools. 400 students usually enrolled. 2012 schedule: June to August. Application deadline: June.

Tuition and Aid Day student tuition: $9800; 5-day tuition and room/board: $20,000; 7-day tuition and room/board: $22,000. Tuition installment plan (FACTS Tuition Payment Plan, individually arranged payment plans). Tuition reduction for siblings, merit scholarship grants, need-based scholarship grants available. In 2011–12, 80% of upper-school students received aid.

Admissions Traditional secondary-level entrance grade is 9. For fall 2011, 250 students applied for upper-level admission, 180 were accepted, 130 enrolled. STS and TOEFL required. Deadline for receipt of application materials: none. Application fee required: $35. Interview recommended.

Athletics Interscholastic: alpine skiing, baseball, basketball, crew, cross-country running, football, freestyle skiing, golf, hockey, ice hockey, indoor track, indoor track & field, jogging, lacrosse, rowing, skiing (downhill), soccer, track and field, wrestling; intramural: aerobics/Nautilus, aquatics, basketball, bicycling, billiards, bowling, broomball, fitness, Frisbee, golf, hockey, ice hockey, ice skating, indoor hockey, indoor soccer, indoor track, jogging, lacrosse, mountain biking, Nautilus, physical fitness, physical training, rowing, running, skeet shooting, skiing (downhill), snowboarding, soccer, strength & conditioning, swimming and diving, table tennis, tennis, weight lifting, weight training, whiffle ball. 2 PE instructors, 25 coaches, 3 athletic trainers.

Computers Computers are regularly used in desktop publishing, drafting, engineering, yearbook classes. Computer network features include on-campus library services, Internet access, Internet filtering or blocking technology. Campus intranet and student e-mail accounts are available to students. Students grades are available online.

Contact Candace Knight, Dean of Admissions. 248-683-0514. Fax: 248-683-1740. E-mail: cknight@stmarysprep.com. Web site: www.stmarysprep.com/.

SAINT MARY'S SCHOOL

900 Hillsborough Street

Raleigh, North Carolina 27603-1689

Head of School: Ms. Theo W. Coonrod

General Information Girls' boarding and day college-preparatory, arts, religious studies, and technology school, affiliated with Episcopal Church. Grades 9–12. Founded: 1842. Setting: urban. Students are housed in single-sex dormitories. 23-acre campus. 26 buildings on campus. Approved or accredited by National Association of Episcopal Schools, North Carolina Association of Independent Schools, Southern Association of Colleges and Schools, Southern Association of Independent Schools, and The Association of Boarding Schools. Member of National Association of Independent Schools and Secondary School Admission Test Board. Total enrollment: 247. Upper school average class size: 12. Upper school faculty-student ratio: 1:8. Upper School students typically attend 5 days per week. The average school day consists of 7 hours.

Upper School Student Profile Grade 9: 56 students (56 girls); Grade 10: 57 students (57 girls); Grade 11: 61 students (61 girls); Grade 12: 73 students (73 girls). 45% of students are boarding students. 78% are state residents. 12 states are represented in upper school student body. 9% are international students. International students from China, Republic of Korea, Spain, United Kingdom, and Viet Nam. 20% of students are members of Episcopal Church.

Faculty School total: 40. In upper school: 10 men, 30 women; 30 have advanced degrees; 36 reside on campus.

Subjects Offered 3-dimensional art, acting, advanced chemistry, advanced math, Advanced Placement courses, algebra, American government, American history, American history-AP, American literature, anatomy, art, astronomy, athletics, ballet, biology, biology-AP, calculus, calculus-AP, ceramics, chemistry, chemistry-AP, choir, choral music, computer science, dance, drama, drama performance, drawing, drawing and design, earth science, ecology, English, English literature, English literature-AP, European history, French, French language-AP, geometry, government, government-AP, government/civics, honors English, honors geometry, honors U.S. history, honors world history, Latin, Latin-AP, mathematics, philosophy, physical education, physics, physics-AP, piano, psychology-AP, religion, senior project, Spanish, Spanish language-AP, speech, U.S. government and politics-AP, U.S. history, U.S. history-AP, Western civilization, world literature, yearbook, yoga.

Graduation Requirements Algebra, arts and fine arts (art, music, dance, drama), biology, electives, English, foreign language, geometry, government, physical education (includes health), physical science, religion (includes Bible studies and theology), social sciences, U.S. history, Western civilization.

Special Academic Programs Advanced Placement exam preparation; honors section; independent study; study at local college for college credit; study abroad.

College Admission Counseling 88 students graduated in 2011; all went to college, including Clemson University; Elon University; North Carolina State University; The University of North Carolina at Chapel Hill; University of Georgia; University of South Carolina.

Student Life Upper grades have specified standards of dress, student council, honor system. Discipline rests equally with students and faculty. Attendance at religious services is required.

Summer Programs Enrichment, sports, art/fine arts, computer instruction programs offered; held on campus; accepts girls; open to students from other schools.

Tuition and Aid Day student tuition: $18,300; 7-day tuition and room/board: $39,144. Tuition installment plan (FACTS Tuition Payment Plan, monthly payment plans). Need-based scholarship grants available. In 2011–12, 42% of upper-school students received aid. Total amount of financial aid awarded in 2011–12: $150,200.

Admissions Traditional secondary-level entrance grade is 9. SSAT and TOEFL required. Deadline for receipt of application materials: none. Application fee required: $100. Interview required.

Athletics Interscholastic: basketball, cross-country running, field hockey, golf, lacrosse, soccer, softball, swimming and diving, tennis, track and field, volleyball; intramural: ballet, dance, dance team, modern dance. 2 PE instructors, 32 coaches, 1 athletic trainer.

Computers Computers are regularly used in dance, English, foreign language, history, introduction to technology, mathematics, newspaper, publications, science, senior seminar, writing, yearbook classes. Computer network features include on-campus library services, online commercial services, Internet access, wireless campus network, Internet filtering or blocking technology. Student e-mail accounts are available to students. Students grades are available online. The school has a published electronic and media policy.

Contact Mrs. Elizabeth Lynnes, Manager of Admission Systems and Data. 919-424-4100. Fax: 919-424-4122. E-mail: admission@sms.edu. Web site: www.sms.edu.

ST. MARY'S SCHOOL

816 Black Oak Drive

Medford, Oregon 97504-8504

Head of School: Mr. Frank Phillips

General Information Coeducational boarding and day college-preparatory, arts, religious studies, and ESL school, affiliated with Roman Catholic Church. Boarding grades 9–12, day grades 6–12. Founded: 1865. Setting: small town. Nearest major city is Eugene. Students are housed in single-sex by floor dormitories. 23-acre campus. 9 buildings on campus. Approved or accredited by National Catholic Education Association, Northwest Association of Schools and Colleges, Pacific Northwest Association of Independent Schools, and Oregon Department of Education. Member of National Association of Independent Schools. Total enrollment: 433. Upper school average class size: 18. Upper school faculty-student ratio: 1:11. There are 180 required school days per year for Upper School students. Upper School students typically attend 5 days per week. The average school day consists of 7 hours and 15 minutes.

Upper School Student Profile Grade 9: 66 students (22 boys, 44 girls); Grade 10: 76 students (37 boys, 39 girls); Grade 11: 81 students (45 boys, 36 girls); Grade 12: 76 students (36 boys, 40 girls). 15% of students are boarding students. 85% are state residents. 2 states are represented in upper school student body. 15% are international students. International students from China, Israel, Mexico, and Republic of Korea; 4 other countries represented in student body. 35% of students are Roman Catholic.

Faculty School total: 48. In upper school: 22 men, 26 women; 21 have advanced degrees; 2 reside on campus.

Subjects Offered Adolescent issues, Advanced Placement courses, algebra, American history, American history-AP, American literature, ancient history, art, art history-AP, biology, biology-AP, calculus-AP, chamber groups, chemistry, chemistry-AP, chorus, community service, computer programming-AP, computer science, creative writing, drama, earth science, economics-AP, English, English-AP, environmental science-AP, ESL, ethics, European history, European history-AP, expository writing, fine arts, general science, geometry, German, government/civics, government/civics-AP, grammar, health, history, human geography - AP, instrumental music, jazz band, Latin, Latin-AP, mathematics, music theory-AP, physical education, physics, physics-AP, religion, science, social sciences, social studies, Spanish, Spanish-AP, speech, studio art-AP, theater, trigonometry, world history, world literature, writing.

Graduation Requirements Arts and fine arts (art, music, dance, drama), electives, English, foreign language, mathematics, physical education (includes health), religion (includes Bible studies and theology), science, social sciences, social studies (includes history), 100 hours of community service (25 each year in Upper School).

Special Academic Programs 18 Advanced Placement exams for which test preparation is offered; independent study; study at local college for college credit; academic accommodation for the gifted, the musically talented, and the artistically talented; ESL (35 students enrolled).

College Admission Counseling 77 students graduated in 2011; 76 went to college, including Oregon State University; Portland State University; Santa Clara University; University of Oregon; University of Portland; University of San Diego. Other: 1 went to work. Mean SAT critical reading: 598, mean SAT math: 586, mean SAT writing: 597, mean combined SAT: 1781.

Student Life Upper grades have specified standards of dress, student council, honor system. Discipline rests equally with students and faculty. Attendance at religious services is required.

Summer Programs Enrichment, advancement, sports programs offered; session focuses on enrichment and SAT prep; held on campus; accepts boys and girls; open to students from other schools. 75 students usually enrolled. 2012 schedule: July 1 to August 27. Application deadline: none.

Tuition and Aid Day student tuition: $11,800. Tuition installment plan (monthly payment plans, annual payment plans). Need-based scholarship grants available. In 2011–12, 47% of upper-school students received aid. Total amount of financial aid awarded in 2011–12: $650,000.

Admissions Traditional secondary-level entrance grade is 9. For fall 2011, 178 students applied for upper-level admission, 158 were accepted. Deadline for receipt of application materials: February 15. Application fee required: $50. Interview required.

Athletics Interscholastic: baseball (boys), basketball (b,g), combined training (b,g), cross-country running (b,g), football (b), golf (b,g), independent competitive sports (b,g), soccer (b,g), softball (g), tennis (b,g), track and field (b,g), volleyball (g); intramural: alpine skiing (b,g), canoeing/kayaking (b,g), equestrian sports (b,g), flag football (g), hiking/backpacking (b,g); coed interscholastic: martial arts; coed intramural: backpacking, fitness, floor hockey, outdoor adventure, skiing (cross-country), strength & conditioning, tennis, weight lifting. 2 PE instructors.

Computers Computers are regularly used in English, history, mathematics, science, speech classes. Computer network features include on-campus library services, online commercial services, Internet access, wireless campus network, Internet filtering or blocking technology, access to homework, daily bulletins, and teachers via email, Wifi. Campus intranet and computer access in designated common areas are available to students. Students grades are available online. The school has a published electronic and media policy.

Contact Rebecca Naumes, Director of Admissions. 541-773-7877. Fax: 541-772-8973. E-mail: admissions@smschool.us. Web site: www.smschool.us.

SAINT MAUR INTERNATIONAL SCHOOL

83 Yamate-cho, Naka-ku

Yokohama 231-8654, Japan

Head of School: Jeanette K. Thomas

General Information Coeducational day college-preparatory, general academic, arts, religious studies, technology, and science school, affiliated with Roman Catholic Church. Grades PK–12. Founded: 1872. Setting: urban. 1-hectare campus. 7 buildings on campus. Approved or accredited by Council of International Schools, East Asia Regional Council of Schools, International Baccalaureate Organization, Ministry of Education, Japan, and New England Association of Schools and Colleges. Language of instruction: English. Total enrollment: 380. Upper school average class size: 15. Upper school faculty-student ratio: 1:4. There are 175 required school days per year for Upper School students. Upper School students typically attend 5 days per week. The average school day consists of 5 hours and 30 minutes.

Upper School Student Profile Grade 9: 32 students (14 boys, 18 girls); Grade 10: 20 students (10 boys, 10 girls); Grade 11: 27 students (12 boys, 15 girls); Grade 12: 25 students (8 boys, 17 girls). 25% of students are Roman Catholic.

Faculty School total: 61. In upper school: 18 men, 16 women; 21 have advanced degrees.

Subjects Offered 20th century history, art, Asian studies, biology, calculus-AP, chemistry, computer science, drama, drama performance, economics, economics-AP, English, fine arts, French, geography, information technology, Japanese, Japanese history, mathematics, music, music performance, physical education, physics, psychology, religious education, religious studies, robotics, science, social studies, Spanish, theory of knowledge, TOEFL preparation, visual arts, world history.

Graduation Requirements Arts and fine arts (art, music, dance, drama), English, foreign language, mathematics, physical education (includes health), religion (includes Bible studies and theology), science, social studies (includes history), graduation requirements for IB diploma differ.

Special Academic Programs International Baccalaureate program; 11 Advanced Placement exams for which test preparation is offered; independent study; academic accommodation for the gifted, the musically talented, and the artistically talented; ESL (49 students enrolled).

College Admission Counseling 39 students graduated in 2011; all went to college, including International Christian University; King's College, University of London; McGill University; Syracuse University; The University of British Columbia; University of Washington. Median combined SAT: 1620. Mean SAT critical reading: 506, mean SAT math: 610, mean SAT writing: 534. 22% scored over 1800 on combined SAT.

Student Life Upper grades have uniform requirement, student council. Discipline rests primarily with faculty. Attendance at religious services is required.

Summer Programs Enrichment, advancement, ESL, sports, art/fine arts, computer instruction programs offered; session focuses on TOEFL and SAT preparation; held both on and off campus; held at various off-campus locations; accepts boys and girls; open to students from other schools. 60 students usually enrolled. 2012 schedule: June 18 to July 6. Application deadline: May 15.

Tuition and Aid Day student tuition: ¥2,045,000.

Admissions For fall 2011, 27 students applied for upper-level admission, 24 were accepted, 24 enrolled. School's own test required. Deadline for receipt of application materials: none. Application fee required: ¥20,000. On-campus interview required.

Athletics Interscholastic: baseball (boys), basketball (b,g), cross-country running (b,g), soccer (b,g), volleyball (g); intramural: soccer (b); coed interscholastic: table tennis; coed intramural: hiking/backpacking, tennis. 2 PE instructors.

Computers Computers are regularly used in computer applications, economics, English, foreign language, French, geography, information technology, mathematics, media, music, SAT preparation, science, social studies, Spanish classes. Computer network features include on-campus library services, Internet access, wireless campus network, Internet filtering or blocking technology. Campus intranet and computer access in designated common areas are available to students. Students grades are available online. The school has a published electronic and media policy.

Contact Jeanette K. Thomas, School Head. 81-(0) 45-641-5751. Fax: 81-(0) 45-641-6688. E-mail: jthomas@stmaur.ac.jp. Web site: www.stmaur.ac.jp.

ST. MICHAEL'S COLLEGE SCHOOL

1515 Bathurst Street

Toronto, Ontario M5P 3H4, Canada

Head of School: Fr. Joseph Redican, CSB

General Information Boys' day college-preparatory and religious studies school, affiliated with Roman Catholic Church. Grades 7–12. Founded: 1852. Setting: urban. 10-acre campus. 2 buildings on campus. Approved or accredited by Ontario Ministry of Education and Ontario Department of Education. Member of Secondary School Admission Test Board. Language of instruction: English. Total enrollment: 1,054. Upper school average class size: 24. Upper school faculty-student ratio: 1:16. There are 184 required school days per year for Upper School students. Upper School students typically attend 5 days per week. The average school day consists of 6 hours and 10 minutes.

Upper School Student Profile Grade 9: 222 students (222 boys); Grade 10: 222 students (222 boys); Grade 11: 226 students (226 boys); Grade 12: 192 students (192 boys). 90% of students are Roman Catholic.

Faculty School total: 73. In upper school: 59 men, 13 women; 20 have advanced degrees.

Subjects Offered Advanced Placement courses, all academic, American history, anatomy and physiology, ancient history, art, biology, calculus, calculus-AP, Canadian geography, Canadian history, Canadian law, Canadian literature, career and personal planning, career education, chemistry, civics, computer multimedia, economics, English, English composition, English literature, finite math, French, functions, geography, history, history-AP, Italian, Latin, leadership, mathematics, media arts, modern Western civilization, outdoor education, physical education, religion, science, Spanish, theology, world religions.

Special Academic Programs Advanced Placement exam preparation.

College Admission Counseling 196 students graduated in 2011; all went to college, including Queen's University at Kingston; The University of Western Ontario; University of Guelph; University of Toronto; University of Waterloo; York University.

Student Life Upper grades have uniform requirement, student council, honor system. Discipline rests primarily with faculty. Attendance at religious services is required.

Tuition and Aid Day student tuition: CAN$16,050. Tuition installment plan (monthly payment plans, individually arranged payment plans, all up front-$300 discount, three monthly installments (March, June, August)-$100 discount). Bursaries, merit scholarship grants, need-based scholarship grants available. In 2011–12, 16% of upper-school students received aid; total upper-school merit-scholarship money awarded: CAN$105,000. Total amount of financial aid awarded in 2011–12: CAN$1,700,000.

Admissions Traditional secondary-level entrance grade is 9. For fall 2011, 235 students applied for upper-level admission, 171 were accepted, 130 enrolled. SSAT required. Deadline for receipt of application materials: none. Application fee required: CAN$100.

Athletics Interscholastic: alpine skiing, aquatics, archery, badminton, baseball, basketball, cross-country running, football, golf, ice hockey, lacrosse, mountain biking, nordic skiing, skiing (cross-country), skiing (downhill), snowboarding, soccer, softball, swimming and diving, tennis, track and field, volleyball; intramural: archery, badminton, ball hockey, basketball, flag football, ice hockey, indoor soccer, outdoor education, power lifting, soccer.

Computers Computers are regularly used in all academic, media arts classes. Computer network features include on-campus library services, Internet access, wireless campus network, Internet filtering or blocking technology. Student e-mail accounts are available to students. The school has a published electronic and media policy.

Contact Ms. Marilyn Furgiuele, Admissions Assistant. 416-653-3180 Ext. 438. Fax: 416-653-7704. E-mail: furgiuele@smcsmail.com. Web site: www.stmichaelscollegeschool.com.

ST. MICHAEL'S PREPARATORY SCHOOL OF THE NORBERTINE FATHERS

19292 El Toro Road

Silverado, California 92676-9710

Head of School: Rev. Gabriel D. Stack, OPRAEM

General Information Boys' boarding college-preparatory and religious studies school, affiliated with Roman Catholic Church. Grades 9–12. Founded: 1961. Setting: suburban. Nearest major city is Los Angeles. Students are housed in single-sex dormitories. 35-acre campus. 4 buildings on campus. Approved or accredited by National Catholic Education Association, Western Association of Schools and Colleges, and California Department of Education. Total enrollment: 62. Upper school average class size: 10. Upper school faculty-student ratio: 1:3. Upper School students typically attend 5 days per week. The average school day consists of 7 hours.

Upper School Student Profile Grade 9: 21 students (21 boys); Grade 10: 19 students (19 boys); Grade 11: 14 students (14 boys); Grade 12: 8 students (8 boys). 100% of students are boarding students. 90% are state residents. 4 states are represented in upper school student body. 4% are international students. International students from Hong Kong and Spain; 2 other countries represented in student body. 98% of students are Roman Catholic.

Faculty School total: 20. In upper school: 18 men, 2 women; 18 have advanced degrees; 13 reside on campus.

Subjects Offered Algebra, American history, American history-AP, American literature, ancient history, art history, Bible studies, biology, calculus-AP, chemistry, chorus, economics, economics-AP, English, English literature, ethics, fine arts, geography, geometry, government-AP, government/civics, Greek, health, history, Latin, Latin-AP, mathematics, philosophy, physical education, physical science, physics, pre-calculus, religion, science, social studies, Spanish, Spanish-AP, theology, trigonometry, world literature.

Graduation Requirements Arts and fine arts (art, music, dance, drama), English, foreign language, mathematics, physical education (includes health), religion (includes Bible studies and theology), science, social studies (includes history), Senior Matura.

Special Academic Programs Advanced Placement exam preparation; honors section; independent study; ESL (1 student enrolled).

College Admission Counseling 11 students graduated in 2011; all went to college, including California State Polytechnic University, Pomona; California State University, Fullerton; California State University, Long Beach; Thomas Aquinas College; University of California, Davis; University of Notre Dame. Mean SAT critical reading: 514, mean SAT math: 530.

Student Life Upper grades have uniform requirement, student council, honor system. Discipline rests equally with students and faculty. Attendance at religious services is required.

Tuition and Aid 5-day tuition and room/board: $17,900. Tuition installment plan (FACTS Tuition Payment Plan, monthly payment plans, individually arranged payment plans). Need-based scholarship grants available. Total amount of financial aid awarded in 2011–12: $350,000.

Admissions Traditional secondary-level entrance grade is 9. High School Placement Test required. Deadline for receipt of application materials: June 30. Application fee required: $100. Interview required.

Athletics Interscholastic: baseball, basketball, cross-country running, football, soccer; intramural: field hockey, outdoor activities, swimming and diving, table tennis, volleyball, weight lifting. 1 PE instructor, 2 coaches.

Computers Computers are regularly used in English, mathematics, science classes. Computer resources include on-campus library services, Internet access, Internet filtering or blocking technology. Computer access in designated common areas is available to students. Students grades are available online.

Contact Mrs. Pamela M. Christian, School Secretary. 949-858-0222 Ext. 237. Fax: 949-858-7365. E-mail: admissions@stmichaelsprep.org. Web site: www.stmichaelsprep.org.

ST. MICHAELS UNIVERSITY SCHOOL

3400 Richmond Road

Victoria, British Columbia V8P 4P5, Canada

Head of School: Robert T. Snowden

General Information Coeducational boarding and day college-preparatory and arts school, affiliated with Church of England (Anglican). Boarding grades 8–12, day grades K–12. Founded: 1906. Setting: suburban. Students are housed in coed dormitories. 20-acre campus. 12 buildings on campus. Approved or accredited by Canadian Association of Independent Schools, Canadian Educational Standards Institute, Pacific Northwest Association of Independent Schools, The Association of Boarding Schools, and British Columbia Department of Education. Language of instruction: English. Endowment: CAN$5 million. Total enrollment: 934. Upper school average class size: 20. Upper school faculty-student ratio: 1:10.

Upper School Student Profile Grade 9: 142 students (54 boys, 88 girls); Grade 10: 145 students (78 boys, 67 girls); Grade 11: 158 students (93 boys, 65 girls); Grade 12: 169 students (76 boys, 93 girls). 42% of students are boarding students. 78% are province residents. 9 provinces are represented in upper school student body. 20% are international students. International students from China, Germany, Mexico, Republic of Korea, Taiwan, and United States; 16 other countries represented in student body. 15% of students are members of Church of England (Anglican).

Faculty School total: 87. In upper school: 40 men, 20 women; 23 have advanced degrees; 15 reside on campus.

Subjects Offered Advanced Placement courses, algebra, art, art history, biology, calculus, career and personal planning, chemistry, computer programming, computer science, creative writing, drama, earth science, economics, English, English literature, environmental science, ESL, European history, fine arts, French, geography, geology, geometry, history, Japanese, mathematics, music, physical education, physics, science, social studies, Spanish, theater, trigonometry.

Graduation Requirements Arts and fine arts (art, music, dance, drama), career and personal planning, computer science, English, foreign language, mathematics, physical education (includes health), science, social studies (includes history), 30 hours of work experience.

Special Academic Programs Advanced Placement exam preparation; honors section; accelerated programs; term-away projects; study abroad; ESL (40 students enrolled).

College Admission Counseling 160 students graduated in 2010; all went to college, including McGill University; Queen's University at Kingston; Simon Fraser University; The University of British Columbia; University of Toronto; University of Victoria. Mean SAT critical reading: 574, mean SAT math: 653.

Student Life Upper grades have uniform requirement, student council, honor system. Discipline rests primarily with faculty. Attendance at religious services is required.

Tuition and Aid Day student tuition: CAN$10,460–CAN$13,000; 7-day tuition and room/board: CAN$28,650–CAN$45,240. Tuition installment plan (Insured Tuition Payment Plan, monthly payment plans, 2-payment plan). Tuition reduction for siblings, bursaries, merit scholarship grants, need-based scholarship grants available. In 2010–11, 10% of upper-school students received aid; total upper-school merit-scholarship money awarded: CAN$100,000. Total amount of financial aid awarded in 2010–11: CAN$620,000.

Admissions Traditional secondary-level entrance grade is 9. For fall 2010, 381 students applied for upper-level admission, 260 were accepted, 210 enrolled. Naglieri Nonverbal School Ability Test, OLSAT, Stanford Achievement Test, SLEP, SSAT, Stanford Achievement Test, Otis-Lennon School Ability Test, Stanford Achievement Test, Otis-Lennon School Ability Test, school's own exam or writing sample required. Deadline for receipt of application materials: none. Application fee required: CAN$250. On-campus interview required.

Athletics Interscholastic: badminton (boys, girls), basketball (b,g), bicycling (b,g), crew (b,g), cricket (b,g), cross-country running (b,g), field hockey (g), rowing (b,g), rugby (b), running (b,g), soccer (b,g), squash (b,g), swimming and diving (b,g), tennis (b,g), track and field (b,g), volleyball (b,g); intramural: aerobics/dance (g), rugby (b,g), squash (b,g), strength & conditioning (b,g), volleyball (b,g); coed interscholastic: badminton, golf, rowing, running, squash; coed intramural: aerobics, aerobics/dance, aerobics/Nautilus, alpine skiing, aquatics, backpacking, badminton, ball hockey, basketball, bowling, canoeing/kayaking, climbing, cricket, cross-country running, dance, dance team, equestrian sports, fitness, floor hockey, fly fishing, hiking/backpacking, ice skating, indoor soccer, kayaking, martial arts, mountain biking, Nautilus, outdoor activities, outdoor education, outdoor skills, physical training, rock climbing, sailing, skiing (downhill), snowboarding, soccer, softball, squash, strength & conditioning, swimming and diving, triathlon, ultimate Frisbee, volleyball, wall climbing, weight lifting, weight training, yoga. 5 PE instructors.

Computers Computers are regularly used in English, foreign language, humanities, library, mathematics, science, social sciences, writing, yearbook classes. Computer network features include on-campus library services, Internet access.

Contact Ms. Maurine McKay, Admissions Assistant. 250-370-6170. Fax: 250-519-7502. E-mail: admissions@smus.bc.ca. Web site: www.smus.bc.ca.

ST. PATRICK CATHOLIC HIGH SCHOOL

18300 St. Patrick Road

Biloxi, Mississippi 39532

Head of School: Mr. Bobby Trosclair

General Information Coeducational day college-preparatory and religious studies school, affiliated with Roman Catholic Church. Grades 7–12. Founded: 2007. Setting: suburban. 32-acre campus. 7 buildings on campus. Approved or accredited by Southern Association of Colleges and Schools and Mississippi Department of Education. Endowment: $400,000. Total enrollment: 474. Upper school average class size: 20. Upper school faculty-student ratio: 1:14. There are 180 required school days per year for Upper School students. Upper School students typically attend 5 days per week. The average school day consists of 6 hours and 45 minutes.

Upper School Student Profile Grade 7: 75 students (38 boys, 37 girls); Grade 8: 102 students (52 boys, 50 girls); Grade 9: 82 students (45 boys, 37 girls); Grade 10: 72 students (37 boys, 35 girls); Grade 11: 73 students (37 boys, 36 girls); Grade 12: 70 students (35 boys, 35 girls). 80% of students are Roman Catholic.

Faculty In upper school: 15 men, 20 women; 18 have advanced degrees.

Subjects Offered Accounting, advanced chemistry, advanced computer applications, advanced math, Advanced Placement courses, algebra, American government, American history, American literature, analytic geometry, anatomy and physiology, art, athletics, band, baseball, Basic programming, basketball, biology, British literature, business applications, business law, calculus, calculus-AP, campus ministry, Catholic belief and practice, cheerleading, chemistry, chemistry-AP, choral music, Christian and Hebrew scripture, church history, civics, college counseling, college placement, college planning, composition-AP, computer applications, creative writing, desktop publishing, drama, driver education, earth science, economics, English, English literature and composition-AP, environmental science, French, geometry, global studies, health, introduction to theater, journalism, keyboarding, law, Life of Christ, marching band, marine biology, marine science, oral communications, physical education, physical science, pre-algebra, pre-calculus, probability and statistics, psychology, softball, Spanish, track and field, trigonometry, U.S. government, U.S. history, U.S. history-AP, volleyball, Web site design, weight fitness, weight training, weightlifting, wood processing, world geography, world history, yearbook.

Graduation Requirements Algebra, American history, American literature, art, biology, British literature, cell biology, chemistry, computer applications, English literature, foreign language, physical education (includes health), state history, U.S. government, U.S. history, world geography, world history, world literature.

Special Academic Programs Advanced Placement exam preparation; study at local college for college credit; remedial reading and/or remedial writing.

College Admission Counseling 72 students graduated in 2011; 71 went to college, including Louisiana State University and Agricultural and Mechanical College; Millsaps College; Mississippi State University; University of Mississippi; University of South Alabama; University of Southern Mississippi. Other: 1 went to work. Mean SAT critical reading: 576, mean SAT math: 619, mean SAT writing: 640, mean composite ACT: 24. 38% scored over 600 on SAT critical reading, 75% scored over 600 on SAT math, 63% scored over 600 on SAT writing, 41% scored over 26 on composite ACT.

Student Life Upper grades have uniform requirement, student council, honor system. Discipline rests primarily with faculty. Attendance at religious services is required.

Tuition and Aid Day student tuition: $5900. Tuition installment plan (monthly payments through local bank). Tuition reduction for siblings, need-based scholarship grants available. In 2011–12, 4% of upper-school students received aid. Total amount of financial aid awarded in 2011–12: $176,590.

Admissions Traditional secondary-level entrance grade is 7. For fall 2011, 402 students applied for upper-level admission, 400 were accepted, 396 enrolled. Deadline for receipt of application materials: none. No application fee required. Interview required.

Athletics Interscholastic: baseball (boys), basketball (b,g), cheering (g), cross-country running (b,g), dance team (g), football (b), golf (b,g), power lifting (b,g), soccer (b,g), softball (g), swimming and diving (b,g), tennis (b,g), track and field (b,g), volleyball (g), weight lifting (b,g), weight training (b,g); intramural: bicycling (b,g); coed interscholastic: sailing; coed intramural: sailing. 3 PE instructors, 18 coaches, 1 athletic trainer.

Computers Computers are regularly used in accounting, business applications, business education, computer applications, desktop publishing, mathematics, newspaper, Web site design, word processing, yearbook classes. Computer network features include on-campus library services, Internet access, Internet filtering or blocking technology. Campus intranet and computer access in designated common areas are available to students. Students grades are available online.

Contact Renee McDaniel, Vice Principal. 228-702-0500. Fax: 228-702-0511. E-mail: rmcdaniel@stpatrickhighschool.net. Web site: www.stpatrickhighschool.net.

SAINT PATRICK HIGH SCHOOL

5900 West Belmont Avenue

Chicago, Illinois 60634

Head of School: Br. Konrad Diebold

General Information Boys' day college-preparatory, arts, and religious studies school, affiliated with Roman Catholic Church. Grades 9–12. Founded: 1861. Setting: urban. 1 building on campus. Approved or accredited by Christian Brothers Association, National Catholic Education Association, North Central Association of Colleges and Schools, and Illinois Department of Education. Endowment: $6.2 million. Total enrollment: 816. Upper school average class size: 22. Upper school faculty-student ratio: 1:17. There are 178 required school days per year for Upper School students. Upper School students typically attend 5 days per week. The average school day consists of 6 hours and 40 minutes.

Upper School Student Profile Grade 9: 217 students (217 boys); Grade 10: 227 students (227 boys); Grade 11: 178 students (178 boys); Grade 12: 194 students (194 boys). 75% of students are Roman Catholic.

Faculty School total: 64. In upper school: 48 men, 16 women; 41 have advanced degrees.

Subjects Offered Accounting, algebra, American history, American literature, anatomy, art, art history, biology, broadcasting, business, business skills, calculus, chemistry, Chinese, chorus, computer graphics, computer science, creative writing, culinary arts, drama, driver education, ecology, economics, English, English literature, ESL, ethics, European history, fine arts, French, geography, geometry, German, government/civics, grammar, health, history, journalism, keyboarding, mathematics, music, physical education, physics, psychology, religion, science, social sciences, social studies, sociology, Spanish, speech, theater, trigonometry, word processing, world history, writing.

Graduation Requirements Arts and fine arts (art, music, dance, drama), business skills (includes word processing), computer science, English, mathematics, physical education (includes health), religion (includes Bible studies and theology), science, service learning/internship, social sciences, social studies (includes history), participation in a retreat program. Community service is required.

Special Academic Programs Advanced Placement exam preparation; honors section; study at local college for college credit; remedial reading and/or remedial writing; remedial math; ESL.

College Admission Counseling 198 students graduated in 2011; 189 went to college, including DePaul University; Lewis University; Northeastern Illinois University; Northern Illinois University; University of Illinois at Chicago; University of Illinois at Urbana–Champaign. Other: 2 went to work, 5 entered military service, 2 had other specific plans. Mean composite ACT: 22. 28% scored over 26 on composite ACT.

Student Life Upper grades have specified standards of dress, student council, honor system. Discipline rests primarily with faculty. Attendance at religious services is required.

Summer Programs Remediation, enrichment, sports, art/fine arts, computer instruction programs offered; session focuses on remediation; held on campus; accepts boys and girls; open to students from other schools. 225 students usually enrolled. 2012 schedule: June 11 to August 3. Application deadline: June 7.

Tuition and Aid Day student tuition: $8890. Tuition installment plan (monthly payment plans, quarterly payment plan). Need-based scholarship grants available. In 2011–12, 40% of upper-school students received aid. Total amount of financial aid awarded in 2011–12: $990,000.

Admissions Traditional secondary-level entrance grade is 9. For fall 2011, 267 students applied for upper-level admission, 261 were accepted, 220 enrolled. ACT-Explore or any standardized test required. Deadline for receipt of application materials: none. No application fee required. On-campus interview required.

Athletics Interscholastic: baseball, basketball, bowling, cross-country running, diving, fishing, football, golf, hockey, soccer, swimming and diving, tennis, track and field, volleyball, water polo, wrestling; intramural: basketball, football, volleyball. 4 PE instructors, 23 coaches, 1 athletic trainer.

Computers Computers are regularly used in business, English, foreign language, geography, graphic arts, graphic design, graphics, history, information technology, introduction to technology, library skills, mathematics, media arts, media production, media services, newspaper, photojournalism, religion, remedial study skills, research skills, science, typing, word processing, yearbook classes. Computer network features include on-campus library services, online commercial services, Internet access, Internet filtering or blocking technology. Students grades are available online. The school has a published electronic and media policy.

Contact Christopher Perez, Director of Curriculum. 773-282-8844 Ext. 228. Fax: 773-282-2361. E-mail: cperez@stpatrick.org. Web site: www.stpatrick.org.

SAINT PATRICK - SAINT VINCENT HIGH SCHOOL

1500 Benicia Road

Vallejo, California 94591

Head of School: Ms. Mary Ellen Ryan

General Information Coeducational day college-preparatory, arts, business, religious studies, and technology school, affiliated with Roman Catholic Church. Grades 9–12. Founded: 1870. Setting: suburban. 31-acre campus. 8 buildings on campus. Approved or accredited by Western Association of Schools and Colleges, Western Catholic Education Association, and California Department of Education. Total enrollment: 534. Upper school average class size: 30. Upper school faculty-student ratio: 1:30. There are 180 required school days per year for Upper School students. Upper School students typically attend 5 days per week. The average school day consists of 6 hours and 15 minutes.

Upper School Student Profile Grade 9: 129 students (65 boys, 64 girls); Grade 10: 129 students (79 boys, 50 girls); Grade 11: 136 students (64 boys, 72 girls); Grade 12: 140 students (66 boys, 74 girls). 80% of students are Roman Catholic.

Faculty School total: 43. In upper school: 20 men, 23 women; 24 have advanced degrees.

Subjects Offered Algebra, art, biology, calculus-AP, campus ministry, Catholic belief and practice, chemistry, chemistry-AP, choir, civics, college counseling, college planning, computer multimedia, computer science-AP, concert bell choir, concert choir, economics, English, English-AP, environmental science, environmental studies, ethnic studies, film appreciation, French, French language-AP, geometry, health, history-AP, honors English, honors world history, human biology, keyboarding, leadership, organic chemistry, physical education, physics, psychology, religion, science, Spanish, Spanish language-AP, statistics, statistics-AP, studio art-AP, theater arts, U.S. history, vocal jazz, world history.

Graduation Requirements English, foreign language, mathematics, physical education (includes health), religion (includes Bible studies and theology), science, social studies (includes history), Christian service.

Special Academic Programs Advanced Placement exam preparation; honors section; academic accommodation for the gifted; remedial math.

College Admission Counseling 144 students graduated in 2011; 142 went to college, including California State University, Sacramento; San Francisco State University; University of California, Berkeley; University of California, Irvine; University of California, Santa Barbara. Other: 2 had other specific plans.

Student Life Upper grades have specified standards of dress, student council, honor system. Discipline rests primarily with faculty. Attendance at religious services is required.

Summer Programs Remediation, enrichment, sports, art/fine arts programs offered; session focuses on enrichment; held on campus; accepts boys and girls; open to students from other schools. 489 students usually enrolled. 2012 schedule: June 18 to July 20. Application deadline: June 8.

Tuition and Aid Day student tuition: $10,990. Tuition installment plan (FACTS Tuition Payment Plan). Tuition reduction for siblings, need-based scholarship grants available. In 2011–12, 23% of upper-school students received aid. Total amount of financial aid awarded in 2011–12: $377,600.

Admissions Traditional secondary-level entrance grade is 9. For fall 2011, 179 students applied for upper-level admission, 165 were accepted, 131 enrolled. High School Placement Test required. Deadline for receipt of application materials: none. Application fee required: $50. Interview required.

Athletics Interscholastic: baseball (boys), basketball (b,g), cross-country running (b,g), golf (b,g), soccer (b,g), softball (g), swimming and diving (b,g), tennis (b,g), track and field (b,g), volleyball (b,g), water polo (b,g), wrestling (b,g); coed interscholastic: cheering, football, yoga. 3 PE instructors, 67 coaches, 1 athletic trainer.

Computers Computers are regularly used in business applications, business education, business studies, career education, career exploration, college planning, computer applications, desktop publishing, drawing and design, economics, English, foreign language, graphic arts, graphic design, history, library, library skills, mathematics, psychology, religious studies, science, social studies, Spanish, theater arts, theology, Web site design, word processing, yearbook classes. Computer network features include on-campus library services, Internet access, wireless campus network, Internet filtering or blocking technology. Student e-mail accounts are available to students. Students grades are available online. The school has a published electronic and media policy.

Contact Mrs. Sheila Williams, Director of Admissions. 707-644-4425 Ext. 448. Fax: 707-644-4770. E-mail: s.williams@spsv.org. Web site: spsv.org.

ST. PATRICK'S REGIONAL SECONDARY

115 East 11th Avenue

Vancouver, British Columbia V5T 2C1, Canada

Head of School: Mr. John V. Bevacqua

General Information Coeducational day college-preparatory, general academic, arts, business, religious studies, and technology school, affiliated with Roman Catholic Church. Grades 8–12. Founded: 1923. Setting: urban. 2 buildings on campus. Approved or accredited by British Columbia Department of Education. Language of instruction: English. Total enrollment: 500. Upper school average class size: 25. The average school day consists of 6 hours.

Upper School Student Profile Grade 8: 98 students (35 boys, 63 girls); Grade 9: 101 students (33 boys, 68 girls); Grade 10: 100 students (36 boys, 64 girls); Grade 11: 101 students (39 boys, 62 girls); Grade 12: 100 students (51 boys, 49 girls). 97% of students are Roman Catholic.

Faculty School total: 35. In upper school: 15 men, 15 women; 5 have advanced degrees.

Special Academic Programs Advanced Placement exam preparation; ESL (15 students enrolled).

College Admission Counseling 100 students graduated in 2011; all went to college, including University of Alaska Fairbanks.

Student Life Upper grades have uniform requirement. Attendance at religious services is required.

Tuition and Aid Tuition installment plan (monthly payment plans).

Admissions Application fee required: CAN$100. Interview required.

Athletics Interscholastic: basketball (boys, girls), soccer (b,g), track and field (b,g), volleyball (g), wrestling (b,g); coed intramural: badminton. 5 PE instructors, 5 coaches.

Contact Mr. John V. Bevacqua, Principal. 604-874-6422. Fax: 604-874-5176. E-mail: administration@stpats.bc.ca. Web site: www.stpats.bc.ca.

ST. PAUL ACADEMY AND SUMMIT SCHOOL

1712 Randolph Avenue

St. Paul, Minnesota 55105

Head of School: Bryn S. Roberts

General Information Coeducational day college-preparatory school. Grades K–12. Founded: 1900. Setting: urban. 32-acre campus. 4 buildings on campus. Approved or accredited by Independent Schools Association of the Central States and Minnesota Department of Education. Member of National Association of Independent Schools. Endowment: $31 million. Total enrollment: 869. Upper school average class size: 14. Upper school faculty-student ratio: 1:7. Upper School students typically attend 5 days per week.

Upper School Student Profile Grade 9: 96 students (47 boys, 49 girls); Grade 10: 95 students (47 boys, 48 girls); Grade 11: 90 students (44 boys, 46 girls); Grade 12: 82 students (34 boys, 48 girls).

Faculty School total: 103. In upper school: 17 men, 20 women; 31 have advanced degrees.

Subjects Offered Algebra, American literature, art, biology, calculus, ceramics, chemistry, Chinese, creative writing, current events, debate, drama, earth science, economics, English, English literature, European history, expository writing, fine arts, French, geometry, German, journalism, law and the legal system, marine biology, mathematics, multicultural studies, music, music theory, newspaper, photography, physical education, physics, psychology, science, senior project, Shakespeare, social psychology, social studies, sociology, space and physical sciences, Spanish, trigonometry, world history, world literature, world religions, yearbook.

Graduation Requirements Arts and fine arts (art, music, dance, drama), English, foreign language, mathematics, physical education (includes health), science, social studies (includes history), month-long senior project, senior speech.

Special Academic Programs Honors section; independent study; term-away projects; study abroad.

College Admission Counseling 87 students graduated in 2011; all went to college, including Boston University; Carleton College; St. Olaf College; University of Chicago; University of Wisconsin–Madison; Washington University in St. Louis. Median SAT critical reading: 620, median SAT math: 650, median SAT writing: 620, median combined SAT: 1890, median composite ACT: 29. 59% scored over 600 on SAT critical reading, 78% scored over 600 on SAT math, 64% scored over 600 on SAT writing, 70% scored over 1800 on combined SAT, 87% scored over 26 on composite ACT.

Student Life Upper grades have specified standards of dress, student council. Discipline rests equally with students and faculty.

Summer Programs Enrichment programs offered; held on campus; accepts boys and girls; open to students from other schools.

Tuition and Aid Day student tuition: $22,650–$24,840. Tuition installment plan (Insured Tuition Payment Plan, monthly payment plans). Need-based scholarship grants available. In 2011–12, 25% of upper-school students received aid. Total amount of financial aid awarded in 2011–12: $1,475,710.

Admissions Traditional secondary-level entrance grade is 9. For fall 2011, 60 students applied for upper-level admission, 42 were accepted, 29 enrolled. SSAT, ERB, PSAT, SAT, PLAN or ACT or writing sample required. Deadline for receipt of application materials: February 1. Application fee required: $75. Interview required.

Athletics Interscholastic: alpine skiing (boys, girls), baseball (b), basketball (b,g), cross-country running (b,g), dance (g), dance team (g), diving (b,g), fencing (b,g), football (b), golf (b,g), ice hockey (b,g), skiing (cross-country) (b,g), skiing (downhill) (b,g), soccer (b,g), softball (g), swimming and diving (b,g), tennis (b,g); intramural: outdoor adventure (b,g); coed interscholastic: lacrosse, strength & conditioning, track and field; coed intramural: hiking/backpacking, physical fitness, snowboarding, table tennis. 1 PE instructor, 85 coaches, 1 athletic trainer.

Computers Computers are regularly used in all academic classes. Computer network features include on-campus library services, online commercial services, Internet access, wireless campus network, Internet filtering or blocking technology, laptop program (beginning in grade 7). Student e-mail accounts and computer access in designated common areas are available to students. The school has a published electronic and media policy.

Contact Mrs. Heather Cameron Ploen, Director of Admission and Financial Aid. 651-698-2451. Fax: 651-698-6787. E-mail: hploen@spa.edu. Web site: www.spa.edu.

ST. PAUL'S EPISCOPAL SCHOOL

161 Dogwood Lane

Mobile, Alabama 36608

Head of School: Mr. F. Martin Lester Jr.

General Information Coeducational day college-preparatory, arts, technology, and honors, Advanced Placement school, affiliated with Episcopal Church. Grades PK–12. Founded: 1947. Setting: suburban. 32-acre campus. 10 buildings on campus. Approved or accredited by National Association of Episcopal Schools, Southern Association of Colleges and Schools, Southern Association of Independent Schools, and Alabama Department of Education. Member of National Association of Independent Schools and Secondary School Admission Test Board. Endowment: $1.6 million. Total enrollment: 1,405. Upper school average class size: 20. Upper school faculty-student ratio: 1:12. There are 177 required school days per year for Upper School students. Upper School students typically attend 5 days per week. The average school day consists of 6 hours and 10 minutes.

Upper School Student Profile Grade 9: 92 students (44 boys, 48 girls); Grade 10: 133 students (69 boys, 64 girls); Grade 11: 132 students (80 boys, 52 girls); Grade 12: 138 students (71 boys, 67 girls).

Faculty School total: 143. In upper school: 21 men, 35 women; 35 have advanced degrees.

Subjects Offered Advanced biology, advanced chemistry, advanced math, Advanced Placement courses, advanced studio art-AP, algebra, American history, American literature, anatomy and physiology, art, arts, band, biology, biology-AP, calculus, calculus-AP, chemistry, chemistry-AP, choir, choral music, civics, composition, computer science, concert choir, digital photography, drama, driver education, economics, economics-AP, English, English literature, English-AP, environmental science, environmental science-AP, European history, European history-AP, fine arts, foreign language, French, French-AP, geometry, government-AP, government/civics, grammar, history, history-AP, honors algebra, honors English, honors geometry, human anatomy, instrumental music, journalism, Latin, marching band, marine biology, mathematics, music, oil painting, painting, photography, physical education, physics, physics-AP, pre-algebra, pre-calculus, public service, Spanish, speech, theater, theater arts, trigonometry, U.S. history-AP, weight training, world history, yearbook.

Graduation Requirements Arts and fine arts (art, music, dance, drama), electives, English, foreign language, history, mathematics, science, 4 years of English, mathematics, social studies, and science, 2 year minimum foreign language, 60 hours of community service. Community service is required.

Special Academic Programs Advanced Placement exam preparation; honors section; study at local college for college credit; special instructional classes for students with diagnosed learning disabilities.

College Admission Counseling 137 students graduated in 2010; 136 went to college, including Auburn University; Birmingham-Southern College; The University of Alabama; Tulane University; University of Mississippi; University of South Alabama. Other: 1 entered military service.

Student Life Upper grades have uniform requirement, student council, honor system. Discipline rests primarily with faculty. Attendance at religious services is required.

Tuition and Aid Tuition installment plan (Insured Tuition Payment Plan, monthly payment plans, individually arranged payment plans, semiannual payment plan). Need-based scholarship grants available. Total amount of financial aid awarded in 2010–11: $353,000.

Admissions Traditional secondary-level entrance grade is 9. For fall 2010, 24 students applied for upper-level admission, 22 were accepted, 18 enrolled. ERB CTP IV or Otis-Lennon and 2 sections of ERB required. Deadline for receipt of application materials: none. Application fee required. Interview required.

Athletics Interscholastic: baseball (boys), basketball (b,g), cheering (g), cross-country running (b,g), diving (b,g), football (b), golf (b,g), indoor track & field (b,g), soccer (b,g), softball (g), strength & conditioning (b,g), swimming and diving (b,g), tennis (b,g), track and field (b,g), volleyball (g), weight training (b), winter (indoor) track (b,g); intramural: basketball (b,g), soccer (b,g), volleyball (g), weight training (b); coed interscholastic: fencing. 6 PE instructors, 13 coaches, 4 athletic trainers.

Computers Computers are regularly used in economics, English, foreign language, history, independent study, journalism, keyboarding, mathematics, newspaper, publications, science, Spanish, writing, yearbook classes. Computer network features include on-campus library services, online commercial services, Internet access, wireless campus network, Internet filtering or blocking technology. Campus intranet, student e-mail accounts, and computer access in designated common areas are available to stu-

dents. Students grades are available online. The school has a published electronic and media policy.
Contact Ms. Julie L. Taylor, Advancement/Admissions Director. 251-461-2129. Fax: 251-342-1844. E-mail: jtaylor@stpaulsmobile.net. Web site: www.stpaulsmobile.net.

ST. PAUL'S HIGH SCHOOL

2200 Grant Avenue

Winnipeg, Manitoba R3P 0P8, Canada

Head of School: Fr. Alan Fogarty, SJ

General Information Boys' day college-preparatory, arts, religious studies, and technology school, affiliated with Roman Catholic Church. Grades 9–12. Founded: 1926. Setting: suburban. 18-acre campus. 5 buildings on campus. Approved or accredited by Jesuit Secondary Education Association and Manitoba Department of Education. Language of instruction: English. Endowment: CAN$6.5 million. Total enrollment: 599. Upper school average class size: 26. Upper school faculty-student ratio: 1:14. There are 193 required school days per year for Upper School students. Upper School students typically attend 5 days per week. The average school day consists of 5 hours and 50 minutes.
Upper School Student Profile Grade 9: 150 students (150 boys); Grade 10: 156 students (156 boys); Grade 11: 142 students (142 boys); Grade 12: 151 students (151 boys). 67% of students are Roman Catholic.
Faculty School total: 44. In upper school: 37 men, 7 women; 15 have advanced degrees.
Subjects Offered Algebra, American history, art, biology, calculus, chemistry, classics, computer science, current events, economics, English, ethics, French, geography, geometry, history, law, mathematics, media, multimedia, multimedia design, music, physical education, physics, political science, psychology, religion, science, social studies, speech, theology, world wide web design.
Graduation Requirements English, mathematics, physical education (includes health), religion (includes Bible studies and theology), science, social studies (includes history), completion of Christian service program.
Special Academic Programs Advanced Placement exam preparation; honors section; remedial math.
College Admission Counseling 136 students graduated in 2011; 129 went to college, including McGill University; Queen's University at Kingston; The University of British Columbia; The University of Winnipeg; University of Manitoba; University of Toronto. Other: 3 went to work, 4 had other specific plans.
Student Life Upper grades have specified standards of dress, student council, honor system. Discipline rests primarily with faculty. Attendance at religious services is required.
Summer Programs Sports programs offered; session focuses on sport skills and relationship building; held on campus; accepts boys; open to students from other schools. 80 students usually enrolled. 2012 schedule: August 21 to September 4.
Tuition and Aid Day student tuition: CAN$6990. Tuition installment plan (Insured Tuition Payment Plan, monthly payment plans, individually arranged payment plans). Bursaries, need-based loans available. In 2011–12, 13% of upper-school students received aid. Total amount of financial aid awarded in 2011–12: CAN$300,000.
Admissions Traditional secondary-level entrance grade is 9. For fall 2011, 320 students applied for upper-level admission, 172 were accepted, 164 enrolled. Achievement tests and STS required. Deadline for receipt of application materials: February 5. Application fee required: CAN$75. On-campus interview required.
Athletics Interscholastic: badminton, basketball, cross-country running, curling, football, golf, ice hockey, indoor track, indoor track & field, rugby, soccer, track and field, volleyball, wrestling; intramural: badminton, basketball, curling, flag football, golf, physical fitness, physical training, skiing (downhill), strength & conditioning, table tennis, volleyball, weight training. 4 PE instructors, 1 athletic trainer.
Computers Computers are regularly used in French, French as a second language, geography, mathematics, multimedia, religious studies, science, Web site design classes. Computer network features include on-campus library services, online commercial services, Internet access, Internet filtering or blocking technology. Campus intranet, student e-mail accounts, and computer access in designated common areas are available to students. Students grades are available online. The school has a published electronic and media policy.
Contact Mr. Tom Lussier, Principal. 204-831-2300. Fax: 204-831-2340. E-mail: tlussier@stpauls.mb.ca. Web site: www.stpauls.mb.ca.

ST. PETER'S PREPARATORY SCHOOL

144 Grand Street

Jersey City, New Jersey 07302

Head of School: Rev. Robert E. Reiser, SJ

General Information Boys' day college-preparatory, arts, technology, and music school, affiliated with Roman Catholic Church. Grades 9–12. Founded: 1872. Setting: urban. Nearest major city is New York, NY. 7-acre campus. 8 buildings on campus. Approved or accredited by Jesuit Secondary Education Association, Middle States Association of Colleges and Schools, and New Jersey Department of Education. Endowment: $18 million. Total enrollment: 966. Upper school average class size: 22. Upper school faculty-student ratio: 1:12. There are 170 required school days per year for Upper School students. Upper School students typically attend 5 days per week. The average school day consists of 6 hours.
Upper School Student Profile Grade 9: 280 students (280 boys); Grade 10: 249 students (249 boys); Grade 11: 209 students (209 boys); Grade 12: 228 students (228 boys). 80% of students are Roman Catholic.
Faculty School total: 80. In upper school: 51 men, 27 women; 46 have advanced degrees.
Subjects Offered Advanced Placement courses, algebra, American history, American history-AP, American legal systems, American literature, Ancient Greek, art, art history, biology, biology-AP, calculus, calculus-AP, ceramics, chemistry, chemistry-AP, choral music, Christian ethics, community service, computer programming, computer science, concert band, creative writing, drawing, English, English language-AP, English literature, English literature-AP, European history, French, geometry, German, government and politics-AP, health, history, human anatomy, Italian, jazz band, Latin, Latin-AP, mathematics, music, music theory, physical education, physics, religion, sculpture, social justice, Spanish, Spanish language-AP, Spanish literature-AP, statistics-AP, studio art, theology, trigonometry, Web site design, world civilizations, world history, world literature, writing.
Graduation Requirements Algebra, American history, American literature, ancient world history, art, Basic programming, biology, British literature, chemistry, computer education, English, geometry, Latin, modern languages, music, physical education (includes health), physics, religion (includes Bible studies and theology), U.S. history, world civilizations, 20 hours of community service in freshman and sophomore years, 60 hours in the third (junior) year.
Special Academic Programs International Baccalaureate program; 13 Advanced Placement exams for which test preparation is offered; honors section; study at local college for college credit; study abroad.
College Admission Counseling 189 students graduated in 2011; 186 went to college, including Boston College; Georgetown University; Rutgers, The State University of New Jersey, Rutgers College; Saint Joseph's University; Saint Peter's College; The College of New Jersey. Other: 2 went to work, 1 entered military service. Median SAT critical reading: 570, median SAT math: 590. Mean SAT writing: 570, mean combined SAT: 1715. 44% scored over 600 on SAT critical reading, 48% scored over 600 on SAT math, 50% scored over 600 on SAT writing, 50% scored over 1800 on combined SAT.
Student Life Upper grades have specified standards of dress, student council, honor system. Discipline rests primarily with faculty.
Summer Programs Remediation, enrichment, sports, art/fine arts programs offered; session focuses on make-up course work for failed classes and enrichment for students trying to advance their studies; held on campus; accepts boys and girls; open to students from other schools. 170 students usually enrolled. 2012 schedule: June 26 to July 27. Application deadline: June 15.
Tuition and Aid Day student tuition: $11,500. Tuition installment plan (SMART Tuition Payment Plan, monthly payment plans). Merit scholarship grants, need-based scholarship grants, paying campus jobs available. In 2011–12, 46% of upper-school students received aid; total upper-school merit-scholarship money awarded: $1,000,000. Total amount of financial aid awarded in 2011–12: $1,000,000.
Admissions Traditional secondary-level entrance grade is 9. For fall 2011, 904 students applied for upper-level admission, 455 were accepted, 280 enrolled. Cooperative Entrance Exam (McGraw-Hill) or SSAT required. Deadline for receipt of application materials: November 15. No application fee required.
Athletics Interscholastic: baseball, basketball, bowling, crew, cross-country running, diving, fencing, football, golf, ice hockey, indoor track, indoor track & field, lacrosse, rugby, soccer, swimming and diving, tennis, track and field, volleyball, water polo, winter (indoor) track, wrestling; intramural: basketball, flag football, Frisbee, handball, indoor soccer, outdoor recreation, team handball, touch football, ultimate Frisbee, weight lifting, whiffle ball. 4 PE instructors, 23 coaches, 1 athletic trainer.
Computers Computers are regularly used in all academic classes. Computer network features include on-campus library services, online commercial services, Internet access, wireless campus network, Internet filtering or blocking technology. Campus intranet and student e-mail accounts are available to students. Students grades are available online. The school has a published electronic and media policy.
Contact Mr. John T. Irvine, Director of Admissions. 201-547-6389. Fax: 201-547-2341. E-mail: Irvinej@spprep.org. Web site: www.spprep.org.

ST. PIUS X CATHOLIC HIGH SCHOOL

2674 Johnson Road NE

Atlanta, Georgia 30345

Head of School: Mr. Steve Spellman

General Information Coeducational day college-preparatory school, affiliated with Roman Catholic Church. Grades 9–12. Founded: 1958. Setting: suburban. 25-acre campus. 8 buildings on campus. Approved or accredited by National Catholic Education Association, Southern Association of Colleges and Schools, The College Board, and Georgia Department of Education. Member of Secondary School Admission Test

Board. Total enrollment: 1,100. Upper school average class size: 21. Upper school faculty-student ratio: 1:12. There are 180 required school days per year for Upper School students.

Upper School Student Profile Grade 9: 295 students (148 boys, 147 girls); Grade 10: 285 students (140 boys, 145 girls); Grade 11: 260 students (130 boys, 130 girls); Grade 12: 260 students (130 boys, 130 girls). 82% of students are Roman Catholic.

Faculty School total: 97. In upper school: 47 men, 50 women; 64 have advanced degrees.

Subjects Offered Accounting, algebra, American history, American literature, anatomy, art, band, biology, business, business law, calculus, ceramics, chemistry, chorus, computer programming, computer science, creative writing, current events, dance, drama, driver education, economics, English, English literature, European history, expository writing, French, geography, geometry, German, government/civics, health, history, instrumental music, journalism, Latin, mathematics, music, physical education, physical science, physics, physiology, psychology, religion, science, social studies, sociology, Spanish, speech, statistics, theater, trigonometry, word processing, world history, world literature.

Graduation Requirements American history, computer science, English, foreign language, mathematics, physical education (includes health), religion (includes Bible studies and theology), science, social studies (includes history).

Special Academic Programs 20 Advanced Placement exams for which test preparation is offered; honors section; special instructional classes for students with learning disabilities and Attention Deficit Disorder.

College Admission Counseling 245 students graduated in 2011; 244 went to college, including Emory University; Georgia Institute of Technology; Georgia Southern University; Georgia State University; University of Georgia; University of Notre Dame. Other: 1 had other specific plans. 60% scored over 600 on SAT critical reading, 60% scored over 600 on SAT math, 50% scored over 26 on composite ACT.

Student Life Upper grades have uniform requirement, student council, honor system. Discipline rests equally with students and faculty. Attendance at religious services is required.

Tuition and Aid Day student tuition: $11,000. Tuition installment plan (FACTS Tuition Payment Plan, monthly payment plans). Tuition reduction for siblings, need-based scholarship grants available. In 2011–12, 18% of upper-school students received aid. Total amount of financial aid awarded in 2011–12: $400,000.

Admissions Traditional secondary-level entrance grade is 9. For fall 2011, 525 students applied for upper-level admission, 330 were accepted, 300 enrolled. SSAT required. Deadline for receipt of application materials: February 1. Application fee required: $100.

Athletics Interscholastic: baseball (boys), basketball (b,g), cheering (b,g), cross-country running (b,g), dance (b), dance squad (g), dance team (g), diving (b,g), drill team (g), football (b), golf (b,g), lacrosse (b,g), soccer (b,g), softball (g), strength & conditioning (b,g), swimming and diving (b,g), tennis (b,g), track and field (b,g), volleyball (g), water polo (b,g), weight training (b,g), wrestling (b); coed interscholastic: sailing, water polo. 4 PE instructors, 33 coaches, 1 athletic trainer.

Computers Computers are regularly used in all academic classes. Computer network features include on-campus library services, online commercial services, Internet access, Internet filtering or blocking technology. Campus intranet, student e-mail accounts, and computer access in designated common areas are available to students. Students grades are available online. The school has a published electronic and media policy.

Contact Terry Sides, Coordinator of Admissions. 404-636-0323 Ext. 291. Fax: 404-636-2118. E-mail: tsides@spx.org. Web site: www.spx.org.

ST. PIUS X HIGH SCHOOL

811 West Donovan

Houston, Texas 77091-5699

Head of School: Sr. Donna M. Pollard, OP

General Information Coeducational day college-preparatory, arts, business, religious studies, and technology school, affiliated with Roman Catholic Church. Grades 9–12. Founded: 1956. Setting: urban. 26-acre campus. 1 building on campus. Approved or accredited by Southern Association of Colleges and Schools, Texas Catholic Conference, Texas Education Agency, The College Board, and Texas Department of Education. Endowment: $2.6 million. Total enrollment: 689. Upper school average class size: 22. Upper school faculty-student ratio: 1:12. There are 180 required school days per year for Upper School students. Upper School students typically attend 5 days per week. The average school day consists of 7 hours.

Upper School Student Profile Grade 9: 170 students (92 boys, 78 girls); Grade 10: 171 students (93 boys, 78 girls); Grade 11: 187 students (105 boys, 82 girls); Grade 12: 161 students (82 boys, 79 girls). 71% of students are Roman Catholic.

Faculty School total: 57. In upper school: 21 men, 36 women; 40 have advanced degrees.

Subjects Offered Advanced chemistry, advanced computer applications, advanced math, Advanced Placement courses, advanced studio art-AP, algebra, American history-AP, American literature, American literature-AP, anatomy and physiology, art, band, biology, biology-AP, business law, calculus, calculus-AP, campus ministry, Catholic belief and practice, chemistry, choir, chorus, Christian ethics, church history, college counseling, community service, computer applications, computer multimedia, computer programming, computer science-AP, cultural geography, dance, death and loss, desktop publishing, earth and space science, economics, English language-AP, English literature-AP, environmental science, film history, fine arts, foreign language, French, geography, geometry, graphic design, health, history of the Catholic Church, honors geometry, honors world history, introduction to theater, Italian, jewelry making, language arts, Latin, Latin-AP, library assistant, marching band, moral and social development, moral theology, musical productions, painting, philosophy, photography, physical education, physics, psychology, reading/study skills, SAT/ACT preparation, Shakespeare, social justice, sociology, Spanish, Spanish language-AP, Spanish-AP, speech, speech communications, stagecraft, student government, student publications, technical theater, theology, U.S. government, U.S. government and politics-AP, U.S. history, U.S. history-AP, Web site design, world history, world religions, yearbook.

Graduation Requirements Advanced math, algebra, American government, American history, ancient world history, art, biology, chemistry, communications, economics, electives, English, geometry, government, health, integrated physics, physical education (includes health), physics, theology, 2 years of foreign language or reading development, Christian Service Learning-100 hours of community service, 4 years of theology.

Special Academic Programs 10 Advanced Placement exams for which test preparation is offered; honors section; study at local college for college credit; remedial reading and/or remedial writing; remedial math; programs in English, mathematics, general development for dyslexic students.

College Admission Counseling 155 students graduated in 2010; all went to college, including St. Edward's University; Texas A&M University; Texas Christian University; Texas Tech University; The University of Texas at San Antonio; University of Houston. Mean SAT critical reading: 545, mean SAT math: 540, mean composite ACT: 22. 27% scored over 600 on SAT critical reading, 26% scored over 600 on SAT math, 19% scored over 26 on composite ACT.

Student Life Upper grades have uniform requirement, student council, honor system. Discipline rests primarily with faculty. Attendance at religious services is required.

Tuition and Aid Day student tuition: $10,100. Tuition installment plan (monthly payment plans, individually arranged payment plans). Tuition reduction for siblings, merit scholarship grants, need-based scholarship grants available. In 2010–11, 28% of upper-school students received aid; total upper-school merit-scholarship money awarded: $21,000. Total amount of financial aid awarded in 2010–11: $704,665.

Admissions Traditional secondary-level entrance grade is 9. For fall 2010, 264 students applied for upper-level admission, 230 were accepted, 186 enrolled. Catholic High School Entrance Examination required. Deadline for receipt of application materials: January 15. Application fee required: $50. Interview required.

Athletics Interscholastic: baseball (boys), basketball (b,g), cheering (g), cross-country running (b,g), dance squad (g), dance team (b,g), drill team (g), football (b), golf (b,g), soccer (b,g), softball (g), swimming and diving (b,g), tennis (b,g), track and field (b,g), volleyball (g). 3 PE instructors, 6 coaches, 1 athletic trainer.

Computers Computers are regularly used in art, career exploration, career technology, desktop publishing, drawing and design, graphic design, journalism, mathematics, multimedia, news writing, newspaper, publications, technology, video film production, yearbook classes. Computer network features include on-campus library services, Internet access, wireless campus network, Internet filtering or blocking technology, faculty Web pages for courses. Student e-mail accounts and computer access in designated common areas are available to students. Students grades are available online. The school has a published electronic and media policy.

Contact Ms. Susie Kramer, Admissions Director. 713-579-7507. Fax: 713-692-5725. E-mail: kramers@stpiusx.org. Web site: www.stpiusx.org.

ST. SCHOLASTICA ACADEMY

7416 North Ridge Boulevard

Chicago, Illinois 60645-1998

Head of School: Ms. Colleen Brewer

General Information Girls' day college-preparatory, arts, and religious studies school, affiliated with Roman Catholic Church. Grades 9–12. Founded: 1865. Setting: urban. 14-acre campus. 1 building on campus. Approved or accredited by International Baccalaureate Organization, National Catholic Education Association, North Central Association of Colleges and Schools, and Illinois Department of Education. Endowment: $3.9 million. Total enrollment: 250. Upper school average class size: 14. Upper school faculty-student ratio: 1:9.

Upper School Student Profile Grade 9: 65 students (65 girls); Grade 10: 50 students (50 girls); Grade 11: 65 students (65 girls); Grade 12: 70 students (70 girls). 60% of students are Roman Catholic.

Faculty School total: 28. In upper school: 5 men, 23 women; 21 have advanced degrees.

Subjects Offered 20th century world history, algebra, American history, American literature, anatomy and physiology, art, arts appreciation, biology, British literature, calculus, ceramics, chemistry, chorus, Christian and Hebrew scripture, consumer economics, consumer education, creative writing, desktop publishing, drama performance, dramatic arts, drawing, English literature, fine arts, French, geometry, graphic arts, graphic design, health, honors algebra, honors English, honors geometry, honors U.S.

history, honors world history, information technology, International Baccalaureate courses, journalism, language arts, Latin, music, painting, peace and justice, philosophy, photography, physical education, physics, pre-calculus, psychology, service learning/internship, Spanish, speech, student publications, theater arts, theology, theory of knowledge, trigonometry, word processing, world cultures, world geography, world history, world literature.

Graduation Requirements Algebra, American literature, arts and fine arts (art, music, dance, drama), biology, British literature, chemistry, electives, foreign language, geography, geometry, health, introduction to literature, keyboarding, speech, theology, U.S. history, world literature.

Special Academic Programs International Baccalaureate program; Advanced Placement exam preparation; honors section; remedial reading and/or remedial writing; remedial math.

College Admission Counseling 77 students graduated in 2011; all went to college, including Benedictine College; DePaul University; Loyola University Chicago; Northeastern Illinois University; University of Illinois at Chicago; University of Illinois at Urbana–Champaign.

Student Life Upper grades have uniform requirement, student council. Discipline rests primarily with faculty. Attendance at religious services is required.

Summer Programs Remediation, advancement, sports, art/fine arts programs offered; session focuses on enabling students to choose additional electives in the academic year; held on campus; accepts boys and girls; open to students from other schools. 100 students usually enrolled. 2012 schedule: June 28 to August 6. Application deadline: June 13.

Tuition and Aid Day student tuition: $10,500. Tuition installment plan (FACTS Tuition Payment Plan). Tuition reduction for siblings, merit scholarship grants, need-based scholarship grants available. In 2011–12, 50% of upper-school students received aid; total upper-school merit-scholarship money awarded: $76,800. Total amount of financial aid awarded in 2011–12: $509,000.

Admissions Traditional secondary-level entrance grade is 9. For fall 2011, 135 students applied for upper-level admission, 129 were accepted, 60 enrolled. STS required. Deadline for receipt of application materials: none. No application fee required.

Athletics Interscholastic: basketball, bowling, cross-country running, indoor track & field, soccer, softball, tennis, track and field, volleyball; intramural: dance. 1 PE instructor, 6 coaches.

Computers Computers are regularly used in English, foreign language, graphic design, journalism, keyboarding, library skills, literary magazine, mathematics, science, social sciences, theology, word processing, writing, yearbook classes. Computer network features include on-campus library services, online commercial services, Internet access, wireless campus network, wireless Internet access. Computer access in designated common areas is available to students. Students grades are available online. The school has a published electronic and media policy.

Contact Ms. Emily Paulus, Director of Pre-Admissions. 773-764-5715 Ext. 356. Fax: 773-764-0304. E-mail: epaulus@scholastica.us. Web site: www.scholastica.us.

ST. SEBASTIAN'S SCHOOL

1191 Greendale Avenue

Needham, Massachusetts 02492

Head of School: Mr. William L. Burke III

General Information Boys' day college-preparatory school, affiliated with Roman Catholic Church. Grades 7–12. Founded: 1941. Setting: suburban. Nearest major city is Boston. 25-acre campus. 5 buildings on campus. Approved or accredited by New England Association of Schools and Colleges and Massachusetts Department of Education. Member of National Association of Independent Schools and Secondary School Admission Test Board. Endowment: $10.4 million. Total enrollment: 360. Upper school average class size: 11. Upper school faculty-student ratio: 1:7.

Upper School Student Profile Grade 9: 66 students (66 boys); Grade 10: 62 students (62 boys); Grade 11: 63 students (63 boys); Grade 12: 66 students (66 boys). 80% of students are Roman Catholic.

Faculty School total: 61. In upper school: 48 men, 13 women; 35 have advanced degrees.

Subjects Offered Algebra, American history, American literature, art, art history, biology, calculus, chemistry, computer science, drama, economics, English, English literature, ethics, European history, fine arts, geography, geometry, government/civics, Greek, history, Latin, mathematics, music, philosophy, photography, physical education, physics, religion, science, social studies, Spanish, speech, theater, trigonometry, world history, world literature, writing.

Graduation Requirements Arts and fine arts (art, music, dance, drama), English, foreign language, mathematics, physical education (includes health), religion (includes Bible studies and theology), science, social studies (includes history), senior service, chapel speaking program.

Special Academic Programs Advanced Placement exam preparation; honors section; independent study; academic accommodation for the gifted, the musically talented, and the artistically talented.

College Admission Counseling 55 students graduated in 2011; 54 went to college, including College of the Holy Cross; Hobart and William Smith Colleges; Loyola University Maryland; Stonehill College; University of Richmond; Villanova University. Median SAT critical reading: 640, median SAT math: 640.

Student Life Upper grades have specified standards of dress, student council, honor system. Discipline rests primarily with faculty. Attendance at religious services is required.

Tuition and Aid Day student tuition: $31,550. Tuition installment plan (Academic Management Services Plan, Key Tuition Payment Plan). Need-based scholarship grants, need-based loans available. In 2011–12, 26% of upper-school students received aid. Total amount of financial aid awarded in 2011–12: $1,750,000.

Admissions Traditional secondary-level entrance grade is 9. For fall 2011, 100 students applied for upper-level admission, 34 were accepted, 17 enrolled. ISEE or SSAT required. Deadline for receipt of application materials: January 15. Application fee required: $40. On-campus interview required.

Athletics Interscholastic: baseball, basketball, cross-country running, football, golf, ice hockey, lacrosse, sailing, skiing (downhill), soccer, squash, swimming and diving, tennis; intramural: strength & conditioning, ultimate Frisbee, weight lifting, whiffle ball, wrestling. 1 athletic trainer.

Computers Computers are regularly used in English, foreign language, mathematics, science, social studies, writing classes. Computer network features include on-campus library services, Internet access, wireless campus network, Internet filtering or blocking technology. Campus intranet is available to students. The school has a published electronic and media policy.

Contact Mrs. Helen Maxwell, Assistant to Dean of Admissions. 781-449-5200 Ext. 125. Fax: 781-449-5630. E-mail: admissions@stsebs.org. Web site: www.saintsebastiansschool.org.

SAINTS PETER AND PAUL HIGH SCHOOL

900 High Street

Easton, Maryland 21601

Head of School: Mr. James Edward Nemeth

General Information Coeducational day college-preparatory school, affiliated with Roman Catholic Church. Grades 9–12. Founded: 1958. Setting: small town. Nearest major city is Baltimore. 4-acre campus. 4 buildings on campus. Approved or accredited by Middle States Association of Colleges and Schools, National Catholic Education Association, and Maryland Department of Education. Endowment: $125,000. Total enrollment: 214. Upper school average class size: 16. Upper school faculty-student ratio: 1:9. There are 183 required school days per year for Upper School students. Upper School students typically attend 5 days per week. The average school day consists of 6 hours and 30 minutes.

Upper School Student Profile Grade 9: 62 students (37 boys, 25 girls); Grade 10: 31 students (29 boys, 22 girls); Grade 11: 49 students (23 boys, 26 girls); Grade 12: 52 students (17 boys, 35 girls). 68% of students are Roman Catholic.

Faculty School total: 22. In upper school: 11 men, 10 women; 15 have advanced degrees.

Subjects Offered Advanced computer applications, algebra, American government, American literature, anatomy and physiology, art and culture, biology, biology-AP, British literature, British literature (honors), calculus, calculus-AP, campus ministry, Catholic belief and practice, chemistry, chemistry-AP, Christian and Hebrew scripture, Christian ethics, Christianity, church history, computer multimedia, computer programming, computer science, conceptual physics, creative writing, drama, earth science, economics, English language and composition-AP, English literature and composition-AP, environmental science, geography, geometry, health and wellness, Hebrew scripture, honors algebra, honors English, honors geometry, honors U.S. history, honors world history, Microsoft, moral theology, music theory, philosophy, physical education, physics, pre-calculus, probability and statistics, Spanish, speech, studio art-AP, theology, U.S. government and politics-AP, U.S. history, U.S. history-AP, Web site design, world history, yearbook.

Graduation Requirements Algebra, American literature, arts and fine arts (art, music, dance, drama), biology, British literature, Catholic belief and practice, chemistry, Christian and Hebrew scripture, Christianity, computer applications, computer science, English, foreign language, geometry, history of the Catholic Church, mathematics, moral theology, physical education (includes health), physics, pre-algebra, social justice, U.S. government, U.S. history, world history.

Special Academic Programs 7 Advanced Placement exams for which test preparation is offered; honors section; independent study.

College Admission Counseling 46 students graduated in 2011; all went to college, including Loyola University Maryland; Salisbury University; University of Maryland, College Park; Washington College. Median SAT critical reading: 530, median SAT math: 520, median SAT writing: 520. 18% scored over 600 on SAT critical reading, 18% scored over 600 on SAT math, 30% scored over 600 on SAT writing.

Student Life Upper grades have uniform requirement. Discipline rests primarily with faculty. Attendance at religious services is required.

Tuition and Aid Day student tuition: $10,600. Tuition installment plan (FACTS Tuition Payment Plan). Tuition reduction for siblings, need-based scholarship grants, parish subsidies available. In 2011–12, 3% of upper-school students received aid. Total amount of financial aid awarded in 2011–12: $6500.

Admissions Traditional secondary-level entrance grade is 9. For fall 2011, 68 students applied for upper-level admission, 62 were accepted, 62 enrolled. Diocesan Entrance Exam required. Deadline for receipt of application materials: none. Application fee required: $50. On-campus interview required.
Athletics Interscholastic: baseball (boys), basketball (b,g), cross-country running (b,g), field hockey (g), golf (b), ice hockey (b), lacrosse (b,g), soccer (b,g), softball (g), swimming and diving (b,g), tennis (b,g). 1 PE instructor, 23 coaches.
Computers Computers are regularly used in all academic classes. Computer network features include on-campus library services, Internet access, wireless campus network, Internet filtering or blocking technology. Students grades are available online. The school has a published electronic and media policy.
Contact Mrs. Carolyn Smith Hayman, Administrative Assistant. 410-822-2275 Ext. 150. Fax: 410-822-1767. E-mail: chayman@ssppeaston.org. Web site: www.ssppeaston.org.

ST. STANISLAUS COLLEGE

304 South Beach Boulevard

Bay St. Louis, Mississippi 39520

Head of School: Br. Bernard Couvillion, SC

General Information Boys' boarding and day college-preparatory, general academic, religious studies, and ESL school, affiliated with Roman Catholic Church. Grades 7–PG. Founded: 1854. Setting: small town. Nearest major city is New Orleans, LA. Students are housed in single-sex dormitories. 54-acre campus. 8 buildings on campus. Approved or accredited by National Catholic Education Association, Southern Association of Colleges and Schools, Southern Association of Independent Schools, and Mississippi Department of Education. Member of Secondary School Admission Test Board. Endowment: $7 million. Total enrollment: 381. Upper school average class size: 20. Upper school faculty-student ratio: 1:23. There are 180 required school days per year for Upper School students. Upper School students typically attend 5 days per week. The average school day consists of 6 hours and 23 minutes.
Upper School Student Profile Grade 9: 63 students (63 boys); Grade 10: 56 students (56 boys); Grade 11: 62 students (62 boys); Grade 12: 87 students (87 boys); Postgraduate: 1 student (1 boy). 22% of students are boarding students. 1% are state residents. 6 states are represented in upper school student body. 17% are international students. International students from China, India, Mexico, Republic of Korea, Thailand, and Viet Nam; 2 other countries represented in student body. 70% of students are Roman Catholic.
Faculty School total: 42. In upper school: 28 men, 14 women; 21 have advanced degrees; 13 reside on campus.
Subjects Offered Accounting, ACT preparation, advanced biology, advanced chemistry, advanced computer applications, advanced math, Advanced Placement courses, algebra, American history, American history-AP, American literature, anatomy, art, astronomy, biology, biology-AP, British literature-AP, business, business education, business law, calculus, calculus-AP, campus ministry, ceramics, chemistry, chemistry-AP, choir, chorus, computer programming, computer science, computer science-AP, creative writing, desktop publishing, drama, economics, economics and history, English, English language and composition-AP, English literature, English literature and composition-AP, environmental science, ESL, European history-AP, finance, French, French as a second language, genetics, geography, geology, geometry, government, government/civics, grammar, guidance, health, health education, history, journalism, law, marine biology, marine science, mathematics, music, music performance, physical education, physics, physics-AP, pre-calculus, psychology, psychology-AP, religion, science, scuba diving, short story, social sciences, social studies, sociology, Spanish, speech, swimming, symphonic band, theater, theater arts, theology, track and field, trigonometry, typing, U.S. history-AP, world history, world literature.
Graduation Requirements Arts and fine arts (art, music, dance, drama), computer science, English, foreign language, mathematics, physical education (includes health), religion (includes Bible studies and theology), science, social sciences, social studies (includes history), service hours are required.
Special Academic Programs 8 Advanced Placement exams for which test preparation is offered; honors section; remedial reading and/or remedial writing; remedial math; programs in English, mathematics, general development for dyslexic students; special instructional classes for students with Attention Deficit Disorder; ESL (10 students enrolled).
College Admission Counseling 77 students graduated in 2010; all went to college, including Louisiana State University and Agricultural and Mechanical College; Mississippi State University; University of Mississippi; University of New Orleans; University of South Alabama; University of Southern Mississippi. Median SAT critical reading: 520, median SAT math: 620, median SAT writing: 570, median composite ACT: 21. 40% scored over 600 on SAT critical reading, 50% scored over 600 on SAT math, 35% scored over 600 on SAT writing, 22% scored over 1800 on combined SAT, 17% scored over 26 on composite ACT.
Student Life Upper grades have uniform requirement, student council. Discipline rests primarily with faculty. Attendance at religious services is required.
Tuition and Aid Day student tuition: $5570; 7-day tuition and room/board: $20,655. Tuition installment plan (monthly payment plans, individually arranged payment plans). Need-based scholarship grants, need-based loans, paying campus jobs available.
Admissions Traditional secondary-level entrance grade is 9. Deadline for receipt of application materials: none. Application fee required: $100. On-campus interview recommended.
Athletics Interscholastic: baseball, basketball, cross-country running, football, golf, power lifting, sailing, soccer, swimming and diving, tennis, track and field; intramural: baseball, basketball, billiards, cheering, fishing, flag football, floor hockey, football, hiking/backpacking, jogging, outdoor activities, outdoor adventure, outdoor education, outdoor recreation, outdoor skills, outdoors, physical fitness, physical training, power lifting, scuba diving, swimming and diving, table tennis, tennis, touch football, volleyball, water polo, water skiing, weight lifting, weight training. 5 PE instructors, 16 coaches, 1 athletic trainer.
Computers Computers are regularly used in accounting, English, mathematics, religion, SAT preparation, science, Spanish classes. Computer network features include on-campus library services, online commercial services, Internet access, wireless campus network, Internet filtering or blocking technology. Campus intranet and computer access in designated common areas are available to students. Students grades are available online.
Contact Mr. John Thibodeaux, Director of Admissions. 228-467-9057 Ext. 226. Fax: 228-466-2972. E-mail: admissions@ststan.com. Web site: www.ststan.com.

ST. STEPHEN'S & ST. AGNES SCHOOL

1000 St. Stephen's Road

Alexandria, Virginia 22304

Head of School: Mrs. Joan G. Ogilvy Holden

General Information Coeducational day college-preparatory, arts, religious studies, and technology school, affiliated with Episcopal Church. Grades JK–12. Founded: 1924. Setting: suburban. Nearest major city is Washington, DC. 35-acre campus. 5 buildings on campus. Approved or accredited by Association of Independent Schools of Greater Washington, National Association of Episcopal Schools, and Virginia Association of Independent Schools. Member of National Association of Independent Schools and Secondary School Admission Test Board. Endowment: $19.5 million. Total enrollment: 1,140. Upper school average class size: 14. Upper school faculty-student ratio: 1:9. There are 170 required school days per year for Upper School students. Upper School students typically attend 5 days per week. The average school day consists of 7 hours and 10 minutes.
Upper School Student Profile Grade 9: 113 students (56 boys, 57 girls); Grade 10: 122 students (66 boys, 56 girls); Grade 11: 113 students (53 boys, 60 girls); Grade 12: 97 students (46 boys, 51 girls). 23% of students are members of Episcopal Church.
Faculty School total: 133. In upper school: 21 men, 31 women; 35 have advanced degrees.
Subjects Offered 1 1/2 elective credits, Advanced Placement courses, algebra, American history, American literature, art, art history, art history-AP, bioethics, biology, biology-AP, calculus, calculus-AP, ceramics, chemistry, chemistry-AP, Christian education, Christian ethics, Christian scripture, Christian testament, comparative government and politics-AP, concert choir, directing, drama, drawing, economics, English, English-AP, ensembles, environmental science-AP, ethics, European history, European history-AP, forensics, French, French language-AP, geometry, government/civics-AP, history, honors English, honors geometry, honors U.S. history, honors world history, instrumental music, jazz ensemble, Latin, Latin-AP, macro/microeconomics-AP, Mandarin, mathematics, medieval history, medieval/Renaissance history, microeconomics-AP, music, music theory-AP, newspaper, painting, physical education, physics, physics-AP, playwriting and directing, pre-calculus, psychology-AP, religion, sculpture, senior project, Spanish, Spanish language-AP, Spanish literature-AP, sports, sports medicine, statistics-AP, studio art, studio art-AP, technical theater, theater, theater arts, trigonometry, U.S. history-AP, world history, writing, yearbook, yoga.
Graduation Requirements Arts and fine arts (art, music, dance, drama), English, family studies, foreign language, history, mathematics, physical education (includes health), religion (includes Bible studies and theology), science, technological applications, senior year independent off-campus project, 40 hours of community service.
Special Academic Programs 22 Advanced Placement exams for which test preparation is offered; honors section; independent study; term-away projects; study abroad; academic accommodation for the gifted, the musically talented, and the artistically talented.
College Admission Counseling 105 students graduated in 2011; all went to college, including Cornell University; Duke University; Georgetown University; The College of William and Mary; University of Virginia; Wake Forest University. Mean SAT critical reading: 627, mean SAT math: 632, mean SAT writing: 629, mean combined SAT: 1888.
Student Life Upper grades have specified standards of dress, student council, honor system. Discipline rests equally with students and faculty. Attendance at religious services is required.
Summer Programs Enrichment, advancement, art/fine arts, computer instruction programs offered; session focuses on enrichment; held both on and off campus; held at Chesapeake Bay, DC, VA and MD area; accepts boys and girls; open to students from other schools. 1,700 students usually enrolled. 2012 schedule: June 18 to August 17. Application deadline: April 9.

Tuition and Aid Day student tuition: $29,582. Tuition installment plan (FACTS Tuition Payment Plan). Need-based scholarship grants available. In 2011–12, 28% of upper-school students received aid. Total amount of financial aid awarded in 2011–12: $2,145,503.
Admissions Traditional secondary-level entrance grade is 9. ISEE or SSAT required. Deadline for receipt of application materials: January 12. Application fee required: $70. Interview required.
Athletics Interscholastic: baseball (boys), basketball (b,g), field hockey (g), football (b), ice hockey (b), lacrosse (b,g), soccer (b,g), softball (g), swimming and diving (b,g), tennis (b,g), track and field (b,g), volleyball (g), winter soccer (g), wrestling (b); intramural: dance team (g), independent competitive sports (b,g); coed interscholastic: cross-country running, diving, golf, winter (indoor) track; coed intramural: basketball, fitness, independent competitive sports, jogging, physical fitness, physical training, strength & conditioning, weight lifting, weight training, yoga. 6 PE instructors, 14 coaches, 2 athletic trainers.
Computers Computers are regularly used in all academic classes. Computer network features include on-campus library services, online commercial services, Internet access, wireless campus network, Internet filtering or blocking technology, computer labs for foreign language, math, technology, library, newspaper, physics, and chemistry, homework assignments posted online, mobile wireless laptop cart (180 laptops), computers available in study hall and library. Campus intranet, student e-mail accounts, and computer access in designated common areas are available to students. Students grades are available online. The school has a published electronic and media policy.
Contact Mr. Jon Kunz, Director of Admission, Grades 6-12. 703-212-2706. Fax: 703-212-2788. E-mail: jkunz@sssas.org. Web site: www.sssas.org.

SAINT STEPHEN'S EPISCOPAL SCHOOL

315 41st Street West

Bradenton, Florida 34209

Head of School: Janet S. Pullen

General Information Coeducational day college-preparatory, arts, religious studies, and marine science school, affiliated with Episcopal Church. Grades PK–12. Founded: 1970. Setting: small town. Nearest major city is Tampa. 35-acre campus. 3 buildings on campus. Approved or accredited by Florida Council of Independent Schools, National Association of Episcopal Schools, Southern Association of Colleges and Schools, and Southern Association of Independent Schools. Member of National Association of Independent Schools. Endowment: $958,000. Total enrollment: 646. Upper school average class size: 16. Upper school faculty-student ratio: 1:10. There are 177 required school days per year for Upper School students. Upper School students typically attend 5 days per week. The average school day consists of 7 hours.
Upper School Student Profile Grade 9: 68 students (35 boys, 33 girls); Grade 10: 71 students (38 boys, 33 girls); Grade 11: 56 students (31 boys, 25 girls); Grade 12: 66 students (31 boys, 35 girls). 15% of students are members of Episcopal Church.
Faculty School total: 85. In upper school: 7 men, 15 women; 20 have advanced degrees.
Subjects Offered 3-dimensional art, Advanced Placement courses, advanced studio art-AP, algebra, American government, American history, American history-AP, American literature, art, art history, art history-AP, art-AP, astronomy, band, biology, biology-AP, British literature, broadcast journalism, calculus, calculus-AP, ceramics, chemistry, chemistry-AP, choir, chorus, community service, comparative religion, composition, composition-AP, computer programming, computer programming-AP, computer science, computer science-AP, conceptual physics, debate, digital art, digital photography, discrete mathematics, drama, economics, English, English language and composition-AP, English language-AP, English literature, English literature and composition-AP, English literature-AP, English-AP, environmental science-AP, European history, European history-AP, French, French language-AP, geometry, graphic design, humanities, international relations, journalism, Latin, Latin-AP, marine biology, marine science, music, newspaper, organic chemistry, painting, photography, physical education, physics, physics-AP, portfolio art, pre-calculus, probability and statistics, psychology, public speaking, science research, Spanish, Spanish language-AP, speech and debate, studio art, studio art-AP, trigonometry, U.S. history, U.S. history-AP, weight training, Western civilization, world history, world history-AP.
Graduation Requirements Arts and fine arts (art, music, dance, drama), electives, English, foreign language, mathematics, physical education (includes health), science, social studies (includes history), senior speech. Community service is required.
Special Academic Programs 17 Advanced Placement exams for which test preparation is offered; honors section.
College Admission Counseling 52 students graduated in 2010; 51 went to college, including Florida State University; University of Central Florida; University of Florida; University of Miami; University of South Florida. Other: 1 had other specific plans. Mean SAT critical reading: 570, mean SAT math: 614, mean SAT writing: 579, mean composite ACT: 25. 39% scored over 600 on SAT critical reading, 56% scored over 600 on SAT math, 36% scored over 600 on SAT writing, 38% scored over 26 on composite ACT.
Student Life Upper grades have specified standards of dress, student council, honor system. Discipline rests primarily with faculty. Attendance at religious services is required.

Tuition and Aid Day student tuition: $16,000. Tuition installment plan (monthly payment plans). Need-based scholarship grants available. In 2010–11, 85% of upper-school students received aid. Total amount of financial aid awarded in 2010–11: $249,000.
Admissions Traditional secondary-level entrance grade is 9. For fall 2010, 48 students applied for upper-level admission, 35 were accepted, 22 enrolled. School's own exam required. Deadline for receipt of application materials: none. Application fee required: $200. Interview recommended.
Athletics Interscholastic: aerobics/dance (girls), aquatics (b,g), baseball (b), basketball (b,g), cheering (g), cross-country running (b,g), dance (g), dance team (g), diving (b,g), football (b), golf (b,g), independent competitive sports (b,g), soccer (b,g), softball (g), swimming and diving (b,g), tennis (b,g), track and field (b,g), volleyball (g), winter soccer (b,g), wrestling (b); intramural: aerobics/dance (g), ballet (g), basketball (b,g), cheering (g), cross-country running (b,g), dance (g), fitness (b,g), horseback riding (b,g), jogging (b,g), lacrosse (b,g), physical fitness (b,g), physical training (b,g), running (b,g), soccer (b,g), softball (b,g), strength & conditioning (b,g), tennis (b,g), track and field (b,g), volleyball (b,g), weight training (b,g), wrestling (b); coed intramural: kayaking, yoga. 8 PE instructors, 14 coaches, 1 athletic trainer.
Computers Computers are regularly used in art, computer applications, foreign language, journalism, library, mathematics, media, science, social sciences, word processing, writing, yearbook classes. Computer network features include on-campus library services, online commercial services, Internet access, wireless campus network, Internet filtering or blocking technology, Microsoft Office. Computer access in designated common areas is available to students. Students grades are available online. The school has a published electronic and media policy.
Contact Linda G. Lutz, Director of Admissions. 941-746-2121 Ext. 568. Fax: 941-345-1237. E-mail: llutz@saintstephens.org. Web site: www.saintstephens.org.

ST. STEPHEN'S EPISCOPAL SCHOOL

6500 St. Stephen's Drive

Austin, Texas 78746

Head of School: Mr. Robert Kirkpatrick

General Information Coeducational boarding and day college-preparatory and theater school, affiliated with Episcopal Church. Boarding grades 8–12, day grades 6–12. Founded: 1950. Setting: suburban. Students are housed in single-sex dormitories. 370-acre campus. 40 buildings on campus. Approved or accredited by Independent Schools Association of the Southwest, National Association of Episcopal Schools, The Association of Boarding Schools, and Texas Department of Education. Member of National Association of Independent Schools and Secondary School Admission Test Board. Endowment: $8.2 million. Total enrollment: 668. Upper school average class size: 17. Upper school faculty-student ratio: 1:8. There are 165 required school days per year for Upper School students. Upper School students typically attend 5 days per week. The average school day consists of 7 hours and 35 minutes.
Upper School Student Profile Grade 9: 109 students (52 boys, 57 girls); Grade 10: 132 students (64 boys, 68 girls); Grade 11: 108 students (61 boys, 47 girls); Grade 12: 113 students (68 boys, 45 girls). 35% of students are boarding students. 80% are state residents. 9 states are represented in upper school student body. 20% are international students. International students from China, Mexico, Republic of Korea, Saudi Arabia, Taiwan, and Thailand; 9 other countries represented in student body. 18% of students are members of Episcopal Church.
Faculty School total: 98. In upper school: 42 men, 43 women; 48 have advanced degrees; 36 reside on campus.
Subjects Offered 3-dimensional design, acting, algebra, American history, American history-AP, anthropology, art, art history, art history-AP, astrophysics, ballet, band, biology, biology-AP, calculus, calculus-AP, ceramics, chamber groups, chemistry, chemistry-AP, Chinese, choreography, classics, computer applications, computer math, computer science, computer studies, creative writing, directing, drama, English, English literature, environmental science, European history, European history-AP, fine arts, French, French-AP, geology, geometry, government/civics, history, jazz band, Latin, mathematics, music, music theory-AP, musical theater, photography, physical education, physics, physics-AP, play/screen writing, pre-calculus, psychology, public policy issues and action, public speaking, religion, science, social studies, Spanish, Spanish-AP, statistics-AP, studio art-AP, theater arts, theology, video, world history, world literature.
Graduation Requirements Arts and fine arts (art, music, dance, drama), electives, English, foreign language, mathematics, physical education (includes health), religion (includes Bible studies and theology), science, social studies (includes history), community service requirement in middle and upper schools.
Special Academic Programs Advanced Placement exam preparation; honors section; independent study; study abroad; ESL (23 students enrolled).
College Admission Counseling 108 students graduated in 2011; all went to college, including The University of Texas at Austin; Washington University in St. Louis. Mean SAT critical reading: 623, mean SAT math: 672, mean SAT writing: 645, mean combined SAT: 1940.
Student Life Upper grades have specified standards of dress, student council. Discipline rests equally with students and faculty. Attendance at religious services is required.

Summer Programs Sports, art/fine arts programs offered; session focuses on soccer, tennis, travel abroad, foreign language/culture, fine arts, community service; held both on and off campus; held at locations in Europe, El Salvador, Nicaragua, Costa Rica, American wilderness areas; accepts boys and girls; open to students from other schools. 120 students usually enrolled. 2012 schedule: June 1 to July 31. Application deadline: none.

Tuition and Aid Day student tuition: $21,970; 7-day tuition and room/board: $41,700. Tuition installment plan (individually arranged payment plans). Merit scholarship grants, need-based scholarship grants, partial tuition remission for children of faculty and staff available. In 2011–12, 15% of upper-school students received aid; total upper-school merit-scholarship money awarded: $30,000. Total amount of financial aid awarded in 2011–12: $1,900,000.

Admissions Traditional secondary-level entrance grade is 9. For fall 2011, 334 students applied for upper-level admission, 239 were accepted, 95 enrolled. ISEE or SSAT required. Deadline for receipt of application materials: February 1. Application fee required: $75. Interview required.

Athletics Interscholastic: baseball (boys), basketball (b,g), cheering (b,g), crew (b,g), cross-country running (b,g), field hockey (g), football (b), golf (b,g), lacrosse (b,g), soccer (b,g), softball (g), swimming and diving (b,g), tennis (b,g), track and field (b,g), volleyball (g), winter soccer (b,g); intramural: bicycling (b,g), climbing (b,g), combined training (b,g), dance (b,g), fitness (b,g), hiking/backpacking (b,g), modern dance (b,g), mountain biking (b,g), mountaineering (b,g), outdoor adventure (b,g), outdoor education (b,g), physical fitness (b,g), rock climbing (b,g), ropes courses (b,g), strength & conditioning (b,g), surfing (b,g), wall climbing (b,g), weight training (b,g). 2 PE instructors, 7 coaches, 1 athletic trainer.

Computers Computer network features include on-campus library services, online commercial services, Internet access, wireless campus network, Internet filtering or blocking technology, online schedules, syllabi, homework, examples, and links to information sources. Campus intranet, student e-mail accounts, and computer access in designated common areas are available to students. Students grades are available online.

Contact Lawrence Sampleton, Director of Admission. 512-327-1213 Ext. 210. Fax: 512-327-6771. E-mail: admission@sstx.org. Web site: www.sstx.org.

ST. STEPHEN'S SCHOOL, ROME

Via Aventina 3

Rome 00153, Italy

Head of School: Ms. Lesley Jane Murphy

General Information Coeducational boarding and day college-preparatory, arts, and bilingual studies school. Grades 9–PG. Founded: 1964. Setting: urban. Students are housed in single-sex by floor dormitories. 2-acre campus. 2 buildings on campus. Approved or accredited by International Baccalaureate Organization, New England Association of Schools and Colleges, and US Department of State. Affiliate member of National Association of Independent Schools; member of European Council of International Schools. Language of instruction: English. Endowment: €2.3 million. Total enrollment: 258. Upper school average class size: 13. Upper school faculty-student ratio: 1:7. There are 175 required school days per year for Upper School students. Upper School students typically attend 5 days per week. The average school day consists of 7 hours.

Upper School Student Profile Grade 9: 56 students (30 boys, 26 girls); Grade 10: 63 students (35 boys, 28 girls); Grade 11: 71 students (26 boys, 45 girls); Grade 12: 66 students (29 boys, 37 girls); Postgraduate: 2 students (1 boy, 1 girl). 14% of students are boarding students. 64% are international students. International students from China, India, Ireland, Kazakhstan, United Kingdom, and United States; 27 other countries represented in student body.

Faculty School total: 45. In upper school: 12 men, 33 women; 39 have advanced degrees; 6 reside on campus.

Subjects Offered Algebra, American literature, art, art history, biology, calculus, chemistry, chorus, classical studies, creative writing, dance, drama, economics, English, English literature, environmental systems, European history, French, geometry, health, Islamic studies, Italian, Latin, music theory, photography, physical education, physics, pre-calculus, Roman civilization, sculpture, Spanish, theory of knowledge, trigonometry, U.S. history, world literature.

Graduation Requirements Arts and fine arts (art, music, dance, drama), English, foreign language, mathematics, physical education (includes health), science, social studies (includes history), senior essay, computer proficiency examination, service.

Special Academic Programs International Baccalaureate program; 7 Advanced Placement exams for which test preparation is offered; domestic exchange program (with Buckingham Browne & Nichols School, Friends Seminary, Choate Rosemary Hall); ESL (9 students enrolled).

College Admission Counseling 58 students graduated in 2011; 49 went to college, including Bard College; Boston University; Brown University; New York University; Northeastern University; University of Pennsylvania. Other: 3 entered a postgraduate year, 6 had other specific plans. Mean SAT critical reading: 584, mean SAT math: 610, mean SAT writing: 598, mean combined SAT: 1792, mean composite ACT: 24.

Student Life Upper grades have student council. Discipline rests equally with students and faculty.

Summer Programs Enrichment, art/fine arts programs offered; session focuses on liberal arts/pre-college; held both on and off campus; held at off campus sites include museum visits and visits to various historical sites within the city; accepts boys and girls; open to students from other schools. 50 students usually enrolled. 2012 schedule: July 3 to August 6. Application deadline: June 20.

Tuition and Aid Day student tuition: €21,700–€22,200; 7-day tuition and room/board: €32,950–€33,450. Tuition installment plan (individually arranged payment plans). Tuition reduction for siblings, merit scholarship grants, need-based scholarship grants available. In 2011–12, 23% of upper-school students received aid; total upper-school merit-scholarship money awarded: €30,000. Total amount of financial aid awarded in 2011–12: €405,150.

Admissions Traditional secondary-level entrance grade is 9. For fall 2011, 178 students applied for upper-level admission, 117 were accepted, 88 enrolled. School's own exam required. Deadline for receipt of application materials: January 16. Application fee required: €150. Interview recommended.

Athletics Interscholastic: soccer (boys, girls), volleyball (b,g); intramural: basketball (b,g), soccer (b,g), tennis (b,g), volleyball (b,g); coed intramural: dance, martial arts, track and field, yoga. 7 coaches.

Computers Computers are regularly used in English, foreign language, mathematics, photography, science, social studies classes. Computer network features include on-campus library services, Internet access, wireless campus network, Internet filtering or blocking technology. Campus intranet, student e-mail accounts, and computer access in designated common areas are available to students. Students grades are available online. The school has a published electronic and media policy.

Contact Ms. Alex Perniciaro, Admissions Coordinator. 39-06-575-0605. Fax: 39-06-574-1941. E-mail: admissions@ststephens-rome.com. Web site: www.sssrome.it.

SAINT TERESA'S ACADEMY

5600 Main Street

Kansas City, Missouri 64113

Head of School: Mrs. Nan Tiehen Bone

General Information Girls' day college-preparatory school, affiliated with Roman Catholic Church. Grades 9–12. Founded: 1866. Setting: urban. 20-acre campus. 4 buildings on campus. Approved or accredited by National Catholic Education Association, North Central Association of Colleges and Schools, and Missouri Department of Education. Member of National Association of Independent Schools. Endowment: $150,000. Total enrollment: 561. Upper school average class size: 21. Upper school faculty-student ratio: 1:12. There are 174 required school days per year for Upper School students. Upper School students typically attend 5 days per week. The average school day consists of 6 hours and 40 minutes.

Upper School Student Profile Grade 9: 151 students (151 girls); Grade 10: 141 students (141 girls); Grade 11: 140 students (140 girls); Grade 12: 129 students (129 girls). 87% of students are Roman Catholic.

Faculty School total: 48. In upper school: 10 men, 38 women; 32 have advanced degrees.

Subjects Offered Advanced chemistry, advanced math, algebra, American government, American history, American literature, analysis, anatomy and physiology, art, athletics, basketball, biology, biology-AP, botany, British literature, calculus, career/college preparation, chamber groups, chemistry, chemistry-AP, choir, chorus, computer graphics, computer programming, computer science-AP, current events, dance, directing, drama, drawing, ecology, English, English language and composition-AP, English language-AP, English literature, European history-AP, fiber arts, fitness, foreign language, forensics, French, French language-AP, French-AP, freshman seminar, geometry, golf, graphic design, health, independent study, journalism, keyboarding, language arts, Latin, Latin History, music-AP, newspaper, painting, physical education, portfolio art, psychology, Shakespeare, social issues, social studies, sociology, softball, Spanish, Spanish language-AP, Spanish-AP, speech, speech and debate, sports conditioning, sports performance development, stagecraft, swimming, tennis, theater, theology and the arts, track and field, trigonometry, U.S. government, U.S. government and politics-AP, U.S. history, volleyball, Western civilization, women spirituality and faith, world geography, world religions, writing, yearbook.

Graduation Requirements Arts and fine arts (art, music, dance, drama), computer science, electives, English, foreign language, mathematics, physical education (includes health), science, social studies (includes history), theology. Community service is required.

Special Academic Programs Advanced Placement exam preparation; honors section; study at local college for college credit.

College Admission Counseling 130 students graduated in 2011; 129 went to college, including Kansas State University; Saint Louis University; The University of Kansas; University of Arkansas; University of Missouri. Other: 1 had other specific plans. Mean SAT critical reading: 600, mean SAT math: 580, mean SAT writing: 610, mean combined SAT: 1780, mean composite ACT: 26.

Student Life Upper grades have uniform requirement, student council. Discipline rests primarily with faculty. Attendance at religious services is required.

Summer Programs Sports, art/fine arts, computer instruction programs offered; session focuses on fine arts, sports and remedial summer school programs; held on campus; accepts girls; open to students from other schools. 100 students usually enrolled. 2012 schedule: June 3 to July 15. Application deadline: May 1.

Tuition and Aid Day student tuition: $9700. Tuition installment plan (SMART Tuition Payment Plan). Tuition reduction for siblings, merit scholarship grants, need-based scholarship grants available. In 2011–12, 25% of upper-school students received aid; total upper-school merit-scholarship money awarded: $125,000. Total amount of financial aid awarded in 2011–12: $130,000.

Admissions Traditional secondary-level entrance grade is 9. For fall 2011, 174 students applied for upper-level admission, 165 were accepted, 150 enrolled. Placement test required. Deadline for receipt of application materials: February 28. No application fee required.

Athletics Interscholastic: aerobics/dance, basketball, cross-country running, diving, drill team, golf, lacrosse, soccer, softball, swimming and diving, tennis, track and field, volleyball; intramural: aerobics/dance, badminton, fitness, fitness walking, jogging, physical fitness, physical training, running, strength & conditioning, table tennis, volleyball, walking, weight lifting, weight training. 1 PE instructor, 25 coaches, 1 athletic trainer.

Computers Computers are regularly used in business education, creative writing, graphics, journalism, library, newspaper, photography, research skills, science, writing, yearbook classes. Computer network features include on-campus library services, Internet access, wireless campus network, Internet filtering or blocking technology. Campus intranet is available to students. Students grades are available online. The school has a published electronic and media policy.

Contact Mrs. Roseann Hudnall, Admissions Director. 816-501-0011 Ext. 135. Fax: 816-523-0232. E-mail: rhudnall@stteresasacademy.org. Web site: www.stteresasacademy.org.

SAINT THOMAS ACADEMY

949 Mendota Heights Road

Mendota Heights, Minnesota 55120

Head of School: Thomas B. Mich, PhD

General Information Boys' day college-preparatory and military school, affiliated with Roman Catholic Church. Grades 7–12. Founded: 1885. Setting: suburban. Nearest major city is St. Paul. 72-acre campus. 3 buildings on campus. Approved or accredited by Independent Schools Association of the Central States. Member of National Association of Independent Schools. Endowment: $17.1 million. Total enrollment: 675. Upper school average class size: 17. Upper school faculty-student ratio: 1:10. There are 173 required school days per year for Upper School students. Upper School students typically attend 5 days per week. The average school day consists of 6 hours and 40 minutes.

Upper School Student Profile Grade 9: 157 students (157 boys); Grade 10: 134 students (134 boys); Grade 11: 146 students (146 boys); Grade 12: 122 students (122 boys). 75% of students are Roman Catholic.

Faculty School total: 58. In upper school: 34 men, 22 women; 43 have advanced degrees.

Subjects Offered Advanced biology, advanced computer applications, advanced math, Advanced Placement courses, algebra, American democracy, American government, American history, American literature, art, art history, band, biology, calculus, campus ministry, chemistry, Chinese, computer science, creative writing, earth science, economics, English, English literature, environmental studies, fine arts, French, geometry, government/civics, health, history, JROTC, Latin, mathematics, military science, music, physical education, physics, psychology, religion, science, social studies, Spanish, trigonometry, world history, world literature, writing.

Graduation Requirements Arts and fine arts (art, music, dance, drama), biology, chemistry, English, foreign language, health education, JROTC or LEAD (Leadership Education and Development), mathematics, physical education (includes health), science, social studies (includes history), theology, U.S. history, world history, 100 hours of community service in 12th grade.

Special Academic Programs 11 Advanced Placement exams for which test preparation is offered; honors section; independent study; study at local college for college credit.

College Admission Counseling 132 students graduated in 2011; 126 went to college, including Iowa State University of Science and Technology; Saint John's University; University of Minnesota, Twin Cities Campus; University of North Dakota; University of St. Thomas; University of Wisconsin–Madison. Other: 3 had other specific plans.

Student Life Upper grades have uniform requirement, student council, honor system. Discipline rests primarily with faculty. Attendance at religious services is required.

Summer Programs Enrichment programs offered; session focuses on study and organizational strategies, time management, test preparation and orientation; held on campus; accepts boys; not open to students from other schools. 120 students usually enrolled. 2012 schedule: July 9 to August 9. Application deadline: May 25.

Tuition and Aid Day student tuition: $17,250. Tuition installment plan (SMART Tuition Payment Plan, monthly payment plans, individually arranged payment plans, quarterly payment plan). Merit scholarship grants, need-based scholarship grants available. In 2011–12, 42% of upper-school students received aid; total upper-school merit-scholarship money awarded: $49,500. Total amount of financial aid awarded in 2011–12: $2,200,000.

Admissions Traditional secondary-level entrance grade is 9. For fall 2011, 285 students applied for upper-level admission, 225 were accepted, 112 enrolled. Cognitive Abilities Test required. Deadline for receipt of application materials: none. No application fee required. On-campus interview recommended.

Athletics Interscholastic: alpine skiing, baseball, basketball, cross-country running, drill team, fitness, football, golf, hockey, ice hockey, JROTC drill, lacrosse, marksmanship, nordic skiing, outdoor skills, physical fitness, riflery, skiing (cross-country), skiing (downhill), soccer, swimming and diving, tennis, track and field, wrestling; intramural: basketball, bowling, football, hockey, physical training, strength & conditioning, table tennis, weight lifting, weight training. 3 PE instructors, 1 athletic trainer.

Computers Computers are regularly used in all academic, art, foreign language, music classes. Computer network features include on-campus library services, online commercial services, Internet access, wireless campus network, Internet filtering or blocking technology. Student e-mail accounts are available to students. Students grades are available online. The school has a published electronic and media policy.

Contact Peggy Mansur, Admissions Assistant. 651-683-1515. Fax: 651-683-1576. E-mail: pmansur@cadets.com. Web site: www.cadets.com.

ST. THOMAS AQUINAS HIGH SCHOOL

2801 Southwest 12th Street

Fort Lauderdale, Florida 33312-2999

Head of School: Mrs. Tina Jones

General Information Coeducational day college-preparatory, arts, religious studies, technology, Campus Ministry, and College Preparatory school, affiliated with Roman Catholic Church. Grades 9–12. Founded: 1936. Setting: suburban. 24-acre campus. 23 buildings on campus. Approved or accredited by National Catholic Education Association, Southern Association of Colleges and Schools, and Florida Department of Education. Total enrollment: 2,190. Upper school average class size: 25. Upper school faculty-student ratio: 1:18. There are 180 required school days per year for Upper School students. Upper School students typically attend 5 days per week. The average school day consists of 6 hours and 30 minutes.

Upper School Student Profile Grade 9: 556 students (277 boys, 279 girls); Grade 10: 549 students (267 boys, 282 girls); Grade 11: 559 students (284 boys, 275 girls); Grade 12: 526 students (253 boys, 273 girls). 96% of students are Roman Catholic.

Faculty School total: 123. In upper school: 52 men, 71 women; 71 have advanced degrees.

Subjects Offered 20th century history, 20th century world history, 3-dimensional art, acting, advanced chemistry, advanced computer applications, advanced math, Advanced Placement courses, algebra, American government, American history, American history-AP, American literature, anatomy and physiology, art, art appreciation, art history-AP, athletics, biology, biology-AP, British literature, British literature (honors), British literature-AP, broadcast journalism, calculus, calculus-AP, chemistry, chemistry-AP, Chinese, choir, choral music, chorus, Christianity, church history, comparative government and politics-AP, comparative political systems-AP, composition-AP, computer art, computer graphics, computer programming-AP, computer science-AP, debate, desktop publishing, digital art, digital imaging, directing, drama, drama performance, drawing, economics-AP, electives, English, English language and composition-AP, English literature, English literature and composition-AP, English literature-AP, English-AP, English/composition-AP, environmental science, environmental science-AP, European history, European history-AP, film and literature, film and new technologies, fitness, food science, forensics, French, French language-AP, French literature-AP, French-AP, general science, geometry, government, government and politics-AP, government-AP, government/civics-AP, grammar, graphic arts, graphic design, health, health and safety, health and wellness, health education, health enhancement, health science, healthful living, Hispanic literature, history, history of drama, history-AP, Holocaust, honors algebra, honors English, honors geometry, honors U.S. history, honors world history, human anatomy, human geography - AP, jazz, jazz band, journalism, keyboarding, lab science, language, language and composition, language arts, language-AP, Latin, Latin-AP, leadership, leadership and service, leadership education training, Life of Christ, literature, literature and composition-AP, literature-AP, macro/microeconomics-AP, macroeconomics-AP, marine biology, marine studies, mathematics-AP, media, microeconomics, microeconomics-AP, model United Nations, modern European history, modern European history-AP, news writing, newspaper, nutrition, oral expression, orchestra, peace and justice, peace education, peace studies, performing arts, photography, photojournalism, physical education, physical fitness, physics, physics-AP, play production, playwriting and directing, poetry, political systems, pottery, pre-algebra, pre-calculus, probability and statistics, psychology, psychology-AP, public speaking, reading, SAT preparation, SAT/ACT preparation, Spanish, Spanish language-AP, Spanish literature, Spanish literature-AP, Spanish-AP, speech, speech and debate, speech and oral interpretations, speech communications, sports team management, stage design, stagecraft, statistics, statistics-AP, student government, student publications, studio art, technical theater, television, trigonometry, U.S. government and politics-AP, U.S. history, U.S. history-AP, United States government-AP, world history, world history-AP.

Graduation Requirements Arts and fine arts (art, music, dance, drama), computer science, electives, English, foreign language, health, mathematics, personal fitness, science, social sciences, theology.

Special Academic Programs Advanced Placement exam preparation; honors section; remedial reading and/or remedial writing; remedial math.

College Admission Counseling 533 students graduated in 2011; all went to college, including Florida Atlantic University; Florida State University; University of Central Florida; University of Florida; University of Miami; University of North Florida. Mean SAT critical reading: 573, mean SAT math: 572, mean SAT writing: 582, mean combined SAT: 1727, mean composite ACT: 24.

Student Life Upper grades have uniform requirement, student council, honor system. Discipline rests primarily with faculty. Attendance at religious services is required.

Summer Programs Remediation, enrichment, advancement, art/fine arts, computer instruction programs offered; session focuses on enrichment; held on campus; accepts boys and girls; open to students from other schools. 1,000 students usually enrolled. 2012 schedule: June 4 to June 27. Application deadline: June 4.

Tuition and Aid Day student tuition: $7200. Need-based scholarship grants available.

Admissions Traditional secondary-level entrance grade is 9. For fall 2011, 800 students applied for upper-level admission, 570 were accepted, 556 enrolled. High School Placement Test required. Deadline for receipt of application materials: March 15. Application fee required: $50. Interview required.

Athletics Interscholastic: baseball (boys), basketball (b,g), bowling (b,g), cheering (g), cross-country running (b,g), dance (b,g), dance squad (g), diving (b,g), drill team (g), football (b), golf (b,g), physical fitness (b,g), soccer (b,g), softball (g), swimming and diving (b,g), tennis (b,g), track and field (b,g), volleyball (b,g), water polo (b,g), wrestling (b); intramural: dance team (g), danceline (g), drill team (g); coed interscholastic: ballet, bowling, ice hockey, indoor hockey, physical training; coed intramural: physical training, running. 3 PE instructors, 25 coaches, 2 athletic trainers.

Computers Computers are regularly used in all academic, data processing, desktop publishing, graphic arts, graphic design, graphics, journalism, keyboarding, lab/keyboard, media, media arts, media production, media services, news writing, newspaper, programming, publications, publishing, technology, video film production, Web site design, word processing classes. Computer network features include on-campus library services, online commercial services, Internet access, Internet filtering or blocking technology. Computer access in designated common areas is available to students. The school has a published electronic and media policy.

Contact Admissions Office. 954-581-2127 Ext. 8623. Fax: 954-327-2193. E-mail: mary.facella@aquinas-sta.org. Web site: www.aquinas-sta.org.

SAINT THOMAS AQUINAS HIGH SCHOOL

11411 Pflumm Road

Overland Park, Kansas 66215-4816

Head of School: Dr. William P. Ford

General Information Coeducational day college-preparatory, religious studies, and technology school, affiliated with Roman Catholic Church. Grades 9–12. Founded: 1988. Setting: suburban. Nearest major city is Kansas City, MO. 44-acre campus. 2 buildings on campus. Approved or accredited by National Catholic Education Association, North Central Association of Colleges and Schools, and Kansas Department of Education. Total enrollment: 982. Upper school average class size: 25. Upper school faculty-student ratio: 1:15. There are 180 required school days per year for Upper School students. Upper School students typically attend 5 days per week. The average school day consists of 7 hours.

Upper School Student Profile Grade 9: 246 students (125 boys, 121 girls); Grade 10: 231 students (110 boys, 121 girls); Grade 11: 248 students (112 boys, 136 girls); Grade 12: 257 students (116 boys, 141 girls). 97% of students are Roman Catholic.

Faculty School total: 70. In upper school: 32 men, 38 women; 60 have advanced degrees.

Graduation Requirements Arts and fine arts (art, music, dance, drama), computer technologies, electives, English, Latin, mathematics, modern languages, physical education (includes health), science, social studies (includes history), speech, theology, service (one fourth credit each of 4 years).

Special Academic Programs Advanced Placement exam preparation; honors section; study at local college for college credit; academic accommodation for the gifted; remedial reading and/or remedial writing; remedial math.

College Admission Counseling 261 students graduated in 2011; 260 went to college, including Benedictine College; Johnson County Community College; Kansas State University; Saint Louis University; The University of Kansas; University of Notre Dame. Other: 1 entered military service. Mean SAT critical reading: 610, mean SAT math: 618, mean SAT writing: 615, mean composite ACT: 25.

Student Life Upper grades have uniform requirement, student council. Discipline rests primarily with faculty. Attendance at religious services is required.

Summer Programs Remediation, advancement, sports, computer instruction programs offered; session focuses on sports camps and selected academic coursework; held on campus; accepts boys and girls; open to students from other schools.

Tuition and Aid Day student tuition: $7475–$8475. Tuition installment plan (SMART Tuition Payment Plan). Need-based scholarship grants available.

Admissions Traditional secondary-level entrance grade is 9. ACT-Explore required. Deadline for receipt of application materials: none. Application fee required: $125. Interview required.

Athletics Interscholastic: baseball (boys), basketball (b,g), bowling (b,g), cross-country running (b,g), dance team (g), diving (b,g), football (b), golf (b,g), soccer (b,g), softball (g), swimming and diving (b,g), tennis (b,g), track and field (b,g), volleyball (g), wrestling (b); intramural: field hockey (g), lacrosse (b); coed interscholastic: cheering; coed intramural: table tennis, ultimate Frisbee. 3 PE instructors, 1 athletic trainer.

Computers Computers are regularly used in all academic, computer applications, desktop publishing, programming, video film production, Web site design classes. Computer network features include on-campus library services, Internet access, wireless campus network, computer labs and laptop carts. Student e-mail accounts are available to students. Students grades are available online. The school has a published electronic and media policy.

Contact Mrs. Diane Pyle, Director of Admissions. 913-319-2423. Fax: 913-345-2319. E-mail: dpyle@stasaints.net. Web site: www.stasaints.net.

ST. THOMAS AQUINAS HIGH SCHOOL

197 Dover Point Road

Dover, New Hampshire 03820

Head of School: Mr. Kevin Collins

General Information Coeducational day college-preparatory and religious studies school, affiliated with Roman Catholic Church. Grades 9–12. Founded: 1960. Setting: small town. Nearest major city is Boston, MA. 11-acre campus. 2 buildings on campus. Approved or accredited by New England Association of Schools and Colleges and New Hampshire Department of Education. Total enrollment: 643. Upper school average class size: 18. Upper school faculty-student ratio: 1:14. There are 185 required school days per year for Upper School students. Upper School students typically attend 5 days per week. The average school day consists of 6 hours and 25 minutes.

Faculty School total: 50. In upper school: 26 men, 24 women; 25 have advanced degrees.

Subjects Offered Algebra, anatomy and physiology, biology, biology-AP, calculus, calculus-AP, chemistry, chorus, Christian ethics, concert band, contemporary studies, drawing, economics, English, environmental science-AP, finite math, French, geography, geometry, honors algebra, honors English, honors geometry, humanities, introduction to technology, Latin, marine biology, math applications, media arts, music appreciation, music theory, painting, physics, prayer/spirituality, pre-calculus, psychology, science, scripture, sculpture, social justice, sociology, Spanish, statistics-AP, studio art, theology, trigonometry, U.S. government and politics-AP, U.S. history, U.S. history-AP, wellness, Western civilization, world religions.

Graduation Requirements Arts and fine arts (art, music, dance, drama), Christian ethics, electives, English, foreign language, freshman seminar, mathematics, prayer/spirituality, science, scripture, social justice, social studies (includes history), theology, world religions, 40 hour community service requirement.

Special Academic Programs Advanced Placement exam preparation; honors section; independent study.

College Admission Counseling 177 students graduated in 2011; 174 went to college, including Boston College; Keene State College; Miami University; Montana State University; Saint Anselm College; University of New Hampshire. Other: 2 entered military service, 1 had other specific plans. Mean SAT critical reading: 565, mean SAT math: 556, mean SAT writing: 560, mean composite ACT: 24.

Student Life Upper grades have specified standards of dress, student council. Discipline rests primarily with faculty. Attendance at religious services is required.

Summer Programs Enrichment, advancement programs offered; held on campus; accepts boys and girls; not open to students from other schools.

Tuition and Aid Day student tuition: $10,100. Tuition installment plan (annual, semi-annual, and 10-month payment plans). Need-based scholarship grants available.

Admissions Traditional secondary-level entrance grade is 9. Scholastic Testing Service High School Placement Test required. Deadline for receipt of application materials: December 31. Application fee required: $40.

Athletics Interscholastic: baseball (boys), basketball (b,g), cross-country running (b,g), field hockey (g), football (b), golf (b,g), ice hockey (b,g), lacrosse (b,g), skiing (downhill) (b,g), soccer (b,g), softball (g), swimming and diving (b,g), tennis (b,g), track and field (b,g), volleyball (g), winter (indoor) track (b,g), wrestling (b); intramural: dance team (g). 51 coaches, 1 athletic trainer.

Computers Computers are regularly used in introduction to technology, media arts classes. Computer network features include on-campus library services, Internet access, wireless campus network. Student e-mail accounts and computer access in designated common areas are available to students. Students grades are available online.

Contact Mr. Scott Rafferty, Director of Admissions. 603-742-3206. Fax: 603-749-7822. E-mail: srafferty@stalux.org. Web site: www.stalux.org.

ST. THOMAS CHOIR SCHOOL

New York, New York

See Junior Boarding Schools section.

ST. THOMAS HIGH SCHOOL

4500 Memorial Drive

Houston, Texas 77007-7332

Head of School: Rev. Patrick Fulton, CSB

General Information Boys' day college-preparatory and religious studies school, affiliated with Roman Catholic Church. Grades 9–12. Founded: 1900. Setting: urban. 37-acre campus. 6 buildings on campus. Approved or accredited by Southern Association of Colleges and Schools, Texas Catholic Conference, Texas Education Agency, and Texas Department of Education. Endowment: $10.5 million. Total enrollment: 738. Upper school average class size: 18. Upper school faculty-student ratio: 1:14. There are 185 required school days per year for Upper School students. Upper School students typically attend 5 days per week. The average school day consists of 7 hours and 20 minutes.

Upper School Student Profile Grade 9: 194 students (194 boys); Grade 10: 190 students (190 boys); Grade 11: 174 students (174 boys); Grade 12: 178 students (178 boys). 75% of students are Roman Catholic.

Faculty School total: 53. In upper school: 36 men, 17 women; 31 have advanced degrees.

Subjects Offered Algebra, American government, American history, American history-AP, American literature, anatomy and physiology, ancient history, art, arts, Basic programming, Bible studies, bioethics, biology, biology-AP, British literature, calculus, calculus-AP, ceramics, chemistry, chemistry-AP, civics/free enterprise, classical civilization, college counseling, comparative government and politics-AP, computer applications, computer information systems, computer programming, computer studies, creative writing, critical thinking, critical writing, decision making skills, desktop publishing, digital photography, drama, drawing, ecology, environmental systems, economics, economics-AP, English, English language-AP, English literature, English literature-AP, environmental education, environmental science, ethics, European history, fine arts, forensics, French, geography, geology, geometry, government and politics-AP, government/civics, grammar, guidance, health, health education, history of the Catholic Church, Holocaust studies, instrumental music, jazz band, journalism, Latin, marine biology, mathematics, military history, oceanography, oral communications, orchestra, painting, photography, physical education, physics, physics-AP, pre-calculus, programming, public speaking, publications, religion, social studies, Spanish, Spanish language-AP, speech, student government, student publications, theater, theology, trigonometry, U.S. government and politics-AP, world history, world literature.

Graduation Requirements Arts and fine arts (art, music, dance, drama), computer applications, English, foreign language, mathematics, physical education (includes health), religion (includes Bible studies and theology), science, social studies (includes history).

Special Academic Programs 10 Advanced Placement exams for which test preparation is offered; honors section.

College Admission Counseling 152 students graduated in 2011; all went to college, including Baylor University; Texas A&M University; Texas Tech University; The University of Texas at Austin; University of Houston; University of Notre Dame. Mean composite ACT: 26.

Student Life Upper grades have specified standards of dress, student council. Discipline rests primarily with faculty. Attendance at religious services is required.

Summer Programs Remediation programs offered; held on campus; accepts boys; not open to students from other schools. 2012 schedule: June 5 to June 26.

Tuition and Aid Day student tuition: $12,300. Tuition installment plan (monthly payment plans). Merit scholarship grants, need-based scholarship grants, middle-income loans available. In 2011–12, 33% of upper-school students received aid; total upper-school merit-scholarship money awarded: $200,000. Total amount of financial aid awarded in 2011–12: $1,300,000.

Admissions Traditional secondary-level entrance grade is 9. For fall 2011, 512 students applied for upper-level admission, 281 were accepted, 229 enrolled. High School Placement Test required. Deadline for receipt of application materials: January 15. Application fee required: $75.

Athletics Interscholastic: baseball, basketball, cross-country running, football, golf, lacrosse, rugby, soccer, swimming and diving, tennis, track and field, wrestling; intramural: basketball, bowling, flag football, Frisbee, roller hockey, table tennis, weight lifting. 2 PE instructors, 2 coaches, 1 athletic trainer.

Computers Computers are regularly used in data processing, desktop publishing, multimedia, newspaper, photography, programming, publications, Web site design, word processing classes. Computer network features include on-campus library services, Internet access, Internet filtering or blocking technology. Computer access in designated common areas is available to students. Students grades are available online. The school has a published electronic and media policy.

Contact Ms. Christine Westman, Assistant Principal. 713-864-6348. Fax: 713-864-5750. E-mail: chris.westman@sths.org. Web site: www.sths.org.

SAINT THOMAS MORE CATHOLIC HIGH SCHOOL

450 East Farrel Road

Lafayette, Louisiana 70508

Head of School: Mrs. Audrey C. Menard

General Information Coeducational day college-preparatory, arts, business, religious studies, bilingual studies, and technology school, affiliated with Roman Catholic Church. Grades 9–12. Founded: 1982. Setting: suburban. Nearest major city is Baton Rouge. 45-acre campus. 1 building on campus. Approved or accredited by Southern Association of Colleges and Schools and Louisiana Department of Education. Endowment: $1.6 million. Total enrollment: 1,029. Upper school average class size: 25. Upper school faculty-student ratio: 1:25. There are 180 required school days per year for Upper School students. Upper School students typically attend 5 days per week. The average school day consists of 7 hours and 4 minutes.

Upper School Student Profile Grade 9: 276 students (129 boys, 147 girls); Grade 10: 262 students (138 boys, 124 girls); Grade 11: 272 students (135 boys, 137 girls); Grade 12: 219 students (108 boys, 111 girls). 89% of students are Roman Catholic.

Faculty School total: 90. In upper school: 27 men, 47 women; 23 have advanced degrees.

Subjects Offered Accounting, advanced chemistry, advanced math, Advanced Placement courses, advanced studio art-AP, algebra, American history, American history-AP, applied music, art, athletics, band, biology, business, calculus-AP, campus ministry, chemistry, chorus, civics/free enterprise, communication skills, computer science, creative writing, debate, desktop publishing, drama, economics, economics and history, English, English literature-AP, English-AP, environmental science, film studies, fine arts, first aid, fitness, French, geography, geometry, health, history, honors algebra, honors English, honors U.S. history, honors world history, independent study, keyboarding, kinesiology, mathematics, newspaper, photography, physical education, physical fitness, physical science, physics, play production, pre-calculus, psychology, public speaking, publications, reading, religion, science, social studies, Spanish, speech and debate, studio art-AP, study skills, theology, trigonometry, U.S. history-AP, Web site design, weight training, word processing, world history, yearbook.

Graduation Requirements Arts and fine arts (art, music, dance, drama), business applications, English, French, keyboarding, mathematics, physical education (includes health), religion (includes Bible studies and theology), science, social studies (includes history), Spanish, world history.

Special Academic Programs 8 Advanced Placement exams for which test preparation is offered; honors section; independent study; study at local college for college credit; academic accommodation for the gifted; remedial reading and/or remedial writing; remedial math.

College Admission Counseling 269 students graduated in 2010; 255 went to college, including Louisiana State University and Agricultural and Mechanical College; University of Louisiana at Lafayette. Other: 2 entered military service, 3 had other specific plans.

Student Life Upper grades have uniform requirement, student council, honor system. Discipline rests primarily with faculty. Attendance at religious services is required.

Tuition and Aid Day student tuition: $6070. Tuition installment plan (monthly payment plans). Merit scholarship grants, need-based scholarship grants, paying campus jobs available. In 2010–11, 20% of upper-school students received aid; total upper-school merit-scholarship money awarded: $500. Total amount of financial aid awarded in 2010–11: $130,000.

Admissions Traditional secondary-level entrance grade is 9. For fall 2010, 1,052 students applied for upper-level admission, 1,040 were accepted, 1,035 enrolled. Achievement tests and ACT-Explore required. Deadline for receipt of application materials: January 19. Application fee required: $350.

Athletics Interscholastic: aquatics (boys, girls), baseball (b), basketball (b,g), bowling (b,g), cheering (g), cross-country running (b,g), dance squad (g), dance team (g), floor hockey (b), football (b), golf (b,g), physical training (b,g), power lifting (b,g), soccer (b,g), softball (g), strength & conditioning (b,g), tennis (b,g), track and field (b,g), volleyball (g), weight lifting (b,g), weight training (b,g), wrestling (b); intramural: flag football (b,g), indoor hockey (b), lacrosse (b); coed interscholastic: Special Olympics. 4 PE instructors, 3 coaches, 1 athletic trainer.

Computers Computers are regularly used in business applications, desktop publishing, English, foreign language, history, keyboarding, lab/keyboard, library, literary magazine, mathematics, newspaper, publications, reading, remedial study skills, science, word processing, yearbook classes. Computer network features include on-campus library services, online commercial services, Internet access, wireless campus network, Internet filtering or blocking technology, computer access in the library before and after school and during lunch. Campus intranet, student e-mail accounts, and computer access in designated common areas are available to students. Students grades are available online. The school has a published electronic and media policy.

Contact Ms. Melanie O. Lauer '96, Director of Admissions. 337-988-7779. Fax: 337-988-2911. E-mail: melanielauer@stmcougars.com. Web site: www.stmcougars.com.

ST. TIMOTHY'S SCHOOL

8400 Greenspring Avenue

Stevenson, Maryland 21153

Head of School: Randy S. Stevens

General Information Girls' boarding and day college-preparatory, arts, and IB (International Baccalaureate diploma program) school, affiliated with Episcopal Church. Grades 9–12. Founded: 1882. Setting: suburban. Nearest major city is Baltimore. Students are housed in single-sex dormitories. 145-acre campus. 23 buildings on campus. Approved or accredited by Association of Independent Maryland Schools, International Baccalaureate Organization, Middle States Association of Colleges and Schools, National Association of Episcopal Schools, The Association of Boarding Schools, and Maryland Department of Education. Member of National Association of Independent Schools and Secondary School Admission Test Board. Endowment: $10 million. Total enrollment: 150. Upper school average class size: 10. Upper school faculty-student ratio: 1:5. Upper School students typically attend 5 days per week. The average school day consists of 6 hours.

Upper School Student Profile Grade 9: 34 students (34 girls); Grade 10: 41 students (41 girls); Grade 11: 40 students (40 girls); Grade 12: 35 students (35 girls). 80% of students are boarding students. 37% are state residents. 15 states are represented in upper school student body. 33% are international students. International students from Afghanistan, China, Germany, Mexico, Republic of Korea, and Spain; 10 other countries represented in student body.

Faculty School total: 39. In upper school: 9 men, 30 women; 21 have advanced degrees; 19 reside on campus.

Subjects Offered Algebra, American literature, art, art history, bell choir, biology, British literature, calculus, chemistry, Chinese, choir, college counseling, comparative politics, creative writing, dance, drama, drama performance, drama workshop, economics, English, English composition, English literature, ESL, ethics, European history, fine arts, foreign language, French, geometry, history, integrated mathematics, International Baccalaureate courses, Latin, Mandarin, mathematics, modern dance, music, photography, physics, piano, religion, SAT preparation, science, Spanish, U.S. history, world history, world literature, writing.

Graduation Requirements Arts and fine arts (art, music, dance, drama), English, foreign language, history, mathematics, physical education (includes health), religion (includes Bible studies and theology), science, Theory of Knowledge course, extended essay, Community, Action, and Service (CAS). Community service is required.

Special Academic Programs International Baccalaureate program; independent study; ESL (9 students enrolled).

College Admission Counseling 44 students graduated in 2011; all went to college, including Brown University; The George Washington University; University of Maryland, College Park; University of Southern California; University of Virginia; Wake Forest University.

Student Life Upper grades have uniform requirement, student council, honor system. Discipline rests equally with students and faculty. Attendance at religious services is required.

Summer Programs Enrichment, ESL programs offered; session focuses on global immersion and intensive language; held on campus; accepts girls; open to students from other schools.

Tuition and Aid Day student tuition: $26,300; 5-day tuition and room/board: $45,200; 7-day tuition and room/board: $45,200. Tuition installment plan (FACTS Tuition Payment Plan). Merit scholarship grants, need-based scholarship grants, need-based loans available. In 2011–12, 45% of upper-school students received aid; total upper-school merit-scholarship money awarded: $71,000. Total amount of financial aid awarded in 2011–12: $2,000,000.

Admissions Traditional secondary-level entrance grade is 9. For fall 2011, 177 students applied for upper-level admission, 87 were accepted, 51 enrolled. ISEE, SLEP for foreign students, SSAT or TOEFL required. Deadline for receipt of application materials: February 1. Application fee required: $50. Interview required.

Athletics Interscholastic: badminton, basketball, dressage, equestrian sports, field hockey, golf, horseback riding, ice hockey, indoor soccer, lacrosse, soccer, softball, squash, tennis, volleyball; intramural: ballet, dance, dance squad, equestrian sports, horseback riding, modern dance, outdoor adventure, weight training, yoga. 3 coaches, 1 athletic trainer.

Computers Computers are regularly used in art, college planning, economics, English, mathematics, publications, SAT preparation, science, yearbook classes. Computer network features include on-campus library services, online commercial services, Internet access, wireless campus network, Internet filtering or blocking technology. Student e-mail accounts are available to students. The school has a published electronic and media policy.

Contact Deborah Haskins, Associate Head for Enrollment Management. 410-486-7401. Fax: 410-486-1167. E-mail: dhaskins@stt.org. Web site: www.stt.org.

SAINT URSULA ACADEMY

4025 Indian Road

Toledo, Ohio 43606

Head of School: Sr. Mary Kay Homan, OP

General Information Girls' day college-preparatory, arts, business, religious studies, bilingual studies, technology, and physical education school, affiliated with Roman Catholic Church. Grades 6–12. Founded: 1854. Setting: suburban. 16-acre campus. 1 building on campus. Approved or accredited by North Central Association of Colleges and Schools, Ohio Catholic Schools Accreditation Association (OCSAA), and Ohio Department of Education. Total enrollment: 549. Upper school average class size: 16. Upper school faculty-student ratio: 1:16. There are 180 required school days per year for Upper School students. Upper School students typically attend 5 days per week. The average school day consists of 7 hours and 20 minutes.

Upper School Student Profile Grade 9: 151 students (151 girls); Grade 10: 121 students (121 girls); Grade 11: 115 students (115 girls); Grade 12: 135 students (135 girls). 75% of students are Roman Catholic.

Faculty School total: 45. In upper school: 8 men, 37 women; 32 have advanced degrees.

Subjects Offered 3-dimensional art, accounting, Advanced Placement courses, advanced studio art-AP, algebra, American government, American history, American history-AP, American literature, anatomy, anatomy and physiology, art, art-AP, ballet, biology, British literature, British literature-AP, business law, calculus-AP, career exploration, Catholic belief and practice, ceramics, chemistry, chemistry-AP, choral music, choreography, chorus, church history, comparative government and politics-AP, comparative religion, composition-AP, computer applications, computer graphics, concert choir, dance, digital photography, drama, drawing, economics, electives, engineering, English language and composition-AP, English literature and composition-AP, fashion, female experience in America, film history, foreign language, French language-AP, geometry, government, government and politics-AP, graphic arts, health, history of the Catholic Church, honors algebra, honors English, honors geometry, honors world history, human geography - AP, instrumental music, Latin, Latin-AP, literature, literature and composition-AP, Mandarin, marketing, mathematics-AP, microeconomics, music, music theory-AP, New Testament, orchestra, painting, personal finance, photography, physical education, physics, physiology, pre-calculus, printmaking, probability and statistics, psychology, psychology-AP, religion and culture, religious education, sculpture, single survival, social psychology, Spanish, Spanish language-AP, speech, statistics, statistics-AP, student publications, studio art-AP, symphonic band, theology, trigonometry, U.S. government and politics, U.S. government and politics-AP, U.S. history, U.S. history-AP, U.S. literature, United States government-AP, vocal music, women's health, women's studies, yearbook.

Graduation Requirements Arts and fine arts (art, music, dance, drama), computers, English, foreign language, mathematics, physical education (includes health), science, social studies (includes history), theology, community service, Career Exploration Experience.

Special Academic Programs 13 Advanced Placement exams for which test preparation is offered; honors section; study at local college for college credit.

College Admission Counseling 125 students graduated in 2011; 123 went to college, including Miami University; The Ohio State University; University of Dayton; University of Michigan. Other: 1 went to work, 1 entered military service. Mean SAT critical reading: 556, mean SAT math: 531, mean SAT writing: 555, mean composite ACT: 24. 38% scored over 600 on SAT critical reading, 23% scored over 600 on SAT math, 50% scored over 600 on SAT writing.

Student Life Upper grades have uniform requirement, student council. Discipline rests primarily with faculty. Attendance at religious services is required.

Summer Programs Enrichment, advancement, sports, art/fine arts, computer instruction programs offered; session focuses on athletics and academics; held both on and off campus; held at golf course; accepts girls; open to students from other schools. 300 students usually enrolled. 2012 schedule: June 6 to July 29. Application deadline: June 1.

Tuition and Aid Day student tuition: $9400. Tuition installment plan (SMART Tuition Payment Plan). Tuition reduction for siblings, merit scholarship grants, need-based scholarship grants, paying campus jobs available. In 2011–12, 68% of upper-school students received aid. Total amount of financial aid awarded in 2011–12: $1,299,000.

Admissions Traditional secondary-level entrance grade is 9. For fall 2011, 160 students applied for upper-level admission, 151 were accepted, 121 enrolled. High School Placement Test or placement test required. Deadline for receipt of application materials: December. Application fee required: $300.

Athletics Interscholastic: aerobics/dance, basketball, bowling, broomball, cheering, crew, cross-country running, dance team, diving, equestrian sports, fencing, golf, gymnastics, horseback riding, independent competitive sports, lacrosse, modern dance, physical fitness, physical training, rowing, soccer, softball, swimming and diving, tennis, track and field, volleyball, water polo, weight training; intramural: badminton, cooperative games, volleyball. 1 PE instructor, 32 coaches, 1 athletic trainer.

Computers Computers are regularly used in accounting, computer applications, graphic arts, newspaper, Web site design, yearbook classes. Computer network features include on-campus library services, Internet access, wireless campus network, Internet filtering or blocking technology. Campus intranet, student e-mail accounts, and computer access in designated common areas are available to students. Students grades are available online. The school has a published electronic and media policy.

Contact Mrs. Kimberly Sofo, Principal. 419-329-2279. Fax: 419-531-4575. E-mail: ksofo@toledosua.org. Web site: www.toledosua.org.

SAINT VIATOR HIGH SCHOOL

1213 East Oakton Street

Arlington Heights, Illinois 60004

Head of School: Rev. Robert M. Egan, CSV

General Information Coeducational day college-preparatory, arts, religious studies, bilingual studies, and technology school, affiliated with Roman Catholic Church. Grades 9–12. Founded: 1961. Setting: suburban. Nearest major city is Chicago. 1 building on campus. Approved or accredited by North Central Association of Colleges and Schools and Illinois Department of Education. Upper school average class size: 25. Upper school faculty-student ratio: 1:18. There are 190 required school days per year for Upper School students.

Faculty School total: 67. In upper school: 25 men, 42 women; 50 have advanced degrees.

Graduation Requirements 25 hours of Christian Service each year (100 total hours).

College Admission Counseling 288 students graduated in 2011; 282 went to college, including DePaul University; Indiana University Bloomington; Loyola University Chicago; The University of Iowa; University of Dayton; University of Illinois at Urbana–Champaign. Other: 2 entered military service, 1 entered a postgraduate year, 3 had other specific plans. Mean composite ACT: 25.

Student Life Upper grades have specified standards of dress, student council, honor system. Discipline rests primarily with faculty. Attendance at religious services is required.

Summer Programs Enrichment, advancement, sports, art/fine arts, computer instruction programs offered; held on campus; accepts boys and girls; not open to students from other schools. 2012 schedule: June 11 to July 27.

Tuition and Aid Day student tuition: $10,950. Tuition installment plan (monthly payment plans). Need-based scholarship grants available. In 2011–12, 27% of upper-school students received aid. Total amount of financial aid awarded in 2011–12: $1,200,000.

Admissions Traditional secondary-level entrance grade is 9. ETS high school placement exam required. Application fee required: $400.

Athletics Interscholastic: baseball (boys), basketball (b,g), cheering (g), cross-country running (b,g), football (b), golf (b,g), ice hockey (b), lacrosse (b,g), pom squad (g), soccer (b,g), softball (g), swimming and diving (b,g), tennis (b,g), track and field (b,g), volleyball (b,g), water polo (b,g), wrestling (b); coed intramural: outdoor adventure. 3 PE instructors, 101 coaches, 2 athletic trainers.

Computers Computer network features include Internet access, faculty Web pages. Students grades are available online. The school has a published electronic and media policy.

Contact Mrs. Eileen Manno, Principal. 847-392-4050 Ext. 229. Fax: 847-392-4101. E-mail: emanno@saintviator.com. Web site: www.saintviator.com.

ST. VINCENT PALLOTTI HIGH SCHOOL

113 St. Mary's Place

Laurel, Maryland 20707

Head of School: Mr. Stephen J. Edmonds

General Information Coeducational day college-preparatory and religious studies school, affiliated with Roman Catholic Church. Grades 9–12. Founded: 1921. Setting: suburban. Nearest major city is Washington, DC. 6-acre campus. 5 buildings on campus. Approved or accredited by Association of Independent Maryland Schools, The College Board, and Maryland Department of Education. Total enrollment: 500. Upper school average class size: 18. Upper school faculty-student ratio: 1:18.

Upper School Student Profile Grade 9: 100 students (55 boys, 45 girls); Grade 10: 120 students (60 boys, 60 girls); Grade 11: 150 students (70 boys, 80 girls); Grade 12: 136 students (70 boys, 66 girls). 70% of students are Roman Catholic.

Faculty School total: 60.

Graduation Requirements 80 hours of community service.

Special Academic Programs Advanced Placement exam preparation; honors section; independent study; study at local college for college credit; academic accommodation for the musically talented; programs in English, mathematics, general development for dyslexic students; special instructional classes for deaf students, blind students.

College Admission Counseling 139 students graduated in 2010; 136 went to college, including Mount St. Mary's University; Shepherd University; Towson University; University of Maryland, College Park; West Virginia University; York College of Pennsylvania. Other: 1 went to work, 2 entered military service. Mean SAT critical reading: 560, mean SAT math: 580, mean SAT writing: 570.

Student Life Upper grades have uniform requirement, student council, honor system. Discipline rests primarily with faculty. Attendance at religious services is required.

Tuition and Aid Day student tuition: $11,595. Tuition installment plan (FACTS Tuition Payment Plan). Tuition reduction for siblings, merit scholarship grants, need-based scholarship grants available. Total amount of financial aid awarded in 2010–11: $400,000.

Admissions Traditional secondary-level entrance grade is 9. For fall 2010, 325 students applied for upper-level admission, 250 were accepted, 105 enrolled. Archdiocese of Washington Entrance Exam required. Deadline for receipt of application materials: December 15. Application fee required: $100. On-campus interview required.

Athletics Interscholastic: baseball (boys), basketball (b,g), dance squad (g), field hockey (g), football (b), lacrosse (b,g), pom squad (g), soccer (b,g), softball (g), volleyball (g), wrestling (b); coed interscholastic: cheering, cross-country running, dance, golf, tennis; coed intramural: mountain biking, skiing (downhill), snowboarding. 1 PE instructor, 30 coaches, 1 athletic trainer.

Computers Computer network features include on-campus library services, Internet access, wireless campus network, Internet filtering or blocking technology. Campus intranet and student e-mail accounts are available to students. Students grades are available online. The school has a published electronic and media policy.

Contact Mrs. Kelly Hawse, Director of Admissions. 301-725-3228 Ext. 202. Fax: 301-776-4343. E-mail: khawse@pallottihs.org. Web site: www.pallottihs.org.

SALEM ACADEMY

500 Salem Avenue

Winston-Salem, North Carolina 27101-0578

Head of School: Mr. Karl Sjolund

General Information Girls' boarding and day college-preparatory and arts school, affiliated with Moravian Church. Grades 9–12. Founded: 1772. Setting: urban. Students are housed in single-sex dormitories. 60-acre campus. 4 buildings on campus. Approved or accredited by Southern Association of Colleges and Schools, The Association of Boarding Schools, and North Carolina Department of Education. Member of National Association of Independent Schools and Secondary School Admission Test Board. Endowment: $7 million. Total enrollment: 167. Upper school average class size: 10. Upper school faculty-student ratio: 1:7. There are 172 required school days per year for Upper School students. Upper School students typically attend 5 days per week. The average school day consists of 7 hours and 30 minutes.

Upper School Student Profile Grade 9: 36 students (36 girls); Grade 10: 45 students (45 girls); Grade 11: 42 students (42 girls); Grade 12: 44 students (44 girls). 60% of students are boarding students. 12 states are represented in upper school student body. 33% are international students. International students from China, Germany, and Republic of Korea; 2 other countries represented in student body. 4% of students are Moravian.

Faculty School total: 24. In upper school: 2 men, 22 women; 13 have advanced degrees; 3 reside on campus.

Subjects Offered Algebra, American history, art, biology, calculus, chemistry, dance, drama, economics, English, European history, fine arts, French, geometry, government/civics, Latin, mathematics, music, physical education, physics, pre-calculus, psychology, religion, science, social sciences, social studies, Spanish, theater, trigonometry, world history.

Graduation Requirements Arts and fine arts (art, music, dance, drama), English, foreign language, mathematics, physical education (includes health), religion (includes Bible studies and theology), science, social sciences, social studies (includes history), completion of January term.

Special Academic Programs 8 Advanced Placement exams for which test preparation is offered; honors section; term-away projects; study at local college for college credit; study abroad; ESL (8 students enrolled).

College Admission Counseling 35 students graduated in 2011; all went to college, including Boston University; Purdue University; The University of North Carolina at Chapel Hill. Mean SAT critical reading: 618, mean SAT math: 627, mean SAT writing: 631, mean combined SAT: 1876.

Student Life Upper grades have specified standards of dress, student council, honor system. Discipline rests equally with students and faculty.

Tuition and Aid Day student tuition: $18,990; 7-day tuition and room/board: $39,030. Tuition installment plan (Key Tuition Payment Plan, monthly payment plans). Merit scholarship grants, need-based scholarship grants available. In 2011–12, 45% of upper-school students received aid; total upper-school merit-scholarship money awarded: $123,100. Total amount of financial aid awarded in 2011–12: $1,033,794.

Admissions Traditional secondary-level entrance grade is 9. For fall 2011, 160 students applied for upper-level admission, 85 were accepted, 65 enrolled. ACT, PSAT, SAT, SSAT or TOEFL required. Deadline for receipt of application materials: none. Application fee required: $50. Interview required.

Athletics Interscholastic: basketball, cross-country running, fencing, field hockey, golf, soccer, softball, swimming and diving, tennis, track and field, volleyball; intramural: aerobics/dance, archery, badminton, dance, fitness, flag football, floor hockey, golf, horseback riding, indoor hockey, indoor soccer, self defense. 2 PE instructors, 15 coaches, 1 athletic trainer.

Computers Computers are regularly used in all academic classes. Computer network features include on-campus library services, online commercial services, Internet access, wireless campus network. Student e-mail accounts and computer access in designated common areas are available to students. Students grades are available online.
Contact C. Lucia Higgins, Director of Admissions. 336-721-2643. Fax: 336-917-5340. E-mail: academy@salem.edu. Web site: www.salemacademy.com.

SALEM ACADEMY

942 Lancaster Drive NE

Salem, Oregon 97301

Head of School: Tina deVries

General Information Coeducational day college-preparatory, general academic, arts, vocational, religious studies, bilingual studies, and technology school, affiliated with Protestant Church. Grades K–12. Founded: 1945. Setting: suburban. 34-acre campus. 6 buildings on campus. Approved or accredited by Association of Christian Schools International, Northwest Accreditation Commission, and Oregon Department of Education. Total enrollment: 594. Upper school average class size: 20. Upper school faculty-student ratio: 1:9. Upper School students typically attend 5 days per week. The average school day consists of 7 hours and 15 minutes.
Upper School Student Profile 90% of students are Protestant.
Faculty School total: 48. In upper school: 16 men, 15 women; 4 have advanced degrees.
Subjects Offered Advanced chemistry, Advanced Placement courses, algebra, American history, American literature, anatomy and physiology, art, athletics, auto mechanics, baseball, Bible, Bible studies, biology, business, calculus, ceramics, cheerleading, chemistry, choir, college counseling, college writing, computer programming, computer science, drama, drama performance, economics, English, English literature, English literature and composition-AP, English literature-AP, ESL, foods, geography, geometry, government/civics, grammar, health, history, history-AP, home economics, honors English, industrial arts, Japanese, jazz ensemble, mathematics, music, physical education, physical science, physics, psychology, religion, SAT preparation, science, shop, social sciences, social studies, softball, Spanish, speech, track and field, typing, U.S. history-AP, vocal music, volleyball, weight training, woodworking, world history, world literature, writing.
Graduation Requirements English, foreign language, mathematics, physical education (includes health), religion (includes Bible studies and theology), science, social sciences, social studies (includes history), one credit in biblical studies for each year attended, 40 hours of community service (high school).
Special Academic Programs Advanced Placement exam preparation; honors section; independent study; study at local college for college credit; academic accommodation for the musically talented and the artistically talented; ESL (23 students enrolled).
College Admission Counseling 72 students graduated in 2011; 65 went to college, including Chemeketa Community College; Corban University; George Fox University; Oregon State University; University of Oregon. Other: 3 went to work. Mean SAT critical reading: 530, mean SAT math: 503, mean SAT writing: 514, mean combined SAT: 1547.
Student Life Upper grades have specified standards of dress, student council, honor system. Discipline rests primarily with faculty.
Tuition and Aid Tuition reduction for siblings, need-based scholarship grants available. In 2011–12, 25% of upper-school students received aid.
Admissions Traditional secondary-level entrance grade is 9. Math Placement Exam, Reading for Understanding, school's own exam and writing sample required. Deadline for receipt of application materials: none. Application fee required: $50. On-campus interview required.
Athletics Interscholastic: baseball (boys), basketball (b,g), cheering (g), cross-country running (b,g), football (b), golf (b,g), softball (g), track and field (b,g), volleyball (g); coed interscholastic: equestrian sports; coed intramural: racquetball. 2 PE instructors.
Computers Computers are regularly used in computer applications, design, digital applications, media, media production, multimedia, music technology, photography, photojournalism, video film production, yearbook classes. Computer network features include on-campus library services, Internet access, wireless campus network. The school has a published electronic and media policy.
Contact Mr. Shannon deVries, Dean of Students. 503-378-1211. Fax: 503-375-3265. E-mail: sdevries@salemacademy.org. Web site: www.salemacademy.org.

SALEM BAPTIST CHRISTIAN SCHOOL

429 South Broad Street

Winston-Salem, North Carolina 27101

Head of School: Ms. Martha Drake

General Information Coeducational day college-preparatory school, affiliated with Baptist Church. Grades P3–12. Founded: 1950. Setting: urban. 6-acre campus. 13 buildings on campus. Approved or accredited by Association of Christian Schools International, Southern Association of Colleges and Schools, and North Carolina Department of Education. Total enrollment: 391. Upper school average class size: 17. Upper school faculty-student ratio: 1:10.
Upper School Student Profile 50% of students are Baptist.
Faculty School total: 35. In upper school: 5 men, 5 women; 3 have advanced degrees.
Subjects Offered Advanced computer applications, advanced math, Advanced Placement courses, algebra, American government, American history, American history-AP, American literature, anatomy and physiology, ancient world history, art, art history, band, Bible, biology, biology-AP, business mathematics, calculus-AP, campus ministry, chemistry, choir, Christian doctrine, church history, civics, computer applications, consumer mathematics, drama, earth science, economics, English composition, English literature, English literature-AP, European history, fine arts, geography, geometry, government, honors algebra, honors English, honors geometry, honors U.S. history, honors world history, Life of Christ, music, personal money management, psychology, theater, U.S. history, U.S. history-AP, world history, world wide web design.
Special Academic Programs Advanced Placement exam preparation; honors section; study at local college for college credit; academic accommodation for the gifted.
College Admission Counseling 26 students graduated in 2010; 24 went to college, including Cedarville University; North Carolina State University; The University of North Carolina at Charlotte; The University of North Carolina at Greensboro. Other: 1 went to work, 1 entered military service.
Student Life Upper grades have specified standards of dress, student council, honor system. Discipline rests primarily with faculty.
Admissions Traditional secondary-level entrance grade is 9. Application fee required: $125. Interview required.
Athletics Interscholastic: baseball (boys), basketball (b,g), cheering (g), golf (b,g), soccer (b,g), swimming and diving (g), track and field (b,g), volleyball (g). 1 PE instructor, 8 coaches.
Computers Computer network features include on-campus library services, Internet access, Internet filtering or blocking technology. Students grades are available online.
Contact 336-725-6113. Fax: 336-725-8455. Web site: www.mysbcs.com.

SALESIAN HIGH SCHOOL

2851 Salesian Avenue

Richmond, California 94804

Head of School: Mr. Timothy J. Chambers

General Information Coeducational day college-preparatory, arts, and religious studies school, affiliated with Roman Catholic Church. Grades 9–12. Founded: 1960. Setting: urban. Nearest major city is San Francisco. 25-acre campus. 3 buildings on campus. Approved or accredited by National Catholic Education Association, Western Association of Schools and Colleges, Western Catholic Education Association, and California Department of Education. Endowment: $200,000. Total enrollment: 527. Upper school average class size: 27. Upper school faculty-student ratio: 1:23. There are 177 required school days per year for Upper School students. Upper School students typically attend 5 days per week. The average school day consists of 6 hours and 50 minutes.
Upper School Student Profile Grade 9: 134 students (63 boys, 71 girls); Grade 10: 117 students (56 boys, 61 girls); Grade 11: 132 students (72 boys, 60 girls); Grade 12: 144 students (81 boys, 63 girls). 62% of students are Roman Catholic.
Faculty School total: 36. In upper school: 19 men, 17 women; 27 have advanced degrees.
Subjects Offered Advanced math, advanced studio art-AP, algebra, American history-AP, American literature, American literature-AP, anatomy, ancient world history, art, art history, art history-AP, biology, calculus, calculus-AP, Catholic belief and practice, Christian scripture, Christianity, classical language, computer literacy, drama, dramatic arts, economics, English, English composition, English language and composition-AP, English literature, English literature-AP, English-AP, environmental science, French, French language-AP, French-AP, geometry, government, government/civics, health and wellness, history of the Catholic Church, history-AP, honors U.S. history, mathematics, mathematics-AP, performing arts, physical education, physics, pre-algebra, pre-calculus, psychology, religion, SAT preparation, science, Spanish, Spanish language-AP, Spanish-AP, U.S. government, U.S. history, visual and performing arts, world history, world religions.
Graduation Requirements Arts and fine arts (art, music, dance, drama), English, foreign language, mathematics, physical education (includes health), religion (includes Bible studies and theology), science, social sciences, 20 hours of Christian service per year.
Special Academic Programs 8 Advanced Placement exams for which test preparation is offered; honors section; remedial reading and/or remedial writing; remedial math.
College Admission Counseling 144 students graduated in 2011; 142 went to college, including San Francisco State University; University of California, Berkeley; University of California, Davis; University of California, Santa Cruz. Other: 2 entered military service.
Student Life Upper grades have uniform requirement, student council. Discipline rests primarily with faculty. Attendance at religious services is required.

Summer Programs Remediation, enrichment, advancement, sports, art/fine arts, computer instruction programs offered; session focuses on enrichment, remediation and recruitment of 6, 7, and 8th grade students; held on campus; accepts boys and girls; open to students from other schools. 280 students usually enrolled. 2012 schedule: June 20 to July 29. Application deadline: June 17.
Tuition and Aid Day student tuition: $12,500. Tuition installment plan (SMART Tuition Payment Plan). Merit scholarship grants, need-based scholarship grants available. In 2011–12, 48% of upper-school students received aid; total upper-school merit-scholarship money awarded: $50,000. Total amount of financial aid awarded in 2011–12: $1,000,000.
Admissions Traditional secondary-level entrance grade is 9. For fall 2011, 280 students applied for upper-level admission, 180 were accepted, 134 enrolled. High School Placement Test and High School Placement Test (closed version) from Scholastic Testing Service required. Deadline for receipt of application materials: none. Application fee required: $75. On-campus interview required.
Athletics Interscholastic: baseball (boys), basketball (b,g), cheering (g), cross-country running (b,g), football (b), physical training (b), soccer (b,g), softball (g), swimming and diving (b,g), volleyball (b,g), weight training (b), winter soccer (b,g); intramural: basketball (b,g), floor hockey (b,g), football (b), weight training (b); coed interscholastic: golf, track and field. 1 PE instructor, 25 coaches.
Computers Computers are regularly used in all academic, computer applications, history, library, yearbook classes. Computer network features include on-campus library services, Internet access, wireless campus network, Internet filtering or blocking technology. Student e-mail accounts and computer access in designated common areas are available to students. Students grades are available online. The school has a published electronic and media policy.
Contact Mrs. Connie Decuir, Director of Admissions. 510-234-4433 Ext. 1128. Fax: 510-236-4636. E-mail: cdecuir@salesian.com. Web site: www.salesian.com.

SALESIANUM SCHOOL

1801 North Broom Street

Wilmington, Delaware 19802-3891

Head of School: Rev. J. Christian Beretta, OSFS

General Information Boys' day college-preparatory school, affiliated with Roman Catholic Church. Grades 9–12. Founded: 1903. Setting: suburban. 22-acre campus. 1 building on campus. Approved or accredited by Middle States Association of Colleges and Schools and Delaware Department of Education. Total enrollment: 981. Upper school average class size: 20. Upper school faculty-student ratio: 1:12.
Upper School Student Profile Grade 9: 247 students (247 boys); Grade 10: 235 students (235 boys); Grade 11: 237 students (237 boys); Grade 12: 262 students (262 boys). 88% of students are Roman Catholic.
Faculty School total: 92. In upper school: 67 men, 25 women; 53 have advanced degrees.
Subjects Offered Algebra, American history, American history-AP, American literature, anatomy, architecture, art, art-AP, band, biology, biology-AP, business, business law, calculus, calculus-AP, career/college preparation, chemistry, chemistry-AP, chorus, community service, computer applications, computer programming, computer science, computer science-AP, drafting, driver education, ecology, economics, English, English literature, English-AP, ensembles, environmental science-AP, European history-AP, fine arts, foreign policy, French, French-AP, geometry, German-AP, government/civics, health, journalism, Latin, law, literature, marketing, mathematics, physical education, physics, physics-AP, pre-calculus, psychology, psychology-AP, religion, science, social sciences, social studies, Spanish, Spanish-AP, statistics, statistics-AP, television, trigonometry, U.S. government and politics-AP, video, Western literature, world affairs, world history, world literature.
Graduation Requirements Arts and fine arts (art, music, dance, drama), college planning, computer science, driver education, electives, English, foreign language, mathematics, physical education (includes health), religion (includes Bible studies and theology), science, social sciences, social studies (includes history). Community service is required.
Special Academic Programs Advanced Placement exam preparation; honors section; independent study; study at local college for college credit; domestic exchange program (with Ursuline Academy, Padua Academy); academic accommodation for the gifted; remedial reading and/or remedial writing; remedial math.
College Admission Counseling 262 students graduated in 2011; 259 went to college, including Penn State University Park; Saint Joseph's University; University of Delaware; Villanova University; Virginia Polytechnic Institute and State University. Other: 2 went to work, 1 entered military service. Mean SAT critical reading: 574, mean SAT math: 589, mean SAT writing: 558, mean combined SAT: 1721. 32% scored over 600 on SAT critical reading, 41% scored over 600 on SAT math, 27% scored over 600 on SAT writing.
Student Life Upper grades have specified standards of dress, student council. Discipline rests primarily with faculty. Attendance at religious services is required.
Summer Programs Enrichment, computer instruction programs offered; session focuses on freshman transition and technology; held on campus; accepts boys; not open to students from other schools.
Tuition and Aid Day student tuition: $12,000. Tuition installment plan (Insured Tuition Payment Plan, monthly payment plans, semester payment plan, annual payment plan, monthly payment plan). Merit scholarship grants, need-based scholarship grants, paying campus jobs available. In 2011–12, 18% of upper-school students received aid; total upper-school merit-scholarship money awarded: $315,000. Total amount of financial aid awarded in 2011–12: $500,000.
Admissions Traditional secondary-level entrance grade is 9. Scholastic Testing Service High School Placement Test required. Deadline for receipt of application materials: December 1. Application fee required: $65.
Athletics Interscholastic: baseball, basketball, cross-country running, diving, football, golf, ice hockey, lacrosse, soccer, swimming and diving, tennis, track and field, volleyball, wrestling; intramural: basketball, bowling, flag football, Frisbee, lacrosse, roller hockey, rowing, skateboarding, tennis, ultimate Frisbee, weight lifting. 4 PE instructors, 58 coaches, 1 athletic trainer.
Computers Computers are regularly used in architecture, college planning, drafting, English, foreign language, mathematics, science, social studies, yearbook classes. Computer network features include on-campus library services, online commercial services, Internet access, wireless campus network, Internet filtering or blocking technology. Campus intranet and computer access in designated common areas are available to students. Students grades are available online.
Contact Mrs. Barbara Palena, Administrative Assistant to the Admissions Office. 302-654-2495 Ext. 148. Fax: 302-654-7767. E-mail: bpalena@salesianum.org. Web site: www.salesianum.org.

SALTUS GRAMMAR SCHOOL

PO Box HM 2224

Hamilton HM JX, Bermuda

Head of School: Mr. E.G. (Ted) Staunton

General Information Coeducational day college-preparatory, general academic, arts, business, and technology school, affiliated with Church of England (Anglican). Grades K–12. Founded: 1888. Setting: suburban. 6 buildings on campus. Approved or accredited by Canadian Association of Independent Schools. Affiliate member of National Association of Independent Schools. Language of instruction: English. Endowment: 5 million Bermuda dollars. Total enrollment: 961. Upper school average class size: 17. Upper school faculty-student ratio: 1:13. There are 195 required school days per year for Upper School students. Upper School students typically attend 5 days per week. The average school day consists of 5 hours and 30 minutes.
Upper School Student Profile Grade 9: 53 students (30 boys, 23 girls); Grade 10: 47 students (24 boys, 23 girls); Grade 11: 51 students (28 boys, 23 girls); Grade 12: 47 students (25 boys, 22 girls).
Faculty School total: 95. In upper school: 18 men, 18 women; 20 have advanced degrees.
Subjects Offered Advanced Placement courses, American history, art, art history, biology, business, chemistry, computer programming, computer science, design, drama, earth science, economics, electronics, English, English literature, environmental science, European history, French, geography, health, history, mathematics, music, photography, physical education, physics, psychology, social studies, sociology, Spanish, speech, statistics, theater, trigonometry, world history.
Graduation Requirements English, mathematics. Community service is required.
Special Academic Programs 17 Advanced Placement exams for which test preparation is offered.
College Admission Counseling 69 students graduated in 2011; 68 went to college, including Acadia University; Dalhousie University; McGill University; Queen's University at Kingston; The University of Western Ontario; University of Guelph. Other: 1 went to work.
Student Life Upper grades have uniform requirement, student council, honor system. Discipline rests primarily with faculty.
Tuition and Aid Day student tuition: 17,980 Bermuda dollars–18,900 Bermuda dollars. Tuition installment plan (monthly payment plans, One Payment Plan, Two payment plan). Bursaries, merit scholarship grants, need-based scholarship grants available. In 2011–12, 16% of upper-school students received aid; total upper-school merit-scholarship money awarded: 268,302 Bermuda dollars. Total amount of financial aid awarded in 2011–12: 359,400 Bermuda dollars.
Admissions Traditional secondary-level entrance grade is 11. Admissions testing, grade equivalent tests, school placement exam or writing sample required. Deadline for receipt of application materials: none. Application fee required: 50 Bermuda dollars. On-campus interview required.
Athletics Interscholastic: badminton (boys, girls), basketball (b,g), cricket (b), cross-country running (b,g), field hockey (g), netball (g), rugby (b), running (b,g), soccer (b,g), softball (b,g), swimming and diving (b,g), track and field (b,g), volleyball (b,g); intramural: badminton (b,g), basketball (b,g), cricket (b), cross-country running (b,g), field hockey (b,g), gymnastics (b,g), indoor soccer (b), lacrosse (b,g), netball (g), physical fitness (b,g), physical training (b,g), rowing (b,g), rugby (b), running (b,g), sailing (b,g), scuba diving (b,g), soccer (b,g), softball (b,g), squash (b,g), strength & conditioning (b,g), swimming and diving (b,g), table tennis (b,g), tennis (b,g), touch football (b,g), track and field (b,g), volleyball (b,g), wall climbing (b,g), weight training (b,g); coed interscholastic: badminton, basketball, field hockey, running, swimming and

diving, water polo; coed intramural: badminton, field hockey, gymnastics, running, scuba diving, swimming and diving, table tennis, water polo. 5 PE instructors.

Computers Computers are regularly used in all classes. Computer network features include on-campus library services, Internet access, wireless campus network, Internet filtering or blocking technology. Campus intranet and student e-mail accounts are available to students. The school has a published electronic and media policy.

Contact Mr. Malcolm J. Durrant, Deputy Headmaster. 441-292-6177. Fax: 441-295-4977. E-mail: mdurrant@saltus.bm. Web site: www.saltus.bm.

SANDIA PREPARATORY SCHOOL

532 Osuna Road NE

Albuquerque, New Mexico 87113

Head of School: B. Stephen Albert

General Information Coeducational day college-preparatory and arts school. Grades 6–12. Founded: 1966. Setting: suburban. 27-acre campus. 13 buildings on campus. Approved or accredited by Independent Schools Association of the Southwest and New Mexico Department of Education. Member of National Association of Independent Schools. Endowment: $4 million. Total enrollment: 659. Upper school average class size: 17. Upper school faculty-student ratio: 1:10. There are 180 required school days per year for Upper School students. The average school day consists of 7 hours and 30 minutes.

Upper School Student Profile Grade 9: 92 students (44 boys, 48 girls); Grade 10: 90 students (38 boys, 52 girls); Grade 11: 86 students (42 boys, 44 girls); Grade 12: 101 students (58 boys, 43 girls).

Faculty School total: 74. In upper school: 40 men, 33 women; 47 have advanced degrees.

Subjects Offered 20th century American writers, 3-dimensional art, adolescent issues, advanced biology, advanced chemistry, advanced computer applications, advanced math, algebra, American history, American literature, American politics in film, anatomy and physiology, ancient world history, art, astronomy, band, biology, calculus, ceramics, chemistry, chorus, computer programming, computer science, creative writing, drawing, earth science, ecology, environmental systems, economics, English, English literature, environmental science, film, film history, filmmaking, fine arts, foreign language, French, French as a second language, geology, geometry, global issues, grammar, guitar, healthful living, history, jazz band, journalism, language arts, library skills, life science, mathematics, media communications, modern world history, music, newspaper, orchestra, outdoor education, painting, performing arts, personal development, philosophy, photography, physical education, physics, pottery, pre-algebra, pre-calculus, science, Shakespearean histories, social studies, Spanish, state history, statistics, technical theater, technology, theater, trigonometry, women in world history, world history, world literature, World War I, World War II, yearbook.

Graduation Requirements Arts and fine arts (art, music, dance, drama), electives, English, foreign language, mathematics, physical education (includes health), science, social studies (includes history), completion of a one-month volunteer Senior Experience in a professional, academic or volunteer area of interest during May of the Senior year.

Special Academic Programs Independent study; study at local college for college credit; study abroad; academic accommodation for the gifted.

College Admission Counseling 91 students graduated in 2010; all went to college, including Carnegie Mellon University; Duke University; Knox College; Lake Forest Academy; Trinity University; University of New Mexico. Median SAT critical reading: 660, median SAT math: 610, median composite ACT: 27. 65% scored over 600 on SAT critical reading, 59% scored over 600 on SAT math, 60% scored over 26 on composite ACT.

Student Life Upper grades have specified standards of dress, student council. Discipline rests primarily with faculty.

Tuition and Aid Day student tuition: $16,400. Tuition installment plan (FACTS Tuition Payment Plan). Need-based scholarship grants available. In 2010–11, 20% of upper-school students received aid. Total amount of financial aid awarded in 2010–11: $950,000.

Admissions Traditional secondary-level entrance grade is 9. For fall 2010, 332 students applied for upper-level admission, 275 were accepted, 136 enrolled. Deadline for receipt of application materials: February 6. Application fee required: $40. On-campus interview required.

Athletics Interscholastic: baseball (boys), basketball (b,g), cross-country running (b,g), dance squad (g), golf (b,g), soccer (b,g), softball (g), swimming and diving (b,g), table tennis (b), tennis (b,g), track and field (b,g), volleyball (g); intramural: basketball (b,g), self defense (g); coed interscholastic: archery, dance, kickball; coed intramural: backpacking, bocce, canoeing/kayaking, climbing, Frisbee, hiking/backpacking, kayaking, lacrosse, modern dance, nordic skiing, ocean paddling, outdoor adventure, outdoor education, outdoor skills, rock climbing, yoga. 5 PE instructors, 40 coaches, 1 athletic trainer.

Computers Computers are regularly used in art, college planning, graphic arts, history, information technology, journalism, library skills, literacy, mathematics, multimedia, newspaper, photography, publications, science, study skills, technology, typing, word processing, yearbook classes. Computer network features include on-campus library services, online commercial services, Internet access, Internet filtering or blocking technology, individual student accounts, productivity software. Students grades are available online. The school has a published electronic and media policy.

Contact Ester Tomelloso, Director of Admissions. 505-338-3000. Fax: 505-338-3099. E-mail: etomelloso@sandiaprep.org. Web site: www.sandiaprep.org.

SANDY SPRING FRIENDS SCHOOL

16923 Norwood Road

Sandy Spring, Maryland 20860

Head of School: Thomas R. Gibian

General Information Coeducational boarding and day college-preparatory, arts, and ESL school, affiliated with Society of Friends. Boarding grades 9–12, day grades PK–12. Founded: 1961. Setting: suburban. Nearest major city is Washington, DC. Students are housed in single-sex by floor dormitories. 140-acre campus. 15 buildings on campus. Approved or accredited by Association of Independent Maryland Schools, Association of Independent Schools of Greater Washington, Friends Council on Education, The Association of Boarding Schools, and Maryland Department of Education. Member of National Association of Independent Schools and Secondary School Admission Test Board. Endowment: $1.1 million. Total enrollment: 572. Upper school average class size: 14. Upper school faculty-student ratio: 1:8. There are 171 required school days per year for Upper School students. Upper School students typically attend 5 days per week. The average school day consists of 7 hours and 30 minutes.

Upper School Student Profile Grade 9: 57 students (19 boys, 38 girls); Grade 10: 59 students (30 boys, 29 girls); Grade 11: 75 students (33 boys, 42 girls); Grade 12: 72 students (47 boys, 25 girls). 11% of students are boarding students. 82% are state residents. 7 states are represented in upper school student body. 8% are international students. International students from China, Ethiopia, Republic of Korea, Taiwan, Thailand, and Viet Nam; 2 other countries represented in student body. 11% of students are members of Society of Friends.

Faculty School total: 74. In upper school: 17 men, 16 women; 21 have advanced degrees; 17 reside on campus.

Subjects Offered Algebra, American history, American literature, art, biology, British literature-AP, calculus, calculus-AP, ceramics, chemistry, chemistry-AP, choral music, creative writing, cultural geography, dance, dance performance, desktop publishing, drama, drawing, English, English as a foreign language, English literature and composition-AP, English literature-AP, environmental science-AP, ESL, ESL, French, French language-AP, geology, geometry, grammar, history, mathematics, music, music theory-AP, Native American history, painting, photography, physical education, physics, poetry, Quakerism and ethics, Russian literature, science, Spanish, Spanish language-AP, statistics-AP, trigonometry, U.S. history-AP, weaving, Western civilization, world literature.

Graduation Requirements Art, English, foreign language, history, mathematics, physical education (includes health), religion (includes Bible studies and theology), science. Community service is required.

Special Academic Programs 15 Advanced Placement exams for which test preparation is offered; honors section; independent study; academic accommodation for the gifted, the musically talented, and the artistically talented; ESL (25 students enrolled).

College Admission Counseling 76 students graduated in 2011; all went to college, including Bowdoin College; Connecticut College; Dickinson College; Haverford College; The College of Wooster; University of Maryland, College Park. Median SAT critical reading: 620, median SAT math: 610, median SAT writing: 620, median combined SAT: 1850, median composite ACT: 27.

Student Life Upper grades have specified standards of dress, student council, honor system. Discipline rests equally with students and faculty. Attendance at religious services is required.

Summer Programs Enrichment, ESL, sports, art/fine arts programs offered; session focuses on recreational and enrichment; held on campus; accepts boys and girls; open to students from other schools. 1,200 students usually enrolled. 2012 schedule: June 21 to August 21. Application deadline: May 1.

Tuition and Aid Day student tuition: $27,500; 5-day tuition and room/board: $40,500; 7-day tuition and room/board: $50,700. Tuition installment plan (FACTS Tuition Payment Plan). Need-based scholarship grants available. In 2011–12, 31% of upper-school students received aid. Total amount of financial aid awarded in 2011–12: $3,035,000.

Admissions Traditional secondary-level entrance grade is 9. For fall 2011, 198 students applied for upper-level admission, 106 were accepted, 57 enrolled. SSAT or TOEFL or SLEP required. Deadline for receipt of application materials: January 15. Application fee required: $75. Interview required.

Athletics Interscholastic: baseball (boys), basketball (b,g), cross-country running (b,g), lacrosse (b,g), soccer (b,g), softball (g), tennis (b,g), volleyball (g); coed interscholastic: cooperative games, modern dance, running, track and field; coed intramural: dance, fitness, flag football, Frisbee, hiking/backpacking, jogging, outdoor activities, outdoor adventure, outdoor education, outdoor recreation, outdoor skills, outdoors, physical fitness, physical training, rappelling, rock climbing, ropes courses, running, skiing (downhill), strength & conditioning, table tennis, track and field, ultimate Frisbee, walking, wall climbing, weight lifting, weight training, wilderness, wilderness survival, wrestling, yoga. 5 PE instructors, 3 coaches, 1 athletic trainer.

Computers Computers are regularly used in all academic classes. Computer network features include on-campus library services, Internet access, wireless campus network. Student e-mail accounts and computer access in designated common areas are available to students. Students grades are available online.

Contact Yasmin McGinnis, Director of Enrollment Management. 301-774-7455 Ext. 182. Fax: 301-924-1115. E-mail: yasmin.mcginnis@ssfs.org. Web site: www.ssfs.org.

See Display below and Close-Up on page 674.

SANFORD SCHOOL

6900 Lancaster Pike

PO Box 888

Hockessin, Delaware 19707-0888

Head of School: Mark J. Anderson

General Information Coeducational day college-preparatory school. Grades PK–12. Founded: 1930. Setting: suburban. Nearest major city is Wilmington. 100-acre campus. 6 buildings on campus. Approved or accredited by Middle States Association of Colleges and Schools and Delaware Department of Education. Member of National Association of Independent Schools and Secondary School Admission Test Board. Endowment: $7 million. Total enrollment: 599. Upper school average class size: 14. Upper school faculty-student ratio: 1:8. There are 169 required school days per year for Upper School students. Upper School students typically attend 5 days per week. The average school day consists of 5 hours and 15 minutes.

Upper School Student Profile Grade 9: 65 students (28 boys, 37 girls); Grade 10: 52 students (22 boys, 30 girls); Grade 11: 61 students (30 boys, 31 girls); Grade 12: 61 students (28 boys, 33 girls).

Faculty School total: 82. In upper school: 11 men, 19 women; 20 have advanced degrees.

Subjects Offered Algebra, American literature, anatomy and physiology, art, biology, biology-AP, calculus-AP, ceramics, chemistry, chemistry-AP, choir, Civil War, collage and assemblage, computer art, computer graphics, computer science-AP, concert band, drawing, driver education, ecology, ecology, environmental systems, economics, engineering, English, English language-AP, English literature, English literature-AP, environmental science-AP, fine arts, French, French-AP, functions, geometry, German, German-AP, graphic design, health, history, jazz band, Latin, Latin-AP, mathematics, music, music appreciation, painting, photography, physics, physics-AP, pre-calculus, printmaking, psychology, social studies, Spanish, Spanish-AP, statistics, statistics-AP, studio art-AP, technology, trigonometry, U.S. history, U.S. history-AP, video film production, visual arts, vocal ensemble, voice, world civilizations, world history, world history-AP, world literature, writing, yearbook.

Graduation Requirements Arts and fine arts (art, music, dance, drama), athletics, computer science, electives, English, foreign language, health, lab science, mathematics, music, social sciences, 2-week senior project/internship in May.

Special Academic Programs Advanced Placement exam preparation; honors section; independent study.

College Admission Counseling 54 students graduated in 2011; all went to college, including College of the Holy Cross; High Point University; Syracuse University; Towson University; University of Delaware; Washington College.

Student Life Upper grades have specified standards of dress, student council, honor system. Discipline rests equally with students and faculty.

Summer Programs Remediation, enrichment, advancement, art/fine arts, computer instruction programs offered; session focuses on enrichment; held on campus; accepts boys and girls; open to students from other schools. 2012 schedule: June 25 to August 3. Application deadline: none.

Tuition and Aid Day student tuition: $20,350–$22,000. Tuition installment plan (Tuition Management System (TMS)). Need-based scholarship grants available. In 2011–12, 44% of upper-school students received aid. Total amount of financial aid awarded in 2011–12: $1,375,825.

Admissions Traditional secondary-level entrance grade is 9. For fall 2011, 73 students applied for upper-level admission, 62 were accepted, 36 enrolled. ERB CTP IV, ISEE or SSAT required. Deadline for receipt of application materials: January 6. Application fee required: $40. On-campus interview required.

Athletics Interscholastic: baseball (boys), basketball (b,g), cross-country running (b,g), field hockey (g), lacrosse (b,g), soccer (b,g), swimming and diving (b,g), tennis (b,g), volleyball (g), wrestling (b); coed interscholastic: golf, indoor track; coed intramural: physical fitness. 27 coaches, 1 athletic trainer.

Computers Computers are regularly used in art, computer applications, English, foreign language, history, mathematics, newspaper, science, yearbook classes. Computer network features include on-campus library services, online commercial services, Internet access, Internet filtering or blocking technology. Campus intranet and student e-mail accounts are available to students. Students grades are available online. The school has a published electronic and media policy.

Contact Ceil Baum, Admission Administrative Assistant. 302-239-5263 Ext. 265. Fax: 302-239-1912. E-mail: admission@sanfordschool.org. Web site: www.sanfordschool.org.

SAN MARCOS BAPTIST ACADEMY

2801 Ranch Road Twelve

San Marcos, Texas 78666-9406

Head of School: Dr. John H. Garrison

General Information Coeducational boarding and day college-preparatory, general academic, arts, business, religious studies, technology, learning skills, and ESL school, affiliated with Baptist Church. Grades 7–12. Founded: 1907. Setting: small town. Nearest major city is Austin. Students are housed in single-sex dormitories. 220-acre campus. 9 buildings on campus. Approved or accredited by Accreditation Commission of the Texas Association of Baptist Schools, Southern Association of Colleges and Schools, and Texas Department of Education. Member of National Association of Independent Schools. Endowment: $5 million. Total enrollment: 294. Upper school average class size: 12. Upper school faculty-student ratio: 1:6. There are 180 required school days per year for Upper School students. Upper School students typically attend 5 days per week. The average school day consists of 6 hours.

Upper School Student Profile Grade 9: 45 students (25 boys, 20 girls); Grade 10: 60 students (39 boys, 21 girls); Grade 11: 65 students (45 boys, 20 girls); Grade 12: 72 students (44 boys, 28 girls). 60% of students are boarding students. 57% are state residents. 6 states are represented in upper school student body. 39% are international students. International students from Angola, China, Mexico, Republic of Korea, Saudi Arabia, and Taiwan; 10 other countries represented in student body. 15% of students are Baptist.

Faculty School total: 42. In upper school: 19 men, 18 women; 20 have advanced degrees; 6 reside on campus.

Subjects Offered Advanced math, Advanced Placement courses, algebra, American government, American history, American literature, analysis and differential calculus, analytic geometry, anatomy and physiology, ancient world history, applied arts, applied music, art, athletic training, athletics, band, baseball, Basic programming, basketball, Bible, Bible studies, biology, biology-AP, British literature, British literature (honors), British literature-AP, business applications, calculus, calculus-AP, career/college preparation, character education, cheerleading, chemistry, choir, Christian scripture, Christian testament, Christianity, civics, civics/free enterprise, clayworking, college admission preparation, college counseling, college planning, communication skills, community service, comparative religion, computer applications, computer information systems, computer programming, computer science, computers, concert band, concert choir, contemporary art, critical thinking, desktop publishing, digital photography, drama, drama performance, drama workshop, dramatic arts, drawing, driver education, earth and space science, earth science, economics, economics and history, English, English as a foreign language, English composition, English literature, English literature and composition-AP, English literature-AP, English-AP, ESL, family and consumer science, fine arts, foreign language, French, geography, geometry, golf, government/civics, grammar, guidance, health, health education, history, history of the Americas, honors algebra, honors geometry, honors U.S. history, honors world history, HTML design, human anatomy, human biology, instrumental music, instruments, intro to computers, introduction to theater, jazz band, journalism, JROTC, JROTC or LEAD (Leadership Education and Development), keyboarding, language and composition, language arts, leadership, leadership education training, learning strategies, library, library skills, library studies, Life of Christ, life skills, literature, literature and composition-AP, literature-AP, logic, mathematical modeling, mathematics, mathematics-AP, military science, music, music appreciation, music performance, music theory, musical productions, musical theater, musicianship, New Testament, news writing, newspaper, novels, painting, participation in sports, personal and social education, personal fitness, personal growth, photography, photojournalism, physical education, physical fitness, physical science, physics, piano, play production, pottery, prayer/spirituality, pre-calculus, psychology, public speaking, reading, reading/study skills, religion, religious education, remedial study skills, research skills, SAT preparation, SAT/ACT preparation, science, social skills, social studies, society and culture, sociology, softball, Spanish, speech, speech and debate, speech communications, sports, sports conditioning, sports performance development, sports team management, state government, state history, stock market, student government, student publications, study skills, swimming, tennis, Texas history, theater, theater arts, theater production, theology, TOEFL preparation, track and field, U.S. government, U.S. government and politics, U.S. history, U.S. literature, visual arts, vocal ensemble, vocal jazz, vocal music, voice, voice and diction, voice ensemble, volleyball, Web authoring, Web site design, weight training, weightlifting, Western civilization, world civilizations, world cultures, world geography, world history, world issues, world literature, world religions, world religions, world studies, world wide web design, World-Wide-Web publishing, yearbook.

Graduation Requirements Arts and fine arts (art, music, dance, drama), computer science, economics, electives, English, foreign language, JROTC or LEAD (Leadership Education and Development), mathematics, physical education (includes health), religion (includes Bible studies and theology), science, social studies (includes history), speech.

Special Academic Programs Advanced Placement exam preparation; honors section; accelerated programs; independent study; study at local college for college credit; academic accommodation for the gifted, the musically talented, and the artistically talented; remedial reading and/or remedial writing; remedial math; programs in English, mathematics, general development for dyslexic students; special instructional classes for deaf students, students with Section 504 learning disabilities, Attention Deficit Disorder, and dyslexia; ESL (51 students enrolled).

College Admission Counseling 51 students graduated in 2011; 44 went to college, including Baylor University; Syracuse University; Texas State University–San Marcos; Texas Tech University; The University of Texas at Austin; University of Illinois at Urbana–Champaign. Other: 3 entered military service, 4 had other specific plans. Mean SAT critical reading: 461, mean SAT math: 547, mean SAT writing: 447, mean combined SAT: 1455. 5% scored over 600 on SAT critical reading, 42% scored over 600 on SAT math, 2% scored over 600 on SAT writing, 15% scored over 1800 on combined SAT.

Student Life Upper grades have uniform requirement, student council, honor system. Discipline rests primarily with faculty. Attendance at religious services is required.

Tuition and Aid Day student tuition: $8565; 7-day tuition and room/board: $27,595. Guaranteed tuition plan. Tuition installment plan (monthly payment plans, individually arranged payment plans). Need-based scholarship grants available. In 2011–12, 30% of upper-school students received aid. Total amount of financial aid awarded in 2011–12: $320,000.

Admissions Traditional secondary-level entrance grade is 9. Deadline for receipt of application materials: none. Application fee required: $100. Interview required.

Athletics Interscholastic: baseball (boys), basketball (b,g), cross-country running (b,g), flag football (b), football (b), golf (b,g), JROTC drill (b,g), power lifting (b,g), softball (g), swimming and diving (b,g), tennis (b,g), track and field (b,g), volleyball (g), weight lifting (b,g); coed interscholastic: cheering, drill team, equestrian sports, marksmanship, soccer, winter soccer; coed intramural: billiards, fitness walking, Frisbee, horseback riding, soccer, table tennis, weight lifting, weight training, winter soccer. 11 coaches, 1 athletic trainer.

Computers Computers are regularly used in computer applications, desktop publishing, information technology, keyboarding, newspaper, photojournalism, technology, typing, Web site design, yearbook classes. Computer network features include on-campus library services, Internet access, wireless campus network, Internet filtering or blocking technology. Student e-mail accounts are available to students. Students grades are available online. The school has a published electronic and media policy.

Contact Mr. Jeffrey D. Baergen, Director of Admissions. 800-428-5120. Fax: 512-753-8031. E-mail: admissions@smba.org. Web site: www.smabears.org.

SANTA CATALINA SCHOOL

1500 Mark Thomas Drive

Monterey, California 93940-5291

Head of School: Sr. Claire Barone

General Information Girls' boarding and day college-preparatory and liberal arts school, affiliated with Roman Catholic Church. Grades 9–12. Founded: 1950. Setting: small town. Nearest major city is San Francisco. Students are housed in single-sex dormitories. 36-acre campus. 21 buildings on campus. Approved or accredited by California Association of Independent Schools, The Association of Boarding Schools, The College Board, Western Association of Schools and Colleges, and California Department of Education. Member of National Association of Independent Schools and Secondary School Admission Test Board. Endowment: $24 million. Total enrollment: 244. Upper school average class size: 12. Upper school faculty-student ratio: 1:7. There are 165 required school days per year for Upper School students. Upper School students typically attend 5 days per week. The average school day consists of 5 hours and 25 minutes.

Upper School Student Profile Grade 9: 55 students (55 girls); Grade 10: 79 students (79 girls); Grade 11: 62 students (62 girls); Grade 12: 48 students (48 girls). 47% of students are boarding students. 80% are state residents. 11 states are represented in upper school student body. 14% are international students. International students from Canada, China, Democratic People's Republic of Korea, Germany, Mexico, and Taiwan; 4 other countries represented in student body. 45% of students are Roman Catholic.

Faculty School total: 34. In upper school: 16 men, 18 women; 28 have advanced degrees; 19 reside on campus.

Subjects Offered Algebra, American literature, art, art history-AP, ballet, biology, biology-AP, calculus, calculus-AP, ceramics, chemistry, chemistry-AP, Chinese, choir, college counseling, conceptual physics, dance, digital art, drama, drama performance, English, English language-AP, English literature, English literature-AP, ensembles, environmental science-AP, European history, fine arts, French, French language-AP, geometry, health, honors algebra, honors English, honors geometry, jazz dance, Latin, Latin-AP, Mandarin, marine science, media arts, music, music performance, peace and justice, philosophy, photography, physical education, physics, physics-AP, pre-calculus, Spanish, Spanish language-AP, Spanish literature-AP, studio art, studio art-AP, theater, theology, trigonometry, U.S. history, U.S. history-AP, women spirituality and faith, world history, world history-AP, world issues, world literature, world religions.

Graduation Requirements Arts, English, foreign language, history, lab science, mathematics, physical education (includes health), religious studies.

Special Academic Programs 16 Advanced Placement exams for which test preparation is offered; honors section; academic accommodation for the gifted, the musically talented, and the artistically talented.

College Admission Counseling 61 students graduated in 2011; all went to college, including New York University; Santa Clara University; Syracuse University; The Uni-

versity of Arizona; University of Notre Dame; University of San Francisco. Mean SAT critical reading: 603, mean SAT math: 583, mean SAT writing: 605.
Student Life Upper grades have uniform requirement, student council. Discipline rests equally with students and faculty. Attendance at religious services is required.
Tuition and Aid Day student tuition: $29,000; 7-day tuition and room/board: $44,600. Tuition installment plan (monthly payment plans, Tuition Management Systems). Merit scholarship grants, need-based scholarship grants available. In 2011–12, 42% of upper-school students received aid. Total amount of financial aid awarded in 2011–12: $1,977,080.
Admissions Traditional secondary-level entrance grade is 9. For fall 2011, 189 students applied for upper-level admission, 137 were accepted, 76 enrolled. ISEE, SSAT or TOEFL required. Deadline for receipt of application materials: February 1. Application fee required: $75. Interview required.
Athletics Interscholastic: basketball, cross-country running, diving, equestrian sports, field hockey, golf, lacrosse, soccer, softball, swimming and diving, tennis, track and field, volleyball, water polo; intramural: ballet, canoeing/kayaking, dance, fencing, fitness, horseback riding, kayaking, modern dance, outdoor activities, physical fitness, rafting, rock climbing, self defense, strength & conditioning, surfing, weight training, yoga. 2 PE instructors, 26 coaches.
Computers Computers are regularly used in English, foreign language, mathematics, media arts, science, yearbook classes. Computer network features include on-campus library services, Internet access, wireless campus network, Internet filtering or blocking technology. Campus intranet, student e-mail accounts, and computer access in designated common areas are available to students. The school has a published electronic and media policy.
Contact Mrs. Jamie Buffington Browne '85, Director of Admission. 831-655-9356. Fax: 831-655-7535. E-mail: jamie.brown@santacatalina.org. Web site: www.santacatalina.org.

SANTA FE PREPARATORY SCHOOL

1101 Camino Cruz Blanca

Santa Fe, New Mexico 87505

Head of School: Mr. James W. Leonard

General Information Coeducational day college-preparatory, arts, and community service school. Grades 7–12. Founded: 1961. Setting: suburban. 13-acre campus. 4 buildings on campus. Approved or accredited by Independent Schools Association of the Southwest and New Mexico Department of Education. Member of National Association of Independent Schools. Endowment: $4.3 million. Total enrollment: 323. Upper school average class size: 13. Upper school faculty-student ratio: 1:10. There are 171 required school days per year for Upper School students. Upper School students typically attend 5 days per week. The average school day consists of 6 hours and 25 minutes.
Upper School Student Profile Grade 7: 45 students (22 boys, 23 girls); Grade 8: 70 students (30 boys, 40 girls); Grade 9: 50 students (31 boys, 19 girls); Grade 10: 59 students (23 boys, 36 girls); Grade 11: 51 students (29 boys, 22 girls); Grade 12: 48 students (25 boys, 23 girls).
Faculty School total: 47. In upper school: 24 men, 23 women; 21 have advanced degrees.
Subjects Offered Acting, advanced chemistry, advanced computer applications, advanced math, algebra, American Civil War, American culture, American democracy, American government, American history, American history-AP, American literature, analytic geometry, art, art appreciation, art history, art history-AP, arts, athletics, basketball, biology, calculus, calculus-AP, ceramics, chemistry, chemistry-AP, chorus, clayworking, college counseling, community service, computer applications, computer graphics, computer literacy, computer programming, computer science, conceptual physics, creative writing, drama, drama performance, dramatic arts, driver education, earth science, English, English literature, European history, fine arts, French, geography, geometry, health, history, humanities, journalism, keyboarding, Latin, mathematics, music, photography, physical education, physics, psychology, science, social studies, Spanish, theater, trigonometry, world history, world literature, writing.
Graduation Requirements Arts and fine arts (art, music, dance, drama), computer science, English, foreign language, humanities, mathematics, music appreciation, physical education (includes health), science, social studies (includes history), senior seminar program. Community service is required.
Special Academic Programs 5 Advanced Placement exams for which test preparation is offered; honors section; independent study; study at local college for college credit; study abroad.
College Admission Counseling 52 students graduated in 2010; 51 went to college, including Lewis & Clark College; Middlebury College; The Colorado College; University of Colorado Boulder; University of Denver; University of New Mexico. Other: 1 went to work. Mean SAT critical reading: 626, mean SAT math: 596, mean SAT writing: 636, mean combined SAT: 1857, mean composite ACT: 27. 56% scored over 600 on SAT critical reading, 49% scored over 600 on SAT math, 60% scored over 600 on SAT writing, 64% scored over 1800 on combined SAT, 50% scored over 26 on composite ACT.
Student Life Upper grades have specified standards of dress, student council. Discipline rests equally with students and faculty.
Tuition and Aid Day student tuition: $17,820. Tuition installment plan (individually arranged payment plans, Tuition Management Systems Plan). Need-based scholarship grants, tuition remission for faculty available. In 2010–11, 26% of upper-school students received aid. Total amount of financial aid awarded in 2010–11: $781,128.
Admissions Traditional secondary-level entrance grade is 9. For fall 2010, 27 students applied for upper-level admission, 23 were accepted, 14 enrolled. Placement test required. Deadline for receipt of application materials: none. Application fee required: $55. On-campus interview required.
Athletics Interscholastic: baseball (boys), basketball (b,g), cross-country running (b,g), diving (b,g), lacrosse (b,g), soccer (b,g), softball (g), swimming and diving (b,g), tennis (b,g), track and field (b,g), volleyball (g); intramural: basketball (b,g), cross-country running (b,g), football (b,g), soccer (b,g), tennis (b,g), track and field (b,g), volleyball (g); coed interscholastic: aerobics/dance, dance team; coed intramural: basketball, bowling, skiing (downhill), swimming and diving. 1 PE instructor, 16 coaches, 1 athletic trainer.
Computers Computers are regularly used in current events, English, French, freshman foundations, geography, graphic arts, history, humanities, journalism, library, literary magazine, mathematics, newspaper, photography, photojournalism, science, social sciences, writing, yearbook classes. Computer network features include on-campus library services, Internet access, wireless campus network, Internet filtering or blocking technology. Campus intranet, student e-mail accounts, and computer access in designated common areas are available to students. The school has a published electronic and media policy.
Contact Marta M. Miskolczy, Director of Admissions. 505-982-1829 Ext. 1212. Fax: 505-982-2897. E-mail: admissions@sfprep.org. Web site: www.santafeprep.org.

SAYRE SCHOOL

194 North Limestone Street

Lexington, Kentucky 40507

Head of School: Mr. Clayton G. Chambliss

General Information Coeducational day college-preparatory, arts, and technology school. Grades PK–12. Founded: 1854. Setting: urban. 60-acre campus. 10 buildings on campus. Approved or accredited by Independent Schools Association of the Central States and Kentucky Department of Education. Member of National Association of Independent Schools and Secondary School Admission Test Board. Endowment: $64 million. Total enrollment: 549. Upper school average class size: 14. Upper school faculty-student ratio: 1:9. There are 179 required school days per year for Upper School students. Upper School students typically attend 5 days per week. The average school day consists of 6 hours and 15 minutes.
Upper School Student Profile Grade 9: 56 students (29 boys, 27 girls); Grade 10: 52 students (28 boys, 24 girls); Grade 11: 57 students (26 boys, 31 girls); Grade 12: 49 students (26 boys, 23 girls).
Faculty School total: 32. In upper school: 12 men, 16 women; 22 have advanced degrees.
Subjects Offered Algebra, American history, American literature, art, art history, biology, calculus, chemistry, community service, computer science, creative writing, drama, earth science, English, English literature, fine arts, French, geometry, government/civics, health, history, journalism, mathematics, music, photography, physical education, physics, public speaking, science, social studies, Spanish, speech, statistics, theater, U.S. constitutional history, world history, writing.
Graduation Requirements Arts and fine arts (art, music, dance, drama), computer science, creative writing, English, foreign language, mathematics, physical education (includes health), public speaking, science, social studies (includes history), senior project internship, senior seminars. Community service is required.
Special Academic Programs 13 Advanced Placement exams for which test preparation is offered; honors section; independent study; term-away projects; study at local college for college credit; academic accommodation for the gifted and the artistically talented.
College Admission Counseling 65 students graduated in 2011; all went to college, including Centre College; Miami University; University of Georgia; University of Kentucky; Vanderbilt University. Median SAT critical reading: 570, median SAT math: 580, median SAT writing: 580, median combined SAT: 1760, median composite ACT: 25. 38% scored over 600 on SAT critical reading, 42% scored over 600 on SAT math, 44% scored over 600 on SAT writing, 41% scored over 1800 on combined SAT, 41% scored over 26 on composite ACT.
Student Life Upper grades have specified standards of dress, student council, honor system. Discipline rests equally with students and faculty.
Tuition and Aid Day student tuition: $18,020–$19,520. Tuition installment plan (Insured Tuition Payment Plan, monthly payment plans, individually arranged payment plans). Merit scholarship grants, need-based scholarship grants available. In 2011–12, 21% of upper-school students received aid. Total amount of financial aid awarded in 2011–12: $6,000,000.
Admissions Traditional secondary-level entrance grade is 9. For fall 2011, 36 students applied for upper-level admission, 27 were accepted, 25 enrolled. Admissions testing, Math Placement Exam, PSAT and SAT for applicants to grade 11 and 12, school's own exam or writing sample required. Deadline for receipt of application materials: none. Application fee required: $75. On-campus interview required.

Athletics Interscholastic: baseball (boys), basketball (b,g), cheering (g), diving (b,g), golf (b,g), lacrosse (b), physical fitness (b), physical training (b,g), soccer (b,g), softball (g), swimming and diving (b,g), tennis (b,g); coed interscholastic: cross-country running. 5 PE instructors, 10 coaches, 1 athletic trainer.

Computers Computers are regularly used in English, foreign language, history, mathematics, music, science classes. Computer network features include on-campus library services, online commercial services, Internet access, wireless campus network, Internet filtering or blocking technology. Student e-mail accounts are available to students. Students grades are available online. The school has a published electronic and media policy.

Contact Mr. John W. Hackworth, Director of Admission. 859-254-1361 Ext. 207. Fax: 859-254-5627. E-mail: jwhackworth@sayreschool.org. Web site: www.sayreschool.org.

SCECGS REDLANDS

272 Military Road

Cremorne 2090, Australia

Head of School: Dr. Peter Lennox

General Information Coeducational day college-preparatory school, affiliated with Church of England (Anglican). Grades PK–12. Founded: 1884. Setting: suburban. Nearest major city is Sydney, Australia. 14-acre campus. 11 buildings on campus. Approved or accredited by New South Wales Department of School Education. Language of instruction: English. Total enrollment: 1,500. Upper school average class size: 20.

Upper School Student Profile 60% of students are members of Church of England (Anglican).

Faculty School total: 111.

Subjects Offered Ancient history, art, ballet, biology, business studies, chemistry, computer math, computer science, computer studies, creative arts, dance, drama, economics, English, ESL, French, geography, geology, German, government/civics, Greek, health, history, industrial arts, information processing, information technology, Japanese, JROTC, language, Latin, Mandarin, mathematics, modern history, music, personal development, photography, physical education, physics, religion, science, social studies, software design, speech, textiles, theater, visual arts.

Graduation Requirements English, foreign language, mathematics, physical education (includes health), religion (includes Bible studies and theology), science, social studies (includes history).

Special Academic Programs International Baccalaureate program; honors section; accelerated programs; independent study; remedial reading and/or remedial writing; remedial math; programs in English, mathematics, general development for dyslexic students; special instructional classes for students with learning disabilities; ESL.

College Admission Counseling 173 students graduated in 2010; 136 went to college, including Macquarie University; University of New South Wales.

Student Life Upper grades have uniform requirement, student council, honor system. Discipline rests equally with students and faculty. Attendance at religious services is required.

Tuition and Aid Day student tuition: 16,780 Australian dollars–22,560 Australian dollars. Merit scholarship grants available.

Admissions For fall 2010, 364 students applied for upper-level admission, 119 were accepted. Deadline for receipt of application materials: none. Application fee required. On-campus interview recommended.

Athletics Interscholastic: basketball (boys, girls), crew (b), cricket (b), cross-country running (b,g), diving (b), golf (b), riflery (b), rugby (b), soccer (b,g), squash (b), swimming and diving (b,g), tennis (b,g), track and field (b); intramural: badminton (b,g), basketball (b,g), crew (b), cricket (b), cross-country running (b,g), diving (b), equestrian sports (b,g), riflery (b), rugby (b), sailing (b,g), soccer (b,g), softball (b,g), squash (b), swimming and diving (b,g), tennis (b,g), touch football (b), track and field (b), water polo (b,g).

Computers Computer resources include on-campus library services, wireless campus network. Student e-mail accounts are available to students.

Contact Ms. Terese Kielt, Registrar. 61-2-9968-9890. Fax: 61-2-9909-3228. E-mail: registrar@redlands.nsw.edu.au. Web site: www.redlands.nsw.edu.au.

SCHOLAR'S HALL PREPARATORY SCHOOL

888 Trillium Drive

Kitchener, Ontario N2R 1K4, Canada

Head of School: Dr. Frederick T. Gore

General Information Coeducational day college-preparatory, general academic, arts, and business school. Grades JK–12. Founded: 1997. Setting: small town. Nearest major city is Toronto, Canada. 10-acre campus. 1 building on campus. Approved or accredited by Ontario Department of Education. Language of instruction: English. Total enrollment: 105. Upper school average class size: 10. Upper school faculty-student ratio: 1:10. There are 200 required school days per year for Upper School students. Upper School students typically attend 5 days per week. The average school day consists of 7 hours.

Upper School Student Profile Grade 6: 10 students (5 boys, 5 girls); Grade 7: 10 students (5 boys, 5 girls); Grade 8: 10 students (5 boys, 5 girls); Grade 9: 10 students (5 boys, 5 girls); Grade 10: 10 students (5 boys, 5 girls); Grade 11: 10 students (5 boys, 5 girls); Grade 12: 10 students (5 boys, 5 girls).

Faculty School total: 10. In upper school: 5 men, 5 women; 5 have advanced degrees.

Special Academic Programs ESL (20 students enrolled).

College Admission Counseling 10 students graduated in 2011; 2 went to college, including The University of Western Ontario; University of Waterloo; Wilfrid Laurier University. Other: 8 entered a postgraduate year.

Student Life Upper grades have uniform requirement, student council, honor system. Discipline rests primarily with faculty.

Summer Programs Remediation, advancement, ESL programs offered; session focuses on acdemic; held on campus; accepts boys and girls; open to students from other schools. 100 students usually enrolled. 2012 schedule: July 1 to August 30. Application deadline: May 30.

Tuition and Aid Day student tuition: CAN$10,900. Guaranteed tuition plan. Tuition installment plan (The Tuition Plan, monthly payment plans, individually arranged payment plans). Tuition reduction for siblings, bursaries available. In 2011–12, 10% of upper-school students received aid. Total amount of financial aid awarded in 2011–12: CAN$20,000.

Admissions Traditional secondary-level entrance grade is 9. For fall 2011, 20 students applied for upper-level admission, 15 were accepted, 15 enrolled. Woodcock-Johnson Educational Evaluation, WISC III required. Deadline for receipt of application materials: June 1. No application fee required. Interview required.

Athletics Coed Interscholastic: badminton, ball hockey, baseball, basketball, cross-country running, fencing, fitness, fitness walking, flag football, floor hockey, Frisbee, golf, independent competitive sports, martial arts, outdoor activities, outdoor education, physical fitness, self defense, soccer, softball, table tennis, volleyball; coed intramural: badminton, ball hockey, baseball, basketball, bowling, cross-country running, fencing, fitness, fitness walking, flag football, floor hockey, Frisbee, golf, martial arts, outdoor activities, outdoor education, physical fitness, self defense, soccer, softball, table tennis, volleyball. 2 PE instructors.

Computers Computers are regularly used in all classes. Computer network features include Internet access, wireless campus network, Internet filtering or blocking technology. Campus intranet is available to students. The school has a published electronic and media policy.

Contact 519-888-6620. Fax: 519-884-0316. Web site: www.scholarshall.com.

SCHOOL OF THE HOLY CHILD

2225 Westchester Avenue

Rye, New York 10580

Head of School: Ann F. Sullivan

General Information Girls' day college-preparatory school, affiliated with Roman Catholic Church. Grades 5–12. Founded: 1904. Setting: suburban. Nearest major city is White Plains. 17-acre campus. 2 buildings on campus. Approved or accredited by New York State Association of Independent Schools, The College Board, and New York Department of Education. Member of National Association of Independent Schools and Secondary School Admission Test Board. Endowment: $3 million. Total enrollment: 345. Upper school average class size: 14. Upper school faculty-student ratio: 1:7. Upper School students typically attend 5 days per week. The average school day consists of 7 hours.

Upper School Student Profile Grade 9: 58 students (58 girls); Grade 10: 70 students (70 girls); Grade 11: 59 students (59 girls); Grade 12: 63 students (63 girls). 85% of students are Roman Catholic.

Faculty School total: 53. In upper school: 6 men, 36 women; 36 have advanced degrees.

Subjects Offered Algebra, American history, American literature, anatomy, art, art history, art history-AP, arts, arts and crafts, astronomy, Bible studies, bioethics, biology, biology-AP, calculus, ceramics, chamber groups, chemistry, chorus, community service, computer programming, computer science, creative writing, dance, design, drama, drawing, driver education, economics, English, English literature, ethics, European history, expository writing, film, fine arts, French, French-AP, geometry, government/civics, grammar, health, history, illustration, Latin, Mandarin, mathematics, music, music theory-AP, physical education, physics, psychology, religion, science, Shakespeare, social studies, Spanish, Spanish-AP, speech, statistics, studio art-AP, theater, trigonometry, world history, writing.

Graduation Requirements Arts and fine arts (art, music, dance, drama), English, foreign language, independent study, mathematics, physical education (includes health), religion (includes Bible studies and theology), science, social studies (includes history), senior internship project, life skills for 9th and 10th grades, guidance for 11th and 12th grades, 100 hours of community service.

Special Academic Programs Advanced Placement exam preparation; honors section; independent study; term-away projects; domestic exchange program; study abroad.

College Admission Counseling 62 students graduated in 2010; all went to college, including Boston College; Georgetown University; Lehigh University; The Johns Hopkins University; University of Chicago; Villanova University.
Student Life Upper grades have uniform requirement, student council. Discipline rests primarily with faculty. Attendance at religious services is required.
Tuition and Aid Day student tuition: $26,000–$27,000. Tuition installment plan (Key Tuition Payment Plan, monthly payment plans). Merit scholarship grants, need-based scholarship grants, need-based loans, merit-based scholarships/grants (9th grade only) available. In 2010–11, 23% of upper-school students received aid.
Admissions Traditional secondary-level entrance grade is 9. Catholic High School Entrance Examination, ISEE or SSAT required. Deadline for receipt of application materials: January 4. Application fee required: $50. On-campus interview required.
Athletics Interscholastic: basketball, cross-country running, field hockey, golf, indoor track & field, lacrosse, soccer, softball, squash, swimming and diving, tennis, track and field, volleyball, winter (indoor) track; intramural: basketball, dance, dance squad, dance team, fitness, fitness walking, modern dance, volleyball, winter (indoor) track. 2 PE instructors, 37 coaches, 1 athletic trainer.
Computers Computers are regularly used in all academic classes. Computer network features include on-campus library services, online commercial services, Internet access, wireless campus network, Internet filtering or blocking technology. Campus intranet, student e-mail accounts, and computer access in designated common areas are available to students. The school has a published electronic and media policy.
Contact Admission Office. 914-967-5622 Ext. 227. Fax: 914-967-6476. E-mail: admission@holychildrye.org. Web site: www.holychildrye.org.

SCICORE ACADEMY

120 Main Street
Hightstown, New Jersey 08520

Head of School: Arthur T. Poulos, PhD

General Information Coeducational day college-preparatory school. Grades K–12. Founded: 2002. Setting: small town. Nearest major city is Trenton. 5-acre campus. 1 building on campus. Approved or accredited by Middle States Association of Colleges and Schools. Total enrollment: 95. Upper school average class size: 13. Upper school faculty-student ratio: 1:7. There are 170 required school days per year for Upper School students. Upper School students typically attend 5 days per week. The average school day consists of 6 hours and 30 minutes.
Faculty School total: 16. In upper school: 9 men, 5 women; 6 have advanced degrees.
Subjects Offered 3-dimensional design, advanced biology, advanced chemistry, advanced math, algebra, American government, American history, American literature, anatomy and physiology, art, Basic programming, biology, biology-AP, biotechnology, British literature, calculus, chemistry, chemistry-AP, Chinese, choir, drafting, drama, electronics, English composition, French, history of science, Italian, Japanese, lab science, logic, rhetoric, and debate, microcomputer technology applications, moral reasoning, music appreciation, optics, physics, pre-calculus, programming, public speaking, SAT preparation, science project, senior project, Spanish, speech and debate, U.S. history, Western civilization, world literature.
Graduation Requirements Advanced math, algebra, American government, American history, American literature, biology, British literature, chemistry, civics, computer programming, English composition, foreign language, geometry, lab science, logic, rhetoric, and debate, physical education (includes health), physics, programming, SAT preparation, science project, U.S. history, Western civilization, world literature.
Special Academic Programs 3 Advanced Placement exams for which test preparation is offered; honors section; independent study; academic accommodation for the gifted and the artistically talented; ESL (4 students enrolled).
College Admission Counseling 5 students graduated in 2011; all went to college, including Bryn Mawr College; Drexel University; New Jersey Institute of Technology; University of Chicago; University of Connecticut.
Student Life Upper grades have specified standards of dress, honor system. Discipline rests primarily with faculty.
Summer Programs Enrichment, advancement, computer instruction programs offered; session focuses on science, math, writing, and computer camps; held on campus; accepts boys and girls; open to students from other schools. 100 students usually enrolled. 2012 schedule: June 21 to August 20. Application deadline: none.
Tuition and Aid Day student tuition: $9120. Tuition installment plan (monthly payment plans). Tuition reduction for siblings available.
Admissions Traditional secondary-level entrance grade is 9. Admissions testing required. Deadline for receipt of application materials: none. No application fee required. Interview required.
Athletics Interscholastic: basketball (boys); intramural: aerobics/dance (g); coed interscholastic: cross-country running, golf, soccer; coed intramural: cross-country running, equestrian sports, fencing, horseback riding. 2 PE instructors, 1 coach.
Computers Computers are regularly used in English, foreign language, French, programming, science, Spanish, yearbook classes. Computer resources include Internet access, wireless campus network. Computer access in designated common areas is available to students. The school has a published electronic and media policy.
Contact Mrs. Danette N. Poulos, Vice Principal. 609-448-8950. Fax: 609-448-8952. E-mail: atpoulos@scicore.org. Web site: www.scicore.org/.

SCOTTSDALE CHRISTIAN ACADEMY

14400 North Tatum Boulevard
Phoenix, Arizona 85032

Head of School: Mr. Tim Hillen

General Information Coeducational day college-preparatory and religious studies school, affiliated with Christian faith. Grades PK–12. Founded: 1968. Setting: suburban. 15-acre campus. 6 buildings on campus. Approved or accredited by Association of Christian Schools International and North Central Association of Colleges and Schools. Total enrollment: 934. Upper school average class size: 25. Upper school faculty-student ratio: 1:25. There are 180 required school days per year for Upper School students. Upper School students typically attend 5 days per week. The average school day consists of 6 hours and 30 minutes.
Upper School Student Profile 99% of students are Christian.
Faculty School total: 30. In upper school: 14 men, 14 women.
Subjects Offered Advanced Placement courses, algebra, American history, American history-AP, American literature, American sign language, anatomy, art, Bible studies, biology, biology-AP, calculus, chemistry, creative writing, drama, economics, English, English-AP, fine arts, French, geography, geometry, government/civics, graphic design, guitar, history, honors geometry, honors U.S. history, mathematics, music, physical education, physical science, physics, physics-AP, religion, science, social studies, Spanish, speech, trigonometry, world history.
Graduation Requirements American government, American history, ancient world history, arts and fine arts (art, music, dance, drama), Bible, biology, chemistry, Christian ethics, economics, English, foreign language, government, mathematics, physical education (includes health), religion (includes Bible studies and theology), science, social sciences, social studies (includes history), speech, U.S. history, world history.
Special Academic Programs Advanced Placement exam preparation; honors section; independent study; study at local college for college credit.
College Admission Counseling 75 students graduated in 2010; 74 went to college, including Arizona Christian University; Arizona State University; Baylor University; Grand Canyon University; Paradise Valley Community College; The University of Arizona. Other: 1 entered military service.
Student Life Upper grades have specified standards of dress, student council. Discipline rests primarily with faculty. Attendance at religious services is required.
Tuition and Aid Day student tuition: $10,000. Tuition installment plan (Academic Management Services Plan). Need-based scholarship grants available.
Admissions Deadline for receipt of application materials: none. Application fee required: $100. On-campus interview required.
Athletics Interscholastic: baseball (boys), basketball (b,g), cheering (g), cross-country running (b,g), football (b), golf (b,g), soccer (b,g), softball (g), swimming and diving (b,g), tennis (b,g), track and field (b,g), volleyball (g), winter soccer (b); intramural: weight lifting (b); coed intramural: martial arts. 3 PE instructors, 10 coaches.
Computers Computer resources include on-campus library services, Internet access, wireless campus network, Internet filtering or blocking technology, EXPAN. Student e-mail accounts are available to students. Students grades are available online. The school has a published electronic and media policy.
Contact Joan Rockwell, Admissions. 602-992-5100. Fax: 602-992-0575. E-mail: jrockwell@scottsdalechristian.org. Web site: www.scottsdalechristian.org.

SCOTUS CENTRAL CATHOLIC HIGH SCHOOL

1554 18th Avenue
Columbus, Nebraska 68601-5132

Head of School: Mr. Wayne Morfeld

General Information Coeducational day college-preparatory, arts, business, religious studies, and technology school, affiliated with Roman Catholic Church. Grades 7–12. Founded: 1884. Setting: small town. Nearest major city is Omaha. 1-acre campus. 1 building on campus. Approved or accredited by National Catholic Education Association, North Central Association of Colleges and Schools, and Nebraska Department of Education. Endowment: $68 million. Total enrollment: 401. Upper school average class size: 20. Upper school faculty-student ratio: 1:14. The average school day consists of 6 hours and 40 minutes.
Upper School Student Profile Grade 7: 72 students (37 boys, 35 girls); Grade 8: 72 students (40 boys, 32 girls); Grade 9: 60 students (31 boys, 29 girls); Grade 10: 66 students (33 boys, 33 girls); Grade 11: 65 students (27 boys, 38 girls); Grade 12: 65 students (36 boys, 29 girls). 97% of students are Roman Catholic.
Faculty School total: 28. In upper school: 10 men, 18 women; 9 have advanced degrees.
Subjects Offered Accounting, advanced math, Advanced Placement courses, algebra, American history, art, astronomy, Bible studies, biology, bookkeeping, calculus, campus ministry, career/college preparation, character education, chemistry, choir, computer applications, CPR, digital applications, drama, earth science, economics, English, family and consumer science, guidance, jazz band, keyboarding, life skills, modern world history, personal fitness, physical science, physics, physiology, psychology, sociology, Spanish, speech, speech and debate, textiles, theater, vocal ensemble, yearbook.

Special Academic Programs Advanced Placement exam preparation; study at local college for college credit.

College Admission Counseling 54 students graduated in 2011; all went to college, including Creighton University; University of Nebraska–Lincoln; University of Nebraska at Kearney; University of Nebraska at Omaha. Median composite ACT: 25. 48% scored over 26 on composite ACT.

Student Life Upper grades have uniform requirement, student council. Discipline rests equally with students and faculty. Attendance at religious services is required.

Tuition and Aid Day student tuition: $2330–$2430. Tuition installment plan (monthly payment plans). Need-based scholarship grants available. In 2011–12, 27% of upper-school students received aid. Total amount of financial aid awarded in 2011–12: $102,667.

Admissions Traditional secondary-level entrance grade is 9. Deadline for receipt of application materials: none. No application fee required.

Athletics Interscholastic: baseball (boys), basketball (b,g), cross-country running (b,g), football (b), golf (b,g), soccer (b,g), softball (g), swimming and diving (b,g), tennis (b,g), track and field (b,g), volleyball (g), wrestling (b); coed interscholastic: weight training. 3 PE instructors, 15 coaches, 2 athletic trainers.

Computers Computers are regularly used in business, newspaper, Web site design, word processing, yearbook classes. Computer network features include Internet access, wireless campus network, Internet filtering or blocking technology. Campus intranet, student e-mail accounts, and computer access in designated common areas are available to students. Students grades are available online. The school has a published electronic and media policy.

Contact Mrs. Pamela K. Weir, 7-12 Guidance Counselor. 402-564-7165. Fax: 402-564-6004. E-mail: pweir@esu7.org. Web site: www.scotuscc.org.

SEABURY HALL

480 Olinda Road

Makawao, Hawaii 96768-9399

Head of School: Mr. Joseph J. Schmidt

General Information Coeducational day college-preparatory, arts, and technology school, affiliated with Episcopal Church. Grades 6–12. Founded: 1964. Setting: rural. Nearest major city is Kahului. 55-acre campus. 8 buildings on campus. Approved or accredited by Western Association of Schools and Colleges. Member of National Association of Independent Schools and Secondary School Admission Test Board. Endowment: $18.7 million. Total enrollment: 444. Upper school average class size: 18. Upper school faculty-student ratio: 1:11. There are 175 required school days per year for Upper School students. Upper School students typically attend 5 days per week. The average school day consists of 7 hours and 30 minutes.

Upper School Student Profile Grade 9: 82 students (27 boys, 55 girls); Grade 10: 77 students (30 boys, 47 girls); Grade 11: 78 students (35 boys, 43 girls); Grade 12: 73 students (35 boys, 38 girls). 5% of students are members of Episcopal Church.

Faculty School total: 56. In upper school: 23 men, 15 women; 23 have advanced degrees.

Subjects Offered Acting, algebra, American history, American literature, art, band, biology, biology-AP, calculus-AP, ceramics, chemistry, chorus, community service, comparative religion, computer programming, dance, drawing, economics, English, English literature, ethics, European history-AP, expository writing, fine arts, geometry, global studies, government, history, Japanese, keyboarding, mathematics, mythology, painting, philosophy, physical education, physical science, physics, physics-AP, political science, pre-algebra, pre-calculus, religion, science, set design, social studies, Spanish, Spanish-AP, speech, studio art-AP, yearbook.

Graduation Requirements Arts and fine arts (art, music, dance, drama), English, foreign language, mathematics, physical education (includes health), religion (includes Bible studies and theology), science, social studies (includes history), speech. Community service is required.

Special Academic Programs 13 Advanced Placement exams for which test preparation is offered; honors section; independent study; academic accommodation for the gifted.

College Admission Counseling 72 students graduated in 2011; all went to college, including Chaminade University of Honolulu; Santa Clara University; School of the Art Institute of Chicago; The University of British Columbia; University of Colorado Boulder; University of Hawaii at Manoa. Mean SAT critical reading: 580, mean SAT math: 570, mean SAT writing: 590, mean combined SAT: 1740, mean composite ACT: 25.

Student Life Upper grades have specified standards of dress, student council, honor system. Discipline rests primarily with faculty.

Summer Programs Enrichment, sports, art/fine arts programs offered; session focuses on enrichment; held on campus; accepts boys and girls; open to students from other schools. 170 students usually enrolled. 2012 schedule: June 11 to July 6. Application deadline: June 13.

Tuition and Aid Day student tuition: $16,990. Tuition installment plan (FACTS Tuition Payment Plan). Need-based scholarship grants available. In 2011–12, 38% of upper-school students received aid. Total amount of financial aid awarded in 2011–12: $848,440.

Admissions Traditional secondary-level entrance grade is 9. For fall 2011, 107 students applied for upper-level admission, 64 were accepted, 42 enrolled. ERB CTP III, ISEE or SSAT required. Deadline for receipt of application materials: February 18. Application fee required: $65. Interview required.

Athletics Interscholastic: basketball (boys, girls), cross-country running (b,g), dance (g), golf (b,g), paddling (b,g), physical fitness (b,g), soccer (b,g), swimming and diving (b,g), tennis (b,g), track and field (b,g), volleyball (b,g); intramural: basketball (b,g), dance (g), fitness (b,g), strength & conditioning (b,g); coed interscholastic: baseball, dance, paddling, physical fitness; coed intramural: ballet, baseball, cross-country running, dance, fitness, track and field, volleyball. 4 PE instructors, 12 coaches, 1 athletic trainer.

Computers Computers are regularly used in art, economics, English, foreign language, history, journalism, mathematics, newspaper, science, speech, yearbook classes. Computer network features include on-campus library services, online commercial services, Internet access, wireless campus network, Internet filtering or blocking technology. Campus intranet, student e-mail accounts, and computer access in designated common areas are available to students. Students grades are available online. The school has a published electronic and media policy.

Contact Elaine V. Nelson, Director of Admissions. 808-572-0807. Fax: 808-572-2042. E-mail: enelson@seaburyhall.org. Web site: www.seaburyhall.org.

SEATTLE ACADEMY OF ARTS AND SCIENCES

1201 East Union Street

Seattle, Washington 98122

Head of School: Joe Puggelli

General Information Coeducational day college-preparatory, arts, and technology school. Grades 6–12. Founded: 1983. Setting: urban. 3-acre campus. 5 buildings on campus. Approved or accredited by Northwest Accreditation Commission, Northwest Association of Schools and Colleges, Pacific Northwest Association of Independent Schools, and Washington Department of Education. Member of National Association of Independent Schools. Endowment: $9.8 million. Total enrollment: 648. Upper school average class size: 18. Upper school faculty-student ratio: 1:9. There are 174 required school days per year for Upper School students. Upper School students typically attend 5 days per week. The average school day consists of 6 hours and 45 minutes.

Upper School Student Profile Grade 9: 106 students (53 boys, 53 girls); Grade 10: 112 students (58 boys, 54 girls); Grade 11: 104 students (53 boys, 51 girls); Grade 12: 87 students (32 boys, 55 girls).

Faculty School total: 93. In upper school: 44 men, 49 women; 75 have advanced degrees.

Subjects Offered Acting, advanced chemistry, algebra, American history, American literature, Asian studies, biology, biotechnology, calculus, chemistry, choir, civics, community service, dance, debate, drawing, economics, English, environmental systems, French, geometry, health, history, humanities, independent study, instrumental music, lab science, literature, Mandarin, marine science, math analysis, musical productions, painting, physical education, physics, printmaking, robotics, sculpture, Spanish, speech, stagecraft, statistics, visual arts, vocal music, world literature, yearbook.

Graduation Requirements Arts and fine arts (art, music, dance, drama), English, foreign language, history, mathematics, physical education (includes health), science, social studies (includes history). Community service is required.

Special Academic Programs Honors section; independent study; term-away projects; study abroad; academic accommodation for the gifted, the musically talented, and the artistically talented; remedial reading and/or remedial writing; remedial math; programs in English, mathematics, general development for dyslexic students.

College Admission Counseling 75 students graduated in 2011; 73 went to college, including New York University; Occidental College; The George Washington University; University of Southern California; University of Washington; Whitman College. Other: 2 had other specific plans. Mean SAT critical reading: 620, mean SAT math: 594, mean SAT writing: 627, mean combined SAT: 1841, mean composite ACT: 25. 67% scored over 600 on SAT critical reading, 50% scored over 600 on SAT math, 73% scored over 600 on SAT writing, 64% scored over 1800 on combined SAT, 60% scored over 26 on composite ACT.

Student Life Upper grades have student council, honor system. Discipline rests equally with students and faculty.

Summer Programs Enrichment, sports, art/fine arts programs offered; held both on and off campus; held at Outdoor Trips to Various National and International Locations; accepts boys and girls; open to students from other schools. 100 students usually enrolled. 2012 schedule: June 18 to August 10.

Tuition and Aid Day student tuition: $26,112. Tuition installment plan (Academic Management Services Plan, monthly payment plans). Need-based scholarship grants available. In 2011–12, 20% of upper-school students received aid.

Admissions Traditional secondary-level entrance grade is 9. ISEE required. Deadline for receipt of application materials: January 12. Application fee required: $50. Interview required.

Athletics Interscholastic: basketball (boys, girls), cross-country running (b,g), golf (b,g), soccer (b,g), tennis (b,g), track and field (b,g), ultimate Frisbee (b,g), volleyball (g); coed interscholastic: dance, dance squad, dance team, Frisbee; coed intramural: bowling, in-line skating, outdoor activities, paint ball, roller blading, roller skating, skateboarding, skiing (cross-country), skiing (downhill), snowboarding, squash. 5 PE instructors, 30 coaches, 2 athletic trainers.

Computers Computers are regularly used in all academic, computer applications, English, foreign language, graphic design, history, mathematics, newspaper, science, speech, study skills, theater arts, video film production, Web site design, yearbook classes. Computer network features include on-campus library services, online commercial services, Internet access, wireless campus network, Internet filtering or blocking technology. Student e-mail accounts are available to students. The school has a published electronic and media policy.

Contact Jim Rupp, Admission Director. 206-324-7227. Fax: 206-323-6618. E-mail: jrupp@seattleacademy.org. Web site: www.seattleacademy.org.

SEATTLE CHRISTIAN SCHOOLS

18301 Military Road South

Seattle, Washington 98188

Head of School: Ms. Gloria Hunter

General Information Coeducational day college-preparatory, general academic, and religious studies school, affiliated with Christian faith. Grades K–12. Founded: 1946. Setting: suburban. 13-acre campus. 1 building on campus. Approved or accredited by Association of Christian Schools International, Northwest Accreditation Commission, and Washington Department of Education. Endowment: $987,200. Total enrollment: 538. Upper school average class size: 17. Upper school faculty-student ratio: 1:10. There are 180 required school days per year for Upper School students. Upper School students typically attend 5 days per week. The average school day consists of 7 hours.

Upper School Student Profile Grade 9: 59 students (29 boys, 30 girls); Grade 10: 45 students (24 boys, 21 girls); Grade 11: 51 students (25 boys, 26 girls); Grade 12: 58 students (31 boys, 27 girls). 100% of students are Christian faith.

Faculty School total: 21. In upper school: 11 men, 10 women; 16 have advanced degrees.

Subjects Offered Algebra, American literature, anatomy and physiology, art, band, Bible, biology, business mathematics, calculus, calculus-AP, chemistry, Christian education, Christian studies, civics, desktop publishing, English-AP, ensembles, geometry, Greek, health, language arts, Latin, Life of Christ, math analysis, multimedia, music, Pacific Northwest seminar, physical education, physics, physics-AP, psychology, Spanish, theater arts, U.S. history, U.S. history-AP, weight training, world history, world literature, yearbook.

Graduation Requirements Algebra, arts and fine arts (art, music, dance, drama), Bible, biology, chemistry, civics, foreign language, geometry, language arts, Life of Christ, mathematics, occupational education, Pacific Northwest seminar, physical education (includes health), physics, science, U.S. history, world history, UTT-Understanding the Times, Acts and Paul and Life of Christ, Bible Survey.

Special Academic Programs 4 Advanced Placement exams for which test preparation is offered; honors section; study at local college for college credit; remedial reading and/or remedial writing; programs in English for dyslexic students.

College Admission Counseling 50 students graduated in 2011; all went to college, including Bellevue College; Biola University; Green River Community College; Highline Community College; Seattle Pacific University; South Seattle Community College. Median SAT critical reading: 540, median SAT math: 510, median SAT writing: 530, median combined SAT: 1580, median composite ACT: 24. 17% scored over 600 on SAT critical reading, 23% scored over 600 on SAT math, 27% scored over 600 on SAT writing, 22% scored over 1800 on combined SAT, 48% scored over 26 on composite ACT.

Student Life Upper grades have specified standards of dress, student council, honor system. Discipline rests primarily with faculty. Attendance at religious services is required.

Tuition and Aid Day student tuition: $9180. Tuition installment plan (FACTS Tuition Payment Plan, monthly payment plans). Tuition reduction for siblings, need-based scholarship grants available. In 2011–12, 47% of upper-school students received aid. Total amount of financial aid awarded in 2011–12: $110,098.

Admissions Traditional secondary-level entrance grade is 9. For fall 2011, 16 students applied for upper-level admission, 14 were accepted, 13 enrolled. Stanford Achievement Test or WRAT required. Deadline for receipt of application materials: none. Application fee required: $75. On-campus interview required.

Athletics Interscholastic: baseball (boys), basketball (b,g), cheering (g), cross-country running (b,g), golf (b,g), soccer (b,g), softball (g), track and field (b,g), volleyball (g); coed interscholastic: cross-country running, track and field; coed intramural: archery, badminton, baseball, basketball, field hockey, fitness, floor hockey, juggling, lacrosse, softball, strength & conditioning, touch football, weight training. 1 PE instructor.

Computers Computers are regularly used in art, library, mathematics, multimedia, reading, science, social studies, Web site design, yearbook classes. Computer network features include on-campus library services, Internet access, Internet filtering or blocking technology, accelerated reading and math program. Computer access in designated common areas is available to students. Students grades are available online. The school has a published electronic and media policy.

Contact Fran Hubeek, Admissions Coordinator. 206-246-8241 Ext. 1301. Fax: 206-246-9066. E-mail: admissions@seattlechristian.org. Web site: www.seattlechristian.org.

SECOND BAPTIST SCHOOL

6410 Woodway Drive

Houston, Texas 77057

Head of School: Dr. Jeff Williams

General Information Coeducational day college-preparatory and religious studies school, affiliated with Baptist Church. Grades PK–12. Founded: 1946. Setting: suburban. 42-acre campus. 4 buildings on campus. Approved or accredited by Southern Association of Colleges and Schools, Southern Association of Independent Schools, and Texas Department of Education. Upper school average class size: 13.

Upper School Student Profile 65% of students are Baptist.

Faculty In upper school: 49 have advanced degrees.

Subjects Offered 3-dimensional art, Advanced Placement courses, algebra, American literature, anatomy and physiology, art, art-AP, band, Bible, biology, biology-AP, British literature, British literature-AP, broadcasting, calculus, calculus-AP, chemistry, chemistry-AP, choir, computer programming, computer programming-AP, computer science, computer science-AP, concert band, concert choir, debate, desktop publishing, drama, economics, English, English-AP, European history-AP, French, French language-AP, French literature-AP, geometry, government, health, honors algebra, honors geometry, jazz ensemble, journalism, Latin, marching band, music theory-AP, photography, physical education, physics, physics-AP, pre-calculus, Spanish, Spanish language-AP, Spanish literature-AP, speech, statistics-AP, U.S. history, U.S. history-AP, world geography, world history.

Graduation Requirements Arts and fine arts (art, music, dance, drama), Bible, computer science, economics, electives, English, foreign language, government, mathematics, physical education (includes health), science, social studies (includes history), speech.

Special Academic Programs Advanced Placement exam preparation; honors section; accelerated programs; independent study; term-away projects; study at local college for college credit; study abroad.

College Admission Counseling 81 students graduated in 2010; all went to college.

Student Life Upper grades have specified standards of dress, student council. Discipline rests primarily with faculty. Attendance at religious services is required.

Tuition and Aid Day student tuition: $13,116. Tuition installment plan (monthly payment plans). Merit scholarship grants, need-based scholarship grants available. In 2010–11, 20% of upper-school students received aid.

Admissions ISEE and writing sample required. Deadline for receipt of application materials: none. Application fee required: $100. Interview required.

Athletics Interscholastic: baseball (boys), basketball (b,g), cross-country running (b,g), diving (b,g), drill team (g), fitness (b,g), football (b), golf (b,g); coed interscholastic: cheering. 9 PE instructors, 37 coaches, 2 athletic trainers.

Computers Computers are regularly used in all academic classes. Computer network features include on-campus library services, online commercial services, Internet access, wireless campus network, Internet filtering or blocking technology, science student interactive programs and computer-based labs. The school has a published electronic and media policy.

Contact Mrs. Andrea Prothro, Director of Admissions. 713-365-2314. Fax: 713-365-2445. E-mail: aprothro@secondbaptistschool.org. Web site: www.secondbaptistschool.org.

SEISEN INTERNATIONAL SCHOOL

12-15 Yoga 1-chome, Setagaya-ku

Tokyo 158-0097, Japan

Head of School: Sr. Concesa Martin

General Information Coeducational day (boys' only in lower grades) college-preparatory school, affiliated with Roman Catholic Church. Boys grade K, girls grades K–12. Founded: 1962. Setting: urban. 1-hectare campus. 3 buildings on campus. Approved or accredited by Council of International Schools, Department of Defense Dependents Schools, International Baccalaureate Organization, Ministry of Education, Japan, National Catholic Education Association, and New England Association of Schools and Colleges. Member of Secondary School Admission Test Board. Language of instruction: English. Total enrollment: 628. Upper school average class size: 20. Upper school faculty-student ratio: 1:3. There are 176 required school days per year for Upper School students. Upper School students typically attend 5 days per week. The average school day consists of 6 hours.

Upper School Student Profile Grade 9: 42 students (42 girls); Grade 10: 41 students (41 girls); Grade 11: 34 students (34 girls); Grade 12: 41 students (41 girls). 20% of students are Roman Catholic.

Faculty School total: 84. In upper school: 12 men, 38 women; 30 have advanced degrees.

Subjects Offered 3-dimensional art, advanced math, art, bell choir, biology, business, career planning, chemistry, choir, college planning, computer graphics, computers, drama, English, environmental studies, ESL, French, geography, geometry, German, health education, history, honors algebra, honors geometry, information technology, International Baccalaureate courses, Japanese, journalism, Korean, library, math methods, mathematics, model United Nations, music, music composition, music performance, painting, performing arts, personal and social education, physical education, physics, pottery, psychology, religion, science, social sciences, social studies, Spanish, speech, theory of knowledge, trigonometry, visual arts, world history, yearbook.

Graduation Requirements Electives, English, foreign language, mathematics, physical education (includes health), religion (includes Bible studies and theology), science, social studies (includes history).

Special Academic Programs International Baccalaureate program; honors section; independent study; remedial reading and/or remedial writing; remedial math; ESL (6 students enrolled).

College Admission Counseling 38 students graduated in 2011; all went to college, including Princeton University; Temple University; The George Washington University; University of Sussex, University of Toronto. Mean SAT critical reading: 554, mean SAT math: 502, mean SAT writing: 539, mean combined SAT: 1595. 12.5% scored over 600 on SAT critical reading, 37.5% scored over 600 on SAT math, 15.6% scored over 600 on SAT writing, 25% scored over 1800 on combined SAT.

Student Life Upper grades have uniform requirement, student council, honor system. Discipline rests primarily with faculty.

Summer Programs Remediation, ESL programs offered; session focuses on high school remedial work only; held on campus; accepts girls; not open to students from other schools. 8 students usually enrolled. 2012 schedule: June 11 to June 28. Application deadline: May 1.

Tuition and Aid Day student tuition: ¥1,940,000. Tuition installment plan (monthly payment plans, individually arranged payment plans). Tuition reduction for siblings, need-based scholarship grants available. In 2011–12, 1% of upper-school students received aid. Total amount of financial aid awarded in 2011–12: ¥1,480,000.

Admissions Traditional secondary-level entrance grade is 9. For fall 2011, 14 students applied for upper-level admission, 13 were accepted, 9 enrolled. Admissions testing, mathematics proficiency exam, Reading for Understanding or writing sample required. Deadline for receipt of application materials: none. Application fee required: ¥20,000. On-campus interview required.

Athletics Interscholastic: basketball, cross-country running, running, soccer, swimming and diving, tennis, track and field, volleyball; intramural: badminton, outdoor activities, running, soccer, table tennis, tennis, winter soccer. 2 PE instructors, 1 coach.

Computers Computers are regularly used in art, business studies, career education, college planning, English, foreign language, graphic design, history, information technology, journalism, mathematics, music, psychology, science, study skills, writing, yearbook classes. Computer network features include on-campus library services, online commercial services, Internet access, wireless campus network, Internet filtering or blocking technology. Campus intranet and computer access in designated common areas are available to students.

Contact Sr. Concesa Martin, School Head. 81-3-3704-2661. Fax: 81-3-3701-1033. E-mail: sisinfo@seisen.com. Web site: www.seisen.com.

See Display on this page and Close-Up on page 676.

SELWYN HOUSE SCHOOL

95 chemin Côte St-Antoine

Westmount, Quebec H3Y 2H8, Canada

Head of School: Mr. Hal Hannaford

General Information Boys' day college-preparatory, bilingual studies, and technology school. Grades K–11. Founded: 1908. Setting: urban. Nearest major city is Montreal, Canada. 2-acre campus. 3 buildings on campus. Approved or accredited by Canadian Association of Independent Schools, Canadian Educational Standards Institute, International Coalition of Boys Schools, National Institute of Independent Schools, Quebec Association of Independent Schools, and Quebec Department of Education. Affiliate member of National Association of Independent Schools; member of Secondary School Admission Test Board. Languages of instruction: English and French. Endowment: CAN$8.1 million. Total enrollment: 546. Upper school average class size: 15. Upper school faculty-student ratio: 1:8.

Upper School Student Profile Grade 9: 54 students (54 boys); Grade 10: 66 students (66 boys); Grade 11: 64 students (64 boys).

Faculty School total: 66. In upper school: 21 men, 14 women; 12 have advanced degrees.

Subjects Offered Art, biology, calculus, Canadian history, chemistry, computer multimedia, computer programming, computer science, creative writing, current events, debate, digital art, drama, drawing, economics, English, English literature, environmental science, French, geography, golf, history, jazz band, jazz ensemble, law, leadership, mathematics, model United Nations, music, outdoor education, photography, physical education, physics, public speaking, publishing, robotics, social justice, Spanish, U.S. history, world history, world issues, yearbook.

Graduation Requirements English, French, history, mathematics, physical science.

Special Academic Programs 4 Advanced Placement exams for which test preparation is offered; honors section.

College Admission Counseling 61 students graduated in 2010; all went to college, including Choate Rosemary Hall; Kent School; Phillips Exeter Academy; St. Paul's School; The Hotchkiss School.
Student Life Upper grades have uniform requirement, student council, honor system. Discipline rests primarily with faculty.
Tuition and Aid Day student tuition: CAN$18,225. Guaranteed tuition plan. Tuition installment plan (monthly payment plans, individually arranged payment plans, 2- and 4-installment plans, credit card payments). Bursaries, merit scholarship grants, need-based scholarship grants, three-year merit-based scholarship to a new Grade 9 student, staff tuition discount, some 50 percent bursaries available for students who qualify for financial assistance available. In 2010–11, 16% of upper-school students received aid; total upper-school merit-scholarship money awarded: CAN$33,000. Total amount of financial aid awarded in 2010–11: CAN$145,830.
Admissions For fall 2010, 16 students applied for upper-level admission, 13 were accepted, 8 enrolled. English, French, and math proficiency required. Deadline for receipt of application materials: October 22. Application fee required: CAN$75. Interview required.
Athletics Interscholastic: badminton, ball hockey, baseball, basketball, cross-country running, curling, fitness, football, golf, ice hockey, rock climbing, rowing, rugby, skiing (cross-country), soccer, tennis, track and field, wrestling; intramural: badminton, ball hockey, fitness, golf, ice hockey, rowing, rugby, skiing (cross-country), soccer, tennis, track and field, weight lifting. 7 PE instructors, 7 coaches, 1 athletic trainer.
Computers Computers are regularly used in all classes. Computer network features include on-campus library services, online commercial services, Internet access, wireless campus network, Internet filtering or blocking technology, one-to-one laptop program for grades 7 to 11, course conferences, Lon Capa—online tutorial for grades 9 to 11 math and science students. Student e-mail accounts are available to students. Students grades are available online. The school has a published electronic and media policy.
Contact Ms. Nathalie Gervais, Director of Admission. 514-931-2775. Fax: 514-932-8776. E-mail: admission@selwyn.ca. Web site: www.selwyn.ca.

SEOUL FOREIGN SCHOOL

55 Yonhi-Dong
Sodaemun-Gu
Seoul 120-113, Republic of Korea

Head of School: Dr. John Engstrom

General Information Coeducational day college-preparatory and International Baccalaureate school, affiliated with Christian faith. Grades PK–12. Founded: 1912. Setting: urban. 25-acre campus. 8 buildings on campus. Approved or accredited by International Baccalaureate Organization and Western Association of Schools and Colleges. Affiliate member of National Association of Independent Schools; member of European Council of International Schools. Language of instruction: English. Endowment: $3.5 million. Total enrollment: 1,414. Upper school average class size: 18. Upper school faculty-student ratio: 1:10.
Upper School Student Profile Grade 9: 116 students (60 boys, 56 girls); Grade 10: 106 students (46 boys, 60 girls); Grade 11: 110 students (59 boys, 51 girls); Grade 12: 101 students (55 boys, 46 girls). 80% of students are Christian faith.
Faculty School total: 162. In upper school: 18 men, 32 women; 41 have advanced degrees.
Subjects Offered 3-dimensional art, algebra, American history, art, art history, Bible studies, biology, business, calculus, chemistry, computer science, creative writing, drama, economics, English, ESL, European history, expository writing, French, health, integrated mathematics, International Baccalaureate courses, international relations, Korean, Korean culture, mathematics, music, philosophy, photography, physical education, physics, psychology, religion, Spanish, speech, theory of knowledge, world history, world literature.
Graduation Requirements Arts and fine arts (art, music, dance, drama), biology, computers, English, foreign language, Korean culture, mathematics, physical education (includes health), physical science, religion (includes Bible studies and theology), social studies (includes history).
Special Academic Programs International Baccalaureate program; 1 Advanced Placement exam for which test preparation is offered; honors section; academic accommodation for the gifted, the musically talented, and the artistically talented; ESL (15 students enrolled).
College Admission Counseling 110 students graduated in 2010; 104 went to college, including Babson College; Boston University; Carnegie Mellon University; New York University; Northwestern University; Tufts University. Other: 6 had other specific plans. Mean SAT critical reading: 610, mean SAT math: 670, mean SAT writing: 640.
Student Life Upper grades have specified standards of dress, student council, honor system. Discipline rests primarily with faculty.
Tuition and Aid Day student tuition: $24,600. Tuition installment plan (individually arranged payment plans, 2-payment plan with final payment due in January). Need-based scholarship grants available. In 2010–11, 12% of upper-school students received aid. Total amount of financial aid awarded in 2010–11: $395,000.
Admissions Traditional secondary-level entrance grade is 9. For fall 2010, 90 students applied for upper-level admission, 47 were accepted, 45 enrolled. Deadline for receipt of application materials: none. Application fee required: $250. On-campus interview required.
Athletics Interscholastic: basketball (boys, girls), cross-country running (b,g), dance team (g), soccer (b,g), swimming and diving (b,g), tennis (b,g), volleyball (b,g); coed interscholastic: aerobics/dance, badminton, cheering; coed intramural: badminton, lacrosse, weight lifting. 2 PE instructors.
Computers Computers are regularly used in English, history, mathematics, music, science classes. Computer network features include on-campus library services, Internet access, wireless campus network, Internet filtering or blocking technology.
Contact Mrs. Nicole Oakes, Admissions Director. 822-330-3100 Ext. 121. Fax: 822-335-2045. E-mail: admissions@seoulforeign.org. Web site: www.seoulforeign.org.

SETON CATHOLIC CENTRAL HIGH SCHOOL

70 Seminary Avenue
Binghamton, New York 13905

Head of School: Mr. Richard Bucci

General Information Coeducational day college-preparatory, arts, business, vocational, religious studies, technology, and cybersecurity school, affiliated with Roman Catholic Church. Grades 7–12. Founded: 1963. Setting: suburban. Nearest major city is Syracuse. 4-acre campus. 1 building on campus. Approved or accredited by Middle States Association of Colleges and Schools, National Catholic Education Association, New York State Board of Regents, The College Board, and New York Department of Education. Total enrollment: 380. Upper school average class size: 23. Upper school faculty-student ratio: 1:23. There are 200 required school days per year for Upper School students. Upper School students typically attend 5 days per week. The average school day consists of 6 hours and 45 minutes.
Upper School Student Profile 90% of students are Roman Catholic.
Faculty School total: 43. In upper school: 16 men, 19 women; 27 have advanced degrees.
Subjects Offered 3-dimensional design, accounting, advanced computer applications, Advanced Placement courses, advertising design, algebra, alternative physical education, American government, American history-AP, American legal systems, American literature, American literature-AP, ancient world history, applied music, architectural drawing, art-AP, band, Bible, biology, biology-AP, business, business law, business mathematics, calculus, calculus-AP, chemistry, chemistry-AP, chorus, Christian scripture, church history, comparative religion, computer applications, computer programming, computer programming-AP, creative drama, criminal justice, dramatic arts, economics, English, English language and composition-AP, English literature and composition-AP, entrepreneurship, environmental science, ethical decision making, ethics and responsibility, European history-AP, food and nutrition, foreign language, forensics, French, government/civics, guitar, health, honors English, honors geometry, instrumental music, integrated mathematics, keyboarding, Latin, Latin-AP, law and the legal system, literature and composition-AP, math applications, mathematics-AP, music theater, music theory, performing arts, photography, physical education, physics, physics-AP, pre-algebra, religion, social psychology, Spanish, Spanish-AP, studio art-AP, theater arts, theology, U.S. history, U.S. history-AP, wood processing, work-study, world history-AP, world religions.
Graduation Requirements Arts and fine arts (art, music, dance, drama), English, foreign language, mathematics, physical education (includes health), science, social studies (includes history), theology.
Special Academic Programs 18 Advanced Placement exams for which test preparation is offered; honors section; study at local college for college credit; academic accommodation for the gifted and the artistically talented; remedial reading and/or remedial writing; remedial math.
College Admission Counseling 82 students graduated in 2011; all went to college, including Le Moyne College; Marywood University; State University of New York at Binghamton; The University of Scranton; Villanova University. Mean SAT critical reading: 561, mean SAT math: 587, mean SAT writing: 561.
Student Life Upper grades have specified standards of dress, student council, honor system. Discipline rests primarily with faculty.
Summer Programs Sports programs offered; session focuses on athletics; held on campus; accepts boys and girls; open to students from other schools. 200 students usually enrolled.
Tuition and Aid Tuition installment plan (monthly payment plans). Tuition reduction for siblings, merit scholarship grants, need-based scholarship grants available. In 2011–12, 40% of upper-school students received aid. Total amount of financial aid awarded in 2011–12: $200,000.
Admissions Traditional secondary-level entrance grade is 7. Deadline for receipt of application materials: none. Application fee required: $100. Interview required.
Athletics Interscholastic: baseball (boys), basketball (b,g), cross-country running (b,g), field hockey (g), football (b), ice hockey (b), indoor track & field (b,g), lacrosse (b,g), soccer (b,g), softball (g), swimming and diving (b,g), tennis (b,g), track and field (b,g), winter (indoor) track (b,g); intramural: snowboarding (b,g), strength & conditioning (b,g), weight training (b,g); coed interscholastic: cheering, golf; coed intramural: alpine skiing. 2 PE instructors, 25 coaches, 1 athletic trainer.

Computers Computers are regularly used in business applications, computer applications, desktop publishing, economics, English, foreign language, history, keyboarding, Latin, mathematics, science, social studies, Spanish, technology, yearbook classes. Computer network features include on-campus library services, online commercial services, Internet access, wireless campus network, Internet filtering or blocking technology. Computer access in designated common areas is available to students. The school has a published electronic and media policy.
Contact Guidance Office. 607-723-5307. Fax: 607-723-4811. E-mail: secathb@syrdiocese.org. Web site: www.setonccs.com.

SETON CATHOLIC HIGH SCHOOL

1150 North Dobson Road

Chandler, Arizona 85224

Head of School: Patricia L. Collins

General Information Coeducational day college-preparatory, arts, religious studies, technology, and dual enrollment with Seton Hill Univ. in specific classes school, affiliated with Roman Catholic Church. Grades 9–12. Founded: 1954. Setting: suburban. Nearest major city is Phoenix. 30-acre campus. 11 buildings on campus. Approved or accredited by North Central Association of Colleges and Schools, Western Catholic Education Association, and Arizona Department of Education. Endowment: $342,000. Total enrollment: 553. Upper school average class size: 22. Upper school faculty-student ratio: 1:13. There are 182 required school days per year for Upper School students. Upper School students typically attend 5 days per week. The average school day consists of 5 hours and 30 minutes.
Upper School Student Profile Grade 9: 145 students (69 boys, 76 girls); Grade 10: 158 students (82 boys, 76 girls); Grade 11: 113 students (60 boys, 53 girls); Grade 12: 110 students (54 boys, 56 girls). 95% of students are Roman Catholic.
Faculty School total: 42. In upper school: 19 men, 23 women; 29 have advanced degrees.
Subjects Offered Aerobics, algebra, American government, American history, anatomy, art, athletic training, Basic programming, biology, biology-AP, calculus, chemistry, chemistry-AP, choir, Christian and Hebrew scripture, Christian scripture, church history, computer applications, dance, drama, drawing, economics, English, English-AP, European history-AP, fitness, foreign language, French, geometry, government, guitar, health, honors English, honors geometry, honors U.S. history, keyboarding, Latin, Latin-AP, personal fitness, photography, physics, pre-calculus, psychology, reading/study skills, religion, scripture, social justice, Spanish, Spanish-AP, study skills, television, theology, U.S. government, U.S. history, video film production, weight training, world history, world religions, yearbook.
Graduation Requirements Arts and fine arts (art, music, dance, drama), computer applications, computer literacy, English, foreign language, mathematics, physical education (includes health), religion (includes Bible studies and theology), science, social studies (includes history), study skills.
Special Academic Programs 11 Advanced Placement exams for which test preparation is offered; honors section.
College Admission Counseling 123 students graduated in 2011; 122 went to college, including Arizona State University; Northern Arizona University; The University of Arizona. Other: 1 had other specific plans. Mean SAT critical reading: 565, mean SAT math: 572, mean SAT writing: 543, mean composite ACT: 24. 26% scored over 600 on SAT critical reading, 31% scored over 600 on SAT math, 20% scored over 600 on SAT writing.
Student Life Upper grades have uniform requirement, student council, honor system. Discipline rests primarily with faculty. Attendance at religious services is required.
Summer Programs Enrichment, advancement, sports programs offered; session focuses on academic support for incoming students and athletic camps; held on campus; accepts boys and girls; open to students from other schools. 60 students usually enrolled. 2012 schedule: June 1 to June 30. Application deadline: May 30.
Tuition and Aid Day student tuition: $11,880. Tuition installment plan (FACTS Tuition Payment Plan, monthly payment plans). Merit scholarship grants, need-based scholarship grants, Catholic Tuition Organization of Diocese of Phoenix available. In 2011–12, 34% of upper-school students received aid; total upper-school merit-scholarship money awarded: $44,000. Total amount of financial aid awarded in 2011–12: $705,000.
Admissions Traditional secondary-level entrance grade is 9. For fall 2011, 249 students applied for upper-level admission, 185 were accepted, 164 enrolled. Catholic High School Entrance Examination or Scholastic Testing Service High School Placement Test required. Deadline for receipt of application materials: January 31. Application fee required: $75. Interview required.
Athletics Interscholastic: baseball (boys), basketball (b,g), cheering (g), cross-country running (b,g), dance squad (g), danceline (g), diving (b,g), football (b), golf (b,g), soccer (b,g), swimming and diving (b,g), tennis (b,g), track and field (b,g), volleyball (b,g), wrestling (b); coed interscholastic: aerobics/dance, dance, dance team, football, physical fitness, strength & conditioning, weight training. 2 PE instructors, 1 athletic trainer.
Computers Computers are regularly used in all academic, religious studies, yearbook classes. Computer network features include on-campus library services, Internet access, wireless campus network, Internet filtering or blocking technology, Turnitin®. Campus intranet and student e-mail accounts are available to students. Students grades are available online. The school has a published electronic and media policy.
Contact Mr. Chris Moore, Director of Admissions. 480-963-1900 Ext. 2008. Fax: 480-963-1974. E-mail: cmoore@setonchs.org. Web site: www.setoncatholic.org.

THE SEVEN HILLS SCHOOL

5400 Red Bank Road

Cincinnati, Ohio 45227

Head of School: Mr. Christopher P. Garten

General Information Coeducational day college-preparatory, arts, and technology school. Grades PK–12. Founded: 1974. Setting: suburban. 35-acre campus. 16 buildings on campus. Approved or accredited by Ohio Department of Education. Member of National Association of Independent Schools and Secondary School Admission Test Board. Endowment: $19.2 million. Total enrollment: 1,000. Upper school average class size: 15. Upper school faculty-student ratio: 1:9. There are 178 required school days per year for Upper School students. Upper School students typically attend 5 days per week. The average school day consists of 7 hours and 5 minutes.
Upper School Student Profile Grade 9: 77 students (45 boys, 32 girls); Grade 10: 61 students (29 boys, 32 girls); Grade 11: 81 students (39 boys, 42 girls); Grade 12: 61 students (29 boys, 32 girls).
Faculty School total: 128. In upper school: 20 men, 25 women; 40 have advanced degrees.
Subjects Offered Acting, advanced computer applications, Advanced Placement courses, algebra, American history, American literature, ancient history, art, art history, biology, British literature, calculus, ceramics, chemistry, computer programming, computer science, economics, English, European history, fine arts, French, geometry, journalism, Latin, linear algebra, Mandarin, medieval/Renaissance history, modern political theory, music, physical education, physics, pre-calculus, psychology, Spanish, speech, theater, world history, world literature, writing.
Graduation Requirements Algebra, arts and fine arts (art, music, dance, drama), biology, chemistry, computer science, English, foreign language, geometry, performing arts, physical education (includes health), physics, U.S. history, U.S. literature, completion of a personal challenge project, successfully pass writing competency exam, 30 hours of community service.
Special Academic Programs 16 Advanced Placement exams for which test preparation is offered; honors section; independent study; term-away projects; study abroad; academic accommodation for the gifted.
College Admission Counseling 70 students graduated in 2011; all went to college, including Duke University; Massachusetts Institute of Technology; Miami University; Northwestern University; Tufts University; Washington University in St. Louis. Median SAT critical reading: 661, median SAT math: 663, median SAT writing: 666, median composite ACT: 29. 74% scored over 600 on SAT critical reading, 87% scored over 600 on SAT math, 84% scored over 600 on SAT writing.
Student Life Upper grades have specified standards of dress, student council. Discipline rests primarily with faculty.
Summer Programs Enrichment programs offered; session focuses on SAT review, sports clinics, and acting workshop; held on campus; accepts boys and girls; open to students from other schools. 400 students usually enrolled. 2012 schedule: June 14 to August 13. Application deadline: none.
Tuition and Aid Day student tuition: $19,911–$20,426. Tuition installment plan (monthly payment plans, individually arranged payment plans). Merit scholarship grants, need-based scholarship grants available. In 2011–12, 17% of upper-school students received aid; total upper-school merit-scholarship money awarded: $157,900. Total amount of financial aid awarded in 2011–12: $530,000.
Admissions Traditional secondary-level entrance grade is 9. ISEE required. Deadline for receipt of application materials: December 2. Application fee required: $50. On-campus interview required.
Athletics Interscholastic: baseball (boys), basketball (b,g), cheering (g), cross-country running (b,g), golf (b), gymnastics (g), lacrosse (b,g), soccer (b,g), softball (g), swimming and diving (b,g), tennis (b,g), volleyball (g); coed interscholastic: track and field. 3 PE instructors, 9 coaches.
Computers Computers are regularly used in foreign language, mathematics, science classes. Computer network features include on-campus library services, online commercial services, Internet access, wireless campus network. Computer access in designated common areas is available to students.
Contact Mrs. Janet S. Hill, Director of Admission and Financial Aid. 513-728-2405. Fax: 513-728-2409. E-mail: janet.hill@7hills.org. Web site: www.7hills.org.

SEVERN SCHOOL

201 Water Street

Severna Park, Maryland 21146

Head of School: Douglas H. Lagarde

General Information Coeducational day college-preparatory, arts, and technology school. Grades 6–12. Founded: 1914. Setting: suburban. Nearest major city is

Annapolis. 19-acre campus. 8 buildings on campus. Approved or accredited by Association of Independent Maryland Schools, Middle States Association of Colleges and Schools, and Maryland Department of Education. Member of National Association of Independent Schools and Secondary School Admission Test Board. Endowment: $6 million. Total enrollment: 582. Upper school average class size: 15. Upper school faculty-student ratio: 1:8. There are 175 required school days per year for Upper School students. Upper School students typically attend 5 days per week. The average school day consists of 6 hours and 35 minutes.

Upper School Student Profile Grade 9: 99 students (43 boys, 56 girls); Grade 10: 105 students (47 boys, 58 girls); Grade 11: 94 students (51 boys, 43 girls); Grade 12: 89 students (48 boys, 41 girls).

Faculty School total: 81. In upper school: 27 men, 30 women; 38 have advanced degrees.

Subjects Offered Algebra, American history, American literature, art, biology, calculus, ceramics, chemistry, community service, computer programming, computer science, CPR, creative writing, dance, desktop publishing, digital art, digital imaging, digital photography, discrete mathematics, drama, drama performance, dramatic arts, drawing, drawing and design, earth science, ecology, economics, economics-AP, English, English literature, environmental science, environmental systems, European civilization, European history, European history-AP, expository writing, fine arts, forensics, French, French language-AP, French literature-AP, geometry, government/civics, grammar, graphic arts, health, history, journalism, Latin, marine biology, mathematics, multimedia, music, photography, physical education, physics, psychology, science, social studies, Spanish, speech, theater, trigonometry, world history, world literature, writing.

Graduation Requirements Arts and fine arts (art, music, dance, drama), computer science, CPR, English, foreign language, mathematics, physical education (includes health), science, social studies (includes history). Community service is required.

Special Academic Programs Advanced Placement exam preparation; honors section; independent study; study abroad; academic accommodation for the gifted, the musically talented, and the artistically talented.

College Admission Counseling 100 students graduated in 2011; all went to college, including Boston University; Elon University; The George Washington University; The Johns Hopkins University; The University of Alabama; University of Maryland, College Park. Median SAT critical reading: 600, median SAT math: 630, median SAT writing: 620, median combined SAT: 1860, median composite ACT: 26. 47% scored over 600 on SAT critical reading, 56% scored over 600 on SAT math, 55% scored over 600 on SAT writing, 58% scored over 1800 on combined SAT, 47% scored over 26 on composite ACT.

Student Life Upper grades have uniform requirement, student council, honor system. Discipline rests primarily with faculty.

Summer Programs Remediation, enrichment, advancement, sports, art/fine arts, computer instruction programs offered; session focuses on advanced math, day camp, and sports camps; held both on and off campus; held at SPY Swimming Pool; accepts boys and girls; open to students from other schools. 250 students usually enrolled. 2012 schedule: June 23 to August 1.

Tuition and Aid Day student tuition: $22,150. Tuition installment plan (Academic Management Services Plan). Need-based scholarship grants available. In 2011–12, 22% of upper-school students received aid. Total amount of financial aid awarded in 2011–12: $1,115,305.

Admissions Traditional secondary-level entrance grade is 9. For fall 2011, 105 students applied for upper-level admission, 55 were accepted, 44 enrolled. ISEE required. Deadline for receipt of application materials: January 20. Application fee required: $55. On-campus interview required.

Athletics Interscholastic: baseball (boys), basketball (b,g), combined training (b,g), dance team (g), field hockey (g), football (b), lacrosse (b,g), soccer (b,g), tennis (b,g); coed interscholastic: cross-country running, dance, diving, golf, sailing, strength & conditioning, swimming and diving, track and field, weight training; coed intramural: aerobics/dance, ice hockey, outdoor adventure, paint ball, table tennis. 4 PE instructors, 56 coaches, 2 athletic trainers.

Computers Computers are regularly used in all academic classes. Computer network features include on-campus library services, online commercial services, Internet access, Internet filtering or blocking technology. Campus intranet, student e-mail accounts, and computer access in designated common areas are available to students. Students grades are available online. The school has a published electronic and media policy.

Contact Ellen Murray, Associate Director of Admissions. 410-647-7701 Ext. 2266. Fax: 410-544-9451. E-mail: e.murray@severnschool.com. Web site: www.severnschool.com.

SEWICKLEY ACADEMY

315 Academy Avenue

Sewickley, Pennsylvania 15143

Head of School: Mr. Kolia J. O'Connor

General Information Coeducational day college-preparatory, arts, and technology school. Grades PK–12. Founded: 1838. Setting: suburban. Nearest major city is Pittsburgh. 30-acre campus. 10 buildings on campus. Approved or accredited by National Independent Private Schools Association and Pennsylvania Department of Education. Member of National Association of Independent Schools and Secondary School Admission Test Board. Endowment: $27.8 million. Total enrollment: 702. Upper school average class size: 15. Upper school faculty-student ratio: 1:7. There are 167 required school days per year for Upper School students. Upper School students typically attend 5 days per week. The average school day consists of 7 hours.

Upper School Student Profile Grade 9: 75 students (38 boys, 37 girls); Grade 10: 81 students (36 boys, 45 girls); Grade 11: 63 students (25 boys, 38 girls); Grade 12: 75 students (39 boys, 36 girls).

Faculty School total: 106. In upper school: 28 men, 28 women; 32 have advanced degrees.

Subjects Offered Advanced chemistry, advanced studio art-AP, African studies, algebra, American history, American history-AP, American literature, American literature-AP, art, art-AP, astronomy, band, biology, biology-AP, calculus, calculus-AP, ceramics, chemistry, chemistry-AP, choral music, chorus, clayworking, computer applications, computer art, computer programming, computer science, computer science-AP, concert band, concert choir, contemporary issues, creative writing, dance, dance performance, digital art, drama, drama performance, drama workshop, drawing, driver education, economics, English, English literature, environmental science, ethics, European history, European history-AP, expository writing, fine arts, French, French language-AP, French literature-AP, geometry, German, German-AP, government/civics, health, health education, history, Italian, keyboarding, Mandarin, music, musical theater, performing arts, photography, physical education, physics, physics-AP, pre-calculus, psychology, psychology-AP, senior project, Spanish, Spanish literature, Spanish-AP, speech and debate, statistics, statistics-AP, studio art, theater, trigonometry, U.S. history-AP, U.S. literature, Vietnam War, world history, world literature, writing.

Graduation Requirements Arts and fine arts (art, music, dance, drama), English, foreign language, health education, mathematics, physical education (includes health), science, social studies (includes history), U.S. history, world cultures, world studies. Community service is required.

Special Academic Programs Advanced Placement exam preparation; honors section; independent study; term-away projects; study at local college for college credit; study abroad.

College Admission Counseling 75 students graduated in 2011; all went to college, including Boston University; Bucknell University; Colgate University; Dartmouth College; Emory University; Princeton University.

Student Life Upper grades have specified standards of dress, student council, honor system. Discipline rests equally with students and faculty.

Summer Programs Enrichment, advancement, sports, art/fine arts programs offered; session focuses on academics, athletics, and musical theater; held on campus; accepts boys and girls; open to students from other schools. 150 students usually enrolled. 2012 schedule: June 11 to August 10. Application deadline: none.

Tuition and Aid Day student tuition: $22,025. Tuition installment plan (monthly payment plans). Need-based scholarship grants available. In 2011–12, 20% of upper-school students received aid. Total amount of financial aid awarded in 2011–12: $600,000.

Admissions Traditional secondary-level entrance grade is 9. For fall 2011, 66 students applied for upper-level admission, 43 were accepted, 26 enrolled. ISEE or SSAT required. Deadline for receipt of application materials: February 8. Application fee required: $50. Interview required.

Athletics Interscholastic: baseball (boys), basketball (b,g), cross-country running (b,g), golf (b,g), ice hockey (b), lacrosse (b,g), physical fitness (b,g), soccer (b,g), softball (g), tennis (b,g); coed interscholastic: bowling, diving, field hockey, physical fitness, swimming and diving, track and field. 5 PE instructors, 5 coaches, 1 athletic trainer.

Computers Computers are regularly used in all academic classes. Computer network features include on-campus library services, online commercial services, Internet access, wireless campus network, Internet filtering or blocking technology. Campus intranet, student e-mail accounts, and computer access in designated common areas are available to students. The school has a published electronic and media policy.

Contact Ms. Wendy Berns, Admission Assistant. 412-741-2235. Fax: 412-741-1411. E-mail: wberns@sewickley.org. Web site: www.sewickley.org.

SHADES MOUNTAIN CHRISTIAN SCHOOL

2290 Old Tyler Road

Hoover, Alabama 35226

Head of School: Mr. Laird Crump

General Information Coeducational day college-preparatory and Biblical studies school, affiliated with Christian faith. Grades K–12. Founded: 1974. Setting: suburban. Nearest major city is Birmingham. 30-acre campus. 3 buildings on campus. Approved or accredited by Association of Christian Schools International, Southern Association of Colleges and Schools, and Alabama Department of Education. Total enrollment: 408. Upper school average class size: 20. Upper school faculty-student ratio: 1:10. There are 180 required school days per year for Upper School students. Upper School students typically attend 5 days per week. The average school day consists of 6 hours and 50 minutes.

Upper School Student Profile Grade 9: 33 students (17 boys, 16 girls); Grade 10: 38 students (22 boys, 16 girls); Grade 11: 24 students (14 boys, 10 girls); Grade 12: 24 students (9 boys, 15 girls). 50% of students are Christian faith.

Faculty School total: 36. In upper school: 9 men, 9 women; 7 have advanced degrees.

Subjects Offered Advanced chemistry, advanced math, algebra, American government, American literature, anatomy and physiology, ancient world history, art, band, Bible studies, business applications, calculus-AP, character education, chemistry, choir, choral music, Christian doctrine, Christian education, Christian ethics, Christian scripture, Christian studies, Christianity, civics, competitive science projects, composition, composition-AP, computer applications, computer literacy, consumer economics, CPR, creative thinking, creative writing, decision making skills, driver education, earth and space science, economics, English, English composition, English language and composition-AP, English literature, ensembles, ethics and responsibility, finance, first aid, general science, geography, geometry, government/civics, guitar, instruments, jazz band, junior and senior seminars, keyboarding, leadership, Life of Christ, marching band, math applications, math methods, math review, mathematics, mathematics-AP, music appreciation, mythology, news writing, personal finance, philosophy, physical education, physical science, physics, pre-algebra, pre-calculus, psychology, reading/study skills, relationships, religion, research and reference, research skills, rhetoric, science, science project, science research, social sciences, social skills, social studies, Spanish, sports medicine, technology, trigonometry, typing, U.S. government and politics, U.S. history, values and decisions, world history, yearbook.

Graduation Requirements American history, Bible, computers, economics, English, foreign language, government, mathematics, philosophy, physical education (includes health), science, world history.

Special Academic Programs 2 Advanced Placement exams for which test preparation is offered; honors section; independent study; programs in English, mathematics, general development for dyslexic students; special instructional classes for students with learning disabilities.

College Admission Counseling 34 students graduated in 2010; 30 went to college, including Auburn University; Samford University; The University of Alabama; The University of Alabama at Birmingham; University of Montevallo. Other: 3 went to work, 1 entered military service. Mean composite ACT: 22. 21% scored over 26 on composite ACT.

Student Life Upper grades have specified standards of dress, student council, honor system. Discipline rests primarily with faculty. Attendance at religious services is required.

Tuition and Aid Day student tuition: $6000. Tuition installment plan (monthly payment plans, individually arranged payment plans). Tuition reduction for siblings, need-based scholarship grants available. In 2010–11, 15% of upper-school students received aid. Total amount of financial aid awarded in 2010–11: $13,000.

Admissions Any standardized test required. Deadline for receipt of application materials: none. Application fee required: $500. Interview required.

Athletics Interscholastic: baseball (boys), basketball (b,g), cheering (g), cross-country running (b,g), football (b), golf (b,g), independent competitive sports (b,g), physical fitness (b,g), physical training (b,g), soccer (b,g), softball (g), strength & conditioning (b,g), swimming and diving (b,g), tennis (b,g), volleyball (g), wrestling (b). 2 PE instructors, 2 coaches, 1 athletic trainer.

Computers Computers are regularly used in keyboarding classes. Computer resources include on-campus library services, Internet access, Internet filtering or blocking technology. Students grades are available online. The school has a published electronic and media policy.

Contact Mrs. Beth Buyck, School Secretary. 205-978-6001. Fax: 205-978-9120. E-mail: bethbuyck@smcs.org.

SHADY SIDE ACADEMY

423 Fox Chapel Road

Pittsburgh, Pennsylvania 15238

Head of School: Mr. Thomas Cangiano

General Information Coeducational boarding and day college-preparatory school. Boarding grades 9–12, day grades PK–12. Founded: 1883. Setting: suburban. Students are housed in single-sex dormitories. 130-acre campus. 26 buildings on campus. Approved or accredited by Middle States Association of Colleges and Schools, The Association of Boarding Schools, and Pennsylvania Department of Education. Member of National Association of Independent Schools. Endowment: $50 million. Total enrollment: 928. Upper school average class size: 13. Upper school faculty-student ratio: 1:8. There are 172 required school days per year for Upper School students. Upper School students typically attend 5 days per week.

Upper School Student Profile Grade 9: 113 students (57 boys, 56 girls); Grade 10: 127 students (62 boys, 65 girls); Grade 11: 119 students (70 boys, 49 girls); Grade 12: 128 students (77 boys, 51 girls). 12% of students are boarding students. 99% are state residents. 3 states are represented in upper school student body.

Faculty School total: 118. In upper school: 33 men, 30 women; 33 have advanced degrees; 15 reside on campus.

Subjects Offered Advanced Placement courses, algebra, American history, American literature, architectural drawing, architecture, art, art history, biology, calculus, calculus-AP, ceramics, chemistry, Chinese, Chinese history, computer graphics, computer math, computer programming, computer science, computer science-AP, creative writing, drama, driver education, economics, English, English literature, ethics, European history, expository writing, fine arts, fractal geometry, French, French-AP, gender issues, geography, geometry, German, German-AP, health, history, Latin, linear algebra, logic, mathematics, music, music technology, musical theater, philosophy, photography, physical education, physics, religion and culture, science, social studies, Spanish, Spanish-AP, speech, statistics, studio art, technical theater, trigonometry, world history, world literature, writing.

Graduation Requirements Arts and fine arts (art, music, dance, drama), athletics, computer science, English, foreign language, mathematics, physical education (includes health), science, social studies (includes history), participation in five seasons of athletics.

Special Academic Programs 6 Advanced Placement exams for which test preparation is offered; honors section; accelerated programs; independent study; term-away projects; study at local college for college credit; study abroad; academic accommodation for the gifted, the musically talented, and the artistically talented.

College Admission Counseling 116 students graduated in 2011; 115 went to college, including Carnegie Mellon University; Cornell University; The George Washington University; University of Pennsylvania; University of Pittsburgh; University of Richmond. Other: 1 had other specific plans. Median SAT critical reading: 620, median SAT math: 650, median SAT writing: 640, median combined SAT: 1910, median composite ACT: 26. 59% scored over 600 on SAT critical reading, 75% scored over 600 on SAT math, 74% scored over 600 on SAT writing, 68% scored over 1800 on combined SAT, 86% scored over 26 on composite ACT.

Student Life Upper grades have specified standards of dress, student council. Discipline rests primarily with faculty.

Summer Programs Remediation, enrichment, advancement, sports, art/fine arts, computer instruction programs offered; session focuses on academic and non-academic enrichment; held on campus; accepts boys and girls; open to students from other schools. 1,170 students usually enrolled. 2012 schedule: June 20 to August 13. Application deadline: none.

Tuition and Aid Day student tuition: $26,000; 5-day tuition and room/board: $36,500. Tuition installment plan (monthly payment plans, Tuition Refund Plan available through Dewar's). Tuition reduction for siblings, merit scholarship grants, need-based scholarship grants, merit-based scholarships are for boarding students, FAME awards (Fund for the Advancement of Minorities Through Education), partial tuition remission for children of full-time employees available. In 2011–12, 22% of upper-school students received aid; total upper-school merit-scholarship money awarded: $95,000. Total amount of financial aid awarded in 2011–12: $1,825,900.

Admissions Traditional secondary-level entrance grade is 9. For fall 2011, 148 students applied for upper-level admission, 104 were accepted, 69 enrolled. ISEE, SSAT or TOEFL required. Deadline for receipt of application materials: February 6. Application fee required: $50. On-campus interview required.

Athletics Interscholastic: baseball (boys), basketball (b,g), crew (g), cross-country running (b,g), field hockey (g), football (b), golf (b,g), ice hockey (b,g), lacrosse (b,g), soccer (b,g), softball (g), squash (b,g), swimming and diving (b,g), tennis (b,g), track and field (b,g), wrestling (b); intramural: cheering (g), volleyball (g); coed intramural: aerobics/dance, backpacking, badminton, bowling, cricket, ultimate Frisbee, weight lifting. 1 PE instructor, 47 coaches, 2 athletic trainers.

Computers Computers are regularly used in all classes. Computer network features include on-campus library services, online commercial services, Internet access, wireless campus network, Internet filtering or blocking technology. Student e-mail accounts and computer access in designated common areas are available to students. The school has a published electronic and media policy.

Contact Ms. Katherine H. Mihm, Director of Enrollment Management and Marketing. 412-968-3179. Fax: 412-968-3213. E-mail: kmihm@shadysideacademy.org. Web site: www.shadysideacademy.org.

SHANNON FOREST CHRISTIAN SCHOOL

829 Garlington Road

Greenville, South Carolina 29615

Head of School: Mr. Bob Collins

General Information Coeducational day college-preparatory, arts, religious studies, and technology school, affiliated with Presbyterian Church. Grades PK–12. Founded: 1968. Setting: small town. 50-acre campus. 7 buildings on campus. Approved or accredited by Association of Christian Schools International and Southern Association of Colleges and Schools. Endowment: $200,000. Total enrollment: 445. Upper school average class size: 17. Upper school faculty-student ratio: 1:17. There are 180 required school days per year for Upper School students. The average school day consists of 7 hours.

Upper School Student Profile Grade 6: 27 students (21 boys, 6 girls); Grade 7: 38 students (23 boys, 15 girls); Grade 8: 47 students (19 boys, 28 girls); Grade 9: 35 students (15 boys, 20 girls); Grade 10: 30 students (13 boys, 17 girls); Grade 11: 29 students (13 boys, 16 girls); Grade 12: 29 students (11 boys, 18 girls). 3% of students are Presbyterian.

Faculty School total: 49. In upper school: 7 men, 20 women; 16 have advanced degrees.

Subjects Offered Algebra, American literature, art, Bible, Bible studies, biology, biology-AP, calculus, calculus-AP, career/college preparation, chemistry, choir, college planning, computer science, drama, economics, English, English literature-AP, English-AP, European history-AP, French, geometry, government, health, journalism, keyboarding, literature, music, physical education, physical science, physics, pre-algebra, pre-calculus, psychology, SAT preparation, sociology, Spanish, theater arts, U.S. history, U.S. history-AP, world geography, world history, yearbook.
Graduation Requirements Computer science, English, foreign language, mathematics, physical education (includes health), religion (includes Bible studies and theology), SAT preparation, science, social sciences, social studies (includes history), annual attendance at two fine arts programs (grades 9 - 12), 30 hours of community service per year.
Special Academic Programs Advanced Placement exam preparation; honors section; programs in English, mathematics, general development for dyslexic students; special instructional classes for students with emotional/behavioral problems, learning disabilities, Attention Deficit Hyperactivity Disorder.
College Admission Counseling 29 students graduated in 2010; all went to college, including Anderson University; Clemson University; Furman University; Presbyterian College; University of South Carolina; Wofford College.
Student Life Upper grades have uniform requirement, student council, honor system. Discipline rests primarily with faculty. Attendance at religious services is required.
Tuition and Aid Day student tuition: $7200. Tuition installment plan (FACTS Tuition Payment Plan). Need-based scholarship grants, Scholar loans available. In 2010–11, 19% of upper-school students received aid. Total amount of financial aid awarded in 2010–11: $15,000.
Admissions Traditional secondary-level entrance grade is 7. For fall 2010, 80 students applied for upper-level admission, 51 were accepted, 40 enrolled. Stanford Achievement Test required. Deadline for receipt of application materials: none. Application fee required: $100. Interview required.
Athletics Interscholastic: baseball (boys), basketball (b,g), cheering (g), cross-country running (b,g), golf (b,g), soccer (b,g), softball (g), swimming and diving (b,g), tennis (b,g), volleyball (g); intramural: baseball (b), flag football (b,g), soccer (b,g), tennis (b,g). 3 PE instructors, 18 coaches, 1 athletic trainer.
Computers Computers are regularly used in English, journalism, keyboarding, yearbook classes. Computer network features include on-campus library services, online commercial services, Internet access, wireless campus network, Internet filtering or blocking technology. Campus intranet is available to students. Students grades are available online. The school has a published electronic and media policy.
Contact Mrs. Lynn Pittman, Admissions Coordinator. 864-414-1308. Fax: 864-281-9372. E-mail: lpittman@shannonforest.com. Web site: www.shannonforest.com.

SHATTUCK-ST. MARY'S SCHOOL

1000 Shumway Avenue

PO Box 218

Faribault, Minnesota 55021

Head of School: Nicholas J.B. Stoneman

General Information Coeducational boarding and day college-preparatory, arts, and BioScience, STEM Education school, affiliated with Episcopal Church. Grades 6–PG. Founded: 1858. Setting: small town. Nearest major city is Minneapolis/St. Paul. Students are housed in single-sex dormitories. 250-acre campus. 10 buildings on campus. Approved or accredited by Independent Schools Association of the Central States, Midwest Association of Boarding Schools, National Association of Episcopal Schools, The Association of Boarding Schools, and Minnesota Department of Education. Member of National Association of Independent Schools and Secondary School Admission Test Board. Total enrollment: 438. Upper school average class size: 12. Upper school faculty-student ratio: 1:9. There are 167 required school days per year for Upper School students. The average school day consists of 7 hours.
Upper School Student Profile Grade 9: 63 students (41 boys, 22 girls); Grade 10: 102 students (69 boys, 33 girls); Grade 11: 124 students (74 boys, 50 girls); Grade 12: 105 students (60 boys, 45 girls); Postgraduate: 4 students (1 boy, 3 girls). 75% of students are boarding students. 25% are state residents. 44 states are represented in upper school student body. 32% are international students. International students from Canada, China, Japan, Republic of Korea, Sweden, and Taiwan; 26 other countries represented in student body.
Faculty In upper school: 25 men, 30 women; 60 reside on campus.
Subjects Offered 20th century world history, Advanced Placement courses, advanced studio art-AP, advanced TOEFL/grammar, algebra, American Civil War, American history, American history-AP, American literature, American sign language, anatomy and physiology, art, art history, astronomy, ballet, band, Bible studies, bioethics, biology, British literature, calculus, calculus-AP, ceramics, chamber groups, chemistry, chemistry-AP, choir, choral music, community service, composition, dance, digital photography, drama, drawing, economics, English, English language and composition-AP, English literature, English literature and composition-AP, environmental science-AP, ESL, ethics, European civilization, European history, European history-AP, expository writing, field ecology, film studies, fine arts, French, French language-AP, geography, geometry, government/civics, grammar, Greek, high adventure outdoor program, history, human anatomy, Latin, Latin American history, Mandarin, mathematics, microbiology, Middle Eastern history, music, Native American history, oil painting, orchestra, painting, physics, physics-AP, piano, pottery, pre-algebra, pre-calculus, psychology, psychology-AP, public speaking, religion, robotics, Roman civilization, science, social studies, South African history, Spanish, Spanish-AP, speech, statistics, statistics-AP, theater, trigonometry, U.S. history-AP, world geography, world history, world history-AP, writing.
Graduation Requirements Arts and fine arts (art, music, dance, drama), English, foreign language, mathematics, religion (includes Bible studies and theology), science, social studies (includes history), 20 hours of community service per year.
Special Academic Programs 14 Advanced Placement exams for which test preparation is offered; honors section; independent study; academic accommodation for the gifted and the musically talented; remedial reading and/or remedial writing; remedial math; programs in English, mathematics, general development for dyslexic students; ESL (85 students enrolled).
College Admission Counseling 104 students graduated in 2011; 100 went to college, including Butler University; Cornell University; University of Illinois at Urbana–Champaign; University of Minnesota, Twin Cities Campus; University of Rochester; University of Wisconsin–Madison. Other: 2 entered a postgraduate year, 2 had other specific plans.
Student Life Upper grades have specified standards of dress, student council. Discipline rests primarily with faculty. Attendance at religious services is required.
Summer Programs ESL, sports, art/fine arts programs offered; session focuses on challenging, diversified instruction in the arts and athletics; ESL summer program; held on campus; accepts boys and girls; open to students from other schools.
Tuition and Aid Day student tuition: $24,950; 7-day tuition and room/board: $38,450. Tuition installment plan (Insured Tuition Payment Plan, monthly payment plans). Merit scholarship grants, need-based scholarship grants, Performing arts scholarship, Headmasters Scholarship available. In 2011–12, 44% of upper-school students received aid. Total amount of financial aid awarded in 2011–12: $3,900,000.
Admissions Traditional secondary-level entrance grade is 9. For fall 2011, 688 students applied for upper-level admission, 247 were accepted, 157 enrolled. SLEP, SSAT or TOEFL required. Deadline for receipt of application materials: none. Application fee required: $75. Interview required.
Athletics Interscholastic: baseball (boys), basketball (b,g), fencing (b,g), golf (b,g), ice hockey (b,g), indoor hockey (b,g), indoor soccer (b,g), lacrosse (b,g), soccer (b,g), tennis (b,g), track and field (b,g), volleyball (g); intramural: drill team (b,g), weight training (b,g); coed interscholastic: figure skating, soccer; coed intramural: aerobics/dance, badminton, basketball, dance, dance team, Frisbee, ice skating, jogging, martial arts, outdoor activities, outdoor recreation, ropes courses, strength & conditioning, table tennis, ultimate Frisbee. 29 coaches, 3 athletic trainers.
Computers Computers are regularly used in animation, college planning, creative writing, English, ESL, foreign language, history, independent study, mathematics, photography, SAT preparation, science, senior seminar, speech, writing, writing, yearbook classes. Computer network features include on-campus library services, Internet access, wireless campus network, Internet filtering or blocking technology. Campus intranet, student e-mail accounts, and computer access in designated common areas are available to students. Students grades are available online. The school has a published electronic and media policy.
Contact Mr. Jesse W. Fortney, Director of Admissions. 800-421-2724. Fax: 507-333-1661. E-mail: admissions@s-sm.org. Web site: www.s-sm.org.

SHAWE MEMORIAL JUNIOR/SENIOR HIGH SCHOOL

201 West State Street

Madison, Indiana 47250-2899

Head of School: Mr. Philip J. Kahn

General Information Coeducational day college-preparatory and religious studies school, affiliated with Roman Catholic Church. Grades 7–12. Founded: 1954. Setting: small town. 30-acre campus. 1 building on campus. Approved or accredited by North Central Association of Colleges and Schools and Indiana Department of Education. Total enrollment: 342. Upper school average class size: 11. Upper school faculty-student ratio: 1:9. There are 180 required school days per year for Upper School students. Upper School students typically attend 5 days per week. The average school day consists of 8 hours and 15 minutes.
Upper School Student Profile Grade 9: 25 students (12 boys, 13 girls); Grade 10: 23 students (11 boys, 12 girls); Grade 11: 41 students (22 boys, 19 girls); Grade 12: 19 students (11 boys, 8 girls). 70% of students are Roman Catholic.
Faculty School total: 22. In upper school: 4 men, 17 women; 10 have advanced degrees.
Special Academic Programs International Baccalaureate program; Advanced Placement exam preparation; honors section; independent study; study at local college for college credit; academic accommodation for the gifted; remedial reading and/or remedial writing; special instructional classes for deaf students, some special needs students can be accommodated on an individual basis.

College Admission Counseling 27 students graduated in 2011; all went to college, including Ball State University; Indiana University Bloomington; Purdue University; University of Kentucky. Mean SAT critical reading: 539, mean SAT math: 506, mean SAT writing: 504, mean combined SAT: 1549.

Student Life Upper grades have specified standards of dress, student council. Discipline rests primarily with faculty. Attendance at religious services is required.

Tuition and Aid Day student tuition: $5915. Tuition installment plan (The Tuition Plan, FACTS Tuition Payment Plan, individually arranged payment plans, multiple options). Tuition reduction for siblings, need-based scholarship grants available. In 2011–12, 35% of upper-school students received aid. Total amount of financial aid awarded in 2011–12: $161,537.

Admissions Traditional secondary-level entrance grade is 9. For fall 2011, 23 students applied for upper-level admission, 19 were accepted, 19 enrolled. Deadline for receipt of application materials: none. Application fee required: $150. Interview required.

Athletics Interscholastic: archery (boys), baseball (b), basketball (b,g), cheering (g), cross-country running (b,g), fencing (b), golf (b,g), soccer (b,g), softball (g), tennis (b,g), track and field (b,g), volleyball (g). 2 PE instructors, 10 coaches, 1 athletic trainer.

Computers Computer network features include on-campus library services, Internet access, wireless campus network, Internet filtering or blocking technology. Campus intranet is available to students. Students grades are available online.

Contact Mr. Philip J. Kahn, President. 812-273-5835 Ext. 245. Fax: 812-273-8975. E-mail: poppresident@popeace.org.

SHAWNIGAN LAKE SCHOOL

1975 Renfrew Road

Postal Bag 2000

Shawnigan Lake, British Columbia V0R 2W1, Canada

Head of School: Mr. David Robertson

General Information Coeducational boarding and day college-preparatory, fine arts, athletics, leadership, citizenship, and entrepreneurship, and language studies school. Grades 8–12. Founded: 1916. Setting: rural. Nearest major city is Victoria, Canada. Students are housed in single-sex dormitories. 300-acre campus. 50 buildings on campus. Approved or accredited by British Columbia Independent Schools Association, Canadian Association of Independent Schools, The Association of Boarding Schools, Western Boarding Schools Association, and British Columbia Department of Education. Affiliate member of National Association of Independent Schools. Languages of instruction: English and French. Endowment: CAN$7.5 million. Total enrollment: 453. Upper school average class size: 15. Upper school faculty-student ratio: 1:8. Upper School students typically attend 6 days per week.

Upper School Student Profile Grade 8: 46 students (30 boys, 16 girls); Grade 9: 55 students (34 boys, 21 girls); Grade 10: 105 students (56 boys, 49 girls); Grade 11: 122 students (66 boys, 56 girls); Grade 12: 125 students (67 boys, 58 girls). 91% of students are boarding students. 65% are province residents. 17 provinces are represented in upper school student body. 22% are international students. International students from China, Democratic People's Republic of Korea, Germany, Hong Kong, Mexico, and United States; 19 other countries represented in student body.

Faculty School total: 59. In upper school: 39 men, 20 women; 22 have advanced degrees; 45 reside on campus.

Subjects Offered Advanced Placement courses, advanced studio art-AP, algebra, art, art history, art history-AP, biology, biology-AP, business skills, calculus, calculus-AP, career and personal planning, chemistry, chemistry-AP, computer science, computer science-AP, creative writing, earth science, economics, English, English language and composition-AP, English literature, English literature and composition-AP, English-AP, environmental science, European history-AP, expository writing, fine arts, French, French language-AP, French literature-AP, French-AP, geography, geometry, German, health, history, human geography - AP, industrial arts, mathematics, media studies, music, physical education, physics, physics-AP, religion, science, social studies, Spanish, sports science, study skills, trigonometry, U.S. history-AP, writing.

Graduation Requirements Acting, arts and fine arts (art, music, dance, drama), athletics, band, biology, career and personal planning, chemistry, drama, English, foreign language, geography, mathematics, music, physical education (includes health), physics, science, social studies (includes history), Graduation requirements are mandated by the BC Provincial Government and include English 12 plus 4 additonal grade 12 courses, and 30 hours of work experience, refer to the curriculum courses to see the subject offerings.

Special Academic Programs Advanced Placement exam preparation; honors section; academic accommodation for the gifted; remedial reading and/or remedial writing; remedial math; special instructional classes for students with learning disabilities; ESL (10 students enrolled).

College Admission Counseling 97 students graduated in 2011; 94 went to college, including McGill University; Queen's University at Kingston; The University of British Columbia; The University of Western Ontario; University of Alberta; University of Victoria. Other: 1 went to work, 1 entered military service, 1 had other specific plans.

Student Life Upper grades have uniform requirement, student council, honor system. Discipline rests equally with students and faculty. Attendance at religious services is required.

Summer Programs Sports programs offered; session focuses on rugby; held on campus; accepts boys and girls; open to students from other schools. 2012 schedule: July 1 to July 6. Application deadline: June 1.

Tuition and Aid Day student tuition: CAN$20,410; 7-day tuition and room/board: CAN$37,900–CAN$50,370. Tuition installment plan (Insured Tuition Payment Plan, individually arranged payment plans). Tuition reduction for siblings, bursaries, merit scholarship grants available. In 2011–12, 25% of upper-school students received aid; total upper-school merit-scholarship money awarded: CAN$200,000. Total amount of financial aid awarded in 2011–12: CAN$800,000.

Admissions Traditional secondary-level entrance grade is 8. For fall 2011, 341 students applied for upper-level admission, 167 were accepted, 153 enrolled. English entrance exam and Math Placement Exam required. Deadline for receipt of application materials: none. Application fee required: CAN$200. Interview required.

Athletics Interscholastic: basketball (boys, girls), crew (b,g), cross-country running (b,g), field hockey (g), golf (b,g), hockey (b), ice hockey (b), rowing (b,g), rugby (b,g), soccer (b,g), squash (b,g), tennis (b,g), volleyball (g); intramural: alpine skiing (b,g), ballet (g), basketball (b,g), crew (b,g), field hockey (g), golf (b,g), rowing (b,g), rugby (b,g), soccer (b,g), squash (b,g), strength & conditioning (b,g), tennis (b,g), volleyball (g), weight training (b,g), winter soccer (g); coed interscholastic: hockey, ice hockey, track and field; coed intramural: aerobics, aerobics/dance, alpine skiing, aquatics, backpacking, badminton, canoeing/kayaking, climbing, cross-country running, dance, fitness, golf, hiking/backpacking, jogging, kayaking, modern dance, nordic skiing, ocean paddling, outdoor activities, outdoor adventure, outdoor education, outdoor recreation, outdoor skills, outdoors, physical fitness, riflery, running, swimming and diving, track and field, wilderness survival, yoga. 4 PE instructors, 20 coaches, 2 athletic trainers.

Computers Computers are regularly used in animation, art, business, computer applications, creative writing, design, drawing and design, English, foreign language, graphic arts, history, library, mathematics, photography, research skills, science, social studies, video film production, yearbook classes. Computer network features include on-campus library services, online commercial services, Internet access, wireless campus network, Internet filtering or blocking technology. Campus intranet and student e-mail accounts are available to students. Students grades are available online. The school has a published electronic and media policy.

Contact Ms. Margot Allen, Associate Director of Admission. 250-743-6207. Fax: 250-743-6280. E-mail: admissions@shawnigan.ca. Web site: www.shawnigan.ca.

SHELTON SCHOOL AND EVALUATION CENTER

Dallas, Texas

See Special Needs Schools section.

SHERIDAN ACADEMY

4948 Kootenai Street

Boise, Idaho 83705

Head of School: Greg P. Norton

General Information Coeducational day college-preparatory, general academic, business, vocational, and bilingual studies school. Grades 1–12. Founded: 1995. Setting: small town. 1-acre campus. 1 building on campus. Approved or accredited by Northwest Accreditation Commission. Total enrollment: 19. Upper school average class size: 12. Upper school faculty-student ratio: 1:10. There are 180 required school days per year for Upper School students. Upper School students typically attend 5 days per week.

Upper School Student Profile Grade 9: 6 students (5 boys, 1 girl); Grade 10: 2 students (1 boy, 1 girl); Grade 11: 3 students (1 boy, 2 girls); Grade 12: 4 students (3 boys, 1 girl).

Faculty School total: 3. In upper school: 1 man, 2 women; all have advanced degrees.

Subjects Offered Art, computers, economics, English, government, history, humanities, literature, mathematics, physical education, reading, science, Spanish-AP.

Graduation Requirements Economics, English, government, history, humanities, mathematics, reading, science, speech.

Special Academic Programs Accelerated programs; independent study; term-away projects; academic accommodation for the gifted; remedial reading and/or remedial writing; remedial math; programs in English, general development for dyslexic students; special instructional classes for students with Attention Deficit Disorder.

College Admission Counseling 3 students graduated in 2010; all went to college, including Boise State University.

Student Life Upper grades have specified standards of dress, honor system. Discipline rests primarily with faculty.

Tuition and Aid Day student tuition: $4500. Tuition installment plan (monthly payment plans, individually arranged payment plans). Tuition reduction for siblings, merit scholarship grants available.

Admissions Traditional secondary-level entrance grade is 9. For fall 2010, 10 students applied for upper-level admission, 10 were accepted. Deadline for receipt of application materials: none. Application fee required: $100. Interview required.

Athletics Coed Interscholastic: baseball, basketball, fishing, fly fishing, jogging, kickball, mountain biking, skateboarding, snowboarding, softball, touch football, walking, winter soccer, winter walking.

Computers Computer resources include Internet access.

Contact 208-331-2044. Fax: 208-331-7724.

THE SHIPLEY SCHOOL

814 Yarrow Street

Bryn Mawr, Pennsylvania 19010-3525

Head of School: Dr. Steven S. Piltch

General Information Coeducational day college-preparatory school. Grades PK–12. Founded: 1894. Setting: suburban. Nearest major city is Philadelphia. 36-acre campus. 4 buildings on campus. Approved or accredited by Middle States Association of Colleges and Schools and Pennsylvania Association of Independent Schools. Member of National Association of Independent Schools and Secondary School Admission Test Board. Endowment: $27 million. Total enrollment: 838. Upper school average class size: 12. Upper school faculty-student ratio: 1:7. There are 167 required school days per year for Upper School students. Upper School students typically attend 5 days per week. The average school day consists of 7 hours and 30 minutes.

Upper School Student Profile Grade 9: 99 students (48 boys, 51 girls); Grade 10: 75 students (39 boys, 36 girls); Grade 11: 83 students (43 boys, 40 girls); Grade 12: 87 students (43 boys, 44 girls).

Faculty School total: 125. In upper school: 26 men, 38 women; 44 have advanced degrees.

Subjects Offered Advanced studio art-AP, algebra, American history, American literature, ancient world history, art, art history, athletic training, athletics, band, bioethics, biology, calculus, chamber groups, chemistry, chorus, classical language, college admission preparation, college counseling, conceptual physics, concert bell choir, CPR, drama, drama performance, dramatic arts, ecology, environmental systems, economics, economics and history, English, English literature, European history, film studies, fine arts, forensics, French, geometry, global issues, global studies, grammar, health, health and wellness, health education, Homeric Greek, honors English, honors geometry, honors U.S. history, honors world history, independent study, introduction to theater, jazz band, Latin, leadership, library skills, Mandarin, mathematics, medieval history, Middle East, model United Nations, music, music theory, musical productions, orchestra, performing arts, philosophy, photography, physical education, physical fitness, physics, pre-calculus, research skills, science, senior project, senior seminar, service learning/internship, Shakespeare, Spanish, speech and debate, statistics, student publications, studio art-AP, theater, theater arts, urban studies, wind ensemble, world history, world literature.

Graduation Requirements English, foreign language, mathematics, performing arts, physical education (includes health), research skills, science, senior project, senior seminar, social studies (includes history), studio art, 40 hours of community service/service learning.

Special Academic Programs 2 Advanced Placement exams for which test preparation is offered; honors section; accelerated programs; independent study; term-away projects; study abroad; academic accommodation for the gifted.

College Admission Counseling 85 students graduated in 2011; 84 went to college, including Franklin & Marshall College; Penn State University Park; Skidmore College; University of Michigan; University of Pennsylvania; University of Richmond. Other: 1 entered a postgraduate year. Mean SAT critical reading: 629, mean SAT math: 626, mean SAT writing: 641, mean combined SAT: 1896, mean composite ACT: 27.

Student Life Upper grades have specified standards of dress, student council, honor system. Discipline rests equally with students and faculty.

Summer Programs Sports programs offered; session focuses on sports; held on campus; accepts boys and girls; open to students from other schools. 29 students usually enrolled. 2012 schedule: June 20 to July 29.

Tuition and Aid Day student tuition: $30,450. Tuition installment plan (monthly payment plans). Need-based scholarship grants available. In 2011–12, 25% of upper-school students received aid. Total amount of financial aid awarded in 2011–12: $2,231,695.

Admissions Traditional secondary-level entrance grade is 9. For fall 2011, 312 students applied for upper-level admission, 209 were accepted, 128 enrolled. ISEE, SSAT or WISC-R or WISC-III required. Deadline for receipt of application materials: January 13. Application fee required: $60. On-campus interview required.

Athletics Interscholastic: baseball (boys), basketball (b,g), crew (b,g), cross-country running (b,g), field hockey (g), independent competitive sports (b,g), lacrosse (b,g), rowing (b,g), soccer (b,g), softball (g), squash (b,g), tennis (b,g), volleyball (g), weight training (b,g); intramural: aerobics (b,g), aerobics/Nautilus (b,g), dance (g), modern dance (g), Nautilus (b,g); coed interscholastic: diving, golf, independent competitive sports, swimming and diving, weight training; coed intramural: aerobics, aerobics/Nautilus, fitness, Nautilus, physical fitness, yoga. 11 PE instructors, 51 coaches, 2 athletic trainers.

Computers Computers are regularly used in all classes. Computer network features include on-campus library services, online commercial services, Internet access, wireless campus network, Internet filtering or blocking technology, all progress, midterm, and final reports are online, 3-D printer. Campus intranet, student e-mail accounts, and computer access in designated common areas are available to students. Students grades are available online. The school has a published electronic and media policy.

Contact Mrs. Zoe Marshall, Assistant to the Director of Admissions. 610-525-4300 Ext. 4118. Fax: 610-525-5082. E-mail: zmarshall@shipleyschool.org. Web site: www.shipleyschool.org.

SHOORE CENTRE FOR LEARNING

Toronto, Ontario, Canada

See Special Needs Schools section.

SHORELINE CHRISTIAN

2400 Northeast 147th Street

Shoreline, Washington 98155

Head of School: Mr. Timothy E. Visser

General Information Coeducational day college-preparatory and general academic school, affiliated with Christian faith. Grades PS–12. Founded: 1952. Setting: suburban. Nearest major city is Seattle. 7-acre campus. 2 buildings on campus. Approved or accredited by Christian Schools International, Northwest Accreditation Commission, Northwest Association of Schools and Colleges, and Washington Department of Education. Endowment: $271,600. Total enrollment: 222. Upper school average class size: 20. Upper school faculty-student ratio: 1:7.

Upper School Student Profile Grade 9: 16 students (11 boys, 5 girls); Grade 10: 25 students (11 boys, 14 girls); Grade 11: 14 students (12 boys, 2 girls); Grade 12: 21 students (14 boys, 7 girls). 100% of students are Christian faith.

Faculty School total: 28. In upper school: 8 men, 5 women; 8 have advanced degrees.

Subjects Offered 20th century history, advanced computer applications, advanced math, Advanced Placement courses, algebra, American history, American literature, art, band, Bible, biology, British literature, calculus, chemistry, choir, Christian doctrine, college writing, composition, computer applications, consumer education, creative writing, current events, current history, drama, drawing, English, film, film appreciation, geometry, global studies, government, health, human anatomy, jazz band, keyboarding, life science, life skills, literature, media, music appreciation, physical education, physical science, physics, pre-calculus, psychology, sculpture, sociology, Spanish, speech, study skills, Washington State and Northwest History, weight training, Western civilization, world literature, world religions, yearbook.

Graduation Requirements American government, American literature, Bible, British literature, college writing, composition, electives, English, foreign language, global issues, keyboarding, life skills, mathematics, occupational education, physical education (includes health), science, social sciences, speech, U.S. history, Washington State and Northwest History, Western civilization, world literature.

Special Academic Programs Independent study; study at local college for college credit; remedial reading and/or remedial writing.

College Admission Counseling 21 students graduated in 2011; 20 went to college, including Azusa Pacific University; Calvin College; Dordt College; Seattle Pacific University; University of Washington; Western Washington University. Other: 1 went to work. Median SAT critical reading: 520, median SAT math: 540, median SAT writing: 560, median composite ACT: 26. 80% scored over 26 on composite ACT.

Student Life Upper grades have specified standards of dress, student council. Discipline rests primarily with faculty. Attendance at religious services is required.

Tuition and Aid Day student tuition: $9650–$10,505. Tuition installment plan (monthly payment plans, individually arranged payment plans, prepaid cash tuition discount, quarterly or semi-annual payment plans). Tuition reduction for siblings, need-based scholarship grants, discount for qualifying Pastor families available. In 2011–12, 29% of upper-school students received aid. Total amount of financial aid awarded in 2011–12: $307,000.

Admissions Traditional secondary-level entrance grade is 9. For fall 2011, 14 students applied for upper-level admission, 6 were accepted, 6 enrolled. Deadline for receipt of application materials: none. Application fee required: $100. Interview required.

Athletics Interscholastic: baseball (boys), basketball (b,g), soccer (b), volleyball (g); coed interscholastic: golf, soccer, track and field. 1 PE instructor.

Computers Computers are regularly used in all academic, art, library, media, music, occupational education, research skills, yearbook classes. Computer network features include on-campus library services, Internet access. Students grades are available online.

Contact Mrs. Laurie Dykstra, Director of Development. 206-364-7777 Ext. 308. Fax: 206-364-0349. E-mail: ldykstra@shorelinechristian.org. Web site: www.shorelinechristian.org.

SIGNET CHRISTIAN SCHOOL

95 Jonesville Crescent

North York, Ontario M4A 1H2, Canada

Head of School: Mr. Martin D. Sandford

General Information Coeducational day college-preparatory and business school, affiliated with Christian faith. Grades JK–12. Founded: 1975. Setting: urban. Nearest major city is Toronto, Canada. 1-acre campus. 1 building on campus. Approved or accredited by Association of Christian Schools International and Ontario Department of Education. Language of instruction: English. Total enrollment: 78. Upper school average class size: 12. Upper school faculty-student ratio: 1:7. There are 178 required school days per year for Upper School students. Upper School students typically attend 5 days per week. The average school day consists of 6 hours and 30 minutes.

Upper School Student Profile Grade 9: 13 students (4 boys, 9 girls); Grade 10: 6 students (2 boys, 4 girls); Grade 11: 9 students (5 boys, 4 girls); Grade 12: 21 students (9 boys, 12 girls). 50% of students are Christian.

Faculty School total: 15. In upper school: 3 men, 4 women.

Subjects Offered Biology, business studies, calculus, Canadian geography, Canadian history, career education, chemistry, civics, English, ESL, French as a second language, math analysis, math applications, physics, science, visual arts.

Graduation Requirements English, Ontario Ministry of Education requirements.

Special Academic Programs Independent study; ESL (4 students enrolled).

Student Life Upper grades have uniform requirement, student council. Discipline rests primarily with faculty. Attendance at religious services is required.

Tuition and Aid Day student tuition: CAN$6120. Tuition installment plan (individually arranged payment plans). Tuition reduction for siblings available. In 2010–11, 20% of upper-school students received aid.

Admissions Traditional secondary-level entrance grade is 9. SLEP required. Deadline for receipt of application materials: none. No application fee required.

Athletics Coed Intramural: basketball, bowling, cross-country running, ice skating, skiing (downhill), snowboarding, soccer, track and field.

Computers Computers are regularly used in English, mathematics, technology classes. Computer network features include Internet access.

Contact Admissions. 416-750-7515. Fax: 416-750-7720. E-mail: scs@titan.tcn.net. Web site: www.signetschool.ca.

SMITH SCHOOL

New York, New York

See Special Needs Schools section.

SOLOMON COLLEGE

#228, 10621 100th Avenue

Edmonton, Alberta T5J 0B3, Canada

Head of School: Ms. Ping Ping Lee

General Information Coeducational day and distance learning college-preparatory, general academic, vocational, bilingual studies, and ESL school. Grades 10–12. Distance learning grades 10–12. Founded: 1994. Setting: urban. 1 building on campus. Approved or accredited by Association of Independent Schools and Colleges of Alberta and Alberta Department of Education. Language of instruction: English. Total enrollment: 25. Upper school average class size: 10. Upper school faculty-student ratio: 1:10. There are 225 required school days per year for Upper School students. Upper School students typically attend 5 days per week. The average school day consists of 4 hours and 30 minutes.

Upper School Student Profile Grade 10: 3 students (3 boys); Grade 11: 1 student (1 boy); Grade 12: 21 students (16 boys, 5 girls).

Faculty School total: 5. In upper school: 2 men, 3 women; 2 have advanced degrees.

Subjects Offered Biology, calculus, career and personal planning, chemistry, Chinese, computer information systems, computer skills, computer technologies, English literature, ESL, keyboarding, mathematics, physics, social studies.

Special Academic Programs ESL (80 students enrolled).

College Admission Counseling 20 students graduated in 2011; 10 went to college, including University of Alberta; University of Calgary; University of Lethbridge.

Student Life Discipline rests equally with students and faculty.

Tuition and Aid Day student tuition: CAN$5800.

Admissions Traditional secondary-level entrance grade is 10. For fall 2011, 25 students applied for upper-level admission, 25 were accepted, 25 enrolled. Placement test required. Deadline for receipt of application materials: August 1. Application fee required: CAN$200.

Computers Computer network features include Internet access, wireless campus network, Internet filtering or blocking technology. Campus intranet is available to students.

Contact Mr. Sunny Ip, Registrar. 780-431-1516. Fax: 780-431-1644. E-mail: sunnyi@solomoncollege.ca.

SONOMA ACADEMY

2500 Farmers Lane

Santa Rosa, California 95404

Head of School: Janet Durgin

General Information Coeducational day college-preparatory and Environmental Leadership & Global Citizenship concentrations school. Grades 9–12. Founded: 1999. 34-acre campus. 3 buildings on campus. Approved or accredited by Western Association of Schools and Colleges and California Department of Education. Member of National Association of Independent Schools. Total enrollment: 236. Upper school average class size: 15. Upper school faculty-student ratio: 1:12. Upper School students typically attend 5 days per week. The average school day consists of 7 hours.

Upper School Student Profile Grade 9: 65 students (34 boys, 31 girls); Grade 10: 57 students (28 boys, 29 girls); Grade 11: 45 students (23 boys, 22 girls); Grade 12: 59 students (32 boys, 27 girls).

Faculty School total: 24. In upper school: 10 men, 14 women; 17 have advanced degrees.

Special Academic Programs 7 Advanced Placement exams for which test preparation is offered; honors section; independent study; study abroad.

College Admission Counseling 63 students graduated in 2011; 60 went to college. Other: 3 had other specific plans.

Student Life Upper grades have student council. Discipline rests equally with students and faculty.

Tuition and Aid Day student tuition: $33,800. Tuition installment plan (Insured Tuition Payment Plan, monthly payment plans). Need-based scholarship grants available. In 2011–12, 50% of upper-school students received aid. Total amount of financial aid awarded in 2011–12: $2,000,000.

Admissions Traditional secondary-level entrance grade is 9. SSAT required. Deadline for receipt of application materials: January 12. Application fee required: $85. Interview required.

Athletics Interscholastic: baseball (boys), basketball (b,g), cross-country running (b,g), lacrosse (b,g), soccer (b,g), track and field (b,g), volleyball (g); coed intramural: aerobics/dance, combined training, dance, fencing, fitness, flag football, kickball, martial arts, outdoor education, physical fitness, physical training, power lifting, softball, strength & conditioning, tai chi, ultimate Frisbee, weight training, whiffle ball, yoga. 9 coaches.

Computers Computers are regularly used in all classes. Computer network features include on-campus library services, online commercial services, Internet access, wireless campus network, Internet filtering or blocking technology, digital technology center. Campus intranet and student e-mail accounts are available to students. The school has a published electronic and media policy.

Contact Sandy Stack, Director of Enrollment and Marketing. 707-545-1770. Fax: 707-636-2474. E-mail: sandy.stack@sonomaacademy.org. Web site: www.sonomaacademy.org/.

SOUNDVIEW PREPARATORY SCHOOL

370 Underhill Avenue

Yorktown Heights, New York 10598

Head of School: W. Glyn Hearn

General Information Coeducational day college-preparatory, arts, and technology school. Grades 6–PG. Founded: 1989. Setting: suburban. Nearest major city is New York. 13-acre campus. 7 buildings on campus. Approved or accredited by New York State Association of Independent Schools and New York Department of Education. Total enrollment: 75. Upper school average class size: 7. Upper school faculty-student ratio: 1:5. Upper School students typically attend 5 days per week. The average school day consists of 6 hours and 13 minutes.

Upper School Student Profile Grade 9: 12 students (4 boys, 8 girls); Grade 10: 14 students (7 boys, 7 girls); Grade 11: 15 students (10 boys, 5 girls); Grade 12: 23 students (18 boys, 5 girls).

Faculty School total: 16. In upper school: 1 man, 12 women; 12 have advanced degrees.

Subjects Offered Advanced Placement courses, algebra, American history, American literature, anatomy and physiology, art, biology, calculus, chemistry, computer literacy, creative writing, drama, earth science, English, English literature, European history-AP, French, geometry, grammar, health, Italian, Latin, mathematics, philosophy, physical education, physics, psychology, science, sculpture, social studies, Spanish, U.S. government, U.S. history-AP, world history.

Graduation Requirements Art, electives, English, foreign language, health, history, mathematics, physical education (includes health), science.

Special Academic Programs Advanced Placement exam preparation; honors section; accelerated programs; independent study; academic accommodation for the gifted and the artistically talented; special instructional classes for students needing wheelchair accessibility.

College Admission Counseling 6 students graduated in 2010; all went to college, including Barnard College; Dickinson College; Drew University; Muhlenberg College; Pace University; Rhode Island School of Design. Median SAT critical reading: 595, median SAT math: 560, median SAT writing: 523, median composite ACT: 24.

Student Life Discipline rests primarily with faculty.

Tuition and Aid Day student tuition: $31,100–$32,200. Need-based scholarship grants available. In 2010–11, 28% of upper-school students received aid. Total amount of financial aid awarded in 2010–11: $470,000.

Admissions Traditional secondary-level entrance grade is 9. For fall 2010, 52 students applied for upper-level admission, 26 were accepted, 24 enrolled. ERB (CTP-Verbal, Quantitative) or ERB Mathematics required. Deadline for receipt of application materials: none. Application fee required: $50. On-campus interview required.

Athletics Interscholastic: basketball (girls); coed interscholastic: basketball, soccer, tennis, ultimate Frisbee; coed intramural: cheering, sailing, skiing (downhill), volleyball. 1 PE instructor, 1 coach.

Computers Computers are regularly used in all academic classes. Computer network features include Internet access, wireless campus network, Internet filtering or blocking technology. Campus intranet and student e-mail accounts are available to students. The school has a published electronic and media policy.

Contact Mary E. Ivanyi, Assistant Head. 914-962-2780. Fax: 914-302-2769. E-mail: mivanyi@soundviewprep.org. Web site: www.soundviewprep.org.

See Display below and Close-Up on page 678.

SOUTHERN ONTARIO COLLEGE

430 York Boulevard

Hamilton, Ontario L8R 3K8, Canada

Head of School: Susan J. Woods

General Information Coeducational day college-preparatory school. Grades 9–12. Founded: 1980. Setting: urban. 1 building on campus. Approved or accredited by Ontario Ministry of Education and Ontario Department of Education. Language of instruction: English. Upper school average class size: 20. Upper school faculty-student ratio: 1:15. Upper School students typically attend 5 days per week.

Faculty School total: 7. In upper school: 5 men, 2 women; 3 have advanced degrees.

Special Academic Programs ESL (15 students enrolled).

College Admission Counseling 50 students graduated in 2010; 5 went to college, including Penn State University Park. Other: 45 entered a postgraduate year.

Student Life Upper grades have uniform requirement, honor system. Discipline rests primarily with faculty.

Tuition and Aid Guaranteed tuition plan.

Admissions Application fee required: CAN$150.

Computers Computers are regularly used in accounting, career education, computer applications classes. Computer resources include Internet access, wireless campus network, Internet filtering or blocking technology.

Contact Mr. Robert Glaister, Admissions Officer. 905-546-1501. Fax: 905-546-5415. E-mail: admin@mysoc.ca. Web site: www.mysoc.ca.

SOUTHFIELD CHRISTIAN HIGH SCHOOL

28650 Lahser Road

Southfield, Michigan 48034-2099

Head of School: Mrs. Margie Baldwin

General Information Coeducational day college-preparatory, arts, religious studies, and technology school, affiliated with Christian faith, Evangelical faith. Grades K–12. Founded: 1970. Setting: suburban. Nearest major city is Detroit. 28-acre campus. 1 building on campus. Approved or accredited by Association of Christian Schools International, Independent Schools Association of the Central States, North Central Association of Colleges and Schools, and Michigan Department of Education. Endowment: $1.5 million. Total enrollment: 547. Upper school average class size: 22. Upper school faculty-student ratio: 1:20. There are 175 required school days per year for Upper School students. Upper School students typically attend 5 days per week. The average school day consists of 6 hours and 30 minutes.

Upper School Student Profile Grade 9: 43 students (23 boys, 20 girls); Grade 10: 52 students (23 boys, 29 girls); Grade 11: 44 students (17 boys, 27 girls); Grade 12: 43 students (20 boys, 23 girls). 100% of students are Christian faith, members of Evangelical faith.

Faculty School total: 20. In upper school: 10 men, 10 women; 18 have advanced degrees.

Subjects Offered Accounting, Advanced Placement courses, algebra, American government, American history, American history-AP, American literature, American literature-AP, ancient world history, art, band, Bible, biology, biology-AP, British literature, calculus-AP, chemistry, chemistry-AP, choir, chorus, communication arts, composition-AP, computer applications, computer programming, conceptual physics, creative writing, drawing and design, economics, English language-AP, English literature and composition-AP, film and literature, French, geography, geometry, government, graphic design, health, instrumental music, Life of Christ, literature and composition-AP, Middle Eastern history, New Testament, organic chemistry, photography, physical education, physics-AP, pre-calculus, probability and statistics, Russian history, senior project, Spanish, speech and debate, U.S. history, vocal music, Web site design, world studies, yearbook.

Special Academic Programs Advanced Placement exam preparation; honors section; independent study.

College Admission Counseling 53 students graduated in 2011; all went to college, including Grand Valley State University; Hope College; Michigan State University; Oakland University; University of Michigan; Wheaton College. Median SAT critical reading: 460, median SAT math: 430, median SAT writing: 480, median composite ACT: 23. 21% scored over 26 on composite ACT.

Student Life Upper grades have uniform requirement, student council. Discipline rests primarily with faculty. Attendance at religious services is required.

Summer Programs Rigorous outdoor training programs offered; session focuses on physical education; held on campus; accepts boys and girls; not open to students from other schools. 10 students usually enrolled. 2012 schedule: June 11 to July 1. Application deadline: May 1.

Tuition and Aid Day student tuition: $8420. Tuition installment plan (FACTS Tuition Payment Plan). Tuition reduction for siblings, need-based scholarship grants available. In 2011–12, 10% of upper-school students received aid.

Admissions Traditional secondary-level entrance grade is 9. For fall 2011, 70 students applied for upper-level admission, 50 were accepted, 39 enrolled. Any standardized test required. Deadline for receipt of application materials: none. No application fee required. On-campus interview required.

Athletics Interscholastic: baseball (boys), cheering (g), football (b), softball (g), volleyball (g); coed interscholastic: basketball, cross-country running, golf, soccer, track and field; coed intramural: archery, backpacking, badminton, bicycling, flag football, floor hockey, Frisbee, skiing (cross-country), weight lifting. 1 PE instructor, 1 athletic trainer.

Computers Computers are regularly used in art, commercial art, computer applications, creative writing, drawing and design, graphic arts, graphic design, independent study, media production, programming, publishing, Web site design, writing, yearbook classes. Computer network features include on-campus library services, Internet access, wireless campus network, Internet filtering or blocking technology. Student e-mail accounts are available to students. Students grades are available online. The school has a published electronic and media policy.

Contact Mrs. Sue Hoffenbacher, High School Principal. 248-357-3660 Ext. 278. Fax: 248-357-5271. E-mail: shoffenbacher@southfieldchristian.org. Web site: www.southfieldchristian.org.

SOUTH KENT SCHOOL

40 Bulls Bridge Road

South Kent, Connecticut 06785

Head of School: Mr. Andrew J. Vadnais

General Information Boys' boarding and day college-preparatory, arts, and technology school, affiliated with Episcopal Church. Grades 9–PG. Founded: 1923. Setting: rural. Nearest major city is New York, NY. Students are housed in single-sex dormitories. 320-acre campus. 30 buildings on campus. Approved or accredited by National Association of Episcopal Schools, New England Association of Schools and Colleges, The Association of Boarding Schools, and Connecticut Department of Education. Member of National Association of Independent Schools and Secondary School Admission Test Board. Endowment: $4 million. Total enrollment: 163. Upper school average class size: 7. Upper school faculty-student ratio: 1:5. Upper School students typically attend 6 days per week. The average school day consists of 6 hours.

Upper School Student Profile Grade 9: 13 students (13 boys); Grade 10: 33 students (33 boys); Grade 11: 40 students (40 boys); Grade 12: 54 students (54 boys); Postgraduate: 23 students (23 boys). 83% of students are boarding students. 28% are state residents. 17 states are represented in upper school student body. 38% are international students. International students from Brazil, Canada, China, Japan, Republic of Korea, and Taiwan; 10 other countries represented in student body. 35% of students are members of Episcopal Church.

Faculty School total: 34. In upper school: 23 men, 11 women; 11 have advanced degrees; 25 reside on campus.

Subjects Offered Advanced biology, Advanced Placement courses, advanced studio art-AP, algebra, American history, American literature, art, biology, calculus, calculus-AP, chemistry, creative writing, digital applications, driver education, ecology, economics-AP, English, English language and composition-AP, English literature, entrepreneurship, environmental science, environmental studies, ESL, European history, expository writing, finance, fine arts, French, French-AP, functions, geography, geometry, government and politics-AP, grammar, history, Latin, marketing, mathematics, Native American history, photography, physics, physiology, pre-calculus, psychology, psychology-AP, robotics, science, Spanish, Spanish-AP, statistics, statistics-AP, trigonometry, U.S. history-AP, world history, writing.

Graduation Requirements Art, English, foreign language, lab science, mathematics, U.S. history.

Special Academic Programs Advanced Placement exam preparation; honors section; independent study; ESL (35 students enrolled).

College Admission Counseling 56 students graduated in 2010; 54 went to college, including Charleston Southern University; Clemson University; Hobart and William Smith Colleges; Lafayette College; Northeastern University; Purdue University. Other: 2 entered a postgraduate year. Median SAT critical reading: 520, median SAT math: 500. 18% scored over 600 on SAT critical reading, 24% scored over 600 on SAT math.

Student Life Upper grades have specified standards of dress, student council, honor system. Discipline rests primarily with faculty. Attendance at religious services is required.

Tuition and Aid Day student tuition: $26,000; 7-day tuition and room/board: $43,000. Tuition installment plan (The Tuition Plan, Insured Tuition Payment Plan, monthly payment plans). Merit scholarship grants, need-based scholarship grants available. In 2010–11, 40% of upper-school students received aid. Total amount of financial aid awarded in 2010–11: $1,900,000.

Admissions Traditional secondary-level entrance grade is 9. For fall 2010, 190 students applied for upper-level admission, 139 were accepted, 90 enrolled. SSAT and writing sample required. Deadline for receipt of application materials: none. Application fee required: $50. Interview required.

Athletics Interscholastic: baseball, basketball, crew, cross-country running, golf, ice hockey, lacrosse, ropes courses, soccer, tennis; intramural: alpine skiing, baseball, basketball, bicycling, canoeing/kayaking, climbing, crew, golf, hiking/backpacking, ice hockey, outdoor activities, skiing (cross-country), skiing (downhill), snowboarding, soccer, strength & conditioning, ultimate Frisbee, wall climbing, weight lifting, weight training. 28 coaches, 2 athletic trainers.

Computers Computers are regularly used in art classes. Computer network features include on-campus library services, online commercial services, Internet access, wireless campus network, Internet filtering or blocking technology. Student e-mail accounts are available to students. The school has a published electronic and media policy.

Contact Mr. Richard A. Brande, Director of Enrollment and Financial Aid. 860-927-3539 Ext. 202. Fax: 888-803-0140. E-mail: brander@southkentschool.org. Web site: www.southkentschool.org.

SOUTHLAND ACADEMY, INC.

PO Box 1127

Americus, Georgia 31709

Head of School: Mr. William E. Stubbs

General Information Coeducational day college-preparatory school. Grades PK–12. Setting: small town. 4 buildings on campus. Approved or accredited by Southern Association of Colleges and Schools and Georgia Department of Education. Member of National Association of Independent Schools. Total enrollment: 565. Upper school average class size: 18. There are 180 required school days per year for Upper School students. Upper School students typically attend 5 days per week. The average school day consists of 5 hours.

Upper School Student Profile Grade 9: 50 students (29 boys, 21 girls); Grade 10: 47 students (24 boys, 23 girls); Grade 11: 38 students (18 boys, 20 girls); Grade 12: 44 students (26 boys, 18 girls).

College Admission Counseling 40 students graduated in 2011; all went to college.

Student Life Upper grades have specified standards of dress, student council, honor system.

Admissions No application fee required. Interview required.

Athletics Interscholastic: baseball (boys), basketball (b,g), cheering (g), cross-country running (b,g), dance squad (g), football (b), golf (b), soccer (g), softball (g), swimming and diving (b,g), tennis (b,g), track and field (b,g), wrestling (b). 4 PE instructors, 8 coaches.

Contact 912-924-4406. Fax: 912-924-2996.

SOUTHWEST CHRISTIAN SCHOOL, INC.

7001 Benbrook Lake Drive

Fort Worth, Texas 76132

Head of School: Dr. Penny Armstrong

General Information Coeducational day college-preparatory, arts, religious studies, and technology school, affiliated with Christian faith. Grades PK–12. Founded: 1969. Setting: suburban. 24-acre campus. 3 buildings on campus. Approved or accredited by Association of Christian Schools International, Southern Association of Colleges and Schools, Texas Education Agency, and Texas Department of Education. Total enrollment: 929. Upper school average class size: 16. Upper school faculty-student ratio: 1:11. There are 176 required school days per year for Upper School students. Upper School students typically attend 5 days per week. The average school day consists of 7 hours.

Upper School Student Profile Grade 7: 59 students (24 boys, 35 girls); Grade 8: 76 students (35 boys, 41 girls); Grade 9: 83 students (42 boys, 41 girls); Grade 10: 71 students (34 boys, 37 girls); Grade 11: 80 students (29 boys, 51 girls); Grade 12: 80 students (39 boys, 41 girls).

Faculty School total: 45. In upper school: 12 men, 33 women; 20 have advanced degrees.

Subjects Offered 1 1/2 elective credits, advanced math, algebra, American government, American literature, American literature-AP, anatomy and physiology, art, Bible studies, biology, biology-AP, British literature, British literature-AP, calculus, calculus-AP, chemistry, chemistry-AP, choir, drama, English, English literature-AP, English-AP, foreign language, French, geometry, government, history, honors algebra, honors English, honors geometry, honors U.S. history, honors world history, journalism, keyboarding, lab science, leadership, literature and composition-AP, physics, physics-AP, pre-algebra, pre-calculus, psychology, SAT preparation, Spanish, speech, technology, U.S. history, U.S. history-AP, Web site design.
Graduation Requirements 4 years of Bible courses.
Special Academic Programs Advanced Placement exam preparation; honors section; accelerated programs; study at local college for college credit; study abroad; academic accommodation for the gifted.
College Admission Counseling 81 students graduated in 2010; 79 went to college, including Abilene Christian University; Baylor University; Texas A&M University; Texas Christian University; University of North Texas. Other: 1 went to work, 1 entered military service. Median SAT critical reading: 533, median SAT math: 530, median SAT writing: 530, median combined SAT: 1595, median composite ACT: 24. 31% scored over 600 on SAT critical reading, 20% scored over 600 on SAT math, 18% scored over 600 on SAT writing, 15% scored over 1800 on combined SAT, 31% scored over 26 on composite ACT.
Student Life Upper grades have uniform requirement, student council, honor system. Discipline rests primarily with faculty. Attendance at religious services is required.
Tuition and Aid Day student tuition: $11,050–$11,500. Tuition installment plan (FACTS Tuition Payment Plan). Need-based scholarship grants available. In 2010–11, 20% of upper-school students received aid. Total amount of financial aid awarded in 2010–11: $455,000.
Admissions Traditional secondary-level entrance grade is 9. For fall 2010, 106 students applied for upper-level admission, 99 were accepted, 62 enrolled. Stanford 9 required. Deadline for receipt of application materials: March 30. No application fee required. Interview required.
Athletics Interscholastic: aerobics/dance (girls), baseball (b), basketball (b,g), cheering (g), cross-country running (b,g), dance team (g), equestrian sports (b,g), football (b), golf (b,g), soccer (b,g), softball (g), track and field (b,g), volleyball (g), wrestling (b); intramural: physical training (b,g); coed interscholastic: aquatics, equestrian sports, paint ball, rodeo; coed intramural: aquatics, fitness, strength & conditioning, weight training. 2 PE instructors, 12 coaches, 1 athletic trainer.
Computers Computers are regularly used in all academic classes. Computer network features include on-campus library services, online commercial services, Internet access, wireless campus network, Internet filtering or blocking technology, computer carts for classroom use. Student e-mail accounts and computer access in designated common areas are available to students. Students grades are available online. The school has a published electronic and media policy.
Contact Mrs. Libby Madison, Prep Campus Admissions Associate. 817-294-9596 Ext. 252. Fax: 817-292-3644. E-mail: lmadison@southwestchristian.org. Web site: www.southwestchristian.org.

SOUTHWESTERN ACADEMY

Beaver Creek Ranch Campus

Rimrock, Arizona 86335

Head of School: Mr. Kenneth Veronda

General Information Coeducational boarding and day college-preparatory and general academic school. Grades 9–PG. Founded: 1963. Setting: rural. Nearest major city is Sedona. Students are housed in single-sex dormitories. 180-acre campus. 24 buildings on campus. Approved or accredited by Arizona Association of Independent Schools, The Association of Boarding Schools, and Arizona Department of Education. Endowment: $9.2 million. Total enrollment: 32. Upper school average class size: 6. Upper school faculty-student ratio: 1:3. Upper School students typically attend 5 days per week. The average school day consists of 8 hours.
Upper School Student Profile Grade 9: 7 students (3 boys, 4 girls); Grade 10: 5 students (3 boys, 2 girls); Grade 11: 12 students (5 boys, 7 girls); Grade 12: 5 students (3 boys, 2 girls); Postgraduate: 3 students (2 boys, 1 girl). 100% of students are boarding students. 3% are state residents. 5 states are represented in upper school student body. 53% are international students. International students from China, Japan, Republic of Korea, Serbia and Montenegro, Taiwan, and Thailand; 3 other countries represented in student body.
Faculty School total: 12. In upper school: 5 men, 7 women; 4 have advanced degrees; 7 reside on campus.
Subjects Offered Advanced math, Advanced Placement courses, algebra, American history, American literature, American literature-AP, art, art appreciation, art history, astronomy, biology, biology-AP, British literature, calculus, chemistry, earth science, ecology, economics, English, English composition, environmental education, environmental science, environmental studies, ESL, fashion, fine arts, general math, geometry, health, integrated science, Latin, math review, mathematics, music, music appreciation, outdoor education, physics, pre-algebra, Spanish, studio art, U.S. government, world cultures, yearbook.
Graduation Requirements Algebra, American government, American history, American literature, British literature, computer literacy, economics, electives, English, foreign language, geometry, lab science, mathematics, physical education (includes health), visual and performing arts, world cultures. Community service is required.
Special Academic Programs Advanced Placement exam preparation; honors section; accelerated programs; independent study; term-away projects; study at local college for college credit; ESL (6 students enrolled).
College Admission Counseling 8 students graduated in 2010; all went to college, including Arizona State University; California State University, Long Beach; Pacific Lutheran University; Trent University. Median SAT critical reading: 450, median SAT math: 600, median SAT writing: 550.
Student Life Upper grades have specified standards of dress, student council, honor system. Discipline rests primarily with faculty.
Tuition and Aid Day student tuition: $14,900; 7-day tuition and room/board: $30,700. Tuition installment plan (monthly payment plans, individually arranged payment plans). Need-based scholarship grants available. In 2010–11, 43% of upper-school students received aid. Total amount of financial aid awarded in 2010–11: $392,300.
Admissions Traditional secondary-level entrance grade is 9. For fall 2010, 33 students applied for upper-level admission, 24 were accepted, 11 enrolled. Deadline for receipt of application materials: none. Application fee required: $100. Interview recommended.
Athletics Interscholastic: basketball (boys, girls), volleyball (g); coed interscholastic: golf, soccer; coed intramural: alpine skiing, archery, backpacking, ballet, baseball, basketball, bicycling, billiards, climbing, cross-country running, equestrian sports, fishing, fitness, golf, hiking/backpacking, horseback riding, horseshoes, ice skating, mountain biking, outdoor activities, outdoor adventure, outdoor education, outdoor recreation, outdoor skills, paint ball, rock climbing, ropes courses, skiing (cross-country), skiing (downhill), snowboarding, soccer, softball, swimming and diving, table tennis, tennis, track and field, volleyball. 1 PE instructor, 2 coaches.
Computers Computers are regularly used in all classes. Computer network features include on-campus library services, Internet access, wireless campus network, Internet filtering or blocking technology. Student e-mail accounts and computer access in designated common areas are available to students.
Contact Office of Admissions. 626-799-5010 Ext. 5. Fax: 626-799-0407. E-mail: bthomas@southwesternacademy.edu. Web site: www.southwesternacademy.edu.

See Display on next page and Close-Up on page 680.

SOUTHWESTERN ACADEMY

2800 Monterey Road

San Marino, California 91108

Head of School: Kenneth R. Veronda

General Information Coeducational boarding and day college-preparatory, general academic, arts, and ESL school. Grades 6–PG. Founded: 1924. Setting: suburban. Nearest major city is Pasadena. Students are housed in single-sex dormitories. 8-acre campus. 9 buildings on campus. Approved or accredited by The Association of Boarding Schools, Western Association of Schools and Colleges, and California Department of Education. Member of Secondary School Admission Test Board. Endowment: $15 million. Total enrollment: 139. Upper school average class size: 12. Upper school faculty-student ratio: 1:6. Upper School students typically attend 5 days per week. The average school day consists of 8 hours.
Upper School Student Profile Grade 9: 19 students (13 boys, 6 girls); Grade 10: 29 students (18 boys, 11 girls); Grade 11: 44 students (29 boys, 15 girls); Grade 12: 48 students (32 boys, 16 girls); Postgraduate: 1 student (1 girl). 72% of students are boarding students. 29% are state residents. 7 states are represented in upper school student body. 55% are international students. International students from China, Hong Kong, Japan, Republic of Korea, Taiwan, and Viet Nam; 10 other countries represented in student body.
Faculty School total: 29. In upper school: 12 men, 11 women; 12 have advanced degrees; 10 reside on campus.
Subjects Offered Algebra, American history, American literature, animation, art, art history, audio visual/media, biology, calculus, calculus-AP, chemistry, college counseling, creative writing, drama, earth science, economics, English, English literature, ESL, European history, expository writing, fashion, fine arts, geography, geology, geometry, government/civics, grammar, health, history, journalism, mathematics, music, photography, physical education, physics, psychology, science, social sciences, social studies, Spanish, speech, world cultures, world history, world literature, writing.
Graduation Requirements Algebra, American government, American history, American literature, British literature, computer literacy, economics, electives, English, foreign language, geometry, lab science, mathematics, physical education (includes health), visual and performing arts, world cultures, 100 hours of community service. Community service is required.
Special Academic Programs Advanced Placement exam preparation; honors section; accelerated programs; independent study; study at local college for college credit; ESL (27 students enrolled).
College Admission Counseling 30 students graduated in 2010; all went to college, including Occidental College; Pepperdine University; University of California, Irvine;

University of California, Los Angeles; University of California, San Diego; University of La Verne.

Student Life Upper grades have specified standards of dress, student council, honor system. Discipline rests primarily with faculty.

Tuition and Aid Day student tuition: $14,900; 7-day tuition and room/board: $30,700. Tuition installment plan (monthly payment plans, individually arranged payment plans). Need-based scholarship grants available. In 2010–11, 20% of upper-school students received aid. Total amount of financial aid awarded in 2010–11: $750,000.

Admissions Traditional secondary-level entrance grade is 9. For fall 2010, 189 students applied for upper-level admission, 94 were accepted, 68 enrolled. Deadline for receipt of application materials: none. Application fee required: $100. Interview recommended.

Athletics Interscholastic: baseball (boys), basketball (b,g), track and field (b,g), volleyball (b,g); intramural: baseball (b), basketball (b,g), track and field (b,g), volleyball (b,g); coed interscholastic: baseball, bowling, climbing, cross-country running, fishing, horseback riding, soccer, tennis; coed intramural: archery, backpacking, baseball, bicycling, bowling, climbing, cross-country running, fishing, golf, hiking/backpacking, horseback riding, outdoor activities, physical fitness, skiing (downhill), snowboarding, soccer, table tennis, tennis, weight training. 2 PE instructors, 4 coaches, 1 athletic trainer.

Computers Computers are regularly used in art, English, ESL, foreign language, history, mathematics, music, science, yearbook classes. Computer network features include on-campus library services, online commercial services, Internet access, wireless campus network, Internet filtering or blocking technology. Student e-mail accounts and computer access in designated common areas are available to students. The school has a published electronic and media policy.

Contact Ms. Maia Moore, Assistant Director. 626-799-5010 Ext. 1204. Fax: 626-799-0407. E-mail: admissions@southwesternacademy.edu. Web site: www.SouthwesternAcademy.edu.

See Display on next page and Close-Up on page 682.

SPARTANBURG DAY SCHOOL

1701 Skylyn Drive

Spartanburg, South Carolina 29307

Head of School: Mr. Christopher A. Dorrance

General Information Coeducational day college-preparatory and arts school. Grades PK–12. Founded: 1957. Setting: suburban. Nearest major city is Greenville. 52-acre campus. 10 buildings on campus. Approved or accredited by Southern Association of Colleges and Schools and Southern Association of Independent Schools. Member of National Association of Independent Schools. Endowment: $4.1 million. Total enrollment: 449. Upper school average class size: 12. Upper school faculty-student ratio: 1:9. There are 175 required school days per year for Upper School students. Upper School students typically attend 5 days per week. The average school day consists of 8 hours.

Upper School Student Profile Grade 9: 38 students (17 boys, 21 girls); Grade 10: 35 students (16 boys, 19 girls); Grade 11: 34 students (19 boys, 15 girls); Grade 12: 27 students (11 boys, 16 girls).

Faculty School total: 56. In upper school: 9 men, 10 women; 15 have advanced degrees.

Subjects Offered Advanced chemistry, advanced math, Advanced Placement courses, algebra, American government, American history, American history-AP, American literature, applied music, art, art history-AP, arts appreciation, band, biology, biology-AP, calculus, calculus-AP, career/college preparation, character education, chemistry, chemistry-AP, chorus, college counseling, college placement, college writing, community service, computer education, concert band, creative drama, creative writing, critical thinking, critical writing, cultural arts, debate, drama performance, drawing, drawing and design, earth science, English, English composition, English literature, English literature-AP, European history, fine arts, French, French language-AP, geometry, government/civics, history, jazz band, keyboarding, Latin, Latin-AP, mathematics, modern European history-AP, music, music theory, philosophy, physics, physics-AP, science, Spanish, Spanish language-AP, speech, statistics, statistics-AP, studio art-AP, trigonometry, U.S. government and politics-AP, world history.

Graduation Requirements Algebra, arts and fine arts (art, music, dance, drama), biology, chemistry, English, foreign language, geometry, ancient or European history, one additional lab science, participation in one sport per year.

Special Academic Programs Advanced Placement exam preparation; honors section; study at local college for college credit; academic accommodation for the gifted and the artistically talented; programs in English, mathematics, general development for dyslexic students.

College Admission Counseling 44 went to college, including Clemson University; College of Charleston; Furman University; University of Georgia. Mean SAT critical reading: 585, mean SAT math: 604, mean SAT writing: 607. 59% scored over 600 on SAT critical reading, 46% scored over 600 on SAT math.

Student Life Upper grades have specified standards of dress, student council, honor system. Discipline rests primarily with faculty.

Summer Programs Enrichment, sports, art/fine arts, computer instruction programs offered; session focuses on enrichment; held on campus; accepts boys and girls; open to students from other schools. 10 students usually enrolled. 2012 schedule: June 4 to August 4. Application deadline: May 1.

Tuition and Aid Day student tuition: $14,000. Tuition installment plan (monthly payment plans, tuition insurance). Merit scholarship grants, need-based scholarship grants, tuition reduction for children of faculty and staff, tuition reduction for children of benefit-receiving employees of Wofford College, Converse College, UCSUpstate available. In 2011–12, 26% of upper-school students received aid; total upper-school merit-scholarship money awarded: $45,810. Total amount of financial aid awarded in 2011–12: $182,000.

Admissions Traditional secondary-level entrance grade is 9. For fall 2011, 35 students applied for upper-level admission, 26 were accepted, 9 enrolled. ERB, Kaufman Test of Educational Achievement, Metropolitan Test, ITBS, Otis Lennon School Ability Test, Stanford Achievement Test or writing sample required. Deadline for receipt of application materials: none. Application fee required: $50. On-campus interview recommended.

Athletics Interscholastic: aquatics (boys, girls), baseball (b), basketball (b,g), cheering (g), lacrosse (b), soccer (b,g), swimming and diving (b,g), tennis (b,g), volleyball (g); coed interscholastic: cooperative games, cross-country running, golf, martial arts, physical fitness, track and field, weight training. 4 PE instructors, 8 coaches, 1 athletic trainer.

Computers Computers are regularly used in art, English, history, mathematics classes. Computer network features include on-campus library services, Internet access, wireless campus network, Internet filtering or blocking technology, multimedia presentation stations. Student e-mail accounts are available to students. The school has a published electronic and media policy.

Contact Mrs. Susan J. Jeffords, Director of Admissions. 864-582-7539 Ext. 2906. Fax: 864-948-0026. E-mail: susan.jeffords@sdsgriffin.org. Web site: www.spartanburgdayschool.org.

THE SPENCE SCHOOL

22 East 91st Street

New York, New York 10128-0657

Head of School: Ellanor N. (Bodie) Brizendine

General Information Girls' day college-preparatory and arts school. Grades K–12. Founded: 1892. Setting: urban. 1 building on campus. Approved or accredited by New York State Association of Independent Schools. Member of National Association of Independent Schools and Secondary School Admission Test Board. Endowment: $82.1 million. Total enrollment: 704. Upper school average class size: 14. Upper school faculty-student ratio: 1:3. There are 160 required school days per year for Upper School students. Upper School students typically attend 5 days per week. The average school day consists of 6 hours.

Upper School Student Profile Grade 9: 58 students (58 girls); Grade 10: 58 students (58 girls); Grade 11: 59 students (59 girls); Grade 12: 48 students (48 girls).

Faculty School total: 124. In upper school: 24 men, 62 women; 72 have advanced degrees.

Subjects Offered Acting, advanced math, African literature, African-American literature, algebra, American literature, art, art history, art-AP, Asian literature, astronomy, biology, calculus, ceramics, chemistry, Chinese history, computer science, critical writing, design, drama, dramatic arts, earth science, English, European history, exercise science, fiber arts, French, geometry, health, history, Indian studies, Japanese history, Latin, Latin American history, Latin American literature, Latin American studies, Mandarin, mathematics, Middle East, music, music composition, non-Western literature, novels, painting, performing arts, photo shop, photography, physical education, physics, poetry, pre-algebra, robotics, science, sculpture, Shakespeare, Spanish, Spanish literature, speech, statistics, technology, theater production, U.S. history, visual and performing arts, women's studies, world religions, world religions, world studies.

Graduation Requirements Advanced math, algebra, American literature, art, biology, chemistry, computer science, dance, drama, English, European history, foreign language, geometry, history, music, non-Western societies, physical education (includes health), physics, pre-algebra, science, Shakespeare, speech, technology, U.S. history, visual and performing arts, world religions, world studies.

Special Academic Programs 1 Advanced Placement exam for which test preparation is offered; independent study; term-away projects; study abroad.

College Admission Counseling 54 students graduated in 2011; 53 went to college, including Brown University; Cornell University; Dartmouth College; Harvard University; University of Pennsylvania; Yale University. Median SAT critical reading: 710, median SAT math: 720, median SAT writing: 750, median combined SAT: 2180, median composite ACT: 30. 98% scored over 600 on SAT critical reading, 98% scored over 600 on SAT math, 96% scored over 600 on SAT writing, 98% scored over 1800 on combined SAT, 87% scored over 26 on composite ACT.

Student Life Upper grades have uniform requirement, student council. Discipline rests primarily with faculty.

Tuition and Aid Day student tuition: $37,500. Tuition installment plan (Academic Management Services Plan). Need-based scholarship grants, prepGATE loans, Academic Management Services Private Loans available. In 2011–12, 30% of upper-school students received aid. Total amount of financial aid awarded in 2011–12: $2,055,580.

Admissions Traditional secondary-level entrance grade is 9. For fall 2011, 131 students applied for upper-level admission, 52 were accepted, 16 enrolled. ISEE, school's own test and SSAT required. Deadline for receipt of application materials: December 1. Application fee required: $65. On-campus interview required.

Athletics Interscholastic: badminton, basketball, cross-country running, field hockey, lacrosse, soccer, softball, squash, swimming and diving, tennis, track and field, volleyball; intramural: fencing. 8 PE instructors, 29 coaches, 2 athletic trainers.

Computers Computers are regularly used in art, computer applications, creative writing, design, economics, foreign language, history, independent study, journalism, mathematics, science, technology classes. Computer network features include on-campus library services, online commercial services, Internet access, wireless campus network, Internet filtering or blocking technology, iPads. Campus intranet, student e-mail accounts, and computer access in designated common areas are available to students. The school has a published electronic and media policy.

Contact Susan Parker, Director of Admissions. 212-710-8140. Fax: 212-289-6025. E-mail: sparker@spenceschool.org. Web site: www.spenceschool.org.

SPRINGSIDE CHESTNUT HILL ACADEMY

500 West Willow Grove Avenue

Philadelphia, Pennsylvania 19118

Head of School: Dr. Priscilla Sands

General Information Coeducational day college-preparatory, arts, technology, science, and math school. Grades PK–12. Founded: 1861. Setting: suburban. 65-acre campus. 4 buildings on campus. Approved or accredited by Pennsylvania Association of Independent Schools and Pennsylvania Department of Education. Member of National Association of Independent Schools and Secondary School Admission Test Board. Endowment: $36 million. Total enrollment: 1,129. Upper school average class size: 16. Upper school faculty-student ratio: 1:6. There are 174 required school days per year for Upper School students. Upper School students typically attend 5 days per week. The average school day consists of 7 hours and 30 minutes.

Upper School Student Profile Grade 9: 107 students (53 boys, 54 girls); Grade 10: 112 students (55 boys, 57 girls); Grade 11: 101 students (48 boys, 53 girls); Grade 12: 128 students (59 boys, 69 girls).

Faculty School total: 137. In upper school: 27 men, 34 women; 40 have advanced degrees.

Subjects Offered Advanced math, Advanced Placement courses, African studies, algebra, American history, art, art history, biology, biology-AP, calculus, calculus-AP, ceramics, chamber groups, chemistry, Chinese, choral music, college counseling, community service, comparative government and politics-AP, computer animation, computer programming, computer science, dance, dance performance, drama, drawing and design, East Asian history, English, English literature, English-AP, environmental science, European history, European history-AP, fine arts, forensics, French, French language-AP, geometry, handbells, health, history-AP, independent study, jazz ensemble, Latin, mathematics, music, oceanography, orchestra, peer counseling, photography, physical education, physics, physics-AP, physiology, printmaking, robotics, science, senior project, social studies, Spanish, Spanish-AP, statistics, statistics-AP, theater, trigonometry, U.S. government and politics-AP, U.S. history, weight reduction, woodworking, world history, world history-AP, writing, writing workshop, yearbook.

Graduation Requirements English, foreign language, health, history, mathematics, music, physical education (includes health), science, senior project, sports, Senior speech. Community service is required.

Special Academic Programs 9 Advanced Placement exams for which test preparation is offered; honors section; independent study.

College Admission Counseling 106 students graduated in 2011; all went to college, including Franklin & Marshall College; Lehigh University; The George Washington University; Trinity College; University of Pennsylvania; Yale University. Mean SAT critical reading: 612, mean SAT math: 611, mean SAT writing: 624, mean composite ACT: 25.

Student Life Upper grades have uniform requirement, student council, honor system. Discipline rests equally with students and faculty.

Summer Programs Remediation, enrichment, sports, art/fine arts, computer instruction programs offered; session focuses on to offer a variety of interesting opportunities for kids of all ages and interests; held on campus; accepts boys and girls; open to students from other schools. 180 students usually enrolled. 2012 schedule: June 14 to August 21.

Tuition and Aid Day student tuition: $27,400. Tuition installment plan (monthly payment plans, Higher Education Service, Inc). Merit scholarship grants, need-based scholarship grants available. In 2011–12, 38% of upper-school students received aid. Total amount of financial aid awarded in 2011–12: $3,146,250.

Admissions Traditional secondary-level entrance grade is 9. For fall 2011, 177 students applied for upper-level admission, 88 were accepted, 46 enrolled. ACT-Explore or SSAT required. Deadline for receipt of application materials: January 15. Application fee required: $50. On-campus interview required.

Athletics Interscholastic: basketball (boys, girls), crew (b,g), cross-country running (b,g), field hockey (g), golf (b,g), ice hockey (b), independent competitive sports (g), lacrosse (b,g), rowing (b,g), soccer (b,g), softball (g), squash (b,g), swimming and diving (b,g), tennis (b,g), track and field (b,g), volleyball (g), winter (indoor) track (b,g), wrestling (b); intramural: aerobics (g), aerobics/dance (g), badminton (g), basketball (g), dance (g), fitness (g), golf (g), outdoor activities (g), physical fitness (g), physical training (g), power lifting (g), ropes courses (g), soccer (g), softball (g), volleyball (g), weight training (g), yoga (g). 9 PE instructors, 53 coaches, 2 athletic trainers.

Computers Computers are regularly used in all classes. Computer network features include on-campus library services, online commercial services, Internet access, wireless campus network, Internet filtering or blocking technology. Student e-mail accounts and computer access in designated common areas are available to students. Students grades are available online. The school has a published electronic and media policy.

Contact Ms. Murielle Telemaque, Admissions Office Manager. 215-247-7007. Fax: 215-247-7308. E-mail: mtelemaque@sch.org. Web site: www.sch.org.

SQUAW VALLEY ACADEMY

235 Squaw Valley Road

Olympic Valley, California 96146

Head of School: Mr. Donald Rees

General Information Coeducational boarding and day college-preparatory and arts school. Grades 9–12. Founded: 1978. Setting: rural. Nearest major city is Reno, NV. Students are housed in single-sex by floor dormitories and single-sex dormitories. 3-acre campus. 4 buildings on campus. Approved or accredited by Western Association of Schools and Colleges and California Department of Education. Total enrollment: 100. Upper school average class size: 8. Upper school faculty-student ratio: 1:8. Upper School students typically attend 5 days per week. The average school day consists of 8 hours.

Upper School Student Profile 100% of students are boarding students. 75% are international students. International students from Armenia, China, Germany, Republic of Korea, Russian Federation, and Saudi Arabia; 8 other countries represented in student body.

Faculty School total: 12. In upper school: 9 men, 3 women; 6 have advanced degrees; 4 reside on campus.

Subjects Offered Addiction, advanced biology, advanced chemistry, advanced math, Advanced Placement courses, advanced TOEFL/grammar, algebra, American democracy, American government, American history, American history-AP, American literature, American literature-AP, anatomy, applied arts, applied music, art, art education, art history, backpacking, band, biology, biology-AP, calculus, calculus-AP, ceramics, chemistry, civics, college admission preparation, college counseling, college placement, college planning, college writing, computer science, computers, creative writing, drama, English, English literature, environmental science, expository writing, fine arts, French, geography, geometry, government/civics, grammar, health, history, history-AP, instruments, Internet, Internet research, jazz, language-AP, linear algebra, literature-AP, martial arts, mathematics, mathematics-AP, music, music appreciation, music history, music performance, music theory, novels, outdoor education, photography, physical education, physics, physics-AP, pre-calculus, psychology, publications, research and reference, SAT preparation, SAT/ACT preparation, science, social sciences, social studies, Spanish, Spanish-AP, student government, student publications, studio art, surfing, swimming, TOEFL preparation, travel, trigonometry, typing, video, visual and performing arts, weight fitness, world history, world history-AP, writing, yearbook, yoga.

Graduation Requirements Arts and fine arts (art, music, dance, drama), college admission preparation, English, foreign language, mathematics, physical education (includes health), science, social sciences, participation in skiing and snowboarding, seniors must gain acceptance into a minimum of one (1) college or university.

Special Academic Programs 9 Advanced Placement exams for which test preparation is offered; honors section; accelerated programs; independent study; study at local college for college credit; academic accommodation for the gifted, the musically talented, and the artistically talented; programs in English, mathematics for dyslexic students; special instructional classes for students with ADD and dyslexia; ESL (15 students enrolled).

College Admission Counseling 17 students graduated in 2011; all went to college, including Michigan State University; Penn State University Park; The Johns Hopkins University; University of California, Davis; University of Colorado Boulder; University of Oregon. Median SAT critical reading: 410, median SAT math: 550, median SAT writing: 445, median combined SAT: 1405. 20% scored over 600 on SAT critical reading, 40% scored over 600 on SAT math, 20% scored over 600 on SAT writing, 20% scored over 1800 on combined SAT.

Student Life Upper grades have uniform requirement, student council, honor system. Discipline rests primarily with faculty.

Summer Programs Remediation, enrichment, advancement, ESL, sports, art/fine arts programs offered; session focuses on academics and mountain sports; held both on and off campus; held at Lake Tahoe; accepts boys and girls; open to students from other schools. 25 students usually enrolled. 2012 schedule: July 3 to August 12. Application deadline: none.

Tuition and Aid Day student tuition: $17,010; 7-day tuition and room/board: $44,298. Tuition installment plan (individually arranged payment plans). Tuition reduction for siblings, need-based scholarship grants available. In 2011–12, 10% of upper-school students received aid.

Admissions Traditional secondary-level entrance grade is 10. For fall 2011, 120 students applied for upper-level admission, 110 were accepted, 100 enrolled. Math Placement Exam and writing sample required. Deadline for receipt of application materials: none. Application fee required: $100. Interview required.

Athletics Interscholastic: alpine skiing (boys, girls), freestyle skiing (b,g), golf (b,g), skiing (downhill) (b,g), snowboarding (b,g); intramural: aerobics (b,g), aerobics/Nautilus (b,g), alpine skiing (b,g), aquatics (b,g), backpacking (b,g), badminton (b,g), basketball (b,g), bicycling (b,g), billiards (b,g), blading (b,g), bowling (b,g), canoeing/kayaking (b,g), climbing (b,g), combined training (b,g), croquet (b,g), cross-country running (b,g), field hockey (b,g), fishing (b,g), fitness (b,g), fitness walking (b,g), flag football (b,g), fly fishing (b,g), freestyle skiing (b,g), Frisbee (b,g), golf (b,g), hiking/backpacking (b,g), horseback riding (b,g), ice skating (b,g), jogging (b,g), kayaking (b,g), mountain biking (b,g), mountaineering (b,g), nordic skiing (b,g), outdoor activities (b,g), outdoor adventure (b,g), outdoor education (b,g), outdoor recreation (b,g), outdoor skills (b,g), outdoors (b,g), paddling (b,g), paint ball (b,g), physical fitness (b,g), physical training (b,g), rafting (b,g), rock climbing (b,g), ropes courses (b,g), running (b,g), self defense (b,g), skateboarding (b,g), skiing (cross-country) (b,g), skiing (downhill) (b,g), snowboarding (b,g), snowshoeing (b,g), strength & conditioning (b,g), swimming and diving (b,g), table tennis (b,g), telemark skiing (b,g), tennis (b,g), ultimate Frisbee (b,g), volleyball (b,g), walking (b,g), wall climbing (b,g), weight lifting (b,g), weight training (b,g), yoga (b,g); coed interscholastic: alpine skiing, freestyle skiing, golf, skiing (downhill), snowboarding, soccer; coed intramural: aerobics, aerobics/Nautilus, alpine skiing, aquatics, backpacking, badminton, baseball, basketball, bicycling, billiards, blading, bowling, canoeing/kayaking, climbing, combined training, croquet, cross-country running, field hockey, fishing, fitness, fitness walking, flag football, fly fishing, freestyle skiing, Frisbee, golf, hiking/backpacking, horseback riding, ice skating, jogging, kayaking, mountain biking, mountaineering, nordic skiing, outdoor activities, outdoor adventure, outdoor education, outdoor recreation, outdoor skills, outdoors, paddling, paint ball, physical fitness, physical training, rafting, rock climbing, ropes courses, running, self defense, skateboarding, skiing (cross-country), skiing (downhill), snowboarding, snowshoeing, soccer, softball, strength & conditioning, swimming and diving, table tennis, telemark skiing, tennis, ultimate Frisbee, volleyball, walking, wall climbing, weight lifting, weight training, yoga.

Computers Computers are regularly used in all academic classes. Computer network features include on-campus library services, online commercial services, Internet access, wireless campus network, Internet filtering or blocking technology. Computer access in designated common areas is available to students.

Contact Adrienne Forbes, M.Ed., Admissions Director. 530-583-9393 Ext. 105. Fax: 530-581-1111. E-mail: enroll@sva.org. Web site: www.sva.org.

THE STANWICH SCHOOL

257 Stanwich Road

Greenwich, Connecticut 06830

Head of School: Mrs. Patricia G. Young

General Information Coeducational day college-preparatory, arts, and technology school. Grades PK–12. Founded: 1998. Approved or accredited by Connecticut Department of Education. Total enrollment: 407. Upper school faculty-student ratio: 1:10. The average school day consists of 8 hours and 30 minutes.

Upper School Student Profile Grade 7: 40 students (24 boys, 16 girls); Grade 8: 50 students (24 boys, 26 girls); Grade 9: 19 students (10 boys, 9 girls).

Faculty School total: 100. In upper school: 5 men, 2 women; 7 have advanced degrees.

Special Academic Programs International Baccalaureate program; 12 Advanced Placement exams for which test preparation is offered; honors section; accelerated programs; independent study; study abroad; academic accommodation for the gifted.

Tuition and Aid Day student tuition: $21,000–$30,000. Tuition installment plan (Insured Tuition Payment Plan, monthly payment plans). Merit scholarship grants, need-based scholarship grants available. Total upper-school merit-scholarship money awarded for 2010–11: $30,000.

Admissions Traditional secondary-level entrance grade is 7. For fall 2010, 36 students applied for upper-level admission, 23 were accepted, 12 enrolled. ISEE required. Deadline for receipt of application materials: January 15. Application fee required: $75. Interview required.

Athletics Interscholastic: baseball (boys), basketball (b), field hockey (g), football (b); intramural: softball (g); coed interscholastic: tennis; coed intramural: dance, fitness, flag football, golf, ice hockey, physical fitness, running.

Computers Computers are regularly used in all classes. Computer network features include on-campus library services, Internet access, wireless campus network, Internet filtering or blocking technology. Student e-mail accounts are available to students. Students grades are available online. The school has a published electronic and media policy.

Contact Ms. May Rawls, Director of Admissions, Grades 4-12. 203-542-0055. Fax: 203-869-4641. E-mail: mrawls@stanwichschool.org. Web site: http://www.stanwichschool.org/.

STEPHEN T. BADIN HIGH SCHOOL

571 New London Road

Hamilton, Ohio 45013

Head of School: Mr. Brian Pendergest

General Information Coeducational day college-preparatory, general academic, arts, business, vocational, religious studies, and technology school, affiliated with Roman Catholic Church. Grades 9–12. Founded: 1966. Setting: urban. Nearest major city is Cincinnati. 22-acre campus. 2 buildings on campus. Approved or accredited by National Catholic Education Association, North Central Association of Colleges and Schools, Ohio Catholic Schools Accreditation Association (OCSAA), and Ohio Department of Education. Endowment: $120,000. Total enrollment: 455. Upper school average class size: 24. Upper school faculty-student ratio: 1:18. There are 182 required school days per year for Upper School students. Upper School students typically attend 5 days per week. The average school day consists of 6 hours and 55 minutes.

Upper School Student Profile Grade 9: 125 students (74 boys, 51 girls); Grade 10: 121 students (65 boys, 56 girls); Grade 11: 105 students (63 boys, 42 girls); Grade 12: 104 students (54 boys, 50 girls). 92% of students are Roman Catholic.

Faculty School total: 34. In upper school: 20 men, 14 women; 20 have advanced degrees.

Subjects Offered Accounting, algebra, American history, American literature, art, band, biology, British literature, calculus, calculus-AP, chemistry, chorus, computer programming, computer resources, consumer economics, consumer mathematics, economics, English, English literature, English-AP, French, geometry, government-AP, government/civics, grammar, history, integrated science, intro to computers, journalism, Latin, marketing, mathematics, music, music theory, physical education, physical science, physics, physiology, pre-calculus, publications, religion, science, social studies, Spanish, trigonometry, Web site design, Western literature, world history.

Graduation Requirements Computer science, English, mathematics, physical education (includes health), religion (includes Bible studies and theology), science, social studies (includes history), 15 hours of community service per year for seniors.

Special Academic Programs 8 Advanced Placement exams for which test preparation is offered; honors section; study at local college for college credit; study abroad; remedial reading and/or remedial writing; remedial math; special instructional classes for blind students.

College Admission Counseling 124 students graduated in 2011; 120 went to college, including College of Mount St. Joseph; Miami University; The Ohio State University; University of Cincinnati; Wright State University; Xavier University. Other: 2 went to work, 2 entered military service. Median SAT critical reading: 519, median SAT math: 526, median SAT writing: 529, median combined SAT: 1574, median composite ACT: 22. 22% scored over 600 on SAT critical reading, 12% scored over 600 on SAT math, 17% scored over 600 on SAT writing, 22% scored over 1800 on combined SAT, 27% scored over 26 on composite ACT.

Student Life Upper grades have uniform requirement, student council. Discipline rests primarily with faculty. Attendance at religious services is required.

Tuition and Aid Day student tuition: $7500. Tuition installment plan (monthly payment plans, individually arranged payment plans, quarterly payment plan). Merit scholarship grants, need-based scholarship grants, paying campus jobs available. In 2011–12, 32% of upper-school students received aid; total upper-school merit-scholarship money awarded: $23,000. Total amount of financial aid awarded in 2011–12: $2,950,000.

Admissions Deadline for receipt of application materials: none. No application fee required. On-campus interview recommended.

Athletics Interscholastic: aquatics (boys, girls), baseball (b), basketball (b,g), bowling (b,g), cheering (g), diving (b,g), football (b), golf (b,g), gymnastics (g), hockey (b), ice hockey (b), rowing (b), soccer (b,g), softball (g), swimming and diving (b,g), tennis (g), volleyball (b,g); coed interscholastic: fishing. 2 PE instructors, 35 coaches, 1 athletic trainer.

Computers Computers are regularly used in mathematics, music, science, Web site design classes. Computer network features include on-campus library services, Internet access, wireless campus network, Internet filtering or blocking technology, scanners, travelling laptops, digital cameras. Students grades are available online.

Contact Mrs. Angie Gray, Director of Recruitment. 513-863-3993 Ext. 145. Fax: 513-785-2844. E-mail: agray@mail.badinhs.org. Web site: www.badinhs.org/index.asp.

STERNE SCHOOL

San Francisco, California

See Special Needs Schools section.

STEVENSON SCHOOL

3152 Forest Lake Road

Pebble Beach, California 93953

Head of School: Mr. Joseph E. Wandke

General Information Coeducational boarding and day college-preparatory, arts, and technology school. Boarding grades 9–12, day grades K–12. Founded: 1952. Setting: suburban. Nearest major city is San Francisco. Students are housed in single-sex by floor dormitories. 70-acre campus. 22 buildings on campus. Approved or accredited by Western Association of Schools and Colleges and California Department of Education. Member of National Association of Independent Schools and Secondary School Admission Test Board. Endowment: $21 million. Total enrollment: 745. Upper school average class size: 14. Upper school faculty-student ratio: 1:10. Upper School students typically attend 5 days per week. The average school day consists of 6 hours.

Upper School Student Profile Grade 9: 105 students (60 boys, 45 girls); Grade 10: 143 students (70 boys, 73 girls); Grade 11: 135 students (66 boys, 69 girls); Grade 12: 135 students (70 boys, 65 girls). 50% of students are boarding students. 71% are state residents. 16 states are represented in upper school student body. 20% are international students. International students from China, Hong Kong, Republic of Korea, Singapore, Taiwan, and Thailand; 10 other countries represented in student body.

Faculty School total: 65. In upper school: 37 men, 17 women; 36 have advanced degrees; 28 reside on campus.

Subjects Offered 3-dimensional art, advanced chemistry, Advanced Placement courses, algebra, American history, American literature, American literature-AP, architecture, art, art history, art-AP, biology, biology-AP, broadcasting, calculus, calculus-AP, ceramics, chemistry, chemistry-AP, Chinese, computer programming, computer science, concert band, creative writing, dance, dance performance, drama, drama performance, drama workshop, dramatic arts, drawing, drawing and design, driver education, economics, economics-AP, English, English literature, English-AP, environmental science, environmental science-AP, ethics, European civilization, European history, expository writing, fine arts, French, French-AP, geometry, German-AP, government/civics, grammar, history of ideas, history-AP, honors algebra, honors English, honors geometry, honors U.S. history, Japanese, jazz, jazz band, jazz ensemble, jazz theory, journalism, Latin, Latin-AP, macroeconomics-AP, marine biology, mathematics, mathematics-AP, microbiology, music, musical productions, musical theater, ornithology, photography, physical education, physics, physics-AP, portfolio art, pre-calculus, psychology, science, social studies, Spanish, Spanish-AP, speech, stage design, stagecraft, studio art-AP, tap dance, theater, trigonometry, U.S. history-AP, visual and performing arts, visual arts, vocal ensemble, wilderness education, wilderness experience, wind ensemble, world cultures, world history, world literature, world studies, writing, yearbook.

Graduation Requirements Arts and fine arts (art, music, dance, drama), English, foreign language, mathematics, physical education (includes health), science, social studies (includes history).

Special Academic Programs Advanced Placement exam preparation; honors section; independent study; term-away projects; study abroad.

College Admission Counseling 152 students graduated in 2011; all went to college, including Boston University; New York University; University of California, Davis; University of California, Los Angeles; University of Oregon; University of Pennsylvania. Mean SAT critical reading: 615, mean SAT math: 668, mean SAT writing: 652, mean combined SAT: 1935, mean composite ACT: 25. 52% scored over 600 on SAT critical reading, 60% scored over 600 on SAT math, 52% scored over 600 on SAT writing, 58% scored over 1800 on combined SAT, 50% scored over 26 on composite ACT.

Student Life Upper grades have specified standards of dress, student council, honor system. Discipline rests equally with students and faculty.

Summer Programs Enrichment programs offered; held on campus; accepts boys and girls; open to students from other schools. 140 students usually enrolled. 2012 schedule: June 28 to July 30. Application deadline: none.

Tuition and Aid Day student tuition: $29,900; 7-day tuition and room/board: $49,100. Tuition installment plan (Insured Tuition Payment Plan). Need-based scholarship grants available. In 2011–12, 21% of upper-school students received aid. Total amount of financial aid awarded in 2011–12: $2,800,000.

Admissions Traditional secondary-level entrance grade is 9. For fall 2011, 499 students applied for upper-level admission, 264 were accepted, 162 enrolled. SSAT required. Deadline for receipt of application materials: February 1. Application fee required: $75. Interview required.

Athletics Interscholastic: baseball (boys), basketball (b,g), cross-country running (b,g), diving (b,g), field hockey (g), football (b), golf (b,g), lacrosse (b,g), sailing (b,g), soccer (b,g), softball (g), swimming and diving (b,g), tennis (b,g), track and field (b,g), volleyball (g), water polo (b,g); intramural: dance (b,g), golf (b,g), horseback riding (b,g), kayaking (b,g), modern dance (b,g), mountaineering (b,g), outdoor education (b,g), outdoors (b,g), power lifting (b,g), rock climbing (b,g), strength & conditioning (b,g), table tennis (b,g), weight lifting (b,g), wilderness (b,g), yoga (b,g); coed interscholastic: sailing; coed intramural: basketball, bicycling, climbing, dance, equestrian sports, fencing, horseback riding, kayaking, modern dance, mountaineering, outdoor education, outdoors, rock climbing, sailing, softball, strength & conditioning, table tennis, weight lifting, wilderness, yoga. 22 coaches.

Computers Computers are regularly used in all classes. Computer network features include on-campus library services, online commercial services, Internet access, wireless campus network, Internet filtering or blocking technology. Campus intranet and student e-mail accounts are available to students. Students grades are available online. The school has a published electronic and media policy.

Contact Mr. Thomas W. Sheppard, Director of Admission. 831-625-8309. Fax: 831-625-5208. E-mail: info@stevensonschool.org. Web site: www.stevensonschool.org.

STONELEIGH–BURNHAM SCHOOL

574 Bernardston Road

Greenfield, Massachusetts 01301

Head of School: Sally Mixsell

General Information Girls' boarding and day college-preparatory and arts school. Grades 7–PG. Founded: 1869. Setting: small town. Nearest major city is Boston. Students are housed in single-sex dormitories. 100-acre campus. 7 buildings on campus. Approved or accredited by Association of Independent Schools in New England, International Baccalaureate Organization, New England Association of Schools and Colleges, The Association of Boarding Schools, and Massachusetts Department of Education. Member of National Association of Independent Schools. Endowment: $2.8 million. Total enrollment: 127. Upper school average class size: 10. Upper school faculty-student ratio: 1:6. Upper School students typically attend 5 days per week. The average school day consists of 7 hours and 30 minutes.

Upper School Student Profile Grade 9: 18 students (18 girls); Grade 10: 24 students (24 girls); Grade 11: 27 students (27 girls); Grade 12: 23 students (23 girls). 71% of students are boarding students. 35% are state residents. 12 states are represented in upper school student body. 38% are international students. International students from China, Japan, Mexico, Republic of Korea, and Taiwan.

Faculty School total: 33. In upper school: 7 men, 16 women; 14 have advanced degrees; 13 reside on campus.

Subjects Offered Acting, Advanced Placement courses, algebra, American history, art, band, biology, biology-AP, calculus, calculus-AP, ceramics, chemistry, Chinese, conceptual physics, dance, desktop publishing, drama, drawing, ecology, English, English-AP, environmental science-AP, equine science, ESL, ethical decision making, European history, European history-AP, fine arts, French, French-AP, geometry, graphic arts, history, International Baccalaureate courses, mathematics, music, music theory, photography, physics, poetry, psychology, public speaking, science, senior seminar, social studies, Spanish, Spanish-AP, sports medicine, theater, U.S. history-AP, values and decisions, water color painting, weaving, yearbook.

Graduation Requirements Art, arts and fine arts (art, music, dance, drama), English, foreign language, history, mathematics, physical education (includes health), science, U.S. history.

Special Academic Programs International Baccalaureate program; Advanced Placement exam preparation; honors section; independent study; ESL (9 students enrolled).

College Admission Counseling Colleges students went to include Brown University; Georgetown University; Mount Holyoke College; Smith College; The George Washington University; Tufts University.

Student Life Upper grades have specified standards of dress, student council, honor system. Discipline rests equally with students and faculty.

Summer Programs Enrichment, sports, art/fine arts programs offered; session focuses on debate, dance, riding, soccer; held on campus; accepts girls; open to students from other schools. 210 students usually enrolled. 2012 schedule: June to August. Application deadline: none.

Tuition and Aid Day student tuition: $28,890; 7-day tuition and room/board: $48,443. Tuition installment plan (monthly payment plans). Merit scholarship grants, need-based scholarship grants available. In 2011–12, 22% of upper-school students received aid; total upper-school merit-scholarship money awarded: $20,000. Total amount of financial aid awarded in 2011–12: $904,000.

Admissions Traditional secondary-level entrance grade is 9. For fall 2011, 107 students applied for upper-level admission, 44 were accepted, 15 enrolled. ISEE, SAT, SSAT or TOEFL or SLEP required. Deadline for receipt of application materials: February 15. Application fee required: $50. Interview required.

Athletics Interscholastic: aerobics/dance, ballet, basketball, cross-country running, dance, dressage, equestrian sports, horseback riding, lacrosse, modern dance, soccer, softball, tennis, volleyball; intramural: alpine skiing, cross-country running, fitness, golf, horseback riding, ice skating, skiing (downhill), snowboarding, strength & conditioning, tennis. 1 athletic trainer.

Computers Computers are regularly used in all classes. Computer network features include on-campus library services, Internet access, wireless campus network, Internet filtering or blocking technology. Campus intranet, student e-mail accounts, and computer access in designated common areas are available to students. The school has a published electronic and media policy.

Contact Laura Lavallee, Associate Director of Admissions. 413-774-2711 Ext. 257. Fax: 413-772-2602. E-mail: admissions@sbschool.org. Web site: www.sbschool.org.

STONE MOUNTAIN SCHOOL

Black Mountain, North Carolina

See Special Needs Schools section.

STORM KING SCHOOL

314 Mountain Road

Cornwall-on-Hudson, New York 12520-1899

Head of School: Mrs. Helen S. Chinitz

General Information Coeducational boarding and day college-preparatory and arts school. Grades 8–12. Founded: 1867. Setting: small town. Nearest major city is New York. Students are housed in single-sex dormitories. 55-acre campus. 24 buildings on campus. Approved or accredited by Middle States Association of Colleges and Schools, The Association of Boarding Schools, and New York Department of Education. Member of National Association of Independent Schools and Secondary School Admission Test Board. Endowment: $1 million. Total enrollment: 132. Upper school average class size: 12. Upper school faculty-student ratio: 1:6. There are 170 required school days per year for Upper School students. Upper School students typically attend 5 days per week. The average school day consists of 9 hours.

Upper School Student Profile Grade 9: 13 students (9 boys, 4 girls); Grade 10: 33 students (17 boys, 16 girls); Grade 11: 37 students (21 boys, 16 girls); Grade 12: 42 students (30 boys, 12 girls). 80% of students are boarding students. 34% are state residents. 9 states are represented in upper school student body. 45% are international students. International students from China, Italy, Japan, Kazakhstan, Republic of Korea, and Viet Nam; 17 other countries represented in student body.

Faculty School total: 36. In upper school: 20 men, 16 women; 20 have advanced degrees; 19 reside on campus.

Subjects Offered Acting, Advanced Placement courses, advanced studio art-AP, advanced TOEFL/grammar, algebra, American history, American literature, American sign language, art, art history-AP, art-AP, athletics, biology, calculus, calculus-AP, ceramics, chemistry, Chinese, choral music, college counseling, community service, computer science-AP, creative writing, dance, diversity studies, drama, drawing, earth science, economics, economics-AP, English, English literature, English literature-AP, environmental science, ESL, fine arts, foreign language, geometry, government/civics, guitar, health, high adventure outdoor program, history, humanities, literature, Mandarin, mathematics, mechanical drawing, music, music composition, musical productions, outdoor education, painting, performing arts, photography, physical education, physics, physics-AP, piano, playwriting, playwriting and directing, pre-calculus, psychology, psychology-AP, SAT preparation, science, social studies, Spanish, stage design, stagecraft, statistics-AP, student government, studio art-AP, theater, U.S. history, world history, world literature, writing, yearbook.

Graduation Requirements English, foreign language, Internet, mathematics, performing arts, physical education (includes health), public speaking, science, social studies (includes history), visual arts, at least two community service, outdoor adventure, and cultural experiences per year. Community service is required.

Special Academic Programs 10 Advanced Placement exams for which test preparation is offered; honors section; academic accommodation for the musically talented and the artistically talented; remedial reading and/or remedial writing; programs in English, mathematics, general development for dyslexic students; ESL (40 students enrolled).

College Admission Counseling 32 students graduated in 2011; all went to college, including Boston University; University of California, Los Angeles. Mean SAT critical reading: 473, mean SAT math: 555, mean SAT writing: 503, mean combined SAT: 1532.

Student Life Upper grades have specified standards of dress, student council, honor system. Discipline rests equally with students and faculty.

Tuition and Aid Day student tuition: $21,500; 7-day tuition and room/board: $40,100. Tuition installment plan (individually arranged payment plans). Tuition reduction for siblings, merit scholarship grants, need-based scholarship grants available. In 2011–12, 28% of upper-school students received aid; total upper-school merit-scholarship money awarded: $110,000. Total amount of financial aid awarded in 2011–12: $401,000.

Admissions Traditional secondary-level entrance grade is 9. For fall 2011, 180 students applied for upper-level admission, 123 were accepted, 56 enrolled. Admissions testing, SSAT or TOEFL or SLEP required. Deadline for receipt of application materials: none. Application fee required: $85. Interview required.

Athletics Interscholastic: basketball (boys, girls), lacrosse (b), soccer (b,g), softball (g), volleyball (g), wrestling (b); coed interscholastic: crew, cross-country running, Frisbee, golf, jogging, skiing (downhill), snowboarding, tennis, ultimate Frisbee; coed intramural: aerobics/dance, aerobics/Nautilus, alpine skiing, backpacking, ballet, bicycling, billiards, blading, bocce, bowling, canoeing/kayaking, climbing, dance, fitness, fitness walking, flag football, freestyle skiing, golf, hiking/backpacking, ice skating, jogging, modern dance, mountain biking, Nautilus, outdoor activities, outdoor adventure, outdoor education, outdoor recreation, paddle tennis, paint ball, physical fitness, power lifting, rafting, rappelling, rock climbing, ropes courses, running, skiing (cross-country), skiing (downhill), snowboarding, strength & conditioning, table tennis, tai chi, tennis, touch football, track and field, ultimate Frisbee, volleyball, weight lifting, wilderness, yoga. 3 coaches, 1 athletic trainer.

Computers Computers are regularly used in computer applications, drawing and design, music technology, photography, yearbook classes. Computer network features include on-campus library services, online commercial services, Internet access, wireless campus network, parent/student/teacher communication portal. Student e-mail accounts and computer access in designated common areas are available to students. Students grades are available online. The school has a published electronic and media policy.

Contact Mrs. Joanna Evans, Associate Director of Admissions. 845-534-9860 Ext. 236. Fax: 845-534-4128. E-mail: admissions@sks.org. Web site: www.sks.org.

See Display on next page and Close-Up on page 684.

STRAKE JESUIT COLLEGE PREPARATORY

8900 Bellaire Boulevard

Houston, Texas 77036

Head of School: Fr. Dan Lahart, SJ

General Information Boys' day college-preparatory school, affiliated with Roman Catholic Church (Jesuit order). Grades 9–12. Founded: 1960. Setting: suburban. 44-acre campus. 21 buildings on campus. Approved or accredited by Jesuit Secondary Education Association, Southern Association of Colleges and Schools, Texas Catholic Conference, Texas Education Agency, and Texas Department of Education. Endowment: $8 million. Total enrollment: 904. Upper school average class size: 25. Upper school faculty-student ratio: 1:11. There are 180 required school days per year for Upper School students. Upper School students typically attend 5 days per week. The average school day consists of 7 hours.

Upper School Student Profile Grade 9: 249 students (249 boys); Grade 10: 220 students (220 boys); Grade 11: 229 students (229 boys); Grade 12: 206 students (206 boys). 74% of students are Roman Catholic Church (Jesuit order).

Faculty School total: 80. In upper school: 59 men, 21 women; 26 have advanced degrees.

Subjects Offered Accounting, algebra, American history, American literature, art, art history, band, biology, broadcasting, calculus, chemistry, chorus, community service, computer science, debate, drama, drawing, economics, English, English literature, French, geography, geometry, government/civics, health, journalism, Latin, mathematics, music, music theory, oceanography, orchestra, painting, physical education, physical science, physics, physiology, pre-calculus, reading, religion, science, social studies, Spanish, speech, television, theater, theology, trigonometry, video, word processing, world history, world literature.

Graduation Requirements Arts and fine arts (art, music, dance, drama), business skills (includes word processing), computer science, English, foreign language, geography, health, mathematics, physical education (includes health), religion (includes Bible studies and theology), science, social studies (includes history), speech. Community service is required.

Special Academic Programs Advanced Placement exam preparation; honors section; study at local college for college credit.

College Admission Counseling 208 students graduated in 2011; 206 went to college, including Louisiana State University in Shreveport; Rice University; Texas A&M University; The University of Texas at Austin; The University of Texas at San Antonio; University of Notre Dame. Other: 2 had other specific plans. Median SAT critical reading: 630, median SAT math: 650, median SAT writing: 640, median combined SAT: 1910, median composite ACT: 28. 74% scored over 26 on composite ACT.

Student Life Upper grades have specified standards of dress, student council, honor system. Discipline rests primarily with faculty. Attendance at religious services is required.

Summer Programs Remediation, enrichment, sports programs offered; held on campus; accepts boys and girls; open to students from other schools.

Tuition and Aid Day student tuition: $15,150. Tuition installment plan (monthly payment plans). Need-based scholarship grants available. In 2011–12, 14% of upper-school students received aid. Total amount of financial aid awarded in 2011–12: $1,350,000.

Admissions Traditional secondary-level entrance grade is 9. For fall 2011, 554 students applied for upper-level admission, 357 were accepted, 249 enrolled. High School Placement Test (closed version) from Scholastic Testing Service required. Deadline for receipt of application materials: January 15. Application fee required: $50.

Athletics Interscholastic: baseball, basketball, cross-country running, football, golf, lacrosse, rugby, soccer, swimming and diving, tennis, track and field, water polo, wrestling. 4 PE instructors, 33 coaches, 2 athletic trainers.

Computers Computer network features include on-campus library services, online commercial services, Internet access. Student e-mail accounts are available to students. Students grades are available online. The school has a published electronic and media policy.

Contact Mrs. Patti McNeil, Assistant to the Director of Admissions. 713-490-8113. Fax: 713-272-4300. E-mail: pledesma@strakejesuit.org. Web site: www.strakejesuit.org.

STRATFORD ACADEMY

6010 Peake Road

Macon, Georgia 31220-3903

Head of School: Dr. Robert E. Veto

General Information Coeducational day college-preparatory, arts, and technology school. Founded: 1960. Setting: suburban. Nearest major city is Atlanta. 70-acre campus. 4 buildings on campus. Approved or accredited by Georgia Independent School Association, Southern Association of Colleges and Schools, Southern Association of Independent Schools, and Georgia Department of Education. Member of National Association of Independent Schools. Endowment: $1 million. Total enrollment: 934. Upper school average class size: 17. Upper school faculty-student ratio: 1:13. There are 180 required school days per year for Upper School students. Upper School students typically attend 5 days per week. The average school day consists of 6 hours.

Faculty School total: 89. In upper school: 25 men, 22 women; 25 have advanced degrees.

Subjects Offered Advanced Placement courses, algebra, American history, American literature, anatomy, art, art history, art-AP, athletics, baseball, basketball, biology, biology-AP, calculus, calculus-AP, chemistry, chemistry-AP, community service, comparative government and politics-AP, computer programming, computer science, creative writing, drama, drama performance, driver education, earth science, economics, English, English literature, English literature-AP, English-AP, European history, European history-AP, expository writing, French, French-AP, geography, geometry, government/civics, grammar, history, history-AP, humanities, journalism, keyboarding, Latin, Latin-AP, madrigals, mathematics, mathematics-AP, music, physical education, physical science, physics, pre-calculus, science, social sciences, social studies, sociology, Spanish, Spanish-AP, speech, theater, trigonometry, U.S. government and politics-AP, water color painting, world history, world literature, writing.

Graduation Requirements English, foreign language, math applications, mathematics, science, senior seminar, social sciences, social studies (includes history). Community service is required.

Special Academic Programs Advanced Placement exam preparation; independent study; special instructional classes for students with learning disabilities, Attention Deficit Disorder, and dyslexia.

College Admission Counseling 60 students graduated in 2011; all went to college, including Auburn University; Georgia Institute of Technology; Georgia Southern University; Harvard University; Northwestern University; University of Georgia.

Student Life Upper grades have uniform requirement, student council, honor system. Discipline rests primarily with faculty.

Tuition and Aid Day student tuition: $12,623. Tuition installment plan (Insured Tuition Payment Plan, monthly payment plans, individually arranged payment plans). Merit scholarship grants, need-based scholarship grants available. Total upper-school merit-scholarship money awarded for 2011–12: $12,623.

Admissions Traditional secondary-level entrance grade is 9. ERB required. Deadline for receipt of application materials: none. Application fee required: $50. On-campus interview required.

Athletics Interscholastic: aerobics (girls), aquatics (b,g), baseball (b), basketball (b,g), cheering (g), cross-country running (b,g), dance team (g), drill team (g), football (b), physical training (b,g), soccer (b,g), tennis (b,g), volleyball (g), wrestling (b), yoga (g); coed interscholastic: badminton, golf. 8 PE instructors, 6 coaches, 1 athletic trainer.

Computers Computers are regularly used in art, creative writing, English, French, graphics, information technology, Spanish classes. Computer network features include on-campus library services, Internet access, wireless campus network. Computer access in designated common areas is available to students. The school has a published electronic and media policy.

Contact Ms. Marilyn Holton-Walker, Registrar/Admissions Assistant. 478-477-8073 Ext. 205. Fax: 478-477-0299. E-mail: marilyn.walker@stratford.org. Web site: www.stratford.org.

STRATTON MOUNTAIN SCHOOL

World Cup Circle

Stratton Mountain, Vermont 05155

Head of School: Christopher G. Kaltsas

General Information Coeducational boarding and day college-preparatory, arts, bilingual studies, and technology school. Boarding grades 7–PG, day grades 6–PG. Founded: 1972. Setting: rural. Nearest major city is Albany, NY. Students are housed in single-sex by floor dormitories. 12-acre campus. 7 buildings on campus. Approved or accredited by New England Association of Schools and Colleges and Vermont Department of Education. Member of National Association of Independent Schools. Endowment: $2.4 million. Total enrollment: 140. Upper school average class size: 10. Upper school faculty-student ratio: 1:6. There are 170 required school days per year for

Upper School students. Upper School students typically attend 5 days per week. The average school day consists of 5 hours.

Upper School Student Profile Grade 9: 27 students (18 boys, 9 girls); Grade 10: 16 students (7 boys, 9 girls); Grade 11: 25 students (11 boys, 14 girls); Grade 12: 23 students (11 boys, 12 girls); Postgraduate: 15 students (13 boys, 2 girls). 54% of students are boarding students. 46% are state residents. 22 states are represented in upper school student body. 5% are international students. International students from Australia, Canada, Italy, Japan, and New Zealand.

Faculty School total: 21. In upper school: 7 men, 10 women; 8 have advanced degrees; 8 reside on campus.

Subjects Offered Algebra, American history, American literature, art, biology, calculus, chemistry, computer science, English, English literature, environmental science, French, geography, geometry, grammar, health, history, journalism, mathematics, nutrition, physical education, physics, science, social studies, Spanish, world history.

Graduation Requirements Arts and fine arts (art, music, dance, drama), computer education, English, foreign language, health education, mathematics, science, social studies (includes history), superior competence in winter sports (skiing/snowboarding). Community service is required.

Special Academic Programs Independent study; ESL (3 students enrolled).

College Admission Counseling 25 students graduated in 2011; 18 went to college, including Dartmouth College; Middlebury College; St. Lawrence University; University of Colorado Boulder; University of New Hampshire; University of Vermont. Other: 1 went to work, 6 entered a postgraduate year. Mean SAT critical reading: 580, mean SAT math: 570, mean SAT writing: 600, mean combined SAT: 1750. 32% scored over 600 on SAT critical reading, 21% scored over 600 on SAT math, 47% scored over 600 on SAT writing, 42% scored over 1800 on combined SAT.

Student Life Upper grades have specified standards of dress, student council, honor system. Discipline rests primarily with faculty.

Tuition and Aid Day student tuition: $30,250; 7-day tuition and room/board: $41,500. Tuition installment plan (choice of one or two tuition installments plus advance deposit). Need-based scholarship grants, need-based loans available. In 2011–12, 44% of upper-school students received aid. Total amount of financial aid awarded in 2011–12: $737,000.

Admissions Traditional secondary-level entrance grade is 9. For fall 2011, 55 students applied for upper-level admission, 31 were accepted, 29 enrolled. Mathematics proficiency exam required. Deadline for receipt of application materials: March 15. Application fee required: $100. On-campus interview required.

Athletics Interscholastic: alpine skiing (boys, girls), bicycling (b,g), cross-country running (b,g), freestyle skiing (b,g), golf (b,g), lacrosse (b,g), nordic skiing (b,g), skiing (cross-country) (b,g), skiing (downhill) (b,g), snowboarding (b,g), soccer (b,g), tennis (b,g); intramural: strength & conditioning (b,g), tennis (b,g), yoga (b,g); coed intramural: skateboarding, tennis, yoga. 24 coaches, 1 athletic trainer.

Computers Computers are regularly used in computer applications, graphic design, mathematics, media production, research skills, science, Web site design, yearbook classes. Computer network features include on-campus library services, online commercial services, Internet access, Internet filtering or blocking technology. Student e-mail accounts are available to students. The school has a published electronic and media policy.

Contact Mrs. Kate Nolan Joyce, Director of Admissions. 802-856-1124. Fax: 802-297-0020. E-mail: knolan@gosms.org. Web site: www.gosms.org.

THE SUDBURY VALLEY SCHOOL

2 Winch Street

Framingham, Massachusetts 01701

Head of School: Michael Sadofsky

General Information Coeducational day college-preparatory and general academic school. Grades PS–12. Founded: 1968. Setting: suburban. Nearest major city is Boston. 10-acre campus. 2 buildings on campus. Approved or accredited by Massachusetts Department of Education. Total enrollment: 160. Upper school faculty-student ratio: 1:16. There are 180 required school days per year for Upper School students. Upper School students typically attend 5 days per week. The average school day consists of 6 hours.

Faculty School total: 10. In upper school: 4 men, 6 women; 3 have advanced degrees.

Subjects Offered Algebra, American history, American literature, anatomy, anthropology, archaeology, art, art history, Bible studies, biology, botany, business, calculus, ceramics, chemistry, computer programming, computer science, creative writing, dance, drama, economics, English, English literature, ethics, European history, expository writing, French, geography, geometry, German, government/civics, grammar, Hebrew, history, history of ideas, history of science, home economics, Latin, mathematics, music, philosophy, photography, physical education, physics, physiology, psychology, religion, social studies, Spanish, speech, theater, trigonometry, typing, world history, world literature, writing.

Graduation Requirements Students must successfully defend the thesis that they have taken responsibility for preparing themselves to be an effective adult in the community.

Special Academic Programs Independent study.

College Admission Counseling 15 students graduated in 2011; 9 went to college. Other: 1 went to work, 5 had other specific plans.

Student Life Upper grades have student council, honor system. Discipline rests equally with students and faculty.

Tuition and Aid Day student tuition: $7400.

Admissions Deadline for receipt of application materials: none. Application fee required: $30. On-campus interview required.

Computers Computer network features include on-campus library services, Internet access. Student e-mail accounts are available to students. The school has a published electronic and media policy.

Contact Hanna Greenberg, Admissions Clerk. 508-877-3030. Fax: 508-788-0674. E-mail: office@sudval.org. Web site: www.sudval.org.

SUFFIELD ACADEMY

185 North Main Street

Suffield, Connecticut 06078

Head of School: Mr. Charles Cahn III

General Information Coeducational boarding and day college-preparatory, arts, technology, and leadership school. Grades 9–PG. Founded: 1833. Setting: small town. Nearest major city is Hartford. Students are housed in single-sex dormitories. 340-acre campus. 49 buildings on campus. Approved or accredited by Connecticut Association of Independent Schools, New England Association of Schools and Colleges, and The Association of Boarding Schools. Member of National Association of Independent Schools and Secondary School Admission Test Board. Endowment: $31 million. Total enrollment: 412. Upper school average class size: 10. Upper school faculty-student ratio: 1:5. There are 180 required school days per year for Upper School students. Upper School students typically attend 6 days per week. The average school day consists of 5 hours and 35 minutes.

Upper School Student Profile Grade 9: 82 students (43 boys, 39 girls); Grade 10: 106 students (58 boys, 48 girls); Grade 11: 101 students (56 boys, 45 girls); Grade 12: 108 students (51 boys, 57 girls); Postgraduate: 15 students (14 boys, 1 girl). 66% of students are boarding students. 36% are state residents. 17 states are represented in upper school student body. 23% are international students. International students from China, Jamaica, Norway, Republic of Korea, Thailand, and United Kingdom; 20 other countries represented in student body.

Faculty School total: 81. In upper school: 45 men, 36 women; 54 have advanced degrees; 65 reside on campus.

Subjects Offered Acting, Advanced Placement courses, algebra, American history, American literature, anatomy and physiology, archaeology, art, art history, biology, biology-AP, calculus, calculus-AP, ceramics, chemistry, chemistry-AP, Chinese, computer math, computer programming, computer science, constitutional law, dance, drama, economics, economics-AP, English, English literature, English-AP, environmental science, ESL, ethics, European history, expository writing, fine arts, French, French-AP, geometry, government-AP, government/civics, grammar, health, history, jazz band, leadership, mathematics, mechanical drawing, music, music theory, news writing, philosophy, photography, physical education, physics, physics-AP, probability and statistics, religion, science, senior seminar, short story, social studies, sociology, Spanish, Spanish-AP, statistics, statistics-AP, technology, theater, theater arts, trigonometry, U.S. history, U.S. history-AP, visual and performing arts, visual arts, voice ensemble, wilderness education, wind ensemble, wind instruments, woodworking, world history, writing.

Graduation Requirements Arts and fine arts (art, music, dance, drama), English, foreign language, leadership, mathematics, physical education (includes health), religion (includes Bible studies and theology), science, social studies (includes history), technology portfolio.

Special Academic Programs 17 Advanced Placement exams for which test preparation is offered; honors section; independent study; academic accommodation for the gifted, the musically talented, and the artistically talented; ESL (12 students enrolled).

College Admission Counseling 131 students graduated in 2011; 130 went to college, including Bentley University; Boston College; Georgetown University; Gettysburg College; Southern Methodist University; Trinity College. Other: 1 entered a postgraduate year. Mean SAT critical reading: 553, mean SAT math: 577, mean SAT writing: 554, mean combined SAT: 1684, mean composite ACT: 24. 27% scored over 600 on SAT critical reading, 43% scored over 600 on SAT math, 30% scored over 600 on SAT writing, 33% scored over 1800 on combined SAT, 52% scored over 26 on composite ACT.

Student Life Upper grades have specified standards of dress, student council, honor system. Discipline rests primarily with faculty.

Summer Programs Enrichment, ESL, art/fine arts, computer instruction programs offered; session focuses on academics; held on campus; accepts boys and girls; open to students from other schools. 125 students usually enrolled. 2012 schedule: June 24 to July 27. Application deadline: June 1.

Tuition and Aid Day student tuition: $32,900; 7-day tuition and room/board: $46,500. Tuition installment plan (monthly payment plans). Need-based scholarship grants, tuition remission for children of faculty and staff who meet years of service

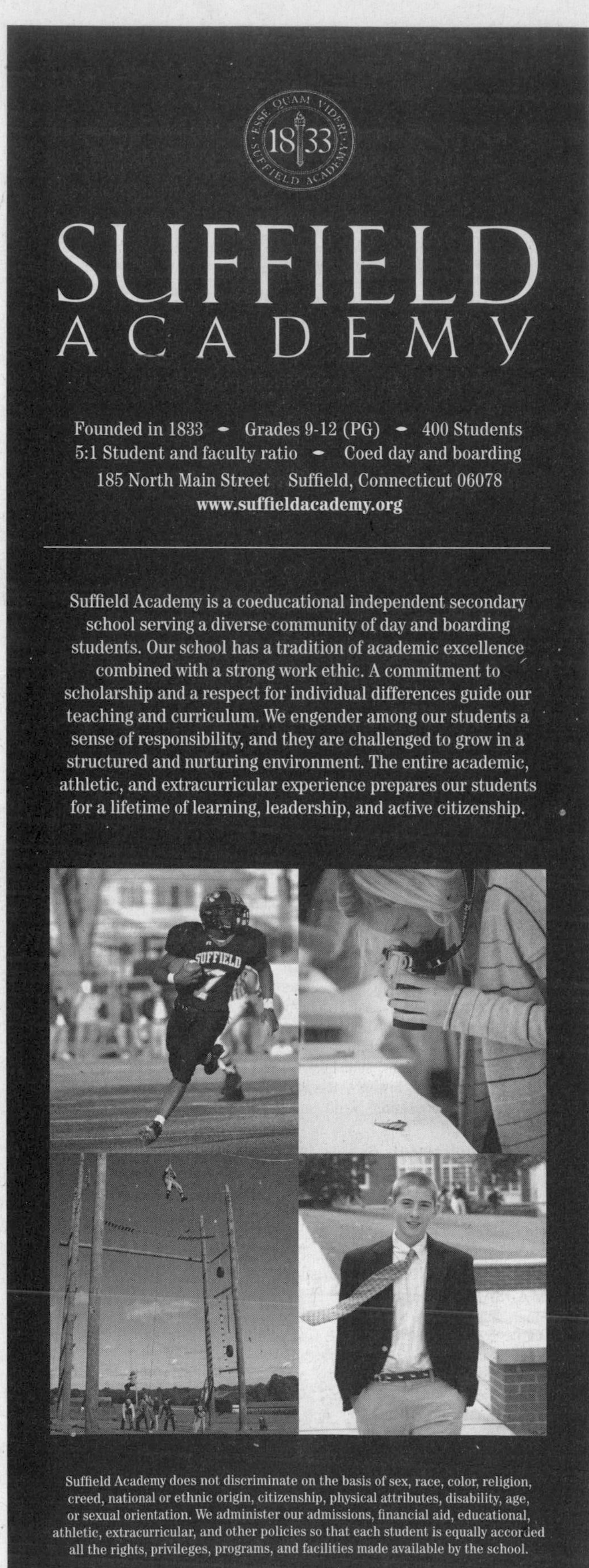

requirement available. In 2011–12, 33% of upper-school students received aid. Total amount of financial aid awarded in 2011–12: $3,500,000.

Admissions Traditional secondary-level entrance grade is 9. For fall 2011, 934 students applied for upper-level admission, 287 were accepted, 145 enrolled. PSAT or SAT, SSAT or TOEFL required. Deadline for receipt of application materials: January 15. Application fee required: $50. Interview required.

Athletics Interscholastic: aquatics (boys, girls), baseball (b), basketball (b,g), cross-country running (b,g), field hockey (g), football (b), lacrosse (b,g), soccer (b,g), softball (g), squash (b,g), swimming and diving (b,g), tennis (b,g), track and field (b,g), volleyball (g), water polo (b,g); coed interscholastic: alpine skiing, backpacking, canoeing/kayaking, climbing, dance, diving, fitness, golf, outdoors, riflery, rock climbing, ropes courses, skiing (downhill), snowboarding, wrestling; coed intramural: rock climbing, ropes courses, weight lifting. 3 coaches, 2 athletic trainers.

Computers Computers are regularly used in architecture, art, English, foreign language, history, mathematics, science classes. Computer network features include on-campus library services, online commercial services, Internet access, wireless campus network. Student e-mail accounts are available to students. The school has a published electronic and media policy.

Contact Terry Breault, Director of Admissions and Financial Aid. 860-386-4440. Fax: 860-668-2966. E-mail: saadmit@suffieldacademy.org. Web site: www.suffieldacademy.org.

See Display on this page and Close-Up on page 686.

SUMMERFIELD WALDORF SCHOOL

655 Willowside Road

Santa Rosa, California 95401

Head of School: Ms. Renate Lundberg

General Information Coeducational day college-preparatory, arts, and Waldorf curriculum school. Grades K–12. Founded: 1974. Setting: rural. 38-acre campus. 8 buildings on campus. Approved or accredited by Association of Waldorf Schools of North America, Western Association of Schools and Colleges, and California Department of Education. Total enrollment: 390. Upper school average class size: 28. Upper school faculty-student ratio: 1:7. Upper School students typically attend 5 days per week. The average school day consists of 7 hours.

Upper School Student Profile Grade 9: 25 students (11 boys, 14 girls); Grade 10: 25 students (13 boys, 12 girls); Grade 11: 23 students (7 boys, 16 girls); Grade 12: 26 students (13 boys, 13 girls).

Faculty School total: 23. In upper school: 11 men, 12 women; all have advanced degrees.

Subjects Offered Advanced chemistry, arts, history, humanities, literature, mathematics, music, science.

Graduation Requirements All , Senior Thesis Project.

Special Academic Programs Honors section; study abroad.

College Admission Counseling 15 students graduated in 2011; 12 went to college, including Bard College; Rhode Island School of Design; University of California, Berkeley; University of California, San Diego; University of California, Santa Cruz; University of Colorado Boulder. Other: 1 went to work, 2 had other specific plans.

Student Life Upper grades have specified standards of dress, student council. Discipline rests primarily with faculty.

Tuition and Aid Day student tuition: $16,250. Tuition installment plan (FACTS Tuition Payment Plan, monthly payment plans). Tuition reduction for siblings, need-based scholarship grants available. In 2011–12, 40% of upper-school students received aid.

Admissions Traditional secondary-level entrance grade is 9. For fall 2011, 34 students applied for upper-level admission, 30 were accepted, 30 enrolled. Deadline for receipt of application materials: January 12. Application fee required: $75. On-campus interview required.

Athletics Interscholastic: baseball (boys), basketball (b,g), soccer (b,g); intramural: volleyball (b,g); coed interscholastic: tennis. 5 PE instructors, 5 coaches.

Computers The school has a published electronic and media policy.

Contact Ms. Sallie Miller, Admissions Director. 707-575-7194 Ext. 102. Fax: 707-575-3217. E-mail: sallie@summerfieldwaldof.org. Web site: www.summerfieldwaldorf.org.

SUNHAWK ADOLESCENT RECOVERY CENTER

St. George, Utah

See Special Needs Schools section.

SUNSHINE BIBLE ACADEMY

400 Sunshine Drive

Miller, South Dakota 57362-6821

Head of School: Jason Watson

General Information Coeducational boarding and day college-preparatory, general academic, arts, business, vocational, religious studies, bilingual studies, and technology school, affiliated with Christian faith. Boarding grades 8–12, day grades K–12. Founded: 1951. Setting: rural. Nearest major city is Pierre. Students are housed in single-sex dormitories. 160-acre campus. 20 buildings on campus. Approved or accredited by Association of Christian Schools International and South Dakota Department of Education. Total enrollment: 100. Upper school average class size: 22. Upper school faculty-student ratio: 1:9. There are 180 required school days per year for Upper School students. Upper School students typically attend 5 days per week. The average school day consists of 6 hours and 40 minutes.

Upper School Student Profile Grade 9: 18 students (12 boys, 6 girls); Grade 10: 16 students (6 boys, 10 girls); Grade 11: 23 students (15 boys, 8 girls); Grade 12: 20 students (10 boys, 10 girls). 91% of students are boarding students. 70% are state residents. 7 states are represented in upper school student body. 19% are international students. International students from Ethiopia and Republic of Korea. 100% of students are Christian faith.

Faculty School total: 12. In upper school: 7 men, 5 women; 3 have advanced degrees; 11 reside on campus.

Subjects Offered Accounting, advanced math, algebra, American history, American literature, band, bell choir, Bible, Bible studies, biology, chemistry, choir, Christian doctrine, Christian ethics, computer science, creative writing, drama, drama performance, economics, English, English literature, ethics, fine arts, geography, geometry, government/civics, grammar, health, history, HTML design, journalism, mathematics, music, music appreciation, music composition, music history, music performance, newspaper, physical education, physics, science, social sciences, social studies, Spanish, speech, speech and oral interpretations, trigonometry, typing, U.S. government, U.S. history, vocal music, world geography, world history, writing, yearbook.

Graduation Requirements Arts and fine arts (art, music, dance, drama), Bible, computer science, English, mathematics, science, social sciences, social studies (includes history).

Special Academic Programs Independent study; academic accommodation for the musically talented; remedial math.

College Admission Counseling 10 students graduated in 2011; 10 went to college. Other: 7 went to work, 1 entered military service. Median composite ACT: 23. 8% scored over 26 on composite ACT.

Student Life Upper grades have specified standards of dress, student council, honor system. Discipline rests primarily with faculty. Attendance at religious services is required.

Tuition and Aid Day student tuition: $5460; 5-day tuition and room/board: $7800; 7-day tuition and room/board: $7800. Guaranteed tuition plan. Tuition installment plan (monthly payment plans). Tuition reduction for siblings, need-based scholarship grants available. In 2011–12, 25% of upper-school students received aid. Total amount of financial aid awarded in 2011–12: $31,500.

Admissions Traditional secondary-level entrance grade is 9. For fall 2011, 80 students applied for upper-level admission, 79 were accepted, 77 enrolled. Deadline for receipt of application materials: none. Application fee required: $50. On-campus interview required.

Athletics Interscholastic: basketball (boys, girls), cheering (g), cross-country running (b,g), football (b), track and field (b,g), volleyball (g), wrestling (b); intramural: physical fitness (b,g), physical training (b,g), strength & conditioning (b,g), weight lifting (b,g), weight training (b,g). 1 PE instructor, 6 coaches.

Computers Computers are regularly used in journalism, newspaper, publications, publishing, research skills, speech, typing, Web site design, writing, yearbook classes. Computer resources include on-campus library services, Internet access, wireless campus network, Internet filtering or blocking technology. Student e-mail accounts are available to students.

Contact Andrew Boersma, Dean of Students. 605-853-3071. Fax: 605-853-3072. Web site: www.sunshinebible.org.

TABOR ACADEMY

66 Spring Street

Marion, Massachusetts 02738

Head of School: Mr. Jay S. Stroud

General Information Coeducational boarding and day college-preparatory and arts school. Grades 9–12. Founded: 1876. Setting: suburban. Nearest major city is Boston. Students are housed in single-sex dormitories. 85-acre campus. 42 buildings on campus. Approved or accredited by Association of Independent Schools in New England, New England Association of Schools and Colleges, and The Association of Boarding Schools. Member of National Association of Independent Schools and Secondary School Admission Test Board. Endowment: $36.5 million. Total enrollment: 519. Upper school average class size: 12. Upper school faculty-student ratio: 1:6. There are 157 required school days per year for Upper School students. Upper School students typically attend 5 days per week. The average school day consists of 7 hours.

Upper School Student Profile Grade 9: 92 students (47 boys, 45 girls); Grade 10: 141 students (78 boys, 63 girls); Grade 11: 129 students (74 boys, 55 girls); Grade 12: 157 students (92 boys, 65 girls). 69% of students are boarding students. 58% are state residents. 20 states are represented in upper school student body. 18% are international students. International students from China, Germany, Japan, Republic of Korea, Taiwan, and Viet Nam; 13 other countries represented in student body.

Faculty School total: 90. In upper school: 52 men, 38 women; 55 have advanced degrees; 59 reside on campus.

Subjects Offered Algebra, American history, American literature, ancient history, architecture, art, art history, astronomy, biology, calculus, celestial navigation, ceramics, chemistry, creative writing, drama, ecology, economics, English, English literature, European history, fine arts, French, freshman foundations, geology, geometry, German, Greek, health, history, Latin, maritime history, mathematics, meteorology, microbiology, music, navigation, oceanography, photography, physics, physiology, science, social sciences, social studies, Spanish, speech, statistics, theater, trigonometry, world history, world literature.

Graduation Requirements Algebra, arts and fine arts (art, music, dance, drama), biology, English, foreign language, geometry, mathematics, science, social sciences, social studies (includes history).

Special Academic Programs Advanced Placement exam preparation; honors section; independent study; term-away projects; academic accommodation for the gifted, the musically talented, and the artistically talented; ESL (12 students enrolled).

College Admission Counseling 132 students graduated in 2011; 127 went to college, including Boston College; Boston University; Hobart and William Smith Colleges; The George Washington University; University of Colorado Boulder; University of Vermont. Other: 1 entered a postgraduate year, 4 had other specific plans. Mean SAT critical reading: 592, mean SAT math: 619, mean SAT writing: 592, mean combined SAT: 1812.

Student Life Upper grades have specified standards of dress, student council, honor system. Discipline rests primarily with faculty.

Summer Programs Enrichment programs offered; session focuses on summer camp; held on campus; accepts boys and girls; open to students from other schools. 500 students usually enrolled. 2012 schedule: June 26 to August 7. Application deadline: none.

Tuition and Aid Day student tuition: $34,000; 7-day tuition and room/board: $47,500. Tuition installment plan (Academic Management Services Plan, Key Tuition Payment Plan, monthly payment plans, Tuition Management Systems Plan). Need-based scholarship grants available. In 2011–12, 30% of upper-school students received aid. Total amount of financial aid awarded in 2011–12: $3,650,000.

Admissions Traditional secondary-level entrance grade is 9. For fall 2011, 806 students applied for upper-level admission, 415 were accepted, 160 enrolled. ISEE, PSAT or SSAT required. Deadline for receipt of application materials: January 31. Application fee required: $50. Interview required.

Athletics Interscholastic: baseball (boys), basketball (b,g), crew (b,g), cross-country running (b,g), field hockey (g), football (b), ice hockey (b,g), lacrosse (b,g), sailing (b,g), soccer (b,g), softball (g), squash (b,g), tennis (b,g), track and field (b,g), wrestling (b); intramural: crew (b,g), ice hockey (g), squash (b,g), tennis (b,g); coed interscholastic: dance, dance team, golf; coed intramural: aerobics, canoeing/kayaking, combined training, dance, fitness, Frisbee, kayaking, physical training, sailing, strength & conditioning, weight training. 2 athletic trainers.

Computers Computers are regularly used in English, foreign language, history, literary magazine, mathematics, newspaper, photography, publications, science, yearbook classes. Computer network features include on-campus library services, online commercial services, Internet access, wireless campus network, Internet filtering or blocking technology, digital media labs. Campus intranet, student e-mail accounts, and computer access in designated common areas are available to students. The school has a published electronic and media policy.

Contact Leslie Geil, Admissions Assistant. 508-291-8300. Fax: 508-291-8301. E-mail: admissions@taboracademy.org. Web site: www.taboracademy.org.

THE TAFT SCHOOL

110 Woodbury Road

Watertown, Connecticut 06795

Head of School: Mr. William R. MacMullen

General Information Coeducational boarding and day college-preparatory, arts, and humanities school. Grades 9–PG. Founded: 1890. Setting: small town. Nearest major city is Waterbury. Students are housed in single-sex dormitories. 224-acre campus. 20 buildings on campus. Approved or accredited by Connecticut Association of Independent Schools, New England Association of Schools and Colleges, The Association of Boarding Schools, The College Board, and Connecticut Department of Education.

Member of National Association of Independent Schools and Secondary School Admission Test Board. Endowment: $206 million. Total enrollment: 585. Upper school average class size: 12. Upper school faculty-student ratio: 1:5. Upper School students typically attend 6 days per week. The average school day consists of 7 hours.

Upper School Student Profile Grade 9: 94 students (50 boys, 44 girls); Grade 10: 155 students (79 boys, 76 girls); Grade 11: 155 students (76 boys, 79 girls); Grade 12: 166 students (78 boys, 88 girls); Postgraduate: 17 students (15 boys, 2 girls). 80% of students are boarding students. 36% are state residents. 37 states are represented in upper school student body. 15% are international students. International students from Canada, China, Hong Kong, Japan, Republic of Korea, and Taiwan; 24 other countries represented in student body.

Faculty School total: 127. In upper school: 70 men, 57 women; 91 have advanced degrees; 112 reside on campus.

Subjects Offered Acting, adolescent issues, advanced biology, advanced chemistry, advanced computer applications, advanced math, Advanced Placement courses, advanced studio art-AP, African-American literature, algebra, American history, American history-AP, American literature, anatomy, anatomy and physiology, animal behavior, architectural drawing, architecture, art, art history, art history-AP, astronomy, biology, biology-AP, calculus, calculus-AP, ceramics, chamber groups, character education, chemistry, chemistry-AP, Chinese, computer math, computer programming, computer science, computer science-AP, concert choir, creative writing, dance, design, digital imaging, drama, drawing, ecology, economics, economics-AP, English, English literature, English literature-AP, environmental science, environmental science-AP, ethics, European history, European history-AP, expository writing, film studies, fine arts, forensics, French, French language-AP, geography, geology, geometry, government-AP, government/civics, grammar, Greek, history, history of rock and roll, history of science, honors algebra, honors English, honors geometry, human rights, humanities, Islamic studies, Japanese, jazz band, Latin, Mandarin, marine biology, mathematics, music, music theory-AP, philosophy, photography, physical education, physics, physics-AP, physiology, pre-calculus, psychology, religion, science, senior project, senior thesis, service learning/internship, sex education, South African history, Spanish, Spanish literature-AP, Spanish-AP, speech, statistics, statistics-AP, studio art-AP, theater, theology, trigonometry, U.S. government and politics-AP, U.S. history-AP, video film production, world history, world literature, writing, zoology.

Graduation Requirements American history, arts and fine arts (art, music, dance, drama), English, foreign language, mathematics, science, social studies (includes history), three semesters of arts, senior thesis.

Special Academic Programs 27 Advanced Placement exams for which test preparation is offered; honors section; independent study; term-away projects; study abroad; academic accommodation for the gifted, the musically talented, and the artistically talented.

College Admission Counseling 154 students graduated in 2011; 152 went to college, including Amherst College; Cornell University; The George Washington University; Trinity College; University of Pennsylvania; Wake Forest University. Other: 1 entered a postgraduate year, 1 had other specific plans. Mean SAT critical reading: 647, mean SAT math: 656, mean SAT writing: 662, mean combined SAT: 1964. 75% scored over 600 on SAT critical reading, 75% scored over 600 on SAT math, 76% scored over 600 on SAT writing, 78% scored over 1800 on combined SAT.

Student Life Upper grades have specified standards of dress, student council, honor system. Discipline rests equally with students and faculty.

Summer Programs Enrichment, ESL, sports, art/fine arts programs offered; session focuses on academic enrichment; held on campus; accepts boys and girls; open to students from other schools. 150 students usually enrolled. 2012 schedule: June 28 to August 1. Application deadline: none.

Tuition and Aid Day student tuition: $34,400; 7-day tuition and room/board: $46,500. Tuition installment plan (Key Tuition Payment Plan). Need-based scholarship grants, need-based loans available. In 2011–12, 37% of upper-school students received aid. Total amount of financial aid awarded in 2011–12: $6,700,000.

Admissions Traditional secondary-level entrance grade is 9. For fall 2011, 1,620 students applied for upper-level admission, 382 were accepted, 199 enrolled. SSAT required. Deadline for receipt of application materials: January 15. Application fee required: $50. Interview required.

Athletics Interscholastic: alpine skiing (boys, girls), baseball (b), basketball (b,g), crew (b,g), cross-country running (b,g), field hockey (g), football (b), golf (b,g), hockey (b,g), ice hockey (b,g), lacrosse (b,g), rowing (b,g), soccer (b,g), softball (g), squash (b,g), tennis (b,g), track and field (b,g), ultimate Frisbee (b,g), volleyball (g), wrestling (b); coed interscholastic: dressage, equestrian sports, horseback riding; coed intramural: aerobics, aerobics/dance, ballet, basketball, climbing, cross-country running, dance, dressage, equestrian sports, figure skating, fitness, fitness walking, Frisbee, hockey, horseback riding, ice hockey, ice skating, jogging, martial arts, modern dance, outdoor activities, physical fitness, rock climbing, rowing, running, soccer, squash, strength & conditioning, tennis, track and field, ultimate Frisbee, walking, wall climbing, weight lifting, weight training, yoga. 1 coach, 3 athletic trainers.

Computers Computers are regularly used in art, English, foreign language, geography, history, mathematics, music, science classes. Computer network features include on-campus library services, online commercial services, Internet access, wireless campus network. Campus intranet, student e-mail accounts, and computer access in designated common areas are available to students. The school has a published electronic and media policy.

Contact Mr. Peter A. Frew, Director of Admissions. 860-945-7700. Fax: 860-945-7808. E-mail: admissions@taftschool.org. Web site: www.taftschool.org.

TAIPEI AMERICAN SCHOOL

800 Chung Shan North Road, Section 6

Taipei 11152, Taiwan

Head of School: Dr. Sharon Hennessy

General Information Coeducational day college-preparatory school. Grades PK–12. Founded: 1949. Setting: urban. 15-acre campus. 4 buildings on campus. Approved or accredited by International Baccalaureate Organization, US Department of State, and Western Association of Schools and Colleges. Affiliate member of National Association of Independent Schools; member of European Council of International Schools. Language of instruction: English. Endowment: $29 million. Total enrollment: 2,192. Upper school average class size: 17. Upper school faculty-student ratio: 1:10. There are 180 required school days per year for Upper School students. Upper School students typically attend 5 days per week. The average school day consists of 6 hours and 40 minutes.

Upper School Student Profile Grade 9: 221 students (115 boys, 106 girls); Grade 10: 218 students (96 boys, 122 girls); Grade 11: 231 students (117 boys, 114 girls); Grade 12: 216 students (95 boys, 121 girls).

Faculty School total: 240. In upper school: 52 men, 50 women; 83 have advanced degrees.

Subjects Offered Advanced math, Advanced Placement courses, advanced studio art-AP, algebra, American literature, art history, Asian studies, biology, business, calculus, ceramics, chemistry, chemistry-AP, Chinese, choir, computer science, computer science-AP, contemporary history, current history, dance, digital photography, drawing, earth science, English, English language-AP, English literature-AP, environmental science-AP, European history-AP, expository writing, fitness, French, French-AP, geography, geometry, health, International Baccalaureate courses, Japanese, jazz ensemble, journalism, linear algebra, macro/microeconomics-AP, macroeconomics-AP, microeconomics-AP, music theory-AP, orchestra, physical education, physics, physics-AP, pre-algebra, pre-calculus, psychology, research seminar, rhetoric, robotics, Spanish, Spanish-AP, speech and debate, statistics-AP, theater, theory of knowledge, trigonometry, U.S. history, U.S. history-AP, video film production, visual arts, wind ensemble, world cultures, world history, world literature, yearbook.

Graduation Requirements English, mathematics, modern languages, physical education (includes health), public speaking, science, social studies (includes history).

Special Academic Programs International Baccalaureate program; 26 Advanced Placement exams for which test preparation is offered; honors section; ESL.

College Admission Counseling 206 students graduated in 2011; 204 went to college, including New York University; University of California, Berkeley; University of California, Los Angeles; University of California, San Diego; University of Southern California; University of Toronto. Other: 2 had other specific plans. Mean SAT critical reading: 596, mean SAT math: 691, mean SAT writing: 624, mean combined SAT: 1911.

Student Life Upper grades have specified standards of dress, student council, honor system. Discipline rests primarily with faculty.

Summer Programs Remediation, enrichment, advancement, computer instruction programs offered; session focuses on internships, advancement, and make-up courses; honors math and science, robotics, writing, public speaking; held on campus; accepts boys and girls; open to students from other schools. 400 students usually enrolled. 2012 schedule: June 4 to July 1. Application deadline: May 30.

Tuition and Aid Day student tuition: 534,560 Taiwan dollars. Tuition installment plan (individually arranged payment plans).

Admissions Traditional secondary-level entrance grade is 9. For fall 2011, 170 students applied for upper-level admission, 110 were accepted, 83 enrolled. California Achievement Test, English for Non-native Speakers, ERB CTP IV, Iowa Tests of Basic Skills, ISEE, latest standardized score from previous school, PSAT, SAT, SSAT or Stanford Achievement Test required. Deadline for receipt of application materials: none. Application fee required: 10,000 Taiwan dollars.

Athletics Interscholastic: badminton (boys, girls), basketball (b,g), cross-country running (b,g), dance (b,g), golf (b,g), rugby (b,g), soccer (b,g), softball (b,g), swimming and diving (b,g), tennis (b,g), track and field (b,g), volleyball (b,g); intramural: swimming and diving (b,g).

Computers Computers are regularly used in all academic classes. Computer network features include on-campus library services, online commercial services, Internet access, wireless campus network, Internet filtering or blocking technology. Campus intranet, student e-mail accounts, and computer access in designated common areas are available to students. Students grades are available online. The school has a published electronic and media policy.

Contact Dr. Winnie Tang, Admissions Officer. 886-2-2873-9900 Ext. 328. Fax: 886-2-2873-1641. E-mail: admissions@tas.edu.tw. Web site: www.tas.edu.tw.

TAKOMA ACADEMY

8120 Carroll Avenue

Takoma Park, Maryland 20912-7397

Head of School: Mr. David Daniels

General Information Coeducational day college-preparatory and religious studies school, affiliated with Seventh-day Adventist Church. Grades 9–12. Founded: 1904. Setting: urban. 10-acre campus. 1 building on campus. Approved or accredited by Middle States Association of Colleges and Schools and Maryland Department of Education. Endowment: $400,000. Total enrollment: 230. Upper school average class size: 20. Upper school faculty-student ratio: 1:12. There are 180 required school days per year for Upper School students. Upper School students typically attend 5 days per week. The average school day consists of 5 hours and 20 minutes.

Upper School Student Profile Grade 9: 55 students (23 boys, 32 girls); Grade 10: 59 students (35 boys, 24 girls); Grade 11: 47 students (32 boys, 15 girls); Grade 12: 68 students (25 boys, 43 girls). 80% of students are Seventh-day Adventists.

Faculty School total: 20. In upper school: 9 men, 11 women; 8 have advanced degrees.

Subjects Offered Accounting, Advanced Placement courses, algebra, American government, American history, anatomy and physiology, art, art and culture, auto mechanics, band, Bible, biology, calculus-AP, career and personal planning, chemistry, choir, computer applications, computer skills, conceptual physics, drama performance, earth science, English, English-AP, geography, geometry, handbells, health education, honors algebra, honors English, honors geometry, honors U.S. history, honors world history, personal finance, physical education, physics, pre-calculus, Spanish, U.S. government and politics, U.S. government and politics-AP, world history.

Special Academic Programs Advanced Placement exam preparation; honors section; study at local college for college credit; remedial reading and/or remedial writing.

College Admission Counseling 70 students graduated in 2011.

Student Life Upper grades have uniform requirement, student council, honor system. Discipline rests primarily with faculty. Attendance at religious services is required.

Summer Programs Remediation, enrichment programs offered; held on campus; accepts boys and girls.

Tuition and Aid Tuition installment plan (FACTS Tuition Payment Plan). Tuition reduction for siblings, merit scholarship grants, need-based scholarship grants, paying campus jobs available.

Admissions Traditional secondary-level entrance grade is 9. Application fee required: $75. On-campus interview recommended.

Athletics Interscholastic: basketball (boys, girls), cross-country running (b,g), flag football (b); intramural: basketball (b,g). 1 PE instructor.

Computers Computer resources include on-campus library services, Internet access, wireless campus network, Internet filtering or blocking technology. Campus intranet and student e-mail accounts are available to students. Students grades are available online.

Contact Mrs. Leah Daniels, Assistant Registrar. 301-434-4700. Fax: 301-434-4814. E-mail: ldaniels@ta.edu. Web site: www.ta.edu.

TANDEM FRIENDS SCHOOL

279 Tandem Lane

Charlottesville, Virginia 22902

Head of School: Andy Jones-Wilkins

General Information Coeducational day college-preparatory and arts school, affiliated with Society of Friends. Grades 5–12. Founded: 1970. Setting: small town. Nearest major city is Richmond. 23-acre campus. 7 buildings on campus. Approved or accredited by Friends Council on Education and Virginia Association of Independent Schools. Member of National Association of Independent Schools. Endowment: $3.3 million. Total enrollment: 196. Upper school average class size: 12. Upper school faculty-student ratio: 1:6. There are 180 required school days per year for Upper School students. Upper School students typically attend 5 days per week. The average school day consists of 7 hours.

Upper School Student Profile Grade 9: 20 students (11 boys, 9 girls); Grade 10: 27 students (9 boys, 18 girls); Grade 11: 28 students (12 boys, 16 girls); Grade 12: 35 students (18 boys, 17 girls). 3% of students are members of Society of Friends.

Faculty School total: 40. In upper school: 8 men, 9 women; 10 have advanced degrees.

Subjects Offered Algebra, American literature, anatomy, art, bioethics, biology, biology-AP, calculus, calculus-AP, ceramics, chemistry, chemistry-AP, college counseling, computer applications, creative writing, cultural geography, discrete mathematics, drama, economics, economics and history, English, English-AP, environmental science-AP, expository writing, fine arts, French, French-AP, geometry, health and wellness, jazz ensemble, Latin, Latin-AP, marine biology, media studies, modern world history, music, musical productions, performing arts, photo shop, photography, physics, Quakerism and ethics, senior project, Spanish, Spanish-AP, statistics, statistics-AP, student government, student publications, studio art, theater, trigonometry, U.S. government, U.S. history, U.S. history-AP, weaving, world history, world literature, writing, yearbook.

Graduation Requirements Arts and fine arts (art, music, dance, drama), computer science, English, foreign language, government/civics, history, mathematics, science, senior year independent experiential learning project. Community service is required.

Special Academic Programs Advanced Placement exam preparation; independent study; academic accommodation for the gifted; remedial reading and/or remedial writing; remedial math.

College Admission Counseling 36 students graduated in 2011; 32 went to college, including Dartmouth College; George Mason University; Guilford College; Temple University; The College of William and Mary; University of Virginia. Other: 4 had other specific plans. Median SAT critical reading: 634, median SAT math: 622, median SAT writing: 651, median combined SAT: 1256, median composite ACT: 26.

Student Life Upper grades have student council, honor system. Discipline rests equally with students and faculty. Attendance at religious services is required.

Tuition and Aid Day student tuition: $16,750. Tuition installment plan (Insured Tuition Payment Plan, monthly payment plans, individually arranged payment plans). Need-based scholarship grants, tuition remission for children of full-time faculty available. In 2011–12, 30% of upper-school students received aid. Total amount of financial aid awarded in 2011–12: $379,110.

Admissions Traditional secondary-level entrance grade is 9. For fall 2011, 17 students applied for upper-level admission, 15 were accepted, 13 enrolled. Woodcock-Johnson required. Deadline for receipt of application materials: none. Application fee required: $50. Interview required.

Athletics Interscholastic: basketball (boys, girls), field hockey (g), lacrosse (b,g), soccer (b,g), tennis (b,g), volleyball (g); coed interscholastic: cross-country running, fencing, golf, mountain biking; coed intramural: fencing. 2 PE instructors, 16 coaches.

Computers Computers are regularly used in all academic classes. Computer network features include on-campus library services, online commercial services, Internet access, wireless campus network, Internet filtering or blocking technology, virtual classroom. Student e-mail accounts and computer access in designated common areas are available to students. Students grades are available online. The school has a published electronic and media policy.

Contact Louise DeCamp Cole, Director of Admissions. 434-951-9314. Fax: 434-296-1886. E-mail: lcole@tandemfs.org. Web site: www.tandemfs.org.

TASIS THE AMERICAN SCHOOL IN ENGLAND

Coldharbour Lane

Thorpe, Surrey TW20 8TE, United Kingdom

Head of School: Mr. Michael McBrien

General Information Coeducational boarding and day college-preparatory and arts school. Boarding grades 9–13, day grades N–13. Founded: 1976. Setting: rural. Nearest major city is London, United Kingdom. Students are housed in single-sex dormitories. 46-acre campus. 26 buildings on campus. Approved or accredited by Council of International Schools, International Baccalaureate Organization, New England Association of Schools and Colleges, Office for Standards in Education (OFSTED), The Association of Boarding Schools, and state department of education. Affiliate member of National Association of Independent Schools; member of Secondary School Admission Test Board and European Council of International Schools. Language of instruction: English. Total enrollment: 750. Upper school average class size: 15. Upper school faculty-student ratio: 1:8. There are 171 required school days per year for Upper School students. Upper School students typically attend 5 days per week. The average school day consists of 6 hours.

Upper School Student Profile Grade 9: 70 students (38 boys, 32 girls); Grade 10: 85 students (47 boys, 38 girls); Grade 11: 115 students (60 boys, 55 girls); Grade 12: 120 students (60 boys, 60 girls). 46% of students are boarding students. 39% are international students. International students from China, Russian Federation, Saudi Arabia, Spain, Taiwan, and United States; 36 other countries represented in student body.

Faculty School total: 112. In upper school: 24 men, 27 women; 38 have advanced degrees; 23 reside on campus.

Subjects Offered 20th century history, acting, algebra, American history, American history-AP, American literature, ancient history, art, art history, art history-AP, biology, biology-AP, calculus-AP, ceramics, chemistry, chemistry-AP, choir, computer graphics, computer science-AP, debate, drawing, economics, economics-AP, English, English language and composition-AP, English literature, English literature and composition-AP, ensembles, environmental science, environmental science-AP, ESL, European history, European history-AP, French, French-AP, geometry, German, government and politics-AP, health and wellness, humanities, international affairs, international relations, Internet, journalism, keyboarding, Latin, Latin-AP, mathematics, music, music technology, music theory, music theory-AP, painting, photography, physical education, physical science, physics, physics-AP, pre-calculus, printmaking, psychology, public speaking, Russian, sculpture, senior humanities, Shakespeare, Spanish, Spanish-AP, statistics-AP, theater arts, theory of knowledge, visual arts, Web site design, Western civilization, word processing, world history, yearbook.

Graduation Requirements Arts and fine arts (art, music, dance, drama), computer science, English, foreign language, history, lab science, mathematics, physical education (includes health), senior humanities, sports. Community service is required.

Special Academic Programs International Baccalaureate program; 21 Advanced Placement exams for which test preparation is offered; independent study; academic accommodation for the gifted; remedial reading and/or remedial writing; ESL (76 students enrolled).

College Admission Counseling 107 students graduated in 2011; 106 went to college, including McGill University; Texas A&M University; University of Richmond; University of South Carolina; University of Southern California. Other: 1 had other specific plans.

Student Life Upper grades have uniform requirement, student council. Discipline rests primarily with faculty.

Summer Programs Remediation, enrichment, advancement, ESL, sports, art/fine arts, computer instruction programs offered; session focuses on ESL, academics, enrichment, and theater; held on campus; accepts boys and girls; open to students from other schools. 420 students usually enrolled. 2012 schedule: June 23 to August 4. Application deadline: none.

Tuition and Aid Day student tuition: £19,210; 7-day tuition and room/board: £32,130. Tuition installment plan (monthly payment plans, individually arranged payment plans). Need-based scholarship grants available.

Admissions TOEFL or SLEP required. Deadline for receipt of application materials: none. Application fee required: £125. Interview recommended.

Athletics Interscholastic: baseball (boys), basketball (b,g), cross-country running (b,g), rugby (b), soccer (b,g), softball (g), tennis (b,g), volleyball (b,g); intramural: aerobics (g), aerobics/dance (g), badminton (b,g), ballet (g), cricket (b,g), dance (g), dance team (g), field hockey (b,g), fitness (b,g), floor hockey (b,g), gymnastics (b,g), handball (b,g), indoor soccer (b,g), jump rope (b,g), lacrosse (b,g), modern dance (b,g), outdoor activities (b,g), outdoor adventure (b,g), physical fitness (b,g), physical training (b,g), rhythmic gymnastics (b,g), rugby (b), running (b,g), scooter football (b,g), soccer (b,g), softball (b,g), strength & conditioning (b,g), team handball (b,g), weight training (b,g), winter soccer (b,g); coed interscholastic: cheering, golf; coed intramural: basketball, bicycling, golf, gymnastics, handball, horseback riding, indoor soccer, lacrosse, martial arts, outdoor activities, outdoor adventure, squash, strength & conditioning, swimming and diving, table tennis, team handball, tennis, track and field, volleyball, weight training, winter soccer. 5 PE instructors, 10 coaches, 1 athletic trainer.

Computers Computers are regularly used in all academic classes. Computer network features include on-campus library services, online commercial services, Internet access, wireless campus network, Internet filtering or blocking technology. Campus intranet, student e-mail accounts, and computer access in designated common areas are available to students. The school has a published electronic and media policy.

Contact Ms. Karen House, Director of Admissions. 44-1932-582316. Fax: 44-1932-564644. E-mail: ukadmissions@tasisengland.org. Web site: www.tasis.com/England/.

See Display below and Close-Up on page 688.

TASIS, THE AMERICAN SCHOOL IN SWITZERLAND

Via Collina d'Oro

Montagnola-Lugano CH-6926, Switzerland

Head of School: Mr. Michael Ulku-Steiner

General Information Coeducational boarding and day college-preparatory, arts, and sports school. Boarding grades 7–PG, day grades 1–PG. Founded: 1956. Setting: small town. Nearest major city is Lugano, Switzerland. Students are housed in single-sex dormitories. 9-acre campus. 19 buildings on campus. Approved or accredited by New England Association of Schools and Colleges and Swiss Federation of Private Schools. Affiliate member of National Association of Independent Schools; member of Secondary School Admission Test Board. Language of instruction: English. Total enrollment: 642. Upper school average class size: 14. Upper school faculty-student ratio: 1:5. Upper School students typically attend 5 days per week.

Upper School Student Profile Grade 9: 61 students (30 boys, 31 girls); Grade 10: 82 students (41 boys, 41 girls); Grade 11: 114 students (57 boys, 57 girls); Grade 12: 78 students (32 boys, 46 girls); Postgraduate: 4 students (4 girls). 80% of students are boarding students. 82% are international students. International students from Brazil, Germany, Italy, and United States; 4 other countries represented in student body.

Faculty In upper school: 30 men, 39 women; 39 have advanced degrees; 32 reside on campus.

Subjects Offered Advanced Placement courses, algebra, American history, American literature, ancient history, art, art history, art history-AP, biology, biology-AP, calculus, calculus-AP, ceramics, chemistry, chemistry-AP, digital photography, drama, economics, economics-AP, English, English language and composition-AP, English literature, English literature and composition-AP, environmental science, ESL, European history, European history-AP, fine arts, French, French language-AP, geography, geometry, German-AP, graphic design, health, history, international relations, Italian, mathematics, medieval/Renaissance history, music, photography, physical education, physics, science, social studies, Spanish, Spanish language-AP, theater, theory of knowledge, U.S. government, U.S. history-AP, world cultures, world history, world literature.

Graduation Requirements Arts, English, European history, foreign language, mathematics, science, senior humanities, sports, U.S. history. Community service is required.

Special Academic Programs International Baccalaureate program; Advanced Placement exam preparation; honors section; ESL (235 students enrolled).

College Admission Counseling 72 students graduated in 2011; 70 went to college, including Pace University; The American University of Paris; The George Washington

University. Other: 2 entered a postgraduate year. Median SAT critical reading: 570, median SAT math: 570. 30% scored over 600 on SAT critical reading, 22% scored over 600 on SAT math.

Student Life Upper grades have specified standards of dress, student council, honor system. Discipline rests equally with students and faculty.

Summer Programs ESL, sports, art/fine arts programs offered; session focuses on languages, sports, and arts; held both on and off campus; held at TASIS Lugano Campus and Chateau d'Oex; accepts boys and girls; open to students from other schools. 650 students usually enrolled. 2012 schedule: June 25 to August 13. Application deadline: none.

Tuition and Aid Day student tuition: 43,140 Swiss francs; 7-day tuition and room/board: 69,000 Swiss francs. Tuition installment plan (individually arranged payment plans). Need-based scholarship grants available. In 2011–12, 15% of upper-school students received aid.

Admissions Traditional secondary-level entrance grade is 11. TOEFL or SLEP required. Deadline for receipt of application materials: none. Application fee required: 300 Swiss francs. Interview recommended.

Athletics Interscholastic: basketball (boys, girls), golf (b), rugby (b), soccer (b,g), swimming and diving (b,g), tennis (b,g), track and field (b,g), volleyball (b,g); intramural: basketball (b,g), rugby (b); coed interscholastic: softball, swimming and diving, track and field; coed intramural: aerobics, aerobics/dance, aerobics/Nautilus, basketball, climbing, combined training, cross-country running, dance, fitness, flag football, floor hockey, golf, horseback riding, indoor soccer, jogging, lacrosse, martial arts, modern dance, physical fitness, physical training, rock climbing, running, sailing, soccer, softball, squash, strength & conditioning, swimming and diving, tennis, ultimate Frisbee, volleyball, weight lifting, weight training. 2 PE instructors.

Computers Computers are regularly used in art, English, ESL, foreign language, history, photography, science classes. Computer network features include on-campus library services, Internet access, wireless campus network, Internet filtering or blocking technology. Student e-mail accounts are available to students. Students grades are available online. The school has a published electronic and media policy.

Contact William E. Eichner, Director of Admissions. 41-91-960-5151. Fax: 41-91-993-2979. E-mail: admissions@tasis.ch. Web site: www.tasis.com.

See Display below, Close-Up on page 690, and Summer Program Close-Up on page 778.

TELLURIDE MOUNTAIN SCHOOL

200 San Miguel River Drive

Telluride, Colorado 81435

Head of School: Mr. Joseph Stefani

General Information Coeducational day college-preparatory, arts, technology, and music, visual and dramatic arts school. Grades PK–12. Founded: 1999. Setting: small town. Nearest major city is Denver. 1 building on campus. Approved or accredited by Association of Colorado Independent Schools and Colorado Department of Education. Member of National Association of Independent Schools. Upper school average class size: 8.

Subjects Offered Algebra, alternative physical education, American Civil War, American history, American literature, ancient world history, applied music, art, backpacking, biology, calculus, character education, chemistry, civil rights, college admission preparation, college counseling, college planning, community service, computer education, computer literacy, computer multimedia, computer music, CPR, creative writing, critical thinking, critical writing, digital music, drama, dramatic arts, English composition, English literature, environmental education, European history, film studies, geography, geology, geometry, grammar, guitar, history, history of rock and roll, instrumental music, Internet research, keyboarding, Latin American literature, leadership, leadership and service, music, music performance, music technology, outdoor education, painting, portfolio writing, pre-algebra, pre-calculus, public speaking, reading/study skills, Spanish, Spanish literature, studio art, trigonometry, video film production, visual arts, white-water trips, wilderness education, world history.

Graduation Requirements Algebra, biology, chemistry, college admission preparation, college counseling, dramatic arts, English, English composition, English literature, geometry, grammar, history, music, physics, pre-calculus, Spanish, trigonometry, U.S. history, visual arts, wilderness education, world history.

Special Academic Programs Study abroad.

College Admission Counseling 4 students graduated in 2011; 2 went to college. Other: 2 had other specific plans.

Student Life Upper grades have specified standards of dress.

Tuition and Aid Day student tuition: $17,250. Tuition installment plan (monthly payment plans, individually arranged payment plans). Need-based scholarship grants available. In 2011–12, 30% of upper-school students received aid.

Admissions Traditional secondary-level entrance grade is 9. Deadline for receipt of application materials: none. Application fee required: $50. Interview required.

Athletics Interscholastic: alpine skiing (boys, girls), freestyle skiing (b,g), skiing (cross-country) (b,g), skiing (downhill) (b,g), snowboarding (b,g), soccer (b); coed interscholastic: backpacking, canoeing/kayaking, climbing, cooperative games, fly fishing, hiking/backpacking, hockey, kayaking, mountaineering, nordic skiing, outdoor activities, outdoor adventure, outdoor education, outdoor recreation, outdoor skills, outdoors, rafting, rappelling, rock climbing, wilderness, wilderness survival, yoga; coed intramural: alpine skiing, ice hockey, lacrosse, rock climbing, snowshoeing, telemark skiing, wilderness. 1 PE instructor, 5 coaches.

Computers Computers are regularly used in all classes. Computer network features include Internet access, wireless campus network. Campus intranet, student e-mail accounts, and computer access in designated common areas are available to students. The school has a published electronic and media policy.

Contact Mrs. Robin Hope, Program Coordinator. 970-728-1969. Fax: 970-369-4412. E-mail: rhope@telluridemtnschool.org. Web site: www.telluridemtnschool.org/.

THE TENNEY SCHOOL

2055 South Gessner

Houston, Texas 77063

Head of School: Mr. Michael E. Tenney

General Information Coeducational day college-preparatory and general academic school; primarily serves students with learning disabilities and individuals with Attention Deficit Disorder. Grades 6–12. Founded: 1973. Setting: suburban. 1-acre campus. 1 building on campus. Approved or accredited by Southern Association of Colleges and Schools and Texas Department of Education. Total enrollment: 62. Upper school average class size: 1. Upper school faculty-student ratio: 1:2. There are 170 required school days per year for Upper School students. Upper School students typically attend 5 days per week. The average school day consists of 5 hours and 30 minutes.

Upper School Student Profile Grade 9: 9 students (6 boys, 3 girls); Grade 10: 12 students (7 boys, 5 girls); Grade 11: 16 students (12 boys, 4 girls); Grade 12: 12 students (5 boys, 7 girls).

Faculty School total: 25. In upper school: 3 men, 22 women; 13 have advanced degrees.

Subjects Offered Accounting, algebra, American history, American literature, biology, British literature, business law, calculus, chemistry, computer programming, computer studies, creative writing, economics, English, fine arts, geometry, government, health, independent study, journalism, keyboarding, mathematics, microcomputer technology applications, physical education, physical science, physics, precalculus, psychology, science, social studies, sociology, Spanish, studio art, theater arts, world geography, world history, world literature, yearbook.

Graduation Requirements American government, American history.

Special Academic Programs Advanced Placement exam preparation; honors section; academic accommodation for the gifted, the musically talented, and the artistically talented; remedial reading and/or remedial writing; remedial math; special instructional classes for deaf students; ESL (10 students enrolled).

College Admission Counseling 10 students graduated in 2011; all went to college, including Houston Baptist University; Texas A&M University; The University of Texas at Austin; University of Houston.

Student Life Upper grades have specified standards of dress. Discipline rests primarily with faculty.

Summer Programs Remediation, enrichment, advancement, computer instruction programs offered; session focuses on academic course work; held on campus; accepts boys and girls; open to students from other schools. 45 students usually enrolled. 2012 schedule: June 6 to June 28. Application deadline: June 1.

Tuition and Aid Day student tuition: $23,000. Tuition reduction for siblings available.

Admissions Traditional secondary-level entrance grade is 9. For fall 2011, 40 students applied for upper-level admission, 26 were accepted, 24 enrolled. Naglieri Nonverbal School Ability Test or Scholastic Achievement Test required. Deadline for receipt of application materials: none. No application fee required. On-campus interview required.

Athletics 1 PE instructor.

Computers Computers are regularly used in computer applications, creative writing, desktop publishing, English, foreign language, journalism, keyboarding, speech, word processing, yearbook classes. Computer network features include on-campus library services, Internet access, wireless campus network, Internet filtering or blocking technology. Campus intranet and computer access in designated common areas are available to students. Students grades are available online.

Contact Mr. Michael E. Tenney, Director. 713-783-6990. Fax: 713-783-0786. E-mail: mtenney@tenneyschool.com. Web site: www.tenneyschool.com.

TEURLINGS CATHOLIC HIGH SCHOOL

139 Teurlings Drive

Lafayette, Louisiana 70501-3832

Head of School: Mr. Michael Harrison Boyer

General Information Coeducational day and distance learning college-preparatory and religious studies school, affiliated with Roman Catholic Church. Grades 9–12. Distance learning grades 10–12. Founded: 1955. Setting: urban. Nearest major city is Baton Rouge. 25-acre campus. 13 buildings on campus. Approved or accredited by National Catholic Education Association, Southern Association of Colleges and Schools, and Louisiana Department of Education. Endowment: $140,000. Total enrollment: 658. Upper school average class size: 21. Upper school faculty-student ratio: 1:21. There are 179 required school days per year for Upper School students. Upper School students typically attend 5 days per week. The average school day consists of 6 hours and 50 minutes.

Upper School Student Profile Grade 9: 161 students (78 boys, 83 girls); Grade 10: 179 students (91 boys, 88 girls); Grade 11: 165 students (86 boys, 79 girls); Grade 12: 153 students (69 boys, 84 girls). 94% of students are Roman Catholic.

Faculty School total: 44. In upper school: 16 men, 25 women; 13 have advanced degrees.

Subjects Offered 20th century history, accounting, acting, advanced chemistry, advanced computer applications, advanced math, algebra, American history, American literature, anatomy and physiology, art, biology, business applications, business law, calculus, campus ministry, chemistry, choral music, civics/free enterprise, computer science, drama, earth science, English, entrepreneurship, environmental science, fine arts, food and nutrition, French, geography, geometry, health, honors algebra, honors English, honors geometry, honors U.S. history, honors world history, interpersonal skills, keyboarding, Latin, music, newspaper, physical education, physical science, physics, psychology, public speaking, publications, Spanish, speech, sports medicine, theology, Web site design, world history.

Graduation Requirements Advanced math, algebra, American history, American literature, biology, chemistry, civics, civics/free enterprise, electives, English, geometry, literature, physical education (includes health), physical science, theology, world geography, world history.

Special Academic Programs Honors section; study at local college for college credit.

College Admission Counseling 166 students graduated in 2011; 158 went to college, including Centenary College of Louisiana; Louisiana State University and Agricultural and Mechanical College; Louisiana State University at Eunice; Northwestern State University of Louisiana; Spring Hill College; University of Louisiana at Lafayette. Other: 2 went to work, 3 entered military service, 3 had other specific plans. Median composite ACT: 21. 12% scored over 26 on composite ACT.

Student Life Upper grades have uniform requirement, student council. Discipline rests equally with students and faculty. Attendance at religious services is required.

Tuition and Aid Day student tuition: $5400. Tuition installment plan (monthly payment plans). Need-based scholarship grants, paying campus jobs available. In 2011–12, 20% of upper-school students received aid. Total amount of financial aid awarded in 2011–12: $84,000.

Admissions Traditional secondary-level entrance grade is 9. For fall 2011, 202 students applied for upper-level admission, 181 were accepted, 151 enrolled. ACT, ACT-Explore, Explore or Stanford Achievement Test required. Deadline for receipt of application materials: January 27. No application fee required.

Athletics Interscholastic: baseball (boys), basketball (b,g), bowling (b,g), cheering (b,g), cross-country running (b,g), dance team (g), football (b), golf (b,g), gymnastics (b), indoor track & field (b,g), soccer (b,g), softball (g), strength & conditioning (b,g), swimming and diving (b,g), tennis (b,g), track and field (b,g), volleyball (g), winter (indoor) track (b,g), wrestling (b); intramural: cheering (g); coed interscholastic: riflery, skeet shooting, trap and skeet. 3 coaches.

Computers Computer network features include on-campus library services, Internet access, wireless campus network, Internet filtering or blocking technology. Student e-mail accounts and computer access in designated common areas are available to students. Students grades are available online. The school has a published electronic and media policy.

Contact Mrs. Kathy Dodson, Administrative Secretary. 337-235-5711 Ext. 101. Fax: 337-234-8057. E-mail: kdodson@tchs.net. Web site: www.tchs.net.

THE THACHER SCHOOL

5025 Thacher Road

Ojai, California 93023

Head of School: Michael K. Mulligan

General Information Coeducational boarding and day college-preparatory, arts, and technology school. Grades 9–12. Founded: 1889. Setting: small town. Nearest major city is Santa Barbara. Students are housed in single-sex dormitories. 450-acre campus. 89 buildings on campus. Approved or accredited by California Association of Independent Schools, The Association of Boarding Schools, Western Association of Schools and Colleges, and California Department of Education. Member of National Association of Independent Schools and Secondary School Admission Test Board.

Endowment: $100 million. Total enrollment: 250. Upper school average class size: 11. Upper school faculty-student ratio: 1:6.
Upper School Student Profile Grade 9: 57 students (28 boys, 29 girls); Grade 10: 67 students (33 boys, 34 girls); Grade 11: 63 students (32 boys, 31 girls); Grade 12: 63 students (31 boys, 32 girls). 90% of students are boarding students. 52% are state residents. 28 states are represented in upper school student body. 10% are international students. International students from Australia, Canada, Hong Kong, Japan, Saudi Arabia, and Taiwan; 5 other countries represented in student body.
Faculty School total: 45. In upper school: 23 men, 20 women; 37 have advanced degrees; 42 reside on campus.
Subjects Offered 3-dimensional art, ACT preparation, acting, advanced chemistry, advanced math, Advanced Placement courses, advanced studio art-AP, algebra, American history, American history-AP, American literature, art, art history, art history-AP, astronomy, biology, biology-AP, calculus, calculus-AP, ceramics, chemistry, chemistry-AP, Chinese, computer math, computer science, computer science-AP, conceptual physics, creative writing, dance, drama, ecology, economics, economics and history, electronic music, English, English literature, English literature-AP, English/composition-AP, environmental science, environmental science-AP, European history, European history-AP, film, fine arts, French, French language-AP, French literature-AP, geography, geometry, health, history, journalism, Latin, logic, marine biology, mathematics, music, music theory-AP, philosophy, photography, physical education, physics, physics-AP, psychology, religion, science, social studies, Spanish, Spanish language-AP, Spanish literature-AP, statistics, studio art-AP, theater, trigonometry, U.S. history-AP, world history, world literature, writing
Graduation Requirements Arts and fine arts (art, music, dance, drama), English, foreign language, mathematics, physical education (includes health), science, social studies (includes history), senior exhibition program (students choose an academic topic of interest and study it for one year, culminating in a school-wide presentation).
Special Academic Programs 17 Advanced Placement exams for which test preparation is offered; honors section; independent study; study abroad; academic accommodation for the gifted, the musically talented, and the artistically talented.
College Admission Counseling 59 students graduated in 2011; all went to college, including Brown University; Columbia College; Dartmouth College; Massachusetts Institute of Technology; Stanford University; University of California, Berkeley. Mean SAT critical reading: 650, mean SAT math: 620, mean SAT writing: 650, mean combined SAT: 1950.
Student Life Upper grades have specified standards of dress, student council, honor system. Discipline rests equally with students and faculty.
Tuition and Aid Day student tuition: $30,400; 7-day tuition and room/board: $45,900. Tuition installment plan (monthly payment plans). Need-based scholarship grants available. In 2011–12, 30% of upper-school students received aid. Total amount of financial aid awarded in 2011–12: $2,001,400.
Admissions Traditional secondary-level entrance grade is 9. For fall 2011, 487 students applied for upper-level admission, 85 were accepted, 67 enrolled. ACT-Explore, ISEE, PSAT or SSAT required. Deadline for receipt of application materials: January 15. Application fee required: $75. Interview required.
Athletics Interscholastic: baseball (boys), basketball (b,g), cross-country running (b,g), dance (b,g), football (b), lacrosse (b,g), soccer (b,g), tennis (b,g), track and field (b,g), volleyball (g); intramural: backpacking (b,g), ballet (b,g), bicycling (b,g), canoeing/kayaking (b,g), climbing (b,g), dance (b,g), horseback riding (b,g), outdoor activities (b,g), weight training (b,g), wilderness (b,g), wilderness survival (b,g), yoga (b,g); coed interscholastic: dance, equestrian sports, coed intramural: backpacking, ballet, bicycling, bowling, canoeing/kayaking, climbing, dance, equestrian sports, fencing, golf, handball, hiking/backpacking, horseback riding, modern dance, outdoor activities, pistol, polo, Polocrosse, riflery, rock climbing, rodeo, skiing (downhill), surfing, trap and skeet, ultimate Frisbee, wall climbing, weight lifting, yoga. 18 coaches, 1 athletic trainer.
Computers Computers are regularly used in English, foreign language, history, mathematics, science classes. Computer network features include on-campus library services, online commercial services, Internet access, wireless campus network, Internet filtering or blocking technology. Campus intranet and student e-mail accounts are available to students. Students grades are available online. The school has a published electronic and media policy.
Contact Mr. William P. McMahon, Director of Admission. 805-640-3210. Fax: 805-640-9377. E-mail: admission@thacher.org. Web site: www.thacher.org.

THETFORD ACADEMY

PO Box 190

Thetford, Vermont 05074

Head of School: Torrelee Fisher-Sass

General Information Coeducational day college-preparatory, arts, and vocational school. Grades 7–12. Founded: 1819. Setting: rural. Nearest major city is Montpelier. 240-acre campus. 4 buildings on campus. Approved or accredited by Association of Independent Schools in New England, Commission on Independent Schools, New England Association of Schools and Colleges, and Vermont Department of Education. Endowment: $2 million. Total enrollment: 300. Upper school average class size: 15. Upper school faculty-student ratio: 1:7. There are 176 required school days per year for Upper School students. Upper School students typically attend 5 days per week. The average school day consists of 6 hours and 30 minutes.
Upper School Student Profile Grade 9: 49 students (23 boys, 26 girls); Grade 10: 67 students (32 boys, 35 girls); Grade 11: 63 students (30 boys, 33 girls); Grade 12: 59 students (28 boys, 31 girls).
Faculty School total: 34. In upper school: 16 men, 18 women; 17 have advanced degrees.
Subjects Offered Acting, advanced math, algebra, anatomy, art, art history, biology, British history, calculus, ceramics, chemistry, community service, computer science, current events, drama, driver education, English, forestry, French, geometry, government, health, history, horticulture, industrial arts, Latin, mathematics, music, painting, physical education, physics, physiology, study skills, U.S. history, voice, world cultures, world history.
Special Academic Programs Independent study; term-away projects; study at local college for college credit; ESL (4 students enrolled).
College Admission Counseling 53 went to college, including Plymouth State University. Other: 6 went to work, 2 entered military service, 44 entered a postgraduate year, 1 had other specific plans.
Student Life Upper grades have specified standards of dress, student council, honor system. Discipline rests primarily with faculty.
Tuition and Aid Day student tuition: $17,890.
Admissions Traditional secondary-level entrance grade is 9. For fall 2011, 22 students applied for upper-level admission, 21 were accepted, 20 enrolled. Canada Quick Individual Educational Test required. Deadline for receipt of application materials: none. No application fee required. Interview recommended.
Athletics Interscholastic: alpine skiing (boys, girls), baseball (b), basketball (b,g), cross-country running (b,g), skiing (downhill) (b,g), soccer (b,g), softball (g), track and field (b,g); coed interscholastic: cross-country running; coed intramural: archery, nordic skiing, skiing (cross-country). 2 PE instructors, 7 coaches, 1 athletic trainer.
Computers Computers are regularly used in all classes. Computer network features include on-campus library services, Internet access, wireless campus network, Internet filtering or blocking technology. Campus intranet, student e-mail accounts, and computer access in designated common areas are available to students. The school has a published electronic and media policy.
Contact Marceny Bourne, Director of Counseling. 802-785-4805 Ext. 212. Fax: 802-785-4085. E-mail: marceny.bourne@thet.net. Web site: www.thetfordacademy.org.

THOMAS JEFFERSON SCHOOL

4100 South Lindhergh Boulevard

St. Louis, Missouri 63127

Head of School: Mr. William C. Rowe

General Information Coeducational boarding and day college-preparatory and Classical education school. Grades 7–PG. Founded: 1946. Setting: suburban. Students are housed in single-sex dormitories. 20-acre campus. 12 buildings on campus. Approved or accredited by Independent Schools Association of the Central States, Midwest Association of Boarding Schools, and The Association of Boarding Schools. Member of National Association of Independent Schools and Secondary School Admission Test Board. Endowment: $1.5 million. Total enrollment: 89. Upper school average class size: 14. Upper school faculty-student ratio: 1:6. There are 130 required school days per year for Upper School students. Upper School students typically attend 5 days per week. The average school day consists of 8 hours and 30 minutes.
Upper School Student Profile Grade 9: 19 students (11 boys, 8 girls); Grade 10: 17 students (10 boys, 7 girls); Grade 11: 17 students (8 boys, 9 girls); Grade 12: 19 students (5 boys, 14 girls). 63% of students are boarding students. 47% are state residents. 7 states are represented in upper school student body. 33% are international students. International students from Canada, China, Japan, Poland, and Republic of Korea.
Faculty School total: 18. In upper school: 6 men, 7 women; 8 have advanced degrees; 7 reside on campus.
Subjects Offered Advanced Placement courses, algebra, American history-AP, ancient history, ancient world history, art, art history, biology, biology-AP, calculus, calculus-AP, ceramics, chemistry, chemistry-AP, dance, earth science, English, English language-AP, English literature-AP, ESL, fine arts, French, geography, geometry, government and politics-AP, government/civics, Greek, history, Homeric Greek, Italian, Latin, life science, mathematics, music, physical science, physics, physics-AP, science, social studies, trigonometry, U.S. history-AP, world history, world history-AP.
Graduation Requirements Arts and fine arts (art, music, dance, drama), English, foreign language, mathematics, science, social studies (includes history). Community service is required.
Special Academic Programs 10 Advanced Placement exams for which test preparation is offered; honors section; academic accommodation for the gifted; ESL (17 students enrolled).
College Admission Counseling 13 students graduated in 2010; all went to college, including Boston University; Case Western Reserve University; The Johns Hopkins University. Median SAT critical reading: 710, median SAT math: 690, median SAT writing: 700, median combined SAT: 2100.
Student Life Upper grades have specified standards of dress, student council, honor system. Discipline rests equally with students and faculty.

Tuition and Aid Day student tuition: $21,200; 5-day tuition and room/board: $34,000; 7-day tuition and room/board: $36,500. Tuition installment plan (monthly payment plans, individually arranged payment plans, Sallie Mae TuitionPay). Merit scholarship grants, need-based scholarship grants, paying campus jobs available. In 2010–11, 39% of upper-school students received aid; total upper-school merit-scholarship money awarded: $10,000. Total amount of financial aid awarded in 2010–11: $507,000.

Admissions Traditional secondary-level entrance grade is 9. For fall 2010, 63 students applied for upper-level admission, 17 were accepted, 15 enrolled. SSAT or TOEFL or SLEP required. Deadline for receipt of application materials: February 15. Application fee required: $40. Interview required.

Athletics Interscholastic: basketball (boys, girls), soccer (b,g), volleyball (b,g); intramural: basketball (b,g), soccer (b,g), volleyball (b,g); coed interscholastic: soccer; coed intramural: dance, fitness, physical fitness, tennis, weight training, yoga.

Computers Computers are regularly used in foreign language, mathematics, science, yearbook classes. Computer network features include Internet access, wireless campus network, Internet filtering or blocking technology. Campus intranet, student e-mail accounts, and computer access in designated common areas are available to students. The school has a published electronic and media policy.

Contact Mrs. Jane Roth, Co-Director of Admissions. 314-843-4151 Ext. 133. Fax: 314-843-3527. E-mail: admissions@tjs.org. Web site: www.tjs.org.

See Display below and Close-Up on page 692.

TIDEWATER ACADEMY

217 Church Street

Post Office Box 1000

Wakefield, Virginia 23888

Head of School: Mr. Rodney L. Taylor

General Information Coeducational day college-preparatory, arts, religious studies, and technology school. Grades PK–12. Founded: 1964. Setting: rural. Nearest major city is Richmond. 10-acre campus. 4 buildings on campus. Approved or accredited by Virginia Association of Independent Schools. Total enrollment: 179. Upper school average class size: 15. Upper school faculty-student ratio: 1:15. There are 180 required school days per year for Upper School students. Upper School students typically attend 5 days per week. The average school day consists of 6 hours and 50 minutes.

Upper School Student Profile Grade 8: 12 students (6 boys, 6 girls); Grade 9: 12 students (5 boys, 7 girls); Grade 10: 10 students (6 boys, 4 girls); Grade 11: 16 students (11 boys, 5 girls); Grade 12: 24 students (12 boys, 12 girls).

Faculty School total: 25. In upper school: 4 men, 9 women; 2 have advanced degrees.

Subjects Offered Algebra, American history, American literature, art, arts, biology, calculus, chemistry, computer applications, creative writing, driver education, earth science, English, English literature, English-AP, fine arts, geography, geometry, government/civics, grammar, health, history, journalism, life skills, mathematics, music, physical education, science, social sciences, social studies, Spanish, world history, world literature, writing.

Graduation Requirements Arts and fine arts (art, music, dance, drama), business skills (includes word processing), computer science, English, foreign language, mathematics, physical education (includes health), science, social sciences, social studies (includes history).

Special Academic Programs 5 Advanced Placement exams for which test preparation is offered; honors section; independent study.

College Admission Counseling 22 students graduated in 2011; 20 went to college, including James Madison University; Radford University; Randolph-Macon College; Virginia Polytechnic Institute and State University. Other: 1 went to work, 1 entered military service. Median SAT critical reading: 516, median SAT math: 501. 5% scored over 600 on SAT critical reading.

Student Life Upper grades have specified standards of dress, student council, honor system. Discipline rests primarily with faculty.

Tuition and Aid Day student tuition: $6450. Tuition installment plan (FACTS Tuition Payment Plan, monthly payment plans, individually arranged payment plans). Need-based scholarship grants available. In 2011–12, 35% of upper-school students received aid. Total amount of financial aid awarded in 2011–12: $125,000.

Admissions Traditional secondary-level entrance grade is 11. For fall 2011, 10 students applied for upper-level admission, 6 were accepted, 6 enrolled. Any standardized test required. Deadline for receipt of application materials: none. Application fee required: $25. On-campus interview required.

Athletics Interscholastic: baseball (boys), basketball (b,g), cheering (g), football (b), softball (g), tennis (b,g), volleyball (g). 2 PE instructors, 2 coaches.

Computers Computers are regularly used in yearbook classes. Computer resources include on-campus library services, Internet access, wireless campus network.

Contact Robyn Croft, Admissions Counselor. 757-899-5401. Fax: 757-899-2521. E-mail: r_croft@tidewateracademy-pvt-va.us. Web site: www.tawarriors.org.

TILTON SCHOOL

30 School Street

Tilton, New Hampshire 03276

Head of School: James R. Clements

General Information Coeducational boarding and day college-preparatory school. Grades 9–PG. Founded: 1845. Setting: small town. Nearest major city is Concord. Students are housed in single-sex by floor dormitories and single-sex dormitories. 150-acre campus. 30 buildings on campus. Approved or accredited by Association of Independent Schools in New England, Independent Schools of Northern New England, New England Association of Schools and Colleges, The Association of Boarding Schools, and New Hampshire Department of Education. Member of National Association of Independent Schools and Secondary School Admission Test Board. Endowment: $14.6 million. Total enrollment: 250. Upper school average class size: 12. Upper school faculty-student ratio: 1:6. There are 187 required school days per year for Upper School students. Upper School students typically attend 6 days per week. The average school day consists of 7 hours.

Upper School Student Profile Grade 9: 30 students (19 boys, 11 girls); Grade 10: 55 students (40 boys, 15 girls); Grade 11: 85 students (54 boys, 31 girls); Grade 12: 56 students (31 boys, 25 girls); Postgraduate: 20 students (17 boys, 3 girls). 76% of students are boarding students. 35% are state residents. 23 states are represented in upper school student body. 20% are international students. International students from Canada, China, Germany, Republic of Korea, Spain, and Taiwan; 6 other countries represented in student body.

Faculty School total: 43. In upper school: 29 men, 14 women; 18 have advanced degrees; 40 reside on campus.

Subjects Offered Advanced chemistry, advanced math, advanced studio art-AP, algebra, American history, American literature, anatomy and physiology, art, band, biology, biology-AP, calculus, chemistry, chemistry-AP, chorus, clay-working, college counseling, computer graphics, criminal justice, debate, drama, drawing, ecology, economics, English, English language and composition-AP, English literature-AP, ESL, European history-AP, forensics, French, French-AP, functions, geology, geometry, honors algebra, honors English, honors geometry, independent study, integrated mathematics, integrated science, leadership, marine ecology, music, music appreciation, music theory, musical productions, newspaper, painting, photography, physics, physics-AP, politics, pre-calculus, psychology-AP, SAT preparation, sociology, Spanish, Spanish-AP, statistics, studio art, studio art-AP, theater, trigonometry, wilderness education, world cultures, world literature, world religions, yearbook.

Graduation Requirements American history, arts and fine arts (art, music, dance, drama), English, foreign language, history, lab science, mathematics, science, annual participation in Plus/5 (including activities in art and culture, athletics, community service, leadership, and outdoor experience).

Special Academic Programs 11 Advanced Placement exams for which test preparation is offered; honors section; independent study; ESL (22 students enrolled).

College Admission Counseling 85 students graduated in 2011; 80 went to college, including Bates College; Rollins College; Stonehill College; University of Connecticut; University of New Hampshire; University of Rhode Island. Other: 2 entered military service, 1 entered a postgraduate year, 2 had other specific plans. Mean SAT critical reading: 520, mean SAT math: 536, mean SAT writing: 522, mean combined SAT: 1578.

Student Life Upper grades have specified standards of dress, student council, honor system. Discipline rests primarily with faculty.

Tuition and Aid Day student tuition: $259,000; 7-day tuition and room/board: $44,900. Tuition installment plan (FACTS Tuition Payment Plan, individually arranged payment plans). Merit scholarship grants, need-based scholarship grants, need-based loans available. In 2011–12, 49% of upper-school students received aid; total upper-school merit-scholarship money awarded: $379,000. Total amount of financial aid awarded in 2011–12: $2,034,450.

Admissions Traditional secondary-level entrance grade is 9. For fall 2011, 469 students applied for upper-level admission, 308 were accepted, 106 enrolled. PSAT or SAT for applicants to grade 11 and 12, SSAT, TOEFL or SLEP or writing sample required. Deadline for receipt of application materials: February 1. Application fee required: $50. Interview required.

Athletics Interscholastic: baseball (boys), basketball (b,g), field hockey (g), football (b), ice hockey (b,g), lacrosse (b,g), soccer (b,g), softball (g), tennis (b,g); coed interscholastic: alpine skiing, cross-country running, golf, mountain biking, skiing (downhill), snowboarding, weight lifting, weight training, wrestling; coed intramural: canoeing/kayaking, hiking/backpacking, outdoor activities, outdoor education, outdoor skills, rock climbing, squash, strength & conditioning, wall climbing, weight training, wilderness survival. 1 athletic trainer.

Computers Computers are regularly used in English, foreign language, graphic arts, history, mathematics, newspaper, science, yearbook classes. Computer network features include on-campus library services, online commercial services, Internet access, wireless campus network, Internet filtering or blocking technology, USB Ports, Smart Media Readers. Campus intranet, student e-mail accounts, and computer access in designated common areas are available to students. The school has a published electronic and media policy.

Contact Jessica W. Dade, Admissions Assistant for Communications and Special Projects. 603-286-1776. Fax: 603-286-1733. E-mail: admissions@tiltonschool.org. Web site: www.tiltonschool.org.

See Display on next page and Close-Up on page 694.

TIMOTHY CHRISTIAN HIGH SCHOOL

1061 South Prospect Avenue

Elmhurst, Illinois 60126

Head of School: Mr. Clyde Rinsema

General Information Coeducational day college-preparatory, general academic, arts, business, vocational, religious studies, and technology school, affiliated with Christian faith. Grades K–12. Founded: 1911. Setting: suburban. Nearest major city is Chicago. 26-acre campus. 1 building on campus. Approved or accredited by Christian Schools International, North Central Association of Colleges and Schools, and Illinois Department of Education. Total enrollment: 1,051. Upper school average class size: 13. Upper school faculty student ratio: 1:13. Upper School students typically attend 5 days per week. The average school day consists of 6 hours and 45 minutes.

Upper School Student Profile 99% of students are Christian.

Faculty School total: 30. In upper school: 18 men, 12 women; 25 have advanced degrees.

Subjects Offered Advanced math, algebra, American literature, anatomy and physiology, art, band, Bible, biology, British literature, business studies, calculus-AP, ceramics, chemistry, child development, choir, Christian doctrine, Christian ethics, church history, communication skills, community service, computer applications, computer art, computer graphics, computer-aided design, concert choir, desktop publishing, drafting, drawing and design, economics, electives, English, English literature-AP, expository writing, food and nutrition, French, geometry, German, health, home economics, honors algebra, honors geometry, human anatomy, independent living, industrial arts, industrial technology, instrumental music, interior design, jazz ensemble, media arts, music, music appreciation, music theory, New Testament, oral communications, orchestra, parent/child development, photography, physical education, physics, physics-AP, pre-calculus, psychology, sewing, Spanish, trigonometry, U.S. government, U.S. history, U.S. history-AP, United States government-AP, Western civilization, world cultures, world literature.

Graduation Requirements Computer processing, English, mathematics, music, physical education (includes health), religious studies, science, social studies (includes history), senior service retreat at end of 12th grade, service requirement in grades 9-11 (10 hours per year).

Special Academic Programs 6 Advanced Placement exams for which test preparation is offered; honors section; remedial reading and/or remedial writing.

College Admission Counseling 97 students graduated in 2011; 95 went to college, including Baylor University; Calvin College; Trinity Christian College. Other: 2 had other specific plans. Mean composite ACT: 24. 60% scored over 26 on composite ACT.

Student Life Upper grades have specified standards of dress, student council, honor system. Discipline rests primarily with faculty. Attendance at religious services is required.

Summer Programs Sports, art/fine arts programs offered; session focuses on athletics; held on campus; accepts boys and girls; open to students from other schools. 136 students usually enrolled.

Tuition and Aid Day student tuition: $8335. Tuition installment plan (FACTS Tuition Payment Plan, FACTS is required unless paying the total tuition at once). Need-based scholarship grants, some need-based financial assistance available through school foundation available. In 2011–12, 10% of upper-school students received aid.

Admissions Traditional secondary-level entrance grade is 9. Scholastic Testing Service High School Placement Test, school's own exam or SLEP for foreign students required. Deadline for receipt of application materials: none. Application fee required: $50. On-campus interview required.

Athletics Interscholastic: baseball (boys), basketball (b,g), cross-country running (b,g), pom squad (g), soccer (b,g), softball (g), tennis (b,g), track and field (b,g), volleyball (g); intramural: basketball (b), flag football (b); coed interscholastic: cheering, golf; coed intramural: volleyball. 2 PE instructors, 1 athletic trainer.

Computers Computers are regularly used in art, computer applications, English, graphic design, industrial technology, keyboarding, science, writing classes. Computer network features include on-campus library services, Internet access, wireless campus network, Internet filtering or blocking technology. Student e-mail accounts are available to students. Students grades are available online. The school has a published electronic and media policy.

Contact Mr. Rudi Gesch, Marketing Director. 630-782-4043. Fax: 630-833-9238. E-mail: gesch@timothychristian.com. Web site: www.timothychristian.com.

TMI - THE EPISCOPAL SCHOOL OF TEXAS

20955 West Tejas Trail

San Antonio, Texas 78257

Head of School: Dr. James A. Freeman

General Information Coeducational boarding and day college-preparatory, arts, and religious studies school, affiliated with Episcopal Church, Christian faith. Boarding grades 9–12, day grades 6–12. Founded: 1893. Setting: suburban. Students are housed in single-sex dormitories. 80-acre campus. 17 buildings on campus. Approved or accredited by Independent Schools Association of the Southwest, National Association of Episcopal Schools, Southwest Association of Episcopal Schools, The Association of Boarding Schools, and Texas Department of Education. Total enrollment: 428. Upper school average class size: 15. Upper school faculty-student ratio: 1:15. There are 168 required school days per year for Upper School students. Upper School students typically attend 5 days per week. The average school day consists of 6 hours and 10 minutes.

Upper School Student Profile Grade 9: 77 students (44 boys, 33 girls); Grade 10: 78 students (54 boys, 24 girls); Grade 11: 67 students (43 boys, 24 girls); Grade 12: 58 students (34 boys, 24 girls). 17% of students are boarding students. 96% are state residents. 5 states are represented in upper school student body. 3% are international students. International students from China, Mexico, Panama, Republic of Korea, and Viet Nam; 2 other countries represented in student body. 83% of students are members of Episcopal Church, Christian.

Faculty School total: 60. In upper school: 26 men, 16 women; 26 have advanced degrees; 13 reside on campus.

Subjects Offered 20th century history, acting, Advanced Placement courses, advanced studio art-AP, algebra, American Civil War, American history, American literature, anatomy and physiology, astronomy, athletics, biology, British literature, calculus, ceramics, chemistry, choir, computer programming, conceptual physics, earth science, economics, English, English literature, environmental science, fine arts, geometry, government, Greek, history, JROTC, Latin, meteorology, military history, philosophy, photography, physics, playwriting, religion, Spanish, statistics, studio art, theater arts, theater design and production, world history, writing.

Graduation Requirements Arts and fine arts (art, music, dance, drama), electives, English, foreign language, history, mathematics, philosophy, physical education (includes health), religion (includes Bible studies and theology), science, students must pass the Assessment of Basic English Skills, senior chapel talk, community service requirement.

Special Academic Programs Advanced Placement exam preparation; honors section; independent study.

College Admission Counseling 62 students graduated in 2010; all went to college, including Baylor University; Harvard University; Rice University; Southern Methodist University; Texas A&M University; Texas Christian University. Median SAT critical reading: 600, median SAT math: 590, median SAT writing: 610, median combined SAT: 1800.

Student Life Upper grades have uniform requirement, student council, honor system. Discipline rests equally with students and faculty. Attendance at religious services is required.

Tuition and Aid Day student tuition: $17,995; 5-day tuition and room/board: $32,495; 7-day tuition and room/board: $36,740. Tuition installment plan (Academic Management Services Plan, FACTS Tuition Payment Plan, monthly payment plans). Merit scholarship grants, need-based scholarship grants, tuition remission for children of faculty available. In 2010–11, 25% of upper-school students received aid; total upper-school merit-scholarship money awarded: $55,000. Total amount of financial aid awarded in 2010–11: $555,500.

Admissions Traditional secondary-level entrance grade is 9. For fall 2010, 75 students applied for upper-level admission, 71 were accepted, 60 enrolled. ISEE required. Deadline for receipt of application materials: January 15. Application fee required: $75. Interview required.

Athletics Interscholastic: baseball (boys), basketball (b,g), cheering (g), cross-country running (b,g), diving (b,g), fitness (b,g), football (b), golf (b,g), lacrosse (b,g), soccer (b,g), softball (g), strength & conditioning (b,g), swimming and diving (b,g), tennis (b,g), track and field (b,g), volleyball (g), weight training (b,g); coed interscholastic: JROTC drill, marksmanship, physical training, riflery, strength & conditioning. 10 coaches, 1 athletic trainer.

Computers Computers are regularly used in journalism, language development, literary magazine, newspaper, programming, science, yearbook classes. Computer network features include on-campus library services, online commercial services, Internet access, Internet filtering or blocking technology. Campus intranet, student e-mail accounts, and computer access in designated common areas are available to students. Students grades are available online. The school has a published electronic and media policy.

Contact Mr. Aaron Hawkins, Associate Director. 210-564-6152. Fax: 210-698-0715. E-mail: a.hawkins@tmi-sa.org. Web site: www.tmi-sa.org.

TORONTO DISTRICT CHRISTIAN HIGH SCHOOL

377 Woodbridge Avenue

Woodbridge, Ontario L4L 2V7, Canada

Head of School: Mr. William Groot

General Information Coeducational day college-preparatory, general academic, arts, business, religious studies, bilingual studies, and technology school, affiliated with Christian faith, Christian faith. Grades 9–12. Founded: 1963. Setting: urban. Nearest major city is Toronto, Canada. 12-acre campus. 1 building on campus. Approved or accredited by Association of Christian Schools International, Christian Schools International, Ontario Ministry of Education, and Ontario Department of Education. Language of instruction: English. Endowment: CAN$100,000. Total enrollment: 430. Upper school average class size: 22. Upper school faculty-student ratio: 1:14. The average school day consists of 5 hours and 20 minutes.

Upper School Student Profile Grade 9: 94 students (46 boys, 48 girls); Grade 10: 100 students (51 boys, 49 girls); Grade 11: 121 students (57 boys, 64 girls); Grade 12: 122 students (59 boys, 63 girls). 99% of students are Christian faith, Christian.

Faculty School total: 33. In upper school: 21 men, 12 women; 8 have advanced degrees.

Subjects Offered 20th century history, advanced math, ancient history, art, athletic training, Bible, biology, bookkeeping, business applications, business education, business mathematics, business technology, cabinet making, calculus, Canadian geography, Canadian history, career and personal planning, chemistry, choir, civics, computer applications, computer multimedia, computer programming, concert band, creative writing, discrete mathematics, dramatic arts, economics, English, English literature, environmental studies, ESL, family living, family studies, French, geography, global issues, guitar, health, history, industrial arts, keyboarding, law, media studies, modern Western civilization, music, philosophy, physical education, physics, remedial study skills, science, social justice, theater arts, video film production, visual arts, Western civilization, world issues, world religions.

Graduation Requirements Ontario Ministry of Education requirements.

Special Academic Programs Honors section; term-away projects; study abroad; remedial reading and/or remedial writing; remedial math; programs in English, mathematics, general development for dyslexic students; ESL (21 students enrolled).

College Admission Counseling 109 students graduated in 2011; 87 went to college, including McMaster University; Redeemer University College; University of Guelph; University of Toronto; University of Waterloo; York University. Other: 10 went to work, 12 had other specific plans.

Student Life Upper grades have specified standards of dress, student council, honor system. Discipline rests equally with students and faculty.

Summer Programs Sports programs offered; session focuses on entry level sports for incoming grade 9 students; held on campus; accepts boys and girls; not open to students from other schools. 24 students usually enrolled.

Tuition and Aid Day student tuition: CAN$9250–CAN$12,020. Tuition installment plan (monthly payment plans, individually arranged payment plans). Tuition reduction for siblings, need-based scholarship grants available.

Admissions Traditional secondary-level entrance grade is 9. Deadline for receipt of application materials: none. Application fee required: CAN$400. On-campus interview required.

Athletics Interscholastic: badminton (boys, girls), basketball (b,g), hockey (b), soccer (b,g), volleyball (b,g), water badminton (b); intramural: badminton (b,g), water badminton (b); coed interscholastic: badminton, cross-country running, track and field, ultimate Frisbee; coed intramural: badminton, ice hockey. 5 PE instructors, 5 coaches.

Computers Computers are regularly used in accounting, all academic, business applications, programming, technology, video film production, yearbook classes. Computer network features include on-campus library services, Internet access, wireless campus network, Internet filtering or blocking technology. Campus intranet, student e-mail accounts, and computer access in designated common areas are available to students. Students grades are available online. The school has a published electronic and media policy.

Contact Mr. Tim Bentum, Vice Principal, Students and Admissions. 905-851-1772 Ext. 202. Fax: 905-851-9992. E-mail: bentum@tdchristian.ca. Web site: www.tdchristian.ca.

TOWER HILL SCHOOL

2813 West 17th Street

Wilmington, Delaware 19806

Head of School: Dr. Christopher D. Wheeler

General Information Coeducational day college-preparatory, arts, and technology school. Grades PS–12. Founded: 1919. Setting: suburban. Nearest major city is Philadelphia, PA. 44-acre campus. 4 buildings on campus. Approved or accredited by Middle States Association of Colleges and Schools and Delaware Department of Education. Member of National Association of Independent Schools and Secondary School Admission Test Board. Endowment: $27 million. Total enrollment: 753. Upper school average class size: 14. Upper school faculty-student ratio: 1:6. There are 162 required school days per year for Upper School students. Upper School students typically attend 5 days per week. The average school day consists of 7 hours.

Upper School Student Profile Grade 9: 69 students (35 boys, 34 girls); Grade 10: 59 students (35 boys, 24 girls); Grade 11: 56 students (29 boys, 27 girls); Grade 12: 53 students (23 boys, 30 girls).

Faculty School total: 111. In upper school: 21 men, 19 women; 33 have advanced degrees.

Subjects Offered Acting, advanced biology, advanced chemistry, advanced computer applications, advanced math, advanced studio art-AP, algebra, American history, American literature, art, art history, band, biology, British literature, calculus, chemistry, China/Japan history, chorus, classical Greek literature, community service, computer science, creative writing, current events, DNA, drama, drawing, driver education, English, English literature, ethics, European history, film, fine arts, French, geometry, historical research, history, human anatomy, jazz band, Latin, mathematics, music, music theory, organic chemistry, painting, photography, physical science, physics, poetry, pre-calculus, psychology, Russian literature, science, Shakespeare, Spanish, Spanish literature, strings, theater, theater design and production, U.S. constitutional history, Vietnam War, Web authoring, woodworking, world history, writing.

Graduation Requirements Arts and fine arts (art, music, dance, drama), athletics, English, foreign language, mathematics, science, social studies (includes history). Community service is required.

Special Academic Programs Advanced Placement exam preparation; honors section; independent study, academic accommodation for the gifted, the musically talented, and the artistically talented.

College Admission Counseling 55 students graduated in 2011; all went to college, including American University; Boston College; Columbia University; Lehigh University; Stanford University; University of Delaware. Mean SAT critical reading: 633, mean SAT math: 661, mean SAT writing: 643. 75% scored over 600 on SAT critical reading, 81% scored over 600 on SAT math, 66% scored over 600 on SAT writing.

Student Life Upper grades have specified standards of dress, student council, honor system. Discipline rests equally with students and faculty.

Summer Programs Enrichment, sports programs offered; session focuses on sports camps and science enrichments; held on campus; accepts boys and girls; open to students from other schools. 60 students usually enrolled. 2012 schedule: June 11 to August 10. Application deadline: May 1.

Tuition and Aid Day student tuition: $24,400–$24,950. Tuition installment plan (The Tuition Plan, monthly payment plans, individually arranged payment plans). Merit scholarship grants, need-based scholarship grants available. In 2011–12, 19% of upper-school students received aid; total upper-school merit-scholarship money awarded: $30,000. Total amount of financial aid awarded in 2011–12: $866,842.

Admissions Traditional secondary-level entrance grade is 9. For fall 2011, 85 students applied for upper-level admission, 57 were accepted, 25 enrolled. ERB CTP IV, PSAT or SAT for applicants to grade 11 and 12, SSAT or writing sample required. Deadline for receipt of application materials: January 2. Application fee required: $40. On-campus interview required.

Athletics Interscholastic: baseball (boys), basketball (b,g), cross-country running (b,g), field hockey (g), football (b), indoor track (b,g), lacrosse (b,g), soccer (b,g), swimming and diving (b,g), tennis (b,g), track and field (b,g), volleyball (g), winter (indoor) track (b,g), wrestling (b); intramural: fitness (g), self defense (g), yoga (g); coed interscholastic: golf; coed intramural: aerobics/Nautilus, strength & conditioning, weight lifting. 10 coaches, 2 athletic trainers.

Computers Computers are regularly used in all academic classes. Computer network features include on-campus library services, Internet access, wireless campus network, Internet filtering or blocking technology. Student e-mail accounts and computer access in designated common areas are available to students. Students grades are available online. The school has a published electronic and media policy.

Contact Mr. William R. Ushler, Associate Director of Admission. 302-657-8350. Fax: 302-657-8377. E-mail: wushler@towerhill.org. Web site: www.towerhill.org.

TOWN CENTRE PRIVATE HIGH SCHOOL

155 Clayton Drive

Markham, Ontario L3R 7P3, Canada

Head of School: Mr. Patrick McCarthy

General Information Coeducational day college-preparatory school. Grades PS–12. Founded: 1986. Setting: suburban. Nearest major city is Toronto, Canada. 5-acre campus. 1 building on campus. Approved or accredited by Ontario Ministry of Education and Ontario Department of Education. Language of instruction: English. Upper school average class size: 15. Upper school faculty-student ratio: 1:15. There are 178 required school days per year for Upper School students. Upper School students typically attend 5 days per week. The average school day consists of 5 hours and 20 minutes.

Upper School Student Profile Grade 9: 42 students (22 boys, 20 girls); Grade 10: 41 students (18 boys, 23 girls); Grade 11: 57 students (27 boys, 30 girls); Grade 12: 45 students (23 boys, 22 girls).

Faculty School total: 17. In upper school: 11 men, 6 women; 6 have advanced degrees.

Subjects Offered Accounting, advanced chemistry, advanced computer applications, advanced math, Advanced Placement courses, algebra, anthropology, art, band, biology,

biology-AP, business, business applications, business studies, calculus, calculus-AP, Canadian geography, Canadian history, Canadian law, career education, chemistry, civics, computer information systems, computer programming, discrete mathematics, economics, English, English as a foreign language, English-AP, ESL, family living, French, geography, health education, health science, history, history-AP, keyboarding, macroeconomics-AP, microeconomics-AP, music, music theory, physics, religion, science, sociology, statistics-AP, visual arts, world religions.

Graduation Requirements Arts, Canadian geography, Canadian history, English, French, mathematics, physical education (includes health), science, technology/design, Ontario Secondary School's Literacy Test, 40 hours community service.

Special Academic Programs 7 Advanced Placement exams for which test preparation is offered; ESL (27 students enrolled).

College Admission Counseling 57 students graduated in 2010; all went to college, including McMaster University; The University of Western Ontario; University of Guelph; University of Toronto; University of Waterloo; York University.

Student Life Upper grades have uniform requirement, student council, honor system. Discipline rests primarily with faculty.

Tuition and Aid Day student tuition: CAN$13,400. Tuition installment plan (monthly payment plans, individually arranged payment plans, 2 installments and full payment). Tuition reduction for siblings available.

Admissions Traditional secondary-level entrance grade is 9. For fall 2010, 23 students applied for upper-level admission, 17 were accepted, 16 enrolled. High School Placement Test required. Deadline for receipt of application materials: none. Application fee required: CAN$200. Interview recommended.

Athletics Interscholastic: badminton (boys, girls), ball hockey (b,g), basketball (b,g), flag football (b), floor hockey (b,g), soccer (b,g), volleyball (b,g); intramural: ball hockey (b), ballet (g), basketball (b,g), soccer (b,g), volleyball (b,g); coed interscholastic: cooperative games, golf, physical fitness, softball, ultimate Frisbee; coed intramural: archery, badminton, ball hockey, baseball, bowling, cricket, cross-country running, fitness, flag football, floor hockey, golf, softball, table tennis, tennis, ultimate Frisbee. 2 PE instructors.

Computers Computers are regularly used in accounting, business, computer applications, information technology, mathematics classes. Computer network features include Internet access, Internet filtering or blocking technology. The school has a published electronic and media policy.

Contact Ms. Patricia Ego, Admissions. 905-470-1200. Fax: 905-470-1721. E-mail: pat.ego@tcphs.com. Web site: www.tcphs.com.

TRAFALGAR CASTLE SCHOOL

401 Reynolds Street

Whitby, Ontario L1N 3W9, Canada

Head of School: Mr. Adam de Pencier

General Information Girls' boarding and day college-preparatory, arts, business, bilingual studies, and technology school. Boarding grades 7–12, day grades 5–12. Founded: 1874. Setting: small town. Nearest major city is Toronto, Canada. Students are housed in single-sex dormitories. 28-acre campus. 2 buildings on campus. Approved or accredited by Canadian Association of Independent Schools, Canadian Educational Standards Institute, Conference of Independent Schools of Ontario, Ontario Ministry of Education, The Association of Boarding Schools, and Ontario Department of Education. Language of instruction: English. Endowment: CAN$153,000. Total enrollment: 181. Upper school average class size: 15. Upper school faculty-student ratio: 1:9. There are 170 required school days per year for Upper School students. Upper School students typically attend 5 days per week. The average school day consists of 7 hours and 30 minutes.

Upper School Student Profile Grade 9: 28 students (28 girls); Grade 10: 32 students (32 girls); Grade 11: 39 students (39 girls); Grade 12: 24 students (24 girls). 38% of students are boarding students. 75% are province residents. 2 provinces are represented in upper school student body. 25% are international students. International students from Bahamas, Barbados, China, Democratic People's Republic of Korea, Mexico, and Republic of Korea; 1 other country represented in student body.

Faculty School total: 27. In upper school: 7 men, 20 women; 9 have advanced degrees; 5 reside on campus.

Subjects Offered Algebra, art, art history, biology, business skills, calculus, chemistry, computer math, computer science, creative writing, drama, earth science, economics, English, English literature, environmental science, ESL, European history, fine arts, French, geography, geometry, grammar, Latin, law, mathematics, music, photography, physical education, physics, science, social studies, world history, world literature, writing.

Graduation Requirements Arts and fine arts (art, music, dance, drama), business skills (includes word processing), computer science, English, foreign language, mathematics, physical education (includes health), science, social studies (includes history).

Special Academic Programs Advanced Placement exam preparation; honors section; independent study; term-away projects; domestic exchange program; special instructional classes for students with slight learning disabilities; ESL (20 students enrolled).

College Admission Counseling 34 students graduated in 2011; all went to college, including McGill University; Queen's University at Kingston; The University of Western Ontario; University of Toronto; University of Waterloo; Wilfrid Laurier University.

Student Life Upper grades have uniform requirement, student council. Discipline rests primarily with faculty.

Tuition and Aid Day student tuition: CAN$18,700–CAN$21,700; 5-day tuition and room/board: CAN$36,000–CAN$37,600; 7-day tuition and room/board: CAN$39,000–CAN$44,900. Tuition installment plan (monthly payment plans, individually arranged payment plans, early payment discounts). Tuition reduction for siblings, bursaries, merit scholarship grants, need-based scholarship grants available. In 2011–12, 3% of upper-school students received aid; total upper-school merit-scholarship money awarded: CAN$16,000. Total amount of financial aid awarded in 2011–12: CAN$43,000.

Admissions Traditional secondary-level entrance grade is 9. For fall 2011, 75 students applied for upper-level admission, 70 were accepted, 64 enrolled. Cognitive Abilities Test required. Deadline for receipt of application materials: none. Application fee required: CAN$2500. Interview required.

Athletics Interscholastic: badminton, baseball, basketball, cross-country running, field hockey, gymnastics, ice hockey, independent competitive sports, soccer, softball, swimming and diving, synchronized swimming, tennis, track and field, volleyball; intramural: badminton, baseball, basketball, cross-country running, dance team, field hockey, fitness, fitness walking, gymnastics, ice hockey, outdoor activities, outdoor adventure, outdoor education, physical fitness, ropes courses, rowing, running, skiing (cross-country), skiing (downhill), snowboarding, soccer, softball, swimming and diving, synchronized swimming, tennis, track and field, volleyball, yoga. 3 PE instructors.

Computers Computers are regularly used in all academic classes. Computer network features include on-campus library services, Internet access, wireless campus network, Internet filtering or blocking technology. Campus intranet and student e-mail accounts are available to students. Students grades are available online. The school has a published electronic and media policy.

Contact Irene Talent, Admissions Officer. 905-668-3358 Ext. 227. Fax: 905-668-4136. E-mail: talenti@castle-ed.com. Web site: www.castle-ed.com.

TRI-CITY CHRISTIAN SCHOOLS

1737 West Vista Way

Vista, California 92083

Head of School: Mr. Clark Gilbert

General Information Coeducational day college-preparatory, general academic, arts, vocational, religious studies, bilingual studies, and technology school, affiliated with Christian faith. Grades PK–12. Founded: 1971. Setting: suburban. Nearest major city is San Diego. 4-acre campus. 4 buildings on campus. Approved or accredited by Association of Christian Schools International and Western Association of Schools and Colleges. Endowment: $100,000. Total enrollment: 614. Upper school average class size: 22. Upper school faculty-student ratio: 1:12. There are 180 required school days per year for Upper School students. Upper School students typically attend 5 days per week. The average school day consists of 7 hours and 25 minutes.

Upper School Student Profile Grade 9: 62 students (29 boys, 33 girls); Grade 10: 59 students (27 boys, 32 girls); Grade 11: 72 students (29 boys, 43 girls); Grade 12: 63 students (33 boys, 30 girls). 25% of students are Christian faith.

Faculty School total: 37. In upper school: 14 men, 23 women; 12 have advanced degrees.

Subjects Offered Algebra, American literature, American sign language, art, Bible studies, biology, biology-AP, British literature (honors), business mathematics, calculus, calculus-AP, chemistry, civics, computer science, drama, economics, English, English language-AP, English literature, English literature-AP, environmental science, European history, geometry, government/civics, guitar, health education, history, honors English, honors U.S. history, honors world history, journalism, library studies, mathematics, philosophy, physical education, physical science, physiology, religion, science, social studies, Spanish, speech, trigonometry, U.S. history, U.S. history-AP, world history, world literature.

Graduation Requirements Arts and fine arts (art, music, dance, drama), computer studies, English, foreign language, mathematics, physical education (includes health), religion (includes Bible studies and theology), science, social studies (includes history), speech, student portfolio. Community service is required.

Special Academic Programs International Baccalaureate program; Advanced Placement exam preparation; honors section; independent study.

College Admission Counseling 77 students graduated in 2011; all went to college, including MiraCosta College; Palomar College; Vanguard University of Southern California. Mean SAT critical reading: 546, mean SAT math: 532, mean SAT writing: 544.

Student Life Upper grades have specified standards of dress, student council. Discipline rests primarily with faculty. Attendance at religious services is required.

Summer Programs Remediation, advancement, sports programs offered; session focuses on development; held both on and off campus; held at other area schools; accepts boys and girls; open to students from other schools. 60 students usually enrolled. 2012 schedule: June 15 to August 31.

Tuition and Aid Day student tuition: $7100–$9100. Tuition installment plan (monthly payment plans, individually arranged payment plans). Tuition reduction for siblings, need-based scholarship grants, paying campus jobs, church affiliation grants

available. In 2011–12, 5% of upper-school students received aid. Total amount of financial aid awarded in 2011–12: $50,000.
Admissions Traditional secondary-level entrance grade is 9. Any standardized test, English entrance exam and Math Placement Exam required. Deadline for receipt of application materials: none. Application fee required: $425. On-campus interview required.
Athletics Interscholastic: aerobics/dance (girls), baseball (b), basketball (b,g), cheering (g), cross-country running (b,g), flag football (b), football (b), golf (b), soccer (b,g), softball (g), tennis (b,g), touch football (b), track and field (b,g), volleyball (b,g), weight training (b,g); intramural: dance (g), physical fitness (b,g); coed interscholastic: equestrian sports, golf, horseback riding, lacrosse, martial arts, snowboarding. 2 PE instructors, 20 coaches, 1 athletic trainer.
Computers Computers are regularly used in animation, business applications, career exploration, computer applications, media production, news writing, science, video film production classes. Computer network features include on-campus library services, Internet access, Internet filtering or blocking technology. Campus intranet and student e-mail accounts are available to students. Students grades are available online. The school has a published electronic and media policy.
Contact Mrs. Terri Montano, Registrar. 760-806-8247 Ext. 200. Fax: 760-906-9002. E-mail: Terri.Montano@tccs.org. Web site: www.tccs.org.

TRINITY CHRISTIAN ACADEMY

10 Windy City Road
Jackson, Tennessee 38305

Head of School: Mr. Nelson Piercey

General Information Coeducational day college-preparatory school. Grades K4–12. Founded: 1986. Setting: small town. Nearest major city is Memphis. 30-acre campus. 1 building on campus. Approved or accredited by Association of Christian Schools International, Southern Association of Colleges and Schools, and Tennessee Department of Education. Total enrollment: 734. Upper school average class size: 22. Upper school faculty-student ratio: 1:9. There are 176 required school days per year for Upper School students. Upper School students typically attend 5 days per week. The average school day consists of 5 hours and 20 minutes.
Faculty School total: 48. In upper school: 6 men, 11 women; 6 have advanced degrees.
Subjects Offered Algebra, art, Bible studies, biology, biology-AP, British literature, British literature (honors), calculus-AP, chemistry, choir, computers, drama, economics, English, etymology, fine arts, forensics, geography, geometry, government, physical science, physics, physics AP, pre calculus, U.S. history, U.S. history-AP, wellness, world history, yearbook.
Graduation Requirements Arts and fine arts (art, music, dance, drama), Bible, computers, English, foreign language, history, mathematics, science, wellness.
Special Academic Programs Honors section.
College Admission Counseling 61 students graduated in 2011; 58 went to college, including Jackson State Community College; The University of Tennessee at Chattanooga; The University of Tennessee at Martin; Union University. Other: 3 went to work. Median composite ACT: 23.
Student Life Upper grades have uniform requirement, student council, honor system. Discipline rests primarily with faculty. Attendance at religious services is required.
Tuition and Aid Day student tuition: $7480. Tuition installment plan (FACTS Tuition Payment Plan, monthly payment plans). Need-based scholarship grants available.
Admissions Traditional secondary-level entrance grade is 9. SAT required. Deadline for receipt of application materials: none. Application fee required: $200. On-campus interview required.
Athletics Interscholastic: baseball (girls), basketball (b,g), cheering (b), cross-country running (b,g), football (g), golf (g), softball (b), tennis (b,g), track and field (b,g), volleyball (b); coed interscholastic: soccer. 2 PE instructors, 6 coaches.
Computers Computer resources include Internet access, Internet filtering or blocking technology. Students grades are available online.
Contact Mrs. Andrea Moody, Admissions Director. 731-668-8500 Ext. 107. Fax: 731-668-3232. E-mail: amoody@tcalions.com. Web site: www.tcalions.com.

TRINITY COLLEGE SCHOOL

55 Deblaquire Street North
Port Hope, Ontario L1A 4K7, Canada

Head of School: Mr. Stuart K.C. Grainger

General Information Coeducational boarding and day college-preparatory school, affiliated with Church of England (Anglican). Boarding grades 9–12, day grades 5–12. Founded: 1865. Setting: small town. Nearest major city is Toronto, Canada. Students are housed in single-sex dormitories. 100-acre campus. 15 buildings on campus. Approved or accredited by Canadian Association of Independent Schools, Canadian Educational Standards Institute, Conference of Independent Schools of Ontario, The Association of Boarding Schools, and Ontario Department of Education. Affiliate member of National Association of Independent Schools; member of Secondary School Admission Test Board. Language of instruction: English. Endowment: CAN$24 million. Total enrollment: 545. Upper school average class size: 16. Upper school faculty-student ratio: 1:8. There are 165 required school days per year for Upper School students. Upper School students typically attend 5 days per week. The average school day consists of 6 hours.
Upper School Student Profile 60% of students are boarding students. 61% are province residents. 8 provinces are represented in upper school student body. 33% are international students. International students from Bahamas, Bermuda, China, Germany, Mexico, and Republic of Korea; 23 other countries represented in student body. 30% of students are members of Church of England (Anglican).
Faculty School total: 86. In upper school: 37 men, 29 women; 17 have advanced degrees; 11 reside on campus.
Subjects Offered Algebra, art, art history-AP, astronomy, biology, biology-AP, calculus, calculus-AP, Canadian geography, Canadian history, career education, career/college preparation, chemistry, chemistry-AP, civics, classical civilization, classics, community service, computer programming, computer science, creative writing, dramatic arts, earth science, economics, English, English literature, English-AP, environmental science, environmental studies, ESL, European history, fine arts, finite math, French, French-AP, general science, geography, geometry, German, guidance, health, history, independent study, Latin, law, mathematics, modern Western civilization, music, philosophy, physical education, physics, physics-AP, political science, science, social sciences, social studies, Spanish.
Graduation Requirements Arts and fine arts (art, music, dance, drama), Canadian geography, Canadian history, civics, English, French, guidance, mathematics, physical education (includes health), science, social sciences, technology, minimum 40 hours of community service.
Special Academic Programs Advanced Placement exam preparation; independent study; term-away projects; study abroad; ESL (15 students enrolled).
College Admission Counseling 138 students graduated in 2011; 134 went to college, including Dalhousie University; McGill University; Queen's University at Kingston; The University of Western Ontario; University of Guelph; University of Toronto. Other: 4 had other specific plans. 25.5% scored over 600 on SAT critical reading, 30% scored over 600 on SAT math, 23% scored over 600 on SAT writing, 30% scored over 1800 on combined SAT.
Student Life Upper grades have uniform requirement, student council, honor system. Discipline rests primarily with faculty. Attendance at religious services is required.
Summer Programs Advancement, art/fine arts, computer instruction programs offered; session focuses on advancement through cultural enrichment; held off campus; held at England; accepts boys and girls; open to students from other schools. 30 students usually enrolled. 2012 schedule: July 3 to July 25. Application deadline: April 12.
Tuition and Aid Day student tuition: CAN$26,490; 7-day tuition and room/board: CAN$49,150–CAN$49,650. Tuition installment plan (monthly payment plans, quarterly payment plan). Bursaries, need-based scholarship grants available. In 2011–12, 26% of upper-school students received aid. Total amount of financial aid awarded in 2011–12: CAN$1,000,000.
Admissions Traditional secondary-level entrance grade is 9. For fall 2011, 198 students applied for upper-level admission, 198 were accepted, 134 enrolled. Otis-Lennon Ability or Stanford Achievement Test, SSAT, ERB, PSAT, SAT, PLAN or ACT or TOEFL required. Deadline for receipt of application materials: none. Application fee required: CAN$200. Interview required.
Athletics Interscholastic: baseball (boys), basketball (b,g), cricket (b), field hockey (g), football (b), ice hockey (b,g), rugby (b,g), soccer (b,g), softball (g), squash (b,g), tennis (b,g), volleyball (b,g); coed interscholastic: badminton, cross-country running, dressage, equestrian sports, golf, nordic skiing, outdoor education, rowing, skiing (cross-country), swimming and diving, track and field; coed intramural: aerobics, aerobics/dance, alpine skiing, badminton, basketball, bicycling, cricket, cross-country running, dance, equestrian sports, fitness, golf, horseback riding, ice hockey, jogging, mountain biking, paddling, skiing (downhill), snowboarding, soccer, softball, squash, strength & conditioning, swimming and diving, table tennis, tennis, water polo, weight lifting, weight training, yoga. 4 PE instructors, 5 coaches, 2 athletic trainers.
Computers Computers are regularly used in career education, college planning, English, ESL, foreign language, French, geography, history, humanities, independent study, information technology, mathematics, music, science, technology classes. Computer network features include on-campus library services, Internet access, wireless campus network. Student e-mail accounts are available to students. The school has a published electronic and media policy.
Contact Ms. Kathryn A. LaBranche, Director of Admissions. 905-885-3209. Fax: 905-885-7444. E-mail: admissions@tcs.on.ca. Web site: www.tcs.on.ca.

TRINITY HIGH SCHOOL

4011 Shelbyville Road
Louisville, Kentucky 40207-9427

Head of School: Robert J. Mullen, EdD

General Information Boys' day college-preparatory, arts, business, religious studies, and technology school, affiliated with Roman Catholic Church. Grades 9–12. Founded: 1953. Setting: suburban. 110-acre campus. 11 buildings on campus. Approved or accredited by National Catholic Education Association, Southern Association of Colleges and Schools, Southern Association of Independent Schools, and Kentucky

Department of Education. Member of National Association of Independent Schools. Endowment: $10 million. Total enrollment: 1,333. Upper school average class size: 21. Upper school faculty-student ratio: 1:12. There are 175 required school days per year for Upper School students. Upper School students typically attend 5 days per week. The average school day consists of 6 hours and 45 minutes.

Upper School Student Profile Grade 9: 365 students (365 boys); Grade 10: 350 students (350 boys); Grade 11: 326 students (326 boys); Grade 12: 292 students (292 boys). 84% of students are Roman Catholic.

Faculty School total: 118. In upper school: 88 men, 30 women; 110 have advanced degrees.

Subjects Offered 20th century history, 3-dimensional art, accounting, acting, adolescent issues, advanced chemistry, advanced computer applications, advanced math, Advanced Placement courses, advanced studio art-AP, algebra, American Civil War, American democracy, American foreign policy, American government, American history, American history-AP, American literature, American literature-AP, analysis and differential calculus, analysis of data, anatomy and physiology, ancient history, ancient world history, applied arts, applied music, art, art and culture, art appreciation, art education, art history, art-AP, arts, arts appreciation, athletic training, athletics, band, banking, Basic programming, Bible as literature, biology, biology-AP, broadcasting, business, business education, business law, business mathematics, business studies, business technology, calculus, calculus-AP, campus ministry, career exploration, career planning, career/college preparation, cell biology, character education, cheerleading, chemistry, chemistry-AP, choir, choral music, chorus, Christian doctrine, Christian ethics, Christian scripture, church history, cinematography, civics, Civil War, classical civilization, classical Greek literature, classical music, college admission preparation, college awareness, college counseling, college placement, college planning, communication arts, communication skills, community service, comparative cultures, comparative government and politics, composition-AP, computer animation, computer applications, computer art, computer education, computer graphics, computer information systems, computer literacy, computer math, computer multimedia, computer music, computer processing, computer programming, computer science, computer skills, computer studies, computer technologies, computer technology certification, computer tools, computers, concert band, concert choir, conflict resolution, constitutional law, contemporary art, CPR, creative writing, critical studies in film, critical thinking, critical writing, data analysis, data processing, death and loss, decision making skills, developmental math, digital photography, DNA research, drama, drama performance, drawing, drawing and design, earth and space science, earth science, ecology, economics, economics and history, economics-AP, English, English language and composition-AP, English literature, English-AP, environmental studies, European civilization, European history, evolution, family living, fencing, film, film studies, finite math, first aid, forensics, French, general science, geography, geometry, German, health, health science, Hebrew scripture, Holocaust studies, HTML design, humanities, independent study, information technology, instrumental music, integrated mathematics, interdisciplinary studies, Internet, jazz band, journalism, keyboarding, language arts, leadership and service, literature, literature-AP, martial arts, mathematics, modern civilization, moral and social development, multimedia design, music performance, musical theater, New Testament, news writing, newspaper, oil painting, painting, peace and justice, philosophy, photography, photojournalism, physical education, physical fitness, physical science, physics, physics-AP, post-calculus, pottery, pre-algebra, precalculus, probability and statistics, programming, psychology, public speaking, religion, religious studies, Roman civilization, Romantic period literature, Russian history, SAT/ACT preparation, science, sculpture, senior seminar, social justice, social psychology, social sciences, social studies, sociology, software design, space and physical sciences, Spanish, Spanish literature, Spanish-AP, speech and debate, sports medicine, sports nutrition, stage design, stained glass, statistics, student government, student publications, technology, trigonometry, U.S. government and politics-AP, U.S. history-AP, video film production, Web site design, weight training, Western civilization, work-study, world civilizations, world history, world history-AP, yearbook.

Graduation Requirements Communication arts, English, foreign language, humanities, lab science, mathematics, physical education (includes health), religion (includes Bible studies and theology), science, social studies (includes history), several elective offerings. Community service is required.

Special Academic Programs Advanced Placement exam preparation; honors section; independent study; study at local college for college credit; study abroad; academic accommodation for the gifted, the musically talented, and the artistically talented; remedial reading and/or remedial writing; remedial math; programs in English, mathematics, general development for dyslexic students; special instructional classes for deaf students, blind students.

College Admission Counseling 361 students graduated in 2011; 355 went to college, including Bellarmine University; Eastern Kentucky University; Indiana University Bloomington; University of Dayton; University of Kentucky; University of Louisville. Other: 6 had other specific plans. Mean combined SAT: 1854, mean composite ACT: 23.

Student Life Upper grades have specified standards of dress, student council, honor system. Discipline rests primarily with faculty. Attendance at religious services is required.

Summer Programs Remediation, enrichment, advancement, sports, art/fine arts, computer instruction programs offered; session focuses on academic advancement and enrichment/sports camps; held on campus; accepts boys; not open to students from other schools. 1,000 students usually enrolled. 2012 schedule: June 1 to August 3. Application deadline: May 15.

Tuition and Aid Day student tuition: $10,825. Guaranteed tuition plan. Tuition installment plan (monthly payment plans, individually arranged payment plans, Tuition Management Systems). Merit scholarship grants, need-based scholarship grants, paying campus jobs available. In 2011–12, 40% of upper-school students received aid. Total amount of financial aid awarded in 2011–12: $2,000,000.

Admissions Traditional secondary-level entrance grade is 9. High School Placement Test required. Deadline for receipt of application materials: none. Application fee required: $75. Interview required.

Athletics Interscholastic: archery, baseball, basketball, bicycling, bowling, cheering, crew, cross-country running, diving, football, golf, hockey, ice hockey, lacrosse, power lifting, rugby, soccer, swimming and diving, tennis, track and field, volleyball, weight lifting, wrestling; intramural: alpine skiing, basketball, bocce, climbing, cricket, fencing, fishing, flag football, freestyle skiing, Frisbee, golf, hiking/backpacking, indoor soccer, kickball, life saving, martial arts, mountain biking, paddle tennis, rock climbing, skiing (downhill), snowboarding, soccer, softball, strength & conditioning, table tennis, ultimate Frisbee, volleyball, water polo, weight lifting, weight training; coed intramural: bowling. 5 PE instructors, 30 coaches, 3 athletic trainers.

Computers Computers are regularly used in all classes. Computer network features include on-campus library services, online commercial services, Internet access, wireless campus network, Internet filtering or blocking technology. Campus intranet, student e-mail accounts, and computer access in designated common areas are available to students. Students grades are available online. The school has a published electronic and media policy.

Contact Mr. Joseph M. Porter Jr., Vice President for Advancement. 502-736-2119. Fax: 502-899-2052. E-mail: porter@thsrock.net. Web site: www.trinityrocks.com.

TRINITY HIGH SCHOOL

581 Bridge Street

Manchester, New Hampshire 03104

Head of School: Mr. Denis Mailloux

General Information Coeducational day college-preparatory, arts, religious studies, and technology school, affiliated with Roman Catholic Church. Grades 9–12. Founded: 1886. Setting: urban. Nearest major city is Boston, MA. 5-acre campus. 2 buildings on campus. Approved or accredited by New England Association of Schools and Colleges and New Hampshire Department of Education. Total enrollment: 417. Upper school average class size: 15. Upper school faculty-student ratio: 1:12. There are 180 required school days per year for Upper School students. Upper School students typically attend 5 days per week. The average school day consists of 6 hours and 30 minutes.

Upper School Student Profile Grade 9: 104 students (61 boys, 43 girls); Grade 10: 121 students (59 boys, 62 girls); Grade 11: 102 students (51 boys, 51 girls); Grade 12: 90 students (55 boys, 35 girls). 80% of students are Roman Catholic.

Faculty School total: 35. In upper school: 19 men, 16 women; 19 have advanced degrees.

Subjects Offered 3-dimensional art, advanced biology, advanced math, Advanced Placement courses, algebra, American government, American history, American history-AP, American literature, analysis, anatomy and physiology, art, Bible studies, biology, calculus, calculus-AP, chemistry, computer science, driver education, English, English literature, English-AP, ethics, French, geometry, grammar, health, history, human development, journalism, Latin, mathematics, physical education, physics, psychology, religion, science, social studies, sociology, Spanish, theology, trigonometry, U.S. history-AP, world history, world literature.

Special Academic Programs 5 Advanced Placement exams for which test preparation is offered; honors section; study at local college for college credit.

College Admission Counseling 105 students graduated in 2011; 104 went to college, including Saint Anselm College; University of New Hampshire; Worcester Polytechnic Institute. Other: 1 went to work.

Student Life Upper grades have specified standards of dress, student council, honor system. Discipline rests primarily with faculty. Attendance at religious services is required.

Tuition and Aid Day student tuition: $8940. Tuition installment plan (FACTS Tuition Payment Plan). Need-based scholarship grants available. In 2011–12, 10% of upper-school students received aid.

Admissions Traditional secondary-level entrance grade is 9. STS required. Deadline for receipt of application materials: none. Application fee required: $50. Interview recommended.

Athletics Interscholastic: baseball (boys), basketball (b,g), cheering (g), cross-country running (b,g), football (b), gymnastics (g), hockey (b), ice hockey (b), indoor track & field (b,g), lacrosse (b), skiing (cross-country) (b,g), skiing (downhill) (b,g), soccer (b,g), softball (g), swimming and diving (b,g), tennis (b,g), volleyball (g), winter (indoor) track (b,g), wrestling (b); coed interscholastic: alpine skiing, golf, track and field; coed intramural: gymnastics. 1 PE instructor, 25 coaches, 1 athletic trainer.

Computers Computers are regularly used in English, journalism, science, social sciences, yearbook classes. Computer resources include Internet access, wireless campus network. Student e-mail accounts are available to students. Students grades are available online.

Contact Mr. Patrick Smith, Admissions Director. 603-668-2910 Ext. 18. Fax: 603-668-2913. E-mail: psmith@trinity-hs.org. Web site: www.trinity-hs.org.

TRINITY HIGH SCHOOL

12425 Granger Road

Garfield Heights, Ohio 44125

Head of School: Mrs. Linda Bacho

General Information Coeducational day college-preparatory, arts, business, religious studies, technology, technical, and medical school, affiliated with Roman Catholic Church. Grades 9–12. Founded: 1926. Setting: suburban. Nearest major city is Cleveland. 26-acre campus. 3 buildings on campus. Approved or accredited by National Catholic Education Association, North Central Association of Colleges and Schools, Ohio Catholic Schools Accreditation Association (OCSAA), and Ohio Department of Education. Total enrollment: 330. Upper school average class size: 17. Upper school faculty-student ratio: 1:10. There are 199 required school days per year for Upper School students. Upper School students typically attend 5 days per week. The average school day consists of 7 hours.

Upper School Student Profile Grade 9: 69 students (23 boys, 46 girls); Grade 10: 91 students (43 boys, 48 girls); Grade 11: 93 students (42 boys, 51 girls); Grade 12: 77 students (38 boys, 39 girls). 89% of students are Roman Catholic.

Faculty School total: 35. In upper school: 14 men, 21 women; 16 have advanced degrees.

Subjects Offered 3-dimensional art, accounting, advanced biology, advanced chemistry, advanced computer applications, advanced math, Advanced Placement courses, advanced studio art-AP, algebra, American government, American history, American history-AP, American literature, analysis and differential calculus, anatomy and physiology, animation, art, athletics, automated accounting, band, Bible, Bible studies, biology, bookkeeping, British literature, British literature (honors), business applications, business skills, business technology, calculus-AP, campus ministry, career and personal planning, career education, career education internship, career experience, career exploration, career planning, career/college preparation, Catholic belief and practice, ceramics, chemistry, choir, Christian and Hebrew scripture, Christian doctrine, Christian ethics, Christian scripture, Christian testament, church history, college admission preparation, college awareness, college counseling, college placement, college planning, college writing, communication skills, community service, comparative religion, competitive science projects, computer animation, computer applications, computer art, computer education, computer graphics, computer information systems, computer multimedia, computer technologies, computer technology certification, computer-aided design, concert band, concert choir, consumer economics, creative writing, critical thinking, critical writing, culinary arts, digital applications, drama performance, drawing and design, earth science, economics and history, electives, English, English literature and composition-AP, environmental science, ethics, European history, food and nutrition, foods, foreign language, four units of summer reading, geometry, global studies, government-AP, graphic arts, graphic design, graphics, guidance, health education, honors algebra, honors English, honors geometry, human anatomy, human biology, instrumental music, integrated mathematics, Internet research, internship, lab science, library, life issues, Life of Christ, marching band, marine biology, Microsoft, moral theology, musical theater, neuroscience, oral communications, participation in sports, peace and justice, peer ministry, personal finance, photo shop, physical education, physics, play production, portfolio art, prayer/spirituality, pre-algebra, pre-calculus, psychology, public speaking, SAT/ACT preparation, speech, sports, studio art-AP, study skills, symphonic band, theology, U.S. government and politics-AP, video, video and animation, vocal ensemble, Web site design, wind ensemble, word processing, world history, yearbook.

Graduation Requirements Arts and fine arts (art, music, dance, drama), electives, English, government, human relations, mathematics, physical education (includes health), science, social studies (includes history), theology, Western civilization, service hours, internship.

Special Academic Programs Advanced Placement exam preparation; honors section; independent study; academic accommodation for the gifted and the artistically talented; remedial math; programs in English, mathematics, general development for dyslexic students.

College Admission Counseling 72 students graduated in 2011; 69 went to college, including John Carroll University; Kent State University; Miami University; Ohio University; The Ohio State University; University of Dayton. Other: 3 had other specific plans. Median SAT critical reading: 500, median SAT math: 520, median SAT writing: 520, median combined SAT: 1540, median composite ACT: 23. 27% scored over 600 on SAT critical reading, 18% scored over 600 on SAT math, 18% scored over 600 on SAT writing, 10% scored over 1800 on combined SAT, 23% scored over 26 on composite ACT.

Student Life Upper grades have uniform requirement, student council. Discipline rests primarily with faculty. Attendance at religious services is required.

Summer Programs Enrichment, advancement, sports, art/fine arts programs offered; session focuses on recruitment; held both on and off campus; held at other schools; accepts boys and girls; open to students from other schools. 125 students usually enrolled. 2012 schedule: June to August. Application deadline: May.

Tuition and Aid Day student tuition: $9600. Tuition installment plan (individually arranged payment plans, private bank loans). Tuition reduction for siblings, need-based scholarship grants, middle-income loans, private bank loans available. In 2011–12, 25% of upper-school students received aid. Total amount of financial aid awarded in 2011–12: $138,000.

Admissions Traditional secondary-level entrance grade is 9. For fall 2011, 90 students applied for upper-level admission, 80 were accepted, 69 enrolled. Scholastic Testing Service High School Placement Test required. Deadline for receipt of application materials: none. Application fee required: $20. On-campus interview required.

Athletics Interscholastic: baseball (boys), basketball (b,g), cheering (g), cross-country running (b,g), danceline (g), football (b), soccer (g), softball (g), track and field (b,g), volleyball (g), wrestling (b); intramural: danceline (g); coed interscholastic: golf, indoor track & field; coed intramural: skiing (downhill), snowboarding. 1 PE instructor, 34 coaches, 1 athletic trainer.

Computers Computers are regularly used in all academic classes. Computer network features include on-campus library services, online commercial services, Internet access, wireless campus network, Internet filtering or blocking technology, Citrix, network printing, personal storage on network, weekly email grade reports, electronic newsletters, remote access, school Web site, online homework tracking system. Computer access in designated common areas is available to students. Students grades are available online. The school has a published electronic and media policy.

Contact Sr. Dian Majsterek, Administrative Assistant, Admissions and Marketing. 216-581-1061. Fax: 216-581-9348. E-mail: SisterDian@ths.org. Web site: www.ths.org.

TRINITY-PAWLING SCHOOL

700 Route 22

Pawling, New York 12564

Head of School: Mr. Archibald A. Smith III

General Information Boys' boarding and day college-preparatory, arts, religious studies, technology, and ESL school, affiliated with Episcopal Church. Boarding grades 9–PG, day grades 7–PG. Founded: 1907. Setting: small town. Nearest major city is New York. Students are housed in single-sex dormitories. 140-acre campus. 23 buildings on campus. Approved or accredited by New York State Association of Independent Schools, New York State Board of Regents, and The Association of Boarding Schools. Member of National Association of Independent Schools and Secondary School Admission Test Board. Endowment: $32 million. Total enrollment: 272. Upper school average class size: 12. Upper school faculty-student ratio: 1:8. There are 186 required school days per year for Upper School students. Upper School students typically attend 6 days per week. The average school day consists of 6 hours and 30 minutes.

Upper School Student Profile Grade 9: 38 students (38 boys); Grade 10: 58 students (58 boys); Grade 11: 69 students (69 boys); Grade 12: 68 students (68 boys); Postgraduate: 15 students (15 boys). 80% of students are boarding students. 20% are state residents. 19 states are represented in upper school student body. 25% are international students. International students from Canada, China, Japan, Republic of Korea, Saudi Arabia, and Viet Nam; 12 other countries represented in student body. 20% of students are members of Episcopal Church.

Faculty School total: 53. In upper school: 36 men, 15 women; 40 have advanced degrees; 50 reside on campus.

Subjects Offered Advanced Placement courses, advanced studio art-AP, algebra, American government, American history, American legal systems, American literature, American studies, anatomy, anatomy and physiology, architectural drawing, art, art history, art history-AP, Asian history, Asian studies, astronomy, Bible, biology, biology-AP, calculus, calculus-AP, ceramics, chemistry, chemistry-AP, choir, chorus, Christian ethics, civil rights, composition-AP, computer applications, computer information systems, computer math, computer music, computer programming, computer science, computer science-AP, computer technologies, constitutional history of U.S., data analysis, drafting, drama, drama performance, earth science, East Asian history, ecology, economics, economics-AP, English, English language-AP, English literature, English literature-AP, English-AP, English/composition-AP, environmental science, environmental science-AP, environmental studies, ESL, ethics, European history, European history-AP, fine arts, French, French language-AP, French studies, geology, geometry, government, government and politics-AP, government/civics, grammar, health science, history, honors algebra, honors English, honors geometry, honors U.S. history, honors world history, human anatomy, keyboarding, Latin, Latin American literature, Latin-AP, law and the legal system, literature, literature and composition-AP, Mandarin, mathematics, mechanical drawing, model United Nations, music, philosophy, photography, physical education, physics, physics-AP, physiology, political science, pre-calculus, probability and statistics, psychology, public speaking, reading/study skills, religion, religious education, religious studies, SAT preparation, science, Shakespeare, social justice, social sciences, social studies, Spanish, Spanish language-AP, Spanish literature-AP, statistics-AP, studio art, studio art-AP, study skills, theater, theology, trigonometry, U.S. government and politics, U.S. history, U.S. history-AP, Vietnam War, word processing, world history, writing, yearbook.

Graduation Requirements Arts and fine arts (art, music, dance, drama), English, foreign language, mathematics, physical education (includes health), religion (includes Bible studies and theology), science, social studies (includes history).

Special Academic Programs 17 Advanced Placement exams for which test preparation is offered; honors section; remedial reading and/or remedial writing; programs in English for dyslexic students; ESL (25 students enrolled).

College Admission Counseling 88 students graduated in 2011; all went to college, including Boston University; Hobart and William Smith Colleges; Syracuse University; The Johns Hopkins University; The University of Arizona; University of New Hampshire. Mean SAT critical reading: 580, mean SAT math: 570.

Student Life Upper grades have specified standards of dress, student council, honor system. Discipline rests equally with students and faculty. Attendance at religious services is required.

Tuition and Aid Day student tuition: $32,000; 7-day tuition and room/board: $45,000. Tuition installment plan (Insured Tuition Payment Plan, Academic Management Services Plan, individually arranged payment plans, payment plans arranged directly with the school business office). Need-based scholarship grants, need-based loans available. In 2011–12, 35% of upper-school students received aid. Total amount of financial aid awarded in 2011–12: $3,000,000.

Admissions Traditional secondary-level entrance grade is 9. For fall 2011, 348 students applied for upper-level admission, 240 were accepted, 116 enrolled. PSAT or SAT, SSAT, TOEFL, Wechsler Intelligence Scale for Children III or WISC-R required. Deadline for receipt of application materials: February 1. Application fee required: $50. On-campus interview required.

Athletics Interscholastic: alpine skiing, baseball, basketball, cross-country running, football, golf, hockey, ice hockey, lacrosse, ropes courses, skiing (downhill), soccer, squash, strength & conditioning, tennis, track and field, weight lifting, weight training, wrestling; intramural: alpine skiing, basketball, bicycling, climbing, fishing, fitness, floor hockey, fly fishing, Frisbee, golf, hiking/backpacking, ice skating, mountain biking, outdoor education, outdoor recreation, physical training, rock climbing, running, skiing (downhill), snowboarding, soccer, softball, squash, strength & conditioning, tennis, trap and skeet, ultimate Frisbee, wall climbing, weight lifting. 30 coaches, 2 athletic trainers.

Computers Computers are regularly used in English, history, mathematics, remedial study skills, science classes. Computer network features include on-campus library services, online commercial services, Internet access, wireless campus network, Internet filtering or blocking technology. Campus intranet, student e-mail accounts, and computer access in designated common areas are available to students. Students grades are available online. The school has a published electronic and media policy.

Contact Mr. MacGregor Robinson, Assistant Headmaster for External Affairs. 845-855-4825. Fax: 845-855-4827. E-mail: grobinson@trinitypawling.org. Web site: www.trinitypawling.org.

See Display below and Close-Up on page 696.

TRINITY PREPARATORY SCHOOL

5700 Trinity Prep Lane

Winter Park, Florida 32792

Head of School: Craig S. Maughan

General Information Coeducational day college-preparatory, arts, and technology school, affiliated with Episcopal Church. Grades 6–12. Founded: 1966. Setting: suburban. Nearest major city is Orlando. 100-acre campus. 12 buildings on campus. Approved or accredited by National Association of Episcopal Schools, The College Board, and Florida Department of Education. Member of National Association of Independent Schools and Secondary School Admission Test Board. Endowment: $7.3 million. Total enrollment: 836. Upper school average class size: 17. Upper school faculty-student ratio: 1:10. There are 175 required school days per year for Upper School students. Upper School students typically attend 5 days per week. The average school day consists of 5 hours and 45 minutes.

Upper School Student Profile Grade 9: 130 students (64 boys, 66 girls); Grade 10: 133 students (65 boys, 68 girls); Grade 11: 124 students (72 boys, 52 girls); Grade 12: 114 students (64 boys, 50 girls). 7% of students are members of Episcopal Church.

Faculty School total: 78. In upper school: 24 men, 35 women; 40 have advanced degrees.

Subjects Offered 20th century American writers, 20th century world history, 3-dimensional art, advanced math, Advanced Placement courses, advanced studio art-AP, algebra, American history, American literature, anatomy, animal science, art, athletic training, audio visual/media, band, Basic programming, Bible, biology, biology-AP, calculus, calculus-AP, character education, chemistry, chemistry-AP, chorus, civics, Civil War, comparative religion, computer graphics, computer multimedia, computer processing, computer programming, computer programming-AP, concert band, concert choir, creative writing, critical studies in film, digital photography, drama, drawing, economics, economics-AP, English, English language and composition-AP, English literature, English literature and composition-AP, environmental science, environmental science-AP, ethics, European history, European history-AP, filmmaking, fine arts, forensics, French, French language-AP, French literature-AP, geography, geometry, government and politics-AP, health, honors algebra, honors English, honors geometry, journalism, Latin, Latin-AP, life management skills, mathematics, music, music theory-AP, newspaper, painting, physical education, physics, physics-AP, portfolio art, pottery, pre-algebra, pre-calculus, probability and statistics, psychology, psychology-AP, science, sculpture, social studies, Spanish, Spanish language-AP, Spanish literature-AP, speech, strings, studio art-AP, theater, trigonometry, U.S. government and politics-AP, U.S. history-AP, weight training, world history, world wide web design, writing, yearbook.

Graduation Requirements Arts and fine arts (art, music, dance, drama), computer science, electives, English, foreign language, life management skills, mathematics, physical education (includes health), science, social sciences, 1/2 additional social studies credit.

Special Academic Programs 25 Advanced Placement exams for which test preparation is offered; honors section; independent study; study at local college for college credit; academic accommodation for the gifted, the musically talented, and the artistically talented.

College Admission Counseling 117 students graduated in 2011; all went to college, including Auburn University; Duke University; Florida State University; Furman University; University of Florida. Mean SAT critical reading: 647, mean SAT math: 662, mean SAT writing: 637, mean combined SAT: 1956, mean composite ACT: 28. 74% scored over 600 on SAT critical reading, 79% scored over 600 on SAT math, 76% scored over 600 on SAT writing, 79% scored over 1800 on combined SAT, 80% scored over 26 on composite ACT.

Student Life Upper grades have specified standards of dress, student council, honor system. Discipline rests primarily with faculty. Attendance at religious services is required.

Summer Programs Remediation, enrichment, advancement, sports, art/fine arts, computer instruction programs offered; session focuses on enrichment; held on campus; accepts boys and girls; open to students from other schools. 300 students usually enrolled. 2012 schedule: June 14 to August 8. Application deadline: none.

Tuition and Aid Day student tuition: $16,800. Tuition installment plan (Insured Tuition Payment Plan, monthly payment plans, semiannual and annual payment plans). Need-based scholarship grants, middle-income loans available. In 2011–12, 25% of upper-school students received aid. Total amount of financial aid awarded in 2011–12: $1,185,990.

Admissions Traditional secondary-level entrance grade is 9. For fall 2011, 73 students applied for upper-level admission, 47 were accepted, 29 enrolled. CTP, ISEE, PSAT, SAT or SSAT required. Deadline for receipt of application materials: February 6. Application fee required: $50. Interview required.

Athletics Interscholastic: baseball (boys), basketball (b,g), bowling (b,g), cheering (g), cross-country running (b,g), diving (b,g), fitness (b,g), football (b), golf (b,g), lacrosse (b,g), physical fitness (b,g), soccer (b,g), softball (g), strength & conditioning (b,g), swimming and diving (b,g), tennis (b,g), track and field (b,g), volleyball (g), weight lifting (b,g), weight training (b,g); intramural: ropes courses (b,g), strength & conditioning (b,g). 5 PE instructors, 48 coaches, 1 athletic trainer.

Computers Computers are regularly used in all classes. Computer network features include on-campus library services, online commercial services, Internet access, wireless campus network, Internet filtering or blocking technology. Student e-mail accounts and computer access in designated common areas are available to students. Students grades are available online. The school has a published electronic and media policy.

Contact Sherryn M. Hay, Director of Admission. 321-282-2523. Fax: 407-671-6935. E-mail: hays@trinityprep.org. Web site: www.trinityprep.org

TRINITY SCHOOL

139 West 91st Street

New York, New York 10024

Head of School: Allman John

General Information Coeducational day college-preparatory school, affiliated with Episcopal Church. Grades K–12. Founded: 1709. Setting: urban. 1 building on campus. Approved or accredited by National Association of Private Schools for Exceptional Children, New York State Association of Independent Schools, and New York Department of Education. Member of National Association of Independent Schools. Endowment: $50 million. Total enrollment: 990. Upper school average class size: 16. Upper school faculty-student ratio: 1:7. Upper School students typically attend 5 days per week.

Upper School Student Profile Grade 9: 110 students (55 boys, 55 girls); Grade 10: 110 students (55 boys, 55 girls); Grade 11: 110 students (55 boys, 55 girls); Grade 12: 110 students (55 boys, 55 girls). 15% of students are members of Episcopal Church.

Faculty School total: 163. In upper school: 50 men, 43 women; 72 have advanced degrees.

Subjects Offered Algebra, American history, American literature, art, art history, biology, calculus, ceramics, chemistry, computer math, computer programming, computer science, creative writing, dance, drama, driver education, economics, English, English literature, environmental science, ethics, European history, expository writing, fine arts, French, geometry, German, government/civics, Greek, history, Latin, marine biology, mathematics, music, photography, physical education, physics, psychology, religion, science, social studies, Spanish, speech, statistics, theater, trigonometry.

Graduation Requirements Arts and fine arts (art, music, dance, drama), English, foreign language, mathematics, physical education (includes health), religion (includes Bible studies and theology), science, social studies (includes history).

Special Academic Programs Advanced Placement exam preparation; honors section; independent study.

College Admission Counseling 110 students graduated in 2010; all went to college, including Brown University; Columbia College; Harvard University; Princeton University; University of Pennsylvania.

Student Life Upper grades have specified standards of dress, student council. Discipline rests equally with students and faculty.

Tuition and Aid Day student tuition: $36,120. Middle-income loans, need-based grants available. In 2010–11, 20% of upper-school students received aid. Total amount of financial aid awarded in 2010–11: $2,500,000.

Admissions Traditional secondary-level entrance grade is 9. For fall 2010, 400 students applied for upper-level admission, 90 were accepted, 55 enrolled. SSAT required. Deadline for receipt of application materials: January 15. Application fee required: $60. On-campus interview required.

Athletics Interscholastic: baseball (boys), basketball (b,g), golf (b,g), indoor track & field (b,g), lacrosse (b,g), soccer (b,g), softball (g), tennis (b,g), track and field (b,g), volleyball (g), winter (indoor) track (b,g), wrestling (b); coed interscholastic: cross-country running, swimming and diving, water polo. 16 PE instructors, 45 coaches, 1 athletic trainer.

Computers Computers are regularly used in art, mathematics, science classes. Computer network features include on-campus library services, Internet access. The school has a published electronic and media policy.

Contact Hannah Trooboff McCollum, Associate Director of Admission. 212-932-6823. Fax: 212-932-6812 Ext. 6819. E-mail: hannah.mccollum@trinityschoolnyc.org. Web site: www.trinityschoolnyc.org.

TRINITY SCHOOL AT GREENLAWN

107 South Greenlawn Avenue

South Bend, Indiana 46617

Head of School: Mr. John A. Lee

General Information Coeducational day college-preparatory, general academic, and Classical curriculum school, affiliated with Protestant faith, Roman Catholic Church. Grades 7–12. Founded: 1981. Setting: suburban. 4-acre campus. 3 buildings on campus. Approved or accredited by Independent Schools Association of the Central States and Indiana Department of Education. Upper school average class size: 15. Upper school faculty-student ratio: 1:7. Upper School students typically attend 5 days per week. The average school day consists of 5 hours.

Upper School Student Profile 90% of students are Protestant, Roman Catholic.

Faculty School total: 23. In upper school: 10 men, 13 women; 12 have advanced degrees.

Subjects Offered Acting, advanced biology, advanced chemistry, advanced math, algebra, American history, American literature, analysis and differential calculus, anatomy, ancient history, applied arts, applied music, art, art history, Bible as literature, biology, British history, British literature, calculus, calligraphy, Catholic belief and practice, chemistry, choral music, Christian and Hebrew scripture, Christian doctrine, classical Greek literature.

College Admission Counseling 26 students graduated in 2010; 25 went to college, including Indiana University Bloomington; Purdue University; Saint Mary's College; University of Notre Dame. Other: 1 went to work. Mean SAT critical reading: 646, mean SAT math: 600, mean SAT writing: 646, mean combined SAT: 1892.

Student Life Upper grades have uniform requirement. Discipline rests primarily with faculty.

Tuition and Aid Day student tuition: $9100. Tuition installment plan (individually arranged payment plans). Need-based scholarship grants available. In 2010–11, 40% of upper-school students received aid.

Admissions Deadline for receipt of application materials: none. Application fee required: $50. Interview required.

Athletics Interscholastic: basketball (boys, girls), soccer (b,g), volleyball (g); coed intramural: golf.

Computers Computer access in designated common areas is available to students. The school has a published electronic and media policy.

Contact Ms. Gina Massa, Director of Community Relations. 574-850-7168. E-mail: gmassa@trinityschools.org. Web site: www.trinitygreenlawn.org.

TRINITY SCHOOL OF TEXAS

215 Teague Street

Longview, Texas 75601

Head of School: Mr. Richard L. Beard

General Information Coeducational day and distance learning college-preparatory, arts, religious studies, and technology school, affiliated with Episcopal Church. Grades PK–12. Distance learning grades 10–12. Founded: 1957. Setting: small town. Nearest major city is Dallas. 14-acre campus. 4 buildings on campus. Approved or accredited by National Association of Episcopal Schools, Southern Association of Colleges and Schools, Southwest Association of Episcopal Schools, and Texas Department of Education. Endowment: $315,000. Total enrollment: 300. Upper school average class size: 12. Upper school faculty-student ratio: 1:8. There are 174 required school days per year for Upper School students. Upper School students typically attend 5 days per week. The average school day consists of 6 hours and 20 minutes.

Upper School Student Profile Grade 9: 15 students (9 boys, 6 girls); Grade 10: 15 students (6 boys, 9 girls); Grade 11: 11 students (7 boys, 4 girls); Grade 12: 12 students (4 boys, 8 girls). 11% of students are members of Episcopal Church.

Faculty School total: 38. In upper school: 3 men, 13 women; 3 have advanced degrees.
Subjects Offered Advanced studio art-AP, algebra, American history, art, astronomy, athletics, biology, biology-AP, calculus, calculus-AP, Central and Eastern European history, character education, chemistry, chemistry-AP, choir, choral music, college admission preparation, college writing, community service, computer applications, computer literacy, conflict resolution, creative writing, desktop publishing, digital photography, drama performance, earth science, economics, English-AP, environmental science, environmental studies, European history-AP, geography, geometry, government, government/civics, grammar, health, junior and senior seminars, keyboarding, language and composition, language arts, leadership and service, library, life science, literature and composition-AP, mathematics, modern European history, modern Western civilization, modern world history, music, music performance, mythology, newspaper, participation in sports, personal finance, photography, photojournalism, physical education, physical fitness, physical science, physics, pre-algebra, pre-calculus, probability and statistics, psychology, psychology-AP, religious studies, research seminar, research skills, SAT preparation, SAT/ACT preparation, sociology, Spanish, Spanish language-AP, sports, statistics, strings, student publications, studio art, Texas history, U.S. government, U.S. history, world geography, world history, world religions, yearbook.
Graduation Requirements Arts and fine arts (art, music, dance, drama), computers, English, government/civics, languages, mathematics, physical education (includes health), science, social sciences, speech, theology.
Special Academic Programs Advanced Placement exam preparation; accelerated programs; independent study; term-away projects; study at local college for college credit; study abroad; academic accommodation for the gifted, the musically talented, and the artistically talented; programs in English, mathematics for dyslexic students.
College Admission Counseling 16 students graduated in 2011; all went to college, including LeTourneau University; Morehouse College; Northeastern University; Texas A&M University; The University of Texas at Arlington; The University of Texas at Austin. Median SAT critical reading: 530, median SAT math: 620, median SAT writing: 535, median combined SAT: 1690, median composite ACT: 23. 18% scored over 600 on SAT critical reading, 23% scored over 600 on SAT math, 13% scored over 600 on SAT writing, 42% scored over 26 on composite ACT.
Student Life Upper grades have specified standards of dress, student council, honor system. Discipline rests primarily with faculty. Attendance at religious services is required.
Summer Programs Remediation, enrichment, advancement, sports, art/fine arts, computer instruction programs offered; session focuses on broad, age-appropriate opportunities for child development; held both on and off campus; held at a wide variety of excursions related to weekly themes; accepts boys and girls; open to students from other schools. 47 students usually enrolled. 2012 schedule: May 31 to July 29. Application deadline: April 15.
Tuition and Aid Day student tuition: $7139–$7897. Tuition installment plan (FACTS Tuition Payment Plan, monthly payment plans, individually arranged payment plans, semester payment plan). Merit scholarship grants, need-based scholarship grants available. In 2011–12, 12% of upper-school students received aid; total upper-school merit-scholarship money awarded: $74,497. Total amount of financial aid awarded in 2011–12: $99,875.
Admissions Traditional secondary-level entrance grade is 9. For fall 2011, 12 students applied for upper-level admission, 12 were accepted, 12 enrolled. Otis-Lennon, Stanford Achievement Test, PSAT or SAT for applicants to grade 11 and 12, Woodcock-Johnson Revised Achievement Test and writing sample required. Deadline for receipt of application materials: none. Application fee required: $850. On-campus interview required.
Athletics Interscholastic: baseball (boys), basketball (b,g), cheering (g), football (b), golf (b,g), physical fitness (b), power lifting (b), tennis (b,g), track and field (b,g), volleyball (g); intramural: football (b), physical fitness (b,g), tennis (b,g), volleyball (g); coed interscholastic: soccer; coed intramural: soccer, track and field, weight training. 2 PE instructors, 4 coaches.
Computers Computers are regularly used in college planning, computer applications, creative writing, English, geography, history, journalism, keyboarding, library, mathematics, newspaper, photography, photojournalism, psychology, publications, publishing, research skills, SAT preparation, science, senior seminar, Spanish, technology, writing, yearbook classes. Computer network features include on-campus library services, online commercial services, Internet access, Internet filtering or blocking technology. The school has a published electronic and media policy.
Contact Mrs. Jill Galvez, Director of Admission. 903-753-0612 Ext. 236. Fax: 903-753-4812. E-mail: jgalvez@trinityschooloftexas.com. Web site: www.trinityschooloftexas.com.

TRINITY VALLEY SCHOOL

7500 Dutch Branch Road

Fort Worth, Texas 76132

Head of School: Dr. Gary Krahn

General Information Coeducational day college-preparatory school. Grades K–12. Founded: 1959. Setting: urban. 75-acre campus. 7 buildings on campus. Approved or accredited by Independent Schools Association of the Southwest and Texas Department of Education. Member of National Association of Independent Schools. Endowment: $28.7 million. Total enrollment: 957. Upper school average class size: 16. Upper school faculty-student ratio: 1:8. There are 176 required school days per year for Upper School students. Upper School students typically attend 5 days per week. The average school day consists of 5 hours and 30 minutes.
Upper School Student Profile Grade 9: 85 students (42 boys, 43 girls); Grade 10: 86 students (40 boys, 46 girls); Grade 11: 74 students (31 boys, 43 girls); Grade 12: 91 students (45 boys, 46 girls).
Faculty School total: 110. In upper school: 18 men, 23 women; 36 have advanced degrees.
Subjects Offered Algebra, American culture, American history, American history-AP, ancient history, ancient world history, art, Asian history, biology, biology-AP, British history, calculus, calculus-AP, ceramics, chemistry, chemistry-AP, Chinese, choir, computer graphics, computer science, computer science-AP, constitutional law, creative writing, debate, digital imaging, economics, economics-AP, English, English language-AP, English literature-AP, environmental science, French, French-AP, geometry, government/civics, humanities, Latin, Latin-AP, leadership, modern European history, photography, physical education, physics, physics-AP, psychology-AP, Spanish, Spanish-AP, statistics, statistics-AP, technical theater, theater arts, U.S. government, U.S. government and politics-AP, video film production, writing workshop, yearbook.
Graduation Requirements Algebra, American government, American history, arts and fine arts (art, music, dance, drama), biology, chemistry, economics, English, foreign language, geometry, physical education (includes health), physics, pre-calculus, Western civilization, students must complete 60 hours of community service in the U.S.. Community service is required.
Special Academic Programs 22 Advanced Placement exams for which test preparation is offered; honors section; academic accommodation for the gifted, the musically talented, and the artistically talented.
College Admission Counseling 88 students graduated in 2011; all went to college, including Southern Methodist University; Texas A&M University; Texas Christian University; The University of Alabama; The University of Texas at Austin; University of Oklahoma.
Student Life Upper grades have uniform requirement, student council, honor system. Discipline rests equally with students and faculty.
Summer Programs Enrichment, sports, art/fine arts, rigorous outdoor training, computer instruction programs offered; session focuses on enrichment; held both on and off campus; held at New Mexico and Colorado (backpacking); accepts boys and girls; open to students from other schools. 200 students usually enrolled. 2012 schedule: June 4 to July 27. Application deadline: May 15.
Tuition and Aid Day student tuition: $17,560. Tuition installment plan (monthly payment plans). Need-based scholarship grants available. In 2011–12, 14% of upper-school students received aid. Total amount of financial aid awarded in 2011–12: $511,265.
Admissions Traditional secondary-level entrance grade is 9. For fall 2011, 46 students applied for upper-level admission, 29 were accepted, 15 enrolled. ISEE required. Deadline for receipt of application materials: March 2. Application fee required: $75. Interview required.
Athletics Interscholastic: baseball (boys), basketball (b,g), cross-country running (b,g), field hockey (g), football (b), golf (b,g), soccer (b,g), softball (g), tennis (b,g), track and field (b,g), volleyball (b,g). 5 PE instructors, 6 coaches, 2 athletic trainers.
Computers Computers are regularly used in all academic classes. Computer network features include on-campus library services, online commercial services, Internet access, wireless campus network, Internet filtering or blocking technology. Campus intranet, student e-mail accounts, and computer access in designated common areas are available to students. Students grades are available online. The school has a published electronic and media policy.
Contact Judith Kinser, Director of Admissions and Financial Aid. 817-321-0116. Fax: 817-321-0105. E-mail: kinserj@trinityvalleyschool.org. Web site: www.trinityvalleyschool.org.

TURNING WINDS ACADEMIC INSTITUTE

Bonners Ferry, Idaho

See Special Needs Schools section.

TUSCALOOSA ACADEMY

420 Rice Valley Road North

Tuscaloosa, Alabama 35406

Head of School: Dr. Jeffrey Mitchell

General Information Coeducational day college-preparatory, arts, bilingual studies, technology, and ESL school. Grades PK–12. Founded: 1967. Setting: suburban. Nearest major city is Birmingham. 35-acre campus. 2 buildings on campus. Approved or accredited by Southern Association of Colleges and Schools and Southern Association of Independent Schools. Member of National Association of Independent Schools. Total enrollment: 418. Upper school average class size: 15. Upper school faculty-student ratio: 1:15. There are 177 required school days per year for Upper School students. Upper School students typically attend 5 days per week. The average school day consists of 6 hours and 55 minutes.

Upper School Student Profile Grade 9: 28 students (17 boys, 11 girls); Grade 10: 32 students (18 boys, 14 girls); Grade 11: 35 students (17 boys, 18 girls); Grade 12: 24 students (12 boys, 12 girls).

Faculty School total: 56. In upper school: 10 men, 12 women; 11 have advanced degrees.

Subjects Offered ACT preparation, advanced math, Advanced Placement courses, algebra, American government, American history, American history-AP, American literature, American literature-AP, anatomy, art, art history, art-AP, baseball, basketball, biology, biology-AP, calculus, calculus-AP, cheerleading, chemistry, chemistry-AP, choir, choral music, chorus, college counseling, computer programming, computer science, computer studies, creative writing, drama, earth science, economics, English, English literature, English-AP, English/composition-AP, European history, expository writing, fine arts, French, French language-AP, French-AP, geography, geometry, German, golf, government-AP, government/civics, grammar, health, history, history-AP, journalism, Latin, Latin-AP, literature-AP, mathematics, mathematics-AP, music, physical education, pre-calculus, psychology, psychology-AP, SAT preparation, SAT/ACT preparation, science, senior thesis, social studies, sociology, softball, Spanish, Spanish language-AP, Spanish-AP, speech, sports conditioning, studio art, studio art-AP, theater, track and field, trigonometry, U.S. history-AP, world history, world literature, yearbook.

Graduation Requirements Algebra, American government, American history, arts and fine arts (art, music, dance, drama), biology, chemistry, computer science, electives, English, foreign language, geometry, literature, mathematics, modern European history, physical education (includes health), physical science, pre-calculus, science, social studies (includes history), speech, U.S. history, 80 community service hours.

Special Academic Programs Advanced Placement exam preparation; honors section; independent study; study at local college for college credit; study abroad; academic accommodation for the gifted; ESL (81 students enrolled).

College Admission Counseling 31 students graduated in 2011; all went to college, including Auburn University; Birmingham-Southern College; Shelton State Community College; The University of Alabama; University of Mississippi.

Student Life Upper grades have specified standards of dress, student council, honor system. Discipline rests primarily with faculty.

Summer Programs Enrichment, sports, art/fine arts, computer instruction programs offered; session focuses on enrichment and sports; held on campus; accepts boys and girls; open to students from other schools. 250 students usually enrolled. 2012 schedule: June 1 to July 30. Application deadline: none.

Tuition and Aid Day student tuition: $7334–$8792. Guaranteed tuition plan. Tuition installment plan (Insured Tuition Payment Plan, monthly payment plans, semester payment plan, annual payment plan). Tuition reduction for siblings, merit scholarship grants, need-based scholarship grants available. In 2011–12, 20% of upper-school students received aid; total upper-school merit-scholarship money awarded: $27,000. Total amount of financial aid awarded in 2011–12: $160,000.

Admissions Traditional secondary-level entrance grade is 9. For fall 2011, 25 students applied for upper-level admission, 23 were accepted, 18 enrolled. Any standardized test, Star-9 and writing sample required. Deadline for receipt of application materials: none. Application fee required: $75. Interview required.

Athletics Interscholastic: baseball (boys), basketball (b,g), cheering (g), cross-country running (b,g), dance team (g), football (b), golf (b,g), softball (g), strength & conditioning (b), tennis (b,g), track and field (b,g), volleyball (g), weight training (b); coed interscholastic: soccer. 2 coaches, 6 athletic trainers.

Computers Computers are regularly used in journalism, keyboarding, yearbook classes. Computer network features include on-campus library services, online commercial services, Internet access, wireless campus network, Internet filtering or blocking technology, laptop program. Campus intranet, student e-mail accounts, and computer access in designated common areas are available to students. Students grades are available online. The school has a published electronic and media policy.

Contact Anne D. Huffaker, Director of Admission. 205-758-4462 Ext. 202. Fax: 205-758-4418. E-mail: ahuffaker@tuscaloosaacademy.org. Web site: www.tuscaloosaacademy.org or www.WhyTa.org.

TYLER STREET CHRISTIAN ACADEMY

915 West 9th Street

Dallas, Texas 75208

Head of School: Dr. Karen J. Egger

General Information Coeducational day college-preparatory, general academic, arts, religious studies, and technology school, affiliated with Christian faith. Grades P3–12. Founded: 1972. Setting: urban. 5-acre campus. 2 buildings on campus. Approved or accredited by Association of Christian Schools International, Southern Association of Colleges and Schools, Texas Private School Accreditation Commission, and Texas Department of Education. Endowment: $120,000. Total enrollment: 198. Upper school average class size: 10. Upper school faculty-student ratio: 1:17. There are 176 required school days per year for Upper School students. Upper School students typically attend 5 days per week. The average school day consists of 7 hours and 40 minutes.

Upper School Student Profile Grade 9: 32 students (14 boys, 18 girls); Grade 10: 12 students (8 boys, 4 girls); Grade 11: 10 students (4 boys, 6 girls); Grade 12: 12 students (7 boys, 5 girls). 82% of students are Christian faith.

Faculty School total: 31. In upper school: 6 men, 8 women; 6 have advanced degrees.

Subjects Offered Advanced Placement courses, algebra, American government, American history, art, art appreciation, art history, arts and crafts, athletic training, band, bell choir, Bible studies, biology, British literature, British literature (honors), calculus, calculus-AP, cheerleading, chemistry, choir, choral music, Christian education, college admission preparation, college counseling, college planning, community service, composition, computer applications, computer literacy, computer skills, computer technologies, computer-aided design, concert band, concert bell choir, CPR, critical writing, economics, English literature, family living, freshman seminar, geography, geometry, government, grammar, guidance, health, history, Holocaust studies, honors algebra, honors English, honors geometry, human anatomy, human biology, integrated physics, keyboarding, lab science, lab/keyboard, leadership, leadership and service, literature, mathematics-AP, musical productions, physical education, physical science, physics, physiology, pre-calculus, religion, science, social studies, Spanish, speech communications, student government, track and field, U.S. government, U.S. history, U.S. literature, volleyball, weight training, world geography, world history, world literature, yearbook.

Graduation Requirements Algebra, American government, arts and fine arts (art, music, dance, drama), Bible, biology, calculus, chemistry, computer science, economics, English, geometry, physical education (includes health), physical science, physics, Spanish, speech communications, U.S. history, world geography, world history.

Special Academic Programs International Baccalaureate program; 1 Advanced Placement exam for which test preparation is offered; honors section; independent study; study at local college for college credit.

College Admission Counseling 12 students graduated in 2011; all went to college, including Baylor University; Rice University; Texas A&M University; Texas Tech University; The University of Texas at Arlington; University of North Texas. Mean SAT critical reading: 564, mean SAT math: 506, mean composite ACT: 25. 43% scored over 600 on SAT critical reading, 15% scored over 600 on SAT math, 28% scored over 600 on SAT writing, 15% scored over 1800 on combined SAT, 9% scored over 26 on composite ACT.

Student Life Upper grades have uniform requirement, student council, honor system. Discipline rests primarily with faculty. Attendance at religious services is required.

Tuition and Aid Day student tuition: $6450. Tuition installment plan (FACTS Tuition Payment Plan). Merit scholarship grants, need-based scholarship grants available. In 2011–12, 55% of upper-school students received aid; total upper-school merit-scholarship money awarded: $2500. Total amount of financial aid awarded in 2011–12: $157,000.

Admissions Traditional secondary-level entrance grade is 9. For fall 2011, 51 students applied for upper-level admission, 49 were accepted, 34 enrolled. Admissions testing, English entrance exam, mathematics proficiency exam and writing sample required. Deadline for receipt of application materials: none. Application fee required: $50. On-campus interview required.

Athletics Interscholastic: basketball (boys, girls), cheering (g), football (b), life saving (b,g), modern dance (g), physical training (b,g), strength & conditioning (b,g), track and field (b,g), volleyball (g), weight lifting (b,g), weight training (b,g); coed interscholastic: cooperative games, life saving, physical training. 1 PE instructor, 4 coaches.

Computers Computers are regularly used in business applications, career exploration, computer applications, data processing, desktop publishing, graphic arts, information technology, introduction to technology, keyboarding, lab/keyboard, library, library skills, literacy, photojournalism, reading, technology, word processing, yearbook classes. Computer network features include on-campus library services, Internet access, Internet filtering or blocking technology, on-campus library services for Accelerated Reader Program. Computer access in designated common areas is available to students. Students grades are available online. The school has a published electronic and media policy.

Contact Mrs. Perla Gonzalez, Registrar. 214-941-9717 Ext. 200. Fax: 214-941-0324. E-mail: perlagonzalez@tsca.org. Web site: www.tsca.org.

UNITED MENNONITE EDUCATIONAL INSTITUTE

614 Mersea Road 6, RR 5

Leamington, Ontario N8H 3V8, Canada

Head of School: Mrs. Sonya A. Bedal

General Information Coeducational day college-preparatory, arts, and religious studies school, affiliated with Mennonite Church USA. Grades 9–12. Founded: 1945. Setting: rural. Nearest major city is Windsor, Canada. 12-acre campus. 3 buildings on campus. Approved or accredited by Ontario Department of Education. Language of instruction: English. Total enrollment: 50. Upper school average class size: 18. Upper school faculty-student ratio: 1:15.

Upper School Student Profile Grade 9: 9 students (4 boys, 5 girls); Grade 10: 11 students (4 boys, 7 girls); Grade 11: 11 students (6 boys, 5 girls); Grade 12: 21 students (6 boys, 15 girls). 65% of students are Mennonite Church USA.

Faculty School total: 9. In upper school: 3 men, 6 women; 1 has an advanced degree.

Subjects Offered 20th century physics, advanced chemistry, advanced math, algebra, American history, ancient world history, art, Bible, biology, business studies, career exploration, chemistry, choir, choral music, Christian ethics, church history, civics, communication arts, computer applications, computer studies, computer technologies, English, environmental geography, family studies, film and new technologies, foreign language, French as a second language, German, instrumental music, introduction to theater, mathematics, orchestra, parenting, religious studies, society challenge and change, theater arts.

Graduation Requirements Arts, Canadian geography, Canadian history, careers, civics, English, French, mathematics, physical education (includes health), science.

College Admission Counseling 11 students graduated in 2011; 10 went to college. Other: 1 went to work.

Student Life Upper grades have specified standards of dress, student council. Discipline rests equally with students and faculty. Attendance at religious services is required.

Tuition and Aid Day student tuition: CAN$6300. Tuition installment plan (monthly payment plans). Tuition reduction for siblings, bursaries, need-based scholarship grants, need-based loans available. In 2011–12, 5% of upper-school students received aid. Total amount of financial aid awarded in 2011–12: CAN$4000.

Admissions Traditional secondary-level entrance grade is 9. Deadline for receipt of application materials: none. No application fee required.

Athletics Interscholastic: badminton (boys, girls), baseball (b,g), basketball (b,g), cross-country running (b,g), floor hockey (b,g), golf (b), softball (g), volleyball (b,g); intramural: badminton (b,g), baseball (b,g), basketball (b,g), bicycling (b), football (b), indoor soccer (b,g), volleyball (b,g); coed intramural: skiing (downhill), ultimate Frisbee. 1 PE instructor.

Computers Computers are regularly used in all classes. Computer network features include on-campus library services, Internet access, Internet filtering or blocking technology.

Contact Mrs. Sonya A. Bedal, Principal. 519-326 7448. Fax: 519-326 0278. E-mail: umeiadm@gmail.com. Web site: www.umei.on.ca.

UNITED NATIONS INTERNATIONAL SCHOOL

24-50 Franklin Roosevelt Drive

New York, New York 10010-4046

Head of School: Mr. George Dymond

General Information Coeducational day college-preparatory, arts, technology, English as Second Language and Eight Mother Tongue programs, and International Baccalaureate, Eight 3rd Language Programs school. Grades K–12. Founded: 1947. Setting: urban. 3-acre campus. 1 building on campus. Approved or accredited by International Baccalaureate Organization, New York State Association of Independent Schools, New York State Board of Regents, and New York Department of Education. Member of National Association of Independent Schools. Endowment: $13.3 million. Total enrollment: 1,542. Upper school average class size: 20. Upper school faculty-student ratio: 1:3. There are 172 required school days per year for Upper School students. Upper School students typically attend 5 days per week. The average school day consists of 6 hours and 40 minutes.

Upper School Student Profile Grade 9: 110 students (57 boys, 53 girls); Grade 10: 114 students (58 boys, 56 girls); Grade 11: 117 students (57 boys, 60 girls); Grade 12: 117 students (51 boys, 66 girls).

Faculty School total: 221. In upper school: 64 men, 82 women; 44 have advanced degrees.

Subjects Offered 3-dimensional art, algebra, American history, American literature, American studies, anthropology, Arabic, art, biology, calculus, chemistry, Chinese, community service, computer applications, computer science, creative writing, drama, economics, English, English literature, ESL, European history, expository writing, film, film studies, fine arts, French, geometry, German, history, humanities, Italian, Japanese, journalism, languages, library, mathematics, media production, modern languages, music, philosophy, photography, physical education, physics, psychology, Russian, science, social sciences, social studies, Spanish, theater arts, theory of knowledge, United Nations and international issues, video, video and animation, video communication, video film production, world history, world literature, writing.

Graduation Requirements Art, electives, English, health and wellness, humanities, independent study, mathematics, modern languages, music, physical education (includes health), science, International Baccalaureate, Theory of Knowledge, extended essay, Creative Aesthetic Service, individual project. Community service is required.

Special Academic Programs International Baccalaureate program; independent study; academic accommodation for the gifted, the musically talented, and the artistically talented; ESL (185 students enrolled).

College Admission Counseling 126 students graduated in 2011; 121 went to college, including Barnard College; Boston College; Cornell University; Northeastern University; Syracuse University; University of Chicago. Other: 1 entered military service, 4 had other specific plans. Median SAT critical reading: 600, median SAT math: 600, median SAT writing: 610, median combined SAT: 1810, median composite ACT: 26. 56% scored over 600 on SAT critical reading, 57% scored over 600 on SAT math, 66% scored over 600 on SAT writing, 58% scored over 1800 on combined SAT, 64% scored over 26 on composite ACT.

Student Life Upper grades have student council. Discipline rests primarily with faculty.

Summer Programs Enrichment, ESL, sports, art/fine arts, computer instruction programs offered; session focuses on recreational program for 4 to 14 years old students; held on campus; accepts boys and girls; open to students from other schools. 300 students usually enrolled. 2012 schedule: June 25 to July 27. Application deadline: May 15.

Tuition and Aid Day student tuition: $24,900–$25,450. Tuition installment plan (Tuition Management System (formerly Key Tuition Plan)). Bursaries available. In 2011–12, 7% of upper-school students received aid. Total amount of financial aid awarded in 2011–12: $286,290.

Admissions Traditional secondary-level entrance grade is 9. For fall 2011, 75 students applied for upper-level admission, 46 were accepted, 36 enrolled. ISEE, PSAT and SAT for applicants to grade 11 and 12 or SSAT required. Deadline for receipt of application materials: November 15. Application fee required: $75. On-campus interview required.

Athletics Interscholastic: baseball (boys), basketball (b,g), indoor track (b,g), indoor track & field (b,g), soccer (b,g), softball (g), track and field (b,g), volleyball (b,g); intramural: volleyball (b,g); coed interscholastic: swimming and diving; coed intramural: aerobics, aerobics/dance, aerobics/Nautilus, aquatics, badminton, ball hockey, basketball, canoeing/kayaking, climbing, cooperative games, dance, field hockey, fitness, flag football, floor hockey, gymnastics, handball, hiking/backpacking, independent competitive sports, indoor hockey, indoor soccer, indoor track, indoor track & field, jogging, jump rope, life saving, martial arts, modern dance, outdoor activities, physical fitness, physical training, rock climbing, ropes courses, rounders, running, soccer, softball, strength & conditioning, swimming and diving, table tennis, team handball, tennis, touch football, track and field, volleyball, wall climbing, weight training. 10 PE instructors, 26 coaches.

Computers Computers are regularly used in all academic, animation, art, basic skills, career education, career exploration, career technology, classics, college planning, computer applications, creative writing, current events, data processing, desktop publishing, desktop publishing, ESL, digital applications, drawing and design, economics, English, ESL, foreign language, French, French as a second language, graphic arts, graphic design, graphics, health, history, humanities, independent study, information technology, introduction to technology, journalism, keyboarding, lab/keyboard, learning cognition, library, library science, library skills, life skills, literacy, literary magazine, mathematics, media, media arts, media production, media services, multimedia, music, music technology, news writing, newspaper, philosophy, photography, photojournalism, programming, publications, publishing, research skills, science, social sciences, social studies, Spanish, study skills, technology, theater, theater arts, video film production, Web site design, writing, yearbook classes. Computer network features include on-campus library services, online commercial services, Internet access, wireless campus network, Internet filtering or blocking technology, media lab, TV studio, Web portal, film production, digital video streaming, digital video editing. Campus intranet, student e-mail accounts, and computer access in designated common areas are available to students. Students grades are available online.

Contact Admissions Office. 212-584-3071. Fax: 212-685-5023. E-mail: admissions@unis.org. Web site: www.unis.org.

THE UNITED WORLD COLLEGE - USA

PO Box 248

State Road 65

Montezuma, New Mexico 87731

Head of School: Lisa A. H. Darling

General Information Coeducational boarding college-preparatory, arts, bilingual studies, wilderness, search and rescue, conflict resolution, and service, science, humanities school. Grades 11–12. Founded: 1982. Setting: small town. Nearest major city is Santa Fe. Students are housed in single-sex dormitories. 320-acre campus. 20 buildings on campus. Approved or accredited by Independent Schools Association of the Southwest, International Baccalaureate Organization, and New Mexico Department of Education. Member of National Association of Independent Schools. Languages of instruction: English, Spanish, and French. Endowment: $91 million. Upper school average class size: 9. Upper school faculty-student ratio: 1:9. There are 245 required school days per year for Upper School students. Upper School students typically attend 5 days per week. The average school day consists of 6 hours and 30 minutes.

Upper School Student Profile Grade 11: 106 students (52 boys, 54 girls); Grade 12: 106 students (54 boys, 52 girls). 100% of students are boarding students. 5% are state residents. 37 states are represented in upper school student body. 82% are international students. International students from Canada, China, Germany, Mexico, Spain, and Venezuela; 81 other countries represented in student body.

Faculty School total: 28. In upper school: 14 men, 12 women; 20 have advanced degrees; 17 reside on campus.

Subjects Offered Anthropology, art, biology, calculus, chemistry, community service, conflict resolution, economics, English, English literature, environmental geography, environmental science, environmental studies, environmental systems, ESL, fine arts, French, German, history, information technology, International Baccalaureate courses, mathematics, music, physics, science, social sciences, social studies, Spanish, theater arts, theory of knowledge, world history, world literature, world religions.

Graduation Requirements American history, arts and fine arts (art, music, dance, drama), biology, calculus, chemistry, comparative religion, economics, English literature, environmental geography, environmental systems, European history, foreign language, French, French as a second language, geography, German, German literature, global issues, global studies, history of the Americas, International Baccalaureate courses, literature, math methods, mathematics, music, music theory, organic chemistry, peace studies, physics, post-calculus, pre-algebra, pre-calculus, research, science, senior thesis, social justice, social sciences, Spanish, Spanish literature, statistics, studio art, theater, theater arts, theory of knowledge, visual arts, wilderness education, wilderness experience, world religions, extended essay, independent research, theory of knowledge. Community service is required.
Special Academic Programs International Baccalaureate program; honors section; independent study; academic accommodation for the musically talented and the artistically talented; ESL (43 students enrolled).
College Admission Counseling 100 students graduated in 2011; 94 went to college, including Brown University; Dartmouth College; Earlham College; Harvard University; Princeton University; Trinity College. Other: 3 entered military service, 3 entered a postgraduate year. 25% scored over 600 on SAT critical reading, 75% scored over 600 on SAT math, 95% scored over 26 on composite ACT.
Student Life Upper grades have student council, honor system. Discipline rests equally with students and faculty.
Tuition and Aid 7-day tuition and room/board: $18,000. Guaranteed tuition plan. Tuition installment plan (all accepted U.S. students are awarded full merit scholarships, need-based aid available to all other students). Merit scholarship grants, need-based scholarship grants, full tuition merit scholarships awarded to all admitted U.S. citizens available. In 2011–12, 85% of upper-school students received aid; total upper-school merit-scholarship money awarded: $2,800,000. Total amount of financial aid awarded in 2011–12: $2,800,000.
Admissions Traditional secondary-level entrance grade is 11. For fall 2011, 440 students applied for upper-level admission, 52 were accepted, 52 enrolled. ACT, PSAT or SAT or PSAT, SAT, or ACT for applicants to grade 11 and 12 required. Deadline for receipt of application materials: January 10. No application fee required. Interview required.
Athletics Coed Intramural: aerobics, aerobics/dance, aerobics/Nautilus, alpine skiing, aquatics, backpacking, badminton, ballet, baseball, basketball, bicycling, billiards, canoeing/kayaking, climbing, combined training, cooperative games, cricket, cross-country running, dance, fitness, Frisbee, hiking/backpacking, jogging, modern dance, mountaineering, nordic skiing, outdoor activities, physical training, racquetball, ropes courses, running, sailing, skiing (cross-country), skiing (downhill), snowboarding, snowshoeing, soccer, softball, squash, strength & conditioning, swimming and diving, table tennis, tennis, volleyball, walking, weight lifting, weight training, wilderness, wilderness survival, yoga. 1 PE instructor, 12 athletic trainers.
Computers Computers are regularly used in art, English, ESL, foreign language, mathematics, music, science classes. Computer network features include on-campus library services, Internet access, wireless campus network, Internet filtering or blocking technology. Campus intranet, student e-mail accounts, and computer access in designated common areas are available to students. Students grades are available online.
Contact Mr. Tim Smith, Director of Admissions. 505-454-4201. Fax: 505-454-4294. E-mail: tim.smith@uwc-usa.org. Web site: www.uwc-usa.org.

UNIVERSITY CHRISTIAN PREPARATORY SCHOOL

4800 Mooringsport Road
Shreveport, Louisiana 71107

Head of School: Ms. Beryl Cowthran

General Information Coeducational day college-preparatory, general academic, arts, religious studies, and technology school, affiliated with Christian faith. Grades K–12. Founded: 1970. Setting: urban. Nearest major city is Bossier City. 25-acre campus. 14 buildings on campus. Approved or accredited by Southern Association of Colleges and Schools and Louisiana Department of Education. Total enrollment: 59. Upper school average class size: 14. Upper school faculty-student ratio: 1:14. There are 178 required school days per year for Upper School students. Upper School students typically attend 5 days per week. The average school day consists of 7 hours.
Upper School Student Profile Grade 9: 5 students (3 boys, 2 girls); Grade 10: 1 student (1 boy); Grade 11: 5 students (5 boys); Grade 12: 8 students (6 boys, 2 girls). 98% of students are Christian faith.
Faculty School total: 12. In upper school: 2 men, 4 women; 1 has an advanced degree.
Subjects Offered Algebra, American history, art, Bible, biology, business mathematics, chemistry, civics/free enterprise, computer applications, computer literacy, general math, general science, geography, geometry, health, Internet research, language arts, mathematics, physical education, physical science, reading, reading/study skills, student teaching, world geography, world history, yearbook.
Graduation Requirements Advanced math, algebra, American history, American literature, Bible, biology, chemistry, civics/free enterprise, computer applications, earth and space science, electives, foreign language, geometry, grammar, language arts, life science, literature, physical education (includes health), physical science, world geography, world history.
College Admission Counseling 13 students graduated in 2010; 11 went to college, including Louisiana State University in Shreveport. Other: 1 went to work, 1 entered military service.
Student Life Upper grades have uniform requirement, student council, honor system. Discipline rests primarily with faculty. Attendance at religious services is required.
Tuition and Aid Day student tuition: $4500. Tuition installment plan (individually arranged payment plans). Tuition reduction for siblings, need-based scholarship grants available. In 2010–11, 13% of upper-school students received aid.
Admissions Traditional secondary-level entrance grade is 9. For fall 2010, 7 students applied for upper-level admission, 4 were accepted, 4 enrolled. Deadline for receipt of application materials: none. No application fee required. Interview recommended.
Athletics Interscholastic: basketball (boys, girls); intramural: basketball (b,g), weight training (b,g).
Computers Computers are regularly used in library, yearbook classes. Computer network features include Internet access. Computer access in designated common areas is available to students.
Contact Mrs. Catherine Johnson, Office Manager. 318-221-2697. Fax: 318-221-2790. Web site: www.universitychristianprep.com.

THE UNIVERSITY OF CHICAGO LABORATORY SCHOOLS

1362 East 59th Street
Chicago, Illinois 60637

Head of School: Dr. David W. Magill

General Information Coeducational day college-preparatory school. Grades N–12. Founded: 1896. Setting: urban. 11-acre campus. 3 buildings on campus. Approved or accredited by Independent Schools Association of the Central States, North Central Association of Colleges and Schools, and Illinois Department of Education. Member of National Association of Independent Schools. Endowment: $17.3 million. Total enrollment: 1,819. Upper school average class size: 16. Upper school faculty-student ratio: 1:10. There are 170 required school days per year for Upper School students. Upper School students typically attend 5 days per week. The average school day consists of 7 hours and 5 minutes.
Upper School Student Profile Grade 9: 130 students (67 boys, 63 girls); Grade 10: 126 students (57 boys, 69 girls); Grade 11: 133 students (52 boys, 81 girls); Grade 12: 121 students (54 boys, 67 girls).
Faculty School total: 215. In upper school: 29 men, 39 women; 63 have advanced degrees.
Subjects Offered Acting, advanced biology, advanced chemistry, African-American history, algebra, American history, art, art history, biology, calculus, calculus-AP, chemistry, Chinese, community service, computer science, computer science-AP, CPR, creative writing, discrete mathematics, drama, drawing, driver education, English, English literature, European history, expository writing, fine arts, French, French-AP, geometry, German, German-AP, government/civics, history, Holocaust, jazz band, journalism, Latin, Mandarin, mathematics, modern European history, music, music theory-AP, newspaper, orchestra, painting, photography, photojournalism, physical education, physics, play production, post-calculus, science, sculpture, social studies, Spanish, Spanish language-AP, Spanish-AP, statistics, statistics-AP, studio art, theater, trigonometry, U.S. history, Web site design, Western civilization, world history, writing, yearbook.
Graduation Requirements Arts and fine arts (art, music, dance, drama), computer science, English, foreign language, mathematics, music, physical education (includes health), science, social studies (includes history). Community service is required.
Special Academic Programs 8 Advanced Placement exams for which test preparation is offered; accelerated programs; independent study; study at local college for college credit.
College Admission Counseling 117 students graduated in 2011; 116 went to college, including Northwestern University; Tufts University; University of Chicago; University of Illinois at Urbana–Champaign; University of Michigan; Yale University. Other: 1 had other specific plans. Median SAT critical reading: 681, median SAT math: 675, median SAT writing: 668, median combined SAT: 2024, median composite ACT: 30. 78% scored over 600 on SAT critical reading, 75% scored over 600 on SAT math, 78% scored over 600 on SAT writing, 82% scored over 1800 on combined SAT, 81% scored over 26 on composite ACT.
Student Life Upper grades have student council. Discipline rests primarily with faculty.
Summer Programs Enrichment, advancement, sports programs offered; session focuses on advancement of placement in courses; held on campus; accepts boys and girls; open to students from other schools. 100 students usually enrolled. 2012 schedule: June 18 to July 27. Application deadline: May 15.
Tuition and Aid Day student tuition: $23,928. Tuition installment plan (monthly payment plans, quarterly payment plan). Need-based scholarship grants available. In 2011–12, 20% of upper-school students received aid. Total amount of financial aid awarded in 2011–12: $1,178,003.
Admissions Traditional secondary-level entrance grade is 9. For fall 2011, 197 students applied for upper-level admission, 61 were accepted, 35 enrolled. ISEE required.

Deadline for receipt of application materials: November 15. Application fee required: $80. On-campus interview required.
Athletics Interscholastic: baseball (boys), basketball (b,g), cross-country running (b,g), indoor track & field (b,g), soccer (b,g), swimming and diving (b,g), tennis (b,g), track and field (b,g), volleyball (g), winter (indoor) track (b,g); intramural: dance squad (g), weight training (b,g); coed interscholastic: cross-country running, fencing, flag football, golf; coed intramural: life saving. 12 PE instructors, 31 coaches, 1 athletic trainer.
Computers Computers are regularly used in mathematics, music, newspaper, science, yearbook classes. Computer network features include on-campus library services, Internet access, wireless campus network. Student e-mail accounts are available to students. The school has a published electronic and media policy.
Contact Irene Reed, Executive Director of Admissions and Financial Aid. 773-702-9451. Fax: 773-702-7455. E-mail: ireed@ucls.uchicago.edu. Web site: www.ucls.uchicago.edu/.

See Close-Up on page 698.

UNIVERSITY OF DETROIT JESUIT HIGH SCHOOL AND ACADEMY

8400 South Cambridge Avenue
Detroit, Michigan 48221

Head of School: Mr. Anthony Trudel

General Information Boys' day college-preparatory, arts, religious studies, and technology school, affiliated with Roman Catholic Church (Jesuit order); primarily serves individuals with Attention Deficit Disorder. Grades 7–12. Founded: 1877. Setting: urban. 12-acre campus. 1 building on campus. Approved or accredited by Jesuit Secondary Education Association, Michigan Association of Non-Public Schools, North Central Association of Colleges and Schools, and Michigan Department of Education. Endowment: $15 million. Total enrollment: 882. Upper school average class size: 22. Upper school faculty-student ratio: 1:14. There are 183 required school days per year for Upper School students. Upper School students typically attend 5 days per week. The average school day consists of 6 hours and 45 minutes.
Upper School Student Profile Grade 9: 212 students (212 boys); Grade 10: 212 students (212 boys); Grade 11: 160 students (160 boys); Grade 12: 155 students (155 boys). 72% of students are Roman Catholic Church (Jesuit order).
Faculty School total: 60. In upper school: 40 men, 18 women; 38 have advanced degrees.
Subjects Offered Acting, African-American history, algebra, American history, American history-AP, American literature, anatomy, art, Bible studies, biochemistry, biology, biology-AP, calculus, calculus-AP, ceramics, chemistry, chemistry-AP, Chinese, Christian and Hebrew scripture, Christian doctrine, Christian education, Christian ethics, Christian studies, Christian testament, church history, comparative religion, computer applications, computer programming, computer-aided design, drawing, earth science, economics, English, English literature, English literature-AP, English-AP, environmental science, ethics, European history, expository writing, French, geography, geometry, government-AP, government/civics, history, history of the Catholic Church, history-AP, Latin, Latin-AP, Mandarin, mathematics, music, physical education, physical science, physics, physics-AP, psychology, public speaking, religion, science, social studies, sociology, Spanish, Spanish-AP, speech, theology, trigonometry, U.S. government and politics-AP, U.S. history, U.S. history-AP, world history, world literature, writing.
Graduation Requirements Arts and fine arts (art, music, dance, drama), business skills (includes word processing), English, foreign language, mathematics, physical education (includes health), public speaking, religion (includes Bible studies and theology), science, social studies (includes history), senior community service program.
Special Academic Programs 14 Advanced Placement exams for which test preparation is offered; honors section; independent study; study at local college for college credit.
College Admission Counseling 176 students graduated in 2011; 174 went to college, including Michigan State University; University of Dayton; University of Michigan; University of Michigan–Dearborn; University of Notre Dame; Wayne State University. Other: 2 had other specific plans.
Student Life Upper grades have specified standards of dress, student council, honor system. Discipline rests primarily with faculty. Attendance at religious services is required.
Summer Programs Art/fine arts, computer instruction programs offered; session focuses on computer applications and art; held on campus; accepts boys; not open to students from other schools. 50 students usually enrolled. 2012 schedule: June 20 to July 22.
Tuition and Aid Day student tuition: $10,600. Tuition installment plan (FACTS Tuition Payment Plan). Merit scholarship grants, need-based scholarship grants available. In 2011–12, 34% of upper-school students received aid; total upper-school merit-scholarship money awarded: $250,000. Total amount of financial aid awarded in 2011–12: $1,610,000.
Admissions Traditional secondary-level entrance grade is 9. For fall 2011, 500 students applied for upper-level admission, 360 were accepted, 212 enrolled. Scholastic Testing Service High School Placement Test or STS - Educational Development Series required. Deadline for receipt of application materials: none. No application fee required. On-campus interview recommended.
Athletics Interscholastic: baseball, basketball, bowling, cross-country running, diving, football, golf, ice hockey, lacrosse, skiing (downhill), soccer, swimming and diving, tennis, track and field, wrestling; intramural: basketball, bowling, flag football, football, Frisbee, soccer, ultimate Frisbee. 2 PE instructors, 15 coaches, 2 athletic trainers.
Computers Computers are regularly used in all academic, art, history, mathematics, science, speech classes. Computer network features include on-campus library services, online commercial services, Internet access, wireless campus network, Internet filtering or blocking technology. Student e-mail accounts are available to students. Students grades are available online. The school has a published electronic and media policy.
Contact Mr. Atif Lodhi, Director of Admissions. 313-862-5400 Ext. 2380. Fax: 313-862-3299. E-mail: atif.lodhi@uofdjesuit.org. Web site: www.uofdjesuit.org/.

UNIVERSITY PREP

8000 25th Avenue NE
Seattle, Washington 98115

Head of School: Erica L. Hamlin

General Information Coeducational day college-preparatory, arts, bilingual studies, technology, and global education school. Grades 6–12. Founded: 1976. Setting: urban. 6-acre campus. 5 buildings on campus. Approved or accredited by Northwest Association of Schools and Colleges, Pacific Northwest Association of Independent Schools, and Washington Department of Education. Member of National Association of Independent Schools. Endowment: $5.5 million. Total enrollment: 510. Upper school average class size: 17. Upper school faculty-student ratio: 1:9. There are 169 required school days per year for Upper School students. Upper School students typically attend 5 days per week. The average school day consists of 6 hours and 50 minutes.
Upper School Student Profile Grade 9: 79 students (43 boys, 36 girls); Grade 10: 83 students (44 boys, 39 girls); Grade 11: 68 students (34 boys, 34 girls); Grade 12: 68 students (38 boys, 30 girls).
Faculty School total: 60. In upper school: 26 men, 28 women; 54 have advanced degrees.
Subjects Offered 3-dimensional art, advanced chemistry, advanced math, African drumming, African-American studies, algebra, American government, American history, American literature, applied arts, applied music, art, art and culture, art history, Asian literature, Asian studies, astronomy, athletics, audio visual/media, band, biology, British literature, calculus, career and personal planning, career planning, career/college preparation, chemistry, Chinese, Chinese studies, choir, chorus, civil rights, classical civilization, college counseling, college placement, college planning, community service, comparative government and politics, comparative religion, composition, computer art, computer literacy, computer science, conceptual physics, creative dance, creative drama, creative writing, critical thinking, critical writing, dance, decision making skills, democracy in America, design, digital art, digital photography, diversity studies, drafting, drama, drama performance, dramatic arts, drawing, ecology, economics, electives, English, English composition, English literature, ensembles, environmental education, environmental science, environmental studies, ethnic studies, European history, expository writing, film studies, fine arts, fitness, foreign language, French, freshman seminar, geography, geometry, global studies, golf, government, government/civics, graphic design, health, history, history of religion, independent study, information technology, introduction to technology, Japanese, Japanese history, Japanese studies, jazz ensemble, journalism, languages, Latin American studies, library, life skills, literary magazine, mathematics, media, medieval/Renaissance history, minority studies, multicultural studies, music, music performance, music theory, orchestra, Pacific Northwest seminar, painting, performing arts, personal fitness, philosophy, photography, physical education, physical fitness, physics, play production, play/screen writing, poetry, political science, politics, programming, psychology, public policy, publishing, research, Russian studies, science, senior thesis, social justice, Spanish, stagecraft, statistics, student publications, theater, theater arts, theater design and production, trigonometry, vocal ensemble, weight training, weightlifting, wilderness education, wilderness experience, women in society, world literature, yearbook.
Graduation Requirements American history, arts and fine arts (art, music, dance, drama), biology, chemistry, English, foreign language, life skills, mathematics, Pacific Northwest seminar, physical education (includes health), physics, science, senior thesis, social studies (includes history). Community service is required.
Special Academic Programs Advanced Placement exam preparation; independent study; term-away projects; study abroad; programs in English, mathematics, general development for dyslexic students; special instructional classes for college-bound students with high intellectual potential who have diagnosed specific learning disability.
College Admission Counseling 70 students graduated in 2011; all went to college, including Chapman University; Dartmouth College; Santa Clara University; University of Pennsylvania; University of Washington; Whittier College. Median SAT critical reading: 600, median SAT math: 620, median SAT writing: 590, median combined SAT: 1810, median composite ACT: 28. 58% scored over 600 on SAT critical reading, 63% scored over 600 on SAT math, 50% scored over 600 on SAT writing, 58% scored over 1800 on combined SAT, 74% scored over 26 on composite ACT.
Student Life Upper grades have student council, honor system. Discipline rests equally with students and faculty.

Tuition and Aid Day student tuition: $27,150. Tuition installment plan (Insured Tuition Payment Plan, Key Tuition Payment Plan, monthly payment plans, individually arranged payment plans, Dewar Tuition Refund Plan). Need-based scholarship grants available. In 2011–12, 20% of upper-school students received aid. Total amount of financial aid awarded in 2011–12: $1,976,682.
Admissions Traditional secondary-level entrance grade is 9. For fall 2011, 188 students applied for upper-level admission, 42 were accepted, 25 enrolled. ISEE required. Deadline for receipt of application materials: January 12. Application fee required: $75. On-campus interview required.
Athletics Interscholastic: baseball (boys), basketball (b,g), cross-country running (b,g), flag football (b), Frisbee (b,g), soccer (b,g), softball (g), tennis (b,g), track and field (b,g), volleyball (g); intramural: golf (b,g), ultimate Frisbee (b,g); coed interscholastic: ultimate Frisbee; coed intramural: aerobics, aerobics/dance, backpacking, climbing, dance, fitness, hiking/backpacking, modern dance, outdoor activities, outdoor adventure, outdoor education, outdoor skills, outdoors, rock climbing, skiing (downhill), snowboarding, strength & conditioning, ultimate Frisbee, wall climbing, weight training, wilderness, yoga. 5 PE instructors, 65 coaches.
Computers Computers are regularly used in all academic, art, creative writing, English, foreign language, history, information technology, journalism, library, mathematics, media, music, photography, publications, science, technology, yearbook classes. Computer network features include on-campus library services, online commercial services, Internet access, wireless campus network, Internet filtering or blocking technology. Campus intranet, student e-mail accounts, and computer access in designated common areas are available to students. Students grades are available online. The school has a published electronic and media policy.
Contact Melaine Taylor, Associate Director of Admission. 206-523-6407. Fax: 206-525-5320. E-mail: admissionoffice@universityprep.org. Web site: www.universityprep.org.

UNIVERSITY SCHOOL OF JACKSON

232/240 McClellan Road

Jackson, Tennessee 38305

Head of School: Clay Lilienstern

General Information Coeducational day college-preparatory, arts, and technology school. Grades PK–12. Founded: 1970. Setting: suburban. 140-acre campus. 3 buildings on campus. Approved or accredited by Southern Association of Colleges and Schools and Tennessee Department of Education. Member of National Association of Independent Schools. Endowment: $85,000. Total enrollment: 1,232. Upper school average class size: 20. Upper school faculty-student ratio: 1:13. There are 180 required school days per year for Upper School students. Upper School students typically attend 5 days per week. The average school day consists of 7 hours and 10 minutes.
Upper School Student Profile Grade 9: 68 students (35 boys, 33 girls); Grade 10: 91 students (51 boys, 40 girls); Grade 11: 105 students (60 boys, 45 girls); Grade 12: 84 students (44 boys, 40 girls).
Faculty School total: 95. In upper school: 12 men, 22 women; 25 have advanced degrees.
Subjects Offered 3-dimensional art, 3-dimensional design, accounting, acting, advanced biology, advanced chemistry, advanced math, Advanced Placement courses, advanced studio art-AP, algebra, American history, American literature, anatomy, anatomy and physiology, art, band, biology, biology-AP, broadcast journalism, calculus, calculus-AP, character education, chemistry, chemistry-AP, chorus, computer applications, computer programming, computer science, creative writing, current events, dramatic arts, ecology, economics, economics and history, English, English language-AP, English literature and composition-AP, English literature-AP, environmental science, environmental science-AP, European history, European history-AP, fine arts, French, geography, geology, geometry, government, government/civics, honors algebra, honors English, honors geometry, humanities, keyboarding, mathematics, music theory, music theory-AP, music-AP, performing arts, photography, physical education, physical science, physics, pre-calculus, psychology, science, social studies, Spanish, Spanish language-AP, studio art-AP, trigonometry, U.S. history, U.S. history-AP, vocal ensemble, world history, world religions, yearbook.
Graduation Requirements Arts and fine arts (art, music, dance, drama), computer science, English, foreign language, mathematics, science, social studies (includes history), 50 hours of community service.
Special Academic Programs Advanced Placement exam preparation; honors section; academic accommodation for the gifted, the musically talented, and the artistically talented; ESL (10 students enrolled).
College Admission Counseling 80 students graduated in 2011; all went to college, including Middle Tennessee State University; Mississippi State University; Rhodes College; The University of Tennessee; Union University; University of Mississippi. Median SAT critical reading: 540, median SAT math: 560, median SAT writing: 540, median combined SAT: 1640, median composite ACT: 23. 25% scored over 600 on SAT critical reading, 35% scored over 600 on SAT math, 27% scored over 600 on SAT writing, 20% scored over 1800 on combined SAT, 40% scored over 26 on composite ACT.
Student Life Upper grades have uniform requirement, student council, honor system. Discipline rests equally with students and faculty.
Summer Programs Remediation, enrichment, sports, art/fine arts, computer instruction programs offered; session focuses on enrichment and remediation; held on campus; accepts boys and girls; open to students from other schools. 500 students usually enrolled. 2012 schedule: June 1 to July 31. Application deadline: none.
Tuition and Aid Day student tuition: $5890–$7795. Tuition installment plan (monthly payment plans, quarterly payment plan). Tuition reduction for siblings, need-based scholarship grants, need-based financial aid available. In 2011–12, 3% of upper-school students received aid. Total amount of financial aid awarded in 2011–12: $130,000.
Admissions Traditional secondary-level entrance grade is 9. For fall 2011, 37 students applied for upper-level admission, 32 were accepted, 27 enrolled. Math Placement Exam, Otis-Lennon School Ability Test, SCAT and writing sample required. Deadline for receipt of application materials: none. Application fee required: $50. On-campus interview required.
Athletics Interscholastic: baseball (boys), basketball (b,g), cheering (g), cross-country running (b,g), football (b), golf (b,g), soccer (b,g), softball (g), tennis (b,g), track and field (b,g), volleyball (g), weight lifting (b,g), weight training (b,g); intramural: bowling (b,g), in-line hockey (b); coed intramural: bowling. 2 coaches.
Computers Computers are regularly used in art, English, foreign language, history, journalism, keyboarding, music, science, technology, theater arts, word processing, writing, yearbook classes. Computer network features include on-campus library services, online commercial services, Internet access. Students grades are available online. The school has a published electronic and media policy.
Contact Kay Shearin, Director of Admissions. 731-660-1692. Fax: 731-668-6910. E-mail: kshearin@usjbruins.org. Web site: www.usjbruins.org.

UNIVERSITY SCHOOL OF MILWAUKEE

2100 West Fairy Chasm Road

Milwaukee, Wisconsin 53217

Head of School: Laura J. Fuller

General Information Coeducational day college-preparatory, arts, and technology school. Grades PK–12. Founded: 1851. Setting: suburban. 131-acre campus. 2 buildings on campus. Approved or accredited by Independent Schools Association of the Central States and Wisconsin Department of Education. Member of National Association of Independent Schools and Secondary School Admission Test Board. Endowment: $47 million. Total enrollment: 1,058. Upper school average class size: 15. Upper school faculty-student ratio: 1:9. There are 178 required school days per year for Upper School students. Upper School students typically attend 5 days per week. The average school day consists of 6 hours and 45 minutes.
Upper School Student Profile Grade 9: 81 students (40 boys, 41 girls); Grade 10: 96 students (50 boys, 46 girls); Grade 11: 72 students (36 boys, 36 girls); Grade 12: 93 students (42 boys, 51 girls).
Faculty School total: 102. In upper school: 21 men, 17 women; 29 have advanced degrees.
Subjects Offered Algebra, American history, American literature, art, art history, band, biology, calculus, chemistry, computer programming, computer science, concert choir, discrete mathematics, drama, drawing, economics, English, English literature, European history, expository writing, French, geometry, health, Latin, mathematics, music, orchestra, painting, photography, physical education, physics, printmaking, psychology, SAT/ACT preparation, sculpture, Spanish, statistics, theater, U.S. history, world history, world literature.
Graduation Requirements Arts and fine arts (art, music, dance, drama), English, foreign language, history, mathematics, physical education (includes health), science, 40 hours of community service.
Special Academic Programs Advanced Placement exam preparation; honors section; independent study; study at local college for college credit.
College Admission Counseling 92 students graduated in 2011; 86 went to college, including Emory University; Northwestern University; Stanford University; University of Chicago; University of Missouri–St. Louis; University of Wisconsin–Madison. Other: 2 entered a postgraduate year, 4 had other specific plans. Median SAT critical reading: 680, median SAT math: 690, median SAT writing: 680, median combined SAT: 2070, median composite ACT: 30. 83% scored over 600 on SAT critical reading, 83% scored over 600 on SAT math, 81% scored over 600 on SAT writing, 81% scored over 1800 on combined SAT, 77% scored over 26 on composite ACT.
Student Life Upper grades have specified standards of dress, student council, honor system. Discipline rests equally with students and faculty.
Summer Programs Enrichment, sports, art/fine arts, computer instruction programs offered; session focuses on reading, writing, math, science, sports, visual arts, music, drama, and computer enrichment/instruction; held on campus; accepts boys and girls; open to students from other schools. 1,500 students usually enrolled. 2012 schedule: June 13 to August 19. Application deadline: none.
Tuition and Aid Day student tuition: $20,425. Tuition installment plan (SMART Tuition Payment Plan). Need-based scholarship grants available. In 2011–12, 24% of upper-school students received aid. Total amount of financial aid awarded in 2011–12: $937,475.
Admissions Traditional secondary-level entrance grade is 9. For fall 2011, 45 students applied for upper-level admission, 32 were accepted, 28 enrolled. ERB Achievement

Test required. Deadline for receipt of application materials: none. Application fee required: $50. Interview required.
Athletics Interscholastic: baseball (boys), basketball (b,g), cross-country running (b,g), dance team (g), diving (b,g), field hockey (g), football (b), golf (b), ice hockey (b,g), lacrosse (b), skiing (downhill) (b,g), soccer (b,g), swimming and diving (b,g), tennis (b,g), track and field (b,g), volleyball (g). 2 PE instructors, 50 coaches, 2 athletic trainers.
Computers Computers are regularly used in college planning, creative writing, English, foreign language, history, journalism, mathematics, science, yearbook classes. Computer network features include on-campus library services, online commercial services, Internet access, wireless campus network, Internet filtering or blocking technology. Student e-mail accounts are available to students. Students grades are available online. The school has a published electronic and media policy.
Contact Kathleen Friedman, Director of Admissions. 414-540-3321. Fax: 414-352-8076. E-mail: kfriedman@usmk12.org. Web site: www.usmk12.org.

UNIVERSITY SCHOOL OF NOVA SOUTHEASTERN UNIVERSITY

3375 SW 75 Avenue
Lower School Building
Fort Lauderdale, Florida 33314

Head of School: Dr. Jerome S. Chermak

General Information Coeducational day college-preparatory school. Grades PK–12. Founded: 1970. Setting: suburban. 300-acre campus. 4 buildings on campus. Approved or accredited by Association of Independent Schools of Florida, Southern Association of Colleges and Schools, and Florida Department of Education. Member of National Association of Independent Schools. Endowment: $750,000. Total enrollment: 1,897. Upper school average class size: 20. Upper school faculty-student ratio: 1:11. There are 180 required school days per year for Upper School students. Upper School students typically attend 5 days per week. The average school day consists of 6 hours.
Upper School Student Profile Grade 9: 192 students (104 boys, 88 girls); Grade 10: 184 students (96 boys, 88 girls); Grade 11: 181 students (96 boys, 85 girls); Grade 12: 157 students (87 boys, 70 girls).
Faculty School total: 181. In upper school: 26 men, 35 women; 43 have advanced degrees.
Subjects Offered Advanced Placement courses, advanced studio art-AP, algebra, American government, American history, American literature, anatomy, art, band, biology, calculus, ceramics, chemistry, chorus, community service, computer programming, computer science, concert choir, creative writing, debate, directing, drawing and design, economics, English, English literature, environmental science, expository writing, fine arts, forensics, French, geometry, grammar, guitar, Internet, journalism, keyboarding, Latin, media production, music, music appreciation, music theory, orchestra, performing arts, personal fitness, physical education, physics, portfolio art, pre-calculus, psychology, public speaking, Spanish, speech, theater, trigonometry, video film production, world geography, world history, world literature, writing.
Graduation Requirements Art, computer science, electives, English, expository writing, foreign language, health education, journalism, mathematics, music, personal fitness, physical education (includes health), public speaking, science, social studies (includes history), speech and debate. Community service is required.
Special Academic Programs Advanced Placement exam preparation; honors section; accelerated programs; independent study; term-away projects; study at local college for college credit; academic accommodation for the gifted, the musically talented, and the artistically talented; remedial reading and/or remedial writing.
College Admission Counseling 166 students graduated in 2011; all went to college, including Boston University; Florida State University; University of Central Florida; University of Florida; University of Miami; University of Pennsylvania.
Student Life Upper grades have uniform requirement, student council. Discipline rests primarily with faculty.
Summer Programs Remediation, enrichment, advancement, sports, art/fine arts programs offered; session focuses on sports, arts, and academics; held on campus; accepts boys and girls; open to students from other schools. 400 students usually enrolled. 2012 schedule: June 4 to August 11. Application deadline: none.
Tuition and Aid Day student tuition: $19,845. Tuition installment plan (Key Tuition Payment Plan). Tuition reduction for siblings, need-based scholarship grants available. In 2011–12, 15% of upper-school students received aid. Total amount of financial aid awarded in 2011–12: $1,500,000.
Admissions Traditional secondary-level entrance grade is 9. For fall 2011, 204 students applied for upper-level admission, 146 were accepted, 103 enrolled. SSAT required. Deadline for receipt of application materials: none. Application fee required: $100. Interview required.
Athletics Interscholastic: baseball (boys), basketball (b,g), cheering (g), crew (b,g), cross-country running (b,g), dance team (g), diving (b,g), football (b), golf (b,g), ice hockey (b), lacrosse (g), roller hockey (b), soccer (b,g), softball (g), swimming and diving (b,g), tennis (b,g), track and field (b,g), volleyball (b,g), wrestling (b); coed interscholastic: cross-country running, dance. 3 PE instructors, 43 coaches, 1 athletic trainer.
Computers Computers are regularly used in all classes. Computer network features include on-campus library services, Internet access, wireless campus network, Internet filtering or blocking technology. Student e-mail accounts and computer access in designated common areas are available to students. Students grades are available online. The school has a published electronic and media policy.
Contact Ms. Allison Musso, Coordinator of Admissions. 954-262-4405. Fax: 954-262-3691. E-mail: amusso@nova.edu. Web site: www.uschool.nova.edu.

URSULINE ACADEMY

85 Lowder Street
Dedham, Massachusetts 02026-4299

Head of School: Ms. Rosann Whiting

General Information Girls' day college-preparatory school, affiliated with Roman Catholic Church. Grades 7–12. Founded: 1946. Setting: suburban. Nearest major city is Boston. 28-acre campus. 3 buildings on campus. Approved or accredited by Association of Independent Schools in New England, National Catholic Education Association, New England Association of Schools and Colleges, The College Board, and Massachusetts Department of Education. Member of National Association of Independent Schools. Total enrollment: 397. Upper school average class size: 18. Upper school faculty-student ratio: 1:9. Upper School students typically attend 5 days per week. The average school day consists of 5 hours and 45 minutes.
Upper School Student Profile Grade 7: 56 students (56 girls); Grade 8: 63 students (63 girls); Grade 9: 73 students (73 girls); Grade 10: 68 students (68 girls); Grade 11: 74 students (74 girls); Grade 12: 63 students (63 girls). 88% of students are Roman Catholic.
Faculty School total: 38. In upper school: 6 men, 31 women; 34 have advanced degrees.
Subjects Offered Algebra, American history, American literature, anatomy and physiology, art, art history, biology, biology-AP, British literature (honors), calculus, calculus-AP, chemistry, chemistry-AP, communication arts, computer studies, English, English literature, English-AP, French, geography, geometry, government/civics, grammar, history, Latin, life science, mathematics, modern European history-AP, music, physical education, physical science, physics, pre-algebra, pre-calculus, psychology, public speaking, social studies, Spanish, Spanish language-AP, studio art, study skills, theology, trigonometry, U.S. history, U.S. history-AP, world history, world literature.
Graduation Requirements Arts and fine arts (art, music, dance, drama), computer science, English, foreign language, mathematics, physical education (includes health), public speaking, religion (includes Bible studies and theology), science, social studies (includes history), study skills, senior year community service field project.
Special Academic Programs 7 Advanced Placement exams for which test preparation is offered; honors section.
College Admission Counseling 62 students graduated in 2010; all went to college, including Boston College; Boston University; College of the Holy Cross; Harvard University; Quinnipiac University; Wake Forest University. Mean SAT critical reading: 626, mean SAT math: 595, mean SAT writing: 631, mean combined SAT: 1853.
Student Life Upper grades have uniform requirement, student council, honor system. Discipline rests primarily with faculty. Attendance at religious services is required.
Tuition and Aid Day student tuition: $13,000. Tuition installment plan (Insured Tuition Payment Plan, FACTS Tuition Payment Plan, monthly payment plans, individually arranged payment plans, semester, quarterly and monthly payment plans). Need-based scholarship grants available. In 2010–11, 15% of upper-school students received aid.
Admissions Traditional secondary-level entrance grade is 9. Archdiocese of Boston or STS or school's own exam required. Deadline for receipt of application materials: December 15. Application fee required: $30.
Athletics Interscholastic: alpine skiing, basketball, cross-country running, diving, field hockey, golf, ice hockey, lacrosse, soccer, softball, swimming and diving, tennis, track and field, volleyball, winter (indoor) track; intramural: dance, golf, skiing (downhill), tennis. 2 PE instructors, 26 coaches.
Computers Computers are regularly used in all classes. Computer network features include on-campus library services, Internet access, Internet filtering or blocking technology. Campus intranet, student e-mail accounts, and computer access in designated common areas are available to students. Students grades are available online. The school has a published electronic and media policy.
Contact Catherine Spencer, Director of Admissions. 781-326-6161 Ext. 107. Fax: 781-329-3926. E-mail: admissions@ursulineacademy.net. Web site: www.ursulineacademy.net.

THE URSULINE ACADEMY OF DALLAS

4900 Walnut Hill Lane
Dallas, Texas 75229

Head of School: Ms. Elizabeth Bourgeois

General Information Girls' day college-preparatory, arts, religious studies, and technology school, affiliated with Roman Catholic Church. Grades 9–12. Founded: 1874. Setting: urban. 26-acre campus. 5 buildings on campus. Approved or accredited by

Independent Schools Association of the Southwest, National Catholic Education Association, Texas Catholic Conference, The College Board, and Texas Department of Education. Total enrollment: 800. Upper school average class size: 18. Upper school faculty-student ratio: 1:10.
Upper School Student Profile Grade 9: 200 students (200 girls); Grade 10: 200 students (200 girls); Grade 11: 200 students (200 girls); Grade 12: 200 students (200 girls). 85% of students are Roman Catholic.
Faculty School total: 91. In upper school: 15 men, 76 women; 68 have advanced degrees.
Subjects Offered 20th century history, Advanced Placement courses, algebra, anatomy, anatomy and physiology, Arabic, band, biology, bookbinding, calculus, ceramics, chemistry, choir, Christian and Hebrew scripture, community service, comparative government and politics, comparative religion, computer programming, computer science, concert choir, creative writing, current events, dance, design, digital imaging, digital photography, discrete mathematics, drama, drawing, economics, English literature, environmental science, ethics, European history, fitness, French, geography, geology, geometry, government, government/civics, graphic design, health and wellness, journalism, Latin, Latin American literature, Mandarin, newspaper, oceanography, orchestra, painting, peer ministry, photography, physical education, physics, pre-calculus, printmaking, psychology, social justice, Spanish, speech, statistics, theater, theology, U.S. history, U.S. literature, Web authoring, Western civilization, world history, world literature, yearbook.
Graduation Requirements Arts and fine arts (art, music, dance, drama), computer science, English, foreign language, mathematics, physical education (includes health), religion (includes Bible studies and theology), science, social studies (includes history), speech. Community service is required.
Special Academic Programs Advanced Placement exam preparation; honors section; independent study.
College Admission Counseling 191 students graduated in 2010; all went to college, including Louisiana State University and Agricultural and Mechanical College; Southern Methodist University; Texas A&M University; Texas Christian University; The University of Texas at Austin; University of Oklahoma. Mean SAT critical reading: 614, mean SAT math: 608, mean SAT writing: 619, mean combined SAT: 1841, mean composite ACT: 28.
Student Life Upper grades have uniform requirement, student council, honor system. Discipline rests equally with students and faculty. Attendance at religious services is required.
Tuition and Aid Day student tuition: $14,975. Tuition installment plan (individually arranged payment plans, annual, semi-annual, and monthly (by bank draft) payment plans). Merit scholarship grants, need-based scholarship grants available. In 2010–11, 23% of upper-school students received aid. Total amount of financial aid awarded in 2010–11: $851,300.
Admissions Traditional secondary-level entrance grade is 9. For fall 2010, 411 students applied for upper-level admission, 215 enrolled. ISEE required. Deadline for receipt of application materials: January 7. Application fee required: $60. Interview required.
Athletics Interscholastic: basketball, cheering, crew, cross-country running, diving, drill team, golf, lacrosse, soccer, softball, swimming and diving, tennis, track and field, volleyball; intramural: crew, drill team. 3 PE instructors, 15 coaches, 1 athletic trainer.
Computers Computers are regularly used in all classes. Computer network features include on-campus library services, online commercial services, Internet access, wireless campus network. Campus intranet and student e-mail accounts are available to students. Students grades are available online.
Contact Mrs. Mary Campise, Assistant Director of Admission. 469-232-1839. Fax: 469-232-1836. E-mail: mcampise@ursulinedallas.org. Web site: www.ursulinedallas.org.

VAIL MOUNTAIN SCHOOL

3000 Booth Falls Road
Vail, Colorado 81657

Head of School: Mr. Peter M. Abuisi

General Information Coeducational day college-preparatory school. Grades K–12. Founded: 1962. Setting: small town. Nearest major city is Denver. 10-acre campus. 2 buildings on campus. Approved or accredited by Association of Colorado Independent Schools, National Independent Private Schools Association, and Colorado Department of Education. Member of National Association of Independent Schools. Endowment: $1.5 million. Total enrollment: 349. Upper school average class size: 15. Upper school faculty-student ratio: 1:8. There are 175 required school days per year for Upper School students. Upper School students typically attend 5 days per week. The average school day consists of 7 hours.
Upper School Student Profile Grade 9: 36 students (16 boys, 20 girls); Grade 10: 25 students (12 boys, 13 girls); Grade 11: 24 students (15 boys, 9 girls); Grade 12: 21 students (9 boys, 12 girls).
Faculty School total: 37. In upper school: 10 have advanced degrees.
Subjects Offered Advanced Placement courses, algebra, American history, American literature, art, arts, biology, calculus, chemistry, computer math, computer science, creative writing, drama, earth science, English, English literature, environmental science, ethics, European history, expository writing, fine arts, geography, geometry, government/civics, grammar, history, Latin, Latin American literature, mathematics, photography, physical education, physics, poetry, psychology, science, Shakespeare, social sciences, social studies, Spanish, theater, trigonometry, world history, writing.
Graduation Requirements Arts and fine arts (art, music, dance, drama), English, foreign language, mathematics, physical education (includes health), psychology, science, social sciences, social studies (includes history), Spanish, acceptance into a four-year college or university.
Special Academic Programs 8 Advanced Placement exams for which test preparation is offered; ESL (6 students enrolled).
College Admission Counseling 22 students graduated in 2011; all went to college, including Cornell University; University of Colorado Boulder; University of Southern California; Washington University in St. Louis.
Student Life Upper grades have specified standards of dress, honor system. Discipline rests primarily with faculty.
Summer Programs Remediation, enrichment, advancement, sports, art/fine arts programs offered; session focuses on math and English enrichment for Hispanic students; held on campus; accepts boys and girls; open to students from other schools. 75 students usually enrolled. 2012 schedule: June 15 to July 31.
Tuition and Aid Day student tuition: $18,500. Tuition installment plan (monthly payment plans, individually arranged payment plans). Need-based scholarship grants, need-based loans available. In 2011–12, 33% of upper-school students received aid. Total amount of financial aid awarded in 2011–12: $390,000.
Admissions Traditional secondary-level entrance grade is 9. For fall 2011, 18 students applied for upper-level admission, 10 were accepted, 7 enrolled. Any standardized test required. Deadline for receipt of application materials: January 28. Application fee required: $50. Interview required.
Athletics Interscholastic: alpine skiing (boys, girls), freestyle skiing (b,g), golf (b,g), nordic skiing (b,g), skiing (cross-country) (b,g), skiing (downhill) (b,g), soccer (b,g), tennis (g); intramural: backpacking (b,g), basketball (b,g), dance team (g), ice hockey (b), independent competitive sports (b,g), indoor soccer (b,g), jogging (b,g), outdoor activities (b,g), outdoor adventure (b,g), outdoor education (b,g), physical fitness (b,g), physical training (b,g), rock climbing (b,g), skiing (cross-country) (b,g), skiing (downhill) (b,g), strength & conditioning (b,g), telemark skiing (b,g), volleyball (g), weight lifting (b,g); coed interscholastic: freestyle skiing, nordic skiing, snowboarding; coed intramural: backpacking, basketball, canoeing/kayaking, climbing, fishing, fitness, Fives, fly fishing, Frisbee, hiking/backpacking, indoor soccer, jogging, jump rope, kayaking, mountain biking, mountaineering, outdoor activities, outdoor adventure, outdoor education, physical fitness, physical training, rafting, rock climbing, ropes courses, running, snowboarding, snowshoeing, strength & conditioning, telemark skiing, touch football, ultimate Frisbee, weight lifting, wilderness survival, yoga. 1 PE instructor, 15 coaches, 1 athletic trainer.
Computers Computers are regularly used in all academic, art, basic skills, college planning, computer applications, creative writing, desktop publishing, English, ethics, foreign language, graphic arts, history, humanities, independent study, introduction to technology, keyboarding, library, library skills, music technology, photography, reading, research skills, senior seminar, social sciences, social studies, Spanish, study skills, technology, Web site design, word processing, writing, writing, yearbook classes. Computer network features include on-campus library services, online commercial services, Internet access, wireless campus network, Internet filtering or blocking technology. Campus intranet and student e-mail accounts are available to students. Students grades are available online. The school has a published electronic and media policy.
Contact Mr. Jeremy Thelen, Director of Admission. 970-477-7164. Fax: 970-476-3860. E-mail: admissions@vms.edu. Web site: www.vms.edu.

VALLE CATHOLIC HIGH SCHOOL

40 North Fourth Street
Ste. Genevieve, Missouri 63670

Head of School: Ms. Sara C. Menard

General Information Coeducational day college-preparatory, arts, business, vocational, religious studies, and technology school, affiliated with Roman Catholic Church. Grades 9–12. Founded: 1837. Setting: small town. Nearest major city is St. Louis. 3-acre campus. 3 buildings on campus. Approved or accredited by North Central Association of Colleges and Schools and Missouri Department of Education. Endowment: $2 million. Total enrollment: 137. Upper school average class size: 15. Upper school faculty-student ratio: 1:9. There are 171 required school days per year for Upper School students. Upper School students typically attend 5 days per week. The average school day consists of 5 hours and 50 minutes.
Upper School Student Profile Grade 9: 41 students (20 boys, 21 girls); Grade 10: 41 students (15 boys, 26 girls); Grade 11: 24 students (12 boys, 12 girls); Grade 12: 28 students (14 boys, 14 girls). 98% of students are Roman Catholic.
Faculty School total: 15. In upper school: 6 men, 9 women; 7 have advanced degrees.
Subjects Offered 20th century American writers, accounting, advanced chemistry, advanced computer applications, advanced math, algebra, American democracy, American history, American literature, analysis and differential calculus, anatomy and physiology, architectural drawing, art, art history, arts, band, biology, British literature, business, business applications, business communications, business law, business math-

ematics, business skills, business studies, calculus, calculus-AP, Catholic belief and practice, chemistry-AP, Christian and Hebrew scripture, Christian scripture, church history, civics, civics/free enterprise, classics, communications, comparative religion, composition, computer applications, computer multimedia, computer science, computer skills, concert band, consumer economics, consumer education, consumer law, consumer mathematics, drafting, drama, drama performance, dramatic arts, drawing, earth science, ecology, environmental systems, economics, economics and history, English, entrepreneurship, environmental science, environmental systems, foreign language, freshman seminar, geography, geometry, history of the Catholic Church, honors algebra, honors English, honors U.S. history, human anatomy, journalism, keyboarding, marching band, math analysis, mathematics, media communications, moral theology, novels, orchestra, painting, peace and justice, physical education, physics, practical arts, psychology, religion, science, social studies, sociology, Spanish, technical drawing, U.S. government, values and decisions, visual arts, Western civilization, yearbook.

Graduation Requirements Advanced math, algebra, American history, American literature, biology, Catholic belief and practice, chemistry, Christian and Hebrew scripture, civics, English, English composition, ethical decision making, foreign language, geometry, government/civics, history of the Catholic Church, mathematics, physical education (includes health), practical arts, religion (includes Bible studies and theology), science, senior composition, social justice, social studies (includes history), Spanish, 80 hours of community service.

Special Academic Programs 1 Advanced Placement exam for which test preparation is offered; honors section; study at local college for college credit; academic accommodation for the gifted and the artistically talented; remedial reading and/or remedial writing; remedial math.

College Admission Counseling 34 students graduated in 2011; 33 went to college, including Missouri State University; Saint Louis University; Southeast Missouri State University; Truman State University; University of Missouri. Mean SAT critical reading: 720, mean SAT math: 780, mean composite ACT: 24. 100% scored over 600 on SAT critical reading, 100% scored over 600 on SAT math, 26% scored over 26 on composite ACT.

Student Life Upper grades have uniform requirement, student council, honor system. Discipline rests primarily with faculty. Attendance at religious services is required.

Summer Programs Remediation, enrichment, advancement programs offered; session focuses on advancement and remediation/make-up; held on campus; accepts boys and girls; not open to students from other schools. 5 students usually enrolled. 2012 schedule: June 3 to July 31.

Tuition and Aid Day student tuition: $4500. Tuition installment plan (The Tuition Plan, monthly payment plans, individually arranged payment plans, tuition assistance through the St. Louis Archdiocese and Scholarships available through the School). Tuition reduction for siblings, merit scholarship grants, need-based scholarship grants, tuition relief funds available from St. Louis Archdiocese available. In 2011–12, 20% of upper-school students received aid; total upper-school merit-scholarship money awarded: $10,000. Total amount of financial aid awarded in 2011–12: $165,000.

Admissions Traditional secondary-level entrance grade is 9. For fall 2011, 11 students applied for upper-level admission, 11 were accepted, 11 enrolled. Any standardized test, school placement exam and writing sample required. Deadline for receipt of application materials: none. Application fee required: $25. Interview recommended.

Athletics Interscholastic: baseball (boys), basketball (b,g), dance team (g), drill team (g), football (b), track and field (b,g), volleyball (g), weight training (b); coed interscholastic: cheering, cross-country running, golf, physical training, strength & conditioning, weight lifting. 1 PE instructor.

Computers Computers are regularly used in accounting, business, career exploration, classics, college planning, economics, English, foreign language, geography, history, humanities, journalism, mathematics, psychology, religion, science, Spanish, writing, yearbook classes. Computer network features include Internet access, Internet filtering or blocking technology. Student e-mail accounts and computer access in designated common areas are available to students. The school has a published electronic and media policy.

Contact Mrs. Dawn C. Basler, Principal. 573-883-7496 Ext. 242. Fax: 573-883-9142. E-mail: baslerd@valleschools.org. Web site: www.valleschools.org.

VALLEY CHRISTIAN HIGH SCHOOL

7500 Inspiration Drive

Dublin, California 94568

Head of School: Mr. Larry Lopez

General Information Coeducational day college-preparatory, arts, and religious studies school, affiliated with Assemblies of God. Grades 6–12. Founded: 1981. Setting: suburban. Nearest major city is Pleasanton. 49-acre campus. 3 buildings on campus. Approved or accredited by Association of Christian Schools International, Western Association of Schools and Colleges, and California Department of Education. Total enrollment: 471. Upper school average class size: 22. Upper school faculty-student ratio: 1:13. Upper School students typically attend 5 days per week. The average school day consists of 5 hours and 36 minutes.

Upper School Student Profile 10% of students are Assemblies of God.

Faculty School total: 39. In upper school: 11 men, 27 women; 7 have advanced degrees.

Subjects Offered Acting, advanced math, Advanced Placement courses, advanced studio art-AP, algebra, American government, American history, American history-AP, American literature, American sign language, anatomy and physiology, art, arts, ASB Leadership, athletics, baseball, basketball, Bible, Bible studies, biology, British literature, business mathematics, calculus, calculus-AP, campus ministry, career and personal planning, career education, career exploration, career planning, career/college preparation, careers, ceramics, character education, cheerleading, chemistry, choir, choral music, Christian doctrine, Christian ethics, Christian scripture, Christian studies, Christian testament, church history, college admission preparation, college awareness, college counseling, college planning, competitive science projects, composition, computer graphics, computer literacy, computer resources, conceptual physics, constitutional history of U.S., creation science, creative writing, critical thinking, critical writing, debate, decision making skills, digital photography, directing, drama, drama performance, drama workshop, earth science, economics, electives, English, English language and composition-AP, English literature, English literature and composition-AP, English literature-AP, English-AP, English/composition-AP, epic literature, ESL, ethical decision making, ethics, European literature, expository writing, expressive arts, fiction, fine arts, fitness, foreign language, geography, geometry, German, German-AP, golf, government, grammar, graphic design, great books, Harlem Renaissance, health, health and wellness, health education, history, history of religion, history-AP, Holocaust, honors algebra, honors English, honors geometry, human anatomy, humanities, ideas, illustration, improvisation, journalism, keyboarding, lab science, language arts, language structure, language-AP, languages, leadership, leadership and service, library, Life of Christ, life science, literary genres, literature, literature and composition-AP, literature-AP, macro/microeconomics-AP, marine biology, math analysis, math applications, mathematics, mathematics-AP, mechanics of writing, medieval literature, methods of research, modern history, modern languages, moral theology, music, music appreciation, music theory, newspaper, novels, oral communications, oral expression, painting, participation in sports, performing arts, physical education, physical fitness, physics, physics-AP, play production, poetry, pre-algebra, pre-calculus, pre-college orientation, psychology, public speaking, reading, reading/study skills, regional literature, religion, religious education, religious studies, remedial study skills, research and reference, research skills, Russian literature, science fiction, science project, scripture, Shakespeare, Shakespearean histories, short story, softball, Spanish, Spanish language-AP, Spanish-AP, speech, sports, sports conditioning, statistics-AP, student government, studio art, studio art-AP, study skills, swimming, tennis, theater, theater arts, theater design and production, U.S. government, U.S. government and politics, U.S. history, U.S. history-AP, U.S. literature, values and decisions, visual and performing arts, volleyball, weight training, world geography, world history, world history-AP, world literature, world religions, world wide web design, yearbook.

Graduation Requirements Art, Christian doctrine, Christian ethics, Christian scripture, composition, economics, foreign language, geography, grammar, health, history, keyboarding, literature, mathematics, moral reasoning, religious studies, science, U.S. government, World War II.

Special Academic Programs Honors section; independent study; academic accommodation for the gifted; programs in English, general development for dyslexic students.

College Admission Counseling 71 students graduated in 2011; 69 went to college, including Arizona State University; Azusa Pacific University; University of California, Davis; University of California, Irvine; University of California, San Diego. Other: 2 had other specific plans. Median SAT critical reading: 574, median SAT math: 570, median SAT writing: 561, median composite ACT: 24.

Student Life Upper grades have specified standards of dress, student council, honor system. Discipline rests primarily with faculty. Attendance at religious services is required.

Tuition and Aid Day student tuition: $11,550. Tuition installment plan (FACTS Tuition Payment Plan). Tuition reduction for siblings, need-based scholarship grants available. In 2011–12, 10% of upper-school students received aid. Total amount of financial aid awarded in 2011–12: $30,000.

Admissions Traditional secondary-level entrance grade is 9. For fall 2011, 50 students applied for upper-level admission, 47 were accepted, 41 enrolled. SSAT, TOEFL or SLEP or writing sample required. Deadline for receipt of application materials: none. Application fee required: $375. On-campus interview required.

Athletics Interscholastic: baseball (boys), basketball (b,g), cheering (g), cross-country running (b,g), flag football (b), football (b), golf (b), soccer (b,g), softball (g), tennis (b,g), track and field (b,g), volleyball (b,g), weight training (b,g), wrestling (b). 4 PE instructors, 20 coaches, 3 athletic trainers.

Computers Computers are regularly used in business skills, graphic design, journalism, keyboarding, lab/keyboard, media arts, publications, Web site design, yearbook classes. Computer network features include on-campus library services, online commercial services, Internet access, wireless campus network. Campus intranet is available to students. Students grades are available online. The school has a published electronic and media policy.

Contact Mrs. Lori Umidon, Admissions Administrative Assistant. 925-560-6256. Fax: 925-828-5658. E-mail: lumidon@dublinvcc.org. Web site: www.valleychristianschools.org.

VALLEY CHRISTIAN HIGH SCHOOL

100 Skyway Drive

San Jose, California 95111

Head of School: Dr. Clifford Daugherty

General Information Coeducational day and distance learning college-preparatory, arts, religious studies, technology, Conservatory of the Arts, and Applied Math, Science and Engineering Institute school, affiliated with Christian faith. Grades K–12. Distance learning grades 8–12. Founded: 1960. Setting: suburban. 53-acre campus. 4 buildings on campus. Approved or accredited by Association of Christian Schools International, Western Association of Schools and Colleges, and California Department of Education. Total enrollment: 2,280. Upper school average class size: 28. Upper school faculty-student ratio: 1:17. There are 174 required school days per year for Upper School students. Upper School students typically attend 5 days per week. The average school day consists of 6 hours and 45 minutes.

Upper School Student Profile Grade 9: 344 students (172 boys, 172 girls); Grade 10: 332 students (170 boys, 162 girls); Grade 11: 329 students (173 boys, 156 girls); Grade 12: 313 students (168 boys, 145 girls). 85% of students are Christian.

Faculty School total: 142. In upper school: 37 men, 49 women; 24 have advanced degrees.

Subjects Offered 20th century American writers, acting, advanced chemistry, advanced computer applications, advanced math, Advanced Placement courses, advanced studio art-AP, algebra, American history, American literature, American sign language, anatomy and physiology, ancient world history, applied music, art, audio visual/media, Basic programming, Bible, Bible studies, biology, biology-AP, British literature-AP, broadcasting, calculus-AP, career and personal planning, cheerleading, chemistry, chemistry-AP, Chinese, choir, choral music, choreography, Christian doctrine, Christian ethics, Christian scripture, Christian studies, college admission preparation, college counseling, college planning, comparative political systems-AP, composition-AP, computer art, computer literacy, computer music, computer science-AP, concert choir, consumer mathematics, critical studies in film, dance, dance performance, digital art, drama, drama performance, dramatic arts, electronics, engineering, English, English language and composition-AP, English literature-AP, environmental science-AP, European history-AP, filmmaking, finite math, foreign language, French, French studies, geometry, global studies, government, grammar, health education, health science, history, history of music, honors English, honors U.S. history, honors world history, HTML design, instrumental music, introduction to theater, Japanese, Japanese as Second Language, jazz band, jazz dance, jazz ensemble, journalism, keyboarding, Latin, leadership, leadership and service, literature and composition-AP, macro/microeconomics-AP, Mandarin, marching band, mathematics, mathematics-AP, Microsoft, music theater, music theory-AP, musical productions, musical theater, photo shop, photojournalism, physical science, physics, physics-AP, play/screen writing, pre-algebra, pre-calculus, radio broadcasting, SAT preparation, sign language, Spanish, Spanish-AP, stage design, statistics, statistics-AP, student government, studio art-AP, symphonic band, tap dance, technical theater, telecommunications, theater arts, theater production, trigonometry, typing, U.S. government, U.S. government and politics-AP, U.S. history, U.S. history-AP, video film production, vocal ensemble, weight training, wind ensemble, world history, yearbook.

Graduation Requirements Arts and fine arts (art, music, dance, drama), biology, Christian and Hebrew scripture, Christian doctrine, Christian studies, computers, economics, economics and history, English, English composition, English literature, global studies, mathematics, physical education (includes health), physical science, science, technology, U.S. government, U.S. history, world geography, world history.

Special Academic Programs 22 Advanced Placement exams for which test preparation is offered; honors section; programs in English, mathematics, general development for dyslexic students.

College Admission Counseling 286 students graduated in 2011; 284 went to college, including Azusa Pacific University; California Polytechnic State University, San Luis Obispo; California State University, Chico; San Jose State University; University of California, Berkeley; University of California, Davis. Other: 1 went to work, 1 entered military service. Median SAT critical reading: 540, median SAT math: 530, median SAT writing: 590, median combined SAT: 1660. 35% scored over 600 on SAT critical reading, 38% scored over 600 on SAT math, 32% scored over 600 on SAT writing, 31% scored over 1800 on combined SAT.

Student Life Upper grades have specified standards of dress, student council, honor system. Discipline rests primarily with faculty.

Summer Programs Remediation, enrichment, advancement, sports, art/fine arts, computer instruction programs offered; session focuses on advancement, remediation, and enrichment; held on campus; accepts boys and girls; open to students from other schools. 400 students usually enrolled. 2012 schedule: June 21 to July 30. Application deadline: none.

Tuition and Aid Day student tuition: $14,418. Tuition installment plan (FACTS Tuition Payment Plan). Tuition reduction for siblings, need-based scholarship grants available. In 2011–12, 20% of upper-school students received aid. Total amount of financial aid awarded in 2011–12: $1,250,000.

Admissions Traditional secondary-level entrance grade is 9. For fall 2011, 405 students applied for upper-level admission, 315 were accepted, 246 enrolled. Admissions testing, essay, Iowa Subtests, mathematics proficiency exam, school's own test or TOEFL or SLEP required. Deadline for receipt of application materials: none. Application fee required: $70. Interview required.

Athletics Interscholastic: aquatics (boys, girls), baseball (b), basketball (b,g), cheering (b,g), cross-country running (b,g), dance squad (b,g), dance team (b), diving (b,g), football (b), golf (b,g), ice hockey (b,g), soccer (b,g), softball (g), swimming and diving (b,g), tennis (b,g), track and field (b,g), volleyball (b,g), water polo (b,g), weight training (b,g), wrestling (b); intramural: weight training (b,g). 3 PE instructors, 23 coaches, 2 athletic trainers.

Computers Computers are regularly used in Bible studies, computer applications, digital applications, foreign language, graphic arts, graphic design, journalism, keyboarding, lab/keyboard, library, mathematics, media arts, music, music technology, news writing, newspaper, photography, photojournalism, science, technology, typing, video film production, Web site design, word processing, writing, yearbook classes. Computer network features include on-campus library services, Internet access, wireless campus network, Internet filtering or blocking technology, ten online classes, through two online learning labs. Campus intranet and computer access in designated common areas are available to students. Students grades are available online. The school has a published electronic and media policy.

Contact Alana James, High School Admissions Coordinator. 408-513-2512. Fax: 408-513-2517. E-mail: ajames@vcs.net. Web site: www.vcs.net.

VALLEY FORGE MILITARY ACADEMY & COLLEGE

1001 Eagle Road

Wayne, Pennsylvania 19087-3695

General Information Boys' boarding and day college-preparatory, arts, business, religious studies, bilingual studies, technology, music, and military school. Boarding grades 7–PG, day grades 7–12. Founded: 1928. Setting: suburban. Nearest major city is Philadelphia. Students are housed in single-sex dormitories. 120-acre campus. 83 buildings on campus. Approved or accredited by Middle States Association of Colleges and Schools, The Association of Boarding Schools, and Pennsylvania Department of Education. Member of National Association of Independent Schools and Secondary School Admission Test Board. Endowment: $12 million. Total enrollment: 248. Upper school average class size: 12. Upper school faculty-student ratio: 1:11. There are 175 required school days per year for Upper School students. Upper School students typically attend 5 days per week. The average school day consists of 5 hours and 50 minutes.

See Display on next page and Close Up on page 700.

VALLEY LUTHERAN HIGH SCHOOL

5199 North 7th Avenue

Phoenix, Arizona 85013-2043

Head of School: Mr. Robert Koehne

General Information Coeducational day college-preparatory, arts, religious studies, and technology school, affiliated with Lutheran Church–Missouri Synod. Grades 9–12. Founded: 1981. Setting: urban. 10-acre campus. 4 buildings on campus. Approved or accredited by National Lutheran School Accreditation, North Central Association of Colleges and Schools, and Arizona Department of Education. Total enrollment: 184. Upper school average class size: 15. Upper school faculty-student ratio: 1:10. There are 180 required school days per year for Upper School students. Upper School students typically attend 5 days per week. The average school day consists of 6 hours and 45 minutes.

Upper School Student Profile Grade 9: 37 students (20 boys, 17 girls); Grade 10: 45 students (23 boys, 22 girls); Grade 11: 60 students (38 boys, 22 girls); Grade 12: 42 students (23 boys, 19 girls). 56% of students are Lutheran Church–Missouri Synod.

Faculty School total: 18. In upper school: 10 men, 8 women; 7 have advanced degrees.

Subjects Offered Advanced Placement courses, advanced studio art-AP, algebra, American government, American history, American history-AP, American literature, American politics in film, anatomy and physiology, art, athletics, band, Bible, biology, British literature, British literature (honors), calculus, calculus-AP, career and personal planning, chemistry, choir, choral music, chorus, Christian doctrine, Christian education, Christian ethics, computer skills, concert band, consumer mathematics, creative writing, current history, economics, English, English literature and composition-AP, environmental science, film history, foreign language, freshman seminar, geography, government, government-AP, honors algebra, honors geometry, human biology, intro to computers, music, music appreciation, New Testament, oral communications, physical education, physical fitness, physics, portfolio art, pre-algebra, pre-calculus, psychology, religion, SAT preparation, SAT/ACT preparation, Spanish, speech, speech communications, trigonometry, U.S. government, U.S. history-AP, United States government-AP, weightlifting, world geography, world history, world literature, World-Wide-Web publishing, yearbook.

Special Academic Programs 4 Advanced Placement exams for which test preparation is offered; honors section; term-away projects; academic accommodation for the gifted; remedial math; special instructional classes for deaf students.

College Admission Counseling 47 students graduated in 2011; 46 went to college, including Arizona State University; Azusa Pacific University; Concordia University; Grand Canyon University; Northern Arizona University; The University of Arizona. Other: 1 went to work. Median SAT critical reading: 550, median SAT math: 560, median SAT writing: 500, median combined SAT: 1610, median composite ACT: 24.

Student Life Upper grades have specified standards of dress, student council, honor system. Discipline rests primarily with faculty. Attendance at religious services is required.

Tuition and Aid Day student tuition: $8500. Tuition installment plan (monthly payment plans, individually arranged payment plans, Vanco Services online payments). Merit scholarship grants, need-based scholarship grants, association grants, Christian worker discounts available. In 2011–12, 30% of upper-school students received aid. Total amount of financial aid awarded in 2011–12: $166,770.

Admissions Traditional secondary-level entrance grade is 9. For fall 2011, 68 students applied for upper-level admission, 68 were accepted, 64 enrolled. High School Placement Test and school's own test required. Deadline for receipt of application materials: none. Application fee required: $50. On-campus interview required.

Athletics Interscholastic: baseball (boys), basketball (b,g), cheering (g), cross-country running (b,g), football (b), pom squad (g), soccer (b,g), softball (g), track and field (b,g), volleyball (g), wrestling (b); coed interscholastic: golf, running, strength & conditioning, tennis, weight training. 13 coaches.

Computers Computers are regularly used in computer applications, desktop publishing, photography, Web site design, word processing, yearbook classes. Computer network features include Internet access, Internet filtering or blocking technology. Students grades are available online. The school has a published electronic and media policy.

Contact Mr. Robert Koehne, Principal. 602-230-1600 Ext. 120. Fax: 602-230-1602. E-mail: rkoehne@vlhs.org. Web site: www.vlhs.org/.

THE VALLEY SCHOOL

5255 S. Linden Rd.

Swartz Creek, Michigan 48473

Head of School: Kaye C. Panchula

General Information Coeducational day college-preparatory and arts school. Grades PK–12. Founded: 1970. Setting: urban. Nearest major city is Flint. 5-acre campus. 1 building on campus. Candidate for accreditation by Independent Schools Association of the Central States. Total enrollment: 57. Upper school average class size: 18. Upper school faculty-student ratio: 1:8. There are 180 required school days per year for Upper School students. Upper School students typically attend 5 days per week. The average school day consists of 5 hours and 30 minutes.

Upper School Student Profile Grade 9: 1 student (1 boy); Grade 10: 6 students (5 boys, 1 girl); Grade 11: 6 students (3 boys, 3 girls); Grade 12: 4 students (2 boys, 2 girls).

Faculty School total: 12. In upper school: 4 men, 3 women; 4 have advanced degrees.

Subjects Offered Algebra, American history, American literature, art, art history, biology, ceramics, chemistry, current events, earth science, English, English literature, European history, expository writing, fine arts, geometry, government/civics, grammar, history, mathematics, music, physical education, physics, probability and statistics, SAT/ACT preparation, science, social sciences, Spanish, trigonometry, world cultures, world history, world literature, writing.

Graduation Requirements Arts and fine arts (art, music, dance, drama), English, foreign language, mathematics, physical education (includes health), science, social sciences, social studies (includes history), senior project off campus.

Special Academic Programs Independent study; term-away projects; study at local college for college credit; academic accommodation for the gifted and the artistically talented.

College Admission Counseling 6 students graduated in 2011; all went to college, including Baylor University; Eastern Michigan University; Kalamazoo College; University of Chicago; University of Michigan. Mean composite ACT: 27.

Student Life Upper grades have student council. Discipline rests equally with students and faculty.

Tuition and Aid Day student tuition: $9399. Tuition installment plan (FACTS Tuition Payment Plan). Tuition reduction for siblings, merit scholarship grants, need-based scholarship grants available. In 2011–12, 83% of upper-school students received aid; total upper-school merit-scholarship money awarded: $28,199. Total amount of financial aid awarded in 2011–12: $51,376.

Admissions Traditional secondary-level entrance grade is 9. For fall 2011, 20 students applied for upper-level admission, 20 were accepted, 17 enrolled. School's own exam required. Deadline for receipt of application materials: none. No application fee required. On-campus interview required.

Athletics Interscholastic: baseball (boys), basketball (b,g), golf (b), outdoor skills (b,g), outdoors (b,g), physical fitness (b,g), soccer (b,g), tennis (g), volleyball (g). 1 PE instructor, 3 coaches.

Computers Computers are regularly used in art, English, mathematics, science, social sciences, stock market, study skills, writing classes. Computer resources include

Internet access, wireless campus network. Computer access in designated common areas is available to students.
Contact Ms. Minka Owens, Director of Admissions. 810-767-4004. Fax: 810-655-0853. E-mail: email@valleyschool.org. Web site: www.valleyschool.org.

VALLEY VIEW SCHOOL

North Brookfield, Massachusetts

See Special Needs Schools section.

THE VANGUARD SCHOOL

Lake Wales, Florida

See Special Needs Schools section.

VENTA PREPARATORY SCHOOL

2013 Old Carp Road

Ottawa, Ontario K0A 1L0, Canada

Head of School: Ms. Marilyn Mansfield

General Information Coeducational boarding and day college-preparatory, arts, and music school. Grades 1–10. Founded: 1981. Setting: small town. Students are housed in single-sex by floor dormitories. 50-acre campus. 8 buildings on campus. Approved or accredited by Ontario Department of Education. Language of instruction: English. Total enrollment: 96. Upper school average class size: 12. Upper school faculty-student ratio: 1:6. Upper School students typically attend 5 days per week.
Upper School Student Profile Grade 8: 13 students (7 boys, 6 girls); Grade 9: 8 students (4 boys, 4 girls); Grade 10: 7 students (5 boys, 2 girls). 40% of students are boarding students. 90% are province residents. 5 provinces are represented in upper school student body. International students from Bermuda, China, Hong Kong, Mexico, and United States.
Faculty School total: 18. In upper school: 6 men, 12 women; 3 have advanced degrees; 6 reside on campus.
Special Academic Programs Independent study; academic accommodation for the gifted; remedial reading and/or remedial writing; remedial math; programs in English, mathematics, general development for dyslexic students.
Student Life Upper grades have uniform requirement, honor system. Discipline rests primarily with faculty.
Tuition and Aid Day student tuition: CAN$17,070–CAN$18,585; 5-day tuition and room/board: CAN$24,290; 7-day tuition and room/board: CAN$25,680. Tuition installment plan (monthly payment plans, individually arranged payment plans). Tuition reduction for siblings, merit scholarship grants available.
Admissions Traditional secondary-level entrance grade is 9. Psychoeducational evaluation required. Deadline for receipt of application materials: none. Application fee required: CAN$75. On-campus interview required.
Athletics Coed Intramural: ball hockey, baseball, basketball, canoeing/kayaking, fitness, ice hockey, jogging, outdoor recreation. 4 PE instructors.
Computers Computers are regularly used in current events, geography, keyboarding, mathematics, research skills, science, Web site design classes. Computer network features include Internet access, wireless campus network, Internet filtering or blocking technology. The school has a published electronic and media policy.
Contact Mr. Cory Awde, Director of Marketing and Admissions. 613-839-2175 Ext. 240. Fax: 613-839-1956. E-mail: info@ventaprep.com. Web site: www.ventapreparatoryschool.com.

VERDALA INTERNATIONAL SCHOOL

Fort Pembroke

Pembroke PBK1641, Malta

Head of School: Mr. Nollaig Mac an Bhaird

General Information Coeducational boarding and day college-preparatory and general academic school. Boarding grades 9–12, day grades PK–12. Founded: 1977. Setting: suburban. Nearest major city is Valletta, Malta. Students are housed in host family homes. 6-acre campus. 6 buildings on campus. Approved or accredited by International Baccalaureate Organization and Middle States Association of Colleges and Schools. Member of European Council of International Schools. Language of instruction: English. Endowment: €91,000.. Total enrollment: 310. Upper school average class size: 15. Upper school faculty-student ratio: 1:7. There are 176 required school days per year for Upper School students. Upper School students typically attend 5 days per week. The average school day consists of 5 hours and 30 minutes.
Upper School Student Profile Grade 9: 28 students (15 boys, 13 girls); Grade 10: 31 students (14 boys, 17 girls); Grade 11: 33 students (16 boys, 17 girls); Grade 12: 27 students (11 boys, 16 girls). 12% of students are boarding students. 90% are international students. International students from Germany, Russian Federation, Sweden, United Kingdom, and United States; 32 other countries represented in student body.
Faculty School total: 48. In upper school: 5 men, 18 women; 7 have advanced degrees.
Subjects Offered Algebra, art, art history, biology, calculus, chemistry, computer science, drama, English, English literature, fine arts, French, geography, geometry, grammar, health, history, Italian, mathematics, music, physical education, physics, psychology, science, social studies, Spanish, theory of knowledge, trigonometry, world history, world literature, writing.
Graduation Requirements Arts and fine arts (art, music, dance, drama), computer science, English, foreign language, mathematics, physical education (includes health), science, social studies (includes history).
Special Academic Programs International Baccalaureate program; ESL (52 students enrolled).
College Admission Counseling 28 students graduated in 2010; 25 went to college. Other: 3 went to work. Median SAT critical reading: 500, median SAT math: 640, median SAT writing: 520.
Student Life Upper grades have specified standards of dress, student council, honor system. Discipline rests primarily with faculty.
Tuition and Aid Day student tuition: €6780; 7-day tuition and room/board: €7260. Tuition installment plan (monthly payment plans, individually arranged payment plans). Tuition reduction for siblings, need-based scholarship grants available. In 2010 11, 64% of upper-school students received aid. Total amount of financial aid awarded in 2010–11: $18,750.
Admissions Traditional secondary-level entrance grade is 9. Academic Profile Tests required. Deadline for receipt of application materials: none. No application fee required. On-campus interview required.
Athletics Interscholastic: basketball (boys), volleyball (b,g); intramural: physical fitness (b,g), soccer (b,g), swimming and diving (b,g), track and field (b,g); coed intramural: physical fitness, swimming and diving. 2 coaches, 1 athletic trainer.
Computers Computer resources include on-campus library services, online commercial services, Internet access. Computer access in designated common areas is available to students.
Contact Mrs. Daphne Baldacchino, Secretary. 356-21375133. Fax: 356-21372387. E-mail: vis1@verdala.org. Web site: www.verdala.org.

VIANNEY HIGH SCHOOL

1311 South Kirkwood Road

St. Louis, Missouri 63122

Head of School: Mr. Lawrence D. Keller

General Information Boys' day college-preparatory, arts, business, religious studies, and technology school, affiliated with Roman Catholic Church. Grades 9–12. Founded: 1960. Setting: suburban. 37-acre campus. 6 buildings on campus. Approved or accredited by National Catholic Education Association, North Central Association of Colleges and Schools, and The College Board. Total enrollment: 622. Upper school average class size: 22. Upper school faculty-student ratio: 1:12. There are 165 required school days per year for Upper School students. Upper School students typically attend 5 days per week. The average school day consists of 6 hours and 5 minutes.
Upper School Student Profile Grade 9: 178 students (178 boys); Grade 10: 150 students (150 boys); Grade 11: 150 students (150 boys); Grade 12: 144 students (144 boys). 98% of students are Roman Catholic.
Faculty School total: 50. In upper school: 42 men, 8 women; 49 have advanced degrees.
Subjects Offered Accounting, advanced chemistry, Advanced Placement courses, algebra, American government, American history, American literature, analysis, analytic geometry, architectural drawing, art, art education, art history, arts appreciation, athletic training, band, British literature (honors), business law, business mathematics, calculus, calculus-AP, Catholic belief and practice, chemistry, Christian and Hebrew scripture, Christian ethics, Christian studies, college writing, communication skills, composition, computer applications, computer programming, computer skills, constitutional history of U.S., consumer education, current events, drama, economics, English composition, English literature, European history, expository writing, foreign language, fractal geometry, French, geometry, German, German literature, government, health and wellness, honors algebra, honors English, honors geometry, honors U.S. history, journalism, keyboarding, leadership, mythology, probability and statistics, publications, research skills, scripture, sex education, Shakespeare, Spanish, Spanish literature, sports conditioning, stage design, stagecraft, technical drawing, technology, technology/design, the Web, theater arts, theater design and production, theater history, trigonometry, U.S. government, U.S. history, U.S. literature, Web site design, weight training, world civilizations, world history, writing.
Graduation Requirements American history, American literature, arts and fine arts (art, music, dance, drama), biology, English, English composition, foreign language, government/civics, history, keyboarding, mathematics, physical education (includes health), physical fitness, religious studies, science, social issues, 100 hours of community service.
Special Academic Programs 3 Advanced Placement exams for which test preparation is offered; honors section; study at local college for college credit; special

instructional classes for students with learning disabilities, Attention Deficit Disorder, dyslexia, emotional and behavioral problems.

College Admission Counseling 133 students graduated in 2010; 130 went to college, including Missouri State University; Saint Louis University; Southeast Missouri State University; St. Louis Community College at Meramec; University of Missouri. Other: 2 went to work, 1 entered military service. Median composite ACT: 23. 25% scored over 26 on composite ACT.

Student Life Upper grades have specified standards of dress, student council, honor system. Discipline rests equally with students and faculty. Attendance at religious services is required.

Tuition and Aid Day student tuition: $10,350. Tuition installment plan (The Tuition Plan, FACTS Tuition Payment Plan, monthly payment plans, individually arranged payment plans). Tuition reduction for siblings, merit scholarship grants, need-based scholarship grants, paying campus jobs available. In 2010–11, 27% of upper-school students received aid; total upper-school merit-scholarship money awarded: $135,127. Total amount of financial aid awarded in 2010–11: $316,127.

Admissions Traditional secondary-level entrance grade is 9. For fall 2010, 187 students applied for upper-level admission, 184 were accepted, 178 enrolled. High School Placement Test (closed version) from Scholastic Testing Service required. Deadline for receipt of application materials: none. No application fee required. On-campus interview required.

Athletics Interscholastic: aquatics, baseball, basketball, cross-country running, diving, football, golf, ice hockey, lacrosse, racquetball, roller hockey, soccer, swimming and diving, tennis, track and field, volleyball, wrestling; intramural: bowling, flag football, paint ball, Special Olympics, touch football. 3 PE instructors, 40 coaches, 1 athletic trainer.

Computers Computers are regularly used in all academic, architecture, computer applications, creative writing, drafting, journalism, yearbook classes. Computer network features include on-campus library services, online commercial services, Internet access, wireless campus network, Internet filtering or blocking technology. Campus intranet, student e-mail accounts, and computer access in designated common areas are available to students. Students grades are available online. The school has a published electronic and media policy.

Contact Mr. Terry Cochran, Director of Admissions. 314-965-4853 Ext. 142. Fax: 314-965-1950. E-mail: tcochran@vianney.com. Web site: www.vianney.com.

VICKSBURG CATHOLIC SCHOOL

1900 Grove Street

Vicksburg, Mississippi 39183

Head of School: Mrs. Michele Connelly

General Information Coeducational day college-preparatory and religious studies school, affiliated with Roman Catholic Church. Grades PK–12. Founded: 1860. Setting: urban. Nearest major city is Jackson. 8-acre campus. 2 buildings on campus. Approved or accredited by National Catholic Education Association, Southern Association of Colleges and Schools, and Mississippi Department of Education. Endowment: $350,000. Total enrollment: 569. Upper school average class size: 16. Upper school faculty-student ratio: 1:10. There are 180 required school days per year for Upper School students. Upper School students typically attend 5 days per week. The average school day consists of 5 hours and 50 minutes.

Upper School Student Profile Grade 7: 51 students (28 boys, 23 girls); Grade 8: 40 students (24 boys, 16 girls); Grade 9: 51 students (25 boys, 26 girls); Grade 10: 40 students (24 boys, 16 girls); Grade 11: 38 students (20 boys, 18 girls); Grade 12: 38 students (20 boys, 18 girls). 50% of students are Roman Catholic.

Faculty School total: 50. In upper school: 11 men, 15 women; 7 have advanced degrees.

Subjects Offered Accounting, algebra, American government, American history, anatomy, anatomy and physiology, art, band, biology, biology-AP, calculus-AP, ceramics, chemistry, chemistry-AP, choir, computer applications, creative writing, desktop publishing, drama, earth science, economics, English, English language and composition-AP, environmental science, foreign language, geography, geology, geometry, global studies, government and politics-AP, health, honors algebra, honors English, honors geometry, humanities, keyboarding, law, learning lab, minority studies, music, personal finance, physical education, physics, physics-AP, pre-algebra, pre-calculus, psychology, public speaking, sociology, Spanish, state history, theology, trigonometry, U.S. government, U.S. history, world geography, world history, yearbook.

Graduation Requirements Algebra, American government, American history, biology, computer skills, economics, English, geography, geometry, government, health, history, lab science, law, physical education (includes health), Spanish, theology, U.S. government, U.S. history, world history, Mississippi state requirements.

Special Academic Programs 6 Advanced Placement exams for which test preparation is offered; honors section; special instructional classes for students with learning disabilities, Attention Deficit Disorder, dyslexia, emotional and behavioral problems.

College Admission Counseling 37 students graduated in 2011; all went to college, including Delta State University; Hinds Community College; Louisiana State University and Agricultural and Mechanical College; Mississippi State University; University of Mississippi; University of Southern Mississippi.

Student Life Upper grades have uniform requirement, student council, honor system. Discipline rests primarily with faculty. Attendance at religious services is required.

Tuition and Aid Day student tuition: $5800. Tuition installment plan (FACTS Tuition Payment Plan). Tuition reduction for siblings, need-based scholarship grants available. In 2011–12, 12% of upper-school students received aid. Total amount of financial aid awarded in 2011–12: $100,000.

Admissions Traditional secondary-level entrance grade is 7. For fall 2011, 22 students applied for upper-level admission, 22 were accepted, 20 enrolled. Deadline for receipt of application materials: none. Application fee required: $50. Interview required.

Athletics Interscholastic: baseball (boys), basketball (b,g), cheering (g), cross-country running (b,g), dance squad (g), football (b), golf (b), power lifting (b), soccer (b,g), softball (g), swimming and diving (b,g), tennis (b,g), track and field (b,g), weight lifting (b); coed interscholastic: swimming and diving, tennis. 2 PE instructors, 4 coaches.

Computers Computers are regularly used in accounting, computer applications, desktop publishing, keyboarding classes. Computer network features include on-campus library services, online commercial services, Internet access, Internet filtering or blocking technology. Students grades are available online. The school has a published electronic and media policy.

Contact Mrs. Patricia Rabalais, Registrar. 601-636-2256 Ext. 16. Fax: 601-631-0430. E-mail: patricia.rabalais@vicksburgcatholic.org. Web site: www.vicksburgcatholic.org.

VILLA DUCHESNE AND OAK HILL SCHOOL

801 South Spoede Road

St. Louis, Missouri 63131

Head of School: Sr. Lucie Nordmann, RSCJ

General Information Coeducational day college-preparatory, arts, religious studies, and technology school, affiliated with Roman Catholic Church. Boys grades JK–6, girls grades JK–12. Founded: 1929. Setting: suburban. 60-acre campus. 2 buildings on campus. Approved or accredited by Independent Schools Association of the Central States, National Catholic Education Association, Network of Sacred Heart Schools, North Central Association of Colleges and Schools, and Missouri Department of Education. Member of National Association of Independent Schools. Total enrollment: 680. Upper school average class size: 15. Upper school faculty-student ratio: 1:9. There are 180 required school days per year for Upper School students. Upper School students typically attend 5 days per week. The average school day consists of 7 hours.

Upper School Student Profile 88% of students are Roman Catholic.

Faculty School total: 89. In upper school: 13 men, 44 women; 40 have advanced degrees.

Subjects Offered American government, American literature, American literature-AP, anatomy and physiology, art, biology, biology-AP, British literature, calculus, calculus-AP, campus ministry, ceramics, chemistry, chorus, civics, computers, creative writing, discrete mathematics, drawing, economics, English, European history, European history-AP, Far Eastern history, French, geography, geometry, health, integrated physics, math analysis, Middle East, music, newspaper, painting, personal development, physical education, physics, pre-algebra, pre-calculus, printmaking, psychology, public speaking, religion, scripture, sculpture, social justice, Spanish, studio art, studio art-AP, theater arts, U.S. history, U.S. history-AP, Western civilization, women's studies, world literature, yearbook.

Graduation Requirements Students must perform community service to graduate.

Special Academic Programs International Baccalaureate program; 11 Advanced Placement exams for which test preparation is offered; honors section; independent study; term-away projects; study at local college for college credit; domestic exchange program (with Network of Sacred Heart Schools); study abroad; remedial reading and/or remedial writing; remedial math.

College Admission Counseling 81 students graduated in 2011; all went to college, including Fordham University; Georgetown University; Miami University; Saint Louis University; Southern Methodist University; University of Missouri. Mean combined SAT: 1823, mean composite ACT: 27.

Student Life Upper grades have uniform requirement, student council, honor system. Discipline rests primarily with faculty. Attendance at religious services is required.

Summer Programs Enrichment, advancement, sports, art/fine arts, computer instruction programs offered; session focuses on enrichment and college preparation; held on campus; accepts boys and girls; open to students from other schools. 150 students usually enrolled. 2012 schedule: June 6 to June 24. Application deadline: May 30.

Tuition and Aid Day student tuition: $17,375. Tuition installment plan (monthly payment plans, individually arranged payment plans, 8-month plan, trimester plan, or full-payment plan). Tuition reduction for siblings, need-based scholarship grants available. In 2011–12, 18% of upper-school students received aid. Total amount of financial aid awarded in 2011–12: $1,026,583.

Admissions Traditional secondary-level entrance grade is 9. Deadline for receipt of application materials: November 16. Application fee required: $40. On-campus interview required.

Athletics Interscholastic: basketball (girls), cross-country running (g), diving (g), field hockey (g), golf (g), lacrosse (g), racquetball (g), soccer (g), softball (g), swimming and diving (g), tennis (g), track and field (g), volleyball (g). 7 PE instructors, 34 coaches, 1 athletic trainer.

Computers Computers are regularly used in all academic classes. Computer network features include on-campus library services, online commercial services, Internet access, wireless campus network, Internet filtering or blocking technology, students in grades 7 to 12 have personal HP tablet PCs. Campus intranet, student e-mail accounts, and computer access in designated common areas are available to students. Students grades are available online. The school has a published electronic and media policy.

Contact Mrs. Elaine Brooks, Admissions Assistant. 314-810-3566. Fax: 314-432-0199. E-mail: ebrooks@vdoh.org. Web site: www.vdoh.org.

VILLAGE CHRISTIAN SCHOOLS

8930 Village Avenue

Sun Valley, California 91352

Head of School: Mr. Tom Konjoyan

General Information Coeducational day college-preparatory, general academic, arts, religious studies, and technology school, affiliated with Christian faith. Grades K–12. Founded: 1949. Setting: suburban. Nearest major city is Los Angeles. 110-acre campus. 7 buildings on campus. Approved or accredited by Association of Christian Schools International, Western Association of Schools and Colleges, and California Department of Education. Total enrollment: 1,091. Upper school average class size: 25. Upper school faculty-student ratio: 1:25. There are 169 required school days per year for Upper School students. Upper School students typically attend 5 days per week. The average school day consists of 6 hours and 30 minutes.

Upper School Student Profile 75% of students are Christian faith.

Faculty School total: 87. In upper school: 20 men, 15 women; 10 have advanced degrees.

Subjects Offered Algebra, American history-AP, American literature, anatomy, art, ASB Leadership, band, Bible studies, biology, biology-AP, British literature, calculus-AP, career education, careers, ceramics, chemistry, choir, choral music, church history, clayworking, computer graphics, computer literacy, drama, earth science, economics, English, English language and composition-AP, English literature and composition-AP, English-AP, environmental science-AP, geometry, health education, history-AP, honors English, jazz band, leadership, library assistant, Life of Christ, marching band, mathematics, music theory-AP, painting, physical education, physics, physiology, pre-calculus, Spanish, Spanish language-AP, Spanish literature-AP, statistics, statistics-AP, strings, theater arts, trigonometry, U.S. government, U.S. government and politics-AP, U.S. history, world history, world religions, yearbook.

Graduation Requirements Arts and fine arts (art, music, dance, drama), computer science, English, foreign language, mathematics, physical education (includes health), religion (includes Bible studies and theology), science, social sciences, social studies (includes history).

Special Academic Programs Advanced Placement exam preparation; honors section; study at local college for college credit.

College Admission Counseling 127 students graduated in 2010; 125 went to college, including Azusa Pacific University; California State University, Northridge; San Diego State University; University of California, Irvine; University of California, Los Angeles; University of Southern California. Other: 1 went to work, 1 entered military service. Mean SAT critical reading: 597, mean SAT math: 582.

Student Life Upper grades have uniform requirement, student council. Discipline rests equally with students and faculty.

Tuition and Aid Day student tuition: $9500. Tuition installment plan (monthly payment plans, individually arranged payment plans). Tuition reduction for siblings, merit scholarship grants, need-based scholarship grants, short-term emergency help for continuing families, fine arts scholarships to current students available.

Admissions Traditional secondary-level entrance grade is 9. Deadline for receipt of application materials: February 1. Application fee required: $100. On-campus interview required.

Athletics Interscholastic: baseball (boys), basketball (b,g), cheering (g), cross-country running (b,g), dance team (g), football (b), physical fitness (b,g), physical training (b,g), soccer (b,g), softball (g), tennis (b,g), track and field (b,g), volleyball (b,g); intramural: basketball (b,g), cross-country running (b,g), physical fitness (b,g), physical training (b,g); coed interscholastic: equestrian sports, golf; coed intramural: equestrian sports. 6 PE instructors, 15 coaches, 1 athletic trainer.

Computers Computers are regularly used in English, graphic arts, history, mathematics, science, Spanish, technology, yearbook classes. Computer network features include on-campus library services, online commercial services, Internet access, Internet filtering or blocking technology. Student e-mail accounts and computer access in designated common areas are available to students. The school has a published electronic and media policy.

Contact Co-Director sof Admissions. 818-767-8382. Fax: 818-768-2006. E-mail: admissions@villagechristian.org. Web site: www.villagechristian.org.

VILLA JOSEPH MARIE HIGH SCHOOL

1180 Holland Road

Holland, Pennsylvania 18966

Head of School: Mrs. Mary T. Michel

General Information Girls' day college-preparatory, arts, religious studies, and drama school, affiliated with Roman Catholic Church. Grades 9–12. Founded: 1932. Setting: suburban. Nearest major city is Philadelphia. 55-acre campus. 3 buildings on campus. Approved or accredited by Middle States Association of Colleges and Schools and Pennsylvania Department of Education. Total enrollment: 366. Upper school average class size: 15. Upper school faculty-student ratio: 1:14. Upper School students typically attend 5 days per week. The average school day consists of 6 hours and 45 minutes.

Upper School Student Profile Grade 9: 93 students (93 girls); Grade 10: 95 students (95 girls); Grade 11: 90 students (90 girls); Grade 12: 88 students (88 girls). 98% of students are Roman Catholic.

Faculty School total: 37. In upper school: 6 men, 28 women; 30 have advanced degrees.

Subjects Offered Algebra, American government, American history, American history-AP, anatomy and physiology, ancient history, art, art appreciation, biology, biology-AP, business mathematics, calculus-AP, chemistry, chemistry-AP, chorus, conceptual physics, dance, drama, earth science, English, English literature-AP, environmental science, environmental science-AP, European history-AP, film and literature, forensics, French, geometry, health, Latin, music, physical education, physics, physics-AP, pre-calculus, psychology, psychology-AP, sociology, Spanish, speech, studio art, theology, trigonometry, world history, writing.

Graduation Requirements Arts and fine arts (art, music, dance, drama), English, foreign language, mathematics, physical education (includes health), religion (includes Bible studies and theology), science, social sciences, social studies (includes history), service hours requirement.

Special Academic Programs 13 Advanced Placement exams for which test preparation is offered; honors section; independent study; study at local college for college credit; academic accommodation for the gifted, the musically talented, and the artistically talented.

College Admission Counseling 88 students graduated in 2011; all went to college, including La Salle University; Penn State University Park; Saint Joseph's University; The University of Scranton; Villanova University. Mean SAT critical reading: 580, mean SAT math: 555, mean SAT writing: 603.

Student Life Upper grades have uniform requirement, student council, honor system. Discipline rests primarily with faculty. Attendance at religious services is required.

Summer Programs Enrichment, sports programs offered; session focuses on enrichment; held on campus; accepts girls; open to students from other schools. 45 students usually enrolled. 2012 schedule: July to July.

Tuition and Aid Day student tuition: $11,150. Tuition installment plan (monthly payment plans). Tuition reduction for siblings, merit scholarship grants, need-based scholarship grants available. Total upper-school merit-scholarship money awarded for 2011–12: $160,000.

Admissions Traditional secondary-level entrance grade is 9. For fall 2011, 200 students applied for upper-level admission, 130 were accepted, 93 enrolled. High School Placement Test required. Deadline for receipt of application materials: November 11. Application fee required: $55. On-campus interview required.

Athletics Interscholastic: basketball, cheering, cross-country running, field hockey, golf, indoor track, lacrosse, soccer, softball, tennis, track and field, volleyball, winter (indoor) track. 1 PE instructor, 14 coaches, 1 athletic trainer.

Computers Computers are regularly used in art, English, foreign language, history, library, literary magazine, mathematics, religion, science, yearbook classes. Computer network features include on-campus library services, online commercial services, Internet access, wireless campus network, Internet filtering or blocking technology. Computer access in designated common areas is available to students. Students grades are available online. The school has a published electronic and media policy.

Contact Mrs. Maureen Cleary, Director of Institutional Advancement. 215-357-8810 Ext. 124. Fax: 215-357-9410. E-mail: mclea@vjmhs.org. Web site: www.vjmhs.org.

VILLA MARIA ACADEMY

2403 West Eighth Street

Erie, Pennsylvania 16505-4492

Head of School: Fr. Scott Jabo

General Information Coeducational day college-preparatory school, affiliated with Roman Catholic Church. Boys grade 12, girls grades 9–12. Founded: 1892. Setting: suburban. 4 buildings on campus. Approved or accredited by Middle States Association of Colleges and Schools and National Catholic Education Association. Total enrollment: 301. Upper school average class size: 16. Upper school faculty-student ratio: 1:10. There are 180 required school days per year for Upper School students. Upper School students typically attend 5 days per week. The average school day consists of 6 hours.

Upper School Student Profile Grade 9: 97 students (97 girls); Grade 10: 70 students (70 girls); Grade 11: 76 students (76 girls); Grade 12: 58 students (6 boys, 52 girls). 85% of students are Roman Catholic.

Faculty School total: 30. In upper school: 11 men, 19 women; 13 have advanced degrees.

Subjects Offered 3-dimensional art, advanced math, Advanced Placement courses, algebra, aquatics, art, arts, athletics, audio visual/media, biology, ceramics, community service, computer science, English, fine arts, geometry, graphic arts, health, keyboarding, Latin, mathematics, newspaper, photography, physical education, physical fitness, physics, practical arts, psychology, religious education, SAT preparation, science, senior project, social studies, Spanish, speech, student government, theology, trigonometry, U.S. history, U.S. history-AP, word processing, world history, yearbook.

Graduation Requirements Arts and fine arts (art, music, dance, drama), English, foreign language, mathematics, physical education (includes health), religion (includes Bible studies and theology), science, social studies (includes history). Community service is required.

Special Academic Programs 6 Advanced Placement exams for which test preparation is offered; honors section; accelerated programs; independent study; study at local college for college credit.

College Admission Counseling 76 students graduated in 2011; 72 went to college, including Edinboro University of Pennsylvania; Gannon University; Kent State University; Mercyhurst College; Penn State Erie, The Behrend College. Other: 3 went to work, 1 entered military service.

Student Life Upper grades have uniform requirement, student council, honor system. Discipline rests primarily with faculty.

Summer Programs Remediation programs offered; held on campus; accepts girls; not open to students from other schools. 16 students usually enrolled.

Tuition and Aid Day student tuition: $6915–$7240. Tuition installment plan (FACTS Tuition Payment Plan). Tuition reduction for siblings, merit scholarship grants, need-based scholarship grants available. In 2011–12, 55% of upper-school students received aid; total upper-school merit-scholarship money awarded: $58,000. Total amount of financial aid awarded in 2011–12: $247,334.

Admissions Traditional secondary-level entrance grade is 9. For fall 2011, 185 students applied for upper-level admission, 172 were accepted, 97 enrolled. Placement test required. Deadline for receipt of application materials: none. No application fee required.

Athletics Interscholastic: basketball (girls), bowling (g), cheering (g), cross-country running (g), golf (g), lacrosse (g), soccer (g), softball (g), swimming and diving (g), tennis (g), track and field (g), volleyball (g), water polo (g). 1 PE instructor.

Computers Computers are regularly used in all academic classes. Computer network features include on-campus library services, online commercial services, Internet access, wireless campus network, Internet filtering or blocking technology. Campus intranet, student e-mail accounts, and computer access in designated common areas are available to students. Students grades are available online. The school has a published electronic and media policy.

Contact Ms. Amy Oldach, Admissions Coordinator. 814-838-2061 Ext. 3239. Fax: 814-836-0881. E-mail: aoldach@villamaria.com. Web site: www.villamaria.com.

VILLA MARIA ACADEMY

370 Old Lincoln Highway

Malvern, Pennsylvania 19355

Head of School: Sr. Marita Carmel McCarthy, IHM

General Information Girls' day college-preparatory, arts, religious studies, and technology school, affiliated with Roman Catholic Church. Grades 9–12. Founded: 1872. Setting: suburban. Nearest major city is Philadelphia. 28-acre campus. 4 buildings on campus. Approved or accredited by Middle States Association of Colleges and Schools, The College Board, and Pennsylvania Department of Education. Total enrollment: 425. Upper school average class size: 15. Upper school faculty-student ratio: 1:9. There are 172 required school days per year for Upper School students. Upper School students typically attend 5 days per week. The average school day consists of 6 hours and 30 minutes.

Upper School Student Profile Grade 9: 102 students (102 girls); Grade 10: 104 students (104 girls); Grade 11: 106 students (106 girls); Grade 12: 113 students (113 girls). 95% of students are Roman Catholic.

Faculty School total: 51. In upper school: 9 men, 41 women; 40 have advanced degrees.

Subjects Offered Accounting, advanced chemistry, advanced math, algebra, American government, American literature, analysis, art, Bible, biology, biology-AP, British literature, British literature (honors), calculus, calculus-AP, Catholic belief and practice, chemistry, chemistry-AP, choral music, church history, college counseling, computer applications, computer literacy, discrete mathematics, drama, driver education, English, English composition, English language-AP, English literature, English literature-AP, environmental science, European history, European history-AP, first aid, French, French-AP, geography, geometry, government-AP, grammar, guidance, health education, history of the Catholic Church, honors algebra, honors English, honors geometry, honors U.S. history, honors world history, information design technology, keyboarding, Latin, library skills, literary magazine, modern European history, modern European history-AP, music performance, music theory, music-AP, orchestra, physical education, physics, physics-AP, piano, psychology-AP, religious studies, social studies, Spanish, Spanish language-AP, statistics, statistics-AP, studio art, studio art-AP, trigonometry, U.S. history, U.S. history-AP, vocal ensemble, voice, Western civilization, world issues.

Graduation Requirements Catholic belief and practice, college admission preparation, computer applications, English, foreign language, mathematics, physical education (includes health), science, social studies (includes history), theology.

College Admission Counseling 111 students graduated in 2011; 109 went to college, including Drexel University; Penn State University Park; Saint Joseph's University; University of Delaware; University of Pittsburgh; Villanova University. Other: 1 went to work, 1 entered military service. 38% scored over 600 on SAT critical reading, 39% scored over 600 on SAT math, 49% scored over 600 on SAT writing, 47% scored over 1800 on combined SAT, 42% scored over 26 on composite ACT.

Student Life Upper grades have uniform requirement, student council, honor system. Discipline rests equally with students and faculty. Attendance at religious services is required.

Tuition and Aid Day student tuition: $14,100. Tuition installment plan (monthly payment plans). Tuition reduction for siblings, merit scholarship grants, need-based scholarship grants available. In 2011–12, 28% of upper-school students received aid; total upper-school merit-scholarship money awarded: $248,600. Total amount of financial aid awarded in 2011–12: $506,986.

Admissions Traditional secondary-level entrance grade is 9. For fall 2011, 226 students applied for upper-level admission, 185 were accepted, 102 enrolled. High School Placement Test required. Deadline for receipt of application materials: December 8. Application fee required: $50. On-campus interview recommended.

Athletics Interscholastic: basketball, cross-country running, dance team, field hockey, golf, indoor track, indoor track & field, lacrosse, soccer, softball, swimming and diving, tennis, track and field, volleyball, winter (indoor) track. 2 PE instructors, 12 coaches, 1 athletic trainer.

Computers Computers are regularly used in accounting, art, Bible studies, Christian doctrine, college planning, economics, English, French, geography, health, history, humanities, Latin, library skills, mathematics, music, psychology, publications, religious studies, science, social studies, Spanish, theology, writing, yearbook classes. Computer network features include on-campus library services, online commercial services, Internet access, wireless campus network, Internet filtering or blocking technology. Campus intranet, student e-mail accounts, and computer access in designated common areas are available to students. Students grades are available online. The school has a published electronic and media policy.

Contact Mrs. Mary Kay D. Napoli, Director of Admissions. 610-644-2551 Ext. 1020. Fax: 610-644-2866. E-mail: mknapoli@vmahs.org. Web site: www.vmahs.org.

VILLA VICTORIA ACADEMY

376 West Upper Ferry Road

Ewing, New Jersey 08628

Head of School: Sr. Lillian Harrington, MPF

General Information Girls' day college-preparatory, arts, religious studies, and technology school, affiliated with Roman Catholic Church. Grades PK–12. Founded: 1933. Setting: suburban. Nearest major city is Trenton. 44-acre campus. 7 buildings on campus. Approved or accredited by Middle States Association of Colleges and Schools, National Catholic Education Association, and New Jersey Department of Education. Member of National Association of Independent Schools and Secondary School Admission Test Board. Total enrollment: 202. Upper school average class size: 12. Upper school faculty-student ratio: 1:6. There are 180 required school days per year for Upper School students. Upper School students typically attend 5 days per week. The average school day consists of 6 hours and 20 minutes.

Upper School Student Profile Grade 9: 16 students (16 girls); Grade 10: 16 students (16 girls); Grade 11: 17 students (17 girls); Grade 12: 18 students (18 girls). 79% of students are Roman Catholic.

Faculty School total: 31. In upper school: 5 men, 15 women; 13 have advanced degrees.

Subjects Offered Algebra, American literature, art, art history, art-AP, arts, arts appreciation, athletics, Bible studies, biology, calculus, calculus-AP, campus ministry, career and personal planning, career exploration, career planning, career/college preparation, Catholic belief and practice, ceramics, character education, chemistry, chemistry-AP, Chinese studies, choir, choral music, chorus, Christian education, Christian ethics, Christianity, church history, clayworking, college admission preparation, college awareness, college counseling, college placement, college planning, college writing, communication skills, community service, computer science, concert band, concert choir, creative thinking, creative writing, critical thinking, critical writing, cultural arts, current events, drama, drawing, drawing and design, earth science, English, English composition, English language and composition-AP, English literature, English literature-AP, English-AP, ethics and responsibility, European history, fiction, fine arts, French, French language-AP, French studies, French-AP, gender and religion, general business, general math, general science, geography, geometry, global issues, government, government and politics-AP, government-AP, government/civics, government/civics-AP, grammar, health, health and safety, health and wellness, health education, history, history of music, history of religion, history of the Americas, history of the Catholic Church, history-AP, honors algebra, honors English, honors geometry, honors U.S. history, honors world history, humanities, independent study, interdisciplinary studies, Internet, Internet research, interpersonal skills, language and composition, Latin, leadership, leadership and service, library research, library skills, life management skills, Life of Christ, linguistics, literary magazine, literature, literature-AP, math analysis, math applications, math methods, math review, mathematics, mathematics-AP, mechanics of writing, modern history, modern languages, modern world history, money management, moral and social development, moral reasoning, moral theology, multimedia, music, music appreciation, music history, music performance, music theater, music theory, musical productions, musical theater, musical theater dance, oil painting, painting, participation in sports, peer ministry, performing arts, personal development, personal finance, personal fitness, personal money management, photography, physical education, physics, physics-AP, play production, poetry, portfolio art, pottery, prayer/spirituality, pre-algebra, pre-calculus, public service, public speaking, qualitative analysis, reading/study skills, religion, religion and culture, religious education, research, research skills, rhetoric, SAT preparation, SAT/ACT preparation, science, science and technology, sculpture, senior humanities, senior project, senior seminar, set design, Shakespeare, skills for success, social skills, social studies, society and culture, Spanish, Spanish language-AP, Spanish-AP, sports, sports conditioning, stage design, stagecraft, strategies for success, student government, student publications, theater, theater design and production, trigonometry, U.S. history, United States government-AP, values and decisions, visual and performing arts, visual arts, vocal ensemble, world civilizations, world cultures, world history, world issues, world literature, world religions, writing.

Graduation Requirements American literature, art history, arts and fine arts (art, music, dance, drama), biology, British literature, chemistry, computer science, English, foreign language, mathematics, physical education (includes health), physics, religion (includes Bible studies and theology), SAT/ACT preparation, science, social studies (includes history), world cultures, world literature, interdisciplinary humanities. Community service is required.

Special Academic Programs Advanced Placement exam preparation; honors section; independent study; academic accommodation for the gifted, the musically talented, and the artistically talented.

College Admission Counseling 17 students graduated in 2011; all went to college, including Boston University; Carnegie Mellon University; Drexel University; Duke University; Duquesne University; New York University. Median combined SAT: 1814.

Student Life Upper grades have uniform requirement, student council, honor system. Discipline rests primarily with faculty. Attendance at religious services is required.

Summer Programs Enrichment, art/fine arts programs offered; session focuses on art and theatre, enrichment; held on campus; accepts boys and girls; open to students from other schools. 25 students usually enrolled. 2012 schedule: June to July.

Tuition and Aid Day student tuition: $11,500. Tuition installment plan (FACTS Tuition Payment Plan, individually arranged payment plans, 2-payment plan). Tuition reduction for siblings, merit scholarship grants, need-based scholarship grants available. In 2011–12, 30% of upper-school students received aid; total upper-school merit-scholarship money awarded: $50,000.

Admissions Traditional secondary-level entrance grade is 9. School placement exam or SSAT required. Deadline for receipt of application materials: December 15. Application fee required: $50. On-campus interview required.

Athletics Interscholastic: basketball, cross-country running, soccer, softball, tennis, track and field; intramural: dance, outdoor activities, outdoor education, walking. 1 PE instructor, 4 coaches.

Computers Computers are regularly used in art, English, foreign language, history, mathematics, music, SAT preparation, science, theater classes. Computer network features include on-campus library services, Internet access, wireless campus network, Internet filtering or blocking technology, each student in 9-11 grade have their own netbook for use in-school and home. Computer access in designated common areas is available to students. Students grades are available online. The school has a published electronic and media policy.

Contact Mrs. Karen M. O'Donnell, Director of Advancement. 609-882-1700 Ext. 19. Fax: 609-882-8421. E-mail: kodonnell@villavictoria.org. Web site: www.villavictoria.org.

VILLA WALSH ACADEMY

455 Western Avenue

Morristown, New Jersey 07960

Head of School: Sr. Patricia Pompa

General Information Girls' day college-preparatory, arts, religious studies, and technology school, affiliated with Roman Catholic Church. Grades 7–12. Founded: 1967. Setting: suburban. Nearest major city is New York, NY. 130-acre campus. 3 buildings on campus. Approved or accredited by Middle States Association of Colleges and Schools, National Catholic Education Association, and New Jersey Department of Education. Endowment: $5 million. Total enrollment: 257. Upper school average class size: 12. Upper school faculty-student ratio: 1:8. There are 176 required school days per year for Upper School students. Upper School students typically attend 5 days per week. The average school day consists of 6 hours and 30 minutes.

Upper School Student Profile Grade 9: 60 students (60 girls); Grade 10: 59 students (59 girls); Grade 11: 57 students (57 girls); Grade 12: 54 students (54 girls). 90% of students are Roman Catholic.

Faculty School total: 35. In upper school: 3 men, 32 women; 20 have advanced degrees.

Subjects Offered Advanced Placement courses, algebra, American history, American literature, anatomy and physiology, art, Bible as literature, biology, biology-AP, British literature, British literature (honors), calculus, calculus-AP, career/college preparation, chemistry, chemistry-AP, choral music, chorus, church history, college admission preparation, computer applications, computer graphics, computer literacy, computer processing, computer programming, computer science, computer skills, CPR, creative writing, desktop publishing, driver education, economics, economics and history, English, English language and composition-AP, English literature, ethics, European civilization, European history-AP, family living, finite math, first aid, French, French language-AP, French-AP, geometry, health education, honors English, honors geometry, honors U.S. history, Italian, keyboarding, life science, mathematics, modern European history, moral theology, philosophy, physical education, physics, physics-AP, pre-algebra, pre-calculus, psychology, psychology-AP, religion, Spanish, Spanish-AP, statistics-AP, studio art, theology, U.S. government and politics, U.S. history, U.S. history-AP, voice ensemble, Web site design, world history, world literature.

Graduation Requirements Arts and fine arts (art, music, dance, drama), English, foreign language, mathematics, physical education (includes health), science, social studies (includes history), theology.

Special Academic Programs 12 Advanced Placement exams for which test preparation is offered; honors section; independent study; academic accommodation for the gifted, the musically talented, and the artistically talented.

College Admission Counseling Colleges students went to include Boston College; Boston University; College of the Holy Cross; Cornell University; University of Pennsylvania; Villanova University.

Student Life Upper grades have uniform requirement, student council, honor system. Discipline rests primarily with faculty. Attendance at religious services is required.

Tuition and Aid Day student tuition: $16,900. Tuition installment plan (Insured Tuition Payment Plan, Key Tuition Payment Plan, individually arranged payment plans). Merit scholarship grants, need-based scholarship grants available. In 2011–12, 12% of upper-school students received aid; total upper-school merit-scholarship money awarded: $10,000. Total amount of financial aid awarded in 2011–12: $140,000.

Admissions Traditional secondary-level entrance grade is 9. For fall 2011, 180 students applied for upper-level admission, 70 were accepted, 61 enrolled. Math, reading, and mental ability tests and writing sample required. Deadline for receipt of application materials: none. Application fee required: $50. On-campus interview required.

Athletics Interscholastic: basketball, cross-country running, indoor track, lacrosse, soccer, softball, swimming and diving, tennis, track and field, volleyball, winter (indoor) track. 1 PE instructor, 32 coaches, 2 athletic trainers.

Computers Computers are regularly used in college planning, desktop publishing, independent study, keyboarding, library science, mathematics, newspaper, programming, SAT preparation, science, technology, Web site design, word processing, yearbook classes. Computer network features include on-campus library services, Internet access, wireless campus network, Internet filtering or blocking technology. Campus intranet is available to students. The school has a published electronic and media policy.

Contact Sr. Doris Lavinthal, Director. 973-538-3680 Ext. 175. Fax: 973-538-6733. E-mail: lavinthald@aol.com. Web site: www.villawalsh.org.

VISITATION ACADEMY OF ST. LOUIS COUNTY

3020 North Ballas Road

St. Louis, Missouri 63131

Head of School: Mrs. Rosalie Henry

General Information Coeducational day (boys' only in lower grades) college-preparatory, arts, and technology school, affiliated with Roman Catholic Church. Boys grade PK, girls grades PK–12. Founded: 1833. Setting: suburban. 30-acre campus. 1 building on campus. Approved or accredited by Independent Schools Association of the Central States, National Catholic Education Association, North Central Association of Colleges and Schools, and Missouri Department of Education. Member of National Association of Independent Schools. Endowment: $7 million. Total enrollment: 633. Upper school average class size: 18. Upper school faculty-student ratio: 1:9. There are 176 required school days per year for Upper School students. Upper School students typically attend 5 days per week. The average school day consists of 7 hours.

Upper School Student Profile Grade 7: 54 students (54 girls); Grade 8: 77 students (77 girls); Grade 9: 96 students (96 girls); Grade 10: 96 students (96 girls); Grade 11: 64 students (64 girls); Grade 12: 71 students (71 girls). 85% of students are Roman Catholic.

Faculty School total: 52. In upper school: 8 men, 44 women; 31 have advanced degrees.

Subjects Offered Adolescent issues, advanced biology, advanced chemistry, advanced math, Advanced Placement courses, algebra, American history, American history-AP, American literature, American literature-AP, anatomy, anatomy and physiology, art, art appreciation, art history, bell choir, Bible studies, biology, biology-AP, calculus, calculus-AP, ceramics, character education, chemistry, chemistry-AP, choral music, chorus, Christian studies, Christian testament, church history, civics, classical language, computer art, computer math, computer programming, computer science, concert choir, creative writing, drama, earth science, economics, economics and history, English, English literature, English literature-AP, environmental science, European history, European history-AP, expository writing, fine arts, French, French-AP, genetics, geography, geometry, government/civics, grammar, health, history, independent study, journalism, keyboarding, Latin, mathematics, music, New Testament, photo shop, photography, physical education, physical science, physics, pre-calculus, psychology, science, social studies, Spanish, speech, statistics-AP, theater, theology, trigonometry, U.S. history-AP, world geography, world literature.

Graduation Requirements Arts and fine arts (art, music, dance, drama), computers, electives, English, foreign language, mathematics, physical education (includes health), science, social studies (includes history), theology, 120 hours of community service.

Special Academic Programs 12 Advanced Placement exams for which test preparation is offered; honors section; independent study; study at local college for college credit; special instructional classes for mild learning differences.

College Admission Counseling 88 students graduated in 2011; all went to college, including Auburn University; Indiana University Bloomington; Saint Louis University; Spring Hill College; University of Missouri; Washington University in St. Louis. Median SAT critical reading: 605, median SAT math: 620, median SAT writing: 610, median combined SAT: 1840, median composite ACT: 29.

Student Life Upper grades have uniform requirement, student council. Discipline rests primarily with faculty. Attendance at religious services is required.

Summer Programs Sports programs offered; session focuses on athletics—basketball, soccer, volleyball, cheerleading; held on campus; accepts girls; open to students from other schools. 200 students usually enrolled.

Tuition and Aid Day student tuition: $15,775. Tuition installment plan (FACTS Tuition Payment Plan). Need-based scholarship grants available. In 2011–12, 10% of upper-school students received aid.

Admissions Traditional secondary-level entrance grade is 7. For fall 2011, 92 students applied for upper-level admission, 90 were accepted, 71 enrolled. SSAT required. Deadline for receipt of application materials: January 20. Application fee required: $75. On-campus interview required.

Athletics Interscholastic: basketball, cheering, cross-country running, dance, diving, field hockey, golf, lacrosse, racquetball, soccer, softball, swimming and diving, tennis, track and field, volleyball; intramural: cheering, dance. 4 PE instructors, 17 coaches, 1 athletic trainer.

Computers Computers are regularly used in art, English, foreign language, history, mathematics, science, theology classes. Computer network features include on-campus library services, Internet access, wireless campus network, Internet filtering or blocking technology. Campus intranet and student e-mail accounts are available to students. Students grades are available online. The school has a published electronic and media policy.

Contact Mrs. Ashley Giljum, Director of Admission. 314-625-9102. Fax: 314-432-7210. E-mail: agiljum@visitationacademy.org. Web site: www.visitationacademy.org.

WAKEFIELD SCHOOL

4439 Old Tavern Road

PO Box 107

The Plains, Virginia 20198

Head of School: Mr. Peter A. Quinn

General Information Coeducational day college-preparatory and arts school. Grades PS–12. Founded: 1972. Setting: rural. Nearest major city is Washington, DC. 65-acre campus. 6 buildings on campus. Approved or accredited by Association of Independent Schools of Greater Washington, Virginia Association of Independent Schools, and Virginia Department of Education. Total enrollment: 432. Upper school average class size: 16. Upper school faculty-student ratio: 1:16. There are 180 required school days per year for Upper School students. Upper School students typically attend 5 days per week. The average school day consists of 7 hours.

Upper School Student Profile Grade 9: 38 students (15 boys, 23 girls); Grade 10: 28 students (15 boys, 13 girls); Grade 11: 35 students (13 boys, 22 girls); Grade 12: 40 students (22 boys, 18 girls).

Faculty School total: 83. In upper school: 15 men, 13 women; 13 have advanced degrees.

Subjects Offered Acting, Advanced Placement courses, algebra, American government, American history-AP, American literature, art, art history, bell choir, biology, biology-AP, British history, British literature, calculus, calculus-AP, chemistry, chemistry-AP, chorus, classical language, composition, computer applications, computer programming, conservation, drama, dramatic arts, earth science, Eastern world civilizations, ecology, English language and composition-AP, English literature and composition-AP, environmental science, environmental science-AP, European history-AP, French, French language-AP, geometry, geopolitics, government and politics-AP, government/civics, Latin, Latin-AP, model United Nations, music, music composition, music history, music theory, music theory-AP, physical fitness, physics, physics-AP, political science, psychology, publications, Spanish, Spanish language-AP, statistics, statistics-AP, studio art, studio art-AP, U.S. history, world civilizations.

Graduation Requirements Advanced math, algebra, American history, American literature, arts, biology, British literature, chemistry, computer literacy, English, geometry, government/civics, grammar, language, physical education (includes health), pre-calculus, world civilizations, 2 interdisciplinary compositions, 2 thesis and portfolio projects, including senior thesis.

Special Academic Programs 11 Advanced Placement exams for which test preparation is offered; honors section; independent study; programs in general development for dyslexic students.

College Admission Counseling 31 students graduated in 2011; all went to college, including University of Mary Washington; University of Virginia; Virginia Polytechnic Institute and State University. Mean SAT critical reading: 590, mean SAT math: 560, mean SAT writing: 590, mean combined SAT: 1740.

Student Life Upper grades have uniform requirement, student council, honor system. Discipline rests equally with students and faculty.

Summer Programs Enrichment, sports, art/fine arts, computer instruction programs offered; session focuses on academics, athletics, fine arts; held both on and off campus; held at various locations; accepts boys and girls; open to students from other schools. 200 students usually enrolled. 2012 schedule: June 18 to July 27.

Tuition and Aid Day student tuition: $2790–$21,520. Tuition installment plan (FACTS Tuition Payment Plan, monthly payment plans, The Tuition Refund Plan). Need-based scholarship grants available. In 2011–12, 18% of upper-school students received aid. Total amount of financial aid awarded in 2011–12: $1,000,000.

Admissions Traditional secondary-level entrance grade is 9. Admissions testing or SSAT required. Deadline for receipt of application materials: none. Application fee required: $60. Interview required.

Athletics Interscholastic: basketball (boys, girls), field hockey (g), lacrosse (b,g), soccer (b,g), squash (b), strength & conditioning (b,g), tennis (b,g), volleyball (g); intramural: field hockey (g), fitness (b,g), lacrosse (b,g), outdoor activities (b,g), soccer (b,g), squash (b), strength & conditioning (b,g), tennis (b,g), volleyball (g), weight training (b,g); coed interscholastic: aquatics, cross-country running, fitness, golf, physical fitness, squash, swimming and diving; coed intramural: aquatics, cross-country running, squash, swimming and diving. 4 PE instructors, 3 coaches, 1 athletic trainer.

Computers Computers are regularly used in computer applications, English, independent study, publications, writing, yearbook classes. Computer network features include on-campus library services, online commercial services, Internet access, wireless campus network, Internet filtering or blocking technology, new Science and Technology building opened in January 2007, student center login/password protected portal for students on new Website. Campus intranet, student e-mail accounts, and computer access in designated common areas are available to students. Students grades are available online. The school has a published electronic and media policy.

Contact Office of Admissions. 540-253-7600. Fax: 540-253-5492. E-mail: admissions@wakefieldschool.org. Web site: www.wakefieldschool.org.

WALDORF HIGH SCHOOL OF MASSACHUSETTS BAY

160 Lexington Street

Belmont, Massachusetts 02478

Head of School: Mara D. White

General Information Coeducational day college-preparatory and arts school. Grades 9–12. Founded: 1996. Setting: suburban. Nearest major city is Boston. 1 building on campus. Approved or accredited by Association of Independent Schools in New England, Association of Waldorf Schools of North America, New England Association of Schools and Colleges, and Massachusetts Department of Education. Total enrollment: 50. Upper school average class size: 12. Upper school faculty-student ratio: 1:4. There are 165 required school days per year for Upper School students. Upper School students typically attend 5 days per week. The average school day consists of 6 hours and 30 minutes.

Upper School Student Profile Grade 9: 9 students (3 boys, 6 girls); Grade 10: 7 students (2 boys, 5 girls); Grade 11: 20 students (10 boys, 10 girls); Grade 12: 9 students (1 boy, 8 girls).

Faculty School total: 12. In upper school: 6 men, 6 women; 4 have advanced degrees.

Subjects Offered Algebra, American history, American literature, American studies, analysis and differential calculus, anatomy and physiology, ancient history, ancient world history, art, art history, astronomy, athletics, Bible as literature, biology, bookbinding, botany, calculus, chamber groups, chemistry, child development, chorus, classical Greek literature, college admission preparation, college counseling, college placement, community service, computer applications, computer programming, computer resources, creative writing, current events, digital art, drama, drama performance, earth science, electives, English, English literature, epic literature, European history, expository writing, fine arts, fitness, geography, geometry, global studies, grammar, history of architecture, history of music, Internet research, jazz ensemble, mathematics, medieval/Renaissance history, model United Nations, modern history, music, Native American history, painting, photography, physical education, physics, play production, poetry, projective geometry, Russian literature, SAT preparation, senior internship, senior seminar, Spanish, theory of knowledge, trigonometry, U.S. government, woodworking, world history, world literature, writing, yearbook, zoology.

Graduation Requirements Algebra, arts and fine arts (art, music, dance, drama), chemistry, English, English literature, foreign language, geometry, global studies, mathematics, music, performing arts, physical education (includes health), physics, practical arts, science, social studies (includes history). Community service is required.
Special Academic Programs Honors section; independent study; term-away projects; study abroad.
College Admission Counseling 13 students graduated in 2011; 8 went to college, including Boston University; Connecticut College; Oberlin College; University of California, Santa Barbara; Wheaton College. Other: 5 went to work.
Student Life Upper grades have specified standards of dress, student council. Discipline rests primarily with faculty.
Tuition and Aid Day student tuition: $24,500. Tuition installment plan (Insured Tuition Payment Plan, monthly payment plans, individually arranged payment plans). Tuition reduction for siblings, merit scholarship grants, need-based scholarship grants available. In 2011–12, 44% of upper-school students received aid; total upper-school merit-scholarship money awarded: $4000. Total amount of financial aid awarded in 2011–12: $357,455.
Admissions Traditional secondary-level entrance grade is 9. For fall 2011, 20 students applied for upper-level admission, 19 were accepted, 13 enrolled. Essay, grade equivalent tests or math and English placement tests required. Deadline for receipt of application materials: none. Application fee required: $50. Interview required.
Athletics Interscholastic: basketball (boys, girls), soccer (b,g); coed intramural: running, ultimate Frisbee. 2 coaches.
Computers Computers are regularly used in college planning, creative writing, current events, independent study, mathematics, research skills, SAT preparation, Spanish, yearbook classes. Computer network features include Internet access, Internet filtering or blocking technology. Computer access in designated common areas is available to students. The school has a published electronic and media policy.
Contact Susan Morris, Enrollment Coordinator. 617-489-6600 Ext. 11. Fax: 617-489-6619. E-mail: s.morris@waldorfhighschool.org. Web site: www.waldorfhighschool.org.

THE WALKER SCHOOL

700 Cobb Parkway North

Marietta, Georgia 30062

Head of School: Jack Hall

General Information Coeducational day college-preparatory, arts, bilingual studies, and technology school. Grades PK–12. Founded: 1957. Setting: suburban. Nearest major city is Atlanta. 32-acre campus. 7 buildings on campus. Approved or accredited by Southern Association of Colleges and Schools and Southern Association of Independent Schools. Member of National Association of Independent Schools and Secondary School Admission Test Board. Endowment: $1.8 million. Total enrollment: 1,049. Upper school average class size: 15. Upper school faculty-student ratio: 1:15. There are 178 required school days per year for Upper School students. Upper School students typically attend 5 days per week. The average school day consists of 7 hours.
Upper School Student Profile Grade 9: 96 students (46 boys, 50 girls); Grade 10: 86 students (43 boys, 43 girls); Grade 11: 103 students (55 boys, 48 girls); Grade 12: 94 students (52 boys, 42 girls).
Faculty School total: 130. In upper school: 28 men, 17 women; 42 have advanced degrees.
Subjects Offered Acting, algebra, American history, American literature, analysis, anatomy, ancient world history, art, art-AP, band, biology, biology-AP, calculus, calculus-AP, chemistry, chemistry-AP, chorus, comparative government and politics-AP, computer science, computer science-AP, dance, drama, economics, economics-AP, English, English composition, English language and composition-AP, English literature, English literature and composition-AP, English-AP, European history, expository writing, fine arts, fitness, French, French language-AP, French literature-AP, genetics, geometry, German, German-AP, government and politics-AP, government-AP, government/civics, grammar, history, history-AP, honors English, honors geometry, Latin, Latin-AP, law, linear algebra, literature and composition-AP, macro/microeconomics-AP, mathematics, modern world history, multimedia design, music, music theory-AP, musical theater, newspaper, oceanography, orchestra, personal finance, philosophy, physical education, physics, physics-AP, play production, post-calculus, psychology, public speaking, science, science research, social studies, Spanish, Spanish-AP, stagecraft, statistics, statistics-AP, trigonometry, U.S. history-AP, Web site design, world history, world history-AP, world literature, writing.
Graduation Requirements Advanced Placement courses, American government, arts and fine arts (art, music, dance, drama), computer science, English, English composition, English literature, foreign language, mathematics, physical education (includes health), science, social studies (includes history).
Special Academic Programs 25 Advanced Placement exams for which test preparation is offered; honors section; independent study; study abroad; academic accommodation for the gifted, the musically talented, and the artistically talented.
College Admission Counseling 80 students graduated in 2011; all went to college, including Auburn University; Elon University; Georgia College & State University; Georgia Institute of Technology; Georgia Southern University; University of Georgia. 49% scored over 600 on SAT critical reading, 53% scored over 600 on SAT math, 43% scored over 600 on SAT writing, 43% scored over 1800 on combined SAT, 41% scored over 26 on composite ACT.
Student Life Upper grades have specified standards of dress, student council, honor system. Discipline rests equally with students and faculty.
Summer Programs Enrichment programs offered; session focuses on prep for school for new students; held on campus; accepts boys and girls; open to students from other schools. 25 students usually enrolled. 2012 schedule: June 1 to August 10. Application deadline: May 31.
Tuition and Aid Day student tuition: $17,950. Tuition installment plan (school's own payment plan (1, 3, or 7 payments)). Need-based scholarship grants available. In 2011–12, 17% of upper-school students received aid. Total amount of financial aid awarded in 2011–12: $480,600.
Admissions Traditional secondary-level entrance grade is 9. For fall 2011, 93 students applied for upper-level admission, 73 were accepted, 49 enrolled. Otis-Lennon School Ability Test, SSAT or WISC III or Stanford Achievement Test required. Deadline for receipt of application materials: February 20. Application fee required: $75. On-campus interview required.
Athletics Interscholastic: aquatics (boys, girls), baseball (b), basketball (b,g), cheering (g), cross-country running (b,g), football (b), golf (b,g), physical training (b,g), soccer (b,g), softball (g), swimming and diving (b,g), tennis (b,g), track and field (b,g), volleyball (g), wrestling (b); intramural: aerobics (g), cross-country running (g), strength & conditioning (b,g), weight training (b,g); coed interscholastic: cross-country running, diving, golf, swimming and diving; coed intramural: fishing, fly fishing, rugby. 3 PE instructors, 3 coaches, 2 athletic trainers.
Computers Computers are regularly used in art, drawing and design, English, foreign language, history, information technology, introduction to technology, literary magazine, mathematics, news writing, newspaper, science, writing classes. Computer network features include on-campus library services, online commercial services, Internet access, wireless campus network, Internet filtering or blocking technology. Student e-mail accounts are available to students. Students grades are available online. The school has a published electronic and media policy.
Contact Patricia H. Mozley, Director of Admission. 678-581-6921. Fax: 770-514-8122. E-mail: patty.mozley@thewalkerschool.org. Web site: www.thewalkerschool.org.

WALNUT HILL SCHOOL

12 Highland Street

Natick, Massachusetts 01760-2199

Head of School: Mr. Antonio Viva

General Information Coeducational boarding and day college-preparatory and arts school. Grades 9–PG. Founded: 1893. Setting: suburban. Nearest major city is Boston. Students are housed in single-sex dormitories. 30-acre campus. 19 buildings on campus. Approved or accredited by New England Association of Schools and Colleges and Massachusetts Department of Education. Member of National Association of Independent Schools and Secondary School Admission Test Board. Endowment: $12 million. Total enrollment: 298. Upper school average class size: 14. Upper school faculty-student ratio: 1:6.
Upper School Student Profile Grade 9: 43 students (15 boys, 28 girls); Grade 10: 71 students (19 boys, 52 girls); Grade 11: 86 students (27 boys, 59 girls); Grade 12: 98 students (36 boys, 62 girls). 80% of students are boarding students. 31% are state residents. 32 states are represented in upper school student body. 32% are international students. International students from Canada, China, Republic of Korea, Taiwan, Thailand, and United Kingdom; 6 other countries represented in student body.
Faculty School total: 51. In upper school: 24 men, 27 women; 47 have advanced degrees; 20 reside on campus.
Subjects Offered 20th century world history, 3-dimensional art, acting, advanced chemistry, advanced math, algebra, American history, American literature, art history, arts, ballet, ballet technique, biology, calculus, ceramics, chemistry, choral music, choreography, chorus, classical music, college counseling, community service, creative writing, dance, directing, drama, drawing, English, English literature, environmental science, ESL, fine arts, French, geometry, health, history, history of dance, jazz dance, mathematics, modern dance, music history, music theory, musical theater, musical theater dance, opera, orchestra, painting, photography, physics, piano, poetry, pre-calculus, research seminar, science, sculpture, set design, Shakespeare, social studies, Spanish, stage design, technical theater, theater, theater design and production, theater production, U.S. history, visual and performing arts, visual arts, vocal music, voice, voice ensemble, world history, writing.
Graduation Requirements Arts, English, foreign language, mathematics, science, social studies (includes history), U.S. history, completion of arts portfolio, body of writing, or participation in performing arts ensembles and/or solo recital.
Special Academic Programs Advanced Placement exam preparation; honors section; independent study; academic accommodation for the gifted, the musically talented, and the artistically talented; ESL (35 students enrolled).
College Admission Counseling 96 students graduated in 2011; 90 went to college, including New England Conservatory of Music; New York University; Peabody Conservatory of The Johns Hopkins University; Pratt Institute; School of the Art Institute of Chicago; The Juilliard School. Other: 6 had other specific plans. Median SAT critical

reading: 590, median SAT math: 580, median SAT writing: 580, median composite ACT: 26.

Student Life Upper grades have student council. Discipline rests equally with students and faculty.

Summer Programs Art/fine arts programs offered; session focuses on theater, ballet, writing, and opera; held both on and off campus; held at Italy (opera); accepts boys and girls; open to students from other schools. 300 students usually enrolled. 2012 schedule: June to August. Application deadline: none.

Tuition and Aid Day student tuition: $35,000; 7-day tuition and room/board: $45,900. Tuition installment plan (Insured Tuition Payment Plan, Academic Management Services Plan, monthly payment plans). Need-based scholarship grants available. In 2011–12, 50% of upper-school students received aid. Total amount of financial aid awarded in 2011–12: $2,900,000.

Admissions Traditional secondary-level entrance grade is 10. For fall 2011, 407 students applied for upper-level admission, 178 were accepted, 119 enrolled. Any standardized test, audition, TOEFL or SLEP or writing sample required. Deadline for receipt of application materials: February 1. Application fee required: $65. Interview recommended.

Athletics Intramural: self defense (girls); coed intramural: aerobics, aerobics/dance, ballet, dance, fitness, modern dance, outdoor activities, physical fitness, physical training, self defense, yoga. 3 athletic trainers.

Computers Computer network features include on-campus library services, Internet access, wireless campus network, Internet filtering or blocking technology. Campus intranet, student e-mail accounts, and computer access in designated common areas are available to students. The school has a published electronic and media policy.

Contact Lorie K. Komlyn '88, JD, Dean of Admission. 508-650-5020. Fax: 508-655-3726. E-mail: admissions@walnuthillarts.org. Web site: why.walnuthillarts.org/.

WARING SCHOOL

35 Standley Street

Beverly, Massachusetts 01915

Head of School: Mr. Peter L. Smick

General Information Coeducational day college-preparatory school. Grades 6–12. Founded: 1972. Setting: suburban. Nearest major city is Boston. 32-acre campus. 6 buildings on campus. Approved or accredited by Association of Independent Schools in New England and New England Association of Schools and Colleges. Endowment: $4 million. Total enrollment: 152. Upper school average class size: 14. Upper school faculty-student ratio: 1:8. There are 170 required school days per year for Upper School students. Upper School students typically attend 5 days per week. The average school day consists of 9 hours.

Upper School Student Profile Grade 9: 31 students (14 boys, 17 girls); Grade 10: 27 students (12 boys, 15 girls); Grade 11: 26 students (15 boys, 11 girls); Grade 12: 21 students (7 boys, 14 girls).

Faculty School total: 45. In upper school: 14 men, 16 women; 17 have advanced degrees.

Subjects Offered Adolescent issues, advanced biology, advanced math, Advanced Placement courses, African studies, algebra, American studies, athletics, biology, calculus, calculus-AP, chemistry, chorus, college counseling, drama, drawing, earth science, European history, European literature, fine arts, French, French language-AP, functions, geometry, graphic design, great books, music appreciation, music performance, music theory, photography, physics, statistics, theater, theater arts, trigonometry, writing, yearbook.

Graduation Requirements Advanced math, algebra, arts and fine arts (art, music, dance, drama), biology, chemistry, drawing, English, foreign language, French, geometry, history, literature, mathematics, music, physical education (includes health), physics, science, social sciences, writing, musical performance.

Special Academic Programs 2 Advanced Placement exams for which test preparation is offered; honors section; independent study; term-away projects; study abroad; academic accommodation for the gifted, the musically talented, and the artistically talented.

College Admission Counseling 24 students graduated in 2011; 23 went to college, including Brown University; Colby College; Ithaca College; Kenyon College; Skidmore College; University of Chicago. Median SAT critical reading: 690, median SAT math: 630, median SAT writing: 690, median combined SAT: 2010. 90% scored over 600 on SAT critical reading, 60% scored over 600 on SAT math, 80% scored over 600 on SAT writing, 82% scored over 1800 on combined SAT.

Student Life Upper grades have student council, honor system. Discipline rests primarily with faculty.

Summer Programs Art/fine arts programs offered; session focuses on arts camp & music camp; held on campus; accepts boys and girls; open to students from other schools. 115 students usually enrolled. 2012 schedule: July 6 to August 15. Application deadline: February 1.

Tuition and Aid Day student tuition: $25,171. Tuition installment plan (Insured Tuition Payment Plan, monthly payment plans, TMS). Need-based scholarship grants available. In 2011–12, 36% of upper-school students received aid. Total amount of financial aid awarded in 2011–12: $588,000.

Admissions Traditional secondary-level entrance grade is 9. For fall 2011, 91 students applied for upper-level admission, 40 were accepted, 31 enrolled. Deadline for receipt of application materials: January 20. Application fee required: $50. On-campus interview required.

Athletics Interscholastic: basketball (boys, girls), lacrosse (b,g), soccer (b,g); coed interscholastic: cross-country running; coed intramural: basketball, dance, fitness, lacrosse, mountain biking, running, soccer, yoga. 15 coaches, 1 athletic trainer.

Computers Computers are regularly used in all academic, literary magazine, mathematics, music, publications, science, writing, yearbook classes. Computer network features include on-campus library services, Internet access, wireless campus network, Internet filtering or blocking technology. Campus intranet and computer access in designated common areas are available to students. The school has a published electronic and media policy.

Contact Ms. Dorothy Wang, Assistant Head of School and Director of Admissions. 978-927-8793 Ext. 226. Fax: 978-921-2107. E-mail: dwang@waringschool.org. Web site: www.waringschool.org.

WASATCH ACADEMY

120 South 100 West

Mt. Pleasant, Utah 84647

Head of School: Mr. Joseph Loftin

General Information Coeducational boarding and day college-preparatory, arts, bilingual studies, technology, and debate school. Grades 8–12. Founded: 1875. Setting: small town. Nearest major city is Provo. Students are housed in single-sex dormitories. 30-acre campus. 19 buildings on campus. Approved or accredited by Northwest Association of Schools and Colleges, Pacific Northwest Association of Independent Schools, The Association of Boarding Schools, and Utah Department of Education. Member of National Association of Independent Schools. Endowment: $1 million. Total enrollment: 285. Upper school average class size: 13. Upper school faculty-student ratio: 1:10.

Upper School Student Profile Grade 8: 7 students (4 boys, 3 girls); Grade 9: 29 students (18 boys, 11 girls); Grade 10: 63 students (38 boys, 25 girls); Grade 11: 98 students (62 boys, 36 girls); Grade 12: 88 students (50 boys, 38 girls); Postgraduate: 1 student (1 boy). 98% of students are boarding students. 19% are state residents. 24 states are represented in upper school student body. 45% are international students. International students from China, Germany, Mali, Republic of Korea, Taiwan, and Viet Nam; 29 other countries represented in student body.

Faculty School total: 53. In upper school: 25 men, 26 women; 19 have advanced degrees; 48 reside on campus.

Subjects Offered Acting, advanced studio art-AP, advanced TOEFL/grammar, algebra, anatomy, ballet, biology, biology-AP, calculus-AP, ceramics, chemistry, chemistry-AP, choir, college counseling, college placement, comedy, community garden, community service, dance, design, drama, drawing, drawing and design, driver education, earth science, electronic music, English, English-AP, equine science, ESL, European history-AP, fencing, film, filmmaking, fine arts, forensics, French, geography, geology, global issues, golf, guitar, honors algebra, honors English, honors U.S. history, Japanese, jewelry making, Latin, learning strategies, math applications, music, music theory, outdoor education, painting, performing arts, philosophy, photography, physical education, physical science, physics, piano, play production, pottery, pre-calculus, reading, SAT/ACT preparation, Spanish, Spanish-AP, speech and debate, stained glass, statistics-AP, study skills, theater, TOEFL preparation, U.S. history, U.S. history-AP, weightlifting, Western civilization, woodworking, world religions, yoga.

Graduation Requirements Arts and fine arts (art, music, dance, drama), computer literacy, English, foreign language, mathematics, physical education (includes health), science, social sciences, social studies (includes history), U.S. history, outdoor, cultural, community service, and recreational requirements.

Special Academic Programs Advanced Placement exam preparation; honors section; accelerated programs; independent study; study at local college for college credit; programs in English, mathematics, general development for dyslexic students; ESL (29 students enrolled).

College Admission Counseling 69 students graduated in 2011; 66 went to college, including Boston University; Lewis & Clark College; University of California, Berkeley; University of Pennsylvania; University of San Diego; University of Utah. Other: 1 went to work, 1 entered a postgraduate year, 1 had other specific plans. Median SAT critical reading: 500, median SAT math: 480, median composite ACT: 22. Mean SAT writing: 564, mean combined SAT: 1892. 13% scored over 600 on SAT critical reading, 9% scored over 600 on SAT math, 27% scored over 26 on composite ACT.

Student Life Upper grades have specified standards of dress, student council, honor system. Discipline rests primarily with faculty.

Summer Programs Remediation, enrichment, advancement, ESL programs offered; session focuses on boarding program transition; held on campus; accepts boys and girls; open to students from other schools. 25 students usually enrolled.

Tuition and Aid Day student tuition: $23,800; 5-day tuition and room/board: $40,000; 7-day tuition and room/board: $43,000. Tuition installment plan (Key Tuition Payment Plan, monthly payment plans, individually arranged payment plans). Merit scholarship grants, need-based scholarship grants, need-based loans available. In 2011–12, 40% of upper-school students received aid; total upper-school merit-scholarship

money awarded: $55,000. Total amount of financial aid awarded in 2011–12: $2,010,000.
Admissions Traditional secondary-level entrance grade is 11. For fall 2011, 304 students applied for upper-level admission, 285 were accepted, 285 enrolled. ACT, ISEE, SSAT, Stanford Achievement Test or TOEFL or SLEP required. Deadline for receipt of application materials: none. Application fee required: $75. Interview required.
Athletics Interscholastic: alpine skiing (boys, girls), baseball (b), basketball (b,g), climbing (b,g), cross-country running (b,g), dance (b,g), dressage (b,g), equestrian sports (b,g), fencing (b,g), golf (b,g), horseback riding (b,g), outdoor activities (b,g), outdoor education (b,g), paint ball (b,g), physical training (b,g), rodeo (b,g), running (b,g), skiing (cross-country) (b,g), skiing (downhill) (b,g), snowboarding (b,g), snowshoeing (b,g), soccer (b,g), tennis (b,g), track and field (b,g), volleyball (g), weight training (b,g); intramural: dance (g), skiing (downhill) (b,g), soccer (b,g), table tennis (b,g); coed interscholastic: aerobics/dance, archery, backpacking, ballet, bicycling, canoeing/kayaking, cheering, climbing, combined training, cross-country running, dance, dressage, equestrian sports, fencing, fishing, fly fishing, golf, hiking/backpacking, horseback riding, kayaking, life saving, martial arts, modern dance, mountain biking, nordic skiing, outdoor activities, paint ball, physical training, rock climbing, rodeo, running, ski jumping, skiing (cross-country), skiing (downhill), snowboarding, snowshoeing, swimming and diving, table tennis, telemark skiing, tennis, track and field, weight training, yoga; coed intramural: aerobics/dance, aquatics, archery, backpacking, badminton, ballet, bicycling, billiards, blading, bowling, canoeing/kayaking, climbing, combined training, cooperative games, dance team, equestrian sports, fishing, fitness, flag football, fly fishing, freestyle skiing, Frisbee, golf, hiking/backpacking, horseback riding, horseshoes, jogging, lacrosse, life saving, modern dance, mountain biking, nordic skiing, outdoor activities, paint ball, physical training, power lifting, rafting, rappelling, rock climbing, running, skateboarding, skiing (downhill), snowshoeing, swimming and diving, table tennis, telemark skiing, ultimate Frisbee, volleyball, weight lifting, weight training, yoga. 2 coaches, 1 athletic trainer.
Computers Computers are regularly used in all academic classes. Computer network features include on-campus library services, online commercial services, Internet access, wireless campus network, Internet filtering or blocking technology. Campus intranet and student e-mail accounts are available to students. Students grades are available online.
Contact Mrs. Carol Reeve, Director of Admissions. 435-462-1415. Fax: 435-462-1450. E-mail: carolreeve@wasatchacademy.org. Web site: www.wasatchacademy.org.

WASHINGTON WALDORF SCHOOL

4800 Sangamore Road
Bethesda, Maryland 20816

Head of School: Mrs. Natalie Adams
General Information Coeducational day college-preparatory and arts school. Grades PS–12. Founded: 1969. Setting: suburban. Nearest major city is Washington, DC. 6-acre campus. 1 building on campus. Approved or accredited by Association of Independent Schools of Greater Washington, Association of Waldorf Schools of North America, Middle States Association of Colleges and Schools, and Maryland Department of Education. Member of National Association of Independent Schools. Total enrollment: 236. Upper school average class size: 18. Upper school faculty-student ratio: 1:7. There are 175 required school days per year for Upper School students. Upper School students typically attend 5 days per week. The average school day consists of 7 hours.
Upper School Student Profile Grade 9: 9 students (5 boys, 4 girls); Grade 10: 10 students (3 boys, 7 girls); Grade 11: 11 students (2 boys, 9 girls); Grade 12: 17 students (6 boys, 11 girls).
Faculty School total: 38. In upper school: 8 men, 8 women; 9 have advanced degrees.
Subjects Offered 3-dimensional art, African-American history, algebra, American Civil War, American literature, anatomy and physiology, ancient world history, art, art and culture, art history, biochemistry, biology, bookbinding, botany, British literature, calculus, calculus-AP, chamber groups, chemistry, choir, chorus, civil rights, classical civilization, crafts, critical thinking, critical writing, drama performance, ecology, epic literature, eurythmy, fine arts, general math, general science, geology, geometry, German, grammar, history of architecture, history of music, human anatomy, human development, lab science, medieval literature, metalworking, modern history, modern world history, mythology, oil painting, optics, physical education, pre-calculus, printmaking, research skills, sculpture, Shakespeare, Spanish, stone carving, trigonometry, U.S. constitutional history, weaving, Western literature, writing, zoology.
Graduation Requirements Arts and fine arts (art, music, dance, drama), comparative religion, constitutional history of U.S., crafts, English, eurythmy, foreign language, history of drama, history of music, mathematics, physical education (includes health), science, social studies (includes history).
Special Academic Programs 1 Advanced Placement exam for which test preparation is offered; study abroad; academic accommodation for the musically talented and the artistically talented.
College Admission Counseling 15 students graduated in 2011; all went to college, including Bard College; Bowdoin College; Clemson University; Rochester Institute of Technology; Sarah Lawrence College; The University of North Carolina at Chapel Hill. Median SAT critical reading: 648, median SAT math: 578, median SAT writing: 652.
Student Life Upper grades have specified standards of dress, student council. Discipline rests primarily with faculty.
Summer Programs Sports programs offered; session focuses on basketball camps; held on campus; accepts boys and girls; open to students from other schools. 18 students usually enrolled.
Tuition and Aid Day student tuition: $22,300. Tuition installment plan (FACTS Tuition Payment Plan, monthly payment plans, individually arranged payment plans, self-insured tuition insurance). Tuition reduction for siblings, need-based scholarship grants, need-based assistance grants, tuition remission for children of faculty, one full scholarship for an inner-city student available. In 2011–12, 25% of upper-school students received aid. Total amount of financial aid awarded in 2011–12: $38,000.
Admissions Traditional secondary-level entrance grade is 9. For fall 2011, 9 students applied for upper-level admission, 7 were accepted, 5 enrolled. Math and English placement tests required. Deadline for receipt of application materials: none. Application fee required: $60. On-campus interview required.
Athletics Interscholastic: baseball (boys), basketball (b,g), cross-country running (b,g), soccer (b,g), softball (g); coed intramural: golf, outdoor education, table tennis, volleyball, yoga. 1 PE instructor, 3 coaches.
Computers Computers are regularly used in graphic design, technology classes. Computer resources include Internet access.
Contact Ms. Lezlie Lawson, Admissions/Enrollment Director. 301-229-6107 Ext. 154. Fax: 301-229-9379. E-mail: llawson@washingtonwaldorf.org. Web site: www.washingtonwaldorf.org.

THE WATERFORD SCHOOL

1480 East 9400 South
Sandy, Utah 84093

Head of School: Mrs. Nancy M. Heuston
General Information Coeducational day college-preparatory, arts, technology, and visual arts, music, photography, dance, and theater school. Grades PK–12. Founded: 1981. Setting: suburban. Nearest major city is Salt Lake City. 45-acre campus. 10 buildings on campus. Approved or accredited by Northwest Accreditation Commission, Northwest Association of Schools and Colleges, Pacific Northwest Association of Independent Schools, and Utah Department of Education. Member of National Association of Independent Schools. Total enrollment: 900. Upper school average class size: 16. Upper school faculty-student ratio: 1:5.
Upper School Student Profile Grade 9: 70 students (37 boys, 33 girls); Grade 10: 59 students (26 boys, 33 girls); Grade 11: 61 students (30 boys, 31 girls); Grade 12: 55 students (24 boys, 31 girls).
Faculty School total: 137. In upper school: 40 men, 32 women; 56 have advanced degrees.
Subjects Offered 20th century history, 3-dimensional design, acting, advanced math, Advanced Placement courses, aerobics, algebra, American history, American history-AP, American literature, art, Asian history, baseball, basketball, biology, biology-AP, British literature, calculus, calculus-AP, ceramics, chemistry, chemistry-AP, chorus, computer applications, computer art, computer graphics, computer programming, computer science, computer science-AP, creative writing, debate, drama, drama performance, drama workshop, drawing, ecology, economics, English-AP, European history, European history-AP, French, French-AP, geology, geometry, German, German-AP, Japanese, jazz ensemble, Latin, Latin American literature, music history, music performance, music theater, newspaper, outdoor education, painting, philosophy, photography, physical education, physics, physics-AP, pre-calculus, probability and statistics, psychology, sculpture, Spanish, Spanish-AP, statistics-AP, strings, studio art-AP, trigonometry, voice ensemble, volleyball, weight training, wind ensemble, world literature, writing workshop, yearbook, zoology.
Graduation Requirements 20th century world history, algebra, American history, American literature, biology, British literature, calculus, chemistry, computer science, English, European history, foreign language, geometry, music performance, physics, pre-calculus, trigonometry, visual arts, world history, writing workshop, six terms of physical education or participation on athletic teams.
Special Academic Programs Advanced Placement exam preparation; honors section; independent study; term-away projects; academic accommodation for the gifted, the musically talented, and the artistically talented.
College Admission Counseling 69 students graduated in 2011; all went to college. Mean SAT critical reading: 612, mean SAT math: 616, mean SAT writing: 613, mean combined SAT: 1841, mean composite ACT: 26.
Student Life Upper grades have uniform requirement, student council, honor system. Discipline rests equally with students and faculty.
Summer Programs Enrichment, advancement, sports, art/fine arts, computer instruction programs offered; session focuses on enrichment and advancement; held both on and off campus; held at various locations in Utah and abroad; accepts boys and girls; not open to students from other schools. 100 students usually enrolled. 2012 schedule: June 10 to August 10. Application deadline: March 15.
Tuition and Aid Day student tuition: $18,500. Guaranteed tuition plan. Tuition installment plan (Insured Tuition Payment Plan, monthly payment plans). Tuition reduction for siblings, need-based scholarship grants available. In 2011–12, 10% of upper-school students received aid.

Admissions Traditional secondary-level entrance grade is 9. For fall 2011, 41 students applied for upper-level admission, 29 were accepted, 23 enrolled. ERB CTP IV required. Deadline for receipt of application materials: none. Application fee required: $35. On-campus interview required.

Athletics Interscholastic: basketball (boys, girls), crew (b,g), cross-country running (b,g), golf (b,g), lacrosse (b,g), soccer (b,g), tennis (b,g), volleyball (g); intramural: indoor soccer (b,g); coed interscholastic: alpine skiing, ballet, dance, Frisbee, outdoor education, racquetball, skiing (downhill); coed intramural: aerobics, alpine skiing, backpacking, climbing, crew, mountain biking, nordic skiing, outdoor recreation, rock climbing, wall climbing, weight training. 7 PE instructors, 6 coaches.

Computers Computers are regularly used in animation, college planning, graphic design, library, literary magazine, newspaper, photography, publications, yearbook classes. Computer network features include on-campus library services, Internet access.

Contact Mr. Todd Winters, Director of Admissions. 801-816-2213. Fax: 801-572-1787. E-mail: toddwinters@waterfordschool.org. Web site: www.waterfordschool.org.

WATKINSON SCHOOL

180 Bloomfield Avenue

Hartford, Connecticut 06105

Head of School: Mr. John W. Bracker

General Information Coeducational day college-preparatory, arts, technology, and athletics, global studies school. Grades 6–PG. Founded: 1881. Setting: suburban. 40-acre campus. 5 buildings on campus. Approved or accredited by Association of Independent Schools in New England, New England Association of Schools and Colleges, and Connecticut Department of Education. Member of National Association of Independent Schools and Secondary School Admission Test Board. Endowment: $3.5 million. Total enrollment: 247. Upper school average class size: 12. Upper school faculty-student ratio: 1:6. There are 165 required school days per year for Upper School students. Upper School students typically attend 5 days per week. The average school day consists of 7 hours and 30 minutes.

Upper School Student Profile Grade 9: 40 students (26 boys, 14 girls); Grade 10: 47 students (26 boys, 21 girls); Grade 11: 30 students (16 boys, 14 girls); Grade 12: 43 students (24 boys, 19 girls); Postgraduate: 3 students (2 boys, 1 girl).

Faculty School total: 50. In upper school: 13 men, 25 women; 19 have advanced degrees.

Subjects Offered African history, algebra, American history, American literature, American sign language, anatomy, ancient world history, art, Asian history, biology, calculus, ceramics, chemistry, creative writing, dance, drama, drawing, earth science, English, English literature, environmental science, European history, expository writing, fine arts, forensics, French, geography, geometry, health, history, internship, mathematics, modern European history, painting, photography, physics, pottery, science, social studies, Spanish, theater, U.S. history, world history, world literature, writing.

Graduation Requirements Arts and fine arts (art, music, dance, drama), English, foreign language, health and wellness, mathematics, science, social studies (includes history), technology.

Special Academic Programs Independent study; study at local college for college credit; academic accommodation for the gifted, the musically talented, and the artistically talented; programs in English, mathematics, general development for dyslexic students; special instructional classes for deaf students.

College Admission Counseling 43 students graduated in 2011; 41 went to college, including Lynn University; McDaniel College; Mitchell College. Other: 2 had other specific plans. Median SAT critical reading: 580, median SAT math: 570, median SAT writing: 560, median combined SAT: 1670, median composite ACT: 26. 47% scored over 600 on SAT critical reading, 26% scored over 600 on SAT math, 26% scored over 600 on SAT writing, 35% scored over 1800 on combined SAT, 43% scored over 26 on composite ACT.

Student Life Upper grades have specified standards of dress, student council. Discipline rests equally with students and faculty.

Summer Programs Remediation, enrichment programs offered; session focuses on academics; held on campus; accepts boys and girls; open to students from other schools. 28 students usually enrolled. 2012 schedule: June 27 to August 5. Application deadline: none.

Tuition and Aid Day student tuition: $32,500. Tuition installment plan (Insured Tuition Payment Plan, Sallie Mae). Need-based scholarship grants available. In 2011–12, 51% of upper-school students received aid. Total amount of financial aid awarded in 2011–12: $1,328,120.

Admissions Traditional secondary-level entrance grade is 9. For fall 2011, 93 students applied for upper-level admission, 50 were accepted, 35 enrolled. ISEE or SSAT required. Deadline for receipt of application materials: February 1. Application fee required: $50. On-campus interview required.

Athletics Interscholastic: baseball (boys), basketball (b,g), crew (b,g), cross-country running (b,g), lacrosse (b,g), soccer (b,g), softball (g), tennis (b,g), volleyball (g); coed interscholastic: crew, cross-country running, tennis, ultimate Frisbee; coed intramural: alpine skiing, ballet, Circus, climbing, combined training, dance, fencing, fitness, juggling, martial arts, outdoor activities, outdoor adventure, physical fitness, physical training, skiing (downhill), snowboarding, street hockey, strength & conditioning, tennis, ultimate Frisbee, volleyball, weight lifting, yoga. 6 coaches, 1 athletic trainer.

Computers Computers are regularly used in computer applications, desktop publishing classes. Computer network features include on-campus library services, online commercial services, Internet access, wireless campus network, Internet filtering or blocking technology. Campus intranet, student e-mail accounts, and computer access in designated common areas are available to students. The school has a published electronic and media policy.

Contact Mrs. Cathy Batson, Admissions Office Assistant. 860-236-5618 Ext. 136. Fax: 860-233-8295. E-mail: cathy_batson@watkinson.org. Web site: www.watkinson.org.

WAYNFLETE SCHOOL

360 Spring Street

Portland, Maine 04102

Head of School: Dr. Mark Segar

General Information Coeducational day college-preparatory school. Grades PK–12. Founded: 1898. Setting: urban. Nearest major city is Boston, MA. 37-acre campus. 11 buildings on campus. Approved or accredited by Association of Independent Schools in New England, Independent Schools of Northern New England, New England Association of Schools and Colleges, The College Board, and Maine Department of Education. Member of National Association of Independent Schools. Endowment: $17.9 million. Total enrollment: 555. Upper school average class size: 13. Upper school faculty-student ratio: 1:12. There are 172 required school days per year for Upper School students. Upper School students typically attend 5 days per week. The average school day consists of 7 hours and 15 minutes.

Upper School Student Profile Grade 9: 71 students (33 boys, 38 girls); Grade 10: 63 students (28 boys, 35 girls); Grade 11: 61 students (27 boys, 34 girls); Grade 12: 58 students (28 boys, 30 girls).

Faculty School total: 77. In upper school: 18 men, 26 women; 28 have advanced degrees.

Subjects Offered 20th century American writers, 20th century history, advanced biology, algebra, American history, American literature, ancient/medieval philosophy, art appreciation, art history, bioethics, biology, calculus, ceramics, chemistry, composition, computer science, constitutional history of U.S., creative writing, drama, drama workshop, English, English composition, English literature, environmental science, equality and freedom, European history, expository writing, film and literature, fine arts, French, geometry, government/civics, grammar, health, jazz ensemble, Latin, Mandarin, marine biology, modern European history, music, physical education, physics, pre-calculus, printmaking, psychology, senior project, Spanish, studio art, theater, trigonometry, U.S. constitutional history, Vietnam, world history, world literature, writing.

Graduation Requirements Arts, biology, English, foreign language, geometry, history, mathematics, performing arts, science, sports, U.S. history. Community service is required.

Special Academic Programs Independent study; term-away projects; study abroad.

College Admission Counseling 61 students graduated in 2011; 60 went to college, including Bates College; Bowdoin College; Brown University; Connecticut College; Northwestern University; University of Maine. Other: 1 had other specific plans. Median SAT critical reading: 620, median SAT math: 600, median SAT writing: 610, median combined SAT: 1840, median composite ACT: 26. 55% scored over 600 on SAT critical reading, 52% scored over 600 on SAT math, 60% scored over 600 on SAT writing, 58% scored over 1800 on combined SAT, 54% scored over 26 on composite ACT.

Student Life Upper grades have student council. Discipline rests primarily with faculty.

Summer Programs Enrichment, sports, art/fine arts programs offered; session focuses on sports, gymnastics, fine arts, performing arts, leadership, digital media, and sustainable ocean studies; held both on and off campus; held at Fore River Fields, Portland, ME and Casco Bay, Darling Marine Center, Damariscotta River; accepts boys and girls; open to students from other schools. 600 students usually enrolled. 2012 schedule: June 11 to July 27. Application deadline: July 1.

Tuition and Aid Day student tuition: $24,325. Tuition installment plan (Insured Tuition Payment Plan, monthly payment plans). Need-based scholarship grants available. In 2011–12, 38% of upper-school students received aid. Total amount of financial aid awarded in 2011–12: $1,319,762.

Admissions Traditional secondary-level entrance grade is 9. For fall 2011, 83 students applied for upper-level admission, 46 were accepted, 37 enrolled. Writing sample required. Deadline for receipt of application materials: February 10. Application fee required: $40. Interview required.

Athletics Interscholastic: baseball (boys), basketball (b,g), cross-country running (b,g), field hockey (g), golf (b,g), lacrosse (b,g), skiing (cross-country) (b,g), soccer (b,g), tennis (b,g); intramural: backpacking (b,g); coed interscholastic: crew, nordic skiing, rowing, swimming and diving, track and field; coed intramural: dance, fitness walking, modern dance, physical fitness, sailing, swimming and diving, tennis, weight lifting, weight training, yoga. 4 PE instructors, 20 coaches, 1 athletic trainer.

Computers Computers are regularly used in all academic classes. Computer network features include on-campus library services, online commercial services, Internet access, wireless campus network, Internet filtering or blocking technology, academic data bases, including JSTOR, MARVEL, Infotrac, Noodle Tools, and URSUS. Student e-mail accounts and computer access in designated common areas are available to students. The school has a published electronic and media policy.

Contact Admission Office. 207-774-5721 Ext. 224. Fax: 207-772-4782. E-mail: admissionoffice@waynflete.org. Web site: www.waynflete.org.

THE WEBB SCHOOL

319 Webb Road East

PO Box 488

Bell Buckle, Tennessee 37020

Head of School: Mr. Ray Broadhead

General Information Coeducational boarding and day college-preparatory, arts, technology, wilderness leadership, and ethics school. Boarding grades 7–12, day grades 6–12. Founded: 1870. Setting: rural. Nearest major city is Nashville. Students are housed in single-sex dormitories. 145-acre campus. 17 buildings on campus. Approved or accredited by Southern Association of Colleges and Schools, Southern Association of Independent Schools, The Association of Boarding Schools, and Tennessee Department of Education. Member of National Association of Independent Schools and Secondary School Admission Test Board. Endowment: $22 million. Total enrollment: 304. Upper school average class size: 12. Upper school faculty-student ratio: 1:7. There are 175 required school days per year for Upper School students. Upper School students typically attend 5 days per week. The average school day consists of 6 hours and 30 minutes.

Upper School Student Profile Grade 9: 43 students (23 boys, 20 girls); Grade 10: 66 students (37 boys, 29 girls); Grade 11: 63 students (30 boys, 33 girls); Grade 12: 56 students (21 boys, 35 girls). 33% of students are boarding students. 85% are state residents. 11 states are represented in upper school student body. 15% are international students. International students from Bahamas, China, Jamaica, Republic of Korea, Taiwan, and Viet Nam; 6 other countries represented in student body.

Faculty School total: 46. In upper school: 18 men, 28 women; 31 have advanced degrees; 17 reside on campus.

Subjects Offered Advanced Placement courses, algebra, American Civil War, American government, American history, American literature, American literature-AP, anatomy, art, art appreciation, art education, art history, arts appreciation, biology, biology-AP, calculus, calculus-AP, ceramics, chemistry, chemistry-AP, choir, chorus, computer programming, computer science, creative writing, drama, driver education, earth science, ecology, economics, economics-AP, English, English literature, English literature-AP, English-AP, ESL, ESL, ethical decision making, ethics, European history, European history-AP, fine arts, French, geography, geometry, German, government/civics, grammar, health, history, history of rock and roll, history-AP, honors algebra, honors English, honors geometry, honors U.S. history, journalism, Latin, macroeconomics-AP, mathematics, microeconomics-AP, modern European history-AP, music, music appreciation, music history, music performance, music theory, outdoor education, physical education, physics, physics-AP, physiology, piano, poetry, pre-algebra, pre-calculus, psychology, religion, Russian history, science, Shakespeare, social sciences, social studies, Spanish, speech, speech communications, statistics, statistics-AP, technology, theater, theater arts, trigonometry, U.S. history, U.S. history-AP, Western civilization, wilderness education, world geography, world history, world literature.

Graduation Requirements American government, American history, arts and fine arts (art, music, dance, drama), computer science, economics, English, ethics, foreign language, mathematics, physical education (includes health), science, senior thesis, social sciences, social studies (includes history), speech, Public Exhibition Program—declamation, oration, performance piece, original creative work.

Special Academic Programs 13 Advanced Placement exams for which test preparation is offered; honors section; independent study; study abroad; academic accommodation for the gifted; programs in English, mathematics, general development for dyslexic students; special instructional classes for deaf students, blind students; ESL (21 students enrolled).

College Admission Counseling 48 students graduated in 2011; 47 went to college, including Belmont University; Clemson University; Sewanee: The University of the South; The University of Tennessee; The University of Tennessee at Chattanooga; Vanderbilt University. Other: 1 entered military service. Mean SAT critical reading: 626, mean SAT math: 623, mean SAT writing: 600, mean combined SAT: 1849, mean composite ACT: 26.

Student Life Upper grades have uniform requirement, student council, honor system. Discipline rests equally with students and faculty.

Tuition and Aid Day student tuition: $16,500; 5-day tuition and room/board: $29,950; 7-day tuition and room/board: $38,500. Tuition installment plan (FACTS Tuition Payment Plan, monthly payment plans, individually arranged payment plans). Merit scholarship grants, need-based scholarship grants available. In 2011–12, 40% of upper-school students received aid; total upper-school merit-scholarship money awarded: $154,000. Total amount of financial aid awarded in 2011–12: $1,200,000.

Admissions Traditional secondary-level entrance grade is 9. For fall 2011, 82 students applied for upper-level admission, 54 were accepted, 33 enrolled. ISEE, SSAT or TOEFL required. Deadline for receipt of application materials: February 15. Application fee required: $50. Interview required.

Athletics Interscholastic: baseball (boys), basketball (b,g), cross-country running (b,g), football (b), golf (b,g), lacrosse (b,g), soccer (b,g); intramural: aerobics (g), aerobics/Nautilus (b,g), volleyball (g); coed interscholastic: marksmanship, running, trap and skeet; coed intramural: aerobics/Nautilus, aquatics, backpacking, badminton, ballet, bowling, canoeing/kayaking, climbing, combined training, fishing, fitness, fitness walking, fly fishing, Frisbee, hiking/backpacking, horseback riding, kayaking, outdoor activities, physical fitness, physical training, rock climbing, ropes courses, skeet shooting, table tennis, ultimate Frisbee, wall climbing, weight lifting, weight training, wilderness survival, yoga. 1 PE instructor, 17 coaches, 1 athletic trainer.

Computers Computers are regularly used in computer applications, English, foreign language, history, mathematics, science, writing classes. Computer network features include on-campus library services, online commercial services, Internet access, wireless campus network, Internet filtering or blocking technology. Campus intranet, student e-mail accounts, and computer access in designated common areas are available to students. Students grades are available online. The school has a published electronic and media policy.

Contact Mrs. Julie Harris, Director of Admissions. 931-389-6003. Fax: 931-389-6657. E-mail: admissions@webbschool.com. Web site: www.thewebbschool.com.

WEBB SCHOOL OF KNOXVILLE

9800 Webb School Drive

Knoxville, Tennessee 37923-3399

Head of School: Mr. Scott L. Hutchinson

General Information Coeducational day college-preparatory, arts, religious studies, and technology school. Grades K–12. Founded: 1955. Setting: urban. Nearest major city is Chattanooga. 108-acre campus. 8 buildings on campus. Approved or accredited by Southern Association of Colleges and Schools, Southern Association of Independent Schools, and Tennessee Department of Education. Member of National Association of Independent Schools and Secondary School Admission Test Board. Endowment: $6.2 million. Total enrollment: 1,047. Upper school average class size: 15. Upper school faculty-student ratio: 1:10. There are 175 required school days per year for Upper School students. Upper School students typically attend 5 days per week. The average school day consists of 8 hours and 5 minutes.

Upper School Student Profile Grade 9: 132 students (74 boys, 58 girls); Grade 10: 121 students (64 boys, 57 girls); Grade 11: 105 students (46 boys, 59 girls); Grade 12: 119 students (56 boys, 63 girls).

Faculty School total: 96. In upper school: 19 men, 27 women; 36 have advanced degrees.

Subjects Offered 20th century world history, 3-dimensional design, advanced math, algebra, American sign language, anatomy and physiology, anthropology, art history-AP, astronomy, biology, biology-AP, calculus, calculus-AP, ceramics, chamber groups, chemistry, chemistry-AP, civil war history, computer science-AP, concert choir, creative writing, digital imaging, drama, dramatic arts, drawing, economics, English, English composition, English language and composition-AP, English literature, English literature and composition-AP, English-AP, environmental science-AP, French, French-AP, freshman foundations, geometry, government and politics-AP, Greek, history of music, honors algebra, honors English, honors geometry, honors world history, independent study, journalism, Latin, Latin-AP, Mandarin, mathematics-AP, modern European history-AP, modern world history, music theory-AP, painting, photography, physics, physics-AP, pre-calculus, printmaking, probability and statistics, psychology, psychology-AP, science research, Shakespeare, Spanish, Spanish-AP, speech communications, stage design, strings, studio art-AP, theater arts, U.S. government and politics, U.S. government and politics-AP, U.S. history, U.S. history-AP, video film production, wind ensemble, world history, world history-AP, world religions, yearbook.

Graduation Requirements Algebra, American history, arts and fine arts (art, music, dance, drama), biology, chemistry, English, foreign language, freshman foundations, geometry, mathematics, physical education (includes health), public service, science, world history, world religions, public speaking (two chapel talks), 25 hours of community service per year.

Special Academic Programs 22 Advanced Placement exams for which test preparation is offered; honors section; independent study; study abroad; remedial reading and/or remedial writing; remedial math.

College Admission Counseling 108 students graduated in 2011; all went to college, including Auburn University; Belmont University; Georgia Institute of Technology; The University of Alabama at Birmingham; The University of Tennessee; University of Mississippi. Mean SAT critical reading: 606, mean SAT math: 587, mean SAT writing: 604, mean composite ACT: 27. 75% scored over 600 on SAT critical reading, 75% scored over 600 on SAT math, 75% scored over 600 on SAT writing, 60% scored over 26 on composite ACT.

Student Life Upper grades have uniform requirement, student council, honor system. Discipline rests equally with students and faculty.

Summer Programs Remediation, enrichment, advancement, sports, art/fine arts programs offered; session focuses on academic and sports-oriented fun; held on campus; accepts boys and girls; open to students from other schools. 2012 schedule: June 4 to August 3. Application deadline: June 4.

Tuition and Aid Day student tuition: $15,990. Tuition installment plan (monthly payment plans, individually arranged payment plans, Tuition Payments can also be paid in two installments-last calendar day in July and November). Need-based scholarship grants available. In 2011–12, 13% of upper-school students received aid. Total amount of financial aid awarded in 2011–12: $646,250.

Admissions Traditional secondary-level entrance grade is 9. For fall 2011, 58 students applied for upper-level admission, 46 were accepted, 37 enrolled. ISEE required. Deadline for receipt of application materials: January 9. Application fee required: $75. On-campus interview required.

Athletics Interscholastic: baseball (boys), basketball (b,g), bowling (b,g), cheering (g), climbing (b,g), cross-country running (b,g), field hockey (g), football (b), golf (b,g), lacrosse (b), soccer (b,g), softball (g), swimming and diving (b,g), tennis (b,g), track and field (b,g), volleyball (g), wrestling (b); coed interscholastic: sailing. 21 coaches, 1 athletic trainer.

Computers Computers are regularly used in art, English, foreign language, graphic design, history, journalism, mathematics, music, science, technology, yearbook classes. Computer network features include on-campus library services, Internet access, wireless campus network, Internet filtering or blocking technology, all students in grades 4-12 own/lease iPads for school. Student e-mail accounts are available to students. Students grades are available online. The school has a published electronic and media policy.

Contact Mrs. Christy Widener, Admissions Administrative Assistant. 865-291-3830. Fax: 865-291-1532. E-mail: christy_widener@webbschool.org. Web site: www.webbschool.org.

THE WELLINGTON SCHOOL

3650 Reed Road

Columbus, Ohio 43220

Head of School: Mr. Robert D. Brisk

General Information Coeducational day college-preparatory, arts, and bilingual studies school. Grades PK–12. Founded: 1982. Setting: suburban. 21-acre campus. 1 building on campus. Approved or accredited by Independent Schools Association of the Central States, Ohio Association of Independent Schools, and Ohio Department of Education. Member of National Association of Independent Schools. Total enrollment: 621. Upper school average class size: 15. Upper school faculty-student ratio: 1:12. Upper School students typically attend 5 days per week. The average school day consists of 7 hours.

Upper School Student Profile Grade 9: 45 students (25 boys, 20 girls); Grade 10: 56 students (24 boys, 32 girls); Grade 11: 48 students (25 boys, 23 girls); Grade 12: 48 students (29 boys, 19 girls).

Faculty School total: 56. In upper school: 15 men, 16 women; 24 have advanced degrees.

Subjects Offered Algebra, art and culture, band, biology, biology-AP, calculus-AP, ceramics, chemistry, chemistry-AP, choir, chorus, computer graphics, creative arts, drama, drawing, earth and space science, economics, English, English-AP, European history-AP, film, finite math, French, French-AP, geometry, government, issues of the 90's, journalism, Latin, Latin-AP, mathematics, modern history, music appreciation, music theory-AP, painting, photography, physical education, physics, printmaking, Spanish, Spanish-AP, speech, strings, studio art-AP, U.S. history, U.S. history-AP, visual arts, voice, Western civilization, word processing, writing, yearbook.

Graduation Requirements 3-dimensional art, arts and fine arts (art, music, dance, drama), English, foreign language, government, lab science, mathematics, physical education (includes health), science, social sciences, social studies (includes history), speech, senior independent project. Community service is required.

Special Academic Programs Advanced Placement exam preparation; honors section; accelerated programs; independent study; study at local college for college credit; study abroad; academic accommodation for the gifted, the musically talented, and the artistically talented; ESL.

College Admission Counseling 49 students graduated in 2010; all went to college, including Elon University; Georgetown University; Miami University; The Ohio State University.

Student Life Upper grades have specified standards of dress, student council. Discipline rests equally with students and faculty.

Tuition and Aid Day student tuition: $17,825–$18,575. Tuition installment plan (Key Tuition Payment Plan, monthly payment plans, individually arranged payment plans, 2-, 6-, and 10-month payment plans). Merit scholarship grants, need-based scholarship grants, need-based loans available.

Admissions Traditional secondary-level entrance grade is 9. Admissions testing or ERB required. Deadline for receipt of application materials: none. Application fee required: $50. On-campus interview required.

Athletics Interscholastic: baseball (boys), basketball (b,g), diving (b,g), fencing (b,g), golf (b,g), lacrosse (b,g), soccer (b,g), softball (g), tennis (b,g); intramural: basketball (b,g), independent competitive sports (g), lacrosse (g); coed interscholastic: fencing, swimming and diving; coed intramural: canoeing/kayaking, climbing, flag football, martial arts. 2 PE instructors, 15 coaches, 1 athletic trainer.

Computers Computers are regularly used in English, foreign language, library, mathematics, music, newspaper, research skills, science, senior seminar, theater arts, typing, yearbook classes. Computer network features include on-campus library services, online commercial services, Internet access, wireless campus network, Internet filtering or blocking technology, SmartBoards. Campus intranet, student e-mail accounts, and computer access in designated common areas are available to students. Students grades are available online. The school has a published electronic and media policy.

Contact Ms. Lynne Steger, Assistant Director of Admission. 614-324-1647. Fax: 614-442-3286. E-mail: steger@wellington.org. Web site: www.wellington.org.

WELLSPRING FOUNDATION

Bethlehem, Connecticut

See Special Needs Schools section.

WELLSPRINGS FRIENDS SCHOOL

3590 West 18th Avenue

Eugene, Oregon 97402

Head of School: Dennis Hoerner

General Information Coeducational day college-preparatory and general academic school, affiliated with Society of Friends; primarily serves underachievers. Grades 9–12. Founded: 1994. Setting: small town. Nearest major city is Portland. 4-acre campus. 2 buildings on campus. Approved or accredited by Northwest Association of Schools and Colleges and Oregon Department of Education. Endowment: $8,000. Total enrollment: 60. Upper school average class size: 10. Upper school faculty-student ratio: 1:8. The average school day consists of 6 hours.

Upper School Student Profile Grade 9: 7 students (7 girls); Grade 10: 12 students (5 boys, 7 girls); Grade 11: 24 students (13 boys, 11 girls); Grade 12: 18 students (7 boys, 11 girls); Grade 13: 1 student (1 girl).

Faculty School total: 10. In upper school: 5 men, 5 women; 4 have advanced degrees.

Subjects Offered 20th century world history, advanced math, algebra, creative writing, English, film, finance, fine arts, geometry, German, government, human sexuality, life science, personal finance, physical education, physical science, poetry, pre-algebra, reading, Spanish, U.S. history.

Graduation Requirements English, foreign language, mathematics, science, social studies (includes history). Community service is required.

Special Academic Programs Independent study; remedial reading and/or remedial writing; remedial math.

College Admission Counseling 21 students graduated in 2010; 8 went to college, including Lane Community College; University of Oregon. Other: 6 went to work, 2 entered military service, 5 had other specific plans.

Student Life Upper grades have student council. Discipline rests equally with students and faculty.

Tuition and Aid Day student tuition: $6000. Tuition installment plan (monthly payment plans, individually arranged payment plans). Need-based scholarship grants available.

Admissions Traditional secondary-level entrance grade is 9. For fall 2010, 15 students applied for upper-level admission, 15 were accepted, 14 enrolled. Deadline for receipt of application materials: none. No application fee required. Interview required.

Athletics Coed Intramural: basketball, bocce, football, Frisbee, hiking/backpacking, physical fitness, skateboarding, table tennis, yoga. 1 PE instructor.

Computers Computers are regularly used in career education, career exploration, music, writing, yearbook classes. Computer network features include Internet access, wireless campus network.

Contact Office Manager. 541-686-1223. Fax: 541-687-1493. E-mail: info@wellspringsfriends.org. Web site: www.wellspringsfriends.org.

WESLEYAN ACADEMY

PO Box 1489

Guaynabo, Puerto Rico 00970-1489

Head of School: Mrs. Nívea E. Dávila

General Information Coeducational day college-preparatory school, affiliated with Wesleyan Church. Grades PK–12. Founded: 1955. Setting: urban. Nearest major city is San Juan. 6-acre campus. 1 building on campus. Approved or accredited by Association of Christian Schools International, Middle States Association of Colleges and Schools, and Puerto Rico Department of Education. Total enrollment: 922. Upper school average class size: 25. Upper school faculty-student ratio: 1:23. There are 180 required school days per year for Upper School students. Upper School students typically attend 6 days per week. The average school day consists of 6 hours and 15 minutes.

Upper School Student Profile Grade 7: 70 students (36 boys, 34 girls); Grade 8: 50 students (27 boys, 23 girls); Grade 9: 56 students (24 boys, 32 girls); Grade 10: 52 students (26 boys, 26 girls); Grade 11: 42 students (22 boys, 20 girls); Grade 12: 47 students (26 boys, 21 girls). 50% of students are members of Wesleyan Church.

Faculty School total: 72. In upper school: 7 men, 14 women; 5 have advanced degrees.

Subjects Offered Accounting, algebra, American history, anatomy and physiology, art, Bible, biology, calculus, career and personal planning, choir, college planning, computer skills, critical writing, dance, drama, English, French, general math, general science, geography, geometry, global studies, golf, guidance, guitar, handbells, health, history, Internet, intro to computers, keyboarding, lab science, library, mathematics, music, music appreciation, personal development, piano, poetry, pre-algebra, pre-calculus, pre-college orientation, Puerto Rican history, science, social sciences, Spanish, swimming, trigonometry, U.S. government, volleyball, world affairs, world history, yearbook.

Graduation Requirements American government, American history, Bible, computer science, electives, English, foreign language, mathematics, physical education (includes health), science, social sciences, social studies (includes history), Spanish, 84 acomulative hours of community service during high school years.

Special Academic Programs Advanced Placement exam preparation; honors section; independent study.

College Admission Counseling 39 students graduated in 2011; 38 went to college, including Boston University; The University of Arizona; University of Florida; University of Puerto Rico, Cayey University College; University of Puerto Rico, Río Piedras. Other: 1 entered military service. Mean SAT critical reading: 533, mean SAT math: 501, mean SAT writing: 471, mean combined SAT: 1505. 24% scored over 600 on SAT critical reading, 14% scored over 600 on SAT math, 48% scored over 600 on SAT writing, 14% scored over 1800 on combined SAT.

Student Life Upper grades have uniform requirement, student council, honor system. Discipline rests primarily with faculty.

Summer Programs Remediation, enrichment, advancement programs offered; session focuses on remediation and enrichment classes; held on campus; accepts boys and girls; open to students from other schools. 100 students usually enrolled. 2012 schedule: June 2 to June 29. Application deadline: May 31.

Tuition and Aid Day student tuition: $6700. Guaranteed tuition plan. Tuition installment plan (monthly payment plans, full-payment discount plan, semester payment plan). Need-based scholarship grants, need-based financial aid available. In 2011–12, 2% of upper-school students received aid. Total amount of financial aid awarded in 2011–12: $10,000.

Admissions For fall 2011, 147 students applied for upper-level admission, 115 were accepted, 107 enrolled. Academic Profile Tests, admissions testing, mathematics proficiency exam and Metropolitan Achievement Test required. Deadline for receipt of application materials: none. Application fee required: $100. On-campus interview required.

Athletics Interscholastic: basketball (boys, girls), cross-country running (b), golf (b), indoor soccer (b,g), soccer (b,g), swimming and diving (b,g), tennis (b,g), track and field (b,g), volleyball (b,g); intramural: basketball (b,g), cross-country running (b), indoor soccer (b,g), soccer (b,g), track and field (b,g), volleyball (b,g); coed interscholastic: tennis. 3 PE instructors, 3 coaches.

Computers Computers are regularly used in all academic classes. Computer network features include on-campus library services, Internet access, wireless campus network, Internet filtering or blocking technology. Computer access in designated common areas is available to students. The school has a published electronic and media policy.

Contact Mrs. Mae Ling Cardona, Admissions Clerk. 787-720-8959 Ext. 235. Fax: 787-790-0730. E-mail: mcardona@wesleyanacademy.org. Web site: www.wesleyanacademy.org.

WESTBURY CHRISTIAN SCHOOL

10420 Hillcroft

Houston, Texas 77096

Head of School: Mr. Greg J. Glenn

General Information Coeducational day college-preparatory, arts, business, and religious studies school, affiliated with Church of Christ. Grades PK–12. Founded: 1975. Setting: urban. 13-acre campus. 1 building on campus. Approved or accredited by National Christian School Association, Southern Association of Colleges and Schools, Texas Private School Accreditation Commission, The College Board, and Texas Department of Education. Endowment: $300,000. Total enrollment: 545. Upper school average class size: 22. Upper school faculty-student ratio: 1:10. There are 180 required school days per year for Upper School students. Upper School students typically attend 5 days per week. The average school day consists of 7 hours and 45 minutes.

Upper School Student Profile Grade 9: 61 students (41 boys, 20 girls); Grade 10: 55 students (32 boys, 23 girls); Grade 11: 65 students (30 boys, 35 girls); Grade 12: 61 students (29 boys, 32 girls). 18% of students are members of Church of Christ.

Faculty School total: 55. In upper school: 19 men, 20 women; 9 have advanced degrees.

Subjects Offered Accounting, algebra, anatomy and physiology, art, athletics, band, basketball, Bible, biology, biology-AP, business, calculus-AP, cheerleading, chemistry, chemistry-AP, community service, computer applications, drama, economics, English, English language and composition-AP, English literature and composition-AP, entrepreneurship, geography, geometry, government, government-AP, health, human geography - AP, macro/microeconomics-AP, marketing, photography, physical education, physical science, physics, pre-calculus, psychology-AP, Spanish, speech, statistics-AP, studio art-AP, U.S. history, U.S. history-AP, vocal music, weight training, world history, world history-AP, yearbook.

Graduation Requirements Arts and fine arts (art, music, dance, drama), Bible, electives, English, foreign language, geometry, mathematics, physical education (includes health), science, social studies (includes history), speech, continuous participation in student activities programs, community service each semester.

Special Academic Programs 15 Advanced Placement exams for which test preparation is offered; independent study.

College Admission Counseling 74 students graduated in 2011; 72 went to college, including Baylor University; Houston Baptist University; Houston Community College System; Texas A&M University; The University of Texas at Austin; University of Houston. Other: 1 went to work, 1 entered military service. Mean SAT critical reading: 473, mean SAT math: 526, mean SAT writing: 470, mean combined SAT: 1470, mean composite ACT: 22. 5% scored over 600 on SAT critical reading, 15% scored over 600 on SAT math, 5% scored over 600 on SAT writing, 5% scored over 1800 on combined SAT, 4% scored over 26 on composite ACT.

Student Life Upper grades have uniform requirement, student council, honor system. Discipline rests primarily with faculty.

Summer Programs Sports programs offered; session focuses on week-long basketball, football, and volleyball instruction camps; held on campus; accepts boys and girls; open to students from other schools. 150 students usually enrolled. 2012 schedule: June 4 to July 27. Application deadline: none.

Tuition and Aid Day student tuition: $9291. Tuition installment plan (FACTS Tuition Payment Plan). Tuition reduction for siblings, merit scholarship grants, need-based scholarship grants available. In 2011–12, 20% of upper-school students received aid; total upper-school merit-scholarship money awarded: $14,000. Total amount of financial aid awarded in 2011–12: $260,000.

Admissions Traditional secondary-level entrance grade is 9. For fall 2011, 128 students applied for upper-level admission, 90 were accepted, 76 enrolled. ISEE, Otis-Lennon School Ability Test, SLEP for foreign students or Stanford Achievement Test required. Deadline for receipt of application materials: none. Application fee required: $75. Interview required.

Athletics Interscholastic: baseball (boys), basketball (b,g), cheering (g), cross-country running (b,g), football (b), golf (b,g), soccer (b,g), softball (g), strength & conditioning (b,g), swimming and diving (b,g), tennis (b,g), track and field (b,g), volleyball (g); intramural: weight training (b). 1 PE instructor, 10 coaches.

Computers Computers are regularly used in all academic classes. Computer network features include on-campus library services, online commercial services, Internet access, wireless campus network, Internet filtering or blocking technology. Student e-mail accounts are available to students. Students grades are available online. The school has a published electronic and media policy.

Contact Mrs. Phylis Frye, Director of Admissions. 713-551-8100 Ext. 1018. Fax: 713-551-8117. E-mail: admissions@westburychristian.org. Web site: www.westburychristian.org.

WEST CATHOLIC HIGH SCHOOL

1801 Bristol Avenue NW

Grand Rapids, Michigan 49504

Head of School: Mrs. Cynthia Kneibel

General Information Coeducational day college-preparatory and religious studies school, affiliated with Roman Catholic Church. Grades 9–12. Founded: 1962. Setting: urban. 20-acre campus. 1 building on campus. Approved or accredited by National Catholic Education Association, North Central Association of Colleges and Schools, and Michigan Department of Education. Endowment: $1 million. Total enrollment: 506. Upper school average class size: 28. Upper school faculty-student ratio: 1:28. There are 181 required school days per year for Upper School students. Upper School students typically attend 5 days per week. The average school day consists of 6 hours.

Upper School Student Profile Grade 9: 115 students (57 boys, 58 girls); Grade 10: 115 students (70 boys, 45 girls); Grade 11: 122 students (61 boys, 61 girls); Grade 12: 154 students (83 boys, 71 girls). 95% of students are Roman Catholic.

Faculty School total: 27. In upper school: 10 men, 17 women; 20 have advanced degrees.

Subjects Offered 20th century world history, acting, advanced chemistry, advanced computer applications, advanced math, American government, American literature, anatomy, art, band, Basic programming, biology, biology-AP, calculus, calculus-AP, career planning, chemistry, chemistry-AP, choir, Christian doctrine, composition, composition-AP, computer applications, computer programming, concert band, desktop publishing, drama, drawing, earth science, economics, economics-AP, English, English language and composition-AP, English literature, English literature and composition-AP, English literature-AP, environmental science, family living, French, general math, geometry, government, government and politics-AP, government-AP, government/civics, history, history of the Catholic Church, honors algebra, honors English, honors geometry, honors world history, human anatomy, intro to computers, jazz band, journalism, marching band, physics, pre-algebra, pre-calculus, psychology, sexuality, social justice, sociology, Spanish, U.S. government and politics-AP, U.S. history, Web site design, world history, yearbook.

Graduation Requirements Economics, electives, English composition, foreign language, government, health, mathematics, religion (includes Bible studies and theology), science, social studies (includes history), U.S. history, visual arts.

Special Academic Programs Advanced Placement exam preparation; honors section; independent study.

College Admission Counseling 137 students graduated in 2011; 135 went to college, including Central Michigan University; Grand Valley State University; Michigan State University; Western Michigan University. Other: 1 went to work, 1 entered military service. 4% scored over 600 on SAT critical reading, 8% scored over 600 on SAT math, 5% scored over 600 on SAT writing, 6% scored over 1800 on combined SAT, 30.7% scored over 26 on composite ACT.

Student Life Upper grades have uniform requirement, student council, honor system. Discipline rests primarily with faculty. Attendance at religious services is required.

Summer Programs Remediation, sports programs offered; session focuses on sports enrichment; held on campus; accepts boys and girls; not open to students from other schools. 130 students usually enrolled. 2012 schedule: June 18 to July 31. Application deadline: June 1.

Tuition and Aid Day student tuition: $7855. Tuition installment plan (Tuition Management Systems). Need-based scholarship grants available. In 2011–12, 25% of upper-school students received aid.

Admissions Traditional secondary-level entrance grade is 9. Essay, High School Placement Test and Math Placement Exam required. Deadline for receipt of application materials: February 1. Application fee required: $150. Interview required.

Athletics Interscholastic: baseball (boys), basketball (b,g), bowling (b,g), cheering (g), cross-country running (b,g), diving (b,g), football (b), golf (b,g), gymnastics (g), hockey (b), ice hockey (b), pom squad (g), skiing (downhill) (b,g), soccer (b,g), softball (g), swimming and diving (b,g), tennis (b,g), track and field (b,g), volleyball (g), weight lifting (b), weight training (b), wrestling (b); intramural: basketball (b,g). 1 PE instructor, 66 coaches, 2 athletic trainers.

Computers Computers are regularly used in all academic classes. Computer network features include Internet access, wireless campus network, Internet filtering or blocking technology. Student e-mail accounts and computer access in designated common areas are available to students. Students grades are available online. The school has a published electronic and media policy.

Contact Mrs. Lauri Ford, Guidance Secretary. 616-233-5909. Fax: 616-453-4320. E-mail: lauriford@grcss.org. Web site: www.grwestcatholic.org.

WESTCHESTER COUNTRY DAY SCHOOL

2045 North Old Greensboro Road

High Point, North Carolina 27265

Head of School: Mr. Cobb Atkinson

General Information Coeducational day college-preparatory, arts, bilingual studies, and technology school. Grades K–12. Founded: 1967. Setting: rural. 53-acre campus. 6 buildings on campus. Approved or accredited by North Carolina Association of Independent Schools, Southern Association of Colleges and Schools, and Southern Association of Independent Schools. Member of National Association of Independent Schools. Endowment: $2.5 million. Total enrollment: 396. Upper school average class size: 16. Upper school faculty-student ratio: 1:6. There are 173 required school days per year for Upper School students. Upper School students typically attend 5 days per week. The average school day consists of 5 hours and 40 minutes.

Upper School Student Profile Grade 9: 31 students (11 boys, 20 girls); Grade 10: 42 students (16 boys, 26 girls); Grade 11: 45 students (27 boys, 18 girls); Grade 12: 32 students (9 boys, 23 girls).

Faculty School total: 54. In upper school: 7 men, 17 women; 16 have advanced degrees.

Subjects Offered Advanced chemistry, Advanced Placement courses, advanced studio art-AP, algebra, American history, American literature, American literature-AP, art, art history-AP, art-AP, athletics, biology, biology-AP, British literature, calculus, calculus-AP, chamber groups, character education, chemistry, chemistry-AP, choral music, chorus, college admission preparation, college counseling, college placement, college planning, college writing, computer science, creative writing, dance, debate, earth science, economics, English, English language-AP, English literature, English literature-AP, environmental science, European history, European history-AP, exercise science, film and literature, fine arts, French, geography, geometry, global studies, government/civics, grammar, health, health education, history, Mandarin, mathematics, music, physical education, physics, probability and statistics, science, social studies, Spanish, Spanish language-AP, statistics-AP, theater, U.S. history-AP, voice ensemble, Web site design, world history, world literature, writing.

Graduation Requirements Arts and fine arts (art, music, dance, drama), civics, English, foreign language, mathematics, physical education (includes health), science, social studies (includes history), community service project, senior speech.

Special Academic Programs 12 Advanced Placement exams for which test preparation is offered; honors section; independent study.

College Admission Counseling 40 students graduated in 2011; all went to college, including East Carolina University; North Carolina State University; The University of North Carolina at Chapel Hill; The University of North Carolina at Charlotte; University of Georgia; University of South Carolina. Median SAT critical reading: 560, median SAT math: 580, median SAT writing: 570.

Student Life Upper grades have specified standards of dress, student council, honor system. Discipline rests primarily with faculty.

Summer Programs Enrichment, sports, art/fine arts, computer instruction programs offered; session focuses on academics, sports, hobby-related; held on campus; accepts boys and girls; open to students from other schools. 200 students usually enrolled. 2012 schedule: June 13 to August 12. Application deadline: none.

Tuition and Aid Day student tuition: $13,600–$13,920. Guaranteed tuition plan. Tuition installment plan (FACTS Tuition Payment Plan, monthly payment plans). Tuition reduction for siblings, need-based scholarship grants available. In 2011–12, 31% of upper-school students received aid. Total amount of financial aid awarded in 2011–12: $930,325.

Admissions Traditional secondary-level entrance grade is 9. Brigance Test of Basic Skills, ERB CTP IV, grade equivalent tests, Metropolitan Achievement Test, Wide Range Achievement Test or Woodcock-Johnson Revised Achievement Test required. Deadline for receipt of application materials: none. Application fee required: $75. Interview recommended.

Athletics Interscholastic: baseball (boys), basketball (b,g), cheering (g), dance (g), dance team (g), soccer (b,g), softball (g), tennis (b,g), volleyball (g); coed interscholastic: aquatics, cross-country running, golf, physical fitness, swimming and diving, track and field. 2 PE instructors, 12 coaches.

Computers Computers are regularly used in English, foreign language, history, library science, mathematics, science, Web site design, yearbook classes. Computer network features include on-campus library services, Internet access, wireless campus network, Internet filtering or blocking technology. Campus intranet, student e-mail accounts, and computer access in designated common areas are available to students. Students grades are available online. The school has a published electronic and media policy.

Contact Mrs. Kerie Beth Scott, Director of Admissions. 336-822-4005. Fax: 336-869-6685. E-mail: keriebeth.scott@westchestercds.org. Web site: www.westchestercds.org.

WESTERN CHRISTIAN SCHOOLS

100 W 9th Street

Upland, California 91786

Head of School: Robert Yovino

General Information Coeducational day college-preparatory, arts, and religious studies school, affiliated with Christian faith. Grades 9–12. Founded: 1920. Setting: suburban. Nearest major city is Los Angeles. 8 buildings on campus. Approved or accredited by Association of Christian Schools International, Western Association of Schools and Colleges, and California Department of Education. Member of European Council of International Schools. Total enrollment: 475. Upper school average class size: 17. Upper school faculty-student ratio: 1:17. There are 175 required school days per year for Upper School students. Upper School students typically attend 5 days per week. The average school day consists of 6 hours and 50 minutes.

Upper School Student Profile 75% of students are Christian.

Faculty School total: 27. In upper school: 12 men, 15 women.

Subjects Offered Advanced Placement courses, aerobics, algebra, American history, anatomy, art, band, Bible studies, biology, biology-AP, calculus, calculus-AP, ceramics, chemistry, chorus, computer science, consumer mathematics, creative writing, drama, economics, English, English-AP, environmental science-AP, ESL, film, French, French-AP, geography, geometry, government-AP, government/civics, health, journalism, math analysis, mathematics, physical education, physics, physiology, psychology, sociology, Spanish, Spanish-AP, speech and debate, theater, world history.

Special Academic Programs 7 Advanced Placement exams for which test preparation is offered.

College Admission Counseling 132 students graduated in 2010; 82 went to college, including Azusa Pacific University; California State Polytechnic University, Pomona; California State University, Fullerton; University of California, Irvine; University of California, Los Angeles; University of Southern California.

Student Life Upper grades have uniform requirement. Discipline rests primarily with faculty.

Tuition and Aid Financial aid available to upper-school students. In 2010–11, 50% of upper-school students received aid. Total amount of financial aid awarded in 2010–11: $150,000.

Admissions School's own test required. Deadline for receipt of application materials: none. No application fee required. On-campus interview required.

Athletics Interscholastic: baseball (boys), basketball (b,g), cheering (g), cross-country running (b,g), football (b), soccer (b,g), softball (g), track and field (b,g), volleyball (g); coed interscholastic: golf. 2 PE instructors, 9 coaches.

Contact John Attwood, Vice Principal. 909-920-5858. Fax: 909-985-3449.

WESTERN MENNONITE SCHOOL

9045 Wallace Road NW

Salem, Oregon 97304-9716

Head of School: Darrel Camp

General Information Coeducational boarding and day college-preparatory, general academic, and religious studies school, affiliated with Mennonite Church USA. Boarding grades 9–12, day grades 6–12. Founded: 1945. Setting: rural. Students are housed in single-sex dormitories. 45-acre campus. 10 buildings on campus. Approved or accredited by Mennonite Education Agency, Mennonite Schools Council, Northwest Association of Schools and Colleges, and Oregon Department of Education. Endowment: $1 million. Total enrollment: 230. Upper school average class size: 16. Upper school faculty-student ratio: 1:14. There are 173 required school days per year for Upper School students. Upper School students typically attend 5 days per week. The average school day consists of 5 hours and 25 minutes.

Upper School Student Profile Grade 9: 35 students (17 boys, 18 girls); Grade 10: 35 students (18 boys, 17 girls); Grade 11: 33 students (16 boys, 17 girls); Grade 12: 51 students (26 boys, 25 girls). 12% of students are boarding students. 85% are state residents. 3 states are represented in upper school student body. 12% are international students. International students from China, Germany, Hong Kong, Japan, Republic of Korea, and Taiwan; 7 other countries represented in student body. 18% of students are Mennonite Church USA.

Faculty School total: 26. In upper school: 12 men, 14 women; 8 have advanced degrees; 10 reside on campus.

Subjects Offered Accounting, advanced math, algebra, anatomy and physiology, art, Bible studies, biology, calculus, career and personal planning, career education, chemistry, choral music, Christian education, Christian scripture, church history, computer applications, computer programming, drawing and design, economics, English, English composition, English literature, general math, geography, geometry, government, health education, human anatomy, instrumental music, intro to computers, keyboarding, mathematics, music, music performance, novels, physical education, physical fitness, physical science, physics, pre-algebra, pre-calculus, psychology, religious education, religious studies, research, science, Spanish, U.S. government, U.S. history, U.S. literature, woodworking, yearbook.

Graduation Requirements Algebra, applied arts, Bible studies, biology, career education, chemistry, choir, economics, English, English literature, geometry, global studies, music, physical education (includes health), Spanish, U.S. government, U.S. history, U.S. literature, world geography, Mini-Term—one week of co-curricular activity at end of academic year (sophomore through senior year).

Special Academic Programs Independent study; term-away projects; study at local college for college credit.

College Admission Counseling 42 students graduated in 2011; 38 went to college, including Chemeketa Community College; Corban University; Eastern Mennonite University; Oregon State University; Seattle Pacific University; Western Oregon University. Median SAT math: 520, median composite ACT: 27. 11% scored over 600 on SAT math, 50% scored over 26 on composite ACT.

Student Life Upper grades have specified standards of dress, student council, honor system. Discipline rests primarily with faculty. Attendance at religious services is required.

Summer Programs Sports programs offered; session focuses on soccer, volleyball, basketball; held on campus; accepts boys and girls; open to students from other schools. 25 students usually enrolled. 2012 schedule: June to August. Application deadline: June.

Tuition and Aid Day student tuition: $7700; 5-day tuition and room/board: $11,748; 7-day tuition and room/board: $13,431. Tuition installment plan (monthly payment plans, individually arranged payment plans). Tuition reduction for siblings, merit scholarship grants, need-based scholarship grants, paying campus jobs available. In 2011–12, 41% of upper-school students received aid.

Admissions Traditional secondary-level entrance grade is 9. Deadline for receipt of application materials: none. Application fee required: $50. Interview recommended.

Athletics Interscholastic: baseball (boys, girls), basketball (b,g), cross-country running (b), soccer (b,g), volleyball (g); coed intramural: softball. 5 PE instructors, 8 coaches.

Computers Computers are regularly used in independent study, introduction to technology, keyboarding, yearbook classes. Computer network features include on-campus library services, online commercial services, Internet access, wireless campus network, Internet filtering or blocking technology. Campus intranet, student e-mail accounts, and computer access in designated common areas are available to students. Students grades are available online. The school has a published electronic and media policy.

Contact Mr. Rich Martin, Admissions Coordinator. 503-363-2000 Ext. 121. Fax: 503-370-9455. E-mail: rmartin@westernmennoniteschool.org. Web site: www.westernmennoniteschool.org.

WESTERN RESERVE ACADEMY

115 College Street

Hudson, Ohio 44236

Head of School: Christopher D. Burner

General Information Coeducational boarding and day college-preparatory and arts school. Grades 9–PG. Founded: 1826. Setting: small town. Nearest major city is Cleveland. Students are housed in single-sex dormitories. 190-acre campus. 49 buildings on campus. Approved or accredited by Independent Schools Association of the Central States, Midwest Association of Boarding Schools, North Central Association of Colleges and Schools, Ohio Association of Independent Schools, The Association of Boarding Schools, and Ohio Department of Education. Member of National Association of Independent Schools and Secondary School Admission Test Board. Endowment: $97.7 million. Total enrollment: 389. Upper school average class size: 12. Upper school faculty-student ratio: 1:6. There are 182 required school days per year for Upper School students. Upper School students typically attend 6 days per week. The average school day consists of 7 hours and 15 minutes.

Upper School Student Profile Grade 9: 84 students (40 boys, 44 girls); Grade 10: 115 students (62 boys, 53 girls); Grade 11: 100 students (61 boys, 39 girls); Grade 12: 90 students (39 boys, 51 girls). 68% of students are boarding students. 70% are state residents. 20 states are represented in upper school student body. 18% are international students. International students from Canada, China, Germany, Republic of Korea, Saudi Arabia, and Taiwan; 10 other countries represented in student body.

Faculty School total: 64. In upper school: 39 men, 25 women; 53 have advanced degrees; 58 reside on campus.

Subjects Offered Algebra, American history, American literature, architecture, art, art history, astronomy, band, biology, calculus, ceramics, chemistry, chorus, computer programming, creative writing, dance, drafting, drama, economics, engineering, English, English literature, environmental science, European history, fine arts, French, geometry, German, health, history, humanities, independent study, industrial arts, Latin, Mandarin, mathematics, mechanical drawing, music, music history, music theory, orchestra, photography, physical education, physics, science, social studies, Spanish, speech, statistics, theater, trigonometry, world history, zoology.

Graduation Requirements Arts and fine arts (art, music, dance, drama), English, foreign language, history, mathematics, physical education (includes health), science, senior seminar, senior thesis.

Special Academic Programs 19 Advanced Placement exams for which test preparation is offered; honors section; independent study; study at local college for college credit; study abroad; academic accommodation for the gifted, the musically talented, and the artistically talented.

College Admission Counseling 110 students graduated in 2010; all went to college, including Boston College; Case Western Reserve University; Cornell University; Dartmouth College; New York University; The Ohio State University.

Student Life Upper grades have specified standards of dress, student council. Discipline rests equally with students and faculty.

Tuition and Aid Day student tuition: $28,900; 7-day tuition and room/board: $40,700. Tuition installment plan (The Tuition Plan, Insured Tuition Payment Plan, Key Tuition Payment Plan, monthly payment plans, individually arranged payment plans). Merit scholarship grants, need-based scholarship grants, need-based loans available. In 2010–11, 34% of upper-school students received aid. Total amount of financial aid awarded in 2010–11: $3,600,000.

Admissions Traditional secondary-level entrance grade is 9. For fall 2010, 364 students applied for upper-level admission, 229 were accepted, 154 enrolled. ISEE, SSAT or TOEFL required. Deadline for receipt of application materials: January 15. Application fee required: $50. Interview required.

Athletics Interscholastic: baseball (boys), basketball (b,g), cross-country running (b,g), diving (b,g), field hockey (g), football (b), golf (b), ice hockey (b), lacrosse (b,g), soccer (b,g), softball (g), swimming and diving (b,g), tennis (b,g), track and field (b,g), volleyball (g), wrestling (b); intramural: basketball (b); coed interscholastic: marksmanship, riflery; coed intramural: aerobics, aerobics/dance, aerobics/Nautilus, backpacking, bicycling, dance, fitness, hiking/backpacking, jogging, martial arts, modern dance, Nautilus, outdoor recreation, paddle tennis, physical fitness, physical training, running, skeet shooting, skiing (downhill), snowboarding, soccer, strength & conditioning, weight lifting, weight training, winter (indoor) track, yoga. 1 coach, 2 athletic trainers.

Computers Computers are regularly used in architecture, drawing and design, economics, engineering, English, foreign language, history, mathematics, science, technical drawing classes. Computer network features include on-campus library services, online commercial services, Internet access, wireless campus network, Internet filtering or blocking technology. Campus intranet and student e-mail accounts are available to students. The school has a published electronic and media policy.

Contact Mrs. Anne F. Sheppard, Dean of Admission and Financial Aid. 330-650-9717. Fax: 330-650-5858. E-mail: admission@wra.net. Web site: www.wra.net.

See Display on next page and Close-Up on page 702.

WESTGATE MENNONITE COLLEGIATE

86 West Gate

Winnipeg, Manitoba R3C 2E1, Canada

Head of School: Mr. Bob Hummelt

General Information Coeducational day college-preparatory, general academic, arts, religious studies, technology, and music, German, and French school, affiliated with Mennonite Church USA. Grades 7–12. Founded: 1958. Setting: urban. 3-acre campus. 1 building on campus. Approved or accredited by Canadian Association of Independent Schools and Manitoba Department of Education. Language of instruction: English. Total enrollment: 340. Upper school average class size: 25. Upper school faculty-student ratio: 1:15. Upper School students typically attend 5 days per week. The average school day consists of 6 hours and 30 minutes.

Upper School Student Profile Grade 10: 71 students (36 boys, 35 girls); Grade 11: 48 students (24 boys, 24 girls); Grade 12: 64 students (39 boys, 25 girls). 55% of students are Mennonite Church USA.

Faculty School total: 27. In upper school: 15 men, 11 women; 5 have advanced degrees.

Special Academic Programs Advanced Placement exam preparation; independent study; term-away projects.

College Admission Counseling 51 students graduated in 2011; they went to The University of Winnipeg; University of Manitoba.

Student Life Upper grades have specified standards of dress, student council. Discipline rests primarily with faculty. Attendance at religious services is required.

Tuition and Aid Day student tuition: CAN$4800. Tuition installment plan (monthly payment plans, individually arranged payment plans). Tuition reduction for siblings, bursaries, merit scholarship grants, need-based scholarship grants available. In 2011–12, 10% of upper-school students received aid; total upper-school merit-scholarship money awarded: CAN$5000. Total amount of financial aid awarded in 2011–12: CAN$36,000.

Admissions Traditional secondary-level entrance grade is 10. Deadline for receipt of application materials: March 10. Application fee required: CAN$50. Interview required.

Athletics Interscholastic: badminton (boys, girls), baseball (b,g), basketball (b,g), bowling (b,g), cheering (b,g), cross-country running (b,g), curling (b,g), floor hockey (b,g), golf (b), gymnastics (b,g), outdoor education (b,g), outdoor skills (b,g), rock climbing (b,g), running (b,g), soccer (b,g), strength & conditioning (b,g), volleyball (b,g); intramural: aerobics/dance (b,g), backpacking (b,g), badminton (b,g), basketball (b,g), bicycling (b,g), broomball (b,g), canoeing/kayaking (b,g), cross-country running (b,g), curling (b,g), field hockey (b,g), floor hockey (b,g), football (b,g), gymnastics (b,g), hiking/backpacking (b,g), ice hockey (b,g), ice skating (b,g), outdoor education (b,g), paddle tennis (b,g), racquetball (b,g), rock climbing (b,g), running (b,g), soccer (b,g), strength & conditioning (b,g), swimming and diving (b,g), volleyball (b,g), wall climbing (b,g); coed interscholastic: badminton, baseball, basketball, bowling, cheering, cross-country running, curling, floor hockey, gymnastics, outdoor education, outdoor skills, rock climbing, running, soccer, strength & conditioning, ultimate Frisbee, volleyball; coed intramural: aerobics/dance, backpacking, badminton, basketball, bicycling, broomball, canoeing/kayaking, cross-country running, curling, field hockey, floor hockey, football, gymnastics, hiking/backpacking, ice hockey, ice skating, outdoor education, paddle tennis, racquetball, rock climbing, running, soccer, strength & conditioning, swimming and diving, volleyball, wall climbing. 3 PE instructors, 7 coaches.

Computers Computer network features include on-campus library services, online commercial services, Internet access. The school has a published electronic and media policy.

Contact Mr. Bob Hummelt, Principal. 204-775-7111 Ext. 202. Fax: 204-786-1651. E-mail: westgate@westgatemennonite.ca. Web site: www.westgatemennonite.ca.

WEST ISLAND COLLEGE

7410 Blackfoot Trail SE

Calgary, Alberta T2H IM5, Canada

Head of School: Ms. Carol Grant-Watt

General Information Coeducational day college-preparatory, arts, business, bilingual studies, technology, and advanced placement school. Grades 7–12. Founded: 1982. Setting: urban. 18-acre campus. 2 buildings on campus. Approved or accredited by Canadian Association of Independent Schools and Alberta Department of Education. Languages of instruction: English, Spanish, and French. Total enrollment: 463. Upper school average class size: 18. Upper school faculty-student ratio: 1:17. There are 185 required school days per year for Upper School students. Upper School students typically attend 5 days per week. The average school day consists of 6 hours and 13 minutes.

Upper School Student Profile Grade 10: 102 students (50 boys, 52 girls); Grade 11: 66 students (31 boys, 35 girls); Grade 12: 71 students (39 boys, 32 girls).

Faculty School total: 44. In upper school: 20 men, 21 women; 15 have advanced degrees.

Subjects Offered Advanced Placement courses, anthropology, art, arts, biology, business, chemistry, choral music, communications, debate, drama, English, European history, experiential education, French, French studies, health, information processing, information technology, leadership, literature, mathematics, modern languages, music, outdoor education, philosophy, physical education, physics, political thought, politics, psychology, public speaking, science, social sciences, social studies, sociology, Spanish, standard curriculum, study skills, world geography, world history, world religions.

Graduation Requirements Alberta education requirements.

Special Academic Programs 10 Advanced Placement exams for which test preparation is offered; honors section; independent study; study abroad; academic accommodation for the gifted.

College Admission Counseling 67 students graduated in 2011; 66 went to college, including McGill University; Queen's University at Kingston; The University of British Columbia; University of Alberta; University of Calgary; University of Victoria. Other: 1 had other specific plans.

Student Life Upper grades have uniform requirement, student council, honor system. Discipline rests equally with students and faculty.

Summer Programs Enrichment, advancement, sports, computer instruction programs offered; session focuses on study skills and academic preparedness; held both on and off campus; held at various public parks in the city; accepts boys and girls; not open to students from other schools. 50 students usually enrolled. 2012 schedule: August 21 to August 25. Application deadline: April 30.

Tuition and Aid Day student tuition: CAN$12,410. Tuition installment plan (monthly payment plans).

Admissions Traditional secondary-level entrance grade is 10. For fall 2011, 38 students applied for upper-level admission, 27 were accepted, 26 enrolled. 3-R Achievement Test, CCAT, CTBS, OLSAT, Gates MacGinite Reading Tests and Otis-Lennon IQ Test required. Deadline for receipt of application materials: none. Application fee required: CAN$100. Interview required.

Athletics Interscholastic: basketball (boys, girls), field hockey (g), rugby (b), track and field (b,g), volleyball (b,g); intramural: aquatics (b,g), basketball (b,g), floor hockey (b,g), track and field (b,g), volleyball (b,g); coed interscholastic: badminton, climbing, cross-country running, soccer; coed intramural: alpine skiing, backpacking, badminton, bicycling, bowling, canoeing/kayaking, climbing, cross-country running, curling, dance, fitness, golf, hiking/backpacking, kayaking, mountaineering, nordic skiing, outdoor activities, outdoor education, physical fitness, physical training, rock climbing, sailing, skiing (cross-country), skiing (downhill), snowboarding, soccer, wilderness survival, wildernessways. 4 PE instructors, 10 coaches, 2 athletic trainers.

Computers Computers are regularly used in business, career education, career exploration, career technology, economics, English, French, independent study, mathematics, media arts, media production, multimedia, science, social studies, technology, word processing classes. Computer network features include on-campus library services, online commercial services, Internet access, wireless campus network, Internet filtering or blocking technology. Campus intranet, student e-mail accounts, and computer access in designated common areas are available to students. Students grades are available online. The school has a published electronic and media policy.

Contact Ms. Nicole Bernard, Director of Admissions. 403-444-0023. Fax: 403-444-2820. E-mail: admissions@westislandcollege.ab.ca. Web site: www.westislandcollege.ab.ca.

WESTMARK SCHOOL

Encino, California

See Special Needs Schools section.

WEST MEMPHIS CHRISTIAN HIGH SCHOOL

1101 North Missouri

West Memphis, Arkansas 72301

Head of School: Dr. Loretta Dale

General Information Coeducational day college-preparatory school, affiliated with Church of Christ, Christian faith. Grades 7–12. Founded: 1970. Setting: small town. Nearest major city is Memphis, TN. 1 building on campus. Approved or accredited by Mississippi Private School Association and Arkansas Department of Education. Candidate for accreditation by North Central Association of Colleges and Schools. Total enrollment: 208. Upper school average class size: 20. Upper school faculty-student ratio: 1:12. There are 180 required school days per year for Upper School students. Upper School students typically attend 5 days per week. The average school day consists of 6 hours and 8 minutes.

Upper School Student Profile Grade 7: 19 students (10 boys, 9 girls); Grade 8: 21 students (13 boys, 8 girls); Grade 9: 21 students (12 boys, 9 girls); Grade 10: 31 students (25 boys, 6 girls); Grade 11: 18 students (7 boys, 11 girls); Grade 12: 17 students (11 boys, 6 girls). 80% of students are members of Church of Christ, Christian faith.

Faculty School total: 20. In upper school: 10 men, 10 women; 10 have advanced degrees.

College Admission Counseling 19 students graduated in 2010; all went to college, including Arkansas State University; Harding University; University of Arkansas; University of Memphis. Mean composite ACT: 23.

Student Life Upper grades have specified standards of dress, student council, honor system. Discipline rests primarily with faculty. Attendance at religious services is required.

Admissions No application fee required.

Athletics 3 PE instructors, 4 coaches.

Contact Mary Anne Pike, Director of Admissions. 870-400-4000. Fax: 870-735-0570. E-mail: mpike@wmcs.com. Web site: www.wmcs.com.

WESTMINSTER CHRISTIAN ACADEMY

237 Johns Road

Huntsville, Alabama 35806

Head of School: Mr. Craig L. Bouvier

General Information Coeducational day college-preparatory, general academic, arts, religious studies, and technology school, affiliated with Presbyterian Church in America. Grades K–12. Founded: 1964. Setting: suburban. Nearest major city is Birmingham. 42-acre campus. 5 buildings on campus. Approved or accredited by Christian Schools International, Southern Association of Colleges and Schools, and Alabama Department of Education. Member of Secondary School Admission Test Board. Endowment: $243,000. Total enrollment: 733. Upper school average class size: 17. Upper school faculty-student ratio: 1:13. There are 180 required school days per year for Upper School students. Upper School students typically attend 5 days per week. The average school day consists of 7 hours and 10 minutes.

Upper School Student Profile Grade 9: 73 students (34 boys, 39 girls); Grade 10: 70 students (41 boys, 29 girls); Grade 11: 70 students (42 boys, 28 girls); Grade 12: 44 students (19 boys, 25 girls). 15% of students are Presbyterian Church in America.

Faculty School total: 62. In upper school: 16 men, 21 women; 9 have advanced degrees.

Subjects Offered Advanced computer applications, algebra, American history, American history-AP, art, band, Bible studies, biology, botany, business mathematics, business skills, calculus, calculus-AP, chemistry, choir, civics, computer programming, computer programming-AP, concert choir, consumer mathematics, CPR, drama, drama performance, economics-AP, English, English-AP, ensembles, environmental science, first aid, fitness, French, geography, geometry, government, government-AP, health education, home economics, interior design, journalism, keyboarding, Latin, modern dance, painting, photography, physical education, physical science, physics, physiology, pre-calculus, psychology, Spanish, Web site design, world history, yearbook.

Graduation Requirements Arts and fine arts (art, music, dance, drama), computer applications, electives, English, foreign language, mathematics, physical education (includes health), religion (includes Bible studies and theology), science, social studies (includes history).

Special Academic Programs Advanced Placement exam preparation; honors section; independent study; study at local college for college credit.

College Admission Counseling 57 students graduated in 2011; 55 went to college, including Auburn University; The University of Alabama; The University of Alabama in Huntsville. Other: 1 went to work, 1 entered military service. 35% scored over 600 on SAT critical reading, 50% scored over 600 on SAT math, 65% scored over 26 on composite ACT.

Student Life Upper grades have specified standards of dress, student council. Discipline rests primarily with faculty. Attendance at religious services is required.

Tuition and Aid Day student tuition: $7484. Guaranteed tuition plan. Tuition installment plan (monthly payment plans, Semi-Annual Payments, Annual Payments). Tuition reduction for siblings, need-based scholarship grants, reduced tuition for children of faculty available. In 2011–12, 4% of upper-school students received aid. Total amount of financial aid awarded in 2011–12: $35,149.

Admissions Traditional secondary-level entrance grade is 9. For fall 2011, 57 students applied for upper-level admission, 33 were accepted, 30 enrolled. Any standardized test, school's own test or writing sample required. Deadline for receipt of application materials: none. Application fee required: $75. Interview required.

Athletics Interscholastic: baseball (boys), basketball (b,g), cheering (g), cross-country running (b,g), drill team (g), football (b), golf (b,g), physical training (b,g), soccer (b,g), softball (g), swimming and diving (b,g), track and field (b,g), volleyball (g), weight training (b,g), wrestling (b); intramural: physical fitness (b,g), physical training (b,g), strength & conditioning (b,g), weight training (b,g); coed interscholastic: cheering; coed intramural: weight training. 2 PE instructors, 6 coaches, 1 athletic trainer.

Computers Computers are regularly used in all academic classes. Computer network features include on-campus library services, Internet access, wireless campus network, Internet filtering or blocking technology. Student e-mail accounts and computer access in designated common areas are available to students. Students grades are available online. The school has a published electronic and media policy.

Contact Mrs. Leslie Parker, Admissions Director. 256-705-8229. Fax: 256-705-8001. E-mail: leslie.parker@wca-hsv.org. Web site: www.wca-hsv.org.

WESTMINSTER CHRISTIAN ACADEMY

186 Westminster Drive

Opelousas, Louisiana 70570

Head of School: Mrs. Merida Brooks

General Information Coeducational day college-preparatory, arts, religious studies, bilingual studies, and technology school, affiliated with Protestant-Evangelical faith, Christian faith. Grades PK–12. Founded: 1978. Setting: rural. Nearest major city is Lafayette. 30-acre campus. 6 buildings on campus. Approved or accredited by Louisiana Department of Education. Endowment: $170,044. Total enrollment: 1,042. Upper school average class size: 23. Upper school faculty-student ratio: 1:13. There are 175 required school days per year for Upper School students. Upper School students typically attend 5 days per week. The average school day consists of 7 hours.

Upper School Student Profile Grade 6: 61 students (27 boys, 34 girls); Grade 7: 74 students (35 boys, 39 girls); Grade 8: 72 students (32 boys, 40 girls); Grade 9: 61 students (25 boys, 36 girls); Grade 10: 58 students (26 boys, 32 girls); Grade 11: 58 students (32 boys, 26 girls); Grade 12: 49 students (35 boys, 14 girls). 95% of students are Protestant-Evangelical faith, Christian faith.

Faculty School total: 66. In upper school: 13 men, 12 women; 5 have advanced degrees.

Subjects Offered Advanced math, algebra, American history, art, biology, calculus, calculus-AP, ceramics, chemistry, chemistry-AP, civics, concert choir, creative writing, drama, economics, English, English-AP, fine arts, French, geometry, guitar, history-AP, Latin, music, physics, religion, Spanish, world history, yearbook.

Graduation Requirements Arts and fine arts (art, music, dance, drama), computer literacy, English, foreign language, mathematics, physical education (includes health), religion (includes Bible studies and theology), science, social studies (includes history).

Special Academic Programs Advanced Placement exam preparation; honors section; accelerated programs; special instructional classes for students with mild learning disabilities and Attention Deficit Disorder.

College Admission Counseling 47 students graduated in 2010; 46 went to college, including Louisiana State University and Agricultural and Mechanical College; Louisiana Tech University; Loyola University New Orleans; Olivet Nazarene University; University of Louisiana at Lafayette. Other: 1 entered military service. Mean composite ACT: 26.

Student Life Upper grades have uniform requirement, student council. Discipline rests primarily with faculty. Attendance at religious services is required.

Tuition and Aid Day student tuition: $5235. Guaranteed tuition plan. Tuition installment plan (FACTS Tuition Payment Plan, monthly payment plans, annual and biannual payment plans). Need-based scholarship grants, pastor discounts available. In 2010–11, 10% of upper-school students received aid. Total amount of financial aid awarded in 2010–11: $36,981.

Admissions Traditional secondary-level entrance grade is 9. School's own exam and Stanford Achievement Test required. Deadline for receipt of application materials: none. Application fee required: $100. On-campus interview required.

Athletics Interscholastic: baseball (boys), basketball (b,g), cheering (g), football (b), golf (b), hiking/backpacking (b,g), soccer (b), softball (g), swimming and diving (b,g), tennis (b,g), track and field (b,g), volleyball (g).

Computers Computers are regularly used in literacy classes. Computer network features include on-campus library services, Internet access. Student e-mail accounts are available to students. Students grades are available online.

Contact Mrs. Michelle Nezat, Admissions Director. 337-948-4623 Ext. 123. Fax: 337-948-4090. E-mail: mnezat@wcala.org. Web site: www.wcala.org.

WESTMINSTER SCHOOL

995 Hopmeadow Street

Simsbury, Connecticut 06070

Head of School: Mr. William V.N. Philip

General Information Coeducational boarding and day college-preparatory, arts, and technology school. Grades 9–PG. Founded: 1888. Setting: suburban. Nearest major city is Hartford. Students are housed in single-sex dormitories. 230-acre campus. 38 buildings on campus. Approved or accredited by Connecticut Association of Independent Schools, New England Association of Schools and Colleges, The Association of Boarding Schools, and Connecticut Department of Education. Member of National Association of Independent Schools and Secondary School Admission Test Board. Endowment: $80 million. Total enrollment: 390. Upper school average class size: 12. Upper school faculty-student ratio: 1:6. There are 185 required school days per year for Upper School students. Upper School students typically attend 6 days per week. The average school day consists of 6 hours and 30 minutes.

Upper School Student Profile Grade 9: 71 students (35 boys, 36 girls); Grade 10: 106 students (56 boys, 50 girls); Grade 11: 99 students (55 boys, 44 girls); Grade 12: 102 students (57 boys, 45 girls); Postgraduate: 12 students (12 boys). 69% of students are boarding students. 49% are state residents. 26 states are represented in upper school student body. 13% are international students. International students from Bahamas, Bermuda, Canada, China, Hong Kong, and Republic of Korea; 17 other countries represented in student body.

Faculty School total: 61. In upper school: 34 men, 27 women; 51 have advanced degrees; 49 reside on campus.

Subjects Offered Acting, advanced chemistry, advanced computer applications, advanced math, Advanced Placement courses, advanced studio art-AP, African American history, algebra, American history, American history-AP, American literature, American literature-AP, anatomy and physiology, Ancient Greek, architecture, art, art history, art history-AP, art-AP, Asian history, astronomy, athletics, band, biology, biology-AP, calculus, calculus-AP, character education, chemistry, chemistry-AP, Chinese, choir, choral music, comparative government and politics-AP, computer programming, computer science-AP, creative writing, dance, discrete mathematics, drama, drama workshop, drawing, drawing and design, driver education, ecology, economics, economics-AP, English, English literature, English-AP, English/composition-AP, environmental science-AP, ethics, ethics and responsibility, European history, European history-AP, female experience in America, fine arts, French, French language-AP, French literature-AP, geology, geometry, graphic design, health, history, honors algebra, honors English, honors geometry, illustration, Latin, Latin-AP, literature and composition-AP, macro/microeconomics-AP, mathematics, mathematics-AP, mechanical drawing, modern European history-AP, music, music appreciation, music composition, music theory-AP, musical theater, Native American history, painting, philosophy, photography, physics, physics-AP, pre-calculus, probability and statistics, psychology-AP, SAT preparation, SAT/ACT preparation, science, set design, social studies, Spanish, Spanish language-AP, Spanish literature, Spanish literature-AP, stagecraft, statistics, statistics-AP, studio art-AP, theater, trigonometry, U.S. history-AP, world history, writing.

Graduation Requirements Arts, English, foreign language, history, mathematics, science.

Special Academic Programs 23 Advanced Placement exams for which test preparation is offered; honors section; independent study; term-away projects; study abroad.

College Admission Counseling 113 students graduated in 2011; 100 went to college, including Boston College; Trinity College; University of Richmond; University of Vermont; Yale University. Median SAT critical reading: 611, median SAT math: 635, median SAT writing: 637, median combined SAT: 1868.

Student Life Upper grades have specified standards of dress, student council. Discipline rests primarily with faculty.

Summer Programs Enrichment, sports programs offered; session focuses on soccer, science; held on campus; accepts boys and girls; open to students from other schools. 350 students usually enrolled. 2012 schedule: July 9 to August 3.

Tuition and Aid Day student tuition: $35,000; 7-day tuition and room/board: $47,300. Tuition installment plan (Academic Management Services Plan). Need-based scholarship grants available. In 2011–12, 30% of upper-school students received aid. Total amount of financial aid awarded in 2011–12: $3,940,000.

Admissions Traditional secondary-level entrance grade is 9. For fall 2011, 1,028 students applied for upper-level admission, 291 were accepted, 129 enrolled. PSAT and SAT for applicants to grade 11 and 12, SSAT or TOEFL required. Deadline for receipt of application materials: January 15. Application fee required: $75. On-campus interview required.

Athletics Interscholastic: baseball (boys), basketball (b,g), cross-country running (b,g), diving (b,g), field hockey (g), football (b), golf (b,g), hockey (b,g), ice hockey (b,g), lacrosse (b,g), soccer (b,g), softball (g), squash (b,g), swimming and diving (b,g), tennis (b,g), track and field (b,g); intramural: strength & conditioning (b,g); coed interscholastic: dance, martial arts, modern dance; coed intramural: aerobics/dance, ballet, bowling, canoeing/kayaking, dance, fly fishing, freestyle skiing, ice skating, modern dance, mountain biking, outdoor activities, rugby, skiing (cross-country), skiing (downhill), table tennis, unicycling. 2 athletic trainers.

Computers Computers are regularly used in English, foreign language, history, mathematics, science classes. Computer network features include on-campus library services, online commercial services, Internet access, wireless campus network, Internet filtering or blocking technology. Campus intranet, student e-mail accounts, and computer access in designated common areas are available to students. The school has a published electronic and media policy.

Contact Mrs. Rhonda Smith, Admissions Assistant. 860-408-3060. Fax: 860-408-3042. E-mail: admit@westminster-school.org. Web site: www.westminster-school.org.

WESTOVER SCHOOL

1237 Whittemore Road

Middlebury, Connecticut 06762

Head of School: Mrs. Ann S. Pollina

General Information Girls' boarding and day college-preparatory, arts, technology, and mathematics and science school. Grades 9–12. Founded: 1909. Setting: small town. Nearest major city is New York, NY. Students are housed in single-sex dormitories. 145-acre campus. 11 buildings on campus. Approved or accredited by Association of Independent Schools in New England, New England Association of Schools and Colleges, The Association of Boarding Schools, and Connecticut Department of Education. Member of National Association of Independent Schools and Secondary School Admission Test Board. Endowment: $48 million. Total enrollment: 209. Upper school average class size: 11. Upper school faculty-student ratio: 1:8. There are 183 required

school days per year for Upper School students. Upper School students typically attend 6 days per week. The average school day consists of 6 hours.
Upper School Student Profile Grade 9: 44 students (44 girls); Grade 10: 59 students (59 girls); Grade 11: 46 students (46 girls); Grade 12: 60 students (60 girls). 62% of students are boarding students. 53% are state residents. 17 states are represented in upper school student body. 16% are international students. International students from China, Japan, Netherlands, Republic of Korea, Russian Federation, and Turkey; 12 other countries represented in student body.
Faculty School total: 37. In upper school: 13 men, 24 women; 29 have advanced degrees; 20 reside on campus.
Subjects Offered Advanced chemistry, Advanced Placement courses, African-American studies, algebra, American history, American history-AP, American literature, art, art history, art-AP, astronomy, ballet technique, bell choir, biology, biology-AP, calculus, calculus-AP, ceramics, chemistry, clayworking, community service, computer literacy, computer science, computer science-AP, creative writing, dance, drama, drawing, English, English language and composition-AP, English literature, environmental science, ESL, etymology, European history, European history-AP, filmmaking, fine arts, French, French-AP, geography, geometry, grammar, health and wellness, journalism, Latin, mathematics, model United Nations, music, music theory-AP, musical productions, painting, performing arts, photo shop, photography, physics, physics-AP, poetry, politics, portfolio art, pre-calculus, religion, robotics, science, sculpture, Shakespeare, short story, social studies, Spanish, Spanish-AP, speech, studio art-AP, theater, trigonometry, wilderness education, women's studies, world history, writing.
Graduation Requirements Art, athletics, English, foreign language, general science, mathematics, science, summer reading. Community service is required.
Special Academic Programs 15 Advanced Placement exams for which test preparation is offered; honors section; independent study; term-away projects; study abroad; academic accommodation for the gifted, the musically talented, and the artistically talented; special instructional classes for deaf students; ESL (5 students enrolled).
College Admission Counseling 48 students graduated in 2011; all went to college, including Barnard College; Bates College; Brown University; Columbia University; University of California, Santa Cruz; University of Notre Dame. Median composite ACT: 27. Mean SAT critical reading: 597, mean SAT math: 594, mean SAT writing: 621. 61% scored over 600 on SAT critical reading, 59% scored over 600 on SAT math, 64% scored over 600 on SAT writing, 54% scored over 1800 on combined SAT, 56% scored over 26 on composite ACT.
Student Life Upper grades have specified standards of dress, student council, honor system. Discipline rests equally with students and faculty.
Tuition and Aid Day student tuition: $32,500; 7-day tuition and room/board: $45,500. Tuition installment plan (The Tuition Plan, Insured Tuition Payment Plan, FACTS Tuition Payment Plan, monthly payment plans). Need-based scholarship grants, need-based loans, middle-income loans available. In 2011–12, 40% of upper-school students received aid. Total amount of financial aid awarded in 2011–12: $2,700,000.
Admissions Traditional secondary-level entrance grade is 9. For fall 2011, 226 students applied for upper level admission, 113 were accepted, 56 enrolled. ISEE, SSAT or TOEFL required. Deadline for receipt of application materials: January 14. Application fee required: $50. On-campus interview required.
Athletics Interscholastic: basketball, cross-country running, field hockey, golf, independent competitive sports, lacrosse, outdoor activities, soccer, softball, squash, swimming and diving, tennis, volleyball; intramural: aerobics, aerobics/dance, alpine skiing, backpacking, ballet, canoeing/kayaking, climbing, dance, fitness, fitness walking, Frisbee, hiking/backpacking, jogging, kayaking, modern dance, outdoor activities, outdoor education, outdoor skills, outdoors, paddle tennis, physical fitness, physical training, rappelling, rock climbing, running, self defense, skiing (downhill), snowboarding, strength & conditioning, tennis, ultimate Frisbee, walking, wall climbing, weight lifting, weight training, wilderness, yoga. 2 PE instructors, 10 coaches, 1 athletic trainer.
Computers Computers are regularly used in all academic classes. Computer network features include on-campus library services, online commercial services, Internet access, wireless campus network, Internet filtering or blocking technology. Campus intranet, student e-mail accounts, and computer access in designated common areas are available to students. Students grades are available online. The school has a published electronic and media policy.
Contact Mrs. Laura Volovski, Director of Admission. 203-577-4521. Fax: 203-577-4588. E-mail: admission@westoverschool.org. Web site: www.westoverschool.org.

WESTRIDGE SCHOOL

324 Madeline Drive

Pasadena, California 91105-3399

Head of School: Ms. Elizabeth J. McGregor

General Information Girls' day college-preparatory, arts, and technology school. Grades 4–12. Founded: 1913. Setting: suburban. Nearest major city is Los Angeles. 9-acre campus. 11 buildings on campus. Approved or accredited by California Association of Independent Schools, National Independent Private Schools Association, The College Board, Western Association of Schools and Colleges, and California Department of Education. Member of National Association of Independent Schools. Endowment: $16.2 million. Total enrollment: 487. Upper school average class size: 14. Upper school faculty-student ratio: 1:6. Upper School students typically attend 5 days per week. The average school day consists of 6 hours and 30 minutes.
Upper School Student Profile Grade 9: 66 students (66 girls); Grade 10: 75 students (75 girls); Grade 11: 67 students (67 girls); Grade 12: 71 students (71 girls).
Faculty School total: 68. In upper school: 12 men, 24 women; 25 have advanced degrees.
Subjects Offered Acting, Advanced Placement courses, algebra, American history, American literature, art, art history, biology, calculus, cell-biology, ceramics, chemistry, Chinese, chorus, classical language, college counseling, computer applications, computer graphics, computer science, creative writing, dance, directing, drama, earth science, English, English literature, environmental science, European history, fine arts, French, geometry, government/civics, history, Latin, life science, Mandarin, mathematics, modern languages, music, orchestra, photography, physical education, physical science, physics, physiology, pre-calculus, science, Spanish, Spanish literature, statistics, studio art, theater, trigonometry, video, visual and performing arts, visual arts, world history, world literature.
Graduation Requirements Art, college counseling, cultural arts, English, foreign language, history, mathematics, music, physical education (includes health), science, senior project, statistics. Community service is required.
Special Academic Programs Advanced Placement exam preparation; honors section; independent study.
College Admission Counseling 65 students graduated in 2011; all went to college, including Carnegie Mellon University, Emerson College; New York University; University of California, Santa Barbara; University of Pennsylvania; University of Southern California. Median SAT critical reading: 620, median SAT math: 600, median SAT writing: 650, median combined SAT: 1900. Mean composite ACT: 29.
Student Life Upper grades have uniform requirement, student council. Discipline rests primarily with faculty.
Summer Programs Art/fine arts programs offered; session focuses on performing arts; held on campus; accepts girls; open to students from other schools. 60 students usually enrolled. 2012 schedule: June 18 to July 23. Application deadline: May 25.
Tuition and Aid Day student tuition: $29,200. Tuition installment plan (monthly payment plans, full payment, two payment plan, 10-month tuition payment). Need-based scholarship grants available. In 2011–12, 33% of upper-school students received aid. Total amount of financial aid awarded in 2011–12: $1,725,550.
Admissions Traditional secondary-level entrance grade is 9. For fall 2011, 68 students applied for upper-level admission, 47 were accepted, 18 enrolled. ISEE, school's own exam or writing sample required. Deadline for receipt of application materials: February 1. Application fee required: $85. On-campus interview required.
Athletics Interscholastic: aerobics/dance, basketball, cross-country running, dance, diving, fencing, golf, lacrosse, martial arts, modern dance, physical fitness, soccer, softball, swimming and diving, tennis, track and field, volleyball, water polo, yoga. 4 PE instructors, 22 coaches, 1 athletic trainer.
Computers Computers are regularly used in art, English, foreign language, history, mathematics, science classes. Computer network features include on-campus library services, online commercial services, Internet access, wireless campus network, Internet filtering or blocking technology, course Web sites, remote access to email and files, school Internet portal/Web site. Student e-mail accounts are available to students. The school has a published electronic and media policy.
Contact Ms. Helen V. Hopper, Director of Admissions. 626-799-1153 Ext. 213. Fax: 626-799-7068. E-mail: hhopper@westridge.org. Web site: www.westridge.org.

WEST SOUND ACADEMY

16571 Creative Drive NE

Poulsbo, Washington 98370

Head of School: Barrie Hillman

General Information Coeducational boarding and day college-preparatory, arts, and International Baccalaureate school. Boarding grades 9–12, day grades 6–12. Founded: 1998. Setting: rural. Nearest major city is Seattle. Students are housed in coed dormitories. 20-acre campus. 4 buildings on campus. Approved or accredited by International Baccalaureate Organization, Northwest Accreditation Commission, and Washington Department of Education. Total enrollment: 76. Upper school average class size: 11. Upper school faculty-student ratio: 1:7. There are 178 required school days per year for Upper School students. Upper School students typically attend 5 days per week. The average school day consists of 6 hours and 15 minutes.
Upper School Student Profile Grade 9: 14 students (8 boys, 6 girls); Grade 10: 12 students (4 boys, 8 girls); Grade 11: 10 students (5 boys, 5 girls); Grade 12: 8 students (5 boys, 3 girls). 7% of students are boarding students. 70% are state residents. 2 states are represented in upper school student body. 27% are international students. International students from Brazil, China, Germany, Indonesia, Iran, and Spain.
Faculty School total: 16. In upper school: 8 men, 8 women; 11 have advanced degrees.
Subjects Offered Advanced biology, advanced chemistry, advanced math, advanced TOEFL/grammar, algebra, American history, American literature, analytic geometry, ancient world history, art, art history, biology, calculus, chemistry, college counseling, college planning, contemporary issues, dance, drama, drawing, earth science, electives, English, English as a foreign language, ESL, fitness, four units of summer reading, French, geometry, global issues, guitar, history, International Baccalaureate courses,

linear algebra, literary magazine, logarithms, marine biology, model United Nations, music, music performance, non-Western literature, non-Western societies, outdoor education, painting, photography, physics, poetry, portfolio art, portfolio writing, SAT preparation, senior thesis, Spanish, sports, studio art, technology, theory of knowledge, U.S. history, visual arts, Washington State and Northwest History, Western civilization, Western literature, wilderness experience, world cultures, world history, world literature, yearbook.

Graduation Requirements Biology, chemistry, English, foreign language, history, International Baccalaureate courses, mathematics, senior thesis, service learning/internship, theory of knowledge, visual arts, West Sound Academy has a 4-1-4 academic calendar; students are required to complete a Jan-Term, courses are 3-week-long short courses of intense study in a variety of subjects outside the usual curriculum, Fall and Spring trips to varied locations teach leadership, environmental ethics, and technical skills.

Special Academic Programs International Baccalaureate program; independent study; term-away projects; academic accommodation for the gifted; ESL (4 students enrolled).

College Admission Counseling 12 students graduated in 2011; 11 went to college, including Eckerd College; Linfield College; University of Puget Sound; University of Rhode Island; University of Washington; Willamette University. Other: 1 entered a postgraduate year. Median SAT critical reading: 550, median SAT math: 630, median SAT writing: 510, median combined SAT: 1610. 33% scored over 600 on SAT critical reading, 56% scored over 600 on SAT math, 11% scored over 600 on SAT writing, 33% scored over 1800 on combined SAT.

Student Life Upper grades have specified standards of dress, honor system. Discipline rests primarily with faculty.

Summer Programs ESL programs offered; session focuses on ESL for international students; held both on and off campus; held at International students stay in Murphy International House, West Sound Academy's off-campus dormitory, program includes both on-campus classes and off-campus field trips to various places of interest, and Seattle, Mount Rainier, Olympic National Park, Mt. St. Helens; accepts boys and girls; open to students from other schools. 15 students usually enrolled. 2012 schedule: July 9 to August 10. Application deadline: March 1.

Tuition and Aid Day student tuition: $15,805; 7-day tuition and room/board: $38,500. Tuition installment plan (Insured Tuition Payment Plan). Merit scholarship grants, need-based scholarship grants available. In 2011–12, 50% of upper-school students received aid; total upper-school merit-scholarship money awarded: $110,225. Total amount of financial aid awarded in 2011–12: $254,180.

Admissions Traditional secondary-level entrance grade is 9. For fall 2011, 47 students applied for upper-level admission, 40 were accepted, 36 enrolled. International English Language Test or TOEFL required. Deadline for receipt of application materials: none. Application fee required: $60. Interview required.

Athletics Coed Intramural: bowling, hiking/backpacking, kayaking, outdoor education, rock climbing.

Computers Computers are regularly used in all classes. Computer network features include on-campus library services, Internet access, wireless campus network. Student e-mail accounts are available to students. The school has a published electronic and media policy.

Contact Lisa Gsellman, Office Manager. . 360-598-5954. Fax: 360-598-5494. E-mail: jkolb@westsoundacademy.org. Web site: www.westsoundacademy.org/.

WEST VALLEY CHRISTIAN CHURCH SCHOOLS

22450 Sherman Way

West Hills, California 91307

Head of School: Dr. Robert Lozano

General Information Coeducational day college-preparatory and religious studies school, affiliated with Christian faith, Christian Church (Disciples of Christ). Grades K–12. Founded: 1978. Setting: suburban. Nearest major city is Los Angeles. 5-acre campus. 6 buildings on campus. Approved or accredited by Association of Christian Schools International, Western Association of Schools and Colleges, and California Department of Education. Total enrollment: 204. Upper school average class size: 25. Upper school faculty-student ratio: 1:15. There are 179 required school days per year for Upper School students. Upper School students typically attend 5 days per week. The average school day consists of 6 hours and 15 minutes.

Upper School Student Profile Grade 6: 14 students (5 boys, 9 girls); Grade 7: 21 students (14 boys, 7 girls); Grade 8: 18 students (6 boys, 12 girls); Grade 9: 9 students (4 boys, 5 girls); Grade 10: 15 students (8 boys, 7 girls); Grade 11: 13 students (6 boys, 7 girls); Grade 12: 26 students (11 boys, 15 girls). 60% of students are Christian, Christian Church (Disciples of Christ).

Faculty School total: 13. In upper school: 6 men, 7 women; 4 have advanced degrees.

Subjects Offered Bible, English, fine arts, history, mathematics, physical education, science, Spanish, technical arts.

Graduation Requirements Arts and fine arts (art, music, dance, drama), career and personal planning, economics, English, government, health, history, mathematics, physical education (includes health), religion (includes Bible studies and theology), science, Spanish.

Special Academic Programs Advanced Placement exam preparation; honors section; study at local college for college credit; academic accommodation for the gifted; remedial math.

College Admission Counseling 11 students graduated in 2010; all went to college, including Azusa Pacific University; Biola University; California State University, Northridge; The University of Arizona; University of California, Riverside; Westmont College. Mean SAT critical reading: 480, mean SAT math: 490, mean SAT writing: 490, mean composite ACT: 21.

Student Life Upper grades have uniform requirement, student council, honor system. Discipline rests primarily with faculty. Attendance at religious services is required.

Tuition and Aid Day student tuition: $8260. Tuition installment plan (monthly payment plans, individually arranged payment plans). Tuition reduction for siblings, need-based scholarship grants available. In 2010–11, 45% of upper-school students received aid. Total amount of financial aid awarded in 2010–11: $150,000.

Admissions Traditional secondary-level entrance grade is 9. For fall 2010, 20 students applied for upper-level admission, 19 were accepted, 19 enrolled. BASIS or TAP required. Deadline for receipt of application materials: none. Application fee required: $150. Interview recommended.

Athletics Interscholastic: basketball (boys, girls), flag football (b), football (b), physical fitness (b,g), track and field (b,g), volleyball (b,g); coed interscholastic: cross-country running; coed intramural: martial arts, outdoor education. 2 PE instructors, 4 coaches.

Computers Computers are regularly used in word processing, yearbook classes. Computer resources include on-campus library services, Internet access. Students grades are available online.

Contact Lisa Kabelitz, School Secretary. 818-884-4710 Ext. 221. Fax: 818-884-4749. Web site: www.westvalleychristianschool.com.

WHEATON ACADEMY

900 Prince Crossing Road

West Chicago, Illinois 60185

Head of School: Dr. Gene Frost

General Information Coeducational day college-preparatory and religious studies school, affiliated with Christian faith. Grades 9–12. Founded: 1853. Setting: suburban. Nearest major city is Chicago. 43-acre campus. 8 buildings on campus. Approved or accredited by Association of Christian Schools International, North Central Association of Colleges and Schools, and Illinois Department of Education. Total enrollment: 640. Upper school average class size: 20. Upper school faculty-student ratio: 1:15. There are 175 required school days per year for Upper School students. Upper School students typically attend 5 days per week. The average school day consists of 6 hours and 30 minutes.

Upper School Student Profile Grade 9: 155 students (72 boys, 83 girls); Grade 10: 171 students (82 boys, 89 girls); Grade 11: 171 students (83 boys, 88 girls); Grade 12: 143 students (67 boys, 76 girls). 98% of students are Christian faith.

Faculty School total: 48. In upper school: 26 men, 22 women; 34 have advanced degrees.

Subjects Offered 20th century history, ACT preparation, algebra, art, arts and crafts, band, Bible, Bible studies, biology, biology-AP, British literature, business, business applications, calculus, calculus-AP, ceramics, chemistry, chemistry-AP, child development, choir, Christian doctrine, Christian education, classics, comparative government and politics-AP, computer art, computer education, computer graphics, computer multimedia, computer processing, computer programming-AP, computer science, concert choir, consumer economics, creative writing, debate, desktop publishing, drama, drama workshop, drawing, driver education, earth science, economics, English, English language and composition-AP, English literature, English literature and composition-AP, environmental science, European history, European history-AP, family living, fiber arts, fine arts, foods, French, French language-AP, freshman seminar, geology, geometry, government/civics, graphic design, Greek, health, health and wellness, history, honors English, honors geometry, honors U.S. history, industrial arts, internship, journalism, keyboarding, leadership, literature, mathematics, multimedia design, music, music theory-AP, novels, orchestra, personal growth, physical education, physics, physics-AP, portfolio art, pre-algebra, psychology, publications, science, social sciences, social studies, sociology, Spanish, Spanish language-AP, speech, statistics, statistics-AP, student publications, theater, theology, trigonometry, U.S. government, U.S. government and politics-AP, U.S. history, U.S. history-AP, U.S. literature, world history, world history-AP, world literature, writing.

Graduation Requirements Arts and fine arts (art, music, dance, drama), English, mathematics, physical education (includes health), religion (includes Bible studies and theology), science, social sciences, social studies (includes history), Winterim (3-week period during January allowing students to take two classes beyond the typical curriculum).

Special Academic Programs 16 Advanced Placement exams for which test preparation is offered; honors section; independent study; term-away projects; study at local college for college credit; academic accommodation for the gifted, the musically talented, and the artistically talented; remedial reading and/or remedial writing; remedial math; special instructional classes for students with learning disabilities.

College Admission Counseling 163 students graduated in 2011; 156 went to college, including Baylor University; Calvin College; Hope College; Taylor University; University of Illinois at Urbana–Champaign; Wheaton College. Other: 2 went to work, 5 had other specific plans. Median composite ACT: 25. 45% scored over 26 on composite ACT.
Student Life Upper grades have specified standards of dress, honor system. Discipline rests primarily with faculty. Attendance at religious services is required.
Summer Programs Enrichment, advancement, sports, art/fine arts, computer instruction programs offered; held on campus; accepts boys and girls; open to students from other schools. 75 students usually enrolled. 2012 schedule: June 11 to June 25.
Tuition and Aid Day student tuition: $12,500. Tuition installment plan (monthly payment plans, semester payment plan). Tuition reduction for siblings, merit scholarship grants, need-based scholarship grants, paying campus jobs available. In 2011–12, 30% of upper-school students received aid; total upper-school merit-scholarship money awarded: $15,000. Total amount of financial aid awarded in 2011–12: $500,000.
Admissions Traditional secondary-level entrance grade is 9. ACT-Explore or placement test required. Deadline for receipt of application materials: none. Application fee required: $50. On-campus interview required.
Athletics Interscholastic: baseball (boys), basketball (b,g), cheering (g), cross-country running (b,g), dance team (g), football (b), golf (b,g), ice hockey (b), pom squad (g), soccer (b,g), softball (g), tennis (b,g), track and field (b,g), volleyball (b,g); intramural: aerobics (g), flagball (g), ice hockey (b), wilderness survival (b); coed interscholastic: modern dance, physical training, running; coed intramural: climbing, floor hockey, hiking/backpacking, outdoor education, outdoor skills, power lifting, project adventure, rock climbing, skiing (cross-country), strength & conditioning, wall climbing, weight lifting, weight training. 2 PE instructors, 6 coaches.
Computers Computers are regularly used in Bible studies, graphic design, independent study, mathematics, multimedia, writing, yearbook classes. Computer network features include on-campus library services, online commercial services, Internet access, wireless campus network, Internet filtering or blocking technology. Student e-mail accounts are available to students. Students grades are available online. The school has a published electronic and media policy.
Contact Mr. Ryan Hall, Admissions Counselor. 630-562-7500 Ext. 7501. Fax: 630-231-0842. E-mail: rhall@wheatonacademy.org. Web site: www.wheatonacademy.org.

THE WHEELER SCHOOL

216 Hope Street

Providence, Rhode Island 02906

Head of School: Mr. Dan Miller, PhD

General Information Coeducational day college-preparatory, arts, Community Action Program (service-based learning), and AERIE Program (individual academic enrichment grades 9-12) school. Grades N–12. Founded: 1889. Setting: urban. 5-acre campus. 8 buildings on campus. Approved or accredited by Association of Independent Schools in New England, New England Association of Schools and Colleges, and Rhode Island Department of Education. Member of National Association of Independent Schools. Endowment: $20.6 million. Total enrollment: 801. Upper school average class size: 15. Upper school faculty-student ratio: 1:6. There are 165 required school days per year for Upper School students. Upper School students typically attend 5 days per week. The average school day consists of 6 hours and 25 minutes.
Upper School Student Profile Grade 9: 84 students (42 boys, 42 girls); Grade 10: 80 students (41 boys, 39 girls); Grade 11: 81 students (38 boys, 43 girls); Grade 12: 72 students (35 boys, 37 girls).
Faculty School total: 125. In upper school: 22 men, 30 women; 41 have advanced degrees.
Subjects Offered 20th century world history, acting, Advanced Placement courses, advanced studio art-AP, algebra, American history, anatomy, art, art history, biology, biology-AP, biotechnology, Black history, broadcasting, business skills, calculus, calculus-AP, ceramics, chemistry, Chinese, Chinese studies, choral music, civil rights, computer programming, computer science, contemporary issues, dance, drama, drawing, economics, engineering, English, English literature, English-AP, environmental science, environmental science-AP, European history, film studies, fine arts, forensics, French, geometry, guitar, Japanese, jazz ensemble, kinesiology, Latin, Latin American history, Latin American studies, mathematics, Middle Eastern history, music, nutrition, photography, physical education, physics, physiology, pre-calculus, printmaking, psychology, research, science, sculpture, social studies, Spanish, statistics, theater, trigonometry, Web site design, Western civilization.
Graduation Requirements Arts and fine arts (art, music, dance, drama), English, foreign language, history, mathematics, performing arts, physical education (includes health), science, community service, Unity and Diversity curriculum.
Special Academic Programs 17 Advanced Placement exams for which test preparation is offered; honors section; accelerated programs; independent study; term-away projects; study at local college for college credit; study abroad; academic accommodation for the gifted; programs in general development for dyslexic students.
College Admission Counseling 95 students graduated in 2011; 94 went to college, including Amherst College; Boston College; Brown University; Princeton University; Vassar College; Yale University. Other: 1 entered a postgraduate year. Mean SAT critical reading: 636, mean SAT math: 643, mean SAT writing: 649, mean combined SAT: 1928, mean composite ACT: 28.
Student Life Upper grades have specified standards of dress, student council. Discipline rests equally with students and faculty.
Summer Programs Session focuses on jazz camp; held on campus; accepts boys and girls; open to students from other schools. 34 students usually enrolled. 2012 schedule: June 25 to June 29. Application deadline: April 23.
Tuition and Aid Day student tuition: $27,670. Tuition installment plan (Insured Tuition Payment Plan, Key Tuition Payment Plan, monthly payment plans). Need-based scholarship grants available. In 2011–12, 25% of upper-school students received aid. Total amount of financial aid awarded in 2011–12: $1,300,563.
Admissions Traditional secondary-level entrance grade is 9. For fall 2011, 157 students applied for upper-level admission, 77 were accepted, 38 enrolled. ISEE or SSAT required. Deadline for receipt of application materials: January 31. Application fee required: $60. On-campus interview required.
Athletics Interscholastic: baseball (boys), basketball (b,g), cross-country running (b,g), field hockey (g), football (b), ice hockey (b,g), lacrosse (b,g), soccer (b,g), softball (g), tennis (b,g), track and field (b,g), winter (indoor) track (b,g); coed interscholastic: golf, squash. 6 PE instructors, 30 coaches, 1 athletic trainer.
Computers Computers are regularly used in health, mathematics, science, Spanish classes. Computer network features include on-campus library services, online commercial services, Internet access, wireless campus network. Campus intranet and student e-mail accounts are available to students. The school has a published electronic and media policy.
Contact Jeanette Epstein, Director of Admission. 401-421-8100. Fax: 401-751-7674. E-mail: jeanetteepstein@wheelerschool.org. Web site: www.wheelerschool.org.

WHITEFIELD ACADEMY

7711 Fegenbush Lane

Louisville, Kentucky 40228

Head of School: Mr. Chip Evans

General Information Coeducational day college-preparatory, arts, religious studies, and technology school, affiliated with Baptist Church. Grades PS–12. Founded: 1976. Setting: suburban. 30-acre campus. 2 buildings on campus. Approved or accredited by Association of Christian Schools International, CITA (Commission on International and Trans-Regional Accreditation), Council of Accreditation and School Improvement, Southern Association of Colleges and Schools, and Kentucky Department of Education. Total enrollment: 731. Upper school average class size: 20. Upper school faculty-student ratio: 1:20. There are 178 required school days per year for Upper School students. Upper School students typically attend 5 days per week. The average school day consists of 6 hours and 25 minutes.
Upper School Student Profile Grade 9: 50 students (30 boys, 20 girls); Grade 10: 52 students (23 boys, 29 girls); Grade 11: 55 students (25 boys, 30 girls); Grade 12: 43 students (20 boys, 23 girls). 45% of students are Baptist.
Faculty School total: 55. In upper school: 11 men, 11 women; 9 have advanced degrees.
Subjects Offered Adolescent issues, advanced math, algebra, anatomy, art, arts, band, Bible studies, biology, calculus, calculus-AP, chemistry, choir, choral music, chorus, Christian education, Christian studies, college placement, college planning, college writing, communication skills, composition, computer applications, computer education, computers, current events, drama, drama performance, economics, English, English composition, English literature, English literature-AP, foreign language, geometry, history, honors English, library, mathematics, music, political science, pre-calculus, reading, SAT/ACT preparation, science, science project, sex education, social sciences, Spanish, speech and debate, student government, student publications, U.S. history, U.S. history-AP.
Graduation Requirements Arts and fine arts (art, music, dance, drama), Bible, electives, English, foreign language, health, mathematics, physical education (includes health), science, social studies (includes history).
Special Academic Programs 6 Advanced Placement exams for which test preparation is offered; honors section; independent study; academic accommodation for the gifted.
College Admission Counseling 54 students graduated in 2011; 52 went to college, including Bellarmine University; Eastern Kentucky University; Jefferson Community and Technical College; University of Kentucky; University of Louisville; Western Kentucky University. Other: 1 went to work, 1 entered military service. Median composite ACT: 23. 31% scored over 26 on composite ACT.
Student Life Upper grades have uniform requirement, student council, honor system. Discipline rests primarily with faculty. Attendance at religious services is required.
Summer Programs Enrichment, sports programs offered; held on campus; accepts boys and girls; open to students from other schools. 60 students usually enrolled.
Tuition and Aid Day student tuition: $6300. Tuition installment plan (FACTS Tuition Payment Plan, annual payment in full plan). Tuition reduction for siblings, need-based scholarship grants available. In 2011–12, 13% of upper-school students received aid. Total amount of financial aid awarded in 2011–12: $42,175.
Admissions Traditional secondary-level entrance grade is 9. For fall 2011, 16 students applied for upper-level admission, 16 were accepted, 16 enrolled. Stanford

Achievement Test required. Deadline for receipt of application materials: none. Application fee required: $350. On-campus interview required.

Athletics Interscholastic: aquatics (boys, girls), baseball (b), basketball (b,g), cheering (b,g), cross-country running (b,g), golf (b,g), soccer (b,g), softball (g), swimming and diving (b,g), tennis (b,g), track and field (b,g), volleyball (g); intramural: aerobics (g), fitness (b,g), outdoor activities (b,g), physical fitness (b,g), volleyball (g), weight lifting (b,g). 3 PE instructors.

Computers Computers are regularly used in all academic, college planning, library, newspaper, SAT preparation, theater arts, yearbook classes. Computer network features include on-campus library services, Internet access, wireless campus network, Internet filtering or blocking technology. Computer access in designated common areas is available to students. Students grades are available online. The school has a published electronic and media policy.

Contact Mrs. Diane Fow, Director of Admissions. 502-231-6261. Fax: 502-239-3144. E-mail: dfow@whitefield.org.

THE WHITE MOUNTAIN SCHOOL

371 West Farm Road

Bethlehem, New Hampshire 03574

Head of School: Tim Breen, PhD

General Information Coeducational boarding and day college-preparatory, arts, and sustainability studies school, affiliated with Episcopal Church. Grades 9–PG. Founded: 1886. Setting: rural. Nearest major city is Concord. Students are housed in single-sex dormitories. 250-acre campus. 13 buildings on campus. Approved or accredited by Association for Experiential Education, National Association of Episcopal Schools, New England Association of Schools and Colleges, The Association of Boarding Schools, and New Hampshire Department of Education. Member of National Association of Independent Schools and Secondary School Admission Test Board. Endowment: $1.5 million. Total enrollment: 99. Upper school average class size: 9. Upper school faculty-student ratio: 1:5. Upper School students typically attend 5 days per week. The average school day consists of 5 hours and 45 minutes.

Upper School Student Profile 85% of students are boarding students. 25% are state residents. 22 states are represented in upper school student body. 30% are international students. International students from China, Ethiopia, Kenya, Republic of Korea, Ukraine, and Zambia; 5 other countries represented in student body. 5% of students are members of Episcopal Church.

Faculty School total: 28. In upper school: 15 men, 13 women; 15 have advanced degrees; 24 reside on campus.

Subjects Offered Algebra, American literature, American studies, anatomy and physiology, biology, calculus, Caribbean history, ceramics, chemistry, Chinese history, college counseling, community garden, community service, creative writing, drawing and design, earth science, economics, English, environmental education, environmental science, environmental studies, ESL, ethics, French, geometry, health, human development, independent study, Japanese history, jazz theory, learning strategies, literature, Middle Eastern history, music history, painting, philosophy, photography, physics, precalculus, printmaking, senior project, social justice, Spanish, studio art, theater arts, theater production, U.S. history, Vietnam, world history, writing.

Graduation Requirements Algebra, American history, arts and fine arts (art, music, dance, drama), English, geometry, health, literature, non-Western societies, physical science, theology, Western civilization, writing, field courses, sustainability studies, community service. Community service is required.

Special Academic Programs 4 Advanced Placement exams for which test preparation is offered; honors section; independent study; term-away projects; academic accommodation for the gifted, the musically talented, and the artistically talented; programs in English, mathematics, general development for dyslexic students; special instructional classes for students with dysgraphia and other learning differences; ESL (19 students enrolled).

College Admission Counseling 27 students graduated in 2010; all went to college, including Fort Lewis College; St. Lawrence University; The College of Wooster; University of Vermont; Warren Wilson College; Western State College of Colorado. 10% scored over 600 on SAT critical reading, 24% scored over 600 on SAT math.

Student Life Upper grades have specified standards of dress, student council, honor system. Discipline rests primarily with faculty.

Tuition and Aid Day student tuition: $22,100; 7-day tuition and room/board: $43,600. Tuition installment plan (Insured Tuition Payment Plan, Academic Management Services Plan, 2-payment plan). Merit scholarship grants, need-based scholarship grants available. In 2010–11, 47% of upper-school students received aid. Total amount of financial aid awarded in 2010–11: $1,412,000.

Admissions For fall 2010, 126 students applied for upper-level admission, 65 were accepted, 39 enrolled. TOEFL or SLEP, WISC III or other aptitude measures; standardized achievement test or writing sample required. Deadline for receipt of application materials: February 1. Application fee required: $50. Interview required.

Athletics Interscholastic: basketball (boys), lacrosse (b,g), soccer (b,g); intramural: dance (g); coed interscholastic: climbing, freestyle skiing, mountain biking, rock climbing; coed intramural: aerobics/Nautilus, alpine skiing, backpacking, bicycling, canoeing/kayaking, climbing, combined training, fitness, freestyle skiing, Frisbee, hiking/backpacking, kayaking, martial arts, mountain biking, mountaineering, Nautilus, nordic skiing, outdoor activities, outdoor adventure, outdoor education, outdoor recreation, outdoor skills, outdoors, paddling, physical fitness, physical training, rappelling, rock climbing, running, skiing (cross-country), skiing (downhill), snowboarding, snowshoeing, strength & conditioning, telemark skiing, tennis, ultimate Frisbee, wall climbing, wilderness, wilderness survival, yoga. 1 athletic trainer.

Computers Computers are regularly used in college planning, foreign language, library skills, mathematics, media arts, science, yearbook classes. Computer network features include on-campus library services, online commercial services, Internet access, wireless campus network, Internet filtering or blocking technology. Student e-mail accounts and computer access in designated common areas are available to students. The school has a published electronic and media policy.

Contact Beth Towle, Director of Admission. 603-444-2928 Ext. 19. Fax: 603-444-5568. E-mail: beth.towle@whitemountain.org. Web site: www.whitemountain.org.

THE WILLIAMS SCHOOL

182 Mohegan Avenue

New London, Connecticut 06320-4110

Head of School: Mark Fader

General Information Coeducational day college-preparatory and arts school. Grades 7–12. Founded: 1891. Setting: urban. 25-acre campus. 2 buildings on campus. Approved or accredited by New England Association of Schools and Colleges and Connecticut Department of Education. Member of National Association of Independent Schools and Secondary School Admission Test Board. Endowment: $4 million. Total enrollment: 259. Upper school average class size: 13. Upper school faculty-student ratio: 1:6. There are 165 required school days per year for Upper School students. Upper School students typically attend 5 days per week. The average school day consists of 6 hours and 48 minutes.

Upper School Student Profile Grade 9: 41 students (20 boys, 21 girls); Grade 10: 55 students (27 boys, 28 girls); Grade 11: 54 students (23 boys, 31 girls); Grade 12: 67 students (30 boys, 37 girls).

Faculty School total: 34. In upper school: 16 men, 18 women; 29 have advanced degrees.

Subjects Offered Algebra, American history, art, band, biology, biology-AP, calculus, calculus-AP, chemistry, chemistry-AP, chorus, dance, digital art, drama, economics, English, English literature, English-AP, environmental science, European history, expository writing, fine arts, French, French-AP, geography, geometry, Greek, history, jazz, journalism, Latin-AP, mathematics, modern European history, music, music composition, music history, music theory, music theory-AP, physical education, physics, physics-AP, pre-calculus, science, social studies, Spanish, Spanish-AP, theater, trigonometry, world history, world literature.

Graduation Requirements Arts and fine arts (art, music, dance, drama), classical language, English, foreign language, mathematics, physical education (includes health), science, senior project, social studies (includes history), at least one year of Latin, four years of math in Upper School.

Special Academic Programs 10 Advanced Placement exams for which test preparation is offered; honors section; independent study; study at local college for college credit; study abroad; academic accommodation for the gifted, the musically talented, and the artistically talented.

College Admission Counseling 49 students graduated in 2011; 47 went to college, including Boston University; Connecticut College; Trinity College; Tufts University; University of Connecticut; Wheaton College. Other: 1 went to work, 1 had other specific plans. Mean SAT critical reading: 623, mean SAT math: 612, mean SAT writing: 610, mean combined SAT: 1845, mean composite ACT: 29. 62% scored over 600 on SAT critical reading, 4% scored over 600 on SAT math, 59% scored over 600 on SAT writing, 63% scored over 1800 on combined SAT, 60% scored over 26 on composite ACT.

Student Life Upper grades have specified standards of dress, student council. Discipline rests primarily with faculty.

Summer Programs Sports programs offered; session focuses on lacrosse and basketball; held on campus; accepts boys and girls; open to students from other schools. 160 students usually enrolled. 2012 schedule: June 21 to August 20. Application deadline: June 15.

Tuition and Aid Day student tuition: $25,835. Tuition installment plan (Insured Tuition Payment Plan, FACTS Tuition Payment Plan, monthly payment plans, individually arranged payment plans). Need-based scholarship grants available. In 2011–12, 40% of upper-school students received aid. Total amount of financial aid awarded in 2011–12: $1,270,680.

Admissions Traditional secondary-level entrance grade is 9. For fall 2011, 105 students applied for upper-level admission, 100 were accepted, 56 enrolled. SSAT required. Deadline for receipt of application materials: February 1. Application fee required: $50. On-campus interview required.

Athletics Interscholastic: baseball (boys), basketball (b,g), cross-country running (b,g), field hockey (g), lacrosse (b,g), sailing (b,g), soccer (b,g), squash (b,g), swimming and diving (b,g), tennis (b,g); intramural: dance (b,g), dance team (b,g), fencing (b,g), fitness (b,g), yoga (b); coed interscholastic: cross-country running, golf, sailing, swimming and diving; coed intramural: basketball, dance, dance team, fencing,

fitness, golf, modern dance, weight training. 2 PE instructors, 19 coaches, 1 athletic trainer.
Computers Computers are regularly used in creative writing, English, French, graphic design, history, journalism, Latin, mathematics, music, newspaper, photography, SAT preparation, science, social studies, Spanish, study skills, theater, writing, yearbook classes. Computer network features include on-campus library services, online commercial services, Internet access, wireless campus network, Internet filtering or blocking technology. Campus intranet, student e-mail accounts, and computer access in designated common areas are available to students. The school has a published electronic and media policy.
Contact Cristan Harris, Director of Admission. 860-439-2789. Fax: 860-439-2796. E-mail: charris@williamsschool.org. Web site: www.williamsschool.org.

THE WILLISTON NORTHAMPTON SCHOOL

19 Payson Avenue
Easthampton, Massachusetts 01027

Head of School: Mr. Robert W. Hill

General Information Coeducational boarding and day college-preparatory school. Boarding grades 9–PG, day grades 7–12. Founded: 1841. Setting: small town. Nearest major city is Northampton. Students are housed in single-sex dormitories. 125-acre campus. 57 buildings on campus. Approved or accredited by Association of Independent Schools in New England, New England Association of Schools and Colleges, and The Association of Boarding Schools. Member of National Association of Independent Schools and Secondary School Admission Test Board. Endowment: $36 million. Total enrollment: 529. Upper school average class size: 13. Upper school faculty-student ratio: 1:7. There are 160 required school days per year for Upper School students. Upper School students typically attend 5 days per week. The average school day consists of 8 hours and 30 minutes.
Upper School Student Profile Grade 9: 83 students (43 boys, 40 girls); Grade 10: 102 students (53 boys, 49 girls); Grade 11: 114 students (54 boys, 60 girls); Grade 12: 130 students (64 boys, 66 girls); Postgraduate: 12 students (12 boys). 64% of students are boarding students. 50% are state residents. 22 states are represented in upper school student body. 16% are international students. International students from Bermuda, China, Hong Kong, Japan, Republic of Korea, and Taiwan; 23 other countries represented in student body.
Faculty School total: 90. In upper school: 41 men, 40 women; 60 have advanced degrees; 59 reside on campus.
Subjects Offered African-American history, algebra, American history, American literature, anatomy and physiology, animal behavior, art, art history, astronomy, biology, biology-AP, calculus, calculus-AP, chemistry, chemistry-AP, China/Japan history, Chinese, choral music, choreography, Christian and Hebrew scripture, comparative government and politics-AP, comparative politics, computer math, computer programming, computer science, computer science-AP, constitutional law, creative writing, dance, discrete mathematics, drama, economics, economics and history, economics-AP, English, English language-AP, English literature, English literature-AP, environmental science, ESL, ethics, European history, expository writing, fine arts, French, French language-AP, French literature-AP, French-AP, genetics, geometry, global studies, government/civics, health, history, history of jazz, honors algebra, honors English, honors geometry, Islamic studies, Latin, Latin American history, Latin-AP, mathematics, music, music theory, organic biochemistry, organic chemistry, philosophy, photography, photojournalism, physics, physics-AP, play production, playwriting, poetry, psychology, psychology-AP, religion, religion and culture, Russian history, science, sculpture, social studies, Spanish, Spanish language-AP, Spanish literature-AP, statistics-AP, theater, theology, trigonometry, U.S. history-AP, world history, world literature, writing workshop.
Graduation Requirements Arts and fine arts (art, music, dance, drama), English, foreign language, history, mathematics, philosophy, religion (includes Bible studies and theology), science, participation in the athletic program.
Special Academic Programs 18 Advanced Placement exams for which test preparation is offered; honors section; independent study; term-away projects; study abroad; academic accommodation for the gifted, the musically talented, and the artistically talented; special instructional classes for deaf students; ESL (12 students enrolled).
College Admission Counseling 130 students graduated in 2010; all went to college, including Bates College; Boston College; Boston University; Colby College; Connecticut College; University of Vermont. Mean SAT critical reading: 580, mean SAT math: 608, mean SAT writing: 589, mean combined SAT: 1777. 42% scored over 600 on SAT critical reading, 47% scored over 600 on SAT math, 43% scored over 600 on SAT writing.
Student Life Upper grades have specified standards of dress, student council, honor system. Discipline rests equally with students and faculty.
Tuition and Aid Day student tuition: $33,000; 7-day tuition and room/board: $46,600. Tuition installment plan (Academic Management Services Plan, monthly payment plans). Need-based scholarship grants, need-based loans available. In 2010–11, 46% of upper-school students received aid. Total amount of financial aid awarded in 2010–11: $5,855,400.
Admissions Traditional secondary-level entrance grade is 9. For fall 2010, 621 students applied for upper-level admission, 274 were accepted, 118 enrolled. ACT, ISEE, PSAT or SAT for applicants to grade 11 and 12, SSAT or TOEFL required. Deadline for receipt of application materials: February 1. Application fee required: $50. Interview required.
Athletics Interscholastic: alpine skiing (boys, girls), baseball (b), basketball (b,g), crew (b,g), cross-country running (b,g), field hockey (g), football (b), golf (b,g), ice hockey (b,g), lacrosse (b,g), soccer (b,g), softball (g), squash (b,g), swimming and diving (b,g), tennis (b,g), track and field (b,g), volleyball (g), water polo (b,g), wrestling (b); intramural: self defense (g); coed interscholastic: dance, diving; coed intramural: aerobics, aerobics/dance, dance, dance team, equestrian sports, fitness, Frisbee, horseback riding, judo, martial arts, modern dance, mountain biking, snowboarding, weight lifting, weight training, yoga. 1 PE instructor, 5 coaches, 2 athletic trainers.
Computers Computers are regularly used in college planning, geography, graphic design, history, library, mathematics, newspaper, photography, photojournalism, programming, science, yearbook classes. Computer network features include on-campus library services, online commercial services, Internet access, wireless campus network, Internet filtering or blocking technology. Campus intranet, student e-mail accounts, and computer access in designated common areas are available to students. The school has a published electronic and media policy.
Contact Ms. Caitlin E. Church, Assistant Director of Admission. 413-529-3401. Fax: 413-527-9494. E-mail: admission@williston.com. Web site: www.williston.com.

See Display on next page and Close-Up on page 704.

THE WILLOWS ACADEMY

1012 Thacker Street
Des Plaines, Illinois 60016

Head of School: Mary J. Keenley

General Information Girls' day college-preparatory, arts, religious studies, and technology school, affiliated with Roman Catholic Church. Grades 6–12. Founded: 1974. Setting: suburban. Nearest major city is Chicago. 4-acre campus. 1 building on campus. Approved or accredited by Illinois Department of Education. Total enrollment: 225. Upper school average class size: 18. Upper school faculty-student ratio: 1:10. Upper School students typically attend 5 days per week. The average school day consists of 6 hours and 30 minutes.
Upper School Student Profile Grade 9: 36 students (36 girls); Grade 10: 32 students (32 girls); Grade 11: 45 students (45 girls); Grade 12: 36 students (36 girls). 85% of students are Roman Catholic.
Faculty School total: 35. In upper school: 1 man, 23 women; 15 have advanced degrees.
Subjects Offered Algebra, American history, American literature, art, biology, calculus, chemistry, choir, choral music, computer graphics, computer programming, computer science, economics, English, English literature, ethics, European history, fine arts, four units of summer reading, French, geography, geometry, government/civics, grammar, health, history, instrumental music, Latin, mathematics, music, music history, music theory, musical productions, philosophy, physical education, physics, pre-calculus, science, social studies, Spanish, statistics, theology, visual arts, vocal music, world history, world literature, writing.
Graduation Requirements Arts and fine arts (art, music, dance, drama), English, foreign language, four units of summer reading, mathematics, physical education (includes health), religion (includes Bible studies and theology), science, social studies (includes history), 40 hours of service work per year.
Special Academic Programs Advanced Placement exam preparation; honors section.
College Admission Counseling 29 students graduated in 2011; all went to college, including Marquette University; Northwestern University; Purdue University; University of Dallas; University of Illinois at Urbana–Champaign; University of Notre Dame. Mean SAT critical reading: 654, mean SAT math: 663, mean SAT writing: 660, mean composite ACT: 26.
Student Life Upper grades have uniform requirement, student council, honor system. Discipline rests primarily with faculty.
Summer Programs Enrichment, sports programs offered; session focuses on athletic camps and enrichment; held on campus; accepts girls; open to students from other schools. 30 students usually enrolled. 2012 schedule: June 1 to July 31. Application deadline: none.
Tuition and Aid Day student tuition: $13,000. Tuition installment plan (Insured Tuition Payment Plan, monthly payment plans, quarterly, semiannual, and annual payment plans). Tuition reduction for siblings, need-based scholarship grants available. In 2011–12, 30% of upper-school students received aid.
Admissions Traditional secondary-level entrance grade is 9. For fall 2011, 26 students applied for upper-level admission, 26 were accepted, 23 enrolled. Any standardized test, ISEE or school's own exam required. Deadline for receipt of application materials: none. Application fee required: $50. On-campus interview required.
Athletics Interscholastic: basketball, cross-country running, dance team, soccer, softball, swimming and diving, volleyball. 1 PE instructor, 8 coaches.
Computers Computers are regularly used in graphic design, history, mathematics, music, music technology, science classes. Computer network features include Internet access. Students grades are available online.

Contact Stephanie Sheffield, Director of Admissions. 847-824-6900. Fax: 847-824-7089. E-mail: sheffield@willowsacademy.org. Web site: www.willowsacademy.org.

WILLOW WOOD SCHOOL

55 Scarsdale Road

Don Mills, Ontario M3B 2R3, Canada

Head of School: Ms. Joy Kurtz

General Information Coeducational day college-preparatory, general academic, arts, technology, and sports school; primarily serves students with learning disabilities and individuals with Attention Deficit Disorder. Grades 1–12. Founded: 1980. Setting: suburban. Nearest major city is Toronto, Canada. 3-acre campus. 1 building on campus. Approved or accredited by Ontario Ministry of Education and Ontario Department of Education. Languages of instruction: English, Spanish, and French. Total enrollment: 190. Upper school average class size: 16. Upper school faculty-student ratio: 1:7. There are 185 required school days per year for Upper School students. Upper School students typically attend 5 days per week. The average school day consists of 7 hours and 15 minutes.

Upper School Student Profile Grade 9: 27 students (24 boys, 3 girls); Grade 10: 25 students (17 boys, 8 girls); Grade 11: 35 students (27 boys, 8 girls); Grade 12: 35 students (23 boys, 12 girls).

Faculty School total: 35. In upper school: 9 men, 7 women; 4 have advanced degrees.

Subjects Offered 20th century world history, accounting, advanced chemistry, advanced math, algebra, ancient world history, applied arts, art, art history, biology, business applications, business mathematics, calculus, Canadian geography, Canadian history, Canadian law, Canadian literature, career and personal planning, careers, chemistry, civics, computer applications, computer graphics, computer information systems, computer literacy, computer multimedia, computer science, creative writing, data processing, dramatic arts, economics, English, English composition, English literature, environmental science, ESL, family studies, film studies, finite math, French as a second language, geography, geometry, global issues, guidance, health education, history, independent study, keyboarding, learning strategies, mathematics, media studies, medieval history, modern Western civilization, philosophy, photography, physical education, physics, politics, psychology, reading/study skills, remedial/makeup course work, research skills, science and technology, skills for success, social skills, society challenge and change, society, politics and law, Spanish, study skills, The 20th Century, visual arts, world history, world religions, yearbook.

Graduation Requirements Arts, business, Canadian geography, Canadian history, career education, civics, computer technologies, electives, English, French, history, mathematics, physical education (includes health), science, social sciences, Provincial Literacy Test requirement, community service hours.

Special Academic Programs Accelerated programs; independent study; study abroad; academic accommodation for the gifted and the artistically talented; remedial reading and/or remedial writing; remedial math; programs in English, mathematics, general development for dyslexic students; special instructional classes for students with learning disabilities and Attention Deficit Disorder; ESL (12 students enrolled).

College Admission Counseling 22 students graduated in 2011; all went to college, including Brock University; Queen's University at Kingston; Trent University; University of Guelph; University of Toronto; York University.

Student Life Upper grades have uniform requirement, student council, honor system. Discipline rests primarily with faculty.

Summer Programs Remediation, enrichment, advancement, ESL, computer instruction programs offered; session focuses on skill building and acquiring secondary school credits; held on campus; accepts boys and girls; open to students from other schools. 40 students usually enrolled. 2012 schedule: July 3 to August 3. Application deadline: June 1.

Tuition and Aid Day student tuition: CAN$17,100. Tuition installment plan (individually arranged payment plans, 10% due upon acceptance; balance divided into three equal payments due June 1, October 1, December 1). Tuition reduction for siblings available. In 2011–12, 5% of upper-school students received aid. Total amount of financial aid awarded in 2011–12: CAN$60,000.

Admissions Traditional secondary-level entrance grade is 9. For fall 2011, 25 students applied for upper-level admission, 15 were accepted, 15 enrolled. Achievement/Aptitude/Writing, CTBS, Stanford Achievement Test, any other standardized test, grade equivalent tests, non-standardized placement tests, school's own test, Wechsler Individual Achievement Test or writing sample required. Deadline for receipt of application materials: none. No application fee required. On-campus interview required.

Athletics Interscholastic: badminton (boys, girls), ball hockey (b,g), basketball (b,g), cooperative games (b,g), croquet (b,g), flag football (b,g), floor hockey (b,g), hockey (b), track and field (b,g), volleyball (b,g); intramural: ball hockey (b,g), basketball (b,g), cooperative games (b,g), flag football (b,g), floor hockey (b,g), indoor hockey (b,g), track and field (b,g); coed interscholastic: badminton, ball hockey, baseball, bowling, cross-country running, curling, fitness walking, Frisbee, golf, hockey, ice hockey, indoor soccer, jogging, outdoor education, outdoor recreation, physical fitness, physical training, running, soccer, softball, table tennis, ultimate Frisbee, walking; coed intramural: aerobics, badminton, ball hockey, baseball, bowling, curling, fitness, fitness walking, hockey, ice hockey, indoor soccer, jogging, outdoor education, outdoor recreation, physical fitness, physical training, running, soccer, softball, strength & conditioning, table tennis, ultimate Frisbee, volleyball, walking. 2 PE instructors, 1 athletic trainer.

Computers Computers are regularly used in accounting, business applications, career exploration, college planning, creative writing, data processing, English, ESL, geography, graphic arts, independent study, learning cognition, publishing, remedial study skills, typing, Web site design, writing, yearbook classes. Computer network features include on-campus library services, online commercial services, Internet access, wireless campus network, Internet filtering or blocking technology. Computer access in designated common areas is available to students. Students grades are available online. The school has a published electronic and media policy.

Contact Ms. Joy Kurtz, Director. 416-444-7644. Fax: 416-444-1801. E-mail: joykurtz@willowwoodschool.ca. Web site: www.willowwoodschool.ca.

WILMINGTON CHRISTIAN SCHOOL

825 Loveville Road

Hockessin, Delaware 19707

Head of School: Mr. William F. Stevens Jr.

General Information Coeducational day college-preparatory, arts, religious studies, and technology school, affiliated with Protestant faith. Grades PK–12. Founded: 1946. Setting: suburban. Nearest major city is Wilmington. 15-acre campus. 1 building on campus. Approved or accredited by Association of Christian Schools International, Middle States Association of Colleges and Schools, and Delaware Department of Education. Endowment: $400,000. Total enrollment: 476. Upper school average class size: 25. Upper school faculty-student ratio: 1:15. There are 177 required school days per year for Upper School students. Upper School students typically attend 5 days per week. The average school day consists of 6 hours and 40 minutes.

Upper School Student Profile Grade 9: 56 students (28 boys, 28 girls); Grade 10: 53 students (31 boys, 22 girls); Grade 11: 56 students (34 boys, 22 girls); Grade 12: 40 students (17 boys, 23 girls). 90% of students are Protestant.

Faculty School total: 51. In upper school: 7 men, 16 women; 9 have advanced degrees.

Subjects Offered Accounting, advanced math, algebra, American history, American history AP, American minority experience, anatomy and physiology, art, band, biology, calculus, calculus-AP, chemistry, chorus, Christian doctrine, Christian ethics, church history, civics, computer applications, consumer mathematics, creative writing, democracy in America, driver education, ecology, economics, English, geometry, German, health, honors algebra, honors English, honors geometry, information processing, journalism, lab science, library assistant, marine biology, modern history, music theory, novels, physical education, physical science, physics, pre-calculus, Spanish, speech, study skills, trigonometry, world civilizations, world religions, yearbook.

Graduation Requirements Bible studies, English, foreign language, health education, mathematics, physical education (includes health), science, social studies (includes history), 40 hours of community service.

Special Academic Programs Advanced Placement exam preparation; honors section; study at local college for college credit; remedial reading and/or remedial writing; remedial math; ESL (9 students enrolled).

College Admission Counseling 52 students graduated in 2011; all went to college, including Drexel University; Eastern University; Gordon College; Liberty University; Messiah College; University of Delaware.

Student Life Upper grades have uniform requirement, student council, honor system. Discipline rests primarily with faculty. Attendance at religious services is required.

Summer Programs Remediation, advancement programs offered; session focuses on to get students "caught-up" to be put in an academic track; held on campus; accepts boys and girls; open to students from other schools. 7 students usually enrolled. 2012 schedule: June 15 to August 5.

Tuition and Aid Day student tuition: $11,470. Tuition installment plan (STEP Plan (monthly deduction from a checking account)). Tuition reduction for siblings, need-based scholarship grants available. In 2011–12, 47% of upper-school students received aid. Total amount of financial aid awarded in 2011–12: $292,720.

Admissions Traditional secondary-level entrance grade is 9. For fall 2011, 44 students applied for upper-level admission, 40 were accepted, 30 enrolled. Stanford Achievement Test required. Deadline for receipt of application materials: August 1. Application fee required: $125. On-campus interview required.

Athletics Interscholastic: baseball (boys), basketball (b,g), cheering (g), field hockey (g), lacrosse (b), soccer (b,g), softball (g), volleyball (g), wrestling (b); coed interscholastic: cross-country running, golf, running. 2 PE instructors, 16 coaches, 1 athletic trainer.

Computers Computers are regularly used in accounting, business education, data processing, information technology, newspaper, yearbook classes. Computer network features include on-campus library services, Internet access. The school has a published electronic and media policy.

Contact Mrs. Kim Connell, Admissions/Headmaster's Assistant. 302-239-2121 Ext. 3205. Fax: 302-239-2778. E-mail: kconnell@wilmingtonchristian.org. Web site: www.wilmingtonchristian.org.

WILSON HALL

520 Wilson Hall Road

Sumter, South Carolina 29150

Head of School: Mr. Frederick B. Moulton Sr.

General Information Coeducational day college-preparatory, arts, and technology school. Grades PS–12. Founded: 1966. Setting: small town. Nearest major city is Columbia. 17-acre campus. 6 buildings on campus. Approved or accredited by Southern Association of Colleges and Schools, Southern Association of Independent Schools, and South Carolina Department of Education. Endowment: $280,000. Total enrollment: 837. Upper school average class size: 18. Upper school faculty-student ratio: 1:13. There are 180 required school days per year for Upper School students. Upper School students typically attend 5 days per week. The average school day consists of 6 hours and 20 minutes.

Upper School Student Profile Grade 9: 63 students (42 boys, 21 girls); Grade 10: 74 students (37 boys, 37 girls); Grade 11: 53 students (27 boys, 26 girls); Grade 12: 60 students (34 boys, 26 girls).

Faculty School total: 80. In upper school: 15 men, 27 women; 21 have advanced degrees.

Subjects Offered 3-dimensional design, algebra, anatomy, biology-AP, calculus-AP, chemistry-AP, computer applications, computer programming, computer programming-AP, drawing, economics, English, English language-AP, English literature-AP, environmental science, European history-AP, French, French language-AP, government, government-AP, journalism, Latin, Latin-AP, Middle Eastern history, multimedia, music theory-AP, philosophy, physical education, physical science, physics-AP, pottery, Spanish, Spanish language-AP, studio art-AP, trigonometry, U.S. history-AP, world history.

Graduation Requirements Arts and fine arts (art, music, dance, drama), computer science, English, foreign language, mathematics, physical education (includes health), science, social studies (includes history), acceptance into four-year college or university, 20 hours community service.

Special Academic Programs Advanced Placement exam preparation; honors section.

College Admission Counseling 48 students graduated in 2011; all went to college, including Clemson University; College of Charleston; Duke University; The Citadel, The Military College of South Carolina; University of South Carolina; University of Virginia.

Student Life Upper grades have specified standards of dress, honor system. Discipline rests primarily with faculty.

Summer Programs Enrichment, sports, art/fine arts, computer instruction programs offered; session focuses on enrichment; held on campus; accepts boys and girls; not open to students from other schools. 100 students usually enrolled. 2012 schedule: June 1 to July 15. Application deadline: May 20.

Tuition and Aid Day student tuition: $5175–$5845. Tuition installment plan (monthly payment plans). Need-based scholarship grants available. In 2011–12, 7% of upper-school students received aid. Total amount of financial aid awarded in 2011–12: $135,000.

Admissions Traditional secondary-level entrance grade is 9. For fall 2011, 153 students applied for upper-level admission, 110 were accepted, 106 enrolled. ACT, CTBS, OLSAT, Iowa Tests of Basic Skills, PSAT and SAT for applicants to grade 11 and 12, school's own test or Stanford Achievement Test, Otis-Lennon School Ability Test required. Deadline for receipt of application materials: none. Application fee required: $150. Interview recommended.

Athletics Interscholastic: baseball (boys), basketball (b,g), bowling (b,g), cheering (g), cross-country running (b,g), equestrian sports (g), fishing (b), football (b), golf (b,g), marksmanship (b), Nautilus (b,g), riflery (b), running (b,g), skeet shooting (b), softball (g), strength & conditioning (b,g), swimming and diving (b,g), tennis (b,g), track and field (b,g), trap and skeet (b), volleyball (g), wrestling (b); intramural: table tennis (b), weight lifting (b,g), weight training (b,g); coed interscholastic: climbing, outdoor adventure, outdoor education, paint ball, riflery, skeet shooting, soccer; coed intramural: outdoor adventure, rafting, rock climbing, ropes courses, table tennis. 4 PE instructors, 12 coaches.

Computers Computers are regularly used in computer applications, English, journalism, literary magazine, technology, yearbook classes. Computer network features include on-campus library services, online commercial services, Internet access, Internet filtering or blocking technology. Students grades are available online. The school has a published electronic and media policy.

Contact Mr. Sean Hoskins, Director of Admissions and Public Relations. 803-469-3475 Ext. 107. Fax: 803-469-3477. E-mail: sean_hoskins@hotmail.com. Web site: www.wilsonhall.org.

WINCHESTER THURSTON SCHOOL

555 Morewood Avenue

Pittsburgh, Pennsylvania 15213-2899

Head of School: Mr. Gary J. Niels

General Information Coeducational day college-preparatory and arts school. Grades PK–12. Founded: 1887. Setting: urban. 5-acre campus. 2 buildings on campus. Approved or accredited by Middle States Association of Colleges and Schools, Pennsylvania Association of Independent Schools, The College Board, and Pennsylvania Department of Education. Member of National Association of Independent Schools. Endowment: $9 million. Total enrollment: 643. Upper school average class size: 15. Upper school faculty-student ratio: 1:8. There are 175 required school days per year for Upper School students. Upper School students typically attend 5 days per week. The average school day consists of 6 hours and 50 minutes.

Upper School Student Profile Grade 9: 61 students (32 boys, 29 girls); Grade 10: 65 students (40 boys, 25 girls); Grade 11: 62 students (26 boys, 36 girls); Grade 12: 56 students (34 boys, 22 girls).

Faculty School total: 91. In upper school: 16 men, 16 women; 16 have advanced degrees.

Subjects Offered Algebra, American history, American history-AP, American literature, animal behavior, art, art history, biology, biology-AP, calculus, calculus-AP, ceramics, chemistry, Chinese, choir, chorus, classics, composition-AP, computer programming, computer science, computer science-AP, creative writing, dance, drama, drawing, economics, economics-AP, English, English literature, English literature-AP, English-AP, European history, European history-AP, expository writing, filmmaking, French, French-AP, geometry, government/civics, health, history, journalism, Latin, Latin-AP, mathematics, music, music theory, philosophy, photography, physical education, physics, physics-AP, psychology, SAT preparation, science, social studies, Spanish, Spanish-AP, speech, statistics-AP, visual arts, world history, world literature, writing, yearbook.

Graduation Requirements Arts and fine arts (art, music, dance, drama), computer science, English, foreign language, mathematics, physical education (includes health), science, social studies (includes history), speech, City As Our Campus coursework, a unique program which connects our students with various educational opportunities within the city of Pittsburgh, (examples of these opportunities include internships, research programs, and service learning options).

Special Academic Programs Advanced Placement exam preparation; independent study; term-away projects; study at local college for college credit; study abroad; academic accommodation for the gifted, the musically talented, and the artistically talented; ESL (2 students enrolled).

College Admission Counseling 63 students graduated in 2011; 62 went to college, including Boston University; Carnegie Mellon University; Haverford College; Haverford College; Lehigh University; University of Pittsburgh. Other: 1 had other specific plans. Mean SAT math: 611, mean SAT writing: 640, mean combined SAT: 1884, mean composite ACT: 26. 49% scored over 600 on SAT critical reading, 42% scored over 600 on SAT math, 46% scored over 600 on SAT writing, 66% scored over 1800 on combined SAT, 67% scored over 26 on composite ACT.

Student Life Upper grades have specified standards of dress, student council. Discipline rests equally with students and faculty.

Summer Programs Enrichment, sports, art/fine arts programs offered; session focuses on adventure and play, sports and physical fitness, creative arts, and academics; held on campus; accepts boys and girls; open to students from other schools. 500 students usually enrolled. 2012 schedule: June 22 to July 31. Application deadline: May 15.

Tuition and Aid Day student tuition: $22,600–$24,600. Tuition installment plan (monthly payment plans). Need-based scholarship grants available. In 2011–12, 31% of upper-school students received aid. Total amount of financial aid awarded in 2011–12: $1,249,000.

Admissions Traditional secondary-level entrance grade is 9. For fall 2011, 98 students applied for upper-level admission, 63 were accepted, 40 enrolled. ISEE or TOEFL or SLEP required. Deadline for receipt of application materials: December 15. Application fee required: $50. Interview required.

Athletics Interscholastic: basketball (boys, girls), drill team (g), field hockey (g), lacrosse (b,g), rowing (b,g), running (b,g), tennis (b,g); intramural: squash (b); coed interscholastic: crew, cross-country running, fencing, golf, soccer, squash, track and field; coed intramural: basketball, dance, Frisbee, independent competitive sports, outdoor activities, physical fitness, physical training, soccer, strength & conditioning, ultimate Frisbee, weight training, winter soccer, yoga. 4 PE instructors, 24 coaches, 1 athletic trainer.

Computers Computers are regularly used in art, college planning, computer applications, creative writing, English, foreign language, history, library, mathematics, music, photography, science, senior seminar, social studies, writing, writing, yearbook classes. Computer network features include on-campus library services, online commercial services, Internet access, wireless campus network, Internet filtering or blocking technology. Campus intranet, student e-mail accounts, and computer access in designated common areas are available to students. Students grades are available online. The school has a published electronic and media policy.

Contact Mr. Scot Lorenzi, Associate Director of Admission. 412-578-3738. Fax: 412-578-7504. E-mail: lorenzis@winchesterthurston.org. Web site: www.winchesterthurston.org.

WINDERMERE PREPARATORY SCHOOL

6189 Winter Garden-Vineland Road

Windermere, Florida 34786

Head of School: Mrs. Donna Montague-Russell

General Information Boys' boarding and coeducational day college-preparatory, arts, and technology school. Boarding boys grades 9–12, day boys grades PK–12, day girls grades PK–12. Founded: 2000. Setting: small town. Nearest major city is Orlando. Students are housed in single-sex dormitories. 48-acre campus. 3 buildings on campus. Approved or accredited by Association of Independent Schools of Florida, International Baccalaureate Organization, National Independent Private Schools Association, Southern Association of Colleges and Schools, Southern Association of Independent Schools, and Florida Department of Education. Total enrollment: 1,043. Upper school average class size: 18. Upper school faculty-student ratio: 1:11. There are 180 required school days per year for Upper School students. Upper School students typically attend 5 days per week. The average school day consists of 7 hours and 15 minutes.

Upper School Student Profile Grade 9: 60 students (30 boys, 30 girls); Grade 10: 97 students (46 boys, 51 girls); Grade 11: 96 students (48 boys, 48 girls); Grade 12: 64 students (31 boys, 33 girls). 9% of students are boarding students. 91% are state residents. 9% are international students. International students from Austria, Canada, China, Germany, Switzerland, and Turkey; 8 other countries represented in student body.

Faculty School total: 103. In upper school: 20 men, 20 women; 30 have advanced degrees; 3 reside on campus.

Subjects Offered 20th century history, 3-dimensional art, acting, Advanced Placement courses, algebra, American government, American history, American literature, art, biology, biology-AP, business, calculus, calculus-AP, ceramics, chemistry, chemistry-AP, choir, chorus, composition-AP, creative writing, dance, dance performance, drama, drama performance, economics, economics-AP, electives, engineering, English, English composition, English language and composition-AP, English literature, English literature and composition-AP, environmental science, ethics, film, forensics, French, geometry, graphic design, honors algebra, honors English, honors U.S. history, honors world history, Latin, music, music theory, personal fitness, physical education, physics, physics-AP, pre-calculus, psychology, psychology-AP, Spanish, speech and debate, theory of knowledge, world history, world history-AP, world literature, yearbook.

Graduation Requirements Arts and fine arts (art, music, dance, drama), electives, English, foreign language, history, mathematics, performing arts, physical fitness, science, 6 additional elective credits. Community service is required.

Special Academic Programs International Baccalaureate program; 11 Advanced Placement exams for which test preparation is offered; honors section; independent study; academic accommodation for the musically talented and the artistically talented.

College Admission Counseling 54 students graduated in 2011; all went to college, including Boston College; Elon University; Rollins College; University of Central Florida; University of Florida; University of North Florida. Median SAT critical reading: 578, median SAT math: 592, median SAT writing: 563.

Student Life Upper grades have uniform requirement, student council, honor system. Discipline rests primarily with faculty.

Summer Programs Enrichment, sports, art/fine arts, computer instruction programs offered; session focuses on enrichment, academics, and athletics; held on campus; accepts boys and girls; open to students from other schools. 200 students usually enrolled. 2012 schedule: June to August. Application deadline: May.

Tuition and Aid Day student tuition: $14,025; 7-day tuition and room/board: $38,950. Tuition installment plan (monthly payment plans). Need-based scholarship grants available. In 2011–12, 9% of upper-school students received aid. Total amount of financial aid awarded in 2011–12: $126,672.

Admissions Traditional secondary-level entrance grade is 9. For fall 2011, 100 students applied for upper-level admission, 75 were accepted, 70 enrolled. Achievement tests or SSAT, ERB, PSAT, SAT, PLAN or ACT required. Deadline for receipt of application materials: none. Application fee required: $100. Interview recommended.

Athletics Interscholastic: ballet (girls), baseball (b), basketball (b,g), cheering (g), dance (g), dance team (g), golf (b,g), lacrosse (b), modern dance (g), physical fitness (b,g), physical training (b,g), soccer (b,g), softball (g), strength & conditioning (g), swimming and diving (b), tennis (b,g), track and field (b,g), volleyball (g), weight training (g); coed interscholastic: crew, cross-country running, equestrian sports, track and field; coed intramural: flag football, golf. 8 PE instructors, 25 coaches, 2 athletic trainers.

Computers Computers are regularly used in all academic classes. Computer network features include on-campus library services, Internet access, wireless campus network, Internet filtering or blocking technology. Student e-mail accounts are available to students. Students grades are available online. The school has a published electronic and media policy.

Contact Mrs. Carol Riggs, Director of Admissions. 407-905-7737. Fax: 407-905-7710. E-mail: carol.riggs@windermereprep.com. Web site: www.windermereprep.com.

THE WINDSOR SCHOOL

Administration Building

136-23 Sanford Avenue

Flushing, New York 11355

Head of School: Mr. James Seery

General Information Coeducational day college-preparatory and arts school. Grades 6–PG. Founded: 1968. Setting: urban. Nearest major city is New York. 2-acre campus. 3 buildings on campus. Approved or accredited by Middle States Association of Colleges and Schools, New York Department of Education, New York State Association of Independent Schools, New York State Board of Regents, The College Board, and US Department of State. Total enrollment: 160. Upper school average class size: 12. Upper school faculty-student ratio: 1:14. There are 185 required school days per year for Upper School students. Upper School students typically attend 5 days per week. The average school day consists of 6 hours.

Upper School Student Profile Grade 9: 15 students (8 boys, 7 girls); Grade 10: 26 students (16 boys, 10 girls); Grade 11: 48 students (27 boys, 21 girls); Grade 12: 60 students (33 boys, 27 girls).

Faculty School total: 15. In upper school: 8 men, 7 women; 12 have advanced degrees.

Subjects Offered Advanced Placement courses, algebra, American history, American literature, art, basic skills, biology, business, business applications, calculus, ceramics, chemistry, computer programming, computer science, computer skills, computer studies, creative writing, driver education, economics, English, English literature, environmental science, ESL, European history, fine arts, French, geometry, government/civics, grammar, health, marketing, mathematics, music, physical education, physics, pre-calculus, psychology, science, social sciences, social studies, Spanish, trigonometry, world affairs, world history.

Graduation Requirements Arts and fine arts (art, music, dance, drama), English, foreign language, mathematics, physical education (includes health), science, social sciences, social studies (includes history).

Special Academic Programs Advanced Placement exam preparation; honors section; accelerated programs; independent study; academic accommodation for the gifted, the musically talented, and the artistically talented; remedial reading and/or remedial writing; remedial math; ESL (40 students enrolled).

College Admission Counseling 43 students graduated in 2011; all went to college, including New York University; Queens College of the City University of New York; St. John's University; State University of New York at Binghamton. Median SAT critical reading: 440, median SAT math: 550, median SAT writing: 460. 10% scored over 600 on SAT critical reading, 23% scored over 600 on SAT math, 10% scored over 600 on SAT writing.

Student Life Upper grades have specified standards of dress. Discipline rests primarily with faculty.

Summer Programs Remediation, enrichment, advancement, ESL, art/fine arts, computer instruction programs offered; session focuses on advancement, enrichment, remediation; held on campus; accepts boys and girls; open to students from other schools. 600 students usually enrolled. 2012 schedule: July 1 to August 18. Application deadline: June 30.

Tuition and Aid Day student tuition: $19,600. Tuition installment plan (individually arranged payment plans). Financial aid available to upper-school students. In 2011–12, 10% of upper-school students received aid. Total amount of financial aid awarded in 2011–12: $30,000.

Admissions Traditional secondary-level entrance grade is 9. For fall 2011, 70 students applied for upper-level admission, 62 were accepted, 55 enrolled. School's own exam required. Deadline for receipt of application materials: none. No application fee required. On-campus interview required.

Athletics Interscholastic: basketball (boys, girls), soccer (b,g), softball (b,g); intramural: aerobics (b,g), basketball (b,g), cooperative games (b,g), fitness (b,g), jump rope (g), physical fitness (b,g), soccer (b,g), softball (b,g), tennis (b,g), volleyball (b,g); coed interscholastic: basketball, soccer, softball; coed intramural: basketball, fitness, jump rope, physical fitness, soccer, softball, table tennis, tennis, volleyball. 2 PE instructors, 2 coaches.

Computers Computers are regularly used in art, business applications, mathematics, research skills, typing, yearbook classes. Computer resources include Internet access.

Contact Dr. Philip A. Stewart, Director of Admissions. 718-359-8300. Fax: 718-359-1876. E-mail: admin@thewindsorschool.com. Web site: www.windsorschool.com.

WINDWARD SCHOOL

11350 Palms Boulevard

Los Angeles, California 90066

Head of School: Tom Gilder

General Information Coeducational day college-preparatory school. Grades 7–12. Founded: 1971. Setting: urban. 9-acre campus. 11 buildings on campus. Approved or accredited by California Association of Independent Schools and Western Association of Schools and Colleges. Member of National Association of Independent Schools. Total enrollment: 541. Upper school average class size: 16. Upper school faculty-student ratio: 1:7. There are 165 required school days per year for Upper School students. Upper School students typically attend 5 days per week. The average school day consists of 7 hours.

Upper School Student Profile Grade 9: 80 students (38 boys, 42 girls); Grade 10: 94 students (46 boys, 48 girls); Grade 11: 91 students (48 boys, 43 girls); Grade 12: 89 students (43 boys, 46 girls).

Faculty School total: 65. In upper school: 32 men, 27 women; 37 have advanced degrees.

Subjects Offered 3-dimensional art, acting, advanced biology, advanced chemistry, Advanced Placement courses, algebra, American history, American literature, art, art history, ballet, biology, calculus, ceramics, chemistry, Chinese, chorus, computer science, creative writing, dance, drama, English, English literature, environmental science, European history, fine arts, French, geometry, government/civics, health, history, journalism, Latin, marine biology, mathematics, music, performing arts, photography, photojournalism, physical education, physiology, robotics, science, senior internship, social studies, Spanish, theater, trigonometry, world history.

Graduation Requirements Arts and fine arts (art, music, dance, drama), English, foreign language, mathematics, physical education (includes health), science, social studies (includes history).

Special Academic Programs 16 Advanced Placement exams for which test preparation is offered; honors section; independent study; study at local college for college credit.

College Admission Counseling 89 students graduated in 2011; all went to college, including Dartmouth College; Northwestern University; Tufts University; University of California, Berkeley; Williams College; Yale University. Mean SAT critical reading: 650, mean SAT math: 645, mean SAT writing: 671, mean combined SAT: 1966.

Student Life Upper grades have specified standards of dress, student council, honor system. Discipline rests primarily with faculty.

Summer Programs Sports programs offered; session focuses on skill development and team play; held on campus; accepts boys and girls; open to students from other schools. 75 students usually enrolled. 2012 schedule: June 18 to August 19.

Tuition and Aid Day student tuition: $33,505. Tuition installment plan (Key Tuition Payment Plan, monthly payment plans). Need-based scholarship grants, need-based loans available. In 2011–12, 17% of upper-school students received aid. Total amount of financial aid awarded in 2011–12: $1,367,106.

Admissions Traditional secondary-level entrance grade is 9. For fall 2011, 149 students applied for upper-level admission, 30 were accepted, 23 enrolled. ISEE required. Deadline for receipt of application materials: December 14. Application fee required: $100. On-campus interview required.

Athletics Interscholastic: baseball (boys), basketball (b,g), football (b); coed interscholastic: cross-country running, flag football. 5 PE instructors, 15 coaches, 2 athletic trainers.

Computers Computers are regularly used in art, English, history, mathematics, science classes. Computer network features include on-campus library services, online commercial services, Internet access, wireless campus network, Internet filtering or blocking technology. Student e-mail accounts are available to students. The school has a published electronic and media policy.

Contact Sharon Pearline, Director of Admissions. 310-391-7127. Fax: 310-397-5655. Web site: www.windwardschool.org.

See Display on next page and Close-Up on page 706.

THE WINSOR SCHOOL

103 Pilgrim Road

Boston, Massachusetts 02215

Head of School: Mrs. Rachel Friis Stettler

General Information Girls' day college-preparatory school. Grades 5–12. Founded: 1886. Setting: urban. 8-acre campus. 2 buildings on campus. Approved or accredited by Association of Independent Schools in New England, New England Association of Schools and Colleges, and Massachusetts Department of Education. Member of National Association of Independent Schools. Endowment: $62.5 million. Total enrollment: 434. Upper school average class size: 13. Upper school faculty-student ratio: 1:5. There are 163 required school days per year for Upper School students. Upper School students typically attend 5 days per week. The average school day consists of 6 hours and 30 minutes.

Upper School Student Profile Grade 9: 65 students (65 girls); Grade 10: 66 students (66 girls); Grade 11: 59 students (59 girls); Grade 12: 51 students (51 girls).

Faculty School total: 72. In upper school: 11 men, 38 women; 39 have advanced degrees.

Subjects Offered Acting, advanced studio art-AP, African history, African literature, algebra, architecture, art, art history, astronomy, biology, biology-AP, British literature (honors), calculus, calculus-AP, ceramics, chemistry, chemistry-AP, Chinese, computer programming, contemporary history, creative writing, digital art, drama, engineering, English, environmental science-AP, expository writing, fine arts, French, French-AP, geometry, health, Islamic history, Latin, Latin-AP, literature, macroeconomics-AP,

marine biology, Middle Eastern history, music, photography, physical education, physics, physics-AP, pre-calculus, sculpture, senior project, Spanish, Spanish-AP, statistics, statistics-AP, theater, U.S. history, U.S. literature, Web site design.
Graduation Requirements Algebra, art, biology, chemistry, English, foreign language, geometry, health and wellness, health education, non-Western literature, non-Western societies, physical education (includes health), physics, pre-calculus, senior project, U.S. history, world history, 1 semester quantitative course senior year.
Special Academic Programs 11 Advanced Placement exams for which test preparation is offered; honors section; term-away projects.
College Admission Counseling 54 students graduated in 2011; all went to college, including Boston College; Dartmouth College; Harvard University; The Johns Hopkins University; Vanderbilt University; Yale University. Median SAT critical reading: 710, median SAT math: 700, median SAT writing: 750, median combined SAT: 2160, median composite ACT: 30. 93% scored over 600 on SAT critical reading, 93% scored over 600 on SAT math, 98% scored over 600 on SAT writing, 96% scored over 1800 on combined SAT.
Student Life Upper grades have specified standards of dress, student council, honor system. Discipline rests primarily with faculty.
Tuition and Aid Day student tuition: $35,500. Tuition installment plan (Tuition Management Systems). Need-based scholarship grants available. In 2011–12, 24% of upper-school students received aid. Total amount of financial aid awarded in 2011–12: $1,735,291.
Admissions Traditional secondary-level entrance grade is 9. For fall 2011, 104 students applied for upper-level admission, 19 were accepted, 12 enrolled. ISEE or SSAT required. Deadline for receipt of application materials: December 17. Application fee required: $45. On-campus interview required.
Athletics Interscholastic: basketball, crew, cross-country running, field hockey, ice hockey, lacrosse, sailing, soccer, softball, squash, swimming and diving, tennis, track and field. 4 PE instructors, 4 coaches, 1 athletic trainer.
Computers Computers are regularly used in photography, programming, Web site design classes. Computer network features include on-campus library services, Internet access, wireless campus network, Internet filtering or blocking technology. Campus intranet and student e-mail accounts are available to students. The school has a published electronic and media policy.
Contact Mrs. Pamela Parks McLaurin, Director of Admission. 617-735-9503. Fax: 617-912-1381. Web site: www.winsor.edu/.

See Display on next page and Close-Up on page 708.

WINSTON PREPARATORY SCHOOL
New York, New York

See Special Needs Schools section.

THE WINSTON SCHOOL SAN ANTONIO
San Antonio, Texas

See Special Needs Schools section.

THE WOODHALL SCHOOL
PO Box 550
58 Harrison Lane
Bethlehem, Connecticut 06751

Head of School: Matthew C. Woodhall
General Information Boys' boarding and day college-preparatory, arts, and ESL school; primarily serves students with above-average intellectual ability who have had difficulties in traditional school environments. Grades 9–PG. Founded: 1983. Setting: rural. Nearest major city is Waterbury. Students are housed in single-sex dormitories. 38-acre campus. 5 buildings on campus. Approved or accredited by Association of Independent Schools in New England, New England Association of Schools and Colleges, and Connecticut Department of Education. Member of National Association of Independent Schools. Endowment: $120,000. Total enrollment: 38. Upper school average class size: 4. Upper school faculty-student ratio: 1:4. There are 184 required school days per year for Upper School students. Upper School students typically attend 6 days per week.
Upper School Student Profile Grade 9: 6 students (6 boys); Grade 10: 10 students (10 boys); Grade 11: 15 students (15 boys); Grade 12: 8 students (8 boys). 100% of students are boarding students. 12% are state residents. 22 states are represented in upper school student body. International students from Switzerland.
Faculty School total: 16. In upper school: 13 men, 3 women; 11 have advanced degrees; 11 reside on campus.
Subjects Offered Algebra, American history, anatomy, art, biology, calculus, chemistry, comparative government and politics, drama, English, environmental science, geometry, Greek, language and composition, Latin, physics, pre-calculus, Spanish, world civilizations.

Graduation Requirements Arts and fine arts (art, music, dance, drama), communication skills, English, foreign language, mathematics, physical education (includes health), science, social studies (includes history).

Special Academic Programs Advanced Placement exam preparation; independent study; special instructional classes for students with Attention Deficit Disorder and nonverbal learning disabilities; ESL.

College Admission Counseling 14 students graduated in 2011; all went to college, including Guilford College; Ithaca College; Keene State College; Lynchburg College; Northeastern University; University of Vermont. Median SAT critical reading: 652, median SAT math: 500, median SAT writing: 569, median combined SAT: 574.

Student Life Upper grades have specified standards of dress, student council, honor system. Discipline rests primarily with faculty.

Tuition and Aid Day student tuition: $45,000; 7-day tuition and room/board: $58,400. Tuition installment plan (individually arranged payment plans).

Admissions Traditional secondary-level entrance grade is 10. Deadline for receipt of application materials: none. Application fee required: $100. On-campus interview required.

Athletics Interscholastic: basketball, cross-country running, lacrosse, soccer; intramural: alpine skiing, basketball, bicycling, bowling, canoeing/kayaking, cross-country running, fishing, fitness, fitness walking, Frisbee, hiking/backpacking, ice skating, jogging, lacrosse, mountain biking, outdoor activities, outdoor education, outdoor recreation, physical fitness, physical training, rafting, running, skiing (cross-country), skiing (downhill), snowboarding, soccer, street hockey, strength & conditioning, table tennis, volleyball, walking, wall climbing, weight lifting, winter walking, wrestling.

Computers Computers are regularly used in art, English, foreign language, history, mathematics, science, social sciences classes. Computer resources include Internet access. The school has a published electronic and media policy.

Contact Matthew C. Woodhall, Head of School. 203-266-7788. Fax: 203-266-5896. E-mail: mwoodhall@woodhallschool.org. Web site: www.woodhallschool.org.

WOODLYNDE SCHOOL

445 Upper Gulph Road

Strafford, Pennsylvania 19087

Head of School: Christopher M. Fulco, EdD

General Information Coeducational day college-preparatory, arts, and technology school; primarily serves individuals with Attention Deficit Disorder, dyslexic students, and language-based learning disabilities. Grades 1–12. Founded: 1976. Setting: suburban. Nearest major city is Philadelphia. 8-acre campus. 2 buildings on campus. Approved or accredited by Pennsylvania Association of Independent Schools and Pennsylvania Department of Education. Member of National Association of Independent Schools. Endowment: $559,699. Total enrollment: 262. Upper school average class size: 10. Upper school faculty-student ratio: 1:5. There are 168 required school days per year for Upper School students. Upper School students typically attend 5 days per week. The average school day consists of 6 hours and 55 minutes.

Upper School Student Profile Grade 6: 24 students (16 boys, 8 girls); Grade 7: 21 students (13 boys, 8 girls); Grade 8: 35 students (18 boys, 17 girls); Grade 9: 22 students (12 boys, 10 girls); Grade 10: 22 students (12 boys, 10 girls); Grade 11: 26 students (14 boys, 12 girls); Grade 12: 28 students (20 boys, 8 girls).

Faculty School total: 62. In upper school: 11 men, 10 women; 7 have advanced degrees.

Subjects Offered Algebra, American history, American literature, art, art-AP, arts, biology, chemistry, creative writing, earth science, English, English literature, English-AP, European history, fine arts, French, geometry, government/civics, health, history, journalism, mathematics, music, photography, physical education, physics, political science, psychology, science, social studies, Spanish, studio art, world history, world literature, writing.

Graduation Requirements Arts and fine arts (art, music, dance, drama), English, foreign language, mathematics, physical education (includes health), science, social studies (includes history), community service, senior project, senior speech.

Special Academic Programs Honors section; remedial reading and/or remedial writing.

College Admission Counseling 29 students graduated in 2010; 28 went to college, including Johnson & Wales University; Penn State University Park. Other: 1 went to work.

Student Life Upper grades have specified standards of dress, student council. Discipline rests primarily with faculty.

Tuition and Aid Day student tuition: $28,300. Tuition installment plan (FACTS Tuition Payment Plan). Need-based scholarship grants available. In 2010–11, 35% of upper-school students received aid. Total amount of financial aid awarded in 2010–11: $525,475.

Admissions Traditional secondary-level entrance grade is 9. For fall 2010, 19 students applied for upper-level admission, 10 were accepted, 6 enrolled. Individual IQ required. Deadline for receipt of application materials: none. Application fee required: $100. On-campus interview required.

Athletics Interscholastic: basketball (boys, girls), lacrosse (b,g), soccer (b,g), softball (g), tennis (b,g), volleyball (g); coed interscholastic: cross-country running. 4 PE instructors, 10 coaches, 1 athletic trainer.
Computers Computers are regularly used in all academic, art, creative writing, drawing and design, English, foreign language, French, graphic arts, graphic design, history, music, newspaper, publications, social studies, Spanish, study skills, technology, word processing, writing, yearbook classes. Computer network features include on-campus library services, Internet access, wireless campus network, Internet filtering or blocking technology. Student e-mail accounts are available to students. The school has a published electronic and media policy.
Contact Karen Duffy, Assistant Director of Admissions. 610-687-9660 Ext. 534. Fax: 610-293-6680. E-mail: duffy@woodlynde.org. Web site: www.woodlynde.org.

WOODSTOCK SCHOOL

Landour
Mussoorie
Uttarakhand 248 179, India

Head of School: Dr. David Laurenson

General Information Coeducational boarding and day college-preparatory, music, and science school, affiliated with Christian faith. Boarding grades 3–12, day grades N–12. Founded: 1854. Setting: rural. Nearest major city is New Delhi, India. Students are housed in single-sex dormitories. 290-acre campus. 7 buildings on campus. Approved or accredited by CITA (Commission on International and Trans-Regional Accreditation) and Middle States Association of Colleges and Schools. Member of European Council of International Schools. Language of instruction: English. Total enrollment: 522. Upper school average class size: 17. Upper school faculty-student ratio: 1:17. There are 180 required school days per year for Upper School students. Upper School students typically attend 5 days per week. The average school day consists of 6 hours and 30 minutes.
Upper School Student Profile Grade 7: 44 students (28 boys, 16 girls); Grade 8: 55 students (32 boys, 23 girls); Grade 9: 73 students (36 boys, 37 girls); Grade 10: 76 students (39 boys, 37 girls); Grade 11: 90 students (49 boys, 41 girls); Grade 12: 81 students (37 boys, 44 girls). 93% of students are boarding students. 63% are international students. International students from Bhutan, Democratic People's Republic of Korea, Japan, Nepal, Thailand, and United States; 21 other countries represented in student body. 47% of students are Christian.
Faculty School total: 70. In upper school: 18 men, 16 women; 17 have advanced degrees; all reside on campus.
Subjects Offered Algebra, American history, American history-AP, American literature, American studies, art, art history, Asian studies, Bible, Bible studies, biology, biology-AP, calculus, calculus-AP, ceramics, chemistry, chemistry-AP, choir, choral music, Christianity, community service, comparative religion, computer science, concert band, drama, economics, English, English language-AP, English literature, English-AP, environmental science, environmental science-AP, ethics, European history, fine arts, French, French-AP, geometry, government, government and politics-AP, health education, Hindi, Indian studies, jazz band, journalism, macro/microeconomics-AP, macroeconomics-AP, mathematics, mathematics-AP, microeconomics-AP, music, philosophy, physical education, physics, physics-AP, religion, science, social studies, theater, trigonometry, U.S. government and politics-AP, vocal music, world history, world history-AP, world literature, world religions, writing, yearbook.
Graduation Requirements Arts and fine arts (art, music, dance, drama), Christian studies, computer literacy, English, foreign language, mathematics, physical education (includes health), science, social studies (includes history). Community service is required.
Special Academic Programs 17 Advanced Placement exams for which test preparation is offered; independent study; study abroad; academic accommodation for the gifted, the musically talented, and the artistically talented; ESL (23 students enrolled).
College Admission Counseling 62 students graduated in 2010; 60 went to college, including Bard College; Columbia University; Mercyhurst College; Middlebury College; Northeastern University; Stanford University. Other: 2 had other specific plans. Median SAT critical reading: 566, median SAT math: 630, median SAT writing: 590, median combined SAT: 1810, median composite ACT: 27. 37% scored over 600 on SAT critical reading, 60% scored over 600 on SAT math, 48% scored over 600 on SAT writing, 56% scored over 1800 on combined SAT, 33% scored over 26 on composite ACT.
Student Life Upper grades have specified standards of dress, student council, honor system. Discipline rests equally with students and faculty. Attendance at religious services is required.
Tuition and Aid Day student tuition: $17,400; 7-day tuition and room/board: $17,400. Tuition installment plan (individually arranged payment plans). Need-based scholarship grants available. In 2010–11, 20% of upper-school students received aid.
Admissions Traditional secondary-level entrance grade is 11. For fall 2010, 310 students applied for upper-level admission, 74 were accepted, 68 enrolled. Any standardized test or TOEFL or SLEP required. Deadline for receipt of application materials: none. Application fee required: $80. Interview recommended.
Athletics Interscholastic: basketball (boys, girls), cricket (b), cross-country running (b,g), field hockey (b,g), soccer (b,g), strength & conditioning (b,g), swimming and diving (b,g), track and field (b,g); intramural: aerobics/dance (g), backpacking (b,g), badminton (b,g), basketball (b,g), climbing (b,g), cricket (b), cross-country running (b,g), field hockey (b,g), gymnastics (b,g), hiking/backpacking (b,g), hockey (b,g), outdoor activities (b,g), outdoor education (b,g), physical fitness (b,g), physical training (b,g), rock climbing (b,g), running (b,g), soccer (b,g), squash (b,g), strength & conditioning (b,g), swimming and diving (b,g), table tennis (b,g), tennis (b,g), track and field (b,g), volleyball (b,g), walking (b,g), wall climbing (b,g), weight training (b,g), wilderness survival (b,g); coed intramural: backpacking, hiking/backpacking, outdoor education, physical fitness, physical training, rock climbing. 4 PE instructors.
Computers Computers are regularly used in all academic classes. Computer network features include on-campus library services, Internet access, wireless campus network, Internet filtering or blocking technology. Campus intranet, student e-mail accounts, and computer access in designated common areas are available to students. Students grades are available online. The school has a published electronic and media policy.
Contact Ms. Kirsten Bradby, Director of Admissions. 91-135-661-5104. Fax: 91-135-263-0897. E-mail: admissions@woodstock.ac.in. Web site: www.woodstock.ac.in.

WOODWARD ACADEMY

1662 Rugby Avenue
College Park, Georgia 30337

Head of School: Mr. Stuart Gulley, PhD

General Information Coeducational day college-preparatory and arts school. Grades PK–12. Founded: 1900. Setting: suburban. Nearest major city is Atlanta. 90-acre campus. 50 buildings on campus. Approved or accredited by Georgia Independent School Association, Southern Association of Colleges and Schools, and Georgia Department of Education. Member of National Association of Independent Schools and Secondary School Admission Test Board. Endowment: $120.7 million. Total enrollment: 2,662. Upper school average class size: 17.
Faculty School total: 384. In upper school: 45 men, 68 women; 85 have advanced degrees.
Subjects Offered 20th century world history, 3-dimensional art, 3-dimensional design, acting, Advanced Placement courses, algebra, American government, American history, American history-AP, anatomy and physiology, art, astronomy, audio visual/media, band, biology, biology-AP, calculus, calculus-AP, ceramics, chemistry, chemistry-AP, choir, choral music, chorus, comparative religion, computer education, computer programming, computer programming-AP, computer science, computer science-AP, concert band, contemporary history, contemporary issues, creative writing, dance, debate, digital music, drama, drama performance, drawing, drawing and design, earth science, ecology, economics, economics and history, economics-AP, English, English language and composition-AP, English literature, English literature and composition-AP, English-AP, environmental science, environmental science-AP, European history, European history-AP, fine arts, French, French language-AP, French-AP, geography, geometry, government and politics-AP, government/civics, grammar, health, history, history-AP, honors English, honors geometry, honors U.S. history, honors world history, independent study, Japanese, jewelry making, journalism, Latin, literature and composition-AP, marching band, marine ecology, mathematics, meteorology, microeconomics-AP, Middle East, modern European history-AP, multicultural literature, music, oceanography, performing arts, personal fitness, photography, physical education, physics, physics-AP, pre-calculus, probability and statistics, science, social studies, Spanish, Spanish language-AP, Spanish-AP, speech communications, statistics, statistics-AP, television, the Sixties, theater, trigonometry, U.S. government and politics, U.S. government and politics-AP, U.S. history, U.S. history-AP, video, voice ensemble, world history, world literature, world religions, yearbook.
Graduation Requirements Arts and fine arts (art, music, dance, drama), computer science, English, foreign language, mathematics, physical education (includes health), religion (includes Bible studies and theology), science, social studies (includes history).
Special Academic Programs 22 Advanced Placement exams for which test preparation is offered; honors section; independent study.
College Admission Counseling 269 students graduated in 2011; all went to college, including Auburn University; Georgia Institute of Technology; Georgia Southern University; The University of Alabama; University of Georgia.
Student Life Upper grades have uniform requirement, student council, honor system. Discipline rests primarily with faculty.
Tuition and Aid Day student tuition: $21,300. Tuition installment plan (SMART Tuition Payment Plan, Your Tuition Solution—Springstone Financial, Sallie Mae). Need-based scholarship grants available. In 2011–12, 10% of upper-school students received aid.
Admissions Traditional secondary-level entrance grade is 9. SSAT required. Deadline for receipt of application materials: March 1. Application fee required: $75. On-campus interview required.
Athletics Interscholastic: baseball (boys), basketball (b,g), cheering (g), cross-country running (b,g), diving (b,g), football (b), golf (b,g), lacrosse (b,g), soccer (b,g), softball (g), swimming and diving (b,g), tennis (b,g), track and field (b,g), volleyball (g); intramural: basketball (b,g), cheering (g), football (b), soccer (b,g), softball (g), swimming and diving (b,g), tennis (b,g), track and field (b,g), volleyball (g); coed interscholastic: Frisbee, power lifting, ultimate Frisbee, weight lifting; coed intramural: fencing, horseback riding. 4 PE instructors, 34 coaches, 1 athletic trainer.

Computers Computers are regularly used in creative writing, English, foreign language, graphic design, journalism, literary magazine, mathematics, media production, newspaper, science, yearbook classes. Computer network features include on-campus library services, online commercial services, Internet access, wireless campus network. Student e-mail accounts are available to students. Students grades are available online.
Contact Russell L. Slider, Vice President/Dean of Admissions. 404-765-4001. Fax: 404-765-4009. E-mail: rusty.slider@woodward.edu. Web site: www.woodward.edu.

THE WOODWARD SCHOOL

1102 Hancock Street

Quincy, Massachusetts 02169

Head of School: Carol Andrews, JD

General Information Girls' day college-preparatory, arts, and technology school. Grades 6–12. Founded: 1869. Setting: urban. Nearest major city is Boston. 2-acre campus. 2 buildings on campus. Approved or accredited by Association of Independent Schools in New England, New England Association of Schools and Colleges, and Massachusetts Department of Education. Total enrollment: 140. Upper school average class size: 12. Upper school faculty-student ratio: 1:8. There are 165 required school days per year for Upper School students. Upper School students typically attend 5 days per week. The average school day consists of 6 hours and 35 minutes.
Upper School Student Profile Grade 9: 22 students (22 girls); Grade 10: 25 students (25 girls); Grade 11: 27 students (27 girls); Grade 12: 24 students (24 girls).
Faculty School total: 19. In upper school: 3 men, 16 women; 12 have advanced degrees.
Subjects Offered Advanced computer applications, algebra, American history, American literature, anatomy, art, arts, biology, calculus, calculus-AP, chemistry, classical studies, classics, community service, computer graphics, computer science, constitutional law, drama, ecology, English, English language and composition-AP, environmental science, filmmaking, fine arts, French, health and wellness, health science, language arts, Latin, Latin-AP, law and the legal system, literature, literature and composition-AP, mathematics, media studies, physics, physics-AP, physiology, political science, portfolio art, pre-algebra, psychology, science, social sciences, social studies, Spanish, theater arts, U.S. government, U.S. history, Web authoring, Web site design, world history, world literature, World War II, writing.
Graduation Requirements Arts and fine arts (art, music, dance, drama), computer science, English, foreign language, mathematics, science, social studies (includes history), Senior Project. Community service is required.
Special Academic Programs 6 Advanced Placement exams for which test preparation is offered; honors section; independent study; ESL (11 students enrolled).
College Admission Counseling 20 students graduated in 2011; all went to college, including Boston College; Boston University; College of the Holy Cross; Northeastern University; Providence College; University of Massachusetts Amherst.
Student Life Upper grades have specified standards of dress, student council, honor system. Discipline rests primarily with faculty.
Tuition and Aid Day student tuition: $12,200. Tuition installment plan (SMART Tuition Payment Plan, monthly payment plans, individually arranged payment plans). Tuition reduction for siblings, merit scholarship grants, need-based scholarship grants, prepGate K-12 Education Loan available. In 2011–12, 47% of upper-school students received aid; total upper-school merit-scholarship money awarded: $27,000. Total amount of financial aid awarded in 2011–12: $185,240.
Admissions Traditional secondary-level entrance grade is 9. For fall 2011, 52 students applied for upper-level admission, 45 were accepted, 28 enrolled. ISEE, school's own exam, SSAT or writing sample required. Deadline for receipt of application materials: none. Application fee required: $40. Interview required.
Athletics Interscholastic: basketball, soccer, softball. 2 PE instructors, 6 coaches, 1 athletic trainer.
Computers Computers are regularly used in all academic classes. Computer network features include on-campus library services, Internet access, wireless campus network, Internet filtering or blocking technology. Computer access in designated common areas is available to students. The school has a published electronic and media policy.
Contact Sarah Jacobs, Director of Admissions. 617-773-5610. Fax: 617-770-1551. E-mail: sjacobs@thewoodwardschool.org. Web site: www.thewoodwardschool.org.

WORCESTER ACADEMY

81 Providence Street

Worcester, Massachusetts 01604

Head of School: Dexter P. Morse

General Information Coeducational boarding and day college-preparatory, arts, technology, and ESL school. Boarding grades 9–PG, day grades 6–12. Founded: 1834. Setting: urban. Nearest major city is Boston. Students are housed in single-sex dormitories. 60-acre campus. 14 buildings on campus. Approved or accredited by Association of Independent Schools in New England, New England Association of Schools and Colleges, and The Association of Boarding Schools. Member of National Association of Independent Schools and Secondary School Admission Test Board. Endowment: $22 million. Total enrollment: 651. Upper school average class size: 13. Upper school faculty-student ratio: 1:8. There are 160 required school days per year for Upper School students. Upper School students typically attend 5 days per week. The average school day consists of 6 hours and 45 minutes.
Upper School Student Profile Grade 6: 30 students (19 boys, 11 girls); Grade 7: 59 students (37 boys, 22 girls); Grade 8: 71 students (31 boys, 40 girls); Grade 9: 94 students (47 boys, 47 girls); Grade 10: 128 students (63 boys, 65 girls); Grade 11: 115 students (58 boys, 57 girls); Grade 12: 127 students (70 boys, 57 girls); Postgraduate: 27 students (26 boys, 1 girl). 33% of students are boarding students. 72% are state residents. 15 states are represented in upper school student body. 20% are international students. International students from China, Hong Kong, Japan, Republic of Korea, Taiwan, and Viet Nam; 15 other countries represented in student body.
Faculty School total: 113. In upper school: 58 men, 45 women; 61 have advanced degrees; 27 reside on campus.
Subjects Offered Acting, advanced studio art-AP, algebra, American history, American history-AP, American literature, American studies, anatomy, Ancient Greek, architecture, art, art-AP, band, biology, biology-AP, British literature, calculus, calculus-AP, ceramics, chemistry, chemistry-AP, Chinese, choral music, chorus, computer programming, computer science-AP, contemporary issues, creative writing, directing, economics, English, English language-AP, English literature, English literature-AP, English-AP, environmental science, environmental studies, ESL, ESL, ethics, European history, European history-AP, French, geography, geometry, government-AP, health, history, Holocaust studies, honors English, honors world history, human anatomy, journalism, Latin, mathematics, music, music theory, physical education, physics, post-calculus, pre-algebra, pre-calculus, sculpture, Spanish, statistics, studio art-AP, U.S. government and politics-AP, U.S. history-AP, world history, world history-AP, world religions, World War II.
Graduation Requirements Algebra, American literature, arts and fine arts (art, music, dance, drama), biology, chemistry, English, foreign language, geometry, health and wellness, mathematics, physical education (includes health), social sciences, U.S. history, world literature, writing, senior projects, community service.
Special Academic Programs 16 Advanced Placement exams for which test preparation is offered; honors section; independent study; ESL (8 students enrolled).
College Admission Counseling 148 students graduated in 2010; all went to college, including Boston College; Bowdoin College; College of the Holy Cross; Emory University; University of Illinois at Urbana–Champaign; Worcester Polytechnic Institute. Mean SAT critical reading: 560, mean SAT math: 620, mean composite ACT: 26. 35% scored over 600 on SAT critical reading, 40% scored over 600 on SAT math, 50% scored over 26 on composite ACT.
Student Life Upper grades have specified standards of dress, student council, honor system. Discipline rests equally with students and faculty.
Tuition and Aid Day student tuition: $26,610; 5-day tuition and room/board: $40,060; 7-day tuition and room/board: $47,070. Tuition installment plan (Academic Management Services Plan). Need-based scholarship grants, paying campus jobs available. In 2010–11, 36% of upper-school students received aid. Total amount of financial aid awarded in 2010–11: $4,400,000.
Admissions Traditional secondary-level entrance grade is 9. For fall 2010, 428 students applied for upper-level admission, 229 were accepted, 117 enrolled. ACT, ISEE, PSAT or SAT for applicants to grade 11 and 12, SSAT or TOEFL required. Deadline for receipt of application materials: January 15. Application fee required: $50. Interview required.
Athletics Interscholastic: baseball (boys), basketball (b,g), cross-country running (b,g), field hockey (g), football (b), ice hockey (b,g), lacrosse (g), skiing (downhill) (b,g), soccer (b,g), softball (g), tennis (b,g), track and field (b,g), volleyball (g), wrestling (b); coed interscholastic: crew, golf, swimming and diving; coed intramural: aerobics/dance, dance team, paddle tennis. 3 PE instructors, 5 coaches, 3 athletic trainers.
Computers Computers are regularly used in all academic, art, college planning, library, media arts, music, theater arts, video film production, yearbook classes. Computer network features include on-campus library services, online commercial services, Internet access, wireless campus network, Internet filtering or blocking technology. Campus intranet, student e-mail accounts, and computer access in designated common areas are available to students. Students grades are available online. The school has a published electronic and media policy.
Contact Gregory Cappello, Director of Admission. 508-754-5302 Ext. 199. Fax: 508-752-2382. E-mail: gregory.cappello@worcesteracademy.org. Web site: www.worcesteracademy.org.

WORCESTER PREPARATORY SCHOOL

508 South Main Street

PO Box 1006

Berlin, Maryland 21811

Head of School: Dr. Barry W. Tull

General Information Coeducational day college-preparatory, arts, and technology school. Grades PK–12. Founded: 1970. Setting: small town. Nearest major city is Ocean City. 45-acre campus. 7 buildings on campus. Approved or accredited by Association of Independent Maryland Schools, Middle States Association of Colleges and

Schools, and Maryland Department of Education. Member of National Association of Independent Schools. Total enrollment: 535. Upper school average class size: 14. Upper school faculty-student ratio: 1:9. There are 173 required school days per year for Upper School students. Upper School students typically attend 5 days per week. The average school day consists of 6 hours and 30 minutes.

Upper School Student Profile Grade 9: 54 students (24 boys, 30 girls); Grade 10: 52 students (25 boys, 27 girls); Grade 11: 49 students (28 boys, 21 girls); Grade 12: 57 students (24 boys, 33 girls).

Faculty School total: 62. In upper school: 13 men, 21 women; 29 have advanced degrees.

Subjects Offered Advanced Placement courses, algebra, American history, American literature, art, art history, biology, biology-AP, calculus, calculus-AP, chemistry, chemistry-AP, computer programming, computer science, creative writing, dance, dance performance, drama, earth science, economics, English, English literature, English literature and composition-AP, English-AP, European history, fine arts, French, geography, geometry, government/civics, Latin, literature and composition-AP, literature-AP, mathematics, military history, music, music theory, physical education, physics, physics-AP, psychology, SAT preparation, science, social sciences, social studies, Spanish, speech, statistics, technological applications, technology/design, theater, typing, U.S. history-AP, vocal music, world history, world history-AP, world literature, writing.

Graduation Requirements Art appreciation, arts and fine arts (art, music, dance, drama), computer science, English, foreign language, mathematics, music appreciation, physical education (includes health), science, social sciences.

Special Academic Programs 8 Advanced Placement exams for which test preparation is offered; honors section; independent study; academic accommodation for the gifted.

College Admission Counseling 39 students graduated in 2011; all went to college, including American University; College of Charleston; Duke University; University of Maryland, College Park; Wake Forest University; Yale University.

Student Life Upper grades have uniform requirement, student council, honor system. Discipline rests primarily with faculty.

Tuition and Aid Day student tuition: $11,490. Tuition installment plan (Key Tuition Payment Plan, monthly payment plans, individually arranged payment plans). Need-based scholarship grants available. In 2011–12, 1% of upper-school students received aid.

Admissions Traditional secondary-level entrance grade is 9. For fall 2011, 16 students applied for upper-level admission, 13 were accepted, 11 enrolled. Achievement/Aptitude/Writing and writing sample required. Deadline for receipt of application materials: none. Application fee required: $50. On-campus interview required.

Athletics Interscholastic: basketball (boys, girls), field hockey (g), lacrosse (b,g), soccer (b,g), tennis (b,g), volleyball (g), weight training (b,g), winter soccer (b,g); intramural: basketball (b,g), dance (b,g), dance squad (b,g), flag football (b,g), soccer (b,g); coed interscholastic: cheering, golf, tennis; coed intramural: dance, dance squad. 3 PE instructors, 3 coaches, 1 athletic trainer.

Computers Computers are regularly used in all classes. Computer network features include on-campus library services, online commercial services, Internet access, wireless campus network, Internet filtering or blocking technology. Campus intranet, student e-mail accounts, and computer access in designated common areas are available to students. The school has a published electronic and media policy.

Contact Tara F. Becker, Director of Admissions. 410-641-3575 Ext. 107. Fax: 410-641-3586. E-mail: tbecker@worcesterprep.org. Web site: www.worcesterprep.org.

WYOMING SEMINARY

201 North Sprague Avenue

Kingston, Pennsylvania 18704-3593

Head of School: Dr. Kip P. Nygren

General Information Coeducational boarding and day college-preparatory school, affiliated with United Methodist Church. Boarding grades 9–PG, day grades PK–PG. Founded: 1844. Setting: suburban. Nearest major city is Wilkes-Barre. Students are housed in single-sex dormitories. 22-acre campus. 12 buildings on campus. Approved or accredited by Middle States Association of Colleges and Schools, Pennsylvania Association of Independent Schools, The Association of Boarding Schools, The College Board, and Pennsylvania Department of Education. Member of National Association of Independent Schools and Secondary School Admission Test Board. Endowment: $39 million. Total enrollment: 771. Upper school average class size: 14. Upper school faculty-student ratio: 1:10. There are 170 required school days per year for Upper School students. Upper School students typically attend 5 days per week. The average school day consists of 7 hours.

Upper School Student Profile Grade 9: 84 students (45 boys, 39 girls); Grade 10: 96 students (47 boys, 49 girls); Grade 11: 116 students (64 boys, 52 girls); Grade 12: 112 students (54 boys, 58 girls); Postgraduate: 19 students (18 boys, 1 girl). 45% of students are boarding students. 50% are state residents. 16 states are represented in upper school student body. 20% are international students. International students from China, Germany, Japan, Republic of Korea, Thailand, and Viet Nam; 15 other countries represented in student body. 10% of students are United Methodist Church.

Faculty School total: 124. In upper school: 37 men, 25 women; 35 have advanced degrees; 30 reside on campus.

Subjects Offered 20th century world history, 3-dimensional design, advanced computer applications, African American history, African history, algebra, alternative physical education, American Civil War, American history, American literature, analysis, analysis and differential calculus, analytic geometry, anatomy and physiology, ancient world history, animal behavior, art, art appreciation, art history, art history-AP, astronomy, Bible studies, biology, biology-AP, botany, British literature, calculus, calculus-AP, ceramics, chemistry, chemistry-AP, choral music, civil rights, college admission preparation, college counseling, community service, computer education, computer graphics, computer programming, computer science, conceptual physics, creative writing, critical writing, dance, discrete mathematics, drama, drawing and design, ecology, economics, economics and history, English, English literature, environmental science, environmental science-AP, ESL, European history, European history-AP, expository writing, fine arts, forensics, French, French-AP, geometry, health education, history, history of music, honors geometry, independent study, Judaic studies, Latin, Latin-AP, marine biology, mathematics, microeconomics, music, music theory, music theory-AP, philosophy, photography, physical education, physics, poetry, pre-calculus, printmaking, psychology, psychology-AP, public speaking, religion, Russian, Russian literature, science, science research, Shakespeare, social studies, sociology, Spanish, Spanish-AP, statistics, statistics-AP, studio art-AP, theater, trigonometry, U.S. government and politics-AP, U.S. history-AP, women in literature, world civilizations, world geography, world history, world literature, world religions, World War II, zoology.

Graduation Requirements Art history, Bible as literature, biology, computer science, English, foreign language, health education, mathematics, music history, physical education (includes health), public speaking, science, social studies (includes history), U.S. history, world civilizations, 40 hours of community service, extracurricular participation.

Special Academic Programs 25 Advanced Placement exams for which test preparation is offered; honors section; independent study; term-away projects; study at local college for college credit; study abroad; ESL (37 students enrolled).

College Admission Counseling 128 students graduated in 2010; 127 went to college, including Boston College; Boston University; Bucknell University; Drexel University; Fordham University; New York University. Other: 1 entered a postgraduate year. Mean SAT critical reading: 568, mean SAT math: 597, mean SAT writing: 571, mean combined SAT: 1736, mean composite ACT: 25.

Student Life Upper grades have specified standards of dress, student council, honor system. Discipline rests equally with students and faculty.

Tuition and Aid Day student tuition: $20,500; 7-day tuition and room/board: $40,550. Tuition installment plan (FACTS Tuition Payment Plan, monthly payment plans). Merit scholarship grants, need-based scholarship grants, need-based loans, prepGATE loans available. In 2010–11, 50% of upper-school students received aid; total upper-school merit-scholarship money awarded: $400,000. Total amount of financial aid awarded in 2010–11: $6,000,000.

Admissions Traditional secondary-level entrance grade is 9. For fall 2010, 346 students applied for upper-level admission, 199 were accepted, 118 enrolled. ACT, PSAT or SAT for applicants to grade 11 and 12, SSAT or TOEFL or SLEP required. Deadline for receipt of application materials: none. Application fee required: $75. Interview required.

Athletics Interscholastic: baseball (boys), basketball (b,g), cross-country running (b,g), diving (b,g), field hockey (g), football (b), ice hockey (b,g), lacrosse (b,g), soccer (b,g), softball (g), swimming and diving (b,g), tennis (b,g), wrestling (b); intramural: paint ball (b), power lifting (b); coed interscholastic: golf, strength & conditioning; coed intramural: alpine skiing, backpacking, badminton, ballet, bowling, combined training, dance, fencing, fitness, flag football, Frisbee, martial arts, modern dance, Nautilus, outdoor activities, outdoor recreation, physical training, skiing (downhill), tai chi, wall climbing, yoga. 2 PE instructors, 4 coaches, 2 athletic trainers.

Computers Computers are regularly used in art, English, foreign language, history, mathematics, music, science classes. Computer network features include on-campus library services, online commercial services, Internet access, wireless campus network, Internet filtering or blocking technology. Campus intranet, student e-mail accounts, and computer access in designated common areas are available to students. The school has a published electronic and media policy.

Contact Mr. David R. Damico, Director of Admission. 570-270-2160. Fax: 570-270-2191. E-mail: admission@wyomingseminary.org. Web site: www.wyomingseminary.org.

XAVERIAN HIGH SCHOOL

7100 Shore Road

Brooklyn, New York 11209

Head of School: Mr. Robert Alesi

General Information Boys' day college-preparatory, religious studies, and technology school, affiliated with Roman Catholic Church; primarily serves students with learning disabilities. Grades 9–12. Founded: 1957. Setting: urban. 1 building on campus. Approved or accredited by Middle States Association of Colleges and Schools and New York Department of Education. Total enrollment: 1,200. Upper school average class size: 27. There are 180 required school days per year for Upper School students. Upper School students typically attend 5 days per week. The average school day consists of 6 hours.

Special Academic Programs Advanced Placement exam preparation; study at local college for college credit; academic accommodation for the gifted and the musically talented; remedial reading and/or remedial writing; remedial math.

Student Life Upper grades have uniform requirement. Attendance at religious services is required.

Summer Programs Remediation, enrichment, sports programs offered; session focuses on academic enrichment and recreation; held on campus; accepts boys; open to students from other schools. 60 students usually enrolled. 2012 schedule: June 27 to July 27. Application deadline: May 1.

Tuition and Aid Merit scholarship grants, need-based scholarship grants, need-based loans available.

Admissions New York Archdiocesan Cooperative Entrance Examination required. Application fee required: $250.

Athletics Interscholastic: aquatics, baseball, basketball, billiards, bowling, cross-country running, diving, fitness, football, golf, handball, ice hockey, indoor track, indoor track & field, lacrosse, physical fitness, physical training, power lifting, running, soccer, strength & conditioning, swimming and diving, team handball, track and field, volleyball, weight lifting, weight training, winter (indoor) track, wrestling.

Computers Computers are regularly used in all classes. Computer network features include on-campus library services, online commercial services, Internet access, wireless campus network, Internet filtering or blocking technology, students are issued iPad 2's when they enter the school. Campus intranet and student e-mail accounts are available to students. Students grades are available online. The school has a published electronic and media policy.

Contact Deacon Kevin McCormack, Principal. 718-836-7100. Fax: 718-836-7114. E-mail: kmccormack@xaverian.org. Web site: www.xaverian.org.

YOKOHAMA INTERNATIONAL SCHOOL

258 Yamate-cho, Naka-ku

Yokohama 231-0862, Japan

Head of School: Mr. James MacDonald

General Information Coeducational day college-preparatory, arts, bilingual studies, and technology school. Grades N–12. Founded: 1924. Setting: urban. 3-acre campus. 8 buildings on campus. Approved or accredited by International Baccalaureate Organization and New England Association of Schools and Colleges. Language of instruction: English. Total enrollment: 670. Upper school average class size: 16. Upper school faculty-student ratio: 1:8. There are 174 required school days per year for Upper School students. Upper School students typically attend 5 days per week. The average school day consists of 7 hours.

Upper School Student Profile Grade 6: 50 students (30 boys, 20 girls); Grade 7: 54 students (29 boys, 25 girls); Grade 8: 56 students (33 boys, 23 girls); Grade 9: 58 students (34 boys, 24 girls); Grade 10: 62 students (22 boys, 40 girls); Grade 11: 57 students (26 boys, 31 girls); Grade 12: 61 students (29 boys, 32 girls).

Faculty School total: 90. In upper school: 30 men, 20 women; 23 have advanced degrees.

Subjects Offered Advanced chemistry, advanced math, art, band, biology, ceramics, chemistry, choir, computer programming, drama, Dutch, economics, English, English literature, environmental science, French, geography, German, information technology, International Baccalaureate courses, Japanese, mathematics, modern languages, music composition, music theory, physical education, physics, Spanish, studio art, theater, theater arts, theory of knowledge, world history, world literature.

Graduation Requirements Arts, English, foreign language, information technology, mathematics, physical education (includes health), science, senior thesis, social studies (includes history), theory of knowledge, 50 hours of community service.

Special Academic Programs International Baccalaureate program; ESL.

College Admission Counseling 59 students graduated in 2010; 54 went to college, including New York University; The University of British Columbia; University of Toronto. Other: 5 had other specific plans. Mean SAT critical reading: 550, mean SAT math: 586, mean SAT writing: 556.

Student Life Upper grades have specified standards of dress, student council. Discipline rests primarily with faculty.

Tuition and Aid Day student tuition: ¥2,250,000. Tuition installment plan (individually arranged payment plans).

Admissions Traditional secondary-level entrance grade is 9. For fall 2010, 50 students applied for upper-level admission, 24 were accepted, 18 enrolled. School's own test required. Deadline for receipt of application materials: none. Application fee required: ¥20,000. Interview recommended.

Athletics Interscholastic: baseball (boys), basketball (b,g), cross-country running (b,g), field hockey (g), soccer (b,g), track and field (b,g), volleyball (g); coed interscholastic: tennis; coed intramural: backpacking, ball hockey, bicycling, canoeing/kayaking, diving, floor hockey, gymnastics, hiking/backpacking, kayaking, netball, outdoor education, skateboarding, skiing (downhill), yoga. 4 PE instructors.

Computers Computers are regularly used in all academic classes. Computer network features include on-campus library services, online commercial services, Internet access, wireless campus network, Internet filtering or blocking technology. Campus intranet, student e-mail accounts, and computer access in designated common areas are available to students. Students grades are available online. The school has a published electronic and media policy.

Contact Ms. Susan Chen, Administrative Officer. 81-45-622-0084. Fax: 81-45-621-0379. E-mail: admissions@yis.ac.jp. Web site: www.yis.ac.jp.

YORK CATHOLIC HIGH SCHOOL

601 East Springettsbury Avenue

York, Pennsylvania 17403

Head of School: Mr. George E. Andrews Jr.

General Information Coeducational day college-preparatory and general academic school, affiliated with Roman Catholic Church. Grades 7–12. Founded: 1927. Setting: suburban. 19-acre campus. 1 building on campus. Approved or accredited by Middle States Association of Colleges and Schools, National Catholic Education Association, and Pennsylvania Department of Education. Total enrollment: 636. Upper school average class size: 21. The average school day consists of 6 hours and 45 minutes.

Upper School Student Profile Grade 9: 99 students (40 boys, 59 girls); Grade 10: 106 students (49 boys, 57 girls); Grade 11: 136 students (60 boys, 76 girls); Grade 12: 99 students (52 boys, 47 girls). 89% of students are Roman Catholic.

College Admission Counseling 110 students graduated in 2011; 104 went to college. Other: 6 entered military service. Median SAT critical reading: 557, median SAT math: 528, median SAT writing: 560, median combined SAT: 1645.

Student Life Upper grades have uniform requirement, student council, honor system. Discipline rests primarily with faculty. Attendance at religious services is required.

Tuition and Aid Day student tuition: $4875. Tuition installment plan (SMART Tuition Payment Plan). Tuition reduction for siblings, need-based scholarship grants available. In 2011–12, 28% of upper-school students received aid. Total amount of financial aid awarded in 2011–12: $250,000.

Admissions Deadline for receipt of application materials: none. No application fee required. Interview required.

Athletics Interscholastic: baseball (boys), basketball (b,g), cross-country running (b,g), diving (b,g), football (b), golf (b,g), lacrosse (b,g), running (b,g), soccer (b,g), softball (g), swimming and diving (b,g), tennis (b,g), track and field (b,g), volleyball (g), wrestling (b); intramural: strength & conditioning (b); coed intramural: bowling, ice hockey, skiing (downhill), table tennis.

Computers Computer resources include on-campus library services, Internet access, Internet filtering or blocking technology. Campus intranet is available to students. Students grades are available online. The school has a published electronic and media policy.

Contact Ms. Heather Hoffman, Director of Admissions. 717-846-8871 Ext. 20. Fax: 717-843-4588. E-mail: hhoffman@yorkcatholic.org. Web site: www.yorkcatholic.org.

YORK COUNTRY DAY SCHOOL

1071 Regents Glen Boulevard

York, Pennsylvania 17403

Head of School: Nathaniel W. Coffman

General Information Coeducational day college-preparatory, arts, and bilingual studies school. Grades PS–12. Founded: 1953. Setting: suburban. Nearest major city is Baltimore, MD. 15-acre campus. 1 building on campus. Approved or accredited by Middle States Association of Colleges and Schools, Pennsylvania Association of Independent Schools, and Pennsylvania Department of Education. Member of National Association of Independent Schools. Endowment: $1.3 million. Total enrollment: 217. Upper school average class size: 12. Upper school faculty-student ratio: 1:6. There are 170 required school days per year for Upper School students. Upper School students typically attend 5 days per week. The average school day consists of 7 hours and 30 minutes.

Upper School Student Profile Grade 9: 14 students (5 boys, 9 girls); Grade 10: 13 students (9 boys, 4 girls); Grade 11: 18 students (12 boys, 6 girls); Grade 12: 16 students (7 boys, 9 girls).

Faculty School total: 42. In upper school: 10 men, 8 women; 12 have advanced degrees.

Subjects Offered Advanced biology, advanced chemistry, advanced studio art-AP, algebra, American history, American history-AP, American literature, art, art history, biochemistry, biology, calculus, calculus-AP, chemistry, choral music, community service, computer programming, computer science, creative writing, drama, English, English literature, English literature-AP, European history, fine arts, French, French-AP, geography, geometry, government/civics, health, history, Latin, literature, mathematics, music, physical education, physics, psychology, public speaking, science, social studies, Spanish, Spanish language-AP, studio art-AP, theater, world history, world history-AP.

Graduation Requirements Arts and fine arts (art, music, dance, drama), English, foreign language, history, independent study, mathematics, physical education (includes health), public speaking, science, visual arts, independent study (3 semesters) through our Magnet Program, two semester classes. Community service is required.

Special Academic Programs Advanced Placement exam preparation; honors section; independent study; term-away projects; study at local college for college credit; study abroad; academic accommodation for the gifted, the musically talented, and the artistically talented.
College Admission Counseling 14 students graduated in 2011; all went to college, including Gettysburg College; Penn State University Park; University of Pittsburgh; University of Richmond; Ursinus College; York College of Pennsylvania. Median SAT critical reading: 540, median SAT math: 510.
Student Life Upper grades have specified standards of dress, student council, honor system. Discipline rests equally with students and faculty.
Summer Programs Sports, art/fine arts programs offered; session focuses on provide sports, arts, crafts, and swimming; held off campus; held at York College of Pennsylvania; accepts boys and girls; open to students from other schools. 35 students usually enrolled. 2012 schedule: June 20 to July 31. Application deadline: June 15.
Tuition and Aid Day student tuition: $16,850. Tuition installment plan (Insured Tuition Payment Plan, monthly payment plans, semester payment plan). Need-based scholarship grants available. In 2011–12, 39% of upper-school students received aid. Total amount of financial aid awarded in 2011–12: $306,250.
Admissions Traditional secondary-level entrance grade is 9. 3-R Achievement Test, Academic Profile Tests, California Achievement Test, ISEE, Otis-Lennon Ability or Stanford Achievement Test or PSAT and SAT for applicants to grade 11 and 12 required. Deadline for receipt of application materials: none. Application fee required: $35. On-campus interview required.
Athletics Interscholastic: baseball (boys), basketball (b,g), bowling (b,g), cross-country running (b,g), field hockey (g), football (b), golf (b,g), soccer (b,g), softball (g), swimming and diving (b,g), tennis (b,g), volleyball (g), wrestling (b); intramural: basketball (b,g), soccer (b,g); coed intramural: soccer. 2 PE instructors, 6 coaches.
Computers Computers are regularly used in all academic classes. Computer network features include on-campus library services, online commercial services, Internet access, Internet filtering or blocking technology. Student e-mail accounts are available to students.
Contact Ms. Alison C. Greer, Director of Admission and Communication. 717-843-9805. Fax: 717-815-6769. E-mail: agreer@ycds.org. Web site: www.ycds.org.

YORK PREPARATORY SCHOOL

40 West 68th Street

New York, New York 10023-6092

Head of School: Ronald P. Stewart

General Information Coeducational day college-preparatory, arts, technology, music (practical and theory), and drama school. Grades 6–12. Founded: 1969. Setting: urban. 1 building on campus. Approved or accredited by Middle States Association of Colleges and Schools, National Independent Private Schools Association, New York State Board of Regents, and New York Department of Education. Member of National Association of Independent Schools. Total enrollment: 351. Upper school average class size: 15. Upper school faculty-student ratio: 1:6. There are 158 required school days per year for Upper School students. Upper School students typically attend 5 days per week. The average school day consists of 6 hours and 30 minutes.
Upper School Student Profile Grade 9: 66 students (36 boys, 30 girls); Grade 10: 61 students (33 boys, 28 girls); Grade 11: 70 students (43 boys, 27 girls); Grade 12: 53 students (31 boys, 22 girls).
Faculty School total: 64. In upper school: 20 men, 41 women; 48 have advanced degrees.
Subjects Offered 20th century history, 20th century world history, 3-dimensional art, advanced chemistry, advanced computer applications, Advanced Placement courses, advanced studio art-AP, algebra, American history, American history-AP, American literature, anatomy, animation, anthropology, art, art appreciation, astronomy, biology, calculus, calculus-AP, ceramics, chemistry, chemistry-AP, comparative religion, computer math, computer programming, computer science, computer skills, concert band, creative writing, current events, drama, drama performance, driver education, earth science, economics, English, English literature, English-AP, environmental science, ethics, European history, expository writing, filmmaking, fine arts, French, genetics, geography, geology, geometry, government/civics, grammar, health education, Holocaust studies, law, literary magazine, mathematics, music, music history, philosophy, photography, physical education, physics, physiology, political science, politics, pre-calculus, psychology, reading/study skills, research skills, SAT preparation, science, science project, social studies, Spanish, statistics, theater, trigonometry, typing, world history, world literature, writing, zoology.
Graduation Requirements Arts and fine arts (art, music, dance, drama), English, foreign language, mathematics, physical education (includes health), science, social studies (includes history), 100 hours of community service. Community service is required.
Special Academic Programs Advanced Placement exam preparation; honors section; accelerated programs; independent study; study at local college for college credit; academic accommodation for the gifted, the musically talented, and the artistically talented; programs in English, mathematics, general development for dyslexic students; special instructional classes for students with mild learning issues (extra tutoring program); ESL (4 students enrolled).

College Admission Counseling 66 students graduated in 2011; all went to college, including Cornell University; Hobart and William Smith Colleges; New York University; Syracuse University; University of Vermont; Vassar College.

Student Life Upper grades have specified standards of dress, student council, honor system. Discipline rests primarily with faculty.

Summer Programs Remediation, advancement programs offered; held on campus; accepts boys and girls; not open to students from other schools. 30 students usually enrolled. 2012 schedule: June 15 to July 31. Application deadline: none.

Tuition and Aid Day student tuition: $38,750–$39,350. Tuition installment plan (Insured Tuition Payment Plan, monthly payment plans, individually arranged payment plans). Tuition reduction for siblings, bursaries, merit scholarship grants, need-based scholarship grants available. In 2011–12, 20% of upper-school students received aid. Total amount of financial aid awarded in 2011–12: $750,000.

Admissions Traditional secondary-level entrance grade is 9. ISEE required. Deadline for receipt of application materials: January 15. Application fee required: $50. On-campus interview required.

Athletics Interscholastic: baseball (boys), basketball (b,g), cross-country running (b,g), softball (b,g), volleyball (b,g); intramural: volleyball (b,g); coed interscholastic: basketball, cross-country running, golf, soccer, tennis, track and field; coed intramural: aerobics, aerobics/dance, aquatics, backpacking, basketball, bowling, cross-country running, dance, fitness, Frisbee, golf, indoor track, judo, lacrosse, roller hockey, skiing (downhill), soccer, softball, swimming and diving, ultimate Frisbee, weight training, yoga. 6 PE instructors, 6 coaches, 2 athletic trainers.

Computers Computers are regularly used in all academic classes. Computer network features include on-campus library services, online commercial services, Internet access, wireless campus network, Internet filtering or blocking technology. Computer access in designated common areas is available to students. Students grades are available online. The school has a published electronic and media policy.

Contact Ms. Cathy Minaudo, Director of Admissions. 212-362-0400 Ext. 106. Fax: 212-362-7424. E-mail: cminaudo@yorkprep.org. Web site: www.yorkprep.org.

See Display on previous page and Close-Up on page 710.

YORK SCHOOL

9501 York Road

Monterey, California 93940

Head of School: Chuck Harmon

General Information Coeducational day college-preparatory, arts, bilingual studies, and technology school, affiliated with Episcopal Church. Grades 8–12. Founded: 1959. Setting: suburban. Nearest major city is San Jose. 126-acre campus. 6 buildings on campus. Approved or accredited by National Association of Episcopal Schools, Western Association of Schools and Colleges, and California Department of Education. Member of National Association of Independent Schools. Endowment: $5.8 million. Total enrollment: 230. Upper school average class size: 13. Upper school faculty-student ratio: 1:8. Upper School students typically attend 5 days per week. The average school day consists of 7 hours.

Upper School Student Profile Grade 8: 18 students (7 boys, 11 girls); Grade 9: 62 students (34 boys, 28 girls); Grade 10: 56 students (28 boys, 28 girls); Grade 11: 43 students (17 boys, 26 girls); Grade 12: 50 students (27 boys, 23 girls).

Faculty School total: 31. In upper school: 17 men, 14 women; 24 have advanced degrees.

Subjects Offered Advanced studio art-AP, algebra, American history-AP, anatomy, ancient history, art, art history, Asian history, band, biology, biology-AP, calculus, calculus-AP, chemistry, chemistry-AP, choir, community service, computer science, creative writing, digital art, drama, English, English-AP, environmental science, film, fine arts, French, French language-AP, geometry, Greek, jazz, Latin, Latin-AP, marine biology, mathematics, music, music theory-AP, orchestra, painting, philosophy, photography, physical education, physical science, physics, physics-AP, physiology, pre-calculus, psychology-AP, science, social studies, Spanish, Spanish language-AP, studio art, U.S. history, U.S. history-AP, world history, yearbook.

Graduation Requirements Arts and fine arts (art, music, dance, drama), computer science, English, foreign language, mathematics, physical education (includes health), science, social studies (includes history), ensemble participation. Community service is required.

Special Academic Programs Advanced Placement exam preparation; honors section.

College Admission Counseling 54 students graduated in 2011; all went to college, including Stanford University; The George Washington University; University of California, Berkeley; University of Puget Sound. Mean SAT critical reading: 681, mean SAT math: 666, mean SAT writing: 666, mean combined SAT: 2013, mean composite ACT: 28.

Student Life Upper grades have specified standards of dress, student council, honor system. Discipline rests primarily with faculty.

Tuition and Aid Day student tuition: $26,375. Tuition installment plan (individually arranged payment plans, 2 Payments, 10 Payments). Need-based scholarship grants available. In 2011–12, 46% of upper-school students received aid. Total amount of financial aid awarded in 2011–12: $1,429,100.

Admissions Traditional secondary-level entrance grade is 9. For fall 2011, 133 students applied for upper-level admission. Admissions testing required. Deadline for receipt of application materials: February 15. Application fee required: $75. Interview required.

Athletics Interscholastic: basketball (boys, girls), cross-country running (b,g), diving (b,g), field hockey (g), golf (b,g), soccer (b,g), softball (g), swimming and diving (b,g), tennis (b,g), volleyball (g); coed interscholastic: lacrosse; coed intramural: badminton, basketball, fitness walking, independent competitive sports, jogging, soccer, ultimate Frisbee, volleyball, walking, weight training, yoga. 18 coaches.

Computers Computers are regularly used in computer applications, technology, yearbook classes. Computer network features include on-campus library services, Internet access, wireless campus network. The school has a published electronic and media policy.

Contact Rachel Gaudoin, Admission Associate. 831-372-7338 Ext. 116. Fax: 831-372-8055. E-mail: rachel@york.org. Web site: www.york.org.

AMERICAN HERITAGE SCHOOL

Plantation and Delray Beach, Florida

Type: Coeducational, day, independent, nonsectarian
Grades: PK-3–grade 12
Enrollment: 2,400, Plantation campus; 1,008, Boca/Delray campus
Head of School: William Laurie, President and Founder

THE SCHOOL

American Heritage School's mission is to graduate students who are prepared in mind, body, and spirit to meet the requirements of the colleges of their choice. To this end, the School strives to offer a challenging college preparatory curriculum, opportunities for leadership, and superior programs in the arts and athletics. American Heritage is committed to providing a safe and nurturing environment for learning so that children of average to gifted intelligence may achieve their full potential to be intelligent, creative, and contributing members of society. Students receive a well-rounded education that provides opportunities for leadership and character building and extensive opportunities for growth in the arts, athletics, and new technology.

ACADEMIC PROGRAMS

The curriculum for the preprimary child is developmental and age appropriate at each level. Daily language, speech, and auditory development activities help children to listen, understand, speak, and learn effectively. The program seeks to maximize the academic potential of each child, while fostering a positive self-image and providing the skills necessary for the next level of education.

The Lower School is committed to developing a student's basic skills, helping the student master content areas, and maintaining the student's enthusiasm for learning. Students learn the fundamentals of reading, process writing, mathematics, and English through a logical progressive sequence, and they learn social studies, handwriting, spelling, science, and health, with an emphasis on the development of good study skills. In math and reading, students are grouped according to ability. Enrichment classes in computer education, art, media center, music, Spanish, Chinese, physical education, and investigative science lab are offered. Field trips, special projects and events, and assemblies supplement the work introduced in class.

Math, reading, grammar, literature, social studies, and science are the core subjects of the junior high curriculum, where critical-thinking skills become increasingly important. Writing skills are emphasized, helping students become literate and articulate thinkers and writers. Enrichment courses are an important part of the junior high curriculum, with courses rotated on a nine-week basis. Honors classes are available in all core subject areas.

At the high school level, emphasis is placed on college preparation and on higher-level thinking skills. Students are challenged by required research and speech and writing assignments in all subject areas. An extensive variety of classes in all areas of the fine arts is available. A selection of electives—from marine biology to Advanced Placement Chinese to stagecraft—rounds out the students' schedules, allowing them to explore other interests and talents. In addition to traditional lecture and discussion, teachers supplement the text curriculum with activities, projects, and field trips that make subjects more relevant and meaningful to the students.

Honors and Advanced Placement (AP) courses are available to qualified students. Students may gain college credit as a benefit of the successful completion of AP courses, which include American government, American history, biology, calculus, chemistry, economics, English language, English literature, environmental studies, European history, French, music theory, physics, psychology, Spanish, and world history.

American Heritage School offers unique pre-medical, prelaw, and pre-engineering programs to qualified high school students. The programs challenge those ninth- through twelfth-grade students who have an interest in these fields of study and encourage students to consider these areas as potential career choices. The many course offerings are most often taught by working professionals in each area. In addition to course work for both programs, there are required internships that match students with professionals in their area of study.

In 2010, the school had 31 National Merit Scholarship Semifinalists and was the top-ranked private school at the National Mu Alpha Theta (mathematics honor society) annual conference.

Through the international program, in addition to an international student's regular academic classes, one to two hours of English language instruction is provided daily. Living with an American family produces more opportunity for language development and practice.

FACULTY AND ADVISERS

The students at American Heritage are served by 211 teachers, counselors, and administrators at the Plantation location and 112 teachers, counselors, and administrators at the Delray campus. Sixty-two percent hold master's or doctoral degrees. Teachers actively seek out both school-year and summer workshops to attend, and they return with creative ideas for their teaching. Faculty turnover is minimal. The faculty is also committed to the Heritage philosophy of developing good character and self-esteem as well as the reinforcement of traditional values in students. Teachers maintain close communication with parents regarding their child's progress, with frequent written progress reports, phone calls, and scheduled conference days. The school provides a Web-based service, Edline, on which students and parents can access information ranging from general school, club, and sports topics to specific content for individual classes. Classes are small, with a 17:1 student-teacher ratio.

COLLEGE ADMISSION COUNSELING

At American Heritage, the goal is to send seniors to colleges that match their goals and expectations for college life. There are 10 full-time guidance counselors in the high school, including a Director of College Placement and a Scholarship Specialist.

The college placement process begins in seventh grade with academic advising about curriculum and course selection and continues through high school with college-preparation advising. The counselors keep abreast of current admissions trends through attendance at national and local conferences and frequent contact with college admissions representatives.

The preparation for college intensifies as students in grades 9 through 12 follow a program designed to help them score well on the SATs. The program includes SAT prep mini-exercises in their English and math classes. In tenth grade and above, students may take an intensive daily SAT prep class taught on campus during the regular school day.

At this level, academic counseling gives consideration to graduation requirements and course selection, study skills and time management, leadership and club involvement, and referral to mentoring or professional tutoring, if needed. College advising is offered in the classroom on topics such as standardized test taking, the college application process, resume and essay writing, and searching for colleges and majors. The School reviews all college applications sent, writes letters of recommendation, finds scholarships for students, prepares students for college interviews, invites college admission representatives to campus, hosts a college fair, and proctors AP exams.

Virtually all graduates continue their educations and are admitted to the nation's finest colleges and universities. In recent years, graduates have been admitted to such schools as Boston College, Colgate, Columbia, Cornell, Duke, Harvard, Georgetown, MIT, NYU, Pepperdine, Princeton, Rutgers, Tufts, Wake Forest, West Point, Yale, and the Universities of Connecticut, Maryland, Pennsylvania, and Southern California.

STUDENT BODY AND CONDUCT

In the Lower School, the PK-3 classes enroll about 16 students; PK-4, 17; Kindergarten, 18; grades 1 and 2, 21; grades 3 and 4, 22; and grades 5 and 6, 23. In preschool through grade six, each class has a teacher and a full-time assistant. Grades 7 through 12 in the Upper School average 17 students.

The Plantation campus has 2,400 students, with 810 in the Lower School and 1,590 in the Upper School. The Boca/Delray student population totals 1,008, with 233 students in the Lower School and 775 in the Upper School. The School's day population is culturally diverse, with students representing forty-three countries from around the world.

ACADEMIC FACILITIES

The Plantation campus includes a fully equipped science lab, ten state-of-the-art computer rooms, and a $25-million Center for the Arts that houses a state-of-the-art 800-seat theater, a black-box theater, spacious art studios, a graphic design lab, choral and band rooms, and individual practice rooms. There are two new library/media centers, one that services the Lower School and another that meets all the technological requirements of students in the Upper School. Heritage has an excellent physical education center that includes an Olympic-sized swimming and diving facility, a gymnasium, six tennis courts, a track, four modern locker rooms, a weight-training room, and acres of well-maintained athletic fields.

The American Heritage Boca/Delray campus provides four state-of-the-art iMac computer labs, fully equipped science labs, art studios, a college guidance computer lab, a library/media center and research lab, a new $20 million center for the arts, an Olympic-sized swimming pool with eight racing lanes, a 2,600-square-foot teaching pool, a 25,000-square-foot gymnasium/auditorium, six lighted tennis courts, a football and soccer field, fully equipped weight training room, locker rooms, two well-equipped playgrounds, acres of well-maintained baseball and softball fields, practice fields for soccer and football, and beautifully landscaped grounds and courtyards.

ATHLETICS

The athletic program is an important part of the sense of community that has developed at Heritage. Parents, teachers, administrators, and students develop a special kind of camaraderie while cheering on the Patriot teams. Awards evenings are held for athletes and parents at the conclusion of each season. Heritage offers a complete competitive sports program. A "no-cut" policy allows every student who wants to participate an opportunity to play on the Patriot team of his or her choice. Coaches provide high-quality instruction in all sports. Sportsmanship, team-work, recognition of effort, and thorough training and preparation are the goals toward which the School works every day. Each year, a number of student-athletes receive financial help for their college education based on their athletic ability and their performance. More importantly, however, for those who do not have the ability—or maybe the desire—to participate at the collegiate level, athletic opportunities offer a very enjoyable and memorable experience, with accomplishments and relationships that last a lifetime. American Heritage competes as a member of the Florida High School Activities Association, and the athletics programs are consistently ranked in the top ten in the state of Florida.

EXTRACURRICULAR OPPORTUNITIES

The extensive activities offered at Heritage serve several purposes. Primarily, they assist in the growth and development of students, but they also provide opportunities for leadership and excellence, which are increasingly required for college admission. Among the activities and clubs offered to high school students are the National Honor Society; Student Council; Spanish/French Honor Society; Premed, Prelaw, and Pre-engineering Clubs; the Modern Language Club; Mu Alpha Theta (math club); SADD; the computer club; yearbook; the student newspaper; thespians; marching band; orchestra; jazz band; and chorus. Lower School students can take after-school classes in art, dance, instrumental music, karate, cooking, computers, and other areas of interest. Students may also participate in Student Council, Junior Thespians, or Math Superstars.

American Heritage School provides an outstanding fine arts program to students in PK-3 through grade 12. The Center for the Arts is a beautiful, specially designed facility that enhances the arts program. Students participating in art, music, and drama programs have won awards at local, state, and national levels of competition in recent years. This recognition includes the Florida Vocal Association (superior ratings for choir, solo, and ensemble), Florida Orchestra Association (superior ratings for solo and ensemble/guitar and strings), American Choral Directors Award, and National Scholastic Art Competition (gold and silver medals).

Many students participate in enrichment and leadership programs offered in Broward County, including the National Conference for Community and Justice, Leadership Broward, Boys and Girls Clubs, Silver Knights, and the Institute for Math and Computer Science. Nationally, students have participated in Hugh O'Brian Youth Foundation, Freedoms Foundation, Presidential Classroom, and Global Young Leaders Conference. In addition, American Heritage School is home to two nonprofit organizations: Mosaic Theatre, an organization committed to promoting the dramatic arts, where students are able to work alongside professional actors, and the Center for the Arts Scholarship Foundation, a fund-raising organization that awards scholarships to talented students in the arts.

SUMMER PROGRAMS

American Heritage has provided summer fun for young campers since 1981. Summer camp provides activities that help build confidence and self-esteem. Campers enjoy the challenges and rewards of teamwork as they work and play. Through the numerous activities that are offered, campers continue to develop the socialization skills begun in school. Campers enjoy good relationships with the high school and college counselors, who serve as role models for them. American Heritage Day Camp sessions are available for students 13 years old and under.

For students who have failed a credit course in high school or have been required by their current school to attend summer school in order to pass to the next grade level, summer school is a necessity. However, many others can benefit from American Heritage's summer academic program, including preschoolers who need readiness skills to succeed in kindergarten or first grade; elementary and junior high students who need practice and development of basic skills in math, reading, and language arts; any students who perform one or two years below grade level; students for whom English is a second language; high school students who want to advance themselves academically by earning extra credits during the summer; and high school students who will soon take the SAT or ACT tests for college admission. More information can be obtained by contacting the American Heritage School.

COSTS AND FINANCIAL AID

In 2011–12, tuition and fees total between $17,494 for preschoolers and $22,019 for twelfth-grade students. An international program is available at additional cost for the academic school year—August through May—and includes tuition, housing, three meals a day, books, uniforms, and 2 hours a day of English language.

American Heritage offers financial aid to parents who qualify.

ADMISSIONS INFORMATION

Enrollment at American Heritage School is limited to students who are above average to gifted in intelligence and who are working at or above grade level. Math, reading, vocabulary, and IQ tests are administered and are used to determine if the student has the background and basic skills necessary to be successful. The results of these entrance exams are discussed with the parents at a conference following the testing. I-20 visas are granted to international students who are accepted. Details are available from the Director of Admissions. Students are admitted without regard to race, creed, or national origin.

For acceptance into American Heritage's international program, families must supply complete academic records from the age of 12, translated into English; two teacher letters of recommendation, translated into English; copies of the student's passport; and a completed American Heritage School application form. The American Heritage Admissions Committee reviews the student's records and determines suitable placement. Full tuition for the school year is due upon acceptance. After tuition has been received, the School issues an I-20 form, which must be taken to the U.S. Embassy in the student's country to obtain a student visa.

APPLICATION TIMETABLE

First-semester classes begin in mid-August. For information regarding specific deadlines, students should contact American Heritage School's Plantation campus.

ADMISSIONS CORRESPONDENCE

Attn: Admissions
American Heritage School
12200 West Broward Boulevard
Plantation, Florida 33325

Phone: 954-472-0022
E-mail: admissions@ahschool.com
Web site: http://www.ahschool.com

American Heritage School Boca/Delray
6200 Linton Boulevard
Delray Beach, Florida 33484

Phone: 561-495-7272
E-mail: admissions@mailhost.ahschoolbd.com
Web site: http://www.ahschool.com

THE AMERICAN SCHOOL IN LONDON

London, England

The American School in London

Type: Coeducational day college-preparatory school
Grades: PK–12: Lower School, Prekindergarten–4; Middle School, 5–8; High School, 9–12
Enrollment: School total: 1,350; High School: 468
Head of School: Mrs. Coreen R. Hester

THE SCHOOL

The American School in London (ASL), the oldest American-curriculum school in the U.K., was founded by Stephen L. Eckard in 1951 to provide an American curriculum for children of American business and government personnel on assignment in London. The School aims to provide a challenging academic program that allows graduates a wide choice of colleges and universities and the continuity of an American curriculum for students coming from and returning to American and international schools. Students of all nationalities who can meet the scholastic standards, including non-English speakers below the age of 11, are welcome to apply.

The School is situated in St. John's Wood, a residential area of London just north of Regent's Park. Underground transport and public buses are available in the neighborhood, and the School offers a door-to-door transport service. Visits to the museums, theaters, and art galleries of London are a regular part of the curriculum, and historic sites in England and Wales are easily accessible from the School. London's central location and well-connected transportation system permit easy travel for student field studies, and student trips are regularly taken in London, the U.K., and Europe.

The School is owned by the American School in London Educational Trust and is registered as a charity in the United Kingdom and as a nonprofit foundation in the United States. It is governed by a Board of Trustees with 26 full-time members from the community. The plant is owned by the School.

The School enjoys an enthusiastic response and avid support from more than 4,000 alumni and friends of ASL.

The School is accredited by the Middle States Association of Colleges and Schools and the Council of International Schools (CIS) and is a member of the National Association of Independent Schools, the European Council of International Schools, the Council for the Advancement and Support of Education, the Educational Records Bureau, and CIS.

ACADEMIC PROGRAMS

The curriculum of the High School is college preparatory. To graduate, a student must complete at least 18 credits, including 4 years of English; 3 each of social sciences and one modern language; 2 each of mathematics, science, and visual arts and/or performing arts; 1 of physical education; ½ of computer science; and ½ of health. The School recommends at least 1 additional year of modern language, science, mathematics, and fine arts. Freshmen, sophomores, and juniors must take five academics (English, modern language, history, mathematics, science) per year, and five are recommended for seniors. Elective courses are available in all subject areas. Some examples are Shakespeare, world literature, journalism, band, play production, digital imaging, psychology, photography, Japanese, human geography, and astronomy.

ASL offers the largest selection of Advanced Placement courses (more than twenty) outside the U.S.; they include American history, European history, calculus (2), statistics, economics, computer science, biology, chemistry, physics (2), art history, French (2), Spanish (2), studio art, and music theory. Other courses can be taken on an independent-study basis.

Classes in basic academic courses are not usually grouped by grade level but tend toward ability grouping in each academic discipline. In modern languages, all classes are grouped by ability. The average class size is 15, and the student-teacher ratio is 11:1.

The school year is divided into two semesters. Grade reports are sent out at the end of each semester. The grading system uses letter grades of A to F. Students who receive two unsatisfactory grades (below C–) or one failing grade for any one marking period are put on academic probation.

Once a year, High School students have a three- to five-day program called Alternatives, which is an experiential learning program. Students can choose a course from among twenty-eight options, including tours, outdoor/indoor activities, travel, and community service activities.

FACULTY AND ADVISERS

The High School faculty consists of 17 men and 30 women. Most hold graduate degrees.

Coreen R. Hester became the seventh head at the American School in London in 2007. Most recently, Mrs. Hester was the head of the Hamlin School in San Francisco, California, for ten years. Prior to her appointment at Hamlin she was ASL's High School Principal, from 1995 to 1997. Early in her career, Mrs. Hester taught English at University Liggett School in Grosse Pointe, Michigan. Later, she spent ten years at the Branson School as teacher, dean, college counselor, Assistant Head, and Interim Head of School. Mrs. Hester was also previously Director of the Western Region of Independent Educational Services. Mrs. Hester holds an A.B. in English and an A.M. in education from Stanford University.

The School hires teachers who are willing to devote the extra time required for excellence and are interested in working with the individual student, within a program that calls for imaginative instruction.

Sabbaticals can be applied for after seven years; three are awarded each year. The School encourages teacher exchanges.

COLLEGE ADMISSION COUNSELING

The High School has 3 class deans, 3 college counselors, and 1 personal counselor, who are available to students for a range of counseling services. The class deans oversee the adviser program for grades 9 through 11, and every student in grade 12 is assigned to a college counselor. A wide selection of reference materials and catalogs is constantly updated to aid students in their college choices. The college search begins with a college information session that is held midyear for the parents of juniors. A junior class meeting in February after receipt of the PSAT results establishes a schedule for seminars and individual sessions on the application process. Individual interviews are held with each student, and summer visits to selected colleges are recommended. In addition, more than 80 college admissions representatives visit the School each year. Students may take the full range of tests required for admission to colleges at the School.

The mean scores on the SAT for the class of 2011 were 659 critical reading, 669 writing, and 669 math. ASL graduates are attending Brown, Georgetown, NYU, and Princeton, among others. In 2011, scores of 3 or higher were obtained on 92 percent of AP exams taken.

STUDENT BODY AND CONDUCT

There are currently 468 students in the High School. The distribution is as follows: grade 9, 127; grade 10, 123; grade 11, 115; and grade 12, 103. There are nearly equal numbers of boys and girls in all grades. Although the majority of the students are U.S. citizens, more than forty-five nationalities are represented in the student body.

The School has a well-defined code of conduct concerning such issues as drugs, alcohol, theft, and plagiarism. Serious violations, although rare, may result in suspension or expulsion.

ACADEMIC FACILITIES

The School building is of modular design and houses all three divisions. There are eighty classrooms and nine science laboratories, seven computer centers, five music rooms, five art studios, two theaters, two gymnasiums, a writing lab, a ceramics room, and two libraries containing more than 50,000 volumes, a large media center, and a recording studio. A computer network with 1,600 network outlets, a state-of-the-art high-speed server, and a high-speed Internet connection were installed in 1996, linking more than 500 computers in the building.

A renovation project began in 1999 and was completed in 2001, adding 24,000 square feet of classroom space and an additional gymnasium; ventilation and lighting were upgraded for the whole school.

ATHLETICS

The physical education program is directed toward recreational and lifetime sports, with an emphasis on fitness.

The School's varsity athletics teams compete against local British and American schools as well as American and international schools in Europe. Boys' teams and girls' teams are organized in basketball, crew, cross-country, golf, soccer, swimming, tennis, track and field, and volleyball. In addition, boys compete in baseball and rugby, and there are girls' teams in cheerleading, dance, field hockey, and softball.

The School's playing fields, located in nearby Canons Park, comprise 21 acres and include soccer and rugby pitches, tennis courts, and a baseball diamond. Neighbourhood facilities include running tracks, tennis courts, and a swimming pool.

EXTRACURRICULAR OPPORTUNITIES

Elected officers and representatives serve on the Student Council, which conveys the interests and concerns of students to the administration and organizes social activities. The council sponsors dances, public service activities, movies, and other events. Concerts and plays are scheduled regularly. Special events include a biannual winter auction and international festival, sponsored by the Parent Community Association; a yearly alumni reception; the senior prom; and the annual music tour, which takes the student orchestra, band, and choir to a European city.

Regular student activities include the yearbook; newspaper; literary magazine; drama productions; Prom Committee; Model United Nations; instrumental and choral groups; the Robotics, Writers, and Debate Clubs; Amnesty International; and Model U.S. Senate. Volunteer groups serve in hospitals and work with children and other groups in the local community.

DAILY LIFE

The school day begins at 8:05 a.m. and ends at 3:05 p.m., except on Wednesdays, which are early release days, ending at 2:10 p.m. The schedule is an eight-day rotating block schedule, with 80-minute periods divided over every two days. Because the periods rotate, classes meet at different times of the day over the course of an eight-day cycle. Lunch can be purchased in the cafeteria, which is open from 11 to 1. Snacks, sandwiches, and drinks can also be purchased on campus throughout the day. The School's open campus policy also allows students to buy their lunch at nearby establishments. Sports and club activities usually take place after school; some sports tournaments are held over weekends.

SUMMER PROGRAM

An active summer program enrolls students ranging from kindergarten through grade 8. A summer program director administers the session.

COSTS AND FINANCIAL AID

Tuition is £22,550 for grades 9–12. Financial aid is awarded on the basis of need.

ADMISSIONS INFORMATION

Applicants are considered on the basis of previous academic records, standardized test results, and recommendations from the previous school. There is a nonrefundable £150 application fee, and a £1000 tuition deposit is required upon admission. The School invites each candidate to spend a day at ASL with a student host to meet teachers and prospective classmates. The American School in London does not discriminate on the basis of race, nationality, creed, or sex.

APPLICATION TIMETABLE

Applications are accepted at any time throughout the year.

ADMISSIONS CORRESPONDENCE

Jodi Coats, Dean of Admissions
The American School in London
One Waverley Place
London NW8 0NP
England
Phone: 020-7449-1221
Fax: 020-7449-1350
Web site: http://www.asl.org

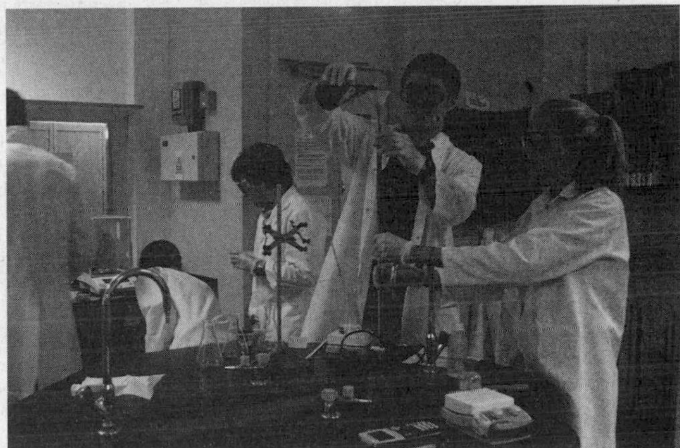

THE ATHENIAN SCHOOL

Danville, California

Type: Coeducational day and boarding college-preparatory school
Grades: 6–12: Middle School, 6–8; Upper School, 9–12
Enrollment: School total: 450; Upper School: 306
Head of School: Eric Niles, Head

THE SCHOOL

Founded in 1965 by Dyke Brown, a graduate of Yale Law School and Vice President of the Ford Foundation, Athenian has as its goal the development of each student for a life of purpose and personal fulfillment as a citizen of the world. An Athenian education equips graduates with a deep understanding of themselves, extraordinary skills for achievement, and the compassion to make a positive difference in the world.

With distinctive programs, Athenian goes far beyond preparing students for outstanding colleges by engaging them in their education. Meaningful hands-on classes and programs make learning exciting and motivating. Classes average 15 to 16 students, so teachers know each student and involve them in discussion and activities. Athenian's diverse student body comes from throughout the East Bay and more than ten other countries. The international programs broaden students' perspectives, with opportunities across the globe for exchanges, service projects, interim trips, and conferences. Students build important skills in activities such as an electric car project, a championship robotics team, athletics, and art, music, chorus, and theater. All students participate in community service each year and, in grade 11, complete the Athenian Wilderness Experience. Few schools offer an experience as academically and personally enriching as Athenian's.

Nearly 100 percent of Athenian graduates are admitted to an outstanding array of four-year colleges and universities. Athenian helps students find the colleges that fit them best. Most importantly, Athenian inspires students to become lifelong learners and confident, successful adults.

Athenian's beautiful 75-acre campus of rolling hills is located 32 miles east of San Francisco at the base of Mt. Diablo. Athenian students access the cultural and educational resources of the San Francisco Bay Area via Athenian's shuttles, buses, and nearby BART stations (the Bay Area rapid transit system). Students also enjoy activities on the nearby Pacific Coast and the majestic Sierra mountains.

A nonprofit institution, Athenian is governed by a 25-member Board of Trustees. The School's operating budget was $12.5 million for 2010–11. The endowment is $7 million.

The Athenian School is fully accredited by the Western Association of Schools and Colleges. It is a member of the National Association of Independent Schools, the California Association of Independent Schools, the National Network of Complementary Schools, A Better Chance, Western Boarding Schools, the College Board, the National Association for College Admission Counseling, and the Round Square Conference of International Schools.

ACADEMIC PROGRAMS

Athenian's exciting broad curriculum develops analytical thinking and communication skills in all disciplines, offering a wide variety of enriching courses in English, history, math, science, fine arts, foreign language, and physical education. The ninth-grade humanities program studies major world cultures through literature, history, and art courses. The sophomore humanities program focuses on American studies in history and literature. Juniors and seniors choose enriching and varied seminars in history and literature. Athenian's mathematics program features statistics and AP statistics courses in addition to two yearlong AP calculus courses. Science features first-year and second-year courses in physics, chemistry, and biology in addition to environmental science, geology, applied science, and the art of science and making. Modern languages offer courses with honors and/or AP options in French, Mandarin Chinese, and Spanish. Fine and performing arts feature courses in drawing, painting, sculpture, pottery, stained glass, photography, dance, musical performance, drama, theater tech, and several arts and society courses. Many honors or Advanced Placement and/or honors options are offered.

The academic year is divided into two semesters. The daily schedule includes six academic periods ranging from 50 to 85 minutes each. Each course meets four times a week.

Courses required for graduation are as follows: English, 4 years; laboratory science, 3 years; mathematics, 3 years; history, 3 years (including freshman humanities, American studies, and three 1-semester elective history seminars in the junior or senior year); 3 years of a foreign language; and 2.5 years of fine arts. Most students exceed these requirements. Students also fulfill graduation requirements in community service each year and must participate in the Athenian Wilderness Experience in grade 11.

Some of the electives offered are studio arts, drama workshops, instrumental ensembles, and additional courses in academic subjects. Required seminars (chosen by students) for English and history may include Shakespeare, science fiction, Russian fiction, Latin American fiction, African American studies, creative writing, or women writers. Science offers inspiring applied science, geology, and environmental science courses and extracurricular programs in building an electric car and robotics. Mathematics courses go beyond two Advanced Placement calculus courses to offer statistics and AP statistics yearlong courses.

Class size varies from 8 to 20, and the average class has 15 students. The overall student-teacher ratio is 10:1. Study for boarding students is supervised by faculty members assigned to dormitories during the evenings.

Athenian offers intermediate and advanced English learning courses to students for whom English is not the first language. ESL students take part in the in the regular curriculum for subjects other than English and history. Field trips help familiarize international students with northern California and U.S. culture.

Opportunities for independent study are provided for selected students by the academic departments. Student exchanges can be arranged either domestically or internationally. The Athenian School is a founding member of a notable consortium of international schools, The Round Square, which offers students academic exchanges, international community service opportunities, and participation in an annual international student conference. Athenian also belongs to the National Network of Complementary Schools, which arranges short-term exchanges of students across the country between member schools that have diverse strengths and resources.

Class field trips in the San Francisco Bay Area are frequent. Students may also participate in off-campus internships oriented toward community service and career exploration. Qualified seniors may take advantage of an accelerated high school program arrangement at the University of California at Berkeley.

A distinctive element of the curriculum is the Athenian Wilderness Experience, required of all students in their junior year. AWE enhances self-confidence, communication skills, and perseverance in addition to fostering an appreciation of the environment.

FACULTY AND ADVISERS

There are 55 full-time and 15 part-time faculty members, 42 of whom hold advanced degrees. Twenty-five faculty members live on-campus with their families.

Eric Niles, Head since 2009, has graduated from the University of Pennsylvania, Wharton School of Economics, and UCLA Law School. Prior to his career in education, he served as counsel to a member of the House of Representatives. Beginning in 1995 he taught and served as Dean of Students at Midland School and then Emma Willard School, where he became Assistant Head in 2005. In 2009 the Athenian Board of Trustees and community selected Mr. Niles as Athenian's Head of School.

The Athenian School maintains an excellent faculty by seeking the most talented people in their respective fields, by encouraging teachers to continue their education, and by providing financial support for professional growth. Enthusiasm for teaching and teaching skills for this age group are qualities also sought in faculty members.

Faculty members perform dormitory supervision, take charge of activities several weekends a year, organize community service activities, and lead adventurous trips and activities during Interim period each spring. Each faculty member also acts as an adviser for 8 to 10 students.

COLLEGE ADMISSION COUNSELING

Two college counselors provide expert advice to students choosing colleges. College counseling starts in the junior year and includes sessions with each student and with parents, as well as preparation for the PSAT and SAT. Trips to campuses throughout the country are available. The Athenian School is visited by numerous college representatives each year.

The following is a representative list of the institutions to which graduates have been admitted: Amherst, Brown, Columbia, Cornell, Dartmouth, Duke, Evergreen State, Georgetown, Johns Hopkins, MIT, NYU, Occidental, Pomona, Princeton, Reed, Stanford, USC, Yale, and the Universities of California (all campuses), Chicago, and Pennsylvania.

STUDENT BODY AND CONDUCT

In 2011–12, there were 74 freshmen (37 boys and 37 girls), 78 sophomores (39 boys and 39 girls), 79 juniors (36 boys and 43 girls), and 75 seniors (37 boys and 38 girls). Of these 306 students, 40 (19 boys and 21 girls) were boarders and 266 (130 boys and 136 girls) were day students.

Eighty-nine percent of the students are from California, and 10 percent are international students from more than ten different countries. Forty-three percent are members of ethnic minority groups.

Living as a community—especially a community as democratic as the one at Athenian—requires cooperation, social responsibility, and a sense of having a real influence on the quality of life and the decision-making process. An informal atmosphere promotes a good rapport between students and faculty members, and faculty members help students behave with respect toward themselves, others, and the school community.

The rules encourage high ethical standards and the ability to live with others harmoniously. The use of tobacco, alcohol, and illegal drugs is prohibited. Cheating and stealing are also major rule violations. Infractions of these rules often result either in referral by the Dean of Students to the Student Discipline Committee or expulsion. Town Meeting is the student government of the School and provides a forum for the discussion of community issues and standards.

ACADEMIC FACILITIES

Academic facilities include classrooms; a science building with four labs; a library holding 16,000 print volumes, forty-three periodical subscriptions, and six electronic subscriptions; a Center for the Arts with gallery, black box theater, drawing and painting, sculpture and pottery, and a dance studio; a new music and multipurpose building, which houses large choral and instrumental rooms, an ensemble room, and two smaller practice rooms; several computer labs; and the improved and renamed Maker's Studio, a significant facility for applied science and robotics.

BOARDING AND GENERAL FACILITIES

There are two dormitories and eleven faculty homes. A number of faculty members reside in apartments or town houses on campus.

Returning students in grades 11 and 12 generally choose single rooms. The Director of the Boarding Program and dormitory parents match the new and younger students with roommates for the double rooms. Ninth graders receive support and guidance from carefully selected seniors through this all-important transition. Supervision of each dorm at the School is the responsibility of a faculty dorm head, assisted by older students who act as proctors.

Students most often arrange to spend the two-week winter and spring vacations with nearby relatives or friends, if they do not travel back to their homes. If needed, the School assists international students in finding suitable homestays during shorter vacation periods. Some trips are also provided during vacations.

The Fuller Commons Building serves as the student recreation and meeting center. The Dyke Brown Main Hall contains the kitchen, dining area, and administrative offices. The Boarding Center provides a gathering place for resident students.

The School nurse visits the dorms each day and advises what action should be taken for any students reported ill. She is available for emergencies as well as drop-in visits during scheduled hours. The School counselor is also available as a resource if needed.

ATHLETICS

Physical education, interscholastic sport, or dance is required of all students.

Athenian teams compete with other schools in the North Bay Conference of the California Interscholastic Federation. The School fields interscholastic teams in thirteen sports—seven for boys and six for girls. These are soccer, volleyball, basketball, tennis, swimming, cross-country, and baseball (for boys). There are also junior varsity teams in soccer, basketball, and girls' volleyball. Athenian's teams have won league championships in a number of sports in recent years.

Noncompetitive activities include rock-climbing, hiking, downhill and cross-country skiing, bicycling, and jazz dance.

Campus facilities include a gym, two tennis courts, a 25-meter pool, a soccer field, a second playing field, and baseball and softball diamonds.

EXTRACURRICULAR OPPORTUNITIES

The School plans occasional trips to museums, plays, the opera, concerts, art exhibits, and lectures in the Bay Area. There are also skiing trips to the Sierra Nevada and excursions to spots on the coast.

On-campus activities include the School newspaper, debate, Interweave, yearbook, and Multicultural Alliance, among many others.

Community service is required of all students. Service projects include cross-country skiing with the visually handicapped, running the scholarship auction, helping at soup kitchens in San Francisco, working with disadvantaged children or the elderly, and working on environmental projects.

DAILY LIFE

A typical day begins with breakfast between 7:30 and 8. Day students arrive in time for classes, which begin at 8:10. A hot lunch prepared at the School is served at noon. Classes end at 2:40 and are followed by sports and performing arts. Dinner is at 6. Clubs, activities, School meetings, and study occupy a portion of each day.

Faculty-supervised evening study hours are from 7:30 to 9:30, when the dormitories are kept quiet. All boarding students are in their dorms by 10:30 p.m., Sunday through Thursday, and by midnight on Friday and Saturday.

WEEKEND LIFE

Weekend activities are arranged by faculty members on duty. They may include hikes on Mt. Diablo, visits to San Francisco and Berkeley, trips to the coast or the Sierra, and an attendance of the Oregon Shakespeare Festival. Boarding students may spend weekends off campus with permission from the Dean of Students and their parents.

Day students are encouraged to participate in all activities available to boarding students and to spend the night on campus from time to time. An outdoor education program is available throughout the year.

COSTS AND FINANCIAL AID

Tuition for 2011–12 was $31,750 for day students and $48,500 for boarding students. Additional expenditures are estimated at $1000. They include such expenses as books, music lessons, field trips, and athletic uniforms. Tuition insurance and a tuition payment plan are available.

Financial aid is based on need; eligibility is determined by the School and Student Service for Financial Aid. For 2011–12, scholarship aid of over $2 million was awarded to 90 students.

ADMISSIONS INFORMATION

Admission is open to all qualified and motivated persons without regard to race, creed, or color. Athenian seeks students who will prosper in an informal, caring environment, want a rigorous academic course of studies, support Athenian's mission, and will contribute to the on-campus community. Admission is selective and based upon the applicant's intellectual ability, academic achievement, character, motivation, creativity, talents, and interests. The School seeks a student body that includes a diversity of geographical, economic, cultural, and ethnic backgrounds.

Each applicant must submit an application, including transcripts and recommendations, have a personal interview, and take an entrance examination, the ISEE, or the SSAT. ESL candidates must take the TOEFL, IELTS, or SLEP.

Priority is given to ninth graders and then to tenth graders. Admission is granted to a smaller number of eleventh graders and occasionally to a twelfth grader.

APPLICATION TIMETABLE

Initial inquiries should be made in the fall of the year preceding anticipated entrance. The School catalog and application forms are available from the Admission Office upon request. Campus visits and interviews may be arranged at any time during the academic year on weekdays between 8:30 and 3. The application deadline is January 15, and notification of admission is given no later than March 19. After this date, applications may still be received and reviewed until all places are filled.

ADMISSIONS CORRESPONDENCE

Christopher Beeson, Director of Admission
The Athenian School
2100 Mt. Diablo Scenic Boulevard
Danville, California 94506
Phone: 925 362-7223
Fax: 925-362-7228
E-mail: admission@athenian.org
Web site: http://www.athenian.org

THE BEEKMAN SCHOOL AND THE TUTORING SCHOOL

New York, New York

Type: Coeducational day college-preparatory and general academic school
Grades: 9–12, postgraduate year
Enrollment: 80
Head of School: George Higgins, Headmaster

THE SCHOOL

The Beekman School/The Tutoring School of New York was founded by George Matthew in 1925. The School was organized to offer a college-preparatory curriculum with the advantage of highly individualized instruction. Since each student has different abilities, learning issues, or goals, teaching is geared to the needs of the individual student. Thus, classes are limited to a maximum of 10 students in The Beekman School and a maximum of 3 students in The Tutoring School.

In addition to having small classes, The Beekman School combines a traditional academic education with a flexible yet structured approach. For instance, some students are eager to complete high school in less than four years for reasons that range from having been retained in a grade earlier in their education to feeling a natural desire to move ahead to college. If there appears (to all concerned) to be a readiness to accomplish this, the School proceeds with a program that will achieve this goal. This is done by adding one or two extra classes to the student's schedule and/or through attendance in the summer session.

In order for students to move effectively at their own pace, the School provides them with the proper level of classes in as many subjects as seems appropriate. Some students require more support to facilitate their learning in the state-mandated academic curriculum. Teachers have several periods free each day to meet with students, and there are supervised study halls each period throughout the day until 5 p.m. In addition, all homework assignments are posted on the School's Web site daily. Upon request, tutors are available through The Tutoring School.

The Tutoring School is a program within The Beekman School. This program specializes in educating students who require private or semiprivate classes. The Tutoring School teaches college-level courses as well as standard courses. Its mission is to provide a supportive environment in which students can realize their academic potential and achieve their educational goals. Generally, incoming students follow The Beekman School's college-preparatory curriculum and receive credit from The Beekman School. However, if necessary, The Tutoring School can follow any school's course syllabus, and course credit is granted by that school upon successful completion of all course work. After-school or home tutoring is available for midterm and final-exam preparation, SAT preparation, or academic support in any subject. In addition, The Tutoring School can arrange at-home schooling, if necessary.

The Beekman School is registered by the Board of Regents of the State of New York and is a member of the College Entrance Examination Board and the Educational Records Bureau.

ACADEMIC PROGRAMS

The requirements of the Board of Regents of the State of New York form the core of the college-preparatory curriculum at The Beekman School and The Tutoring School. It is strongly advised, however, that students exceed these requirements, especially in the areas of mathematics, the sciences, and humanities. In addition to the requirements, The Beekman School faculty has developed many interesting and challenging elective courses from which students may choose. Some of these are psychology, bioethics, ecology, computer animation, creative writing, modern politics, filmmaking, darkroom photography, Eastern and Western philosophy, poetry, and art. Students also participate in after-school activities, such as the literary magazine, yearbook projects, and the School's volunteer program. Students can elect to study music, music theory, voice, various musical instruments, or composition at the Turtle Bay Music School, which is a 2-block walk from The Beekman School. If 6 or more students wish to form a particular course, the administration will offer the course at The Beekman School. If 1 to 3 students wish to take a particular course, it will be offered through The Tutoring School. Otherwise, students are encouraged to take specialized elective courses at various institutions throughout the city.

If students take an elective course off campus, they must complete 48 course hours to earn a semester credit and 96 course hours to earn a full-year credit. For the college-bound student, the suggested academic high school program consists of the following courses: 4 years of English, 4 years of history (including a senior-year program that consists of a semester of U.S. government and a semester of economics), 3 years of mathematics (through algebra II/trigonometry), 3 years of science (including 1 year of a lab science), 3 years of a foreign language, 1 year of art or music, several elective courses, and 1 semester of health education and computer science.

The grading system of the School is A to D (passing) and F (failing). Sixty percent is the minimum passing grade. Midway through each quarter, an interim progress report is mailed home to any student who is earning below 70 percent in any course. Weekly updates by phone can be arranged so that parents always know the academic status of their child.

Because of the independent nature and small size of the School community, the scheduling of classes and the number of classes in which a student enrolls are flexible. Students can begin their day with the first, second, or third period. For the same reasons of independence and adaptability, the School also tries to accommodate any reasonable requests of the students for additional courses. Similarly, tutoring for study and organizational skills and remediation courses in English and math are offered through The Tutoring School.

FACULTY AND ADVISERS

There are 14 full-time members of The Beekman School faculty.

The current Headmaster, George Higgins, has been at the School since 1980, first as a teacher, then as Assistant Headmaster, before serving the School as Headmaster.

All faculty members have graduate degrees or are enrolled in a graduate degree program. In addition to teaching, faculty members also act as advisers to small groups of students. Faculty advisers review progress reports with students and hold meetings periodically to listen to student concerns and discuss upcoming events. Parent conferences are held as frequently as they are needed or requested. Twice during the school year, parents are invited to the School to attend open-house evenings, at which time they can discuss their child's progress with the teachers. When necessary, the Headmaster or classroom teacher calls parents to keep them informed of their child's homework and general behavior.

The School's offices are open to the students almost all day, every day. Students feel welcome to visit the Headmaster to talk, complain, laugh, or ask questions.

COLLEGE ADMISSION COUNSELING

Each year, approximately 96 percent of the graduating class attends college. The aim of the School's college guidance program is to find the right college for each graduating senior. Major considerations include how competitive an environment the student wants, what area of study the student is leaning toward, what size of school would be conducive to success, and where the student would like to live (i.e., city, suburb, East Coast, West Coast). In the past five years, graduates of the School have been accepted at the following colleges and universities: Bard, Boston University, Bennington, Cornell, Duke, Vassar, Fordham, Chapman, NYU, Sarah Lawrence, School of Visual Arts, SUNY at Purchase, and the University of Colorado, to name a few. The Beekman School's staff and faculty members make every effort to examine not just where a student will likely be admitted but where that student will learn, grow, and feel successful for the next four years.

The senior class numbers approximately 25 students. Each student is carefully guided through the college application process, as are his or her parents. A Parents' College Evening, hosted by the School's college guidance counselor, is held each fall for the parents of seniors. It is always an informative evening for parents; the guest speaker is an administrator from the admissions office of a nearby university, who is also there to answer questions. The college guidance counselor schedules several individual appointments with all seniors in order to help them navigate the college application process.

STUDENT BODY AND CONDUCT

Each year, The Beekman School begins the fall term with approximately 70 students. Its rolling admissions policy means that the School adds members to the student body until it reaches its maximum enrollment of 80 students. The enrollment is generally evenly divided between boys and girls. All students are from the immediate tristate area of Connecticut, New Jersey, and New York and its suburbs. The success of The Beekman School's philosophy is proven by the distance students gladly travel in order to be in a school where the enrollment and class size are small, the faculty is supportive and caring, and the education is challenging yet can be paced according to the student's abilities and needs.

There is a School code of behavior that has been shaped by the students and teachers of the School. The main tenet of the code is based on the Golden Rule—"Do unto others as you would have others do unto you." The small, intimate environment makes any type of behavior problem untenable; if the code of the School is violated, there is always an appropriate response. There have been no serious discipline or behavior issues at the School; Beekman students respect their school and its philosophy and recognize the need for tolerance, compassion, and respect in this global community.

ACADEMIC FACILITIES

The School is located in an East Side Manhattan town house. There are eight classrooms; a small library; a state-of-the-art laboratory for biology, chemistry, and physics; a darkroom; a computer lab updated with the latest technology; a study hall equipped with computers; a beautifully landscaped garden; and a student lounge where students can eat lunch and socialize. Rapid Internet access is available throughout the School. Each administrator and teacher has an e-mail address, so parents and students can easily communicate with staff members.

ATHLETICS

The Beekman School meets the New York State requirements for physical education by providing a gym program at a nearby athletic facility. Students may participate in the School's program or design their own program; for example, they may wish to attend their neighborhood gym while being supervised by a private trainer, or they may decide to take dance lessons, karate lessons, or other lessons. Students must exercise for 2 hours each week. In the School's program, an instructor is provided, and students begin the year with aerobics and weight training. Activities in the gym program vary throughout the year and include swimming, volleyball, basketball, cardiovascular exercise, and track. If a student is seriously involved in an intramural activity outside the School, such as soccer or tennis, he or she may be excused from the School's sports program.

EXTRACURRICULAR OPPORTUNITIES

The School's Manhattan location gives it the opportunity to use New York City and its immediate environs as an extension of the classroom. Groups from the School attend plays, films, operas, and dance performances and visit various museums, exhibitions, historical sites, and other points of interest in and around Manhattan and as far away as Philadelphia.

Any student who wants to work on the yearbook or school literary magazine is welcome to do so, and about one third of the student body participates in one way or another. Additional after-school activities include the drama club, photography club, and film club. Upperclassmen can also take part in a community volunteer program if the desire and maturity are present.

DAILY LIFE

Students' schedules reflect their individual needs. The school day begins at 8:45 a.m. and continues until 3:50 p.m. When possible, students who have a long commuting distance are scheduled to begin classes at 9:30 or 10:15. Students with professional programs outside of school can have classes arranged for mornings or afternoons. Supervised study halls are provided throughout the day from 8:45 a.m. to 5 p.m. Lunch periods are scheduled throughout the day on a staggered basis.

SUMMER PROGRAMS

The Beekman School is in session almost year-round. In June, when the academic year is over, the School begins a three-week mini-session of intensive work for students who want or need private tutoring in a specific subject area, who need to make up work in a course for which they received an incomplete, or who exceeded the School's attendance policy (sixteen absences are allowed in a year course, and eight are allowed in a semester course).

Following the mini-session, The Beekman School operates a six-week summer session, which is attended by the School's students and by students from boarding and other private day schools who wish to accelerate in any major academic course, enrich their knowledge of a particular subject, or repeat a course. Each summer class is 2 hours long; there are four classes each day, and the program lasts for twenty-four days. The Beekman School's summer session is approved by the New York State Education Department.

COSTS AND FINANCIAL AID

The annual tuition is $33,000, which is divided into four payments. In addition, an activity fee and an administrative fee ($250 each) are charged. All twelfth-grade students pay a senior fee of $500.

The tuition for the mini-session depends upon the individual's length of study. The tuition for the six-week summer session is $2300 per 2-hour course.

If a student wishes to take a course in The Tutoring School (average student-teacher ratio is 2:1), tuition is $8800 for each yearlong course and $4700 for each semester course. Activity and administration fees are included. Currently, there is no financial aid.

ADMISSIONS INFORMATION

It is a reflection of the School's philosophy that it does not use admissions tests as a means to determine a prospective student's eligibility to attend the School. The Headmaster or Director meets with each prospective student and his or her parents in an intensive interview so that all may better understand each other. Together, they try to assess whether the School would be a good match for the student. Previous school transcripts and records of testing are reviewed but are not solely used to determine a course of study. Prospective students are also welcome to observe for a half or full day so they can gain a clearer understanding of the style of the School. Informal evaluations in math and English may be administered to determine the best course placement for various students.

APPLICATION TIMETABLE

Since there are several different types of secondary schools offering many different programs, it is advisable that interviews take place during the early spring of the year prior to entry. Selecting a school in which to study and socialize is an important process, and students and their families should take the time to look closely at several schools before coming to a final decision. Occasionally, students choose a school that is not a good fit for them. Because Beekman has a rolling admissions policy, even if the traditional day program is filled, students can begin their day in the afternoon and take classes into the late afternoon or early evening. These courses are usually semiprivate and cost more than the regular Beekman tuition. The School believes that a successful secondary education is of vital importance to all young adults; its goal is to make the School available to any student who wishes to actively participate in his or her education.

ADMISSIONS CORRESPONDENCE

George Higgins, Headmaster
The Beekman School
220 East 50th Street
New York, New York 10022

Phone: 212-755-6666
Fax: 212-888-6085
E-mail: georgeh@beekmanschool.org
Web site: http://www.beekmanschool.org

BERKSHIRE SCHOOL

Sheffield, Massachusetts

Type: Coeducational boarding and day college-preparatory school
Grades: 9–12 (Forms III–VI), postgraduate year
Enrollment: 380
Head of School: Michael J. Maher

THE SCHOOL

Berkshire School is a coed college preparatory boarding school offering a rigorous academic program. Pioneering programs—such as Advanced Math/Science Research, Sustainability and Resource Management, Advanced Humanities Research, and Aviation Science (including flight training and FAA Ground School certification)—are available along with advanced sections and AP offerings in all disciplines. With a range of artistic and athletic offerings, a state-of-the-art academic building, brand new facilities for music and dance, and national recognition for its efforts in environmental conservation, Berkshire is an extraordinary setting in which students are encouraged to learn, in the words of the school motto, "Not just for school, but for life."

In 1907, Mr. and Mrs. Seaver B. Buck, graduates of Harvard and Smith respectively, rented the building of Glenny Farm at the foot of Mt. Everett and founded Berkshire School. For thirty-five years, the Bucks devoted themselves to educating young men to the values of academic excellence, physical vigor, and high personal standards. In 1969, this commitment to excellence was extended to include girls.

Situated at the base of Mt. Everett, the second-highest mountain in Massachusetts, Berkshire's campus spans 500 acres. It is a 75-minute drive to both Albany International Airport and Hartford's Bradley International Airport, and just over 2 hours from Boston and New York City.

Berkshire School is incorporated as a not-for-profit institution, governed by a 28-member self-perpetuating Board of Trustees. The School has a $94-million endowment. Annual operating expenses exceed $25 million. Annual Giving in 2010–11 exceeded $2.8 million. The Berkshire Chapter of the Cum Laude Society was established in 1942.

Berkshire School is accredited by the New England Association of Schools and Colleges and holds memberships in the Independent School Association of Massachusetts, the National Association of Independent Schools, the College Entrance Examination Board, the National Association for College Admission Counseling, the Secondary School Admission Test Board, and the Association of Boarding Schools.

ACADEMIC PROGRAMS

Berkshire's academic program is firmly rooted in a college-preparatory curriculum that features advanced and AP courses across all disciplines. In addition, unique opportunities to excel in math/science research, student-directed independent study, and electives in science, history, and fine arts allow students to pursue advanced study at Berkshire. As creative and agile problem solvers, strong critical thinkers, persuasive communicators, and active global citizens, Berkshire's students are equipped with the skills required to excel in the twenty-first century. The School's balance between academic rigor and possibility allows students to flourish as independent learners, community members, and professionals.

Believing that the best preparation for college is the acquisition of knowledge from a variety of disciplines, Berkshire requires the following credits: 4 years of English; 3 years each of mathematics, a foreign language, and history; 2 years of science; and 1 year of the visual or performing arts. All departments provide for accelerated sections, and students are placed at a level commensurate with their skills and talent. Many students take one or more of the sixteen Advanced Placement courses offered.

Most students carry five courses. The average number of students in a class is 12, and the student-teacher ratio is 6:1. The academic year is divided into two semesters, each culminating with an assessment period. Students receive grades, teacher comments, and adviser letters twice each semester. Berkshire uses a traditional letter-grading system of A–F (D is passing).

In 2007, Berkshire introduced its Advanced Math/Science Research course in which students use the strong foundation of knowledge acquired in the regular Berkshire curriculum as a springboard for beyond-the-curriculum projects in areas of cutting-edge research and other fields. Students intern with a professional scientist to conduct research in facilities located in the nearby Hartford, Connecticut and Albany, New York areas. Students work closely with their mentor in the field of their choice for 4 to 8 hours a week. The course culminates with a critical review paper and a research paper, both in scientific format.

FACULTY AND ADVISERS

The Berkshire teaching faculty numbers 61, 49 of whom live on campus. Thirty-four teachers hold a master's degree and 5 hold doctorates. Faculty members contribute to both the academic and personal development of each student. The small size of the Berkshire community permits faculty members to become involved in students' lives outside, as well as inside, the classroom. Each student is paired with a faculty adviser who provides guidance, monitors academic progress, and serves as a liaison with the student's family. Berkshire also retains the services of 4 pediatricians, a nurse practitioner, 4 registered nurses, and 2 certified athletic trainers.

Michael J. Maher was named Berkshire's fifteenth head of school in the spring of 2004. He holds a bachelor's degree in political science from the University of Vermont and a master's degree in liberal studies from Wesleyan University. Mr. Maher is in his eighth year at Berkshire; previously he held positions as administrator, teacher, and hockey coach. He and his wife, Jean, an associate director of admission and a member of the Foreign Language Department, have 3 children, 2 of whom attend Berkshire.

COLLEGE ADMISSION COUNSELING

College counseling at Berkshire is the responsibility of 3 full-time and 2 part-time professionals who assist students and their parents in the search for an appropriate college or university. The formal process begins in the Fifth Form, with individual conferences with the college counselors, and the opportunity to meet with some of the approximately 100 college admissions representatives who visit the campus. In February, Fifth Formers and their parents attend a two-day seminar on the college admission process. Admission strategies are discussed and specific institutions are identified for each student's consideration. During the summer, students are encouraged to visit colleges and write the first draft of their college application essay. The application process is generally completed by winter vacation in the Sixth Form year.

Members of the classes of 2009, 2010, and 2011 enrolled at a variety of four-year colleges or universities, including Bard, Bates, Berkeley, Boston College, Boston University, Bowdoin, Brown, Carnegie Mellon, Colby, Colgate, Cornell, Dartmouth, Denison, Dickinson, Emory, Johns Hopkins, Kenyon, Lehigh, Middlebury, MIT, NYU, Northeastern, Northwestern, SMU, St. Lawrence, Syracuse, Union, Villanova, Williams, and the Universities of Connecticut, Maine, Massachusetts, Michigan, New Hampshire, Wisconsin, and Vermont

STUDENT BODY AND CONDUCT

In the 2011–12 academic year, there were 333 boarders and 47 day students; with 3 students studying abroad in the first semester. The student body is drawn from twenty-four states and twenty-four countries.

Students contribute directly to the life of the school community through involvement in the Student Government, the Prefect Program, dormitory life, and various clubs and activities. Participation gives students a positive growth experience supporting the School motto of learning "not just for school, but for life." The rules at Berkshire are simple and straightforward and are consistent with the values and ideals of the School. They are designed to help students live orderly lives within an environment of mutual trust and respect.

ACADEMIC FACILITIES

Berkshire Hall, the primary academic facility built in 1930 and the centerpiece of the campus, reopened in the fall of 2008 after a full renovation. It now features larger classrooms with state-of-the-art technology, new administrative offices, a two-story atrium, and a Great Room for student study and special functions. A new music center opened in the fall of 2010, featuring two specially designed classrooms to meet the needs of the instrumental, choral, and chamber music programs. The center has five practice rooms, plenty of spacious storage cabinets for instruments, a recording studio, and storage and office space for the music program. A new dance studio also opened in the fall of 2010 as part of the existing gymnasium. Godman House is home to several darkrooms and a digital art and electronic music studio, and deWindt Dormitory houses a visual arts studio. In 2009, the School opened its Center for Writing and Critical Thinking, which is home to a nightly writing tutoring program. The center also hosts faculty forums and 4 visiting writers each year.

In the fall of 2011, Allen Theater reopened after a complete renovation. The Allen renovation also included new academic spaces for the Kenefick Center for Learning, new classrooms for the theater and film department and the SAT tutoring program, and a new studio for WBSL, the School's own radio station. A new building devoted to math and science is scheduled to open in the fall of 2012.

The Geier Library contains approximately 43,000 volumes in open stacks, an extensive reference collection in both print and electronic format, numerous periodicals, and a fine audiovisual collection. The library has wireless Internet access, as well as twenty computers with Internet access and an online card catalog for student use. ProQuest Direct, the Expanded Academic Index ASAP, the *New York Times* full text (1994 to present), and the current ninety days' full text of 150 Northeastern newspapers, including the *Wall Street Journal* online, keep the library fully up-to-date on breaking information. In addition, in 2011 the Library acquired access to JSTOR, an online database of more than 1,000 academic journals, containing literally millions of peer-reviewed articles, images, reviews, and primary sources.

At the Dixon Observatory, computer synchronized telescopes make it possible to view and photograph objects in the solar system and beyond. Given the combination of equipment, software, and location, Berkshire's observatory is among the best in New England.

BOARDING AND GENERAL FACILITIES

Berkshire has ten residential houses, including two girls' dormitories that were completed in the fall of 2002. Three faculty families, many with small children, generally reside in each house along with a prefect—Sixth Formers whose primary responsibility is to assist dorm parents with daily routines, such as study hall and room inspection. Dorm rooms all have Internet access and private phone lines. There is a common room in each house, where students may relax or study. Benson Commons, the school center, features a dining hall capable of seating the entire School, a post office, the School bookstore, the Music Center, the Student Life office, the Center for Writing and Critical Thinking, and recreational spaces. In 2011 an 8-acre solar field was built on campus that is expected to provide up to 40 percent of the School's electricity needs.

ATHLETICS

Berkshire enjoys a proud tradition of athletic excellence. The School provides competition in twenty-seven interscholastic sports, including baseball, basketball, crew, cross-country running, field hockey, football, golf, ice hockey, lacrosse, mountain biking, skiing, soccer, softball, squash, tennis, track and field, and volleyball. Students may also participate in the Ritt Kellogg Mountain Program, a program that utilizes Berkshire's natural environment and its proximity to the Appalachian Trail to present athletic challenges, teach leadership, and foster environmental responsibility.

In January 2009 the 117,000-square-foot Jackman L. Stewart Athletic Center opened. The facility offers two ice rinks (one Olympic-size), fourteen locker rooms, seating for 800 spectators, a 34-machine fitness center and athletic training rooms. It can also be used for indoor tennis and can accommodate all-school functions. A second athletic center features full-size courts for basketball and volleyball, four international squash courts, a climbing wall, and a dance studio. Other facilities include the new Thomas H. Young Field for baseball, new softball fields, an all-weather track, a lighted football field, and two synthetic-turf fields. A new twelve-court tennis facility was completed in the fall of 2010.

EXTRACURRICULAR OPPORTUNITIES

Berkshire offers students a variety of opportunities to express their talents and passions. Students publish a newspaper, a yearbook, and a literary magazine that features student writing, art, and photography. The Ritt Kellogg Mountain Program offers backcountry skills, boatbuilding, fly fishing, hiking, kayaking, rock climbing, and winter mountaineering.

There are a number of active clubs, including the Drama Club, the International Club, the Investment Club, the Maple Syrup Program, the Philanthropy Society, and a Student Activities Committee.

Berkshire's student-run FM radio station, WBSL, operates with a power of 250 watts and is capable of reaching 10,000 listeners. Berkshire is one of the few secondary schools to hold membership in the Intercollegiate Broadcasting System and the only one affiliated with both the Associated Press wire service and its radio service.

Berkshire students pursue the arts in the classroom and in extracurricular activities. The theater program offers two plays in the fall and spring as well as a winter musical. There are three choral groups: Ursa Major, an all-school chorus; Ursa Minor, a girls' a cappella group; and Greensleeves, an all male chorus. There are two music groups: a jazz band and a chamber music ensemble. Students can also take private voice and instrumental lessons. Each season the Berkshire community looks forward to various performances, such as dance and music recitals, a jazz café, and poetry readings. Visual arts include painting, drawing, sculpture, digital art, photography, and ceramics. Students display their work in galleries in the Student Center and in Berkshire Hall.

DAILY LIFE

The first of the six class periods in a school day begins at 8 a.m., and the final class concludes at 2:45 p.m., except on Wednesday and Saturday, when the last class ends by 11:35 a.m. Berkshire follows a rotating schedule in which classes meet at different times each day.

Athletics, outdoor experiences, and art activities occupy the afternoon. Clubs often meet after dinner, before the 2 hour supervised study period that begins at 8 p.m.

WEEKEND LIFE

Weekend activities are planned by a Director of Student Activities and include first-run movies, dances with live bands, and other dances hosted by DJs. There are trips to local amusement parks and theaters as well as shopping trips to Hartford and Albany. In addition, students and faculty members journey to New York and Boston to visit museums, attend theater and music productions, or take in professional sports events.

COSTS AND FINANCIAL AID

For the 2011–12 academic year, tuition is $48,100 for boarding students and $38,100 for day students. For most students, $100 a month is sufficient personal spending money. Ten percent of the tuition is paid upon enrollment, 50 percent is payable on July 1, and 40 percent is payable on November 30. Various tuition payment plans are available.

Financial aid is awarded on the basis of need to about 32 percent of the student body. The total financial aid spent in 2011–12 was $4.1 million. The School and Student Service (SSS) Parents Financial Statement and a 1040 form are required.

ADMISSIONS INFORMATION

Berkshire adheres to the principle that in diversity there is strength and, therefore, actively seeks students from a broad range of geographic, ethnic, religious, and socioeconomic backgrounds. Admission is most frequent in the Third and Fourth Forms, and the School enrolls a small number of postgraduates each year.

In order to assess the student's academic record, potential, character, and contributions to his or her school, Berkshire requires a personal interview, a transcript, test scores, and recommendations from English and mathematics teachers, along with the actual application. Candidates should have their Secondary School Admission Test (SSAT) scores forwarded to Berkshire School (school code 1612).

APPLICATION TIMETABLE

Interested families are encouraged to visit the campus in the fall or winter preceding the September in which admission is desired. Visits are arranged according to the academic schedule, Monday through Friday, from 8 a.m. to 2 p.m. and Saturday from 8 to 10:45 a.m. January 15 is the deadline for submitting applications; late applications are accepted as long as space is anticipated. Berkshire adheres to the standard notification date of March 10 and the families' reply date of April 10. Depending on availability, late applications are processed on a rolling basis. Applications for admission are available online at the School's Web site. http://www.berkshireschool.org.

ADMISSIONS CORRESPONDENCE

Andrew Bogardus, Director of Admission
Berkshire School
245 North Undermountain Road
Sheffield, Massachusetts 01257

Phone: 413-229-1003
Fax: 413-229-1016
E-mail: admission@berkshireschool.org
Web site: http://www.berkshireschool.org

BESANT HILL SCHOOL

Ojai, California

Type: Coeducational boarding and day college-preparatory school with a focus on divergent thinking, creativity, and environmental sustainability
Grades: 9–12
Enrollment: 105
Head of School: Mr. Randy Bertin

THE SCHOOL

Founded in 1946 by Aldous Huxley, J. Krishnamurti, Guido Ferrando, and Rosalind Rajagopal on 520 acres in the resort town of Ojai, California, this residential school community offers a vigorous college-preparatory curriculum with a cornerstone of creative expression, sustainability, and divergent thinking. Besant Hill offers over thirty art electives, competitive athletics, travel and experiential education programs, small classes, and a 4:1 student-teacher ratio.

The School was envisioned as an educational community that would provide an atmosphere where students could develop and discover both their intellectual and creative potential and where they would learn "how to think, not what to think™." This philosophy is still the core of the School today.

In addition to its fine arts and athletic programs, Besant Hill School has an academic program that integrates best practice teaching techniques and universal design. This cutting-edge program prepares students for a lifetime of learning as well as a foundation for their professional career. The School has SmartBoards in all of its classrooms, making the Socratic method of teaching it uses even more accessible to many styles of learners.

Besant Hill School holds membership in the California Association of Independent Schools, the National Association of Independent Schools, and Western Boarding Schools Association. The School is accredited by the Western Association of Schools and Colleges.

ACADEMIC PROGRAMS

The Academic Dean is responsible for the academic life of the School. Courses of study follow the University of California (UC) system and can also be determined by the individual student's future plans and interests. The average load is five academic solids, an elective, an art, and a sport or fitness class.

Class size averages 10 students. Advanced Placement courses are offered in calculus, English, government, physics, and Spanish.

Besant Hill has two academic semesters, and evaluations are sent to parents four times a year. An evening study hall is required.

Graduation requirements are as follows: English, 4 years; Science, 3 years (including 1 year of biology and 1 year of chemistry); Foreign language, 2 years of the same language; Math, 3 years (through algebra II); Social Science, 3 years (including world cultures and American (U.S.) history); Arts, 2 years (visual, theater, music) with at least 1 year of the same art; Fitness, 4 years; and Electives, at least 3 (one must be senior capstone).

English as a second language (ESL) is also offered. This program works to improve the development of English and oral and listening comprehension skills. Concentration on vocabulary expansion, improved pronunciation, and use of idioms aid the students in understanding and participating in class. The full-year course, which requires an additional fee, is two or three periods a day and can include ESL classes in science, social studies, U.S. history, and TOEFL preparation.

FACULTY AND ADVISERS

There are 35 teachers and administrators on the Besant Hill staff. Twenty-one faculty members and administrators reside on campus, and all faculty and staff members are involved in the life of the community beyond the classroom. Of the 25 full-time teachers, half have advanced degrees, 2 of whom hold their doctorates.

COLLEGE ADMISSION COUNSELING

All students take a college-preparatory curriculum and begin their testing program with the Preliminary SAT (PSAT) in the fall of the sophomore year. They take the PSAT again as juniors, in preparation for the SAT, which they take later that same year and then again as seniors. The SAT Subject Tests are administered to those juniors and seniors for whom it is appropriate.

The School receives annual visits from college representatives. The Director of College Counseling is on campus and begins working with students in their sophomore year. In 2011, colleges or universities accepted all of the graduates. Recent graduates are attending colleges such as Bard, Beloit, Berklee School of Music, Bowdoin, Cal Arts, Chicago Institute of the Arts, Columbia, Mills, NYU, University of Washington, and various campuses of the California State University and University of California systems.

STUDENT BODY AND CONDUCT

Of the 105 students attending Besant Hill School this year, one fifth are day students and four fifths are residential. Besant Hill School seeks to instill in students a lifelong love of learning. This goal is reflected in the School motto "Aun Aprendo" ("I am still learning"). The community sets reasonable limits for its members. Elected students participate in a Disciplinary Advisory Committee, along with faculty members and administrators. The School disciplinary system works on a basis of minors and majors. Students may have occasional work crew hours or more serious disciplinary action, depending on the offense.

ACADEMIC FACILITIES

There are twelve buildings on campus. Networked computer stations are available in several buildings. Most of the campus has wireless access. The School houses a science lab, observatory, photography lab, new art studio, theater, recording studio, ceramics studio, and digital media lab. The renowned Zalk Theater houses both the drama and music departments. The School has also recently added four soundproof music practice rooms.

BOARDING AND GENERAL FACILITIES

The Besant Hill School campus offers boarding facilities for both boys and girls. The residents are housed 2 to a room in bedrooms that contain study and storage facilities for each student. Dorm parents live in each wing of the dormitories and supervise the boarding students with the help of student prefects. Other facilities include a modern dining hall, tennis courts, volleyball courts, a baseball field, basketball courts, and a soccer field.

ATHLETICS

Team experience and personal challenges through athletics are a valuable part of any education and are made available to every student. The School competes interscholastically in lacrosse, basketball, cross-country, soccer, and volleyball. Boys varsity basketball is the School's most competitive athletic program, and the team has won back-to-back Southern California Section titles.

EXTRACURRICULAR OPPORTUNITIES

The School's proximity to both the coast and the mountains provides students with a wide range of recreational activities, from surfing to rock climbing. Students can also take advantage of museums, movies, concerts, plays, skating, shopping, and bowling.

DAILY LIFE

Boarding students are responsible for cleaning their rooms and performing assigned crew jobs. Breakfast is served from 7 to 8 a.m. Academic classes are until 2:45 p.m. In the afternoon, fitness and athletics classes are offered. Dinner is at 5:30 p.m., followed by evening study hall.

WEEKEND LIFE

Weekends give students a chance to relax, catch up on their studies, or partake in planned activities by the Residential Life Director. Weekend trips to Los Angeles, Santa Barbara, and Ventura are frequent.

Students who have parental permission may leave the campus on open weekends, provided they are in good standing with the School.

COSTS AND FINANCIAL AID

The cost of tuition, room, and board for the 2011–12 academic year was $43,250. Day student tuition was $20,900. A book and activity fee of $2735 is required to cover the costs of books, trips, and other expenses. The ESL fee for first-year students is $7200. Participation in the School's instructional support program is $7400.

Approximately 20 percent of the School's income is given annually in scholarship and financial aid. Information on aid availability can be obtained from the Admissions Office.

ADMISSIONS INFORMATION

Students are selected on the basis of character and academic promise. Personal interviews and references are used to identify those students who are most likely to benefit from the Besant Hill School experience. Consequently, a visit to the School is strongly urged for each applicant. Acceptance is based upon records, recommendations, and a personal interview.

APPLICATION TIMETABLE

Candidates should schedule an interview with a member of the Besant Hill School admissions team, schedule a class visit, go on a tour of the School, and begin working on the Besant Hill School application for admission in the fall. Students should also begin requesting recommendations, transcripts, and school reports from their current school. The financial aid deadline is January 15, and the application deadline is February 16. Admissions decisions should be mailed by March 10, and new student contracts are due by April 10. Applications received after February 16 are reviewed and acted upon on a space-available basis as soon as the candidate's file is complete. After April 10, remaining spaces will be filled through a rolling admissions policy.

ADMISSIONS CORRESPONDENCE

Terra Furguiel
Besant Hill School
P.O. Box 850
Ojai, California 93024
Phone: 805-646-4343 Ext. 111
800-900-0487 (toll-free)
Fax: 805-646-4371
E-mail: tfurguiel@besanthillschool.org
Web site: http://www.besanthillschool.org

BLAIR ACADEMY

Blairstown, New Jersey

Type: Coeducational boarding and day college-preparatory school
Grades: 9–12, postgraduate year
Enrollment: 450
Head of School: T. Chandler Hardwick III

THE SCHOOL

In its 164th year, Blair Academy continues to offer a superior college-preparatory program while holding firmly to its tradition of being a community fully focused on the development of each individual student. In this environment, students learn to advocate for themselves, become service-minded, and develop the leadership skills necessary for success in college and beyond. Students balance their academic responsibilities with extensive opportunities to develop in theater, music, competitive athletics, and numerous extracurricular activities. The balance between high academic and personal expectations, and a willingness to provide individual focus are among Blair's greatest strengths.

Situated on 423 hilltop acres adjacent to Blairstown in one of New Jersey's most scenic counties, Blair is just 10 minutes from the Appalachian Trail and the Delaware Water Gap, only 60 miles from New York City, and 2 hours from Philadelphia.

Blair maintains an enrollment of 450 students on average, large enough to support a broad program of studies, activities, and athletics, yet small enough so that everyone can receive individualized instruction and ample attention. The average class size is 11 students, and the dual advisory system also makes for close relationships between students and faculty members.

A Board of Trustees directs the school, and alumni are well represented on the Board. The school's endowment is currently estimated at approximately $66.5 million. Blair received $2.5 million in capital gifts for 2010–11 and the Blair Fund raised $2.6 million.

Blair Academy is accredited by the Middle States Association of Colleges and Schools. Its memberships include the Cum Laude Society, New Jersey Association of Independent Schools, National Association of Independent Schools, The Association of Boarding Schools, Council for Advancement and Support of Education, and Secondary School Admission Test Board.

ACADEMIC PROGRAMS

With twenty-three Advanced Placement (AP) courses and a wide range of electives such as Roman history, epidemiology, marine biology, ethical philosophy, architecture, and video production, Blair students enhance their potential and awaken new interests with the guidance of committed teachers. The talented and diverse faculty brings enthusiasm, passion, and global perspective to lessons. Caring and committed to each individual student, the faculty members serve as housemasters, advisers, coaches, and friends while laying the necessary foundation for academic success at Blair and beyond.

Blair boasts a notable fine and performing arts program that is integral to its well-rounded curriculum. From introductory-level to advanced, art courses encourage students to think and express themselves creatively through various mediums, including canvas, dance, music, theater, film, graphic design, and ceramics. In the spring of 2009, the Blair wind symphony and string ensemble joined together to form the first-ever Blair Academy Orchestra, a momentous occasion for the music program. With vocal and instrumental performance tours across Eastern Europe, musicians and vocalists at Blair are able to explore international travel while performing at some of Europe's most historic concert venues.

History teacher Quint Clarke, affectionately known as Q, has taken students to such faraway places as Vietnam, Beijing, and many locations in Africa. A trip to Kenya he conducted several years ago as a community service effort was so successful and meaningful that it has now become Q's annual summer trip with students. Other faculty members have also taken students on trips abroad, most recently to Spain, Tunisia, France, and China. Spring break offers an opportunity to travel to countries like Russia, France, and Greece, while Long Winter Weekend allows marine science students to expand upon their classroom studies in the Cayman Islands.

FACULTY AND ADVISERS

For the 2011–12 academic year, Blair employed 80 full-time faculty members and administrators, more than half of whom hold graduate degrees. Ninety-two percent of faculty members and administrators live on campus, many as houseparents in the dormitories. They also serve as coaches, academic monitors, and advisers. Faculty members have high expectations for their students and seek to provide individual focus in addition to the rigorous and challenging academic program. Encouraging students to excel in a particular area is what motivates every faculty member at Blair. Teachers are exceptionally talented, with diverse and outstanding educational backgrounds and a wide range of interests. This allows each student to cultivate positive relationships with many adults in the Blair community. Through a dual advisory system, faculty advisers and academic monitors guide Blair students' personal growth. Blair is further set apart by allowing each student to choose his or her own adviser, which allows students to develop a strong sense of independence, responsibility, and confidence in engaging the world around them.

T. Chandler Hardwick III was appointed the Academy's fifteenth Headmaster in 1989. A graduate of the University of North Carolina (B.A., 1975) and Middlebury College (M.A., 1983), Mr. Hardwick previously taught English and was Senior Dean at the Taft School, as well as the Director of the Taft Summer School.

COLLEGE ADMISSION COUNSELING

College counselors begin working with students and their families in January of their junior year. Each student is required to have at least five private meetings with a college counselor to map out their college search and application process. Counselors communicate regularly with parents to keep them informed and involved. Parents of juniors are invited to spend a day on campus for an informational introduction to the Blair College Counseling Office and process; in 2010, the guest speaker was Diane McKoy, Senior Associate Director of Admission at Columbia University in New York. In addition, Blair hosts on-campus visits from representatives of at least seventy colleges and universities each year.

Blair works with each individual student to craft an academic program that emphasizes areas of strength while fulfilling the expectations of competitive college admissions. Students from recent graduating classes are attending colleges and universities such as Brown, Colgate, Columbia, Cornell, Davidson, Georgetown, Harvard, Middlebury, NYU, Princeton, Stanford, U.S. Military Academy, U.S. Naval Academy, Williams, Yale, and the Universities of Pennsylvania and Virginia.

STUDENT BODY AND CONDUCT

Blair attempts to maintain a geographically, ethnically, and socioeconomically diverse student body. For 2011–12, Blair welcomed students from twenty-two states and twenty countries, including Zimbabwe, Hong Kong, Spain, South Africa, and Thailand. The composition of the 2011–12 student body was as follows: senior class and postgraduate year, 74 boys, 60 girls; junior class, 76 boys, 54 girls; sophomore class, 55 boys, 40 girls; and freshman class, 44 boys, 43 girls. Of the total enrollment of 450, there are 104 day and 346 boarding students.

ACADEMIC FACILITIES

At the center of the campus are the four major classroom buildings: Clinton Hall, Bogle Hall, Timken Library, and Armstrong-Hipkins Center for the Arts. Bogle Hall, dedicated in 1989, provides laboratories and classrooms for the math and science departments and includes a state-of-the-art computer laboratory and a 150-seat auditorium. Armstrong-Hipkins Center for the Arts was dedicated in 1997 and includes DuBois auditorium, which seats 500 people and is where school meetings are held. Additional arts facilities include a black box theater, outdoor theater, soundproof practice rooms, two dance/yoga studios, various painting/drawing studios, ceramics room, architecture studio, photography darkroom, and digital video laboratory. A renovated Timken Library, which includes classrooms and a computer center, opened in 1998 and houses over 20,000 volumes. The library also subscribes to several excellent databases. These are recognized academic sites with information that has been collected and reviewed specifically for student use.

BOARDING AND GENERAL FACILITIES

The newest additions to the Blair campus were completed in 2009. Several additions were made to the exterior sports facilities including a new turf field, ten new tennis courts, an improved all-weather track, stadium seating to accompany the turf field, and a tennis house. A new interior athletic space houses seven squash courts, a weight-lifting center, a fitness center, three basketball courts, a six-lane swimming pool, a wrestling room, and ample locker space for students and coaches. The bookstore, canteen, and college counseling suite moved to the activities portion of the new building. Both the athletic facility and student activities center have quickly become an integral part of campus life and complement Blair's existing facilities.

There is an ongoing initiative to improve the physical campus as part of Blair's Ever Always campaign. Summer 2010 saw changes to central campus, where only pedestrian traffic is allowed now as part of a plan to develop a parklike setting for recreation and study through improvements to the campus infrastructure and landscaping.

Ten dormitories house boarding students. The housemaster and other dorm faculty members play a unique role in residential life. They help create a community and ensure that students adapt to dorm life and school. They make sure the dorm offers an atmosphere conducive to study but also provides a social liveliness that builds dorm spirit. In addition to having a housemaster and dorm parents in residence, each underclass dormitory unit has prefects who live in the underclass dormitories. Prefects are seniors who are selected by the faculty for their leadership ability and commitment to Blair; they devote their senior year to living with the younger students in order to help them make a smooth transition to Blair, all the while balancing their own college applications, varsity athletics, and demanding course schedules of honors and AP courses.

ATHLETICS

Blair's philosophy is that physical education is beneficial and important; hence all students participate in a program of athletics or supervised recreational sports. Blair fields twenty-eight competitive varsity teams in baseball, basketball, crew, cross-country, field hockey, football, golf, ice hockey, lacrosse, skiing, soccer, softball, squash, swimming, tennis, wrestling, and winter and spring track. Because participation is key to Blair's sports program, most sports field junior varsity and thirds-level competitive teams.

EXTRACURRICULAR OPPORTUNITIES

Blair students are also offered numerous learning opportunities outside of the classroom, ranging from weekly lectures as part of the Society of Skeptics, to travel abroad with faculty and peers. The Society of Skeptics, the longest continuously running high school lecture series in the country (now in its thirty-fourth year), was an outgrowth of the Blair International Society, begun in 1962, and has served as a forum for the discussion and debate of important national and international issues. For more than three decades, under the tutelage of Dr. Martin Miller, the weekly lecture series has featured a wide variety of speakers who are engaging, accomplished in their respective fields, and often controversial.

The Nevett Bartow Series brings to campus some twenty programs each year. The mission of the Bartow Series is to expand the artistic experiences of Blair students by bringing professional performers from far and wide to the Blair stage, including such offerings as Rockapella, Solid Brass, Loudon Wainwright III, the Cincinnati Boychoir, the David Grisman Quintet, Tom Chapin, Judy Collins, Arlo Guthrie, and visiting lecturers. Day trips are arranged to the theater, concerts, opera, ballet, and museums in New York City.

Among popular campus organizations are the Blair Academy Singers, the Blair Academy Players, the String Orchestra, the Wind Symphony and Jazz Ensemble, the Community Service and Environmental Clubs, Model United Nations, and the Investment Club. The outdoor-skills group takes full advantage of Blair's proximity to the Delaware Water Gap and the Appalachian Trail, while the Ski Club utilizes the Pocono Mountains for daily skiing excursions. Students write for the school newspaper, *The Blair Breeze*, compose the yearbook, and publish a literary magazine each year. Service-oriented organizations, such as the Blue and White Key, encourage students to become engaged and active citizens within the Blair community.

DAILY LIFE

Classes are 55 minutes long and meet four times during a six-day week. Four days per week, classes end at 3:10 p.m. Wednesday and Saturday are shortened days, with afternoons dedicated to athletic competitions and extended theater practices.

Afternoons are devoted to athletics practices and games, play rehearsals, recreational sports, or activities. Family-style dinner, a formal dining room meal, is held two to three days per week for boarding students. Each dormitory, including senior dorms, has monitored evening study hours from 8 to 10 p.m. Students who have earned study privileges (known as honor nights) can be in their rooms, the library, the canteen, computer labs, or receive tutoring from an individual faculty member during these hours. Most importantly, faculty members do not disappear into their apartments at the end of the school day but instead are present around campus as mentors, friends, and houseparents.

WEEKEND LIFE

The campus bustles with activity on the weekends. Every Saturday evening, there is a community-focused event, such as athletic competitions, a dance, movie night, open-mic night, musical performances, and student theater productions. In addition, the Residential Life Office sponsors numerous off-campus trips (New York City, movies, mall trips, hikes, local festivals) as well as other low-key entertainment events (Blair intramural games, volleyball tournaments, scavenger hunts) throughout the weekends. Highlights include International Weekend, the midwinter formal, Super Sunday, and Peddie Week. Closed weekends during examinations and the first two weeks of September require all boarding students to remain on campus. Otherwise, students are allowed to take weekends away from campus according to a scale based on their grade in school.

COSTS AND FINANCIAL AID

Tuition for 2011–12 was $47,600 for boarders and $33,000 for day students. Additional deposits or fees are charged for the use of certain equipment, private music lessons, and extra medical services.

Financial aid is awarded on the basis of demonstrated financial need and proven personal and academic merit in accordance with procedures established by the School and Student Service for Financial Aid. Approximately $4.1 million in aid was distributed to 32 percent of the student body for the 2011–12 academic year.

ADMISSIONS INFORMATION

Blair is interested in students who seek the satisfaction of personal achievement through an experience that is both broad and challenging. Blair students are determined to make the most of their secondary school years and to prepare for college and beyond by being active participants in an engaging environment. Academic preparation is only part of being ready for college; Blair also emphasizes social responsibility, involvement, and leadership. Students take on such roles as team captains, dormitory prefects, or members of class council, and play an important part in shaping the Blair experience for those around them. They share in school planning and decision-making, and serve with faculty members on committees involving residential life, discipline, academic honor, multiculturalism, health, and student activities. Each student leader has an opportunity to influence the direction of Blair and impact the experiences of his or her classmates—skills that he or she will carry beyond Blair.

Blair enrolls students in grades 9–11 each year and also admits a limited number of high school graduates who wish to pursue a postgraduate year of study.

In addition to a personal interview, several written components complete the formal application. To complement the school transcript and teachers' recommendations, Blair requests results from a standardized test: the SSAT or ISEE for grades 9–10; and the PSAT, SAT, or ACT for eleventh-grade entry and postgraduates. Application forms must be accompanied by a nonrefundable fee of $50 ($125 for international applicants). The application deadline is February 1.

APPLICATION TIMETABLE

The initial inquiry is welcome at any time. An official inquiry can be made by visiting the Academy's Web site at www.blair.edu. The Admission Office is open for interviews and tours by appointment on weekdays and Saturdays. Applicants who complete the admissions process prior to February 1 are notified of the decision on March 10.

ADMISSIONS CORRESPONDENCE

Ryan M. Pagotto, Dean of Admissions
Blair Academy
P.O. Box 600
Blairstown, New Jersey 07825-0600
Phone: 908-362-2024
800-462-5247 (toll-free)
Fax: 908-362-7975
E-mail: admissions@blair.edu
Web site: http://www.blair.edu

THE BOLLES SCHOOL

Jacksonville, Florida

Type: Coeducational boarding (7–12) and day (PK–12) college-preparatory school
Grades: PK–12: Lower Schools, PK–5; Middle School, 6–8; Upper School, 9–12
Enrollment: School total: 1,648; Lower Schools, 462; Middle School, 405; Upper School, 781
Head of School: John E. Trainer Jr., President and Head of School

THE SCHOOL

Bolles offers a comprehensive college-preparatory program. Bolles prepares students for the future by offering them an education that challenges and guides them in the belief that all things are possible. Moral development is encouraged by an emphasis on respect for self and others, volunteerism, and personal responsibility.

Bolles has served as the educational inspiration for three generations, with a strong and unshakable commitment to providing the finest preparatory education possible for each student. Located in Jacksonville, Florida, Bolles was founded in 1933 as an all-boys military school on the San Jose Campus. In 1962, the School dropped its military status; in 1971, it began admitting girls.

In 1981, the Lower School Whitehurst Campus for grades K–5 was begun. A separate campus for middle schoolers in grades 6–8 was achieved in 1991 with the acquisition of Bartram School, an independent girls' school operating since 1934 and now known as the Bolles Middle School Bartram Campus. In 1998, the Bolles Lower School Ponte Vedra Beach Campus opened its doors to serve students in pre-kindergarten through grade 5.

Today, with nearly 1,700 students on four campuses, Bolles is recognized as one of the finest college-preparatory institutions in the nation. All of its students are college-bound. Bolles students consistently place in the top 10 percent of Advanced Placement scores from throughout the country. The School prepares students for the future by providing them with a variety of activities and a myriad of challenges that promote growth and development in four primary areas: academics, arts, activities, and athletics. Students learn to make decisions and budget time by balancing homework, sports, extracurricular, family, and community service responsibilities.

Students from all walks of life, cultures, religions, and races learn together at Bolles, a microcosm of the world that they will inherit. The School's excellent academic and athletic offerings attracted students from twenty countries and eight states to participate in the resident program for the 2011–12 school year. This blend of cultures and interests sets Bolles apart from other independent college-preparatory institutions in the Southeast and fosters a level of mutual respect that is crucial in learning how to meet global challenges.

The School's locations are in suburban neighborhoods. The Upper School San Jose Campus and the Lower School Whitehurst Campus occupy 52 acres on the St. Johns River. Five miles to the northeast, the Middle School Bartram Campus is set on 23 acres. The Bolles Lower School Ponte Vedra Beach Campus is located on 12 acres in Ponte Vedra Beach, east of Jacksonville.

Jacksonville, a major metropolitan area in northeast Florida, is home to the Jaguars National Football League team and many cultural associations, such as the Jacksonville Symphony, the Florida Ballet, several professional theater companies, three major museums, the Jacksonville Zoo, and several professional sports teams. Downtown Jacksonville is located approximately 35 minutes from the Jacksonville Beach area, which includes Ponte Vedra Beach, and about an hour from St. Augustine, the oldest city in the United States.

A not-for-profit institution, Bolles is governed by a self-perpetuating board of 33 trustees. The School also works with a 20-member Board of Visitors and an Alumni Board that represents more than 8,000 living graduates.

The School's operating budget is more than $30 million. The annual giving goal for 2011–12 was $1.68 million, which included more than $500,000 in unrestricted funds. The School's endowment is more than $11.3 million.

The School is accredited by the Southern Association of Colleges and Schools and the Florida Council of Independent Schools and holds membership in the National Association of Independent Schools, the Council for Spiritual and Ethical Education, the Secondary School Admission Test Board, and the Southeastern Association of Boarding Schools.

ACADEMIC PROGRAMS

The Middle School curriculum includes English, government, world cultures, world geography, U.S. history, mathematics through algebra, and science. Students may select from a varied fine and performing arts program and may choose among band, chorus, drama, dance, graphics, drawing and painting, ceramics and sculpture, computers, foreign language, and language arts on a rotating basis throughout the year. Each student has an adviser, and a full-time, on-campus guidance counselor assists with decision-making skills, peer relations, and alcohol- and drug-abuse awareness.

Upper School students must earn 22 credits for graduation, with a college-certifying grade of at least C-. Specific requirements are 4 years of English; 2 of a single foreign language; 3 of social studies, including U.S. and world history; 3 of mathematics through algebra II; 3 of science, including biology and chemistry; 2 of physical education; 1 of fine arts; ½ year of life management skills; and 3½ years of additional electives. The average class size is 15 students.

Among the full-year courses are English, French, Latin, Spanish, German, Japanese, Chinese, world and U.S. history, algebra, geometry, precalculus, physical science, biology, chemistry, marine science, environmental science, band, introduction to dance, intermediate dance, upper-level dance, AP drawing, AP portfolio 2-D, AP portfolio 3-D, advanced acting, portfolio development honors, men's chorus, women's chorus, concert choir, and symphonic band. There are honors sections in English, geometry, algebra, biology, chemistry, physics, neurobiology, languages, and social studies. Courses designed to prepare students for Advanced Placement examinations are available in English, U.S. and European history, American and comparative government, languages, calculus, biology, chemistry, physics, computer science, statistics, portfolio art, and art history. A postgraduate program is available to students seeking an additional year of academics prior to entering college.

Students choose from such semester electives as foundations of studio art, drawing and painting, ceramics and sculpture, creative writing, acting, directing, production, public speaking, computer applications, AP statistics, algebra III, introduction to programming, Web site development, American government and politics, economics, human anatomy, marine science, and driver education.

Opportunities for off-campus projects sponsored directly by the School include the Outdoor Academy and the French, Spanish, and Japanese Exchange Programs.

Grades, with narrative reports from faculty advisers, are sent to parents twice each quarter.

FACULTY AND ADVISERS

Dr. John E. Trainer Jr. was appointed President and Head of School in 2001. He holds a Bachelor of Science degree in biology from Muhlenberg College in Allentown, Pennsylvania; a master's in biology from Wake Forest University in Winston-Salem, North Carolina; and a doctorate in zoology from the University of Oklahoma in Norman, Oklahoma. Dr. Trainer was selected for this position because of his strong people skills and innovative thinking and his extensive experience in working effectively with academic professionals, community leaders, executives, and legislators.

Bolles has 149 full-time faculty members and 16 part-time faculty members; there are 83 professional staff members who hold master's degrees and 7 who hold doctorates.

Each student in the Middle and Upper Schools is assigned to a faculty member, whose primary responsibility is to serve as an adviser. A minimal class load makes the adviser readily accessible to both students and parents. The School maintains an Office of Student Counseling to assist students in addressing issues that fall outside the traditional categories of academic advising.

COLLEGE ADMISSION COUNSELING

The aim of the college counseling program is to help students and their families to find college options and ultimately to find the most appropriate college choice. At the start of the second semester of the junior year, a daylong meeting is held to begin the more structured aspect of the process, and each student is assigned a college-placement adviser. An evening parent meeting provides additional information. The Williams Guidance Center offers a full range of up-to-date college reference materials, which include catalogs, videotapes, and computer search programs. In addition, approximately 100 college representatives visit the campus each year to meet with students, counselors, and parents.

In each of the past five years, 98 percent of graduates have attended four-year colleges and universities. A small number of students defer admission, and a small percentage attends two-year schools.

The middle 50 percent of scores for the last three graduating classes on the SAT Reasoning Test are 1070–1310 on a 1600 scale. The middle 50 percent of ACT scores are 22–28. Teachers in English and mathematics classes work with students in preparation for college admission testing.

STUDENT BODY AND CONDUCT

The Upper School numbers 781 students, with between 190 and 200 students in each grade. There are 86 boarding students.

There is an Honor Code and a Values Statement, and the Honor Council of Upper School students administers the Code and serves as the judiciary court for infractions against the Code. The Student Council is very active and serves as a proactive body for legislation of student privileges, organizes activities, and offers advice to the Upper School administration.

ACADEMIC FACILITIES

On the Upper School San Jose Campus, Bolles Hall houses classrooms, boys' dormitory rooms, a dining room and kitchen, offices, and three meeting rooms. Other academic buildings are Clifford G. Schultz Hall, with seventeen classrooms; the Michael Marco Science Center, which houses three science labs; the Joan W. and Martin E. Stein Computer Laboratory; the Hirsig Life Science Center; Ulmer Hall, which includes fifteen classrooms, a language lab, and two science labs; and a marine science classroom along the St. Johns River.

The Swisher Library houses the Meadow Multimedia Center, with a large-screen television, two satellite dishes, and computer labs. Other facilities include the McGehee Auditorium, which seats more than 600, and the Cindy and Jay Stein Fine Arts Center, which contains the Independent Life Music Building, the Lucy B. Gooding Art Gallery, and the Lynch Theater.

Middle School academic facilities include Murchison-Lane Hall for classrooms and administrative offices, the Art Barn, a marine science classroom along Pottsburg Creek, girls' dormitory rooms, the Pratt Library, and the Betsy Lovett Arts Center, which opened in 2007.

The Lower School Whitehurst Campus houses each grade separately in homelike classrooms set around a natural playground. The Lower School Ponte Vedra Beach Campus is a modern campus that includes an administration/classroom facility as well as the McLauchlan-Evans Building, housing classrooms, and the River Branch Building, which is the location of both the Ullmann Family Art Room and the Loeb-Lovett Family Music Room.

BOARDING AND GENERAL FACILITIES

All boarding students are housed in rooms that accommodate 2 students. Boys and girls reside on separate campuses. Students are assigned roommates based upon age and interests.

Upper School athletic facilities include Collins Stadium at the Donovan Baseball Field, Hodges Field, the Bent Tennis Complex, the Baker-Gate Petroleum Company Track Facility, and Skinner-Barco Stadium. The Davis Sports Complex includes the Huston Student Center, basketball and volleyball courts, the 25-yard Lobrano and 50-meter Uible swimming pools, the Cassidy Aquatic Fitness Center, and the Garces Diving Facility. The Agnes Cain Gymnasium features a wrestling room and athletic offices. The newly constructed Peyton Boathouse and Rice Family Crew Complex, and the Bent Student Center are proud additions to the San Jose Campus.

Among the Middle School athletic facilities are a football and soccer field, the Conroy Athletic Center, and Meninak Field, which includes Collins Baseball Stadium.

ATHLETICS

Bolles is a member of the Florida High School Athletic Association. Boys' teams compete in baseball, basketball, crew, cross-country, football, golf, lacrosse, soccer, swimming, tennis, track, volleyball, and wrestling. Girls' teams compete in basketball, cheerleading, crew, cross-country, golf, soccer, softball, swimming, tennis, track, and volleyball. Middle School boys' teams compete in baseball, basketball, crew, football, lacrosse, soccer, swimming, track, and wrestling. Middle School girls' teams compete in basketball, cheerleading, crew, soccer, softball, swimming, track, and volleyball.

EXTRACURRICULAR OPPORTUNITIES

Extracurricular activities offered include Student Government; National Honor Society; language honor societies; Amnesty International; Interact, a service club; a mentor program; three student afterschool tutoring programs; Student Advocate Council, which promotes community spirit among the students; an array of other community service opportunities; language clubs; special interest clubs; Community Service Leadership Council; Sophomore Leadership Council; class-sponsored activities; *Turris* (yearbook); *The Bugle* (newspaper); and *Perspective* (literary magazine).

DAILY LIFE

The daily schedule for the Upper School, which lasts from 8 a.m. until 3:45 p.m., includes seven 45-minute periods and "Zero Hour," a 30-minute period reserved for individual conferences and extra help. Boarders have evening study in their rooms, with faculty members available for extra help, and supervised study halls are provided for students needing more structured assistance.

WEEKEND LIFE

Resident students are strongly encouraged to take advantage of the excellent recreational facilities at Bolles. On weekends, the waterfront is open for resident students, weather permitting. In addition, regular off-campus trips are organized, as are, from time to time, special trips.

COSTS AND FINANCIAL AID

Upper School tuition costs for the 2010–11 school year were as follows: tuition, room, and meals for boarding students (grades 7–12) totaled $36,000, and tuition for day students (grades 9–12) totaled $17,350. Additional fees include $500–$750 for books, $30–$35 per gym uniform set, $375 for driver education, a one-time $500 facilities fee, and $45–$65 for the yearbook. Essential services fees for boarding students include $250 for the School clinic, $100 for emergency escrow, and an allowance of $40 per week ($1440 per school year) for students in grades 7–8, $45 per week ($1620 per school year) for students in grades 9–11, and $50 per week ($1800 per school year) for students in grade 12. Lunches and snacks are available for purchase by day students.

The School awarded over $2.9 million in financial aid for the 2010–11 academic year.

ADMISSIONS INFORMATION

The School seeks students who demonstrate the ability to meet the requirements of a rigorous college-preparatory curriculum. In addition, special talents and strengths that allow the applicant to achieve distinction within the applicant pool are desired. The ISEE or its equivalent is required of all applicants, as are a personal interview, teacher recommendations, and transcripts. There is a $45 application fee for day students and a $75 application fee for international students.

APPLICATION TIMETABLE

The Admission Office accepts applications beginning in the fall, with an initial deadline of January 10. Applications received after that date are considered on a rolling basis as space becomes available. Upon acceptance, the applicant must respond with a deposit of 10 percent of the total tuition and pay the facilities fee within two weeks.

ADMISSIONS CORRESPONDENCE

The Bolles School
7400 San Jose Boulevard
Jacksonville, Florida 32217

Phone: 904-256-5030
Fax: 904-739-9929
Web site: http://www.Bolles.org

BUXTON SCHOOL

Williamstown, Massachusetts

Type: Coeducational college-preparatory boarding and day school
Grades: 9–12
Enrollment: 90
Head of School: C. William Bennett and Peter Smith '74, Co-Directors

THE SCHOOL

In 1928, Ellen Geer Sangster founded Buxton School as a coeducational day school in Short Hills, New Jersey. In 1947, she moved the high school to her family estate in Williamstown, Massachusetts, and formed it anew as a boarding school.

From the beginning, Buxton has been a progressive school, one devoted to innovation and change. Today, that devotion remains steadfast. At Buxton, students' pursuits help them develop the clear vision they need to comprehend the world they live in and to define their future lives. Each student's bridge to the larger world is the informed, skilled, confident self that he or she develops while at Buxton.

Buxton places great importance on the composition and character of its student body. Foremost, a young person must want to be at Buxton. In addition, Buxton seeks to enroll students who have the intelligence, motivation, creativity, and intellectual curiosity to succeed there. Prior to coming to Buxton, students have experienced positive relationships with adults as well as peers. Buxton students take a responsible and ambitious role in shaping their own lives and wish to make significant and mature social contributions. They are conscious of the importance of being useful and contributory, of serving as an asset to others, and of aiding in others' efforts to enrich the life of the group. One of the first tasks Buxton students encounter is that of developing and maintaining a sound, compassionate, stimulating environment for oneself and for the entire group.

Buxton promotes personal growth and cultivates students' abilities to understand and manage their lives. Presenting a way of life that students can come to understand and manage is of primary importance. The student body is diverse; life at the School is flexible, noninstitutional, and open to change. Opportunities often arise for collective deliberation of life's most pressing challenges. A Buxton education reflects the fundamental premise that a mature individual must be morally and actively committed, each in his or her own way, to the creation and betterment of a healthy society.

The 150-acre campus of Buxton overlooks historic Williamstown, which is located approximately 170 miles north of New York City and 150 miles west of Boston. Williams College, the Clark Art Institute, and the Massachusetts Museum of Contemporary Art (MASS MoCA) are nearby and are all exceptional resources for Buxton students.

Buxton is a nonprofit, nonsectarian institution governed by a 21-member self-perpetuating Board of Trustees. The board includes the Co-Directors, Associate Director, faculty members, alumni, parents of students and alumni, and friends of the School.

The physical plant at Buxton is valued at $7.2 million. The operating budget is $4 million annually. The current endowment is $1.9 million, and the Annual Fund for 2010–11 raised $249,546.

Buxton is accredited by the New England Association of Schools and Colleges and is approved by the Massachusetts Department of Education. It is a member of the Secondary School Admission Test Board, The Association of Boarding Schools, the Association of Independent Schools of New England, the National Association of Independent Schools, and the Small Boarding School Association as well as other professional organizations.

ACADEMIC PROGRAMS

Academic courses, activities, and community life are all essential parts of a Buxton education. Each offers the opportunity for unique and vital growth; therefore, each is of educational significance.

Buxton's academic curriculum is broad and demanding, offering an unusual combination of traditional subjects, courses in the arts, and electives in subjects that are usually only encountered at the college level. Students collaborate with teachers to design their course programs. Although they are advised to design a course schedule that will prepare them for higher education, students have considerable freedom of choice about what courses they take and when they take them.

Sixteen credits are required for graduation. All students are expected to take 4 years of English, 3 years of history, a biological and a physical science, 3 years of a language (French, Spanish, Mandarin, and Indonesian are offered), and 3 years of math. Students are also encouraged to pursue courses in the arts—studio art; ceramics; black-and-white and digital photography; video production; music theory, composition, and performance; and beginning and advanced drama.

Buxton offers a range of elective courses—examples of those offered recently include writing workshops; The Practice of Poetry; Latin American History Through Literature; The Western Tradition; Advanced European Studies; Economics; Media Literacy; Africa; Cultural Anthropology, Cultures of Native North America; Race, Class, and Gender; Film History; Film Art and Analysis; Sound and Music in the Twentieth Century; Psychology, Architectural Thinking, Designing, and Building; Marine Science (oceanography and marine biology); Geology, Astronomy, and Environmental Studies.

Students in their junior year participate in a year-long research project that culminates in a substantial scholarly paper as well as a creative project that grows out of their research. Topics in recent years have included a history of the Israeli/Palestinian conflict, the invention of the steam engine, the worldwide problem of human trafficking, the history and tradition of the Japanese tea ceremony, cowboy history and lore, and an exploration of the life and work of the film and theater director Elia Kazan.

Buxton divides its academic year into two semesters. The School has a 5:1 student-teacher ratio, and class size averages 9 students. Faculty-supervised study periods are held daily during class hours and for 2 hours in the evening. Students may be required to attend.

Each year in March, the entire School travels to a major North American city. Atlanta, Chicago, El Paso, Havana, Mexico City, New Orleans, Philadelphia, San Juan, Toronto, Washington, D.C., and three cities in Nicaragua are among those visited in recent years. This event is of central importance in the school year, and students are involved in all aspects of planning and executing the weeklong trip. Social, economic, and political issues are the focus of project groups, and everyone in the Buxton community takes part in the All-School Play or other performances, which are presented several times during the trip. Upon returning to Buxton, students share their project experiences with the School and archive their reports.

FACULTY AND ADVISERS

There are 22 faculty members—12 men and 10 women. Four hold master's degrees. Fourteen live on campus. C. William Bennett, Director of the School since 1983, is a graduate of Williams College and has been at Buxton since 1969. In 2008, Peter Smith became Co-Director with Mr. Bennett. Mr. Smith graduated from Buxton in 1974, is a graduate of Clark University, and has been working at Buxton since 1984.

Most teaching families and teachers live at the School, interweaving their daily lives with those of the Buxton community. Along with teaching in the classroom, faculty members have advisory, leadership, administrative, and caretaking responsibilities. As advisers, faculty members are in regular contact with parents.

Compassionate adult action and reaction form the foundation of education at Buxton. Teachers seek to motivate students to engage in sincere intellectual commitment and self-evaluation. The adults are available and open to young people and are concerned with their growth in academic disciplines as well as in every other respect. Buxton faculty and staff members react to young people knowledgeably, deeply, and personally. Developing honest and caring friendships between Buxton adults and students is an educational goal in itself.

COLLEGE ADMISSION COUNSELING

Buxton faculty members counsel students as they form their college plans. Students are assigned faculty college advisers in the spring of their junior year. The advisers guide students in making appropriate college choices and help students with the application process.

In recent years, Buxton graduates have attended Amherst, Bard, Barnard, Bennington, Berklee College of Music, Carleton, Cornell, Emory, Hampshire, Lewis and Clark, Middlebury, Mount Holyoke, Oberlin, Reed, St. John's, Sarah Lawrence, Skidmore, Smith, Swarthmore, Wellesley, and Williams.

STUDENT BODY AND CONDUCT

Enrollment at Buxton averages 90 students, with an equal number of boys and girls. In 2011–12, eleven states and the countries of Bermuda, Cameroon, China, Egypt, Japan, Mexico, Rwanda, and Venezuela are represented among the student population.

ACADEMIC FACILITIES

The campus contains four classroom buildings (one housing science labs and a computer lab); a library with Internet-access computers and extra Ethernet ports for students' portable computers; a theater; and a recently completed arts complex for fine arts (including space for photography and video production), music, and ceramics. Designated campus areas are equipped for wireless Internet access.

BOARDING AND GENERAL FACILITIES

In addition to the academic facilities, there are a number of other buildings on campus. The Main House contains a girls' dormitory, the School dining room, and administrative offices. The Gate House serves as an additional girls' dormitory; the boys' dormitory is a converted barn. The School has additional buildings for administrative offices and for faculty and staff housing. Williamstown Medical Associates provides medical services to students.

ATHLETICS

At Buxton, competitive and recreational sports programs do not merely fulfill physical education requirements; they also expose students to the challenges inherent in disciplined physical activity and different kinds of team play. Students acquire personal confidence and a sense of mastery as well as leadership skills through participation in these activities.

Competitive sports are not mandatory, but regular outdoor activity is expected of everyone. Interscholastic soccer and basketball take place on a scheduled and supervised basis. Other activities include skiing and snowboarding at a local facility, biking, hiking, running, horseback riding, yoga classes, indoor soccer, intramural basketball, skating, sledding, softball, spring soccer, skateboarding, squash, tennis, martial arts, table tennis, and Ultimate (Frisbee).

The campus has its own playing fields; a basketball court; a weight room; three ponds for ice skating; and a hill for sledding, skiing, and snowboarding. Hiking trips are scheduled when there is student interest. Riding lessons can be arranged.

EXTRACURRICULAR OPPORTUNITIES

In keeping with the Buxton philosophy that all aspects of School life are valuable to the education of a student, activities play a prominent role. Students of every degree of interest and ability are urged to take part and are counted on to support the efforts of each other as co-participant, audience, or encouraging friend. All of Buxton's activities, which include art, music, drama, dance, drumming, and creative writing, are designed to foster personal expression and commitment through a combination of self-discipline, patient practice, interpersonal skill, and astute observation of life. The art studio has an extensive array of two- and three-dimensional media. Painting, drawing, figure drawing, printmaking, book arts, sculpture, metal fabrication, work with fabric or found objects, mixed media, ceramics, and black-and-white and digital photography are available. Chorus, chamber orchestra, and chamber ensembles are offered at Buxton as music activities. Drama includes acting, working on technical crews, and costuming. The dance and drumming program at Buxton focuses on West African, Afro-Caribbean, and Balinese traditional influences. Students have the chance to study Balinese dance and drumming in the summer program in Bali. Each year, seniors raise funds for and produce the School yearbook, which they present as a gift to the Buxton community.

An essential part of a Buxton education is Work Program, which takes place on Tuesday afternoons and Saturday mornings. At these times, students engage in tasks such as forestry work and gardening, construction projects, office work, and cooking. Administered by volunteer students and faculty members, Work Program requires a great deal of planning, budgeting, and managing. What is done and who does it are always changing, but it is a consistent, direct challenge to everyone that Work Program can and must fill a major part of Buxton's nonprofessional needs.

The annual Fall and Spring Arts Weekends offer students' families the opportunity to share in Buxton life. Over the three days of these events, the School presents performances by the chorus, chamber orchestra, and chamber ensembles; performances of student composers' work; drama productions; and readings of students' creative writing. The School also exhibits new student artwork. Independent and joint science projects are often presented on these weekends as well. In addition, there is ample time for parent-faculty conferences.

The proximity of Williams College is particularly significant, as it provides a source of stimulation and example as well as the opportunity for Buxton students to occasionally attend events and use the college library. Next door to Buxton is one of the finest small art museums in the country, the Clark Art Institute. The museum and its digital-image library enrich the students' lives considerably.

DAILY LIFE

Each day, students clean their rooms and complete minor housekeeping tasks around the School. Classes begin at 8 a.m. and are held until 3 p.m., five days a week. Sports and activities are offered from 3 to 5 p.m. Students attend study hall, study on their own, or participate in rehearsals or other activities from 7 to 9 p.m. Meals are family-style, with student waiters; students attend lunch at 12:30 and dinner at 6 in the School dining room.

WEEKEND LIFE

Weekends at Buxton are considered just as important as weekdays. Students plan and organize Friday night activities, which include outdoor sports and games, dances, swimming, and theme events. On Saturday mornings, everyone in the School participates in Work Program. Students are free to go into Williamstown to buy necessities or attend a movie or cultural event on Saturday afternoons and evenings. All Saturday meals are planned and prepared by students. Sundays begin with brunch and typically are devoted to academic work. Sunday evenings feature a formal dinner and arts events or presentations concerning social issues. Students remain at Buxton on weekends except for a designated Home Weekend each semester.

Students who wish to do so may attend religious services locally.

COSTS AND FINANCIAL AID

Tuition and fees for 2011–12 were $45,500 for boarding students and $28,000 for day students. This included room and board and academic study, plus basic materials for courses, lab fees, field trips, tickets to approved cultural events, athletics (including ski passes), and programs and activities held on campus. Academic supplies, all-school trip fees, laundry fees, some art supplies, weekly allowance, and travel are the family's responsibility. The international student fee was $3500. This included support services plus ESL and/or TOEFL prep.

Buxton is committed to maintaining the diversity of its student body. Approximately 49 percent receive need-based financial aid; $1.3 million was awarded for 2011–12.

ADMISSIONS INFORMATION

Buxton admits students into grades 9 through 11. Interested parents and prospective students may request an information packet by calling or writing the Admissions Office or through the School Web site. An on-campus interview is required, and the student's most recent SSAT, SLEP, or TOEFL scores should accompany the application.

APPLICATION TIMETABLE

Inquiries are welcome any time. Applications are due February 1, although they are accepted later if space is available. The application fee is $50 for U.S. students and $100 for international students.

ADMISSIONS CORRESPONDENCE

Admissions Office
Buxton School
291 South Street
Williamstown, Massachusetts 01267

Phone: 413-458-3919
Fax: 413-458-9428
E-mail: Admissions@BuxtonSchool.org
Web site: http://www.BuxtonSchool.org

CAMPBELL HALL (EPISCOPAL)

North Hollywood, California

Type: Coeducational day college-preparatory school
Grades: K–12: Lower School, K–6; Middle School, 7–8; Upper School, 9–12
Enrollment: School total: 1,086; Upper School: 528
Head of School: The Reverend Canon Julian Bull, Headmaster

THE SCHOOL

Campbell Hall is an independent, K–12, coeducational, nonprofit day school affiliated with the Episcopal Church. It offers college-preparatory academic training within the perspective of the Judeo-Christian tradition. Campbell Hall was founded in 1944 by the Reverend Alexander K. Campbell as a school dedicated not only to the finest in academic education but also to the discovery of the values of a religious heritage. Campbell Hall enrolls students in kindergarten through the twelfth grade.

The school's 15-acre campus is located in a residential suburb 10 miles north of Los Angeles. Students take advantage of the school's proximity to museums, missions, historic sites, science centers, and universities.

The basic structure and operation of the school and the formulation of educational and other school policies are guided by a 26-member Board of Directors. The board is composed of community leaders, alumni, and parents of Campbell Hall students. The Headmaster has traditionally served as a liaison between the board and the various segments of the school community.

The school's advancement programs include annual and capital campaigns.

Campbell Hall is accredited by the Western Association of Schools and Colleges and the California Association of Independent Schools. The school is also accredited by the Episcopal Diocesan Commission on Schools. It holds memberships in the National Association of Independent Schools, National Association of Episcopal Schools, Episcopal Diocesan Commission on Schools, Educational Records Bureau, National Association of College Admission Counselors, Council for Advancement and Support of Education, College Board, Council for Religion in Independent Schools, and Cum Laude Society.

ACADEMIC PROGRAMS

Students at the high school must complete 7½ units in the humanities, including 4 units of the English component, 3 units of the history component, and ½ unit of senior seminar. Other requirements for graduation include 3 units of mathematics, 3 of a world language, 3 of a laboratory science, 2 years of physical education, 1 year of a visual or performing art, ½ year of art history, ½ year of music history, and ½ year of human development. In addition to the graduation requirements, students must complete additional units chosen from electives, such as music theory, creative writing, economics, ethics, physiology, poetry, computer programming, philosophy, psychology, and visual and performing arts. Students must also complete 20 hours of approved community service each year.

A number of special academic options attract qualified students. Twenty-one Advanced Placement courses and eighteen honors courses are offered and include calculus (AB and BC), probability and statistics, English, French, Japanese, Spanish, European history, U.S. history, government/politics, human geography, biology, chemistry, physics, music theory, art history, psychology, economics, and computer science. In addition, qualified seniors may take college-level courses through the Talented High School Student Program of the California State University at Northridge, through local community colleges, through the UCLA High School Scholars' Program, and through approved online course providers.

Classes range in size from 8 or fewer students in advanced courses to 19 in some of the required courses. An online pilot program is available to students who wish to petition for specific courses in which they are particularly interested that are not part of the curriculum.

The school's grading system uses percentages: 100–90 is an A; 89–80 is a B; 79–70 is a C; 69–60 is a D, and no credit is given for a grade of 59 or below. Report cards, which are issued electronically each semester and trimester, include letter grades, as well as evaluations of work habits and cooperation.

At the end of each year, students who earn all A's in all classes are eligible for the Headmaster's List; students who earn a 3.6 academic average qualify for the Honor Roll primarily on the basis of grade point average. Academically outstanding juniors and seniors are eligible for membership in the Cum Laude Society.

FACULTY AND ADVISERS

There are 105 full-time faculty members (67 women and 38 men); 47 hold master's degrees, and 6 have doctorates. Faculty members are encouraged to attend seminars and conferences in their fields. In addition to giving academic and social guidance to individual students, faculty advisers work closely with class officers to ensure unity and success in various class projects and social activities.

The Reverend Canon Julian Bull was appointed Headmaster in 2003. He is a graduate of Dartmouth (B.A., 1982), Boston College (M.A., 1988), and received his M.Div. from Virginia Theological Seminary in 2007. Mr. Bull was formerly Head of School at Trinity Episcopal in New Orleans, Louisiana.

COLLEGE ADMISSION COUNSELING

In October, all sophomores and juniors take the PSAT. Throughout their high school years, students receive extensive college counseling through group workshops and in-depth individual conferences with the college counseling staff members. Throughout the school year, the college counseling office offers a number of programs to help students and parents understand the college admissions process. These programs often include college admission representatives. In recent years, speakers from Brown, California Institute of the Arts, Columbia, Duke, NYU, Northwestern, Pitzer College, Sarah Lawrence, Stanford, UCLA, and USC have participated in these programs. One hundred percent of Campbell Hall graduates are accepted to four-year colleges or universities. They are drawn to a broad range of schools, and in recent years have enrolled at Berklee College of Music, Berkeley, Carnegie Mellon, Claremont McKenna, Columbia, Cornell, Duke, Emory, Georgetown, Grinnell College, Julliard, Middlebury, NYU, Northwestern, Pomona, Rhode Island School of Design, Rice, Scripps, UCLA, USC, Spelman, Stanford, Swarthmore, Tufts, the U.S. Air Force Academy, Vassar, Washington (St. Louis), Wesleyan, Whitman, and the Universities of Chicago, Michigan, and Pennsylvania.

STUDENT BODY AND CONDUCT

Of the 528 boys and girls in the Upper School (grades 9–12), 125 are in the ninth grade, 134 in the tenth, 136 in the eleventh, and 133 in the twelfth. Most students live in the suburban areas of Los Angeles.

Because Campbell Hall is concerned with the formation of character traits and values that reflect a sense of responsibility as well as a concern for the needs of others, misconduct is subject to disciplinary action. Violation of school rules and regulations may result in suspension or expulsion.

ACADEMIC FACILITIES

Campus academic facilities include classroom complexes, seven science labs, four computer labs, the Fine Arts Building, and a theater. A 22,000-square-foot library and academic center serves as the hub for technological resources. The campus is equipped with wireless access and every classroom has computers available, including laptop carts, networked overhead projectors, and SmartBoards. Every student (from grades 3–12) and faculty member has a school-managed e-mail account. All faculty members have school-supplied iPads and significant professional development resources available to them. The school library subscribes to a number of online databases. The new Arts and Education Center is under construction on the campus. This 111,000-square-foot project includes three two-story connected buildings, a multilevel subterranean parking garage, twenty-four state-of-the-art classrooms, an art gallery, a faculty resource center, outdoor learning spaces, terraces, and gardens, with extensive use of multimedia throughout. Designed by Gensler, an architectural firm renowned for its expertise in education design and innovative sustainability practices, the project is slated to be LEED certified at completion.

ATHLETICS

There are two basic components to the athletics program. First, required physical education courses provide basic and advanced instruction for sports that are in season; and second, Campbell Hall is a member of the California Interscholastic Federation (Gold Coast Athletic Association) and field teams in baseball, basketball, cheerleading, cross-country, 11-man tackle football, equestrian, golf, soccer, softball, tennis, track and field, swimming, and volleyball.

The school has two well-equipped gymnasiums, a baseball diamond, an artificial turf football and soccer field, a softball field, and five outdoor basketball/volleyball courts.

EXTRACURRICULAR OPPORTUNITIES

An active student government with elected officers represents each division of the student body. Among the student-planned events are dances; homecoming; the Winter Formal; and the Halloween, Christmas, and Valentine's Day celebrations. The year's social schedule culminates in a spring prom, planned by the student activities committee to honor the senior class.

There are also many curricular field trips and about sixty special interest groups, such as the Speech and Debate Team, Highlanders, the Cultural Awareness Club, the Spirit Club, Thespians, the Creative Writing Club, Amnesty International, Junior Statesmen of America, GSA, the Community Service Committee, and the High School Academic Honor Board.

DAILY LIFE

Monday through Thursday, there are four 75-minute blocks that meet between 8:50 a.m. and 3:40 p.m. Four days per week, 40 minutes are devoted to chapel (every Monday and Thursday), advisee group meetings, or clubs. On Wednesdays, school begins at 9:30 a.m. to allow for student/faculty conferences There is a daily 45 minute lunch break. Interspersed among the academic courses are electives that provide enrichment in the fine arts (painting, drawing, ceramics, sculpture, and photography), the performing arts (chorus, instrumental music, drama, stagecraft, and dance), sports (physical education and team sports), robotics, computer programming, etc. Yearbook, newspaper, and journalism are also available as curricular classes.

SUMMER PROGRAMS

The school offers a full complement of summer programs for students in kindergarten through grade 12, including summer school courses, a creative arts academy, and sports camps. Additional information may be obtained by contacting the Summer Programs Director.

COSTS AND FINANCIAL AID

Tuition for 2011–12, including fees, is $29,380 to $30,380. Tuition payments may be made annually, biannually or, at an additional charge to cover interest costs, in ten monthly installments. Students may either bring their own lunches to school or purchase them at the student store or from a school-sponsored caterer at the school at lunchtime. There is a dress code. Bus service is available from some parts of town.

Financial aid is available and is awarded on the basis of family need. Continuing students have priority for renewal. In 2011–12, 24 percent of Middle and Upper School students received financial aid.

ADMISSIONS INFORMATION

The school seeks students who are able to benefit from a rigorous college preparatory curriculum and who will contribute to extracurricular as well as other community activities. The school does not discriminate against applicants on the basis of race, religion, or national or ethnic origin. Campbell Hall is a diverse school community. Students of color make up 32.7 percent of the student body, and a variety of different faiths and family structures are also represented.

An entrance examination is required, as are recommendations from 2 teachers, a transcript from the school in which the applicant is currently enrolled, and an interview.

APPLICATION TIMETABLE

The Admissions Office is open from 8 a.m. to 4 p.m., Monday through Friday, to answer inquiries and to arrange interviews and campus visits. Applicants for the 2012–13 school year should file an application, accompanied by a $125 fee, by January 27, 2012. Most applications are submitted by December of the year preceding the desired entrance. Applicants take the Independent School Entrance Examination.

The school makes most decisions concerning new admissions by March. Parents are expected to reply to an offer of acceptance within two weeks and to pay a deposit, which is credited toward the first semester's tuition.

ADMISSIONS CORRESPONDENCE

Alice Fleming, Director of Admissions
George White, Associate Director
Campbell Hall
4533 Laurel Canyon Boulevard
P.O. Box 4036
North Hollywood, California 91617-9985
Phone: 818-980-7280
Web site: http://www.campbellhall.org

CANTERBURY SCHOOL

Ft. Myers, Florida

Type: Coeducational, day, college-preparatory
Grades: Prekindergarten–12: Lower School, Pre-K–3; Intermediate School, 4–6; Middle School, 7–8; Upper School, 9–12
Enrollment: 615; Upper School, 203
Head of School: Anthony J. Paulus

THE SCHOOL

Founded in 1964, the Canterbury School sits on 33 acres located on College Parkway between U.S. 41 and McGregor Boulevard. The School is dedicated to academic excellence within a caring and supportive community, preparing students of ability, promise, and diverse backgrounds for selective colleges. Canterbury's motto, "Education, character, leadership, service," defines the focus of the School's program and underscores all that its students do in and out of the classroom.

There are four divisions—Lower (grades prekindergarten–3), Intermediate (grades 4–6), Middle (grades 7–8), and Upper (grades 9–12). At all levels, the academic program emphasizes individual growth, skill development, a high caliber of instruction, collaboration, and high standards. Canterbury provides all students with an opportunity to challenge themselves and take risks in an atmosphere of mutual respect and partnership among students, parents, and teachers. Canterbury's integrated, innovative curriculum emphasizes group and individual study of the liberal arts, in addition to experiential learning and community service opportunities.

The Canterbury School is accredited by the Southern Association of Independent Schools (SAIS), Southern Association of Colleges and Schools/Council on Accreditation and School Improvement (SACS/CASI), Florida Council of Independent Schools (FCIS), the College Board, and the Florida Kindergarten Council (FKC).

ACADEMIC PROGRAMS

All students pursue a demanding schedule of college-preparatory classes for four years in the Upper School, earning a minimum of 26 credits to graduate. Students play an active role in their course of study, and juniors and seniors may pursue advanced work in areas of significant interest or expertise. Although Honors and Advanced Placement courses, as well as independent studies, give students extra challenges, even the standard-level courses thoroughly prepare students for college work. Offering a rigorous and rewarding liberal arts curriculum, the Upper School program is rich in math, science, modern and classical languages, music, visual arts, social sciences, foreign language, and drama, with a special emphasis on writing, research, and the discourse of ideas. Study strategies, self-discipline, academic responsibility, and fluency in technology are underscored in each content area. Students learn academic honesty, competitive fair play, and good citizenship through a respected honor code. Students master key skills that will serve them well in their college careers as they actively participate in intellectual inquiry, analysis, and evaluation.

Middle School students take one course in each of the major disciplines every year—English, mathematics, science, social studies, and foreign language—and classes in the arts and in physical education/health, as well as other electives.

Canterbury's Intermediate School offers instruction in a math, science, and technology triad, as well as the "Writing Across the Curriculum" initiative, which links critical thinking and written expression in every curriculum area. Lower School celebrates childhood in an age-appropriate, developmental learning environment for students in prekindergarten through third grade; a balance between hard work and fun creates an environment where children are encouraged to take risks and assume personal responsibility for their learning as they embark upon their learning journey.

FACULTY AND ADVISERS

There are 80 faculty members, 38 of whom teach in the Upper School. Canterbury's talented and dedicated faculty seeks to inspire young minds through a rigorous and rewarding curriculum. Passionate about ideas and mentoring, instructors understand how students learn most effectively. Teaching is more than facts, figures, and formulas—it's a way of life. Canterbury's teachers personalize their approach to meet individual student needs. Small class sizes allow one-on-one time for personal attention, challenging and supporting students as they stretch their minds and their opportunities.

COLLEGE ADMISSION COUNSELING

College preparation is a primary focus of Canterbury's curriculum, so students receive the highly personalized direction and encouragement they need to choose the undergraduate institution with the right fit. An experienced college counselor guides juniors and seniors, as well as their families, through the process—helping them gain a comprehensive understanding of college acceptance practices. The result? An ongoing tradition of a 100 percent college-acceptance rate among Canterbury graduates. Recent graduates have been accepted to such distinguished institutions as Carnegie Mellon, Dartmouth, Georgetown, Harvard, Princeton, and Yale.

STUDENT BODY AND CONDUCT

Six hundred students are enrolled in grades prekindergarten–12. They come from diverse backgrounds, but the majority live in Fort Myers, Cape Coral, Sanibel, and the surrounding area.

ACADEMIC FACILITIES

The Canterbury School Libraries offer instruction, materials, and technology to promote the skills of information literacy and fluency, the love of reading, and the joy of intellectual discovery. By providing resources for both academic and recreational reading needs, the libraries help students develop research competencies for college and facilitate lifelong learning. The libraries also provide space for individual reflection and creation, as well as a forum for the sharing of ideas within the Canterbury community. The Ellenberg Library (grades 6-12) has established several special collections, in addition to the familiar biography, fiction, nonfiction, periodical, reference, and story collections. The Hilliard Library serves students from pre-K through fifth grade and their teachers. The library collection, of both print and nonprint resources, includes books, videotapes, magazines, Internet access, professional resources, and online subscription databases.

The Lower and Intermediate schools have dedicated art and music classrooms, science laboratories, computer labs and classrooms. They share a library. The Middle and Upper schools share a library, a language listening lab, and music and art classrooms, but they have separate science laboratories, computer labs, classrooms, and commons areas. The entire school shares the dining hall, a gymnasium and a sports center, an outdoor marine biology touch tank and classroom, and the Performing Arts Center.

ATHLETICS

At Canterbury, the life of the mind is complemented by a strong athletic program. Canterbury School fields teams in soccer, basketball, baseball, six-man football, volleyball, swimming, tennis, golf, cross-country, track and field, and lacrosse. Students are encouraged to become involved with athletics; around 85 percent of all Middle and Upper School students participate in interscholastic sports. Canterbury School is a member of the Florida High School Athletic Association (FHSAA) and is accredited by the Southern Association of Schools and Colleges (SACS). The Middle School belongs to the Suncoast Middle School League.

EXTRACURRICULAR OPPORTUNITIES

Clubs and organizations play key roles in student life. Students can choose from more than twenty active clubs on campus, including yearbook, newspaper, chess, mock trial, and Model UN, which meet regularly throughout the year. Students can also participate in a variety of local, state, national, and international scholastic competitions.

DAILY LIFE

Students spend their days in class, followed by after-school activities ranging from community service, student government, and athletics to clubs and study groups.

SUMMER PROGRAMS

Summer academic programs are available to students of all ages. Students can brush up their math, writing, or Spanish skills or take SAT-prep courses. Canterbury provides a recommended summer reading list for prekindergarten to fifth grade students so that they can begin, continue, and support the process of developing comprehension and analytical skills. Students in grades 6–12 receive a required summer reading list to support their academic course selection for the following year.

COSTS AND FINANCIAL AID

Upper School students pay $18,055 plus fees per academic year. Tuition is $13,920 for prekindergarten and kindergarten, $15,650 for grades 1–3, $16,890 for grades 4–6, and $17,485 for Middle School. Fees are additional. In 2011–12, Canterbury provided more than $1.5 million in financial assistance to 22 percent of the student body, with awards ranging from 20 percent to 95 percent of tuition.

Tuition payments include both a nonrefundable deposit and the remaining tuition balance. The nonrefundable 20 percent deposit is due upon enrollment and must accompany the student's enrollment contract. On July 1, another 30 percent of tuition is due, and the remaining 50 percent is due October 1. With this plan, tuition refund insurance is optional. Payment plan options are presented in the addendum to the enrollment contract.

ADMISSIONS INFORMATION

As a college-preparatory school with high academic standards, Canterbury seeks students of demonstrated abilities with potential for intellectual growth. Boys and girls entering prekindergarten through grade eleven are invited to apply, beginning the fall prior to the school year they wish to attend. Applications can be submitted online or by mail and must include the $75 application fee.

Applicants are first evaluated by testing, using the ERB, CTP 4 Test, or the SSAT in grades 3–11. Next, candidates' files are forwarded to the Admission Committee, which assesses each application based on the student's past academic achievement, performance on the admission test, a written essay, personal recommendations, and an interview with the division head and director of admission.

APPLICATION TIMETABLE

Open houses are scheduled October through April; attendees must reserve a space by contacting the admission office. Applications are accepted continually.

ADMISSIONS CORRESPONDENCE

Julie Peters, Director of Admissions
Canterbury School
8141 College Parkway
Fort Myers, Florida 33919
Phone: 239-415-8945
Fax: 239-481-8339
E-mail: jpeters@canterburyfortmyers.org
Web site: http://www.canterburyfortmyers.org/

CHAMBERLAIN-HUNT ACADEMY

Port Gibson, Mississippi

Type: Christian military boarding school for boys
Grades: 7–12
Enrollment: 100
Head of School: Jack West, President

THE SCHOOL

Chamberlain-Hunt is first and foremost a Christian school. It operates on the belief that God made man for His glory, and, therefore, everything that is taught in the classroom, achieved on the playing field, or modeled in relationships is done to the honor and glory of God.

Chamberlain-Hunt is the nation's third-oldest military school and one of the few in the United States that self-consciously maintains its distinctive Christian character and strict military discipline.

Chamberlain-Hunt is also a boarding school. Its cadets are removed from some of the distractions of the usual high school scene and are placed in an environment that supports their academic, physical, and spiritual development.

ACADEMIC PROGRAMS

Chamberlain-Hunt's cadets achieve distinction in the classroom, often for the first time. Class sizes are purposely kept small to allow each cadet to get the attention he needs. The average cadet-teacher ratio is 5:1, with class sizes ranging from 1 to 14 students. There is no danger of a child falling through the cracks at Chamberlain-Hunt. While the Academy's cadre members meet each cadet on his level, they also expect achievement and are always challenging them to reach a higher level of academic success.

Communicating through writing is crucial to achievement in life. Chamberlain-Hunt is committed to training cadets in necessary writing skills. Chamberlain-Hunt employs Excellence in Writing (EiW), a program particularly beneficial to boys that can help them overcome the fear of the blank page. It is designed to teach structure and style in composition. This program is used for writing across the curriculum, and becomes the standard by which all writing is taught and measured. By teaching students to rewrite existing stories and write from pictures, students are given the confidence to write their own material. The program concludes with modules on writing formal essays and critiques.

The caring and highly qualified members of the teaching faculty work to help shape the future for every cadet. Young men who complete the Academy's program enter the nation's top colleges. College-bound Chamberlain-Hunt seniors score an average of 5 points higher than the state average and 4 points higher than the national average on the ACT.

In addition to the educational challenges at Chamberlain-Hunt, cadets have many other opportunities to achieve distinction. These include athletics, military rankings, and extracurricular activities such as chess and gardening. While the Academy issues demerits for failures to meet requisite standards, it always rewards success, which teaches cadets to strive to meet the high goals set for them.

FACULTY AND ADVISERS

The administrators and staff of Chamberlain-Hunt Academy, known as the cadre, are individuals who care deeply about encouraging young men to make the most of their God-given ability. The cadre members are committed to giving cadets everything they need to achieve their educational goals, while also focusing on their emotional and spiritual development. The Academy's staff and faculty members believe that all wisdom stems from God the Heavenly Father, and that true education must be an active, ongoing part of a living faith.

Chamberlain-Hunt utilizes a thorough and comprehensive approach in hiring all members of its cadre. The application process includes questions about the prospect's Christian background, education, work history, and personal spiritual beliefs. Because the cadre members are working with children, background checks are performed to ensure that only the most honorable and reliable individuals are hired.

Chamberlain-Hunt's instructors offer an unparalleled education for young men. All instructors are certified and 80 percent hold advanced degrees.

COLLEGE ADMISSION COUNSELING

Chamberlain-Hunt's guidance counselors are interested in more than helping young men become productive members of society; they also challenge students to consider God's will for their lives and how they are called to serve him in whatever direction he leads.

All juniors and seniors (and select tenth graders) receive six weeks of ACT preparation and several practice tests. The Academy's college-bound senior cadets earn an average ACT score of 23.25, well above state and national averages. Over 90 percent of Chamberlain-Hunt's graduates will enter college or join the military within one year of graduation.

Guidance counseling involves exposing cadets to the variety of postsecondary opportunities, one-on-one counseling sessions to help them assess their abilities and interests, and offering them help understanding the FAFSA and other means of obtaining financial assistance.

Military Service is the goal for typically 25 percent of the cadets. Since 2004, 5 cadets have received appointments to the United States Military Academy at West Point. Other cadets have received ROTC scholarships to colleges and still others have enlisted or joined National Guard or reserve units. A young man who is interested in pursuing a military career can certainly benefit from a secondary education that employs a military structure, such as the program at Chamberlain-Hunt.

STUDENT BODY AND CONDUCT

Chamberlain-Hunt is located in rural Mississippi, so nearly all of the boys are in the boarding program. There are 100 boys from twenty-five states housed in three dormitories. The Academy's racial makeup is 80 percent Caucasian, 13 percent African American, 4 percent Hispanic, and 3 percent Asian. The grade-level breakdown of the Academy's cadet corps is grade7, 6 percent; grade 8, 10 percent; grade 9, 22 percent; grade 10, 20 percent; grade 11, 25 percent; and grade 12, 17 percent.

Chamberlain-Hunt's military structure is one of the School's unique features, which sets it apart from most of the nation's boarding schools. A military model promotes discipline, helping the cadets learn how to live within the boundaries of society. While it provides immediate consequences for infractions, it also rewards achievement. Cadets earn points in four areas of accountability, including consistent observation of procedures, appearance, room inspection, and classroom performance. Accumulation of these points can lead to rewards ranging from an extra treat, like candy or soda, to a pass to go home on a nonscheduled weekend. In addition, cadets work to earn positions of leadership throughout the corps. Through their time at Chamberlain-Hunt, young men learn the benefits of hard work and adherence to rules, as they see these qualities rewarded. This model has proven to have a positive effect on the cadets as they transition into the adult world.

Additional information about the Academy's policies and procedures can be found in the *Cadet Handbook* which can be downloaded from the Academy's Web site, under the "Cadet Life" tab.

ACADEMIC FACILITIES

The Academy has over twenty buildings; a full-size, in-ground pool; four ball fields; a six-lane cork track; a weight-training facility; indoor and outdoor basketball courts; two tennis courts; two beach volleyball courts; a covered outdoor recreational pavilion; an auditorium; library; spacious cafeteria; game room; and air-conditioned residence halls.

BOARDING AND GENERAL FACILITIES

Chamberlain-Hunt Academy is located 3 miles east of the Mississippi River, 27 miles south of Vicksburg, and 35 miles north of Natchez, on U.S. Highway 61 in Mississippi. The Academy campus is approximately 200 acres in size.

The Academy moved to its present campus, in Port Gibson, Mississippi in 1900. The two original campus buildings, McComb Hall and Guthrie Hall, were designed in brick Georgian Revival style by noted New York architect George Palliser and are listed in the National Register of Historic places.

There is a 72-acre wilderness training facility adjacent to campus with two paintball courses, a climbing and rappelling tower, a 30-yard pistol and rifle range, a fitness trail, two confidence courses, and a 4.5-acre fishing pond.

ATHLETICS

Chamberlain-Hunt strongly believes in the benefits of competitive sports. Team sports give cadets an energy outlet; a means for maintaining physical fitness; and a natural way to teach leadership, discipline, and teamwork. An athlete's skills and abilities are gifts from God, and learning to use them in a way that honors him is an important component of sports training at Chamberlain-Hunt.

The competitive athletic program for grades 7–12 includes basketball, cross-country, soccer, track, tennis, and golf.

EXTRACURRICULAR OPPORTUNITIES

A Chamberlain-Hunt cadet will have experiences that many other high school students never have. High-energy activities like swimming, tackling the climbing and rappelling tower, running obstacle courses, and intramural athletics will get them in the best physical shape of their lives. They will have the opportunity to hone shooting skills on the rifle range. The Academy's military structure gives students the chance to be a leader among peers as they rise through the ranks and earn badges and command positions. It's different from the usual high school agenda, but it offers experiences and friendships that will last a lifetime.

DAILY LIFE

Chamberlain-Hunt provides an environment for boys that interrupts their usual lifestyle: haircuts and uniforms change their appearance, schedules change their routines, and accountability changes their behavior. The cadre members and the curricula change what the cadets would otherwise put into their brains. Chamberlain-Hunt is not a monastery or a prison, but it is a place marked by devotion and discipline. Devotion to God and discipline in deportment—this is the tradition.

Undeniably, cadets give up some traditional teenage activities to come to Chamberlain-Hunt. What they get in return—rigorous academics, small class sizes, opportunities to excel, safety, close friendships—is worth sacrificing the dates and dances they miss. The Academy's belief is that the purpose of high school is not having a full social calendar, but rather to prepare students for college and adulthood. Through a structured boarding program, cadets get a change of pace from the usual high school experience and have space to develop academically, physically, and spiritually.

WEEKEND LIFE

Saturday mornings are generally spent working with other cadets on a campus or community project. Saturday afternoons and evenings are reserved for leisure time, with a variety of options including movies and plays, bowling, skating, and paintball. Swimming is another favorite activity, whether in the Chamberlain-Hunt pool or its 4.5-acre lake.

Sundays are devoted to honoring the Lord's Day through worship and rest, as prescribed in the Bible. The cadet corps march from campus to Port Gibson's historic Presbyterian Church for morning worship. After lunch, cadets retire to their dorms and spend the afternoons in rest and reflection as they read, nap, or write letters. Before supper, there is an evening vespers service. After supper, cadets return to their rooms to prepare for a new week.

SUMMER PROGRAMS

Adventure Summer School, for students who will be entering grades 7–12, is the best introduction to military boarding school. The emphasis is on academic remediation in addition to exciting extracurricular activities. Junior high cadets will take focus courses with an emphasis on math, English, writing, and proper study habits. High school cadets will take one subject and earn one academic credit.

Adventure Camp (new in 2012), for students who will be entering grades 6–8 grades, is a nonacademic summer experience with an emphasis on outdoor activities and athletics. The boys will play paintball and other competitive games. Staff members will instruct them in swimming, canoeing, climbing and rappelling, gun safety, and marksmanship (available to rising eighth graders only). Each day will include biblical instruction so that boys may know more about God and his creation while also avoiding the dangers of common temptations.

COSTS AND FINANCIAL AID

The enrollment fee for cadets living within the United States for the 2012–13 academic year is $25,000. The enrollment fee for international cadets for the 2012–13 academic year is $29,000.

Private loan programs, such as Your Tuition Solution, prepGATE and Sallie Mae's K–12 assist many families in making tuition payments more affordable by providing the funds up front and spreading the payments over a longer period of time than tuition payment plans allow. Current fees, rates, and other details are available by contacting Your Tuition Solution, prepGATE or Sallie Mae directly.

The Academy may also be able to offer means-tested financial assistance on a first-come basis to help make a Chamberlain-Hunt education more affordable. Applicants must turn in their request by August 1 for the fall semester and December 15 for the spring semester.

Because Chamberlain-Hunt is a unique school and the needs of its cadets are varied, the first step is to determine whether the Academy is the right choice for a student. Only those who have been interviewed and accepted for admission may apply for financial assistance.

ADMISSIONS INFORMATION

Choosing the right school is a big decision. An interview and tour of the campus is required of all new cadets. To help Chamberlain-Hunt prepare for the interview, applicants are asked to complete Step 1 of the application process. A checklist is found on the first page of the application.

Chamberlain-Hunt Academy does not discriminate on the basis of race, color, or national or ethnic origin in administration of its educational policies, scholarship and loan programs, athletics, or other school-administered programs. Only boys are enrolled as boarding students in both the school year and summer programs.

APPLICATION TIMETABLE

Applications are accepted at any time. The application processing fee is $50.

ADMISSIONS CORRESPONDENCE

Chamberlain-Hunt Academy
124 Macomb Avenue
Port Gibson, Mississippi 39150
Phone: 601-437-8855
Fax: 601-437-4313
E-mail: admissions@chamberlain-hunt.com
Web site: http://www.chamberlain-hunt.com

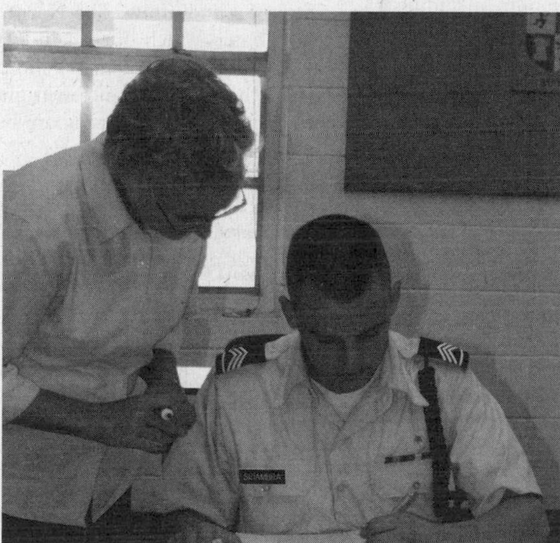

CHARLOTTE LATIN SCHOOL

Charlotte, North Carolina

Type: Independent, college-preparatory, nonsectarian, coeducational day school
Grades: Transitional kindergarten–Grade 12
Enrollment: 1,391
Head of School: Arch N. McIntosh, Jr., Headmaster

THE SCHOOL

Founded in 1970, Charlotte Latin School (CLS) is located on a 122-acre campus in southeast Charlotte, North Carolina. The school community, which includes students, parents, alumni, and faculty and staff members, embraces a shared mission, core values, and a commitment to academic excellence. Latin is a school that is traditional by design yet innovative in implementation. The School's emphasis is for its students to maintain balance in their lives, which is enhanced by a curriculum built upon a foundation of academic rigor, the arts, and athletics. Students are presented with many growth-promoting opportunities to explore and develop their interests, including a variety of co-curricular options and a TK–12 community service program that fosters a lifelong commitment to service through age-appropriate activities. Students also are encouraged to explore their world and are supported in this endeavor through active international sister schools and study-abroad programs.

Charlotte Latin remains true to its founding parents' original vision as a place where a stimulating learning environment is united with a vibrant family life. Named for America's early Latin schools, in which colonial children pursued classical studies under the careful tutelage of their teachers, Charlotte Latin similarly fosters a close relationship between its faculty and students. With their teachers' guidance, students of all ages study and serve the community that surrounds them and the world that beckons them, in preparation to care for and succeed in the global community they will inherit as adults. Their parents, too, are partners with the School in their education and are frequently seen on campus attending special events, cheering on a Hawks athletic team, sharing lunch with their children in Founders' Hall, or serving on the Board of Trustees, Parents' Council, or one of the many volunteer committees that make Charlotte Latin a special place. Alumni, too, often return to campus to visit former teachers, and in some cases, to visit their own children at Latin. More than 3,300 alumni are members of the active CLS Alumni Association.

Charlotte Latin School is accredited by and is a member of the National, Southern, and North Carolina Associations of Independent Schools. The most recent reaccreditation by SAIS-SACS (the Southern Association of Independent Schools and Southern Association of Colleges and Schools) was in 2011. The School is also accredited by the North Carolina Department of Public Instruction. Latin is the youngest school in the United States to receive a Cum Laude chapter, and it has been named a Blue Ribbon School of Excellence three times by the U.S. Department of Education.

ACADEMIC PROGRAMS

Charlotte Latin is organized into three divisions: the Lower School includes transitional kindergarten through fifth grade; the Middle School encompasses the sixth through eighth grades; and the Upper School comprises the ninth through twelfth grades.

The academic program prepares students to succeed in college and beyond by instilling a lifelong love of learning. Charlotte Latin School's curriculum is designed so that each successive grade adds to the students' mastery of skills and continued maturation. Through the leadership of the Division Heads and Curriculum Coordinator, the curriculum is constantly reviewed and refined to ensure that best practices are adopted to create a strong academic foundation.

The class of 2011's SAT scores reflect this academic strength. The middle 50 percent of scores are 570–680 for critical reading, 580–710 for mathematics, and 590–700 for writing. The class's middle 50 percent ACT composite score is 25–31.

While Latin has high expectations for its students, the School provides a nurturing environment and individual support, including a learning resources coordinator and guidance counselor for each division.

FACULTY AND ADVISERS

At Latin's core is a dedicated faculty composed of more than 180 experienced educators. The School's low student-teacher ratios and considerable professional development resources demonstrate that Latin values its teachers and celebrates learning. Active Middle School and Upper School advisory programs foster strong ties between faculty members and students, which enable these adults to serve as positive role models for maturing adolescents.

COLLEGE ADMISSION COUNSELING

As a college preparatory school, Charlotte Latin provides a College Center that guides students and their families through every step of the college admission process. The College Center is staffed by 3 full-time college counselors and a full-time registrar who work actively with both students and their families throughout the Upper School years. The support is individualized and proactive, and designed to empower the student to take ownership of the process. The success of Latin's approach to college admissions is evidenced annually; 100 percent of the School's graduates are accepted to prestigious colleges and universities across the United States and beyond.

STUDENT BODY AND CONDUCT

The Charlotte Latin community is guided by the CLS Honor Code. A plaque bearing the inscription "Honor above all" is posted in every classroom as a constant reminder of the importance of this creed in the life of Charlotte Latin School. Adherence to the Honor Pledge is a condition of enrollment in the Upper School. Students may participate with administrators and faculty members as representatives of the Upper School Honor Council after demonstrating successive levels of leadership and personally modeling honorable conduct.

ACADEMIC FACILITIES

Latin's campus features distinct areas and buildings for each of the three divisions as well as shared facilities, such as the 17,630-square-foot Media Center and 13,275-square-foot Founders' Hall dining facility. Connected by covered walkways, each area of campus is appropriate for the developmental stage of the students while also enhancing a sense of school unity. The Horne Performing Arts Center, which opened in 2011, provides state-of-the-art instructional and performance spaces for the vocal and instrumental music programs. The theater program benefits from the performing arts center's 740-seat Thies Auditorium and Anne's Black Box Theater.

Wired and wireless computer connectivity is available in every building via a campuswide fiber-optic network and a dedicated 10MB line for high-speed data transmission. Computer labs and mobile laptop labs are utilized by students at all grade levels. Internet access via the academic network is filtered by the School to ensure that students view only appropriate online content.

ATHLETICS

Interscholastic athletics have a long and rich tradition at Charlotte Latin School. Throughout its more than forty-year history, students have proven they can compete on the playing field as well as in the classroom. Along with the many conference and state titles earned over the years, the School has always placed a premium on the values instilled and the life lessons learned from athletic competition.

Latin sponsors more than sixty-five athletic teams in seventeen men's and women's sports, and more than 90 percent of students in grades 7–12 participate in at least one sport.

Athletic facilities include three gymnasiums, an all-weather track surrounding the 1,450-seat Patten Stadium; six tennis courts; seven playing fields; an Olympic-quality natatorium; a cross-country course; and the Beck Student Activities Center, which includes an arena, fitness facility, indoor track, and dedicated wrestling room.

The Charlotte Latin Hawks have won the Wachovia Cup for overall excellence in high school athletics every year from 2005 through 2011. A commitment to athletic excellence is not only reflected in the many championship banners collected over the years but also through Latin's adherence to high standards of personal conduct and good sportsmanship on the part of student athletes, coaches, and fans.

EXTRACURRICULAR OPPORTUNITIES

Charlotte Latin offers a balanced program that provides creative outlets for students' intellectual and physical energies. Beginning in the fourth grade, a broad selection of clubs and organizations is available to encourage students to pursue their interests and explore new opportunities. Leadership development is a key component of participation, with students accepting increasing responsibility for managing organizations such as the Student Council, Service Program, and the Mosaic Club, which fosters inclusiveness and promotes awareness of diversity issues.

SUMMER PROGRAMS

The goal of Charlotte Latin Summer Programs is to provide an environment that promotes a joy for learning, where campers can develop cognitively, socially, emotionally, and physically through growth-promoting experiences. A professional and caring staff sustains a safe, structured, and innovative environment that sparks children's excitement about exploring new possibilities. Camps are primarily designed for boys and girls in Lower School and Middle School. Fees vary depending on the camp(s) selected. For more information, call 704-846-7277.

COSTS AND FINANCIAL AID

Tuition for the 2011–2012 school year was as follows: transitional kindergarten and kindergarten, $15,350; grades 1–5, $17,850; and grades 6–12, $19,250.

Charlotte Latin has need-based financial aid funds available for qualified families. Application for financial aid is made during the admissions application process. Charlotte Latin is a Malone Scholar School, and other scholarships are available to students based upon specific qualifying criteria.

ADMISSIONS INFORMATION

Charlotte Latin School's admission policies were established to fulfill the School's philosophy: to initiate in its students a love of and a respect for learning, to help them develop self-discipline, and to encourage creativity. The School seeks to attract a variety of students who demonstrate motivation and the ability to respond to the total School program. Charlotte Latin welcomes students who indicate a willingness to participate and a desire to do their best. The School believes that students with a breadth of talents and interests will contribute to the creation of a dynamic learning environment. Charlotte Latin School does not discriminate on the basis of sex, race, color, religion, or national origin in the administration of its educational programs, admissions policies, financial aid policies, employment practices, or other School-administered programs.

APPLICATION TIMETABLE

Additional information about Charlotte Latin School's admissions process and key dates is available online at www.charlottelatin.org/admissions.

ADMISSIONS CORRESPONDENCE

Charlotte Latin School
9502 Providence Road
Charlotte, North Carolina 28277
Phone: 704-846-1100
E-mail: inquiries@charlottelatin.org
Web site: http://www.charlottelatin.org

CHATHAM HALL

Chatham, Virginia

Type: Girls' boarding and day college-preparatory school
Grades: 9–12
Enrollment: 140
Head of School: Gary J. Fountain, Rector

THE SCHOOL

Since its founding 1894, Chatham Hall, an independent, all-girls boarding and day high school in Chatham, Virginia, has earned a national and international reputation for its broad, strong college-preparatory program and its global educational community. At the center of the School is its honor code and strong Episcopal heritage. Its alumnae have earned positions of prominence in politics, business, education, medicine, engineering, and the arts, and include renowned painter Georgia O'Keeffe and Pulitzer Prize-winning poet Claudia Emerson.

Chatham Hall's unique programming includes annual service trips to South Africa and its Leader in Residence Program, which brings world leaders to campus to meet with students. Recent leaders in residence have included Jane Goodall, well-known anthropologist and primatologist; the late Benazir Bhutto, Prime Minister of Pakistan; Ellen Johnson-Sirleaf, the first female President of Liberia; and Nancy Brinker, founder of Race for the Cure.

Chatham Hall benefits from its proximity to educational and cultural centers in Raleigh, Durham, Chapel Hill, and Greensboro, North Carolina; and Charlottesville, Lynchburg, and Roanoke, Virginia. Located in the Piedmont section of Virginia, its 362-acre campus has rolling countryside with woods, streams, and pasturelands.

Chatham Hall is governed by a national, self-perpetuating Board of Trustees. The school's recorded endowment is valued at $20 million, and the average gift to the school is one of the highest among girls' schools.

Accredited by the Southern Association of Colleges and Schools and the National Association of Independent Schools, Chatham Hall holds memberships in the National Association of Principals of Schools for Girls, the National Association of College Admission Counselors, the National Coalition of Girls' Schools, the Secondary School Admission Test Board, the Council for the Advancement and Support of Education, and the Virginia Association of Independent Schools.

ACADEMIC PROGRAMS

The school's curriculum emphasizes analytical reasoning, expressive abilities, character and vision, and physical vigor. To graduate from Chatham Hall, students must complete their senior year at the school and fulfill the following minimum distribution requirements: 4 years of English, 3 years of mathematics, 3 years of history (1 of which must be U.S. history), 3 years of one foreign language, 3 years of lab science (2 of which must be biology and chemistry), 1 year of fine or performing arts, 1 trimester of religion, and 1 trimester of ethics. In addition, students must participate in the physical fitness program each trimester. A total of 20 credits are required. Advanced Placement courses are offered in each department, and students may apply to the Discovery Challenge independent-study program. Electives include such courses as DNA Science and Veterinary Science.

Classes meet five days per week for 45-, 60-, and 75-minute periods. The average class size is 8 students, and the overall student-teacher ratio is approximately 7:1. Typically, students carry five to six academic courses each trimester. Grading is on a scale of A to F with pluses and minuses. Grade reports with teacher comments are sent home at the middle and end of each trimester. Parents also have regular communication with the student's adviser.

FACULTY AND ADVISERS

The faculty consists of 33 teaching members. Sixty-two percent have advanced degrees. Nearly all faculty members live on campus, and each serves as an adviser to a small group of girls, meeting with each girl individually and helping her to define and realize her goals for the year and for the future.

Dr. Gary Fountain is Chatham Hall's ninth rector in its history. He received an A.B. degree from Brown University, a Master of Arts in Religion from Yale Divinity School, and a Ph.D. from the Department of English and American Literature at Boston University. Prior to coming to Chatham Hal, Fountain was an associate professor of English and Director of English Teacher Education at Ithaca College in New York. He also has served in faculty or administration positions at Saint Joseph's College, Miss Porter's School, and Ethel Walker School.

COLLEGE PLACEMENT

Chatham Hall is a college-preparatory school; as such, students prepare for college from the moment they enter Chatham Hall. Students begin working formally with the school's college counselor early in their Chatham Hall experience and meet frequently with her throughout the process. Recently, Chatham Hall graduates have attended such schools as Colgate, Cornell, Dartmouth, Duke, Georgetown, Johns Hopkins, Stanford, Swarthmore, Wellesley, and the Universities of North Carolina and Virginia.

STUDENT BODY AND CONDUCT

Chatham Hall is one of the few girls' schools in which more than 80 percent of the students are seven-day boarders. In 2011–12, the student body consisted of 140 girls from twenty-one states and eleven other countries.

The entire Chatham Hall community upholds the Honor Code as the foundation upon which the school is built. In matters of daily living, Chatham Hall students also depend on a clear statement of citizenship, known as the Purple and Golden Rule. Chatham Hall does not subscribe to a demerit system. Rather, Chatham Hall students value a system of implicit understandings over explicit and restrictive rules. The school believes in each girl's innate ability to make good choices and to lead herself according to her conscience. Under the Purple and Golden Rule, each girl is responsible for her actions and accepts the consequences of them, and she embraces the concept of White Flag—respect for people and property. The Purple and Golden Rule establishes a framework by which each girl governs herself and her peers throughout the school year. As a custodian of these principles, she sets an example for others and counsels others when they are not living up to these principles.

ACADEMIC FACILITIES

The Chatham Hall Intranet connects the school community electronically. Each dorm room has two data ports and two phone ports. Each classroom and office is also networked. A full-time Director of Instructional Technology works with faculty members on integrating technology into their curricula. Pruden Hall contains offices, formal sitting rooms, two dormitory floors, a nine-bed Health Care Center, and a darkroom facility. Dabney Hall contains eleven classrooms; a computer lab; two dormitory floors; a day student room; and a student center, including a kitchen, a viewing room, mail boxes, the bookstore, and a fitness center. The Shaw Science and Technology building has four state-of-the-art laboratory classrooms, a sophisticated technology classroom, a seminar room, and a wireless computer network. The Holt Language Building has four foreign language classrooms. Boasting award-winning architecture, the Edmund and Lucy Lee Library contains 30,000 holdings, is fully computerized, and allows students online access to virtually every resource in the country through VLIN, Dialog, OCLC, and Internet connections. The Whitner Dance/Art Studio has large, flexible spaces that are well equipped for modern dance and ballet; for painting, pottery, sculpture, and weaving; and for drama in the black box theater. Willis Hall contains two large classrooms and the Advancement Office.

The School has also recently completed construction of the Van Voorhis Lecture Hall. This new lecture hall makes it possible for the entire Chatham Hall community and guests to gather on campus to hear lectures by some of the world's greatest leaders, thinkers and artists. The new 3,788-square-foot lecture hall accommodates an audience of up to 350 people.

Chatham Hall's dining facility, Yardley Hall, received a massive renovation during the summer of 2008. In addition to a state-of-the-art, open-air kitchen, the dining hall has been refurbished with new tables, chairs, and carpeting. The sleek yet comfortable design and layout is a perfect setting for Chatham's community meals.

BOARDING AND GENERAL FACILITIES

Students live on one of four dormitory floors located in Pruden and Dabney. They generally share a room, but some may live in a single. Houseparents live on each floor, as do members of the Student Council. Both dormitories have phone and Internet access and individual heating/air conditioning units in each room. St. Mary's Chapel is a focal point of the school, hosting three weekly services, Senior Chapel Talks, choir rehearsals, and piano and voice lessons. Chatham Hall's forty-stall riding facility features the Mars Riding Arena, a 125-foot by 250-foot indoor riding facility that is among the best on the East Coast. The physical plant is valued at $25.2 million.

ATHLETICS

Physical fitness is a vital part of the Chatham Hall experience. All students participate in athletics each trimester. The school supports varsity teams in basketball, cross-country, field hockey, riding, soccer, swimming, tennis, and volleyball. Chatham Hall's Riding Program offers hunt seat riding and features a competitive, varsity show team that participates in AA shows in USEF Zone 3.

The recently renovated and air-conditioned gymnasium serves as both an athletic facility for basketball and volleyball and as a recreation and performance space for mixers, aerobics, and dance. The school also has three playing fields and six all-weather tennis courts. Riding facilities include forty stalls, a 125-foot by 250-foot indoor arena, a 275-foot by 175-foot show arena, a permanent hunter trial course, three large schooling and teaching fields, and extensive trails.

EXTRACURRICULAR OPPORTUNITIES

Chatham Hall students belong to more than thirty organizations representing a wide range of interests, including FOCUS; various art, language, and riding clubs; the environmental club; and numerous student publications. All students and faculty are members of one of the branches of the Service League: Community Life, School Life, or Church Life.

Students have performance and academic instruction opportunities in theater, dance, and music. The Sherwood Dramatic Club performs two major productions a year. Panache, Chatham Hall's modern dance ensemble, performs on and off campus several times a year. Singers have a variety of performance opportunities to perform in St. Mary's Choir, the Chamber Choir, and Sextet.

DAILY LIFE

Classes begin at 8 a.m. and end at 3:30 p.m. Afternoons are devoted to athletics. Required chapel services are held three times each week. The community gathers in the Well in Pruden on Monday and Thursday mornings for an all-school assembly. The school eats meals together; most meals are buffet-style. There are three seated meals each week: lunch on Wednesday and Thursday and dinner on Monday. Students sit with faculty advisers. Clubs generally meet after dinner. There are required study hours from 7:30 to 9:30 on school nights. Students may study in their rooms, the library, special group study rooms, or one of the computer labs. Room bell in the dormitories is at 10:25 p.m.

WEEKEND LIFE

Chatham Hall is a seven-day boarding school, and offers a variety of fun and enriching activities both on and off campus. Taking advantage of the school's location, Chatham Hall students spend weekends attending concerts and theater and art shows in nearby cities, enjoying a wide variety of outdoor activities such as skiing and hiking, or going out to dinner and movies with friends. Chatham Hall also arranges large trips to Washington D.C. and Baltimore for cultural and shopping excursions. Chatham Hall participates in the Boarding Schools Social Activities Committee (BSSAC), which coordinates mixers and other events with boarding schools throughout Virginia.

COSTS AND FINANCIAL AID

The comprehensive fee for boarders is $39,000, which includes tuition, room, and board. The fee for day students is $16,500. Books, transportation, private music lessons, English as a second language, swimming, and riding carry additional charges.

Chatham Hall is committed to bringing qualified girls to the school. To this end, the school offers financial aid grants to families who demonstrate need under the guidelines of the School and Student Service for Financial Aid.

ADMISSIONS INFORMATION

Chatham Hall admits young women whose character and integrity, academic and intellectual promise, motivation, and enthusiasm for participating in the life of the school will predictably make them successful members of the school community.

APPLICATION TIMETABLE

Chatham Hall's application deadline is February 1. After that date, students are admitted on a rolling basis. Candidates should plan to visit the school early in the process for an interview and tour and to spend the night in a dorm. In addition to completing the application forms, candidates must also submit standardized test scores, such as those from the Secondary School Admission Test (SSAT).

ADMISSIONS CORRESPONDENCE

Vicki Wright
Director of Admission and Financial Aid
Chatham Hall
800 Chatham Hall Circle
Chatham, Virginia 24531
Phone: 434-432-2941
877-644-2941 (toll-free)
Fax: 434-432-2405
E-mail: admission@chathamhall.com
Web site: http://www.chathamhall.org

CHRIST SCHOOL

Arden, North Carolina

Type: Boys' boarding and day college-preparatory school
Grades: 8–12
Enrollment: 248
Head of School: Paul M. Krieger, Headmaster

THE SCHOOL

Founded in 1900 and located just south of Asheville, North Carolina, Christ School is located on a beautiful 500-acre suburban mountain campus. The school is home to 248 students; 175 live on campus and 73 are day students. They come from fifteen states and nine other countries, including Germany, China, Canada, South Korea, Russia, Hong Kong, and the Bahamas.

A traditional college preparatory boarding school for boys, Christ School's focus and offerings center on providing opportunities for boys to simply become a more mature expression of who they are intended to be.

Comfortable, genuine, quality minus pretense—these are ways in which the school is often described. A student sums it up in this way: "Christ School is not a coat and tie school; it's a necktie and shorts school." In short, Christ School is a place where solid academic programming can coexist alongside solid athletic and extracurricular programming—one does not come at the expense of the other.

ACADEMIC PROGRAMS

Preparing boys academically for college is Christ School's primary objective. The curriculum is designed to provide students with a firm foundation in both the academic subjects and the study skills they will need in college. The School's curriculum also stresses the knowledge and skills that will enable a student to become an informed and intelligent citizen of his community. The School has always believed that these objectives can best be fulfilled through a concentration in the traditional arts and sciences.

Small classes and individual attention are the keys to a boy's academic development. A structured program of independent and supervised study enables a student to better achieve his potential.

Requirements for graduation include the completion of 20 credits: English (4); mathematics (4); science (3); history (3); foreign language—Latin, French, or Spanish (2); fine arts (1); religious studies (0.5); technology (0.5); and electives (2). Electives include Advanced Placement courses in the arts, computer programming, English, foreign languages, history, mathematics, and science. General elective courses include choir, economics, government, history of Vietnam, journalism, marine biology, music of Western civilization, music practicum, music theory and composition, studio art I and II, and theater.

Most students carry a course load of five academic subjects, independent or supervised study, and a choice of extracurricular activities.

The average class size is 10–12 students; the student-faculty ratio is 5:1. Students are placed in classes on the basis of their achievement levels, their interests, and the requirements for graduation.

Christ School's Learning Resource Program offers academic support in English, math, and study skills within the context of a rigorous college-preparatory curriculum. The program serves those who can meet the challenges of a full academic schedule while benefiting from the program's supportive techniques.

FACULTY AND ADVISERS

The faculty consists of 43 full-time members, 28 with advanced degrees. Twenty-eight reside on campus.

Paul M. Krieger was appointed the twelfth Headmaster of Christ School in 2003. He had previously served as the school's Principal since August 2000. Before coming to Christ School, he served as Head of the Middle School at Montgomery Academy in Chester Springs, Pennsylvania. Following an extensive career in marketing, much of which was spent in the Eastern Mediterranean and the Middle East, he chose to leave the business field in 1989 for education. At the Hill School, in Pottstown, Pennsylvania, he served as Assistant Director of Development and Alumni Affairs and Assistant Director of Admissions, was Founder and Director of the Hill Sports Camp, and held the Knobloch Chair in Economics, teaching Advanced Placement courses. Mr. Krieger has a Bachelor of Arts degree from Gettysburg College and a Master of Education Leadership from Immaculata College.

The School seeks teachers who are dedicated to the academic, social, and spiritual well-being of students and who share the common interest in self-improvement that sets boys upon the path to maturity and manhood. A student's progress throughout his years at Christ School is monitored closely by the faculty. Each boy has an adviser for guidance, mentorship, and support in his academic and personal life at the School.

A strong relationship between the student and adviser is formed through formal and informal meetings and frequent gatherings for meals and recreation. In addition, each new student is matched with an outstanding upperclassman as a Big Brother to further help the adjustment to boarding school life.

COLLEGE ADMISSION COUNSELING

In a student's sophomore, junior, and senior years, the Dean and College Counselor work with the student and his family to assist him in securing admission to the college most suited to his needs. In addition, college representatives visit the campus in the fall and winter to discuss college admission requirements and procedures with students.

Christ School graduated 56 seniors in 2011, all of whom were accepted at four-year colleges and universities. The School administered sixty Advanced Placement exams.

Graduates have been accepted at a variety of colleges and universities. Among them are the Air Force Academy, Art Institute of Boston, Brown, Clemson, Columbia, Duke, Elon, Furman, George Washington, Georgia Tech, Harvard, Macalester, Morehouse, Northeastern, Presbyterian, Rensselaer, SMU, Stanford, Wake Forest, Washington and Lee, Wheaton, William and Mary, Wofford, the University of North Carolina at Chapel Hill, and the University of the South.

STUDENT BODY AND CONDUCT

Christ School has a boarding student population of 175 boarders and 73 day students. Fifteen states and nine other countries are represented among the student body, and boys come from various religious and socioeconomic backgrounds.

The responsibility for student life and conduct at Christ School is largely in the hands of the students themselves. A student council, composed of prefects appointed by the Headmaster and members elected by the various forms, makes recommendations to the Headmaster regarding discipline and other aspects of School life. Sixth Formers (twelfth graders) guide and help supervise various activities, such as house life and the self-help work program.

ACADEMIC FACILITIES

The academic facilities are housed mainly in Wetmore Hall, which contains classrooms, a computer lab, and a music room. The Information and Media Center houses the main reading and research room, with a state-of-the-art computer center that links an in-house service with the Internet global community. The Pingree Fine Arts Auditorium was dedicated in 1992. In fall 2011 the Mebane Science Center was opened, which contains state-of-the-art chemistry, biology, and physics laboratories with separate lecture areas, as well as a rooftop observatory.

BOARDING AND GENERAL FACILITIES

Christ School students reside in five houses and typically, two boys are assigned to a room. Each house is supervised by prefects and proctors under the direction of a dorm parent. All houses are fully equipped with computer networking capabilities. Students in grades 8 and 9 live separately from students in grades 10 through 12. A student center includes a game room, lounge, fireplace, snack shop, barbershop, bookstore, and forty-seat theater/TV room. Renovations of St. Joseph's chapel, which was built in 1907, were completed in 2006.

ATHLETICS

Physical development, sportsmanship, cooperation, and self-esteem are all fostered by organized athletics. The various levels in all team sports allow each boy to choose those activities that best meet his interests and competence.

On the School grounds are six hard-surfaced tennis courts, a football field, a baseball field, three soccer fields, an all-weather track, a challenging 5K cross-country course, and a 3-acre lake that is used for kayaking, canoeing, fishing, and swimming. Indoor athletics facilities are housed in a modern field house containing a basketball court and three full-sized practice courts. The remodeled Memorial Gymnasium contains a wrestling gym, three racquetball courts, a new weight room, a training room, an equipment room, four locker rooms, and offices for coaches.

The School fields interscholastic teams in football, cross-country, soccer, basketball, wrestling, swimming, lacrosse, baseball, tennis, golf, and track. In lieu of athletics, students have the option to participate in the theater program, debate, an intramural program, or the outdoor program. An outdoor education program provides instruction and trips in white-water canoeing, climbing, hiking, camping, mountain biking, and initiatives on a low-ropes course. The outdoor program is available as an alternative to team sports.

EXTRACURRICULAR OPPORTUNITIES

Daily periods are set aside for extracurricular activities. On weekends, a wide range of planned activities is available for students to explore other interests.

For students who are learning to play musical instruments, private lessons in guitar, drums, keyboards, and other instruments can be arranged. The School yearbook and literary magazine provide opportunities for creative writing, photography, and art. The student newspaper is produced using the latest computer technology and appears on the School Web site. A theater program produces three plays a year, enabling students to express their talents in acting, set designing, and stage managing. The art studio contains tools and equipment for extracurricular painting, woodworking, drawing, and ceramics.

Because of the School's proximity to various winter resorts, there are many opportunities for Christ School students to ski on designated ski days and weekends.

WEEKEND LIFE

Weekends offer a less structured environment that allows participation in sports, planned activities, and free time to pursue a wide variety of interests. Christ School has a student activities director to coordinate weekend and coeducational activities. Weekends provide opportunities for interscholastic athletics; white-water rafting; taking in a concert or a movie; trips to cultural events in Asheville, Atlanta, Charlotte, and Knoxville; attending professional and collegiate sporting events; shopping; dances; and course work.

COSTS AND FINANCIAL AID

For the 2011–12 school year, tuition and room and board are $40,250 for boarders and $21,000 for day students. In addition, a weekly allowance can be arranged through the school bookstore to cover additional expenses for each individual student. Tuition insurance and tuition payment plans are available.

Financial aid and merit scholarships are available to qualified students. For the 2011–12 school year, the School will award $2.1 million in aid and scholarships.

ADMISSIONS INFORMATION

Christ School accepts students in grades 8–11. Admission policies are based on academic ability and personal qualifications. The School seeks students who can realize their full potential in a school that emphasizes the value of structure, community, and personal responsibility. Of paramount importance is the ability of each potential student to fit into and contribute to a small, caring community.

The School requires prospective candidates to schedule a campus visit, and submit teacher recommendations, a transcript, and application essays. The SSAT is required.

Campus visits include a tour of the campus and a personal interview with the admission office, as well as time with the Headmaster.

A small number of students are accepted for the second semester, which begins in January. The School encourages families to set up a campus visit in the fall.

APPLICATION TIMETABLE

For boarding students, the nonbinding, early action application deadline is December 15, and decisions are mailed on January 1. The regular application deadline for boarders is February 15, and decisions are mailed on March 1. For day students, the application deadline is February 15, with decisions mailed on March 1. After March 1, admissions are made on a rolling basis. There are very limited openings after June 1.

ADMISSIONS CORRESPONDENCE

Garrison K. Conner
Director of Admission
Christ School
500 Christ School Road
Arden, North Carolina 28704
Phone: 828-684-6232 Ext. 106
800-422-3212 (toll-free)
Fax: 828-209-0003
E-mail: admission@christschool.org
Web site: http://www.christschool.org

CONVENT OF THE SACRED HEART

Greenwich, Connecticut

Type: Independent, Catholic day school for girls
Grades: P–12: Lower School, Preschool–4; Middle School, 5–8; Upper School, 9–12
Enrollment: School total: 769; Upper School: 285
Head of School: Pamela Juan Hayes, Head of School

THE SCHOOL

Convent of the Sacred Heart is situated on a beautiful 110-acre wooded campus in Greenwich, Connecticut. Greenwich is a suburban town located about 30 miles from New York City and 40 minutes from New Haven. An independent Catholic school for girls in preschool through grade 12, Sacred Heart was first established in New York City in 1848 and moved to Greenwich in 1945. Convent of the Sacred Heart is one of twenty-two Sacred Heart schools in the United States and part of an international network of schools that includes more than 200 schools in twenty-eight countries around the world.

A Sacred Heart education provides a strong academic foundation appropriate to each student's individual talents and abilities within an environment that fosters the development of her spiritual life and a strong sense of personal values. True to its international heritage, the school welcomes students and faculty members of diverse backgrounds and faiths, so that each student will grow in her understanding of different cultures and peoples. Graduates are prepared to become leaders with broad intellectual and spiritual horizons.

Convent of the Sacred Heart is a nonprofit institution governed by a 23-member Board of Trustees, which is responsible to the Society of the Sacred Heart for the implementation of the society's educational philosophy. Parents, religious, alumnae, and educators serve on the board. Sacred Heart benefits from the active involvement and strong support of its parent and alumnae organizations.

The school is accredited by the New England Association of Schools and Colleges and approved by the Connecticut State Board of Education. It is a member of the National Association of Independent Schools, the Connecticut Association of Independent Schools, the Cum Laude Society, the College Board, the National Association of College Admissions Counselors, the National Coalition of Girls' Schools, and the Network of Sacred Heart Schools in the United States.

ACADEMIC PROGRAMS

Sacred Heart is committed to the development of each student's intellectual, physical, spiritual, and emotional well-being. The academic program in the Upper School provides a rigorous educational foundation that enables students to become independent and creative thinkers. Students are active participants in the learning process, expanding their experience through exploration, inquiry, and discovery. Students analyze, critique, evaluate, and make important connections with the concepts they learn.

Sacred Heart's academic program is comprehensive, rigorous, and flexible. Serious study is emphasized, and the development of essential academic skills necessary for success in college and life is encouraged. College-preparatory, honors, and advanced-placement courses are offered throughout the core curriculum, which includes mathematics, science, English, history and social sciences, world languages, theology, and the arts. A student is afforded opportunities for exploration of her own talents and interests through special projects, study abroad, summer programs, and independent study. Emphasizing the connection between the disciplines is critical to learning at Sacred Heart. Faculty collaboration helps students in discovering and understanding the relevance of all subject areas and the importance of their learning in relationship to society and their daily lives.

A student's schedule for the three-term academic year is planned individually. The student plans her course of study with the support of her teachers and her Academic Dean. Course levels are chosen according to academic readiness, ability, and talent in an academic area. Each student typically takes between 6 and 8 credits per school year in a combination of required courses and electives.

Graduation requirements are based on the expectations of highly selective colleges and universities; all of Sacred Heart's graduates choose to attend college. To receive a diploma, students must complete a minimum of 25 credits, although the majority of students complete more than this minimum number. The requirements include 4 credits of English, 4 credits in theology, 3 credits in history, 3 credits in mathematics, 3 credits in a world language, 3 credits in science, and 2 elective credits, at least 1 of which must be in the arts. Students must also complete 2 years of physical education and a 2-year health education requirement.

All academic disciplines employ the computer as a tool for writing, research, analysis, and presentation, including the use of multimedia presentations, spreadsheets and databases for organization and analysis, and desktop publishing. The program also addresses the possibilities and responsibilities associated with the use of technology in today's society. All students in grades 7–12 use laptop computers in the classroom and anywhere else they study or work.

FACULTY AND ADVISERS

High expectations and positive role models are important to the success of girls and young women. A student-faculty ratio of 7:1 and an average class size of approximately 13 students ensure the teachers know every student. Assured of the faculty's support, students are motivated to take risks through which confidence and self-discipline develop. Individual teaching styles are complemented by a common commitment to the goals and criteria of a Sacred Heart education.

Convent of the Sacred Heart has 122 faculty members, with 42 full-time and 7 part-time members teaching in the Upper School. They also serve as academic advisers to small groups of about 10 advisees, and many serve as club moderators and coaches as well. Students meet with their advisers regularly during a special advisory period. Each day begins with an all-school assembly and students and faculty members attend an Upper School chapel service once per cycle.

Teachers regularly participate in workshops, summer study, curriculum development, travel, and research. Approximately 83 percent of the faculty members hold advanced degrees, including 10 who have doctoral degrees. The full-time faculty has an average of fifteen years of teaching experience.

COLLEGE ADMISSION COUNSELING

The College Guidance Department at Sacred Heart believes in the importance of an individualized college process and works hard to find the best match possible for each student. An informational parent meeting in the sophomore year helps to set this tone. The Directors of College Guidance also review PSAT scores, and help their student advisees plan schedules for appropriate SAT Subject Tests.

In junior year, students and parents meet with the Directors of College Guidance to identify goals and discuss expectations about college plans. The college search process is explained at an evening winter program, which features college representatives and the college counselors. Juniors also attend guidance classes that explore issues surrounding the college selection process, including identifying prospective colleges, the campus visit and interview, the college essay, and financial aid and scholarships. Students have access to a variety of college search resources, including guidebooks, Internet search engines, and an internal software program. Students are also encouraged to take advantage of opportunities to meet with the many college representatives who visit Sacred Heart in the fall.

During the senior year, each student and her parents examine the more specific details of the application process: deadlines, the submission of standardized test scores, the college essay, resumes, and financial aid. In the school's 162-year history, Sacred Heart graduates have attended many of the nation's finest colleges and universities. Recent graduates are currently attending schools such as Boston College, Brown, Georgetown, Harvard, Holy Cross, Johns Hopkins, Notre Dame, Stanford, Wellesley, Yale, and the University of Pennsylvania.

STUDENT BODY AND CONDUCT

There are 769 students enrolled in preschool through grade 12, with 285 students enrolled in the Upper School. Students join the high school from more than sixty-seven different communities, coming from public, private, and parochial schools in Connecticut and New York State. The student body includes a diversity of ethnic, socioeconomic, and religious backgrounds that allows for a dynamic community with a wide range of interests, talents, and passions.

School policies and practices foster the acceptance of responsibility, self-discipline, respect for the self and others, and caring for the school and wider community. The student government, student/faculty disciplinary board, and the administration work together to establish and enforce policies and minimal rules that govern the school community.

ACADEMIC FACILITIES

Overlooking Long Island Sound, the campus consists of modern classrooms, science laboratories, an observatory, playgrounds, synthetic-turf fields, a media center, a theater, a chapel, a broadcast journalism studio, a gymnasium, a fitness room, a swimming pool, and a dance studio.

The media center holds a collection of 30,000 books, 1,000 e-books, online databases and encyclopedias, and DVDs and videos in a fully wireless environment.

A 29,000-square-foot science center has state-of-the-art science laboratories for all three divisions, including the Upper School's Science Research Program, in addition to space for the Upper School art studio, special space for drama and music, classrooms, and offices. On campus, there is a free-standing state-of-the-art observatory, which offers students interested in astronomy the opportunity for viewings of the night sky through a computerized, 16-inch telescope with 800x magnification. In addition, outside the observatory there is a pad with ten 8-inch telescopes.

The broadcast journalism studio consists of control, editing, and recording rooms. Students learn how to operate camera, audio, lighting, and editing equipment to tell their stories. This state-of-the-art space provides students with the opportunity to practice media literacy in a meaningful, hands-on fashion.

Students studying art, environmental science, and ecology make frequent use of the school's acres of woods, trails, fields, and a working vegetable garden. The campus is further enlivened by traditions and events unique to Convent of the Sacred Heart.

ATHLETICS

The energy of the Sacred Heart community extends beyond the walls of the school buildings. The indoor competition swimming pool, tennis courts, and the synthetic and grass playing fields outside are showcases for girls accepting challenges, testing limits, and cooperating with teammates. Sacred Heart provides a full schedule of varsity, junior varsity, and thirds sports, including basketball, crew, cross-country, field hockey, golf, lacrosse, soccer, softball, squash, swimming and diving, tennis, and volleyball. The teams are supported with the very best facilities and equipment, including two synthetic-turf fields. Convent of the Sacred Heart is a member of the twelve-school Fairchester League and the New England Preparatory School Athletic Council (NEPSAC). A certified athletic trainer services both the Middle and Upper School student-athletes.

The physical education program is designed to develop skills for a healthy and active life. Opportunities are provided for competition, excellence, and fun in a variety of activities for all students.

EXTRACURRICULAR OPPORTUNITIES

A wide range of clubs, committees, and activities provide opportunities for students to contribute to the school community, pursue their interests, and develop leadership and team skills. Students produce major theatrical productions, govern the student body through extensive collaboration with student-elected representatives, and produce award-winning publications, which include a school newspaper and a literary and art magazine in English and another in a variety of world languages. Sacred Heart students participate in local, regional, and national competitions with their peers from other schools through programs such as forensics/speech and debate, science research, broadcast journalism, and Model United Nations. These programs are designed to promote self-expression, intellectual challenge, and individual leadership opportunities.

Music, dramatic readings, and gallery art shows are an important part of the Upper School experience. Diverse curricular offerings in visual arts, theater, and music provide opportunities for interdisciplinary study, and core academic classes often collaborate on thematic projects with the arts departments.

Recognizing that one's own creative development emerges from exposure to the creativity of others, Sacred Heart emphasizes a balance between performance and appreciation. Guest artists, performers, and lecturers regularly visit the school. Proximity to New York City creates opportunities to investigate unlimited cultural resources, while student exhibitions and performances showcase the talents cultivated in the school's classes and studios.

The Community Service Program is also an integral part of the Upper School experience at Sacred Heart. Using age-appropriate tools, students study a wide range of issues, including racism, poverty, housing, and education. Analysis of social injustices helps the students recognize that they can use their talents to be agents of change in the world. The Community Service Program explores domestic and global issues and includes guest speakers, individual yearly projects, service trips, and retreats. While service is required for Upper School students, most exceed the graduation requirement of 100 hours with extra volunteer work. The Barat Foundation is a student-run philanthropic organization that awards grants to community nonprofits and teaches financial literacy to students.

The Sacred Heart Exchange Program allows students to experience different cultures in the United States and around the world. Upper School students may complete an academic exchange of two to ten weeks at another Sacred Heart school. Convent of the Sacred Heart also welcomes exchange students to its campus. Recently, Sacred Heart students have studied in California, Chicago, Houston, Miami, New Orleans, and Seattle and abroad in England, France, Spain, Australia, Chile, Mexico, and Nova Scotia. Upon graduating, students are given an international Sacred Heart Passport listing the Sacred Heart schools throughout the world where they are always welcome.

DAILY LIFE

The first academic period begins at 8:25 a.m. The school day includes six academic periods with time built in for advisory periods, assembly periods, and activities and club meetings. The day concludes at 3:25 p.m. Sports and a variety of activities occur after school. Students may buy or bring their lunch. A hot lunch is provided for a yearly fee.

SUMMER PROGRAMS

Sacred Heart hosts an annual Summer Outreach Program for 250 boys and girls in grades 2 through 9 from low-income families. The academic program is augmented with extracurricular activities, including team sports, swimming lessons, and hands-on experience with a vegetable garden. The Summer Science Academy is for girls who show interest and promise in science and math entering grades 6 through 9 from low-income families. The five-week program includes traditional classroom experiences as well as guided scientific activities, independent investigations, and field trips.

As part of the Summer Outreach, the Summer Humanities Academy, which began in 2002, accepts girls entering grades 7 and 8 and offers a curriculum focused on writing, literature, and art. Students refined their writing skills, enhanced their reading and analytical skills, and had hands-on experiences that allowed them to understand the distinction between and the union of art and craft. Students used computers to create a literary magazine. Artists-in-residence offered workshops in writing, dance, and music. In addition, students received swimming instruction and participated in the farm program.

COSTS AND FINANCIAL AID

An education at Sacred Heart is an investment that provides many important and valuable opportunities. Tuition for 2011–12 was $33,300 for grades 9–12. The Financial Aid Committee is committed to helping families find ways to make an education at Convent of the Sacred Heart affordable. The Financial Aid Committee works with families to determine personalized need-based assistance and financial planning. Applying for financial aid has no bearing on admission to Convent of the Sacred Heart.

ADMISSIONS INFORMATION

Sacred Heart admits students without regard to race, religion, nationality, or ethnic origin. Applicants are considered on the basis of their school records, teacher recommendations, admission test scores, class visit, and personal interview. Entrance exams are administered at the school in November and January and at other local independent schools throughout the fall.

Families are encouraged to attend the All-School Open House in November or Thursday morning Tour Day programs (October, November, December, and January). Sacred Heart also hosts an evening Upper School Open House in October for students interested in grades 9–12. Specific dates for these events will be available on the School's Web site at http://www.cshgreenwich.org. Individual tours and interviews are also available.

APPLICATION TIMETABLE

All application materials and visits must be completed by February 1. Decision letters are mailed by March 1. Applications for financial aid with supporting documentation are due by February 15.

ADMISSIONS CORRESPONDENCE

Catherine Cullinane, Director of Admission and Financial Aid
Convent of the Sacred Heart
1177 King Street
Greenwich, Connecticut 06831
Phone: 203-532-3534
Fax: 203-532-3301
E-mail: admission@cshgreenwich.org
Web site: http://www.cshgreenwich.org

CRANBROOK SCHOOLS

Bloomfield Hills, Michigan

Type: Coeducational day and boarding college-preparatory school
Grades: PK–12: Brookside Lower School, Prekindergarten–5; Cranbrook Kingswood Middle School, 6–8; Cranbrook Kingswood Upper School, 9–12
Enrollment: School total: 1,655; Upper School: 799; Middle School: 343; Lower School: 515
Head of School: Arlyce M. Seibert, Director of Schools

THE SCHOOL

First established in 1922, Cranbrook Schools seek to prepare young men and women from diverse backgrounds to develop intellectually, morally, and physically; to move into higher education with competence and confidence; and to appreciate the arts. The Schools also strive to instill in their students a strong sense of social responsibility and the ability to contribute in an increasingly complex world.

Its founders, George and Ellen Scripps Booth, believed that "a life without beauty is only half lived." Critics have called the 315-acre Cranbrook campus "a masterpiece of American architecture." The buildings, gardens, and fountains were designed by Finnish architect, Eliel Saarinen, and offer students an exquisite environment in which to live and learn.

The Schools are a division of Cranbrook Educational Community, which also includes Cranbrook Institute of Science (a natural history and science museum serving Michigan and the Great Lakes region) and Cranbrook Academy of Art, known worldwide for its prestigious graduate programs in fine arts and architecture as well as its Art Museum. The entire complex has been designated a National Historic Landmark.

Cranbrook offers a comprehensive college-preparatory education that commences with Brookside (PK–5), continues in Cranbrook Kingswood Middle School (6–8, separate programs for boys and girls), and culminates in the opportunity and possibility that is provided by graduation from Cranbrook Kingswood Upper School (day and boarding, 9–12).

Bloomfield Hills is a residential suburb (population 3,985) approximately 25 minutes northwest of Detroit and 5 minutes from Birmingham.

A nonprofit corporation, Cranbrook is directed by a 21-member, self-perpetuating Board of Trustees, which meets four times a year. The corporation has a $217 million endowment.

Cranbrook Kingswood is accredited by the Independent Schools Association of the Central States. It is a member of the National Association of Independent Schools.

ACADEMIC PROGRAMS

The school year, from September to early June, is divided into semesters. Classes, which enroll an average of 16 students each, meet five days a week. Eight academic periods are scheduled daily. All boarding students participate in supervised evening study hours from Sunday through Thursday. Grades are sent to parents quarterly, written evaluations are given semiannually, and progress reports for new students are issued in October.

Promotion from one class level to another is contingent upon faculty recommendations and is necessary for graduation. Each student is expected to take five academic classes each semester, along with a class chosen from the fine arts, performing arts, or computer departments. In order to graduate, students must complete the following minimum unit requirements: English, 4; mathematics, 4; foreign language, 2; social science/history, 2½; science, 3; religion/philosophy, 1; and performing or fine arts, 1. (One unit is the equivalent of a full-year course.)

In addition to sixty-eight full-year courses, Cranbrook Kingswood Upper School offers seventy-six semester courses, including anatomy, astronomy, Eastern religious traditions, ethics, genetics, geology, heroes in British literature and film, human geography, principles of macroeconomics, principles of psychology, and Russia and Eastern Europe. An extensive fine and performing arts program includes basic design, drawing, painting, sculpture, metalsmithing, ceramics, weaving, photography, dance, concert band, symphony orchestra, madrigals, jazz band, mastersingers, concert choir, acting, speech, and stagecraft.

Sixteen Advanced Placement (AP) courses are available in English, foreign languages, mathematics, and social sciences. Honors courses and directed-study programs are also offered for qualified students. ESL is offered for international students who demonstrate a strong academic record and a high intermediate level of English proficiency.

The Tennessee Wilderness Expedition (modeled on Outward Bound) is available to tenth graders each March. Seniors can participate in Senior May (off-campus internships) during the spring term.

Students are graded on an A–E scale, although some elective courses are pass/fail. Students must maintain a minimum C- average to avoid academic probation. Classes are generally grouped by ability within grade level. The student-teacher ratio is 8:1.

FACULTY AND ADVISERS

More than 70 percent of the 95 full-time Cranbrook Kingswood Upper School faculty members reside on campus; 50 are men and 45 are women; 85 percent of the Upper School faculty members hold master's degrees or Ph.D.'s in the subject area that they teach. The average tenure of a Cranbrook Schools teacher is more than fourteen years.

In selecting its faculty, Cranbrook Kingswood seeks men and women with educational and intellectual curiosity. Faculty members are encouraged to explore special interests and talents that extend beyond their academic discipline. They are continually involved in professional advancement programs—course work, conferences, and workshops, the cost of which Cranbrook Kingswood largely underwrites. All faculty members are involved in some type of extracurricular activity, and each is an adviser to an average of 8 students, helping them in all aspects of school life from course selection to peer relationships.

Arlyce M. Seibert was appointed Vice President of Cranbrook Educational Community and the Director of Schools in 1996. Mrs. Seibert joined the Upper School in 1970 and has served in many capacities in her thirty-nine years with the Schools.

COLLEGE ADMISSION COUNSELING

Four full-time counselors help students select colleges, and representatives from more than 140 colleges visit Cranbrook Kingswood each year. The selection process begins in the junior year, involving both students and parents.

Among Cranbrook Kingswood's 2011 graduates, the mean SAT scores were 631 critical reading, 666 math, and 646 writing. A total of 205 graduates are attending such colleges and universities as Amherst, Brown, Carnegie Mellon, Cornell, Dartmouth, Duke, Emory, Georgetown, Harvard, Johns Hopkins, MIT, Northwestern, Oberlin, Princeton, Wellesley, Williams, Yale, and the Universities of Michigan and Pennsylvania.

STUDENT BODY AND CONDUCT

The 2011–12 Upper School was composed of 159 boarding boys, 247 day boys, 99 boarding girls, and 294 day girls, distributed as follows: 195 in the ninth grade, 205 in tenth, 210 in eleventh, and 189 in twelfth. Twenty-four states and twenty countries were represented. Twenty-eight percent of students identified themselves as members of minority groups, and international students made up 11 percent of the student body.

Cranbrook Kingswood's disciplinary system is designed to be educative, not punitive. Honest conduct, regular attendance, punctual completion of assignments and thoughtful adherence to school policies and rules are the minimum commitments expected of students. A Discipline Committee, consisting of faculty members, the deans, and elected students, assumes responsibility in matters of conduct. Major offenses may result in dismissal.

Students participate in several committees that help to shape life at Cranbrook Schools, such as the Conduct Review Board, the Dormitory Council, the Athletic Committee, the Diversity Committee, the Student Leadership Task Force, and the President's Council.

ACADEMIC FACILITIES

Students have the advantage of full access to two educational campuses. Kingswood's world-famous, Saarinen-designed building is a single continuous unit that includes a library with 23,500 volumes, a gymnasium, and six separate art studios. A new girls' middle school was completed during the 2010–11 school year.

Cranbrook's classrooms are located around a quadrangle in Lindquist Hall (1927) and Hoey Hall (1927). Other facilities that compose the quadrangle complex are a library with more than 21,500 volumes, a dining hall, boys' dormitories, and a student center. A recently renovated performing arts center and the Gordon Science Center are located adjacent to the quadrangle.

Students take shuttle buses from one campus to another according to their class schedules. Students also have access to the museums and other resources at the Cranbrook Institute of Science and the Cranbrook Art Museum.

BOARDING AND GENERAL FACILITIES

Cranbrook Kingswood maintains single-sex boarding facilities. The campus buildings are linked by a fiber-optic network and provide telephone, computer, and video access in each dormitory room, classroom, lab, and faculty and student work area. The campus is equipped with more than ninety SmartBoards.

The Kingswood dormitory for girls, adjacent to Kingswood Lake, houses 102 girls. Most live in suites that contain two single or double bedrooms with adjoining bath. The dormitory has two lounges with televisions, stereo equipment, and a piano. Two kitchenettes and laundry facilities are available, in addition to a four-lane bowling alley.

At the Cranbrook campus, there are single rooms for 158 boys, who are divided according to their grade. The student activity center has a dance floor, a snack bar, a performance space, recently renovated kitchen, and a small theater for videotape recording and viewing.

Many Cranbrook Kingswood faculty members live in the dormitories with their families. Others live in faculty homes clustered throughout the grounds. Resident Advisers (senior students) live on each floor and act as confidants and helpmates to their fellow boarders.

ATHLETICS

Cranbrook Kingswood Upper School provides the opportunity for participation in eighteen interscholastic sports, including baseball, basketball, cross-country, crew, fencing, field hockey, football, golf, ice hockey, lacrosse, skiing, soccer, softball, swimming, tennis, track, volleyball, and wrestling. Recent state championships include boys' and girls' tennis, girls' golf, boys' lacrosse, and boys' and girls' hockey. Among the intramural and noncompetitive athletic activities are martial arts, modern dance, rock climbing, strength and fitness, and walking for fitness.

Athletics facilities include a football stadium, a track, fifteen outdoor tennis courts, a dance studio, an indoor ice arena, three gymnasiums, and numerous playing fields. The School's award-winning natatorium was designed by a Cranbrook graduate.

EXTRACURRICULAR OPPORTUNITIES

Cranbrook Kingswood offers thirty-nine student organizations, including Model UN, forensics, ethnic clubs, dramatics, community service, and publications including a newspaper and an arts and literary publication. Other clubs meet to discuss topics as varied as politics and racial diversity.

The cultural and educational events on campus include the exhibitions, lectures, films, and concerts offered through the science and art museums, highlighted by regular planetarium and laser shows, a world-class collection of modern American and European paintings, and traveling exhibits. The spacious grounds, wooded areas, lakes and indoor and outdoor theaters provide a serene setting for cross-country skiing, biking, jogging, swimming, and canoeing, as well as the Cranbrook Music Festival, the American Artists Series, the Cranbrook Kingswood Film Program, the Symposium Series, and the Cranbrook Retreat for Writers and Artists.

DAILY LIFE

The school day is divided into eight 45-minute classes between 8 a.m. and 3:20 p.m., including lunch, Monday through Friday. After-school activities such as class meetings, extra-help sessions, and athletics follow. Dinner for boarders begins at 5:30 weekdays, followed by a study period from 8 to 10 p.m.

WEEKEND LIFE

Boarding students have an unusual opportunity to take part in urban and rural activities on the weekends. Although students may go home some weekends with parental permission, there are weekends during the year when all boarding students must stay on the campus for special activities. Shuttle buses drive students to nearby Birmingham for shopping and entertainment, and groups can go to places such as Detroit and Ann Arbor for professional sporting events and cultural activities. There are frequent weekend camping, hiking, rock climbing, and skiing trips during the year. On-campus activities include dances, concerts, exhibits, lectures, sporting events, and recent movies at the student center.

SUMMER PROGRAMS

The Cranbrook Educational Community conducts several summer programs for day and boarding students and the community at large. These include day camps, a theater school, a soccer clinic, a film-making seminar, a compensatory educational program for youngsters from low-income families, a jazz ensemble, and ice hockey, lacrosse, and tennis camps.

COSTS AND FINANCIAL AID

The 2011–12 fees were $37,900 for boarding students and $27,450 for day students. Other expenses are for books ($500) and a room deposit fee ($200). A tuition-payment plan, health insurance plan, and tuition insurance are offered.

In 2011–12, 32 percent of the Upper School students received some amount of tuition aid, some as much as 50 percent of day or boarding tuition. Aid is based on financial need, following procedures established by the School and Student Service for Financial Aid.

ADMISSIONS INFORMATION

Cranbrook admits day students in preschool through grade 12 and boarding students in grades 9 through 12. The Schools accept students without regard to race, religion, national origin, sex, or handicap. Admission is based on recommendations, past performance, a personal interview, a writing sample, and results of the SSAT or other standardized examinations. Recommended grades for entrance are all A's or A's and B's.

APPLICATION TIMETABLE

An initial inquiry is welcome at any time. Campus tours and interviews are arranged on weekdays through the admissions office. Notification of acceptance begins in February. The application fee is $50.

ADMISSIONS CORRESPONDENCE

Drew Miller
Dean of Admission and Financial Aid
Cranbrook Schools
39221 Woodward Avenue
P.O. Box 801
Bloomfield Hills, Michigan 48303-0801
Phone: 248-645-3610
Fax: 248-645-3025
E-mail: admission@cranbrook.edu
Web site: http://www.schools.cranbrook.edu

CUSHING ACADEMY

Ashburnham, Massachusetts

Type: Coeducational boarding and day college-preparatory school
Grades: 9–12, postgraduate year
Enrollment: 445
Head of School: Dr. James Tracy, Ph.D., M.B.A.

THE SCHOOL

Cushing Academy, founded in 1865, opened as a coeducational boarding school with funds provided by Thomas Parkman Cushing. Since its founding, Cushing Academy has prepared boys and girls in grades 9 through 12 and postgraduate to be contributing members of colleges and universities and of the modern world. Students live and learn with students from over thirty countries and twenty-eight states in a quiet, safe, and supportive community 1 hour northwest of Boston. At Cushing Academy, students are prepared for the technological, political, artistic, environmental, scientific, cultural, and ethical issues already present in their lives—the big questions of this new century that frame their academics, athletics, activities, and life on campus. Cushing builds students' global awareness, helps them to fulfill their aspirations, and enables them to learn the skills they will need to succeed throughout their lives.

Cushing's 162-acre campus lies in the small, rural town of Ashburnham in north-central Massachusetts, 55 miles west of Boston and 10 miles south of the New Hampshire border. Proximity to Boston permits extensive use of the city's cultural, entertainment, and commercial resources.

The Academy is governed by a 13-member Board of Trustees, 6 of whom are alumni. The operating budget for 2011–12 was $24.4 million, and the endowment was estimated at $29.2 million. Total voluntary support received in 2010–11 exceeded $3.4 million.

Cushing is accredited by the New England Association of Schools and Colleges. The Academy is a member of the National Association of Independent Schools, the Association of Independent Schools in New England, the Secondary School Admission Test Board, and the Cum Laude Society.

ACADEMIC PROGRAMS

The hub of Cushing's academic program is the Cushing Institute for 21st Century Leadership, founded in 2007. Designed to help high-school students understand the world of today and tomorrow at their academic level, the Institute brings current issues into every classroom, drives curriculum, facilitates global travel experiences, and brings a range of speakers to campus—including the twice-yearly Oxford-Cushing Panel Discussions—in order to deliver the world to Cushing students. The institute also provides leadership and entrepreneurial opportunities on campus; experiential opportunities off campus; and coordinates the Cushing Scholars, an enrichment program for students selected on the basis of intellectual, athletic, and artistic promise, as well as leadership potential.

The Academy offers more than 150 full-year courses and seminars, including ten laboratory courses and fifteen advanced-level courses. Advanced independent study programs may be arranged through the Dean of Academics.

Typically, Cushing Academy students carry five major courses every trimester, in addition to a required elective in the visual or performing arts. To satisfy Cushing's diploma requirements, students must earn a minimum of 18 credits distributed as follows: English, 4; mathematics, 4; foreign language, 2; history and social science, 2; and science, 2. The remaining requirements may be filled by choosing from numerous electives, including ethics, creative writing, visual and performing arts, ecology, marine biology, economics, comparative religions, global diplomacy, and leadership.

All teachers are available in their classrooms during a daily extra-help period. Informal tutoring may also take place after dinner or during free time.

The Academy offers a structured academic support program staffed by 6 educational specialists who work with students on a variety of strategies to assist them with their studies. Students who enroll in the academic support program, either through the admissions process or who are identified as needing additional support after they arrive at Cushing, take one or more courses with the academic support specialists, concurrent with their other classes, for an additional fee. With students from thirty countries, Cushing also has a thriving international community. Students entering Cushing in need of English as a second language enroll in the ESL program for one or more years and then transition into the standard academic offerings.

The academic year is divided into three terms of twelve, ten, and nine weeks in length. Cumulative final exams are given at the end of fall and spring terms in all academic courses. Evaluations are sent home six times each year. Letters warning of academic difficulty are written at the discretion of the Academic Dean.

Cushing uses a letter grading system that follows a 4.0 scale; 1.2 is passing, 3.3–3.6 is honors, and 3.7 and above is high honors. Class placement is determined by demonstrated ability and past performance in each subject area. The average class size is 12 students. The student-teacher ratio is approximately 8:1. On weeknights from 8 to 10 p.m., students work quietly in their rooms during supervised study hall.

FACULTY AND ADVISERS

In 2011–12, the faculty and administration consisted of 92 full-time teachers and administrators—45 women and 47 men, of whom 52 had master's degrees, and 7 had earned their Ph.D.'s. Seventy percent of faculty members live on campus, and all faculty members are involved in the daily life of students beyond the classroom experience. Each teacher is responsible for the academic, social, extracurricular, and dorm life for 5 to 7 student advisees.

The Headmaster, Dr. James Tracy, joined the Cushing community in 2006. He received an M.A. from the University of Massachusetts, a Ph.D. from Stanford University, and an M.B.A. from Boston University.

COLLEGE ADMISSION COUNSELING

Staffed by 5 experienced professionals, the Cushing Academy College Counseling Office is a resource available to all students and parents. The counseling process begins when a student enters the school, at which time a comprehensive College Counseling Guide is presented to each student and his or her parents. Cushing believes in engaging the students at all levels and that the college advising process should focus on each student's particular needs, aspirations, and abilities. The goal is to provide students and parents with information that will help all to feel knowledgeable, confident, and organized as they move through this exciting time.

Group meetings are held regularly for each of the various grade levels on such topics as summer activities, college research, campus visits, athletic recruitment, interviews, financial aid, applications, and standardized tests. Workshops for parents are presented during family weekends in the fall and spring. During the winter and spring trimesters, juniors meet individually with a member of the college counseling staff to establish a prospective list of colleges. The following fall, a new round of group meetings and individual interviews take place to aid the seniors in completing their applications to universities of responsible choice.

Standardized tests, including the SAT and the ACT, are administered on-site at Cushing throughout the year, beginning with the PSAT in October. Individual tutoring and group test preparation is available for an additional fee.

The College Counseling Office utilizes Naviance, a Web-based counseling tool and database that aids the students and the office in the research process as well as in the organization and management of the application process. In addition, a library of college counseling books, course catalogs, viewbooks, DVDs, and other college materials are available in the College Counseling Office.

Recent college enrollments include Boston College, Boston University, Bowdoin, Brown, Cornell, College of the Holy Cross, Dartmouth, George Washington, Hofstra, Parsons School of Design, Purdue, Syracuse, University of Virginia, Vanderbilt, and Wellesley. Admissions representatives from over eighty colleges and universities visit the Cushing Academy campus each fall to meet with the students and college counseling staff.

STUDENT BODY AND CONDUCT

The 2011–12 student body consisted of 41 boys and 24 girls in the freshman class; 67 boys and 40 girls in the sophomore class; 71 boys and 69 girls in the junior class; 70 boys and 40 girls in the senior class; and 20 boys and 3 girls in the postgraduate class.

Of these 445 students, 374 were boarders. Students were predominantly from Massachusetts (136) and other parts of New England (59), as well as from New Jersey (16), New York (11), Florida (11), and Georgia (7), and Texas (7). Twenty-eight states and Puerto Rico, as well as thirty countries, ranging from Indonesia to Germany, were represented. Of the total enrollment, 8 percent were African American.

Students play an active role in school governance through their participation in the school's thriving student organizations, such as student proctors, class officers, student-faculty senate, and tour guides, and through participation in the school's discipline committee process. Through these and other organizations, students influence decision making at the school and serve as leaders for the community.

ACADEMIC FACILITIES

At the center of Cushing's campus is the Main Building, which houses classrooms, offices, and Cowell Chapel where members of the community gather for all-school meetings and performing arts productions. Also in the Main Building is the Fisher-Watkins Library, which was transformed in 2009 to a digital learning center. In addition to its collection of e-readers and online data sources, the library features collaborative instruction space, large-screen monitors for viewing interactive data and news feeds from around the world, quiet study carrels, and a cyber café. The Joseph R. Curry Academic Center houses mathematics, the sciences, and the performing arts. This state-of-the-art facility of more than 56,000 square feet includes instructional laboratories, studios, student project rooms, and seminar space. The English Building houses seven newly renovated classrooms. The Emily Fisher Landau Center for Visual Arts has both studio and gallery space for students to create and display professional-quality work in a variety of media, including fused and stained glass, silver, ceramics, photography, painting, and sculpture. Cushing Academy students have been invited to display their works in galleries in Santa Fe, New York, and at Oxford University.

The Cushing Network, a campuswide wireless computer network, may be accessed throughout the school, including all classrooms and dormitory rooms. CushNet and MyCushing, the school's intranet systems, allow students to send e-mail, join bulletin-board discussions for classes, communicate with teachers and friends, follow campus happenings, monitor homework and submit assignments. Parents and guardians of Cushing students may log in to a separate portal where they may access their students' course syllabi, school news items, calendars, and events. SmartBoard technology is available in all classrooms and the Academy is rolling out its newly designed interactive iClass Tables in various departments.

BOARDING AND GENERAL FACILITIES

The Academy houses more than 350 students in seven dormitories and six student-faculty houses that vary in capacity from 3 to 81 students each. Almost all rooms are doubles, and returning students select rooms through a room-draw system that favors seniority. New students are assigned rooms by the Co-Directors of Admission and the Student Life Office. The ratio of faculty to students in the dormitories is generally 1:12.

Cushing's dining commons houses a student center on the lower level, which includes a recreational area, snack bar, bookstore, and post office. Formal family-style dinners are served once a month.

ATHLETICS

In the belief that physical fitness and agility enrich both the individual and the community, Cushing's renowned athletic program is designed to involve everyone in physical endeavors. There are boys' interscholastic teams in baseball, basketball, cross-country, football, golf, ice hockey, lacrosse, skiing, soccer, tennis, and track; girls compete in basketball, cross-country, field hockey, ice hockey, lacrosse, skiing, soccer, softball, tennis, track, and volleyball. Organized recreational sports include aerobics, dance, figure skating, horseback riding, skiing, snowboarding, tennis, and weight lifting.

The Heslin Gymnasium contains four locker rooms, the John Biggs Jr. Memorial Fitness Center, a training room, and a basketball/volleyball court. There are also six playing fields and six tennis courts. In addition to year-round ice skating, the Theodore Iorio Ice Arena offers boys' and girls' locker rooms, workout facilities, a multipurpose function room, and a snack bar. Cushing's Athletic Leadership Program further challenges student-athletes who wish to take their drive beyond the playing fields through workshops, guest speakers, and off-campus opportunities.

EXTRACURRICULAR OPPORTUNITIES

In addition to their commitments in the classroom and on the playing fields, Cushing students take advantage of the many opportunities to join or start up clubs and to organize campus events. Always based on student interest, clubs in recent years have included Open Doors, International Club, Environmental Club, Cushing Academy Music Association, Literary Magazine, Radio Station, Mock Trial, Model United Nations, and Book Club. Students are also involved in coordinating campus events.

Cushing's proximity to Boston enables students to have access to the city's resources—museums, sporting events, shopping, theater— and regular trips to take advantage of these opportunities are scheduled throughout the year. Students interested in exploring opportunities in business, the arts, law, or other fields can also pursue internships with Boston-area professionals.

DAILY LIFE

The Monday-through-Friday schedule, which begins with classes at 8 a.m., provides time for an extra-help period, activities, and athletics before evening study hall at 8 p.m. Lights-out is at 10:30 p.m. for underclassmen and 11 for seniors and postgraduates. Classes are 40 minutes long on Mondays and Fridays and 55 minutes long on Tuesdays, Wednesdays, and Thursdays. Courses, activities, and athletics are all centrally scheduled to avoid unnecessary conflicts. On weekdays, the hours from 3 to 5 p.m. are reserved for athletics, arts, and activities; interscholastic competitions occur on Wednesday, Friday (occasionally), and Saturday.

WEEKEND LIFE

On a typical weekend at the Academy, students enjoy many off-campus trips with faculty chaperones. Movies are shown on campus each weekend, while dances and concerts are often scheduled in the evening. Students are permitted to spend a number of weekends off campus, but on any given weekend 70 to 75 percent of the boarding population chooses to remain at school. One weekend each month is designated an on-campus weekend, during which students remain at Cushing to enjoy performances and sporting events, and participate in special activities as a community.

SUMMER PROGRAMS

During the five-week summer session, Cushing offers a unique boarding school experience for girls and boys ages 12–18 from throughout the United States and around the world. The program features Prep for Success for middle school students, regular and advanced college-preparatory courses for high school students, intensive art, and extensive English as a second language instruction. Each program is combined with interesting artistic and athletic electives as well as exciting excursions throughout New England. For further information, students should contact Margaret Lee, Director of Summer Programs at mlee@cushing.org or 978-827-7700.

COSTS AND FINANCIAL AID

Tuition and required fees for 2011–12 were $49,600 for boarding students and $34,900 for day students. There are optional fees for skiing, music lessons, and fine arts materials. A $4960 nonrefundable enrollment deposit ($3490 for day students) is credited toward the balance due; half of the remaining total is due on July 1 and the balance on December 1.

In 2011–12, 26 percent of the student body received $3.2 million in financial aid. Funds are awarded on the basis of need as demonstrated by established criteria of the School and Student Service for Financial Aid. Financial aid is renewed annually, subject to continued need and availability of funds.

ADMISSIONS INFORMATION

Cushing Academy seeks students who are interested in taking an active role in promoting their own academic and social growth. Cushing values strong character, motivation, diversity, and strength in extracurricular activities. Candidates are evaluated based on school performance, SSAT, PSAT, SAT, ACT, TOEFL, or other tests, and a personal interview. If travel is too difficult, international applicants may request a video interview via Skype.

APPLICATION TIMETABLE

Initial inquiries are welcome at any time. Application materials are available online and are provided, along with the school's viewbook, upon request. Interviews and campus tours are scheduled Monday through Friday and some Saturdays.

Completed applications should be submitted, along with the $50 nonrefundable application fee ($100 for international students), by February 1. Applications may be submitted after February1, and will be acted on after March 10, subject to the availability of spaces in the classes. Decisions are mailed out on March 10 for students submitting applications by the deadline and for others on a rolling basis as space permits.

ADMISSIONS CORRESPONDENCE

Deborah Gustafson, Co-Director of Admission
Adam Payne, Co-Director of Admission
Cushing Academy
39 School Street
P.O. Box 8000
Ashburnham, Massachusetts 01430
Phone: 978-827-7300
Fax: 978-827-6253
E-mail: admission@cushing.org
Web site: http://www.cushing.org

DEERFIELD ACADEMY

Deerfield, Massachusetts

Type: Coeducational boarding and day college-preparatory school
Grades: 9–12, postgraduate year
Enrollment: 630
Head of School: Dr. Margarita O'Byrne Curtis

THE SCHOOL

Since its founding in 1797, Deerfield Academy has provided a unique and challenging opportunity for young people. Deerfield Academy is a vibrant learning community nurturing high standards of scholarship, citizenship, and personal responsibility. Through a demanding liberal arts curriculum, extensive cocurricular program, and supportive residential environment, Deerfield encourages each student to develop an inquisitive and creative mind, sound body, strong moral character, and commitment to service. The setting of the campus, which is rich in tradition and beauty, inspires reflection, study and play, the cultivation of friendships, and the growth of a defining community spirit.

The school's 280-acre campus is located in the center of Historic Deerfield, a restored Colonial village in western Massachusetts, 90 miles from Boston and 55 miles from Hartford. Only 20 minutes south is the five-college area that includes Amherst, Smith, Mount Holyoke, and Hampshire Colleges and the University of Massachusetts, providing rich cultural and intellectual resources.

A 30-member Board of Trustees is the Academy's governing body. The endowment is valued at approximately $368 million. In 2010–11, operating expenses totaled $50.7 million, capital gifts amounted to $19.8 million, and Annual Giving was $5.2 million, with 48 percent of the 9,323 alumni participating.

Deerfield is accredited by the New England Association of Schools and Colleges. It is a member of the National Association of Independent Schools, the Independent School Association of Massachusetts, and the Secondary School Admission Test Board.

ACADEMIC PROGRAMS

Deerfield's curriculum is designed to enable its students to assume active and intelligent roles in the world community. Courses and teaching methods are aimed at developing logical and imaginative thinking, systematic approaches to problem solving, clear and correct expression in writing and speech, and the confidence to pursue creatively one's interests and talents. Students take five courses per trimester. Their schedules are planned individually in consultation with advisers and the Academic Dean.

Graduation requirements include English, 4 years; mathematics, 3 years; foreign language, 3 years of a language (Arabic, Chinese, French, Greek, Latin, or Spanish); history, 2 years (including 1 year of U.S. history); laboratory science, 2 years; fine arts, two terms; and philosophy and religious studies, one term. All sophomores take a one-term course in health issues. In addition, all new students take a required course in library skills. Honors and Advanced Placement (AP) courses are offered in nineteen subject areas. Last year, 330 students sat for 823 AP exams. Ninety percent of the tests received qualifying scores of 3 or better. Independent study is offered in all departments.

During the spring term, seniors may engage in off-campus alternate-studies projects, ranging from working in a local hospital to serving as an intern for a member of Congress. Juniors may spend half of their year at the Maine Coast Semester, which combines regular classes with studies of environmental issues; at the Mountain School in Vermont; or at a boarding school in South Africa, Botswana, or Kenya. Sophomores and juniors may spend a semester at the Island School on Eleuthera in the Bahamas. The Swiss Semester in Zermatt is a program that gives sophomores an opportunity to study geology, European history, and foreign language at the foot of the Matterhorn. Deerfield participates in the School Year Abroad program in China, France, Italy, Japan, Spain, and Vietnam, which is available for juniors and seniors. Students may also choose from many exchange programs, including programs in Australia, Hong Kong, Jordan, and New Zealand. Summer opportunities are available in China, the Dominican Republic, France, Greece, Italy, Spain, and Uruguay.

The average class size is 12. The overall faculty-student ratio is 1:6. Placement in AP courses, honors sections, and accelerated courses is based upon preparedness, ability, and interest. All students have study hours Sunday through Thursday evenings.

The school year is divided into three 11-week terms. Grades are sent at the end of each term and at midterm. In the fall and spring, the student's academic adviser prepares a formal written report, commenting extensively on the student's academic performance, attitude, work habits, dormitory life, and participation in athletics and cocurricular activities and as a citizen of the school.

Grading is based on a numerical scale of 0 to 100; 60 is passing. The honor roll is made up of students with minimum averages of 87, and the high honor roll recognizes students with averages of 93 and above. Students in academic difficulty are reviewed by the Academic Standing Committee at the end of each term. Teachers are available during evenings, weekends, and free periods to assist students individually. Students can also get help from the Study Skills Coordinator.

FACULTY AND ADVISERS

The high quality of Deerfield's faculty is the school's greatest endowment. The faculty consists of 119 members (57 women and 62 men); 75 percent hold advanced degrees. Ninety percent reside on campus or live in the village of Deerfield. All faculty members act as advisers to students, coach sports, head tables in the dining hall, and serve on various committees. Teachers receive summer grants and time away from the Academy for advanced study, travel, and exchange teaching.

Dr. Margarita O'Byrne Curtis was appointed Head of School in July 2006. She earned her B.A. from Tulane, her B.S. from Mankato State, and a Ph.D. in Romance languages and literature from Harvard.

COLLEGE ADMISSION COUNSELING

College advising is coordinated by 4 college advisers. Beginning in their junior year, all students attend small-group discussions that help them make informed decisions about college. In mid-winter, every junior is assigned to an individual college adviser, who further develops, with parental consultation, a list of prospective colleges. In the fall of the senior year, college advisers assist students in narrowing their college choices and in making the most effective presentation of their strengths. During the fall, representatives of approximately 160 colleges visit the Academy for presentations and interviews.

Normally, sophomores and juniors take the PSAT in October. Juniors take the SAT in January; SAT Subject Tests in December, May, and June; and Advanced Placement (AP) tests in May. Seniors, whenever advisable, take the SAT in the fall and additional AP tests later in the year. The midrange of SAT scores for the class of 2011 was 620–700 critical reading, 620–720 math, and 620–720 writing.

Of the 189 graduates in 2011, 175 are attending college; 14 students deferred admission to college for a year. Colleges attended by 5 or more students are: Middlebury (12); Georgetown (10); Dartmouth (8); Bowdoin and Virginia (7 each); Cornell, Princeton, Stanford, and Yale (6 each); and Bucknell, Duke, Harvard, Trinity, and NYU (5 each).

STUDENT BODY AND CONDUCT

In fall 2011, Deerfield enrolled 630 students: 311 girls and 319 boys. There were 82 boarders and 19 day students in the ninth grade, 133 boarders and 17 day students in the tenth grade, 163 boarders and 17 day students in the eleventh grade, and 175 boarders and 24 day students in the twelfth grade (including 20 postgraduates). Recognizing that diversity enriches the school, the Academy seeks to foster an appreciation of difference. To that end, international students make up 14 percent of the student body, and those from minority groups make up 27 percent. Deerfield students come from thirty-nine states and thirty-one countries.

In all communities, a healthy tension exists between the need for individuality and the need for common values and standards. A community's shared values define the place, giving it a distinct sense of itself. In all facets of school life, Deerfield strives to teach that honesty, tolerance, compassion, and responsibility are essential to the well-being of the individual, the school, and society. Deerfield Academy is a residential community in which students learn to conduct themselves according to high standards of citizenship. Expectations for students are clear, and the response to misbehavior is timely and as supportive as possible of the students involved.

ACADEMIC FACILITIES

Deerfield's campus has eighty-one buildings. The Frank L. Boyden Library has a collection of more than 85,000 books, periodicals, and films. Most of the library's collection is accessible via a fully integrated online catalog. The Koch Center, a new, state-of-the-art 80,000-square-foot center for science, mathematics, and technology, includes a new planetarium; thirty classroom and laboratory spaces, including dedicated spaces for independent research; a 225-seat auditorium; the Star Terrace; and a central atrium.

The Memorial Building contains the main auditorium, Hilson Gallery, Russell Gallery, art studios, a black-box theater, a dance facility, and music recital and practice rooms.

BOARDING AND GENERAL FACILITIES

There are eighteen dormitories. Faculty members live in apartments attached to each dorm corridor and maintain a close, supportive relationship with students. Two senior proctors also live on the freshman and sophomore corridors. Eighty-five percent of the boarding students have single rooms.

The fifteen-bed health center, Dewey House, is staffed full-time by a physician and registered nurses.

ATHLETICS

Participation in sports—at the student's level of ability—is the athletic program's central focus. The Academy fields interscholastic teams in baseball, basketball, crew, cross-country, cycling, diving, field hockey, football, golf, ice hockey, lacrosse, skiing, soccer, softball, squash, swimming, tennis, track, volleyball, water polo, and wrestling. Supervised recreational activities include aerobics, cycling, dance, skiing, squash, strength training, tennis, and an outdoor skills program.

Deerfield's gymnasium complex contains three basketball courts; a wrestling arena; an indoor hockey rink; a new 5,500-square-foot fitness center with state-of-the-art cardiovascular and weight lifting equipment, trainer's room, and locker rooms; the Dewey Squash Center, a 16,000-square-foot facility housing ten international squash courts and tournament seating; and the largest preparatory school natatorium in New England, which includes an indoor, eight-lane, 25-yard pool with a separate diving well. Ninety acres of playing fields include three football fields, twelve soccer/lacrosse fields, three field hockey fields, eighteen tennis courts, a major-league-quality baseball field, a softball field, paddle tennis courts, a new boathouse and crew facility, and a new eight-lane track. Two synthetic turf fields were added in the summer of 2008.

EXTRACURRICULAR OPPORTUNITIES

Deerfield students and faculty members are extraordinarily productive in the performing and visual arts. Musical groups include wind ensemble, chamber music, string orchestra, jazz ensemble, brass choir, madrigal singers, a cappella groups, and the Academy Chorus. Many opportunities exist for acting as well. In addition to the three major theater productions each year, plays and scenes are also performed by advanced acting classes. Students who are interested in dance may explore modern, jazz, and ballet, with the opportunity to perform all three terms.

Cocurricular organizations include Peer Counselors, the Diversity Task Force, Amnesty International, and debate, photography, and political clubs. Outing groups offer opportunities to ski, rock climb, and bike on weekends. Publications include an award-winning campus newspaper, the yearbook, and literary publications.

Students provide service as tutors, dormitory proctors, tour guides, and waiters in the dining hall. Students serve responsibly on various standing and ad hoc administrative committees and play an especially important role on the disciplinary committee. Students are also involved in various community service projects. The Community Service program encourages Deerfield students and faculty members to broaden their perspectives by sharing with and learning from people of different ages, abilities, cultures, and economic backgrounds. Ongoing projects include mentoring at nearby schools, volunteering in shelters and day-care centers, tutoring, organic farming and on-campus recycling, visiting nursing homes, and sponsoring Red Cross blood drives. Some students also serve as Big Brothers or Big Sisters to local youth. In addition, each sophomore also participates in Deerfield Perspectives, an on-campus service program.

DAILY LIFE

Students normally take five courses each term, and each course meets four times per week. The length of a class period ranges from 45 to 70 minutes. Classes begin at 8:30 and end at 3, except on Wednesday, when classes end at 12:45 and are followed by interscholastic athletics and cocurricular activities. Classes do not meet on Saturdays. One morning a week, students and faculty members gather together for a school meeting, and students and faculty members attend seven family-style meals per week. All sports and drama activities take place after classes. Clubs and cocurricular groups meet between dinner and study hours or on weekends.

Students study in their dormitory rooms between 7:45 and 9:45 p.m., Sunday through Thursday. They may also study in the library, perform laboratory experiments, or seek help from a faculty member or the student tutoring service. During the school week, the curfew for freshmen and sophomores is 7:45; for juniors and seniors, it is 9:45.

WEEKEND LIFE

In addition to athletic events on Saturday afternoon, there are films, theatrical productions, and musical performances. Social activities, sponsored by the Student Activities Committee and chaperoned by faculty members, include coffeehouses, talent shows, concerts, and dances. Deerfield's rural setting and extensive athletic facilities are ideal for recreational hiking, rock climbing, skiing, swimming, ice skating, and other activities.

The Academy Events Committee plans and sponsors events throughout the school year. The Robert Crow Lecture Series brings to the Academy leaders in politics, government, education, science, and journalism. Students attend concerts and film series. Art exhibitions and numerous dramatic productions provide recognition for promising young artists, photographers, and actors. Students also have access to cultural programs in the five-college area.

Freshmen may take two weekends off campus in the fall term and three each in the winter and spring terms; sophomores may take two weekends in fall, three in winter, and an unlimited number in spring; juniors and seniors in good standing may take unlimited weekends. On weekends, the curfew for freshmen and sophomores is at 10:30 p.m. on Friday and 11 on Saturday. For juniors and seniors, Friday curfew is at 11; Saturday curfew is at 11:30.

COSTS AND FINANCIAL AID

For 2011–12, the cost for boarding students was $45,450; for day students, it was $32,575. Additional fees include $2045 for books, infirmary, and technology. Tuition is payable in two installments, on August 1 and December 1. A $2500 deposit (credited to the August tuition bill) is due within four weeks of the student's acceptance by Deerfield.

Deerfield awards financial aid to 35 percent of its students. Financial aid totaled more than $7 million for the 2011–12 academic year; grants, based on demonstrated need and procedures established by the School and Student Service for Financial Aid, range from $2500 to full tuition.

ADMISSIONS INFORMATION

Deerfield maintains rigorous academic standards and seeks a diverse student body—geographic, socioeconomic, and racial. Selection is based upon academic ability and performance, character and maturity, and promise as a positive community citizen. The Admission Committee closely examines candidates' teacher and school recommendations and personal essays.

The SSAT or ISEE is required of applicants for grades 9 and 10 and should be taken during an applicant's current academic year. The SSAT, ISEE, or PSAT is required for eleventh-grade applicants, and the PSAT, SAT or ACT is required for twelfth-grade and postgraduate candidates. The TOEFL may be taken in place of the aforementioned tests by students for whom English is not their first language.

Deerfield Academy does not discriminate on the basis of race, color, creed, handicap, sexual orientation, or national or ethnic origin in its admission policies or financial aid program.

APPLICATION TIMETABLE

Applicants normally visit the Academy in the year prior to the proposed date of entrance. Campus tours and interviews are conducted from 8:30 to 2:20 on Monday, Tuesday, Thursday, and Friday; from 8:15 to noon on Wednesday; and at 9, 10, and 11 on Saturday. Weekdays are preferable, since there are no Saturday classes. The completed application—including teacher recommendations, the school transcript, and essays—should be submitted no later than the deadline, which is usually in mid-January. Applicants receive notification of the admission decision in early to mid-March. The candidate reply date is in early to mid-April. Specific dates can be found on the Academy's Web site at http://deerfield.edu/apply/how-to-apply.

ADMISSIONS CORRESPONDENCE

Patricia L. Gimbel
Dean of Admission and Financial Aid
Deerfield Academy
Deerfield, Massachusetts 01342

Phone: 413-774-1400
E-mail: admission@deerfield.edu
Web site: http://www.deerfield.edu

THE DERRYFIELD SCHOOL

Manchester, New Hampshire

Type: Coeducational, college-preparatory day school
Grades: Grades 6–12
Enrollment: Total: 365; Middle School: 120; Upper School: 248
Head of School: Craig N. Sellers, Head of School

THE SCHOOL

The Derryfield School, an independent, coeducational, college-preparatory day school, was founded by local citizens in 1964 to provide an outstanding secondary education for students who want to live at home.

Derryfield inspires bright, motivated young people to be their best, and provides them with the skills and experiences needed to be valued, dynamic, confident, and purposeful members of any community.

The School is governed by a 20-member Board of Trustees and, in addition to tuition, is supported financially through annual giving and an endowment fund of more than $4.4 million.

Derryfield is accredited by the New England Association of Schools and Colleges and is a member of the National Association of Independent Schools (NAIS), the Association of Independent Schools of New England (AISNE), and the Independent Schools Association of Northern New England (ISANNE).

ACADEMIC PROGRAMS

Derryfield's challenging academic program combines a seriousness of purpose with a sense of spirit. A core college-preparatory curriculum is enhanced by more than seventy elective classes and independent learning opportunities.

Students entering Derryfield in the Middle School participate in a curriculum that provides a firm background in skills and basic discipline areas in preparation for Upper School courses. All students in grades 6, 7, and 8 take English, mathematics, science, history, and a foreign language. In addition, all Middle School students participate in drama, music, wellness, physical education, and art.

Students entering the Upper School (grades 9–12) plan their course of study in the context of graduation requirements, college plans, and interests. A total of 18 academic credits is required with the following departmental distribution: 4 credits in English, 2 credits in history, 3 credits in mathematics, 3 credits in a world language, 2⅓ credits in science, 1 credit in fine arts, and participation in either the alternative sports program or a team sport two seasons per year. Each student carries a minimum of five courses each term. The academic year consists of three terms.

The Independent Senior Project is an option for seniors during the final six weeks of the spring term. The project allows students to explore their interests and to gain practical experience outside of the classroom.

FACULTY AND ADVISERS

The Derryfield faculty consists of 37 members (21 men and 27 women). Master's degrees are held by 16 members and Ph.D.'s are held by 3 members. Eighteen faculty members have taught at Derryfield for ten or more years, and annual faculty turnover is low. The student-faculty ratio is 8:1.

Faculty members are hired on the basis of a high level of expertise in their academic areas as well as enthusiasm to contribute to the overall success of their students and the School. In addition to their classroom obligations, faculty members advise approximately 8 students, coach Derryfield's athletic and academic teams, advise student activities, and make themselves available to counsel students in other areas of student life.

COLLEGE ADMISSION COUNSELING

A dedicated college counselor begins working with students in February of their junior year. College counseling is an active process that includes group seminars and individual meetings with students and their families. More than 50 college representatives visit Derryfield each year.

The average SAT scores for the class of 2011 were 633 in critical reading, 611 in math, and 625 in the writing section. Sixty-four students graduated in 2011, with 100 percent of the class going to college. A sampling of the colleges and universities currently attended by 2 or more Derryfield graduates includes Bates, Boston College, Brandeis, Brown, Carnegie Mellon, Colby, George Washington, Hamilton, Johns Hopkins, Lehigh, Middlebury, Rensselaer, Smith, Trinity, Tufts, Wellesley, Wesleyan, and the Universities of Chicago, Delaware, New Hampshire, and Vermont.

STUDENT BODY AND CONDUCT

Of the 368 students enrolled at The Derryfield School, 120 students attend the Middle School program and 248 students attend the Upper School program. Students come from over forty local communities.

Violations of School rules are handled by the Discipline Committee, which consists of elected students and faculty members who evaluate discipline issues and make recommendations to the Head of School.

ACADEMIC FACILITIES

Derryfield's academic facilities include classroom buildings with five fully equipped science laboratories, a technology center with workstations and laptops, a 95-seat multimedia lyceum, a 17,000-volume library with a large subscription database, two art studios, an art gallery, and a 400-seat performing arts center. Outdoor classroom facilities include several miles of cross-country trails, high and low ropes courses, and many acres of woods. A turf field, a full-sized gymnasium, weight-training area, and trainer's room are also valuable learning sites for courses in physical education and health and wellness. In addition, the School opened the new 8,000-square-foot Gateway Building in 2011, which houses administrative offices, the Breakthrough Manchester Program, and two additional teaching spaces.

ATHLETICS

"A healthy mind in a healthy body" defined the Greek ideal and is the concept at the core of Derryfield's physical education, health and wellness, and athletics philosophy.

All Middle Schoolers (grades 6–8) take physical education and health and wellness. Seventh and eighth graders also have competitive athletic requirements. Offerings include baseball, basketball, cross-country running, field hockey, lacrosse, Nordic and Alpine skiing, soccer, softball, and tennis.

In the Upper School (grades 9–12), two levels of competitive sports teams (junior varsity and varsity), as well as some alternative physical activities (e.g., yoga, weight training) are offered. Upper School athletics include baseball, basketball, crew, cross-country running, field hockey, golf, lacrosse, Nordic and Alpine skiing, soccer, softball, and tennis. The School also honors areas of physical interest that it does not offer on site; students may request that an independent physical activity be a replacement for one of the two required seasons.

Derryfield is a member of the New Hampshire Interscholastic Athletic Association, participating in Divisions I, III, and IV, according to sport. Derryfield currently has the most athletic offerings of any Division IV school in New Hampshire and has garnered more than twenty-five state championships in the last ten years.

EXTRACURRICULAR OPPORTUNITIES

Derryfield's commitment to the arts is evident. High school students perform two large-scale drama productions each year, while seventh and eighth graders take part in their own musical. Each sixth grade drama class produces its own junior musical. Instrumental ensembles that include classical, jazz, and orchestral instruments are active in both the Middle and Upper School. There are vocal groups in both schools, and Upper School students may audition for a select chorus. All musicians participate in two concerts per year and frequently in talent shows and assemblies. Students are encouraged to audition for the New Hampshire All-State Chorus and Band. Visual art students regularly submit materials to the New Hampshire Student Artist Awards and the Boston Globe Scholastic Art Awards, and help organize displays of their own work in Derryfield's art gallery openings.

In each of the two schools, Middle and Upper, students participate in more than a dozen student-organized clubs. Choices include School Council, Conservation Club, Art Club, Gay/Straight Alliance, Cartooning Club, Robotics Club, and Chinese Culture Club, among others. Derryfield also offers competitive clubs, including Math Team, Debate Team, Mock Trial, Granite State Challenge, and Model United Nations. Student publications include newspapers, literary magazines, academic journals, and a yearbook.

Field trips, organized through classes or clubs, include regular visits to New York City, Boston, and Manchester museums, theaters, courtrooms, and outdoor areas of interest. Each year, different faculty members lead groups of students on cultural or service-learning outings. Recent trips have been led to Europe, the Dominican Republic, and the Galapagos Islands.

In its dedication to local and global communities, Derryfield's Key Club actively partners with the National Honor Society and more than a dozen organizations, including the New Hampshire Food Bank, Heifer International, New Horizons Soup Kitchen, Boys and Girls Club, and local immigrant relocation programs.

Breakthrough Manchester, a year-round, tuition-free academic program, is also an important part of The Derryfield School. Breakthrough offers motivated students from Manchester's public elementary schools the opportunity to learn from outstanding high school and college students. Several Derryfield faculty members work as mentor teachers, while a large number of Derryfield students teach for Breakthrough.

Traditional Derryfield events and celebrations include Founders' Day, Winter Carnival, Grandparents' Day, Head's Holiday, Country Fair, Moose Revue talent show, and the Prom.

DAILY LIFE

Because Derryfield students come from approximately forty different surrounding towns, the School itself becomes a hub for learning, playing, serving, and socializing.

A full Derryfield School day begins at 7:55 a.m. and ends between 2:45 and 3:20 p.m. Departure times vary, depending on grade, a student's level of involvement in extracurricular activities or desire to obtain extra help from a teacher, use the library, or attend study hall.

Homeroom gatherings occur two mornings per week, and advisories meet three times per week. The Tuesday and Friday class schedules allow time for an activities period, during which clubs meet. A 30-minute all-school assembly takes place each Monday morning. The class schedule is a seven period, seven-"day," rotating schedule.

SUMMER PROGRAMS

Derryfield offers several summer camps, including tennis and two drama camps.

COSTS AND FINANCIAL AID

Tuition and fees for 2011–12 were $26,435. In addition to the Financial Aid Program, which offers direct grants, the School offers installment payment options.

The Financial Aid Program is designed to make a Derryfield education accessible to qualified students who could not otherwise afford the cost of attending. On average, Derryfield provides financial assistance to 26 percent of the student body, with awards that vary from 5 to 95 percent of tuition. Derryfield awards nearly $1.5 million in financial aid grants annually.

The Merit Scholarship Program is designed to recognize students who demonstrate qualities that will add meaning and vitality to Derryfield's core values or are distinguished by a commitment to purposeful involvement in both the local and global community. Awards of up to $15,000 are made annually.

ADMISSIONS INFORMATION

The Admission Committee considers applications from students entering grades 6 through 12. Although the largest number of students enters in grades 6, 7, and 9, spaces are often available in other grades as well.

Applicants are required to complete an on-campus interview and a written application. The SSAT is required for all applications to grades 6 through 9. Applicants to grade 10, 11, and 12 have the option to submit their PSAT or SAT scores.

APPLICATION TIMETABLE

The priority deadline for applications is February 1. Tours and interviews are offered through the Admission Office. There is a $50 preliminary application fee for applicants.

Notification of acceptance is mailed on March 10, and families are expected to reply by April 10.

ADMISSIONS CORRESPONDENCE

Admission Office
The Derryfield School
2108 River Road
Manchester, New Hampshire 03104-1396
Phone: 603-669-4524
Fax: 603-641-9521
E-mail: admission@derryfield.org
Web site: http://www.derryfield.org

ELGIN ACADEMY

Elgin, Illinois

Type: Independent, coeducational, college-preparatory day school
Grades: PS (age 3) through Grade 12
Enrollment: 460
Head of School: Dr. John W. Cooper

THE SCHOOL

Elgin Academy is a preschool through grade 12, independent, college-preparatory, coeducational day school committed to developing the full potential of each of its students. Through a proactive partnership among faculty, parents, and students in a nurturing, dynamic, challenging, and diverse community, Elgin Academy creates an environment where students may acquire the knowledge, skills, and attitudes necessary to become intellectually engaged and confident about their place in the world.

Elgin Academy is dedicated to its challenging liberal arts and college-preparatory curriculum, a belief in equal standards for both genders, the development of high moral character, and a true spirit of community. Admission is selective and focuses on commitment to learning, academic record, entrance examination, and personal interviews.

The 18-acre campus is located 35 miles northwest of Chicago. The school draws families from Elgin, Barrington, St. Charles, Dundee, Algonquin, and approximately thirty-five other communities, thus creating a culturally and economically diverse student body.

Average SAT scores for the 2011–12 academic year were as follows: Math 618; Critical Reading 610, and Writing 616. The average ACT score was 26. Two years in a row, the National Merit Scholarship program recognized 3 Elgin Academy seniors. The Class of 2011 had an average SAT score of 1846, much higher than the national average of 1509.

Elgin Academy is accredited by ISACS (Independent Schools Association of the Central States) and is a proud member of the following associations: NAIS (National Association of Independent Schools), ISACS (Independent Schools Association of the Central States) [ISACS Accreditation Certificate], LMAIS (Lake Michigan Association of Independent Schools), ISM (Independent School Management), ICNS (Illinois Coalition of Non-Public Schools), CAPE (Council for American Private Education), IHSA (Illinois High School Association), and the Cum Laude Society (founded in 1906; honors scholastic achievement in secondary schools). This is Elgin Academy.

ACADEMIC PROGRAMS

Elgin Academy's approach to its Early Childhood curriculum is not complex. The Academy constantly seeks to provide children with opportunities to find learning joyful. Elgin Academy's approach is integrated and holistic, offering developmental opportunities not only in cognitive areas but also in the social, emotional, and physical aspects of the child's growth. The Academy's philosophy includes an enduring respect for developing the individuality, creativity, and self-esteem of each child. Material presented to children is developmentally appropriate at all times. The Academy believes rote learning concepts (the alphabet, counting, etc.) are possible, and meaningful learning does not take place for young children unless the information presented is relevant to the child's experience. A child's initiative comes from a natural curiosity about the world around them. If learning is relevant, children are highly likely to be motivated and persistent.

While the Lower School (Grades K–4) curriculum provides significant structure and ensures a core background for all students, it also allows each individual the flexibility of a program that is appropriate, challenging, and of particular interest. Students are required to take language arts, mathematics, science, social studies, the arts, a foreign language, and physical education.

Elgin Academy's Middle School (Grades 5–8) students are required to take mathematics, English, science, social studies, mythology, computer, humanities, a foreign language (French, Spanish, or Latin), the arts (music, visual arts, and theater),and physical education. Underlying the core curriculum is an acknowledgment of the importance of character education. The Academy agrees with the words of Socrates that the goal of education is to enable children to be both smart and good.

The Upper School (Grades 9–12) curriculum is structured with college preparation in mind. A series of courses provides all students with the depth and breadth expected by the finest colleges. Advanced Placement (AP) courses are offered in the following eight subjects: American history, biology, calculus AB, calculus BC, chemistry, European history, psychology, and studio art. Students may choose to prepare for AP examinations in the following thirteen subjects: comparative government and politics, computer science, English language, English literature, environmental science, French language, French literature, Latin, music theory, physics, Spanish language, Spanish literature, and U.S. government and politics. Honors courses are offered in chemistry and physics. For graduation, students must complete 24½ credit hours. While the program provides significant structure and ensures a core background for all students, it also allows each individual the flexibility needed to build a selection of courses that is appropriate, challenging, and of particular interest.

FACULTY AND ADVISERS

The faculty is recruited nationally, with an average of seventeen years of teaching experience. Of the Upper School faculty members, 88 percent hold advanced degrees. 100 percent have at least five years of teaching experience, and 92 percent have at least fifteen years of teaching experience. The student-teacher ratio is 7:1.

COLLEGE ADMISSION COUNSELING

Elgin Academy has two college counselors and an administrative assistant, all of whom have many opportunities to get to know students in a variety of different ways. As a result, the process is first and foremost a personal one built upon solid relationships. Nationally, the ratio of high school students to counselors who provide college counseling is approximately 300:1. The comparable figure at the Academy is 30:1.

The college counseling office provides the following services: the availability of a counselor who knows each student at all points in the process; Sophomore College Night, an evening geared to introduce each family to the college process and the components of each student's application; College Night for Juniors, the formal beginning of the process during which families receive the extensive "College Handbook," a complete resource for every aspect of the process and discuss with representatives from local colleges and universities, the college search and application process; and many college visits by representatives from schools all over the country that come to recruit Elgin Academy students.

One hundred percent of Academy graduates are admitted to four-year colleges, with most students admitted to highly selective colleges and universities (as classified by *U.S. News & World Report*). Of the 29 members of the Class of 2011, 83 percent received merit-based scholarship offers totaling $2 million; they were accepted to 123 colleges and universities, including Augustana, Arizona State, Beloit, Boston University, Bradley, Case Western Reserve, Catholic University, Chapman, Colby, Colgate, Cornell College, Davidson, Dayton, Denison, DePaul, Dickinson, Drake, Earlham, Fordham, Furman, Georgetown, George Washington, Illinois Wesleyan, Iowa State, Ithaca, Knox, Lawrence, Macalester, Marquette, Miami (Ohio), NYU, Penn State, Rollins, Seton Hall, Tulane, Wake Forest, Washington (St. Louis), Wheaton (Massachusetts), Xavier, and the Universities of Alabama, Cincinnati, Colorado, Denver, Edinburgh (UK), Illinois, Iowa, Manchester (UK), Rochester, St. Andrews (Scotland), and Wisconsin.

STUDENT BODY AND CONDUCT

Elgin Academy is coed and nonsectarian, with an enrollment of 461 students consisting of 214 boys and 247 girls. The school's population of students has had the honor of representing over twenty states and such countries as Brazil, China, India, Japan, Pakistan, Vietnam, Portugal, France, and the United Kingdom.

ACADEMIC FACILITIES

The campus contains the following buildings: Old Main (special rooms for select Upper School classes and Elgin Historical Society), Raymond House (Business Office), Penney House (Offices of Admissions & Marketing, Development, and

Alumni Relations), Sears Gallery and Theatre, North Hall (Lower School, PS–4), Sears Hall (Middle School, Grades 5–8), Edwards Hall (Upper School, Grades 9–12), the Gymnasium, and the Harold D. Rider Family Media, Science, and Fine Arts Center (Media Center/Library, Kimball Street Theatre, Fine Arts classrooms, and Liautaud-Lyons Upper School Accelerated classes), which earned LEED Gold certification from the U.S. Green Building Council. The Rider Center is now a "living laboratory" for science and math students interested in technology, materials, and design/construction techniques. The Rider Center is one of the most environmentally friendly school facilities in the nation.

ATHLETICS

An extensive selection of interscholastic sports is offered to Middle and Upper School students in grades 6–12. Sports offered to both girls and boys include basketball, cross-country, golf, soccer, tennis, track, and volleyball; girls' field hockey is offered as well. The Academy competes against other schools in the Independent School League, including North Shore Country Day School, Latin School, The University of Chicago Lab School, and Francis Parker School.

The Athletics facilities include the on-campus Gymnasium, off-campus athletic fields (on Franklin Boulevard), and regular use of The Centre of Elgin (the recreation center of the City of Elgin).

EXTRACURRICULAR OPPORTUNITIES

A long list of options includes Model United Nations, Chinese language classes, mathematics and science competitions, musical and theatrical productions, formal and informal dances, Chess Club, Outdoor Club, Mock Trial, Improvisational Theatre, National Honor Society, and Student Government. There are also several courses to choose from in the Academy's Accelerated Program with the Northwestern University's Center for Talent Development. In the school's Battle of the Books, teams read books chosen by local librarians. Scores are kept, and winners are recognized; emphasis is placed on the fun of participation and the satisfaction that comes from reading and from finishing an assignment.

Community service opportunities include projects with local agencies and an annual service trip to volunteer at an orphanage in the Dominican Republic.

DAILY LIFE

Classes take place Monday–Friday, 8:15 a.m. to 2:45 p.m. Office Hours are Monday–Friday, 8 a.m. to 4:30 p.m. Younger students have frequent field trips, and students in grades 6–12 participate in extended educational trips, including many high-adventure outdoor education experiences. All trips include faculty members and focus on team building. Recent trips have included the Canadian boundary waters; the Apostle Islands; the Appalachian Mountains; Montana's Missouri River; Texas' Big Bend; the Pine Ridge Indian Reservation; Washington, DC; Costa Rica; and Italy.

SUMMER PROGRAMS

The following camps are offered in conjunction with Summer at the Academy programs and are available to both Elgin Academy and non-Elgin Academy students: Health World Summer Camps, Basketball, Summer Art, Music Adventures, and Indoor Soccer Camp. The Accelerated Summer camps include Academic Enrichment Review Recreational, which runs six weeks. Summer camps are also available with Center for Talent Development through Northwestern University.

COSTS AND FINANCIAL AID

Tuition for Elgin Academy is estimated to be between $11,750 and $21,735. In order to keep Elgin Academy diversified, 198 need-based scholarships are awarded, the value totaling $1,600,000. Financial aid grants can help cover the tuition cost.

ADMISSIONS INFORMATION

To start the admissions process, prospective families should request an information packet by completing the online inquiry form. The Admission Office will then contact students and their families and give further details on applying for admission. For domestic students, the application fee is $50, which is submitted with the completed application. The Academy recommends that families schedule a screening/visit and parent tour. After receiving the student's Teacher Recommendation Forms, report cards, and Entrance Exam scores (Middle and Upper School), the Admission Office will notify parents of the admit/deny status. For international admissions information, international students should e-mail the Admissions Office directly at admissions@elginacademy.org.

APPLICATION TIMETABLE

Elgin Academy utilizes a rolling admission process until the grade is at optimum enrollment. March 1 is the deposit deadline for all freshmen. March 1 is also the early deposit deadline for returning non-aided students. March 15 is the final deadline to deposit as well as the deadline for selection of payment options. Prospective families should contact the Academy to inquire about particular grades and available space.

ADMISSIONS CORRESPONDENCE

Office of Admissions
Elgin Academy
350 Park Street
Elgin, Illinois
Phone: 847-695-0303
E-mail: admissions@elginacademy.org
Web site: www.elginacademy.org

EMMA WILLARD SCHOOL

Troy, New York

Type: Girls' boarding and day college-preparatory school
Grades: 9–12, postgraduate year
Enrollment: 322
Head of School: Trudy E. Hall

THE SCHOOL

In 1814, Emma Hart Willard founded the school that now bears her name, making it the oldest institution for the higher education of young women in the United States. Her belief in women's intellectual capabilities, a radical idea for the time, is the cornerstone of a curriculum that has challenged Emma Willard students for nearly 200 years.

The exceptionally beautiful 137-acre campus has forty-two buildings. Emma Willard School is located on the edge of the city of Troy, 7 miles from Albany, at the crossroads of the Berkshires, the Adirondacks, and the Catskills.

The 31-member Board of Trustees includes 16 alumnae, 4 parents, and 1 faculty member. An operating budget of $18 million is supported in part through a $78.5-million endowment and Annual Giving that exceeds $1.8 million.

Emma Willard School (EWS) is accredited by the New York State Association of Independent Schools and by the New York State Board of Regents. It is a member of the National Association of Independent Schools, the New York State Association of Independent Schools, the Cum Laude Society, and the National Coalition of Girls Schools.

ACADEMIC PROGRAMS

The Emma Willard curriculum develops those abilities and qualities of mind that are essential to the successful woman. The rigorous college-preparatory curriculum ensures a strong foundation in all major academic areas in addition to extensive exposure to the arts. Emma Willard celebrates leadership, rewards successes, offers appropriate support, and reminds girls of the limitless possibilities the world presents an educated woman.

Each student's faculty adviser helps her plan her courses in coordination with the Director of College Counseling and the Academic Office. Graduation requirements include a minimum of 4 years of English; 3 years of mathematics, history, and foreign language; 2 years of lab science (including biology and chemistry); and 2 years of visual and performing arts. All students are required to participate in physical education.

The School offers more than 130 courses, including Advanced Placement (AP) preparation in all academic departments, including art and computer science. A student who wishes to study subjects beyond the curriculum offerings may arrange individualized tutorials with faculty supervision.

All boarding underclass women are assigned to a supervised study hall each evening during the fall term; students in good academic standing are excused from this study hall at the end of the term. There is a 2-hour evening study period Sunday through Thursday for all boarding students all year. Students may be assigned by their advisers to a supervised evening study hall. The library is open 15 hours a day, seven days a week. At least one professional librarian is on duty 66 hours a week.

Emma Willard students may take courses for credit at nearby universities. In addition, the School is a member of the National Network of Complementary Schools, which offers students an opportunity to pursue special programs on an exchange basis. Practicum, Emma Willard's independent study program, provides opportunities to earn credit and explore a career interest through hands-on experience in many industries, organizations, and professions. Recent Practicum projects have focused on broadcasting, publishing, microbiology, veterinary medicine, law, environmental engineering, photojournalism, advertising, government, and architecture. Vacation trips abroad, as well as work with Habitat for Humanity, are undertaken by students with faculty chaperones each year; groups have traveled to Austria, Belize, England, Ethiopia, France, Germany, Greece, Ireland, Italy, Russia, and Spain.

The grading system uses letter grades with plus and minus notations. A few courses are graded Credit/No Credit. Grades and comments are issued to parents and students at midterm and at the end of each semester.

FACULTY AND ADVISERS

The faculty numbers 46 (40 full-time and 6 part-time); 74 percent are women and 26 percent are men. The student-faculty ratio is 6:1. Most faculty members reside on campus. Thirty-six percent of the faculty members hold a master's or doctoral degree. The faculty members hold degrees from institutions such as Amherst, Bard, Boston College, Boston University, Brown, Bucknell, Carnegie Mellon, Colby, Colgate, Connecticut, Cornell, Dartmouth, Davidson, Dickinson, Fordham, Kenyon, Middlebury, Mount Holyoke, New England Conservatory, RPI, Smith, St. Lawrence, Trinity (Dublin), Trinity (Hartford), Union (New York), Vassar, Virginia, Wellesley, Wesleyan, Williams, and Yale.

Trudy E. Hall was appointed Head of School in 1999. She holds a B.S. from St. Lawrence University, an M.Ed. from Harvard University, and an M.A.L.S. from Duke University.

In selecting its teachers, Emma Willard looks for adults who are dedicated to enriching the lives of young people in and out of the classroom. Faculty development grants are available to those who wish to pursue advanced degrees or enrich their current areas of study and to those who wish to develop new courses. Sabbaticals and travel funds are available to all faculty members. Most dormitory staff members are full-time residence personnel and do not teach. All faculty members act as advisers to 3–6 students each. Faculty members chaperone weekend activities, sit on School committees, and advise student organizations. Annual faculty turnover is typically less than 10 percent.

COLLEGE ADMISSION COUNSELING

Formal college counseling begins in the junior year. The director of college counseling supervises all college placement testing (the PSAT, the SAT, and Subject Tests), coordinates visits to Emma Willard by college admissions officers, assists students in college planning and college applications, and writes a comprehensive recommendation for each senior, based on the student's academic record and teachers' written evaluations.

Eighty-four students in the class of 2011 have enrolled in colleges and universities, including Amherst, Bryn Mawr, Carnegie Mellon, Colby, Colgate, Columbia, Cornell, George Washington, Hamilton, MIT, Middlebury, Mount Holyoke, NYU, NYU–Abu Dhabi, Occidental, Pitzer, Sarah Lawrence, Scripps, Skidmore, Smith, St. Lawrence, Stanford, Swarthmore, Tufts, Union (New York), UCLA, Wellesley, Williams, and the Universities of Pennsylvania, Rhode Island, and Rochester. The average SAT scores for the class of 2011 were 1897: 620 (critical reading), 635 (math), and 642 (writing).

STUDENT BODY AND CONDUCT

In 2011–12, Emma Willard has 204 boarding and 118 day students, as follows: grade 9, 58; grade 10, 89; grade 11, 90; and grade 12, 85. Students come from twenty states and thirty-two countries; 20 percent are students of color.

The School seeks to enroll girls who are responsible and mature enough not to require rigid structure, but all are expected to abide by the fundamental rules that govern major issues of discipline.

Students do not wear uniforms, but they are expected to meet standards of neatness and cleanliness in dress code during the academic day or in the dormitories. Dress for plays, concerts, and academic convocations is more formal.

ACADEMIC FACILITIES

The oldest buildings, of Tudor Gothic design, include the Alumnae Chapel and Slocum Hall, which contains classrooms, offices, Kiggins Hall, the main auditorium, a lab theater, and a dance studio. The Hunter Science Center, an addition to Weaver Hall, opened in 1996. Hunter includes computer equipment integrated with revolutionary fractal laboratories. Completing the main quadrangle is the art, music, and library complex designed by Edward Larabee Barnes and constructed from 1967 to 1971. Other campus buildings house an additional auditorium and dance studio, ten music practice rooms, twenty-one grand pianos, six science laboratories, an audiovisual center, two photography darkrooms, a microcomputer center, and a weaving studio.

The William Moore Dietel Library holds more than 35,000 volumes in addition to a growing collection of e-books, CDs, DVDs, and an impressive variety of periodicals. Students have access to many online databases that augment the journal collection. The school archives contain school records dating back to the early 1800s. Some of the collections include nineteenth-century photographs and student manuscripts, and Emma Willard's papers.

BOARDING AND GENERAL FACILITIES

Students reside in three connected dormitories, Sage, Hypen, and Kellas. Sophomores, juniors, and seniors live together on various halls; ninth grade students live together on the same hall. There are single rooms, doubles, and suites. Professional residential faculty members supervise student life in the dormitories. A team of faculty affiliates, student proctors, and peer educators shares in dormitory responsibilities. Day students are assigned to residence halls to facilitate their integration into the residential program.

In 2004, the School embarked on a $32-million adaptive reuse project of the first and garden levels of the residence halls to create new community spaces. The design included a new state-of-the-art dining hall, student center, student study lounge, e-café, admissions suite, and student services offices. The project was completed in fall 2007. Other campus buildings include a variety of on-campus faculty residences.

ATHLETICS

Emma Willard encourages students to combine lifetime sports with competition; students can fulfill the physical activities requirement through team sports, individual sports, or dance. Emma Willard teams compete in a league with local public and private schools in basketball, crew, cross-country, field hockey, lacrosse, soccer, softball, swimming, tennis, track, and volleyball. Recreational activities include cross-country skiing, dance, skating, swimming, tennis, volleyball, weight conditioning, and yoga. In addition to the Mott Gymnasium, which includes two indoor tennis courts and full facilities for basketball, volleyball, and fitness training, facilities include six outdoor tennis courts, three large playing fields, and an all-weather 400-meter track. In 1998, the Helen S. Cheel Aquatics and Fitness Center opened with a competition-size swimming pool and state-of-the-art fitness equipment.

EXTRACURRICULAR OPPORTUNITIES

The Serving and Shaping Her World Speakers Series and the 175th Anniversary Speakers Series bring prominent individuals to campus for lectures, classroom interaction, and residencies. Speakers have included Poet Laureate Billy Collins; mathematician and author Edward Burger; ABC news correspondent Lynn Sherr; science writer Margaret Wertheim; Pulitzer Prize–winning authors Nicholas Kristof and Sheryl WuDunn; artist, slam poet, and filmmaker Kip Fulbeck; and award-winning novelist Tobias Wolff. The EWS arts calendar features an impressive array of renowned chamber groups, dance companies, artists, and exhibitions.

The surrounding region offers performances at the historic Troy Music Hall, the Saratoga Performing Arts Center, and Tanglewood; events at the Empire State Performing Arts Center in Albany; ethnic festivals; sports events; theater; and activities at nearby colleges and universities. The School sponsors a world-class chamber music series and all students are required to attend at least two cultural events each term.

Among the many clubs and organizations are the Outing Club, Slavery No More, Student Organization for Animal Rights, EMMA Green (environmental group), Quiz Team, Fair Trade, Foreign and American Student Organization, Black and Hispanic Awareness, Phila (charitable service club), and various singing groups. There are also three student publications: *Triangle*, the arts and literary magazine; *The Clock*, the School newspaper; and *Gargoyle*, the yearbook. Through Interact, girls may serve the community in volunteer projects such as Big Brothers/Big Sisters. Traditions include the opening of-school Academic Convocation, fall and spring senior dinners, holiday Eventide, Revels, the surprise holiday Principal's Play Day, May Day, and the Flame Ceremony.

DAILY LIFE

Classes are held Monday through Friday from 8 to 3:30, in time blocks of 50-minute and 75-minute periods. On Wednesdays, students and teachers gather to participate in schoolwide academic activities, such as the service program and the Serving and Shaping Her World Speakers Series. A mid-morning all-school meeting is held three times a week. Team sports, choir, some dance classes, and drama rehearsals meet after 3:30. Dinner is served from 5:30 to 7 p.m., and quiet study hours are 7:30 to 9:30. All students must be on their floor by 10:30 and in their rooms by 11 p.m.

WEEKEND LIFE

An extensive weekend activities program is developed and coordinated by the Director of Student Activities. The Emma Willard campus is at the crossroads of New England, the Adirondacks, the Catskills, and the Berkshires. This location gives students an exciting array of cultural and recreational venues. Weekend activities include sports events, dances with boys' schools, dinner in the Capital District, movies on and off campus, and trips to Boston, New York, and Montreal. Generally, 75 to 80 percent of the boarders remain on campus during the weekend, and day students are encouraged to participate in weekend activities. Transportation to area events and places of worship is provided upon request.

COSTS AND FINANCIAL AID

Tuition, room, and board in 2011–12 were $43,650. Day student tuition was $27,700. A SmartCard fee of $600 for boarding students in grades 9–11 ($650 for seniors) and $400 for day students in grades 9–11 ($450 for seniors) covers testing, field trips, and other class-related expenses. A technology fee of $350 per year is required to cover all technology services, including the use of the computer and access to all of the services available over the wired and wireless networks. Emma Willard requires all students to have a laptop computer.

Families purchase text books directly from the School's online vendor. The average cost of books per year is $500. Special-fee courses include private music lessons, ballet, skiing, and horseback riding. A 10 percent deposit is required to confirm enrollment; School fees are billed in July and December, and families may elect to pay 60 percent in August, with the remainder due in January. Families that wish to make monthly tuition payments may do so through the School's ten-month installment plan.

The School is committed to maintaining the diversity of its student body and allocated more than $3.9 million in financial aid to 54 percent of the student body during 2011–12. Aid is awarded on the basis of academic promise and family financial need, as determined by the parents' financial statement of the School and Student Service for Financial Aid. Applications for financial aid must be submitted by February 1. As long as a student is in good standing and family circumstances warrant continued assistance, grants are renewed from year to year.

ADMISSIONS INFORMATION

Emma Willard seeks students of above-average to superior academic ability who are self-motivated, responsible, interested in learning, and involved in activities outside the classroom. All candidates for admission must submit an application, a personal essay, transcripts, three recommendations, and the results of the SSAT. Students for whom English is not their first language should submit the results of the TOEFL in lieu of the SSAT. An interview is strongly encouraged. Applicants for the postgraduate year should submit SAT scores.

APPLICATION TIMETABLE

Initial inquiries are welcome at any time. Campus visits include tours for parents and daughters, interviews, a class visit, and occasionally a meal. On weekdays, office hours are 8 a.m. to 4 p.m. Appointments may be made at any time of year, but October through April visits are strongly recommended. Open house programs are scheduled in the fall.

The application fee of $50 ($100 for international students) is nonrefundable. The application deadline is February 1. Prospective students and their parents are notified of the Admission Committee's decision in March. Applications received after that time are accepted on a space-available basis.

ADMISSIONS CORRESPONDENCE

Director of Admissions
Emma Willard School
285 Pawling Avenue
Troy, New York 12180
Phone: 518-833-1320
Fax: 518-833-1805
E-mail: admissions@emmawillard.org
Web site: http://www.emmawillard.org

THE EPISCOPAL ACADEMY

Newtown Square, Pennsylvania

Type: Coeducational day college-preparatory school
Grades: Lower School, Prekindergarten–5; Middle School, 6–8; Upper School, 9–12
Enrollment: School total: 1,227; Upper School: 511
Head of School: Mr. L. Hamilton Clark, The Greville Haslam Head of School

THE SCHOOL

The Episcopal Academy is a coeducational day school that has educated the whole child—Mind, Body, and Spirit—for over 225 years. Founded in 1785 by The Right Reverend William White, the first Bishop of Pennsylvania, Episcopal's original purpose was to teach Anglican doctrine and train the clergy. However, Bishop White believed in free education for the poor, and in 1789, the Academy set up free schools for more than 100 children. After moving to a number of sites in Philadelphia, the Academy moved to the suburbs of Merion in 1921. Originally all boys, in 1974, Episcopal became coed and opened a second campus in Devon.

In 2001, Episcopal Academy's Board of Trustees launched an initiative to provide its community with the facilities it needed to do its best work, to experience a greater sense of unity, and to accommodate future plans. This endeavor was to build a new school, uniting two campuses, on 123 acres in Newtown Square, Pennsylvania. In August of 2008, Episcopal opened one of the finest day school campuses in the country. The facilities allow academic, athletic, and arts programs to flourish and Episcopal to stay at the forefront of curricular development and expansion for decades to come. The campus is valued at $195 million.

Hamilton Clark, The Greville Haslam Head of School, has led Episcopal for almost ten years. A fundamental value of being an Episcopalian school is religious openness and acceptance, in every way respectful of all faiths, and the recognition that the presence of students, families, and faculty members of varied religions and backgrounds is vital to the vibrancy of the Academy's diverse community. Episcopal students are drawn from wide geographic and demographic backgrounds. There are over 1,200 students currently on the Newtown Square campus.

The Episcopal Academy takes every opportunity to keep alumni integrated in the life of the school, most specifically in counselor and mentor programs. Passing on the rich history and traditions to current students is part of the school's legacy.

Episcopal also has a very active parents association that sponsors events and provides services throughout the community. Through association activities, parents become involved in the day-to-day life of the school and contribute time and effort on behalf of their children and those of others.

The Episcopal Academy is accredited by the Middle States Association of Colleges and Secondary Schools and the Pennsylvania Association of Private Academic Schools. It holds membership in the National Association of Independent Schools, the Pennsylvania Association of Independent Schools, the National Association of Episcopal Schools, the National Association of Principals of Schools for Girls, the Association of Delaware Valley Schools, and the National Association of College Admission Counselors in compliance with the NACAC Statement of Principles of Good Practice.

ACADEMIC PROGRAMS

The Episcopal Academy is renowned for its classical education, which combines the humanities and sciences with a focus on social responsibility and an individual approach to each child. The development of each student's Mind, Body, and Spirit begins in pre-kindergarten and continues through senior year.

The Upper School curriculum stresses clear, concise writing; reading; mathematics; the natural sciences; social studies; the arts; and foreign language proficiency. Added emphasis is also placed on preparing students for college and postgraduate study and in teaching students to take personal responsibility for their own education. All graduates go off to a four-year college, and a significant number of seniors are honored each year in the National Merit Scholarship competition.

To graduate, a student must acquire 19 credits (1 credit equals one full-year course). Graduation requirements include 4 credits in English, 3 credits in mathematics, 3 credits in science, 3 credits in history, 2 credits in foreign language, 1 credit in religion, 1 credit in the arts distributed among at least two of the three arts areas (music, theater and dance, and visual art), and successful participation in after-school athletic programs. Advanced Placement courses in French and Spanish language, Latin (Vergil), calculus (AB and BC), statistics, Computer Science AB, biology, chemistry, physics, U.S history, U.S. government and politics, and macroeconomics are complemented by courses in English, art history, and studio art that also prepare students for the AP exams. In addition to AP courses, students may take honors courses in Latin, Greek, Algebra II, geometry, precalculus (AB and BC), Mandarin, Spanish, French, biology, chemistry, physics, and art.

Each student has a faculty adviser who supervises his or her progress and provides counsel in times of difficulty. The adviser and parents are encouraged to remain in close touch on both academic and nonacademic matters. In addition, each grade has a dean who remains with them for all four years.

The Upper School operates on a twelve-day rotating schedule. The school year consists of two semesters. The recommended course load for all students is six courses during each semester. Teacher reports are sent out at mid-points of each semester.

Chapel is an important part of the Episcopal community. Upper and Middle School attend every other day, and Lower School students attend twice every twelve days. It is an affirmation of a wide range of faiths, cultures, and traditions and the powerful conservations that enrich individual understanding.

FACULTY AND ADVISERS

Episcopal's faculty (7:1 student-teacher ratio) is committed to each students' educational and individual growth. Close contact with faculty members enhances the quality of learning. In their roles as educators, advisers, and coaches, the Academy's teachers take notice and action—the "teacher-counselor-coach."

New faculty members are hired for their academic credentials, experience, and ability to contribute to school life beyond the classroom. Salaries are competitive, and turnover is low. Of the 176 faculty in the entire school, many hold advanced degrees as well as have served the school for ten years or more. The school provides continuing education, enrichment, collaborative summer work, travel grants, and a sabbatical program for faculty members to continue study in their field.

COLLEGE PLACEMENT

The college planning process begins in the ninth grade. College guidance counselors meet with parents and begin to guide students through a process of self-evaluation in both individual conferences and class meetings. During their junior year, students build their Episcopal resume and begin the application process. More than 100 schools send admission representatives to Episcopal each year to meet with students. Through this guidance process, students and their families choose the most appropriate college, university, or program.

Episcopal students are consistently accepted by the nation's most selective colleges. Eight or more members of the classes of 2007–2011 have gone to Boston College, Boston University,

Bucknell, Colgate, Cornell, Duke, Franklin & Marshall, Georgetown, Harvard, Johns Hopkins, Penn State, Princeton, Syracuse, Trinity College, Vanderbilt, Villanova, and Wake Forest, and the Universities of Delaware, Pennsylvania, Pittsburgh, and Richmond.

STUDENT BODY AND CONDUCT

In 2011–12, the Upper School has 511 students: 271 boys and 240 girls. Eighteen percent are members of minority groups. Students come from Philadelphia, its northern and western suburbs as far as Lancaster, and nearby New Jersey. Students from Europe, China, and Australia have enrolled at Episcopal through various exchange programs.

The Student Council (2 faculty members and 24 students) is the elected Upper School student government. They represent a voice for the entire student body and serve in an advisory role for the administration while promoting school spirit, morale, and extracurricular activities.

ACADEMIC FACILITIES

At the Newtown Square campus, there is an individual building for Lower, Middle, and Upper School; an athletic center; a chapel; a campus center; a science center; a greenhouse; the Sherrerd Alumni House; a maintenance facility; an outdoor playground and basketball courts; turf fields; grass fields; tennis courts; and a cross-country course as well as parking for 600. There are also two state-of-the-art libraries.

With more than 800 computers on campus, students and faculty and staff members have access to educational technology throughout the school. The entire campus is fully networked.

ATHLETICS

Episcopal has a strong physical education curriculum for pre-kindergarten through fifth grade. Athletics are required for grades 6–12. There are twenty-nine varsity sports, and Episcopal's student-athletes compete at the highest levels. On the field, students learn honor in victory and grace in defeat, as well as how to accomplish a common goal by relying on others. Weight training, fitness, and dance options are also offered.

EXTRACURRICULAR OPPORTUNITIES

The Community Service Program is entirely voluntary yet enormously successful. Everyone, including faculty and staff, is encouraged to get involved. Approximately 97 percent of all students participate in the program.

In the Arts, students are able to participate in instrumental, vocal, drama, and dance groups during the school year. They can also work on the newspaper, yearbook, and literary arts magazine.

There are a multitude of clubs developed from student and faculty interest, including debate, television production, photography, poetry, stock market, cooking, chess, French, Student Council, Vestry, Social Impact, robotics, World Affairs, PRISM, science, and Community Connections, to name a few.

DAILY LIFE

The Upper School academic day begins with homeroom at 8:05 a.m. There is a 35-minute lunch at midday. Students attend Chapel every other day. Required athletics begin at 3:40 p.m. daily and end at 4:45 p.m. for those in intramural sports and approximately 5:15 p.m. for those on interscholastic teams.

SUMMER PROGRAMS

The Episcopal Academy offers a coeducational summer program for students entering grades K–12 that features personal and academic enrichment activities including visual and performing arts, athletics, science, and technology. Students can also take courses for credit to fulfill graduation requirements.

COSTS AND FINANCIAL AID

Episcopal Academy is committed to enrolling a diverse student body from varying economic backgrounds. Financial aid and admission are two separate processes; financial aid requests have no impact on the admission decisions made by the Admission Committees.

Upper School tuition for 2011–12 is $28,120. Additional costs vary by student. All financial aid is based on demonstrated financial need, as determined by the information families provide the Student and School Service (SSS), an independent scholarship processing center. A copy of the most recent 1040 form(s) is also needed, in addition to completing The Episcopal Academy Application for Financial Aid.

ADMISSIONS INFORMATION

Through a review of academic records, testing, and interviews, the family and the school carefully examine whether Episcopal will meet the needs of the student. The process helps establish the candidate's potential to benefit from the academic, physical, spiritual, and social/emotional atmosphere at Episcopal.

APPLICATION TIMETABLE

Application can be made by mail or online. Decisions on admission are made by an Admission Committee, which considers all the information, including the candidate's academic ability, achievements, and other interests. Early application is advised.

ADMISSIONS CORRESPONDENCE

Rachel G. Tilney, Director of Enrollment Management
The Episcopal Academy
1785 Bishop White Drive
Newtown Square, Pennsylvania 19073
Phone: 610-414-1445
Fax: 484-424-1604
E-mail: rtilney@episcopalacademy.org
Web site: http://www.episcopalacademy.org/

FOUNTAIN VALLEY SCHOOL OF COLORADO

Colorado Springs, Colorado

FOUNTAIN VALLEY SCHOOL
— OF COLORADO —

Type: Coeducational boarding and day college-preparatory school
Grades: 9–12
Enrollment: 244
Head of School: Craig W. Larimer Jr. '69, Headmaster

THE SCHOOL

Fountain Valley School of Colorado (FVS) was established in 1930 and was opened the following year led by a group of visionary men and women who were philanthropists, statesmen, scientists, entrepreneurs, and educators. Many had personal and professional ties to the East; all shared the conviction that the Eastern independent school tradition of academic excellence, progressive ideals, self-reliance, and intellectual curiosity would thrive in the expansiveness of the Rocky Mountain West. John Dewey, the notable American educational reformer, was on the first Board of Trustees, and his grandson graduated with the class of 1940.

The School's mission remains unchanged: FVS is dedicated to providing a rigorous college-preparatory curriculum in academics, athletics, and the arts. The community endeavors to foster a lifelong love of challenge and learning in an environment of diversity and mutual respect and to prepare adolescents to become individuals who are open-minded, curious, courageous, self-reliant, and compassionate.

The School is situated at the base of Pikes Peak on the former Bradley Ranch on 1,100 acres of rolling prairie in southeastern Colorado Springs. The School's 40-acre Mountain Campus is located 115 miles west of the main campus, in the San Isabel National Forest.

Fountain Valley School of Colorado is a nonprofit corporation governed by a 23-member Board of Trustees, 18 of whom are alumni. The School's endowment is valued at more than $32 million. In 2010–11, annual giving was $1.2 million. More than 2,600 alumni maintain contact with FVS, and many are actively involved. In June 2005, more than 600 alumni returned to campus to celebrate the School's seventy-fifth anniversary. In 2003, FVS completed a $24-million capital campaign, the largest in Colorado independent-school history.

FVS is accredited by the Association of Colorado Independent Schools and holds memberships in the National Association of Independent Schools, the Secondary School Admission Test Board, the College Board, the Association of Boarding Schools, the Western Boarding School Association, the Council for Advancement and Support of Education, the Colorado High School Activities Association, and the Cum Laude Society.

ACADEMIC PROGRAMS

Fountain Valley's academic program is rigorous and comprehensive, offering honors and Advanced Placement courses in all disciplines and providing a flexible approach to placing students in courses appropriate to their abilities. More than 80 courses were offered by seven departments in the 2011–12 year.

The school year is divided into two semesters; major semester courses receive ½ credit. Twenty credits in major courses are required for graduation (most seniors graduate with more than 22 credits), with the following minimum departmental expectations: 4 credits of English; completion of the third-year level of one foreign language (French, Mandarin Chinese, or Spanish); 3 credits of high school mathematics, with the minimum successful completion of algebra II, 3 credits of science (including 1 credit of biology); 3½ credits of history (including 1 credit of world societies, 1 credit of global studies, 1 credit of U.S. history and 1 credit of senior history elective); 1 credit of visual and performing arts; ½ credit of computer skills; ½ credit of human development; and 4 credits of physical education. Most students take one minor and five major courses per semester. In addition, English as a second language (ESL) is offered at the intermediate and advanced levels. Qualified seniors, with the approval of the Curriculum Committee, design Independent Study Projects to supplement their advanced studies. All seniors participate in the Senior Seminar, a weeklong service project culminating their FVS education. Freshmen are required to take the Freshman Transitions class, which seeks to help students adjust to life at FVS, and Freshman Arts, a yearlong introduction to all the arts.

The Western Immersion Program (WIP) is a signature interdisciplinary program for all FVS sophomores. Weaving together the disciplines of literature, history, science, and art, WIP explores how the Western landscape shaped the people, history, and culture of the region. Sophomores also take Career Development.

The student-teacher ratio is 5:1, and the average core class size is 11 students. The small classes allow for personal attention and provide an intimate learning environment characterized by mutual respect and active participation.

Grades (letters A through E) are given at midterm and at the conclusion of each semester. Written comments are provided for each course at the fall midterm for all new students and at the end of the term for all students.

FACULTY AND ADVISERS

FVS has a 44-member teaching faculty, with 34 teaching full-time. Seventy-four percent of faculty members hold advanced degrees; 22 live on campus, with 8 in residence halls; 34 are advisers; and 25 are coaches.

Fountain Valley's seventh headmaster, Craig W. Larimer Jr. '69, assumed the leadership of the School in 2007. He graduated from Pomona College and earned his M.A. from Johns Hopkins School of Advanced International Studies. Prior to his appointment as headmaster, Larimer served for five years as president of the FVS Board of Trustees, where he coauthored the School's current Strategic Plan. Professionally, he worked for twenty-two years in international capital markets with the First National Bank of Chicago and Bank One. Larimer began his career in government, where he served in the U.S. Treasury Department's office at the U.S. Embassy in London as well as the Office of International Monetary Affairs in Washington, D.C.

Because all faculty members share responsibility for the residential and cocurricular programs at the School, Fountain Valley seeks to recruit teachers with personal idealism, a genuine respect for students, and high professional competence. An endowment and annually budgeted funds ensure continued faculty professional development.

COLLEGE ADMISSION COUNSELING

Students begin to prepare for college in their first year at Fountain Valley through course choice and careful planning with the Academic Dean. College counseling starts in the sophomore year. Sessions are planned to help students understand the complexities of the college application process and learn about the range of colleges offering programs in which they are interested.

Each fall, Fountain Valley holds a college fair to give juniors and seniors an opportunity to talk with representatives from approximately 150 colleges and universities. Students gather firsthand information from the Director of College Counseling, college Web sites and other college Internet resources, an extensive library of college catalogs and media, and a workbook designed to help them with the college application process.

FVS has a detailed section on its own Web site devoted to college counseling. The section includes information on college programs, summer programs and scholarships, financial aid, and detailed Web listings to help the college-bound student.

The Director of College Counseling begins working with individual students and small groups during the junior year, while other staff members work with sophomores. She creates an individual list of college possibilities for each junior tailored to their expressed interests and needs. She continues to work closely with each senior in refining his or her college plans.

The classes of 2009 through 2011 had an SAT range of scores (middle 50 percent) of critical reading, 510–640; math, 540–680; and writing, 503–650. From 2007 through 2011, FVS graduates were admitted to 321 four-year colleges and universities.

STUDENT BODY AND CONDUCT

In 2011–12 the School's enrollment is 162 boarding students and 82 day students from twenty-seven states and twenty-one countries.

The School works to create and maintain an environment for learning in which goodwill and mutual trust exist among all members of the campus community. At the same time, it adheres to the belief that every strong community must have a clear set of standards and defined values for all its members to uphold. If a student is found to be involved in a serious disciplinary matter, the case is heard by an honor council composed of elected student representatives and faculty members. The council considers all facets of each case and recommends a course of action to the Headmaster.

A Community Council chaired by the president of the student body provides a forum in which any members of the School community can make recommendations regarding the operation of the School.

ACADEMIC FACILITIES

The majority of classes are conducted in the Froelicher Academic Building, which includes a state-of-the-art science annex and two computer labs (with both PCs and Macintosh computers). There are also clusters of computers in other parts of campus that students can use, including in the library and the Learning Center.

The William Thayer Tutt Art Center (Art Barn) houses art, jewelry, and ceramics studios; an art gallery; a photo laboratory; and production rooms for the School's publications. The John B. Hawley, Jr. Library has forty-one study carrels, two seminar rooms, and a film editing and projection room. The library has an online catalog of more than 25,000 volumes and a collection of periodicals on microfilm.

The FVS Learning Center offers important education support for students, parents, and teachers. Students who need help with study skills, personal organization, time management, or test anxiety can meet with a trained staff member individually or in small groups.

Students who need continued, regular support for their learning issues can be enrolled by their parents in the Learning Assistance Program. There is an additional charge for the program; enrollment is limited.

BOARDING AND GENERAL FACILITIES

Fountain Valley School's four residence halls include ten individual houses where 162 students and 13 houseparent families live. Spacious double and triple bedrooms, common rooms, a kitchen, dining area, bathrooms, laundry facilities, and a computer lab are laid out in floor plans unique to each house.

The Hacienda, Fountain Valley's original ranch house, has dining facilities for 300, private dining rooms for meetings, and a living room for meetings and quiet conversation. The dining room was renovated in 2008 to provide a better atmosphere and a wider selection of menu choices for students and faculty. The Chase Stone Infirmary is a recently renovated ten-bed facility with a nurse on call at all times.

The Frautschi Campus Center has a student-operated snack bar, a campus bookstore, a post office, lounge and recreation facilities, a faculty lounge, a multimedia viewing room, and a meeting space.

The Lewis Perry Jr. Chapel, currently being expanded to accommodate the School's increased student population, houses weekly All-School meetings, concerts, and other regular activities. The Performing Arts Center contains a small black-box type theater that houses the School's three yearly productions.

ATHLETICS

Fountain Valley believes strongly in the value of sports for building physical fitness, self-confidence, and character. Most students fulfill their requirement by participating in a variety of interscholastic sports, including basketball, climbing, cross-country, golf, ice hockey, lacrosse, soccer, tennis, track, and volleyball for boys and basketball, climbing, cross-country, lacrosse, soccer, swimming, tennis, track, and volleyball for girls.

Students may also earn physical education credit for horseback riding, skiing, snowboarding, and outdoor education. The School provides suitable levels of competition for students of varying abilities. FVS offers a comprehensive horsemanship program that provides diverse training in both English and Western riding. Riding facilities include the largest outdoor arena in the Colorado Springs area, a covered arena, a barn, stables, and more than 1,000 acres of open prairie. In 2007 and 2010, the English riding team earned the hunt seat national title at the Interscholastic Equestrian Association championships. A new state-of-the-art indoor riding facility that includes stables, tack rooms, offices, and classroom space opened in 2008.

The Penrose Sports Center includes a gymnasium, two squash courts, a newly renovated strength and conditioning facility, and a five-lane, 25-yard indoor swimming pool. FVS athletic fields are some of the finest in Colorado for soccer and lacrosse. Also, the School's first-ever outdoor track opened in 2008. Nine tennis courts and a climbing wall complete the facilities.

EXTRACURRICULAR OPPORTUNITIES

Extracurricular activities vary from season to season. Students can perform in three major drama productions annually, including a winter musical. Guest speakers and artists regularly visit the campus for formal presentations and lectures. There are three student publications (newspaper, poetry book, and yearbook) and about twenty student activity clubs.

Special annual events include gymkhanas in which a riding team from Fountain Valley competes with teams from local riding clubs, Earth Day, Mountain Bike Weekend, Ski Weekend, Stupid Night Out, and Unity Day.

During Interim, traditional classes are suspended, and students participate in a variety of on- and off-campus programs. Recent Interims have included learning about French culture while in Paris, discovering southern culture and the blues in Memphis, kayaking in Georgia, and connecting with American musical theater in New York. Freshman Interim introduces students to the central premise of Interim—learning by doing. Organized in small groups, Freshman Interim focuses on the history of Colorado by exploring subjects such as ranching, Colorado wildlife, Native American heritage, Hispanic heritage, and pioneer heritage.

DAILY LIFE

Classes meet five days per week in six 50-minute sessions between 8 and 3. Afternoon activities (athletics or theater) are scheduled from 3:15 to 5:30. One period each week is used for student-adviser and All-School meetings. Students and teachers generally have at least one free period daily.

Dinner is at 5:30, and study hours run from 7 to 8:30 p.m. and 9 to 10 p.m. All boarding students are expected to observe study hours, although seniors in good academic standing may be excused in the spring of their senior year.

Day students are expected to be on campus before their first commitment and to remain until 5:30 p.m. on weekdays. Day students may stay overnight in a residence hall with permission from the houseparent and the student's parents.

WEEKEND LIFE

Weekends are time for relaxation and taking advantage of campus resources and a host of opportunities in the surrounding mountain region.

Student and faculty teams sponsor recreational activities throughout the weekend. Events include mountain climbing, skiing, and pack trips, often based at the Mountain Campus; excursions to Colorado Springs and Denver for movies, theater, concerts, dinner, and shopping; and dances, barbecues, movies, and athletics on campus.

Students with parental permission may request a weekend away from the campus. Many students visit friends or relatives or are invited to another student's home.

COSTS AND FINANCIAL AID

In 2011–12, tuition was $44,100 for boarding students; the cost (including all meals and bus transportation) for day students was $23,900. A book fee of $1300 covers textbooks, art supplies, lab fees, and one yearbook.

Interim, a required weeklong experiential learning opportunity, varies in cost according to the student's choice of trip. There are also fees for optional activities such as music lessons, horseback riding, and horse boarding. Tuition insurance and a tuition payment plan are available.

In 2011–12, 41 percent of students received approximately $1.87 million in merit- and need-based financial aid. Fountain Valley School adheres to the principles of good practice in its need-based aid distribution as part of the National Association of Independent Schools. All first-round applicants for ninth and tenth grade are considered for merit scholarships through the School's Summit Scholarship program.

ADMISSIONS INFORMATION

Students are admitted without regard to race, religion, or nationality. Fountain Valley School of Colorado seeks students who have the potential to benefit from a rigorous academic program and contribute to the School community. Students are admitted in grades 9 through 11 (in some cases grade 12) on the basis of previous school records, three academic recommendations, results of the Secondary School Admission Test (SSAT), an essay, and a personal interview.

APPLICATION TIMETABLE

Fountain Valley subscribes to the March 10 notification date endorsed by the SSAT Board. The application deadline is February 1. Applications are processed after that date if openings remain. The application fee is $50 for applicants residing in the United States and $100 for applicants living outside the United States.

ADMISSIONS CORRESPONDENCE

Randy Roach
Director of Admission and Financial Aid
Fountain Valley School of Colorado
6155 Fountain Valley School Road
Colorado Springs, Colorado 80911

Phone: 719-390-7035 Ext. 251
Fax: 719-390-7762
E-mail: admission@fvs.edu
Web site: http://www.fvs.edu

THE GRIER SCHOOL

Tyrone, Pennsylvania

Type: Girls' boarding and day college-preparatory school
Grades: 7–PG: Middle School, 7–8; Upper School: 9–12, postgraduate year
Enrollment: School total: 263
Heads of School: Douglas A. Grier, Director; Andrew Wilson, Headmaster; Gina Borst, Head of School

THE SCHOOL

The Grier School was founded in 1853 as the Mountain Female Seminary and was reincorporated in 1857 under the direction of Dr. Lemuel Grier. The School has been successfully operated under the management of four generations of the Grier family. In 1957, the School was reincorporated as a nonprofit foundation administered by an alumnae Board of Trustees. Grier is located on a 300-acre campus in the country, 3 miles from Tyrone, Pennsylvania, and halfway between State College (where Penn State University is located) and Altoona.

The School is committed to a highly supportive philosophy aimed at developing each girl's full potential as an individual. Competitive sports are offered but do not overshadow the many intramural, life-sports, and creative arts opportunities available to each girl. Grier does not seek an elitist or high-pressure label and is proud of its familylike environment. "Friendliness" is the word most often used by visitors to describe the atmosphere.

The current endowment stands at approximately $12 million, supplemented by $500,000 raised through the most recent Annual and Capital Giving program.

The Grier School is accredited by the Middle States Association of Colleges and Schools. It has memberships in the National Association of Independent Schools, the Pennsylvania Association of Independent Schools, and the Secondary School Admission Test Board.

ACADEMIC PROGRAMS

Grier offers a multitrack academic program. The Elite Scholars Program is well suited for high-achieving students interested in honors and AP courses. AP courses are offered in all subject areas as sixteen class offerings. While all classes are college preparatory in nature, the LEAP! program ensures that all students receive the support they need to empower themselves as learners. Every attempt is made to pace the curriculum to the needs of individual students, and crossover is permitted between the academic tracks according to the abilities of the students.

Learning Skills, a course taught by 3 specialists, is available for students who require additional academic structure and offered as part of LEAP! to provide opportunities for tutoring and the development of strong study habits. This program serves the needs of approximately 40 students at Grier. A comprehensive English as a second language program is offered to international students. Girls who test below 60 on the TOEFL Internet-based test are required to attend an intensive summer session.

Students are encouraged to take at least one elective in the arts each year. The variety of course offerings is designed to provide students with the opportunity to pursue areas of interest and to develop and enhance their individual talents. Strong programs are offered in studio art, ceramics, jewelry making, photography, weaving, costume design, dance, music, and drama. Art faculty members help students assemble portfolios in preparation for higher education.

FACULTY AND ADVISERS

The full-time faculty consists of 13 men and 40 women, more than half of whom have received advanced degrees.

Douglas A. Grier, Director of the School for the past twenty-nine years, is a graduate of Princeton and has an M.A. and a Ph.D. from the University of Michigan. Andrew Wilson and Gina Borst are co-heads of the School. Headmaster Andrew Wilson has a B.A. from Middlebury College and has worked at Grier for twenty-five years. Head of School Gina Borst has a B.S. and an M.Ed. from Penn State University. She has worked at Grier for nineteen years.

Fifty percent of the faculty members live on campus, and 18 housemothers supervise the dormitories. Faculty members are available for extra academic help on a daily basis. Faculty members also serve as advisers to students and participate in various clubs and sports activities.

COLLEGE ADMISSION COUNSELING

The School has a full-time college counselor who works with students in their junior and senior years. College counseling begins in the winter term of the junior year with class discussions about colleges, admissions requirements, and application procedures. The college counselor then discusses specific colleges with each student individually and helps the student develop a preliminary list of colleges to investigate and visit over the summer, thus refining the list. In the fall of the senior year, the counselor reviews each student's list again and encourages the student to apply to at least six colleges. Applications are usually sent by Thanksgiving (or before Christmas break at the latest).

Graduates of the class of 2011 were accepted at various colleges and universities, including Berkley, Boston College, Carnegie Mellon, Cornell, Maryland Institute College of Art, Michigan, Penn State, Rhode Island School of Design, Savannah College of Art and Design, and Smith.

STUDENT BODY AND CONDUCT

Students come from fifteen states and fourteen other countries.

Students are expected to follow the rules as defined in the student handbook. A Discipline Committee composed of students, faculty members, and administrators handles all infractions. Grier believes that good citizenship should be encouraged through incentive, and girls earn merits for good conduct, honors grades, and academic effort.

The student government consists of a Student Council with representatives from each class. The council serves as a forum for student concerns and helps plan the weekend programs.

ACADEMIC FACILITIES

Trustees Building is a modern classroom facility that was completely remodeled in summer 2002. It houses classrooms, two science labs, a supervised study room, and studios for ceramics, batik, and photo printmaking. Adjoining buildings house computer studios, language classrooms, and the Landon Library, which houses 16,000 volumes. The Fine Arts Center, housing extensive facilities for music and art classes, opened in January 2002. The Science Center opened in August 2003. Grier's Performing Arts Center, containing practice and performance space for dance and drama, opened in June 2006.

BOARDING AND GENERAL FACILITIES

The living quarters consist of five dormitory areas and seven cottages. The dorms provide a modern private bath for every two rooms. Two girls share a room, and each combination of two rooms and bath is called a suite. All students must leave the campus for Thanksgiving, Christmas, and spring break, though the School does sponsor trips during Thanksgiving and spring break.

Multiple student lounges with TVs and games are available, and a School-operated snack bar is located in a remodeled eighteenth-century log cabin.

The Health Center is located on the campus and is staffed at all times for emergencies or any medical concern that may arise.

ATHLETICS

Students of all ability levels are encouraged to participate in either the interscholastic sports program, which includes riding, dance, basketball, soccer, volleyball, and tennis, or the life-sports program of riding, dance, swimming, tennis, fencing, archery, badminton, yoga, body sculpting, scuba diving, and skiing/snowboarding. Grier has an excellent horseback riding program with 2 full-time instructors and 1 part-time instructor. Four stables accommodate 35 School horses and up to 15 privately owned horses. One indoor and two outdoor rings are located on the campus within an easy walking distance of the dorm. Grier's indoor ring was completed in December 2007. It is a spacious building of 22,500 square feet.

The School's gymnasium is well suited for basketball and volleyball. Grier's state-of-the-art fitness center opened in September 2006. Five tennis courts and ample playing fields round out the School's physical education facilities.

EXTRACURRICULAR OPPORTUNITIES

Student groups active on campus include Grier Dance; the Athletic Association; drama, outing, Spanish, essence, and gourmet cooking clubs; and the yearbook, literary magazine, and School newspaper. In addition, students participate in "Green and Gold" intramural sports, which often include soccer, volleyball, basketball, softball, and horseback riding.

Creative arts play an important part in School life, and girls can participate in several activities for enjoyment and credit, including drama, photography, art, piano, voice, and dance.

Nearby Penn State University provides many cultural, social, and educational opportunities. A wide variety of field trips are offered each year, ranging from rock concerts to ski weekends to trips to Washington, D.C., Pittsburgh, and New York City. A regular schedule of visiting artists and a movie series complete the social activities.

DAILY LIFE

Classes begin at 8 and run until 2:37, Monday through Friday; sports activities are scheduled during the next 3 hours. A 40-minute period is set aside daily for student-teacher conferences, and an all-School meeting is held daily. Students have a 105-minute supervised study period in the dormitories Sunday through Thursday nights.

WEEKEND LIFE

Because most of Grier's students are boarders, a comprehensive program of weekend activities is planned. Approximately eight dances are planned annually, usually for Saturday evenings. The Outing Club uses the nearby facilities of Raystown Lake for camping and hiking, and canoeing and white-water rafting on the Youghiogheny River are also popular. Tussey Mountain Ski Resort, near Penn State University, is 40 minutes away.

COSTS AND FINANCIAL AID

Tuition, room, and board for the 2011–12 school year was $45,800. Books cost approximately $400 per year. Off campus entertainment is optional, with additional costs charged based on individual participation. A deposit of $4000 is due with the Enrollment Contract. Parents may elect to pay the entire tuition by July 1 or pay 80 percent in July and the balance in December.

Financial aid is based primarily on need. To apply, parents must submit the Parents' Financial Statement to the School and Student Service for Financial Aid in Princeton, New Jersey. In 2010–11, 35 percent of the student body received a total of $1.5 million in financial aid.

ADMISSIONS INFORMATION

Grier seeks college-bound students of average to above-average ability who possess interest in sports and the arts as well as a desire to work in a challenging yet supportive academic atmosphere. Applicants are accepted in grades 7 through 12 (and occasionally for a postgraduate year) on the basis of previous record, recommendations, and an interview. The Grier School admits students of any race, nationality, religion, or ethnic background.

Approximately 65 percent of all applicants are accepted for admission.

APPLICATION TIMETABLE

Grier has rolling admissions, and the Admissions Committee meets on a regular basis to consider students whose files are complete. Candidates are asked to file an application and transcript release form with a $50 application fee, submit two teacher's recommendations, and have a personal interview on campus. The Admissions Office is open for interviews and tours during both the academic year and the summer.

ADMISSIONS CORRESPONDENCE

Andrew Wilson, Director of Admissions
The Grier School
Tyrone, Pennsylvania 16686
Phone: 814 684-3000
Fax: 814-684-2177
E-mail: admissions@grier.org
Web site: http://www.grier.org

GRIGGS INTERNATIONAL ACADEMY

Berrien Springs, Michigan

Type: Christian distance education school
Grades: Preschool–Grade 12
Enrollment: Approximately 2,000
Head of School: La Ronda Forsey, K–12 Principal

THE SCHOOL

For parents seeking academic excellence for their children in a nontraditional educational setting, the distance education programs offered by Griggs International Academy (GIA) could very well be their answer. Griggs is the only Christian online high school in America with dual accreditation—both regional (the same as classroom schools) and national (for distance education programs).

Since 1909 Griggs International Academy, together with Griggs University, has enrolled more than a quarter-million students from around the world. In July 2011 Griggs International Academy moved its main operations to Berrien Springs, Michigan. Griggs is now owned and operated by Andrews University, the premier university in the Seventh-day Adventist global education system. Identified by *U.S. News & World Report* to be one of the most culturally and internationally diverse universities in the nation, Andrews University is also listed as one of the top 650 colleges and universities in the country by *Forbes* magazine.

Griggs offers both online and print-based distance education courses, with reasonable tuition and a flexible schedule to fit the needs of the distance-learning student. Studies can be completed at a pace that fits the student's schedule with open enrollment allowing twelve months to finish any course.

In addition to a full diploma program, single courses are available as make-up credits or as supplements to a traditional classroom education. Thanks to Griggs' regional accreditation, most credits can be transferred to Griggs from a student's current school. Credits can also be transferred from GIA to schools in the United States as long as they are approved by the school's registrar.

Most of the school's junior and senior high school courses are available online, and both college prep and general high school curricula are offered. Dual enrollment is possible for academically advanced high school students. The school's teachers and administrative staff are readily available for aid and support as needed by each student and his or her parent.

Full-semester tuition amounts may be paid over several months with no interest charges. Griggs also offers a tuition refund policy for its diploma-seeking students, should they need to withdraw from courses.

Griggs has numerous accreditations and recognitions that reflect the high level of academic excellence in all of its programs and courses. No other Christian online high school in America has the distinction of being dually accredited—both regionally and nationally. Griggs' elementary through high school programs are regionally accredited by the Southern Association of Colleges and Schools (SACS) Commissions on Elementary, Middle, and Secondary Schools. This is the same accrediting organization recognized by the U.S. Department of Education for accrediting traditional classroom schools across the Southeastern United States. Because Griggs is regionally accredited, the diploma its high school graduates earn is widely recognized for college enrollment. In addition, Griggs is nationally accredited for its distance education programs by the Distance Education and Training Council, recognized by the U.S. Department of Education for accrediting online schools. The elementary program also has a second regional accreditation, that of the Middle States Association of Colleges and Schools (MSA) Commission on Elementary Schools. Griggs is also accredited by the Commission on International and Trans-Regional Accreditation (CITA) and the Accrediting Association of Seventh-day Adventist Schools, Colleges, and Universities (AAA). The School is approved as a nonpublic school by the State of Maryland.

From its humble beginnings in a one-room school in 1909, Griggs International Academy has grown into a worldwide Christian school that maintains high academic standards with solid accreditations, and teachers who truly care about their students.

ACADEMIC PROGRAMS

GIA offers a basic high school diploma and a college-preparatory diploma, with many courses offered both online and in print-based formats. The basic diploma requires 21 Carnegie units, which must include 4 units of English, 3 units of math, 3 units of social studies (one of which must be U.S. history), 2 units of science, and 4 units of Bible study (students may be excused from the Bible requirement if their personal convictions and familial belief systems so dictate). One half-credit is given toward a Griggs diploma for a student who has taken driver's education.

The college-preparatory diploma requires 24 units, including those listed for the basic diploma plus an additional unit in science and 2 units of a second language.

Many parents prefer homeschooling because it gives them more opportunities to interact and build solid relationships with their children. GIA is designed so that parents can manage what their children learn and when they learn it. Parents can also limit negative influences that children might be exposed to in a local school. Another advantage of homeschooling is that the family is not bound by typical school restrictions; families can travel and engage in experiential learning while still following a basic curriculum.

Each Griggs course comes equipped with a "teacher on paper"—the course instructional guide. All learning objectives, instructional sections, reading assignments, supplemental information, self-diagnostic tools, and lessons/submissions are included. The student also receives a full set of supplies, including a textbook and, when needed, additional electronic materials, lab equipment, and reading supplements. Experienced teachers are assigned to each course to provide positive, individual interaction with students. Students receive contact information for each of their teachers.

For most courses, two examinations are required each semester—a midterm and a semester examination. All examinations must be supervised by a school or community official (such as a teacher or registrar) or by a responsible adult who is not related to the student. If a student is enrolled in another school while taking GIA courses, the examinations should be taken under the direction of that school's registrar or testing department. Final grades are issued as A, B, C, D, or F. At the high school level, pluses and minuses (e.g., B+ and B–) are also used.

Because GIA's high school program offers year-round registration and self-paced instruction, students may adapt their class schedules to meet learning needs. The structure of the instructional materials engenders self-discipline and motivation as well as academic excellence.

FACULTY AND ADVISERS

The writers for GIA courses are exceptional professionals in their specialties, and most hold degrees at the master's or doctoral level. The courses are intellectually stimulating and designed to foster the student's academic growth and curiosity. Griggs has dozens of faculty members and nonteaching professionals to provide assistance to students and parents. The majority of Griggs' faculty members have advanced degrees.

Faculty members are chosen on the basis of their expertise in their disciplines and their ability to counsel, advise, and instruct an international, multicultural student body in an online and distance-education environment.

COLLEGE ADMISSION COUNSELING

Graduates of GIA attend colleges and universities throughout the world. High school and college advisers provide guidance counseling and college placement information to all interested students.

STUDENT BODY AND CONDUCT

The GIA student body includes thousands of students across the United States as well as thirty other countries.

Because Griggs is not limited to a traditional school year, enrollment figures may vary from month to month as new students enroll and others finish their programs. Griggs also provides opportunities for supplementing and augmenting programs for students attending traditional secondary schools.

DAILY LIFE

Distance education students benefit from being able to progress at their own speed, and have the flexibility to plan the study portion of their day in shorter blocks of time than a traditional school. This allows for holistic personal development, providing time for greater physical, social, and spiritual development, and integrating academic learning into daily life activities and service to others. Full-time Griggs students can enjoy intramural sport groups and have extra time to use libraries, museums, and faith-based activities in their communities. On average, full-time students spend 4 to 5 hours a day on their studies.

COSTS AND FINANCIAL AID

GIA offers two options (grades K–8)—the Accredited Plan and the Non-Accredited Plan.

The Accredited Plan is state approved and includes tuition, textbooks and instructional guides, daily lesson plans, exams, teacher assistance, grading services, record keeping, report cards, and transcript services. In the 2011–12 school year, the costs for core subjects for one full year, including a $20 enrollment fee, were kindergarten, $293; grade 1, $1040; grade 2, $1090; grade 3, $992; grade 4, $1039; grade 5, $1114; and grade 6, $989. The grade 6 curriculum is also available online for $965.

The junior high program (grades 7 and 8) allows for more immediate interaction between parent and student. The programs are available online or in print-based formats. The 2011–12 prices for the four core courses, including an $80 enrollment fee, were $1034 for grade 7 and $1042 for grade 8. This does not include the cost of shipping and handling. Sales tax is added if shipping to Maryland or Michigan.

The 2011–12 high school tuition was $230 per course per semester, plus the cost of books and supplies, an $80 enrollment fee, and shipping.

Because of its reasonable tuition and fees, Griggs does not offer financial aid. Parents are offered a payment plan that allows tuition to be paid over a period of three months. The school also offers a generous tuition refund policy for students who must withdraw from semesters or courses before they are completed. Please visit the Griggs Web site for details.

The Non-Accredited Plan (K–8 only) is for those who choose not to use Griggs International Academy's teaching, grading, advising, or record-keeping services. However, this plan does offer instructional guides, activity sheets, tests (no answer keys for tests), and placement advising for the student (if necessary). Prices for the Non-Accredited Plan are substantially lower, and financial aid is not available. For the 2011–12 school year, costs for the core curriculum were preschool, $57; kindergarten, $143; grade 1, $621; grade 2, $640; grade 3, $557; grade 4, $494; grade 5, $665; and grade 6, $535. Online courses are not available in the Non-Accredited Plan.

All prices are subject to change July 1 each year.

ADMISSIONS INFORMATION

Griggs accepts applications for admission at any time. Applications can be completed online at www.griggs.edu. Questions can be e-mailed to enrollgia@andrews.edu.

ADMISSIONS CORRESPONDENCE

Gabriela Melgar, Enrollment Counselor
Griggs International Academy
8903 U.S. Highway 31
Berrien Springs, Michigan 49104
Phone: 269-471-6570
800-782-4769 (toll-free; inquiries only)
E-mail: enrollgia@andrews.edu
Web site: http://www.griggs.edu

THE HARKER SCHOOL

San Jose, California

Type: Coeducational day college-preparatory school
Grades: K–12: Lower School, Kindergarten–5; Middle School, 6–8; Upper School, 9–12
Enrollment: School total: 1,791; Lower School: 591; Middle School: 485; Upper School: 715
Head of School: Christopher Nikoloff

THE SCHOOL

The origins of The Harker School belong in the city of Palo Alto where two schools, Manzanita Hall and Miss Harker's School, were established in 1893 to provide incoming Stanford University students with the finest college-preparatory education available.

Harker's three campuses are located minutes from each other in the heart of California's famed Silicon Valley. The campuses are well maintained, beautifully landscaped, and secured with an emphasis on student safety. The Upper School campus is 16 acres, the Middle School campus is 40 acres, and the Lower School campus is 10 acres. The Harker Upper School opened in 1998 and graduated its first senior class in 2002.

Harker's suburban San Jose location attracts day students from surrounding communities, such as Los Gatos, Saratoga, Cupertino, Los Altos, and Fremont.

Harker operates as a nonprofit organization, governed by a board of directors composed of business leaders, educators, and parents. With strong support from parent volunteers, the School's Annual Fund raised more than $1 million during the 2010–11 school year. Funds are used to enhance programs such as computer science and fine arts.

Harker is accredited by the Western Association of Schools and Colleges and is a member of the California Association of Independent Schools.

ACADEMIC PROGRAMS

The Harker School is a coeducational day school for students in kindergarten through grade 12. Harker students are highly motivated, creative young people who come from families with strong commitments to educational values. The exceptional faculty, caring and qualified support staff, and modern, safe campuses give students a definite advantage in becoming top achievers. For example, students consistently score among the highest percentiles in nationally normed achievement tests. Each year, an impressive number of seventh-grade students qualify for academic recognition as Johns Hopkins University Scholars by scoring above 500 on the SAT. Small class sizes, with an average of 16 students, enable teachers to form flexible ability groupings so that children's needs are constantly evaluated and met.

The Upper School curriculum offers a full array of academic courses, from introductory-level to Advanced Placement and honors-level courses in every discipline, from sciences and math to English, foreign language, and the fine arts. The Upper School offers a complete athletic program for boys and girls as well as a full extracurricular program, including yearbook, performing arts, newspaper, and debate.

The use of technology in teaching is an important facet of the academic program, and every student takes a semester of technology as a graduation requirement. A unique aspect of the program is Harker's requirement that every student have Internet access at home. The Internet is utilized for academic research through the Harker Library's online periodical databases and access to faculty help after school hours. Grades 6–12 are also required to have a personal laptop that is linked to the School's wireless network. A Middle School laptop program was implemented in fall 2007.

Graduation requirements include 4 years of English, third-year proficiency in a foreign language (French, Spanish, Japanese, or Latin), 3 years of science (physics, chemistry, and biology), 3 years of mathematics (with a strong recommendation to take 4 years), 3 years of history, 2 years of physical education, 1 year of fine arts, and 1 semester of computer science.

The Lower and Middle Schools' solid curriculum in both the core subjects of math and language arts and the enriching opportunities with specialists in science, expository writing, Spanish, French, Japanese, computer science, physical education, art, music, dance, and drama provides a solid foundation for the Upper School academic program.

The Lower School's full-day program allows all students ample time for learning through games, dancing, and other physical activities. Harker kindergarteners have access to teaching specialists and campus resources such as extensively equipped computer science labs and the library. In grades 1–5 the curriculum is strongly academic. In keeping with the School's commitment to treat each child as an individual, students who show special promise have ample opportunity to go beyond the standard curriculum through Harker's advanced placement grouping. Study-travel trips to Marin Headlands and California's Gold Country add field experience to the academic science offerings.

Harker's Middle School program offers students a safe and trusting atmosphere in which to grow through the challenging times of early adolescence. Special courses aid students in gaining a sense of self-worth, dealing with anxiety, understanding the risks of substance abuse, and learning about other major health issues. Student performances, field trips, art exhibitions, and assembly presentations enliven the School atmosphere. Study-travel trips to Yosemite, the Grand Canyon, and Washington, D.C., are meaningful Middle School experiences.

FACULTY AND ADVISERS

The Harker faculty is composed of 187 professionals, 114 of whom hold advanced degrees. Christopher Nikoloff, Head of School, earned his B.A. in English literature and his M.A.T. in education at Boston University. Faculty members serve as advisers to students on a daily basis. Many participate in after-school athletics as well as academic and arts enrichment activities. Continuing education is facilitated with monthly meetings and individual incentives for professional growth. Harker seeks highly qualified candidates who reflect the School's commitment to academic excellence and diversity.

COLLEGE ADMISSION COUNSELING

Harker is a college-preparatory school whose rigorous curriculum prepares students for top universities. Four college counselors provide extensive guidance to students and parents in the junior and senior years regarding preparation for college admission. Over the four years of high school, there are parent workshops, family interviews, individual student interviews, classes for students, visits from college representatives, and special speakers from college admission offices.

STUDENT BODY AND CONDUCT

During the 2011–12 academic year, there were 1,790 students enrolled in kindergarten through grade 12. The student body reflects the dynamic and diverse Bay Area population, and the international programs further prepare the students as global citizens.

Harker Lower and Middle School students are required to wear uniforms. Upper School students adhere to a dress code. Students are expected to comply with rules defined in the *Student/Parent Handbook.* Good citizenship, along with academic and athletic achievement, is frequently rewarded. Discipline rests primarily with the faculty.

With leadership from its Student Council, the entire School communicates its views on codes and policies and works on community service projects. Students participate in a variety of leadership opportunities, spirit commission, and service volunteer programs.

ACADEMIC FACILITIES

Harker's strong sense of community ties three campuses into one school, while allowing children close contact with their peers. The Lower, Middle, and Upper School campuses are within 3 miles of each other. Modern, extensively equipped facilities such as computer and science labs and art and dance studios provide enhanced learning opportunities for students at all grade levels. A new state-of-the-art Science and Technology Center opened in 2008.

The library system has 44,900 items among the three campuses. Each campus has its own library facility, staffed by full-time professional librarians, and equipped with an array of quality print and digital resources. With over 80 subscription databases, students have 24/7 access to materials from Gale, ProQuest, EBSCO, Oxford University Press, JSTOR, Project MUSE, LexisNexis, and others. Librarians and instructional technologists team with classroom teachers to select appropriate technology tools to support twenty-first-century learning.

Harker has extensive student support services. The full-time staff includes licensed school counselors, college counselors, registered school nurses, certified lifeguards, and a professional chef.

ATHLETICS

Students of all ability levels are encouraged to participate in the School's extensive athletics program. Baseball, basketball, cross-country, football, golf, soccer, softball, tennis, track, and volleyball are popular Upper School sports. Combined athletic facilities include two competition-sized pools, eight tennis courts, three wood-floored gymnasiums, a new lighted football/soccer field with synthetic turf, and expansive playing fields.

EXTRACURRICULAR OPPORTUNITIES

While the basic goal is to prepare students for future schooling by introducing them to a large body of knowledge, the focus on academics is balanced with numerous opportunities for personal development, including school spirit, sports and arts activities, and community service projects. Students take an active role in their school community, including planning school dances and rallies and participation in more than forty clubs. Harker's proximity to San Francisco makes frequent field trips to major cultural attractions and performances possible for students at all grade levels.

DAILY LIFE

Students can arrive on campus as early as 7 a.m. The school day begins and ends at staggered times between 8 a.m. and 3:30 p.m. The campus closes at 6 p.m. Supervised after-school recreation and athletics programs are available to all students at no additional cost. A professional chef supervises food service on all campuses, providing nutritious lunch selections of hot meals, fresh fruits, salad bars, and vegetarian options.

SUMMER PROGRAMS

Harker Summer Programs offers an intriguing variety of activities for boys and girls ages 4½ to 18. For students in grades K–6, day camp choices offer academic enrichment combined with sports, recreation, and computer science for a total of eight weeks. Field trips to local natural and cultural attractions such as Santa Cruz beaches, local redwood forests, and San Francisco are a popular aspect of the program. Harker's Summer Institute for students in grades 6–12 runs for 6 weeks during the summer. Students attend academic credit courses to hone existing skills or learn new topics. Offerings have included the Summer Conservatory program of music, theater, and dance; Speech and Debate Camp; rigorous math and science courses; and an enrichment courses in expository writing, Spanish, and PSAT/SAT. Annual enrollment is approximately 1,300. Enrollment in Harker's academic program is not required. Harker Summer Programs is accredited by the American Camping Association and the Western Association of Independent Camps. Further information can be obtained by contacting Summer Programs Director Kelly Espinosa at the Harker School office.

COSTS AND FINANCIAL AID

For the 2011–12 school year, tuition ranged from $25,060 to $36,435. An $1100 to $1200 lunch fee is added to tuition for Middle and Upper Schools. Estimated extra costs are as follows: $400 to $550 plus lunch fee for Lower School and $700 to $850 for Middle and Upper School students. Financial aid based on need is available.

ADMISSIONS INFORMATION

Harker seeks a diversified student body that reflects a range of backgrounds, aptitudes, and interests. Students performing at average to above-average levels are considered for acceptance. Student motivation and the ability to adjust comfortably to a close-knit and congenial educational community are also important factors. The specific criteria used in admissions are entrance exams, school records, character evaluations by a teacher or principal, and extracurricular experiences.

APPLICATION TIMETABLE

An initial inquiry is welcome at any time, and students should visit the Web site for School and application information. Potential students and their families are encouraged to attend an open house or schedule a visit because there is no better way to appreciate Harker's warmth and vitality. A visit may be arranged by contacting the School offices, which are open from 8 a.m. to 5 p.m.

ADMISSIONS CORRESPONDENCE

Ms. Nan Nielsen
Director of Admission and Financial Aid
The Harker School, Saratoga Campus

Lower School (K–5)
4300 Bucknall Road
San Jose, California 95130
Phone: 408-871-4600
Fax: 408-871-4320

Middle School (6–8)
3800 Blackford Avenue
San Jose, California 95117
Phone: 408-248-2510
Fax: 408-248-2502

Upper School (9–12)
500 Saratoga Avenue
San Jose, California 95129
Phone: 408-249-2510
Fax: 408-984-2325
E-mail: admissions@harker.org
Web site: http://www.harker.org

THE HILL SCHOOL

Pottstown, Pennsylvania

The Hill School

Type: Coeducational boarding and day college-preparatory school
Grades: 9–PG (Forms III–VI)
Enrollment: 500
Head of School: David R. Dougherty, Headmaster

THE SCHOOL

The Hill School was founded in 1851 by Matthew Meigs, and the Meigs family was instrumental in guiding the course of the School for three generations. In 1920, ownership was transferred to the alumni, who now operate the School as a not-for-profit institution through a 28-member Board of Trustees. In 1998, the School began admitting young women and became a coeducational institution.

The Hill School continues to emphasize both structure and guidance in the quest for academic excellence. The School's mission is to prepare students well for college, careers, and life. The Hill also strives to instill an awareness of accountability for all decisions and to teach those standards of personal conduct that are expected throughout life.

The Hill's 200-acre campus in Pottstown is located 37 miles northwest of Philadelphia and 15 miles from Valley Forge National Park. Because of its Middle Atlantic location, students at The Hill can take advantage of a balanced climate, including warm autumn weather and a winter season that makes possible such activities as skiing in the nearby Pocono Mountains.

The School's endowment is approximately $130 million. The amount of Annual Giving for 2010–11 was more than $2.3 million, with approximately 20 percent of the living alumni participating.

The Hill School is accredited by the Middle States Association of Colleges and Schools and is a member of the Secondary School Admission Test Board and the National Association of Independent Schools.

ACADEMIC PROGRAMS

The Hill School's principal academic goal is to instill in each student the capacity and desire to learn. The School maintains a student-faculty ratio of approximately 7:1 and an average class size of 12 students.

Sixteen academic credits in grades 9 through 12 are required to earn a diploma, and the distribution of courses includes no fewer than four in English (4 years), three in mathematics (algebra I, geometry, and algebra II), three in one foreign language (or two in each of two languages), two in history, two in laboratory science (biology, chemistry, or physics), and a course in the arts as well as one in theology or philosophy. Foreign language offerings include 6 years of Latin, 5 years of Spanish and French, and 4 years of Chinese, German, and Greek. Courses offered within the Department of History include world history, European history, and U.S. history; U.S. Civil War, World War II, and Vietnam history; Islamic, Latin American, and Native American civilizations; economics; and other electives. Department of Mathematics offerings include algebra I and II, geometry, pre-calculus, functions and discrete math, calculus, graph theory, and advanced topics. Science courses include 2 years of biology, 2 years of chemistry, 2 years of physics, and 2 years of computer science as well as environmental science, astronomy, human physiology, kinesiology, and psychology. Twenty-three Advanced Placement (AP) courses are offered; in 2011, 182 students took 368 AP exams.

Academic reports are sent home at the conclusion of each of the three terms. Comments from instructors, the dorm parent, and the academic adviser are mailed to parents after the fall and spring terms. Students have seven-day-a-week access to the teaching faculty, nearly all of whom live on campus; many faculty members live in the residence halls as dormitory parents. The School library is open 12 hours each school day as well as weekends.

FACULTY AND ADVISERS

The Hill has 68 teaching faculty members. Seventy-five percent hold or are working toward advanced degrees. Nearly all reside in dormitories serving as dorm parents or live in homes on campus with their families.

David R. Dougherty was appointed Headmaster in 1993. He received a B.A. in English from Washington and Lee University in 1968. He earned an M.A. in English from Georgetown University and a master's in literature from Middlebury College's Bread Loaf School of English at Lincoln College, Oxford. Prior to becoming The Hill's tenth Headmaster, Mr. Dougherty had been Headmaster of North Cross School in Roanoke, Virginia, since 1987. From 1982 to 1987, he was Assistant Headmaster of Episcopal High School in Alexandria, Virginia. He began his teaching career at Episcopal High School in 1968.

COLLEGE ADMISSION COUNSELING

For more than 155 years, the Hill School has prepared students for outstanding colleges and universities throughout the United States. The College Advising Office, staffed by 5 individuals, is devoted exclusively to helping students select appropriate colleges and universities and to helping them plan and prepare college admission materials.

Each year, more than 100 college and university representatives visit The Hill to present information about their institutions. Interested students are invited to attend these sessions, and Sixth Form students may schedule formal interviews with college representatives. During the Fifth Form year, students participate in a college forum class, which addresses the college application process. Topics covered include decision making, career interest identification, essay writing, interview techniques, methods of quality assessment, and SAT practice tests.

A complete range of standardized tests is administered on campus, including SAT and SAT Subject Tests, ACT, Advanced Placement, and TOEFL; students generally take those exams at regular intervals during the Fifth and Sixth Form years. The middle 50 percent ranges on the SAT for the class of 2011 were 580–680 critical reading, 570–700 math, and 550–680 writing.

Recent graduates are attending such colleges and universities as Amherst, Brown, Bowdoin, Bucknell, Colgate, Cornell, Dickinson, George Washington, Georgetown, Harvard, Princeton, Tufts, the United States Naval Academy, Wellesley, William and Mary, Yale, and the Universities of Pennsylvania, Richmond, St. Andrews (Scotland), and the South.

STUDENT BODY AND CONDUCT

In the Third Form, there are 64 boarding and 44 day students; in the Fourth Form, there are 77 boarding and 46 day students; in the Fifth Form, there are 79 boarding and 36 day students; in the Sixth Form, there are 124 students; and in the PG class, there are 22 students. Students come from twenty-nine states and twenty-one other countries. Sixty-nine percent of the students come from Middle Atlantic states, with the rest of the students coming in equal measure from New England, the Southeast, and Midwestern and Western states. Thirty-six percent of Hill's student body is multicultural.

In 1997, the Hill School students and faculty members adopted a student-initiated Honor Code to promote an environment of mutual trust and respect and to uphold the School's principles of trust, honor, and integrity in all intellectual, athletic, and social pursuits. Most disciplinary matters are handled by either the Discipline Committee or Honor Council, depending on the nature of the offense. Both groups consist of students and faculty members who have been chosen by their peers.

ACADEMIC FACILITIES

The Hill School's fifty-five academic buildings include the 40,000-volume John P. Ryan Library, the Alumni Chapel, Harry Elkins Widener Memorial Science Building, Theodore N. Danforth Computer Center, the 31,000-square-foot Center for the Arts, the $12-million Academic and Student Center, and the McIlvain Multimedia Learning Classroom, a state-of-the-art, twenty-four-computer digital language lab.

BOARDING AND GENERAL FACILITIES

The Hill School's eleven major dormitory structures are divided into residential units that most often house 12 students and one faculty family. Housing has been designed for 2 students per dormitory room. Two selected Sixth Form prefects, who share some supervisory responsibilities with the residential faculty family, live on each dormitory corridor. New students are assigned roommates by the Residential Life and Admission

Offices; in subsequent years, however, roommate selections are made by each student. There is a formal dining room where students and faculty families enjoy seated family-style and buffet meals.

The Student Health Service is staffed by full-time registered nurses and 2 physicians who are on call around the clock.

ATHLETICS

Athletics are an integral part of The Hill's educational offering. A program of twenty-nine sports enables each student to compete and develop expertise in the sports of their choice.

The athletic facilities at The Hill include a 34,000-square-foot field house and seven squash courts, a gymnasium complex, four basketball courts, a six-lane swimming pool, and a fitness center that includes twenty cardiovascular machines, Body Masters strength training equipment, and free weights. Additional structures include a new 92-foot by 200-foot collegiate-sized indoor ice-hockey arena and a wrestling room. The Hill shares an eighteen-hole golf course and owns eleven tennis courts and 90 acres of playing fields for baseball, cross-country, field hockey, football, lacrosse, and soccer.

EXTRACURRICULAR OPPORTUNITIES

Students at The Hill are involved in many pursuits that take them well beyond the classroom and frequently beyond the campus itself. The students publish a newspaper, a literary magazine, and a yearbook. Students fulfill a community service requirement, which includes a written reflection, and also initiate a variety of community-wide service projects. For students interested in music, there are several instrumental and vocal groups, including the Hilltones and Hilltrebles (a cappella groups), jazz band, orchestra, men's glee club, women's chorus, and more. Other student organizations include the Hill Athletic Association, Student Government Association, Ellis Theatre Guild, and numerous clubs that reflect special interests.

The Hill School Humanities Fund provides students with tickets and transportation to hear the Philadelphia Orchestra and makes possible other cultural excursions as well. In addition, numerous on-campus lectures, concerts, plays, and exhibits are scheduled to stimulate and enrich students' cultural life.

DAILY LIFE

Classes are held six days a week, with a mid-morning chapel service on Monday and Thursday. A full academic day is divided into eight 40-minute periods, beginning at 8:25 a.m. and ending at 3:30 p.m. Wednesday and Saturday classes meet in the morning only. Athletic practice takes place between 3:45 and 5:45 p.m. Additional help with faculty members can be scheduled during free periods and in the evening. Student organizations meet after dinner. Evening study hours are supervised by faculty members and prefects.

Every Hill student "gives back" to the School by completing specifically assigned jobs within the School community several times each week for approximately 40 minutes each session.

WEEKEND LIFE

The Student Activities Office organizes weekend activities for Hill students. Off-campus activities include trips to movie theaters and malls, sporting events, amusement parks, outdoor activities (skiing, snow tubing, paintball), and excursions to Baltimore, Philadelphia, the Jersey shore, New York City, and Washington, D.C. Special on-campus events include concerts, dances, karaoke night, outdoor movie nights, the International Food Fair, and Spring Fling, where student participate in schoolwide volleyball competitions and rock climbing, listen to live bands, and more.

COSTS AND FINANCIAL AID

The annual charge for boarding students in 2011–12 is $47,500. This fee covers instruction, board, room, concerts, lectures, movies, athletic contests, services of the School physician and nurses at daily dispensaries, and athletic equipment on an issue basis. It also includes subscriptions for the newspaper and the literary magazine. There is an optional laundry service for an additional fee.

The day student tuition in 2011–12 is $32,800, which includes lunch for every day except Sunday. All day students are required to board for one year.

Financial aid is awarded to students whose parents are unable to meet the full cost of tuition. Aid is granted without regard to race, color, or ethnic origin. Financial aid grants are based on the guidelines established by the School and Student Service for Financial Aid. Grants are renewed annually; parents must submit the School and Student Service for Financial Aid form each year. About 40 percent of students receive financial aid. Applications for financial aid should be submitted by December 15.

ADMISSIONS INFORMATION

The Hill School seeks to enroll students who show academic promise, intellectual curiosity, and strong character. The School encourages applications from students who demonstrate involvement in the arts, athletics, and community service. The following credentials are required for admission: a formal application; a writing sample; a transcript of grades; results from the SSAT, ISEE, PSAT, SAT, or ACT; a letter of recommendation from the school counselor and English and mathematics teachers; and an interview.

APPLICATION TIMETABLE

During the year preceding the applicant's proposed entrance, a formal application for admission should be filed, accompanied by a nonrefundable application fee of $50 ($100 for international students). January 31 is the deadline for consideration in the first round; late applications are considered on a space-available basis.

Families are encouraged to visit The Hill during the school term to meet members of the faculty and student body. An appointment should be made in advance.

ADMISSIONS CORRESPONDENCE

Thomas Eccleston IV, '87
Assistant Headmaster for Admission and External Affairs
The Hill School
717 East High Street
Pottstown, Pennsylvania 19464
Phone: 610-326-1000
Fax: 610-705-1753
E-mail: admission@thehill.org
Web site: http://www.thehill.org

THE HOCKADAY SCHOOL

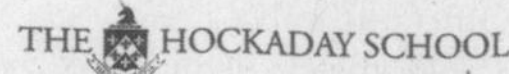

Dallas, Texas

Type: Girls' day college-preparatory (Prekindergarten to grade 12) and boarding (grades 8–12) school
Grades: Prekindergarten–12: Lower School, Prekindergarten–4; Middle School, 5–8; Upper School, 9–12 (Forms I–IV)
Enrollment: School total: 1,086
Head of School: Kim Wargo, Eugene McDermott Headmistress

THE SCHOOL

The Hockaday School, founded in 1913, provides a nationally recognized college-preparatory education for bright girls of strong potential who will assume positions of responsibility and leadership in a rapidly changing world. Ela Hockaday dedicated herself to giving each girl a foundation for living based on scholarship, character, courtesy, and athletics—the traditional Four Cornerstones that remain the dominant influence in the School's educational philosophy.

Hockaday's campus encompasses almost 100 acres of open fields and wooded creeks in residential northwest Dallas. The School's contemporary architectural setting features an academic quadrangle built to provide views of exterior gardens and landscaped terraces. The science center and Clements Lecture Hall opened in 1983, the Ashley Priddy Lower School Building in 1984, the Biggs Dining Room and Whittenburg Dining Terrace in 1985, the Fine Arts Wing in 1987, the Lower School addition in 2001, the Liza Lee Academic Research Center in 2002, the renovated Middle and Upper Schools in 2005, and the renovated Clements Lecture Hall in 2007.

A Board of Trustees is the governing body. The School's endowment is more than $100 million, and the operating income is supplemented by Annual Fund giving of more than $2 million. The Alumnae Association, with more than 7,000 graduates and former students, contributes significantly to the ongoing programs of the School.

The Hockaday School is accredited by the Independent Schools Association of the Southwest. It holds membership in the National Association of Independent Schools, the National Association of Principals of Schools for Girls, the College Board, the National Association for College Admission Counseling, the Educational Records Bureau, the National Coalition of Girls' Schools, and the Secondary School Admission Test Board.

ACADEMIC PROGRAMS

Students are exposed to a rigorous academic curriculum that offers core educational subjects as well as unique offerings in technology, the arts, and leadership and personal development. Graduation requirements (in years) include English, 4; mathematics, 3; history, 2.5; foreign language, 2; laboratory science, 3; fine arts, 1.5; physical education and health, 4; and academic electives from any department, 2, plus basic proficiency in computer usage. Hockaday offers 121 courses, including many honors courses. Advanced Placement courses are offered in eighteen subjects, including English, modern European history, U.S. history, AB and BC calculus, statistics, physics, chemistry, biology, studio art, Latin, French, Spanish, computer science, and economics. For some selected courses, Hockaday has a cooperative program with St. Mark's School of Texas, a boys' school in Dallas. Private lessons are available in cello, flute, guitar, piano, violin, and voice.

A one-year English as a second language (ESL) program is offered to students on intermediate and advanced levels. Intensive language training in writing, reading, listening, and speaking skills is the focus of the program. Students may continue at Hockaday after the first year, following acceptance into the regular academic program. International students with intermediate or advanced English proficiency may study at Hockaday. Along with these special classes, students may study math, science, fine arts, and other courses in the mainstream curriculum. First-year students travel to the Texas Hill Country and Washington, D.C.

Class sizes average 15 students, with an overall student-teacher ratio of 10:1.

The grading system in grades 7–12 uses A to F designations with pluses and minuses. Reports are sent to parents at the end of each quarter period. High achievement in the Upper School is recognized by inclusion on the Headmistress's List and by initiation into a number of honor societies, including the Cum Laude Society.

Each student receives careful counseling throughout her Hockaday career. Academic counseling begins even in the admissions process and continues under the supervision of the counseling office, which coordinates the faculty adviser system and general counseling program. Each student has an interested, concerned faculty adviser to assist her with academic or personal matters on a daily basis.

FACULTY AND ADVISERS

The Hockaday faculty is represented by accomplished individuals, most of whom have advanced degrees, with 9 holding doctoral degrees.

Hockaday's teachers are chosen for their depth of knowledge in their fields of specialization, personal integrity, and the ability to facilitate the progress of individual students. Many are successful writers, lecturers, artists, musicians, photographers, or composers. Summer study grants are awarded to faculty members to encourage both research and professional development.

Ms. Kim Wargo, Eugene McDermott Headmistress, holds a bachelor's degree in journalism from Louisiana State University, where she graduated summa cum laude with minors in history and English. She earned a master's degree in history from Tulane University.

COLLEGE ADMISSION COUNSELING

The college counselors work directly with Upper School students in their college planning. Each student participates with her parents in conferences with the counselor concerning applications and final selection.

In 2011, SAT scores ranged from 600 to 720 in critical reading, 620 to 740 in math, and 620 to 730 in writing. The class of 2011 had 15 National Merit Finalists, 15 National Merit Semifinalists, 26 National Merit Commended Students, 1 National Achievement Finalist, 1 National Achievement Scholar, 3 National Achievement Outstanding Participants, and 2 National Hispanic Honorable Mention Finalists. Hockaday alumnae include Hesburgh-Yusko Scholars (Notre Dame), Jefferson-Echols Scholars (Virginia), Marshall Scholars, Morehead-Cain Scholars (UNC-CH), a Rhodes Scholar, and Truman Scholars. They have received the Michael C. Rockefeller Memorial Fellowship at Harvard and have been named to the Gates Millennium Scholars Program. Traditionally, 100 percent of Hockaday graduates attend four-year colleges or universities. The 122 members of the class of 2011 were accepted for admission by 182 institutions, including Brown, Carnegie Mellon, Claremont McKenna, Duke, George Washington, Harvard, McGill (Canada), Middlebury, Northwestern, Oxford (England), Princeton, SMU, Stanford, Vanderbilt, Wake Forest, Washington (St. Louis), Yale, and the Universities of Chicago and Texas at Austin, among others.

STUDENT BODY AND CONDUCT

The student body is composed of 1,086 girls (79 of whom board) from ten states and eleven countries besides the United States. Thirty-seven percent of the girls are members of minority groups.

The Upper School Student Council and the Honor Council exert strong, active, and responsible leadership in student affairs. In addition to planning activities, allocating funds, and serving as a forum for student concerns, these councils promote and exemplify the School's written Honor Code.

Students are expected to abide by the guidelines set forth in the Upper School manual. Disciplinary measures rest primarily with the Head of the Upper School and the Headmistress.

ACADEMIC FACILITIES

The campus includes twelve buildings. The Liza Lee Academic Research Center is 52,000-square-feet and hosts two expansive libraries, several computer labs, breakout rooms, and a versatile hall that doubles as a lecture facility and audiovisual theater. In the academic area are classrooms; laboratories for languages, computers, and reading; and a study center. The campus is fully wireless, and Middle and Upper School classrooms are equipped with SmartBoard technology for use in conjunction with students' laptops, required for every girl in grades 6–12. The Fine Arts facilities include a 600-seat auditorium, instrumental and voice studios, practice rooms, a painting studio, ceramics facilities with outdoor kilns, a photography laboratory, printmaking facilities, and an electronic music studio. The Science Center contains a recently renovated lecture hall, study lounges, classrooms, ten major laboratories, a computer lab, and a greenhouse. The Wellness Center includes the 5,000-square-foot Hill Family Fitness Center, an 1,800-square-foot aerobics room with state-of-the-art aerobic and resistance equipment, and athletic training facilities fully equipped for the treatment of sports-related injuries.

BOARDING AND GENERAL FACILITIES

Accommodations for boarding students are comfortable dormitories, updated study areas, and lounges. Girls of similar grades are normally housed on a separate hall, each with its own lounge, kitchen, large-screen plasma television, DVR, and laundry room. The dormitories are wireless and all laptops are equipped with Skype. An additional common lounge has also been updated with a large-screen television, kitchen, and fireplace, and overlooks an outdoor swimming pool and tennis courts. Rooms are shared by two students, and each hall contains a small suite for the adult counselor in charge. The dormitories are closed for Thanksgiving, Christmas, and spring vacations.

An infirmary is located on the ground floor of the dormitory area, with a registered nurse on duty at all times and the School doctor on call. Campus security is maintained 24 hours a day.

The Wellness Center features an aerobics center, a fitness testing area, a trainer's facility, and the Hill Fitness Center, a 5,000-square-foot facility offering aerobic, resistance, and circuit training equipment.

ATHLETICS

Athletic facilities include two gymnasiums housing basketball courts (convertible to volleyball and indoor tennis courts), a climbing wall, two racquetball courts, a swimming pool, and a dance studio. On the grounds are six athletic fields, a softball complex, an all-weather track, a tennis center with ten courts and seating for 90 people. Interscholastic sports include basketball, crew, cross-country, fencing, field hockey, golf, lacrosse, soccer, softball, swimming and diving, tennis, track, and volleyball.

EXTRACURRICULAR OPPORTUNITIES

The Hockaday educational experience includes far more than just the classroom. There is a vast range of extracurricular opportunities for students to take part in: more than fifty student clubs, community service projects that impact the world beyond the campus, class bonding trips that build lifelong friendships, world-renowned speakers who expand students' perspectives, talent showcases at the Coffeehouse, and more.

To encourage student creativity, the Upper School sponsors a literary and journalistic magazine, a newspaper, and the Hockaday yearbook. These publications are edited by students with the guidance of faculty advisers. The literary magazine, *Vibrato,* won a gold medal with one all-Columbian honor from the Columbia Scholastic Press Association (CSPA). *Vibrato* has won top distinctions in ten of the last eleven years. Hockaday's student newspaper, *The Fourcast,* was awarded a gold medal with three all-Columbian honors, the highest score possible. NSPA rated the magazine first class with two marks of distinction. The yearbook, *Cornerstones,* was featured in a full-page treatment in the 2010 edition of Taylor Publishing's *Yearbook Yearbook.* All three of Hockaday's scholastic press publications were featured in the NSPA's *Best of the High School Press.*

Service to the School and its surrounding community is an important part of a girl's life at Hockaday. Each Upper School student is required to contribute a minimum of 15 volunteer hours per year in service to the wider community.

DAILY LIFE

Upper School classes begin at 8 a.m. and end at 3:45 p.m. Monday through Friday. The daily schedule provides time for academic help sessions and club meetings.

Varsity sports meet after the close of the regular school day. Boarding students have a 2-hour required study time, Sunday through Thursday nights.

WEEKEND LIFE

Off-campus activities each weekend enable resident students to take advantage of the many cultural and recreational resources in the Dallas–Fort Worth area. Faculty members are frequently involved in boarding activities, as are families of the Hockaday Parents' Association, who sponsor girls who are new to Hockaday and include them in family activities. Each resident student is matched with a local Dallas family through the Host Family Program. The host families offer local support for the girls and encourage their participation in social activities outside of school.

SUMMER PROGRAMS

A six-week coed academic summer session is offered for day and boarding students. Students may attend three- or six-week sessions beginning in June and July. Summer boarding is limited to girls ages 12–17. Programs in language immersion, math and science enrichment, computers, sports, SAT preparation, study skills, English, creative writing, and arts/theater are offered. Academic courses focus on enrichment opportunities. English as a second language, an international program lasting three weeks, begins in July. Information on the summer session is available in late spring. Applications are accepted until all spaces are filled, although students are encouraged to apply early to ensure their preferred course selection.

COSTS AND FINANCIAL AID

In 2011–12, tuition for Upper School day students averaged $24,000. For resident students, costs were approximately $42,000 for tuition, room, and board. Additional expenses for both day and resident students include, among others, those for books and uniforms. A deposit of $1000 is due with the signed enrollment contract, and the balance of tuition and fees is due by July 1, prior to entrance in August. Partial payment for room and board for resident students is also made at this time. The room and board balance for resident students is payable by December 1 following entrance in August.

The Hockaday Financial Aid Program offers assistance based on financial need. Parents of all applicants for financial aid must provide financial information as required by the Financial Aid Committee. Over $3 million was awarded to students in 2011–12. Details of the programs are available from the Admission Office.

ADMISSIONS INFORMATION

Applicants to Hockaday's Upper School are considered on the basis of their previous academic records, results of aptitude and achievement testing, teacher and head of school evaluations, and, in most cases, a personal interview. There is no discrimination because of race, creed, or nationality. Because the School requires a student to attend the School for at least two years to be eligible for graduation, new students are not normally admitted to the senior class. In order to qualify for admission and have a successful experience at Hockaday, girls need to possess strong potential and a desire to learn.

APPLICATION TIMETABLE

Initial inquiries are welcome at any time, and applications are received continuously. There is a nonrefundable application fee for both day-student and boarding-student applications. Entrance tests are scheduled in December, January, and February and periodically throughout the spring and summer. Campus tours are available at convenient times during the year. Notification of the admission decision is made approximately six weeks after testing. Parents are expected to reply to an offer of admission within two weeks.

ADMISSIONS CORRESPONDENCE

Jen Liggitt, Assistant Head for Enrollment Management
The Hockaday School
11600 Welch Road
Dallas, Texas 75229-2999
Phone: 214-363-6311
Fax: 214-265-1649
E-mail: admissions@mail.hockaday.org
Web site: http://www.hockaday.org

IDYLLWILD ARTS ACADEMY

Idyllwild, California

Type: Coeducational boarding and day college-preparatory school emphasizing the performing and visual arts
Grades: 9–12, postgraduate year
Enrollment: 291
Head of School: Brian D. Cohen, President

THE SCHOOL

The Idyllwild Arts Academy is a boarding and day academy offering preprofessional arts training and academic preparation for colleges and conservatories to boys and girls in grades 9 through 12 and to those taking a postgraduate year.

Dr. Max Krone and Beatrice Krone founded the Idyllwild Arts Foundation in 1946 and established the Academy as a summer program in 1950. The summer program opened for 100 students that year. The summer program, which reached an enrollment of more than 1,300 children and adults, was the Academy's focus for much of its history.

The Idyllwild Arts Academy seeks to prepare students for further education, for advanced arts studies, and for adult life as contributing, productive members of society. The Academy believes in an education of high quality that places demands on both faculty members and students, who in turn must be committed to the good of the school community.

The Academy is situated on 205 acres at an elevation of more than 5,000 feet in the San Jacinto Mountains. Strawberry Creek borders the campus, which is surrounded by more than 20,000 acres of protected forest and parkland. The village of Idyllwild, a community of 2,500 year-round residents, is a center for wilderness enthusiasts, who use the hundreds of miles of trails for hiking and mountain biking and the nearby lakes and creeks for boating and fishing. Idyllwild is about 100 miles from San Diego and 125 miles from Los Angeles. Its location near the junction of Routes 74 and 243 makes it accessible from all directions over freeway and highway routes. Motels, inns, campgrounds, and bed-and-breakfast facilities are available for visitors.

The Idyllwild Arts Foundation, which administers the Academy, is a nonprofit corporation governed by a 50-member self-perpetuating Board of Trustees. The trustees elect 18 of their members to a Board of Governors, which meets four times a year to conduct the foundation's affairs.

The Idyllwild Arts Academy is accredited by the Western Association of Schools and Colleges and is a member of the Secondary School Admission Test Board, Western Boarding Schools, NAFSA: Association of International Educators, the Network of Performing and Visual Arts Schools, the National Association of Independent Schools, California Association of Independent Schools, and the Federation of American and International Schools.

ACADEMIC PROGRAMS

In order to stimulate young people intellectually and to advance their knowledge in all areas, the Arts Academy provides an exciting and challenging academic program. In accordance with the thesis that artistically inclined young people tend to learn best by experiencing and doing rather than by simply reading or listening to information, the Academy's program of studies is designed to motivate students to think for themselves and to use disciplined inquiry to explore concepts in the various domains of knowledge.

Upon graduation, Arts Academy students have met or exceeded the admission requirements of the University of California System and are prepared to enter selective colleges, universities, and conservatories across the nation. Students must complete 17 academic units in addition to their arts curriculum. The academic units must include 4 units of English, 3 of mathematics, 2 of foreign language, 2 of laboratory sciences, 3 of social studies, 2 of physical education, and 1 of academic electives. In addition, students must meet the Academy's requirement for computer literacy. Postgraduates engage in a one-year intensive program in academics and the arts.

Students choose a major and plan individual schedules with faculty members and the Dean of the Arts and Dean of Academics. Placement in arts courses is by level of ability and experience; students then advance according to their performance. Areas of study include creative writing, music (including classical, voice, piano, and jazz), dance, acting, theatrical production and design, musical theater, moving pictures, interdisciplinary arts, and the visual arts. Each program incorporates courses in four categories: theory, history, and fundamentals of the form; creation, production, presentation, or performance; specialized master classes and private instruction; and field trips to arts communities of southern California to observe professionals at work.

Among the regular courses offered are tap, ballet, modern dance, pointe, jazz, men's class, pas de deux, and dance composition; music fundamentals, introduction to music literature, ear training/sight singing, music theory, music history, voice class, chamber music, orchestra, class piano, piano proficiency, accompaniment, and repertoire class; acting, voice and diction, musical theater, technical theater, drama history and literature, movement, playwriting, directing, and stage design; drawing and painting, art history, ceramics, sculpture, design and aesthetics, computer graphics illustration, and photography; and creative writing I and II, individual critique, and visiting artist workshops.

The academic year is divided into two semesters. Teachers are available to provide extra help in both the academic and the arts programs. Grades are issued and sent to parents four times a year.

FACULTY AND ADVISERS

Brian D. Cohen holds an M.F.A. in painting from the University of Washington and a B.A. from Haverford College. Prior to his appointment as President of Idyllwild Arts, he had been the Dean of Faculty at the Putney School in Vermont, chaired the arts department for eight years, and was the Founding Director of the Putney School Summer Program.

The full-time faculty, including administrators who teach, numbers 39 members. All have distinguished themselves as teachers and professional artists. They hold baccalaureate and graduate degrees from such institutions as California Institute of the Arts, Catawba, DePaul, Harvard, Juilliard, New England Conservatory of Music, Oberlin, Royal College of Music (London), San Francisco Conservatory of Music, Stanford, UCLA, USC, Yale, and the Universities of California, Santa Cruz; New Mexico; and Texas at Austin. Private instructors are appointed on a part-time or short-term basis to meet special needs. Prominent performing artists are scheduled to be in residence at various times during the academic year to conduct master classes and give performance examples.

COLLEGE ADMISSION COUNSELING

College guidance for students is provided by their advisers and one full-time college counselor. Students take the SAT and ACT and receive coaching on auditions and portfolio presentation.

More than 95 percent of Arts Academy graduates have gone on to attend a wide range of colleges and conservatories, including Art Center College of Design, Berkeley, Boston Conservatory, California Institute of the Arts, Carnegie Mellon, Cornish College of the Arts, Curtis Institute, Harvard, Indiana University, Juilliard, New England Conservatory, NYU (Tisch School of the Arts, Steinhardt School of Education, Gallatin School of Individualized Study, College of General Studies, and the College of Arts and Science), Oberlin College Conservatory of Music, Peabody Conservatory of Music, Rice, Sarah Lawrence, Stanford, UCLA, USC, Yale, and the Universities of California at San Diego and Santa Cruz, Hartford (Hartt School of Music), and Michigan.

Other graduates of the Arts Academy have gone directly to positions with institutions such as the San Francisco Ballet, BalletMet, and Circle Repertory Company.

STUDENT BODY AND CONDUCT

In 2010–11, the Academy enrolled 185 girls and 106 boys. The student body represents thirty states and twenty-two other countries.

The Dean of Students is responsible for students' residential life. The Judicial Committee, comprising 2 faculty members, 1 dorm parent, and 3 students, works in cooperation with the Dean of Students to oversee the rules and regulations instituted by the Academy. There is no formal dress code.

ACADEMIC FACILITIES

The campus of the Idyllwild Arts Academy is designed to be in harmony with its forested surroundings. Lecture halls, science laboratories, classrooms, art and dance studios, and three theaters are among the many campus facilities that enable Arts Academy students to live, study, practice, and perform in this special high school environment. The Bruce Ryan soundstage opened in 2002 for students in the moving pictures (film and video) major. Nelson Hall, a dining facility, opened in May 2006.

The Max and Bee Krone Library, a state-of-the-art multimedia center, opened in 2000. It includes a museum, a 6,000-volume music library, 6,564 books, and a computer graphics lab.

The Idyllwild Arts Foundation Theater, seating 300 people, is ideal for concerts, recitals, and mainstage plays.

Three dance facilities, complete with barres, mirrors, and resilient flooring, are in constant use throughout the year.

Music facilities include excellent recital and performance areas as well as practice rooms and several studios for ensemble rehearsals.

Studios for painting and drawing, design, sculpture, and photography are located near the center of the campus. A large ceramics studio has separate facilities for throwing on the wheel and hand building. A variety of kilns, including raku, Anagama, salt, gas, and wood, are available for student use.

Parks Exhibition Center, which opened in 2002, provides a spacious, well-lighted facility where students, faculty members, and guest exhibitors show their work.

BOARDING AND GENERAL FACILITIES

For most of the nine-month academic year, the dormitories are home to the Academy's boarding students. They share double rooms in four modern, comfortable dormitories supervised by faculty members and dorm parents. The close knit family atmosphere provides a strong base of support for the artistic, academic, and social life of the students.

A registered nurse is available at all times, and a physician in Idyllwild is on call. Emergency medical care is available at nearby hospitals.

ATHLETICS

Owing to the type of curriculum offered at the Arts Academy, the physical education program tends to be more creative than typical standardized course offerings. Physical education courses are intended to inspire a lifelong commitment to fitness.

Although students are required to complete 2 years of physical education, including one semester of health education, it is recommended that they take a physical education course each semester they are enrolled.

Health education serves to promote knowledge of nutrition and weight control as well as an understanding of stress in work and recreation, substance abuse, family issues, sexuality and relationships, and values in the decision-making process.

Idyllwild's current Physical Education facility includes a swimming pool, small gym with Universal weights and cardio equipment, tennis court, and playing field.

EXTRACURRICULAR OPPORTUNITIES

Extracurricular activities are planned by the student government and Student Services personnel. All students and faculty members are invited to make suggestions for these activities. Students sometimes go off campus for skiing, skating, and rock climbing and for trips to concerts, art museums, dance performances, theater productions, conferences, sports events, and beaches. Students who sign up for an off-campus trip are charged according to the cost of that particular event, including the costs of transportation, food consumed away from school, and entrance fees/tickets.

Students are also encouraged to become involved in Peer Ears, a student counseling group; and student publications, including the yearbook and *Parallax*, a literary and visual art publication.

DAILY LIFE

Academic classes begin at 8 a.m. and are held Monday through Saturday mornings. Arts classes are held in the afternoons, Monday through Friday, until dinner at 6:30. Evenings are set aside for rehearsals, study halls, and studio time.

WEEKEND LIFE

On weekend field trips, students enjoy the outstanding cultural attractions of Los Angeles and San Diego—museums, theaters, art galleries, and concert halls—and the many world-famous recreational areas nearby, including Disneyland, Knott's Berry Farm, Magic Mountain, Sea World, and the San Diego Zoo. In addition, southern California offers a wide variety of world-class sports attractions. The Arts Academy seeks to offer its students both the renewing serenity of the mountains and the bright lights and cultural stimulation of the city—the best of two worlds.

SUMMER PROGRAMS

The Summer Arts Program offers a wide variety of courses ranging in length from a weekend to two weeks for students of all ages. These include a Children's Arts Center, Creative Writing and Poetry (for junior high and high school students and adults), Native American arts, and comprehensive offerings in dance, music, theater and musical theater, and the visual arts. Steven Fraider is the Vice President and Director of the Summer Program.

COSTS AND FINANCIAL AID

For the 2011–12 school year, boarding tuition is $52,000 and day tuition is $34,800. The Academy subscribes to the School and Student Service for Financial Aid and awards more than $5 million in financial aid annually on the basis of talent and financial need. A tuition payment plan is available.

ADMISSIONS INFORMATION

The Idyllwild Arts Academy seeks dedicated, motivated, and talented students. Students are admitted in grades 9 through 12 and for a postgraduate year on the basis of academic transcripts, recommendations, a personal interview, and a demonstration of potential in the performing or visual arts through audition or portfolio.

APPLICATION TIMETABLE

Application deadlines begin February 1, and applicants are accepted until quotas are filled in each major. Students may be admitted at midyear, if space is available. The priority deadline for financial aid is February 1. The application fee is $50 for U.S. citizens and $100 for international applicants.

ADMISSIONS CORRESPONDENCE

Marek Pramuka, Dean of Admission and Financial Aid
Academy Admission Office
Idyllwild Arts Academy
52500 Temecula Road
P.O. Box 38
Idyllwild, California 92549-0038
Phone: 951-659-2171 Ext. 2223
Fax: 951-659-3168
E-mail: admission@idyllwildarts.org
Web site: http://www.idyllwildarts.org

THE LAWRENCEVILLE SCHOOL

Lawrenceville, New Jersey

Type: Coeducational boarding and day college-preparatory school
Grades: 9–PG (Second–Fifth Forms): Lower School, Second Form; Circle/Crescent Level, Third–Fourth Forms; Fifth Form
Enrollment: 810
Head of School: Elizabeth A. Duffy, Head Master

THE SCHOOL

The Lawrenceville School was founded in 1810 by Isaac Van Arsdale Brown as the Maidenhead Academy. Throughout the 1900s, Lawrenceville continued to develop as a leader in academic innovation, including early adoption of Advanced Placement (AP) courses and the introduction of nationally and internationally known guest speakers designed to broaden the intellectual horizons of young Lawrentians. Among the most-lasting changes was the introduction in 1936 of the Harkness method of education, which sought to bring the benefits of the House system to the classroom by providing an intimate environment for intellectual discourse.

Discussion of coeducation began in earnest in the 1970s, and after a lengthy, but thoughtful analysis of what it would mean both pedagogically and practically to the school, the Board elected to accept female students in 1985. The first girls arrived on campus in 1987 and brought a new vitality to the campus community. As the twentieth century drew to a close, the School embraced the ever-increasing diversity of its students in gender, geography, faith, race, and socioeconomic status, focusing on the need for a Lawrentian education to include broad exposure to all facets of the global community and an appreciation for and understanding of multiculturalism.

For more than 200 years, Lawrenceville graduates have gone on to success in their chosen fields, prepared by their education for the changing world around them. As the School enters its third century of educating students, it welcomes new students to join the legacy of Lawrenceville and discover what it means to be a Lawrentian in the twenty-first century.

The Lawrenceville School is located on 700 acres in the historic village of Lawrenceville, New Jersey.

The mission of the School is to inspire and educate promising young people from diverse backgrounds for responsible leadership, personal fulfillment, and enthusiastic participation in the world. Through its unique House system, collaborative Harkness approach to teaching and learning, close mentoring relationships, and extensive cocurricular opportunities, Lawrenceville helps students to develop high standards of character and scholarship; a passion for learning; an appreciation for diversity; a global perspective; and strong commitments to personal, community, and environmental responsibility.

Lawrenceville is accredited by the Middle States Association of Colleges and Schools and is a member of the Secondary School Admission Test Board, the National Association of Independent Schools, the New Jersey Association of Independent Schools, and the Council for Religion in Independent Schools.

ACADEMIC PROGRAMS

In fall 2006, after an 18-month curriculum review, the School adopted new graduation requirements that are designed to ensure students receive a strong foundation in all disciplines during their first two years that can be built upon in the upper forms. The requirements meet NCAA standards and are aligned with standard requirements for college admissions.

The requirements for entering Second Formers are: arts, 3 terms; English, 9 terms; history, 6 terms; humanities–English, 3 terms; humanities–cultural studies, 3 terms; interdisciplinary, 2 terms (at the advanced level); language through unit 9 (foundational level–through unit 6)*; mathematics through advanced algebra or precalculus (foundational level–through math 3)*; religion and philosophy, 2 terms; and science, 9 terms (foundational level–6 terms)*. Students are also required to give at least 40 hours of community service before they graduate. (*Students may opt to finish their course work in one of these disciplines at the foundational level with approval.)

Individual participation is encouraged in small classroom sections that average 12 students. Classes are grouped randomly and are taught around a large oval table called the Harkness table. Evening study periods, held in the Houses, are supervised by the Housemaster, the Assistant Housemaster, or an Associate Housemaster.

Students may also apply for independent study, off-campus projects, or the Lawrenceville international programs. Recent destinations include China, the Dominican Republic, Mexico, Japan, France, Peru, Nicaragua, Ghana, the Galapagos, Great Britain, South Africa, and Tanzania. Other opportunities include language immersion trips, where students reside with host families. Driver's education is also available.

Lawrenceville uses a letter grading system (A–F) in which D– is passing and B+ qualifies for honors.

The school year is divided into three 10-week terms. Full reports are sent home at the end of each term, with interim reports at midterm. The full reports include comments and grades from each of a student's teachers indicating his or her accomplishments, efforts, and attitudes. Less formal progress reports are also written by teachers throughout the term as needed. Students in academic difficulty are placed on academic review, which entails close supervision and additional communication with parents.

FACULTY AND ADVISERS

There are 139 full-time faculty members who hold numerous degrees: bachelor's, 33; master's 86; doctorates 2; Ph.D., 18; J.D., 1; and professional, 1. Most faculty members reside on the campus, and many serve as residential Housemasters, coaches, and club advisers. All are active in advising and counseling students.

Elizabeth A. Duffy was appointed the twelfth Head Master of the Lawrenceville School in 2003. Ms. Duffy graduated magna cum laude from Princeton University in 1988 with an A.B. in molecular biology. In 1993, she received an M.B.A. from the Graduate School of Business at Stanford University and an A.M. in administration and policy analysis from the School of Education there. She has spent her entire career working with educators at all levels.

COLLEGE ADMISSION COUNSELING

The College Counseling Office supports, informs, and encourages students and their families as they navigate the exciting, complex, and ever-changing process of college admissions. The counselors educate students and families about the nuances of admissions, advise students about college options that best suit their individual needs, and support and encourage students as they complete the application process.

Lawrenceville's college counselors offer students decades of professional experience as college counselors and college admissions officers. The counseling staff provides valuable and timely advice to families as the process unfolds and helps students present their abilities, talents, and experiences to colleges in the most appropriate manner. The 5 counselors carry a small average case load of 45 students, which allows for personal attention and sustained involvement in all aspects of the residential school community. Over the course of their Lawrenceville careers, families and students receive information through form-specific newsletters, classwide meetings, and Parent Weekend programming. They also have access to Naviance, an online college admission management tool. All of these resources help ensure that students and their families are well prepared to embrace the college counseling process when students are officially assigned to individual counselors in the middle of their Fourth Form year.

The class of 2011's median SAT scores were: 676 critical reading, 694 math, and 698 writing. Between 2009 and 2011, the twenty colleges most attended by Lawrenceville students were Princeton, 42; Georgetown, 28; Pennsylvania, 27; Duke, 24; NYU, 24; Columbia, 21; Trinity (Hartford), 19; Stanford, 16; Johns Hopkins, 15; Yale, 15; Cornell, 14; Dartmouth, 14; Brown, 13; George Washington, 12; Boston College, 11; Middlebury, 10; Wesleyan, 8; Williams, 8; Vanderbilt, 8; and Virginia, 8.

STUDENT BODY AND CONDUCT

For 2011–12, there are 810 students: boarding 548, day 262; boys 425, and girls 385. Students are from twenty-nine states and thirty-five countries.

Lawrenceville expects its students to achieve good records and develop self-control, systematic study habits, and a clear sense of responsibility. The School has a high regard for energy, initiative, a positive attitude, and active cooperation. Students accepting this premise have no trouble following the basic regulations.

The student body elects 5 governing officers from among students in the Fifth Form, and each House elects its own Student Council.

ACADEMIC FACILITIES

Lawrenceville's first rate, state-of-the art academic facilities, which include the Kirby Arts Center, Gruss Center of Visual Arts, the F.M. Kirby Science Center, the Juliet Lyell Staunton Clark Music Center, Bunn Library, and the Noyes History Center, offer a unique opportunity for all students. Each building houses an entire academic discipline, so students are immersed within a particular subject from the minute they enter the building until the minute they leave.

Lawrenceville supports excellent teaching with outstanding educational and campus resources. The Bicentennial Campaign, completed in 2010 in honor of the School's 200th anniversary, demonstrated the intense willingness of alumni, parents, and friends to provide the absolute best facilities and support for students and faculty. This most ambitious campaign raised $218.5 million, exceeding the $200 million goal, for student financial aid, faculty support, academic programs, and student life. Among the campaign's successes were the new Al Rashid Health and Wellness Center, a state-of-the-art facility for both treatment and prevention; Carter House, a Fifth girls' residential house (opened fall 2010); and lighted turf fields of the Getz Sports Complex.

BOARDING AND GENERAL FACILITIES

Lawrenceville's most distinguishing feature is its House system. In each of the twenty Houses, the Housemaster maintains close contact with the residents. House athletics teams compete intramurally, and

House identity is maintained through separate dining rooms in the Irwin Dining Center for the underformers. This distinctive system provides a small social environment in which each student's contribution is important and measurable.

Services in the Edith Memorial Chapel are nondenominational. The Al Rashid Health and Wellness Center offers inpatient and outpatient medical care, including psychological counseling services, and a consulting staff who offer gynecological care, orthopedic/sports medicine, and nutrition. Certified athletic trainers provide rehabilitation services for injuries. The Center's health professionals seek to educate and encourage students to develop the knowledge and skills needed to sustain a lifetime of healthy function.

ATHLETICS

Lawrenceville regards athletics as yet another educational opportunity for students and a valuable complement to the School's rigorous academic expectations. The importance of commitment; satisfaction of teamwork; hard lessons of failure; courage to surmount pain, fatigue, and frustration for a common goal; the virtue of physical conditioning; imperatives of sportsmanship; and the sheer joy of healthy competition are values Lawrenceville's athletic program is uniquely suited to teach. In addition, the School's proud interscholastic tradition and comprehensive intramural program, along with instruction in lifetime sports, ensure that each student experiences the challenge and reward of athletic competition.

The School takes pride in its first-class outdoor sports facilities: two FieldTurf artificial playing surfaces with lights for field hockey, lacrosse, and soccer; and eighteen other multipurpose natural grass athletic fields, including five intramural fields and two softball and two baseball diamonds. There are also twelve tennis courts, a nine-hole golf course, and a quarter-mile all-weather track. The crew program enjoys the use of a bay and other facilities at the Mercer Lake Rowing Association boathouse.

The Edward J. Lavino Field House is one of the finest in any independent school. The main arena has a Mondo surface with three combination basketball-volleyball-tennis courts; a four-lane 200-meter banked indoor track, with an eight-lane straightaway; and long jump, shot put, pole vault, and high jump areas. Along each side of the arena are two gymnasiums, a six-lane competition swimming pool, a wrestling room, a performance center, and an athletic training wellness room. A modern, enclosed ice hockey rink is attached to the Lavino Field House, and there are ten Anderson international squash courts. Nearby, a separate building houses the state-of-the-art, 4,500-square-foot Al Rashid Strength and Conditioning Center that is supervised by 2 certified coaches.

Students must participate in an approved form of athletic activity each term. Rehabilitation of athletic injuries and fitness testing are an important part of the athletic program and are available to students by Lawrenceville's 2 certified athletic trainers.

The School's outdoor, experientially based programs and initiatives educate students in responsible leadership, community membership, and character development and provide interactions in the outdoor environment, enhancing both academic and nonacademic skills development. Lawrentians have traveled the globe through outdoor program courses, scaling glaciers in Patagonia, trekking through the desert in South Africa, and sea kayaking among icebergs in Newfoundland. Athletic credit is given to participants.

Lawrenceville's ropes course offers students the opportunity to accept a challenge and work toward conquering it as a group. The course, created and built by an outdoor experiential education expert, is designed to help students listen to each other, trust each other, and work toward a common goal.

EXTRACURRICULAR OPPORTUNITIES

Lawrenceville provides a numerous opportunities for students to explore outside the classroom. There are more than eighty clubs and organizations specializing in interests such as writing, acting, debate, music, art, history, religion, science, photography, woodworking, and scuba diving.

Through the required Community Service Program, students serve as tutors, elementary school study center supervisors, and group activity counselors. The School sponsors organized educational and cultural trips to New York City and Washington, D.C.

Exhibits occur throughout the year. Several lecture programs bring speakers and artists to the campus. Annual events include Parents' Weekend in the fall, Parents' Winter Gathering, and Alumni Weekend in the spring.

DAILY LIFE

Lawrenceville students have their schedules packed full of classes, study hours, athletic practice, rehearsals, and time for friends, special events, eating, and sleeping. Students learn to manage their time, meet their commitments, and enjoy their friendships.

Classes begin at 8 a.m. on most days, and the dining center opens at 7 a.m. for breakfast. Each class meets four times a week for 55-minute sessions. Science and advanced classes have an additional 55-minute period each week for labs, extended discussions, test practice, writing workshops, etc. There also are three 40-minute periods each week for student-teacher consultations. Students are highly encouraged to take advantage of consultation periods.

The entire School eats lunch at the same time, and each House dines together. This tradition is yet another example of how the House system defines the Lawrenceville experience. On Mondays, students take lunch with their academic advisers. Each advisee group shares a table, and time is spent discussing both individual and group concerns; if needed, students can schedule a private meeting with their adviser.

The entire School assembles once a week for an all-School community meeting. These gatherings feature readings, reflections, and announcements. School meeting agendas include outside speakers, special guests, musical presentations, and opportunities to examine student issues.

Classes end at 3:05 p.m., but then there is more to do—sports or community service. On Wednesdays, classes end at 12:20 p.m., and students have the option of studying, rehearsing, practicing sports, working on publications, or fulfilling their community service requirement. Saturday classes end at 11:30 a.m..

Dinner is served from 5:30 to 7 p.m. All Forms eat in the Irwin Dining Center, except for the Fifth Form, which takes meals in the Abbott Dining Room in the Upper House. After dinner, there is time for clubs, activities, homework, and socializing. Check-in is at 8 p.m. for Lower School, 8:30 p.m. for Crescent Circle Houses, and 9 p.m. for the Fifth Form, Sunday–Friday. Permission to leave the House after check-in to go to the library, rehearsals, club meetings, or to meet a teacher for consultation is granted after check-in time, but students must check back in with the Housemaster on duty by 10 p.m. (11 p.m. on Saturday).

WEEKEND LIFE

On weekends, at least one House sponsors an all-School social event, which may include carnivals, concerts, formal dinners, and dances. Faculty members are on hand to take trips to local shopping areas and movie theaters. Reach Out to the Arts is a faculty-led club that takes weekly trips to cultural events in New York. Day students are encouraged to attend all-campus activities.

COSTS AND FINANCIAL AID

The annual charges for 2011–12 were $48,800 for boarding students and $39,960 for day students.

Through the generosity of alumni, friends, and foundations, approximately $9.7 million in funds are available to provide financial assistance to qualified students. Currently, 29 percent of the student body receives assistance. Awards are made on the basis of character, ability, past performance, and future promise. Amounts are based solely on need and are determined by procedures established by the School and Student Service for Financial Aid.

ADMISSIONS INFORMATION

All students who enter must be able to meet the academic standards. Lawrenceville also looks for students who possess the potential to become vitally interested members of the student body—students who make individual contributions.

Selection is based on all-around qualifications without regard to race, creed, or national origin. Character, seriousness of purpose, and future promise as well as past performance, the recommendation of a headmaster or principal, and SSAT results are all taken into consideration by the Admission Committee.

For fall 2011, there were 1,940 formal applications for grades 9–12, of which 240 enrolled. Thirty-nine percent were from public schools, 40 percent from private schools, 7 percent from international schools, and 14 percent from church-related schools.

Required for admission is the formal application, which includes a written essay, a transcript of the applicant's school record, a letter of recommendation from the head of the current school, three reference letters, SSAT or ISEE and/or TOEFL scores, and an on-campus interview.

APPLICATION TIMETABLE

Campus interviews are conducted during the week from 9 to 2 Monday, Tuesday, Thursday, and Friday. Applicants can also interview on Wednesdays from 9 to 10:30 and on Saturdays from 8:30 to10:30. Interviews are not conducted on Saturdays during the summer months.

The application deadline is January 31 for boarding students and January 14 for day students, at which time all application materials must be submitted and interviews completed. The notification date is March 10, and parents reply by April 10.

ADMISSIONS CORRESPONDENCE

Dean of Admission
The Lawrenceville School
2500 Main Street
P.O. Box 6008
Lawrenceville, New Jersey 08648
Phone: 609-895-2030
800-735-2030 (toll-free outside New Jersey)
Fax: 609-895-2217
E-mail: admissions@lawrenceville.org
Web site: http://www.lawrenceville.org

LINSLY SCHOOL

Wheeling, West Virginia

Type: Independent, coeducational, college-preparatory boarding and day school
Grades: 5–12
Enrollment: 450 students; 103 boarding students
Head of School: Chad Barnett

THE SCHOOL

Founded in 1814, the Linsly School is a private, independent day and boarding school for students in grades 5 through 12. Located in Wheeling, West Virginia, the School offers a college-preparatory curriculum that combines the traditional values of hard work, respect, honor, honesty, and self-discipline within a challenging academic program designed to unlock the potential of each student.

The family-like atmosphere at Linsly helps students grow and develop under the guidance of faculty members who know them by name and care about their future. Learning is not limited to the classroom—it happens over lunch, dinner, evening study hall, and at any time—learning at Linsly never ends.

Linsly is a place where lifelong friendships between students and faculty are formed. Students wear uniforms, not to encourage conformity, but to ensure that they are known for their unique ideas and abilities. Linsly is a school where long-forgotten traditional values live on in everyday curriculum.

With 100 percent college placement, Linsly's record as an excellent college-preparatory academy speaks for itself. But the School also teaches that there is more to education than test scores and college acceptance letters. Every day, students learn by living many of life's most important principles: responsibility, commitment, time management, sportsmanship, maturity, and even disappointment. The School's "no-quit" policy teaches students to finish what they start and to follow through with their commitments.

The education a student earns at Linsly is both deep and lasting because life's lessons continually emerge. The experience fosters lifelong learning to prepare students for college and life.

ACADEMIC PROGRAMS

At Linsly, academic excellence has always been developed through a traditional curriculum enhanced with contemporary courses. While some schools claim to go back to basics, Linsly is proud to have never left them.

The academic program is rigorous and challenging to every student. Advanced-level courses are available in both the high school and the middle school curriculum, ensuring that even the most gifted students will be intellectually challenged.

Class grades are computed on a numerical basis. All grades below 70 percent are considered failing. Certain grades are indicated by letter grade (92 and up, A; 83–91, B; 74–82, C; 70–73, D). Report cards are mailed home four times a year at the end of every grading period. Students receive a separate report for each subject. A student having attained an average of 92 percent has earned second honors. A student having received an average of 95 percent has earned first honors. In addition, deficiency reports and/or progress reports are mailed to parents at the midpoint of each grading period. Lower School students receive letter grades in computer and physical education/health twice a year, at the end of each semester. Lower School students receive letter grades in fine arts courses every grading period.

A full program of college preparatory subjects is offered at Linsly. All students must carry a five-course per semester class load (excluding physical education). Full credit courses meet five times weekly for the entire year. However, there are certain half-credit courses which meet three times weekly for a year, or every day for a semester. Twenty credits are required for graduation and must include the following minimums: 4 credits of English, 4 credits of mathematics, 3 credits of history, 3 credits of the same foreign language, 2 credits of science, physical education, ¼ credit of art appreciation, ¼ credit of music appreciation, ½ credit of computer science, and the Senior Research Essay.

FACULTY AND ADVISERS

Linsly teachers share a common calling. They are not individuals who see education as an 8-to-3 job. They are not individuals who see themselves as specialists in a very narrow area, uninterested in broadening the education of their students. Linsly teachers are interested in the complete development of their students. They are diverse in their talents, varied in their interests, and committed to a model of education that places the relationship with their students at the heart of the teaching experience.

Many of Linsly's faculty members live on campus, making them readily accessible for extra help and counsel. As advisers, the faculty members build strong and lasting relationships with their students. This strong sense of community is felt in all aspects of school life at Linsly. The School is extremely proud of its accomplished and respected faculty and administrative team.

Linsly's Advisory Program provides guidance from the faculty members in both academic and personal matters and allows a small group of students and a faculty mentor to get to know one another personally outside of the academic environment. Students meet daily for the first 10 minutes of the academic day with other advisees. While this is an ideal time for group discussions, students may call upon their faculty adviser for help or advice whenever needed. The average advisory group consists of 10 students. New students are assigned advisers, and returning students choose their adviser at the end of every year. The adviser becomes the student's close personal contact with the School, and advisers are available to offer assistance in all areas of a student's life.

COLLEGE ADMISSION COUNSELING

Linsly's college counseling office seeks to find the best college or university to match each individual student's needs and interests. The School's director of college counseling conducts a thorough program of testing and interviews with both students and parents throughout each high school student's Linsly career. College counseling begins in the sophomore year when students sit for their first PSAT and SAT tests. Taking these exams early allows students to become familiar with their test-taking abilities and provides instructors with the data necessary to help meet the academic needs of a particular individual or body of students.

A multiyear, comprehensive SAT-preparation program begins in the sophomore year and concludes prior to the student's first senior SAT. In addition to regular administration of the PSAT, SAT, and SAT Subject Tests, each student goes through a thorough interview process including the Strong Interest Inventory to help them discover academic and career interests. This individual attention and concern helps students gain an understanding of their academic and personal priorities when selecting institutions of higher learning.

STUDENT BODY AND CONDUCT

There are approximately 450 students enrolled at the Linsly School during the academic year. Students in grades 5 through 8 are considered members of Linsly's Lower School. The Upper School is comprised of students in grades 9 through 12.

Daily life at Linsly is based on principles of mutual respect and cooperation. Students are encouraged to accept responsibility, express themselves openly, and develop a strong sense of self-awareness and self-confidence. Boys and girls adhere to a dress code designed to distinguish themselves by their accomplishments rather than by their appearance.

ACADEMIC FACILITIES

Linsly's scenic 65-acre campus offers an ideal setting for a safe and vibrant learning community. Tucked behind Wheeling's historic National Road, and bordered by Wheeling Creek, the Linsly campus functions as an extensive classroom. The School's location makes it an attractive educational option for families throughout West Virginia, Pennsylvania, Ohio, and beyond.

With nearly twenty faculty residences situated throughout campus, Linsly's neighborhood feeling provides all students an encouraging and attentive place to grow and learn.

Linsly's Banes Hall serves as the School's primary academic building. The 80,000-square-foot structure houses twenty-seven classrooms, modern science laboratories, upgraded computer centers, a technology-rich library, music room, swimming pool, and cafeteria. The Williams Visual Arts Center provides top-quality studio, classroom, and gallery space, while the Hess Center offers equipment for students interested in woodworking.

The Dlesk Conference Center is a unique place for meetings or searching the Linsly history archives housed there.

BOARDING AND GENERAL FACILITIES

Any student living outside the day student area (as defined by the School) must live in a Linsly dormitory. Weiss Hall, Merriman Hall, Yost Hall, and the Dicke Dorm are operated for those students who reside outside the Wheeling area and who have a strong desire to participate in the Linsly education program.

The layout of each of the dormitories is different. Within each dormitory there are faculty members assigned a specific section or wing. The Dormitory Master for that section is responsible for prescribing specific rules and the conduct of the residents. Students are not permitted in other dormitories or in other wings without consent.

The Linsly campus is located approximately 1 hour from the Pittsburgh International Airport. If necessary, the School can help parents arrange transportation to and from the airport for boarding students.

ATHLETICS

At Linsly, athletics are an important part of a well-rounded education; they not only contribute to physical well-being, but they also teach valuable lessons. Through athletics, students learn that hard work, perseverance, sportsmanship, and teamwork count at least as much as winning.

Every Linsly student is encouraged to participate in athletics. Lower School students can play on interscholastic teams, and all participate in a spring intramural sports program. The Upper School athletic program includes more than twenty interscholastic teams, which compete in both the Ohio Valley Athletic Conference (OVAC) and the Interstate Prep School League. Even students who are not athletically inclined can choose an appropriate sport and work with a coach to gain satisfaction of meeting the sport's physical and mental challenges.

EXTRACURRICULAR OPPORTUNITIES

Linsly provides a wide range of extracurricular options considered essential to the overall educational process. The Student Life program gives each student the opportunity to express his or her individuality through participation in activities that meet a variety of needs and interests.

Throughout the year, the School sponsors dances, fun activities, and on-campus events that highlight the talents of the diverse student body. A weekly all-school meeting is held to recognize accomplishments both in and outside of school.

Linsly offers a variety of special interest and community service clubs and organizations to give students the opportunity to participate in areas where they have interests and abilities. Participation helps each student develop a sense of responsibility for their community that is important to the individual and the school. Once a student begins a commitment, they must finish the commitment. The clubs and organizations meet regularly during specified times during the school day or after school. Some of the extracurricular activities offered include animal shelter club, Lower School band, yearbook, newspaper, chorus, Upper and Lower School drama, stage band, forensics, French club, German club, Fellowship of Christian Athletes, Key Club, Shakespeare club, Spanish club, Upper School math club, chess club, Lower School newspaper, classical club, puzzlemaniacs, history club, Princeton Model Congress, Model United Nations, environmental club, outdoor adventure club, multicultural club, technology club, Scrabble club, and Students Against Destructive Decisions.

DAILY LIFE

The school day begins at 8 a.m. when students meet in adviser groups for 10 minutes. Fifty-minute academic periods begin at 8:10. At 9:50 there is a half-hour flexible period to allow School clubs and class meetings to take place. The five remaining 50-minute periods are broken up by a half-hour lunch period. The Lower School eats at noon, and the Upper School eats at 12:50.

COSTS AND FINANCIAL AID

Tuition for the 2011–12 academic year is $14,280 for day students and $29,320 for boarding students. The cost of books, uniforms, and supplies is approximately $1000.

The Linsly School seeks to attract and maintain a highly capable and diverse student body. To help meet that commitment the School offers financial aid to qualified students on the basis of the demonstrated financial need of the family and the availability of funds. Families should not be discouraged from applying because of limited financial resources. For the 2011–12 academic year, 44 percent of Linsly students received awards totaling $1.8 million.

The Linsly School does not offer merit scholarships; the financial aid program is need-based. It is the School's expectation that families receiving financial assistance embrace the value of a Linsly education and make it a priority in their financial planning.

Financial aid decisions are made independent of admission decisions. Once students who have applied for financial aid are accepted in the admission process, they are referred to the Financial Aid Committee, which reviews the family's financial information, calculates their demonstrated need, and determines their financial aid awards.

Questions or concerns about financial aid or the financial aid application process should be directed to Craig Tredenick, Linsly's Director of Admissions and Financial Aid.

ADMISSIONS INFORMATION

Families interested in learning more about Linsly can request information by calling the Admissions Office at 304-233-1436 or e-mailing admit@linsly.org. In addition, families can submit an inquiry form via the Linsly School's Web site at www.linsly.org/admissions.

There are three main steps to Linsly's admissions process. The first is to schedule a visit by contacting the Admissions Office, Monday–Friday, 8 to 4. Weekend visits are also available. A campus visit will last approximately 2 hours and will include a tour of campus, an interview with the admissions director, and the completion of the School's admissions test. Interested students may also attend a Campus Visit Day.The second step is to complete and submit an application and supporting materials (two essays, teacher recommendations, standardized test scores, and a parent survey). Finally, if the applicant family plans to apply for financial aid, they need to notify the admissions office; the application information will be forwarded to them.

Once an application for admission is completed, the admissions committee meets to discuss each applicant. When a decision is made, the admissions office will notify the applicant of the decision.

APPLICATION TIMETABLE

An application for admissions and all supporting documents should be submitted to the admissions office by mid-December (decision by mid-January) or mid-February (decision by mid-March). Specific deadline dates for each year are available on the School's Web site. The deadline for International Student applications is usually the end of January.

ADMISSIONS CORRESPONDENCE

Craig Tredenick
Director of Admissions
Linsly School
60 Knox Lane
Wheeling, West Virginia 26003
Phone: 304-233-1436
E-mail: admit@linsly.org
Web site: http://www.linsly.org/admissions

LYNDON INSTITUTE

Lyndon Center, Vermont

Type: College-preparatory and general academic coeducational day and boarding school
Grades: 9–12
Enrollment: 600 (approximate)
Head of School: Richard D. Hilton, Headmaster

THE SCHOOL

Lyndon Institute (LI) was founded in 1867 in the tradition of the New England academy. The Institute still shows the effects of the shaping hand of T. N. Vail, founder of AT&T, who served as president of LI in the early 1900s and was responsible for considerable growth in its programs and facilities.

An accomplished faculty that includes published authors, noted artists, college faculty members, and others active in their professional fields provides a challenging, comprehensive educational program in a picturesque Vermont village setting. Lyndon students enjoy personal attention from the faculty members, genuine respect for their individuality and unique talents, a truly inclusive environment, and outstanding preparation for their choices of colleges and careers.

Lyndon Institute consists of three campuses on 150 acres centered on the village green of historic Lyndon Center, Vermont. It is a safe, supportive community of exceptional beauty.

LI is located 10 miles north of St. Johnsbury on Interstate 91. Boston and Hartford are 3–4 hours away by car. Burlington, Vermont, and Montreal are only 2 hours from the campus. Airline service to Burlington; Manchester, New Hampshire; or Boston, Massachusetts, provides easy access. Burke Mountain Ski Area is 7 miles away.

The school's operating budget is $10.1 million; parents, friends, and an active alumni group raise about $250,000 in annual support. The endowment is $8 million.

Lyndon Institute is accredited by the New England Association of Schools and Colleges and approved by the Vermont Department of Education. Memberships include the Independent School Association of Northern New England, the Vermont Independent School Association, the Secondary School Admission Test Board, and The Association of Boarding Schools.

ACADEMIC PROGRAMS

Lyndon Institute is a comprehensive secondary school offering college-preparatory and fine arts programs of study as well as business, information, and technical education areas. Twenty-two credits are required for graduation, with the following distribution: English, 4 credits; social studies, 3 credits; mathematics, 3 credits; science, 3 credits; fine arts, 1 credit; health and physical education, 2½ credits; and electives, 4½ credits.

Other course offerings include French, 4 years; Japanese, 4 years; Latin, 4 years; Spanish, 4 years; Russian, 4 years; band and chorus, 4 years; art and theater, 4 years; advanced math, 2 years; algebra, 2 years; geometry, 1 year; Calculus, 2 years; biology, 2 years; chemistry, 2 years; physics, 2 years; computer science, 7 courses; technology, 14 courses; drafting, 5 courses, including computer-aided design; word processing, 3 courses; and office technology, 3 courses. Honors courses are offered in American literature, English literature, algebra 1 and 2, geometry, world geography, U.S. history, contemporary U.S. history, world civilizations, biology, advanced biology, chemistry, physics, and advanced art. LI offers Advanced Placement courses in English composition, English literature, chemistry, physics, environmental science, European history, U.S. history, calculus A/B and B/C, and studio art in both drawing and design.

The fine and performing arts program allows students to take a series of courses within the fine arts concentration, which includes concert band, jazz band, improvisation, music theory, chorus, select chorus, art, art 4, advanced art, book arts, painting, printmaking, design, 2-D and 3-D art, photography, dance, jazz dance, lyrical ballet, four years of acting, and theater production.

Classes are grouped on the basis of ability. The student-teacher ratio is 10:1, with an average class size of 18. The grading system ranges from A to F and is calculated on a 4-point scale: A, 4.0; B, 3.0; C, 2.0; D, 1.0; and F, 0.0. The academic year is divided into two semesters consisting of two quarters each. Exchange trips are available during vacation times, and many opportunities for class travel are offered throughout the year.

FACULTY AND ADVISERS

There are 61 full-time and part-time faculty members at Lyndon Institute. Thirty-one percent have earned a master's degree or higher.

Richard D. Hilton was appointed Headmaster in 1999. He holds a B.A. in English from Notre Dame and a master's degree from Villanova.

COLLEGE ADMISSION COUNSELING

College planning is accomplished through individual and small-group counseling beginning in the freshman year. Two full-time counselors work in concert with students and families to develop postsecondary plans. In a student's junior year, counselors from the Student Services Office help with coordinating college applications and essay writing.

Representatives from more than thirty colleges visit Lyndon Institute annually. LI cosponsors the Northeast Kingdom College Night program each spring with representatives from more than 100 colleges and universities in attendance.

Last year, 86 percent of LI graduates pursued postsecondary options. Recent graduates have attended Berkeley, Boston College, Boston University, Brown, Clarkson, Cornell, Dartmouth, Fordham, Georgia Tech, Harvard, Indiana, Michigan State, Northeastern, Parsons, Penn State, Purdue, Rensselaer, Smith, St. Lawrence, Syracuse, and the Universities of Arizona, Connecticut, Illinois, Maine, Massachusetts, Michigan, New Hampshire, Vermont, Washington, and Wisconsin.

STUDENT BODY AND CONDUCT

The total enrollment is approximately 600 students, who come from the surrounding communities in Vermont and New Hampshire and from countries around the globe. The school implemented a boarding program in 2003–04, which included 106 students in grades 9–12 during the 2010–11 school year. Countries represented in the international program in the last five years include Afghanistan, China, Germany, Jamaica, Japan, Kazakhstan, Korea, Mexico, Pakistan, Spain, Sweden, Taiwan, and the Bahamas.

The Code of Conduct is established by the faculty members, the administration, and the Board of Trustees and is based on common courtesy, mutual respect, and socially acceptable behavior.

ACADEMIC FACILITIES

Lyndon Institute comprises three campuses. The Darling Campus consists of the Main Building, containing ten classrooms, four science labs, a small performing arts space, administrative offices, and a multilevel media center; Pierce Hall, containing seven classrooms, a computer lab, and a 250-seat cafeteria; Alumni Wing, which houses a 550-seat gymnasium and a 650-seat auditorium; and Lewis Field.

The Harris Campus consists of five main buildings, including the school's health center, and Sanborn Hall, which provides locker rooms, athletic training facilities, and a full-size auxiliary gymnasium.

The Vail Campus comprises eleven buildings, eight of which house technology classrooms, laboratories, and workshops, including a fully networked computer-aided design (CAD) lab and drafting studio, a newly dedicated art center (2003), and four residence dormitories.

BOARDING AND GENERAL FACILITIES

Seven dorms make up the housing for boarding students at Lyndon Institute, including a new dormitory for 20 students. The dormitories can accomodate 106 students in single (seventy-six) or double rooms (fifteen), as well as 15 resident dorm parents.

ATHLETICS

In the 2009–10 school year, roughly 45 percent of the student body participated in the fall sports program. Lyndon Institute is involved in sixteen interscholastic sports as well as six club sports and students can use the multiple game and practice fields; the Fenton Chester Ice Arena, which is adjacent to the school; and Burke Mountain Ski Area, just 7 miles from campus. The golf team practices at nearby St. Johnsbury Country Club's championship golf course. In the last five years, LI teams have won state championships in baseball, cross-country running, golf, Nordic skiing, softball, and track.

EXTRACURRICULAR OPPORTUNITIES

Student clubs and organizations include Student Council, National Honor Society, Future Business Leaders of America, and USA Skills/Vocational Industrial Clubs of America. Students may join the jazz ensemble; choral and drama groups; French, Latin, and Spanish clubs; the forensics team, and the scholars bowl team. The award-winning art and literature magazine, *Janus*; the *Viking Voice*, LI's student newspaper; *Cynosure*, the yearbook; and the Writers Workshop offer students writing, editing, and desktop publishing opportunities.

The French and Spanish clubs organize trips abroad in alternating years. Students can take advantage of the cultural events and concerts at LSC, the Catamount Film and Arts Center in St. Johnsbury, and the Hopkins Center at Dartmouth College. The Music, Dance, and Art Departments offer students opportunities to work and perform with guest artists-in-residence. In addition to dances, plays, concerts, and athletics events, Spirit Week and Winter Carnival are two schoolwide events that engage the entire student body. Kingdom Trails offers a network of trails in the region for mountain biking in the summer and fall, and cross-country skiing and snowshoeing in the winter. Numerous field trips throughout Vermont, New England, and Canada are offered throughout the year.

DAILY LIFE

Classes begin each day at 7:55 a.m. and end at 2:45 p.m. There are eight class periods of 47 minutes each. Faculty members remain in their classrooms until 3 p.m. to assist students. Activities are scheduled at 3 p.m. or later to allow students additional time to meet with faculty members as needed. The library is open from 7:30 a.m. to 4:30 p.m.

WEEKEND LIFE

Weekends in the Northeast Kingdom are always an adventure. Many interscholastic events take place on Saturday. Trips are scheduled to nearby ski areas and to the urban centers of Burlington; Hanover, New Hampshire; and Montreal. Catamount Film and Arts Center in St. Johnsbury frequently hosts special events or series in the area, some of which are scheduled at LI and Lyndon State College. Students in good standing and with advance permission have the option to spend the weekend with a host family in the area or to travel home.

SUMMER PROGRAMS

Lyndon Institute sponsors day camps for football, basketball, and soccer in late July and August, and it sponsors camps for dance and theater in July.

COSTS AND FINANCIAL AID

Tuition for boarding students for 2012–13 is $42,570. A deposit of $2000 is due by May 31 to reserve a place. The Institute works with parents to arrange alternative payment schedules when needed.

Financial aid is based on need as determined by the School's Financial Aid Committee.

ADMISSIONS INFORMATION

Acceptance to Lyndon Institute is based on academic performance and potential, school citizenship, and motivation. The SSAT is required for domestic students. The TOEFL or SLEP is required for international students whose native language is not English. A minimum score of 50 on the SLEP is necessary for acceptance.

Lyndon Institute admits students of any race, color, or national or ethnic origin to all the rights, privileges, programs, and activities generally accorded or made available to students at the school. LI does not discriminate on the basis of race, color, or national or ethnic origin in the administration of its educational policies, admission policies, scholarships, and loan programs or athletics and other school-administered programs.

APPLICATION TIMETABLE

Inquiries are welcome at any time. An interview is strongly suggested. Interviews and tours are scheduled between 10 a.m. and 2 p.m., Monday through Friday. Weekend appointments are available by special arrangement. Admissions decisions are made on a rolling basis. Since the boarding program is limited in enrollment, early application (by March 31) is recommended.

ADMISSIONS CORRESPONDENCE

Mary B. Thomas, Assistant Head for Admissions
Donald F. Steen, Assistant Director of Admissions
Lyndon Institute
P.O. Box 127
Lyndon Center, Vermont 05850-0127
Phone: 802-626-5232
Fax: 802-626-6138
E-mail: admissions@lyndon.institute.org
Web site: http://www.lyndoninstitute.org

MAINE CENTRAL INSTITUTE

Pittsfield, Maine

Type: Coeducational traditional boarding and day college-preparatory and comprehensive curriculum
Grades: 9–12, postgraduate year
Enrollment: 460
Head of School: Christopher Hopkins

THE SCHOOL

Founded in 1866 by Free Will Baptists, Maine Central Institute (MCI) retains the inventive spirit and philosophy of its founders but no longer has a formal affiliation with the church. During the school's pioneer years, MCI served as a feeder school to Bates College in nearby Lewiston, Maine. Although adhering to upstanding and traditional educational values, MCI is progressive and broadminded, pledging to provide a comprehensive college-preparatory education to a multicultural student body diverse in talents, abilities, and interests.

MCI regards each student as an individual with individual needs and aspirations. In keeping with its belief in individuality, MCI strives to foster an overall environment of mutual respect, cooperation, and tolerance among all of its members and with the surrounding community. In a safe and caring atmosphere, students are encouraged to develop a moral and social consciousness, self-esteem, and social responsibility and to become globally aware, lifelong learners.

The rural town of Pittsfield (population 4,500) is nestled in between the Atlantic Ocean and the mountains of western Maine. The region of central Maine provides prime opportunities for hiking, skiing, biking, fishing, skating, and snowmobiling. The campus is within walking distance of local eateries, recreational parks, shopping, hiking trials, and a movie theater.

Maine Central Institute is accredited by the New England Association of Schools and Colleges and approved by the State of Maine Department of Education. MCI is also a member of the College Board and the National Association of Independent Schools.

ACADEMIC PROGRAMS

MCI offers a rigorous comprehensive curriculum to accommodate various learning styles and academic abilities. MCI fosters the intellectual curiosities of its student body by offering accelerated and advanced placement courses in all core subject areas.

For grades 9–12, 20 credits are required for graduation. Students must successfully complete units in English (4), mathematics (4), social studies (3, including U.S. history), science (4), physical education (1), fine arts (1), computer science (½), and health (½). Students are required to take the equivalent of at least 5 units each semester. MCI also offers a postgraduate academic year with college prep and, more specifically, SAT prep.

MCI's math and science programs exceed national standards and utilize state-of-the-art technology and academic facilities. Students in MCI's well-known humanities program understand the culture of an era through a study of its history, literature, and art. The Institute has an award-winning music program.

The foreign language program includes four levels of French and Spanish. In 2009, MCI added a Chinese Mandarin program to the foreign languages, which is taught by an exchange teacher from China. In addition to the traditional offerings, students may take courses in psychology, music composition, the Internet, sociology, child development, computer-assisted drawing, personal finance, vocational subjects, and philosophy.

MCI offers a structured ESL program for the international student who is planning for a university education. Students receive individual testing before placement at one of three levels of ESL. The extensive ESL program includes American history for international students and carefully structured math classes that focus on the development of math language skills. MCI also offers a four-week summer program for ESL.

FACULTY AND ADVISERS

The 2011–12 faculty consists of 42 full-time members. More than a quarter of the faculty and staff members reside on campus, while the rest live in nearby towns such as Newport, Waterville, and Bangor.

Faculty members are selected on the basis of three main criteria. They must possess a strong subject-matter background, the ability to relate to students, and an educational philosophy consistent with that of the institution and its mission. Faculty members are also expected to become actively involved in coaching, supervising dormitories, advising, counseling, and student affairs.

COLLEGE ADMISSION COUNSELING

A guidance team of 4 professionals is available for students. Counselors are responsible primarily for helping students with postsecondary placement and academic program planning. Approximately 75 college admissions representatives visit MCI's campus annually. Career counseling is also an integral part of the guidance department. Financial aid workshops for seniors, postgraduates, and their parents are offered. Preparation for the SAT and ACT is offered within the math and English curricula.

MCI has a strong history of placing students in postsecondary school. Schools attended by recent graduates include Bates, Boston University, Colby, Cornell, Emerson, Emory, George Mason, Gettysburg, Hofstra, Husson, Maine Maritime Academy, Michigan State, Muhlenberg, Northeastern, Syracuse, Tufts, Worcester Polytechnic, and the Universities of Connecticut, Maine, New England, New Hampshire, and Rhode Island.

STUDENT BODY AND CONDUCT

The 2011–12 enrollment of 460 includes day and boarding students. Students come to MCI from eleven states and seventeen countries.

Students at MCI are expected to be good citizens and are held responsible for their behavior. The rules that provide the structure for the school community are written in the student handbook. Disciplinary issues are the responsibility of the administration, the faculty, and the residence hall staff.

ACADEMIC FACILITIES

There are seventeen buildings housed on the 23-acre campus. Visitors are greeted upon entrance with the stoic simplicity of the campus with its brick-front buildings and the historic bell tower of Founder's Hall.

The Math and Science Center is a 23,000-square-foot recent addition to MCI, including fourteen instructional spaces, two computer classrooms, and a botany area. More than 210 computers are available for student use campuswide, many of which have Internet and e-mail access. The 12,000-volume Powell Memorial Library has a computerized card catalogue as well as Internet access. The Pittsfield Public Library is also available for school use.

BOARDING AND GENERAL FACILITIES

Boarding students reside in single-sex residence halls on campus, supervised by resident faculty and staff members. Each residence hall has its own recreation room and laundry facilities. MCI celebrated the opening in fall 2007 of an Honors Dormitory, converted from a home owned by the school to reward the highest-achieving residential students. Construction of the Donna Leavitt Furman Student Center was a second notable addition to the MCI campus in 2007. It is home to the dining hall, student lounge, and garden sitting area, including a performance stage, food court, garden benches, and game room.

Weymouth Hall houses the Student Services Center, consisting of the student union, snack machines, the Wellness Center, and the school bookstore.

MCI offers a unique Host Family Program. Participating students are paired with a family from the community that makes the student a part of its family for the school year. Students may spend time with their host family on weekends, after school, and during vacations, if so desired.

ATHLETICS

MCI believes that athletics not only provide a wholesome outlet for youthful energies but also help students apply and further develop their skills in various sports. The school strives to furnish opportunities for participation by students of all abilities by offering JV, varsity, and club-level sports. MCI also provides an opportunity for postgraduate basketball, and many alumni have gone on to play in the NCAA Division 1 and 9 and also in the NBA.

There are seventeen sports teams for boys and girls, including baseball, basketball, cheering, field hockey, football, golf, rifle, skiing, soccer, softball, tennis, track, and wrestling.

Wright Gymnasium and Parks Gymnasium are multiple-use athletic facilities, and each contains a weight room and locker facilities. Located on the main campus are a football field, a practice field, a ¼-mile track, two tennis courts, and a rifle range. Manson Park has fields for soccer, field hockey, baseball, and softball as well as three tennis courts. The school has the use of a local golf course and ski areas for competitive teams and recreation.

EXTRACURRICULAR OPPORTUNITIES

MCI students may choose from among more than thirty campus organizations, which represent some of the following interests: drama production; foreign languages and travel to places such as Spain, England, and Russia; chess; hiking; weight lifting; Future Problem Solvers; Key Club, which is the school's community service organization; computer science; and public speaking. Students may participate in Student Council; MCI's strong, award-winning music program includes concert band, concert choir, chamber choir, vocal jazz ensemble, instrumental jazz ensemble, jazz combo, percussion ensemble, and pep band; and the Math Team and the Science Olympiad, which compete locally and statewide.

Bossov Ballet Theatre offers MCI students a unique opportunity to study classical ballet as part of the academic curriculum. Ballet classes are taught by Andrei Bossov, a world-renowned teacher who previously taught at the Vaganova Academy in Saint Petersburg, Russia. The program consists of a preprofessional-level syllabus that prepares students for a professional ballet career.

DAILY LIFE

The school day begins at 7:40 a.m. and ends at 2:36 p.m., with a 42-minute lunch break beginning at 11:30. Classes run from Monday through Friday, with dinner served from 5 to 6:30 p.m.

Sunday through Thursday, there is a mandatory supervised study hall from 7 to 8:30 p.m. for all boarding students.

WEEKEND LIFE

Supervised weekend activities include trips to Canada, Boston, the nearby capital of Augusta, the city of Portland, historic ports, lighthouses and coastal towns along the Atlantic shoreline, and cultural and athletic events both on and off campus. Activities such as whale watching, white-water rafting, and skiing at Sugarloaf Resort are also offered. With parental permission, students are allowed to go home on weekends or visit the home of their host family.

COSTS AND FINANCIAL AID

The 2011–12 tuition, room, and board are $39,900 for boarding students, and tuition is $10,000 for private day students. The cost for ESL support is $2500 for the first class and $1500 for each additional class. The nonrefundable deposit of $3000 is due within two weeks of an offer of admission. A variety of payment plans are available.

Financial aid is awarded on a need basis, determined by information shown on the Parents' Confidential Statement and any additional financial information that is requested.

ADMISSIONS INFORMATION

MCI's Admissions Committee screens all applicants to determine their compatibility with MCI's philosophy that students should assume a mature responsibility for their own education. No entrance tests are required, but an on-campus interview with each student and his or her parents is strongly recommended. School transcripts and results of standardized tests are used to determine academic ability and appropriate academic placement in classes in accordance with the student's individual needs, abilities, and interests.

Maine Central Institute does not discriminate on the basis of race, sex, age, sexual preference, disability, religion, or national or ethnic origin in the administration of its educational and admission policies, financial aid programs, and athletic or other school-administered programs and activities.

APPLICATION TIMETABLE

Inquiries and applications are welcome at any time; however, applying by June 1 is recommended. Visits may be scheduled at any time during the year but are most effective when school is in session. Tours and interviews can be arranged by calling the Admissions Office, which is open Monday through Friday from 8 to 4:30. A nonrefundable application fee of $50 is required.

ADMISSIONS CORRESPONDENCE

Clint M. Williams, Director of Admission
Maine Central Institute
295 Main Street
Pittsfield, Maine 04967
Phone: 207-487-2282
Fax: 207-487-3512
E-mail: cwilliams@mci-school.org
Web site: http://www.mci-school.org

MARYMOUNT SCHOOL OF NEW YORK

New York, New York

Type: Girls' independent college-preparatory Catholic day school
Grades: N–12: Lower School, Nursery–3; Middle School, 4–7; Upper School, 8–12
Enrollment: School total: 643; Upper School: 248
Head of School: Concepcion R. Alvar

THE SCHOOL

Marymount School of New York is an independent Catholic day school that educates girls in a tradition of academic excellence and moral values. The School promotes in each student a respect for her own unique abilities and provides a foundation for exploring and acting on questions of integrity and ethical decision-making. Founded by Mother Joseph Butler in 1926 as part of a worldwide network of schools directed by the Religious of the Sacred Heart of Mary, Marymount remains faithful to its mission "to educate young women who question, risk, and grow; young women who care, serve, and lead; young women prepared to challenge, shape, and change the world." Committed to its Catholic heritage, the School welcomes and values the religious diversity of its student body and seeks to give all students a deeper understanding of the role of the spiritual in life. The School also has an active social service program and integrates social justice and human rights into the curriculum.

Marymount occupies three adjoining landmark Beaux Arts mansions, located on Fifth Avenue's historic Museum Mile, and a fourth mansion on East 82nd Street. The School has recently expanded to include an additional facility with 42,000-square-feet of space on East 97th Street. The Metropolitan Museum of Art and Central Park, both located directly across the street from the School, provide resources that are integral to the School's academic and extracurricular programs. Middle School art classes meet once a week in studios at the Museum. As part of the Class IX humanities curriculum, and in AP Art History, Upper School students visit the Museum as often as twice a week. Central Park is used for science and physical education classes as well as extracurricular activities. Other city sites, such as the United Nations, the Tenement Museum, Ellis Island, the New York Zoological Society, the American Museum of Natural History, the Rose Planetarium, the Frick and Guggenheim Museums, and El Museo Del Barrio are also frequent extensions of the classroom for Marymount students.

Since 1969, the School has been independently incorporated under the direction of a 30-member Board of Trustees made up of parents, alumnae, educators, and members of the founding order. The School benefits from a strong Parents' Association; an active Alumnae Association; the involvement of parents, alumnae, and student volunteers; and a successful Annual Giving Program.

Marymount is accredited by the New York State Association of Independent Schools (NYSAIS). The School holds membership in the National Association of Independent Schools (NAIS), NYSAIS, the Independent Schools Admissions Association of Greater New York, the National Catholic Education Association, the National Coalition of Girls' Schools (NCGS), and the Educational Records Bureau.

ACADEMIC PROGRAMS

Emphasizing classic disciplines and scientific inquiry, the challenging college-preparatory curriculum provides students with the skills necessary to succeed in competitive colleges and in life beyond the classroom. Through its rigorous academic program and its focus on the education of young women, Marymount seeks to instill in its students self-confidence, leadership ability, a risk-taking spirit, and a love of learning.

A commitment to the study of science, technology, engineering, and mathematics (STEM) is reflected in Marymount's curriculum, which fully integrates information and communication technologies into all subject areas. Students have access to desktop and laptop computers, iPads, and other mobile computing devices throughout the School. Students in Classes VI through XII and staff members have individual e-mail accounts and use digital media to carry out research, create presentations, publish work, communicate, and demonstrate ideas and concepts. Students learn a wide variety of authoring tools as well as programming languages to create and publish digital media. Using an array of interactive media, students extend discussions and collaborations beyond the classroom. Using Web-based tools and video-conferencing, students collaborate on projects with other Marymount Schools and with students and researchers around the globe.

Marymount's position at the forefront of educational technology relies on more than the investment in laptops, iPads, SmartBoards, software, and networks. To maintain its cutting-edge program, recognized for excellence by NAIS and NCGS, the School offers technology seminars every summer and workshops during the school year for the faculty and other NAIS-school faculty members.

High school graduation requirements include satisfactory completion of 4 years of English, 3 years of history, 3 years of math, 3 years of laboratory science, 3 years of a world language, 4 years of religious studies, 4 years of physical education, 1 year of studio art, 1 year of computer science, 6 semesters of health/guidance, and 1 semester of speech. These requirements provide a broad, solid base of knowledge while sharpening problem-solving and research skills and promoting critical and creative thinking.

The School offers honors and Advanced Placement courses as well as electives such as AP art history, economics, classical Greek, music history, history of theater, two AP studio art courses, African studies, Latin American studies, Middle Eastern studies, history of modern China, and programming languages. In senior English, students choose from seminars that cover topics from Shakespeare's history plays to contemporary American drama to the literature of African-American and Asian-American women writers. Most students elect to take a fourth year of math; advanced offerings include AP calculus AB, AP calculus BC, AP statistics, and calculus. Fourth-year science courses include AP biology, AP chemistry, AP physics C, advanced physics, and atmospheric science. Class XII students may elect to take AP psychology or other advanced courses through Marymount's affiliate membership in Online School for Girls. The science program connects with and utilizes the research of numerous institutions, including the New York Academy of Sciences and Princeton University, as well as participating in the STEM Internship Program and the STEM Research Program.

While a leader in science and technological education, Marymount is also committed to the study of humanities. All Class IX students take part in the Integrated Humanities Program, an interdisciplinary curriculum that focuses on history, literature, art history, and world religions in the study of ancient civilizations. Classes are held at the Metropolitan Museum of Art at least once a week. The program includes a World Civilizations Festival and collaborative research projects in history and art history. Seniors must submit a writing portfolio of selected work from their last three years of high school.

The visual arts department offers studio art, AP 2-D design, and AP drawing. The performing arts program includes a school chorus, a chamber choir, courses in music history and the history of theater, speech classes, and a rich extracurricular program in forensics and dramatic arts.

The religious studies program includes comparative religions, Hebrew scriptures, the New Testament, social justice, and ethics. With a focus on moral and ethical decision making, students analyze systemic social issues and immerse themselves in the community through numerous service projects, as well as the Youth and Philanthropy Initiative. The Catholic-Jewish Initiative provides students with a deeper understanding of the Judeo-Christian tradition and includes Holocaust studies and a trip to the National Holocaust Museum in Washington, D.C.

During the last four weeks of the academic year, seniors participate in an off-campus internship to gain exposure to a career of interest. Students have interned at hospitals, research laboratories, law firms, financial organizations, theaters, schools, nonprofit organizations, and corporations. They also attend a career day, with visiting alumnae as guest speakers. A financial literacy program prepares graduates for the financial challenges of college and life.

As members of a worldwide network of schools, students may opt to spend the second semester of their sophomore year at a Marymount International School in London or Rome. Annual concert and study tours and service trips extend the curriculum. Recent study tours have included the scientists and poets in England and Scotland, mathematics and culture of ancient Greece, the ecology of the Galapagos Islands, the theater and literature of Shakespeare's London and Stratford-upon-Avon, and the music, language, and culture of Italy, France, and Spain. Recent service trips have brought students to work with disabled orphans in Jamaica, rebuild homes in New Orleans, and promote justice for trafficked women in New York City. The Marymount Singers enjoys an annual concert tour every spring and have performed in Italy, France, Austria, the Czech Republic, Ireland, Portugal, and Spain.

Upper School students are formally evaluated four times a year, using an A–F grading system. The evaluation process includes written reports and biannual parent/student/teacher conferences.

The Middle School curriculum welcomes the diverse interests of young adolescents and is structured to channel their energy and natural love of learning. The integrated core curriculum gradually increases in the degree of departmentalization at each grade level, and challenging learning activities and flexible groupings in main subject areas ensure that the students achieve their full potential. In Class IV, students study a trimester of French, Latin, and Spanish; in Class V, students choose to pursue a three-year sequence in one of these languages. The Middle School years culminate in a study tour to France and Spain; the integration of language, mathematics, social studies, science, architecture, religious studies, and art makes the study tour a rich intellectual experience as well as accentuating the relevance of the students' classroom study to the world at large. All students enjoy regular visits to the Metropolitan Museum of Art, including weekly studio art classes. Technology enhances all aspects of the curriculum; students at East 82nd Street have a one-to-one laptop program.

Twice-weekly speech classes prepare the girls for dramatic presentations reflective of their social studies and literature curriculum: *Revolutionary Voices, Greek Mythology,* and scenes from *The Canterbury Tales* and *A Midsummer Night's Dream*. Uptown Broadway, an extracurricular option offered each semester, allows the students to participate in a full-scale musical production. The Middle School celebrates music and voice at its annual spring concert.

The Lower School provides child-centered, creative learning within a challenging, structured environment. The curriculum focuses on the acquisition of foundational skills, often through an interdisciplinary approach. Programs engage students in the exciting process of learning about themselves, their surroundings, and the larger world. Introductory lessons in Spanish complement the social studies curriculum. A hands-on science program, an emphasis on technology integration, a study of robotics, a popular School chorus, and an extensive after-school program are some highlights of the Lower School.

FACULTY AND ADVISERS

There are 103 full-time and 6 part-time faculty members, allowing for a 6:1 student-teacher ratio. Eighty-three percent of the faculty members hold master's degrees, and 11 percent hold doctoral degrees. In Nursery through Class I, each class has a head teacher and at least one assistant teacher. Classes II and III have two co-head teachers in each classroom. In the Middle School, students make the transition from having homeroom teachers to having advisers. In Classes IV and V, each class has two homeroom teachers. In Classes V–XII, each student has a homeroom teacher and an adviser, usually one of her teachers, who follows her academic progress and provides guidance and support. Technologists, learning resource specialists, school nurses, an athletic trainer, artists-in-residence, a school counselor, and school psychologists work with students throughout the School.

Concepcion R. Alvar was appointed Headmistress in 2004 after serving thirteen years as the Director of Admissions and three years as a head teacher. She also served as the Director and Supervisor of Marymount Summer for sixteen years. Mrs. Alvar holds a B.S. from Maryknoll College (Philippines) and an M.A. from Columbia University, Teachers College.

COLLEGE ADMISSION COUNSELING

Under the guidance of the Director of College Counseling, Marymount's formal college counseling program begins during the junior year. In the second semester, two College Nights are held for students and parents. Individual counseling throughout the semester directs each student to those colleges that best match her achievements and interests. Students participate in weekly guidance classes to learn about general requirements for college admission, the application process, and standardized tests. During the fall of their senior year, students continue the weekly sessions, focusing on essay writing, admissions interviews, and financial aid applications.

Graduates from recent classes are attending the following colleges and universities: Amherst, Barnard, Boston College, Boston University, Bowdoin, Brown, Columbia, Cooper Union, Connecticut, Cornell, Dartmouth, Davidson, Duke, Fairfield, Fordham, George Washington, Georgetown, Harvard, Holy Cross, Kenyon, Middlebury, NYU, Oberlin, Princeton, Skidmore, Smith, Stanford, Trinity, Tufts, Vanderbilt, Villanova, Wake Forest, Wellesley, Wesleyan, Wheaton, Williams, Yale, and the Universities of Notre Dame, Pennsylvania, St. Andrew's (Scotland), and Virginia.

STUDENT BODY AND CONDUCT

Marymount's enrollment is 643 students in Nursery through Class XII, with 248 girls in the Upper School. Most students reside in the five boroughs of New York City; however, Upper School students also commute from Long Island, New Jersey, and Westchester County. Students wear uniforms, except on special days; participate in athletic and extracurricular activities; and attend weekly chapel services, all-school masses, and annual class retreats.

Marymount encourages students to be active participants in their education and in the life of the School community. Students seek out leadership and volunteer opportunities, serving as advocates for one another through peer mentoring, retreat teams, and the Big Sister/Little Sister program. Student government and campus ministry provide social and service opportunities that enable students to broaden their perspectives, develop as leaders, sharpen public-speaking skills, and form lasting friendships.

Teachers and administrators encourage each student to respect herself and others and to be responsible members of the community. While there are relatively few rules, those that exist are consistently enforced to promote freedom and growth for the individual and the entire School community.

ACADEMIC FACILITIES

The Beaux Arts mansions provide rooms for the Nursery–Class XII educational program. Facilities include wired and wireless classrooms with SmartBoards, a networked library complex, five science laboratories, two computer centers, a math laboratory, an art suite, a chapel, a language lab, an auditorium, a courtyard playground, two gymnasiums, and the Middle School multipurpose Commons.

ATHLETICS

The athletic program promotes good health, physical fitness, coordination, skill development, confidence, and a spirit of competition and collaboration through its physical education classes, the electives program for Classes X–XII, and individual and team sports.

Marymount provides a full schedule for varsity and junior varsity sports, as well as Middle School teams at the V/VI and VII/VIII class levels. Participants in Classes V/VI stay two days per week for an after-school sports program; students in Classes VII/VIII commit to three afternoons per week. The junior varsity and varsity teams compete within the Athletic Association of Independent Schools League (AAIS) in badminton, basketball, cross-country, fencing, field hockey, lacrosse, soccer, softball, swimming, tennis, track and field, and volleyball.

In addition to its gymnasiums, Marymount uses the facilities of nearby Catholic schools, the Harlem Armory, Riverbank State Park, and Roberto Clemente State Park. Central Park, Randall's Island, and Van Cortland Park are sites for field sports. Tennisport, Riverbank State Park, and Flushing Meadows are competitive sites for the tennis and swim teams. Additional facilities are used throughout New York City.

EXTRACURRICULAR OPPORTUNITIES

A wide range of clubs and activities complement the academic program and provide students with the opportunity to contribute to the School community, pursue their individual interests, and develop communication, cooperation, and leadership skills. Upper School activities and clubs offered include Amnesty International, art club, book club, campus ministry, chamber choir, cultural awareness, digital photography, science and the environment club, film club, finance club, forensics team, Mathletes, Marymount Singers, Marymount Players, Mock Trial (2006 state champions, 2009 NYC finalists), Model United Nations, National Honor Society, philosophy club, set design/tech crew, student government, and women in action. Student publications include a yearbook (*Marifia*), a newspaper (*Joritan*), and an award-winning literary/arts journal (*Muse*). A wide range of Friday noontime clubs in the Middle School includes Student Council; Italian, Latin, and French clubs; altar servers; handbells; environmental science; art; drama; handwork; and the literary magazine, *Chez Nous*.

Each year, the Upper School presents two dramatic productions, including a musical; organizes either a Bias Awareness Day or Harambee Celebration during Black History Month; sponsors an Art Festival Week; and participates in numerous community service projects, local and national competitions, and conferences with other schools.

The School brings people of stature and high achievement to address students, including Nobel Peace Prize winner Leymah Gbowee, former poet laureate Billy Collins, athlete Tegla Laroupe, author Jhumpa Lahiri, bioethicist Ronald Green, nanotechnologist Dr. Susan Arney, African American painter Philomena Williamson, feminist Gloria Steinem, Sr. Helen Prejean, author of *Dead Man Walking*, and Sheryl WuDunn, coauthor of *Half the Sky*. The Maggie Murray Fund supports a series of writing-related events to enrich the students' literary experiences and has given students the opportunity to attend conversations with such celebrated writers as Toni Morrison and Chinua Achebe.

Students have the opportunity to interact with boys from neighboring schools through exchange days, dramatic productions, community service projects, walkathons, dances, and other student-run social activities.

DAILY LIFE

Upper School classes are held from 8:20 a.m. to 3:30 p.m. on Monday, Tuesday, and Thursday. To accommodate electives, extracurricular activities, and team sports, classes end at 2:45 p.m. on Wednesdays and Fridays. Class periods are each 45 minutes in length and typically meet nine out of ten days in a two-week cycle, with a double period each week in each course. Students meet daily with their advisory group, gather with the entire Upper School every Friday for assembly, and frequently meet individually with their classroom teachers. After classes have ended, most students remain for sports, extracurricular activities, and/or independent study.

COSTS AND FINANCIAL AID

The tuition for the 2011–12 academic year ranged from $21,835 for Nursery to $37,975 for Class XII. In February, parents are required to make a deposit of $5000, which is credited toward the November tuition. The Key Education Resources Payment Plan is available.

Nearly $3 million in financial aid was awarded in 2010–11 to students after establishing need through School and Student Services. Over 21 percent of Marymount students receive financial aid.

ADMISSIONS INFORMATION

As a college-preparatory school, Marymount aims to enroll young women of academic promise and sound character who seek a challenging educational environment and opportunities for learning outside the classroom. Educational Records Bureau tests, school records, and interviews are used in selecting students.

The School admits students of any race, color, and national or ethnic origin to all the rights, privileges, programs, and activities generally accorded or made available to students at the School and does not discriminate on these bases in the administration of its educational policies, admissions policies, scholarship or loan programs, athletic programs, or other School programs.

APPLICATION TIMETABLE

Interested students are encouraged to contact the Admissions Office as early as possible in the fall for admission the following year. The application deadline is November 30, but may be changed at the discretion of the Director of Admissions. Notification of admissions decisions is sent during February and March, according to the dates established by the Independent School Admissions Association of Greater New York.

ADMISSIONS CORRESPONDENCE

Lillian Issa
Deputy Head/Director of Admissions
Marymount School of New York
1026 Fifth Avenue
New York, New York 10028

Phone: 212-744-4486
Fax: 212-744-0163 (general)
212-744-0716 (admissions)
E-mail: admissions@marymountnyc.org
Web site: http://marymountnyc.org

MILTON ACADEMY

Milton, Massachusetts

Type: Coeducational boarding and day college-preparatory school
Grades: K–12: (Lower School: K–8; Upper School: 9–12)
Enrollment: School total: 980; Upper School: 675
Head of School: Todd Bland

THE SCHOOL

The Academy received its charter in 1798 under the Massachusetts land-grant policy. It bequeathed to the school a responsibility to "open the way for all the people to a higher order of education than the common schools can supply." Milton's motto, "Dare to be true," not only states a core value, it describes Milton's culture. Milton fosters intellectual inquiry and encourages initiative and the open exchange of ideas. Teaching and learning at Milton are active processes that recognize the intelligence, talents, and potential of each member of the Academy.

For more than 200 years, Milton has developed confident, independent thinkers in an intimate, friendly setting where students and faculty members understand that the life of the mind is the pulse of the school. A gifted and dedicated faculty motivates a diverse student body, providing students with the structure to learn and the support to take risks. The faculty's teaching expertise and passion for scholarship generates extraordinary growth in students who learn to expect the most of themselves. The Milton community connects purposefully with world issues. Students graduate with a clear sense of themselves, their world, and how to contribute.

From Milton Academy's suburban 125-acre campus, 8 miles south of Boston in the town of Milton (population 26,000), students and faculty members access the vast cultural resources of Boston and Cambridge. Minutes from campus is the Blue Hills Reservation, 6,000 wooded acres of hiking trails and ski slopes.

Milton Academy is a nonprofit organization with a self-perpetuating Board of Trustees. Its endowment is $167 million (as of June 1, 2011).

Milton Academy is accredited by the New England Association of Schools and Colleges and holds memberships in the National Association of Independent Schools, the Cum Laude Society, and the Association of Independent Schools in New England.

ACADEMIC PROGRAMS

Milton students and faculty members are motivated participants in the world of ideas, concepts, and values. Milton's curriculum provides rigorous preparation for college and includes more than 182 courses in nine academic departments. For students entering Milton in the ninth grade, a minimum of 18 credits are required for graduation. This includes 4 years of English, 2 years of history (including U.S. and modern world history), 2 years of science, 1 year of an arts course, and successful completion of algebra II, geometry, and a level III foreign language course. Noncredit requirements include current events/public speaking, physical education, a ninth-grade arts course (music/drama/visual arts), and a four-year affective education curriculum that includes health, values, social awareness, and senior transitions.

Electives are offered in all academic areas. Examples of electives include computer programming, comparative government, performing literature, Spanish film and social change, advanced architecture, philosophy and literature, choreography, film and video production, psychology, engineering, nuclear physics, issues in environmental science, creative writing, music theory, observational astronomy, and marine biology. Students may petition to take independent study courses, and Advanced Placement courses leading to college credit are offered in most subject areas.

In January, seniors submit a proposal for a five-week spring independent project, on or off campus. Senior projects give students the opportunity to pursue in-depth interests stemming from their work at Milton.

The typical class size is 14 students, and the overall student-teacher ratio is 5:1. Nightly 2-hour study periods in the houses are supervised for boarding students.

Faculty members are available for individual help throughout the day and in the houses at night. Students seeking assistance with assignments or help with specific skills, organization, and/or time management visit the Academic Skills Center, which is staffed throughout the day.

The school year, which is divided into two semesters, runs from early September to early June with an examination period at the end of January. Students typically take five courses per semester. Students earn letter grades from E (failure) through A+, and comments prepared by each student's teachers and adviser are sent to parents three times a year in November, February, and June.

All academic buildings and residential houses are part of a campuswide computer network. MiltONline, the Academy's e-mail and conferencing system, allows students to join conference discussions for many classes and extracurricular activities, communicate with faculty members and friends, and submit assignments. Students have access to the Milton Intranet as well as the Internet.

Class II students (eleventh graders) may apply to spend either the fall or spring semester at the Mountain School Program of Milton Academy (an interdisciplinary academic program set on a working 300-acre farm in Vermont); at CITYterm at the Master's School in Dobbs Ferry, New York; or at the Maine Coast Semester at Chewonki. Through School Year Abroad, Milton provides opportunities in Spain, France, Italy, and China. Milton also offers six- to eight-week exchange programs with schools in Spain, France, and China.

FACULTY AND ADVISERS

The deep commitment of a learned and experienced group of teachers is Milton's greatest treasure. Teaching in Classes IV-I (grades 9–12) are 127 full-time faculty members, 78 percent of whom hold advanced degrees (Ph.D. and master's degrees). Eighty-five percent of faculty members live on campus.

In addition to teaching, faculty members also serve as house parents and coaches, as well as advisers to student clubs, organizations, publications, and activities. Each faculty member is an adviser to a group of 6 to 8 students and supports the students' emotional, social, and academic well-being at Milton.

COLLEGE ADMISSION COUNSELING

Four college counselors work one-on-one with students, beginning in their Class II (eleventh grade) year, in a highly personal and effective approach toward the college admissions process.

For the graduating classes of 2009, 2010, and 2011, the top college enrollments were Harvard (26), Tufts (20), Brown (19), Columbia (18), Boston College (17), Georgetown (15), and Cornell (15).

STUDENT BODY AND CONDUCT

Of the 675 students in the Upper School, 50 percent are boys and 50 percent are girls; 50 percent are boarding students and 50 percent are day students. Forty-five percent of Milton's enrolled students are students of color. Ten percent of the Upper School students are international, coming from twenty-one countries across the globe. Thirty-two percent of Milton students receive financial aid, and the average grants account for 75 percent of tuition.

All Upper School students from Classes IV-I (grades 9–12) participate in the Self-Governing Association, led by 2 elected student representatives, 1 senior girl and 1 senior boy. Elected class representatives serve with faculty members on the Discipline Committee, which recommends to the Head of School appropriate responses when infractions of major school rules occur. Rules at Milton Academy foster the cohesion and morale of the community and enhance education by upholding standards of conduct developed by generations of students and faculty members.

ACADEMIC FACILITIES

Among the prominent buildings on the Milton campus are three primarily academic buildings: Warren Hall (English), Wigglesworth Hall (history), and Ware Hall (math and foreign languages); the Kellner Performing Arts Center, with a 350-seat teaching theater, a studio theater, dressing rooms, scene shop, practice rooms, orchestral rehearsal room, dance studio, and speech/debate room; the Athletic and Convocation Center, with a hockey rink, a fitness center, three basketball courts, and an indoor track; the Williams Squash Courts; the Ayer Observatory; and Apthorp Chapel. The new Pritzker Science Center, which opened in 2010, integrates classroom areas with laboratory tables and equipment to create an environment that allows students to work collaboratively and move seamlessly between discussion and hands-on lab work. The Art and Media Center is home to numerous visual art studios and public display spaces, including the Nesto Gallery and the Greely auditorium.

Cox Library contains more than 46,000 volumes, more than 150 periodicals with back issues on microfilm, and a newspaper collection dating back to 1704. It also provides CD-ROM sources, Internet access and online search capabilities. Within Cox Library is one of several computer laboratories.

BOARDING AND GENERAL FACILITIES

Milton Academy students live in one of eight single-sex houses ranging in size from 31 to 48 students; four for boys and four for girls. Single rooms house one third of the students, while the other two thirds of the students reside in double rooms. Milton houses include all four classes as well as faculty members' families. Students spend all their Milton years in one house, experiencing a family-at-school context for developing close relationships with valued adults, learning about responsibility to the community, taking leadership roles with peers, and sharing social and cultural traditions. All rooms are networked, and school computers are available for student use in the house common rooms.

The Health and Counseling Center and the Academic Skills Center, as well as house parents in each residential house, class deans, and the office of the school chaplain, are available to meet students' needs.

ATHLETICS

Milton believes that teamwork, sportsmanship, and the pursuit of excellence are important values and that regular vigorous exercise is a foundation of good health. Milton offers a comprehensive athletic program that includes physical education classes and a range of intramural and interscholastic sports geared to the needs and interests of every student.

The school's offerings in interscholastic sports are Alpine skiing, baseball, basketball, cross-country, field hockey, football, golf, ice hockey, lacrosse, sailing, soccer, softball, squash, swimming and diving, tennis, track, volleyball, and wrestling.

Intramural offerings include the outdoor program, pilates, soccer, squash, strength and conditioning, tennis, Ultimate (Frisbee), and yoga.

Sports facilities include four athletic buildings, an ice hockey rink and fitness center, two indoor climbing walls, twelve playing fields, seventeen tennis courts, seven international squash courts, an all-weather track, a cross-country course, and a ropes course.

EXTRACURRICULAR OPPORTUNITIES

The breadth of extracurricular opportunities means that every student finds a niche—a comfortable place to develop new skills, take on leadership, show commitment, make friends, and have fun. Clubs and organizations include cultural groups such as the Asian Society, Latino Association, Onyx, and Common Ground (an umbrella organization for the various groups); the Arts Board; Dance Workshop; the Outdoor Club; the Chinese, French, and Spanish clubs; the debate, math, and speech teams; and Students for Gender Equality. There are eleven student publications, among them *The Asian, La Voz, MAGUS/MABUS, Mille Tonnes, Milton Measure, Milton Paper,* and the yearbook. Music programs include the chamber singers, the gospel choir, the glee club, the orchestra, improvisational jazz combos, and five a cappella groups. The performing arts are an important part of the extracurricular offerings at Milton. Main stage theater productions, studio theater productions, play readings, and speech and debate team are a few of the available opportunities. Milton stages twelve major theater productions each year, including a Class IV (ninth grade) play, student directed one-act plays, a dance concert, and a biennial musical. Service opportunities include the audio-visual crew, community service, Lorax (environmental group), Orange and Blue Key (admission tour guides and leaders), and the Public Issues Board.

DAILY LIFE

The academic day runs from 8 a.m. to 2:55 p.m., except on Wednesday, when classes end at 1:15 p.m. There are no classes on Saturday or Sunday. Cafeteria-style lunch is served from 11 a.m. to 1:30 p.m., and students eat during a free period within that time. The students' activities period is from 3 to 3:30 p.m. Athletics and extracurricular activities take place from 3:30 to 5:30 p.m. Family-style dinner is at 6 p.m., and the evening study period runs from 7:30 to 9:30 p.m. Lights-out time depends on the grade level of each student.

WEEKEND LIFE

Interscholastic games are held on Wednesday, Friday, and Saturday afternoons. Social activities on Friday and Saturday evenings are planned by the Student Activities Association. Day students join boarders every weekend for events such as dances with live or recorded music, classic and new films, concerts, plays, drama readings, dormitory open houses, and trips to professional sports events, arts events, or local museums.

Prior to leaving campus, students must check their plans with house parents, who must approve their whereabouts and any overnight plans.

SUMMER PROGRAMS

Milton Academy does not run its own summer programs on campus. Professional development opportunities are made available to faculty members, including the Cultural Diversity Institute and the Boarding Staff Conference for teachers from across the country. In addition, Milton hosts many outside programs, including sports camps and academic enrichment programs.

COSTS AND FINANCIAL AID

For the 2011–12 academic year, tuition was $45,720 for boarding students and $37,530 for day students.

Milton seeks to enroll the most qualified applicants regardless of their financial circumstances. To that end, more than $8 million in financial aid will be provided to students in the 2012–13 school year. All financial aid at Milton is awarded on the basis of need. In addition to the program of direct grants, the school offers installment payment options and two low-interest loan programs.

ADMISSIONS INFORMATION

Milton Academy seeks students who are able, energetic, intellectually curious, and have strong values and a willingness to grow. Applicants must submit the Secondary School Admission Test (SSAT) scores (students applying for eleventh grade may submit PSAT or SAT scores if applicable). All applicants must also submit a school transcript, teacher recommendations, parental statement, and two essays. An interview, on or off campus, is also required.

APPLICATION TIMETABLE

The deadline for applying is January 15. Notification letters are sent out March 10; the reply date is April 10. There is a $50 application fee for U.S. applicants and a $100 fee for international applicants.

ADMISSIONS CORRESPONDENCE

Paul Rebuck, Dean of Admission
Milton Academy
170 Centre Street
Milton, Massachusetts 02186

Phone: 617-898-2227
Fax: 617-898-1701
E-mail: admissions@milton.edu
Web site: http://www.milton.edu

MORAVIAN ACADEMY

Bethlehem, Pennsylvania

Type: Day college-preparatory school
Grades: PK–12: Lower School, Prekindergarten–5; Middle School, 6–8; Upper School, 9–12
Enrollment: School total: 764; Upper School: 285
Head of School: George N. King Jr., Headmaster

THE SCHOOL

Moravian Academy (MA) traces its origin back to 1742 and the Moravians who settled Bethlehem. Guided by the wisdom of John Amos Comenius, Moravian bishop and renowned educator, the Moravian Church established schools in every community in which it settled. Moravian Academy became incorporated in 1971 when Moravian Seminary for Girls and Moravian Preparatory School were merged. The school has two campuses: the Lower–Middle School campus in the historic downtown area of Bethlehem and the Upper School campus on a 120-acre estate 6 miles to the east.

For more than 269 years, Moravian Academy has encouraged sound innovations to meet contemporary challenges while recognizing the permanence of basic human values. The school seeks to promote young people's full development in mind, body, and spirit by fostering a love for learning, respect for others, joy in participation and service, and skill in decision making. Preparation for college occurs in an atmosphere characterized by an appreciation for the individual.

Moravian Academy is governed by a Board of Trustees. Six members are representatives of the Moravian Church. The school is valued at $35.1 million, of which $15.3 million is endowment. In 2010–11, Annual Giving was $440,494, and operating expenses were $14.2 million.

Moravian Academy is accredited by the Middle States Association of Colleges and Schools and the Pennsylvania Association of Independent Schools. The school is a member of the National Association of Independent Schools, the Association of Delaware Valley Independent Schools, the College Board, the Council for Spiritual and Ethical Education, the School and Student Service for Financial Aid, and the Secondary School Admission Test Board.

Moravian Academy does not discriminate on the basis of race, nationality, sex, sexual orientation, religious affiliation, or ethnic origin in the administration of its educational and admission policies, financial aid awards, and athletic or other school-administered programs. Applicants who are disabled (or applicants' family members who are disabled) and require any type of accommodation during the application process, or at any other time, are encouraged to identify themselves and indicate what type of accommodation is needed.

ACADEMIC PROGRAMS

Students are required to carry five major courses per year. Minimum graduation requirements include English, 4 credits; mathematics, 3 credits; lab sciences, 3 credits; global language, 3 credits; social studies, 3 credits; fine arts, 2 credits; and physical education and health. All students must successfully complete a semester course in world religions or ethics. Community service is an integral part of the curriculum. Electives are offered in many areas, such as fine and performing arts, sciences, English, math, history, and global language. Moravian Academy offers Advanced Placement courses, numerous honors courses, and the opportunity to pursue an honors independent study project under the mentorship of a faculty member. The Academy also participates in a high school scholars program that enables a small number of highly qualified students to take college courses at no cost. The overall student-faculty ratio is about 9:1, with classes ranging from 10 to 18 students.

Grades in most courses are A–F; D is a passing grade. However, a C- is required to advance to the next level in math and global languages. Reports are sent to parents on a monthly basis, and parent-conference opportunities are scheduled in the fall semester. Faculty and staff members are available for additional conferences whenever necessary. Examinations are held at the end of each seventeen-week semester in all major subjects. In the senior year, final examinations are given in May to allow seniors time for a two-week Post Term Experience before graduation.

FACULTY AND ADVISERS

The Upper School has 39 full-time and 3 part-time faculty members. Ninety-two percent of the full-time Upper School faculty members have advanced degrees. Several faculty members have degrees in counseling in addition to other subjects, and the entire faculty shares in counseling through the Faculty-Student Adviser Program.

George N. King Jr. was appointed Headmaster in 2007. He previously served as the Head of the Wooster School in Danbury, Connecticut. Mr. King received his B.A. from Murray State University and his M.A. from the New England Conservatory of Music.

COLLEGE ADMISSION COUNSELING

The Director of Academic Counseling begins group work in college guidance in the tenth grade. Tenth graders take the PSAT as practice and repeat it the following year. Sophomore Seminar encourages students to familiarize themselves with the college application process; the focus is on understanding academic options and participation in school and community life. College Night is held annually for juniors and their parents. Junior Seminar meets weekly in small groups for college counseling during the second semester and includes an individual family conference in the spring. They take the PSAT, SAT, and SAT Subject Tests. Some students also elect to take the ACT in their junior or senior year. Senior Seminar meets twice weekly in small groups during the first semester for additional guidance and seniors are guided through the college application process. They take the SAT and SAT Subject Tests again, if necessary. In recent years, approximately 85 to 90 percent of the senior class takes at least one Advanced Placement course and earns a score of 3 or higher.

Average SAT scores of 2011 graduates were 656 critical reading, 658 math, and 655 writing. Graduates of 2011 are attending Boston College, Boston University, Bryn Mawr, Bucknell, Carnegie Mellon, Colgate, Cornell, Dartmouth, Emory, Georgetown, George Washington, Harvard, Lafayette, Lehigh, NYU, Penn State, Pennsylvania, Pittsburgh, Richmond, Scripps College, Vanderbilt, Villanova, Wake Forest, Washington (St. Louis), Wellesley, William and Mary, and Yale. Some students participate in travel abroad or gap year programs before attending college.

STUDENT BODY AND CONDUCT

The Upper School has 285 students. The school understands the value of diversity in the educational setting. In all divisions, students and faculty members from a variety of ethnic, cultural, religious, and socioeconomic backgrounds carry on this commitment. Through classroom activities, nondenominational chapel services discussing many faiths, and active engagement with each other, students at Moravian Academy are encouraged to appreciate one another's individuality.

Students enjoy the small classes and the opportunity for participation in sports and other activities. Students are expected to wear clothing that is neat and appropriate for school. Denim is not permitted during the school day, and a school uniform is required for members of performing groups. Students participate actively in a Student Council. Serious matters of discipline come before a faculty-student discipline committee.

ACADEMIC FACILITIES

Snyder House, Walter Hall, Couch Fine Arts Center, and the Heath Science Complex hold the classrooms, studios, and laboratories (chemistry, physics, biology, and computer). In September 2007, the Academy dedicated the new Van S. Merle-Smith Woodworking Studio. All of the library's resources are integrated with the instructional program to intensify and individualize the educational experience. Technology plays an important role in enhancing learning and students get hands-on experience with the latest equipment in classrooms and labs. There are dedicated computer labs, additional computers in the library, portable wireless labs, and a computer in every classroom. SmartBoards are used in all divisions to enhance the learning process. The Couch Fine Arts Center houses the studio arts department. A 350-seat auditorium enhances the music and theater programs. Students can also use the resources and facilities of the seven colleges and universities in the area.

ATHLETICS

A strong athletics program meets the guidelines of the school's philosophy that a person must be nurtured in body, as well as in mind and spirit, and that respect for others and participation are important goals. A large gymnasium, eight athletics fields, and six tennis courts provide the school with facilities for varsity and junior varsity teams in boys' lacrosse and baseball; girls' field hockey; boys' and girls' basketball, cross-country, soccer, swimming, and tennis; coeducational golf; and a girls' varsity softball team. Students also have the opportunity to participate in girls' volleyball, football, track, and wrestling in co-operative programs with a local school. A gymnasium that includes a weight room complements the physical education facilities in Walter Hall. An outdoor recreational pool is available for special student functions as well as the Academy's summer day camp program for younger children.

All students take part in team sports. In any given athletic season, more than one third of the Upper School student body participates in after-school athletics at the Academy.

In addition to the on-campus programs, students may take advantage of the golf courses in the Lehigh Valley, along with an indoor rock-climbing facility, a bicycle velodrome, and indoor stables. Many students belong to the Academy's ski club, which offers weekly ski excursions to local ski areas over five consecutive Fridays during the winter.

EXTRACURRICULAR OPPORTUNITIES

Moravian Academy's activity program provides opportunities for varied interests and talents. Included are service projects, outdoor education, International Club, *Legacy* (yearbook), *The Moravian Star* (newspaper), *Green Ponderer* (literary magazine), Model Congress, Model UN, PJAS, Scholastic Scrimmage, and a variety of activities that change in response to student interests. A fine arts series combines music, art, drama, and dance. In addition, the Academy's outdoor education program offers a variety of off-campus experiences in hiking, rock climbing, and white water rafting/kayaking. The annual Country Fair gives students an opportunity to work with the Parents' Association to create a family fun day for the school and Lehigh Valley community. Rooted in Moravian tradition, a strong appreciation of music has continued. There are several student musical groups, including chorale, MA Chamber Singers, a cappella group, handbell choirs, and instrumental ensembles. Highlights of the year include the Christmas Vespers Service and the spring concert.

DAILY LIFE

A typical school day begins at 8 a.m., and classes run until 3:15 p.m. on Monday, Tuesday, Wednesday, and Friday. On Thursday, classes conclude at 2:45. The average length of class periods is about 40 minutes. Students usually take six classes a day.

A weekly nondenominational chapel service is held on Thursday mornings. On Monday, Tuesday, Wednesday, and Friday, there is a period for class, school, or advisory meetings.

COSTS AND FINANCIAL AID

Tuition for 2011–12 is $22,540. There is an additional dining fee for students. An initial deposit of $1000 is required upon acceptance, and the remainder of the fee is to be paid in two installments, unless other arrangements are made. An additional fee for tuition insurance is recommended for all new students.

Financial aid is available. Moravian Academy uses the services of the School and Student Service for Financial Aid by NAIS. Aid is awarded on the basis of demonstrated financial need. Aid is received by approximately 20 percent of Upper School students.

ADMISSIONS INFORMATION

Students are admitted in grades 9–11. Each applicant is carefully considered. Students who demonstrate an ability and willingness to handle a rigorous academic program as well as such qualities as intellectual curiosity, responsibility, creativity, and cooperation, are encouraged to apply. Scores on tests administered by the school are also used in the admission process. In addition, school records, recommendations, and a personal interview are required. Admissions are usually completed by May, but there are sometimes openings available after that time.

APPLICATION TIMETABLE

Inquiries are welcome at any time. The Admission Office makes arrangements for tours and classroom visits during the school week. If necessary, other arrangements for tours can be made. The application fee is $65. Test dates are scheduled on specified Saturday mornings from January through March. Notifications are sent after February 15, and families are asked to respond within two weeks.

ADMISSIONS CORRESPONDENCE

Daniel J. Axford
Director of Admissions, Upper School
Moravian Academy
4313 Green Pond Road
Bethlehem, Pennsylvania 18020
Phone: 610-691-1600
Web site: http://www.moravianacademy.org

MUNICH INTERNATIONAL SCHOOL

Starnberg, Germany

Type: Coeducational day college-preparatory school
Grades: PK–12: Junior School, Early Childhood (ages 4 and 5)–grade 4; Middle School, grades 5–8; Senior School, grades 9–12
Enrollment: School total: 1,213; Junior School: 421, Middle School: 384, Senior School: 408
Head of School: Simon Taylor

THE SCHOOL

Munich International School (MIS) is a non-profit coeducational primary and secondary day school that serves students from early childhood (ages 4 and 5) through grade 12, with English as the language of instruction. A total of 1,213 students who represent about fifty countries and nationalities attend MIS. Students are accepted without regard to race, creed, nationality, or religion. The 26-acre MIS campus lies in an environmentally protected area of woodlands and farmland near scenic Lake Starnberg, some 20 kilometres (12 miles) south of Munich. School buses serve the cities of Munich and Starnberg and the surrounding region.

Founded in 1966, the School serves the international community in and around Munich, Germany, as well as those from the local community who wish to take advantage of the unique MIS educational experience. As an exemplary English language International Baccalaureate (I.B.) World School, MIS inspires students to be interculturally aware and achieve their potential within a stimulating and caring learning environment. The curriculum follows the frameworks of the I.B. Primary Years Programme (IBPYP) and the I.B. Middle Years Programme (IBMYP), which culminate in the final two years with the International Baccalaureate Diploma (IBDP) or the American high school diploma.

MIS regards the acquisition of knowledge, concepts, and skills as essential. They are seen as part of a broad and significant process of personal development toward independence, understanding, and tolerance. Learning is a lifelong process, and students are encouraged to cultivate a respect for learning and the ability and wisdom to use it well. Furthermore, since the School is an international and multicultural community, it seeks to develop in young people an active and lasting commitment to international cooperation.

All parents whose children attend MIS constitute the membership of the MIS Association, a tax-exempt, nonprofit organisation that elects a Board of Directors from its membership to operate the School in accordance with its Articles of Association.

Munich International School is fully accredited by the Council of International Schools (CIS) and the New England Association of Schools and Colleges (NEASC) and is approved by the German and Bavarian Educational Authorities.

ACADEMIC PROGRAMME

The academic programme throughout the School covers English language and literature, mathematics, humanities (including history, business and management, economics, geography, and social studies), sciences (including biology, chemistry, and physics), foreign languages, computer science, the fine arts, and film studies.

In the belief that students best benefit from the experience of living in Germany if they are able to communicate effectively and take part in local culture, MIS offers German language instruction to all students in early childhood classes through grade 12. Furthermore, comprehensive instruction in English as a second language (ESL) is offered to students who come to MIS with minimal or no English language skills. In the Senior School, however, English language competence is required for admission.

The School programme is designed so that all students have the opportunity to pursue studies in the fine arts (art, music, drama, and film studies) and computing, athletic, and recreational skills.

The Junior School (early childhood–grade 4) follows the curriculum of the IBPYP, which emphasises an inquiry-based approach to learning across all core academic subjects. The children are taught in self-contained classes in a nurturing environment. The early childhood classes prepare the students for successful entry into grade 1.

The Middle School (grades 5–8) provides a caring, stable environment with a balance of challenging academic studies and opportunities for curricular and extracurricular skill development. The curriculum conforms to the frameworks of the IBMYP in grades 6, 7, and 8. The IBMYP is also part of the curriculum in grades 9 and 10. Studies emphasise the development of skills that involve moral reasoning, aesthetic judgement, and the use of scientific method. The Middle School is committed to providing students with the knowledge, learning strategies, and study skills necessary for the demanding Senior School programme. Food technology and ethics are introduced in grade 6, and French and Spanish are offered as electives from grade 6 onwards. Additional programmes that focus on health, design and technology, social skills, and the importance of the environment are also provided.

The academic programme of the Senior School (grades 9–12) is designed to prepare students for higher education. The guidance counselor especially encourages career planning to make students aware of the education and skills necessary to pursue lifetime goals. The academic programme culminates in grades 11 and 12, with studies leading to a full International Baccalaureate Diploma or an American high school diploma.

FACULTY AND ADVISERS

At MIS, more than 160 teachers from twenty-three nations are part of this broad international experience, coming from such countries as Australia, Canada, France, Germany, Great Britain, Hungary, Ireland, the Netherlands, New Zealand, Sri Lanka, and the United States. The faculty members are fully qualified; many have taught overseas and hold advanced degrees.

COLLEGE ADMISSION COUNSELING

Students have the opportunity to prepare and sit for the American PSAT, SAT, and ACT—tests normally needed for U.S. college entrance. About 90 percent of MIS graduates continue their education at universities and colleges in the world, including Columbia, Duke, the London School of Economics and Political Science, Middlebury, Politecnico Milano (Italy), Sciences Po (France), Tokyo Institute of Technology, Universita Bocconi (Italy), University of Munich, and the University of St. Andrews (Scotland), to cite some recent examples.

STUDENT BODY AND CONDUCT

The strong MIS community of students, teachers, and parents works together. MIS teachers and administrators understand the uncertainties and complexities that accompany a student's transition from one country to another and from one school to another, as well as the normal challenges of growing up. A coordinated support system across the School consists of homeroom teachers, grade coordinators, year coordinators, year advisers, IBPYP/IBMYP/IB coordinators, and guidance counselors.

ACADEMIC FACILITIES

The Junior School is housed in a modern facility, with spacious, light-filled classrooms that radiate from a central multipurpose activity area. There are rooms for computing, German, ESL, learning support, art, and music classes as well as a large, well-equipped library. The Health Office and the School cafeteria, which serves hot meals, are also located in this building.

The Middle School is also located in a modern building. The architectural concept maximizes the use of windows, allowing students to feel close to the natural beauty of the campus. In addition to the spacious classrooms, there are two science laboratories, and a multipurpose auditorium as well as rooms for ESL, academic support, music, and food technology.

The Senior School combines a new building and a traditional Bavarian-style building. Multipurpose classrooms are enhanced by five science laboratories, music and computer rooms, a library, a student lounge, and a performing arts center.

Stately Schloss Buchhof, an original manor house of the area that dates back to 1875, has been renovated to house the Middle and Senior School fine arts departments as well as the administrative offices of the School.

ATHLETICS

Sports activities, which play an important role at MIS, are conducted for all ages after school and during weekends. Soccer, skiing, volleyball, basketball, track and field, tennis, cross-country, and softball are the main sports offered. Tennis courts, several sports fields, and a well-equipped triple gymnasium are available on campus.

The School competes in several ISST tournaments and participates in local leagues and events under the auspices of a School-sponsored sports club. Middle and Senior School teams represent MIS at various international school competitions across Europe.

EXTRACURRICULAR OPPORTUNITIES

In order to take advantage of the experience of living in Germany and Europe, there is a wide range of half- or full-day field trips at all school levels. There are overnight trips for the Middle and Senior School, when teachers and students travel both within Germany and beyond for educational and cultural experiences.

Students may select from a variety of activities in the fine arts, ranging from painting, drawing, and ceramics to handicrafts, drama, and dance. There are several School choirs, bands, and an orchestra. Private instrumental instruction is available. A number of student drama productions are performed throughout the year. Senior and Middle School students participate in the International School Theatre Festival, the Speech and Debate Team, and several international school tournaments. Students in grades 11 and 12 have a weekly period set aside for recreational sports and service activities. They may take part in the Business@School and Model United Nations programmes.

Each year, a group of 8 to 10 students travels to Tanzania to visit project sites funded by donations from the MIS community. The travelling students present their findings at special assemblies held in each division of the School.

An active Parent-Teacher Organisation (PTO) operates as a voluntary support group for the School and fellow parents. The PTO organises a wide range of activities throughout the year, including a Ski Swap, Winterfest, and, in the spring, Frühlingsfest.

DAILY LIFE

The school year begins at the end of August and ends in late June. It is interspersed with short vacations, usually a week at the end of October, two weeks at Christmas, a Ski Week, and two weeks for Spring Break.

The school day starts at 9:10 a.m.; it ends at 3:15 p.m. for Junior School students and at 4 p.m. for Middle and Senior School students. Buses organised by the School and serving most areas in and around Munich provide transportation for nearly 80 percent of the students.

SUMMER PROGRAMMES

A two-week daytime sports programme at the beginning of July includes a week of camping in the Dolomite Mountains in northern Italy.

COSTS AND FINANCIAL AID

In the school year 2011–12, tuition was €14,000–€14,150 for pre-reception–grade 5, €15,900–€16,050 for grades 6–8, and €17,400 for grades 9–12. There is also an entrance fee of €5500 per child upon initial admission and an additional €3000 per child in each of the following two school years.

ADMISSIONS INFORMATION

Applicants are advised that the School does not have the facilities to serve the educational needs of students who have mental, emotional, or physical handicaps or severe learning disabilities. The School does not have boarding facilities.

APPLICATION TIMETABLE

Interested students are required to submit a completed MIS application packet. Following submission of all required documentation, applicants are screened. Based on the School's judgment of the suitability of the educational programme for the prospective student and on space availability, applicants are admitted throughout the year. Earliest acceptance of application material is six months prior to attendance and/or January of that particular year. A nonrefundable application fee is paid in advance of admission decisions being made.

ADMISSIONS CORRESPONDENCE

Admissions Office
Munich International School
Schloss Buchhof
D-82319 Starnberg
Germany
Phone: 49-8151-366-120
Fax: 49-8151-366-129
E-mail: admissions@mis-munich.de
Web site: http://www.mis-munich.de

THE NEWMAN SCHOOL

Boston, Massachusetts

Type: Coeducational day college-preparatory school
Grades: 9–12
Enrollment: 250
Head of School: J. Harry Lynch, Headmaster

THE SCHOOL

The Newman School provides a diverse student body with a college-preparatory, liberal arts education based on Judeo-Christian values, intellectual rigor, and trust, guided by the spirit and philosophy of John Henry Cardinal Newman. Located in the heart of Boston's historic Back Bay district, the Newman School, near Copley Square and the Prudential Center, is convenient to railroad stations, bus terminals, and MBTA stations. Newman's motto "Let heart speak to heart" establishes the tone for each day, encouraging students to form mature and stimulating relationships with teachers and peers and to recognize their individual gifts.

The Newman School, which was named in honor of John Henry Cardinal Newman, was founded in 1945 by Dr. J. Harry Lynch to provide a year of college-preparatory work. Since then, the Newman School has grown into a four-year high school. Classes are offered in fall, winter, and summer sessions, enabling students to attend the School year-round, if desired. Intensive instruction for international students is also available.

Newman is incorporated as a not-for-profit organization and directed by a self-perpetuating 10-member Board of Trustees, which meets quarterly and includes several alumni.

The Newman School is approved by the Boston School Committee and the Department of Education of the Commonwealth of Massachusetts and is accredited by the New England Association of Schools and Colleges. The School holds membership in the Association of Independent Schools of New England (AISNE), the National Association of Secondary School Principals, the Massachusetts Secondary School Principals Association, the National Association of College Admission Counselors, and the Secondary School Admission Test Board. It is approved by the U.S. Immigration and Naturalization Service for the teaching of international students.

ACADEMIC PROGRAMS

The Newman School is recognized by the International Baccalaureate Organization as a World School, offering the International Baccalaureate (I.B.) Diploma Programme in the eleventh and twelfth grades. Freshmen and sophomores pursue a course of pre-I.B. studies in language, mathematics, English literature and composition, and lab science leading to I.B. studies in the junior and senior years.

Transfer credit may be accepted for high school work completed in other schools; however, diploma candidates must take a minimum of 6 credits at Newman. To graduate, a student must complete 22 credits as follows: 4 English, 3 social studies (including U.S. history), 4 mathematics, 3 laboratory science, 2 foreign language, 1 fine/applied arts, 1 computer science, and 4 electives.

The International Student Adviser and the School's Guidance Department aid students from other countries who are preparing for entrance to American colleges and universities. Intermediate and advanced English courses for international students are offered in an intensive program of six classes per day for sixteen weeks in the fall and spring semesters and ten weeks in the summer session. Special attention is given to preparing for the Test of English as a Foreign Language and for College Board tests.

FACULTY AND ADVISERS

J. Harry Lynch, the Headmaster, is a graduate of the College of the Holy Cross (B.A., 1974) and Northeastern University (M.B.A., 1976). He has been Headmaster of Newman since 1985.

The faculty includes 22 full-time teachers and 2 part-time teachers. These 9 men and 13 women hold twenty-two baccalaureate degrees, thirteen master's degrees, and one doctorate.

Members of the faculty are available each day to give students extra help with their course work.

COLLEGE ADMISSION COUNSELING

The College and Career Reference Area provides students with information regarding college admissions and the employment outlook in various fields.

An average graduating class has approximately 65 students, of whom more than 95 percent attend four-year colleges and universities. Recent graduates from Newman have been accepted to the following four-year colleges and universities, among others: American, Assumption, Babson, Bates, Boston College, Boston University, California Institute of Technology, Clark, Columbia, Emerson, Fairfield, Georgetown, Grinnell, Harvard, Holy Cross, McGill, MIT, NYU, Oberlin, Regis, St. Anselm, Smith, Stonehill, Tufts, Tulane, the U.S. Air Force Academy, Vassar, Wellesley, Wheaton, Worcester Polytechnic, and the Universities of Connecticut, Delaware, Maryland, Massachusetts, Miami, New Hampshire, and Rhode Island.

STUDENT BODY AND CONDUCT

The Newman School enrolls approximately 250 day students ranging from 14 to 19 years of age. About 50 of them are out-of-town residents who are temporarily living in Boston. Current and recent students have come from California, Connecticut, Florida, Illinois, Massachusetts, New Hampshire, New Jersey, New York, Ohio, Austria, France, Germany, Greece, India, Iran, Ireland, Italy, Japan, Korea, the People's Republic of China, Poland, Russia, Saudi Arabia, Thailand, Spain, Vietnam, the West Indies, and several Central and South American countries.

Admission to and continuance in the Newman School is to be regarded as a privilege and not a right; the Board of Trustees requires the withdrawal of any student for disciplinary or scholastic reasons that it deems sufficiently grave to warrant such action. The board is the final judge in matters of admission and retention of students. Each student has the responsibility of being thoroughly informed at all times concerning the regulations and requirements of Newman; these are outlined in the School brochure and student handbook.

ACADEMIC FACILITIES

The School plant consists of two nineteenth-century town houses located on Marlborough Street that contain libraries, laboratories, classrooms, and offices. Both buildings are wireless-network accessible. The School does not maintain boarding facilities but does assist out-of-town students in finding homestay families.

ATHLETICS

The School competes interscholastically with other independent schools in sports such as boys' and girls' basketball, crew, and soccer; girls' softball; and boys' baseball and cross-country. Intramural sports, which include competitive cheerleading, flag football, rugby, sailing, and tennis, are available according to student interest but may not be available each term.

EXTRACURRICULAR OPPORTUNITIES

Extracurricular activities that are available each year include a yearbook and a newspaper *(247)*. There are drama, dance, student government, community services, peer leadership, robotics, photography, film, recreation and outing, and science clubs, as well as chorus, ensembles, and bands that perform throughout the year. Other activities may be organized based on student interest. The School has sponsored study-abroad as well as student exchange programs with Spain, Italy, and Colombia.

DAILY LIFE

The academic year is divided into semesters and each semester has four marking periods. At the end of each quarter, grade reports are mailed home. Academic alerts are mailed any time when faculty members observe poor performance by a student. Semesters begin in September and January and a ten-week session begins in June. The school day starts at 8:10 and ends by 3. Classes are held five days a week; to permit completion of a year's work in one fall or spring session, many courses meet for two periods each day.

The summer session incorporates the same amount of work in extended class periods. Thus, summer students may earn a full year's credit for courses not previously taken.

SUMMER PROGRAMS

Newman students may continue their studies during the summer session, receiving academic credit for regular high school courses. In addition, refresher and makeup courses are offered for students from other schools who need to correct deficiencies. International students may attend the Newman School's summer program to work on their English skills and to experience many aspects of American culture within the city of Boston.

COSTS AND FINANCIAL AID

Day tuition was estimated at $15,500 to $25,000 for the 2011–12 school year, depending on the individual schedule. Additional expenses include books (approximately $300 per semester). Estimated living expenses for out-of-town students were $10,600 for the 2011–12 school year.

Entering ninth graders may be given scholarships, depending on the result of the entrance examinations. The School awarded $75,000 in scholarship aid for 2011–12. Financial aid is also available.

ADMISSIONS INFORMATION

Applicants are accepted for enrollment in September, January, and June. Transcripts of any previous high school work, a personal interview, and a character reference letter from the previous school are all part of the requirements to determine acceptance. Applicants must also take a placement test that is administered at the School.

It has always been the policy of the Newman School to admit students without distinction as to race, color, creed, sex, age, ethnic background, or national origin.

APPLICATION TIMETABLE

Candidates for admission should file an application on the required form at the earliest feasible date preceding the session in which they wish to enroll. There is a $40 application fee for American students and a $300 application and processing fee for international students.

ADMISSIONS CORRESPONDENCE

Mrs. Patricia Lynch, Ph.D.
Director of Admissions
The Newman School
247 Marlborough Street
Boston, Massachusetts 02116
Phone: 617-267-4530
Fax: 617-267-7070
E-mail: @newmanboston.org
Web site: http://www.newmanboston.org

NORTHWOOD SCHOOL

Lake Placid, New York

Type: Independent, coeducational, college-preparatory boarding and day school
Grades: 9–12, postgraduate
Enrollment: 182
Head of School: Edward M. Good

THE SCHOOL

Founded in 1905, Northwood is located in the heart of the Adirondack Mountains in Lake Placid, a small village that twice hosted the Winter Olympics (1932 and 1980). It is also the home of the Lake Placid Center for the Arts; consequently, the area offers unique outdoor, athletic, and cultural opportunities. The School is 2 hours from Montreal, Ontario, Canada; Albany, New York; and Burlington, Vermont. The 85-acre campus is nestled in the heart of the village and at the base of Cobble Mountain. The Adirondack Mountains surround the village and are a beautiful backdrop for the School.

Northwood is dedicated to sound scholarship in a diverse environment. It endeavors to stimulate intellectual curiosity in its students and encourages them to learn for themselves through the guidance of its faculty and the examples set by all in the Northwood community. In addition to its academic rigor, the School also stresses responsibility to self and community, asking students to discuss and establish core values, respect different perspectives, and contribute to both the School and its surroundings through various student activities and community services.

Northwood has a wide variety of athletic opportunities, in both competitive team sports and intense outdoor experiences. All students are asked to challenge themselves and display their talents through concerts and theater productions, presentation of darkroom and studio work in art shows and the annual Artsfest, and writing for the School newspaper and literary magazine. Informed by their active lives, Northwood students are independent young men and women who are prepared to lead and achieve in college.

Northwood School is accredited by the New York State Association of Independent Schools (NYSAIS) and the New York State Board of Regents.

ACADEMIC PROGRAMS

Graduation requirements include 19½ units in the following areas: English (4 years), social science (3 years), U.S. history (1 year), science (3 years), mathematics (3 years), language (2 years), fine arts (1 year), and health (½ year). The required number of courses per year is five.

Advanced Placement courses include biology, calculus, English literature, English language, and U.S. history.

Honors courses include algebra II, biology, chemistry, English III, physics, precalculus, and U.S. history.

Elective courses include art exploration, art history, anthropology, ceramics, constitutional law, drama, drawing and painting I and II, economics, ethics, fiber arts, geology, government, Great Issues, instrumental ensemble, Irish history, photography, political geography, psychology, sculpture, and steel drums.

The average class size is 9, and the overall student-teacher ratio is 5:1. Study hall conditions are in effect for room study Sunday through Thursday evenings from 7 to 9 p.m. Ample time is given to all students for laboratory work and library study. Lectures and workshops are scheduled on a regular basis with nearby colleges (St. Lawrence and Middlebury, for example). Trips are scheduled to museums and art centers in Ottawa, Ontario, and other cities near the School.

Many opportunities are available for trips to other countries, especially for the language department. The English as a second language (ESL) program is designed for nonnative English speakers.

The grading system is based on letter grades from A to F. Academic reports go home to parents and to advisers four times per year.

FACULTY AND ADVISERS

There are 35 full-time faculty members, 20 of whom reside on campus. Fifteen of the 35 faculty members have master's degrees. Mr. Edward M. Good, the Headmaster, comes from thirty years of experience in education. He holds a bachelor's degree from Bowdoin, a master's degree from Brown, and a CAGS from the University of Massachusetts. Mr. Good has been at Northwood since 1997. He teaches one current events course. Faculty turnover is very low at Northwood. Faculty members serve as advisers to students, with whom they meet periodically. The adviser communicates any issues to the parents.

COLLEGE ADMISSION COUNSELING

The Director of College Guidance is John Spear. Mr. Spear works with each senior on a regular basis until the student is accepted by a college or university. He assists students and parents with the college application process. Three other faculty members also assist with the college application process. The SAT average is 1670 and the SAT range is 1580–1840.

Of last year's 68 graduates, 95 percent were accepted and enrolled at four-year colleges or universities. Last year, Northwood seniors chose to attend schools such as Amherst College, Boston College, Brown, Harvard, Hobart and William Smith, Illinois at Urbana-Champaign, Penn State, Princeton, Purdue, and Skidmore.

STUDENT BODY AND CONDUCT

Northwood has 182 students. Of these, 145 are boarders and 37 are day students. Thirty percent of the student population is international, coming from countries such as Canada, China, Finland, France, Korea, New Zealand, Norway, Russia, Scotland, Spain, and Vietnam.

ACADEMIC FACILITIES

Northwood has twelve classrooms, a lecture hall, a fine arts studio, four science laboratories, a theater, and a library. The library is student friendly and provides many resources for both academic and personal growth.

The fine arts department has been renovated to provide a photography studio, a fiber arts room, and first-rate painting and drawing facilities as well as a pottery studio. The living room was remodeled in the summer of 2011.

BOARDING AND GENERAL FACILITIES

Residential facilities include one main-building dormitory for boys, separated on three floors. A girls' dorm is located away from the main building.

The Student Center is complete with pool tables and video games, as well as vending machines and a separate television lounge. The bookstore and student mailboxes are also located in the student lounge area.

A state-of-the-art fitness center has been built, complete with all new fitness/weight machines, an indoor climbing wall, and a racquetball/squash court.

Four outdoor tennis courts, three soccer/lacrosse fields, and an outdoor adventure cabin and lean-to make up the outside facilities for athletics. Northwood also has two indoor tennis courts to complete the on-campus facilities. The School uses the Olympic Center for all figure skating and hockey practices and home games.

ATHLETICS

True to the credo on its seal, "Power Through Health and Knowledge," Northwood has a wide variety of athletics opportunities in both competitive team sports and intense outdoor experiences through the Outdoor Adventure Program. A full-time athletics trainer resides on campus.

Girls' sports include Alpine/Nordic skiing, crew, cycling, figure skating, freestyle skiing, golf, ice hockey, lacrosse, soccer, and tennis. Boys' sports include Alpine/Nordic skiing, crew, cycling, freestyle skiing, golf, ice hockey, lacrosse, soccer, and tennis. Coed athletics offerings include canoeing, conditioning, four-season camping, hiking, kayaking, orienteering, rock/ice climbing, telemarking/backcountry skiing, and wilderness first aid.

Northwood also has access to other Olympic facilities for sports such as bobsledding, luge, ski jumping, and speed skating.

EXTRACURRICULAR OPPORTUNITIES

There are various extracurricular activities at Northwood. The yearbook is created mostly by upperclass students. The literary magazine focuses on publishing student works and entering literary accomplishments in local writing competitions. The newly formed student-faculty steel drums band performs both on campus and for the community. Trips to nearby cities for cultural or sporting events are frequent. Students are encouraged to join one of the many on campus clubs or groups, such as the French club or the food committee.

Learning at Northwood School happens in many ways and on many levels. One of the most significant lessons students learn is their responsibility to the greater community. Over the years, students have adopted many service projects as expressions of this sense of responsibility. They run blood drives for the Red Cross, maintain several miles of cross-country ski and hiking trails, and organize annual fundraisers for the Myelin Project and breast cancer research. Students work one-on-one as athletes' assistants for the Special Olympics winter events, and they offer a certified group of search-and-rescue volunteers to help the New York State forest rangers.

Northwood School's faculty members and students are ever mindful of their obligation to serve beyond the boundaries of their campus.

DAILY LIFE

Breakfast starts at 6:50 a.m. and finishes at 7:20. Students attend class from 7:45 until 2:30 p.m., Monday through Friday. A two-week rotating academic schedule incorporates a work program, daily School meeting, and lunch within the 40-minute class periods. Friday evenings are often used for outside presentations and lectures.

Sports and activities meet each afternoon from 3 to 5 p.m. After dinner there is a supervised 2-hour study hall from 7:15 to 9:15 p.m.

During the winter schedule, classes, which normally take place after lunch, are moved to 4:15 p.m. to allow skiers and other winter athletes to train at appropriate times.

WEEKEND LIFE

Weekends are full of diverse events. There are trips to Montreal for hockey or baseball games and trips to nearby colleges, such as Middlebury College or St. Lawrence University. The movie theater, bowling alley, and Main Street shopping in town or in nearby cities are popular weekend activities. Friday evenings often include on-campus activities and visiting musical groups as well as talent night and trivia night. A weekend might also include an overnight camping trip or snowshoeing to a cabin in the woods. Students and faculty members together enjoy planning weekend events at Northwood.

SUMMER PROGRAMS

The Northwood School campus is home to the Can/Am Hockey camp and various other athletic and cultural programs that make Lake Placid their home in the summer.

COSTS AND FINANCIAL AID

The 2011–12 tuition for boarding students was $44,425. Day student tuition was $25,450. There is an additional fee of $1000 for international students and $2000 for those needing ESL.

Fifty-five percent of Northwood School students receive financial assistance.

ADMISSIONS INFORMATION

Northwood School accepts students on a rolling admissions basis. Upon receipt of the application and all required admissions material, the admissions committee meets to discuss acceptance. Admission to Northwood School is based upon evaluation of the applicant's academic record and aptitude test results received from his or her present school. Each candidate is required to take the Secondary School Admission Test, which is published by the Educational Testing Service, Princeton, New Jersey, and is administered numerous times each year at various centers. Northwood may designate other testing according to need. A short essay exercise is required of all candidates who visit the campus.

APPLICATION TIMETABLE

Persons interested can call, write, or visit the School's Web site for information. The Web site has much information and pictures of the facilities and students. Prospective students can download an application or apply online from the admissions page of the Web site.

ADMISSIONS CORRESPONDENCE

Timothy Weaver
Director of Admissions and Financial Aid
Northwood School
92 Northwood Road
P.O. Box 1070
Lake Placid, New York 12946

Phone: 518-523-3357
E-mail: admissions@northwoodschool.com
Web site: http://www.northwoodschool.com

THE OXFORD ACADEMY

Westbrook, Connecticut

Type: Boys' boarding college-preparatory school whose mission is to provide young men with a successful educational experience through one-to-one instruction
Grades: 9–12, postgraduate year
Enrollment: 48
Head of School: Philip B. Cocchiola, Headmaster

THE SCHOOL

The Oxford Academy was founded in 1906 by Dr. Joseph M. Weidberg, who was appalled by the seeming lack of interest on the part of traditional schools in educating young men with good potential who were experiencing academic problems. He knew that some young men who do not always do well in a classroom situation can achieve acceptable, and sometimes extraordinary, academic success when given individualized attention.

After investigating different types of pedagogy, Dr. Weidberg decided to use the Socratic method of teaching. He taught his students by questioning them and stimulating them to know themselves, to think, to understand, to use initiative, and to express themselves. The school continues to do this for young men between the ages of 14 and 20 who have experienced learning difficulties in a traditional school setting. A special feature of the school is that all teaching is one-to-one—1 teacher to 1 student per class.

The school, originally located in Pleasantville, New Jersey, was destroyed by fire in 1971 and moved to a 12-acre site in Westbrook, Connecticut, along the state's shoreline. Since then, campus improvements include the Corthouts Gymnasium, Hoskins Hall, and a recreation hall as well as an academic wing built in 1999. In addition, two playing fields were developed and three tennis courts completed.

Westbrook is a 5-minute drive from Old Saybrook, which has Amtrak train service from Boston and New York, each approximately 2 hours away. Bradley International Airport, in Hartford, is an hour from the school.

The school's physical plant is valued at $3.7 million.

The Oxford Academy is accredited by the New England Association of Schools and Colleges and approved by the Connecticut Department of Education. It is a member of the Connecticut Association of Independent Schools and the National Association of Independent Schools and is an associate member of the International Council of Schools.

ACADEMIC PROGRAMS

Because of its pedagogical approach, unique among boarding schools, the Oxford Academy admits students whenever there is an opening, and a boy begins his course of studies at the point dictated by his academic needs, which are determined after extensive testing. A curriculum is planned to compensate for each student's deficiencies, taking into account his individual academic needs and psychological makeup. The curriculum is geared to high school and postgraduate students and consists of courses in the five traditional academic subject areas: English, mathematics, science, social studies, and foreign languages. In addition, courses in developmental reading and mathematics, language arts, studio art, English as a second language, and other curricular areas of need can be incorporated into a boy's program.

Although the vast majority of students follow a college-preparatory curriculum, provision is made for a course of study leading to a general high school diploma. Many types of developmental learning disabilities can be addressed, but boys with severe learning disabilities are not accepted. A boy must have at least average intelligence in order to be admitted.

Every week, each student's program is evaluated, and grades for achievement and effort are handed in to the Dean of Studies. Standardized testing is used periodically to evaluate a boy's progress, and sufficient help is given to enable students to take the ACT, SAT, and TOEFL in order to make the transition from the Academy to a traditional preparatory school or to college.

FACULTY AND ADVISERS

In 2011–12, the Oxford Academy faculty had 20 full-time members; 35 percent of them have master's degrees. Teachers at the Oxford Academy receive special instruction and supervision in one-to-one pedagogy from the Headmaster and the Dean of Studies.

Most faculty members live on campus and thus are in constant contact with the boys to advise them not only on academic matters but also on personal and social problems.

COLLEGE ADMISSION COUNSELING

The Academy offers individual help in college placement. A quarter of the school population normally stays at the Academy for up to twelve months before seeking placement in a traditional preparatory school. The remaining students, who tend to stay at the Academy for less than three years, are usually college bound. Educational consultants are kept abreast of a student's progress and thus are in a good position to evaluate college needs after a year or two at the Oxford Academy.

Graduating seniors were accepted by the following colleges and universities in 2011: Fordham, Green Mountain, Skidmore, Suffolk, and the University of Colorado.

STUDENT BODY AND CONDUCT

The Oxford Academy has a limited number of places. Forty-eight students is the maximum number that can be accommodated with the present facilities and staff. In September 2011, the ages of the students ranged from 14 to 19, and they came from twelve states and five other countries. These boys and their parents were attracted to the Academy because of its individualized instruction and the cultural and geographical diversity of the student body, which enhances the general educational atmosphere.

ACADEMIC FACILITIES

The main academic building, Knight Hall, named after a former Headmaster, is more than 6,500 square feet and includes offices, classrooms, a general reference library, and a state-of-the-art computer facility as well as an art studio and a darkroom. There is also a science laboratory, with a greenhouse, fully equipped for general science, biology, chemistry, and physics. The Westbrook Public Library is located directly across from the Academy.

Hoskins Hall, named in honor of an Oxford teacher who was at the school for thirty-eight years, houses three additional classrooms.

BOARDING AND GENERAL FACILITIES

The Academy has two dormitory buildings, each with facilities for 24 students. Resident faculty members live in each dormitory building with the students. Most rooms are double occupancy, and there is a common bathroom for each dormitory. One dormitory houses the dining room. Hill House, an eighteenth-century Colonial building, contains business offices, a reception center, and the admissions office. Next door is the nineteenth-century Post House, which houses faculty members. The Headmaster's residence, built in 1800, is located on the western property line next to the skating pond, which adjoins the beach area on Long Island Sound. Completing the plant is a former barn, which has been converted into a recreation center for the students.

ATHLETICS

Oxford's daily sports program aims neither to attract students nor to discourage them. Students come to Oxford for what it can do for them academically. The athletics program is designed to provide the physical activity necessary to maintain each student at his physical and psychological best. The Academy offers three varsity sports including soccer, basketball, and tennis. All other sports and games—golf, karate, paintball, and bowling—are played on either an intramural or individual basis.

Corthouts Gymnasium was built in 1983. The foyer to the gymnasium and a weight room are located in Hoskins Hall.

EXTRACURRICULAR OPPORTUNITIES

A darkroom is available for students interested in photography. In addition to participating in the interscholastic sports program, students enjoy swimming, skiing, golf, and riding near the school. Occasional field trips are sponsored.

DAILY LIFE

Breakfast is served from 7 to 7:55 a.m., and classes begin at 8. Classes end at 3 and are followed by a scheduled athletic period. Dinner is served at 6, and the evening study period runs from 7:30 to 8:45. Lights-out is at 11 p.m.

WEEKEND LIFE

Because of the location of the Oxford Academy, students are able to take advantage of cultural events in New Haven and Hartford. Often, weekend day trips are planned to Boston and New York.

Students who have met their academic and social obligations may leave the campus after testing on Saturday, with parental permission, and return by 7 p.m. on Sunday.

SUMMER PROGRAMS

In the summer, Oxford runs a program that offers the same type of work as its winter session. The program is intended primarily for students enrolled in the regular program who would like to accelerate their studies, but the Academy does accept students for the summer session only.

COSTS AND FINANCIAL AID

Tuition for the 2011–12 school year was $53,500. A security deposit of $1000 for domestic students and $2000 for international students is required. Additional expenses may include those for testing ($400), laundry, books, and field trips.

ADMISSIONS INFORMATION

Admission to the Oxford Academy is selective. The school accepts young men between the ages of 14 and 20 who have yet to realize their academic potential, wish to make up for lost time, or are international students seeking entrance into American colleges and universities. The Oxford Academy does not discriminate on the basis of race, color, or creed. The admissions policy excludes youngsters of below-normal intelligence and students who are emotionally disturbed in the medical sense. As Oxford is not a therapeutic facility, other schools are recommended to students with severe learning disabilities or significant behavioral issues.

APPLICATION TIMETABLE

Application for admission to Oxford can be made at any time. A student begins his program the day he arrives, since he is in a class by himself. The limited number of spaces may necessitate waiting one or two months before the student begins, but the school has rolling admissions procedures. No student is accepted until all previous school records have been received and he and his parents have had an interview at the school. Exceptions have been made for international students who cannot travel to the United States but who have been interviewed by parents of former students or by alumni in their home countries.

ADMISSIONS CORRESPONDENCE

Mr. Philip B. Cocchiola
Headmaster
The Oxford Academy
1393 Boston Post Road
Westbrook, Connecticut 06498

Phone: 860-399-6247
Fax: 860-399 6805
E-mail: admissions@oxfordacademy.net
Web site: http://www.oxfordacademy.net

THE PENNINGTON SCHOOL

Pennington, New Jersey

Type: Coeducational day and boarding college-preparatory school
Grades: 6–12: Middle School, 6–8; Upper School, 9–12
Enrollment: School total: 485; Middle School, 95; Upper School: 390
Head of School: Stephanie G. Townsend, Head of School

THE SCHOOL

The Pennington School is an independent coeducational school for students in grades 6 through 12, with both day and boarding programs. The curriculum is college preparatory, with an emphasis on fostering the development of the whole student through academics, athletics, community service, and the creative and performing arts. There are also specialized programs within the curriculum for international students and for students with learning differences. Founded in 1838, Pennington values both tradition and innovation, applying the values gleaned from centuries of learning along with the most up-to-date knowledge, to a rapidly changing world. The School's faculty members focus not only on what they can teach the students but also on what the varied perspectives of the student body can impart to the overall educational experience.

The 54-acre campus is strategically located in a suburban setting just 60 miles from New York City, 40 miles from Philadelphia, and within 8 miles of Princeton. This location makes it convenient for cultural and educational field trips.

The governing body is a 36-member Board of Trustees. Pennington's endowment currently stands at $27 million.

The Pennington School is accredited by the Middle States Association of Colleges and Schools and approved by the New Jersey State Department of Education. It is a member of the National Association of Independent Schools, the New Jersey Association of Independent Schools, and the Secondary School Admission Test Board. Pennington is affiliated with the University Senate and the Board of Higher Education and Ministry of the United Methodist Church.

ACADEMIC PROGRAMS

Pennington's objectives are to offer a challenging and broad academic program that best prepares its students for life as college students.

Middle School students concentrate on five major subject areas: math, English, social studies, science, and foreign language. All students rotate through a series of exploratory courses during the year, including art/drama, music, health, technology, writing workshop, and ethics.

Students in the Upper School usually take six classes per day. The minimum number of credits necessary for graduation is 20. Requirements include the following: English, 4; mathematics, 3; history, 3; science, 3; foreign language, 2; religion, 1; art, 1; health, 1; technology, ½; and public speaking, ¼. Honors and Advanced Placement courses are offered in all disciplines.

The student-teacher ratio is 8:1, and the average class size is 13, with a maximum of 18 students in any one class. A 2-hour evening study period for boarders is supervised. The School library is open a half-hour before the school day begins until the conclusion of study hall on school nights and for limited hours on weekends.

The School uses the semester system, but, with midterm evaluations, there are four marking periods. Parent-teacher or parent-adviser-student conferences are held twice a year. Individual conferences are arranged as required.

Official grades are issued at the conclusion of each semester. Pennington uses a letter grading system in which D– (60) is the passing grade and C– (70) the minimum grade for a course to count toward graduation requirements.

The Pennington School has two unique programs: a Center for Learning, a program designed for academically talented students with language-based learning differences, and an English as a second language (ESL) program.

FACULTY AND ADVISERS

The faculty consists of 100 men and women, about half of whom live on campus. The faculty holds thirty-five baccalaureate, sixty master's, and four doctoral degrees. Faculty members serve as advisers for 6 to 8 students. Other counseling is available from trained counselors. Teachers also serve as hall parents, providing the basis for yet another kind of close relationship.

Stephanie (Penny) Townsend, appointed Head of School in 2006, earned her bachelor's degree from the University of Connecticut and her master's degree from Middlebury College. Before coming to Pennington, she taught Spanish at Northfield Mount Hermon School in Massachusetts and at the Taft School in Connecticut. Most recently, Townsend served as the Dean of Faculty at the Taft School.

COLLEGE ADMISSION COUNSELING

College guidance is the responsibility of trained counselors who coordinate all aspects of the college planning and placement process, including the taking of PSAT, SAT, TOEFL, and Advanced Placement tests. Representatives from almost 200 colleges visit Pennington to meet with students. Juniors and seniors meet individually with their college counselors and attend college admission panels. Juniors attend special college programs, including two spring on-campus college fairs, and take a college admission seminar.

Among the schools recent graduates attended are American, Boston College, Boston University, Brown, Bucknell, Columbia, Emory, Georgetown, Harvey Mudd, Hofstra, Lafayette, Lehigh, NYU, Parsons, Rutgers, Syracuse, Trinity (Hartford), Villanova, Williams, and the Universities of Pennsylvania and Saint Andrews (Scotland).

STUDENT BODY AND CONDUCT

Of Pennington's 485 students, 95 are in the Middle School and 390 are in the Upper School; 360 are day students, and 125 are boarding students. The ratio of girls to boys in the Upper School is approximately 4:5. Current students represent five states and come from a number of countries, including the Bahamas, Bulgaria, China, Korea, Russia, Spain, Taiwan, Uzbekistan, and the West Indies. Twenty percent of the students belong to minority groups.

There is a student government, elected by the student body. Students are expected to follow the rules defined in the *Student/Parent Handbook.* Violations may be dealt with by the Behavior Review Board, which is made up of students and faculty members.

During class hours, Upper School boys must wear collared shirts, slacks, and dress shoes; on certain days, shirts and ties are required. Upper School girls must wear slacks or skirts with collared shirts or blouses. Middle School students wear Pennington polo shirts and khakis. Monday dinner and certain programs call for jackets and ties for boys and dresses or skirts and blouses for girls. The dress code permits jeans, T-shirts, and sneakers to be worn by students after class hours and on weekends but not during class time.

ACADEMIC FACILITIES

The centers of academic activities are Stainton Hall, a classroom/administration building; the Campus Center, containing art and music studios, a theater, foreign language classrooms, and the Student Center; Meckler Library, which contains the academic book collection, online databases, and the Computer Center; and Old Main, which houses classrooms and five residence halls.

BOARDING AND GENERAL FACILITIES

In addition to Old Main, there are two dormitories containing another five residence halls: Becher Hall, a one-story residence with ten student rooms and two faculty apartments, and Buck Hall, containing four halls with double rooms and private bathrooms. There are eight faculty apartments in this building. The School has an attractive dining facility and a health center, with 2 registered nurses in residence. Boarding facilities close for the Thanksgiving, Christmas, and spring holidays, so all students must leave the campus during those vacation periods.

ATHLETICS

The Pennington School believes that the lessons learned through athletics involvement are valuable ones. Thus, every student is expected to participate in a team or individual sport that fits his or her own ability level. Although Pennington's athletic teams are very successful and frequently win state championships, the emphasis is on participation, collective effort, sportsmanship, and personal growth. All students must participate in at least one sport per year. Boarders must take three terms of activities. When boarding students are not involved in a sport, they must be involved in other extracurricular activities.

The sports available for boys and girls in grades 9 to 12 are basketball, cheerleading, cross-country, golf, lacrosse, soccer, swimming, tennis, track and field, and water polo. In addition, field hockey and softball are available for girls, and baseball, football, and ice hockey are offered for boys.

In addition to a gymnasium/swimming pool complex, Pennington has five tennis courts, 30 acres of playing fields, an all-weather-surface track, and a lighted artificial turf field lined for lacrosse, soccer, and football.

EXTRACURRICULAR OPPORTUNITIES

Life at Pennington is more than classrooms, laboratories, and the library, essential as these are. Opportunities exist for participation in a wide range of extracurricular activities.

Apart from the athletics program, there are many clubs and organizations that students may join. These include three drama productions a year, the Pennington Singers, Mock Trial, Peer Leadership, National Honor Society, Photography Club, International Club, International Thespian Society, Model United Nations, Pennington Sports News, Youth Service Fellowship, Campus Guides, United People of Many Colors, jazz ensemble, chamber ensemble, Junior Proctors, foreign language clubs, and staffs of the yearbook, newspaper, and literary magazine, which contains creative writing and artistic work of students. All students are encouraged to do community service during the year. Students do volunteer work for hospitals and charitable organizations in Pennington, Princeton, and Trenton and travel on service related trips during School vacations.

A student activities program provides for social events such as dances, ski trips, movies, theater presentations, and visits to area places of interest.

Life at Pennington also includes a weekly chapel service.

DAILY LIFE

The day's activities begin at 8 a.m. and conclude at 2:45. There is an activities period on Fridays and a bimonthly community meeting on Wednesdays. There are two lunch periods. An extra-help conference period follows the class day. Sports practice takes place from 3:15 to 5:15, and dinner follows at 5:30. A monitored study period for boarders from 7:30 to 9:30 completes the day. Lights are out at 10:30 p.m. on weekdays.

WEEKEND LIFE

Day students and boarders are encouraged to participate in weekend activities. These include functions on campus as well as trips off campus to attend plays, museums, festivals, and professional sports contests. The library, swimming pool, and gymnasium are open on weekends. Transportation is also provided to shopping centers, where students may shop, eat, or see a movie.

COSTS AND FINANCIAL AID

The 2011–12 charges were $29,750 for day students, $44,310 for boarding students, with additional charges for Center for Learning and ESL classes. Additional costs are a book deposit of $500 or $600, and an activity fee of $150 or $350. There are special fees for private music lessons and tutoring. An allowance of $15 to $25 per week is recommended for spending money for residential students.

When an enrollment contract is signed, a nonrefundable deposit of 10 percent of tuition for day students and boarders is required to hold a space for the student; it is applied toward the year's tuition. The remainder of the tuition may be paid in installments of one half on July 15 and the remaining half on November 1, or tuition may be paid through a ten-month payment plan. Enrollment in school tuition insurance is required.

Financial aid is based on demonstrated need. Parents applying for aid must submit the required paperwork and forms through TADS. Financial aid is granted on an annual basis. Thirty percent of the students received financial aid for the 2011–12 school year.

ADMISSIONS INFORMATION

Pennington seeks students who have strong academic ability, as demonstrated on the SSAT, good character, and a record of good citizenship. Approximately 37 percent of the applicants are accepted for admission.

The School does not discriminate on the basis of race, color, religion, gender, or national or ethnic origin in the administration of its admission or educational policies or the financial aid, athletic, or other School-administered programs.

APPLICATION TIMETABLE

Students should begin the application process for Pennington early in the fall. The School uses a March 10 notification date, an April 10 reply date, and then rolling admissions as space is available. Students who wish to be considered in March should have all materials and the $50 application fee submitted and the interview completed by February 1. The Admission Office is open throughout the year for interviews and tours of the campus from 8:15 to 2, Monday through Friday, by appointment.

ADMISSIONS CORRESPONDENCE

Mark Saunders
Director of Admission and Financial Aid
The Pennington School
Pennington, New Jersey 08534
Phone: 609-737-6128
Fax: 609-730-1405
E-mail: admiss@pennington.org
Web site: http://www.pennington.org

PRESBYTERIAN PAN AMERICAN SCHOOL

Kingsville, Texas

Type: Coeducational college-preparatory boarding school and day school
Grades: 9–12 plus a fifth "bridge" year
Enrollment: 150
Head of School: James. H. Matthews, Ph.D.

THE SCHOOL

Founded in 1911 on land from the world-renowned King Ranch, Presbyterian Pan American School (Pan Am) has distinguished itself over the past century for its commitment to preparing international students, along with racial and ethnic minorities, for a university-level education. Although students come from many countries in addition to the United States, all classroom instruction is in English. English as a second language (ESL) is the foundation of an international student's first year, with faculty and classes assigned on the basis of proficiency testing administered during the first week on campus.

Pan Am seeks applicants who show clear evidence of a lively intelligence—students who are at ease communicating with others, open to experiencing the wider world, and eager to discover and explore the possibilities it holds for them.

Enrollment at Pan Am averages 150, with approximately the same number of boys and girls. In recent years students have come from South Korea, Mexico, China, Japan, Rwanda, Ecuador, Peru, Bolivia, Hong Kong, Taiwan, Guatemala, Coast Rica, Spain, Equatorial Guinea, and the United States.

As a mission school of the Presbyterian Church (U.S.A.), Pan Am offers a generous program of financial aid. The majority of students come from Christian families, either Protestant or Roman Catholic; however, the admissions process is blind to both religion and a family's economic situation. All students attend chapel services and take elective courses in Bible. In their upper-class semesters they participate in usually spirited seminars that require critical thinking about selected topics in ethics, economic justice, and human rights, particularly as informed by the teachings and ideals of the Protestant Reformation. However, the School does not attempt to proselytize and indeed prizes and teaches a wholesome respect for the reality and diversity of God's creation.

Pan Am is located on a 670-acre working cattle ranch in Kingsville, Texas, less than an hour's drive from the Corpus Christi International Airport and about an hour and a half north of the U.S. border with Mexico.

The School is accredited by the Southern Association of Colleges and Schools (SACS) as well as by the Texas Education Association (TEA).

ACADEMIC PROGRAMS

Classroom instruction, along with a student's social formation, is designed to equip the student for success in college and eventually in a satisfying career. A student who fully utilizes Pan American School's many resources should be able to achieve a minimum average grade of 85 in college. Each student is coached to attain a score of 550 on the standardized Test of English as a Foreign Language (TOEFL).

In addition to traditional high school subjects, Pan Am offers instruction in speech, journalism, economics, fine arts, computers, agronomy and agriculture, health and hygiene, physical education, and religious studies. Practical experience in robotics is offered when instructors are available. For those students eager for the experience, the School offers a supervised 4-H program in which participants raise their own steer or lamb, which will eventually be sold at the annual livestock show and auction. No previous ranch experience is required.

Classes average about 16 students each. The student- faculty ratio is 9:1.

Senior students who score well on a college placement exam have the option of taking college-level classes for dual credit. In a typical year, up to one third of the senior class graduates with college credits in math, English, government, or economics.

Pan Am also offers a fifth "bridge" year for international students who are academically strong but whose command of English might place them at a competitive disadvantage in a U.S. college classroom. The emphasis of the bridge year is strengthening a student's English reading, speaking, writing, and listening skills.

FACULTY AND ADVISERS

The professional staff includes classroom teachers; resource specialists; specialists in art, music, and physical education; a school principal (or dean); academic and psychological counselors; a computer network engineer; and a library and media specialist. Many are graduates of Texas A&M University–Kingsville and/or are working toward advanced degrees on that campus.

Several staff members, including the president and spiritual life director, live on campus. Parents are invited to visit, phone, or e-mail faculty members. Each student's family receives an online password to access their child's grades, along with comments and observations from teachers and counselors.

COLLEGE ADMISSION COUNSELING

Academic counselors advise each student regarding options for college. Each senior is required to apply to a minimum of three colleges or universities, which may be in the United States, the student's home country, or elsewhere in the world. Many choose to study in Texas before returning home.

Presbyterian Pan American School is proud of its nearly 100 percent college acceptance rate among senior class students. In recent years, Pan Am's graduates have been accepted by The Art Institute of Atlanta, Baylor, Dordt, Schreiner, Technológico de Monterrey, Texas A&M, Trinity (San Antonio), Universidad Autónoma de Nuevo León, Universidad Iberoamericana, Universidad Nacional Autónoma de México, University of Houston, The University of Texas at Austin, and other locations in The University of Texas system.

ACADEMIC FACILITIES

The campus includes four classroom buildings offering science labs, an art studio, choir room, and computer lab; and a library with a computer section. The campus is served by two T-1 broadband Internet lines.

BOARDING AND GENERAL FACILITIES

In addition to the academic facilities, there are a number of other buildings on the 50-acre campus. A kitchen and dining hall serves three meals daily to the student body and staff. Morris Chapel is the center of worship and spiritual life and is also the location for all-school assemblies. Boys and girls live in their respective dormitory complexes, each with lounge facilities and a resident adult staff of dorm parents and assistants. An indoor field house contains basketball and volleyball courts. In addition there are administrative offices, a teachers' lounge and offices, a student union building, and on-campus guest quarters where parents and other visitors can arrange for private accommodations.

ATHLETICS

Presbyterian Pan American School points proudly to a string of Texas state championships in boys' soccer. In addition, the School offers both boys' and girls' basketball, girls' volleyball, cheerleading, and girls' and boys' track. There is also an outdoor basketball court, a tennis court, a soccer field and track, and a newly renovated swimming pool. Student lifeguards are Red Cross–trained and certified. The boys' dorm complex includes a weight room. The School plans to add a baseball program in 2011–12.

EXTRACURRICULAR OPPORTUNITIES

Pan Am firmly believes that social and personal formation is at least as vital as academic information in preparing young people to take their places in the world. While athletics offer the most obvious extracurricular outlets, the School provides additional activities as well. A professionally led choir affords training and vocal coaching. Several students each year qualify to compete at various levels of Texas All-State Choir. A traveling show choir visits around the state and serves as a powerful outreach for the School. The 4-H Club presents opportunities to participate in raising cattle and sheep on the School's extensive ranch. Quilting and photography are also taught through 4-H. Student Council, drama club, yearbook, and National Honor Society further develop leadership and organizational ability. The chapel's praise band offers students the opportunity to perform on keyboard, percussion, and guitar. Student-led committees abound, ranging from worship to waste recycling, and there are frequent class fund-raising projects, opportunities to contribute to the student-produced newspaper, and outings to NCAA Division II athletic events.

DAILY LIFE

Students clean their rooms each morning in preparation for inspection. Breakfast is at 7:15 on weekdays and later on weekends. The first class of the day begins at 7:50. The work program and athletic activities take over at 3 p.m. Choir rehearsals are toward the end of the afternoon. Computer lab is held on alternate evenings for boys and girls. Free time for informal athletics, board games, jogging, and other pursuits is available following dinner. There is a required chapel worship service every Wednesday at 11 a.m., with students working alongside the director of spiritual life to plan and lead the worship. Students typically have several hours of homework to complete before lights-out at 10:30 p.m.

Since the School's founding in 1911, the student work program has been an integral component of the weekday routine. Each student is required to perform 6 hours per week of supervised on-campus work, which may include cleaning the library or public areas of the dorms, assisting in the kitchen, sanitizing tables in the dining hall, collecting trash, gardening, or other routine tasks.

Weekends at Pan Am are as important as weekdays and begin just as the last class ends on Friday. There is no work program on Fridays. Students are free to use that afternoon as they wish. Friday evening activities are usually in the Student Union Building (SUB), where there are movies and dances, cards and chess, and pool and ping-pong. Saturdays and Sundays are also times when students may be driven into Kingsville or the malls in Corpus Christi to shop and hang out together. Weekend activities also include occasional barbecues over native mesquite cut from the ranch, or gatherings at the swimming pool in season. Many students enjoy the tree-covered campus as a pleasant place to come together to play the guitar, sing, and be with friends. Sunday mornings there is worship in the chapel at 11, which all students attend. Students who live within driving distance of the campus can sign out of the dorm with parental permission and spend an occasional weekend at home, often inviting friends and roommates to go with them.

COSTS AND FINANCIAL AID

Tuition and fees in 2011–12 were $14,500 for boarding students and $8500 for day students. This included room, board, tuition, and test fees for PSAT, SAT, and TOEFL. Costs for the 2012–13 school year are likely to be several hundred dollars higher.

The School offers a tuition installment plan and is able to accept online payments via credit card. As a mission school of the Presbyterian Church (U.S.A.), Pan Am remains committed to being financially accessible to families with modest financial resources. Most years, about 85 percent of the student body receives some degree of need-based financial aid. Nearly $1,000,000 was awarded for the 2010–11 school year.

ADMISSIONS INFORMATION

Presbyterian Pan American School admits students into grades 9 through 12 and also offers a post–high school year of intensive English language studies for international students who are preparing to apply to a U.S. college. Interested parents and prospective students may find further information online at www.ppas.org. Admission packets are available on the Web site or by contacting the Office of Admissions. Visits to the campus are recommended, although they may be impractical for families who live far from the United States. When indicated, the director of admissions can conduct a Webcam interview over the Internet.

Once an international student has been admitted, the School will issue a United States Homeland Security Form I-20, which is the application for an F-1 Student Visa. Once the Form I-20 has been received, students must make an appointment with the U.S. embassy or a consular office in their home country, where they will be interviewed regarding their reasons for wishing to study in the United States and their future plans back home.

APPLICATION TIMETABLE

Inquiries are welcome at any time. The School begins receiving applications in January of each year but cannot make an admissions decision until the applicant's file is complete. Applications should be submitted by May 31 of each year, although they may be accepted later if space is available. The application fee is $35, payable either in cash or online.

ADMISSIONS CORRESPONDENCE

Mr. Joe L. Garcia, Director of Admissions
Presbyterian Pan American School
Post Office Box 1578
223 North FM Road 772
Kingsville, Texas 78363

Phone: 361-592-4307
Fax: 361-592-6126
E-mail: jlgarcia@ppas.org
Web site: http://www.ppas.org

RANNEY SCHOOL

Tinton Falls, New Jersey

Type: Coeducational college-preparatory day school
Grades: BG (3 years old)–grade 12: Lower School, BG–Grade 5; Middle School, Grades 6–8; Upper School, Grades 9–12
Enrollment: School total: 821
Head of School: Lawrence S. Sykoff, Ed.D.

THE SCHOOL

Ranney School was founded in 1960 by Russell G. Ranney for the purpose of fostering high academic achievement. A former Associate Director of the New York University Reading Institute, Mr. Ranney was a firm believer in the three R's. A 19-member Board of Trustees, plus the Head of School, supervises the School's operation on its campus of more than 60 acres in a residential neighborhood located approximately 45 miles south of New York City.

Ranney School is dedicated to engaging its students in an exemplary, well-rounded education, one that promotes the development of every child's intellectual, personal, creative, and moral promise. By serving a diverse community that values a rigorous, wide-ranging program of study, Ranney students are inspired to reach their full potential. Guided by dedicated and compassionate professionals, the Ranney experience is distinguished by the heartfelt bond between student and teacher—the hallowed principle celebrating the unique nature of every child. In an environment with contemporary learning resources, students learn the value of contributing to their local and global communities through leadership and service. The School's motto, "Knowledge, vision, honor," is as much an inspiration as it is a social imperative, one that informs the thinking and actions the School's students. Awakening students' intellectual potential and encouraging them to communicate with confidence in their own unique voice remains fundamental to the Ranney experience. The ultimate success of Ranney students is the result of a simple yet powerful mission-promise, that every child will be known and valued.

The Board of Trustees is the School's governing body. During 2010–11, annual giving totaled $713,000; annual operating expenses average $22 million.

Ranney School alumni number approximately 1,670. An Alumni Council oversees alumni activities.

Ranney School is accredited by the Middle States Association of Colleges and Schools. The School maintains active membership in the National Association of Independent Schools (NAIS), the New Jersey Association of Independent Schools (NJAIS), the Council for Advancement and Support of Education (CASE), the Educational Records Bureau (ERB), and the National Association for College Admission Counseling (NACAC).

ACADEMIC PROGRAMS

The Lower School (Beginners (age 3) through grade 5) curriculum is designed to stimulate a child's natural love of learning. Goals are set forth in a program consistent with the early stages of child development. The primary goal is to maximize the growth of each individual. The curriculum remains rooted in the development of language arts. Course time is allotted to vocabulary building, spelling, grammar usage, reading, and the development of writing skills. Strong programs in mathematics, science, social studies, instrumental music, and computer education complement these courses. Students are also introduced to studies in the fine arts, music, and world languages. Aquatics and physical education complete the course of study. Teaching strategies include cooperative learning, interdisciplinary arrangements, and individual attention.

The Middle School (grades 6 through 8) curriculum is designed to provide a special community in which students can grow, learn about themselves, develop personal and group values, and prepare for the challenges of higher learning, particularly within the Ranney Upper School. The comprehensive English and mathematics programs initiated in the Lower School continue through the middle years, along with additional concentrations in science, history, and world languages, including Mandarin Chinese. A one-to-one laptop program begins in Middle School, with courses in computer fundamentals, art, music, drama, word processing, physical education, and aquatics. To provide flexibility in instruction, some classes in math, history, and world languages are arranged to cover the curriculum over a two-year period.

The Upper School (grades 9 through 12) graduation requirements include a minimum of 20 academic credits, plus 4 units in health and physical education. All students are expected to take 5 full credits of course work each year. Specific requirements include English (4 credits), world language (3 credits), history (3 credits, 2 of which must be American history), mathematics (3 credits), science (2 credits with lab, including biology and either chemistry or physics), art (1 credit), and physical education (4 credits). In addition to required courses, a number of single-semester and full-year electives are available to sophomores, juniors, and seniors. The Upper School curriculum also offers many honors and college-level Advanced Placement (AP) courses. Nineteen AP units are available to students who are capable of accelerated study. All Upper School students receive a laptop computer in addition to the digital media center on campus.

Ranney utilizes a numeric grading system with a 100-point scale. The school year consists of two semesters and four marking periods, with grades and written evaluations being sent home at the end of the first and third marking periods. Report cards with grades only are sent at the end of each semester. Midterm exams are given in January and final exams in June.

FACULTY AND ADVISERS

There are 92 full-time faculty members, plus 3 part-time instructors. Fifty-one faculty members have master's degrees or higher. Each Middle and Upper School faculty member serves as an adviser to an average of 6 to 8 students. Ranney faculty members are accomplished and recognized professionals whose contributions to the growth and status of their calling often extend outside the School community.

Dr. Lawrence S. Sykoff was appointed Headmaster in June 1993. He holds degrees from the University of San Diego (Ed.D. and M.Ed.) and Baruch College of Business Administration of the City University of New York (B.B.A.).

COLLEGE ADMISSION COUNSELING

The College Guidance Office is one of the distinguishing features of Ranney School. It all starts in ninth grade, where all student schedules pass through the college guidance office for review. Staff members then work closely with students, parents, and advisers throughout the Upper School years to ensure that each student follows an appropriate academic course, with clear and achievable goals. Beginning in tenth grade, students take the PSAT and the PLAN test and are guided by their college counselor to focus on either the ACT or SAT exam.

During the junior year, Ranney's college counselors meet one-on-one with students and parents to discuss all the variables in the college selection process and help focus each student's priorities, goals, and aspirations. Students enter the admission process well-prepared and well-informed, benefiting from individualized counseling designed to ensure success. Ranney's success is evident: 100 percent of graduates go on to attend four-year schools, 80 percent are admitted to their first- or second-choice college, and Ranney students regularly earn more than $2 million in scholarships.

All seniors receive direction from the College Guidance Office in writing college essays, interviewing skills, and preparing their final applications.

The mean SAT scores for 2011 graduates were 630 critical reading, 650 writing, and 620 math.

The senior class of 2011 achieved 100 percent college acceptance at schools such as Boston University, Cornell, Georgetown, Johns Hopkins, NYU, Notre Dame, and Williams.

STUDENT BODY AND CONDUCT

The 2011–12 student body consisted of 821 students, as follows: 182 boys and 187 girls in the Lower School, 106 boys and 93 girls in the Middle School, and 118 boys and 135 girls in the Upper School.

Ranney's families represent many countries, including China, India, Japan, and Russia. The School sponsors an International Week of Celebration each year in all three divisions.

A Judicial Board handles routine disciplinary issues in the Upper School. The board consists of 2 faculty members and 2 students and is chaired by the Dean of Students. Recommendations are given to the Principal and the Headmaster for review and decision.

ACADEMIC FACILITIES

The Lower School is comprised of three buildings and has its own computer lab, two science labs, and library. Ranney is a completely wireless campus with over fifty laptops and 100 iPads available in the Lower School. In addition, each classroom is equipped with two computers. The Middle School and Upper School are housed in Ranney's modern and high-tech academic complex. The facility offers thirty-three classrooms; state-of-the-art biology, chemistry, physics, and robotics laboratories; a world language laboratory; a college guidance center; a modern library with digital media center; student assembly areas; 300 computers; and a unique Distance Learning Center. The entire building offers wireless Internet access. In addition, the Middle and Upper Schools have their own dining hall.

ATHLETICS

Ranney School encourages students to participate in sports and views athletics as an important part of the educational program. All students are eligible to participate regardless of ability. Ranney School offers twenty-five varsity-level sport teams, as well as a coed squash club. Ranney School also offers fourteen interscholastic teams on the middle school level, along with four club sports, including winter track, fencing, crew, and golf. Ranney competes against other accredited public and private schools in the area and maintains active membership in the Shore Conference of High Schools, the New Jersey Independent School Athletic Association, and the New Jersey State Interscholastic Athletic Association. Interscholastic competition begins in the sixth grade. The School has two gymnasiums; a newly renovated 25-meter indoor swimming pool; five new tennis courts; a baseball and softball field; and brand-new athletic facilities, including a synthetic turf field and all-weather track. In addition, there is a new fitness center with a certified athletic trainer on duty.

EXTRACURRICULAR OPPORTUNITIES

Ranney Plus is a robust, all inclusive, after-school program that enriches opportunities for students of all ages at the School. Across the divisions, Ranney Plus plays an important role for students. It provides opportunities for students to explore activities that encompass global perspectives in the areas of performing arts, technology, science, math, and athletics, and also allows them to receive teacher-supported assistance with homework, study skills, or preparation for a specific subject assessment or project. Each division offers an array of selections for students to explore after school, such as clubs, specialized student activities, and athletic teams and interscholastic sports. Ranney Plus also provides complimentary after-care programs for students in the Lower and Middle Schools and late bus transportation for students in all divisions, grades 3–12. More information about Ranney Plus, registration forms, and transportation permission slips are available on the School's Web site.

In addition to Ranney Plus, the Lower School offers a variety of extracurricular and after school activities for grades 2 through 5, including computers, art instruction, creative writing, chorus, band, cooking, swimming, and other sports.

Both the Middle and Upper Schools have a broad selection of student organizations in which to participate. Both schools have a student council, world language clubs, and excellent forensics teams. Students in grades 6 through 9 are eligible to join the Science Olympiad Team, which travels to Rider University for participation in the New Jersey State Science Olympiad.

The Upper School has an active chapter of the National Honor Society, seven academic honor societies, and a Cum Laude Society chapter. Students can also participate in Mock Trial, math, chess, and academic bowl teams. Chorus and drama clubs offer students an opportunity to perform for friends, parents, and peers. Publications include *Horizons* (the School's award-winning yearbook), *The Torch, The Beacon* (college guidance magazine), and *RSVP (Ranney School Verse & Prose)*, which showcases the talents of Ranney's young artists and authors.

Throughout the year, the Ranney School Fine Arts Department and Thespian Troupe present art exhibitions, music recitals, and two major drama productions. Traditional events include Spirit Day/Homecoming, International Week, Halloween Parade, Grandparents' Thanksgiving Feast, Parents' Day Tea, and Lower, Middle, and Upper School Carnivals (fund-raisers). Field trips, both interstate and intrastate, offer cultural exposure outside the Ranney campus for students in the middle and upper divisions. International student travel takes place each year, with students immersed in the culture of countries such as England, France, Italy, and Spain.

DAILY LIFE

The typical school day consists of six 45-minute academic periods and one 60-minute period, with a 10-minute break between second and third periods, plus a lunch period. Assemblies are held throughout the year. Each week, grades 6–12 meet with their advisers for approximately 20 minutes during an adviser period. School begins at 8:25 a.m. and ends at 3:25 p.m. The cafeteria serves hot and cold lunches. Bus transportation is available to most students.

SUMMER PROGRAMS

Students can enroll for two through six weeks to take enhancement and/or credit courses in several academic subject areas. Most courses are taught by Ranney School faculty members. In addition, an eight-, six-, or four-week summer day camp program is available for boys and girls ages 3 through 13. Ranney-in-the Summer is fully accredited by the American Camping Association.

COSTS AND FINANCIAL AID

Tuition for 2011–12 ranged from $10,550 to $25,440. Extras include books (Lower School: $150–$550; Middle School: $400–$650; Upper School: $600–$900) and transportation ($4500–$5000). Parents of students in grades pre-K through 12 are required to purchase a $1000 bond, which is redeemed when the child either graduates or leaves Ranney School.

Ranney School is committed to awarding financial aid to those students who demonstrate a financial need. Families who feel that a need for assistance exists are encouraged to apply. The Financial Aid Committee of the Board of Trustees bases financial aid decisions on the formula provided by the School and Student Service for Financial Aid (SSS) in Princeton, New Jersey. The Financial Aid Committee diligently reviews each application in order to distribute available funds equitably. All applications are held in strict confidence. Each student applying for aid must be in good standing in all aspects of student life. Parents must complete the SSS financial aid form annually and should send it to Princeton as early as possible. Inquiries should be directed to the Associate Head for Admissions and Marketing.

Parents can arrange to pay the tuition over a ten-month period through Tuition Management Services. An enrollment deposit must be paid directly to the School upon registration.

ADMISSIONS INFORMATION

Standardized placement tests are administered on an individual or small-group basis. Transferring students should forward a completed application and appropriate school records to the Admission Office prior to the scheduled date of the placement exam. All candidates must complete an interview with appropriate members of the Admission Committee. Ranney School does not discriminate on the basis of sex, race, religion, ethnic origin, or disabilities in the administration of its education, hiring, and admission policies; financial aid program; and athletic or other School-administered programs.

APPLICATION TIMETABLE

Ranney School does not stipulate a formal application deadline, but it strongly recommends that parents contact the Admission Office during the fall to enroll for the next academic year. There is a $75 application fee.

ADMISSIONS CORRESPONDENCE

Joseph M. Tweed, Director of Admissions and Financial Aid
Ranney School
235 Hope Road
Tinton Falls, New Jersey 07724
Phone: 732-542-4777 Ext. 1107
Fax: 732-460-1078
E-mail: jtweed@ranneyschool.org
Web site: http://www.ranneyschool.org

RIDLEY COLLEGE

St. Catharines, Ontario, Canada

Type: Coeducational, college-preparatory, boarding and day school
Grades: Lower School, JK–8; Upper School, 9–12/PG
Enrollment: School total: 636; Upper School, 460; Lower School, 176
Head of School: Jonathan Leigh, Headmaster

THE SCHOOL

Established in 1889, Ridley College was founded by a group of Anglican clergymen intending to provide boys in Ontario with an education that emphasized strong academic and religious values. Named after Bishop Nicholas Ridley, a sixteenth-century churchman in England martyred during the Protestant Reformation, the School was originally known as Bishop Ridley College. Ridley became coeducational in 1973. Ridley's school life philosophy embraces four essential qualities: academics, athletics, citizenship, and faith.

Ridley College is a university preparatory school that offers junior kindergarten through grade 12 with a postgraduate option. The campus is built on 100 acres of land near Lake Ontario, a few minutes from Niagara Falls. It is conveniently located 45 minutes from the Toronto Airport and Buffalo Airport.

Ridley College is accredited to the Canadian Association of Independent Schools (CAIS) and the Canadian Educational Standards Institute (CESI) under the Ridley College Board of Governors. Ridley's endowment is currently $21.9 million. Ridley is a member of the National Association of Boarding Schools (NAIS), Conference of Independent Schools of Ontario (CIS), The Association of Boarding Schools (TABS), Canadian Association of Independent Schools (CAIS) and the Headmasters' and Headmistresses' Conference (HMC).

ACADEMIC PROGRAMS

In September 2012, Ridley College is slated to begin offering the International Baccalaureate Diploma Programme alongside the Ontario Secondary School Diploma. Ridley College offers eighteen Advanced Placement courses. The average class size is 16 students, and the student-teacher ratio is 7:1. During weeknights there is mandatory study time set aside in the houses for boarding students. Evening study is also open to day students who wish to stay. Students have an opportunity to meet with their teachers after school and in the evening for tutorial sessions. Ridley College offers English language development classes and individual learning skills sessions for students with specific learning needs. Students can participate in an exchange program in their tenth-grade year; Ridley students have travelled to Australia, South Africa, Scotland, and Spain on exchange. The school year is divided into three trimesters, known as the Michaelmas, Lent, and Trinity terms. Progress reports are distributed throughout the term, and a final report is given at the end of each term. Teachers, coaches, housemasters, and academic advisers contribute individual comments to the reports.

FACULTY AND ADVISERS

There are 52 full-time and 12 part-time faculty members at Ridley College. Twenty-eight percent of the faculty members have master's degrees. Twenty-two of the faculty members live on campus. Each faculty member at Ridley is an academic adviser to approximately 5 students. Advisers meet with their students on a regular basis and ensure that they are doing well academically, physically, and emotionally. Faculty members also coach sports, coordinate activities and community service, and supervise students in the boarding house several times a month.

Mr. Jonathan Leigh has been headmaster of Ridley College since 2005. He has been involved in independent boarding education for thirty-five years. He was a head of history, housemaster, and Second Master at Cranleigh School in Surrey, UK, and then headmaster of Blundell's School, in Devon, UK, for twelve years. A Fellow of the Royal Society of Arts, Mr. Leigh was educated at Eton and Corpus Christi College, Cambridge, where he held a tenor choral award.

COLLEGE ADMISSION COUNSELING

The Ridley College Guidance Department works to assist students with their academic progression through the School and with gaining entry to college or university. The department maintains a current and comprehensive library of career and educational resources and a Web site of guidance-related links and maintains academic records in compliance with the Ontario Ministry of Education and Training. The department can also provide personal counseling when the need arises and refer students to specialists or agencies if warranted.

Ninety-nine percent of Ridley College students are university-bound. Alumni pursue postsecondary degrees at top Canadian universities, including Dalhousie, McGill, McMaster, Queen's, Toronto, Waterloo, and Western as well as top schools in the United States and Europe including Cambridge, Cornell, Durham, Georgetown, Harvard, Imperial College, London School of Economics, Newcastle, Oxford, Princeton, Spelman, St. Andrew's, Yale, and the Universities of Edinburgh and London.

STUDENT BODY AND CONDUCT

The Upper School is composed of 460 students: 282 boys and 178 girls, 278 boarding students and 182 day students. The Lower School is composed of 176 students: 102 boys and 74 girls, 17 boarding students and 159 day students

There are 193 international students attending Ridley College, representing more than twenty countries, including the Bahamas, Bangladesh, Barbados, Bermuda, the Cayman Islands, China, France, Germany, Hong Kong, Japan, Republic of Korea, Mexico, Nigeria, Russian Federation, Saudi Arabia, Taiwan, the United States, and Venezuela.

Social discipline in the residential setting is based on the demerit system, and accumulations of demerits lead to the imposition of "gatings," during which students are prohibited from leaving the campus and must check-in with the faculty member on duty each half-hour, on the half-hour, when not engaged in classroom work or having meals.

ACADEMIC FACILITIES

The Upper School, or School House, building has a campus co-op store, a computer help desk, a dining hall, and classrooms. The Second Century Building (2CB) houses the science department, art department, and music and drama department. The latter includes several labs and various studio rooms. The Mandeville Theatre, with a capacity of 350 guests, serves as an auditorium for various local public schools and production companies. The Memorial Chapel was built during the 1920s and is dedicated to the memory of Ridley alumni who died in World War I.

The Lower School is located across the campus from the Upper School. The Lower School has a JK/SK class, one class each for grades 1 through 6, and two classes each for grades 7 and 8. The Lower School building also offers a design shop; an art room; a resource centre; and a junior boarding residence for students in grades 5–8

BOARDING AND GENERAL FACILITIES

Ridley has ten boarding houses. A unique feature of the Ridley boarding experience is the fact that all day students have study and storage space within the houses and opportunities for overnight stays when necessary. The residences are home base for the term. Here belongings are kept, pictures put up, and study time is observed. Recreational areas also exist for students. Much emphasis has been put into the public areas where students relax, visit, and socialize with their friends.

Each house has a housemaster living in a family home adjacent to the house as well as an assistant housemaster. A full-duty team of advisers watches over the welfare and personal and academic progress of every student in their care. This team is the main point of contact for parents. North American students typically return to their families during School holidays, and international students who choose not to return to their home countries (or are unable to due to time constraints) are often billeted with Ridley families or go on school trips.

The Schmon Health Centre is dedicated to the promotion of health and the total well-being of the Ridley community. It is located behind Upper School and the Athletic Therapy Clinic is located in the field house. A registered practical nurse and/or a registered nurse are on duty during regular hours of operation. A nurse is available for emergencies during overnight hours. A physician is also on campus four days a week, and is available by phone 24 hours a day for emergencies. The Athletic Therapy Clinic is open Monday through Saturday in the mid-afternoon. The St. Catharines General Hospital is located about 2 kilometres from the campus, should a student require additional medical evaluation and/or treatment.

ATHLETICS

Sport is an integral part of the fabric of the Ridley community. The College believes that physical fitness and active participation are a crucial part of student life. Ridley annually fields more than forty-five competitive teams. The variety of competitive sport offered at Ridley is unparalleled in the independent system, and the annual competitive success rivals that of any comparable-size high school in the country. Ridley College has four program development sports: basketball, ice hockey, rowing, and soccer. Ridley also fields teams for all ages in field hockey, gymnastics, rugby, squash, swimming, tennis, and volleyball, with Upper School teams in cross-country and track and field. Each program has represented the school at the provincial championships in the last decade. While Ridley students do enjoy winning, the athletic program pushes its athletes toward being "triple impact competitors," with a focus on personal mastery of skill, developing leadership and interpersonal skills, and honouring the game that they play. Ridley College's athletic facilities include two gyms, a new arena and field-house built in 2010, a swimming pool, five outdoor tennis courts, three indoor squash courts, a dance studio and fitness/strength training centre, Concept 2 rowing ergometer room, and five natural turf playing fields.

EXTRACURRICULAR OPPORTUNITIES

Ridley College offers a wide range of extracurricular activities including computer club, dance club, debate club, drama club, international club, math club, Model

UN, peer tutoring, photography club, quiz bowl, radio station, running club, school band, ski club, student government, student publications, tour guides, and yearbook.

One of Ridley's most notable traditions is the Snake Dance, a school spirit-building celebration to inaugurate the fall sports season. Other traditions include an annual cross-country run, intramural competition among dormitory residences for the Bradley Shield (girls) and Bermuda Cup (boys) trophies, the Chimes Challenge (a sprinting contest held during the midday chimes of the clock tower), and the annual Prize Day that concludes the school year. Ridley's motto is *Terar dum prosim*—"may I be consumed in service"—and students take this to heart. Ridley students participate in community service on a regular basis and raise money and awareness for their house charities.

DAILY LIFE

Ridley College has a balanced day schedule. From 6:30 to 8 a.m. on Monday, Tuesday, Thursday, Friday and Saturday, students may have practice for one of the four major sports (rowing, ice hockey, basketball, or soccer), music or band practice, fitness class, or community service, depending on their involvement. From 6:15 to 8:15 a.m., breakfast is available in the dining hall. Chapel is held on Monday and Tuesday mornings and Friday afternoons. There is an assembly to share news on Thursday morning. Classes run from 8:45 a.m. to 3:45 p.m. on Monday, Tuesday, Thursday, and Friday. There are two nutrition breaks and a lunch period from 11:30 a.m. to 12:30 p.m. There is also a tutorial period during the day where students can receive academic assistance from their teachers. Sports, community service, and other activities begin at 4 p.m., except on Wednesdays and Saturdays, when they begin at 2:15 and 1 p.m., respectively. On Wednesdays, breakfast begins at 8 a.m., and classes start at 9:30 a.m. and finish at 2:15 p.m. On Saturdays, classes begin at 8:30 and finish at 10 a.m., with community service, sports, or activities taking place until 5:30 p.m. Dinner is served in the dining hall every evening from approximately 5:15 to 7:15 p.m., depending on the day. Evening study is from 7:30 to 9:30 p.m. on weekdays. Sunday is a day to rest and catch up on homework. Sunday afternoons are designated for residential programs or free time.

WEEKEND LIFE

There is a varied and comprehensive weekend program planned for students on campus. All varsity athletes are engaged each weekend in practices or games. The Sport for Life group involves intramural athletics, and also meets for scheduled fitness activities on Saturdays. Most of the fun, supervised weekend activities take place in the afternoon or evening and participation is voluntary. Students are required to sign-in with the faculty member who is on duty in their house on the weekends. Each grade is given a curfew time and places that they are allowed to visit on weekends. There is a movie bus on most weekends that takes students to the local theatre and many students go to restaurants and coffee shops near the campus. Day students are more than welcome to join in activities on campus over the weekend. Junior boarders go on weekend trips with their housemaster and housemates. Past trips have included Canada's Wonderland, go-karting, Sugar Bush, and movies. On long weekend breaks, Duke of Edinburgh trips are offered for those students working towards their Bronze, Silver, or Gold certification. During the November midterm break, a trip to Ottawa and Montreal is offered in order to tour historical Canadian landmarks. In February, a ski trip to Mont Tremblant, Quebec, allows students to experience a true Canadian winter wonderland and to ski at a top-ranked ski resort.

COSTS AND FINANCIAL AID

Tuition is Can$46,250 for seven-day boarding students, Can$34,500 for five-day boarding students, and Can$26,200 for day students. The standard payment plan allows tuition to be paid in four installments; a monthly payment plan is available for families living in Canada or the United States, using preauthorized payments or postdated cheques.

Students in grades 9–12 are required to purchase a laptop equipment bundle (Can$2310 in 2010–11). A technology fee is charged each year for software upgrades and technical support. General expenses include campus store purchases, textbooks, athletic uniforms, dry cleaning and mending, prescriptions, tutoring, theatre tickets, school ski trip, school pictures, courier charges, dances, and September camp. Other estimated fees for Upper School students are Can$3000–$3500 for boarders and Can$2000–$2500 for day students. This amount does not include the laptop bundle, major trips, or some tournament travel for sports teams. Lower School charges are generally less than those noted. Boarding students in grades 5–8 are allocated pocket money each week and parents are billed at the end of each term. Pocket money for boarding students in grades 9–12/PG is not provided.

In the 2010–11 academic year, approximately 225 students (representing over one third of the total school enrollment) received financial assistance. Ridley attempts to meet the needs of all students with academic promise and worthy character through merit-based scholarships, need-based bursaries, and a deferred payment plan. The average merit scholarship was Can$7000.

Merit scholarships are available only to new students seeking entrance to Ridley. These scholarships offer awards up to Can$15,000 annually. Merit scholarships are awarded according to the following criteria: past academic achievement; the score from the SSAT; and the potential to contribute to the Ridley community either through the arts, athletics, community service, or leadership. Scholarship awards are renewed annually during a student's Ridley career, conditional upon maintaining academic honours (80 percent and above) and continuing a positive contribution to school life.

Need-based bursaries are offered to assist with a family's financial contribution to Ridley. These bursaries are based on the family's ability to afford a Ridley education and do not need to be repaid. In order to apply for a bursary, families are required to complete the FACS (Financial Aid for Canadian Students) application. This application requests information on family assets, liabilities, income, expenses, and special circumstances.

Deferred payment or loans are also available to families with demonstrated need.

ADMISSIONS INFORMATION

Ridley College admits students who are well rounded. Admissions officers look for students who are involved in a wide range of activities from music to athletics to community service—students who thrive on being engaged and involved. Ridley no longer requires standardized admissions testing as a part of the application process. Applicants interested in applying for a merit-based scholarship are required to write the SSAT (Secondary School Admission Test). Ridley's SSAT number is 6036. Registration and more SSAT information is available at www.ssat.org/ontario. Ridley reserves the right to require results from standardized admissions testing in certain circumstances, particularly from candidates for whom English is a second language.

Applicants to grade 2 and above are asked to submit their most recent school reports as well as transcripts including grades from the previous two years. All accepted students are asked to submit their final year grades as well.

APPLICATION TIMETABLE

While admission to Ridley is on a rolling basis, the Admissions Office encourages families to begin the process during the fall and spring of the preceding academic year.

A campus visit can be scheduled Monday through Friday between 8:15 a.m. and 3:30 p.m. The Admissions Office is also open for visits on select Saturday mornings throughout the academic year. A campus visit or interview can be scheduled by calling the Admissions Office at 905-684-1889 Ext. 2207 or e-mailing admissions@ridleycollege.com.

The Ridley College application can be completed online at https://apply.ridleycollege.com. The application fee for domestic students is Can$100 and Can$150 for international boarding students. Once an application is complete, a prospective student will typically receive an answer from the Admissions Committee in two to three weeks.

ADMISSIONS CORRESPONDENCE

Dr. Andrew Weller, Director of Admissions
Ridley College
2 Ridley Road
St. Catharines, Ontario L2R7C3
Canada

Phone: 905-684-1889 Ext. 2207
866-603-1889 (toll-free in North America only)
E-mail: admissions@ridleycollege.com
Web site: http://www.ridleycollege.com

RYE COUNTRY DAY SCHOOL

Rye, New York

Type: Coeducational day college-preparatory school
Grades: P–12: Lower School, Prekindergarten–4; Middle School, 5–8; Upper School, 9–12
Enrollment: School total: 887; Upper School: 394
Head of School: Scott A. Nelson, Headmaster

THE SCHOOL

Founded in 1869, Rye Country Day School (RCDS) is entering its 142nd year. Reflecting and reaffirming the School's purposes, the RCDS mission statement states, "Rye Country Day School is a coeducational, college-preparatory school dedicated to providing students from Pre-Kindergarten through Grade Twelve with an excellent education using both traditional and innovative approaches. In a nurturing and supportive environment, we offer a challenging program that stimulates individuals to achieve their maximum potential through academic, athletic, creative, and social endeavors. We are actively committed to diversity. We expect and promote moral responsibility, and strive to develop strength of character within a respectful school community. Our goal is to foster a lifelong passion for learning, understanding, and service in an ever-changing world."

Rye Country Day School acts consciously and deliberately in order to create and sustain an inclusive community. According to the School's diversity mission statement, "At Rye Country Day, we believe that diversity is the existence of human variety. As such, each one of us is diverse in multiple ways and in a variety of contexts. We recognize diversity as including, but not limited to, differences in ability/disability, age, ethnicity, family structures, gender, geographic origin, life experiences, physical appearance, race, religion, sexual orientation, and socioeconomic status. As educators, we are committed to creating and sustaining a school community that is diverse and inclusive, one in which all members can participate fully and maximize their potential. We believe that only an inclusive school community can be equitable and just. We are proactive about teaching our students the importance of diversity and inclusion in an increasingly interconnected, multicultural, and ever-changing world. As we prepare our students for leadership in the world beyond Rye Country Day, we are responsible for teaching them how to communicate with and be respectful of others—beginning with those in our school community and extending to those who live beyond our nation's borders. Every global citizen should be able to thrive in a diverse and interconnected society. Our commitment to inclusion enriches our community with diverse ideas and perspectives. Students grow and flourish in this type of environment, where they can safely explore their individual identity while developing and exercising strength of character, healthy self-esteem, and confidence. Through our commitment to diversity and inclusion, we strive to be good role models for the individuals in our care so that their present and future actions and choices may positively impact the world."

The 26-acre campus is located in Rye at the junction of routes I-95 and I-287, one block from the train station. The School's location, 25 miles from Manhattan, provides easy access to both New York City and to a suburban setting with ample playing fields and open spaces. Through frequent field trips, internships, and community service projects, the School takes considerable advantage of the cultural opportunities in the New York metropolitan area.

A nonprofit, nonsectarian institution, Rye Country Day is governed by a 26-member Board of Trustees that includes parents and alumni. The annual operating budget is $26.5 million, and the physical plant assets have a book value in excess of $54.4 million. Annual gifts from parents, alumni, and friends amount to more than $3.2 million. The endowment of the School is valued at more than $29.1 million.

Rye Country Day School is accredited by the Middle States Association of Colleges and Schools and the New York State Association of Independent Schools and is chartered and registered by the New York State Board of Regents. It is a member of the National Association of Independent Schools, the New York State Association of Independent Schools, the Educational Records Bureau, the College Board, and the National Association for College Admission Counseling.

ACADEMIC PROGRAMS

Leading to the college-preparatory program of the Upper School, the program in the Middle School (grades 5–8) emphasizes the development of skills and the acquisition of information needed for success at the secondary school level by exposing students to a wide range of opportunities. The academic program is fully departmentalized. Spanish or French is offered to all students in grades 2–5. Starting in grade 6 students may choose Latin or Mandarin Chinese or continue with Spanish or French. The math, foreign language, and writing programs lead directly into the Upper School curriculum. Programs in art, music (vocal and instrumental), computer use, and dramatics are offered in all grades. Students in kindergarten through grade 6 are scheduled for sports for 45 to 75 minutes daily, and a full interscholastic sports program is available to both boys and girls in grades 7 and 8, and in the Upper School.

Sixteen courses are required for Upper School graduation, including 4 years of English, 3 years of mathematics, 3 years of one foreign language, 2 years of science, and 2 years of history. Students entering the School by grade 9 must complete ½ unit in art and music survey, and ½ unit in the arts. Seniors must successfully complete an off-campus Senior Term community service program in June. In addition, seniors must satisfactorily complete 1 unit in the senior humanities seminar. Students are expected to carry five academic courses per year.

Full-year courses in English include English 9, 10, and 11; major American writers; English and American literature; and creative and expository writing. Required mathematics courses are algebra I, algebra II, trigonometry, and geometry. Regular course work extends through calculus BC, and tutorials are available for more advanced students. Yearlong courses in science are environmental science, biology, chemistry, and physics. Science courses are laboratory based. The computer department offers beginning and advanced programming, software applications courses, desktop publishing, and independent study opportunities.

The modern language department offers five years of Mandarin Chinese, French, and Spanish, and the classics department teaches five years of Latin. History courses include world civilizations, U.S. history, government, and modern European history. Semester electives in the humanities include philosophy, psychology, government, and economics.

In the arts, full-year courses in studio art, art history, and music theory are available. Participation in the Concert Choir and Wind Ensemble earns students full academic credit. Semester courses in drawing, printmaking, sculpture, graphic design, ceramics, and photography are available. The drama department offers electives in technique, history, oral presentation, technical theater, and dance.

Advanced Placement courses leading to the AP examinations are offered in biology, psychology, environmental science, chemistry, physics, statistics, calculus, English, government, U.S. and modern European history, French, Spanish, Latin, music theory, art, and computer science. Honors sections are scheduled in tenth- and eleventh-grade English, math, physics, biology, and chemistry, and in foreign languages at all levels. Independent study is available in grades 11 and 12 in all disciplines.

The student-teacher ratio is 8:1, and the average class size in the Upper School is 12. Extra help is provided for students as needed.

The year is divided into two semesters. Examinations are given in March. Grades are scaled from A to F and are given four times a year. Written comments accompany grades at the end of each quarter.

Academic classes travel to New York City and other areas to supplement classroom work. Although not a graduation requirement, all students are involved in community service programs. Semester class projects as well as individual experiences involve work with local charities and schools, YMCA, Midnight Run, United Cerebral Palsy, Big Brother-Big Sister, Doctors Without Borders, AmeriCares, and numerous local organizations.

Students in grades 7–12 are required to have laptop computers. The campus supports wireless Internet connection and provides appropriate filters for student and faculty educational use. A technology department supports and updates the network and assists students with software and hardware issues. Students receiving financial aid awards receive new laptop computers from the school which are replaced every three years.

FACULTY AND ADVISERS

The Upper School faculty consists of 65 full-time teachers—35 men and 30 women, the large majority of whom hold at least one advanced degree. The average length of service is eight years, and annual faculty turnover averages fewer than 6 teachers.

Scott A. Nelson became Headmaster in 1993. He holds a B.A. from Brown University and an M.A. from Fordham University. Prior to his appointment at Rye, he served as Upper School Director both at the Marlborough School in Los Angeles and at the Hackley School in Tarrytown, New York. Mr. Nelson and his family reside on campus.

Nearly all faculty members in the Middle and Upper Schools serve as advisers for 5 to 12 students each. In addition to helping students select courses, faculty advisers monitor the students' progress in all areas of school life and provide ongoing support. The advisers also meet with students' parents at various times throughout the year.

Rye Country Day seeks faculty members who are effective teachers in their field and who, by virtue of their sincere interest in the students' overall well-being, will further the broad goals of the School's philosophy. The School supports the continuing education of its faculty through grants and summer sabbaticals totaling more than $380,000 a year.

COLLEGE ADMISSION COUNSELING

The college selection process is supervised by a full-time Director of College Counseling and an Associate Director, and support is provided by an administrative assistant. Advising is done in groups and on an individual basis, with the staff meeting with both students and their families. More than 100 college representatives visit the campus each year.

The 97 graduates of the class of 2011 enrolled in fifty colleges and universities, including Amherst, Barnard, Brown, Chicago, Colgate, Columbia, Cornell, Dartmouth, Duke, Emory, Georgetown, Harvard, Johns Hopkins, Michigan, Northwestern, Notre Dame, Pomona, Princeton, Stanford, Tufts, Vanderbilt, Washington (St. Louis), Wellesley, Wesleyan, Williams, Yale, and the University of Pennsylvania.

STUDENT BODY AND CONDUCT

The Upper School enrollment for 2011–12 totaled 394: 193 boys and 201 girls. There were 102 students in grade 9, 107 in grade 10, 87 in grade 11, and 98 in grade 12. Members of minority groups represented 29 percent of the student body in grades 5–12. Students came from roughly forty different school districts in Westchester and Fairfield counties as well as New York City. Students holding citizenship in eighteen countries were enrolled.

While School regulations are few, the School consciously and directly emphasizes a cooperative, responsible, and healthy community life. The Student Council plays a major role in administering School organizations and activities. Minor disciplinary problems are handled by the Division Principal or Grade Level Dean; more serious matters in the Upper School may be brought before the Disciplinary Committee. There is student representation on the Academic Affairs and other major committees.

ACADEMIC FACILITIES

Academic facilities at Rye Country Day School include the Main Building (1927) and Main Building Addition (2002), with separate areas for kindergarten through grade 4, grades 5 and 6, and grades 7 and 8. The Lower and Middle School divisions have separate art, computer, and science facilities.

The Upper School is housed in the Pinkham Building (1964), which was completely renovated in 2010. The new 14,000-square-foot addition includes a 140-seat auditorium, a college counseling center, faculty offices, classrooms, and three science labs.

There are two libraries on campus—the Lower School Library (2002) and the Klingenstein Library (1984), which serves the Middle and Upper School divisions. The Klingenstein Library contains more than 25,000 volumes with fully automated circulation and collection management technology. Resources include significant periodical and reference materials that are available via direct online services and the Internet, CD-ROM, and substantial videotape collection.

The school has invested in technology infrastructure and classroom SmartBoards in all three divisions. Laptop computers, which are required for all students in grades 7 through 12, are used extensively throughout the curriculum. Access to the RCDS network and Internet is via a campuswide wireless network. In total, there are 650 networked computers on campus.

The performing arts programs are housed in the Dunn Performing Arts Center (1990), which includes a 400-seat theater-auditorium and classroom spaces for vocal music, instrumental music, and a dance studio. There also are five music practice rooms which adjunct faculty use for private music lessons.

ATHLETICS

Rye Country Day's athletic program offers seventy-two interscholastic teams for students in grades 7 through 12. Varsity competition includes boys' and girls' teams in soccer, cross-country, basketball, ice hockey, fencing, squash, tennis, golf, track and field, sailing, and lacrosse, as well as football, field hockey, wrestling, baseball, and softball. Approximately 70 percent of the students participate in at least one team sport.

The physical education department offers classes throughout the year in fitness center training, yoga, boot camp, kickboxing, Zumba, tennis, squash, dance, running, and skating.

Athletic facilities include the LaGrange Field House (1972) with its indoor ice rink/tennis courts; a multipurpose gymnasium which serves as the home for the wrestling and fencing programs; the Nelson Athletic Center (2000), which houses a two-court gymnasium, four squash courts, four locker rooms, and an athletic training facility; and a state-of-the-art fitness center. Between 2007 and 2009, the School installed four artificial turf fields, making it the premier outdoor athletic facility in the area.

EXTRACURRICULAR OPPORTUNITIES

More than fifty extracurricular activities are available. Students can choose vocal music (Concert Choir, Madrigal Singers, and solfeggio classes) and instrumental music (Wind Ensemble, Concert Band, and Jazz Band). Many of these offerings have curricular status. The performance groups give local concerts and occasionally travel to perform at schools and universities here and abroad. In addition, professional instructors offer private instrumental and voice lessons during and after the school day. The drama department presents major productions three times a year. Recent productions have included *The Laramie Project, South Pacific, Dark of the Moon, The Mystery of Edwin Drood, Macbeth, The Pajama Game, The Arabian Nights, Anything Goes, Alice in Wonderland, Urinetown, Museum, Bye Bye Birdie,* and *The Comedy of Errors.*

Student publications include a yearbook, newspaper, literary magazine, graphic arts and photography magazines, and a public affairs journal, each of which is composed using student publications desktop publishing facilities. The School's Web site (http://www.ryecountryday.org) is an ever-changing location for student- and staff-provided information on and perspectives of the School. Students participate in Model Congress programs on campus and at other schools and colleges.

The School's new focus on public purpose goes beyond community service by challenging community members to identify, examine, and research social inequities in order to plan a course of action that is responsive, that is partnership-based, and that utilizes rich and varied methods. Using a service-learning approach, the School encourages students to strengthen their skills and realize their potential to empower others and themselves. Rye Country Day is committed to leveraging its human and educational resources to co-create sustainable solutions to real-world problems. The Schools public purpose mission statement reads: "Since 1869, Rye Country Day School's motto, 'Not for self, but for service,' has been integral to the culture of the School. The Rye Country Day School philosophy states, 'A superior education embraces the concept that to educate is to do more than to teach.' Through service learning, we will provide transformative educational opportunities that prepare our students to be responsible citizens with an ethic of service and empathy for our shared human experience. We believe that meaningful and mutually beneficial partnerships emanate from a curriculum enhanced by community engagement. Rye Country Day School's sustained commitment to making a positive impact on the community and contributing to the common good defines our public purpose."

DAILY LIFE

Beginning each day at 8:05, the Upper School utilizes a six-day schedule cycle. Most courses meet five of the six days, with one or two longer, 70-minute periods per cycle. The day includes an activity/meeting period and two lunch periods as well as seven class periods. Class periods end at 2:50, and team sport practices and games begin at 3:30. Breakfast and lunch may be purchased in the school dining room; seniors may have lunch off campus. Study halls are required for grade 9.

SUMMER PROGRAMS

The Rye Country Day Summer School enrolls approximately 100 students—grades 6 to postgraduate—in remedial, enrichment, and advanced-standing courses. Some courses prepare students for the New York State Regents exams that may be taken at the local public schools. The program is six weeks long and runs on a five-period schedule from 8 a.m. to noon, Monday through Friday. Tuition averages $1300 per course. A brochure is available after April 1 from the Director of the Summer School or on the School's Web site.

In addition to the Summer School, Rye conducts a summer program, ACTION, an academic enrichment program at Rye for gifted and motivated public school students from underserved populations who will be entering grades 7, 8, and 9. ACTION seeks to expand the academic and intellectual horizons of very capable and responsible students through educational challenges both on and off campus. The program promotes confidence and strength of character while helping students to grow academically and develop as leaders.

The ACTION program runs for four weeks in July. It consists of core academic classes including history, math, English, science, and leadership. Students also have the opportunity to express their creative selves through photography, manual art, public speaking, and computer courses, and take various field trips.

COSTS AND FINANCIAL AID

Tuition for grade 9 for 2011–12 was $32,800. Additional charges are made for textbooks, lunches, sports, field trips, and private music lessons, as appropriate.

Tuition aid is available on a need basis. For the 2010–11 academic year, 123 students received a total of more than $3.6 million in aid. All aid applications are processed through the School and Student Service for Financial Aid.

ADMISSIONS INFORMATION

Students are accepted in all grades. In 2011–12, 26 new students enrolled in the ninth grade, 12 in the tenth grade, and 3 in the eleventh grade. Academic readiness is a prerequisite; a diversity of skills and interests, as well as general academic aptitude, is eagerly sought. The School seeks and enrolls students of all backgrounds; a diverse student body is an important part of the School's educational environment.

Required in the admissions process are the results of the Educational Records Bureau's ISEE or the Secondary School Admission Test (SSAT); the student's school record; and school and faculty recommendations. A visit to the campus and an interview are also required.

APPLICATION TIMETABLE

Inquiries are welcome throughout the year. Interviews and tours of the campus begin in late September. To be considered in initial admissions decisions, applicants must fully complete the Application by December 15. All other parts of the Application Folder (transcripts, testing, recommendation forms, interview, etc.) are due by January 15. Candidates whose Application Folders are complete by that date are notified by approximately February 15. Applications received after December 15 are evaluated on a rolling basis.

ADMISSIONS CORRESPONDENCE

Matthew J. M. Suzuki, Director of Admissions
Rye Country Day School
Cedar Street
Rye, New York 10580-2034
Phone: 914-925-4513
Fax: 914-921-2147
E-mail: matt_suzuki@ryecountryday.org
Web site: http://www.ryecountryday.org

ST. ANDREW'S SCHOOL

Barrington, Rhode Island

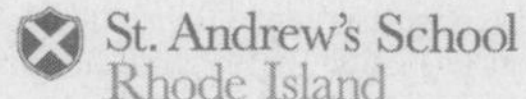

Type: Coeducational boarding and day college-preparatory school
Grades: 3–12: Lower School, 3–5; Middle School, 6–8; Upper School and Boarding, 9–12
Enrollment: School total: 218; Upper School: 173
Head of School: John D. Martin

THE SCHOOL

St. Andrew's School is a coeducational boarding and day school for students in grades 3–12, with the boarding program starting in the ninth grade. The School is located on a 100-acre campus in Barrington (population 16,000), a suburban community 10 miles southeast of Providence on Narragansett Bay. The campus contains open space and woodlands. Its proximity to Providence and Newport, as well as Boston, offers a wide variety of cultural opportunities for students.

St. Andrew's School was founded in 1893 by Rev. William Merrick Chapin as a school for homeless boys. From these simple beginnings through its years as a working farm school to its present role as a coeducational boarding and day college preparatory school, St. Andrew's steadfastly maintains the same sense of purpose and concern for the individual. The curriculum is designed primarily to prepare students for college, with emphasis on helping them to develop stronger academic skills, study habits, and self-esteem.

Every St. Andrew's teacher is trained to teach using a multisensory approach for the different ways students may learn. St. Andrew's students find that when they get to college, they are well prepared to handle the course work because they have a true understanding of how they learn and an awareness of the tools they need to achieve their best.

St. Andrew's School is a nonsectarian, nonprofit corporation. A Board of Trustees governs the School; this 21-member board meets five times a year. The School's physical plant is valued at approximately $25 million. The School's endowment is currently valued at more than $17 million.

St. Andrew's is accredited by the New England Association of Schools and Colleges. It is a member of the National Association of Independent Schools, the Association of Independent Schools in New England, the Association of Boarding Schools, and the Independent Schools Association of Rhode Island.

ACADEMIC PROGRAMS

St. Andrew's School believes that every student can find success in the classroom. With a 5:1 student-teacher ratio, the average class size at St. Andrew's is 10 to 12 students. Small classes, along with twice-daily adviser meetings, help to ensure that no student is overlooked. The homelike community, nurturing environment, and hands-on approach to learning and teaching help maintain close student-teacher relationships.

To graduate from the Upper School, a student must complete 26 credits: 24 academic credits and 2 credits in physical education. Students are expected to take course work in English, math, science, social studies, and physical education each year. Preparation in a foreign language is also highly recommended. Students may only have one study hall in their schedule. Seniors must pass the equivalent of five full-credit courses in order to graduate. Specific minimum requirements for Upper School students are 4 credits in English, 3 credits in social studies (including 1 in U.S. history), 3 credits in mathematics, 3 credits in science (including 2 in a lab science), 2 credits in physical education, 1 credit in art, and 10 elective credits. An English as a Second Language (ESL) Program is provided for international students. The School's computer network, which is available to all students, provides Internet access from all classrooms, dorm rooms, and offices.

The School's Learning Services program (certified by the State of Rhode Island and Providence Plantations) for students who have been identified with language-based learning differences or attentional challenges is taught by certified learning support teachers. All students enrolled in a program receive instruction and support to enable academic success in the School's college-preparatory course of study. An Individual Education Plan is designed and updated annually with input from the student, family, and each teacher. This plan identifies both the skills and support to be provided throughout the year to guide learning success. Individualized programs are available to support the advancement of reading, writing, speech and language, and study skills (e.g., materials management, test preparation, focus and homework strategies, time management, organization, and planning).

The school year runs on a semester basis. Students are evaluated frequently by their teachers so that each student's progress is monitored closely throughout the year. Each advisee meets twice a day with his or her adviser to discuss issues pertaining to the student's academic progress and his or her involvement in the School community. Advisers communicate with families every three weeks by phone or e-mail.

FACULTY AND ADVISERS

The faculty numbers 47, with 20 men and 27 women. Twenty-one reside with their families on campus and seven of them serve as dorm parents. All full-time faculty members serve as advisers. John D. Martin was appointed Head of School on July 1, 1996, and has an extensive background in independent schools, including teaching and administrative positions at Sewickley Academy, Peddie School, and Tabor Academy. He holds a Master of Divinity degree from Yale University, a Master of Education degree from American International College, and a Bachelor of Arts degree from Tufts University.

COLLEGE ADMISSION COUNSELING

All of St. Andrew's graduates enter four-year colleges, two-year colleges, post-graduate programs, or technical schools upon graduation each year. Goal setting, short- and long-term planning, and informal discussions about careers and postsecondary plans are ongoing between students and advisers from the moment a student enters the Upper School. Formal college counseling begins in the eleventh grade. The college counselor works with students and their parents to assist in determining the best steps for each student. The advisers and other faculty members assist the college counselor in assessing each student's options. PSATs are given in the fall of sophomore year and again at the start of junior year. SATs should be taken during the junior and senior years. College representatives visit the campus throughout the year to meet with interested students.

St. Andrew's graduates have matriculated to the following colleges and universities in the last three years: Boston College, Boston University, Bryant, Emmanuel, Emory, George Washington, Iona, Ithaca, Michigan State, Mount Holyoke, New England College, Parsons, Penn State, Providence, Purdue, Ringling College of Art and Design, Rhode Island College, Roger Williams, Savannah College of Art and Design, Seton Hall, Simmons, Syracuse, Tulane, and the Universities of Hawaii, Illinois, Louisville, Maine, Massachusetts, Minnesota, Rhode Island, Vermont, and Wisconsin.

STUDENT BODY AND CONDUCT

The School enrolls both boarding and day students. Approximately one third of the Upper School population boards. Approximately 21 percent of the School's population is enrolled in the Lower and Middle Schools, and less than 40 percent of the School's population participates in the Resource/Focus Programs.

Over the years, St. Andrew's School has attracted boarding students from all corners of the United States and other countries, including Canada, China, France, Germany, Greece, India, Israel, Jamaica, Japan, Montenegro, Senegal, South Korea, and Taiwan.

Each student is required to read the *Parent and Student Handbook,* which defines expectations for students within the community. Difficulties, if they arise, are handled according to degree; minor issues are handled by teachers and dorm parents, while major offenses are handled by the Director of Student Life in conjunction with a joint student-faculty disciplinary committee. Faculty advisers play a major role in working with students to help them understand the expectations of them as members of the community.

ACADEMIC FACILITIES

Stone Academic Center (1988) houses fifteen classrooms, a newly renovated resource wing with five classrooms for instruction, a computer lab, academic offices, and a faculty workroom. It is also the site of a new library, which features study carrels, meeting rooms, and computer workstations. Hardy Hall (1898) was renovated in 2008 and houses the Middle School (6–8) and new Lower School (3–5). The classrooms are designed for interactive learning in groups of 5 to 12 students. The George M. Sage Gymnasium (2001) and the Karl P. Jones Gymnasium (1965) each house a full-size gymnasium and locker room facilities. The Annie Lee Steele Adams Memorial Student Service Center (1997) houses the Health Center, classrooms, and additional office space. The David A. Brown '52 Science Center houses four science labs, two regular classrooms, and the office of the Director of College Counseling. The Norman E. and Dorothy R. McCulloch Center for the Arts (2004) houses a 287-seat theater, two visual art classrooms, a ceramics lab, a music classroom, music practice rooms, a black-box/theater classroom, a computer graphics lab, storage, and theater scene shop.

BOARDING AND GENERAL FACILITIES

Upper School girls live in Cady House (1969) and Coleman House (circa 1795). Upper School boys live in Bill's House (1970) and Perry Hall (1927). Students are assigned to single or double rooms. Each dormitory is supervised by faculty dorm parents, who are aided by the Director of Residential Life and the Director of Student Life. Each dorm has a common room, laundry facilities, access to a kitchen area, and ample storage space. Gardiner Hall (1926) houses the Herbert W. Spink Dining Room and the Headmaster's Dining Room. McVickar Hall (1913) contains the Admissions office, the Headmaster's office, the Development and Communications department, and reception area. Peck Hall (circa 1895) contains the Business office. Clark Hall (1899) houses the Student Center, offering students space for entertainment and relaxation. The second floor provides faculty housing.

Coleman House and the Rectory, the Headmaster's house, are late-eighteenth-century buildings that were acquired by the School from two local estates. Both buildings are said to have been stops for travelers on the Underground Railroad. The Rectory has a hidden back staircase and room.

ATHLETICS

Upper School students participate in athletics at the completion of each class day. St. Andrew's fields varsity teams in boys' and girls' basketball, cross-country, golf, lacrosse, soccer, and tennis. Intramural sports programs are also offered and include fitness training, weight training, yoga, biking, lawn games, and Project Adventure Ropes Course. St. Andrew's also offers an extensive health and fitness center that comprises separate cardio and weight-training facilities.

EXTRACURRICULAR OPPORTUNITIES

The School's proximity to Providence, Newport, and Boston provides a myriad of cultural and recreational activities. Students may take advantage of museums, movies, concerts, plays, rock climbing, skating, bowling, skiing, and professional and collegiate sporting events. Among the on-campus extracurricular activities are theater, photography, debate club, and yearbook. The St. Andrew's Parent Association (SAPA) organizes a wide variety of social activities for students throughout the year, from dances to laser tag to paintball to barbecues.

DAILY LIFE

Boarding students generally rise at about 7 a.m. and are responsible for making their beds, cleaning their rooms, and performing other assorted dorm chores. Breakfast is served at 7:30 and is a favorite gathering time for day and boarding students alike. Students assemble for Morning Meeting at 8 and then meet in their advising groups. Classes begin at 8:30. Adviser meetings are held again at the end of the day. Activities and athletics begin at 3 p.m. and run until approximately 4. Students may leave the campus between athletics and dinner if they are in good standing in the community. Dinner is at 5:30, and evening study hall is from 7:30 to 9:30. All study halls are proctored by faculty members, who are able to provide extra academic assistance if needed. During study hall, the library is open for those students who need to conduct research.

The Student Center is open on weekdays from 11 a.m. to 1 p.m., all day Saturday, and at other times depending on scheduled special activities.

WEEKEND LIFE

Weekend activities are planned by the Director of Student Life and the Coordinator of Weekend Activities, with student and faculty input. Students choose from an array of on- and off-campus activities, including sporting events, concerts, movies, plays, hayrides, open gymnasium, bicycle riding, skiing, attending performances by special guests on campus, dances, skating, festivals and fairs, hiking, and shopping. Visits to nearby cities and other places of interest are also offered. Boarders may leave for the weekend, with parental permission, either to go home or to visit a day student's family. Each weekend, about 75 percent of the boarding community remains on campus.

COSTS AND FINANCIAL AID

Tuition for a boarder in 2011–12 was $44,700; for a day student, it was $29,800. Additional costs for the Resource and Focus Programs are $10,000. The yearly book fee is about $600. Parents of a boarding student should plan to set up an account in the on campus bank for weekly allowance needs. The amount varies from family to family and student to student.

Approximately 48 percent of students received financial aid for the 2011–12 academic year, with more than $2 million offered in grants and loans. Financial aid is based solely on need. St. Andrew's School is affiliated with School and Student Services by NAIS in Randolph, Massachusetts for financial aid and works in conjunction with this organization to provide an objective and fair basis for awarding financial aid. All required information is due to the School by February 10. Final awards are determined by the School's Financial Aid Committee.

ADMISSIONS INFORMATION

In order to assess the match between student and school and to plan an appropriate academic program, the School requires a tour, a personal interview, an application with a fee of $50 ($100 for international students), a school transcript covering the last three years, three teacher recommendations, and standardized test scores. For applicants to the Resource Program, an educational evaluation and a psychological evaluation (both within eighteen months of potential enrollment) and a current Individualized Education Plan (if applicable) are required. A student applying to the Focus Program must establish a history of attention difficulties and supply the School with a medical diagnosis from a physician and appropriate testing results. International students must also submit results from an SLEP or TOEFL evaluation.

APPLICATION TIMETABLE

Parents and prospective students are encouraged to contact the Admissions Office for information during the fall semester. Because the School considers a visit to the campus and a personal interview with the candidate to be such a critical part of the admissions process, it asks that all families call for an appointment. It is best to visit the School during the fall if considering enrollment for the following September, although the School welcomes campus visitors throughout the year.

St. Andrew's School does not discriminate on the basis of race, creed, gender, or handicap in the administration of policies, practices, and procedures.

Applications are due by January 31. Students are notified of acceptance by March 9, and the School holds a place for accepted students until April 10. Depending on available space, rolling admission may be offered thereafter. A nonrefundable deposit of $1000 is due when students agree to attend and is credited toward tuition.

ADMISSIONS CORRESPONDENCE

R. Scott Telford
Director of Admissions
St. Andrew's School
63 Federal Road
Barrington, Rhode Island 02806
Phone: 401-246-1230
Fax: 401-246-0510
E-mail: inquiry@standrews-ri.org
Web site: http://www.standrews-ri.org

ST. MARK'S SCHOOL OF TEXAS

Dallas, Texas

Type: Boys' day college-preparatory school
Grades: 1–12: Lower School, 1–4; Middle School, 5–8; Upper School, 9–12
Enrollment: School total: 851; Upper: 373; Middle: 328; Lower: 150
Head of School: Arnold E. Holtberg, Eugene McDermott Headmaster

THE SCHOOL

St. Mark's is the descendant of three former Dallas boys' schools: Terrill School (1906–1944), Texas Country Day School (1933–1950), and Cathedral School (1944–1950). St. Mark's was organized in 1950 on the Preston Road campus of Texas Country Day School (TCD) when the Cathedral School merged with TCD. The campus is located on 43 acres in the residential area of North Dallas.

St. Mark's college-preparatory program is synchronized to the unique learning styles and maturity rates of boys. Free from traditional gender assumptions, boys are encouraged to discover and develop their intellectual, academic, and artistic interests. Challenging studies in the sciences, arts, and humanities form the basis of a St. Mark's education. Teachers work to instill an enthusiasm for learning, encourage independent and critical judgment, and demonstrate the methods for making sound inquiries and for using effective communication. St. Mark's aims to prepare young men for responsible lives of leadership and service.

St. Mark's Lower School (grades 1–4) is housed in a single building and has approximately 25 faculty members. The program offers diverse learning activities, including academic instruction in Spanish language and culture, language arts, mathematics, science, and social studies; regular instruction in the arts (visual arts, music, creative dramatics); and a developmental physical education program that teaches fundamental skills at a level geared to the age and abilities of the child.

St. Mark's School of Texas is accredited by the Independent Schools Association of the Southwest. Its memberships include the National Association of Independent Schools, the Cum Laude Society, the International Boys' School Coalition, and the College Board.

ACADEMIC PROGRAMS

The academic program in the Upper School is designed to satisfy the most exacting requirements for admission to colleges and universities across the country, but the program is more broadly defined by the School and the faculty as preparation for personal independence, enlightenment, and maturity.

There are required courses, Advanced Placement courses, and many electives available. Graduation requirements are 4 years of English, 3 years of a foreign language, 3 years of mathematics, 4 years of physical education or athletics, 3 years of social studies, 3 years of a laboratory science, 1 year in fine arts, a senior exhibition, and 15 hours of community service each Upper School year. Each student takes five classes per year, and some students, with the permission of the Head of the Upper School, may take more.

The individual teaching sections average about 14 students. In most classes, the students are randomly grouped; the notable exceptions are in honors and Advanced Placement courses.

The School operates on a trimester system. Grade reports are given three times a year and are made available to the parents with written comments. Interim reports are also written to help ensure adequate reporting to the parents. Parents are encouraged to communicate at any time with their son's adviser. Only final grades in Upper School classes are recorded for transcript purposes.

FACULTY AND ADVISERS

For the academic year 2011–12, the nonadministrative faculty consisted of 98 full-time members; 72 hold master's degrees, and 6 have earned doctoral degrees.

The Eugene McDermott Headmaster, Arnold E. Holtberg, graduated cum laude from Princeton University in 1970 with a baccalaureate degree in sociology. He also received a master's degree in pastoral care and counseling in 1976 from the Lutheran Theological Seminary in Philadelphia, Pennsylvania.

The School seeks to employ faculty members who are willing to participate fully in the many areas of school life. The School compensates teachers in the top 10 percent of independent schools nationally and supports fourteen endowed teaching positions.

COLLEGE ADMISSION COUNSELING

The Director of College Counseling and staff members coordinate college planning and counseling. All Upper School students are encouraged to attend the College Previews, held in September, and are welcome to utilize the college office. Several required college conferences are scheduled with students and parents, beginning in the junior year. The SAT mean scores for the class of 2012 were critical reading, 680; math, 715; and writing, 680. The mean ACT scores were 31.

St. Mark's graduates attend major universities throughout the country. Ten or more students in the Classes of 2007–2011 have enrolled at Dartmouth, Duke, Harvard, Northwestern, Princeton, Southern Methodist, Stanford, Vanderbilt, Washington (St. Louis), Yale, and the Universities of Pennsylvania, Southern California, and Texas at Austin.

STUDENT BODY AND CONDUCT

In 2011–12, there were 96 boys in grade 9, 94 in grade 10, 94 in grade 11, and 90 in grade 12. Since St. Mark's is a day school, almost all of the boys come from the Dallas area. Approximately 40 percent of the boys are students of color.

While the rules that govern the School are published by the School, these rules or guidelines provide only a part of the criteria that determine student behavior. Students are also encouraged to take responsibility for their own actions, with the guidance of the faculty and class sponsors. A faculty- and student-led Discipline Council deals with some disciplinary problems.

Each boy has a faculty adviser who is available for personal counseling and advice and is responsible for reporting to the parents and the School on the student's overall performance.

ACADEMIC FACILITIES

Among the campus buildings are Centennial Hall and the Robert K. Hoffman Center, both new facilities for fall 2008; the Green-McDermott Science and Mathematics Center; the Cecil and Ida Green Library; Nearburg Hall; the H. Ben Decherd Center for the Arts; the St. Mark's Chapel;

Thomas O. Hicks Family Athletic Center; Mullen Family Fitness Center; the A. Earl Cullum, Jr., Alumni Commons; and the Athletic Center, which includes the Morris G. Spencer Gymnasium and the Ralph B. Rogers Natatorium.

The Cecil and Ida Green Library houses 56,000 volumes and a state-of-the-art computer laboratory for research and Internet access, which includes online subscription databases. Three professional librarians and a technical assistant staff the library. The School has an integrated campuswide technology network that includes video projection systems in more than 90 percent of the classrooms and numerous labs and access to extensive advanced information systems.

ATHLETICS

Every boy at St. Mark's is required to participate daily in some form of athletics. Upper School boys may select either the physical education program or one of the sports teams.

In physical education, the School is concerned with students' neuromuscular and cardiovascular development, as well as their development of an appreciation of physical fitness, through the specialty classes and intramural program.

The School provides many levels of interscholastic team sports to fit the needs of each student. There are sixteen different sports that are available to Middle and Upper School students, including baseball, basketball, crew, cross-country, cheerleading, fencing, football, golf, lacrosse, soccer, swimming, tennis, track and field, volleyball, water polo, and wrestling. For the 2010–11 school year, St. Mark's was awarded its tenth consecutive Athletic Director's trophy for the best overall boys' athletic program in the Southwest Preparatory Conference.

EXTRACURRICULAR OPPORTUNITIES

Students at St. Mark's are encouraged to do more than excel in their academic subjects. Boys have the opportunity to participate in speech and debate, the Student Council, the mathematics team, the robotics team, the School's yearbook and newspaper, drama activities, the environmental club, the letterman's club, the Cum Laude Society, the Lion and Sword Society, the tutorial program, the astronomy club, the School's literary magazine, and many other activities.

DAILY LIFE

The school day begins at 8 a.m. for all boys and ends at 3:55 p.m. for grades 9–12. Most of the classes, except science and fine arts, last 45 minutes. Sports and extracurricular activities for grades 9–12 are from 4 to 6 p.m.

COSTS AND FINANCIAL AID

In 2011–12, tuition, including textbooks and supplies, lunches, and fees, was $25,186 for grade 9, $23,636 for grades 10 and 11, and $24,399 for grade 12. At the time of enrollment, a deposit of $1000 is due with the signed enrollment contract, and the balance of the tuition is due by July 1 prior to entrance in August.

Financial aid awards are based on need and require annual qualification. Approximately 19 percent of the students receive financial aid. Parents are expected to furnish all of the financial information, as requested by the financial aid committee. Specific details are available from the Office of Admission.

ADMISSIONS INFORMATION

Applicants receive information about the School upon request or at the School's Web site at http://www.smtexas.org. Parents are asked to file an application, obtain a teacher's recommendation, and send a transcript of the applicant's prior work. Applicants take general aptitude, reading comprehension, vocabulary, and mathematics tests. A writing sample and on-campus interviews are also required. The application fee is $50 for grade 1 and $125 for grades 2–12.

APPLICATION TIMETABLE

Inquiries are welcome at any time. Group tours and individual tours are recommended. Applications should be submitted by December for grade 1 and by November for grades 2 through 4. Applications for grades 5 through 12 are due in January. Testing and interviewing are completed in February, and decision letters are mailed in mid-March.

ADMISSIONS CORRESPONDENCE

David Baker
Director of Admission
St. Mark's School of Texas
10600 Preston Road
Dallas, Texas 75230-4047
Phone: 214-346-8700
Fax: 214-346-8701
E-mail: admission@smtexas.org
Web site: http://www.smtexas.org

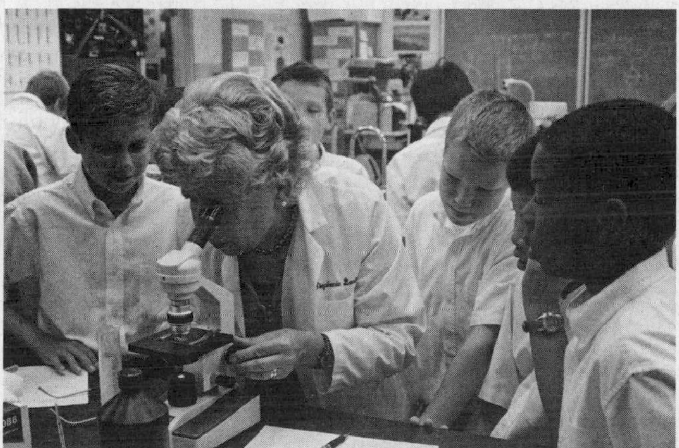

SANDY SPRING FRIENDS SCHOOL

Sandy Spring, Maryland

SANDY SPRING FRIENDS SCHOOL

Type: Coeducational day and five- and seven-day boarding college-preparatory school
Grades: PK –12: Lower School, PK–5; Middle School 6–8; Upper School 9–12
Enrollment: School total: 572; Lower School: 170; Middle School: 139; Upper School: 263
Head of School: Thomas R. Gibian

THE SCHOOL

Sandy Spring Friends School (SSFS) was founded by Brook Moore in 1961 under the care of the Sandy Spring Monthly Meeting of Friends. The School provides a college-preparatory liberal arts curriculum for students of varying ethnic, economic, and religious backgrounds. It is situated on a 140-acre campus that contains woodlands, a pond and stream, walking and biking paths, playing fields, and one of the largest aerial ropes courses in the United States, the Adventure Park of Sandy Spring. Sandy Spring is in Montgomery County and is located approximately 35 minutes from both Washington, D.C., and Baltimore.

As a Quaker school, Sandy Spring Friends School shares the Quaker philosophy for the unique worth of the individual. Intellectual traits along with qualities of sensitivity, inventiveness, persistence, and humor are valued. The School's goal is to help each student develop a sense of personal integrity while growing academically and learning to be a responsible member of the community. The School offers a diverse liberal arts curriculum, with courses ranging from college-preparatory to Advanced Placement courses. Performing and fine arts courses and athletics are an important part of the curriculum.

The 24-member Board of Trustees includes appointments by the Baltimore Yearly Meeting, the Sandy Spring Monthly Meeting, and Sandy Spring Friends School. The 2011–12 budget exceeds $15 million, with a growing endowment program that began in 1989.

The School is accredited by the Association of Independent Maryland Schools and approved by the State of Maryland Department of Education. It is a member of the National Association of Independent Schools, the Association of Independent Maryland Schools, the Association of Independent Schools of Greater Washington, the Association of Boarding Schools, the Friends Council on Education, the Secondary School Admission Test Board, the Education Records Bureau, A Better Chance, the National Association for College Admission Counseling, the Black Student Fund, the Potomac and Chesapeake Association of College Admissions Counselors, and the College Board.

ACADEMIC PROGRAMS

The curriculum at Sandy Spring Friends School is intended to prepare students for college as well as for being valuable citizens of the world. It focuses on Quaker values, academic excellence, and personal growth in an environment that values personal responsibility. The school year, from early September to early June, includes Thanksgiving, winter, and spring vacations. A typical daily schedule includes six academic periods, jobs, lunch, an electives period, and sports. The school day is from 8 to 3:20, with sports and activities after school. Boarding students are required to attend dinner at 6 and study hall from 7:30 to 9:30 p.m. The average class size is 14, with a faculty-student ratio of 1:8.

Meeting for Worship is required once a month for Lower School children and once a week for Middle and Upper School students.

The required academic load for an Upper School student is six courses. To graduate, students must earn 24 credits, including English, 4; foreign language, 3; history, 3 (including United States history); mathematics, 3; science, 3; fine arts, 3; and electives, 3. Additional requirements are participating in a physical activity two times per year, passing a semester course on Quakerism, and community service. Advanced Placement courses are available in English, Spanish, French, history, math, art, and science. The ESL program is open to students in grades 9–12; currently, 61 students are enrolled.

Intersession week in March gives Upper School students an opportunity to participate in off-campus activities that supplement the standard curriculum. Projects have included trips to countries such as Belize, Brazil, France, Greece, Italy, Korea, Senegal, and Turkey after intensive study; community service projects in Georgia, Maryland, New York, North Carolina, Tennessee, Virginia, and Washington, D.C.; intensive arts workshops in modern dance, improvisational theater, spinning and weaving, and other arts; and numerous opportunities for outdoor exploration by foot, bike, and boat.

The Upper School operates on a semester schedule, and the grading systems vary by division according to the developmental needs of the students in the age group. The Lower School works within the framework of parent and teacher conferences with extensive comments; the Middle and Upper Schools use letter grades, with additional comments and parent-teacher conferences.

FACULTY AND ADVISERS

There are 69 full-time and 7 part-time teachers and administrators who teach. Seventeen live on campus, 6 with their families. Twenty-eight faculty members hold advanced degrees.

Tom Gibian, the seventh Head of School, came to Sandy Spring Friends School in July, 2010 after ten years as CEO, managing director, and founding partner of Emerging Capital Partners, the largest fund manager working across the African continent. Prior to returning to the Washington D.C. area, he was Executive Director in the Asia-Pacific region of Goldman Sachs (Asia) Limited from 1992 to 1995, having joined Goldman Sachs in 1987 as vice president. Throughout his career, he has focused on staying true to his Quaker values and using them in the business world. He has served on both the Sandy Spring Friends School and the Sidwell School Boards, and has dedicated his volunteer efforts to the governance of Quaker schools.

Mr. Gibian grew up in Sandy Spring, Maryland, and is a member of Sandy Spring Monthly Meeting. He received a bachelor's degree with honors from the College of Wooster in Ohio, and an M.B.A. in finance from the University of Pennsylvania's Wharton School of Business. As a college senior, his independent study project at College of Wooster was entitled "Dissent and Experimentation in American Schools, 1900–1960." He taught at Wooster High School and received a secondary school teaching certificate. After college he was a community organizer and, later, an administrator in a local anti-poverty agency.

Sandy Spring faculty members share a variety of nonacademic duties, including supervising student activities, proctoring the dorms, and advising students. The School encourages and supports faculty members in the pursuit of educational interests by providing funding and by supporting a professional development committee of the School.

Middle and Upper School students have a strong adviser-advisee relationship that is based on developing a mutual trust and respect. It provides parents with a personal contact when they have questions or concerns about their child's progress.

COLLEGE ADMISSION COUNSELING

Active college planning begins in the junior year with individual meetings with the College Guidance Director to discuss the general admissions process and to identify colleges of interest. Parents and students attend College Night Programs that include information regarding common admission and application for financial aid procedures. Also, many college representatives make personal visits to the School each year. The School's goal is to match the student with the right school.

One hundred percent of the students in the class of 2011 were accepted to college. They are attending institutions such as American, Bowdoin, Boston Conservatory, College of Wooster, Dartmouth, Dickinson, Earlham, Emerson, Georgia Tech, Haverford, Johns Hopkins, Penn State, St. Mary's (Maryland), Tufts, Xavier, and the Universities of Delaware, Maryland, Pittsburgh, Vermont, Virginia, and Washington.

STUDENT BODY AND CONDUCT

In 2011–12, the Upper School enrolled 263 students, 129 boys and 134 girls, as follows: 56 in grade 9, 59 in grade 10, 76 in grade 11, and 72 in grade 12. The boarding program enrolled 61 students from the mid-Atlantic region and eight countries. Nine percent are members of the Religious Society of Friends, and 40 percent are students of color. International students represent 17 percent of the Upper School student body.

The Torch Committee, the student government organization, includes day and boarding students as well as faculty and administration representatives. The committee, operating by consensus, considers student concerns and makes recommendations to faculty committees and to the administration. A student member of Torch is invited to attend faculty and business meetings and meetings of the Board of Trustees.

ACADEMIC FACILITIES

The School's physical plant, which is valued at more than $41 million, includes a science center; a Lower School building and a Middle School building; a dormitory and dining hall; three major classroom buildings and an administration building; a performing arts center with a fine arts wing; an athletic complex; and Yarnall Hall, a $1.75-million resource center that houses a 20,000-volume library, a gymnasium, and an observatory. Computers are integrated into many aspects of the curriculum. Every division of the School is equipped with its own computer lab, and every classroom includes at least one computer and is wired for network and Internet access. The School's library includes computers for online research through the public library system, subscription to online reference tools, and the Internet. A fiber-optic backbone connects the network, and a T1 line connects the Internet and e-mail accounts to students and faculty members. All faculty members and students use Moodle (a course management software).

BOARDING AND GENERAL FACILITIES

All of the boarding students live with their roommates in one 2-story dormitory. Boys and girls each have a separate floor. Community life for boarders includes regular dorm meetings (with decisions reached by consensus), committee-style sponsored activities, family-style dinners with resident staff members, and visits to the homes of day student friends. The dorm staff members (6 adults for 61 boarders in 2010–11) all reside in either apartments or town houses located near the Westview dormitory.

The School nurse assists with the appropriate care for students who may become ill. The School's infirmary is open all day for the entire school year.

ATHLETICS

Sandy Spring Friends School is a member of the Potomac Valley Athletic Conference. The Middle and Upper School teams compete in the following interscholastic sports: baseball, basketball, cross-country, golf, lacrosse, soccer, softball, tennis, track and field, and volleyball. Other activities include weight lifting and outdoor exploration.

The athletic facilities include a complex with a 9,000-square-foot gymnasium, a fully equipped fitness center, and state-of-the-art training and locker room facilities. The 140-acre campus includes four soccer and lacrosse fields, baseball and softball fields, and a 5-kilometer cross-country course. A new 40-foot by 50-foot teaching climbing wall was added in 2011.

EXTRACURRICULAR OPPORTUNITIES

Getting involved is made easy at Sandy Spring Friends by a weekly activities period that allows students to participate in clubs such as Amnesty International (now in its tenth year at SSFS), the Multicultural Club, the International Student Club, the Open Door Club, the ski club (eight weeks of Friday-night skiing plus other trips), the chess club, and the outdoor exploration club. The yearbook and the award-winning literary magazine are also popular activities for students.

The Community Service Program at Sandy Spring Friends School seeks to respond to the needs of others and enrich the School community and the lives of its members. Every student at the School completes 100 community service hours as a requirement for graduation. The service programs are diverse and allow for individual interests to be pursued.

DAILY LIFE

Breakfast for the boarding community begins at 7. Classes begin at 8 and end at 3:20. Advisory and tutorial periods occur once a week, Meeting for Worship occurs once each week, and a "jobs" period is scheduled daily for dorm students. Lunch is served cafeteria-style daily.

Athletics take place between 3:30 and 5:30, and dinner is served family-style at 6. Dorm meetings or activity groups frequently meet before the study hours, which begin nightly at 7:30, Sunday through Thursday.

WEEKEND LIFE

Weekends at the School are relaxed. Activities, which are frequently designed by both students and faculty members, have included adventures such as day trips into Washington, D.C., for a museum visit, a march on the Mall, lunch at Planet Hollywood and a show at the Kennedy Center, or shopping in Georgetown. In addition, the students have visited Baltimore's Inner Harbor, Harper's Ferry, and various hot spots around the School. While boarding students are not required to stay at the School on weekends, all students can choose the weekend activities in which they wish to participate (day students and five-day boarders are charged an appropriate fee for the off-campus activities). One third of the weekends during the school year include on-campus activities such as School dances; student performances in theater, music, and modern dance; art shows; and special concerts and symposiums in the areas of science and the arts.

COSTS AND FINANCIAL AID

In 2011–12, tuition ranged from $19,900 to $22,400 in the Lower School, $24,800 in the Middle School, and $27,500 in the Upper School. Boarding tuition was $40,000 for five days and $50,700 for seven days. A hot lunch is provided beginning in the first grade. Additional costs include an incidental account for the School store, student allowances, laboratory fees, and art supplies.

Sandy Spring Friends School offers financial aid on the basis of need. The financial aid decisions for applications submitted by January 15 are made by mid-March for the following year. Thirty-three percent of the students received financial aid for the 2011–12 school year. The average award was $30,250 for boarders and $14,750 for day students in the Upper School.

ADMISSIONS INFORMATION

Sandy Spring Friends School actively seeks a diverse, curious, and enthusiastic community of students. The student body is diverse in race, creed, and economic and social background. The admissions process allows prospective students and their families to become familiar with as many aspects of the School as possible. New students enter at all grade levels as space permits.

APPLICATION TIMETABLE

Inquiries are welcome at any time. The Admissions Office is open from 8 a.m. to 4:30 p.m., Monday through Friday. Application forms are due by January 15. The application process must be completed by February 1 to ensure first-round consideration. Applications received after January 15 are reviewed as space permits.

ADMISSIONS CORRESPONDENCE

Yasmin McGinnis, Director of Enrollment Management
Sandy Spring Friends School
16923 Norwood Road
Sandy Spring, Maryland 20860-1199
Phone: 301-774-7455 Ext. 182
Fax: 301-924-1115
E-mail: admissions@ssfs.org
Web site: http://www.ssfs.org

SEISEN INTERNATIONAL SCHOOL

Tokyo, Japan

Type: Girls' Catholic college-preparatory day school with a coeducational Montessori Kindergarten
Grades: K–12: Montessori Kindergarten; Elementary School, 1–6; Middle School, 7–8; High School, 9–12
Enrollment: School total: 640; High School: 158
Head of School: Sr. Concesa Martin, School Head

THE SCHOOL

Seisen International School began in 1949 as a kindergarten with only 4 American children. When the School moved to Gotanda in 1962, it enrolled 70 students and started a first-grade program as well. By 1970, the School included nine grades; in 1973, when Seisen moved to its present location, its curriculum was extended to grade 12. The School has an enrollment of over 600 students representing more than fifty nationalities.

Seisen is operated by the Handmaids of the Sacred Heart of Jesus under the auspices of the Seisen Jogakuin Educational Foundation. The order was founded in 1877 by St. Raphaela Maria Porras to dedicate its efforts to educational activities. As a Catholic school with a Christian atmosphere in which students of all races, nationalities, and creeds can thrive, Seisen has high expectations for the students' character development, particularly in respect, compassion, and international understanding.

Seisen offers a Montessori kindergarten, which is designed to take full advantage of young children's self-motivation and their sensitivity to their environment. In this program, the teacher observes each child's interests and needs and offers the stimulation and guidance that will enable him or her to experience the excitement of learning by choice. The Montessori equipment helps in the development of concentration, coordination, good working habits, and basic skills according to each child's capacities and in a noncompetitive atmosphere.

Seisen's Elementary School strives to create a Christian environment that welcomes and respects children of all nationalities and faiths. Seisen, an authorized International Baccalaureate (I.B.) Primary Years Programme (PYP) school, follows the PYP model in elementary school, grades 1–6. The PYP is a transdisciplinary program of international education designed to foster the development of the whole child, touching hearts and minds, and encourage students to be inquirers and critical thinkers.

In addition to academics, PYP encompasses social, physical, emotional, and cultural aspects of learning. PYP strives to give children a strong foundation in all the major areas of knowledge: social studies, science, language, the arts, math, and personal, social, and physical education. The heart of the PYP program is grounded in the use of inquiry to foster knowledge and skills. Teachers and students work together in a PYP classroom to create an environment that encourages the inquiry process. The goal is to enable students to gain essential knowledge and skills and to engage in responsible action.

The High School program prepares young women to face the challenges of a global society with excellent academic preparation, a strong program of athletics, advanced preparation in the visual and performing arts, and an emphasis on community service. From the time the I.B. Diploma Programme was adopted at Seisen in 1988, Seisen students have consistently scored higher than the worldwide I.B. mean each year.

Seisen is accredited by the New England Association of Schools and Colleges, the Council of International Schools, and the Japanese Ministry of Education. The School is also a member of the Japan Council of Overseas Schools, the Kanto Plain Association of Secondary School Principals, and the East Asia Regional Council of Overseas Schools.

The School is located in Tokyo's largest residential area, Setagaya-ku. It is easily accessible from downtown Tokyo and surrounding cities by public transportation. Seisen also operates ten school buses, which cover different routes throughout Tokyo.

ACADEMIC PROGRAMS

Seisen requires that students earn 22 credits in grades 9 through 12. Graduation requirements are as follows: English, 4 credits; social sciences, 4 credits; mathematics, 3 credits; science, 3 credits; foreign language, 3 credits; religion, 2 credits; physical education, 1 credit; and academic electives, 2 credits. Academic electives in high school include art, music, math, history, foreign language, and an introduction to Montessori teachings. Other electives are yearbook, journalism, survival Japanese, computer graphics, choir, drama, 2-D art, and pottery. In grades 9 and 10, students are required to take a performing/visual arts block, drama, music, pottery, or 2-D art. The Personal Social Health Education course is also a requirement at the ninth and tenth grade levels. Special instruction in English as an additional language is available.

Class size varies according to subject. The grading system uses letter grades (A to F) for all subjects. Reports are sent to parents at the end of each quarter.

Students are grouped heterogeneously, except in mathematics, in which there are regular, honors, and accelerated groups. The average course load is five or six classes in academic subjects and one elective. The library is open during the school day and before and after school.

To fully serve the needs of a university-bound, international student body, Seisen offers a program of studies in grades 11 and 12 that can culminate in either a full International Baccalaureate diploma or certificates in individual subjects. These attainments are recognized for admission by over 2,000 universities in more than seventy countries, including many American colleges that accept the I.B. for advanced standing. The I.B. diploma is considered equivalent to most European university entrance requirements. Seisen offers the following I.B. subjects: English A1 higher level (HL) and standard level (SL), Japanese A2 HL and SL, Japanese B HL, Japanese ab initio SL, French B HL and SL, Spanish B HL and SL, biology HL and SL, chemistry HL and SL, physics HL and SL, mathematics HL and SL, math studies SL, arts/design HL and SL, music HL and SL, business and management HL, history HL and SL, psychology HL and SL, and Theory of Knowledge.

The following are administered in the School: PSAT/NMSQT, SAT and SAT Subject Tests, selected IGCSE, the Iowa Test of Basic Skills, and the Iowa Test of Educational Development.

FACULTY AND ADVISERS

The faculty consists of 68 full-time members, of whom 51 are women. Approximately 55 percent of the faculty members hold a master's degree or higher.

The administration and faculty members endeavor to educate the students in academic areas and to foster their spiritual and emotional growth. Teachers are involved in counseling and advising students. The personal counselor helps students with life strategies, and teachers assist through the homeroom and teacher-adviser system.

COLLEGE ADMISSION COUNSELING

The college adviser helps students in college selection and career orientation. Many college representatives visit the School each year, and some Seisen graduates return to give juniors and seniors information about various colleges.

During the junior year, all students take the PSAT and SAT. The SAT middle 50 percent range of scores for last year's graduates was 440–530 for verbal, 470–580 for mathematics, and 470–550 for writing.

All Seisen graduates move on to higher education. A representative list of schools in which Seisen graduates have been matriculated in the past three years includes Universiteit van Amsterdam (Netherlands); Art Institute of Chicago; Ateneo de Manila University (Philippines); Barnard; University of Bath (UK); University of Birmingham (UK); Blanche McDonald Center (Canada); Arts University College Bournemouth (UK); University of British Columbia (Canada); California, San Diego; Central St. Martins College of Art and Design (UK); Chelsea College of Art and Design (UK); Copenhagen Business School (Denmark); Denison; University of Durham (UK); University of Exeter (UK); Fordham; Georgetown; George Washington; International Christian University (Japan); Kingston University (UK); Kutztown; Loughborough University (UK); Loyola Marymount; Manhattanville; University of Melbourne (Australia); McGill University (Canada); Miami (Florida); Miriam College (Philippines); University of Montpelier (France); Nagoya University (Japan); NYU; Northeastern; Osaka University (Japan), Oxford Brookes University (UK); Pacific Lutheran; Penn State; Pepperdine; Princeton; Reed; San Francisco; Sophia University (Japan); USC; SUNY College at Postdam; University of Sussex (UK); Temple University (Japan); University of Toronto (Canada); University of Toronto Scarborough (Canada); Virginia; University of Warwick (UK); Waseda University (Japan); and Washington (Seattle).

STUDENT BODY AND CONDUCT

The 2011–12 student body included 42 in the ninth grade, 41 in the tenth, 34 in the eleventh, and 41 in the twelfth. The largest percentages of students are from the United States, Korea, the United Kingdom, India, and Japan, but nationalities from all over the world are represented.

ACADEMIC FACILITIES

In addition to classrooms, the School has a chapel, three science laboratories, a computer center, a music room, two art rooms, a media center, a gymnasium, two tennis courts, playgrounds, and a cafeteria.

The School's libraries have a collection of more than 25,000 volumes of books and subscribe to sixty periodicals and two newspapers. The High School library houses a multimedia center, two color printers, ten computer workstations, and twenty laptops. Students are able to access the library homepage as well as various online references and databases from outside the School.

ATHLETICS

In addition to the physical education program, Seisen offers badminton, basketball, cross-country, futsal, soccer, swimming, tennis, track and field, and volleyball. Basketball, tennis, and volleyball are offered at varsity and junior varsity levels.

EXTRACURRICULAR OPPORTUNITIES

As a member of the Kanto Plain Association of Secondary School Principals, Seisen is active in various competitions (debate, speech, Brain Bowl, Math Field Day). There are vocal and instrumental groups and a drama club. Other organizations and activities include the National Honor Society, the Student Council, student publications, Alleluia Club, Bell Choir, Booster Club, Model United Nations (MUN), social service groups, and the Girls' Athletic Association (GAA).

Seisen After School Activities (SASA), which are offered to elementary school students, include sports, art, computer graphics, music, dance, cooking, sewing, science, and language classes.

DAILY LIFE

Students have eight 40-minute classes, which include study halls and activity periods. The School cafeteria serves hot lunches, but students may choose to bring their own lunch from home. Classes begin at 8:20 a.m. and end at 3:20 p.m. There are no Saturday classes. Students are encouraged to participate in competitive sports and other activities after school.

SUMMER PROGRAMS

A three-week program of remedial studies is offered in June. Enrichment programs and sports are offered on a limited basis.

COSTS AND FINANCIAL AID

School fees are quoted in Japanese yen. For the 2011–12 school year, the High School tuition was 1.94 million yen. Transportation and lunches are available for additional costs. A registration fee of 300,000 yen and a land and building development fee of 400,000 yen are payable when a student registers.

ADMISSIONS INFORMATION

Seisen International School serves the needs of diplomatic, business, and professional families of the international community. It also provides education for Japanese children who have lived abroad and wish to continue their education in English.

A completed application form and Confidential Counselor Recommendation, transcripts from the school(s) previously attended, and payment of the application fee are required of all applicants in the initial process of admission. An interview with the principal or the School Head of Seisen International School and an entrance examination are required in the final phase of the admission process.

APPLICATION TIMETABLE

Applications are welcome at any time. Parents and prospective students are encouraged to visit the School.

ADMISSIONS CORRESPONDENCE

Sr. Concesa Martin, School Head
Seisen International School
12-15, Yoga 1-chome
Setagaya-ku
Tokyo
Japan 158-0097
Phone: 81-3-3704-2661
Fax: 81-3-3701-1033
E-mail: sisadmissions@seisen.com
Web site: http://www.seisen.com

SOUNDVIEW PREPARATORY SCHOOL

Yorktown Heights, New York

Type: Coeducational day college-preparatory school
Grades: Middle School, 6–8; Upper School, 9–12
Enrollment: Total, 70; Middle School, 13; Upper School, 57
Head of School: W. Glyn Hearn, Headmaster

THE SCHOOL

Soundview Preparatory School, a coeducational, college-preparatory school for grades 6 through 12, was founded in 1989 on the belief that the best environment for students is one where classes are small, teachers know the learning style and interests of each student, and an atmosphere of mutual trust prevails. At Soundview, students and teachers work in close collaboration in classes with an average size of 7 students.

The School's mission is to provide a college-preparatory education in a supportive and non-competitive environment that requires rigorous application to academics, instills respect for ethical values, and fosters self-confidence by helping each student feel recognized and valued. Soundview empowers students to develop their potential and reach their own goals in a setting that promotes respect for others and a sense of community.

Soundview Prep opened its doors with 13 students in the spring of 1989. In the spring of 1998, having outgrown its original quarters in Pocantico Hills, New York, the School moved to a larger facility in Mount Kisco, New York. On January 14, 2008, Soundview moved to its first permanent home, a 13.8-acre campus in Yorktown Heights, New York. New York City, only an hour away, provides a wealth of cultural opportunities for Soundview students to explore on class trips.

The School is governed by a 10-member Board of Trustees. The current operating budget is $2.46 million. In 2010–11, Soundview raised a gross total amount of $185,838 through the Annual Fund and fund-raising events, and from parents, alumni families, grandparents, friends, foundations, and corporations.

Soundview is chartered by the New York State Board of Regents and is accredited by the New York State Association of Independent Schools. The School is a member of the National Association of Independent Schools, the Education Records Bureau, and the Council for Advancement and Support of Education.

ACADEMIC PROGRAMS

Soundview provides a rigorous academic program to ensure that students not only develop the skills and acquire the knowledge needed for college work but also have the opportunity to pursue their own personal goals.

The academic day is carefully structured but informal, with nurture a crucial ingredient. Soundview's student-teacher ratio of 5:1 guarantees that students are monitored closely and receive the support they need. At the same time, the School provides advanced courses for students who wish to go beyond the high school level or take a subject that is not usually offered, allowing students to soar academically and truly develop their potential.

The Middle School curriculum is designed to establish a foundation of knowledge and skills in each academic discipline, strong comprehension and communication skills, good work habits and study skills, confidence in using technology, and creativity in the arts.

The Upper School curriculum provides a traditional college-preparatory education in academics and the arts. In addition to the core subjects—English, history, math, and science—Soundview offers four languages (Latin, French, Spanish, and Italian), studio art, and electives such as history of philosophy, drama, forensics, psychology, creative writing, journalism, environmental science, and a three-year individual science research project.

AP courses are made available according to students' abilities and interests. Recently, AP courses have been offered in calculus, biology, physics, U.S. history, European history, government, art, French, and Spanish.

Academic requirements for graduation are 4 years each of English and history, 3 years each of math and science, 3 years of one foreign language or 2 years each of two different languages, 1 year of art, and ½ year of health.

Computer technology at Soundview is integrated into the curriculum. Teachers post assignments on the School's Web site, and students upload completed work into teachers' folders. The School is wired for wireless technology and has a well-equipped computer lab.

The School's annual two-week trips abroad (to Argentina, Russia, China, England, and Italy over the last few years) offer students experience with other cultures.

The school year is divided into two semesters, with letter grades sent out at the end of each. Individual conferences with parents, students, faculty members, and the Headmaster are arranged throughout the year.

Students take the Educational Records Bureau (ERB) standardized tests every year for use by the School in monitoring each student's progress.

FACULTY AND ADVISERS

The faculty consists of 16 teachers (12 women and 4 men); the majority hold advanced degrees. Three teachers are part-time; the rest, full-time. Turnover is low, with an average of one or two replacements per year.

Each teacher serves as adviser to up to 5 students. Most faculty members supervise a club or publication or coach an athletic team.

W. Glyn Hearn has served as Headmaster since the School was founded in 1989. He obtained his B.A. in English at the University of Texas at Austin and his M.A. in American literature at Texas Tech University. He spent twelve years at the Awty International School of Houston, Texas, where he served as Principal of the Lower, Middle, and Upper Schools and Head of the American Section, before becoming Assistant Headmaster and then Headmaster of the American Renaissance School in Westchester County in 1987.

COLLEGE ADMISSION COUNSELING

College placement at Soundview is directed by Carol Gill, president of Carol Gill Associates and one of the nation's leading college counseling experts. The process starts early on, when eighth, ninth, and tenth graders plan and refine a course sequence that is appropriate for a competitive college. In the junior year, students and their parents begin meeting with Ms. Gill to discuss the college application process, develop lists of colleges, and plan college visits. The meetings continue through the senior year to complete applications. Representatives from approximately twenty colleges visit Soundview every year to speak with students.

Because of the School's small size, the faculty and staff members know each student well and are able to assist students in selecting colleges that are the right match for them. The Headmaster writes a personal recommendation for each senior.

College acceptances in recent years include Allegheny, Bard, Barnard, Bates, Brandeis, Brown, Carnegie Mellon, Clark, Columbia, Dickinson, Drew, Duke, Franklin & Marshall, Gettysburg, Hampshire, Hartwick, Hobart and William Smith, Manhattanville, Maryland Institute College of Art, Muhlenberg, Northeastern, NYU, Oberlin, Reed, Rensselaer, Rhode Island School of Design, Roger Williams, Sarah Lawrence, SUNY, Susquehanna, Vassar, Williams, and the Universities of Maine and Vermont.

STUDENT BODY AND CONDUCT

Soundview reflects the diversity—ethnic, religious, and economic—of American society. The 34 boys and 38 girls come from Westchester, Fairfield, and Rockland Counties and New York City. Approximately 11 percent of the student body are members of minority groups.

Respect for ethical values such as kindness, honesty, and respect for others are paramount at Soundview, where individual responsibility and a sense of community are stressed.

The School's disciplinary structure is informal, since it is based on the assumption that students attending the School desire to be there and are therefore willing to adhere to a code of conduct that demonstrates awareness that the community is based upon a shared sense of purpose and commitment. Despite the cordiality of its atmosphere, Soundview has high expectations of personal conduct. The result of this policy is a remarkably cooperative, considerate group of students who value each other and who appreciate their teachers.

Attire appropriate for a school is expected of all students, although there is no formal dress code.

ACADEMIC FACILITIES

Soundview's campus consists of 13.8 rustic acres with a historic main house, numerous outbuildings, a large pond, meadows, and woods, all in the heart of the village of Yorktown Heights, New York. The main house, the former Underhill mansion built by Yorktown's leading family in the nineteenth century, contains classrooms, administrative offices, the computer lab, and meeting rooms. A large barn houses the science lab, art studios, additional classrooms, and a cafeteria-meeting hall, while a third building is home to the Middle School. A fourth building provides another large meeting space, while a small former chapel is used seasonally for drama rehearsals. Woodland paths and footbridges lead across streams and around the property.

ATHLETICS

Physical education and sports at Soundview offer students the opportunity to develop leadership and teamwork skills as well as to excel in individual sports. Students participate on coed soccer, coed basketball, girls' basketball, and Ultimate Frisbee teams that compete against other independent schools in the Hudson Valley region. Depending upon student interest in a given year, other sports, such as tennis, softball, and baseball are also offered. Any student who wishes to play is accepted, regardless of ability.

The Ski and Snowboard Club offers opportunities for noncompetitive sports. For physical education, students play intramural sports, work out on exercise equipment, and participate in the Outdoors Club, clearing trails and planting gardens on school property.

Soundview's home gym is the Solaris Sports Club in Yorktown Heights, a state-of-the-art multisport center just blocks from the School. The facility includes tennis courts, a large indoor basketball court, and exercise equipment.

EXTRACURRICULAR OPPORTUNITIES

Soundview offers a wide range of clubs and activities, with additional choices added each year by students themselves.

Drama is important at Soundview. Students perform at School functions, attend plays on Broadway, and meet backstage with theater professionals. The School sponsors activities to expose students to other cultures, such as trips to art exhibitions, dance performances, concerts, and plays. The Community Service Club works on such projects as collecting food for local food banks and toys for the children of women incarcerated at a nearby correctional facility.

Other activities students are likely to sign up for include yearbook, literary magazine, student newspaper, mock trials, Outdoors Club, Chess Club, Politics Club, Art Club, Music Club and New York! New York (that explores New York's architectural and historical sites on foot).

Major annual functions at Soundview include the Back-to-School Picnic; the Spring Gala, a dinner and fund-raiser for the Soundview community; the Talent Show, which involves every student in the School; Texas Day, a lighthearted event featuring a barbecue, games, and spoofs on the Headmaster's home state; and the Graduation Dinner, an evening for Soundview parents to honor the graduating class.

DAILY LIFE

The school day begins at 8:10 with Morning Meeting, when the entire student body, faculty, and staff assemble to hear announcements about ongoing activities, listen to presentations by clubs, and discuss the day's national and international news. The Head of School encourages students to express their views and helps them to assess events that are unfolding in the world around them.

Classes begin at 8:25 and end at 3:25. There are eight academic periods plus lunch.

SUMMER PROGRAMS

Soundview offers a small summer school on an as-needed basis, with classes that vary each year. A typical offering includes English, writing, math, history, a science, and a language. Students have the opportunity to work one-on-one with a teacher or in small classes to skip ahead in a given subject or fulfill a requirement.

COSTS AND FINANCIAL AID

Tuition and fees for 2011–12 were $33,600 for Middle School and $34,700 for Upper School. Fees include gym, books, art and lab fees, ERB exams, and literary publications.

In 2010–11, the School provided a total of $494,400 in financial aid to approximately 30 percent of the student body.

ADMISSIONS INFORMATION

Soundview operates on a rolling admissions policy, with students accepted throughout the year in all grades except twelfth. Families of prospective students meet with the Admissions Director, after which the student spends a day at the School. The SSAT is not required, but portions of the ERB standardized examination are administered (unless the applicant provides the School with sufficient, current test data).

Students of all backgrounds are welcomed. The academic program is demanding, but the School's small size allows it to work with each individual student in order to develop strategies for success.

APPLICATION TIMETABLE

Soundview accepts applications on a rolling basis throughout the year. The application fee is $50.

ADMISSIONS CORRESPONDENCE

Mary E. Ivanyi
Director of Admissions and Assistant Head
Soundview Preparatory School
370 Underhill Road
Yorktown Heights, New York 10598
Phone: 914-962-2780
E-mail: info@soundviewprep.org
Web site: http://www.soundviewprep.org

SOUTHWESTERN ACADEMY

Beaver Creek Ranch, Arizona

Type: Coeducational boarding and day college-preparatory and general academic school
Grades: 9–12, postgraduate year
Enrollment: 45
Head of School: Kenneth R. Veronda, Headmaster

THE SCHOOL

Southwestern Academy offers achievement-based, departmentalized, and supportively structured classes limited to 9 to 12 students. Small classes allow for individualized attention in a noncompetitive environment. Southwestern was founded by Maurice Veronda in 1924 as a college-preparatory program "for capable students who could do better" in small, supportive classes. While maintaining that commitment, Southwestern Academy includes U.S. and international students with strong academic abilities who are eager to learn and strengthen English-language skills as well as pursue a general scholastic program in a small, supportive school structure. Southwestern Academy is accredited by the Western Association of Schools and Colleges (WASC).

Southwestern Academy offers students the opportunity to study at either of two distinctly different and beautiful campuses. The Arizona campus, which is known as Beaver Creek Ranch, is located deep in a red-rock canyon in northern Arizona. The San Marino, California, campus is situated in a historic orange grove area near Pasadena. Students may attend either campus and, if space permits, may divide the academic year between the two.

The Beaver Creek campus is a 180-acre ranch located 100 miles north of Phoenix, 12 miles from the resort community of Sedona, and 45 miles south of Flagstaff. The San Marino campus occupies 8 acres in a residential suburb 10 miles from downtown Los Angeles and immediately south of Pasadena, home to the renowned Tournament of Roses Parade. Although the program and philosophies are the same at both campuses, each offers a very different learning environment. Students studying at the Beaver Creek Ranch campus enjoy a living and learning environment that takes full advantage of the rich cultural, scenic, and environmentally significant region. Students at the California campus draw on the offerings of the urban setting.

A mix of U.S. and international students from several countries offers a unique blend of cultural, social, and educational opportunities for all. Every effort is made to enroll a well-balanced student body that represents the rich ethnic diversity of U.S. citizens and students from around the world. The student body consists of college-bound students who prefer a small, personalized education; above-average students who have the potential to become excellent academic achievers in the right learning environment; and average students who, with a supportive structure, can achieve academic success.

Southwestern Academy is incorporated as a not-for-profit organization. Operating expenses are approximately $4.5 million per annum and are met by tuition (93 percent) and grants and annual giving (7 percent). The Academy has no indebtedness.

ACADEMIC PROGRAMS

Middle school students are placed in classes based on individual achievement levels. High school classes are divided by grade level, and students are assigned based on ability and achievement.

High school graduation requirements are based on University of California requirements and include completion of a minimum of 200 academic credits plus 40 credit hours of physical education. The academic term is mid-September through mid-June, with a summer quarter offered at both campuses. Requirements include 4 years of English, 3 years of mathematics, 2 years of a foreign language, 2 years of laboratory sciences, and 1 year each of U.S. history and world cultures, plus one semester of U.S. government and economics and 2 years of visual/performing arts. Proficiency exams in English, mathematics, and computer literacy, as well as community service hours, are also required for graduation.

A typical semester of course work includes six classes plus physical education. Advanced Placement classes are available in English, history, language, math, and science. Review and remedial classes are made available to students who need additional instruction. International students are offered three levels of classes in English as a second language (ESL), including an introductory class, to prepare them to enter and succeed in other academic areas.

Teachers are available daily during a midafternoon study period to work individually with students and meet with parents. There is no extra charge for this tutoring. Boarding students are required to attend a monitored evening study hall, where additional teacher assistance is available.

Student achievement is recognized with a grading system that ranges from A to F. Progress letters are sent monthly to parents and report cards are sent quarterly. The minimum college-recommending grade upon completion of academic requirements is C.

Students studying at the Beaver Creek Ranch campus attend classes on a block schedule, Monday through Thursday. Each Friday, students participate in educational, project-oriented, and assignment-based field trips. Experiential learning allows students to apply knowledge from the classroom. It also supports an integrated academic element that links core subject areas in a practical, applied manner, promoting understanding and retention of key concepts.

FACULTY AND ADVISERS

Headmaster Kenneth Veronda was born at the San Marino campus that his father founded. Mr. Veronda attended classes at Southwestern, graduated, and completed undergraduate and graduate work in American history and foreign relations at Stanford University. The majority of 31 faculty members, 9 in Arizona and 22 in California, hold advanced degrees in their subject areas. Each teacher serves as a faculty adviser to a few students and meets with them individually throughout the school year. On-campus college and career counselors are also available to meet with and assist students in making post–high school graduation plans.

COLLEGE ADMISSION COUNSELING

The college counselors closely monitor the advisement and placement needs of each student. Beginning in the ninth grade, every effort is made to assist students in researching a variety of colleges and universities that match their interests and academic achievement levels. Students are provided a college planning handbook that offers helpful hints and suggestions regarding college application processes. A variety of college representatives are invited annually to visit each campus and meet with students.

Approximately 35 students graduate each year from Southwestern Academy. Almost all enter a U.S. college or university. Some choose to attend a local two-year community college before transferring to a four-year college or university. In recent years, Southwestern Academy graduates have been accepted to the following schools: American; Arizona State; Art Center College of Design; Azusa Pacific; Boston University; Brown; Butler; California State, Fullerton, Monterey Bay, and Northridge; California State Polytechnic, Pomona; Columbia; Hampton; Howard; Loyola; Marymount; Menlo College; Mills; Occidental; Oregon State; Parsons; Penn State; Pepperdine; Pitzer; Temple; USC, Whittier; Woodbury; Wooster; Xavier; and the Universities of California, La Verne, Nevada, New Orleans, the Pacific, San Diego, San Francisco, and Washington (Seattle).

ACADEMIC FACILITIES

At the Beaver Creek Ranch campus, newly renovated classrooms, a learning resource center, and the dormitories blend into the picturesque setting. The campus also includes recreation rooms, a gymnasium, several large activity fields, and an indoor, solar-heated swimming pool.

The San Marino campus includes seven buildings encircling a large multisport athletic field. Lincoln Hall, the main academic building, houses morning assembly and study hall, ten classrooms, science and computer labs, and the library. Pioneer Hall includes several classrooms, a kitchen, dining rooms, and business offices. A separate building is home to large music and art studios and an additional science classroom and lab.

BOARDING AND GENERAL FACILITIES

The Beaver Creek Ranch Campus offers dorm rooms that accommodate 1 to 4 people. Meals are served in the dining room and sometimes in the charming courtyard. Picnics are also popular. A lounge with a huge fireplace is a favorite spot for students to watch movies and DirectTV®.

Seven stone cottages are home to faculty and staff members and sometimes upperclassmen and are set along the trout-filled Beaver Creek. Two fishing ponds, pastures, prehistoric Indian caves, and a favorite swimming hole in the creek are found on campus. Even in this remote, rugged environment, students can e-mail friends and surf the Internet, thanks to the T-1 wireless connectivity.

Four dormitory halls are located on the San Marino campus. Each is designed to accommodate up to 20 boys in double and single rooms. Two off-campus dormitories (located within a mile) house a total of 32 girls. Dorm parents live in apartments adjoining each hall.

ATHLETICS

Gyms and playing fields are available to all students at both campuses, where sports opportunities exist for physical education requirements and recreation. As a member of federated leagues in Arizona and California, Southwestern Academy fields teams at both campuses in all major sports except tackle football. Athletic events are held in late afternoon following the regular school day.

EXTRACURRICULAR OPPORTUNITIES

At the Beaver Creek Ranch campus, students can learn to ride and care for horses or swing on a rope over the creek—and drop in for a swim! The indoor pool is heated for those who prefer warmer water. The campus offers a full program of sports, including golf, and a full range of art classes. Wildlife, including mule deer, bighorn sheep, and javelina, can be seen on hikes. Other recreation opportunities include camping, hiking, mountain biking, fishing, and backpacking.

Southwestern offers a wide range of co-curricular and extracurricular activities and opportunities, including art, drama, music, journalism, student government, and student clubs. Current clubs include chess, Interact, International, the Southwestern Arts Society, Southwestern Environmental Associates, and tennis. Frequent class trips to southern California and northern Arizona places of interest, such as tide pools, museums, archaeological sites, art galleries, and live theater, are great learning experiences for students at both campuses.

DAILY LIFE

Boarding students begin each school day with a breakfast buffet at 7:30. Following breakfast, day and boarding students meet for a required assembly at 8:10, with classes following from 8:30 to 2:45. Required study halls and optional clubs and athletic events are held between 2:50 and 4:30. Dinner is served at 6 and is followed by a monitored study hall lasting until 8. Lights out is at 10:30 for middle school students and 11 for those in high school.

SUMMER PROGRAMS

Summer school sessions are offered at both campuses. Both offer intensive yet enjoyable individualized classes in English and other subjects, plus educational and recreational trips to interesting places in northern Arizona and southern California.

Summer sessions at Beaver Creek Ranch combine review and enrichment courses with experiential learning and high-adventure activities in classwork, camp-type activities, and travel in northern Arizona. ESL is offered at the Beaver Creek campus during the summer.

The summer program in San Marino is an excellent opportunity for domestic students to catch up, if needed, or to move ahead academically in order to take more advanced courses before graduation. For non-English-speaking international students, the summer session can provide an entire semester of the appropriate ESL level necessary to successfully complete a college-preparatory curriculum.

COSTS AND FINANCIAL AID

Tuition for a 2011–12 U.S. boarding student was $30,700. International student tuition was $36,750. The cost for a day student (U.S. citizens and permanent residents only) was $14,900. An incidental account containing $2000 for boarding students or $1000 for day students is required of all students to cover expenses such as books, school supplies, physical education uniforms, and discretionary spending money. Payment is due in advance unless other arrangements are made with the business office.

Financial aid is awarded based on financial need. More than $740,000 was awarded in 2011–12.

ADMISSIONS INFORMATION

Southwestern Academy admits students of any race, color, national and ethnic origin, creed, or sex. A completed application packet is required, followed by a personal on-campus interview with students and parents. A daylong visit to classes (and an overnight for prospective boarding students) is strongly encouraged for prospective students already living in the United States. Interviews with prospective international students and parents are scheduled by the international admissions director and do not require a campus visit.

Each campus offers exceptional learning opportunities. Prospective students are encouraged to seriously consider both campuses and apply to the one that seems better suited to them.

Admission materials and other information can be downloaded from the Southwestern Academy Web site. It can also be obtained by contacting the Office of Admissions.

APPLICATION TIMETABLE

Admission offers are made throughout the year, as space permits. Appointments are required for interviews and campus tours at both locations. The admissions office for both campus locations is located in San Marino. Students should write or call the San Marino office for information on either campus.

ADMISSIONS CORRESPONDENCE

Office of Admissions
Southwestern Academy
2800 Monterey Road
San Marino, California 91108
Phone: 626-799-5010 Ext. 4
Fax: 626-799-0407
E-mail: admissions@southwesternacademy.edu
Web site: http://www.southwesternacademy.edu

SOUTHWESTERN ACADEMY

San Marino, California

Type: Coeducational boarding and day college-preparatory and general academic school
Grades: 6–12, postgraduate year
Enrollment: 140
Head of School: Kenneth R. Veronda, Headmaster

THE SCHOOL

Southwestern Academy offers achievement-based, departmentalized, and supportively structured classes limited to 9 to 12 students. Small classes allow for individualized attention in a noncompetitive environment. Southwestern was founded by Maurice Veronda in 1924 as a college-preparatory program "for capable students who could do better" in small, supportive classes. While maintaining that commitment, Southwestern Academy includes U.S. and international students with strong academic abilities who are eager to learn and strengthen English-language skills as well as pursue a general scholastic program in a small, supportive school structure. Southwestern Academy is accredited by the Western Association of Schools and Colleges (WASC).

Southwestern Academy offers students the opportunity to study at either of two distinctly different and beautiful campuses. The San Marino, California, campus is situated in a historic orange grove area near Pasadena. The Arizona campus, which is known as Beaver Creek Ranch, is located deep in a red-rock canyon in northern Arizona. Students may attend either campus and, if space permits, may divide the academic year between the two.

The San Marino campus occupies 8 acres in a residential suburb 10 miles from downtown Los Angeles and immediately south of Pasadena, home to the renowned Tournament of Roses Parade. The Beaver Creek campus is a 180-acre ranch located 100 miles north of Phoenix, 12 miles from the resort community of Sedona, and 45 miles south of Flagstaff. Although the program and philosophies are the same at both campuses, each offers a very different learning environment. Students at the California campus draw on the offerings of the urban setting. Students studying at the Beaver Creek Ranch campus enjoy a living and learning environment that takes full advantage of the rich cultural, scenic, and environmentally significant region.

A mix of U.S. and international students from several countries offers a unique blend of cultural, social, and educational opportunities for all. Every effort is made to enroll a well-balanced student body that represents the rich ethnic diversity of U.S. citizens and students from around the world. The student body consists of college-bound students who prefer a small, personalized education; above-average students who have the potential to become excellent academic achievers in the right learning environment; and average students who, with a supportive structure, can achieve academic success.

Southwestern Academy is incorporated as a not-for-profit organization. Operating expenses are approximately $4.5 million per annum and are met by tuition (93 percent) and grants and annual giving (7 percent). The Academy has no indebtedness.

ACADEMIC PROGRAMS

Middle school students are placed in classes based on individual achievement levels. High school classes are divided by grade level, and students are assigned based on ability and achievement.

High school graduation requirements are based on University of California requirements and include completion of a minimum of 200 academic credits plus 40 credit hours of physical education. The academic term is mid-September through mid-June, with a summer quarter offered at both campuses. Requirements include 4 years of English, 3 years of mathematics, 2 years of a foreign language, 2 years of laboratory sciences, and 1 year each of U.S. history and world cultures, plus one semester of U.S. government and economics and 2 years of visual/performing arts. Proficiency exams in English, mathematics, and computer literacy, as well as community service hours, are also required for graduation.

A typical semester of course work includes six classes plus physical education. Advanced Placement classes are available in English, history, language, math, and science. Review and remedial classes are made available to students who need additional instruction. International students are offered three levels of classes in English as a second language (ESL), including an introductory class, to prepare them to enter and succeed in other academic areas.

Teachers are available daily during a midafternoon study period to work individually with students and meet with parents. There is no extra charge for this tutoring. Boarding students are required to attend a monitored evening study hall, where additional teacher assistance is available.

Student achievement is recognized with a grading system that ranges from A to F. Progress letters are sent monthly to parents and report cards are sent quarterly. The minimum college-recommending grade upon completion of academic requirements is C.

While studying at the Beaver Creek Ranch campus, students attend classes on a block schedule, Monday through Thursday. Each Friday, students participate in educational, project-oriented, and assignment-based field trips. Experiential learning allows students to apply knowledge from the classroom. It also supports an integrated academic element that links core subject areas in a practical, applied manner, promoting understanding and retention of key concepts.

FACULTY AND ADVISERS

Headmaster Kenneth Veronda was born at the San Marino campus that his father founded. Mr. Veronda attended classes at Southwestern, graduated, and completed undergraduate and graduate work in American history and foreign relations at Stanford University. The majority of 31 faculty members, 22 in California and 9 in Arizona, hold advanced degrees in their subject areas. Each teacher serves as a faculty adviser to a few students and meets with them individually throughout the school year. On-campus college and career counselors are also available to meet with and assist students in making post–high school graduation plans.

COLLEGE ADMISSION COUNSELING

The college counselors closely monitor the advisement and placement needs of each student. Beginning in the ninth grade, every effort is made to assist students in researching a variety of colleges and universities that match their interests and academic achievement levels. Students are provided a college planning handbook that offers helpful hints and suggestions regarding college application processes. A variety of college representatives are invited annually to visit each campus and meet with students.

Approximately 35 students graduate each year from Southwestern Academy. Almost all enter a U.S. college or university. Some choose to attend a local two-year community college before transferring to a four-year college or university. In recent years, Southwestern Academy graduates have been accepted to the following schools: American; Arizona State; Art Center College of Design; Azusa Pacific; Boston University; Brown; Butler; California State, Fullerton, Monterey Bay, and Northridge; California State Polytechnic, Pomona; Columbia; Hampton; Howard; Loyola; Marymount; Menlo College; Mills; Occidental; Oregon State; Parsons; Penn State; Pepperdine; Pitzer; Temple; USC, Whittier; Woodbury; Wooster; Xavier; and the Universities of California, La Verne, Nevada, New Orleans, the Pacific, San Diego, San Francisco, and Washington (Seattle).

ACADEMIC FACILITIES

The San Marino campus includes seven buildings encircling a large multisport athletic field. Lincoln Hall, the main academic building, houses morning assembly and study hall, ten classrooms, science and computer labs, and the library. Pioneer Hall includes several classrooms, a kitchen, dining rooms, and business offices. A separate building is home to large music and art studios and an additional science classroom and lab.

Newly renovated classrooms, a learning resource center, and the dormitories blend into the picturesque setting along Beaver Creek.

BOARDING AND GENERAL FACILITIES

Four dormitory halls are located on the San Marino campus. Each is designed to accommodate up to 20 boys in double and single rooms. Two off-campus dormitories (located within a mile) house a total of 32 girls. Dorm parents live in apartments adjoining each hall.

At Beaver Creek, seven stone cottages encircle the main campus area and provide faculty/staff housing. Four recently renovated residence halls accommodate up to 56 students. The Beaver Creek

Ranch campus includes recreation rooms, a gymnasium, several large activity fields, and an indoor, solar-heated swimming pool.

ATHLETICS

Gyms and playing fields are available to all students at both campuses, where sports opportunities exist for physical education requirements and recreation. As a member of federated leagues in California and Arizona, Southwestern Academy fields teams at both campuses in all major sports except tackle football. Athletic events are held in late afternoon, following the regular school day.

EXTRACURRICULAR OPPORTUNITIES

Southwestern offers a wide range of cocurricular and extracurricular activities and opportunities, including art, drama, music, journalism, student government, and student clubs. Current clubs include chess, Interact, International, the Southwestern Arts Society, Southwestern Environmental Associates, and tennis. Frequent class trips to southern California and northern Arizona places of interest, such as tide pools, museums, archaeological sites, art galleries, and live theater, are great learning experiences for students at both campuses.

DAILY LIFE

Boarding students begin each school day with a breakfast buffet at 7:30. Following breakfast, day and boarding students meet for a required assembly at 8:10, with classes following from 8:30 to 2:45. Required study halls and optional clubs and athletic events are held between 2:50 and 4:30. Dinner is served at 6 and is followed by a monitored study hall lasting until 8. Lights out is at 10:30 for middle school students and 11 for high schoolers.

WEEKEND LIFE

Students in good standing may leave the campus, with permission, during any weekend. Many students take advantage of the planned activities that are arranged for them, including theater performances, shopping at the malls and Old Town Pasadena, barbecues, beach parties, and movies. Visits are planned to Disneyland, Magic Mountain, and Big Surf, and the other attractions of the two-state areas are a part of the social program at Southwestern Academy. Day students are welcome to attend all weekend activities if space permits.

SUMMER PROGRAMS

Summer school sessions are offered at both campuses. Both offer intensive yet enjoyable individualized classes in English and other subjects, plus educational and recreational trips to interesting places in southern California and northern Arizona.

The summer program in San Marino is an excellent opportunity for domestic students to catch up, if needed, or to move ahead academically in order to take more advanced courses before graduation. For non-English-speaking international students, the summer session can provide an entire semester of the appropriate ESL level necessary to successfully complete a college-preparatory curriculum.

Summer sessions at Beaver Creek Ranch combine review and enrichment courses with experiential learning and high-adventure activities in classwork, camp-type activities, and travel in northern Arizona. ESL is offered at the Beaver Creek campus during the summer.

COSTS AND FINANCIAL AID

Tuition for the 2011–12 U.S. boarding student was $30,700. International student tuition was $36,750. The cost for a day student (U.S. citizens and permanent residents only) was $14,900. An incidental account containing $2000 for boarding students or $1000 for day students is required of all students to cover expenses such as books, school supplies, physical education uniforms, and discretionary spending money. Payment is due in advance unless other arrangements are made with the business office.

Financial aid is awarded based on financial need. More than $740,000 was awarded in 2011–12.

ADMISSIONS INFORMATION

Southwestern Academy admits students of any race, color, national and ethnic origin, creed, or sex. A completed application packet is required, followed by a personal on-campus interview with students and parents. A daylong visit to classes (and an overnight for prospective boarding students) is strongly encouraged for prospective students already living in the United States. Interviews with prospective international students and parents are scheduled by the international admissions director and do not require a campus visit.

Each campus offers exceptional learning opportunities. Prospective students are encouraged to seriously consider both campuses and apply to the one that seems better suited to them.

Admission materials and other information can be downloaded from the Southwestern Academy Web site. It can also be obtained by contacting the Office of Admissions.

APPLICATION TIMETABLE

Admission offers are made throughout the year, as space permits. Appointments are required for interviews and campus tours at both locations. The admissions office for both campus locations is located in San Marino. Students should write or call the San Marino office for information on either campus.

ADMISSIONS CORRESPONDENCE

Office of Admissions
Southwestern Academy
2800 Monterey Road
San Marino, California 91108
Phone: 626-799-5010 Ext. 4
Fax: 626-799-0407
E-mail: admissions@southwesternacademy.edu
Web site: http://www.southwesternacademy.edu

THE STORM KING SCHOOL

Cornwall-on-Hudson, New York

Type: Coeducational boarding and day college-preparatory school
Grades: 8–12
Enrollment: 135
Head of School: Helen Stevens Chinitz

THE SCHOOL

The Storm King School was founded in 1867 as a college-preparatory school by the Reverend Louis P. Ledoux. In 1928, it was chartered by the Board of Regents of the State University of New York as a nonprofit institution governed by a self-perpetuating 18-member Board of Trustees. The School has an endowment of $1 million and an active Annual Giving campaign.

The Storm King School seeks to provide a caring, structured residential life and an academic program that prepares students for college. The School helps students stretch themselves by building upon their strengths while realistically acknowledging and addressing their weaknesses. Storm King believes that art, theater, music, and athletics are components of a good education. Therefore, they are a part of daily life at the School. Central to Storm King's philosophy is the belief that the School is a learning community striving to help students live as productive members.

The School is located near the crest of Storm King Mountain on the west bank of the Hudson River. The 55-acre campus offers a serene setting and a magnificent view of a sweeping bend of the river, the Shawangunk Mountains, and the distant Catskills. The 4,000-acre Black Rock Forest, a wilderness preserved by environmentalists, adjoins the campus to the south; West Point Military reservation and Bear Mountain Preserve are nearby, as are the estates of several long-established Hudson Highlands families. New York City, about 50 miles away, is within easy reach via the Palisades Parkway or via the Metro-North Hudson Line.

The Storm King School has a Middle School program for grade 8. The focus of this program is to help students develop and retain a sense of responsibility and individuality. The Middle School curriculum offers the basic core courses as well as technology, physical education, and performing and visual arts. Students are allowed to be creative and self-exploring while fulfilling an educationally intensive program.

The School is accredited by the Middle States Association of Colleges and Schools. It is a member of the Cum Laude Society, the National Honor Society, the New York State Association of Independent Schools, the National Association of Independent Schools, and the College Board.

ACADEMIC PROGRAMS

College preparation is a goal of The Storm King School; therefore, the School emphasizes the development of present skills and talents as the best way to prepare for the future. The School seeks to discover and extend what a student has learned and to identify and develop what he or she has not. The curriculum focuses on skill development as well as content knowledge. The English and history programs stress reading and writing skills and include both required and elective courses; offerings range from creative writing to the British novel and from contemporary world history to psychology and economics. To graduate, a student must also complete a course in health and in public speaking.

The School believes that all students can improve their mathematical skills and reasoning ability. The flexible curriculum encourages students to remedy any past deficiencies in mathematics and to move forward. Courses range from algebra and geometry to Advanced Placement (AP) calculus. The science program includes biology, chemistry, physics, environmental science, and other electives. The foreign language program ensures that all students become familiar with the language, history, and culture of other countries. The School offers Spanish, Mandarin Chinese, and American Sign Language (ASL).

The fine, performing, and creative arts programs encourage students' creative potential through the exploration of artistic expression. All students are required to take one performing arts (theater or music) and one visual arts course. Students who are interested in pursuing the arts at the university level are given advanced, individualized attention in their area of interest to develop their creative repertoire and portfolios. The Department of Fine Arts offers courses in ceramics, design, drawing, painting, photography, sculpture, and AP Studio Art: Drawing, among others. Excellent faculty members encourage and inspire students to create works of art that far exceed students' personal expectations. The Department of Music offers chorus, digital recording and studio production, as well as individual instruction in piano, guitar, and other instruments by special arrangement. Students learn performance techniques and are prepared for public recitals. The Dance Department offers instruction in classical ballet, tap, jazz, and modern dance. Dance students present their work in public recitals. The Department of Theatre Arts offers performance, stage craft, theater history, theater appreciation, and courses in design and production. Students apply classroom instruction in rehearsals and production work through the two or three Storm King Theatre Ensemble productions, on which the entire division collaborates. Arts education and training at The Storm King School enhance a student's education and development through academic courses in the arts and are supported by opportunities for practical application in every creative area.

The Learning Center (TLC) helps selected students develop the skills and self-confidence that are essential for academic independence. TLC emphasizes the development of strong executive functioning skills. TLC works collaboratively with teachers in order to plan instruction that is directly related to classroom curriculum. The Learning Center focuses on building current strengths while improving academics and organization. Study skills work includes note-taking, outlining, researching, test taking, and time management.

In 2004, The Storm King School established a small school-within-a-school called the Mountain Center, using the same curriculum as the Upper School. This program is designed for bright, college-bound students who have an Individual Education Plan (IEP), or the equivalent, developed to address the need for different learning styles. The program does not accept students who have significant emotional or behavioral problems. The Mountain Center presents core subjects (English, math, science, social studies) in a 5:1 ratio setting. The center uses a variety of methods that are appropriate to the needs of each student to accomplish the desired outcome.

Graduation requirements include 4 years each of English and history, 3 years of mathematics, 3 years of science, 2 years or the equivalent of a foreign language, 1 year each in the visual and performing arts, 1 credit public speaking, ½ credit in health, and community service.

Grades are based on a numeric system. These grades are sent to parents four times a year, but, for guidance purposes, progress reports are sent out in the middle of each marking period.

FACULTY AND ADVISERS

Sixty-five percent of the faculty members live on campus—either in the dormitories or in campus housing—and are available for extra help, especially in the evening. All faculty members are active in advising and counseling students and provide a critical link between the family and the School. Of the 30 full-time and 6 part-time faculty members, 24 hold advanced degrees. The School provides funds for continuing education.

Helen Stevens Chinitz was appointed the fifteenth Head of School in July 2004. She is the first female head of The Storm King School.

COLLEGE ADMISSION COUNSELING

Guidance is a continuing process that takes place throughout a student's entire stay at Storm King and quite often even after graduation. College guidance begins in the sophomore year. In group meetings, students and their advisers discuss what lies ahead; individual conferences take place frequently and often include parents. There are many "right" colleges for each student. In recent years, 2 or more graduates have attended the following colleges, among others: Bennington, Boston University, Bucknell, Emerson, George Washington, Hamilton, Iona, Northeastern, NYU, NYU-SVA, Parsons, Pratt, Roger Williams, Skidmore, Smith, several campuses of the State University of New York, Syracuse, Tufts, Virginia Tech, and the Universities of Colorado, Hartford, Illinois at Urbana-Champaign, Massachusetts, Miami, Southern California, and Vermont. In recent years, the senior class has consistently been offered more than $1 million in scholarships.

STUDENT BODY AND CONDUCT

The Storm King School student body represents a wide spectrum of socioeconomic backgrounds from nine states and fifteen other countries. The student body includes 110 boarding and 25 day students. About 50 new students enroll annually.

A disciplinary committee and the Head of School determine consequences for disciplinary infractions. Major offenses may result in withdrawal. Student and faculty groups are consulted in policy formation. Students are expected to be supportive of School policies and to take an active and positive part in the School's programs and activities.

ACADEMIC FACILITIES

Stillman Hall contains mathematics and science classrooms, laboratories, a darkroom, and department offices. There is a greenhouse located down the hill from Stillman Hall. Dyar Hall provides humanities classrooms. The Ogden Library is a split-level learning center with study carrels, an audiovisual room, and the Computer Center, which is equipped with seventeen microcomputer workstations. The Walter Reade Jr. Theatre was dedicated in 1984. The Cobb-Matthiessen Astronomy Observatory was dedicated in 1990. The Allison Vladimir Art Center, a converted carriage house, is a beautiful facility with a spectacular view of the Black Rock wilderness area. The center was dedicated in 1994.

BOARDING AND GENERAL FACILITIES

There are four dormitories: Highmount, McConnell, Dempsey, and Cottage. Each dormitory has two faculty apartments. Most of the rooms are doubles; there are a few triples for girls and several singles available to student leaders. Orr Commons contains a video room, music practice studios, and modern kitchen and dining room facilities. The health center is on the ground floor of Stillman Hall. An admissions/development complex opened in 1992. Also on campus are several faculty residences; the Administration Building, the second floor of which has a faculty apartment; and Spy Rock House, the Head's residence. New faculty residences were completed in December 2003.

ATHLETICS

Athletics at Storm King include recreational and competitive activities as well as an outdoor adventure program (including activities such as hiking, rock climbing, and kayaking).

Each student must participate in a sport in at least two of the three seasons each year. Students may elect to take sports in all three seasons.

The gymnasium provides a basketball court, weight-lifting and fitness equipment, and a dance studio.

With sixteen teams across eleven sports, the School offers students lots of choices in its athletic program. In the fall, students may select from soccer, volleyball, crew, and cross-country. In winter, choices include basketball, wrestling, and ski/snowboarding club. Springtime offerings are lacrosse, softball, golf, tennis, crew, and Ultimate (Frisbee). Students are also encouraged to take advantage of opportunities for outdoor adventure such as hiking, rock climbing, and kayaking. For one season each year, a student may select a club instead of a sport or theater.

EXTRACURRICULAR OPPORTUNITIES

The Student Activities Committee oversees many extracurricular activities. Among the student activities are the yearbook, photography, art, the literary magazine, the environmental club, and recycling club. A work program involves students in routine chores on campus. Service learning opportunities are available on and off campus.

DAILY LIFE

Classes are 45 minutes long and meet five times a week. The day begins with breakfast from 7:15 to 7:50, followed by a morning meeting and classes, which end by 4. This is followed by required activities from 4 to 5:30. Thursday dinners are served family style, with formal dress required every four to six weeks. A 2-hour supervised study hall, either in the dorm or in the library, and some free time cap off the evening. The day ends at 9:30 p.m. Students are quiet and in their rooms by 10:30; lights are out by 11 p.m.

WEEKEND LIFE

The School's location provides various opportunities for social, cultural, and entertainment activities. Students may attend theater performances and concerts in New York City. The activities director and a student committee plan weekend activities, such as movies, dances, intramural athletics, hikes, skiing, horseback riding, visits to museums, and trips to special events and points of interest in the Northeast and as far south as Washington, D.C. The School plans an international trip each year; most recently, students have visited Ireland and Scotland, and Italy. Students may go home any weekend after their obligations have been met.

COSTS AND FINANCIAL AID

For 2011–12, costs for Upper School boarding students totaled $40,100; for Upper School day students, costs totaled $21,500. There are additional fees for English as a second language (ESL), the Learning Center (TLC), and the Mountain Center. Costs for books, insurance, and laundry are additional. Students pay for transportation to and from the School. Families may establish student accounts at the School, from which spending money may be drawn.

Financial assistance totaling about $511,000 is awarded annually according to guidelines determined by the School and Student Service for Financial Aid, to about 28 percent of the student body.

ADMISSIONS INFORMATION

The School accepts students in grades 8 through 12 as well as a few academic postgraduates. Selections are made without regard to race or creed and are based upon the applicant's promise of success and past record. An interview at the School is highly desirable. The School also offers prospective students the opportunity to participate in the student-for-a-day program to help them feel more comfortable and to enable them to learn about the School directly from their peers. The Director of Admission recommends candidates for consideration to the Admissions Committee.

APPLICATION TIMETABLE

Initial inquiries are welcome at any time, and campus interviews can be arranged from 8:30 to 3:30 during the week. A nonrefundable $85 fee ($125 for international applications) must accompany the application. Acceptance notifications are sent as soon as all information is complete and the Admissions Committee makes a decision.

ADMISSIONS CORRESPONDENCE

David Flynn
Director of Admissions
The Storm King School
314 Mountain Road
Cornwall-on-Hudson, New York 12520-1899
Phone: 845-534-9860
800-225-9144 (toll free)
Fax: 845-534-4128
E-mail: admissions@sks.org
Web site: http://www.sks.org

SUFFIELD ACADEMY

Suffield, Connecticut

Type: Coeducational boarding and day college-preparatory school
Grades: 9–12, postgraduate year
Enrollment: 410
Head of School: Charles Cahn III, Headmaster

THE SCHOOL

Challenge, structure, support, and a strong sense of community characterize Suffield Academy. A rigorous college-preparatory program in academics is supported by an extensive emphasis on leadership training. Beautiful new facilities for academics, athletics, and the arts support each student's education. The school has a tradition of academic and athletic excellence and a deep sense of community spirit.

Founded as the Connecticut Literary Institution in 1833, the school became coeducational in 1843 and provided a traditional education for 100 years as both a private academy and the town's only public high school. It took the name of Suffield Academy in 1916 and after World War II became a fully independent boarding and day school for boys. In 1974, Suffield Academy returned to coeducation.

Suffield's strength lies in the personal concern and support shown for each student. The school emphasizes small classes and a structured academic program. In this setting, faculty members encourage students to take an active role in their education and to seek creative insights and solutions.

Each student is challenged intellectually, ethically, and physically to make the best use of his or her talents while developing a sound system of personal and social values.

The Academy's beautiful 350-acre campus is located in the historic residential town of Suffield, Connecticut, a community of 15,000 people located in a region that offers excellent opportunities for bicycling and hiking. Concerts, museums, theaters, and other city offerings are easily accessible in Springfield, Massachusetts, 10 miles north of Suffield, and Hartford, Connecticut, 17 miles to the south. New York is 135 miles to the south, and Boston is 90 miles to the northeast. Bradley International Airport is 5 miles from the campus.

A nonprofit institution, Suffield is governed by a self-perpetuating 30-member Board of Trustees. It has an endowment of $35 million. The School has raised over $55 million since 2002 and the annual budget is more than $17 million.

Suffield is accredited by the New England Association of Schools and Colleges (NEASC). In 2011, the association awarded its highest possible ratings to Suffield Academy in twelve out of fourteen accreditation categories and the second-highest marks in the other two categories.

Suffield is a member of or is affiliated with each of the following organizations: the Connecticut Association of Independent Schools, the National Association of Independent Schools, the Cum Laude Society, American Secondary Schools for International Students and Teachers (ASSIST), the Secondary School Admission Test Board, A Better Chance, the Council for Advancement and Support of Education, Hartford Area Boarding Schools, the Hartford Youth Scholars Foundation, the SPHERE Consortium, and the WALKS Foundation.

ACADEMIC PROGRAMS

Suffield offers a college-preparatory curriculum that is grounded in the liberal arts. The academic program stresses acquiring the fundamental skills and knowledge needed to succeed in a variety of academic disciplines and in college. With careful guidance, students select a program of study designed to meet special interests and needs.

The school year is divided into three terms. Classes are held six days a week but end at noon on Wednesday and at 11 a.m. on Saturday, when athletics contests are scheduled in the afternoon. Classes average 10 students, and each class meets four times per week (two 45-minute periods and two extended 70-minute periods). Teachers are available for extra help on an individual basis. Students also have the support of faculty advisers and a walk-in counseling office. The student-faculty ratio is 7:1.

The Suffield Leadership program is a distinguishing characteristic of the school. The program is required for all students and emphasizes seven core elements which each student is exposed to in direct ways: (1) personal mastery, (2) moral foundation, (3) goal-setting, (4) communication skills, (5) problem-solving, (6) self-awareness, and (7) inspiring and mobilizing others. The overarching goal is to help students build the skills and habits that lend themselves to effective leadership. The program is housed in a beautiful academic building (Centurion Hall) and also makes use of the Courtney Robinson '88 Outdoor Leadership Center. This facility, located on 40 acres, houses an indoor climbing wall and outdoor high ropes course.

Students may choose from course offerings in the visual arts (painting, sculpture, woodworking, architecture, computer graphics, and more) or the performing arts (instrument ensembles, choral groups, dance, and private instruction in voice or instrument) to satisfy the requirement of a year's study in the arts. Artists wishing to pursue these areas in an in-depth fashion will also have this opportunity at Suffield, as a gifted faculty and extensive facilities are dedicated to the arts.

The Academic Support Office provides resources for students who have different learning styles or challenges, as shown by their prior academic evaluation. The Director of Academic Support meets regularly with each student to create strategies that will sharpen their focus and strengthen their academic performance in the classroom. The Director also works with faculty members to communicate specific student needs so that Academy teachers are better able to meet the needs of students who have a broad range of learning styles.

To earn a Suffield diploma, each student must successfully complete the program and uphold the school's expectations of good citizenship. Students must earn 18 credits to earn a diploma, including the following particular academic requirements: 4 credits in English, 4 credits in mathematics, 2 credits in foreign language (including study through Level II), 2 credits in science, 2 credits in history (including U.S. History and Regional Studies), and 1 credit in the arts. In addition each student must: take a leadership course each year, meet the Technology Portfolio requirement (one in grade 9 or 10 if enrolled at Suffield, the second in grade 11 or 12), take a minimum of four courses each term, successfully complete each course taken in the senior year, and pass all term-length classes in the spring of the senior year.

All major departments offer honors-level courses. Advanced Placement courses are offered in computer science, English, foreign languages, history, math, and science. Interest in a course may lead to individual work with a teacher. In the senior year, students may select an independent study project for credit.

Grades, based on a minimum passing grade of D-, are recorded every five weeks. Effort also plays a significant part in the grading system. Academic reports from teachers (including grade, effort rating, and detailed comments), along with an evaluation from the adviser, are sent to parents at the end of each term and at the first midterm.

Ample time is provided for uninterrupted study, both during the day and in the evening. All boarding students study in their rooms, in the library, or in the computer lab in the evening from 8 to 10. Unsatisfactory effort necessitates attendance at supervised study halls during the day and evening until the student's effort improves.

FACULTY AND ADVISERS

There are 81 dedicated men and women on the faculty at Suffield Academy, over 56 of whom have or are working toward graduate degrees. Faculty members and their families live on campus and all serve as advisers, coaches, dormitory parents, activity supervisors, and trip leaders. They engage in training programs and workshops as well as graduate programs leading to advanced degrees and professional expertise in their academic discipline.

Charles Cahn III is in his eighth year as Headmaster. He has been a leader at Suffield for sixteen years. Mr. Cahn is a respected, dynamic person with great enthusiasm for Suffield Academy. He is widely admired in the independent school community and is a tremendous asset for Suffield. Prior to being appointed headmaster in 2003, Mr. Cahn served as an English teacher, varsity lacrosse coach, dorm parent, director of admissions, dean of faculty, and associate headmaster. He is familiar with all aspects of the school. A native of Baltimore, Maryland, Mr. Cahn is a graduate of Gilman School, the University of Michigan, and Wesleyan University. His wife, Hillary Rockwell Cahn ('88) teaches photography and coaches Suffield's alpine ski team. They live on the Suffield campus with their 2 children.

Suffield is above all a caring school, and its faculty members reflect this attitude. All faculty members serve as advisers, with an average advisee group of 5 students. Students select their advisers, meet with them on a regular basis, and confer with them when needed. Two traditional annual events, Parents' Day in the fall and Spring Parents' Weekend, feature parental conferences with teachers and advisers that enable parents to share the results of their son's or daughter's experience at Suffield. Advisers are available to meet with parents and teachers as needed concerning a student's progress.

COLLEGE ADMISSION COUNSELING

Suffield's mission includes readying students for success at the next level and beyond. As part of this effort, the school's unique college counseling program includes material designed to appropriately challenge students of each grade. Housed in the new 3,000-square-foot Hoffman College Counseling Center, built in 2011, Suffield Academy's innovative college counseling program is a model for independent schools across the United States. The latest distinctive, forward-looking initiative by Suffield, the four-year program has generous staffing, modern space, significant financial resources, and dedicated time in the school day. With this step, Suffield aims to provide comprehensive and effective college counseling marked by individual attention and extensive services.

The goals of the College Counseling Office at Suffield Academy are threefold: to help students understand the college admissions process; to represent each student fairly and responsibly, with his or her uniqueness and potential appropriately identified; and to enable each student to find a match between his or her ambitions and talents and a college's resources and style.

A student's involvement in the college admissions process offers them the opportunity to gain a better sense of who they are as they evaluate their achievements and expectations, research schools, and begin to assume some responsibility for the next phase of their education. Meeting deadlines, making and keeping appointments, filling out applications, and working to their potential in the classroom are all steps the students themselves can take to achieve the desired results of the college selection process. The process can be challenging, but it does not have to be difficult if students are organized and begin their search early, a year or more in advance.

In 2011, graduates enrolled at over eighty colleges and universities, including Amherst, Bates, Columbia, Cornell, Emory, Georgetown, Johns Hopkins, Middlebury, Northwestern, NYU, and the Universities of Pennsylvania and Virginia.

STUDENT BODY AND CONDUCT

The student community of 2011–12 had an enrollment of 410 students; 155 were boarding boys, 125 were boarding girls, 60 were day boys, and 70 were day girls. Students came from twenty states and twenty-six other countries. A wealth of understanding and enrichment is fostered through this diversity of cultural backgrounds.

Although all students are encouraged to become constructively involved in the extracurricular life of the school, class representatives contribute to the decision-making process through participation in the Student Council and Discipline Committee. Cooperation and consideration of the rights of others are important factors in the decision-making process of each student. Each student holds at least one leadership position as part of the school's four-year leadership program.

The School Work Program and off-campus Community Service Program are vital parts of Suffield Academy life, promoting pride in the school and respect for other people. Everyone in the Suffield community performs a daily job that contributes to the general well-being of the school. A number of seniors and faculty members oversee this program.

ACADEMIC FACILITIES

The school occupies over twenty major buildings, including Centurion Hall, the main classroom building for leadership, math, and history courses. Memorial Building is where English and language courses are held; this facility also houses the technology center and Academic Support Office. There is a dedicated science building with several labs, and a beautiful, historic library. The Jeanice H. Seaverns Performing Arts Center and Guttag Music Center include a 200-seat theater, an art gallery, a set design studio and scene shop, a recording studio, practice rooms, and space for Suffield's dance and choral programs. The Emily Hall Tremaine Visual Arts Center features a multipurpose art studio, ceramics studio, graphics lab, photography lab, library office, and gallery. Nondenominational chapel services are held once a week in the town's Second Baptist Church. The new wellness center opened in fall 2007, and renovations in the music and performing arts center were completed in winter 2008.

BOARDING AND GENERAL FACILITIES

Twelve dormitories provide double rooms for 280 students. All dorm rooms are wired for both telephone and Internet use. Five new cottage-style dorms opened in September 1998. The newest dorm, Rockwell Hall, opened in 2008. It also houses a state-of-the-art health center. Fuller and Spencer Halls are larger dormitories housing 46 and 50 students, respectively. There are also four homes, each shared by between 6 and 12 students. All dormitories have faculty residents, including families, and student proctors.

The downstairs part of Brewster Hall contains the school dining room, the kitchen, and the student union with lounge, TV room, game room, snack area, bookstore, and post office. Other buildings are the Fuller Hall administration building and the historic Gay Mansion, the official residence of the Headmaster.

ATHLETICS

With more than thirty-five interscholastic teams, as well as various other athletics options, all students participate in sports on a level of competition that matches individual experience and ability. Athletics at Suffield stress good sportsmanship, acquisition of skills, and leadership development. The new Tisch Field House, opened in 2009, is a gorgeous, 30,000-square-foot facility housing two multipurpose courts, a squash center, and a new athletic training facility. It complements Sherman Perry Gymnasium, which has a newly renovated fitness center and wrestling room, a riflery range, and a classic wood basketball court. The campus includes a football field, five soccer fields, two baseball diamonds and a softball diamond, ten tennis courts, a hockey field, three lacrosse fields, a sand volleyball pit, and an all-weather track. Facilities for skiing and golf are available nearby. Fitness programs, outdoor programs, team management, volunteer service, or play production may be undertaken in lieu of interscholastic sports. A new synthetic turf field was constructed in 2008.

EXTRACURRICULAR OPPORTUNITIES

Suffield believes that every student should become constructively involved in the life of the school outside of the classroom. In addition to weekly chapel and a varied program of assemblies, both required, the school sponsors visiting artists and professionals who share experiences with the student body that often provoke new interests.

Students may choose from more than twenty-five activities, including concert and theater series, bicycling, bands, the yearbook, drama productions, the school newspaper, photography, chess, horseback riding, community service, and computers. Suffield Outdoor Leadership Opportunities (S.O.L.O.) maintains an active program, including rock-climbing, caving, backpacking, hiking, canoeing, camping, and other seasonal activities. The school opened an outdoor leadership center in 2000 with a rock-climbing wall and high and low ropes courses. Suffield's location gives students access to plays, concerts, and museums in two major cities.

DAILY LIFE

Classes begin at 8 a.m. and conclude at 3:05 p.m. on Monday, Tuesday, Thursday, and Friday. Athletics follow the end of the academic day. Only morning classes are scheduled on Wednesday and Saturday; the afternoons are reserved for interscholastic athletics contests. Most clubs meet after dinner.

WEEKEND LIFE

The Student Union was expanded, redesigned, and renovated in 1992. The Weekend Activities and Film committees, as well as the Student Union Board of Governors, use this facility as the center of social life at the school.

On-campus weekend activities include dances, live entertainment, films, plays, and special events, such as Chill on the Hill and Luau. Off-campus options include movies, ski and shopping trips, indoor tennis, and activities sponsored by the Weekend Committee.

Boarding students in good standing may, with parental permission, take an unlimited number of weekends. Rapport between day and boarding students is close, with day students sharing campus activities and many boarding students visiting day students' homes on weekends.

COSTS AND FINANCIAL AID

Charges for 2011–12 were $46,500 for boarders and $32,900 for day students. Additional expenses include books and supplies ($550–$700), spending money ($25/week), laundry, and travel. The required, subsidized computer purchase ranges in cost from $1500 to $3000.

For 2011–12, 146 scholarships with a total value of almost $3.5 million were awarded.

ADMISSIONS INFORMATION

The Admissions Committee seeks students who are committed to serious study and who have a sense of purpose, a good previous record both academically and personally, and supportive recommendations from persons who know the student well. Admissions requirements include the application form with a written essay; an academic transcript from the current school; letters of recommendation from the student's guidance counselor or placement officer, English and mathematics teachers, and a third teacher of the student's choice; and SSAT, SAT, PSAT, or WISC results. TOEFL is required from students for whom English is not their spoken language.

APPLICATION TIMETABLE

When classes are in session, campus interviews and tours are conducted daily from 8 a.m. to 2 p.m., (8 to 10 a.m. on Wednesday and Saturday). Prospective students are encouraged to visit the campus. Visits can also be arranged at times when school is not in session by contacting the Admissions Office.

Applications are due January 15 and should be accompanied by a $50 fee for domestic applicants, and a $100 fee for international applicants. The mailing of acceptances is March 10, and students are asked to reply by April 10.

ADMISSIONS CORRESPONDENCE

Terry Breault
Director of Admissions and Financial Aid
Suffield Academy
185 North Main Street
Suffield, Connecticut 06078

Phone: 860-386-4440
Fax: 860-668-2966
E-mail: saadmit@suffieldacademy.org
Web site: http://www.suffieldacademy.org

TASIS THE AMERICAN SCHOOL IN ENGLAND

Thorpe, Surrey, England

Type: Coeducational boarding and day college-preparatory school
Grades: Nursery–13: Lower School, Nursery–4; Middle School, 5–8; Upper School, 9–13
Enrollment: School total: 750; Upper School: 390
Head of School: Mr. Michael McBrien, Headmaster

THE SCHOOL

TASIS England was founded in 1976 by Mrs. M. Crist Fleming and is a sister school of The American School in Switzerland (TASIS), which she established in 1956. The 46-acre campus is set in a country village in the Thames valley, only 18 miles from central London and 6 miles from Heathrow Airport.

The School offers a traditional, college-preparatory program. While academics are emphasized, a wide variety of sports, extracurricular activities, cultural excursions, and weekend trips ensure a balanced education. The program takes full advantage of its location and the opportunities that England and Europe offer as extensions to classroom learning. The TASIS Schools and Summer Programs are owned and fully controlled by the TASIS Foundation, a Swiss, independent, not-for-profit educational foundation, registered in Delémont, Switzerland.

TASIS England is an IB World School; is accredited by the Council of International Schools (CIS) and the New England Association of Schools and Colleges (NEASC); and is a member of the National Association of Independent Schools (NAIS) and The Association of Boarding Schools (TABS). It was inspected by the British Office for Standards in Education (Ofsted) in November 2008, and it received high ratings for its academic, arts, athletics, and extracurricular programs; student care; and facilities.

ACADEMIC PROGRAMS

The upper school encompasses grades 9 to 13. The minimum requirements for graduation from the upper school are 4 years of English, 3 years of history (including U.S. history at the eleventh- or twelfth-grade level), a third-level proficiency in a foreign language, 3 years of mathematics (through algebra II), three laboratory sciences (including a biological and a physical science), and 1 year of fine arts. All seniors are required to take a full-year humanities course. Students who have attended TASIS England for three years or more are expected to complete 19 credits. A normal course load consists of six courses per year. Advanced Placement courses are offered for qualified students and include art history, biology, calculus, chemistry, computer science, economics, English, environmental science, French, government and politics, history, Latin, music theory, physics, statistics, and Spanish.

TASIS also offers the International Baccalaureate (IB) diploma. Students may apply to this program for their final two years at TASIS, and successful IB diploma candidates can earn both the IB diploma and the TASIS England high school diploma. Entry into the IB Program is made in consultation between the School, student, and family and is open to highly motivated students with strong academic, time management, and study skills.

With an average class size of 15, and a teacher-student ratio of 1:8, the School provides an intimate learning environment that can challenge a young person to realize his or her full potential. The Advisory Program enhances this aspect of a TASIS education, as the advisers are charged with the social and academic well-being of each advisee.

A student's day is fully structured. Participation in supervised evening study hall for boarding students is a requirement for all but those who have earned the privilege of independent study in their rooms.

The academic year is divided into two semesters, ending in January and June, respectively. Grades and comments are mailed home to parents four times a year at mid-semester and end-of-semester breaks, together with a summary report from the adviser. The grading system uses A to F, indicating achievement levels, and 1 to 5 as a measure of a student's attitude and application to his or her work.

An educational travel program during the October break is required for all boarding students and is included in the tuition. Past trips have included such destinations as Austria, France, Germany, Greece, Hungary, Italy, Poland, Romania, Russia, Spain, and Switzerland. These school trips are also an option for day students.

FACULTY AND ADVISERS

Mr. Michael McBrien was appointed as headmaster of TASIS England in 2010. He holds a master's degree in education and a Bachelor of Arts in counseling, psychology, and communication. He has twenty-four years of experience in education and has worked as an administrator at the University of California, Berkeley, and at Babson College and Frontier Academy, in Colorado. Mr. McBrien was previously Head of Baylor School in Tennessee, an independent, coeducational college preparatory, day, and boarding school.

The faculty represents one of the School's strongest assets. Its members are dedicated professionals with a true sense of vocation. Duties are not limited to teaching but encompass the responsibilities of advisors, sports coaches, dorm parents, community service aides, and trip chaperones. There are 112 full-time faculty members—42 men and 70 women—and 21 part-time teachers. Approximately half of them have advanced degrees and 23 live on campus. In addition, music specialists visit the School for private instruction by arrangement.

COLLEGE ADMISSION COUNSELING

TASIS England employs 4 college counselors who provide guidance about university choices and assist in managing the details of the search/application process. They meet individually with students in their junior and senior years to discuss academic programs, careers, and college plans. Support programs include student seminars, career day, transition workshops, and a case study night. The counselors maintain a reference library of college catalogs, videos, and computer software and familiarize students with the range of opportunities available to them. The counselors coordinate visits to the School by college admissions officers from universities in the United States and Europe and administer the college admissions testing program. TASIS England is a test center for the PSAT, ACT, and SAT for juniors and seniors and all Advanced Placement examinations.

TASIS graduates are accepted by universities around the world and have recently attended such schools as Boston University, Brown, Bryn Mawr, Cambridge, Cornell, Dartmouth, Duke, Georgetown, George Washington, Imperial College of London, King's College London, London School of Economics, MIT, Northwestern, Notre Dame, Princeton, Rhode Island School of Design, Rice, Stanford, Tufts, University College London, and the Universities of Pennsylvania (U.S.); Bristol, Durham, and Edinburgh (U.K.); McGill (Canada); and Waseda (Japan). TASIS believes that students should be encouraged to think deeply about the purposes of higher education, about the intangible benefits of genuine intellectual activity, and about the range of philosophical options offered by educational institutions. The major responsibility for college choices lies with each student, but the School provides as much advice and support as possible.

STUDENT BODY AND CONDUCT

For the 2011–12 academic year, there were 390 students in the upper school (grades 9–13): 120 seniors, 115 juniors, 85 sophomores, and 70 freshmen. Overall, the ratio of boys to girls in each grade level is close to 1:1. In some cases, boarding students' parents are expatriates undertaking assignments overseas, such as in Saudi Arabia, Africa, Europe, and various parts of the British Isles. The student body is culturally diverse, with about half of the students in the upper school representing approximately fifty other countries. In the lower school, there are 170 children, and the middle school (grades 5–8) has 190 students

TASIS England promotes a purposeful environment for learning and growing, including demonstrating respect for one's self and for others. The *Student Handbook* clearly identifies the accepted codes of conduct within the School community. A uniform is required for upper school students. Lower and middle school students wear white and navy blue. An infraction of a major school rule is dealt with by the upper school administration with the Disciplinary Advisory Board. TASIS England reserves the right to dismiss at any time a student who has proved to be an unsatisfactory member of the school community, even though there may have been no infraction of a specific rule.

In the upper school, the Student Council is made up of representatives from all grade levels and is the vehicle of student government. Prefects, as student leaders, carry special responsibilities in dormitory and general school life.

ACADEMIC FACILITIES

Two large Georgian mansions and purpose-built classrooms are the focal points of the campus. There are computer centers and a library for each school division, art studios, a darkroom, music rooms, a language laboratory, a 24-hour health center, two multipurpose gymnasiums, a fitness center, two drama/dance studios, and a 350-seat theater. TASIS England is implementing a ten-year master plan to enhance all campus facilities. The most recent development, a state-of-the-art Science Center with three floors of classrooms and well-equipped laboratories, opened in 2011 and augments the School's vibrant science program. Wi-Fi is available throughout the campus.

BOARDING AND GENERAL FACILITIES

Approximately 180 boarding students (grades 9–13) are accommodated in single-sex dormitories supervised by a faculty resident dorm parent, assisted by prefects. Each unit holds 13–16 students, usually in 2-, 3-, or 4-person rooms, which are located in the top floors of the main buildings as well as in the adjacent cottages, such as Tudor House, Orchard, Shepherd's Cottage, and Vicarage Mews. The Boarding Program is coordinated by two staff members, both of whom are experienced in providing boarding care and serving the needs of young people. All meals are provided, and the campus Health Center has an experienced 24-hour nursing staff, and a school doctor on call.

ATHLETICS

An awareness of physical fitness, the discipline of training the body as well as the mind, and the spirit of competition are viewed as important elements in a student's education at TASIS England. All upper school students participate in the afternoon sports/activities program, which operates on a three-term basis, reflecting seasonal sports. The minimum requirement is participation for two afternoons a week.

Varsity sports include basketball, cross-country, dance, golf, lacrosse, soccer, tennis, and volleyball as well as boys' teams in rugby and baseball and girls' teams in cheering and softball. Recreational sports include badminton, basketball, golf, horseback riding, lacrosse, running, soccer, squash, swimming, tennis, and a conditioning program.

There are four large playing fields on campus, six all-weather tennis courts, two gymnasiums, and a fitness center that offers a complete weight-training circuit and a wide variety of cardiovascular machines. The nearby Egham Sports Center offers fine supplementary facilities.

Besides participating in local sports events, the School competes in International Schools Sports Tournaments (ISSTs) with other international schools throughout Europe and the Middle East.

EXTRACURRICULAR OPPORTUNITIES

England's capital city, London, only 18 miles away, provides an unrivaled opportunity for students to enjoy such pleasures as theater, opera, concerts, art galleries, and museums. Through course-related study or School-chaperoned trips, in the evenings and on weekends, students are regularly encouraged to participate in as many educational experiences as possible.

On-campus activities include drama productions; musical groups; choir; the School newspaper; Model UN; the Duke of Edinburgh Award Program; art, debate, and drama clubs; and the yearbook committee, as well as School dances and movies.

A committee of students and teachers coordinates and plans on-campus and off-campus recreational activities, including day trips (sightseeing, for example) and weekends away. Traditionally, the International Festival, Christmas Dinner Dance, Spring Prom, and May Fair are the highlights of the year.

The Community Service Program aims to help each student to develop skills leading to a sense of involvement and greater responsibility for others. The minimum commitment involves approximately 1 hour a week. Students may serve the School community in a variety of ways, e.g., by helping in the library or tutoring younger children. They may serve the local community by visiting homes for the elderly, working with the disabled, participating in conservation projects, and raising funds for local charities. Special summer projects are also available.

DAILY LIFE

Classes commence at 8:20 (9:15 on Wednesdays) and end at 3:15. Each Upper School class meets four times a week, allowing a structured advisory and tutorial period during the day. Sports/activities time is between 3:30 and 5 p.m. each day, except Fridays. An upper school meeting is regularly scheduled for Wednesdays. No classes are held on Saturday or Sunday.

WEEKEND LIFE

Day students as well as boarders participate freely in organized social events on the weekends. These can include trips to the theater and concerts, the ballet, and professional sports events. The Activities Coordinator and Student Council members collaborate to develop a wide variety of activities. Day trips are organized to such destinations as Stratford-upon-Avon, Salisbury, Cambridge, Oxford, Canterbury, and Bath in the U.K., Lille in France, and a weekend trip to Christmas markets in Germany.

Organized excursions are chaperoned by members of the faculty.

SUMMER PROGRAMS

During the summer, six-week credit-based academic courses are offered in such subjects as math and English literature and composition, as well as enrichment courses such as the ShakespeareXperience, Theater in London, SAT Review, English as a Second Language, Film Production, Photography in London, and Art. Some 420 students regularly participate from schools in the United States and from international schools all over the world. Qualified teachers and counselors from the United States and around the world make up the summer programs administration and faculty. Weekend travel is included in the program.

In addition to the courses in England, TASIS offers a variety of summer programs in France, Spain, and Switzerland to students from all over the world. From intensive study of painting, photography, and architecture at Les Tapies in the Ardèche to learning Spanish in Salamanca or French at Chateaux d'Oex in Switzerland, TASIS summer courses enrich the talents, skills, and interests of its participants.

COSTS AND FINANCIAL AID

In 2011–12, tuition and fees for day students were £5925–£19,210 per annum. Fees include lunches, loan of textbooks, IT and laboratory fees, some classroom materials, and the cost of most curriculum-related activities and field trips. Optional expenses, including costs for music lessons and horseback riding, are by private arrangement. Boarding fees were £32,130 and include tuition, room, full board, loan of textbooks, IT and laboratory fees, annual laptop maintenance, some classroom materials, the cost of most curriculum-related activities and field trips, weekly laundry service for bed linen and towels, and travel insurance for school-sponsored trips. Costs for the October Travel Week are also included in the boarding fees. A recommended personal allowance is £50 per week.

There is a one-time-only Development Fund Fee of £750 per student for on campus building projects and an enrollment deposit of £1000 for day students and £2000 for boarders. The balance of fees becomes payable for each semester by June 1 and November 15.

Students are invited to apply for financial aid, which is granted on the basis of merit, need, and available funds. Early application for financial help is recommended. Each year the School awards approximately £200,000 in financial aid.

ADMISSIONS INFORMATION

Applications for admission are considered by the Admissions Committee upon receipt of a completed application form together with the application fee, three teachers' recommendations, and a transcript. Standardized test scores are requested, and a student questionnaire is required. An interview is recommended unless distance is a prohibiting factor. A decision is reached on the basis of a student's academic and behavioral acceptability to the TASIS England School community. A student's nationality, religion, ethnic background, and gender play no part in the committee's decision, although availability of space in the dormitories (all are grouped by gender) is sometimes a limiting factor.

APPLICATION TIMETABLE

Applications are processed throughout the year. Visitors are welcome on campus at any time of the year other than the period between Christmas and New Year, when the School is closed. An interview by prior arrangement, even on very short notice, is recommended. It is preferable for visitors to choose days when school is in session in order to appreciate the working atmosphere of the community.

While early applications are encouraged, there is no final deadline, since a rolling admissions policy exists. Acceptances are made with the provision that students complete their current year in good standing. There is an application fee of £125.

ADMISSIONS CORRESPONDENCE

Karen House, Director of Admissions
TASIS The American School in England
Coldharbour Lane
Thorpe, Nr Egham
Surrey TW20 8TE
England
Phone: 44-1932-582316
Fax: 44-1932-564644
E-mail: ukadmissions@tasisengland.org

TASIS Schools and Summer Programs in Europe
112 South Royal Street
Alexandria, Virginia 22314
Phone: 703-299-8150
800-442-6005 (toll-free)
Fax: 703-299-8157
E-mail: usadmissions@tasis.com
Web site: http://www.tasis.com

TASIS THE AMERICAN SCHOOL IN SWITZERLAND

Montagnola-Lugano, Switzerland

Type: Coeducational boarding and day college-preparatory school
Grades: Pre-K–12, PG: Elementary School, pre-K–5; Middle School, 6–8; High School, 9–12, postgraduate year
Enrollment: School total: 635; High School: 334; Middle School: 114; Elementary School: 186
Head of School: Michael Ulku-Steiner, Headmaster

THE SCHOOL

TASIS The American School in Switzerland was founded in 1956 by Mrs. M. Crist Fleming to offer a strong American college-preparatory education in a European setting. TASIS was the first American boarding school established in Europe. Over time, it has become a school for students from more than fifty countries seeking an American independent school experience. The International Baccalaureate (I.B.) Program is also offered within this setting.

The objective of the School is to foster both a vital enthusiasm for learning and habits that are essential to a full realization of each student's moral and intellectual potential. The curriculum gives special emphasis to the achievements of the Western heritage, many elements of which are easily accessible from the School's location. By providing an international dimension to education, the School stresses the need for young people to mature with confidence and competence in an increasingly interrelated world.

The beautiful campus is in the village of Montagnola, overlooking the city and the lake of Lugano, nestled among the southernmost of the Swiss Alps in the Italian-speaking canton of Ticino. Ideally situated in the heart of Europe, the School makes the most of its location by introducing students to European cultures and languages through extensive travel programs.

The TASIS Foundation, a not-for-profit Swiss foundation, owns the School. The TASIS Foundation also has a school near London and offers summer programs in England, Spain, and Italy as well as Switzerland. Alumni provide enthusiastic support for the School's activities and participate in annual reunions and other special events.

TASIS is accredited by the Council of International Schools (CIS) and the New England Association of Schools and Colleges (NEASC) and is a member of the National Association of Independent Schools and the Swiss Group of International Schools.

ACADEMIC PROGRAMS

The minimum requirements for graduation from the high school college-preparatory program are 4 years of English, 3 years of history (including European and U.S. history), a third-year proficiency in a modern foreign language, 3 years of mathematics (through algebra II), 3 years of laboratory science (including physical and biological sciences), and 1 year of fine arts, plus senior humanities, sports/physical education, and community service requirements. Students must satisfactorily complete a minimum of 19 credits. Students are required to enroll in a minimum of five full-credit courses per year or the equivalent. A normal course load for students consists of six courses.

TASIS offers an extensive English as an additional language program that focuses on oral and written academic English skills and competence in a high school curriculum leading to the TASIS college-preparatory diploma.

TASIS offers a diverse and challenging curriculum, including the Advanced Placement Program (AP), the International Baccalaureate (I.B.) Diploma Programme, and a wide range of required and elective courses. In 2011, 22 students took fifty-two AP exams in eleven subject areas; 23 percent of the scores were 4 or above and 8 percent earned the top score of 5. Students may also select I.B. courses and can earn subject-specific certificates or the full diploma.

The average class size is 12; the teacher-student ratio is 1:6. The student's day is fully structured, including time for academics, sports and activities, meals and socializing, and supervised evening study hours. The grading system uses A to F for performance and assigns effort grades of 1 to 5, reflecting students' attitudes and application to their work. The academic year is divided into two semesters and grades and comment reports are e-mailed to parents five times a year.

The postgraduate year presents an additional opportunity to high school graduates who wish to spend an interim year in Europe before going on to college. Each postgraduate student can design a tailor-made course of study with the assistance and approval of the Academic Dean that enables him or her to explore and develop new interests, strengthen academic weaknesses, or concentrate in areas of strength or particular interest. It includes a course-related Academic Travel program.

FACULTY AND ADVISERS

The faculty represents one of the School's strongest assets. Its members are a group of dedicated professionals who are enthusiastic about working with young people. The TASIS faculty includes 91 full-time teaching administrators and faculty members, of whom 51 are women and 40 are men. Seventy-two percent of the faculty members have advanced degrees. Thirty-two faculty members live on campus; the rest live nearby and participate in most campus activities. In addition to teaching, faculty members act as advisers, sports coaches, trip chaperones, and dormitory residents and help to create a warm, family-like atmosphere.

COLLEGE ADMISSION COUNSELING

The School employs 3 full-time college counselors, who meet with students individually and in groups during their junior and senior years. The college counseling office maintains a reference library of university catalogs from around the world so that students can familiarize themselves with the wide variety of opportunities that are open to them. As a counseling resource, the School provides a small computer lab for college research. Many college admissions officers from universities in the U.S. and Europe visit the School and speak to students. TASIS is an official testing center for the PSAT, SAT, SAT Subject Tests, ACT, PLAN, and all AP and I.B. examinations.

Recent graduates attend such institutions as Edinburgh, Reading, and Nottingham Universities in the U.K. and Boston University, Colorado College, George Washington, Notre Dame, Stanford, and Tufts in the United States.

STUDENT BODY AND CONDUCT

Each student is honor bound to abide by the rules, as defined in the TASIS *Student Handbook*. The School employs a variety of counseling, disciplinary, and administrative responses to rules violations, determined on a case-by-case basis. The School administration and Conduct Review Board handle more serious offenses. All responses take into account the seriousness of the offense, the number of previous offenses, any mitigating circumstances, and the student's record as a member of the TASIS community.

Students at TASIS bear a serious responsibility to conduct themselves not only in a way that does credit to them, to their School, and to their country of origin, but also in a way that is consistent with the high standards set by the citizens of the European countries they visit. For this reason, TASIS has established reasonable but definitive standards of behavior, attitude, and appearance for all of its students. The School reserves the right to ask any student to withdraw for failure to maintain these standards.

ACADEMIC FACILITIES

The campus comprises twenty-two buildings, a combination of historical villas restored for school use and new, purpose-built facilities. The seventeenth century Villa De Nobili was the School's original building and houses the dining hall, dormitories, administrative offices, and science laboratories. Hadsall House contains classrooms and dormitories. Villa Monticello contains modern classrooms, a computer center, a computer-based language lab, and dormitories. Next to Villa Monticello is the 22,000-volume M. Crist Fleming Library. Villa Aurora provides new classrooms for the Middle School. The fine arts program is housed in Ca'Gioia, and the Coach House has additional art and photography studios. Classes are also held in the dormitories of Belvedere and Villa Del Sole. The Palestra houses a sports complex with a gymnasium, fitness center, dance studio, locker rooms, student lounge with café, and music rooms. The School recently completed the John E. Palmer Cultural Center, which includes a state-of-the-art theater, and Fiammetta, which houses classrooms. Lanterna is the newest building, which includes classrooms and the health center. The newly renovated Casa Al Focolare houses Elementary School students from prekindergarten to first grade. A second gymnasium and new arts center is slated for completion in September 2012.

BOARDING AND GENERAL FACILITIES

The campus includes ten dormitories, each of which houses from 6 to 43 students. Dormitories are located in Villa De Nobili, Villa Monticello, Hadsall House, Villa Del Sole, Balmelli, Giani, Belvedere, and Lanterna. All dormitories are supervised, and some faculty members live in the dormitories. Rooms accommodate from 2 to 4 students each. Although School facilities are closed during the winter and spring vacations, optional faculty-chaperoned trips are offered for students who are unable to return home.

Two recreation centers and a snack bar serve as focal points for student social activities. Three fully qualified nurses are in residence.

ATHLETICS

Students are required to participate in either a varsity sport three days a week or recreational sports after classes. Sports available include soccer, basketball, fitness training, mountain biking, volleyball, rugby, tennis, track and field, squash, swimming, rock climbing, and aerobics. Horseback riding and tennis are available at an extra cost. On weekends, students often go on hiking and mountain-climbing trips in the Swiss Alps during the fall and spring and go skiing during the winter. During Ski Week in Crans-Montana (High School) or Verbier (Middle School), every student takes lessons in downhill or cross-country skiing or snowboarding. The Fleming Cup ski race and a faculty versus students hockey game are held during the Crans-Montana week.

Varsity sports give students the opportunity to compete against many schools in Switzerland and other countries and to take part in tournaments sponsored by the Swiss Group of International Schools. Varsity sports include soccer, volleyball, basketball, tennis, and track and field. Students also have the opportunity to enroll in the AC Milan soccer program, run by the coaches of the renowned Italian soccer team AC Milan.

Facilities include a playing field, a gym, and an outdoor basketball/volleyball area. The newly constructed Palestra sports complex includes a gymnasium with seating for up to 400 spectators, a dance studio, a fitness center, changing rooms, and a student lounge with a café.

EXTRACURRICULAR OPPORTUNITIES

The School's location in central Europe offers an enviable range of cultural opportunities. Trips to concerts, art galleries, and museums in Lugano, Locarno, and Milan extend education beyond the classroom. All students participate in the the Academic Travel program, a four-day, faculty-chaperoned trip in the fall and a seven-day, faculty-chaperoned trip in the spring to such cities as Athens, Barcelona, Florence, Madrid, Munich, Nice, Paris, Prague, Rome, Venice, and Vienna.

On-campus activities include drama productions, choral and instrumental music, Model Congress, Environmental Club, Student Council, yearbook, and the Student Weekend Activities Team (SWAT). The Service Learning program focuses on the TASIS community, the local community, the interschool community, and the global community. Opportunities include peer tutoring, volunteering at a local domestic violence shelter, participating in Model UN, and work with Habitat for Humanity. TASIS also offers an annual summer service trip to Africa. Special annual social events include Family Weekend, dinner dances at the beginning of the academic year and at Christmas, prom, and the spring arts festival, along with a special graduation banquet and ceremony for seniors.

DAILY LIFE

Classes start at 8 a.m. and follow a rotating schedule. Classes meet from 50 to 65 minutes. There are weekly all-School assemblies, and students meet with their advisers every day. Sports and activities take place after school until 5:30 p.m. Meals are served buffet-style except for Wednesday evenings, when students share a formal dinner with their adviser group. Evening study is from 7 until 10.

WEEKEND LIFE

Both day and boarding students are encouraged to participate in organized events on weekends, including mountain-climbing and camping trips to scenic areas in Switzerland, shopping trips to open-air markets in northern Italy, and sightseeing excursions to Zurich, Milan, Venice, or Florence. On-campus events include talent shows, open-mic coffeehouse afternoons, films, and discotheque dances.

On weekends, students have Lugano town privileges if they have no School commitments and are in good academic and social standing. All excursions beyond Lugano are chaperoned by a member of the faculty, except those for seniors and some juniors, who, with parental permission, enjoy the privilege of independent travel in groups of 2 or more.

COSTS AND FINANCIAL AID

The all-inclusive tuition fee for boarding students was CHF 69,000 for the 2011–12 academic year, with an enrollment deposit of CHF 3000. This includes all fees that are necessary for attendance: room, board, tuition, eleven days of academic travel, Ski Week, all textbooks, laundry, activities, and most lab fees. A monthly personal allowance of CHF 250–300 is recommended. Seventy percent of the tuition is due by July 1 and the remainder by November 15.

Students may apply for financial aid, which is granted on the basis of merit, need, and the student's ability to contribute to the School community.

ADMISSIONS INFORMATION

All applicants are considered on the basis of previous academic records, three teachers' evaluations, a personal statement, and a parental statement. The SSAT is recommended, and the SLEP test is required for students whose native language is not English. TASIS does not discriminate on the basis of race, color, nationality, or ethnic origin in its admissions policies and practices.

Application for entrance is recommended only for those students with sufficient academic interest and motivation to benefit from the program. The School accepts students from prekindergarten to grade 12 and at the postgraduate level.

APPLICATION TIMETABLE

TASIS has a rolling admissions policy and considers applications throughout the year. Applicants are encouraged to make an appointment to visit the campus. Within ten days of receipt of a completed application, the CHF 300 application fee, an official transcript from the previous school, and three teachers' evaluations, the Admissions Committee notifies the parents of its decision.

ADMISSIONS CORRESPONDENCE

Mr. William E. Eichner, Director of Admissions
TASIS The American School in Switzerland
CH-6926 Montagnola-Lugano
Switzerland
Phone: 41-91-960-5151
Fax: 41-91-993-2979
E-mail: admissions@tasis.ch
Web site: http://www.tasis.com

or

The TASIS Schools
112 South Royal Street
Alexandria, Virginia 22314
Phone: 703-299-8150
Fax: 703-299-8157
E-mail: usadmissions@tasis.com

THOMAS JEFFERSON SCHOOL

St. Louis, Missouri

Type: Coeducational boarding and day college-preparatory school
Grades: 7–12
Enrollment: 92
Head of School: Elizabeth L. Holekamp, Ph.D.

THE SCHOOL

Thomas Jefferson School was founded in 1946. It has received national attention for its academic excellence and its teacher-trustee system, the two guiding ideas of the founders. It became coeducational in 1971. The campus is a 20-acre estate in Sunset Hills, a suburb 15 miles southwest of downtown St. Louis.

The School's mission is to give its students the strongest possible academic background through a classical education. Within a nurturing community, students develop a responsibility for their own learning and a desire to lift up the world with beauty and intellect. Many of the School's distinctive features, such as the daily schedule, are outgrowths of this mission.

The School is unique in its business organization. A majority of the members of its Board of Trustees must be teachers in the School; moreover, no one may teach full-time for more than five years without becoming a trustee. The Headmaster and the other teacher-trustees make up the administration of the School, with the exception of the Director of Development, who is not a faculty member. This structure gives teachers a greater stake in the School and a breadth of experience that produces better teaching.

Thomas Jefferson School is a member of the National Association of Independent Schools, the Association of Boarding Schools, the Independent Schools Association of the Central States, Midwest Boarding Schools, the School and Student Service for Financial Aid, and the Educational Records Bureau.

ACADEMIC PROGRAMS

Thomas Jefferson offers a challenging approach to learning, with the emphasis on the student's own efforts. Classes are short, and the teachers seldom lecture; instead, all students are called on to answer questions and generate discussion. During afternoon and evening study time, the students have a good deal of freedom in choosing when and where to do their homework, with help readily available from faculty members.

Seventh and eighth graders take English, mathematics, science, social studies, and Latin. In the ninth through twelfth grades, students take 4 years of English; 4 years of mathematics through calculus; 2 years of Greek (ninth and tenth grades); 2 years of Italian or French (tenth and eleventh); at least 3 years of science, including an AP course; and at least 2 years of history, including AP American history. Electives include additional language, science, and history courses. Advanced Placement exams are a standard part of the courses in American history, government and politics, calculus, biology, advanced French, junior and senior English, physics, and chemistry. The faculty members also help students work toward AP exams in Latin, computer science, and studio art.

The English curriculum gives students intensive training in grammar, vocabulary, and writing skills. They also read and discuss a great deal of literature, including recognized classics (Shakespeare, the Bible, and epics), time-tested authors (Austen, Dickens, Dostoyevsky, Fitzgerald, Manzoni, Melville, and Shaw), and more recent major authors, such as Amy Tan, Ralph Ellison, and Chaim Potok.

A special feature is the study of classical Greek, which contributes to intellectual development (including concrete benefits such as enhanced vocabulary) and cultural background. This subject, in which the School is a national leader, continues to stir curiosity and ambition. A number of graduates continue to study it in college; others do so independently or later in life.

The average class size is 15, and the overall student-teacher ratio is 7:1. During the day, teachers are accessible to everyone and are ready to help; one teacher is on duty each evening and visits the students' rooms to assist with homework. Younger new students and those having academic difficulty are placed in afternoon or evening study halls.

The grading system uses letter grades of A, B, C, D, and E. An average of B– is Honors; an average of A– is High Honors. To remain in good standing, a student must have no more than one D in any marking period; students in their first year, however, are allowed extra time to adjust. One-hour examinations are given at the end of the first and third quarters (October and April), and 2- to 3-hour examinations are given at midyear and at the end of the year. Following each exam period, a student's adviser sends the parents a letter discussing the student's progress and giving the latest grades and teachers' comments.

The unusually long winter and spring vacations (about one month each) give students an opportunity to unwind, spend time with their families, and do independent work for extra credit.

FACULTY AND ADVISERS

The faculty, including the Head of School, consists of 8 women and 5 men. Faculty members hold thirteen baccalaureate degrees, twelve master's degrees, one law degree, and three Ph.D.'s.

Dr. Elizabeth Holekamp became the fourth Head of School in the summer of 2011, succeeding William Rowe. Dr. Holekamp attended the University of Missouri and holds a Ph.D. from Indiana University.

All faculty members are expected to continue educating themselves by regular reading, both within and outside the subject areas they teach. They meet periodically to report on their reading and to discuss it.

Currently, 6 of the 13 faculty members live on the campus, along with 2 resident assistants and one staff member. Each teacher, whether resident or not, has several duties besides teaching, such as athletics supervision, evening study help, and advising students. Teachers meet with each of their advisees regularly to check the student's grades and to keep in touch with his or her personal development.

COLLEGE ADMISSION COUNSELING

Three experienced faculty members serve as college advisers, guiding the seniors through the process, helping them develop a realistic list of choices, and offering advice on writing personal essays. They also spend many hours following up with colleges by phone and e-mail.

In sixty-five years, the School has had 594 graduates; all have gone to college—most to well-known, selective institutions. Among the colleges and universities attended by Thomas Jefferson graduates in the past nine years are Boston University (6), Brown (2), Caltech (2), Carnegie Mellon (1), Carleton (1), Claremont-McKenna (2), Columbia (2), Duke (3), Emory (3), Harvard (1), Haverford (5), Johns Hopkins (4), Lake Forest (3), Northwestern (6), Pitzer (2), Pomona (3), Reed (3), Rensselaer (2), Rhodes (4), Smith (2), Stanford (1), Swarthmore (2), Vanderbilt (4), Washington (St. Louis) (10), Wesleyan (3), and the Universities of Missouri (6) and Chicago (4).

Ten-year medians for the SAT are 710 critical reading and 670 math.

STUDENT BODY AND CONDUCT

In 2011–12, the School has 92 students (53 boarding, 39 day). Most students come from the region between the Appalachians and the Great Plains. Approximately one third are international students from various countries (ESL instruction is available, although knowledge of English is required for admission). Most grades have girls and boys in about equal numbers.

A Student Council, whose members are elected twice a year, brings student concerns before the faculty and helps maintain a healthy, studious atmosphere. Collectively, the council has one vote in faculty meetings on any decision concerning student life.

Demerits are given for misconduct, lateness, and other routine matters; a student who receives too many demerits in one week has to do chores around the campus on Saturday. Students may appeal any demerits, even those given by the Head of School, before a Student Appeals Court.

ACADEMIC FACILITIES

The Main Building, a former residence, provides a comfortable, homelike setting for classes and meals; it also contains faculty and administrative offices, the library, computer terminals, and an art gallery. Sayers Hall, next to the Main Building, provides science laboratories, classrooms, and a library/computer annex. In 2008, the School opened a new art facility and built an addition onto the gymnasium.

BOARDING AND GENERAL FACILITIES

Boarders live in the Gables—a smaller building from the original estate—and in five modern one-story houses, built in 1960, plus one additional, similar house added in 1994. Each house has four double rooms; each room has an outside entrance, a private bath, large windows, wall-to-wall carpeting, and air conditioning. The houses were designed to provide quiet, privacy, and independence. Normally, 2 or 3 boarding students share a room with 1 or 2 day students. All dorm rooms provide phone and Internet access.

ATHLETICS

Thomas Jefferson School athletics are meant to help students relax, stay healthy and in good condition, and study better. Outdoor sports include intramural tennis (five courts), varsity soccer, and fitness; indoor sports are volleyball and basketball, both varsity and JV. Athletics are required on Monday, Tuesday, Thursday, and Friday afternoons. Teams compete with other local schools in basketball, soccer, and volleyball.

EXTRACURRICULAR OPPORTUNITIES

St. Louis has a wealth of resources in art, music, and theater, as well as an excellent zoo, a science museum, and a world-renowned botanical garden. The faculty members keep the students informed about opportunities around town and help provide them with transportation and tickets whenever possible. Teachers often take groups of students on informal weekend field trips. In recent years, groups have gone to the Ozarks for camping, to the Mississippi River to see bald eagles, and to many symphony concerts, ballets, and plays. Students also attend movies, sports events, and concerts.

Volunteer service is a required part of the program, and the School helps students find opportunities for service. All students must plan and complete a required amount of voluntary community service before they graduate. Students are encouraged to pursue their own interests, such as music lessons, and the School helps make arrangements. A piano is available. Over the years, students have initiated and sustained major activities, such as the School yearbook, a student newspaper, mock trial, and the all-school play.

DAILY LIFE

A school day begins with breakfast at 7:45. Eight 35-minute class periods (and lunch) take place between 8:30 and 1:10. In grades 11 and 12, students take four classes and in grades 7 through 10, they take five. Classes meet daily, but AP classes, which have longer assignments, may meet only four days a week. After lunch, a student may have a science lab, a language lab, or other supplementary academic work. Then they have an hour of athletics, perhaps a meeting with their adviser or study help from another teacher, and some independent time in which they are expected to start their homework for the next day. Dinner is at 5:45, and evenings are devoted to study. On Wednesday and Friday afternoons, there are fine-arts classes in such subjects as drawing, photography, ceramics, and art and music appreciation, and students may leave the campus for nearby shopping centers. Day students are on campus from about 8:30 to 5.

WEEKEND LIFE

Weekends are leisure time. As long as students are in good standing academically, they have considerable freedom and may leave the campus for movies, shopping, dates, and overnights. Older students may keep cars on campus at the discretion of the faculty, and a school driver provides transportation for students as well. The sports facilities are available for weekend use. Dances are organized periodically by the Student Council.

SUMMER PROGRAMS

The School organizes summer trips to Europe for students in grades 10–12, often led by the Head of School or other experienced faculty members. Students in grades 7–9 may participate in a weeklong trip to London in the spring.

COSTS AND FINANCIAL AID

Charges for 2011–12 are $38,000 for full boarding, $36,500 for weekday boarding, and $22,000 for day students. This includes room plus all meals for boarders and all lunches for day students. Approximately $2000 covers books, school supplies, and other expenses related to School activities. Optional off-campus activities such as music lessons (and the necessary transportation) cost extra.

A $2000 deposit, nonrefundable but credited to tuition, is required when a student enrolls. The balance of the tuition is paid through Sallie Mae's TuitionPay program.

Financial aid is available, based on a family's need. About 40 percent of the student body currently receives some financial aid; the total amount awarded is more than $625,000. An applicant's family must file a statement with the School and Student Service, and this information is used in judging need. Many middle-income families receive some assistance.

ADMISSIONS INFORMATION

The School looks for signs of native intelligence, liveliness, energy, ambition, and curiosity. Strong grades and test scores are important considerations but not always the deciding ones. A candidate should submit the results of the Secondary School Admission Test (SSAT); international students submit the results of the SLEP or TOEFL. About 40 percent of those who complete the application process are accepted.

APPLICATION TIMETABLE

Inquiries and applications are welcome at any time, but the School has three rounds of admissions: early decision applicants submit their materials by mid-December and receive an answer in early January; regular decision applicants submit their materials by mid-February and receive an answer in early March; after April, applications for any remaining openings are considered as they are received. As part of the application process, prospective students usually spend a day at the School visiting classes, having lunch, and spending time with the admissions staff to ask questions and have an interview. There is a $40 fee for domestic applications, and a $100 fee for international applications.

ADMISSIONS CORRESPONDENCE

Jane Roth and Ken Colston, Co-Directors of Admissions
Thomas Jefferson School
4100 South Lindbergh Boulevard
St. Louis, Missouri 63127
Phone: 314-843-4151
Fax: 314-843-3527
E-mail: admissions@tjs.org
Web site: http://www.tjs.org

TILTON SCHOOL

Tilton, New Hampshire

Type: Coeducational boarding and day college-preparatory
Grades: 9–12, postgraduate year
Enrollment: 250
Head of School: James R. Clements

THE SCHOOL

Tilton School challenges students to embrace and navigate a world marked by diversity and change. Through the quality of human relationships, Tilton School's faculty cultivates in its students the curiosity, the skills, the knowledge and understanding, the character, and the integrity requisite for the passionate pursuit of lifelong personal success and service.

Tilton School values education—the active pursuit of knowledge and the growth of intellectual curiosity. The rigorous academic program is designed to prepare graduates to be successful college students and contributing members of society. Various pathways to learning are supported; the acquisition of genuine understanding is the goal. Tilton is committed to the principle that all students can excel. Through a broad range of learning experiences, students discover the power of their potential by developing problem-solving skills and self confidence while becoming independent and critical thinkers.

A nonprofit corporation, Tilton is governed by the Head of School and a 26-member Board of Trustees. Annual expenses of $8.8 million are met through tuition, endowment, and annual giving. The endowment currently totals $15.2 million. More than 5,200 living alumni have a beneficial impact on fund raising, with pledges and gifts to the School of more than $1.7 million annually for both annual and restricted purposes.

Tilton School is accredited by the New England Association of Schools and Colleges and is a member of the National Association of Independent Schools, the Independent Schools Association of Northern New England, the Cum Laude Society, the National Honor Society, the Secondary School Admission Test Board, and the Council for Religion in Independent Schools.

ACADEMIC PROGRAMS

Tilton's academic program offers a traditional college-preparatory curriculum framed within a twenty-first century skills-based program, supporting the student's intellectual maturation and encouraging the development of academic and personal competencies. The School seeks to produce students who have a genuine interest in intellectual pursuits, to teach students self-discipline, and to reinforce in students the sound moral and ethical judgment that are needed to successfully navigate the complex and changing world of the twenty-first century.

The school year is divided into two semesters. During each term, students at Tilton take a minimum of five full-credit courses. Required credits include English, mathematics, world language, fine arts, laboratory science, and social science (history), for a total of 18.

Interdisciplinary standards in the five essential domains of critical thinking, communication, creativity, community, and character are the cornerstones of the curriculum.

The program of study for ninth grade students is a team-taught integrated program (F.I.R.S.T.—foundation, integrity, respect, service, team) emphasizing a strong academic foundation and supportive intellectual, personal, and social development.

Additional grade-level programs are designed from grade 10 through grades 11, 12, and the postgraduate (PG) year to support student growth and development in a purposefully designed program. At the end of the tenth grade year, and prior to graduation, all students must provide evidence of learning that meets benchmark curriculum standards through participation in performance assessment programs, the Gateway Program (grade 10), and the Capstone Project (graduating class).

The average class size is 12 students, and the student-teacher ratio is 6:1. Evening study hall is supervised. Evening study hours are designed to allow for availability of resources and a quiet, uninterrupted study atmosphere where reinforcement of learned skills can be emphasized under direct supervision by faculty members. Academic focus is the primary purpose of evening study hall, which provides a balance of structure and self-directed study.

At Tilton School, student learning is assessed by measuring demonstrated performance of learned skills and knowledge against specific standards developed for grade levels, departments, and specific courses that have been structured within the School's twenty-first century skills-curriculum framework, with reference to national and state standards for specific academic disciplines. Within this system, letter grades mean the following; A = significantly exceeds the standard; B = exceeds the standard; C = meets the standard; D = does not yet meet the standard.

The Learning Center serves approximately 30 percent of the students, complementing their regular academic instruction by identifying individual needs and helping to devise strategies that enable them to achieve academic success. The center provides specialized instructional support for students whose academic progress is limited by deficiencies in basic skills or study habits, or by distinct learning-style differences. A 2:1 SAT tutorial is also offered through the center.

The English as a Second Language Program serves students who need intermediate and advanced English language support skills.

FACULTY AND ADVISERS

Tilton's faculty consists of 68 members. All of the faculty members hold bachelor's degrees, and there are also twenty-five advanced degrees among them, including two Ph.D.'s and a Juris Doctor. Most members of the faculty and administration live on campus with their families.

Faculty members must have not only a high level of expertise in their academic areas but also an enthusiastic commitment to students' interests and student life. In addition to dormitory and afternoon coaching and activity duties, most faculty members have 6 to 8 student advisees. The adviser is responsible for monitoring academic progress and for counseling in other areas of school life.

James R. Clements, appointed Head of School in 1998, is a graduate of the University of New Hampshire (B.A., 1972; M.B.A., 1998). Prior to joining Tilton, Mr. Clements spent twenty-one years at the Chapel Hill–Chauncy Hall School in Waltham, Massachusetts, most recently as Head of School from 1993–98.

COLLEGE ADMISSION COUNSELING

Three full-time counselors guide students in the selection of colleges and coordinate the application process, beginning in the junior year. College admissions officers visit the School each year to talk with groups of students or to interview individual students.

Members of the classes of 2007–11 were accepted at numerous colleges and universities, including Bates, Bowdoin, Boston University, Carnegie Mellon, Clarkson, Colby, Cornell, Denison, Hobart and William Smith, Holy Cross, Lake Forest, Middlebury, Notre Dame, Syracuse, Trinity, Tufts, Union, Vassar, Wesleyan, and the Universities of Massachusetts, New Hampshire, and Vermont.

STUDENT BODY AND CONDUCT

In 2011–12, Tilton enrolled 250 students—75 percent are boarders and 25 percent are day students. There are 163 boys and 87 girls. Tilton students represent many racial, religious, and socioeconomic backgrounds; eighteen states are represented, with approximately 60 percent of the students coming from New England, 20 percent from other parts of the United States, and 20 percent from thirteen other countries.

Expectations at Tilton are high and are thoroughly communicated. Although the immediate goal of School rules and regulations is to promote order, mutual respect, and academic excellence, this structure serves, in the long range, to prepare students for productive and responsible roles in a changing society. At Tilton, there is a basic faith in young people. Guided by the attitude that students can learn and want to learn, faculty members are eager to inspire commitment, pride, and responsibility in their students.

ACADEMIC FACILITIES

Plimpton Hall and the academic building create the academic quad on the West side of campus. Plimpton Hall houses ten classrooms for English, social science, and English as a second language (ESL), the Center for Leadership room, the computer center, admissions, college counseling, the business office, and the school store. The academic building is home to three state-of-the-art science classrooms/labs, three math classrooms, four world language classrooms, a world language lab, the ninth grade seminar room, a solarium, the Learning Center, and the Davis Lecture Hall that seats 100. All classrooms include wireless access and electronic interactive whiteboards.

Two music classrooms, two practice rooms and the art gallery are contained in the lower level of the chapel. The Helene Grant Daly Art Center provides excellent facilities for art classes, including ceramics, graphic arts, studio art, printmaking, sculpture, silk-screening, and photography. The Lucien Hunt Memorial Library contains approximately 17,500 volumes, including subscriptions to numerous periodicals, newspapers, encyclopedias, and an online periodical index. The library features ten computers; several Kindles, iPods, and iPads; reading and conference rooms; and extensive facilities for research. Drama and musical productions are performed in the Rome Theater in Hamilton Hall.

The Tilton campus is connected by a fiber-optic backbone that supports the School's intranet and access to the Internet. All classrooms and dormitories are connected to the network via a combination of wired and wireless networks. All students have their own account, accessible through a password. The network supports both Windows and MAC OS environments. The world language lab is a state-of-the-art digital lab with twenty-four workstations. There is also a student computer lab, two laptop carts with twenty-one laptops, and iPads available for classroom use. The Daly Art Center has both iMacs and computers for graphic arts and photography instruction.

BOARDING AND GENERAL FACILITIES

Nine dormitories, each housing 18 to 48 students and 1 to 4 faculty members and their families, are located on campus. Students live in double or single rooms. Returning students may state their preference for room assignments.

The new Maloney Hall is a 15,000-square-foot dormitory housing 20 students and includes three faculty apartments. Highlights of the new facility include a two-story common room, a group study room, suite-style rooms (two double rooms that share a common bathroom), a recreation room, a laundry area, and storage space.

The school store, MARC Student Center, and the snack bar are open at various times of the day and evening. There is a six-bed health center operated by LRGH (Lakes Region General Hospital), with a resident nurse and a doctor on call.

ATHLETICS

The School believes that people of all ages perform best when they are active and healthy and that organized sports promote physical development, physical courage, self-discipline, and a sense of team spirit. All students must participate in an afternoon activity. Students must play at least one sport each year to fulfill their annual athletic requirement.

Boys' sports include baseball, basketball, football, ice hockey, lacrosse, soccer, and tennis. Girls' sports are basketball, field hockey, ice hockey, lacrosse, soccer, softball, and tennis. Coed sports include Alpine skiing, cross-country running, cycling, golf, mountain biking, snowboarding, and wrestling.

Facilities include 22 acres of outstanding playing fields, 3 miles of cross-country trails, three tennis courts, a gymnasium, a field house with an indoor ice rink, and an outdoor swimming pool. The golf team uses a nearby eighteen-hole course.

EXTRACURRICULAR OPPORTUNITIES

Tilton's +5 Program, distinctive among independent secondary schools, requires that all students involve themselves in five areas of nonacademic campus life: art and culture; outdoor experiences; community service; leadership roles; and ethical, moral, and spiritual development. These learning experiences enhance self-confidence and self-esteem.

By structuring extracurricular activities, the School broadens students' interests, enables them to develop skills that enhance their self-worth, and provides enjoyment during their free time. Faculty members' commitment to excellence and their guidance encourage and reassure students who may be doubtful of their abilities. As a result, strong relationships develop, and students and teachers work together more effectively in the classroom.

Offerings in art and culture include drama, musical theater, tech crew, ceramics, graphic arts, studio art, photography, music studio, and chorus.

Throughout the school year, there are opportunities to participate in outdoor trips for canoeing, mountain biking, Alpine skiing, fishing, rock climbing, hiking, snowshoeing, or cross-country skiing. An afternoon outdoor program is offered as an activity in the fall and winter seasons.

Community service opportunities are available both on campus and in the Tilton community. This division of the +5 Program encourages students to commit themselves to helping others. Other projects include helping at a soup kitchen; reading to patients at the New Hampshire Veterans' Home; tutoring local children; raising funds for UNICEF, Oxfam, and Toys for Tots; and teaching in a learn-to-skate program for young children.

Leadership may be the most important of the five areas. Experience as an admissions ambassador, dorm proctor, work-program supervisor, Student Council officer, editor, or team captain offers a rigorous challenge.

Movies, plays, lectures, and concerts are regular events on campus, while trips to museums and theaters in Boston are regular off-campus activities.

DAILY LIFE

Class periods are approximately 45 minutes long, with each class meeting once a week for a 75-minute double period. Mid-morning each day, there is a meeting either with advisee groups, special committees, or the entire School at School Meeting, which is held two times per week. Conference period, X-Period, and campus service programs are also part of student life. The conference period is an opportunity to meet teachers for extra help or to make an appointment to meet a teacher later in the evening for more extensive work. X-Period is held once a week and was developed to cement a time where student clubs and organizations could meet.

After classes, all students participate in an afternoon activity. Each of the three seasons, fall, winter, and spring, will offer a number of different sports or programs for the students to choose from. Wednesday and Saturday schedules are half days, which allows time for athletic competitions and program activities.

WEEKEND LIFE

Faculty and staff teams plan all weekend activities with student support. Saturday events include sports competitions, movies, dances, concerts, and trips to shopping areas and movie theaters. The gym, field house, student center, and art center are periodically open both Saturday and Sunday. Sunday is for scheduled activities, both on and off the campus. Day students are invited to participate and are active in weekend life.

COSTS AND FINANCIAL AID

For 2011–12, tuition, room, and board cost $44,900; tuition for day students was $25,900. Additional expenses, such as those for books and laundry, range from $600 to $1000. Private music or voice lessons, skiing, snowboarding, learning center sessions, and ESL classes are charged separately. Tuition may be paid in full in mid-July, or families can take advantage of one of Tilton's payment plan options.

Forty percent of the students receive financial aid in the form of direct grants and/or loans. For 2011–12, more than $2 million in aid was granted. Applications for aid, which should be made before February 15, are reviewed separately from admission decisions.

ADMISSIONS INFORMATION

The Admissions Committee seeks to admit students who will benefit from and contribute to Tilton and those of diverse backgrounds and individual personal strengths. Students with various academic abilities who seek to challenge themselves and take advantage of Tilton's programs within and outside the classroom are excellent candidates for admission. Candidates for the ninth and tenth grades should take the SSAT and have the results sent to Tilton. Eleventh and twelfth graders and postgraduates should take the PSAT or SAT. Additional application requirements for admission include the student's school transcript and current teacher recommendations. All prospective students are expected to visit the School and interview with the Admissions Office. Students may enter at all grade levels; entry in the eleventh or twelfth grade or the postgraduate year is more competitive.

APPLICATION TIMETABLE

Initial inquiries are welcome at any time but are recommended before the late spring prior to the year in which admission is sought. Ideally, applications (accompanied by a $50 application fee or $100 international application fee) should be filed by February 1. The Admissions Office is open for interviews on weekdays and on selected Saturday mornings. It is best to plan a visit while school is in session.

Admissions decisions for applications received by February 1 are made on March 10. After March 10 decisions are made on a rolling basis. The School adheres to the Parents' Reply Date of April 10. A nonrefundable deposit is required to hold a place at Tilton and is applied to tuition for the year.

ADMISSIONS CORRESPONDENCE

Beth Skoglund
Director of Admissions
Tilton School
Tilton, New Hampshire 03276
Phone: 603-286-1733
Fax: 603-286-1705
E-mail: admissions@tiltonschool.org
Web site: http://www.tiltonschool.org

TRINITY–PAWLING SCHOOL

Pawling, New York

Type: Boys' boarding (9–PG) and day (7–PG) college-preparatory school
Grades: 7–12, postgraduate year
Enrollment: 310
Head of School: Archibald A. Smith III, Headmaster

THE SCHOOL

The Pawling School was founded in 1907 by Dr. Frederick Gamage. In 1946, it was renamed Trinity-Pawling School in recognition of its ties with Trinity School of New York City. In 1978, Trinity-Pawling School became a separate educational and corporate entity. Trinity-Pawling's Episcopal background is reflected in daily chapel services and course offerings in religion, ethics, and psychology.

The School is located 68 miles north of New York City along the Connecticut border; regular train service is available from Grand Central Station to Pawling (population 5,000). The campus, set on 140 acres of rolling hills, is just over an hour's drive from New York's major airports. On vacations, the School transports students to and from the airports and train stations.

It is Trinity-Pawling's belief that an appreciation of one's own worth can best be discovered by experiencing the worth of others, by understanding the value of one's relationship with others, and by acquiring a sense of self-confidence that comes through living and working competently at the level of one's own potential. Trinity-Pawling respects and recognizes the differences in individuals and the different processes required to achieve their educational potential.

The School is governed by a self-perpetuating 26-member Board of Trustees. The School raises more than $1 million in annual giving, in part from its more than 5,000 alumni. The School's endowment exceeds $30 million, and its operating budget for 2011–12 is more than $10 million.

Trinity-Pawling is accredited by the New York State Association of Independent Schools and chartered by the New York State Board of Regents. It is a member of the National Association of Independent Schools, the Secondary School Admission Test Board, the New York State Association of Independent Schools (NYSAIS), and the National Association of Episcopal Schools.

ACADEMIC PROGRAMS

To graduate from Trinity-Pawling, a student must obtain a minimum of 112 credits in eight disciplines to earn a diploma. A full-year course is worth 6 credits, and a term course (trimester) is worth 2 credits. If a student enters after grade 9, his school record is evaluated and translated into Trinity-Pawling's system.

Students are required to complete 90 credits in the following subjects: 24 credits in English; 18 credits in mathematics; 18 credits in a laboratory science; 18 credits in history; 12 credits in a foreign language (excluding Language Program students); 6 credits in fine, performing, or studio arts (music, art, drafting, or drama); 4 credits in religion or philosophy; and 2 credits in health. Additionally, students must take 22 credits of elective courses. Advanced Placement courses are offered in English, U.S. history, European history, economics, chemistry, physics, biology, environmental science, mathematics, computer science, Latin, French, and Spanish.

Students carry a minimum of five courses per term. Evening study periods, held in student residences, are supervised by dorm masters. Students with academic difficulty have a formally supervised study hall. Teachers are available to give students extra help at any time that is agreeable to both. Reports are posted online for parents three times per term. Trinity-Pawling uses a number grading system (0–100) in which 60 is passing, 80 qualifies for honors, and 85 qualifies for high honors.

In addition to academic grades, the School utilizes a unique effort system to rank students based on overall effort in many aspects of School life, including academics, athletics, clubs, and dormitory life. A student's privileges are then tied to his overall effort ranking. This program is designed to work in conjunction with the School's philosophy of encouraging each student to work toward his own personal potential.

The Language Program, open to a maximum of 40 students, is initiated in the ninth and tenth grades. A modification of the Orton-Gillingham method, it strives to retrain students with developmental dyslexia. First-year students work in pairs with tutors. In addition, they take a skills-oriented language arts course. Phonetics, sequencing ideas, handwriting, memorization, and other language skills are emphasized. The second-year student is placed in an analytical writing class in addition to a skills-level English class. All students in the program also take basic history, mathematics, and science courses. The program's goal is to enable students to complete Trinity-Pawling's regular college-preparatory curriculum. Students in the program are not required to take a foreign language but may elect to do so.

FACULTY AND ADVISERS

There are 58 full-time members of the faculty, all of whom reside on the campus. Members of the teaching faculty hold fifty-eight baccalaureate and thirty-five graduate degrees. All participate in counseling and advising students. The School actively supports advanced study for its teachers during summers and other holidays.

Archibald A. Smith III was appointed Headmaster in 1990, after having served at Trinity-Pawling as a chemistry teacher, Director of College Placement, and Assistant Headmaster at various times since 1975. He is a graduate of St. John's School in Houston, Texas; Trinity College (Hartford) (B.S., 1972); and Wesleyan University (M.S., 1980). His career also includes teaching at the Northwood School in Lake Placid, New York. Mr. Smith is the past president of the New York State Association of Independent Schools and a member of the Accreditation Council of NYSAIS. He is a trustee of Dutchess Day School, a trustee of the International Boys School Coalition, a trustee of the Parents' League of New York, and is a member of the Headmasters Association.

COLLEGE ADMISSION COUNSELING

Trinity-Pawling's Director of College Counseling works closely with other administrators and faculty members to advise and aid students and their families with college placement. Individual meetings and group workshops are held on a regular basis, and more than 100 college representatives visit the campus each fall for presentations and interviews. More than 95 percent of the class of 2011 gained admission to their first- or second-choice college.

All of the 2010 graduates earned college or university acceptances. Among those they attend are Bucknell, Berkeley, Carnegie Mellon, George Washington, Johns Hopkins, Northwestern, Occidental, Princeton, Purdue, Salve Regina, Skidmore, Syracuse, Trinity, Tulane, U.S. Military Academy at West Point, and Vermont.

STUDENT BODY AND CONDUCT

Boarding students number 240, and day students number 70. Students come from twenty-nine states and thirteen countries. Students from minority groups make up 18 percent of the total enrollment. Students who choose Trinity-Pawling tend to desire a reasonably structured community that is dedicated to individual growth. A strong academic program in harmony with fine athletics and activities programs brings the School together. The School seeks students who want to actively pursue their academic and social development in a caring atmosphere.

Major violations of community rules are handled by a Faculty-Student Disciplinary Committee, which makes recommendations to the Headmaster. Less serious breaches are handled by the Dean of Students and others.

The Student-Faculty Senate is composed of School prefects and elected student and faculty representatives. The senate works to develop self-government, plans School activities, and fosters a bond between the students and the faculty. It consists of six committees, each with a responsibility for specific areas of School life.

ACADEMIC FACILITIES

The Dann Building (1964) and the Science and Technology Center (2002) house classrooms and science and computer labs. The Art Building, completed in 2004, houses the fine arts, theater, and music programs. This building contains a theater that is used for student productions, lectures, and visiting professional performances. The library features an online catalog, more than 28,000 volumes, and available computers. It is located in the historic Cluett Building, which also contains administrative offices and the student center.

BOARDING AND GENERAL FACILITIES

Students reside in single or double rooms in eighteen dormitory units located in eight buildings, including Starr Hall (1984), Starr East (1987), and Cluett (renovated 1995). Each is under the supervision of 1 or more faculty members aided by senior proctors. Students are allowed to choose roommates, and, whenever possible, housing choice is granted. Students are grouped in housing units according to grade level. A student's dorm master is usually his adviser, so a strong personal relationship often develops. Trinity-Pawling stresses the value of close student-faculty relationships.

Students enjoy a School store and snack bar that are open daily. The Scully Dining Hall was completed in 2009. Medical services are provided by the Health Center, staffed by a resident nurse and a doctor who makes daily visits. Several hospitals serve the area. Trinity-Pawling is within walking distance of the village of Pawling.

ATHLETICS

Trinity-Pawling is a member of the New England Private School Athletic Conference and the Founders League, which affords it the opportunity to play schools in New England, such as Avon, Choate, Hotchkiss, Kent, Loomis Chaffee, Salisbury, Taft, and Westminster. Because the School believes that athletics and physical development are key ingredients in a student's growth, all students are required to participate in the program during the school year. Three or four levels of teams are formed in each interscholastic sport, including baseball, basketball, cross country, football, golf, hockey, lacrosse, soccer, squash, tennis, track and field, and wrestling. Also offered at both the interscholastic and intramural levels are running, skiing, and weight training.

The Carleton Gymnasium contains a 50-foot by 90-foot basketball court with two cross courts for practice. The lower floor and wing contain weight-training rooms, five international squash courts, and locker rooms. There are also six soccer fields, a new football field, baseball fields, an all-weather track, twelve tennis courts, three lacrosse fields, ponds for skating and fishing, the McGraw wrestling pavilion, and the enclosed Tirrell Hockey Rink, which underwent a $1 million renovation in 2007.

EXTRACURRICULAR OPPORTUNITIES

Each student is encouraged to participate in one or more of the twenty-four activities offered on the campus. These activities are often initiated and directed by the students with the guidance of an interested faculty adviser. Among the offerings are the student newspaper, Model United Nations, the Minority Student Union, the yearbook, the choir, the photography club, the dramatic club, the chess club, the computer club, the fishing club, foreign language clubs, jazz groups, and the outing club. Trinity-Pawling encourages student initiative in starting new activities.

The School sponsors regular trips to nearby areas of educational and cultural interest, including museums and theaters in New York City. Annual events include Parents' Weekend, Junior Parents' Weekend, and several alumni functions. The concert series, offering five concerts annually, brings a rich variety of musical talent to the campus during the school year.

Each student participates in the work program that emphasizes the School's policy of self-responsibility and economy of operation. Boys assist with parts of the routine maintenance work throughout the buildings and on the grounds.

DAILY LIFE

At 8 a.m., three mornings a week, a brief community chapel service is held for all students. A more formal Episcopal service is held for the entire school mid-morning on Tuesdays. Classes are scheduled from 8:20 until 2:40 four days a week and until noon on Wednesdays and Saturdays. Wednesday and Saturday afternoons are reserved for interscholastic sports events. Athletic practices take place in the afternoon, while most extracurricular activities are scheduled in the evening. Lunches are generally served cafeteria-style, dinners sit-down family-style. Students are required to study from 7:30 to 9:30 in their rooms, the library, or the study hall, depending upon their academic status.

WEEKEND LIFE

Dances, plays, concerts, trips to New York City, and informal activities are planned for weekends. The Student-Faculty Senate organizes and plans many of the weekend activities. Social activities are also arranged with girls' schools in the area. Weekend leaves from the School are based upon a group rating, which encompasses a student's record in academic effort and achievement, general citizenship, and dormitory life. In general, as the group rating increases, so do the amount and nature of privileges. Students are evaluated twice per term.

COSTS AND FINANCIAL AID

Charges for 2011–12 are $47,000 for boarding students, $33,500 for day students in ninth through twelfth grade, and $23,000 for day students in seventh and eighth grade. Extra expenses total approximately $2000 per year. The Language Program is an additional $5250–$7500 per year, depending on the grade. A tuition payment plan and tuition insurance are available.

Thirty-five percent of the students receive a total of over $3 million in financial aid each year. Trinity-Pawling subscribes to the School and Student Service for Financial Aid and grants aid on the basis of need.

ADMISSIONS INFORMATION

Trinity-Pawling seeks the well-rounded student who will both gain from and give to the School. New students are accepted in all grades; a limited number are accepted for the postgraduate year. Selection is based upon all-around qualifications without regard to race, color, creed, or national origin. Candidates must submit a complete transcript plus two or three teachers' recommendations, have a personal interview at the School, and take the SSAT. Candidates for the Language Retraining Program are asked to have completed a Wechsler Test (WISC-R).

In 2011, there were 350 applicants, of whom 250 were accepted and 110 enrolled.

APPLICATION TIMETABLE

Initial inquiries are welcome at any time. Campus tours and interviews (allow 1½–2 hours) can be arranged by appointment, Monday through Friday, 8:30–1:30, and on Saturday, 8:30–11. All candidates must have an interview. The completed forms must be accompanied by a nonrefundable fee of $50 ($100 for international students).

Fall is the usual time for applying, and notification of acceptance begins in early March. Parents are expected to reply to acceptances one month after notification.

ADMISSIONS CORRESPONDENCE

MacGregor Robinson
Assistant Headmaster for External Affairs
Trinity-Pawling School
Pawling, New York 12564
Phone: 845-855-4825
Fax: 845-855-4827
E-mail: pmccracken@trinitypawling.org
Web site: http://www.trinitypawling.org

THE UNIVERSITY OF CHICAGO LABORATORY SCHOOLS

Chicago, Illinois

Type: Coeducational, day, college-preparatory school
Grades: N–12
Enrollment: 1,780
Head of School: Dr. David W. Magill

THE SCHOOL

The University of Chicago Laboratory Schools (Lab) is an independent, coeducational day school enrolling approximately 1,780 students from nursery school through twelfth grade. Founded in 1896 by John Dewey, Lab's progressive education is broad and deep, with an emphasis on the arts, humanities, math, and science. Lab is a division of the University of Chicago, and Lab students benefit from access to University professors, classes, and facilities. Lab prepares students to be critical thinkers who are equipped to handle the rigors of a complex and changing world. Each year, Lab graduates matriculate at top four-year colleges throughout the United States and abroad.

Lab is approved or accredited by the Independent Schools Association of the Central States, North Central Association of Colleges and Schools, and the Illinois Department of Education. Lab is a member of the National Association of Independent Schools.

ACADEMIC PROGRAMS

The Laboratory Schools do not specialize in a particular academic area. Rather, Lab prepares students to be creative, in-depth thinkers who are lifelong learners, ready to face the challenges of an increasingly complex global society.

Lab's curriculum is both broad and deep. All students are required to take math, science, English, history, a world language (French, German, Spanish, Latin, and Chinese), computer science, physical education, music, community learning, and fine arts. In addition, high school students may enroll in University of Chicago classes, utilize University libraries, and intern with University of Chicago faculty members. Lab graduates enter a variety of fields, including education, law, medicine, and others.

Students at University High (U-High) pursue a comprehensive liberal arts program that emphasizes analytical reading, writing, research, and strong math and science skills. Through discussion, hands-on lab work, research, and other school work, Lab students learn to read closely, form independent ideas, and write analytically. Approximately 90 percent enroll in at least one of the eight Advanced Placement or ten advanced topics courses.

FACULTY AND ADVISERS

Approximately 200 teachers, counselors, librarians, and assistant teachers comprise the faculty at the Laboratory Schools. Most have higher degrees and many have doctoral degrees.

A total of 8 current or former teachers throughout the Laboratory Schools have won the coveted Golden Apple Award for excellence in teaching, awarded by Illinois' Golden Apple Foundation, more than any other school.

COLLEGE ADMISSION COUNSELING

Two full-time college placement counselors provide step-by-step guidance to juniors, seniors, and their parents as they navigate the college admission and selection process. This includes conducting workshops on various college topics and directing families to appropriate information at each stage of the process. In 2008, the *New York Times* named the Laboratory School's college placement office the fifth best in the nation.

STUDENT BODY AND CONDUCT

Lab enrolls approximately 1,780 students from nursery school through twelfth grade, with a largely equal number of boys and girls. Lab students speak more than forty languages at home, and identify themselves as having fifty-nine different nationalities. The Nursery/Kindergarten program enrolls approximately 340 students, while the Lower School (grades 1–4) and Middle School (grades 5–8) enroll approximately 470 students each. Lab's high school, U-High, enrolls approximately 500 students. Lab students live throughout the greater Chicago area, with approximately half coming from the Hyde Park/Kenwood area. Approximately 50 percent of Lab students have parents who are affiliated with the University of Chicago.

ACADEMIC FACILITIES

Lab's campus consists of Blaine Hall (the Lower School), Belfield (the Middle School), and the University High building. Judd Hall contains Lab's administrative offices, as well as some additional classrooms. The lower, middle, and high school libraries together contain more than 100,000 volumes. Lab has art studios, a darkroom, music classrooms and practice rooms, a state-of-the-art language lab, a dance studio, and a theater. Wireless Internet access is available for students and faculty throughout the school.

Athletic facilities are located in Sunny and Kovler Gymnasium, steps away from the main buildings. In addition, Lab students have access to the academic and athletic facilities at the University of Chicago.

In 2013, Lab anticipates opening an early childhood center, which will house students from Nursery 3 through second grade.

ATHLETICS

The 2011–12 school year marks the 108th year that the Laboratory Schools have offered students interscholastic athletic competition. During the previous year, 660 students from middle through high school competed in the athletic program on one or more of Lab's forty-four different teams. Over the last three years Lab's varsity teams have won six sectional and fourteen regional championships in nine different sports. All told, Lab has 57 coaches currently, 24 of whom are faculty members. Lab's no-cut policy ensures that all students may participate in any sport they choose. The Laboratory Schools are part of the Illinois High School Association (IHSA) as a nonbounded school.

EXTRACURRICULAR OPPORTUNITIES

In the high school, students run more than forty school-sponsored organizations, ranging from religious and ethnic clubs to activities in the arts, culture, academics, philanthropy, and social activism. University High students devote significant time to many different extracurricular activities: joining sports, math, science, debate, or Model UN teams; writing and publishing the School's newspaper or yearbook; serving in student government or community service roles; and participating in theater productions or musical performances. Many of these extracurricular activities begin in the Middle School.

DAILY LIFE

Because Lab begins with children who are 3 years old, and slightly over half continue at Lab until they graduate from U-High in twelfth grade, there are enormous variances in the students' daily schedules and activities.

The nursery and kindergarten classrooms at Lab are busy, with many different activities going on at one time. This is Lab's negotiated curriculum in action: teachers prepare an environment filled with possibilities and encourage choice, initiative, exploration, and collaboration.

Lab's Lower School curriculum (first through fourth grades) is designed to help children master the skills that will serve as the foundation to their intellectual life. Children entering the Middle School years (fifth through eighth grade) begin an intense period of social, emotional, physical, moral, and intellectual growth.

U-Highers are an independent group whose high expectations go hand in hand with a demanding workload and a great deal of personal freedom. Each year, Lab students are better able to think for themselves, challenge assumptions, and, most importantly, take on increasing levels of responsibility for their own education.

SUMMER PROGRAMS

Summer Lab is a six-week program that includes Summer School, Adventure Kids Day Camp, sports camps, Fun in the Sun, and Summer Lab on Stage. Summer Lab Field Study stages domestic and international summer travel. Summer Lab embodies the notion that love of learning never goes on vacation. Approximately 900 students, from ages 3 to 18, participated last summer in the rich and diverse program, mixing Labbies with children from all around the city of Chicago, the United States, and the world.

COSTS AND FINANCIAL AID

Tuition costs for the 2011–12 academic year are as follows: $14,814 for the nursery school half-day program; $21,060 for the nursery and kindergarten full-day program; $21,876 for grades 1–4; $23,676 for grades 5–8; and $24,870 for grades 9–12.

Each year, Lab provides financial assistance to help meet the needs of deserving students and their families. Lab does not have a specific income threshold for financial aid. Rather, the Financial Aid Committee reviews a family's entire financial picture, including income, expenses, and other circumstances. Financial aid awards are not automatically renewed; families are required to reapply for aid each year. Awards are recalculated annually based on the most recent financial data.

ADMISSIONS INFORMATION

Every applicant family receives personal attention, including a meeting with an admissions representative, a tour of the schools, and an opportunity to interact with other students and faculty. Lab believes that each applicant is unique and possesses special qualities, which cannot always be captured by test scores and applications alone. Lab learns about its applicants through playgroups, classroom visits, interviews, shadow days, and tours. Applicant families also learn more about Lab's special character through this process.

APPLICATION TIMETABLE

Historically, most students enter Lab at either Nursery 3 (3 years old) or ninth grade and begin the application process in August or September of the year prior to enrollment. Applicants to the Nursery 3 program must be two years old prior to September 1 of the year of application. The Nursery 3 application deadline is September 30 of the year prior to enrollment. Admissions deadlines and details on the application process are available on Lab's Web site at www.ucls.uchicago.edu.

ADMISSIONS CORRESPONDENCE

Irene M. Reed, Executive Director
Admissions and Financial Aid
University of Chicago Laboratory Schools
1362 East 59th Street
Chicago, Illinois 60637
Phone: 773-702-9451
Fax: 773-702-1520
E-mail: admissions@ucls.uchicago.edu
Web site: http://www.ucls.uchicago.edu

VALLEY FORGE MILITARY ACADEMY & COLLEGE

Wayne, Pennsylvania

Type: Boys' college-preparatory and coeducational transfer college military boarding school
Grades: 7–PG: Middle School, 7–8; Upper School, 9–PG
Enrollment: 565
Head of School: Col. David R. Gray, Ph.D., USA (Ret.), President

THE SCHOOL

The 100-acre campus of Valley Forge Military Academy includes a boys' boarding preparatory high school and a coeducational transfer college, located 15 miles west of Philadelphia. The mission of Valley Forge is to educate individuals to be fully prepared to meet their responsibilities, alert in mind, sound in body, and considerate of others and to have a high sense of duty, honor, loyalty, and courage. Valley Forge fosters these goals through a comprehensive system that is built on the five cornerstones of academic excellence, character development, personal motivation, physical development, and leadership.

The Academy is accredited by the Middle States Association of Colleges and Schools. It holds memberships in the Association of Military Colleges and Schools of the United States, the Council for Religion in Independent Schools, the Boarding School Headmasters' Association, the International Boys School Coalition (IBSC), and the National Association of Independent Schools. The U.S. Department of the Army designates Valley Forge as an honor unit with distinction.

ACADEMIC PROGRAMS

Valley Forge seeks to educate and develop students for college entrance, career success, and responsible citizenship. A challenging curriculum, dedicated faculty members, small classes, individual attention, and faculty-supervised evening study hall provide cadets with an environment conducive to attaining academic success. The acquisition of knowledge, the development of skills, and the shaping of attitudes are emphasized to enable cadets to excel academically and to inspire them to pursue education throughout life.

The school year extends from late August to early June and is divided into two semesters; each has two marking periods. At the end of each marking period, grades are sent to parents. Unsatisfactory grades result in special afternoon help and extra study hall, with biweekly evaluations forwarded to parents. Evening study hall is required of all students. Cadets are placed in one of three college-preparatory curricula—honors, intermediate, or standard—according to aptitude level or achievement. The grading system uses A to F with pluses and minuses. Class periods (eight per day) normally cover 45 minutes each, with double periods for laboratory courses. Twenty and a half credits are required for graduation, distributed as follows: English, 4; mathematics, 4; social studies, 3 (1 of which must be U.S. history); foreign language, 2; science, 2; laboratory science, 1; and electives, 4.5.

The average Academy class size is 13; the student-teacher ratio is approximately 10:1. Opportunities for independent study, off-campus field trips, and enrollment in courses at Valley Forge Military College are available to eligible cadets.

FACULTY AND ADVISERS

There are 52 full-time and 13 part-time teachers at the Academy. Thirty-one members hold master's degrees; currently, 2 have doctorates.

Col. David R. Gray, USA (ret.), is a 1980 Distinguished Military Graduate of Western Illinois University where he majored in history. He is a graduate of the Infantry Officer Basic and Advanced Courses, the Command and General Staff College, the Armed Forces Staff College (JPME II), and the U.S. Army War College. He has earned a master's degree in strategic studies from the U.S. Army War College and master's and doctorate degrees in military history from Ohio State University. He has published articles in several professional journals including *Parameters, Military Review, Army History,* and *Army Magazine.*

Experienced teachers, dedicated to educating young men, are selected primarily for their professional ability and concern for young people. Faculty members perform additional duties as athletic coaches, study hall supervisors, and advisers for extracurricular activities. Ongoing professional development is strongly encouraged.

COLLEGE ADMISSION COUNSELING

The Guidance Department has 4 full-time counselors and gives continual assistance and counseling to each cadet. The department follows each cadet's academic progress and keeps in close contact with parents. College orientation and parent involvement begin during the second semester of the junior year and continue throughout the cadet's residence. College orientation sessions cover college selection, nomination to service academies, financial aid, the Army ROTC program, and contacts with college placement representatives. College test requirements are reviewed, and cadets are counseled in college application preparation and interview procedures. Ninety-nine percent of the class of 2010 went on to college, with the greatest representation at Embry-Riddle, Holy Cross, Penn State, Purdue, the U.S. Air Force Academy, the U.S. Naval Academy, and Villanova.

STUDENT BODY AND CONDUCT

The 2010–11 Upper School student body was comprised of 300 boarding cadets. The student body is diverse, and this year cadets came from thirty-three states and thirty-one countries. Eight percent were African American, 11 percent were Hispanic, 13 percent were Asian/Pacific Islanders, and 13 percent were international students.

The military structure of Valley Forge provides extraordinary opportunities for students to develop and exercise their leadership abilities in a safe environment. The Valley Forge experience is designed to foster the development of individual responsibility, self-discipline, and sound leadership skills by providing opportunities for the practical application of leadership theories in positions of increasing responsibility.

The Corps of Cadets is a self-administering body organized in eight company units along military lines, with a cadet officer and noncommissioned officer organization for cadet control and administration. Cadet leadership and positive peer encouragement within this structured setting result in a brotherhood and camaraderie among cadets. Through their student representatives, cadets cooperate with the administration in enforcing regulations regarding student conduct. A Student Advisory Council represents the cadets in the school administration. The Dean's Council meets regularly to discuss aspects of academic life.

Character development and personal motivation are integral parts of the Valley Forge experience. The character development program includes weekly chapel and vesper services and monthly character development seminars that are facilitated by peer/faculty teams. Valley Forge emphasizes time-proven standards of conduct, ethical behavior, integrity, spiritual values, and service to community and country. It also motivates young men to strive for excellence, both as individuals and as members of an organization, in all areas of endeavor. Motivation is encouraged through positive competition, recognition, loyalty, teamwork, organizational pride, and the establishment of personal goals.

ACADEMIC FACILITIES

Shannon Hall is the principal academic building. In addition to classrooms, it includes biology, chemistry, and physics laboratories; a computer complex; and the military science department. The Friedman Auditorium, adjacent to Shannon Hall, serves as a large study hall, a conference and instructional center, and a center for SAT and other testing procedures. The May H. Baker Library provides more than 70,000 books, 500 video titles, more than 60 periodical subscriptions, and more than 30 subscriptions to online research resources. To integrate library resources into the curriculum, the library faculty collaborates with the classroom faculty in implementing information literacy instruction in two fully networked computer classrooms and two seminar rooms. The educational psychologists of the Cadet Achievement Center, housed in the library, counsel and advise cadets concerning learning and personal issues.

A fiber-optic, Internet-capable network connects all classrooms, laboratories, and library and dormitory rooms on the campus.

BOARDING AND GENERAL FACILITIES

Cadets are housed by their military companies in individual dormitories, 2 cadets to a room, under the supervision of adult Tactical Officers and their cadet leaders. Cadets eat together in the Regimental Mess. The Health Center has a resident physician and a 24-hour staff; special consultants are always available. The Alumni Chapel of St. Cornelius the Centurion seats 1,500. The service is nondenominational but Christian in format, and services are available for all faiths. Mellon Hall provides a parents' reception room, a ballroom, piano and instrument practice rooms, a photography laboratory, a 10-point rifle and pistol range, and meeting rooms. Other facilities include the student center, the cadet laundry, the tailor shop, and the Cadet Store. Price Athletic Center and Trainer Hall house three full-size and six intermediate-size basketball courts, a five-lane swimming pool, locker rooms, weight rooms, meeting rooms, administrative offices, and the L. Maitland Blank Hall of Fame. Also on campus are six athletic fields, nine outdoor tennis courts, an outdoor Olympic-size swimming pool, the cavalry stables, and the Mellon Polo Pavilion.

ATHLETICS

Athletics and physical well-being are important elements in a Valley Forge education. The aim of the program is to develop all-around fitness, alertness, character, esprit de corps, leadership, courage, competitive spirit, and genuine desire for physical and mental achievement. There is competition at three levels: varsity, junior varsity, and intramural. To have every cadet on a team is the constant goal. Sports opportunities include baseball, basketball, cross-country, equestrian jumping, football, golf, lacrosse, rugby, soccer, swimming, tennis, track, and wrestling.

Valley Forge has a strong athletic tradition. Since 1986, the VFMA&C football program has sent more than 140 cadets to Division I schools on full football scholarships. Seven VF alumni currently play in the NFL. One alumnus currently plays for a major league baseball team. In 2003, the equestrian show jumping team participated in the Junior Olympics.

EXTRACURRICULAR OPPORTUNITIES

Clubs, honor societies, publications, intramurals, the Regimental Choir, the Anthony Wayne Legion Guard, and some thirty-five other organizations (forensic, literary, language, science, and Boy Scouts, to name a few) attract about 75 percent of the Corps. Publications include the *Legionnaire* (the newspaper) and *Crossed Sabres* (the yearbook).

Outside lecturers visit the Academy regularly. The band and choir travel widely and have performed at the Kennedy Center, Carnegie Hall, Westminster Abbey, Lincoln Center, and the White House and have participated in inaugural events for several U.S. presidents. Various cadet units assist local communities in parades, community events, and horse shows. Cadets participate in various public service activities in the surrounding communities; several cadet groups pay regular visits during the year to local children's homes, centers for the disabled, and nursing homes. Important traditional events are Parents' and Grandparents' Weekend, Regimental Mounted Parades, Dunaway Oratorical Contest, and frequent band and choir concerts.

DAILY LIFE

Classes (45 minutes each) are held five days a week from 7:30 a.m. to 3:30 p.m. The average number of classes per student is six in an eight-period day. An extra instruction period is available after the last class period. Athletics and other activities are held between 3 and 5:45 p.m. daily. Evening study hours extend from 7:30 to 9:30 p.m. Taps sounds at 10 p.m. Monday afternoon is reserved for drill, company meetings, and special activities, such as the ropes course and rappelling.

WEEKEND LIFE

Special or afternoon leaves as well as overnight and weekend privileges may be earned. Ample opportunities exist for cadets to take advantage of the cultural and entertainment opportunities in the Philadelphia area. Cadets desiring to stay at school can use all facilities and attend movies on Friday and Saturday nights in the student center. The cadets frequently enjoy mixers, formal dances, plays, band concerts, special sports events, and polo matches with students from neighboring schools. All events are chaperoned by faculty members.

Gold and Silver Star cadets are those who have earned academic achievement. They are granted trips into town on Wednesday afternoons and evenings. On Friday, Saturday, and Sunday, those not restricted for academic or other reasons may visit town after their last duty until early evening. Periodically during the year, weekend leaves are authorized for the entire corps; other times there are special weekend leaves for Gold and Silver Star honor students. The leaves help reinforce positive peer pressure to excel in both academics and leadership tasks. Following chapel and Regimental Parade on Sunday, cadets may leave the grounds on special dinner leave with their parents or other authorized adults.

SUMMER PROGRAMS

A four-week residential summer camp is available for boys and girls ages 7–17. A day camp is available for boys and girls ages 9–17. These programs provide them with the very best in recreational and educational opportunities.

COSTS AND FINANCIAL AID

The annual charge for 2011–12 was $39,265. This charge includes tuition, room and board, uniforms, and all other fees. There is an optional charge for private music lessons, developmental reading, and driver's education. Health center stays for each period of more than 24 hours' duration are also an additional expense. A nonrefundable application fee of $100 is required with an application. At the time of acceptance, a $500 validation fee is required.

In 2010–11, approximately 35 percent of the students received financial aid totaling more than $1 million. Merit-based scholarships are offered for academic excellence and performance in athletics, the band, and the choir. Through the generosity of many friends of Valley Forge, some special and endowed scholarships, with varying need and/or merit-based criteria, are available.

ADMISSIONS INFORMATION

Admission is based on academic aptitude as measured by the Otis-Lennon Mental Ability Test and/or the SSAT, information pertaining to grade level, personal character and scholastic references, and the recommendation of the Admissions Counselor based on a personal interview with the applicant. Applicants must present evidence of being capable of meeting the demands of a college-preparatory curriculum.

The admission policies of Valley Forge Military Academy & College are nondiscriminatory with respect to race, color, creed, and national or ethnic origin and are in compliance with federal laws.

APPLICATION TIMETABLE

Inquiries are always welcome. Those seeking further information are invited to attend periodic Sunday Campus Visitations; everyone is encouraged to contact the admissions office to make an appointment to visit the campus. New cadets are enrolled in late August, and limited openings also exist for January, or midyear, entry. While there is no application deadline, it is recommended that applications be submitted three months before the desired entry date.

ADMISSIONS CORRESPONDENCE

Dean of Admissions
Valley Forge Military Academy & College
Wayne, Pennsylvania 19087-3695

Phone: 610-989-1490
866-923-VFMA (toll-free)
Fax: 610-688-1545
E-mail: admissions@vfmac.edu
Web site: http://academy.vfmac.edu

WESTERN RESERVE ACADEMY

Hudson, Ohio

Type: Coeducational, boarding and day, college-preparatory
Grades: 9–12, postgraduate year
Enrollment: 402
Head of School: Christopher D. Burner, Head of School

THE SCHOOL

Founded in 1826 as a preparatory school for Western Reserve College, Western Reserve Academy (WRA) is one of the oldest boarding schools in the nation and the premier school of its kind in the Midwest. WRA offers a challenging curriculum that prepares students for future academic success and for leading purposeful, fulfilling lives. Attending WRA is a transformational experience; students learn to strive for excellence, live with integrity, and act with compassion.

WRA is a traditional college-preparatory school that is committed to maintaining academic excellence and to offering its students a well-rounded program so that they may develop into interesting, knowledgeable, and sensitive adults. The academic part of the day is not overly structured, but an atmosphere of academic seriousness prevails. Close relationships among the adults and students are an essential and natural part of daily life.

Hudson lies between Cleveland (30 minutes away) and Akron (25 minutes away), just off the Ohio Turnpike (U.S. 80). The main part of the Western Reserve Academy campus is located one block from downtown Hudson, but most of its 190 acres extend into the surrounding countryside. Thus, outdoor activities are as much a part of life at WRA as are those kinds of activities associated with major urban areas. Concerts (classical and otherwise), drama, art museums, outdoor activities, and cinema are a functional part of a student's life at the school.

Western Reserve Academy is governed by a board of 30 trustees who supervise the school's \$106.5-million endowment. The annual budget of more than \$23.4 million is fortified by the interest from that endowment as well as by funds from the Annual Fund. Parent organizations such as the Dads Club and the Pioneer Women's Association are actively involved in campus events as well. Approximately \$4.8 million is allocated for financial aid, providing an opportunity for students who otherwise would be unable to attend.

Western Reserve Academy is accredited by the Independent Schools Association of the Central States. It is a member of the National Association of Independent Schools, the Association of Boarding Schools, the Secondary School Admission Test Board, the School and Student Service for Financial Aid, the Committee on Boarding Schools, the Midwest Boarding Schools, the Association of Boarding Schools, and the Ohio Association of Independent Schools.

ACADEMIC PROGRAMS

The academic program at WRA offers an exceptional college preparatory education, giving its students a strong foundation in the arts, humanities, natural sciences, and social sciences. The faculty at WRA employs a variety of teaching styles, centered on the Harkness table system, helping students to recognize their strengths and overcome their weaknesses. By the end of their senior year, WRA students are able to engage in intellectual debate with their peers; analyze and synthesize data to support an argument or thesis; use language to express themselves with lucidity and conviction; and pursue independent research, using both primary and secondary sources. Western Reserve Academy offers fifteen Advanced Placement (AP) courses. On occasion, students have the opportunity to take as many as twenty-one exams including Spanish Language and a second physics exam.

To graduate, a student must complete the equivalent of 21 credits, carrying a minimum load of 6 credits in the freshman year and 5 or more credits each marking period in grades 10 through 12, in schedules arranged with their faculty advisers. The classes are small, with an average size of 12, although classes for advanced-level courses are typically smaller in size. There are no formal opportunities for remedial studies in any academic discipline.

Advisers work closely with students and parents to determine academic programs, daily schedules, preparation for final exams, and the need for academic enrichment.

FACULTY AND ADVISERS

Western Reserve Academy has 61 full- and part-time faculty members, of whom all but a few live on campus in school houses or in apartments in dormitories. Many administrators teach at least one course. All faculty members have a bachelor's degree, and 84 percent have advanced degrees.

Only the third alumnus to serve as Head of School since the school's founding in 1826, Christopher D. Burner '80, was appointed in 2008 and is a graduate of Franklin & Marshall College (B.A.), Dartmouth College (M.A.L.S.), and Harvard University (M.Ed.). Mr. Burner has taught at Western Reserve Academy on two separate occasions. During his first term (1986) at WRA, Mr. Burner served as the Assistant Dean of Students, taught Latin, and coached varsity wrestling, football, and lacrosse. He also held faculty positions at Saint James School in Maryland and Westminster School in Connecticut. After returning to WRA (1992), Mr. Burner served as the Director of Admission and most recently as the Dean of Faculty and Administration, in addition to teaching Latin and coaching.

The average faculty member at Western Reserve Academy has more than nineteen years of teaching experience. Almost all teachers coach a sport, serve evening duty in dormitories, supervise an activity, and advise students.

COLLEGE ADMISSION COUNSELING

College counseling begins when a student enters WRA. Its small size allows the counseling staff to know students well and thus provide effective, individualized counseling. Throughout their WRA careers, students receive counseling about making course selections, building a strong academic and extracurricular profile, and standardized testing. WRA's counseling staff meets with freshmen and sophomores in group settings, and then individually with juniors to prepare a preliminary list of colleges that fit each student's ability, interests, and goals. Students continue to meet with their counselor on a regular basis throughout their senior year as they navigate the latter stages of the process.

The College Counseling Office maintains a strong rapport with college admission officers across the country. The counseling staff travels extensively throughout the year, visiting college campuses and attending conferences. In addition, students have the unique opportunity to meet with over 80 college admission representatives who visit the WRT campus every fall. The college counseling staff works hard to build and maintain strong relationships with the admission offices of America's top colleges and universities.

Of WRA's graduates, 100 percent attend colleges or universities each year. SAT averages are consistently very high. Recent graduates are attending such institutions as Case Western Reserve, Georgetown, Harvard, Miami (Ohio), Middlebury, Northwestern, Princeton, Stanford, the U.S. Naval Academy, Vanderbilt, Yale, and the Universities of Chicago and Pennsylvania.

STUDENT BODY AND CONDUCT

Two thirds of all students are boarders, and slightly more than half are boys. Students at WRA come from many parts of this country and the world. Western Reserve Academy is dedicated to creating and maintaining a healthy and pluralistic composition in its student body. Currently, 28 percent of the students represent minority groups (African American, Hispanic American, and Asian American).

Student government officers, dorm prefects, and various other student leaders contribute their views in most matters of student conduct and general rule determination, although the school behavior and dress code is generally considered conservative.

ACADEMIC FACILITIES

Almost every building at Western Reserve Academy has an academic function, but there are seven principal academic buildings: Seymour Hall, the Chapel, Hayden Hall, Wilson Hall, the Knight Fine Arts Center, Metcalf Center, and the John D. Ong Library. The seven buildings house classrooms, labs, music practice rooms, a lecture hall, a recital hall, dance rooms, a student lounge, woodworking and metalworking shops, a photography studio, a computer center, art studios, a publications room, administrative offices, and the school library of 38,000 volumes. The Wilson Hall Science Center was completely renovated in 2001.

Visually dominating the campus is the Chapel, modeled, as were most of the buildings, on the architectural style of Yale College. Some of the buildings, such as the Loomis Observatory (circa 1838), are more than 100 years old.

BOARDING AND GENERAL FACILITIES

Western Reserve Academy has nine dormitories and one large dining hall for its boarding students. Two times per week, evening meals are served family-style, as are lunches on Thursdays. Other meals during the week are buffet-style. Students can also purchase items at the campus store, or they can sign out to eat at one of Hudson's many restaurants. Most boys' dorm rooms are doubles, with some triples, and a few single rooms are available. Girls have dorms with doubles and a few singles. There are laundry facilities in five dorms.

The school's Health Services building is state-of-the-art and has a dispensary, examination and waiting rooms, and six sick-bay rooms. A nurse is on duty during the day and on call at night, unless needed on duty when a student must stay in the Health Services center overnight. The school doctor visits the campus every weekday to examine and talk to students.

The Student Center, which is located in the lower level of Ellsworth Hall, contains the newly renovated Green Key snack bar, booths for eating and talking, a wide-screen television, Ping-Pong, pool, and video games. A broadcasting center is also in this area.

ATHLETICS

Western Reserve Academy emphasizes athletic competition and believes student participation in team sports is an essential part of the daily program. There are two or three levels of interschool competition for boys and girls in tennis, basketball, ice hockey, diving, swimming, cross-country, track, golf, lacrosse, soccer, football, wrestling, baseball, rifle team, volleyball, softball, and field hockey. WRA is a member of the Interstate Prep School League.

WRA's athletics facilities include a ProTurf stadium with a six-lane all-weather track, a competition swimming pool and separate diving well with 3- and 1-meter boards, a state-of-the-art fitness center with Nautilus equipment, two football fields, four soccer/lacrosse fields, a 3.1-mile cross-country course, two field-hockey fields, a wrestling arena, and twelve all-weather tennis courts. An indoor athletic complex features a 45,000-square-foot field house housing a 200-meter indoor track, varsity and four practice basketball courts, and a complete training facility.

EXTRACURRICULAR OPPORTUNITIES

Aside from participating in the Student Council, student publications, and services already mentioned, students may join a diverse and changing group of clubs and organizations: photography, debate, chess, REACH (a community service club), Green Key (the student center), skiing, drama, Green Campus Action Team, Culinary Club, and the Junior Engineering Technical Society (JETS). The school's coordinator of student activities, in conjunction with the Dean's Office, organizes dances and weekend activities on campus as well as in Cleveland and Akron.

DAILY LIFE

The typical class day at Western Reserve Academy begins at 8 a.m. There are six 55-minute periods each day. From 3:30 to 5:45, most students participate in athletics. Dinner begins at 6 or 6:30 p.m., and study halls in dorms are from 7:30 until 10. Classes meet on Saturday from 8 a.m. until noon.

WEEKEND LIFE

A wide variety of activities are presented to the student body (for both day and boarding students) each weekend.

Western Reserve Academy is located in a thriving geographic area. Nestled in the quaint village of Hudson, which was recently named among 2011's 100 Best Communities for Young People in America, WRA is within easy walking distance of attractive shops, restaurants, and community activities. Beyond Hudson, Cleveland and Akron offer major cultural events. The world-famous Cleveland Orchestra, the Rock and Roll Hall of Fame, E. J. Thomas Hall, Playhouse Square, the Ohio Ballet, the Cleveland Institute of Art, and the Museum of Natural History are easily accessible. Weekend programs also include downhill skiing at nearby slopes, concerts, off-campus movies, trips to the Gateway Sports Complex to see professional athletics teams, and outdoor activities at the nearby Cuyahoga Valley National Recreation Area. Western Reserve Academy's proximity to Case Western Reserve University, Hiram College, Kent State, Oberlin, and the University of Akron makes the resources of these colleges and universities available as well.

SUMMER PROGRAMS

Western Reserve Academy provides students a variety of instructive and athletic summer opportunities. Among them are numerous sports camps and enrichment courses in the areas of science, visual art, music, acting, leadership, math, and test-taking skills. Adventure Camp at WRA combines outdoor activities and sports with engaging classroom experiences.

COSTS AND FINANCIAL AID

Fees for 2011–12 were $43,000 for boarders and $30,500 for day students. Extra fees of about $600 cover books and other incidental expenses. Payments are made in three installments: July, September, and November. WRA offers a payment and tuition refund plan.

For 2011–12, more than $4.8 million in financial aid was awarded to over 34 percent of WRA's students. Awards are made on the basis of family need (as established by the School and Student Service for Financial Aid).

ADMISSIONS INFORMATION

Western Reserve Academy admits students of any race, sex, color, disability, or national or ethnic origin to all rights, privileges, programs, and activities generally accorded or made available to students at WRA. It does not discriminate on the basis of race, sex, color, disability, or national or ethnic origin in the administration of its educational policies, admissions policies, scholarship and loan programs, and athletics or other school-administered programs.

Western Reserve Academy requires that all applicants submit SSAT, ISEE, TOEFL, or SAT scores and recommendations from 2 current teachers, the school counselor, and an additional recommendation. Applicants average in the top three deciles on the SSAT and have achieved A's and B's at their previous schools. Most students enter in grade 9 or 10. WRA enrolls approximately 100 freshmen per year.

APPLICATION TIMETABLE

Most inquiries are made in the fall, with applications ($50 fee for students within the United States and $150 for international students) completed by January 15 (day students, December 1). Applicants and their families should have a campus tour and an interview. After an application is submitted, it is reviewed by the Admission Committee; families are notified after March 10 (day students, January 15) and are usually allowed two to four weeks to notify the school of their intentions.

ADMISSIONS CORRESPONDENCE

Admission Office
Western Reserve Academy
115 College Street
Hudson, Ohio 44236

Phone: 330-650-9717
Fax: 330-650-5858
E-mail: admission@wra.net
Web site: http://wra.net

THE WILLISTON NORTHAMPTON SCHOOL

Easthampton, Massachusetts

Type: Coeducational boarding and day college-preparatory school
Grades: 7–PG: Middle School, 7–8; Upper School, 9–12, postgraduate year
Enrollment: School total: 528; Upper School: 447
Head of School: Robert W. Hill III, Head of School

THE SCHOOL

Williston Seminary was founded in 1841 by Samuel and Emily Williston. Initially coeducational, Williston Seminary later became a college-preparatory school for boys only. The Willistons amassed a great fortune from the production of cloth-covered buttons and the manufacture of rubber webbing and thread. They also supported the local colleges both financially and personally.

In 1924, Sarah B. Whitaker and Dorothy M. Bement founded the academic Northampton School for Girls.

In 1971, the two schools merged to form the Williston Northampton School, a coeducational school offering a strong secondary education to prepare interested students for the rigorous academic programs of colleges today and the demands and complexities in life afterward. Today, the Williston Northampton School inspires students to live with purpose, passion, and integrity.

The School is located on 125 acres in the heart of the Pioneer Valley near the base of Mount Tom, 85 miles west of Boston, and 150 miles north of New York. Within a 15-mile radius are the Five Colleges: Smith, Mount Holyoke, Hampshire, and Amherst Colleges, and the University of Massachusetts.

The current endowment is estimated at $37 million. The School's 10,000 alumni contributed more than $1.47 million in Annual Giving last year.

Williston is accredited by the New England Association of Schools and Colleges and is affiliated with the National Association of Independent Schools, the Association of Independent Schools of New England, the College Board, the School and College Conference on English, the Art Association of New England Preparatory Schools, and the Council for Advancement and Support of Education.

ACADEMIC PROGRAMS

Williston's outstanding facilities and the magnificent recreational and cultural offerings nearby provide the setting for an outstanding education. Through its unique Williston+ Program, the School provides superior college preparation by bringing the rich resources of the nearby five colleges (Amherst, Hampshire, Mount Holyoke, and Smith Colleges and the University of Massachusetts, Amherst) into the classroom to enrich the School's curriculum and provide professional development opportunities for the faculty. The proximity of the five colleges gives Williston students and faculty unparalleled opportunities to engage in and explore a variety of subjects.

At the heart of the School is a strong and varied academic program that seeks to strengthen, expand, and encourage students' skills and interests in the essential disciplines. Care is taken to place each student in the courses and sections most appropriate to his or her abilities. An average class size of 13 students enables faculty members to learn each student's abilities, and the flexibility of the program makes it possible for the School to structure programs that can best meet every individual student's needs. In addition, Williston offers numerous opportunities in competitive athletics, the arts, and leadership.

The School believes that each student should experience as many academic and creative disciplines as possible while they are at Williston. Therefore, Williston expects each of its students not only to satisfy the minimum basic requirements of 4 years of English, 3 years of math, 2 of science, 2 of a foreign language, and 2 in the social sciences, but also to select two trimester courses from the area of fine arts and one trimester course from the area of religion and philosophy. Williston also offers 37 Advanced Placement (AP) and honors classes. Qualified students may elect to complete extra work in consultation with the teacher to prepare to take the AP exam in two additional subject areas. Of the Williston students who took the AP exams in 2011, which is required of all AP students at the School, 54 percent received scores of 4 or higher, earning college credit at participating institutions.

The Writing Center plays a central part in Williston's academic program. Located in the library, the Writing Center is staffed by members of the English department, as well as by highly qualified student writers. The Writing Center provides support for students at all levels, on any writing assignment, so they can build critical thinking skills and clarity of expression, crucial tools that will be used again, in college and beyond. The Writing Center has over 1,000 visits annually.

Williston also offers a Writers' Workshop series every fall. Founded by Williston parents and accomplished authors Madeleine Blais and Elinor Lipman in 1998, Williston's Writers' Workshop Series has hosted a variety of distinguished writers who give a public reading and then work with Williston's Readers and Writers Master Class students on the craft of writing. Authors who have participated include Augusten Burroughs, Gregory Maguire, Elinor Lipman, Sue Miller, Richard Russo, and Curtis Sittenfeld.

During the winter and spring trimesters, Williston hosts the Photographers' Lecture series. Begun in 2000, this lecture series features internationally acclaimed photojournalists, filmmakers, and commercial photographers who share their work and ideas with the community and Williston's advanced photography students. Past distinguished visiting photographers have included John Willis, Sean Kerman, Lori Grinker, Nina Berman, and David Burnett.

Most students choose to complete work beyond the basic requirements established by each department. To graduate, a student at Williston must complete a minimum of 57 academic credits in grades 9–12. Because Williston places a high value on a well-rounded college-preparatory experience, students are also responsible for 3 fine arts credits. Students may also choose a 1-credit directed studies course on a special topic not included in the regular curriculum. Students generally take five courses per trimester.

Students attaining honor grades are recognized at the end of each term. The highest honor is election to the Cum Laude Society. Williston's chapter of Cum Laude is one of the oldest in the nation, founded in 1906.

FACULTY AND ADVISERS

The Williston Northampton School teaching faculty numbers 67 full-time members. Sixty hold master's degrees, and 5 have doctorates. Thirty live in dorms. The School has established programs to counsel students about academic work, personal problems, class performance, and future educational goals and opportunities. Each boarding student has a faculty adviser who is also a dorm parent and may be easily consulted on academic or personal matters. Students can also consult with the Dean of Students, Chaplain, and Academic Dean. The School also employs the services of professional counselors.

In 2008, Williston instituted its Ninth Grade Program, which is designed to ease the transition for students from middle school to secondary school and to build camaraderie among ninth graders. The program includes an overnight orientation, special advisers, assemblies, and academic monitoring. The cornerstone of the program is C.O.R.E. (curiosity, organizations, reflection, and empathy). Each of these concepts is the focus of a special ninth grade–only assembly where Williston adults and upperclass students address the ninth graders and discuss how these principles have helped them succeed. In addition, at the end of each trimester, the program holds final exam preparation clinics, where advisers outline for students the expectations for exam week and help the ninth graders fill out an hour-by-hour study schedule.

On July 1, 2010, Robert W. Hill III became Williston's nineteenth head of school. Mr. Hill comes to Williston from Carolina Day School in Asheville, North Carolina, where he had served as Associate Head of School and Principal of the Upper School since 2007. There, he successfully focused on building the school's community culture as well as faculty and curriculum development. Prior to 2007, he served for nine years at St. Paul's School (Concord, New Hampshire) in a variety of roles, including Academic Dean, Director of College Advising, and Associate Dean of Faculty. His tenure there also included responsibilities as an English teacher, varsity girls' squash coach, and dorm resident. Hill started his teaching career at Westminster School (Simsbury, Connecticut), where he taught for fifteen years. He received his B.A. cum laude from Middlebury College (Vermont) and earned his M.A. in English literature from Middlebury's Bread Loaf School of English.

COLLEGE ADMISSION COUNSELING

Williston provides a thorough and personalized college counseling program for every student, beginning in their junior year. Four full-time counselors work with the junior and senior class. From the beginning, the counseling process draws in both parents and students to establish a dialogue between the School and the family. During the junior year, counselors and faculty members meet with students to acquaint them with standardized test-taking, financial aid, roles and functions of college officials, and campus lifestyles. In addition, all juniors visit the five colleges and participate in mock interviews at the different campuses.

The 122 members of the class of 2011 were accepted at over 450 colleges and universities, including Brown, Colby, Connecticut College, Harvard, Hobart and William Smith, NYU, Northwestern, Skidmore, the University of Chicago, and Williams College.

STUDENT BODY AND CONDUCT

Most students enter Williston during the freshman or sophomore year. In 2011–12, grade 9 had 89 members (45 boys, 44 girls), of whom 53 were day students. Grade 10 had 118 members (61 boys, 57 girls), of whom 49 were day students. Grade 11 had 111 members (60 boys, 51 girls), of whom 43 were day students. Grade 12 had 129 members (76 boys, 53 girls), of whom 40 were day students. There were 15 postgraduate students. Sixteen percent of the students are members of minority groups. Students came from twenty-two states and twenty-four countries.

The rules and regulations of the School have evolved from experience and lengthy discussion and provide clear guidelines for everyone living in the School community. It is expected that students will follow both the spirit and the letter of these regulations as described in the *Student Handbook*, which is provided to all enrolling students.

Students who are reported to have violated School rules and regulations meet with the Discipline Committee, made up of faculty and student representatives. The committee's decisions and recommendations are reviewed by the head of school, who makes the final decision in disciplinary matters.

ACADEMIC FACILITIES

The campus is located on approximately 125 acres. The School's thirty-eight buildings include the Reed Campus Center, the Scott Hall Science Building, the Boardman Theater, the Robert A. Ward Schoolhouse, the Robert Clapp Library, the Philip Stevens Chapel, and the Whitaker-Bement Middle School Building. Renovations to the old gymnasium to create a new Campus Center that includes music and fine arts classrooms were completed in 1996. The Technology and Student Publications Center, the Science Tech Lab, the library, and the math floor house four student computer labs.

BOARDING AND GENERAL FACILITIES

The buildings on campus include the Head's House, the Zachs Admission Center at the Homestead, the Chapel, the Birch Dining Commons, five dormitories with facilities for 25 to 50 students, five residence houses with boarding facilities for 8 to 12 students, and faculty homes. Ford Hall and Memorial Dorm each house 50 boys. Ford Hall received a million-dollar renovation in 1999, adding sun-splashed common rooms and other enhancements. All dorm rooms are wired into the campus computer network and have voice mail. A new ninth grade boys' dorm with housing for 32 students and three faculty families opened in 2008. The dorm, which is heated and cooled via seventeen geothermal wells, is the centerpiece of a planned residential quad.

Each dormitory or house is supervised by resident faculty houseparents to create an environment conducive to academic achievement and a warm and pleasant home atmosphere.

ATHLETICS

Sports are an integral part of student life at Williston, whether interscholastic or recreational. The School requires that each student be involved in the athletics program in each of the three sports seasons. The athletics department instills the principles of fair play, good sportsmanship, teamwork, and respect for rules and authority. Most of the academic faculty members also coach competitive teams, and the Director of Athletics oversees the program.

Interscholastic teams for girls include crew, cross-country, field hockey, soccer, and volleyball in the fall; basketball, ice hockey, skiing, squash, swimming and diving, and wrestling in the winter; and crew, golf, lacrosse, softball, tennis, track, and water polo in the spring. Boys may elect crew, cross-country, football, soccer, or water polo; basketball, ice hockey, skiing, squash, swimming and diving, or wrestling; and baseball, crew, golf, lacrosse, tennis, or track. Horseback riding at a nearby stable and modern dance are available every season. Fitness training, aerobics, yoga, and self-defense are choices open to upperclass students.

The Athletic Center houses two basketball courts, a six-lane pool with a diving well, five international squash courts, a weight room and fitness center, and a wrestling room. Other facilities include a lighted, synthetic-surface football/lacrosse field with stadium seating; a dance studio; facility renovated hockey rink; twelve tennis courts; an all-weather running track that surrounds a synthetic surface field for field hockey, soccer, and lacrosse; more than 30 acres of playing fields; and a 3.4-mile cross-country course. In addition, the School's golf teams play on several golf courses in the Easthampton area, and the ski team competes on the slopes in the eastern Berkshires.

EXTRACURRICULAR OPPORTUNITIES

The countryside offers excellent climbing, biking, and skiing opportunities, and the proximity of the Five Colleges provides a culturally rich environment of fine museums, libraries, and theater programs as well. The cities of Northampton and Springfield, Massachusetts, and Hartford, Connecticut, are near enough so that concerts and activities there are as readily available as those at the local colleges.

DAILY LIFE

The academic day runs from 8:30 a.m. until 1:50 or 2:50 p.m. on Monday, Tuesday, Thursday, and Friday and until 12:25 on Wednesday. Classes are held every other Saturday morning as well. Students take five courses in a six-period schedule, with classes lasting 45 or 70 minutes, depending on the day. All-School assemblies for announcements and special presentations are held once each week. Athletics are scheduled from the end of the class day until dinnertime. Except for theme-based formal dinners, most meals are served buffet-style. A free period from 6:30 to 8 p.m. is frequently used for meetings of extracurricular organizations, library work, theater or music rehearsals, visiting between dormitories, or simply relaxing. Supervised evening study hours run from 8 to 10 p.m. Ninth grade students have lights out at 10:30 p.m. All students are checked into the dorms at 8 p.m. by the dorm faculty.

WEEKEND LIFE

While the vast majority of students remain on campus, weekends at home or at the home of a friend are permitted with parental approval after all school obligations have been met. The Student Activities Director and students on the Activity Committee organize a variety of weekly activities, and students may take advantage of the events listed in the five college calendar. Students travel off campus for college and professional athletic events, films, plays, dance performances, and concerts and to go skiing in Vermont. The many on-campus activities include dances and coffeehouse entertainment, talent shows, lectures by invited speakers, and a film series.

SUMMER PROGRAMS

Throughout the year, students have the opportunity to take part in several international excursions that enrich their studies. Trips to Canada and France during school vacations offer real-life practice for French language skills. A trip to Honduras allows students to perform community service while honing their Spanish. Ed Hing '77, Williston's photography instructor, helps students capture the beauty of locations in Italy, France, China, and other international destinations during summer photo trips. In the summer, the School also offers an intensive four-week Spanish program in Mexico and hosts many outside camps, offering theater, music, and athletics.

COSTS AND FINANCIAL AID

Tuition for boarders for 2011–12 was $47,900; for day students, it was $32,800. Additional expenses include books, insurance, laundry, and other incidental expenses. Tuition payment and insurance plans are recommended upon request.

Financial aid is awarded on the basis of need. The grants totaled $6.4 million for 2011–11.

ADMISSIONS INFORMATION

Williston seeks students who are interested in a challenging academic program, who can demonstrate solid academic achievement and outstanding personal character. Students should also be involved and caring contributors to life beyond the classroom. Admission is based upon an evaluation of these traits, a personal interview, and satisfactory scores on the SSAT or TOEFL. In 2011–12, 169 new students were enrolled in the Upper School.

APPLICATION TIMETABLE

The fall or winter prior to a candidate's prospective admission is usually the best time for a visit, which includes a faculty and student-guided tour of the School and an interview. The Admission Office is open Monday through Friday, from 8:30 a.m. to 4:30 p.m. during the academic year and 8 a.m. to 4 p.m. in the summer months, and on alternate Saturday mornings during the academic year.

An application for admission should be submitted by February 1 along with a nonrefundable fee of $50 ($100 for international students). The School abides by the March 10 notification date. After that date, a rolling admission plan is in effect.

ADMISSIONS CORRESPONDENCE

Ann C. Pickrell, Director of Admission
The Williston Northampton School
19 Payson Avenue
Easthampton, Massachusetts 01027
Phone: 413-529-3241
Fax: 413-527-9494
E-mail: admissions@williston.com
Web site: http://www.williston.com

WINDWARD SCHOOL

Los Angeles, California

Type: Coeducational day college-preparatory school
Grades: 7–12; Middle School 7–8; Upper School 9–12
Enrollment: 540
Head of School: Thomas W. Gilder

THE SCHOOL

A dynamic education, a nurturing community—that's the mission of Windward School. Founded in 1971 in order to provide a unique educational opportunity for Westside young people, the School takes its name from Shirley Windward, one of Windward's founders, whose dedication to the School has become legendary.

Under the leadership of Tom Gilder, who became Head of School in 1987, the School has continued to broaden its academic programs and to incorporate areas of social concern and global awareness into the classroom and extracurricular activities.

From its founding, two concepts have been fundamental to Windward School. The first, that educators and young people should work together in an environment that encourages them to be responsible, caring, well informed, ethical, and prepared. Secondly, education should provide a basis for lifelong growth, and the School should therefore concern itself with every facet of the student's life.

Today, Windward School stands as a living tribute to its many graduates and the hard work of innumerable individuals. Windward students attend the colleges of their choice around the country, and as working adults they have shown that they can succeed and prosper. Never content to rest on its laurels, Windward continues to pursue innovation, even as it remains faithful to the vision of its founders.

A not-for-profit corporation, Windward is governed by a 25-member Board of Trustees and an administrative team centered by the Head of School. The Western Association of Schools and Colleges accredits Windward. The School holds membership in the National Association of Independent Schools, the Independent School Alliance for Minority Affairs, A Better Chance, Independent School Management, the Educational Records Bureau, and the California Association of Independent Schools.

ACADEMIC PROGRAMS

Fundamental to the Windward School philosophy is the belief that secondary education must engage more than the mind alone. Allowing young people to participate in a range of academic and extracurricular experiences fosters social growth and responsibility, as well as personal development. Woven through the traditional college-preparatory courses—English language and literature, a complex social studies curriculum, mathematics, science, and foreign languages—are opportunities that enable students to be actively involved in their own education.

Windward's comprehensive and rigorous course of study teaches students to think independently, to reason with care and logic, to write and speak with clarity, and to identify and develop their aesthetic talents. This strong academic preparation is complemented by the development of ethics, character, and people skills. The School hopes its graduates will go forth from Windward with a strong sense of personal integrity, self-confidence, and pride in their particular talents, inspired by learning, and prepared for college and for life in the twenty-first century.

At Windward, the average class size is 15 students. In academic areas, courses are sectioned on the basis of interest and ability, and Advanced Placement courses are offered in every discipline. The minimum course load for students in grades 7–10 is six. Students in grades 11–12 may opt for an alteration of this pattern, though approval of the grade-level deans is required, and students are actively encouraged to take six or seven classes.

In the Upper School, minimum course requirements are one English course each year through grade 12, one history course each year through grade 12 (seniors who wish to take two courses in another discipline may petition to waive the grade 12 history requirement), one mathematics course each year through grade 11, one science course each year through grade 10, one science course in either grade 11 or grade 12 (this must include one year of laboratory science), completion of Level III in one foreign language or completion of Level II in each of two foreign languages (continuation of foreign language through grade 11 is required), one arts course each year through grade 10, and one physical education course each year through grade 10 (students in grades 9 and 10 who compete in an interscholastic team sport are excused from physical education during that sport's season).

Community service has long been at the heart of the Windward tradition. Beginning in Middle School, service learning is a core component of the program, and in the Upper School, all students are required to complete two separate and extensive community service projects prior to graduation.

Windward maintains a sister school relationship with two schools in Spain and France. Students are able to attend a sister school for a three-week academic exchange once they have mastered an appropriate level of linguistic fluency. Generally, the schools exchange 15 to 20 students at a time. The culminating academic experience of a Windward education is the School's annual senior trip for one week at the School's expense. This "classroom in the field" is the capstone of six years of work and allows for an appropriate opportunity to say goodbye to one another.

FACULTY AND ADVISERS

The Windward faculty consists of 75 full- and part-time members (37 women and 38 men). Seventy-three percent have advanced degrees, with 11 possessing doctorates. Thomas W. Gilder, Head of School, was appointed in 1987.

In selecting its faculty members, Windward looks for individuals who enjoy the art of teaching, who are enthusiastic about working with adolescents, who will involve themselves in the nonacademic life of the School, and who have lively personal interests of their own. Every faculty member at Windward is an integral component in the life of the School. Faculty benefits at Windward are generous on all accounts and include financial support for continuing education and the funding of faculty-generated betterment opportunities.

COLLEGE ADMISSION COUNSELING

The college counseling program is directly linked to Windward's mission of providing a dynamic education in a nurturing environment. As such, the School works closely to support its students and their families through every stage of the college search process, beginning in the tenth grade. Windward's college counselors not only serve students as academic-schedule advisers, but also help them explore extracurricular and summer options. The counseling program reflects both the depth and the breadth of students' interests, and the School strives to find the best colleges for Windward students. Representatives of more than 100 different colleges and universities come to Windward each year to meet its students. Additional support in exploring college options is provided through an East Coast college trip for eleventh grade students and workshops with topics ranging from interview tips to the college essay.

Last year's graduating class of 89 students matriculated to more than fifty different colleges and universities. Students in the last several graduating classes chose between such diverse opportunities as Barnard, Berkeley, Boston College, Colby, Columbia, Emory, George Washington, Harvard, Kenyon, Michigan, Princeton, Rhode Island School of Design, Rice, Stanford, Tufts, Vassar, Washington (St. Louis), Wesleyan, Yale, and the Universities of Pennsylvania, Texas, and Wisconsin. Windward places the utmost importance upon each senior having options from which to choose, and its college counselors seek to guide students to discover the college or university best suited to their individual needs and aspirations.

STUDENT BODY AND CONDUCT

Windward has 540 students in grades 7–12. The average class size is 15 students, allowing teachers to offer individualized attention.

The student government is directed by a group of 20 prefects, selected on the basis of community respect, personal integrity, and the ability to positively affect the life in the community. By working closely with the adults at Windward, acting as intermediaries, organizing School activities, and leading by example, the prefects help to set the tone of the School. Of primary importance is the cultivation of respect and consideration for others and their property, the enhancement of relationships between faculty members and students, and the general well-being of the student body. The prefects are expected to respect Windward's standards in their personal conduct and in the way in which they lead others.

At Windward, the breaking of major School rules (lying, cheating, stealing, or using or possessing drugs or alcohol) is a pressing matter and typically leads to dismissal. A committee headed by the appropriate division-level Dean of Students handles disciplinary matters and refers matters to the appropriate division head for final consideration. Beyond rules and regulations, however, the School's deeply ingrained code of honor expects all students to offer both civility and compassion to other students and to teachers, staff members, and their own families. In fact, this expectation is one of the defining characteristics of Windward School.

Under the oversight of the Head of School, the Middle and Upper School Directors oversee the successful operation of the School and ensure that appropriate procedures are in place for students to enjoy their Windward experience and to be safe in the knowledge that discipline is expected of all community members.

ACADEMIC FACILITIES

Windward moved to its present 9-acre site in 1982, envisioning then the pastoral campus familiar to today's Windward students. As the School's programs have expanded, new facilities have been added to the campus. In 2002, the School constructed a ten-room classroom building, the Lewis Jackson Memorial Sports Center, the Student Pavilion, the Arts Center, and renovated the playing fields. A state-of-the-art library/learning center with performing arts studios and broadcast production center and a science/math center opened in 2009.

ATHLETICS

There is a suitable level of athletics for every student. Some students seek out competitive accomplishment in one sport through years of participation, while others take advantage of Windward's breadth of offerings to begin new sports at the introductory level. The physical education and athletic programs emphasize acquiring lifetime skills, shaping confident attitudes about oneself as an individual and a contributing member of a group, and developing along the way a true sense of integrity and fairness.

There are junior varsity and varsity offerings in most sports, including football, soccer, baseball, cross-country, tennis, volleyball, basketball, and golf.

The Lewis Jackson Memorial Sports Center houses a weight training facility, meeting space, and trophy room display, while the gymnasium offers basketball and volleyball courts. The beauty of the playing fields, which are built to university and professional specifications, offers all participating students a chance to play at their best.

EXTRACURRICULAR OPPORTUNITIES

An array of extracurricular opportunities is available to students through period eight activity programs. Period eight is a block of scheduled time that is set aside twice a week for clubs, study hall, and other activities that provide extracurricular opportunities for Upper School students. Students choose from a wide variety of activities that include robotics, debate, yoga, ceramics, chorus, the yearbook, the newspaper, junior senate, and comedy sports. Students are encouraged to participate and to explore interests that support the development of talents and strengths that are not just limited to academic success.

DAILY LIFE

Beginning at 8 each morning and ending at 3 p.m., both Middle and Upper Schools utilize a five-day schedule cycle. Monday mornings offer an all-School meeting for both Middle and Upper School students and faculty members, and there is a morning nutrition period five days a week. Seniors may take lunch off campus.

COSTS AND FINANCIAL AID

Tuition for 2011–12 was $33,500. The School's philosophy is to avoid extra charges for sports, field trips, or other activities offered through the School. Approximately 19 percent of the students at the School receive need-based scholarship opportunities.

ADMISSIONS INFORMATION

In every year, more students wish to become members of the Windward community than can be admitted. The admissions office works diligently to ensure that students who are accepted offer positive contributions to the community and succeed in Windward's challenging academic environment. The School seeks qualified students of diverse economic, social, ethnic, and racial backgrounds. The ISEE, grades, recommendations from the previous school, and an interview with Windward admissions personnel are required for all applicants. Openings exist traditionally for grades 7 and 9, although students may apply for grades 8 and 10 with permission of the admissions office. Applicants to Windward should all possess admirable strengths of character, be positive contributors to school and community, and attain high grades at their present schools.

APPLICATION TIMETABLE

Inquiries are welcome throughout the year, though the deadline for application for the following year is in December. Interviews and tours of the campus begin as soon as all faculty and staff members have returned in September.

ADMISSIONS CORRESPONDENCE

Sharon Pearline
Director of Admission
Windward School
11350 Palms Boulevard
Los Angeles, California 90066
Phone: 310-391-7127
Fax: 310-397-5655
Web site: http://www.windwardschool.org

THE WINSOR SCHOOL

Boston, Massachusetts

Type: Girls' college-preparatory day school
Grades: 5–12 (Lower School, 5–8; Upper School, 9–12)
Enrollment: 430
Head of School: Rachel Friis Stettler, Director

THE SCHOOL

The Winsor School is an independent day school for academically promising girls in grades 5 through 12.

Located in Boston's Longwood Medical area, the School mirrors its vibrant urban setting. Founded in 1886, the School moved from Boston's Beacon Hill to its current location in 1910. Winsor's historic campus is a 7-acre oasis, nestled amid Simmons and Wheelock Colleges, Harvard Medical School, and many of Boston's renowned teaching hospitals. Classes make frequent use of nearby resources, including the State House, Boston Public Library, African American Meeting House, Museum of Science, and Museum of Fine Arts.

The School's superb faculty encourages girls to think logically, creatively, and compassionately—and to think for themselves. As a community, Winsor cherishes integrity and generosity of spirit, and its mission underscores a commitment to diversity and global responsibility. The School's small size means girls build lasting friendships, and Winsor encourages each girl to realize her own uniqueness and promise.

The Lower School comprises grades 5 through 8. In this supportive environment, teachers foster natural curiosity through active, hands-on lessons. Winsor's Upper School is an energetic learning community of ninth through twelfth graders. Special programs augment academics, ranging from global exchanges to a summer science internship program to culminating Independent Learning Experiences. Winsor wants girls to thrive, and it helps them become their best selves through a coordinated system of wellness, counseling, and academic support.

While college is the next step for graduates, Winsor prepares young women not only for college but for life. The lives of alumnae are the true measure of the School's strength. One hundred twenty five years after its founding, The Winsor School holds firm to a vision of preparing girls to see their futures as open to boundless possibilities.

Winsor is accredited by the New England Association of Schools and Colleges, and it holds membership in the National Association of Independent Schools, the Association of Independent Schools of New England, the Head Mistresses Association of the East, the National Coalition of Girls' Schools, the National Association of College Admission Counseling, and the National Association of Principals of Schools for Girls.

ACADEMIC PROGRAMS

Winsor's reputation for academic excellence has drawn families for generations. The School encourages and expects the best from every girl. Girls expect no less from Winsor.

As spelled out in the School's Philosophy of Curriculum, Winsor defines curriculum as the total classroom learning experience for all students. The curricular philosophy is based on understandings about student learning, the pedagogies practiced in response to these understandings, the ways that teachers assess learning, and the qualities of character that students are encouraged to develop—as well as the skills and content more commonly associated with "curriculum." The curriculum is a designed continuum of developmentally appropriate learning experiences across departments.

Winsor believes that students learn best when their ideas, skills, and experiences are reinforced across the disciplines and through the grade levels in a connected curriculum. Core skills are integrated into the curriculum in a spiraling model.

Independent thinking and learning is a core principle of Winsor's curricular philosophy. At every grade level, the curriculum guides students toward independence through age-appropriate experiences that lead them to take increasing responsibility for their own learning. As a culminating educational experience, seniors undertake an Independent Learning Experience in the last month of senior year, challenging them to apply important skills they have gained in solving problems and making decisions.

The School also believes that a critical aspect of academic excellence in the twenty-first century is preparation for responsible participation in the global community. The Principles of Diversity and its Principles of Global Responsibility articulate a commitment to "foster a global consciousness."

Graduation requirements include the following: English (4 years, including one semester of Expository Writing in Class V, 1 year of U.S. literature in Class VI, and one semester of non-Western literature in Class VII); Fine Arts (2½ years); History (2½ years, including 1 year of Modern World History, 1 year of U.S. History, and one semester of non-Western history in Class VII.); Language (3 years); Mathematics (3 years); Physical Education (seven semesters of physical activity and three semesters of health and wellness); Science (2½ years); Senior Year (one semester of a quantitative course and an Independent Learning Experience in the second semester).

Also broadening girls' perspectives are off-campus programs, including student exchanges to China and France and concert tours and speaking competitions around the world. Closer to home, some students enjoy a semester away at two of the country's leading educational programs: the Mountain School in Vermont and CITYterm, which uses New York City as its classroom.

FACULTY AND ADVISERS

Winsor's teachers are bright, creative, and caring individuals. They make their subjects come alive for students in small classes, with an average class size of 13 students. Nearly 20 percent have taught at Winsor for twenty or more years, and 89 percent have advanced degrees. More than 10 percent have doctoral degrees, including several members of the science and mathematics faculty. Faculty members are much more than teachers; they are advisers, coaches, club leaders, and role models. They care deeply about their students—not only as learners but also as people.

Each student has a faculty adviser who is the primary liaison between the student, her parents, and the rest of the faculty. The adviser keeps track of the student's academic progress and of her general well-being.

COLLEGE ADMISSION COUNSELING

The college choices of Winsor graduates reflect the academic strength of the girls and the School. Throughout the college search, Winsor's College Counseling Office offers information, structure, and support to juniors and seniors and their families.

The majority of students go on to attend the nation's most selective colleges and universities. In the last five years, the students' most common college choices were Boston College, Brown, Columbia, Dartmouth, Duke, Georgetown, George Washington, Harvard, MIT, Pennsylvania, Vanderbilt, Wesleyan, and Yale.

STUDENT BODY AND CONDUCT

The School enrolls approximately 430 students from diverse cultural, racial, and ethnic backgrounds. They hail from more than fifty different communities in and around the city of Boston.

ACADEMIC FACILITIES

Winsor facilities include eight science labs, three computer labs, a media lab and recording studio, an updated digital language lab, and three art studios. The School has continued to invest significantly in technology facilities and equipment. Winsor's experienced technology staff supports students with wireless access, school e-mail, and 150 computers for their daily use in labs, the library, and classrooms.

ATHLETICS

Winsor fields more than thirty teams in thirteen different seasonal sports. The School is one of ten independent schools that belong to the Eastern Independent League (EIL).

Girls may try out for a variety of interscholastic sports teams in grades 7 through 12. Sports are a central aspect of students' development, helping girls at many skill levels to build a positive self-image and teamwork skills. The program encourages all students to pursue a physically active life beyond their years at Winsor. In addition to athletics, the School provides physical education and health classes that are required for graduation.

EXTRACURRICULAR OPPORTUNITIES

The Winsor experience shapes girls in every possible way. While classroom learning is the core, it is just the beginning. Girls are not only thinkers and scholars but also artists, athletes, community volunteers, club members, leaders, and mentors.

Girls also shape Winsor. They give fresh life to time-honored traditions, making them their own. Girls lead everything. They speak their minds, giving voice to student issues, and often presenting or performing at weekly assemblies.

At Winsor, girls approach co-curricular activities passionately and have won national honors in crew, debate, engineering, and choral competitions.

Winsor offers more than thirty student clubs. Winsor builds time for them into all students' weekly schedules. Clubs allow girls to explore issues, develop new skills, or simply relax and have fun in the middle of a busy day. Several clubs also meet after school and on weekends, such as community service, Model United Nations, debate, drama, and engineering. The menu changes from year to year, with girls often suggesting and starting their own.

Girls also work with boys from Belmont Hill and The Roxbury Latin Schools on coordinated drama, music, and newspaper activities.

DAILY LIFE AND COMMUNITY

Winsor knows girls. It's small enough that every girl is known—by teachers, advisers, counselors, class coordinators, and deans. Students also get to know each other, creating strong friendships and bonds with classmates.

A tight-knit, caring community is part of Winsor's culture. The School encourages respect, personal responsibility, and generosity of spirit. The care with which girls and teachers live these values enriches the Winsor experience.

To cultivate a healthy educational community, Winsor's Community Wellness and Support (CWS) team integrates health and wellness initiatives, counseling, peer resources, and academic support. Embracing a holistic approach, CWS aims to support students as they learn to balance academic achievement with social, emotional, and physical well-being.

In addition to supporting students, the office organizes and facilitates parent forums that address varying issues of adolescence. Regularly scheduled parent discussion groups address different stages of girls' psycho-social development and offer parents strategies that can help them to support their daughter during this time.

COSTS AND FINANCIAL AID

For the 2011–12 academic year, Winsor's comprehensive tuition was $35,500. The School welcomes applications for tuition assistance and offers a variety of payment plans. It is Winsor's philosophy to keep the School within reach of many girls. Having talented students from diverse socioeconomic backgrounds strengthens Winsor in every way. Approximately 25 percent of Winsor students receive tuition assistance. Last year the School awarded $2.7 million in financial aid.

ADMISSIONS INFORMATION

Winsor welcomes applications for grades 5 through 7 in its Lower School and for grades 9 through 11 in the Upper School. Most students enter Winsor in the fifth or sixth grade. Openings in grades 7, 9, 10, and 11 are more limited.

APPLICATION TIMETABLE

Inquiries are welcome anytime. The admission process begins in September and ends in January for admission during the following school year. For detailed information, prospective families should check the "Important Dates and Deadlines" page on the School's Web site. Admission decisions are mailed out in March.

ADMISSIONS CORRESPONDENCE

Admissions Office
The Winsor School
103 Pilgrim Road
Boston, Massachusetts 02215

Phone: 617-735-9503
Fax: 617-912-1381
E-mail: admissions@winsor.edu
Web site: http://www.winsor.edu/admission

YORK PREPARATORY SCHOOL

New York, New York

Type: Coeducational day college-preparatory school
Grades: 6–12: Middle School, 6–8; Upper School, 9–12
Enrollment: 351
Head of School: Ronald P. Stewart, Headmaster

THE SCHOOL

York Prep is a college-preparatory school where contemporary methods enliven a strong, academically challenging, traditional curriculum. In a city known for its diversity of private schools, York Prep has developed a unique program that leads students to their highest potential. The School's approach emphasizes independent thought, builds confidence, and sends graduates on to the finest colleges and universities. At York, every student finds opportunities to flourish. York Prep believes that success breeds success, and excellence in academics, arts, or sports creates self-confidence that enhances all aspects of life, both in and out of the classroom.

York Prep was established in 1969 by its current Headmaster, Ronald P. Stewart, and his wife, Jayme Stewart, Director of College Guidance. Situated on West 68th Street between Columbus Avenue and Central Park West, the School is well served by public transportation. Consequently, it attracts students from all over the metropolitan area. York Prep takes full advantage of the prime location, with regular visits to museums, parks, and theaters, all of which are easily accessible.

York Prep is approved by the New York State Board of Regents and accredited by the Middle States Association of Colleges and Schools.

ACADEMIC PROGRAMS

The curriculum is designed to develop the superior academic skills necessary for future success. Close attention to each student's needs ensures that progress toward personal excellence is carefully guided.

Students must complete 21 credits for graduation: 4 in English, 4 in math, 4 in science, 4 in history, a minimum of 3 in foreign language, 1 in art or music, ½ in health, and ½ in community service.

Eleventh and twelfth graders choose from a number of course offerings in every subject area. In addition to selecting one course from each required category, a student must choose an elective from a variety of options that range from the creative and performing arts to the analytical sciences. Students are required to carry at least five major subjects a year plus physical education.

York Prep pioneered the requirement of community service for graduation from high school. The School requires 100 hours of structured and supervised community service with a final end-of-year paper. York Prep is in close contact with the charitable agencies where its students serve the community.

Independent study courses and Advanced Placement courses are offered. When it is appropriate, students may graduate early or enroll at local colleges for specific classes.

Classes at York are small—the average class has 15 students. There are close student-teacher relations and all students begin their day with a morning "house" period. Each student's academic and social progress is carefully monitored by the teachers, advisers, and deans of the Upper and Middle Schools. The deans, in turn, keep the Headmaster and the Principal informed at weekly meetings. In addition, the Headmaster and Principal maintain close relationships with the students. All of York's administrators, including the Headmaster and Principal, teach courses and are readily available to students and parents alike. At the close of each day, there is a period when students may go to faculty members or advisers for help.

Parents are kept informed of a student's progress through individual reports posted on "Edline," a component of the York Prep Web site, every Friday. Each family signs in with a unique password to see their child's progress in all academic subjects. The annual Curriculum Night, in which parents become students for an evening by attending their child's truncated classes, provides a good overview of the course work and the faculty members. Parent involvement is encouraged, and there is an active Parents' Association.

FACULTY AND ADVISERS

York Prep is proud of having maintained a stable faculty of outstanding and dedicated individuals. New teachers join the staff periodically, creating a nice balance between youth and experience.

There are 64 full-time faculty members, including 2 college guidance counselors, 13 reading and learning specialists, 2 computer specialists, and a librarian.

Mr. Ronald P. Stewart, the founding Headmaster, is a graduate of Oxford University (B.A., 1965; M.A., 1966; B.C.L., 1968), where he also taught.

COLLEGE ADMISSION COUNSELING

York Prep has a notable college guidance program. Mrs. Jayme Stewart, the Director of College Guidance, is well known for her expertise, experience, and authorship of *How to Get into the College of Your Choice.* She meets with all tenth graders to outline the program and then meets individually with eleventh graders and their parents. Extensive meetings continue through the twelfth grade on an individual basis. In addition, the eleventh and twelfth graders take college guidance as a course where they write their essays, research colleges, and complete their applications during school hours.

One hundred percent of York Prep's graduating students attend college. The ultimate aim of the college guidance program is the placement of each student in the college best suited to him or her. More than 85 percent of York Prep graduates are accepted to, attend, and finish at their first- or second-choice college. Graduates are currently attending schools that include Barnard, Berkeley, Bowdoin, Colgate, Columbia, Cornell, Franklin and Marshall, Hamilton, Harvard, Hobart, Pennsylvania, Skidmore, Vassar, Wesley, and the University of Michigan. Numerous college representatives visit the School regularly to meet with interested students.

STUDENT BODY AND CONDUCT

There are 351 students enrolled at York Prep. York Prep students reside in all five boroughs of New York City as well as Long Island, northern New Jersey, and Westchester County. The School has a student code of conduct and a dress code. The elected student council is also an integral part of life at York Prep.

ACADEMIC FACILITIES

Located steps from Central Park at 40 West 68th Street, York Prep is a seven-story granite building housing two modern science laboratories, state-of-the-art computer equipment, performance and art studios, and a sprung hardwood gymnasium with weight and locker room facilities. The classrooms are spacious and airy, carpeted, and climate controlled. All classrooms have computers and audiovisual (AV) projectors. High-speed Internet access is available for the entire School and enables students to e-mail their teachers and review homework assignments. The building is wheelchair accessible and is located near Lincoln Center on a safe and lovely tree-lined street.

ATHLETICS

All students are required to take courses in physical education and health each year. A varied and extensive program and after-school selection offer students the opportunity to participate in competitive, noncompetitive, team, and individual sports. York Prep is a playing member of several athletics leagues.

EXTRACURRICULAR OPPORTUNITIES

The Student Council organizes regular social events and trips. The School provides a wide range of extracurricular activities, including Model UN, golf, electric blues band, bee-keeping, and a drama club.

DAILY LIFE

The School day begins at 8:40 with a 10-minute house period. Academic classes of 42-minute duration begin at 8:56. There is a midmorning break at 10:24. Lunch period is from 12:08 to 12:58, Mondays through Thursdays, and classes end at 3:12. Following dismissal, teachers are available for extra help. During this time, clubs and sports teams also meet. On Fridays the school day ends at 1:35.

SUMMER PROGRAMS

The School provides workshops during the summer, both in study skills and in academic courses, most of which are set up on an individual tutorial basis. In addition, the athletic department provides summer sports camps.

COSTS AND FINANCIAL AID

Tuition for the 2011–12 academic year ranged from $36,500 to $37,100. More than 30 percent of the student body receives some financial assistance. During the previous year, $1 million was offered in scholarship assistance.

ADMISSIONS INFORMATION

York Prep seeks to enroll students of above-average intelligence with the will and ability to complete college-preparatory work. Students are accepted on the basis of their applications, ISEE test scores, writing samples, and interviews.

APPLICATION TIMETABLE

York conforms to the notification guidelines established by the Independent Schools Admissions Association of Greater New York. Subsequent applications are processed on a rolling admissions basis. Requests for financial aid should be made at the time of application for entrance.

ADMISSIONS CORRESPONDENCE

Elizabeth Norton, Director of Enrollment
Cathy Minaudo, Director of Admissions
York Preparatory School
40 West 68th Street
New York, New York 10023
Phone: 212-362-0400
Fax: 212-362-7424
E-mail: enorton@yorkprep.org
cminaudo@yorkprep.org
Web site: http://www.yorkprep.org

Special Needs Schools

AMERICAN ACADEMY

12200 West Broward Boulevard
Plantation, Florida 33325

Head of School: William R. Laurie

General Information Coeducational day college-preparatory, arts, and technology school; primarily serves underachievers, students with learning disabilities, individuals with Attention Deficit Disorder, dyslexic students, and slow learners, and those with lowered self-esteem and confidence. Grades 1–12. Founded: 1965. Setting: suburban. Nearest major city is Fort Lauderdale. 40-acre campus. 10 buildings on campus. Approved or accredited by Association of Independent Schools of Florida, Southern Association of Colleges and Schools, and Florida Department of Education. Total enrollment: 306. Upper school average class size: 14. Upper school faculty-student ratio: 1:12. There are 175 required school days per year for Upper School students. Upper School students typically attend 5 days per week. The average school day consists of 7 hours and 15 minutes.

Upper School Student Profile Grade 9: 35 students (27 boys, 8 girls); Grade 10: 43 students (35 boys, 8 girls); Grade 11: 33 students (20 boys, 13 girls); Grade 12: 36 students (26 boys, 10 girls).

Faculty School total: 32. In upper school: 3 men, 18 women; 14 have advanced degrees.

Subjects Offered Algebra, American history, American literature, anatomy, art, band, biology, business mathematics, ceramics, chemistry, chorus, computer graphics, computer science, creative writing, drafting, drama, drawing, earth science, English, English literature, environmental science, fine arts, French, geometry, health, jazz, mathematics, music appreciation, oceanography, orchestra, photography, physical education, physical science, science, sculpture, Spanish, theater, vocal music, weight training, word processing, world geography, world history, world literature, writing, yearbook.

Graduation Requirements 20th century history, arts and fine arts (art, music, dance, drama), computer science, English, mathematics, physical education (includes health), science, social studies (includes history), must be accepted to a college, 120 community service hours over 4 years of high school. Community service is required.

Special Academic Programs Honors section; independent study; academic accommodation for the gifted, the musically talented, and the artistically talented; remedial reading and/or remedial writing; remedial math; programs in English, mathematics, general development for dyslexic students; ESL (1 student enrolled).

College Admission Counseling 40 students graduated in 2011; all went to college, including Broward College; Florida Atlantic University; Lynn University; Nova Southeastern University; Palm Beach State College.

Student Life Upper grades have uniform requirement, student council. Discipline rests primarily with faculty.

Summer Programs Remediation, enrichment, advancement, ESL, art/fine arts, computer instruction programs offered; session focuses on remediation and make-up courses; held on campus; accepts boys and girls; open to students from other schools. 400 students usually enrolled. 2012 schedule: June 11 to August 10. Application deadline: none.

Tuition and Aid Day student tuition: $24,632–$28,463. Tuition installment plan (monthly payment plans, semester payment plan, annual payment plan). Tuition reduction for siblings, need-based scholarship grants available.

Admissions Traditional secondary-level entrance grade is 9. Psychoeducational evaluation, SAT and Slosson Intelligence required. Deadline for receipt of application materials: none. Application fee required: $100. On-campus interview required.

Athletics Interscholastic: baseball (boys), basketball (b,g), cheering (g), cross-country running (b,g), dance (g), dance squad (g), diving (b,g), football (b), golf (b,g), lacrosse (b,g), roller hockey (b), soccer (b,g), softball (g), swimming and diving (b,g), tennis (b,g), track and field (b,g), volleyball (b,g), weight lifting (b), weight training (b,g), winter soccer (b,g), wrestling (b). 7 PE instructors, 4 coaches.

Computers Computers are regularly used in graphic arts, literary magazine, newspaper, Web site design, word processing, writing, yearbook classes. Computer network features include on-campus library services, online commercial services, Internet access, Internet filtering or blocking technology, Questia. Student e-mail accounts and computer access in designated common areas are available to students. Students grades are available online. The school has a published electronic and media policy.

Contact William R. Laurie, President. 954-472-0022. Fax: 954-472-3088. Web site: www.ahschool.com.

ARROWSMITH SCHOOL

245 St. Clair Avenue West
Toronto, Ontario M4V 1R3, Canada

Head of School: Ms. Barbara Arrowsmith Young

General Information Coeducational day school; primarily serves underachievers, students with learning disabilities, and dyslexic students. Ungraded, ages 6–20. Founded: 1980. Setting: urban. 1 building on campus. Approved or accredited by Ontario Ministry of Education and Ontario Department of Education. Language of instruction: English. Total enrollment: 75. Upper school average class size: 20. Upper school faculty-student ratio: 1:10. Upper School students typically attend 5 days per week. The average school day consists of 7 hours and 30 minutes.

Faculty School total: 9. In upper school: 2 men, 2 women.

Special Academic Programs Remedial reading and/or remedial writing; remedial math; programs in English, mathematics for dyslexic students.

College Admission Counseling 10 students graduated in 2011; 8 went to college, including University of Toronto; York University. Other: 2 went to work.

Student Life Upper grades have specified standards of dress. Discipline rests primarily with faculty.

Tuition and Aid Day student tuition: CAN$22,000. Tuition installment plan (monthly payment plans).

Admissions Traditional secondary-level entrance age is 14. For fall 2011, 20 students applied for upper-level admission, 20 were accepted, 20 enrolled. Achievement tests, Cognitive Abilities Test, Differential Aptitude Test, Oral and Written Language Scales, Otis-Lennon Mental Ability Test, Raven (Aptitude Test); school's own exam, Reading for Understanding, school's own test, Wide Range Achievement Test, WISC/Woodcock-Johnson or writing sample required. Deadline for receipt of application materials: none. No application fee required. Interview required.

Computers Computer resources include Internet access.

Contact Ms. Daina Luszczek, Receptionist. 416-963-4962. Fax: 416-963-5017. E-mail: dluzchek@arrowsmithprogram.ca. Web site: www.arrowsmithschool.org.

ASPEN RANCH

1090 North Aspen Road
PO Box 369
Loa, Utah 84747

Head of School: Dr. Thomas Vitale

General Information Coeducational boarding college-preparatory, general academic, arts, and bilingual studies school; primarily serves underachievers, students with learning disabilities, individuals with Attention Deficit Disorder, individuals with emotional and behavioral problems, and dyslexic students. Grades 8–12. Founded: 1995. Setting: rural. Nearest major city is Salt Lake City. Students are housed in single-sex dormitories and family-style, single-sex dormitories. 80-acre campus. 9 buildings on campus. Approved or accredited by California Association of Independent Schools, Northwest Association of Schools and Colleges, and Utah Department of Education. Total enrollment: 72. Upper school average class size: 8. Upper school faculty-student ratio: 1:8. There are 280 required school days per year for Upper School students. Upper School students typically attend 5 days per week. The average school day consists of 7 hours and 45 minutes.

Upper School Student Profile Grade 9: 11 students (7 boys, 4 girls); Grade 10: 23 students (14 boys, 9 girls); Grade 11: 18 students (11 boys, 7 girls); Grade 12: 14 students (8 boys, 6 girls). 100% of students are boarding students. 3% are state residents. 48 states are represented in upper school student body.

Faculty School total: 11. In upper school: 4 men, 4 women; 4 have advanced degrees.

Subjects Offered Algebra, American literature, art, athletics, biology, business mathematics, calculus, career education, chemistry, creative writing, criminal justice, earth science, economics, English, English literature, environmental science, equestrian sports, equine science, fine arts, French, geometry, guitar, health, history, information technology, life saving, mathematics, physical education, physical science, poetry, pre-algebra, pre-calculus, psychology, reading, science, social skills, social studies, Spanish, study skills, trigonometry, U.S. government, U.S. history, weight training, world civilizations.

Graduation Requirements Art, career education, English, information technology, mathematics, physical education (includes health), science, social studies (includes history), teen living.

Special Academic Programs Honors section; accelerated programs; independent study; study at local college for college credit; academic accommodation for the gifted; remedial reading and/or remedial writing; remedial math.

College Admission Counseling 17 students graduated in 2010; 10 went to college.

Student Life Upper grades have uniform requirement, student council, honor system. Discipline rests equally with students and faculty.

Tuition and Aid Tuition installment plan (monthly payment plans, individually arranged payment plans). Middle-income loans available.

Admissions Traditional secondary-level entrance grade is 10. For fall 2010, 95 students applied for upper-level admission, 71 were accepted, 57 enrolled. Kaufman Test of Educational Achievement required. Deadline for receipt of application materials: none. No application fee required.

Athletics Intramural: backpacking (boys, girls), basketball (b,g), bicycling (b,g), equestrian sports (b,g), fishing (b,g), fitness (b,g), flag football (b,g), horseback riding (b,g), mountain biking (b,g), mountaineering (b,g), outdoor activities (b,g), outdoor adventure (b,g), outdoor education (b,g), outdoor recreation (b,g), outdoor skills (b,g), physical fitness (b,g), physical training (b,g), rappelling (b,g), ropes courses (b,g); coed intramural: basketball, bicycling, canoeing/kayaking, equestrian sports, fishing, fitness, flag football, hiking/backpacking, horseback riding, life saving, mountain biking, mountaineering, outdoor activities, outdoor adventure, outdoor education, outdoor recreation, outdoor skills, physical fitness, physical training, rappelling, ropes courses, skiing (downhill), softball, ultimate Frisbee, volleyball, water skiing, weight training, wilderness. 2 PE instructors.

Computers Computers are regularly used in creative writing, English, history, psychology, science classes. Computer resources include online commercial services, Internet access, desktop publishing. Students grades are available online.

Contact Aspen Ranch Admissions. 877-231-0734. Fax: 435-836-2277. Web site: www.aspenranch.com.

ASSETS SCHOOL

One Ohana Nui Way
Honolulu, Hawaii 96818

Head of School: Mr. Paul Singer

General Information Coeducational day college-preparatory, arts, and technology school; primarily serves students with learning disabilities, individuals with Attention Deficit Disorder, dyslexic students, and gifted/talented students. Grades K–12. Founded: 1955. Setting: urban. 3-acre campus. 5 buildings on campus. Approved or accredited by The Hawaii Council of Private Schools, Western Association of Schools and Colleges, and Hawaii Department of Education. Member of National Association of Independent Schools. Endowment: $607,632. Total enrollment: 349. Upper school average class size: 7. Upper school faculty-student ratio: 1:8. There are 169 required school days per year for Upper School students. Upper School students typically attend 5 days per week. The average school day consists of 5 hours and 58 minutes.

Upper School Student Profile Grade 9: 24 students (19 boys, 5 girls); Grade 10: 35 students (25 boys, 10 girls); Grade 11: 28 students (18 boys, 10 girls); Grade 12: 24 students (20 boys, 4 girls).

Faculty School total: 68. In upper school: 9 men, 17 women; 18 have advanced degrees.

Subjects Offered 1 1/2 elective credits, algebra, American history, art, biology, business skills, calculus, chemistry, computer science, consumer education, creative writing, current events, earth science, economics, English, fine arts, fitness, general science, geometry, government/civics, health, humanities, independent study, integrated science, keyboarding, literature, marine biology, marine science, mathematics, music, music appreciation, philosophy, physical education, physics, pre-calculus, psychology, sign language, social studies, Spanish, statistics, theater, trigonometry, women's health, woodworking, word processing, world history, world literature.

Graduation Requirements Arts and fine arts (art, music, dance, drama), biology, business skills (includes word processing), computer science, English, foreign language, mathematics, physical education (includes health), science, social studies (includes history), study skills, participation in mentorship program in 10th-12th grades.

Special Academic Programs Academic accommodation for the gifted; remedial reading and/or remedial writing; remedial math; programs in English, mathematics, general development for dyslexic students.

College Admission Counseling 24 students graduated in 2011; 23 went to college, including Chaminade University of Honolulu; Hawai`i Pacific University; McMaster University; Oregon State University; University of Hawaii at Manoa. Other: 1 went to work.

Student Life Upper grades have specified standards of dress, student council, honor system. Discipline rests primarily with faculty.

Summer Programs Advancement programs offered; session focuses on learning strategies for students in the 9th and 10th grades; held on campus; accepts boys and girls; open to students from other schools. 40 students usually enrolled. 2012 schedule: June 14 to July 15. Application deadline: none.

Tuition and Aid Day student tuition: $21,625. Tuition installment plan (monthly payment plans, semester payment plan). Need-based scholarship grants, partial tuition remission for children of staff available. In 2011–12, 33% of upper-school students received aid. Total amount of financial aid awarded in 2011–12: $170,000.

Admissions Traditional secondary-level entrance grade is 9. For fall 2011, 23 students applied for upper-level admission, 11 were accepted, 8 enrolled. WISC III or other aptitude measures; standardized achievement test required. Deadline for receipt of application materials: none. Application fee required: $75. On-campus interview required.

Athletics Interscholastic: baseball (boys), basketball (b,g), bowling (b,g), canoeing/kayaking (b,g), cheering (g), cross-country running (b,g), diving (b,g), football (b), golf (b,g), gymnastics (g), judo (b,g), kayaking (b,g), sailing (b,g), soccer (b,g), softball (g), swimming and diving (b,g), tennis (b,g), track and field (b,g), volleyball (b,g), water polo (b,g), wrestling (b,g); intramural: basketball (b,g), volleyball (b,g); coed intramural: basketball, dance, flag football, kickball, Newcombe ball, soccer, softball, tai chi, touch football, ultimate Frisbee, volleyball, whiffle ball, yoga. 2 PE instructors, 4 coaches.

Computers Computers are regularly used in English, mathematics, photography, science classes. Computer network features include on-campus library services, Internet access, wireless campus network, assistive technology for learning differences. The school has a published electronic and media policy.

Contact Ms. Sandi Tadaki, Director of Admissions. 808-423-1356. Fax: 808-422-1920. E-mail: stadaki@assets-school.net. Web site: www.assets-school.net.

ATLANTIS ACADEMY

9600 Southwest 107th Avenue
Miami, Florida 33176

Head of School: Mr. Carlos Aballi

General Information Coeducational day general academic school; primarily serves underachievers, students with learning disabilities, individuals with Attention Deficit Disorder, individuals with emotional and behavioral problems, dyslexic students, and Autism Spectrum Disorder. Ungraded, ages 5–18. Founded: 1976. Setting: suburban. 3-acre campus. 1 building on campus. Approved or accredited by Florida Council of Independent Schools, Southern Association of Colleges and Schools, and Florida Department of Education. Total enrollment: 156. Upper school average class size: 9. Upper school faculty-student ratio: 1:8. The average school day consists of 6 hours and 15 minutes.

Faculty School total: 26. In upper school: 5 men, 9 women; 3 have advanced degrees.

Subjects Offered Art, computer skills, French, language arts, mathematics, physical education, reading, science, social studies, Spanish.

Special Academic Programs Remedial reading and/or remedial writing; remedial math; programs in English, mathematics, general development for dyslexic students; ESL (3 students enrolled).

College Admission Counseling 12 students graduated in 2011; 8 went to college, including Florida International University; Lynn University; Miami Dade College; New York Institute of Technology. Other: 4 went to work.

Student Life Upper grades have uniform requirement. Discipline rests primarily with faculty.

Summer Programs Remediation, ESL, art/fine arts, computer instruction programs offered; session focuses on remediation; held on campus; accepts boys and girls; open to students from other schools. 60 students usually enrolled. 2012 schedule: June 4 to August 11. Application deadline: March 1.

Tuition and Aid Day student tuition: $14,000–$16,000. Tuition installment plan (monthly payment plans, semi-annual and annual payment plans). Need-based scholarship grants available. In 2011–12, 90% of upper-school students received aid. Total amount of financial aid awarded in 2011–12: $12,000.

Admissions Traditional secondary-level entrance age is 14. For fall 2011, 15 students applied for upper-level admission, 15 were accepted, 15 enrolled. Psychoeducational evaluation or school's own exam required. Deadline for receipt of application materials: none. No application fee required. On-campus interview required.

Athletics Interscholastic: basketball (boys, girls), flag football (b), tennis (b,g), volleyball (b,g); intramural: flag football (b); coed interscholastic: softball; coed intramural: golf, tennis. 1 PE instructor, 2 coaches.

Computers Computers are regularly used in art, English, foreign language, history, mathematics, science, social sciences classes. Computer network features include Internet access.

Contact Mr. Eric Smith, Assistant Director/Director of Admissions. 305-271-9771. Fax: 305-271-7078. E-mail: esmith@esa-education.com. Web site: miami.atlantisacademy.com.

BACHMAN ACADEMY

414 Brymer Creek Road
McDonald, Tennessee 37353

Head of School: Mr. Mark A. Frizzell, M.Ed.

General Information Coeducational boarding and day college-preparatory, general academic, and vocational school; primarily serves underachievers, students with learning disabilities, individuals with Attention Deficit Disorder, and dyslexic students. Grades 6–PG. Founded: 1999. Setting: rural. Nearest major city is Chattanooga. Students are housed in single-sex dormitories. 210-acre campus. 6 buildings on campus. Approved or accredited by Southern Association of Colleges and Schools, Southern Association of Independent Schools, and Tennessee Department of Education. Member of National Association of Independent Schools. Total enrollment: 31. Upper school average class size: 5. Upper school faculty-student ratio: 1:3. There are 169 required school days per year for Upper School students. Upper School students typically attend 5 days per week. The average school day consists of 7 hours and 30 minutes.

Upper School Student Profile Grade 9: 3 students (3 boys); Grade 10: 6 students (3 boys, 3 girls); Grade 11: 11 students (8 boys, 3 girls); Grade 12: 2 students (2 boys); Grade 13: 1 student (1 boy); Postgraduate: 2 students (1 boy, 1 girl). 51% of students are boarding students. 50% are state residents. 11 states are represented in upper school student body. 6% are international students. International students from Canada and Nigeria.

Faculty School total: 10. In upper school: 5 men, 5 women; 1 has an advanced degree.

Subjects Offered ACT preparation, agriculture, art, biology, calculus, carpentry, chemistry, English, equine management, equitation, leadership and service, mathematics, mechanics, personal finance, physics, pre-algebra, SAT preparation, social studies, Spanish, wellness, woodworking.

Graduation Requirements All courses as required by the State of TN Department of Education, Preparation for College Life I&II, Success and Leadership.

Special Academic Programs Academic accommodation for the gifted; remedial reading and/or remedial writing; remedial math; programs in English, mathematics, general development for dyslexic students.

College Admission Counseling 4 students graduated in 2011; 1 went to college, including Messiah College. Other: 1 went to work, 1 entered a postgraduate year, 1 had other specific plans.
Student Life Upper grades have uniform requirement, student council, honor system. Discipline rests primarily with faculty.
Summer Programs Remediation, enrichment, sports programs offered; session focuses on learning disabilities; held on campus; accepts boys and girls; open to students from other schools. 150 students usually enrolled. 2012 schedule: July 1 to July 31. Application deadline: April 1.
Tuition and Aid Day student tuition: $18,779; 5-day tuition and room/board: $38,846; 7-day tuition and room/board: $48,275. Tuition installment plan (monthly payment plans, bi-annual payment plan). Need-based scholarship grants available. In 2011–12, 48% of upper-school students received aid. Total amount of financial aid awarded in 2011–12: $145,160.
Admissions Traditional secondary-level entrance grade is 9. For fall 2011, 183 students applied for upper-level admission, 72 were accepted, 25 enrolled. Any standardized test, Individual IQ, Achievement and behavior rating scale or WISC III or other aptitude measures; standardized achievement test required. Deadline for receipt of application materials: none. Application fee required: $100. Interview required.
Athletics Coed Intramural: backpacking, basketball, billiards, bowling, canoeing/kayaking, equestrian sports, fishing, fitness, fitness walking, hiking/backpacking, horseback riding, JROTC drill, kickball, outdoor activities, outdoor education, outdoor recreation, outdoor skills, outdoors, paddling, physical fitness, physical training, rafting, strength & conditioning, swimming and diving, table tennis, volleyball, walking.
Computers Computers are regularly used in economics, English, foreign language, mathematics, social studies, writing classes. Computer network features include Internet access, wireless campus network, Internet filtering or blocking technology. Student e-mail accounts and computer access in designated common areas are available to students. The school has a published electronic and media policy.
Contact Mrs. Bridgette Owen, Director of Admissions. 423-479-4523 Ext. 41. Fax: 423-472-2718. E-mail: admissions@bachmanacademy.org. Web site: www.bachmanacademy.org/.

BRIDGES ACADEMY

3921 Laurel Canyon Boulevard
Studio City, California 91604

Head of School: Carl Sabatino

General Information Coeducational day college-preparatory, arts, technology, and music, drama, talent development school; primarily serves gifted students with nonverbal learning differences. Grades 5–12. Founded: 1994. Setting: suburban. Nearest major city is Los Angeles. 4-acre campus. 3 buildings on campus. Approved or accredited by Western Association of Schools and Colleges and California Department of Education. Total enrollment: 129. Upper school average class size: 9. Upper school faculty-student ratio: 1:8. There are 174 required school days per year for Upper School students. Upper School students typically attend 5 days per week. The average school day consists of 5 hours and 15 minutes.
Upper School Student Profile Grade 9: 25 students (20 boys, 5 girls); Grade 10: 20 students (18 boys, 2 girls); Grade 11: 17 students (14 boys, 3 girls); Grade 12: 15 students (14 boys, 1 girl).
Faculty School total: 22. In upper school: 14 men, 8 women; 12 have advanced degrees.
Subjects Offered 20th century history, algebra, American government, American literature, anatomy and physiology, art, biology, calculus, chemistry, drama, economics, European history, European literature, film, genetics, geometry, Japanese, modern European history, music, non-Western literature, photography, physics, pre-calculus, senior project, Spanish, statistics, study skills, technology, U.S. history, world history.
Graduation Requirements Economics, English, foreign language, government, history, mathematics, performing arts, science, senior seminar, visual arts.
Special Academic Programs Honors section; academic accommodation for the gifted.
College Admission Counseling 15 students graduated in 2011; 13 went to college, including California State University, Northridge. Other: 2 had other specific plans. 56% scored over 600 on SAT critical reading, 24% scored over 600 on SAT math.
Student Life Discipline rests primarily with faculty.
Summer Programs Enrichment, sports, art/fine arts, computer instruction programs offered; session focuses on enrichment; held on campus; accepts boys and girls; open to students from other schools. 2012 schedule: June 1 to July 31. Application deadline: none.
Tuition and Aid Day student tuition: $31,411. Tuition installment plan (Insured Tuition Payment Plan, monthly payment plans). Need-based scholarship grants available. In 2011–12, 10% of upper-school students received aid.
Admissions Traditional secondary-level entrance grade is 9. For fall 2011, 12 students applied for upper-level admission, 9 were accepted, 6 enrolled. Deadline for receipt of application materials: March 1. Application fee required: $150. On-campus interview required.
Athletics Coed Interscholastic: basketball, cross-country running, track and field. 2 PE instructors, 1 coach.
Computers Computers are regularly used in all classes. Computer network features include Internet access, wireless campus network, Internet filtering or blocking technology. Campus intranet and student e-mail accounts are available to students. Students grades are available online.
Contact Doug Lenzini, Director of Admissions. 818-506-1091. Fax: 818-506-8094. E-mail: doug@bridges.edu. Web site: www.bridges.edu.

CAMPHILL SPECIAL SCHOOL

1784 Fairview Road
Glenmoore, Pennsylvania 19343

Head of School: Mr. Bernard Wolf

General Information Coeducational boarding and day general academic, arts, and vocational school; primarily serves underachievers, intellectual and developmental disabilities, and mental retardation. Grades K–13. Founded: 1963. Setting: rural. Nearest major city is Philadelphia. Students are housed in on-campus single family homes. 82-acre campus. 1 building on campus. Approved or accredited by Association of Waldorf Schools of North America, Middle States Association of Colleges and Schools, National Council for Private School Accreditation, and Pennsylvania Department of Education. Total enrollment: 110. Upper school average class size: 11. Upper school faculty-student ratio: 1:5. There are 180 required school days per year for Upper School students. Upper School students typically attend 5 days per week. The average school day consists of 9 hours.
Upper School Student Profile Grade 9: 10 students (6 boys, 4 girls); Grade 10: 10 students (5 boys, 5 girls); Grade 11: 10 students (7 boys, 3 girls); Grade 12: 12 students (10 boys, 2 girls); Grade 13: 17 students (15 boys, 2 girls). 85% of students are boarding students. 68% are state residents. 9 states are represented in upper school student body. 2% are international students. International students from Nigeria; 2 other countries represented in student body.
Faculty In upper school: 2 men, 2 women; 70 reside on campus.
Subjects Offered 20th century American writers, 20th century history, 20th century physics, 20th century world history, acting, agriculture, American Civil War, American culture, American democracy, American history, Ancient Greek, ancient history, ancient world history, animal husbandry, art, art and culture, art appreciation, astronomy, bell choir, biology, body human, botany, chemistry, choir, drama, drama performance, ecology, environmental education, eurythmy, gardening, geography, geometry, government, handbells, health and wellness, history, instruments, life skills, mathematics, medieval history, medieval literature, medieval/Renaissance history, meteorology, music, mythology, natural history, painting, physics, poetry, pottery, reading, science, Shakespeare, woodworking, zoology.
Special Academic Programs Remedial reading and/or remedial writing; remedial math.
Student Life Upper grades have student council. Discipline rests primarily with faculty.
Summer Programs Enrichment programs offered; session focuses on Extended School Year (ESY); held on campus; accepts boys and girls; not open to students from other schools. 45 students usually enrolled. 2012 schedule: June 30 to July 28.
Tuition and Aid Need-based scholarship grants available.
Admissions Traditional secondary-level entrance grade is 9. Deadline for receipt of application materials: none. No application fee required. On-campus interview required.
Contact 610-469-9236. Web site: www.camphillspecialschool.org.

CEDAR RIDGE ACADEMY

4270 West 5625 N.
Roosevelt, Utah 84066

Head of School: Christine Haggerty

General Information Coeducational boarding and day college-preparatory, general academic, and arts school; primarily serves underachievers, students with learning disabilities, individuals with Attention Deficit Disorder, individuals with emotional and behavioral problems, dyslexic students, and Credit Deficient. Grades 9–12. Founded: 1996. Setting: rural. Nearest major city is Salt Lake City. Students are housed in single-sex dormitories. 100-acre campus. 8 buildings on campus. Approved or accredited by National Council for Private School Accreditation, Northwest Accreditation Commission, Northwest Association of Schools and Colleges, and Utah Department of Education. Upper school average class size: 10. Upper school faculty-student ratio: 1:15. There are 250 required school days per year for Upper School students. Upper School students typically attend 5 days per week. The average school day consists of 6 hours and 30 minutes.
Upper School Student Profile Grade 9: 4 students (2 boys, 2 girls); Grade 10: 10 students (10 boys); Grade 11: 18 students (9 boys, 9 girls); Grade 12: 9 students (5 boys, 4 girls). 100% of students are boarding students. 1% are state residents. 16 states are represented in upper school student body. 1% are international students.
Faculty School total: 7. In upper school: 5 men, 2 women; 3 have advanced degrees; 2 reside on campus.
Subjects Offered 1 1/2 elective credits, 20th century American writers, 20th century history, 20th century world history, ACT preparation, algebra, American government, American history, American literature, anatomy, ancient world history, art, art appreci-

ation, biology, British literature, business mathematics, career and personal planning, career/college preparation, ceramics, character education, computer literacy, consumer mathematics, drawing, electives, English, geometry, government/civics, health education, independent living, keyboarding, language arts, life management skills, martial arts, peer counseling, personal fitness, physics, pre-algebra, pre-calculus, psychology, reading, SAT/ACT preparation, Shakespeare, studio art.
Graduation Requirements 20th century history, 20th century world history, algebra, American government, American history, ancient world history, art appreciation, biology, British literature, computer literacy, consumer economics, earth systems analysis, English, environmental science, geometry, government, health, keyboarding, life management skills, martial arts, reading/study skills, U.S. history, visual arts, world history, writing.
Special Academic Programs Accelerated programs; remedial reading and/or remedial writing; remedial math.
College Admission Counseling 14 students graduated in 2010; all went to college, including Christopher Newport University; Foothill College; Fort Lewis College; The University of Arizona; The University of Kansas; University of Colorado Boulder. Median composite ACT: 23. 22% scored over 26 on composite ACT.
Student Life Upper grades have specified standards of dress, student council, honor system. Discipline rests primarily with faculty.
Tuition and Aid Day student tuition: $24,000; 7-day tuition and room/board: $36,000. Guaranteed tuition plan. Tuition installment plan (monthly payment plans). Tuition reduction for siblings, need-based scholarship grants, paying campus jobs available. In 2010–11, 15% of upper-school students received aid. Total amount of financial aid awarded in 2010–11: $45,000.
Admissions Traditional secondary-level entrance grade is 11. For fall 2010, 53 students applied for upper-level admission, 50 were accepted, 48 enrolled. Deadline for receipt of application materials: none. Application fee required: $50. Interview required.
Athletics Intramural: basketball (boys), volleyball (g), weight training (b,g); coed intramural: martial arts, outdoor activities, physical training, softball, strength & conditioning, yoga. 3 athletic trainers.
Computers Computers are regularly used in all academic classes. Computer resources include Internet access, wireless campus network. Student e-mail accounts and computer access in designated common areas are available to students.
Contact Shirley Page, Receptionist. 435-353-4498 Ext. 100. Fax: 435-353-4898. E-mail: staff@ccdaridge.net. Web site: www.cedarridgeacademy.net.

CHATHAM ACADEMY

4 Oglethorpe Professional Boulevard
Savannah, Georgia 31406

Head of School: Mrs. Carolyn M. Hannaford

General Information Coeducational day college-preparatory, general academic, and technology school; primarily serves underachievers, students with learning disabilities, individuals with Attention Deficit Disorder, dyslexic students, and different learning styles. Grades 1–12. Founded: 1978. Setting: suburban. 5-acre campus. 1 building on campus. Approved or accredited by Georgia Independent School Association, Southern Association of Colleges and Schools, and Georgia Department of Education. Endowment: $100,000. Total enrollment: 78. Upper school average class size: 10. Upper school faculty-student ratio: 1:10. There are 180 required school days per year for Upper School students. Upper School students typically attend 5 days per week. The average school day consists of 6 hours.
Upper School Student Profile Grade 9: 4 students (3 boys, 1 girl); Grade 10: 4 students (4 boys); Grade 11: 9 students (5 boys, 4 girls); Grade 12: 11 students (9 boys, 2 girls).
Faculty School total: 18. In upper school: 2 men, 8 women; 6 have advanced degrees.
Subjects Offered Algebra, American history, American literature, art, biology, earth science, economics, English, English literature, expository writing, geology, geometry, government/civics, grammar, history, keyboarding, mathematics, physical education, physical science, reading, SAT/ACT preparation, science, social studies, world history, world literature, writing.
Graduation Requirements Algebra, American government, American history, biology, British literature, chemistry, civics, composition, consumer economics, earth science, economics, electives, English, English composition, English literature, foreign language, French, grammar, marine biology, mathematics, physical education (includes health), physical science, reading/study skills, science, social studies (includes history), U.S. history.
Special Academic Programs Independent study; study at local college for college credit; remedial reading and/or remedial writing; remedial math; programs in English, mathematics, general development for dyslexic students.
College Admission Counseling 9 students graduated in 2011; 5 went to college, including Armstrong Atlantic State University; Savannah College of Art and Design. Other: 2 went to work, 2 had other specific plans.
Student Life Upper grades have uniform requirement, student council, honor system. Discipline rests primarily with faculty.
Tuition and Aid Day student tuition: $15,050. Tuition installment plan (monthly payment plans, individually arranged payment plans). Tuition reduction for siblings, need-based scholarship grants, Georgia Special Needs Scholarship available. In 2011–12, 33% of upper-school students received aid. Total amount of financial aid awarded in 2011–12: $90,200.
Admissions Traditional secondary-level entrance grade is 10. For fall 2011, 10 students applied for upper-level admission, 7 were accepted, 5 enrolled. Achievement tests, Individual IQ, Achievement and behavior rating scale, school's own test, Stanford Binet, Wechsler Individual Achievement Test, Wechsler Intelligence Scale for Children III, WISC or WAIS, WISC-R, Woodcock-Johnson Revised Achievement Test or writing sample required. Deadline for receipt of application materials: none. Application fee required: $50. Interview required.
Athletics Interscholastic: flag football (boys, girls), football (b), yoga (g); intramural: football (b), soccer (b,g); coed interscholastic: baseball, basketball, cheering, fitness, fitness walking, flag football; coed intramural: canoeing/kayaking, cheering, cooperative games, fitness, fitness walking, flag football, football, jump rope, kickball, Newcombe ball, outdoor activities, outdoor recreation, paddle tennis, physical fitness, physical training, soccer, whiffle ball. 1 PE instructor, 2 coaches.
Computers Computers are regularly used in all academic classes. Computer network features include Internet access, Internet filtering or blocking technology. The school has a published electronic and media policy.
Contact Mrs. Carolyn M. Hannaford, Principal. 912-354-4047. Fax: 912-354-4633. E-mail: channaford@chathamacademy.com. Web site: www.chathamacademy.com.

CHELSEA SCHOOL

711 Pershing Avenue
Silver Spring, Maryland 20910

Head of School: Katherine Fedalen

General Information Coeducational day college-preparatory, general academic, arts, bilingual studies, and technology school; primarily serves students with learning disabilities, individuals with Attention Deficit Disorder, and dyslexic students. Grades 5–12. Founded: 1976. Setting: suburban. 10-acre campus. 3 buildings on campus. Approved or accredited by Maryland Department of Education. Total enrollment: 71. Upper school average class size: 8. Upper school faculty-student ratio: 1:8. There are 180 required school days per year for Upper School students. Upper School students typically attend 5 days per week. The average school day consists of 6 hours and 30 minutes.
Upper School Student Profile Grade 9: 13 students (10 boys, 3 girls); Grade 10: 12 students (11 boys, 1 girl); Grade 11: 17 students (11 boys, 6 girls); Grade 12: 17 students (12 boys, 5 girls)
Faculty School total: 19. In upper school: 10 men, 9 women.
Subjects Offered Algebra, American history, American literature, art, biology, calculus, career/college preparation, chemistry, community service, composition, computer graphics, computer technologies, computers, conceptual physics, earth and space science, earth science, English, English literature, environmental science, foreign language, geometry, health, health and wellness, independent study, information technology, math review, music, personal fitness, physical education, physics, pre-algebra, pre-calculus, reading, reading/study skills, remedial study skills, science, social skills, Spanish, state government, U.S. government, U.S. history, U.S. literature, wellness.
Graduation Requirements 20th century world history, algebra, American government, American history, art, biology, career/college preparation, chemistry, earth science, electives, English, English composition, English literature, general math, geometry, health and wellness, physical education (includes health), pre-algebra, Spanish, U.S. history.
Special Academic Programs Remedial reading and/or remedial writing; remedial math; programs in English, mathematics, general development for dyslexic students.
College Admission Counseling 25 students graduated in 2011; they went to Macalester College.
Student Life Upper grades have student council. Discipline rests primarily with faculty.
Summer Programs Remediation, enrichment, computer instruction programs offered; session focuses on remediation; held on campus; accepts boys and girls; not open to students from other schools. 30 students usually enrolled. 2012 schedule: July to August. Application deadline: none.
Tuition and Aid Day student tuition: $35,610. Tuition installment plan (individually arranged payment plans). Need-based scholarship grants available. In 2011–12, 14% of upper-school students received aid.
Admissions Traditional secondary-level entrance grade is 9. For fall 2011, 28 students applied for upper-level admission, 22 were accepted, 13 enrolled. Academic Profile Tests, Wechsler Individual Achievement Test, Wide Range Achievement Test, WISC III or other aptitude measures; standardized achievement test, WISC or WAIS, WISC-R or Woodcock-Johnson required. Deadline for receipt of application materials: none. Application fee required: $50. On-campus interview required.
Athletics Interscholastic: basketball (boys, girls), flagball (b); coed interscholastic: soccer, softball, track and field. 1 PE instructor.
Computers Computer network features include on-campus library services, Internet access, wireless campus network, Internet filtering or blocking technology. Campus intranet, student e-mail accounts, and computer access in designated common areas are available to students. The school has a published electronic and media policy.
Contact Debbie Lourie, Director of Admissions. 301-585-1430 Ext. 303. Fax: 301-585-0245. E-mail: dlourie@chelseaschool.edu. Web site: www.chelseaschool.edu.

COMMUNITY HIGH SCHOOL

1135 Teaneck Road
Teaneck, New Jersey 07666

Head of School: Dennis Cohen

General Information Coeducational day college-preparatory school; primarily serves students with learning disabilities, individuals with Attention Deficit Disorder, and dyslexic students. Ungraded, ages 14–19. Founded: 1968. Setting: suburban. Nearest major city is Hackensack. 1 building on campus. Approved or accredited by New Jersey Association of Independent Schools, New York Department of Education, and New Jersey Department of Education. Total enrollment: 184. There are 180 required school days per year for Upper School students. Upper School students typically attend 5 days per week. The average school day consists of 6 hours and 30 minutes.

Subjects Offered Algebra, American history, American literature, art, biology, business, calculus, chemistry, computer science, creative writing, drama, driver education, English, English literature, European history, expository writing, fine arts, geography, geometry, government/civics, grammar, history, journalism, mathematics, music, photography, physical education, physics, psychology, science, social sciences, social studies, sociology, Spanish, speech, study skills, theater, trigonometry, writing.

Graduation Requirements Arts and fine arts (art, music, dance, drama), English, mathematics, physical education (includes health), science, social sciences, social studies (includes history).

Special Academic Programs Remedial reading and/or remedial writing; remedial math; programs in English, mathematics, general development for dyslexic students.

College Admission Counseling 50 students graduated in 2010.

Student Life Upper grades have specified standards of dress. Discipline rests primarily with faculty.

Tuition and Aid Day student tuition: $38,437.

Admissions Traditional secondary-level entrance grade is 9. Traditional secondary-level entrance age is 14. For fall 2010, 195 students applied for upper-level admission, 57 were accepted, 54 enrolled. Deadline for receipt of application materials: none. Application fee required: $65. On-campus interview required.

Athletics Interscholastic: baseball (boys), basketball (b), soccer (b), softball (g); intramural: baseball (b), basketball (b,g), softball (g), table tennis (b,g), track and field (b,g), volleyball (b,g). 5 PE instructors, 8 coaches.

Computers Computers are regularly used in all academic classes. Computer network features include online commercial services, voice recognition systems. The school has a published electronic and media policy.

Contact Toby Braunstein, Director of Education. 201-862-1796. Fax: 201-862-1791. E-mail: tbraunstein@communityhighschool.org. Web site: communityschool.k12.nj.us.

COPPER CANYON ACADEMY

PO Box 230
Rimrock, Arizona 86335

Head of School: Paul Taylor

General Information Girls' boarding college-preparatory and general academic school; primarily serves individuals with Attention Deficit Disorder and individuals with emotional and behavioral problems. Grades 9–12. Founded: 1998. Setting: rural. Nearest major city is Sedona. Students are housed in single-sex dormitories. 29-acre campus. 8 buildings on campus. Approved or accredited by CITA (Commission on International and Trans-Regional Accreditation), North Central Association of Colleges and Schools, and Arizona Department of Education. Total enrollment: 95. Upper school average class size: 10. Upper school faculty-student ratio: 1:10. Upper School students typically attend 5 days per week. The average school day consists of 6 hours.

Upper School Student Profile Grade 9: 20 students (20 girls); Grade 10: 25 students (25 girls); Grade 11: 25 students (25 girls); Grade 12: 25 students (25 girls). 100% of students are boarding students. 10% are state residents. 33 states are represented in upper school student body. 5% are international students.

Faculty School total: 12. In upper school: 5 men, 7 women; 3 have advanced degrees; 2 reside on campus.

Subjects Offered ACT preparation, acting, adolescent issues, advanced math, algebra, American Civil War, American government, American history, American literature, ancient history, ancient world history, applied arts, applied music, art, art and culture, art appreciation, art education, art history, arts, athletic training, athletics, ballet, ballet technique, basketball, biology, botany, British literature, business, business communications, business mathematics, calculus, career planning, character education, chemistry, child development, choir, chorus, civics, Civil War, civil war history, college admission preparation, college awareness, college counseling, college placement, college planning, college writing, communication skills, communications, community garden, community service, comparative civilizations, composition, computer applications, computer education, computer graphics, computer literacy, computer math, computer science, computer skills, computers, consumer mathematics, contemporary art, contemporary history, contemporary issues, creative arts, creative dance, creative writing, current events, dance, dance performance, decision making skills, drama, drama performance, drama workshop, dramatic arts, drawing, drawing and design, earth science, economics, economics and history, electives, English, English composition, English literature, equality and freedom, equestrian sports, equine management, equine science, ethical decision making, European history, European literature, experiential education, female experience in America, film appreciation, fine arts, fitness, food and nutrition, foreign language, foreign policy, French, gender issues, general science, geography, geology, geometry, global studies, government, government/civics, grammar, graphic arts, health, health and safety, health and wellness, health education, health science, heritage of American Women, history, history of dance, history of drama, home economics, human biology, human development, human sexuality, independent living, international studies, intro to computers, jazz dance, journalism, lab/keyboard, language, language and composition, language arts, leadership, leadership education training, learning strategies, library, life issues, life management skills, life skills, linear algebra, literature, literature by women, math applications, mathematics, modern dance, modern languages, moral and social development, music, music appreciation, music composition, music history, music performance, musical productions, musical theater, nature study, news writing, newspaper, non-Western literature, nutrition, oil painting, parenting, participation in sports, peer counseling, performing arts, personal development, personal growth, physical education, physics, play production, poetry, political science, political systems, portfolio art, pre-calculus, psychology, SAT preparation, SAT/ACT preparation, science, sex education, sexuality, Shakespeare, Shakespearean histories, social issues, sociology, softball, Spanish, Spanish literature, speech, speech and debate, sports, sports conditioning, stage and body movement, state history, statistics, student government, student publications, studio art, study skills, tap dance, theater, theater arts, theater history, theater production, trigonometry, U.S. government, U.S. government and politics, U.S. history, U.S. literature, visual and performing arts, visual arts, vocal music, volleyball, water color painting, weight fitness, weightlifting, wellness, Western literature, women in literature, women's health, women's literature, world civilizations, world cultures, world geography, world history, world studies, writing, writing, yoga.

Graduation Requirements Option of traditional academic graduation as well as graduation from the therapeutic side of school.

Special Academic Programs Accelerated programs; independent study; study at local college for college credit; academic accommodation for the gifted, the musically talented, and the artistically talented; programs in English, mathematics for dyslexic students.

Student Life Upper grades have uniform requirement, student council, honor system. Discipline rests primarily with faculty.

Tuition and Aid 7-day tuition and room/board: $6800. Middle-income loans, Keybank, prepGATE and Sallie Mae loans available. In 2011–12, 80% of upper-school students received aid. Total amount of financial aid awarded in 2011–12: $81,600.

Admissions Traditional secondary-level entrance grade is 10. For fall 2011, 400 students applied for upper-level admission, 150 were accepted, 90 enrolled. Deadline for receipt of application materials: none. No application fee required.

Athletics Interscholastic: basketball, soccer, softball, volleyball; intramural: aerobics, aerobics/dance, badminton, ballet, basketball, cross-country running, dance, fitness, fitness walking, horseback riding, jogging, modern dance, physical fitness, physical training, soccer, softball, walking, yoga. 2 PE instructors, 1 coach, 1 athletic trainer.

Computers Computers are regularly used in all academic classes. Computer network features include Internet access, Internet filtering or blocking technology. Student e-mail accounts are available to students. Students grades are available online. The school has a published electronic and media policy.

Contact Stephanie Coleman, Admissions Counselor. 877-617-1222 Ext. 116. Fax: 928-567-1323. E-mail: stephaniecoleman@coppercanyonacademy.com. Web site: www.coppercanyonacademy.com.

CROSS CREEK PROGRAMS

150 North State Street
LaVerkin, Utah 84745

Head of School: Karr Farnsworth

General Information Coeducational boarding college-preparatory, general academic, arts, and business school; primarily serves underachievers, students with learning disabilities, individuals with Attention Deficit Disorder, and individuals with emotional and behavioral problems. Grades 7–12. Founded: 1987. Setting: small town. Nearest major city is St. George. Students are housed in single-sex dormitories. 5-acre campus. 4 buildings on campus. Approved or accredited by Northwest Accreditation Commission, Northwest Association of Schools and Colleges, and Utah Department of Education. Total enrollment: 86. Upper school average class size: 7. Upper school faculty-student ratio: 1:15. There are 128 required school days per year for Upper School students. Upper School students typically attend 3 days per week. The average school day consists of 6 hours and 30 minutes.

Upper School Student Profile Grade 7: 6 students (2 boys, 4 girls); Grade 8: 14 students (7 boys, 7 girls); Grade 9: 19 students (9 boys, 10 girls); Grade 10: 21 students (8 boys, 13 girls); Grade 11: 18 students (7 boys, 11 girls); Grade 12: 8 students (5 boys, 3 girls).

Faculty School total: 7. In upper school: 3 men, 3 women; 3 have advanced degrees.

Subjects Offered 20th century American writers, 20th century world history, advanced chemistry, advanced math, algebra, American government, American history, American literature, art, art appreciation, art history, athletic training, athletics, baseball, basketball, biology, business, business applications, business technology, calculus, career/college preparation, careers, chemistry, child development, choir, chorus, computer applications, computer technologies, consumer mathematics, drawing, early childhood, earth science, electives, English, English composition, English literature, fitness, food and nutrition, general math, general science, geography, geometry, government, health, health education, honors algebra, honors English, honors geometry, honors U.S. history, honors world history, human biology, intro to computers, introduction to theater, keyboarding, language and composition, language arts, mathematics, parenting, pre-algebra, pre-calculus, projective geometry, psychology, reading/study skills, SAT preparation, SAT/ACT preparation, science, Spanish, sports, state history, U.S. government, U.S. history, world civilizations, world cultures.

Graduation Requirements 20th century world history, American government, American history, arts and fine arts (art, music, dance, drama), business skills (includes word processing), business technology, English, geography, keyboarding, mathematics, physical education (includes health), science, social sciences, social studies (includes history), senior project (including 90 hours of community or school service).

Special Academic Programs Honors section; accelerated programs; independent study; study at local college for college credit; remedial reading and/or remedial writing; remedial math; programs in English, mathematics, general development for dyslexic students.

College Admission Counseling 80 students graduated in 2010; 73 went to college. Other: 5 went to work, 2 entered military service.

Student Life Upper grades have uniform requirement, student council, honor system. Discipline rests primarily with faculty.

Tuition and Aid 7 day tuition and room/board: $53,940. Guaranteed tuition plan. Tuition installment plan (monthly payment plans, discount for one year paid in-advance tuition). Tuition reduction for siblings available.

Admissions Traditional secondary-level entrance grade is 10. Deadline for receipt of application materials: none. No application fee required. Interview required.

Athletics Interscholastic: backpacking (boys, girls), baseball (b,g), basketball (b,g), bowling (b,g), cooperative games (b,g), cross-country running (b,g), danceline (b,g), fitness (b,g), fitness walking (b,g), Frisbee (b,g), hiking/backpacking (b,g), outdoor activities (b,g), physical fitness (b,g), physical training (b,g), running (b,g), softball (b,g), strength & conditioning (b,g), track and field (b,g), volleyball (b,g), walking (b,g), water skiing (b,g), winter walking (b,g); intramural: basketball (b,g), cross-country running (b,g), track and field (b,g); coed interscholastic: baseball, softball. 1 PE instructor, 2 coaches.

Computers Computers are regularly used in business, career education, college planning, computer applications, economics, English, foreign language, geography, health, history, mathematics, reading, science classes. Computer resources include on-campus library services.

Contact Kami Farnsworth, Admissions Representative. 800-514-7438. Fax: 435-635-2331. E-mail: kami@crosscreekprograms.com. Web site: www.crosscreekprograms.com.

DELAWARE VALLEY FRIENDS SCHOOL

19 East Central Avenue
Paoli, Pennsylvania 19301-1345

Head of School: Dr. Daniel Kahn

General Information Coeducational day college-preparatory, arts, technology, and Orton-Gillingham based reading instruction school, affiliated with Society of Friends; primarily serves students with learning disabilities, individuals with Attention Deficit Disorder, and dyslexic students. Grades 6–12. Founded: 1986. Setting: suburban. Nearest major city is Philadelphia. 8-acre campus. 1 building on campus. Approved or accredited by Pennsylvania Association of Independent Schools. Endowment: $3.6 million. Total enrollment: 187. Upper school average class size: 8. Upper school faculty-student ratio: 1:5. There are 170 required school days per year for Upper School students. Upper School students typically attend 5 days per week. The average school day consists of 6 hours and 17 minutes.

Upper School Student Profile Grade 9: 25 students (11 boys, 14 girls); Grade 10: 45 students (25 boys, 20 girls); Grade 11: 34 students (23 boys, 11 girls); Grade 12: 44 students (27 boys, 17 girls). 6% of students are members of Society of Friends.

Faculty School total: 38. In upper school: 14 men, 23 women; 23 have advanced degrees.

Subjects Offered 20th century world history, algebra, American history, Asian studies, astronomy, biology, calculus, ceramics, chemistry, college counseling, college placement, computer-aided design, crafts, culinary arts, electives, English, first aid, geometry, human development, language arts, music, photography, physical education, physics, pre-calculus, printmaking, Spanish, studio art, trigonometry, video and animation, world history, writing.

Graduation Requirements Arts and fine arts (art, music, dance, drama), English, lab science, language arts, mathematics, physical education (includes health), senior internship, social studies (includes history), at least one Adventure Based Learning (A.B.L.E.) course, community service hours. Community service is required.

Special Academic Programs Remedial reading and/or remedial writing; remedial math; programs in English, mathematics, general development for dyslexic students.

College Admission Counseling 45 students graduated in 2010; 42 went to college, including American University; La Salle University; McDaniel College; University of Delaware; University of Pennsylvania. Other: 3 had other specific plans.

Student Life Upper grades have specified standards of dress, student council. Discipline rests primarily with faculty. Attendance at religious services is required.

Tuition and Aid Day student tuition: $35,200. Tuition installment plan (monthly payment plans, 2-payment plan (66% due May 1, 34% due January 1)). Tuition reduction for siblings, need-based scholarship grants available. In 2010–11, 31% of upper-school students received aid. Total amount of financial aid awarded in 2010–11: $756,000.

Admissions Traditional secondary-level entrance grade is 9. For fall 2010, 46 students applied for upper-level admission, 34 were accepted, 25 enrolled. Psychoeducational evaluation and WISC or WAIS required. Deadline for receipt of application materials: none. Application fee required: $100. On-campus interview required.

Athletics Interscholastic: basketball (boys, girls), cross-country running (b,g), Frisbee (b), lacrosse (b,g), soccer (b,g); coed interscholastic: Frisbee, golf, soccer, tennis, ultimate Frisbee; coed intramural: backpacking, bicycling, hiking/backpacking, rock climbing, sailing, skiing (cross-country), volleyball. 2 PE instructors, 5 coaches.

Computers Computers are regularly used in all classes. Computer network features include online commercial services, Internet access, wireless campus network, Internet filtering or blocking technology, adaptive technologies such as Kurzweil, Dragon/Mac Speech Dictate, etc., homework site, all students have school-supplied laptops. Student e-mail accounts and computer access in designated common areas are available to students. Students grades are available online. The school has a published electronic and media policy.

Contact Mary Ellen Trent, Director of Admissions. 610-640-4150 Ext. 2162. Fax: 610-560-4336. E-mail: maryellen.trent@dvfs.org. Web site: www.dvfs.org.

EAGLE HILL-SOUTHPORT

214 Main Street
Southport, Connecticut 06890

Head of School: Leonard Tavormina

General Information Coeducational day arts school; primarily serves underachievers, students with learning disabilities, individuals with Attention Deficit Disorder, and dyslexic students. Ungraded, ages 7–15. Founded: 1985. Setting: small town. Nearest major city is Bridgeport. 2-acre campus. 1 building on campus. Approved or accredited by Connecticut Association of Independent Schools and Connecticut Department of Education. Member of National Association of Independent Schools. Endowment: $7.7 million. Total enrollment: 112. Upper school average class size: 5. Upper school faculty-student ratio: 1:4. There are 180 required school days per year for Upper School students. Upper School students typically attend 5 days per week. The average school day consists of 7 hours and 15 minutes.

Faculty School total: 27. In upper school: 6 men, 21 women; 20 have advanced degrees.

Subjects Offered Algebra, art, biology, computer skills, creative writing, earth science, English, grammar, history, literature, mathematics, physical education, reading, social studies, writing.

Special Academic Programs Remedial reading and/or remedial writing; remedial math; programs in English, mathematics, general development for dyslexic students.

Student Life Upper grades have uniform requirement, student council. Discipline rests primarily with faculty.

Summer Programs Remediation programs offered; session focuses on academic skills reinforcement; held on campus; accepts boys and girls; open to students from other schools. 72 students usually enrolled. 2012 schedule: June 27 to July 31. Application deadline: none.

Tuition and Aid Day student tuition: $40,700. Tuition installment plan (monthly payment plans, individually arranged payment plans). Need-based scholarship grants available. In 2011–12, 23% of upper-school students received aid. Total amount of financial aid awarded in 2011–12: $130,095.

Admissions For fall 2011, 1 student applied for upper-level admission, 1 was accepted, 1 enrolled. Wechsler Intelligence Scale for Children required. Deadline for receipt of application materials: none. Application fee required: $100. On-campus interview required.

Athletics Interscholastic: cheering (girls); intramural: cheering (g); coed interscholastic: baseball, basketball, cross-country running, fitness, outdoor adventure, physical fitness, soccer, softball; coed intramural: baseball, basketball, soccer.

Computers Computers are regularly used in English, mathematics, writing classes.

Contact Carolyn Lavender, Director of Admissions. 203-254-2044. Fax: 203-255-4052. E-mail: info@eaglehillsouthport.org. Web site: www.eaglehillsouthport.org.

FAIRHILL SCHOOL

16150 Preston Road
Dallas, Texas 75248

Head of School: Ms. Jane Sego

General Information Coeducational day college-preparatory, arts, and technology school; primarily serves students with learning disabilities, individuals with Attention Deficit Disorder, and dyslexic students. Grades 1–12. Founded: 1971. Setting: suburban. 16-acre campus. 2 buildings on campus. Approved or accredited by Southern

Association of Colleges and Schools and Texas Department of Education. Endowment: $4 million. Total enrollment: 219. Upper school average class size: 12. Upper school faculty-student ratio: 1:12. There are 175 required school days per year for Upper School students. Upper School students typically attend 5 days per week. The average school day consists of 7 hours and 30 minutes.

Upper School Student Profile Grade 9: 23 students (12 boys, 11 girls); Grade 10: 24 students (17 boys, 7 girls); Grade 11: 25 students (17 boys, 8 girls); Grade 12: 18 students (12 boys, 6 girls).

Faculty School total: 32. In upper school: 6 men, 10 women; 4 have advanced degrees.

Subjects Offered American history, American literature, art, biology, British literature, chemistry, computer science, economics, English, government, health, journalism, mathematics, music, performing arts, physical education, physical science, physics, psychology, reading, Spanish, speech, study skills, world geography.

Graduation Requirements Arts and fine arts (art, music, dance, drama), computer science, English, mathematics, physical education (includes health), science, social studies (includes history), 60 hours of volunteer service for seniors.

Special Academic Programs Honors section; remedial reading and/or remedial writing; remedial math; programs in English, mathematics, general development for dyslexic students.

College Admission Counseling 18 students graduated in 2011; 16 went to college, including Collin County Community College District; Southern Methodist University; St. Edward's University; Texas Tech University; University of Oklahoma. Other: 1 went to work, 1 entered military service.

Student Life Upper grades have uniform requirement, student council. Discipline rests primarily with faculty.

Summer Programs Remediation, computer instruction programs offered; session focuses on academics; held on campus; accepts boys and girls; open to students from other schools. 50 students usually enrolled. 2012 schedule: June 1 to June 26. Application deadline: none.

Tuition and Aid Day student tuition: $15,000. Need-based scholarship grants available. In 2011–12, 6% of upper-school students received aid. Total amount of financial aid awarded in 2011–12: $50,000.

Admissions Traditional secondary-level entrance grade is 9. For fall 2011, 7 students applied for upper-level admission, 5 were accepted, 5 enrolled. Psychoeducational evaluation required. Deadline for receipt of application materials: none. Application fee required: $1500. Interview required.

Athletics Interscholastic: baseball (boys), basketball (b,g), cheering (b,g), golf (b,g), soccer (b,g), tennis (b,g), volleyball (g); intramural: cheering (b,g), jump rope (b,g); coed interscholastic: cheering, golf, soccer, tennis. 3 coaches.

Computers Computers are regularly used in college planning, English, technology, yearbook classes. Computer network features include on-campus library services, Internet access, wireless campus network, Internet filtering or blocking technology. The school has a published electronic and media policy.

Contact Mrs. Melinda Cameron, Head of Upper School. 972-233-1026. Fax: 972-233-8205. E-mail: mcameron@fairhill.org. Web site: www.fairhill.org.

THE FAMILY FOUNDATION SCHOOL

431 Chapel Hill Road
Hancock, New York 13783

Head of School: Mr. Emmanuel A. Argiros

General Information Coeducational boarding college-preparatory, arts, religious studies, and character education school, affiliated with Christian faith, Jewish faith; primarily serves underachievers, individuals with Attention Deficit Disorder, individuals with emotional and behavioral problems, and alcohol and drug abuse. Grades 9–12. Founded: 1987. Setting: rural. Nearest major city is Binghamton. Students are housed in single-sex dormitories. 158-acre campus. 14 buildings on campus. Approved or accredited by Joint Commission on Accreditation of Healthcare Organizations, Middle States Association of Colleges and Schools, New York State Board of Regents, and New York Department of Education. Total enrollment: 120. Upper school average class size: 12. There are 210 required school days per year for Upper School students. Upper School students typically attend 5 days per week. The average school day consists of 6 hours and 20 minutes.

Upper School Student Profile Grade 9: 10 students (8 boys, 2 girls); Grade 10: 23 students (18 boys, 5 girls); Grade 11: 38 students (25 boys, 13 girls); Grade 12: 49 students (34 boys, 15 girls). 100% of students are boarding students. 40% are state residents. 22 states are represented in upper school student body. 1% are international students. International students from Canada. 97% of students are Christian, Jewish.

Faculty School total: 36. In upper school: 19 men, 17 women; 13 have advanced degrees; 5 reside on campus.

Subjects Offered Advanced chemistry, algebra, American government, American history, analysis and differential calculus, ancient world history, applied music, art, biology, British literature, character education, chemistry, choir, chorus, college writing, community service, dance, debate, drama, earth science, economics, English, family living, geometry, global studies, government, health and safety, health education, Jewish studies, journalism, modern dance, photography, physical education, physics, pre-calculus, religious education, Russian, sociology, Spanish, tap dance, trigonometry, woodworking, work-study, world history, World-Wide-Web publishing, yearbook.

Graduation Requirements Character education, English, foreign language, life skills, mathematics, physical education (includes health), science, social studies (includes history), New York State Board of Regents requirements, completion of character education program.

Special Academic Programs Study at local college for college credit; remedial reading and/or remedial writing.

College Admission Counseling 35 students graduated in 2011; 32 went to college, including Marywood University; Montclair State University; Nassau Community College; St. John's University; State University of New York at Binghamton; The University of Scranton. Other: 3 had other specific plans. Mean SAT critical reading: 517, mean SAT math: 518, mean SAT writing: 502, mean combined SAT: 1537, mean composite ACT: 22.

Student Life Upper grades have specified standards of dress, student council, honor system. Discipline rests equally with students and faculty. Attendance at religious services is required.

Summer Programs Remediation, enrichment, sports programs offered; held on campus; accepts boys and girls; not open to students from other schools. 120 students usually enrolled. 2012 schedule: June 28 to August 16.

Tuition and Aid 7-day tuition and room/board: $75,600. Tuition installment plan (monthly payment plans). Need-based scholarship grants, paying campus jobs available. In 2011–12, 15% of upper-school students received aid. Total amount of financial aid awarded in 2011–12: $500,000.

Admissions Iowa Tests of Basic Skills required. Deadline for receipt of application materials: none. Application fee required. On-campus interview required.

Athletics Interscholastic: basketball (boys, girls), soccer (b,g), softball (g); intramural: basketball (b,g), lacrosse (b), strength & conditioning (b,g); coed interscholastic: dance, golf; coed intramural: aerobics/dance, ballet, basketball, fishing, fitness, fitness walking, flag football, fly fishing, Frisbee, hiking/backpacking, horseback riding, horseshoes, ice skating, outdoor activities, outdoors, running, skateboarding, soccer, softball, tennis, ultimate Frisbee, volleyball, weight training, yoga. 3 PE instructors, 4 coaches.

Computers Computers are regularly used in English, history, journalism, science, Spanish, yearbook classes. Computer network features include on-campus library services, online commercial services, Internet access, wireless campus network, Internet filtering or blocking technology. Computer access in designated common areas is available to students.

Contact Mr. Jeff Brain, MA, CTS, CEP, Dean of Admissions. 845-887-5213 Ext. 499. Fax: 845-887-4939. E-mail: jbrain@thefamilyschool.com. Web site: www.thefamilyschool.com.

FOOTHILLS ACADEMY

745 37th Street NW
Calgary, Alberta T2N 4T1, Canada

Head of School: Mr. G.M. Bullivant

General Information Coeducational day college-preparatory, general academic, and technology school; primarily serves underachievers, students with learning disabilities, individuals with Attention Deficit Disorder, dyslexic students, and Asperger's Syndrome. Grades 3–12. Founded: 1979. Setting: urban. 7-acre campus. 1 building on campus. Approved or accredited by Association of Independent Schools and Colleges of Alberta and Alberta Department of Education. Language of instruction: English. Endowment: CAN$3 million. Total enrollment: 200. Upper school average class size: 12. Upper school faculty-student ratio: 1:12. There are 177 required school days per year for Upper School students. Upper School students typically attend 5 days per week. The average school day consists of 6 hours and 10 minutes.

Upper School Student Profile Grade 9: 36 students (20 boys, 16 girls); Grade 10: 26 students (10 boys, 16 girls); Grade 11: 24 students (18 boys, 6 girls); Grade 12: 29 students (19 boys, 10 girls).

Faculty School total: 40. In upper school: 10 men, 15 women; 6 have advanced degrees.

Subjects Offered Algebra, art, athletics, basic skills, biology, career and personal planning, career education, chemistry, college admission preparation, college awareness, college planning, community service, computer animation, computer applications, computer education, computer literacy, computer multimedia, computer skills, conflict resolution, consumer mathematics, decision making skills, digital photography, drama, drama performance, dramatic arts, electives, English composition, English literature, environmental studies, expository writing, food and nutrition, grammar, health education, information processing, Internet research, interpersonal skills, keyboarding, language arts, leadership, leadership and service, learning strategies, library research, library skills, mathematics, mechanics of writing, oral communications, painting, personal and social education, photography, physical fitness, poetry, reading, reading/study skills, remedial study skills, research and reference, research skills, science, Shakespeare, short story, social skills, social studies, speech therapy, study skills, technological applications, track and field, writing.

Graduation Requirements Athletics, career and personal planning, English, English composition, English literature, expository writing, grammar, keyboarding, language arts, learning strategies, mathematics, mechanics of writing, physical fitness, reading/study skills, research skills, science, social studies (includes history), study skills, Alberta education standards.

Special Academic Programs Remedial reading and/or remedial writing; remedial math; programs in English, mathematics, general development for dyslexic students.
College Admission Counseling 24 students graduated in 2011; 18 went to college, including Macalester College; Mount Allison University; Mount Royal University; The University of Winnipeg; University of Calgary; University of Victoria. Other: 6 went to work.
Student Life Upper grades have specified standards of dress, student council, honor system. Discipline rests primarily with faculty.
Summer Programs Remediation, enrichment programs offered; session focuses on remedial reading, language, organization skills; held on campus; accepts boys and girls; open to students from other schools. 50 students usually enrolled. 2012 schedule: July 4 to August 21. Application deadline: June 1.
Tuition and Aid Day student tuition: CAN$13,500–CAN$26,500. Tuition installment plan (The Tuition Plan, monthly payment plans, individually arranged payment plans). Bursaries, need-based scholarship grants available. In 2011–12, 60% of upper-school students received aid. Total amount of financial aid awarded in 2011–12: CAN$500,000.
Admissions Traditional secondary-level entrance grade is 9. For fall 2011, 30 students applied for upper-level admission, 10 were accepted, 10 enrolled. Achievement tests, CTBS, Stanford Achievement Test, any other standardized test, math, reading, and mental ability tests, Wechsler Intelligence Scale for Children or writing sample required. Deadline for receipt of application materials: none. Application fee required: CAN$50. On-campus interview required.
Athletics Interscholastic: badminton (boys, girls), basketball (b,g); intramural: badminton (b,g), basketball (b,g), football (b); coed interscholastic: cross-country running, golf, indoor track & field, tennis, track and field, volleyball; coed intramural: badminton, ball hockey, baseball, climbing, cooperative games, cross-country running, curling, fitness, flag football, floor hockey, golf, gymnastics, handball, hiking/backpacking, in-line skating, indoor soccer, indoor track & field, jogging, kickball, life saving, outdoor activities, outdoor adventure, outdoor education, outdoor recreation, outdoor skills, physical fitness, physical training, roller blading, running, skiing (downhill), snowboarding, snowshoeing, soccer, softball, strength & conditioning, tennis, touch football, track and field, volleyball, walking, weight training, wilderness, wilderness survival, wrestling. 1 PE instructor, 10 coaches, 2 athletic trainers.
Computers Computers are regularly used in all academic, animation, basic skills, career education, career exploration, computer applications, creative writing, desktop publishing, keyboarding, library skills, mentorship program, research skills, social studies, Web site design, word processing, writing, yearbook classes. Computer network features include on-campus library services, online commercial services, Internet access, wireless campus network, Internet filtering or blocking technology. Computer access in designated common areas is available to students. The school has a published electronic and media policy.
Contact Ms. A. Rose, Student Applications. 403-270-9400. Fax: 403-270-9438. E-mail: arose@foothillsacademy.org. Web site: www.foothillsacademy.org.

FRANKLIN ACADEMY

106 River Road
East Haddam, Connecticut 06423

Head of School: A. Frederick Weissbach

General Information Coeducational boarding and day college-preparatory school; primarily serves students with learning disabilities and non-verbal learning differences (NLD) and Asperger's Syndrome. Grades 9–PG. Founded: 2000. Setting: rural. Nearest major city is Hartford. Students are housed in single-sex by floor dormitories and single-sex dormitories. 75-acre campus. 18 buildings on campus. Approved or accredited by New England Association of Schools and Colleges and Connecticut Department of Education. Total enrollment: 92. Upper school average class size: 8. Upper school faculty-student ratio: 1:3. There are 180 required school days per year for Upper School students. Upper School students typically attend 6 days per week. The average school day consists of 6 hours and 15 minutes.
Upper School Student Profile Grade 9: 19 students (8 boys, 11 girls); Grade 10: 15 students (13 boys, 2 girls); Grade 11: 21 students (16 boys, 5 girls); Grade 12: 31 students (21 boys, 10 girls); Postgraduate: 6 students (3 boys, 3 girls). 94% of students are boarding students. 18% are state residents. 22 states are represented in upper school student body. 3% are international students.
Faculty School total: 40. In upper school: 20 men, 20 women; 25 have advanced degrees; 20 reside on campus.
Special Academic Programs Honors section; term-away projects; study abroad; academic accommodation for the gifted.
College Admission Counseling 21 students graduated in 2010; 20 went to college, including Guilford College; Hampshire College; Rochester Institute of Technology; University of Vermont. Other: 1 had other specific plans.
Student Life Upper grades have student council, honor system. Discipline rests equally with students and faculty.
Tuition and Aid Day student tuition: $64,500; 7-day tuition and room/board: $76,800. Tuition installment plan (monthly payment plans, individually arranged payment plans).
Admissions Traditional secondary-level entrance grade is 9. Achievement tests, psychoeducational evaluation, Wechsler Intelligence Scale for Children and writing sample required. Deadline for receipt of application materials: none. Application fee required: $75. On-campus interview required.
Athletics Coed Intramural: aerobics/dance, aquatics, basketball, bicycling, bowling, canoeing/kayaking, climbing, cooperative games, dance, fishing, fitness, fitness walking, Frisbee, golf, horseback riding, kayaking, martial arts, mountain biking, outdoor recreation, outdoors, paddling, paint ball, physical fitness, physical training, running, sailing, scuba diving, soccer, softball, swimming and diving, tai chi, tennis, ultimate Frisbee, walking, yoga.
Computers Computers are regularly used in all classes. Computer network features include on-campus library services, Internet access, wireless campus network, Internet filtering or blocking technology. Campus intranet, student e-mail accounts, and computer access in designated common areas are available to students. The school has a published electronic and media policy.
Contact Sandra Mahan, Assistant Director of Admissions. 860-873-2700 Ext. 154. Fax: 860-873-9345. E-mail: smahan@fa-ct.org. Web site: www.fa-ct.org.

FRASER ACADEMY

2294 West 10th Avenue
Vancouver, British Columbia V6K 2H8, Canada

Head of School: Mrs. Maureen Steltman

General Information Coeducational day college-preparatory, general academic, arts, technology, and BC Ministry of Education curriculum school; primarily serves students with learning disabilities and dyslexic students. Grades 1–12. Founded: 1982. Setting: urban. 1 building on campus. Approved or accredited by Canadian Association of Independent Schools and British Columbia Department of Education. Language of instruction: English. Total enrollment: 191. Upper school average class size: 8. Upper school faculty-student ratio: 1:3. There are 178 required school days per year for Upper School students. Upper School students typically attend 5 days per week. The average school day consists of 7 hours and 40 minutes.
Upper School Student Profile Grade 6: 11 students (7 boys, 4 girls); Grade 7: 22 students (16 boys, 6 girls); Grade 8: 26 students (20 boys, 6 girls); Grade 9: 18 students (12 boys, 6 girls); Grade 10: 28 students (15 boys, 13 girls); Grade 11: 22 students (14 boys, 8 girls); Grade 12: 22 students (15 boys, 7 girls).
Faculty School total: 71. In upper school: 9 men, 48 women; 6 have advanced degrees.
Graduation Requirements British Columbia Ministry of Education requirements.
Special Academic Programs Academic accommodation for the gifted; programs in English, mathematics, general development for dyslexic students; special instructional classes for Orton Gillingham tutoring program.
College Admission Counseling 19 students graduated in 2010.
Student Life Upper grades have uniform requirement, honor system. Discipline rests primarily with faculty.
Tuition and Aid Day student tuition: CAN$23,980. Tuition installment plan (quarterly payment plan). Tuition reduction for siblings, bursaries available.
Admissions Traditional secondary-level entrance grade is 8. For fall 2010, 49 students applied for upper-level admission, 48 were accepted, 46 enrolled. Academic Profile Tests, admissions testing and writing sample required. Deadline for receipt of application materials: none. Application fee required: CAN$250. Interview required.
Athletics Interscholastic: volleyball (girls); intramural: volleyball (g); coed interscholastic: alpine skiing, basketball, canoeing/kayaking, cross-country running, field hockey, flag football, kickball, martial arts, outdoor activities, outdoor education, physical fitness, running, skiing (downhill), snowboarding, soccer, softball, track and field; coed intramural: alpine skiing, ball hockey, basketball, bicycling, climbing, cross-country running, martial arts, mountain biking, rock climbing, running, scuba diving, skiing (downhill), snowboarding, soccer, softball, track and field, wall climbing. 1 PE instructor, 1 coach.
Computers Computers are regularly used in all academic classes. Computer network features include Internet access, Internet filtering or blocking technology, various learning disabilities/dyslexic-specific software.
Contact Ms. Brooke Ellison, Executive Assistant and Admissions Coordinator. 604-736-5575 Ext. 222. Fax: 604-736-5578. E-mail: bellison@fraseracademy.ca. Web site: www.fraseracademy.ca.

THE FROSTIG SCHOOL

971 North Altadena Drive
Pasadena, California 91107

Head of School: Dr. Chris Schnieders

General Information Coeducational day arts, vocational, and technology school; primarily serves underachievers, students with learning disabilities, individuals with Attention Deficit Disorder, and dyslexic students. Grades 1–12. Founded: 1951. Setting: suburban. Nearest major city is Los Angeles. 2-acre campus. 1 building on campus. Approved or accredited by National Association of Private Schools for Exceptional Children, Western Association of Schools and Colleges, and California Department of Education. Endowment: $3 million. Total enrollment: 91. Upper school average class size: 12. Upper school faculty-student ratio: 1:6. There are 180 required school days per

year for Upper School students. Upper School students typically attend 5 days per week. The average school day consists of 6 hours and 10 minutes.
Upper School Student Profile Grade 9: 10 students (6 boys, 4 girls); Grade 10: 11 students (8 boys, 3 girls); Grade 11: 12 students (7 boys, 5 girls); Grade 12: 8 students (6 boys, 2 girls).
Faculty School total: 25. In upper school: 4 men; 2 have advanced degrees.
Subjects Offered Spanish.
Special Academic Programs Remedial reading and/or remedial writing; remedial math; programs in English, mathematics, general development for dyslexic students.
College Admission Counseling 19 students graduated in 2011; 14 went to college, including Glendale Community College; Moorpark College; Pasadena City College; Santa Monica College. Other: 1 went to work, 1 entered military service, 2 had other specific plans.
Student Life Upper grades have specified standards of dress, student council. Discipline rests equally with students and faculty.
Summer Programs Remediation, sports, art/fine arts programs offered; session focuses on maintaining skills obtained during the regular term, work experience for high school students; held on campus; accepts boys and girls; not open to students from other schools. 36 students usually enrolled. 2012 schedule: July 1 to July 29.
Tuition and Aid Day student tuition: $27,000. Tuition installment plan (monthly payment plans, individually arranged payment plans). Need-based scholarship grants available. In 2011–12, 5% of upper-school students received aid. Total amount of financial aid awarded in 2011–12: $50,000.
Admissions Traditional secondary-level entrance grade is 9. For fall 2011, 25 students applied for upper-level admission, 20 were accepted, 16 enrolled. Admissions testing required. Deadline for receipt of application materials: none. Application fee required: $100. On-campus interview required.
Athletics Coed Interscholastic: basketball, flag football, softball, touch football. 1 PE instructor, 2 coaches.
Computers Computers are regularly used in art, basic skills, career education, career exploration, college planning, computer applications, creative writing, current events, English, geography, health, history, keyboarding, lab/keyboard, library, library skills, life skills, mathematics, media, music, occupational education, photography, psychology, reading, remedial study skills, research skills, science, social sciences, social studies, study skills, technology, video film production, Web site design, word processing, writing, writing, yearbook classes. Computer network features include on-campus library services, Internet access, Internet filtering or blocking technology, assistive technology services.
Contact Ms. Jacquie Knight, IEP and Admissions Administrator. 626-791-1255. Fax: 626-798-1801. E-mail: admissions@frostig.org. Web site: www.frostig.org.

GATEWAY SCHOOL

2570 NW Green Oaks Boulevard
Arlington, Texas 76012

Head of School: Mrs. Harriet R. Walber

General Information Coeducational day college-preparatory, general academic, arts, and technology school; primarily serves underachievers, students with learning disabilities, individuals with Attention Deficit Disorder, and dyslexic students. Grades 5–12. Founded: 1980. Setting: urban. 7-acre campus. 1 building on campus. Approved or accredited by Southern Association of Colleges and Schools, Southern Association of Independent Schools, Texas Education Agency, and Texas Department of Education. Upper school average class size: 10. Upper school faculty-student ratio: 1:8. The average school day consists of 7 hours.
Faculty School total: 6. In upper school: 1 man, 5 women; 5 have advanced degrees.
Subjects Offered Algebra, American literature, art, biology, British literature, career planning, chemistry, college awareness, college counseling, community service, composition, computer education, computer literacy, computer science, computer skills, developmental math, drama, earth science, economics, English, English composition, English literature, environmental science, geometry, government, government/civics, grammar, health, health education, history, intro to computers, introduction to theater, journalism, keyboarding, language arts, literature, mathematics, music, music performance, music theater, newspaper, physical education, pre-algebra, reading, reading/study skills, science, social studies, Spanish, speech, state history, theater, U.S. government, U.S. history, word processing, world history, world literature, writing, writing workshop, yearbook.
Graduation Requirements Computer science, English, foreign language, mathematics, physical education (includes health), science, social studies (includes history). Community service is required.
Special Academic Programs Independent study; study at local college for college credit; remedial reading and/or remedial writing; remedial math; programs in English, mathematics, general development for dyslexic students.
College Admission Counseling 6 students graduated in 2010; 4 went to college, including Lon Morris College; Tarrant County College District; Texas Wesleyan University; The University of Texas at Arlington. Other: 1 went to work, 1 entered military service.
Student Life Upper grades have uniform requirement, student council. Discipline rests primarily with faculty.
Tuition and Aid Day student tuition: $13,500. Guaranteed tuition plan. Merit scholarship grants, need-based scholarship grants available.
Admissions Traditional secondary-level entrance grade is 9. School's own test, Wechsler Intelligence Scale for Children and Woodcock-Johnson required. Deadline for receipt of application materials: none. Application fee required: $150. On-campus interview required.
Athletics Interscholastic: basketball (boys, girls), golf (g); intramural: basketball (b,g), bowling (b,g), golf (b,g), jogging (b,g); coed interscholastic: fitness walking, golf, jogging, scuba diving; coed intramural: bowling. 1 PE instructor.
Computers Computers are regularly used in basic skills, English, mathematics, science classes. Computer network features include Internet access. The school has a published electronic and media policy.
Contact Harriet R. Walber, Executive Director. 817-226-6222. Fax: 817-226-6225. E-mail: walberhr@aol.com. Web site: www.gatewayschool.com.

GLEN EDEN SCHOOL

8665 Barnard Street
Vancouver, British Columbia V6P 5G6, Canada

Head of School: Dr. Rick Brennan

General Information Coeducational day school; primarily serves underachievers, students with learning disabilities, individuals with Attention Deficit Disorder, individuals with emotional and behavioral problems, and Autism Spectrum Disorders. Grades K–12. Founded: 1976. Setting: urban. 1 building on campus. Approved or accredited by British Columbia Department of Education. Language of instruction: English. Upper school average class size: 4. Upper school faculty-student ratio: 1:5.
Faculty School total: 5. In upper school: 2 men, 1 woman; 2 have advanced degrees.
Special Academic Programs Remedial reading and/or remedial writing; remedial math.
Summer Programs Remediation programs offered; session focuses on outreach/group dynamics; held on campus; accepts boys and girls; not open to students from other schools. 10 students usually enrolled. 2012 schedule: July 1 to August 31. Application deadline: June 1.
Admissions Deadline for receipt of application materials: none. Application fee required: CAN$1000. Interview required.
Computers Computers are regularly used in journalism classes. Computer resources include Internet access.
Contact Dr. Rick Brennan, Director. 604-267-0394. Fax: 604-267-0544. E-mail: glenedenschool@gleneden.org. Web site: www.gleneden.org.

THE GLENHOLME SCHOOL, DEVEREUX CONNECTICUT

81 Sabbaday Lane
Washington, Connecticut 06793

Head of School: Maryann Campbell

General Information Coeducational boarding and day college-preparatory, arts, vocational, technology, social coaching and motivational management, and self-discipline strategies and character development school; primarily serves underachievers, students with learning disabilities, individuals with Attention Deficit Disorder, individuals with emotional and behavioral problems, Aspergers Syndrome, ADHD, PDD, OCD, and anxiety disorders. Founded: 1968. Setting: rural. Nearest major city is Hartford. Students are housed in single-sex dormitories. 105-acre campus. 30 buildings on campus. Approved or accredited by Association of Independent Schools in New England, Connecticut Association of Independent Schools, Connecticut Department of Children and Families, Council of Accreditation and School Improvement, Massachusetts Department of Education, National Association of Private Schools for Exceptional Children, New England Association of Schools and Colleges, New Jersey Department of Education, New York Department of Education, US Department of State, and Connecticut Department of Education. Member of National Association of Independent Schools. Total enrollment: 88. Upper school average class size: 10. Upper school faculty-student ratio: 1:10. There are 215 required school days per year for Upper School students. The average school day consists of 5 hours and 45 minutes.
Upper School Student Profile Grade 9: 12 students (10 boys, 2 girls); Grade 10: 20 students (15 boys, 5 girls); Grade 11: 18 students (14 boys, 4 girls); Grade 12: 10 students (9 boys, 1 girl); Postgraduate: 14 students (8 boys, 6 girls). 92% of students are boarding students. 16% are state residents. 12 states are represented in upper school student body. 5% are international students. International students from Bermuda, Bermuda, Egypt, India, Russian Federation, and United Kingdom.
Faculty School total: 21. In upper school: 5 men, 16 women; 12 have advanced degrees; 3 reside on campus.
Subjects Offered ADL skills, adolescent issues, aerobics, algebra, art, basketball, biology, career and personal planning, career education, career exploration, career/college preparation, character education, chemistry, choral music, chorus, college admission preparation, college planning, communication skills, community service, computer animation, computer applications, computer art, computer education, computer graphics, computer literacy, computer skills, creative arts, creative dance, creative drama, creative thinking, creative writing, culinary arts, dance, decision making skills,

digital photography, drama, drama performance, earth science, English, equine management, fine arts, geometry, graphic arts, guidance, health, health and wellness, health education, Internet research, interpersonal skills, keyboarding, library, life skills, mathematics, media arts, moral and social development, music, participation in sports, performing arts, personal fitness, photography, physical education, piano, play production, radio broadcasting, SAT preparation, science, social sciences, Spanish, theater, U.S. history, video and animation, world history, writing, yearbook.

Graduation Requirements Art, electives, English, language, mathematics, physical education (includes health), science, social studies (includes history), students must meet either Glenholme graduation requirements or the requirements of their home state, depending on the funding source.

Special Academic Programs Academic accommodation for the gifted; remedial reading and/or remedial writing; remedial math; programs in English, mathematics, general development for dyslexic students.

College Admission Counseling 12 students graduated in 2011; 5 went to college, including California College of the Arts; Meredith College; Western Connecticut State University. Other: 4 went to work, 3 entered a postgraduate year.

Student Life Upper grades have uniform requirement, student council, honor system. Discipline rests primarily with faculty.

Summer Programs Remediation, enrichment, sports, art/fine arts, computer instruction programs offered; session focuses on strengthening social skills and boosting academic proficiency; held on campus; accepts boys and girls; open to students from other schools. 90 students usually enrolled. 2012 schedule: July 5 to August 24.

Admissions Individual IQ, Achievement and behavior rating scale or psychoeducational evaluation required. Deadline for receipt of application materials: none. Application fee required: $150. On-campus interview required.

Athletics Intramural: aerobics (boys, girls), aerobics/dance (b,g), aquatics (b,g), archery (b,g), artistic gym (b,g), basketball (b,g), cheering (b,g), combined training (b,g), cooperative games (b,g), cross-country running (b,g), dance (b,g), dance squad (b,g), dance team (b,g), equestrian sports (b,g), figure skating (b,g), fishing (b,g), fitness (b,g), fitness walking (b,g), flag football (b,g), Frisbee (b,g), golf (b,g), hiking/backpacking (b,g), horseback riding (b,g), ice skating (b,g), jogging (b,g), jump rope (b,g), kickball (b,g), modern dance (b,g), outdoor activities (b,g), outdoor recreation (b,g), paddle tennis (b,g), physical fitness (b,g), physical training (b,g), roller blading (b,g), ropes courses (b,g), soccer (b,g), softball (b,g), strength & conditioning (b,g), tennis (b,g), ultimate Frisbee (b,g), volleyball (b,g), walking (b,g), weight training (b,g), yoga (b,g); coed interscholastic: basketball, cross-country running, soccer, softball, tennis; coed intramural: aerobics, aerobics/dance, aquatics, archery, artistic gym, basketball, cheering, combined training, cooperative games, cross-country running, dance, dance squad, dance team, equestrian sports, figure skating, fishing, fitness, fitness walking, flag football, Frisbee, golf, hiking/backpacking, horseback riding, ice skating, jogging, jump rope, kickball, modern dance, outdoor activities, outdoor recreation, paddle tennis, physical fitness, physical training, roller blading, ropes courses, soccer, softball, strength & conditioning, tennis, ultimate Frisbee, volleyball, walking, weight training, yoga. 1 PE instructor, 2 coaches, 1 athletic trainer.

Computers Computers are regularly used in all academic, technology classes. Computer network features include on-campus library services, Internet access, wireless campus network, Internet filtering or blocking technology, online learning, Web cam parent communications. Campus intranet, student e-mail accounts, and computer access in designated common areas are available to students. Students grades are available online. The school has a published electronic and media policy.

Contact Stephanie Daniels, Admissions. 860-868-7377 Ext. 285. Fax: 860-868-7413. E-mail: sdaniel2@devereux.org. Web site: www.theglenholmeschool.org.

HARMONY HEIGHTS RESIDENTIAL AND DAY SCHOOL

PO Box 569
Oyster Bay, New York 11771

Head of School: Ellen Benson

General Information Girls' boarding and day college-preparatory school; primarily serves underachievers, students with learning disabilities, individuals with Attention Deficit Disorder, individuals with emotional and behavioral problems, and students with psychological problems. Grades 9–12. Founded: 1974. Approved or accredited by Commission on Secondary Schools and New York Department of Education. Total enrollment: 70. Upper school faculty-student ratio: 1:12. Upper School students typically attend 5 days per week.

Faculty School total: 16. In upper school: 3 men, 13 women; 8 have advanced degrees.

Subjects Offered Art, computer science, English, general science, mathematics, music, physical education, social studies.

Special Academic Programs Remedial reading and/or remedial writing; remedial math; programs in English, mathematics for dyslexic students; special instructional classes for deaf students, blind students.

Tuition and Aid Guaranteed tuition plan.

Admissions Deadline for receipt of application materials: none. No application fee required. On-campus interview required.

Computers Computers are regularly used in all classes.

Contact Ms. Lori Neazer, Clinical Director. 516-922-6688. Fax: 516-922-6126. E-mail: ellen.benson@harmonyheights.org.

THE HILL CENTER, DURHAM ACADEMY

3200 Pickett Road
Durham, North Carolina 27705

Head of School: Dr. Sharon Maskel

General Information Coeducational day college-preparatory school; primarily serves underachievers, students with learning disabilities, individuals with Attention Deficit Disorder, and dyslexic students. Grades K–12. Founded: 1977. Setting: small town. 5-acre campus. 1 building on campus. Approved or accredited by National Association of Private Schools for Exceptional Children, Southern Association of Colleges and Schools, Southern Association of Independent Schools, and North Carolina Department of Education. Member of National Association of Independent Schools. Endowment: $3.5 million. Total enrollment: 135. Upper school average class size: 4. Upper school faculty-student ratio: 1:4. There are 175 required school days per year for Upper School students. Upper School students typically attend 5 days per week. The average school day consists of 3 hours.

Upper School Student Profile Grade 9: 11 students (9 boys, 2 girls); Grade 10: 14 students (8 boys, 6 girls); Grade 11: 13 students (8 boys, 5 girls), Grade 12: 10 students (5 boys, 5 girls).

Faculty School total: 22. In upper school: 9 women; 7 have advanced degrees.

Subjects Offered Algebra, American literature, calculus, English, English literature, expository writing, geometry, grammar, mathematics, mechanics of writing, pre-algebra, pre-calculus, Spanish, writing.

Graduation Requirements Graduation requirements are determined by the student's home-based school.

Special Academic Programs Remedial reading and/or remedial writing; remedial math; programs in English, mathematics, general development for dyslexic students.

College Admission Counseling 14 students graduated in 2011; 12 went to college, including East Carolina University; The University of North Carolina at Asheville; The University of North Carolina at Charlotte; The University of North Carolina at Greensboro; The University of North Carolina Wilmington; University of Mississippi. Other: 2 went to work.

Student Life Upper grades have student council. Discipline rests primarily with faculty.

Tuition and Aid Day student tuition: $15,950. Guaranteed tuition plan. Tuition installment plan (The Tuition Plan, Key Tuition Payment Plan, monthly payment plans, The Tuition Refund Plan). Need-based scholarship grants available. In 2011–12, 18% of upper-school students received aid. Total amount of financial aid awarded in 2011–12: $59,700.

Admissions Traditional secondary-level entrance grade is 9. For fall 2011, 21 students applied for upper-level admission, 18 were accepted, 15 enrolled. WISC-III and Woodcock-Johnson required. Deadline for receipt of application materials: March 15. Application fee required: $50. On-campus interview required.

Computers Computers are regularly used in English, foreign language, mathematics, writing classes. Computer network features include Internet access, wireless campus network. Campus intranet is available to students.

Contact Ms. Wendy Speir, Director of Admissions. 919-489-7464 Ext. 7545. Fax: 919-489-7466. E-mail: wspeir@hillcenter.org. Web site: www.hillcenter.org.

HILLCREST SCHOOL

3510 North A Street
Building C
Midland, Texas 79705

Head of School: Mrs. Betty Noble Starnes

General Information Coeducational day college-preparatory, general academic, and technology school; primarily serves students with learning disabilities, individuals with Attention Deficit Disorder, and dyslexic students. Grades 1–12. Founded: 1993. Setting: small town. 2-acre campus. 1 building on campus. Approved or accredited by Southern Association of Colleges and Schools, Texas Education Agency, and Texas Department of Education. Endowment: $300,000. Total enrollment: 34. Upper school average class size: 10. Upper school faculty-student ratio: 1:10. There are 180 required school days per year for Upper School students. Upper School students typically attend 5 days per week. The average school day consists of 7 hours and 30 minutes.

Upper School Student Profile Grade 9: 5 students (3 boys, 2 girls); Grade 10: 8 students (5 boys, 3 girls); Grade 11: 5 students (5 boys); Grade 12: 5 students (3 boys, 2 girls).

Faculty School total: 10. In upper school: 8 women; 1 has an advanced degree.

Subjects Offered 3-dimensional design.

Graduation Requirements Computers, electives, English, history, mathematics, physical education (includes health), science, senior methods course.

Special Academic Programs Accelerated programs; independent study; remedial reading and/or remedial writing; remedial math; programs in English, mathematics, general development for dyslexic students.

College Admission Counseling 5 students graduated in 2010; 4 went to college. Other: 1 went to work.
Student Life Upper grades have uniform requirement. Discipline rests primarily with faculty.
Tuition and Aid Day student tuition: $8000. Tuition reduction for siblings, need-based scholarship grants available. In 2010–11, 25% of upper-school students received aid. Total amount of financial aid awarded in 2010–11: $21,000.
Admissions Traditional secondary-level entrance grade is 9. For fall 2010, 7 students applied for upper-level admission, 6 were accepted, 5 enrolled. Deadline for receipt of application materials: none. Application fee required: $100. Interview required.
Athletics Coed Intramural: badminton, baseball, basketball, fitness, flag football, football, jump rope, kickball, outdoor activities, outdoor education, physical fitness, soccer, track and field, volleyball.
Computers Computers are regularly used in all classes. Computer network features include on-campus library services, Internet access, Internet filtering or blocking technology. The school has a published electronic and media policy.
Contact Mrs. Sharel Sims, Program Coordinator. 915-570-7444. Fax: 915-570-7361. Web site: www.hillcrestschool.org.

THE HILL TOP PREPARATORY SCHOOL

737 South Ithan Avenue
Rosemont, Pennsylvania 19010

Head of School: Mr. Thomas W. Needham

General Information Coeducational day college-preparatory, arts, and technology school; primarily serves students with learning disabilities, individuals with Attention Deficit Disorder, and Aspergers. Grades 5–12. Founded: 1971. Setting: suburban. Nearest major city is Philadelphia. 25-acre campus. 4 buildings on campus. Approved or accredited by Middle States Association of Colleges and Schools and Pennsylvania Department of Education. Member of National Association of Independent Schools. Total enrollment: 75. Upper school average class size: 8. Upper school faculty-student ratio: 1:4. Upper School students typically attend 5 days per week.
Upper School Student Profile Grade 10: 17 students (14 boys, 3 girls); Grade 11: 12 students (10 boys, 2 girls); Grade 12: 16 students (15 boys, 1 girl).
Faculty School total: 27. In upper school: 6 men, 8 women.
Subjects Offered Algebra, American history, American literature, art, biology, ceramics, chemistry, civics, college counseling, computer math, computer science, computers, creative writing, drama, earth science, economics, electives, English, English literature, environmental science, European history, geography, geometry, government/civics, grammar, health, history, journalism, keyboarding, mathematics, media studies, music appreciation, Native American studies, photography, physical education, physics, psychology, public speaking, science, senior project, social studies, study skills, theater, trigonometry, U.S. history, woodworking, world cultures, world history, writing.
Graduation Requirements Business skills (includes word processing), computer science, English, mathematics, physical education (includes health), science, senior project, social sciences, social studies (includes history), study skills.
Special Academic Programs Independent study; study at local college for college credit; academic accommodation for the gifted and the artistically talented; remedial reading and/or remedial writing; remedial math; programs in English, mathematics, general development for dyslexic students.
College Admission Counseling 16 students graduated in 2011; 14 went to college, including Cabrini College; Landmark College; Mitchell College; Montgomery County Community College; Temple University; West Chester University of Pennsylvania. Other: 1 entered a postgraduate year, 1 had other specific plans. Median SAT critical reading: 490, median SAT math: 540, median SAT writing: 540, median combined SAT: 1570. 25% scored over 600 on SAT critical reading, 33% scored over 600 on SAT math, 14% scored over 600 on SAT writing, 25% scored over 1800 on combined SAT.
Student Life Upper grades have specified standards of dress, student council, honor system. Discipline rests primarily with faculty.
Summer Programs Remediation, enrichment programs offered; session focuses on remediation, enrichment, and recreation; held on campus; accepts boys and girls; open to students from other schools. 30 students usually enrolled. 2012 schedule: June 25 to August 3. Application deadline: none.
Tuition and Aid Day student tuition: $36,850. Tuition installment plan (monthly payment plans, payment in full, 60% due June 1 and 40% due December 1, monthly payments over 10 months). Tuition reduction for siblings, need-based scholarship grants available. In 2011–12, 15% of upper-school students received aid.
Admissions Traditional secondary-level entrance grade is 10. For fall 2011, 11 students applied for upper-level admission, 6 were accepted, 5 enrolled. Achievement tests, psychoeducational evaluation, Rorschach or Thematic Apperception Test, WISC or WAIS and WISC/Woodcock-Johnson required. Deadline for receipt of application materials: none. Application fee required: $75. On-campus interview required.
Athletics Interscholastic: wrestling (boys); intramural: wall climbing (b,g), weight lifting (b,g); coed interscholastic: basketball, golf, soccer, tennis, track and field; coed intramural: aerobics/Nautilus, badminton, ball hockey, basketball, bicycling, climbing, combined training, cooperative games, Cosom hockey, cross-country running, fitness, flag football, floor hockey, Frisbee, indoor hockey, indoor soccer, martial arts, Newcombe ball, outdoor activities, outdoor adventure, outdoor recreation, outdoor skills, paint ball, physical fitness, physical training, rock climbing, running, skiing (downhill), snowboarding, soccer, strength & conditioning, team handball, tennis, touch football, wall climbing, weight lifting, yoga. 2 PE instructors, 5 coaches.
Computers Computers are regularly used in English, mathematics, science, study skills classes. Computer network features include on-campus library services, Internet access, wireless campus network, Internet filtering or blocking technology, one-to-one student and faculty laptop initiative, online student information system, ACTIVBoards, projectors, and audio in all classrooms. Campus intranet, student e-mail accounts, and computer access in designated common areas are available to students. Students grades are available online. The school has a published electronic and media policy.
Contact Ms. Cindy Falcone, Assistant Headmaster. 610-527-3230 Ext. 697. Fax: 610-527-7683. E-mail: cfalcone@hilltopprep.org. Web site: www.hilltopprep.org.

THE HOWARD SCHOOL

1192 Foster Street
Atlanta, Georgia 30318

Head of School: Ms. Marifred Cilella

General Information Coeducational day college-preparatory, general academic, arts, and technology school; primarily serves students with learning disabilities, individuals with Attention Deficit Disorder, dyslexic students, and students with language learning disabilities and differences. Grades PK–12. Founded: 1950. Setting: urban. 15-acre campus. 2 buildings on campus. Approved or accredited by Georgia Independent School Association, Southern Association of Colleges and Schools, Southern Association of Independent Schools, and Georgia Department of Education. Member of National Association of Independent Schools. Total enrollment: 232. Upper school average class size: 9. Upper school faculty-student ratio: 1:8.
Upper School Student Profile Grade 9: 26 students (11 boys, 15 girls); Grade 10: 19 students (15 boys, 4 girls); Grade 11: 23 students (18 boys, 5 girls); Grade 12: 8 students (6 boys, 2 girls).
Faculty School total: 60. In upper school: 4 men, 9 women; 11 have advanced degrees.
Subjects Offered Algebra, American history, American literature, art, biology, communications, computer science, creative writing, drama, ecology, economics, English, English literature, European history, film studies, geography, geometry, government/civics, grammar, history, journalism, mathematics, music, physical education, physical science, psychology, reading, science, service learning/internship, social studies, Spanish, study skills, trigonometry, world history, world literature, writing.
Graduation Requirements English, foreign language, mathematics, physical education (includes health), science, social studies (includes history).
Special Academic Programs Independent study; academic accommodation for the artistically talented; remedial reading and/or remedial writing; remedial math; programs in English, mathematics, general development for dyslexic students.
College Admission Counseling Colleges students went to include Brevard College; Georgia State University; Johnson & Wales University; Lynn University.
Student Life Upper grades have specified standards of dress, student council, honor system. Discipline rests equally with students and faculty.
Summer Programs Remediation, advancement programs offered; session focuses on make-up of academic courses; held on campus; accepts boys and girls; open to students from other schools. 19 students usually enrolled. 2012 schedule: June 20 to July 27. Application deadline: June 1.
Tuition and Aid Day student tuition: $25,750. Tuition installment plan (individually arranged payment plans, 1-, 2-, 3- and 8-payment plans). Need-based scholarship grants available. In 2011–12, 30% of upper-school students received aid.
Admissions Psychoeducational evaluation required. Deadline for receipt of application materials: none. Application fee required: $150. On-campus interview required.
Athletics Interscholastic: basketball (boys, girls), soccer (b), track and field (b,g), volleyball (g), weight training (b,g); coed interscholastic: golf, soccer, track and field. 3 PE instructors, 6 coaches.
Computers Computers are regularly used in all classes. Computer network features include online commercial services, Internet access. The school has a published electronic and media policy.
Contact Ms. Dawn Splinter, Assistant to the Director of Admissions and Registrar. 404-377-7436 Ext. 259. Fax: 404-377-0884. E-mail: dsplinter@howardschool.org. Web site: www.howardschool.org.

HUMANEX ACADEMY

2700 South Zuni Street
Englewood, Colorado 80110

Head of School: Ms. Tracy Wagers

General Information Coeducational day college-preparatory, general academic, and arts school; primarily serves underachievers, students with learning disabilities, individuals with Attention Deficit Disorder, individuals with emotional and behavioral problems, dyslexic students, and Asperger's Disorder, High Functioning Autism. Grades 6–12. Founded: 1983. Setting: suburban. Nearest major city is Denver. 1-acre campus. 1 building on campus. Approved or accredited by North Central Association of Colleges and Schools and Colorado Department of Education. Total enrollment: 63.

Upper school average class size: 5. Upper school faculty-student ratio: 1:7. The average school day consists of 6 hours and 30 minutes.

Upper School Student Profile Grade 9: 10 students (7 boys, 3 girls); Grade 10: 10 students (10 boys); Grade 11: 10 students (6 boys, 4 girls); Grade 12: 26 students (19 boys, 7 girls).

Faculty School total: 11. In upper school: 5 men, 6 women; 8 have advanced degrees.

Subjects Offered 1 1/2 elective credits, 1968, 20th century American writers, 20th century history, 20th century physics, 20th century world history, 3-dimensional art, 3-dimensional design, ACT preparation, addiction, ADL skills, adolescent issues, advanced biology, advanced math, advanced studio art-AP, advanced TOEFL/grammar, aerobics, American Civil War, American culture, American democracy, American foreign policy, American government, American history, American legal systems, American literature, American politics in film, anatomy, anatomy and physiology, ancient world history, animal behavior, animation, anthropology, art, art appreciation, art history, arts and crafts, athletic training, athletics, biology, British literature, calculus, career and personal planning, career exploration, cartooning/animation, chemistry, civics, civics/free enterprise, Civil War, civil war history, college counseling, college placement, comedy, composition, computer art, computer graphics, conflict resolution, consumer mathematics, creative writing, critical thinking, current events, drawing, English, English literature, epic literature, evolution, existentialism, expository writing, film, film and literature, fitness, foreign language, general, general math, general science, geography, geology, geometry, government, government/civics, grammar, graphic arts, graphic design, great books, Greek drama, guitar, Harlem Renaissance, health, health education, history, Holocaust, honors algebra, honors English, honors geometry, honors U.S. history, honors world history, human anatomy, human biology, human sexuality, illustration, independent living, keyboarding, language, language arts, language structure, languages, literacy, literary genres, literary magazine, literature, mathematics, media literacy, military history, newspaper, non-Western literature, North American literature, novels, nutrition, peer counseling, philosophy, physical fitness, physics, physiology, play/screen writing, poetry, politics, pottery, pre-algebra, pre-calculus, psychology, public speaking, reading, reading/study skills, remedial study skills, remedial/makeup course work, research, research skills, SAT preparation, SAT/ACT preparation, science, science fiction, sculpture, sexuality, Shakespeare, short story, speech, speech and debate, sports, statistics, U.S. government, U.S. government and politics, U.S. history, U.S. literature, Vietnam history, Vietnam War, weight fitness, weight training, weightlifting, Western civilization, Western literature, world geography, world governments, world history.

Graduation Requirements Research, speech.

Special Academic Programs Honors section; academic accommodation for the gifted; remedial reading and/or remedial writing; remedial math; programs in English, mathematics, general development for dyslexic students; special instructional classes for deaf students, blind students.

College Admission Counseling 23 students graduated in 2011; 17 went to college, including Colorado School of Mines; Colorado State University; Fort Lewis College; University of Colorado Boulder; University of Denver; University of Northern Colorado. Other: 3 went to work, 3 had other specific plans. Median composite ACT: 24. 33% scored over 26 on composite ACT.

Student Life Upper grades have specified standards of dress, student council. Discipline rests equally with students and faculty.

Summer Programs Remediation, advancement programs offered; session focuses on academics; held on campus; accepts boys and girls. 30 students usually enrolled. 2012 schedule: June 6 to June 24. Application deadline: June 5.

Tuition and Aid Day student tuition: $17,900. Guaranteed tuition plan. Tuition installment plan (FACTS Tuition Payment Plan). Tuition reduction for siblings, need-based scholarship grants, middle-income loans, paying campus jobs, Sallie Mae available. In 2011–12, 13% of upper-school students received aid. Total amount of financial aid awarded in 2011–12: $5000.

Admissions Traditional secondary-level entrance grade is 10. For fall 2011, 10 students applied for upper-level admission, 9 were accepted, 9 enrolled. Deadline for receipt of application materials: none. Application fee required: $500. On-campus interview required.

Athletics Coed Intramural: aerobics, ball hockey, basketball, bocce, bowling, cooperative games, fitness, flag football, Frisbee, handball, kickball, physical training, power lifting, ultimate Frisbee, weight lifting, weight training. 1 PE instructor.

Computers Computers are regularly used in art, English, health, history, literacy, mathematics, philosophy, psychology, reading, research skills, social studies, Spanish, speech, study skills, writing, writing classes. Computer resources include on-campus library services, online commercial services, Internet access, Internet filtering or blocking technology. Campus intranet is available to students. Students grades are available online. The school has a published electronic and media policy.

Contact 303-783-0137. Fax: 303-783-5901. Web site: www.humanexacademy.com.

THE JOHN DEWEY ACADEMY

389 Main Street
Great Barrington, Massachusetts 01230

Head of School: Dr. Kenneth M. Steiner

General Information Coeducational boarding college-preparatory and arts school; primarily serves underachievers, students with learning disabilities, individuals with Attention Deficit Disorder, individuals with emotional and behavioral problems, and gifted, underachieving, self-destructive adolescents. Grades 10–PG. Founded: 1985. Setting: small town. Nearest major city is Hartford, CT. Students are housed in single-sex by floor dormitories. 90-acre campus. 3 buildings on campus. Approved or accredited by New England Association of Schools and Colleges and Massachusetts Department of Education. Member of Secondary School Admission Test Board. Total enrollment: 20. Upper school average class size: 6. Upper school faculty-student ratio: 1:3. There are 330 required school days per year for Upper School students. Upper School students typically attend 7 days per week. The average school day consists of 6 hours.

Upper School Student Profile Grade 10: 3 students (3 boys); Grade 11: 10 students (7 boys, 3 girls); Grade 12: 7 students (5 boys, 2 girls). 100% of students are boarding students. 10% are state residents. 11 states are represented in upper school student body. 10% are international students. International students from Jordan and Russian Federation.

Faculty School total: 10. In upper school: 5 men, 5 women; 9 have advanced degrees; 2 reside on campus.

Subjects Offered Adolescent issues, algebra, American literature, art, art history, biology, calculus, chemistry, creative writing, drama, English, English literature, environmental science, ethics, European history, fine arts, French, geometry, government/civics, grammar, health, history, Italian, moral reasoning, philosophy, physical education, physics, psychology, sociology, Spanish, statistics, theater, trigonometry, world history, world literature, writing.

Graduation Requirements American history, arts and fine arts (art, music, dance, drama), biology, English, English literature, European history, foreign language, leadership, literature, mathematics, moral reasoning, physical education (includes health), science, social studies (includes history), moral leadership qualities, minimum 18 months residency.

Special Academic Programs Honors section; accelerated programs; independent study; study at local college for college credit; academic accommodation for the gifted and the artistically talented; remedial reading and/or remedial writing; remedial math; programs in general development for dyslexic students.

College Admission Counseling 7 students graduated in 2011; all went to college, including Carleton College; Clark University; Columbia University; Peabody Conservatory of The Johns Hopkins University; Vassar College; Wheaton College. 95% scored over 600 on SAT critical reading, 95% scored over 600 on SAT math, 95% scored over 600 on SAT writing, 95% scored over 1800 on combined SAT.

Student Life Upper grades have specified standards of dress, student council, honor system. Discipline rests equally with students and faculty.

Summer Programs Session focuses on continuing college preparatory program; held on campus; accepts boys and girls; not open to students from other schools. 25 students usually enrolled.

Tuition and Aid 7-day tuition and room/board: $92,000. Tuition installment plan (monthly payment plans, individually arranged payment plans). Need-based scholarship grants available. In 2011–12, 25% of upper-school students received aid.

Admissions Traditional secondary-level entrance grade is 10. Deadline for receipt of application materials: none. No application fee required. On-campus interview required.

Computers Computer resources include Internet access. Computer access in designated common areas is available to students.

Contact Dr. Lisa Sinsheimer, Parent Liaison/Admissions Counselor. 917-597-7814. E-mail: lisa@sinsheimer.net. Web site: www.jda.org.

THE JUDGE ROTENBERG EDUCATIONAL CENTER

250 Turnpike Street
Canton, Massachusetts 02021-2341

Head of School: Glenda Crookes

General Information Coeducational boarding general academic and vocational school; primarily serves underachievers, students with learning disabilities, individuals with Attention Deficit Disorder, individuals with emotional and behavioral problems, dyslexic students, and autism and developmental disabilities. Founded: 1971. Setting: suburban. Nearest major city is Boston. 2 buildings on campus. Approved or accredited by Massachusetts Department of Education and Massachusetts Office of Child Care Services. Upper school average class size: 10. Upper School students typically attend 5 days per week. The average school day consists of 6 hours.

Special Academic Programs Remedial reading and/or remedial writing; remedial math; special instructional classes for deaf students, blind students.

Student Life Upper grades have specified standards of dress, honor system. Discipline rests primarily with faculty.

Admissions Deadline for receipt of application materials: none. No application fee required. Interview recommended.

Athletics Intramural: basketball (boys, girls); coed intramural: aerobics/dance, physical fitness. 2 PE instructors.

Computers Computers are regularly used in all academic classes. Computer network features include Internet access, Internet filtering or blocking technology. Student e-mail accounts are available to students.

Contact Julie Gomes, Director of Admissions. 781-828-2202 Ext. 4275. Fax: 781-828-2804. E-mail: j.gomes@judgerc.org. Web site: www.judgerc.org.

THE KARAFIN SCHOOL

40-1 Radio Circle
PO Box 277
Mount Kisco, New York 10549

Head of School: Bart A. Donow, PhD

General Information Coeducational day college-preparatory and general academic school; primarily serves underachievers, students with learning disabilities, individuals with Attention Deficit Disorder, individuals with emotional and behavioral problems, emotionally disabled students, and Tourette's Syndrome. Grades 9–12. Founded: 1958. Setting: suburban. Nearest major city is New York. 1 building on campus. Approved or accredited by New York Department of Education and New York Department of Education. Total enrollment: 78. Upper school average class size: 6. Upper school faculty-student ratio: 1:6. There are 180 required school days per year for Upper School students. Upper School students typically attend 5 days per week. The average school day consists of 5 hours and 30 minutes.

Upper School Student Profile Grade 9: 15 students (7 boys, 8 girls); Grade 10: 21 students (11 boys, 10 girls); Grade 11: 21 students (10 boys, 11 girls); Grade 12: 21 students (11 boys, 10 girls).

Faculty School total: 25. In upper school: 9 men, 16 women; all have advanced degrees.

Subjects Offered Algebra, American history, American literature, art, art history, arts, biology, business, business skills, calculus, chemistry, computer math, computer programming, computer science, creative writing, earth science, ecology, economics, English, English literature, environmental science, European history, expository writing, fine arts, French, geography, geology, geometry, government/civics, grammar, history of science, Italian, Latin, mathematics, music, photography, physical education, physics, psychology, science, social sciences, social studies, sociology, Spanish, speech, trigonometry, typing, world history, world literature, writing, zoology.

Graduation Requirements Arts and fine arts (art, music, dance, drama), business skills (includes word processing), computer science, English, foreign language, mathematics, physical education (includes health), science, social sciences, social studies (includes history).

Special Academic Programs 1 Advanced Placement exam for which test preparation is offered; academic accommodation for the gifted, the musically talented, and the artistically talented; remedial reading and/or remedial writing; remedial math; programs in English, mathematics, general development for dyslexic students; special instructional classes for deaf students.

College Admission Counseling 20 students graduated in 2011; 15 went to college, including City College of the City University of New York; Hampshire College; John Jay College of Criminal Justice of the City University of New York; Manhattanville College; Purchase College, State University of New York; Westchester Community College. Other: 2 went to work, 1 entered a postgraduate year, 2 had other specific plans. Mean SAT critical reading: 500, mean SAT math: 550, mean SAT writing: 500.

Student Life Upper grades have student council. Discipline rests primarily with faculty.

Tuition and Aid Day student tuition: $27,945. Tuition installment plan (monthly payment plans).

Admissions Traditional secondary-level entrance grade is 9. For fall 2011, 350 students applied for upper-level admission, 50 were accepted, 25 enrolled. Deadline for receipt of application materials: none. No application fee required. On-campus interview required.

Athletics Coed Intramural: aerobics, aerobics/dance, archery, badminton, ball hockey, baseball, basketball, billiards, bowling, cooperative games, fitness, fitness walking, floor hockey, football, Frisbee, golf, gymnastics, jump rope, kickball, paddle tennis, physical fitness, physical training, pillo polo, power lifting, project adventure, racquetball, soccer, strength & conditioning, table tennis, team handball, tennis, touch football, volleyball, weight lifting, whiffle ball, wrestling. 1 PE instructor.

Computers Computers are regularly used in all academic classes. Computer resources include Internet access, Internet filtering or blocking technology. The school has a published electronic and media policy.

Contact Bart A. Donow, PhD, Director. 914-666-9211. Fax: 914-666-9868. E-mail: karafin@optonline.net. Web site: www.karafinschool.com.

KEY SCHOOL

3947 East Loop 820 South
Fort Worth, Texas 76119

Head of School: Mary Ann Key

General Information Coeducational day college-preparatory, general academic, and technology school; primarily serves underachievers, students with learning disabilities, individuals with Attention Deficit Disorder, and dyslexic students. Grades K–12. Founded: 1966. Setting: suburban. Nearest major city is Dallas. 2-acre campus. 1 building on campus. Approved or accredited by Council of Accreditation and School Improvement, Southern Association of Colleges and Schools, and Texas Department of Education. Total enrollment: 87. Upper school average class size: 9. Upper school faculty-student ratio: 1:4. There are 140 required school days per year for Upper School students. Upper School students typically attend 4 days per week. The average school day consists of 6 hours and 45 minutes.

Upper School Student Profile Grade 9: 7 students (7 boys); Grade 10: 8 students (6 boys, 2 girls); Grade 11: 4 students (1 boy, 3 girls); Grade 12: 7 students (6 boys, 1 girl).

Faculty School total: 35. In upper school: 6 men, 29 women; 7 have advanced degrees.

Subjects Offered Algebra, art history, aviation, biology, chemistry, composition, current events, desktop publishing, economics, electives, English, geometry, government, grammar, journalism, keyboarding, language arts, life science, life skills, literature, mathematics, mathematics-AP, mechanics of writing, microbiology, novels, physical science, physics, pre-algebra, pre-calculus, reading, reading/study skills, SAT/ACT preparation, science, science fiction, social studies, Spanish, speech, speech communications, study skills, Texas history, U.S. history, world geography, world history, yearbook.

Graduation Requirements Graduation speech.

Special Academic Programs Study at local college for college credit; remedial reading and/or remedial writing; remedial math; programs in English, mathematics, general development for dyslexic students; special instructional classes for students with academic deficits, speech and auditory deficits, and ADD/ADHD; ESL (1 student enrolled).

College Admission Counseling 7 students graduated in 2011; all went to college, including Tarrant County College District; Texas Wesleyan University; Weatherford College; WyoTech Laramie. Median SAT critical reading: 420, median SAT math: 490, median SAT writing: 410.

Student Life Upper grades have specified standards of dress, honor system. Discipline rests primarily with faculty.

Summer Programs Remediation, enrichment, advancement, computer instruction programs offered; session focuses on academic enrichment; held on campus; accepts boys and girls; open to students from other schools. 125 students usually enrolled. 2012 schedule: June 4 to June 28. Application deadline: none.

Tuition and Aid Tuition installment plan (individually arranged payment plans, quarterly and semester payment plans). Need-based tuition assistance available. In 2011–12, 18% of upper-school students received aid. Total amount of financial aid awarded in 2011–12: $30,000.

Admissions For fall 2011, 23 students applied for upper-level admission, 23 were accepted, 23 enrolled. Deadline for receipt of application materials: none. No application fee required. On-campus interview required.

Computers Computers are regularly used in desktop publishing, journalism, keyboarding, newspaper, writing, yearbook classes. Computer network features include Internet access, wireless campus network, Internet filtering or blocking technology. The school has a published electronic and media policy.

Contact Patricia Banks, Registrar. 817-446-3738. Fax: 817-446-8471. E-mail: registrar@ksfw.org. Web site: www.keyschoolfortworth.org.

KILDONAN SCHOOL

425 Morse Hill Road
Amenia, New York 12501

Head of School: Benjamin N. Powers

General Information Coeducational boarding and day college-preparatory, general academic, arts, and technology school; primarily serves students with learning disabilities, dyslexic students, and language-based learning differences. Boarding grades 7–PG, day grades 2–PG. Founded: 1969. Setting: rural. Nearest major city is New York. Students are housed in single-sex dormitories. 350-acre campus. 19 buildings on campus. Approved or accredited by Academy of Orton-Gillingham Practitioners and Educators, New York State Association of Independent Schools, The Association of Boarding Schools, and New York Department of Education. Member of National Association of Independent Schools and Secondary School Admission Test Board. Endowment: $579,300. Total enrollment: 91. Upper school average class size: 8. Upper school faculty-student ratio: 1:2. The average school day consists of 7 hours.

Upper School Student Profile Grade 6: 5 students (1 boy, 4 girls); Grade 7: 8 students (5 boys, 3 girls); Grade 8: 7 students (3 boys, 4 girls); Grade 9: 12 students (10 boys, 2 girls); Grade 10: 12 students (9 boys, 3 girls); Grade 11: 9 students (7 boys, 2 girls); Grade 12: 16 students (11 boys, 5 girls). 68% of students are boarding students. 44% are state residents. 15 states are represented in upper school student body. 9% are international students. International students from Bermuda, Brazil, France, Mexico, Puerto Rico, and United Arab Emirates; 1 other country represented in student body.

Faculty School total: 56. In upper school: 26 men, 28 women; 11 have advanced degrees; 48 reside on campus.

Subjects Offered Algebra, American history, American literature, anthropology, art, art history, biology, botany, business skills, calculus, ceramics, chemistry, computer programming, computer science, creative writing, earth science, ecology, economics, English, English literature, environmental science, European history, expository writing, fine arts, geography, geology, geometry, government/civics, grammar, health, history, mathematics, photography, physical education, physics, science, social studies, trigonometry, typing, world history, world literature, zoology.

Graduation Requirements Arts and fine arts (art, music, dance, drama), English, mathematics, physical education (includes health), science, social studies (includes history).

Special Academic Programs Independent study; remedial reading and/or remedial writing; programs in English, mathematics, general development for dyslexic students.

College Admission Counseling 14 students graduated in 2010; 8 went to college, including Curry College; Landmark College; Mitchell College; Rhode Island School of Design; Xavier University.

Student Life Upper grades have uniform requirement, student council, honor system. Discipline rests primarily with faculty.

Tuition and Aid Day student tuition: $43,000; 5-day tuition and room/board: $57,500; 7-day tuition and room/board: $60,000. Tuition installment plan (Tuition Management Systems). Need-based scholarship grants available. In 2010–11, 46% of upper-school students received aid. Total amount of financial aid awarded in 2010–11: $300,000.

Admissions Traditional secondary-level entrance grade is 9. For fall 2010, 60 students applied for upper-level admission, 43 were accepted, 23 enrolled. Wechsler Individual Achievement Test, WISC or WAIS, WISC/Woodcock-Johnson or Woodcock-Johnson Revised Achievement Test required. Deadline for receipt of application materials: none. Application fee required: $50. On-campus interview required.

Athletics Interscholastic: basketball (boys, girls); intramural: aerobics (g), basketball (b,g), dance (g); coed interscholastic: alpine skiing, lacrosse, skiing (downhill), snowboarding, soccer, softball, tennis, yoga; coed intramural: archery, basketball, bicycling, canoeing/kayaking, cross-country running, dressage, equestrian sports, fitness, fitness walking, flag football, freestyle skiing, golf, hiking/backpacking, horseback riding, ice skating, lacrosse, martial arts, mountain biking, outdoor activities, physical fitness, rock climbing, running, skiing (cross-country), skiing (downhill), snowboarding, soccer, strength & conditioning, table tennis, touch football, walking, water skiing, weight lifting, weight training.

Computers Computers are regularly used in English, mathematics, multimedia classes. Computer network features include on-campus library services, Internet access, wireless campus network. Student e-mail accounts and computer access in designated common areas are available to students. Students grades are available online. The school has a published electronic and media policy.

Contact Beth Rainey, Director of Student Recruitment and Financial Aid. 845-373-2017. Fax: 845-373-2004. E-mail: brainey@kildonan.org.

KINGSHILL SCHOOL

RR 1, Box 6125
Kingshill
St. Croix, Virgin Islands 00850

Head of School: Mrs. Janie M. Koopmans

General Information Coeducational day college-preparatory, general academic, arts, vocational, and technology school; primarily serves underachievers, students with learning disabilities, individuals with Attention Deficit Disorder, dyslexic students, cerebral palsy, and Asperger's Syndrome. Grades 7–12. Founded: 1997. Setting: rural. Nearest major city is Christiansted, U.S. Virgin Islands. 6-acre campus. 2 buildings on campus. Approved or accredited by Middle States Association of Colleges and Schools and Virgin Islands Department of Education. Total enrollment: 30. Upper school average class size: 6. Upper school faculty-student ratio: 1:5. There are 180 required school days per year for Upper School students. Upper School students typically attend 5 days per week. The average school day consists of 6 hours and 30 minutes.

Upper School Student Profile Grade 9: 4 students (2 boys, 2 girls); Grade 10: 10 students (5 boys, 5 girls); Grade 11: 7 students (4 boys, 3 girls); Grade 12: 7 students (4 boys, 3 girls).

Faculty School total: 6. In upper school: 2 men, 4 women; 4 have advanced degrees.

Subjects Offered Algebra, American government, American history, American literature, ancient world history, applied arts, architecture, art appreciation, arts appreciation, athletics, auto mechanics, biology, bowling, career exploration, career planning, career/college preparation, Caribbean history, chemistry, civics, college admission preparation, college counseling, community service, composition, computer skills, computer technologies, consumer mathematics, current events, earth science, electives, English, English literature, entrepreneurship, environmental science, geography, geometry, health, health education, history of the Americas, keyboarding, learning lab, learning strategies, marine biology, math applications, music appreciation, photography, physical education, pre-algebra, remedial/makeup course work, SAT preparation, scuba diving, Spanish, world geography, world history.

Graduation Requirements Algebra, American government, American history, American literature, art history, biology, Caribbean history, chemistry, creative writing, geometry, health, physical science, Spanish, transition mathematics, world civilizations, world history, world literature.

Special Academic Programs Accelerated programs; independent study; study at local college for college credit; remedial reading and/or remedial writing; remedial math; programs in English, mathematics, general development for dyslexic students.

College Admission Counseling 3 students graduated in 2011; 2 went to college. Other: 1 entered military service. Median SAT critical reading: 420, median SAT math: 420.

Student Life Upper grades have specified standards of dress, student council, honor system. Discipline rests equally with students and faculty.

Summer Programs Advancement programs offered; session focuses on transition skills; held both on and off campus; held at with local businesses and exploration of St. Croix; accepts boys and girls; open to students from other schools. 20 students usually enrolled. 2012 schedule: June 18 to July 30. Application deadline: June 1.

Tuition and Aid Day student tuition: $9975. Tuition installment plan (monthly payment plans, individually arranged payment plans). Tuition reduction for siblings, merit scholarship grants, need-based scholarship grants, paying campus jobs available. In 2011–12, 68% of upper-school students received aid; total upper-school merit-scholarship money awarded: $9500. Total amount of financial aid awarded in 2011–12: $82,000.

Admissions Traditional secondary-level entrance grade is 9. For fall 2011, 31 students applied for upper-level admission, 12 were accepted, 10 enrolled. WISC or WAIS, Woodcock-Johnson Educational Evaluation, WISC III or WRAT required. Deadline for receipt of application materials: none. No application fee required. Interview required.

Athletics Intramural: football (boys), volleyball (g); coed intramural: aerobics/dance, baseball, basketball, bowling, canoeing/kayaking, cooperative games, fitness walking, flag football, Frisbee, hiking/backpacking, horseback riding, independent competitive sports, kayaking, outdoor activities, physical fitness, scuba diving, Special Olympics, surfing, swimming and diving, table tennis, touch football, walking, yoga. 2 PE instructors.

Computers Computers are regularly used in all academic, animation, art, basic skills, career exploration, college planning, computer applications, independent study, music, photography, SAT preparation, Web site design, yearbook classes. Computer resources include Internet access, wireless campus network, Internet filtering or blocking technology. Computer access in designated common areas is available to students. The school has a published electronic and media policy.

Contact Mrs. Janie M. Koopmans, Director. 340-778-6564. Fax: 340-778-0520. E-mail: kingshillschool@gmail.com. Web site: kingshillschool.org.

LANDMARK SCHOOL

PO Box 227
429 Hale Street
Prides Crossing, Massachusetts 01965-0227

Head of School: Robert J. Broudo

General Information Coeducational boarding and day college-preparatory, general academic, and language arts tutorial, skill based curriculum school, primarily serves students with learning disabilities, dyslexic students, and language-based learning disabilities. Boarding grades 9–12, day grades 2–12. Founded: 1971. Setting: suburban. Nearest major city is Boston. Students are housed in single-sex dormitories. 50-acre campus. 22 buildings on campus. Approved or accredited by Association of Independent Schools in New England, Massachusetts Department of Education, National Association of Private Schools for Exceptional Children, New England Association of Schools and Colleges, and Massachusetts Department of Education. Member of National Association of Independent Schools. Endowment: $10 million. Total enrollment: 459. Upper school average class size: 8. Upper school faculty-student ratio: 1:3. There are 180 required school days per year for Upper School students. Upper School students typically attend 5 days per week. The average school day consists of 7 hours.

Upper School Student Profile Grade 9: 72 students (27 boys, 45 girls); Grade 10: 69 students (20 boys, 49 girls); Grade 11: 82 students (39 boys, 43 girls); Grade 12: 76 students (24 boys, 52 girls). 54% of students are boarding students. 49% are state residents. 21 states are represented in upper school student body. 3% are international students. International students from Colombia, Mexico, Saudi Arabia, and United Kingdom.

Faculty School total: 232. In upper school: 72 men, 88 women; 125 have advanced degrees; 22 reside on campus.

Subjects Offered Advanced math, algebra, American government, American history, American literature, anatomy and physiology, art, auto mechanics, basketball, biology, boat building, calculus, calculus-AP, chemistry, chorus, communications, composition, computer programming, computer science, consumer mathematics, creative writing, cultural geography, dance, drama, early childhood, environmental science, expressive arts, filmmaking, geometry, grammar, integrated mathematics, language and composition, language arts, literature, marine science, modern world history, multimedia design, newspaper, oral communications, oral expression, photography, physical education, physical science, portfolio art, pragmatics, pre-algebra, pre-calculus, reading, reading/study skills, senior thesis, sociology, study skills, technical theater, technology, U.S. history, woodworking, world history, yearbook.

Graduation Requirements English, mathematics, physical education (includes health), science, social studies (includes history), Landmark School competency tests, minimum grade equivalents on standardized tests in reading and reading comprehension.

Special Academic Programs Study at local college for college credit; remedial reading and/or remedial writing; remedial math; programs in English, mathematics, general development for dyslexic students; special instructional classes for deaf students.

College Admission Counseling 72 students graduated in 2011; 69 went to college, including Curry College; Lynn University; The University of Arizona; University of Denver; Westfield State University. Other: 2 went to work, 1 entered a postgraduate year. Mean SAT critical reading: 448, mean SAT math: 430, mean SAT writing: 441.

Student Life Upper grades have specified standards of dress, student council. Discipline rests primarily with faculty.

Summer Programs Remediation programs offered; session focuses on academic remediation and study skills; held on campus; accepts boys and girls; open to students from other schools. 140 students usually enrolled. 2012 schedule: July 8 to August 3. Application deadline: May 15.

Tuition and Aid Day student tuition: $39,975–$46,575; 7-day tuition and room/board: $55,400–$62,000. Tuition installment plan (Key Tuition Payment Plan). Need-based scholarship grants, community and staff grants available. In 2011–12, 5% of upper-school students received aid. Total amount of financial aid awarded in 2011–12: $362,041.

Admissions Traditional secondary-level entrance grade is 9. For fall 2011, 317 students applied for upper-level admission, 196 were accepted, 121 enrolled. Achievement tests, psychoeducational evaluation and WISC or WAIS required. Deadline for receipt of application materials: none. Application fee required: $150. On-campus interview required.

Athletics Interscholastic: baseball (boys), basketball (b,g), dance (g), lacrosse (b,g), soccer (b,g), tennis (b,g), wrestling (b); intramural: basketball (b,g), floor hockey (b), volleyball (b,g); coed interscholastic: cross-country running, golf, swimming and diving, track and field; coed intramural: ropes courses, skateboarding, skiing (downhill). 5 PE instructors, 1 athletic trainer.

Computers Computers are regularly used in all academic, programming, publishing, technology, yearbook classes. Computer network features include on-campus library services, Internet access, wireless campus network, Internet filtering or blocking technology. Student e-mail accounts are available to students. The school has a published electronic and media policy.

Contact Carol Bedrosian, Admission Liaison. 978-236-3420. Fax: 978-927-7268. E-mail: cbedrosian@landmarkschool.org. Web site: www.landmarkschool.org.

See Display below, Close-Up on page 740, and Summeer Program Close-Up on page 776.

THE LAUREATE ACADEMY

100 Villa Maria Place
Winnipeg, Manitoba R3V 1A9, Canada

Head of School: Mr. Gregory D. Jones

General Information Coeducational day college-preparatory school; primarily serves students with learning disabilities, individuals with Attention Deficit Disorder, and dyslexic students. Grades 1–12. Founded: 1987. Setting: suburban. 10-acre campus. 1 building on campus. Approved or accredited by Manitoba Department of Education. Language of instruction: English. Total enrollment: 95. Upper school average class size: 10. Upper school faculty-student ratio: 1:6. There are 183 required school days per year for Upper School students. Upper School students typically attend 5 days per week. The average school day consists of 6 hours and 15 minutes.

Faculty School total: 16. In upper school: 6 men, 3 women; 3 have advanced degrees.

Subjects Offered All academic.

Graduation Requirements Algebra, biology, Canadian geography, Canadian history, chemistry, communication skills, composition, computer skills, English, English literature, geometry, life issues, mathematics, physical education (includes health), physics, public speaking, science, social studies (includes history), writing, Department of Manitoba Education requirements, Classical Studies. Community service is required.

Special Academic Programs Academic accommodation for the gifted; remedial reading and/or remedial writing; remedial math; programs in English, mathematics for dyslexic students.

College Admission Counseling 4 students graduated in 2010; all went to college, including The University of Winnipeg; University of Manitoba.

Student Life Upper grades have specified standards of dress, student council, honor system. Discipline rests primarily with faculty.

Tuition and Aid Day student tuition: CAN$16,800. Tuition installment plan (monthly payment plans, quarterly payment plan). Tuition reduction for siblings, bursaries available. In 2010–11, 14% of upper-school students received aid. Total amount of financial aid awarded in 2010–11: CAN$61,000.

Admissions Traditional secondary-level entrance grade is 9. For fall 2010, 17 students applied for upper-level admission, 10 were accepted, 9 enrolled. WISC or WAIS and WISC-III and Woodcock-Johnson required. Deadline for receipt of application materials: none. Application fee required: CAN$75. Interview required.

Athletics Interscholastic: basketball (boys), volleyball (b); intramural: badminton (b), ball hockey (b), basketball (b); coed interscholastic: badminton, cross-country running, soccer, track and field, volleyball; coed intramural: aerobics, alpine skiing, badminton, ball hockey, basketball, broomball, combined training, cooperative games, fitness, flag football, floor hockey, Frisbee, jogging, martial arts, outdoor activities, outdoor adventure, outdoor education, outdoor recreation, paddle tennis, physical fitness, physical training, running, self defense, skiing (downhill), snowboarding, soccer, softball, strength & conditioning, table tennis, touch football, track and field, ultimate Frisbee, volleyball, weight lifting, weight training. 2 PE instructors, 2 coaches.

Computers Computers are regularly used in career education, career exploration, computer applications, creative writing, English, mathematics, research skills, science, social studies, writing, yearbook classes. Computer network features include Internet access, wireless campus network, Internet filtering or blocking technology. Campus intranet, student e-mail accounts, and computer access in designated common areas are available to students. The school has a published electronic and media policy.

Contact Mrs. Dora Lawrie, Admissions Coordinator. 204-831-7107. Fax: 204-885-3217. E-mail: dlawrie@laureateslanding.ca. Web site: www.laureateacademy.com.

LAWRENCE SCHOOL

Upper School
10036 Olde Eight Road
Sagamore Hills, Ohio 44067

Head of School: Mr. Lou Salza

General Information Coeducational day college-preparatory school; primarily serves students with learning disabilities, individuals with Attention Deficit Disorder, and dyslexic students. Grades 1–12. Founded: 1969. Setting: suburban. Nearest major city is Cleveland. 47-acre campus. 1 building on campus. Approved or accredited by Independent Schools Association of the Central States, North Central Association of Colleges and Schools, and Ohio Department of Education. Endowment: $2 million. Total enrollment: 291. Upper school average class size: 11. Upper school faculty-student ratio: 1:11. There are 185 required school days per year for Upper School students. Upper School students typically attend 5 days per week. The average school day consists of 6 hours.

Faculty School total: 34. In upper school: 12 men, 18 women; 10 have advanced degrees.

Subjects Offered 20th century history, accounting, Advanced Placement courses, algebra, American history, American sign language, anatomy, art, astronomy, biology, calculus, choir, chorus, college counseling, computer applications, consumer economics, creative writing, debate, drama, earth science, economics, English, English composition, forensics, geography, geometry, global studies, government, graphic arts, graphic design, health, integrated mathematics, journalism, keyboarding, language arts, Latin, law, life science, life skills, mathematics, meteorology, military history, music, mythology, painting, physical education, physical science, physics, physics-AP, poetry, pre-algebra, psychology, research skills, sign language, society, politics and law, sociology, Spanish, speech, speech communications, The 20th Century, U.S. history, U.S. history-AP, video, video communication, Web site design, weight training, world geography, world history, yearbook.

Graduation Requirements Independent study project for seniors, community service project.

Special Academic Programs Honors section; independent study; remedial reading and/or remedial writing; remedial math; programs in English, mathematics, general development for dyslexic students.

College Admission Counseling 37 students graduated in 2011; 30 went to college, including John Carroll University; Kent State University; Ohio University; University of Connecticut; Valparaiso University; Xavier University. Other: 1 entered military service, 5 entered a postgraduate year, 1 had other specific plans.

Student Life Upper grades have specified standards of dress, student council, honor system. Discipline rests equally with students and faculty.

Tuition and Aid Day student tuition: $18,205–$19,475. Tuition installment plan (FACTS Tuition Payment Plan, monthly payment plans, individually arranged payment plans). Need-based scholarship grants available. In 2011–12, 31% of upper-school students received aid. Total amount of financial aid awarded in 2011–12: $800,000.

Admissions Traditional secondary-level entrance grade is 9. Admissions testing required. Deadline for receipt of application materials: none. Application fee required: $100. Interview required.

Athletics Interscholastic: baseball (boys), basketball (b,g), cross-country running (b,g); coed interscholastic: golf; coed intramural: badminton, bowling, cooperative games, fishing, flag football, floor hockey, outdoor activities. 1 PE instructor.

Computers Computers are regularly used in all academic classes. Computer network features include on-campus library services, Internet access, wireless campus network, Internet filtering or blocking technology, one-to-one notebook laptop program for grades 9 to 12, laptop program for grades 7-8, school-wide social networking through Saywire. Student e-mail accounts are available to students. Students grades are available online. The school has a published electronic and media policy.

Contact Mrs. Janet Robinson, Admissions Assistant. 440-526-0717. Fax: 440-526-0595. E-mail: jrobinson@lawrenceschool.org.

LITTLE KESWICK SCHOOL

PO Box 24
Keswick, Virginia 22947

Head of School: Marc J. Columbus

General Information Boys' boarding arts school; primarily serves underachievers, students with learning disabilities, individuals with Attention Deficit Disorder, individuals with emotional and behavioral problems, and dyslexic students. Founded: 1963. Setting: small town. Nearest major city is Washington, DC. Students are housed in single-sex dormitories. 30-acre campus. 10 buildings on campus. Approved or accredited by Virginia Association of Independent Specialized Education Facilities and Virginia Department of Education. Total enrollment: 34. Upper school average class size: 7. Upper school faculty-student ratio: 1:4. There are 247 required school days per year for Upper School students. Upper School students typically attend 5 days per week. The average school day consists of 5 hours and 30 minutes.

Upper School Student Profile 100% of students are boarding students. 17 states are represented in upper school student body. 10% are international students. International students from China and Mexico.

Faculty School total: 6. In upper school: 3 men, 3 women; 4 have advanced degrees; 2 reside on campus.

Subjects Offered Algebra, American history, biology, computer applications, earth science, English, geography, government/civics, health, industrial arts, mathematics, physical education, practical arts, social studies, world history.

Special Academic Programs Academic accommodation for the gifted; remedial math; programs in English, mathematics, general development for dyslexic students.

Student Life Upper grades have specified standards of dress, student council. Discipline rests primarily with faculty.

Summer Programs Remediation, enrichment, sports, art/fine arts, rigorous outdoor training, computer instruction programs offered; session focuses on remediation and therapy; held on campus; accepts boys; open to students from other schools. 34 students usually enrolled. 2012 schedule: July 1 to August 3. Application deadline: none.

Tuition and Aid 7-day tuition and room/board: $101,546. Need-based scholarship grants available. In 2011–12, 2% of upper-school students received aid. Total amount of financial aid awarded in 2011–12: $20,000.

Admissions WISC-III and Woodcock-Johnson required. Deadline for receipt of application materials: none. Application fee required: $350. On-campus interview required.

Athletics Interscholastic: basketball (boys), combined training (b), soccer (b); intramural: basketball (b), bicycling (b), climbing (b), cross-country running (b), equestrian sports (b), fishing (b), fitness (b), gymnastics (b), hiking/backpacking (b), horseback riding (b), lacrosse (b), outdoor activities (b), soccer (b), softball (b), swimming and diving (b), volleyball (b). 1 PE instructor, 2 coaches.

Computers Computer resources include Internet access. Computer access in designated common areas is available to students.

Contact Ms. Terry Columbus, Director. 434-295-0457 Ext. 14. Fax: 434-977-1892. E-mail: tcolumbus@littlekeswickschool.net. Web site: www.littlekeswickschool.net.

MAPLEBROOK SCHOOL

5142 Route 22
Amenia, New York 12501

Head of School: Donna M. Konkolics

General Information Coeducational boarding and day general academic, vocational, and technology school; primarily serves underachievers, students with learning disabilities, individuals with Attention Deficit Disorder, and low average cognitive ability (minimum I.Q. of 70). Ungraded, ages 11–18. Founded: 1945. Setting: small town. Nearest major city is Poughkeepsie. Students are housed in single-sex dormitories. 95-acre campus. 22 buildings on campus. Approved or accredited by Middle States Association of Colleges and Schools, National Association of Private Schools for Exceptional Children, New York Department of Education, New York State Association of Independent Schools, New York State Board of Regents, US Department of State, and New York Department of Education. Member of National Association of Independent Schools. Endowment: $500,000. Total enrollment: 70. Upper school average class size: 6. Upper school faculty-student ratio: 1:8. There are 180 required school days per year for Upper School students. Upper School students typically attend 7 days per week. The average school day consists of 6 hours and 5 minutes.

Upper School Student Profile 98% of students are boarding students. 15% are state residents. 24 states are represented in upper school student body. 20% are international students. International students from Bermuda, Canada, Mexico, Morocco, Nigeria, and South Africa; 6 other countries represented in student body.

Faculty School total: 55. In upper school: 12 men, 14 women; 26 have advanced degrees; 50 reside on campus.

Subjects Offered Algebra, American history, art, biology, business skills, computer science, consumer mathematics, creative writing, drama, driver education, earth science, English, geography, global studies, government/civics, health, home economics, industrial arts, integrated mathematics, keyboarding, mathematics, music, occupational education, performing arts, photography, physical education, physical science, science, social skills, speech, theater, world history, writing.

Graduation Requirements Career and personal planning, computer science, English, mathematics, physical education (includes health), science, social sciences, social skills, social studies (includes history), attendance at Maplebrook School for a minimum of 2 years.

Special Academic Programs Study at local college for college credit; remedial reading and/or remedial writing; remedial math; programs in English, mathematics, general development for dyslexic students.

College Admission Counseling 19 students graduated in 2010; 8 went to college, including Dutchess Community College; Mitchell College. Other: 11 entered a postgraduate year.

Student Life Upper grades have specified standards of dress, student council, honor system. Discipline rests primarily with faculty.

Tuition and Aid Day student tuition: $34,350; 5-day tuition and room/board: $50,200; 7-day tuition and room/board: $54,700. Tuition installment plan (Key Tuition Payment Plan, individually arranged payment plans, Tuition Management Systems Plan, Sallie Mae loans). Merit scholarship grants, need-based scholarship grants, need-based loans, middle-income loans, paying campus jobs, minority and cultural diversity scholarships, day-student scholarships available. In 2010–11, 15% of upper-school students received aid; total upper-school merit-scholarship money awarded: $10,000. Total amount of financial aid awarded in 2010–11: $157,000.

Admissions Traditional secondary-level entrance age is 15. For fall 2010, 190 students applied for upper-level admission, 60 were accepted, 35 enrolled. Achievement tests, Bender Gestalt, TerraNova, Test of Achievement and Proficiency or WISC or WAIS required. Deadline for receipt of application materials: none. No application fee required. Interview required.

Athletics Interscholastic: basketball (boys, girls), cheering (g), field hockey (g); coed interscholastic: cooperative games, cross-country running, equestrian sports, fitness, freestyle skiing, horseback riding, running, skiing (cross-country), skiing (downhill), soccer, softball, swimming and diving, tennis, track and field, weight lifting, weight training; coed intramural: aerobics/dance, alpine skiing, basketball, bicycling, bowling, cooperative games, cricket, dance, figure skating, fitness, fitness walking, flag football, floor hockey, freestyle skiing, golf, hiking/backpacking, horseback riding, ice skating, indoor hockey, martial arts, outdoor education, outdoor recreation, roller blading, skiing (cross-country), skiing (downhill), soccer, softball, Special Olympics, swimming and diving, table tennis, tennis, volleyball, weight lifting, weight training, wrestling. 1 PE instructor, 12 coaches.

Computers Computers are regularly used in all academic classes. Computer network features include on-campus library services, Internet access, wireless campus network, Internet filtering or blocking technology. Campus intranet, student e-mail accounts, and computer access in designated common areas are available to students. Students grades are available online. The school has a published electronic and media policy.

Contact Jennifer L. Scully, Dean of Admissions. 845-373-8191. Fax: 845-373-7029. E-mail: admissions@maplebrookschool.org. Web site: www.maplebrookschool.org.

MILL SPRINGS ACADEMY

13660 New Providence Road
Alpharetta, Georgia 30004

Head of School: Mr. Robert W. Moore

General Information Coeducational day college-preparatory and arts school; primarily serves students with learning disabilities, individuals with Attention Deficit Disorder, and dyslexic students. Grades 1–12. Founded: 1981. Setting: suburban. Nearest major city is Atlanta. 85-acre campus. 5 buildings on campus. Approved or accredited by Georgia Association of Private Schools for Exceptional Children, Georgia Independent School Association, Southern Association of Colleges and Schools, and Southern Association of Independent Schools. Member of National Association of Independent Schools. Endowment: $140,000. Total enrollment: 305. Upper school average class size: 10. Upper school faculty-student ratio: 1:4. There are 180 required school days per year for Upper School students. Upper School students typically attend 5 days per week. The average school day consists of 7 hours.

Upper School Student Profile Grade 9: 43 students (36 boys, 7 girls); Grade 10: 29 students (19 boys, 10 girls); Grade 11: 30 students (23 boys, 7 girls); Grade 12: 10 students (5 boys, 5 girls).

Faculty School total: 49. In upper school: 12 men, 10 women; 13 have advanced degrees.

Subjects Offered Algebra, American history, American literature, anatomy and physiology, art, band, biology, British literature, British literature (honors), calculus, career/college preparation, chemistry, chorus, composition, creative writing, diversity studies, drama, ecology, economics, film, geometry, government, health, history, honors algebra, honors English, honors geometry, honors U.S. history, honors world history, journalism, literature, media, music theater, performing arts, physical education, physics, play production, play/screen writing, playwriting and directing, political science, pre-algebra, pre-calculus, psychology, sculpture, senior project, set design, Spanish, state government, studio art, symphonic band, technology, theater, theater design and production, trigonometry, U.S. history, values and decisions, visual and performing arts, voice, world literature, yearbook.

Graduation Requirements Algebra, American history, American literature, anatomy and physiology, biology, British literature, British literature (honors), calculus, chemistry, civics, ecology, economics, geometry, physical education (includes health), physics, Spanish, trigonometry, world history, world literature, senior English, 6 units of electives.

Special Academic Programs Honors section; study at local college for college credit; academic accommodation for the gifted, the musically talented, and the artistically talented; programs in English, mathematics, general development for dyslexic students.

College Admission Counseling 40 students graduated in 2011; 32 went to college, including Andrew College; Georgia College & State University; Georgia Perimeter College; Reinhardt University; Valdosta State University; Young Harris College. Other: 1 entered military service, 4 entered a postgraduate year, 3 had other specific plans. Mean SAT critical reading: 459, mean SAT math: 436, mean SAT writing: 426, mean composite ACT: 18. 4% scored over 600 on SAT critical reading, 3% scored over 600 on SAT math, 1% scored over 600 on SAT writing, 1% scored over 26 on composite ACT.

Student Life Upper grades have uniform requirement, student council, honor system. Discipline rests equally with students and faculty.

Summer Programs Sports programs offered; session focuses on skills development or course credit; held on campus; accepts boys and girls; open to students from other schools. 160 students usually enrolled. 2012 schedule: June 4 to August 10. Application deadline: June 3.

Tuition and Aid Day student tuition: $20,069. Tuition installment plan (FACTS Tuition Payment Plan). Tuition reduction for siblings, need-based scholarship grants available. In 2011–12, 14% of upper-school students received aid. Total amount of financial aid awarded in 2011–12: $77,000.

Admissions Traditional secondary-level entrance grade is 9. For fall 2011, 31 students applied for upper-level admission, 21 were accepted, 20 enrolled. Psychoeducational evaluation required. Deadline for receipt of application materials: none. Application fee required: $100. On-campus interview required.

Athletics Interscholastic: baseball (boys), basketball (b,g), golf (b), lacrosse (b), tennis (b,g), volleyball (g), wrestling (b); intramural: cheering (g), strength & conditioning (b), weight lifting (b); coed interscholastic: cross-country running, soccer, swimming and diving, track and field; coed intramural: archery, dance, fencing, fishing, golf, mountain biking, outdoor activities, physical fitness, scuba diving, yoga. 2 coaches.

Computers Computers are regularly used in all academic classes. Computer network features include on-campus library services, Internet access, wireless campus network, Internet filtering or blocking technology, all students 4-12th grades have laptops, electronic textbooks/literature books, assignments online. Student e-mail accounts are available to students. Students grades are available online. The school has a published electronic and media policy.

Contact Mrs. Sheila FitzGerald, Admissions Director. 770-360-1336 Ext. 1707. Fax: 770-360-1341. E-mail: sfitzgerald@millsprings.org. Web site: www.millsprings.org.

See Display on next page and Close-Up on page 742.

NOBLE ACADEMY

3310 Horse Pen Creek Road
Greensboro, North Carolina 27410

Head of School: Laura Blackburn

General Information Coeducational day college-preparatory, arts, and technology school; primarily serves students with learning disabilities, individuals with Attention Deficit Disorder, and dyslexic students. Grades K–12. Founded: 1987. Setting: suburban. Nearest major city is Greensboro/Winston-Salem. 40-acre campus. 3 buildings on campus. Approved or accredited by North Carolina Department of Exceptional Children, Southern Association of Colleges and Schools, Southern Association of Independent Schools, and North Carolina Department of Education. Endowment: $2.1 million. Total enrollment: 150. Upper school average class size: 9. Upper school faculty-student ratio: 1:9. There are 180 required school days per year for Upper School students. Upper School students typically attend 5 days per week. The average school day consists of 6 hours and 45 minutes.

Upper School Student Profile Grade 10: 11 students (8 boys, 3 girls); Grade 11: 8 students (7 boys, 1 girl); Grade 12: 14 students (7 boys, 7 girls).

Faculty School total: 34. In upper school: 4 men, 5 women; 5 have advanced degrees.

Subjects Offered Algebra, American history, art, basic skills, biology, career and personal planning, career exploration, chemistry, civics, college counseling, drama, earth science, economics, English, environmental science, geometry, health, journalism, life management skills, political systems, pre-algebra, pre-calculus, reading, reading/study skills, Spanish, world history, world history-AP, yearbook.

Graduation Requirements Algebra, American history, biology, earth science, economics, English, environmental science, geometry, physical education (includes health), Spanish, world history, 8th grade end-of-grade test, 20th percentile score on standardized reading test, North Carolina Computer Competency Test.

Special Academic Programs Study at local college for college credit; remedial reading and/or remedial writing; remedial math; programs in English, mathematics, general development for dyslexic students.

College Admission Counseling 14 students graduated in 2011; 10 went to college, including Brevard College; Elon University; Guilford College; St. Andrews Presbyterian College; The University of North Carolina at Greensboro; William Peace University. Other: 3 went to work, 1 had other specific plans. Median SAT critical reading: 510, median SAT math: 420, median SAT writing: 480. Mean combined SAT: 1458. 12% scored over 600 on SAT critical reading, 12% scored over 600 on SAT math, 12% scored over 600 on SAT writing.

Student Life Upper grades have student council, honor system. Discipline rests primarily with faculty.
Summer Programs Remediation, advancement, computer instruction programs offered; session focuses on courses for credit; held on campus; accepts boys and girls; open to students from other schools. 25 students usually enrolled. 2012 schedule: June 20 to August 4. Application deadline: June 4.
Tuition and Aid Day student tuition: $15,850. Tuition installment plan (monthly payment plans, individually arranged payment plans). Need-based scholarship grants available. In 2011–12, 12% of upper-school students received aid. Total amount of financial aid awarded in 2011–12: $33,000.
Admissions Traditional secondary-level entrance grade is 10. For fall 2011, 12 students applied for upper-level admission, 6 were accepted, 6 enrolled. WISC/Woodcock-Johnson required. Deadline for receipt of application materials: none. Application fee required: $75. On-campus interview required.
Athletics Interscholastic: cheering (girls); coed interscholastic: basketball, cross-country running, flag football, golf, soccer, tennis, volleyball; coed intramural: tennis. 1 PE instructor, 7 coaches.
Computers Computers are regularly used in art, career education, career exploration, career technology, college planning, computer applications, current events, graphic arts, graphic design, history, information technology, introduction to technology, journalism, keyboarding, lab/keyboard, photography, social studies, Spanish, study skills, word processing, writing, writing, yearbook classes. Computer network features include Internet access, wireless campus network, Internet filtering or blocking technology. Student e-mail accounts are available to students. Students grades are available online. The school has a published electronic and media policy.
Contact Tim Montgomery, Assistant Head and Director of Admissions. 336-282-7044. Fax: 336-282-2048. E-mail: tmontgomery@nobleknights.org. Web site: www.nobleknights.org.

OAKLAND SCHOOL

Boyd Tavern
Keswick, Virginia 22947

Head of School: Ms. Carol Williams

General Information Coeducational boarding and day general academic school, primarily serves underachievers, students with learning disabilities, dyslexic students, processing difficulties, and organizational challenges. Boarding grades 2–9, day grades 1–9. Founded: 1950. Setting: rural. Nearest major city is Richmond. Students are housed in single-sex dormitories. 450-acre campus. 25 buildings on campus. Approved or accredited by Virginia Association of Independent Specialized Education Facilities and Virginia Department of Education. Upper school average class size: 5. Upper school faculty-student ratio: 1:5. There are 180 required school days per year for Upper School students. The average school day consists of 6 hours and 30 minutes.
Upper School Student Profile 60% of students are boarding students. 40% are state residents. 8 states are represented in upper school student body. 10% are international students.
Faculty School total: 18. In upper school: 4 men, 13 women; 9 have advanced degrees; 8 reside on campus.
Subjects Offered Algebra, American history, earth science, English, expository writing, geometry, grammar, health, history of the Americas, keyboarding, life science, mathematics, physical education, physical science, remedial study skills, study skills, world history.
Graduation Requirements Skills must be at or above grade/ability level.
Special Academic Programs Remedial reading and/or remedial writing; remedial math; programs in English, mathematics for dyslexic students.
College Admission Counseling 18 students graduated in 2011.
Student Life Upper grades have specified standards of dress, student council, honor system. Discipline rests primarily with faculty.
Summer Programs Remediation, sports, art/fine arts, computer instruction programs offered; session focuses on academics; held on campus; accepts boys and girls; open to students from other schools. 135 students usually enrolled. 2012 schedule: June 24 to August 3.
Tuition and Aid Day student tuition: $26,850; 7-day tuition and room/board: $46,975. Tuition installment plan (SMART Tuition Payment Plan, individually arranged payment plans). Need-based scholarship grants available. In 2011–12, 20% of upper-school students received aid.
Admissions Wechsler Intelligence Scale for Children III required. Deadline for receipt of application materials: none. No application fee required. Interview required.
Athletics Interscholastic: basketball (boys, girls), cheering (g), cross-country running (b,g), equestrian sports (b,g), fishing (b,g), fitness (b,g), golf (b,g), handball (b,g), horseback riding (b,g), outdoor activities (b,g), outdoor adventure (b,g), outdoor education (b,g), outdoor recreation (b,g), outdoor skills (b,g), outdoors (b,g), physical fitness (b,g), physical training (b,g), roller skating (b,g), running (b,g), soccer (b,g), softball (b,g), table tennis (b,g), tennis (b,g), volleyball (b,g), weight training (b,g), wilderness (b,g), wildernessways (b,g); intramural: soccer (b,g), yoga (g); coed interscholastic: aerobics/dance, archery, basketball, bicycling, cross-country running, equestrian sports, fishing, fitness, golf, handball, horseback riding, outdoor activities, outdoor adventure, outdoor education, outdoor skills, outdoors, physical training, roller skating, running, soccer, softball, table tennis, tennis, volleyball, weight training, wilderness,

wildernessways; coed intramural: archery, basketball, bicycling, billiards, cooperative games, cross-country running, equestrian sports, fishing, fitness, Frisbee, golf, hiking/backpacking, horseback riding, in-line skating, indoor soccer, kickball, lacrosse, mountain biking, outdoor activities, outdoor recreation, outdoors, paddle tennis, physical fitness, roller blading, roller skating, running, skateboarding, soccer, softball, swimming and diving, table tennis, tennis. 1 PE instructor.

Computers Computers are regularly used in English classes.

Contact Mrs. Amanda S. Baber, Admissions Director. 434-293-9059. Fax: 434-296-8930. E-mail: admissions@oaklandschool.net. Web site: www.oaklandschool.net.

THE OLIVERIAN SCHOOL

PO Box 98
Mount Moosilauke Highway
Haverhill, New Hampshire 03765

Head of School: Mr. Randy Richardson

General Information Coeducational boarding and day and distance learning college-preparatory, arts, technology, and experiential education school; primarily serves students with learning disabilities, individuals with Attention Deficit Disorder, individuals with emotional and behavioral problems, and minor emotional and behavioral problems. Grades 9–PG. Distance learning grade X. Founded: 2002. Setting: rural. Nearest major city is Boston, MA. Students are housed in single-sex dormitories. 1,800-acre campus. 10 buildings on campus. Approved or accredited by Independent Schools of Northern New England and New Hampshire Department of Education. Candidate for accreditation by New England Association of Schools and Colleges. Member of National Association of Independent Schools and Secondary School Admission Test Board. Endowment: $50,000. Total enrollment: 50. Upper school average class size: 6. Upper school faculty-student ratio: 1:2. There are 180 required school days per year for Upper School students. Upper School students typically attend 5 days per week. The average school day consists of 7 hours and 30 minutes.

Upper School Student Profile Grade 9: 4 students (2 boys, 2 girls); Grade 10: 9 students (5 boys, 4 girls); Grade 11: 16 students (8 boys, 8 girls); Grade 12: 18 students (10 boys, 8 girls); Postgraduate: 3 students (2 boys, 1 girl). 100% of students are boarding students. 5% are state residents. 10 states are represented in upper school student body. 10% are international students. International students from Bermuda, Canada, Germany, Israel, and Kuwait.

Faculty School total: 19. In upper school: 9 men, 9 women; 10 have advanced degrees; 18 reside on campus.

Special Academic Programs 10 Advanced Placement exams for which test preparation is offered; honors section; accelerated programs; independent study; term-away projects; study at local college for college credit; study abroad; academic accommodation for the gifted and the artistically talented; remedial reading and/or remedial writing; remedial math; ESL (5 students enrolled).

College Admission Counseling 22 students graduated in 2011; 19 went to college, including St. Olaf College. Other: 1 went to work, 2 entered a postgraduate year.

Student Life Upper grades have specified standards of dress, student council, honor system. Discipline rests primarily with faculty.

Summer Programs Remediation, enrichment, advancement, ESL, art/fine arts, computer instruction programs offered; session focuses on academics; held on campus; accepts boys and girls; open to students from other schools. 20 students usually enrolled. 2012 schedule: June 20 to August 7. Application deadline: June 20.

Tuition and Aid 7-day tuition and room/board: $60,000. Tuition installment plan (FACTS Tuition Payment Plan). Merit scholarship grants, need-based scholarship grants available. In 2011–12, 20% of upper-school students received aid; total upper-school merit-scholarship money awarded: $50,000. Total amount of financial aid awarded in 2011–12: $200,000.

Admissions Traditional secondary-level entrance grade is 11. Deadline for receipt of application materials: none. Application fee required: $75. Interview required.

Athletics Intramural: flag football (boys, girls); coed interscholastic: soccer; coed intramural: alpine skiing, backpacking, basketball, bicycling, billiards, bowling, canoeing/kayaking, climbing, cooperative games, cross-country running, equestrian sports, fishing, fitness, Frisbee, golf, hiking/backpacking, horseback riding, indoor soccer, juggling, martial arts, mountain biking, mountaineering, nordic skiing, outdoor activities, outdoor adventure, outdoor education, outdoor recreation, outdoor skills, outdoors, physical fitness, physical training, rappelling, rock climbing, ropes courses, running, skateboarding, skiing (cross-country), skiing (downhill), snowboarding, snowshoeing, strength & conditioning, table tennis, touch football, triathlon, ultimate Frisbee, volleyball, walking, wall climbing, weight training, wilderness, wildernessways, yoga.

Computers Computer network features include online commercial services, Internet access, wireless campus network, Internet filtering or blocking technology. Campus intranet, student e-mail accounts, and computer access in designated common areas are available to students. Students grades are available online. The school has a published electronic and media policy.

Contact Mr. Barclay Mackinnon Jr., Director of Admissions/Headmaster Emeritus. 603-989-5100 Ext. 7103. Fax: 603-989-3055. E-mail: bmackinnon@oliverianschool.org. Web site: www.oliverianschool.org.

THE PATHWAY SCHOOL

162 Egypt Road
Norristown, Pennsylvania 19403

Head of School: David Maola

General Information Coeducational day Life Skills/Functional Academics and Pre-vocational/Career Education school; primarily serves underachievers, students with learning disabilities, individuals with Attention Deficit Disorder, individuals with emotional and behavioral problems, neurologically impaired students, students with neuropsychiatric disorders, Asperger's Syndrome, Emotional Disturbance, and students needing speech/language therapy and occupational therapy. Ungraded, ages 7–21. Founded: 1961. Setting: suburban. Nearest major city is Philadelphia. 12-acre campus. 12 buildings on campus. Approved or accredited by Pennsylvania Department of Education. Endowment: $1 million. Upper school average class size: 9. Upper school faculty-student ratio: 1:6. There are 181 required school days per year for Upper School students. Upper School students typically attend 5 days per week. The average school day consists of 5 hours and 30 minutes.

Faculty School total: 23. In upper school: 4 men, 5 women; 4 have advanced degrees.

Subjects Offered Algebra, art, biology, career education, career experience, career/college preparation, computer skills, consumer mathematics, creative arts, drama, earth science, electives, English, environmental science, general math, geometry, health education, history, horticulture, interpersonal skills, language arts, mathematics, money management, physical education, pre-vocational education, senior seminar, social skills, social studies, work experience, world history.

Graduation Requirements Graduation requirements are as specified by the sending school district.

Special Academic Programs Study at local college for college credit; remedial reading and/or remedial writing; remedial math; programs in general development for dyslexic students; special instructional classes for Emotional Support Program.

College Admission Counseling 18 students graduated in 2011; 6 went to college. Other: 10 went to work, 2 had other specific plans.

Student Life Upper grades have specified standards of dress, student council, honor system. Discipline rests equally with students and faculty.

Summer Programs Remediation programs offered; session focuses on providing consistency for the entire calendar year; held on campus; accepts boys and girls; open to students from other schools. 85 students usually enrolled. 2012 schedule: July 9 to August 17.

Tuition and Aid Day student tuition: $44,000. Tuition installment plan (individually arranged payment plans).

Admissions Traditional secondary-level entrance age is 16. For fall 2011, 10 students applied for upper-level admission, 5 were accepted, 4 enrolled. Deadline for receipt of application materials: none. No application fee required. On-campus interview required.

Athletics Interscholastic: basketball (boys, girls), softball (b,g), Special Olympics (b,g); coed interscholastic: soccer, Special Olympics; coed intramural: basketball, flag football, soccer. 2 PE instructors, 2 coaches.

Computers Computers are regularly used in basic skills, business education, business skills, career education, data processing, design, newspaper, typing classes. Computer network features include on-campus library services, Internet access, Internet filtering or blocking technology, computer access in classroom. Computer access in designated common areas is available to students. The school has a published electronic and media policy.

Contact Diana Phifer, Director of Admissions. 610-277-0660 Ext. 289. Fax: 610-539-1493. E-mail: dphifer@pathwayschool.org. Web site: www.pathwayschool.org.

PINEHURST SCHOOL

10 Seymour Avenue
St. Catharines, Ontario L2P 1A4, Canada

Head of School: Mr. Dave Bird

General Information Coeducational boarding college-preparatory, arts, business, and technology school; primarily serves students with learning disabilities, individuals with Attention Deficit Disorder, and individuals with emotional and behavioral problems. Grades 7–12. Founded: 2000. Setting: urban. Students are housed in single-sex by floor dormitories. 5-acre campus. 1 building on campus. Approved or accredited by Ontario Ministry of Education, Virginia Association of Independent Specialized Education Facilities, and Ontario Department of Education. Language of instruction: English. Total enrollment: 23. Upper school average class size: 10. Upper school faculty-student ratio: 1:10. There are 158 required school days per year for Upper School students. Upper School students typically attend 5 days per week. The average school day consists of 5 hours and 50 minutes.

Upper School Student Profile Grade 11: 2 students (1 boy, 1 girl); Grade 12: 12 students (9 boys, 3 girls). 100% of students are boarding students. 90% are province residents. 2 provinces are represented in upper school student body. 10% are international students. International students from Bermuda, Oman, Saudi Arabia, and United States.

Faculty School total: 5. In upper school: 3 men, 2 women; 2 have advanced degrees.

Graduation Requirements 20th century world history, art, business applications, Canadian geography, English, French, geography, health education, history, math applications, mathematics, outdoor education, science.

Special Academic Programs Honors section; accelerated programs; independent study; remedial reading and/or remedial writing; remedial math.
College Admission Counseling 9 students graduated in 2011; 2 went to college, including Zion Bible College. Other: 6 entered a postgraduate year, 1 had other specific plans.
Student Life Upper grades have uniform requirement, student council, honor system. Discipline rests primarily with faculty.
Tuition and Aid 7-day tuition and room/board: CAN$35,000. Tuition installment plan (monthly payment plans).
Admissions Traditional secondary-level entrance grade is 11. For fall 2011, 5 students applied for upper-level admission, 5 were accepted, 5 enrolled. Deadline for receipt of application materials: none. No application fee required. On-campus interview required.
Athletics Coed Intramural: alpine skiing, aquatics, archery, backpacking, badminton, ball hockey, baseball, basketball, bicycling, billiards, blading, bocce, bowling, canoeing/kayaking, climbing, cooperative games, cricket, croquet, curling, field hockey, fishing, fitness, fitness walking, flag football, floor hockey, football, golf, hiking/backpacking, hockey, ice hockey, ice skating, in-line skating, indoor hockey, indoor soccer, kayaking, mountain biking, outdoor activities, outdoor education, paddling, physical fitness, physical training, rock climbing, roller blading, ropes courses, scuba diving, skateboarding, skiing (cross-country), skiing (downhill), snowboarding, snowshoeing, soccer, softball, street hockey, strength & conditioning, swimming and diving, table tennis, touch football, volleyball, walking, wall climbing, weight lifting, weight training, wilderness, wilderness survival, wildernessways, winter soccer, winter walking, yoga. 1 PE instructor, 1 coach, 1 athletic trainer.
Computers Computers are regularly used in all classes. Computer network features include on-campus library services, Internet access, wireless campus network, Internet filtering or blocking technology. Student e-mail accounts are available to students.
Contact Mrs. Donna MacDonald, Admissions/Office Coordinator. 905-641-0993. Fax: 905-641-0399. E-mail: pinedonna@sympatico.ca. Web site: www.pinehurst.on.ca.

ROBERT LAND ACADEMY

6727 South Chippawa Road
Wellandport, Ontario L0R 2J0, Canada

Head of School: Lt. Col. G. Scott Bowman

General Information Boys' boarding college-preparatory, arts, business, English and Math foundational building, and military school; primarily serves underachievers, students with learning disabilities, individuals with Attention Deficit Disorder, individuals with emotional and behavioral problems, dyslexic students, Oppositional Defiant Disorder, and Attention Deficit Hyperactive Disorder. Grades 6–12. Founded: 1978. Setting: rural. Nearest major city is Hamilton, Canada. Students are housed in single-sex dormitories and barracks. 168-acre campus. 14 buildings on campus. Approved or accredited by Ontario Ministry of Education and Ontario Department of Education. Language of instruction: English. Total enrollment: 125. Upper school average class size: 14. Upper school faculty-student ratio: 1:14. Upper School students typically attend 7 days per week. The average school day consists of 6 hours and 30 minutes.
Upper School Student Profile Grade 11: 15 students (15 boys); Grade 12: 6 students (6 boys). 100% of students are boarding students. 65% are province residents. 9 provinces are represented in upper school student body. 20% are international students. International students from Bahamas, China, Hong Kong, Japan, United Kingdom, and United States; 5 other countries represented in student body.
Faculty School total: 14. In upper school: 13 men, 1 woman; 7 have advanced degrees.
Subjects Offered Advanced biology, advanced chemistry, advanced math, algebra, all academic, American history, ancient history, art, art history, athletic training, athletics, band, basic language skills, biology, bookkeeping, British history, business, calculus, Canadian geography, Canadian history, Canadian literature, career planning, career/college preparation, chemistry, civics, computer applications, computer art, computer education, computer graphics, computer information systems, computer processing, computer programming, computer science, computer skills, computer studies, computers, consumer education, creative writing, culinary arts, economics, English, English literature, environmental geography, environmental science, environmental studies, ethical decision making, ethics, ethics and responsibility, European history, French, functions, geography, health education, history, keyboarding, language, language arts, leadership, life management skills, martial arts, military history, navigation, nutrition, personal fitness, physical education, physical fitness, physics, reading, science, scuba diving, sports, statistics, survival training, values and decisions, volleyball, weight fitness, weight training, weightlifting, wilderness education, wilderness experience, world literature, wrestling.
Graduation Requirements Ontario Literacy Equivalence Test, minimum 40 hours of community service.
Special Academic Programs Honors section; independent study; remedial reading and/or remedial writing; remedial math; programs in general development for dyslexic students.
College Admission Counseling 16 students graduated in 2011; 14 went to college, including Brock University; McMaster University; University of Guelph; University of Toronto; Wilfrid Laurier University. Other: 2 went to work.
Student Life Upper grades have uniform requirement, student council, honor system. Discipline rests primarily with faculty.
Tuition and Aid 7-day tuition and room/board: CAN$39,950. Tuition installment plan (monthly payment plans, individually arranged payment plans). Bursaries, merit scholarship grants, need-based scholarship grants, middle-income loans available. In 2011–12, 10% of upper-school students received aid.
Admissions Traditional secondary-level entrance grade is 11. Deadline for receipt of application materials: none. Application fee required: CAN$250. Interview required.
Athletics Interscholastic: badminton, basketball, cross-country running, ice hockey, rugby, running, soccer, track and field, volleyball, wall climbing, wrestling; intramural: aerobics/Nautilus, archery, backpacking, badminton, ball hockey, baseball, basketball, bicycling, boxing, canoeing/kayaking, climbing, cross-country running, drill team, fishing, fitness, fitness walking, flag football, floor hockey, Frisbee, hiking/backpacking, hockey, ice hockey, ice skating, indoor hockey, indoor soccer, jogging, JROTC drill, life saving, marksmanship, martial arts, mountain biking, mountaineering, Nautilus, outdoor activities, outdoor adventure, outdoor education, outdoor recreation, outdoor skills, outdoors, paddling, paint ball, physical fitness, physical training, rafting, rappelling, riflery, rock climbing, ropes courses, rugby, running, scuba diving, self defense, skydiving, soccer, softball, street hockey, strength & conditioning, touch football, track and field, ultimate Frisbee, volleyball, walking, wall climbing, weight lifting, weight training, wilderness, wilderness survival, winter walking, wrestling. 3 PE instructors, 10 coaches.
Computers Computer network features include on-campus library services, Internet access, Internet filtering or blocking technology.
Contact Admissions Officer. 905-386-6203. Fax: 905-386-6607. E-mail: admissions@rla.ca. Web site: www.robertlandacademy.com.

ROBERT LOUIS STEVENSON SCHOOL

24 West 74th Street
New York, New York 10023

Head of School: Douglas Herron

General Information Coeducational day college-preparatory school; primarily serves underachievers, students with learning disabilities, individuals with Attention Deficit Disorder, individuals with emotional and behavioral problems, and dyslexic students. Grades 7–PG. Founded: 1908. Setting: urban. 1 building on campus. Approved or accredited by New York Department of Education. Member of National Association of Independent Schools. Total enrollment: 60. Upper school average class size: 8. Upper school faculty-student ratio: 1:5. There are 165 required school days per year for Upper School students. Upper School students typically attend 5 days per week. The average school day consists of 6 hours and 30 minutes.
Upper School Student Profile Grade 7: 1 student (1 boy); Grade 8: 4 students (3 boys, 1 girl); Grade 9: 6 students (3 boys, 3 girls); Grade 10: 12 students (8 boys, 4 girls); Grade 11: 18 students (10 boys, 8 girls); Grade 12: 19 students (11 boys, 8 girls).
Faculty School total: 16. In upper school: 6 men, 8 women; 8 have advanced degrees.
Subjects Offered Algebra, American history, American literature, anatomy, ancient history, ancient world history, ancient/medieval philosophy, art, biology, calculus, ceramics, chemistry, creative writing, current history, drama, earth and space science, earth science, English, English literature, environmental science, European civilization, European history, expository writing, film appreciation, geometry, government/civics, grammar, health, history, history of ideas, mathematics, philosophy, physical education, physics, physiology, poetry, political science, political thought, pre-algebra, pre-calculus, psychology, robotics, science, senior project, sex education, Shakespeare, social sciences, social studies, theater, trigonometry, world literature, writing.
Graduation Requirements American history, computer literacy, English, health education, mathematics, physical education (includes health), science, social sciences, social studies (includes history), portfolio of work demonstrating readiness to graduate.
Special Academic Programs Accelerated programs; independent study; academic accommodation for the gifted; remedial reading and/or remedial writing; remedial math; programs in English, mathematics, general development for dyslexic students.
College Admission Counseling 18 students graduated in 2011; 16 went to college, including City University of New York System; Pace University; State University of New York System. Other: 1 went to work, 1 had other specific plans.
Student Life Upper grades have student council. Discipline rests primarily with faculty.
Summer Programs Remediation, enrichment, advancement programs offered; session focuses on tutorial work; held on campus; accepts boys and girls; open to students from other schools. 18 students usually enrolled. 2012 schedule: July 1 to July 29. Application deadline: June 22.
Tuition and Aid Day student tuition: $49,000. Tuition installment plan (individually arranged payment plans). Need-based scholarship grants, need-based loans available. In 2011–12, 4% of upper-school students received aid. Total amount of financial aid awarded in 2011–12: $50,000.
Admissions Traditional secondary-level entrance grade is 10. For fall 2011, 65 students applied for upper-level admission, 43 were accepted, 38 enrolled. Psychoeducational evaluation required. Deadline for receipt of application materials: none. No application fee required. On-campus interview required.
Athletics Coed Interscholastic: basketball, bowling, cross-country running, fitness, floor hockey, jogging, soccer, softball, yoga; coed intramural: aerobics, ball hockey, basketball, bicycling, blading, bowling, cooperative games, fitness, flag football, floor hockey, jogging, judo, juggling, martial arts, physical fitness, physical training, soccer,

softball, strength & conditioning, table tennis, tennis, touch football, volleyball, weight lifting, weight training, yoga. 1 PE instructor.

Computers Computers are regularly used in art, English, history, mathematics, science, technology classes. Computer network features include Internet access, wireless campus network, Internet filtering or blocking technology. Student e-mail accounts and computer access in designated common areas are available to students. The school has a published electronic and media policy.

Contact Dr. Dayana Jimenez, Clinical Director. 212-787-6400. Fax: 212-873-1872. E-mail: djimenez@stevenson-school.org. Web site: www.stevenson-school.org.

SHELTON SCHOOL AND EVALUATION CENTER

15720 Hillcrest Road
Dallas, Texas 75248

Head of School: Linda Kneese

General Information Coeducational day college-preparatory and general academic school; primarily serves students with learning disabilities, individuals with Attention Deficit Disorder, and dyslexic students. Grades PS–12. Founded: 1976. Setting: suburban. 1-acre campus. 1 building on campus. Approved or accredited by Independent Schools Association of the Southwest and Southern Association of Independent Schools. Endowment: $6.7 million. Total enrollment: 868. Upper school average class size: 8. Upper school faculty-student ratio: 1:8. There are 168 required school days per year for Upper School students. Upper School students typically attend 5 days per week. The average school day consists of 7 hours.

Upper School Student Profile Grade 9: 71 students (45 boys, 26 girls); Grade 10: 67 students (44 boys, 23 girls); Grade 11: 71 students (43 boys, 28 girls); Grade 12: 47 students (29 boys, 18 girls).

Faculty School total: 159. In upper school: 15 men, 25 women; 26 have advanced degrees.

Subjects Offered All academic, American sign language, ethics, Spanish, theater arts.

Graduation Requirements Arts and fine arts (art, music, dance, drama), computers, English, ethics, foreign language, mathematics, physical education (includes health), reading, science, social studies (includes history), speech.

Special Academic Programs Programs in English, mathematics, general development for dyslexic students.

College Admission Counseling 53 students graduated in 2011; 49 went to college, including Collin County Community College District; Texas A&M University; The University of Arizona; University of Arkansas; University of Colorado Boulder; University of Oklahoma. Other: 4 had other specific plans.

Student Life Upper grades have uniform requirement, student council, honor system. Discipline rests primarily with faculty.

Summer Programs Enrichment programs offered; session focuses on enrichment; held on campus; accepts boys and girls; open to students from other schools. 39 students usually enrolled. 2012 schedule: June 25 to July 20. Application deadline: May 11.

Tuition and Aid Day student tuition: $19,350. Tuition installment plan (SMART Tuition Payment Plan, Sallie Mae). Need-based scholarship grants available. In 2011–12, 2% of upper-school students received aid. Total amount of financial aid awarded in 2011–12: $43,500.

Admissions Traditional secondary-level entrance grade is 9. For fall 2011, 43 students applied for upper-level admission, 25 were accepted, 22 enrolled. WISC/Woodcock-Johnson required. Deadline for receipt of application materials: none. No application fee required. Interview required.

Athletics Interscholastic: baseball (boys), basketball (b,g), cheering (g), cross-country running (b,g), football (b), golf (b), tennis (b,g), track and field (b,g), volleyball (g). 3 PE instructors, 4 coaches.

Computers Computers are regularly used in all academic, English, foreign language, information technology, lab/keyboard, library, research skills, SAT preparation, video film production classes. Computer network features include on-campus library services, Internet access, wireless campus network, Internet filtering or blocking technology. Campus intranet and student e-mail accounts are available to students. Students grades are available online. The school has a published electronic and media policy.

Contact Diann Slaton, Director of Admissions. 972-774-1772. Fax: 972-991-3977. E-mail: dslaton@shelton.org. Web site: www.shelton.org.

SHOORE CENTRE FOR LEARNING

801 Eglinton Avenue West
Suite 201
Toronto, Ontario M5N 1E3, Canada

Head of School: Mr. Michael I. Shoore

General Information Coeducational day general academic school; primarily serves underachievers, students with learning disabilities, individuals with Attention Deficit Disorder, individuals with emotional and behavioral problems, and dyslexic students. Grades 8–12. Setting: urban. Approved or accredited by Ontario Department of Education. Language of instruction: English. Total enrollment: 30. Upper school average class size: 6. Upper school faculty-student ratio: 1:6.

Faculty School total: 8. In upper school: 5 men, 2 women.

Subjects Offered Advanced math, anthropology, art, business studies, calculus, Canadian geography, Canadian history, Canadian law, career education, chemistry, civics, drama, dramatic arts, earth science, English, general science, health and safety, history, independent study, law, mathematics, media arts, parenting, physical education, physics, science, science and technology, technology, visual arts, writing.

Special Academic Programs Remedial reading and/or remedial writing; remedial math; programs in English, mathematics, general development for dyslexic students.

College Admission Counseling 6 students graduated in 2010. Other: 4 entered a postgraduate year.

Student Life Upper grades have specified standards of dress. Discipline rests primarily with faculty.

Tuition and Aid Day student tuition: CAN$22,100. Tuition installment plan (monthly payment plans, individually arranged payment plans).

Admissions Deadline for receipt of application materials: none. No application fee required. Interview required.

Computers Computer resources include Internet access.

Contact Mr. Michael I. Shoore, Director. 416-781-4754. Fax: 416-781 0163. E-mail: shoore@shoorecentre.com. Web site: www.shoorecentre.com.

SMITH SCHOOL

131 West 86 Street
New York, New York 10024

Head of School: Karen Smith

General Information Coeducational day college-preparatory and music and art programs school; primarily serves students with learning disabilities, individuals with Attention Deficit Disorder, and depression or anxiety disorders; emotional and/or motivational issues. Grades 7–12. Founded: 1990. Setting: urban. 1 building on campus. Approved or accredited by Middle States Association of Colleges and Schools, New York State Board of Regents, and New York Department of Education. Total enrollment: 53. Upper school average class size: 4. Upper school faculty-student ratio: 1:4. There are 160 required school days per year for Upper School students. Upper School students typically attend 5 days per week. The average school day consists of 6 hours and 30 minutes.

Upper School Student Profile Grade 9: 10 students (4 boys, 6 girls); Grade 10: 11 students (4 boys, 7 girls); Grade 11: 9 students (4 boys, 5 girls); Grade 12: 13 students (5 boys, 8 girls).

Faculty School total: 14. In upper school: 5 men, 9 women; all have advanced degrees.

Subjects Offered Algebra, American history, art, biology, chemistry, computer skills, earth science, English, environmental science, European history, film, French, geometry, lab science, life science, physical science, physics, pre-calculus, Spanish, trigonometry, U.S. government, U.S. history, world history.

Graduation Requirements Algebra, American history, art, biology, chemistry, conceptual physics, earth science, English, environmental science, European history, geometry, government, health education, languages, physical education (includes health), physical science, pre-algebra, pre-calculus, trigonometry, world history, community service/20 hours per year.

Special Academic Programs Accelerated programs; independent study; study at local college for college credit; remedial reading and/or remedial writing; remedial math; special instructional classes for peer mediation, socialization, and motivational issues.

College Admission Counseling 14 students graduated in 2011; all went to college, including Fashion Institute of Technology; Fordham University; John Jay College of Criminal Justice of the City University of New York; Landmark College; State University of New York at New Paltz; Syracuse University. Median SAT critical reading: 600, median SAT math: 620, median SAT writing: 620, median combined SAT: 600. 50% scored over 600 on SAT critical reading, 40% scored over 600 on SAT math, 50% scored over 600 on SAT writing, 45% scored over 1800 on combined SAT, 60% scored over 26 on composite ACT.

Student Life Upper grades have student council, honor system. Discipline rests primarily with faculty.

Summer Programs Remediation, enrichment, advancement, computer instruction programs offered; session focuses on academic courses for enrichment, remediation, or credit; held both on and off campus; held at local colleges; accepts boys and girls; open to students from other schools. 25 students usually enrolled. 2012 schedule: June 18 to August 21. Application deadline: June 1.

Tuition and Aid Day student tuition: $31,000–$44,000. Tuition installment plan (monthly payment plans, individually arranged payment plans, quarterly payment plan). Tuition reduction for siblings available. In 2011–12, 10% of upper-school students received aid. Total amount of financial aid awarded in 2011–12: $30,000.

Admissions Traditional secondary-level entrance grade is 9. For fall 2011, 45 students applied for upper-level admission, 28 were accepted, 22 enrolled. Comprehensive educational evaluation, psychoeducational evaluation, school placement exam, Wide Range Achievement Test or writing sample required. Deadline for receipt of application materials: none. Application fee required: $50. On-campus interview required.

Athletics Coed Interscholastic: basketball, dance, martial arts, physical fitness, running, volleyball, yoga. 2 PE instructors, 2 coaches.

Computers Computers are regularly used in English, history, research skills, writing, yearbook classes. Computer network features include Internet access, wireless campus network, Internet filtering or blocking technology, yearbook and monthly newsletter. Computer access in designated common areas is available to students. The school has a published electronic and media policy.
Contact Jennifer Sudary-Narine, Executive Assistant. 212-879-6317. Fax: 212-879-0962. E-mail: jsudary@smithschool.org. Web site: www.smithschool.org.

STERNE SCHOOL

2690 Jackson Street
San Francisco, California 94115

Head of School: Edward J. McManis

General Information Coeducational day college-preparatory, general academic, and vocational school; primarily serves underachievers, students with learning disabilities, individuals with Attention Deficit Disorder, and dyslexic students. Grades 6–12. Founded: 1976. Setting: urban. 1 building on campus. Approved or accredited by Western Association of Schools and Colleges and California Department of Education. Endowment: $900,000. Total enrollment: 43. Upper school average class size: 10. Upper school faculty-student ratio: 1:8. There are 176 required school days per year for Upper School students. Upper School students typically attend 5 days per week. The average school day consists of 7 hours.
Upper School Student Profile Grade 9: 7 students (5 boys, 2 girls); Grade 10: 7 students (5 boys, 2 girls); Grade 11: 5 students (3 boys, 2 girls); Grade 12: 4 students (2 boys, 2 girls).
Faculty School total: 11. In upper school: 4 men, 3 women; 5 have advanced degrees.
Subjects Offered Algebra, American history, American literature, art, biology, computer science, driver education, earth science, economics, English, English literature, environmental science, geography, geometry, government/civics, mathematics, physical education, science, social sciences, social studies, world history, world literature.
Graduation Requirements Computer science, English, mathematics, physical education (includes health), science, social sciences, social studies (includes history).
Special Academic Programs Remedial reading and/or remedial writing; remedial math; programs in English, mathematics, general development for dyslexic students.
College Admission Counseling 5 students graduated in 2010; 4 went to college, including Mitchell College. Other: 1 went to work.
Student Life Upper grades have uniform requirement, student council. Discipline rests primarily with faculty.
Tuition and Aid Day student tuition: $22,100. Tuition installment plan (individually arranged payment plans, TMS Tuition Management System). Need-based scholarship grants, Your Tuition Solution available. In 2010–11, 28% of upper-school students received aid. Total amount of financial aid awarded in 2010–11: $50,000.
Admissions Cognitive Abilities Test, Kaufman Test of Educational Achievement, Stanford Binet, Wechsler Individual Achievement Test, Wechsler Intelligence Scale for Children III or Woodcock-Johnson required. Deadline for receipt of application materials: none. No application fee required. On-campus interview required.
Athletics Interscholastic: basketball (boys, girls), cross-country running (b,g), soccer (b,g); intramural: basketball (b,g), swimming and diving (b,g), yoga (b,g); coed interscholastic: soccer; coed intramural: basketball, bowling, cooperative games, fitness, swimming and diving, tennis, volleyball, walking, yoga. 2 PE instructors.
Computers Computers are regularly used in all academic classes. Computer network features include online commercial services, Internet access, Internet filtering or blocking technology, Photoshop, assistive technology. Student e-mail accounts and computer access in designated common areas are available to students. The school has a published electronic and media policy.
Contact Edward McManis, Head of School. 415-922-6081 Ext. 21. Fax: 415-922-1598. E-mail: emcmanis@sterneschool.org. Web site: www.sterneschool.org.

STONE MOUNTAIN SCHOOL

126 Camp Elliott Road
Black Mountain, North Carolina 28711

Head of School: Susan Hardy

General Information Boys' boarding arts and vocational school; primarily serves underachievers, students with learning disabilities, individuals with Attention Deficit Disorder, individuals with emotional and behavioral problems, dyslexic students, NLD, and Asperger's Syndrome. Grades 6–12. Founded: 1990. Setting: rural. Nearest major city is Asheville. Students are housed in single-sex dormitories. 100-acre campus. 19 buildings on campus. Approved or accredited by CITA (Commission on International and Trans-Regional Accreditation), North Carolina Department of Exceptional Children, Southern Association of Colleges and Schools, and North Carolina Department of Education. Total enrollment: 58. Upper school average class size: 5. Upper school faculty-student ratio: 1:4. There are 180 required school days per year for Upper School students. Upper School students typically attend 4 days per week.
Upper School Student Profile Grade 9: 17 students (17 boys); Grade 10: 14 students (14 boys); Grade 11: 6 students (6 boys); Grade 12: 2 students (2 boys). 100% of students are boarding students. 10% are state residents. 24 states are represented in upper school student body. 3% are international students. International students from Canada; 3 other countries represented in student body.
Faculty School total: 11. In upper school: 8 men, 3 women; 3 have advanced degrees; all reside on campus.
Subjects Offered 1 1/2 elective credits, algebra, art, biology, earth science, English, geography, geometry, government/civics, history, keyboarding, mathematics, natural resources management, physical education, physical science, pre-algebra, science, social studies, Spanish, U.S. history, world history.
Graduation Requirements English, mathematics, physical education (includes health), science, social studies (includes history).
Special Academic Programs International Baccalaureate program; academic accommodation for the gifted; remedial reading and/or remedial writing; remedial math; programs in English, mathematics, general development for dyslexic students; special instructional classes for Orten Gillingham instruction.
College Admission Counseling 3 students graduated in 2010; 2 went to college. Other: 1 went to work.
Student Life Upper grades have specified standards of dress, student council. Discipline rests primarily with faculty.
Tuition and Aid 7-day tuition and room/board: $84,600. Guaranteed tuition plan. Tuition installment plan (monthly payment plans). Need-based loans, middle-income loans available. In 2010–11, 13% of upper-school students received aid. Total amount of financial aid awarded in 2010–11: $80,000.
Admissions Traditional secondary-level entrance grade is 9. Achievement tests or Wechsler Intelligence Scale for Children III required. Deadline for receipt of application materials: none. Application fee required: $3500. Interview recommended.
Athletics Interscholastic: backpacking, canoeing/kayaking, climbing, fishing, fly fishing, Frisbee, hiking/backpacking, kayaking, martial arts, mountaineering, outdoor activities, outdoor adventure, outdoor skills, paddling, physical fitness, rafting, rappelling, rock climbing, ropes courses, skiing (downhill), snowboarding, soccer, swimming and diving, ultimate Frisbee, volleyball, wall climbing, weight lifting, wilderness, wilderness survival; intramural: baseball, basketball, bicycling, billiards, crew, football, paddle tennis, sailing, skiing (downhill), soccer, swimming and diving, table tennis, track and field, volleyball. 5 coaches.
Computers Computer network features include Internet access, wireless campus network, Internet filtering or blocking technology. Student e-mail accounts are available to students. The school has a published electronic and media policy.
Contact Shannon Wheat, Admissions Director. 828-669-8639. Fax: 888-218-5262. E-mail: swheat@stonemountainschool.com. Web site: www.stonemountainschool.com.

SUNHAWK ADOLESCENT RECOVERY CENTER

948 North 1300 West
St. George, Utah 84770

Head of School: Mr. Benjamin G. Harris

General Information Coeducational boarding college-preparatory and arts school; primarily serves underachievers, students with learning disabilities, individuals with Attention Deficit Disorder, dyslexic students, and drug and alcohol involvement. Grades 8–12. Founded: 1996. Setting: suburban. Nearest major city is Las Vegas, NV. Students are housed in single-sex dormitories. 3-acre campus. 1 building on campus. Approved or accredited by Northwest Accreditation Commission and Utah Department of Education. Total enrollment: 52. Upper school average class size: 10. Upper school faculty-student ratio: 1:7. Upper School students typically attend 6 days per week. The average school day consists of 6 hours.
Upper School Student Profile Grade 8: 2 students (1 boy, 1 girl); Grade 9: 3 students (2 boys, 1 girl); Grade 10: 5 students (3 boys, 2 girls); Grade 11: 17 students (12 boys, 5 girls); Grade 12: 22 students (15 boys, 7 girls). 100% of students are boarding students. 3% are state residents. 15 states are represented in upper school student body. 1% are international students. International students from Canada.
Faculty School total: 7. In upper school: 5 men, 2 women; 6 have advanced degrees.
Subjects Offered Algebra, American government, art, biology, calculus, chemistry, earth science, economics, fine arts, geometry, language arts, physical science, physics, U.S. history, visual arts, world civilizations, world geography.
Special Academic Programs Accelerated programs; independent study; academic accommodation for the gifted and the artistically talented; remedial reading and/or remedial writing; remedial math.
College Admission Counseling 56 students graduated in 2010; 12 went to college, including Hofstra University; Linn-Benton Community College; Mitchell College; Northern Illinois University. Other: 2 entered military service, 12 entered a postgraduate year. Median composite ACT: 23. 1% scored over 26 on composite ACT.
Student Life Upper grades have uniform requirement, student council. Discipline rests equally with students and faculty.
Tuition and Aid 7-day tuition and room/board: $225. Tuition installment plan (individually arranged payment plans, Clark Custom Loans).
Admissions Traditional secondary-level entrance grade is 10. Iowa Tests of Basic Skills required. Deadline for receipt of application materials: none. No application fee required. Interview required.
Athletics Coed Intramural: baseball, basketball, flag football, Frisbee, kickball, martial arts, outdoor activities, outdoor adventure, outdoor recreation, ropes courses, snowboarding, soccer, softball, volleyball. 1 PE instructor.

Computers Computer resources include on-campus library services, Internet filtering or blocking technology. Students grades are available online.

Contact Mr. Jeff Johnson, Admissions Director. 435-705-9989 Ext. 235. Fax: 435-656-3213. E-mail: jjohnson@sunhawkrecovery.com. Web site: www.sunhawkrecovery.com.

TURNING WINDS ACADEMIC INSTITUTE

6885 Bauman Street
Bonners Ferry, Idaho 83805

Head of School: Gordon Newell

General Information Coeducational boarding college-preparatory, religious studies, bilingual studies, and technology school; primarily serves individuals with Attention Deficit Disorder and individuals with emotional and behavioral problems. Founded: 2002. Setting: rural. Nearest major city is Troy, MT. Students are housed in single-sex dormitories. 149-acre campus. 4 buildings on campus. Approved or accredited by National Independent Private Schools Association and Northwest Accreditation Commission. Upper school average class size: 15. Upper school faculty-student ratio: 1:2. There are 260 required school days per year for Upper School students. Upper School students typically attend 5 days per week. The average school day consists of 6 hours.

Upper School Student Profile 100% of students are boarding students. 10% are state residents. 35 states are represented in upper school student body. 5% are international students.

Faculty In upper school: 3 men, 3 women.

Subjects Offered ACT preparation, advanced biology, advanced chemistry, advanced math, Advanced Placement courses, algebra, art and culture, biology, calculus, chemistry, Christian scripture, classical studies, college planning, computer science, fitness, gardening, geography, geology, geometry, health, history, honors English, mathematics, music appreciation, nutrition, physics, poetry, political science, pre-algebra, pre-calculus, pre-college orientation, psychology, radio broadcasting, Russian, SAT/ACT preparation, stock market, theater.

Student Life Upper grades have specified standards of dress, honor system. Discipline rests primarily with faculty.

Tuition and Aid Tuition installment plan (individually arranged payment plans, Quarterly payments are required). Financial aid available to upper-school students. In 2010–11, 10% of upper-school students received aid.

Admissions Deadline for receipt of application materials: none. Application fee required: $495.

Athletics 4 PE instructors.

Computers Computer network features include on-campus library services, Internet access. Campus intranet is available to students. Students grades are available online.

Contact Joyce Drush, Office Manager. 208-267-1500. Fax: 208-267-1600. E-mail: info@fsni.org. Web site: www.turningwinds.com.

VALLEY VIEW SCHOOL

91 Oakham Road
PO Box 338
North Brookfield, Massachusetts 01535

Head of School: Dr. Philip G. Spiva

General Information Boys' boarding college-preparatory, general academic, arts, and vocational school; primarily serves underachievers, students with learning disabilities, individuals with Attention Deficit Disorder, individuals with emotional and behavioral problems, and difficulty socially adjusting to family and surroundings. Grades 5–12. Founded: 1970. Setting: rural. Nearest major city is Worcester. Students are housed in single-sex dormitories. 215-acre campus. 9 buildings on campus. Approved or accredited by Massachusetts Office of Child Care Services. Endowment: $530,000. Total enrollment: 56. Upper school average class size: 6. Upper school faculty-student ratio: 1:6. Upper School students typically attend 5 days per week.

Upper School Student Profile 100% of students are boarding students. 15% are state residents. 25 states are represented in upper school student body. 15% are international students. International students from Canada, France, Kenya, and Mexico; 2 other countries represented in student body.

Faculty School total: 11. In upper school: 5 men, 4 women; 4 have advanced degrees; 3 reside on campus.

Subjects Offered Algebra, American literature, anatomy, art, biology, chemistry, civics, composition, computer math, computer science, creative writing, drama, drama performance, drama workshop, dramatic arts, drawing, drawing and design, driver education, earth and space science, earth science, Eastern world civilizations, ecology, environmental systems, economics, economics and history, economics-AP, electronics, English, English composition, English language and composition-AP, English language-AP, English literature, English literature and composition-AP, English literature-AP, English-AP, English/composition-AP, environmental education, environmental geography, environmental science, environmental science-AP, epic literature, ethics and responsibility, ethnic studies, European history, European history-AP, general science, geography, geometry, government, grammar, health, history, life science, literature, mathematics, music, physical education, physical science, science, social studies, Spanish, study skills, theater, U.S. history, Western civilization, world history, world literature, writing, zoology.

Graduation Requirements English, mathematics, physical education (includes health), science, social studies (includes history).

Special Academic Programs Remedial reading and/or remedial writing; remedial math.

College Admission Counseling 1 student graduated in 2011.

Student Life Upper grades have specified standards of dress, student council, honor system. Discipline rests primarily with faculty.

Tuition and Aid 7-day tuition and room/board: $65,900. Tuition installment plan (quarterly payment plan).

Admissions Academic Profile Tests required. Deadline for receipt of application materials: none. No application fee required. On-campus interview required.

Athletics Interscholastic: basketball, cross-country running, golf, lacrosse, soccer, softball, tennis, ultimate Frisbee; intramural: alpine skiing, archery, backpacking, baseball, basketball, bicycling, billiards, blading, bowling, canoeing/kayaking, climbing, fishing, fitness, flag football, floor hockey, Frisbee, golf, hiking/backpacking, ice skating, in-line skating, mountain biking, outdoor recreation, riflery, rock climbing, roller blading, skateboarding, skiing (cross-country), skiing (downhill), snowboarding, softball, street hockey, swimming and diving, table tennis, touch football, ultimate Frisbee, volleyball, wall climbing, weight lifting, whiffle ball. 2 PE instructors.

Computers Computers are regularly used in English, mathematics, science classes. Computer network features include Internet access. Student e-mail accounts are available to students.

Contact Dr. Philip G. Spiva, Director. 508-867-6505. Fax: 508-867-3300. E-mail: valview@aol.com. Web site: www.valleyviewschool.org.

THE VANGUARD SCHOOL

22000 Highway 27
Lake Wales, Florida 33859-6858

Head of School: Dr. Cathy Wooley-Brown, PhD

General Information Coeducational boarding and day and distance learning college-preparatory and general academic school; primarily serves underachievers, students with learning disabilities, individuals with Attention Deficit Disorder, dyslexic students, non-verbal learning disabilities, and higher functioning Asperger's Syndrome. Grades 5–PG. Distance learning grades 9–PG. Founded: 1966. Setting: small town. Nearest major city is Orlando. Students are housed in single-sex by floor dormitories, coed dormitories, and single-sex dormitories. 75-acre campus. 13 buildings on campus. Approved or accredited by Florida Council of Independent Schools, Southern Association of Colleges and Schools, The Association of Boarding Schools, and Florida Department of Education. Member of National Association of Independent Schools and Secondary School Admission Test Board. Endowment: $3.8 million. Total enrollment: 109. Upper school average class size: 7. Upper school faculty-student ratio: 1:7. There are 180 required school days per year for Upper School students. Upper School students typically attend 5 days per week. The average school day consists of 7 hours and 15 minutes.

Upper School Student Profile Grade 9: 13 students (7 boys, 6 girls); Grade 10: 25 students (18 boys, 7 girls); Grade 11: 31 students (24 boys, 7 girls); Grade 12: 25 students (17 boys, 8 girls); Grade 13: 4 students (2 boys, 2 girls). 76% of students are boarding students. 34% are state residents. 22 states are represented in upper school student body. 38% are international students. International students from Bahamas, Belize, Bermuda, Jamaica, Puerto Rico, and United Arab Emirates; 18 other countries represented in student body.

Faculty School total: 20. In upper school: 6 men, 12 women; 6 have advanced degrees; 3 reside on campus.

Subjects Offered Algebra, American history, American legal systems, American literature, art, basic skills, biology, British literature, business mathematics, calculus-AP, chemistry, creative writing, culinary arts, driver education, economics, economics and history, English, English literature, environmental science, environmental studies, film and literature, fine arts, forensics, geometry, government, government/civics, grammar, history, industrial arts, journalism, language arts, life management skills, mathematics, music, photography, physical education, physical science, physics, pre-calculus, psychology, reading, science, sign language, social studies, Spanish, speech, study skills, television, world history, world literature, yearbook.

Graduation Requirements Arts and fine arts (art, music, dance, drama), biology, economics, English, government, life management skills, literature, mathematics, physical education (includes health), reading, science, social studies (includes history).

Special Academic Programs Honors section; accelerated programs; independent study; study at local college for college credit; academic accommodation for the gifted; remedial reading and/or remedial writing; remedial math; programs in English, mathematics, general development for dyslexic students; special instructional classes for deaf students.

College Admission Counseling 42 students graduated in 2010; 29 went to college, including Florida Gulf Coast University; Johnson & Wales University; Lynn University; Nova Southeastern University; Santa Fe College; Warren Wilson College. Other: 4 went to work, 1 entered military service, 3 entered a postgraduate year, 5 had other specific plans.

Student Life Upper grades have specified standards of dress, student council, honor system. Discipline rests equally with students and faculty.
Tuition and Aid Day student tuition: $22,500; 7-day tuition and room/board: $42,500. Tuition installment plan (monthly payment plans, individually arranged payment plans, Your Tuition Solution). Tuition reduction for siblings, merit scholarship grants, need-based scholarship grants, Presidential Scholarship (one per year) available. In 2010–11, 42% of upper-school students received aid; total upper-school merit-scholarship money awarded: $5000. Total amount of financial aid awarded in 2010–11: $500,800.
Admissions Traditional secondary-level entrance grade is 9. For fall 2010, 76 students applied for upper-level admission, 45 were accepted, 37 enrolled. Wechsler Intelligence Scale for Children required. Deadline for receipt of application materials: none. Application fee required: $100. Interview required.
Athletics Interscholastic: basketball (boys, girls), football (b), golf (b), running (b,g), soccer (b), tennis (b), track and field (b,g), volleyball (g), weight lifting (b); intramural: basketball (b,g), flag football (b,g), floor hockey (b,g); coed interscholastic: cheering, cross-country running, golf, soccer, tennis; coed intramural: basketball, broomball, canoeing/kayaking, fishing, fitness, fitness walking, golf, paint ball, physical fitness, scuba diving, skateboarding, soccer, walking, weight lifting, weight training, yoga. 5 coaches.
Computers Computers are regularly used in all classes. Computer resources include on-campus library services, online commercial services, Internet access, wireless campus network, Internet filtering or blocking technology. Computer access in designated common areas is available to students. Students grades are available online. The school has a published electronic and media policy.
Contact Melanie Anderson, Director of Admissions. 863-676-6091. Fax: 863-676-8297. E-mail: vanadmin@vanguardschool.org. Web site: www.vanguardschool.org.

WELLSPRING FOUNDATION

21 Arch Bridge Road
PO Box 370
Bethlehem, Connecticut 06751

Head of School: Harvey I. Newman

General Information Coeducational boarding and day college-preparatory and general academic school; primarily serves students with learning disabilities, individuals with Attention Deficit Disorder, individuals with emotional and behavioral problems, and depression, mood disorders, eating disorders, and bipolar disorder. Boarding boys grades 1–6, boarding girls grades 1–12, day boys grades 1–12, day girls grades 1–12. Founded: 1977. Setting: rural. Nearest major city is Litchfield. Students are housed in single-sex dormitories. 13-acre campus. 6 buildings on campus. Approved or accredited by Connecticut Department of Education. Candidate for accreditation by New England Association of Schools and Colleges. Total enrollment: 52. Upper school average class size: 6.
Faculty School total: 20.
Special Academic Programs Independent study.
Student Life Upper grades have specified standards of dress.
Summer Programs Enrichment programs offered; held on campus; accepts boys and girls; open to students from other schools. 36 students usually enrolled.
Admissions Deadline for receipt of application materials: none. No application fee required. On-campus interview required.
Computers Computer network features include Internet access, Internet filtering or blocking technology. Campus intranet is available to students. The school has a published electronic and media policy.
Contact Nancy Thurston. 203-266-8002. Fax: 203-266-8030. E-mail: nancy.thurston@wellspring.org. Web site: www.wellspring.org.

WESTMARK SCHOOL

5461 Louise Avenue
Encino, California 91316

Head of School: Muir Meredith

General Information Coeducational day college-preparatory, general academic, arts, and technology school; primarily serves students with learning disabilities, individuals with Attention Deficit Disorder, dyslexic students, and students with language-based learning disabilities. Grades 4–12. Founded: 1982. Setting: suburban. Nearest major city is Los Angeles. 4.6-acre campus. 6 buildings on campus. Approved or accredited by California Association of Independent Schools, Western Association of Schools and Colleges, and California Department of Education. Member of National Association of Independent Schools. Upper school average class size: 12. Upper school faculty-student ratio: 1:12.
Faculty School total: 50.
Subjects Offered Algebra, American history, American literature, anatomy, art, biology, career exploration, chemistry, community service, computer science, creative writing, drama, earth science, economics, English, environmental science, European history, fine arts, general science, geography, geometry, health, history, home economics, literature, mathematics, music, physical education, physical science, physics, physiology, science, sign language, social sciences, social studies, Spanish, theater, trigonometry, video, world history, writing.
Graduation Requirements Arts and fine arts (art, music, dance, drama), English, foreign language, mathematics, physical education (includes health), science, social sciences, social studies (includes history), educational career plan. Community service is required.
Special Academic Programs Independent study; study at local college for college credit; remedial reading and/or remedial writing; remedial math; programs in English, mathematics, general development for dyslexic students.
College Admission Counseling 19 students graduated in 2011; all went to college, including The University of Arizona; University of Colorado Boulder; Whittier College.
Student Life Upper grades have uniform requirement, student council, honor system. Discipline rests equally with students and faculty.
Summer Programs Remediation, enrichment, advancement, art/fine arts, computer instruction programs offered; session focuses on academic and social development; held on campus; accepts boys and girls; open to students from other schools. 40 students usually enrolled. 2012 schedule: July 7 to August 1. Application deadline: May 30.
Tuition and Aid Day student tuition: $31,000. Tuition installment plan (The Tuition Plan, individually arranged payment plans, Tuition Management Systems Plan). Need-based scholarship grants, sending district special education funding available.
Admissions Traditional secondary-level entrance grade is 9. Wechsler Intelligence Scale for Children III required. Deadline for receipt of application materials: none. Application fee required: $125. On-campus interview required.
Athletics Interscholastic: baseball (boys), basketball (b,g), cheering (b,g), equestrian sports (g), football (b,g), softball (g), volleyball (g); intramural: outdoor education (g); coed interscholastic: equestrian sports, flag football, golf, soccer, swimming and diving; coed intramural: basketball, outdoor education. 3 PE instructors, 6 coaches.
Computers Computers are regularly used in English, history, science classes. Computer network features include on-campus library services, Internet access.
Contact Polly Brophy, Director of Admissions. 818-986-5045 Ext. 306. Fax: 818-380-1377. Web site: www.westmarkschool.org.

WINSTON PREPARATORY SCHOOL

126 West 17th Street
New York, New York 10011

Head of School: Mr. William DeHaven

General Information Coeducational day college-preparatory, general academic, and arts school, primarily serves underachievers, students with learning disabilities, individuals with Attention Deficit Disorder, dyslexic students, and non-verbal learning difficulties. Grades 6–12. Founded: 1981. Setting: urban. 2 buildings on campus. Approved or accredited by New York State Association of Independent Schools. Member of National Association of Independent Schools. Total enrollment: 197. Upper school average class size: 11. Upper school faculty-student ratio: 1:3. There are 170 required school days per year for Upper School students. Upper School students typically attend 5 days per week. The average school day consists of 7 hours.
Faculty School total: 62. In upper school: 22 men, 40 women; 55 have advanced degrees.
Subjects Offered Algebra, American history, American literature, art, biology, community service, creative writing, drama, economics and history, English, English literature, European history, expository writing, fine arts, geography, geometry, grammar, health, history, mathematics, music, physical education, physics, science, social skills, social studies, speech, theater, trigonometry, U.S. history, world history, world literature, writing.
Graduation Requirements Art, English, history, mathematics, physical education (includes health), science.
Special Academic Programs Remedial reading and/or remedial writing; remedial math; programs in English, mathematics, general development for dyslexic students.
College Admission Counseling 39 students graduated in 2011; 30 went to college, including Adelphi University; Clark University; Keene State College; Mitchell College; Parsons The New School for Design; The University of Arizona. Other: 4 entered a postgraduate year, 5 had other specific plans.
Student Life Upper grades have student council. Discipline rests primarily with faculty.
Summer Programs Remediation, enrichment, art/fine arts programs offered; session focuses on emphasis on reading, writing, and math skill development as well as study skills; held on campus; accepts boys and girls; open to students from other schools. 30 students usually enrolled. 2012 schedule: June 30 to August 20. Application deadline: none.
Tuition and Aid Day student tuition: $49,000. Tuition installment plan (SMART Tuition Payment Plan, individually arranged payment plans). Need-based scholarship grants available. In 2011–12, 20% of upper-school students received aid. Total amount of financial aid awarded in 2011–12: $500,000.
Admissions Achievement tests, battery of testing done through outside agency, Wechsler Intelligence Scale for Children and writing sample required. Deadline for receipt of application materials: none. Application fee required: $70. On-campus interview required.

Athletics Interscholastic: basketball (boys, girls); intramural: boxing (b,g); coed interscholastic: cross-country running, golf, soccer, softball, track and field; coed intramural: judo, outdoor education, physical fitness, physical training, sailing, strength & conditioning, weight training, yoga. 3 PE instructors, 3 coaches.
Computers Computers are regularly used in art, English, history, mathematics, science, writing classes. Computer network features include Internet access, wireless campus network, Internet filtering or blocking technology. The school has a published electronic and media policy.
Contact Ms. Medry Rodriguez, Assistant to Director of Admissions. 646-638-2705 Ext. 619. Fax: 646-839-5457. E-mail: mrodriguez@winstonprep.edu. Web site: www.winstonprep.edu.

THE WINSTON SCHOOL SAN ANTONIO

8565 Ewing Halsell Drive
San Antonio, Texas 78229

Head of School: Dr. Charles J. Karulak

General Information Coeducational day college-preparatory, general academic, arts, and technology school; primarily serves students with learning disabilities, individuals with Attention Deficit Disorder, and dyslexic students. Grades K–12. Founded: 1985. Setting: urban. 16-acre campus. 2 buildings on campus. Approved or accredited by Independent Schools Association of the Southwest, Southern Association of Colleges and Schools, and Texas Education Agency. Total enrollment: 185. Upper school average class size: 10. Upper school faculty-student ratio: 1:8. There are 174 required school days per year for Upper School students. Upper School students typically attend 5 days per week. The average school day consists of 7 hours and 5 minutes.
Upper School Student Profile Grade 9: 19 students (13 boys, 6 girls); Grade 10: 23 students (16 boys, 7 girls); Grade 11: 26 students (13 boys, 13 girls); Grade 12: 15 students (14 boys, 1 girl).
Faculty School total: 29. In upper school: 7 men, 9 women; 7 have advanced degrees.
Subjects Offered Algebra, American history, American literature, anatomy and physiology, art, athletics, basketball, biology, calculus, cheerleading, chemistry, college counseling, college planning, community service, computer graphics, computer literacy, computer multimedia, drama, economics, English, English composition, English literature, environmental science, geography, geometry, government, graphic design, health, health education, journalism, mathematical modeling, multimedia, music, photography, physical education, physical science, physics, pre-calculus, reading, Spanish, speech, student publications, world geography, world history, yearbook.
Graduation Requirements Arts and fine arts (art, music, dance, drama), computer science, English, foreign language, history, mathematics, physical education (includes health), science, social sciences, 20 hours of community service per year.
Special Academic Programs Independent study; study at local college for college credit; remedial reading and/or remedial writing; programs in English, mathematics, general development for dyslexic students.
College Admission Counseling 21 students graduated in 2011; 17 went to college, including Concordia University Texas; Johnson & Wales University; San Antonio College; St. Mary's University; The University of Texas at San Antonio; University of the Incarnate Word. Other: 4 went to work.
Student Life Upper grades have uniform requirement, student council, honor system. Discipline rests primarily with faculty.
Summer Programs Remediation, advancement, sports, computer instruction programs offered; session focuses on high school classes for credit; held on campus; accepts boys and girls; open to students from other schools. 50 students usually enrolled. 2012 schedule: June 11 to July 6. Application deadline: May 30.
Tuition and Aid Day student tuition: $15,500. Tuition installment plan (monthly payment plans, individually arranged payment plans). Need-based scholarship grants available. In 2011–12, 25% of upper-school students received aid.
Admissions Traditional secondary-level entrance grade is 9. For fall 2011, 13 students applied for upper-level admission, 12 were accepted, 11 enrolled. Achievement tests, battery of testing done through outside agency, comprehensive educational evaluation, Individual IQ, Individual IQ, Achievement and behavior rating scale, psychoeducational evaluation, Wechsler Individual Achievement Test, Wechsler Intelligence Scale for Children, Wide Range Achievement Test or WISC or WAIS required. Deadline for receipt of application materials: none. Application fee required: $100. On-campus interview required.
Athletics Interscholastic: baseball (boys), basketball (b,g), cheering (g), football (b), softball (g), volleyball (g); intramural: strength & conditioning (b); coed interscholastic: cross-country running, golf, track and field; coed intramural: cheering, golf, outdoor education, physical fitness, physical training, tennis, track and field. 2 PE instructors.
Computers Computers are regularly used in all academic classes. Computer network features include on-campus library services, online commercial services, Internet access, wireless campus network, Internet filtering or blocking technology. Campus intranet is available to students. Students grades are available online. The school has a published electronic and media policy.
Contact Ms. Julie A. Saboe, Director of Admissions. 210-615-6544. Fax: 210-615-6627. E-mail: saboe@winston-sa.org. Web site: www.winston-sa.org.

Special Needs Schools Close-Ups

LANDMARK SCHOOL

Prides Crossing, Massachusetts

Type: Coeducational boarding and day college-preparatory and general academic school for students with language-based learning disabilities, such as dyslexia
Grades: Grades 2–12
Enrollment: 451
Head of School: Robert J. Broudo, M.Ed.

THE SCHOOL

Landmark School was founded in 1971 by Dr. Charles "Chad" Drake with the goal of educating students whose reading, writing, spelling, and mathematical skills did not match their thinking and problem-solving capacities. Most call these children dyslexic or learning disabled. Chad saw their promise, and called them bright and capable. Landmark opened its doors with 40 students and a small group of teachers on one campus in Prides Crossing, Massachusetts. Since then, Landmark has grown to 450 students on two North Shore campuses and a faculty and staff of more than 300. Today Landmark is recognized as a leader in the field of language-based learning disabilities.

Landmark is a coeducational boarding and day school offering a full range of customized programs for students in grades 2 to 12. With a college-preparatory high school, a middle school, and an elementary school, Landmark is one of the most comprehensive schools serving students with language-based learning disabilities in the United States. Landmark personalizes instruction for each student, emphasizing the development of language and learning skills, and cultivates a uniquely supportive and structured living and learning environment.

Landmark offers day and residential programs and enrolls students from across the United States and around the world. The School accepts bright students who have been diagnosed with a language-based learning disability, such as dyslexia. Successful candidates should be emotionally healthy and motivated to learn but need remedial help with reading, writing, spelling, listening, and speaking, as well as mathematics.

Landmark teachers are committed to the success of every student. The faculty is at the core of the School's innovative, effective program of remediation. Landmark's teaching principles and practices are based on forty years of front-line experience. Practical, classroom-tested methods are influenced by the latest research on human intelligence, cognitive development, and learning disabilities.

With a 1:3 teacher-student ratio, teaching at Landmark is concentrated and dynamic. Teachers, tutors, and case managers meet and share information about students every morning. The entire team is focused on the progress of each student.

Landmark School is located on Boston's North Shore, overlooking the ocean, in an area rich in historic sites and recreational opportunities. The high school and administration offices are located in the Prides Crossing section of Beverly, Massachusetts, just 25 miles north of Boston. The elementary–middle school campus is 3 miles to the northeast, nestled in the woods on an estate in Manchester-by-the-Sea.

Landmark is a nonprofit, nonsectarian educational organization. It is governed by a 26-member Board of Trustees. The School's operating expenses for 2010–11 were $23 million. Contributions and grants totaled $2.577 million.

Landmark is accredited by the New England Association of Schools and Colleges. It is a member of the Massachusetts Association of 766 Approved Private Schools, the National Association of Independent Schools, and the Association of Independent Schools of New England and is approved as a school for children with language-based learning disabilities by the Division of Special Education of the State Department of Education in the Commonwealth of Massachusetts. It is licensed as a residential facility by the Massachusetts Office of Child Care Services.

ACADEMIC PROGRAMS

The key to Landmark's successful model is the daily one-to-one tutorial. Students meet and work closely with one tutor for the entire year. A personalized tutorial curriculum is designed to remediate specific language needs, which may encompass decoding, fluency, phonological awareness, written composition, and organizational skills. The tutorial has a distinct curriculum and provides a personal connection between the student and teacher.

At Landmark high school, preparation for college and beyond is the goal of the program. Focus is placed on skill acquisition and achievement; a personalized program is designed for each student. The curriculum addresses the spectrum of student needs. Based on their unique abilities and skill levels, students are assigned to a schedule of courses.

The curriculum is designed to teach the students to become independent learners. Individual assessments are made continually to determine the appropriate approach of remediation.

Core subjects are math, social studies, science, language arts, oral expression, study skills, and electives. Computer technology is integrated across the entire curriculum.

For students who need intensive help with oral and written communication, Landmark offers courses in expressive language skills. Rigorous remediation is provided through an integrated curriculum to reinforce the relationship between listening, speaking, reading, and writing. Landmark teachers receive supervision from certified speech-language pathologists.

When a student progresses to within one year of grade level, their case manager may consider transitioning them to a more advanced level of course work. The pace is likely to be a bit faster and the classes slightly larger (8–12 students). For some students, the daily one-to-one tutorial is replaced by a study skills class. Mathematics is assigned based on skill level.

The elementary school program, for ages 7 to 10 (grades 2–5), is a self-contained model in which children are assigned to a small group of less than 8 students and matched with a key teacher for their academic day. Every child receives a daily individual language arts tutorial specifically attuned to diagnosed needs in the areas of reading, spelling, writing, and handwriting. The group stays together for the remaining classes: language arts, oral expression/literature, social studies, and science. Math classes are grouped separately according to each student's needs. Enrichment and elective offerings include arts and crafts, music, physical education, woodworking, computers, and small-engine repair.

The middle school program serves students ages 10–14 (grades 6–8), and each student receives a daily individual language arts tutorial as well as a schedule of small-group classes (4–8 students) consisting of language arts, math, science, social studies, auditory/oral expression, literature, and study skills. Computer competencies and keyboarding skills are incorporated into the class schedule, and electives (physical education, art, computer graphics, woodworking, and small-engine repair) complete the daily schedule.

FACULTY AND ADVISERS

Landmark employs 280 educational personnel made up of teaching faculty members, case managers, supervisors, and department heads. More than 65 percent hold advanced degrees.

In addition to teaching, staff members support the residential team after school hours and on weekends.

Through the Landmark School Outreach Program, faculty members present graduate courses and workshops at schools and conferences nationwide. Faculty members have published books on teaching study skills, writing, and mathematics. A professional development institute and lectures are presented each summer on the Landmark campus.

COLLEGE ADMISSION COUNSELING

Landmark's Guidance Department works with juniors and seniors. Counselors meet individually with seniors to help them select a successful path to the future and specifically work with preparing applications, interviewing, and completing the SAT, with accommodations as needed.

Over the past five years, the average rate of Landmark high school graduates attending two- or four-year colleges was 92 percent, which is 29 percent higher than the national average. Graduates from the class of 2011 were accepted to competitive colleges, including Northeastern, Ithaca, and Simmons.

STUDENT BODY AND CONDUCT

The 2011–12 student body has 451 students. The high school has 305 students; 142 day students (80 boys and 62 girls) and 163 boarding students (110 boys and 53 girls). The elementary–middle school has 146 day students. Students came from twenty-one states and seven other countries.

Approximately 19 percent of the students are members of a minority group.

Landmark provides a safe and positive environment for its students, teaching respect, honesty, and commitment. Programs are structured to help students acquire and improve academic and social skills. The Dean of Students and a Standards Committee composed of faculty and staff members address individual conduct issues as needed.

The Student Council, which is elected by all grade levels and includes dormitory representatives, helps plan community service activities, parties, dances, lectures, and trips.

ACADEMIC FACILITIES

Landmark's high school campus is located in an estate setting on 30 acres that overlook the Atlantic Ocean. The Alexander Academic Center contains a library containing 8,000 volumes, a newly renovated dining room, and a tutorial center. Classes are conducted in Governor's Landing Academic Center, Prep Building, Classroom Building, Computer Center, and Early Literacy Tutorial Center. Science labs, the health center, and a girls' dormitory are in Bain Hall. Performing arts, visual arts, woodshop/boat building, auto shop, the Alice Ansara Athletic Center, Collins Athletic Field, and Tot Spot Childcare Center are all located on the main campus.

Lopardo Center contains boys' living space and the student center. Student residences are Williston Hall and Woodside Hall (both girls' dorms), Porter House, and the Campus Cottage.

The elementary and middle school (EMS) campus has a main building with classrooms, a newly renovated dining hall, a meeting room, a library, and offices. Three additional buildings house the tutorial center, art center, woodworking shop, small-engine shop, gymnasium, and more classrooms.

BOARDING AND GENERAL FACILITIES

Landmark has a fully staffed Residential Life Program that provides a round-the-clock living and teaching environment. Students learn how to manage their schoolwork; support their friends and roommates; and enjoy a wide range of planned activities, outings, and social events. The program incorporates a structured-level-based system that gives students the opportunity to earn privileges as they demonstrate their developing abilities in time management, organization, and peer mediation and to consistently manage their responsibilities.

ATHLETICS

Fitness, health, competition, and recreation are all part of Landmark's athletic program. Students are encouraged to stay active and healthy. Eighty percent of Landmark high school students participate in organized team sports, and 95 percent of Landmark coaches are teachers at Landmark. Landmark competes in the Eastern Independent League and the Independent Girls Conference.

Landmark offers varsity and junior varsity baseball, basketball, cross-country, golf, lacrosse, soccer, swimming, tennis, and wrestling. Intramural programs include basketball, dodgeball, floor hockey, and volleyball. Supervised recreational clubs and activities typically include downhill skiing, mountain biking, skateboarding, and weight training.

EXTRACURRICULAR OPPORTUNITIES

In addition to intramural sports, the School also offers student council, gay/straight alliance, auto mechanics, visual arts, and the performing arts. Support of the greater community is encouraged; Landmark students have completed thousands of community service hours to support local and national charities.

DAILY LIFE

Classes are held Monday through Friday from 8 a.m. to 2:50 p.m., with seven 45-minute classes. After-school activities are encouraged. On weeknights, high school boarding students are required to attend a supervised study hall.

WEEKEND LIFE

Landmark's Residential Life Program emphasizes responsibility, respect, and independence. Students enjoy a great range of planned activities, outings, and social events, including movies, cultural trips, and skiing. Home visits are arranged individually on request. Transportation to attend religious services is provided.

SUMMER PROGRAMS

Landmark's Summer Program offers academic skill development and exciting afternoon activities in a supportive environment for grades 1 to 12 (boarding 8 to 12). Landmark faculty members provide a personalized program designed to improve reading, writing, spelling, and composition skills for each student. Full- and half-day academic programs feature daily one-to-one tutorials and small classes that can be combined with recreational or hands-on activities that foster personal growth. Choices vary by grade and age but have included marine science, kayaking, adventure ropes, and practical arts such as woodworking and small engines. Admission criteria are similar to the academic year programs.

COSTS AND FINANCIAL AID

The 2011–12 tuition for the academic program for day students is $46,575 and $62,000 for boarding students. Enrollment deposits ranging from $6700 to $9000, depending on the program, are due on acceptance. Half of the balance of the tuition is due July 1, and the remainder by December 1. Parents have the option of a ten-month payment plan.

More than 50 percent of Landmark's students receive financial aid through various agencies, mainly local departments of education.

ADMISSIONS INFORMATION

Landmark programs are designed for students with average to above-average intellectual ability; well-developed thinking, problem-solving, and comprehension skills; difficulty decoding, spelling, and writing; difficulty processing language; and no apparent primary emotional, social, or behavioral issues. Prior to admission, Landmark must receive a diagnostic evaluation as well as educational and medical records.

APPLICATION TIMETABLE

Landmark accepts applications and admits students throughout the year as space permits. Early application for summer programs is recommended.

Students who meet admission criteria are invited to visit Landmark with at least one parent or guardian. The half-day visit includes an interview, individual testing, tour, discussion of test results, and a decision regarding acceptance.

A fee of $150 must accompany the application form.

ADMISSIONS CORRESPONDENCE

Carolyn Orsini Nelson, Director of Admission
Landmark School
P.O. Box 227
Prides Crossing, Massachusetts 01965-0227
Phone: 978-236-3000
Fax: 978-927-7268
E-mail: admission@landmarkschool.org
Web site: http://www.landmarkschool.org

MILL SPRINGS ACADEMY

Alpharetta, Georgia

Type: Coeducational college-preparatory day school for ADHD/LD students
Grades: 1–12
Enrollment: 305
Head of School: Robert. W. Moore, Headmaster

THE SCHOOL

Since 1981 Mill Springs Academy has been providing children with learning differences and/or ADHD an inviting and effective alternative to the traditional educational setting. Mill Springs is located on an 85-acre campus nestled in the beautiful rolling hills and pastureland of North Atlanta.

Mill Springs Academy is a values-based educational community dedicated to the academic, physical, and social growth of those students who have not realized their full potential in traditional classroom settings. The Academy's philosophy is summarized by its founder, Tweetie L. Moore: "If a student can't learn the way we teach...we should teach the way a student can learn."

Mill Springs Academy is a not-for-profit, 501c3 independent, college-preparatory, coeducational school for grades 1 through 12. Small classes are offered in a nurturing, structured environment that enhances instruction and each student's appreciation for learning. Mill Springs' unique program addresses the student's various needs, complemented by supportive services for parents that include consistent communication with professionals who are working with the individual student.

The Technology for Learning program is an important aspect of Mill Springs. The school was the first in the area to enact a one-to-one laptop program, beginning with Toshiba laptops in 1998. Today, students in grades 4 through 12 use Lenovo ThinkPad laptops to help bridge any gaps that may exist, allowing students to produce written work they are proud of, many for the first time. The student's laptops come equipped with several assistive technology programs that display and read student textbooks, fiction books, and teacher-created assignments. Students use their laptops and the Internet to expand available resources beyond the textbook; create innovative presentations and artwork; view grades, assignments, and teacher notes anytime, anyplace; and communicate with their teachers. Mill Springs has on-site technical and educational support to ensure that students' experiences with technology are as stress-free and productive as possible. Students in first through third grades begin with desktop computers to learn keyboarding skills. Microsoft Word, Excel, and PowerPoint are used by all students for organizing, writing, editing, and turning in assignments.

Mill Springs Academy offers a broad range of college preparatory and fine arts postsecondary options, along with college and fine arts placement support. One of the school's objectives is to help the student identify the tools and skills necessary for ongoing academic success, equivalent to his or her abilities across the spectrum of multiple intelligences. Typically more than 95 percent of Mill Springs graduates are accepted to a college.

Mill Springs Academy holds dual accreditation with the Southern Association of Independent Schools (SAIS) and Southern Association of Colleges and Schools (SACS). Mill Springs Academy is a member of the following organizations: Southern Association of Independent Schools (SAIS), Southern Association of Colleges and Schools (SACS), Georgia Association of Independent Schools (GISA), Atlanta Area Association of Independent Schools (AAAIS), National Association of Independent Schools (NAIS), International Dyslexia Association (IDA), Georgia Association of Private Schools for Exceptional Children (GAPSEC), Learning Disabilities Association of Georgia (LDGA), Atlanta Athletic Conference, and Association for Supervision and Curriculum Development (ASCD).

The Annual Fund is the most important gift the members of the school family (parents, grandparents, Board of Trustees, faculty/staff) are asked to make to Mill Springs each year.

Capital campaigns are held as needed to help fund capital development on the campus. Among other developments, previous capital campaigns have supported the addition of a permanent building for the Upper, Communication Arts and PreUpper Schools; the Student Activity Center (which houses the fine arts and physical education departments); the track; and baseball and soccer fields.

Both the Annual Fund and the periodic capital campaigns benefit the school, but in different ways. The Annual Fund provides resources by which Mill Springs lives, and capital campaigns provide resources by which Mill Springs grows.

ACADEMIC PROGRAMS

Mill Springs Academy provides a carefully structured environment within a warm, supportive atmosphere. Learning strategies are based upon Academic Plans, which are developed individually for each student by Mill Springs' multidisciplinary staff. Learning strategies are generated from psychoeducational evaluations, previous school records, diagnostic skills assessment, observations, and communication with other professionals involved with the student and the school's continuing experiences with the student. Mill Springs Academy is committed to a comprehensive program design that is multifaceted to meet the needs of each child. Conferences with parents are scheduled throughout the term and others are based on the immediate needs of the student as defined by the student, family, or school.

Mill Springs Academy divides the academic year into two semesters. The school has a 6:1 student to teacher ratio and classes average 8–12 students.

In the Lower School Program (grades 1–4) core academic subjects of reading, language arts, and math are taught in the morning between 8:30 and 11:30 a.m., when students are rested and can concentrate better. Morning classes include phonics, reading, spelling, written expression, comprehension, grammar, math computation and concepts, word-problem solving, and library skills. Higher interest subjects of science, social studies, computers, art, values, music, drama, and physical education are taught in the afternoon when attention may be decreasing. The afternoon classes involve less reading and are more discussion- and project-oriented.

The Middle School (grades 5–6) utilizes a modified block schedule. This approach involves three, 90-minute classes per day and allows for more intensive individual attention to the instructional needs of each student and more in-depth coverage of the class topics. The curriculum is challenging and the design is innovative and individualized, with a variety of approaches for presenting material and information, including focusing on the multiple intelligences and individual learning styles. Courses include reading, language arts, mathematics, science, U.S. history, world geography, technology, physical education, art, drama, Spanish, band, and chorus.

The PreUpper (grades 7–8), Upper (grades 9–12) and Communication Arts (grades 7–12) schools include a designed block schedule that involves three, 2-hour classes per day and allows for more intensive individual attention to the instructional needs of each students. The curriculum is challenging, with emphasis on college preparatory courses. Instruction includes a variety of approaches for presenting material and information, including focusing on individual learning styles.

FACULTY AND ADVISERS

There are 51 faculty members; 18 men and 33 women. Twenty-seven hold master's degrees, and one has earned a doctorate. All are members of the Council for Exceptional Children. Each faculty member assumes an advisory role to a small group of students in a morning and afternoon advisory class. The goal of this time period is to enhance communication and disseminate information. Advisers routinely call the parents of their students in order to keep them current with their student's progress.

COLLEGE ADMISSION COUNSELING

Mill Springs Academy has a college counselor that guides students to colleges that best meet their individual needs, goals, and interests. Freshmen and sophomores begin defining goals for college and are encouraged to select appropriate courses and extracurricular activities. All freshmen take the EXPLORE test and all sophomores take the PLAN test.

Juniors take the PSAT test in the fall and enroll in the Junior Transition class for spring semester in which they continue defining and clarifying goals for college. As they register for the ACT and SAT tests, the school psychometrist works individually with each student to arrange appropriate accommodations based on recommendations from psychoeducational evaluations.

Seniors enroll in the Senior Transition class where they are guided through the college application process, and plan college visits and interviews to colleges of their choice.

In recent years, Mill Springs Academy's graduates have been accepted to Auburn, Brigham Young, Clemson, Elon, Georgia, Georgia Tech, Georgia State, Kennesaw State, Miami (Florida), North Carolina, Savannah College of Art and Design, SMU, UCLA, and various other colleges throughout the United States.

STUDENT BODY AND CONDUCT

Mill Springs' population includes college-bound students with average to superior abilities who have been diagnosed with learning differences, dyslexia and/or attention deficit. The goal of Mill Springs Academy is to enable students to learn about and achieve mastery of themselves and the world around them. Students are encouraged to become enthusiastic independent, lifelong learners. Self-respect, self-discipline, and regard for others are engendered in an atmosphere of individual acceptance, respect, and commitment. Mill Springs offers a unique community and a school-wide, reality-based structure that clearly defines student responsibilities. This structure allows the student to make fully informed choices and to assume personal responsibility for those choices. Weekly meetings, which all students must attend, incorporate peer and faculty feedback. Students also participate in values groups focusing on character development.

ACADEMIC FACILITIES

The campus contains Lower School, Middle School, PreUpper School, and Communication Arts/Upper School buildings; a library; a gymnasium; three art studios; a theater; two music/drama classroom buildings; and technology and administration buildings. The entire campus is Wi-Fi accessible to accommodate the Technology for Learning program.

In addition to the academic facilities, Mill Springs Academy's 85-acre campus includes a track and field complex, soccer field, baseball field, tennis courts, lacrosse fields, a 1.7 mile cross-country trail, and a 5-kilometer cross-country course with multiple trail options.

ATHLETICS

Mill Springs Academy's athletics program plays a large role in building self-esteem; therefore, it is a vital part of student life. The school's indoor and outdoor facilities afford the perfect setting for a variety of organized competitive activities for boys and girls. Mill Springs operates under the belief that athletics are important to help develop an interest in an activity that will provide a lifelong positive experience. Athletics also help build skills such as teamwork, self-discipline, communication, and confidence, all of which promote a healthy lifestyle. Experienced and dedicated coaches work hard to promote a positive team atmosphere for the student-athletes. Mill Springs' athletes are students first, so study halls are incorporated and the academic progress is monitored to keep students current with their subjects. Competitive offerings for seventh through twelfth graders include varsity baseball, cross-country, girls' volleyball, soccer, JV/varsity girls' and boys' basketball, golf, tennis, track and field, swimming, lacrosse, and wrestling.

EXTRACURRICULAR OPPORTUNITIES

A variety of activities of after-school options are offered for Lower and Middle School students. Some of those activities have included archery, tennis, arts and crafts, golf, an explorers club, and weird science. These activities change seasonally and vary accordingly.

The Fine Arts Department includes 2 art teachers, a band director, a chorus/music teacher, one theater/drama teacher, and a technical director. This allows Mill Springs to offer a wide variety of courses for talented students in art, band, chorus, drama, and theater tech as a part of the curriculum. The Fine Arts Department shines with professionalism and creativity with every performance and event.

During two weeks in January, seventh through twelfth grade students participate in the Winter Learning Program instead of their regular class schedule. Various on-site learning and field trip opportunities are offered, so students can explore, discover, and enjoy new experiences. Previous Winter Learning sessions have included touring historic cities, a trip to Kenya, visiting New York for Broadway plays, college visits, SCUBA diving and ecology lessons, a Galapagos Islands trip, career exploration, a Marine Lab trip to Florida, a visit to the Grand Canyon, or various internships.

SUMMER PROGRAMS

Mark Trail Camp serves all students between the ages of 6 and 14 with an activity based program. There is a choice of morning, afternoon, or full-day activities.

The High School Summer Program serves rising ninth through twelfth graders who lack necessary credits or who choose to accelerate their progression through high school.

Sport camps are specific skills-development opportunities during the summer and are led by Mill Springs coaches. Basketball, soccer, wrestling, or volleyball camps may be some of the offerings available.

COSTS AND FINANCIAL AID

The tuition for the 2011–12 school year was $20,069 for Lower, Middle, PreUpper, and Upper Schools and $21,327 for the Communication Arts School. Mill Springs offers a ten-month tuition installment plan through FACTS. Financial aid is available based on need through the school and through a Student Scholarship Organization (SSO). In addition, Mill Springs Academy is an approved school for participation in the Georgia Special Needs Scholarship Program (SB10). Uniforms, student laptops, transportation and overnight field trips are additional expenses. Optional expenses include lunch, after school programs, and athletic fees.

ADMISSIONS INFORMATION

Mill Springs Academy admits qualified students of any sex, race, color, national or ethnic origin. The population includes students with average to superior abilities who have been diagnosed with learning differences, dyslexia, and/or attention deficit. Open houses are held throughout the year for prospective parents. Applications are available online at http://www.millsprings.org/Admissions. A current psychoeducational evaluation is required at the initial parent interview. Students are interviewed and receive a tour once their school records have been received by Mill Springs. Parents are notified of a student's acceptance by phone and a letter.

APPLICATION TIMETABLE

Mill Springs has a rolling admissions policy that allows students to be admitted throughout the year, depending on space and availability.

ADMISSIONS CORRESPONDENCE

Sheila FitzGerald, Admissions Director
Mill Springs Academy
13660 New Providence Road
Alpharetta, Georgia 30004
Phone: 770-360-1336
E-mail: sfitzgerald@millsprings.org
Web site: http://www.millsprings.org

Junior Boarding Schools

THE AMERICAN BOYCHOIR SCHOOL

19 Lambert Drive
Princeton, New Jersey 08540

Head of School: Ms. Lisa Eckstrom

General Information Boys' boarding and day college-preparatory, arts, choral music, and music theory and literacy school. Grades 4–8. Founded: 1937. Setting: small town. Students are housed in single-sex dormitories. 17-acre campus. 5 buildings on campus. Approved or accredited by Middle States Association of Colleges and Schools. Member of Secondary School Admission Test Board. Endowment: $4 million. Total enrollment: 51. Upper school average class size: 11. Upper school faculty-student ratio: 1:5. Upper School students typically attend 5 days per week. The average school day consists of 8 hours.

Student Profile Grade 6: 12 students (12 boys); Grade 7: 18 students (18 boys); Grade 8: 12 students (12 boys). 70% of students are boarding students. 60% are state residents. 13 states are represented in upper school student body. 8% are international students. International students from Republic of Korea, Switzerland, and Taiwan.

Faculty School total: 13. In upper school: 5 men, 7 women; 6 have advanced degrees; 4 reside on campus.

Subjects Offered Computer music, computer skills, English, general science, health, mathematics, music, music performance, music theory, music theory-AP, physical education, physical fitness, social studies, Spanish.

Graduation Requirements Algebra, applied music, character education, choir, choral music, concert choir, English, eurythmics (guard), eurythmy, general science, geography, mathematics, music, music appreciation, music composition, music performance, music technology, music theory, musicianship, physical education (includes health), piano, pre-algebra, social studies (includes history), Spanish, values and decisions, vocal music, voice, participation in the concert choir.

Special Academic Programs Academic accommodation for the musically talented.

Secondary School Placement 13 students graduated in 2011; they went to St. Paul's School; The Hotchkiss School; The Lawrenceville School; The Pennington School.

Student Life Uniform requirement, student council, honor system. Discipline rests equally with students and faculty.

Tuition and Aid Day student tuition: $23,300; 7-day tuition and room/board: $29,550. Tuition installment plan (individually arranged payment plans). Tuition reduction for siblings, need-based scholarship grants available. In 2011–12, 70% of students received aid. Total amount of financial aid awarded in 2011–12: $38,000.

Admissions For fall 2011, 26 students applied for admission, 22 were accepted, 13 enrolled. Audition or standardized test scores required. Deadline for receipt of application materials: none. No application fee required. On-campus interview required.

Athletics Intramural: baseball, basketball. 1 PE instructor.

Computers Computers are regularly used in English, history, mathematics, music, science classes. Computer resources include Internet access, wireless campus network, Internet filtering or blocking technology. Computer access in designated common areas is available to students. The school has a published electronic and media policy.

Contact Ms. Lori Hoffman, Admissions Associate. 609-924-5858 Ext. 34. Fax: 801-934-5858. E-mail: lhoffman@americanboychoir.org. Web site: www.americanboychoir.org.

ARTHUR MORGAN SCHOOL

60 AMS Circle
Burnsville, North Carolina 28714

Head of School: Michelle Rehfield

General Information Coeducational boarding and day college-preparatory, general academic, arts, service learning, and outdoor experiential learning school. Grades 7–9. Founded: 1962. Setting: rural. Nearest major city is Asheville. Students are housed in coed boarding homes. 100-acre campus. 7 buildings on campus. Approved or accredited by North Carolina Department of Non-Public Schools and North Carolina Department of Education. Member of Small Boarding School Association. Endowment: $1 million. Total enrollment: 22. Upper school average class size: 9. Upper school faculty-student ratio: 1:2. There are 180 required school days per year for Upper School students. Upper School students typically attend 5 days per week. The average school day consists of 8 hours.

Student Profile Grade 7: 7 students (4 boys, 3 girls); Grade 8: 10 students (4 boys, 6 girls); Grade 9: 5 students (3 boys, 2 girls). 75% of students are boarding students. 75% are state residents. 6 states are represented in upper school student body.

Faculty School total: 15. In upper school: 7 men, 8 women; 1 has an advanced degree; 14 reside on campus.

Subjects Offered 3-dimensional art, 3-dimensional design, acting, ADL skills, adolescent issues, African American history, African American studies, African history, agriculture, agroecology, algebra, alternative physical education, American culture, American government, American history, American literature, American minority experience, American studies, anatomy, ancient/medieval philosophy, animal behavior, animal husbandry, anthropology, art, arts and crafts, astronomy, athletics, audio visual/media, audition methods, auto mechanics, backpacking, baseball, biology, bookbinding, botany, career education, career education internship, carpentry, ceramics, character education, chemistry, civics, civil rights, clayworking, communication skills, community garden, community service, comparative cultures, comparative politics, composition, computer skills, computers, conflict resolution, conservation, constitutional history of U.S., consumer education, crafts, creative arts, creative dance, creative drama, creative thinking, creative writing, critical thinking, culinary arts, current events, dance, debate, decision making skills, democracy in America, design, drama, drama performance, dramatic arts, drawing, earth science, ecology, English, English composition, English literature, entrepreneurship, ethical decision making, ethics, ethics and responsibility, evolution, experiential education, expressive arts, fabric arts, family and consumer science, family living, family studies, fiber arts, first aid, fitness, food and nutrition, foreign language, forestry, gardening, gender issues, general science, geography, geology, geometry, global issues, global studies, grammar, guitar, health and wellness, health education, high adventure outdoor program, history, horticulture, human rights, human sexuality, humanities, independent living, integrated mathematics, interpersonal skills, jewelry making, journalism, language arts, leadership, leadership and service, life issues, mathematics, media studies, medieval/Renaissance history, meditation, mentorship program, metalworking, music, mythology, Native American studies, natural history, natural resources management, nature study, North Carolina history, oil painting, organic gardening, outdoor education, painting, peace and justice, peace education, peace studies, peer counseling, permaculture, personal growth, photo shop, photography, physical education, physics, piano, playwriting, poetry, politics, pottery, practical living, printmaking, probability and statistics, reading/study skills, relationships, sex education, shop, social justice, social sciences, social skills, social studies, socioeconomic problems, Spanish, sports, stained glass, study skills, swimming, travel, values and decisions, Vietnam War, visual and performing arts, visual arts, weaving, wilderness education, woodworking, work experience, writing, yearbook, yoga.

Graduation Requirements Annual 18-day field service learning trip, annual 3-, 6- and 8-day outdoor education trips.

Secondary School Placement 6 students graduated in 2010; they went to Carolina Friends School; George School; The Meeting School; Westtown School.

Student Life Honor system. Discipline rests primarily with faculty.

Tuition and Aid Day student tuition: $11,495; 5-day tuition and room/board: $21,945; 7-day tuition and room/board: $21,945. Tuition installment plan (40% by 8/15, 60% by Dec. 15; monthly payment 10% interest; full payment by 8/15- 2% discount). Need-based scholarship grants, individually negotiated barter arrangements may be made available. In 2010–11, 90% of students received aid. Total amount of financial aid awarded in 2010–11: $93,000.

Admissions Traditional entrance grade is 7. For fall 2010, 18 students applied for admission, 16 were accepted, 13 enrolled. Deadline for receipt of application materials: none. Application fee required: $35. On-campus interview required.

Athletics Coed Interscholastic: soccer; coed intramural: aquatics, backpacking, bicycling, billiards, blading, canoeing/kayaking, climbing, cooperative games, cross-country running, dance, fishing, Frisbee, hiking/backpacking, jogging, mountain biking, outdoor activities, rafting, running, skateboarding, soccer, swimming and diving, ultimate Frisbee, wilderness, winter walking, wrestling, yoga.

Computers Computers are regularly used in writing classes. Computer resources include supervised student access to computers for Web research, word processing, spreadsheet. Computer access in designated common areas is available to students.

Contact Meghan Lundy-Jones, Admissions Coordinator. 828-675-4361. Fax: 828-675-0003. E-mail: admissions@arthurmorganschool.org. Web site: www.arthurmorganschool.org.

THE BEMENT SCHOOL

94 Old Main Street
PO Box 8
Deerfield, Massachusetts 01342

Head of School: Mrs. Shelley Borror Jackson

General Information Coeducational boarding and day college-preparatory and arts school. Boarding grades 3–9, day grades K–9. Founded: 1925. Setting: small town. Nearest major city is Springfield. Students are housed in single-sex dormitories. 18-acre campus. 11 buildings on campus. Approved or accredited by Association of Independent Schools in New England, Junior Boarding Schools Association, and The Association of Boarding Schools. Member of National Association of Independent Schools and Secondary School Admission Test Board. Endowment: $4.4 million. Total enrollment: 246. Upper school average class size: 12. Upper school faculty-student ratio: 1:6. There are 163 required school days per year for Upper School students. Upper School students typically attend 5 days per week. The average school day consists of 8 hours and 30 minutes.

Student Profile Grade 6: 27 students (15 boys, 12 girls); Grade 7: 31 students (19 boys, 12 girls); Grade 8: 44 students (25 boys, 19 girls); Grade 9: 24 students (10 boys, 14 girls). 30% of students are boarding students. 80% are state residents. 8 states are represented in upper school student body. 21% are international students. International students from Bahamas, Brazil, China, Japan, Mexico, and Republic of Korea; 3 other countries represented in student body.

Faculty School total: 40. In upper school: 12 men, 12 women; 17 have advanced degrees; 10 reside on campus.

Subjects Offered Algebra, American history, art, art history, biology, chemistry, Chinese, community service, creative writing, dance, drama, earth science, English, English literature, fine arts, French, geography, geometry, grammar, health, history,

Latin, literature, mathematics, music, music history, physical education, physical science, physics, science, social studies, Spanish, theater, theater history, typing, world history, world literature, writing.
Graduation Requirements Algebra, American history, art history, arts and fine arts (art, music, dance, drama), athletics, drama, English, foreign language, health, mathematics, music history, physics, science, social studies (includes history). Community service is required.
Special Academic Programs Honors section; study abroad; special instructional classes for deaf students; ESL (12 students enrolled).
Secondary School Placement 24 students graduated in 2010; they went to Deerfield Academy; Kent School; Northfield Mount Hermon School; Suffield Academy; The Williston Northampton School.
Student Life Specified standards of dress. Discipline rests primarily with faculty.
Tuition and Aid Day student tuition: $19,395; 5-day tuition and room/board: $35,385; 7-day tuition and room/board: $42,740. Tuition installment plan (Academic Management Services Plan, monthly payment plans, individually arranged payment plans, 60%/40% payment plan). Need-based scholarship grants available. In 2010–11, 31% of students received aid.
Admissions Traditional entrance grade is 7. For fall 2010, 79 students applied for admission, 45 were accepted, 26 enrolled. SSAT or WISC III or Wechsler Intelligence Scale for Children required. Deadline for receipt of application materials: none. Application fee required: $50. On-campus interview required.
Athletics Interscholastic: alpine skiing (boys, girls), baseball (b), basketball (b,g), field hockey (g), lacrosse (b,g), skiing (downhill) (b,g), soccer (b,g), softball (g), swimming and diving (b,g), track and field (b,g); coed interscholastic: cross-country running, diving, golf, ice hockey, squash, ultimate Frisbee; coed intramural: aerobics/dance, ballet, dance, fitness walking, indoor soccer, jogging, martial arts, modern dance, nordic skiing, outdoor activities, outdoor education, physical fitness, skiing (cross-country), skiing (downhill), snowboarding, strength & conditioning, swimming and diving, table tennis, tennis. 3 coaches.
Computers Computers are regularly used in art, English, foreign language, history, mathematics, science classes. Computer resources include on-campus library services, Internet access. Computer access in designated common areas is available to students. The school has a published electronic and media policy.
Contact Ms. Kimberly Caldwell Loughlin, Director of Admission. 413-774-7061 Ext. 104. Fax: 413-774-7863. E-mail: admit@bement.org. Web site: www.bement.org/.

CARDIGAN MOUNTAIN SCHOOL

62 Alumni Drive
Canaan, New Hampshire 03741-9307

Head of School: Mr. David J. McCusker Jr.

General Information Boys' boarding and day college-preparatory, arts, and technology school. Grades 6–9. Founded: 1945. Setting: rural. Nearest major city is Manchester. Students are housed in single-sex dormitories. 525-acre campus. 18 buildings on campus. Approved or accredited by Association of Independent Schools in New England, Independent Schools of Northern New England, Junior Boarding Schools Association, New England Association of Schools and Colleges, The Association of Boarding Schools, and New Hampshire Department of Education. Member of National Association of Independent Schools and Secondary School Admission Test Board. Endowment: $13.2 million. Total enrollment: 195. Upper school average class size: 12. Upper school faculty-student ratio: 1:4. There are 165 required school days per year for Upper School students. Upper School students typically attend 6 days per week. The average school day consists of 4 hours.
Student Profile Grade 6: 18 students (18 boys); Grade 7: 38 students (38 boys); Grade 8: 89 students (89 boys); Grade 9: 50 students (50 boys). 89% of students are boarding students. 24% are state residents. 16 states are represented in upper school student body. 41% are international students. International students from Canada, China, Hong Kong, Japan, Mexico, and Republic of Korea; 4 other countries represented in student body.
Faculty School total: 45. In upper school: 35 men, 10 women; 20 have advanced degrees; 39 reside on campus.
Subjects Offered Algebra, American history, American literature, art, biology, ceramics, computer math, computer science, creative writing, drama, earth science, ecology, English, English literature, environmental science, ethics, European history, expository writing, fine arts, French, geography, geology, geometry, grammar, health, history, industrial arts, Latin, life skills, mathematics, music, physical science, reading, science, social studies, Spanish, speech, study skills, theater, trigonometry, typing, world history, world literature, writing.
Graduation Requirements Arts and fine arts (art, music, dance, drama), computer science, English, foreign language, mathematics, reading, science, social studies (includes history), study skills.
Special Academic Programs Honors section; independent study; academic accommodation for the gifted; remedial reading and/or remedial writing; remedial math; ESL (12 students enrolled).
Secondary School Placement 70 students graduated in 2010; they went to Avon Old Farms School; Berkshire School; Kent School; Salisbury School; St. Paul's School.
Student Life Specified standards of dress, student council, honor system. Discipline rests primarily with faculty.
Tuition and Aid Day student tuition: $25,600; 7-day tuition and room/board: $44,100. Tuition installment plan (The Tuition Plan, Insured Tuition Payment Plan, Academic Management Services Plan, Key Tuition Payment Plan, monthly payment plans). Need-based scholarship grants, need-based loans, prepGATE loans available. In 2010–11, 25% of students received aid. Total amount of financial aid awarded in 2010–11: $981,000.
Admissions For fall 2010, 220 students applied for admission, 155 were accepted, 80 enrolled. ISEE, SLEP for foreign students, SSAT or Wechsler Intelligence Scale for Children III required. Deadline for receipt of application materials: none. Application fee required: $50. Interview required.
Athletics Interscholastic: alpine skiing, baseball, basketball, cross-country running, football, freestyle skiing, ice hockey, independent competitive sports, lacrosse, mountain biking, nordic skiing, outdoor activities, physical training, rock climbing, running, sailing, skiing (cross-country), skiing (downhill), snowboarding, soccer, strength & conditioning, tennis, track and field, wall climbing, weight training, wrestling; intramural: archery, bicycling, bowling, boxing, climbing, equestrian sports, fitness, golf, ice hockey, martial arts, mountain biking, outdoor activities, physical training, riflery, rock climbing, ropes courses, sailing, skiing (downhill), snowboarding, swimming and diving, tennis, trap and skeet, weight lifting, whiffle ball. 1 coach, 1 athletic trainer.
Computers Computers are regularly used in English, history, mathematics, science, writing classes. Computer network features include on-campus library services, online commercial services, Internet access, wireless campus network, Internet filtering or blocking technology. Campus intranet, student e-mail accounts, and computer access in designated common areas are available to students. Students grades are available online. The school has a published electronic and media policy.
Contact Mrs. Jessica Bayreuther, Admissions Coordinator. 603-523-3548. Fax: 603-523-3565. E-mail: jebay@cardigan.org. Web site: www.cardigan.org.

EAGLEBROOK SCHOOL

Pine Nook Road
Deerfield, Massachusetts 01342

Head of School: Mr. Andrew C. Chase

General Information Boys' boarding and day college-preparatory, arts, and technology school. Grades 6–9. Founded: 1922. Setting: rural. Nearest major city is Springfield. Students are housed in single-sex dormitories. 750-acre campus. 26 buildings on campus. Approved or accredited by Association of Independent Schools in New England and The Association of Boarding Schools. Member of National Association of Independent Schools and Secondary School Admission Test Board. Endowment: $75 million. Total enrollment: 265. Upper school average class size: 10. Upper school faculty-student ratio: 1:4.
Student Profile Grade 6: 19 students (19 boys); Grade 7: 55 students (55 boys); Grade 8: 103 students (103 boys); Grade 9: 88 students (88 boys). 75% of students are boarding students. 35% are state residents. 28 states are represented in upper school student body. 25% are international students. International students from Bermuda, Hong Kong, Mexico, Republic of Korea, Taiwan, and Venezuela; 20 other countries represented in student body.
Faculty School total. 76. In upper school: 44 men, 24 women; 30 have advanced degrees; 50 reside on campus.
Subjects Offered Acting, African-American history, algebra, American studies, anthropology, architectural drawing, architecture, art, astronomy, band, batik, biology, ceramics, Chinese history, chorus, Civil War, civil war history, community service, computer art, computer science, computer-aided design, concert band, CPR, creative writing, current events, desktop publishing, digital music, digital photography, drafting, drama, drawing, drawing and design, earth science, ecology, English, English literature, environmental science, ESL, European history, expository writing, fine arts, first aid, French, general science, geography, geometry, grammar, health, history, industrial arts, instrumental music, journalism, keyboarding, Latin, mathematics, medieval history, music, newspaper, photography, physical education, pottery, pre-algebra, public speaking, publications, Russian history, science, sex education, social sciences, social studies, Spanish, study skills, swimming, theater, typing, U.S. history, Web site design, woodworking, world history, writing.
Graduation Requirements Arts and fine arts (art, music, dance, drama), English, foreign language, mathematics, physical education (includes health), science, social sciences, social studies (includes history). Community service is required.
Special Academic Programs Honors section; academic accommodation for the gifted, the musically talented, and the artistically talented; ESL (30 students enrolled).
Secondary School Placement 86 students graduated in 2011; they went to Choate Rosemary Hall; Deerfield Academy; Northfield Mount Hermon School; Phillips Exeter Academy; The Hotchkiss School; The Taft School.
Student Life Specified standards of dress, student council. Discipline rests primarily with faculty.
Summer Programs Enrichment, advancement, ESL, sports, art/fine arts, rigorous outdoor training, computer instruction programs offered; session focuses on enrichment; held on campus; accepts boys and girls; open to students from other schools. 60 students usually enrolled. 2012 schedule: July 2 to July 31. Application deadline: none.

Tuition and Aid Day student tuition: $30,600; 7-day tuition and room/board: $47,800. Tuition installment plan (individually arranged payment plans). Need-based scholarship grants available. In 2011–12, 30% of students received aid. Total amount of financial aid awarded in 2011–12: $1,650,000.

Admissions Wechsler Intelligence Scale for Children required. Deadline for receipt of application materials: none. Application fee required: $50. On-campus interview required.

Athletics Interscholastic: alpine skiing, aquatics, baseball, basketball, cross-country running, diving, football, Frisbee, golf, hiking/backpacking, hockey, ice hockey, ice skating, in-line hockey, indoor hockey, indoor soccer, lacrosse, mountain biking, outdoor activities, outdoor recreation, ski jumping, skiing (downhill), snowboarding, soccer, squash, strength & conditioning, swimming and diving, tennis, track and field, triathlon, ultimate Frisbee, water polo, wrestling; intramural: backpacking, bicycling, broomball, canoeing/kayaking, climbing, fishing, fitness, floor hockey, fly fishing, hiking/backpacking, hockey, ice hockey, ice skating, in-line hockey, in-line skating, indoor hockey, indoor soccer, juggling, kayaking, life saving, mountain biking, nordic skiing, outdoor activities, physical training, rafting, riflery, rock climbing, roller blading, roller hockey, roller skating, ropes courses, scuba diving, ski jumping, skiing (cross-country), street hockey, table tennis, volleyball, wallyball, weight lifting, weight training, wilderness survival. 1 athletic trainer.

Computers Computer network features include on-campus library services, Internet access, wireless campus network, Internet filtering or blocking technology. Student e-mail accounts are available to students. The school has a published electronic and media policy.

Contact Mr. Theodore J. Low, Director of Admission. 413-774-9111. Fax: 413-774-9119. E-mail: tlow@eaglebrook.org. Web site: www.eaglebrook.org.

See Display on this page and Close-Up on page 756.

FAY SCHOOL

48 Main Street
Southborough, Massachusetts 01772-9106

Head of School: Robert J. Gustavson

General Information Coeducational boarding and day college-preparatory, arts, and technology school. Boarding grades 7–9, day grades PK–9. Founded: 1866. Setting: small town. Nearest major city is Boston. Students are housed in single-sex dormitories. 66-acre campus. 26 buildings on campus. Approved or accredited by Association of Independent Schools in New England and Massachusetts Department of Education. Member of National Association of Independent Schools and Secondary School Admission Test Board. Endowment: $35 million. Total enrollment: 461. Upper school average class size: 12. Upper school faculty-student ratio: 1:8. There are 166 required school days per year for Upper School students. Upper School students typically attend 5 days per week. The average school day consists of 6 hours and 15 minutes.

Student Profile Grade 7: 71 students (35 boys, 36 girls); Grade 8: 90 students (43 boys, 47 girls); Grade 9: 49 students (28 boys, 21 girls). 54% of students are boarding students. 53% are state residents. 8 states are represented in upper school student body. 36% are international students. International students from China, Hong Kong, Mexico, Mexico, Republic of Korea, and Thailand; 11 other countries represented in student body.

Faculty School total: 77. In upper school: 21 men, 32 women; 35 have advanced degrees; 41 reside on campus.

Subjects Offered Algebra, American history, American literature, art, astronomy, biology, ceramics, computer science, creative writing, drama, English, English literature, environmental science, ethics, European history, expository writing, fine arts, French, geography, geometry, government/civics, grammar, Latin, Mandarin, mathematics, music, photography, physical education, science, social studies, Spanish, world history, writing.

Graduation Requirements Art, English, history, mathematics, music, science, technology.

Special Academic Programs Honors section; independent study; term-away projects; academic accommodation for the gifted, the musically talented, and the artistically talented; ESL (35 students enrolled).

Secondary School Placement 46 students graduated in 2011; they went to Choate Rosemary Hall; New Hampton School; Phillips Exeter Academy; Saint Mark's School; St. George's School; The Lawrenceville School.

Student Life Specified standards of dress, student council. Discipline rests primarily with faculty.

Summer Programs Enrichment, ESL, sports, art/fine arts, computer instruction programs offered; session focuses on ESL and Enrichment; held on campus; accepts boys and girls; open to students from other schools. 70 students usually enrolled. 2012 schedule: June 25 to August 3. Application deadline: April 1.

Tuition and Aid Day student tuition: $27,750–$28,750; 7-day tuition and room/board: $47,200–$55,800. Tuition installment plan (monthly payment plans, individually arranged payment plans). Need-based scholarship grants available. In 2011–12, 19% of students received aid. Total amount of financial aid awarded in 2011–12: $1,110,900.

Admissions Traditional entrance grade is 7. For fall 2011, 266 students applied for admission, 108 were accepted, 80 enrolled. Wechsler Intelligence Scale for Children required. Deadline for receipt of application materials: none. Application fee required: $50. Interview required.

Athletics Interscholastic: baseball (boys), basketball (b,g), cross-country running (b,g), field hockey (g), football (b), golf (b,g), hockey (b,g), ice hockey (b,g), independent competitive sports (b,g), lacrosse (b,g), soccer (b,g), softball (g), tennis (b,g), track and field (b,g), volleyball (g), wrestling (b); intramural: basketball (b,g), climbing (b,g), cooperative games (b,g), dance (b,g), fitness (b,g), golf (b,g), horseback riding (b,g), physical fitness (b,g), rock climbing (b,g), ropes courses (b,g), skiing (downhill) (b,g), snowboarding (b,g), soccer (b,g), strength & conditioning (b,g), tennis (b,g), trap and skeet (b,g), wall climbing (b,g), weight training (b,g), yoga (b,g); coed interscholastic: basketball, cross-country running, golf, hockey, ice hockey, independent competitive sports, lacrosse, soccer, tennis, track and field, volleyball; coed intramural: aerobics/Nautilus, alpine skiing, backpacking, basketball, bicycling, climbing, cooperative games, dance, fitness, golf, horseback riding, outdoor activities, outdoor adventure, outdoors, physical fitness, rock climbing, ropes courses, skiing (downhill), snowboarding, soccer, squash, strength & conditioning, tennis, trap and skeet, wall climbing, weight training, yoga. 2 PE instructors, 17 coaches, 1 athletic trainer.

Computers Computers are regularly used in art, English, foreign language, history, information technology, mathematics, music, science classes. Computer network features include on-campus library services, Internet access, wireless campus network, Internet filtering or blocking technology. Campus intranet, student e-mail accounts, and computer access in designated common areas are available to students. Students grades are available online. The school has a published electronic and media policy.

Contact Tarah Breed, Admission Associate. 508-490-8201. Fax: 508-481-7872. E-mail: tbreed@fayschool.org. Web site: www.fayschool.org.

See Display below, Close-Up on page 758, and Summer Program Close-Up on page 774.

THE FESSENDEN SCHOOL

250 Waltham Street
West Newton, Massachusetts 02465-1750

Head of School: Mr. David Stettler

General Information Boys' boarding and day college-preparatory, general academic, and arts school. Boarding grades 5–9, day grades K–9. Founded: 1903. Setting: suburban. Nearest major city is Boston. Students are housed in single-sex dormitories. 41-acre campus. 25 buildings on campus. Approved or accredited by Association of Independent Schools in New England, National Independent Private Schools Association, The Association of Boarding Schools, and Massachusetts Department of Education. Member of National Association of Independent Schools and Secondary School Admission Test Board. Endowment: $33 million. Total enrollment: 475. Upper school average class size: 12. Upper school faculty-student ratio: 1:7. There are 162 required school days per year for Upper School students. Upper School students typically attend 5 days per week. The average school day consists of 8 hours.

Student Profile Grade 7: 68 students (68 boys); Grade 8: 87 students (87 boys); Grade 9: 42 students (42 boys). 50% of students are boarding students. 70% are state residents. 17 states are represented in upper school student body. 19% are international students. International students from Bermuda, China, Mexico, Republic of Korea, Taiwan, and Thailand; 7 other countries represented in student body.

Faculty School total: 91. In upper school: 40 men, 51 women; 54 have advanced degrees; 43 reside on campus.

Subjects Offered Algebra, American history, American literature, anatomy, art, astronomy, biology, ceramics, chemistry, computer math, computer programming, computer science, creative writing, drama, earth science, English, English literature, European history, expository writing, fine arts, French, geography, geometry, government/civics, grammar, health, history, human sexuality, Latin, library studies, mathematics, music, photography, physical education, physics, science, social sciences, social studies, Spanish, theater, typing, world history, writing.

Graduation Requirements Arts and fine arts (art, music, dance, drama), computer science, English, foreign language, mathematics, science, social sciences, social studies (includes history).

Special Academic Programs Honors section; academic accommodation for the gifted, the musically talented, and the artistically talented; remedial reading and/or remedial writing; remedial math; ESL (14 students enrolled).

Secondary School Placement 49 students graduated in 2011; they went to Middlesex School; Milton Academy; Noble and Greenough School; Tabor Academy.

Student Life Specified standards of dress, student council, honor system. Discipline rests primarily with faculty.

Summer Programs ESL programs offered; held on campus; accepts boys and girls; open to students from other schools. 40 students usually enrolled. 2012 schedule: June 27 to July 31. Application deadline: none.

Tuition and Aid Day student tuition: $23,775–$33,750; 5-day tuition and room/board: $42,750–$43,600; 7-day tuition and room/board: $48,750–$49,600. Tuition installment plan (Academic Management Services Plan, monthly payment plans). Need-based scholarship grants available. In 2011–12, 74% of students received aid. Total amount of financial aid awarded in 2011–12: $1,043,947.

Admissions Traditional entrance grade is 7. For fall 2011, 84 students applied for admission, 43 were accepted, 34 enrolled. ISEE, SLEP for foreign students, SSAT, Wechsler Intelligence Scale for Children or writing sample required. Deadline for receipt of application materials: February 1. Application fee required: $50. On-campus interview required.

Athletics Interscholastic: baseball, basketball, cross-country running, football, ice hockey, lacrosse, soccer, squash, tennis, track and field, wrestling; intramural: alpine skiing, baseball, basketball, canoeing/kayaking, fencing, football, golf, ice hockey, mountain biking, racquetball, sailing, skiing (cross-country), skiing (downhill), snowboarding, soccer, strength & conditioning, swimming and diving, tennis, weight training. 3 PE instructors, 1 athletic trainer.

Computers Computers are regularly used in English, mathematics, science classes. Computer network features include on-campus library services, Internet access, Internet filtering or blocking technology. Campus intranet and student e-mail accounts are available to students. The school has a published electronic and media policy.

Contact Mr. Caleb Thomson, Director of Admissions. 617-630-2300. Fax: 617-630-2303. E-mail: admissions@fessenden.org. Web site: www.fessenden.org.

See Display below and Close-Up on page 760.

THE GREENWOOD SCHOOL

14 Greenwood Lane
Putney, Vermont 05346

Head of School: Mr. Stewart Miller

General Information Boys boarding and day arts, woodshop, and music school; primarily serves underachievers, students with learning disabilities, individuals with Attention Deficit Disorder, dyslexic students, and Executive Functioning Difficulties. Founded: 1978. Setting: rural. Nearest major city is Boston, MA. Students are housed in single-sex dormitories. 100-acre campus. 13 buildings on campus. Approved or accredited by Independent Schools of Northern New England, Junior Boarding Schools Association, National Association of Private Schools for Exceptional Children, New England Association of Schools and Colleges, The Association of Boarding Schools, and Vermont Department of Education. Member of National Association of Independent Schools. Endowment: $840,000. Total enrollment: 45. Upper school average class size: 5. Upper school faculty-student ratio: 1:2. There are 199 required school days per year for Upper School students. Upper School students typically attend 7 days per week. The average school day consists of 7 hours and 30 minutes.

Student Profile Grade 6: 3 students (3 boys); Grade 7: 6 students (6 boys); Grade 8: 10 students (10 boys); Grade 9: 18 students (18 boys); Grade 10: 8 students (8 boys). 93% of students are boarding students. 16% are state residents. 16 states are represented in upper school student body. 9% are international students. International students from Canada, Hong Kong, and Panama; 2 other countries represented in student body.

Faculty School total: 33. In upper school: 15 men, 14 women; 20 have advanced degrees; 15 reside on campus.

Subjects Offered American history, American literature, art, biology, crafts, creative writing, drama, earth science, ecology, English, geography, grammar, history, mathematics, music, physical education, pragmatics, speech, theater, woodworking, writing.

Special Academic Programs Academic accommodation for the gifted, the musically talented, and the artistically talented; remedial reading and/or remedial writing; remedial math; programs in English, mathematics, general development for dyslexic students; ESL.

Secondary School Placement 12 students graduated in 2011; they went to Dublin School; The Gow School.

Student Life Specified standards of dress, student council, honor system. Discipline rests primarily with faculty.

Tuition and Aid Day student tuition: $52,000; 7-day tuition and room/board: $65,870. Tuition installment plan (individually arranged payment plans). Need-based scholarship grants available. In 2011–12, 12% of students received aid. Total amount of financial aid awarded in 2011–12: $249,290.

Admissions Traditional entrance grade is 9. For fall 2011, 30 students applied for admission, 15 were accepted, 12 enrolled. Wechsler Intelligence Scale for Children III or Woodcock-Johnson Revised Achievement Test required. Deadline for receipt of application materials: none. Application fee required: $75. On-campus interview required.

Athletics Interscholastic: baseball, basketball, cross-country running, soccer, wrestling; intramural: alpine skiing, archery, backpacking, badminton, ball hockey, basketball, bicycling, billiards, canoeing/kayaking, climbing, cooperative games, cricket, equestrian sports, fishing, fitness, flag football, floor hockey, fly fishing, football, freestyle skiing, Frisbee, golf, hiking/backpacking, hockey, horseback riding, horseshoes, ice hockey, ice skating, in-line skating, indoor hockey, indoor soccer, jogging, judo, juggling, jump rope, kayaking, kickball, lacrosse, mountain biking, mountaineering, nordic skiing, outdoor activities, outdoor adventure, outdoor education, outdoor recreation, outdoor skills, outdoors, physical fitness, rock climbing, roller blading, ropes courses, running, skateboarding, skiing (cross-country), skiing (downhill), snowboarding, snowshoeing, telemark skiing, tennis, ultimate Frisbee, volleyball, walking, wilderness, winter soccer. 1 PE instructor, 6 coaches.

Computers Computers are regularly used in English, mathematics, science, social studies, writing classes. Computer network features include Internet access, wireless campus network, Internet filtering or blocking technology, individual laptop for each student. Campus intranet and student e-mail accounts are available to students. Students grades are available online. The school has a published electronic and media policy.

Contact Mrs. Melanie Miller, Director of Admissions. 802-387-4545 Ext. 199. Fax: 802-387-5396. E-mail: mmiller@greenwood.org. Web site: www.greenwood.org.

HAMPSHIRE COUNTRY SCHOOL

28 Patey Circle
Rindge, New Hampshire 03461

Head of School: Bernd Foecking

General Information Boys' boarding college-preparatory and general academic school; primarily serves underachievers, individuals with Attention Deficit Disorder, and non-verbal learning disabilities and Asperger's Syndrome. Grades 3–12. Founded: 1948. Setting: rural. Nearest major city is Boston, MA. Students are housed in single-sex dormitories. 1,700-acre campus. 8 buildings on campus. Approved or accredited by New England Association of Schools and Colleges and New Hampshire Department of Education. Member of National Association of Independent Schools. Endowment: $1 million. Total enrollment: 23. Upper school average class size: 4. Upper school faculty-student ratio: 1:2. There are 180 required school days per year for Upper School students. Upper School students typically attend 5 days per week. The average school day consists of 5 hours and 30 minutes.

Student Profile Grade 9: 3 students (3 boys); Grade 10: 1 student (1 boy); Grade 11: 1 student (1 boy); Grade 12: 2 students (2 boys). 100% of students are boarding students. 4% are state residents. 14 states are represented in upper school student body. 12% are international students. International students from Australia and Saudi Arabia.

Faculty School total: 15. In upper school: 8 men, 7 women; 3 have advanced degrees; 14 reside on campus.

Subjects Offered Algebra, American history, ancient history, biology, English, environmental science, French, geometry, history, life science, mathematics, pre-algebra, science, world history.

Graduation Requirements English, language arts, mathematics, science, social studies (includes history).

Special Academic Programs Academic accommodation for the gifted; remedial reading and/or remedial writing; remedial math.

Secondary School Placement 3 students graduated in 2011; all went to college.

Student Life Specified standards of dress. Discipline rests primarily with faculty.

Tuition and Aid 7-day tuition and room/board: $48,000.

Admissions Academic Profile Tests, any standardized test or Individual IQ required. Deadline for receipt of application materials: none. No application fee required. On-campus interview required.

Athletics Intramural: alpine skiing, backpacking, basketball, bicycling, canoeing/kayaking, cooperative games, fishing, flag football, floor hockey, hiking/backpacking, ice skating, kickball, outdoor activities, outdoor recreation, skiing (downhill), snowshoeing, soccer, softball, tennis, touch football, walking, wall climbing, whiffle ball, winter walking.

Computers Computers are regularly used in writing classes.

Contact William Dickerman, Admissions Director. 603-899-3325. Fax: 603-899-6521. E-mail: admissions@hampshirecountryschool.net. Web site: www.hampshirecountryschool.org.

NORTH COUNTRY SCHOOL

4382 Cascade Road
Lake Placid, New York 12946

Head of School: David Hochschartner

General Information Coeducational boarding and day college-preparatory, general academic, and arts school. Grades 4–9. Founded: 1938. Setting: rural. Nearest major city is Albany. Students are housed in residential houses. 200-acre campus. 11 buildings on campus. Approved or accredited by New York Department of Education. Member of National Association of Independent Schools and Secondary School Admission Test Board. Endowment: $7 million. Total enrollment: 88. Upper school average class size: 12. Upper school faculty-student ratio: 1:3.

Student Profile Grade 6: 8 students (2 boys, 6 girls); Grade 7: 16 students (6 boys, 10 girls); Grade 8: 22 students (12 boys, 10 girls); Grade 9: 22 students (14 boys, 8 girls). 90% of students are boarding students. 30% are state residents. 19 states are represented in upper school student body. 18% are international students. International students from Bahamas, Bermuda, China, Colombia, Mexico, and Republic of Korea; 2 other countries represented in student body.

Faculty School total: 33. In upper school: 13 men, 20 women; 9 have advanced degrees; 20 reside on campus.

Subjects Offered Algebra, American history, biology, ceramics, computer science, creative writing, earth science, English, mathematics, music, performing arts, photography, physical education, social studies, Spanish, studio art.

Special Academic Programs Remedial reading and/or remedial writing; remedial math; ESL (10 students enrolled).

Secondary School Placement 23 students graduated in 2011; they went to Dublin School; Gould Academy; Northwood School; Vermont Academy.

Student Life Specified standards of dress, student council. Discipline rests primarily with faculty.

Summer Programs Session focuses on recreation, arts, ESL, and outdoor programs; held on campus; accepts boys and girls; open to students from other schools. 150 students usually enrolled. 2012 schedule: June 27 to August 19. Application deadline: December 16.

Tuition and Aid Day student tuition: $21,700; 7-day tuition and room/board: $52,500. Tuition installment plan (monthly payment plans, individually arranged payment plans, 2-payment plan). Need-based scholarship grants available. In 2011–12, 30% of students received aid. Total amount of financial aid awarded in 2011–12: $450,000.

Admissions Deadline for receipt of application materials: none. No application fee required. On-campus interview required.

Athletics Coed Interscholastic: aerobics/dance, alpine skiing, artistic gym, backpacking, basketball, bicycling, climbing, curling, drill team, equestrian sports, field hockey, fishing, fitness walking, Frisbee, hiking/backpacking, horseback riding, lacrosse, modern dance, mountain biking, mountaineering, nordic skiing, outdoor activities, outdoor adventure, outdoor education, outdoor recreation, outdoor skills, outdoors, physical fitness, rappelling, rock climbing, running, skateboarding, ski jumping, skiing (cross-country), skiing (downhill), snowboarding, snowshoeing, swimming and diving, telemark skiing, volleyball, walking, wall climbing, wilderness survival, yoga; coed intramural: basketball, biathlon, cross-country running, skiing (cross-country), skiing (downhill), soccer.

Computers Computer resources include on-campus library services, Internet access. Student e-mail accounts are available to students.

Contact Christine LeFevre, Director of Admissions. 518-523-9329 Ext. 6000. Fax: 518-523-4858. E-mail: admissions@northcountryschool.org. Web site: www.northcountryschool.org.

See Display on next page and Close-Up on page 762.

THE RECTORY SCHOOL

528 Pomfret Street
Pomfret, Connecticut 06258

Head of School: Fred Williams

General Information Coeducational boarding and day college-preparatory, general academic, arts, technology, and music school, affiliated with Episcopal Church; primarily serves underachievers. Boarding grades 5–9, day grades K–9. Founded: 1920. Setting: rural. Nearest major city is Hartford. Students are housed in single-sex dormitories. 138-acre campus. 24 buildings on campus. Approved or accredited by Connecticut Association of Independent Schools, Junior Boarding Schools Association, and The Association of Boarding Schools. Member of National Association of Independent Schools and Secondary School Admission Test Board. Endowment: $8.3 million. Total enrollment: 248. Upper school average class size: 10. Upper school faculty-student ratio: 1:4. There are 172 required school days per year for Upper School students. Upper School students typically attend 5 days per week. The average school day consists of 7 hours and 45 minutes.

Student Profile Grade 6: 23 students (16 boys, 7 girls); Grade 7: 46 students (27 boys, 19 girls); Grade 8: 69 students (44 boys, 25 girls); Grade 9: 63 students (43 boys, 20 girls). 69% of students are boarding students. 30% are state residents. 14 states are represented in upper school student body. 45% are international students. International students from Bermuda, China, Japan, Mexico, Nigeria, and Republic of Korea; 5 other countries represented in student body. 11% of students are members of Episcopal Church.

Faculty School total: 65. In upper school: 27 men, 38 women; 25 have advanced degrees; 26 reside on campus.

Subjects Offered Algebra, American Civil War, American history, American literature, ancient world history, art, biology, chorus, creative arts, creative writing, drama, earth science, ecology, English, English as a foreign language, English literature, environmental science, European history, expository writing, fine arts, foreign language, general science, geography, geometry, grammar, history, journalism, Latin, life science, mathematics, medieval history, medieval/Renaissance history, music, photography, physical education, physical science, reading, science, social studies, Spanish, study skills, theater, vocal music, world history, world literature, writing.

Graduation Requirements Arts and fine arts (art, music, dance, drama), literature, mathematics, physical education (includes health), science, social studies (includes history).

Special Academic Programs Honors section; academic accommodation for the gifted; remedial reading and/or remedial writing; remedial math; programs in English, mathematics, general development for dyslexic students; special instructional classes for students with learning disabilities, Attention Deficit Disorder, and dyslexia; ESL.

Secondary School Placement 47 students graduated in 2011; they went to Brewster Academy; Choate Rosemary Hall; Pomfret School; Suffield Academy; Tabor Academy.

Student Life Specified standards of dress, student council, honor system. Discipline rests primarily with faculty. Attendance at religious services is required.

Summer Programs Remediation, enrichment, ESL, sports, art/fine arts programs offered; session focuses on study skills, academic enrichment, sports , music, off campus trips; held on campus; accepts boys and girls; open to students from other schools. 60 students usually enrolled. 2012 schedule: June 26 to July 23. Application deadline: none.

Tuition and Aid Day student tuition: $21,450; 7-day tuition and room/board: $42,950. Tuition installment plan (Key Tuition Payment Plan). Need-based scholarship grants available. In 2011–12, 31% of students received aid. Total amount of financial aid awarded in 2011–12: $1,389,020.

Admissions Traditional entrance grade is 8. For fall 2011, 203 students applied for admission, 159 were accepted, 86 enrolled. Deadline for receipt of application materials: none. Application fee required: $50. Interview required.
Athletics Interscholastic: baseball (boys), basketball (b,g), cross-country running (b,g), football (b), golf (b,g), soccer (b,g), softball (g), wrestling (b); intramural: basketball (b,g), dance (g), soccer (b); coed interscholastic: cross-country running, equestrian sports, fencing, golf, ice hockey, lacrosse, soccer, tennis, track and field; coed intramural: basketball, bowling, climbing, cooperative games, cross-country running, equestrian sports, fencing, fitness, flag football, golf, ice hockey, lacrosse, life saving, outdoor adventure, ropes courses, skiing (downhill), snowboarding, snowshoeing, soccer, softball, squash, street hockey, strength & conditioning, table tennis, tennis, touch football, ultimate Frisbee, volleyball, weight training, whiffle ball, yoga. 4 coaches, 2 athletic trainers.
Computers Computers are regularly used in English, history, mathematics, multimedia, music, science, writing, yearbook classes. Computer network features include on-campus library services, online commercial services, Internet access, wireless campus network, Internet filtering or blocking technology. Campus intranet and student e-mail accounts are available to students. Students grades are available online. The school has a published electronic and media policy.
Contact Vincent Ricci, Director of Admissions and Marketing. 860-928-1328. Fax: 860-928-4961. E-mail: admissions@rectoryschool.org. Web site: www.rectoryschool.org.

RUMSEY HALL SCHOOL

201 Romford Road
Washington Depot, Connecticut 06794

General Information Coeducational boarding and day college-preparatory, general academic, and arts school. Boarding grades 5–9, day grades K–9. Founded: 1900. Setting: rural. Nearest major city is Hartford. Students are housed in single-sex dormitories. 147-acre campus. 29 buildings on campus. Approved or accredited by Connecticut Association of Independent Schools, National Independent Private Schools Association, The Association of Boarding Schools, and Connecticut Department of Education. Member of National Association of Independent Schools and Secondary School Admission Test Board. Endowment: $5.7 million. Total enrollment: 303. Upper school average class size: 14. Upper school faculty-student ratio: 1:8. There are 180 required school days per year for Upper School students. Upper School students typically attend 6 days per week. The average school day consists of 6 hours and 40 minutes.

See Display on next page and Close-Up on page 764.

ST. CATHERINE'S ACADEMY

215 North Harbor Boulevard
Anaheim, California 92805

Head of School: Sr. Johnellen Turner, OP

General Information Boys' boarding and day college-preparatory, general academic, religious studies, leadership/military tradition, ESL, and military school, affiliated with Roman Catholic Church. Boarding grades 4–8, day grades K–8. Founded: 1889. Setting: suburban. Nearest major city is Los Angeles. Students are housed in single-sex dormitories. 8-acre campus. 8 buildings on campus. Approved or accredited by Military High School and College Association, National Catholic Education Association, The Association of Boarding Schools, Western Association of Schools and Colleges, Western Catholic Education Association, and California Department of Education. Total enrollment: 161. Upper school average class size: 16. Upper school faculty-student ratio: 1:8. There are 180 required school days per year for Upper School students. Upper School students typically attend 5 days per week. The average school day consists of 7 hours and 45 minutes.
Student Profile Grade 6: 17 students (17 boys); Grade 7: 40 students (40 boys); Grade 8: 46 students (46 boys). 43% of students are boarding students. 73% are state residents. 4 states are represented in upper school student body. 19% are international students. International students from Hong Kong, Mexico, Puerto Rico, Republic of Korea, and Taiwan. 58% of students are Roman Catholic.
Faculty School total: 21. In upper school: 4 men, 17 women; 7 have advanced degrees; 6 reside on campus.
Subjects Offered Art, band, Catholic belief and practice, character education, choir, Civil War, computer applications, computer literacy, computer skills, conflict resolution, decision making skills, English, environmental systems, ESL, ethical decision making, ethics and responsibility, fine arts, fitness, grammar, guidance, guitar, health and wellness, health education, healthful living, history, instrumental music, instruments, interpersonal skills, keyboarding, lab/keyboard, leadership, leadership education training, life skills, marching band, mathematics, military history, military science, moral and social development, music, music appreciation, music history, music performance, participation in sports, personal development, personal fitness, personal growth, physical education, physical fitness, piano, pre-algebra, reading/study skills, religion, religious education, science, service learning/internship, single survival, social studies, Spanish, sports, survival training, swimming, volleyball, wind instruments, word processing, yearbook.

Special Academic Programs Special instructional classes for students with Attention Deficit Disorder and learning disabilities; ESL (14 students enrolled).

Secondary School Placement 44 students graduated in 2011; they went to Army and Navy Academy; Mater Dei High School; New Mexico Military Institute; Servite High School.

Student Life Uniform requirement, honor system. Discipline rests equally with students and faculty. Attendance at religious services is required.

Summer Programs Remediation, enrichment, ESL, sports, art/fine arts, computer instruction programs offered; session focuses on academics and athletic activities; held both on and off campus; held at local attractions, (e.g., beach, aquarium, water park); accepts boys; open to students from other schools. 120 students usually enrolled. 2012 schedule: July 1 to July 31. Application deadline: none.

Tuition and Aid Day student tuition: $10,395; 5-day tuition and room/board: $29,540; 7-day tuition and room/board: $39,111. Tuition installment plan (FACTS Tuition Payment Plan, monthly payment plans, individually arranged payment plans, 4 payments). Need-based scholarship grants available. In 2011–12, 45% of students received aid. Total amount of financial aid awarded in 2011–12: $260,000.

Admissions Any standardized test required. Deadline for receipt of application materials: none. Application fee required: $100. Interview required.

Athletics Interscholastic: basketball, flag football, volleyball; intramural: ball hockey, baseball, basketball, bowling, cooperative games, cross-country running, drill team, equestrian sports, field hockey, fitness, flag football, golf, handball, life saving, physical fitness, physical training, soccer, softball, swimming and diving, touch football, track and field, volleyball, water volleyball, weight lifting. 1 PE instructor, 7 coaches.

Computers Computers are regularly used in English, history, science, social studies classes. Computer network features include Internet access, Internet filtering or blocking technology. Students grades are available online.

Contact Graciela Salvador, Director of Admissions. 714-772-1363 Ext. 103. Fax: 714-772-3004. E-mail: admissions@stcatherinesacademy.org. Web site: www.StCatherinesAcademy.org.

ST. THOMAS CHOIR SCHOOL

202 West 58th Street
New York, New York 10019-1406

Head of School: Rev. Charles Wallace

General Information Boys' boarding college-preparatory, general academic, arts, religious studies, technology, music, and pre-preparatory school, affiliated with Episcopal Church. Grades 3–8. Founded: 1919. Setting: urban. Students are housed in single-sex dormitories. 1 building on campus. Approved or accredited by National Association of Episcopal Schools, The Association of Boarding Schools, and New York Department of Education. Member of National Association of Independent Schools and Secondary School Admission Test Board. Endowment: $18 million. Total enrollment: 35. Upper school average class size: 8. Upper school faculty-student ratio: 1:5.

Student Profile Grade 6: 9 students (9 boys); Grade 7: 8 students (8 boys); Grade 8: 7 students (7 boys). 100% of students are boarding students. 10% are state residents. 12 states are represented in upper school student body. 67% of students are members of Episcopal Church.

Faculty School total: 7. In upper school: 5 men, 2 women; 6 have advanced degrees; all reside on campus.

Subjects Offered Algebra, applied music, art, choir, computers, English, French, Greek, history, Latin, mathematics, music theory, physical education, science, study skills, theology, visual arts.

Graduation Requirements Arts and fine arts (art, music, dance, drama), English, foreign language, mathematics, physical education (includes health), religion (includes Bible studies and theology), science, social studies (includes history).

Special Academic Programs Academic accommodation for the gifted and the musically talented; remedial reading and/or remedial writing; remedial math; programs in general development for dyslexic students.

Secondary School Placement 3 students graduated in 2011.

Student Life Uniform requirement. Discipline rests primarily with faculty. Attendance at religious services is required.

Tuition and Aid 7-day tuition and room/board: $13,500. Tuition installment plan (monthly payment plans, individually arranged payment plans). Need-based scholarship grants available. In 2011–12, 70% of students received aid. Total amount of financial aid awarded in 2011–12: $187,950.

Admissions Admissions testing and audition required. Deadline for receipt of application materials: none. No application fee required. On-campus interview required.

Athletics Interscholastic: basketball, soccer, softball; intramural: baseball, basketball, fitness, flag football, floor hockey, independent competitive sports, indoor hockey, indoor soccer, kickball, lacrosse, Newcombe ball, outdoor recreation, physical fitness, running, soccer, softball, strength & conditioning, table tennis, track and field, ultimate Frisbee, volleyball. 1 PE instructor.

Computers Computers are regularly used in art, English, foreign language, history, library, mathematics, music, science classes.

Contact Ms. Ruth S. Cobb, Director of Admissions, Alumni Relations, and Development. 212-247-3311 Ext. 304. Fax: 212-247-3393. E-mail: rcobb@choirschool.org. Web site: www.choirschool.org.

Junior Boarding Schools Close-Ups

EAGLEBROOK SCHOOL

Deerfield, Massachusetts

Type: Boys' day and boarding school
Grades: 6–9
Enrollment: 250
Head of School: Andrew C. Chase, Headmaster

THE SCHOOL

Eaglebrook School was opened in 1922 by its Headmaster and founder, Howard B. Gibbs, a former faculty member of Deerfield Academy. One of the earliest members of his faculty was C. Thurston Chase. When Mr. Gibbs died in 1928, Mr. Chase became Headmaster, a position he held for thirty-eight years. From 1966 to 2002, Stuart and Monie Chase assumed leadership of the School. While continuing to foster the School's traditional commitment to excellence, the Chases have encouraged and developed many components of a vital school: expansion of both academic and recreational facilities, emphasis on the arts, increased endowment and financial aid, student and faculty diversity, and a balanced, healthful diet. Stuart and Monie's son, Andrew C. Chase, now assumes leadership duties as Headmaster. Eaglebrook's goals are simple—to help each boy come into full and confident possession of his innate talents, to improve the skills needed for the challenges of secondary school, and to establish values that will allow him to be a person who acts with thoughtfulness and humanity.

The School owns more than 750 acres on Mt. Pocumtuck, overlooking the Deerfield Valley and the historic town of Deerfield. It is located 100 miles west of Boston and 175 miles north of New York City.

The Allen-Chase Foundation was chartered in 1937 as a charitable, educational trust. It is directed by a 40-member self-perpetuating Board of Trustees, representing alumni, parents, and outside professionals in many fields.

Eaglebrook is a member of the National Association of Independent Schools, the Association of Independent Schools of New England, the Valley Independent School Association, the Junior Boarding School Association, and the Secondary School Admissions Test Board.

ACADEMIC PROGRAMS

Sixth graders are taught primarily in a self-contained setting. Subjects include English, mathematics, reading, Latin, history, science, and trimester-length courses in studio art, computers, music, and woodworking. Required classes for grades 7 through 9 each year include foreign language study in Latin, French, Mandarin Chinese, or Spanish; a full year of mathematics; a full year of Colonial history in seventh grade, followed by a self-selected history the next two years; a full year of English; two trimesters of geography; two trimesters of science in seventh grade, followed by a full-year laboratory course; one trimester of human sexuality in eighth grade; and one trimester of ethics in the ninth grade. The School offers extensive trimester electives, including band and instrumental instruction, computer skills, word processing, current events, conditioning, chess, film classics, drama, public speaking, industrial field trips, music appreciation, first aid, publications, and an extensive variety of studio arts. Drug and alcohol education is required of all students in every grade.

Class enrollment averages 8 to 12 students. Teachers report directly to a student's adviser any time the student's work is noteworthy, either for excellence or deficiency. This allows the adviser to communicate praise or concern effectively and initiate appropriate follow-up. Midway through each trimester, teachers submit brief written evaluations to the advisers of each of their students. Advisers stay in close touch with the parents of their advisees. Grades, along with full academic reports from each of the student's teachers, are given to advisers each trimester and then sent home. The reports are accompanied by a letter from the adviser discussing the student's social adjustment progress, athletic and activity accomplishments, and academic progress and study habits.

FACULTY AND ADVISERS

Andrew C. Chase, the current Headmaster, is a graduate of Deerfield Academy and Williams College. Along with his wife, Rachel Blain, a graduate of Phillips Andover Academy and Amherst College, Andrew succeeded his father as Headmaster in 2002.

Eaglebrook's full- and part-time faculty consists of 72 men and women, 46 of whom live on campus, many with families of their own. Seventy hold undergraduate degrees, and 30 also hold graduate degrees. Leaves of absence, sabbaticals, and financial assistance for graduate study are available. The ratio of students to faculty members is 4.9:1.

Teachers endeavor to make learning an adventure and watch over each boy's personal growth. They set the academic tone, coach the teams, serve as dorm parents, and are available for a boy when he needs a friend. They help each individual establish lifelong study habits and set standards for quality. Eaglebrook's teachers have the skill not only to challenge the very able but also to make learning happen for those who need close supervision. Faculty members are chosen primarily for their appreciation of boys this age, their character and integrity as role models, and competence in their subject areas. The fact that many are married and have children of their own helps to create a warm, experienced family atmosphere.

SECONDARY SCHOOL PLACEMENT

The Director of Placement assists families in selecting, visiting, and applying to secondary schools. He meets with parents and students in the spring of a boy's eighth-grade year to discuss which schools might be appropriate based on each boy's aptitude, interests, achievements, and talent. He arranges visits from secondary schools and helps with applications. Parents and the Director of Placement work together until the boy has decided upon his secondary school in April of his ninth-grade year.

Schools frequently attended by Eaglebrook School graduates include Deerfield Academy, Choate Rosemary Hall, the Hotchkiss School, Loomis Chaffee, Northfield Mount Hermon School, Phillips Andover Academy, Phillips Exeter Academy, Pomfret School, St. George's School, St. Paul's School, Taft School, and Westminster School.

STUDENT BODY AND CONDUCT

In the 2011–12 school year, of the 196 boarding students and 54 day students, 20 were in grade 6, 46 in grade 7, 93 in grade 8, and 91 in grade 9. Twenty-two states and twenty-three countries were represented.

There are specified standards of dress, which are neat and informal most of the time. Discipline is handled on an individual basis by those faculty members who are closely involved with the student.

ACADEMIC FACILITIES

The C. Thurston Chase Learning Center contains classrooms, an audiovisual center, and an assembly area. It also houses the Copley Library, which contains 18,000 volumes and subscriptions to eighty-five publications, books on tape, newspapers, CD-ROMs, and Internet access. The computer room is equipped with state-of-the-art computers, color printers, scanners, digital cameras, and a projection board. The Bartlett Assembly Room is an all-purpose area with seats for the entire School. The Jean Flagler Matthews Science Building houses three laboratories, classrooms, a project room, a library, an online computerized weather station, and teachers' offices. The Bryant Arts Building houses studios for drawing, painting, stained glass, architectural design, computer-aided design, stone carving, ceramics, silk-screening, printmaking, and computer art; a darkroom for photography; a woodworking shop; a band rehearsal room; a publications office; a piano studio; piano practice rooms; and a drama rehearsal room. The campus has a high-speed fiber-optic network with e-mail and access to the World Wide Web for research.

BOARDING AND GENERAL FACILITIES

Dormitories are relatively small; the five dormitories house between 18 and 36 students each, with at least one faculty family to every 8 to 10 boys.

Most students live in double rooms. A limited number of single rooms are available. After the first year, a boy may request a certain dormitory and adviser.

ATHLETICS

The athletics program is suitable for boys of all sizes and abilities. Teams are small enough to allow each boy a chance to play in the games, master skills, and develop a good sense of sportsmanship. The School's Athletic Director arranges a competitive schedule to ensure games with teams of equal ability. Fall sports include cross-country, tennis, hiking, football, water polo, and soccer. Winter sports include ice hockey, basketball, recreational and competitive skiing, swimming and diving, snowboarding, squash, and wrestling. The School maintains the Easton Ski Area, consisting of several ski trails, the Macomber Chair Lift, and snowmaking equipment. Spring sports are baseball, track and field, golf, Ultimate Disc, lacrosse, triathlon, mountain and road biking, and tennis. The School plays host to numerous students throughout the year in seasonal tournaments in ice hockey, soccer, skiing, basketball, Ultimate Disc, swimming, and wrestling. The Schwab Family Pool is a six-lane facility for both competitive and recreational swimming. The McFadden Rink at Alfond Arena features a state-of-the-art NHL-dimensioned 200-foot by 85-foot indoor ice surface. A multisport indoor surface is installed in the arena in the off-season to enable use of the facility for in-line skating, in-line hockey, soccer, lacrosse, and tennis. The Lewis Track and Field was dedicated in 2002.

EXTRACURRICULAR OPPORTUNITIES

Service and leadership opportunities build a sense of pride in the School and camaraderie in the student body. Elected Student Council representatives meet with the Headmaster as an advisory group and discuss School issues. Boys act as admissions guides, help with recycling, organize dances, serve as proctors in the dormitories and the dining room, act as headwaiters, and give the morning assemblies. Boys also assume responsibility, with faculty guidance, for the School newspaper, yearbook, and literary magazine.

Many of the students participate in numerous outdoor activities that are sponsored by the Mountain Club. They maintain an active weekend schedule that includes camping, hiking, backpacking, canoeing, kayaking, white-water rafting, fishing, rock climbing, and snowshoeing.

DAILY LIFE

On weekdays, students rise at 7:20 a.m.; breakfast is at 8. Academic class periods, including assembly, begin at 8:30. Lunch is at noon, and classes resume at 12:33. Study hall and special appointments begin at 2:15, athletics begin at 3:15, and tutorial periods and other activities begin at 5. Dinner is at 6, and evening activities are scheduled between 6:45 and 7:30; study hall is then held until 9:15 p.m. or later, according to the grade.

WEEKEND LIFE

A wide variety of weekend activities are available at Eaglebrook, both on campus and off, including community service, riflery, museum visits, dances, field trips, tournaments, movies, plays, concerts, town trips, Deerfield Academy games, bicycle trips, ski trips, hiking, camping, and mountain climbing. On Sunday, the Coordinator of Religion supervises a nondenominational and nonsectarian meeting for the student body. Attendance is required for boarding students. The aim is to share different beliefs and ways of worship. Transportation is provided for boys who wish to maintain their own religious commitment by attending local places of worship. Students with permission may leave the School for the weekend; 5–10 percent of the student body normally do so on a given weekend.

COSTS AND FINANCIAL AID

Eaglebrook School's tuition for the 2011–12 school year was $50,800 for boarding students and $31,200 for day students. Eaglebrook seeks to enroll boys from different backgrounds from this country and abroad, regardless of their ability to pay. Approximately 30 percent of the students receive financial aid. To apply for tuition assistance, a candidate must complete the School Scholarship Service's Parents' Financial Statement, which is obtainable from the Financial Aid Office.

ADMISSIONS INFORMATION

Most students enter in either the seventh or eighth grade, although students can be admitted to any grade. Information regarding required testing and transcripts can be obtained from the Admissions Office. A School visit and interview are required.

Eaglebrook welcomes boys of any race, color, religion, nation, or creed, and all share the same privileges and duties.

APPLICATION TIMETABLE

The School accepts applications throughout the year, but it is to the candidate's advantage to make application as early as possible. Decisions and notifications are made whenever a boy's file is complete. There is a $50 application fee ($100 for international students).

ADMISSIONS CORRESPONDENCE

Theodore J. Low
Director of Admissions
Eaglebrook School
Pine Nook Road
Deerfield, Massachusetts 01342

Phone: 413-774-9111 (admissions)
413-774-7411 (main)
Fax: 413-774-9119 (admissions)
413-772-2394 (main)
E-mail: admissions@eaglebrook.org
Web site: http://www.eaglebrook.org

FAY SCHOOL

Southborough, Massachusetts

Type: Coeducational school for grades prekindergarten–9; boarding available for grades 7–9
Grades: Primary School (prekindergarten–2), Lower School (3–6), Upper School (7–9)
Enrollment: School total: 450; Boarding 110
Head of School: Robert J. Gustavson Jr., Head of School; David Liebmann, Assistant Head of School; Marie Beam, Director of Advancement; Matt Evans, Head of Upper School; Lainie Schuster, Head of Lower School; Anne Bishop, Head of Primary School

THE SCHOOL

A dynamic learning environment since 1866, Fay School exemplifies a coeducational tradition of academic excellence coupled with a dedication to maximize the potential of each individual child. With a structured environment that recognizes both effort and achievement, Fay School offers both breadth and depth in academic, artistic, and athletic programs. Multilevel course offerings and the availability of tutorial support ensure each student an appropriate level of academic challenge. In small advisory groups, students receive extensive individualized attention. Relationships between students and teachers mirror those of parent and child. At Fay, faculty members and parents work as partners during the critically important childhood and adolescent years. Fay's comprehensive secondary school placement program not only provides guidance in identifying and applying to model secondary schools but also assists students and their parents in selecting the best environment for continuing their education at the next level. Exceptional facilities and a faculty committed to ongoing professional development create an environment where living and learning thrive.

Established in 1866 by two sisters, Eliza Burnett Fay and Harriet Burnett, the School is situated on 42 acres in semirural surroundings 25 miles west of Boston. Fay School's day students come from thirty surrounding communities, and boarding students are drawn from across the United States and fifteen countries. Fay's graduates go on to thrive at independent secondary schools and area public high schools.

At Fay, each child's voice matters. Through its leadership opportunities, cultural program, comprehensive academic program, community service, arts, and sports offerings, the School caters to a wide range of interests and abilities. Students' endeavors are encouraged and supported by a dedicated and highly qualified faculty and monitored by an effort system that measures the level of engagement each student demonstrates in all aspects of campus life. Particular attention is given to the needs of boarding students and to making life in dormitories a "home away from home."

Fay School is a nonprofit institution and is governed by a self-perpetuating board of 27 trustees. Its endowment stands at $34 million and is supplemented by an annual fund of more than $1 million in total gifts, bridging the gap between tuition and the operating budget. Through its development efforts, the School annually receives support from more than 1,000 alumni, parents, and friends.

ACADEMIC PROGRAMS

Fay's program seeks to achieve far more than a sound foundation in course work; the emphasis is on fostering positive attitudes toward learning and living in the world beyond the campus. By limiting class size to an average of 12 Upper School students, Fay provides an environment in which children are active participants in their own education. Each student's specific needs and academic background are carefully considered when scheduling classes. A rotating block schedule and more than 200 class offerings ensure maximum flexibility in designing programs of study.

The School offers different levels in most subject areas. In the Primary and Lower Schools, the program emphasizes individual growth and the development of sound fundamental skills. Courses of study in the Upper School provide sequential programs grounded in strengthening basic practices in grades 6 and 7, a foundation upon which deeper conceptual understanding and application are built in the high school courses offered in grades 8 and 9. At the eighth and ninth grade levels, honors courses are available for students who qualify for this enriched experience. A full complement of courses within the five main disciplines of mathematics, English, history, science, and world languages is offered in the Upper School. Fay also provides leadership training in grades 1–9 through a full-year program that stresses the leadership skills of conflict management, social responsibility, team building, communication, and positive role modeling.

Fay School offers a comprehensive technology education program. Technology is integrated across the curriculum and throughout the grades. The School also offers technology classes to Upper and Lower School students that are designed to help students use technology to enhance their studies and to become safe, ethical, and effective computer users. Technology offerings range from Lower School introductory courses to information literacy, digital video production, and Web site design in the upper grades. All students must complete at least one term of art each year as well as a yearlong course in music.

To facilitate success in a student's academic endeavors, deliberate attention is paid to the development of study skills through a study skills curriculum administered by Learning Center staff members and reinforced in the classroom. In particular, research skills, note-taking, time management, and test-taking strategies are taught at the appropriate grade levels. In the academic and athletics programs, the School also monitors each student's progress by means of biweekly effort evaluations and by trimester reports at the middle and end of terms. Specialized help is available through the Learning Services Department for children who need support in following their regular course of study.

The International Student Program (ISP) offers English courses for students whose native language is not English. Three levels and small classes afford opportunities to tailor ISP courses to individual needs in the areas of speaking, listening, writing, reading, and skill building. As students' proficiency in English increases, they are integrated into mainstream courses. Full participation in art, music, technology classes, and sports activities helps students adapt quickly to life in their new community.

FACULTY AND ADVISERS

Children entering Fay School are welcomed into a family whose heart is the faculty. Faculty members are selected for their empathy and enthusiasm for working with students at the elementary and junior level, as well as for their expertise in a particular discipline. Students and teachers work, learn, play, and have meals together. In the boarding community they also spend weekends together, sharing many vibrant experiences both on and off campus.

Advisers are teachers and administrators who form the nuclei of small groups of 4 to 6 students, both day and boarding. Advisory groups meet at least three times a week. This peer support, combined with the guidance of a concerned and involved adult, makes advisory groups an important source of nurturing for youngsters at Fay. A major responsibility for advisers is communicating with parents.

SECONDARY SCHOOL PLACEMENT

Ensuring a good match between each graduating student and a secondary school is the primary objective in placement. The Director of Secondary School Placement and a second placement counselor work closely with American students, their families, their advisers, coaches, and teachers in identifying the students' needs, strengths, and talents. The Director of the International Student Program provides the same service for Fay's international students. Throughout the application process, the Placement Office provides counsel in selecting and applying to appropriate schools. Schools currently attended by Fay graduates include Berkshire School, Brooks School, Cate School, Choate Rosemary Hall, Concord Academy, Cushing Academy, Deerfield Academy, Emma Willard, Episcopal High School, Governor Dummer Academy, Groton School, Kent School, Lawrence Academy, Lawrenceville School, Loomis Chaffee School, Middlesex School, Milton Academy, Noble and Greenough School, Phillips Andover Academy, Phillips Exeter Academy, Pomfret School, Proctor Academy, Rivers School, St. George's School, St. Mark's School, St. Paul's School, Salisbury School, Suffield Academy, Tabor Academy, Thacher School, Westminster School, and Worcester Academy.

STUDENT BODY AND CONDUCT

At Fay, every effort is made to establish a balance between freedom and responsibility for the young people in its care. Through small advisory groups and the Leadership Program, unstated School rules such as ethical behavior and respect for others are reinforced. Minor misconduct is dealt with by advisers or by the Head of the Primary, Lower, or Upper Schools, depending on the child's grade. Where infractions of major School rules are involved, the Discipline Committee, composed of the appropriate Head and 5 faculty members, may convene.

ACADEMIC FACILITIES

The Root Academic Center (1984) houses most of the Upper and Lower School classrooms. The Mars Wing (2001) includes the Learning Center, the media lab, four state-of-the-art science labs, a writing lab, and a multimedia lab. The Reinke Building (1971) contains a large auditorium and houses the Fay Extended Day Program, band room, School Counselor's office, and Summer and Special Programs office. The Picardi Art Center (1987) provides outstanding facilities for art classes, including a darkroom and ceramics studio. The Harris Events Center (1995) is home to Fay's Performing Arts Program and includes five music practice rooms, two music classrooms, a dance studio, and a 400-seat theater.

The School is completely networked and runs on PC and Mac technology in each classroom, in the library, the Learning Center, and in three computer labs. In addition, five multimedia carts are outfitted with the equipment necessary to create multimedia presentations, and three mobile laptop labs provide wireless Web connection for full class lessons. The library offers 17,000 volumes and nine computers for student use. The library Web page provides access to a fully automated catalog of Fay holdings, a connection to holdings outside of Fay via the Internet or the

CD-ROM Catalogue of Independent Schools in Eastern Massachusetts, a subscription to 10 different databases to support teachers designing lessons and students accomplishing research, and links to many useful Web sites organized by subject and index. The library functions as a key point in the learning experience at Fay, providing students and faculty members with resources for study, research, and pleasure reading. The library program encourages a love of reading and an appreciation of quality literature, equips students with the knowledge and skills to become lifelong learners, and helps ensure that students are effective and responsible users of information and ideas.

BOARDING AND GENERAL FACILITIES

Boarding boys are housed in the Boys Village Dorm (2008) or Steward Dorm (1978), while girls live on the upper floors of the Girls Village Dorms (2008) and the Dining Room Building (1924), in Webster House (1880), and in East House (circa 1895). Family-style meals are served in the dining room. The Wellness Center, which opened in 2009, is situated in the lower level of the Steward Dorm and serves as the campus medical facility. Additional campus buildings include Brackett House (1860), home of advancement offices; Fay House (1860), the location for the Admission Office; and the Upjohn Building (1895), currently serving as a multiuse space.

ATHLETICS

Characterized by diversity, spirit, and sportsmanship, Fay's competitive athletics program involves all students and offers a wide range of sports and ability levels each term. Fay's interscholastic teams are noted for the high degree of pride and team spirit they bring with them. Fay's ten athletics fields and eight new tennis courts are in constant use for practices and games during the fall and spring terms, while in warmer weather the pool becomes a popular place to cool off. In snowy weather, the Harlow Gymnasium and the Mars Wrestling Room become the centers of activity, with the ice rinks at the nearby New England Sports Center providing facilities for Fay's hockey teams. Participants in the skiing program enjoy the slopes of SkiWard, a local ski area. Fay hosts annual basketball, wrestling, and tennis tournaments, and many individual athletes and teams participate in tournaments hosted by other schools. The following sports and activities are offered: fall—cross-country, field hockey, football, golf, photography, soccer, and tennis; winter—basketball, dance, drama, fitness, ice hockey, skiing, volleyball, woodworking, and wrestling; and spring—baseball, fitness, golf, lacrosse, softball, squash, tennis, and track.

The School's athletics facilities were greatly enhanced with the completion of the Fay School Athletic Campus in 2009. The campus comprises 30 acres of dedicated regulation-sized outdoor fields for soccer, field hockey, baseball, softball, and lacrosse. The campus also features a cross-country course and four batting cages—two for baseball and two for softball. Additional facilities include the Harlow Gymnasium (1993), a facility that incorporates four basketball courts, expanded locker room space, team rooms, a wrestling room, a weight room, and a training room.

EXTRACURRICULAR OPPORTUNITIES

Fay's academic program is augmented by a wide choice of extracurricular activities. Dramatic productions and musical groups such as band, bell ringers, and chorus offer performance opportunities; aspiring journalists, photographers, and artists work on the yearbook and student newspaper; and activities such as videotaping, woodworking, community service, chess, and computers offer something for everyone. In addition, an 800-square-foot textured rock climbing wall has been added to the state-of-the-art gymnasium. The rock wall, 26 feet in height, provides an ideal setting for climbing, bouldering, and rappelling. Full advantage is taken of the School's proximity to Boston, and visits to museums, sports events, and historic sites take place throughout the year.

DAILY LIFE

Classes are held Monday through Friday in flexible blocks, starting at 8 and ending at 2:30 for all students. Grades prekindergarten–2 are dismissed at 3. All other students go on to sports, which continue until 3:30 for grades 3 and 4 and 4:30 for grades 5–9. Boarders have free time after sports until a family-style dinner at 6, followed by free time until 7:30 and a study period until 9. Lights-out is between 9:30 and 10, depending on the student's age.

WEEKEND LIFE

Due to the geographic diversity of Fay's boarding community, few boarding students return home on weekends. Boarders look forward to weekends, when the Weekend Coordinator schedules a wide range of activities, including daylong and weekend-long skiing, white-water rafting, and hiking trips; athletics contests; nature trips; attendance at a wide range of cultural events and performances; and visits to amusement and recreational parks, movies, Boston shops, and community service projects.

Families of day students are warmly supportive of the boarders, opening their homes to youngsters for weekends and some holidays. The number of off-campus weekends is not limited, with the exception of a few closed weekends, but permission must be granted by advisers and teachers.

SUMMER PROGRAMS

Fay School offers a safe, fun-filled co-ed camp for children ages 4 through 12, called Fay Discovery. Campers use the Fay campus and extensive facilities to participate in a variety of summertime activities, including swimming instruction. Four 2-week sessions run Monday through Friday from 9 a.m. to 4 p.m., with extended care available. The School's highly qualified staff members and low camper-to-counselor ratio ensure individualized attention in all activities.

The Summer Session of Fay's International Student Program is designed to enrich international students' use of English and to provide an academic and cultural introduction to Fay School and the United States.

This is a six-week boarding program for students ages 10–15, running from late June to early August each year. The program provides a structured schedule throughout the day, beginning with academic classes in the morning and ending with sports and activities in the afternoon and evening. The weekends include exciting excursions to Boston and surrounding areas.

COSTS AND FINANCIAL AID

Tuition for 2011–12 ranged from $18,500 for day students in pre-K to $26,750 for fifth graders and $28,750 for ninth graders. Tuition for domestic boarding students in grades 7–9 ranged from $47,200 to $47,800; for mainstream international boarding students in grades 7–9 ranged from $49,675 to $50,275; and for international boarding students with ESL ranged from $55,200 to $55,800. Additional fees included $525 (grades 1–5) or $725 (grades 6–9) for books and $1145 for laundry service (boarders only). The School offers several creative payment plans.

Financial aid is awarded on the basis of need to 14 percent of the student body. Amounts, based upon demonstrated need and procedures established by the School and Student Service for Financial Aid, range from $1000 to nearly full tuition.

ADMISSIONS INFORMATION

Fay School accepts day students for prekindergarten to grade 9 and boarding students for grades 7–9. The personal requirements for admission include satisfactory evidence of good character, an acceptable record of previous academic work, and the ability and motivation to successfully complete the work at Fay. All applicants must complete the application form and return it to the Director of Admission with the application fee, a transcript, and teacher recommendations. Applicants must visit the School for a personal interview and tour, on weekdays while classes are in session; interested students should call the Admission Office to arrange a time. Candidates for grades 4–9 must take the WISC-IV.

APPLICATION TIMETABLE

Applications for day students are due on February 15. Decisions on day student candidates whose folders are complete are announced on March 10. Fay continues to accept qualified candidates after this date until the grades are filled. Wait lists are often established. Decisions on boarding students are made once a candidate's folder is complete, beginning in January. Parents are asked to respond to the acceptance within thirty days. To hold a place for a child, a deposit and enrollment contract must be submitted. Information regarding clothing, course selection, and other pertinent items is sent upon enrollment.

ADMISSIONS CORRESPONDENCE

Beth Whitney, Director of Admission
Fay School
48 Main Street
Southborough, Massachusetts 01772-9106
Phone: 508-490-8201
Fax: 508-481-7872
E-mail: admission@fayschool.org
Web site: http://www.fayschool.org

THE FESSENDEN SCHOOL

West Newton, Massachusetts

Type: Boys' boarding and day school
Grades: K–9: Lower School, Kindergarten–4; Middle School, 5–6; Upper School, 7–9
Enrollment: 475
Head of School: David B. Stettler, Headmaster

THE SCHOOL

The Fessenden School of West Newton, Massachusetts, has enjoyed a long and rich history of providing high-quality education for boys in a supportive yet challenging environment. The School was founded in 1903 by Mr. and Mrs. Frederick J. Fessenden. The founders' original educational philosophy was "to train a boy along the right lines, to teach him how to study and form correct habits of work, and to inculcate principles, which are to regulate his daily conduct and guide his future life." The Fessenden School brings out the best in boys by adhering to these same principles today. The Fessenden School also recognizes the special requirements of a boy's elementary education experience and focuses on providing that experience in a nurturing environment where a boy can live up to his potential. Intellectual, physical, and emotional development share equal emphasis at Fessenden.

The mission of The Fessenden School is to teach, nurture, and celebrate growing boys, cultivating each student's individual potential and developing in balance his mind, character, heart, and body in an inclusive and joyful community that, through rigor, friendship, and service, reflects Fessenden's traditional values of honesty, compassion, and respect.

The Fessenden School campus is situated on 41 acres in a residential community just west of Boston. The School's proximity to the city presents a world of exciting possibilities for year-round activity, including well-known historic sites, first-class music and theater, world-renowned museums, and a multitude of professional and collegiate sporting events. The Fessenden campus is convenient to all major highway routes, and Logan International Airport is only a 20-minute drive from campus.

The Fessenden School is a nonprofit organization. The School's endowment currently stands at just over $34 million and is supported by alumni and parents, both past and present, through an Annual Fund.

Fessenden's well-established character education program, based on the principles of honesty, compassion, respect, and commitment to academic and athletic excellence, seeks to ensure that every member of the school community is given the support and nurturing he needs to feel secure in his academic, physical, and social ability.

Fessenden holds membership in many academic associations, including the Association of Independent Schools in New England, the National Association of Independent Schools, the Junior Boarding Schools Association, the Secondary School Admission Test Board, and the Massachusetts Association of Nonprofit Schools and Colleges.

ACADEMIC PROGRAMS

The Fessenden School's traditional curriculum is designed to be challenging yet developmentally appropriate and supportive of each student's learning style, providing him with a foundation of skills that are imperative for the secondary school experience. With an average class size of 12, each student's needs are carefully considered by his teachers, advisers, and division heads prior to placement in grade-level or honors classes.

Fessenden's Lower School (K–4) places a heavy emphasis on skills in reading, oral and written communication, and mathematics. These areas are complemented with additional work in social studies, FLES (foreign language in elementary school), science, computers, library skills, art, drama, music, and sports. A link to Upper School students is maintained through the Big Brother program, peer tutoring, assemblies, and other all-school activities.

In the Middle School grades, students begin the transition from the self-contained classrooms of the Lower School toward the departmentalized structure of the Upper School. Courses in English, math, social studies, geography, science, art, music, and Spanish are required for all Middle School students. Each fifth-grade student is also required to take a reading and study skills course.

The Upper School academic program ensures that each student is properly prepared for the educational programs he will encounter in secondary school. Grades 7–9 focus on the five major academic disciplines of English, history, mathematics, science, and foreign language (Spanish and Latin). Fessenden's commitment to the arts requires each student to choose a class each semester in the fine arts or performing arts. A "help and work" period each day provides additional opportunities for students to consult their teachers on an individual or small-group basis. Students must complete a half-year of computer studies and a course in personal growth and development prior to graduation. In addition, each boy is required to choose from a range of nearly twenty popular electives, including computer studies, student government, theater workshops, art courses at various levels, woodworking, photography, video production, and individual music instruction.

The Fessenden School recognizes that some students may need more specialized help with skill building and therefore offers a Skills Center staffed by professional reading and language specialists. The Skills Center provides individual skills instruction, administers tests, and makes evaluations and recommendations.

Fessenden's English as a second language program (ESL) is offered on both the intermediate and advanced levels to increase English proficiency. ESL students are educated using a variety of appropriate teaching resources. Class trips include visits to historic Plymouth, Massachusetts; Mystic Seaport, Connecticut; Boston's Freedom Trail; Old Sturbridge Village; and whale watches.

Fessenden's academic year is divided into four marking periods. The School acknowledges that a student's effort to learn is as important as standard letter or numerical grades. Teachers give both qualitative and quantitative marks four times during the year.

FACULTY AND ADVISERS

The 120 members of Fessenden's dedicated faculty and staff are committed to creating a family-oriented community by serving as teachers, coaches, advisers, dorm parents, and mentors. Seventy-five percent of the faculty and staff members for students in grades 5–9 live on campus, many with families of their own. The student-faculty ratio is approximately 6:1.

Each student has an academic faculty or staff adviser. Advisers foster close relationships with each student, becoming actively involved in all facets of the student's life at school. Each adviser is responsible for communicating to parents all aspects of their sons' experiences at Fessenden.

SECONDARY SCHOOL PLACEMENT

Fessenden seeks to provide each student with the placement guidance needed to ensure a positive secondary school experience. This is achieved by collaboration between the student and the Director of Placement, advisers, teachers, dorm parents, and coaches. Beginning in the spring of eighth grade, families start selecting an appropriate school based on academic ability, extracurricular activities, and athletic interests. Eighth and ninth grade students are encouraged to take the SSAT preparatory class in English and math. The Placement Director also works with students to teach specific interviewing techniques, including mock interviews. This helps address any placement issues well in advance.

Fessenden graduates have attended a variety of secondary schools, including Avon Old Farms, Belmont Hill, Brooks, Cate School, Choate Rosemary Hall, Cushing, Deerfield, Exeter, Governor's Academy, Holderness, Loomis Chaffee, Middlesex, Noble and Greenough, Phillips Academy, Rivers, Roxbury Latin, Tabor, and Westminster. However, it is ultimately the successful match between student and school that remains essential in the placement process.

STUDENT BODY AND CONDUCT

The Fessenden School seeks boys of solid character who can grow in a supportive environment where a balanced program of academics, athletics, the arts, and social life is vigorously pursued.

Of a total enrollment of 475 students for the academic year 2011–12, 375 were day students and 100 were boarders. Fessenden students come from fifty-eight cities and towns in Massachusetts, seventeen other states, and twelve other countries. International students represent 12 percent of the total student body.

Fessenden's character education program is modeled by its faculty members, who have an extraordinary investment in caring for the boys and setting guidelines for them. Acknowledging boys for being active and positive contributors within the community in turn places an emphasis on the reinforcement of positive role modeling. Teachers, coaches, and advisers handle disciplinary matters on an individual basis as warranted.

ACADEMIC FACILITIES

Fessenden's state-of-the-art academic building houses twenty-five classrooms that provide multiple data points, allowing the expanding world of information into each classroom via technology. The campus features a science center, a library, a study hall, two computer labs, a digital photography lab, a student health center, and a performing arts center that features a theater-size wide-screen projection monitor. The Fessenden School library contains 21,000 volumes, sixteen desktop computers, twenty laptop computers, twenty Chromebooks, Kindles, Nooks, twenty-five digital cameras, a color scanner, and a printer. The School's two computer labs include forty computers, which are networked and have color monitors and an Internet account. Students also have access to 170 laptops. There are two art studios with five electric pottery wheels and two kilns, a printmaking machine, and a music center that features two band rehearsal rooms and five individual practice rooms equipped with pianos. The Skills Center contains eight classrooms for one-to-one tutoring.

BOARDING AND GENERAL FACILITIES

Fessenden's boarding students live in homelike dormitories closely supervised by residential faculty members and their families. Dormitories are made up of students in grades 5–8, with proctors who are in grade 9. There are 11 to 19 students per hallway. Students in grade 9 live in two different dormitories. Weekday meals are served family style, with a buffet on weekends.

Students' everyday health care needs are served at the campus Health Center and a registered nurse is always available. Newton-Wellesley Hospital is located only minutes away.

ATHLETICS

The School offers a variety of seasonal athletics for students of every age and ability level. Fessenden's long-standing tradition in sports embodies the philosophy of fair play, sportsmanship, and equal opportunity for all participants. Students may choose from competitive, intramural, or recreational activities each season. Competitive and intramural sports include baseball, basketball, cross-country, football, hockey, lacrosse, soccer, squash, tennis, track and field, and wrestling. Boys may also choose from an exciting range of recreational sports, such as cross-country skiing, golf, mountain biking, sailing, and weight lifting and conditioning. The Fessenden School participates in several athletic tournaments each year and also hosts annual soccer, wrestling, and tennis tournaments.

Fessenden has a state-of-the-art athletic facility, which houses two indoor basketball courts, a wrestling center with two regulation-size mats, a weight-training suite, and locker rooms for coaches and visiting teams. The facility overlooks Fessenden's six outdoor tennis courts, which are lighted. Rounding out the sports facilities are an indoor hockey rink, thirteen outdoor tennis courts, two outdoor swimming pools, and nine playing fields.

EXTRACURRICULAR OPPORTUNITIES

The Fessenden School provides a variety of opportunities for students to develop leadership skills and exhibit their talents, thus enriching and balancing their academic program. Each year, the theater arts program presents several dramatic and musical productions. Faculty members offer club programs to share specific skills and interests with students, including in-line skating, board games, cooking, floor hockey, billiards, indoor soccer, model building, volleyball, science and aeronautics, and weight lifting.

Fessenden's Student Council is formed of elected officers in grade 9. The Council meets every two weeks for regular business and calls special meetings to discuss important issues. The Student Council has a voice in implementing School rules and planning special events.

DAILY LIFE

Boarding students begin their day with a family-style breakfast. The academic day encompasses eight periods. Athletic activities take place each weekday afternoon. Day students return home after sports; for boarding students, a structured study hall follows. There are also after-dinner study halls and free-time activities.

WEEKEND LIFE

Fessenden's weekend program is exceptionally full, providing the balance between academic and social life by satisfying the boys' many outside interests. The residential life staff works closely with the residential faculty to offer more than twenty exciting and interesting supervised activities every weekend. A sampling of weekend trips includes college and professional sports events, museum trips, ski outings, movie nights, camping and mountain-biking trips, dances, plays, and concerts. The Fessenden School holds no religious affiliation but can provide transportation to services for boys of all faiths.

An indispensable aspect of Fessenden's boarding life is the Welcome Family Program. This program connects all new families with a current Fessenden family that has a boy in the same school division. Boarders may also spend some evenings, weekends, or holidays with their "Welcome Family," creating friendships that can last long after their Fessenden experience is over.

SUMMER PROGRAMS

The Fessenden School's residential summer ESL program provides five weeks of immersion in the English language and American culture. This program is open to international boys and girls, ages 10 to 16.

The classes are offered at beginning, intermediate, and advanced levels and are designed to develop competent conversational skills and expand English vocabulary. Classes are small to enable every student to participate fully.

Fessenden's summer ESL program also offers films, videos, fun projects, and games, reinforcing classroom work and actively engaging students in the learning process. After-school and weekend trips bring students to such sites as Plymouth Plantation, Martha's Vineyard, Mystic Seaport, and Harvard University.

COSTS AND FINANCIAL AID

Day student tuition ranges from $23,775 to $33,750. Boarding tuition ranges from $42,750 to $49,600. Additional charges may be applicable to all students for supplies and laundry services.

The Fessenden School awards approximately $1.3 million in financial assistance to more than 11 percent of the student body each academic year. Scholarships are awarded on the basis of need.

ADMISSIONS INFORMATION

Catalogs, applications, and financial aid material may be obtained by contacting Fessenden's Admissions Office.

APPLICATION TIMETABLE

Admissions inquiries are welcome at any time. The application deadline for day students is February 1. Boarding student applications are processed on a rolling admissions basis.

ADMISSIONS CORRESPONDENCE

Caleb W. Thomson '79, Director of Admissions
The Fessenden School
250 Waltham Street
West Newton, Massachusetts 02465

Phone: 617-630-2300
Fax: 617-630-2303
E-mail: admissions@fessenden.org
Web site: http://www.fessenden.org

NORTH COUNTRY SCHOOL

Lake Placid, New York

NORTH *Opening minds and possibilities*
COUNTRY SCHOOL

Type: Coeducational boarding middle school
Grades: 4–9
Enrollment: 89
Head of School: David Hochschartner

THE SCHOOL

The student body numbered 6 children when Walter and Leonora Clark started North Country School in 1938. Because construction of their new school building had been delayed, this tiny band of children and adults took temporary shelter on the property in a thin-walled summer-camp building that had neither heat nor electricity. Years later, the Clarks delighted in telling these stories about those early days: borrowing a wood stove from an obliging neighbor, hanging blankets over the windows, and breaking ice in kitchen water buckets. Thus North Country School began with children learning lessons about overcoming unexpected difficulties with energy, cooperation, and good humor.

The 200-acre campus, which is located in the Adirondack High Peaks, includes a working farm, organic gardens, and lakeshore and is abutted by wilderness land. Sharing in the daily chores necessary to the maintenance of the School and farm has always been at the core of a child's experience at North Country. The Clarks believed that real responsibilities fostered feelings of purpose and self-worth in children. The school they envisaged was one in which all the experiences of each day, both in the classroom and out, would have the power to teach. That same belief had informed the founding of Camp Treetops seventeen years earlier on the same site, a project in which the Clarks also participated and which to this day complements the School program, making North Country School–Camp Treetops (NCS-CTT) one of the few truly year-round communities for children in the country.

Today, North Country School–Camp Treetops is overseen by a Board of Trustees that meets four times a year on the campus so that members may visit classes, talk with students and staff members, and advance the institution's long-range plan. Gifts to the institution in 2008–09 totaled approximately $750,000, not including capital campaign contributions.

The institution is accredited by the New York State Association of Independent Schools and the American Camping Association and is a member of the Secondary School Admission Test Board, the Educational Records Bureau, and the National Association of Independent Schools.

ACADEMIC PROGRAMS

North Country School was founded on the dictum of John Dewey that "the educative process is fired and sustained by the impulse that comes from the desires, interests, and purposes of the pupil." The School structures children's study of the traditional school subjects but always encourages children to follow their own interests as they emerge. The School believes that all children are in some way gifted and creates a teaching and learning environment that is designed to find and develop those gifts. Education at North Country is a hands-on as well as a conceptual, social, and aesthetic matter. No summative grades are awarded; instead, teachers write comprehensive reports on each child's work twice a year. Ninth graders do receive course grades for their high school transcripts.

Learning environments are highly enriched with manipulative materials and resources. There is one computer for every 2 students, and students are taught how to use the Internet for information retrieval and global conversation. Some classes are taught by 2 or 3 teachers—1 as lead teacher and the others as coaches.

Science and math classes utilize the farm and mountain environment in their curriculum as well as problem-solving techniques that were recently endorsed by the National Council of Teachers of Mathematics.

FACULTY AND ADVISERS

The Head of North Country School–Camp Treetops is David Hochschartner, a graduate of Union College and the Klingenstein Center at Columbia University Teachers College. Mr. Hochschartner has served as the Director of the Presidio Hill School in San Francisco, California, and as Assistant Director of Burgundy Farm Country Day School in Alexandria, Virginia. He has been an instructor at Colorado Outward Bound School, has served as a coach and blind-racer guide for the U.S. Disabled Ski Team, and has an extensive background in outdoor sports.

The faculty members divide their time among teaching, coaching, tutoring, and the outdoors, where much of the School's program occurs year-round. Though many of the faculty members are experts and hold degrees in a particular subject area, they are primarily generalists who are prepared to work with children in all aspects of North Country School's program. A Faculty Enrichment Fund has been established to support summer study among the faculty, and time is taken before school and during the children's vacation periods for workshops and new-program development.

The staff includes a school nurse and a licensed social counselor. The Adirondack Medical Center is 20 minutes from the School.

SECONDARY SCHOOL PLACEMENT

The ninth-grade curriculum at North Country School includes a directed program in planning for transition. Students examine themselves, their interests and skills, and their aspirations as a basis for thinking about their transition to secondary school. They receive instruction and practice in writing essays as well as in interviewing and evaluating schools.

Parents are brought into the process of school selection at the end of the seventh-grade year and stay in contact with the Secondary School Placement Director from then on.

Schools attended by North Country School graduates include Buxton School, Cushing Academy, Darrow School, Dublin School, Emma Willard School, Gould Academy, High Mowing School, Knox School, Masters School, New Hampton School, Northfield Mount Hermon School, Northwood School, Orme School, Phillips Academy (Andover), Proctor Academy, Putney School, Stony Brook School, Tilton School, and Vermont Academy.

STUDENT BODY AND CONDUCT

Of the 89 children enrolled in 2010–11, 66 were boarders and 23 were day students or faculty children. This student community included 37 girls and 52 boys from sixteen states and ten other countries. The children ranged in age from 9 to 15.

Although North Country School is in many ways a highly structured community, it is also an informal one where everyone is on a first-name basis. Respect for one another is a key prerequisite for the success of the School community and is achieved through conversation and care rather than authority.

Candy, junk food, and television are not allowed except on special occasions. Children who feel the need to test limits do so with candy rather than other substances.

The School believes in the direct arbitration of disputes between children by an adult. Houseparents are regularly in touch with the parents of their charges. When a problem exists academically, socially, or personally, conversation about it begins early and parents are asked to participate in its solution if appropriate.

ACADEMIC FACILITIES

Most classes are held in one building, which was built in 1940 and has since been significantly modernized. Windows are large and rooms are sunny; there are slides by three of the staircases. The art, ceramics, weaving, woodworking, and photography studio areas are contiguous and occupy the lower level of the Main Building. A variety of dance, theater, and music classes are held in the spacious, post and beam performing arts building, built in 2001.

The barn, greenhouse, and sugarhouse are also used for teaching at various times in the year. The library, a bright and many-windowed space, contains 5,000 volumes and is filled with comfortable nooks and crannies for reading as well as state-of-the-art computer retrieval and online capabilities.

In recent years the school has added a learning lab to offer assistance to children with mild to moderate language-based learning challenges. In addition, an English as a Second Language (ESL) program is available to international students who require beginning and intermediate English instruction.

BOARDING AND GENERAL FACILITIES

Students live in one of seven "houses" with resident houseparents. There are no more than 12 boarding students to a house. Genders and ages are mixed much as they would be in a family, and most houseparents have young children of their own who complete the family circle. Two other adults are assigned to each house as well, so that there is always plenty of coverage and the 1:3 adult-child ratio is maintained. Houseparents oversee reading period and homework for the younger students. Eighth and ninth graders attend a supervised study hall in the main building. An evening snack is often prepared by a houseparent and 1–2 children. Younger children are tucked into bed and often read to before going to sleep.

ATHLETICS

Part of North Country School's educational philosophy is to encourage cooperation rather than competition; this is reflected in the School's athletics and recreation program. While some soccer and basketball games are played against local schools and North Country School's ski teams compete throughout the winter, the emphasis is on lifelong sports, free-form games, and play and mastery. Children may have riding classes once a week in the fall and spring. Children ski on the School's own ski hill and on adjacent cross-country trails. They ski each Tuesday afternoon at Whiteface Mountain and take advantage of Lake Placid's Olympic ski-jumping, bobsled, and luge venues one or two evenings a week throughout the winter. Children sled, toboggan, build snow caves, and wee-bob most afternoons on the hill by the School's lake. Students also enjoy ice skating at the Olympic speed-skating oval in town and on the School's ponds.

A major activity at North Country School is mountain climbing. Many children aim during their years at NCS-CTT to become Adirondack '46ers. There are expeditions nearly every weekend throughout the year, many on snowshoes. There is also a climbing wall in the main building that prepares children for more technical climbs in the out-of-doors. Dave's Crag, North Country's on-site climbing area, is 40-feet high by 250-feet wide and has twenty-five different routes ranging from beginner to advanced.

EXTRACURRICULAR OPPORTUNITIES

The school year is built around a number of all-School special events, many of which date back fifty years. For Halloween, children make their own costumes for an evening of festivities, including a senior-run spook house and a carnival.

The fall harvests are followed by Thanksgiving, which is attended by the children's families and at which the harvest is served. Music and dramatic performances follow.

The winter holiday celebration spans a week of special meals and treats as children go from one house to another and from one faculty residence to another.

Valentine's Day is again a time for creative manufacture and celebration, as are Box Dinners later in the spring. Mountain Cakes, a month-long escapade of spring mountaineering, is capped off by a big awards dinner, when each house is given a cake whose dimensions reflect the number of miles collectively climbed.

All children study music formally and many informally as well. Sunday dinner may be a special occasion where children dress up and where the meal is followed by a student performance, often of music.

Children are urged to learn to ride, ski, go on at least one overnight a term, and climb Cascade Mountain. A mounted drill team performs in the spring, and there are several horseback expeditions during the fall and spring.

Spring is maple sugar harvest time. The children split wood, gather sap, run the evaporator, and can more than 100 gallons of syrup each year.

A student newspaper and literary journal, a chorus, musical ensembles, and various student-created activities round out the extracurricular program.

DAILY LIFE

Children with barn chores are awakened at 6:30, others at 7 for building chores. All meals are served family-style. Breakfast is at 8, except on weekends, when the day begins a little later. Classes follow at 8:30 Monday through Friday and run through 3 p.m., with a break for lunch at 12:15. There is a 15-minute "council" right after lunch at which announcements are made, afternoon activities planned, recognitions and awards given, and an occasional story told. After lunch, older students choose from a substantial list of elective courses, including photography, wood shop, dance, theater, chorus, and individual music lessons. Sports follow, with various athletic opportunities, depending upon the season. Following sports, children return to their houses to relax and wind down with friends and houseparents before dinner. Occasionally, there are open houses in one living unit or another or at the Head's house. Wednesdays begin with a town meeting and end with an afternoon and evening of house-related activities, including a home-cooked meal.

Dinner is at 6; following that, younger children go to their houses for reading period, study time, and an evening in their houses until bedtime at 8:30. Older children remain in the building for study hall. Bedtime for them is 9:30.

WEEKEND LIFE

Weekends are nonacademic and involve field trips, hikes, sailing, and water activities in the fall and spring as well as games, horseback riding, fort building, off-campus winter competitions, sledding, skating, various homemade entertainments, dances, and free play. Ice cream is served on Saturday nights and followed by a dance or an all-school activity. Children never leave the campus unsupervised but often go 2 or 3 at a time with a faculty member to work on a town-related project, buy fish for the aquarium, get a bicycle fixed, or go in larger groups for an occasional movie.

SUMMER PROGRAMS

North Country School and Camp Treetops are seasonal expressions of the same philosophy. Camp Treetops, which was founded in 1921, provides a seven-week program that, with the exception of the academic component, very much mirrors the School. Children from age 8 to 14 participate in the regular session and children from 14 to 17 in Treetops Expeditions—four- to five-week trips that involve a variety of activities, including hiking, kayaking, cycling, and community service.

COSTS AND FINANCIAL AID

Student tuition for 2011–12 is $52,500. This fee covers such costs as textbooks, art materials, laundry service, field trips, and all ski and recreational passes. ESL is provided at an additional fee.

Financial aid is provided to approximately 35 percent of the students enrolled, the average grant being $18,000. Eligibility for financial aid is based upon the recommendation of the School Schol arship Service and requires submission of a copy of the applicant family's IRS filing for the previous year.

ADMISSIONS INFORMATION

North Country School looks to enroll children who are capable of using the School and the community to their advantage and who are also able to give to others from their own lives. The School is particularly successful with gifted children and children with variant learning styles. A decision to accept is based upon a child's school records, conversations with the child's parents, recommendations from those who have taught the child, the results of Wechsler Intelligence Scale for Children, and an interview with the School administrators. Skype interviews may be arranged for international families.

APPLICATION TIMETABLE

Applications to North Country School Camp Treetops are considered on a rolling admissions basis; midyear enrollment is possible.

ADMISSIONS CORRESPONDENCE

Director of Admissions
North Country School–Camp Treetops
4382 Cascade Road
Lake Placid, New York 12946
Phone: 518-523-9329 Ext. 6000
Fax: 518-523-4858
E-mail: admissions@northcountryschool.org
Web site: http://www.northcountryschool.org

RUMSEY HALL SCHOOL

Washington Depot, Connecticut

Type: Coeducational junior boarding (grades 5–9) and day preparatory school
Grades: K–9: Lower School, K–5; Upper School, 6–9
Enrollment: School total: 321
Head of School: Thomas W. Farmen, Headmaster

THE SCHOOL

Rumsey Hall School was founded in 1900 by Mrs. Lillias Rumsey Sanford. Since its inception, Rumsey Hall School has retained its original philosophy: to help each child develop to his or her maximum stature as an individual, as a member of a family, and as a contributing member of society. The curriculum emphasizes basic academic skills, a complete athletic program, fine arts, computer literacy, and numerous extracurricular offerings, which are all designed to encourage individual responsibility for academic achievement, accomplishment in team sports, and service to the School community. The School believes that "effort is the key to success."

The 147-acre campus on the Bantam River provides landscaped and wooded areas in a rural environment located outside of Washington, Connecticut. Rumsey Hall School is 90 miles from New York City and within an hour of the major Connecticut cities of Hartford and New Haven. The School's location enables students to take advantage of major cultural and athletic events in New York City and Boston throughout the school year.

A nonprofit institution, Rumsey Hall School is governed by a 21-member Board of Trustees that meets quarterly. The 2011–12 operating budget totaled $7.6 million. Revenues include tuition and fees and contributions from alumni, parents, corporations, foundations, and friends of the School. The School's endowment is approximately $8.3 million. Annual fund giving was $1.8 million in 2011.

Rumsey Hall School is a member of the National Association of Independent Schools, the Connecticut Association of Independent Schools, the Junior Boarding Schools Association, the Educational Records Bureau, Western Connecticut Boarding Schools, and the Educational Testing Service, and is a voting member of the Secondary School Admission Test Board.

ACADEMIC PROGRAMS

At Rumsey Hall, effort is as important as academic achievement. Effort as a criterion for success opens a new world to the students. Effort does not start and end with the student. It is a shared responsibility between the student and each faculty member. Just as the faculty members expect maximum effort from each student, they promise in return to give each student their very best effort.

Students in the Upper School (sixth through ninth grades) carry at least five major subjects. There are eight 40-minute periods in each day, including lunch. Extra help is available each day for students who need additional instruction or extra challenges. All classes are departmentalized.

Final examinations are given in all subjects twice a year. Report cards, with numerical grades, are sent home every other week throughout the school year. Anecdotal comments and individualized teacher, adviser, and Headmaster comments are sent home three times each academic year.

A supplementary feature of the academic program is the Language Skills Department, which is directed toward intellectually able students with dyslexia or learning differences. Students in this program carry a regular academic course load, with the exception of a foreign language. In 2011–12, 15 percent of the student body was involved in this program.

English as a Second Language (ESL) is offered to international students and is comprised of two levels with three courses in each level. The courses are designed to help students develop their conversational and academic English, reading comprehension, awareness of social and cultural differences, and to introduce them to American history.

The school year, divided into trimesters, begins in September and runs until the first weekend in June. Vacations are scheduled at Thanksgiving and Christmas and in the spring.

Class size averages 12 students. Honors courses are offered to exceptional ninth grade students who demonstrate talent and whose scholarship indicates a strong sense of responsibility and motivation.

Students have a study hall built into their daily schedules, and there is an evening study hall for all boarding students. Study halls are supervised by faculty members, and there is ample opportunity for assistance. The library and computer facilities adjoin the formal study hall and are available at all study times.

In the Lower School (K through fifth grade), the nine daily academic periods begin at 8 a.m. after class meetings. English, reading, mathematics, science, and social studies are taught by the classroom teachers. Classes in foreign languages, language skills, health, music, art, and physical education vary the students' schedules by requiring them to move to different classrooms with specialized teachers. Normal class size is between 12 and 14 students, which makes for a dynamic learning environment where everyone's voice is heard and encouraged.

FACULTY AND ADVISERS

All 58 full- and part-time faculty members (29 men and 29 women) hold baccalaureate degrees, and half have master's degrees. Forty-two faculty members live on campus, many with their families. This enables Rumsey to provide the close supervision and warm family atmosphere that is an essential part of the School's culture.

Thomas W. Farmen was appointed Headmaster of Rumsey Hall School in 1985. He holds a Bachelor of Arts degree from New England College and a master's in school administration from Western Connecticut State University. He has served as President of the Association of Boarding Schools for the National Association of Independent Schools, President of the Junior Boarding Schools Association, and as a director of the Connecticut Association of Independent Schools.

The Dean of Students supervises and coordinates the advisory program. Each faculty member has 7 or 8 student advisees. Advisers meet with their advisees individually and in a weekly group setting. The adviser is the first link in the line of communication between school and home.

Faculty members at Rumsey Hall are encouraged to continue their professional development by taking postgraduate courses and attending seminars and conferences throughout the year. The School generously funds these programs.

SECONDARY SCHOOL PLACEMENT

The Director of Secondary School Placement supervises all facets of the secondary school search. Beginning in the eighth grade, a process of testing and interviewing with students and parents takes place that enables the placement director to highlight certain schools that seem appropriate. After visits and interviews with the schools, the list is pared down to those to which the student wishes to apply. The 74 graduates of the class of 2011 wrote applications to sixty-two schools, and 80 percent of the students enrolled in their first-choice schools. Members of the 2009–11 classes enrolled in the following prep schools: Asheville School, Avon Old Farms, Berkshire, Brewster, Canterbury School, Cheshire Academy, Dana Hall School, Deerfield Academy, Dwight School, Emma Willard, George School, Governor's Academy, Groton, The Gunnery, Hill, Hotchkiss, Hun School of Princeton, Kent, Kimball Union Academy, Kiski School, Lawrenceville, Liberty Christian Academy, Loomis Chaffee, Masters School, Mercersburg Academy, Middlesex, Millbrook, Milton Academy, Miss Hall's, Miss Porter's, Northfield Mount Hermon, Phillips Academy, Phillips Exeter Academy, Poly Prep, Proctor, Putney, St. Andrew's, St. George's, St. James, St. Johnsbury Academy, St. Margaret's, St. Mark's, St. Paul's, Salisbury, South Kent, Suffield, Taft, Trinity-Pawling, Vermont Academy, Walnut Hill, Westminster, Westover, and Williston Northampton.

STUDENT BODY AND CONDUCT

In 2011–12, Rumsey Hall enrolled 321 students. The Lower School (grades K–5) enrolled 72 day students. The Upper School (grades 6–9) enrolled 249 students: 112 day students and 137 boarders. The School population was 56 percent boys and 44 percent girls.

In 2011–12, Rumsey students came from nineteen states, eleven countries, and thirty-three local communities. International students enrolled in the ESL program composed 8 percent of the community.

The dress code requires jackets, collared shirts, and ties for boys and dresses or skirts and collared shirts or blouses for girls. In the winter term, boys may wear turtlenecks and sweaters and girls may wear slacks.

The School values of honesty, kindness, and respect comprise the yardstick by which Rumsey measures a student's thoughts and actions. Students living outside the spirit of the community are asked to meet with the Disciplinary and Senior Committees. These committees represent a cross section of administrators, faculty members, and students.

ACADEMIC FACILITIES

Situated alongside the Bantam River on a 147-acre campus, the School is housed in thirty buildings, most of which have been constructed since 1950. Nine structures house a total of thirty classrooms, including the Dane W. Dicke Family Math and Science Buildings. Other buildings include the Dicke Family Library; the Sanford House, which houses the study and meeting hall; the J. Seward Johnson Sr. Fine Arts Center, with spacious art and music rooms; and the Satyvati Science Center. Students and faculty members meet as a community for meals in the D. G. Barr Dining Hall.

The Garassino Building is home to three lower school classrooms including an all-day kindergarten. The Maxwell A. Sarofim '05 Performing Arts Center (the MAX) is the setting for student performances, visiting artists, and school assemblies; students' art and exhibits of Rumsey community interest are displayed in the adjacent Allen Finkelson Gallery.

Rumsey has three fully interactive computer labs on campus and more than 120 wireless networked computers throughout the School. The schoolwide intranet system enhances communication within the community.

BOARDING AND GENERAL FACILITIES

The close relationship between teachers and students is a special part of Rumsey Hall School. Students live in dormitories with supportive dorm parents, and students become a part of their dorm parents' families.

Rumsey's boarding students live in one of eight dormitories. Dormitories are assigned by age, and most students have roommates, although single rooms are available in most dorms. Each dormitory has its own common room that is the shared living space for the dorm. A snack bar and store are open every afternoon. Laundry and dry cleaning are sent out on a weekly basis. Four registered nurses staff the School's infirmary, and the School doctor, a local pediatrician, is available on a daily basis. Emergency facilities are available at New Milford Hospital, which is 10 miles away. There are telephones in all dormitories, and every student has an e-mail account.

ATHLETICS

Athletics are a healthy and essential part of the Rumsey experience. On the playing field, lifelong attitudes, values, and habits are born. All students participate at their own level in athletics. Effort is rewarded through athletic letters and certificates at the end of the season.

Rumsey Hall fields thirty-two interscholastic teams throughout the year. Most sports are offered on different levels so that students are able to compete with children of their own size and skill level. Interscholastic teams are fielded in baseball, basketball, crew, cross-country, field hockey, football, boys' ice hockey, girls' ice hockey, lacrosse, skiing, soccer, softball, tennis, volleyball, and wrestling. Other activities available include horseback riding, Outdoor Club, Lower School games and activities, recreational skiing and snowboarding, biking, and ice-skating.

The John F. Schereschewsky, Sr. Memorial Center houses the Magnoli and Blue Dog Gymnasiums where basketball, volleyball, and wrestling activities are held. Recent renovations to the indoor athletic facilities include an indoor climbing wall, boys' and girls' locker rooms, and three new and improved tennis courts. The Cornell Common Room serves as the weight-training room and offers other training machines, as well as housing the athletic director and athletic training staff. Lufkin Rink is the newest of Rumsey Hall's athletic facilities. Opened in late 2008, the rink provides home ice for the boys' and girls' hockey teams. Intramural and recreational activities make the space available to skaters of all abilities.

There are several athletic fields on campus including the Pavek Athletic Field, in honor of Veronica D. and Charles H. Pavek; Scott Evans Seibert '92 Memorial Field; Paul Lincoln Cornell Athletic Field, and Roy Field. There are also three outdoor tennis courts and two ponds for outdoor recreation and winter skating.

Holt Beach at Lake Waramaug is the site for spring crew training. Students who ski and snowboard in the winter term travel to Mohawk Mountain in nearby Cornwall, Connecticut on weekday afternoons.

EXTRACURRICULAR OPPORTUNITIES

Throughout the year, Upper School students may participate in many activities and clubs. The choices include fishing, computers, chorus, art club, bicycling, fly fishing, School newspaper, yearbook, art, swimming, hiking, rocketry, baking, community service, intramural sports, and participation in School dramatic and musical productions.

The Lower School features an exciting afternoon enrichment program for all students in kindergarten through fifth grade after their daily academic curriculum is complete. In keeping with Rumsey Hall's mission to educate the whole child, the varied activities offered each afternoon are organized to cultivate interests that can be nurtured as the children grow. Most activities are led by Rumsey teachers while others enlist the skills of specialists from surrounding communities. Activities include but are not limited to the arts (ceramics, printmaking, theater, crafts), athletics (field/gymnasium sports, martial arts), and recreational and outdoor games.

Traditional annual events for the School community include a Christmas concert, Parents' Day, Grandparents' Day, and Headmaster's Weekend and ski trip to Bromley Mountain, Vermont. Service to the School and to the greater community is encouraged throughout the year by the community service/service learning program. During the 2010–11 academic year the students amassed 1,121 total hours of volunteer service.

The student body is divided into red and blue color teams. These teams enjoy friendly competition throughout the school year in areas of community service, academic achievement, and athletics.

DAILY LIFE

The school day begins at 8 a.m. with an all-School meeting. All administrators, faculty members, and students are in attendance. It is a time to share the news of the School and the world as well as important information and announcements with the whole community. The rest of the academic day consists of eight 40-minute periods and supervised study halls, with a 20-minute recess in the middle of the morning. Extra help is available every day after lunch. Athletic practices or contests take place from 3 to 4:30 p.m. Dinner is served family style at 6 and is followed by study hall from 7 to 8:30. Free time follows, with bedtimes varying depending on the grade of the child.

WEEKEND LIFE

Weekends for boarding students include a variety of activities on and off campus. There are School dances, special theme weekends, off-campus trips, and intramural activities on campus. Rumsey's proximity to four major cities—New York, Boston, Hartford, and New Haven—allows for a wide variety of cultural events, sports events (collegiate and professional), and shopping excursions. All trips are fully supervised, and an appropriate student-teacher ratio is maintained. Day students are encouraged to participate in weekend activities and are also allowed to invite boarding students home with them for the weekend.

SUMMER PROGRAMS

The five-week Rumsey Hall summer session is open to students in the third through ninth grades. The program is designed for students who desire enrichment or need additional work in a subject area in order to move on to the next grade with confidence.

Special emphasis is placed on English, mathematics, study skills, and computer skills. Normal class size ranges from 6 to 10 students with individual attention and help available. Students who need support in language skills or developmental reading work daily with trained specialists. ESL is offered to international students. In the afternoon, students enjoy recreational activities such as swimming, hiking, tennis, fishing, horseback riding, baseball, soccer, lacrosse, and basketball. Off-campus trips to museums, movies, concerts, amusement parks, and sporting events occur each week. Considerable effort is made to cultivate students' interests and to expose them to new experiences. For the 2011 summer session, tuition, room, and board was $6800 for boarding students, $2430 for day students, and $1580 for half-day students. There are additional fees for individual tutoring in language skills and enrollment in ESL.

COSTS AND FINANCIAL AID

In 2011–12, full-year tuition was $17,000 for kindergarten, $17,400 for day students in grades 1 and 2, $21,400 for day students in grades 3–9, and $45,100 for boarding students. Additional fees included books, athletic fees, school supplies, and laundry and dry cleaning. A nonrefundable deposit of $2000 serves as the boarding student's drawing account for the year. The annual fee for language skills was $5020. The annual fee for ESL was $7350. Two thirds of the total tuition is due July 15 and the balance by December 15. A ten-installment payment agreement is available.

Rumsey Hall is a member of the School and Student Service for Financial Aid. In the 2011–12 academic year approximately $1 million in tuition assistance was awarded to one third of the students.

ADMISSIONS INFORMATION

Rumsey Hall welcomes students of average to above-average intelligence and achievement. Students must show evidence of good citizenship and the willingness to live in a boarding community. Acceptance is based on past school performance, scores on standardized achievement tests, and a personal interview. Rumsey is able to accept a limited number of students with learning differences if their learning profile is compatible with the School's Orton-Gillingham–based language skills program. Rumsey Hall School admits students of any race, color, religion, or national or ethnic origin.

APPLICATION TIMETABLE

Inquiries are welcome at any time of the year, with most families beginning the admission process in the fall or winter in anticipation of September enrollment. Admission interviews and tours are scheduled throughout the year. Boarding student applications are accepted on a rolling basis. Day student applicants should complete the application process by February 15. Applicants are notified of acceptance by March 1.

ADMISSIONS CORRESPONDENCE

Matthew S. Hoeniger '81, Director of Admissions
Rumsey Hall School
201 Romford Road
Washington Depot, Connecticut 06794

Phone: 860-868-0535
Fax: 860-868-7907
E-mail: admiss@rumseyhall.org
Web site: http://www.rumseyhall.org

Summer Programs Close-Ups

BESANT HILL SCHOOL

SUMMER INSTITUTE FOR AMERICAN LANGUAGE AND CULTURE

OJAI, CALIFORNIA

TYPE OF PROGRAM: English as a Second Language (ESL)
PARTICIPANTS: International students
PROGRAM DATES: July–August
HEAD OF PROGRAM: Portia Pelow-Dickerson, Director

LOCATION

The Besant Hill Summer Institute for American Language and Culture provides a safe and secure setting on 500 acres at the foot of the beautiful Topa Topa Mountains in the resort town of Ojai, California. The proximity to major cities of Ventura, Santa Barbara, and Los Angeles enables international participants to gain knowledge and understanding of life in the United States. In addition, the program also provides an intensive English language learning experience in the classroom.

BACKGROUND AND PHILOSOPHY

Recognized throughout the world for its commitment to international relations, the Besant Hill Summer Institute for American Language and Culture's six-week immersion summer program in English as a Second Language (ESL) is highly recommended for students who plan to continue their education in the United States. It is also an enrichment program for visiting students interested in improving their English and writing skills.

Besant Hill School has earned a worldwide reputation for being among the finest schools in the United States. Students from the Los Angeles and Ventura areas and from all over the world participate in the School's college-preparatory academic and preprofessional arts programs, which ensure that they are well prepared to enroll in the nation's best colleges and universities.

The students in this summer program have a schedule that mirrors many aspects of the school day at BHS. From academic and art classes in the morning to study hall and dorm crew jobs in the evening, they are able to get used to the duties they are likely to have during the year. In addition, the Institute provides opportunities to have fun and learn about American culture. Outside of classes, students and faculty play games and travel around California—from Ojai to Santa Barbara to San Francisco, and many places in between. As the summer wraps up, the students compile a newsletter highlighting their experiences.

PROGRAM OFFERINGS

The Besant Hill Summer Institute for American Language and Culture offers vigorous academic instruction in English along with travel, recreation, and cultural exchange. For approximately six weeks, from the beginning of July to the middle of August, boys and girls between the ages of 14 and 18 live with faculty members in a close-knit, multicultural community.

A blend of academics, cultural enrichment, language projects, travel experiences, summer camp activities, and total language immersion makes the Besant Hill Summer Institute for American Language and Culture experience truly unique.

English Study Beginner/Intermediate: The ESL Beginner/Intermediate Instruction programs offer different levels of academic instruction for beginning and intermediate English learners. Small class size and skilled supportive teachers are the keys to the success of this programs, which consists of two 2-hour skills classes: one to enhance listening and speaking, the other to focus on reading and writing.

Integrated Skills for Advanced Students Preparing for TOEFL iBT: This 4-hour course is the perfect choice for the summer for the student who is a rising junior (grade 11), senior (grade 12), or postgraduate, who possesses advanced demonstrable proficiency in English and wish to practice intensively for the Internet-based test of English as a Foreign Language (TOEFL iBT); improve English grammar and sentence structure; expand vocabulary; hone reading and listening skills; and refine essay writing skills. In addition to the grade-level and English proficiency criteria needed to enroll in this course, class size is set at appropriately 12 qualified students. Not only do students take pre- and post-assessments in all sections of the TOEFL iBT, they also periodically complete an entire practice (unofficial) test.

ENROLLMENT

In the summer of 2010, there were 14 international students who participated in BHS Institute for American Language and Culture program. Of those students, 13 went on to enroll in BHS for the upcoming academic year.

DAILY SCHEDULE

Students attend academic classes during the morning, participate in a variety of projects and activities in the afternoon, play together in the pool and on the athletic fields, travel throughout the United States visiting major landmarks, and learn to work and live in a global society. The BHS Institute for American Language and Culture places a strong emphasis on respect for the individual and the uniqueness that each student brings to the community.

EXTRA OPPORTUNITIES AND ACTIVITIES

The iBT Test of English as a Foreign Language (TOEFL) is a computerized test that ESL students take before applying to an American college or university. Spaces at official testing sites fill quickly because registration is done electronically. Students who are interested in taking the TOEFL while studying at the Besant Hill Summer Institute for American Language and Culture are able to register in advance for a test date between the months of July and August.

FACILITIES

There are twelve buildings on the Besant Hill campus. Networked computer stations are available in several buildings. Most of the campus has wireless access. The School houses a science lab, observatory, photography lab, new art studio, theater, recording studio, ceramics studio, and digital media lab. The renowned Zalk Theater houses both the drama and music departments. The School has also recently added four soundproof music practice rooms.

The Besant Hill School campus offers boarding facilities for both boys and girls. The residents are housed 2 to a room in bedrooms that contain study and storage facilities for each student. Other facilities include a modern dining hall, tennis courts, volleyball courts, a baseball field, basketball courts, and a soccer field.

STAFF

Portia Pelow-Dickerson, is the Director of Besant Hill Summer Institute for American Language and Culture. She is Chair of the Department of English and teaches English and ESL classes at Besant Hill School during the school year. In addition, she coaches both girls' volleyball and soccer.

MEDICAL CARE

Medical care is provided as needed.

COSTS

Tuition and fees for the Besant Hill Summer Institute for American Language and Culture's approximately six-week program are $8000. The fee includes room, board, tuition, books, student activities, in-program travel, and the issuance of an I-20 if needed. There is an additional $150 application fee. A $500 non-refundable deposit is due with the application by May 15. If an I-20 is needed, it will be issued after the full amount is received. One-on-one tutoring and individualized instruction is available for an additional cost.

TRANSPORTATION

Transportation is provided from the airport to Besant Hill School, as needed.

APPLICATION TIMETABLE

The application along with the nonrefundable deposit must be received by May 15. The remainder of the tuition must be sent by June 15. Applications are available online at www.besanthill.org.

FOR MORE INFORMATION, CONTACT:

Summer Institute for American Language and Culture
Besant Hill School
8585 Ojai-Santa Paula Road
Ojai, California 92023
Phone: 805-646-4343
E-mail: ppelow@besanthill.org
Web site: http://www.besanthill.org

CHAMBERLAIN-HUNT ACADEMY

ADVENTURE SUMMER SCHOOL

PORT GIBSON, MISSISSIPPI

TYPE OF PROGRAM: ACADEMIC ENRICHMENT
PARTICIPANTS: Students entering grades 7–12
ENROLLMENT: 50
PROGRAM DATES: June 4–30, 2012
HEAD OF PROGRAM: Jack West, President

LOCATION

Chamberlain-Hunt Academy is located 3 miles east of the Mississippi River, 27 miles south of Vicksburg, and 35 miles north of Natchez on U.S. Highway 61 in rural Mississippi. The Academy's campus is approximately 200 acres in size.

BACKGROUND AND PHILOSOPHY

Founded in 1879, Chamberlain-Hunt is the third-oldest military boarding school in the United States. The Academy has a rich 134-year tradition, challenging young men toward knowledge and wisdom in submission to God.

Chamberlain-Hunt is first and foremost a Christian school. It operates on the belief that God made man for His glory, and, therefore, everything that is taught in the classroom, achieved on the playing field, or modeled in relationships is done to the honor and glory of God.

Chamberlain-Hunt is one of the few military schools in the United States that self-consciously maintains its distinctive Christian character and strict military discipline.

Chamberlain-Hunt is also a boarding school. Its cadets are removed from some of the distractions of the usual high school scene and are placed in an environment that supports their academic, physical, and spiritual development.

Chamberlain-Hunt's Adventure Summer programs offer several benefits for boys during the summer months. Adventure Summer School is a great way to gain academic credit, and its camp-like setting provides opportunities for many outdoor activities. For families that are considering enrolling their son at Chamberlain-Hunt for the school year, the program can serve as an opportunity to try out the Academy's offerings firsthand.

PROGRAM OFFERINGS

This is no ordinary summer school. Adventure Summer School is a challenging month-long academic, military, and adventure experience for rising seventh through twelfth graders.

The main purpose of Adventure Summer School is academic enrichment. Each weekday, students will attend a supervised study hall followed by five hours of classroom instruction from the Academy's excellent faculty. Junior high cadets will complete an enrichment course in reading and math, study skills, and art. High school cadets can earn a full credit from one of the following courses: algebra 1, geometry, English 1 and 2, world history, U.S. history, biology, or chemistry. These courses may be subject to change or reach enrollment limits. Preference is determined by high school level and individual need.

ENROLLMENT

An interview and campus tour is required of all summer cadets. If potential cadets are unable to travel to Chamberlain-Hunt, a video interview is an option; however, the campus tour is an important component to help the parent and the cadet understand the unique characteristics of the Academy. Upon acceptance, there is a $500 deposit to secure enrollment. Space is limited to 50 cadets.

An Adventure Summer School brochure is available to download, print, and share from the Academy's Web site. Prospective families should visit www.chamberlain-hunt.com/.

MILITARY STRUCTURE

The Academy is proud of its century-long military tradition. Military discipline, dormitory inspections, physical training, and a required uniform provide structure to the program and influence habits long after the summer is over. The one-month format of the Adventure Summer School provides numerous opportunities for the cadets to build character and self-confidence with less time away from home and a lower cost than the full school term.

EXTRA OPPORTUNITIES AND ACTIVITIES

A variety of weekend experiences gives cadets a break from their studies. Cadets can use the rifle range with M4 rifle training, climbing wall, obstacle course, paintball courses, and fishing pond in the 72-acre wilderness facility that adjoins the main campus. Off-campus excursions include a trip to a Mississippi Braves baseball game, an overnight camping/canoe trip, and a bowling competition.

FACILITIES

The Academy has over twenty buildings; a full-size, in-ground pool; four ball fields; a six-lane cork track; a weight-training facility; indoor and outdoor basketball courts; two tennis courts; two beach volleyball courts; a covered outdoor recreational pavilion; an auditorium; library; spacious cafeteria; game room; and four air-conditioned residence halls.

There is a 72-acre wilderness training facility adjacent to campus with two paintball courses, a climbing and rappelling

tower, a 30-yard pistol and rifle range, a fitness trail, two confidence courses, and a 4.5-acre pond.

FACULTY

The administrators and staff of Chamberlain-Hunt, known as the cadre, are individuals who care deeply about encouraging young men to make the most of their God-given ability. Cadre members are committed to giving cadets everything they need to achieve their educational goals, while also focusing on their emotional and spiritual development. The Academy's staff and faculty members believe that all wisdom stems from God the heavenly father, and that true education must be an active, ongoing part of a living faith.

Chamberlain-Hunt utilizes a thorough and comprehensive approach in hiring all members of the cadre. The application process includes questions about the prospect's Christian background, education, work history, and personal spiritual beliefs. Because cadre members are working with children, background checks are performed to ensure that only the most honorable and reliable individuals are hired.

Cadre instructors offer an unparalleled education for young men. All instructors are certified and 80 percent hold advanced degrees. The average classroom cadet-to-instructor ratio is 5:1.

COSTS

The cost for the junior high enrichment course is $3600. The cost for the senior high credit course is $4000. These amounts cover tuition, room, board, uniforms, and a cadet bank account of $250 for incidental expenses. The history courses include a travel component, which requires an additional $200 fee. The science courses include a lab, which requires an additional $50 fee.

FINANCIAL AID

There is no financial aid awarded for the summer programs.

TRANSPORTATION

Parents are responsible for travel to and from campus. Chamberlain-Hunt provides transportation to and from the airport, Amtrak terminal, or bus station on the day of arrival or dismissal. Flight, train, and bus departure times should be scheduled no earlier than 3 hours after the published dismissal time.

APPLICATION TIMETABLE

Families should complete Step One of the application, available online, by May 25, 2012.

FOR MORE INFORMATION, CONTACT:

Chamberlain Hunt Academy
124 McComb Avenue
Port Gibson, Mississippi 39150
Phone: 601-437-8855
E-mail: admissions@chamberlain-hunt.com
Web site: http://www.chamberlain-hunt.com

CUSHING ACADEMY

SUMMER SESSION

ASHBURNHAM, MASSACHUSETTS

TYPE OF PROGRAM: Academic enrichment
PARTICIPANTS: Coeducational, ages 12–18
ENROLLMENT: 350
PROGRAM DATES: July to August, five weeks
HEAD OF PROGRAM: Dr. James Tracy, Headmaster

LOCATION

Located in the hills of north-central Massachusetts, 60 miles from Boston, Cushing Academy's 162-acre campus offers a rural atmosphere with the cultural advantages of a major city only an hour's drive away. The school is situated in and overlooks the picturesque New England town of Ashburnham.

BACKGROUND AND PHILOSOPHY

Established in 1865, Cushing Academy is an accredited boarding school for boys and girls in grades 9 through 12. The Summer Session, offering programs for boys and girls ages 12 to 18, continues the school's approach to education into the summer. The mission of the Summer Session is to allow young people to grow and learn by facing challenges in a secure and supportive environment, thereby successfully developing self-esteem. Cushing strives to develop happy, fair-minded, and productive human beings, and all of its programs are directed toward this goal. The focus is always on the potential of the adolescent, and Cushing helps students discover, develop, and appreciate their own uniqueness and value.

PROGRAM OFFERINGS

Each student is enrolled in one of five major programs: College Prep–Secondary School Level; Critical Skills Across the Curriculum in English, Mathematics, and Study Techniques; English as a Second Language; the Prep for Success Program; or Studio Art. The average class contains 8–12 students, with a purposeful yet friendly atmosphere that encourages questions and discussion. Faculty members prepare two formal evaluations on each student, one in the middle and one at the end of the summer. Written evaluations highlight the progress made by the individual student relative to his or her own needs and placement, and a grade of honors, pass, or fail is given.

College Prep–Secondary School Level For students ages 14–18, this program offers a choice of Geometry, Algebra I and II, Precalculus, Calculus, U.S. History, English: Literature and Writing, Biology, Chemistry, and Physics. A College Advising Workshop is also available for rising juniors and seniors (not for academic credit.) The courses taught in this program prepare students to meet the challenge of a college-level curriculum confidently and successfully. Each of these courses is the equivalent of a year of secondary school course work, and Cushing awards a full year of secondary school academic credit upon successful completion of the program.

Critical Skills Across the Curriculum This program is for students ages 14–18. It aims to accelerate students' learning in two "foundation" subjects that play an essential role in success across the curriculum: English (literature and writing) and mathematics. Each student is given placement tests to assess skills and learning styles, and an individualized learning program is developed. Students are assigned to classes structured to meet their specific learning needs. Each student learns at his or her own pace, mastering progressively higher levels of skills. The schedule is flexible enough to allow a focus on either English or mathematics development or both. Study skills such as time management, research, and strategies for test-taking are taught within the context of the subject matter.

English as a Second Language (ESL) is offered for students ages 14–18. Within the ESL program, classes enhance skills in reading, writing, speaking, and listening. Students can dramatically increase their proficiency in English through this five-week immersion experience. Students are tested at the beginning of the program and placed in a class appropriate to their skill level and needs. Preparation for the Test of English as a Foreign Language (TOEFL) is offered, and the opportunity to take the official TOEFL is offered to students of advanced and high intermediate levels during the final weeks of the program.

Prep for Success For students ages 12–13, this program offers a choice of English, mathematics, and ESL. Each student also has a daily class of technology and study skills. The courses taught in this program prepare students for the academic experiences that lie ahead in secondary school. Featuring hands-on learning, each course has a dual focus on the subject matter and on the skills needed for academic success, including reading comprehension strategies, vocabulary development, word analogies, time management, organizational techniques, and test-taking strategies.

Studio Art This program, for students ages 13–18, is taught in Cushing's state-of-the-art Emily Fisher Landau Center for the Visual Arts, a beautiful facility with five advanced studios and a gallery. Both experienced and beginning art students are provided with opportunities to explore a variety of media, including painting and drawing, pottery and sculpture, stained and fused glass, silversmithing, and photography.

ENROLLMENT

Approximately 350 students, representing more than thirty countries and as many states, attend the session.

DAILY SCHEDULE

Classes in the major programs take place for 4 hours, Monday through Friday, beginning at 8 a.m. Each afternoon, students participate in academic, athletic, and fine arts electives, of which Cushing offers a wide variety. Writing workshop, SAT preparation, computer design, and Algebra I are just a few academic electives offered. Fine arts electives include painting and drawing, photography, jewelry design, pottery, dance, theater, and

videomaking, while athletic activities include aerobics, basketball, golf, soccer, tennis, and volleyball.

EXTRA OPPORTUNITIES AND ACTIVITIES

Each week brings a variety of activities to campus, including dances, sports events, and performances by musical groups and entertainers. Optional excursions are scheduled every Saturday and Sunday to shopping centers, amusement parks, beaches, Red Sox games, local community service opportunities, and other activities that take advantage of recreational and cultural offerings in the Boston area and throughout New England.

On Wednesdays, a variety of class field trips to sites such as Plimoth Plantation, the New England Aquarium, and Mystic Seaport are organized. These excursions are included in the comprehensive fee and are chaperoned by faculty members. College counseling and secondary school placement counseling are available for students who want assistance with educational planning.

During each week, Cushing offers a special all-school activity, including a trip to High Meadow resort and a dinner/dance cruise around Boston Harbor. Among the special events is International Evening, a celebration of the rich cultural diversity present at the Summer Session. In preparation the students bring from home traditional clothing, flags, posters, and recipes. Cushing's dining hall is transformed into an international bazaar, where students view displays and sample foods from other cultures. The evening concludes with student-created performances of songs, dances, and skits representative of their culture. The Cushing Cabaret, a night dedicated to short programs and entertainment by the Cushing community, has also become a well-loved summer tradition. Students and faculty members show off their talent through comedy, music, poetry, skits, and more.

FACILITIES

The campus combines the charm of nineteenth-century buildings with the contemporary style of Cushing's redesigned digital library. Boys and girls live in separate dormitories with roommates, supervised by members of the faculty. Two or three students are assigned to each room. The Joseph R. Curry Academic Center, an outstanding new facility for the study of science, mathematics, and the performing arts, includes a large theater and dance practice rooms and music studios. The spacious dining hall accommodates the entire Cushing community for relaxed and congenial mealtimes. The Student Center, part of the student commons complex, houses the student post office, bookstore, snack bar, and lounge. Athletic facilities include playing fields, tennis courts, a gymnasium with weight room, and a world-class ice arena.

STAFF

Teachers are experienced professionals educated in the theories and methods of teaching. They are also supportive, insightful, caring, good-humored, and kind. A diverse group, they share a willingness to spend their lives with young people. Most have master's degrees, and some have doctorates; all have experience teaching in this country or abroad. The faculty-student ratio is approximately 1:8. In their roles as dorm parents, athletic coaches, and chaperones, Cushing teachers are in an excellent position to know when to offer support, enforce discipline, mediate a dispute, or let students work things out among themselves.

MEDICAL CARE

The Health Center is fully equipped to handle all routine medical needs. Nurses and doctors are available at all times. Cushing uses the Henry Heywood Hospital in nearby Gardner for nonroutine needs.

COSTS

Program tuitions vary, but the five-week fee of $6675 ($3195 for day students) covers the following: tuition for all courses, academic electives, and athletic activities; meals and dormitory housing; required trips and excursions; special all-school activities; books and supplies; athletic uniform; on-campus social activities, dormitory-room supplies; and limited accident insurance. In addition, students have use of the Academy's communications system, which includes a private telephone, voice mail, and Internet access for each student.

TRANSPORTATION

The staff meets flights and provides transportation between Cushing and Logan International Airport (Boston) on scheduled arrival and departure dates. There is a nominal fee for this service.

APPLICATION TIMETABLE

The application form should be completed and mailed with the nonrefundable processing fee of $60 as early as possible. Admissions decisions are made as soon as these materials are in hand. Within four weeks of acceptance, a nonrefundable enrollment deposit of $500 is due. The remainder of the tuition is due on or before May 15.

FOR MORE INFORMATION, CONTACT

Cushing Academy Summer Session
39 School Street
Ashburnham, Massachusetts 01430-8000
Phone: 978-827-7700
Fax: 978-827-6927
E-mail: summersession@cushing.org
Web site: http://www.cushing.org

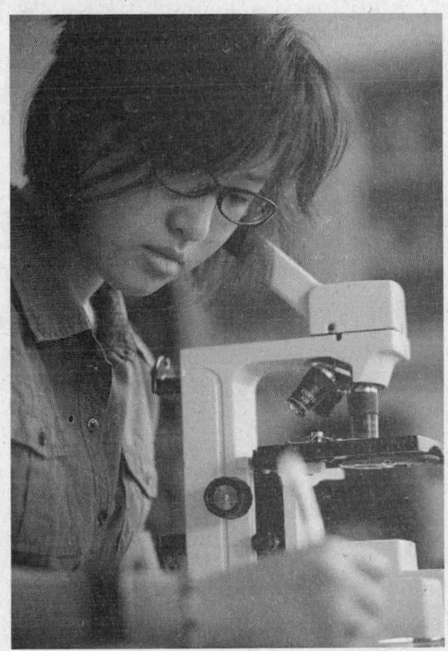

FAY SCHOOL

INTERNATIONAL STUDENT PROGRAM

SOUTHBOROUGH, MASSACHUSETTS

TYPE OF PROGRAM: International families who want their children to be educated in the United States have a unique opportunity at Fay School each summer. The International Student Program offers academic programs in the morning and day camp activities in the afternoon, providing English language immersion and contact with domestic students of a comparable age.

PARTICIPANTS: Coeducational, international boarding students, ages 10–15

ENROLLMENT: 50

PROGRAM DATES: Early July through mid-August

HEAD OF PROGRAM: Liza Gallagher, Director of Auxiliary Programs

LOCATION

Fay School is situated on 42 beautiful acres in semirural surroundings in Southborough, Massachusetts, 25 miles west of Boston.

BACKGROUND AND PHILOSOPHY

The International Student Program (ISP) is integrated into the entire summer Fay experience. In addition to their daily academic program, international students spend part of each day with domestic students of similar age, choosing from a variety of fun and enriching activities that include day camp, athletics, visual and performing arts, trips, cultural experiences, test preparation, and public speaking. Each afternoon, students are immersed in English, putting their language skills to work, all while participating in engaging activities with other campers.

This summer boarding program makes it possible for international students ages 10 to 15 to participate in the Fay experience regardless of their level of English proficiency. It provides a meaningful introduction to Fay for students enrolling full-time in the upcoming academic year as well as an outstanding stand-alone program for international students who wish to focus on developing their English skills during the summer months.

The International Student Program supports students in all aspects of their summer experience. The School provides ground travel arrangements, academic scheduling, and continuous communication with parents. International students learn English by taking academic courses at their appropriate level.

PROGRAM OFFERINGS

Each morning, ISP students take academic classes designed to improve their English writing and speaking skills. There are three levels of classes: beginner (Level I), intermediate (Level II), and advanced (Level III). Students are placed in classes upon their arrival at Fay based on placement tests. At every level, classes emphasize grammar, composition, reading comprehension, and speaking and listening skills. Advanced electives include world geography, U.S. history, general science, and creative writing. As students become more proficient, they may progress to higher levels of the program. In

addition to daily course work, students are expected to complete approximately 1 hour of homework each night.

Students are assessed in class on both effort and achievement. Just as in Fay's regular school year ISP program, students receive effort grades every two weeks in order to provide feedback on their level of engagement. In addition, students receive a midsummer grade and a final grade for each course, along with a written summary from the student's advisers.

Each afternoon, ISP students join children from the local area by participating in day camp or a specialty workshop, which includes academics, art, theater, music, outdoor adventures, and sports. This provides ISP students the opportunity to have an afternoon full of activities of their choice and to meet American friends of the same age.

The day camp activities offered in the afternoons include: archery, art, baseball, basketball, boating, ceramics, climbing wall, computers, cooking, crafts, dodge ball, drawing, fishing, flag football, free swim, gardening, GPS mapping and orienteering, high ropes course, improv, jewelry making, kickball, music, music with computers, nature, outdoor living, painting, photography, puppeteering, robotics and rockets, science, sculpture, sewing and fashion design, soccer, street hockey, swim lessons, tennis, theater, Ultimate (Frisbee), video production, woodshop, and writers' corner.

ENROLLMENT

During the summer of 2011, 50 students enrolled in Fay's Summer ISP program.

DAILY SCHEDULE

Mornings: Academic classes
Noon: Lunch
Afternoons: Day Camp activities
4 p.m.: Evening activities, dinner, and study hall

EXTRA OPPORTUNITIES AND ACTIVITIES

Summer weekends at Fay are a valuable time for students to put their language skills to use. They participate in academic and social activities on campus, explore Boston and the surrounding areas on field trips, and bond with faculty and other students. Weekend activities include Summer Olympics, which highlights students' athletic, artistic, and other talents; a canoe trip down the Charles River; a trip to the New England seashore; an historical scavenger hunt throughout Boston; dance parties; and movie trips.

Students are also required to attend study hall each weekend in order to complete assignments for classes. The combination of trips and on-campus activities ensure that students remain engaged in the American experience while allowing them time to foster lasting relationships with students from all over the world.

FACILITIES

Fay's residential facilities are comfortable and well supervised. An adult is available at all times to answer questions and help resolve any issues that may arise. The School strives to create a family atmosphere based on respect for one's self and for others. Students live, work, and play together with guidance and supervision from dedicated teachers and staff.

The Root Academic Center (1984) houses most of the Upper and Lower School classrooms. The Mars Wing (2001) includes the Learning Center, the media lab, four state-of-the-art science labs, a writing lab, and a multimedia lab. The Picardi Art Center (1987) provides outstanding facilities for art classes, including a darkroom and ceramics studio. The Harris Events Center (1995) is home to Fay's performing arts program and includes five music practice rooms, two music classrooms, a dance studio, and a 400-seat theater.

Family-style meals are served in the dining room. The Wellness Center (2009) is situated in the lower level of the Steward Dorm and serves as the campus medical facility.

The School's athletic facilities were greatly enhanced with the completion of the Fay School athletic campus in 2009. The campus comprises 30 acres of dedicated regulation-sized outdoor fields for soccer, field hockey, baseball, softball, and lacrosse. The campus also features a cross-country course and four batting cages, two for baseball and two for softball. Additional facilities include the Harlow Gymnasium (1993), a facility that incorporates four basketball courts, expanded locker room space, team rooms, a wrestling room, a weight room, and a training room.

STAFF

ISP teachers and residential staff enjoy working with international students and are experienced and skillful instructors and mentors.

MEDICAL CARE

A school nurse is available on campus at all times.

COSTS

Tuition for ISP is $8225, which includes room and board. There is a $1200 incidentals fee (the unused portion is returned to the family).

FINANCIAL AID

Prospective families should contact the Director of Auxiliary Programs to discuss the possible availability of financial aid.

TRANSPORTATION

Fay School will make ground transportation arrangements from and to the airport.

APPLICATION TIMETABLE

Student registration is conducted on a rolling basis throughout the 2011–12 school year.

FOR MORE INFORMATION, CONTACT:

Liza Gallagher, Director of Auxiliary Programs
Fay School
48 Main Street
Southborough, Massachusetts 01772
Phone: 508-485-8247
E-mail: LGallagher@fayschool.org
Web site: http://www.fayschool.org

LANDMARK SCHOOL SUMMER PROGRAM

SUMMER ACADEMIC PROGRAMS

PRIDES CROSSING, MASSACHUSETTS

TYPE OF PROGRAM: Academic skill development and recreation for students with language-based learning disabilities such as dyslexia

PARTICIPANTS: Coeducational, ages 7–20, grades 1–12

ENROLLMENT: 125

PROGRAM DATES: Elementary-Middle: July 5–August 8 and High School: July 8–August 3

HEAD OF PROGRAM: Robert J. Broudo, M.Ed., Head of School

LOCATION

Landmark School has two beautiful campuses on the Atlantic coast just 25 miles north of Boston and close to beaches, fishing ports, and sailing centers. The location is ideal for educational, cultural, and recreational activities, and the School takes full advantage of its setting.

BACKGROUND AND PHILOSOPHY

Landmark's Summer Program offers a chance to learn, relax, and have fun in a supportive environment—whether it's gaining a jump start for the next grade or supplementing gaps in learning—for students with language-based learning disabilities. The program combines intensive, academic skill development with recreational activities and exploration along Boston's beautiful North Shore. Landmark provides a customized program for each student that is designed to improve reading, writing, spelling, and study skills. The program's daily one-to-one tutorial is the cornerstone of its individualized approach. Students are bright, motivated to learn, and emotionally healthy, but they need help to achieve academic excellence.

PROGRAM OFFERINGS

Landmark's Elementary and Middle School Summer Program runs five weeks, from July 5 to August 8. Students have the option of a half-day academic program or a full-day combination program, which includes afternoon activities.

Half-Day Academic Program Students build language arts skills through small classes and a daily one-to-one tutorial. This program for elementary and middle school students is offered in the morning from 8 a.m. to noon. The Half-Day Academic Program is the only option available to first and second graders (afternoon activities are not offered for this age group).

Full-Day Combination Program Students in grades 3–7 start their day with a morning of academic classes, including a daily one-to-one tutorial. In the afternoon they may choose from the Exploration Program or the Sun, Sand, and Speed Program.

Exploration Program Marine Science and Adventure Ropes activities are offered together in consecutive 14-day segments for small groups of students in grades 3–7. Marine Science includes field trips, lab activities, kayaking, an introduction to snorkeling, and exploration of the North Shore's ocean and coastal ecosystems. Adventure Ropes offers younger students use of Landmark's climbing wall and low ropes elements to engage in fun, problem-solving group activities, as well as nature exploration and arts-oriented activities. Older students use the outdoor course, engaging in games and confidence building on the climbing wall and low ropes and high ropes elements.

Sun, Sand, and Speed Landmark introduces students in grades 3–7 to a fun pair of hands-on challenges: Woodworking and the Art of Small-Engine Repair and Design. Basic woodworking skills are presented and reinforced in supervised sessions that allow students to work at their own pace. Ultimately they learn how to build a model boat. Small-Engine Repair and Design teaches students how to research tools, use common tools and computer programs to repair a single-cylinder small engine as well as related computer programs. Participants design and build their own CO_2-powered dragster as a culminating class project.

Landmark High School's **Summer School in a Month** runs from July 8 to August 3. It combines intensive academic-skill development with afterschool programs for students in grades 8–12. High School students have three core requirements which include Language Arts (which focuses on written expression), Mathematics, and a daily one-to-one Language Arts tutorial. Based on individual strengths, each student is also assigned to either Study Skills (to develop a more organized and independent approach to learning) or Reading Literature (for oral reading and comprehension skills). Academic classes will be held in the morning, followed by lunch in the campus dining room and study hall during the week. Day students may stay for study hall or leave at lunch time.

The **2012 Afterschool Activities** for high school students run from 3 to 6 p.m. It is open to day students for an additional fee. Students may choose one of the five following programs:

Marine Science Students can spend their afternoons exploring the seashore and a wide variety of marine life while relaxing with new friends. This program provides discovery through field activities where participants get their hands and feet wet and learn by doing. Students investigate a range of local environments including rocky shores, salt marshes, and sandy beaches through snorkeling and shoreline exploration. The class also visits sites of maritime historic interest. Students should feel comfortable in and around water but do not need to be strong swimmers. Students should have (or plan to purchase), a mask, snorkel, and fins.

Visual Arts This program enables students to explore a variety of art media in depth. It includes both 2-D and 3-D media, such as drawing and painting, digital photography, and ceramics. This is an excellent opportunity for both beginning art students and those interested in pursuing art beyond high school.

Audio/Video Production This program lets students produce their own short films. It offers an introduction to the methods used to create a comprehensive short film. Students learn about film formulas, script writing, and storyboards and then use technology to enhance and edit their product. Students work in groups and participate as members of the video crew and on-screen actors.

Health and Fitness Training Students become members of a local gym for the month of July and work with a health-conscious Landmark-trained teacher to prepare themselves for upcoming athletic seasons or to simply create and advance their personal fitness goals. Students explore the most effective ways to exercise and maintain a healthy lifestyle.

Digital Photography Students will explore various modalities of taking photographs digitally. The course will focus on the art form of photography, from composition and juxtaposition, as well as the technicalities of this craft. The class will use the rambling Landmark campus and selected locations on the North Shore as its studio and will produce a final show of its most noteworthy work at the end of the course.

Sea Kayaking Students will take advantage of the North Shore's beautiful coastline with daily guided kayak tours out of Gloucester Harbor. Students will learn from the professionally certified staff at Discovery Adventures and will also be supported and encouraged by a Landmark staff member with years of kayaking experience. Students will investigate a range of local kayaking destinations while gaining valuable teambuilding experience. The program aims to help students gain a love of the ocean and its challenges, while fostering a safe environment for students to create friendships through trust and communication. Students should feel comfortable in and around water, but do not need to have kayaking experience.

The **Residential Program** for grades 8–12 includes afterschool programs, weeknight events, and special weekend trips. Living at Landmark allows students to acquire the skills they need to be successful in college and beyond while relaxing at our beautiful coastal location. The program encourages independence, individual responsibility, and achievement. Students learn how to manage their schoolwork and organize their time. Students also make new friends and lasting connections with peers who have similar learning styles and experiences. Community Nights and weekend trips have included Beach Barbecue Night, Field Day, movie nights, trips to Boston, local beaches and area attractions.

ENROLLMENT

Landmark's Summer Program attracts students from across the United States and many other countries. The program accepts bright students who have been diagnosed with a language-based learning disability, such as dyslexia. Successful candidates should be emotionally healthy and motivated to learn but need remedial help with reading, writing, spelling, listening, speaking, or mathematics. Prior to admission, Landmark must receive a diagnostic evaluation as well as educational and medical records. Landmark offers day and residential programs to students in grades 9–12 and day programs to students in grades 1–12. Landmark admits grade 8 students to the residential program on a case-by-case basis.

DAILY SCHEDULE

The Elementary and Middle School Half-Day Program runs from 7:45 to 11:55 a.m. with lunch included. Afternoon activities in the full-day program run from noon to 3 p.m. The High School Programs run from 8 a.m. to 1:15 p.m. with lunch included. Extended day and resident students have a required study hall from 1:20 to 2:35 p.m. Academic day students not participating in the afterschool activities are dismissed at 2:35, and resident students return to their dorms from 2:35 to 3 p.m. Afterschool activities run from 3 to 6. Extended day students are dismissed at 6 p.m., and residents complete their day with dinner and special community and dorm nights. Bedtimes vary according to the student's age.

EXTRA OPPORTUNITIES AND ACTIVITIES

Afternoons and weekends offer opportunities for outdoor activities and trips (both day and overnight) to local points of interest, historic sites, and cultural programs. Free time, movies, and social events on campus complement these activities.

FACILITIES

Landmark has two campuses located on Boston's beautiful North Shore. The high school and administrative offices are located in the Prides Crossing section of Beverly, Massachusetts. The elementary/ middle school is nestled in the woods on an estate in Manchester-by-the-Sea.

STAFF

Summer staff members are highly trained teachers and supervisors from the regular school year staff. A student-faculty ratio of 3:1 allows Landmark to provide a customized program for each student.

MEDICAL CARE

The Health Center attends to the medical needs of the Landmark community. The center is available on school days from 7 a.m. to 11 p.m.; the duty staff is in charge at other times. Student medications are dispensed from the Health Center. The school physician, other specialists, and the Beverly Hospital Emergency Room are available at all times for residential student appointments and emergencies. The state requires that immunization history forms be submitted at enrollment. In addition, counselors are available if necessary.

RELIGIOUS LIFE

Students who wish to attend religious services are provided with transportation.

COSTS

Tuition varies according to the program. For 2012, tuition for the elementary and middle school programs is as follows: Half-Day Academic Program, grades 1–7, $4625; Full-Day Combination Program, grades 3–7, $6450. For the 2012 high school programs, tuition is as follows: Day Program with no afternoon activity, $4700; Extended Day Program with an afternoon activity, $5775; and Residential Program (includes day program/afternoon activity), $7625.

TRANSPORTATION

Landmark is located about 25 miles from Boston's Logan Airport and within walking distance of the train from Boston. Scheduled transportation to and from Logan Airport is available.

APPLICATION TIMETABLE

Students are accepted in order of applications received. Early application is advised, as space is limited. Applicants cannot be considered without a full diagnostic report; the School is happy to answer questions about testing and to help guide parents or school counselors to diagnostic sources. A tuition deposit of $500 for day students and $1000 for boarding students must accompany the application.

FOR MORE INFORMATION, CONTACT

Admission Office
Landmark School
429 Hale Street
P.O. Box 227
Prides Crossing, Massachusetts 01965-0227

Phone: 978-236-3000
Fax: 978-927-7268
E-mail: admission@landmarkschool.org
Web site: http://www.landmarkschool.org

TASIS–THE AMERICAN SCHOOL IN SWITZERLAND

LANGUAGES, ART HISTORY, PHOTOGRAPHY, ENGINEERING, AND PAINTING TICINO

LUGANO AND CHÂTEAU D'OEX, SWITZERLAND

TYPE OF PROGRAM: *Lugano:* Intensive foreign language study, art history, digital photography, engineering, and painting Ticino; *Château d'Oex:* Intensive French language instruction

PARTICIPANTS: Coeducational, *Lugano:* ages 4+–18; *Château d'Oex:* ages 11–17

ENROLLMENT: *Lugano:* 300; *Château d'Oex:* 65

PROGRAM DATES: *Lugano:* Four weeks, June–July; three weeks, July–August; *Château d'Oex:* Four weeks in July, plus one optional week in August

HEADS OF PROGRAMS: Betsy Newell, Marc Pierre Jansen, Jim Haley, and Marie-Josée Breton

LOCATION

Lugano, Switzerland: Nestled in the foothills of the southern Swiss Alps, with spectacular views, the TASIS campus is a compact cluster of historic buildings and new facilities. It overlooks the attractive resort town of Lugano and is 2 miles from Agno International Airport and less than an hour's drive from Milan (Malpensa) International Airport in Italy. The idyllic setting allows for a wide range of enjoyable activities, including windsurfing, pleasure cruises to lakeside hamlets, picnics, and hiking to picturesque villages.

Château d'Oex, Switzerland: Located in the French-speaking canton of Vaud, the area offers outstanding opportunities for French language learning and an appreciation of the area's natural beauty.

Bardolino, Italy: Located a few kilometers from Lake Garda, not far from the Verona airport, this new TASIS program, in collaboration with AC Milan Junior Camp, will give middle school students the unique opportunity to study a language, learn soccer techniques and tactics, and discover the beauty of this area of northern Italy.

BACKGROUND AND PHILOSOPHY

Founded in 1956 by Mrs. M. Crist Fleming, TASIS is a coed college-preparatory American boarding school for students in grades 6–12 and postgraduates.

The Summer Programs began thirty-four years ago and were designed to offer American and international students an opportunity to study abroad and a chance to live in a truly international environment. The programs in Château d'Oex, were founded fifteen years ago.

PROGRAM OFFERINGS

TASIS Summer Program (TSP): This program combines languages, arts, and outdoor pursuits, and is based on the campus of The American School in Switzerland in Lugano. Offerings include intensive language courses in English as an additional language, French, and Italian for 14- to 18-year-olds. The program includes artistic activities, a wide choice of sports, alpine activities, and weekend excursions in Switzerland and Italy. Both four- and three-week sessions are available. Besides language courses, the program offers courses in digital photography, drawing and painting, and musical theater.

Middle School Program (MSP): This program, on the Lugano campus, is designed for students aged 11 to 13 to study English as an additional language, French, Italian, or musical theater. The program provides appropriate academic challenges and recreational activities for this transitional age group within a warm and caring community. Students choose special workshops to attend two afternoons a week, including music and drama, art, special sports, or tennis. During the remaining afternoons, students participate in afternoon and weekend activities, sports, and excursions.

Optional intensive afternoon sports activities are offered in both MSP and TSP. TSP students can attend the AC Milan Junior Camp or Armani Junior Basketball Club four afternoons per week, while MSP offers four different special sports tracks that meet three afternoons per week. Students with proven previous experience can also choose the Golf Club or Tennis Academy.

Le Château des Enfants (CDE): This summer program offers learning and fun for 4+ to 10 year olds. Sharing the Lugano campus with TSP and MSP, but with its own separate living and dining facilities, the program teaches English, Italian, or French through lessons, games, activities, sports, and art in a close-knit, caring, family-style community specifically tailored to younger children. Picnics, excursions, and camping trips are also offered. Both four- and three-week sessions are available. Children from 4+ to 6 years of age can attend the Minnows program as day students only.

The Château-d'Oex Summer Language Program (TSLP, ages 14–17): This program offers English- or French-language learning in an intimate alpine setting. Intensive outdoor sports options, arts and crafts workshops, excursions such as climbing and rafting, and special weekend activities make this program ideal for more adventurous students.

The Château-d'Oex Middle School Program (MSPCD, ages 11–13) This program is for students willing to improve or learn either English or French in this alpine setting of the

Pays d'Enhaut. The study of the language is combined with mountain sports, cultural excursions, and a variety of activities which take advantage of the beautiful location.

The TASIS Soccer Academy (TSA, ages 11–14): This program combines language learning with intensive soccer training. Students train five days per week with AC Milan coaches at top-notch facilities near Lake Garda, Italy. The program offers intensive English as an additional language and Italian courses, along with a variety of activities which give children the opportunity to explore this beautiful region.

ENROLLMENT

In Lugano, more than 300 students represent as many as forty different countries. In Château d'Oex, approximately 65 students enroll from all over the world, including the Americas, Europe, and Asia.

EXTRA OPPORTUNITIES AND ACTIVITIES

Lugano: All students participate in afternoon sports and activities. Students choose from a variety of sports, including swimming, aerobic dance, basketball, cross-country running, soccer, softball, tennis, and volleyball. The afternoon activities include art, photography, and computer club. Weekend excursions provide ample opportunity for students to explore local areas of interest. Full-day excursions to Como and Milan, Lucerne, and Valley Verzasca and half-day excursions to nearby places of interest, such as Swiss Miniature in Melide and the antique street markets in Como, are organized. Optional weekend travel destinations (at an extra cost) include such cities as Florence, Nice, Paris, Venice, and Verona. Students ages 11–18 may also choose to attend special sports afternoon tracks such as the AC Milan Junior Camp or the Armani Basketball Club, under the supervision of trained coaches. Middle school students can also participate in the Golf Club or Tennis Academy if they have previous experience in these sports.

Château d'Oex: Hiking, rock climbing, tennis, swimming, basketball, and soccer are offered. Weekend destinations include Geneva, Interlaken, Zermatt, and Gstaad.

FACILITIES

Lugano: The program uses all of the boarding school facilities of the American School in Switzerland. The historic Villa de Nobili houses the administrative offices, dining rooms/ terraces, classrooms, and dormitory areas. Villa Monticello contains classrooms, a computer center, and dormitories. Hadsall House houses an audiovisual lab, a recreation center, and a snack bar, as well as dormitory accommodations. The art and photography studios are adjacent. The M. Crist Fleming Library holds 20,000 volumes. On-campus sports facilities include a gymnasium, an outdoor pool, a fitness center, and two multipurpose hard courts.

Château d'Oex: The historic wood-carved chalets, set in the heart of the village, are home to TASIS students. They house dormitories, classrooms, a dining room, and recreation areas. There are a tennis/basketball court and Ping-Pong tables in the garden of the main chalet. Nearby facilities include a swimming pool, soccer field, and beach volley. Tennis players of intermediate and advanced ability can enroll in the intensive tennis offering to improve their skills under the guidance of certified tennis instructors.

Bardolino, Lake Garda: Sport Hotel Veronello is located in culturally-rich northern Italy, half an hour from the Verona airport, and a few kilometers from stunning Lake Garda. Soccer fields and swimming pools make this location ideal for sports enthusiasts.

STAFF

There are 60 full-time summer staff members (the staff-student ratio is 1:5). Qualified classroom teachers also undertake supervisory responsibilities, including coaching sports, chaperoning trips, dormitory coverage, and the "in loco parentis" role. Counselors work alongside teachers in the dorms, on excursions, on the sports fields, and in recreational activities to help provide a caring environment for students.

Many of the staff members are current or former TASIS faculty members, and counselors are alumni from all TASIS programs.

COSTS

For Lugano and Château d'Oex, Switzerland, the all-inclusive cost for a four-week session in 2012 is CHF 7300. The cost for the three-week session is CHF 5900. The TASIS Summer Program in Château-d'Oex, with the additional optional week to Nice, South of France, amounts to CHF 8500. The cost for the three-week TASIS Soccer Academy is CHF 6300. There are no additional fees, with the exception of long-haul airfare, the optional European weekend travel costs, personal spending money, and medical expenses not covered by TASIS health insurance.

FOR MORE INFORMATION, CONTACT

TASIS U.S. Representative
The TASIS Schools
112 South Royal Street
Alexandria, Virginia 22314
Phone: 703-299-8150
Fax: 703-299-8157
E-mail: usadmissions@tasis.com
Web site: http://www.tasis.com

Specialized Directories

COEDUCATIONAL DAY SCHOOLS

Academy at the Lakes, FL
The Academy for Gifted Children (PACE), ON, Canada
Academy of Holy Angels, MN
Academy of the Sacred Heart, LA
Academy of the Sacred Heart, MI
Académie Ste Cécile International School, ON, Canada
Alexander Dawson School, CO
Allendale Columbia School, NY
Allison Academy, FL
Alpha Omega Academy, IA
American Academy, FL
American Heritage School, FL
The American School Foundation, Mexico
The American School in London, United Kingdom
Anacapa School, CA
Annie Wright School, WA
Archbishop Hoban High School, OH
Archbishop Mitty High School, CA
Arendell Parrott Academy, NC
Armbrae Academy, NS, Canada
Armona Union Academy, CA
Arrowsmith School, ON, Canada
ASSETS School, HI
The Athenian School, CA
Atlanta International School, GA
Atlantis Academy, FL
Augusta Christian School (I), GA
Augusta Preparatory Day School, GA
Bachman Academy, TN
The Baltimore Actors' Theatre Conservatory, MD
Baltimore Lutheran School, MD
Barrie School, MD
Battle Ground Academy, TN
Baylor School, TN
Bayside Academy, AL
Bearspaw Christian School, AB, Canada
The Beekman School, NY
Benet Academy, IL
Ben Franklin Academy, GA
Berean Christian High School, CA
Berkeley Preparatory School, FL
Berkshire School, MA
Beth Haven Christian School, KY
The Birch Wathen Lenox School, NY
Bishop Blanchet High School, WA
Bishop Brady High School, NH
Bishop Eustace Preparatory School, NJ
Bishop Fenwick High School, OH
Bishop Guertin High School, NH
Bishop Ireton High School, VA
Bishop John J. Snyder High School, FL
Bishop Kelly High School, ID
Bishop McGuinness Catholic High School, NC
Bishop McGuinness Catholic High School, OK
Bishop Montgomery High School, CA
Bishop's College School, QC, Canada
The Bishop's School, CA
Bishop Stang High School, MA
Blair Academy, NJ
Blanchet School, OR
Blessed Sacrament Hugenot, VA
Blessed Trinity High School, GA
Blue Mountain Academy, PA
The Bolles School, FL
Boston University Academy, MA
Boylan Central Catholic High School, IL
Breck School, MN
Brentwood School, CA
Brewster Academy, NH
Briarcrest Christian High School, TN
Briarwood Christian High School, AL
Bridgemont High School, CA
Bridges Academy, CA
Brimmer and May School, MA
Brooks School, MA
Brookstone School, GA
Bulloch Academy, GA
Burr and Burton Academy, VT
Butte Central Catholic High School, MT
Buxton School, MA
The Byrnes Schools, SC
Calgary Academy Collegiate, AB, Canada
Calvary Chapel High School, CA
The Calverton School, MD
Calvin Christian High School, CA
The Cambridge School of Weston, MA
Campbell Hall (Episcopal), CA
Camphill Special School, PA
Cannon School, NC
The Canterbury Episcopal School, TX
Canterbury School, FL
Canyonville Christian Academy, OR
Cape Cod Academy, MA
Cape Fear Academy, NC
Cape Henry Collegiate School, VA
Capistrano Valley Christian Schools, CA
Cardinal Mooney Catholic College Preparatory High School, MI
Cardinal Newman High School, FL
Cardinal O'Hara High School, PA
Carlisle School, VA
Carolina Day School, NC
Carrollton Christian Academy, TX
Cascadilla School, NY
The Catlin Gabel School, OR
Central Alberta Christian High School, AB, Canada
Central Catholic High School, CA
Central Catholic High School, MA
Chadwick School, CA
Chamberlain-Hunt Academy, MS
Chaminade College Preparatory, CA
Chaminade-Madonna College Preparatory, FL
Chapel Hill–Chauncy Hall School, MA
Charlotte Christian School, NC
Charlotte Country Day School, NC
Charlotte Latin School, NC
Chatham Academy, GA
Chattanooga Christian School, TN
Chelsea School, MD
Cheshire Academy, CT
Cheverus High School, ME
The Chicago Academy for the Arts, IL
Children's Creative and Performing Arts Academy of San Diego, CA
Chinese Christian Schools, CA
Christ Church Episcopal School, SC
Christchurch School, VA
Christian Brothers Academy, NY
Christian Central Academy, NY
Christian Home and Bible School, FL
Christopher Dock Mennonite High School, PA
Chrysalis School, WA
Cincinnati Country Day School, OH
Clarksville Academy, TN

Clearwater Central Catholic High School, FL
Colegio Nueva Granada, Colombia
Collegedale Academy, TN
The Collegiate School, VA
The Colorado Springs School, CO
Columbia Academy, TN
Columbia International College of Canada, ON, Canada
The Columbus Academy, OH
Commonwealth School, MA
Community Christian Academy, KY
The Community School of Naples, FL
The Concept School, PA
Concord Academy, MA
Concordia Lutheran High School, IN
Copenhagen International School, Denmark
Cotter Schools, MN
The Country Day School, ON, Canada
Covenant Canadian Reformed School, AB, Canada
Crawford Adventist Academy, ON, Canada
Crossroads School for Arts & Sciences, CA
The Culver Academies, IN
Currey Ingram Academy, TN
Cushing Academy, MA
The Dalton School, NY
Darlington School, GA
Davidson Academy, TN
Deerfield Academy, MA
Deerfield-Windsor School, GA
Denver Christian High School, CO
DePaul Catholic High School, NJ
The Derryfield School, NH
Doane Stuart School, NY
The Dr. Miriam and Sheldon G. Adelson Educational Campus, The Adelson Upper School, NV
Donelson Christian Academy, TN
Dublin Christian Academy, NH
DuBois Central Catholic High School/Middle School, PA
Durham Academy, NC
Eagle Hill-Southport, CT
Eastside Catholic School, WA
Eastside Christian Academy, AB, Canada
Edison School, AB, Canada
Edmund Burke School, DC
Eldorado Emerson Private School, CA
Episcopal Collegiate School, AR
Episcopal High School, TX
Escola Americana de Campinas, Brazil
Excel Christian Academy, GA
Ezell-Harding Christian School, TN
Fairhill School, TX
Faith Christian High School, CA
Faith Lutheran High School, NV
Falmouth Academy, MA
Father Lopez High School, FL
Father Ryan High School, TN
Fayetteville Academy, NC
Fay School, MA
The First Academy, FL
First Baptist Academy, TX
First Presbyterian Day School, GA
Flint Hill School, VA
Flintridge Preparatory School, CA
Flint River Academy, GA
Foothills Academy, AB, Canada
Forsyth Country Day School, NC
Fort Lauderdale Preparatory School, FL
Fort Worth Country Day School, TX
Foundation Academy, FL
Fountain Valley School of Colorado, CO
Fowlers Academy, PR
Fox Valley Lutheran High School, WI
Freeman Academy, SD
French-American School of New York, NY
Fresno Christian Schools, CA
Friends Academy, NY
Friends' Central School, PA
Front Range Christian High School, CO
The Frostig School, CA
Fuqua School, VA
Gabriel Richard High School, MI
The Galloway School, GA
Gann Academy (The New Jewish High School of Greater Boston), MA
Garces Memorial High School, CA
Gaston Day School, NC
The Geneva School, FL
George Stevens Academy, ME
George Walton Academy, GA
Germantown Friends School, PA
Gill St. Bernard's School, NJ
Gilmour Academy, OH
Glades Day School, FL
Glen Eden School, BC, Canada
Glenelg Country School, MD
The Glenholme School, Devereux Connecticut, CT
Glenlyon Norfolk School, BC, Canada
Gonzaga Preparatory School, WA
Gould Academy, ME
The Governor French Academy, IL
Grace Brethren School, CA
The Grauer School, CA
Great Lakes Christian High School, ON, Canada
Greenfield School, NC
Greenhill School, TX
Greensboro Day School, NC
Groton School, MA
Guamani Private School, PR
The Gunston School, MD
Hackley School, NY
Hamden Hall Country Day School, CT
Hampton Roads Academy, VA
Harding Academy, TN
Harding Academy, TN
The Harker School, CA
The Harley School, NY
Harrells Christian Academy, NC
Hawaiian Mission Academy, HI
Hawaii Baptist Academy, HI
Hawken School, OH
Hawthorne Christian Academy, NJ
Head-Royce School, CA
Hebrew Academy, CA
Hebrew Academy-the Five Towns, NY
Heritage Christian Academy, AB, Canada
Heritage Christian School, ON, Canada
Highland Hall Waldorf School, CA
The Hill Center, Durham Academy, NC
Hillcrest Christian School, CA
Hillcrest Christian School, MS
The Hill School, PA
Hill School of Fort Worth, TX
The Hill Top Preparatory School, PA
Holy Cross High School, CT
Holy Innocents' Episcopal School, GA

Holyoke Catholic High School, MA
Holy Savior Menard Catholic High School, LA
Holy Trinity Diocesan High School, NY
Holy Trinity High School, IL
Hoosac School, NY
Hopkins School, CT
The Hotchkiss School, CT
Houghton Academy, NY
The Howard School, GA
Humanex Academy, CO
Huntington-Surrey School, TX
Hyde School, CT
Hyde School, ME
Hyman Brand Hebrew Academy of Greater Kansas City, KS
Idyllwild Arts Academy, CA
Immaculata-La Salle High School, FL
Immaculate Conception School, IL
Immaculate Heart High School, AZ
Independent School, KS
Indian Springs School, AL
Interlochen Arts Academy, MI
Intermountain Christian School, UT
International High School, CA
International School Bangkok, Thailand
International School Hamburg, Germany
International School Manila, Philippines
International School of Amsterdam, Netherlands
The International School of London, United Kingdom
Jack M. Barrack Hebrew Academy, PA
Jackson Preparatory School, MS
John Burroughs School, MO
John Paul II Catholic High School, FL
John T. Morgan Academy, AL
Junipero Serra High School, CA
The Karafin School, NY
Kauai Christian Academy, HI
Keith Country Day School, IL
Kentucky Country Day School, KY
Kerr-Vance Academy, NC
The Kew-Forest School, NY
Key School, TX
Kimball Union Academy, NH
King Low Heywood Thomas, CT
Kings Christian School, CA
King's-Edgehill School, NS, Canada
King's High School, WA
Kingshill School, VI
King's Ridge Christian School, GA
Kingswood-Oxford School, CT
La Jolla Country Day School, CA
Lakefield College School, ON, Canada
Lakehill Preparatory School, TX
Lakeside School, WA
Lancaster Mennonite High School, PA
Landmark Christian Academy, KY
Landmark Christian School, GA
Landmark School, MA
Lansdale Catholic High School, PA
La Salle High School, CA
The Latin School of Chicago, IL
Lausanne Collegiate School, TN
Lawrence Academy, MA
Lawrence School, OH
Lehigh Valley Christian High School, PA
Lehman High School, OH
Le Lycee Francais de Los Angeles, CA
Lexington Catholic High School, KY
Liberty Christian School, CA
Lighthouse Christian School, AB, Canada
Lincoln Academy, ME
Linden Christian School, MB, Canada
The Linsly School, WV
Lodi Academy, CA
Long Island Lutheran Middle and High School, NY
The Loomis Chaffee School, CT
Los Angeles Baptist Middle School/High School, CA
Los Angeles Lutheran High School, CA
Louisville Collegiate School, KY
The Lovett School, GA
Lutheran High School, IN
Lutheran High School North, MO
Lutheran High School Northwest, MI
Lutheran High School of Hawaii, HI
Lutheran High School of San Diego, CA
Luther College High School, SK, Canada
MacLachlan College, ON, Canada
Madison Academy, AL
Madison-Ridgeland Academy, MS
Maharishi School of the Age of Enlightenment, IA
Maine Central Institute, ME
Manhattan Christian High School, MT
Maranatha High School, CA
Maret School, DC
Marian Central Catholic High School, IL
Marian High School, IN
The Marin School, CA
Marion Academy, AL
Marist School, GA
Mars Hill Bible School, AL
Martin Luther High School, NY
The Marvelwood School, CT
Marymount International School, Italy
Mary Star of the Sea High School, CA
The Master's School, CT
The Masters School, NY
Matignon High School, MA
McDonogh School, MD
The Meadows School, NV
Menaul School, NM
Mercyhurst Preparatory School, PA
Mesa Grande Seventh-Day Academy, CA
Middlesex School, MA
Mid-Pacific Institute, HI
Millbrook School, NY
Miller School, VA
Mill Springs Academy, GA
Milton Academy, MA
MMI Preparatory School, PA
Monsignor Donovan High School, NJ
Montclair Kimberley Academy, NJ
Moorestown Friends School, NJ
Mooseheart High School, IL
Moravian Academy, PA
Moreau Catholic High School, CA
Morristown-Beard School, NJ
Mount Saint Charles Academy, RI
MPS Etobicoke, ON, Canada
MU High School, MO
Munich International School, Germany
Nazareth Academy, IL
Nebraska Christian Schools, NE
Newark Academy, NJ
New Covenant Academy, MO
New Tribes Mission Academy, ON, Canada

Niagara Christian Community of Schools, ON, Canada
Nichols School, NY
Noble Academy, NC
Noble and Greenough School, MA
The Nora School, MD
Norfolk Academy, VA
North Catholic High School, PA
North Cobb Christian School, GA
North Country School, NY
North Toronto Christian School, ON, Canada
Northwest Academy, OR
Northwest Catholic High School, CT
Northwest Yeshiva High School, WA
Northwood School, NY
The Norwich Free Academy, CT
Notre Dame High School, TN
Notre Dame Junior/Senior High School, PA
Oak Grove School, CA
Oak Hill Academy, VA
Oak Hill School, OR
The Oakland School, PA
Oakland School, VA
Oak Ridge Military Academy, NC
The Oakridge School, TX
Ojai Valley School, CA
The O'Neal School, NC
Oneida Baptist Institute, KY
Oregon Episcopal School, OR
Orinda Academy, CA
Out-Of-Door-Academy, FL
The Overlake School, WA
Pacific Crest Community School, OR
Pacific Hills School, CA
Padua Franciscan High School, OH
The Paideia School, GA
Paradise Adventist Academy, CA
The Park School of Baltimore, MD
The Pathway School, PA
Peddie School, NJ
Peoples Christian Academy, ON, Canada
Philadelphia-Montgomery Christian Academy, PA
Phillips Academy (Andover), MA
Phillips Exeter Academy, NH
Phoenix Country Day School, AZ
Pickens Academy, AL
Pickering College, ON, Canada
Pic River Private High School, ON, Canada
Pinecrest Academy, GA
Pine Crest School, FL
The Pingree School, MA
The Pingry School, NJ
Pioneer Valley Christian School, MA
Pope John XXIII Regional High School, NJ
Porter-Gaud School, SC
The Potomac School, VA
Powers Catholic High School, MI
The Prairie School, WI
Prestonwood Christian Academy, TX
Professional Children's School, NY
Providence Christian School, AB, Canada
Providence Country Day School, RI
Providence Day School, NC
Providence High School, CA
Punahou School, HI
Queen Margaret's School, BC, Canada
Quinte Christian High School, ON, Canada
Rabbi Alexander S. Gross Hebrew Academy, FL
Randolph-Macon Academy, VA
Ranney School, NJ
Ransom Everglades School, FL
Ravenscroft School, NC
Realms of Inquiry, UT
The Rectory School, CT
Redwood Christian Schools, CA
Reitz Memorial High School, IN
Ridley College, ON, Canada
Ripon Christian Schools, CA
Riverdale Country School, NY
Rivermont Collegiate, IA
The Rivers School, MA
Robert Louis Stevenson School, NY
Rock Point School, VT
The Roeper School, MI
Rolling Hills Preparatory School, CA
Rosseau Lake College, ON, Canada
Ross School, NY
Rothesay Netherwood School, NB, Canada
Rowland Hall, UT
Royal Canadian College, BC, Canada
Rundle College, AB, Canada
Rye Country Day School, NY
Sacramento Adventist Academy, CA
Sacramento Country Day School, CA
Sacred Heart/Griffin High School, IL
Sacred Heart School of Halifax, NS, Canada
Saddleback Valley Christian School, CA
Saddlebrook Preparatory School, FL
Sage Hill School, CA
Sage Ridge School, NV
St. Andrew's Regional High School, BC, Canada
St. Andrew's School, RI
St. Andrew's–Sewanee School, TN
St. Anne's–Belfield School, VA
Saint Anthony High School, CA
Saint Anthony High School, IL
St. Anthony's Junior-Senior High School, HI
St. Benedict at Auburndale, TN
St. Bernard High School, CT
St. Bernard's Catholic School, CA
St. Brendan High School, FL
Saint Clement Academy, ON, Canada
St. Croix Country Day School, VI
St. Croix Schools, MN
Saint Dominic Academy, ME
Saint Edward's School, FL
Saint Elizabeth High School, CA
Saint Francis School, HI
St. George's Independent School, TN
St. George's School of Montreal, QC, Canada
St. Gregory College Preparatory School, AZ
Saint John's Preparatory School, MN
St. John's-Ravenscourt School, MB, Canada
St. Joseph Academy, FL
Saint Joseph High School, IL
Saint Joseph High School, NJ
Saint Joseph Junior-Senior High School, HI
St. Joseph's Catholic School, SC
St. Jude's School, ON, Canada
St. Mark's High School, DE
St. Martin's Episcopal School, LA
Saint Mary's College High School, CA
Saint Mary's Hall, TX
Saint Mary's High School, AZ
Saint Mary's High School, MD

St. Mary's School, OR
Saint Maur International School, Japan
St. Patrick Catholic High School, MS
Saint Patrick - Saint Vincent High School, CA
St. Patrick's Regional Secondary, BC, Canada
St. Paul Academy and Summit School, MN
St. Pius X Catholic High School, GA
Saints Peter and Paul High School, MD
St. Stephen's & St. Agnes School, VA
St. Stephen's Episcopal School, TX
St. Stephen's School, Rome, Italy
St. Thomas Aquinas High School, FL
Saint Thomas Aquinas High School, KS
St. Thomas Aquinas High School, NH
Saint Viator High School, IL
Salem Academy, OR
Salesian High School, CA
Saltus Grammar School, Bermuda
Sandy Spring Friends School, MD
Sanford School, DE
San Marcos Baptist Academy, TX
Sayre School, KY
Scholar's Hall Preparatory School, ON, Canada
SciCore Academy, NJ
Scotus Central Catholic High School, NE
Seabury Hall, HI
Seattle Academy of Arts and Sciences, WA
Seattle Christian Schools, WA
Seton Catholic Central High School, NY
Seton Catholic High School, AZ
The Seven Hills School, OH
Severn School, MD
Sewickley Academy, PA
Shady Side Academy, PA
Shattuck-St. Mary's School, MN
Shawe Memorial Junior/Senior High School, IN
Shawnigan Lake School, BC, Canada
Shelton School and Evaluation Center, TX
The Shipley School, PA
Shoreline Christian, WA
Smith School, NY
Solomon College, AB, Canada
Sonoma Academy, CA
Southfield Christian High School, MI
Southland Academy, Inc., GA
Spartanburg Day School, SC
Springside Chestnut Hill Academy, PA
Squaw Valley Academy, CA
Stephen T. Badin High School, OH
Stevenson School, CA
Storm King School, NY
Stratton Mountain School, VT
The Sudbury Valley School, MA
Suffield Academy, CT
Summerfield Waldorf School, CA
Sunshine Bible Academy, SD
Tabor Academy, MA
The Taft School, CT
Taipei American School, Taiwan
Takoma Academy, MD
Tandem Friends School, VA
TASIS The American School in England, United Kingdom
TASIS, The American School in Switzerland, Switzerland
Telluride Mountain School, CO
The Tenney School, TX
Teurlings Catholic High School, LA
The Thacher School, CA
Thetford Academy, VT
Tidewater Academy, VA
Tilton School, NH
Timothy Christian High School, IL
Toronto District Christian High School, ON, Canada
Tower Hill School, DE
Tri-City Christian Schools, CA
Trinity Christian Academy, TN
Trinity College School, ON, Canada
Trinity High School, NH
Trinity High School, OH
Trinity Preparatory School, FL
Trinity School of Texas, TX
Trinity Valley School, TX
Tuscaloosa Academy, AL
Tyler Street Christian Academy, TX
United Mennonite Educational Institute, ON, Canada
United Nations International School, NY
The University of Chicago Laboratory Schools, IL
University Prep, WA
University School of Jackson, TN
University School of Milwaukee, WI
University School of Nova Southeastern University, FL
Vail Mountain School, CO
Valle Catholic High School, MO
Valley Christian High School, CA
Valley Christian High School, CA
Valley Lutheran High School, AZ
The Valley School, MI
Vicksburg Catholic School, MS
Villa Duchesne and Oak Hill School, MO
Villa Maria Academy, PA
Wakefield School, VA
Waldorf High School of Massachusetts Bay, MA
The Walker School, GA
Walnut Hill School, MA
Waring School, MA
Wasatch Academy, UT
Washington Waldorf School, MD
The Waterford School, UT
Watkinson School, CT
Waynflete School, ME
The Webb School, TN
Webb School of Knoxville, TN
Wellspring Foundation, CT
Wesleyan Academy, PR
Westbury Christian School, TX
West Catholic High School, MI
Westchester Country Day School, NC
Western Mennonite School, OR
Westgate Mennonite Collegiate, MB, Canada
West Island College, AB, Canada
Westmark School, CA
Westminster Christian Academy, AL
Westminster School, CT
West Sound Academy, WA
Wheaton Academy, IL
The Wheeler School, RI
Whitefield Academy, KY
The Williams School, CT
Willow Wood School, ON, Canada
Wilmington Christian School, DE
Wilson Hall, SC
Winchester Thurston School, PA
Windermere Preparatory School, FL
The Windsor School, NY
Windward School, CA

Winston Preparatory School, NY
The Winston School San Antonio, TX
Woodward Academy, GA
Worcester Preparatory School, MD
York Catholic High School, PA
York Country Day School, PA
York Preparatory School, NY
York School, CA

BOYS' DAY SCHOOLS

Academy of the New Church Boys' School, PA
The American Boychoir School, NJ*
Archbishop Curley High School, MD
Archbishop Rummel High School, LA
Army and Navy Academy, CA
Belen Jesuit Preparatory School, FL
Benedictine High School, OH
Benedictine High School, VA
Bishop Mora Salesian High School, CA
Brophy College Preparatory, AZ
Brother Rice High School, MI
The Browning School, NY
Brunswick School, CT
Calvert Hall College High School, MD
Central Catholic High School, TX
CFS, The School at Church Farm, PA
Chaminade College Preparatory School, MO
Christian Brothers Academy, NJ
Christopher Columbus High School, FL
Cistercian Preparatory School, TX
Colegio San Jose, PR
Collegiate School, NY
Covington Catholic High School, KY
Damien High School, CA
De La Salle High School, CA
Delbarton School, NJ
DeMatha Catholic High School, MD
Devon Preparatory School, PA
Eaglebrook School, MA
The Fessenden School, MA
Fordham Preparatory School, NY
Georgetown Preparatory School, MD
Gilman School, MD
Gonzaga College High School, DC
Hargrave Military Academy, VA
The Haverford School, PA
Holy Cross High School, NY
Holy Ghost Preparatory School, PA
Iona Preparatory School, NY
Jesuit College Preparatory School, TX
Jesuit High School of New Orleans, LA
Jesuit High School of Tampa, FL
Junipero Serra High School, CA
Landon School, MD
Loyola-Blakefield, MD
Malden Catholic High School, MA
Memphis University School, TN
Merchiston Castle School, United Kingdom
Missouri Military Academy, MO
Montgomery Bell Academy, TN
Mount Michael Benedictine School, NE
Notre Dame College Prep, IL
Palma School, CA
Regis High School, NY
Riverside Military Academy, GA
The Roxbury Latin School, MA
Saint Agnes Boys High School, NY
St. Albans School, DC
St. Andrew's College, ON, Canada
Saint Augustine Preparatory School, NJ
St. Benedict's Preparatory School, NJ
St. Catherine's Academy, CA
St. Christopher's School, VA
St. Francis de Sales High School, OH
Saint Francis High School, CA
St. John's Preparatory School, MA
Saint Joseph's High School, NJ
St. Joseph's Preparatory School, PA
St. Mark's School of Texas, TX
St. Mary's Preparatory School, MI
St. Michael's College School, ON, Canada
Saint Patrick High School, IL
St. Paul's High School, MB, Canada
St. Peter's Preparatory School, NJ
St. Sebastian's School, MA
Saint Thomas Academy, MN
St. Thomas High School, TX
Salesianum School, DE
Strake Jesuit College Preparatory, TX
Trinity High School, KY
Trinity-Pawling School, NY
University of Detroit Jesuit High School and Academy, MI
The Woodhall School, CT
Xaverian High School, NY

GIRLS' DAY SCHOOLS

Academy of Our Lady of Peace, CA
Academy of the Holy Cross, MD
Academy of the New Church Girls' School, PA
Academy of the Sacred Heart, LA
Balmoral Hall School, MB, Canada
Bishop Conaty-Our Lady of Loretto High School, CA
Branksome Hall, ON, Canada
The Brearley School, NY
Carondelet High School, CA
Carrollton School of the Sacred Heart, FL
Cathedral High School, NY
The Catholic High School of Baltimore, MD
Chatham Hall, VA
Columbus School for Girls, OH
Convent of the Sacred Heart, CT
Country Day School of the Sacred Heart, PA
Dana Hall School, MA
Dominican Academy, NY
Elizabeth Seton High School, MD
The Ellis School, PA
Emma Willard School, NY
The Ethel Walker School, CT
Fontbonne Hall Academy, NY
Foxcroft School, VA
Girls Preparatory School, TN
Greenwich Academy, CT
The Grier School, PA
The Hockaday School, TX
Holy Names Academy, WA
Immaculate Conception High School, NJ
Immaculate Heart High School and Middle School, CA
Institute of Notre Dame, MD
Josephinum Academy, IL
Ladywood High School, MI

** Coeducational in lower grades*

Louisville High School, CA
Magnificat High School, OH
Marlborough School, CA
Marylawn of the Oranges, NJ
Marymount High School, CA
Mercy High School, CT
Mercy High School, NE
Mercy High School College Preparatory, CA
Merion Mercy Academy, PA
Miss Edgar's and Miss Cramp's School, QC, Canada
Miss Hall's School, MA
Miss Porter's School, CT
Mother McAuley High School, IL
Mount Saint Joseph Academy, PA
Nerinx Hall, MO
Notre Dame Academy, CA
Our Lady Academy, MS
Our Lady of Mercy Academy, NJ
Our Lady of Mercy High School, NY
Providence Catholic School, The College Preparatory School for Girls Grades 6-12, TX
Roland Park Country School, MD
St. Agnes Academy, TX
St. Andrew's Priory School, HI
Saint Basil Academy, PA
St. Clement's School, ON, Canada
St. Joseph's Academy, LA
St. Mary's Episcopal School, TN
Saint Mary's School, NC
St. Scholastica Academy, IL
Saint Teresa's Academy, MO
St. Timothy's School, MD
Saint Ursula Academy, OH
Salem Academy, NC
Santa Catalina School, CA
The Spence School, NY
Stoneleigh–Burnham School, MA
Trafalgar Castle School, ON, Canada
Villa Joseph Marie High School, PA
Villa Maria Academy, PA
Villa Victoria Academy, NJ
Villa Walsh Academy, NJ
Westover School, CT
Westridge School, CA
The Willows Academy, IL
The Winsor School, MA
The Woodward School, MA

SCHOOLS ACCEPTING BOARDING BOYS AND GIRLS

Académie Ste Cécile International School, ON, Canada†
Alliance Academy, Ecuador
The Athenian School, CA†
Bachman Academy, TN†
Baylor School, TN†
Berkshire School, MA†
Bishop's College School, QC, Canada†
Blair Academy, NJ†
Blue Mountain Academy, PA†
The Bolles School, FL†
Brewster Academy, NH†
Brooks School, MA†
Burr and Burton Academy, VT†
Buxton School, MA†
The Cambridge School of Weston, MA†
Camphill Special School, PA†
Canyonville Christian Academy, OR†
Carlisle School, VA†
Cascadilla School, NY†
Chapel Hill–Chauncy Hall School, MA†
Cheshire Academy, CT†
Children's Creative and Performing Arts Academy of San Diego, CA†
Columbia International College of Canada, ON, Canada†
Concord Academy, MA†
Cotter Schools, MN†
The Culver Academies, IN†
Cushing Academy, MA†
Darlington School, GA†
Deerfield Academy, MA†
Dublin Christian Academy, NH†
Eldorado Emerson Private School, CA†
Episcopal High School, VA
The Family Foundation School, NY
Fay School, MA†
Forest Lake Academy, FL
Fountain Valley School of Colorado, CO†
Freeman Academy, SD†
George Stevens Academy, ME†
Gilmour Academy, OH†
The Glenholme School, Devereux Connecticut, CT
Gould Academy, ME†
The Governor French Academy, IL†
Great Lakes Christian High School, ON, Canada†
Groton School, MA†
Hackley School, NY†
Happy Hill Farm Academy, TX
The Harvey School, NY
Hawaiian Mission Academy, HI†
The Hill School, PA†
Hoosac School, NY†
The Hotchkiss School, CT†
Houghton Academy, NY†
Hyde School, CT†
Hyde School, ME†
Idyllwild Arts Academy, CA†
Indian Springs School, AL†
Interlochen Arts Academy, MI†
The John Dewey Academy, MA
The Judge Rotenberg Educational Center, MA
Kimball Union Academy, NH†
The King's Academy, TN
King's-Edgehill School, NS, Canada†
Lakefield College School, ON, Canada†
Lancaster Mennonite High School, PA†
Landmark School, MA†
Lawrence Academy, MA†
The Linsly School, WV†
The Loomis Chaffee School, CT†
Luther College High School, SK, Canada†
Maharishi School of the Age of Enlightenment, IA†
Maine Central Institute, ME†
The Marvelwood School, CT†
The Masters School, NY†
McDonogh School, MD†
Menaul School, NM†
Middlesex School, MA†
Midland School, CA
Millbrook School, NY†
Miller School, VA†
Milton Academy, MA†
Mooseheart High School, IL†

† Accepts day students

Nebraska Christian Schools, NE†
Neuchatel Junior College, Switzerland
Niagara Christian Community of Schools, ON, Canada†
Noble and Greenough School, MA†
North Country School, NY†
Northwood School, NY†
Oak Grove School, CA†
Oak Hill Academy, VA†
Oakland School, VA†
Oak Ridge Military Academy, NC†
Ojai Valley School, CA†
Oneida Baptist Institute, KY†
Oregon Episcopal School, OR†
Peddie School, NJ†
Phillips Academy (Andover), MA†
Phillips Exeter Academy, NH†
Pickering College, ON, Canada†
Pinehurst School, ON, Canada
Presbyterian Pan American School, TX
Randolph-Macon Academy, VA†
The Rectory School, CT†
Ridley College, ON, Canada†
Rock Point School, VT†
Rosseau Lake College, ON, Canada†
Ross School, NY†
Rothesay Netherwood School, NB, Canada†
Saddlebrook Preparatory School, FL†
St. Andrew's School, DE
St. Andrew's School, RI†
St. Andrew's–Sewanee School, TN†
St. Anne's–Belfield School, VA†
St. Anthony Catholic High School, TX
St. Bernard's Catholic School, CA†
St. Croix Schools, MN†
Saint John's Preparatory School, MN†
St. John's-Ravenscourt School, MB, Canada†
St. Mary's School, OR†
St. Stephen's Episcopal School, TX†
St. Stephen's School, Rome, Italy†
Sandy Spring Friends School, MD†
San Marcos Baptist Academy, TX†
Shady Side Academy, PA†
Shattuck-St. Mary's School, MN†
Shawnigan Lake School, BC, Canada†
Squaw Valley Academy, CA†
Stevenson School, CA†
Storm King School, NY†
Stratton Mountain School, VT†
Suffield Academy, CT†
Sunshine Bible Academy, SD†
Tabor Academy, MA†
The Taft School, CT†
TASIS The American School in England, United Kingdom†
TASIS, The American School in Switzerland, Switzerland†
The Thacher School, CA†
Tilton School, NH†
Trinity College School, ON, Canada†
The United World College - USA, NM
Walnut Hill School, MA†
Wasatch Academy, UT†
The Webb School, TN†
Wellspring Foundation, CT†
Western Mennonite School, OR†
Westminster School, CT†
West Sound Academy, WA†

SCHOOLS ACCEPTING BOARDING BOYS

Academy of the New Church Boys' School, PA†
The American Boychoir School, NJ†
Army and Navy Academy, CA†
The Blue Ridge School, VA
Butte Central Catholic High School, MT†
CFS, The School at Church Farm, PA†
Chamberlain-Hunt Academy, MS†
Chaminade College Preparatory School, MO†
Christchurch School, VA†
Eaglebrook School, MA†
The Fessenden School, MA†
Georgetown Preparatory School, MD†
Hampshire Country School, NH
Hargrave Military Academy, VA†
Little Keswick School, VA
Marine Military Academy, TX
Merchiston Castle School, United Kingdom
Missouri Military Academy, MO†
Mount Michael Benedictine School, NE†
Riverside Military Academy, GA†
Robert Land Academy, ON, Canada
St. Albans School, DC†
St. Andrew's College, ON, Canada†
St. Catherine's Academy, CA†
St. Mary's Preparatory School, MI†
St. Michael's Preparatory School of the Norbertine Fathers, CA
St. Thomas Choir School, NY
Trinity-Pawling School, NY†
Valley View School, MA
Windermere Preparatory School, FL†
The Woodhall School, CT†

SCHOOLS ACCEPTING BOARDING GIRLS

Academy of the New Church Girls' School, PA†
Academy of the Sacred Heart, LA†
Annie Wright School, WA†
Auldern Academy, NC
Balmoral Hall School, MB, Canada†
The Bishop Strachan School, ON, Canada
Branksome Hall, ON, Canada†
Chatham Hall, VA†
Copper Canyon Academy, AZ
Dana Hall School, MA†
Emma Willard School, NY†
The Ethel Walker School, CT†
Foxcroft School, VA†
The Grier School, PA†
The Hockaday School, TX†
Miss Hall's School, MA†
Miss Porter's School, CT†
Queen Margaret's School, BC, Canada†
Saint Mary's School, NC†
St. Timothy's School, MD†
Salem Academy, NC†
Santa Catalina School, CA†
Stoneleigh–Burnham School, MA†
Trafalgar Castle School, ON, Canada†
Westover School, CT†

MILITARY SCHOOLS

Army and Navy Academy, CA
Benedictine High School, VA

† Accepts day students

Chamberlain-Hunt Academy, MS
Hargrave Military Academy, VA
Lyman Ward Military Academy, AL
Marine Military Academy, TX
Missouri Military Academy, MO
Oak Ridge Military Academy, NC
Randolph-Macon Academy, VA
Riverside Military Academy, GA
Robert Land Academy, ON, Canada
St. Catherine's Academy, CA
Saint Thomas Academy, MN

SCHOOLS WITH A RELIGIOUS AFFILIATION

Anglican Church of Canada
The Bishop Strachan School, ON, Canada
Queen Margaret's School, BC, Canada
Rothesay Netherwood School, NB, Canada
St. Clement's School, ON, Canada

Assemblies of God
Valley Christian High School, CA

Baptist Bible Fellowship
New Tribes Mission Academy, ON, Canada

Baptist Church
Berean Christian High School, CA
Beth Haven Christian School, KY
Bulloch Academy, GA
First Baptist Academy, TX
Foundation Academy, FL
Landmark Christian Academy, KY
Liberty Christian School, CA
Linden Christian School, MB, Canada
Los Angeles Baptist Middle School/High School, CA
Oak Hill Academy, VA
San Marcos Baptist Academy, TX
Whitefield Academy, KY

Baptist General Association of Virginia
Hargrave Military Academy, VA

Bible Fellowship Church
Chinese Christian Schools, CA
Dublin Christian Academy, NH

Brethren Church
Grace Brethren School, CA
New Tribes Mission Academy, ON, Canada

Brethren in Christ Church
Niagara Christian Community of Schools, ON, Canada

Calvinist
Providence Christian School, AB, Canada
Ripon Christian Schools, CA

Christian
Academy of the New Church Girls' School, PA
Briarcrest Christian High School, TN
Bulloch Academy, GA
Excel Christian Academy, GA
Faith Christian High School, CA
The Family Foundation School, NY
The First Academy, FL
First Presbyterian Day School, GA
Fowlers Academy, PR
Grace Brethren School, CA
Happy Hill Farm Academy, TX
Harding Academy, TN
Harrells Christian Academy, NC
Hawthorne Christian Academy, NJ
Heritage Christian Academy, AB, Canada
Highroad Academy, BC, Canada
Horizon Christian Academy Junior/Senior High School, CA
Intermountain Christian School, UT
Marion Academy, AL
Mesa Grande Seventh-Day Academy, CA
New Covenant Academy, MO
North Cobb Christian School, GA
Peoples Christian Academy, ON, Canada
Philadelphia-Montgomery Christian Academy, PA
Porter Gaud School, SC
Quinte Christian High School, ON, Canada
Redwood Christian Schools, CA
St. Croix Schools, MN
Timothy Christian High School, IL
Toronto District Christian High School, ON, Canada
Valley Christian High School, CA

Christian Nondenominational
Alliance Academy, Ecuador
Alpha Omega Academy, IA
Bearspaw Christian School, AB, Canada
Bridgemont High School, CA
Calvary Chapel High School, CA
Canyonville Christian Academy, OR
Capistrano Valley Christian Schools, CA
Charlotte Christian School, NC
Chattanooga Christian School, TN
Christian Central Academy, NY
Davidson Academy, TN
Donelson Christian Academy, TN
Dublin Christian Academy, NH
Eastside Christian Academy, AB, Canada
Front Range Christian High School, CO
The Geneva School, FL
Hawthorne Christian Academy, NJ
Hillcrest Christian School, CA
The Hill School, PA
Kauai Christian Academy, HI
King's High School, WA
King's Ridge Christian School, GA
Landmark Christian School, GA
Lyman Ward Military Academy, AL
Madison-Ridgeland Academy, MS
Manhattan Christian High School, MT
Maranatha High School, CA
The Master's School, CT
Merchiston Castle School, United Kingdom
Missouri Military Academy, MO
Riverside Military Academy, GA
Saddleback Valley Christian School, CA
St. Anne's–Belfield School, VA
St. George's Independent School, TN
Seattle Christian Schools, WA
Shoreline Christian, WA
Southfield Christian High School, MI
Sunshine Bible Academy, SD
Toronto District Christian High School, ON, Canada
Tri-City Christian Schools, CA

Tyler Street Christian Academy, TX
Wheaton Academy, IL

Christian Reformed Church
Central Alberta Christian High School, AB, Canada
Denver Christian High School, CO
Manhattan Christian High School, MT

Church of Christ
Christian Home and Bible School, FL
Columbia Academy, TN
Ezell-Harding Christian School, TN
Great Lakes Christian High School, ON, Canada
Madison Academy, AL
Mars Hill Bible School, AL
Westbury Christian School, TX

Church of England (Anglican)
Lakefield College School, ON, Canada
Ridley College, ON, Canada
Saltus Grammar School, Bermuda
Trinity College School, ON, Canada

Church of the New Jerusalem
Academy of the New Church Boys' School, PA
Academy of the New Church Girls' School, PA

Episcopal Church
Annie Wright School, WA
Berkeley Preparatory School, FL
The Bishop's School, CA
The Blue Ridge School, VA
Breck School, MN
Brooks School, MA
Campbell Hall (Episcopal), CA
The Canterbury Episcopal School, TX
CFS, The School at Church Farm, PA
Chatham Hall, VA
Christ Church Episcopal School, SC
Christchurch School, VA
Doane Stuart School, NY
Episcopal Collegiate School, AR
Episcopal High School, TX
Episcopal High School, VA
Groton School, MA
Holy Innocents' Episcopal School, GA
Hoosac School, NY
Oregon Episcopal School, OR
Porter-Gaud School, SC
The Rectory School, CT
Rock Point School, VT
St. Albans School, DC
St. Andrew's Priory School, HI
St. Andrew's School, DE
St. Andrew's–Sewanee School, TN
St. Christopher's School, VA
Saint Edward's School, FL
St. Martin's Episcopal School, LA
St. Mary's Episcopal School, TN
Saint Mary's School, NC
St. Stephen's & St. Agnes School, VA
St. Stephen's Episcopal School, TX
St. Thomas Choir School, NY
St. Timothy's School, MD
Seabury Hall, HI
Shattuck-St. Mary's School, MN
Trinity-Pawling School, NY
Trinity Preparatory School, FL
Trinity School of Texas, TX
York School, CA

Evangelical
Heritage Christian Academy, AB, Canada
Pioneer Valley Christian School, MA
Southfield Christian High School, MI

Evangelical Free Church of America
Intermountain Christian School, UT

Evangelical/Fundamental
Chinese Christian Schools, CA

Evangelical Lutheran Church in America
Faith Lutheran High School, NV

Jewish
The Dr. Miriam and Sheldon G. Adelson Educational Campus, The Adelson Upper School, NV
The Family Foundation School, NY
Gann Academy (The New Jewish High School of Greater Boston), MA
Hebrew Academy, CA
Hebrew Academy-the Five Towns, NY
Hyman Brand Hebrew Academy of Greater Kansas City, KS
Jack M. Barrack Hebrew Academy, PA
Northwest Yeshiva High School, WA
Rabbi Alexander S. Gross Hebrew Academy, FL

Lutheran Church
Long Island Lutheran Middle and High School, NY
Los Angeles Lutheran High School, CA
Lutheran High School North, MO
Lutheran High School of San Diego, CA
Luther College High School, SK, Canada
Martin Luther High School, NY

Lutheran Church&-Missouri Synod
Baltimore Lutheran School, MD
Concordia Lutheran High School, IN
Faith Lutheran High School, NV
Los Angeles Lutheran High School, CA
Lutheran High School, IN
Lutheran High School Northwest, MI
Lutheran High School of Hawaii, HI
Valley Lutheran High School, AZ

Mennonite Church
Christopher Dock Mennonite High School, PA
Freeman Academy, SD
Lancaster Mennonite High School, PA

Mennonite Church USA
United Mennonite Educational Institute, ON, Canada
Western Mennonite School, OR
Westgate Mennonite Collegiate, MB, Canada

Methodist Church
Randolph-Macon Academy, VA

Moravian Church
Moravian Academy, PA
Salem Academy, NC

Pentecostal Church
Community Christian Academy, KY

Presbyterian Church
Blair Academy, NJ
Calvin Christian High School, CA
Chamberlain-Hunt Academy, MS
Menaul School, NM

Presbyterian Church (U.S.A.)
Presbyterian Pan American School, TX

Presbyterian Church in America
Briarwood Christian High School, AL
First Presbyterian Day School, GA
Westminster Christian Academy, AL

Protestant
Landmark Christian School, GA
Liberty Christian School, CA
Mooseheart High School, IL
Pioneer Valley Christian School, MA
Quinte Christian High School, ON, Canada
Wilmington Christian School, DE

Protestant Church
Salem Academy, OR

Protestant-Evangelical
Fresno Christian Schools, CA
Kauai Christian Academy, HI
Lehigh Valley Christian High School, PA
Nebraska Christian Schools, NE
North Toronto Christian School, ON, Canada

Reformed Church
Calvin Christian High School, CA
Chamberlain-Hunt Academy, MS
Covenant Canadian Reformed School, AB, Canada
Heritage Christian School, ON, Canada
Providence Christian School, AB, Canada

Roman Catholic Church
Academy of Holy Angels, MN
Academy of Our Lady of Peace, CA
Academy of the Holy Cross, MD
Academy of the Sacred Heart, LA
Academy of the Sacred Heart, LA
Academy of the Sacred Heart, MI
Académie Ste Cécile International School, ON, Canada
Archbishop Curley High School, MD
Archbishop Hoban High School, OH
Archbishop Mitty High School, CA
Archbishop Rummel High School, LA
Belen Jesuit Preparatory School, FL
Benedictine High School, OH
Benedictine High School, VA
Benet Academy, IL
Bishop Blanchet High School, WA
Bishop Brady High School, NH
Bishop Conaty-Our Lady of Loretto High School, CA
Bishop Eustace Preparatory School, NJ
Bishop Fenwick High School, OH
Bishop Guertin High School, NH
Bishop Ireton High School, VA
Bishop Kelly High School, ID
Bishop McGuinness Catholic High School, NC
Bishop McGuinness Catholic High School, OK
Bishop Montgomery High School, CA
Bishop Mora Salesian High School, CA
Bishop Stang High School, MA
Blanchet School, OR
Blessed Sacrament Hugenot, VA
Blessed Trinity High School, GA
Boylan Central Catholic High School, IL
Brother Rice High School, MI
Butte Central Catholic High School, MT
Calvert Hall College High School, MD
Cardinal Mooney Catholic College Preparatory High School, MI
Cardinal Newman High School, FL
Cardinal O'Hara High School, PA
Carondelet High School, CA
Carrollton School of the Sacred Heart, FL
Cathedral High School, NY
The Catholic High School of Baltimore, MD
Central Catholic High School, CA
Central Catholic High School, MA
Central Catholic High School, TX
Chaminade College Preparatory, CA
Chaminade College Preparatory School, MO
Chaminade-Madonna College Preparatory, FL
Christian Brothers Academy, NJ
Christian Brothers Academy, NY
Christopher Columbus High School, FL
Cistercian Preparatory School, TX
Clearwater Central Catholic High School, FL
Colegio Nueva Granada, Colombia
Colegio San Jose, PR
Convent of the Sacred Heart, CT
Cotter Schools, MN
Country Day School of the Sacred Heart, PA
Covington Catholic High School, KY
Damien High School, CA
De La Salle High School, CA
Delbarton School, NJ
DeMatha Catholic High School, MD
DePaul Catholic High School, NJ
Devon Preparatory School, PA
Dominican Academy, NY
DuBois Central Catholic High School/Middle School, PA
Eastside Catholic School, WA
Elizabeth Seton High School, MD
Father Lopez High School, FL
Father Ryan High School, TN
Fontbonne Hall Academy, NY
Fordham Preparatory School, NY
Gabriel Richard High School, MI
Garces Memorial High School, CA
Georgetown Preparatory School, MD
Gilmour Academy, OH
Gonzaga College High School, DC
Holy Cross High School, CT
Holy Cross High School, NY
Holy Ghost Preparatory School, PA
Holy Names Academy, WA
Holyoke Catholic High School, MA
Holy Savior Menard Catholic High School, LA
Holy Trinity Diocesan High School, NY
Holy Trinity High School, IL
Immaculata-La Salle High School, FL
Immaculate Conception High School, NJ
Immaculate Conception School, IL
Immaculate Heart High School, AZ
Immaculate Heart High School and Middle School, CA

Institute of Notre Dame, MD
Iona Preparatory School, NY
Jesuit High School of New Orleans, LA
Jesuit High School of Tampa, FL
John Paul II Catholic High School, FL
Josephinum Academy, IL
Junipero Serra High School, CA
Junipero Serra High School, CA
Ladywood High School, MI
Lansdale Catholic High School, PA
La Salle High School, CA
Lehman High School, OH
Lexington Catholic High School, KY
Loretto Academy, TX
Louisville High School, CA
Loyola-Blakefield, MD
Magnificat High School, OH
Malden Catholic High School, MA
Marian Central Catholic High School, IL
Marian High School, IN
Marist School, GA
Marylawn of the Oranges, NJ
Marymount High School, CA
Marymount International School, Italy
Mary Star of the Sea High School, CA
Matignon High School, MA
Mercy High School, CT
Mercy High School, NE
Mercy High School College Preparatory, CA
Mercyhurst Preparatory School, PA
Merion Mercy Academy, PA
Monsignor Donovan High School, NJ
Mooseheart High School, IL
Moreau Catholic High School, CA
Mother McAuley High School, IL
Mount Michael Benedictine School, NE
Mount Saint Charles Academy, RI
Mount Saint Joseph Academy, PA
Nativity B.V.M. High School, PA
Nazareth Academy, IL
Nerinx Hall, MO
North Catholic High School, PA
Northwest Catholic High School, CT
Notre Dame Academy, CA
Notre Dame College Prep, IL
Notre Dame High School, TN
Notre Dame Junior/Senior High School, PA
Our Lady Academy, MS
Our Lady of Mercy Academy, NJ
Our Lady of Mercy High School, NY
Padua Franciscan High School, OH
Palma School, CA
Pic River Private High School, ON, Canada
Pinecrest Academy, GA
Pope John XXIII Regional High School, NJ
Powers Catholic High School, MI
Providence Catholic School, The College Preparatory School for Girls Grades 6-12, TX
Providence High School, CA
Regis High School, NY
Reitz Memorial High School, IN
Sacred Heart/Griffin High School, IL
Sacred Heart School of Halifax, NS, Canada
St. Agnes Academy, TX
Saint Agnes Boys High School, NY
St. Andrew's Regional High School, BC, Canada
St. Anthony Catholic High School, TX
Saint Anthony High School, CA
Saint Anthony High School, IL
St. Anthony's Junior-Senior High School, HI
Saint Augustine Preparatory School, NJ
Saint Basil Academy, PA
St. Benedict at Auburndale, TN
St. Benedict's Preparatory School, NJ
St. Bernard High School, CT
St. Bernard's Catholic School, CA
St. Brendan High School, FL
St. Catherine's Academy, CA
Saint Clement Academy, ON, Canada
Saint Dominic Academy, ME
Saint Elizabeth High School, CA
St. Francis de Sales High School, OH
Saint Francis High School, CA
Saint Francis School, HI
St. John's Preparatory School, MA
Saint John's Preparatory School, MN
St. Joseph Academy, FL
Saint Joseph High School, IL
Saint Joseph High School, NJ
Saint Joseph Junior-Senior High School, HI
St. Joseph's Academy, LA
St. Joseph's Catholic School, SC
Saint Joseph's High School, NJ
St. Joseph's Preparatory School, PA
St. Mark's High School, DE
Saint Mary's College High School, CA
Saint Mary's High School, AZ
Saint Mary's High School, MD
St. Mary's Preparatory School, MI
St. Mary's School, OR
Saint Maur International School, Japan
St. Michael's College School, ON, Canada
St. Michael's Preparatory School of the Norbertine Fathers, CA
St. Patrick Catholic High School, MS
Saint Patrick High School, IL
Saint Patrick - Saint Vincent High School, CA
St. Patrick's Regional Secondary, BC, Canada
St. Paul's High School, MB, Canada
St. Peter's Preparatory School, NJ
St. Pius X Catholic High School, GA
St. Scholastica Academy, IL
St. Sebastian's School, MA
Saints Peter and Paul High School, MD
Saint Teresa's Academy, MO
Saint Thomas Academy, MN
St. Thomas Aquinas High School, FL
Saint Thomas Aquinas High School, KS
St. Thomas Aquinas High School, NH
St. Thomas High School, TX
Saint Ursula Academy, OH
Saint Viator High School, IL
Salesian High School, CA
Salesianum School, DE
Santa Catalina School, CA
Scotus Central Catholic High School, NE
Seisen International School, Japan
Seton Catholic Central High School, NY
Seton Catholic High School, AZ
Shawe Memorial Junior/Senior High School, IN
Stephen T. Badin High School, OH
Teurlings Catholic High School, LA
Trinity High School, KY
Trinity High School, NH
Trinity High School, OH

Valle Catholic High School, MO
Vicksburg Catholic School, MS
Villa Duchesne and Oak Hill School, MO
Villa Joseph Marie High School, PA
Villa Maria Academy, PA
Villa Maria Academy, PA
Villa Victoria Academy, NJ
Villa Walsh Academy, NJ
Visitation Academy of St. Louis County, MO
West Catholic High School, MI
The Willows Academy, IL
Xaverian High School, NY
York Catholic High School, PA

Roman Catholic Church (Jesuit Order)
Brophy College Preparatory, AZ
Cheverus High School, ME
Gonzaga Preparatory School, WA
Jesuit College Preparatory School, TX
Strake Jesuit College Preparatory, TX
University of Detroit Jesuit High School and Academy, MI

Seventh-day Adventist Church
Crawford Adventist Academy, ON, Canada
Hawaiian Mission Academy, HI
Lodi Academy, CA
Sacramento Adventist Academy, CA
Takoma Academy, MD

Seventh-day Adventists
Armona Union Academy, CA
Blue Mountain Academy, PA
Collegedale Academy, TN
Forest Lake Academy, FL
Mesa Grande Seventh-Day Academy, CA
Paradise Adventist Academy, CA

Society of Friends
Friends Academy, NY
Friends' Central School, PA
Germantown Friends School, PA
Lincoln School, RI
Moorestown Friends School, NJ
Sandy Spring Friends School, MD
Tandem Friends School, VA

Southern Baptist Convention
First Baptist Academy, TX
Hawaii Baptist Academy, HI
The King's Academy, TN
Oneida Baptist Institute, KY
Prestonwood Christian Academy, TX

United Church of Christ
Mid-Pacific Institute, HI

United Methodist Church
Carrollton Christian Academy, TX

Wesleyan Church
Houghton Academy, NY
Wesleyan Academy, PR

Wisconsin Evangelical Lutheran Synod
Fox Valley Lutheran High School, WI
St. Croix Schools, MN

Worldwide Church of God
Bishop John J. Snyder High School, FL

SCHOOLS BEGINNING AT JUNIOR, SENIOR, OR POSTGRADUATE YEAR

Neuchatel Junior College, Switzerland 12
The United World College - USA, NM 11

SCHOOLS WITH ELEMENTARY DIVISIONS

Academy at the Lakes, FL
Academy of the Sacred Heart, LA
Alexander Dawson School, CO
Allendale Columbia School, NY
The American School Foundation, Mexico
The American School in London, United Kingdom
Annie Wright School, WA
Army and Navy Academy, CA
ASSETS School, HI
The Athenian School, CA
Atlanta International School, GA
Augusta Preparatory Day School, GA
Bachman Academy, TN
Balmoral Hall School, MB, Canada
Barrie School, MD
Battle Ground Academy, TN
Baylor School, TN
Berkeley Preparatory School, FL
The Birch Wathen Lenox School, NY
Bishop's College School, QC, Canada
The Bishop's School, CA
The Bishop Strachan School, ON, Canada
The Bolles School, FL
Branksome Hall, ON, Canada
The Brearley School, NY
Breck School, MN
Brentwood School, CA
Brimmer and May School, MA
Brookstone School, GA
The Browning School, NY
Brunswick School, CT
The Bryn Mawr School for Girls, MD
Bulloch Academy, GA
The Calverton School, MD
Campbell Hall (Episcopal), CA
The Canterbury Episcopal School, TX
Canterbury School, FL
Cape Cod Academy, MA
Cape Fear Academy, NC
Cape Henry Collegiate School, VA
Carlisle School, VA
Carolina Day School, NC
Carrollton School of the Sacred Heart, FL
The Catlin Gabel School, OR
CFS, The School at Church Farm, PA
Chadwick School, CA
Chaminade College Preparatory School, MO
Charlotte Country Day School, NC
Charlotte Latin School, NC
Cheshire Academy, CT
Christ Church Episcopal School, SC
Cincinnati Country Day School, OH
Cistercian Preparatory School, TX
Clarksville Academy, TN

Collegiate School, NY
The Collegiate School, VA
The Colorado Springs School, CO
The Columbus Academy, OH
Columbus School for Girls, OH
The Community School of Naples, FL
Convent of the Sacred Heart, CT
Country Day School of the Sacred Heart, PA
Crossroads School for Arts & Sciences, CA
Currey Ingram Academy, TN
The Dalton School, NY
Dana Hall School, MA
Darlington School, GA
Deerfield-Windsor School, GA
Delbarton School, NJ
The Derryfield School, NH
Devon Preparatory School, PA
Doane Stuart School, NY
The Dr. Miriam and Sheldon G. Adelson Educational Campus, The Adelson Upper School, NV
Durham Academy, NC
Eaglebrook School, MA
Edmund Burke School, DC
The Ellis School, PA
Episcopal Collegiate School, AR
Escola Americana de Campinas, Brazil
The Ethel Walker School, CT
Falmouth Academy, MA
Fayetteville Academy, NC
Fay School, MA
The Fessenden School, MA
Flint Hill School, VA
Flintridge Preparatory School, CA
Forsyth Country Day School, NC
Fort Lauderdale Preparatory School, FL
Fort Worth Country Day School, TX
Friends Academy, NY
Friends' Central School, PA
The Galloway School, GA
Gaston Day School, NC
Germantown Friends School, PA
Gill St. Bernard's School, NJ
Gilman School, MD
Gilmour Academy, OH
Girls Preparatory School, TN
Glenelg Country School, MD
Glenlyon Norfolk School, BC, Canada
Greenfield School, NC
Greenhill School, TX
Greensboro Day School, NC
Greenwich Academy, CT
The Grier School, PA
Groton School, MA
Hackley School, NY
Hamden Hall Country Day School, CT
Hampshire Country School, NH
Hampton Roads Academy, VA
Hargrave Military Academy, VA
The Harker School, CA
The Harley School, NY
The Harvey School, NY
The Haverford School, PA
Hawaii Baptist Academy, HI
Hawken School, OH
Head-Royce School, CA
The Hill Center, Durham Academy, NC
Hill School of Fort Worth, TX
The Hill Top Preparatory School, PA
The Hockaday School, TX
Holy Innocents' Episcopal School, GA
Hoosac School, NY
Hopkins School, CT
Houghton Academy, NY
The Howard School, GA
Indian Springs School, AL
International High School, CA
International School Bangkok, Thailand
International School Manila, Philippines
Jack M. Barrack Hebrew Academy, PA
Jackson Preparatory School, MS
John Burroughs School, MO
Keith Country Day School, IL
Kent Place School, NJ
Kentucky Country Day School, KY
The Kew-Forest School, NY
King Low Heywood Thomas, CT
King's Ridge Christian School, GA
Kingswood-Oxford School, CT
La Jolla Country Day School, CA
Lakefield College School, ON, Canada
Lakehill Preparatory School, TX
Lakeside School, WA
Landmark School, MA
Landon School, MD
The Latin School of Chicago, IL
Lausanne Collegiate School, TN
Lincoln School, RI
The Linsly School, WV
Louisville Collegiate School, KY
The Lovett School, GA
Lyman Ward Military Academy, AL
Maharishi School of the Age of Enlightenment, IA
Maret School, DC
Marist School, GA
Marlborough School, CA
The Masters School, NY
McDonogh School, MD
The Meadows School, NV
Memphis University School, TN
Mid-Pacific Institute, HI
Miller School, VA
Mill Springs Academy, GA
Milton Academy, MA
Miss Edgar's and Miss Cramp's School, QC, Canada
Missouri Military Academy, MO
MMI Preparatory School, PA
Montclair Kimberley Academy, NJ
Montgomery Bell Academy, TN
Moorestown Friends School, NJ
Moravian Academy, PA
Morristown-Beard School, NJ
Munich International School, Germany
Newark Academy, NJ
Nichols School, NY
Noble and Greenough School, MA
Norfolk Academy, VA
North Country School, NY
Northwest Academy, OR
Oak Grove School, CA
Oak Hill School, OR
Oak Ridge Military Academy, NC
The Oakridge School, TX
Ojai Valley School, CA
The O'Neal School, NC

Oregon Episcopal School, OR
Out-Of-Door-Academy, FL
The Overlake School, WA
Pacific Hills School, CA
The Park School of Baltimore, MD
Phoenix Country Day School, AZ
Pickering College, ON, Canada
Pinecrest Academy, GA
Pine Crest School, FL
The Pingry School, NJ
Porter-Gaud School, SC
The Potomac School, VA
The Prairie School, WI
Professional Children's School, NY
Providence Country Day School, RI
Providence Day School, NC
Punahou School, HI
Queen Margaret's School, BC, Canada
Randolph-Macon Academy, VA
Ranney School, NJ
Ransom Everglades School, FL
Ravenscroft School, NC
The Rectory School, CT
Ridley College, ON, Canada
Riverdale Country School, NY
Rivermont Collegiate, IA
Riverside Military Academy, GA
The Rivers School, MA
Robert Louis Stevenson School, NY
The Roeper School, MI
Roland Park Country School, MD
Rolling Hills Preparatory School, CA
Ross School, NY
Rothesay Netherwood School, NB, Canada
Rowland Hall, UT
The Roxbury Latin School, MA
Rye Country Day School, NY
Sacramento Country Day School, CA
St. Albans School, DC
St. Andrew's College, ON, Canada
St. Andrew's Priory School, HI
St. Andrew's School, RI
St. Andrew's–Sewanee School, TN
St. Anne's–Belfield School, VA
St. Anthony's Junior-Senior High School, HI
St. Christopher's School, VA
St. Clement's School, ON, Canada
St. Croix Country Day School, VI
Saint Edward's School, FL
Saint Francis School, HI
St. George's Independent School, TN
St. George's School of Montreal, QC, Canada
St. Gregory College Preparatory School, AZ
Saint John's Preparatory School, MN
Saint Joseph Junior-Senior High School, HI
St. Mark's School of Texas, TX
St. Martin's Episcopal School, LA
St. Mary's Episcopal School, TN
Saint Mary's Hall, TX
St. Mary's School, OR
St. Paul Academy and Summit School, MN
St. Sebastian's School, MA
St. Stephen's & St. Agnes School, VA
St. Stephen's Episcopal School, TX
Saint Thomas Academy, MN
St. Thomas Choir School, NY
Saltus Grammar School, Bermuda
Sandy Spring Friends School, MD
Sanford School, DE
San Marcos Baptist Academy, TX
Sayre School, KY
Seabury Hall, HI
Seattle Academy of Arts and Sciences, WA
The Seven Hills School, OH
Severn School, MD
Sewickley Academy, PA
Shady Side Academy, PA
Shattuck-St. Mary's School, MN
Shawnigan Lake School, BC, Canada
The Shipley School, PA
Southland Academy, Inc., GA
Spartanburg Day School, SC
The Spence School, NY
Springside Chestnut Hill Academy, PA
Stevenson School, CA
Stoneleigh–Burnham School, MA
Storm King School, NY
Stratton Mountain School, VT
Taipei American School, Taiwan
Tandem Friends School, VA
TASIS The American School in England, United Kingdom
TASIS, The American School in Switzerland, Switzerland
Telluride Mountain School, CO
Tower Hill School, DE
Trinity College School, ON, Canada
Trinity-Pawling School, NY
Trinity Preparatory School, FL
Trinity Valley School, TX
Tuscaloosa Academy, AL
United Nations International School, NY
The University of Chicago Laboratory Schools, IL
University Prep, WA
University School of Jackson, TN
University School of Milwaukee, WI
University School of Nova Southeastern University, FL
Vail Mountain School, CO
Villa Duchesne and Oak Hill School, MO
Villa Victoria Academy, NJ
Visitation Academy of St. Louis County, MO
The Walker School, GA
Wasatch Academy, UT
Washington Waldorf School, MD
The Waterford School, UT
Watkinson School, CT
Waynflete School, ME
The Webb School, TN
Webb School of Knoxville, TN
Westchester Country Day School, NC
Westmark School, CA
Westridge School, CA
The Wheeler School, RI
The Williams School, CT
Winchester Thurston School, PA
Windward School, CA
The Winsor School, MA
Winston Preparatory School, NY
Woodward Academy, GA
Worcester Preparatory School, MD
York Country Day School, PA
York Preparatory School, NY
York School, CA

SCHOOLS REPORTING ACADEMIC ACCOMMODATIONS FOR THE GIFTED AND TALENTED

School	
The Academy for Gifted Children (PACE), ON, Canada	G
Academy of Holy Angels, MN	G,M,A
Academy of the Holy Cross, MD	G,A
Academy of the New Church Boys' School, PA	G,M,A
Academy of the New Church Girls' School, PA	G,M,A
Academy of the Sacred Heart, LA	G,M,A
Academy of the Sacred Heart, MI	G,M,A
Académie Ste Cécile International School, ON, Canada	G,M,A
Alexander Dawson School, CO	G,M,A
Alliance Academy, Ecuador	G,A
Allison Academy, FL	G,M,A
American Academy, FL	G,M,A
The American Boychoir School, NJ	M
American Heritage School, FL	G,M,A
Archbishop Hoban High School, OH	G
Archbishop Mitty High School, CA	G,M,A
Armbrae Academy, NS, Canada	A
ASSETS School, HI	G
Augusta Preparatory Day School, GA	G
Auldern Academy, NC	G
Bachman Academy, TN	G
Balmoral Hall School, MB, Canada	G
The Baltimore Actors' Theatre Conservatory, MD	G,M,A
Baltimore Lutheran School, MD	G
Baylor School, TN	G,M,A
The Beekman School, NY	G,M,A
Benedictine High School, VA	G,A
Benet Academy, IL	G
Ben Franklin Academy, GA	G
The Birch Wathen Lenox School, NY	G,M,A
Bishop Brady High School, NH	G
Bishop Eustace Preparatory School, NJ	G,M
Bishop Guertin High School, NH	G
Bishop Ireton High School, VA	M
Bishop McGuinness Catholic High School, OK	G,A
Bishop Mora Salesian High School, CA	M,A
Bishop's College School, QC, Canada	G,M,A
The Bishop Strachan School, ON, Canada	G,M,A
Blue Mountain Academy, PA	M
Blueprint Education, AZ	M,A
Boston University Academy, MA	G
Boylan Central Catholic High School, IL	G,M,A
Branksome Hall, ON, Canada	G,M,A
Breck School, MN	G,M,A
Brentwood School, CA	G,A
Briarcrest Christian High School, TN	G,M,A
Briarwood Christian High School, AL	G
Bridges Academy, CA	G
The Browning School, NY	G,M
Brunswick School, CT	G,M,A
The Bryn Mawr School for Girls, MD	G,M,A
Bulloch Academy, GA	G,M,A
Buxton School, MA	G,M,A
The Byrnes Schools, SC	G
Calvert Hall College High School, MD	G,M,A
Cape Henry Collegiate School, VA	G,M,A
Cardinal Newman High School, FL	G
Cardinal O'Hara High School, PA	M
Carondelet High School, CA	G
Cascadilla School, NY	G,M,A
The Catlin Gabel School, OR	G,M,A
Central Catholic High School, CA	G
CFS, The School at Church Farm, PA	G,M,A
Chadwick School, CA	G,M,A
Chamberlain-Hunt Academy, MS	G,M,A
Chaminade College Preparatory School, MO	G
Chaminade-Madonna College Preparatory, FL	G,M,A
Charlotte Country Day School, NC	G
Charlotte Latin School, NC	G
Chatham Hall, VA	G,M,A
Chattanooga Christian School, TN	G,M,A
Cheshire Academy, CT	M,A
The Chicago Academy for the Arts, IL	M,A
Children's Creative and Performing Arts Academy of San Diego, CA	G,M,A
Chinese Christian Schools, CA	G
Christchurch School, VA	G
Christopher Columbus High School, FL	G
Chrysalis School, WA	G
Colegio Nueva Granada, Colombia	G
The Colorado Springs School, CO	G
Columbia International College of Canada, ON, Canada	G
The Columbus Academy, OH	G
Commonwealth School, MA	G,M,A
The Concept School, PA	G,A
Concord Academy, MA	G,M,A
Convent of the Sacred Heart, CT	G,A
Copper Canyon Academy, AZ	G,M,A
Cotter Schools, MN	G,M,A
Country Day School of the Sacred Heart, PA	M
Crossroads School for Arts & Sciences, CA	G,M,A
The Culver Academies, IN	G,M,A
Currey Ingram Academy, TN	G,M,A
Cushing Academy, MA	G,M,A
Darlington School, GA	M
Deerfield Academy, MA	G,M,A
Deerfield-Windsor School, GA	G,M,A
DeMatha Catholic High School, MD	G,M,A
Doane Stuart School, NY	G,M,A
Donelson Christian Academy, TN	G
Dublin Christian Academy, NH	M,A
Eaglebrook School, MA	G,M,A
Eastside Catholic School, WA	G
Eastside Christian Academy, AB, Canada	G,M
Edison School, AB, Canada	G
Eldorado Emerson Private School, CA	G,M,A
Elizabeth Seton High School, MD	G,M,A
The Ellis School, PA	G
Emma Willard School, NY	G,M,A
Episcopal High School, VA	G,M,A
The Ethel Walker School, CT	G,M,A
Faith Lutheran High School, NV	M
Father Ryan High School, TN	G,M,A
Fay School, MA	G,M,A
The Fessenden School, MA	G,M,A
The First Academy, FL	G
Flint Hill School, VA	M,A
Flintridge Preparatory School, CA	G,M,A
Flint River Academy, GA	M,A
Forsyth Country Day School, NC	G
Fort Lauderdale Preparatory School, FL	G
Fort Worth Country Day School, TX	G,M,A
Fountain Valley School of Colorado, CO	G,M,A
Foxcroft School, VA	G,M,A
Fox Valley Lutheran High School, WI	G
Freeman Academy, SD	M,A
Front Range Christian High School, CO	G
The Galloway School, GA	G,M,A
Gaston Day School, NC	G
The Geneva School, FL	G,M,A

G — gifted; M — musically talented; A — artistically talented

School	
George Stevens Academy, ME	G,M,A
Georgetown Preparatory School, MD	G
George Walton Academy, GA	M,A
Germantown Friends School, PA	G,M,A
Gilman School, MD	G,M,A
Gilmour Academy, OH	G,M,A
Glenelg Country School, MD	G
The Glenholme School, Devereux Connecticut, CT	G
Gonzaga Preparatory School, WA	G
Gould Academy, ME	G,M,A
The Governor French Academy, IL	G,A
The Grauer School, CA	G,M,A
Greenfield School, NC	G
Greensboro Day School, NC	G,A
The Greenwood School, VT	G,M,A
The Grier School, PA	G,M,A
Groton School, MA	G,M,A
The Gunston School, MD	G,M,A
Hamden Hall Country Day School, CT	G
Hampshire Country School, NH	G
Happy Hill Farm Academy, TX	G,M,A
The Harker School, CA	G
The Haverford School, PA	G
Hawken School, OH	G,M
Head-Royce School, CA	G,M,A
Hebrew Academy-the Five Towns, NY	A
The Hill Top Preparatory School, PA	G,A
Hoosac School, NY	M,A
The Hotchkiss School, CT	G,M,A
The Howard School, GA	A
Humanex Academy, CO	G
Huntington-Surrey School, TX	G
Hyde School, ME	G,M,A
Hyman Brand Hebrew Academy of Greater Kansas City, KS	G
Immaculata-La Salle High School, FL	G
Independent School, KS	G,M,A
Indian Springs School, AL	G,M
Institute of Notre Dame, MD	G
Interlochen Arts Academy, MI	G,M,A
International High School, CA	G,M,A
International School of Amsterdam, Netherlands	G,M,A
Iona Preparatory School, NY	G
Jack M. Barrack Hebrew Academy, PA	G
Jackson Preparatory School, MS	G,M,A
The John Dewey Academy, MA	G,A
Junipero Serra High School, CA	G
The Karafin School, NY	G,M,A
Keith Country Day School, IL	G,M,A
Kentucky Country Day School, KY	G,M,A
The Kew-Forest School, NY	G
King Low Heywood Thomas, CT	G,M,A
King's-Edgehill School, NS, Canada	G
Lakefield College School, ON, Canada	G,M,A
Lancaster Mennonite High School, PA	M
Landmark Christian School, GA	G
The Latin School of Chicago, IL	G
Laurel Springs School, CA	G,M,A
Lausanne Collegiate School, TN	G,M,A
Lawrence Academy, MA	M,A
Lehigh Valley Christian High School, PA	G
The Linsly School, WV	G
Little Keswick School, VA	G
Los Angeles Lutheran High School, CA	G,M,A
The Lovett School, GA	G,M,A
Loyola-Blakefield, MD	G,M,A
Lutheran High School of Hawaii, HI	M,A
Luther College High School, SK, Canada	G
Madison-Ridgeland Academy, MS	G
Maharishi School of the Age of Enlightenment, IA	G,M,A
Maine Central Institute, ME	M
Maranatha High School, CA	A
Maret School, DC	G,M,A
Marine Military Academy, TX	G
Marylawn of the Oranges, NJ	G,M,A
The Master's School, CT	G,M,A
The Masters School, NY	G,M,A
The Meadows School, NV	G,M,A
Menaul School, NM	G,A
Merchiston Castle School, United Kingdom	G,M,A
Mercyhurst Preparatory School, PA	G,M,A
Merion Mercy Academy, PA	G,M,A
Middlesex School, MA	G
Mid-Pacific Institute, HI	G,A
Miller School, VA	G,M,A
Mill Springs Academy, GA	G,M,A
Milton Academy, MA	G,M,A
Miss Hall's School, MA	G,M,A
Missouri Military Academy, MO	G,M,A
MMI Preparatory School, PA	G
Monsignor Donovan High School, NJ	G,M,A
Montclair Kimberley Academy, NJ	G
Mount Saint Joseph Academy, PA	G,M,A
MU High School, MO	G
Munich International School, Germany	G
Nativity B.V.M. High School, PA	G
Newark Academy, NJ	G,M,A
Noble and Greenough School, MA	G,M,A
The Nora School, MD	G,A
Norfolk Academy, VA	G,M,A
North Catholic High School, PA	G
North Cobb Christian School, GA	M,A
Northwest Academy, OR	G,M,A
Northwest Yeshiva High School, WA	G
Notre Dame College Prep, IL	G
Oak Hill School, OR	G
The Oakland School, PA	G,A
Oak Ridge Military Academy, NC	G
The Oakridge School, TX	G,M,A
Ojai Valley School, CA	G,A
The Oliverian School, NH	G,A
Oregon Episcopal School, OR	G
Orinda Academy, CA	G
The Overlake School, WA	G,M,A
Pacific Crest Community School, OR	G
The Park School of Baltimore, MD	G,M,A
Philadelphia-Montgomery Christian Academy, PA	G,M,A
Phillips Academy (Andover), MA	G,M,A
Phillips Exeter Academy, NH	G,M,A
The Pingry School, NJ	G
The Prairie School, WI	G,M,A
Prestonwood Christian Academy, TX	G
Providence Country Day School, RI	G,M,A
Providence Day School, NC	G,M,A
Providence High School, CA	M,A
Queen Margaret's School, BC, Canada	G,M,A
Rabbi Alexander S. Gross Hebrew Academy, FL	G
Randolph-Macon Academy, VA	G
Ravenscroft School, NC	G,M,A
Realms of Inquiry, UT	G,M,A
The Rectory School, CT	G
Ridley College, ON, Canada	M,A
Ripon Christian Schools, CA	M,A
Riverdale Country School, NY	G,M,A

G — gifted; M — musically talented; A — artistically talented

Rivermont Collegiate, IA G,M,A
Robert Louis Stevenson School, NY G
The Roeper School, MI G,M,A
Rolling Hills Preparatory School, CA G
Rosseau Lake College, ON, Canada G
Rothesay Netherwood School, NB, Canada G,M,A
The Roxbury Latin School, MA G,M,A
Rye Country Day School, NY G
Sacred Heart/Griffin High School, IL G,M,A
Sage Hill School, CA G,M,A
Sage Ridge School, NV G
St. Andrew's Priory School, HI M,A
St. Andrew's School, DE G,M,A
St. Andrew's–Sewanee School, TN G,M,A
St. Anthony Catholic High School, TX G
Saint Anthony High School, CA G,A
St. Benedict at Auburndale, TN G,M,A
St. Brendan High School, FL G
St. Christopher's School, VA G,M,A
St. Clement's School, ON, Canada G
St. Croix Schools, MN G,M,A
Saint Edward's School, FL G,M,A
St. George's School of Montreal, QC, Canada G,M,A
St. Gregory College Preparatory School, AZ G,M,A
St. John's Preparatory School, MA G,M,A
Saint John's Preparatory School, MN G,M,A
St. Joseph Academy, FL G,A
Saint Joseph High School, IL G,M,A
Saint Joseph High School, NJ G
Saint Joseph Junior-Senior High School, HI G
Saint Joseph's High School, NJ G
St. Joseph's Preparatory School, PA G,M,A
St. Mark's High School, DE G
St. Mark's School of Texas, TX G
St. Mary's Episcopal School, TN G,M,A
Saint Mary's High School, MD G
St. Mary's Preparatory School, MI M,A
St. Mary's School, OR G,M,A
Saint Maur International School, Japan G,M,A
Saint Patrick - Saint Vincent High School, CA G
St. Sebastian's School, MA G,M,A
St. Stephen's & St. Agnes School, VA G,M,A
Saint Thomas Aquinas High School, KS G
St. Thomas Choir School, NY G,M
Salem Academy, OR M,A
Salesianum School, DE G
Sandy Spring Friends School, MD G,M,A
San Marcos Baptist Academy, TX G,M,A
Santa Catalina School, CA G,M,A
Sayre School, KY G,A
SciCore Academy, NJ G,A
Seabury Hall, HI G
Seattle Academy of Arts and Sciences, WA G,M,A
Seton Catholic Central High School, NY G,A
The Seven Hills School, OH G
Severn School, MD G,M,A
Shady Side Academy, PA G,M,A
Shattuck-St. Mary's School, MN G,M
Shawe Memorial Junior/Senior High School, IN G
Shawnigan Lake School, BC, Canada G
The Shipley School, PA G
Spartanburg Day School, SC G,A
Squaw Valley Academy, CA G,M,A
Storm King School, NY M,A
Suffield Academy, CT G,M,A
Sunshine Bible Academy, SD M
Tabor Academy, MA G,M,A
The Taft School, CT G,M,A
Tandem Friends School, VA G
TASIS The American School in England, United Kingdom G
The Tenney School, TX G,M,A
The Thacher School, CA G,M,A
Tower Hill School, DE G,M,A
Trinity High School, KY G,M,A
Trinity High School, OH G,A
Trinity Preparatory School, FL G,M,A
Trinity School of Texas, TX G,M,A
Trinity Valley School, TX G,M,A
Tuscaloosa Academy, AL G
United Nations International School, NY G,M,A
The United World College - USA, NM M,A
University School of Jackson, TN G,M,A
University School of Nova Southeastern University, FL G,M,A
Valle Catholic High School, MO G,A
Valley Christian High School, CA G
Valley Lutheran High School, AZ G
The Valley School, MI G,A
Villa Joseph Marie High School, PA G,M,A
Villa Victoria Academy, NJ G,M,A
Villa Walsh Academy, NJ G,M,A
The Walker School, GA G,M,A
Walnut Hill School, MA G,M,A
Waring School, MA G,M,A
Washington Waldorf School, MD M,A
The Waterford School, UT G,M,A
Watkinson School, CT G,M,A
The Webb School, TN G
West Island College, AB, Canada G
Westover School, CT G,M,A
West Sound Academy, WA G
Wheaton Academy, IL G,M,A
The Wheeler School, RI G
Whitefield Academy, KY G
The Williams School, CT G,M,A
Willow Wood School, ON, Canada G,A
Winchester Thurston School, PA G,M,A
Windermere Preparatory School, FL M,A
The Windsor School, NY G,M,A
Worcester Preparatory School, MD G
Xaverian High School, NY G,M
York Country Day School, PA G,M,A
York Preparatory School, NY G,M,A

SCHOOLS WITH ADVANCED PLACEMENT PREPARATION

Academy at the Lakes, FL
The Academy for Gifted Children (PACE), ON, Canada
Academy of Holy Angels, MN
Academy of Our Lady of Peace, CA
Academy of the Holy Cross, MD
Academy of the New Church Boys' School, PA
Academy of the New Church Girls' School, PA
Academy of the Sacred Heart, LA
Academy of the Sacred Heart, LA
Academy of the Sacred Heart, MI
Académie Ste Cécile International School, ON, Canada
Alexander Dawson School, CO
Allendale Columbia School, NY
Alliance Academy, Ecuador
Allison Academy, FL
American Heritage School, FL

G — gifted; M — musically talented; A — artistically talented

The American School Foundation, Mexico
The American School in London, United Kingdom
Anacapa School, CA
Archbishop Curley High School, MD
Archbishop Hoban High School, OH
Archbishop Mitty High School, CA
Archbishop Rummel High School, LA
Arendell Parrott Academy, NC
Armbrae Academy, NS, Canada
Army and Navy Academy, CA
The Athenian School, CA
Augusta Christian School (I), GA
Auldern Academy, NC
Balmoral Hall School, MB, Canada
The Baltimore Actors' Theatre Conservatory, MD
Baltimore Lutheran School, MD
Barrie School, MD
Battle Ground Academy, TN
Baylor School, TN
Bayside Academy, AL
The Beekman School, NY
Belen Jesuit Preparatory School, FL
Benedictine High School, OH
Benedictine High School, VA
Benet Academy, IL
Ben Franklin Academy, GA
Berean Christian High School, CA
Berkeley Preparatory School, FL
Berkshire School, MA
The Birch Wathen Lenox School, NY
Bishop Blanchet High School, WA
Bishop Brady High School, NH
Bishop Conaty-Our Lady of Loretto High School, CA
Bishop Eustace Preparatory School, NJ
Bishop Fenwick High School, OH
Bishop Guertin High School, NH
Bishop Ireton High School, VA
Bishop John J. Snyder High School, FL
Bishop Kelly High School, ID
Bishop McGuinness Catholic High School, NC
Bishop McGuinness Catholic High School, OK
Bishop Montgomery High School, CA
Bishop's College School, QC, Canada
The Bishop's School, CA
Bishop Stang High School, MA
The Bishop Strachan School, ON, Canada
Blair Academy, NJ
Blanchet School, OR
Blessed Sacrament Hugenot, VA
Blessed Trinity High School, GA
Blue Mountain Academy, PA
Blueprint Education, AZ
The Bolles School, FL
Boylan Central Catholic High School, IL
The Brearley School, NY
Breck School, MN
Brentwood School, CA
Brewster Academy, NH
Briarcrest Christian High School, TN
Briarwood Christian High School, AL
Brimmer and May School, MA
Brooks School, MA
Brookstone School, GA
Brophy College Preparatory, AZ
Brother Rice High School, MI
The Browning School, NY
Brunswick School, CT
The Bryn Mawr School for Girls, MD
Bulloch Academy, GA
Burr and Burton Academy, VT
Butte Central Catholic High School, MT
The Byrnes Schools, SC
Calgary Academy Collegiate, AB, Canada
Calvary Chapel High School, CA
Calvert Hall College High School, MD
The Calverton School, MD
Calvin Christian High School, CA
The Cambridge School of Weston, MA
Campbell Hall (Episcopal), CA
Cannon School, NC
The Canterbury Episcopal School, TX
Canterbury School, FL
Canyonville Christian Academy, OR
Cape Cod Academy, MA
Cape Fear Academy, NC
Cape Henry Collegiate School, VA
Capistrano Valley Christian Schools, CA
Cardinal Mooney Catholic College Preparatory High School, MI
Cardinal Newman High School, FL
Cardinal O'Hara High School, PA
Carlisle School, VA
Carolina Day School, NC
Carondelet High School, CA
Carrollton School of the Sacred Heart, FL
Cascadilla School, NY
Cathedral High School, NY
The Catholic High School of Baltimore, MD
Central Catholic High School, CA
Central Catholic High School, MA
Central Catholic High School, TX
CFS, The School at Church Farm, PA
Chadwick School, CA
Chaminade College Preparatory, CA
Chaminade College Preparatory School, MO
Chaminade-Madonna College Preparatory, FL
Chapel Hill–Chauncy Hall School, MA
Charlotte Christian School, NC
Charlotte Latin School, NC
Chatham Hall, VA
Chattanooga Christian School, TN
Cheshire Academy, CT
Cheverus High School, ME
The Chicago Academy for the Arts, IL
Children's Creative and Performing Arts Academy of San Diego, CA
Chinese Christian Schools, CA
Christchurch School, VA
Christian Brothers Academy, NJ
Christian Brothers Academy, NY
Christian Central Academy, NY
Christian Home and Bible School, FL
Christopher Columbus High School, FL
Christopher Dock Mennonite High School, PA
Cincinnati Country Day School, OH
Cistercian Preparatory School, TX
Clarksville Academy, TN
Clearwater Central Catholic High School, FL
Colegio Nueva Granada, Colombia
Colegio San Jose, PR
Collegedale Academy, TN
Collegiate School, NY
The Collegiate School, VA
The Colorado Springs School, CO
Columbia Academy, TN

Columbia International College of Canada, ON, Canada
The Columbus Academy, OH
Columbus School for Girls, OH
Commonwealth School, MA
The Community School of Naples, FL
Concordia Lutheran High School, IN
Convent of the Sacred Heart, CT
The Country Day School, ON, Canada
Country Day School of the Sacred Heart, PA
Covington Catholic High School, KY
Crawford Adventist Academy, ON, Canada
The Culver Academies, IN
Cushing Academy, MA
The Dalton School, NY
Damien High School, CA
Dana Hall School, MA
Darlington School, GA
Davidson Academy, TN
Deerfield Academy, MA
Deerfield-Windsor School, GA
De La Salle High School, CA
Delbarton School, NJ
DeMatha Catholic High School, MD
DePaul Catholic High School, NJ
The Derryfield School, NH
Devon Preparatory School, PA
Doane Stuart School, NY
Dominican Academy, NY
Donelson Christian Academy, TN
Dublin Christian Academy, NH
Durham Academy, NC
Eastside Catholic School, WA
Edgewood Academy, AL
Edison School, AB, Canada
Edmund Burke School, DC
Eldorado Emerson Private School, CA
Elizabeth Seton High School, MD
The Ellis School, PA
Emma Willard School, NY
Episcopal Collegiate School, AR
Episcopal High School, TX
Episcopal High School, VA
Escola Americana de Campinas, Brazil
The Ethel Walker School, CT
Excel Christian Academy, GA
Ezell-Harding Christian School, TN
Faith Christian High School, CA
Faith Lutheran High School, NV
Falmouth Academy, MA
Father Lopez High School, FL
Father Ryan High School, TN
Fayetteville Academy, NC
The First Academy, FL
First Baptist Academy, TX
First Presbyterian Day School, GA
Flint Hill School, VA
Flintridge Preparatory School, CA
Flint River Academy, GA
Fontbonne Hall Academy, NY
Fordham Preparatory School, NY
Forsyth Country Day School, NC
Fort Lauderdale Preparatory School, FL
Fort Worth Country Day School, TX
Foundation Academy, FL
Fountain Valley School of Colorado, CO
Foxcroft School, VA
French-American School of New York, NY
Fresno Christian Schools, CA
Friends Academy, NY
Front Range Christian High School, CO
Fuqua School, VA
Gabriel Richard High School, MI
The Galloway School, GA
Gann Academy (The New Jewish High School of Greater Boston), MA
Garces Memorial High School, CA
Gaston Day School, NC
The Geneva School, FL
George Stevens Academy, ME
Georgetown Preparatory School, MD
George Walton Academy, GA
Gill St. Bernard's School, NJ
Gilman School, MD
Gilmour Academy, OH
Girls Preparatory School, TN
Glades Day School, FL
Glenelg Country School, MD
Gonzaga College High School, DC
Gonzaga Preparatory School, WA
Gould Academy, ME
The Governor French Academy, IL
Grace Brethren School, CA
The Grauer School, CA
Greenfield School, NC
Greenhill School, TX
Greensboro Day School, NC
Greenwich Academy, CT
The Grier School, PA
Groton School, MA
Guamani Private School, PR
The Gunston School, MD
Hackley School, NY
Hamden Hall Country Day School, CT
Hampton Roads Academy, VA
Harding Academy, TN
Hargrave Military Academy, VA
The Harker School, CA
The Harley School, NY
Harrells Christian Academy, NC
The Harvey School, NY
Hawaii Baptist Academy, HI
Hawken School, OH
Head-Royce School, CA
Hebrew Academy, CA
Hebrew Academy-the Five Towns, NY
Hillcrest Christian School, CA
Hillcrest Christian School, MS
The Hill School, PA
The Hockaday School, TX
Holy Cross High School, CT
Holy Ghost Preparatory School, PA
Holy Innocents' Episcopal School, GA
Holyoke Catholic High School, MA
Holy Savior Menard Catholic High School, LA
Holy Trinity Diocesan High School, NY
Holy Trinity High School, IL
Hoosac School, NY
Hopkins School, CT
The Hotchkiss School, CT
Houghton Academy, NY
Hyde School, CT
Hyman Brand Hebrew Academy of Greater Kansas City, KS
Idyllwild Arts Academy, CA
Immaculata-La Salle High School, FL

Immaculate Conception High School, NJ
Immaculate Conception School, IL
Immaculate Heart High School, AZ
Independent School, KS
Indian Springs School, AL
Institute of Notre Dame, MD
Interlochen Arts Academy, MI
Intermountain Christian School, UT
International School Bangkok, Thailand
International School Manila, Philippines
Iona Preparatory School, NY
Jack M. Barrack Hebrew Academy, PA
Jackson Preparatory School, MS
Jesuit College Preparatory School, TX
Jesuit High School of New Orleans, LA
Jesuit High School of Tampa, FL
John Burroughs School, MO
John Paul II Catholic High School, FL
Josephinum Academy, IL
Junipero Serra High School, CA
Junipero Serra High School, CA
The Karafin School, NY
Keith Country Day School, IL
Kent Place School, NJ
Kentucky Country Day School, KY
Kerr-Vance Academy, NC
The Kew-Forest School, NY
Kimball Union Academy, NH
King Low Heywood Thomas, CT
The King's Academy, TN
Kings Christian School, CA
King's High School, WA
King's Ridge Christian School, GA
Kingswood-Oxford School, CT
Ladywood High School, MI
La Jolla Country Day School, CA
Lakefield College School, ON, Canada
Lakehill Preparatory School, TX
Lancaster Mennonite High School, PA
Landmark Christian School, GA
Landon School, MD
Lansdale Catholic High School, PA
La Salle High School, CA
La Scuola D'Italia Guglielmo Marconi, NY
The Latin School of Chicago, IL
Laurel Springs School, CA
Lausanne Collegiate School, TN
Lawrence Academy, MA
Lehigh Valley Christian High School, PA
Lehman High School, OH
Le Lycee Francais de Los Angeles, CA
Lexington Catholic High School, KY
Liberty Christian School, CA
Lincoln Academy, ME
Lincoln School, RI
The Linsly School, WV
Lodi Academy, CA
Long Island Lutheran Middle and High School, NY
The Loomis Chaffee School, CT
Loretto Academy, TX
Los Angeles Baptist Middle School/High School, CA
Los Angeles Lutheran High School, CA
Louisville Collegiate School, KY
Louisville High School, CA
The Lovett School, GA
Loyola-Blakefield, MD
Lutheran High School, IN
Lutheran High School North, MO
Lutheran High School Northwest, MI
Lutheran High School of Hawaii, HI
Lutheran High School of San Diego, CA
Lyman Ward Military Academy, AL
MacLachlan College, ON, Canada
Madison-Ridgeland Academy, MS
Magnificat High School, OH
Maine Central Institute, ME
Malden Catholic High School, MA
Manhattan Christian High School, MT
Maranatha High School, CA
Maret School, DC
Marian Central Catholic High School, IL
Marian High School, IN
Marine Military Academy, TX
Marist School, GA
Marlborough School, CA
Mars Hill Bible School, AL
Martin Luther High School, NY
The Marvelwood School, CT
Marylawn of the Oranges, NJ
Marymount High School, CA
Mary Star of the Sea High School, CA
The Master's School, CT
The Masters School, NY
Matignon High School, MA
McDonogh School, MD
The Meadows School, NV
Memphis University School, TN
Menaul School, NM
Mercy High School, CT
Mercy High School, NE
Mercy High School College Preparatory, CA
Merion Mercy Academy, PA
Middlesex School, MA
Mid Pacific Institute, HI
Millbrook School, NY
Miller School, VA
Milton Academy, MA
Miss Edgar's and Miss Cramp's School, QC, Canada
Miss Hall's School, MA
Missouri Military Academy, MO
Miss Porter's School, CT
MMI Preparatory School, PA
Monsignor Donovan High School, NJ
Montclair Kimberley Academy, NJ
Montgomery Bell Academy, TN
Moorestown Friends School, NJ
Moravian Academy, PA
Moreau Catholic High School, CA
Morristown-Beard School, NJ
Mother McAuley High School, IL
Mount Michael Benedictine School, NE
Mount Saint Charles Academy, RI
Mount Saint Joseph Academy, PA
MU High School, MO
Nativity B.V.M. High School, PA
Nazareth Academy, IL
Nerinx Hall, MO
Neuchatel Junior College, Switzerland
Newark Academy, NJ
Nichols School, NY
Noble and Greenough School, MA
Norfolk Academy, VA
North Catholic High School, PA
North Cobb Christian School, GA

Northwest Catholic High School, CT
Northwood School, NY
The Norwich Free Academy, CT
Notre Dame Academy, CA
Notre Dame College Prep, IL
Notre Dame High School, TN
Notre Dame Junior/Senior High School, PA
Oak Grove School, CA
Oak Hill School, OR
The Oakridge School, TX
Ojai Valley School, CA
The Oliverian School, NH
The O'Neal School, NC
Oneida Baptist Institute, KY
Oregon Episcopal School, OR
Orinda Academy, CA
Our Lady Academy, MS
Our Lady of Mercy High School, NY
Out-Of-Door-Academy, FL
The Overlake School, WA
Pacific Hills School, CA
Padua Franciscan High School, OH
The Paideia School, GA
Palma School, CA
The Park School of Baltimore, MD
Peddie School, NJ
Philadelphia-Montgomery Christian Academy, PA
Phillips Academy (Andover), MA
Phillips Exeter Academy, NH
Phoenix Country Day School, AZ
Pinecrest Academy, GA
Pine Crest School, FL
The Pine School, FL
The Pingree School, MA
The Pingry School, NJ
Pioneer Valley Christian School, MA
Porter-Gaud School, SC
The Potomac School, VA
Powers Catholic High School, MI
The Prairie School, WI
Prestonwood Christian Academy, TX
Providence Catholic School, The College Preparatory School for Girls Grades 6-12, TX
Providence Country Day School, RI
Providence Day School, NC
Providence High School, CA
Punahou School, HI
Rabbi Alexander S. Gross Hebrew Academy, FL
Randolph-Macon Academy, VA
Ranney School, NJ
Ransom Everglades School, FL
Ravenscroft School, NC
Redwood Christian Schools, CA
Regis High School, NY
Reitz Memorial High School, IN
Ridley College, ON, Canada
Ripon Christian Schools, CA
Rivermont Collegiate, IA
Riverside Military Academy, GA
The Rivers School, MA
The Roeper School, MI
Roland Park Country School, MD
Rolling Hills Preparatory School, CA
Ross School, NY
Rowland Hall, UT
The Roxbury Latin School, MA
Rye Country Day School, NY
Sacramento Adventist Academy, CA
Sacramento Country Day School, CA
Sacred Heart/Griffin High School, IL
Sacred Heart School of Halifax, NS, Canada
Saddleback Valley Christian School, CA
Sage Hill School, CA
Sage Ridge School, NV
St. Agnes Academy, TX
Saint Agnes Boys High School, NY
St. Albans School, DC
St. Andrew's College, ON, Canada
St. Andrew's Priory School, HI
St. Andrew's School, RI
St. Andrew's–Sewanee School, TN
St. Anne's–Belfield School, VA
St. Anthony Catholic High School, TX
Saint Anthony High School, CA
Saint Anthony High School, IL
St. Anthony's Junior-Senior High School, HI
Saint Augustine Preparatory School, NJ
Saint Basil Academy, PA
St. Benedict at Auburndale, TN
St. Bernard's Catholic School, CA
St. Brendan High School, FL
St. Christopher's School, VA
St. Clement's School, ON, Canada
St. Croix Country Day School, VI
St. Croix Schools, MN
Saint Dominic Academy, ME
Saint Edward's School, FL
Saint Elizabeth High School, CA
St. Francis de Sales High School, OH
Saint Francis High School, CA
Saint Francis School, HI
St. George's Independent School, TN
St. George's School of Montreal, QC, Canada
St. Gregory College Preparatory School, AZ
St. John's Preparatory School, MA
Saint John's Preparatory School, MN
St. John's-Ravenscourt School, MB, Canada
St. Joseph Academy, FL
Saint Joseph High School, IL
Saint Joseph Junior-Senior High School, HI
St. Joseph's Academy, LA
St. Joseph's Catholic School, SC
Saint Joseph's High School, NJ
St. Joseph's Preparatory School, PA
St. Mark's High School, DE
St. Mark's School of Texas, TX
St. Martin's Episcopal School, LA
Saint Mary's College High School, CA
St. Mary's Episcopal School, TN
Saint Mary's Hall, TX
Saint Mary's High School, AZ
Saint Mary's High School, MD
St. Mary's Preparatory School, MI
Saint Mary's School, NC
St. Mary's School, OR
Saint Maur International School, Japan
St. Michael's College School, ON, Canada
St. Michael's Preparatory School of the Norbertine Fathers, CA
St. Patrick Catholic High School, MS
Saint Patrick High School, IL
Saint Patrick - Saint Vincent High School, CA
St. Patrick's Regional Secondary, BC, Canada
St. Paul's High School, MB, Canada
St. Peter's Preparatory School, NJ

St. Pius X Catholic High School, GA
St. Scholastica Academy, IL
St. Sebastian's School, MA
Saints Peter and Paul High School, MD
St. Stephen's & St. Agnes School, VA
St. Stephen's Episcopal School, TX
St. Stephen's School, Rome, Italy
Saint Teresa's Academy, MO
Saint Thomas Academy, MN
St. Thomas Aquinas High School, FL
Saint Thomas Aquinas High School, KS
St. Thomas Aquinas High School, NH
St. Thomas High School, TX
Saint Ursula Academy, OH
Salem Academy, NC
Salem Academy, OR
Salesian High School, CA
Salesianum School, DE
Saltus Grammar School, Bermuda
Sandy Spring Friends School, MD
Sanford School, DE
San Marcos Baptist Academy, TX
Santa Catalina School, CA
Sayre School, KY
SciCore Academy, NJ
Scotus Central Catholic High School, NE
Seabury Hall, HI
Seattle Christian Schools, WA
Seton Catholic Central High School, NY
Seton Catholic High School, AZ
The Seven Hills School, OH
Severn School, MD
Sewickley Academy, PA
Shady Side Academy, PA
Shattuck St. Mary's School, MN
Shawe Memorial Junior/Senior High School, IN
Shawnigan Lake School, BC, Canada
The Shipley School, PA
Sonoma Academy, CA
Southfield Christian High School, MI
Spartanburg Day School, SC
The Spence School, NY
Springside Chestnut Hill Academy, PA
Squaw Valley Academy, CA
Stephen T. Badin High School, OH
Stevenson School, CA
Stoneleigh–Burnham School, MA
Storm King School, NY
Strake Jesuit College Preparatory, TX
Stratford Academy, GA
Suffield Academy, CT
Tabor Academy, MA
The Taft School, CT
Taipei American School, Taiwan
Takoma Academy, MD
Tandem Friends School, VA
TASIS The American School in England, United Kingdom
TASIS, The American School in Switzerland, Switzerland
The Tenney School, TX
The Thacher School, CA
Tidewater Academy, VA
Tilton School, NH
Timothy Christian High School, IL
Tower Hill School, DE
Trafalgar Castle School, ON, Canada
Tri-City Christian Schools, CA
Trinity College School, ON, Canada
Trinity High School, KY
Trinity High School, NH
Trinity High School, OH
Trinity-Pawling School, NY
Trinity Preparatory School, FL
Trinity School of Texas, TX
Trinity Valley School, TX
Tuscaloosa Academy, AL
Tyler Street Christian Academy, TX
The University of Chicago Laboratory Schools, IL
University of Detroit Jesuit High School and Academy, MI
University Prep, WA
University School of Jackson, TN
University School of Milwaukee, WI
University School of Nova Southeastern University, FL
Vail Mountain School, CO
Valle Catholic High School, MO
Valley Christian High School, CA
Valley Lutheran High School, AZ
Vicksburg Catholic School, MS
Villa Duchesne and Oak Hill School, MO
Villa Joseph Marie High School, PA
Villa Maria Academy, PA
Villa Victoria Academy, NJ
Villa Walsh Academy, NJ
Visitation Academy of St. Louis County, MO
Wakefield School, VA
The Walker School, GA
Walnut Hill School, MA
Waring School, MA
Wasatch Academy, UT
Washington Waldorf School, MD
The Waterford School, UT
The Webb School, TN
Webb School of Knoxville, TN
Wesleyan Academy, PR
Westbury Christian School, TX
West Catholic High School, MI
Westchester Country Day School, NC
Westgate Mennonite Collegiate, MB, Canada
West Island College, AB, Canada
Westminster Christian Academy, AL
Westminster School, CT
Westover School, CT
Westridge School, CA
Wheaton Academy, IL
The Wheeler School, RI
Whitefield Academy, KY
The Williams School, CT
The Willows Academy, IL
Wilmington Christian School, DE
Wilson Hall, SC
Winchester Thurston School, PA
Windermere Preparatory School, FL
The Windsor School, NY
Windward School, CA
The Winsor School, MA
The Woodhall School, CT
Woodward Academy, GA
The Woodward School, MA
Worcester Preparatory School, MD
Xaverian High School, NY
York Country Day School, PA
York Preparatory School, NY
York School, CA

SCHOOLS REPORTING A POSTGRADUATE YEAR

Bachman Academy, TN
The Beekman School, NY
Berkshire School, MA
Blair Academy, NJ
The Bolles School, FL
Brewster Academy, NH
The Cambridge School of Weston, MA
Cascadilla School, NY
Chapel Hill–Chauncy Hall School, MA
Cheshire Academy, CT
Christchurch School, VA
The Culver Academies, IN
Cushing Academy, MA
Darlington School, GA
Deerfield Academy, MA
Emma Willard School, NY
Gould Academy, ME
The Grier School, PA
Hargrave Military Academy, VA
The Hill School, PA
Hoosac School, NY
The Hotchkiss School, CT
Houghton Academy, NY
Idyllwild Arts Academy, CA
Interlochen Arts Academy, MI
The John Dewey Academy, MA
Kimball Union Academy, NH
The Loomis Chaffee School, CT
Maine Central Institute, ME
Marine Military Academy, TX
Missouri Military Academy, MO
Northwood School, NY
The Oliverian School, NH
Peddie School, NJ
Phillips Academy (Andover), MA
Phillips Exeter Academy, NH
Randolph-Macon Academy, VA
Ridley College, ON, Canada
Robert Louis Stevenson School, NY
Saint John's Preparatory School, MN
St. Stephen's School, Rome, Italy
Shattuck-St. Mary's School, MN
Stoneleigh–Burnham School, MA
Stratton Mountain School, VT
Suffield Academy, CT
The Taft School, CT
TASIS, The American School in Switzerland, Switzerland
Tilton School, NH
Trinity-Pawling School, NY
Walnut Hill School, MA
Watkinson School, CT
Westminster School, CT
The Windsor School, NY
The Woodhall School, CT

SCHOOLS OFFERING THE INTERNATIONAL BACCALAUREATE PROGRAM

Academy of the Holy Cross, MD
Academy of the Sacred Heart, LA
Académie Ste Cécile International School, ON, Canada
The American School Foundation, Mexico
Annie Wright School, WA
Atlanta International School, GA
Branksome Hall, ON, Canada
Calgary Academy Collegiate, AB, Canada
Cardinal Newman High School, FL
Carlisle School, VA
Carrollton School of the Sacred Heart, FL
Chamberlain-Hunt Academy, MS
Charlotte Country Day School, NC
Cheshire Academy, CT
Christ Church Episcopal School, SC
Clearwater Central Catholic High School, FL
Colegio San Jose, PR
Copenhagen International School, Denmark
DePaul Catholic High School, NJ
DuBois Central Catholic High School/Middle School, PA
Fort Lauderdale Preparatory School, FL
Glenlyon Norfolk School, BC, Canada
Hebrew Academy, CA
Immaculate Heart High School, AZ
International High School, CA
International School Bangkok, Thailand
International School Hamburg, Germany
International School Manila, Philippines
International School of Amsterdam, Netherlands
The International School of London, United Kingdom
Kerr-Vance Academy, NC
The Kew-Forest School, NY
King's-Edgehill School, NS, Canada
La Scuola D'Italia Guglielmo Marconi, NY
Lausanne Collegiate School, TN
Le Lycee Francais de Los Angeles, CA
Luther College High School, SK, Canada
Marymount International School, Italy
Mercyhurst Preparatory School, PA
Mid-Pacific Institute, HI
Munich International School, Germany
Newark Academy, NJ
Niagara Christian Community of Schools, ON, Canada
Providence Catholic School, The College Preparatory School for Girls Grades 6-12, TX
Providence Christian School, AB, Canada
Rothesay Netherwood School, NB, Canada
Saint Anthony High School, IL
Saint Dominic Academy, ME
Saint John's Preparatory School, MN
St. Joseph's Preparatory School, PA
Saint Maur International School, Japan
St. Peter's Preparatory School, NJ
St. Scholastica Academy, IL
St. Stephen's School, Rome, Italy
St. Timothy's School, MD
Seisen International School, Japan
Shawe Memorial Junior/Senior High School, IN
Stoneleigh–Burnham School, MA
Taipei American School, Taiwan
TASIS The American School in England, United Kingdom
TASIS, The American School in Switzerland, Switzerland
Tri-City Christian Schools, CA
Tyler Street Christian Academy, TX
United Nations International School, NY
The United World College - USA, NM
Villa Duchesne and Oak Hill School, MO
West Sound Academy, WA
Windermere Preparatory School, FL

SCHOOLS REPORTING THAT THEY AWARD MERIT SCHOLARSHIPS

Academy at the Lakes, FL
Academy of the Holy Cross, MD
Academy of the Sacred Heart, LA
Academy of the Sacred Heart, LA
Academy of the Sacred Heart, MI
Académie Ste Cécile International School, ON, Canada
Allison Academy, FL
American Heritage School, FL
The American School Foundation, Mexico
Anacapa School, CA
Annie Wright School, WA
Archbishop Curley High School, MD
Archbishop Hoban High School, OH
Archbishop Rummel High School, LA
Armbrae Academy, NS, Canada
Balmoral Hall School, MB, Canada
Baltimore Lutheran School, MD
Battle Ground Academy, TN
Baylor School, TN
Benedictine High School, OH
Benedictine High School, VA
The Birch Wathen Lenox School, NY
Bishop Blanchet High School, WA
Bishop Brady High School, NH
Bishop Eustace Preparatory School, NJ
Bishop Fenwick High School, OH
Bishop Guertin High School, NH
Bishop Ireton High School, VA
Bishop Mora Salesian High School, CA
Bishop's College School, QC, Canada
Bishop Stang High School, MA
The Bishop Strachan School, ON, Canada
Blanchet School, OR
The Blue Ridge School, VA
Branksome Hall, ON, Canada
Brookstone School, GA
Brother Rice High School, MI
Calvert Hall College High School, MD
Canterbury School, FL
Canyonville Christian Academy, OR
Cape Fear Academy, NC
Cape Henry Collegiate School, VA
Capistrano Valley Christian Schools, CA
Carolina Day School, NC
Carrollton School of the Sacred Heart, FL
Cascadilla School, NY
Cathedral High School, NY
The Catholic High School of Baltimore, MD
The Catlin Gabel School, OR
Central Catholic High School, CA
Central Catholic High School, MA
Central Catholic High School, TX
Chamberlain-Hunt Academy, MS
Chaminade College Preparatory, CA
Chaminade College Preparatory School, MO
Charlotte Latin School, NC
Chatham Hall, VA
Cheshire Academy, CT
Cheverus High School, ME
The Chicago Academy for the Arts, IL
Children's Creative and Performing Arts Academy of San Diego, CA
Chinese Christian Schools, CA
Christ Church Episcopal School, SC
Christian Brothers Academy, NJ
Christian Brothers Academy, NY
Christian Central Academy, NY
Cincinnati Country Day School, OH
Clearwater Central Catholic High School, FL
The Colorado Springs School, CO
Columbia International College of Canada, ON, Canada
The Columbus Academy, OH
The Community School of Naples, FL
Concordia Lutheran High School, IN
Country Day School of the Sacred Heart, PA
Covington Catholic High School, KY
Crossroads School for Arts & Sciences, CA
The Culver Academies, IN
Cushing Academy, MA
Damien High School, CA
Darlington School, GA
Deerfield-Windsor School, GA
DeMatha Catholic High School, MD
Denver Christian High School, CO
DePaul Catholic High School, NJ
The Derryfield School, NH
Devon Preparatory School, PA
Dominican Academy, NY
DuBois Central Catholic High School/Middle School, PA
Eastside Catholic School, WA
Elizabeth Seton High School, MD
Emma Willard School, NY
Episcopal High School, VA
Falmouth Academy, MA
Father Lopez High School, FL
First Presbyterian Day School, GA
Fontbonne Hall Academy, NY
Fordham Preparatory School, NY
Forest Lake Academy, FL
Fort Lauderdale Preparatory School, FL
Fort Worth Country Day School, TX
Fountain Valley School of Colorado, CO
Foxcroft School, VA
Freeman Academy, SD
Fresno Christian Schools, CA
Fuqua School, VA
Gabriel Richard High School, MI
Garces Memorial High School, CA
Gaston Day School, NC
Gill St. Bernard's School, NJ
Gilmour Academy, OH
Glenelg Country School, MD
Glenlyon Norfolk School, BC, Canada
Gonzaga College High School, DC
Gonzaga Preparatory School, WA
Great Lakes Christian High School, ON, Canada
Greenfield School, NC
The Grier School, PA
The Gunston School, MD
Hargrave Military Academy, VA
The Haverford School, PA
Hawken School, OH
Hawthorne Christian Academy, NJ
Holy Cross High School, CT
Holy Cross High School, NY
Holy Ghost Preparatory School, PA
Holy Savior Menard Catholic High School, LA
Holy Trinity High School, IL
Hoosac School, NY
Hyde School, ME
Immaculate Conception High School, NJ
Immaculate Conception School, IL

Institute of Notre Dame, MD
Interlochen Arts Academy, MI
Iona Preparatory School, NY
Jack M. Barrack Hebrew Academy, PA
Jesuit College Preparatory School, TX
Josephinum Academy, IL
Junipero Serra High School, CA
Junipero Serra High School, CA
Keith Country Day School, IL
Kentucky Country Day School, KY
King's-Edgehill School, NS, Canada
Kingshill School, VI
Kingswood-Oxford School, CT
Ladywood High School, MI
Lancaster Mennonite High School, PA
Lansdale Catholic High School, PA
La Salle High School, CA
Le Lycee Francais de Los Angeles, CA
Lexington Catholic High School, KY
Lodi Academy, CA
Long Island Lutheran Middle and High School, NY
Los Angeles Baptist Middle School/High School, CA
Los Angeles Lutheran High School, CA
Louisville Collegiate School, KY
Louisville High School, CA
Loyola-Blakefield, MD
Lutheran High School North, MO
Lutheran High School Northwest, MI
Lutheran High School of Hawaii, HI
Lutheran High School of San Diego, CA
Luther College High School, SK, Canada
Lyman Ward Military Academy, AL
Madison-Ridgeland Academy, MS
Magnificat High School, OH
Maine Central Institute, ME
Malden Catholic High School, MA
Maranatha High School, CA
Martin Luther High School, NY
The Marvelwood School, CT
Marylawn of the Oranges, NJ
Marymount High School, CA
Mary Star of the Sea High School, CA
The Master's School, CT
Matignon High School, MA
Merchiston Castle School, United Kingdom
Mercy High School, CT
Mercy High School, NE
Mercyhurst Preparatory School, PA
Merion Mercy Academy, PA
Mid-Pacific Institute, HI
Miss Edgar's and Miss Cramp's School, QC, Canada
Miss Hall's School, MA
Missouri Military Academy, MO
Miss Porter's School, CT
MMI Preparatory School, PA
Monsignor Donovan High School, NJ
Moreau Catholic High School, CA
Morristown-Beard School, NJ
Mother McAuley High School, IL
Mount Michael Benedictine School, NE
Mount Saint Joseph Academy, PA
Nativity B.V.M. High School, PA
Nazareth Academy, IL
Nebraska Christian Schools, NE
Niagara Christian Community of Schools, ON, Canada
Northwest Catholic High School, CT
Notre Dame Academy, CA
Notre Dame College Prep, IL
Oak Hill School, OR
The Oakland School, PA
Oak Ridge Military Academy, NC
The Oliverian School, NH
The O'Neal School, NC
Our Lady of Mercy Academy, NJ
Our Lady of Mercy High School, NY
Padua Franciscan High School, OH
Palma School, CA
Peddie School, NJ
Pickering College, ON, Canada
The Pingree School, MA
The Prairie School, WI
Presbyterian Pan American School, TX
Providence Catholic School, The College Preparatory School for Girls Grades 6-12, TX
Providence High School, CA
Punahou School, HI
Queen Margaret's School, BC, Canada
Randolph-Macon Academy, VA
Ravenscroft School, NC
Redwood Christian Schools, CA
Ridley College, ON, Canada
Rivermont Collegiate, IA
Robert Land Academy, ON, Canada
Rolling Hills Preparatory School, CA
Rosseau Lake College, ON, Canada
Rothesay Netherwood School, NB, Canada
Rowland Hall, UT
Royal Canadian College, BC, Canada
Rundle College, AB, Canada
Sacred Heart/Griffin High School, IL
Sacred Heart School of Halifax, NS, Canada
Saddleback Valley Christian School, CA
St. Agnes Academy, TX
St. Andrew's College, ON, Canada
St. Andrew's Priory School, HI
St. Andrew's–Sewanee School, TN
St. Anthony Catholic High School, TX
Saint Anthony High School, CA
St. Anthony's Junior-Senior High School, HI
Saint Augustine Preparatory School, NJ
Saint Basil Academy, PA
St. Benedict at Auburndale, TN
St. Bernard High School, CT
St. Bernard's Catholic School, CA
St. Christopher's School, VA
St. Clement's School, ON, Canada
St. Croix Country Day School, VI
St. Croix Schools, MN
Saint Dominic Academy, ME
Saint Elizabeth High School, CA
St. Francis de Sales High School, OH
Saint Francis High School, CA
Saint Francis School, HI
St. John's Preparatory School, MA
Saint John's Preparatory School, MN
St. John's-Ravenscourt School, MB, Canada
Saint Joseph High School, IL
Saint Joseph High School, NJ
St. Joseph's Catholic School, SC
Saint Joseph's High School, NJ
St. Joseph's Preparatory School, PA
St. Mark's High School, DE
St. Martin's Episcopal School, LA
Saint Mary's College High School, CA

Saint Mary's Hall, TX
Saint Mary's High School, MD
St. Mary's Preparatory School, MI
St. Michael's College School, ON, Canada
St. Peter's Preparatory School, NJ
St. Scholastica Academy, IL
St. Stephen's Episcopal School, TX
St. Stephen's School, Rome, Italy
Saint Teresa's Academy, MO
Saint Thomas Academy, MN
St. Thomas High School, TX
St. Timothy's School, MD
Saint Ursula Academy, OH
Salem Academy, NC
Salesian High School, CA
Salesianum School, DE
Saltus Grammar School, Bermuda
Santa Catalina School, CA
Sayre School, KY
Seton Catholic Central High School, NY
Seton Catholic High School, AZ
The Seven Hills School, OH
Shady Side Academy, PA
Shattuck-St. Mary's School, MN
Shawnigan Lake School, BC, Canada
Spartanburg Day School, SC
Springside Chestnut Hill Academy, PA
Stephen T. Badin High School, OH
Stoneleigh–Burnham School, MA
Storm King School, NY
Stratford Academy, GA
Takoma Academy, MD
Tilton School, NH
Tower Hill School, DE
Trafalgar Castle School, ON, Canada
Trinity High School, KY
Trinity School of Texas, TX
Tuscaloosa Academy, AL
Tyler Street Christian Academy, TX
The United World College - USA, NM
University of Detroit Jesuit High School and Academy, MI
Valle Catholic High School, MO
Valley Lutheran High School, AZ
The Valley School, MI
Villa Joseph Marie High School, PA
Villa Maria Academy, PA
Villa Maria Academy, PA
Villa Victoria Academy, NJ
Villa Walsh Academy, NJ
Waldorf High School of Massachusetts Bay, MA
Wasatch Academy, UT
The Webb School, TN
Westbury Christian School, TX
Western Mennonite School, OR
Westgate Mennonite Collegiate, MB, Canada
West Sound Academy, WA
Wheaton Academy, IL
The Woodward School, MA
Xaverian High School, NY
York Preparatory School, NY

SCHOOLS REPORTING A GUARANTEED TUITION PLAN

Armona Union Academy, CA
Auldern Academy, NC
The Blue Ridge School, VA
Butte Central Catholic High School, MT
Calvary Chapel High School, CA
Central Catholic High School, CA
Chamberlain-Hunt Academy, MS
Community Christian Academy, KY
Concord Academy, MA
Crawford Adventist Academy, ON, Canada
The Culver Academies, IN
Damien High School, CA
Foundation Academy, FL
Glenlyon Norfolk School, BC, Canada
Grace Brethren School, CA
Hawaii Baptist Academy, HI
Hebrew Academy, CA
The Hill Center, Durham Academy, NC
Humanex Academy, CO
Manhattan Christian High School, MT
Marion Academy, AL
Middlesex School, MA
Missouri Military Academy, MO
Nebraska Christian Schools, NE
New Covenant Academy, MO
Pickens Academy, AL
Pope John XXIII Regional High School, NJ
Presbyterian Pan American School, TX
St. George's School of Montreal, QC, Canada
San Marcos Baptist Academy, TX
Scholar's Hall Preparatory School, ON, Canada
Sunshine Bible Academy, SD
Trinity High School, KY
Tuscaloosa Academy, AL
The United World College - USA, NM
The Waterford School, UT
Wesleyan Academy, PR
Westchester Country Day School, NC
Westminster Christian Academy, AL

SCHOOLS REPORTING A TUITION INSTALLMENT PLAN

Academy at the Lakes, FL
The Academy for Gifted Children (PACE), ON, Canada
Academy of Holy Angels, MN
Academy of Our Lady of Peace, CA
Academy of the Holy Cross, MD
Academy of the New Church Boys' School, PA
Academy of the New Church Girls' School, PA
Academy of the Sacred Heart, LA
Academy of the Sacred Heart, LA
Academy of the Sacred Heart, MI
Académie Ste Cécile International School, ON, Canada
Alexander Dawson School, CO
Allendale Columbia School, NY
Alliance Academy, Ecuador
Allison Academy, FL
Alpha Omega Academy, IA
American Academy, FL
The American Boychoir School, NJ
American Heritage School, FL
The American School Foundation, Mexico
The American School in London, United Kingdom
Anacapa School, CA
Annie Wright School, WA
Archbishop Curley High School, MD
Archbishop Hoban High School, OH

Archbishop Mitty High School, CA
Archbishop Rummel High School, LA
Arendell Parrott Academy, NC
Armbrae Academy, NS, Canada
Armona Union Academy, CA
Army and Navy Academy, CA
Arrowsmith School, ON, Canada
ASSETS School, HI
The Athenian School, CA
Atlanta International School, GA
Atlantis Academy, FL
Augusta Christian School (I), GA
Auldern Academy, NC
Bachman Academy, TN
Balmoral Hall School, MB, Canada
The Baltimore Actors' Theatre Conservatory, MD
Baltimore Lutheran School, MD
Barrie School, MD
Battle Ground Academy, TN
Baylor School, TN
Bayside Academy, AL
Bearspaw Christian School, AB, Canada
The Beekman School, NY
Belen Jesuit Preparatory School, FL
Benedictine High School, OH
Benedictine High School, VA
Benet Academy, IL
Ben Franklin Academy, GA
Berkeley Preparatory School, FL
Berkshire School, MA
Beth Haven Christian School, KY
The Birch Wathen Lenox School, NY
Bishop Blanchet High School, WA
Bishop Brady High School, NH
Bishop Conaty-Our Lady of Loretto High School, CA
Bishop Eustace Preparatory School, NJ
Bishop Fenwick High School, OH
Bishop Guertin High School, NH
Bishop Ireton High School, VA
Bishop John J. Snyder High School, FL
Bishop Kelly High School, ID
Bishop McGuinness Catholic High School, NC
Bishop McGuinness Catholic High School, OK
Bishop Montgomery High School, CA
Bishop Mora Salesian High School, CA
Bishop's College School, QC, Canada
The Bishop's School, CA
Bishop Stang High School, MA
The Bishop Strachan School, ON, Canada
Blair Academy, NJ
Blanchet School, OR
Blessed Sacrament Hugenot, VA
Blessed Trinity High School, GA
Blue Mountain Academy, PA
The Blue Ridge School, VA
The Bolles School, FL
Boston University Academy, MA
Boylan Central Catholic High School, IL
Branksome Hall, ON, Canada
The Brearley School, NY
Breck School, MN
Brentwood School, CA
Brewster Academy, NH
Briarcrest Christian High School, TN
Briarwood Christian High School, AL
Bridgemont High School, CA
Bridges Academy, CA
Brimmer and May School, MA
Brooks School, MA
Brookstone School, GA
Brophy College Preparatory, AZ
Brother Rice High School, MI
The Browning School, NY
Brunswick School, CT
The Bryn Mawr School for Girls, MD
Bulloch Academy, GA
Burr and Burton Academy, VT
Butte Central Catholic High School, MT
Buxton School, MA
The Byrnes Schools, SC
Calgary Academy Collegiate, AB, Canada
Calvary Chapel High School, CA
Calvert Hall College High School, MD
The Calverton School, MD
Calvin Christian High School, CA
The Cambridge School of Weston, MA
Campbell Hall (Episcopal), CA
Cannon School, NC
The Canterbury Episcopal School, TX
Canterbury School, FL
Canyonville Christian Academy, OR
Cape Cod Academy, MA
Cape Fear Academy, NC
Cape Henry Collegiate School, VA
Capistrano Valley Christian Schools, CA
Cardinal Mooney Catholic College Preparatory High School, MI
Cardinal Newman High School, FL
Cardinal O'Hara High School, PA
Carlisle School, VA
Carolina Day School, NC
Carondelet High School, CA
Carrollton Christian Academy, TX
Carrollton School of the Sacred Heart, FL
Cascadilla School, NY
Cathedral High School, NY
The Catholic High School of Baltimore, MD
The Catlin Gabel School, OR
Central Alberta Christian High School, AB, Canada
Central Catholic High School, CA
Central Catholic High School, MA
Central Catholic High School, TX
CFS, The School at Church Farm, PA
Chadwick School, CA
Chamberlain-Hunt Academy, MS
Chaminade College Preparatory, CA
Chaminade College Preparatory School, MO
Chaminade-Madonna College Preparatory, FL
Chapel Hill–Chauncy Hall School, MA
Charlotte Christian School, NC
Charlotte Country Day School, NC
Charlotte Latin School, NC
Chatham Academy, GA
Chatham Hall, VA
Chattanooga Christian School, TN
Chelsea School, MD
Cheshire Academy, CT
Cheverus High School, ME
The Chicago Academy for the Arts, IL
Children's Creative and Performing Arts Academy of San Diego, CA
Chinese Christian Schools, CA
Christ Church Episcopal School, SC
Christchurch School, VA
Christian Brothers Academy, NJ

Christian Brothers Academy, NY
Christian Central Academy, NY
Christian Home and Bible School, FL
Christopher Columbus High School, FL
Christopher Dock Mennonite High School, PA
Chrysalis School, WA
Cincinnati Country Day School, OH
Cistercian Preparatory School, TX
Clarksville Academy, TN
Clearwater Central Catholic High School, FL
Colegio Nueva Granada, Colombia
Colegio San Jose, PR
Collegedale Academy, TN
Collegiate School, NY
The Collegiate School, VA
The Colorado Springs School, CO
Columbia Academy, TN
The Columbus Academy, OH
Columbus School for Girls, OH
Commonwealth School, MA
Community Christian Academy, KY
The Community School of Naples, FL
The Concept School, PA
Concord Academy, MA
Concordia Lutheran High School, IN
Convent of the Sacred Heart, CT
Copenhagen International School, Denmark
Cotter Schools, MN
Country Day School of the Sacred Heart, PA
Covenant Canadian Reformed School, AB, Canada
Covington Catholic High School, KY
Crawford Adventist Academy, ON, Canada
Crossroads School for Arts & Sciences, CA
The Culver Academies, IN
Currey Ingram Academy, TN
Cushing Academy, MA
The Dalton School, NY
Damien High School, CA
Dana Hall School, MA
Darlington School, GA
Davidson Academy, TN
Deerfield Academy, MA
Deerfield-Windsor School, GA
De La Salle High School, CA
Delbarton School, NJ
DeMatha Catholic High School, MD
Denver Christian High School, CO
DePaul Catholic High School, NJ
The Derryfield School, NH
Devon Preparatory School, PA
Doane Stuart School, NY
Dominican Academy, NY
Donelson Christian Academy, TN
Dublin Christian Academy, NH
DuBois Central Catholic High School/Middle School, PA
Durham Academy, NC
Eaglebrook School, MA
Eagle Hill-Southport, CT
Eastside Catholic School, WA
Eastside Christian Academy, AB, Canada
Edgewood Academy, AL
Edison School, AB, Canada
Edmund Burke School, DC
Eldorado Emerson Private School, CA
Elizabeth Seton High School, MD
The Ellis School, PA
Emma Willard School, NY
Episcopal Collegiate School, AR
Episcopal High School, TX
Episcopal High School, VA
Escola Americana de Campinas, Brazil
The Ethel Walker School, CT
Excel Christian Academy, GA
Ezell-Harding Christian School, TN
Faith Christian High School, CA
Faith Lutheran High School, NV
The Family Foundation School, NY
Father Lopez High School, FL
Father Ryan High School, TN
Fayetteville Academy, NC
Fay School, MA
The Fessenden School, MA
The First Academy, FL
First Baptist Academy, TX
First Presbyterian Day School, GA
Flint Hill School, VA
Flint River Academy, GA
Fontbonne Hall Academy, NY
Foothills Academy, AB, Canada
Fordham Preparatory School, NY
Forest Lake Academy, FL
Forsyth Country Day School, NC
Fort Lauderdale Preparatory School, FL
Fort Worth Country Day School, TX
Foundation Academy, FL
Fountain Valley School of Colorado, CO
Fowlers Academy, PR
Foxcroft School, VA
Fox Valley Lutheran High School, WI
Freeman Academy, SD
French-American School of New York, NY
Fresno Christian Schools, CA
Friends Academy, NY
Friends' Central School, PA
Front Range Christian High School, CO
The Frostig School, CA
Fuqua School, VA
Gabriel Richard High School, MI
The Galloway School, GA
Gann Academy (The New Jewish High School of Greater Boston), MA
Garces Memorial High School, CA
Gaston Day School, NC
The Geneva School, FL
George Stevens Academy, ME
Georgetown Preparatory School, MD
George Walton Academy, GA
Germantown Friends School, PA
Gill St. Bernard's School, NJ
Gilman School, MD
Gilmour Academy, OH
Girls Preparatory School, TN
Glades Day School, FL
Glenelg Country School, MD
Glenlyon Norfolk School, BC, Canada
Gonzaga College High School, DC
Gonzaga Preparatory School, WA
Gould Academy, ME
The Governor French Academy, IL
Grace Brethren School, CA
The Grauer School, CA
Great Lakes Christian High School, ON, Canada
Greenfield School, NC
Greensboro Day School, NC

Greenwich Academy, CT
The Greenwood School, VT
The Grier School, PA
Groton School, MA
The Gunston School, MD
Hackley School, NY
Hamden Hall Country Day School, CT
Hampton Roads Academy, VA
Happy Hill Farm Academy, TX
Harding Academy, TN
Harding Academy, TN
Hargrave Military Academy, VA
The Harley School, NY
Harrells Christian Academy, NC
The Harvey School, NY
The Haverford School, PA
Hawaiian Mission Academy, HI
Hawaii Baptist Academy, HI
Hawken School, OH
Hawthorne Christian Academy, NJ
Head-Royce School, CA
Hebrew Academy, CA
Hebrew Academy-the Five Towns, NY
Heritage Christian Academy, AB, Canada
Heritage Christian School, ON, Canada
Highland Hall Waldorf School, CA
The Hill Center, Durham Academy, NC
Hillcrest Christian School, CA
Hillcrest Christian School, MS
The Hill School, PA
Hill School of Fort Worth, TX
The Hill Top Preparatory School, PA
Holy Cross High School, CT
Holy Cross High School, NY
Holy Ghost Preparatory School, PA
Holy Innocents' Episcopal School, GA
Holyoke Catholic High School, MA
Holy Savior Menard Catholic High School, LA
Holy Trinity Diocesan High School, NY
Holy Trinity High School, IL
Hoosac School, NY
Hopkins School, CT
The Hotchkiss School, CT
Houghton Academy, NY
The Howard School, GA
Humanex Academy, CO
Huntington-Surrey School, TX
Hyde School, ME
Hyman Brand Hebrew Academy of Greater Kansas City, KS
Idyllwild Arts Academy, CA
Immaculata-La Salle High School, FL
Immaculate Conception High School, NJ
Immaculate Conception School, IL
Immaculate Heart High School, AZ
Independent School, KS
Indian Springs School, AL
Institute of Notre Dame, MD
Interlochen Arts Academy, MI
Intermountain Christian School, UT
International High School, CA
International School Bangkok, Thailand
International School Hamburg, Germany
International School Manila, Philippines
International School of Amsterdam, Netherlands
Iona Preparatory School, NY
Jack M. Barrack Hebrew Academy, PA
Jackson Preparatory School, MS
Jesuit College Preparatory School, TX
Jesuit High School of New Orleans, LA
Jesuit High School of Tampa, FL
John Burroughs School, MO
The John Dewey Academy, MA
John Paul II Catholic High School, FL
John T. Morgan Academy, AL
Josephinum Academy, IL
Junipero Serra High School, CA
Junipero Serra High School, CA
The Karafin School, NY
Kauai Christian Academy, HI
Keith Country Day School, IL
Kent Place School, NJ
Kentucky Country Day School, KY
Kerr-Vance Academy, NC
The Kew-Forest School, NY
Key School, TX
Kimball Union Academy, NH
King Low Heywood Thomas, CT
The King's Academy, TN
Kings Christian School, CA
King's-Edgehill School, NS, Canada
King's High School, WA
Kingshill School, VI
King's Ridge Christian School, GA
Kingswood-Oxford School, CT
Ladywood High School, MI
La Jolla Country Day School, CA
Lakefield College School, ON, Canada
Lakehill Preparatory School, TX
Lakeside School, WA
Lancaster Mennonite High School, PA
Landmark Christian Academy, KY
Landmark Christian School, GA
Landmark School, MA
Landon School, MD
Lansdale Catholic High School, PA
La Salle High School, CA
The Latin School of Chicago, IL
Laurel Springs School, CA
Lausanne Collegiate School, TN
Lawrence Academy, MA
Lawrence School, OH
Lee Academy, MS
Lehigh Valley Christian High School, PA
Lehman High School, OH
Lexington Catholic High School, KY
Liberty Christian School, CA
Lighthouse Christian School, AB, Canada
Lincoln School, RI
Linden Christian School, MB, Canada
The Linsly School, WV
Lodi Academy, CA
Long Island Lutheran Middle and High School, NY
The Loomis Chaffee School, CT
Loretto Academy, TX
Los Angeles Baptist Middle School/High School, CA
Los Angeles Lutheran High School, CA
Louisville Collegiate School, KY
Louisville High School, CA
The Lovett School, GA
Loyola-Blakefield, MD
Lutheran High School, IN
Lutheran High School North, MO
Lutheran High School Northwest, MI
Lutheran High School of Hawaii, HI

Lutheran High School of San Diego, CA
Luther College High School, SK, Canada
Lyman Ward Military Academy, AL
MacLachlan College, ON, Canada
Madison Academy, AL
Madison-Ridgeland Academy, MS
Magnificat High School, OH
Maharishi School of the Age of Enlightenment, IA
Maine Central Institute, ME
Malden Catholic High School, MA
Manhattan Christian High School, MT
Maranatha High School, CA
Maret School, DC
Marian Central Catholic High School, IL
Marian High School, IN
Marine Military Academy, TX
The Marin School, CA
Marist School, GA
Marlborough School, CA
Mars Hill Bible School, AL
Martin Luther High School, NY
The Marvelwood School, CT
Marylawn of the Oranges, NJ
Marymount High School, CA
Mary Star of the Sea High School, CA
The Master's School, CT
The Masters School, NY
Matignon High School, MA
McDonogh School, MD
The Meadows School, NV
Memphis University School, TN
Menaul School, NM
Mercy High School, CT
Mercy High School, NE
Mercy High School College Preparatory, CA
Mercyhurst Preparatory School, PA
Merion Mercy Academy, PA
Mesa Grande Seventh-Day Academy, CA
Middlesex School, MA
Mid-Pacific Institute, HI
Millbrook School, NY
Miller School, VA
Mill Springs Academy, GA
Milton Academy, MA
Miss Edgar's and Miss Cramp's School, QC, Canada
Miss Hall's School, MA
Missouri Military Academy, MO
Miss Porter's School, CT
MMI Preparatory School, PA
Monsignor Donovan High School, NJ
Montclair Kimberley Academy, NJ
Montgomery Bell Academy, TN
Moorestown Friends School, NJ
Moravian Academy, PA
Moreau Catholic High School, CA
Morristown-Beard School, NJ
Mother McAuley High School, IL
Mount Michael Benedictine School, NE
Mount Saint Charles Academy, RI
Mount Saint Joseph Academy, PA
MPS Etobicoke, ON, Canada
Munich International School, Germany
Nativity B.V.M. High School, PA
Nazareth Academy, IL
Nebraska Christian Schools, NE
Nerinx Hall, MO
Newark Academy, NJ
New Covenant Academy, MO
New Tribes Mission Academy, ON, Canada
Niagara Christian Community of Schools, ON, Canada
Nichols School, NY
Noble Academy, NC
Noble and Greenough School, MA
The Nora School, MD
Norfolk Academy, VA
North Catholic High School, PA
North Cobb Christian School, GA
North Country School, NY
North Toronto Christian School, ON, Canada
Northwest Academy, OR
Northwest Catholic High School, CT
Northwest Yeshiva High School, WA
Northwood School, NY
Notre Dame Academy, CA
Notre Dame College Prep, IL
Notre Dame High School, TN
Notre Dame Junior/Senior High School, PA
Oak Grove School, CA
Oak Hill Academy, VA
Oak Hill School, OR
The Oakland School, PA
Oakland School, VA
Oak Ridge Military Academy, NC
The Oakridge School, TX
Ojai Valley School, CA
The Oliverian School, NH
The O'Neal School, NC
Oneida Baptist Institute, KY
Oregon Episcopal School, OR
Orinda Academy, CA
Our Lady Academy, MS
Our Lady of Mercy Academy, NJ
Our Lady of Mercy High School, NY
Out Of Door Academy, FL
The Overlake School, WA
Pacific Crest Community School, OR
Pacific Hills School, CA
Padua Franciscan High School, OH
The Paideia School, GA
Palma School, CA
Paradise Adventist Academy, CA
The Park School of Baltimore, MD
The Pathway School, PA
Peddie School, NJ
Peoples Christian Academy, ON, Canada
Philadelphia-Montgomery Christian Academy, PA
Phillips Academy (Andover), MA
Phillips Exeter Academy, NH
Phoenix Country Day School, AZ
Pickens Academy, AL
Pickering College, ON, Canada
Pine Crest School, FL
Pinehurst School, ON, Canada
The Pingree School, MA
The Pingry School, NJ
Pioneer Valley Christian School, MA
Pope John XXIII Regional High School, NJ
Porter-Gaud School, SC
The Potomac School, VA
Powers Catholic High School, MI
The Prairie School, WI
Presbyterian Pan American School, TX
Prestonwood Christian Academy, TX
Professional Children's School, NY

Providence Catholic School, The College Preparatory School for Girls Grades 6-12, TX
Providence Christian School, AB, Canada
Providence Country Day School, RI
Providence Day School, NC
Providence High School, CA
Punahou School, HI
Queen Margaret's School, BC, Canada
Quinte Christian High School, ON, Canada
Rabbi Alexander S. Gross Hebrew Academy, FL
Randolph-Macon Academy, VA
Ranney School, NJ
Ransom Everglades School, FL
Ravenscroft School, NC
Realms of Inquiry, UT
The Rectory School, CT
Redwood Christian Schools, CA
Reitz Memorial High School, IN
Ridley College, ON, Canada
Ripon Christian Schools, CA
Riverdale Country School, NY
Rivermont Collegiate, IA
Riverside Military Academy, GA
The Rivers School, MA
Robert Land Academy, ON, Canada
Robert Louis Stevenson School, NY
Rock Point School, VT
The Roeper School, MI
Roland Park Country School, MD
Rolling Hills Preparatory School, CA
Rosseau Lake College, ON, Canada
Ross School, NY
Rothesay Netherwood School, NB, Canada
Rowland Hall, UT
The Roxbury Latin School, MA
Rundle College, AB, Canada
Rye Country Day School, NY
Sacramento Adventist Academy, CA
Sacramento Country Day School, CA
Sacred Heart/Griffin High School, IL
Sacred Heart School of Halifax, NS, Canada
Saddleback Valley Christian School, CA
Saddlebrook Preparatory School, FL
Sage Hill School, CA
Sage Ridge School, NV
St. Agnes Academy, TX
Saint Agnes Boys High School, NY
St. Albans School, DC
St. Andrew's College, ON, Canada
St. Andrew's Priory School, HI
St. Andrew's School, DE
St. Andrew's School, RI
St. Andrew's–Sewanee School, TN
St. Anne's–Belfield School, VA
St. Anthony Catholic High School, TX
Saint Anthony High School, CA
Saint Anthony High School, IL
St. Anthony's Junior-Senior High School, HI
Saint Augustine Preparatory School, NJ
Saint Basil Academy, PA
St. Benedict at Auburndale, TN
St. Benedict's Preparatory School, NJ
St. Bernard High School, CT
St. Bernard's Catholic School, CA
St. Brendan High School, FL
St. Catherine's Academy, CA
St. Christopher's School, VA
Saint Clement Academy, ON, Canada
St. Clement's School, ON, Canada
St. Croix Country Day School, VI
St. Croix Schools, MN
Saint Dominic Academy, ME
Saint Edward's School, FL
St. Francis de Sales High School, OH
Saint Francis High School, CA
Saint Francis School, HI
St. George's Independent School, TN
St. George's School of Montreal, QC, Canada
St. Gregory College Preparatory School, AZ
St. John's Preparatory School, MA
Saint John's Preparatory School, MN
St. John's-Ravenscourt School, MB, Canada
St. Joseph Academy, FL
Saint Joseph High School, IL
Saint Joseph High School, NJ
Saint Joseph Junior-Senior High School, HI
St. Joseph's Academy, LA
St. Joseph's Catholic School, SC
Saint Joseph's High School, NJ
St. Joseph's Preparatory School, PA
St. Jude's School, ON, Canada
St. Mark's High School, DE
St. Mark's School of Texas, TX
St. Martin's Episcopal School, LA
Saint Mary's College High School, CA
St. Mary's Episcopal School, TN
Saint Mary's Hall, TX
Saint Mary's High School, AZ
Saint Mary's High School, MD
St. Mary's Preparatory School, MI
Saint Mary's School, NC
St. Mary's School, OR
St. Michael's College School, ON, Canada
St. Michael's Preparatory School of the Norbertine Fathers, CA
St. Patrick Catholic High School, MS
Saint Patrick High School, IL
Saint Patrick - Saint Vincent High School, CA
St. Patrick's Regional Secondary, BC, Canada
St. Paul Academy and Summit School, MN
St. Paul's High School, MB, Canada
St. Peter's Preparatory School, NJ
St. Pius X Catholic High School, GA
St. Scholastica Academy, IL
St. Sebastian's School, MA
Saints Peter and Paul High School, MD
St. Stephen's & St. Agnes School, VA
St. Stephen's Episcopal School, TX
St. Stephen's School, Rome, Italy
Saint Teresa's Academy, MO
Saint Thomas Academy, MN
Saint Thomas Aquinas High School, KS
St. Thomas Aquinas High School, NH
St. Thomas Choir School, NY
St. Thomas High School, TX
St. Timothy's School, MD
Saint Ursula Academy, OH
Saint Viator High School, IL
Salem Academy, NC
Salesian High School, CA
Salesianum School, DE
Saltus Grammar School, Bermuda
Sandy Spring Friends School, MD
Sanford School, DE
San Marcos Baptist Academy, TX

Santa Catalina School, CA
Sayre School, KY
Scholar's Hall Preparatory School, ON, Canada
SciCore Academy, NJ
Scotus Central Catholic High School, NE
Seabury Hall, HI
Seattle Academy of Arts and Sciences, WA
Seattle Christian Schools, WA
Seisen International School, Japan
Seton Catholic Central High School, NY
Seton Catholic High School, AZ
The Seven Hills School, OH
Severn School, MD
Sewickley Academy, PA
Shady Side Academy, PA
Shattuck-St. Mary's School, MN
Shawe Memorial Junior/Senior High School, IN
Shawnigan Lake School, BC, Canada
Shelton School and Evaluation Center, TX
The Shipley School, PA
Shoreline Christian, WA
Smith School, NY
Sonoma Academy, CA
Southfield Christian High School, MI
Spartanburg Day School, SC
The Spence School, NY
Springside Chestnut Hill Academy, PA
Squaw Valley Academy, CA
Stephen T. Badin High School, OH
Stevenson School, CA
Stoneleigh-Burnham School, MA
Storm King School, NY
Strake Jesuit College Preparatory, TX
Stratford Academy, GA
Stratton Mountain School, VT
Suffield Academy, CT
Summerfield Waldorf School, CA
Sunshine Bible Academy, SD
Tabor Academy, MA
The Taft School, CT
Taipei American School, Taiwan
Takoma Academy, MD
Tandem Friends School, VA
TASIS The American School in England, United Kingdom
TASIS, The American School in Switzerland, Switzerland
Telluride Mountain School, CO
Teurlings Catholic High School, LA
The Thacher School, CA
Tidewater Academy, VA
Tilton School, NH
Timothy Christian High School, IL
Toronto District Christian High School, ON, Canada
Tower Hill School, DE
Trafalgar Castle School, ON, Canada
Tri-City Christian Schools, CA
Trinity Christian Academy, TN
Trinity College School, ON, Canada
Trinity High School, KY
Trinity High School, NH
Trinity High School, OH
Trinity-Pawling School, NY
Trinity Preparatory School, FL
Trinity School of Texas, TX
Trinity Valley School, TX
Tuscaloosa Academy, AL
Tyler Street Christian Academy, TX
United Mennonite Educational Institute, ON, Canada
United Nations International School, NY
The United World College - USA, NM
The University of Chicago Laboratory Schools, IL
University of Detroit Jesuit High School and Academy, MI
University Prep, WA
University School of Jackson, TN
University School of Milwaukee, WI
University School of Nova Southeastern University, FL
Vail Mountain School, CO
Valle Catholic High School, MO
Valley Christian High School, CA
Valley Christian High School, CA
Valley Lutheran High School, AZ
The Valley School, MI
Valley View School, MA
Vicksburg Catholic School, MS
Villa Duchesne and Oak Hill School, MO
Villa Joseph Marie High School, PA
Villa Maria Academy, PA
Villa Maria Academy, PA
Villa Victoria Academy, NJ
Villa Walsh Academy, NJ
Visitation Academy of St. Louis County, MO
Wakefield School, VA
Waldorf High School of Massachusetts Bay, MA
The Walker School, GA
Walnut Hill School, MA
Waring School, MA
Wasatch Academy, UT
Washington Waldorf School, MD
The Waterford School, UT
Watkinson School, CT
Waynflete School, ME
The Webb School, TN
Webb School of Knoxville, TN
Wesleyan Academy, PR
Westbury Christian School, TX
West Catholic High School, MI
Westchester Country Day School, NC
Western Mennonite School, OR
Westgate Mennonite Collegiate, MB, Canada
West Island College, AB, Canada
Westmark School, CA
Westminster Christian Academy, AL
Westminster School, CT
Westover School, CT
Westridge School, CA
West Sound Academy, WA
Wheaton Academy, IL
The Wheeler School, RI
Whitefield Academy, KY
The Williams School, CT
The Willows Academy, IL
Willow Wood School, ON, Canada
Wilmington Christian School, DE
Wilson Hall, SC
Winchester Thurston School, PA
Windermere Preparatory School, FL
The Windsor School, NY
Windward School, CA
The Winsor School, MA
Winston Preparatory School, NY
The Winston School San Antonio, TX
The Woodhall School, CT
Woodward Academy, GA
The Woodward School, MA
Worcester Preparatory School, MD

York Catholic High School, PA
York Country Day School, PA
York Preparatory School, NY
York School, CA

SCHOOLS REPORTING THAT THEY OFFER LOANS

Academy of the New Church Boys' School, PA	M
Academy of the New Church Girls' School, PA	M,N
Alexander Dawson School, CO	N
Bishop's College School, QC, Canada	N
Blair Academy, NJ	N
The Brearley School, NY	N
Brookstone School, GA	M,N
The Bryn Mawr School for Girls, MD	M,N
Calvin Christian High School, CA	N
Cheshire Academy, CT	N
Commonwealth School, MA	N
Concord Academy, MA	N
Copper Canyon Academy, AZ	M
Dana Hall School, MA	N
Episcopal High School, TX	M
Falmouth Academy, MA	N
Georgetown Preparatory School, MD	M
Germantown Friends School, PA	N
Gilman School, MD	N
Gilmour Academy, OH	N
Gould Academy, ME	N
Great Lakes Christian High School, ON, Canada	M,N
Greenwich Academy, CT	M
The Grier School, PA	N
Hackley School, NY	N
Hamden Hall Country Day School, CT	N
Hargrave Military Academy, VA	N
The Harker School, CA	N
Hawken School, OH	N
The Hotchkiss School, CT	N
Humanex Academy, CO	M
John Burroughs School, MO	N
The Latin School of Chicago, IL	M,N
Lawrence Academy, MA	N
The Loomis Chaffee School, CT	N
Marian High School, IN	N
McDonogh School, MD	M,N
The Meadows School, NV	N
Merion Mercy Academy, PA	M
Mesa Grande Seventh-Day Academy, CA	M,N
Middlesex School, MA	N
Millbrook School, NY	N
Missouri Military Academy, MO	N
Moorestown Friends School, NJ	N
Mount Michael Benedictine School, NE	N
Noble and Greenough School, MA	N
Ojai Valley School, CA	N
Pacific Hills School, CA	N
Peddie School, NJ	N
Phillips Academy (Andover), MA	M
The Pingree School, MA	N
Ravenscroft School, NC	N
Reitz Memorial High School, IN	N
Ridley College, ON, Canada	N
Robert Land Academy, ON, Canada	M
Robert Louis Stevenson School, NY	N
St. Albans School, DC	N
St. Andrew's Priory School, HI	M
St. Andrew's School, RI	N
St. Anthony's Junior-Senior High School, HI	N
St. Joseph's Preparatory School, PA	M,N
St. Paul's High School, MB, Canada	N
St. Sebastian's School, MA	N
St. Thomas High School, TX	M
St. Timothy's School, MD	N
Stratton Mountain School, VT	N
The Taft School, CT	N
Tilton School, NH	N
Trinity High School, OH	M
Trinity-Pawling School, NY	N
Trinity Preparatory School, FL	M
United Mennonite Educational Institute, ON, Canada	N
Vail Mountain School, CO	N
Wasatch Academy, UT	N
Westover School, CT	M,N
Windward School, CA	N
Xaverian High School, NY	N

TOTAL AMOUNT OF UPPER SCHOOL FINANCIAL AID AWARDED FOR 2011–12

Academy of Holy Angels, MN	$1,000,000
Academy of Our Lady of Peace, CA	$2,100,000
Academy of the New Church Boys' School, PA	$510,000
Academy of the New Church Girls' School, PA	$400,000
Academy of the Sacred Heart, LA	$241,400
Academy of the Sacred Heart, MI	$834,755
Académie Ste Cécile International School, ON, Canada	CAN$15,000
Alexander Dawson School, CO	$905,000
Allendale Columbia School, NY	$645,341
Alliance Academy, Ecuador	$800,000
Allison Academy, FL	$105,000
The American Boychoir School, NJ	$38,000
American Heritage School, FL	$3,800,000
The American School Foundation, Mexico	9,000,000 Mexican pesos
The American School in London, United Kingdom	411,850
Annie Wright School, WA	$300,000
Archbishop Hoban High School, OH	$2,200,000
Archbishop Mitty High School, CA	$2,800,000
Arendell Parrott Academy, NC	$260,000
Armbrae Academy, NS, Canada	CAN$60,000
Armona Union Academy, CA	$50,000
Army and Navy Academy, CA	$377,300
ASSETS School, HI	$170,000
The Athenian School, CA	$2,002,000
Atlantis Academy, FL	$12,000
Bachman Academy, TN	$145,160
Balmoral Hall School, MB, Canada	CAN$135,000
The Baltimore Actors' Theatre Conservatory, MD	$12,000
Baltimore Lutheran School, MD	$70,000
Barrie School, MD	$814,427
Battle Ground Academy, TN	$750,000
Baylor School, TN	$2,500,000
Bearspaw Christian School, AB, Canada	CAN$137,342
Belen Jesuit Preparatory School, FL	$400,000
Benedictine High School, VA	$500,000
Berkshire School, MA	$4,175,000
Beth Haven Christian School, KY	$4450
The Birch Wathen Lenox School, NY	$1,200,000
Bishop Blanchet High School, WA	$1,600,000
Bishop Conaty-Our Lady of Loretto High School, CA	$627,618

M — middle-income loans; N — need-based loans

Bishop Eustace Preparatory School, NJ	$550,000
Bishop Ireton High School, VA	$622,000
Bishop John J. Snyder High School, FL	$250,000
Bishop Kelly High School, ID	$956,077
Bishop McGuinness Catholic High School, NC	$288,550
Bishop McGuinness Catholic High School, OK	$264,300
Bishop Montgomery High School, CA	$30,000
Bishop Mora Salesian High School, CA	$1,548,500
The Bishop's School, CA	$2,900,000
Bishop Stang High School, MA	$500,000
The Bishop Strachan School, ON, Canada	CAN$500,000
Blair Academy, NJ	$4,100,000
Blanchet School, OR	$240,000
Blessed Sacrament Hugenot, VA	$175,000
Blue Mountain Academy, PA	$287,000
The Blue Ridge School, VA	$1,700,000
The Bolles School, FL	$2,368,513
Boston University Academy, MA	$1,089,800
Boylan Central Catholic High School, IL	$425,000
Branksome Hall, ON, Canada	CAN$650,000
The Brearley School, NY	$3,441,395
Brentwood School, CA	$3,500,000
Brewster Academy, NH	$2,700,000
Briarwood Christian High School, AL	$5000
Bridgemont High School, CA	$108,660
Brimmer and May School, MA	$1,467,825
Brooks School, MA	$2,600,000
Brookstone School, GA	$341,100
Brophy College Preparatory, AZ	$2,241,937
Brother Rice High School, MI	$900,000
The Browning School, NY	$953,900
Brunswick School, CT	$1,250,000
The Bryn Mawr School for Girls, MD	$1,241,190
Bulloch Academy, GA	$50,000
Butte Central Catholic High School, MT	$68,000
Buxton School, MA	$1,300,000
The Byrnes Schools, SC	$25,000
Calgary Academy Collegiate, AB, Canada	CAN$300,000
Calvert Hall College High School, MD	$1,142,000
Calvin Christian High School, CA	$225,000
The Cambridge School of Weston, MA	$2,598,100
Campbell Hall (Episcopal), CA	$4,000,000
Cannon School, NC	$310,000
Canterbury School, FL	$709,284
Canyonville Christian Academy, OR	$390,000
Cape Fear Academy, NC	$249,612
Capistrano Valley Christian Schools, CA	$225,000
Carlisle School, VA	$250,000
Carolina Day School, NC	$674,035
Carondelet High School, CA	$1,300,000
Carrollton School of the Sacred Heart, FL	$920,000
Cascadilla School, NY	$60,000
The Catholic High School of Baltimore, MD	$408,150
The Catlin Gabel School, OR	$2,900,000
Central Catholic High School, CA	$196,598
Central Catholic High School, TX	$542,050
CFS, The School at Church Farm, PA	$3,535,445
Chadwick School, CA	$1,985,375
Chamberlain-Hunt Academy, MS	$250,000
Chaminade College Preparatory, CA	$2,171,466
Chaminade College Preparatory School, MO	$1,600,000
Chaminade-Madonna College Preparatory, FL	$400,000
Chapel Hill–Chauncy Hall School, MA	$850,000
Charlotte Christian School, NC	$389,150
Charlotte Country Day School, NC	$1,530,035
Charlotte Latin School, NC	$817,525
Chatham Academy, GA	$90,200
Chattanooga Christian School, TN	$122,300
Cheshire Academy, CT	$2,000,000
Cheverus High School, ME	$1,888,610
Children's Creative and Performing Arts Academy of San Diego, CA	$25,000
Chinese Christian Schools, CA	$120,000
Christ Church Episcopal School, SC	$488,705
Christchurch School, VA	$1,490,200
Christian Central Academy, NY	$54,868
Christopher Columbus High School, FL	$800,000
Christopher Dock Mennonite High School, PA	$533,185
Cincinnati Country Day School, OH	$1,200,000
Cistercian Preparatory School, TX	$320,500
Colegio San Jose, PR	$216,000
Collegedale Academy, TN	$55,000
Collegiate School, NY	$1,630,000
The Collegiate School, VA	$850,330
The Colorado Springs School, CO	$492,602
Columbia Academy, TN	$26,250
The Columbus Academy, OH	$979,150
Columbus School for Girls, OH	$720,655
Commonwealth School, MA	$1,108,002
Community Christian Academy, KY	$9000
The Community School of Naples, FL	$1,091,586
Concord Academy, MA	$3,340,000
Convent of the Sacred Heart, CT	$1,404,800
Copenhagen International School, Denmark	4,000,000 Danish kroner
Copper Canyon Academy, AZ	$81,600
Country Day School of the Sacred Heart, PA	$424,500
Crawford Adventist Academy, ON, Canada	CAN$35,000
Crossroads School for Arts & Sciences, CA	$3,128,946
The Culver Academies, IN	$8,900,000
Currey Ingram Academy, TN	$1,200,000
Cushing Academy, MA	$3,200,000
The Dalton School, NY	$2,938,600
Damien High School, CA	$50,000
Dana Hall School, MA	$3,163,219
Darlington School, GA	$2,801,475
Deerfield Academy, MA	$7,003,000
Deerfield-Windsor School, GA	$350,000
Delbarton School, NJ	$1,574,000
DeMatha Catholic High School, MD	$1,315,308
Denver Christian High School, CO	$72,000
The Derryfield School, NH	$1,041,927
Devon Preparatory School, PA	$700,000
Doane Stuart School, NY	$867,583
Donelson Christian Academy, TN	$125,757
Dublin Christian Academy, NH	$35,000
DuBois Central Catholic High School/Middle School, PA	$448,000
Durham Academy, NC	$805,415
Eaglebrook School, MA	$1,650,000
Eagle Hill-Southport, CT	$130,095
Eastside Christian Academy, AB, Canada	CAN$8400
Edmund Burke School, DC	$978,185
Eldorado Emerson Private School, CA	$50,000
Elizabeth Seton High School, MD	$500,000
The Ellis School, PA	$968,120
Emma Willard School, NY	$3,881,300
Episcopal Collegiate School, AR	$649,000
Episcopal High School, TX	$1,700,000
Episcopal High School, VA	$4,300,000
Escola Americana de Campinas, Brazil	$51,000
The Ethel Walker School, CT	$3,354,000
Fairhill School, TX	$50,000
Faith Christian High School, CA	$50,000

Faith Lutheran High School, NV	$300,000
Falmouth Academy, MA	$650,000
The Family Foundation School, NY	$500,000
Father Lopez High School, FL	$780,000
Father Ryan High School, TN	$536,000
Fayetteville Academy, NC	$477,000
Fay School, MA	$1,110,900
The Fessenden School, MA	$1,043,947
First Presbyterian Day School, GA	$874,000
Flint Hill School, VA	$1,931,144
Fontbonne Hall Academy, NY	$107,500
Foothills Academy, AB, Canada	CAN$500,000
Fordham Preparatory School, NY	$2,200,000
Forest Lake Academy, FL	$378,500
Forsyth Country Day School, NC	$914,455
Fort Lauderdale Preparatory School, FL	$1,000,000
Fort Worth Country Day School, TX	$867,400
Fountain Valley School of Colorado, CO	$1,870,000
Fowlers Academy, PR	$5000
Foxcroft School, VA	$1,200,000
Fox Valley Lutheran High School, WI	$325,000
Freeman Academy, SD	$24,000
French-American School of New York, NY	$188,856
Fresno Christian Schools, CA	$218,577
Friends Academy, NY	$1,169,500
Friends' Central School, PA	$2,694,469
Front Range Christian High School, CO	$180,000
The Frostig School, CA	$50,000
Fuqua School, VA	$44,000
The Galloway School, GA	$312,130
Garces Memorial High School, CA	$312,000
Gaston Day School, NC	$469,262
Georgetown Preparatory School, MD	$2,000,000
Germantown Friends School, PA	$855,950
Gill St. Bernard's School, NJ	$1,200,000
Gilman School, MD	$1,839,100
Gilmour Academy, OH	$3,200,000
Girls Preparatory School, TN	$1,310,040
Glenelg Country School, MD	$1,800,000
Glenlyon Norfolk School, BC, Canada	CAN$129,895
Gonzaga College High School, DC	$2,190,000
Gonzaga Preparatory School, WA	$2,000,000
Gould Academy, ME	$1,355,000
The Grauer School, CA	$90,000
Great Lakes Christian High School, ON, Canada	CAN$150,000
Greenhill School, TX	$1,424,960
Greenwich Academy, CT	$1,351,850
The Greenwood School, VT	$249,290
The Grier School, PA	$1,940,000
Groton School, MA	$4,900,000
The Gunston School, MD	$700,000
Hackley School, NY	$3,500,000
Hamden Hall Country Day School, CT	$1,600,000
Hampton Roads Academy, VA	$800,000
Harding Academy, TN	$191,824
Hargrave Military Academy, VA	$525,000
Harrells Christian Academy, NC	$32,500
The Harvey School, NY	$2,010,500
The Haverford School, PA	$2,614,756
Hawaii Baptist Academy, HI	$229,635
Hawken School, OH	$5,000,000
Hawthorne Christian Academy, NJ	$26,124
Head-Royce School, CA	$2,015,100
Hebrew Academy, CA	$30,000
Highland Hall Waldorf School, CA	$204,600
The Hill Center, Durham Academy, NC	$59,700
Hillcrest Christian School, CA	$20,000
Hillcrest Christian School, MS	$42,824
The Hill School, PA	$4,800,000
The Hockaday School, TX	$1,851,800
Holy Cross High School, CT	$550,000
Holy Ghost Preparatory School, PA	$1,000,000
Holy Innocents' Episcopal School, GA	$1,800,000
Holy Names Academy, WA	$1,005,360
Holyoke Catholic High School, MA	$174,000
Holy Savior Menard Catholic High School, LA	$135,000
Holy Trinity High School, IL	$600,000
Hoosac School, NY	$625,000
Hopkins School, CT	$2,500,000
The Hotchkiss School, CT	$8,282,237
Houghton Academy, NY	$95,000
Humanex Academy, CO	$5000
Hyde School, CT	$258,000
Hyde School, ME	$1,300,000
Hyman Brand Hebrew Academy of Greater Kansas City, KS	$76,850
Idyllwild Arts Academy, CA	$5,054,332
Immaculata-La Salle High School, FL	$165,000
Immaculate Conception High School, NJ	$73,250
Immaculate Conception School, IL	$150,000
Immaculate Heart High School, AZ	$121,000
Indian Springs School, AL	$1,000,000
Institute of Notre Dame, MD	$400,000
Interlochen Arts Academy, MI	$9,400,000
Intermountain Christian School, UT	$18,260
International High School, CA	$748,000
Iona Preparatory School, NY	$325,000
Jack M. Barrack Hebrew Academy, PA	$1,483,690
Jackson Preparatory School, MS	$195,000
Jesuit College Preparatory School, TX	$1,233,850
Jesuit High School of New Orleans, LA	$523,900
Jesuit High School of Tampa, FL	$1,300,000
John Burroughs School, MO	$1,956,000
John Paul II Catholic High School, FL	$40,000
Josephinum Academy, IL	$400,000
Junipero Serra High School, CA	$500,000
Junipero Serra High School, CA	$1,900,000
Kauai Christian Academy, HI	$40,000
Keith Country Day School, IL	$342,664
Kent Place School, NJ	$1,299,061
Kentucky Country Day School, KY	$857,811
Kerr-Vance Academy, NC	$15,000
The Kew-Forest School, NY	$900,000
Key School, TX	$30,000
Kimball Union Academy, NH	$3,465,400
King Low Heywood Thomas, CT	$933,795
The King's Academy, TN	$186,665
Kings Christian School, CA	$175,000
King's-Edgehill School, NS, Canada	CAN$900,000
King's High School, WA	$572,000
Kingshill School, VI	$82,000
Kingswood-Oxford School, CT	$2,300,000
Ladywood High School, MI	$135,000
La Jolla Country Day School, CA	$2,316,168
Lakefield College School, ON, Canada	CAN$170,000
Lakeside School, WA	$2,995,770
Lancaster Mennonite High School, PA	$2,000,000
Landmark School, MA	$362,041
Landon School, MD	$1,443,680
La Salle High School, CA	$1,250,000
The Latin School of Chicago, IL	$1,999,129
Lausanne Collegiate School, TN	$494,108
Lawrence Academy, MA	$3,450,000
Lawrence School, OH	$800,000

Lee Academy, MS	$35,000
Lehigh Valley Christian High School, PA	$2500
Lehman High School, OH	$371,023
Le Lycee Francais de Los Angeles, CA	$63,000
Lexington Catholic High School, KY	$450,000
Liberty Christian School, CA	$300,000
Lincoln School, RI	$2,000,000
The Linsly School, WV	$900,000
Little Keswick School, VA	$20,000
Lodi Academy, CA	$27,000
Long Island Lutheran Middle and High School, NY	$325,000
The Loomis Chaffee School, CT	$7,700,000
Loretto Academy, TX	$220,000
Los Angeles Baptist Middle School/High School, CA	$913,690
Los Angeles Lutheran High School, CA	$100,000
Louisville High School, CA	$623,000
The Lovett School, GA	$1,182,390
Loyola-Blakefield, MD	$2,394,563
Lutheran High School, IN	$160,000
Lutheran High School North, MO	$750,000
Lutheran High School Northwest, MI	$20,000
Lutheran High School of Hawaii, HI	$500,000
Lutheran High School of San Diego, CA	$60,000
Luther College High School, SK, Canada	CAN$165,000
Lyman Ward Military Academy, AL	$50,000
MacLachlan College, ON, Canada	CAN$9000
Madison Academy, AL	$100,000
Madison-Ridgeland Academy, MS	$170,000
Magnificat High School, OH	$900,000
Maine Central Institute, ME	$705,450
Malden Catholic High School, MA	$300,000
Maret School, DC	$2,800,000
Marian Central Catholic High School, IL	$294,625
Marian High School, IN	$350,000
Marine Military Academy, TX	$300,000
Marist School, GA	$1,637,000
Mars Hill Bible School, AL	$150,000
Martin Luther High School, NY	$195,182
The Marvelwood School, CT	$850,000
Marylawn of the Oranges, NJ	$111,850
Marymount High School, CA	$1,125,000
Mary Star of the Sea High School, CA	$145,000
The Master's School, CT	$250,000
The Masters School, NY	$4,000,000
Matignon High School, MA	$110,000
McDonogh School, MD	$2,415,935
The Meadows School, NV	$612,935
Memphis University School, TN	$1,300,000
Menaul School, NM	$307,000
Mercy High School, NE	$1,000,000
Mercyhurst Preparatory School, PA	$578,050
Merion Mercy Academy, PA	$857,600
Mesa Grande Seventh-Day Academy, CA	$35,000
Middlesex School, MA	$4,100,000
Midland School, CA	$1,000,000
Mid-Pacific Institute, HI	$2,900,000
Millbrook School, NY	$2,148,000
Miller School, VA	$525,000
Mill Springs Academy, GA	$77,000
Milton Academy, MA	$7,169,420
Miss Edgar's and Miss Cramp's School, QC, Canada	CAN$105,000
Miss Hall's School, MA	$2,500,000
Missouri Military Academy, MO	$750,000
Miss Porter's School, CT	$3,300,000
MMI Preparatory School, PA	$893,050
Monsignor Donovan High School, NJ	$400,000
Montclair Kimberley Academy, NJ	$1,281,308
Montgomery Bell Academy, TN	$1,632,000
Moorestown Friends School, NJ	$1,550,300
Moravian Academy, PA	$1,006,630
Moreau Catholic High School, CA	$1,400,000
Morristown-Beard School, NJ	$1,800,000
Mother McAuley High School, IL	$900,000
Mount Michael Benedictine School, NE	$611,812
Mount Saint Charles Academy, RI	$700,000
Mount Saint Joseph Academy, PA	$706,460
Munich International School, Germany	31,326
Nativity B.V.M. High School, PA	$155,000
Nazareth Academy, IL	$300,000
Nebraska Christian Schools, NE	$180,000
Nerinx Hall, MO	$505,000
Neuchatel Junior College, Switzerland	90,000 Swiss francs
Newark Academy, NJ	$1,788,634
Niagara Christian Community of Schools, ON, Canada	CAN$400,000
Nichols School, NY	$1,720,000
Noble Academy, NC	$33,000
Noble and Greenough School, MA	$3,077,675
The Nora School, MD	$115,000
North Cobb Christian School, GA	$270,000
North Country School, NY	$450,000
Northwest Catholic High School, CT	$1,300,000
Northwest Yeshiva High School, WA	$465,591
Notre Dame College Prep, IL	$3,600,000
Notre Dame High School, TN	$378,271
Oak Grove School, CA	$60,000
Oak Hill Academy, VA	$370,000
The Oakland School, PA	$40,000
Ojai Valley School, CA	$282,105
The Oliverian School, NH	$200,000
The O'Neal School, NC	$413,315
Oregon Episcopal School, OR	$400,000
Orinda Academy, CA	$300,000
Our Lady Academy, MS	$40,000
Our Lady of Mercy Academy, NJ	$48,000
Our Lady of Mercy High School, NY	$1,200,000
Out-Of-Door Academy, FL	$650,465
The Overlake School, WA	$675,904
Pacific Crest Community School, OR	$50,000
Padua Franciscan High School, OH	$12,500,000
The Paideia School, GA	$1,156,509
Palma School, CA	$229,000
Paradise Adventist Academy, CA	$50,000
The Park School of Baltimore, MD	$1,292,085
Peddie School, NJ	$5,000,000
Peoples Christian Academy, ON, Canada	CAN$30,000
Philadelphia-Montgomery Christian Academy, PA	$500,000
Phillips Academy (Andover), MA	$17,015,000
Phillips Exeter Academy, NH	$15,635,367
Phoenix Country Day School, AZ	$1,016,600
Pickering College, ON, Canada	CAN$112,000
Pine Crest School, FL	$1,888,380
The Pine School, FL	$1,000,000
The Pingree School, MA	$1,310,000
The Pingry School, NJ	$199,259
Pioneer Valley Christian School, MA	$80,400
Porter-Gaud School, SC	$467,620
The Potomac School, VA	$1,293,670
Powers Catholic High School, MI	$450,300
The Prairie School, WI	$120,000
Presbyterian Pan American School, TX	$907,340
Prestonwood Christian Academy, TX	$806,285
Professional Children's School, NY	$692,500

Providence Catholic School, The College Preparatory School for Girls Grades 6-12, TX $200,000
Providence Country Day School, RI $1,500,000
Providence Day School, NC $1,056,585
Providence High School, CA $276,600
Punahou School, HI $2,201,900
Queen Margaret's School, BC, Canada CAN$150,000
Rabbi Alexander S. Gross Hebrew Academy, FL $300,000
Randolph-Macon Academy, VA $460,000
Ranney School, NJ $139,000
Ransom Everglades School, FL $3,643,980
Realms of Inquiry, UT $40,000
The Rectory School, CT $1,389,020
Redwood Christian Schools, CA $356,524
Reitz Memorial High School, IN $264,840
Ridley College, ON, Canada CAN$3,000,000
Ripon Christian Schools, CA $20,000
The Rivers School, MA $3,304,050
Robert Louis Stevenson School, NY $50,000
Rock Point School, VT $150,000
The Roeper School, MI $384,375
Rolling Hills Preparatory School, CA $550,000
Rosseau Lake College, ON, Canada CAN$160,000
Rothesay Netherwood School, NB, Canada CAN$667,845
Rowland Hall, UT $467,658
The Roxbury Latin School, MA $1,918,630
Rundle College, AB, Canada CAN$24,000
Rye Country Day School, NY $2,300,000
Sacramento Adventist Academy, CA $10,000
Sacramento Country Day School, CA $447,850
Sacred Heart/Griffin High School, IL $442,207
Sacred Heart School of Halifax, NS, Canada CAN$138,000
Saddleback Valley Christian School, CA $175,000
Sage Hill School, CA $1,783,170
Sage Ridge School, NV $176,225
St. Agnes Academy, TX $800,000
St. Albans School, DC $2,313,228
St. Andrew's College, ON, Canada CAN$1,944,330
St. Andrew's Priory School, HI $491,650
St. Andrew's School, DE $4,950,000
St. Andrew's School, RI $2,173,820
St. Andrew's–Sewanee School, TN $1,499,125
St. Anne's–Belfield School, VA $1,633,575
St. Anthony Catholic High School, TX $185,000
Saint Augustine Preparatory School, NJ $1,010,000
Saint Basil Academy, PA $268,175
St. Benedict at Auburndale, TN $35,000
St. Benedict's Preparatory School, NJ $1,908,723
St. Bernard High School, CT $354,257
St. Bernard's Catholic School, CA $55,000
St. Catherine's Academy, CA $260,000
St. Christopher's School, VA $783,200
St. Croix Country Day School, VI $265,550
St. Croix Schools, MN $446,000
Saint Edward's School, FL $889,050
Saint Elizabeth High School, CA $980,000
St. Francis de Sales High School, OH $1,672,600
Saint Francis High School, CA $450,000
Saint Francis School, HI $317,000
St. George's Independent School, TN $305,421
St. Gregory College Preparatory School, AZ $1,230,000
St. John's Preparatory School, MA $2,800,000
Saint John's Preparatory School, MN $725,000
St. John's-Ravenscourt School, MB, Canada CAN$262,250
St. Joseph Academy, FL $119,467
Saint Joseph High School, IL $800,000
Saint Joseph High School, NJ $50,000
Saint Joseph Junior-Senior High School, HI $225,000
St. Joseph's Academy, LA $350,000
St. Joseph's Catholic School, SC $376,126
Saint Joseph's High School, NJ $250,000
St. Joseph's Preparatory School, PA $2,000,000
St. Mark's High School, DE $1,000,000
St. Mark's School of Texas, TX $1,194,576
St. Martin's Episcopal School, LA $700,925
Saint Mary's College High School, CA $2,220,840
St. Mary's Episcopal School, TN $318,600
Saint Mary's Hall, TX $621,990
Saint Mary's High School, AZ $1,500,000
Saint Mary's High School, MD $250,000
Saint Mary's School, NC $150,200
St. Mary's School, OR $650,000
St. Michael's College School, ON, Canada CAN$1,700,000
St. Michael's Preparatory School of the Norbertine Fathers, CA $350,000
St. Patrick Catholic High School, MS $176,590
Saint Patrick High School, IL $990,000
Saint Patrick - Saint Vincent High School, CA $377,600
St. Paul Academy and Summit School, MN $1,475,710
St. Paul's High School, MB, Canada CAN$300,000
St. Peter's Preparatory School, NJ $1,000,000
St. Pius X Catholic High School, GA $400,000
St. Scholastica Academy, IL $509,000
St. Sebastian's School, MA $1,750,000
Saints Peter and Paul High School, MD $6500
St. Stephen's & St. Agnes School, VA $2,145,503
St. Stephen's Episcopal School, TX $1,900,000
St. Stephen's School, Rome, Italy 405,150
Saint Teresa's Academy, MO $130,000
Saint Thomas Academy, MN $2,200,000
St. Thomas Choir School, NY $187,950
St. Thomas High School, TX $1,300,000
St. Timothy's School, MD $2,000,000
Saint Ursula Academy, OH $1,299,000
Saint Viator High School, IL $1,200,000
Salem Academy, NC $1,033,794
Salesian High School, CA $1,000,000
Salesianum School, DE $500,000
Saltus Grammar School, Bermuda 359,400 Bermuda dollars
Sandy Spring Friends School, MD $3,035,000
Sanford School, DE $1,375,825
San Marcos Baptist Academy, TX $320,000
Santa Catalina School, CA $1,977,080
Sayre School, KY $6,000,000
Scholar's Hall Preparatory School, ON, Canada CAN$20,000
Scotus Central Catholic High School, NE $102,667
Seabury Hall, HI $848,440
Seattle Christian Schools, WA $110,098
Seisen International School, Japan 1,480,000
Seton Catholic Central High School, NY $200,000
Seton Catholic High School, AZ $705,000
The Seven Hills School, OH $530,000
Severn School, MD $1,115,305
Sewickley Academy, PA $600,000
Shady Side Academy, PA $1,825,900
Shattuck-St. Mary's School, MN $3,900,000
Shawe Memorial Junior/Senior High School, IN $161,537
Shawnigan Lake School, BC, Canada CAN$800,000
Shelton School and Evaluation Center, TX $43,500
The Shipley School, PA $2,231,695
Shoreline Christian, WA $307,000
Smith School, NY $30,000
Sonoma Academy, CA $2,000,000
Spartanburg Day School, SC $182,000

The Spence School, NY	$2,055,580
Springside Chestnut Hill Academy, PA	$3,146,250
Stephen T. Badin High School, OH	$2,950,000
Stevenson School, CA	$2,800,000
Stoneleigh–Burnham School, MA	$904,000
Storm King School, NY	$401,000
Strake Jesuit College Preparatory, TX	$1,350,000
Stratton Mountain School, VT	$737,000
Suffield Academy, CT	$3,500,000
Sunshine Bible Academy, SD	$31,500
Tabor Academy, MA	$3,650,000
The Taft School, CT	$6,700,000
Tandem Friends School, VA	$379,110
Teurlings Catholic High School, LA	$84,000
The Thacher School, CA	$2,004,400
Tidewater Academy, VA	$125,000
Tilton School, NH	$2,034,450
Tower Hill School, DE	$866,842
Trafalgar Castle School, ON, Canada	CAN$43,000
Tri-City Christian Schools, CA	$50,000
Trinity College School, ON, Canada	CAN$1,000,000
Trinity High School, KY	$2,000,000
Trinity High School, OH	$138,000
Trinity-Pawling School, NY	$3,000,000
Trinity Preparatory School, FL	$1,185,990
Trinity School of Texas, TX	$99,875
Trinity Valley School, TX	$511,265
Tuscaloosa Academy, AL	$160,000
Tyler Street Christian Academy, TX	$157,000
United Mennonite Educational Institute, ON, Canada	CAN$4000
United Nations International School, NY	$286,290
The United World College - USA, NM	$2,800,000
The University of Chicago Laboratory Schools, IL	$1,178,003
University of Detroit Jesuit High School and Academy, MI	$1,610,000
University Prep, WA	$1,976,682
University School of Jackson, TN	$130,000
University School of Milwaukee, WI	$937,475
University School of Nova Southeastern University, FL	$1,500,000
Vail Mountain School, CO	$390,000
Valle Catholic High School, MO	$165,000
Valley Christian High School, CA	$30,000
Valley Christian High School, CA	$1,250,000
Valley Lutheran High School, AZ	$166,770
The Valley School, MI	$51,376
Vicksburg Catholic School, MS	$100,000
Villa Duchesne and Oak Hill School, MO	$1,026,583
Villa Maria Academy, PA	$247,334
Villa Maria Academy, PA	$506,986
Villa Walsh Academy, NJ	$140,000
Wakefield School, VA	$1,000,000
Waldorf High School of Massachusetts Bay, MA	$357,455
The Walker School, GA	$480,600
Walnut Hill School, MA	$2,900,000
Waring School, MA	$588,000
Wasatch Academy, UT	$2,010,000
Washington Waldorf School, MD	$38,000
Watkinson School, CT	$1,328,120
Waynflete School, ME	$1,319,762
The Webb School, TN	$1,200,000
Webb School of Knoxville, TN	$646,250
Wesleyan Academy, PR	$10,000
Westbury Christian School, TX	$260,000
Westchester Country Day School, NC	$930,325
Westgate Mennonite Collegiate, MB, Canada	CAN$36,000
Westminster Christian Academy, AL	$35,149
Westminster School, CT	$3,940,000
Westover School, CT	$2,700,000
Westridge School, CA	$1,725,550
West Sound Academy, WA	$254,180
Wheaton Academy, IL	$500,000
The Wheeler School, RI	$1,300,563
Whitefield Academy, KY	$42,175
The Williams School, CT	$1,270,680
Willow Wood School, ON, Canada	CAN$60,000
Wilmington Christian School, DE	$292,720
Wilson Hall, SC	$135,000
Winchester Thurston School, PA	$1,249,000
Windermere Preparatory School, FL	$126,672
The Windsor School, NY	$30,000
Windward School, CA	$1,367,106
The Winsor School, MA	$1,735,291
Winston Preparatory School, NY	$500,000
The Woodward School, MA	$185,240
York Catholic High School, PA	$250,000
York Country Day School, PA	$306,250
York Preparatory School, NY	$750,000
York School, CA	$1,429,100

SCHOOLS REPORTING THAT THEY OFFER ENGLISH AS A SECOND LANGUAGE

Academy at the Lakes, FL
Academy of the New Church Boys' School, PA
Academy of the New Church Girls' School, PA
Academy of the Sacred Heart, LA
Académie Ste Cécile International School, ON, Canada
Alliance Academy, Ecuador
Allison Academy, FL
American Academy, FL
American Heritage School, FL
The American School in London, United Kingdom
Annie Wright School, WA
Army and Navy Academy, CA
The Athenian School, CA
Atlanta International School, GA
Atlantis Academy, FL
Balmoral Hall School, MB, Canada
The Beekman School, NY
Berkshire School, MA
Bishop Brady High School, NH
Bishop's College School, QC, Canada
The Bishop Strachan School, ON, Canada
Blanchet School, OR
The Blue Ridge School, VA
The Bolles School, FL
Branksome Hall, ON, Canada
Brewster Academy, NH
Brimmer and May School, MA
Burr and Burton Academy, VT
Buxton School, MA
The Calverton School, MD
Canyonville Christian Academy, OR
Cape Henry Collegiate School, VA
Capistrano Valley Christian Schools, CA
Carlisle School, VA
Cascadilla School, NY
Chamberlain-Hunt Academy, MS
Chaminade College Preparatory School, MO
Chapel Hill–Chauncy Hall School, MA
Charlotte Country Day School, NC

Chatham Hall, VA
Cheshire Academy, CT
Children's Creative and Performing Arts Academy of San Diego, CA
Chinese Christian Schools, CA
Christ Church Episcopal School, SC
Christchurch School, VA
Colegio Nueva Granada, Colombia
Columbia International College of Canada, ON, Canada
Copenhagen International School, Denmark
Cotter Schools, MN
Crawford Adventist Academy, ON, Canada
The Culver Academies, IN
Cushing Academy, MA
Darlington School, GA
Donelson Christian Academy, TN
Eaglebrook School, MA
Eastside Christian Academy, AB, Canada
Eldorado Emerson Private School, CA
Emma Willard School, NY
Escola Americana de Campinas, Brazil
Father Lopez High School, FL
Fay School, MA
The Fessenden School, MA
First Presbyterian Day School, GA
Forsyth Country Day School, NC
Fort Lauderdale Preparatory School, FL
Fountain Valley School of Colorado, CO
French-American School of New York, NY
George Stevens Academy, ME
Georgetown Preparatory School, MD
Germantown Friends School, PA
Glenlyon Norfolk School, BC, Canada
Gonzaga Preparatory School, WA
Gould Academy, ME
The Governor French Academy, IL
The Grauer School, CA
Great Lakes Christian High School, ON, Canada
Greensboro Day School, NC
The Greenwood School, VT
The Grier School, PA
The Gunston School, MD
Happy Hill Farm Academy, TX
Hargrave Military Academy, VA
Hawaiian Mission Academy, HI
Highroad Academy, BC, Canada
Hillcrest Christian School, CA
The Hockaday School, TX
Holy Trinity High School, IL
Hoosac School, NY
Houghton Academy, NY
Hyde School, CT
Hyde School, ME
Idyllwild Arts Academy, CA
Immaculate Heart High School, AZ
Interlochen Arts Academy, MI
International High School, CA
International School Bangkok, Thailand
International School Hamburg, Germany
International School Manila, Philippines
International School of Amsterdam, Netherlands
The International School of London, United Kingdom
Key School, TX
The King's Academy, TN
King's-Edgehill School, NS, Canada
Lancaster Mennonite High School, PA
La Scuola D'Italia Guglielmo Marconi, NY
Lausanne Collegiate School, TN
Lawrence Academy, MA
Lehigh Valley Christian High School, PA
Le Lycee Francais de Los Angeles, CA
Long Island Lutheran Middle and High School, NY
Los Angeles Baptist Middle School/High School, CA
Los Angeles Lutheran High School, CA
Luther College High School, SK, Canada
MacLachlan College, ON, Canada
Maharishi School of the Age of Enlightenment, IA
Maine Central Institute, ME
Marine Military Academy, TX
The Marvelwood School, CT
Marylawn of the Oranges, NJ
Marymount International School, Italy
The Masters School, NY
Matignon High School, MA
Menaul School, NM
Merchiston Castle School, United Kingdom
Mercyhurst Preparatory School, PA
Mid-Pacific Institute, HI
Miller School, VA
Miss Hall's School, MA
Missouri Military Academy, MO
Miss Porter's School, CT
MPS Etobicoke, ON, Canada
Munich International School, Germany
Nebraska Christian Schools, NE
Niagara Christian Community of Schools, ON, Canada
North Country School, NY
North Toronto Christian School, ON, Canada
Northwest Yeshiva High School, WA
Northwood School, NY
The Norwich Free Academy, CT
Notre Dame College Prep, IL
Oak Grove School, CA
Oak Hill Academy, VA
The Oakland School, PA
Oak Ridge Military Academy, NC
Ojai Valley School, CA
The Oliverian School, NH
Oneida Baptist Institute, KY
Oregon Episcopal School, OR
Orinda Academy, CA
Our Lady Academy, MS
Our Lady of Mercy High School, NY
Pickering College, ON, Canada
Pine Crest School, FL
Pope John XXIII Regional High School, NJ
The Prairie School, WI
Presbyterian Pan American School, TX
Professional Children's School, NY
Providence Christian School, AB, Canada
Queen Margaret's School, BC, Canada
Rabbi Alexander S. Gross Hebrew Academy, FL
Randolph-Macon Academy, VA
The Rectory School, CT
Redwood Christian Schools, CA
Ridley College, ON, Canada
Riverside Military Academy, GA
Rock Point School, VT
Rolling Hills Preparatory School, CA
Rosseau Lake College, ON, Canada
Ross School, NY
Rothesay Netherwood School, NB, Canada
Royal Canadian College, BC, Canada
Sacramento Country Day School, CA

Sacred Heart School of Halifax, NS, Canada
Saddleback Valley Christian School, CA
Saddlebrook Preparatory School, FL
St. Andrew's College, ON, Canada
St. Andrew's Priory School, HI
St. Andrew's School, RI
St. Andrew's–Sewanee School, TN
St. Anne's–Belfield School, VA
St. Anthony Catholic High School, TX
St. Benedict's Preparatory School, NJ
St. Bernard High School, CT
St. Catherine's Academy, CA
Saint Clement Academy, ON, Canada
St. Croix Schools, MN
Saint Edward's School, FL
Saint Francis School, HI
St. George's School of Montreal, QC, Canada
Saint John's Preparatory School, MN
St. John's-Ravenscourt School, MB, Canada
Saint Joseph Junior-Senior High School, HI
St. Jude's School, ON, Canada
St. Mary's Preparatory School, MI
St. Mary's School, OR
Saint Maur International School, Japan
St. Michael's Preparatory School of the Norbertine Fathers, CA
Saint Patrick High School, IL
St. Patrick's Regional Secondary, BC, Canada
St. Stephen's Episcopal School, TX
St. Stephen's School, Rome, Italy
St. Timothy's School, MD
Salem Academy, NC
Salem Academy, OR
Sandy Spring Friends School, MD
San Marcos Baptist Academy, TX
Scholar's Hall Preparatory School, ON, Canada
SciCore Academy, NJ
Seisen International School, Japan
Shattuck-St. Mary's School, MN
Shawnigan Lake School, BC, Canada
Solomon College, AB, Canada
Squaw Valley Academy, CA
Stoneleigh–Burnham School, MA
Storm King School, NY
Stratton Mountain School, VT
Suffield Academy, CT
Tabor Academy, MA
Taipei American School, Taiwan
TASIS The American School in England, United Kingdom
TASIS, The American School in Switzerland, Switzerland
The Tenney School, TX
Thetford Academy, VT
Tilton School, NH
Toronto District Christian High School, ON, Canada
Trafalgar Castle School, ON, Canada
Trinity College School, ON, Canada
Trinity-Pawling School, NY
Tuscaloosa Academy, AL
United Nations International School, NY
The United World College - USA, NM
University School of Jackson, TN
Vail Mountain School, CO
Walnut Hill School, MA
Wasatch Academy, UT
The Webb School, TN
Westover School, CT
West Sound Academy, WA
Willow Wood School, ON, Canada
Wilmington Christian School, DE
Winchester Thurston School, PA
The Windsor School, NY
The Woodhall School, CT
The Woodward School, MA
York Preparatory School, NY

SCHOOLS REPORTING A COMMUNITY SERVICE REQUIREMENT

The Academy for Gifted Children (PACE), ON, Canada
Academy of Our Lady of Peace, CA
Academy of the Sacred Heart, LA
Academy of the Sacred Heart, LA
Academy of the Sacred Heart, MI
Allison Academy, FL
American Academy, FL
American Heritage School, FL
Archbishop Curley High School, MD
Armona Union Academy, CA
The Athenian School, CA
Atlanta International School, GA
Auldern Academy, NC
Barrie School, MD
Battle Ground Academy, TN
Belen Jesuit Preparatory School, FL
Benedictine High School, OH
Benedictine High School, VA
Berkeley Preparatory School, FL
Berkshire School, MA
The Birch Wathen Lenox School, NY
Bishop Brady High School, NH
Bishop Conaty-Our Lady of Loretto High School, CA
Bishop Eustace Preparatory School, NJ
Bishop Fenwick High School, OH
Bishop Guertin High School, NH
Bishop Ireton High School, VA
Bishop Kelly High School, ID
Bishop McGuinness Catholic High School, NC
The Bishop's School, CA
Bishop Stang High School, MA
The Bishop Strachan School, ON, Canada
Blanchet School, OR
Boston University Academy, MA
Boylan Central Catholic High School, IL
Breck School, MN
Brentwood School, CA
Briarwood Christian High School, AL
Brimmer and May School, MA
Brooks School, MA
Brophy College Preparatory, AZ
The Browning School, NY
Brunswick School, CT
The Bryn Mawr School for Girls, MD
Burr and Burton Academy, VT
Butte Central Catholic High School, MT
The Cambridge School of Weston, MA
Campbell Hall (Episcopal), CA
Cannon School, NC
Canterbury School, FL
Cape Cod Academy, MA
Cape Fear Academy, NC
Cape Henry Collegiate School, VA
Cardinal Newman High School, FL
Carrollton School of the Sacred Heart, FL
Cascadilla School, NY

The Catholic High School of Baltimore, MD
The Catlin Gabel School, OR
Central Catholic High School, CA
Central Catholic High School, TX
CFS, The School at Church Farm, PA
Chaminade College Preparatory, CA
Chaminade College Preparatory School, MO
Chaminade-Madonna College Preparatory, FL
Chapel Hill–Chauncy Hall School, MA
Charlotte Country Day School, NC
Chattanooga Christian School, TN
Cheshire Academy, CT
Cheverus High School, ME
Children's Creative and Performing Arts Academy of San Diego, CA
Christian Brothers Academy, NY
Christian Central Academy, NY
Christian Home and Bible School, FL
Christopher Columbus High School, FL
Cincinnati Country Day School, OH
Colegio San Jose, PR
Collegiate School, NY
The Collegiate School, VA
The Colorado Springs School, CO
The Columbus Academy, OH
Commonwealth School, MA
The Community School of Naples, FL
Concordia Lutheran High School, IN
Convent of the Sacred Heart, CT
Cotter Schools, MN
Country Day School of the Sacred Heart, PA
Covington Catholic High School, KY
Crossroads School for Arts & Sciences, CA
The Culver Academies, IN
Currey Ingram Academy, TN
The Dalton School, NY
Dana Hall School, MA
Darlington School, GA
Deerfield-Windsor School, GA
Devon Preparatory School, PA
Donelson Christian Academy, TN
Durham Academy, NC
Eaglebrook School, MA
Eastside Catholic School, WA
Edgewood Academy, AL
Edmund Burke School, DC
Eldorado Emerson Private School, CA
Elizabeth Seton High School, MD
Emma Willard School, NY
Escola Americana de Campinas, Brazil
The Ethel Walker School, CT
Father Lopez High School, FL
First Baptist Academy, TX
Flint Hill School, VA
Flintridge Preparatory School, CA
Forest Lake Academy, FL
Forsyth Country Day School, NC
Fort Worth Country Day School, TX
Fountain Valley School of Colorado, CO
French-American School of New York, NY
Friends Academy, NY
Fuqua School, VA
Garces Memorial High School, CA
Gaston Day School, NC
Georgetown Preparatory School, MD
r Academy, OH
Country School, MD
Glenlyon Norfolk School, BC, Canada
Gonzaga College High School, DC
Gonzaga Preparatory School, WA
The Grauer School, CA
Greenfield School, NC
Greenhill School, TX
Greenwich Academy, CT
Guamani Private School, PR
The Gunston School, MD
Hampton Roads Academy, VA
The Harker School, CA
The Harley School, NY
Harrells Christian Academy, NC
Hawaiian Mission Academy, HI
Hawken School, OH
Head-Royce School, CA
Highland Hall Waldorf School, CA
Hillcrest Christian School, CA
Hillcrest Christian School, MS
The Hockaday School, TX
Holy Ghost Preparatory School, PA
Holy Innocents' Episcopal School, GA
Holyoke Catholic High School, MA
Hopkins School, CT
Hyman Brand Hebrew Academy of Greater Kansas City, KS
Immaculata-La Salle High School, FL
Immaculate Conception High School, NJ
Independent School, KS
Institute of Notre Dame, MD
Intermountain Christian School, UT
International School Bangkok, Thailand
International School of Amsterdam, Netherlands
The International School of London, United Kingdom
Iona Preparatory School, NY
Jack M. Barrack Hebrew Academy, PA
Jesuit College Preparatory School, TX
Jesuit High School of New Orleans, LA
Jesuit High School of Tampa, FL
Josephinum Academy, IL
Junipero Serra High School, CA
Junipero Serra High School, CA
Keith Country Day School, IL
Kerr-Vance Academy, NC
King's Ridge Christian School, GA
Kingswood-Oxford School, CT
La Jolla Country Day School, CA
Lakeside School, WA
Landon School, MD
The Latin School of Chicago, IL
Lawrence School, OH
Lincoln Academy, ME
Lincoln School, RI
Lodi Academy, CA
Louisville High School, CA
Lutheran High School North, MO
Lutheran High School Northwest, MI
MacLachlan College, ON, Canada
Manhattan Christian High School, MT
Maranatha High School, CA
Maret School, DC
The Marin School, CA
Marist School, GA
Mars Hill Bible School, AL
The Marvelwood School, CT
Marylawn of the Oranges, NJ
Marymount High School, CA
Matignon High School, MA

McDonogh School, MD
The Meadows School, NV
Menaul School, NM
Mercy High School, CT
Mesa Grande Seventh-Day Academy, CA
Miller School, VA
Miss Hall's School, MA
Missouri Military Academy, MO
Miss Porter's School, CT
Moorestown Friends School, NJ
Moreau Catholic High School, CA
Morristown-Beard School, NJ
Mount Michael Benedictine School, NE
Munich International School, Germany
Nerinx Hall, MO
Newark Academy, NJ
Noble and Greenough School, MA
The Nora School, MD
Norfolk Academy, VA
North Cobb Christian School, GA
Northwest Academy, OR
Northwest Catholic High School, CT
Northwest Yeshiva High School, WA
Notre Dame Academy, CA
Notre Dame College Prep, IL
Oak Grove School, CA
Oak Hill School, OR
The Oakland School, PA
Oak Ridge Military Academy, NC
The Oakridge School, TX
The O'Neal School, NC
Orinda Academy, CA
Out-Of-Door Academy, FL
The Overlake School, WA
Pacific Hills School, CA
The Paideia School, GA
Palma School, CA
Paradise Adventist Academy, CA
Peddie School, NJ
Phoenix Country Day School, AZ
Pickering College, ON, Canada
The Pingree School, MA
The Pingry School, NJ
Pioneer Valley Christian School, MA
Pope John XXIII Regional High School, NJ
Powers Catholic High School, MI
The Prairie School, WI
Providence Catholic School, The College Preparatory School for Girls Grades 6-12, TX
Providence Country Day School, RI
Punahou School, HI
Queen Margaret's School, BC, Canada
Rabbi Alexander S. Gross Hebrew Academy, FL
Ravenscroft School, NC
Riverdale Country School, NY
The Rivers School, MA
Robert Land Academy, ON, Canada
Rock Point School, VT
Roland Park Country School, MD
Ross School, NY
Sacramento Adventist Academy, CA
Sacramento Country Day School, CA
Sacred Heart School of Halifax, NS, Canada
Sage Ridge School, NV
St. Agnes Academy, TX
St. Albans School, DC
St. Andrew's College, ON, Canada
St. Andrew's Priory School, HI
St. Andrew's School, RI
St. Andrew's–Sewanee School, TN
St. Anne's–Belfield School, VA
Saint Anthony High School, CA
Saint Basil Academy, PA
St. Bernard High School, CT
St. Bernard's Catholic School, CA
St. Brendan High School, FL
St. Christopher's School, VA
St. Croix Country Day School, VI
Saint Edward's School, FL
Saint Elizabeth High School, CA
St. Francis de Sales High School, OH
Saint Francis High School, CA
Saint Francis School, HI
St. George's School of Montreal, QC, Canada
St. Gregory College Preparatory School, AZ
Saint Joseph High School, IL
Saint Joseph High School, NJ
St. Joseph's Catholic School, SC
Saint Joseph's High School, NJ
St. Mark's School of Texas, TX
St. Martin's Episcopal School, LA
Saint Mary's Hall, TX
Saint Mary's High School, AZ
St. Mary's School, OR
Saint Patrick High School, IL
St. Peter's Preparatory School, NJ
St. Stephen's & St. Agnes School, VA
St. Stephen's Episcopal School, TX
Saint Teresa's Academy, MO
Saint Thomas Academy, MN
St. Thomas Aquinas High School, NH
St. Timothy's School, MD
Saint Ursula Academy, OH
Salem Academy, OR
Salesianum School, DE
Saltus Grammar School, Bermuda
Sandy Spring Friends School, MD
Sayre School, KY
Seabury Hall, HI
Seattle Academy of Arts and Sciences, WA
The Seven Hills School, OH
Severn School, MD
Sewickley Academy, PA
Shattuck-St. Mary's School, MN
The Shipley School, PA
Smith School, NY
Springside Chestnut Hill Academy, PA
Stephen T. Badin High School, OH
Storm King School, NY
Strake Jesuit College Preparatory, TX
Stratford Academy, GA
Stratton Mountain School, VT
Tandem Friends School, VA
TASIS The American School in England, United Kingdom
TASIS, The American School in Switzerland, Switzerland
Tilton School, NH
Tower Hill School, DE
Tri-City Christian Schools, CA
Trinity College School, ON, Canada
Trinity High School, KY
Trinity Valley School, TX
Tuscaloosa Academy, AL
United Nations International School, NY
The United World College - USA, NM

The University of Chicago Laboratory Schools, IL
University of Detroit Jesuit High School and Academy, MI
University Prep, WA
University School of Jackson, TN
University School of Milwaukee, WI
University School of Nova Southeastern University, FL
Valle Catholic High School, MO
Villa Duchesne and Oak Hill School, MO
Villa Maria Academy, PA
Villa Victoria Academy, NJ
Visitation Academy of St. Louis County, MO
Waldorf High School of Massachusetts Bay, MA
Wasatch Academy, UT
Waynflete School, ME
Webb School of Knoxville, TN
Wesleyan Academy, PR
Westbury Christian School, TX
Westchester Country Day School, NC
Westmark School, CA
Westover School, CT
Westridge School, CA
The Wheeler School, RI
Willow Wood School, ON, Canada
Wilmington Christian School, DE
Wilson Hall, SC
Windermere Preparatory School, FL
The Winston School San Antonio, TX
The Woodward School, MA
York Country Day School, PA
York Preparatory School, NY
York School, CA

SCHOOLS REPORTING EXCHANGE PROGRAMS WITH OTHER U.S. SCHOOLS

Academy of the Sacred Heart, LA
Academy of the Sacred Heart, LA
Academy of the Sacred Heart, MI
The Athenian School, CA
Carrollton School of the Sacred Heart, FL
Convent of the Sacred Heart, CT
Country Day School of the Sacred Heart, PA
Doane Stuart School, NY
Emma Willard School, NY
Germantown Friends School, PA
La Scuola D'Italia Guglielmo Marconi, NY
Providence Day School, NC
Sacred Heart/Griffin High School, IL
Sacred Heart School of Halifax, NS, Canada
St. Benedict's Preparatory School, NJ
St. Stephen's School, Rome, Italy
Salesianum School, DE
Trafalgar Castle School, ON, Canada
Villa Duchesne and Oak Hill School, MO

SCHOOLS REPORTING PROGRAMS FOR STUDY ABROAD

Academy of Holy Angels, MN
Academy of the Sacred Heart, LA
Alexander Dawson School, CO
Annie Wright School, WA
The Athenian School, CA
Atlanta International School, GA
Baylor School, TN
Bayside Academy, AL
Benedictine High School, OH
Berean Christian High School, CA
Berkeley Preparatory School, FL
Berkshire School, MA
The Birch Wathen Lenox School, NY
Bishop's College School, QC, Canada
The Bishop's School, CA
The Bishop Strachan School, ON, Canada
Blair Academy, NJ
The Brearley School, NY
Brooks School, MA
Brophy College Preparatory, AZ
The Bryn Mawr School for Girls, MD
Burr and Burton Academy, VT
The Cambridge School of Weston, MA
Cape Cod Academy, MA
Cape Fear Academy, NC
Carrollton School of the Sacred Heart, FL
The Catlin Gabel School, OR
Central Catholic High School, TX
CFS, The School at Church Farm, PA
Chadwick School, CA
Charlotte Country Day School, NC
Charlotte Latin School, NC
Chatham Hall, VA
Cheshire Academy, CT
Chinese Christian Schools, CA
Cincinnati Country Day School, OH
Collegiate School, NY
Commonwealth School, MA
The Community School of Naples, FL
Concord Academy, MA
Convent of the Sacred Heart, CT
Cotter Schools, MN
The Country Day School, ON, Canada
Country Day School of the Sacred Heart, PA
Damien High School, CA
Dana Hall School, MA
Deerfield Academy, MA
Doane Stuart School, NY
Emma Willard School, NY
Episcopal High School, VA
Escola Americana de Campinas, Brazil
The Ethel Walker School, CT
Falmouth Academy, MA
Flintridge Preparatory School, CA
Foxcroft School, VA
Gann Academy (The New Jewish High School of Greater Boston), MA
Georgetown Preparatory School, MD
Germantown Friends School, PA
Gill St. Bernard's School, NJ
The Grauer School, CA
Greensboro Day School, NC
Greenwich Academy, CT
The Grier School, PA
Groton School, MA
The Gunston School, MD
Hawken School, OH
Head-Royce School, CA
Hebrew Academy-the Five Towns, NY
Highland Hall Waldorf School, CA
The Hill School, PA
The Hockaday School, TX
Holy Ghost Preparatory School, PA
Holy Innocents' Episcopal School, GA

Hopkins School, CT
The Hotchkiss School, CT
International High School, CA
Iona Preparatory School, NY
Jack M. Barrack Hebrew Academy, PA
Keith Country Day School, IL
Kentucky Country Day School, KY
Kimball Union Academy, NH
King's-Edgehill School, NS, Canada
Kingswood-Oxford School, CT
La Jolla Country Day School, CA
Lakefield College School, ON, Canada
Lakehill Preparatory School, TX
Lakeside School, WA
Landon School, MD
La Scuola D'Italia Guglielmo Marconi, NY
The Latin School of Chicago, IL
Lawrence Academy, MA
Lincoln School, RI
The Loomis Chaffee School, CT
Louisville Collegiate School, KY
The Lovett School, GA
Luther College High School, SK, Canada
Maine Central Institute, ME
Maret School, DC
The Masters School, NY
Matignon High School, MA
Memphis University School, TN
Merchiston Castle School, United Kingdom
Millbrook School, NY
Milton Academy, MA
Miss Porter's School, CT
Montclair Kimberley Academy, NJ
Montgomery Bell Academy, TN
Moorestown Friends School, NJ
Morristown-Beard School, NJ
Neuchatel Junior College, Switzerland
Newark Academy, NJ
Nichols School, NY
Noble and Greenough School, MA
Norfolk Academy, VA
The Oakridge School, TX
Ojai Valley School, CA
The Oliverian School, NH
Oregon Episcopal School, OR
The Overlake School, WA
Padua Franciscan High School, OH
Peddie School, NJ
Phillips Academy (Andover), MA
Phillips Exeter Academy, NH
Phoenix Country Day School, AZ
The Pine School, FL
The Pingry School, NJ
Providence Country Day School, RI
Providence Day School, NC
Punahou School, HI
Randolph-Macon Academy, VA
Ravenscroft School, NC
Realms of Inquiry, UT
Regis High School, NY
Ridley College, ON, Canada
Riverdale Country School, NY
Roland Park Country School, MD
Rosseau Lake College, ON, Canada
Rundle College, AB, Canada
Sacred Heart School of Halifax, NS, Canada
Saddleback Valley Christian School, CA
St. Albans School, DC
St. Andrew's College, ON, Canada
St. Andrew's–Sewanee School, TN
St. Anthony Catholic High School, TX
Saint Augustine Preparatory School, NJ
Saint Edward's School, FL
St. John's Preparatory School, MA
Saint John's Preparatory School, MN
St. Joseph's Preparatory School, PA
St. Mark's High School, DE
Saint Mary's Hall, TX
Saint Mary's High School, MD
Saint Mary's School, NC
St. Paul Academy and Summit School, MN
St. Peter's Preparatory School, NJ
St. Stephen's & St. Agnes School, VA
St. Stephen's Episcopal School, TX
Salem Academy, NC
Seattle Academy of Arts and Sciences, WA
The Seven Hills School, OH
Severn School, MD
Sewickley Academy, PA
Shady Side Academy, PA
The Shipley School, PA
Sonoma Academy, CA
The Spence School, NY
Stephen T. Badin High School, OH
Stevenson School, CA
Summerfield Waldorf School, CA
The Taft School, CT
Telluride Mountain School, CO
The Thacher School, CA
Toronto District Christian High School, ON, Canada
Trinity College School, ON, Canada
Trinity High School, KY
Trinity School of Texas, TX
Tuscaloosa Academy, AL
University Prep, WA
Villa Duchesne and Oak Hill School, MO
Waldorf High School of Massachusetts Bay, MA
The Walker School, GA
Waring School, MA
Washington Waldorf School, MD
Waynflete School, ME
The Webb School, TN
Webb School of Knoxville, TN
West Island College, AB, Canada
Westminster School, CT
Westover School, CT
The Wheeler School, RI
The Williams School, CT
Willow Wood School, ON, Canada
Winchester Thurston School, PA
York Country Day School, PA

SCHOOLS REPORTING SUMMER SESSIONS OPEN TO STUDENTS FROM OTHER SCHOOLS

Academy of Holy Angels, MN	F,S
Academy of Our Lady of Peace, CA	A
Academy of the Holy Cross, MD	A,C,F,S
Academy of the New Church Boys' School, PA	A,C,F,S
Academy of the New Church Girls' School, PA	A,C,F
Academy of the Sacred Heart, LA	R
Academy of the Sacred Heart, MI	A,C,F,S
Académie Ste Cécile International School, ON, Canada	A,F

A — academic; C — computer instruction; F — art/fine arts; R — rigorous outdoor training; S — sports; O — other

Allendale Columbia School, NY	A,F,S
Allison Academy, FL	A
American Academy, FL	A,C,F
American Heritage School, FL	A,C,F
The American School Foundation, Mexico	A
Archbishop Curley High School, MD	A,C,F,S
Archbishop Mitty High School, CA	A,C,F,S
Archbishop Rummel High School, LA	A,C,F,R,S
Army and Navy Academy, CA	A,C,F,R,S
ASSETS School, HI	A
The Athenian School, CA	A,C,F,S
Atlanta International School, GA	A,C,F,S
Atlantis Academy, FL	A,C,F
Augusta Christian School (I), GA	A
Augusta Preparatory Day School, GA	A,F,S
Bachman Academy, TN	A,S
The Baltimore Actors' Theatre Conservatory, MD	A,F
Baltimore Lutheran School, MD	A,S
Barrie School, MD	S
Battle Ground Academy, TN	A,C,F,S
Baylor School, TN	A,C,F,R,S
The Beekman School, NY	A
Benedictine High School, OH	A,C,S
Benedictine High School, VA	A,F,S
Berkeley Preparatory School, FL	A,C,F,S
Bishop Brady High School, NH	A,S
Bishop Conaty-Our Lady of Loretto High School, CA	A,C,F
Bishop Eustace Preparatory School, NJ	A,S
Bishop Ireton High School, VA	A,C,F
Bishop Mora Salesian High School, CA	A,C,F,R,S
Bishop's College School, QC, Canada	A
The Bishop's School, CA	A,C,F,S
Bishop Stang High School, MA	A,C,F,S
The Bishop Strachan School, ON, Canada	A,C,F,R
Blanchet School, OR	A,S
Blessed Sacrament Hugenot, VA	A,C,F,S
Blueprint Education, AZ	A
The Bolles School, FL	A,C,F
Boylan Central Catholic High School, IL	A,F,R,S
Branksome Hall, ON, Canada	A
Brentwood School, CA	A,C,F,S
Brewster Academy, NH	A,C,F,S
Bridgemont High School, CA	S
Bridges Academy, CA	A,C,F,S
Brooks School, MA	A,C,S
Brophy College Preparatory, AZ	A,C,F,S
Brother Rice High School, MI	A,F
Brunswick School, CT	A
The Bryn Mawr School for Girls, MD	A,F,S
Calvert Hall College High School, MD	A,C,F,S
The Calverton School, MD	A,C,F,S
Calvin Christian High School, CA	A,S
The Cambridge School of Weston, MA	F
Campbell Hall (Episcopal), CA	A,C,F,S
Cannon School, NC	A,C,F,S
The Canterbury Episcopal School, TX	A,S
Canterbury School, FL	A,F,S
Cape Fear Academy, NC	A,F,S
Cape Henry Collegiate School, VA	A,C,F,S
Capistrano Valley Christian Schools, CA	A,S
Carlisle School, VA	A,C,F,S
Carolina Day School, NC	A,C,F,S
Cascadilla School, NY	A,F
Cathedral High School, NY	A
The Catholic High School of Baltimore, MD	A,C,F,S
The Catlin Gabel School, OR	A,C,F
Central Catholic High School, CA	A
Central Catholic High School, TX	A,C,S
Chadwick School, CA	C,F,S
Chamberlain-Hunt Academy, MS	A,R,S
Chaminade College Preparatory, CA	A,C,S
Chaminade College Preparatory School, MO	A,F,S
Charlotte Christian School, NC	A,C,F,S
Charlotte Country Day School, NC	A,C,F,S
Charlotte Latin School, NC	A,C,F,S
Chatham Hall, VA	S
Chattanooga Christian School, TN	A,C,F,S
Cheshire Academy, CT	A,R
Cheverus High School, ME	A,S
Children's Creative and Performing Arts Academy of San Diego, CA	A,C,F
Chinese Christian Schools, CA	A,S
Christ Church Episcopal School, SC	A,S
Christchurch School, VA	A,S
Christian Central Academy, NY	S
Chrysalis School, WA	A,C
Cincinnati Country Day School, OH	A,C,F,S
Cistercian Preparatory School, TX	A,F,S
Clarksville Academy, TN	A,C,F,S
Clearwater Central Catholic High School, FL	A,C,S
Colegio San Jose, PR	A
Collegedale Academy, TN	A
The Collegiate School, VA	A,C,F,S
The Colorado Springs School, CO	A,C,F,S
Columbia International College of Canada, ON, Canada	A,C,F,S
The Columbus Academy, OH	A,C,F
Columbus School for Girls, OH	A,C,F,R,S
The Community School of Naples, FL	A,F,S
Concordia Lutheran High School, IN	A,F,S
Cotter Schools, MN	A,F,S
The Country Day School, ON, Canada	A,F,S
Crossroads School for Arts & Sciences, CA	A,C,F,S
The Culver Academies, IN	A,C,F,R,S
Currey Ingram Academy, TN	A,F,S
Cushing Academy, MA	A,C,F,S
Damien High School, CA	A,C,F,S
Dana Hall School, MA	A,S
Darlington School, GA	A,C,F,S
Davidson Academy, TN	A,F,S
Delbarton School, NJ	A,C,S
DeMatha Catholic High School, MD	A,C,F,S
DePaul Catholic High School, NJ	A,C,S
The Derryfield School, NH	F
Dominican Academy, NY	A
Durham Academy, NC	A,C,F,S
Eaglebrook School, MA	A,C,F,R,S
Eagle Hill-Southport, CT	A
Edgewood Academy, AL	O
Edmund Burke School, DC	A,C,F
Elizabeth Seton High School, MD	A,F,S
The Ellis School, PA	O
Episcopal Collegiate School, AR	A,C,F,S
Episcopal High School, TX	A,F
Episcopal High School, VA	A,F,S
The Ethel Walker School, CT	F,S
Fairhill School, TX	A,C
Father Ryan High School, TN	A,C,F,S
Fayetteville Academy, NC	A,C,F,S
Fay School, MA	A,C,F,S
The Fessenden School, MA	A
The First Academy, FL	A,F,S
First Presbyterian Day School, GA	A,F,S
Flint Hill School, VA	A,C,F,R,S

A — academic; C — computer instruction; F — art/fine arts; R — rigorous outdoor training; S — sports; O — other

School	Programs
Flintridge Preparatory School, CA	A,C,F,R,S
Fontbonne Hall Academy, NY	S
Foothills Academy, AB, Canada	A
Forsyth Country Day School, NC	A
Fort Lauderdale Preparatory School, FL	A,C
Fort Worth Country Day School, TX	A,F,S
Foundation Academy, FL	A,F,S
Fountain Valley School of Colorado, CO	A,C,S
Fowlers Academy, PR	A
Friends Academy, NY	F
Friends' Central School, PA	A
Fuqua School, VA	A,F,S
The Galloway School, GA	A,S
Garces Memorial High School, CA	A,C,F,S
Gaston Day School, NC	A,F,S
The Geneva School, FL	A,F,S
George Stevens Academy, ME	A,F,S
Georgetown Preparatory School, MD	A,S
George Walton Academy, GA	A,F,S
Germantown Friends School, PA	A
Gill St. Bernard's School, NJ	A,F,S
Gilman School, MD	A,F,R,S
Gilmour Academy, OH	A,S
Girls Preparatory School, TN	A,C,F,S
Glenelg Country School, MD	S
The Glenholme School, Devereux Connecticut, CT	A,C,F,S
Gonzaga College High School, DC	A
Gonzaga Preparatory School, WA	A,C,F
The Governor French Academy, IL	A
Grace Brethren School, CA	A
The Grauer School, CA	A,C,F,R,S
Great Lakes Christian High School, ON, Canada	A,C,S
Greenfield School, NC	A,C,F,S
Greenhill School, TX	A,C,F,S
Greensboro Day School, NC	A,C,F,S
Greenwich Academy, CT	A,F,S
The Grier School, PA	A,F,S
Guamani Private School, PR	A
The Gunston School, MD	A,C,S
Hackley School, NY	S
Hamden Hall Country Day School, CT	A,C,F,S
Hampton Roads Academy, VA	A,C,F,S
Harding Academy, TN	A,C,F,S
Harding Academy, TN	A,S
Hargrave Military Academy, VA	A,C,R,S
The Harker School, CA	A
The Harley School, NY	A,C,F,S
The Harvey School, NY	A
Hawaii Baptist Academy, HI	A,C,F,S
Hawken School, OH	A,C
Head-Royce School, CA	A
Hill School of Fort Worth, TX	A
The Hill Top Preparatory School, PA	A
The Hockaday School, TX	A,C,F,S
Holy Ghost Preparatory School, PA	A,C,S
Holy Innocents' Episcopal School, GA	A,C,F,S
Hoosac School, NY	A
Hopkins School, CT	A,C,F,R,S
The Hotchkiss School, CT	F
The Howard School, GA	A
Huntington-Surrey School, TX	A
Hyde School, CT	A,F,R,S
Hyde School, ME	A,F,R,S
Idyllwild Arts Academy, CA	A,F
Immaculata-La Salle High School, FL	A
Independent School, KS	A,C,F,S
Indian Springs School, AL	A,F,S

School	Programs
Institute of Notre Dame, MD	A,C,F,R,S
Interlochen Arts Academy, MI	F
International High School, CA	A
International School Bangkok, Thailand	A,F
International School Manila, Philippines	A
Jackson Preparatory School, MS	A,C,F
Jesuit College Preparatory School, TX	A,C,F,S
Junipero Serra High School, CA	A,C,F,R,S
Junipero Serra High School, CA	A,C,S
Kauai Christian Academy, HI	A,C,F
Keith Country Day School, IL	A,F,S
Kentucky Country Day School, KY	A,C,F,R,S
Kerr-Vance Academy, NC	A
The Kew-Forest School, NY	A
Key School, TX	A,C
Kimball Union Academy, NH	A,F,S
King Low Heywood Thomas, CT	A,F,S
King's High School, WA	S
Kingshill School, VI	A
La Jolla Country Day School, CA	A,C,F,S
Lakehill Preparatory School, TX	A,C,F,S
Lakeside School, WA	A,C,F,S
Lancaster Mennonite High School, PA	A,S
Landmark School, MA	A
Landon School, MD	A,F
Lansdale Catholic High School, PA	A,F,S
La Salle High School, CA	A,C,F,S
The Latin School of Chicago, IL	A,C,F,R,S
Laurel Springs School, CA	A,C,F
Lausanne Collegiate School, TN	A,C,F,S
Le Lycee Francais de Los Angeles, CA	O
The Linsly School, WV	A,C
Little Keswick School, VA	A,C,F,R,S
Long Island Lutheran Middle and High School, NY	C,F,S
The Loomis Chaffee School, CT	A
Los Angeles Baptist Middle School/High School, CA	A,C,S
Los Angeles Lutheran High School, CA	A,S
Louisville Collegiate School, KY	A,C,F,S
Louisville High School, CA	S
The Lovett School, GA	A
Loyola-Blakefield, MD	A,S
Lutheran High School of Hawaii, HI	A,C,F,S
Lyman Ward Military Academy, AL	A,R
Madison-Ridgeland Academy, MS	A,S
Maine Central Institute, ME	A,F
Malden Catholic High School, MA	A,S
Maranatha High School, CA	A,F,S
Maret School, DC	A,F,S
Marian Central Catholic High School, IL	S
Marian High School, IN	C,F,S
Marine Military Academy, TX	A,R,S
Marist School, GA	A,F,S
Marlborough School, CA	A,C,F,S
Mars Hill Bible School, AL	A,F,S
Martin Luther High School, NY	A,C
The Marvelwood School, CT	A,C,F
Marylawn of the Oranges, NJ	A,C
Marymount High School, CA	A,C,F,S
Mary Star of the Sea High School, CA	A,F
The Master's School, CT	A,C,F,S
Matignon High School, MA	A
McDonogh School, MD	A,C,F,S
The Meadows School, NV	A,F,S
Memphis University School, TN	A,S
Mercy High School College Preparatory, CA	A
Mercyhurst Preparatory School, PA	A,C,F
Merion Mercy Academy, PA	A,F,S

A — academic; C — computer instruction; F — art/fine arts; R — rigorous outdoor training; S — sports; O — other

Mesa Grande Seventh-Day Academy, CA S
Middlesex School, MA F
Mid-Pacific Institute, HI A,C,F
Mill Springs Academy, GA S
Missouri Military Academy, MO A,R,S
Miss Porter's School, CT A,F
MMI Preparatory School, PA A,C
Montclair Kimberley Academy, NJ A,C,F,S
Montgomery Bell Academy, TN A,C,R,S
Moravian Academy, PA A,F,S
Moreau Catholic High School, CA A,S
Morristown-Beard School, NJ A,C,F,S
Mother McAuley High School, IL A,C,F,S
Mount Saint Charles Academy, RI F,S
MPS Etobicoke, ON, Canada A,C,F,S
Munich International School, Germany R,S
Nazareth Academy, IL A,F,S
Newark Academy, NJ A,C,F,S
Nichols School, NY A,F
Noble Academy, NC A,C
Norfolk Academy, VA A,F,S
North Cobb Christian School, GA A,C,F,S
North Country School, NY O
The Norwich Free Academy, CT A,S
Notre Dame Academy, CA A,C,F,S
Notre Dame College Prep, IL A,C,F,S
Notre Dame High School, TN A,F,S
Oak Grove School, CA A
Oak Hill Academy, VA A
Oakland School, VA A,C,F,S
Oak Ridge Military Academy, NC A
The Oakridge School, TX A,C,F,R,S
Ojai Valley School, CA A,C,F
The Oliverian School, NH A,C,F
Oneida Baptist Institute, KY A
Oregon Episcopal School, OR A,C,F,S
Orinda Academy, CA A
Our Lady of Mercy High School, NY A,C,F,S
Out-Of-Door Academy, FL A,F,S
Pacific Hills School, CA A
Padua Franciscan High School, OH A,C,F,S
The Paideia School, GA A
Palma School, CA A
Paradise Adventist Academy, CA S
The Pathway School, PA A
Peddie School, NJ A,F,S
Phillips Academy (Andover), MA A,C,F
Phillips Exeter Academy, NH A
Phoenix Country Day School, AZ A,C,F,S
Pickering College, ON, Canada A
Pine Crest School, FL A,S
The Pingry School, NJ A,S
Pope John XXIII Regional High School, NJ A,S
The Potomac School, VA A,F,S
The Prairie School, WI A,C,F
Prestonwood Christian Academy, TX A,C,F,R,S
Providence Catholic School, The College Preparatory School for Girls Grades 6-12, TX A,C,F,S
Providence Day School, NC A,C,F,S
Providence High School, CA A,C,F,S
Queen Margaret's School, BC, Canada A,S
Randolph-Macon Academy, VA A,C,F
Ranney School, NJ A,C,F,S
Ransom Everglades School, FL A,C
Ravenscroft School, NC A,C,F,S
Realms of Inquiry, UT R
The Rectory School, CT A,F,S
Reitz Memorial High School, IN A,S
Rivermont Collegiate, IA A,C,F,S
Riverside Military Academy, GA A,C,F,R,S
Robert Louis Stevenson School, NY A
Rock Point School, VT A,F
The Roeper School, MI F
Roland Park Country School, MD A,F,S
Rolling Hills Preparatory School, CA A,F
Rosseau Lake College, ON, Canada A
Ross School, NY A,F,S
Rowland Hall, UT A,C,F,S
The Roxbury Latin School, MA A,C,S
Royal Canadian College, BC, Canada A
Rye Country Day School, NY A,C,F,S
Sacred Heart/Griffin High School, IL A,S
Sacred Heart School of Halifax, NS, Canada A
Saddlebrook Preparatory School, FL A
Sage Hill School, CA A,F,S
Sage Ridge School, NV A,F
Saint Agnes Boys High School, NY A
St. Albans School, DC A,C,F,R,S
St. Andrew's College, ON, Canada A,F,S
St. Andrew's Priory School, HI A,C,F,R,S
St. Andrew's School, RI A,C,F,R,S
St. Anne's–Belfield School, VA A,S
St. Anthony Catholic High School, TX A,C,F,S
Saint Anthony High School, CA A,S
St. Anthony's Junior-Senior High School, HI A
Saint Augustine Preparatory School, NJ A,C,F,R,S
Saint Basil Academy, PA A,S
St. Bernard's Catholic School, CA A
St. Brendan High School, FL A,C
St. Catherine's Academy, CA A,C,F,S
St. Christopher's School, VA A
St. Clement's School, ON, Canada A,F
St. Croix Schools, MN A,S
Saint Edward's School, FL A,C,F,S
Saint Francis High School, CA A,S
Saint Francis School, HI A,C
St. George's Independent School, TN A,C,F,S
St. John's Preparatory School, MA A,C,F,S
Saint John's Preparatory School, MN A,F
Saint Joseph High School, IL A,C,F,S
Saint Joseph High School, NJ A
Saint Joseph Junior-Senior High School, HI A,C,F,S
St. Joseph's Catholic School, SC F,S
Saint Joseph's High School, NJ A,C,S
St. Joseph's Preparatory School, PA A,F
St. Jude's School, ON, Canada O
St. Mark's High School, DE A
St. Martin's Episcopal School, LA A,C,F,S
St. Mary's Episcopal School, TN A,F,S
Saint Mary's Hall, TX A,C,F,S
Saint Mary's High School, AZ A,F,S
St. Mary's Preparatory School, MI A,S
Saint Mary's School, NC A,C,F,S
St. Mary's School, OR A,S
Saint Maur International School, Japan A,C,F,S
Saint Patrick High School, IL A,C,F,S
Saint Patrick - Saint Vincent High School, CA A,F,S
St. Paul Academy and Summit School, MN A
St. Paul's High School, MB, Canada S
St. Peter's Preparatory School, NJ A,F,S
St. Scholastica Academy, IL A,F,S
St. Stephen's & St. Agnes School, VA A,C,F
St. Stephen's Episcopal School, TX F,S
St. Stephen's School, Rome, Italy A,F

A — academic; C — computer instruction; F — art/fine arts; R — rigorous outdoor training; S — sports; O — other

Saint Teresa's Academy, MO	C,F,S
St. Thomas Aquinas High School, FL	A,C,F
Saint Thomas Aquinas High School, KS	A,C,S
St. Timothy's School, MD	A
Saint Ursula Academy, OH	A,C,F,S
Salesian High School, CA	A,C,F,S
Sandy Spring Friends School, MD	A,F,S
Sanford School, DE	A,C,F
Scholar's Hall Preparatory School, ON, Canada	A
SciCore Academy, NJ	A,C
Seabury Hall, HI	A,F,S
Seattle Academy of Arts and Sciences, WA	A,F,S
Seton Catholic Central High School, NY	S
Seton Catholic High School, AZ	A,S
The Seven Hills School, OH	A
Severn School, MD	A,C,F,S
Sewickley Academy, PA	A,F,S
Shady Side Academy, PA	A,C,F,S
Shattuck-St. Mary's School, MN	A,F,S
Shawnigan Lake School, BC, Canada	S
Shelton School and Evaluation Center, TX	A
The Shipley School, PA	S
Smith School, NY	A,C
Spartanburg Day School, SC	A,C,F,S
Springside Chestnut Hill Academy, PA	A,C,F,S
Squaw Valley Academy, CA	A,F,S
Stevenson School, CA	A
Stoneleigh–Burnham School, MA	A,F,S
Strake Jesuit College Preparatory, TX	A,S
Suffield Academy, CT	A,C,F
Tabor Academy, MA	A
The Taft School, CT	A,F,S
Taipei American School, Taiwan	A,C
TASIS The American School in England, United Kingdom	A,C,F,S
TASIS, The American School in Switzerland, Switzerland	A,F,S
The Tenney School, TX	A,C
Timothy Christian High School, IL	F,S
Tower Hill School, DE	A,S
Tri-City Christian Schools, CA	A,S
Trinity College School, ON, Canada	A,C,F
Trinity High School, OH	A,F,S
Trinity Preparatory School, FL	A,C,F,S
Trinity School of Texas, TX	A,C,F,S
Trinity Valley School, TX	A,C,F,R,S
Tuscaloosa Academy, AL	A,C,F,S
United Nations International School, NY	A,C,F,S
The University of Chicago Laboratory Schools, IL	A,S
University School of Jackson, TN	A,C,F,S
University School of Milwaukee, WI	A,C,F,S
University School of Nova Southeastern University, FL	A,F,S
Vail Mountain School, CO	A,F,S
Valley Christian High School, CA	A,C,F,S
Villa Duchesne and Oak Hill School, MO	A,C,F,S
Villa Joseph Marie High School, PA	A,S
Villa Victoria Academy, NJ	A,F
Visitation Academy of St. Louis County, MO	S
Wakefield School, VA	A,C,F,S
The Walker School, GA	A
Walnut Hill School, MA	F
Waring School, MA	F
Wasatch Academy, UT	A
Washington Waldorf School, MD	S
Watkinson School, CT	A
Waynflete School, ME	A,F,S
Webb School of Knoxville, TN	A,F,S
Wellspring Foundation, CT	A
Wesleyan Academy, PR	A
Westbury Christian School, TX	S
Westchester Country Day School, NC	A,C,F,S
Western Mennonite School, OR	S
Westmark School, CA	A,C,F
Westminster School, CT	A,S
Westridge School, CA	F
West Sound Academy, WA	A
Wheaton Academy, IL	A,C,F,S
The Wheeler School, RI	O
Whitefield Academy, KY	A,S
The Williams School, CT	S
The Willows Academy, IL	A,S
Willow Wood School, ON, Canada	A,C
Wilmington Christian School, DE	A
Winchester Thurston School, PA	A,F,S
Windermere Preparatory School, FL	A,C,F,S
The Windsor School, NY	A,C,F
Windward School, CA	S
Winston Preparatory School, NY	A,F
The Winston School San Antonio, TX	A,C,S
Xaverian High School, NY	A,S
York Country Day School, PA	F,S

SCHOOLS REPORTING THAT THEY ACCOMMODATE UNDERACHIEVERS

American Academy, FL
Arrowsmith School, ON, Canada
Atlantis Academy, FL
Auldern Academy, NC
Bachman Academy, TN
The Blue Ridge School, VA
Camphill Special School, PA
Chatham Academy, GA
Eagle Hill-Southport, CT
The Family Foundation School, NY
Foothills Academy, AB, Canada
Fowlers Academy, PR
The Frostig School, CA
Glen Eden School, BC, Canada
The Glenholme School, Devereux Connecticut, CT
The Greenwood School, VT
Hampshire Country School, NH
The Hill Center, Durham Academy, NC
Humanex Academy, CO
The John Dewey Academy, MA
The Judge Rotenberg Educational Center, MA
The Karafin School, NY
Key School, TX
Kingshill School, VI
Little Keswick School, VA
Lyman Ward Military Academy, AL
Mooseheart High School, IL
Oakland School, VA
The Pathway School, PA
Realms of Inquiry, UT
The Rectory School, CT
Robert Land Academy, ON, Canada
Robert Louis Stevenson School, NY
St. Jude's School, ON, Canada
Valley View School, MA
Winston Preparatory School, NY

A — academic; C — computer instruction; F — art/fine arts; R — rigorous outdoor training; S — sports; O — other

SCHOOLS REPORTING PROGRAMS FOR STUDENTS WITH SPECIAL NEEDS

Remedial Reading and/or Writing

Academy of the New Church Boys' School, PA
Academy of the New Church Girls' School, PA
Académie Ste Cécile International School, ON, Canada
Alexander Dawson School, CO
Alliance Academy, Ecuador
Allison Academy, FL
American Academy, FL
The American School Foundation, Mexico
Archbishop Curley High School, MD
Archbishop Hoban High School, OH
Arrowsmith School, ON, Canada
ASSETS School, HI
Atlantis Academy, FL
Auldern Academy, NC
Bachman Academy, TN
The Beekman School, NY
Benedictine High School, OH
Bishop Conaty-Our Lady of Loretto High School, CA
Bishop Mora Salesian High School, CA
Bishop's College School, QC, Canada
Bishop Stang High School, MA
Blue Mountain Academy, PA
Blueprint Education, AZ
The Blue Ridge School, VA
Boylan Central Catholic High School, IL
Brother Rice High School, MI
Burr and Burton Academy, VT
Butte Central Catholic High School, MT
Calvin Christian High School, CA
Camphill Special School, PA
Cardinal Newman High School, FL
Cascadilla School, NY
Cathedral High School, NY
The Catholic High School of Baltimore, MD
Central Catholic High School, CA
Chamberlain-Hunt Academy, MS
Chaminade-Madonna College Preparatory, FL
Chatham Academy, GA
Chattanooga Christian School, TN
Chelsea School, MD
Cheshire Academy, CT
Children's Creative and Performing Arts Academy of San Diego, CA
Chinese Christian Schools, CA
Christopher Columbus High School, FL
Christopher Dock Mennonite High School, PA
Chrysalis School, WA
The Concept School, PA
Cotter Schools, MN
Covenant Canadian Reformed School, AB, Canada
Crawford Adventist Academy, ON, Canada
Currey Ingram Academy, TN
Cushing Academy, MA
Damien High School, CA
Deerfield-Windsor School, GA
DeMatha Catholic High School, MD
DePaul Catholic High School, NJ
Dublin Christian Academy, NH
Eagle Hill-Southport, CT
Eastside Christian Academy, AB, Canada
Fairhill School, TX
The Family Foundation School, NY
The Fessenden School, MA
Foothills Academy, AB, Canada
Fort Lauderdale Preparatory School, FL
Foundation Academy, FL
Fox Valley Lutheran High School, WI
Fresno Christian Schools, CA
Friends Academy, NY
Front Range Christian High School, CO
The Frostig School, CA
George Stevens Academy, ME
Glen Eden School, BC, Canada
The Glenholme School, Devereux Connecticut, CT
Gonzaga Preparatory School, WA
Greenfield School, NC
The Greenwood School, VT
The Grier School, PA
Hampshire Country School, NH
Hargrave Military Academy, VA
The Haverford School, PA
Hebrew Academy, CA
Heritage Christian Academy, AB, Canada
Heritage Christian School, ON, Canada
The Hill Center, Durham Academy, NC
The Hill Top Preparatory School, PA
Holy Trinity High School, IL
Hoosac School, NY
The Howard School, GA
Humanex Academy, CO
Hyde School, CT
Hyde School, ME
Institute of Notre Dame, MD
International School of Amsterdam, Netherlands
Jack M. Barrack Hebrew Academy, PA
The John Dewey Academy, MA
Josephinum Academy, IL
The Judge Rotenberg Educational Center, MA
Junipero Serra High School, CA
The Karafin School, NY
Kauai Christian Academy, HI
Keith Country Day School, IL
Key School, TX
Kings Christian School, CA
Kingshill School, VI
Lancaster Mennonite High School, PA
Landmark Christian School, GA
Landmark School, MA
La Scuola D'Italia Guglielmo Marconi, NY
The Latin School of Chicago, IL
Laurel Springs School, CA
Lawrence School, OH
Le Lycee Francais de Los Angeles, CA
Lutheran High School, IN
Lyman Ward Military Academy, AL
Maharishi School of the Age of Enlightenment, IA
Maine Central Institute, ME
Manhattan Christian High School, MT
Maranatha High School, CA
Marian Central Catholic High School, IL
Marian High School, IN
The Marvelwood School, CT
Marylawn of the Oranges, NJ
Memphis University School, TN
Merchiston Castle School, United Kingdom
Mercy High School, NE
Mercyhurst Preparatory School, PA
Merion Mercy Academy, PA
Missouri Military Academy, MO
Monsignor Donovan High School, NJ

Mooseheart High School, IL
MU High School, MO
Noble Academy, NC
The Nora School, MD
North Catholic High School, PA
North Country School, NY
Northwest Yeshiva High School, WA
Northwood School, NY
The Norwich Free Academy, CT
Notre Dame College Prep, IL
Oak Hill Academy, VA
The Oakland School, PA
Oakland School, VA
Ojai Valley School, CA
The Oliverian School, NH
Oneida Baptist Institute, KY
Padua Franciscan High School, OH
The Pathway School, PA
Pinehurst School, ON, Canada
Pioneer Valley Christian School, MA
Powers Catholic High School, MI
The Prairie School, WI
The Rectory School, CT
Redwood Christian Schools, CA
Robert Land Academy, ON, Canada
Robert Louis Stevenson School, NY
Rosseau Lake College, ON, Canada
Saddleback Valley Christian School, CA
St. Andrew's School, RI
St. Andrew's–Sewanee School, TN
Saint Anthony High School, CA
St. Benedict at Auburndale, TN
St. Benedict's Preparatory School, NJ
St. Bernard's Catholic School, CA
St. Brendan High School, FL
St. Croix Schools, MN
Saint Elizabeth High School, CA
St. George's School of Montreal, QC, Canada
Saint Joseph High School, IL
Saint Joseph High School, NJ
St. Jude's School, ON, Canada
St. Mark's High School, DE
Saint Mary's High School, AZ
St. Patrick Catholic High School, MS
Saint Patrick High School, IL
St. Scholastica Academy, IL
St. Thomas Aquinas High School, FL
Saint Thomas Aquinas High School, KS
St. Thomas Choir School, NY
Salesian High School, CA
Salesianum School, DE
San Marcos Baptist Academy, TX
Seattle Academy of Arts and Sciences, WA
Seattle Christian Schools, WA
Seisen International School, Japan
Seton Catholic Central High School, NY
Shattuck-St. Mary's School, MN
Shawe Memorial Junior/Senior High School, IN
Shawnigan Lake School, BC, Canada
Shoreline Christian, WA
Smith School, NY
Stephen T. Badin High School, OH
Storm King School, NY
Takoma Academy, MD
Tandem Friends School, VA
TASIS The American School in England, United Kingdom
The Tenney School, TX
Timothy Christian High School, IL
Toronto District Christian High School, ON, Canada
Trinity High School, KY
Trinity-Pawling School, NY
University School of Nova Southeastern University, FL
Valle Catholic High School, MO
Valley View School, MA
Villa Duchesne and Oak Hill School, MO
Webb School of Knoxville, TN
Westmark School, CA
Wheaton Academy, IL
Willow Wood School, ON, Canada
Wilmington Christian School, DE
The Windsor School, NY
Winston Preparatory School, NY
The Winston School San Antonio, TX
Xaverian High School, NY

Remedial Math

Academy of the New Church Boys' School, PA
Academy of the New Church Girls' School, PA
Académie Ste Cécile International School, ON, Canada
Alexander Dawson School, CO
Alliance Academy, Ecuador
Allison Academy, FL
Alpha Omega Academy, IA
American Academy, FL
The American School Foundation, Mexico
Archbishop Curley High School, MD
Archbishop Hoban High School, OH
Arrowsmith School, ON, Canada
ASSETS School, HI
Atlantis Academy, FL
Auldern Academy, NC
Bachman Academy, TN
The Beekman School, NY
Benedictine High School, OH
Benedictine High School, VA
Bishop Conaty-Our Lady of Loretto High School, CA
Bishop John J. Snyder High School, FL
Bishop's College School, QC, Canada
Bishop Stang High School, MA
Blue Mountain Academy, PA
Blueprint Education, AZ
The Blue Ridge School, VA
Boylan Central Catholic High School, IL
Brother Rice High School, MI
Burr and Burton Academy, VT
Butte Central Catholic High School, MT
Camphill Special School, PA
Cardinal Newman High School, FL
Cascadilla School, NY
Cathedral High School, NY
The Catholic High School of Baltimore, MD
Central Catholic High School, CA
Chamberlain-Hunt Academy, MS
Chaminade-Madonna College Preparatory, FL
Chatham Academy, GA
Chattanooga Christian School, TN
Chelsea School, MD
Cheshire Academy, CT
Children's Creative and Performing Arts Academy of San Diego, CA
Chrysalis School, WA
The Concept School, PA
Cotter Schools, MN
Covenant Canadian Reformed School, AB, Canada

Cushing Academy, MA
Damien High School, CA
Deerfield-Windsor School, GA
De La Salle High School, CA
DePaul Catholic High School, NJ
Dublin Christian Academy, NH
Eagle Hill-Southport, CT
Eastside Christian Academy, AB, Canada
Fairhill School, TX
The Fessenden School, MA
Flint River Academy, GA
Foothills Academy, AB, Canada
Fort Lauderdale Preparatory School, FL
Foundation Academy, FL
Fox Valley Lutheran High School, WI
Fresno Christian Schools, CA
Friends Academy, NY
Front Range Christian High School, CO
The Frostig School, CA
George Stevens Academy, ME
Glen Eden School, BC, Canada
The Glenholme School, Devereux Connecticut, CT
Gonzaga Preparatory School, WA
Grace Brethren School, CA
The Grauer School, CA
Greenfield School, NC
The Greenwood School, VT
The Grier School, PA
Hampshire Country School, NH
Hargrave Military Academy, VA
The Haverford School, PA
Hebrew Academy, CA
Heritage Christian Academy, AB, Canada
Heritage Christian School, ON, Canada
The Hill Center, Durham Academy, NC
The Hill Top Preparatory School, PA
Hoosac School, NY
The Howard School, GA
Humanex Academy, CO
Hyde School, CT
Hyde School, ME
Institute of Notre Dame, MD
International School of Amsterdam, Netherlands
Jack M. Barrack Hebrew Academy, PA
The John Dewey Academy, MA
Josephinum Academy, IL
The Judge Rotenberg Educational Center, MA
Junipero Serra High School, CA
The Karafin School, NY
Kauai Christian Academy, HI
Key School, TX
Kings Christian School, CA
Kingshill School, VI
Lancaster Mennonite High School, PA
Landmark Christian School, GA
Landmark School, MA
La Scuola D'Italia Guglielmo Marconi, NY
The Latin School of Chicago, IL
Laurel Springs School, CA
Lawrence School, OH
Le Lycee Francais de Los Angeles, CA
Little Keswick School, VA
Lutheran High School, IN
Lyman Ward Military Academy, AL
Maharishi School of the Age of Enlightenment, IA
Maine Central Institute, ME
Manhattan Christian High School, MT
Maranatha High School, CA
Marian Central Catholic High School, IL
Marian High School, IN
Marine Military Academy, TX
The Marvelwood School, CT
Marylawn of the Oranges, NJ
Memphis University School, TN
Merchiston Castle School, United Kingdom
Mercy High School, NE
Mercyhurst Preparatory School, PA
Merion Mercy Academy, PA
Missouri Military Academy, MO
Monsignor Donovan High School, NJ
Mooseheart High School, IL
Munich International School, Germany
Noble Academy, NC
The Nora School, MD
North Country School, NY
Northwest Yeshiva High School, WA
The Norwich Free Academy, CT
Notre Dame College Prep, IL
The Oakland School, PA
Oakland School, VA
Ojai Valley School, CA
The Oliverian School, NH
Oneida Baptist Institute, KY
Padua Franciscan High School, OH
The Pathway School, PA
Pinehurst School, ON, Canada
Pioneer Valley Christian School, MA
Powers Catholic High School, MI
The Rectory School, CT
Redwood Christian Schools, CA
Ripon Christian Schools, CA
Robert Land Academy, ON, Canada
Robert Louis Stevenson School, NY
Rosseau Lake College, ON, Canada
Sacramento Adventist Academy, CA
Saddleback Valley Christian School, CA
St. Andrew's–Sewanee School, TN
Saint Anthony High School, CA
Saint Anthony High School, IL
St. Benedict at Auburndale, TN
St. Benedict's Preparatory School, NJ
St. Bernard's Catholic School, CA
St. Croix Schools, MN
Saint Elizabeth High School, CA
St. George's School of Montreal, QC, Canada
Saint Joseph High School, IL
Saint Joseph Junior-Senior High School, HI
St. Jude's School, ON, Canada
St. Mark's High School, DE
Saint Mary's High School, AZ
Saint Patrick High School, IL
Saint Patrick - Saint Vincent High School, CA
St. Paul's High School, MB, Canada
St. Scholastica Academy, IL
St. Thomas Aquinas High School, FL
Saint Thomas Aquinas High School, KS
St. Thomas Choir School, NY
Salesian High School, CA
Salesianum School, DE
San Marcos Baptist Academy, TX
Seattle Academy of Arts and Sciences, WA
Seisen International School, Japan
Seton Catholic Central High School, NY
Shattuck-St. Mary's School, MN

Shawnigan Lake School, BC, Canada
Smith School, NY
Stephen T. Badin High School, OH
Sunshine Bible Academy, SD
Tandem Friends School, VA
The Tenney School, TX
Toronto District Christian High School, ON, Canada
Trinity High School, KY
Trinity High School, OH
Valle Catholic High School, MO
Valley Lutheran High School, AZ
Valley View School, MA
Villa Duchesne and Oak Hill School, MO
Webb School of Knoxville, TN
Westmark School, CA
Wheaton Academy, IL
Willow Wood School, ON, Canada
Wilmington Christian School, DE
The Windsor School, NY
Winston Preparatory School, NY
Xaverian High School, NY

Deaf Students

Alexander Dawson School, CO
Baylor School, TN
Bishop Fenwick High School, OH
Blanchet School, OR
Boylan Central Catholic High School, IL
Burr and Burton Academy, VT
The Colorado Springs School, CO
The Concept School, PA
Denver Christian High School, CO
DePaul Catholic High School, NJ
Front Range Christian High School, CO
Gonzaga Preparatory School, WA
The Grauer School, CA
Heritage Christian Academy, AB, Canada
Humanex Academy, CO
Jack M. Barrack Hebrew Academy, PA
The Judge Rotenberg Educational Center, MA
The Karafin School, NY
Lancaster Mennonite High School, PA
Landmark School, MA
Lawrence Academy, MA
Merchiston Castle School, United Kingdom
Mercy High School, NE
Northwest Yeshiva High School, WA
Phillips Academy (Andover), MA
Rye Country Day School, NY
Saint Anthony High School, IL
St. Mark's High School, DE
San Marcos Baptist Academy, TX
Shawe Memorial Junior/Senior High School, IN
The Tenney School, TX
Trinity High School, KY
Valley Lutheran High School, AZ
Watkinson School, CT
The Webb School, TN
Westover School, CT

Blind Students

Boylan Central Catholic High School, IL
Burr and Burton Academy, VT
The Concept School, PA
DePaul Catholic High School, NJ
Front Range Christian High School, CO
Gonzaga Preparatory School, WA
Humanex Academy, CO
The Judge Rotenberg Educational Center, MA
Lancaster Mennonite High School, PA
Lawrence Academy, MA
Merchiston Castle School, United Kingdom
Mercy High School, NE
MMI Preparatory School, PA
Phillips Academy (Andover), MA
The Prairie School, WI
St. Mark's High School, DE
Stephen T. Badin High School, OH
Trinity High School, KY
The Webb School, TN

Index

Alphabetical Listing of Schools

In the index that follows, page numbers for school profiles are shown in regular type, page numbers for Close-Ups are shown in **boldface** type, and page numbers for Displays are shown in *italics*.

Special Advertising Section

+ AMIT SOOD | sports business major